D0753662
3½ PIPE
3½ PLUG
3½ GATE VALVE
2X6 NIPPLE
3½X2 BUSHING
3½ PIPE
3½ ELL
3" TYPE "B"
FIELD WELD
NOT THREADED
11'-2
2'-8
12
12
12
12
2'-8
14'-10
5'-8
2'-4⅞
6'-0
3½ PIPE
¾ POP SAFETY VALVE
¾X3½ BUSHING
3½ PLUG
3½ CROSS
3½ TEE
CONDENSER
SPECIAL FLANGE

Engineering Design Graphics

AutoCAD® 2007
Twelfth Edition

James H. Earle

Professor Emeritus
Texas A&M University

Upper Saddle River, New Jersey
Columbus, Ohio

Library of Congress Control Number: 2007920973

Editor in Chief: Vernon R. Anthony
Acquisitions Editor: Jill Jones-Renger
Editorial Assistant: Yvette Schlarman
Production Editor: Louise N. Sette
Production Supervision: Karen Fortgang
Design Coordinator: Diane Ernsberger
Art Coordinator: Jill Horton
Cover Designer: James H. Earle
Production Manager: Deidra M. Schwartz
Director of Marketing: David Gesell
Marketing Manager: Jimmy Stephens
Marketing Coordinator: Alicia Dysert

This book was set by Aptara, Inc. It was printed and bound by Courier Westford, Inc. The cover was printed by Coral Graphic Services, Inc.

Pearson Education Ltd.
Pearson Education Singapore Pte. Ltd.
Pearson Education Canada, Ltd.
Pearson Education—Japan
Pearson Education Australia Pty. Limited
Pearson Education North Asia Ltd.
Pearson Educación de Mexico, S.A. de C.V.
Pearson Education Malaysia Pte. Ltd.

10 9 8 7 6 5 4 3 2 1
ISBN-13: 978-0-13-204356-4
ISBN-10: 0-13-204356-4

Dedicated to my father
Hubert Lewis Earle
October 25, 1900–October 22, 1967

Preface

The Best Yet

Once more, *Engineering Design Graphics* has been revised and refined into a new edition, which we believe is its best yet in all categories: content, format, readability, clarity, quality of illustrations, and economy. Every effort has been made to write and illustrate the book to make it easier for the student to learn and the teacher to teach. The content has been fine-tuned to serve today's courses and fit tomorrow's needs.

It is a daunting task for a single author in the area of engineering design graphics to prepare and refine 2000 illustrations, 1000 problems, and a multitude of topics that must be merged into a cohesive textbook as concisely as possible. Content must include fundamentals, design, computer graphics, industrial applications, and meaningful problems. We have tried our best to meet these goals.

How Many Revised Figures and Problems?

Approximately 200 new figures have been included as additions to or replacements for previous figures, and 129 new design problems have been added. About 600 figures have been modified to make them more readable and more effective as part of the "fine-tuning."

Content

Every paragraph and illustration has been revisited for evaluation, revision, improvement, or elimination so that every item makes a worthwhile contribution to the learning process. No space has been squandered on exotic illustrations that are only vaguely related to the objective of the book. Instead, that valuable space has been used to better illustrate and present concepts in an understandable format to reduce the amount of classroom tutoring needed by the student.

Major content areas covered in this text are:
design and creativity,
computer graphics,
engineering drawing,
descriptive geometry, and
problem solving.

Emphasis on Design and Creativity

Chapters 2 through 9 are devoted to the introduction of design and creativity. Case studies with examples of worksheets and drawings that apply the steps of design guide the student through the design process.

Additional problems have been added to these chapters (especially Chapter 9) to introduce the student to the fun of being creative. Problems range from simple, success-assured to those with real-world challenges. The duration of these problems varies from half-hour quickies to semester-long team projects. Additional design exercises appear at the ends of the chapters throughout the book.

Because the primary objective of design instruction is to teach the *process of design,* meaningful problem assignments are given to make the process fun, to encourage ingenuity, and to stimulate entrepreneurship. Most students have never been assigned projects that ask them to apply their imagination, intuition, and creativity, each of which is a dormant, untapped resource. We hope that these exercises will confirm the need for technical knowledge and the importance of applying one's imagination.

Computer Graphics

AutoCAD® 2007 is presented in a step-by-step format to aid the student in learning how to use this popular software, not just read about it in the abstract. Steps in each illustration show the reader what will be seen on the screen as the example is followed. Chapter 37 gives an introduction to two-dimensional computer graphics, and Chapter 38 covers three-dimensional computer graphics, solid modeling, and rendering.

A primary purpose of *Engineering Design Graphics* is to help students learn the principles of graphics, whether done on the drawing board or on the computer. This book can be used in courses in which the entire course is done by computer, none is done by computer, or is partly done by computer.

Format: Was It Worth It?

Much effort has been devoted to the creation of illustrations separated into multiple steps to present the concepts as clearly and simply as possible. A second color is applied as a functional means of emphasizing sequential steps, key points, and explanations, not just as decoration. Explanatory information and text are closely associated with the steps of each example.

There are no blank pages, wide margins, or unused space in the text. Every effort has been made to avoid waste and to make the best use of the space. All figures have been reproduced with a uniform size of figure labeling that is both functional and readable.

Many illustrations have been drawn, modified, and refined to aid the student in visualizing and understanding the example at hand. Actual industrial parts and products have been merged with explanatory examples of principles being covered.

The author has personally developed and drawn the illustrations in this book, not a team of illustrators who have never taught graphics in the classroom nor tried to explain concepts to a student. Only after years of classroom experience and trial-and-error testing is it possible to present principles of graphics in a format that enables the student and teacher to cover more content with fewer learning obstacles.

The two-color, step-by-step format of presentation with conveniently located text has been classroom tested to validate its effectiveness over a number of years. Its classroom effectiveness is substantially better than that of the conventional format used in other texts, but it required about twice as much effort by the author and more expense by the publisher to produce this textbook in this format.

Do the results in the classroom justify this added effort and expense? Yes.

A Book to Keep

Some material in this book may not be formally covered in the course for which it was adopted owing to variations in courses offered from campus to campus. These lightly covered topics may be the ones that will be needed in later courses or in practice; therefore, this book should be retained as a convenient reference for the engineer, technologist, or technician.

A Teaching System

Engineering Design Graphics, used in combination with the following supplements, makes a complete teaching system.

Textbook problems: Approximately 1000 problems are offered to aid the student in mastering the principles of graphics and design.

Instructor's manual: A manual containing the solutions to most of the problems in this book is available to assist the teacher with grading student solutions.

Problem manuals: Nineteen problem books and teacher's guides (with outlines, problem solutions, tests, and test solutions) that are keyed to this book are available. New problem manuals are in development as well. Fifteen of the problem books are designed to allow problem solution by computer, by sketching, or on the drawing board with instruments. These manuals are listed inside the back cover of this book.

Online Instructor's Manual

To access supplementary materials online, instructors need to request an instructor access code. Go to **www.prenhall.com**, click the **Instructor Resource Center** link, and then click **Register Today** for an instructor access code. Within 48 hours after registering, you will receive a confirming e-mail including an instructor access code. Once you have received your code, go to the site and log on for full instructions on downloading the materials you wish to use.

Autodesk Learning License

Through a recent agreement with AutoCAD publisher Autodesk®, Prentice Hall now offers the option of purchasing *Engineering Design Graphics [with] AutoCAD® 2007,* 12th edition, with either a 180-day or a 1-year student software license agreement. This provides adequate time for a student to complete all the activities in this book. The software is functionally identical with the professional license but is intended **for student personal use only**. It is not for professional use. For more information about this book and the Autodesk Learning License, contact your local Pearson Prentice Hall sales representative, or contact our National Marketing Manager, Jimmy Stephens, at 1(800)228-7854 ×3725 or at Jimmy_Stephens@prenhall.com. For the name and number of your sales rep, please contact Prentice Hall Faculty Services at 1(800)526-0485.

Acknowledgments

We are grateful for the assistance of many who have influenced the development of this volume. Many industries have furnished photographs, drawings, and applications that have been acknowledged in the corresponding legends. The Engineering Design Graphics staff of Texas A&M University has been helpful in making suggestions for the revision of this book over the years.

Professor Tom Pollock provided valuable information on metallurgy for Chapter 19. Professor Leendert Kersten of the University of Nebraska, Lincoln, kindly provided his descriptive geometry computer programs for inclusion; his cooperation is appreciated.

We are indebted to Denis Cadu and Jimm Meloy of Autodesk, Inc. for their assistance and cooperation. We are appreciative of the fine editorial and production team assembled by Jill Jones-Renger at Prentice Hall: Louise Sette and Jill Horton. Barbara Liguori was the best ever as editor and checker of the manuscript. Karen Fortang oversaw the production of a book that involved the management of 2000 illustrations and hundreds of pages of text to ensure that they came together as a cohesive book. Many thanks to them for their efforts.

We would also like to acknowledge the reviewers of this text: Dan Dimitriu, San Antonio College, and Greg Riggs, Elizabethtown Community and Technical College.

Above all, we appreciate the many institutions who have thought enough of our publications to adopt them for classroom use. This is the highest honor that can be paid an author. We are hopeful that this textbook will fill the needs of engineering and technology programs. As always, comments and suggestions for improvement and revision will be appreciated.

JIM EARLE
College Station, Texas

Brief Contents

Contents

1 Engineering and Technology

1.1 Introduction

This book deals with the field of engineering design graphics and its application to the design process. Engineering graphics is the primary medium of design. Essentially all designs begin with pencil sketches and end with precisely executed graphical documents from which products and projects become realities. The solution of most engineering problems requires a combination of organization, analysis, problem-solving principles, graphics, skill, and communication (**Figure 1.1**).

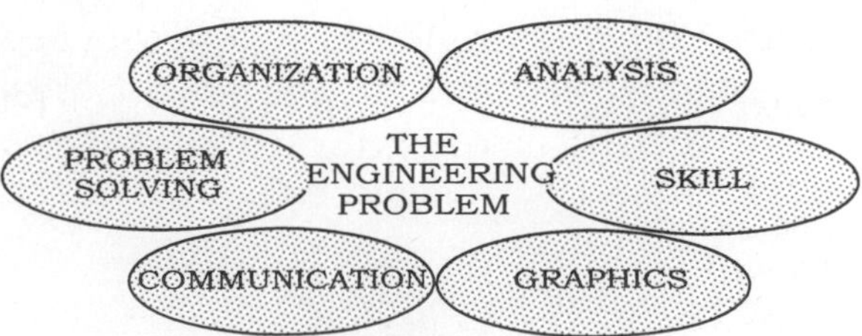

1.1 This text illustrates the total approach to engineering, with the engineering problem as the focal point.

This book is intended to help you use your creativity and develop your imagination because innovation is essential to a successful career in engineering and technology. Albert Einstein said, "Imagination is more important than knowledge, for knowledge is limited, whereas imagination embraces the entire world . . . stimulating progress, or, giving birth to evolution."

You will find that graphics is a powerful means of developing and communicating ideas and concepts whether done by pencil or electronically. Graphics is the language of the technological team.

1.2 Engineering Graphics

Engineering graphics covers the total field of graphical problem solving within two major areas of specialization: **descriptive geometry** and **documentation drawings**. Other areas of application are nomography, graphical illustration, vector graphics, data analysis, and computer graphics. Graphics is one of the designer's most effective tools for developing design concepts and solving three-dimensional problems. It also is the designer's best means of communicating ideas to others.

Descriptive Geometry

Gaspard Monge (1746–1818), the "father of descriptive geometry," used graphical methods to solve design problems related to fortifications and battlements while a military student in France. His headmaster scolded him for not using the usual long, tedious mathematical process. Only after lengthy explanations and demonstrations of his technique was he able to convince his faculty that graphical methods (now called *descriptive geometry*) produced solutions in less time.

Descriptive geometry was such an improvement over mathematical methods that it was kept as a military secret for fifteen years before the authorities allowed it to be taught as part of the civilian curriculum.

Descriptive geometry is the projection of three-dimensional figures on the two-dimensional plane of paper in a manner that allows geometric manipulations to determine lengths, angles, shapes, and other geometric information about the figures.

1.3 Technological Milestones

Many of the technological advancements of the twentieth century are engineering achievements. Since 1900, technology has taken us from the horse-drawn carriage to the moon and back, and more advancements are certain in the future.

Figure 1.2 shows a few of the many technological mileposts since 1900. It identifies products and processes that have provided millions of jobs and a better way of life for all. Other significant achievements were building a railroad from Nebraska to California that met at Promontory Point, Utah, in 1869 in less than 4 years; constructing the Empire State Building with 102 floors in 13.5 months in 1931; and retooling industry in 1942 for World War II to produce 4.5 naval vessels, 3.7 cargo ships, 203 airplanes, and 6 tanks each day while supporting 15 million Americans in the armed forces.

MILESTONES OF THE 20TH CENTURY

1900	Vacuum cleaner Airplane Dial telephone Lightbulb Model T Ford	1950	Atomic bomb tests Optical fibers Soviet satellite Microchip
1910	Washing machine Refrigerator Wireless phone	1960	Commun. satellite Industrial robot Nuclear reactor Heart transplant Man on moon
1920	Radio broadcasts Telephone service 35 mm camera Cartoons & sound	1970	Silicon chip Personal computer Videocassette record. Supersonic jet Neutron bomb
1930	Tape recorder Atom split Jet engine Television	1980	Stealth bomber Space shuttle Artificial heart Soviet space station
1940	Elect. computer Missile Transistor Microwave Polaroid camera	1990	Computer voice recoginition Artificial intelligence E-mail and the Internet

1.2 This chronology lists some of the significant technological advances of the twentieth century.

One "miracle project" of the 1990s was the construction of the 31-mi "Chunnel" that connects England and France under the English Channel for high-speed shuttle trains. It consists of three tunnels drilled 131 ft under the channel floor; two of the tunnels are 24 ft in diameter. The trip from London to Paris can be made in 3-1/2 hours.

1.4 The Technological Team

Technology and design have become so broad and complex that teams of specialists rather than individuals undertake most projects (**Figure 1.3**). Such teams usually consist of one or more scientists, engineers, technologists, technicians, and craftspeople, and may include designers and stylists (**Figure 1.4**).

Scientists

Scientists are researchers who seek to discover new laws and principles of nature through experimentation and scientific testing

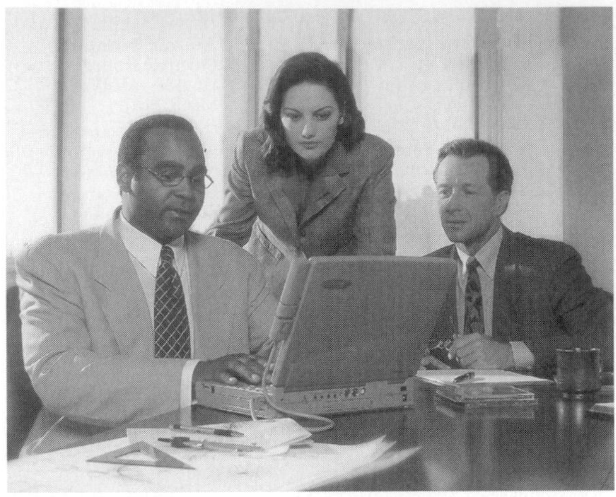

1.3 Technological and design team members with varying experiences and areas of expertise must communicate and interact with one another. (*Courtesy of Toshiba America Information Systems, Inc.*)

1.5 No project has involved such a high degree of research and application as that produced by the scientists and engineers working on the space program. (*Courtesy of NASA.*)

(**Figure 1.5**). They are more concerned with the discovery of scientific principles than with the application of those principles to products and systems. Their discoveries may not find applications until years later.

Engineers

Engineers receive training in science, mathematics, and industrial processes to prepare them to apply the findings of the scientists (**Figure 1.6**). Thus engineers are concerned with converting raw materials and power sources into needed products and services. Creatively applying scientific principles to develop new products and systems is the design process, the engineer's primary function. In general, engineers use known principles and available resources to achieve a practical end at a reasonable cost.

Technologists

Technologists obtain backgrounds in science, mathematics, and industrial processes. Whereas engineers are responsible for analysis, overall design, and research, technologists are

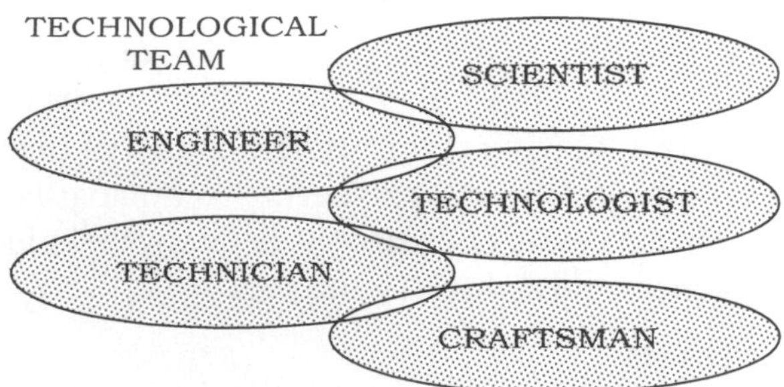

1.4 This ranking of the typical technological team is from the most theoretical level (scientists) to the least technical level (craftspeople).

1.6 The design of an oil refinery is possible through the efforts of the entire technological team, beginning with scientists and engineers, whose plans and specifications are converted into reality. (*Courtesy of the Exxon Mobil Corporation.*)

1.7 An engineering technician works on a phased-array radar antenna. *(Courtesy of Northrop Grumman Corporation.)*

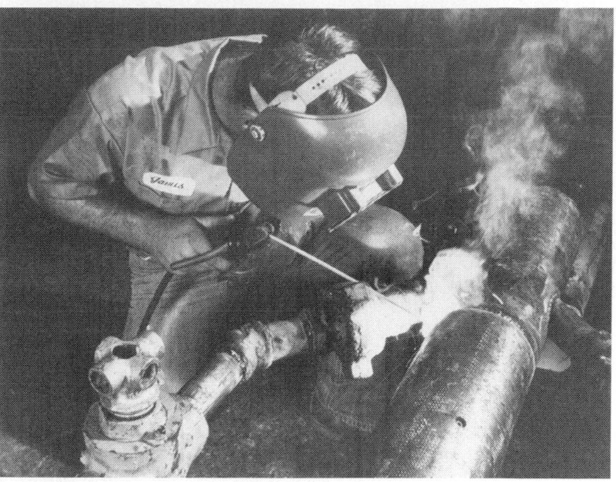

1.8 A welder who is a skilled craftsman assembles a portion of an experimental aircraft. *(Courtesy of Texas Eastern; TE Today; photo by Bob Thigpen.)*

concerned with the application of engineering principles to planning, detail design, and production (**Figure 1.7**). Technologists apply their knowledge of engineering principles, manufacturing, and testing to assist in the implementation of projects and production. They also provide support and act as liaisons between engineers and technicians.

Technicians

Technicians assist engineers and technologists at a less theoretical level than technologists and provide liaison between technologists and craftspeople. They have backgrounds in mathematics, drafting, computer programming, and materials testing. Their work varies from conducting routine laboratory experiments to supervising craftspeople in manufacturing or construction.

Craftspeople

Craftspeople are responsible for implementing designs by fabricating them according to engineers' specifications. They may be machinists who make product parts or electricians who assemble electrical components. Their ability to produce a part according to specifications is as necessary to the success of a project as the engineers' design of it. Craftspeople include electricians, welders, machinists, fabricators, drafters, and members of many other occupational groups (**Figure 1.8**).

Designers

Designers may be engineers, technologists, inventors, or industrial designers who have special talents for devising creative solutions. Designers do not necessarily have engineering backgrounds, especially in newer technologies where there is little design precedent. Thomas A. Edison, for example, had little formal education, but he created some of the world's most significant inventions.

Stylists

Stylists are concerned with the appearance and market appeal of a product rather than its fundamental design. They may design an automobile body or the exterior of an electric iron. Automobile stylists, for example, consider the car's appearance, driver's vision, passengers' enclosure, power unit's space requirement, and so on. However, they are not involved with the design of the car's internal mechanical functions, such as the engine, steering linkage, and brakes. Stylists must have a high degree of aesthetic awareness and an instinct for styling to attract consumers.

2
The Design Process

2.1 Introduction

The design process is the method of devising innovative solutions to problems that will result in new products or systems. Engineering graphics is the primary medium of design that is used for developing designs from initial concepts to final working drawings. Initially, a design consists of sketches, which are refined, analyzed, and developed into precise detail drawings and specifications. They, in turn, become part of the contract documents for the parties involved in funding and implementing a project.

At first glance, the solution of a design problem may appear to involve merely the recognition of a need and the application of effort toward its solution, but most engineering designs are more complex than that. The engineering and design efforts may be the easiest parts of a project.

For example, engineers who develop roadway systems must deal with constraints such as ordinances, historical data, human factors, social considerations, scientific principles, budgeting, and politics (**Figure 2.1**). Engineers can readily design driving surfaces, drainage systems, overpasses, and other components of the system. However, adherence to budgetary limitations is essential, and funding is closely related to politics on public projects.

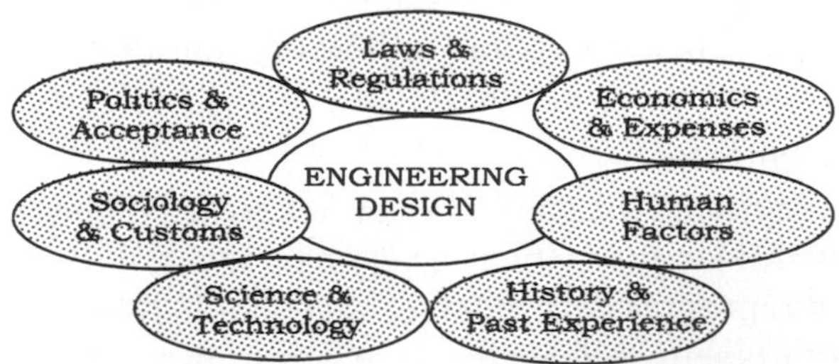

2.1 An engineering project often involves the interaction of people representing many professions and interests, with engineering design as the central function.

Traffic laws, zoning ordinances, environmental impact statements, right-of-way acquisition, and liability clearances are legal aspects of roadway design that engineers must deal with. Past trends, historical data, human factors (including driver characteristics), and safety features affecting the function of the traffic system must be analyzed. Social problems may arise if proposed roadways will be heavily traveled and will attract commercial development such as shopping centers, fast-food outlets, and service stations. Finally, designers must apply engineering principles developed through research and experience to obtain durable roads, economical bridges, and fully functional systems.

2.2 Types of Design Problems

Most design problems fall into one of two categories: **product design** and **systems design**.

Product Design

Product design is the creation, testing, and manufacture of an item that usually will be mass produced, such as appliances, tools, or large products such as automobiles (**Figure 2.2**). In general, a product must have sufficiently broad appeal for meeting a specific need and performing an independent function to warrant its production in quantity. Designers of products, whether automobiles or bicycles, must consider current market needs, production costs, function, sales, distribution methods, profit predictions, and other factors shown in **Figure 2.3**.

Products can perform one or many functions. For instance, the primary function of an automobile is to provide transportation, but it also contains products that provide communications, illumination, comfort, entertainment, and safety. Because it is mass produced for a large consumer market and can be purchased as a unit, the automobile is regarded as a product. However, because it consists of many products that perform various functions, the automobile also is a system.

2.2 Product design seeks to develop a product that meets a specific need, that can function independently, and that can be mass produced.

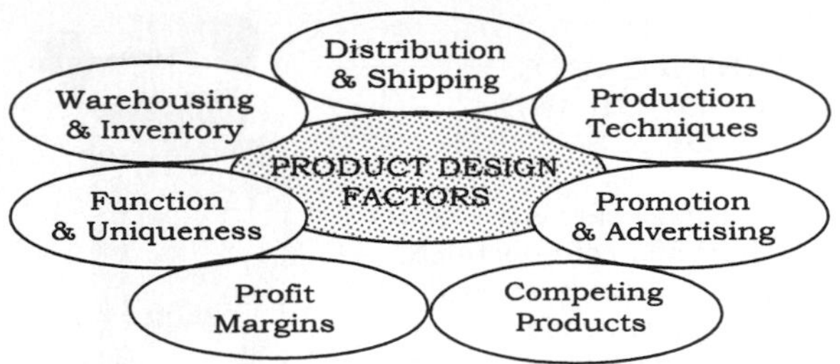

2.3 These are some of the major factors that must be considered when developing a product design.

Systems Design

Systems design combines products and their components into a unique arrangement and provides a method for their operation. A residential building is a system of products consisting of heating and cooling, plumbing, natural gas, electrical power, sewage, appliances, entertainment, and others that form the overall system, as shown in **Figure 2.4**.

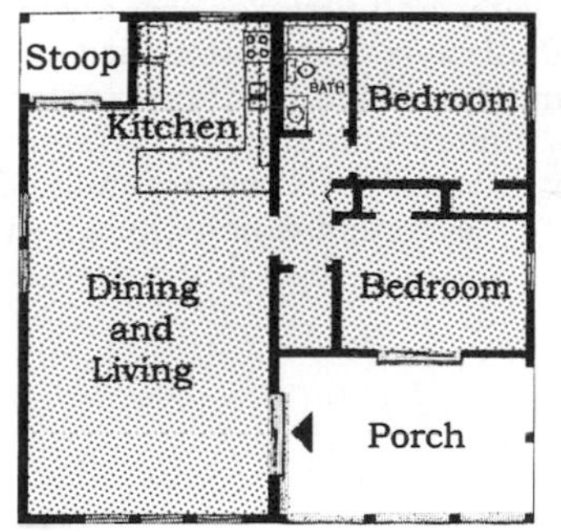

2.4 The typical residence is a system composed of many components and products.

SMARTE CARTE:
A PRODUCT AND
PART OF A SYSTEM

This luggage cart is a product and part of a coin-operated luggage system in airports for the convenience of travelers in managing their baggage.

2.5 The Smarte Carte is a product and part of a system. (*Courtesy of Smarte Carte.*)

Systems-Design Example

Suppose that you were carrying luggage to a faraway gate in an airport terminal. It would be easy for you to recognize the need for a luggage cart that you could use and then leave behind for others to use. If you had this need, then others might, too. The identification of this need could prompt you to design a cart like the one shown in **Figure 2.5** to hold luggage, and even a child, and to make it available to travelers. The cart is a product.

How could you profit from providing such a cart? First, you would need a method of holding the carts and dispensing them to customers, such as the one shown in **Figure 2.6**.

SMARTE CARTE STATION

Luggage stations are located conveniently near entry gates and baggage areas where individual carts and be returned after use and dispensed to other travelers. This combination of cart and a dispenser is the beginning of a system which offers more than just a product.

2.6 Carts plus a dispensing apparatus is the beginning of the development of a system. (*Courtesy of Smarte Carte.*)

COIN-OPERATED
DISPENSER

In addition to releasing a cart, the station makes change, accepts credit cards, and issues baggage cards that can be used at the next airport during the traveler's trip.
These added features constitute a system that is more than just a grouping of products.

2.7 The coin-operated dispenser station releases a cart, makes change for $5, $10, and $20 bills, and issues baggage cards that can be used at the next terminal. (*Courtesy of Smarte Carte.*)

You would also need a method for users to pay for cart rental, so you could design a coin-operated gate for releasing them (**Figure 2.7**).

For an added customer convenience you could provide a vending machine that would both take bills to make change and issue cards entitling customers to multiple use of carts at this and other terminals (**Figure 2.7**). A mechanism to encourage customers to return carts to another, conveniently located dispensing unit would be helpful and efficient. A coin dispenser (**Figure 2.6**) that would give a partial refund on the rental fee to customers returning carts to a dispensing unit at their destination might work.

The combination of these products and the method of using them is a system design, although it is a relatively simple one. Such a system of products is more valuable than the sum of the products alone. An example of a larger, more complex system is the highway system (**Figure 2.8**), which is composed of vehicles, highways, bridges, tunnels, signals, signs, and much more.

2.3 The Design Process

Design is the process of creating a product or system to satisfy a set of requirements that has multiple solutions by using any available

2.8 One of the largest systems is the highway network, which is composed of vehicles, roads, bridges, signals, etc.

resources. In essentially all cases, the final design must be profitable or within a budget.

The steps of the design process shown in **Figure 2.9** are:

1. problem identification,
2. preliminary ideas (ideation),
3. refinement,
4. analysis,
5. decision, and
6. implementation.

Designers should work sequentially from step to step but should review previous steps periodically and rework them if a new approach comes to mind during the process.

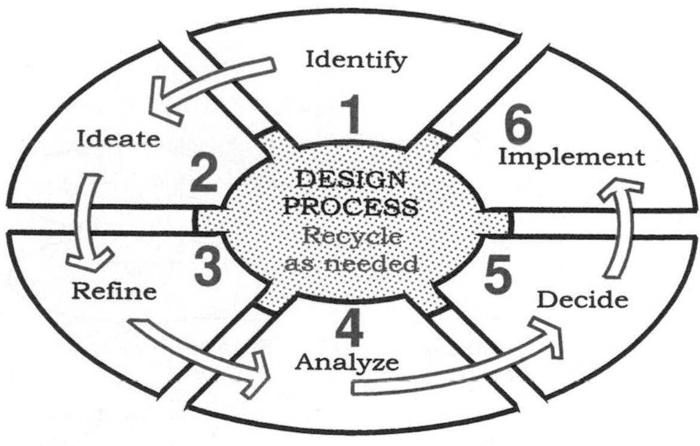

2.9 The design process consists of six steps, each of which can be recycled as needed.

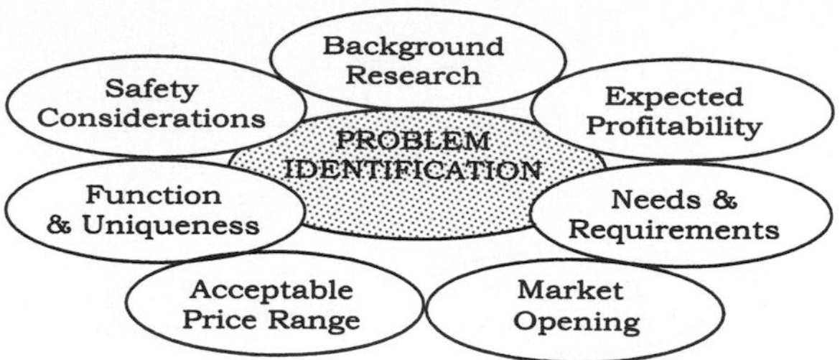

2.10 Problem identification requires that the designer accumulate as much information about a problem as possible before attempting a solution. The designer also should keep product marketing in mind at all times.

Problem Identification

Most engineering problems are not clearly defined at the outset and require identification before an attempt is made to solve them **(Figure 2.10).** For example, air pollution is a concern, but we must identify its causes before we can solve the problem. Is it caused by automobiles, factories, atmospheric conditions that harbor impurities, or geographic features that trap impure atmospheres?

Another example is traffic congestion. When you enter a street where traffic is unusually congested, can you identify the reasons for the congestion? Are there too many cars? Are the signals poorly synchronized? Are there visual obstructions? Has an accident blocked traffic?

Problem identification involves much more than simply stating, "We need to eliminate air pollution." Data of several types are necessary: opinion surveys, historical records, personal observations, experimental data, physical measurements from the field, and more. It is important that the designer resist the temptation to begin developing a solution before the identification step has been completed.

Preliminary Ideas

The second step of the design process is the development of as many ideas for problem

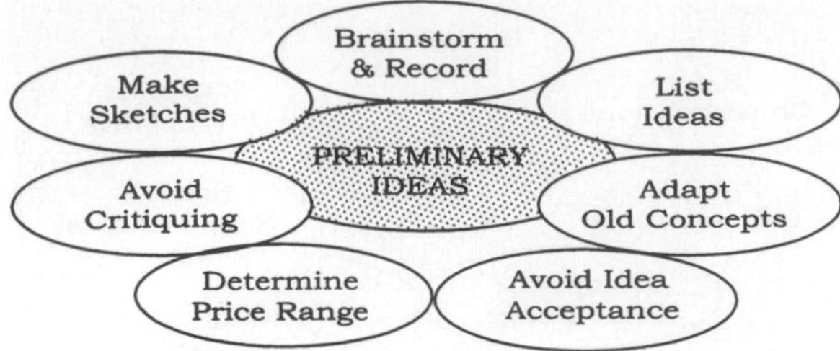

2.11 The designer gathers ideas from a brainstorming session and develops preliminary ideas for problem solution. Ideas should be listed, sketched, and noted to have a broad range of ideas to work with.

solution as possible (**Figure 2.11**). A brainstorming session is a good way to collect ideas at the outset that are highly creative, revolutionary, and even wild. Rough sketches, notes, and comments can capture and preserve preliminary ideas for further refinement. The more ideas the better at this stage.

Refinement

Several of the better preliminary ideas are selected for refinement to determine their merits. The rough preliminary sketches are converted into scale drawings for spatial analysis, determination of critical measurements, and the calculation of areas and volumes affecting the design (**Figure 2.12**). Descriptive geometry aids in determining spatial relationships, angles between planes, lengths of structural members, intersections of surfaces and planes, and other geometric relationships.

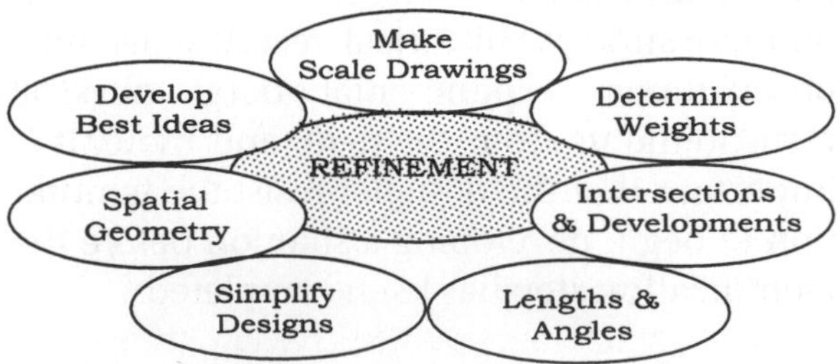

2.12 Refinement begins with the construction of scale drawings of the best preliminary ideas. Descriptive geometry and graphics are used to describe geometric characteristics.

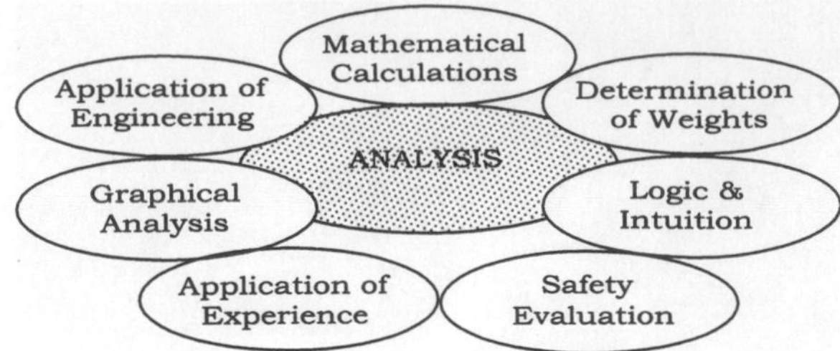

2.13 All available methods, from science to technology to graphics to experience, should be used to analyze a design.

Analysis

Analysis is the step during which engineering and scientific principles are used most intensively to evaluate the best designs and compare their merits with respect to function, strength, safety, cost, and optimization (**Figure 2.13**). Graphical methods play an important role in analysis, also. Data can be analyzed graphically; forces can be analyzed as graphical vectors; and empirical data can be analyzed, integrated, and differentiated by other graphical methods. Analysis is less creative than the previous steps.

Decision

After analysis, a single design, which may be a compromise among several designs, is decided on as the solution to the problem (**Figure 2.14**). The designer alone, or a team, may make the

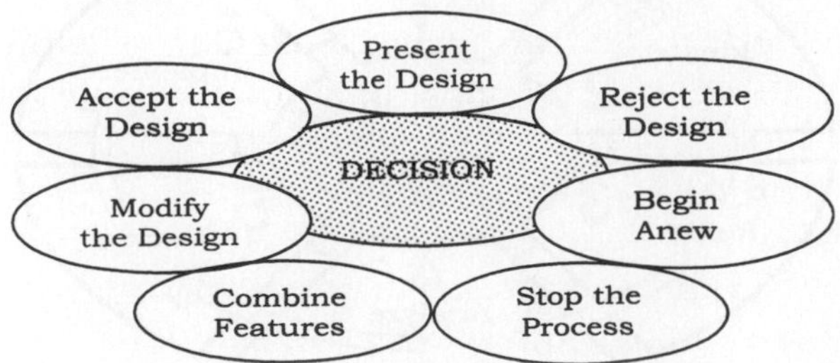

2.14 Decision involves the selection of the best design or design features to implement. This step may require an acceptance, rejection, or a compromise of the proposed solution.

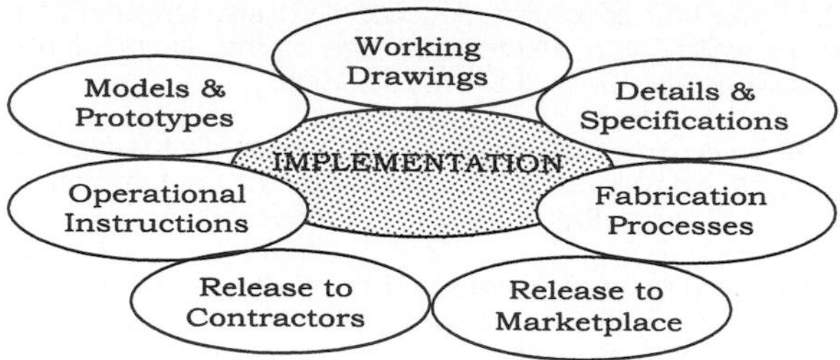

2.15 Implementation is the preparation of drawings, specifications, and documentation from which the product can be made. The product is produced and marketing is begun.

decision. The outstanding aspects of each design usually lend themselves to graphical comparisons of manufacturing costs, weights, operational characteristics, and other data essential in decision making.

Implementation

The final design must be described and detailed in working drawings and specifications from which the project will be built, whether it is a computer chip or a suspension bridge (**Figure 2.15**). Workers must have precise instructions for the manufacture of each component, often measured within thousandths of an inch to ensure proper fabrication assembly. Working drawings must be sufficiently explicit to serve as part of the legal contract with the successful bidder on the job.

2.4 Graphics and Design

Whether used in freehand sketching, with instruments, or on a computer, graphics (drawing) is the medium of design. Engineering, scientific, and analytical principles must be applied throughout the process, and graphics is the medium that is employed in each step from problem identification to implementation.

An example of how graphics was used as a medium of design in the development of the

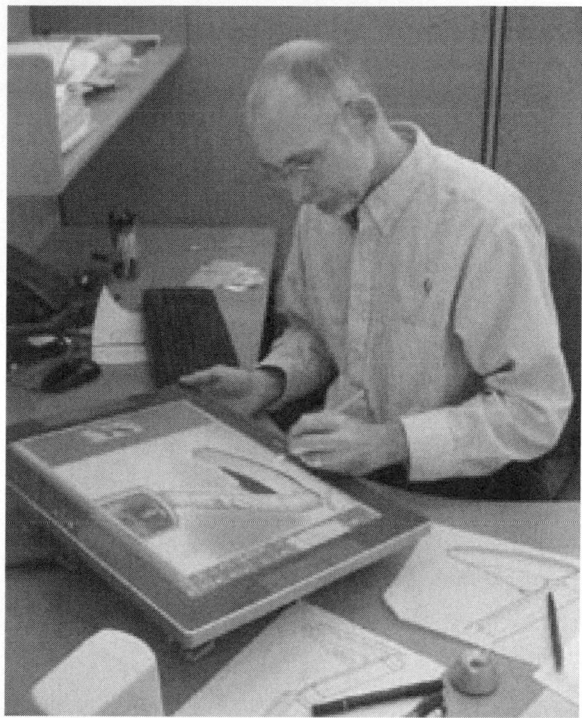

2.16 The designer makes numerous freehand sketches to describe his ideas for a video phone that will enable the transmission of a person's image and voice simultaneously. *(Courtesy Bresslergroup and Worldgate.)*

Worldgate Ojo Videophone by the Bresslergroup is shown in **Figures 2.16** through **2.20**.

The designer made numerous rough freehand sketches of design ideas using paper and pencil. The better ideas were refined on his electronic drawing pad for further development (**Figure 2.16**).

The designer made a series of three-dimensional sketches of the videophone and rendered the best one, as shown in **Figure 2.17**. These drawings represented his thinking process and were a means of recording his ideas and communicating with others.

Additional three-dimensional pictorials (**Figure 2.18**) were drawn to develop and illustrate necessary operational details as the design evolved. The preliminary designs were

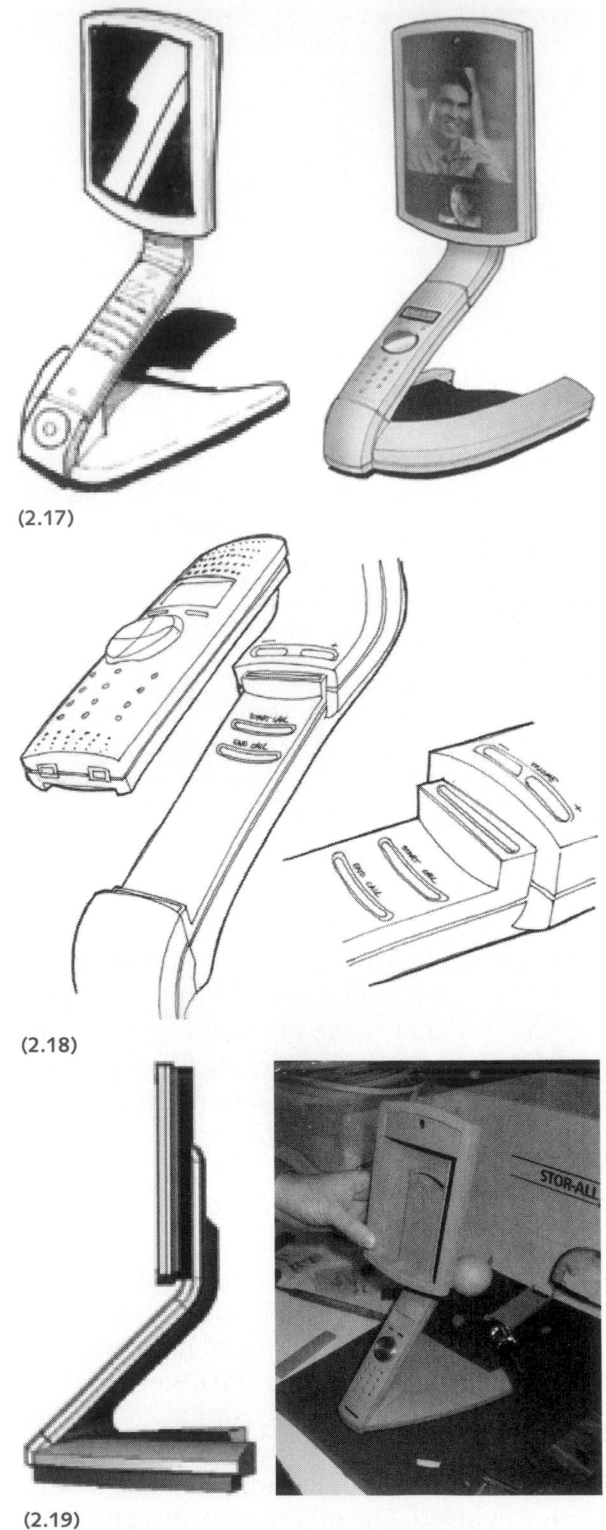

(2.17)

(2.18)

(2.19)

2.17 The best concept is sketched (left) and rendered as a more realistic and descriptive image of the design (right). *(Courtesy Bresslergroup and Worldgate.)*

2.18 Three-dimensional pictorials are used to clarify additional production details that must be refined for the Ojo Videophone device. *(Courtesy Bresslergroup and Worldgate.)*

2.19 Computer models used to develop and present the final design (left) are then converted into a prototype model, shown at the right before painting. *(Courtesy Bresslergroup and Worldgate.)*

studied and evaluated by several designers and engineers to troubleshoot the design and apply all available experience and expertise to it.

Engineering was applied throughout the design process toward its conclusion to assure that the electronics could be properly housed, that manufacturing could be economically performed, and that it functioned in the best manner. Computer models were developed and converted into a rapid model for added realism, as shown in **Figure 2.19**.

The prototype model was painted and finished to simulate the final product so it could be presented to the client for approval (**Figure 2.20**). Once approved, the product

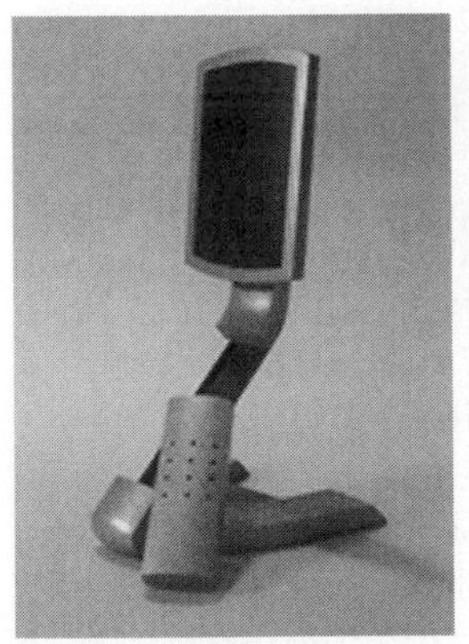

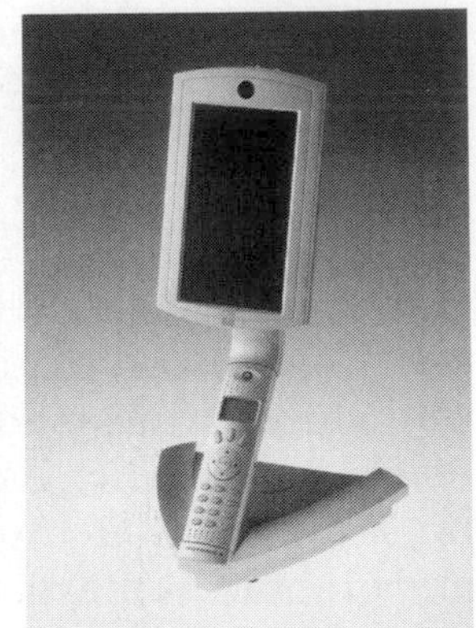

2.20 The prototype is painted to present it as realistically as possible (right). Once approval is given and the design is accepted, the Ojo Videophone is produced in its final form. *(Courtesy Bresslergroup and Worldgate.)*

was detailed for manufacture and produced for the market.

2.5 Application of the Design Process

The following example illustrates the application of the design process to a simple problem.

Hanger Bracket Problem

A bracket is needed to support a 2-in.-diameter hot-water pipe from a beam or column 9 in. from the mounting surface. This design project is typical of an in-house assignment by an engineer of a company specializing in pipe hangers and supports.

Problem Identification

First, write a statement of the problem and a statement of need (**Sheet 1**). List limitations and desirable features and make descriptive sketches to better identify the requirements (**Sheet 2**). Even if much of this information may be obvious, writing statements and making sketches about the problem will help you "warm up" to the problem and begin the creative process. Also, you must begin thinking about sales outlets and marketing methods.

Preliminary Ideas

Brainstorm the problem for possible solutions with others, or alone if necessary. List the ideas obtained on a worksheet (**Sheet 3**), and summarize the best ideas and design features on a separate worksheet (**Sheet 4**), then translate and expand these verbal ideas into rapidly drawn freehand sketches (**Sheets 5** and **6**). You should develop as many ideas as possible during this step, because a large number of ideas represents a high level of creativity. This is the most creative step of the design process.

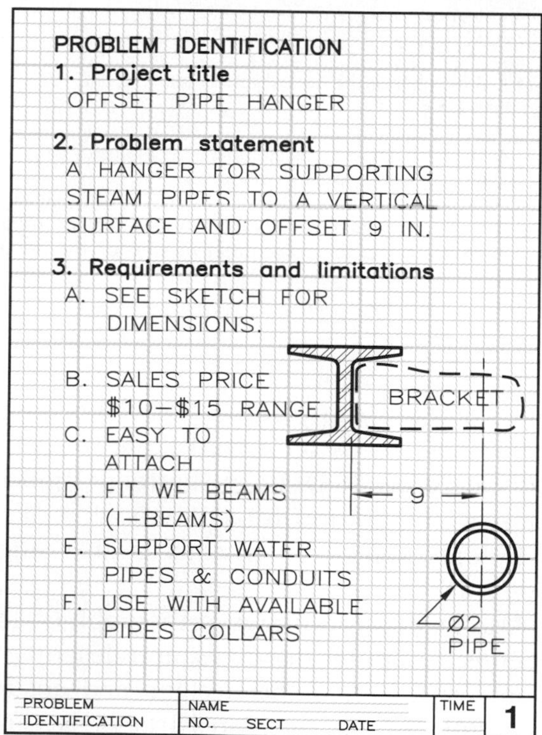

Sheet 1 This worksheet shows aspects of problem identification, the first step of the design process.

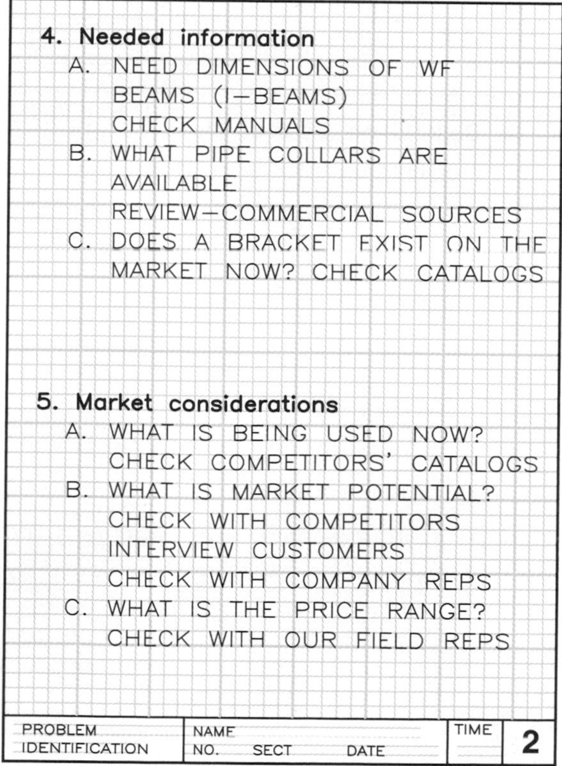

Sheet 2 This worksheet shows information needed before the designer can proceed, including sources from which it can be obtained.

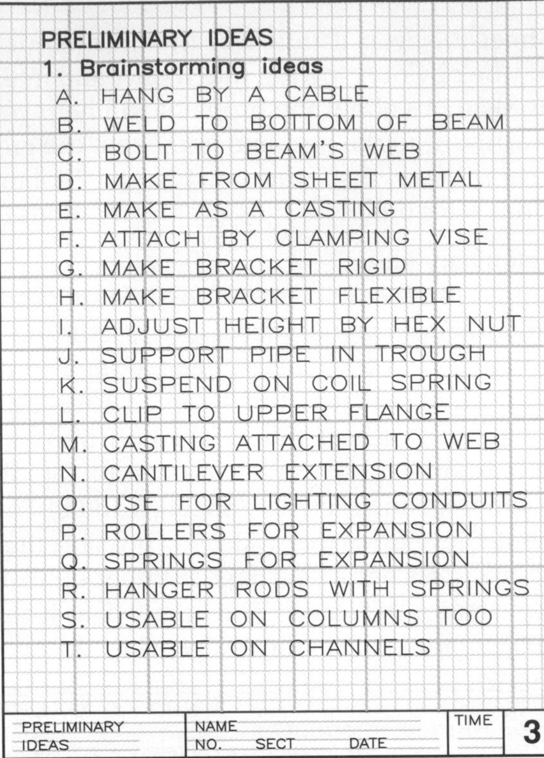
PRELIMINARY IDEAS
1. Brainstorming ideas
A. HANG BY A CABLE
B. WELD TO BOTTOM OF BEAM
C. BOLT TO BEAM'S WEB
D. MAKE FROM SHEET METAL
E. MAKE AS A CASTING
F. ATTACH BY CLAMPING VISE
G. MAKE BRACKET RIGID
H. MAKE BRACKET FLEXIBLE
I. ADJUST HEIGHT BY HEX NUT
J. SUPPORT PIPE IN TROUGH
K. SUSPEND ON COIL SPRING
L. CLIP TO UPPER FLANGE
M. CASTING ATTACHED TO WEB
N. CANTILEVER EXTENSION
O. USE FOR LIGHTING CONDUITS
P. ROLLERS FOR EXPANSION
Q. SPRINGS FOR EXPANSION
R. HANGER RODS WITH SPRINGS
S. USABLE ON COLUMNS TOO
T. USABLE ON CHANNELS
PRELIMINARY IDEAS
NAME
NO. SECT DATE
TIME
3

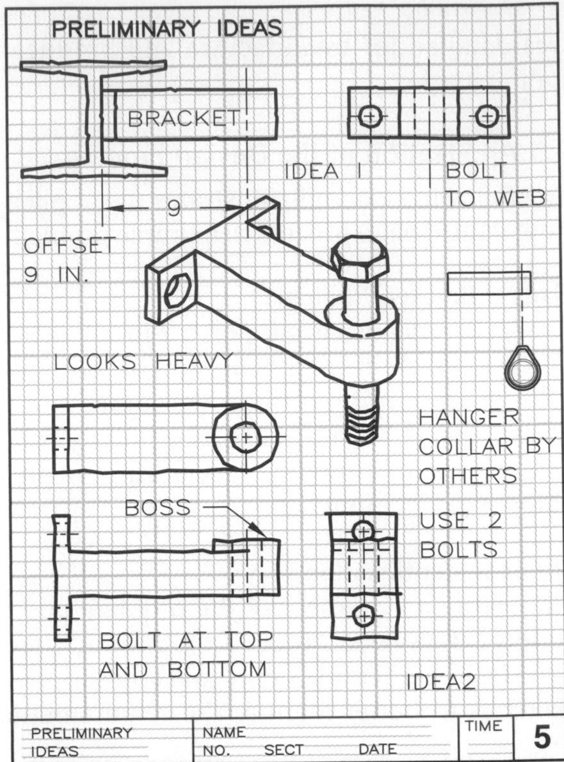
PRELIMINARY IDEAS
BRACKET
IDEA I
BOLT TO WEB
9
OFFSET 9 IN.
LOOKS HEAVY
HANGER COLLAR BY OTHERS
BOSS
USE 2 BOLTS
BOLT AT TOP AND BOTTOM
IDEA2
PRELIMINARY IDEAS
NAME
NO. SECT DATE
TIME
5

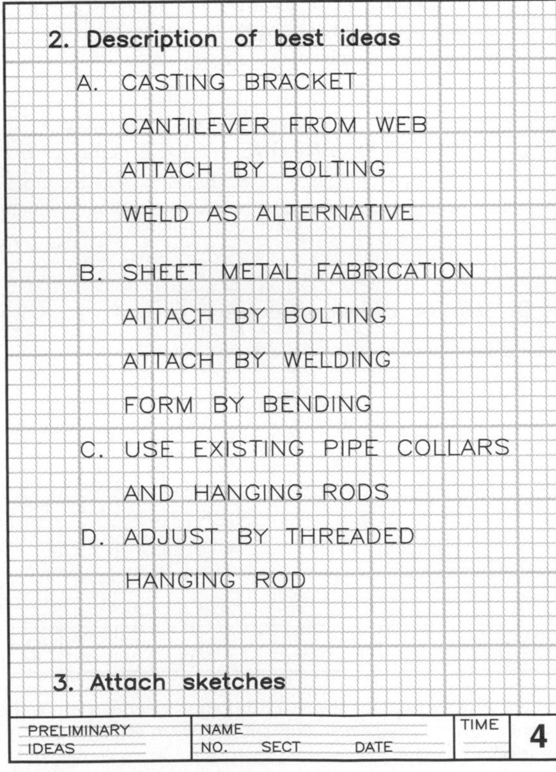
2. Description of best ideas
A. CASTING BRACKET
CANTILEVER FROM WEB
ATTACH BY BOLTING
WELD AS ALTERNATIVE
B. SHEET METAL FABRICATION
ATTACH BY BOLTING
ATTACH BY WELDING
FORM BY BENDING
C. USE EXISTING PIPE COLLARS
AND HANGING RODS
D. ADJUST BY THREADED
HANGING ROD
3. Attach sketches
PRELIMINARY IDEAS
NAME
NO. SECT DATE
TIME
4

Sheet 3 A member of the brainstorming team records the ideas from the session.

Sheet 4 The best ideas are selected from the brainstorming session to be developed as preliminary ideas.

Sheet 5 Preliminary ideas are sketched and noted for further development. This is the most creative step of the design process.

Problem Refinement

Describe the design features of one or more preliminary ideas on a worksheet for comparison (**Sheet 7**). Draw the better designs to scale in preparation for analysis; you need show only a few dimensions at this stage (**Sheet 8**).

Use instrument-drawn orthographic projections, computer drawings, and descriptive geometry to refine the designs and ensure precision. Let's say that you select ideas 3 and 4 for analysis. **Sheet 8** depicts orthographic views of the two designs.

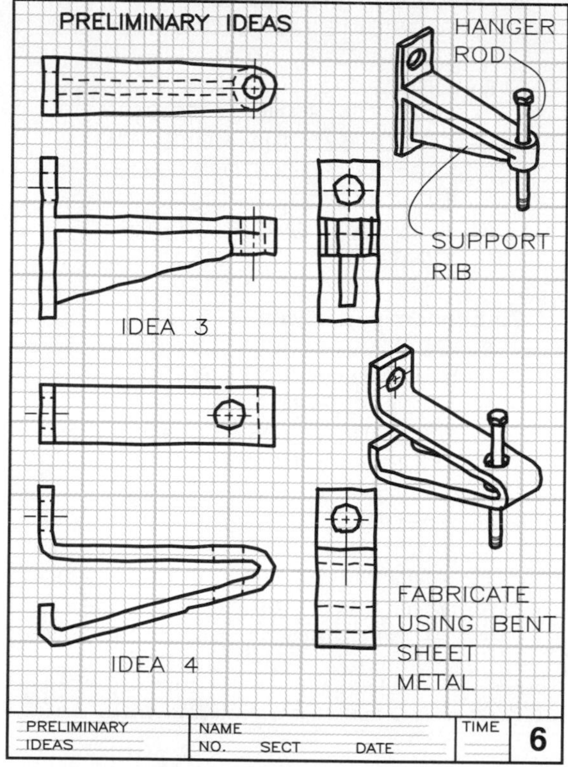

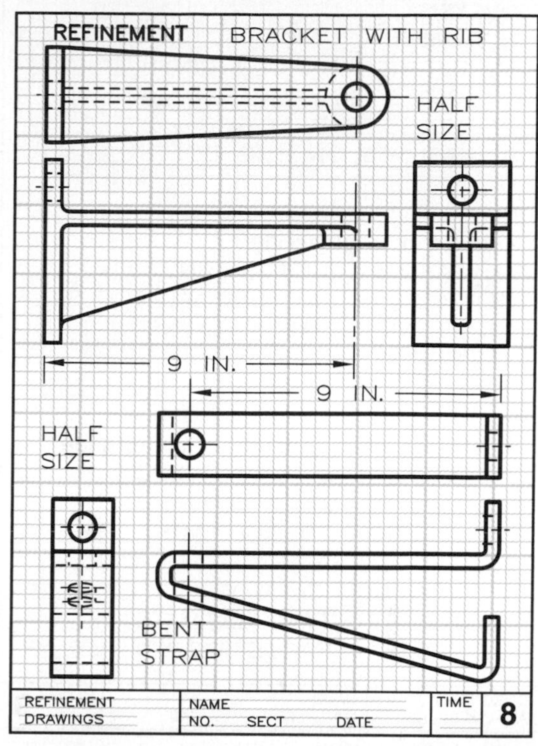

Sheet 6 Additional preliminary design solutions are sketched here.

Sheet 7 Refinement of preliminary ideas begins with written descriptions of the better ideas.

Sheet 8 Scale drawings of two designs are made to describe the designs. Almost no dimensions are needed.

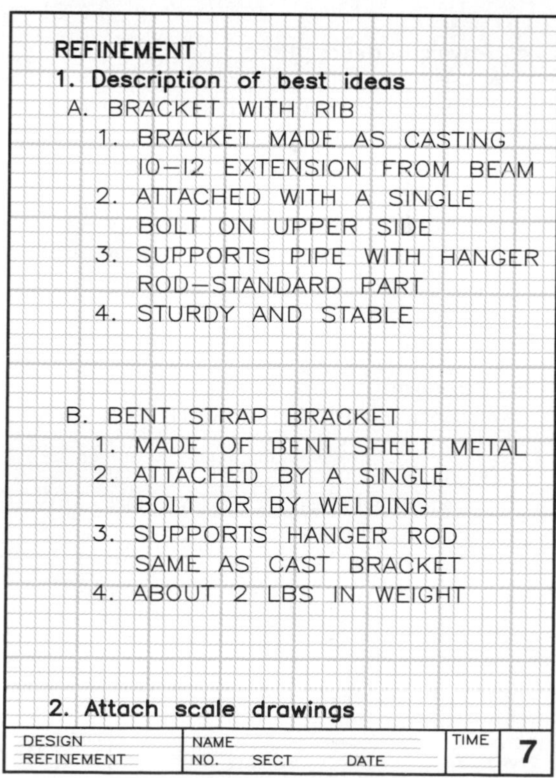

Analysis

Use an analysis worksheet to analyze the cast-iron bracket design (**Sheets 9** through **12**). If you are considering more than one solution, analyze each design.

By using the maximum load of 200 lb and the geometry of the bracket, it is possible to graphically determine the angle of the reaction that the bolt must carry, 456 lb, when the bracket is fully loaded (**Sheet 12**). Again, graphics is used as an important design tool.

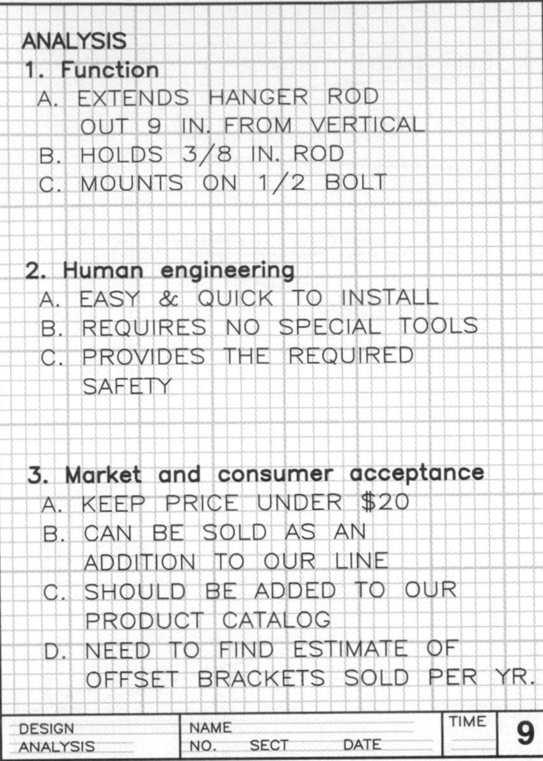

ANALYSIS

1. Function
   A. EXTENDS HANGER ROD OUT 9 IN. FROM VERTICAL
   B. HOLDS 3/8 IN. ROD
   C. MOUNTS ON 1/2 BOLT

2. Human engineering
   A. EASY & QUICK TO INSTALL
   B. REQUIRES NO SPECIAL TOOLS
   C. PROVIDES THE REQUIRED SAFETY

3. Market and consumer acceptance
   A. KEEP PRICE UNDER $20
   B. CAN BE SOLD AS AN ADDITION TO OUR LINE
   C. SHOULD BE ADDED TO OUR PRODUCT CATALOG
   D. NEED TO FIND ESTIMATE OF OFFSET BRACKETS SOLD PER YR.

DESIGN ANALYSIS | NAME NO. SECT DATE | TIME | 9

4. Physical description
   A. BRACKET: 10–11 IN. LONG WITH RIB FOR STRENGTH
   B. ATTACHED WITH A SINGLE BOLT AT UPPER SIDE
   C. WEIGHT: ABOUT 3–4 LBS
   D. BOSS FOR EXTRA STRENGTH WHERE HANGER ROD ATTACHES
   E. FORMED AS A CASTING CAST IRON

5. Strength
   A. WILL SUPPORT ABOUT 200 LBS WITH A SAFETY FACTOR OF 5
   B. 1/2 BOLT SUFFICIENT FOR ATTACHMENT TO BEAM OR OR COLUMN
   C. 3/8 DIA HANGER ROD MORE THAN ADEQUATE TO SUPPORT 200 LBS

DESIGN ANALYSIS | NAME NO. SECT DATE | TIME | 10

6. Production procedures
   A. FABRICATE AS A CASTING USING CAST IRON
   B. DRILL .50 DIA HOLE FOR .375 DIA HANGER ROD
   C. DRILL .625 DIA HOLE FOR .50 DIA BOLT TO ATTACH BRACKET
   D. PAINT TO GIVE RUST–PROOF COATING

7. Economic analysis

A. COSTS			
1. DEVELOPMENT	$0.20		
2. CAST IRON	.50		
3. CASTING COST	1.40	2.50	
4. DRILL 2 HOLES	.20		
5. PAINTING	.20		
B. LABOR			.70
C. PACKAGING			.30
D. PROFIT			2.00
E. WHOLESALE PRICE			6.50
F. RETAIL PRICE			$12.00

DESIGN ANALYSIS | NAME NO. SECT DATE | TIME | 11

Sheet 9 A continuation of the analysis step.

Sheet 10 A continuation of the analysis step.

Sheet 11 This portion of the analysis focuses on the production and economic considerations.

Decision

The decision table (**Sheet 13**) compares two designs: the bracket with a rib and the bent strap. Assign weight factors to be analyzed by assigning points to them that add up to 10. You can then rank the designs by their overall scores from highest to lowest.

Draw conclusions and summarize the features of the recommended design, along with a projection of its marketability (**Sheet 14**). In this case, let's say we decide to implement the bracket with a rib.

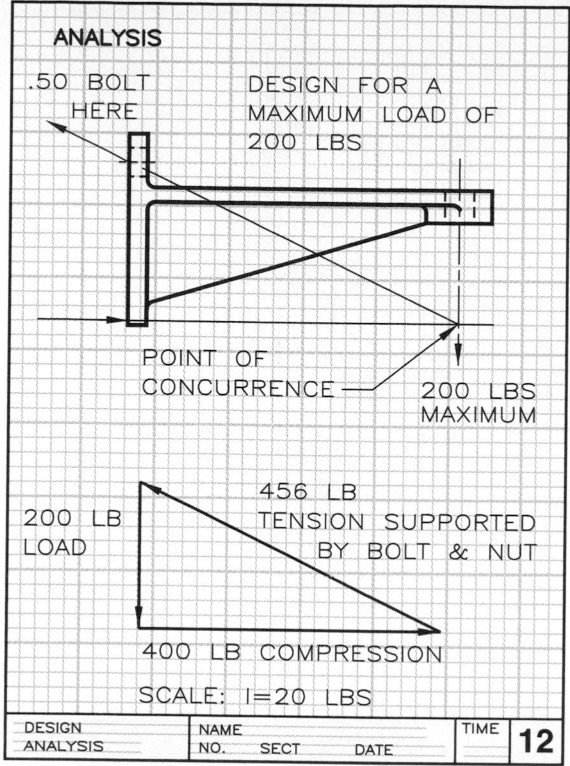

Sheet 12 Graphics and descriptive geometry can be used to determine the load carried by the support bolt.

Sheet 13 A decision table is used to evaluate alternative designs in arriving at the final selection.

Sheet 14 The final step of the decision process is the summary of the conclusions.

Implementation

Detail the bracket with a rib design in a working drawing that graphically describes and dimensions each individual part (**Sheet 15**).

Use notes to specify standard parts—the nuts, bolts, and hanger rod—but it will be unnecessary to draw them because they will be bought as standard parts. This working drawing shows how the bracket will be made. Now, you need to build a prototype or model of the product and test it for function.

CONCLUSIONS

THE BRACKET WITH A RIB DESIGN APPEARS TO BE THE BEST AND MOST MARKETABLE SOLUTION

IT WOULD BE MOST SUITED TO THE MARKET NEEDS

GOOD POSSIBILITY OF SELLING AS ADDITIONAL PRODUCT ACCESSORY

RETAIL	$12.00
SHIPPING EXPENSES	2.00
NUMBER TO SELL TO BREAK EVEN	1000
MANUFACTURED IN HOUSE	$3.50
PROFIT PER UNIT	$2.00

RECOMMEND IMPLEMENTATION AND PRODUCTION OF THE PRODUCT AND ADD TO LINE.

DESIGN DECISION | NAME NO. SECT DATE | TIME | 14

DECISION

1. Decision table for evaluation

DESIGN 1: BRACKET WITH RIB
DESIGN 2: BENT STRAP
DESIGN 3:
DESIGN 4:
DESIGN 5:

MAX	FACTORS	1	2	3	4	5
2	FUNCTION	2	1.5			
2	HUMAN FACT.	1.5	1.5			
1	MARKET ANAL	.5	.2			
1	STRENGTH	1	.5			
1	PRODUCTION	.5	.5			
1	COST	.5	.2			
2	PROFITABILITY	1.0	1.0			
0	APPEARANCE	0	0			
10	TOTALS	7	5.4			

DESIGN DECISION | NAME NO. SECT DATE | TIME | 13

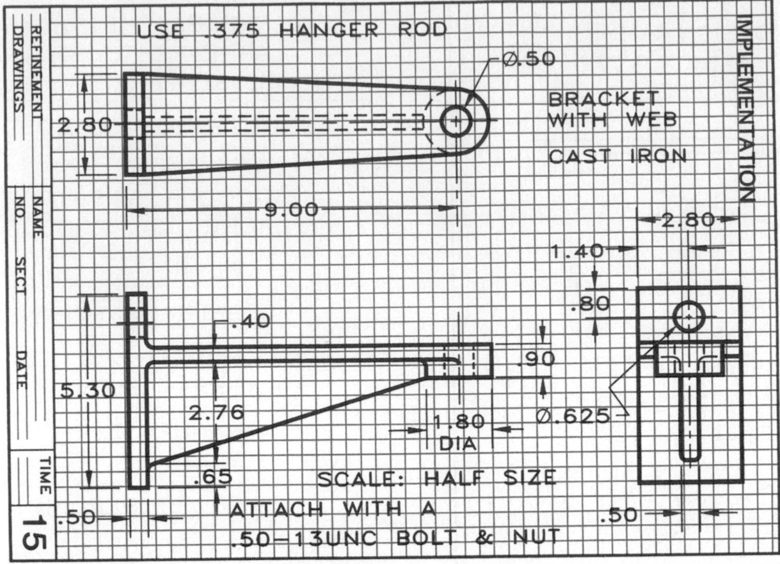

Sheet 15 The final bracket design is drawn as a working drawing ready for production.

Figure 2.21 shows the final product, the cast-iron bracket with a rib. After determining how it will be packaged and distributed, your next task will be to add it to your company's product line, list it in your catalog, and introduce it to the marketplace.

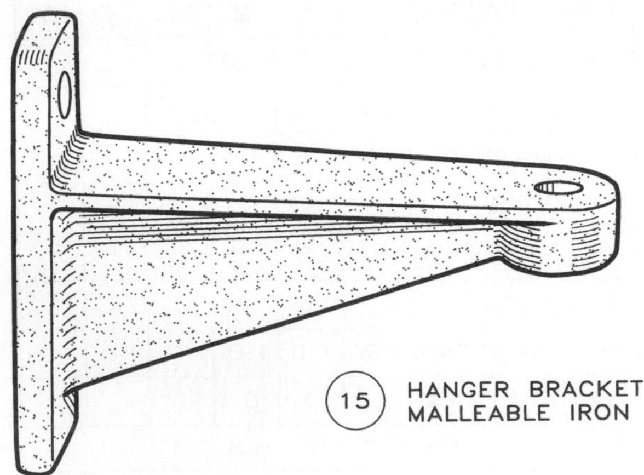

2.21 The completed bracket is shown here ready to be marketed.

Problems

Most problems are to be solved on 8-1/2 × 11-in. paper, using instruments or by sketching freehand as assigned. You may use either plain paper or paper with a printed grid for laying out the problems.

Endorse each problem sheet with your name and file number, date, and problem number. Letter the answers to essay problems with approved single-stroke Gothic lettering. (See Chapter 11.)

1. Outline your plan of activities for the weekend. Indicate aspects of your plans that you feel display creativity or imagination. Explain your reasoning.

2. Write a report not to exceed two pages on an engineer who or engineering achievement that you believe exhibits a high degree of creativity. Outline the creative aspects of your choice.

3. Test your ability to recognize the need for new designs. List as many improvements as you can think of for the typical automobile. Make suggestions for implementing these improvements. Follow the same procedure for another product of your choice.

4. List as many systems as you can that affect your daily life. Separate several of these systems into their components (subsystems).

5. Subdivide the following items into their individual components: (a) a classroom, (b) a wristwatch, (c) a movie theater, (d) an electric motor, (e) a coffee percolator, (f) a golf course, (g) a service station, and (h) a bridge.

6. Indicate which of the items in Problem 5 are systems and which are products. Explain your answers.

7. Make a list of products and systems that you believe would be necessary for life on the moon.

8. You are responsibile for organizing and designing a skateboard installation that will be self-supporting. Write a paragraph on each of the six steps of the design process to explain how you would apply each step to the problem. For example, explain the steps you would take to identify the problem.

9. You are responsible for designing a motorized wheelbarrow to be marketed for home use. Write a paragraph on each of the six steps of the design process, explaining how you would apply each step to the problem. For example, what action would you take to identify the problem?

10. Hanger Bracket identification: Make a worksheet that could follow Sheet 2 to provide additional identification information. For example, how much per linear foot will a 2" XXX pipe weigh (refer to Chapter 35) when it is full of water (refer to the Appendix for the weight of water). Show your calculations on the worksheet. How far apart should hangers be spaced if each is to carry no more than 200 lbs with a safety factor of 5 (the capacity to carry 5 times the design load)? Make sketches to clarify this information.

11. List and explain a sequence of steps that you believe would be adequate for, yet different from, the design process steps given in this chapter. Your version of the design process may contain any of the steps discussed.

12. Design a simple device for holding a fishing pole in a fishing position while the person fishing rows the boat. Make sketches and notes to describe your design.

13. Design a doorstop to keep a door from slamming into the wall behind it. Make rapid freehand sketches and notes using the six design steps. Do not spend more than 30 minutes on this problem. Indicate any information you would need at the decision and implementation steps that you may not have now.

14. List factors to consider during the problem identification step for designing (a) a skillet, (b) a bicycle lock, (c) a handle for a piece of luggage, (d) improving your grades, (e) a child's toy, (f) a stadium seat, (g) a desk lamp, (h) an umbrella, and (i) a hot dog stand.

15. Detection of terrorists and protection from them has become a worldwide problem. Can you make suggestions as to how security can be improved at airports, on campuses, at sports stadiums, dormitories, residences, and others locations? Select one of these areas or one of your own choosing and apply the design process to the development of a solution.

3 Problem Identification

3.1 Introduction

Problem identification is the initial step that a designer takes to solve a problem. Identification involves recognizing a need and then proposing design criteria (**Figure 3.1**).

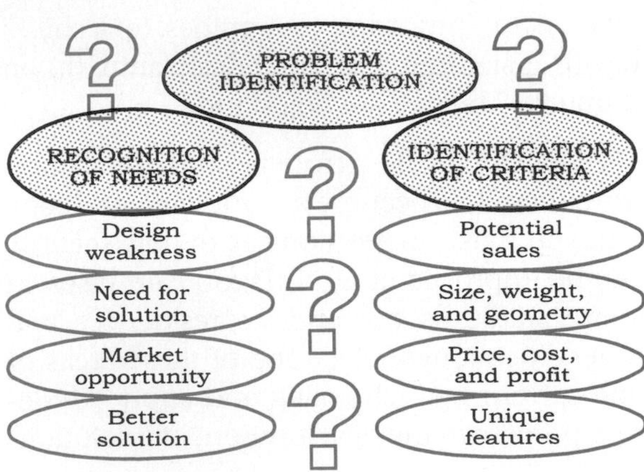

3.1 Problem identification involves the recognition of a need and the identification of design criteria.

Recognizing a need may begin with observation of a problem or a defect in an existing product or a system that needs to be corrected. Or a designer may fortuitously think to him- or herself, "Why hasn't someone invented a gadget that . . . " The need may be for an improved automobile safety belt, a system allowing full wheelchair access to public buildings, or a new exercise apparatus. The solution may be a product or a system improvement to make it more reliable and perhaps more profitable.

Proposing design criteria follows need recognition. Here the designer proposes the specifications a new product or system must meet.

3.2 Example: Hand Truck

A hand truck works well enough for simple applications (**Figure 3.2**). However, wouldn't it be nice if it were adjustable for a variety of

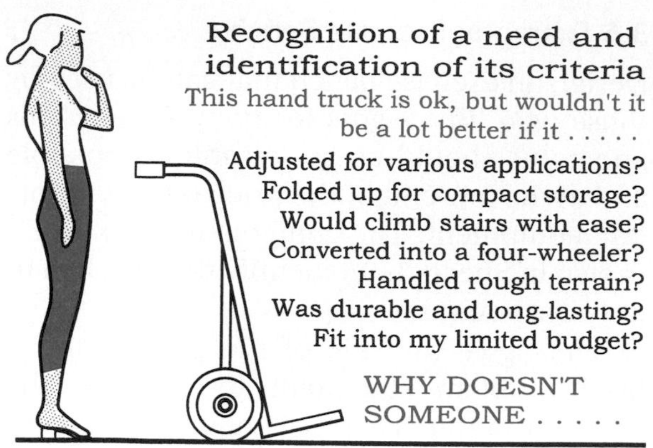

3.2 Development of a product begins with the recognition of a need and the identification of the criteria that must be considered.

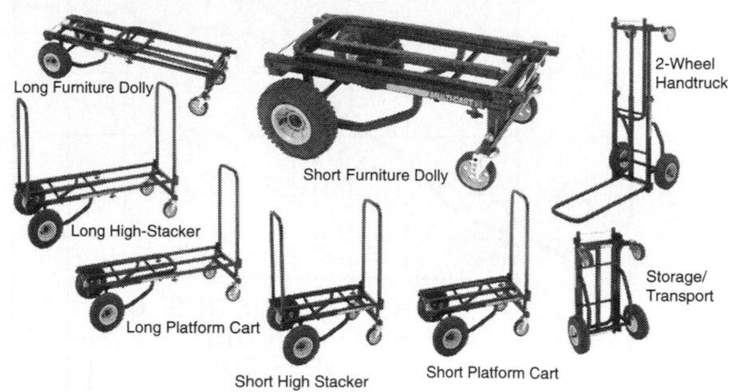

3.3 And someone did meet the design criteria to produce a unique marketable hand truck. *(Courtesy of Michael Dahl, Multi-Cart inventor.)*

applications and could even climb stairs? These are needs that most people recognize promptly after using the standard truck.

Now the designer must determine the design criteria before proceeding with a solution. The designer needs to know the geometry and dimensions of typical applications and the potential market for the solution. Can it be made to fold up for ease of storage?

Figure 3.3 illustrates a truck in which most of the criteria have been merged into a single design that provides greater versatility and marketability. Other solutions are possible, but they all begin with recognizing the need and criteria, as in this example.

3.3 The Identification Process

Problem identification requires the designer to determine requirements, limitations, and other background information before becoming involved in problem solution. The designer should take the following steps during problem identification (**Figure 3.4**).

1. Problem statement. Describe the problem to begin the thinking process.

2. Requirements. List the conditions that the design must satisfy. Most will be questions to be answered after data are gathered.

3. Limitations. List the factors affecting design specifications, such as maximum weight or size.

4. Sketches. Make sketches and add notes and dimensions to identify physical and theoretical characteristics.

5. Existing solutions. Investigate existing solutions that will be your competition in the marketplace.

6. Data collection. Gather data on population trends, related designs, physical characteristics, sales records, and market studies.

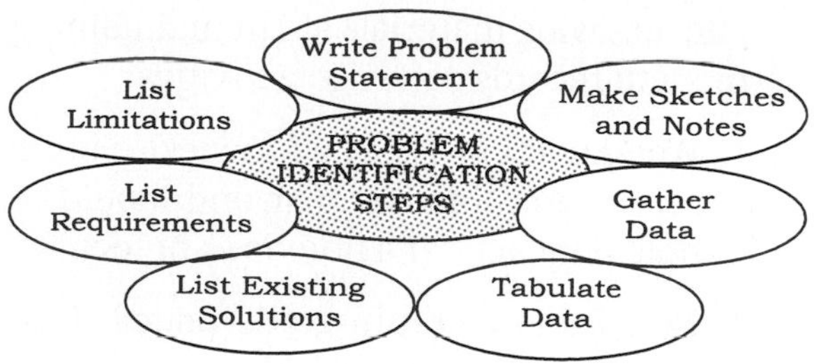

3.4 Problem identification requires a thorough investigation of background factors before attempting a design solution.

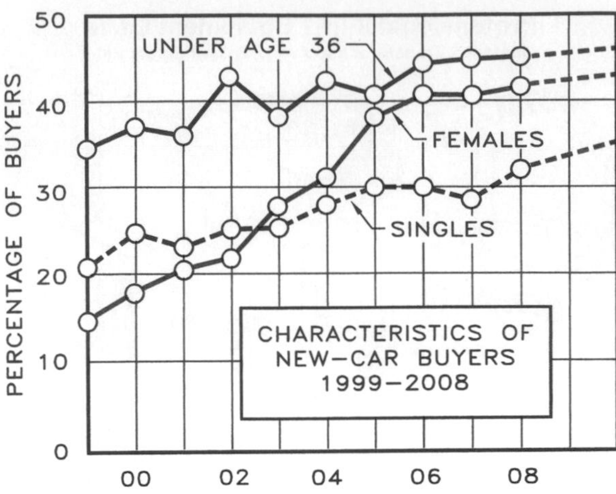

3.5 Data gathered to identify the changing characteristics of new-car buyers can be interpreted more easily when it has been graphed.

7. Tabulate data and findings. Organize and graph the data for ease of interpretation, as was done in **Figure 3.5.**

3.4 Design Worksheets

Designers must make numerous notes and sketches on worksheets throughout the design process. Worksheets serve to document what has been done and allow periodic review of earlier ideas to avoid overlooking previously identified concepts. Moreover, a written and visual record of design work helps establish ownership of patentable ideas.

The following materials aid in maintaining permanent records of design activities.

1. Worksheets (8-1/2 × 11 inches). Sheets can be either grid-lined or plain and should be three-hole punched for a notebook binder.

2. Pencils. A medium-grade pencil (F or HB) is adequate for most purposes.

3. Binder or envelope. Keep worksheets in a binder or envelope for reference.

3.5 Example: Exercise Bench

Design an exercise bench that can be used by those who lift weights for body fitness. This apparatus should be as versatile as possible and at the low end of the price range of exercise equipment. The contents of worksheets shown in **Sheets 1–3A** identify the problem in a typical manner.

First, give the title of the project and a brief problem statement to describe the problem better. Then list requirements and limitations and add sketches as necessary. You will have to list some requirements as questions for the time being, but in all cases make estimates and give sources for the answers (**Sheet 1**). Make estimates as you go

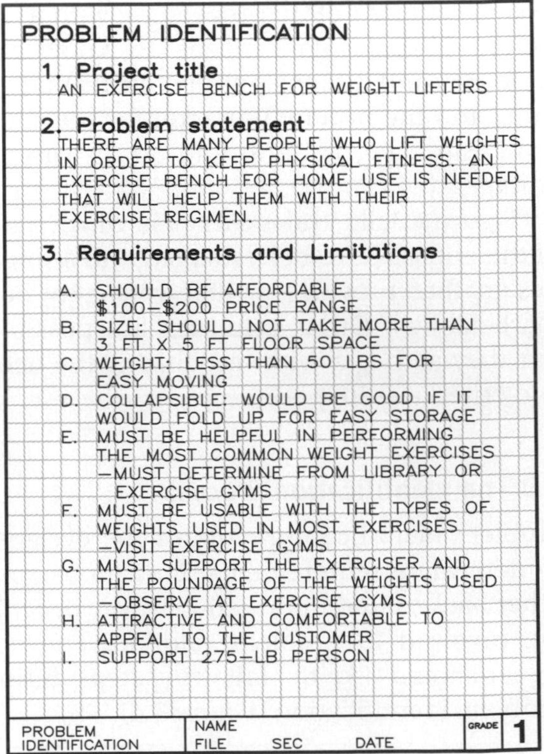

PROBLEM IDENTIFICATION

1. **Project title**
AN EXERCISE BENCH FOR WEIGHT LIFTERS

2. **Problem statement**
THERE ARE MANY PEOPLE WHO LIFT WEIGHTS IN ORDER TO KEEP PHYSICAL FITNESS. AN EXERCISE BENCH FOR HOME USE IS NEEDED THAT WILL HELP THEM WITH THEIR EXERCISE REGIMEN.

3. **Requirements and Limitations**

A. SHOULD BE AFFORDABLE $100–$200 PRICE RANGE
B. SIZE: SHOULD NOT TAKE MORE THAN 3 FT X 5 FT FLOOR SPACE
C. WEIGHT: LESS THAN 50 LBS FOR EASY MOVING
D. COLLAPSIBLE: WOULD BE GOOD IF IT WOULD FOLD UP FOR EASY STORAGE
E. MUST BE HELPFUL IN PERFORMING THE MOST COMMON WEIGHT EXERCISES —MUST DETERMINE FROM LIBRARY OR EXERCISE GYMS
F. MUST BE USABLE WITH THE TYPES OF WEIGHTS USED IN MOST EXERCISES —VISIT EXERCISE GYMS
G. MUST SUPPORT THE EXERCISER AND THE POUNDAGE OF THE WEIGHTS USED —OBSERVE AT EXERCISE GYMS
H. ATTRACTIVE AND COMFORTABLE TO APPEAL TO THE CUSTOMER
I. SUPPORT 275–LB PERSON

PROBLEM IDENTIFICATION | NAME | FILE | SEC | DATE | GRADE | 1

Sheet 1 The problem identification step gives the project a title, describes what the product will be used for, and lists basic requirements and limitations for the design.

along; for example, it must cost between $100 and $200; it must weigh less than 50 lbs; and it must at least support a person weighing 250 lbs. Give estimates as ranges of prices or weights rather than exact numbers. Use catalogs offering similar products as sources for prices, weights, and sizes.

Next, make a list of the questions that need answers. Follow each question with a source for its possible answer and give a preliminary answer. How many people exercise? What are their ages? Do they buy exercise equipment? What are the most popular weight exercises? You may obtain this type of information from interviews, product catalogs, the library, and sporting-goods stores.

Market considerations include the average income of a typical exerciser. How much does he or she spend on physical fitness per year? The opinions of sporting-goods dealers are helpful, and they should be able to direct you to other sources of information (**Sheet 2**).

Record the data that you gather by interviewing gym managers, looking at catalogs, and visiting sporting-goods stores to learn about the people who exercise and the equipment they use (**Sheet 3**). Determine the most popular weight exercises of those for whom this bench is to be designed by surveying users, coaches, and sporting-goods outlets. Sketch those exercises on a worksheet (**Sheet 3A**).

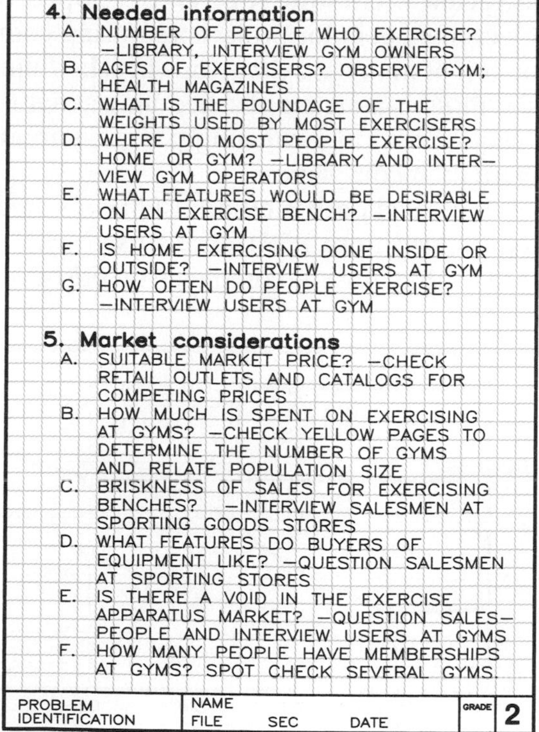

4. Needed information

A. NUMBER OF PEOPLE WHO EXERCISE? —LIBRARY, INTERVIEW GYM OWNERS
B. AGES OF EXERCISERS? OBSERVE GYM; HEALTH MAGAZINES
C. WHAT IS THE POUNDAGE OF THE WEIGHTS USED BY MOST EXERCISERS
D. WHERE DO MOST PEOPLE EXERCISE? HOME OR GYM? —LIBRARY AND INTER—VIEW GYM OPERATORS
E. WHAT FEATURES WOULD BE DESIRABLE ON AN EXERCISE BENCH? —INTERVIEW USERS AT GYM
F. IS HOME EXERCISING DONE INSIDE OR OUTSIDE? —INTERVIEW USERS AT GYM
G. HOW OFTEN DO PEOPLE EXERCISE? —INTERVIEW USERS AT GYM

5. Market considerations

A. SUITABLE MARKET PRICE? —CHECK RETAIL OUTLETS AND CATALOGS FOR COMPETING PRICES
B. HOW MUCH IS SPENT ON EXERCISING AT GYMS? —CHECK YELLOW PAGES TO DETERMINE THE NUMBER OF GYMS AND RELATE POPULATION SIZE
C. BRISKNESS OF SALES FOR EXERCISING BENCHES? —INTERVIEW SALESMEN AT SPORTING GOODS STORES
D. WHAT FEATURES DO BUYERS OF EQUIPMENT LIKE? —QUESTION SALESMEN AT SPORTING STORES
E. IS THERE A VOID IN THE EXERCISE APPARATUS MARKET? —QUESTION SALES—PEOPLE AND INTERVIEW USERS AT GYMS
F. HOW MANY PEOPLE HAVE MEMBERSHIPS AT GYMS? SPOT CHECK SEVERAL GYMS.

PROBLEM IDENTIFICATION | NAME FILE SEC DATE | GRADE | 2

Sheet 2 Continuation of problem identification for the exercise bench includes gathering information on market potential.

PROBLEM IDENTIFICATION

A. CHECK YELLOW PAGES FOR GYMS
—8 GYMS FOR POPULATION OF 100,000
—ONE GYM PER 12,500 PEOPLE

B. GYM MEMBERSHIP FOR STILLMAN'S GYM

YEAR	MEN	WOMEN
1998	75	20
1990	70	36
1992	110	70
2004	175	82
2006	180	120
2008	210	135

C. INTERVIEW RETAILERS OF EQUIPMENT
—3 DEALERS POSITIVE ABOUT BENCH
—2 DEALERS NEUTRAL
—1 DEALER NEGATIVE ABOUT PROSPECTS

D. AGES OF EXERCISERS (BY OBSERVATION)
—20% UNDER 20
—40% BETWEEN 20 AND 30
—30% BETWEEN 30 AND 50
—10% OVER 50

E. PRICES AT STORES

1.	COMPLEX MULTIUSE	$1000
2.	MEDIUM—RANGE EQUIPMENT	700
3.	LIGHTWEIGHT BENCHES	130
4.	WEIGHTS	100

F. TYPICAL BRANDS OF EQUIPMENT ON THE MARKET?
1. WEIDER
2. NAUTILUS
3. BODY WONDERFUL
4. HEALTH PLUS

PROBLEM IDENTIFICATION | NAME FILE SEC DATE | GRADE | 3

Sheet 3 This worksheet shows the data collected for use in designing the exercise bench.

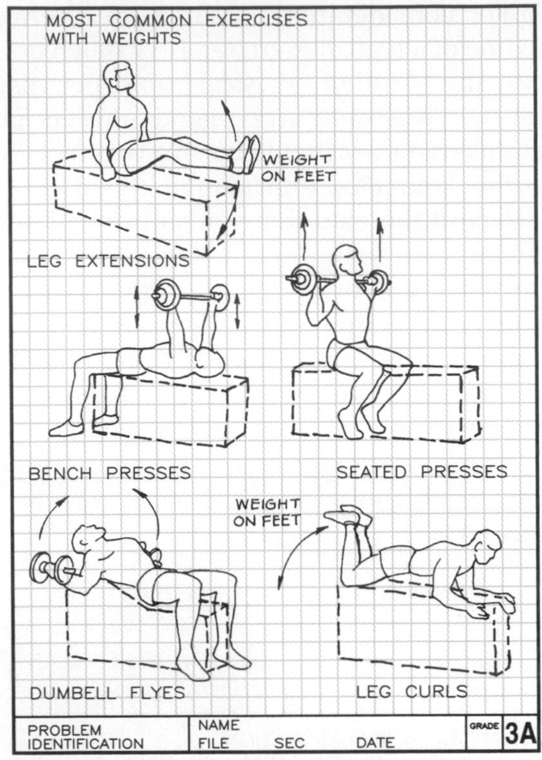

Sheet 3A These sketches illustrate some of the typical exercises with weights.

Think about costs and pricing the product even during problem identification. **Figure 3.6** shows how products may be priced from wholesale to retail, but these percentages vary by product. For instance, profit margins are smaller for food sales than furniture sales. If an item retails for $50, the production and overhead cost cannot be more than about $20 to maintain the necessary margins.

Data are easier to interpret if presented graphically (**Figure 3.7**). Thorough problem identification includes graphs, sketches, and schematics that enhance the communication of your findings.

Problem identification is not complete at this point. However, this example should give you a basic understanding of the process.

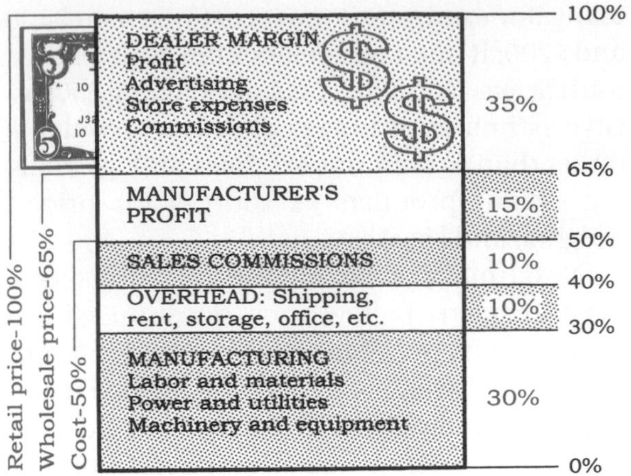

3.6 This chart shows the breakdown of costs involved in the retail price of a product.

3.6 Organization of Effort

The designer should prepare a schedule of required design activities after completing problem identification. The **project evaluation and review technique (PERT)**, developed by project managers for projects requiring coordination of many activities, aids in scheduling tasks. PERT is a means of scheduling activities in sequence and reviewing progress made toward their completion.

The **critical path method (CPM)** of scheduling evolved from PERT and is used with it. The tasks that must be completed before others

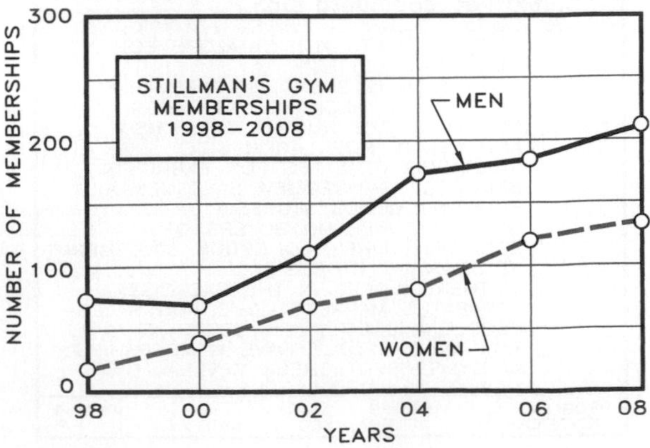

3.7 This graph describes visually the trends in potential customers for the exercise apparatus.

can begin are critical tasks and should be given priority. The critical path is the sequence of tasks requiring the longest time from start to finish and has the least flexibility. Activities not in the critical path receive less emphasis.

3.7 Planning Design Activities

The chart in **Figure 3.8** illustrates the steps involved in planning a job (project): (1) list the tasks on a form called a **Design Schedule and Progress Record**; (2) prepare an **Activities Network Diagram**, arranging the tasks in sequence; and (3) prepare an **Activity Sequence Chart** that graphs the tasks in the sequence shown in the network.

Design Schedule and Progress Record

The designer separates the job into tasks, numbers them, and lists them in the **Design Schedule and Progress Record (DS&PR)** without concern for their sequence (**Figure 3.9**). Next, the designer estimates the amount of time required for each task and enters it in the third column. The designer adjusts the amount of time for each task so that the total matches the time allotted for the job.

Activities Network

The designer prepares an **Activities Network (AN)** by arranging the tasks from the DS&PR in their proper sequence in either note or symbol form. The note form identifies activities by task name (**Figure 3.10**); the symbol form identifies activities by task number. Arrows connect activities, showing their sequence. Labels on the arrows indicate the amount of time needed to complete the activities. For example, the first activity in preparing the technical report is to assemble preliminary notes, which requires 0.5 hour (**Figure 3.10A**).

Dummy activities simply indicate connections between activities that involve no work and no time, because activities must be connected in the network. The two dummy activities (dashed lines) in **Figure 3.11** show sequential connections but no expenditure of time. In other words, the project data and the preliminary sketches and diagrams that were assembled were not needed to complete the draft of Chapter 1 but are available for later use in the project.

Design Schedule & Progress Record

TEAM 4 PROJECT PRODUCT DESIGN

WORK PERIODS 11 MAN HOURS 70 FINISHING DATE 4–15

JOB	ASSIGNMENT	Est. Hrs.	Act. Hrs.	PERCENT COMPLETE 0 20 40 60 80
7	WRITE REPORT–ALL	15		
6	BRAINSTORM–ALL	.5	1	
3	WRITE MFGRS–JHE	2		
10	GRAPH DATA–HLE	2		
5	MARKET ANALYSIS–DL	3	3	
12	COLLECT DATA–TT	2		

3.9 The Design Schedule and Progress Record (DS&PR) shows typical entries for a product design project.

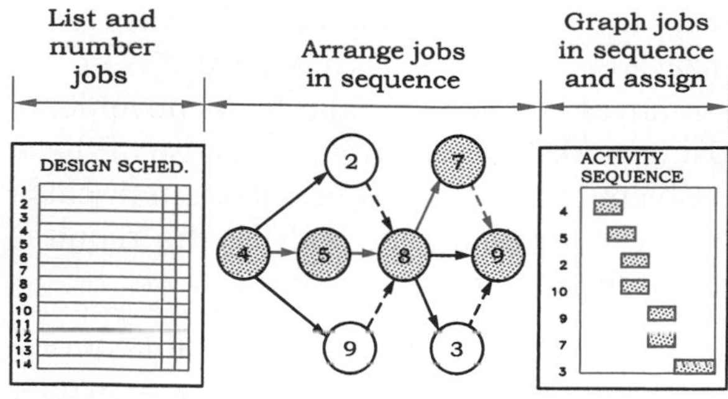

3.8 Planning and scheduling a project involves three steps.

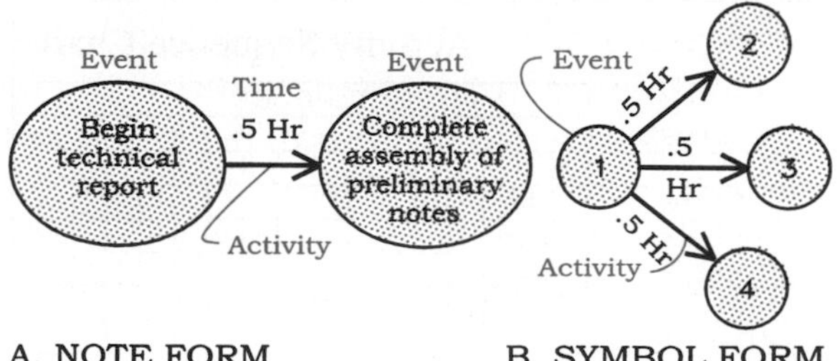

3.10 Two ways of preparing an Activities Network are (A) note form and (B) symbol form, both of which graphically arrange activities in sequence.

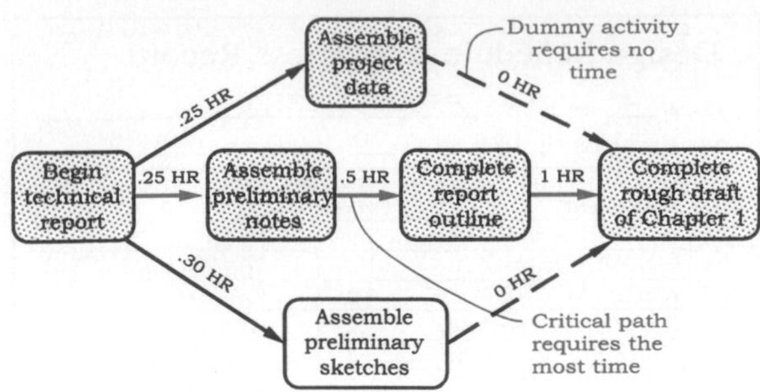

3.11 The critical path is the path from start to end of the project that requires the most time; shown here for a portion of the product design project.

The critical path identified in the Activities Network (**Figure 3.11**) is the longest time path from the project's beginning to its end. For the partial Activities Network shown, 1.75 hours are required to complete the draft of Chapter 1 of the technical report.

Activity Sequence Chart

Next, the designer lists the activities on the **Activity Sequence Chart (ASC)**, shown in **Figure 3.12**, which shows task numbers and team member assignments from the DS&PR. A bar graph shows the sequence of and the time allocated to each task. For example, 0.5 hour is scheduled for brainstorming, or task 2, from the DS&PR and is to be done first. The ASC also is the overall project schedule.

As work progresses, the designer graphs the status of each activity on the DS&PR (**Figure 3.9**). The actual hours required to complete tasks appear in column 4, for easy comparison with the original time estimates. When the extra time required becomes greater than that scheduled, the designer has to make adjustments in the ASC.

Activity Sequence Chart

PROJECT HOURS: 0 2 4 6 8 10 12 14 16

JOB	MEMBER
7	ALL
6	SMITH
3	PRISK
10	REED
5	ALL
12	FLYNN

3.12 The Activity Sequence Chart (ASC) contains tasks, assignments, and initial time estimates from the DS&PR and activity sequence from the Activity Network.

Problems

Problems should be presented on 8-1/2 × 11-in. paper, grid or plain. Notes, sketches, drawings, and graphs should be neatly executed. Written matter should be lettered on paper using 1/8-in. guidelines.

General

1. Identify a need for a design solution that could be completed as a short class assignment in less than 3 hours. Submit a proposal outlining this need and your general plan for its solution. Limit the written proposal to one typed or lettered page.

2. You are marooned on an uninhabited island with no tools or supplies. Identify the major problems that you would be required to solve. List the factors that you would have to consider before attempting a solution for each problem. For example: There is the need for food. Determine (a) available sources of food on island, (b) methods of gathering/catching, (c) methods of storing a food supply, and (d) method of cooking.

3. While you were walking to class today, what irritants or discomforts did you recognize? Were the sidewalks too narrow? Were the entrances to the buildings inconvenient? Using worksheets, identify the cause of these problems, write a problem statement (including need recognition), and list the requirements for and limitations on solutions.

4. Repeat Problem 3, but use irritants or discomforts found in your (a) living quarters, (b) classroom, (c) recreation facilities, (d) dining facilities, or (e) another environment with which you are familiar.

Product-Design Problems

5. Reconstruct the designer's approach to development of the tab-opening can. Even though the problem has been solved and its solution marketed, identify the need for the product and propose specifications for it. Is the existing solution the most appropriate one, or does your problem identification statement suggest others? Explain your answer.

6. Repeat problem 5 for a travel iron for pressing clothes.

7. List the problems involved in designing a motorized wheelbarrow.

8. Suppose that you recognize the need for a device that could be attached to a bicycle to allow it to be ridden over street curbs to sidewalk level. Identify the problems involved in determining the marketability of such a device.

9. Identify the problems you might encounter in developing a portable engineering travel kit to give engineers the capability of making engineering calculations, notes, sketches, and drawings. The kit might include a carrying case, calculator, computer, instruments, paper, reference material, and other accessories.

10. Use Section 3.7 as a guide and prepare a Design Schedule & Progress Record, an Activities Network, and an Activity Sequence Chart for the portion of your design project as assigned below:

- **A.** An overview of the entire project as you anticipate it at the present.
- **B.** The first three steps of the design process.
- **C.** The problem identification step only. Use as many sheets as necessary.

11. Develop your ability to make educated guesses and estimates regarding your world. For example, can you guess how many McDonald's hamburger stores there are in a neighboring city? If you looked in the Yellow Pages of your town, counted the McDonald's there, divided by the local population to find the population per store, would this factor help you with your estimate? Check a phone book from the neighboring city to see.

Using this approach, go to your library, look in the Yellow Pages, and determine the business outlets per 1000 of population for any of the following categories: banks, gas stations, movie theaters, bookstores, fitness centers, restaurants, department stores, or other businesses that are of interest to you. An alternate source could be your computer.

The ability to make intelligent guesses will make you a better engineer and entrepreneur.

12. Pricing products is similar to making estimates covered in problem 11. Use your common sense and instincts (that you may not realize you have) to explain why markup and profit margins vary among various types of products. Give your explanation in a brief outline form that will make your key points easy to process by the reader.

13. Where do you want to be in your career 10 years from now? Want to be successful? Want to be held in high esteem by your associates?

Identify the needs that must be met in order for you to make the achievements that you desire. List the steps that you could make that would enhance your chances of attaining your goals.

14. What disaster preparations should be made in advance for floods, fires, hurricanes, droughts, or terror? Identify the problems by speculating on the conditions that might arise and the preliminary steps that could be made to give the greatest degree of personal safety.

4

Preliminary Ideas

4.1 Introduction

Creativity is highest during the preliminary idea step of the design process because there are no limitations on being innovative, experimental, and daring. During subsequent steps of the design process, creativity diminishes and the need for information and facts increases. **Figure 4.1** shows this relationship between creativity and information accumulation during the design process.

High
Medium
Low
CREATIVITY VS. INFORMATION
Data and Information Development
Design and Creativity
Ideate Refine Analyze Decide Implem't

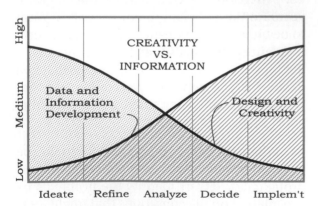

4.1 Creativity is highest during the early stages of the design process and information accumulation is highest at the end of the process.

A unique design is the digital tire gauge used for checking air pressure with greater accuracy and convenience (**Figure 4.2**). It is designed with a light in its nose to find the valve

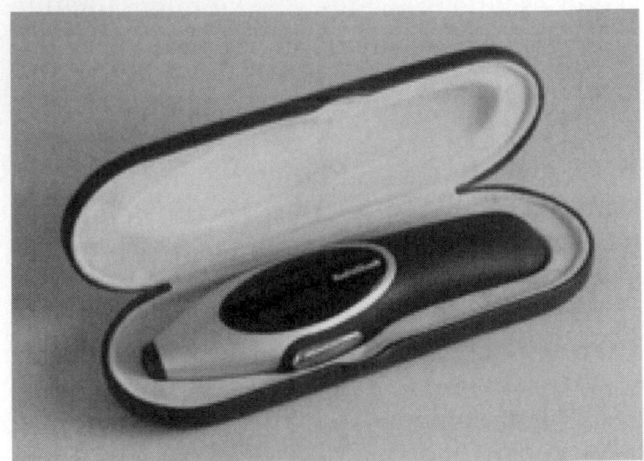

4.2 This battery-operated digital tire gauge was designed to fit in the glove compartment of an automobile. It has a light in its nose to make it easy to find the valve stem in poor light. *(Courtesy Bresslergroup and Measurement Specialties, Inc.)*

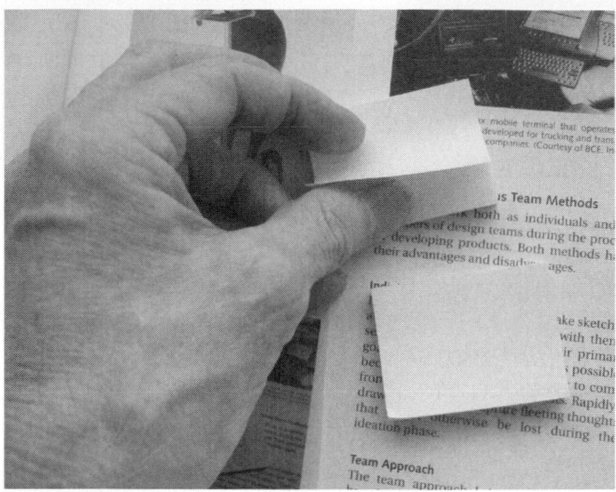

4.3 Unique and profitable design solutions are often brilliant in their simplicity, such as the stick-on note pads used to mark pages for easy access.

stem of a tire even in the dark. Designs such as this in the future will be limited only by our imagination in applying technology.

Although the stick-on tab in **Figure 4.3** is a less technical product, it is a unique design that prompts the question, "Why didn't I think of that?" This product, first developed by the 3M Corporation, became a very successful and profitable item and is found in most offices.

A product that is expected to affect pedestrian traffic is the Segway™ Human Transporter (**Figure 4.4**), a battery-powered vehicle that will truly give the individual "wheels." It has a speed of 12.5 mi/h, a range of 17 mi, and a passenger capacity of 250 lb.

A short time ago these products were considered futuristic fantasies. Progress in the future will be limited only by our imagination in applying technology.

4.2 Individual versus Team

Designers work both as individuals and as members of design teams during the process of developing products. Both methods have their advantages and disadvantages.

4.4 The Segway™ Human Transporter (HT) is expected to revolutionize pedestrian transportation. It is designed to move in response to leaning one's body forward or backward. *(Courtesy of Segway LLC.)*

Individual Approach

Designers working alone must make sketches and notes to communicate first with themselves and then with others. Their primary goal is to generate as many ideas as possible, because better ideas are more likely to come from long lists than from short lists. Rapidly drawn sketches can capture fleeting thoughts that might otherwise be lost during ideation.

Team Approach

The team approach brings diversity and a broad range of ideas to the design process, but along with it come problems of management and coordination. Groups perform better with a leader with the authority to guide their activities and make assignments.

Teams should alternate between individual and group work to take advantage of both approaches. For example, each team member

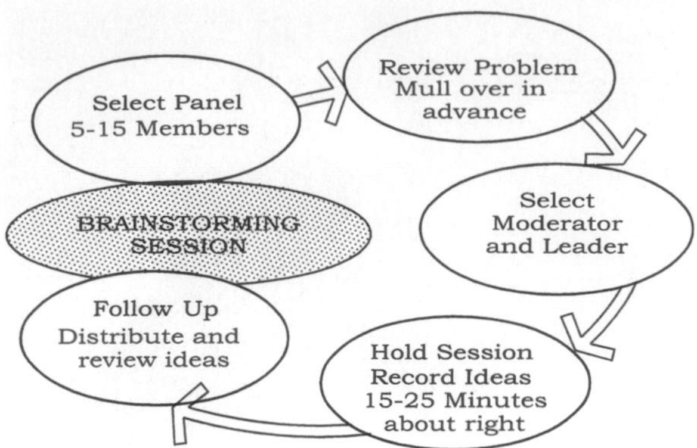

4.5 A plan of action is needed for the preliminary ideas step of the design process, which will probably involve most of the steps shown here.

could individually develop preliminary ideas, bring them to a team meeting, compare solutions, merge ideas, and return to individual work with a renewed outlook.

4.3 Plan of Action

The following steps are suggested for completing the preliminary ideas step of the design process: (1) hold brainstorming sessions (**Figure 4.5**), (2) prepare sketches and notes, (3) research background data, and (4) conduct surveys. Periodically reviewing notes and worksheets made during problem identification ensures that efforts will stay focused on the design objectives.

4.4 Brainstorming

Brainstorming is a problem-solving technique in which members of a group spontaneously contribute ideas. The best session is one that adheres to the following rules.

Rules of Brainstorming

The guidelines for a brainstorming session are as follows:*

1. **Criticism is ruled out.** Judgment of ideas must be withheld until later.
2. **Freewheeling is encouraged.** The wilder the idea, the better; it is easier to tame down than to think up. A good solution may emerge from a suggestion that was made as a joke.
3. **Quantity is wanted.** The larger the number of ideas, the greater will be the likelihood of useful ideas.
4. **Combination and improvement are sought.** Participants should seek ways of improving the ideas of others.

Brainstorming Session Organization The organization of a brainstorming session involves selecting the panel, becoming familiar with the problem, selecting a moderator and recorder, holding the session, and following up (**Figure 4.5**).

Panel Selection The optimum number of participants in a brainstorming session is 12 people. For diversity they should be people both with and without knowledge of the subject. Because supervisors may restrict the flow of ideas, panels should be composed of nonsupervisory professionals of similar status.

Preliminary Work An information sheet about the session should be given to panel members a couple of days before the session to allow ideas to incubate.

The Problem The problem to be brainstormed should be defined concisely. Instead of presenting the problem as "how to improve our campus," it should be presented by category, such as "how to improve student parking," or "how to improve food services."

The Moderator and Recorder The panel selects a moderator to be in charge of the session

*From Alex Osborn, *Applied Imagination*, NYC: Scribner, 1963.

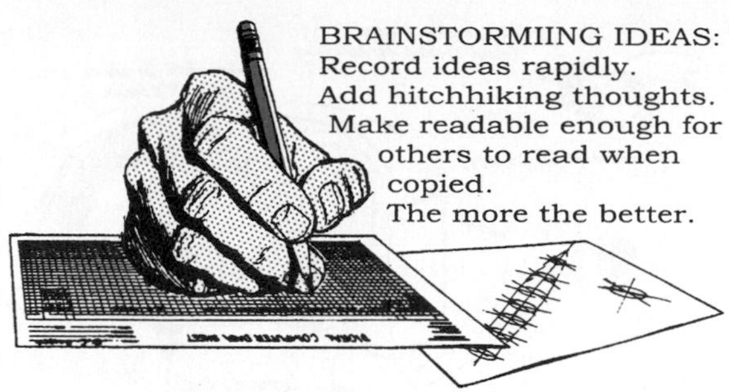
BRAINSTORMIING IDEAS:
Record ideas rapidly.
Add hitchhiking thoughts.
Make readable enough for
others to read when
copied.
The more the better.

4.6 The recorder should make a list of all brainstorming ideas during the session.

and a recorder to keep track of the ideas presented (**Figure 4.6**).

The Session The moderator introduces the problem and recognizes the first member holding up a hand to respond. The person responding should state an idea as briefly as possible. The moderator then recognizes the next person holding up a hand, and the process continues. A suggestion made by one member often stimulates ideas in others, who snap their fingers to signify that they want to "hitchhike" on the previous idea. This interaction is central to a brainstorming session.

The moderator's most important job is to keep the ideas flowing and to prevent participants from giving long, drawn-out responses that dampen the spontaneous and "fun" aspects of the session.

Length A session should move at a brisk pace and end when ideas slow to an unproductive rate. An effective session can last from a few minutes to an hour, but 20 minutes is considered about the best length.

Follow-up The recorder should reproduce the list of ideas gathered during the session and distribute them to the participants. As many as 100 ideas may be gathered during a 20-minute session. The designer should pare them down to those having the most merit.

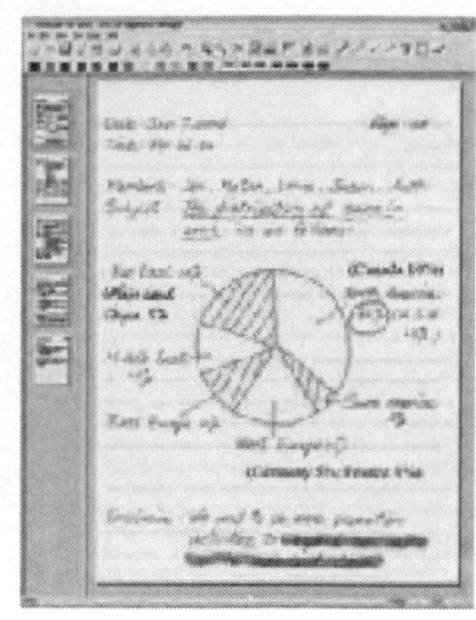

4.7 The DigiMemo A501 is a stand-alone device with storage capability that digitally captures and stores everything written or drawn with ink on ordinary paper, without the use of the computer and special paper. Then, handwritten notes can be viewed, edited, organized, and shared in Windows and transmitted as an e-mail. *(Courtesy of Solidtek USA.)*

4.5 Sketching and Notes

Sketching is an effective medium of design, its development, and its communication whether it is a simple part or a complex product. There are many instances when modification of designs and their descriptions are almost impossible without the ability to make simple and rapid freehand sketches. Sketching allows the designer's ideas to take form as three-dimensional pictorials or as two-dimensional views that are visual extensions of the thinking process. Technology has provided an alternative means of sketching on the DigiMemo notepad (**Figure 4.7**), which digitizes and preserves the designer's sketches for ease of transmission and revision by computer.

The sketches shown in **Figure 4.8** were several of many that were made in developing a design for a point-of-purchase pivoting-sphere scanner. **Figure 4.9** shows one of many sketches that were used in the design of the various components and systems of the space program, one of the most advanced design programs in history.

The preliminary ideas for the Transportable Uni-Lodge (**Figure 4.10**) illustrate the importance of sketches in developing and communicating ideas. These ideas propose that the Uni-Lodge be transported by helicopter to

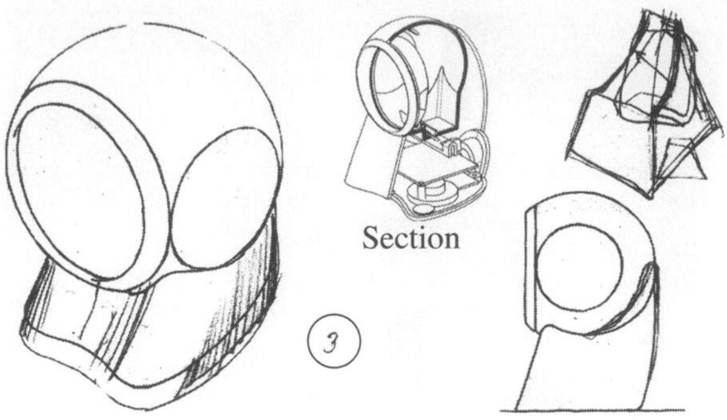

4.8 These preliminary sketches were made during the design of a point-of-purchase pivoting-sphere scanner. *(Courtesy of Bresslergroup and Metrologic Instruments.)*

previously unreachable areas and lowered onto the site or the water. Its retractable legs can be equipped with pontoons, allowing it to float. Additional features are noted on the sketches.

Another concept is a self-contained pipe layer (**Figure 4.11**) for laying irrigation pipe in

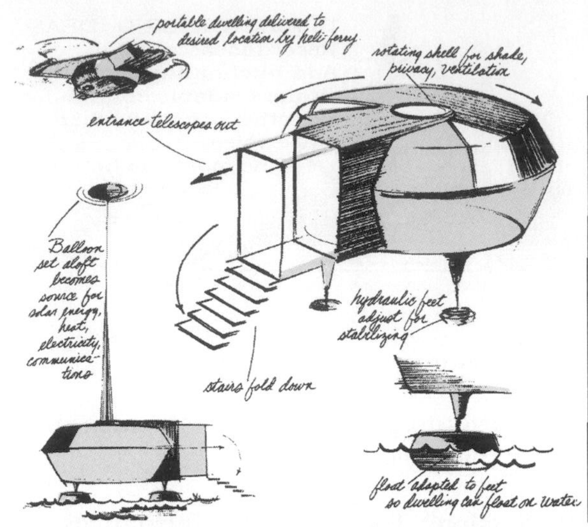

4.10 These preliminary sketches and notes depict a Transportable Uni-Lodge, a mobile dwelling of the future. *(Courtesy of Lippincott and Margulies, Inc., and Charles Bruning Company.)*

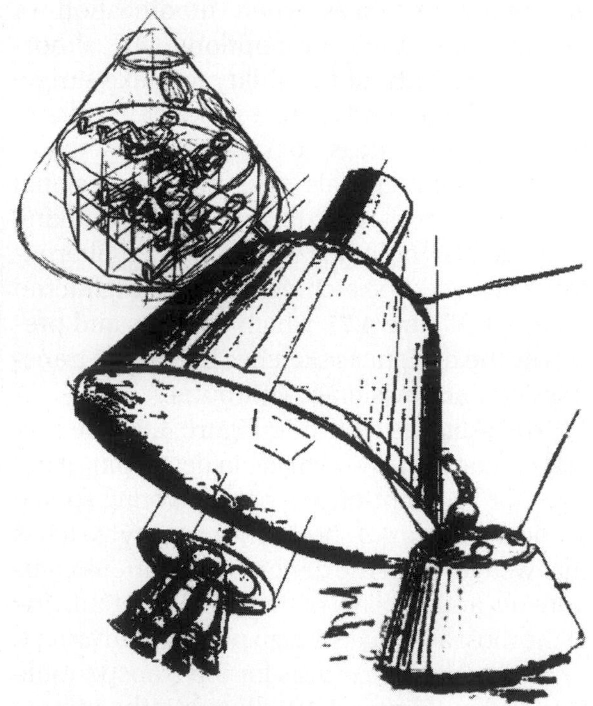

4.9 Sketches are important to the development solutions of the most complex engineering and scientific designs. These sketches illustrate preliminary ideas for the manned space capsule. *(Courtesy of NASA.)*

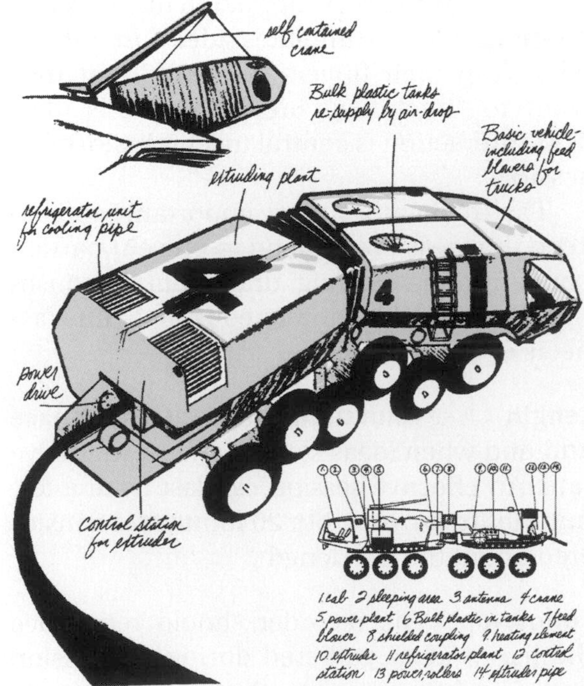

4.11 These sketches show a designer's ideas for a self-contained pipe layer for laying irrigation pipe in large tracts of desert areas. *(Courtesy of Donald Desky Associates, Inc. and Charles Bruning Company.)*

4.12 A flotilla of classrooms controlled from a master tracking center by lasers and computer relays is illustrated by sketches. *(Courtesy of Raymond Loewy/William Snaith, Inc. and Charles Bruning Company.)*

desert areas. The tractor has a cab, sleeping accommodations, radio equipment, power plant, and bulk storage tanks for plastic. The van consists of an extrusion machine, a refrigeration unit, and a control station. The pipe layer transports bulk plastic and machinery that can extrude and lay approximately 2 mi of pipe from each pair of storage tanks. Empty tanks are discarded and replaced by full tanks that are air-dropped to the crew.

Sketches in **Figure 4.12** describe a teaching flotilla, mobile floating classrooms that are connected to a master tracking center from which programs are transmitted by lasers and satellite relays. Each helio-hover craft is equipped with advanced technology including two-dimensional and three-dimensional projectors and televisions. The computerized tracking center can transmit presentations to six different floating classrooms.

The concepts in these examples could not have been developed without the use of sketching as a medium of design and as a means of thinking. Rapid sketches capture a person's thought process, imagination, and creativity in a form that can be shared by others.

4.6 Sketching Application

The previous sketches ranged from simplistic to complicated, but they are typical of the drawings used in creating designs for automobiles, spacecraft, and all other products. Remember that sketching is the medium of developing concepts and details from idea to final design throughout the design process. The designer must develop numerous preliminary solutions to design problems, most of which will be rapidly drawn freehand sketches (**Figure 4.13**).

A series of sketches (**Figures 4.14** through **4.17**) illustrate how sketches are developed from rough sketches to more sophisticated drawings as the preliminary idea process progresses. The product illustrated is a unique design for a shoe brush.

Figure 4.14 shows how rapidly drawn sketches are used as an extension of the brainstorming process to develop initial concepts

4.13 The designer uses sketching as a primary means of developing preliminary design concepts. *(Courtesy I.N. Incorporated.)*

4.14 Design concepts of the shoe brush are brainstormed and sketched as two- and three-dimensional views. *(Courtesy Bresslergroup and Shoe Store Supplies.)*

of the shoe brush. The designer uses sketches to communicate with himself.

Figure 4.15 illustrates another preliminary but better developed concept for the shoe brush. Three-dimensional sketches are used by the designer to develop his design and communicate his ideas to others. Notes are used to clarify significant features. Third and fourth design concepts are sketched in **Figures 4.16** and **4.17**, respectively.

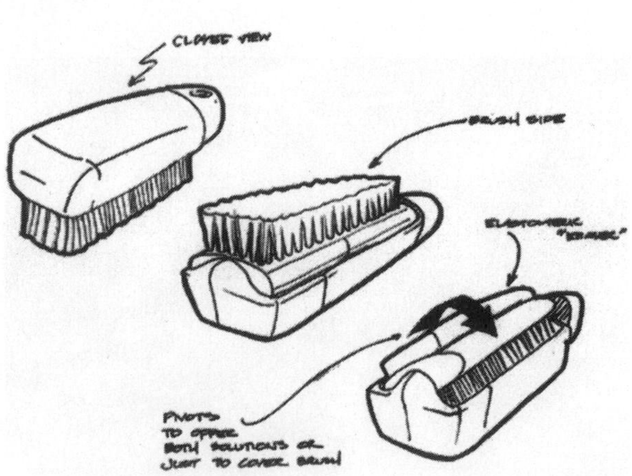

4.15 Second design concept of the shoe brush is sketched in three-dimensional views. *(Courtesy Bresslergroup and Shoe Store Supplies.)*

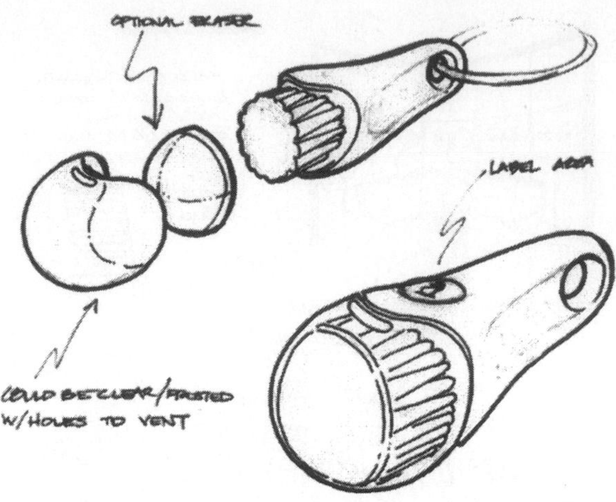

4.16 A third design concept of the shoe brush is sketched in three-dimensional views. *(Courtesy Bresslergroup and Shoe Store Supplies.)*

The final design for the shoe brush is shown as a prototype in **Figure 4.18**. The concepts shown here are but a few of the many sketches that were made during the preliminary phase of the design process. The more concepts you have to choose from, the better are your chances of attaining the best design solution. Most preliminary ideas begin as freehand sketches but soon evolve into computer drawings.

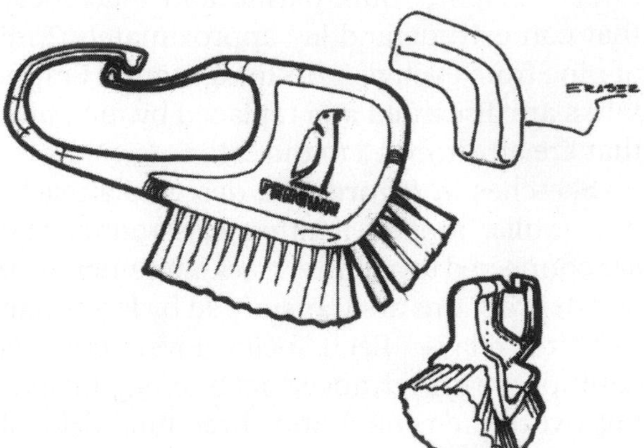

4.17 Another design concept of the shoe brush is sketched in three-dimensional views. *(Courtesy Bresslergroup and Shoe Store Supplies.)*

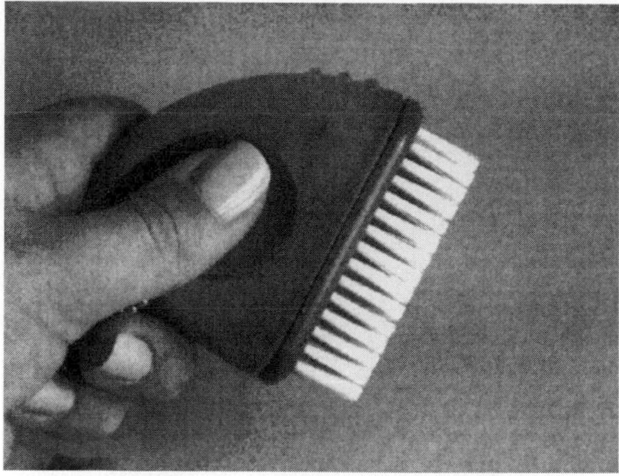

4.18 The final design for the shoe brush is shown here in product form. *(Courtesy Bresslergroup and Shoe Store Supplies.)*

4.7 Quickie Design

Let's assume that we recognize the need for a product to protect walls and doorknobs where doors swing into walls. First, we make sketches on a worksheet to identify the problem and its geometry (**Sheet 1**). If we decide to develop a floor-mounted doorstop, we may begin with sketches (made by hand or by computer) of a design that begins as a basic block, which will do the job (**Sheet 2**). However, we can do better than that; we make additional sketches to refine and develop the design until we find a suitable and marketable solution.

We make more drawings (**Sheet 3**) to develop the doorstop's details, which we show to others for consultation and evaluation. **Sheet 4** shows other solutions to this problem that are products already being marketed. An example of a wall-mounted stop on the market is one that serves as a bumper

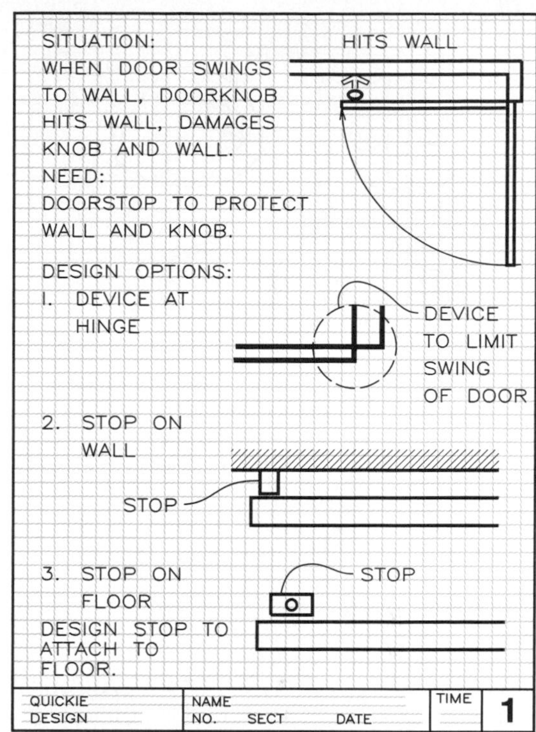

Sheet 1 This worksheet of sketches and notes identifies the need for a device to prevent damage caused by a door swinging into a wall.

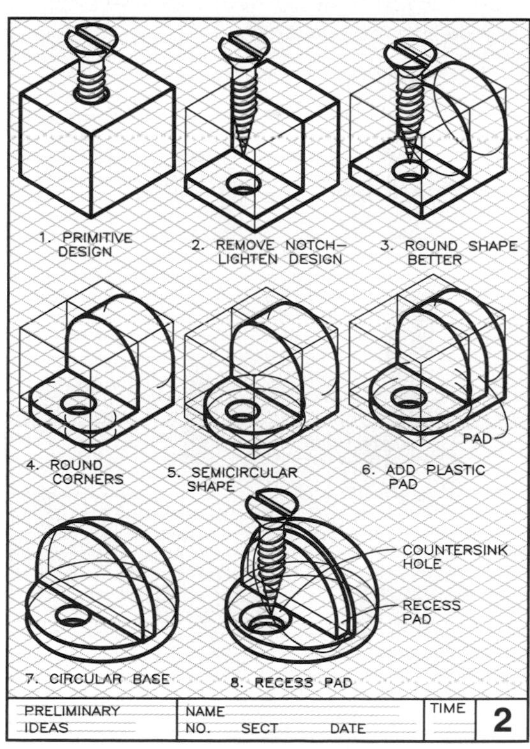

Sheet 2 A series of detailed sketches illustrates the evolution of the doorstop design.

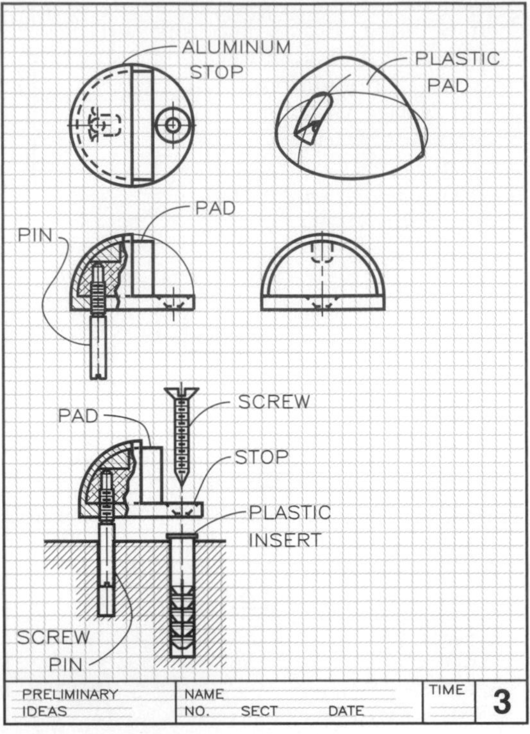

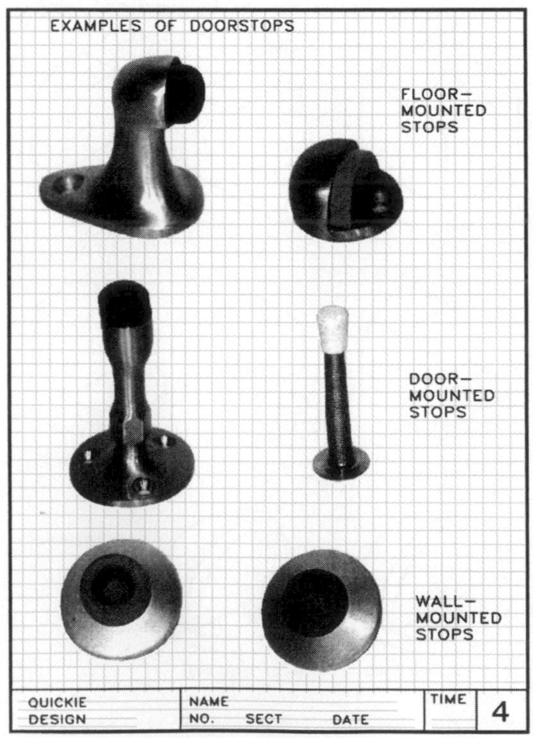

Sheet 3 Detailed sketches are used to refine the design and clarify it for others.

Sheet 4 The doorstops shown here are examples of some that are available on today's market.

4.19 An example of a solution to the doorstop problem that is on the market. It attaches to the wall, where it is struck by the doorknob, preventing wall damage.

for the doorknob (**Figure 4.19**). These products were developed in a similar manner, by designers using graphics as the medium of design.

4.8 Background Information

One way of gathering preliminary ideas is to look for existing products and designs that are similar to the one being considered. Several sources of background information include magazines, patents, and consultants (**Figure 4.20**).

Magazines

Articles in both general and technical magazines often present unique designs, complete with drawings and photographs. Advertisements in these magazines may give helpful information on materials and innovative devices. There are various magazines that specialize in most product areas that your librarian can help you find as a reference.

4.20 The gathering of background information is helpful and necessary to the development of preliminary ideas.

Patents

Patents from the U.S. Patent Office illustrate the details of all designs that were granted a patent. The designer can use them to understand competing products better and to ensure that there is no infringement on existing patents.

Consultants

Complex projects may require specialists in manufacturing, electronics, materials, and instrumentation. Manufacturers' representatives also provide valuable assistance with projects related to their companies' products. Having no knowledge of a project at the outset can prove to be an advantage, since a fresh perspective is what is needed.

4.9 Opinion Surveys

Designers need to know the attitudes of consumers about a new product at the preliminary design stage. Is there a need for the product? Are consumers excited about the prospects for a particular product being designed? Will they buy the product? What features do they like or dislike? What price range would be acceptable to them? What do retailers think it will sell for? Does size, weight, or color matter?

For a survey to be of value, the population for whom the product is being developed should be identified. Is it homeowners, high school males, or single women? A selected sample of the population can be surveyed by a personal interview, telephone survey, or mail questionnaire.

The Personal Interview

A personal interview survey should be organized to obtain and summarize reliable responses quickly and easily. For this reason, questions should be true/false or multiple choice for ease of tabulation.

Interviewers should introduce themselves, explain the purpose of the interview, and ask for permission to proceed. They should make the interview brief, record responses, and thank the interviewee for participating.

The Telephone Interview

If the opinions of the general public are desired, interviewers can talk to people selected from the telephone book. If opinions from a certain group—say, sporting-goods retailers—are needed, the Yellow Pages provide prospective interviewees.

The Mail Questionnaire

An economical method of contacting a large number of people in many locations is by mail questionnaire. To test the suitability of questions to be asked, the questionnaire can be mailed to a small group of people for their response as a test. The final questionnaire should be mailed to at least three times as many people as the number of responses desired. Inserting a self-addressed, stamped envelope will increase responses.

4.10 Preliminary Ideas: Exercise Bench

We introduced the design of an exercise bench in Chapter 3, where we took it through the problem identification step. Recall that it is to be used by those who lift weights to

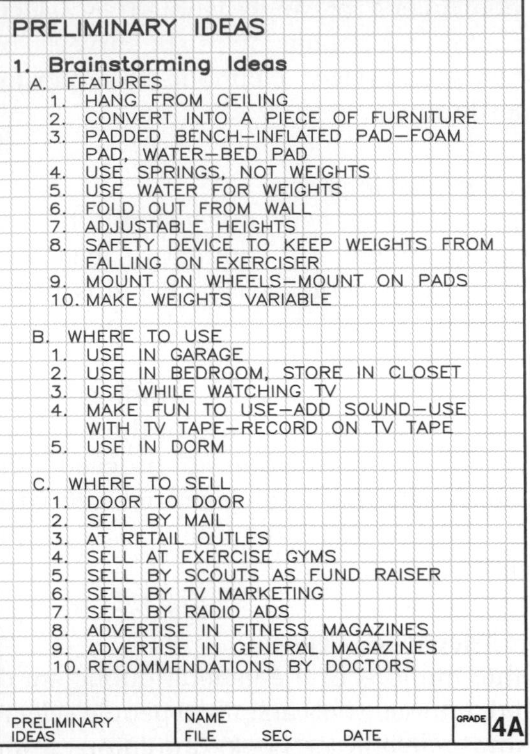

PRELIMINARY IDEAS

1. Brainstorming Ideas

A. FEATURES
1. HANG FROM CEILING
2. CONVERT INTO A PIECE OF FURNITURE
3. PADDED BENCH—INFLATED PAD—FOAM PAD, WATER-BED PAD
4. USE SPRINGS, NOT WEIGHTS
5. USE WATER FOR WEIGHTS
6. FOLD OUT FROM WALL
7. ADJUSTABLE HEIGHTS
8. SAFETY DEVICE TO KEEP WEIGHTS FROM FALLING ON EXERCISER
9. MOUNT ON WHEELS—MOUNT ON PADS
10. MAKE WEIGHTS VARIABLE

B. WHERE TO USE
1. USE IN GARAGE
2. USE IN BEDROOM, STORE IN CLOSET
3. USE WHILE WATCHING TV
4. MAKE FUN TO USE—ADD SOUND—USE WITH TV TAPE—RECORD ON TV TAPE
5. USE IN DORM

C. WHERE TO SELL
1. DOOR TO DOOR
2. SELL BY MAIL
3. AT RETAIL OUTLES
4. SELL AT EXERCISE GYMS
5. SELL BY SCOUTS AS FUND RAISER
6. SELL BY TV MARKETING
7. SELL BY RADIO ADS
8. ADVERTISE IN FITNESS MAGAZINES
9. ADVERTISE IN GENERAL MAGAZINES
10. RECOMMENDATIONS BY DOCTORS

PRELIMINARY IDEAS	NAME FILE SEC DATE	GRADE	4A

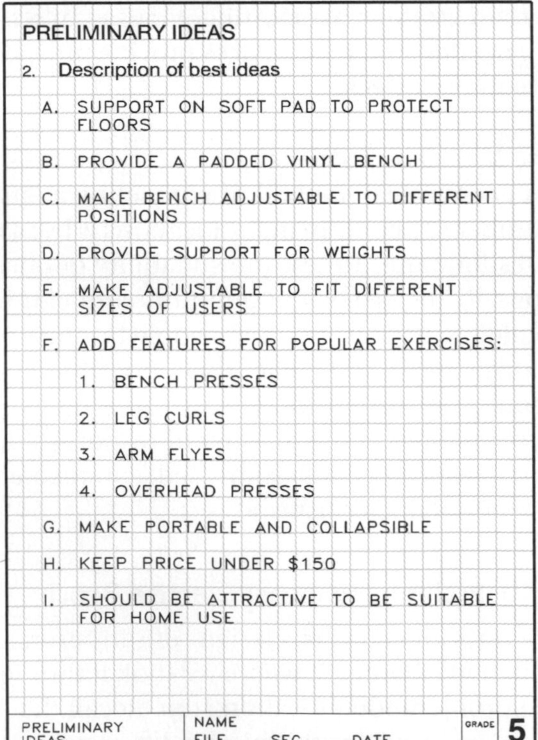

PRELIMINARY IDEAS

2. Description of best ideas

A. SUPPORT ON SOFT PAD TO PROTECT FLOORS

B. PROVIDE A PADDED VINYL BENCH

C. MAKE BENCH ADJUSTABLE TO DIFFERENT POSITIONS

D. PROVIDE SUPPORT FOR WEIGHTS

E. MAKE ADJUSTABLE TO FIT DIFFERENT SIZES OF USERS

F. ADD FEATURES FOR POPULAR EXERCISES:

1. BENCH PRESSES
2. LEG CURLS
3. ARM FLYES
4. OVERHEAD PRESSES

G. MAKE PORTABLE AND COLLAPSIBLE

H. KEEP PRICE UNDER $150

I. SHOULD BE ATTRACTIVE TO BE SUITABLE FOR HOME USE

PRELIMINARY IDEAS	NAME FILE SEC DATE	GRADE	5

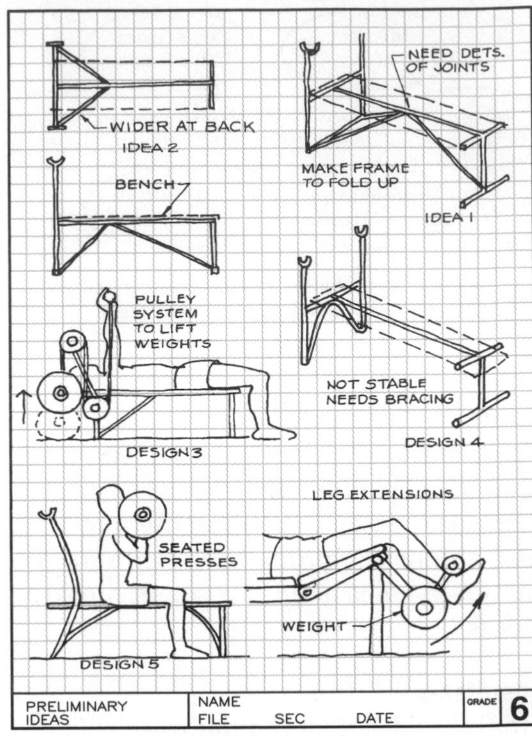

Sheet 4A Ideas gathered during a brainstorming session are listed on a worksheet for future reference.

Sheet 5 The best of the brainstorming ideas are selected and summarized for further development.

Sheet 6 Preliminary concepts for the exercise bench are shown as sketches and notes.

maintain body fitness. This apparatus should be versatile and at the low end of the price range for exercise equipment.

Now, to apply the preliminary ideas step of the design process, hold a brainstorming session with team members to generate and record ideas on a worksheet (**Sheet 4A**). Then, select the better ideas, list their features, and summarize them on a worksheet (**Sheet 5**), even if they have more features than you could possibly use in a single design. The reason is to make sure that you do not forget or lose any concepts.

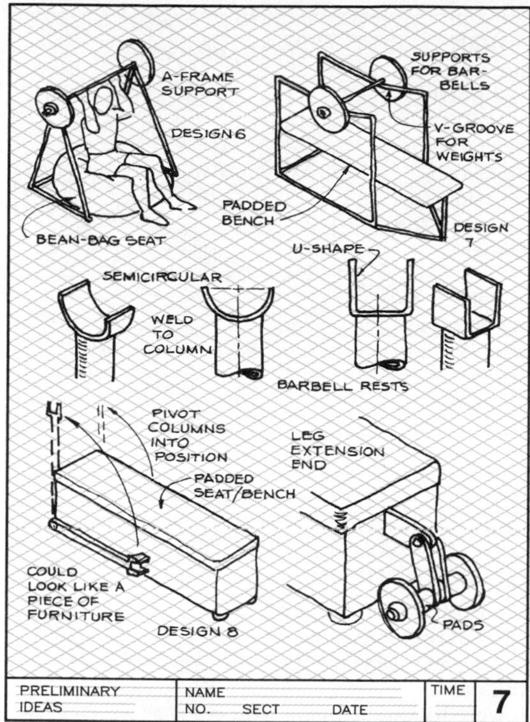

Sheet 7 Sketches and notes describe additional ideas of the exercise bench.

Using rapid freehand sketching techniques, such as orthographic views and three-dimensional pictorial sketches, sketch ideas on worksheets (**Sheet 6**). Note on the drawings any ideas or questions that come to mind while you sketch. Do not erase and modify your sketches; instead, make new sketches that incorporate revisions and modifications. By so doing, you will be able to review your thinking process from idea to idea. You should occasionally go back to previous steps to be sure that usable concepts have not been overlooked.

In **Sheet 7**, note the adaptation of ideas from various types of benches and exercise techniques. A number identifies each idea.

Problems

Additional sketches can be made of specific details of each design: connections, fabrication details, padding, and so forth.

Sketching Problems

Concepts for products are shown in the sketches on the following pages. Make orthographic sketches of the individual parts as if you were the designer, following the guidelines given in each figure. Some of these products have details that are unclear. You must exercise your creativity, judgment, and experience to reveal the necessary details. Give thought as to how you could improve, simplify, or economize on these concepts as you progress.

Design 1: Tool post assembly. This tool post assembly holds the cutting tool in position within the slot of the post when the screw is tightened. The tool rests on the rocker, which is dished to conform to the arc of the wedge. Make sketches of the parts as specified in the figure.

Design 2: Pulley assembly. This assembly of parts is used to keep the proper tension in the belt that engages the circular pulley. Follow the details given in the figure.

Design 3: Pipe roll. Make orthographic sketches of the parts of the pipe roll in accordance with the specifications in the illustration.

Design 4: Chisel-sharpening guide. Sketch the details of the sharpening guide to clarify its details. Follow the instructions given in the figure.

Design 5: Tool holder. This tool holder supports tools that are held in place by two square-head screws. Make sketches of the parts of the holder as specified in the figure.

Design 6: Column anchor design. Design an anchor in accordance with the specifications given in the illustration.

DESIGN 1: TOOL POST

The post assembly holds a cutting tool in place to cut cylinders on a lathe. The screw holds the tool in place on the wedge that fits in the rocker which is dished out. Make sketches of the parts on size A sheets.

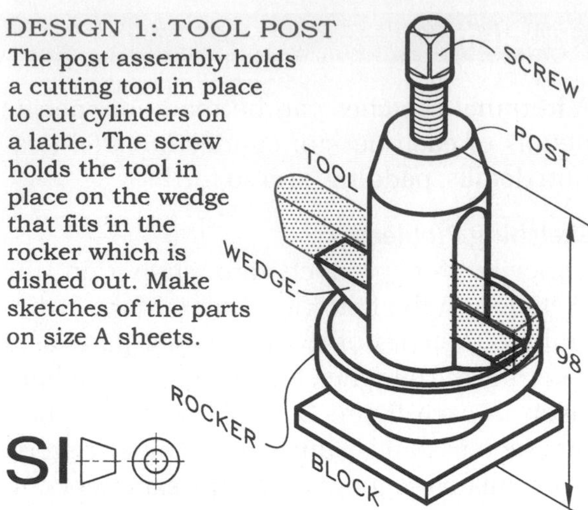

DESIGN 3: PIPE ROLL

Make sketches of of the parts of the pipe roll. Determine the unspecified dimensions as if you were the designer.

Pipe rolls support pipes while allowing them to expand and contract.

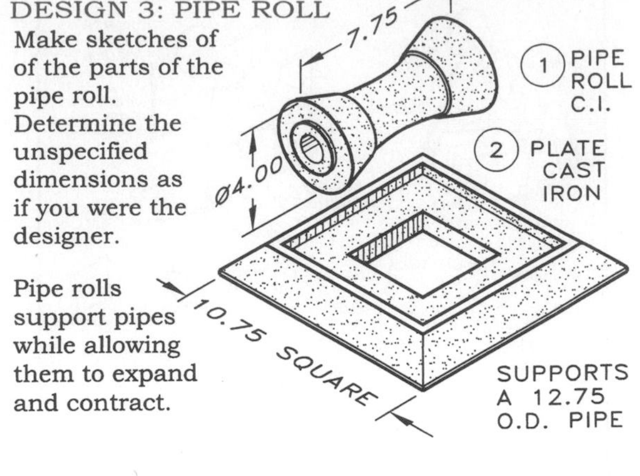

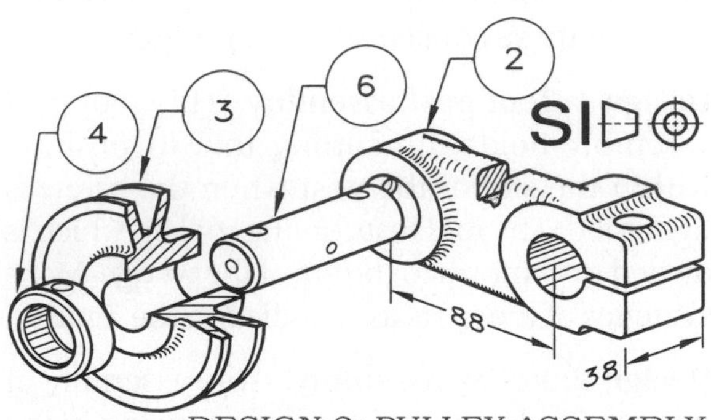

DESIGN 2: PULLEY ASSEMBLY

Sketch views of the parts of this assembly on size A sheets. The shaft has a diameter of 25 and the pulley has an outside diameter of 100.

DESIGN 4: CHISEL-SHARPENING GUIDE

Make sketches of the parts of the sharpening guide on size A sheets. Develop its details as if you were its designer.

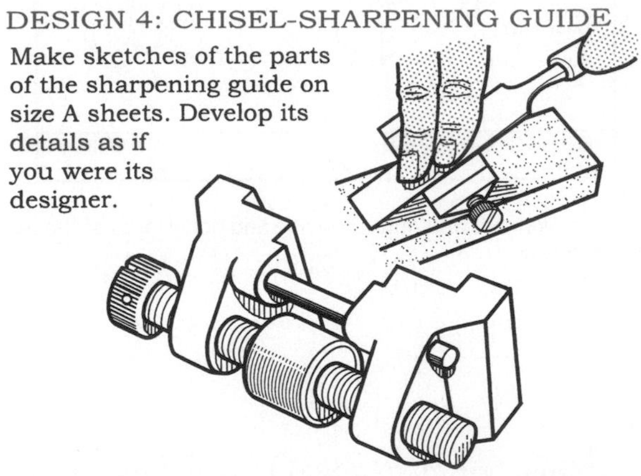

Design 7: Aircraft socket casting. Sketch views of the socket in accordance with the given instructions. There will be a little creativity involved.

Design 8: Aircraft bracket casting. Sketch views of the symmetrical bracket that will be held in place with three bolts. Figure out where the bolt holes are meant be be, and draw descriptive views on a size A sheet.

Creativity Problems

Your most underexercised muscle is your creativity muscle. Get some exercise! Present your solutions on 81/2 × 11-in. paper, grid or

DESIGN 5: TOOL HOLDER

Sketch views of the parts of this tool holder on size A sheets. Play the role of the designer of the holder's details that are unclear. Learn to sketch rapidly.

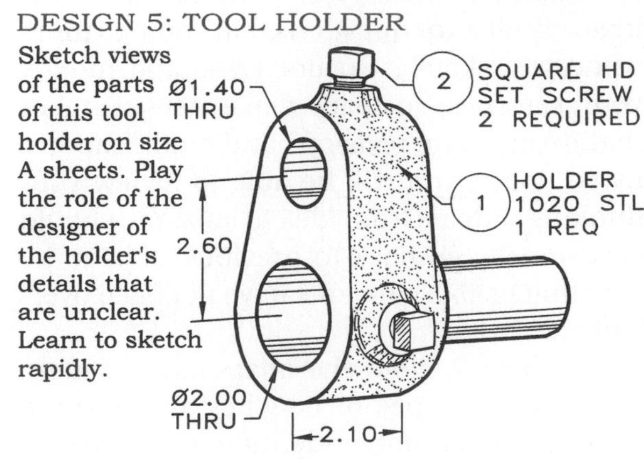

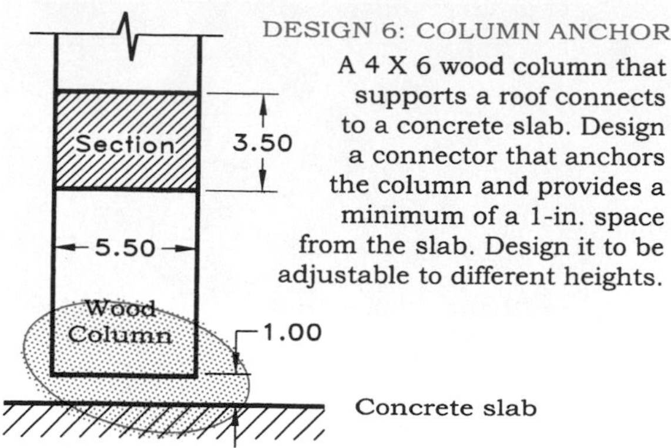

DESIGN 6: COLUMN ANCHOR

A 4 X 6 wood column that supports a roof connects to a concrete slab. Design a connector that anchors the column and provides a minimum of a 1-in. space from the slab. Design it to be adjustable to different heights.

DESIGN 7: LEVER BASE

This aluminum lever base will be used in an aircraft. Make orthographic sketches of it based on its proportions on a size A sheet. The 0.7-in.DIA hole is a through hole. Six screw holes will be drilled to anchor it. Can you locate them?

plain. All notes, sketches, drawings, and graphs should be neat and accurate. Written matter should be legibly lettered, using 1/8-in. guidelines.

9. Select one or more of the following items and list as many of their uses as possible: (a) empty vegetable cans (3-in. diameter by 5 in.), (b) 2,000 sheets of 8-1/2 × 11-in. bond paper, (c) 1 cu yd of dirt, (d) three empty oil drums (24-in. diameter by 36 in.), (e) a load of egg cartons, (f) 25 bamboo poles (10 ft. long), (g) 10 old tires, or (h) old newspapers.

10. If you were going to select an ideal team to develop an engineering solution to a problem, what team member characteristics would you look for? Explain.

11. What are the advantages and disadvantages of working independently on a project? Of working as a member of a team? Explain and give examples in which each approach would have the advantage.

12. Develop a questionnaire to determine the public's attitude toward a particular product of your selection. Explain how you would tabulate the responses to the questionnaire.

DESIGN 8: AIRCRAFT BRACKET CASTING

This unfinished aluminum casting will attach to an aircraft member and support a cylindrical part with a diameter of 0.6 in. Sketch views of the bracket on a size A sheet and locate two holes through both flanges at the right and a 0.3-in. DIA hole through the lug at the upper left end.

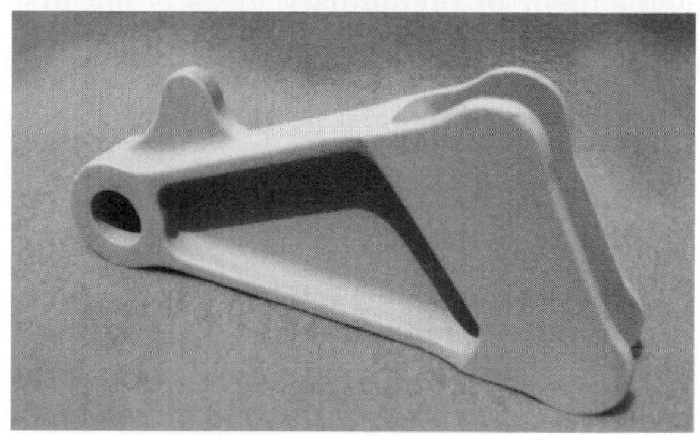

13. Organize a group of classmates and hold a brainstorming session to identify problems in need of solutions. Make a list of the ideas.

5 Refinement

5.1 Introduction

Refinement of preliminary ideas is the first departure from unrestricted creativity and imagination. The designer must now give primary consideration to function, costs, and practicality.

This step of the design process calls for the designer to make scale drawings with instruments to check dimensions and geometry that cannot be accurately measured in unscaled sketches. However, it is unnecessary to fully dimension these drawings. Descriptive geometry has its greatest application as a design tool in the idea refinement step of the design process.

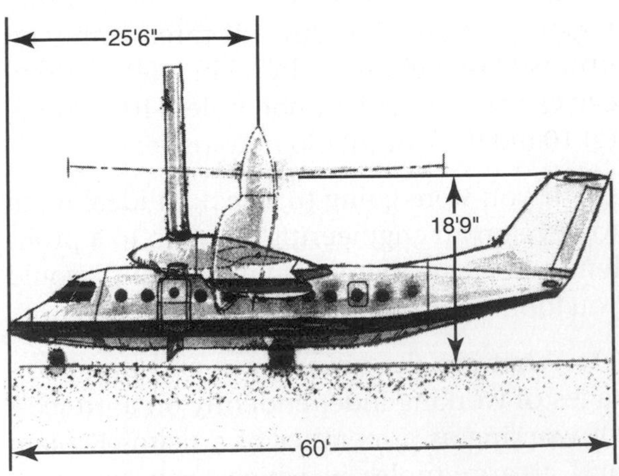

5.1 This scale drawing gives several overall dimensions to describe a helicopter body. It is important that refinement drawings be accurately drawn to scale; only major dimensions need be given on the drawing. (*Courtesy of Bell Helicopter Textron.*)

5.2 Physical Properties

In refining an idea it is important to determine the product's physical properties. An example of a refinement drawing is the profile of a helicopter showing its basic geometry and seat positions (**Figure 5.1**). These dimensions are based on the dimensions of the ultimate user, the average-size person.

Although most refinement drawings will be two-dimensional drawings on which dimensions can be accurately scaled and compared,

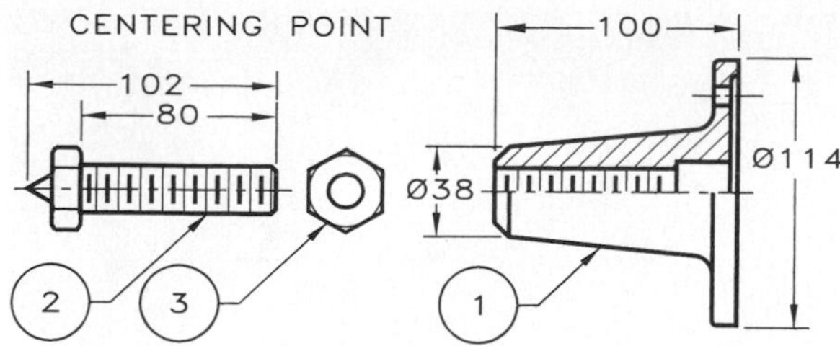

5.2 These views of a centering point are drawn to scale with only primary dimensions given for analysis and evaluation. Most refinement drawings are two-dimensional orthographic views.

three-dimensional drawings can also be used. **Figure 5.2** is an example of two-dimensional orthographic views drawn to scale, so the centering point can be measured on the drawing with only its primary dimensons given.

The configuration of a spacecraft is refined in the same manner as are simpler designs, by beginning with orthographic views, as shown in **Figure 5.3**. The computer is a significant aid to the designer in taking the refinement a step further. Mechanisms with moving parts can be made to operate on the computer's monitor to test their operation. In **Figure 5.4**, the refinement views of three smoke-detector designs are drawn as computer models for ease of comparison. The final design of the smoke detector rendered by computer as a three-dimensional exploded assembly is shown in **Figure 5.5**.

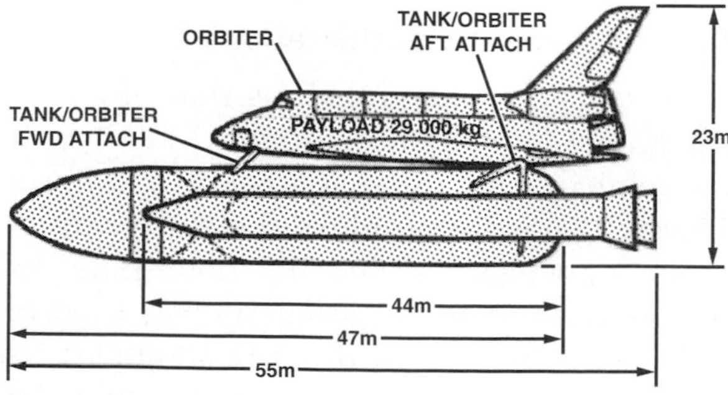

5.3 A two-dimensional, orthographic drawing of the configuration of an aircraft, the space shuttle vehicle. *(Courtesy of NASA.)*

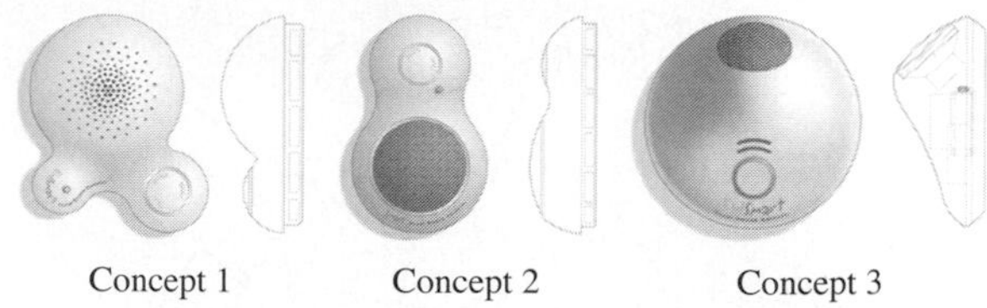

5.4 Two-dimensional orthographic refinement renderings of the Vocal Smoke Detector are created for client presentation. *(Courtesy of Bresslergroup and Kidsmart.)*

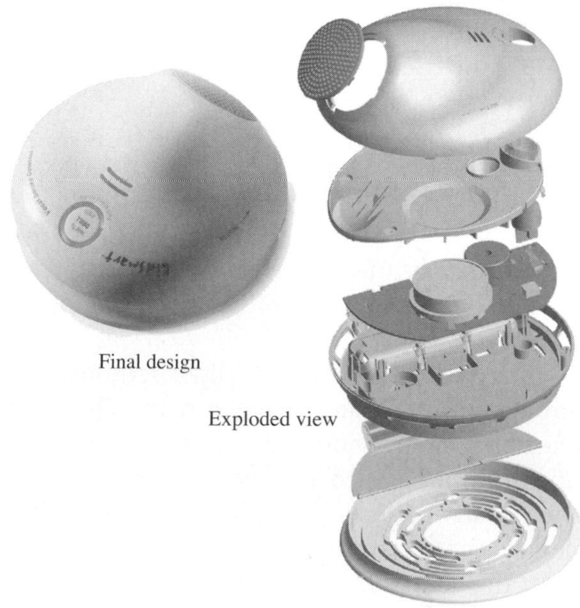

5.5 A three-dimensional view exploded by computer illustrates the Kidsmart Vocal Smoke Detector, which has been honored by *Popular Mechanics* and *CES Innovation. (Courtesy of Bresslergroup and Kidsmart.)*

5.3 Application of Descriptive Geometry

Descriptive geometry is the study of points, lines, and surfaces in three-dimensional space, which are the geometric elements that make up all forms. Before descriptive geometry can be applied, the designer must draw orthographic views to scale, from which auxiliary views can be projected. **Figure 5.6** shows how descriptive geometry is used to determine the clearance between a hydraulic cylinder and the fender of an automobile, where

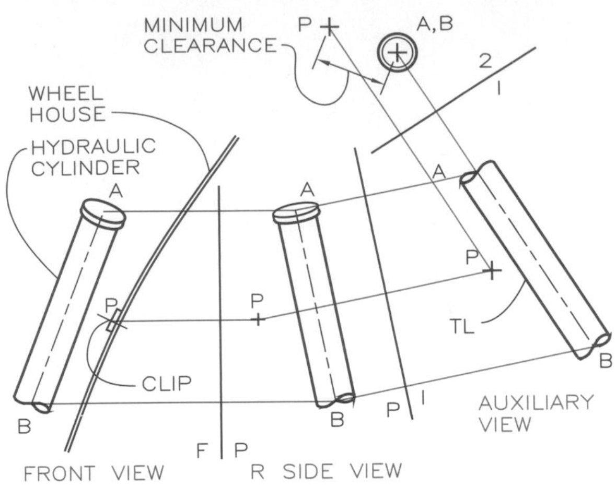

5.6 Descriptive geometry is an effective way to determine clearances between components, such as the clearance between a hydraulic cylinder and a fender.

the cylinder is attached with a clip. This drawing can be constructed either by pencil or by computer.

The design of a surgical light requires the application of descriptive geometry. The light fixture must provide maximum light on the operating area with the least obstruction, as shown in **Figure 5.7**. This scale drawing depicts the converging beams of light emitted from the reflectors, the light's position above the operating area, and approximate positions of the surgeon. The beams are positioned so

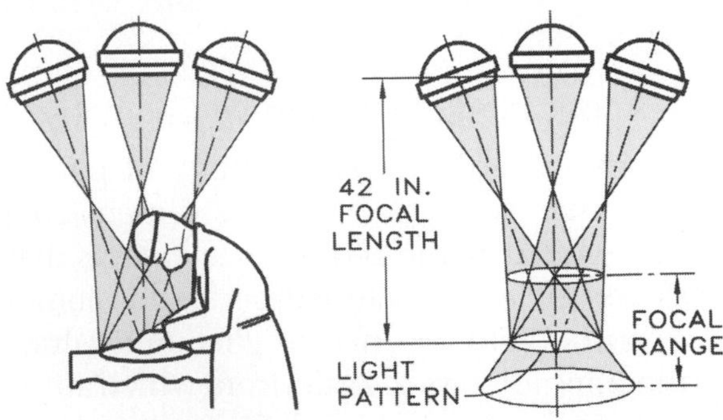

5.7 By using scale drawings developed in the refinement step of the design process, the designer can study the geometry of a surgical lamp. (*Courtesy of Sybron Corporation*.)

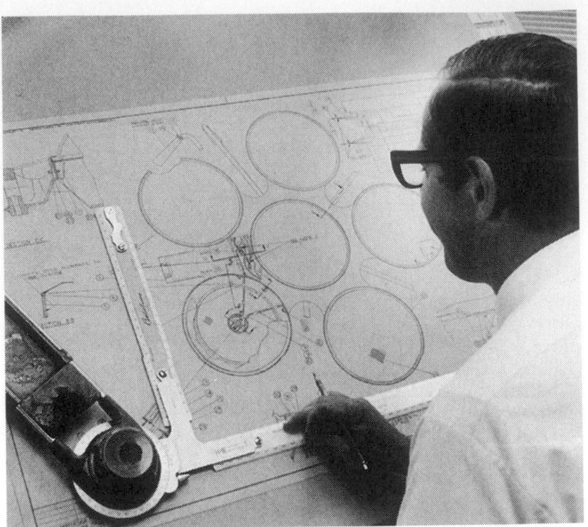

5.8 Refinement drawing shows the overall dimensions of the final design of the surgical lamp. (*Courtesy of Sybron Corporation*.)

their narrowest rays are at shoulder level to minimize shadows cast by the surgeon's shoulders, arms, and hands.

From these scale drawings, lengths, angles, areas, and other geometric relations can be determined by the designer at the drawing board or at the computer (**Figure 5.8**). When the three-dimensional geometric relationships have been determined, the engineering details can be developed for more analysis and testing. The major dimensions of the surgical lamp are shown in the refinement drawing in **Figure 5.9**.

5.4 Refinement Considerations

In advanced designs, such as that of a new model automobile, numerous features must be refined. The exhaust system shown in **Figure 5.10** is the result of the many refinement drawings needed to determine its geometry. Descriptive geometry was used to determine the exhaust pipe's bend angles, its length, and clearances required for fitting it to the chassis without interference (**Figure 5.11**).

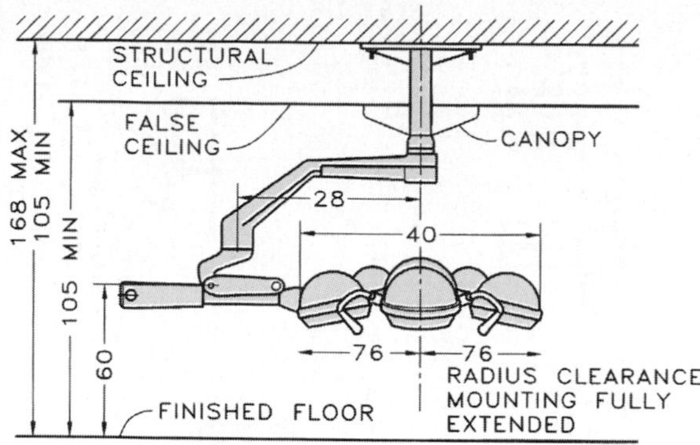

5.9 A well-designed surgical lamp emits light that passes around the surgeon's shoulders with a minimum of shadow. The focal range of this surgical lamp is between 30 and 60 ins. (*Courtesy of Sybron Corporation.*)

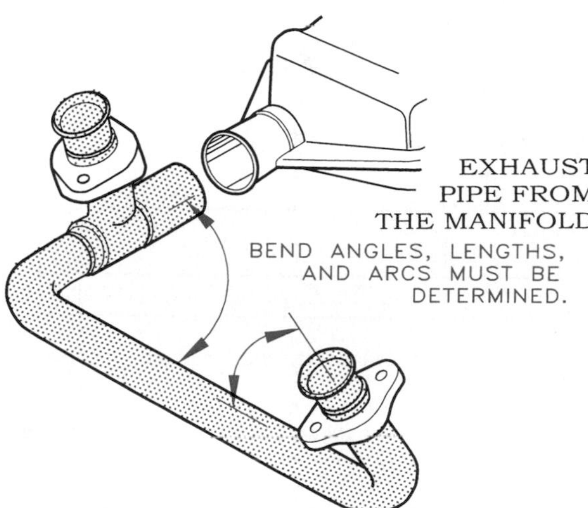

5.10 Descriptive geometry is useful in determining the lengths and angles of an automobile's pipe assembly from the manifold.

A designer's refinement drawing of the fuselage of business jet aircraft is shown as an orthographic section in **Figure 5.12**. This drawing, although simple in concept, is effective in determining clearance, heights, and seat sizes for passengers.

5.5 Refinement: Exercise Bench

The exercise bench design problem was identified in Chapter 3, and preliminary ideas for it were developed in Chapter 4. Now, in this

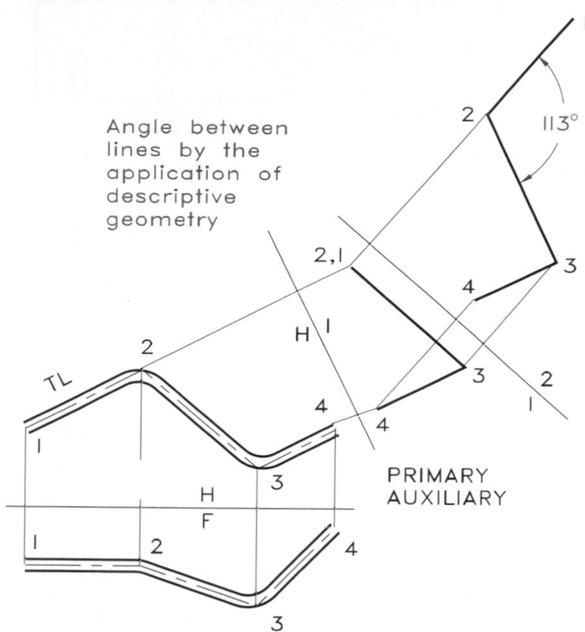

5.11 Descriptive geometry is applied to find the lengths and angles between exhaust pipe segments.

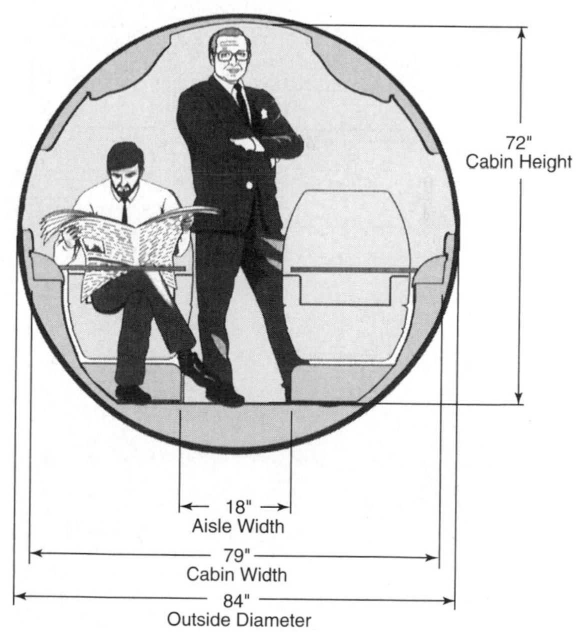

5.12 This refinement drawing is a section drawn through the fuselage of the Hawker Horizon, a business jet aircraft that shows the clearance, heights, and seat sizes of the interior. (*Courtesy of Raytheon Aircraft Corporation.*)

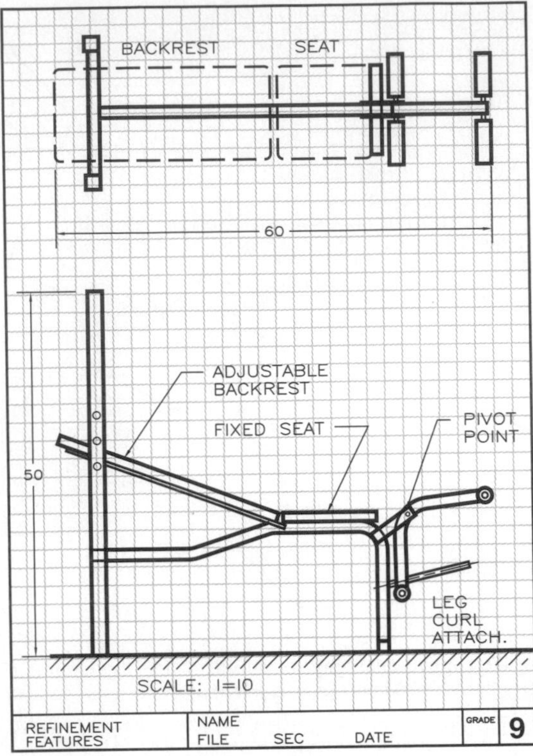

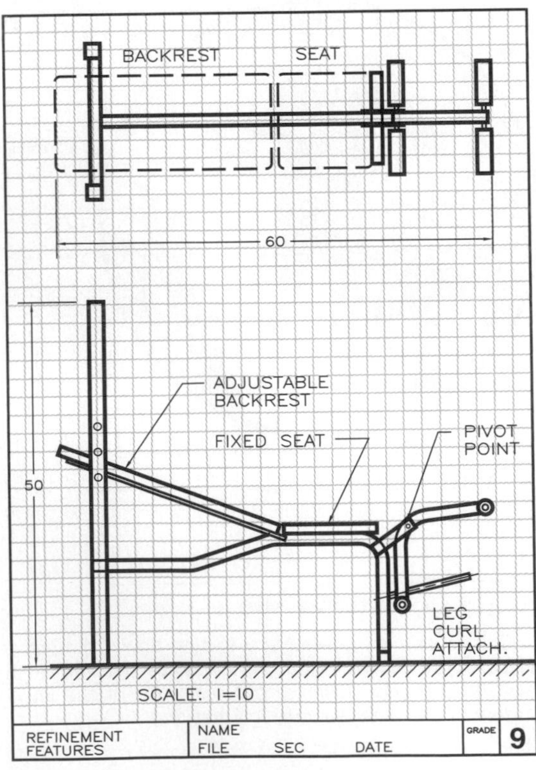

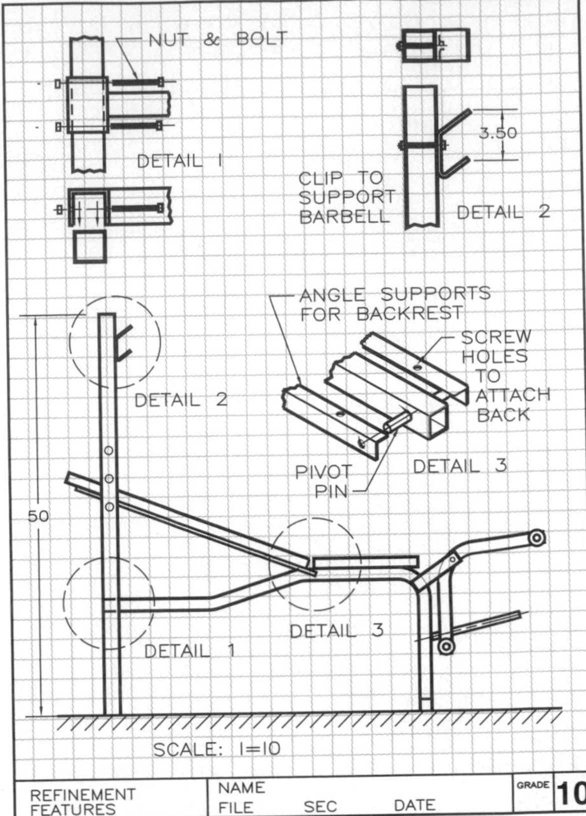

Sheet 8 This list of desirable features is a refinement of the exercise bench.

Sheet 9 This refinement drawing for the exercise bench is a scale drawing with only several of the major dimensions shown.

Sheet 10 This refinement drawing is of another design concept for the exercise bench.

step, we refine the preliminary ideas for the exercise bench with instrument drawings.

First, list the features to be incorporated into the design on a worksheet (**Sheet 8**). Then refine a preliminary idea, say, idea 2 from Chapter 4, in an orthographic scale drawing of the seat (**Sheet 9**). Block in extruded parts, such as the framework members, to expedite the drawing process and omit unneeded hidden lines.

Refinement drawings must be drawn to scale. The use of instruments is important to precisely portray the design from which angles, lengths, shapes, and other geometric elements will be obtained. The drawing shows only overall dimensions, and several connecting joints are detailed to explain the design. **Sheet 10** shows additional design features. These worksheets depict representative types of drawings required to refine a design; additional drawings would be required for a complete refinement of the design.

5.6 Standard Parts

When preparing refinement drawings, specify standard parts whenever possible because they are more economical and readily available. Merchandise catalogs, sales brochures, magazine advertisements, newspapers, and similar sources contain specifications for standard parts.

Make a practice of keeping files on stock items—such as leveling devices and casters (**Figure 5.13**)—that can be used in developing products and specified in refinement drawings by referring to literature from manufacturers and vendors. You can become a better designer by observing how standard parts and devices are made and how they function. When you see a device that you are unfamiliar with, ask yourself, Why is it made the way it is? How is it used? and What application can I use it for in a design?

A. LEVELING DEVICES

B. CASTERS FOR MOVABLE (ROLLING) EQUIPMENT

5.13 A. The leveling devices are standard parts for leveling equipment on uneven floors.
B. Casters are attached to equipment that must be movable about a work area. They range from small sizes for TV sets to those that carry over 1,000 lb. (*Courtesy of Vlier Industries, and Hamilton Casters.*)

Problems

Problems should be presented on 8-1/2 × 11-in. paper, grid or plain. All notes, sketches, drawings, and graphical work should be neatly presented. Written matter should be lettered legibly using 1/8-in. guidelines.

1. When refining a design for a folding lawn chair, what physical properties would a designer need to determine? What physical properties would be needed for a (a) TV set base, (b) golf cart, (c) child's swing set, (d) bicycle rack, (e) shortwave radio, (f) portable camping tent, and (g) warehouse dolly used for moving heavy boxes?

2. Why should scale drawings rather than freehand sketches be used in the refinement of a design?

3. List five examples of problems involving spatial relationships that could be solved by the application of descriptive geometry. Explain your answers.

4. In the refinement step, how many preliminary designs should be refined? Why?

5. Make a list of refinement drawings that would be needed to develop the installation and design of a 100-ft radio antenna. Make rough sketches of the types of drawings needed, with notes to explain their purposes.

6. If a design is eliminated as a possible solution after refinement drawings have been made, what should be the designer's next step? Explain.

7. For the exercise bench discussed in Section 5.5, what refinement drawings are necessary in addition to those presented? Make freehand sketches of the necessary drawings, with notes to explain them.

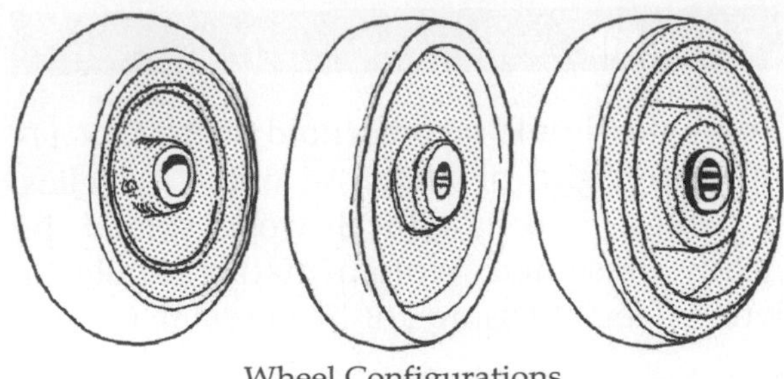

5.14 Problem 8: Why are wheels not disks with a hole through their center? Why do they have raised hubs and bushings?

Refinement Problems

8. Students often draw wheels as disks with holes at their center, but even the simplest wheels have more sophistication in their design. Make refinement drawings of one of the wheels shown in the sketches in **Figure 5.14**. Why do wheels have a raised hub at their center? Why do they have a bushing in the hole through them?

9. Caster refinement. Make scaled refinement drawings of the casters shown in **Figure 5.13** on size A sheets.

10. Pipe hanger. Preliminary sketches for a pipe hanger bracket, used to support steam pipes from overhead beams, are given in **Figure 5.15**. These sketches are sufficient for you to understand the concepts, but they need further refinement. Make refinement drawings of these sketches and make whatever modifications in the design that you think would improve them.

11. Pipe hanger. The preliminary sketches in **Figure 5.16** illustrate another concept for a pipe hanger bracket. Solve this problem by following the steps in problem 10.

12. Pipe hanger 3. The preliminary sketches in **Figure 5.17** illustrate a pipe clamp assembly that attaches to a hanger rod that attaches to a hanger bracket of the type shown in the two previous figures. Solve this problem by following the steps in problem 10.

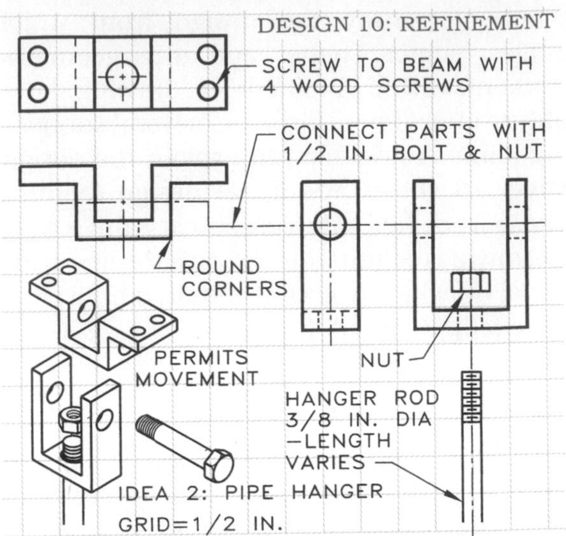

5.15 Problem 10: Preliminary idea sketches of a pipe hanger for supporting steam pipes from an overhead beam on a hanger rod.

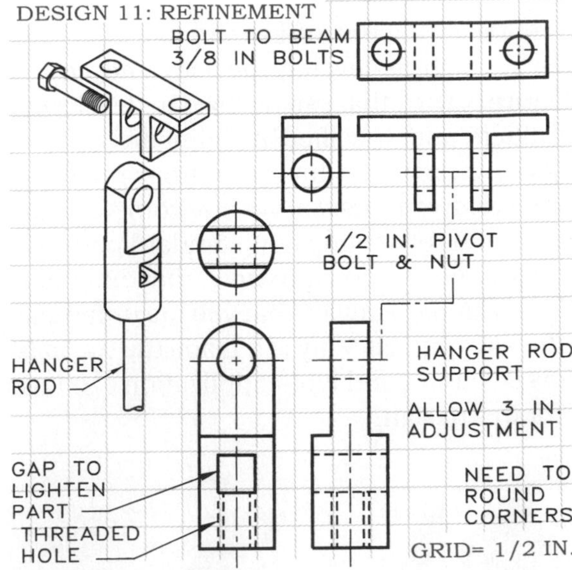

5.16 Problem 11: Preliminary idea sketches of concepts for a hanger rod support for suspending steam pipes.

13. Pipe hanger 4. Make refinement drawings of the pipe hanger sketches given in **Figure 5.18** by following the specification

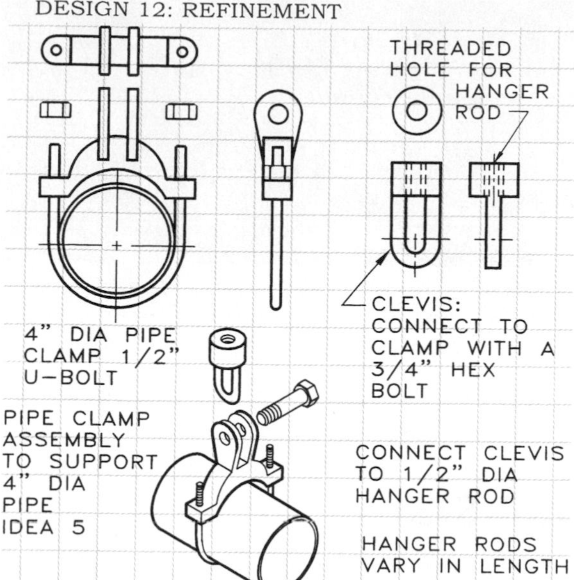

5.17 Problem 12: Preliminary idea sketches of a pipe clamp assembly for holding steam pipes and connecting to an overhead hanger bracket.

DESIGN 13: REFINEMENT -- PIPE HANGER

Develop the preliminary sketches of the hanger into scaled refinement drawings for modification on a size A sheet. Make design improvements as you progress with the drawings. Now is a good time to use your creativity. If not now, when?

9

BRACKET

1/2 IN. BOLT

BOSS

LOOKS HEAVY

BOLT TO I–BEAM

SUPPORTS A HANGING PIPE

5.18 Problem 13: Preliminary ideas for a pipe hanger for supporting steam pipes from an overhead beam.

DESIGN 14: REFINEMENT -- CUP HOLDER

Refine these concept sketches for a cup holder that attaches to a table top on size A sheets and think of improvements in its design as you work. Do you think there's a market for it? What must it sell for? Who would be your best market?

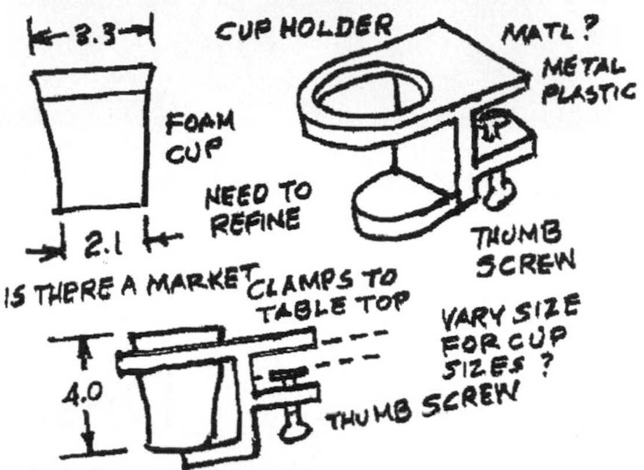

5.19 Problem 14: The preliminary ideas for a holder for a beverage cup were sketched during lunch on a napkin. Could this be the beginning of a financial bonanza?

given and the instructions for problem 10. (Have you had enough of pipe hangers?)

14. Cup holder. Preliminary ideas for a beverage cup holder were sketched on the back of a napkin by two coworkers during lunch (**Figure 5.19**). They thought it a good idea to have a cup holder for the Styrofoam cups that overturned easily at their desks. These sketches represent a start. Refine and design as you go.

15. Exhaust pipe. Make refinement drawings of the exhaust pipe shown in **Figure 5.10** on size A sheets. The pipe has an outside diameter of 2 in. Estimate the other dimensions using your judgment.

6 Design Analysis

6.1 Introduction

Analysis is the development and evaluation of a proposed design by objective thinking and the application of engineering and technology. For example, bridge designs are analyzed for loads, stresses, travel loads, dimensions, materials, sizes, function, economy, and much more. Less creativity is needed during analysis than during the previous steps of the design process. Analysis is the step in the design process most thoroughly covered in engineering courses.

6.2 Graphics and Analysis

Graphics and geometry are effective tools for analyzing a design in addition to the numerical methods normally used in engineering. Empirical data obtained from laboratory experiments and field observation can be transformed into formats suitable for graphical analysis and evaluation (**Figure 6.1**).

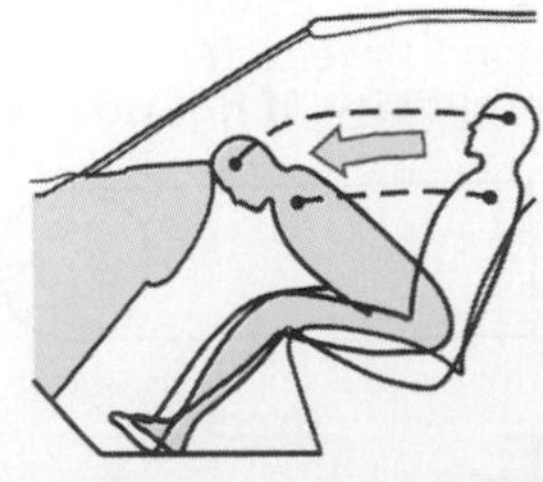

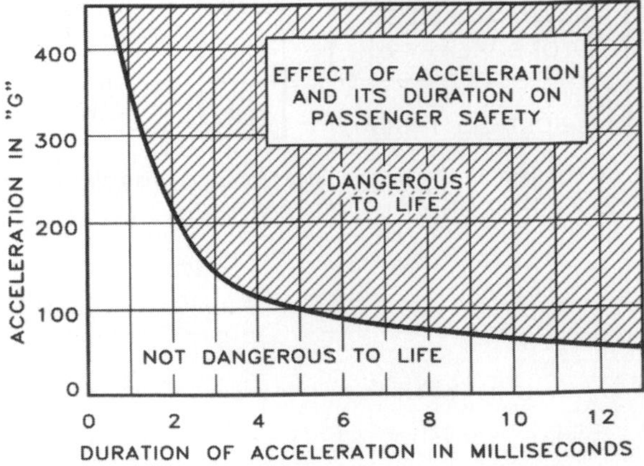

6.1 Designers analyze experimental data and human factors to determine comfortable and safe automobile designs. Graphics is a helpful tool in this step of the design process.

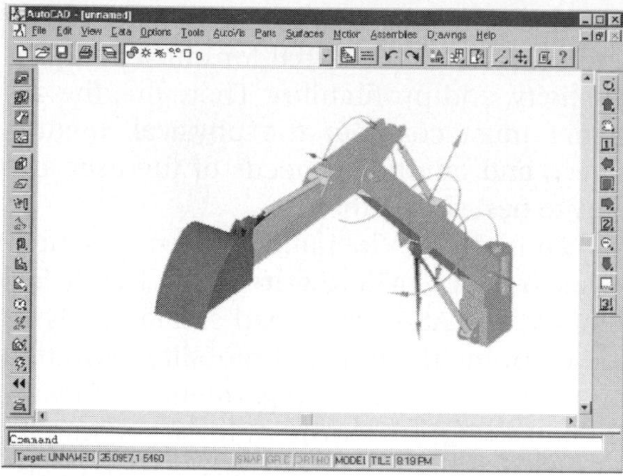

6.2 Clearance between functional parts and linkage systems can be analyzed efficiently with graphical methods by computer. *(Courtesy of Design Technologies International, Inc.)*

Figure 6.2 shows an example of computer graphics applied to the analysis of a linkage system to determine clearances, limits, and velocities of it members. Graphics also is an effective way to present and analyze technical information, background data, market surveys, population trends, and sales projections. A graph shown in **Figure 6.3** enables the designer to quickly select the appropriate conveyor for transporting raw material at the desired rate.

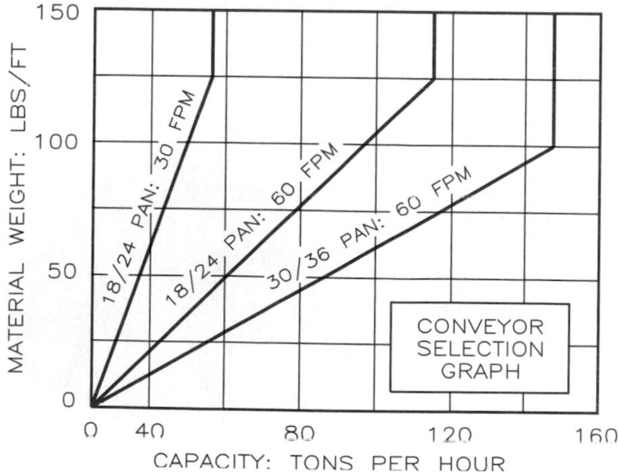

6.3 Graphics can be used to organize and present laboratory and field data to facilitate analysis for design applications.

6.3 Types of Analysis

Analysis includes evaluation of the following attributes:

1. function
2. human factors
3. product market
4. physical specifications
5. strength
6. economic factors
7. models

Function

Function is the most important characteristic of a design because a product that does not function properly is a failure regardless of its other desirable features (**Figure 6.4**). Many products serve a narrow, utilitarian purpose, such as piston linkage of a gasoline engine (**Figure 6.5**). In those cases, the designer is concerned with function to a much greater extent. Functional analysis usually involves the optimization of several aspects of the design, including safety, economics, durability,

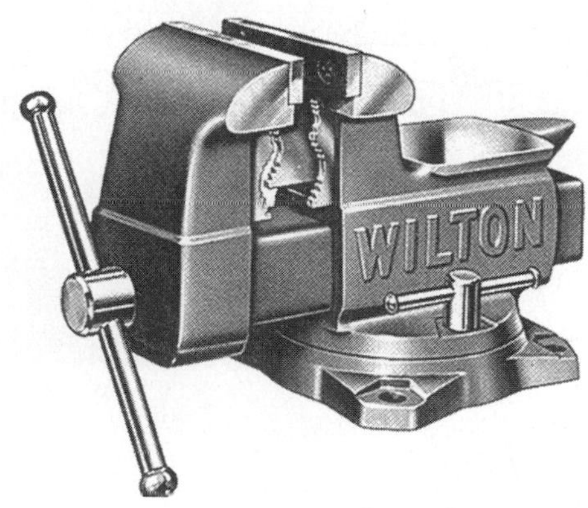

6.4 This vise must function properly to be acceptable. No other features can offset a design that operates poorly. *(Courtesy of Wilton Tool Division.)*

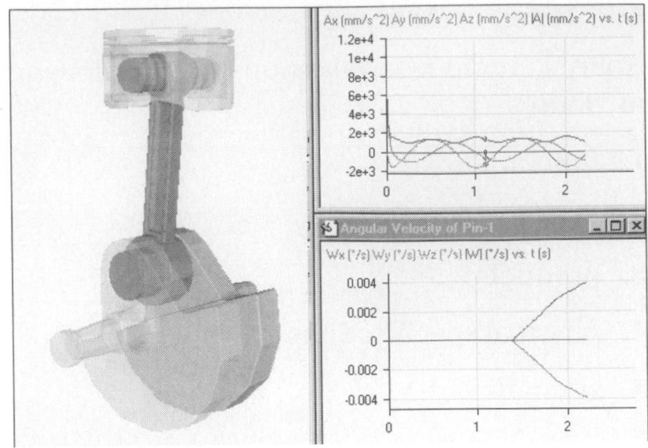

6.5 Graphical analysis is an efficient way to determine operating limits for the piston linkage of a gasoline engine. *(Courtesy Knowledge Revolution, Inc.)*

appearance, and marketability. For example, despite high fuel costs, most consumers will not accept cars designed to get good mileage at the expense of comfort, safety, and styling. Buyers may be willing to give up some features, but few would give up air conditioning, CD players, radios, comfortable seats, and safety features for improved gasoline mileage.

Human Factors

Human engineering (*ergonomics*) is the design of products and workplaces suited to the humans who use and occupy them. Safety and comfort are essential for efficiency, productivity, and profitability. Therefore, the designer must consider the physical, mental, safety, and emotional needs of the user and how to best satisfy them.

Leonardo da Vinci analyzed body dimensions in about 1473 (**Figure 6.6A**). Nearly 500 years later NASA performed similar analyses to determine the range of mobility permitted by a radiation protection garment used by astronauts (**Figure 6.6B**). Analysis of human factors is crucial in the space program because even the simplest, most familiar tasks require training and adaptation when astronauts perform them while in a weightless state. The configuration of the ENV racing bike in **Figure 6.7** shares many similarities with an automobile's interior because it must provide comfort and function, but the bike has the added restriction of less space to work within. At the most basic level, heel height affects a person's posture as shown in **Figure 6.8**, which illustrates the broadness of human engineering.

Dimensions and Ranges A design must take into account the sizes, ranges of movement, senses, and comfort zones of the people using

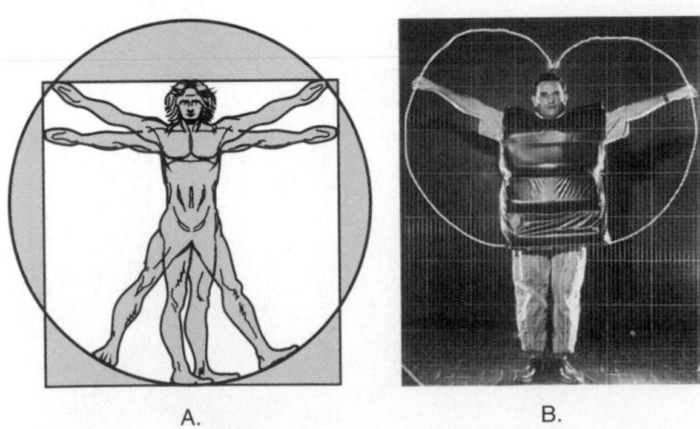

6.6 Human dimensions.
A Leonardo da Vinci analyzed body dimensions and proportions with graphics in 1473.
B Engineers used Leonardo's techniques in the twentieth century to analyze motions by astronauts restricted by radiation protection vests. *(Courtesy of General Dynamics Corporation.)*

6.7 Human factors were a major part of designing the configuration of this ENV racing bike that is sleek, lightweight, and comfortable at high speeds. *(Courtesy of Intelligent Energy.)*

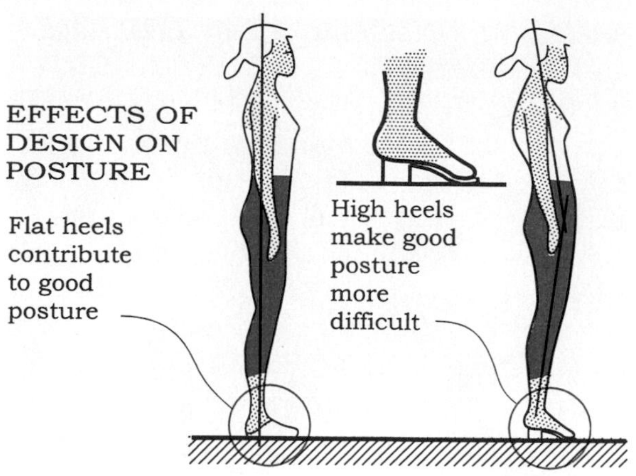

6.8 Shoe heel height affects posture and is part of human engineering at the most basic level.

the finished product (**Figure 6.9**). Variations in people's physical characteristics conform to the normal distribution curve shown in **Figure 6.10**. Designers must use the body dimensions of the average American man (**Figure 6.11**) and the average American woman (**Figure 6.12**) as the bases for industrial

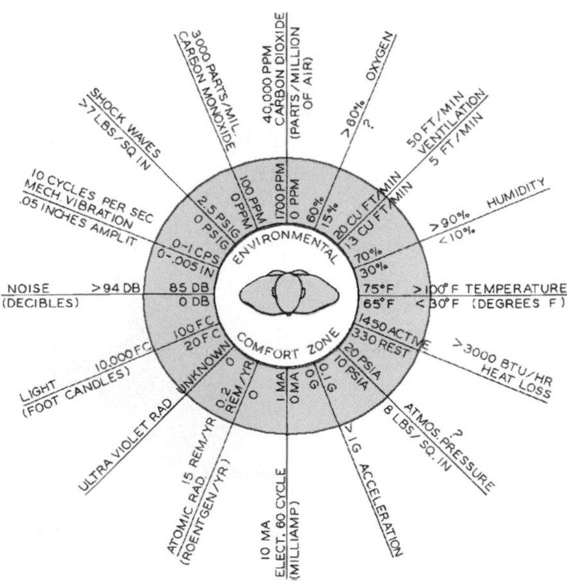

6.9 The inner circle represents the environmental comfort zone, and the outer circle the bearable limit zone of the human environment. *(Courtesy of Henry Dreyfuss, The Measure of Man.)*

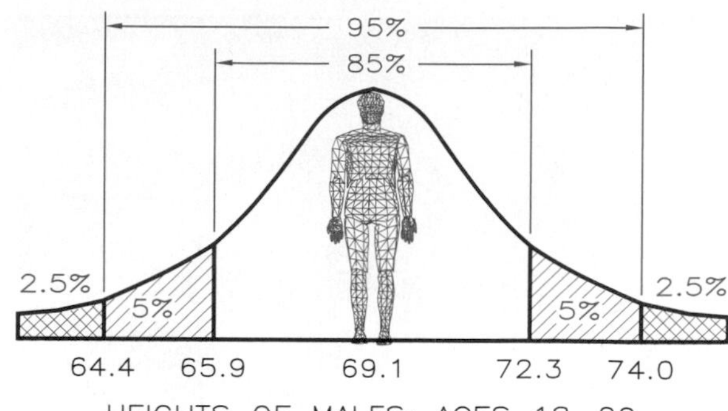

6.10 This chart shows the distribution of average heights in inches of American men from 18 to 22 years of age. Fifty percent of American men in this age range are taller than 69.1 in., and 50% are shorter. *(Courtesy of HumanCAD.)*

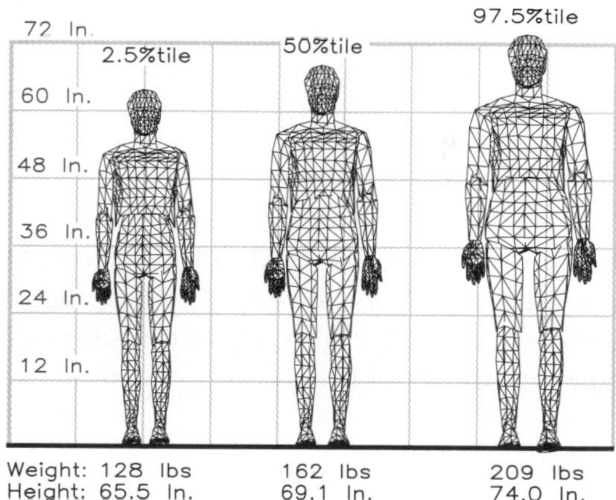

6.11 Men of average build have the body measurements shown. *(Courtesy of HumanCAD.)*

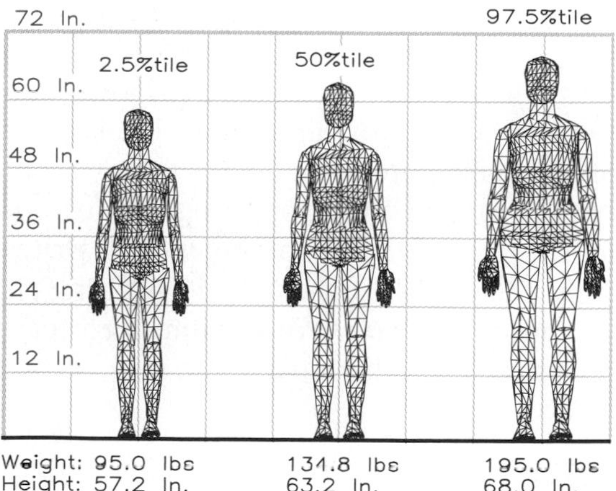

6.12 Women of average build have the body measurements shown. *(Courtesy of HumanCAD.)*

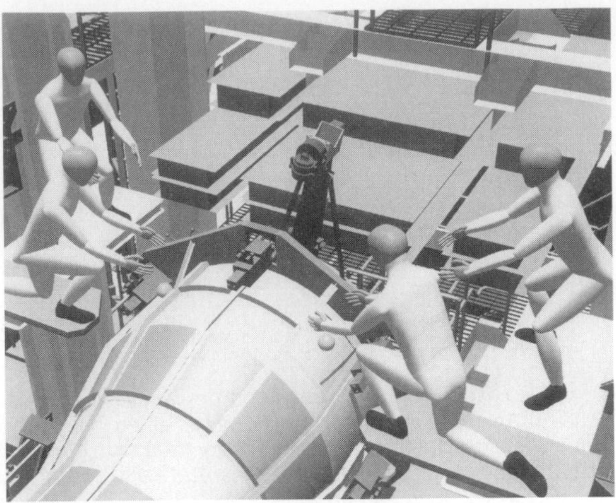

6.13 This computer model permits the analysis of body movements that are required to service a spacecraft. *(Courtesy of McDonnell-Douglas Space & Defense System.)*

6.14 The design of the spacecraft of the Gemini 8 mission was the ultimate challenge in providing physical accommodations and life-support systems for astronauts. *(Courtesy of NASA.)*

designs. It is a challenging assignment to design accommodations that will be comfortable for the smallest as well as the largest subjects. **Figure 6.13** shows ranges of body movements of workers performing maintenance on a spacecraft.

Motion The study of body motion begins with an understanding of the amount of space required for a person to function comfortably, safely, and efficiently. The Gemini 8 spacecraft shown in **Figure 6.14** was the ultimate challenge in designing an environment and life-support systems for astronauts in space. A less critical human design problem, but challenging nonetheless, was the ergonomic pen that was designed to more comfortably fit the hand while writing (**Figure 6.15**). The design of this writing pen is a reminder that there is room for unique designs in even the most common everyday applications.

Vision Designs that include gauges and controls must provide the most visually effective means of aiding the operator. For example, the welding helmet must be equipped with autodarkening lens to protect the welder's eyes. Helmets must permit its user to function safely and efficiently with adequate vision and protection.

Sound Sound must be within specified frequencies so as not to adversely affect a person's stress level and productivity. Many types of sound are stressful *and* contribute to an unsafe work environment.

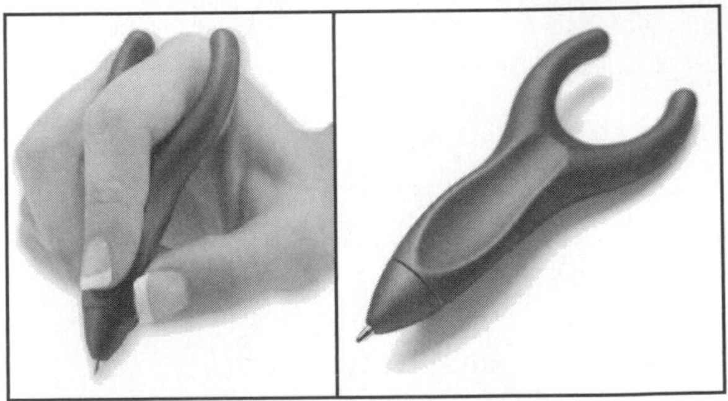

6.15 The PenAgain® is an ergonomic design that has been adapted to grip and movement to enhance writing in a natural and comfortable manner. *(Courtesy of Pacific Writing Instruments, Inc.)*

Environment Working environments may include an entire industrial plant, a particular workstation, or a specialized location, such as the cockpit of a farm machine. Important environmental factors are temperature, lighting, color, sound, and comfort.

Product Market

Designers study the market for a product during all stages of product development (Chapters 3–5) and review it more formally during the analysis step. Areas of product analysis are market prospects, retail outlets, sales features, and advertising.

Market Prospects Market information should be collected to learn about the age groups, income brackets, and geographic locations of prospective purchasers of the product. This information is helpful in planning advertising campaigns to reach potential customers.

Retail Outlets The product may be marketed through existing wholesale and retail channels, from newly established dealerships, or by the manufacturer directly. For example, mainframe computers are not suitable for distribution through retail outlets, so manufacturers' technical representatives work with clients individually. However, an exercise machine can be sold effectively through department stores, television commercials, direct mail, and sporting-goods outlets.

Sales Features The designer should itemize the unique features of a new design that would stimulate interest in the product and attract consumers. The question the designer must continually ask is, What features make this design better than my competitor's?

Advertising Manufacturers, wholesalers, and retailers use several media, including personal contact, direct mail, radio, TV, newspapers, and periodicals, to advertise their products to potential customers. Advertising costs vary widely, and each medium should be analyzed for suitability before one or more are selected.

Physical Specifications

During the refinement step, the designer specified various measurements, such as lengths, areas, shapes, weight, and angles for the product. During the analysis step, the designer uses the product's geometry and measurements to calculate member sizes and dimensions, weights, volumes, capacities, velocities, operating ranges, packaging, shipping requirements, and similar information (**Figure 6.16**).

Sizes and Dimensions The designer must evaluate product sizes and dimensions to ensure that they meet any standards specified, such as permissible widths, lengths, and weights in automobile design. For products that

i180 Specifications at a Glance:

Maximum speed: 12.5 mph
Carrying capacity: 260 lbs
Footprint: 19x25 in
Weight: ~ 83 lbs
Battery type: Two lithium-ion or NiMH battery packs
Motors: Two brushless, DC servomotors
Wheels: 14 in glass-reinforced thermoplastic
Tires: 19 in tubeless, puncture-resistant
Platform height: 8 in
Ground clearance: 3 - 4 in
Display: Multicolor backlit LCD

6.16 Designs must be analyzed to determine their physical properties, including weights, ranges, geometries, and capacities, as shown for the Human Transporter (HT). *(Courtesy of Segway LLC.)*

have moving parts, such as a construction crane, the designer must analyze the size of the product when extended, contracted, or positioned differently, as well as weight and balance requirements.

Ranges Many products have ranges of operation, capacities, and speeds that the designer must analyze before finalizing a design. For example, the designer must determine ranges and maximum limits such as seating capacity, miles per gallon, pounds of laundry per cycle, flows in gallons per minute, or power required.

Packaging and Shipping The designer must also be concerned with product packaging and shipping. Packaging relates both to product protection and consumer appeal: how the product is to be shipped—by air, rail, mail, or truck—and whether it is to be shipped one at a time or in quantity are important considerations. Shipping and marketing a product assembled, partially assembled, or disassembled requires design attention and analysis, as does the cost of each method.

Strength Much of engineering is devoted to analyzing a product's strength to support maximum design loads, withstand specified shocks, and endure necessary repetitive motions. **Figure 6.17** illustrates motion analysis for a moving part on a conveyor. The designer plots the data obtain and then uses graphical calculus to find the conveyor's velocity versus time profile as the first step in determining the strength needed by the part.

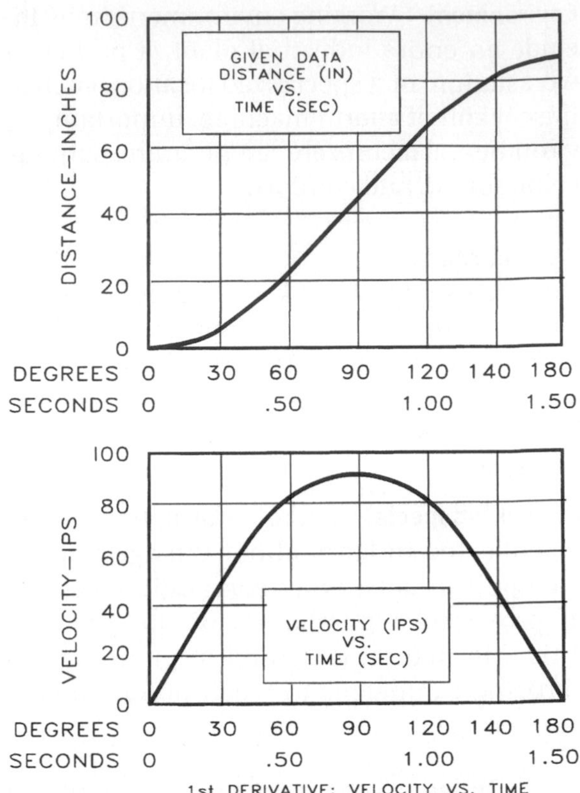

6.17 This graph shows the distance traveled versus the time required for a part on a conveyor. The designer graphically differentiates the plot of the data given to obtain a graph of velocity versus time as the first step in designing parts of sufficient strength for the conveyor.

Economic Factors

Designs must be economically competitive to have a chance of being successful. Therefore, before releasing a product for production, the designer must analyze its cost and expected profit margin. Two methods of pricing a product are **itemizing** and **comparative pricing**.

Itemizing The process of totaling the costs of each part and its related overhead to determine its final cost is the first step in itemizing a product's price. From the working drawings, the designer (or an estimator) can estimate the costs of materials, manufacturing, labor, overhead, and other items to arrive at the total production expense. The wholesale price is production cost plus profit. Dealer margin plus the wholesale cost gives the retail price. One example of an economic model is shown in **Figure 6.18**; these

DEALER MARGIN
Profit
Advertising
Store expenses
Commissions
35%

MANUFACTURER'S PROFIT
15%

SALES COMMISSIONS
10%

OVERHEAD: Shipping, rent, storage, office, etc.
10%

MANUFACTURING
Labor and materials
Power and utilities
Machinery & equipment
30%

100%
65%
50%
40%
30%
0%

Retail price-100%
Wholesale price-65%
Cost-50%

6.18 An economic model that can be used as a guide in the economic analysis and pricing of a product.

percentages vary for different areas of manufacturing, marketing, and retailing.

Comparative Pricing The other method used to estimate the price of a proposed product is to compare it with the prices of similar products. For example, the power tools shown in **Figure 6.19** are priced in the $50 range. These tools are similar: Both use the same type of power source, are made from the same materials, and have the same styling. **Most important, these products will have about the same market size.** Approximately the same number of drills, sanders, and saws are sold; consequently, production costs and retail prices are similar for each.

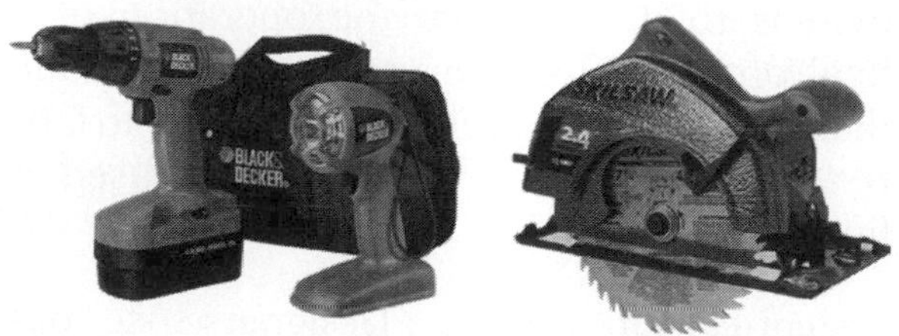

6.19 The cordless drill and the circular saw retail for approximately the same price. They can be priced comparatively because they are similar in design and have essentially the same market size. *(Courtesy of the Black & Decker Company.)*

6.20 This hunting seat and the exercise bench in Figure 6.21 can be comparatively priced at between $90 and $100 because both have similar manufacturing requirements and market volume potential. *(Courtesy of Baker Manufacturing Company, Valdosta, Georgia.)*

The prices of the hunting seat (**Figure 6.20**) and the exercise bench (**Figure 6.21**), which have somewhat equal market sizes, are another example of comparative pricing. Since both products' manufacturing requirements and market volumes are similar, both

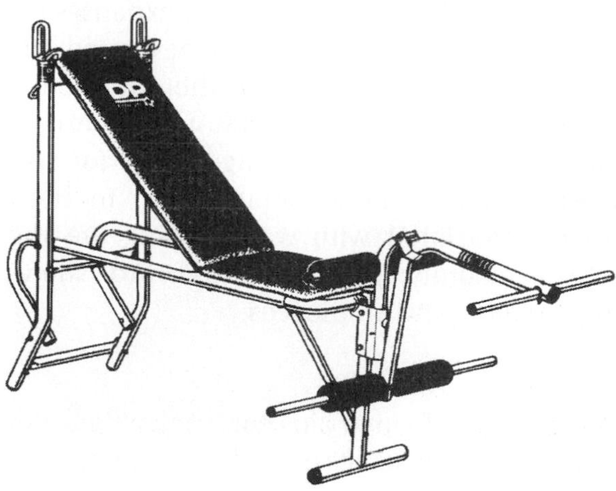

6.21 Priced at $100, this exercise apparatus is similar in manufacture and market appeal to the hunting seat shown in Figure 6.19. *(Courtesy of Diversified Products Corporation.)*

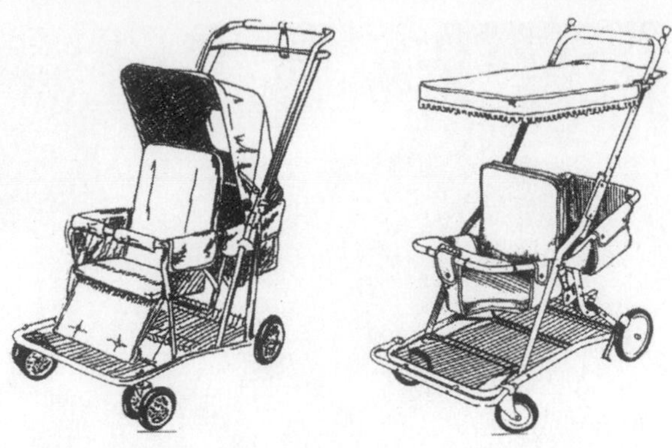

6.22 These baby strollers are priced from $55 to $75, or considerably less than the hunting seat and exercise apparatus, because the stroller market is larger and competition for customers is greater. *(Courtesy of Strolee of California.)*

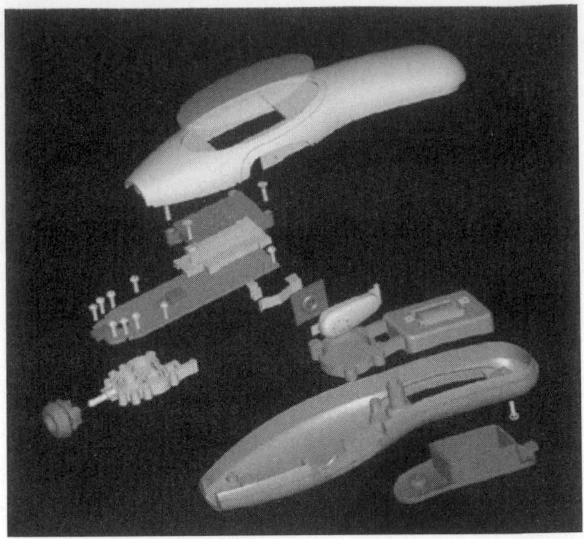

6.23 A computer-generated conceptual model of a digital tire gauge enables the designer to analyze the relationship of the device's components. *(Courtesy Bresslergroup and Measurement Specialties, Inc.)*

sell for about the same price of $90–$100. However, the baby stroller (**Figure 6.22**) sells for about $50 because of its larger and more competitive market, even though it is very similar in configuration to the hunting seat and the exercise bench.

Manufacturers also use comparative pricing to estimate cost per square foot, per mile, per cubic foot, or per day. These factors yield rough cost estimates as a basis for doing more detailed studies.

Miscellaneous Expenses Various expenses incurred in the development of new products can easily be overlooked and thereby affect a product's profitability projections. For example, warehousing and storage costs for finished products must be included in their price. Associated with warehousing are the costs of insurance, temperature control, shelving, forklifts, and employees.

Models

Models are effective aids for analyzing a design in the final stages of its development. Designers use three-dimensional models to study a product's proportion, operation, size, function, and efficiency. Types of models often used are **conceptual models, mock-ups, prototypes**, and **system layout models**.

Conceptual Models Designers use preliminary models or computer models to analyze a preliminary design or feature concept (**Figure 6.23**).

Mock-Ups Designers use full-size dummies of the finished design to demonstrate the product's size, appearance, and component relationships. Mock-ups give a visual impression rather than demonstrate its operation.

Prototypes Designers use full-size working models to demonstrate the operation of a final product. Because prototypes are made mostly by hand, materials that are easy to fabricate are used instead of those to be used in final production.

System-Layout Models Designers use detailed scale models that show the relationships among components of large manufacturing systems, building complexes, and traffic lay-

6.24 This system layout model is used to analyze the details of construction of a refinery. *(Courtesy of E. I. du Pont de Nemours and Company.)*

outs. Designers usually construct system layout models of refineries to supplement working drawings for contractors and construction supervisors during construction (**Figure 6.24**).

Model Materials Designers commonly use balsa wood, cardboard, and clay in model construction because they are easy to shape and require few tools. Standard parts such as wheels, tubing, figures, dowels, and other structural shapes can be purchased, rather than made, to save time and effort. Plexiglas can be used to construct models that illustrate both inside and outside design features. Finished models should give a realistic impression of the design, especially when they are used for sales presentations and displays.

Model Scale A model should be large enough to show the function of the smallest significant moving parts. For example, the student model of a portable home caddy shown in **Figure 6.25** (made of balsa wood) demonstrates a linkage system that permits the wheels to be collapsed for storage. The model's scale is large enough to permit the linkage system to operate as it will in the final product. The transport cart shown in

6.25 A student's model demonstrates how a portable home caddy will fold flat for ease of storage.

Figure 6.26 that is currently on the market shares many of the features developed years earlier by the student design team.

Model Testing Using models to test performance is helpful in determining how well a design meets requirements. Aerodynamic characteristics of the rear styling of an automobile can be evaluated by wind tunnel tests.

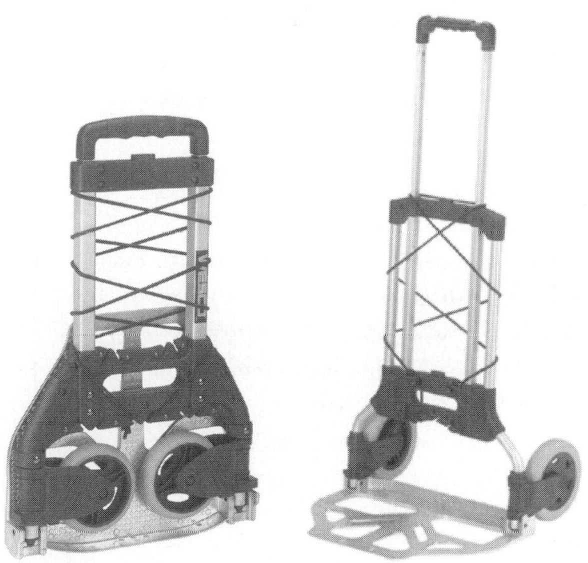

6.26 This folding transport cart folds to a thickness of 2.23 in., weighs 9.9 lb, and has a load capacity of 275 lb. *(Courtesy of Wesco Industrial Products.)*

6.27 Prototypes are full-size models for demonstrating and testing a design's operation. *(Courtesy of General Motors Corporation.)*

Physical relationships and the functional workings of movable components, as for the hatch and storage area of a car, can be tested in a prototype. Products can be tested on the computer screen to economically obtain results of their operation. Designers also use models to test consumer reactions to new products before releasing the design for production (**Figure 6.27**).

6.4 Analysis: Exercise Bench

To illustrate a method of analyzing a product design, we return to our problem example, the exercise bench, which was carried through the first three steps of the design process in Chapters 3–5. The main areas of analysis listed on **Sheets 11** through **14** will assist you in analyzing the design. Additional worksheets

Sheet 11 A worksheet containing an analysis of function, human engineering, and market considerations for the exercise bench.

Sheet 12 A worksheet giving the physical description and strength analysis for the exercise bench.

Sheet 13 A worksheet containing an analysis of the production procedures for and economics of the exercise bench.

Sheet 14 A worksheet that shows graphical analysis of the range of movements for the adjustable parts of the exercise bench.

ANALYSIS

1. Function
   - A. PROVIDES SUPPORT FOR BASIC EXERCISES
   - B. SUPPORTS BAR BELLS
   - C. ADJUSTABLE TO SUIT INDIVIDUAL
2. Human engineering
   - A. PADDED BENCH
   - B. ADJUSTABLE BACKREST
   - C. CONFORMS TO BODY MOTIONS
   - D. BARBELL BRACKETS FOR SAFETY
   - E. FOAM PADS FOR COMFORT
3. Market and consumer acceptance
   - A. POTENTIAL MARKET
     1. STATE–56,000
     2. NATION–7,000,000
   - B. MORE EFFECTIVE EXERCISING
   - C. AFFORDABLE AT $120–$150 RANGE
   - D. USABLE FOR NONWEIGHT EXERCISES ALSO

DESIGN ANALYSIS	NAME FILE SEC DATE	GRADE	11

4. Physical description
   - A. BENCH COMPOSED OF BACKREST & SEAT
   - B. BACKREST ADJUSTABLE FROM 0 DEG. TO +30 DEG. WITH HORIZONTAL
   - C. 2 BAR HOLDER BRACKETS FOR BARBELLS
   - D. 2 BUTTERFLY EXERCISE ATTACHMENTS
   - E. LEG CURL ATTACHMENT
   - F. WEIGHT: 45 LB
   - G. SIZE: 52" LONG X 31" WIDE X 50" TALL
5. Strength
   - A. RECOMMENDED WEIGHT SET: 160 LB
   - B. SUPPORT PERSON WEIGTHING UP TO 300 LB
   - C. CROSS BRACED TO PROVIDE STABILITY
   - D. REPLACEABLE PLASTIC SLEEVES FOR BUTTERFLY ATTACHMENTS
   - E. MAX. LEG CURL WEIGHT: 100 LB.
   - F. MAX. RECOMMENDED BUTTERFLY WEIGHTS: 50 LB EACH

DESIGN ANALYSIS	NAME FILE SEC DATE	GRADE	12

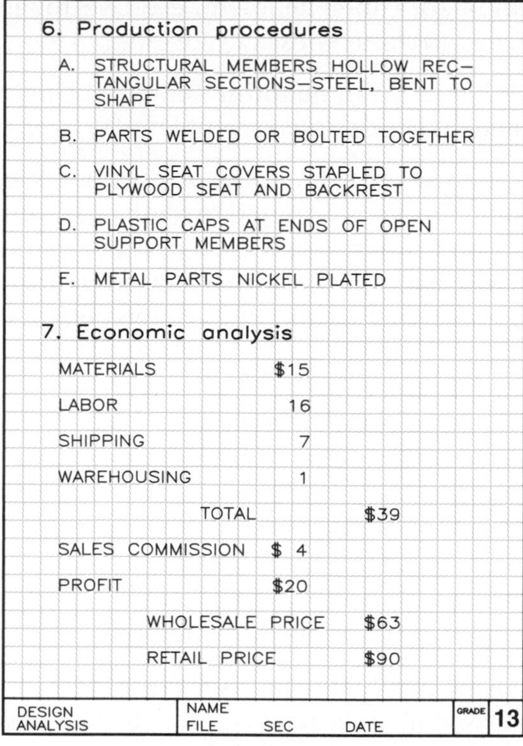

6. Production procedures

A. STRUCTURAL MEMBERS HOLLOW RECTANGULAR SECTIONS—STEEL, BENT TO SHAPE

B. PARTS WELDED OR BOLTED TOGETHER

C. VINYL SEAT COVERS STAPLED TO PLYWOOD SEAT AND BACKREST

D. PLASTIC CAPS AT ENDS OF OPEN SUPPORT MEMBERS

E. METAL PARTS NICKEL PLATED

7. Economic analysis

MATERIALS	$15	
LABOR	16	
SHIPPING	7	
WAREHOUSING	1	
TOTAL		$39
SALES COMMISSION	$ 4	
PROFIT	$20	
WHOLESALE PRICE		$63
RETAIL PRICE		$90

DESIGN ANALYSIS | NAME | FILE | SEC | DATE | GRADE | 13

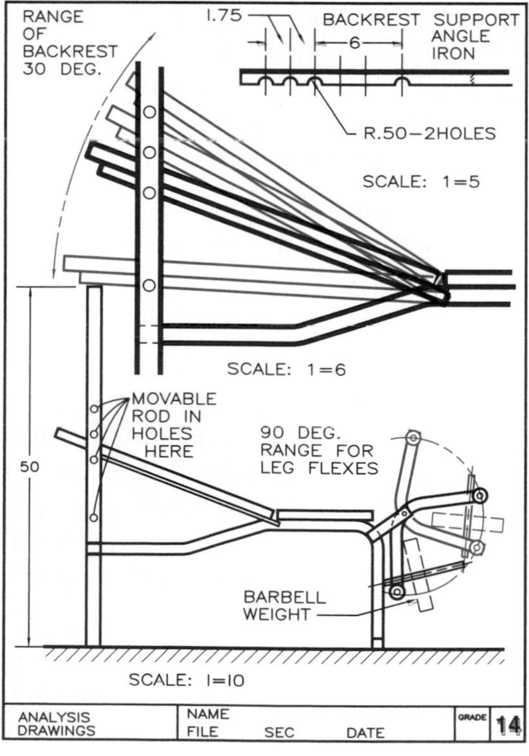

and large sheet sizes for analysis drawings may be used if more space is needed.

Sheet 14 shows how graphics is used to determine the range of positions of the backrest. Those positions affect the design of the angle-iron supports for the backrest and the locations of the semicircular holes in the angle irons for a range of settings of 30°.

The leg-exercising attachment at the end of the bench is designed to move through a 90° arc, which is sufficient for leg extensions. By determining the maximum loads on the backrest and the leg exerciser, you can select the member sizes and materials that provide the strength required. For further analysis, construct a model and test the design for suitability. A product that must support body weight plus weights that are being lifted should be rigorously tested to ensure that it is adequately sturdy.

Figure 6.28 illustrates a model of the exercise bench for testing its functional features. The catalog description of the bench shown in

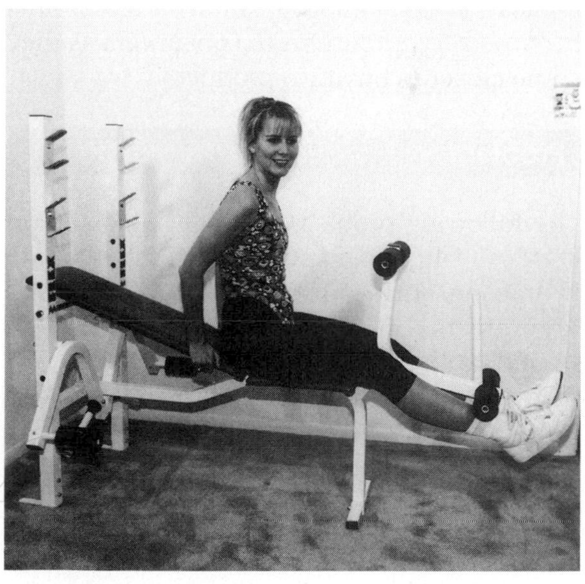

6.28 A full-size model of the exercise bench is tested for function and acceptability.

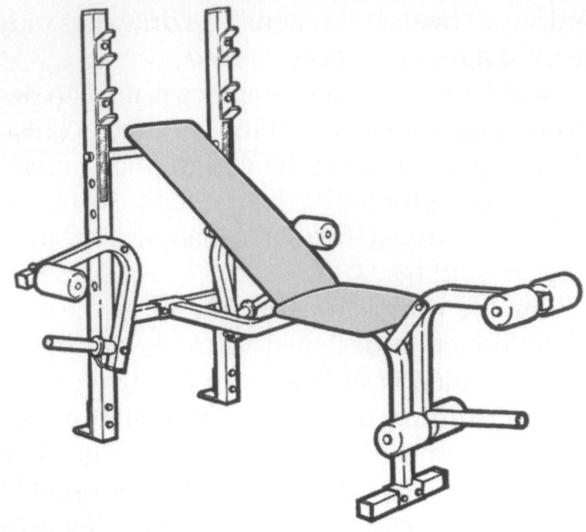

6.29 This catalog description gives the key features of the exercise bench: Weider® bench with butterfly attachment. It features no-pinch supports, multiposition padded back and leg lift, and tubular steel frame. Total weight capacity is 1000 lb; butterfly capacity, 50 lb; leg lift capacity, 65 lb; overall size, 58" × 45" × 41"; weight, 48 lb; and price, $89.99. *(Courtesy of Sears, Roebuck and Company.)*

Figure 6.29 lists the physical properties of the Weider® exercise bench to help the consumer understand its features. You should keep a list of descriptive characteristics of your design for its final catalog specifications. These points become very important to consumers as they come closer to buying a product.

Problems

The following problems should be solved on 8-1/2 × 11-in. paper and the solution presented in drawing, note, and text forms. Answers to essay problems can be typed or lettered. All sheets should be placed in a binder or folder.

General

1. Make a list of human factors that must be considered in designing the following items: (a) canoe, (b) hairbrush, (c) water cooler, (d) automobile, (e) wheelbarrow, (f) drawing table, (g) study desk, (h) pair of binoculars, (i) baby stroller, (j) golf course, (k) seating in a stadium, (l) coffee table, (m) exercise apparatus, and (n) lunch box.

2. What physical quantities have to be determined for the designs in problem 1?

3. Select one of the items in problem 1 and outline the steps required to analyze (a) function, (b) human factors, (c) product market, (d) physical specifications, (e) strength, (f) economic factors, and (g) a prototype model.

Human Engineering

4. Design a computer-graphics table for your body size to meet your own working and comfort needs. Make a drawing indicating the optimum working areas and tilt angle for the computer when you sit at the station. The drawing also should show the most efficient positioning of supplies and manuals.

5. Using the dimensions for the average man and woman (**Figures 6.11** and **6.12**), design stadium benches to meet the optimum needs of spectators. Consider the slope of the stadium seating to allow an adequate view of the playing field. You must also consider spectator comfort and provision for traffic along aisles in front of the benches.

6. Compare the measurements of the male and female students in your class with the averages given in **Figures 6.11** and **6.12**. Tabulate the results and compare them with the percentiles given in **Figure 6.10**.

7. Design a backpack for use on a week-long camping trip. Determine the minimum number of articles a camper should carry; use their weights and volumes in establishing design criteria. Make sketches of the pack and the method of attaching it to the body to provide mobility, comfort, and capacity.

8. State the dimensions, facilities, and provisions needed for a one-person storm shelter to provide protection for 48 hours. Make sketches of the interior in relationship to a person and the supplies.

9. Design a manhole access to an underground facility. Determine the diameter of the manhole required to permit a person to climb a ladder a distance of 10 ft with freedom of movement. Make a sketch of your design and explain your method of solving the problem.

10. Analyze the needs for an observation facility for temporary service in the Arctic. This facility is to be as compact as possible, but it must provide for the needs of one person during a 72-hour duty watch. Make sketches of your design and explain the items considered essential to human survival in that harsh climate.

11. Design an automobile steering wheel that is different from current designs but that is just as functional. Base your design on human factors such as arm position, grip, and vision. Make sketches of your design and list the factors that you considered.

12. Assume that you prefer to alternate between sitting and standing when working at a study desk. Determine the ideal height of the tabletop for working in each position. Indicate how you would devise the table to permit instant conversion from the height for standing to the height for sitting.

Market Analysis

13. Conduct a market analysis for the drill shown in **Figure 6.19**, covering the areas mentioned in the text. Assume that this power tool has never been introduced before. Outline the steps you would take in conducting a product market analysis.

14. Make a market analysis of the hunting seat shown in **Figure 6.20**, following the steps suggested in the text. Determine a reasonable price, potential outlets, and other marketing information for the product.

15. Assume that the costs of producing hunting seats are estimated as follows: 100 seats, $35 each; 200 seats, $20 each; 400 seats, $10 each; 1,000 seats, $8.50 each. Using these figures, determine the price at which you could introduce the seats to consumers on a trial basis and still make some money. Explain your plan.

Strength and Function Analysis

16. Refer to the integral curves plotted in **Figure 6.17** and answer the following questions. At what point (in seconds) is velocity the greatest, and what is this velocity? What is the velocity at 0.25 second? After how many seconds does deceleration begin? What woud be the velocity at 360°?

17. Using the graph in **Figure 6.30**, answer the following questions: (a) For a mat depth of 4 in. and a speed of 120 ft/min, how many tons per hour are transported? (b) To transport 100 tons per hour, what is the slowest conveyor speed that would be safe (would avoid the "caution advised" area)? (c) For a mat depth of 5 in. and a speed of 20 ft/min, what would be the capacity?

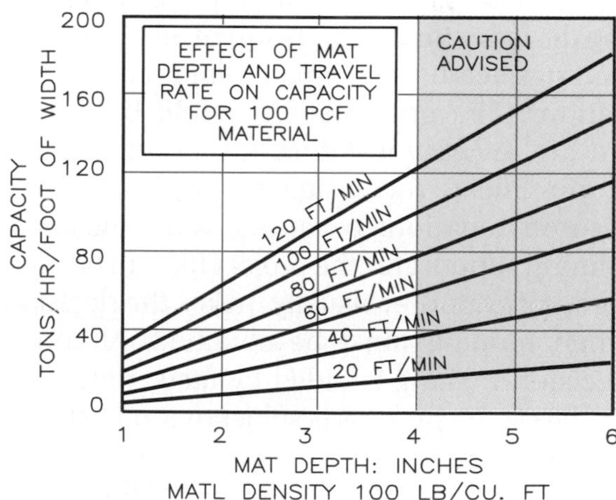

6.30 **Problem 17:** These straight-line curves represent conveyor speeds used for transporting materials of 100 lb/cu ft. The capacity in tons per hour per foot of width of the conveyor is given on the *y*-axis, and mat depth is shown on the *x*-axis. Mat depth is the thickness of the material applied to the conveyor.

7 Decision

7.1 Introduction

After the designer has conceived, developed, refined, and analyzed several designs, one must be selected for implementation. The decision process begins with a presentation by the designer (or design team) of all significant findings, features, estimates, and recommendations. The presentation should be organized in an easy-to-follow form, and it must communicate the designer's conclusions and recommendations because it is the means of gaining support for the project for it to be realized. A committee usually makes the decision when funding must be obtained. Although decision making is aided by facts, data, and analyses, the process is subjective at best.

7.2 Decision

The purpose of oral presentations and written reports is to present the findings of a project so that a decision can be made whether to implement it. One of three types of decisions may be made:

Acceptance. A design may be accepted in its entirety, which indicates success by the designer.

Rejection. A design may be rejected in its entirety, which does not necessarily mean that the designer has failed. Changes in the economic climate, moves by competitors, or other factors beyond the designer's control may make the design obsolete, premature, or unprofitable.

Compromise. Parts of a design may have weaknesses, and compromises may be suggested. For example, the initial production run may be increased or decreased, or various features may be eliminated, modified, merged, or added.

7.3 Decision: Exercise Bench

We have used the exercise bench problem introduced in Chapter 3 to illustrate the first four steps of the design process. We continue to use it here to help explain the decision step.

Decision Table

Use a table like the one shown in **Sheet 16** to compare designs, where each idea is listed and given a number for identification. Assign maximum values for each analysis factor, based on your best judgment, so they total to 10 points. Rate each factor for the competing designs by entering points for each.

Sum the columns of numbers to determine the total for each design, and compare the scores of each design. Your instincts may disagree with the outcome of this numerical analysis. If so, have enough faith in your judgment to go with your intuition. The scores from the decision table are meant to be a guide for you and not the absolute final word in your decision.

Conclusion

After making a decision, state it and the reasons for it clearly (**Sheet 17**). Record any additional information, such as number to be produced initially, selling price per unit, profit per unit, estimated sales during the first year, break-even number, and the product's most marketable features, that will help you prepare your presentation.

If you believe that none of your designs are satisfactory, you should recommend that they not be implemented. A negative recommendation is not a failure of the design process; it means only that the solutions developed so far

DECISION

1. Decision for evaluation

DESIGN 1 A–FRAME

DESIGN 2 U–FRAME

DESIGN 3 2–COLUMN FRAME

DESIGN 4

DESIGN 5

MAX	FACTORS	1	2	3	4
3.0	FUNCTION	2.0	2.3	2.5	
2.0	HUMAN FACTORS	1.6	1.4	1.7	
0.5	MARKET ANALYSIS	0.4	0.4	0.4	
1.0	STRENGTH	1.0	1.0	1.0	
0.5	PRODUCTION EASE	0.3	0.2	0.4	
1.0	COST	0.7	0.6	0.8	
1.5	PROFITABILITY	1.1	1.0	1.3	
0.5	APPEARANCE	0.3	0.4	0.4	
10	TOTALS	7.4	7.3	8.5	

DESIGN DECISION | NAME FILE SEC DATE | GRADE | 16

Sheet 16 This worksheet shows the decision table used to evaluate the design alternatives for the exercise bench.

CONCLUSIONS

THE 2–COLUMN FRAME IS THE BEST SOLUTION FOR IMPLEMENTATION BECAUSE

1. GOOD MARKET POTENTIAL
2. AIDS WELL IN EXERCISING
3. FULFILLS PRODUCT REQUIREMENTS
4. ATTRACTIVE PRICE
5. MANUFACTURED EASILY

RECOMMEND IMPLEMENTATION AND PRODUCTION OF THE DESIGN

ECONOMIC FORECAST

SALES PRICE $ 90

SHIPPING EXPENSES $ 12

CUSTOMER PRICE $102

MANUFACTURER'S PROFIT $ 20 EACH

BREAK–EVEN AT 500 UNITS

PRODUCTION: RECOMMEND THAT BENCHES BE MADE BY QUALIFIED MANUFACTURER ON A CONTRACT BASIS

PROFITABILITY: BENCH SHOULD YIELD AN ATTRACTIVE RETURN ON INVESTMENT

DESIGN CONCLUSION | NAME FILE SEC DATE | GRADE | 17

Sheet 17 This worksheet summarizes the designer's conclusions and recommendations for implementing that design.

are not feasible. Going forward with an inadequate solution could cause both monetary losses and wasted effort.

Presentation

Until now your efforts have been self-directed and mostly free from supervision. The work is your own (or that of your team), you have solved the problem to the best of your ability, and you are ready to make recommendations regarding its implementation.

At this point the project usually involves the input of others besides the designers. These outsiders may be other engineers, managers, administrators, salespeople, company shareholders, investors, or bankers who will loan money for the project. You must prepare a presentation suitable for your audience to communicate the important features of your design, the data you gathered and analyzed, and the benefits to be gained by implementing your design.

Present your findings, conclusions, and recommendations as objectively as possible so that the group can make a valid decision. At no time should your enthusiasm for the project outweigh an impartial presentation of the facts.

7.4 Types of Presentations

Presentations may be made to groups ranging from a few knowledgeable design associates to a large number of laypeople unfamiliar with the project and its objectives. Presentations of the first type usually are informal; the second type, formal.

Informal Presentations

Informal presentations are made to several associates and perhaps a supervisor. Although formally prepared visual aids are unnecessary for presentations to a small group, the designer nevertheless needs to graph data, draw pictorials, sketch schematics, and build models to explain design concepts. Ideas and concepts may be sketched on a blackboard or informally discussed in a one-on-one situation (**Figure 7.1**).

7.1 A decision may be the outcome of an informal presentation to an associate where ideas and designs are discussed one-on-one.

Formal Presentations

Formal presentations usually involve large groups that may include associates, administrators, and/or laypeople, or a combination of these. They may be clients for whom the project is designed, potential investors, or politicians who will vote to approve or disapprove the design (**Figure 7.2**). Function and acceptability of a design are the primary concerns of

7.2 When preparing a presentation assume that you are preparing it for a group of bankers and investors whose support you need.

engineering associates, and profitability is most important to investors.

7.5 Organizing a Presentation

An effective method of planning oral and written reports is to use 3 × 5-in. index cards for the ideas to be presented. Placing the cards on a table or tacking them to a bulletin board (**Figure 7.3**) allows an easy choice of sequence and rearrangement as needed. Each card (**Figure 7.4**) should contain the following information:

1. **Number.** The card's position in the presentation sequence.
2. **Illustration.** A sketch of the illustration, if any.
3. **Text.** A brief outline of the points to be covered for that idea.

7.6 Visual Aids

Visual aids commonly used in presentations are flip charts, photographic slides, overhead visuals, models, computer images, and videotapes. The following suggestions apply to the preparation of visual aids:

1. Limit each visual to a single concept or point.

7.3 Planning cards are useful in preparing the sequence of a presentation. The cards are arranged on a planning board (as shown here) or on a tabletop. *(Courtesy of Eastman Kodak.)*

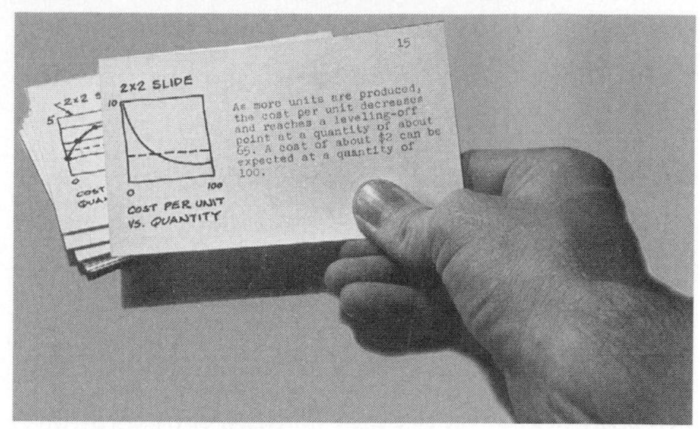

7.4 This layout on a 3 × 5-in. card, showing a sketch of the visual and its accompanying text, illustrates sound planning.

2. Reduce statements to key points to communicate thoughts clearly and concisely.
3. Make visuals containing text large enough to be readable.
4. Use illustrations, color, and attention-getting devices.
5. Prepare enough visuals so that notes are unnecessary.

Flip Charts

Flip charts consist of bold illustrations drawn on sheets (usually 30 × 36 in.) for presentation to groups no larger than about 30 people.

Paper Flip charts may be drawn on brown wrapping paper or white newsprint paper attached to a cardboard backing board. A stand or easel is needed to support the cardboard-backed set of sheets.

Lettering Felt-tipped markers, ink, tempera, or sign paints are fine for lettering. When used correctly, felt-tipped markers can yield bold, visible lines in a variety of colors and with sophisticated effects.

Color Construction paper cutouts mounted with rubber cement are especially effective for adding color to bar graphs. The use of felt-tipped markers and tempera colors also adds color and interest to a chart.

Assembly Flip chart sheets should be arranged in order of presentation with a title page covered by a blank sheet of paper on top to prevent audience anticipation. Fasten the sheets at the top to the backing board.

Presentation Each sheet is flipped in sequence after the presenter has covered the points on it. A pointer should be used to direct the audience's attention to specific items on the sheet. Well-prepared flip charts should require no additional notes.

Photographic Slides

Slides are effective for larger audiences and for showing actual scenes or examples of hardware.

Artwork The method for proportionally sizing artwork for a 35 mm slide is shown in **Figure 7.5**. An 8 × 12-in. size is suitable for most slides. The artwork should contain color to make the slides more attractive and effective in maintaining audience interest. Colored construction paper, mat board, and other poster materials should be used in preparing slides.

Allow at least an inch margin on all artwork so the edges will not show when photographed. Uppercase letters are best for slides, with the space between lines of text equal to the height of the letters. Do not use a white background for slide artwork, because it is tiring to the eyes.

Photographing Layouts To make slides, a camera, copy stand, and lights are required. A 35 mm reflex camera with through-the-lens viewfinder is best because the photographer sees exactly what is being photographed. The copy stand holds the camera steady. If all the artwork is uniform in size, the camera can be left in the same position during photography. Small illustrations can be photographed with a close-up lens. The finished slides are reviewed, arranged in sequence, numbered, and loaded in a tray for showing.

Slide Scripts A slide script is useful when a presentation will be made repeatedly. Photographic copies of the slides attached to the left side of the script serve as prompts for the presenter (**Figure 7.6**).

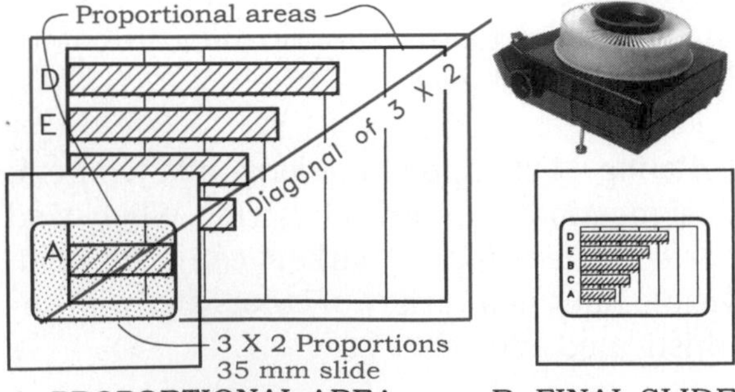

7.5 Use of this method of proportionately sizing artwork ensures that it will properly fill a photographic slide.

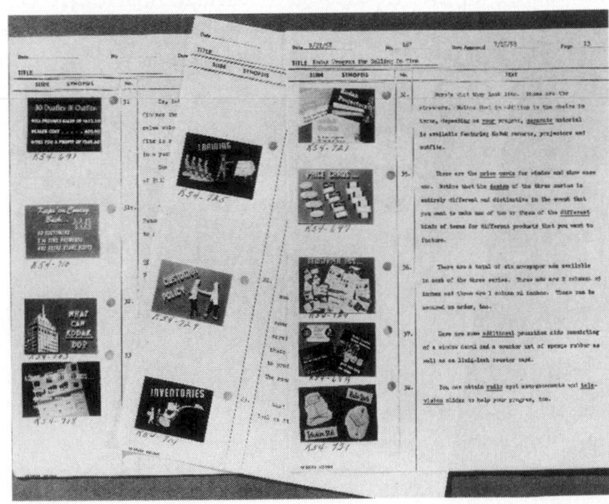

7.6 A slide script is useful for lengthy slide presentations and those that will be given repetitively. *(Courtesy of Eastman Kodak.)*

Overhead Projector Transparencies

Overhead projector transparencies are reproduced on 8 × 10-in. plastic sheets by the heat-transfer or diazo processes, or plotted by the computer. Tracing paper is the most commonly used drawing surface for preparing art from which transparencies are made. Tracing paper can be used in both the heat-transfer and diazo processes (opaque paper cannot be used in the diazo process). Computer plotting can be done directly onto plastic film with special pens. Diazo transparencies are reproduced on plastic film in the same manner as blue-line prints are made.

Drawings should be made in black India ink. Stick-on shapes and graphing tapes can give the drawing a professional appearance. Lettering should be at least 0.20 in. high.

Color Overlays Several color overlays can be hinged to the transparency mount for presentations with multiple steps (**Figure 7.7**). Each color overlay requires a separate piece of artwork, which is drawn on tracing paper placed over the basic layout.

Computer-Plotted Transparencies Computer-generated art and text can be plotted directly on plastic film with fiber-tipped pens, which come in many colors and match the film (**Figure 7.7**). The Romand font of AutoCAD is better suited for large lettering on transparencies than is the Romans font.

Presentation The presenter stands or sits near the projector in a semilighted room and refers to the transparencies while facing the audience. The presenter can emphasize items on the stage of the projector with a pointer, which is projected onto the screen. In the same manner as multiple overlays are hinged to a mount, paper overlays can be attached to mounts to block out parts of the transparency to control audience attention.

Models

A model is the most realistic visual aid for showing a final design. Models should be large enough to be seen by all in the audience. A series of photographic close-ups of the model, taken from different angles, can be used to supplement the presentation. Obviously, a full-size prototype of the completed design (**Figure 7.8**) provides the most accurate description of the product and demonstrates its operation.

Computer Visuals Software programs such as Microsoft's PowerPoint can be used for making

7.7 A transparency used on an overhead projector consists of an 8-1/2 × 11-in. transparency mounted on a 10 × 12-in. frame. The projection area within the frame is about 7-1/2 × 9-1/2-in. To show information sequentially, different-colored overlays can be flipped over, one at a time.

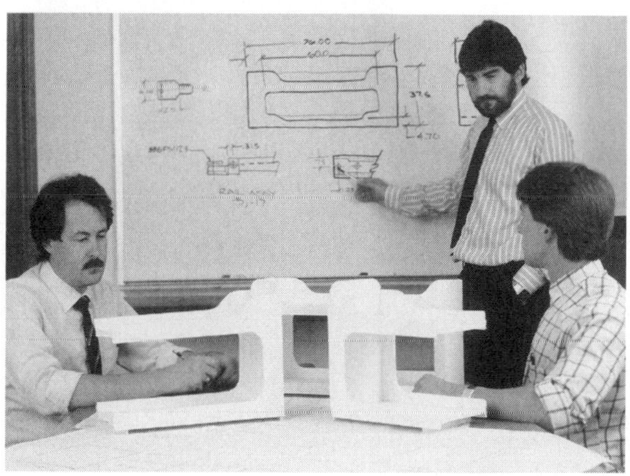

7.8 A model and a blackboard are effective aids in a presentation to a small group.

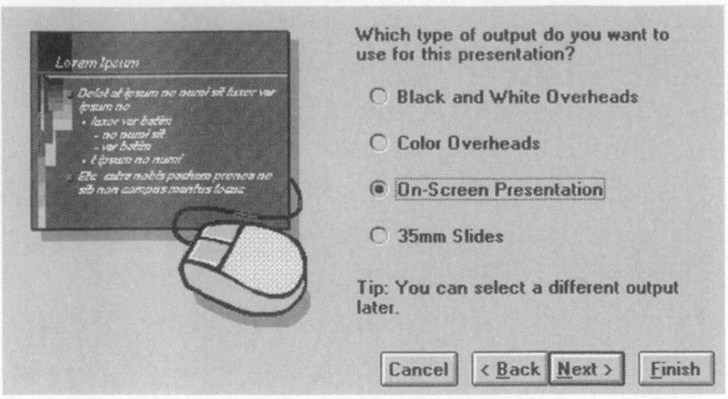

7.9 The dialogue screen illustrates a computer visual and the prompts for composing it. *(Courtesy of PowerPoint.)*

slides that can be viewed on the computer monitor for small groups or projected onto a large screen connected to a computer for large groups. **Figure 7.9** shows a dialogue screen used in composing a computer visual with PowerPoint. Any drawing or photograph that can be seen on the computer monitor can be used as a visual.

When slides are made by the computer, there is no need for special art supplies, storage problems are eliminated, and the entire slide show can be shown on a laptop computer (**Figure 7.10**). Full-color art work, special effects, and animation can be incorporated into these presentations.

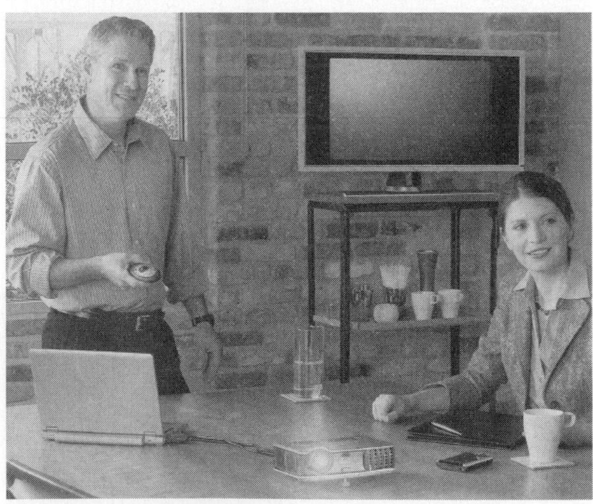

7.10 High-tech presentations can be given with a portable projector and a laptop computer to help the presenter communicate with the audience. *(Courtesy of Dell Inc.)*

7.11 Future presentations may be prepared for the Personal Video Player (PVP) and displayed on its built-in LCD screen or a standard TV. This device is being developed by Sonicblue and the Intel Corporation. *(Courtesy of the Intel Corporation.)*

Video

Videotaping presentations or visuals supplemented by a voice-over narration is an effective and sophisticated method. The videotape may include various special effects such as music, sound effects, close-ups, motion, and precise realism.

Formal presentations in the future will be multimedia shows using video and the computer in combination. The PVP (Personal Video Player), a miniature, handheld player holding up to 10 hours of content, is an example of a device that may revolutionize presentations of the future (**Figure 7.11**).

7.7 Making a Presentation

Inspect the room in which the presentation is to be made prior to the meeting. Check out the visibility of your visuals from various audience locations. Projectors and visual-aid equipment must be positioned and focused before the audience arrives, and remote controls for projectors should be readied for use. Be aware of where to stand so as to not block anyone's view.

Delivery

Progress through the presentation at a moderate pace while emphasizing information on the visual aids with a pointer (**Figure 7.10**). A positive approach in selling ideas should not become deceptive high-pressure salesmanship. You should be frank in pointing out weaknesses in a design and show alternatives that compensate for them.

Conclusions and recommendations should be supported by data and analyses. A recommendation to reject or accept a design should be supported by reasons. A period for questions and answers should follow the presentation for clarification purposes. If available, a technical report should be given to the audience.

Critique

When your team gives a presentation to the class, both your design recommendations and the skill of your presentation will be evaluated and critiqued. The form shown in **Figure 7.12** is typical of the evaluation form that may be used for your critique. It can also be used as a guide in preparing the presentation. The names of the team members are listed at the top of the sheet. As a group, your team must agree on the percentage contribution of each member to the project prior to presentation. The sum of the percentage contributions of all team members must equal 100 percent. The F-factor for each member is the number of members (N) times the contribution of each (C). The chart in the appendix illustrates how an individual's contribution to the project is translated into his or her individual grade by using the F-factor.

Complete this table jointly with your team and leave the grade column blank for completion by your instructor who will use the chart on page 4 and the factor "F" that was computed for each member.

ORAL REPORT

Team No. **5** Project: **TOY MANUFACTURING**

Number members: (N= **7**)	%Contribution (C)	F=NC	GRADE
1. **BROWN, GEORGE**	17	119	91
2. **PRIDE, HELEN**	14.3	100	87
3. **SMITH, ROGER**	20	140	95
4. **REED, RALPH**	5.7	40	63
5. **POTTER, JOYCE**	14.3	100	87
6. **FLYNN, BUNKY**	14.3	100	87
7. **ROSS, LAWRENCE**	14.4	100	87

EVALUATION BY INSTRUCTOR	Max.	
1. Introduction of team members	2	2
2. Proper dress of team members	2	2
3. Statement of purpose of presentation	5	4
4. Use of visuals—point to important points, do not block screen, do not fumble, etc.	10	8
5. Adequate number of visual aids	9	9
6. Quality of visual aids	15	12
7. Clear presentation of recommended design	10	8
8. Coverage of alternative solutions considered	2	2
9. Consideration of human factors	5	5
10. Coverage of economics (manufacturing, shipping, packing, overhead, mark-up, etc.)	10	7
11. Presentation of an effective conclusion	5	4
12. Continuity of presentation	3	3
13. Poise and professionalism	2	2
14. Team participation (perfect score if all participate)	10	10
15. Use of allotted time	10	9
TOTAL	100	87

Comments:

Good introduction to project.

Several visuals were too complicated.

Economic analysis a little weak.

Good conclusion and proposed solution.

Very good professional manner of giving the presentation.

7.12 An evaluation form for grading oral reports.

7.8 A Successful Presentation

The objective of a presenter is to obtain customers, funding, resources, or endorsements, whereas the objective of the audience is to improve profits and find solutions to their problems. Knowing this is the fundamental rule of salesmanship. When a designer is introducing a new product or concept, the presentation must address the needs of the potential buyer.

When seeking acceptance for a new design concept or product, find out in advance what the needs of the customer are and focus on those points during your presentation. Talk to your audience about their needs, not yours, to be most effective.

A successful presentation will likely result in a positive decision enabling you to move to the implementation stage of the design process.

7.9 Written Reports

The three basic types of written reports are **proposals, progress reports,** and **final reports**.

Proposals

Proposals establish the need for projects and are necessary to obtain authorization of funds and support to pursue them. Proposals outline data, costs, specifications, time schedules, personnel requirements, completion dates, and similar information. The project's purpose is stated with emphasis on its benefit to the client.

Proposals should reflect the interests and language of the readers. For instance, investors are interested in profits and returns, whereas engineers are more concerned with function and feasibility. Elements of a proposal are:

Statement of the problem. Identification of the problem and its purpose.

Method of approach. An outline of procedures for attacking the problem.

Personnel needs and facilities. Itemization of requirements for equipment, space, and personnel.

Time schedule. Estimation of completion dates for each phase of the project.

Budget. Itemization of the funds required for each phase of the project.

Summary. A review of the important points.

Progress Reports

Progress reports are periodic summaries of the status of a project. They are brief and may take the form of a letter or memo. They generally review progress and project the outlook for further progress, including the need for increases or decreases in expenditures or time.

Final Reports

The most comprehensive type of reports are final reports that summarize the completion of the project. Typically, they contain the following sections:

1. Project identification
2. Method and approach
3. Body
4. Findings and solution
5. Conclusions and recommendations

Some reports present the conclusions at the beginning and others at the end. The order of presentation will vary with the requirements of your instructor or employer.

Report Format The usual sequence of a report is as follows:

1. **Cover.** The report is inserted in a binder, with its title and author labeled on the cover.

2. **Letter of transmittal** (optional). A letter to the recipient inserted at the front of the report describing the report's contents.

3. **Title page.** A page giving the title of the report, the name of the person or team who prepared it, and the date.

4. **Table of contents.** The major headings in the report and their page numbers.

5. **Table of illustrations** (optional). A list of the illustrations in the report.

6. **Problem identification.** (Actual heading should be appropriate to the report rather than this general term.) An explanation of the importance of and need for a solution to the problem by outlining background information on the problem.

7. **Method.** (Actual heading should be appropriate to the report rather than this general term.) A coverage of the methods used in solving the problem.

8. **Body.** (Actual heading should be appropriate to the report rather than this general term.) This main section describes the data collected, analyses made, and the steps taken to solve the problem. Subheadings emphasize various sections.

9. **Findings.** (Actual heading should be appropriate to the report rather than this general

term.) Findings should relate to the data described in the preceding section.

10. Conclusions. The culmination of the findings and presentation of the solution.

11. Bibliography. References—books, magazines, brochures, interviews—used in the preparation of the report listed alphabetically by author.

12. Appendix. Information (such as drawings, sketches, raw data, brochures, and letters) that supplements (often in more detail) the main sections of the report.

Common Omissions Often omitted from student reports are sales estimates, advertising methods, shipping costs, product packaging, miscellaneous overhead expenses, and recommendation summaries.

Illustrations Reports should be liberally illustrated. Drawings and illustrations should be numbered and given captions that describe them. The text should refer to each figure by number and explain its contents. For example, "Figure 6 shows the number of boats sold between 2000 and 2008" identifies the figure and what it depicts.

Illustrations should be drawn or reproduced on opaque paper rather than tracing paper; ink illustrations are preferred. Position illustrations on the page so that they can be read from the bottom or from the right. Large drawings should fold to 8-1/2 × 11 in. to fit the binder.

Problems

1. Prepare a checklist for evaluating an oral presentation by one of your classmates. List items to consider and develop a grading scale to arrive at an overall evaluation.

2. Use 3 × 5-in. cards to plan a flip-chart presentation that will last no more than 5 minutes. The subject may be of your choosing or one assigned by your instructor. Some examples are (a) your career plans for the first 2 years after graduation, (b) the role of this course in your overall educational program, (c) the importance of effective communication, (d) the need for a design project that you are proposing, and (e) a comparison of engineering with another profession.

3. Prepare graphical aids for an oral presentation using the methods and materials covered in this chapter.

4. Using the planning cards developed in problem 2, prepare a 5-minute briefing on a technique that you choose or are assigned by your instructor.

5. You are an engineer responsible for developing a proposal for a project that could result in a sizable contract for your firm. Make a list of instructions to give to your assistants for their help in preparing a presentation for a group of 20 people, ranging in background from bankers to engineers.

Outline the materials needed, types and number of graphical aids required, method of projection or presentation, assistance needed during the presentation, room seating arrangements, and other factors. Cover the entire presentation for the length of time you think most desirable. Select a topic or use one assigned by your instructor.

6. Many designs and products come onto the market that are mistakes from the beginning—they don't sell and may not function well. Poor decisions were made when the "go ahead" was given. Make a list of as many of these "mistakes" as you can think of. For starters, the Susan B. Anthony dollar is a mistake that was discontinued by the government.

7. Select a commercial advertisement on TV that you regard as successful. Make a list of the points presented and the reasons that they are successful in attracting consumers.

8

Implementation

8.1 Introduction

Implementation is the final step of the design process, in which the design becomes a reality. The designer details the product in working drawings with specifications and notes for its fabrication. Graphical methods are particularly important during implementation, because all products are manufactured from working drawings and specifications. Implementation also involves the packaging, warehousing, distribution, and sales of the manufactured product.

8.2 Working Drawings

Working drawings, with orthographic views, dimensions, and notes, describe how to make the individual parts of a product. The blank hanger in **Figure 8.1** is drawn by computer as a working drawing for implementation in **Figure 8.2.** Properly executed working

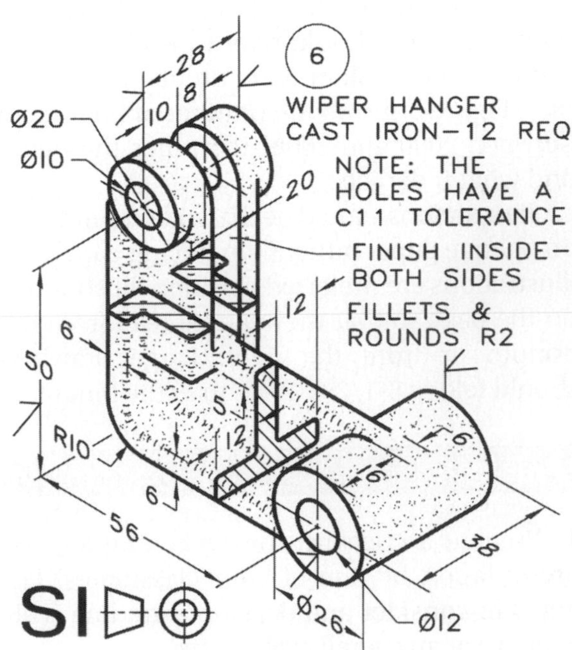

8.1 This wiper hanger is shown in a dimensioned working drawing in Figure 8.2 with three orthographic views.

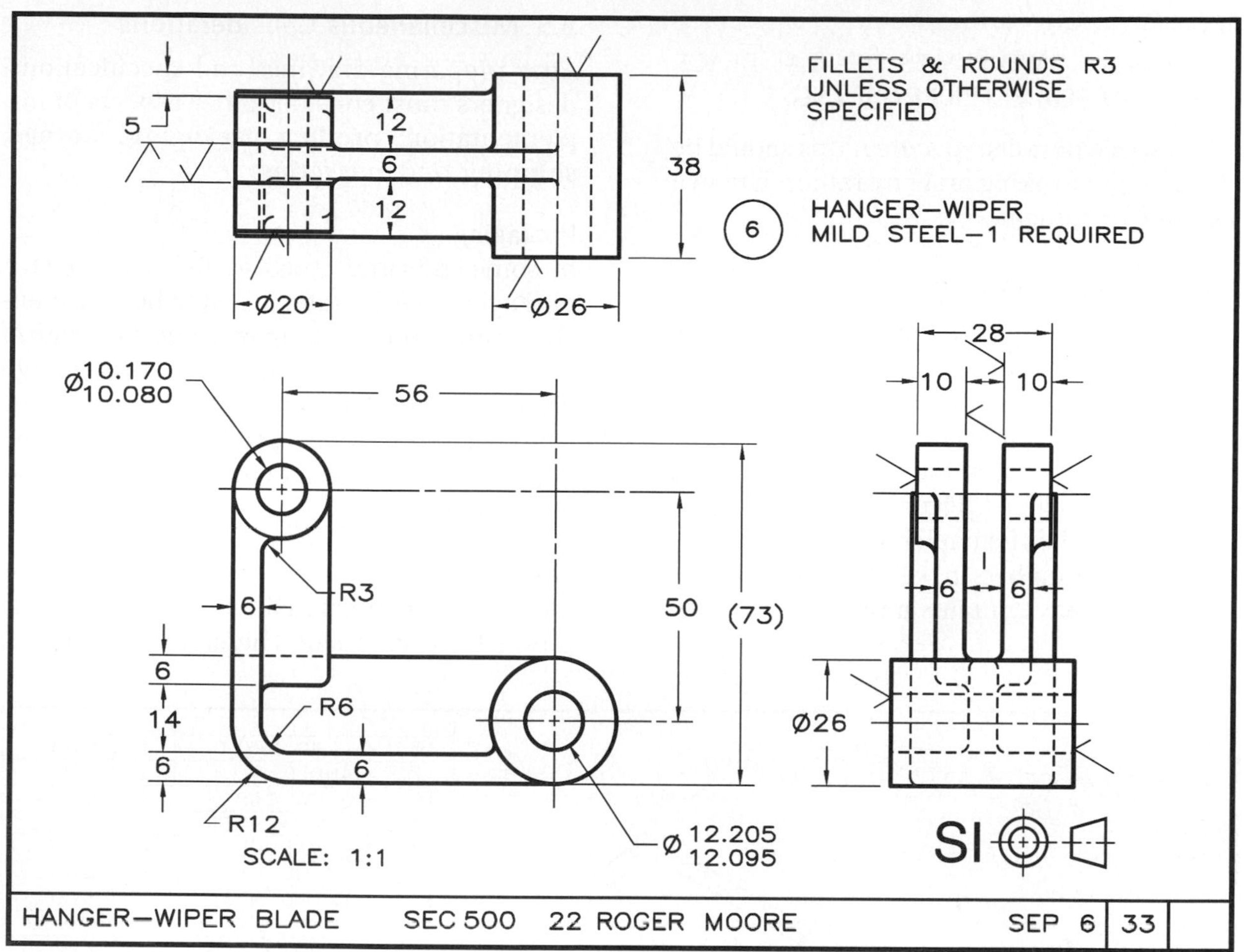

8.2 This computer-drawn working drawing enables the design for this part to be implemented as a final product.

drawings ensure that the resulting products will be identical when the instructions on the drawings are followed regardless of the shop in which they are made.

When making working drawings, designers draw several parts on the same sheet without attempting to arrange them in relationship to one another or in order of their assembly. The names of the parts, their identifying numbers, the quantity required, and the materials to be used in making them are noted near the views.

8.3 Specifications

Specifications are written notes and instructions that supplement the information shown in drawings. Specifications may be prepared as separate typed documents that accompany drawings or that stand alone when graphical representation is unnecessary. Instructional notes such as the following are adequate as written specifications without drawings:

METALLURGICAL INSPECTION IS REQUIRED BEFORE MACHINING.

or

PAINT WITH TWO COATS OF FLAT BLACK PAINT (NO. 780) AFTER FINISHING.

When space permits, specifications should be given on the working drawing rather than in a separate document.

8.4 Assembly Drawings

Assembly drawings illustrate how individual parts are to be put together to become the final product. They can be drawn as three-dimensional pictorials or orthographic views that are fully assembled, fully exploded, or partially exploded. **Figure 8.3** shows a partially exploded orthographic view of an assembly with part numbers in balloons. An assembly drawing usually contains a parts list for easy reference.

8.5 Miscellaneous Considerations

After preparing drawings and specifications, designers must consider other aspects of implementation: **product packaging, storage, shipping**, and **marketing**.

Packaging

In some industries such as the toy industry, packaging is elaborate and may be as expensive as the product. Designers must be aware of packaging problems as they develop a design because a product that is difficult to package will cost more. Many products are shipped partially disassembled to make packaging easier and cheaper.

Storage

Most manufacturers maintain an inventory of products for shipment. Therefore warehousing

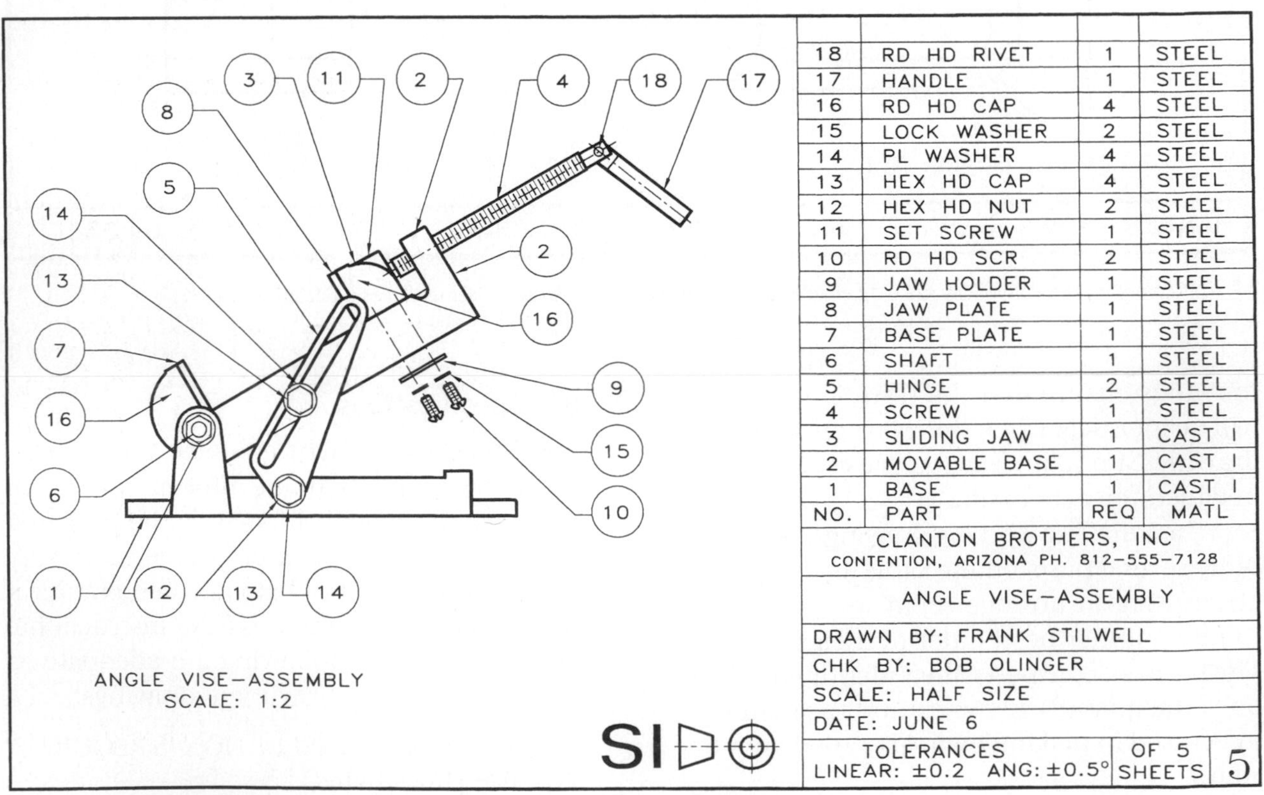

NO.	PART	REQ	MATL
18	RD HD RIVET	1	STEEL
17	HANDLE	1	STEEL
16	RD HD CAP	4	STEEL
15	LOCK WASHER	2	STEEL
14	PL WASHER	4	STEEL
13	HEX HD CAP	4	STEEL
12	HEX HD NUT	2	STEEL
11	SET SCREW	1	STEEL
10	RD HD SCR	2	STEEL
9	JAW HOLDER	1	STEEL
8	JAW PLATE	1	STEEL
7	BASE PLATE	1	STEEL
6	SHAFT	1	STEEL
5	HINGE	2	STEEL
4	SCREW	1	STEEL
3	SLIDING JAW	1	CAST I
2	MOVABLE BASE	1	CAST I
1	BASE	1	CAST I

8.3 An orthographic assembly drawing of a vise shows how the individual parts fit together.

costs must be figured into the product's final selling price.

Shipping

Industries that locate warehouse facilities in the middle of their market areas have lower shipping costs than those with warehouses at the edges of their market areas.

Marketing

Designers must be concerned with all aspects of a product after it enters the marketplace, including its marketability and consumer acceptance. Complaints about a product's reliability and function are important to designers, alerting them to design or manufacturing defects that must be overcome in future versions of the product.

8.6 Implementation: Exercise Bench

To illustrate implementation of a product design, we return to the exercise bench, which was introduced in Chapter 3 and has been used to demonstrate the application of each step in the design process.

Working Drawings

The two working drawings shown in **Figures 8.3** through **8.5** depict some details of the exercise bench design. Additional working drawings are required to show the other parts of the bench, which are dimensioned in decimal inches. Standard parts to be purchased from suppliers are not drawn but are itemized on the drawing, given part numbers,

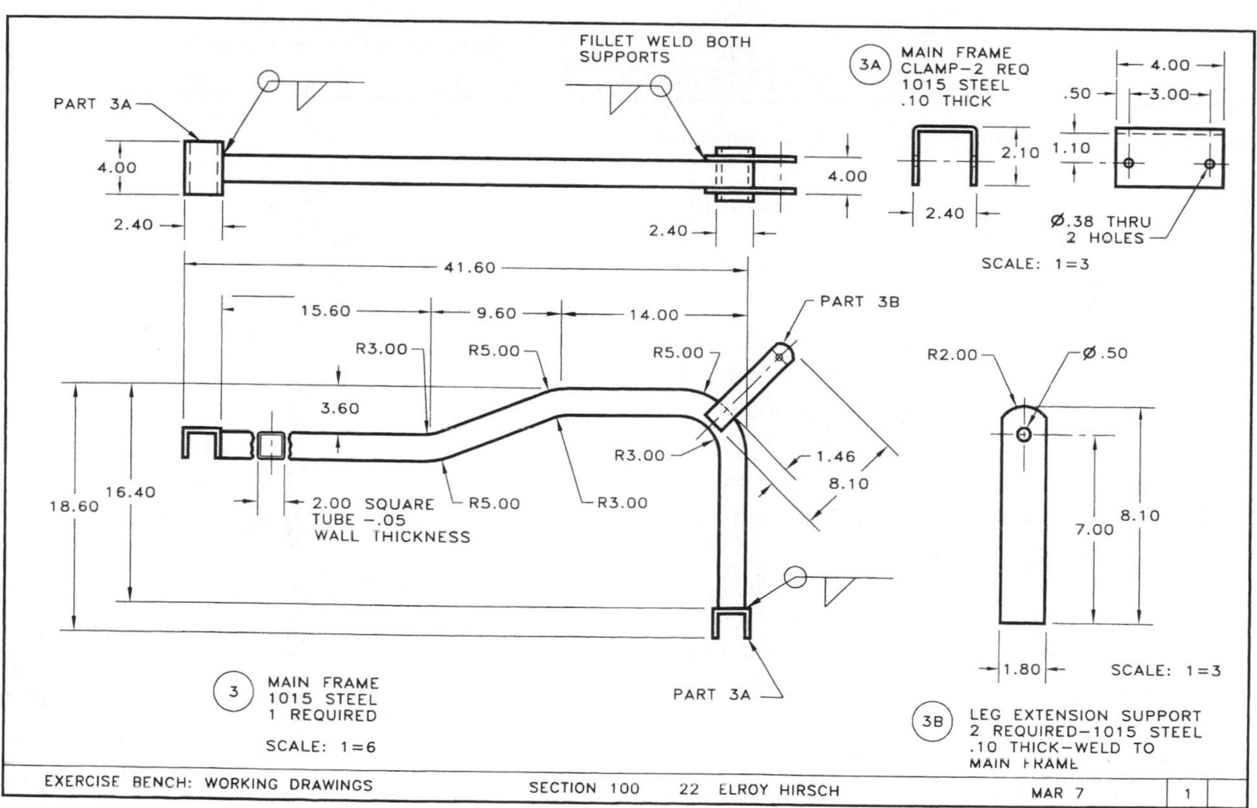

8.4 This working drawing depicts exercise bench parts (sheet 1 of 5).

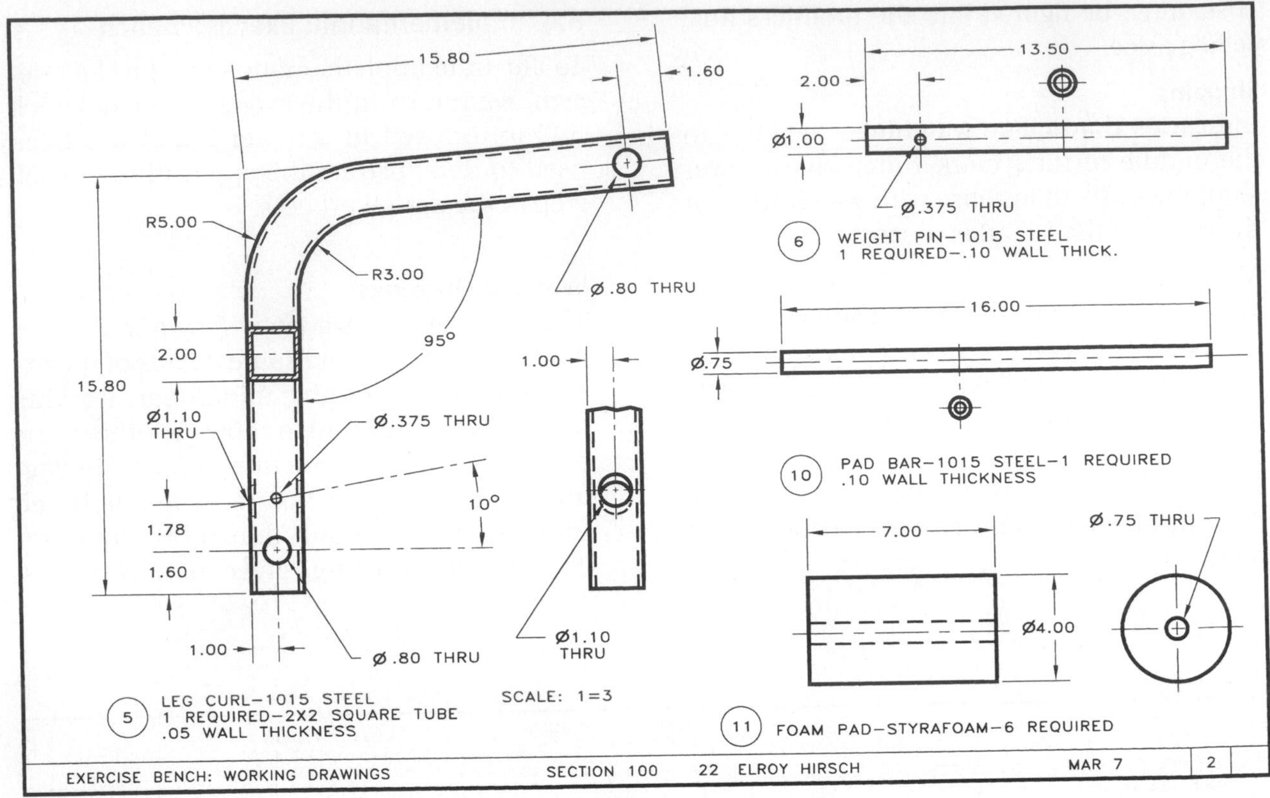

8.5 This working drawing depicts exercise bench parts (sheet 2 of 5).

and listed in the parts list on the assembly drawing.*

Assembly Drawing

Figure 8.6 shows an assembly drawing that illustrates how the parts are to be assembled after they have been made. The assembly is shown pictorially, with the different parts identified by numbered balloons attached to leaders. The parts list identifies each part by number and describes it generally.

Packaging

The Weider exercise bench is packaged in a corrugated cardboard box and weighs approximately 40 lb (**Figure 8.7**). It is shipped unassembled so that it will fit into a smaller carton for ease of handling during shipment.

Storage

An inventory of benches must be maintained to meet retailer demand. The need to hold inventory increases overhead costs for interest payments, warehouse rent, warehouse personnel, and loading equipment.

Shipping

Shipping costs for all types of carriers (rail, motor freight, air delivery, and mail services) must be evaluated. The shipping cost for a Weider bench with its accessories is $15–$20, depending on distance, when shipped one at a time by United Parcel Service. The cost per

*This particular design was developed and patented and is marketed by Weider Health and Fitness, 2100 Erwin Street, Woodland Hills, CA 91367.

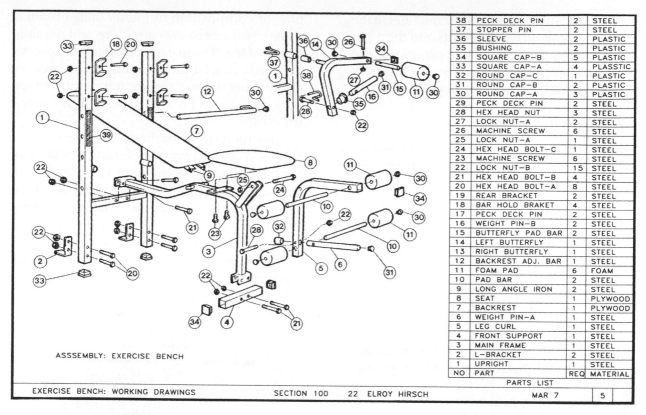

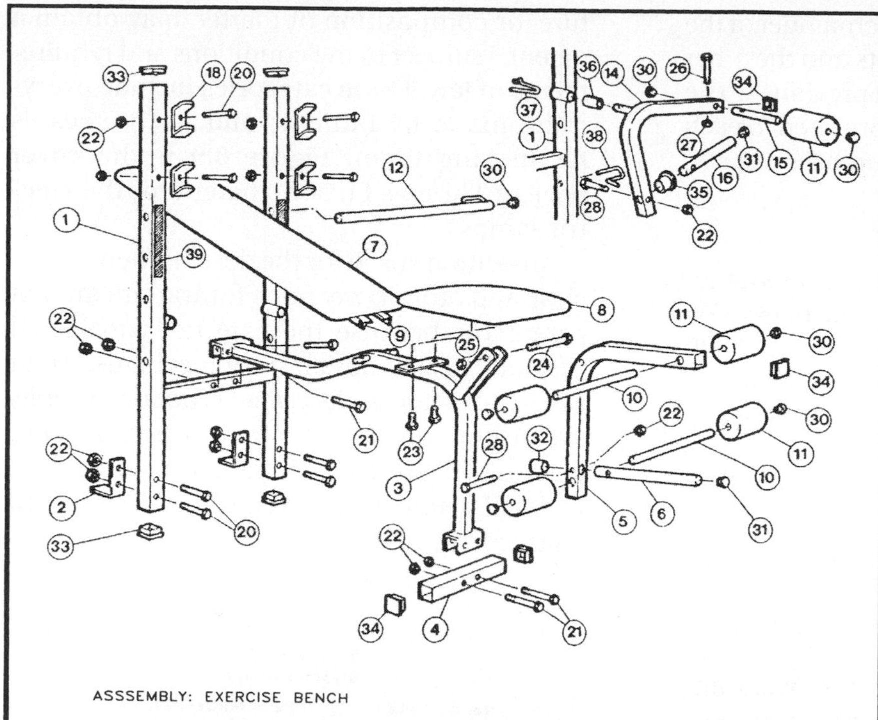

NO	PART	REQ	MATERIAL
38	PECK DECK PIN	2	STEEL
37	STOPPER PIN	2	STEEL
36	SLEEVE	2	PLASTIC
35	BUSHING	2	PLASTIC
34	SQUARE CAP–B	5	PLASTIC
33	SQUARE CAP–A	4	PLASSTIC
32	ROUND CAP–C	1	PLASTIC
31	ROUND CAP–B	2	PLASTIC
30	ROUND CAP–A	3	PLASTIC
29	PECK DECK PIN	2	STEEL
28	HEX HEAD NUT	3	STEEL
27	LOCK NUT–A	2	STEEL
26	MACHINE SCREW	6	STEEL
25	LOCK NUT–A	1	STEEL
24	HEX HEAD BOLT–C	1	STEEL
23	MACHINE SCREW	6	STEEL
22	LOCK NUT–B	15	STEEL
21	HEX HEAD BOLT–B	4	STEEL
20	HEX HEAD BOLT–A	8	STEEL
19	REAR BRACKET	2	STEEL
18	BAR HOLD BRAKET	4	STEEL
17	PECK DECK PIN	2	STEEL
16	WEIGHT PIN–B	2	STEEL
15	BUTTERFLY PAD BAR	2	STEEL
14	LEFT BUTTERFLY	1	STEEL
13	RIGHT BUTTERFLY	1	STEEL
12	BACKREST ADJ. BAR	1	STEEL
11	FOAM PAD	6	FOAM
10	PAD BAR	2	STEEL
9	LONG ANGLE IRON	2	STEEL
8	SEAT	1	PLYWOOD
7	BACKREST	1	PLYWOOD
6	WEIGHT PIN–A	1	STEEL
5	LEG CURL	1	STEEL
4	FRONT SUPPORT	1	STEEL
3	MAIN FRAME	1	STEEL
2	L–BRACKET	2	STEEL
1	UPRIGHT	1	STEEL

PARTS LIST

ASSSEMBLY: EXERCISE BENCH

EXERCISE BENCH: WORKING DRAWINGS SECTION 100 22 ELROY HIRSCH MAR 7 5

8.6 An assembly drawing for the Weider exercise bench (sheet 5 of 5). *(Courtesy of Weider Health and Fitness.)*

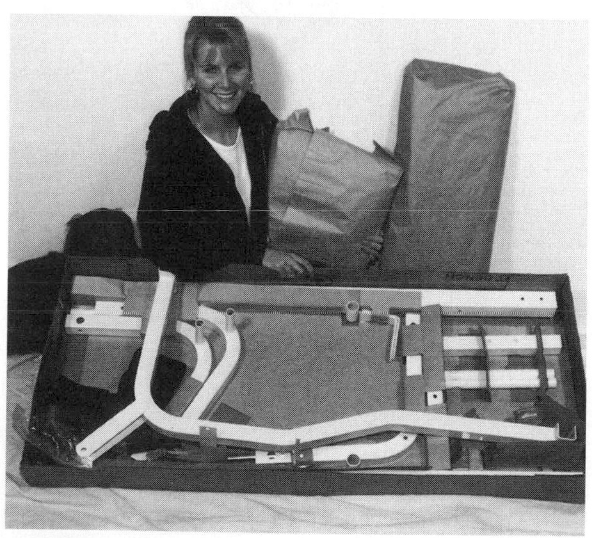

8.7 The exercise bench is packaged unassembled and flat for ease of packaging and handling during shipment.

unit is about 50 percent less when units are shipped in bundles of 10 to the same destination.

Accessories

Examples of accessories, or add-ons, are the butterfly attachments for arm exercises. Accessories enable buyers to upgrade the basic product in stages, which can increase product marketability and sales.

Prices

The retail price of the Weider bench is about $100. This type of product generally retails for about five or six times the cost of manufacturing it (materials and labor). Retailers receive approximately a 40 percent margin, distributors earn about 10 percent, and the remainder of the price represents advertising costs and the other miscellaneous costs mentioned previously. The consumer pays all these costs (prorated to each exercise bench) as part of the purchase price.

8.7 Patents

Inventors of processes or products should investigate the possibility of obtaining patents on them from the U.S. Patent and Trademark Office (PTO) before disclosing their inventions. The PTO issued its first patent in 1836, a patent for traction wheels (**Figure 8.8**). The patent procedure is outlined in *General Information Concerning Patents,* a publication available from the PTO, from which the following material was extracted.

What May Be Patented?

Any person who "invents or discovers any new and useful process, machine, manufacture, or composition of matter, may obtain a patent," subject to the conditions and requirements of law. These categories include everything made by humans and the processes for making them. **Figure 8.9** is the cover page of Thomas Edison's patent for the electric lamp.

Inventions used for the development of nuclear and atomic weapons for warfare are not patentable because they are not considered "useful." Also, a design for a mechanism that will not operate as described is not patentable. An idea or concept for a new invention is not patentable; it must be designed and described in detail before it can be considered for patent registration.

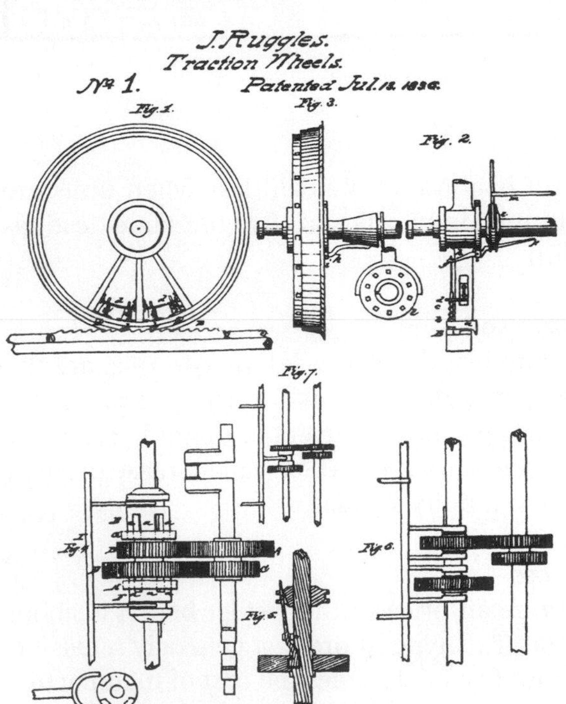

8.8 The U.S. Patent and Trademark Office issued this first patent in 1836.

8.9 Thomas Edison received this patent for the electric lamp in 1880 that began the electrical/electronics revolution.

Who May Apply for a Patent?

Only the inventor may apply for a patent. A patent given to a person who was not the inventor would be void and the recipient subject to prosecution for perjury. However, the executor of a deceased inventor's estate may apply for a patent, and two or more people may apply for a patent as joint inventors.

Patent Rights

An inventor granted a patent has the right to exclude others from making, using, or selling the invention throughout the United States for **20 years** from the time of application. At the end of that time, anyone may make, use, or sell the invention without authorization from the patent holder.

Application for a Patent

An inventor applying for a patent must provide:

1. a completed form that includes a petition, specification (description and claims), and oath or declaration;
2. a drawing, if a drawing is possible; and
3. filing, search, and examination fees.

Petition and Oath In the petition and oath (usually on one form) the inventor asks to be given a patent on the invention and declares that he or she is the original inventor of the device described in the application.

Specification The inventor must submit a written specification, describing the invention in detail so that a person skilled in the field to which the invention pertains can produce the item. Drawings should carry figure numbers and contain part numbers for text references (**Figure 8.10**).

Claims The inventor's claims are brief descriptions of the invention's features that distinguish it from already patented items. The

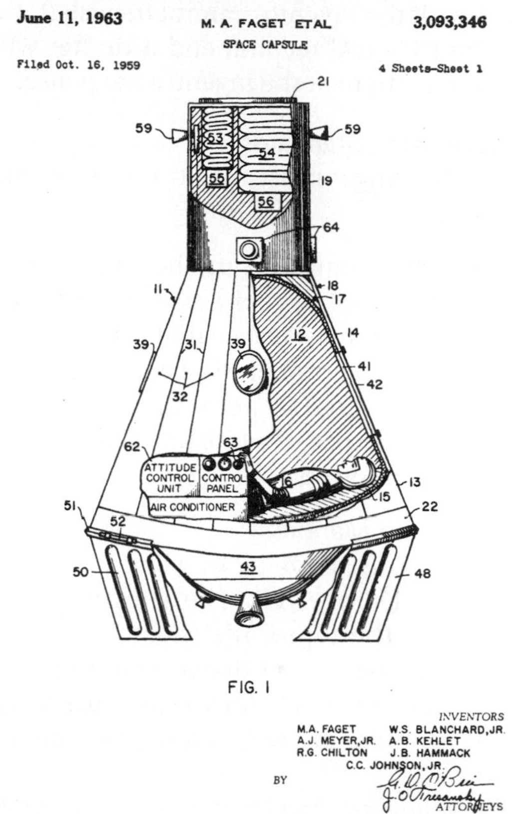

8.10 This patent drawing of a space capsule was developed by the National Aeronautics and Space Administration. *(Courtesy NASA.)*

PTO studies claims to judge the novelty and patentability of an invention.

Fee As part of the application for a patent, the inventor must submit a $300 filing fee. Additional fees can be charged based on additional specifications and claims. An issue fee of $1400 is payable when the PTO grants the patent. As a general rule, patents cost the inventor about $4000–$6000, excluding attorney's fees.

8.8 Patent Drawings

The booklet *Guide for Patent Draftsmen* (available from the U.S. Government Printing Office) outlines the required format for patent drawings. If the inventor cannot furnish drawings, the PTO will recommend a drafter who can prepare them at the inventor's expense.

Patent Drawing Standards

Patent drawings must meet the following standards.

Paper and Ink Drawings must be on pure white paper of the thickness of a two- or three-ply Bristol board with a surface that is calendered and smooth to permit erasure and correction. India ink is required for permanence and solid black lines. The use of white pigment to cover errors is not allowed.

Sheet Size and Margins

Sheet size must be 8-1/2 × 11 in. or 21.0 × 29.7 cm (DIN size A4). The shorter side is regarded as the top of the sheet. The sheets should not have frames drawn around the usable surface but should have crosshairs (target points) printed on two catercorner margin corners.

The following specifications are required:

For 8-1/2 × 11-in. sheets, there must be a top margin of at least 1 in., a left margin of least 1 in., a right margin of at least 5/8 in., and a bottom margin of at least 3/8 in., thereby enclosing an area no greater than 6-15/16 × 9-5/8 in.

For 21.0 × 29.7-cm sheets, there must be a top margin of at least 2.5 cm, a left margin of of at least 2.5 cm, a right margin of at least 1.5 cm, and a bottom margin of at least 1.0 cm, thereby enclosing an area no greater than 17.0 cm × 26.2 cm.

All sheets must be the same size and no holes should be made in the sheets (binder holes or staple holes).

Character of Lines All lines and lettering must be absolutely black regardless of line thickness. Freehand work is to be avoided.

Hatching and Shading Hatching lines used to shade the surface of an object should be parallel

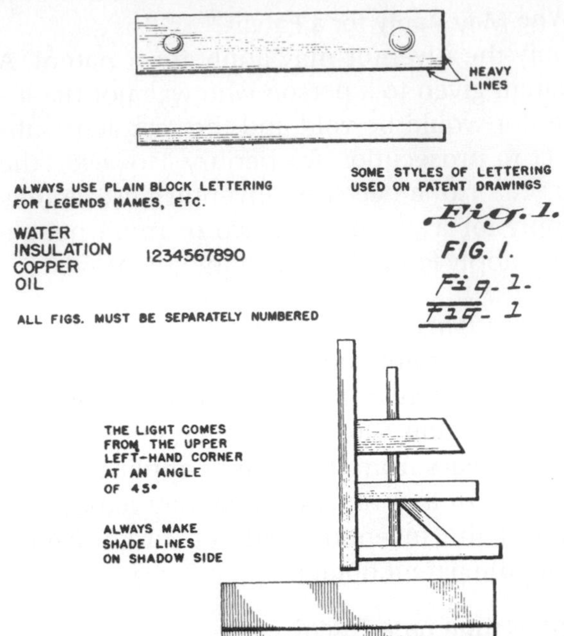

8.11 Typical examples of lines and lettering recommended for patent drawings.

and at least 1/20 in. apart (**Figure 8.11**). Heavy lines are used on the shade side of the views if they do not confuse the drawing. The light is assumed to come from the upper left-hand corner at an angle of 45°. **Figure 8.12** depicts several types of surface delineation.

Scale The scale must be large enough to show the mechanism without crowding when the drawing is reduced for reproduction. Portions of the mechanism may be drawn at a larger scale to show details.

Reference Characters Different views of a mechanism should be identified by consecutive plain, legible numerals at least 1/8-in.-high, not encircled, and placed close to their parts. A blank space should be provided on hatched surfaces if numbers are to be placed on them. The same part appearing in more than one view on the drawing should be labeled with the same numeral.

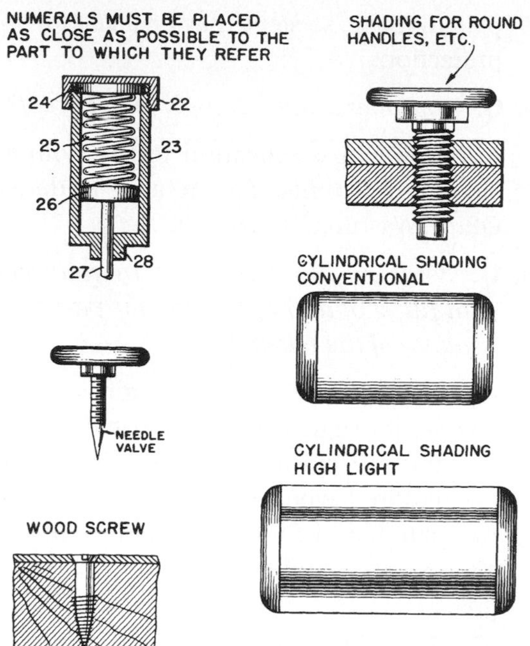

8.12 Several techniques of representing surfaces and beveled planes may be used on patent drawings.

Symbols Symbols used to represent various materials in sections, electrical components, and mechanical devices are recommended by the PTO and conform to engineering drawing standards.

Signature and Names The signature or name of the applicant and the signature of the attorney or agent are placed in the lower right-hand corner of each sheet within the marginal lines or below the lower marginal line.

Views Figures should be numbered consecutively in order of their appearance. Figures may be plan, elevation, section, perspective, or detail views. Exploded views may be used to describe an assembly of multiple parts. Large parts may be broken into sections and drawn on several sheets if this approach is not confusing. Removed sections may be used if the cutting plane is labeled to indicate the section by number. All sheet headings and signatures are to be placed in the same position on the sheet whether the drawing is read from the bottom or the right of the sheet. Completed drawings should be sent flat, protected by heavy board, or rolled in a suitable mailing tube.

8.9 Patent Searches

A patent can be granted only after PTO examiners have searched existing patents to verify that the invention has not been patented previously. With more than 6,000,000 patents on record, a search is the most time-consuming part of obtaining a patent. Most inventors employ patent attorneys or agents to do preliminary searches for possible infringement on other patents.

8.10 Questions and Answers

We used the PTO's pamphlet *Questions and Answers about Patents* to answer the following questions. Additional information can be found on the web at **www.uspto.gov**.

Nature and Duration of Patents

1. **Q.** *What is a patent?*

   A. A patent is a grant issued by the U.S. Government, giving an inventor the right to exclude all others from making, using, or selling his or her invention within the United States, its territories, and possessions.

2. **Q.** *For how long is a patent granted?*

   A. Twenty years from the date on which an application is filed; except for patents on ornamental designs, which are granted for terms of 3-1/2, 7, or 14 years.

3. **Q.** *May the term of a patent be extended?*

   A. Only by special act of Congress, which occurs rarely and only under exceptional circumstances.

4. **Q.** *Does the person granted the patent have any control over the patent after it expires?*

A. No. Anyone has the right to use an invention covered in an expired patent so long as they do not use features covered in other unexpired patents.

5. **Q.** *On what subject matter may a patent be granted?*

A. A patent may be granted to the inventor or discoverer of any new and useful process, machine, manufacture, or composition of matter, or any new and useful improvement thereof, or on any distinct and new variety of plant, or on any new, original, and ornamental design for an article of manufacture.

6. **Q.** *What may not be patented?*

A. A patent may not be granted on a useless device, on printed matter, on a method of doing business, on an improvement in a device that would be obvious to a person skilled in the art, or on a machine that will not operate, particularly on alleged perpetual motion machines.

7. **Q.** *What do "patent pending" and "patent applied for" mean?*

A. They are used by a manufacturer or seller of an article to indicate that a patent application for that article is on file with the U.S. Patent and Trademark Office. Those using these terms falsely to deceive the public can be fined.

8. **Q.** *I have made some changes and improvements in my invention after my patent application was filed with the PTO. May I amend my patent application by adding a description or illustration of these features?*

A. No. The law provides that new matter shall not be introduced into a patent application. You should call to the attention of your patent agent any such changes you may make, or plan to make, so steps may be taken for your protection.

9. **Q.** *How does someone apply for a patent?*

A. By making application to the Commissioner of Patents, Patent and Trademark Office, Washington, DC, 20231.

10. **Q.** *What are the PTO's fees in connection with filing of an application for patent and issuance of the patent?*

A. A filing fee of $300 plus certain additional charges for claims, depending on their number and the manner of their presentation, are required when the application is filed. An issue fee of $1400 plus certain printing charges are required if the patent is to be granted.

11. **Q.** *Are models required as a part of the application?*

A. Only in exceptional cases. The PTO has the authority to require that a model be submitted, but rarely exercises it.

12. **Q.** *Is it necessary for me to go to the PTO in Washington to transact business concerning patent matters?*

A. No. Most business is conducted by correspondence. Interviews regarding pending applications can be arranged with examiners if necessary and often are helpful.

13. **Q.** *Can the PTO give me advice about whether to apply for a patent?*

A. No. It can only consider the patentability of an invention when an application comes before it.

14. **Q.** *Is there any danger that the PTO will give others information contained in my application while it is pending?*

A. No. All patent applications are kept secret until the patent is issued. After the patent is issued, the PTO file containing the application and all correspondence leading to its issuance is made available in the Patent Office Search Room to anyone, and copies may be purchased from the PTO.

15. Q. *May I write to the PTO about my application after it is filed?*

A. The PTO will answer your inquiries about the status of the application and indicate whether the application has been rejected, allowed, or is awaiting action. However, you should forward correspondence through your patent attorney or agent.

16. Q. *What happens when two inventors apply separately for a patent on the same invention?*

A. The PTO declares an "interference" and requires that testimony be submitted to determine which inventor is entitled to the patent.

17. Q. *May applications be examined out of their regular order?*

A. No. All applications are examined in the order in which they are filed, except under special conditions.

When to Apply for a Patent

18. Q. *I have been making and selling my invention for the past 13 months and have not filed any patent application. Is it too late for me to apply?*

A. Yes. A patent may not be obtained if the invention has been in public use or for sale in this country for more than a year prior to application. Your own use and sale of it for more than a year before filing will bar your right to a patent as though someone else had done so.

19. Q. *I published an article describing my invention in a magazine 13 months ago. Is it too late to apply for a patent?*

A. Yes. The inventor is not entitled to a patent if the invention has been described in a printed publication anywhere in the world more than a year before filing an application.

20. Q. *If two or more people work together on an invention, to whom will the patent be granted?*

A. If each had a share in the ideas forming the invention, they are joint inventors and a patent will be issued to them jointly if an application is filed by them jointly. If one person provided all the ideas and the other has only followed instructions in making the device, the person contributing the ideas is the sole inventor and the patent application and patent should be in his or her name only.

21. Q. *If one person furnishes all the ideas for an invention and someone else employs that person or furnishes the money for building and testing the invention, should the patent application be filed by them jointly?*

A. No. The application must be signed, executed, sworn to, and filed in the name of the inventor, who is the person furnishing the ideas, not the employer or the person furnishing the money.

22. Q. *May a patent be granted if an inventor dies before filing an application?*

A. Yes. The application may be filed by the executor or administrator of the inventor's estate.

23. Q. *While in England this summer, I found an ingenious article that has not been introduced into the United States or patented. May I obtain a U.S. patent on it?*

A. No. A U.S. patent may be obtained only by the inventor, not by someone learning of someone else's invention.

9 Design Problems

9.1 Introduction

This chapter offers problems that are suitable for both individual assignments and team projects so as to provide experience in applying the methods of creative problem solving presented in this textbook. Graphics has many applications during the design process: All new products begin with sketches at the preliminary idea step and end with documentation drawings at implementation.

9.2 The Individual Approach

The solution of short problems (1 to 2 hours) is best suited to students working alone. Although simple design problems may involve fewer details and less depth than comprehensive problems, the same steps are involved.

9.3 The Team Approach

An effectively organized team working on a problem has more talent than the typical individual possesses. However, management of talent becomes as much of the process as solving the problem. It is essential that the team process be learned, since most engineering activities in industry are done by teams.

Team Size

Student design teams should have from three to eight members. Three is the minimum number needed for a valid team experience, and four is the number needed to minimize the possibility of domination by one or two members.

Team Composition

In practice, an engineering team often consists of representatives from different departments or even from different firms who may be unacquainted. This situation can be advantageous because it reduces the impact of preconceived notions about individuals. Team members must work toward common goals in a professional manner to utilize their knowledge and talents rather than their personalities.

Team Leader

A leader is necessary for teams to function effectively. The leader is responsible for making assignments, ensuring that deadlines are met, and mediating disagreements.

9.4 Selection of a Problem

The best student design project is one involving familiar and accessible conditions that can be observed, measured, and inspected. A design of a water-ski rack for an automobile is more feasible than a support bracket for an airplane. When a team selects a design problem, they should prepare a written proposal identifying the problem and outlining its limitations. Assignment of problems by the instructor in the classroom is analogous to assignments by a supervisor in the workplace.

9.5 Problem Specifications

An individual or team may be expected to complete any or all of the following tasks.

Short Problems (1 or 2 hours)

1. Worksheets that record development of a design procedure (Chapter 2).
2. Freehand sketches of the development of the design (Chapters 4 and 13).
3. Instrument drawings of the solution (Chapters 8 and 23).
4. Pictorial sketches (or drawings made with instruments or computer) illustrating the design (Chapters 4, 13, and 25).
5. Visual aids, flip charts, or other media for presentation to a group (Chapter 7).

Comprehensive Problems (40 to 100 person hours)

1. A proposal identifying the problem and outlining an approach for solving it (Chapters 2, 3, and 7).
2. Worksheets documenting the preliminary ideas for a solution (Chapter 4).
3. Schematic diagrams, flowcharts, or other graphics to illustrate refinements of the design (Chapter 5).
4. A market survey evaluating the product's possible acceptance and estimated profit (Chapters 3 and 6).
5. A model or prototype for analysis and/or presentation (Chapter 6).
6. Pictorials to illustrate features of the final design solution (Chapters 7 and 25).
7. Dimensioned working drawings and assembly drawings to give details and specifications (Chapters 8 and 23).
8. A written or oral report, illustrated with graphs and diagrams, to explain the method of solution and present conclusions and recommendations (Chapter 7).

9.6 Scheduling Team Activities

Design projects and team activities should be assigned to be completed in stages throughout the semester. Spreading design projects over the school term allows time for thinking about the problem, gathering information, and interacting with team members. Refer to the exercise bench example in Chapters 3 through 8 as an example for completing your assigned project.

9.7 Short Design Problems

The following short design problems can be completed in less than 2 hours.

1. **Lamp bracket.** Design a bracket to attach a desk lamp to a vertical wall for reading in bed. It should be removable for use as a conventional desk lamp.
2. **Towel bar.** Design a towel bar for a kitchen or bathroom. Determine optimum size and

consider styling, ease of use, and method of attachment.

3. **Bicycle carriage rack.** Design for a bicycle a rack (or basket) for carrying books and class materials.
4. **Boot puller.** Design a device for helping you remove cowboy boots from your feet.
5. **Side-mounted mirror.** Design an improved side-mounted rearview mirror for an automobile. Consider aerodynamics, protection from inclement weather, visibility, and other factors.
6. **Pipe column support.** Design a base that can be attached to a concrete slab with bolts that would provide a base for pipe columns of varying diameters.
7. **Motor mount (Figure 9.1).** Design a bracket to support a motor. The plate should be the upper part of the finished bracket.
8. **Paint can holder.** Paint cans held by their wire bails are difficult to access with paint brushes. Design a holding device that can be attached and removed easily from a gallon-size paint can. Consider weight, grip, balance, and function.

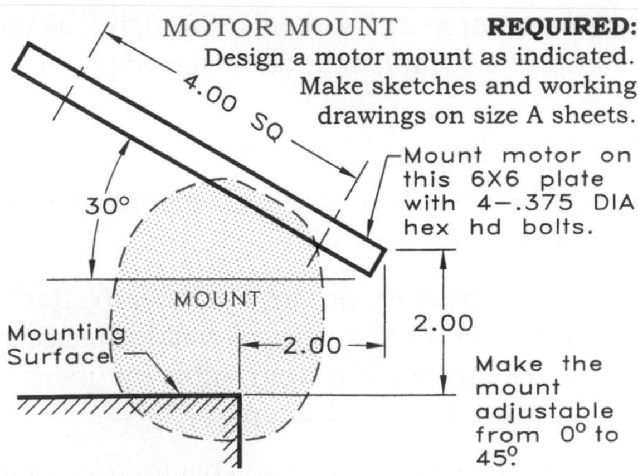

Design a motor mount as indicated.

Mount motor on this 6X6 plate with 4—.375 DIA hex hd bolts.

Make the mount adjustable from 0° to 45°.

9.1 Problem 7.

Attach clamp in this area.

9.2 Problem 9.

9. **Angle pipe clamp (Figure 9.2).** A pipe with a 4-in. diameter must be supported by angles that are spaced 8 ft apart. Design a clamp as specified in the figure.
10. **Foot scraper.** Design a device that can be attached to the sidewalk for scraping mud from your shoes.
11. **CD storage unit.** Design a storage unit for an automobile that will hold several CDs, making them accessible to the driver but not to a thief.
12. **Ladder device (Figure 9.3).** Develop the details of the base flange in accordance with the instructions given in the figure.

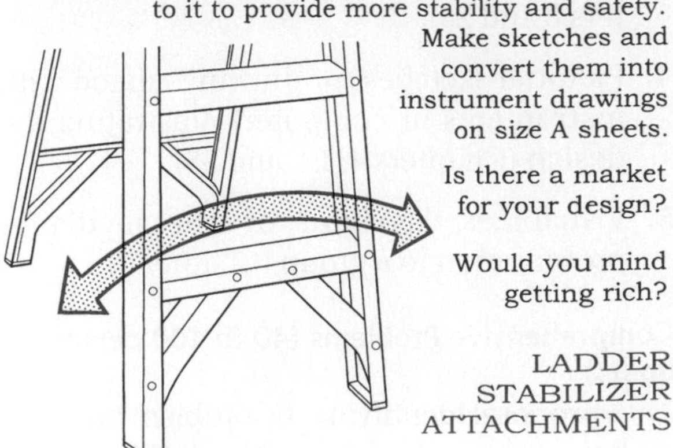

This ladder leans and sinks into soft soil creating a hazard. Design devices that can be easily attached to it to provide more stability and safety.
Make sketches and convert them into instrument drawings on size A sheets.
Is there a market for your design?
Would you mind getting rich?
LADDER STABILIZER ATTACHMENTS

9.3 Problem 12.

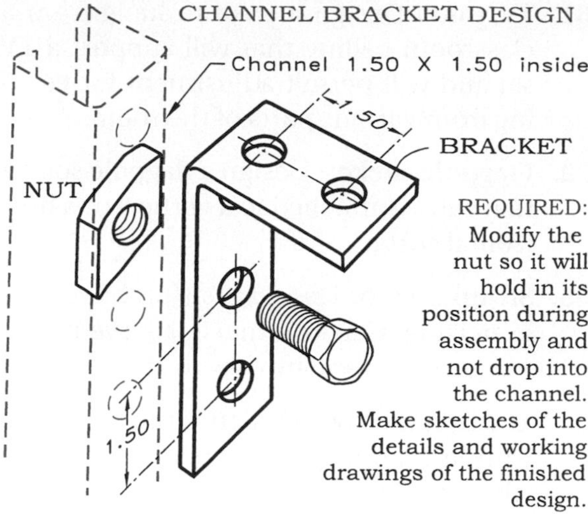
CHANNEL BRACKET DESIGN
Channel 1.50 X 1.50 inside
1.50
BRACKET
NUT
REQUIRED:
Modify the nut so it will hold in its position during assembly and not drop into the channel.
Make sketches of the details and working drawings of the finished design.
1.50

9.4 **Problem 14.**

13. **Slide projector elevator.** Design a device for raising a slide projector to the proper angle for projection on a screen. Consider making it part of the original projector or an accessory to be attached to existing projectors.

14. **Channel bracket (Figure 9.4).** Design an attachment for the conduit to support a channel used as a raceway for electrical wiring as illustrated.

15. **Book holder 1.** Design a holder to support a book for reading in bed.

16. **Book holder 2.** Design a holder to support a textbook or reference book at a workstation for ease of reading and accessibility.

17. **Conduit connector (Figure 9.5).** The bracket shown is designed to fit on the flat side of the channel. Design a method of attaching the bracket to the slotted side so the nut will not drop down inside the channel during attachment.

18. **Table leg design.** Do-it-yourselfers build a variety of tables using commercially available legs. Determine standard heights for various types of tables and design a family of legs that can be attached to tabletops with screws.

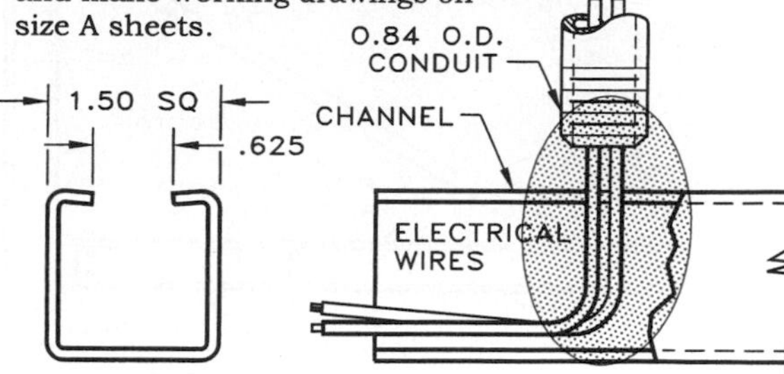
CONDUIT CONNECTOR
REQUIRED: Design a hanger to support a channel and serve as a conduit for electrical wires. Sketch and make working drawings on size A sheets.
0.84 O.D. CONDUIT
1.50 SQ
.625
CHANNEL
ELECTRICAL WIRES

9.5 **Problem 17.**

19. **Lawn cart.** Design a cart or a container that leaves can be raked into and then transported to their final destination. Make it portable, lightweight, and economical.

20. **Toothbrush holder.** Design a toothbrush holder for a cup and two toothbrushes that can be attached to a bathroom wall.

21. **Step stool.** Design a step stool that can be used for reaching various heights as needed for home chores such as changing lightbulbs.

22. **Roller brackets (Figure 9.6).** The rollers are to be positioned as shown so as to

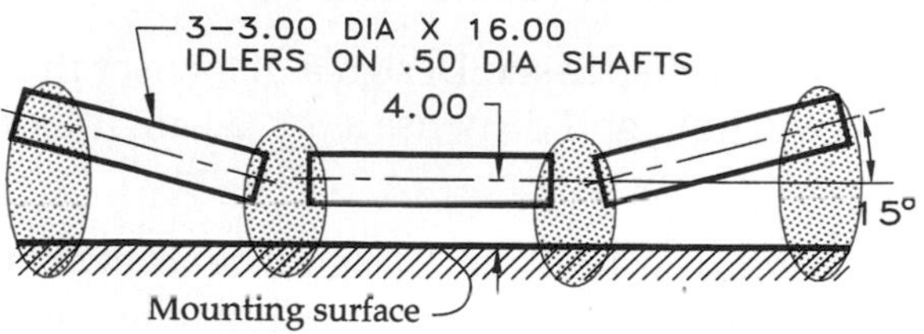
ROLLER SUPPORT BRACKETS
Design brackets to support the three idler rollers and attach to the mounting surface. Use size A sheets.
3—3.00 DIA X 16.00
IDLERS ON .50 DIA SHAFTS
4.00
5°
Mounting surface

9.6 **Problem 22.**

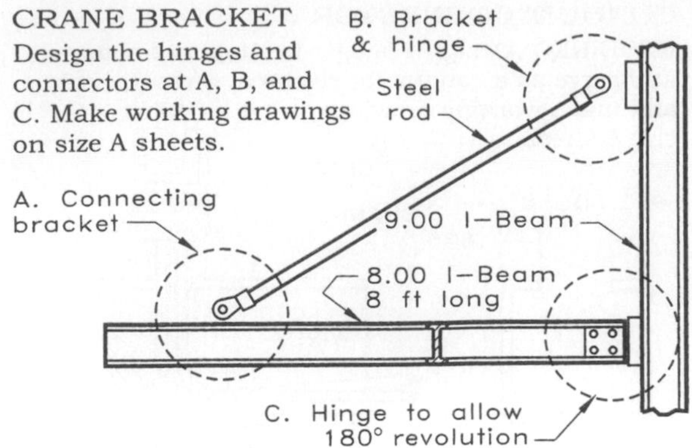

9.7 Problem 25.

support a conveyor belt that carries bulk material. Design brackets to support the rollers.

23. **Clothes hook.** Design a clothes hook that can be attached to a closet door for hanging clothes.

24. **Hammock support.** Design a hammock support that will fold up and require minimal storage space.

25. **Jib crane bracket (Figure 9.7).** Design the hinges and brackets at the joints as specified in the figure.

26. **Doorstop.** Design a doorstop that can be attached to a wall or floor to prevent a door knob from hitting the wall.

27. **Basketball goal.** Design a basketball goal that is easy to install and appropriate for kids in the 8 to 10 age range.

28. **Drawer handle.** Design a handle for a standard file cabinet drawer.

29. **Paper dispenser.** Design a dispenser that will hold and dispense a 6 × 24-in. roll of wrapping paper.

30. **Handrail bracket.** Design a bracket that will support a tubular handrail to be used on a staircase.

31. **TV yoke.** Design a yoke to hang from a classroom ceiling that will support a TV set and will permit adjustment for viewing from various parts of the room.

32. **Flagpole socket.** Design a flagpole socket that can be attached to a vertical or a horizontal surface.

33. **Sit-up bench.** Design a sit-up bench for exercising. Can you make it serve multiple purposes and be easy to store?

34. **Trash-can cover.** Design a functional lid with an appropriate opening through which to put garbage.

35. **Hose spool.** Design a spool rack on which a garden hose can be wound and left neatly near the outside faucet.

36. **Gate hinge.** Design a hinge that can be attached to a 3-in.-diameter tubular post to support a 3-ft-wide wooden gate.

37. **Pipe bracket clamp (Figure 9.8).** Design a clamp that can be attached to an overhead I-beam to support a pipe without welding or drilling holes in the beam.

38. **Emergency ladder.** Design a portable, easy-to-store ladder to be used in case of fire by residents in multistory homes.

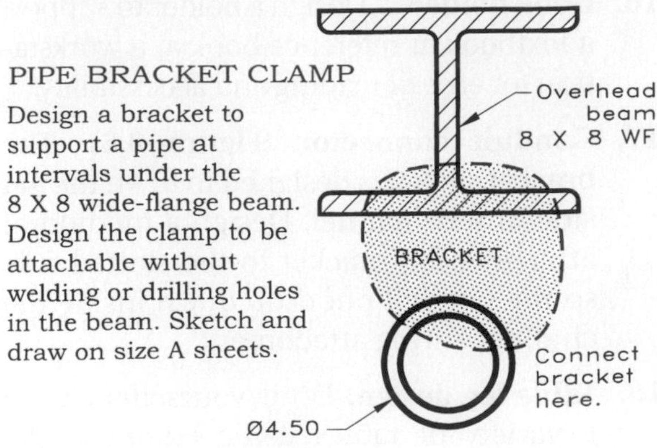

PIPE BRACKET CLAMP
Design a bracket to support a pipe at intervals under the 8 X 8 wide-flange beam. Design the clamp to be attachable without welding or drilling holes in the beam. Sketch and draw on size A sheets.
Overhead beam 8 X 8 WF
BRACKET
Connect bracket here.
Ø4.50

9.8 Problem 37.

9.8 Systems Design Problems

Systems problems require analysis of the interrelationships of various components and products.

39. **Portable bleachers.** Design portable bleachers that can be easily assembled, disassembled, and stored. Identify the uses that would justify their production for the general market.

40. **Archery range.** Determine the feasibility of providing an archery range that can be operated profitably. Investigate the potential market for such a facility and factors such as location, equipment needed, method of operation, utilities, concessions, parking, costs, and fees.

41. **Bicycle rental system.** Investigate the feasibility of a student-operated bicycle rental system. Determine student interest, cost factors, number of bikes needed, prices, personnel needs, storage, maintenance, and so on. Summarize your location, operating cost, and profitability conclusions.

42. **Model-airplane field.** Investigate the need for a model-airplane field, including space requirements, types of surface, sound control, safety factors, and method of operation. Select a site on or near your campus that is adequate for this facility and evaluate the equipment, utilities, and site preparation required.

43. **Overnight campsite.** Analyze the feasibility of converting a vacant tract of land near a major highway into sites for overnight campers. Determine the facilities required by the campers and the venture's profitability.

44. **Skateboard facility study.** Determine the cost of building and operating a skateboard facility on your campus. Consider its location, expected usage, and the amounts of equipment and labor necessary to operate it. Would it be financially feasible?

45. **Hot-water supply.** Your weekend cottage does not have a hot-water supply, but cold water is available from a private well. Design a system that uses the sun's energy in the summer to heat water for bathing and kitchen use. Devise a system for heating the water in the winter by some other source. Determine whether one or both of these systems could be made portable for showers on camping trips. Explain.

46. **Information center.** Design a drive-by information center to help campus visitors find their way around. Determine the best location for it and the informational material needed, such as slides, photographs, maps, sound, and other audiovisual aids.

47. **Golf driving range ball-return system.** Balls at golf driving ranges are usually retrieved by hand or with a specially designed vehicle. Design a system capable of automatically returning balls to the tee area.

48. **Car wash.** Design a car wash facility for your campus that would be self-supporting and would provide the basic needs for washing cars. Think simple and economical.

49. **Instant motel.** Many communities need temporary housing for celebrations and sporting events. Investigate methods of providing an "instant motel" involving the use of tents, vans, trailers, train cars, or other temporary accommodations. Estimate profitability.

50. **Mountain lodge.** Determine the food supply and other provisions needed for a mountain lodge to accommodate six people who might be snowed-in for 2 weeks. Identify and explain the features that should be included in the design of the lodge.

51. **Disaster provisions.** Determine the appropriate items and plans that would be

needed for a community disaster that might be caused by a flood or hurricane.

52. **Drive-in garbage system.** Design a system for leaving wrappers, boxes, and napkins left over after eating in your car at a hamburger drive-in. It would be preferable if it could be used without getting out of your car.

53. **Computer wiring system.** Computer installations become cluttered and inaccessible as more accessories are attached. Design a system to organize the electrical wiring to make it more convenient and accessible.

54. **Injury-proof playground.** Design a playground that permits the greatest degree of participation by children with the least risk of injury.

55. **Modification of an existing facility.** Select a facility on your campus or in your community that is inadequate, such as a street intersection, parking lot, recreational area, or classroom. Identify its deficiencies and propose improvements to it.

56. **Recreational facility.** Analyze the various recreational activities on your campus that could be improved with the construction of a multipurpose facility to accommodate activities such as movies, plays, sports, meetings, and dances. The facility should be designed as an outdoor installation with a minimum of structures.

57. **Production planning.** You are responsible for establishing the production system for manufacturing a product. Select one such as the can crusher in **Figure 9.27** or one of this caliber. Do an analysis on what would be needed to produce 500 units per month—space, raw materials, office facilities, manufacturing facilities, people, warehousing, the workstations required, and so forth. Calculate the cost of producing the item and the selling price necessary to make a profit.

58. **Patio table production.** Proceed as in problem 57 for production of a plywood patio table. Determine the number to be manufactured per month to break even and the selling price. Establish quantity breaks for selling prices for quantities that exceed the break-even level.

9.9 Product-Design Problems

Product design involves developing a device that will perform a specific function, be mass produced, and attract a market that will be profitable.

59. **Chaise lounge (Figure 9.9).** Develop the details of the curvy chaise lounge in accordance with its specifications in the figure.

60. **Hunting blind.** Design a portable hunting blind adequate for hunting game that can be easily taken to its site. Consider making the blind of degradable materials so it can be left at the site.

61. **Mailbox.** Design a residential mailbox that either attaches to the house or is supported on a pole at the street.

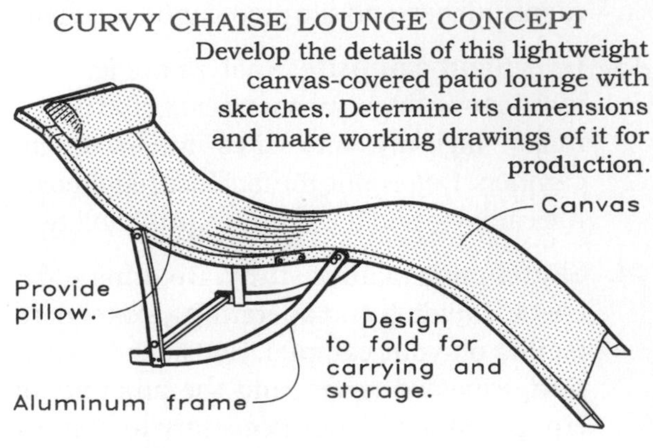

CURVY CHAISE LOUNGE CONCEPT
Develop the details of this lightweight canvas-covered patio lounge with sketches. Determine its dimensions and make working drawings of it for production.
Canvas
Provide pillow.
Design to fold for carrying and storage.
Aluminum frame

9.9 **Problem 59.**

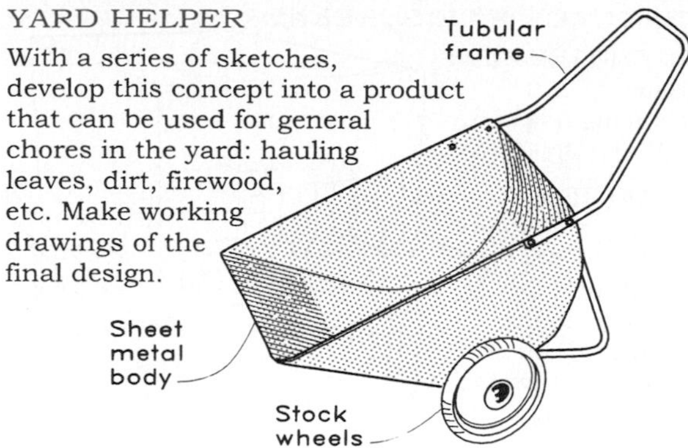

YARD HELPER
With a series of sketches, develop this concept into a product that can be used for general chores in the yard: hauling leaves, dirt, firewood, etc. Make working drawings of the final design.
Tubular frame
Sheet metal body
Stock wheels

9.10 **Problem 64.**

62. **Writing table arm.** Design a writing table arm that can be attached to a folding chair.

63. **Rescue litter.** Design a rescue litter (for carrying wounded victims) that can be folded into a number of positions to provide care for the injured. It should be lightweight and collapsible for convenient storage.

64. **Yard helper (Figure 9.10).** Design a movable container that can be used for gardening and yard work.

65. **Computer mount.** Design a device that can be clamped to a desktop for holding a computer, permitting it to be adjusted to various positions while leaving the desktop free.

66. **Workers' stilts.** Design stilts to give workers access to an 8-ft-high ceiling, permitting them to nail 4 × 8-ft ceiling panels overhead.

67. **Pole-vault uprights.** Pole-vault uprights must be adjusted for each vaulter by moving them forward or backward 18 in. The crossbar must be replaced at heights of over 18 ft by using poles and ladders. Develop a more efficient set of uprights that can be readily adjusted and allow the crossbar to be replaced easily.

68. **Sports chair.** Design a sports chair that can be used for camping, for fishing from a bank or boat, at sporting events, and for other purposes.

69. **Bicycle child carrier.** Design a seat that can be used to carry a small child as a passenger on a bicycle.

70. **Car washer.** Design a garden-hose attachment that can apply water and agitation to wash a car. Suggest other applications for this device.

71. **Power lawn-fertilizer attachment.** The rotary power lawn mower emits a force caused by the rotating blades that might be used to distribute fertilizer during mowing. Design an attachment for a lawn mower that could be used in this manner.

72. **Drum truck (Figure 9.11).** Design a truck that can be used for handling 55-gal drums of turpentine (7.28 lb/gal) one at a time. Drums are stored in a vertical position and used in a horizontal position. The truck should be useful in tipping a drum into a horizontal position (as shown) as well as in moving the drum.

73. **Sawhorse.** Design a portable sawhorse for use in carpentry projects, it should fold up

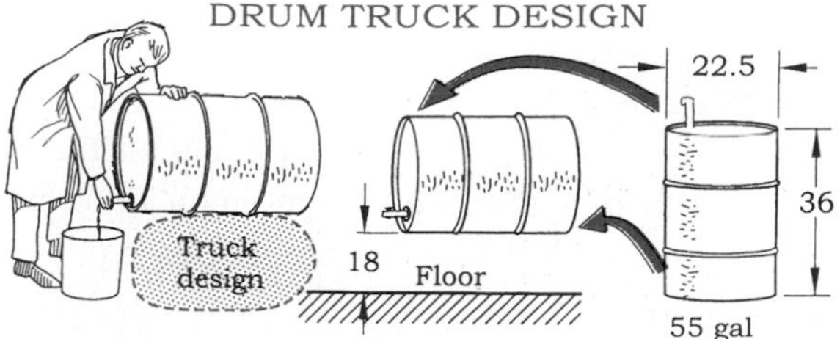

Design a truck for handling 55-gal drums of turpentine (7.28 lb/gal) one at a time. Design the truck to tip the drum from the vertical to the horizontal position as well as for moving the drum about the floor to different locations.

9.11 **Problem 72.**

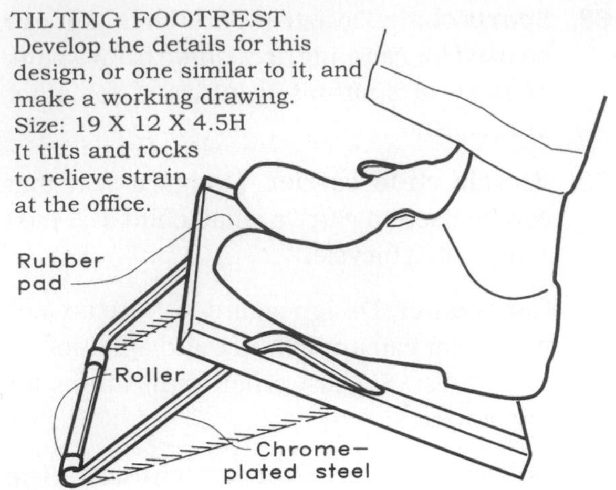

TILTING FOOTREST
Develop the details for this design, or one similar to it, and make a working drawing.
Size: 19 X 12 X 4.5H
It tilts and rocks to relieve strain at the office.
Rubber pad
Roller
Chrome-plated steel

9.12 Problem 74.

for easy storage and should be about 36 in. long and 30 in. high.

74. **Footrest (Figure 9.12).** Develop the design of the footrest that provides comfort to the office worker in accordance with the given specifications.

75. **Projector cabinet.** Design a cabinet to serve as an end table or some other function while housing a slide projector and slide trays ready for use.

76. **Heavy-appliance mover.** Design a device for moving large appliances—stoves, refrigerators, and washers—about the house for the purposes of rearranging, cleaning, and servicing them.

77. **Car jack.** The average car jack does not attach itself adequately to the automobile's frame or bumper, causing a safety problem. Design one that would employ a different method of lifting a car on various types of terrain.

78. **Map holder.** Design a map holder to give a car driver an easy, convenient view of the map while driving. Provide a method of lighting the map that will not distract the driver.

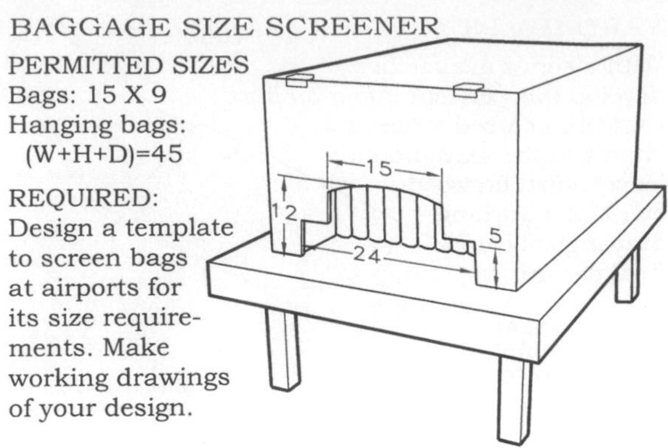

BAGGAGE SIZE SCREENER
PERMITTED SIZES
Bags: 15 X 9
Hanging bags:
(W+H+D)=45
REQUIRED:
Design a template to screen bags at airports for its size requirements. Make working drawings of your design.
15
12
5
24

9.13 Problem 79.

79. **Baggage size screener (Figure 9.13).** In an attempt to limit the size of carry-on luggage, airlines are testing designs for an effective template that can be used to screen luggage at check-in time. Design a template using the specifications shown in the figure.

80. **Tree stump remover.** Design an apparatus that can be attached to a car bumper to remove dead stumps by pushing or pulling.

81. **Elastic exerciser (Figure 9.14).** Design and detail an elastic exerciser as specified in the figure.

82. **Monitor arm (Figure 9.15).** Design a computer monitor arm to support and position the screen for ease of use.

ELASTIC EXERCISER
Design an elastic exerciser that can be held and used as shown.
Sketch your ideas on size A sheets.
ELASTIC EXERCISER
Make working drawings of your final design.

9.14 Problem 81.

MONITOR ARM

Design an arm that will attach to a tabletop and support a flat panel monitor (sizes 18, 19, and 21 in.). Develop your ideas with sketches and finalize your concept with instrument drawings.

How would your design be priced?
Is there a market for it?

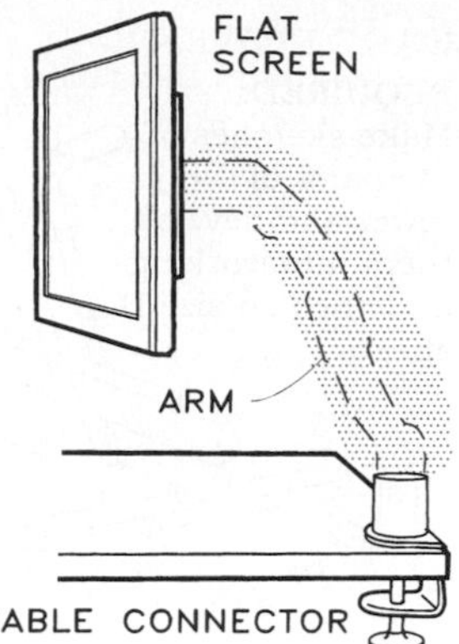

9.15 **Problem 82.**

83. **Bike rack (Figure 9.16).** Develop the design of the bike rack as specified in the illustration.

84. **Gate opener.** An annoyance to farmers and ranchers is the necessity of opening and closing gates. Design a manually operated gate that could be opened and closed by the driver from his or her vehicle.

85. **Paint mixer.** Design a product for use at paint stores or by paint contractors to mix paint quickly in the store or on the job.

86. **Automobile coffee maker.** Design a device that will provide hot coffee from the dashboard of an automobile. Consider the method of changing and adding water, the spigot system, and similar details.

87. **Baby seat (cantilever).** Design a chair to support a child. It should attach to and be cantilevered from a standard tabletop. The chair also should be collapsible for ease of storage.

88. **Miniature-TV support.** Design a device that will support TV sets ranging in size from 6 × 6 in. to 7 × 7 in. for viewing from a bed. Provide adjustments on the device to allow positioning of the set.

89. **Panel applicator.** A worker applying 4 × 8-ft plasterboard to a ceiling needs a helper to hold the panel in place while she nails it. Design a device to hold the panel and eliminate the need for an assistant.

90. **Backpack.** Design a backpack that can be used for carrying camping supplies. Adapt the backpack to the human body for maximum comfort for extended periods of time. Suggest other uses for your design.

91. **Dock light (Figure 9.17).** Develop the design in accordance with the specifications given in the figure.

92. **Computer workstation.** Design a computer workstation that reduces user discomfort and fatigue.

TUBULAR BICYCLE RACK

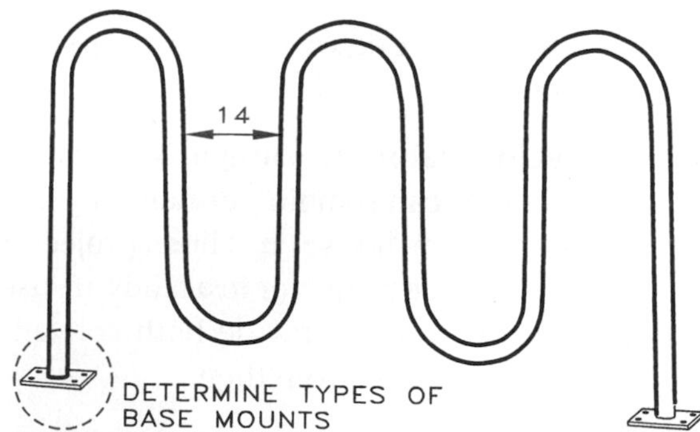

Develop the details for this five-bike tubular rack, giving special attention to the base mounts. Design them to attach to concrete, to the ground, or to be freestanding. Make working drawings on size A sheets.

9.16 **Problem 83.**

ADJUSTABLE DOCK LIGHT

This fixture by ULINE provides light for docks, reaches 40 in., pivots up and down, and uses 300 W bulbs.

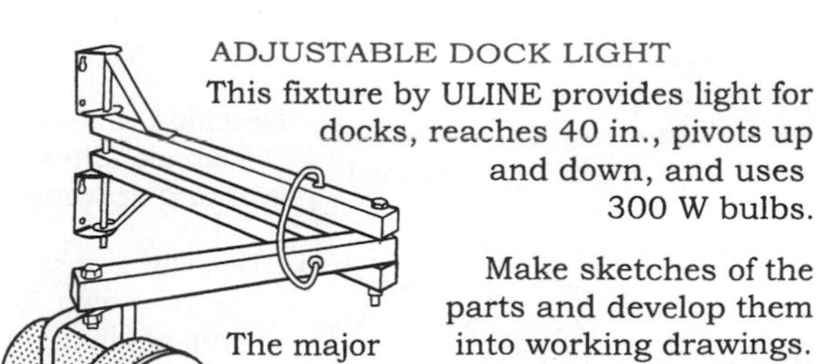

Make sketches of the parts and develop them into working drawings. Develop an alternative design of your own and make working drawings of it.

The major problem will be the design of the movable joints.

9.17 **Problem 91.**

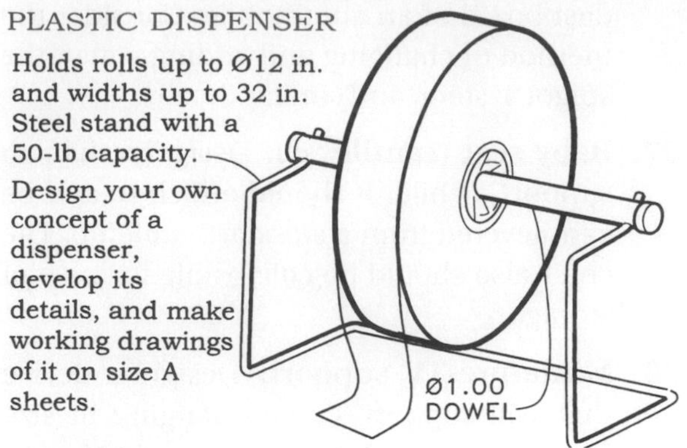

PLASTIC DISPENSER
Holds rolls up to Ø12 in. and widths up to 32 in. Steel stand with a 50-lb capacity.
Design your own concept of a dispenser, develop its details, and make working drawings of it on size A sheets.
Ø1.00 DOWEL

9.18 **Problem 93.**

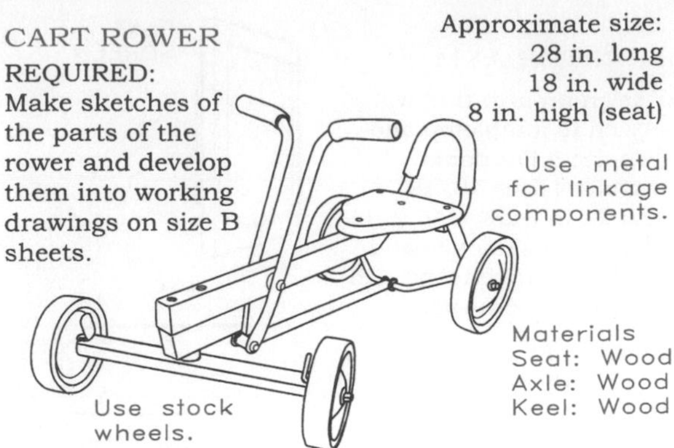

CART ROWER
REQUIRED:
Make sketches of the parts of the rower and develop them into working drawings on size B sheets.
Approximate size:
28 in. long
18 in. wide
8 in. high (seat)
Use metal for linkage components.
Materials
Seat: Wood
Axle: Wood
Keel: Wood
Use stock wheels.

9.20 **Problem 99.**

93. **Plastic dispenser (Figure 9.18).** Develop the design in accordance with the specifications given in the figure.

94. **CD caddy.** Design a container for CDs and DVDs that can be used for storage and filling for easy retrieval of the disks. Can it be designed to work in both the office and automobile?

95. **Specialty vise (Figure 9.19).** A concept for a vise to hold irregular objects while they are being machined is shown here. Develop the design in accordance with the specifications given in the figure.

96. **Automobile controls.** Design driving controls that can be easily attached to the standard automobile to permit a car to be driven without using the legs.

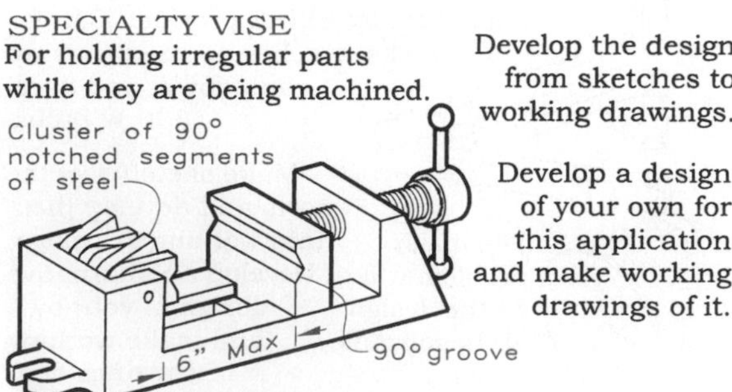

SPECIALTY VISE
For holding irregular parts while they are being machined.
Develop the design from sketches to working drawings.
Develop a design of your own for this application and make working drawings of it.
Cluster of 90° notched segments of steel
6" Max
90° groove

9.19 **Problem 95.**

97. **Bathing apparatus.** Design an apparatus that would help a wheelchair-bound person get in and out of a bathtub without assistance from others.

98. **Adjustable TV base.** Design a base to support full-size TV sets and allow maximum adjustment up and down and rotation about vertical and horizontal axes.

99. **Cart rower (Figure 9.20).** Develop the details of the product as specified in the figure.

100. **Two-wheel pedaler (Figure 9.21).** Develop the details and design of the pedaler as specified in the figure.

101. **Log splitter.** Design a device to aid in splitting logs for firewood.

102. **Projector cabinet.** Design a portable cabinet that can remain permanently in a classroom to house a slide projector and/or a movie projector in a ready-to-use position. It should provide both convenience and security from theft.

103. **Projector eraser.** Design a device to erase grease-pencil markings from the acetate roll of a specially equipped overhead projector as the acetate is cranked past the stage of the projector.

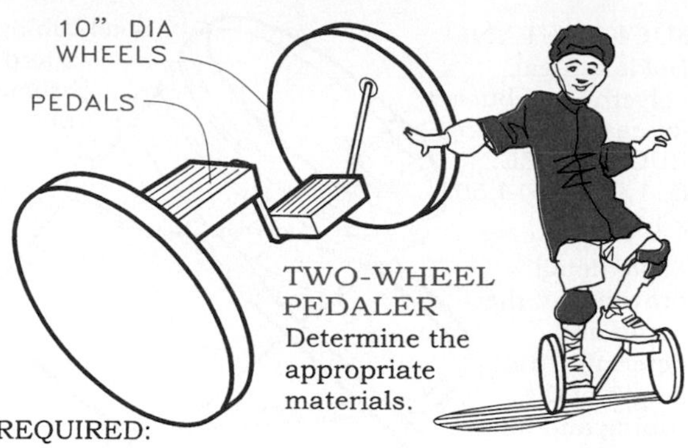

9.21 **Problem 100.**

104. Ash receptacle (Figure 9.22). Develop the details and design of the outdoor receptacle for smokers in accordance with the instructions in the figure.

105. Cement mixer. Design a portable cement mixer that a homeowner can operate manually. Such mixers are used only occasionally, so it also should be affordable to make it marketable.

106. Boat trailer. Design a trailer from which a boat hangs rather than riding on top of it so that the boat can be launched in very shallow water.

107. Washing machine. Design a manually operated washing machine. It may be considered an "undesign" of an electrically powered washing machine.

108. Pickup truck hoist. Design a manual lift that can be attached to the tailgate of a pickup truck for raising and lowering loads from the bed of the truck.

109. Folding clothes hook (Figure 9.23). Develop the details and design of the clothes hook in accordance with the instructions given in the figure.

110. Display booth. Design a portable display booth for use behind or on an 8-ft-long table for displaying your company's name and product information. It must be collapsible so that it can be carried by one person as airplane luggage.

111. Decorative star (Figure 9.24). Develop the details, geometry, and design of the

OUTDOOR ASH RECEPTACLE

Develop the details of this design for an outdoor cigarette ash receptacle. Begin with sketches and make working drawings of your solution on size A sheets.

ALTERNATIVE DESIGN:
Develop design details of an original concept of your own that would serve the purpose as well as the given design. Make working drawings of it.

How would it be emptied?
Does it have a market?
What materials would you recommend?

9.22 **Problem 104.**

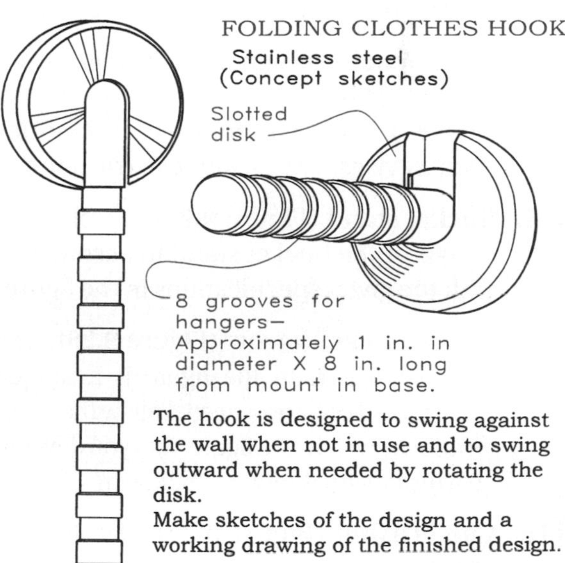

FOLDING CLOTHES HOOK
Stainless steel
(Concept sketches)
Slotted
disk
8 grooves for
hangers—
Approximately 1 in. in
diameter X 8 in. long
from mount in base.
The hook is designed to swing against
the wall when not in use and to swing
outward when needed by rotating the
disk.
Make sketches of the design and a
working drawing of the finished design.

9.23 **Problem 109.**

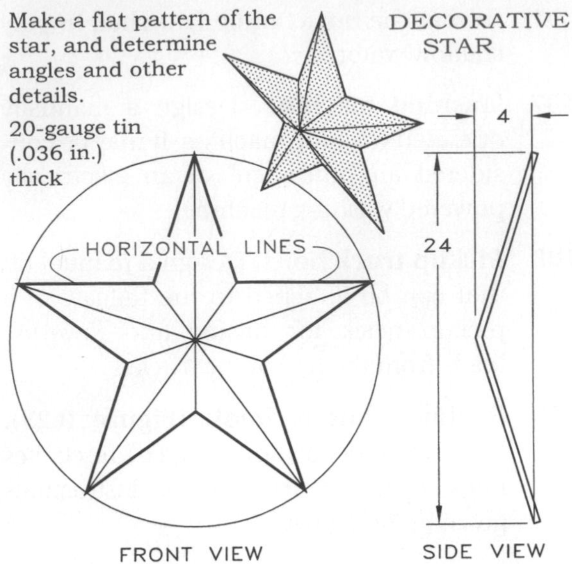

Make a flat pattern of the star, and determine angles and other details.
20-gauge tin (.036 in.) thick

9.24 **Problem 112.**

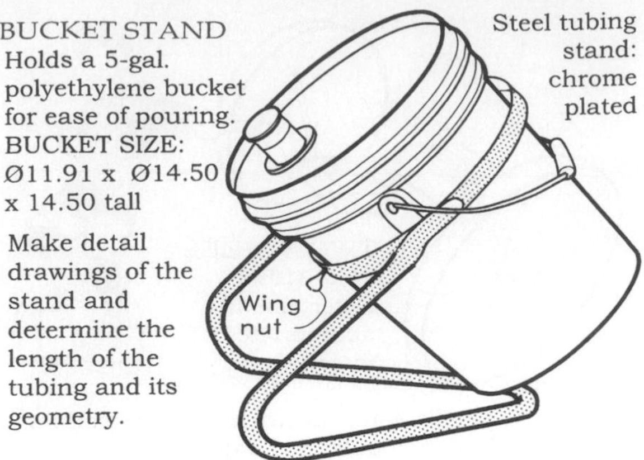

BUCKET STAND
Holds a 5-gal. polyethylene bucket for ease of pouring.
BUCKET SIZE:
Ø11.91 x Ø14.50 x 14.50 tall
Make detail drawings of the stand and determine the length of the tubing and its geometry.
Steel tubing stand: chrome plated
Wing nut

9.25 **Problem 114.**

CANVAS WHEELBARROW
Develop the fabrication details of this canvas wheelbarrow that is lightweight, functional, and portable for yard chores. Determine the size of the canvas. Make working drawings of its parts.

ALTERNATIVE:
Develop a design of your own for a product that would fill the same needs as this one.

9.26 **Problem 131.** *(Courtesy of Allsop Home & Garden.)*

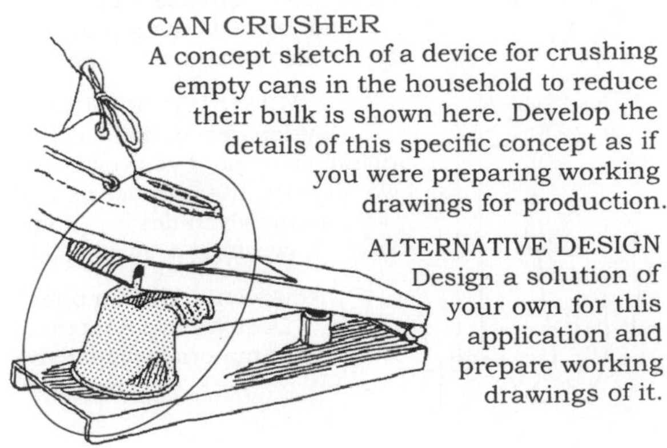

CAN CRUSHER
A concept sketch of a device for crushing empty cans in the household to reduce their bulk is shown here. Develop the details of this specific concept as if you were preparing working drawings for production.
ALTERNATIVE DESIGN
Design a solution of your own for this application and prepare working drawings of it.

9.27 **Problem 121.**

decorative star in accordance with the instructions given in the figure. Make working drawings of your finished details.

112. Patio grill. Design a portable charcoal grill for cooking on the patio. Consider how it would be cleaned, stored, and used. Study competing products already on the market.

113. Shop bench. Design an adjustable shop bench that is collapsible for easy storage. Design it to accommodate accessories such as vises, anvils, and electrical tools.

114. Bucket stand (Figure 9.25). Develop the design of the bucket stand in accordance with the given specifications in the figure.

115. Canvas wheelbarrow (Figure 9.26). The example shown in the figure is a unique solution to a common need. Follow the specifications given in the figure. Can you develop an alternative solution of your own?

116. Can crusher (Figure 9.27). Develop the concept for a can crusher in accordance with the specifications given in the figure.

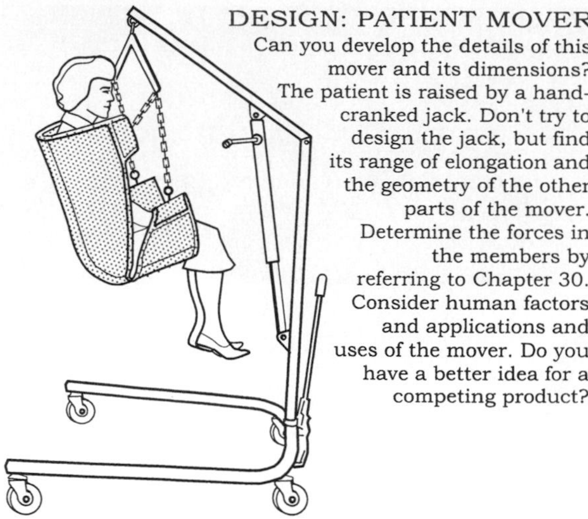

DESIGN: PATIENT MOVER
Can you develop the details of this mover and its dimensions? The patient is raised by a hand-cranked jack. Don't try to design the jack, but find its range of elongation and the geometry of the other parts of the mover. Determine the forces in the members by referring to Chapter 30. Consider human factors and applications and uses of the mover. Do you have a better idea for a competing product?

9.28 **Problem 118.**

117. **Mailbox.** Develop concepts for a mailbox in accordance with the specifications given in the figure.

118. **Patient mover (Figure 9.28).** Develop the design of the patient mover on size B sheets in accordance with the specifications.

119. **Punching bag platform.** Design a platform for a speed punching bag that is adjustable to various heights, is portable, and is suitable for shipping in a flat box.

120. **Firewood rack.** Design a rack for holding firewood inside near the fireplace. Can you give it multiple uses?

121. **Shopping caddy.** Design a portable lightweight caddy that a shopper can use for carrying parcels.

122. **Bed table.** Design a table that can be used for reading, studying, computing, writing, and/or eating in bed.

123. **Aircraft.** Design and build an aircraft of a specified type of paper that will maintain flight when tied to the grill of a buzz fan with a thread. Determine which design supports the most weight, such as pennies taped to the craft.

124. **Fine art crate.** Design a reusable crate/container for shipping valuable paintings from art galleries that would ensure protection while in transit. Sizes (including frames) vary from 36 × 36 to 10 × 10.

125. **Auto safety kit.** Design (or assemble) a compact kit of items that should be available in automobiles to provide support in emergencies: first-aid supplies, multi-use tools, lights, phone numbers, and so on.

126. **Bed rail.** Children tend to roll out of bed while sleeping. Design side rails that can be attached to the sides of a bed to secure the restless sleeper.

10 Drawing Instruments

10.1 Introduction

The preparation of technical drawings requires the ability to use drawing instruments. Even people with little artistic ability can produce professional technical drawings when they learn to use drawing instruments properly.

The drawing instruments covered in this chapter are traditional ones that are used by hand as opposed to computer instruments. Traditional instruments will always have an application in the development of drawings, but to a lesser degree than in the past.

Computer Instruments

Electronic drawing instruments—computers, plotters, scanners, and similar equipment—are covered in Chapter 37. The ability to use computer graphics and its associated hardware is a necessary skill for engineers because of its extensive use in producing graphics for engineering and technology.

10.2 Drawing Media

Pencils

A good drawing begins with the correct pencil grade and its proper use. Pencil grades range from the hardest, 9H, to the softest, 7B (**Figure 10.1**). The pencils in the medium-grade range, 4H–4B, are used most often for drafting work of the type covered in this textbook.

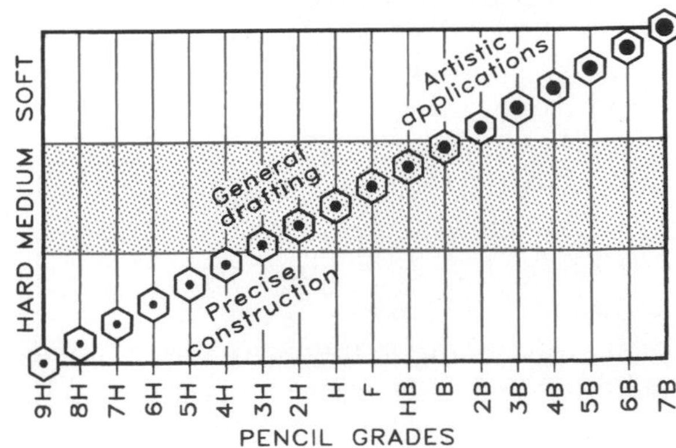

10.1 The hardest pencil lead is 9H, and the softest is 7B. The diameters of the hard leads are smaller than those of the soft leads.

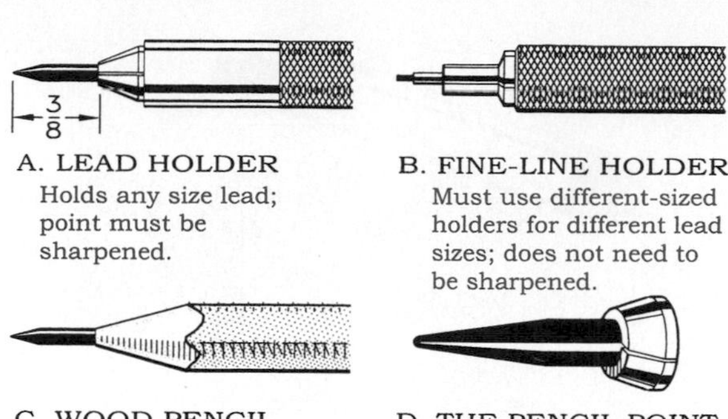
3/8
A. LEAD HOLDER
Holds any size lead; point must be sharpened.
B. FINE-LINE HOLDER
Must use different-sized holders for different lead sizes; does not need to be sharpened.
C. WOOD PENCIL
Wood must be trimmed and lead must be pointed.
D. THE PENCIL POINT
Sharpen to a conical point with a lead pointer or a sandpaper pad.

10.2 Sharpen the drafting pencil to a tapered conical point (not a needle point) with a sandpaper pad or other type of sharpener.

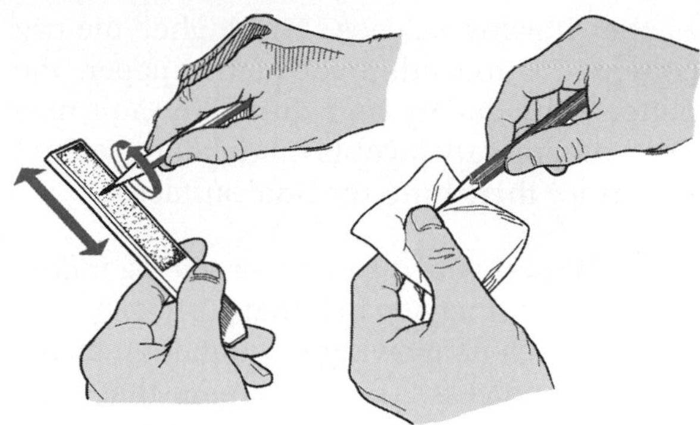

10.3 Rotate the drafting pencil about its axis while stroking the sandpaper pad to form a conical point. Wipe away the graphite from the point with a tissue.

Figure 10.2 shows three standard pencils used for drawing. The leads used in the lead holder shown in **Figure 10.2A** (the best all-around pencil of the three) are marked at their ends to indicate their grade.

The fine-line leads used in the lead holder in **Figure 10.2B** are more difficult to identify because their sizes are smaller and are not marked. A different fine-line holder must be used for each size of lead. The common sizes are 0.3 mm, 0.5 mm, and 0.07 mm, which are the diameters of the leads. A disadvantage of the fine-line pencil is the tendency of the lead to snap off when you apply pressure to it.

Although you have to sharpen it and point its lead, the wood pencil shown in **Figure 10.2C** is a very satisfactory pencil. The grade of the lead is marked on one end of the pencil; therefore, the opposite end should be sharpened so the identity of the grade of lead will be retained. The wood can be sharpened with a knife or a drafter's pencil sharpener to leave about 3/8 in. of lead exposed.

You must sharpen a pencil's lead properly to obtain a point as shown in **Figure 10.2D**. To obtain a conical point, stroke the pencil lead against a sandpaper board and rotate the pencil about it axis in the process (**Figure 10.3**). Wipe excess graphite from the point with a cloth or tissue.

Although sharpening a pencil point with a sandpaper board may seem outdated, it is a very suitable and practical way to sharpen pencil points and about the only way to sharpen compass points. However, a multitude of pencil pointers are available, some of which work well while others do not.

Papers and Films

Sizes Sheet sizes are specified by the letters A–E. These sizes are multiples of either the standard 8-1/2 × 11-in. sheet (used by engineers) or the 9 × 12-in. sheet (used by architects) (**Figure 10.4**). The metric sizes (A4–A0) are equivalent to the 8-1/2 × 11-in. modular sizes.

Detail Paper When drawings are not to be reproduced by the diazo or blue-line process, an opaque paper, called **detail paper**, can be used

	ENGINEERS'	ARCHITECTS'		METRIC
A	11" X 8.5"	12" X 9"	A4	297 X 210
B	17" X 11"	18" X 12"	A3	420 X 297
C	22" X 17"	24" X 18"	A2	594 X 420
D	34" X 22"	36" X 24"	A1	841 X 594
E	44" X 34"	48" X 36"	A0	1189 X 841

10.4 Standard sheet sizes vary by purpose.

as the drawing surface. The higher the rag content (cotton additive) of the paper, the better is its quality and durability. You may draw preliminary layouts on detail paper and then trace them onto the final surface.

Tracing Paper Tracing paper or tracing *vellum* is a thin, translucent paper that permits light to pass through it, allowing reproduction by the blue-line process. Tracing papers that yield the best reproductions are the most translucent ones. Vellum is a tracing paper that is chemically treated to improve its translucency, but vellum does not retain its original quality as long as do high-quality, untreated tracing papers.

Tracing Cloth Tracing cloth is a permanent drafting medium used for both ink and pencil drawings. It is made of cotton fabric and is coated with a starch compound to provide a tough, erasable drafting surface that yields excellent blue-line reproductions. Tracing cloth does not change shape as much as tracing paper does with variations in temperature and humidity. Repeated erasures do not damage the surface of tracing cloth.

Polyester Film An excellent drafting surface is polyester film, which is available under several trade names such as *Mylar.* It is more transparent, stable, and tougher than paper or cloth and is waterproof. Mylar film is used for both pencil and ink drawings. A plastic-lead pencil must be used with some films, whereas standard lead pencils may be used with others.

10.3 Drawing Equipment

Drafting Machine

Most professional drafters prefer the mechanical drafting machine (**Figure 10.5**), which is attached to the drawing tabletop and has fingertip controls for drawing lines at any angle. A modern, fully equipped drafting station is shown in **Figure 10.6**. Today, most offices are equipped with computer graphics stations, which have replaced much of the manual equipment (**Figure 10.7**).

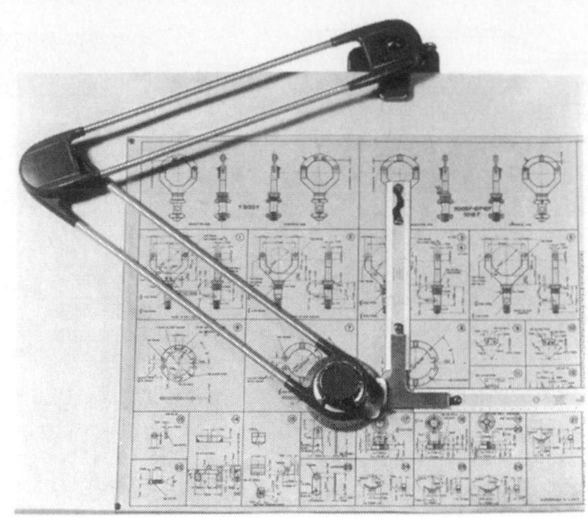

10.5 The drafting machine is used to produce drawings by hand. *(Courtesy of Keuffel & Esser Company.)*

Triangles

The two types of triangles used most often are the 45° triangle and the 30°-60° triangle.

10.6 The professional drafter or engineer may work in this type of environment.

10.7 A typical engineering workstation used in industry. *(Courtesy of Dell Inc.)*

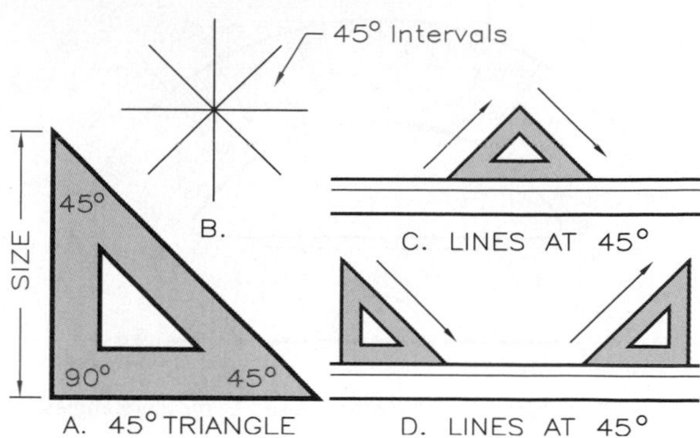

10.9 Use the 45° triangle to draw lines at 45° angles throughout 360°.

The size of a 30°-60° triangle is specified by the longer of the two sides adjacent to the 90° angle (**Figure 10.8**). Standard sizes of 30°-60° triangles range in 2-in. intervals from 4 to 24 in.

The size of a 45° triangle is specified by the length of the sides adjacent to the 90° angle. These range in 2-in. intervals from 4 to 24 in., but the 6-in. and 10-in. sizes are adequate for most classroom applications. **Figure 10.9** shows the various angles that you may draw with this triangle. Using the 45° and 30°-60° triangles in combination allows angles to be drawn at 15° intervals throughout 360° (**Figure 10.10**).

Protractor

A protractor is used (**Figure 10.11**) for drawing or measuring lines at angles other than multiples of 15°. Protractors are available as semicircles (180°) or circles (360°). Adjustable triangles with movable edges that can be set at different angles with thumbscrews also are available.

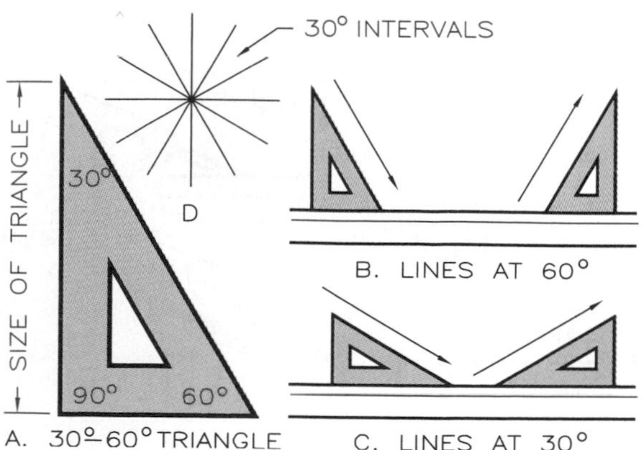

10.8 The 30°-60° triangle is used to draw lines at 30° intervals throughout 360°.

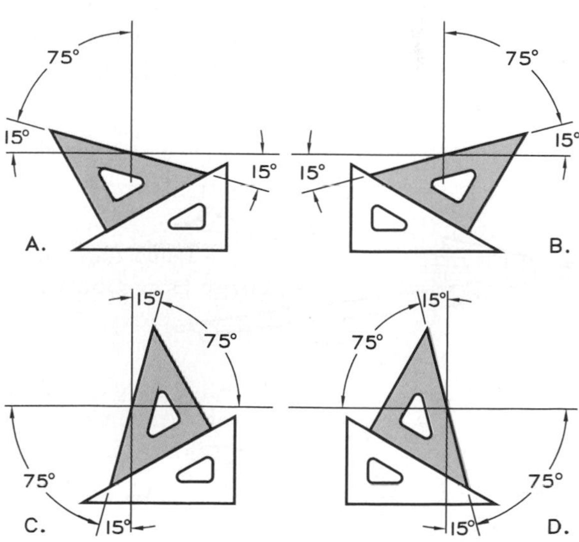

10.10 Using a 30°-60° triangle in combination with a 45° triangle allows angles to be drawn at 15° intervals.

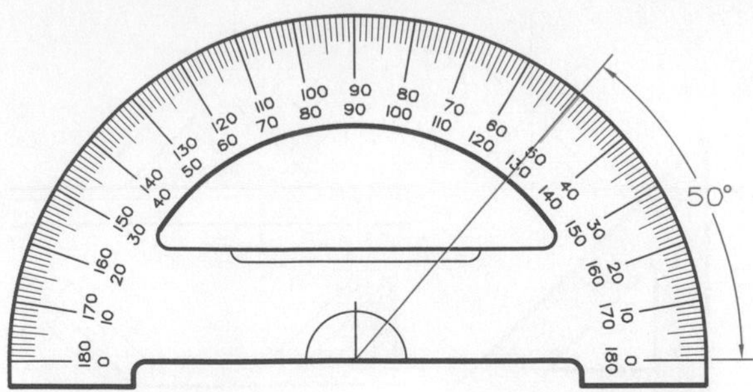

10.11 The semicircular protractor is used to measure angles.

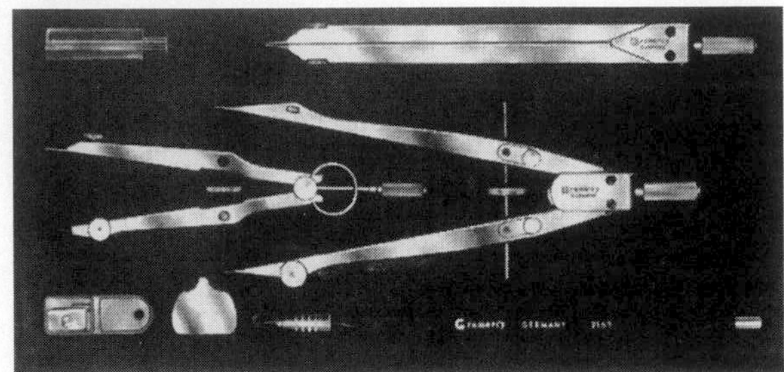

10.12 A typical cased set of drawing instruments. *(Courtesy of Gramercy Guild.)*

Instrument Set

Figure 10.12 shows a cased set of some of the basic drawing instruments that are available individually as well. The three most important instruments for hand drawing are the large compass, small compass, and dividers, shown in **Figure 10.13**.

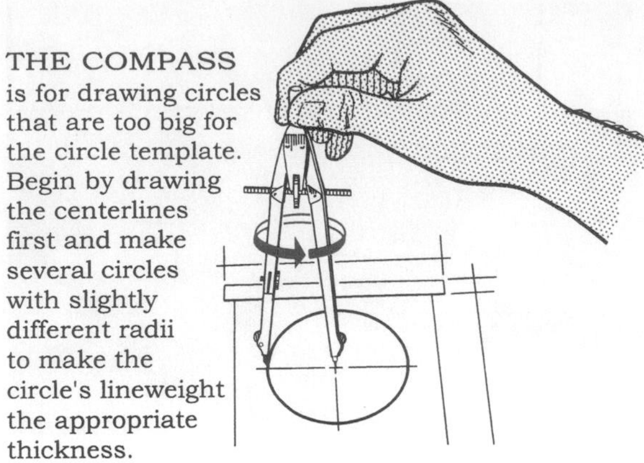

THE COMPASS
is for drawing circles that are too big for the circle template. Begin by drawing the centerlines first and make several circles with slightly different radii to make the circle's lineweight the appropriate thickness.

10.14 Use a compass for drawing large circles.

Compass Use the compass to draw circles and arcs in pencil or ink (**Figure 10.14**). To draw circles well with a pencil compass, sharpen the lead on its outside with a sandpaper board (**Figure 10.15**). A bevel cut of this type gives the best point for drawing circles. You cannot draw a thick arc in pencil with a single sweep; draw a series of thin concentric circles by adjusting the radius of the compass slightly.

When setting the compass pivot point in the drawing surface, insert it just far enough for a firm set, not to the shoulder of the point. When the tabletop has a hard covering, place

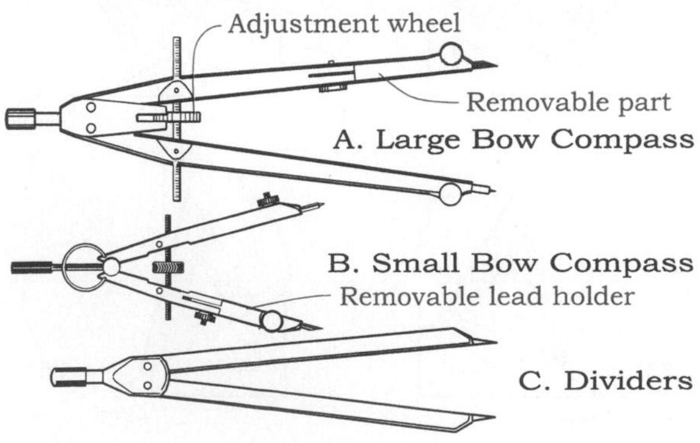

10.13 Drawing instruments can be purchased individually or as a set.

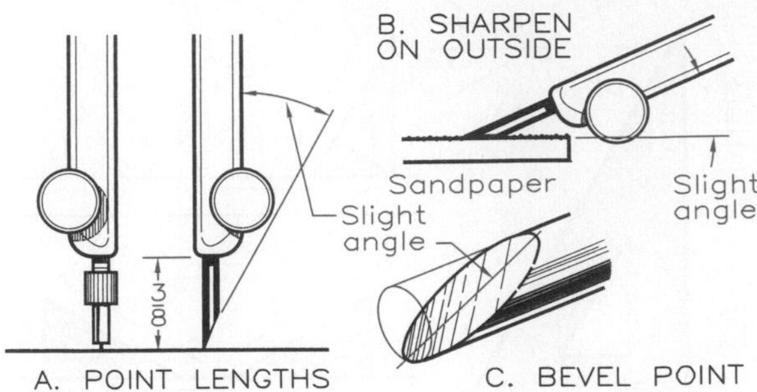

10.15 Compass lead
A Adjust the pencil point to be the same length as the compass point.
B & C Sharpen the lead from the outside with a sandpaper pad.

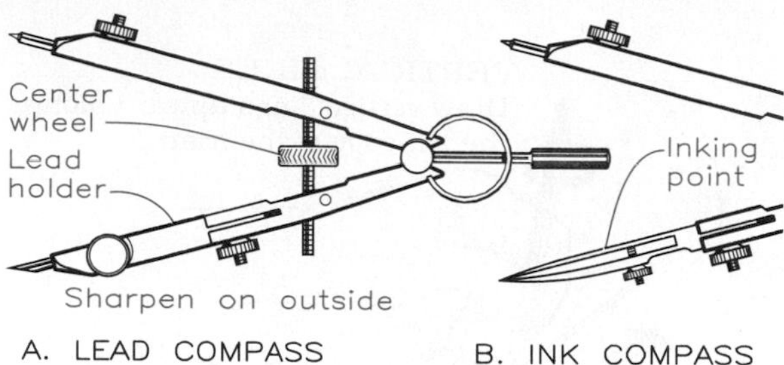

10.16 Use a small bow compass for drawing circles of up to 2-in. radius in pencil or in ink.

several sheets of paper under the drawing to provide a seat for the compass point.

Use a small bow compass (**Figure 10.16**) to draw small circles of up to 2 in. in radius. For larger circles, use an extension bar included in most sets to extend the range of the large bow compass. You may draw small circles conveniently with a circle template aligned with the centerlines of the circles (**Figure 10.17**).

Dividers Dividers look like a compass without a drawing point. They are used for laying off and transferring dimensions onto a drawing. For example, you can step off equal divisions rapidly and accurately along a line (**Figure 10.18**). As you make each measurement, the dividers' points make a slight impression mark in the drawing surface.

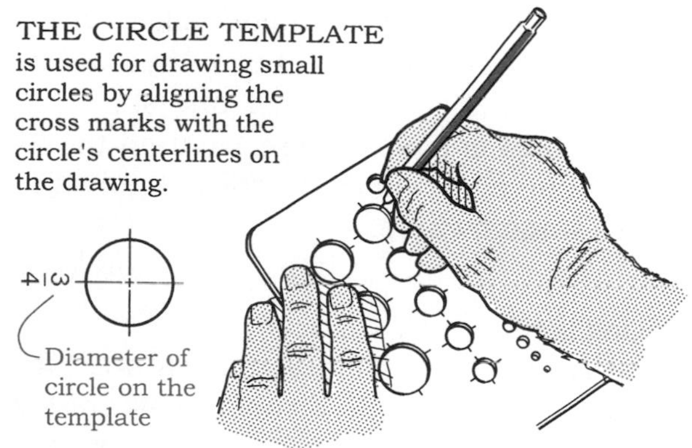

THE CIRCLE TEMPLATE
is used for drawing small circles by aligning the cross marks with the circle's centerlines on the drawing.
3/4
Diameter of circle on the template

10.17 Drawing small circles with a template.

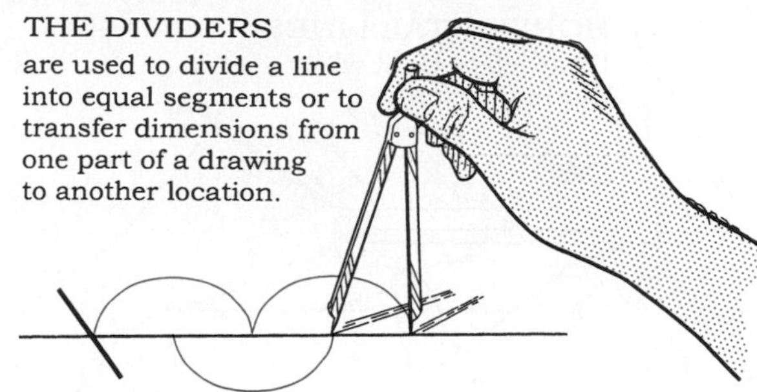

THE DIVIDERS
are used to divide a line into equal segments or to transfer dimensions from one part of a drawing to another location.

10.18 Using dividers to step off measurements.

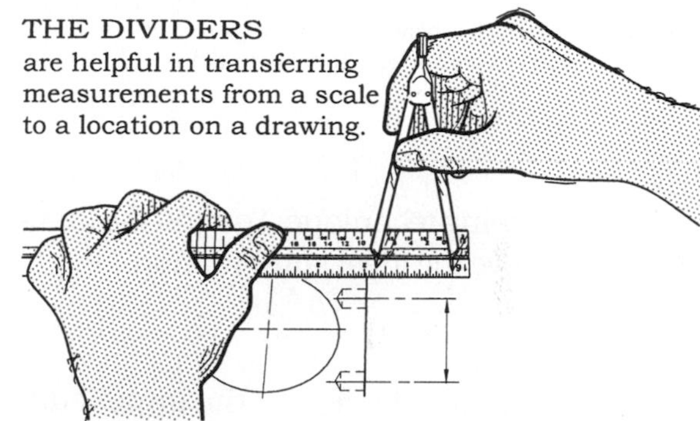

THE DIVIDERS
are helpful in transferring measurements from a scale to a location on a drawing.

10.19 Use dividers to transfer dimensions to a drawing.

Also, use dividers to transfer dimensions from a scale to a drawing (**Figure 10.19**) or to divide a line into a number of equal parts. Bow dividers (**Figure 10.20**) are useful for transferring smaller dimensions, such as the spacing between lettering guidelines.

10.4 Lines

The type of line produced by a pencil depends on the hardness of its lead, the drawing surface,

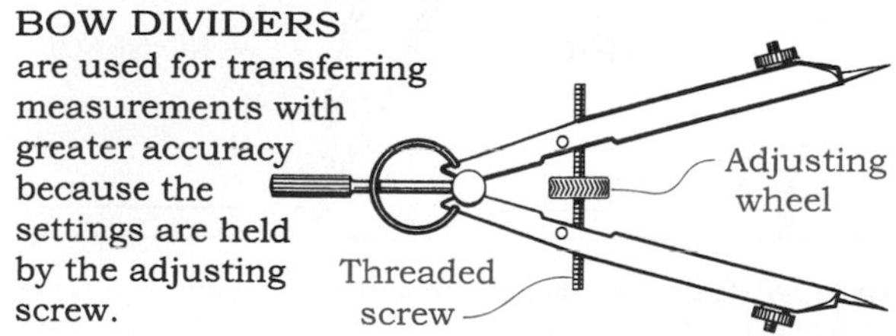

BOW DIVIDERS
are used for transferring measurements with greater accuracy because the settings are held by the adjusting screw.
Adjusting
wheel
Threaded
screw

10.20 Bow dividers are excellent for transfering the spacings of guidelines for lettering.

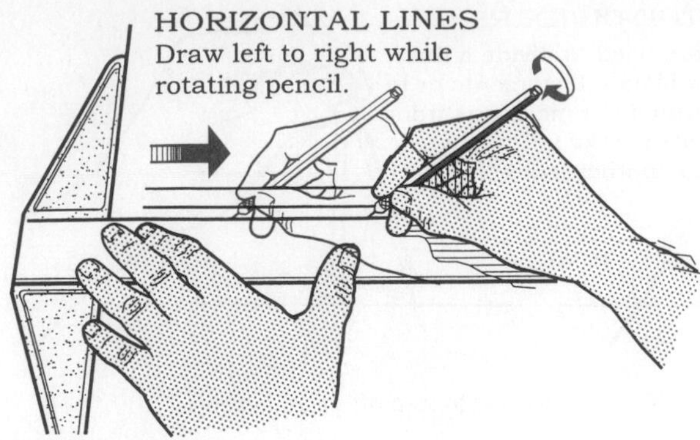

HORIZONTAL LINES
Draw left to right while rotating pencil.

10.21 Draw horizontal lines along the upper edge of a straightedge while holding the pencil in a plane perpendicular to the paper and at 60° to the surface, and rotate the pencil about its axis.

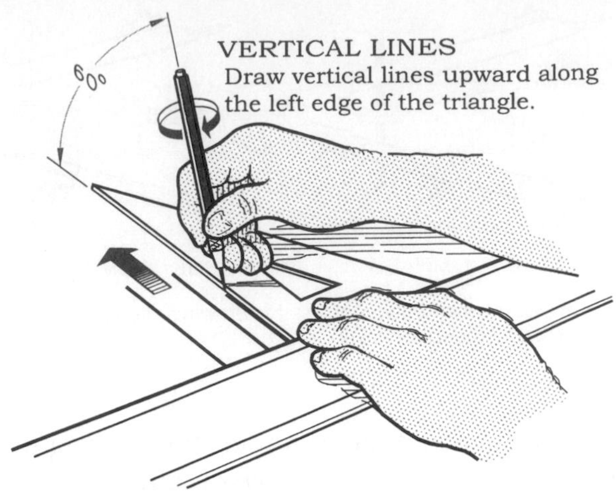

60°
VERTICAL LINES
Draw vertical lines upward along the left edge of the triangle.

10.23 Draw vertical lines along the left side of a triangle (if you are right-handed) in an upward direction, holding the pencil or pen in a plane perpendicular to the paper and at 60° to the surface.

and your drawing technique. You must experiment to achieve the ideal combination.

Horizontal Lines

To draw a horizontal line, use the upper edge of your horizontal straightedge and make strokes from left to right, if you are right-handed (**Figure 10.21**), and from right to left if you are left-handed. Rotate the pencil about its axis so that its point will wear evenly. Darken pencil lines by drawing over them with multiple strokes. For drawing the best line, leave a small space between the straightedge and the pencil or pen point (**Figure 10.22**).

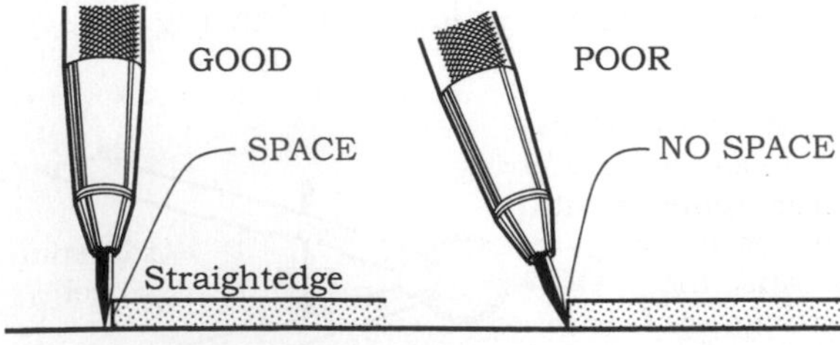

10.22 While drawing, hold the pencil or pen point in a plane perpendicular to the paper, leaving a space between the point and the straightedge.

Vertical Lines

Use a triangle and a straightedge to draw vertical lines. Hold the straightedge firmly with one hand and position the triangle where needed, and draw the vertical lines with the other hand (**Figure 10.23**). Draw vertical lines upward along the left side of the triangle if you are right-handed and upward along the right side of the triangle if you are left-handed.

Irregular Curves

Curves that are not arcs must be drawn with an irregular curve (sometimes called *French curves*). These plastic curves come in a variety of sizes and shapes, but the one shown in **Figure 10.24** is typical. Here, we used the irregular curve to connect a series of points to form a smooth curve.

Erasing Lines

Always use the softest eraser that will do a particular job. For example, do not use ink erasers to erase pencil lines because ink erasers are

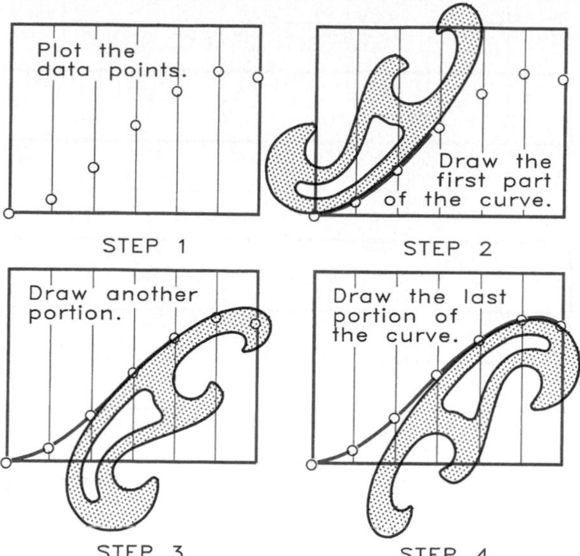

Draw the first part of the curve.

10.24 Using the irregular curve.

Step 1: Plot data points.

Step 2: Position the curve to pass through as many points as possible and draw that portion of the curve.

Step 3: Reposition the irregular curve and draw another portion of the curve.

Step 4: Draw the last portion to complete the curve.

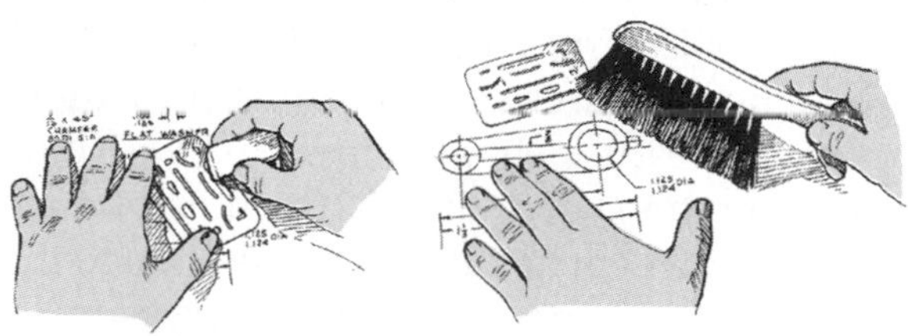

10.25 Use an erasing shield for erasing in tight spots. Use a brush, not your hand, to brush away the erasure crumbs.

coarse and may damage the surface of the paper. When working in small areas, you should use an erasing shield to avoid accidentally erasing adjacent lines (**Figure 10.25**). Follow erasing by brushing away the "crumbs" with a dusting brush. Wiping the crumbs away with your hands will smudge the drawing. A typical cordless electric eraser is

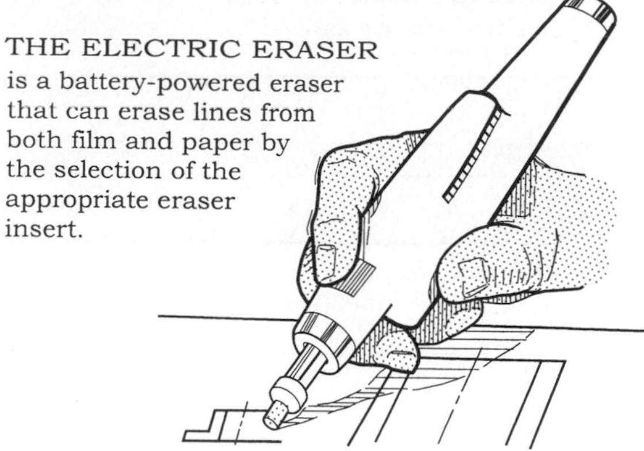

THE ELECTRIC ERASER
is a battery-powered eraser that can erase lines from both film and paper by the selection of the appropriate eraser insert.

10.26 This cordless electric eraser is typical of those used by professional drafters.

shown in **Figure 10.26** that can be used with several grades of erasers to meet your needs.

10.5 Measurements

Scales

All engineering drawings require the use of scales for measuring lengths and sizes. Scales may be flat or triangular and are made of wood, plastic, or metal. **Figure 10.27** shows triangular architects', engineers', and metric scales. Most scales are either 6 or 12 in. long.

Architects' Scale

Drafters use architects' scales to dimension and scale features such as room size, cabinets, plumbing, and electrical layouts. Most indoor measurements are made in feet and inches with the architects' scale. **Figure 10.28** shows how to indicate the scale you are using on a drawing. Place this scale designation in the title block or in a prominent location on the drawing. Because dimensions measured with the architects' scale are in feet and inches, you must convert all dimensions to decimal equivalents (all feet or all inches) before making calculations.

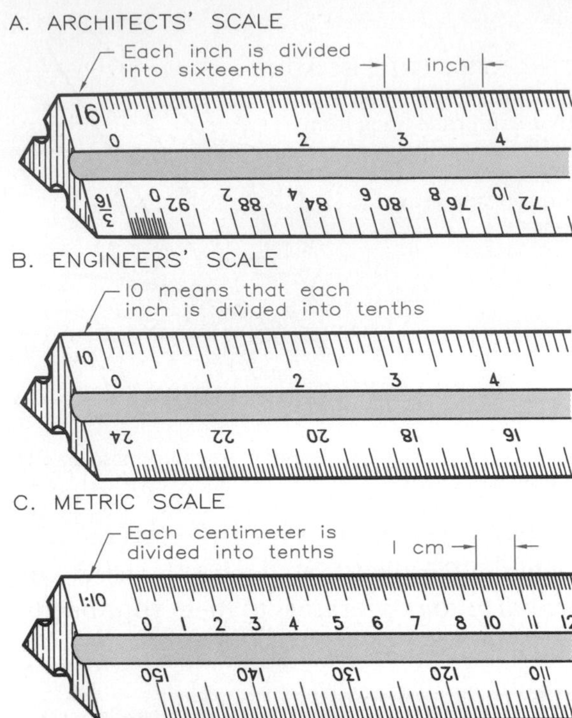

10.27 The architects' scale (A) measures in feet and inches. The engineers' scale (B) and the metric scale (C) are calibrated in decimal units.

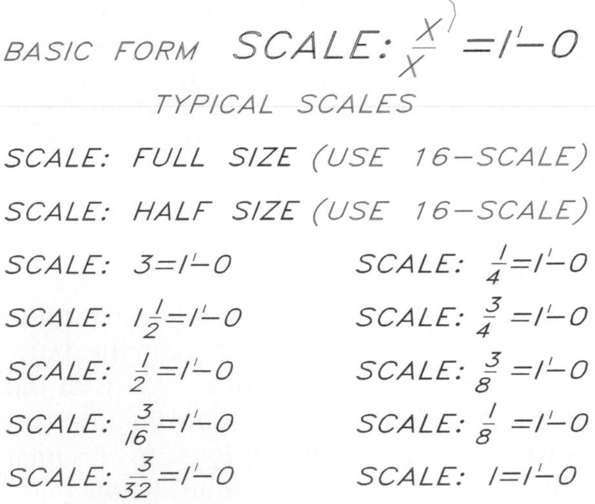

10.28 Use this basic form to indicate the scale on a drawing made with an architects' scale.

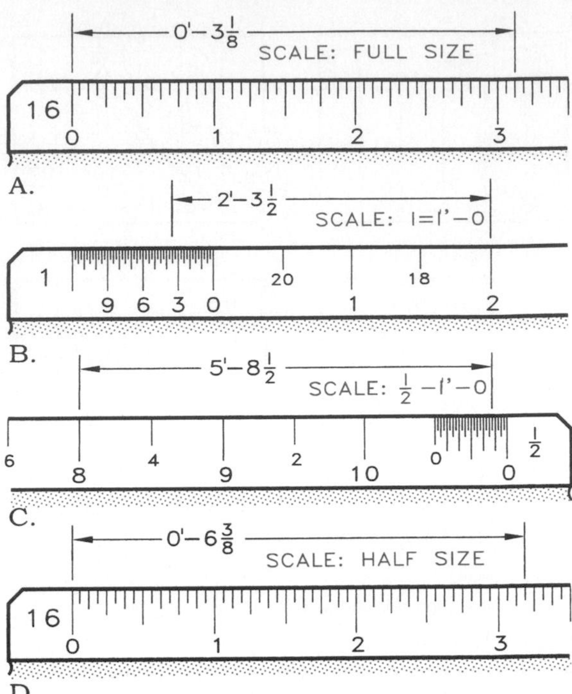

10.29 Lines measured with an architects' scale.

Use the 16 scale for measuring full-size lines (**Figure 10.29A**). An inch on the 16 scale is divided into sixteenths to match the ruler used by carpenters. The measurement shown is 3-1/8″. When the measurement is less than 1 ft, a zero may precede the inch measurements, with inch marks omitted, or 0′-3-1/2. (Inch marks are omitted, since inches are understood to be the units of measurement in the English system.)

Figure 10.29B shows the use of the 1 = 1′-0 scale to measure a line. Read the nearest whole foot (2 ft in this case) and the remainder in inches from the end of the scale (3-1/2 in.) for a total of 2′-3-1/2. Note that, at the end of each scale, a foot is divided into inches for use in measuring fractional parts of feet in inches. The scale 1′ = 1′-0 is the same as saying that 1 in. is equal to 12 in. or that the drawing is 1/12 the actual size of the object.

When you use the 1/2 = 1′-0 scale, 1/2 in. represents 12 in. on a drawing. Thus the line in **Figure 10.29C** measures 5′-8-1/2.

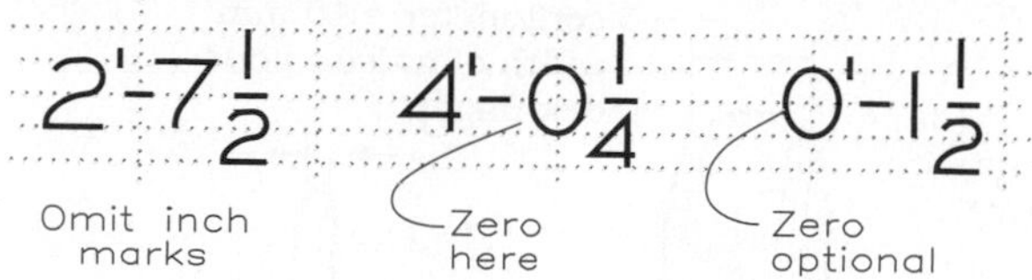

10.30 Omit inch marks but show foot marks (according to current standards). When the inch measurement is less than a whole inch, use a leading zero.

To obtain a half-size measurement divide the full-size measurement by 2 and measure it with the 16 scale. Half size is sometimes specified as SCALE: 6 = 12 (inch marks omitted). The line in **Figure 10.29D** measures 0′-6-3/8.

Letter dimensions in feet and inches as shown in **Figure 10.30**, with fractions twice as tall as whole numerals.

Engineers' Scale

On the engineers' scale, each inch is divided into multiples of 10. Because it is used for making drawings of outdoor projects—streets, structures, tracts of land, and other topographic features—it is sometimes called the civil engineers' scale.

Figure 10.31 shows the form for specifying scales when using the engineers' scale. For example, scale: 1 = 10′. With measurements already in decimal form, performing calculations is easy; there is no need to convert from one unit to another as when you use the architects' scale.

FROM END OF SCALE

BASIC FORM SCALE: 1= XX

EXAMPLE SCALES

10	SCALE: 1=1'	SCALE: 1=1,000
20	SCALE: 1=200'	SCALE: 1=20 LB
30	SCALE: 1=3'	SCALE: 1=3,000'
40	SCALE: 1=4'	SCALE: 1=40'
50	SCALE: 1=50'	SCALE: 1=500'
60	SCALE: 1=6	SCALE: 1=0.6'

10.31 Use this basic form to indicate the scale on a drawing made with an engineers' scale.

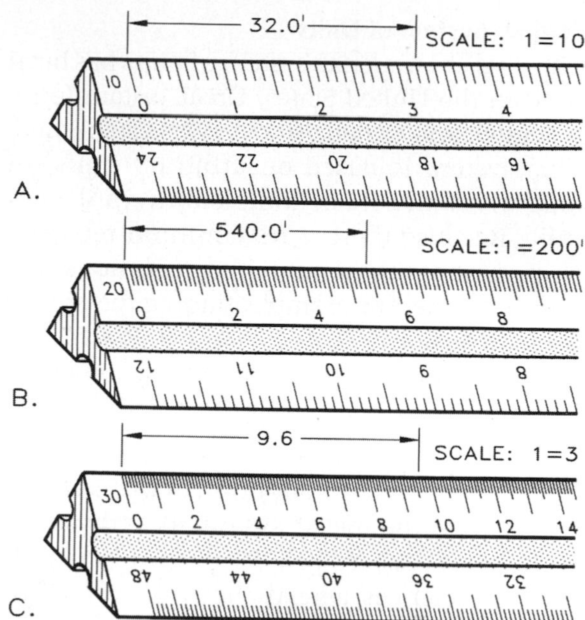

10.32 These lines are measured with engineers' scales.

Each end of the scale is labeled 10, 20, 30, and so on, which indicates the number of units per inch on the scale (**Figure 10.32**). You may obtain many combinations simply by mentally moving the decimal places of a scale.

Figure 10.32A shows the use of the 10 scale to measure a line 32.0 ft long drawn at the scale of 1 = 10′. **Figure 10.32B** shows use of the 20 scale to measure a line 540.0 ft long drawn at a scale of 1 = 200′. **Figure 10.32C** shows use of the 30 scale to measure a line 9.6 in. long at a scale of 1 = 3. **Figure 10.33** shows the proper format for indicating measurements in feet and inches.

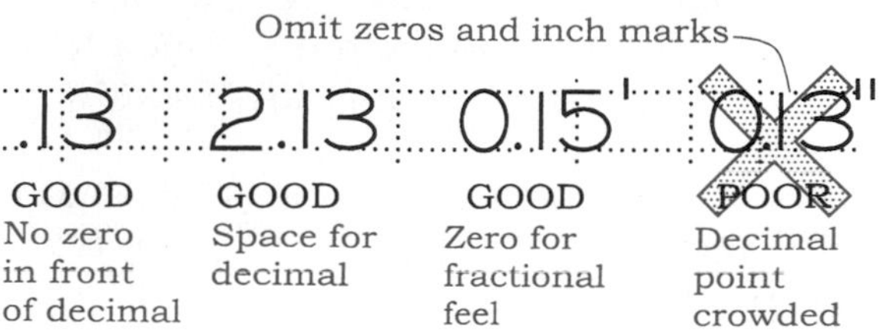

10.33 For decimal fractions in inches, omit leading zeros and inch marks. For feet, leave adequate space for decimal points between numbers and show foot marks.

English System of Units

The English (Imperial) system of units has been used in the United States, Great Britain (until recently), and Canada since it was established. This system is based on arbitrary units (of length) of the inch, foot, cubit, yard, and mile. Because there is no common relationship among these units, calculations are cumbersome. For example, finding the area of a rectangle that measures 25 in. × 6-3/4 yd first requires conversion of one unit to the other.

Metric System (SI) of Units

France proposed the adoption of the meter as the basis of the metric system as early as the eighteenth century. In 1791 the French Academy of Sciences agreed that the meter (m) would be one ten-millionth of the length of the meridian quadrant of the earth through Paris from equator to pole. Fractions of the meter would be expressed as decimal fractions. An international commission officially adopted the metric system in 1875.

The worldwide organization responsible for promoting the metric system is the **International Standards Organization (ISO)**. It has endorsed the Système International d'Unités (International System of Units), abbreviated **SI**. Prefixes to SI units indicate placement of the decimal, as **Figure 10.34** shows.

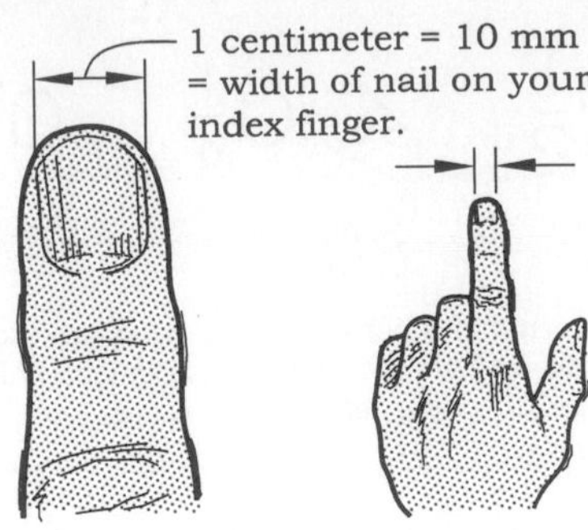

10.35 The nail width of your index finger is approximately equal to 1 centimeter, or 10 millimeters.

Metric Scales

The meter is 39.37 in. The basic metric unit of measurement for an engineering drawing is the millimeter (mm), which is one-thousandth of a meter, or one-tenth of a centimeter. Dimensions on a metric drawing are understood to be in millimeters unless otherwise specified.

The width of the fingernail of your index finger is a convenient way to approximate the dimension of 1 centimeter, or 10 millimeters (**Figure 10.35**). Depicted in **Figure 10.36** is the format for specifying metric scales on a drawing.

Decimal fractions are unnecessary on most drawings dimensioned in millimeters.

Value	Prefix	Sym.	Pronounce
1 000 000 = 10^6	= Mega	M	"Megah"
1 000 = 10^3	= Kilo	k	"Keylow"
100 = 10^2	= Hecto	h	"Heck tow"
10 = 10^1	= Deka	da	"Dekah"
1 =			
0.1 = 10^{-1}	= Deci	d	"Des sigh"
0.01 = 10^{-2}	= Centi	c	"Cen'-ti"
0.001 = 10^{-3}	= Milli	m	"Mill lee"
0.000 001 = 10^{-6}	= Micro	μ	"Microw"

10.34 These prefixes and abbreviations indicate decimal placement for SI measurements.

FROM END OF SCALE

BASIC FORM SCALE: 1 = XX

EXAMPLE SCALES

SCALE: 1:1 (1mm = 1mm; 1cm = 1cm)

SCALE: 1:2 (1mm = 2mm; 1mm = 20mm)

SCALE: 1:3 (1mm = 30mm; 1mm = 0.3mm)

SCALE: 1:4 (1mm = 4mm; 1mm = 40mm)

SCALE: 1:5 (1mm = 5mm; 1mm = 500mm)

SCALE: 1:6 (1mm = 6mm; 1mm = 60mm)

10.36 Use this basic form to indicate the scale of a drawing made with a metric scale.

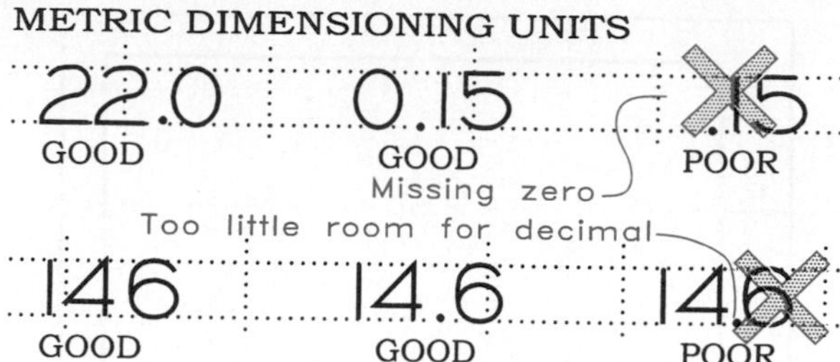

10.37 In the metric system, a zero precedes the decimal. Allow adequate space for it.

Thus dimensions are rounded off to whole numbers except for those measurements dimensioned with specified tolerances. For metric measurements of less than 1, a zero precedes the decimal. In the English system, the zero is omitted from measurements of less than an inch (**Figure 10.37**).

Metric scales are expressed as ratios: 1:20, 1:40, 1:100, 1:500, and so on. These ratios mean that one unit represents the number of units to the right of the colon. For example, 1:10 means that 1 mm equals 10 mm, or 1 cm equals 10 cm, or 1 m equals 10 m. The full-size metric scale (**Figure 10.38**) shows the relationship between the metric units decimeter, centimeter, millimeter, and micrometer. The line shown in **Figure 10.39A** measures 59 mm. Use the 1:2 scale when 1 mm represents 2 mm, 20 mm, 200 mm, and so on. The line shown in

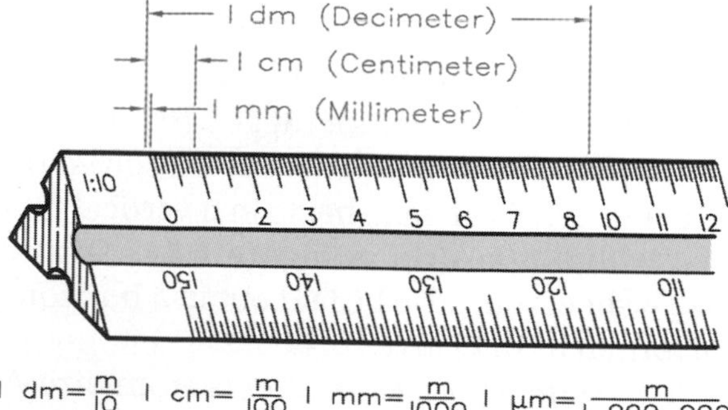

10.38 The decimeter is one tenth of a meter, the centimeter is one hundredth of a meter, a millimeter is one thousandth of a meter, and a micrometer is one millionth of a meter.

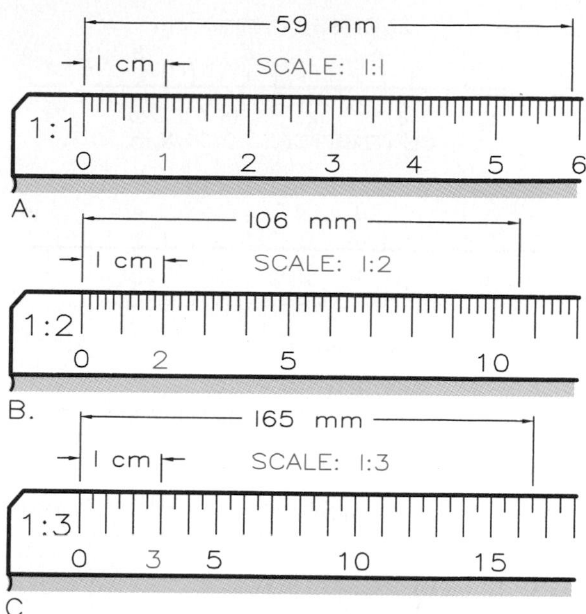

10.39 Measurements with metric scales.

Figure 10.39B measures 106 mm. **Figure 10.39C** shows a line measuring 165 mm, where 1 mm represents 3 mm.

Metric Symbols To indicate that drawings are in metric units, insert SI in or near the title block (**Figure 10.40**). The two views of the partial cone denote whether the orthographic views were drawn in accordance with the U.S. system (third-angle projection) or the European system (first-angle projection).

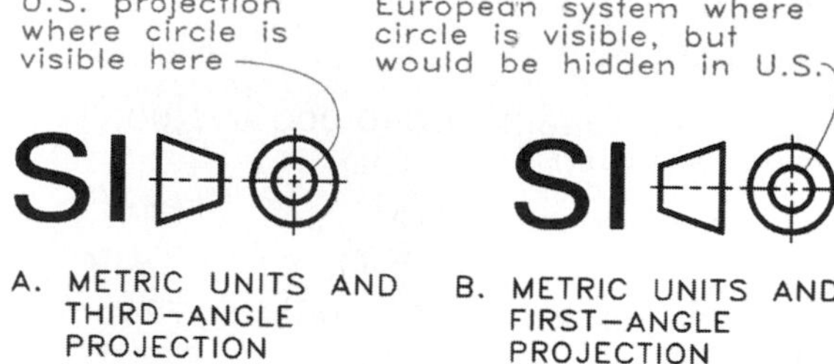

10.40 The large SI indicates that measurements are in metric units. The partial cones indicate whether the views are drawn in (A) third-angle (U.S. system) or (B) first-angle projection (European system).

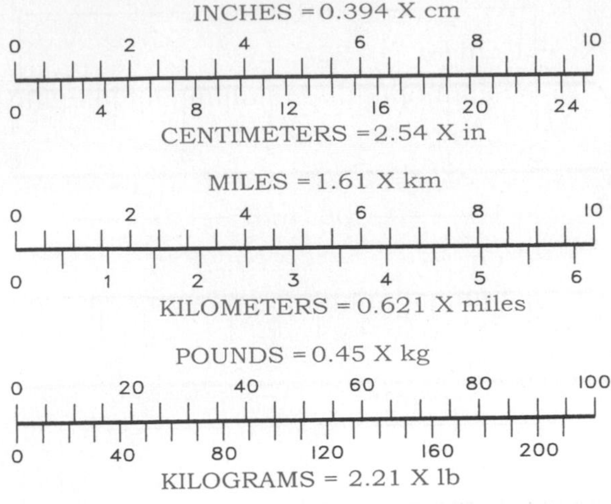

10.41 A comparison of English system units with metric system units

Figure 10.41 shows several comparisons of English and SI units.

Expression of Metric Units The general rules for expressing SI units are given in **Figure 10.42**. Do not use commas to separate digits in large numbers; instead, leave a space between them, as shown.

Scale Conversion

Appendix 2 gives factors for converting English to metric lengths, and vice versa. For example, multiply decimal inches by 25.4 to obtain millimeters, and divide millimeters by 0.394 to obtain inches.

Multiply an architects' scale by 12 to convert it to an approximate metric scale. For example, Scale: 1/8 = 1′-0 is the same as 1/8 in. = 12 in. or 1 in. = 96 in., which closely approximates the metric scale of 1:100. You cannot convert most metric scales exactly to English scales, but the metric scale 1:60 does convert exactly to 1 = 5′, which is the same as 1 in. = 60 in.

Omit commas and group into threes	1 000 000 GOOD		1,000,000 POOR
Use a raised dot for multiplication	N•M GOOD		NM POOR
Precede decimals with zeros	0.72 mm GOOD		.72 mm POOR
Methods of division	kg/m GOOD	or	$kg \cdot m^{-1}$ GOOD

10.42 Follow these general gules for showing SI units.

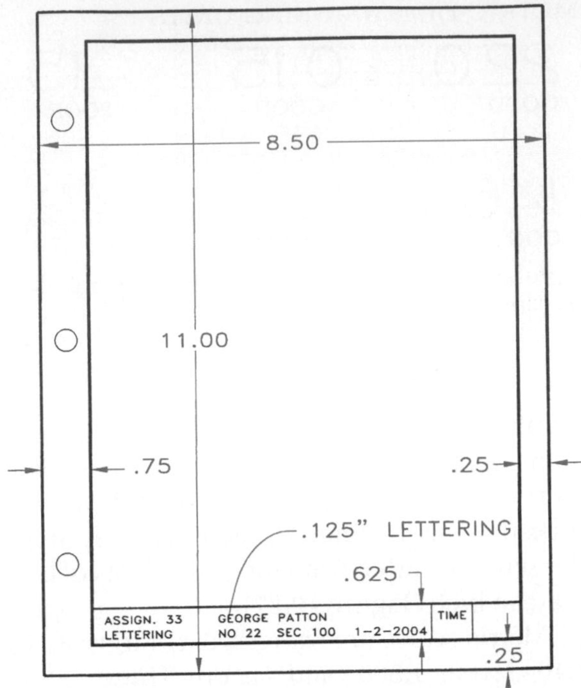

10.43 Use the format and title strip shown for a size A (vertical format) to present the solutions to problems at the end of each chapter.

10.6 Problem Layouts

The following formats are suggested for problem layouts. Most problems can be solved on size A (8-1/2 × 11-in.) sheets in a vertical format with a title strip as **Figure 10.43** shows. Size A sheets can also be laid out in a horizontal format as in **Figure 10.44**.

The standard sizes of sheets from size A through size E and an alternative title strip are shown in **Figure 10.44**. Always use guidelines for lettering title strips.

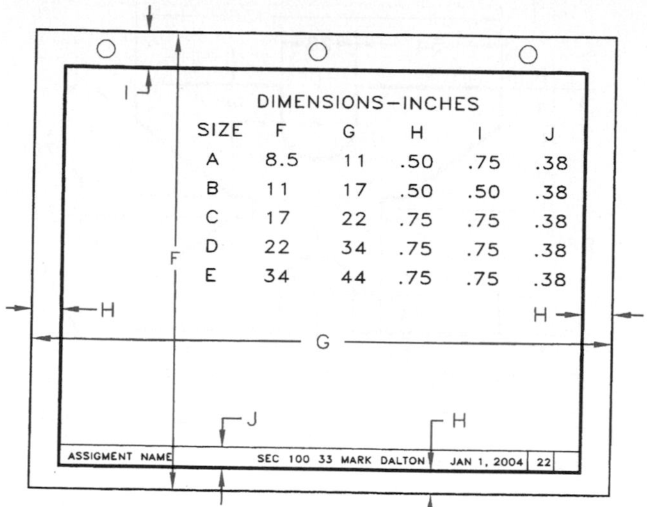

DIMENSIONS—INCHES

SIZE	F	G	H	I	J
A	8.5	11	.50	.75	.38
B	11	17	.50	.50	.38
C	17	22	.75	.75	.38
D	22	34	.75	.75	.38
E	34	44	.75	.75	.38

10.44 This is a horizontal format for size A through size E sheets. The numbers in columns F–J are the various layout dimensions for size A through size E sheets.

Problems

1–9. (**Figures 10.45–10.47**) Draw these problems on size A sheets (plain or with a grid) using the format shown in **Figure 10.45**. Each grid represents 0.25 in., or 6 mm.

10–20. (**Figures 10.48–10.59**) Draw full-size views on size A sheets (horizontal format) and omit the dimensions.

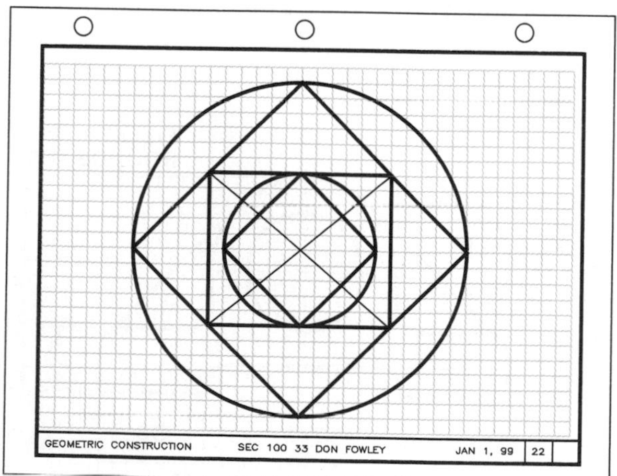

10.45 Problem 1 and sheet format.

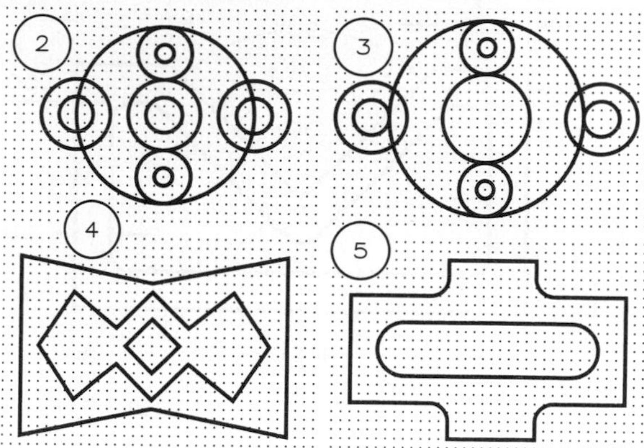

10.46 Problems 2–5.

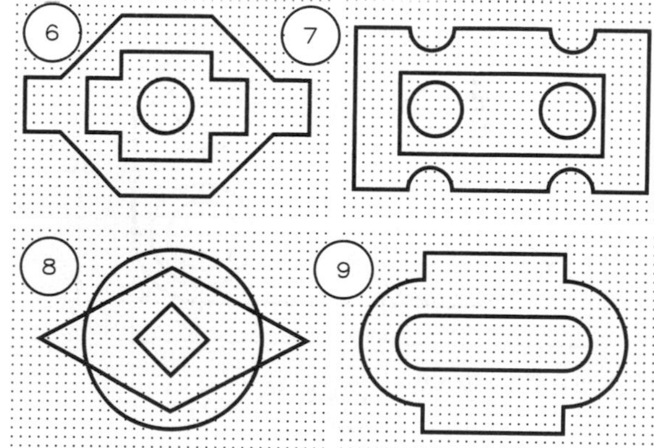

10.47 Problems 6–9.

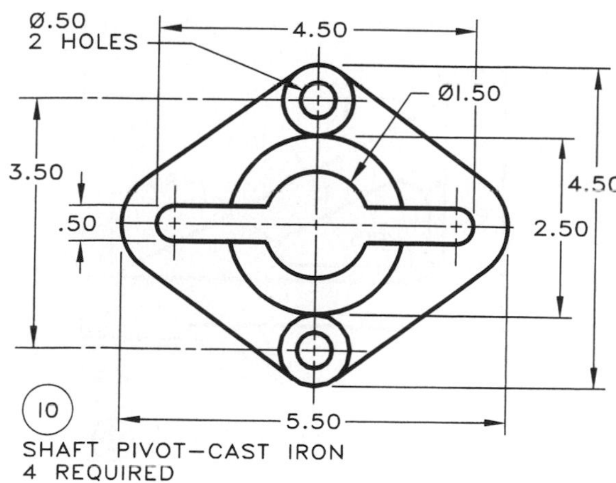

10.48 Problem 10.

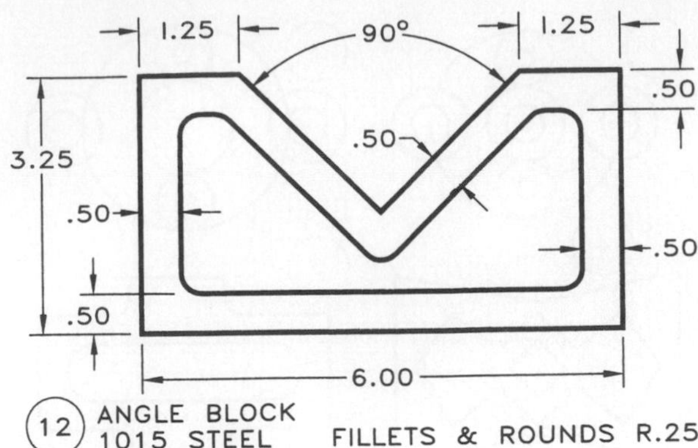

10.49 Problem 11.

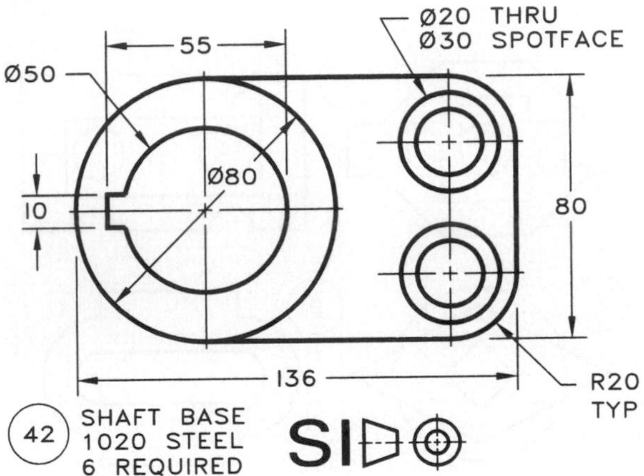

10.50 Problem 12.

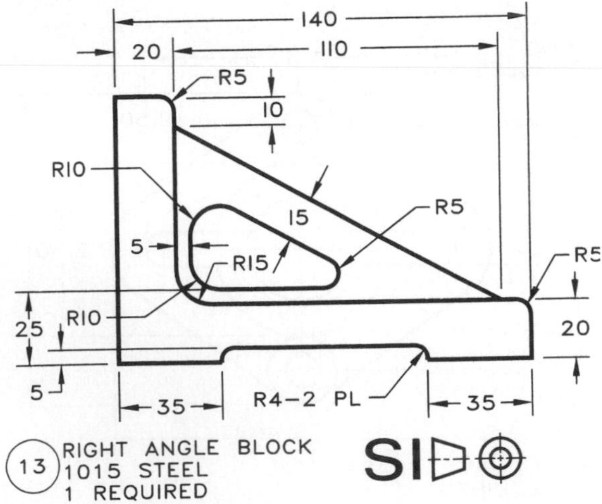

10.51 Problem 13.

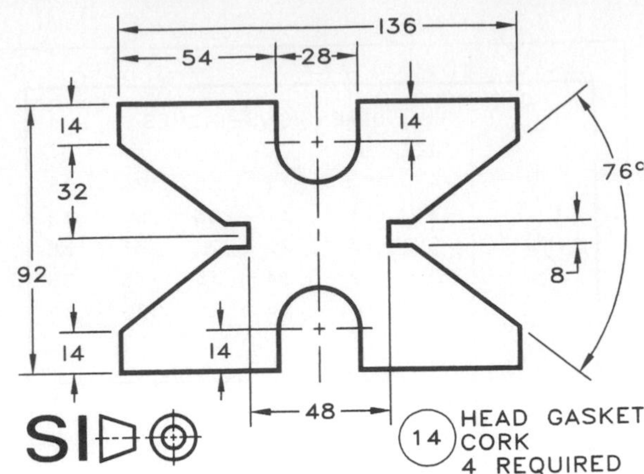

10.52 Problem 14.

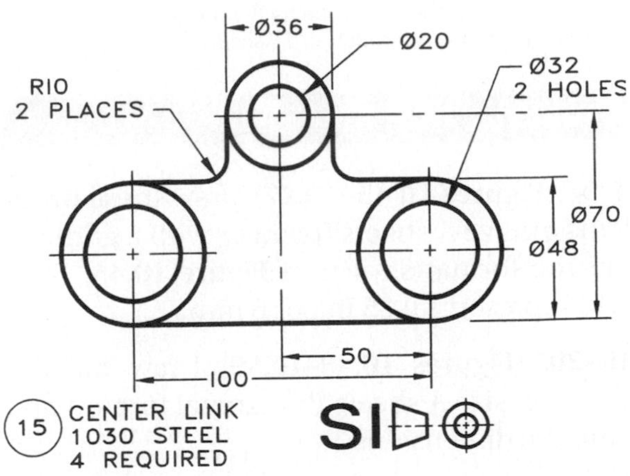

10.53 Problem 15.

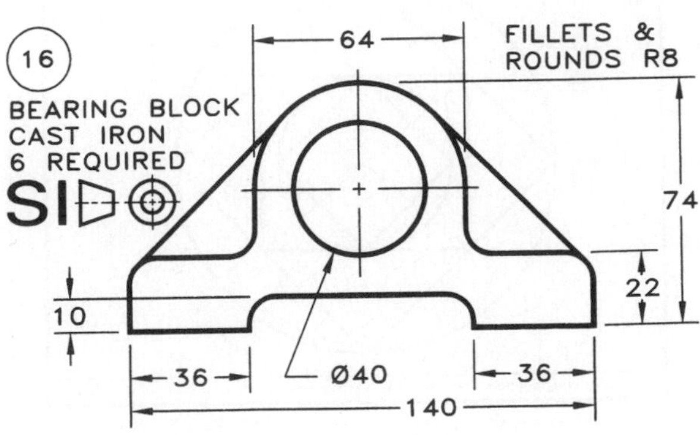

10.54 Problem 16.

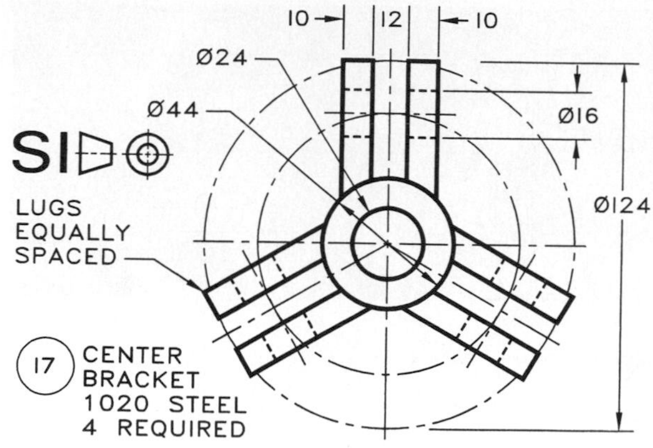

10.55 Problem 17.

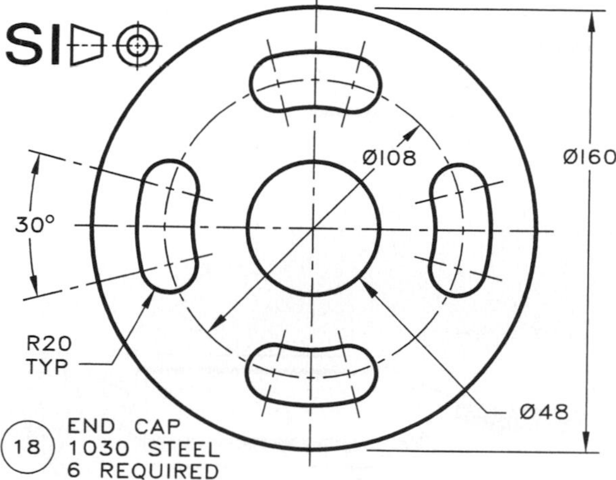

10.56 Problem 18.

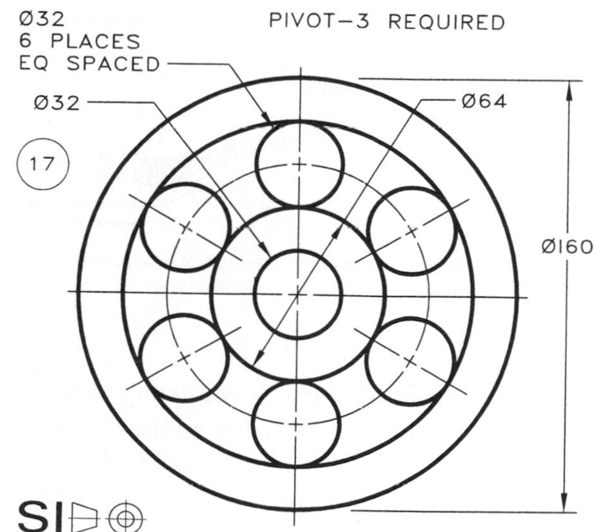

10.57 Problem 19.

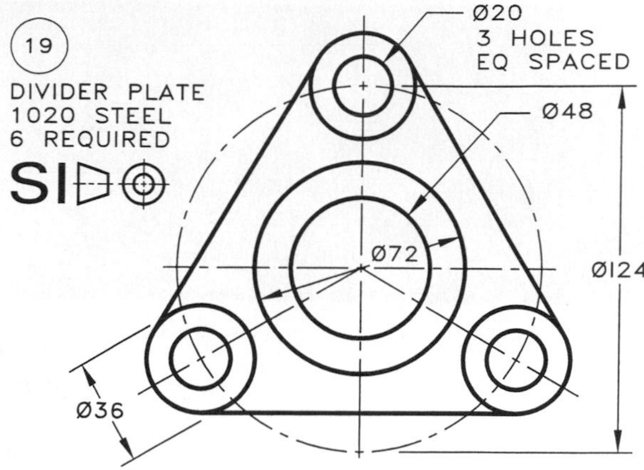

10.58 Problem 20.

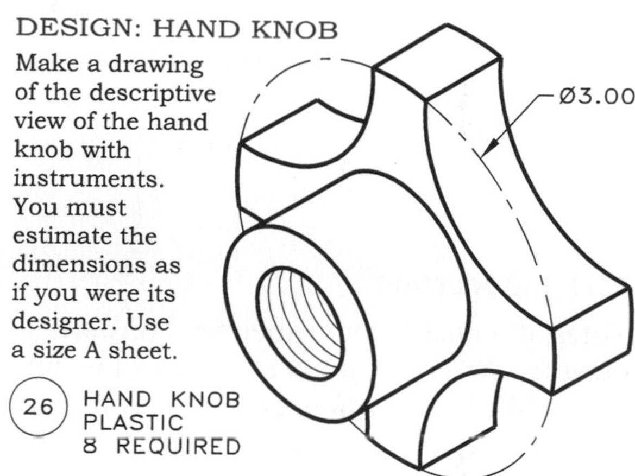

DESIGN: HAND KNOB
Make a drawing of the descriptive view of the hand knob with instruments. You must estimate the dimensions as if you were its designer. Use a size A sheet.
Ø3.00
26
HAND KNOB
PLASTIC
8 REQUIRED

10.59 Problem 21. Follow the same instructions that were given for the design of the hand knob, but instead of having four knob projections, design it to have five.

11 Lettering

11.1 Introduction

Notes, dimensions, and specifications, which must be lettered, supplement all drawings. The ability to letter freehand is an important skill to develop because it affects the use and interpretation of drawings. It also displays an engineer's skill with graphics, and may be taken as an indication of professional competence.

11.2 Lettering Tools

The best pencils for lettering on most surfaces are the H, F, and HB grades, with an F grade pencil being the one most commonly used. Some papers and films are coarser than others and may require a harder pencil lead. To give the desired line width, round the point of the pencil slightly (**Figure 11.1**).

Rotate the pencil about its axis with each stroke so that the lead will wear evenly. For good reproduction, bear down firmly to make letters black and bright with a single stroke. Prevent smudging while lettering by placing a sheet of paper under your hand to protect the drawing (**Figure 11.2**).

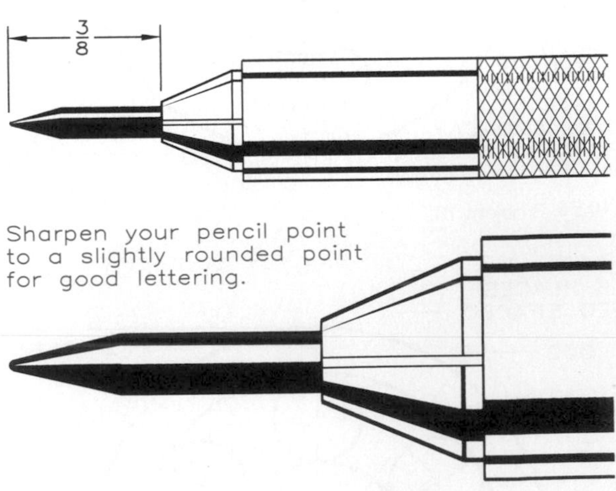

3/8
Sharpen your pencil point
to a slightly rounded point
for good lettering.

11.1 Good lettering begins with a properly sharpened pencil point. The F grade pencil is good for lettering.

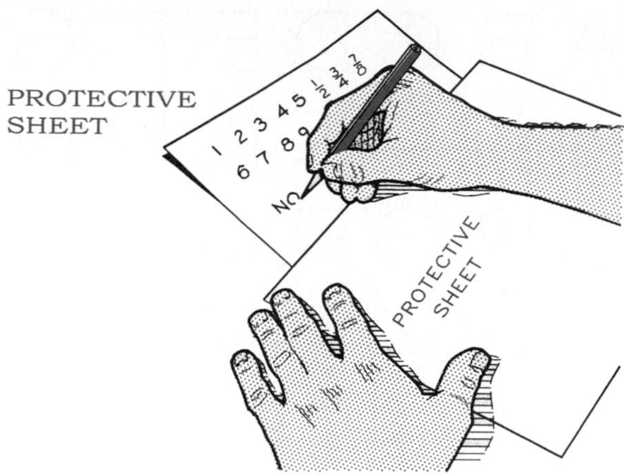

11.2 Place a protective sheet under your hand to prevent smudges, and work from a comfortable position for natural strokes.

11.3 Guidelines

The most important rule of lettering is **use guidelines at all times**, whether you are lettering a paragraph or a single letter. **Figure 11.3** shows how to draw and use guidelines. Use a sharp pencil in the 2H–4H grade range and draw light guidelines, **just dark enough to be seen**.

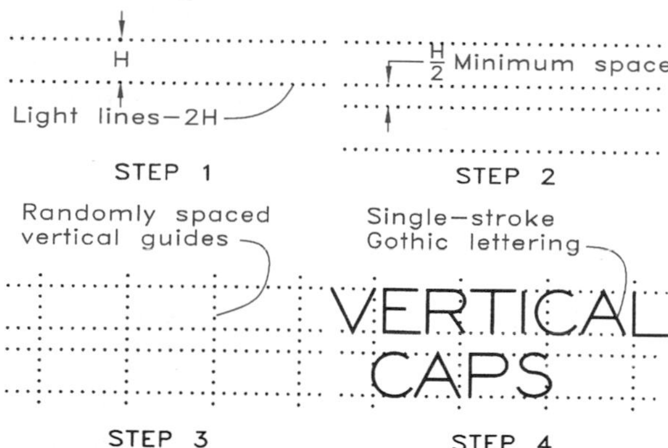

11.3 Method of using lettering guidelines.

Step 1 Lay off letter heights, H, and draw light guidelines with a 2H pencil.

Step 2 Space lines no closer than H/2 apart.

Step 3 Draw vertical guidelines as light, thin, randomly spaced lines.

Step 4 Draw letters with single strokes using a medium-grade pencil: H, F, or HB. Leave the guidelines.

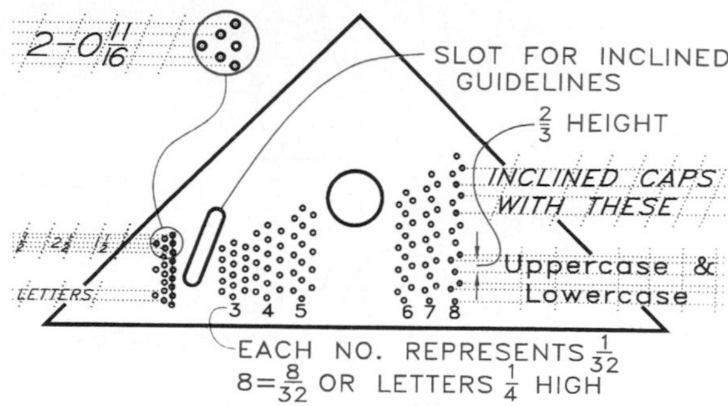

11.4 The Braddock-Rowe triangle also is used for drawing guidelines for lettering. The numbers near the guideline holes represent thirty-seconds of an inch.

Most lettering on an engineering drawing is done with capital letters that are 1/8 in. (3 mm) high. The spacing between lines of lettering should be no closer than half the height of the capital letters, or 1/16 in. in this case.

Lettering Guides

Two instruments for drawing guidelines are the Braddock-Rowe lettering triangle and the Ames lettering instrument.

The **Braddock-Rowe triangle** contains sets of holes for spacing guidelines (**Figure 11.4**). The numbers under each set of holes represent thirty-seconds of an inch. For example, the numeral 4 represents 4/32 in. or 1/8 in. for making uppercase (capital) letters. Some triangles have millimeter markings. Intermediate holes provide guidelines for lowercase letters, which are not as tall as capital letters.

While holding a horizontal straightedge firmly in position, place the Braddock-Rowe triangle against its upper edge. Insert a sharp 2H pencil point in the desired guideline hole to contact the drawing surface and guide the pencil point across the paper, drawing the guideline while the triangle slides along the straightedge. Repeat this procedure by moving the pencil point to each successive hole to draw other guidelines. Use the slanted slot in the triangle to draw guidelines, spaced randomly, for inclined lettering.

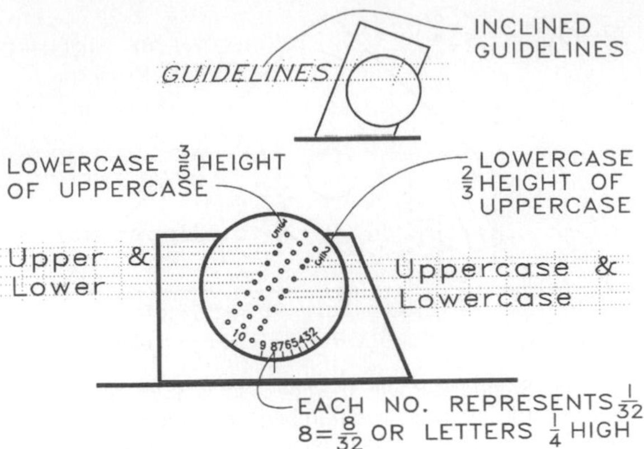

11.5 The Ames lettering guide is used for drawing guidelines for lettering. Set the dial to the desired number of thirty-seconds of an inch for the height of uppercase letters.

The **Ames lettering guide (Figure 11.5)** is a similar device but has a circular dial for selecting guideline spacing. The numbers around the dial represent thirty-seconds of an inch. For example, the number 8 represents 8/32 in., or guidelines for drawing capital letters that are 1/4 in. tall.

11.4 Gothic Lettering

The lettering recommended for engineering drawings is single-stroke Gothic lettering, so called because the letters are a variation of the Gothic style made with a series of single strokes. Gothic lettering may be vertical or inclined.

Vertical Letters

Uppercase The alphabet of the single-stroke Gothic uppercase (capital) letters is shown in **Figure 11.6**. Each letter is drawn inside a square box of guidelines to show their correct proportions. Draw straight lines with a single stroke; for example, draw the letter A with three single strokes. Letters composed of curves can best be drawn in segments; for example, draw the letter O by joining two semicircles. The shape (form) of each letter is important. Small wiggles in strokes will not detract from your lettering if the letter forms are correct.

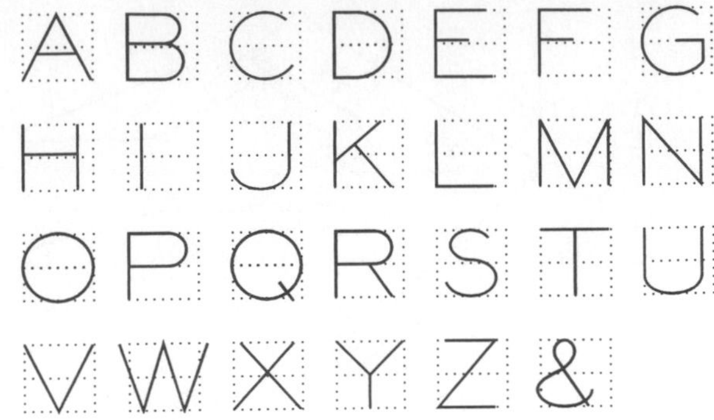

11.6 This alphabet shows the form of single-stroke Gothic vertical uppercase letters. Letters are drawn inside squares to show their proportions.

Lowercase The alphabet of lowercase letters is shown in **Figure 11.7**, which should be either two-thirds or three-fifths as tall as uppercase letters. Both lowercase ratios are labeled on the Ames guide, but only the two-thirds ratio is available on the Braddock-Rowe triangle.

Some lowercase letters, such as the letter *b,* have ascenders that extend above the body of the letter; some, such as the letter *p,* have descenders that extend below the body. Ascenders and descenders should be equal in length.

The guidelines in **Figure 11.7** that form squares about the body of each letter are used

11.7 The alphabet is drawn here in single-stroke Gothic vertical lowercase letters.

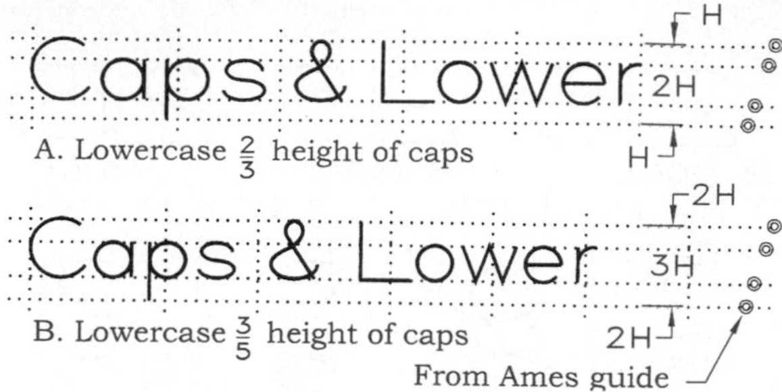

11.8 The ratio of lowercase to uppercase letter height should be either two-thirds (A) or three-fifths (B). The Ames guide has both ratios, but the Braddock-Rowe triangle has only the two-thirds ratio.

to illustrate their proportions. Letters that have circular bodies should extend slightly beyond the sides of the guideline squares. **Figure 11.8** shows examples of upper- and lowercase letters used in combination.

Numerals Vertical numerals used with single-stroke Gothic lettering are shown in **Figure 11.9**. Each numeral is enclosed in a square of guidelines. Numbers should be the same height as the capital letters being used, usually 1/8 in. The numeral 0 (zero) is an oval, whereas the letter O is a circle in vertical lettering.

Inclined Letters

Uppercase Inclined uppercase (capital) letters have the same heights and proportions as vertical letters; the only difference is their 68° inclination **(Figure 11.10).** Guidelines for inclined lettering can be drawn with both the Braddock-Rowe triangle and the Ames guide.

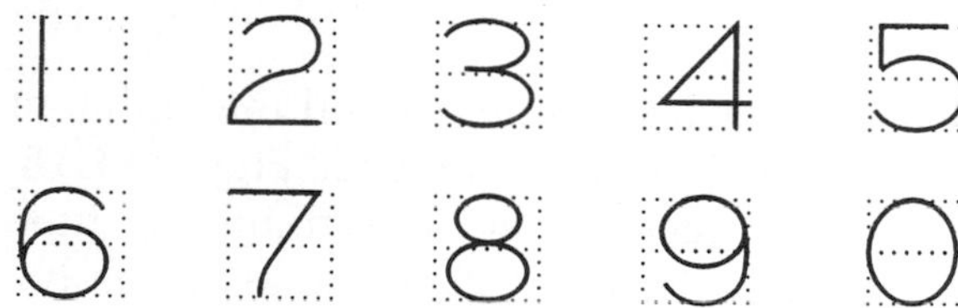

11.9 These numerals are used with single-stroke Gothic vertical letters.

11.10 An alphabet of single-stroke Gothic, inclined uppercase letters.

Lowercase Inclined lowercase letters are drawn in the same manner as vertical lowercase letters **(Figure 11.11)**, but circular features are drawn as ovals (ellipses). The angle of inclination is 68°, the same as for uppercase letters.

Numerals Examples of inclined numerals are shown in **Figure 11.12**, and letters used in combination with numerals are shown in

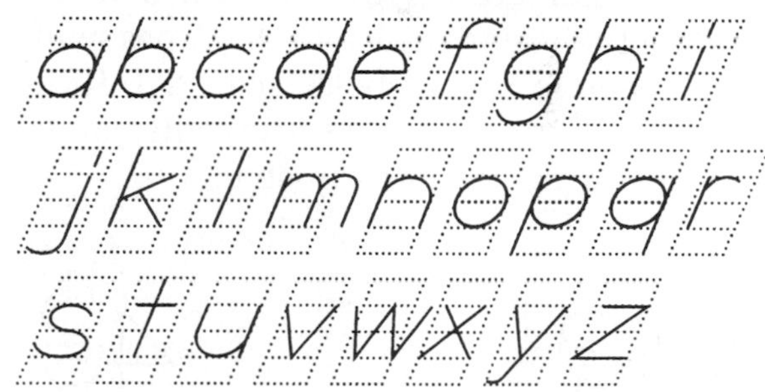

11.11 An alphabet of single-stroke Gothic, inclined lowercase letters.

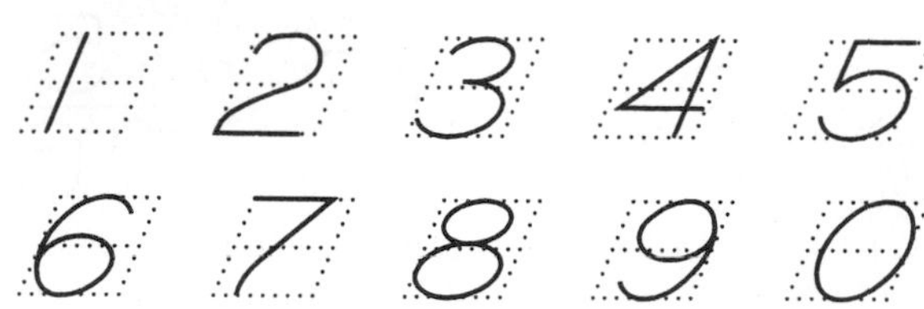

11.12 Single-stroke Gothic inclined numerals.

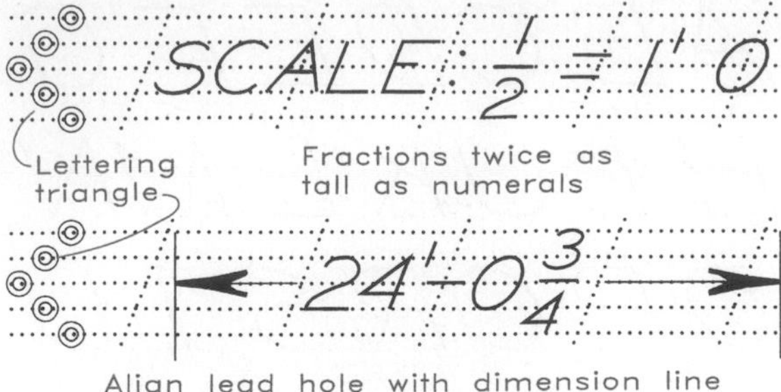

11.13 Inclined common fractions are twice as tall as single numerals. Omit inch marks in dimensions.

Figure 11.13. The ratio of the height of lowercase to uppercase letters should be either two-thirds (A) or three-fifths (B). The Ames guide has both ratios, but the Braddock-Rowe triangle has only the two-thirds ratio. Guidelines are drawn using the Braddock-Rowe triangle or the Ames lettering guide shown in **Figure 11.14**.

Spacing Numerals and Letters

Allow adequate space between numerals for the decimal point and fractions **(Figure 11.15)**. Common fractions are twice as tall as single numerals **(Figure 11.15)**. Both the Braddock-Rowe triangle and the Ames guide have separate sets of holes spaced 1/16 in. apart for common fractions. The center guideline locates the fraction's crossbar.

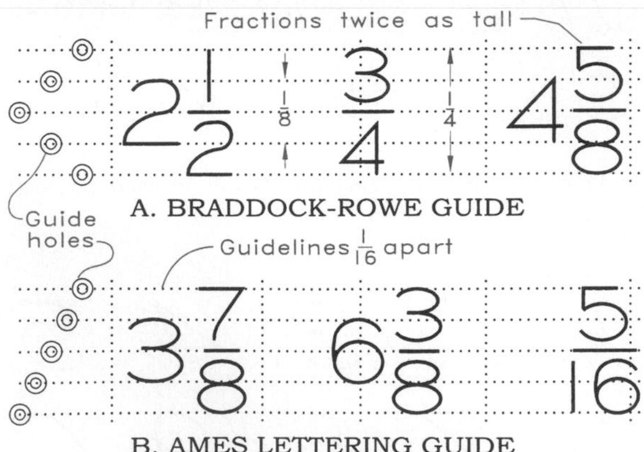

11.14 Guidelines are drawn for fractions so they can be twice as tall as single numerals

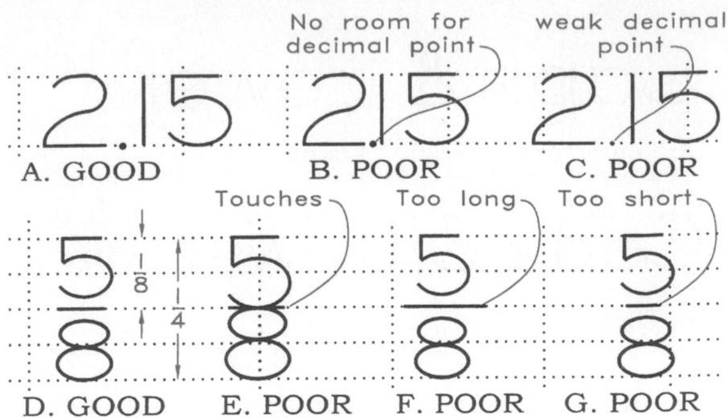

11.15 Avoid making these errors in lettering fractions.

11.16 Letters should be spaced so that the areas between them are about equal.

When grouping letters to spell words, make the areas between the letters approximately equal for the most visually pleasing result, as shown in **Figure 11.16**.

Problems

Complete exercises on size A (11 × 8-1/2-in., horizontal format) plain paper or paper with a grid using the format shown in **Figure 11.17**.

1. Draw the alphabet in vertical uppercase letters as shown in **Figure 11.17**. Draw each letter three times: three As, three Bs, and so on. Use a medium-weight pencil—H, F, or HB.

2. Draw vertical numerals and the alphabet in lowercase letters as shown in **Figure 11.18**. Construct each letter and numeral three times: three 1s, three 2s, three a's, three b's, and so on. Use a medium-weight pencil—H, F, or HB.

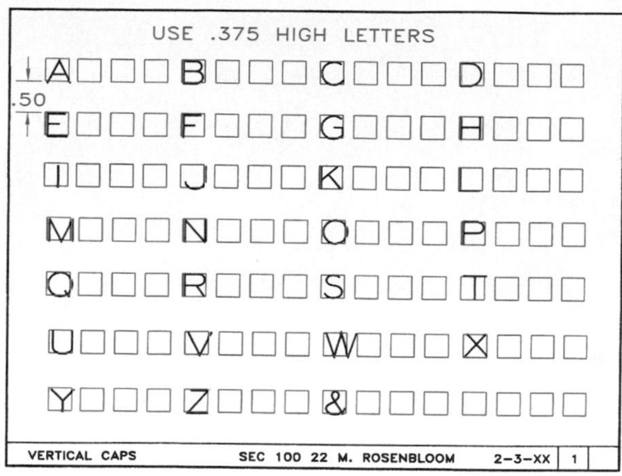

11.17 The sheet layout for lettering assignments.

3. Draw the alphabet in inclined uppercase letters as shown in **Figure 11.10**. Construct each letter four times with a medium-weight pencil—H, F, or HB—as shown in **Figure 11.17**.

4. Draw the vertical numerals and the alphabet in lowercase letters as shown in **Figures 11.7** and **11.9**. Draw each numeral three times and each letter five times (as shown in **Figure 11.18**). Use a medium-weight pencil—H, F, or HB.

5. Construct guidelines for 1/4-in. capital letters starting at the top border of a sheet

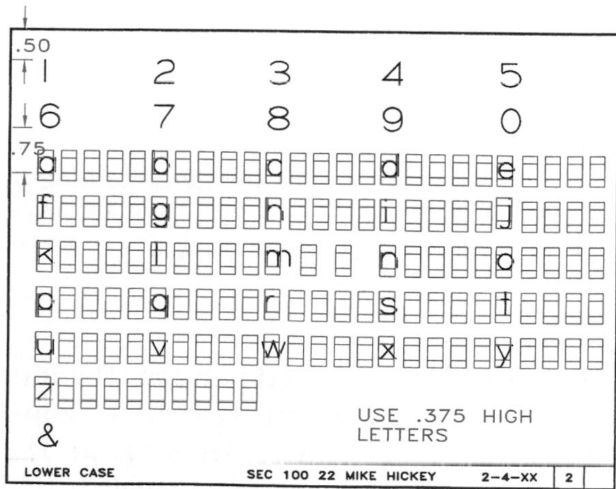

11.18 A typical sheet layout for lettering assignments.

We, the people of the United States, in order to form a more perfect Union, establish justice, insure domestic tranquility, provide for the common defense, promote the general welfare, and secure the blessings of liberty to ourselves and our posterity, do ordain and establish this Constitution for the United States of America.

PREAMABLE: CONSTITUTION | SEC 100 22 TOM JEFFERSON | 2–4–XX | 3

11.19 The preamble to the Constitution of the United States.

similar to **Figure 11.19** and letter the preamble to the U.S. Constitution using all vertical capitals. Spacing between the lines should be 1/4 in.

6. Repeat problem 5, but use inclined capital (uppercase) letters. Use inclined guidelines to help you slant letters uniformly.

7. Repeat problem 5, but use vertical capital and lowercase letters in combination. Capitalize only those words capitalized in the given text.

8. Repeat problem 5, but use inclined capital and lowercase letters in combination. Capitalize only those letters that are capitalized in the text.

12
Geometric Construction

12.1 Introduction

The solution of many graphical problems requires the use of geometry and geometric construction. Because mathematics was an outgrowth of graphical construction, the two areas are closely related. The proofs of many principles of plane geometry and trigonometry can be developed by using graphics. Graphical methods can be applied to solve some types of problems in algebra and arithmetic, and virtually all types of problems in analytical geometry.

12.2 Polygons

A **polygon** is a multisided plane figure of any number of sides. If the sides of a polygon are equal in length, the polygon is a **regular polygon**. A regular polygon can be inscribed in a circle and all its corner points will lie on the circle (**Figure 12.1**). Other regular polygons not pictured are the **heptagon** (7 sides), the **nonagon** (9 sides), the **decagon** (10 sides), and the **dodecagon** (12 sides).

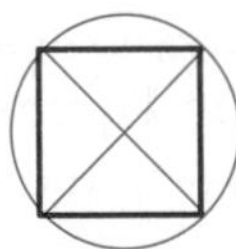

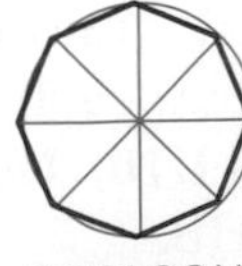

12.1 Regular polygons (polygons with equal-length sides) can be inscribed in circles.

The sum of the angles inside any polygon (interior angles) is $S = (n - 2) \times 180°$, where n is the number of sides of the polygon.

Triangles

A **triangle** is a three-sided polygon. The four types of triangles are **scalene, isosceles, equilateral**, and **right** triangles (**Figure 12.2**). The sum of the interior angles of a triangle is 180° $[(3 - 2) \times 180°]$.

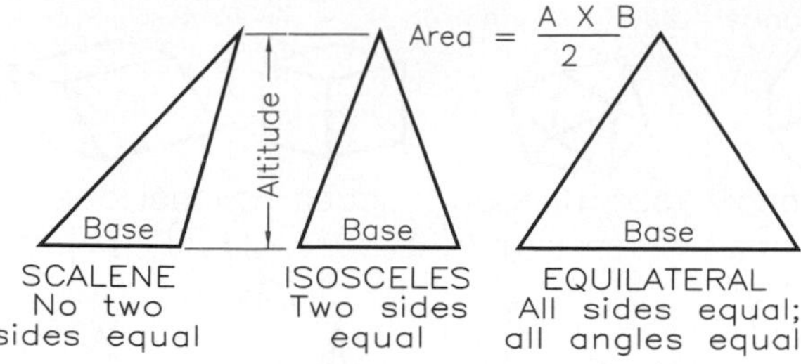

12.2 Standard types of triangles and their definitions.

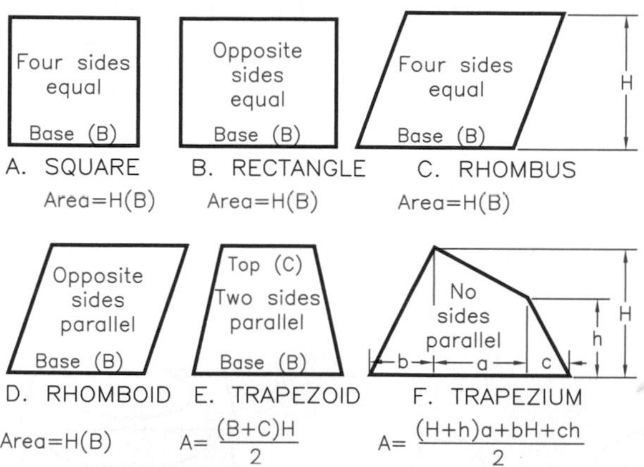

12.3 Types of quadrilaterals, their definitions, and formulas for calculating their areas.

Quadrilaterals

A **quadrilateral** is a four-sided polygon of any shape. The sum of the interior angles of a quadrilateral is 360° [(4 − 2) × 180°]. **Figure 12.3** shows the various types of quadrilaterals and the equations for their areas.

12.3 Circles

Figure 12.4 gives the names of the elements of a circle that are used throughout this textbook. A circle is constructed by swinging a radius from a fixed point through 360°. The area of a circle equals πR^2.

12.4 Geometric Solids

Figure 12.5 illustrates the various types of solid geometric shapes and their characteristics.

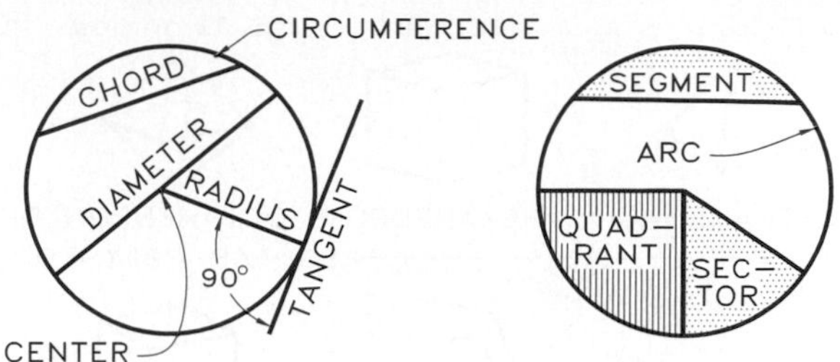

12.4 Elements of a circle and their definitions.

Polyhedra

A **polyhedron** is a multisided solid formed by intersecting planes. If its faces are regular polygons (having sides of equal length), it is a regular polyhedron. Five regular polyhedra are the **tetrahedron** (4 sides), the **hexahedron** (6 sides), the **octahedron** (8 sides), the **dodecahedron** (12 sides), and the **icosahedron** (20 sides).

Prisms

A **prism** has two parallel bases of equal shape connected by sides that are parallelograms. The line from the center of one base to the center of the other is the axis. If its axis is perpendicular to the bases, the prism is a **right prism**. If its axis is not perpendicular to the bases, the prism is an **oblique prism**. A prism that has been cut off to form a base not parallel to the other is a **truncated prism**. A **parallelepiped** is a prism with bases that are either rectangles or parallelograms.

Pyramids

A **pyramid** is a solid with a polygon as a base and triangular faces that converge at a vertex. The line from the vertex to the center of the base is the **axis**. If its axis is perpendicular to the base, the pyramid is a **right pyramid**. If its axis is not perpendicular to the base, the pyramid is an **oblique pyramid**. A truncated pyramid is called a **frustum** of a pyramid.

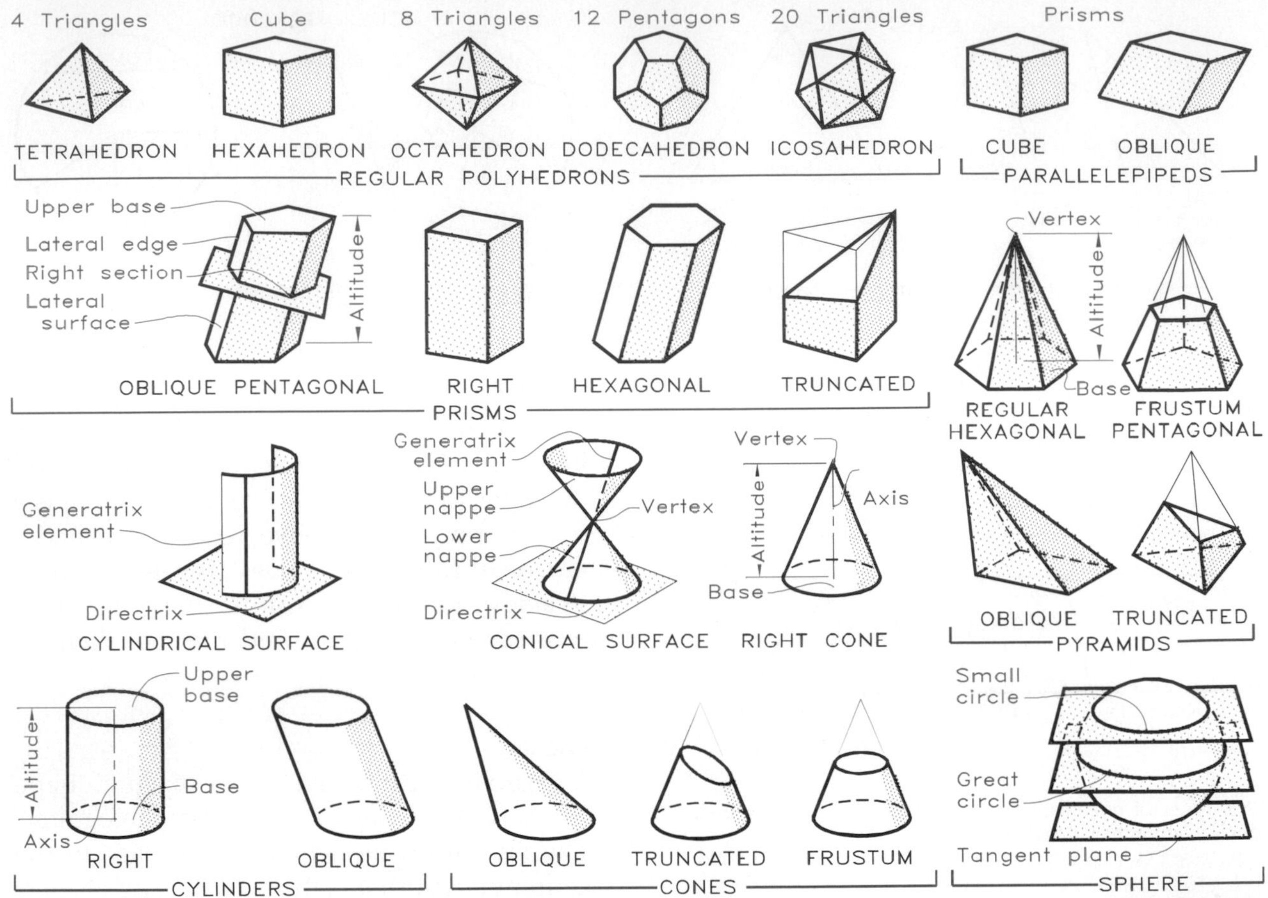

12.5 Various types of geometric solids and their elements.

Cylinders

A **cylinder** is formed by a line or an element (called a *generatrix*) that moves about the circle while remaining parallel to its axis. The axis of a cylinder connects the centers of each end of a cylinder. If the axis is perpendicular to the bases, it is the altitude of a **right cylinder**. If the axis does not make a 90° angle with the base, the cylinder is an **oblique cylinder**.

Cones

A **cone** is formed by a generatrix, one end of which moves about the circular base while the other end remains at a fixed vertex. The line from the center of the base to the vertex is the axis. If its axis is perpendicular to the base, the cone is a **right cone**. A truncated cone is called a **frustum** of a cone.

Spheres

A **sphere** is generated by rotating a circle about one of its diameters to form a solid. The ends of the axis of rotation of the sphere are **poles**.

12.5 Constructing Polygons

A regular polygon (having equal sides) can be inscribed in or circumscribed about a circle.

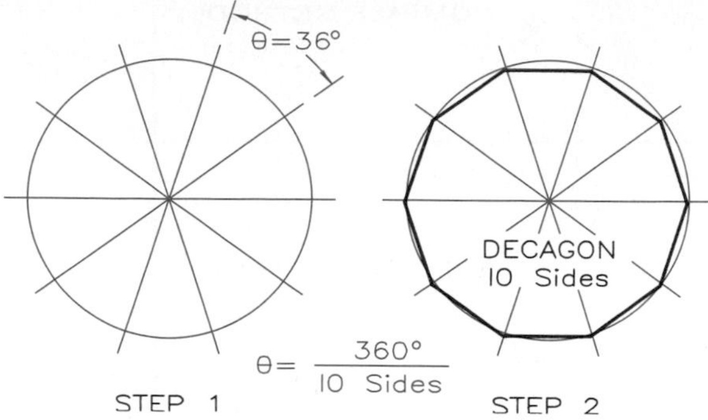

12.6 A regular polygon (sides of equal length).

Step 1 Divide circle into the desired number of sectors.

Step 2 Connect the division points with staight lines where they intersect the circle to form an inscribed polygon.

When the polygon is inscribed, all corner points will lie on the circle. (**Figure 12.6**). For example, constructing a 10-sided polygon involves dividing the circle into 10 sectors and connecting the points to form the polygon.

Hexagons

The **hexagon**, a six-sided regular polygon, can be inscribed in or circumscribed about a circle (**Figure 12.7**). Use a 30°-60° triangle to draw the hexagon. The circle represents the distance from corner to corner for an inscribed hexagon and from flat to flat when the hexagon is circumscribed about a circle.

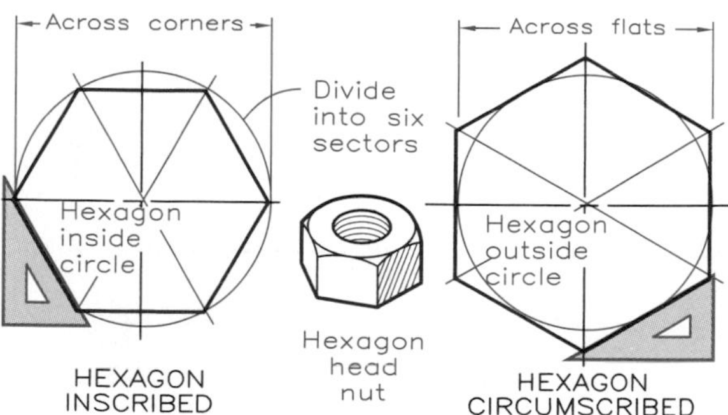

12.7 A hexagon can be inscribed in or circumscribed about a circle with a 30°-60° triangle.

Octagons

The **octagon**, an eight-sided regular polygon, can be inscribed in or circumscribed about a circle (**Figure 12.8**). Use a 45° triangle in both circumscribing and inscribing an octagon about a circle.

Pentagons

The **pentagon**, a five-sided regular polygon, can be inscribed in or circumscribed about a circle. **Figure 12.9** shows the steps of constructing a pentagon with a compass and straightedge where the vertices lie on the circle.

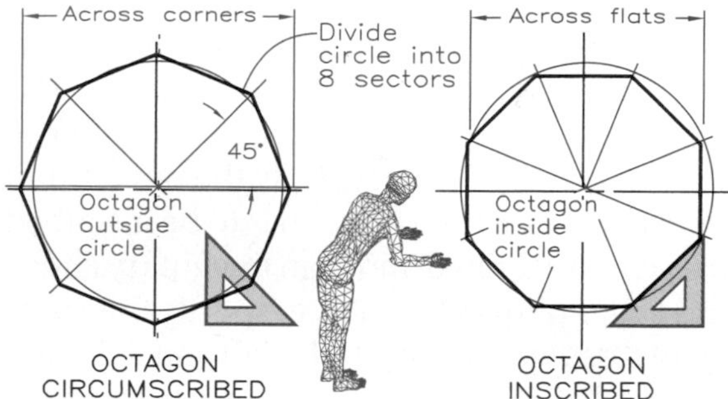

12.8 An octagon can be inscribed in or circumscribed about a circle with a 45° triangle.

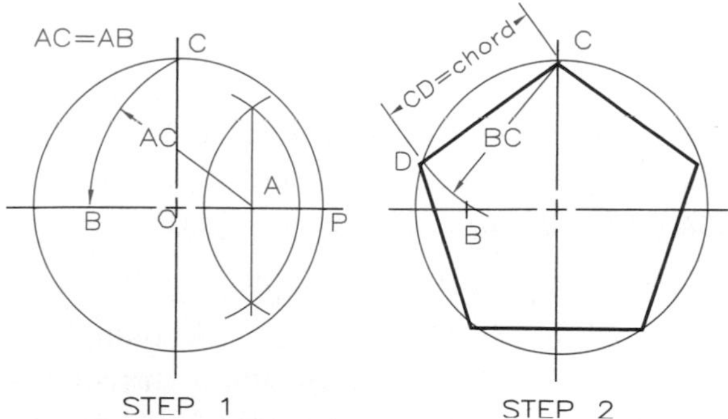

12.9 Constructing an inscribed pentagon.

Step 1 Bisect radius OP to locate point A. With A as the center and radius AC, locate point B on the diameter.

Step 2 With point C as the center and BC as the radius, locate point D. Use line CD as the chord to locate the other corners of the pentagon about the circle.

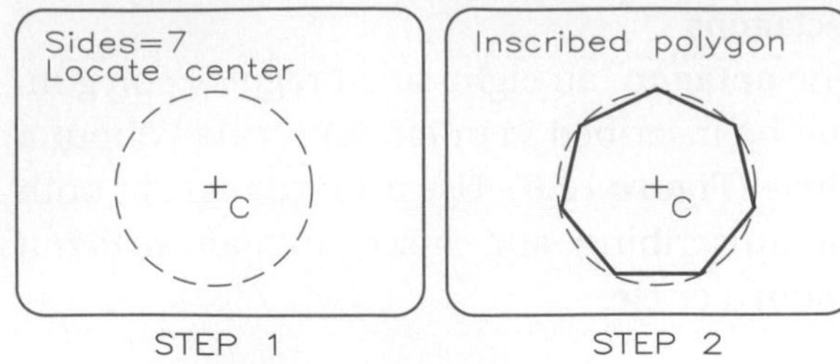

12.10 A polygon by AutoCAD (*Draw* menu).

Step 1 *Command:* Polygon (Enter)
Enter number of sides: 7 (Enter)
Specify center of polygon or [Edge]: (Locate with cursor.)
Enter an option [Inscribed in circle/Circumscribed about circle] <I>: I (Enter)

Step 2 *Specify radius of circle:* (Drag cursor to select R. Polygon is inscribed inside the imaginary circle.)

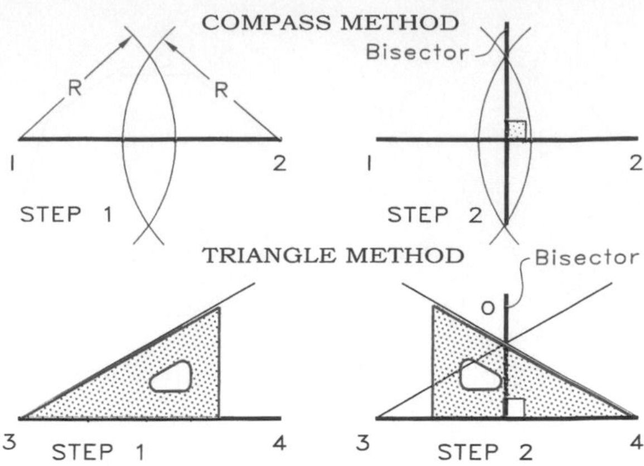

12.11 Bisecting a line.
Method 1 Use a compass and any radius.
Method 2 Use a standard triangle and a straightedge.

AutoCAD Method You may use one of two *Polygon* options from under the *Draw* command to draw polygons (**Figure 12.10**). The *Center* option asks you to give the number of sides, select the center, specify the radius, and indicate whether the polygon is to be inscribed in or circumscribed about an imaginary circle. The *Edge* option allows you to specify the number of sides and specify the length and direction of one edge of the polygon before drawing it.

12.6 Bisecting Lines and Angles

Bisecting Lines

Two methods of finding the midpoint of a line with a perpendicular bisector are shown in **Figure 12.11**. In the first method, a compass is used to construct the perpendicular bisector to the line. In the second method, a standard triangle and a straightedge are used.

AutoCAD Method The midpoint of a line may be found (**Figure 12.12**) by using the *Midpoint* mode of *Osnap* while drawing a line from any point, P, to the line. The line will snap to the line's midpoint.

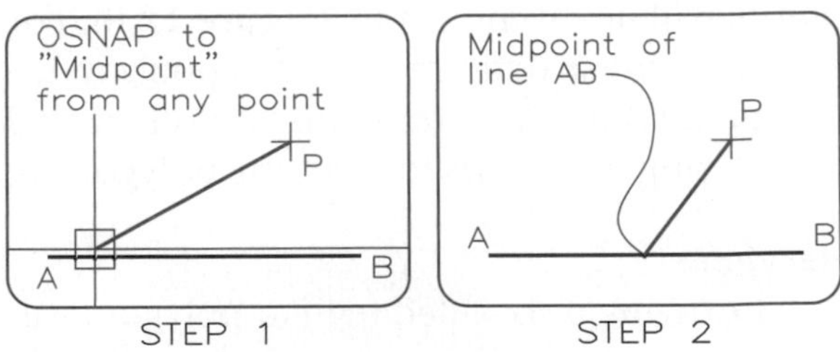

12.12 Midpoint of a line by AutoCAD (*Draw* menu).

Step 1 *Command:* Line (Enter)
Specify first point: P (Locate P anywhere with cursor.)
Specify next point or [Undo]: Mid (Enter) (Midpoint mode.)

Step 2 *of* (Select any point on line AB.) The line from point P is drawn to the midpoint of the line AB.

Bisecting Angles

You may bisect angles by using a compass and drawing three arcs, as shown in **Figure 12.13**.

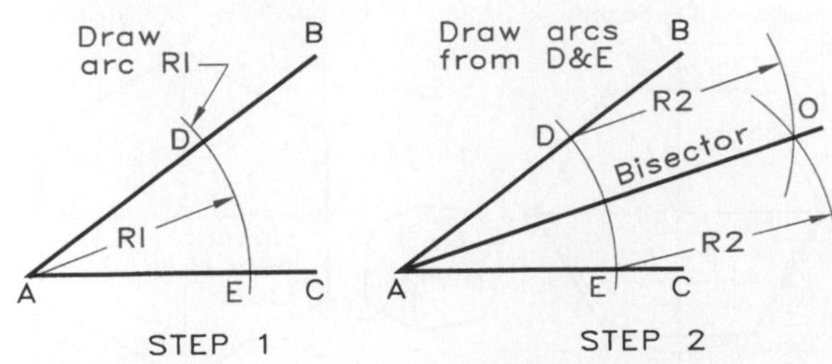

12.13 Bisecting an angle.

Step 1 Swing an arc R1 to locate points D and E.

Step 2 Draw equal arcs from D and E to locate point O. Line AO is the bisector of the angle.

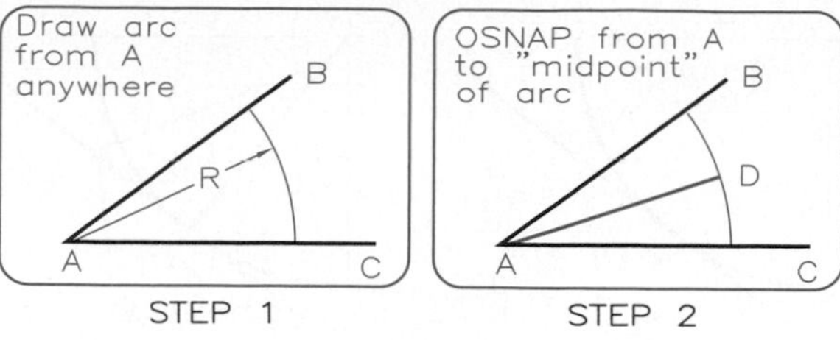

12.14 Bisecting an angle by AutoCAD (*Draw* menu).

Step 1 Use the *Arc* command, any radius, and center A to draw an arc that *Osnaps, Nearest* to AC and AB.

Step 2 *Command:* <u>*Line*</u> *(Enter)*
Specify first point or [Undo]: <u>Mid</u> (Enter) (*Midpoint* option.) (Select arc. Line AD is the bisector of the angle.)

AutoCAD Method Use the *Arc* command (with *Osnap* set to *Midpoint*) and draw an arc of a convenient radius between the two lines, with its center at vertex A (**Figure 12.14**). Use the *Line* command (with *Osnap* set to *Midpoint*) to draw a line from the vertex, A, to the arc's midpoint, D. Line AD is the bisector.

12.7 Division of Lines

Dividing a line into several equal parts often is necessary. **Figure 12.15** shows the method used to solve this type of problem where the line AB is divided into five equal lengths by using a scale to lay off the five divisions.

The same principle applies to locating equally spaced lines on a graph (**Figure 12.16**).

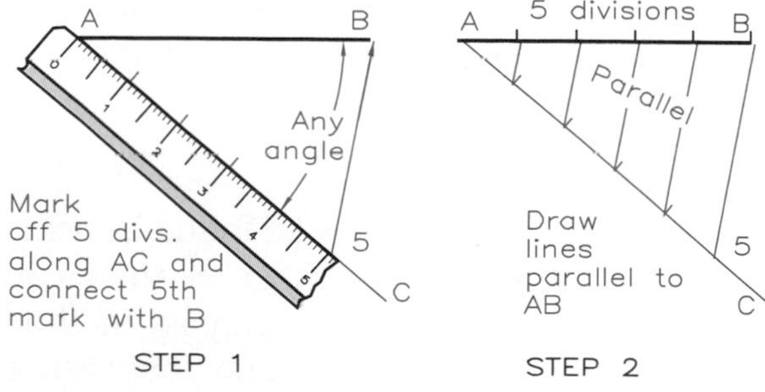

12.15 Dividing a line.

Step 1 To divide line AB into five equal lengths, lay off five equal divisions along line AC (at a convenient angle) and connect point 5 to end B with a construction line.

Step 2 Draw a series of five construction lines parallel to 5B to divide line AB into five divisions.

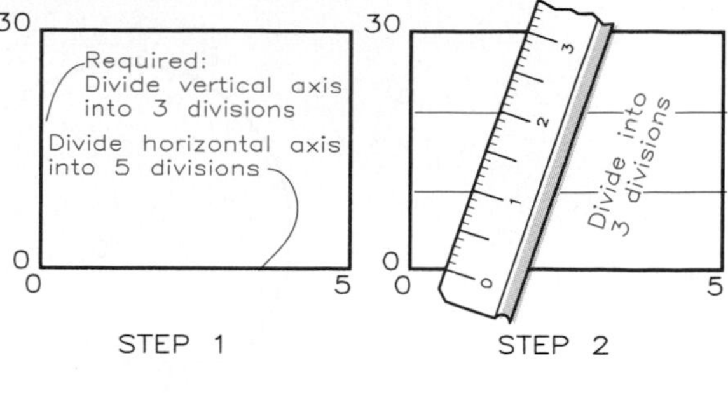

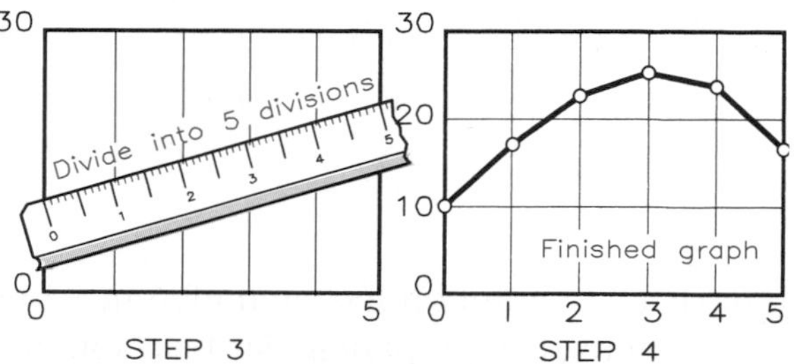

12.16 Dividing axes on a graph.

Step 1 Draw the outline of the graph.

Step 2 To divide the *y*-axis into three equal segments, lay a scale so that three units of measurement span the graph, with the 0 and 3 located on the top and bottom lines. Make marks at points 1 and 2 and draw horizontal lines through them.

Step 3 To divide the *x*-axis into five equal segments, lay a scale so that five units of measurement span the graph, with the 0 and 5 on the left- and right-hand vertical lines. Make marks at points 1, 2, 3, and 4 and draw vertical lines through them.

Step 4 Plot the data points and draw the curve to complete the graph.

Lay scales with the desired number of units (0 to 3 and 0 to 5, respectively) across the graph up and down and then left to right. Make marks at each whole unit and draw vertical and horizontal index lines through these points. These index lines are used to show data in a graph.

12.8 An Arc through Three Points

An arc can be drawn through three points by connecting the points with two lines and drawing perpendicular bisectors through each line to locate the center of the circle at C (**Figure 12.17**). Draw the arc, and lines AB and BD become chords of the arc.

To find the center of a circle or an arc, reverse this process by drawing two chords that

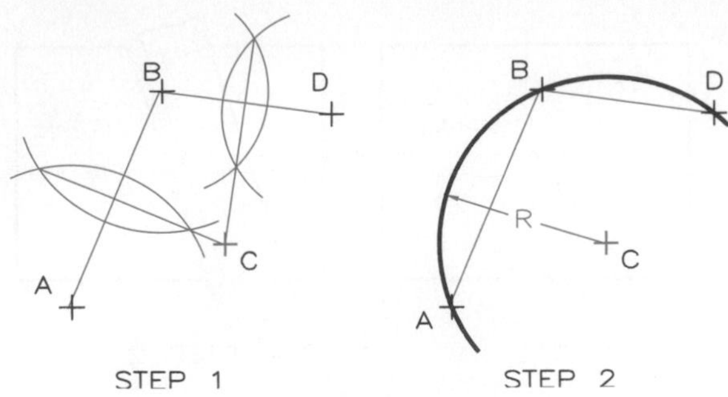

12.17 An arc through three points.

Step 1 Connect points A, B, and D with two lines and construct their perpendicular bisectors, which intersect at the center, C.

Step 2 Using the center C and the distance to the points as the radius, R, draw the arc through the points.

intersect at a point on the circumference and bisect them. The perpendicular bisectors intersect at the center of the circle.

12.9 Parallel Lines

You may draw one line parallel to another by using either method shown in **Figure 12.18**. In the first method, use a compass and draw two arcs having radius R to locate a parallel line at the desired distance (R) from the first line. In the second method, measure the desired perpendicular distance R from the first line, mark it, and draw the parallel line through it with your drafting machine.

COMPASS METHOD

Swing arcs equal to distance between lines

Draw tangent to two arcs

Parallel

STEP 1 STEP 2

TRIANGLE METHOD

Construct perpendicular to AB

Straightedge

Draw parallel line

Parallel

Measure off distance apart

STEP 1 STEP 2

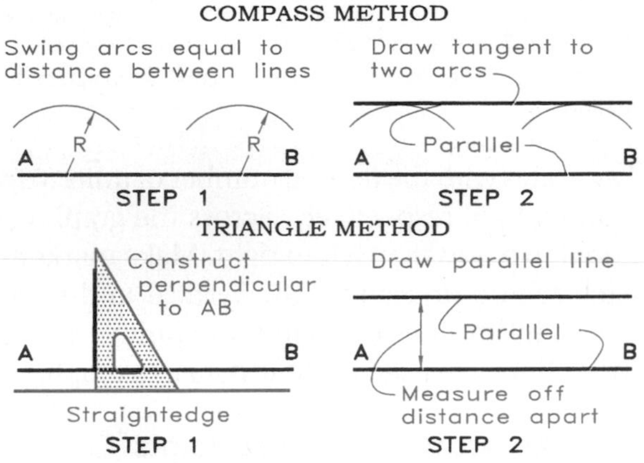

12.18 Drawing parallel lines.

Compass Method

Step 1 Swing two arcs from points on line AB.

Step 2 Draw the parallel line tangent to the arcs.

Triangle Method

Step 1 Draw a line perpendicular to AB.

Step 2 Measure the desired distance along the perpendicular and draw the parallel line through it.

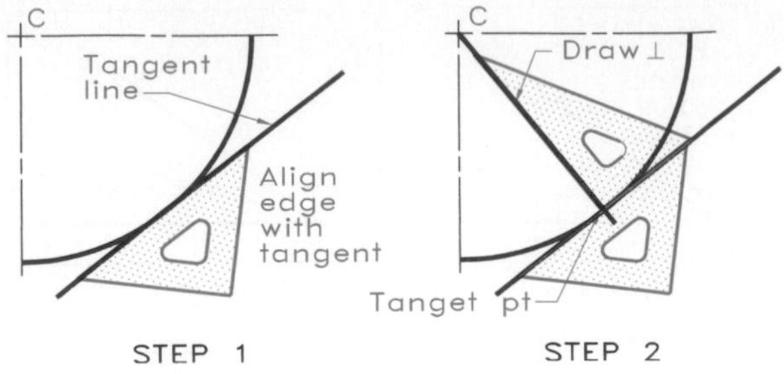

12.19 Locating a tangent point.

Step 1 Align a triangle with the tangent line while holding it against a firmly held straightedge.

Step 2 Hold the triangle in position, position a second triangle perpendicular to it, and draw a line from the center to locate the tangent point.

12.10 Tangents

Marking Points of Tangency

A point of tangency is the theoretical point at which a line joins an arc, or two arcs join without crossing. **Figure 12.19** shows how to find the point of tangency with triangles by constructing a perpendicular line to the tangent line from the arc's center. **Figure 12.20** shows the conventional methods of marking points of tangency.

Line Tangent to an Arc

The point of tangency may be found by using a triangle and a straightedge as shown in **Figure 12.19**. The classical compass method of finding the point of tangency between a line and a point is shown in **Figure 12.21**. Connect point A to the arc's center and bisect line AC (step 1); swing an arc from point M through point C locating tangent point T

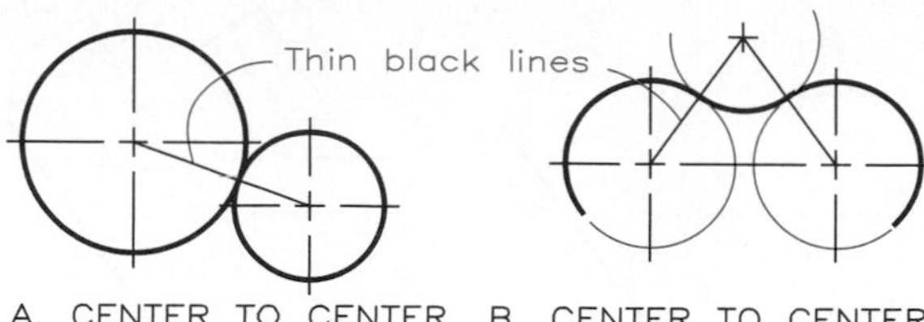

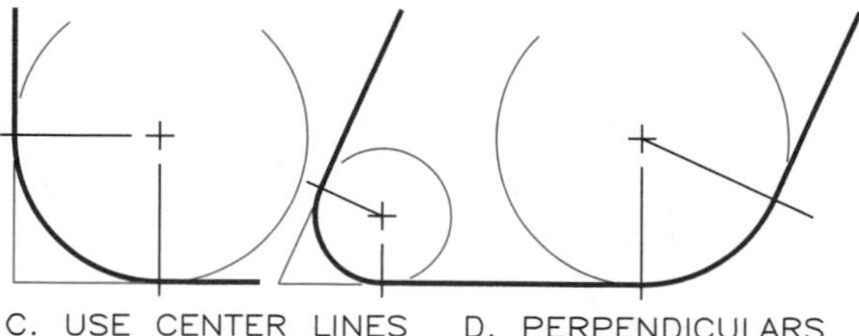

12.20 Use thin, dark lines that extend from the centers slightly beyond the arcs to mark tangency points.

(step 2); draw the tangent to T (step 3); and mark the tangent point (step 4).

AutoCAD Method A line can be drawn from a point tangent to an arc by using the *Osnap*

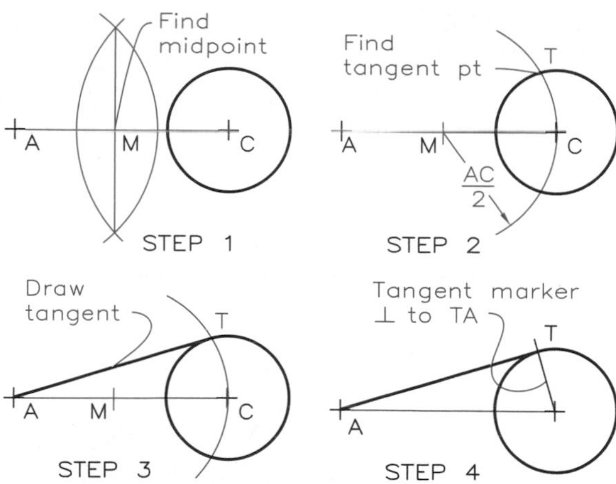

12.21 A line tangent to an arc from a point.

Step 1 Connect point A with center C, and locate point M by bisecting AC.

Step 2 Using point M as the center and MC as the radius, locate point T on the arc.

Step 3 Draw the line from A to T tangent to the arc at T.

Step 4 Draw the tangent marker perpendicular to TA from the center past the arc as a thin, dark line.

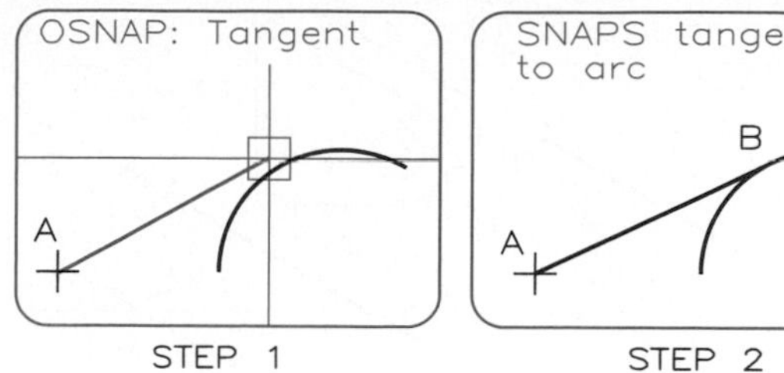

12.22 A line tangent to an arc by AutoCAD.

Step 1 *Command:* Line *(Enter)*

Specify first point or [Undo]: A (Select point A)

Specify next point or [Undo]: Tan *(Enter)*

Step 2 *to:* (Select point on arc near tangent point. Line AB is drawn tangent to the arc.)

Tangent option (**Figure 12.22**). When prompted for the second point, select a point on the arc near the tangent point, and the line will be drawn to the true tangent point.

Arc Tangent to a Line from a Point

To construct an arc that is tangent to line DE at T and that passes through point P (**Figure 12.23**), draw the perpendicular bisector of line TP. Draw a perpendicular to line DE at point T to locate the center at point C, and swing an arc with radius OT.

Arc Tangent to Two Lines

Figure 12.24 shows how to construct an arc of a given radius tangent to two nonparallel lines that form an acute angle. The same steps

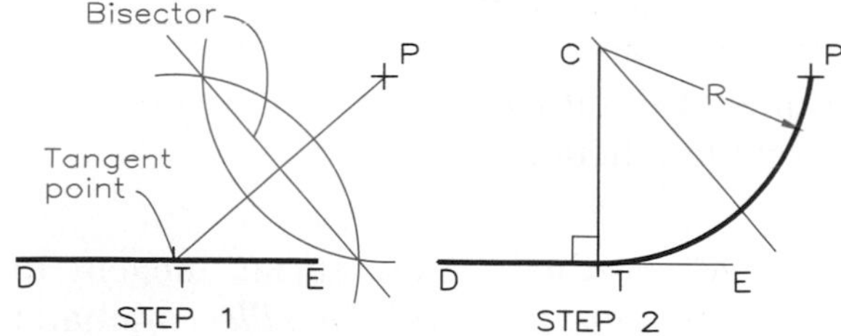

12.23 An arc through two points.

Step 1 To draw an arc through point P tangent to line DE at point T, draw the perpendicular bisector of TP.

Step 2 Construct a perpendicular to line DE at point T to intersect the bisector at point C, and draw the arc from C with radius CT.

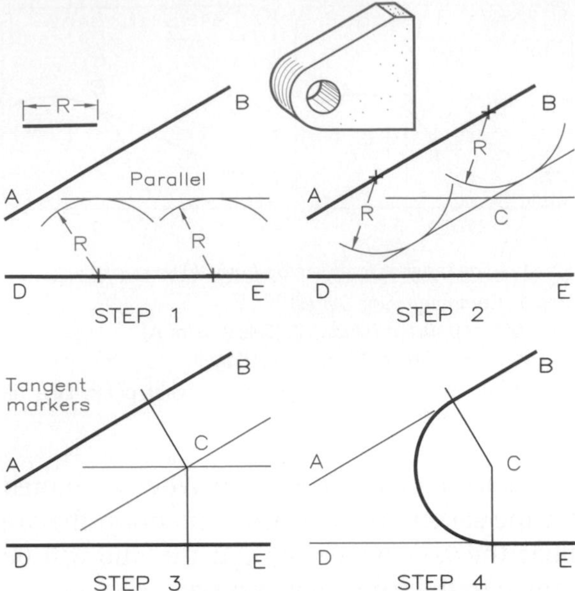

12.24 An arc tangent to lines making an acute angle.

Step 1 Construct a light construction line parallel to line DE with radius R.

Step 2 Draw a second light line parallel to and distance R from line AB to locate center C.

Step 3 Draw thin, dark lines from center C perpendicular to lines AB and DE to locate the tangency points.

Step 4 Draw the tangent arc and darken the lines.

apply to constructing an arc tangent to two lines that form an obtuse angle (**Figure 12.25**). In both cases, the points of tangency are located with thin, dark lines drawn from their centers perpendicular to and past the original lines. **Figure 12.26** shows a technique for finding an arc tangent to lines that are perpendicular.

AutoCAD Method Draw an arc tangent to two nonparallel lines with the *Fillet* command (*Modify* menu) (**Figure 12.27**). When the radius length has been set and a point selected on each line, the arc is drawn and the lines trimmed. To mark tangent points, snap to the center of the arc with the *Center* option of *Osnap* and draw two lines perpendicular (use

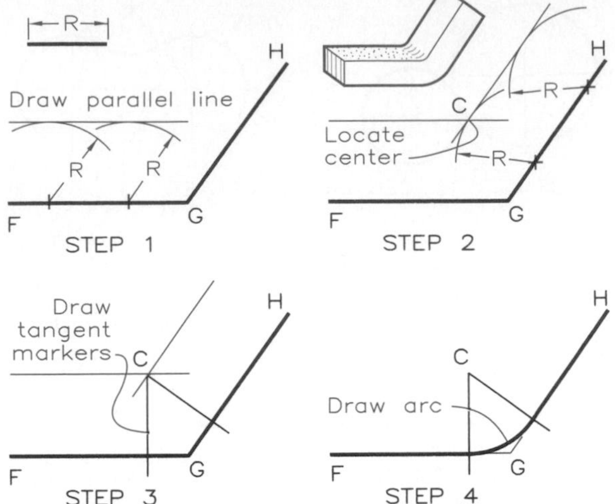

12.25 An arc tangent to lines making an obtuse angle.

Step 1 Using radius R, draw a light line parallel to FG.

Step 2 Construct a light line parallel to line GH that is R distance from it to locate center C.

Step 3 Draw thin lines from center C perpendicular to lines FG and GH to locate the tangency points.

Step 4 Draw the tangent arc and darken your lines.

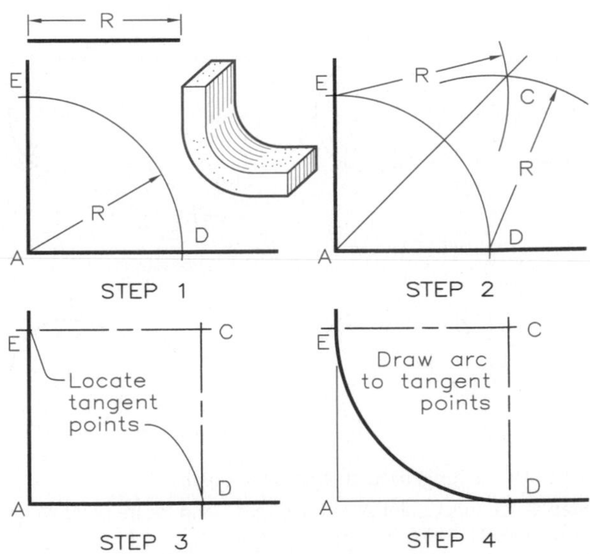

12.26 An arc tangent to perpendicular lines.

Step 1 Using radius R and center A, locate D and E.

Step 2 Find C by swinging two arcs with radius R.

Step 3 Perpendiculars CE and CD locate tangent points.

Step 4 Draw the tangent arc and darken your lines.

the *Osnap Perpend* option) to lines AB and CD from the center.

Arc Tangent to an Arc and a Line

Figure 12.28 shows the steps for constructing an arc tangent to an arc and a line. **Figure 12.29** shows a variation of this technique for an arc drawn tangent to a given arc and line with the arc reversed.

Arc Tangent to Two Arcs

Figure 12.30 shows how to draw an arc tangent to two arcs. Lines drawn between the centers locate the points of tangency. The resulting tangent arc is concave from the top. Drawing a convex arc tangent to the given arcs requires that its radius be greater than the radius of either of the given arcs, as shown in **Figure 12.31**.

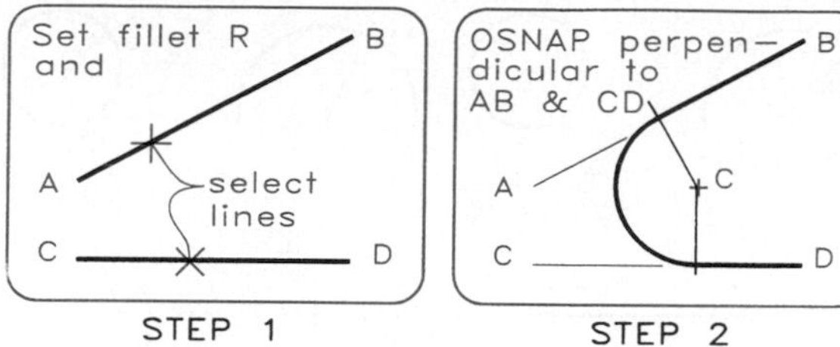

12.27 An arc tangent to two lines by AutoCAD.

Step 1 *Command:* Fillet (Enter)

Select first object or [Polyline/Radius/Trim]: R (Enter)

Specify fillet radius <0.0000>*:* .75 (Enter)

Command: (Enter)

Select first object or [Polyline/Radius/Trim]: (Select points on AB and CD.)

Step 2 *Command:* Line (Enter)

Line from from first point: Center (Enter) *of* (Select point on the arc.)

Specify next point or [Undo]: Perpend (Enter) *to* (Select line AB; a perpendicular is drawn to the point of tangency. Locate the tangent point on CD in the same manner.)

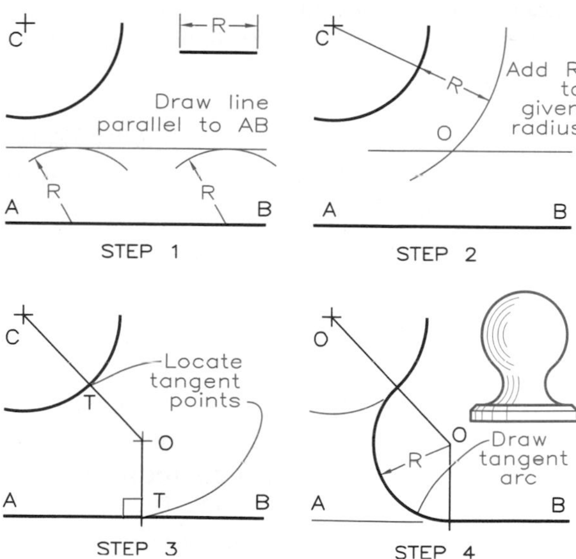

12.28 An arc tangent to an arc and a line.

Step 1 Draw a line parallel to AB distance R from it.

Step 2 Add radius R to the radius from center C. Swing the extended radius to find the center O.

Step 3 Lines OC and OT locate the tangency points.

Step 4 Draw the tangent arc between the points of tangency with radius R and center O.

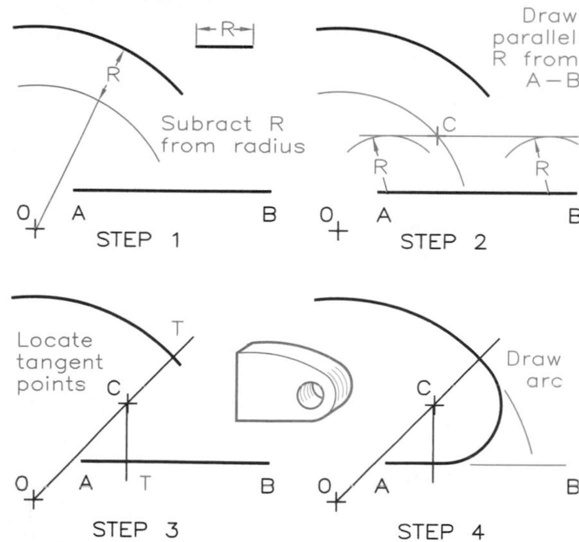

12.29 An arc tangent to an arc and a line.

Step 1 Subtract radius R from the radius through center O. Draw a concentric arc.

Step 2 Draw a line parallel to line 1-2 and distance R from it to locate the center at C.

Step 3 Locate the tangency points with lines OC and from C perpendicular to 1-2.

Step 4 Draw the tangent arc between the tangent points with radius R and center C.

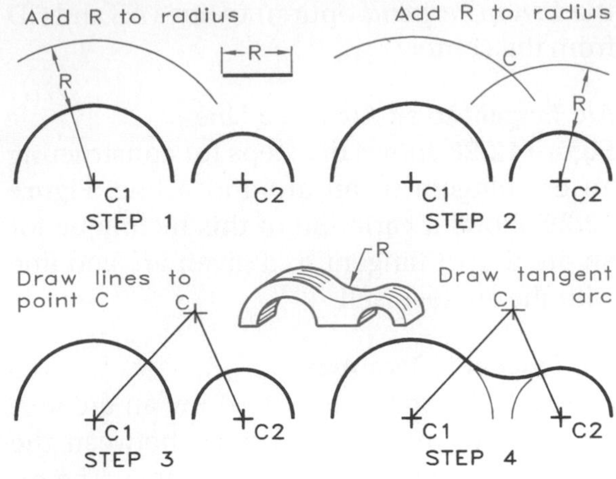

12.30 A concave arc tangent to two arcs.

Step 1 Extend the radius by adding the radius R to it. Draw a concentric arc with the extended radius.

Step 2 Extend the radius of the other circle by adding radius R to it. Use this extended radius to construct a concentric arc to locate center C.

Step 3 Connect center C with centers C1 and C2 with thin, dark lines to locate the tangency points.

Step 4 Draw the tangent arc between the points of tangency using radius R and center C.

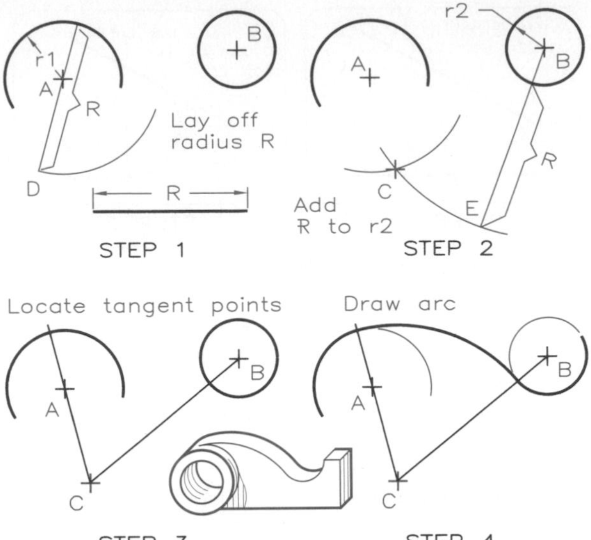

12.32 An arc tangent to two circles.

Step 1 Lay off radius R from the arc along an extended radius to locate point D.

Step 2 Extend the radius from center B and add radius R to it to point E. Use radius BE to locate center C.

Step 3 Draw thin lines from center C through centers A and B to locate the points of tangency.

Step 4 Draw the tangent arc between the tangent points using radius R and center C.

One variation of this problem (**Figure 12.32**) is to draw an arc of a given radius tangent to the top of one arc and the bottom of the other. Another (**Figure 12.33**) is to draw an arc tangent to a circle and a larger arc.

AutoCAD Method Use the *Fillet* command (**Figure 12.34**) to draw an arc tangent to two arcs. After entering the command, specify the radius when prompted. Press the carriage return (Enter) twice to return to the

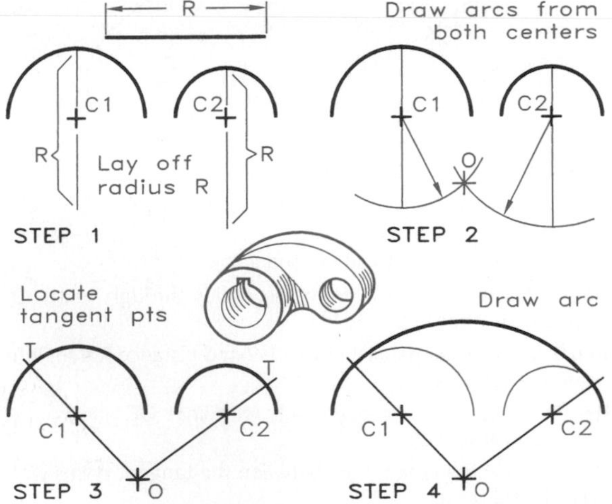

12.31 A convex arc tangent to two arcs.

Step 1 Extend each radius from the arc past its center by a distance R, the radius, along these lines.

Step 2 Use the distance from each center to the ends of the extended radii to swing arcs to locate center O.

Step 3 Draw thin, dark lines from center O through centers C1 and C2 to locate the points of tangency.

Step 4 Draw the tangent arc between the tangent points using radius R and center O.

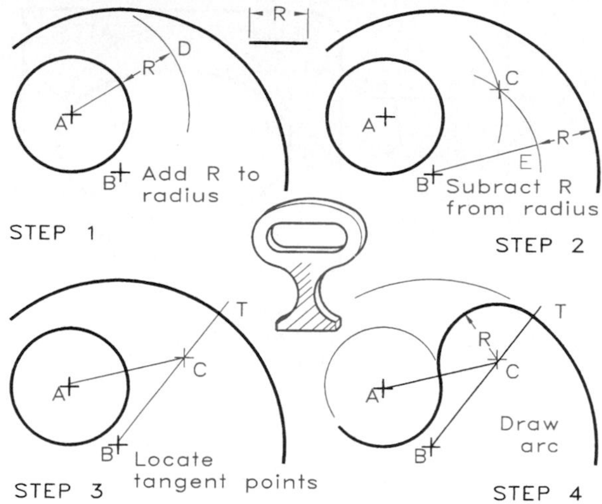

12.33 An arc tangent to two arcs.

Step 1 Add radius R to the radius from A. Use radius AD to draw a concentric arc from center A.

Step 2 Subtract radius R from the radius through B. Use radius BE to draw an arc to locate center C.

Step 3 Draw thin lines to connect the centers, and mark the points of tangency.

Step 4 Draw the tangent arc between the tangency points using radius R and center C.

Command mode, and the *Fillet* command is ready for use.

Select the two arcs with your cursor; the tangent arc is drawn and the arcs are trimmed at the points of tangency. Mark the tangency points by drawing lines from centers C1 and C2.

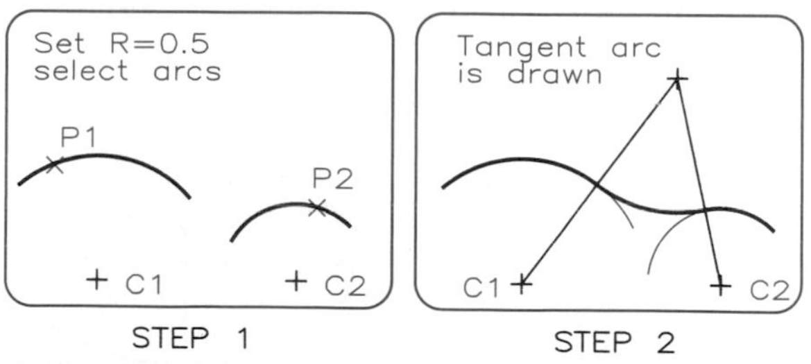

12.34 An arc tangent to two arcs by AutoCAD.

Step 1 *Command:* Fillet *(Enter)*

Select first object or [Polyline/Radius/Trim]: R (Enter) *Specify fillet radius* <0.0000>*:* .5 (Enter)

Step 2 *Command:* (Enter)
Select first object or [Polyline/Radius/Trim]: P1
Select second object or [Polyline/Radius/Trim]: P2 (Tangent arc is drawn. Locate tangent points with lines between the centers.)

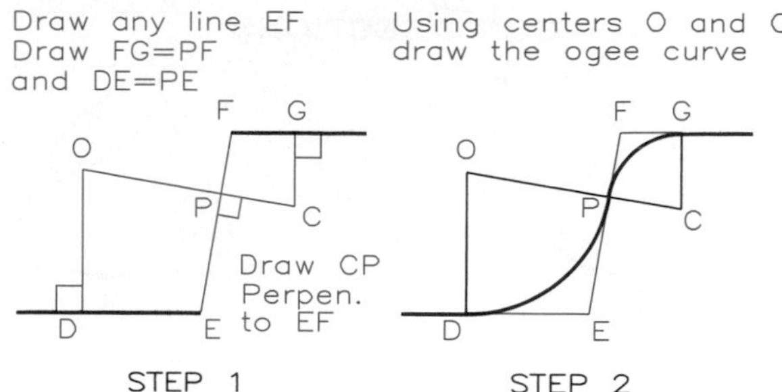

12.35 An ogee curve.

Step 1 To draw an ogee curve between two parallel lines, draw light line EF at any angle. Locate P anywhere on EF. Find the tangent points by making FG equal to FP and DE equal to EP. Draw perpendiculars at G and D to intersect the perpendicular at O and C.

Step 2 Use radii CP and OP at centers O and C to draw two tangent arcs to complete the ogee curve.

Ogee Curves

The **ogee curve** is an S curve formed by tangent arcs. The ogee curve shown in **Figure 12.35** is the result of constructing two arcs tangent to three intersecting lines.

12.11 Conic Sections

Conic sections are plane figures that can be described both graphically and mathematically; they are formed by passing imaginary cutting planes through a right cone, as **Figure 12.36** shows.

Ellipses

The ellipse is a conic section formed by passing a plane through a right cone at an angle (**Figure 12.36B**). Mathematically, the ellipse is the path of a point that moves in such a way that the sum of the distances from two focal points is a constant. The largest diameter of an ellipse—the major diameter—is always the true length. The shortest diameter—the minor diameter—is perpendicular to the major diameter.

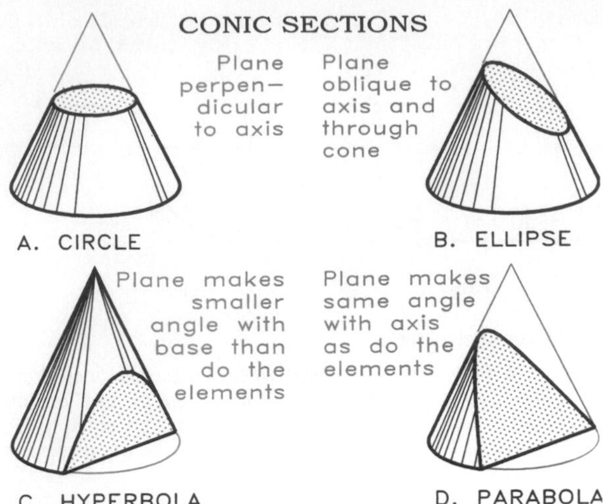

12.36 The conic sections are the (A) circle, (B) ellipse, (C) hyperbola, and (D) parabola. They are formed by passing cutting planes through a right cone.

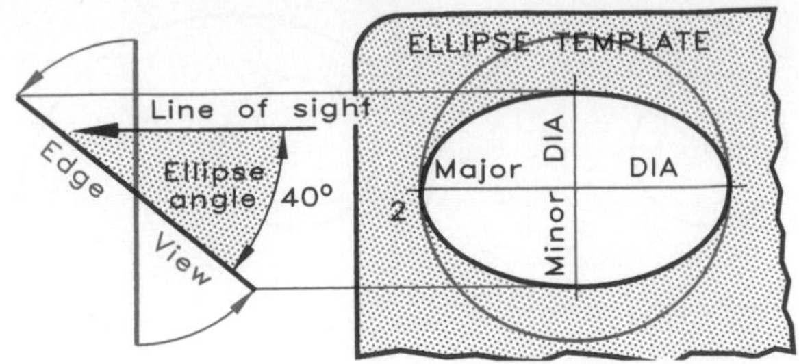

12.38 When the line of sight is not perpendicular to a circle's edge, it appears as an ellipse. The angle between the line of sight and the edge of the circle is the ellipse template angle.

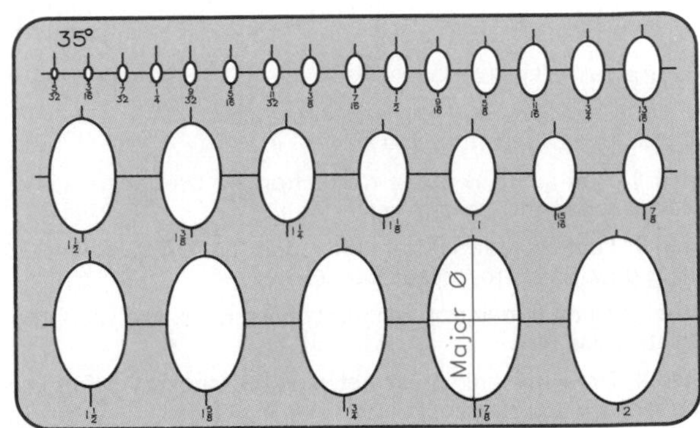

12.39 Ellipse templates are calibrated at 5° intervals from 15° to 60°.

Revolving the edge view of a circle yields an ellipse (**Figure 12.37**). The ellipse template shown in **Figure 12.38** is used to draw the same ellipse. The angle between the line of sight and the edge of the circle is the angle of the ellipse template (or the one closest to this size) that should be used. Ellipse templates are available in 5d intervals and in major diameter sizes that vary in increments of about 1/8 in. (**Figure 12.39**).

You may construct an ellipse inside a rectangle or parallelogram by plotting a series of points to form the ellipse (**Figure 12.40**).

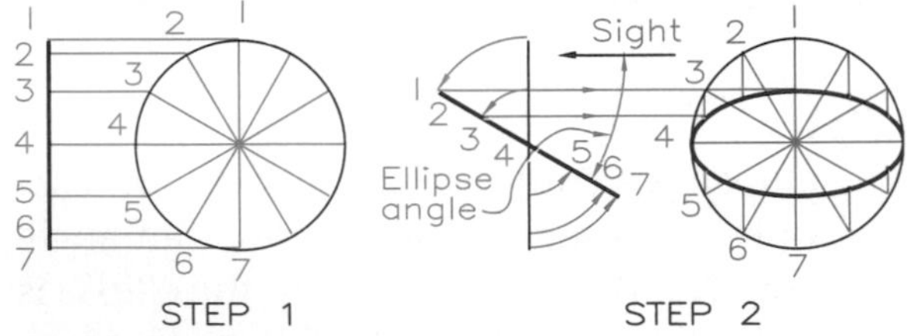

12.37 An ellipse by revolution.

Step 1 When the edge of a circle is perpendicular to the projectors from its adjacent view, it appears as a circle. Mark equally spaced points around the circle's circumference and project them to the edge.

Step 2 Revolve the edge of the circle and project the points to the circular view. Project the points vertically downward to the projectors to obtain the elliptical view.

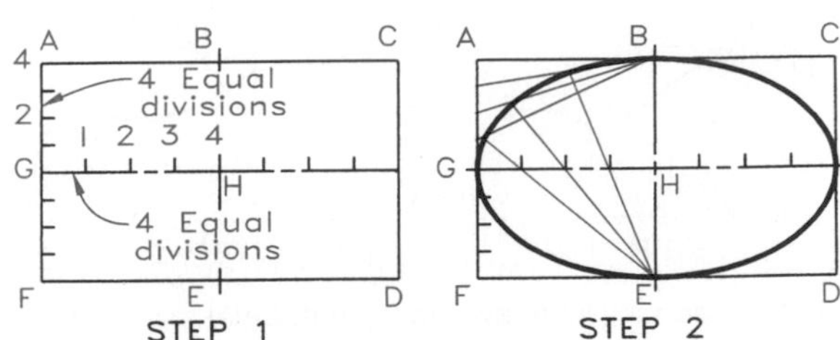

12.40 An ellipse by the parallelogram method.

Step 1 Draw an ellipse inside a rectangle or parallelogram by dividing the horizontal centerline AF, and CD into the same number of equal divisions.

Step 2 The curve construction is shown for one quadrant. Sets of rays from E and B cross at points on the curve.

An ellipse can be drawn on x- and y-axes by plotting x- and y-coordinates from the equation of an ellipse. The mathematical equation of an ellipse is

$$\frac{x^2 + y^2}{a^2 + b^2} = 1, \text{ where } a \text{ and } b \text{ are not } 0$$

Parabolas

The **parabola** is defined as a plane curve, each point of which is equidistant from a straight line (called a *directrix*) and a focal point. The parabola is the conic section formed when the cutting plane and an element on the cone's surface make the same angle with the cone's base as shown in **Figure 12.36D**.

Figure 12.41 shows construction of a parabola by using its mathematical definition, as is done in analytical geometry. A second method of drawing a parabola, which involves the use of a rectangle or parallelogram, is shown in **Figure 12.42**. The mathematical equation of the parabola is:

$$y = ax^2 + bx + c, \text{ where } a \text{ is not } 0$$

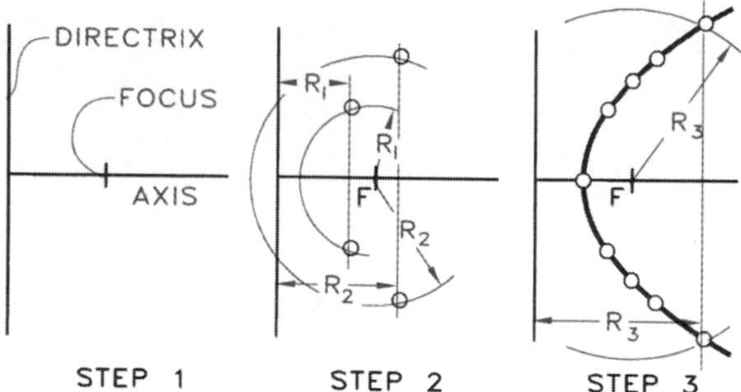

12.41 A parabola by the mathematical method.

Step 1 Draw an axis perpendicular to the directrix (a line). Choose a point for the focus, F.

Step 2 Use a series of selected radii to find points on the curve. For example, draw a line parallel to the directrix and R2 from it. Swing R2 from F to intersect the line and plot the point.

Step 3 Continue the process with a series of arcs of varying radii until you find an adequate number of points to complete the curve.

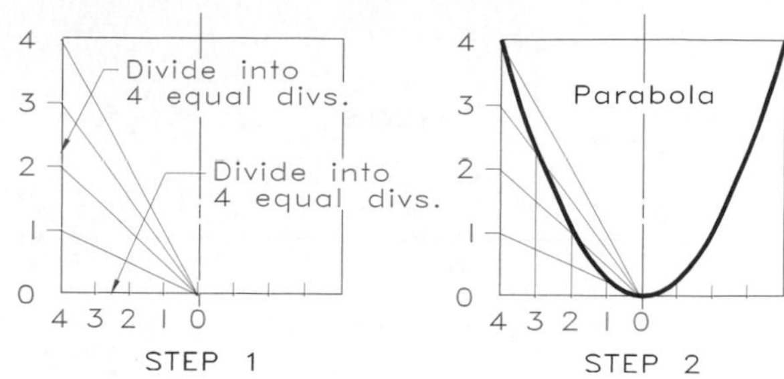

12.42 A parabola by the parallelogram method.

Step 1 Draw a parallelogram or rectangle to contain the parabola; draw its axis parallel to the sides through 0. Divide the sides into equal segments; draw rays from 0.

Step 2 Draw lines parallel to the sides (vertical in this case) to locate points along the rays from 0, and draw a smooth curve through them.

Hyperbolas

The hyperbola is a two-part conic section defined as the path of a point that moves in such a way that the difference of its distances from two focal points is a constant (**Figure 12.36C**). **Figure 12.43** shows construction of a hyperbola according to this definition. By selecting a series of radii until enough points have been located, the hyperbolic curve can be accurately drawn.

12.12 Spirals

The **spiral** is a coil lying in a single plane that begins at a point and becomes larger as it travels around the origin. **Figure 12.44** shows the steps for constructing a spiral. The number of divisions selected in this construction depends on the degree of accuracy desired.

12.13 Helixes

The **helix** is a three-dimensional curve that coils around a cylinder or cone at a constant angle of inclination. Applications of helixes are corkscrews and the threads on a screw. **Figure 12.45** shows the construction of a cylindrical helix. The stairway wrapping around the tank in **Figure 12.46** is an application of helix construction.

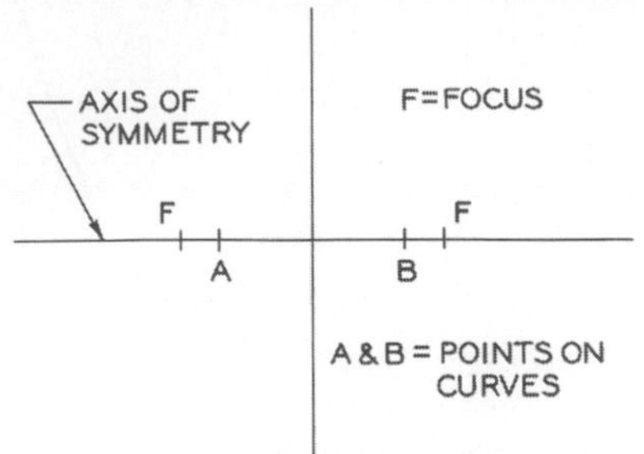

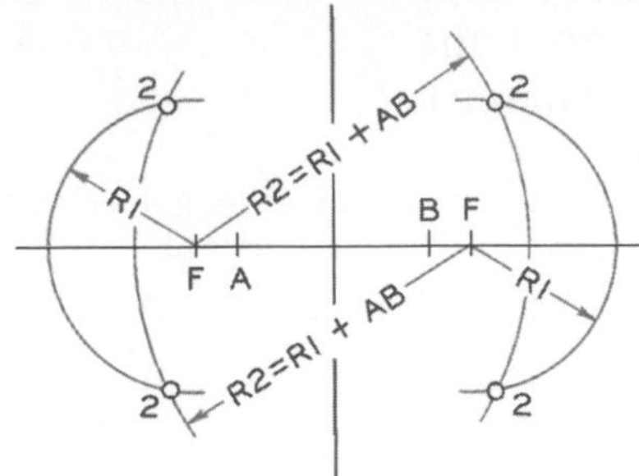

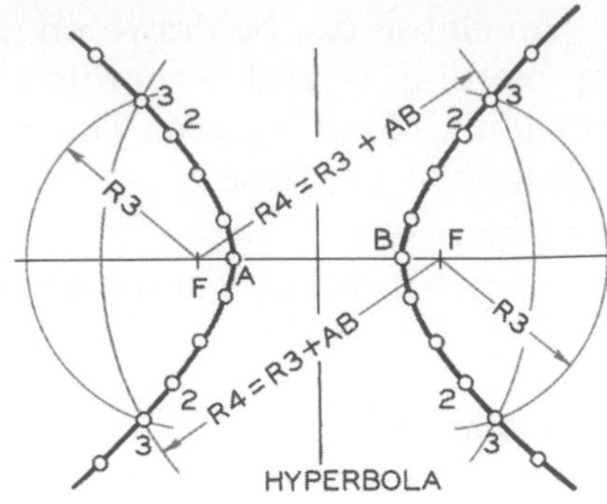

12.43 A hyperbola.

Step 1 Draw a perpendicular through the axis of symmetry. Locate focal points F equidistant from it on both sides. Locate points A and B equidistant from the perpendicular at a distance of your choice but between the focal points.

Step 2 Use radius R1 to draw arcs using focal points F as the centers. Add R1 to AB (the nearest distance between the hyperbolas) to find R2. Draw arcs using radius R2 and the focal points as centers. R1 and R2 locate points labeled 2.

Step 3 Select other radii and add them to AB to locate additional points as shown in step 2. Draw a smooth curve through the points with an irregular curve to form the hyperbola.

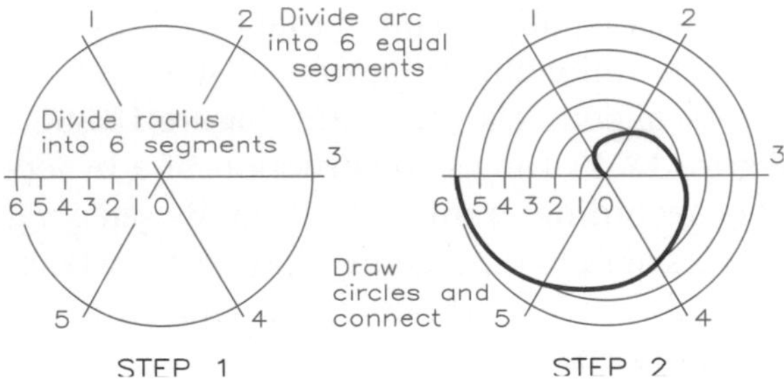

12.44 Constructing a spiral.

Step 1 Draw a circle and divide it into equal parts. Divide the radius into the same number of equal parts (six in this case).

Step 2 Begin inside and draw arc 0-1 to intersect radius 0-1. Then swing arc 0-2 to radius 0-2, and continue to point 6 on the original circle, and connect the points.

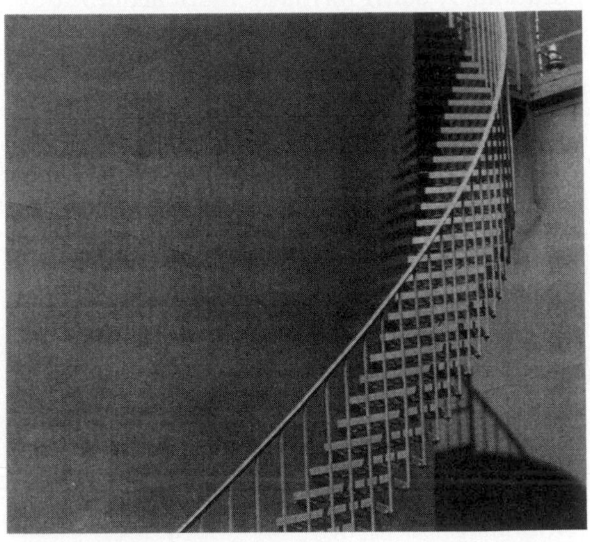

12.46 The path of this stairway around a petroleum storage tank has a helical path as constructed in **Figure 12.45**.

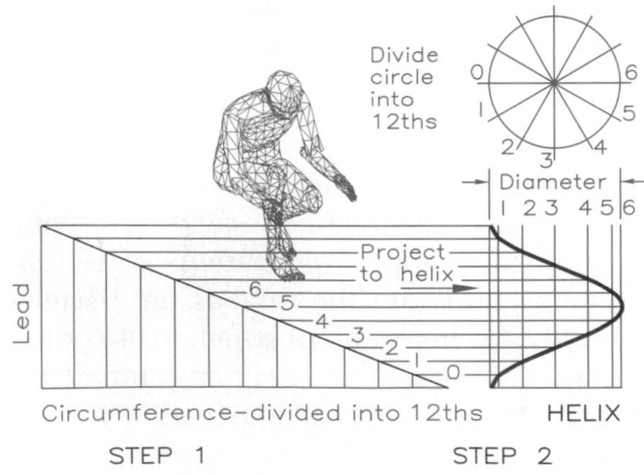

12.45 A cylindrical helix.

Step 1 Divide the top view of the cylinder into equal parts and project them to the front view. Lay out the circumference and the lead (pronounced *leed*) as the cylinder. Divide the circumference into the same number of equal parts transferred from the top view.

Step 2 Project the points along the inclined rise to their respective elements on the diameter, and connect them with a smooth curve.

Problems

Present your problem solutions on size A (8-1/2 × 11-inch) sheets. The printed grid represents 0.20-in. intervals, so you can use your engineers' 10 scale to lay out the problems. By equating each grid interval to 5 mm, you also can use your full-size metric scale to lay out and solve the problems. Show your construction and mark all points of tangency as recommended in the chapter.

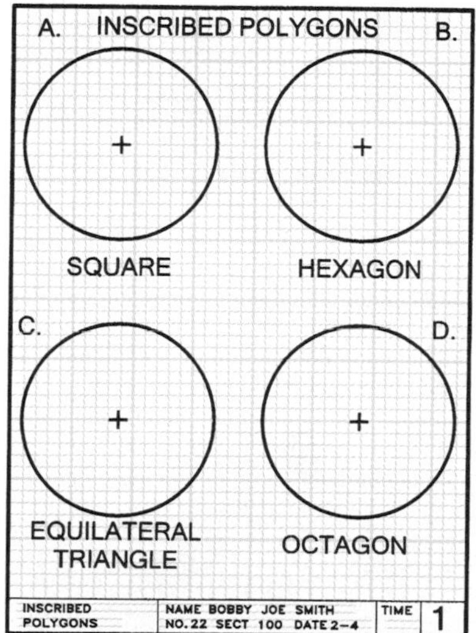

Sheet 1 Regular polygon construction.

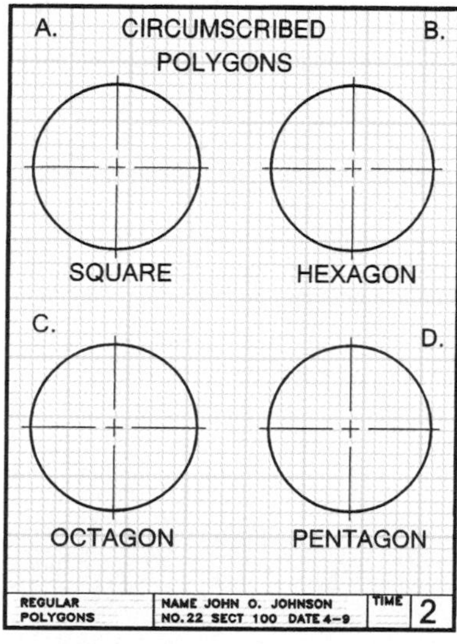

Sheet 2 Regular polygon construction.

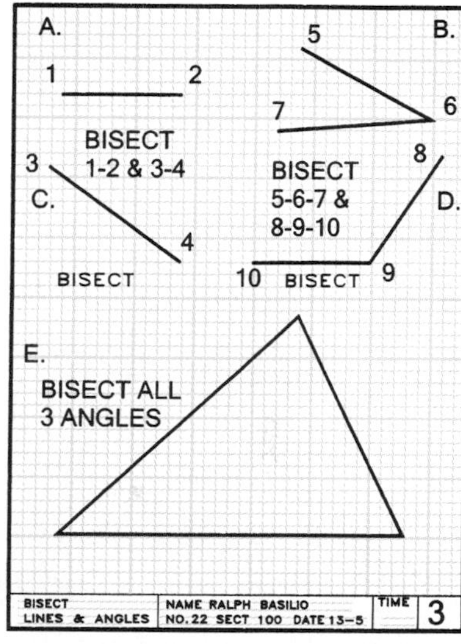

Sheet 3 Bisection of lines and angles.

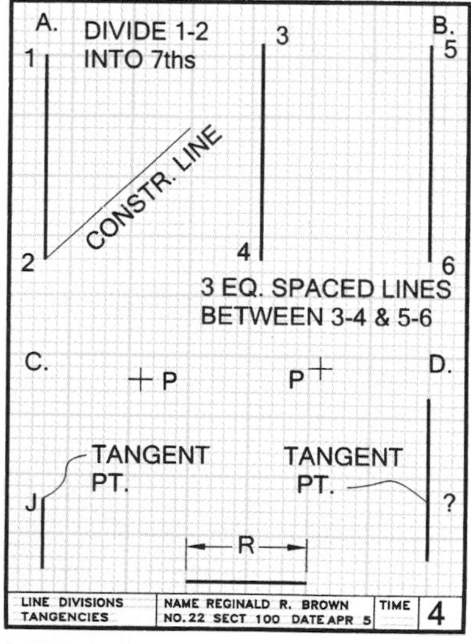

Sheet 4 Division of lines and tangencies.

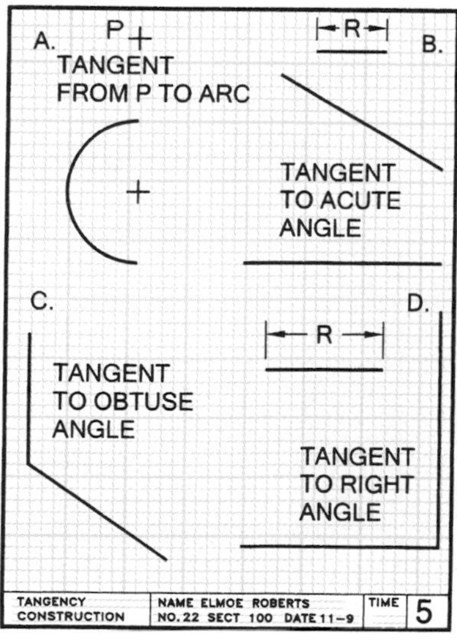

Sheet 5 Tangency constructions.

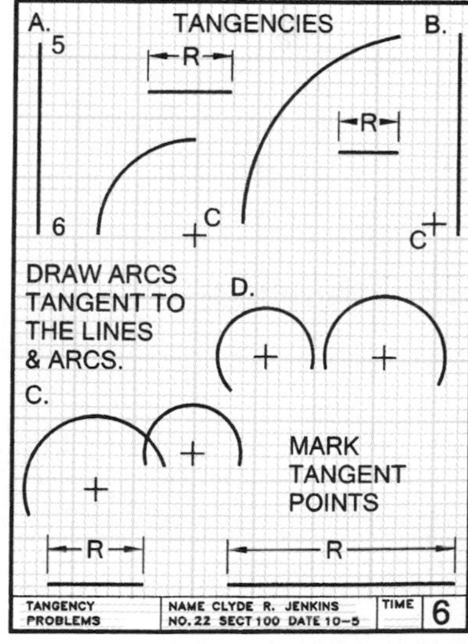

Sheet 6 Tangency constructions.

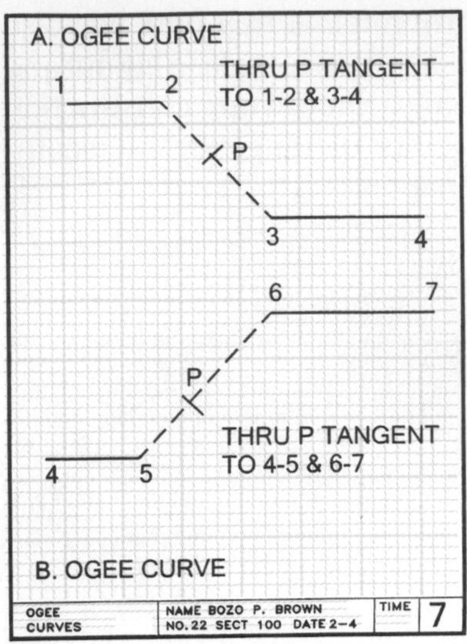

Sheet 7 Construct ogee curves through P and that are tangent to the given lines.

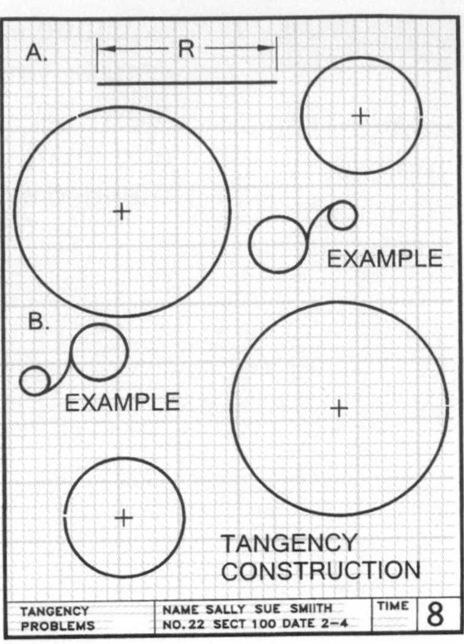

Sheet 8 Connect the circles with the tangent arcs as indicated in the examples.

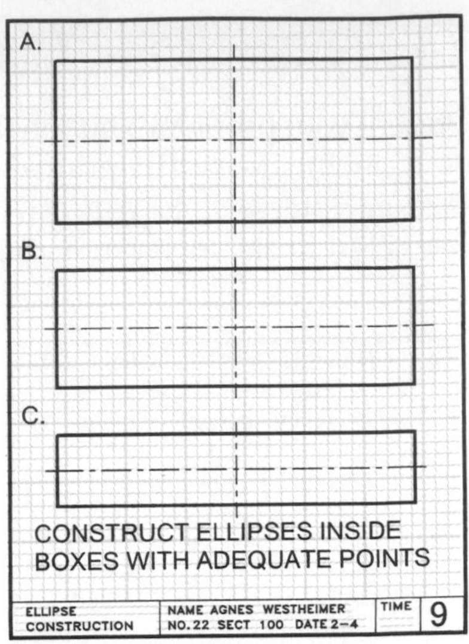

Sheet 9 Construct ellipses inside the rectangles using your irregular curve.

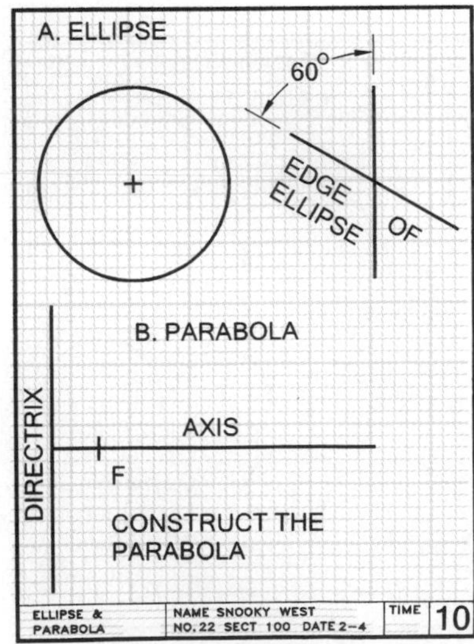

Sheet 10 Construct an ellipse at A and a parabola at B.

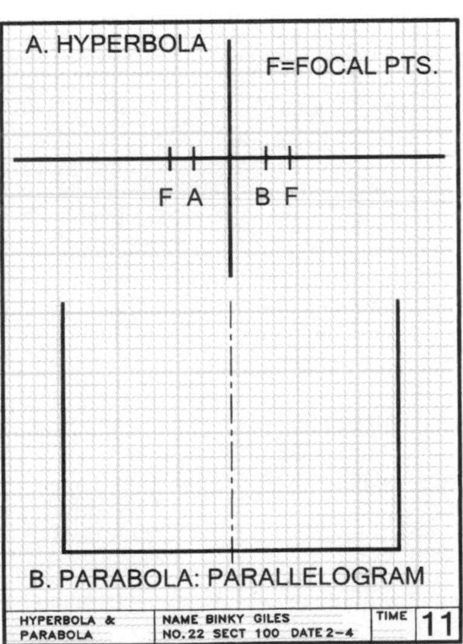

Sheet 11 Construct a hyperbola at A and a parabola at B.

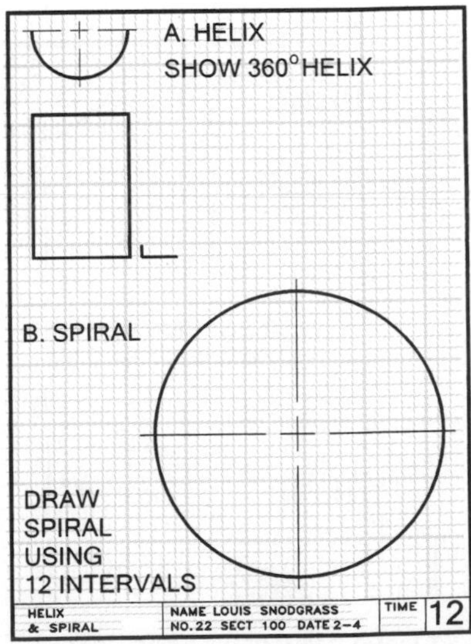

Sheet 12 Construct a helix at A and a spiral at B.

Problems 13–23. Practical Applications

Construct the given shapes on size A sheets, one problem per sheet. Select the scale that will best fit the problem to the sheet. Mark all points of tangency and strive for good line quality.

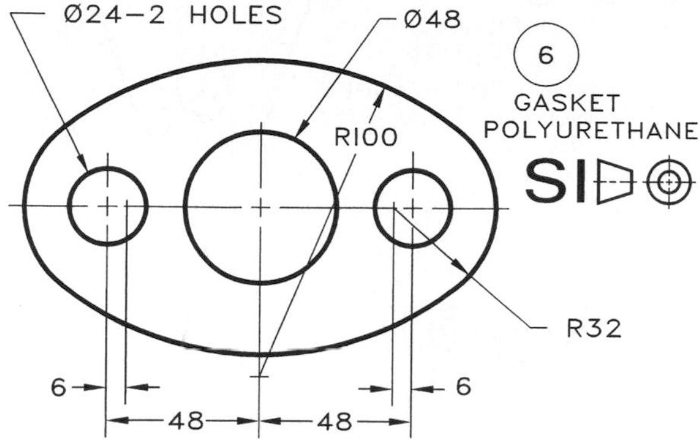

12.47 Problem 13.

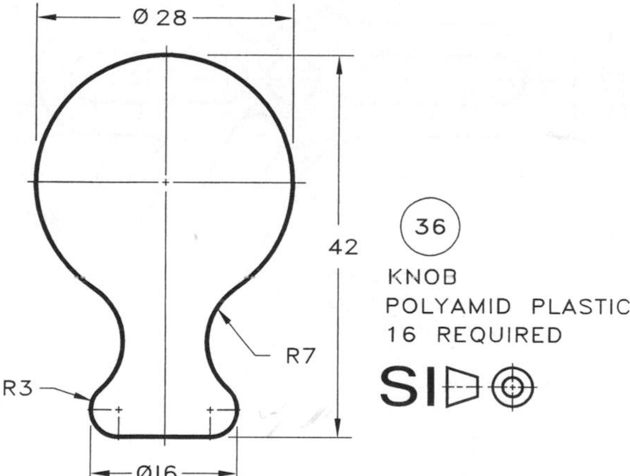

12.48 Problem 14.

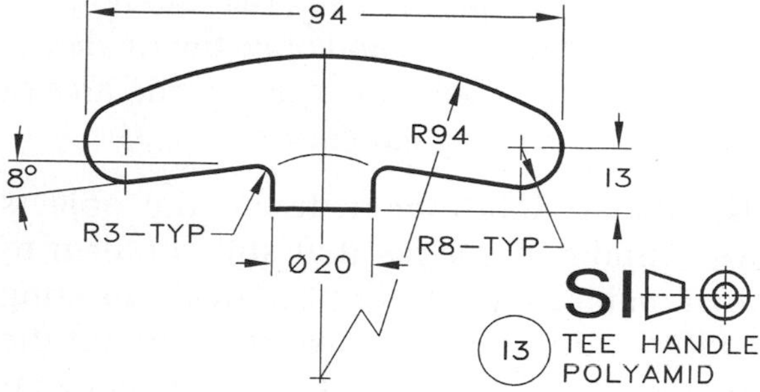

12.49 Problem 15.

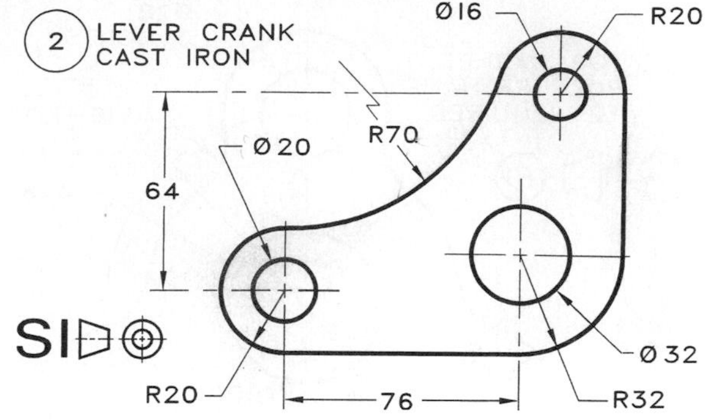

12.50 Problem 16.

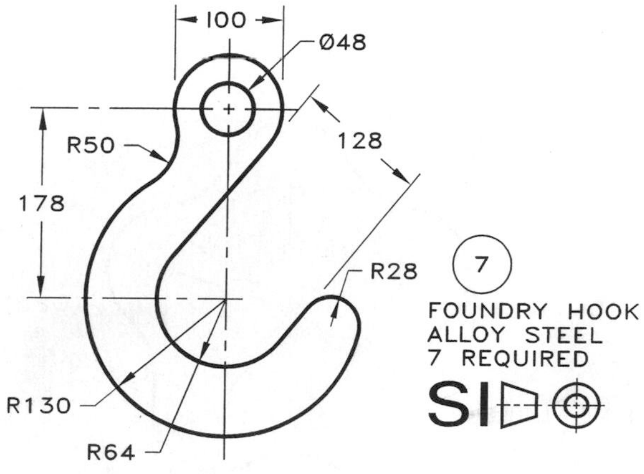

12.51 Problem 17.

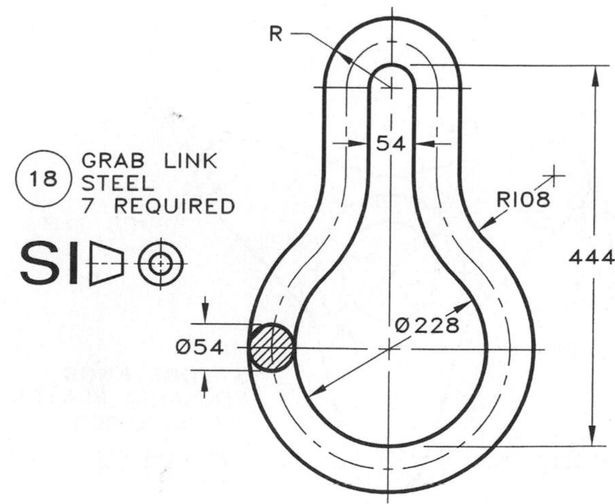

12.52 Problem 18.

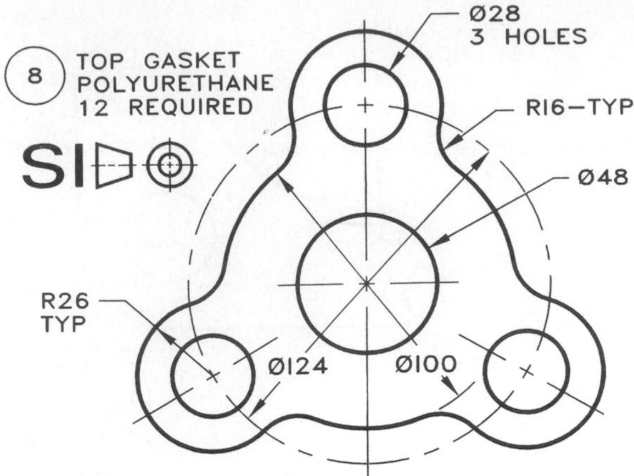

12.53 Problem 19.

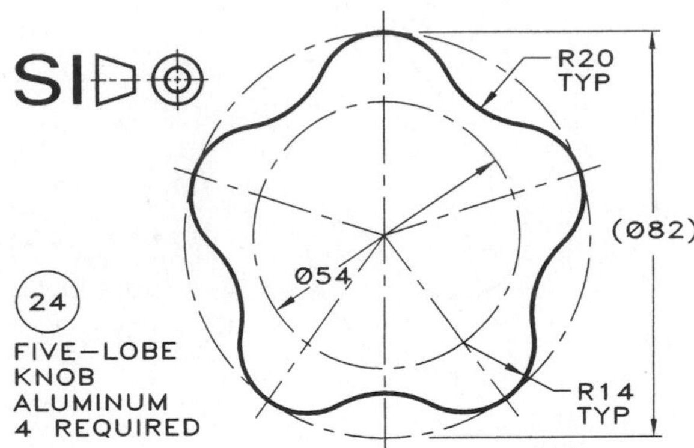

12.54 Problem 20.

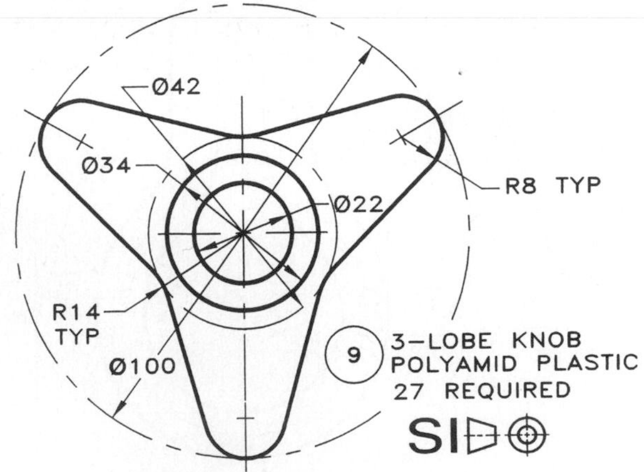

12.55 Problem 21.

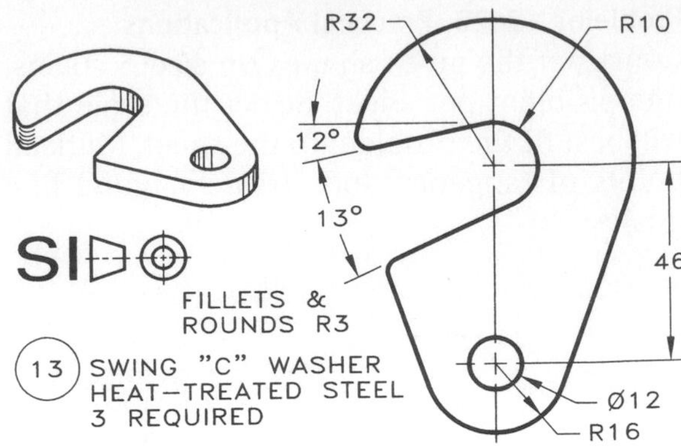

12.56 Problem 22.

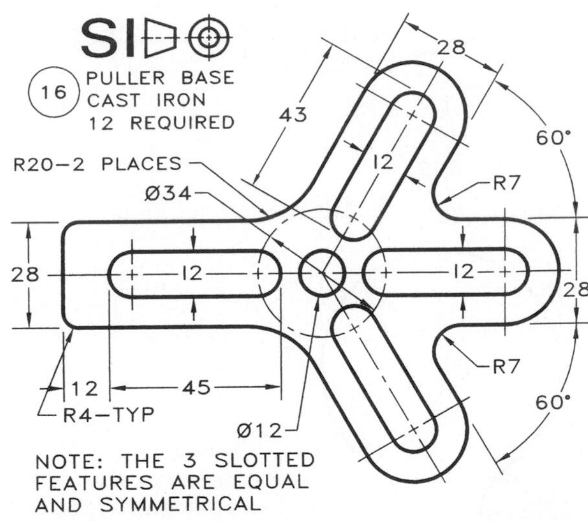

12.57 Problem 23.

Design Problems

Approach design problems 1–4 as if you were the designer. Approximate the missing dimensions and details, and draw the single descriptive view of each part using true arcs of circles with no irregular curves.

Alternative Solution: Redesign the objects with modified shapes that still conform to their major functions implied by the existing configuration. In other words, maintain the existing locations of slots, holes, and specified sizes.

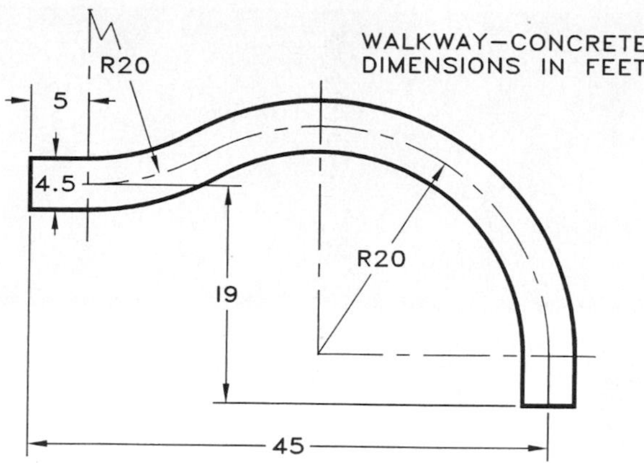

12.58 Problem 24.

DESIGN 1: EYE BOLT

Complete this partially dimensioned assembly as if you were its designer. Draw it on a size A sheet at an appropriate scale.

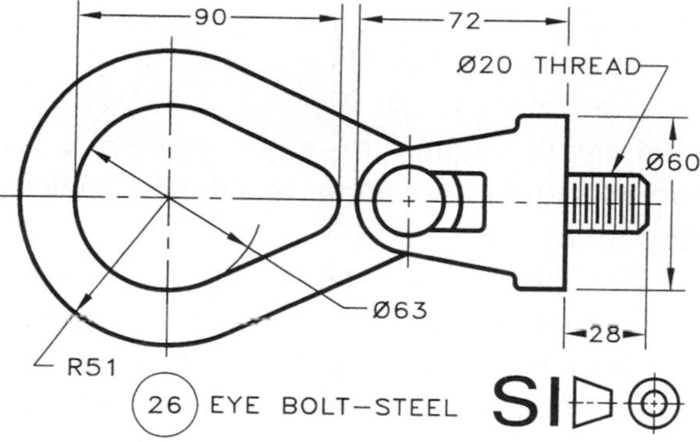

DESIGN 2: CHAIN GRAB

Make a drawing of the grab on a size A sheet using an appropriate scale. All curves are to be arcs of a circle.

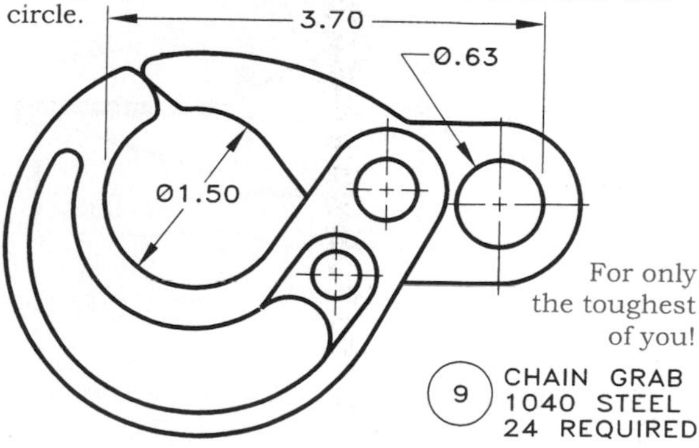

For only the toughest of you!

DESIGN 3: WRENCH

Complete the design of the wrench by supplying the missing dimensions. Make all curves arcs of a circle. Draw on a size A sheet at an appropriate scale.

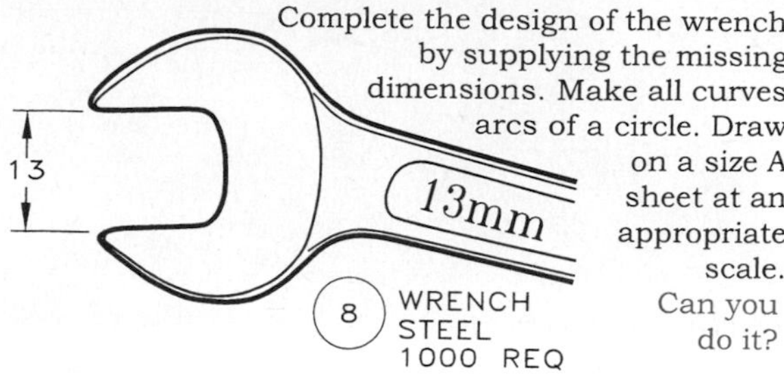

Can you do it?

DESIGN 4: LEVER

Determine the missing dimensions and draw the view of the lever at an appropriate scale on a size A sheet. Use only radii of circles.

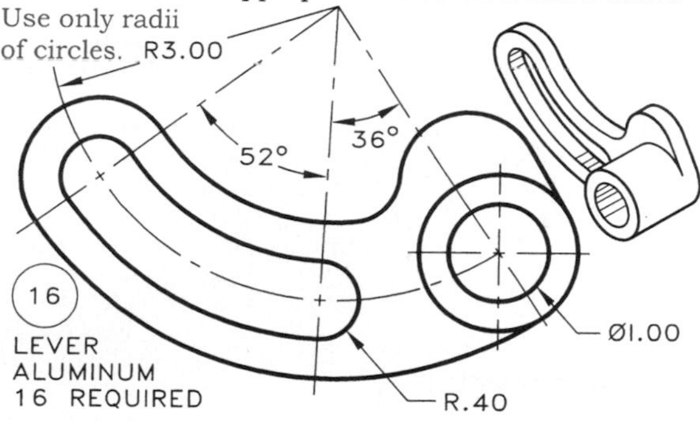

Thought Questions

1. Name the types of conic sections and sketch 3D views of how they are formed in relationship to a cone.

2. What is the purpose of marking points of tangency in geometric construction that involves arcs and circles?

3. Give examples of designs that utilize parabolic shapes.

4. Which AutoCAD commands enable you to draw a line from a point tangent to a line?

5. How is the ellipse template angle for drawing an ellipse determined?

6. Describe the following: frustum, truncated cone, dodecahedron, hexahedron, polyhedron, hyperbola.

13
Freehand Sketching

13.1 Introduction

Sketching is a rapid, freehand method of drawing without the use of drawing instruments. Sketching is also a thinking process as much as it is a method of communication. Designers and engineers make many sketches as a method of developing ideas before arriving at the final solution. Many new products and projects have begun as sketches made on the back of an envelope or on a napkin at a restaurant (**Figure 13.1**). Sketching is used by the engineer throughout the engineering process, including free-body diagrams during analysis (**Figure 13.2**).

The ability to communicate by any means is a great asset, and sketching is one of the best ways to transmit ideas. Engineers must use their sketching skills to explain their ideas before they can delegate assignments and obtain the assistance of their team members.

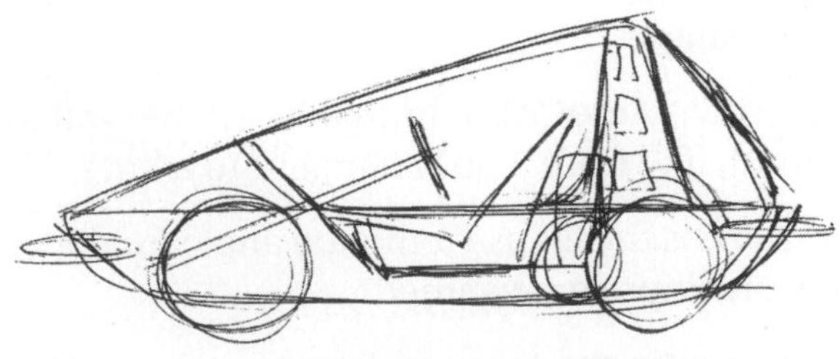

13.1 Designs begin with rough, freehand sketches as a means of developing concepts. (Courtsy of Chrysler Corporation.)

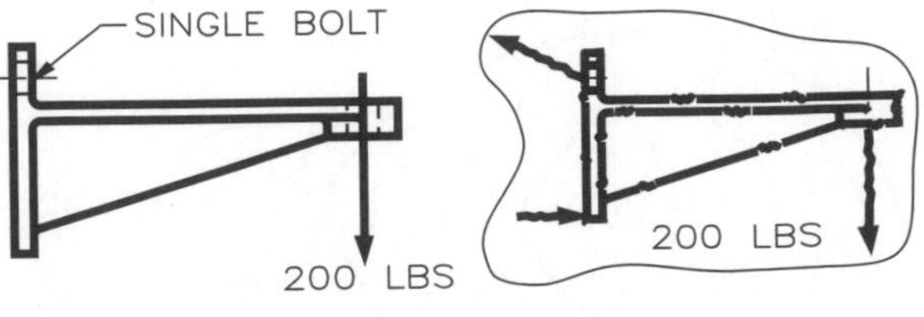

13.2 Sketching is a necessary skill used in all aspects of design, from free-body diagrams through design documentation.

13.2 Shape Description

Although the angle bracket in **Figure 13.3** is a simple three-dimensional object, describing it with words is difficult. Most untrained people would think that drawing it as a three-dimensional pictorial would be a challenge. To make drawing such objects easier, engineers devised a standard system, called **orthographic projection**, for showing objects in different views.

In orthographic projection, separate views represent the object at 90° intervals as the viewer moves about it (**Figure 13.4**). **Figure 13.5** shows two-dimensional views of the bracket from the front, top, and right side. The top view is drawn above the front view, and both share the dimension of width. The right-side view is drawn to the right of the front view, and both share the dimension of height.

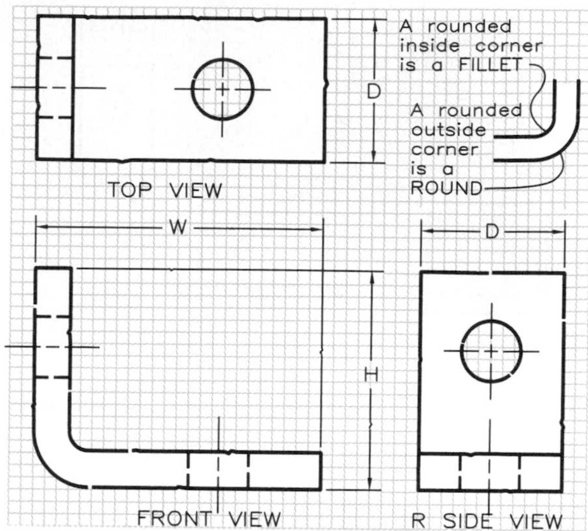

13.5 This sketch shows three orthographic views of the angle bracket.

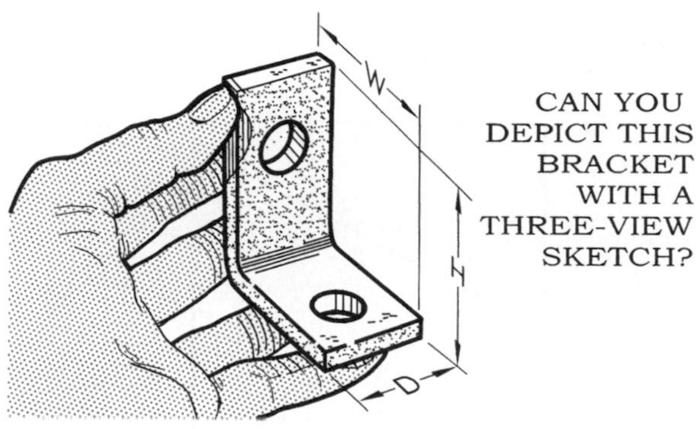

CAN YOU DEPICT THIS BRACKET WITH A THREE-VIEW SKETCH?
W
H
D

13.3 How can you sketch this angle bracket to convey its shape effectively?

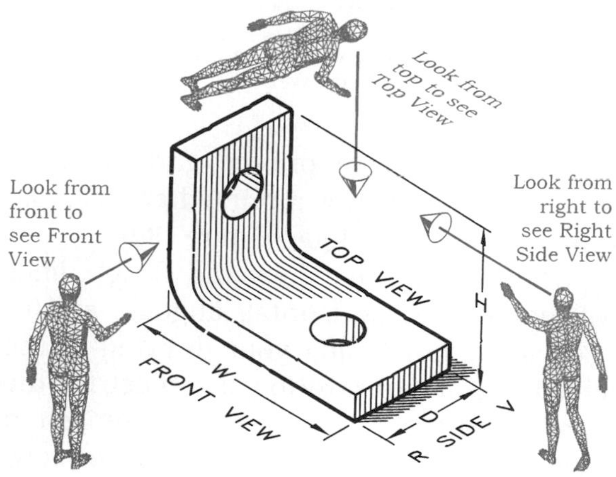

13.4 These positions give the viewpoints for three orthographic views of the angle bracket: top, front, and right side.

The views of the bracket are drawn with three types of lines: **visible lines, hidden lines**, and **centerlines**. Visible lines are the thickest. Thinner hidden lines (dashed lines) represent features that are invisible, or hidden, in a view. The thinnest lines are centerlines, which are imaginary lines composed of long and short dashes to show the centers of arcs and the axes of cylinders.

The space between views may vary, but the views must be positioned as shown here. This arrangement is logical, the views are easiest to interpret in this order, and the drawing process is most efficient because the views project from each other. **Figure 13.6** illustrates the lack of clarity when views are incorrectly positioned, even though each view is properly drawn.

13.3 Sketching Techniques

You need to understand the application of line types used in sketching (freehand) orthographic views before continuing with the

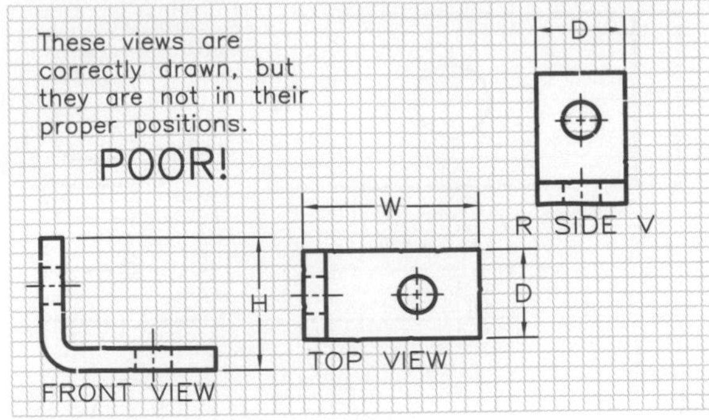

13.6 Views must be sketched in their standard orthographic positions. If they are incorrectly positioned, the object cannot be readily understood.

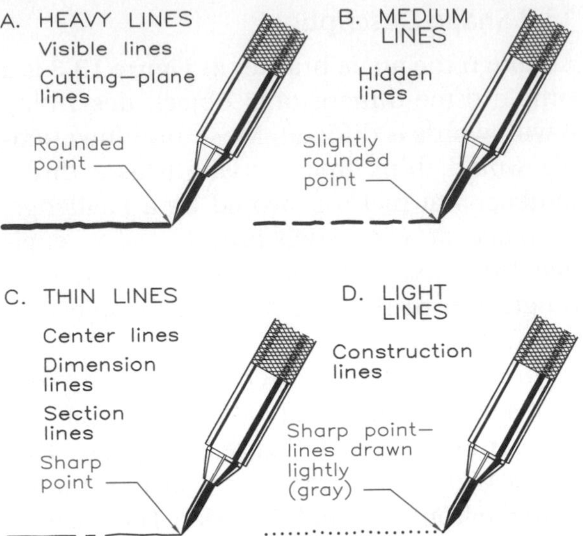

13.8 An F pencil is a good choice for sketching all lines if you sharpen it for varying line widths.

principles of projection. The "alphabet of lines" for sketching is presented in **Figure 13.7**. All lines, except construction lines, should be black and dense. Construction lines are drawn lightly so that they need not be erased. The other lines are distinguished by their line widths (line thicknesses), but they are equal in darkness.

Medium-weight pencils, such as H, F, or HB grades, are best for sketching the lines shown in **Figure 13.8**. By sharpening the pencil point to match the desired line width, you may use the same grade of pencil for all these lines. Lines sketched freehand should have a freehand appearance; do not attempt to make them appear mechanical. Using a printed grid or laying translucent paper over a printed grid can aid your sketching technique (**Figure 13.9**).

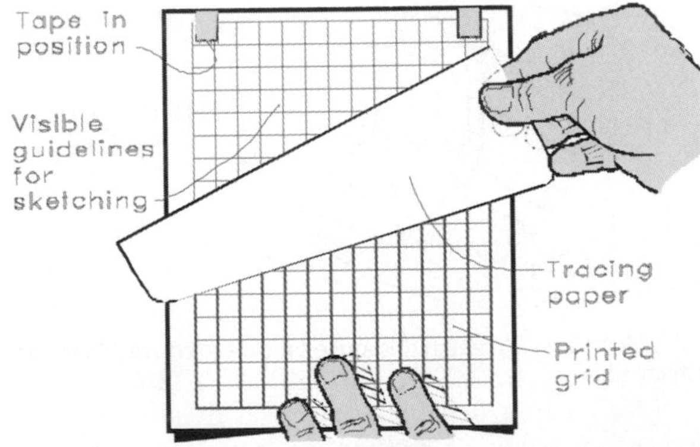

13.9 A grid placed under a sheet of tracing paper will provide guidelines as an aid in freehand sketching.

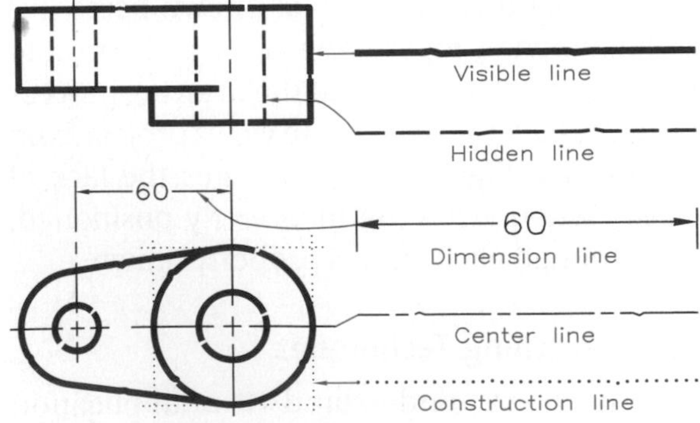

13.7 The alphabet of lines for sketching are shown here. The lines at the right are full size.

When you make a freehand sketch, lines will be vertical, horizontal, angular, and/or circular. By not taping your drawing to the tabletop, you can position the sheet for the most comfortable strokes, usually from left to right (**Figure 13.10**). Examples of correctly sketched lines are contrasted with incorrectly sketched ones in **Figure 13.11**.

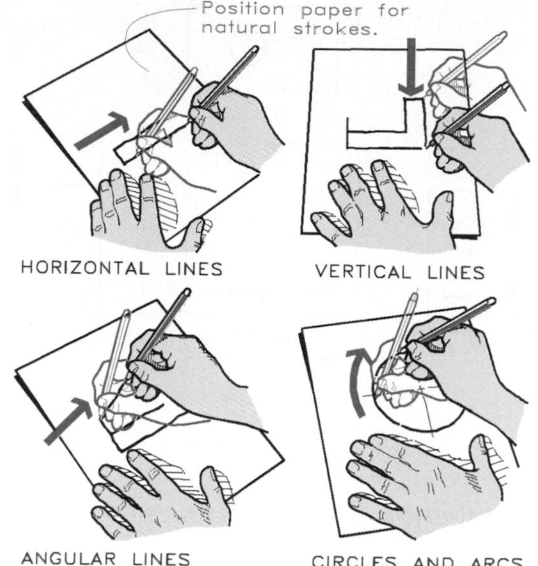

13.10 Sketch lines as shown here for the best results; rotate your drawing sheet for comfortable sketching positions.

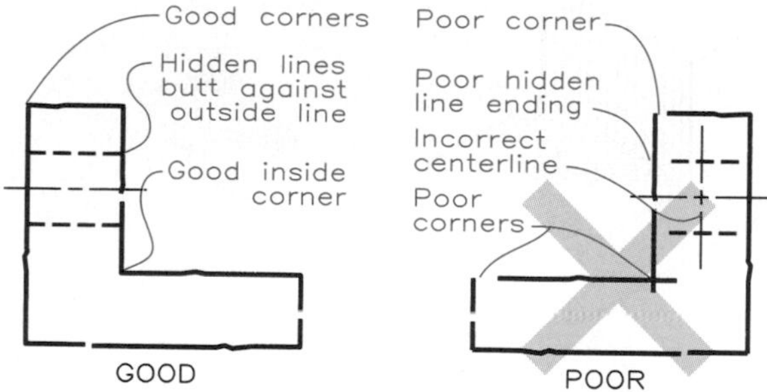

13.11 For good sketches, follow the examples of good technique and avoid the common errors of poor technique shown.

13.4 Six-View Sketching

The maximum number of principal views that can be drawn in orthographic projection is six, as the viewer changes position at 90° intervals (Figure 13.12). In each view, two of the three dimensions of **height**, **width**, and **depth** are seen.

These views must be sketched in their standard positions (**Figure 13.13**). The width dimension is shared by the top, front, and bottom views. The height dimension is shared with the right-side, front, left-side, and rear

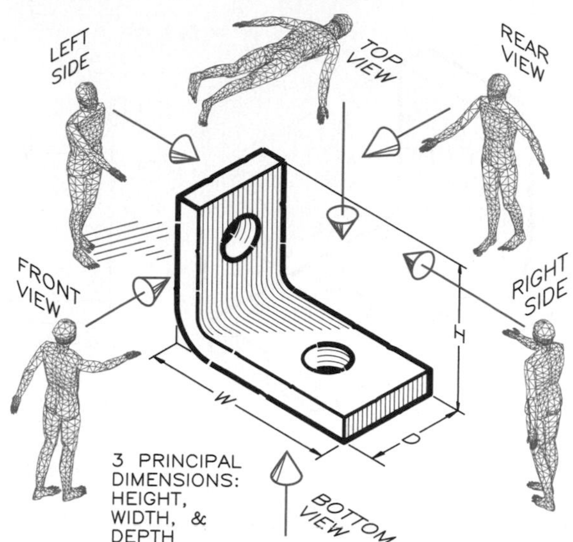

13.12 Six principal views of the angle bracket can be sketched from the viewpoints shown.

views. Note the simple and effective dimensioning of each view with two dimensions. Seldom is an object so complex that it requires six orthographic views.

13.5 Three-View Sketching

You can adequately describe most objects with three orthographic views; usually the top, front, and right-side views. **Figure 13.14** shows a typical three-view sketch of a T-block with height, width, and depth dimensions and the front, top, and right-side views labeled.

The object shown in **Figure 13.15** is represented by three orthographic views on a grid in **Figure 13.16**. To obtain those views, first sketch the overall dimensions of the object, then sketch the slanted surface in the top view and project it to the other views. Finally, darken the lines; label the views; and letter the overall dimensions of height, width, and depth.

Slanted surfaces will appear as **edges** or **foreshortened** (not-true-size) planes in the principal views of orthographic projection

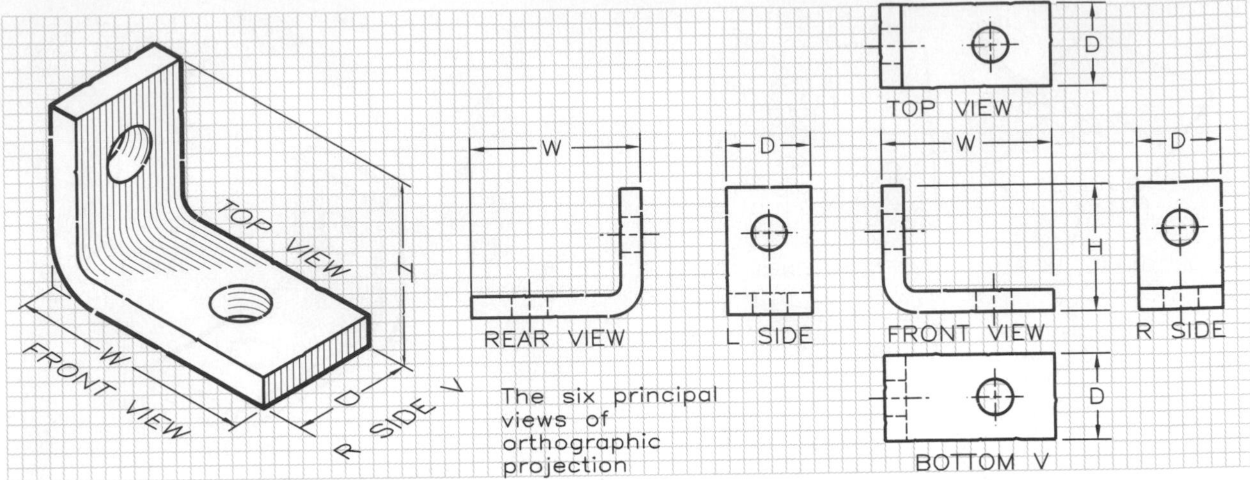

13.13 This six-view sketch of the angle bracket shows the six principal views of orthographic projection. Note the placement of dimensions on the views.

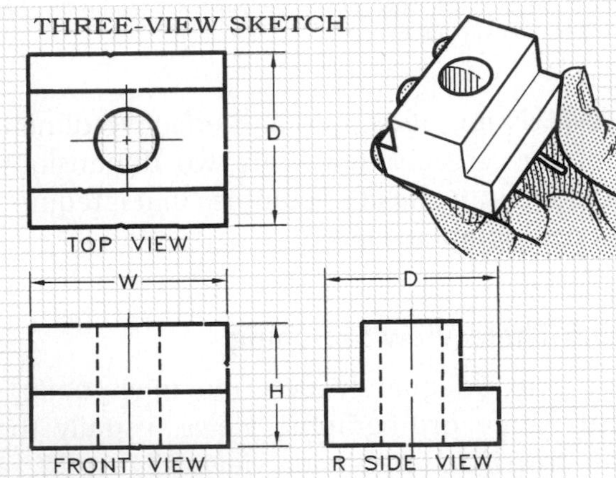

13.14 This sketch shows the standard orthographic arrangement for three views of a jaw nut, with dimensions and labels.

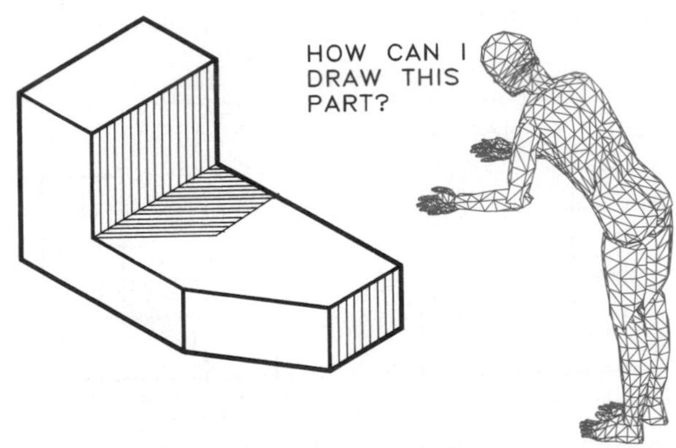

13.15 Sketches of three orthographic views describe this fixture block in **Figure 13.14.**

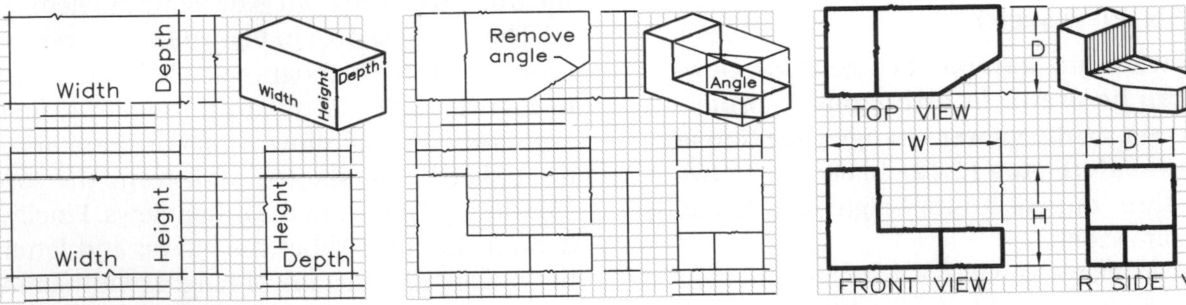

13.16 Three-view sketching.

Step 1 Block in the views with light construction lines. Allow proper spacing for labeling and dimensioning the views.

Step 2 Remove the notches and project from view to view.

Step 3 Check for correctness, darken the lines, and letter the labels and dimensions.

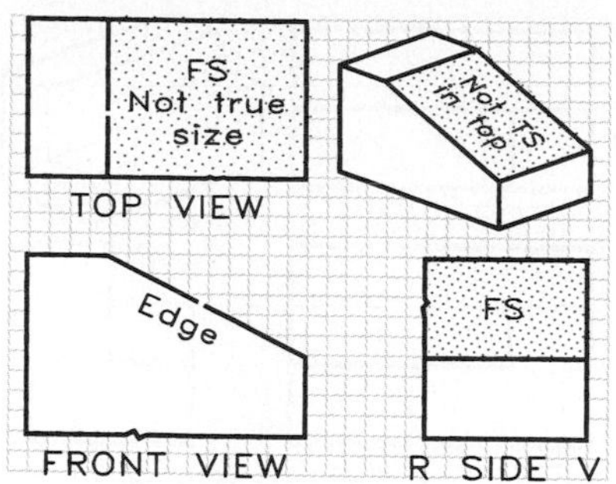

A. FORESHORTENED IN TOP

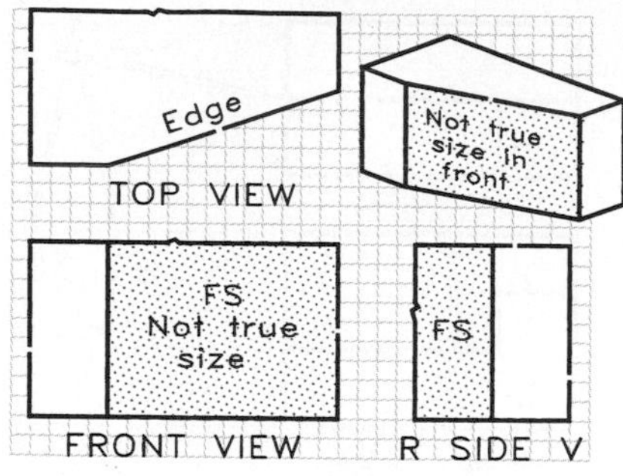

B. FORESHORTENED IN FRONT

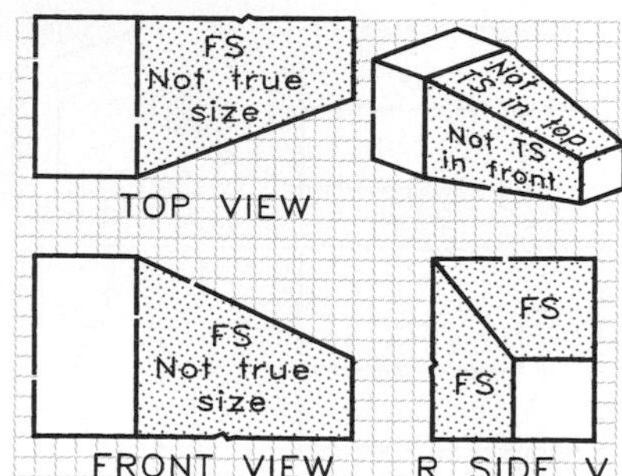

C. FORESHORTENED IN ALL

13.17 Views of planes

The plane appearing as an angular edge in the front view is foreshortened in the top and side views.

The plane appearing as an angular edge in the top view is foreshortened in the front and side views.

Two sloping planes appear foreshortened in the side view, and neither appears as edges in either the top or front views.

(**Figure 13.17**). In **Figure 13.17C**, two intersecting planes of the object slope in two directions; thus both appear foreshortened in the front, top, and right-side views.

A good way to learn orthographic projection is to construct a missing third view (the front view in **Figure 13.18**) when two views are given. In **Figure 13.19**, we construct the missing right-side view from the given top and front views. To obtain the depth dimension for the right-side view, transfer it from the top view with dividers; to obtain the height dimension, project it from the front view.

Figure 13.20 shows a fixture pad sketched in three views. The pad has a **finished surface**, indicated by V marks in the two views where the surface appears as edges, and four **counterbored** holes. Dimension lines for the height, width, and depth labels should be spaced at least three letter heights from the views. For example, when you use 1/8-in. letters, position them at least 3/8-in. from the views.

Apply the finish mark symbol to the edge views of any finished surfaces, visible or hidden, to specify that the surface is to be machined to make it smoother. The surface in **Figure 13.21** is being finished by grinding,

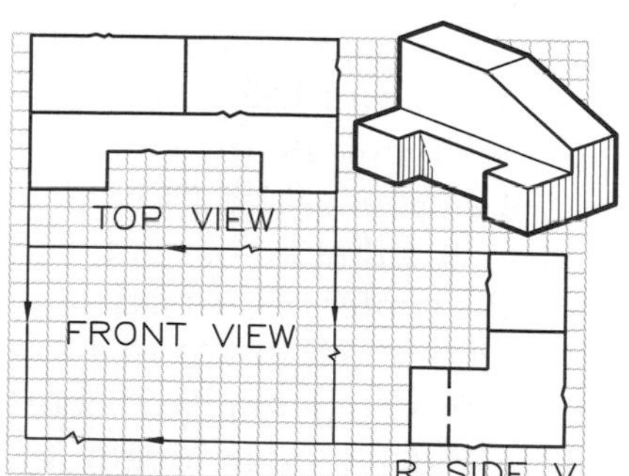

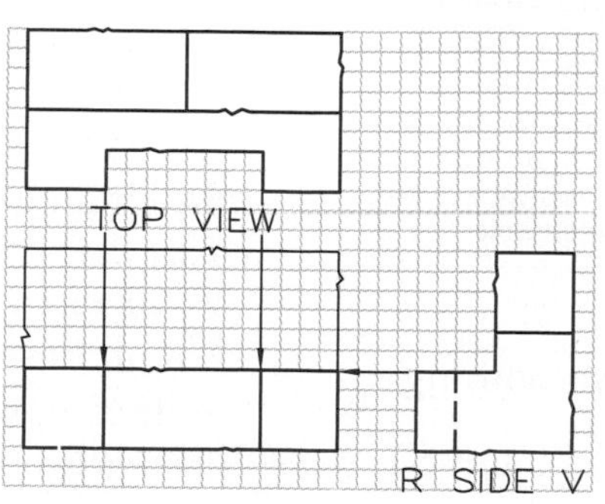

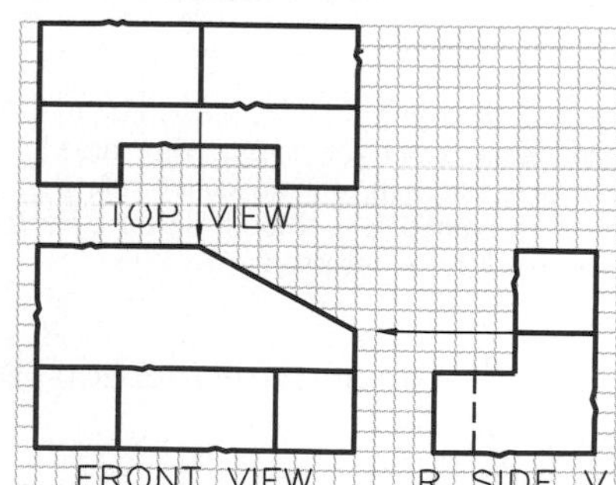

13.18 Sketching a missing front view.

Step 1 Begin by blocking in the front view with light construction lines that will not need to be erased.

Step 2 Project the notch from the top view to the front view and darken these lines as final lines.

Step 3 Project the ends of the angular notch from the top and right-side views, check the views, and darken the lines.

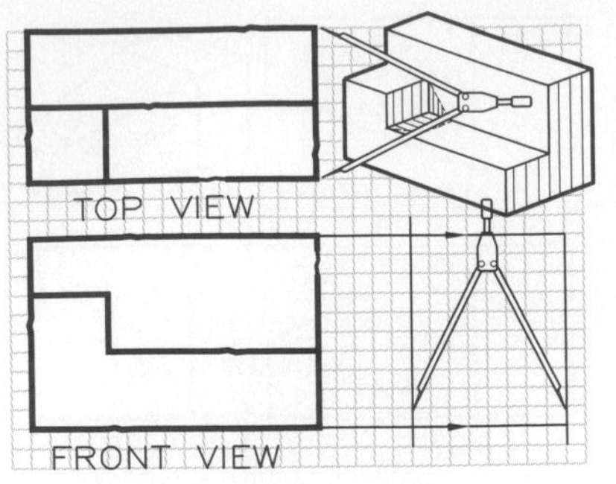

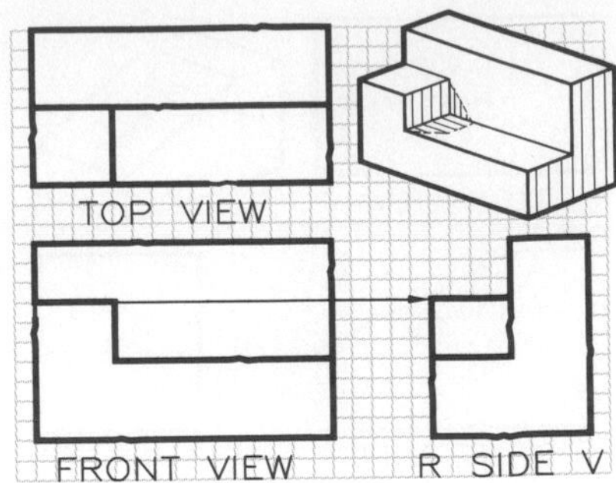

13.19 Sketching a missing side view.

Step 1 Transfer the depth with dividers and project the height from the front. Block in the side view with construction lines.

Step 2 Locate the notch in the side view with your dividers and project its base from the front view. Use light construction lines.

Step 3 Project the top of the notch from the front view, check for correctness, darken the lines, and label the views.

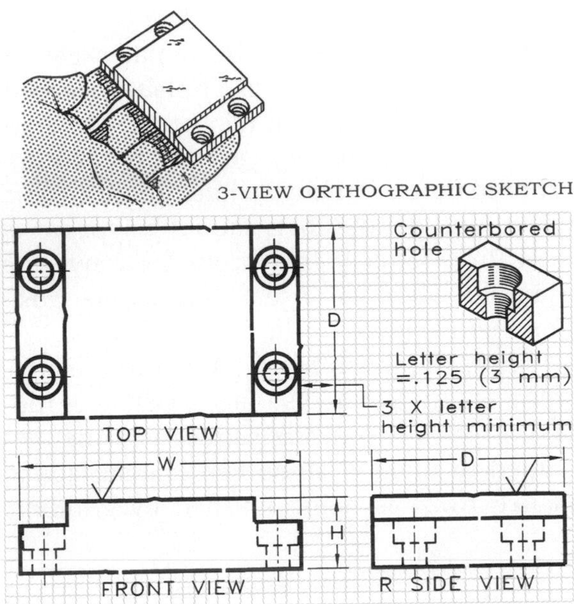

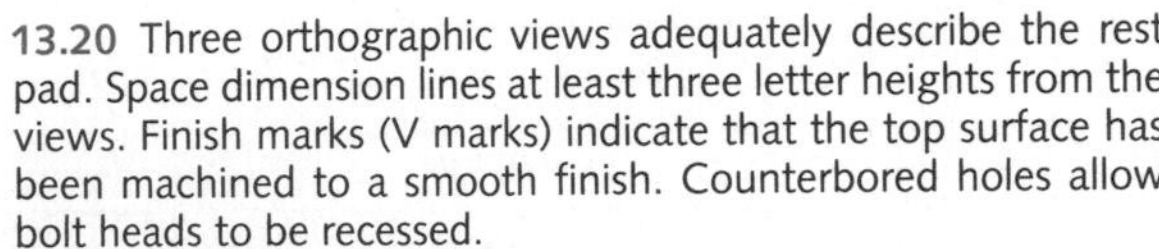

13.20 Three orthographic views adequately describe the rest pad. Space dimension lines at least three letter heights from the views. Finish marks (V marks) indicate that the top surface has been machined to a smooth finish. Counterbored holes allow bolt heads to be recessed.

which is one of many methods of smoothing a surface.

13.6 Circular Features

The pulley shaft depicted in **Figure 13.22** in two views is composed of circular features.

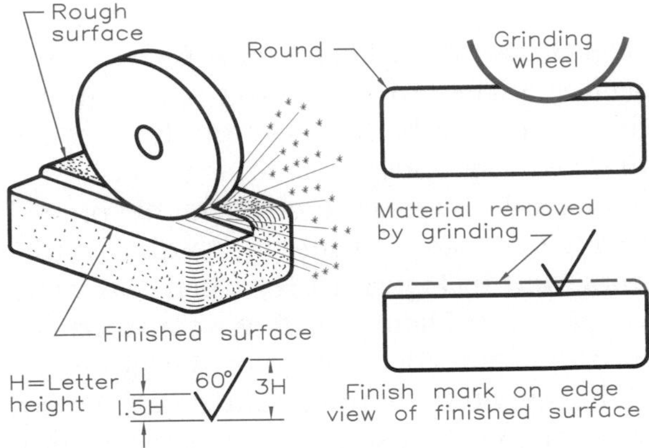

13.21 Place a finish mark on all edge views of a surface (visible or hidden) that has to be smoothed by machining. Grinding is one of the methods used to finish a surface.

Centerlines are added to better identify these cylindrical features. **Figure 13.23** shows how to apply centerlines to indicate the center of the circular ends of a cylinder and its vertical axis. Perpendicular centerlines cross in circular views to locate the center of the circle and extend beyond the arc by about 1/8 in. Centerlines consist of alternating long and short dashes, about 1 in. and 1/8 in. in length, respectively.

When centerlines coincide with visible or hidden lines, the centerline should be omitted because object lines are more important, and

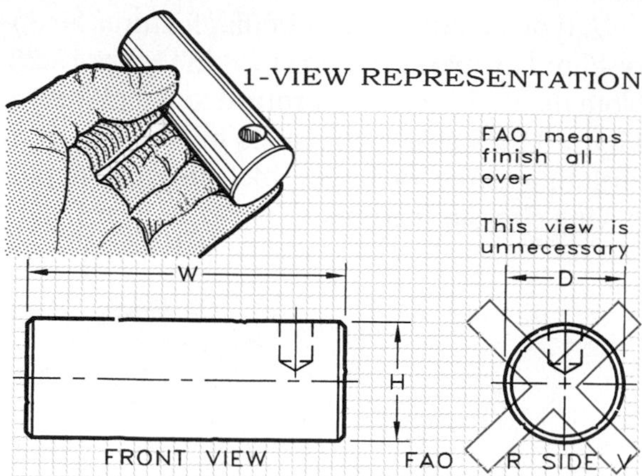

13.22 This pulley shaft is a typical cylindrical part that can be represented adequately by two views.

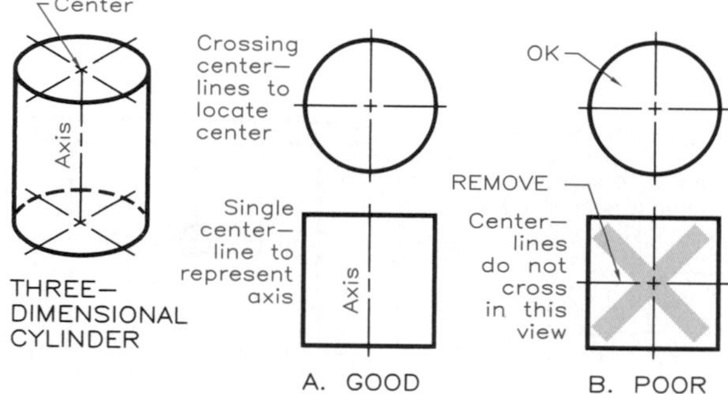

13.23 Centerlines identify the centers of circles and axes of cylinders. Centerlines cross only in the circular view and extend about 1/8 in. beyond the outside lines.

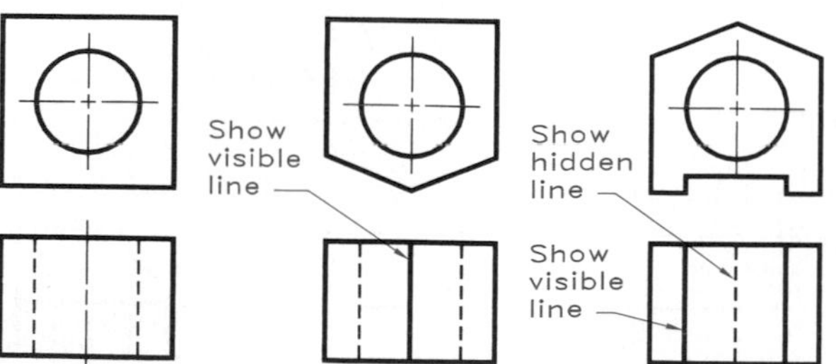

13.24 When visible lines coincide with hidden lines, show the visible lines. When hidden lines coincide with centerlines, show the hidden lines.

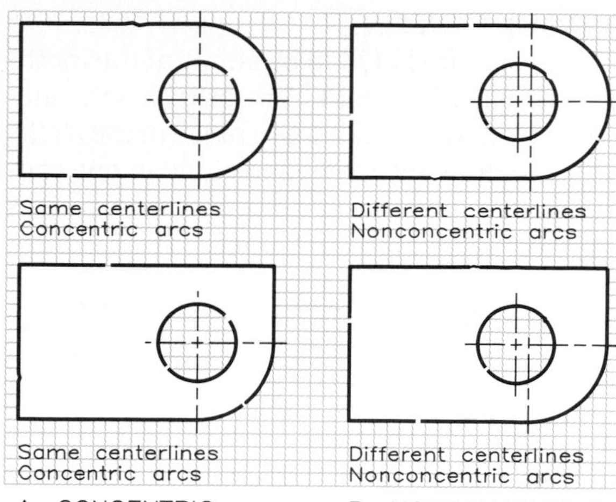

13.25 Centerlines

A Extend centerlines beyond the last arc that has the same center.

B Sketch separate centerlines when the arcs are not concentric.

centerlines are imaginary lines. **Figure 13.24** shows the precedence of lines.

The centerlines shown in **Figure 13.25** clarify whether the circles and arcs are concentric (share the same centers). **Figure 13.26** shows the correct manner of applying centerlines to orthographic views of an object composed of concentric cylinders.

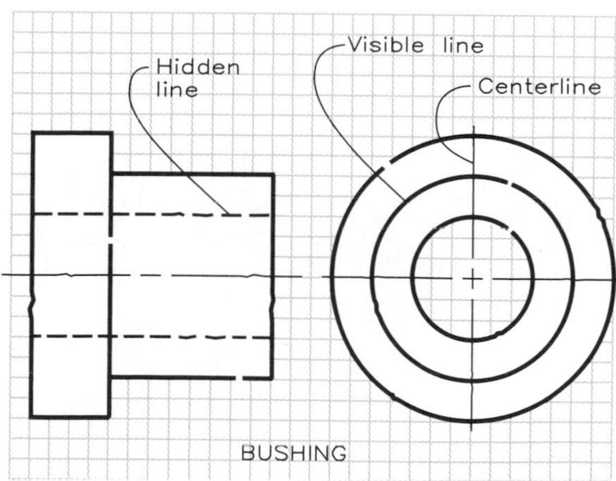

13.26 This orthographic sketch depicts the application of centerlines to concentric cylinders, and the relative weights of various lines.

Sketching Circles

Circles can be sketched by either of the methods shown in **Figure 13.27** by using light guidelines and dark centerlines to block in the circle. Because drawing a freehand circle in one continuous arc is difficult, draw arcs in segments with the help of the guidelines.

A typical part having circular features is represented by two sketched views in **Figure 13.28**. Note the definitions of a **round** and a **chamfer**. **Figure 13.29** shows the steps involved in constructing three orthographic views of a part having circular features.

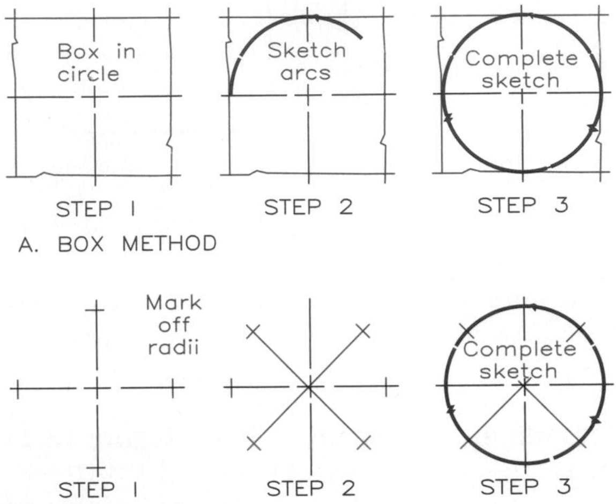

13.27 Sketching circles.

Method 1

Step 1 Block in the diameter of the circle about the centerlines.

Step 2 Sketch an arc tangent through two tangent points.

Step 3 Complete the circle with other arcs.

Method 2

Step 1 Mark off radii on the centerlines.

Step 2 Mark off radii on two construction lines drawn at 45°.

Step 3 Sketch the circles with arcs passing through the marks.

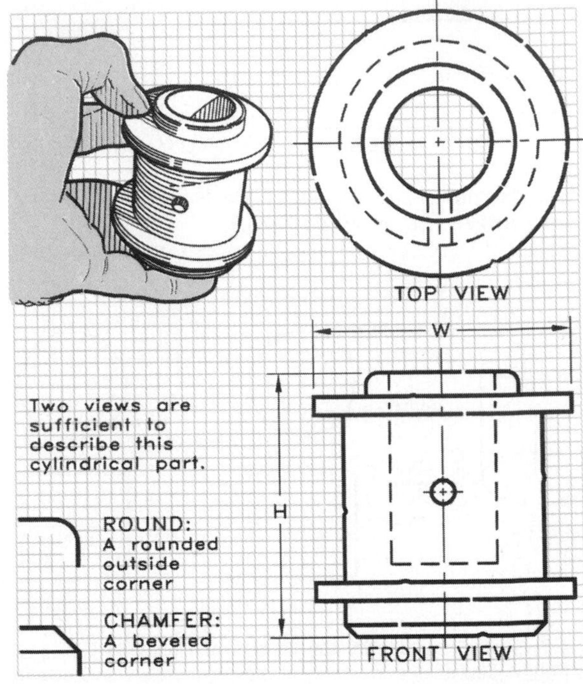

13.28 Two views adequately describe this cylindrical pivot base.

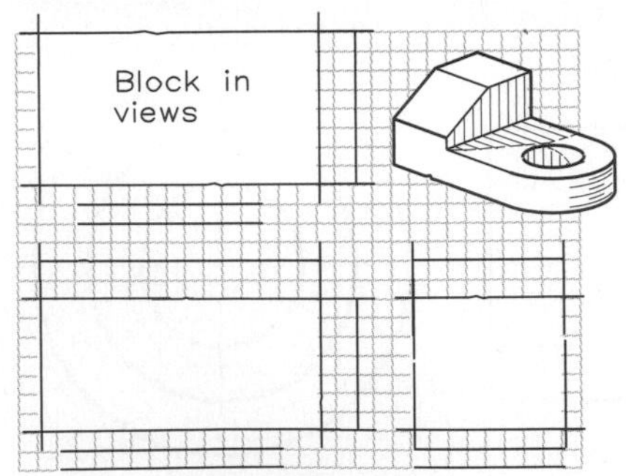

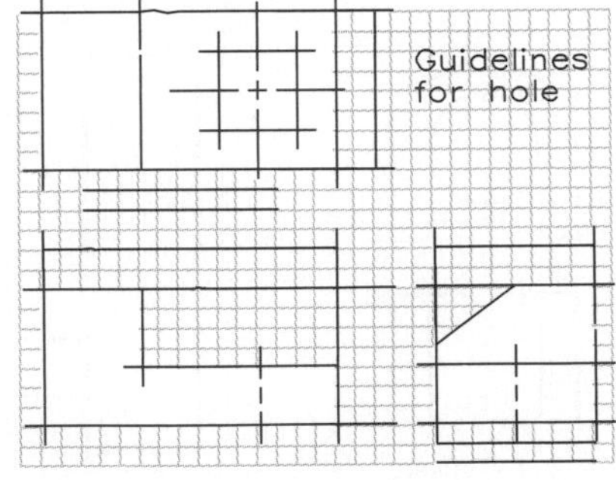

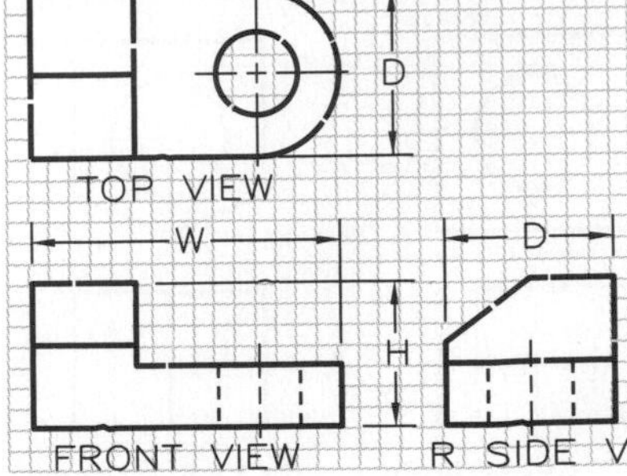

13.29 Sketching circular features.

Step 1 Begin by blocking in the overall dimensions with construction lines. Leave room for labels and dimensions.

Step 2 Draw the centerlines and the squares that block in the diameter of the circle. Find the slanted surface in the side view.

Step 3 Sketch the arcs, darken the lines, label the views, and show the dimensions W, D, and H between the views.

13.7 Pictorial Sketching: Obliques

An oblique pictorial is a three-dimensional representation of an object's height, width, and depth. It approximates a photograph of an object, making the sketch easier to understand at a glance than do orthographic views. Sketch the front of the object as a true-shape orthographic view (**Figure 13.30**). Sketch the receding axes at an angle of between 20° and 60° oblique to the horizontal in the front view. Lay off the depth dimension as its true length along the receding axes. When the depth is true length, the oblique is a **cavalier** oblique.

The major advantage of an oblique pictorial is the ease of sketching circular features as circular arcs on the true-size front plane. **Figure 13.31** shows an oblique sketch of a shaft block. Circular features on the receding planes appear as ellipses, requiring slanted guidelines, as shown.

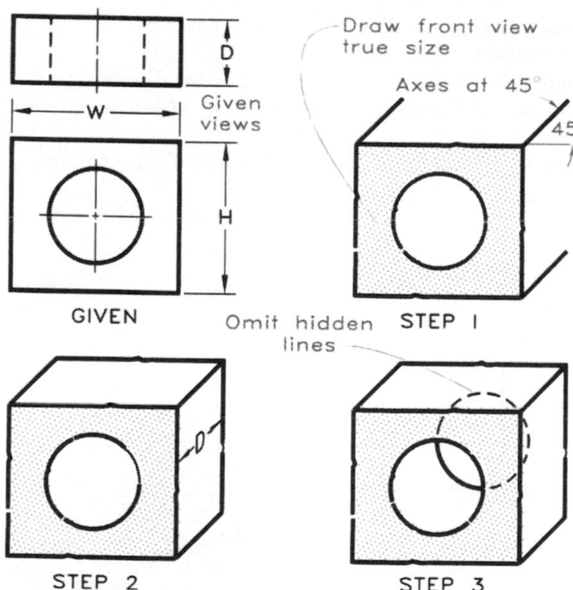

13.30 Sketching oblique pictorials.

Step 1 Sketch the front of the part as an orthographic front view and the receding lines at 45° to show the depth dimension.

Step 2 Measure the depth along the receding axes and sketch the back of the part.

Step 3 Locate the circle on the rear plane, show the visible portion of it, and omit the hidden lines.

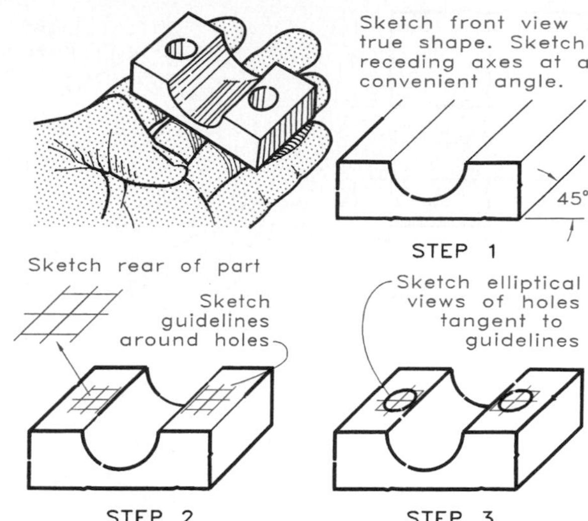

13.31 Sketching arcs in oblique pictorials.

Step 1 Sketch the front view of the mounting bracket saddle as a true front view. Sketch the receding axes from each corner.

Step 2 Sketch the rear of the part by measuring its depth along the receding axes. Sketch guidelines about the holes.

Step 3 Sketch the circular features as ellipses on the upper planes tangent to the guidelines.

13.8 Pictorial Sketching: Isometrics

Another type of three-dimensional representation is the isometric pictorial, in which the axes make 120° angles with one another (**Figure 13.32**). Specially printed isometric grids with

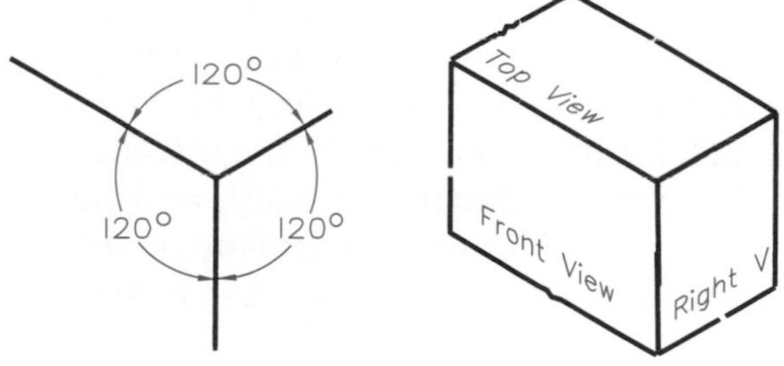

13.32 An isometric sketch.

A Begin an isometric pictorial by sketching three axes spaced 120° apart. One axis usually is vertical.

B Sketch the isometric shape parallel to the three axes and use its true measurements as the dimensions.

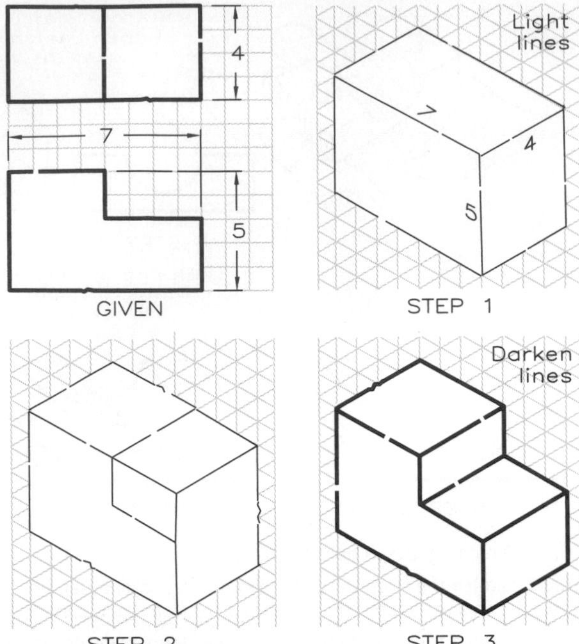

13.33 Sketching isometric pictorials.

Step 1 Use an isometric grid, transfer dimensions from the given views, and sketch a box having those dimensions.

Step 2 Locate the notch by measuring over four squares and down two squares, as shown in the orthographic views.

Step 3 Finish the notch and darken the lines.

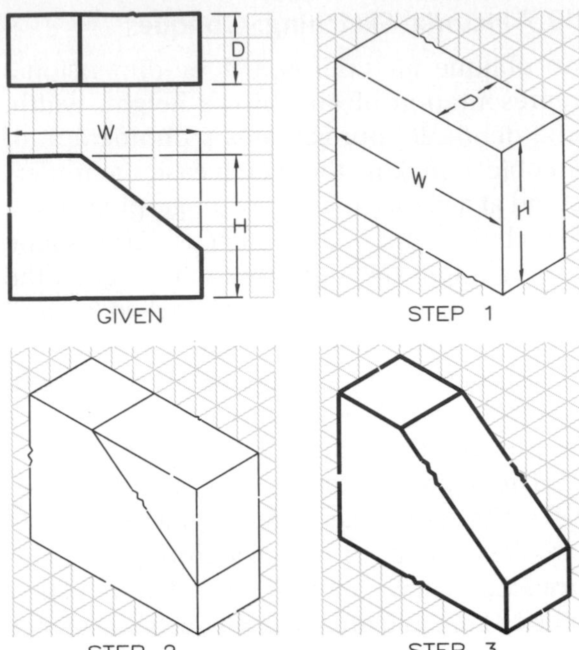

13.34 Sketching angles in isometric pictorials.

Step 1 Sketch a box from the overall dimensions given in the orthographic views.

Step 2 Angles cannot be measured with a protractor. Find each end of the angle with coordinates measured along the axes.

Step 3 Connect the ends of the angle and darken the lines.

lines intersecting at 60° angles make isometric sketching easier (**Figure 13.33**). Simply transfer the dimensions from the squares in the orthographic views to the isometric grid.

You cannot measure angles in isometric pictorials with a protractor; you must find them by connecting coordinates of the angle laid off along the isometric axes. In **Figure 13.34**, locate the ends of the angular plane by using the coordinates for width and height. When a part has two sloping planes that intersect (**Figure 13.35**), you must sketch them one

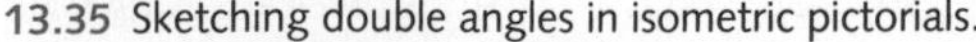

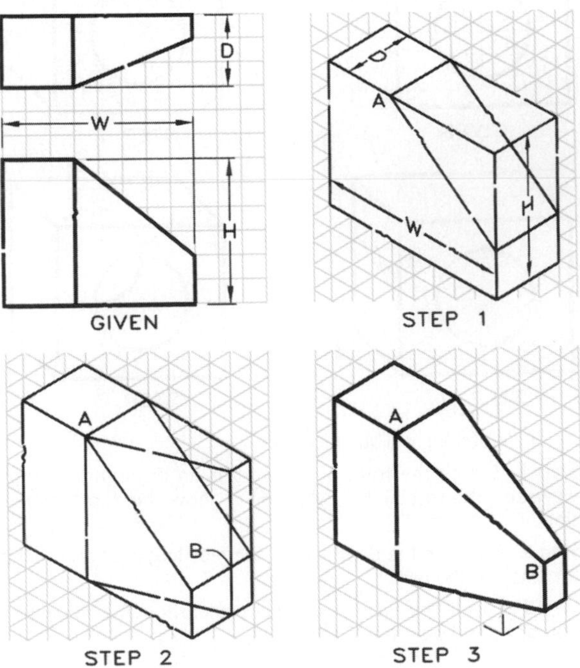

13.35 Sketching double angles in isometric pictorials.

Step 1 This object has two sloping angles that intersect; begin by sketching the overall box and draw one of the angles.

Step 2 Find the second angle, which locates point B, the intersection line between the planes.

Step 3 Connect points A and B and darken the lines. Line AB is the line of intersection between the two sloping planes.

at a time to find point B. Line AB is found as the line of intersection between the planes. Isometric drawing is covered more thoroughly in Chapter 25.

Circles in Isometric

Circles appear as ellipses in isometric pictorials. When you sketch them, begin with their centerlines and construction lines enclosing their diameters, as shown in **Figure 13.36**. The end of the block is semicircular in the front view, so its center must be equidistant from the top, bottom, and end of the front view. Circles and ellipses are easier to sketch if you use construction lines.

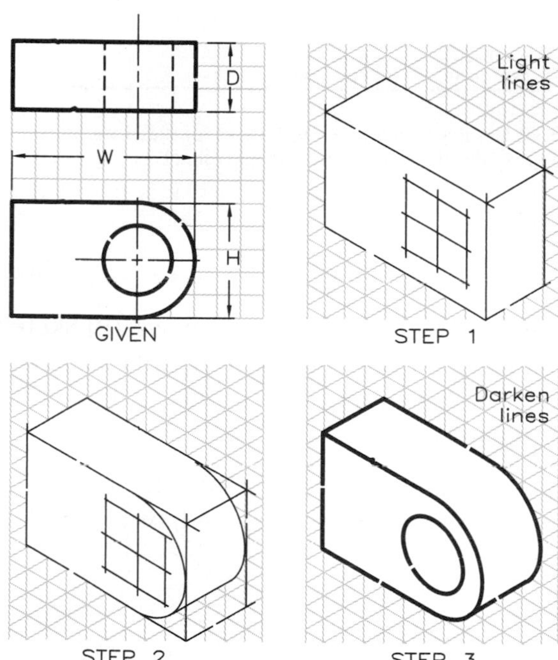

13.36 Sketching circles in isometric pictorials.

Step 1 Sketch a box using the overall dimensions given. Sketch the centerlines and a rhombus blocking in the circular hole.

Step 2 Sketch the isometric arcs tangent to the box. These arcs are elliptical rather than circular.

Step 3 Sketch the hole and darken the lines. Hidden lines usually are omitted in isometric pictorial sketches.

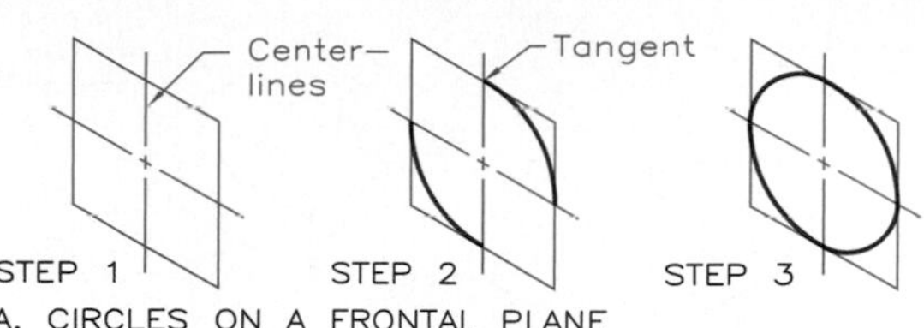

STEP 1 STEP 2 STEP 3

B. CIRCLES ON A HORIZONTAL PLANE

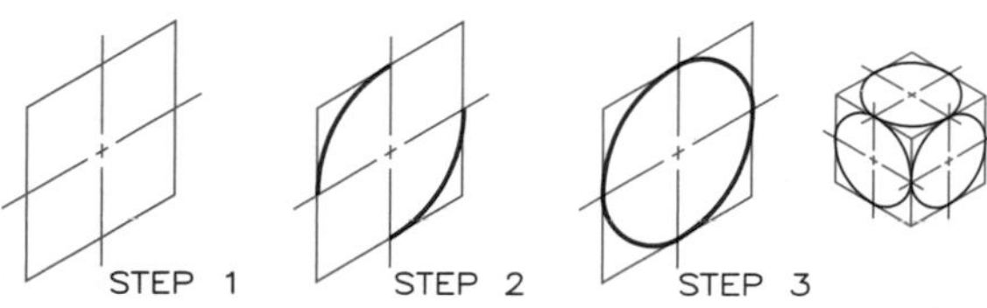

13.37 Sketching circular features in isometric.

Step 1 Lay out centerlines and guidelines.

Step 2 Sketch two opposite arcs.

Step 3 Connect the ends of the arcs to complete the ellipses.

Figure 13.37 shows how to use centerlines and construction lines to draw ellipses in the three isometric planes: frontal, horizontal (top), and profile (side) views. This technique is used to sketch a cylinder in **Figure 13.38**

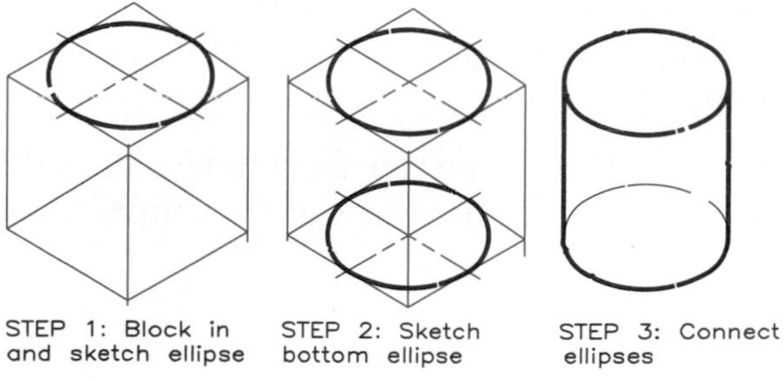

13.38 Sketching a cylinder as an isometric pictorial.

Step 1 Block in the cylinder and sketch the upper ellipse.

Step 2 Sketch the lower ellipse.

Step 3 Connect the ellipses with lines tangent to the elliptical ends and darken the lines.

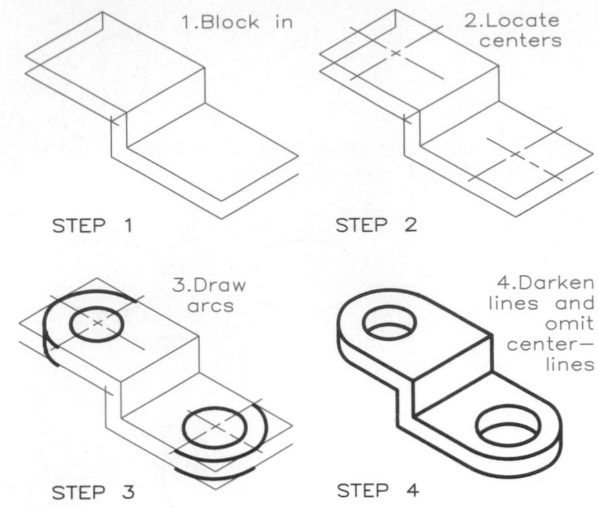

13.39 Sketching circular features in isometric pictorials.

Step 1 Block in the isometric shape of the object with light lines.

Step 2 Locate the centerlines of the holes and the rounded ends.

Step 3 Sketch the semicircular ends of the part and the holes.

Step 4 Draw the bottoms of the holes and darken the lines.

and an object having semicircular ends in **Figure 13.39**. Hidden lines are usually omitted in isometric drawings.

Problems

Sketch the problems in **Figures 13.41–13.43** on size A (8-1/2 × 11-in.) paper, with or without a printed grid as shown in **Figure 13.40**. Each grid is equal to 0.20 in., or approximately 5 mm.

1–24. (A) Sketch the top, front, and right-side views of the problems assigned; supply lines

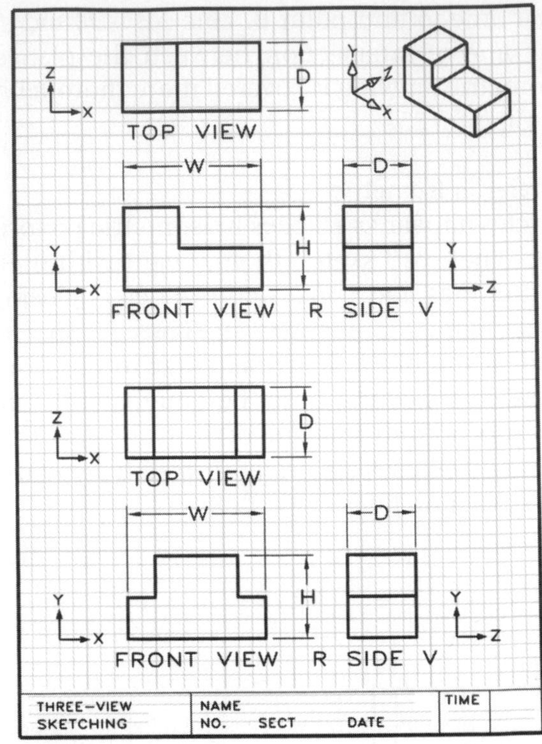

13.40 Use this layout of a size A sheet for sketching problems. You may sketch two problems on each sheet.

that may be missing from all views. (B) Sketch oblique pictorials of the problems assigned. (C) Sketch isometric pictorials of the problems assigned.

25–64. Sketch the top, front, and right-side views of the problems assigned, two problems per sheet.

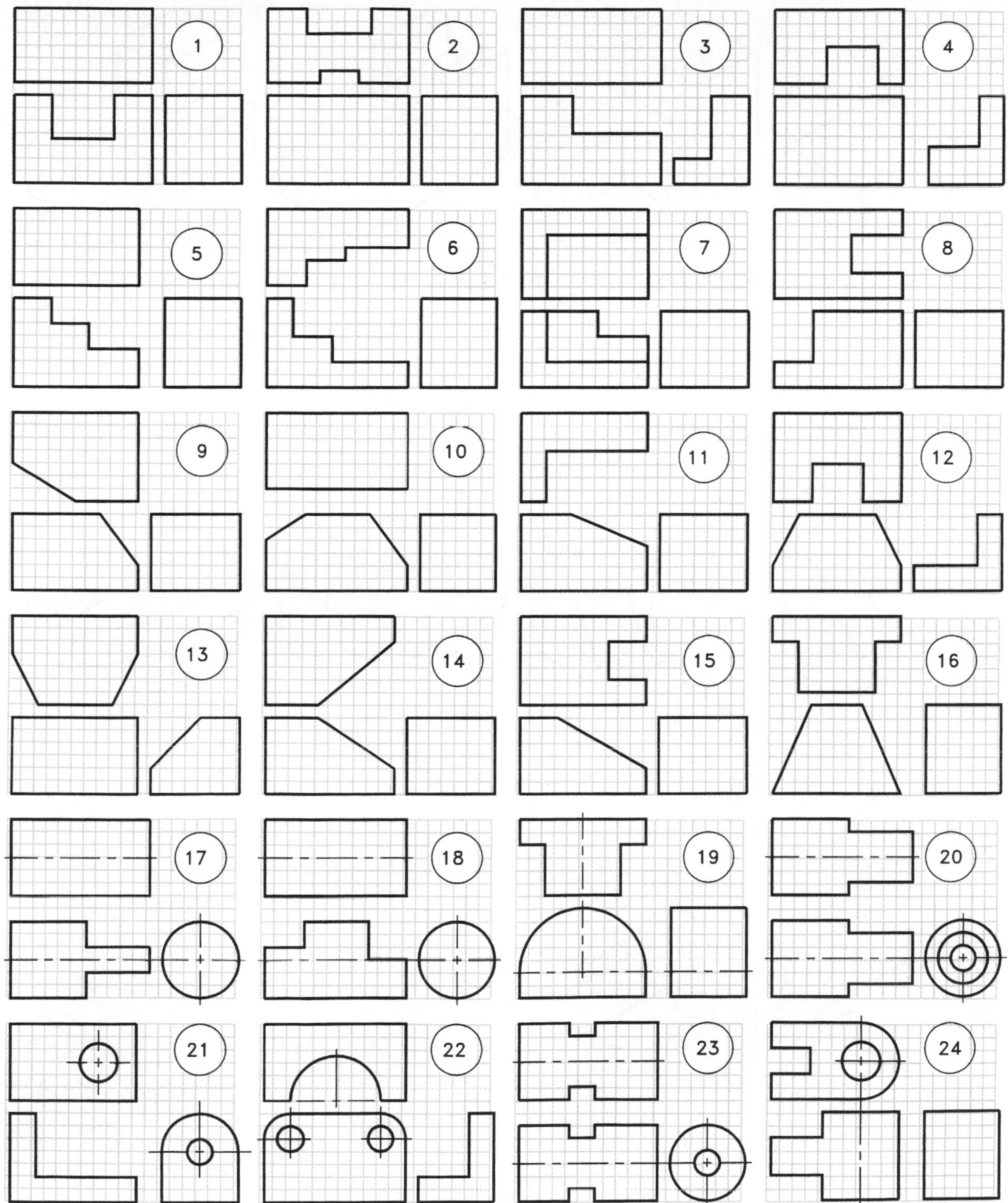

13.41 Problems 1–24.

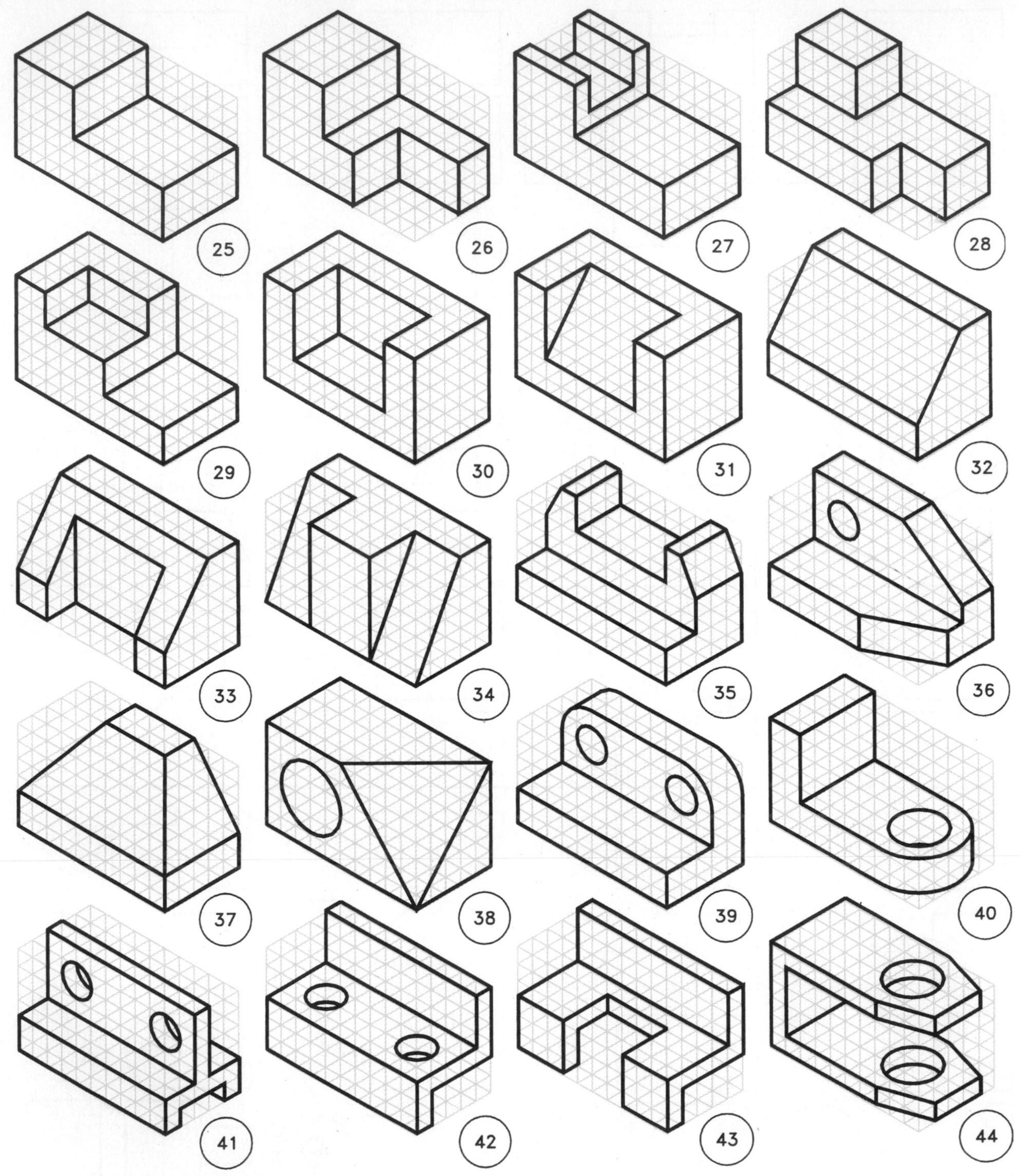

13.42 Problems 25–44.

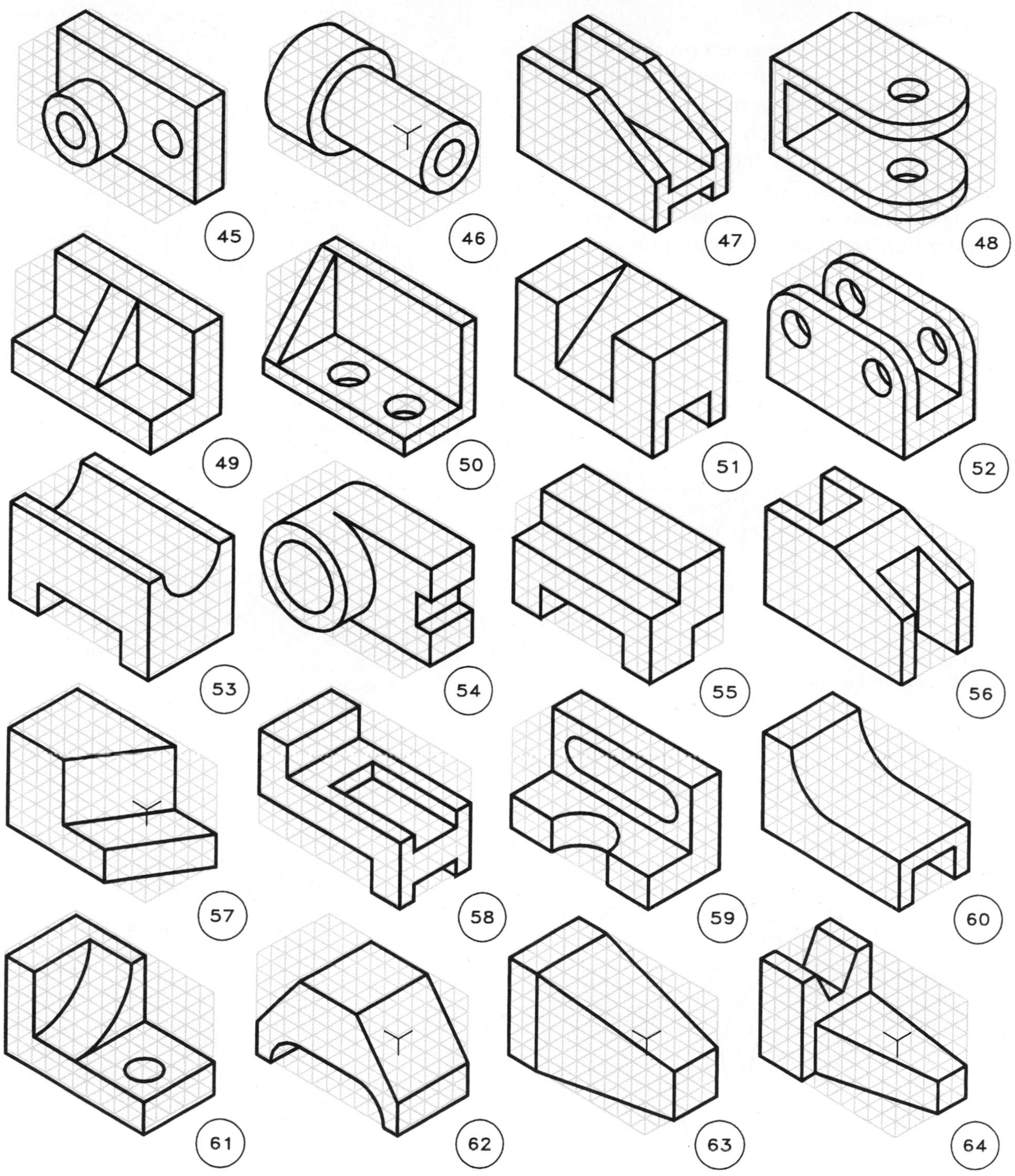

13.43 Problems 45–64.

Design Sketching

General dimensions are given on the following problems. You must determine all missing information as if you were the original designer of the parts. Sketch your solutions on size A sheets (8-1/2 × 11-in.), in either vertical or horizontal format. Consider how you would redesign each example to function as well as or better than the given configuration.

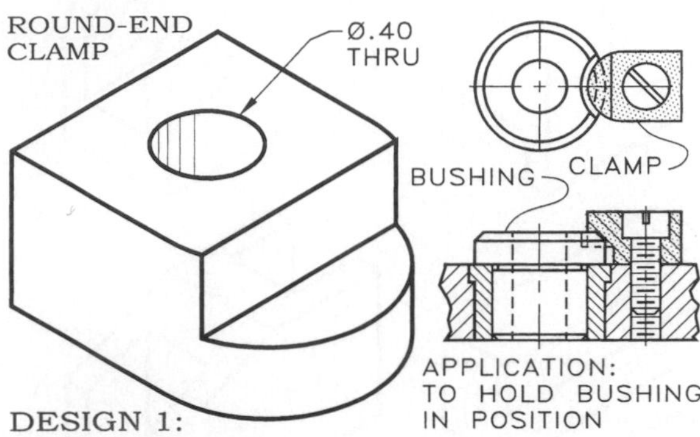

DESIGN 1:

Sketch the necessary views of the clamp on a size A sheet to describe its details. Sketch it as a pictorial as well and label all views.

DESIGN 2: Move the flange to the center of the part and show 6 holes instead of 4 and add 2 ribs on each side. Sketch the necessary views to describe the the new design. Label your sketches as needed.

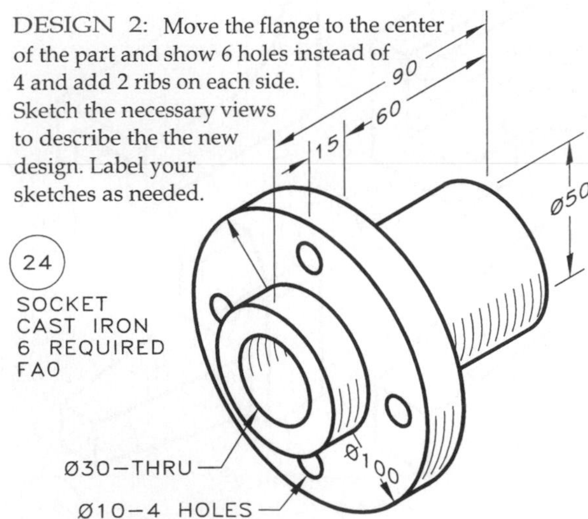

DESIGN 3: Sketch the necessary views of the clamp to describe its details on a size A sheet using the approximate dimensions.

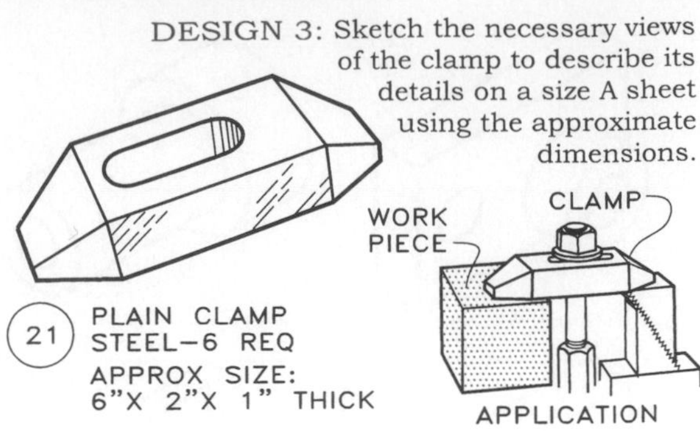

DESIGN 4: Sketch orthographic views of the parts of the hinge assembly on a size A sheet. Consider designing a better one. Estimate missing dimensions.

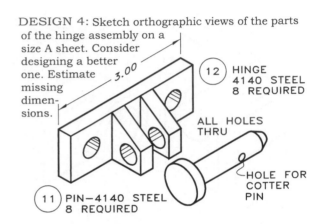

3.00

12 HINGE
4140 STEEL
8 REQUIRED

ALL HOLES
THRU

HOLE FOR
COTTER
PIN

11 PIN—4140 STEEL
8 REQUIRED

DESIGN 5: Reposition the rib of the strut brace to the center of its base. Sketch orthographic views of the modified part on a size A sheet. Approximate the missing dimensions.

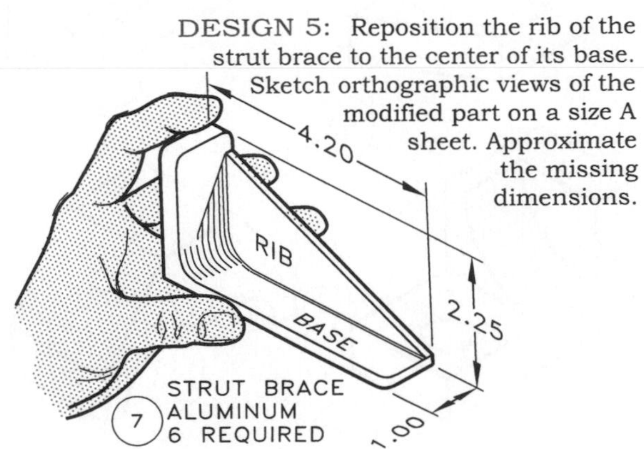

DESIGN 6: Sketch orthographic views necessary to describe the shaft swivel on a size A sheet. Determine the dimensions from the ones that are given.

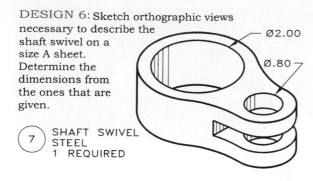

Ø2.00

Ø.80

7 SHAFT SWIVEL
STEEL
1 REQUIRED

DESIGN 7: Sketch the orthographic views of the handle on a size A sheet. Add a threaded hole at the bent end for a set screw to secure the square shaft to it.

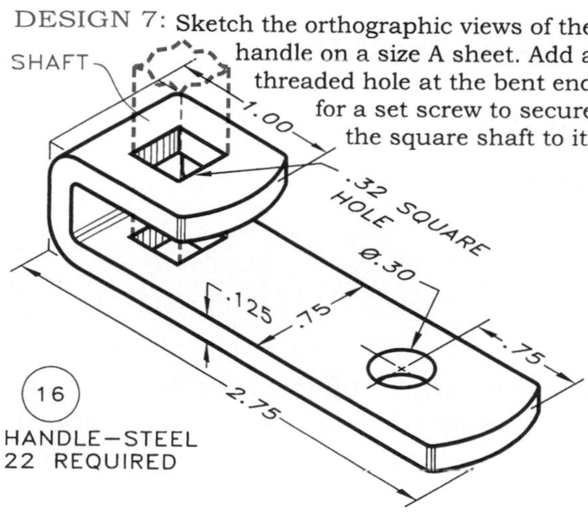

DESIGN 8: Modify the clevis to have semicircular ends about the 1.60 DIA holes and rounded corners concentric with the 4 holes. Sketch the views on a size A sheet.

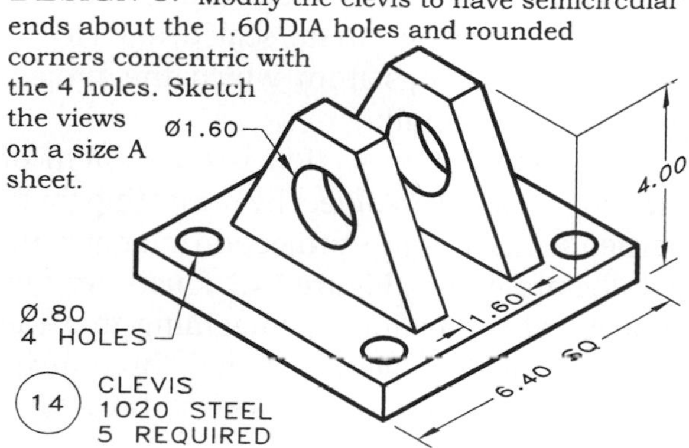

DESIGN 9: PULLEY ASSEMBLY

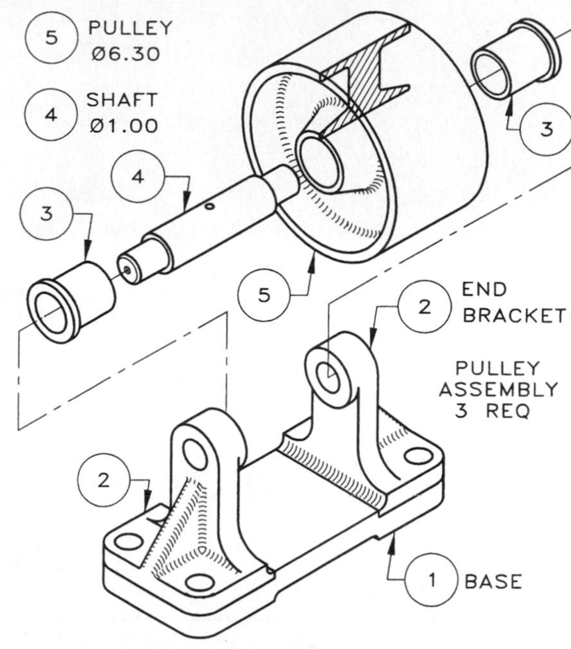

There are five parts in the pulley assembly shown in the design. Part 4 is a shaft with a 1.00-in. diameter, and part 5 is a pulley with a 6.30-in. diameter. Sketch orthographic views of each part on A size sheets following the instructions below.

Option 1: Make a two-view sketch of the shaft (part 4). Do you know why there are two holes in the shaft? Explain.

Option 2: Make a two-view drawing of the bushing (part 3). What are bushings and what is their purpose? Explain.

Option 3: Make a two-view drawing of the base (part 1). How are the brackets (part 2) connected to the base? Explain.

Option 4: Make a three-view drawing of the end brackets (part 2). How do the brackets support the shaft?

Option 5: Make a two-view orthographic drawing of the pulley (part 5).

Option 6: Redesign the bracket (part 2) and show your proposed modification in a three-view sketch. Use as many detail sketches as needed.

14

Orthographic Projection: Instruments

14.1 Introduction

In Chapter 13, you were introduced to orthographic projection by freehand sketching, which is an excellent way to develop a design concept. Now, you must convert these sketches into orthographic views drawn to scale with instruments (or by computer) to more precisely define your design. Afterward, you will add dimensions, notes, and specifications to convert these drawings into working drawings from which the design will become a reality.

Orthographic drawings are representations of three-dimensional objects in separate views arranged in a standard manner that are readily understood by the technological team. Because multiview drawings usually are executed with instruments and drafting aids, they are often called **mechanical drawings**. They are called **working drawings**, or **detail drawings**, when sufficient dimensions, notes, and specifications are added to enable the product to be manufactured or built from the drawings.

14.2 Orthographic Projection

An artist has the option of representing objects impressionistically, but the engineer must represent them precisely. Orthographic projection is used to prepare accurate, scaled, and clearly presented drawings from which the project depicted can be built.

Orthographic projection is the system of drawing views of an object by projecting them perpendicularly onto projection planes with parallel projectors. **Figure 14.1** illustrates this concept of projection by imagining that the object is inside a glass box and three of its views are projected to planes of the box.

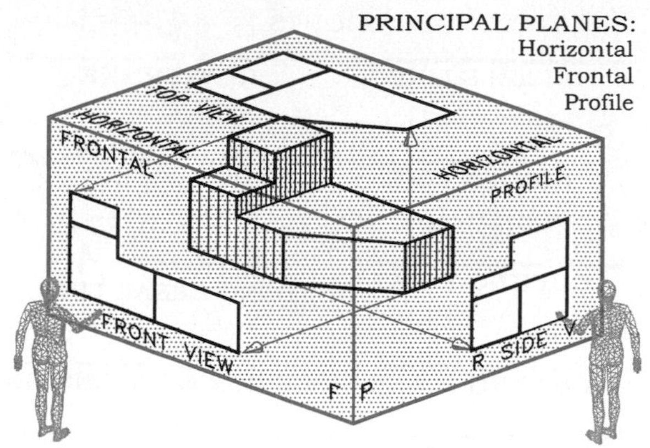

14.1 Orthographic projection is the system of projecting views onto an imaginary glass box with parallel projectors to the three mutually perpendicular projection planes.

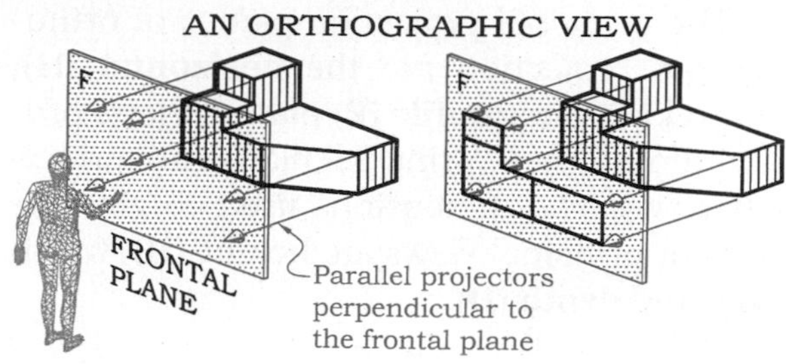

14.2 An orthographic view is found by projecting from the object to a projection plane with parallel projectors that are perpendicular to the projection plane.

Figure14.2 illustrates the principle of orthographic projection in which the front view is projected perpendicularly onto a vertical projection plane, called the *frontal plane,* with parallel projectors. The projected front view is two dimensional because it has only width and height and lies in a single plane.

Similarly, the top view is projected onto a horizontal projection plane, and the side view is projected onto a second vertical projection plane.

Imagine that the box is opened into the plane of the drawing surface. **Figure 14.3A** illustrates how three planes of a glass box are opened into a single plane (**Figure 14.3B**) to yield the standard positions for the three orthographic views. These views are the front, top, and right-side views.

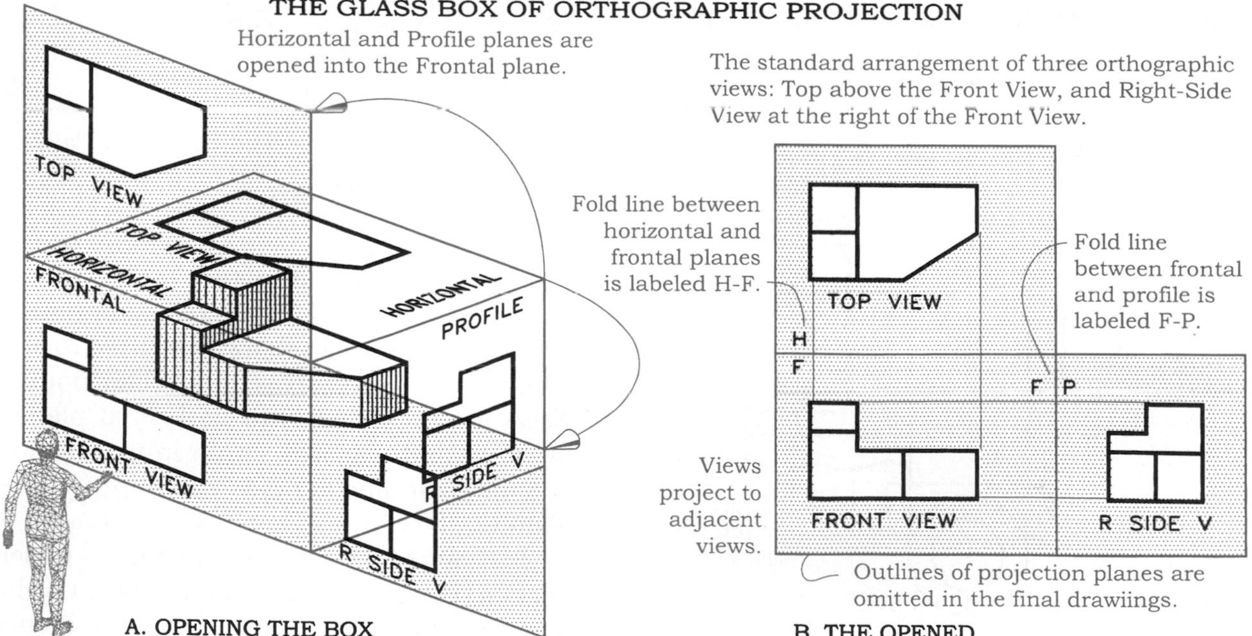

14.3 When the imaginary glass box is opened, the orthographic views and labeling are drawn in this format.

The principal projection planes of orthographic projection are the **horizontal (H)**, **frontal (F)**, and **profile (P)** planes. Views projected onto these principal planes are principal views. The dimensions used to give the sizes of principal views are **height (H)**, **width (W)**, and **depth (D)**.

14.3 Alphabet of Lines

Draw all orthographic views with dark and dense lines as if drawn with ink. Only the line widths should vary, except for guidelines and construction lines, which are drawn very lightly for layout and lettering. **Figure 14.4** gives examples of lines used in orthographic projection and the recommended pencil grades for them. The lengths of dashes in hidden lines and centerlines are drawn longer as a drawing's size increases. **Figure 14.5** further describes these lines.

14.4 Six-View Drawings

When you imagine that an object is inside a glass box, you will see two horizontal planes, two frontal planes, and two profile planes (**Figure 14.6**). Therefore, the maximum number of principal views that can be used to represent an object is six. The top and bottom views are projected onto horizontal planes, the front and rear views onto frontal planes, and the right- and left-side views onto profile planes.

To draw the six views on a sheet of paper, imagine the glass box is opened up into the plane of the drawing paper as shown in **Figure 14.7**. Place the top view over and the bottom view under the front view; place the right-side

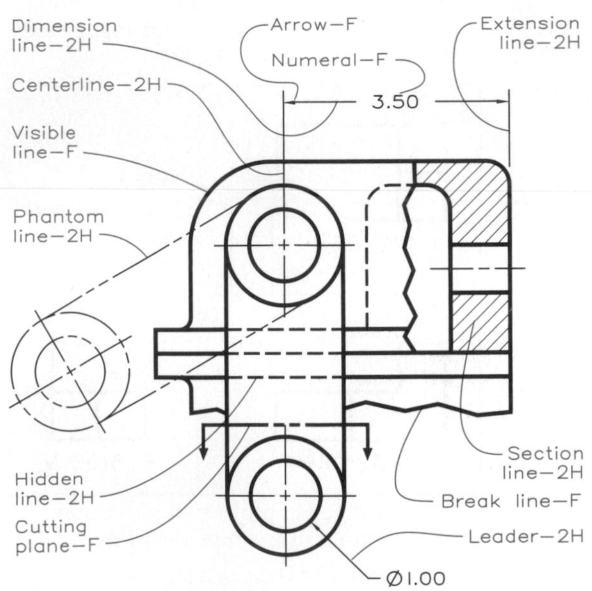

14.4 The alphabet of lines and recommended pencil grades for drawing orthographic views.

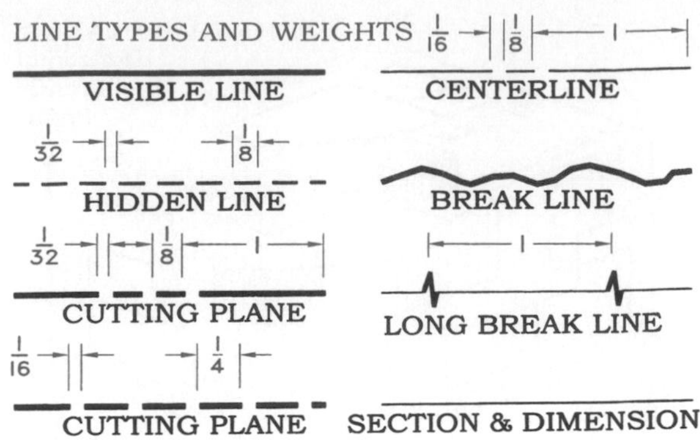

14.5 Full-size line weights are recommended for drawing orthographic views.

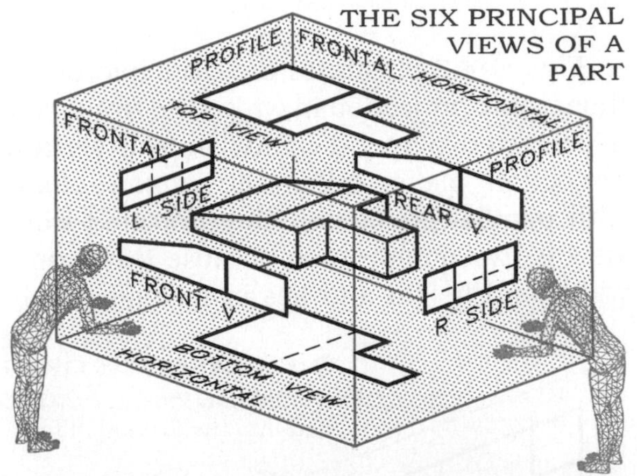

14.6 Six principal views of an object can be drawn in orthographic projection. Imagine that the object is in a glass box with the views projected onto its six planes.

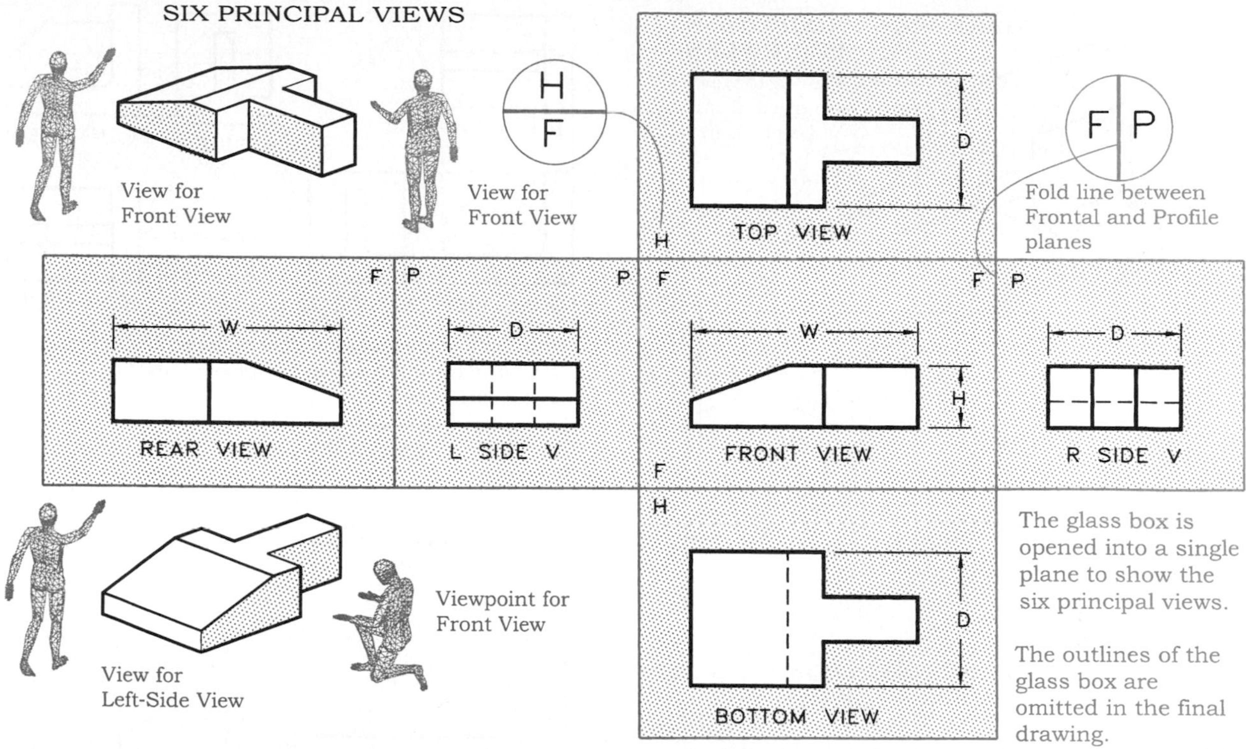

14.7 Opening the box into a single plane positions the six views as shown to describe the object.

view to the right and the left-side view to the left of the front view; and place the rear view to the left of the left-side view.

Projectors align the views both horizontally and vertically about the front view. Each side of the fold lines of the glass box is labeled **H, F,** or **P** (horizontal, frontal, or profile) to identify the projection planes on each side of the imaginary fold lines (**Figure 14.7**).

Height (H), width (W), and depth (D), the three dimensions necessary to dimension an object, are shown in their recommended positions in **Figure 14.7**. The standard arrangement of the six views allows the views to share dimensions by projection. For example, the height dimension, which is shown only once between the front and right-side views, applies to the four horizontally aligned views. The width dimension is placed between the top and front views, but applies to the bottom view also.

14.5 Three-View Drawings

The most commonly used orthographic arrangement of views is the three-view drawing, consisting of front, top, and right-side views. Imagine that the views of the object are projected onto the planes of the glass box (**Figure 14.8**) and the three planes are opened into a single plane, the frontal plane. **Figure 14.9** shows the resulting three-view drawing, in which the views are labeled and dimensioned with H, W, and D.

14.6 Arrangement of Views

Figure 14.10 shows the standard positions for a three-view drawing: The top and side views are projected from and aligned with the front

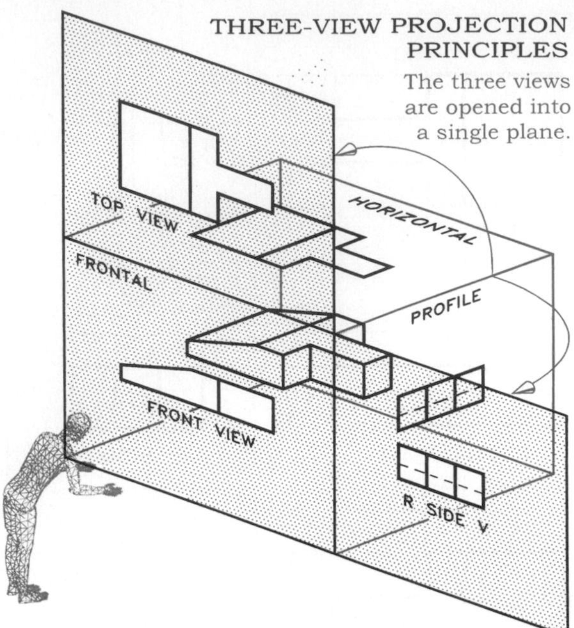

14.8 Three-view drawings are commonly used to describe small objects such as machine parts.

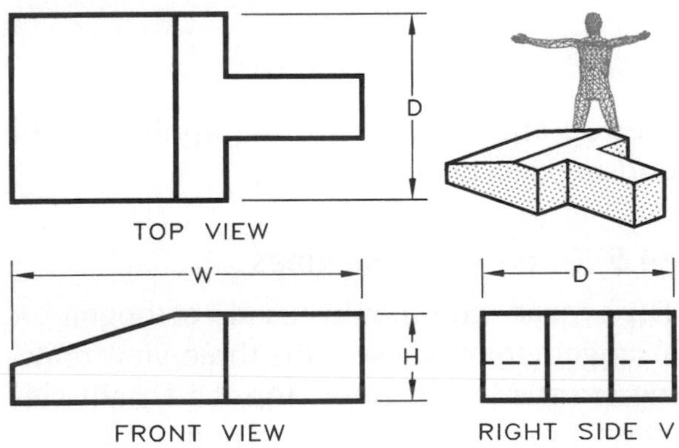

14.9 This three-view drawing depicts the object shown in **Figure 14.8.**

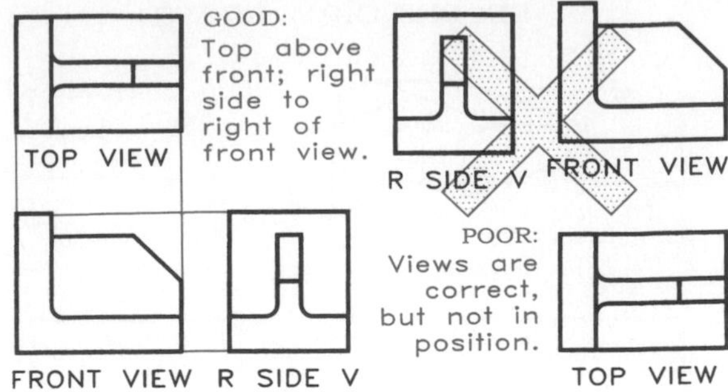

14.10 Orthographic views must be arranged in their proper positions in order for them to be interpreted correctly.

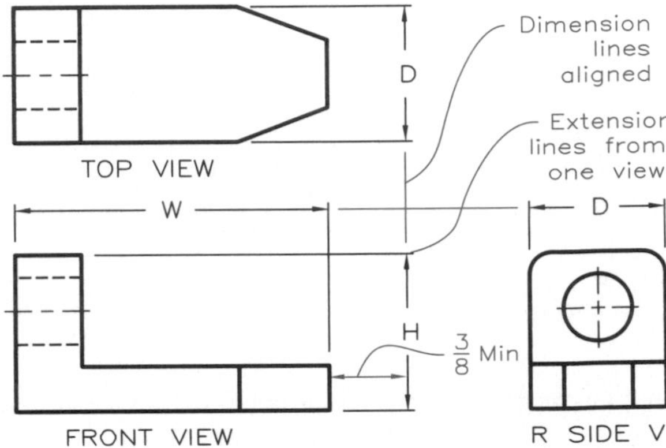

14.11 Dimension and extension lines used in three-view orthographic projection should be aligned. Draw extension lines from only one view when dimensions are placed between views.

view. Improperly arranged views that do not project from view to view are also shown. **Figure 14.11** illustrates the rules of projection and shows the proper alignment of dimensions. Orthographic projection shortens layout time, improves readability, and reduces the number of dimensions required because they are placed between and are shared by the views to which they apply.

14.7 Selection of Views

Select the sequence of orthographic views with the fewest hidden lines. **Figure 14.12A** shows that the right-side view is preferable to the left-side view because it has fewer hidden lines. Although the three-view arrangement of top, front, and right-side views is more commonly used, the top, front, and left-side view arrangement is acceptable (**Figure 14.12B**) if the left-side view has fewer hidden lines than the right-side view.

The most descriptive view usually is selected as the front view. If an object, such as a chair, has predefined views that people generally recognize as the front and top views, you should label the accepted front view as the orthographic front view.

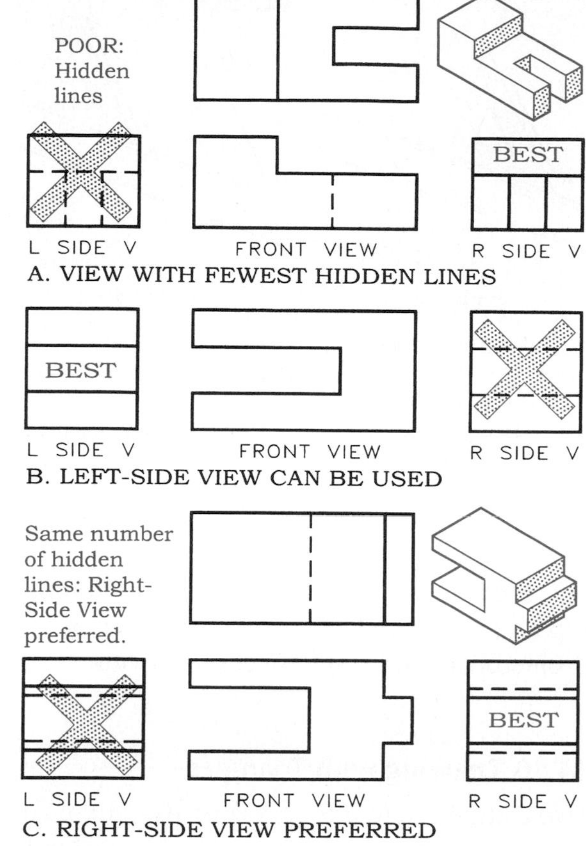

14.12 Selection of views.

A Select the sequence of views with the fewest hidden lines.

B Select the left-side view because it has fewer hidden lines than the right-side view.

C When both views have an equal number of hidden lines, select the right-side view.

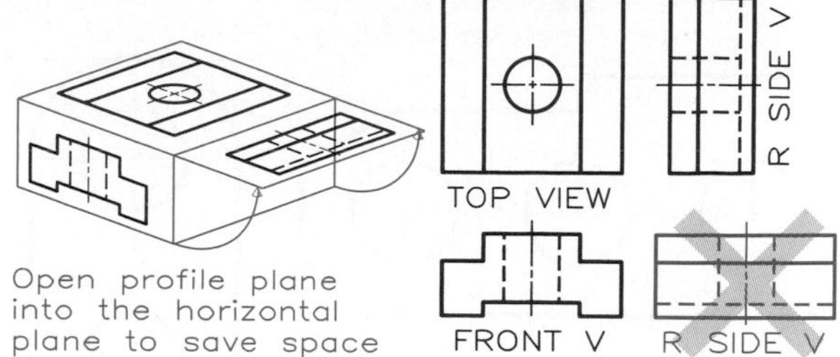

14.13 The side view can be projected from the top view instead of the front view. This alternative position saves space when the depth of an object is considerably greater than its height.

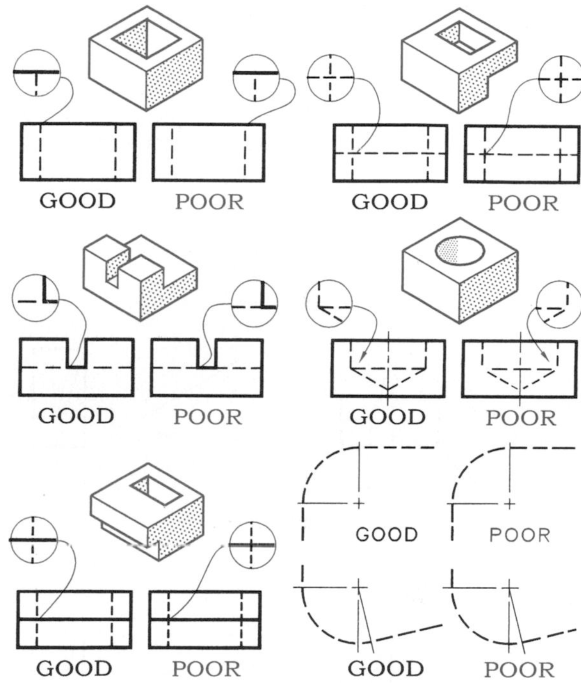

14.14 These drawings show proper intersections and other line techniques in orthographic views.

Although the right-side view usually is placed to the right of the front view, the side view can be projected from the top view (**Figure 14.13**). This alternative position is advisable when the object has a much larger depth than height.

14.8 Line Techniques

Figure 14.14 illustrates techniques for handling most types of intersecting lines, hidden lines, and arcs in combination. Proper application of these principles improves the readability of orthographic drawings.

Become familiar with the order of importance (precedence) of lines (**Figure 14.15**). The most important line, the visible object line, is shown regardless of any other line lying behind it. Of next importance is the hidden line, which is more important than the centerline.

14.9 Point Numbering

Some orthographic views are difficult to draw because of their complexity. Numbering the endpoints of the lines of the parts in each view

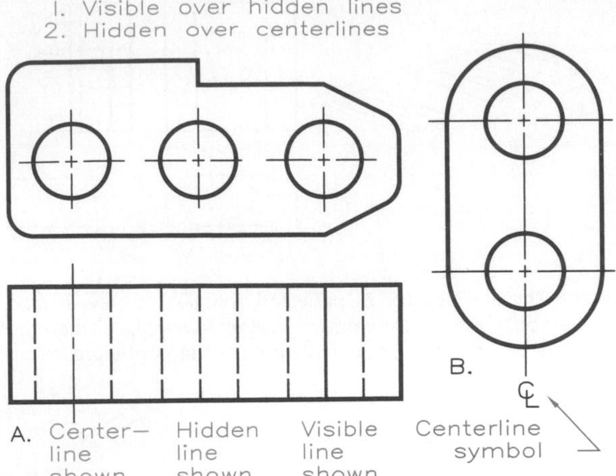

14.15 When lines coincide, the more important lines take precedence (cover up) the other lines. The order of importance is visible lines, hidden lines, and centerlines.

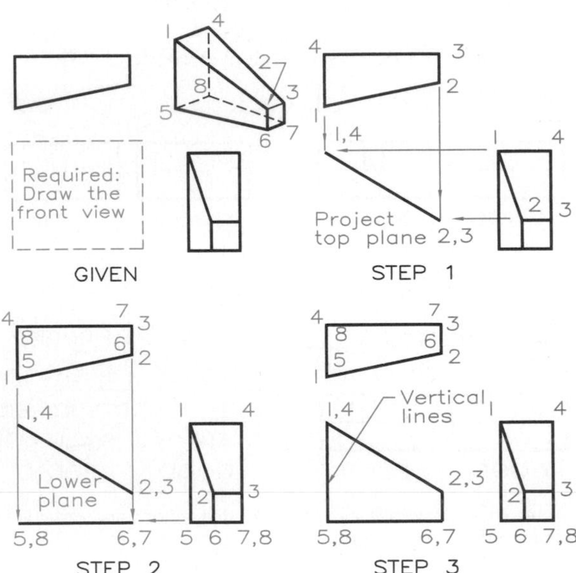

14.16 Point numbering.
Required: Draw the front view.

Step 1 Number the corners of plane 1-2-3-4 in the top and side views and project these points to the front view.

Step 2 Number the corners of plane 5-6-7-8 in the top and side views and project these points to the front view.

Step 3 Connect the numbered lines to complete the front view.

as you construct it (**Figure 14.16**) makes location of the object's features easier. For example, using numbers on the top and side views of this object aids in the construction of the missing front view. Projecting points from the top and side views to the intersections of the projectors locates the object's front view.

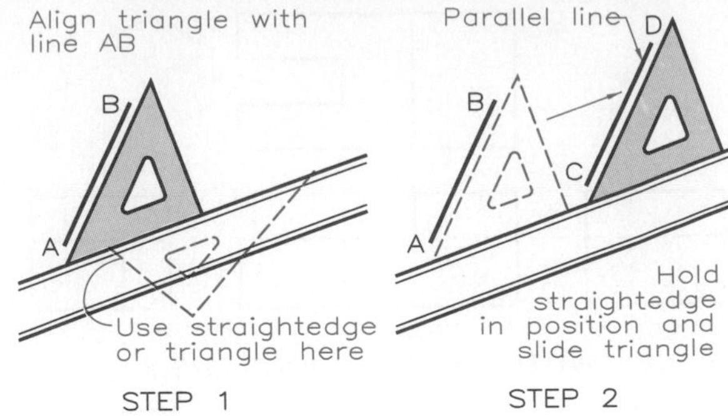

14.17 Drawing parallel lines.

Step 1 Align the upper triangle with AB and in contact with the lower triangle (or straightedge).

Step 2 Hold the lower triangle in position and slide the upper triangle to where CD is drawn parallel to AB.

14.10 Drawing with Triangles

Two triangles can effectively be used to make instrument drawings on 8-1/2 × 11-in. sheets without taping the sheet to the drawing surface. It is better to be able to move the sheet about to comfortably position the triangles.

Parallel lines The 45° triangle or the 30°-60° triangle can be used to draw parallel lines as shown in **Figure 14.17**. One triangle or a straightedge is held in position while the other triangle is moved to where the parallel line is drawn.

Perpendiculars To draw a line perpendicular to AB in **Figure 14.18**, align the hypotenuse side of the 30°-60° triangle with AB and against the lower triangle or straightedge. Hold the lower triangle in position and rotate the triangle so that the hypotenuse side is perpendicular to AB and draw CD.

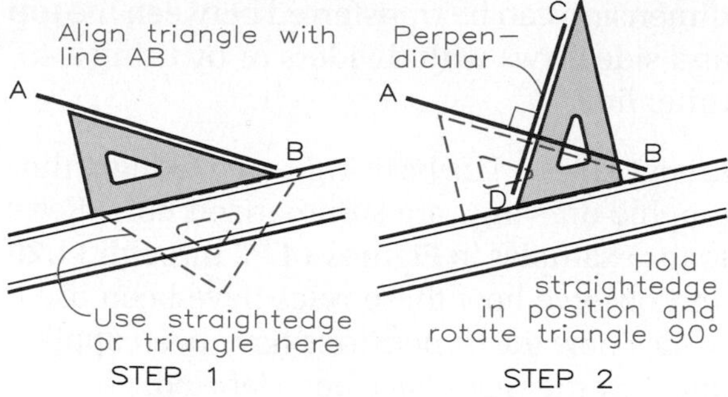

14.18 Drawing perpendiculars.

Step 1 Align your triangle with line AB and in contact with the lower triangle (or straightedge).

Step 2 Hold the lower triangle in position, rotate your triangle, and draw CD perpendicular to AB.

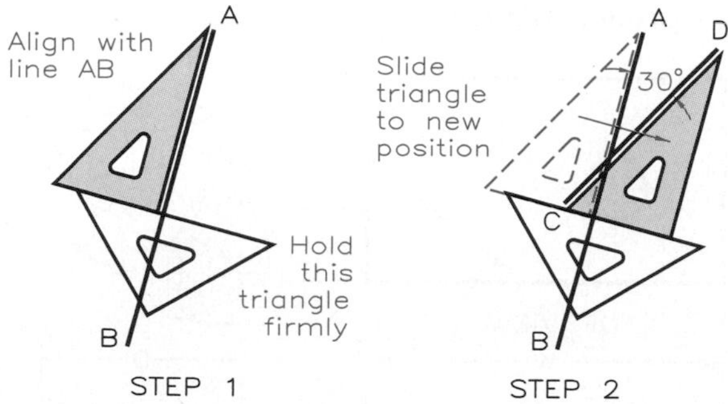

14.19 Drawing a 30° angle.

Step 1 Hold the 30°-60° triangle aligned with AB and in contact with the lower triangle (or straightedge).

Step 2 Hold the straightedge in position and slide the triangle and draw CD at 30° to AB.

Angles To draw a line making 30° with AB, use the steps shown in **Figure 14.19**. Two triangles can be used in other combinations to make instrument drawings in this informal manner yet with a sufficient degree of accuracy.

14.11 Views by Subtraction

Figure 14.20 illustrates how three views of a part are drawn by beginning with a block having the overall height, width, and depth of the finished part and removing volumes from it. This drawing procedure is similar to the steps of making the part in the shop.

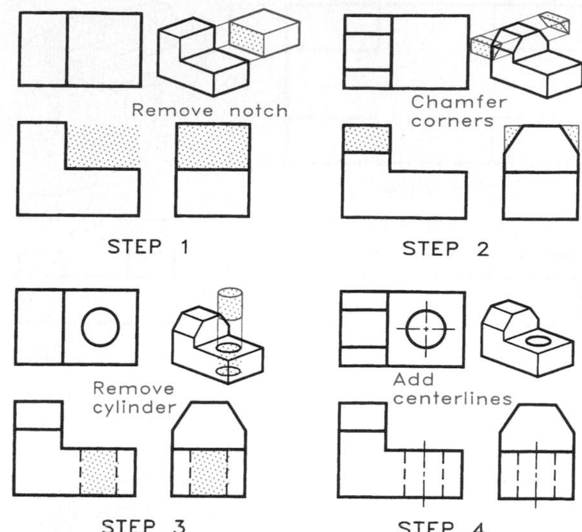

14.20 Views by subtraction.

Step 1 Block in the views of the object using overall dimensions of H, W, and D. Create the notch by removing the block.

Step 2 Remove the triangular volumes at the corners.

Step 3 Form the hole by removing a cylindrical volume.

Step 4 Add centerlines to complete the views.

14.12 Three-View Drawings

The depth dimension applies to both the top and side views, but these views usually are positioned where depth does not project between them (**Figure 14.21**). The depth

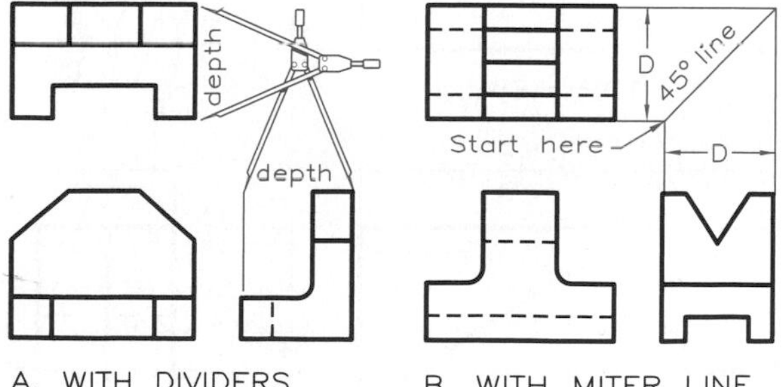

14.21 Transferring depth.

A Transfer the depth dimension to the side view from the top view with your dividers.

B Use a 45° miter line to transfer the depth dimension between the top and side views by projection.

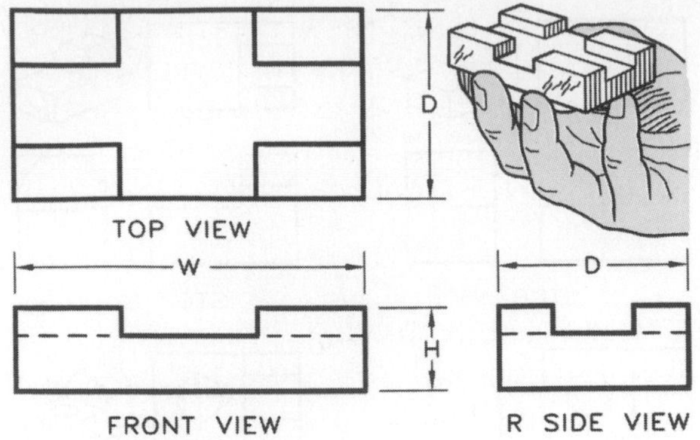

14.22 This three-view drawing depicts an object that has only horizontal and vertical planes.

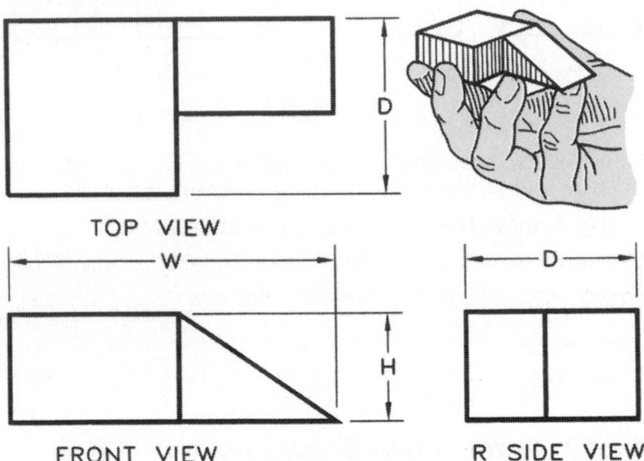

14.23 This three-view drawing shows an object that has a sloping plane.

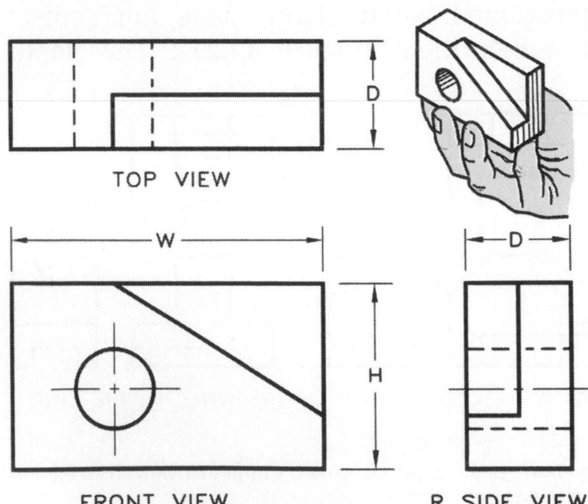

14.24 This three-view drawing shows an object that has a sloping plane with a cylindrical hole through it.

dimension can be transferred between the top and side views with dividers or by using a 45° miter line.

Layout Rules The basic rules of making orthographic drawings are summarized here. Refer to the examples in **Figures 14.22** through **14.26** and observe how these rules have been used. Notice how the dimensions have been applied and how the views have been labeled.

1. **Draw orthographic views in their proper positions.**

2. **Select the most descriptive view as the front view, if the object does not have a predefined front view.**

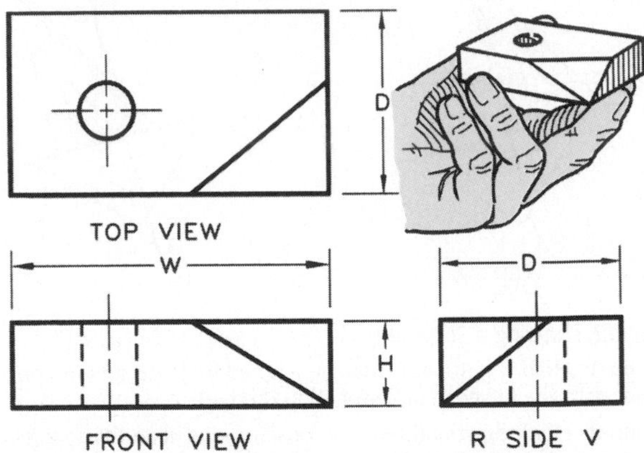

14.25 This three-view drawing depicts an object that has a plane with a compound slope.

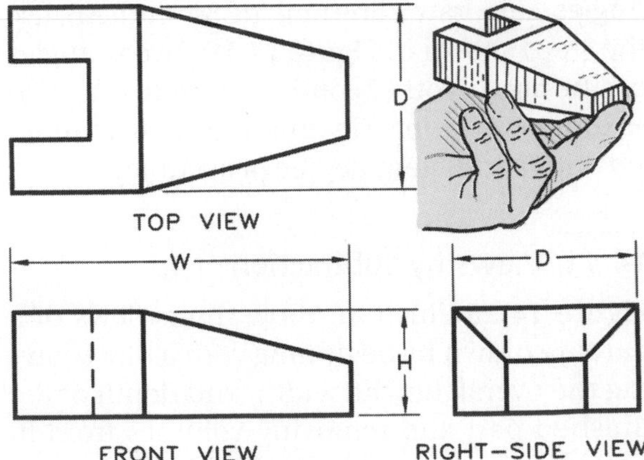

14.26 This three-view drawing shows an object that has planes with compound slopes.

3. **Select the sequence of views with the fewest hidden lines.**
4. **Label the views; for example, top view, front view, and right-side view.**
5. **Place dimensions between the views to which they apply.**
6. **Use the proper alphabet of lines.**
7. **Leave adequate room between the views for labels and dimensions.**
8. **Draw the views necessary to describe a part. Sometimes fewer or more views are required.**

14.13 Views by AutoCAD

The steps of drawing three orthographic views of an object are shown in **Figure 14.27**, where the *Line* command is used to draw the overall outlines of the three views. Other visible and hidden lines are added in by projecting from view to view. The *Dtext* command is used to label the views if this is desired. Additional details of using the *Line* command can be found in Chapter 37.

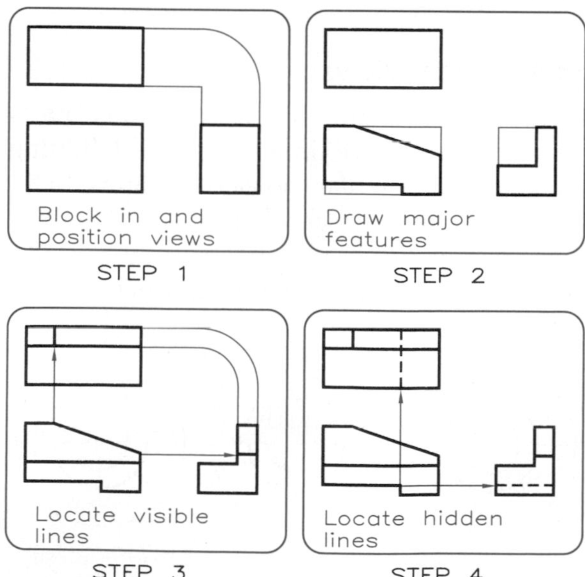

14.27 Three views by AutoCAD.
Step 1 With the *Line* command draw the outlines of the views.
Step 2 Draw the major features as orthographic views.
Step 3 Draw the visible lines.
Step 4 Draw the hidden lines.

14.14 Two-View Drawings

Time and effort can be saved by drawing only the views and features that are necessary to describe a part. **Figure 14.28** shows typical objects that require only two views necessary to be described. The fixture block in **Figure 14.29** is another example of a part needing only two views to be adequately described. You can see that the top and front views are

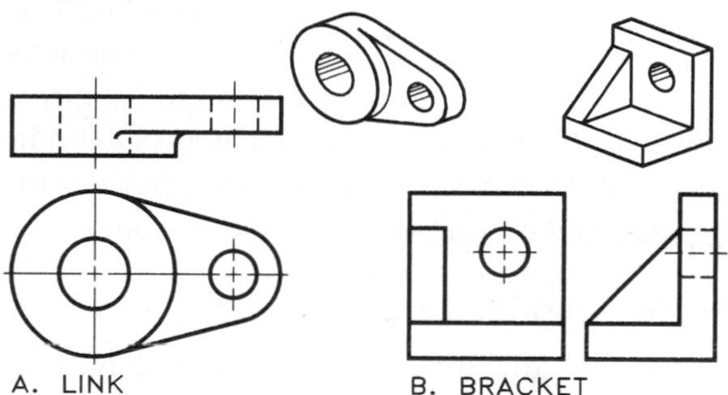

14.28 These objects can be adequately described with two orthographic views.

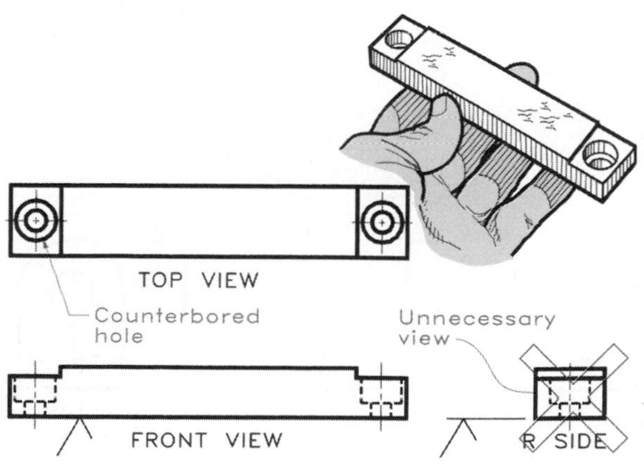

14.29 Two views adequately describe this part.

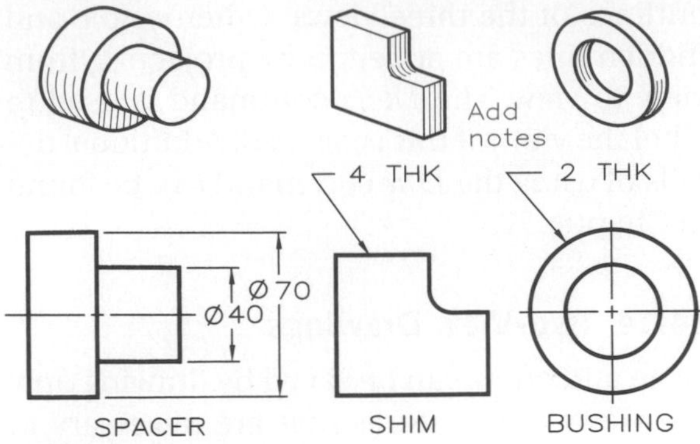

14.30 Objects that are cylindrical or of a uniform thickness can be described with only one orthographic view and supplementary notes.

the best for this part. The front and side views would not be as good.

14.15 One-View Drawings

Simple cylindrical parts and parts of a uniform thickness can be described by only one view, as shown in **Figure 14.30**. Supplementary notes clarify features that would have been shown in the omitted views. Diameters are labeled with diameter signs, and thicknesses are noted.

14.16 Simplified and Removed Views

The right- and left-side views of the part in **Figure 14.31** would be harder to interpret if all hidden lines were drawn by rigorously following the rules of orthographic projection. Simplified views in which confusing and unnecessary lines have been omitted are better and more readable.

When it is difficult to show a feature with a standard orthographic view because of its location, a **removed view** can be drawn (**Figure 14.32**). The removed view, indicated by the directional arrows, is clearer when moved to an isolated position.

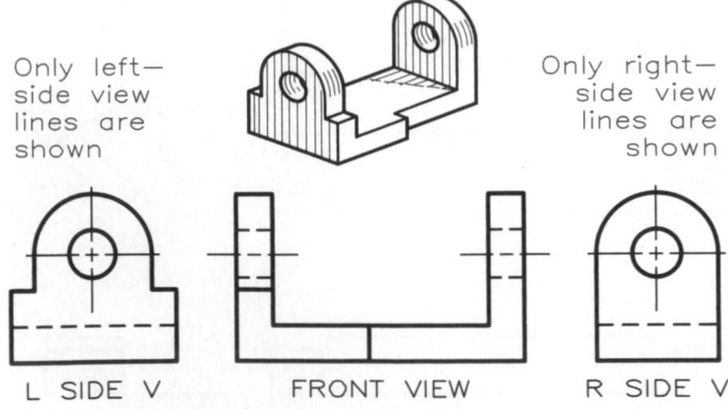

14.31 Use simplified views with unnecessary and confusing hidden lines omitted to improve clarity.

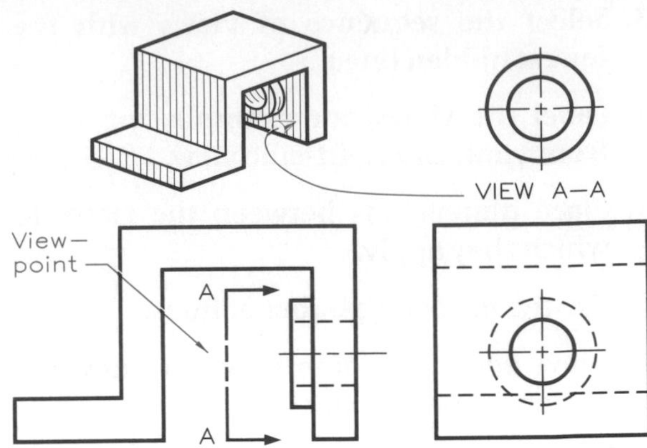

14.32 Use a removed view, indicated by the directional arrows, to show hard-to-see views in removed locations.

14.17 Partial Views

Partial views of symmetrical or cylindrical parts may be used to save time and space. Omitting the rear of the circular top view in **Figure 14.33** saves space without sacrificing clarity. To clarify that a part of the view has been omitted, a conventional break is used in the top view.

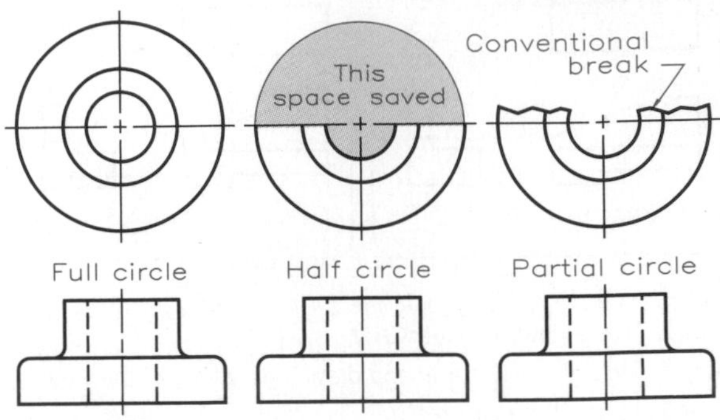

14.33 Save space and time by drawing the circular view of a cylindrical part as a partial view.

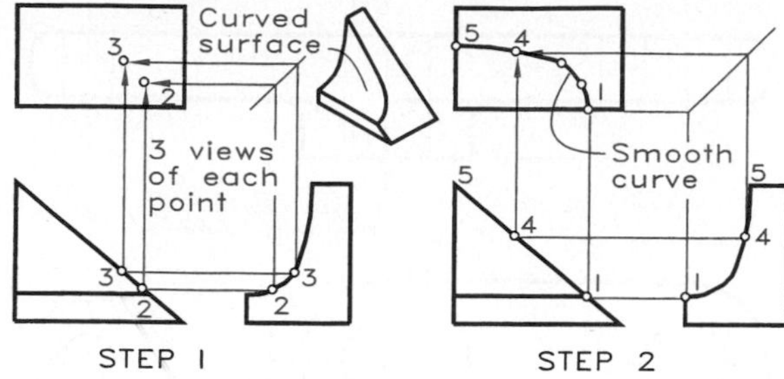

14.34 Curve plotting.

Step 1 Locate points 2 and 3 in the front and side views by projection. Project points 2 and 3 to the top view.

Step 2 Locate the remaining points in the three views and connect the points in the top view with a smooth curve.

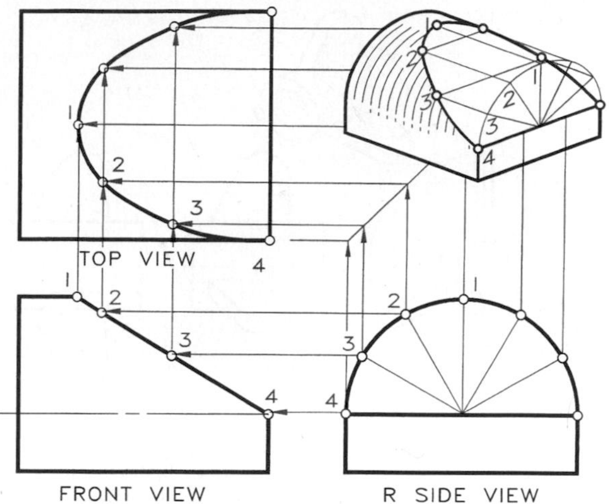

14.35 The ellipse in the top view was found by numbering points in the front and side views and projecting them to the top view.

14.18 Curve Plotting

An irregular curve can be plotted by following the rules of orthographic projection as shown in **Figure 14.34**. Begin by numbering the points in the given front and side views along the curve. Next, project from the points having the same numbers in the front and side views to the top to where the projectors intersect. Continue projecting in this manner, then connect the points in the top view with a smooth curve drawn with an irregular curve. **Figure 14.35** shows an ellipse plotted in the top view by projecting points from front and side views. It is best to number points as they are transferred one at a time to avoid getting lost in your construction.

14.19 Conventional Practices

The readability of an orthographic view may be improved if the rules of projection are violated. Violations of rules customarily made for the sake of clarity are called **conventional practices**.

Symmetrically spaced holes in a circular plate (**Figure 14.36**) are drawn at their true radial distance from the center of the plate in the front view as a conventional practice. Imagine that the holes are revolved to the centerline in the top view before projecting them to the front view.

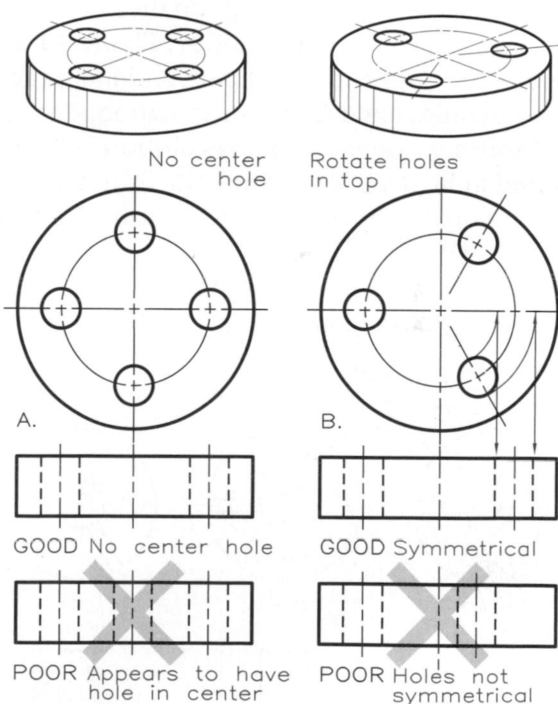

14.36 Placement of holes.

A Omit the center hole found by true projection that gives an impression that a hole passes through the center of the plate.

B Use a conventional view to show the holes located at their true radial distances from the center. They are imagined to be rotated to the centerline in the top view.

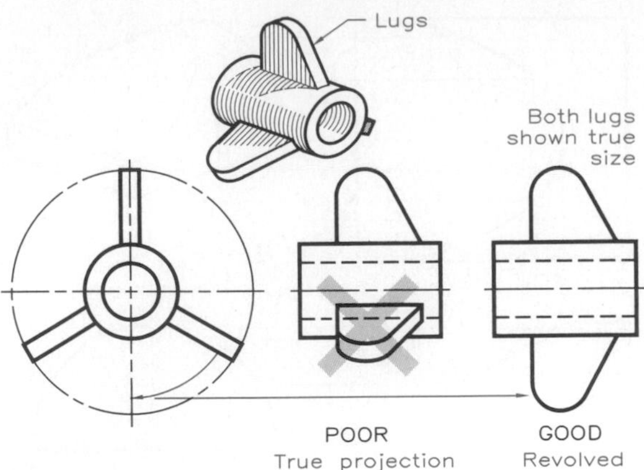

14.37 Symmetrically positioned external features, such as webs, ribs, and these lugs, are imagined to be revolved to their true-size positions for the best views.

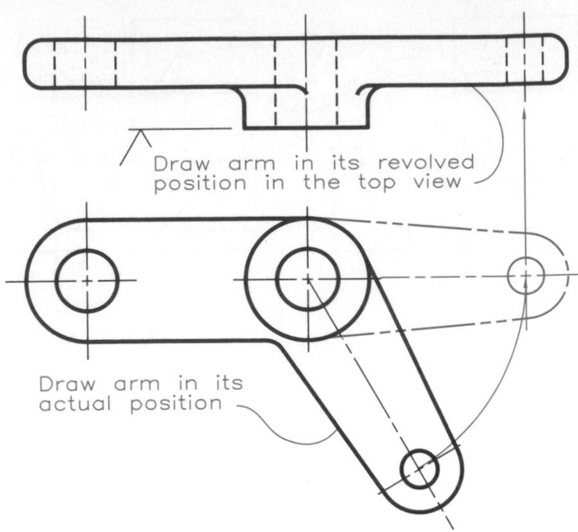

14.39 Imagine that the front view of the arm is revolved so its true length can be drawn in the top view as a conventional practice.

This principle of revolution also applies to symmetrically positioned features such as ribs, webs, and the three lugs on the outside of the part shown in **Figure 14.37**. **Figure 14.38** shows the applications of conventional practices to holes and ribs in combination.

Another conventional revolution is illustrated in **Figure 14.39** where the front view of an inclined arm is revolved to a horizontal position so that it can be drawn true size in the top view. The revolved arm in the front view is not drawn because the revolution is imaginary.

Figure 14.40 shows how to improve views of parts by conventional revolution. By revolving the top views of these parts 45°, slots and holes no longer coincide with the centerlines and can be seen more clearly. Draw the front

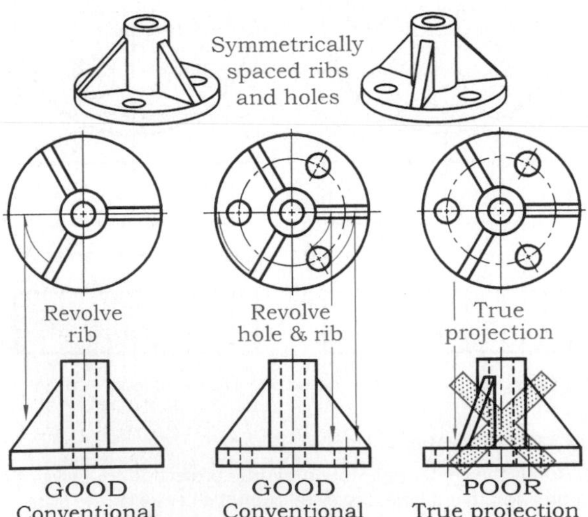

14.38 Conventional methods of revolving holes and ribs in combination improve clarity.

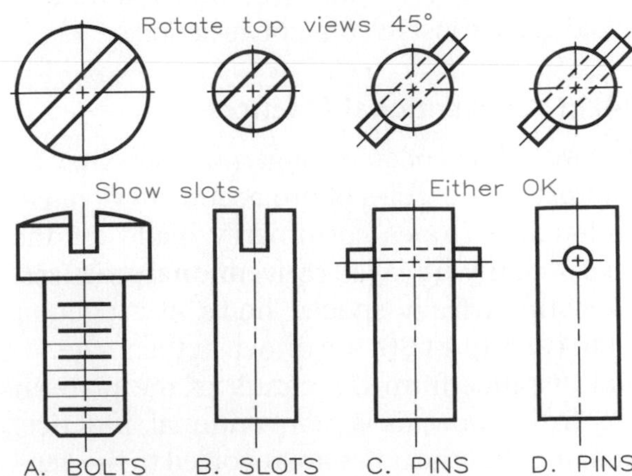

14.40 It is conventional practice to draw the slots and holes at 45° in the top view and true size in the front view.

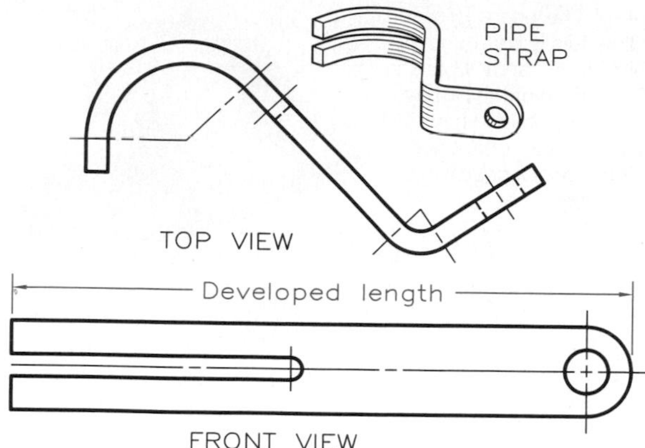

14.41 It is conventional practice to use true-size developed (flattened-out) views of parts made of bent sheet metal.

views of the slots and holes true size by imagining that they have been revolved 45°.

Another type of conventional view is the true-size development of a curved sheet-metal part drawn as a flattened-out view (**Figure 14.41**). The top view shows the part's curvature.

14.20 Conventional Intersections

In orthographic projection, lines are drawn to represent the intersections (fold lines) between planes of an object. Wherever planes intersect, forming an edge, this line of intersection is projected to its adjacent view. Examples showing where lines are required are given in **Figure 14.42**.

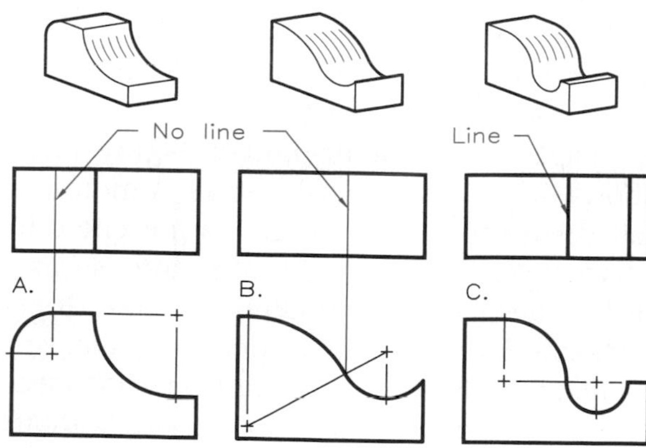

14.42 Object lines are drawn only where there are sharp intersections or where arcs are tangent at their centerlines, as at C.

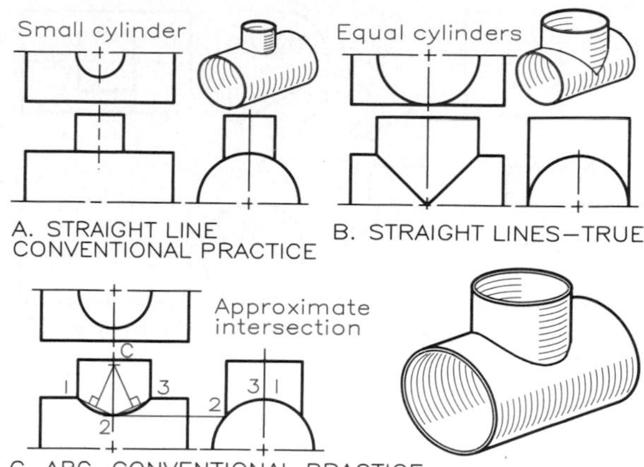

14.43 Intersections between cylinders.
A and **C** Use these methods of construction.
B Equal-size cylinders have straight-line intersections.

Figure 14.43 shows how to draw intersections between cylinders rather than plotting more complex, orthographically correct lines of intersection. **Figures 14.43A** and **C** show conventional intersections, which means they are approximations drawn for ease of construction while being sufficiently representative of the object. **Figure 14.43B** shows an easy-to-draw intersection between cylinders of equal diameters, and this is a true intersection as well. **Figures 14.44** and **14.45** show other cylindrical intersections, and **Figure 14.46** shows conventional practices for depicting intersections formed by holes in cylinders.

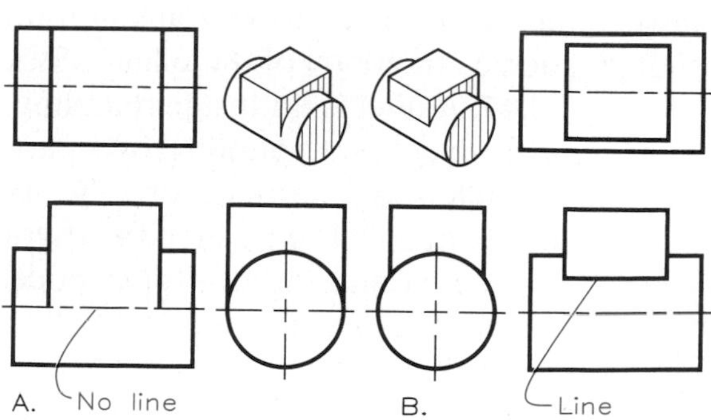

14.44 These are true intersections between cylinders and prisms.

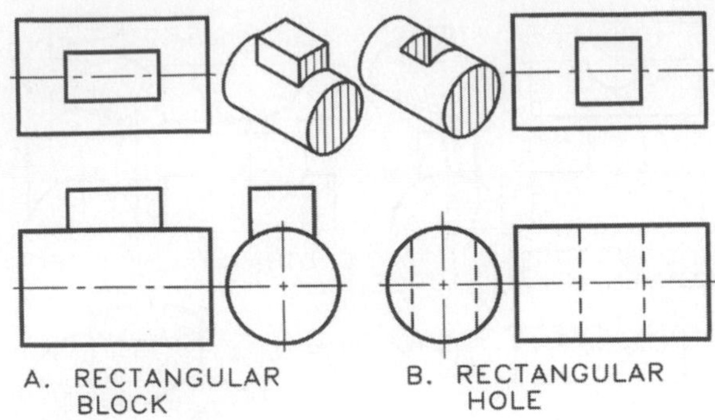

14.45 These are conventional intersections between cylinders and prisms.

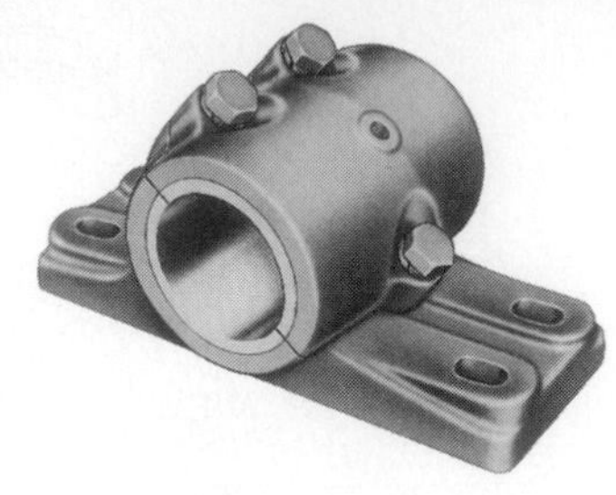

14.47 The edges of this pillow block are rounded with fillets and rounds. The surface of the casting is rough except where it has been machined. *(Courtesy of Dodge Mfgr. Company.)*

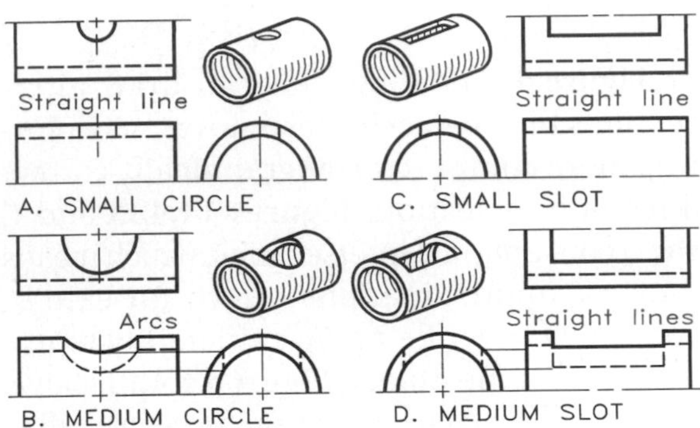

14.46 Conventional methods of describing holes in cylinders are easy to draw and to understand.

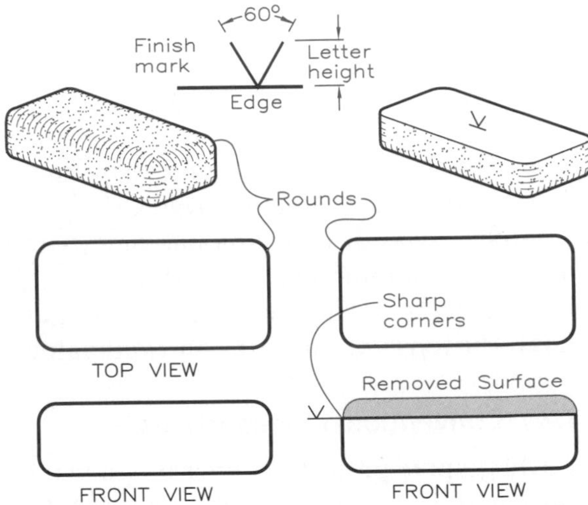

14.48 When a surface is finished (machined), the cut removes the rounded corners and leaves sharp corners. The finish mark is placed on the edge of the surface indicates that it is to be finished.

14.21 Fillets and Rounds

Fillets and **rounds** are rounded intersections between the planes of a part that are used on castings, such as the body of the pillow block in **Figure 14.47**. A fillet is an inside rounding, and a round is an external rounding on a part. The radii of fillets and rounds usually are small, about 1/4 in. Fillets give added strength at inside corners, rounds improve appearance, and both remove sharp edges (**Figure 14.48**).

A casting will have square corners when its surface has been *finished,* which is the process of machining away part of the surface to a smooth finish (**Figure 14.49**). Finished surfaces are indicated by placing a finish mark (V) on all edge views of finished surfaces whether the edges are visible or hidden. **Figure 14.50** shows four types of finish marks. A more detailed surface texture symbol is presented in Chapter 21. **Figure 14.51** illustrates several techniques for showing fillets and rounds on orthographic views with a circle template.

Figure 14.52 gives a comparison of intersections and runouts of parts with and without fillets and rounds. Small runouts are drawn with a circle template. Runouts on orthographic

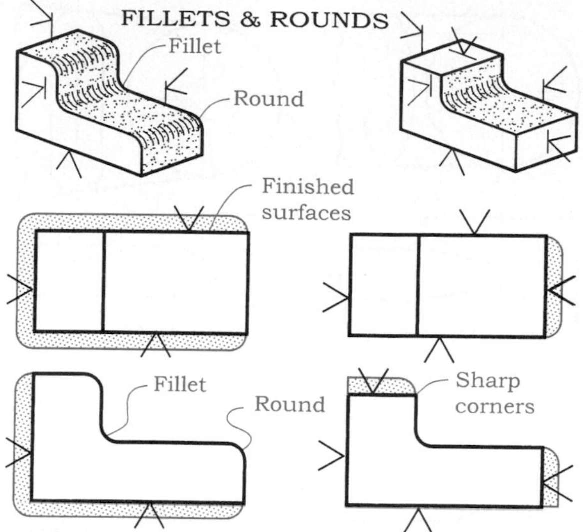

14.49 Fillets and rounds are rounded inside and outside corner respectively, that are standard features on castings. When surfaces are finished, fillets and rounds are removed as shown here.

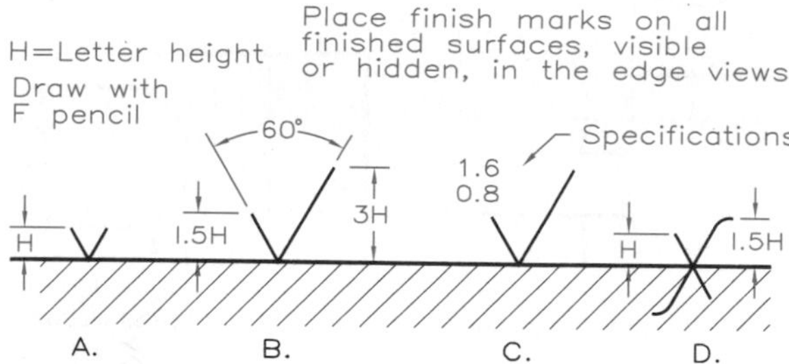

14.50 Any of these finish marks are placed on all views of finished surfaces, visible or hidden.

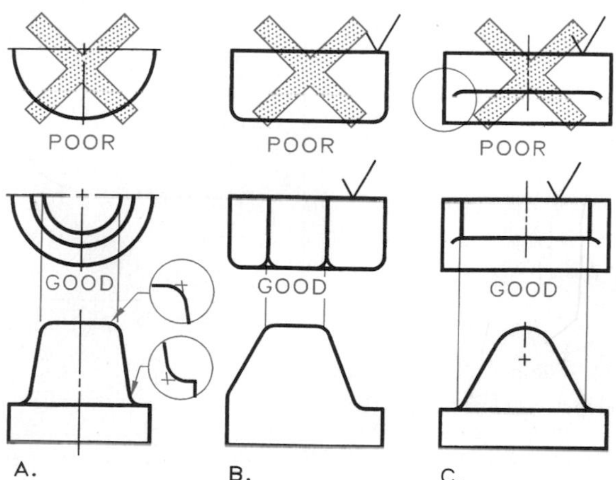

14.51 These examples show both poorly drawn and conventionally drawn fillets and rounds.

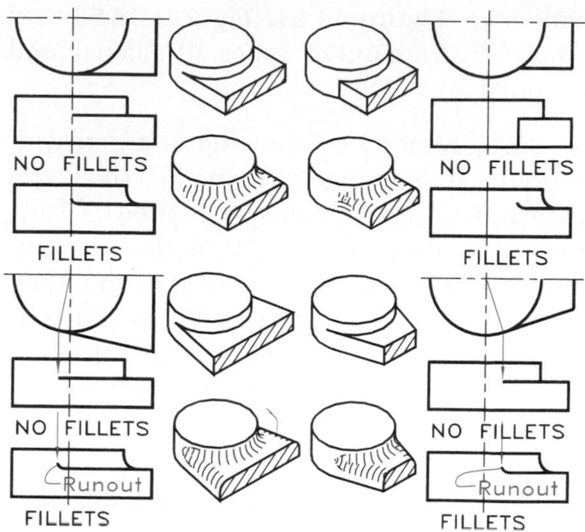

14.52 These examples show conventional intersections and runouts on cylindrical features of parts. Runouts result when fillets and rounds intersect cylinders.

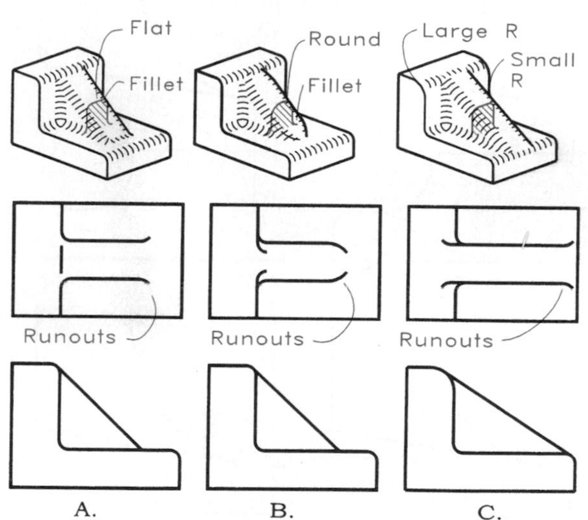

14.53 Examples of typical runouts of edges with fillets and rounds.

views reveal much about the details of an object. For example, the runout in the top view of **Figure 14.53A** tells us that the rib has rounded corners, whereas the top view of **Figure 14.53B** tells us the rib is completely round. Large runouts are constructed as an eighth of a circle with a compass as shown in **Figure 14.54. Figures 14.55** and **14.56** illustrate other types of filleted and rounded intersections.

AutoCAD Method A drawing of a part with runouts at its tangent points is shown in **Figure 14.57**. The runouts are plotted by using the *Line* command, then using the *Arc* command, and finally pressing (Enter) to obtain the first point of an arc tangent to and connected to the end of the line. Locate the other end of the arc to complete the runout.

14.22 Third-Angle Projection

The examples in this chapter are third-angle projections in which the top view is placed

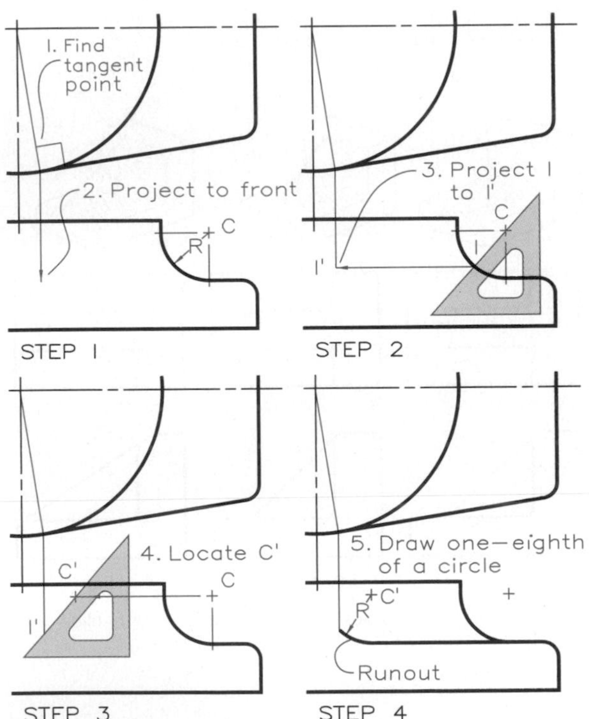

14.54 Plotting runouts.

Step 1 Find the tangency point in the top view and project it to the front view.

Step 2 Find point 1 with a 45° triangle and project it to 1'.

Step 3 Move the 45° triangle to locate point C' on the horizontal projector from center C.

Step 4 Use the radius of the fillet to draw the runout with C' as its center. The runout arc is equal to one-eighth of a circle.

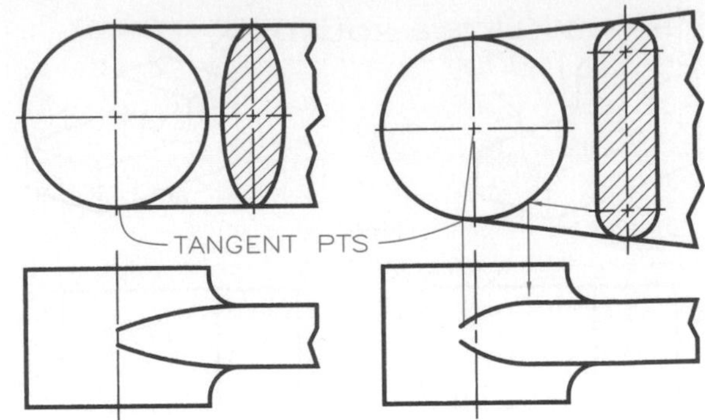

14.55 Conventional representation of runouts.

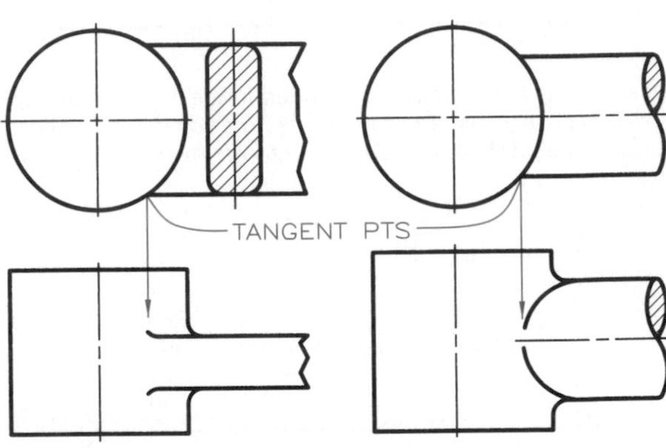

14.56 These are conventional runouts for different cross sections.

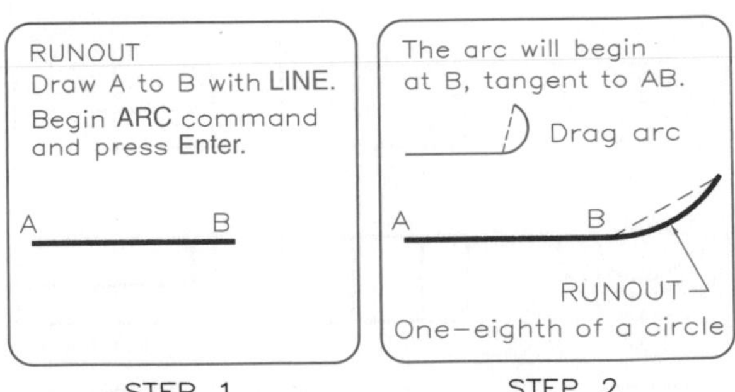

14.57 Runouts by AutoCAD.

Step 1 *Command:* Line (Enter)
Specify first point: A (Enter)
Specify next point or [Undo] : B (Enter)

Step 2 *Command:* Arc (Enter)
Specify start point or arc or [CEnter]: (Enter)
Specify end point of arc: C (Drag to point C.)

over the front view, and the right-side view is placed to the right of the front view, as shown in **Figure 14.58**. This method is used in the United States, Great Britain, and Canada. However, most of the world uses first-angle projection. The first-angle system is illustrated in **Figure 14.59**, in which an object is placed above the horizontal plane and in front of the frontal plane. When these projection planes are opened onto the surface of the drawing paper, the front view projects over the top view, and the right-side view projects to the left of the front view.

The angle of projection used in making a drawing is indicated by placing the truncated cone in or near the title block (**Figure 14.60**).

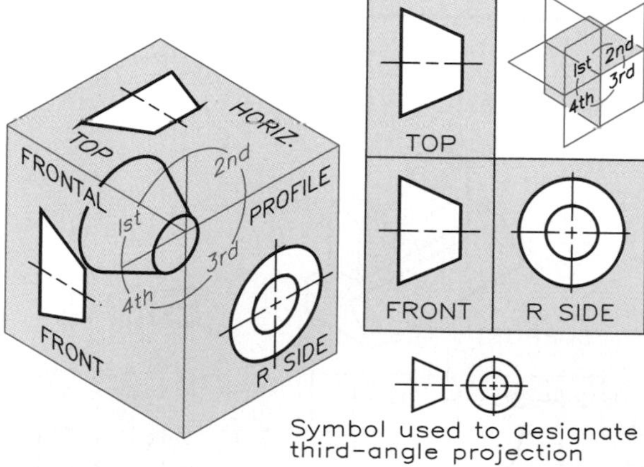

14.58 Third-angle projection is used for drawing orthographic views in the United States, Great Britain, and Canada. The top view is placed over the front view, and the right-side view is placed to the right of the front view. The truncated cone is the symbol used to designate third-angle projection.

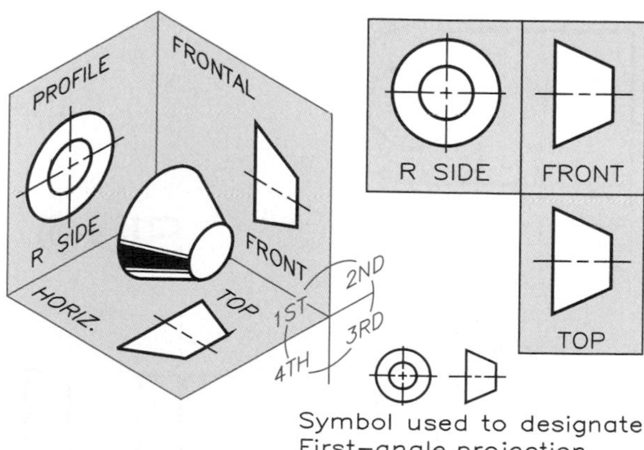

14.59 First-angle projection is used in most of the world. It shows the right-side view to the left of the front view and the top view under the front view. The truncated cone designates first-angle projection.

14.60 These symbols are placed on drawings to specify first-angle or third-angle projection and metric units of measurement.

Problems

1–7. (Figures 14.61–14.67) Draw the given views on size A sheets, two per sheet, using the dimensions given and draw the missing top, front, or right-side views. Lines may be missing in the given views.

8-17. (Figures 14.68–14.90) Draw three views of the objects. Each square gird is equal to 0.20 inches or 5 mm. Two problems can be placed on a size A sheet. Label the views and show the overall dimensions as W, D, and H.

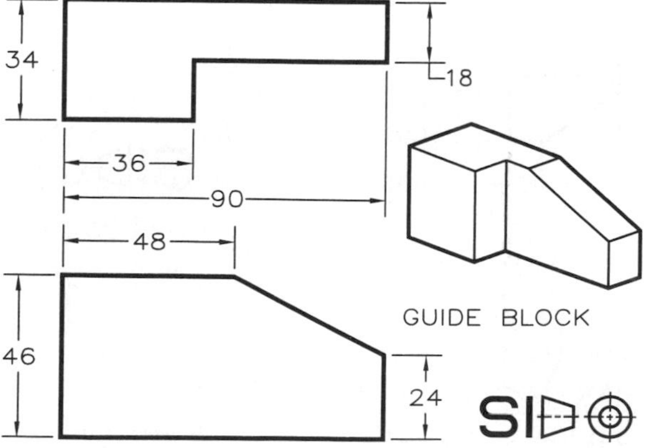

14.61 Problem 1.

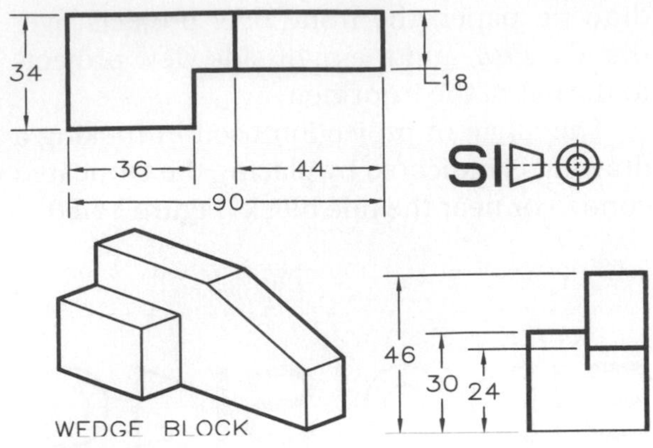

14.62 Problem 2.

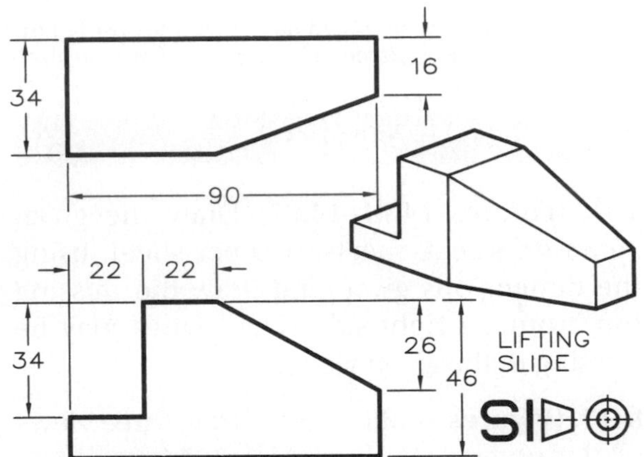

14.63 Problem 3.

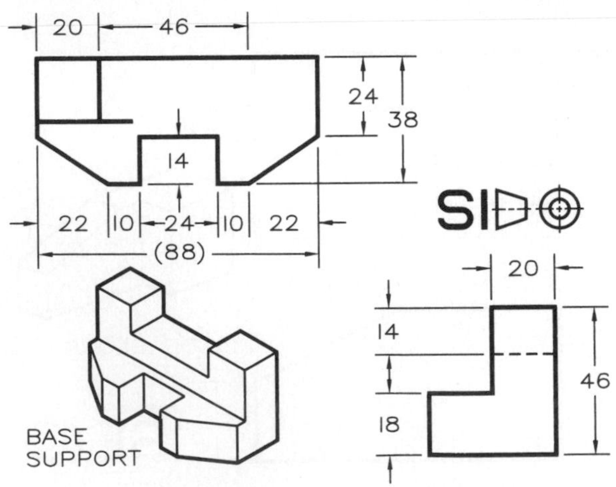

14.64 Problem 4.

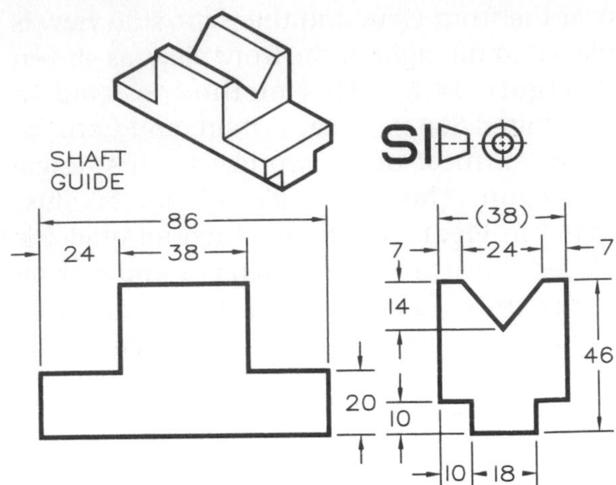

14.65 Problem 5.

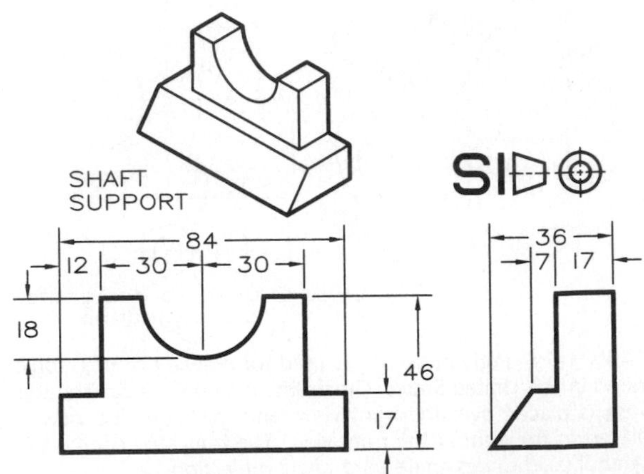

14.66 Problem 6.

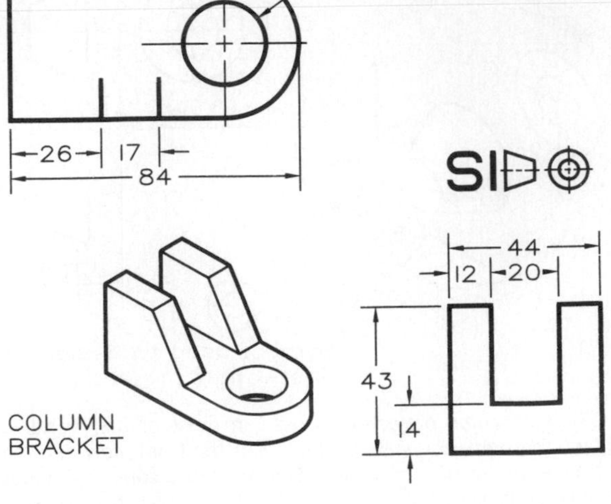

14.67 Problem 7.

8–17. (Figures 14.68–14.90) Draw the necessary orthographic views to describe the objects on B-size sheets at an appropriate scale. Label the views and show the overall dimensions W, D, and H.

Due to space limitations, dimensions on the given pictorials may not conform to the rules of dimensioning that should be applied to orthographic views.

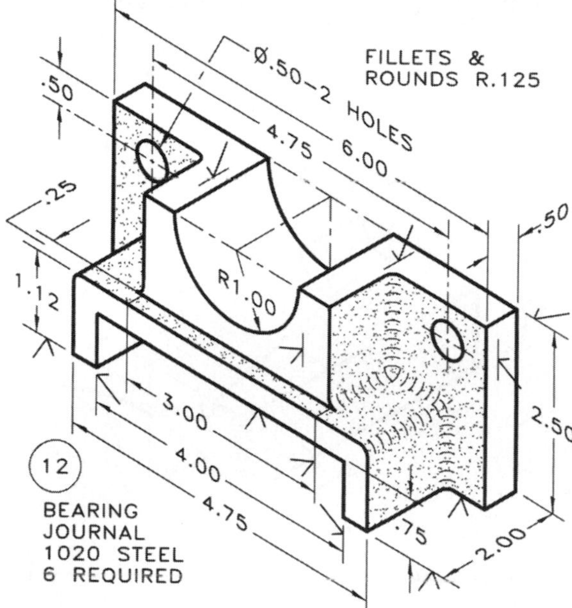

14.68 Problem 8.

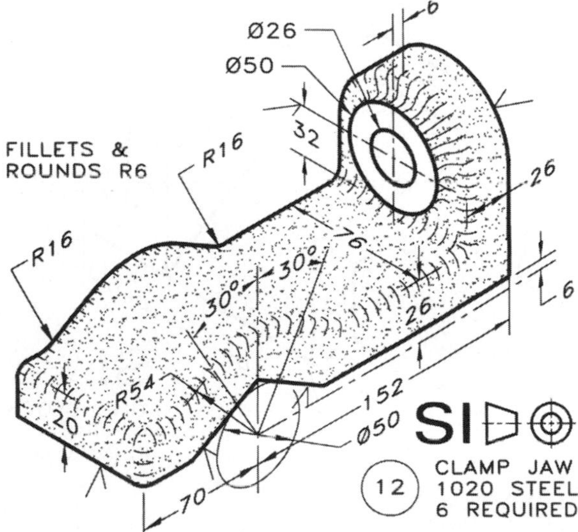

14.69 Problem 9.

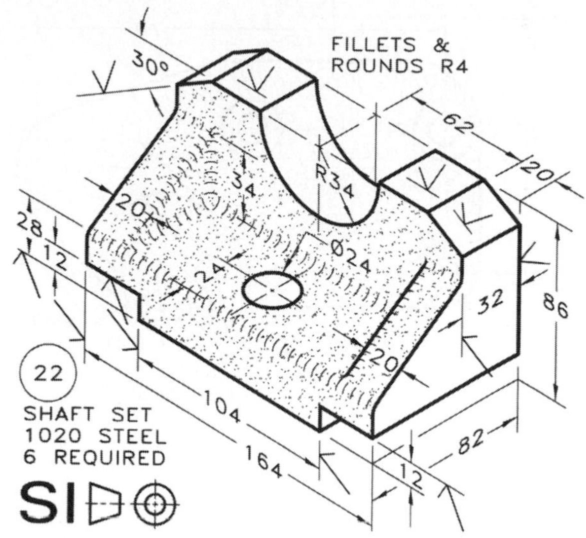

14.70 Problem 10.

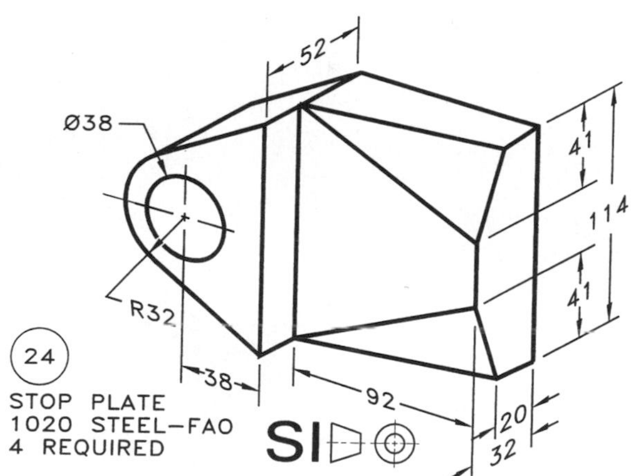

14.71 Problem 11.

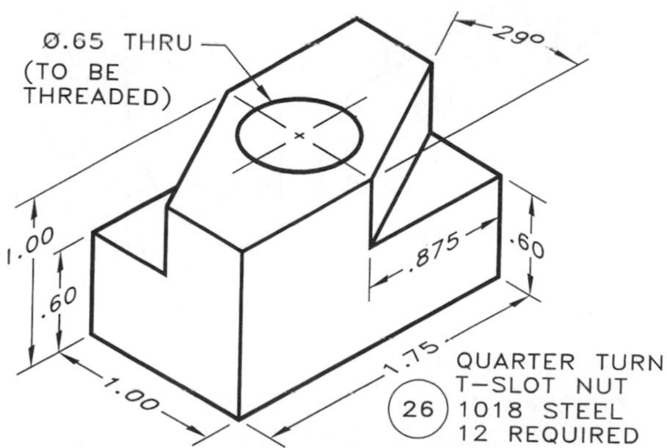

14.72 Problem 12.

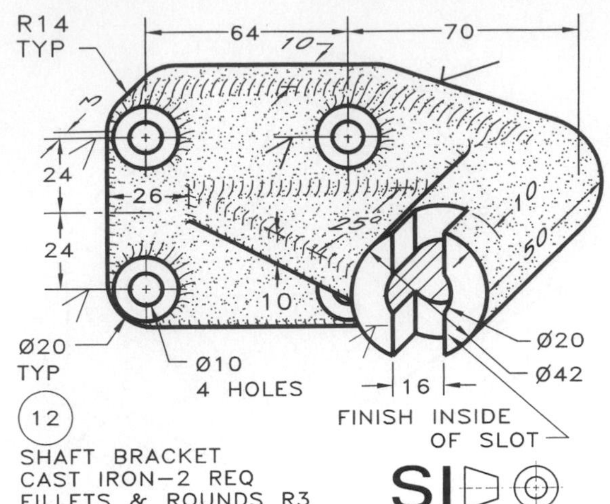

14.73 Problem 13.

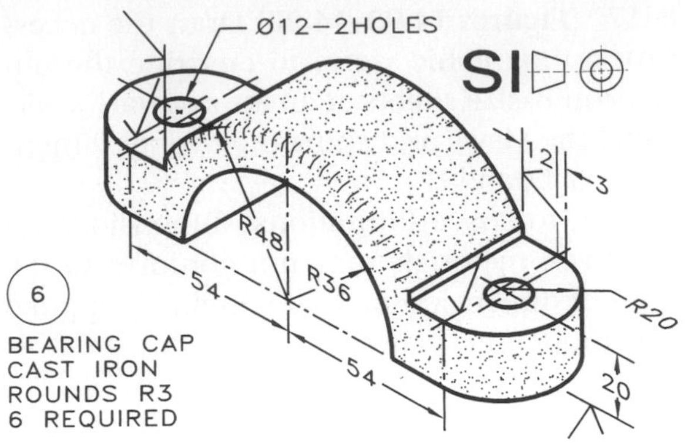

14.75 Problem 14.

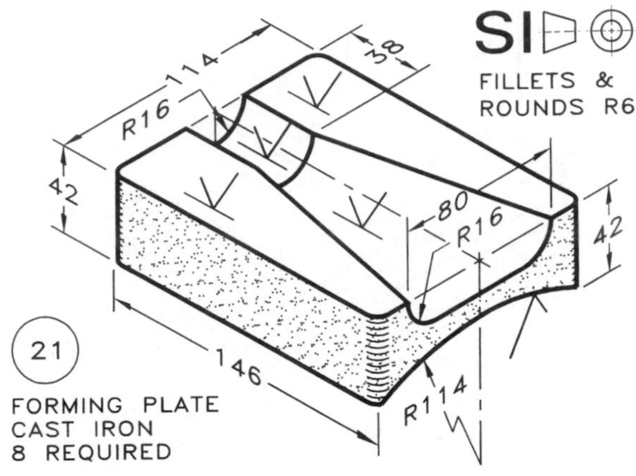

14.76 Problem 16.

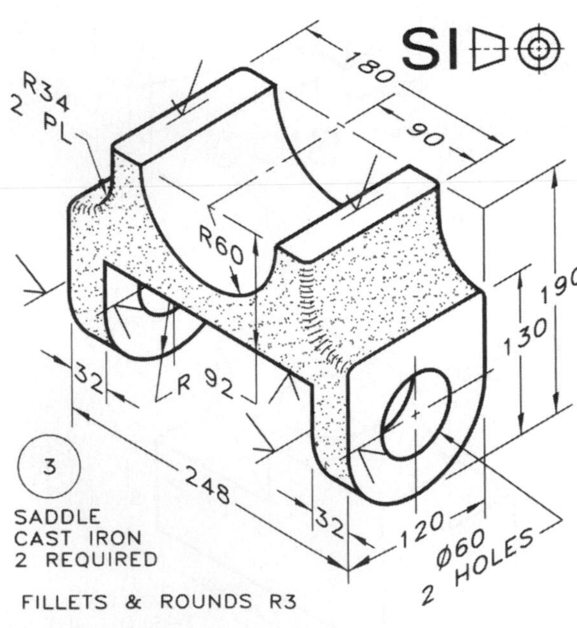

14.74 Problem 14.

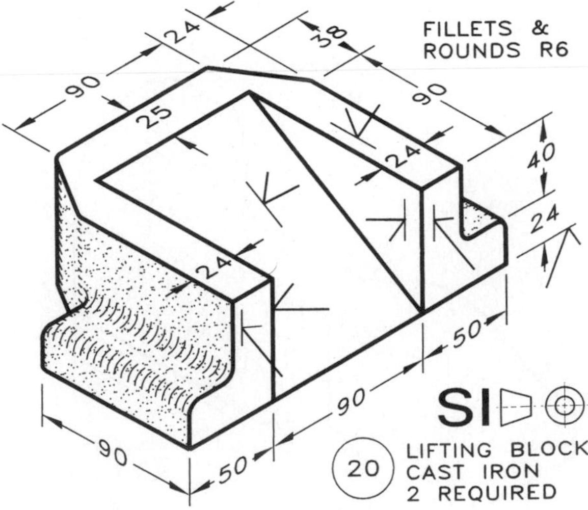

14.77 Problem 17.

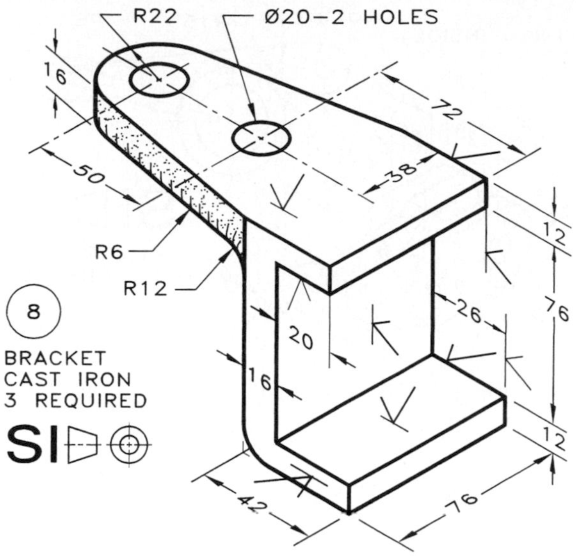

14.78 Problem 18.

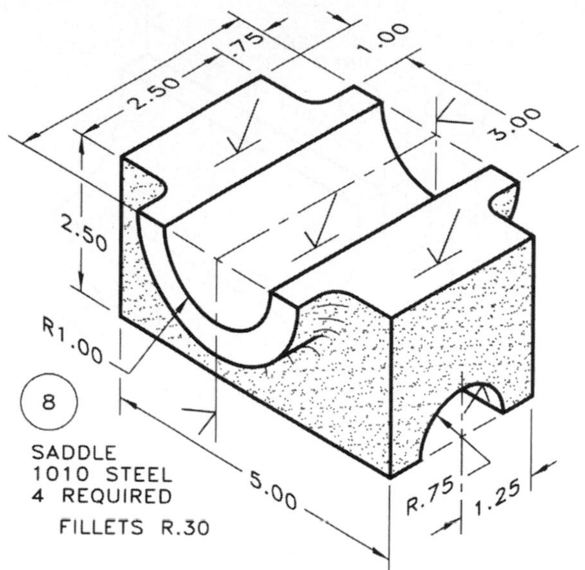

14.80 Problem 20.

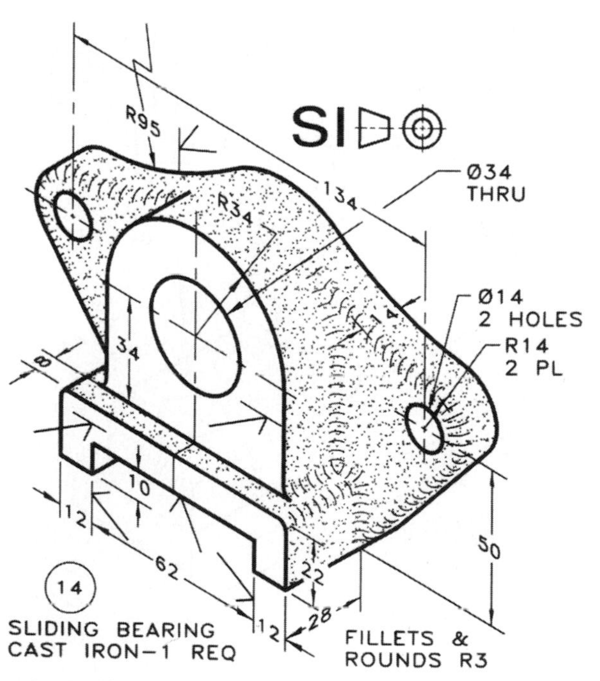

14.79 Problem 19.

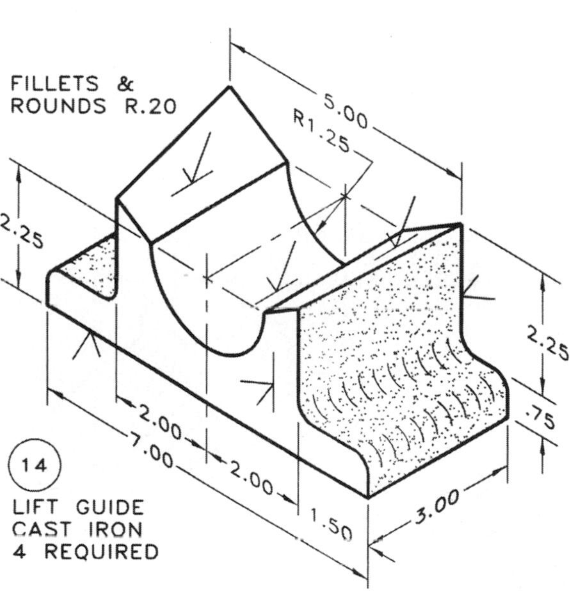

14.81 Problem 21.

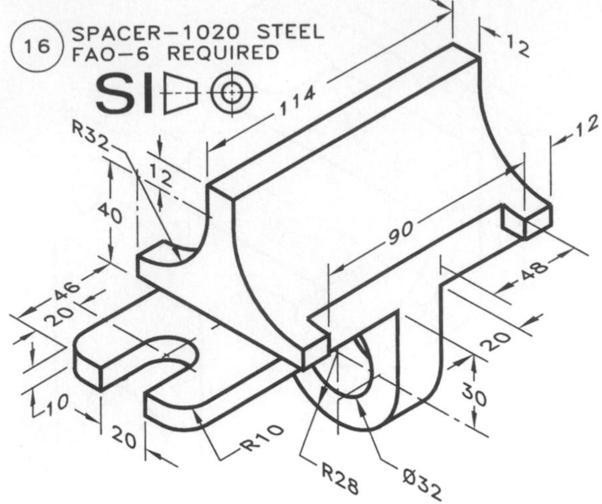

14.82 Problem 22.

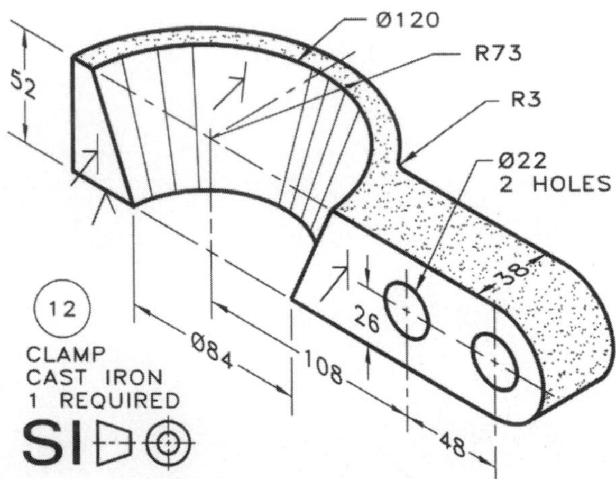

14.83 Problem 23.

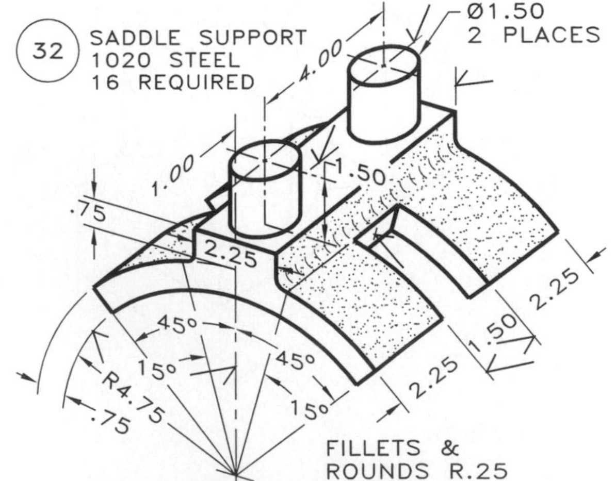

14.84 Problem 24.

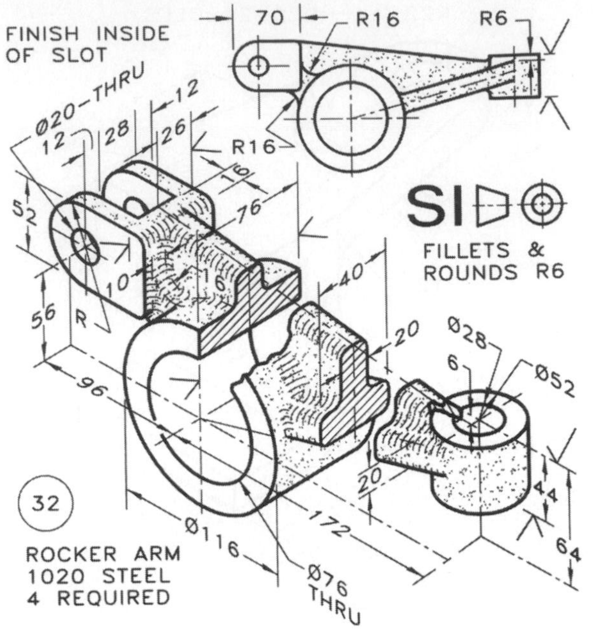

14.85 Problem 25.

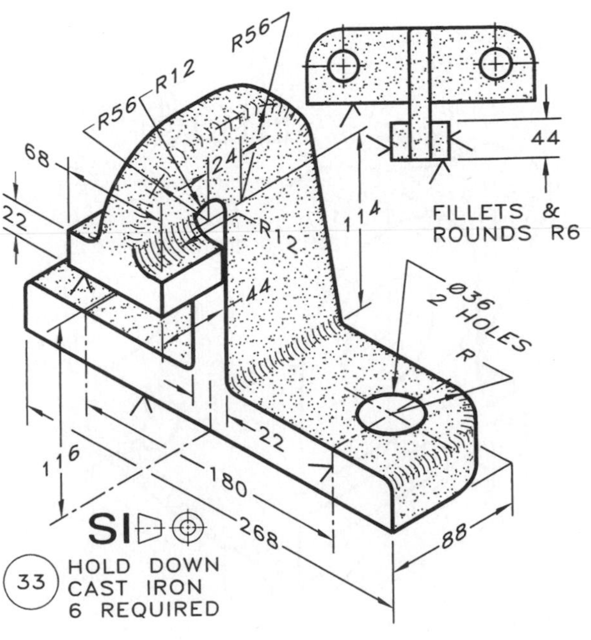

14.86 Problem 26.

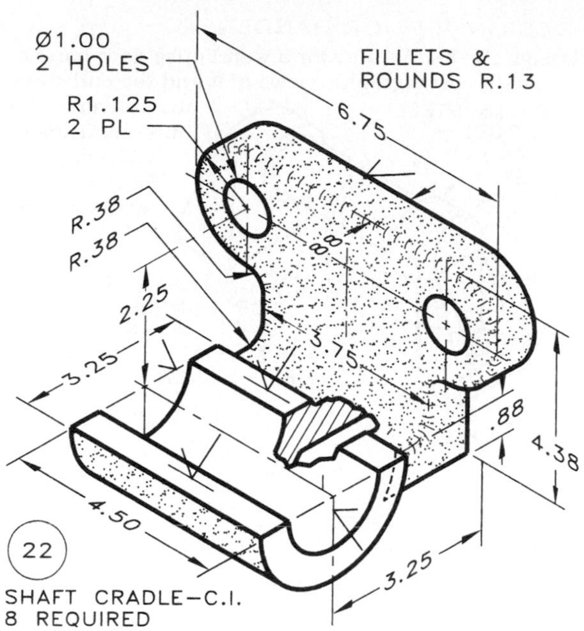

14.87 Problem 27.

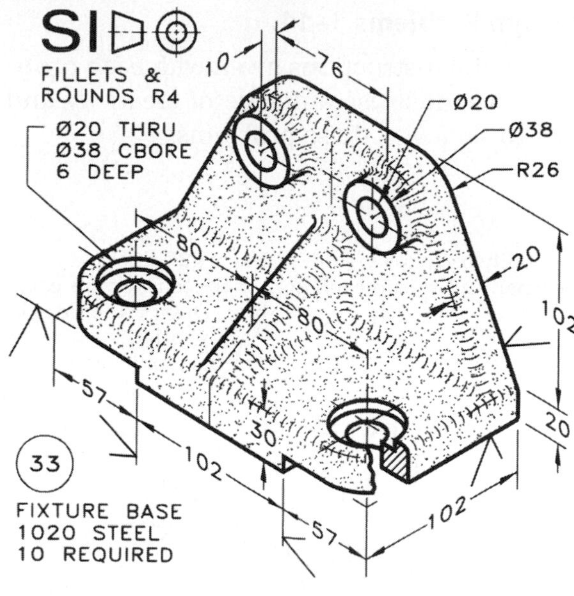

14.89 Problem 29.

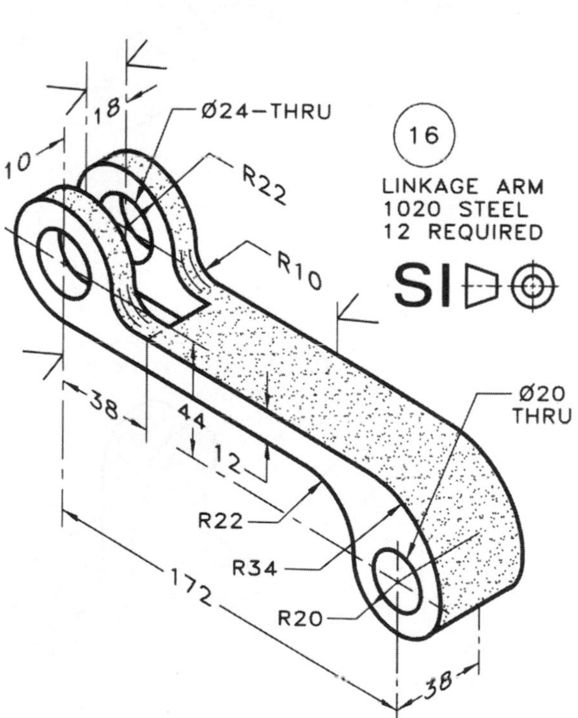

14.88 Problem 28.

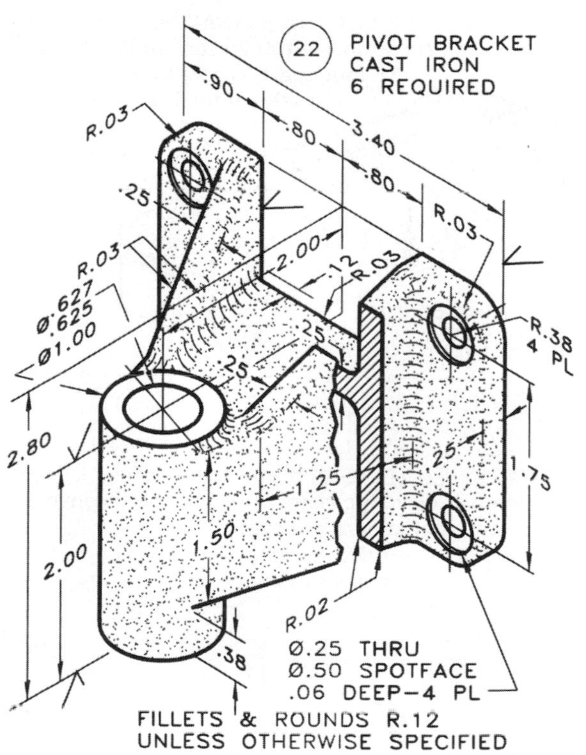

14.90 Problem 30.

Design Problems 1–11:

Follow the instructions given with each problem. You must use a degree of creativity and design skill with these problems.

Modify as follows: Add 4 bosses (.20 thick) at each corner and round each corner concentric with each hole. Draw orthographic views with instruments of the modified part on a size A sheet.

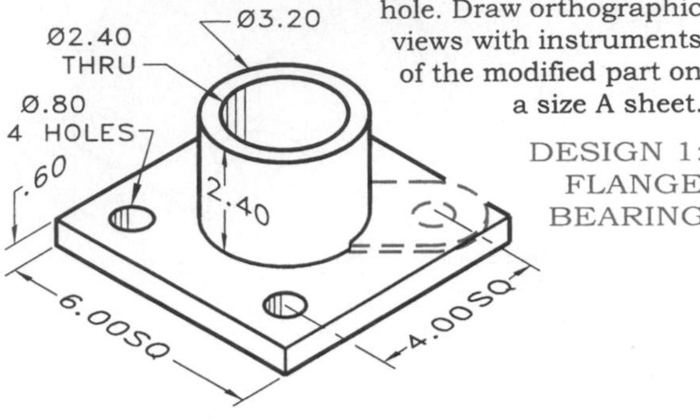

DESIGN 1: FLANGE BEARING

DESIGN 2: TENSIONER ARM

The arm supports two 25-mm shafts that are 88 mm apart, center to center. Draw orthographic views of it with instruments on a size A sheet as if you were its designer.

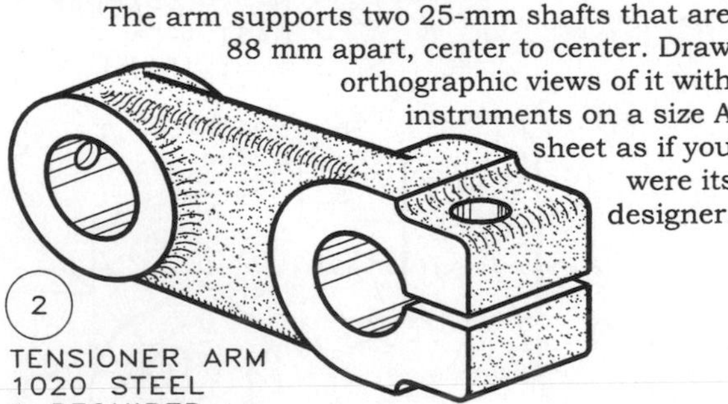

DESIGN 3: ADJUSTING STOP

Sketch orthographic views of the stop and convert them into instrument drawings on a size B sheet. The base is 64 mm x 114 mm x 44 mm from which the dimensions of the other parts must be estimated.

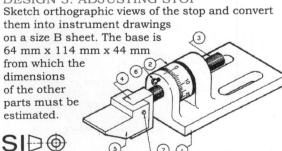

1 2 3 4 5 6 7

SI

DESIGN 4: DOOR HANDLE

Design the middle stay for a warehouse door handle. Sketch orthographic views of it and the end stays and convert them into instrument drawings for fabrication on size A sheets.

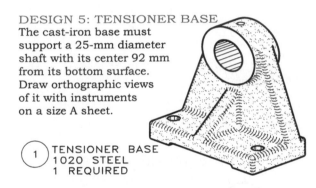

Ø1.18 STEEL TUBE
END STAY
3.15
1.80
1.00
MIDDLE STAY FOR HANDLES OVER 36 IN.
HOLE FOR .25 SOCKET HEAD SCREW

DESIGN 5: TENSIONER BASE

The cast-iron base must support a 25-mm diameter shaft with its center 92 mm from its bottom surface. Draw orthographic views of it with instruments on a size A sheet.

1 TENSIONER BASE
1020 STEEL
1 REQUIRED

DESIGN 6: BRACKET

Two views of a bracket are given that support a 24-mm diameter shaft at a height of 108 mm between two of them. Sketch orthographic views of the bracket and convert them into instrument drawings on a size B sheet.

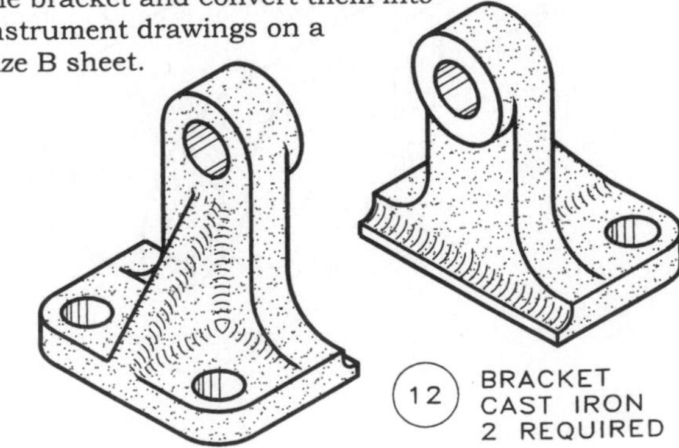

DESIGN 7: BASE FLANGE

Make an instrument drawing of the flange by using the general specifications and your judgment as its designer. Draw details on a size A sheet.

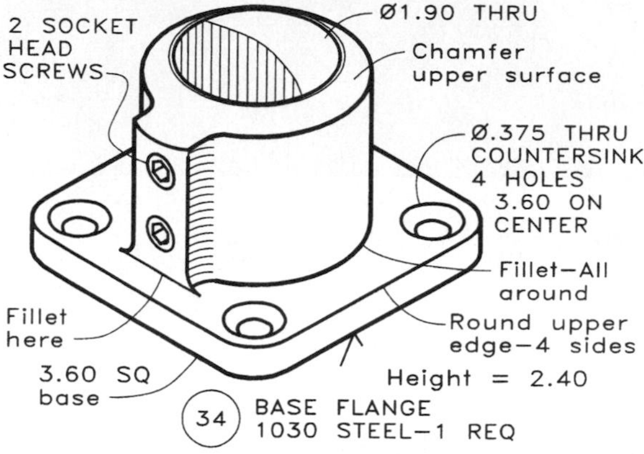

DESIGN 10: STUDY DESK

A concept for a study desk is shown here. Make orthographic sketches of the parts of the desk. Convert your sketches to instrument drawings on a size B sheet as if you were its designer. Determine the best dimensions for comfort and function.

Alternative: Develop a concept of your own to solve this problem.

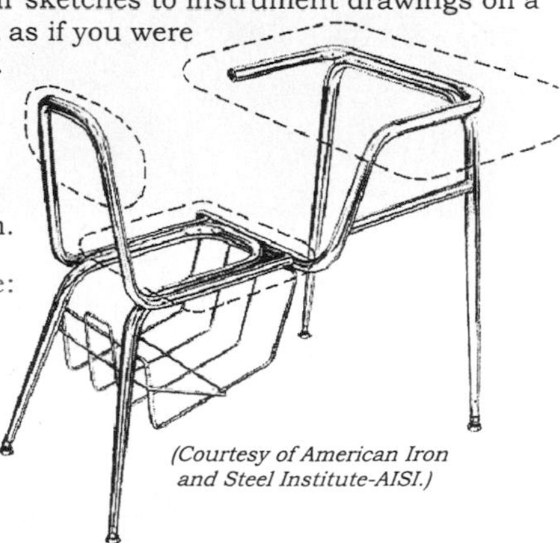

(Courtesy of American Iron and Steel Institute-AISI.)

DESIGN 8: BEARING HANGER

Sketch orthographic views of the hanger and convert them into instrument drawings on a size B sheet. The large hole is 80 mm in diameter and 82 mm deep. The four small holes are 24 mm in diameter. Determine the dimensions as if you were its designer.

DESIGN 11: COLUMN BASE

The base is secured by four .38 DIA anchor bolts to support a 2.38 O.D. steel pipe held in place by two hexagon head set screws. Make instrument drawings of the base on a size A sheet at a suitable scale.

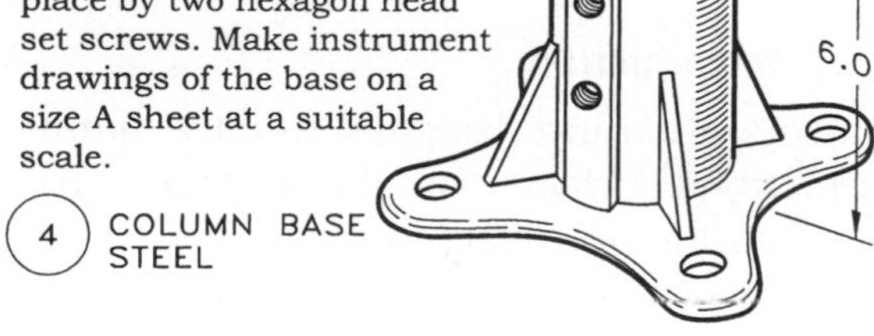

DESIGN 12: YOKE TROLLEY

65 lb weight
90 lb capacity

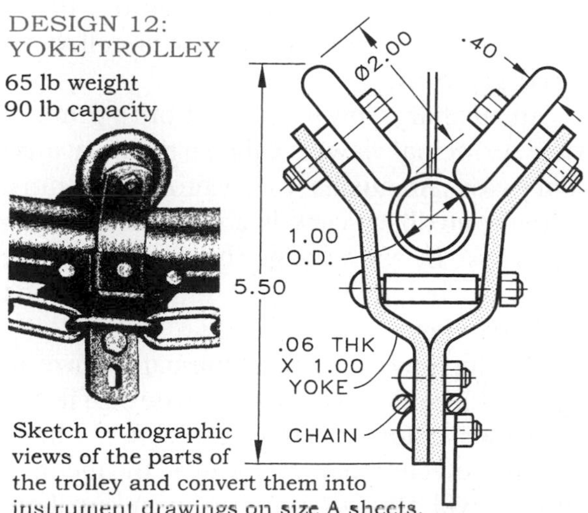

Sketch orthographic views of the parts of the trolley and convert them into instrument drawings on size A sheets.

Sketch and draw orthographic views of the parts with instruments on size A sheets.

ALTERNATIVE APPROACH

Develop a design for your own gate latch and make your first million.

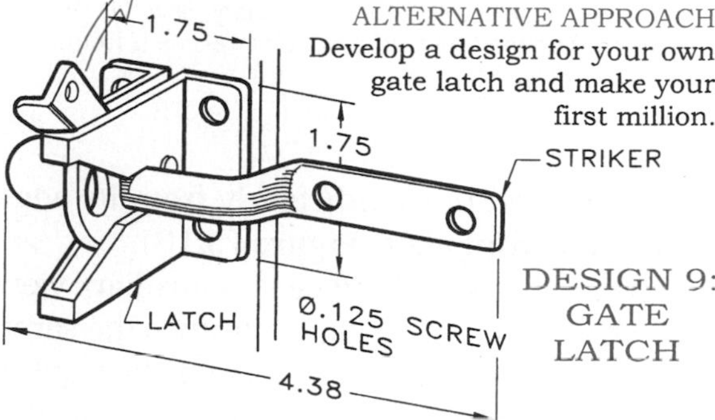

DESIGN 9: GATE LATCH

15

Primary Auxiliary Views

15.1 Introduction

Objects often are designed to have sloping or inclined surfaces that do not appear true size in principal orthographic views. A plane of this type is not parallel to a principal projection plane (horizontal, frontal, or profile) and is, therefore, a **nonprincipal plane**. Its true shape must be projected onto a plane that is parallel to it. This view is called an **auxiliary view**.

An auxiliary view projected from a primary view (principal view) is called a **primary auxiliary view**. An auxiliary view projected from a primary auxiliary view is a **secondary auxiliary view**. By the way, get out your dividers; you must use them all the time in drawing auxiliary views.

The inclined surface of the part shown in **Figure 15.1A** does not appear true size in the top view because it is not parallel to the horizontal projection plane. However, the inclined surface will appear true size in an auxiliary view projected perpendicularly from its edge view in the front view (**Figure 15.1B**).

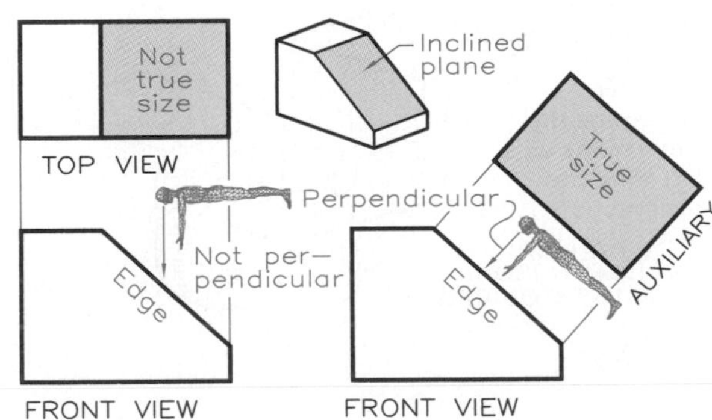

15.1 A surface that appears as an inclined edge in a principal view can be found true size by an auxiliary view. (A) The top view is foreshortened, but (B) the inclined plane is true size in the auxiliary view.

The relationship between an auxiliary view and the view it was projected from is the same as that between any two adjacent orthographic views. **Figure 15.2A** shows an auxiliary view

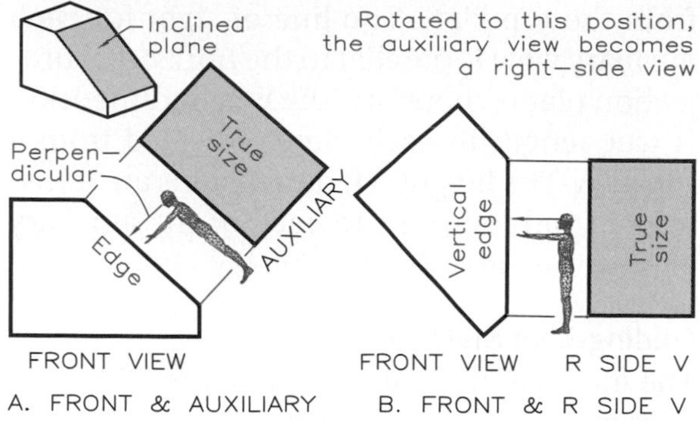

15.2 An auxiliary view has the same relationship with the view it is projected from as that of any two adjacent principal views.

projected perpendicularly from the edge view of the sloping surface. Rotating these views (the front and auxiliary views) so that the projectors are horizontal produces views that have the same relationship as regular front and right-side views (**Figure 15.2B**).

15.2 Folding-Line Principles

The three principal orthographic planes are the **frontal** (F), **horizontal** (H), and **profile** (P) planes. An auxiliary view is projected from a principal orthographic view (a top, front, or side view), and a primary auxiliary plane is perpendicular to one of the principal planes and oblique to the other two.

Think of auxiliary planes as planes that fold into principal planes along a folding line (**Figure 15.3**). The plane in **Figure 15.3A** folds at a 90° angle with the frontal plane and is labeled F-1, where F is an abbreviation for frontal, and 1 represents first, or primary, auxiliary plane. **Figures 15.3B** and **15.3C** illustrate the positions for auxiliary planes that fold from the horizontal and profile planes, labeled H-1 and P-1, respectively.

It is important that reference lines be labeled as shown in **Figure 15.3**, with the numeral 1 placed on the auxiliary side and the letter H, F, or P on the principal-plane side.

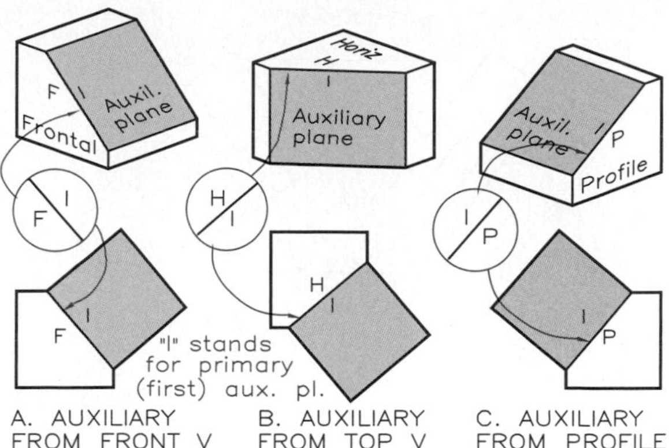

15.3 A primary auxiliary plane can be folded from the frontal, horizontal, or profile planes. The fold lines are labeled F-1, H-1, and P-1, with 1 on the auxiliary plane side and P on the principal-plane side.

15.3 Auxiliaries from the Top View

Moving your position about the top view of a part as shown in **Figure 15.4** makes each line of sight perpendicular to the height dimension. One of the views, the front view, is a principal view, while the other positions see auxiliary views.

Figure 15.5 illustrates how these five views (one of which is a front view) are projected

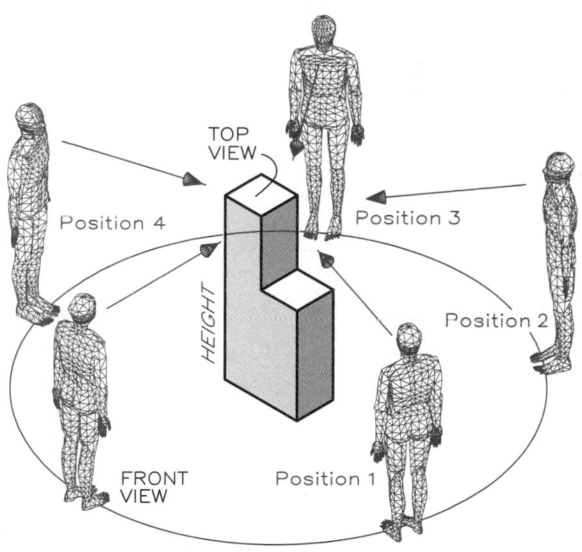

15.4 By moving your viewpoint around the top view of an object, you will see a series of auxiliary views in which the height dimension (H) is true length in all of them.

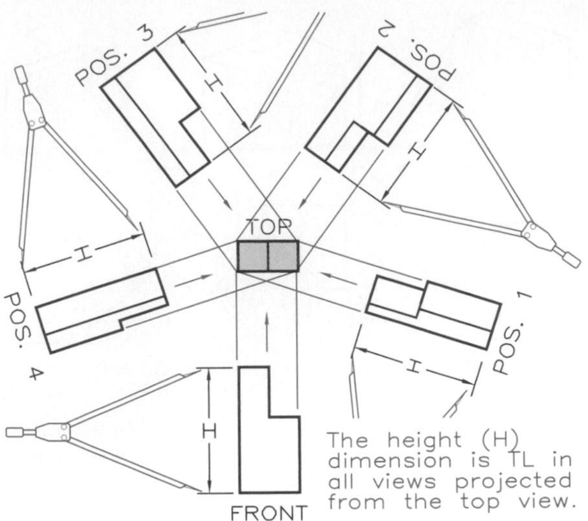

15.5 The views shown in **Figure 15.4** would be drawn as shown here with the same height dimensions common to each view.

from the top view. The line of sight for each auxiliary view is parallel to the horizontal projection plane; therefore, the height dimension is true length in each view projected from a top view. The height (H) dimensions are transferred from the front to each of the auxiliary views by using dividers.

Folding-Line Method

The inclined plane shown in **Figure 15.6** is an edge in the top view and is perpendicular to the horizontal plane. If an auxiliary plane is drawn parallel to the inclined surface, the view projected onto it will be a true-size view of the inclined surface. **A surface must appear as an edge in a principal view for it to be found true size in a primary auxiliary view.** When the auxiliary view is projected from the top view, the height dimensions in the front view must be transferred to the auxiliary view with dividers.

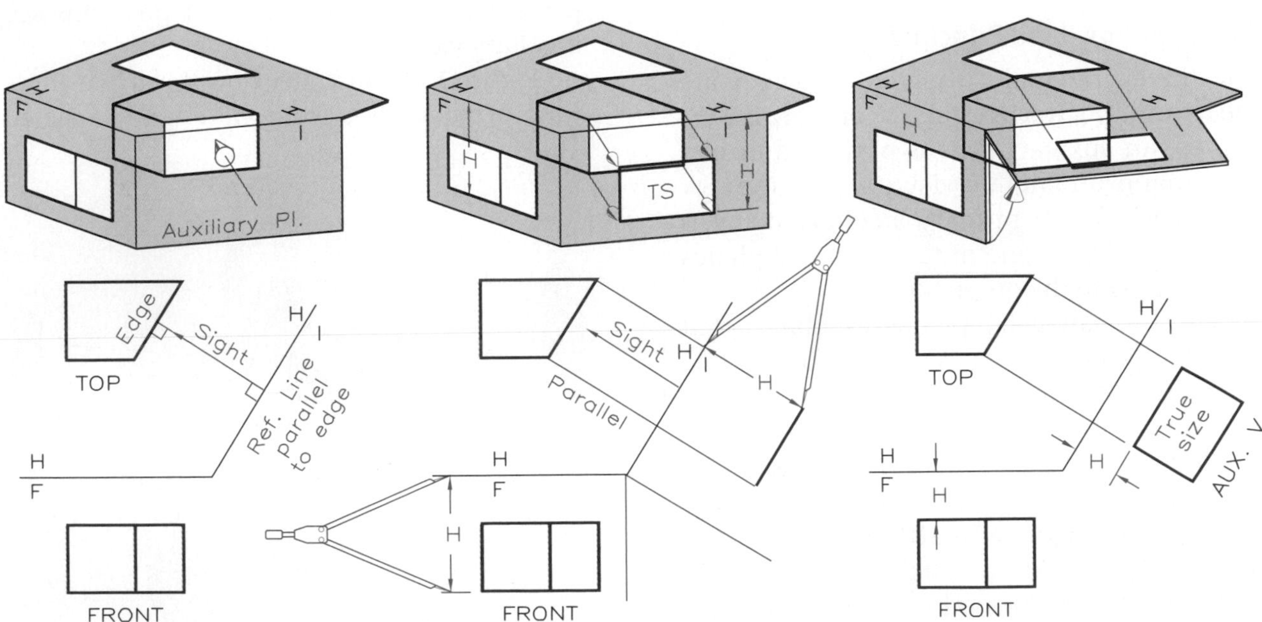

15.6 Auxiliary view from the top.

Step 1 Draw the line of sight perpendicular to the edge view of the inclined surface. Draw the H-1 line parallel to its edge, and draw the H-F reference line between the top and front views.

Step 2 Project from the edge view of the inclined surface parallel to the line of sight. Transfer the H dimensions from the front to locate a line in the auxiliary view.

Step 3 Locate the other corners of the inclined surface by projecting to the auxiliary view and locating the points by transferring the height (H) from the front view.

15.4 Auxiliaries from the Top View: Application

Figure 15.7 illustrates how the folding-line method is used to find an auxiliary view of a part that is imagined to be in a glass box. The semicircular end of the part does not appear true size in front or side views, making these views difficult to draw and interpret if they are drawn. However, because the inclined surface appears as an edge in the top view, it can be found true size in a primary auxiliary view projected from the top view. The height dimension (H) in the frontal view will be the same as in the auxiliary plane, because both planes are perpendicular to the horizontal projection plane. Height is transferred from the front to the auxiliary view with dividers. In **Figure 15.8** the auxiliary plane is rotated about the H-1 fold line into the plane of the top view, the horizontal projection plane. This rotation illustrates how the placement of the views is arrived at when drawing the views.

When drawn on a sheet of paper, the views of this object appear as shown in **Figure 15.9**. The top view is a complete view, but the front view is drawn as a partial view because the omitted portion would have been hard to draw and would not have been true size. The auxiliary view also is drawn as a partial view because the front view shows the omitted features better, which saves drawing time and space on a drawing.

Reference-Plane Method

A second method of locating an auxiliary view uses reference planes instead of the folding-plane method. **Figure 15.10A** shows a horizontal reference plane (HRP) drawn through the center of the front view. Because this view is symmetrical, equal height dimensions on both sides of the HRP can conveniently be transferred from the front view to the auxiliary view and laid off on both sides of the HRP.

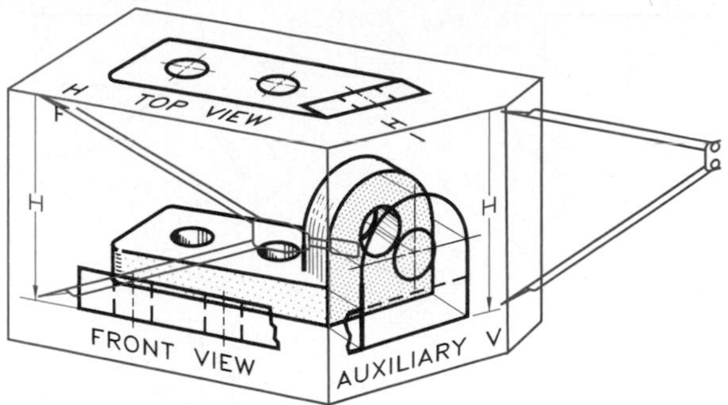

15.7 If you imagine that the object is inside a glass box, you can see the relationship of the auxiliary plane, on which the true-size view is projected, and the horizontal projection plane.

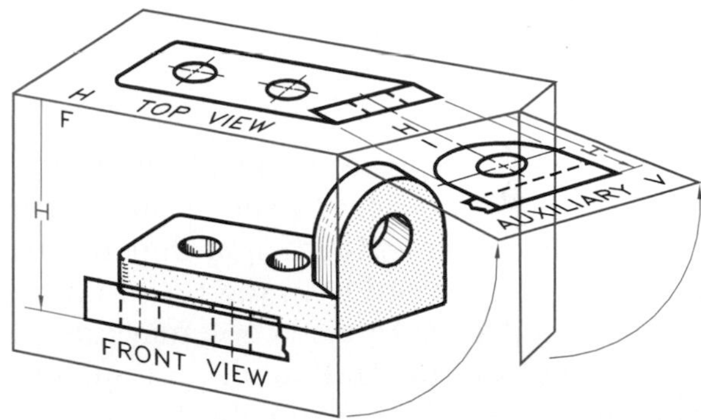

15.8 Fold the auxiliary plane into the horizontal projection plane by rotating it about the H-1 fold line.

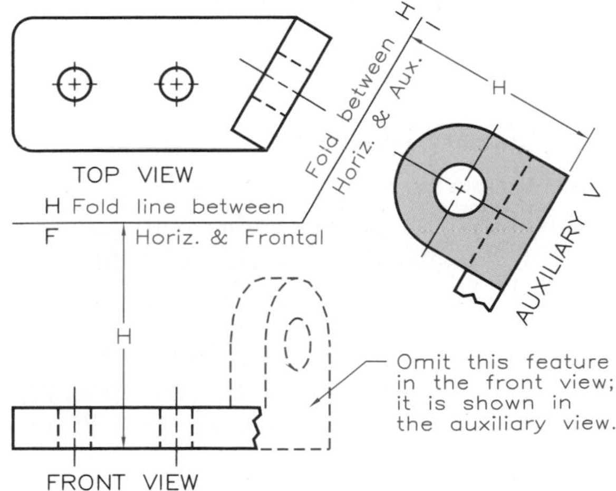

15.9 The front and auxiliary views are drawn as partial views to avoid drawing the object's elliptical features, which are shown in the auxiliary view as true arcs.

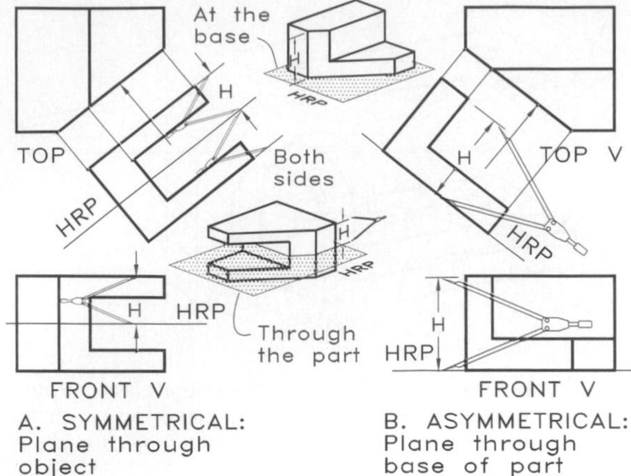

15.10 A horizontal reference plane (HRP) can be positioned through the part or in contact with it. The dimension of height (H) is measured from the HRP and transferred to the auxiliary view with dividers.

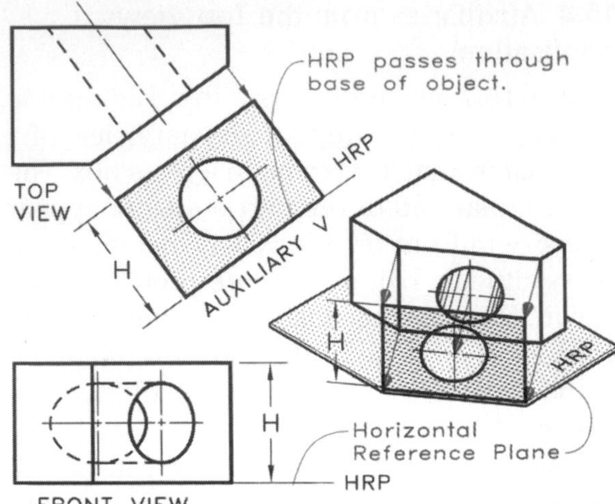

15.11 An auxiliary view projected from the top view is used to draw a true-size view of the inclined surface using a horizontal reference plane. The HRP is drawn through the bottom of the front view.

The reference plane can be placed at the base of the front view as shown in **Figure 15.10B**. In this case, the height dimensions are measured upward from the HRP in both the front and auxiliary views. You may draw a reference plane (the HRP in this example) in any convenient position in the front view: through the part, above it, or below it.

A similar example of an auxiliary view drawn with a horizontal reference plane is shown in **Figure 15.11**. In this example, the hole appears as a true circle in the auxiliary view instead of as an ellipse.

15.5 Rules of Auxiliary Construction

Now that we have discussed several examples of auxiliary views, we summarize the general rules of construction, which are outlined in **Figure 15.12**.

1. An auxiliary view that shows a surface true size must be projected perpendicularly from the edge view of the surface. Usually, the inclined surface, or a partial view, is all that is needed in the auxiliary view, but the entire object can be drawn in the auxiliary view if desired, as shown here.

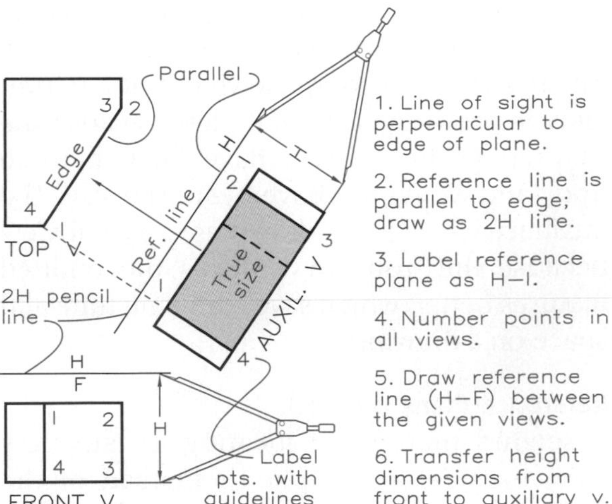

15.12 Rules of auxiliary view construction.

Step 1 Draw a line of sight perpendicular to the edge of the inclined surface. Draw the H-1 fold line parallel to the edge of the inclined surface, and draw an H-F fold line between the given views.

Step 2 Find points 1 and 2 by transferring the height (H) dimensions with your dividers from the front view to the auxiliary view.

Step 3 Find points 3 and 4 in the same manner by transferring the H dimensions.

2. Draw the sight line perpendicular to the inclined edge of the plane you wish to find true size (TS).

3. Draw the reference line, H-1, for example, parallel to the edge view of the inclined plane that will be perpendicular to the line of sight.

4. Draw a reference line between the given views (front and top in this example). Reference lines (fold lines) should be drawn as thin black lines with a 2H or 3H pencil.

5. If an auxiliary is projected from the front view, it will have an F-1 reference line; if it is projected from the horizontal view (top view), it will have an H-1 reference line; and if projected from the side view (profile view), it will have a P-1 reference line.

6. Transfer measurements from the other given view with your dividers (not the view you are projecting from), height in the front view in this example.

7. It is very helpful to number the points one at a time in the primary views and the auxiliary views as they are plotted.

8. Do your lettering in a professional manner with guidelines.

9. Connect the points with light construction lines and use light gray projectors that do not have to be erased with a pencil in the 2H–4H range.

10. Draw the outlines of the auxiliary view as thick visible lines the same as visible lines in principal views, with an F or HB pencil.

15.6 Auxiliaries from the Front View

By moving about the front view of the part as shown in **Figure 15.13**, you will be looking parallel to the edge view of the frontal plane; therefore, the depth dimension (D) will appear true size in each auxiliary view projected

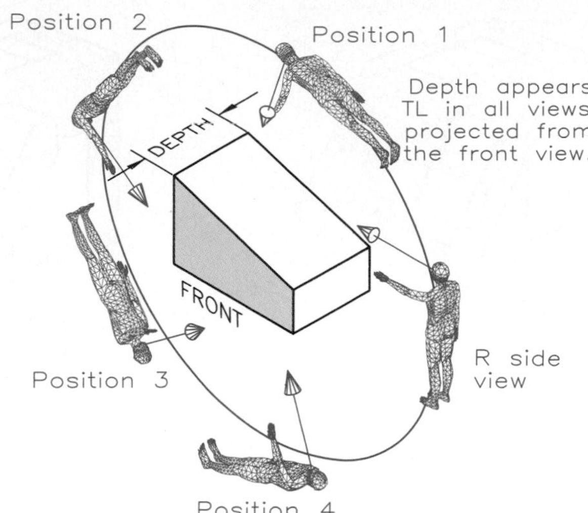

15.13 By moving your viewpoint around the frontal view of an object, you will see a series of auxiliary views in which the depth dimension (D) is true length in all views.

from the front view. One of the positions gives a principal view, the right-side view, and position 1 gives a true-size view of the inclined plane. **Figure 15.14** illustrates the relationship between the auxiliary views projected from the front view.

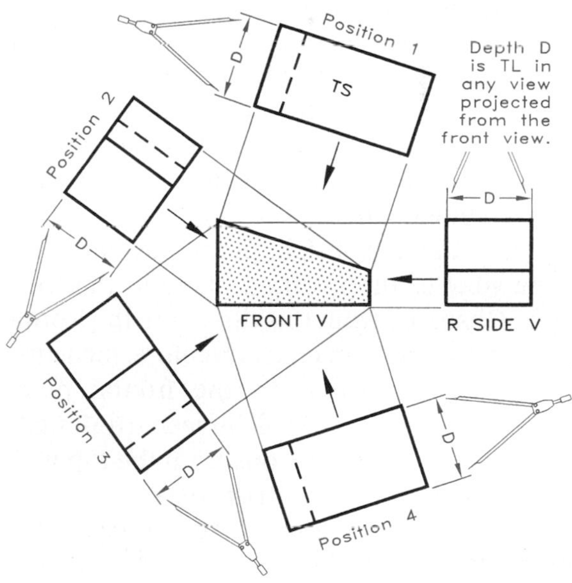

15.14 The auxiliary views shown in **Figure 15.13** would be seen in this arrangement when projected from the front view.

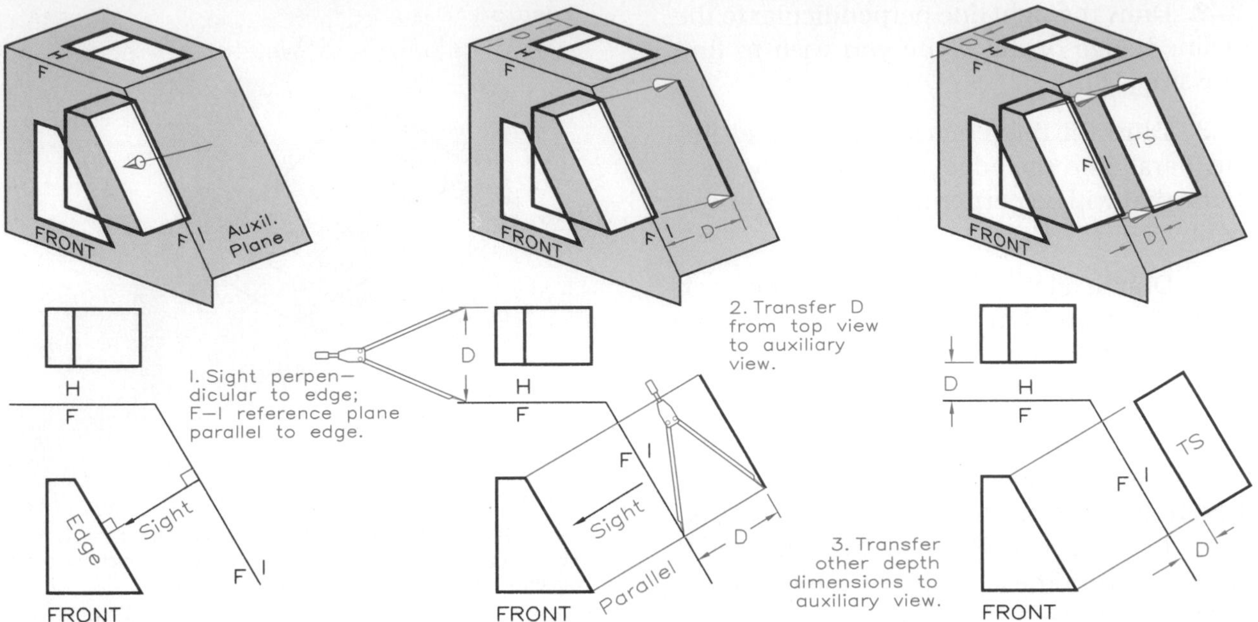

15.15 Auxiliary from the front; folding-plane method.

Step 1 Draw the line of sight perpendicular to the edge of the plane and draw the F-1 line parallel to it. Draw the H-F fold line between the top and front views.

Step 2 Project perpendicularly from the edge view of the inclined surface and parallel to the line of sight. Transfer the depth dimensions (D) from the top to the auxiliary view with your dividers.

Step 3 Locate the other corners of the inclined surface by projecting to the auxiliary view. Locate the points by transferring the depth dimensions (D) from the top to the auxiliary view.

Folding-Plane Method

A plane of an object that appears as an edge in the front view (**Figure 15.15**) is true size in an auxiliary view projected perpendicularly from it. Draw fold line F-1 parallel to the edge view of the inclined plane in the front view at a convenient location.

Draw the line of sight perpendicular to the edge view of the inclined plane in the front view. Observed from this direction, the frontal plane appears as an edge; therefore, measurements perpendicular to the frontal plane depth dimensions (D) will be seen true length. Transfer depth dimensions from the top view to the auxiliary view with dividers.

The object in **Figure 15.16** is imagined to be enclosed in a glass box, and an auxiliary plane is folded from the frontal plane to be

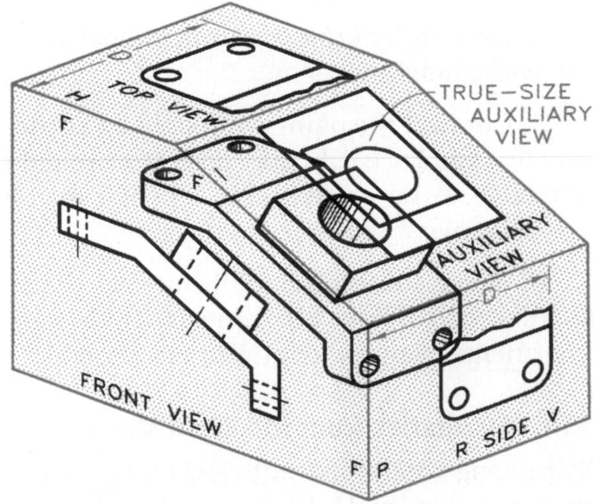

15.16 This part is shown in an imaginary glass box to illustrate the relationship of the auxiliary plane, on which the true-size view of the inclined surface is projected, with the principal planes.

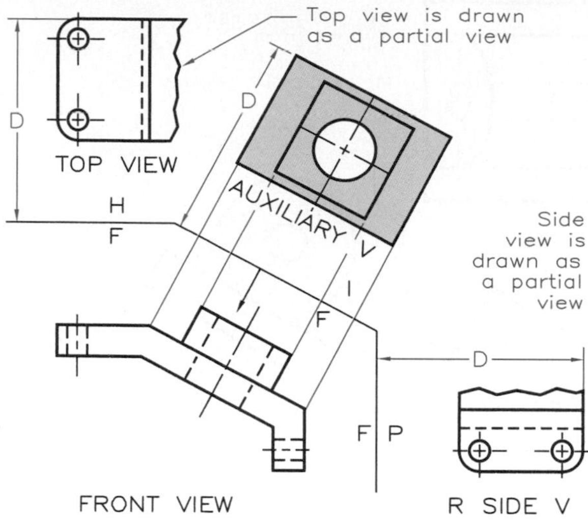

15.17 The layout and construction of an auxiliary view of the object shown in **Figure 15.18.**

parallel to the inclined surface. When drawn on a sheet of paper, the views appear as shown in **Figure 15.17**. The top and side views are drawn as partial views because the auxiliary view eliminates the need for drawing complete views. The auxiliary view, located by transferring the depth dimension measured perpendicularly from the edge view of the frontal plane in the top view and transferred to the auxiliary view, shows the surface's true size.

AutoCAD Method

Find the true-size view of the inclined surface that appears as an edge in the front view (**Figure 15.18**) by using the LISP commands *Parallel* and *Transfer* (see Section 27.2). This program is not a regular part of AutoCAD, but it is an excellent addition to have available for solving auxiliary problems. It was developed

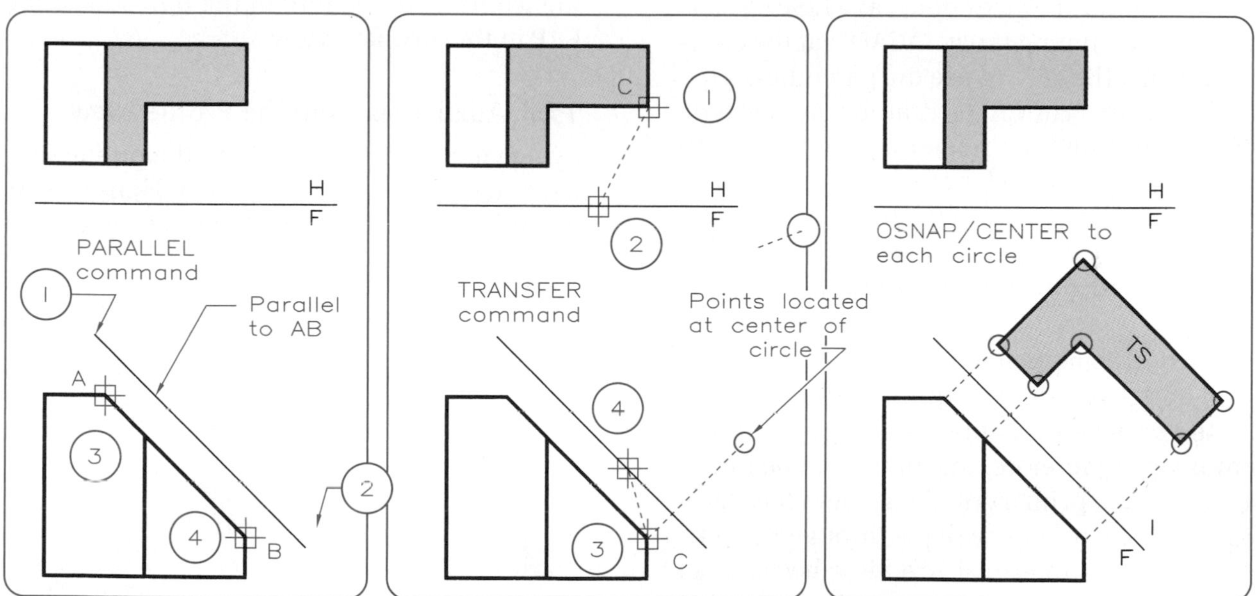

15.18 Auxiliary views by AutoCAD.

Step 1 Type Parallel to receive the prompts for the first end of the reference line (1) and its approximate second endpoint (2). You are then prompted for the ends of line AB, to which the reference line is parallel.

Step 2 Type Transfer; you are prompted for a point in the top view (1) and its distance from the H-F line (2) to transfer. You are prompted for the front view of the point to project (3) and the reference line (4). Point C is projected to the auxiliary view.

Step 3 Continue using *Transfer* to locate the other corner points of the inclined plane. Connect the points using the *Center* option of *Osnap* to snap to the centers of the circles. *Erase* the circles after connecting their centers.

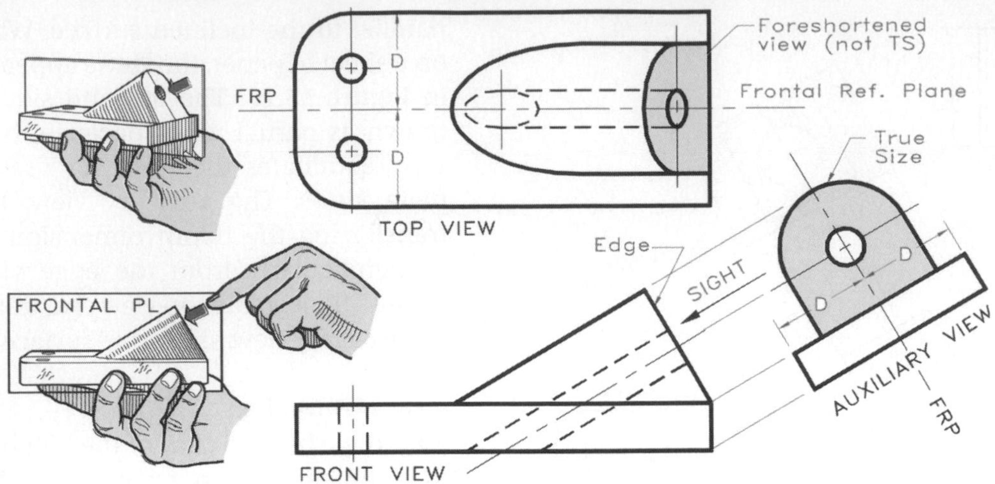

15.19 Because the inclined surface of this part is symmetrical, it is helpful to use a frontal reference plane (FRP) that passes through the object. Project the auxiliary view perpendicularly from the edge view of the plane in the front view. The FRP appears as an edge in the auxiliary view, and depth dimensions (D) are transferred from each side of it in the top view to locate points on the true-size view of the inclined surface.

by Professor Leendert Kersten of the University of Nebraska. Once copied as a LISP file, it is accessed by typing (Load "ACAD") at the command line. (Be sure to use the parentheses.)

While in AutoCAD's drafting mode, type Parallel to draw the reference line parallel to edge AB. Type Transfer to obtain prompts for transferring measurements from the top view as if you were using your dividers. Connect the circular points to complete the auxiliary view.

Reference-Plane Method

The object shown in **Figure 15.19** has an inclined surface that appears as an edge in the front view; therefore, this plane can be found true size in a primary auxiliary view. It is helpful to draw a reference plane through the center of the symmetrical top view because all depth dimensions can be located on each side of the frontal reference plane. Because the reference plane is a frontal plane, it is labeled FRP in the top and auxiliary views. In the auxiliary view, the FRP is drawn parallel to the edge view of the inclined plane at a convenient distance from it. The symmetrical view of the part is drawn by transferring depth dimensions from the FRP in the top view to the FRP in the auxiliary view.

15.7 Auxiliaries from the Profile View

By moving your position about the profile view (side view) of the part as shown in **Figure 15.20**, you will be looking parallel to the edge view of

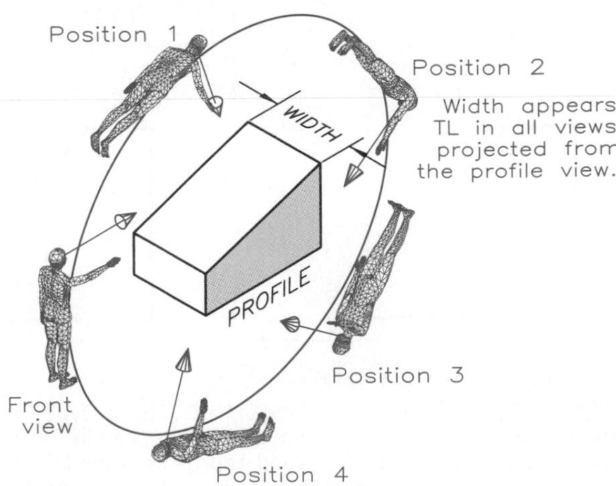

15.20 By moving your viewpoint around a profile (side) view of an object you will obtain a series of auxiliary views in which the width dimension (W) is true length.

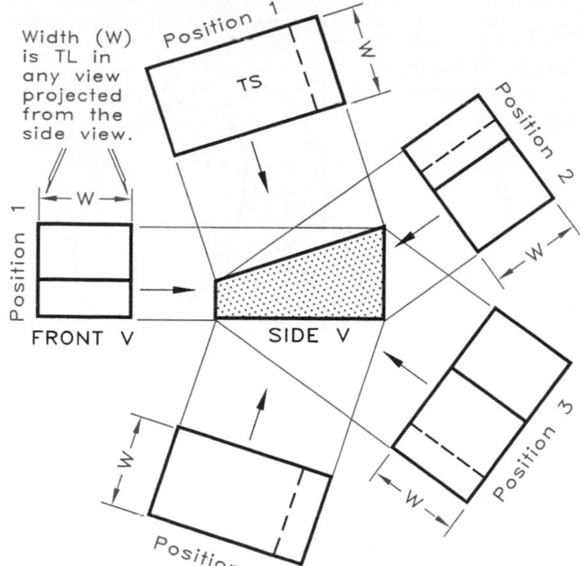

15.21 The auxiliary views shown in **Figure. 15.20** would be seen in this arrangement when projected from the side view.

the profile plane. Therefore, the width dimension will appear true size in each auxiliary view projected from the side view. One of the positions gives a principal view, the front view, and position 1 gives a true-size view of the inclined plane. **Figure 15.21** illustrates the arrangement of the auxiliary views projected from the side view drawn on a sheet of paper.

Folding-Plane Method

Because the inclined surface in **Figure 15.22** appears as an edge in the profile plane, it can be found true size in a primary auxiliary view

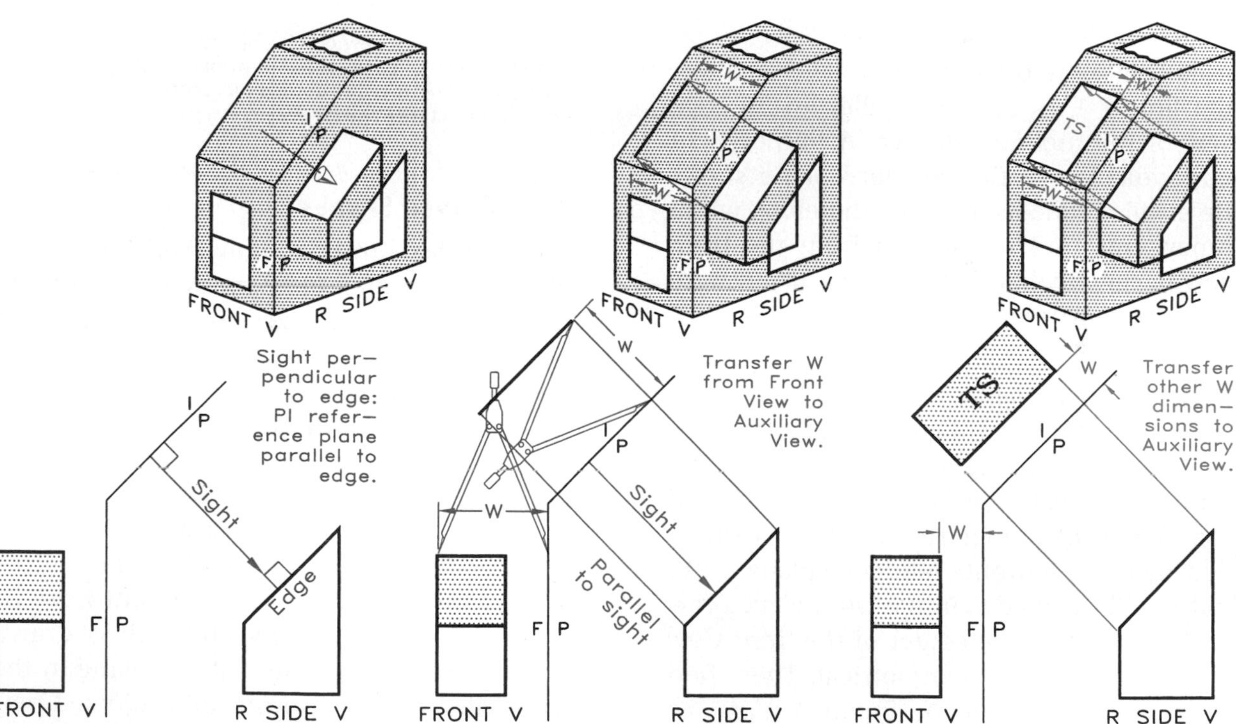

15.22 From the side, folding-plane method.

Step 1 Draw a line of sight perpendicular to the edge of the inclined surface. Draw the P-1 fold line parallel to the edge view, and draw the F-P fold line between the given views.

Step 2 Project the corners of the edge view parallel to the line of sight. Transfer the width dimensions (W) from the front view to locate a line in the auxiliary view.

Step 3 Find the other corners of the inclined surface by projecting to the auxiliary view. Locate the points by transferring the width dimensions (W) from the front view to the auxiliary view.

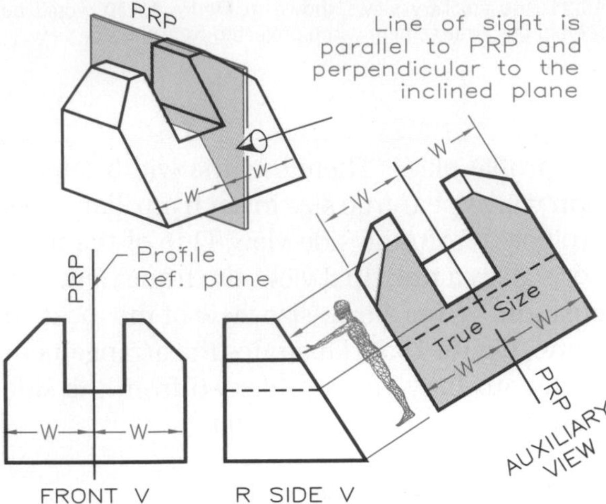

15.23 An auxiliary view is projected from the right-side view by using a profile reference plane (PRP) to show the true-size view of the inclined surface.

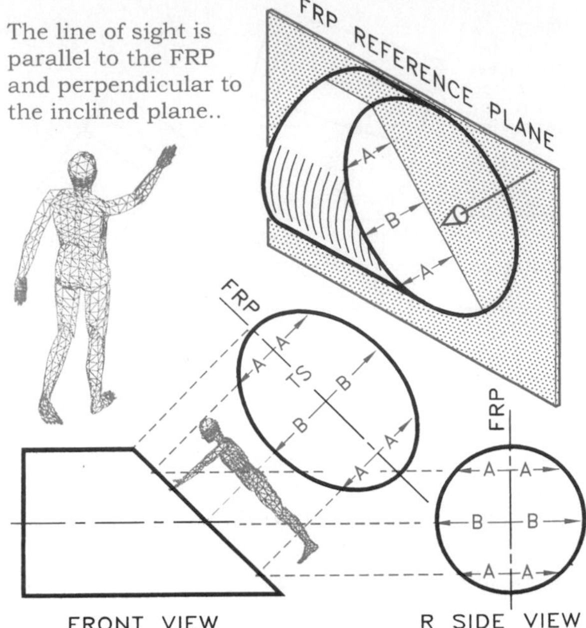

15.24 The auxiliary view of this elliptical surface was found by locating a series of points about its perimeter. The frontal reference plane (FRP) is drawn through its center in the side view, since the object is symmetrical.

projected from the side view. The auxiliary fold line, P-1, is drawn parallel to the edge view of the inclined surface. A line of sight perpendicular to the auxiliary plane shows the profile plane as an edge; therefore, width dimensions (W) transferred from the front view to the auxiliary view appear true length in the auxiliary view.

Reference-Plane Method

The object shown in **Figure 15.23** has an inclined surface that appears as an edge in the right-side view, the profile view. This inclined surface may be drawn true size in an auxiliary view by using a profile reference plane (PRP) that is a vertical edge in the front view. Draw the PRP through the center of the front view because the view is symmetrical. Then, find the true-size view of the inclined plane by transferring equal width dimensions (W) with your dividers from the edge view of the PRP in the front view to both sides of the PRP in the auxiliary view.

15.8 Curved Shapes

The cylinder shown in **Figure 15.24** has an inclined surface that appears as an edge in the front view. The true-size view of this plane can be seen in an auxiliary view projected from the front view.

Because the cylinder is symmetrical, a frontal reference plane (FRP) is drawn through the center of the side view so that equal dimensions can be laid off on both sides of it. Points located about the circular side view are projected to its edge view in the front view.

In the auxiliary view, the FRP is drawn parallel to the edge view of the plane in the front view, and the points are projected perpendicularly from the edge view of the plane. Dimensions A and B are shown as examples of depth dimensions used for locating points in the auxiliary view. To construct a smooth

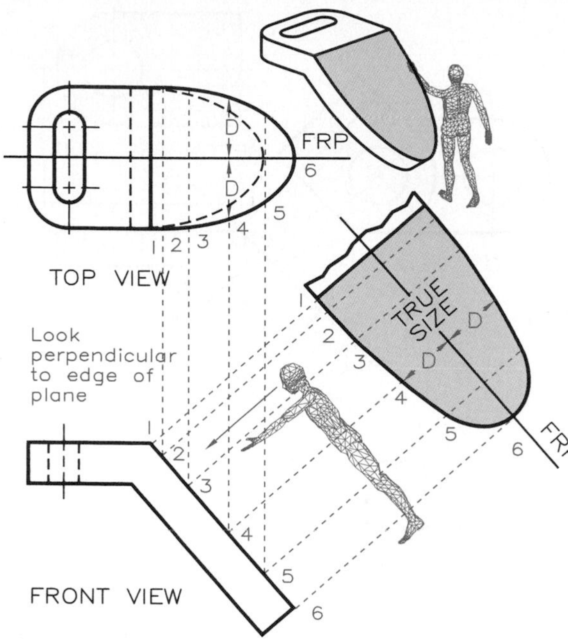

15.25 The auxiliary view of this curved surface required that a series of points be located in the top view, be projected to the front view, and then projected to the auxiliary view. The FRP was passed through the top view.

elliptical curve, more points than shown are needed.

A true-size auxiliary view of a surface bounded by an irregular curve is shown in **Figure 15.25**. Project points from the curve in the top view to the front view. Locate these points in the auxiliary view by transferring depth dimensions (D) from the FRP in the top view to the auxiliary view.

15.9 Partial Views

Auxiliary views are used as supplementary views to clarify features that are difficult to depict with principal views alone. Consequently, portions of principal views and auxiliary views may be omitted, provided that the partial views adequately describe the part. The object shown in **Figure 15.26** is composed of a complete front view, a partial auxiliary view, and a partial top

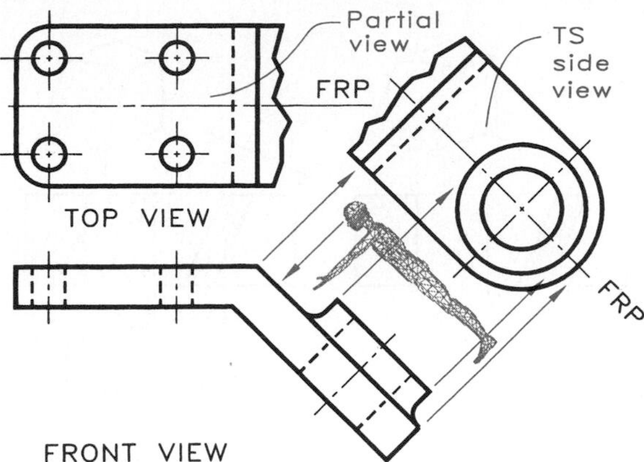

15.26 Partial views with foreshortened portions omitted can be used to represent objects. The FRP reference line is drawn through the center of the object in the top view because the object is symmetrical to make point location easier.

view. These partial views are easier to draw and are more descriptive without sacrificing clarity.

15.10 Auxiliary Sections

In **Figure 15.27**, a cutting plane labeled A-A is passed through the part to obtain the auxiliary section labeled section A-A. The auxiliary

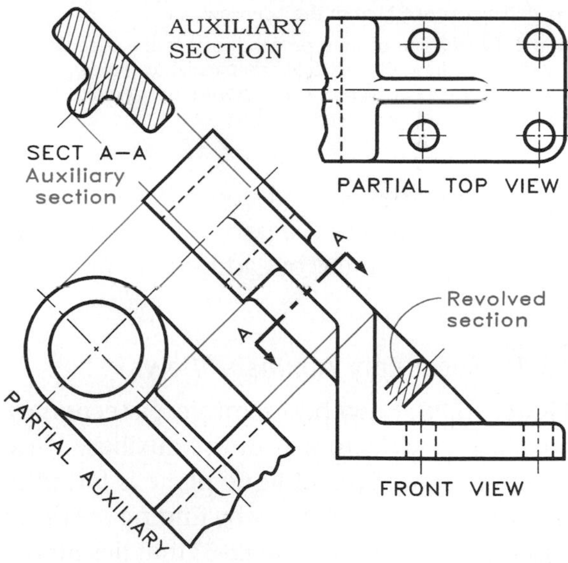

15.27 A cutting plane labeled A-A is passed through the object, and the auxiliary section, section A-A, is drawn as a supplementary view to describe the part. The top and front views are drawn as partial views.

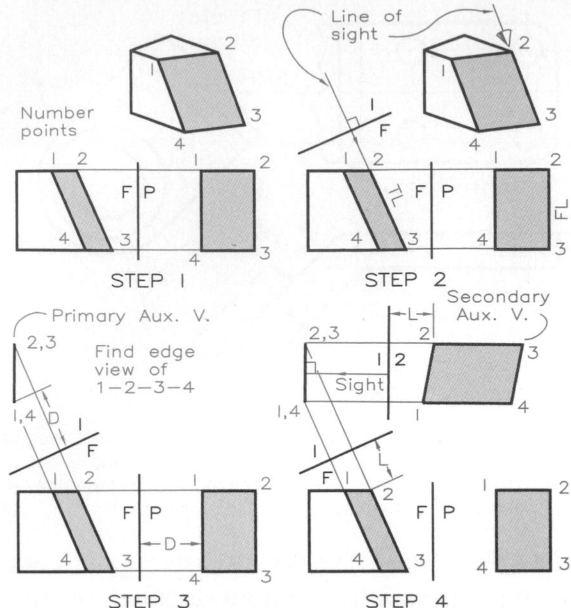

15.28 Secondary auxiliary views.

Step 1 Draw a fold line F-P between the front and side views. Label the corner points in both views.

Step 2 Line 2-3 is a true-length frontal line in the front view. Draw reference line F-1 perpendicular to line 2-3 at a convenient location with a line of sight parallel to line 2-3.

Step 3 Find the edge view of plane 1-2-3-4 by transferring depth dimensions (D) from the side view.

Step 4 Draw a line of sight perpendicular to the edge view of 1-2-3-4 and draw the 1-2 fold line parallel to the edge view. Find the true-size auxiliary view by transferring the dimensions (L) from the front view to the auxiliary view.

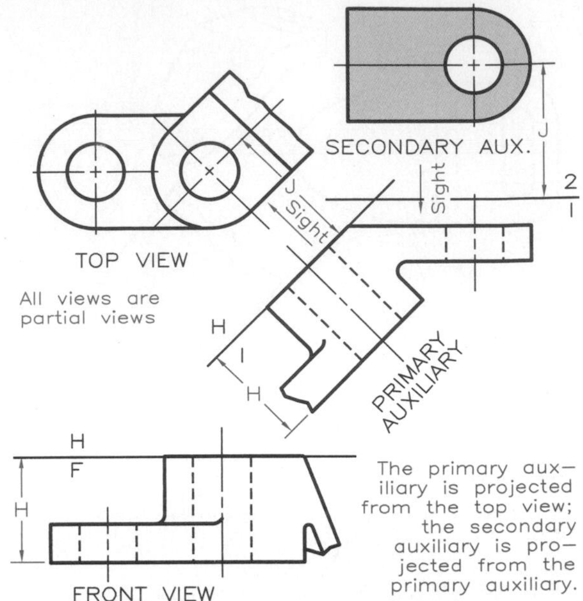

15.29 A secondary auxiliary view projected from a primary auxiliary view that was projected from the top view is shown here. All views are drawn as partial views.

section provides a good and efficient way to describe features of the part that could not be as easily described by additional principal views.

15.11 Secondary Auxiliary Views

Figure 15.28 shows how to project a secondary auxiliary view from a primary auxiliary view. An edge view of the oblique plane is found in the primary auxiliary view by finding the point view of a true-length line (2-3) that lies on the oblique surface. A line of sight perpendicular to the edge view of the plane gives a secondary auxiliary view that shows the oblique plane as true size.

Note that the reference line between the primary auxiliary view and the secondary auxiliary view is labeled 1-2 to represent the fold line between the primary plane (1) and the secondary plane (2). The label 1 is placed on the primary side and the label 2 is placed on the secondary side.

Figure 15.29 illustrates the construction of a secondary auxiliary view that gives the true-size view of a surface on a part using these same principles and a combination of partial views. A secondary auxiliary view must be used in this case because the oblique plane does not appear as an edge in a principal view.

Find the point view of a line on the oblique plane to find the edge view of the plane in the primary auxiliary view. The secondary auxiliary view, projected perpendicularly from the edge view of the plane in the primary auxiliary view, gives a true-size view of the plane. In this example all the views are drawn as partial views.

15.12 Elliptical Features

Occasionally, circular shapes will project as ellipses, which must be drawn with an irregular curve or an ellipse template. The ellipse template (guide) is by far the most convenient method of drawing ellipses. The angle of the ellipse template is the angle the line of sight makes with the edge view of the circular feature. In **Figure 15.30** the angle is found to be 45° where the curve is an edge in the front view, so the right-side view of the curve is drawn as a 45° ellipse.

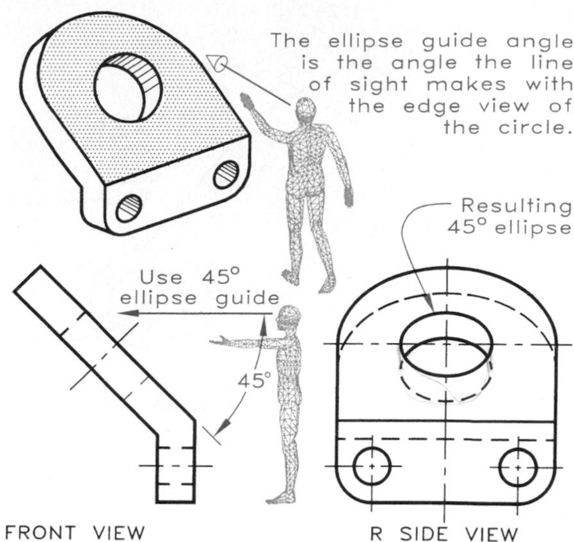

15.30 The ellipse guide angle is the angle that the line of sight makes with the edge view of the circular feature. The ellipse angle for the right-side view is 45°.

Problems

1–13. (**Figure 15.31**) Using the example layout, change the top and front views by substituting the top views given at the right in place of the one given in the example. The angle of inclination in the front view is 45° for all problems, and the height is 38 mm (1.5 in.) in the front view. Construct auxiliary views that show the inclined surface true size. Draw two problems per size A sheet.

14–31. (**Figures 15.32–15.49**) Draw the necessary primary and auxiliary views to describe the objects assigned. Draw one per size A or size B sheet. Adjust the scale of each to utilize the space on the sheet.

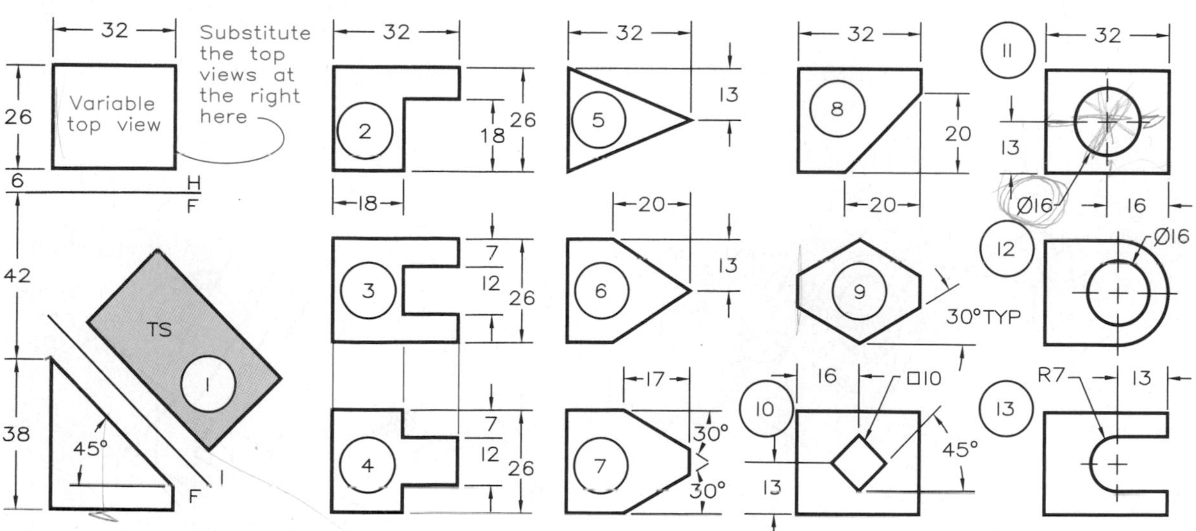

15.31 Problems 1–13. Primary auxiliary views.

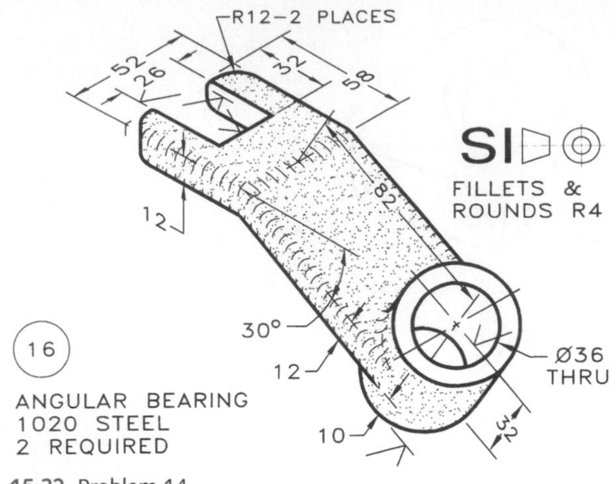

15.32 Problem 14.

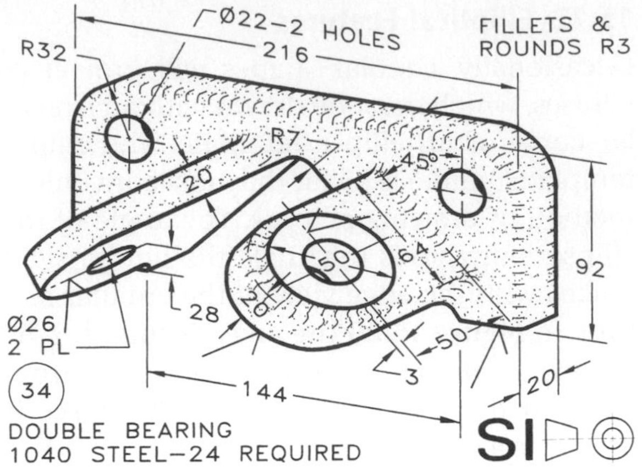

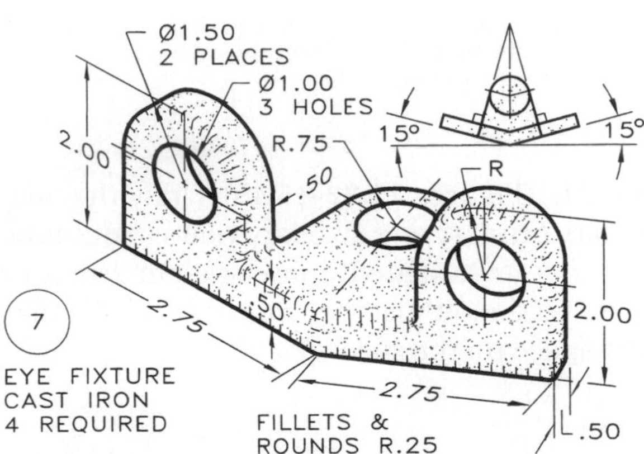

15.33 Problem 15.

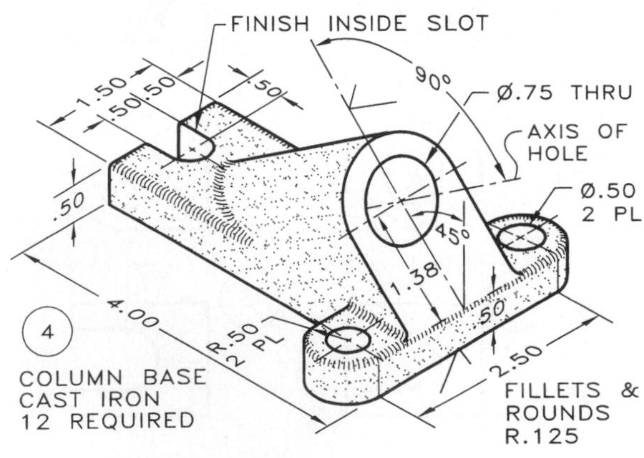

15.34 Problem 16.

15.35 Problem 17.

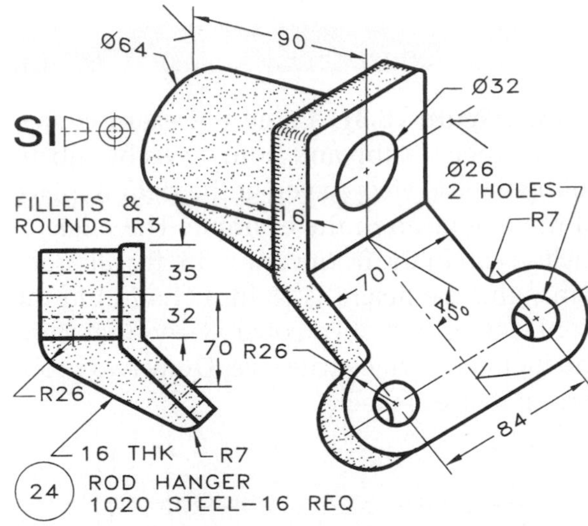

15.36 Problem 18.

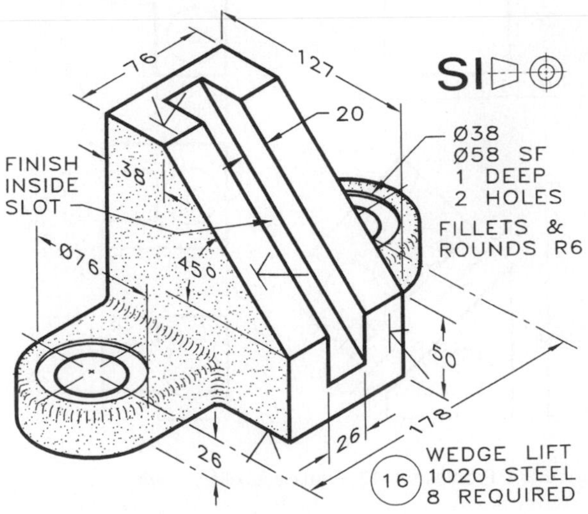

15.37 Problem 19.

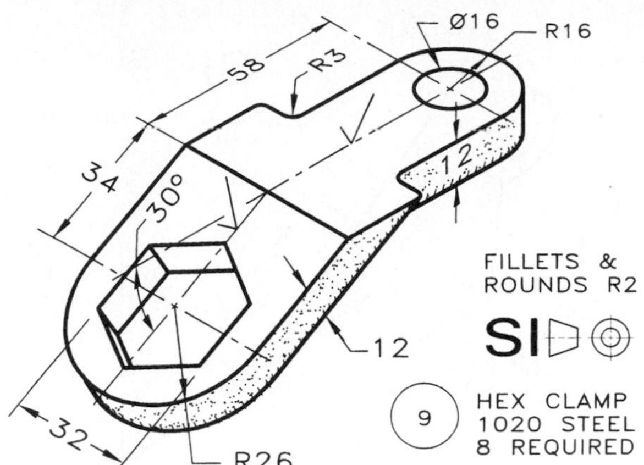

15.38 Problem 20.

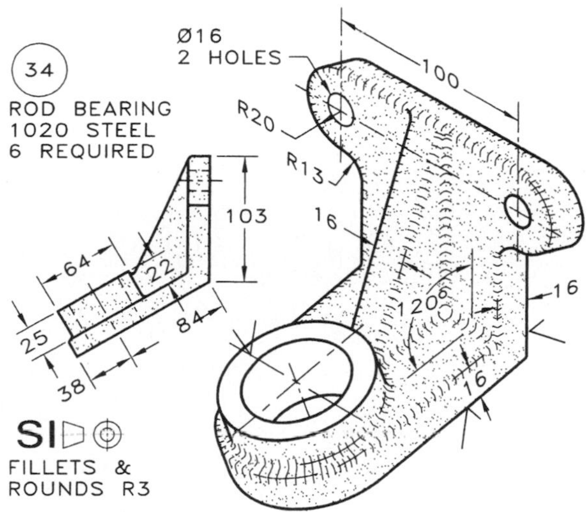

15.39 Problem 21.

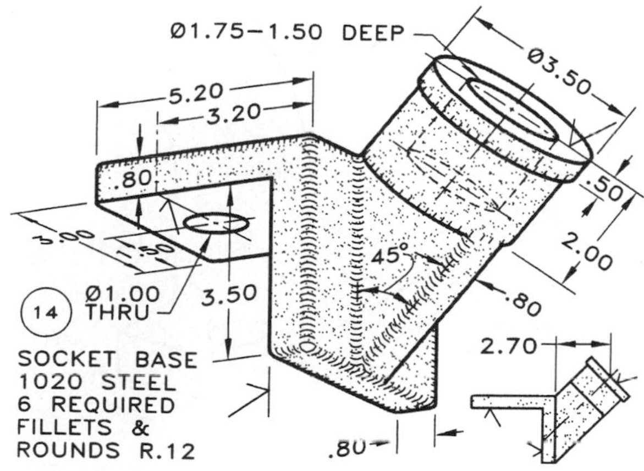

15.40 Problem 22.

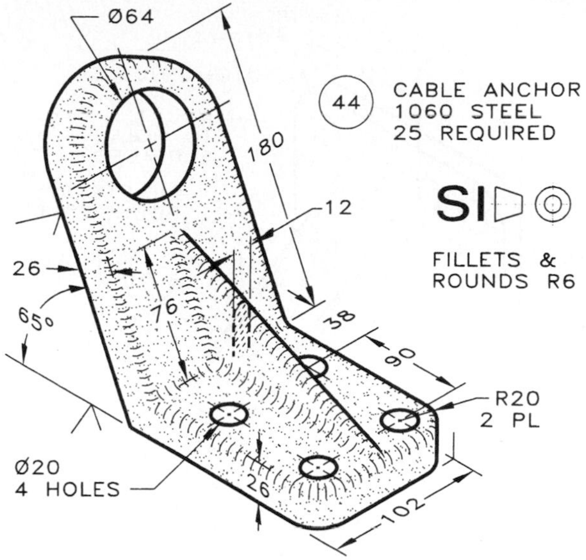

15.41 Problem 23.

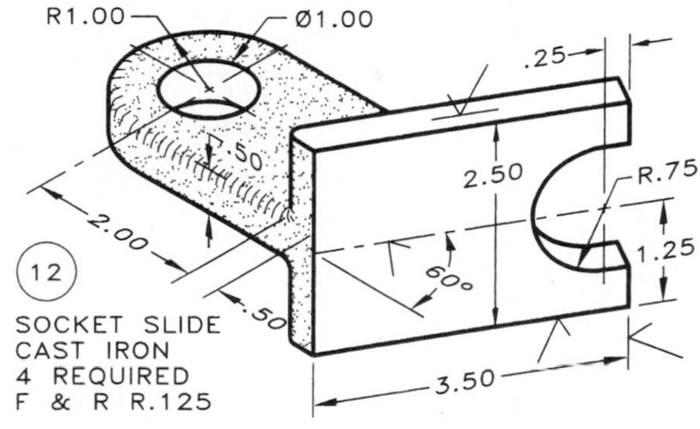

15.42 Problem 24.

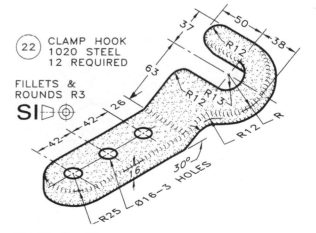

22 CLAMP HOOK
1020 STEEL
12 REQUIRED

FILLETS & ROUNDS R3

SI

50 37 38 R12 63 R13 R12 26 42 42 R R12 16 30° Ø16–3 HOLES R25

15.43 Problem 25.

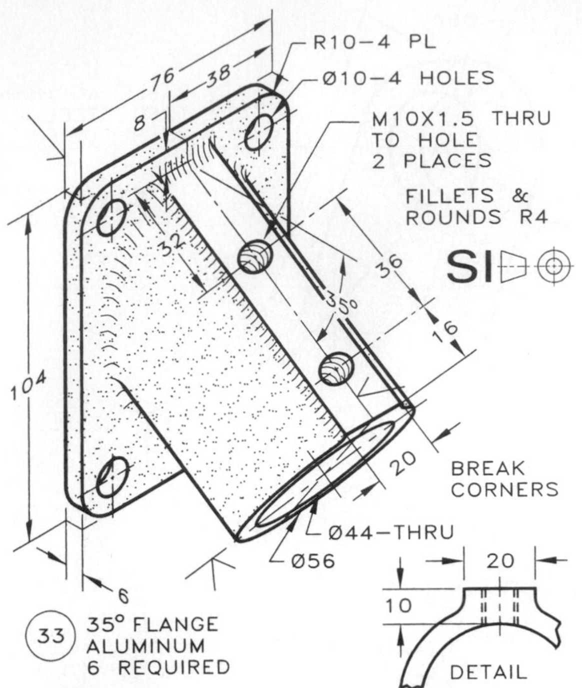

15.44 Problem 26.

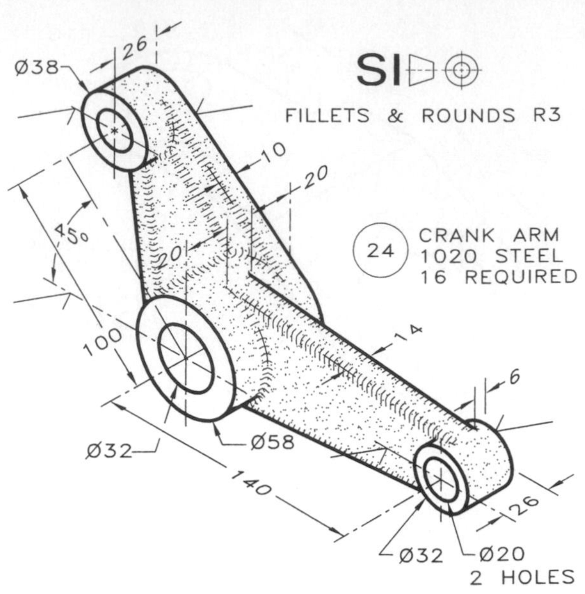

15.46 Problem 28.

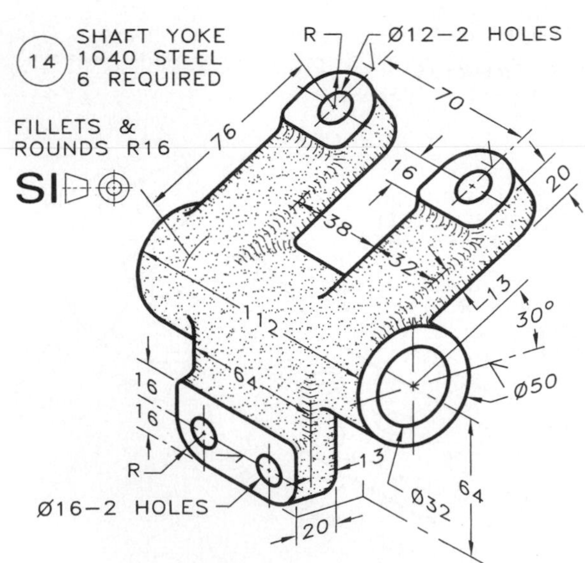

15.45 Problem 27.

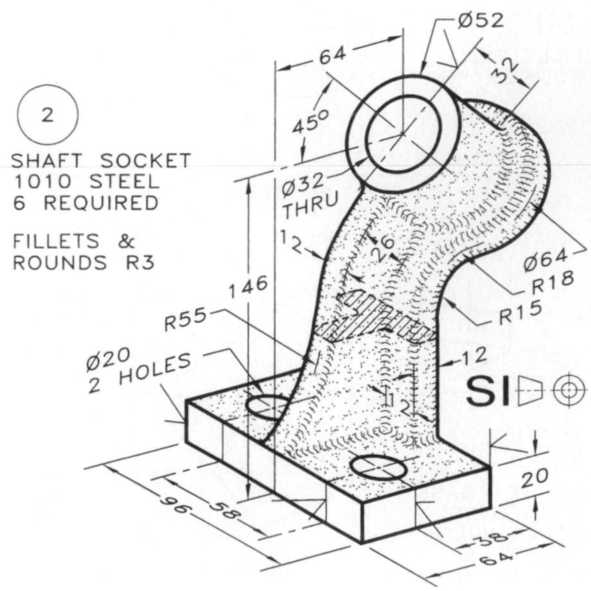

15.47 Problem 29.

15.48 Problem 30. Lay out the necessary orthographic views of the oblique bracket on a size B sheet. Construct the true-size auxiliary view that shows the inclined surface true size. Select the appropriate scale.

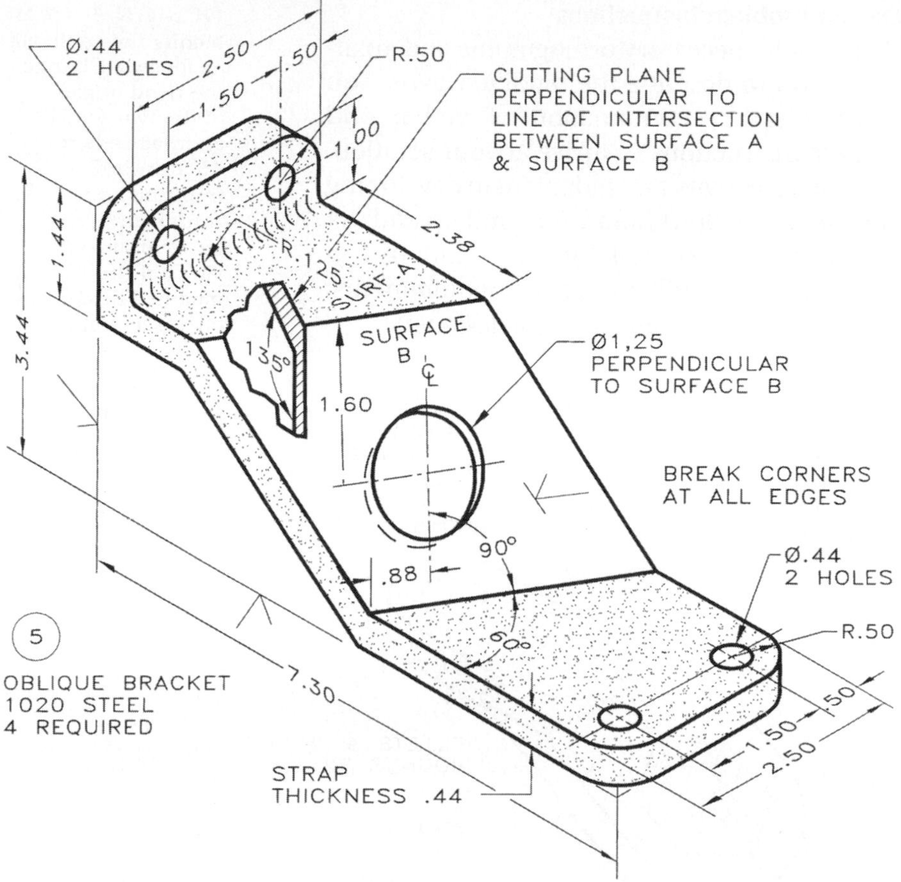

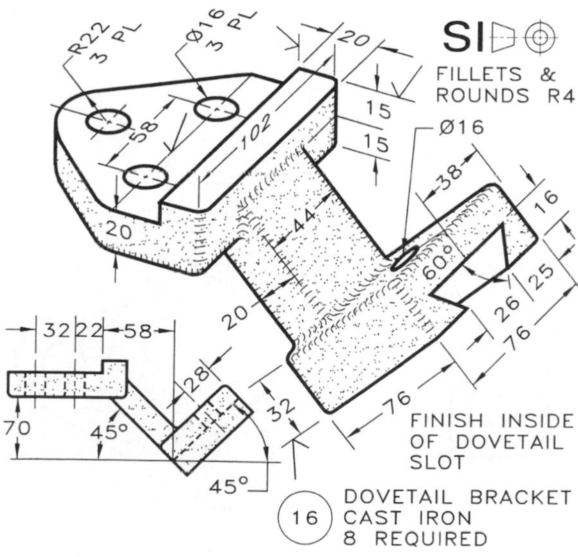

15.49 Problem 31.

Design Problems

Refer to the instructions for design problems at the top of the following page. This problem is to be solved on size A sheets.

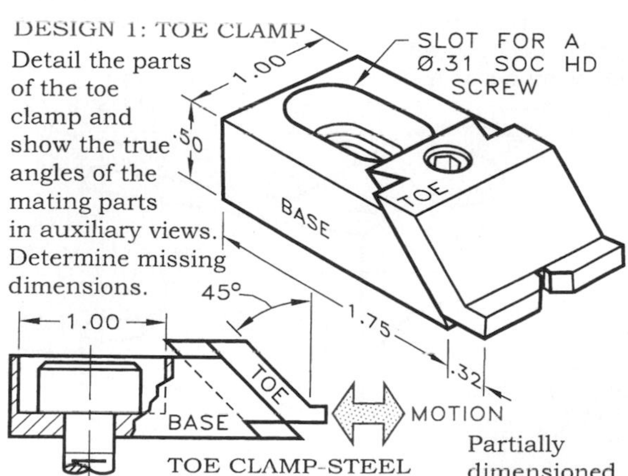

Design Problem Instructions

Develop the necessary orthographic and auxiliary views to describe the modified parts. You must follow a combination of verbal and graphic instructions to arrive at your solution. Use your creativity and judgment in developing your solution; don't hold your hand up and ask your instructor to think for you. Solutions can vary and still fulfill the stated requirements; grab hold, figure it out, and be a designer!

DESIGN 2: HEX CLAMP

Modify the clamp to have a 45° bend instead of 30°, a square hole with corners aligned with the centerlines instead of a hexagon, and a 32 DIA hole instead of a 16 DIA hole. Add a 10 mm thick rib from the edge of each hole for added strength. Draw on a size A sheet. Make other modifications as needed.

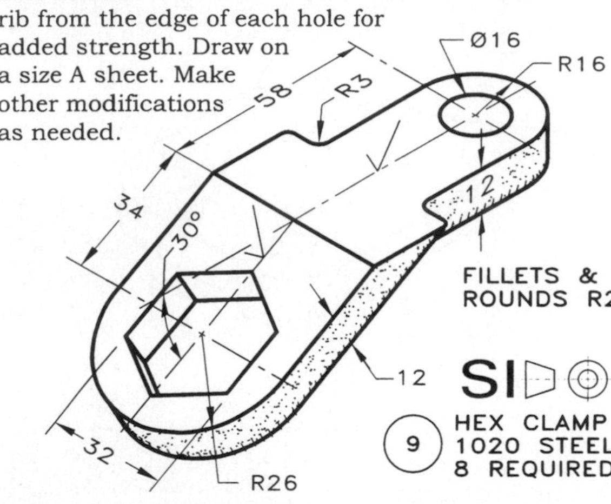

DESIGN 3: SOCKET SLIDE

Modify the slide as follows: Slant the base 45° instead of 60°; using the same center location, convert the semicircular slot into a circular hole of 1.50 DIA and make the end of the base semicircular and concentric with the 1.50 DIA hole. Draw on a size A sheet.

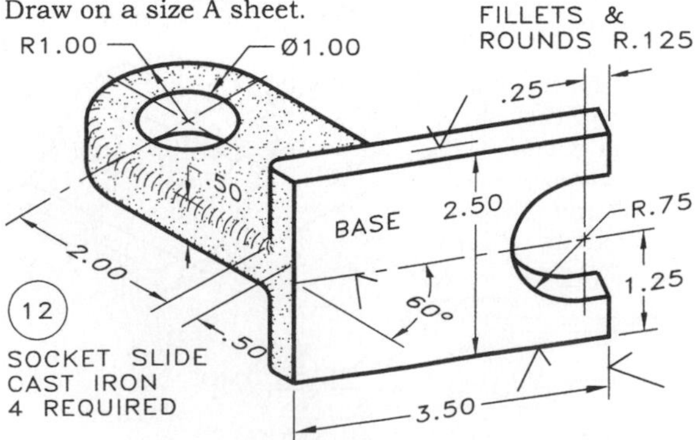

DESIGN 4: CABLE CLIP

Modify the cable clip as follows: Change the bend angles of the two semicircular ends to 45° outward from the horizontal feature. Draw auxiliary views of the modified design on a size A sheet.

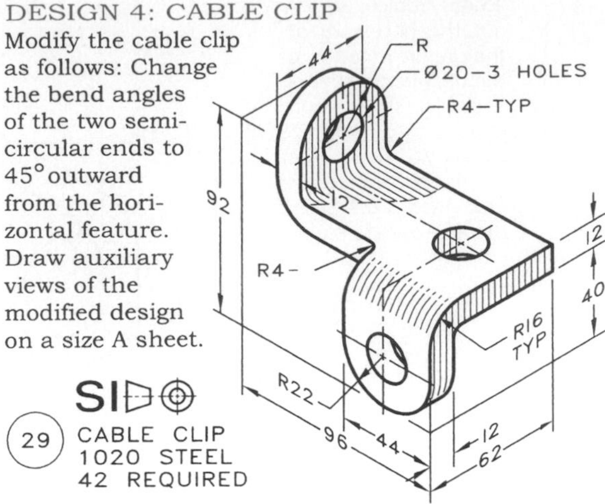

DESIGN 5: ROD HANGER

Modify the hanger as follows: Make the vertical feature semicircular about the 32 DIA hole; add two bosses of 52 DIA about the 26 DIA holes that rise 6 mm above the slanted surface; finish the bosses and eliminate the finishing elsewhere on the slanted surface. Draw on a size A sheet.

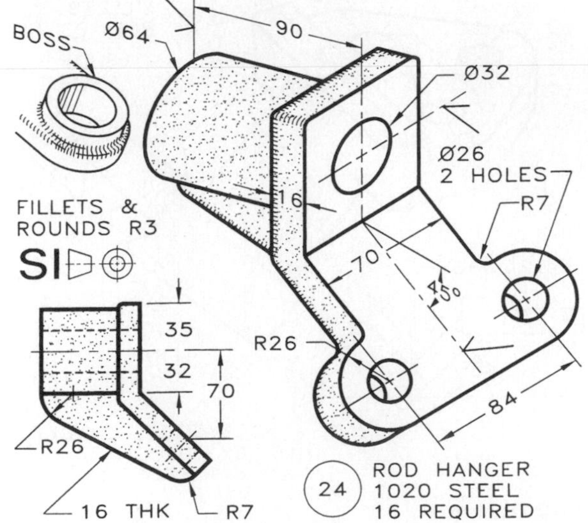

DESIGN 6: CABLE ANCHOR

Change the slope of the inclined feature to 45° from 65°; change the base from rectangular to triangular with 3 holes instead of 4; and modify the rib as necessary. Draw the necessary orthographic views on a size A sheet at an appropriate scale.

(23) CABLE ANCHOR 1010 STEEL 50 REQUIRED

FILLETS & ROUNDS R6

Ø64 180 12 26 65° 76 38 90 R20 2 PL Ø20 4 HOLES 26 102

DESIGN 8: GUIDE

The inclined feature is to have a slope of 25° and three equally spaced holes with the outside ones 30 mm from the edge. Complete the design that joins the inclined feature with the base into a single part. Show the necessary auxiliary views on a size B sheet.

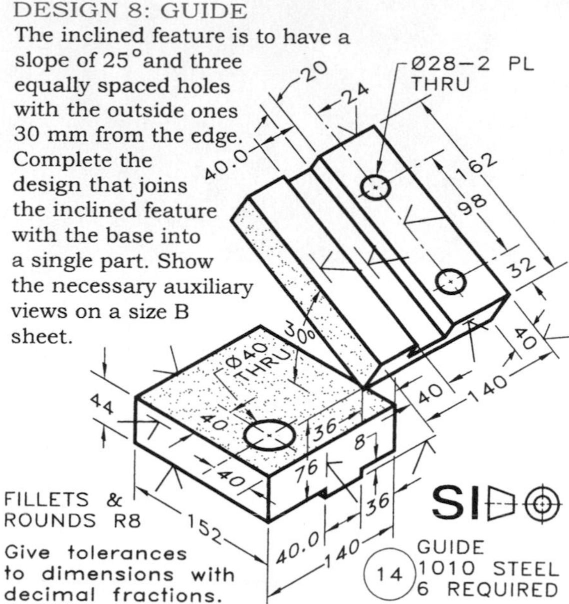

DESIGN 7: CONNECTOR

Modify both vertical sides to make angles of 20° with the vertical (40° apart); make both ends of these panels symmetrical with 10 DIA holes in each end (4 holes total); and make 3 equally spaced 6 DIA holes with the outside holes 20 mm from the ends of the horizontal base. Draw the necessary views on a size A sheet.

Make this end 40 tall also.

Make 3 eq. spaced 6 DIA holes in base

Ø10 2HOLES R12 TYP 114 VERTICAL SIDE VERTICAL SIDE BASE 40 R10 TYP 26 17 34 20

OUTSIDE BEND RADIUS R5

(3) CONNECTOR—1030 STEEL 3 THICK—4 REQUIRED

DESIGN 9: FLANGE COUPLING

Modify the coupling to support a shaft at a 10° angle with the base with its high end 1.40 above the base as shown. Incline the front and rear faces 10° as well. Draw the necessary auxiliary views on a size A sheet to represent the modified part.

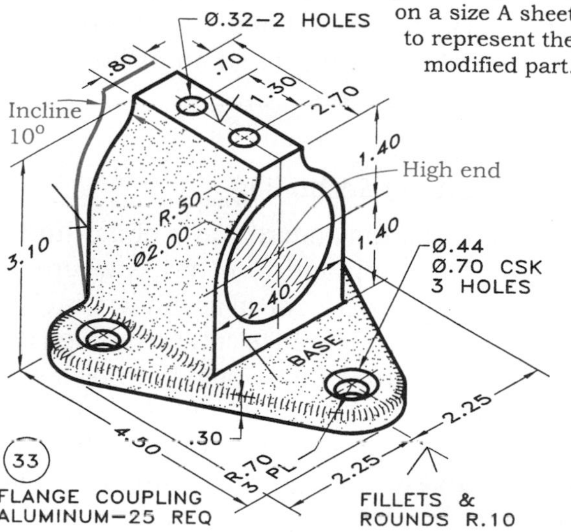

16
Sections

16.1 Introduction

Correctly drawn orthographic views that show all hidden lines may not clearly describe an object's internal details. The gear housing shown in **Figure 16.1** is such an example that is better understood when a section has been cut from it. The technique of constructing imaginary cross-sectional cuts through a drawing of a part results in an orthographic view called a **section**.

16.1 This gear housing has many internal features that cannot be described clearly in a standard orthographic view. Sections are used to clarify interior parts.

16.2 Basics of Sectioning

In **Figure 16.2A** standard views of a cylinder are shown as top and front views where its interior features are drawn as hidden lines. If you imagined a knife edge cutting through the top view, the front view would become a section. This section is a **full section**, since the cutting plane passes fully through the part (**Figure 16.2B**). The portion of the part that was cut by the imaginary plane is cross-hatched, and hidden lines usually are omitted in sectional views because they are not needed.

Figure 16.3 shows two types of cutting planes. Either is acceptable, although the one

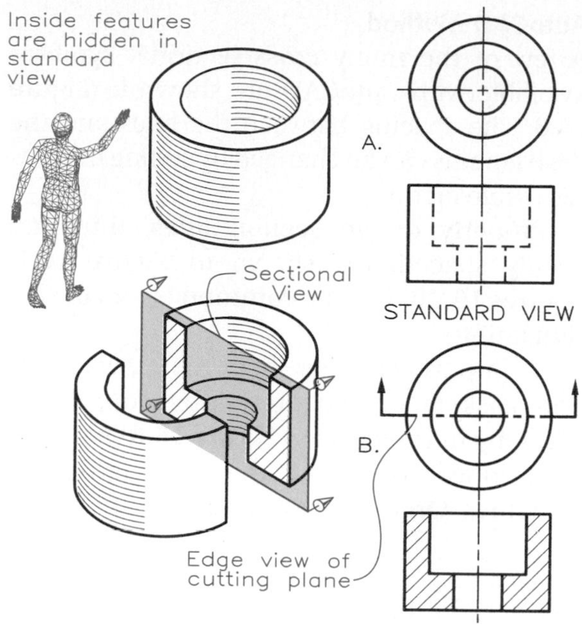

16.2 A part with internal features can be better shown with sectional views than with standard views with hidden lines.

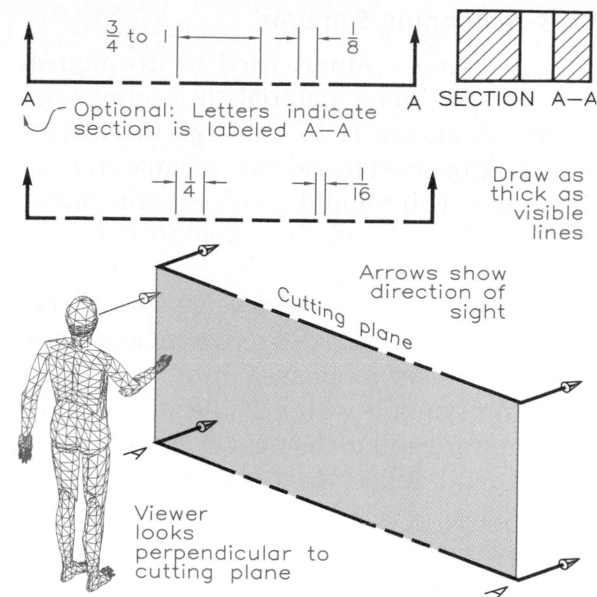

16.3 Cutting planes can be thought of as knife edges that pass through views to reveal interior features in sections. The cutting plane marked A-A results in a section labeled SECTION A-A.

with pairs of short dashes is most often used. The spacing and proportions of the dashes depend on the size of the drawing. The line thickness of the cutting planc is the same as the visible object line. Letters placed at each end of the cutting plane are used to label the sectional view, such as **SECTION A-A**.

The sight arrows at the ends of the cutting plane are always perpendicular to the cutting plane. In the sectional view, the observer is looking in the direction of the sight arrows, perpendicular to the surface of the cutting plane.

Figure 16.4 shows the three basic positions of sections and their respective cutting planes. In each case perpendicular arrows point in the direction of the line of sight. For example, the cutting plane in **Figure 16.4A** passes through and removes the front of the top view, and the line of sight is perpendicular to the remainder of the top view.

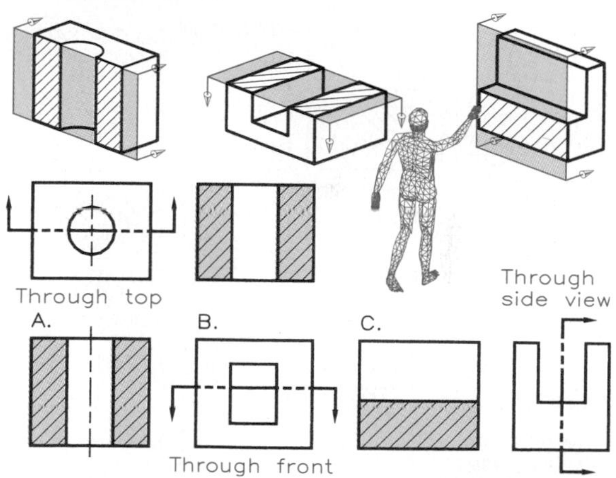

16.4 The three examples of cutting planes that pass through the principal views, (A) top, (B) front, and (C) side views, are shown here. The arrows point in the direction of the line of sight for each section.

The top view appears as a section when the cutting plane passes through the front view and the line of sight is downward (**Figure 16.4B**). When the cutting plane passes vertically through the side view (**Figure 16.4C**), the front view becomes a section.

16.3 Sectioning Symbols

The hatching symbols used to distinguish between different materials in sections are shown in **Figure 16.5**. Although these symbols may be used to indicate the materials in a section, you should provide supplementary notes specifying the materials to ensure clarity.

The cast-iron symbol (evenly spaced section lines) may be used to represent any material and is the symbol used most often. Draw cast-iron symbols with a 2H pencil, slant the lines upward and to the right at 30°, 45°, or 60° angles, and space the lines about 1/16 in. apart (close together in small areas and farther apart in larger areas).

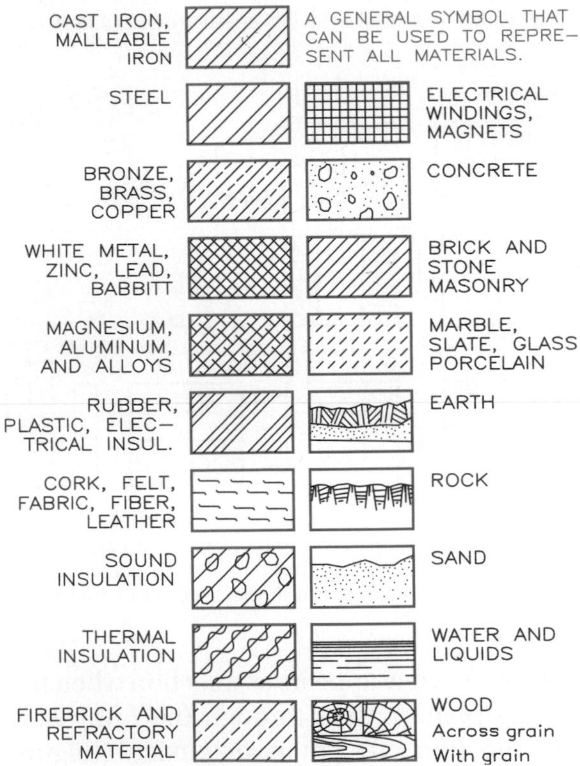

16.5 These symbols are used for hatching parts in section. The cast-iron symbol may be used for any material.

AutoCAD Method

A few of the many cross-sectional symbols available with AutoCAD are shown in **Figure 16.6**. The spacing between the lines and the dash lengths can be changed by setting the pattern scale factor.

Properly drawn section lines, thin and evenly spaced, are shown in **Figure 16.7. Figures 16.7B–F** show common errors of section lining.

Thin parts such as sheet metal, washers, and gaskets are sectioned by completely blacking in their areas (**Figure 16.8**) because space does not permit the drawing of section lines. On the other hand, large parts are

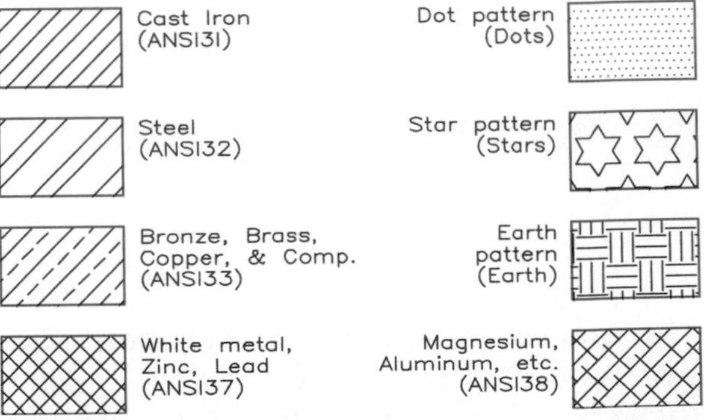

16.6 These are a few of the hatching symbols available in AutoCAD. The spacing and size of the symbols can be varied by setting the pattern scale factor.

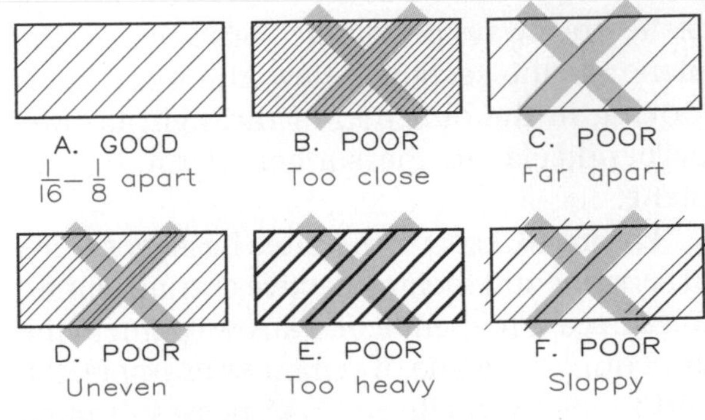

16.7 Hatching techniques.
A Section lines are thin black lines drawn 1/16 to 1/8 in. apart.
B–F Avoid these common errors of section lining.

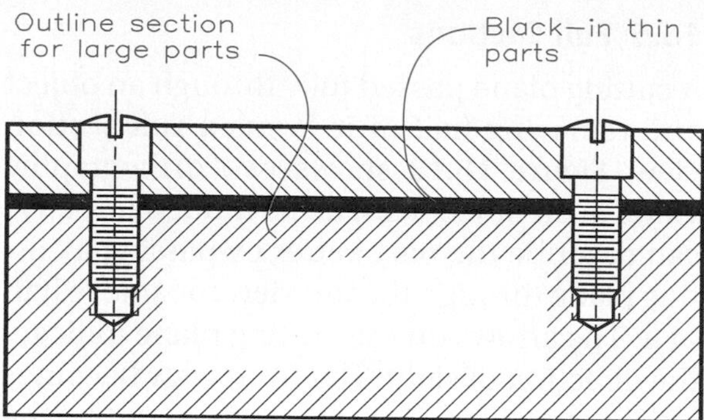

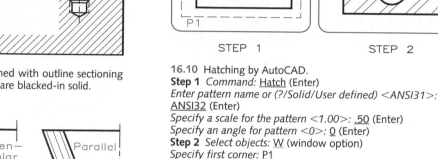

16.8 Large sectional areas are hatched with outline sectioning (around their edges), and thin parts are blacked-in solid.

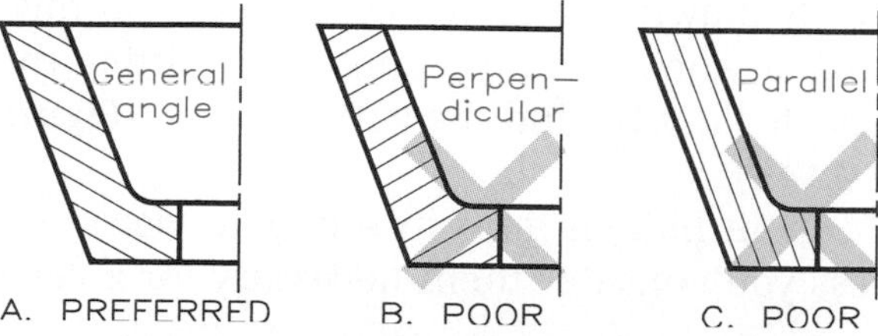

16.9 Draw section lines that are neither parallel nor perpendicular to the outlines of the part, so that they are not misunderstood as machining features.

sectioned with an **outline section** to save time and effort.

Sectioned areas should be hatched with symbols that are neither parallel nor perpendicular to the outlines of the parts lest they be confused with serrations or other machining treatments of the surface (**Figure 16.9**).

The most basic principle of applying section symbols to an area with AutoCAD is shown in **Figure 16.10**. After assigning the proper hatch symbol with the *Hatch* command, select the area to be sectioned with a window, and the hatch lines are drawn. To vary the spacing of the section lines, change the patterns scale of the *Hatch* command. *Bhatch* and other hatching commands are covered in Chapters 37 and 38.

The lines that outline areas to be hatched must intersect perfectly at each corner point;

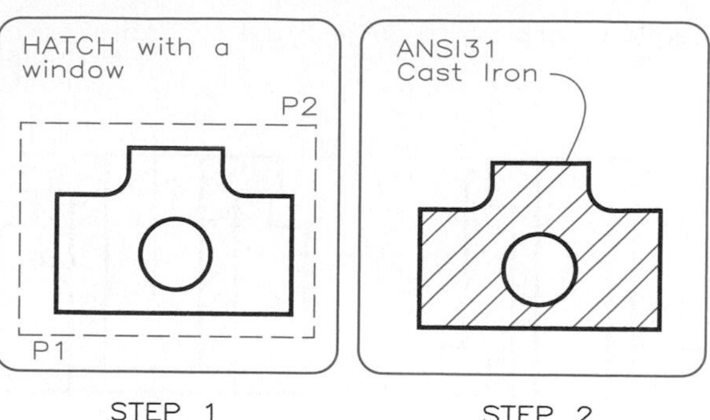

16.10 Hatching by AutoCAD.
Step 1 *Command:* Hatch (Enter)
Enter pattern name or (?/Solid/User defined) <ANSI31>: ANSI32 (Enter)
Specify a scale for the pattern <1.00>: .50 (Enter)
Specify an angle for pattern <0>: 0 (Enter)
Step 2 *Select objects:* W (window option)
Specify first corner: P1
Specify opposite corner: P2 (Enter) (The hatching is applied.)

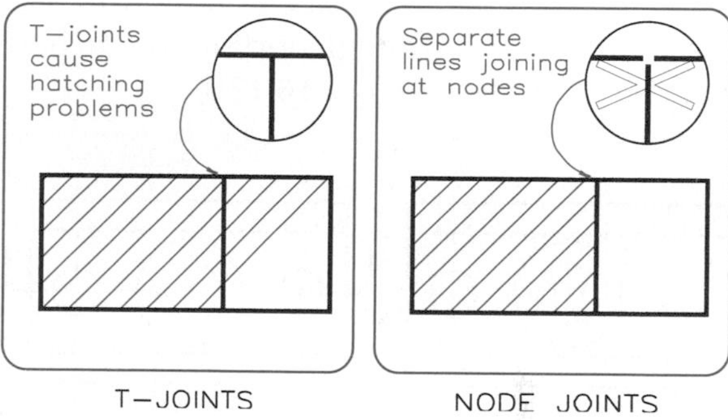

16.11 For the *Hatch* command to work properly, the outlines of areas to be section lined must be drawn with perfect-closing outlines. T-joints, overlaps, or gaps at intersections can result in irregular results.

no T-joints are permitted (**Figure 16.11**). Poor intersections may cause hatching symbols to fill the desired area improperly.

16.4 Sectioning Assemblies of Parts

When sectioning an assembly of several parts, draw section lines at varying angles to distinguish the parts from one another (**Figure 16.12A**). Using different material symbols in

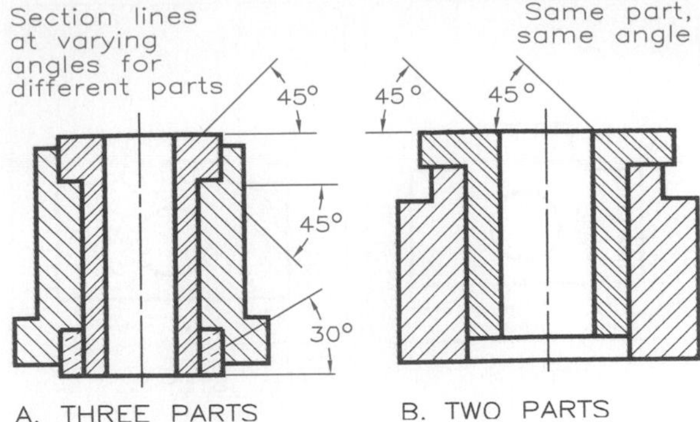

16.12 Hatching parts in assembly.
A Draw section lines of different parts in an assembly at varying angles to distinguish the parts.
B Draw section lines on separated portions of the same part (both sides of a hole here) in the same direction.

an assembly also helps distinguish among the parts and their materials. Crosshatch the same part at the same angle and with the same symbol even though portions of the part may be separated (**Figure 16.12B**).

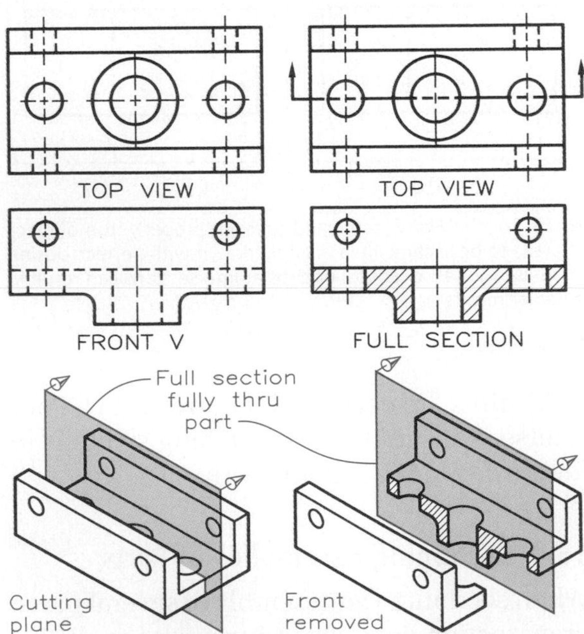

16.13 A full section is found by passing a cutting plane fully through the top view of this part, removing half of it. The arrows on the cutting plane give the direction of the line of sight. The front sectional view shows the internal features clearly.

16.5 Full Sections

A cutting plane passed fully through an object and removing half of it forms a **full section** view. **Figure 16.13** shows two orthographic views of an object with all its hidden lines. We can describe the part better by passing a cutting plane through the top view to remove half of it. The arrows on the cutting plane indicate the direction of sight. The front view becomes a full section, showing the surfaces cut by the cutting plane. **Figure 16.14** shows a full section through a cylindrical part, with half the object removed. **Figure 16.14A** shows the correctly drawn sectional view. A common mistake in constructing sections is omitting the visible lines behind the cutting plane (**Figure 16.14B**).

Omit hidden lines in sectional views unless you consider them necessary for a clear

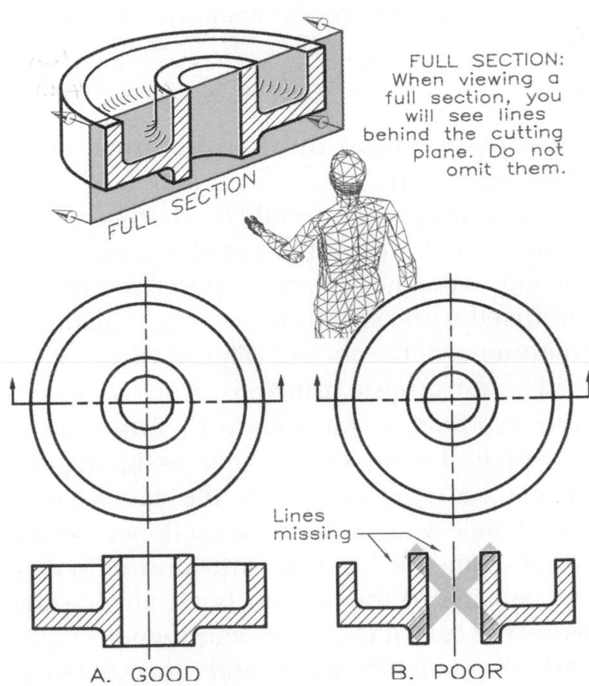

16.14 Full section; cylindrical part.
A When a front view of a cylinder is shown as a full section as shown here, visible lines will be seen behind the cut surface.
B By showing only the lines of the cut surface, the section, the view will be incompete.

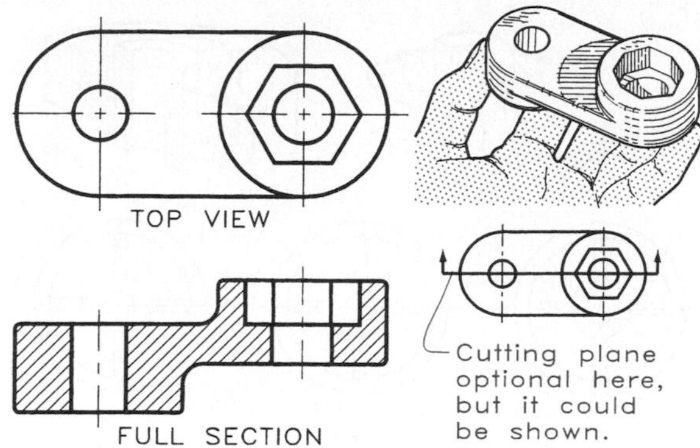

16.15 The cutting plane of a section can be omitted if its location is obvious.

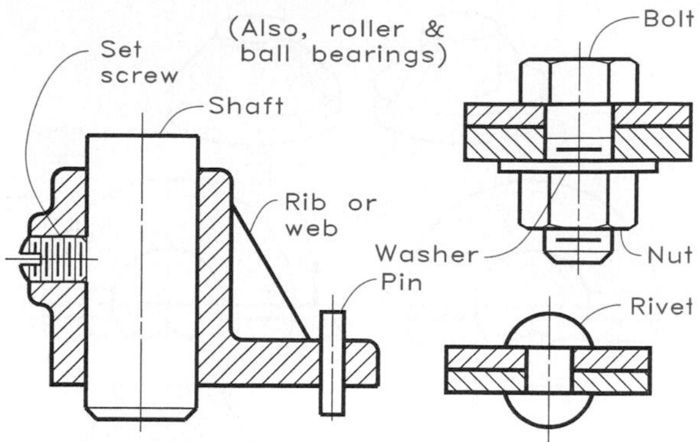

16.16 By conventional practice these parts are not section lined even though cutting planes pass through them.

understanding of the view. Also, omit cutting planes if you consider them unnecessary. **Figure 16.15** shows a full section of a part from which the cutting plane was omitted because its path is obvious.

Parts Not Requiring Section Lining

Many standard parts, such as nuts and bolts, rivets, shafts, and setscrews, do not require section lining even though the cutting plane passes through them (**Figure 16.16**). These parts have no internal features, so sections through them would be of no value. Other parts not requiring section lining are roller bearings, ball bearings, gear teeth, dowels, pins, and washers.

Ribs

Ribs are not section lined when the cutting plane passes flatwise through them (**Figure 16.17A**), because to do so would give a misleading impression of the rib. But ribs do require section lining when the cutting plane passes perpendicularly through them and shows their true thickness (**Figure 16.17B**).

By not section lining the ribs in **Figure 16.18A,** we provided a descriptive section view of the part. Had we hatched the ribs, the section would give the impression that the part was solid and conical (**Figure 16.18B**).

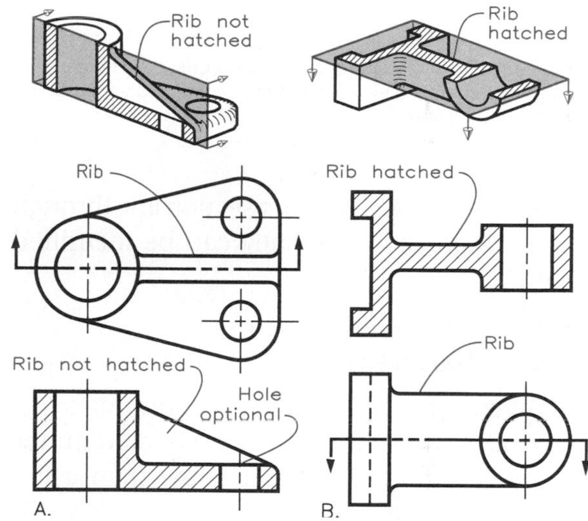

16.17 Ribs in section.
A A rib cut in a flatwise direction is not hatched.
B Ribs are hatched when cutting planes pass through them, showing their true thickesses.

Figure 16.19 shows an alternative method of section lining webs and ribs. The outside ribs in **Figure 16.19A** do not require section lining because the cutting plane passes flatwise through them and they are well identified. As a rule, webs do not require crosshatching, but the webs shown in **Figure 16.19B** are not well identified in the front section and could go unnoticed. Therefore, using alternative section lines as shown in **Figure 16.19C** is preferable.

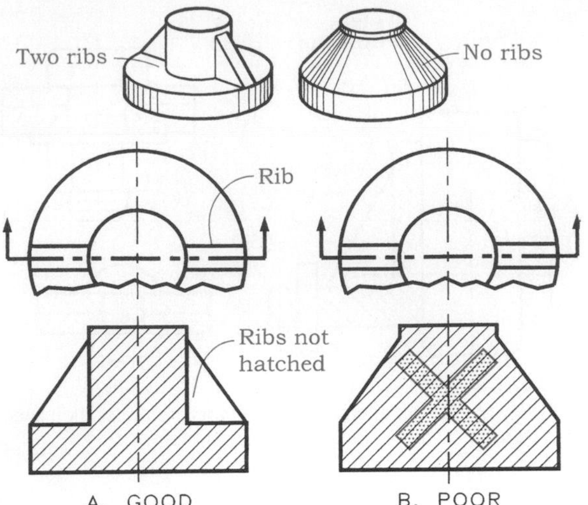

16.18 Ribs in section.
A Ribs are not hatched in section to better describe the part.
B If ribs were hatched in section, a misleading impression of the part would be given.

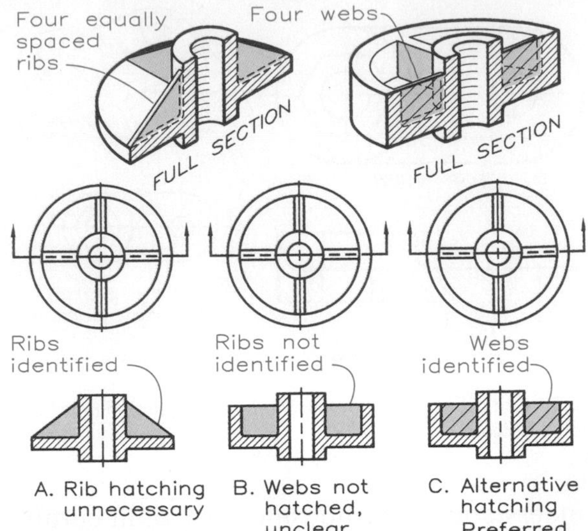

16.19 Ribs and webs in section.
A These ribs are well defined in this section and are not hatched.
B These webs are poorly defined when not hatched in the sectional view.
C Alternative hatch lines call attention to poorly defined webs.

Here, extending every other section line through the webs ensures that they can be identified easily.

16.6 Partial Views

A conventional method of representing symmetrical views is the half view, which requires less space and less time to draw than a full view (**Figure 16.20**). A half top view is sufficient when drawn adjacent to the section view or front view. For half views (not sections), the removed half is away from the adjacent view (**Figure 16.20A**). For full sections, the removed half is the half nearest the section (**Figure 16.20B**). When drawing partial views with half sections, you may omit either the near or the far halves of the partial views.

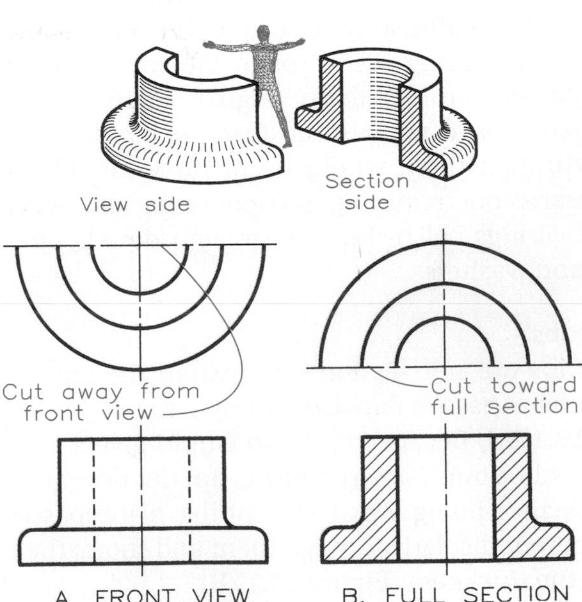

16.20 Half views of symmetrical parts can be used to conserve space and dawing time as an approved conventional practice. (A) The external portion of the half view is toward the front view. (B) The internal portion of the half view is toward the front view when it is a section. In half sections, the omitted half view can be either toward or away from the section.

16.7 Half Sections

A **half section** is a view obtained by passing a cutting plane halfway through an object and removing a quarter of it to show both external and internal features. Half sections are used

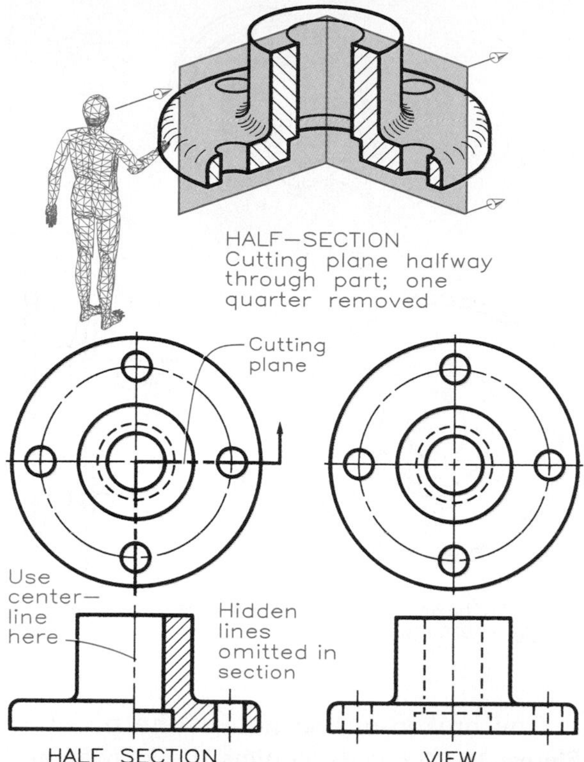

16.21 In a half section the cutting plane passes halfway through the object, removing a quarter of it, to show half the outside and half the inside. Omit hidden lines in sectional views unless they are needed for clarity.

with symmetrical parts and with cylinders, in particular, as shown in **Figure 16.21**. By comparing the half section with the standard front view, you can see that both internal and external features show more clearly in a half section than in a view. Hidden lines are unnecessary, and we've omitted them to simplify the section. **Figure 16.22** shows a half section of a pulley.

Note that the cutting plane is omitted from the half section shown in **Figure 16.23** because the cutting plane's location is obvious. Because the parting line of the half section is not at a centerline, you may use a solid line or a centerline to separate the sectional half from the half that appears as an external view.

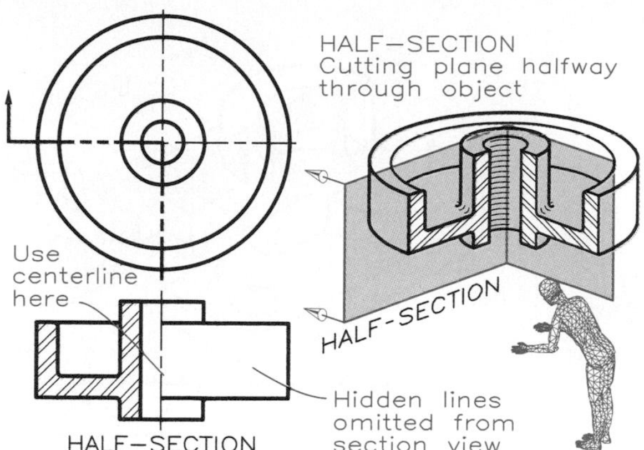

16.22 This half section describes the part that is shown orthographically and pictorially.

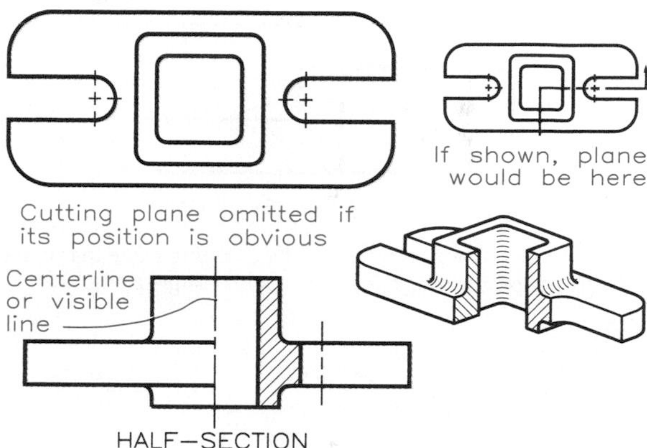

16.23 The cutting plane can be omitted when its location is obvious. The parting line between the section and the view may be a visible line or a centerline if the part is not cylindrical.

16.8 Offset Sections

An **offset section** is a full section in which the cutting plane is offset to pass through important features that do not lie in a single plane. **Figure 16.24** shows an offset section in which the plane is offset to pass through the large hole and one of the small holes. The cut formed by the offset is not shown in the section because it is imaginary.

16.9 Broken-Out Sections

A **broken-out section** shows a partial view of a part's interior features. The broken-out section

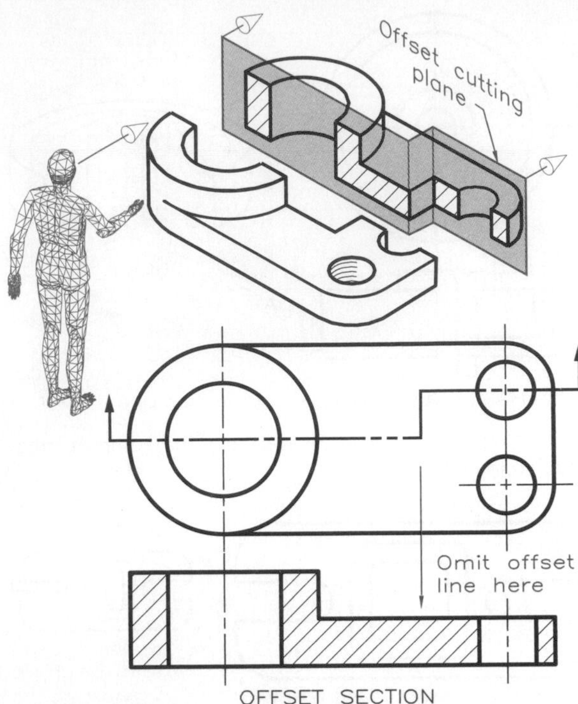

16.24 An offset section is formed by a cutting plane that must be offset to pass through features not in a single plane.

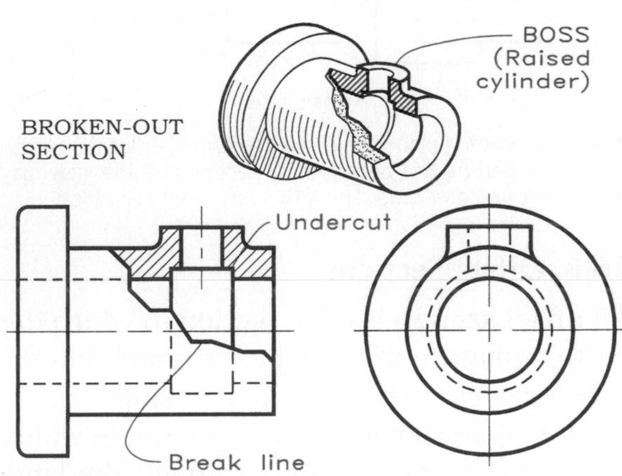

16.25 A broken-out section is one in which a part of the object has been broken away to show internal features.

of the part shown in **Figure 16.25** reveals details of the wall thickness to describe the part better. The irregular lines representing the break are conventional breaks (discussed later in this chapter).

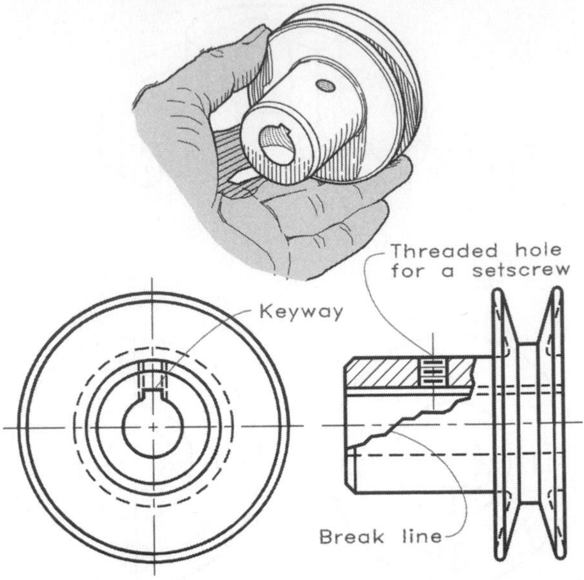

16.26 This broken-out section shows the keyway and the threaded hole for the setscrew in the pulley.

The broken-out section of the pulley in **Figure 16.26** clearly depicts the keyway and threaded hole for a setscrew. This method shows the part efficiently, with a minimum of views.

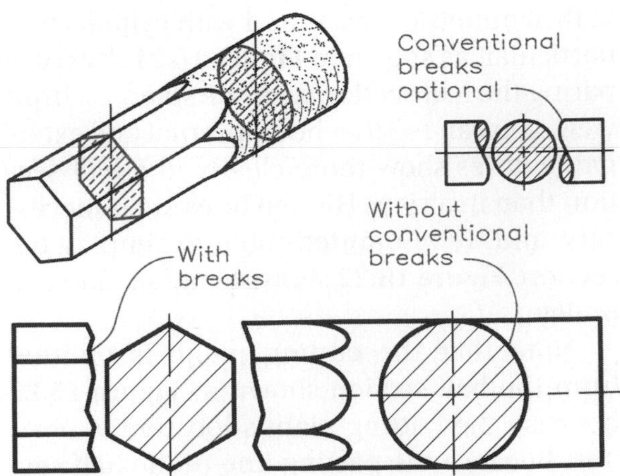

16.27 Revolved sections show cross-sectional features of a part and eliminate the need for additional orthographic views. Revolved sections may be superimposed on the given views, or conventional breaks may be used to separate them from the given view.

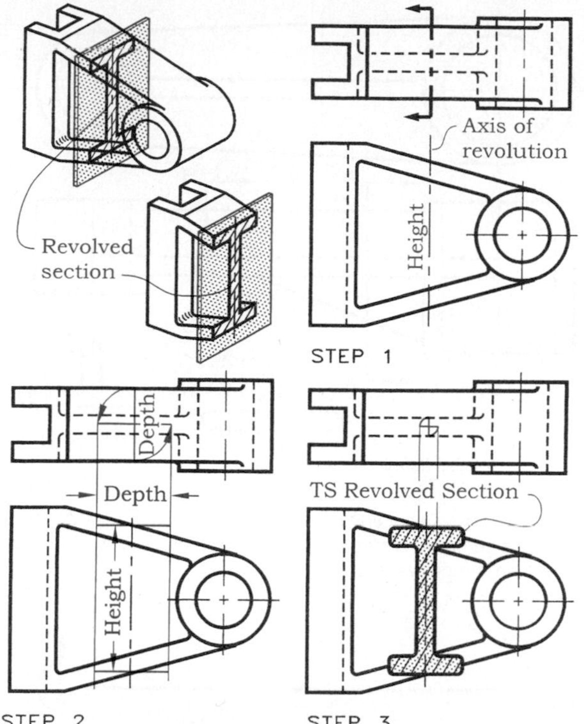

16.28 Revolved section construction.
Given: The part is shown pictorially with a cutting plane that shows the cross section that will be revolved.
Step 1 An imaginary cutting plane is located in the top view, and the axis of revolution is located in the front view.
Step 2 The depth in the top view is rotated in the top view and is projected to the front view. The height and depth in the front view give the overall dimensions of the revolved view.
Step 3 The revolved section is drawn, fillets and rounds are added, and section lines are applied to finish the view.

16.10 Revolved Sections

A **revolved section** describes a cross section that is revolved about an axis of revolution and placed on the view where the revolution occurred. Note the use of revolved sections to explain two cross sections of the shaft shown in **Figure 16.27** (with and without conventional breaks). Conventional breaks are optional; you may draw a revolved section on the view without them.

A revolved section helps describe the part shown in **Figure 16.28**. Imagine passing a cutting plane through the top view of the part (step 1). Then, imagine revolving the cutting plane in the top view and projecting it to the front (step 2). The true-size revolved section is completed in step 3. Conventional breaks could be used on each side of the revolved section.

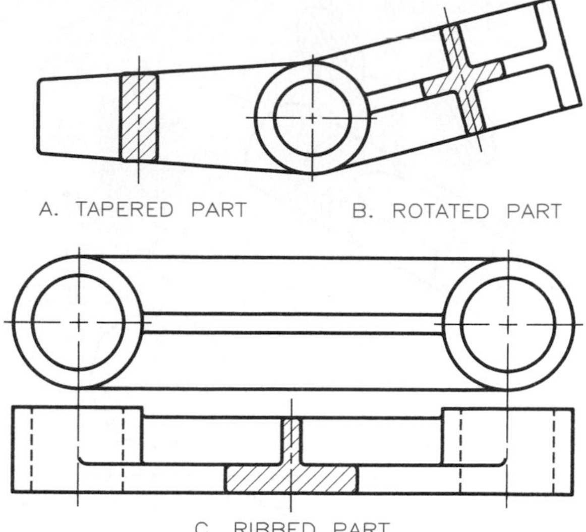

16.29 These revolved sections describe the cross sections of the two parts that would be difficult to depict in supplementary orthographic views, such as a side view.

Figure 16.29 demonstrates how to use typical revolved sections to show cross sections through parts without having to draw additional orthographic views.

16.11 Removed Sections

A **removed section** is a revolved section that is shown outside the view in which it was revolved (**Figure 16.30**). Centerlines are used as axes of revolution to show the locations from which the sections are taken. Where space does not permit revolution on the given view (**Figure 16.31A**), removed sections must be used instead of revolved sections (**Figure 16.31B**).

Removed sections do not have to be positioned directly along an axis of revolution adjacent to the view from which they were revolved. Instead, removed sections can be located elsewhere on a drawing if they are

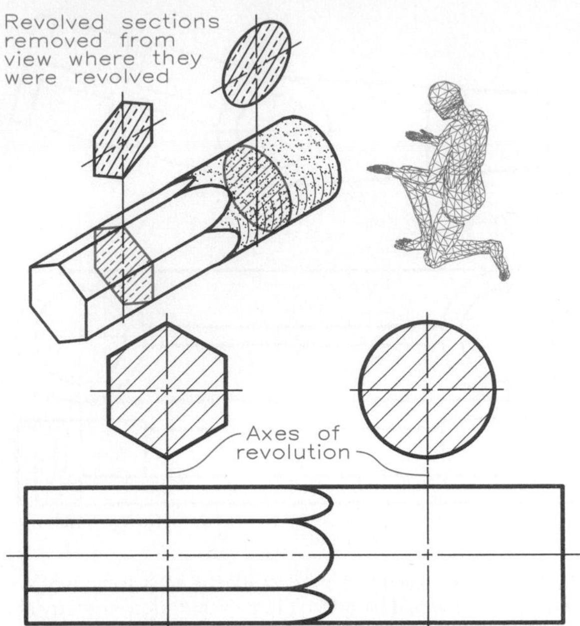

16.30 Removed sections are revolved sections that are drawn outside the object and along their axes of revolution.

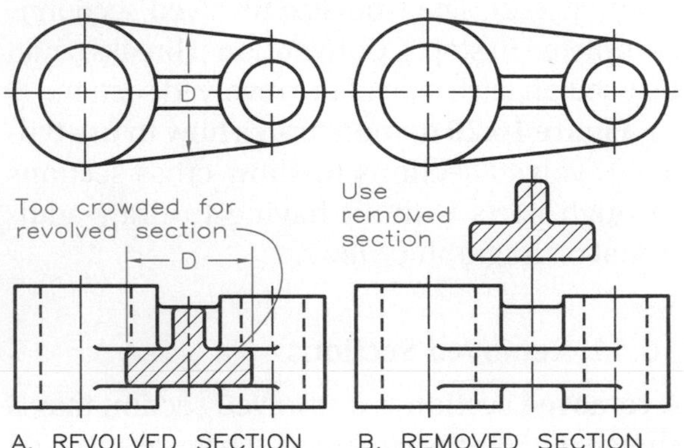

16.31 Removed sections are necessary when space does not permit the revolved section to be superimposed on the part.

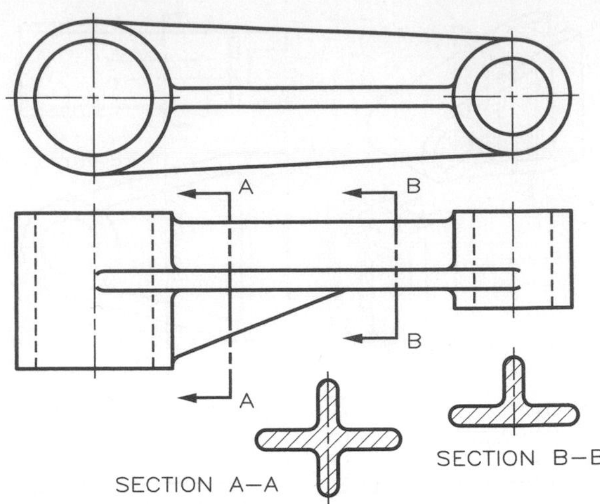

16.32 Lettering each end of a cutting plane (such as A-A) identifies the removed section labeled SECTION A-A drawn elsewhere on the drawing.

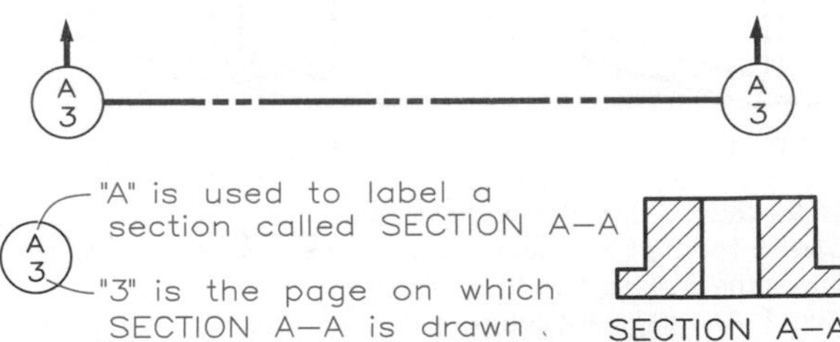

16.33 When placing a removed secion on another page of a set of drawings, label each end of the cutting plane with a letter and a number. The letter identifies the section, and the numeral indicates the page on which it is drawn.

properly labeled (**Figure 16.32**). For example, the plane labeled with an A at each end identifies the location of section A-A; the same applies to section B-B.

When a set of drawings consists of multiple sheets, removed sections and the views from which they are taken may appear on different sheets. When this method of layout is necessary, label the cutting plane in the view from which the section was taken and the sheet on which the section appears (**Figure 16.33**).

16.12 Conventional Revolutions

In **Figure 16.34A**, the middle hole is omitted because it does not pass through the center of the circular plate. However, in **Figure 16.34B**, the hole does pass through the plate's center and is shown in the section. Although the cutting plane does not pass through one of the symmetrically spaced holes in the top view (**Figure 16.34C**), the hole is revolved to the cutting plane to show the full section.

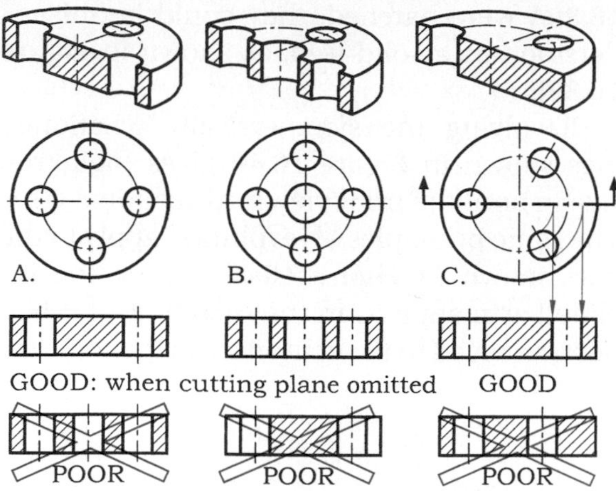

16.34 Symmetrically spaced holes are revolved to show their true radial distance from the center of a circular part in sectional views. (A) Omit the middle hole; it is not at the center of the plate. (B) Show the middle hole; it is at the center of the plate. (C) Rotate the holes to the centerline and project to make a symmetrical section. (Cutting planes are optional when it is obvious where they would be placed.)

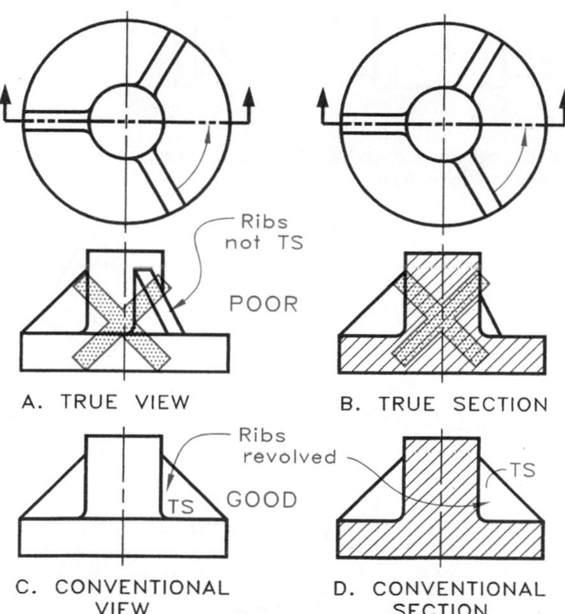

16.35 As a conventional practice, symmetrically spaced ribs are revolved and drawn true size in their orthographic and sectional views to show them true size.

When ribs are symmetrically spaced about a hub (**Figure 16.35**), it is conventional practice to revolve them so that they appear true size in both views and sections. **Figure 16.36** illustrates the conventional practice of revolving both holes and ribs (or webs) of symmetrical parts. Revolution gives a better description of the parts in a manner that is easier to draw.

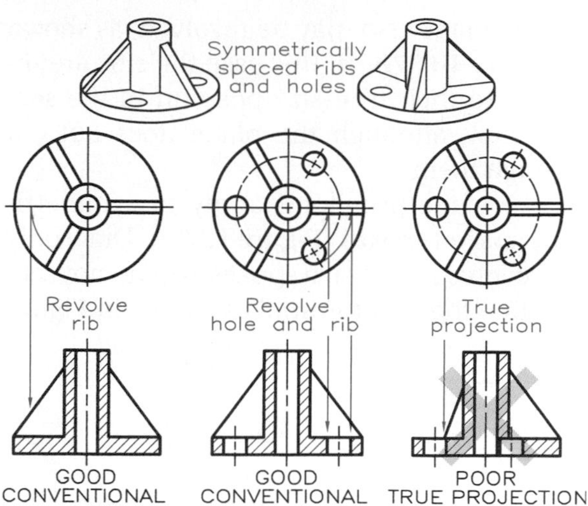

16.36 Symmetrically spaced ribs and holes should be shown in sections with the ribs rotated to show them true size and the holes rotated to show them at their true radial distance from the center.

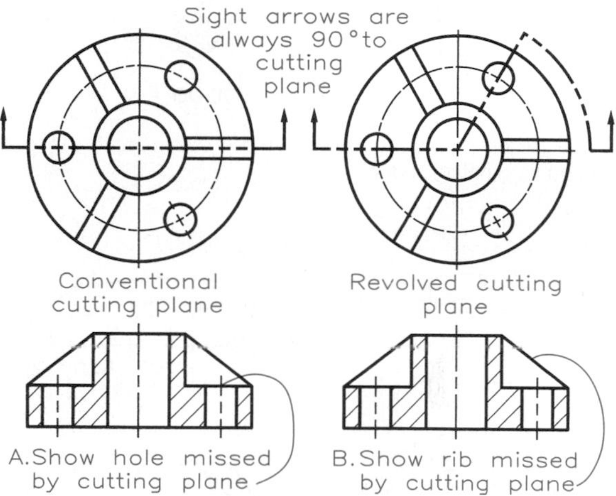

16.37 Show symmetrically spaced ribs true size whether or not the cutting plane pass through them. As an alternative, draw the cutting plane to pass through the ribs for clarity.

A cutting plane may be positioned in either of two ways shown in **Figure 16.37**. Even though the cutting plane does not pass through the ribs and holes in **Figure 16.37A**, they may appear in section as if the cutting plane passed through them. The path of the cutting plane also may be revolved, as shown in **Figure 16.37B**. In this case the ribs are revolved to their true-size position in the section view, although the plane does not cut through them.

The same principles apply to symmetrically spaced spokes (**Figure 16.38**). Draw only the revolved, true-size spokes and do not section line them. If the spokes shown in **Figure 16.39A** were hatched, they could be misunderstood as a solid web, as shown in **Figure 16.39B**.

Revolving the symmetrically positioned lugs shown in **Figure 16.40** gives their true size in both the front view and sectional view. The same principles of revolution apply to the part shown in **Figure 16.41**, where the inclined arm appears in the section as if it had been revolved to the centerline in the top view

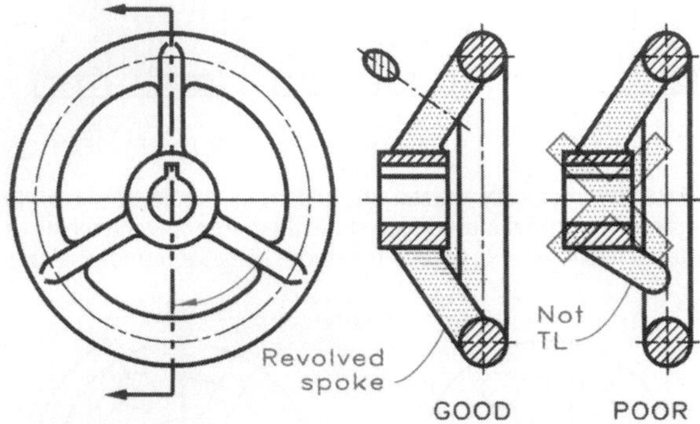

16.38 Revolve spokes to show them true size in section. Do not section line (hatch) spokes.

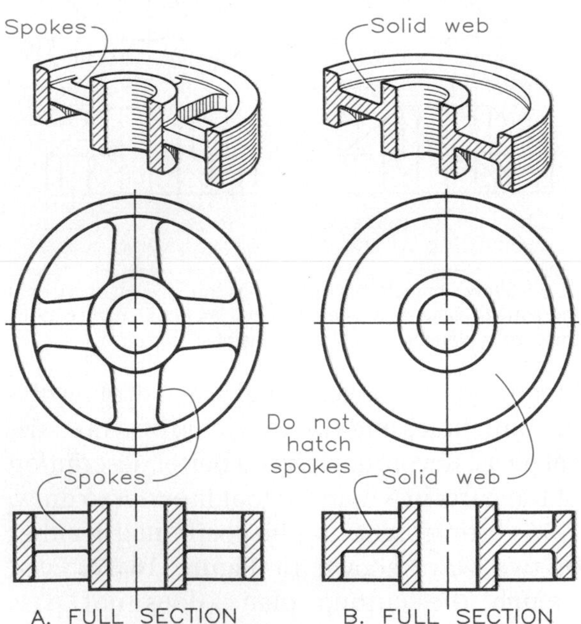

16.39 Spokes and webs in section.
A. Spokes are not hatched even though they have been cut.
B. Webs are hatched when cut by the cutting plane.

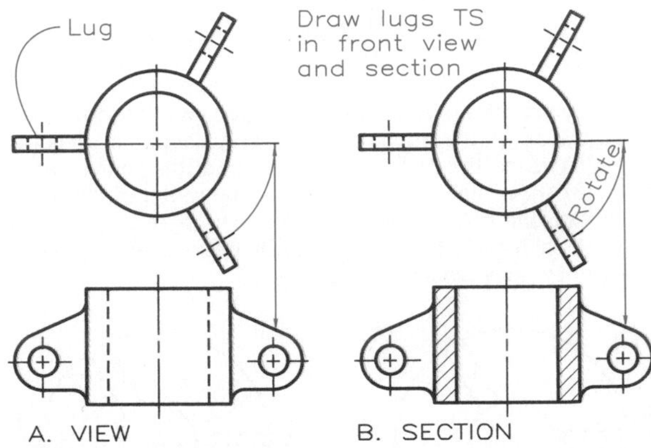

16.40 Lugs are revolved to show their true size in (A) the front view and also in (B) the sectional view.

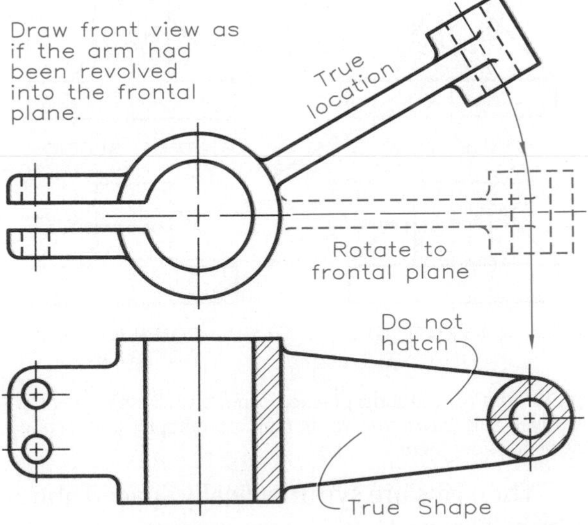

16.41 It is conventional practice to revolve parts with inclined features to show them true size in both sections and regular orthographic views.

and then projected to the sectional view. These conventional practices save time and space on a drawing and also make the views more understandable by the reader.

16.13 Conventional Breaks

Figure 16.42 shows types of conventional breaks to use when you remove portions of an object. You may draw the "figure-eight" breaks used for cylindrical and tubular parts freehand (**Figure 16.43**) or with a compass when they are larger, as shown in **Figure 16.44**.

Conventional breaks can be used to shorten a long piece by removing the portion between the breaks so that it may be drawn at a larger

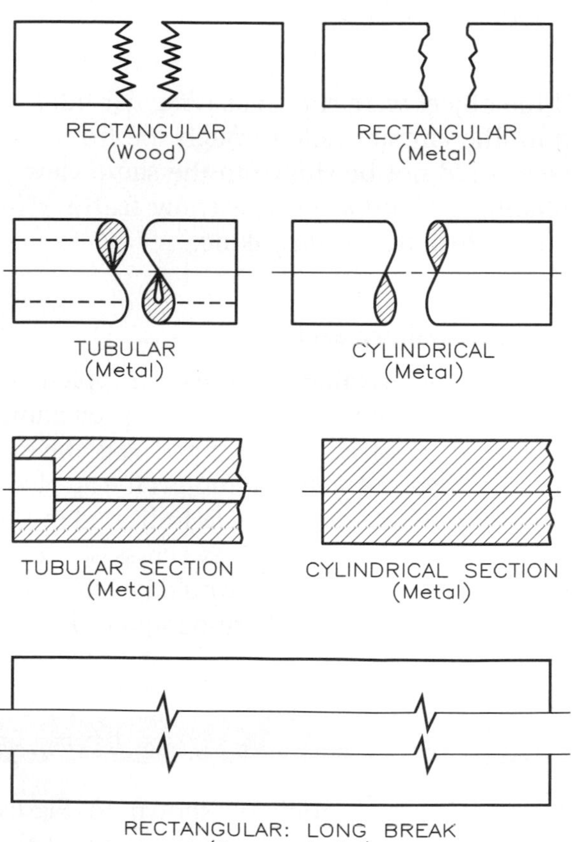

16.42 These conventional breaks indicate that a portion of an object has been omitted.

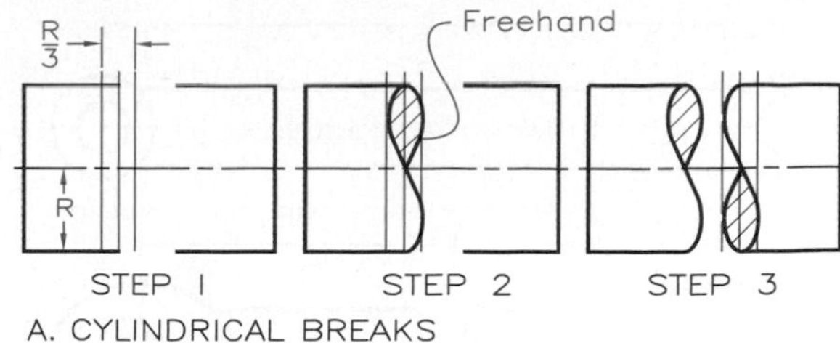

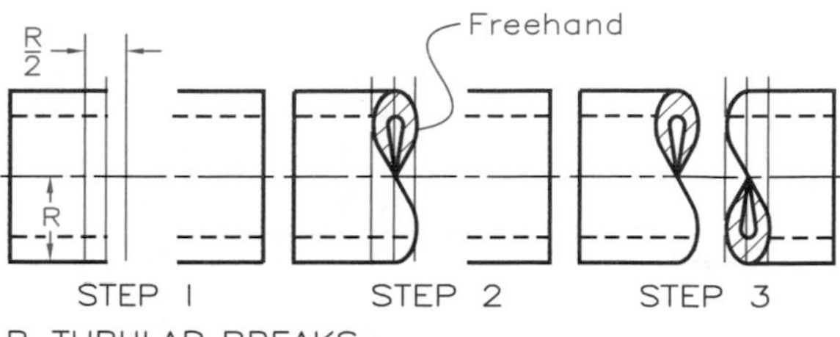

16.43 It is essential that you use guidelines in drawing conventional breaks for both (A) solid cylinders and (B) tubular cylinders freehand. The radius R is used to determine the widths.

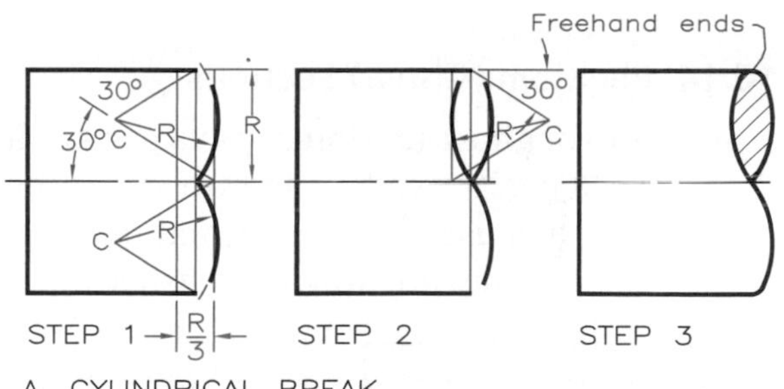

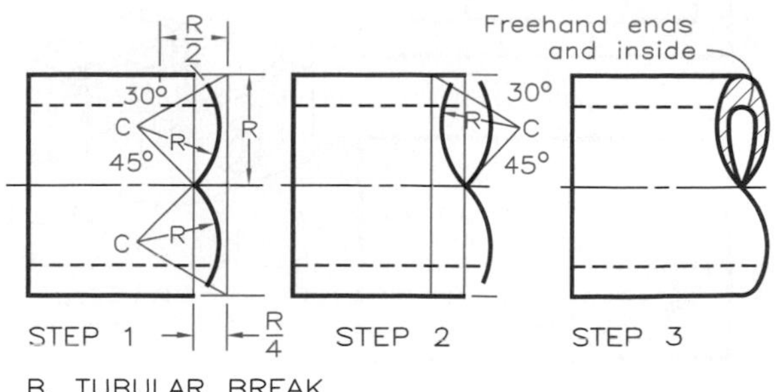

16.44 These steps can be followed to draw conventional breaks with a compass.

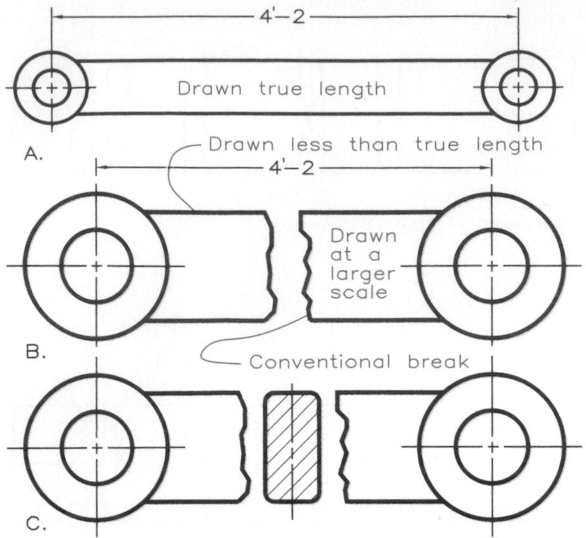

16.45 Using conventional breaks allows part of the object to be removed so the part can be drawn at a larger scale or space can be saved. A revolved section can also be inserted between the breaks to further describe the part.

scale (**Figure 16.45**). The dimension specifies the true length of the part, and the breaks indicate that a portion of the length has been removed.

16.14 Phantom (Ghost) Sections

A **phantom** or **ghost section** depicts parts as if they were being X-rayed. In **Figure 16.46**, the cutting plane is used in the normal manner, but the section lines are drawn as dashed lines.

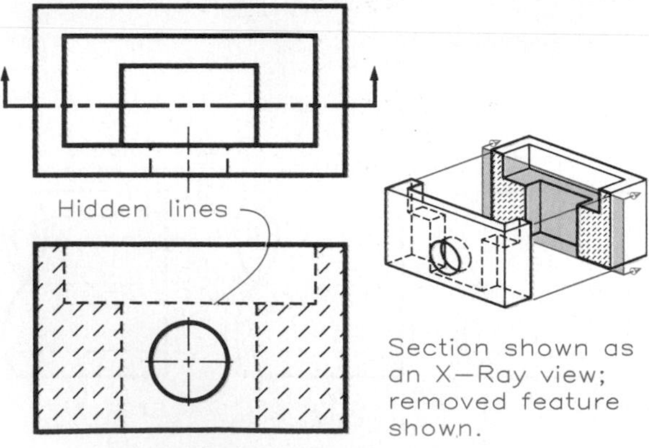

16.46 Phantom sections give an "X-ray" view of a part to show features on both sides of the cutting plane. Section lines are drawn as dashed lines.

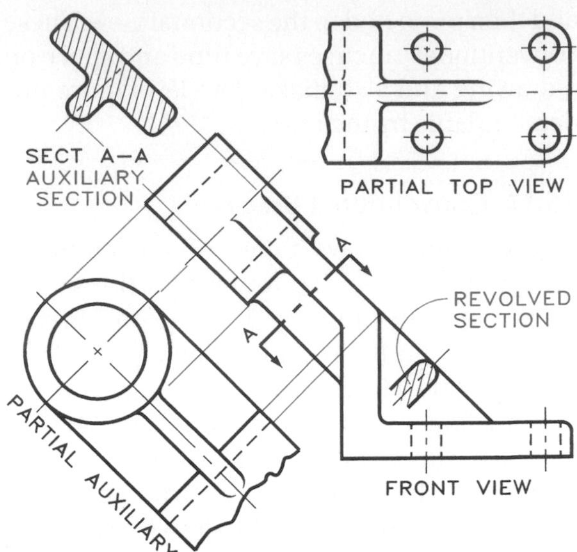

16.47 Auxiliary sections are helpful in clarifying the details of inclined features of a part.

If the object were shown as a regular full section, the circular hole through the front surface could not be shown in the same view. A phantom section lets you show features on both side of the cutting plane.

16.15 Auxiliary Sections

You may use **auxiliary sections** to supplement the principal views of orthographic projections (**Figure 16.47**). Pass auxiliary cutting plane A-A through the front view and project the auxiliary view from the cutting plane as indicated by the sight arrows. Section A-A gives a cross-sectional description of the part that would be difficult to depict by other principal orthographic views.

Problems

1–24. Solve the problems shown in **Figure 16.48** on size A sheets by drawing two solutions per sheet. Each grid space equals 0.20 in., or 5 mm.

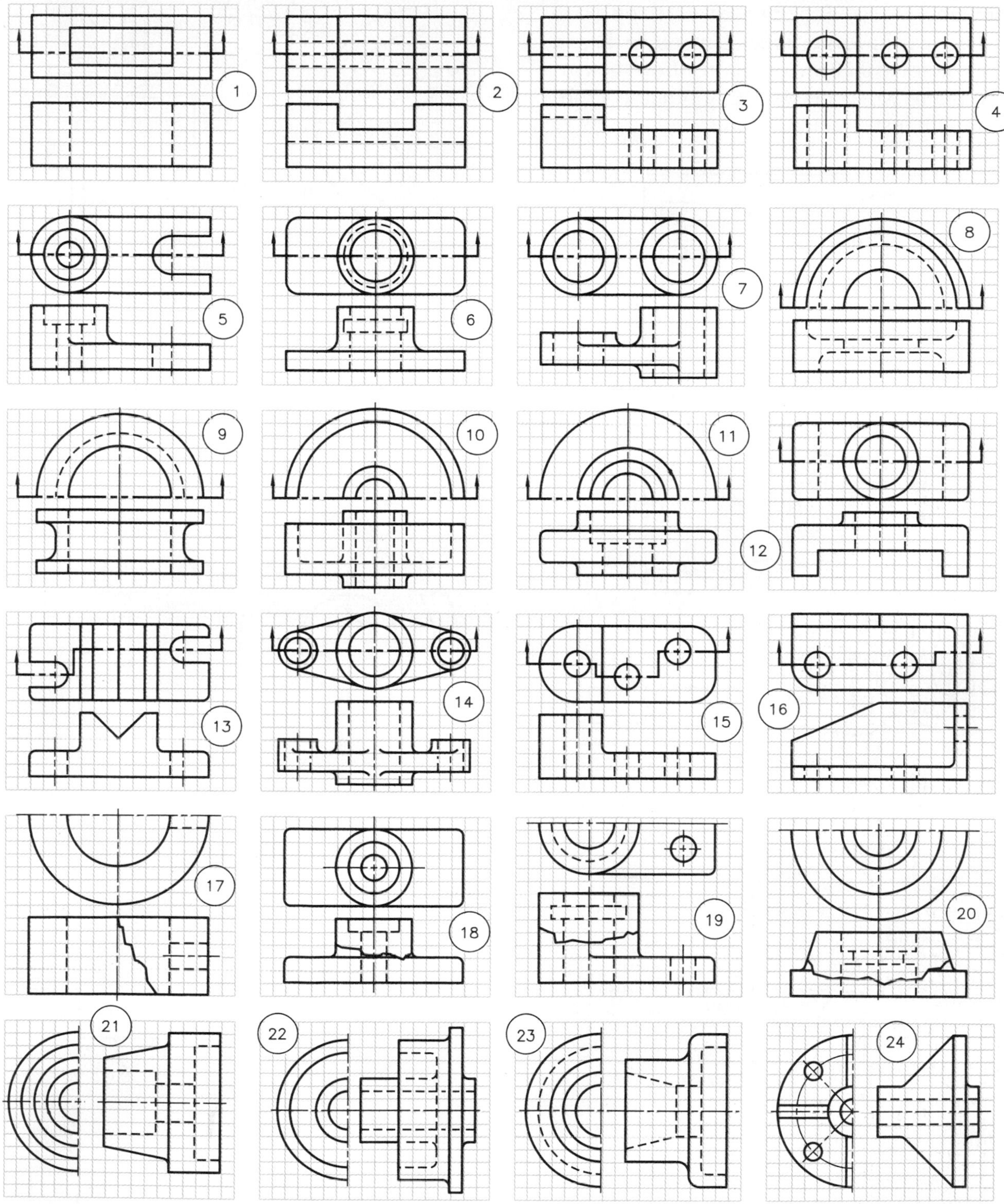

16.48 Problems 1–24. Introductory sections.

25–35. (Figures 16.50–16.55) The following problems are sized so that two will fit on a size A sheet as shown in **Sheet 1** when each grid space is set to 0.20 in., or 5 mm. Show the cutting plane when needed. Lay out the problems with instruments.

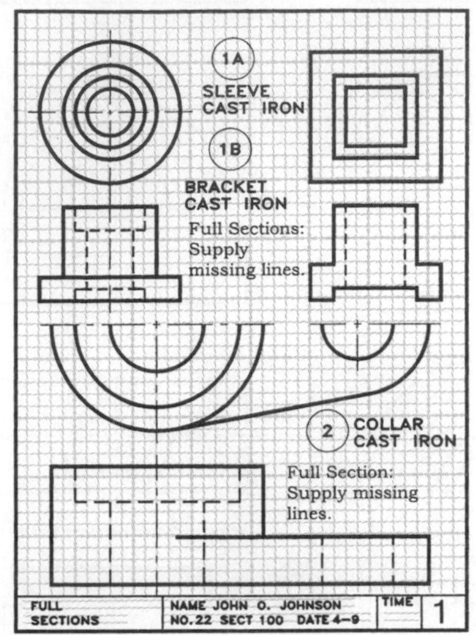

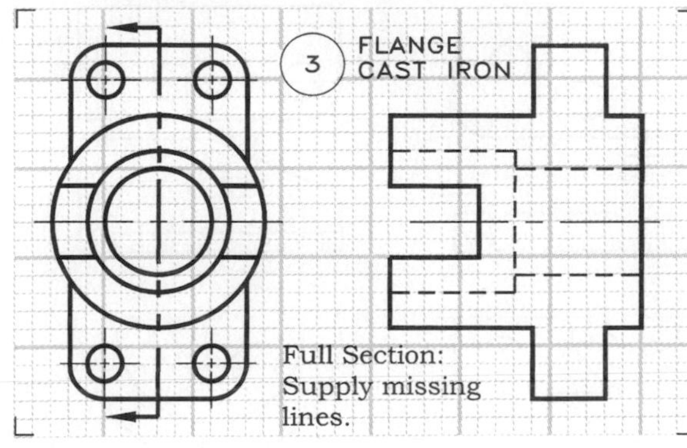

16.49 Problem 3.

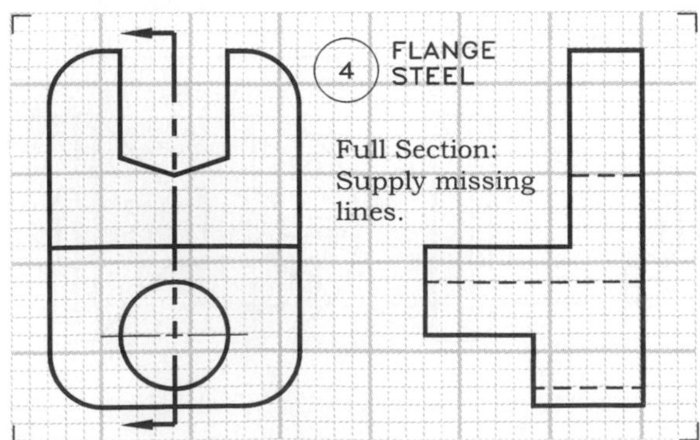

16.50 Problem 4.

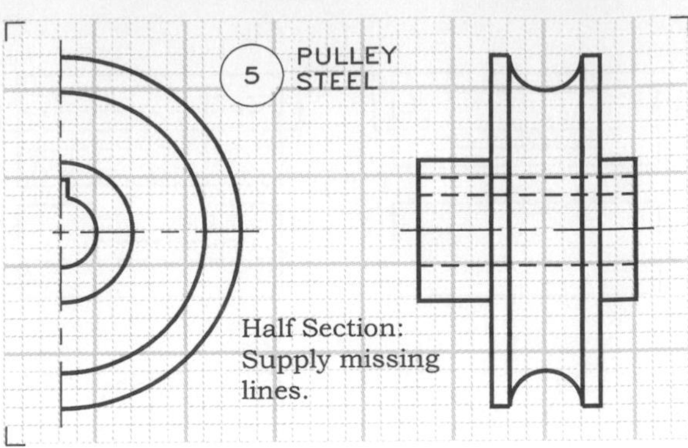

16.51 Problem 5.

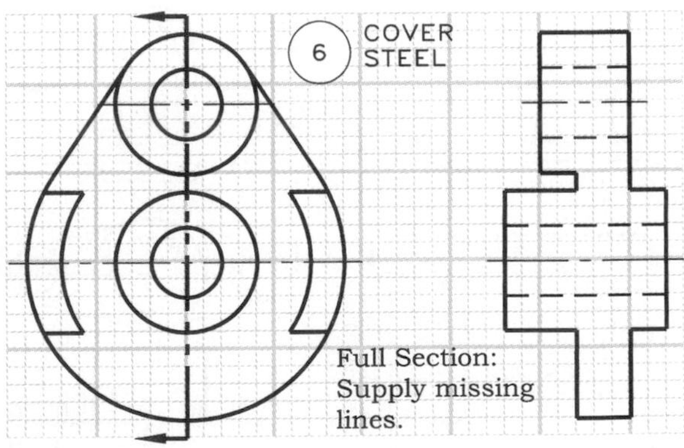

16.52 Problem 6.

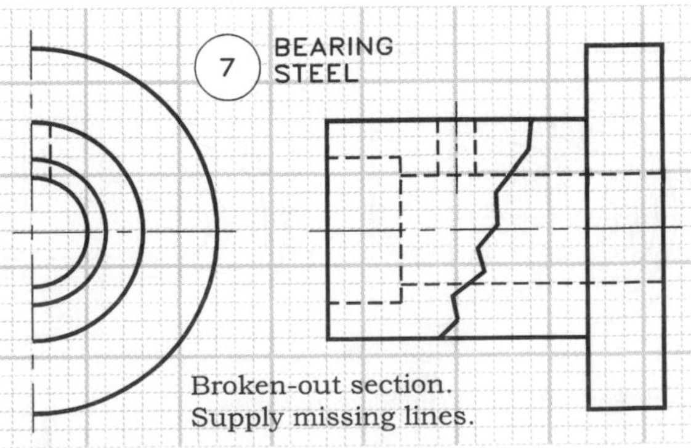

16.53 Problem 7.

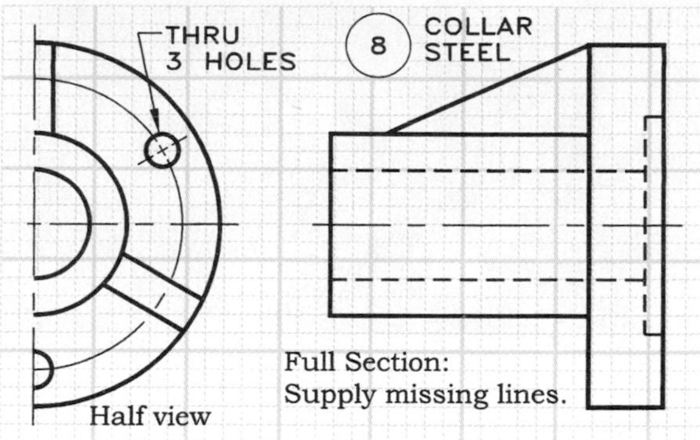

16.54 Problem 8.

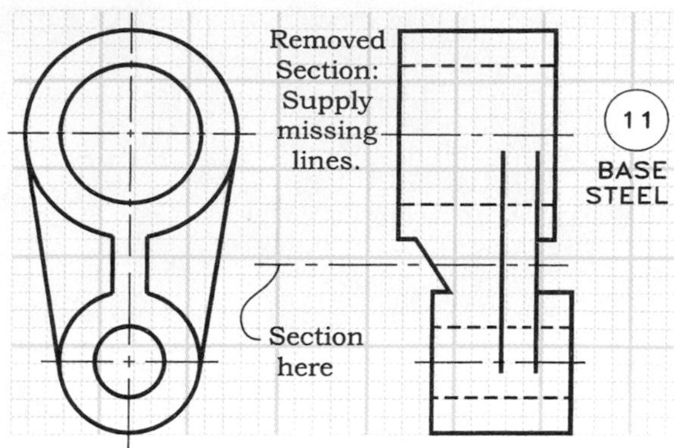

16.57 Problem 11.

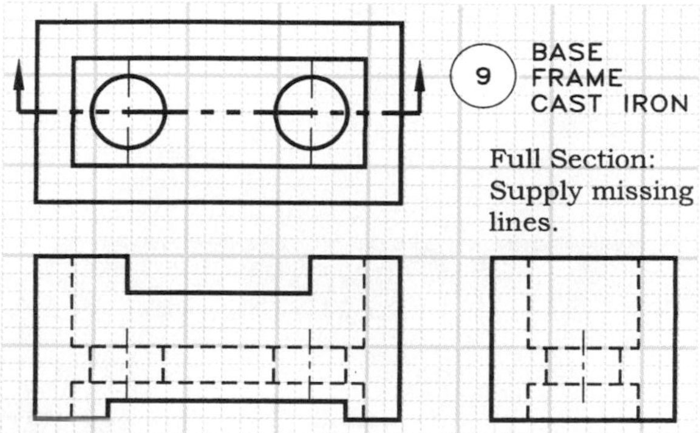

16.55 Problem 9.

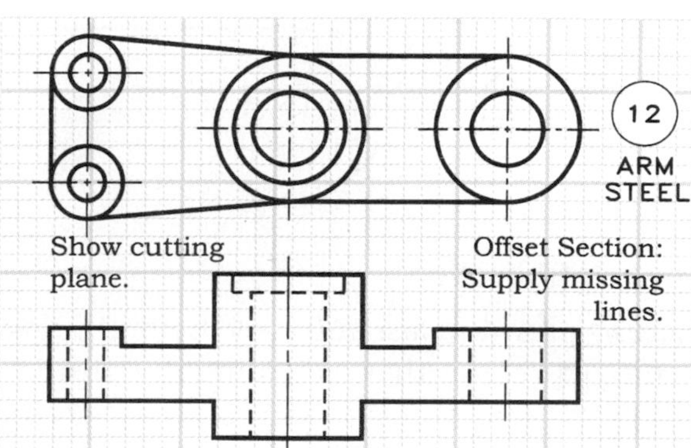

16.58 Problem 12.

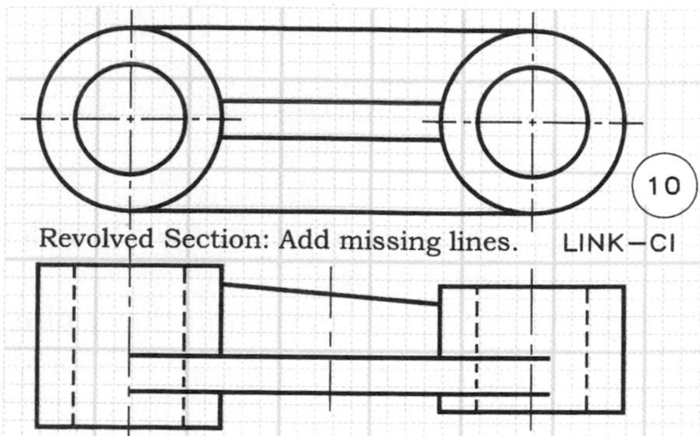

16.56 Problem 10.

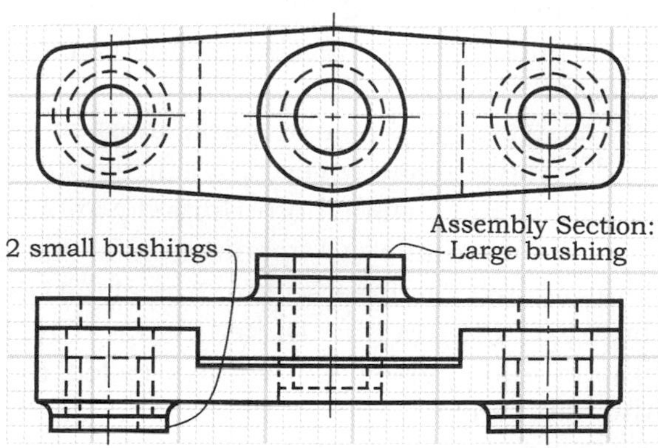

16.59 Problem 13.

17
Screws, Fasteners, and Springs

17.1 Introduction

Screws provide a fast and easy method of fastening parts together, adjusting the position of parts, and transmitting power. **Screws, sometimes called *threaded fasteners,* should be purchased rather than made as newly designed parts for each product**. Screws are available through commercial catalogs in countless forms and shapes for various specialized and general applications (**Figure 17.1**). Such screws are cheap, interchangeable, and easy to replace.

The types of threaded parts most often used in industry are covered by current ANSI Standards and include both Unified National (UN) and International Organization for Standardization (ISO) threads. Adoption of the UN thread in 1948 by the United States, Great Britain, and Canada (sometimes called the ABC Standards), a modification of the American Standard and the Whitworth thread, was a major step in standard threads. The ISO developed metric thread standards for even broader worldwide applications.

17.1 Nuts, bolts, screws, and fasteners of all types are available in a multitude of configurations. Only the threading specifications remain standardized.

Other types of fasteners include **keys**, **pins**, and **rivets**. **Springs** resist and react to forces and have applications varying from pogo sticks to automobiles. Springs also are available in many forms and styles from specialty

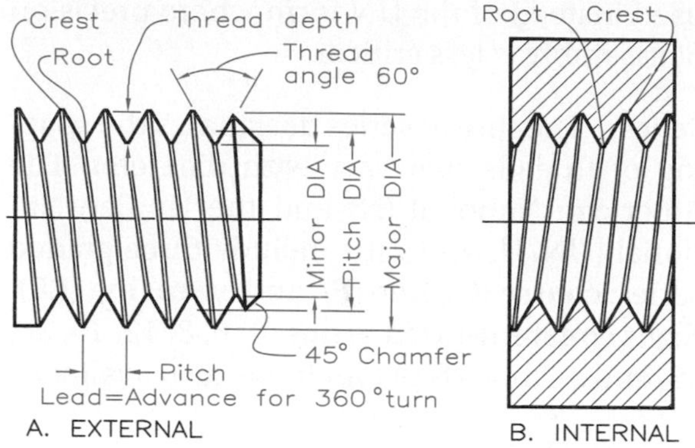

17.2 Most of the definitions of thread terminology are labeled for (A) external and (B) internal threads.

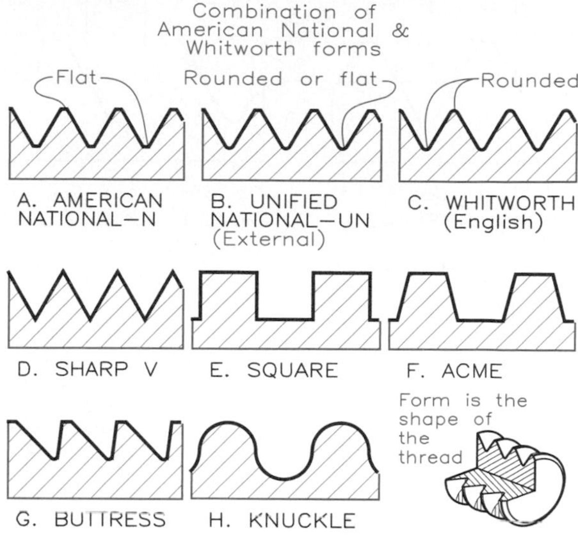

17.3 The various types of thread forms for external threads are shown here.

manufacturers who supply most of them to industry.

17.2 Thread Terminology

Understanding threaded parts begins with learning their terminology, which is used throughout this chapter.

External thread: a thread on the outside of a cylinder, such as a bolt.

Internal thread: a thread cut on the inside of a part, such as a nut.

Major diameter: the largest diameter on an internal or external thread (**Figure 17.2**).

Minor diameter: the smallest diameter on an internal or external thread (**Figure 17.2**).

Crest: the peak edge of a screw thread (**Figure 17.2**).

Root: the bottom of the thread cut into a cylinder to form the minor diameter (**Figure 17.2**).

Depth: the depth of the thread from the major diameter to the minor diameter; also measured as the root diameter (**Figure 17.2**).

Thread angle: the angle between threads cut by the cutting tool, usually 60° (**Figure 17.2**).

Pitch (thread width): the distance between crests of threads, found by dividing 1 in. by the number of threads per inch of a particular thread (**Figure 17.2**).

Pitch diameter: the diameter of an imaginary cylinder passing through the threads at the points where the thread width is equal to the space between the threads (**Figure 17.2** and **Figure 17.4**).

Lead (pronounced *leed*): the distance a screw will advance when turned 360°.

Form: the shape of the thread cut into a threaded part (**Figure 17.3**).

Series: the number of threads per inch for a particular diameter, grouped into coarse, fine, extra fine, and eight constant-pitch thread series.

Class: the closeness of fit between two mating parts. Class 1 represents a loose fit and Class 3 a tight fit.

Right-hand thread: one that will assemble when turned clockwise. A right-hand external thread slopes downward to the right when its axis is horizontal, and in the opposite direction on internal threads.

Left-hand thread: one that will assemble when turned counterclockwise. A left-hand external thread slopes downward to the left

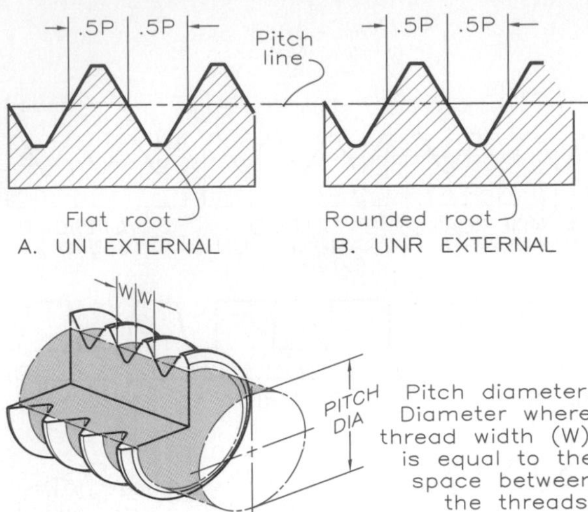

17.4 UN and UNR thread forms.

A The UN external thread has a flat root (rounder root is optional) and a flat crest.

B The UNR thread has a rounded root formed by rolling rather than by cutting. The UNR form does not apply to internal threads.

when its axis is horizontal, and in the opposite direction on internal threads.

17.3 English System Specifications

Form Thread form is the shape of the thread cut into a part (**Figure 17.3**). The Unified National form, denoted by UN in thread notes, is the most widely used form in the United States (**Appendix 5**). The American National form, denoted by N, appears occasionally on older drawings. The sharp V thread is used for setscrews and in applications where friction in assembly is desired. Acme, square, and buttress threads are used in gearing and other machinery applications (**Figure 17.3**).

The Unified National Rolled form, denoted UNR, is used for external threads, never internal threads, because internal threads cannot be formed by rolling. The standard UN form has a flat root (a rounded root is optional) (**Figure 17.4A**), and the UNR form (**Figure 17.4B**) has a rounded root formed by rolling a cylinder across a die. The UNR form can be used instead of the UN form where precision of assembly is less critical.

Series The thread series designates the spacing of threads that vary with diameter. The American National (N) and the Unified National (UN/UNR) forms include three graded series: **coarse (C), fine (F)**, and **extra fine (EF)**. Eight **constant-pitch** series (4, 6, 8, 12, 16, 20, 28, and 32 threads per inch) are also available.

Coarse Unified National forms are denoted UNC or UNRC, which is a combination of form and series designation. The coarse thread (UNC/UNRC or NC) has the largest pitch of any series and is suitable for bolts, screws, nuts, and general use with cast iron, soft metals, and plastics when rapid assembly is desired. An American National (N) form for a coarse thread is written NC.

Fine Threads (NF or UNF/UNRF) are used for bolts, nuts, and screws when a high degree of tightening is required. Fine threads are closer together than coarse threads, and their pitch is graduated to be smaller on smaller diameters.

Extra-Fine Threads (UNEF/UNREF or NEF) are suitable for sheet-metal screws and bolts, thin nuts, ferrules, and couplings when the length of engagement is limited and high stresses must be withstood.

Constant-Pitch Threads (4 UN, 6 UN, 8 UN, 12 UN, 16 UN, 20 UN, 28 UN, and 32 UN) are used on larger diameter threads (beginning near the 1/2-in. size) and have the same pitch size regardless of the diameter size. The most commonly used constant-pitch threads are 8 UN, 12 UN, and 16 UN members of the series, which are used on threads of about 1 in. in diameter and larger. Constant-pitch threads may be specified as UNR or N thread forms. The ANSI table in **Appendix 6** shows constant-pitch threads for larger thread diameters instead of graded pitches of coarse, fine, and extra fine.

Class of Fit The class of fit is the tightness between two mating threads, as between a nut and bolt, and is indicated in the thread note by the numbers 1, 2, or 3 followed by the letters A or B. For UN forms, the letter A represents an external thread, and the letter B represents an internal thread. The letters A and B do not appear in notes for the American National form (N).

Class 1A and **1B** threads are used on parts that assemble with a minimum of binding and precision. **Class 2A** and **2B** threads are general-purpose threads for bolts, nuts, and screws used in general and mass-production applications. **Class 3A** and **3B** threads are used in precision assemblies where a close fit is required to withstand stresses and vibration.

Single and Multiple Threads A single thread (**Figure 17.5A**) is a thread that advances the distance of its pitch in a revolution of 360°; that is, its pitch is equal to its lead. The crest lines have a slope of 1/2 P, since only 180° of the revolution is visible in the view.

Multiple threads are used where quick assembly is required. A double thread is composed of two threads that advance a distance of 2P when turned 360° (**Figure 17.5B**); that is, its lead is equal to 2P. The crest lines have a slope of P because only 180° of the revolution is visible in the view. A triple thread advances 3P in 360° with a crest line slope of 1-1/2 P in the view where 180° of the revolution is visible (**Figure 17.5C**).

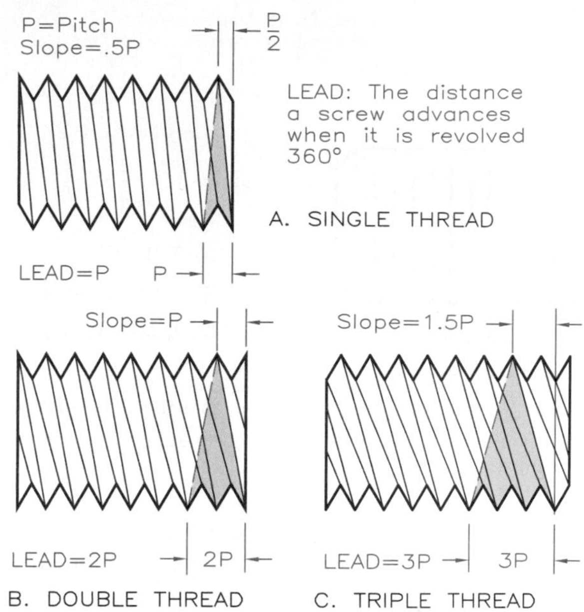

17.5 Threads can be (A) single, (B) double, or (C) triple, which represents the ratio that each advances when turned 360°.

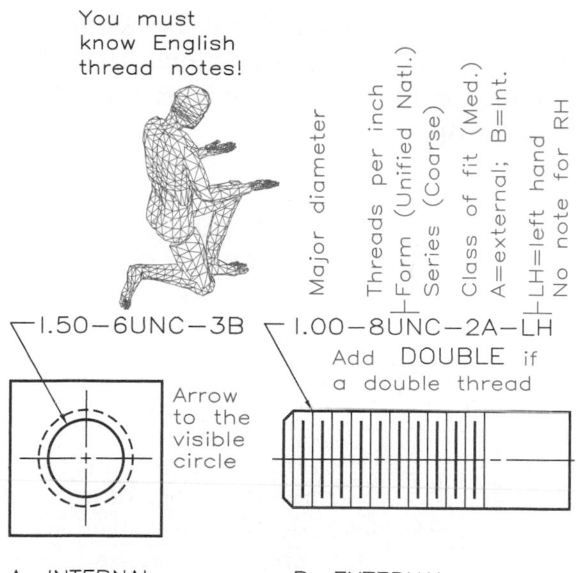

17.6 Thread notes of the English form that are applied to (A) internal and (B) external threads are defined here.

17.4 English Thread Notes

Drawings of threads are only symbolic representations and are inadequate to give the details of a thread unless accompanied by notes (**Figure 17.6**). In a thread note, the major diameter is given first, then the number of threads per inch, the form, series, the class of fit, and the letter A or B to denote external or internal threads, respectively. For a double or triple

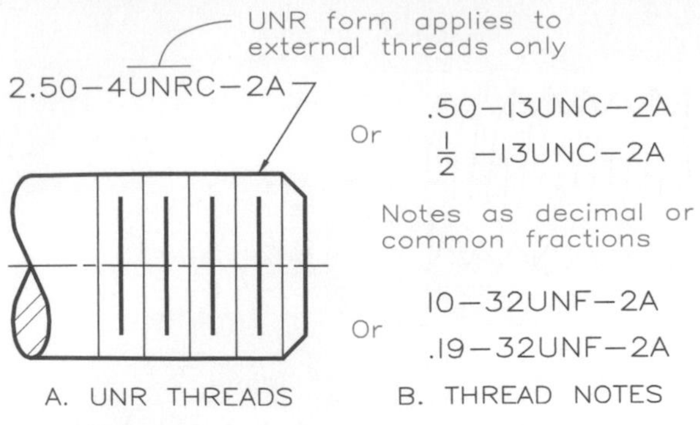

17.7 Thread notes.

A The UNR thread note is applied only to external threads.

B Diameters in thread notes can be given as decimal fractions or common fractions.

thread, the word *double* or *triple* is included in the note, and for left-hand threads the letters LH are added.

Figure 17.7 shows a UNR thread note for the external thread. (UNR does not apply to internal threads.) When inches are the unit of measurement, fractions can be written as decimal or as common fractions. The information for thread notes comes from ANSI tables in **Appendix 5**.

Using Thread Tables

A portion of **Appendix 5** is shown in **Figure 17.8**, which gives the UN/UNR thread table from which specifications for standardized

American National Standards Institute
Unified Inch Threads (UN and UNR)

Nominal Diameter	Basic Diameter	Coarse NC & UNC		Fine NF & UNF		Extra Fine NEF/UNEF	
		Thds per inch	Tap Drill Dia	Thds per inch	Tap Drill Dia	Thds per inch	Tap Drill Dia
1	1.000	8	.875	12	.922	20	.953
1−1/16	1.063	...	...	...	...	18	1.000
1−1/8	1.125	7	.904	12	1.046	18	1.070
1−3/16	1.188	...	...	...	...	18	1.141
1−1/4	1.250	7	1.109	12	1.172	18	1.188
1−5/16	1.313	...	...	...	...	18	1.266
1−3/8	1.375	6	1.219	12	1.297	18	1.313
1−7/16	1.438	...	...	...	...	18	1.375
1−1/2	1.500	6	1.344	12	1.422	18	1.438

17.8 This is a portion of the ANSI tables for UN and UNR threads in Appendix 15.

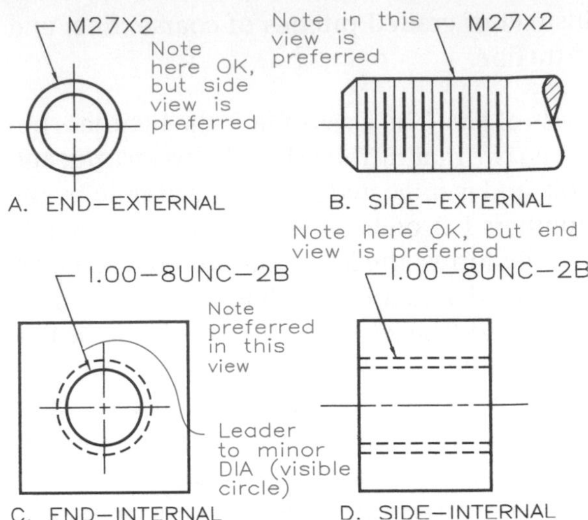

17.9 Notes for external threads are best if they are placed on the rectangular view of the threads. Notes for internal threads are best in the circular view if space permits.

interchangeable threads can be selected. Note that a 1-1/2-in.-diameter bolt with fine thread (UNF) has 12 threads per inch, and its thread note is written as

1.500-12 UNF-2A or 1-1/2-12 UNF-2A.

If the thread were internal (nut), the thread note would be the same but the letter B would be used instead of the letter A. For constant-pitch thread series, selected for larger diameters, write the thread note as

1.750-12 UN-2A or 1-3/4-12 UN-2A.

For the UNR thread form (for external threads only) substitute UNR for UN in the last three columns; for example, UNREF for UNEF (extra fine). **Figure 17.9** shows the preferred placement of thread notes (with leaders) for external and internal threads.

17.5 Metric Thread Notes

Metric thread notes usually given as a basic designation are suitable for general applications. However, for applications where the assembly of threaded parts is crucial, a complete

COARSE		FINE	
Maj. Dia. and Thread Pitch	Tap Drill	Maj. Dia. and Thread Pitch	Tap Drill
M20 X 2.5	17.5	M20 X 1.5	18.5
M22 X 2.5	19.5	M22 X 1.5	20.5
M24 X 3	21.0	M24 X 2	22.0
M27 X 3	24.0	M27 X 2	25.0
M30 X 3.5	26.5	M30 X 2	28.0
M33 X 3.5	29.5	M33 X 2	31.0
M36 X 4	32.0	M36 X 2	33.0
M39 X 4	35.0	M39 X 2	36.0
M42 X 4.5	37.5	M42 X 2	39.0

17.10 This portion of the metric (ISO) thread tables in Appendix 7 shows specifications for metric thread notes.

thread designation should be noted. The ISO thread table in **Appendix 7**, a portion of which is shown in **Figure 17.10**, contains specifications for metric thread notes.

Basic Designation **Figure 17.11** shows examples of metric screw thread notes. Each note begins with the letter M, designating the note as metric, followed by the major diameter size in millimeters and the pitch in millimeters separated by the multiplication sign and the number 3.

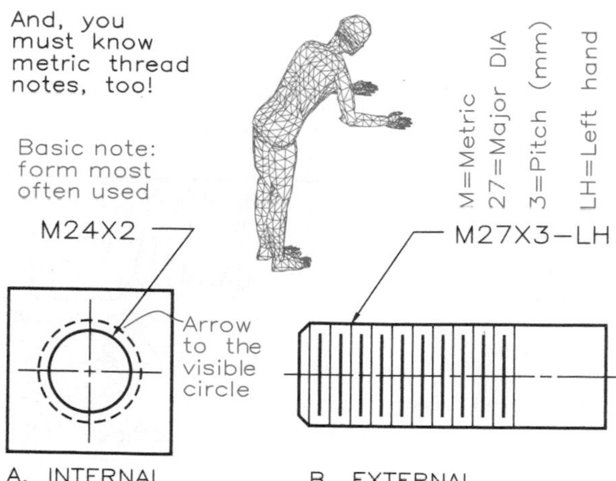

17.11 This is the basic thread note that is used for (A) internal and (B) external threads.

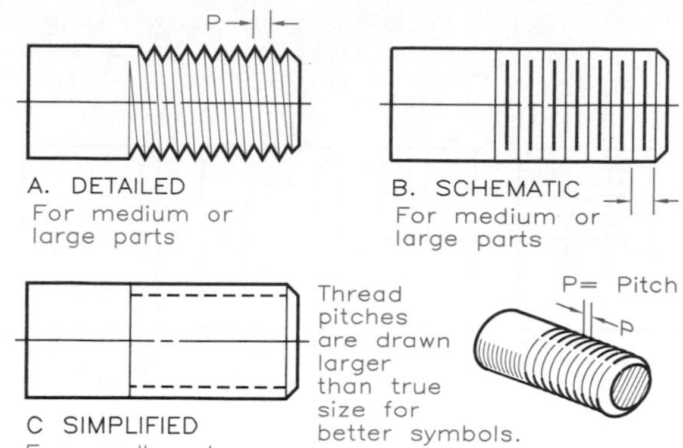

17.12 The three types of thread symbols used for drawing threads are (A) simplified, (B) schematic, and (C) detailed.

17.6 Drawing Threads

Threads may be represented by **detailed, schematic**, and **simplified** symbols (**Figure 17.12**). Detailed symbols represent a thread most realistically, simplified symbols represent a thread least realistically, and the schematic symbols are a compromise between the two. Detailed and schematic symbols can be used for drawing larger threads on a drawing (1/2-in. diameter and larger) and simplified symbols are best for smaller threads.

17.7 Detailed Symbols

UN/UNR Threads Detailed thread symbols for external threads in view and in section are shown in **Figure 17.13**. Instead of helical curves, straight lines are used to depict crest

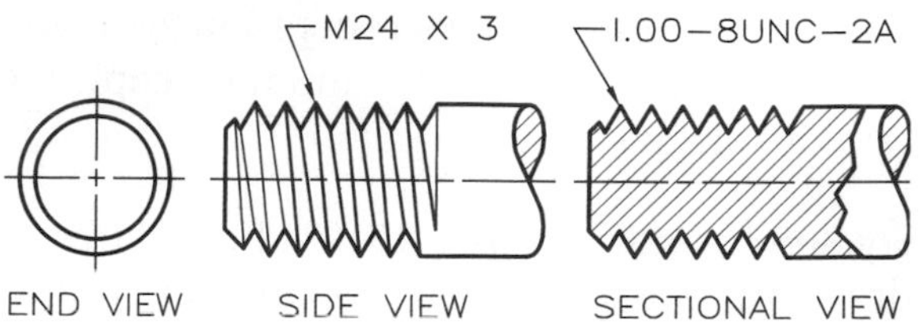

17.13 These detailed symbols represent external threads in view and section.

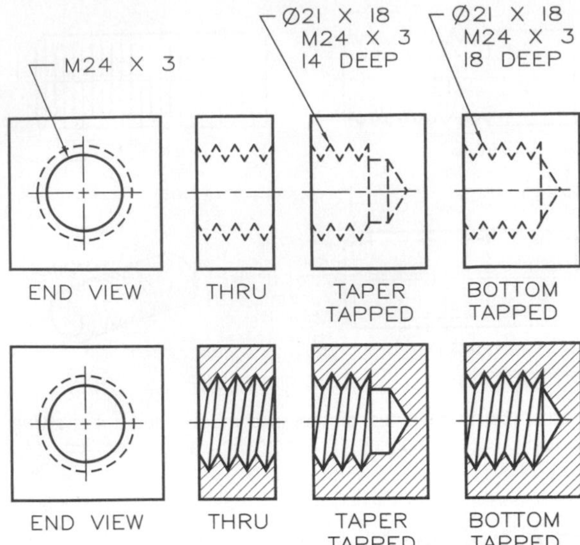

17.14 These detailed symbols represent internal threads. Approximate the minor diameter as 75% of the major diameter. Tap drill diameters (21) are found in the appendix.

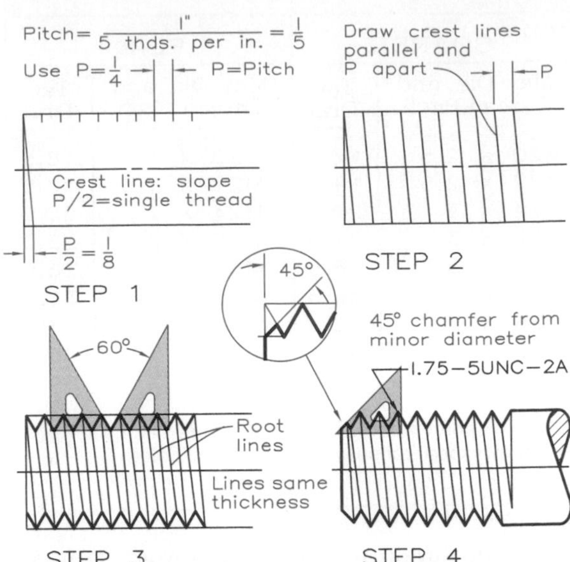

17.15 Detailed representation of threads.

Step 1 To draw a detailed drawing of a 1.75-5 UNC-2A thread, find the pitch by dividing 1 in. by the number of threads per inch, or 5 in this case. Use a pitch of 1/4 instead of 1/5 to space the threads apart. Lay off the pitch along the length of the thread and draw a crest line at a slope of P/2, or 1/8 in. in this case.

Step 2 Draw the other crest lines as dark, visible lines parallel to the first crest line.

Step 3 Find the root lines by constructing 60° vees between the crest lines. Draw the root lines from the bottom of the vees. Root lines are parallel to each other but not to crest lines.

Step 4 Construct a 45° chamfer at the end of the thread from the minor diameter. Darken all lines and add a thread note.

and root lines. Variations of detailed thread symbols for internal threads drawn in views and sections are shown in **Figure 17.14**.

The steps of drawing a detailed thread representation, whether English or metric threads, are shown in **Figure 17.15**. When using the English tables, calculate the pitch by dividing 1 in. by the number of threads per inch. In the metric system, pitch is given in the tables in **Appendix 7**. **Draw the spacing between crest lines larger than the actual pitch size to avoid "clogged-up" lines.**

AutoCAD Method You can draw detailed thread symbols by computer (**Figure 17.16**) and duplicate them with the *Copy* command's *Multiple* option. The program produces a typical set of threads in step 1 and then copies it repetitively in step 2.

Square Threads **Figure 17.17** shows how to draw and note a detailed drawing of a square thread by referring to **Appendix 8**. Follow the same basic steps to draw views and sections of

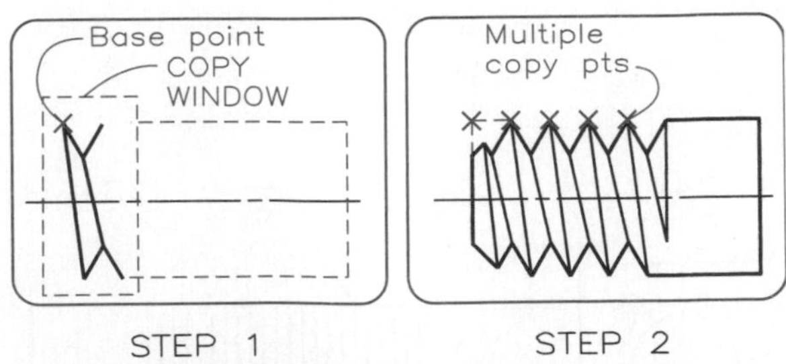

17.16 Detailed thread symbols by AutoCAD.

Step 1 Draw a typical detailed thread symbol at the end of the screw.

Step 2 Duplicate a typical set of threads with the *Copy* command and the *Multiple* option along the predetermined snap points of the screw.

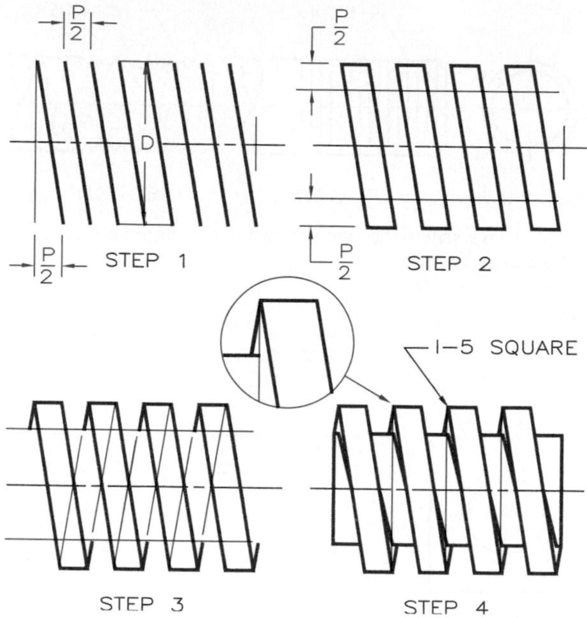

17.17 Drawing a square thread.

Step 1 Lay out the major diameter. Space the crest lines 1/2P apart and slope them downward to the right for right-hand threads. Refer to **Appendix 8**.

Step 2 Connect every other pair of crest lines. Find the minor diameter by measuring 1/2P inward from the major diameter.

Step 3 Connect the opposite crest lines with light construction lines to establish the profile of the thread form.

Step 4 Connect the inside crest lines with light construction lines to locate the points on the minor diameter where the thread wraps around the minor diameter. Darken the final lines.

square internal threads (**Figure 17.18**). In section, draw both the internal crest and root lines, but in a view draw only the outline of the threads. Place thread notes for internal threads in the circular view, whenever possible, with the leader pointing toward the center and stopping at the visible circle.

When a square thread is long, it can be represented by using phantom lines, without drawing all the threads (**Figure 17.19**). This conventional practice saves time and effort without reducing the drawing's effectiveness.

Acme Threads A modified version of the square thread is the Acme thread, which has square threads. The steps involved in drawing

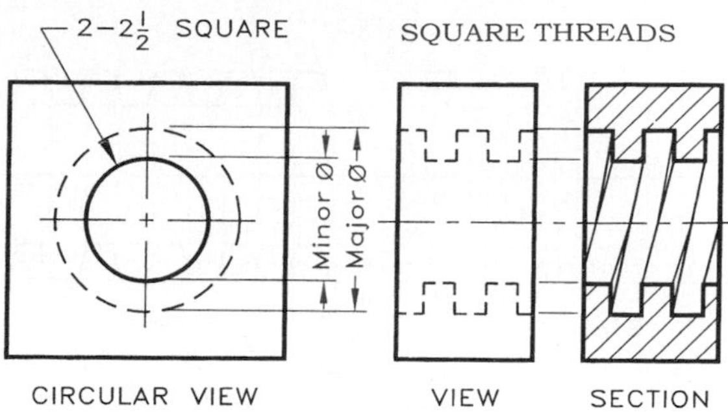

17.18 Internal square threads in view and section.

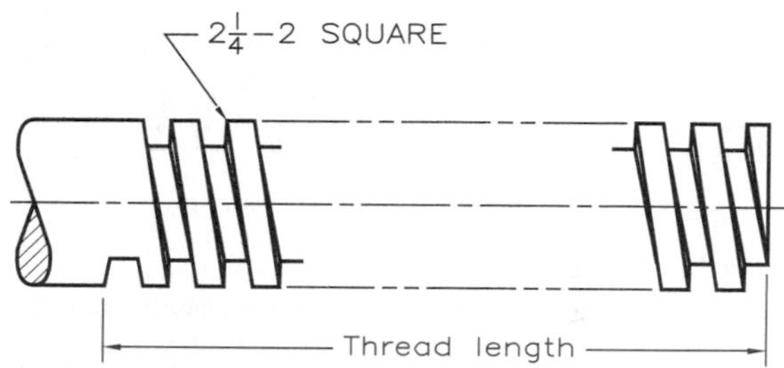

17.19 The conventional method of showing square threads is to draw sample threads at each end and to connect them with phantom lines.

detailed Acme threads are shown in **Figure 17.20**. Acme threads are heavy threads that are used to transmit force and power in mechanisms such as screw jacks, leveling devices, and lathes. **Appendix 8** contains the table for Acme thread specifications.

Internal Acme threads are shown in view and section in **Figure 17.21**. Left-hand internal threads in section appear the same as right-hand external threads.

17.8 Schematic Symbols

Figure 17.22 shows schematic representations of external threads with metric notes from **Appendix 7**. Because schematic symbols are easy to draw and adequately represent threads, it is the thread symbol used most often for medium-size threads. Draw schematic thread symbols by using thin parallel crest lines and thick root lines. Schematic drawings of left-hand

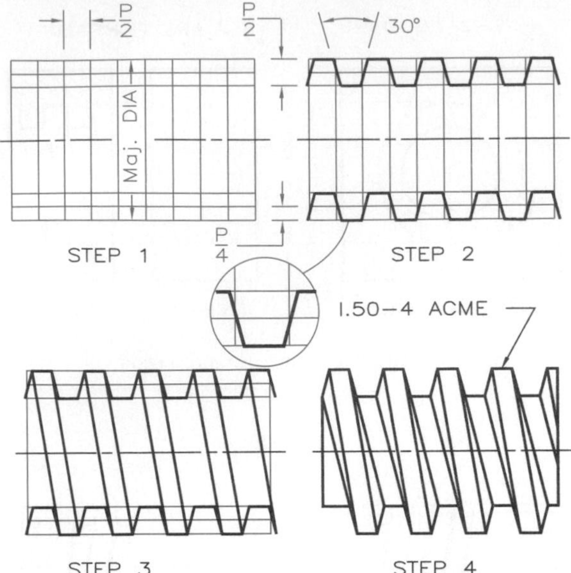

17.20 Drawing the Acme thread.

Step 1 Lay out the major diameter and thread length and divide the shaft into equal divisions 1/2 P apart. Locate the minor and pitch diameters by using distances 1/2P and 1/4P. Refer to **Appendix 8**.

Step 2 Draw construction lines at 15° angles with the vertical along the pitch diameter to make a total angle of 30°.

Step 3 Draw the crest lines across the screw.

Step 4 Darken the lines, draw the root lines, and add the thread note to complete the drawing.

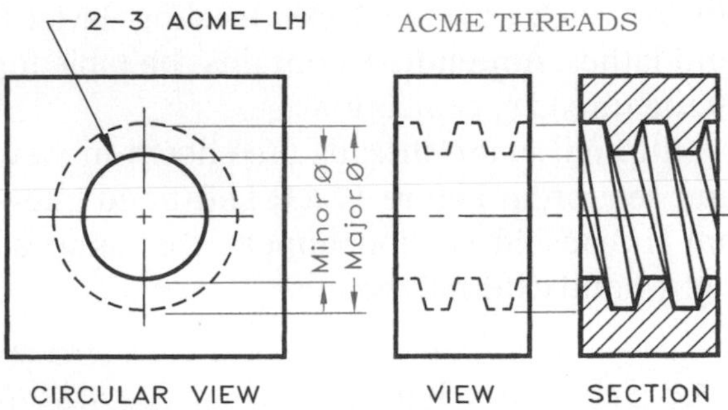

17.21 This drawing shows internal Acme threads in view and section.

and right-hand threads are identical; only the LH in the thread note indicates that a thread is left-handed. Right-hand threads are not marked RH but are understood to be right-hand threads.

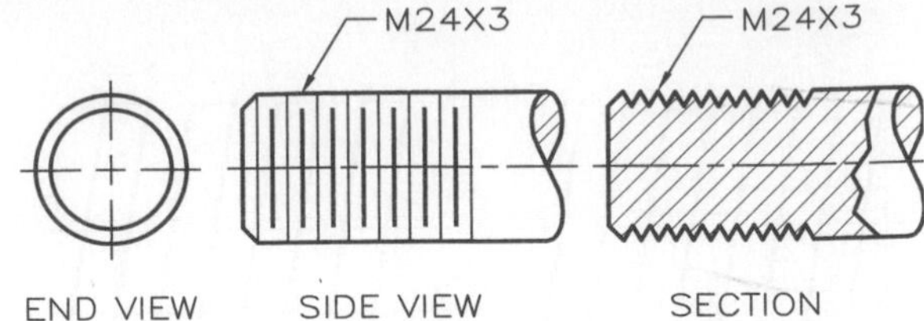

17.22 These schematic symbols represent external threads in view and section.

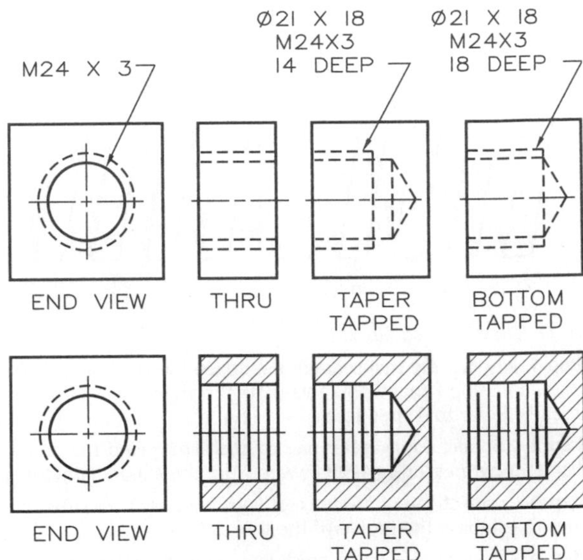

17.23 These schematic symbols represent internal threads in view and section. Tap drill diameters are found in the appendix.

Figure 17.23 shows threaded holes in view and in section drawn with schematic symbols. The size of the tap drill diameter is approximately equal to the major diameter minus the pitch. However, the minor diameter usually is drawn a bit smaller to provide better separation between the lines representing the major and minor diameters.

Figure 17.24 shows how to draw schematic threads using English specifications. Using specifications from **Appendix 5**, draw the minor diameter at approximately 3/4 of the major diameter, and the chamfer (bevel) 45° from the minor diameter. Draw crest lines as thin lines and root lines as thick visible lines.

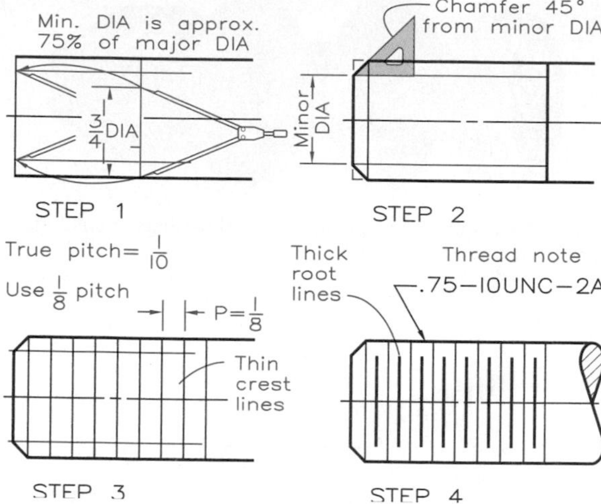

17.24 Schematic representation of threads.

Step 1 Lay out the major diameter and locate the minor diameter (about 3/4 of the major diameter). Draw the minor diameter with light construction lines.

Step 2 Chamfer the end of the threads with a 45° angle from the minor diameter.

Step 3 Find the pitch of a .75-10UNC-2A thread (0.1) by dividing 1 in. by the number of threads per inch (10). Use a larger pitch, 1/8 in. in this case, for spacing the thin crest lines.

Step 4 Draw root lines as thick as the visible lines between the crest lines to the construction lines representing the minor diameter. Add a thread note.

17.9 Simplified Symbols

Examples of external threads drawn with simplified symbols and noted with both metric and English formats are shown in **Figure 17.25**. Simplified symbols are the easiest to draw and are best suited for drawing small threads where drawing using schematic and detailed symbols would be too crowded. Various techniques of applying simplified symbols to threads are shown in **Figure 17.26**. The minor diameter is drawn as hidden lines spaced at about 3/4 the major diameter. **Figure 17.27** shows the steps for drawing simplified threads by referring to **Appendix 5**. With experience, you will be able to approximate the location of the minor diameter of simplified threads by eye.

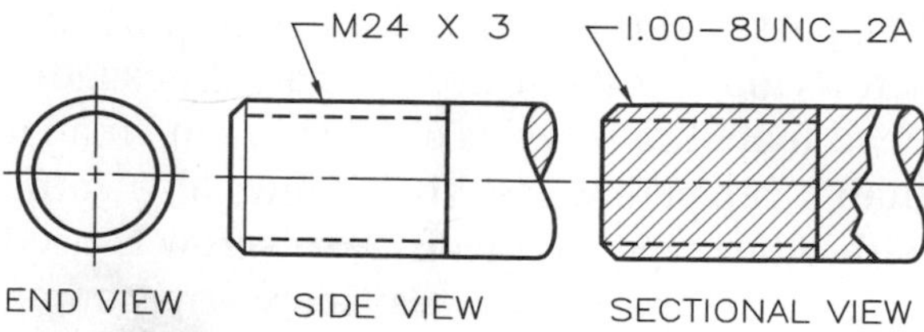

17.25 These simplified thread symbols represent external threads in view and section.

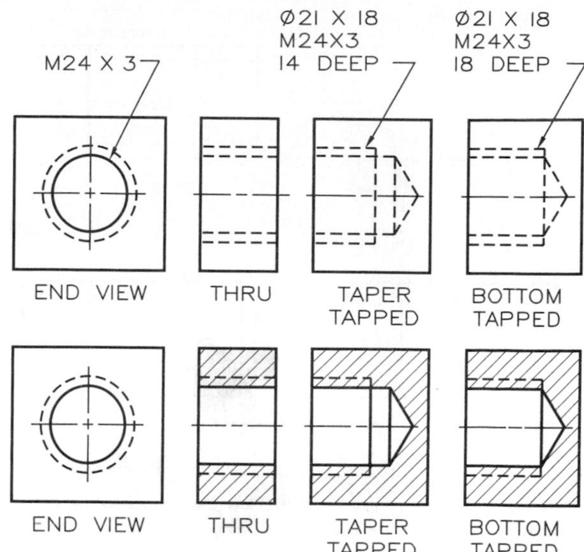

17.26 These simplified thread symbols represent internal threads in view and section. Draw minor diameters at about 3/4 the major diameter.

Drawing Small Threads

Remember, a drawing of a thread is a pictorial symbol; therefore, do not try to draw the true spacing of the threads. True spacing will be too close and too hard to read. Instead, select a wider spacing between root and crest lines for easier reading and drawing (**Figure 17.28**). This conventional practice of enlarging the thread's pitch to separate thread symbols is applied in drawing all three types of symbols (simplified, schematic, and detailed). Add a thread note to the drawing to give the necessary detailed specifications.

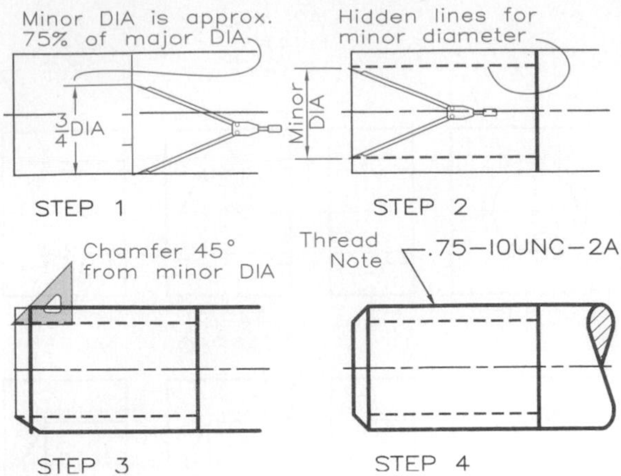

17.27 Simplified representation of threads.

Step 1 Lay out the major diameter. Locate the minor diameter (about 3/4 of the major diameter).

Step 2 Draw hidden lines to represent the minor diameter.

Step 3 Draw a 45° chamfer from the minor diameter to the major diameter.

Step 4 Darken the lines and add a thread note.

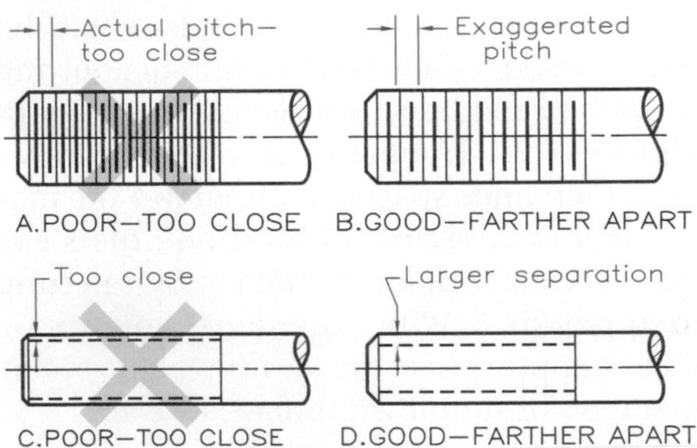

17.28 Most threads must be drawn using exaggerated dimensions instead of actual measurements to avoid having lines drawn too closely together.

17.29 This photo shows a nut, bolt, and washers in combination. *(Courtesy of Lamson & Sessions.)*

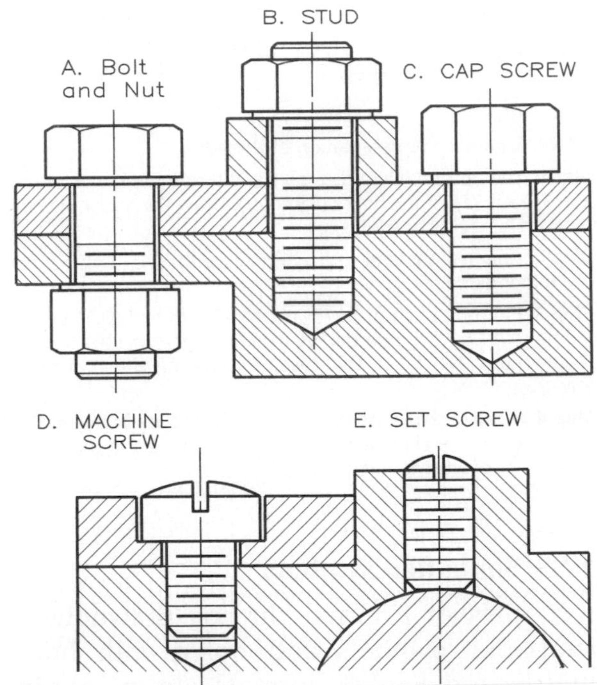

17.30 Types of threaded bolts and several applications.

17.10 Nuts and Bolts

Nuts and **bolts (Figure 17.29)** come in many forms and sizes for many different applications. Some common types of threaded fasteners are shown in **Figure 17.30**. A **bolt** is a threaded cylinder with a head and is used with a nut to hold parts together. A **stud** is a headless bolt, threaded at both ends, that is screwed into one part with a nut attached to the other end.

A **cap screw** usually does not have a nut but passes through a hole in one part and screws into another threaded part. A hexagon-head **machine screw** is similar to but smaller than a cap screw. Machine screws also come with other types of heads. A **setscrew** is used to hold one part fixed in place with another, usually to prevent rotation, as with a pulley on a shaft.

17.31 Examples of types of nuts. *(Courtesy of Russell, Burdsall & Ward Bolt and Nut Company.)*

Types of heads used on **regular** and **heavy** bolts and nuts are shown in **Figure 17.31** and **Figure 17.32**. Heavy bolts have thicker heads than regular bolts, for heavier usage. A **finished head** (or nut) has a 1/64-in.-thick washer face (a circular boss) to provide a bearing surface for smooth contact. **Semifinished bolt heads** and **nuts** are the same as finished bolt heads and nuts. **Unfinished bolt heads** and nuts have no bosses and no machined surfaces.

A **hexagon jam nut** does not have a washer face, but it is chamfered (beveled at its corners) on both sides **(Figure 17.32)**. **Figure 17.33** shows other standard bolt and screw heads for cap screws and machine screws.

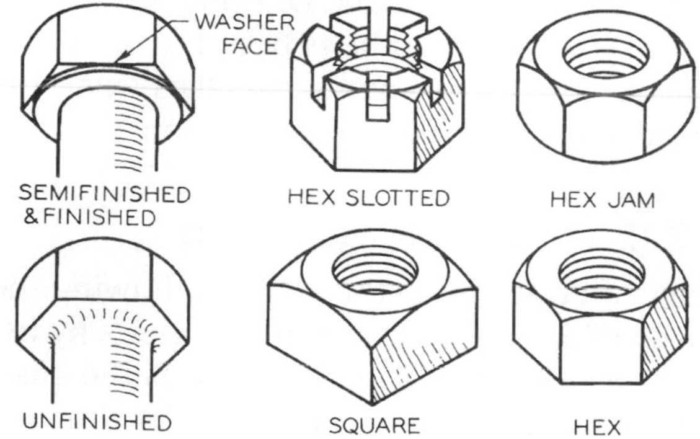

17.32 Finished and semifinished bolts and nuts have raised washer faces. Several types of nuts are shown here also.

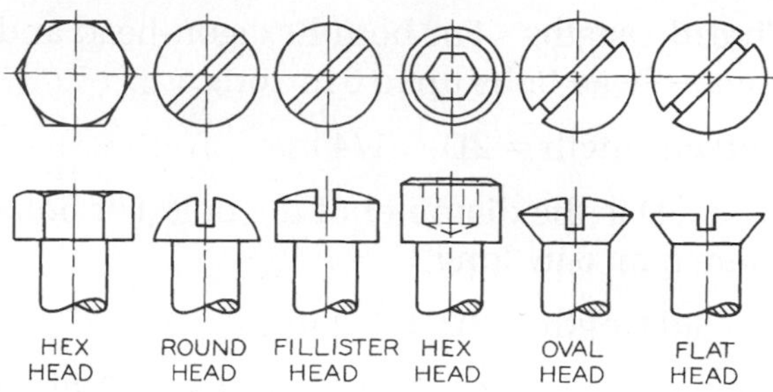

17.33 Standard types of bolt and screw heads.

Dimensions

Figure 17.34 shows a properly dimensioned bolt. The ANSI tables in **Appendixes 10–19** give nut and bolt dimensions, but you may use the following guides for hexagon-head and square-head bolts.

Overall Lengths Hexagon-head bolts are available in 1/4-in. increments up to 8 in. long, in 1/2-in. increments from 8 to 20 in. long, and in 1-in. increments from 20 to 30 in. long. Square-head bolts are available in 1/8-in. increments from 1/2 to 3/4 in. long, in 1/4-in. increments from 3/4 in. to 5 in. long, in 1/2-in. increments from 5 to 12 in. long, and in 1-in. increments from 12 to 30 in. long.

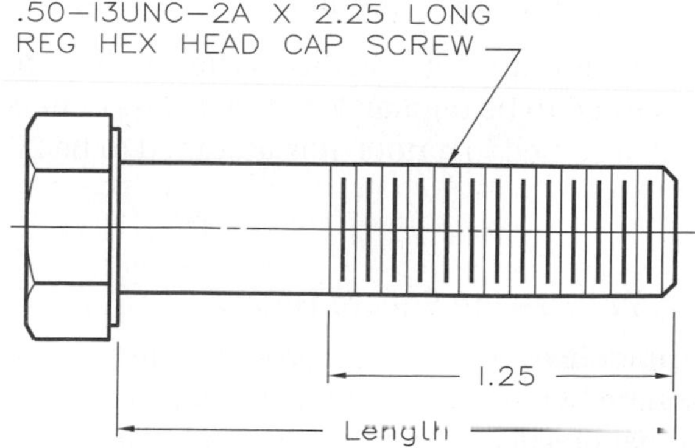

17.34 A properly dimensioned and noted hexagon-head bolt.

Thread Lengths For both hexagon-head and square-head bolts up to 6 in. long,

Thread length = 2D + 1/4 in.

where D is the diameter of the bolt. For bolts more than 6 in. long,

Thread length = 2D + 1/2 in.

Threads for bolts can be coarse, fine, or 8-pitch threads. The class of fit for bolts and nuts is understood to be 2A and 2B if no class is specified in the note.

Dimension Notes

Designate standard square-head and hexagon-head bolts by notes in one of three forms:

3/8-16 × 1-1/2 SQUARE BOLT—STEEL;

1/2-13 × 3 HEX CAP SCREW—SAE GRADE 8—STEEL;

.75 × 10 UNC-2A HEX HD LAG SCREW.

The numbers (left to right) represent bolt diameter, threads per inch (omit for lag screws), bolt length, screw name, and material (material designation is optional). When not specified in a note, each bolt is assumed to have a class 2 fit. Three types of notes for designating nuts are

1/2-13 SQUARE NUT—STEEL;

3/4-16 HEAVY HEX NUT;

1.00-8UNC-2B HEX HD THICK SLOTTED NUT—CORROSION-RESISTANT STEEL.

When nuts are not specified as heavy, they are assumed to be regular. When the class of fit is not specified in a note, it is assumed to be 2B for nuts.

17.11 Drawing Square Heads

Appendixes 10 and **11** give dimensions for square bolt heads and nuts. However, conventional practice is to draw nuts and bolts by using the general proportions shown in **Figure 17.35**. Your first step in drawing a bolt head or nut is to determine whether the view is to be across corners or across flats—that is, whether the lines at either side of the view represent the square's corners or flats. Drawing across corners shows nuts and bolts best, but occasionally you must draw one across flats when the head or nut is truly in this orientation.

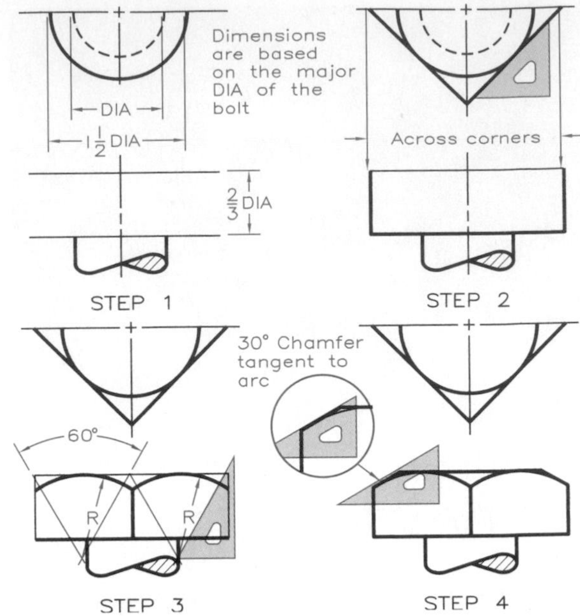

17.35 Drawing the square head.

Step 1 Draw the major diameter, DIA, of the bolt. Use 1.5 DIA to draw the hexagon-head's diameter and 2/3 DIA to establish its thickness.

Step 2 Draw the top view of the square head at a 45° angle to give an across-corners view.

Step 3 Show the chamfer in the front view by using a 30°-60° triangle to find the centers for the radii.

Step 4 Show a 30° chamfer tangent to the arcs in the front view. Darken the lines.

17.12 Drawing Hexagon Heads

Figure 17.36 shows the steps of drawing the head of a hexagon bolt across corners by using the bolt's major diameter, D, as the basis for all other proportions. Begin by drawing the top view of the head as a circle of a diameter of 1-1/2 D. For a regular head, the thickness

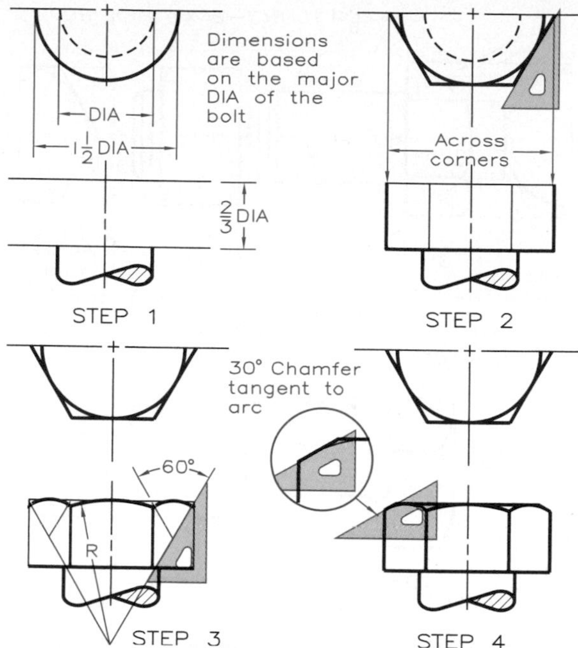

17.36 Drawing the hexagon head.

Step 1 Draw the major diameter, DIA, of the bolt and use it to establish the head diameter (as 1.5 DIA) and thickness (as 2/3 DIA).

Step 2 Construct a hexagon head with a 30°-60° triangle to give an across-corners view.

Step 3 Find arcs in the front view to draw the chamfer of the head.

Step 4 Draw a 30° chamfer tangent to the arcs in the front view. Darken the lines.

is 2/3 D; for a heavy head, it is 7/8 D. Circumscribe a hexagon about the circle. Then, draw outside arcs in the rectangular view and tangent chamfers (bevels) to complete the drawing.

Drawing Nuts

Use the same techniques to draw a square and a hexagon nut (shown across corners in **Figure 17.37**) that you did to draw bolt heads. The difference is that nuts are thicker than bolt heads: The thickness of a regular nut is 7/8 D, and the thickness of a heavy nut is 1 D, where D is the bolt diameter. Hidden lines may be inserted in the front view to indicate threads, or omitted. Exaggerate the thickness

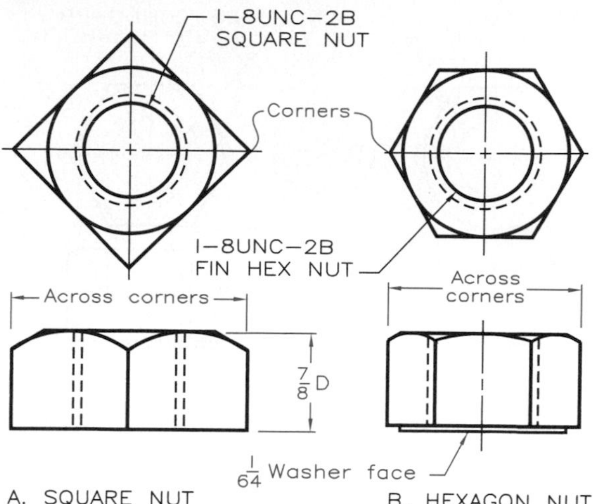

17.37 Drawing square and hexagon nuts across corners involves the same steps used for drawing bolt heads. Add notes to give nut specifications.

of the 1/64-in. washer face on the finished and semifinished hexagon nuts to about 1/32 in. to make it more noticeable. Place thread notes on circular views with leaders when space permits. Square nuts that are not labeled heavy are assumed to be regular nuts.

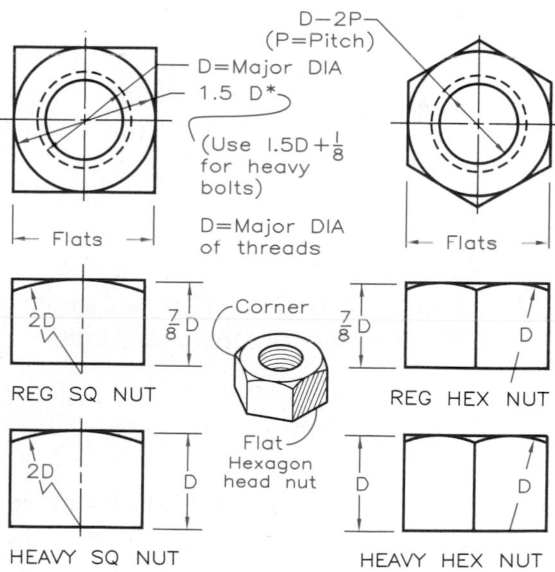

17.38 These square and hexagon nuts are drawn across flats with notes added to give their specifications. Square nuts are unfinished.

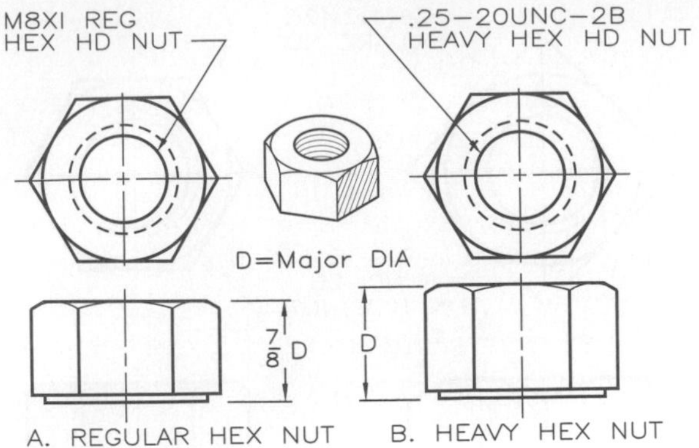

17.39 These regular and heavy hexagon nuts are drawn across corners, with notes added to give their specifications.

Figure 17.38 shows how to construct square and hexagon nuts across flats. For **regular nuts**, the distance across flats is 1-1/2D (D = major diameter of the thread), and 1-5/8 D for **heavy nuts**. Draw the top views in the same way you did across-corner top views, but rotate them to give across-flat front views. **Figure 17.39** depicts dimensioned and noted hexagon regular and heavy nuts drawn across corners.

Drawing Nut-and-Bolt Combinations

Nuts and bolts in assembly are drawn in the same manner as they are drawn individually (**Figure 17.40**). Use the major diameter, D, of the bolt as the basis for other dimensions. Here, the views of the bolt heads are across corners, and the views of the nuts are across flats, although both views could have been drawn across corners. The half-end views are used to find the front views by projection. Add a note to give the specifications of the nut and bolt.

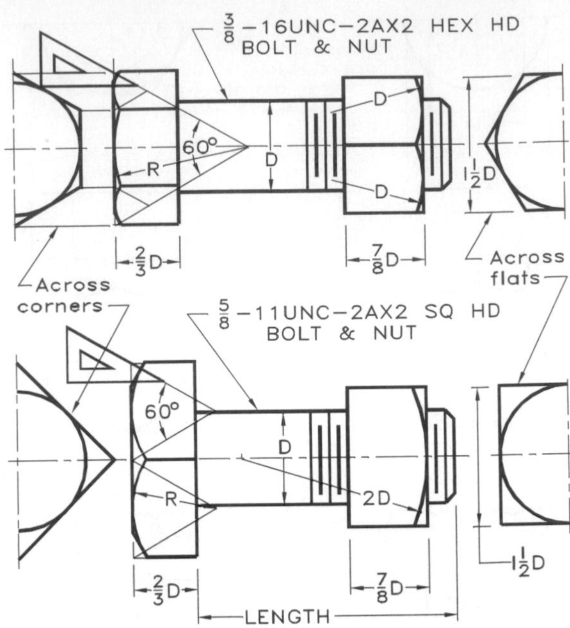

17.40 The proportions and the geometry for drawing square nuts and bolts and hexagon nuts and bolts.

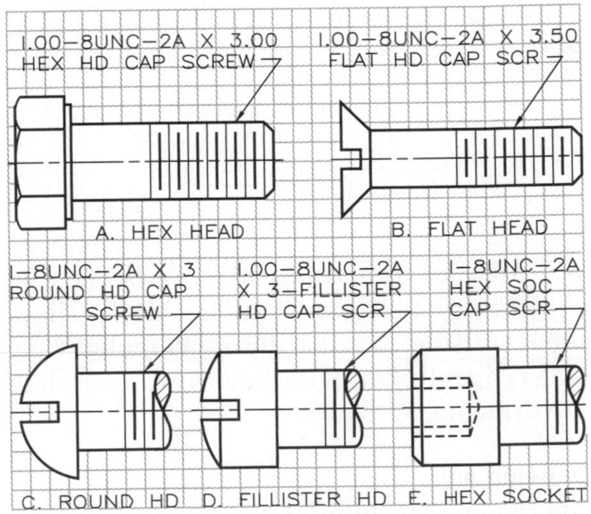

17.41 These cap screws are drawn on a grid to give the proportions for drawing them at different sizes. Notes give thread specifications, length, head type, and bolt name (cap screw).

17.13 Types of Screws

Cap Screws

The **cap screw** passes through a hole in one part and screws into a threaded hole in the other part so the two parts can be held together without a nut. Cap screws are usually larger than machine screws, and they may also be used with nuts. **Figure 17.41** shows the standard types of cap screw heads drawn on a grid that can be used as a guide for drawing cap screws of other sizes. **Appendixes 14–18** give cap screw dimensions, which can aid in drawing them.

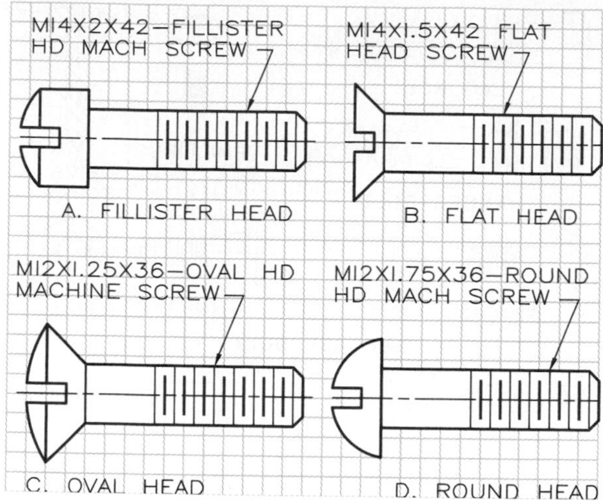

17.42 These are standard types of machine screws. The same proportions may be used to draw machine screws of all sizes.

Machine Screws

Smaller than most cap screws, **machine screws** usually are less than 1 in. in diameter. They screw into a threaded hole in a part or into a nut. Machine screws are fully threaded when their length is 2 in. or less. Longer screws have thread lengths of 2D + 1/4 in. (D = major diameter of the thread). **Figure 17.42** shows four types of machine screws, along with notes, drawn on a grid that may be used as an aid in drawing them without dimensions from a table. Machine screws range in diameter from No. 0 (0.060 in.) to 3/4 in., as shown in **Appendix 19**, which gives the dimensions of round-head machine screws.

Setscrews

Setscrews are used to hold parts together, such as pulleys and handles on a shaft, and prevent rotation. **Figure 17.43** shows various types of setscrews, with dimensions denoted by letters that correspond to the tables of dimensions in **Appendix 20**.

Setscrews are available in combinations of points and heads. The shaft against which the setscrew is tightened may have a machined

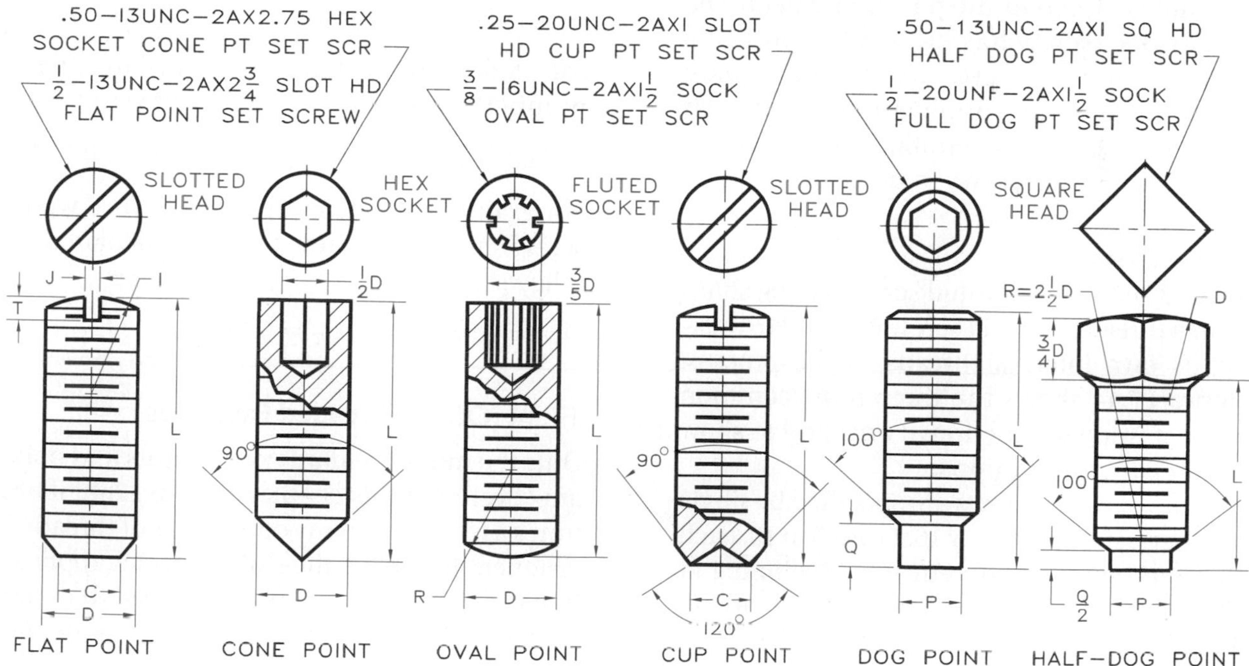

17.43 Setscrews are available with various combinations of heads and points. Notes give their measurements. (See Appendix 20.)

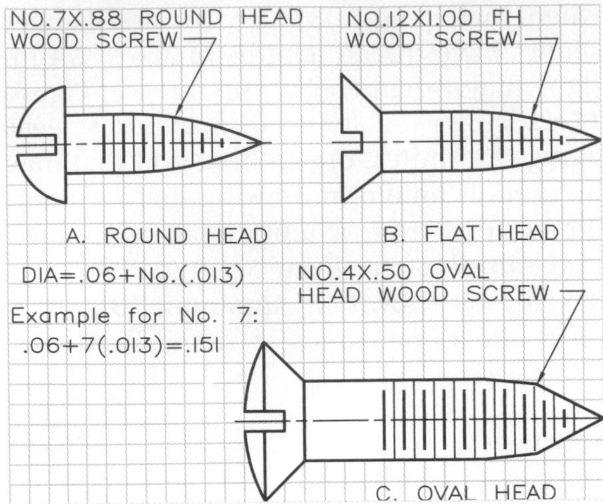

17.44 Standard types of wood screws are drawn on a grid that gives the proportions for drawing them at other sizes.

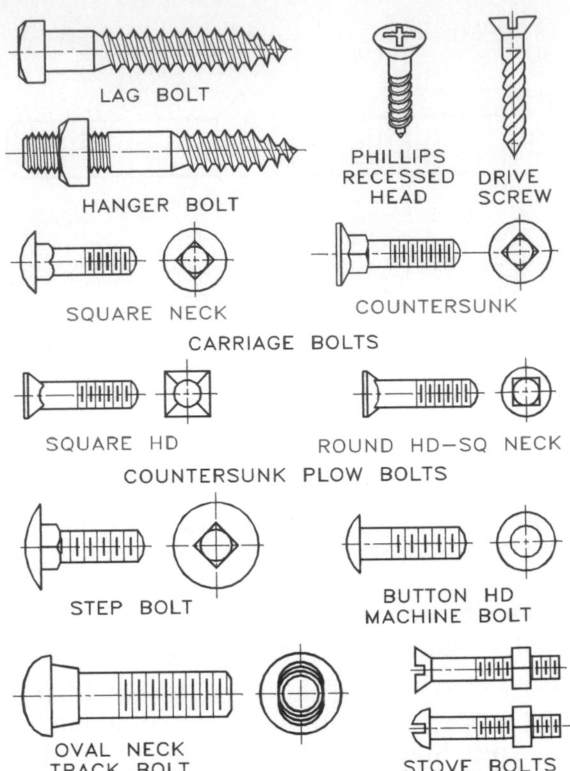

17.45 A few of the many different types of bolts and screws.

flat surface to provide a good bearing surface for a **dog-** or **flat-point** setscrew end to press against. The **cup point** gives good gripping when pressed against round shafts. The **cone point** works best when inserted into holes drilled in the part being held. The **headless setscrew** has no head to protrude above a rotating part. An exterior square head is good for applications in which greater force must be applied with a wrench to hold larger setscrews in position.

Wood Screws

A **wood screw** is a pointed screw having sharp coarse threads that will screw into wood, making its own internal threads in the process. **Figure 17.44** shows the three most common types of wood screws drawn on a grid to show their relative proportions.

Sizes of wood screws are specified by single numbers, such as 0, 6, or 16. From 0 to 10, each digit represents a different size. Beginning at 10, only even-numbered sizes are standard, that is, 10, 12, 14, 16, 18, 20, 22, and 24. Use the following formula to translate these numbers into the actual diameter sizes:

Actual DIA = 0.06 + (screw number × 0.013).

For example, the diameter for the No. 7 wood screw shown in **Figure 17.44** is calculated as follows:

DIA = 0.06 + 7(0.013) = 0.151.

17.14 Other Threaded Fasteners

Only the more standard types of nuts and bolts are covered in this chapter. **Figure 17.45** illustrates a few of the many other types of threaded fasteners that have their own special applications. Three types of wing screws that are turned by hand are available in incremental

DESIGNATION: 10-16 X 2 WING SCREW
TYPE B-STYLE 1-STEEL CADMIUM PLATED

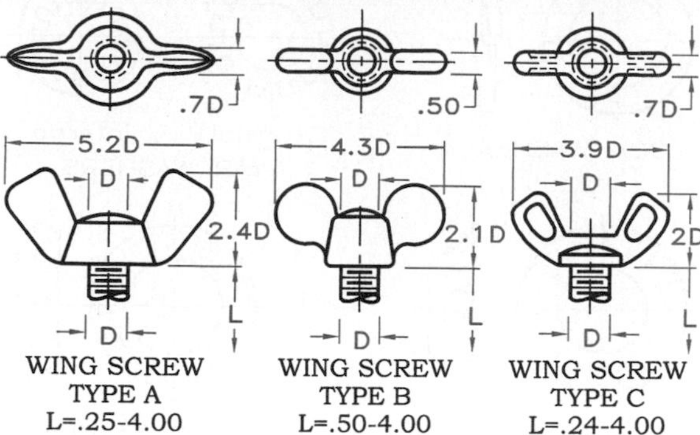

17.46 These wing screw proportions are for screw diameters of about 5/16 inch. The same proportions may be used to draw wing screws of any diameter. Type A screws are available in diameters of 4, 6, 8, 10, 12, 0.25, 0.313, 0.375, 0.438, 0.50, and 0.625 in. Type B screws are available in diameters of 10 to 0.625 in. Type C screws are available in diameters of 6 to 0.375 in.

lengths of 1/8 in. (**Figure 17.46**). **Figure 17.47** shows two types of thumb screws, which serve the same purpose as wing screws, and **Figure 17.48** shows wing nuts that can be screwed together by fingertip without wrenches or screwdrivers.

DESIGNATION: 10-32 X 1.25 THUMB SCREW
TYPE A-REG - STEEL

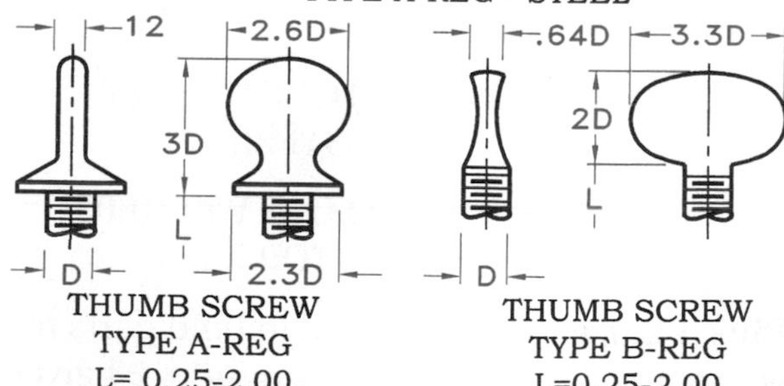

17.47 These thumb screw proportions are for screw diameters of about 1/4 inch. The same proportions may be used to draw thumb screws of any diameter. Type A screws are available in diameters of 6, 8, 10, 12, 0.25, 0.313, and 0.375 in. Type B thumb screws are available in diameters of 6 to 0.50 in.

DESIGNATION: 10-32 TYPE A WING NUT
REG SERIES-STEEL ZINC PLATED

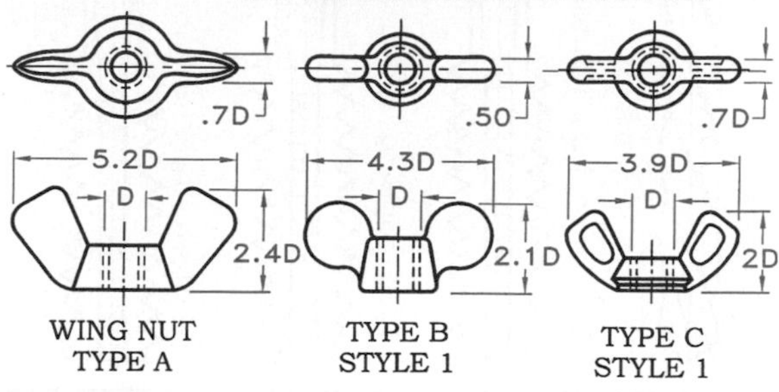

17.48 These wing nut proportions are for screw diameters of 3/8 in. The same proportions may be used to draw thumb screws of any size. Type A wing nuts are available in screw diameters of 3, 4, 5, 6, 8, 10, 12, 0.25, 0.313, 0.375, 0.438, 0.50, 0.583, 0.625, and 0.75 in. Type B nuts are available in sizes from 5 to 0.75 in. Type C nuts are available in sizes from 4 to 0.50 in.

17.15 Tapping a Hole

An internal thread is made by drilling a hole with a tap drill with a 120° point (**Figure 17.49**). The depth of the drilled hole is measured to the shoulder of the conical point, not to the point. The diameter of the drilled hole is approximately equal to the root diameter, calculated as the major diameter of the screw thread minus its pitch (**Appendixes 5–7**). The hole is **tapped**, or threaded, with a tool called a **tap** of one of the types shown.

The **taper, plug**, and **bottoming** hand taps have identical measurements, except for the chamfered portion of their ends. The taper tap has a long chamfer (8 to 10 threads), the plug tap has a shorter chamfer (3 to 5 threads), and the bottoming tap has the shortest chamfer (1 to 1-1/2 threads).

When tapping is to be done by hand in open or "through" holes, the taper tap should be used for coarse threads and in harder metals because it ensures straighter alignment and starting. The plug tap may be used in soft metals and for fine-pitch threads. When a hole is tapped to its bottom, all three

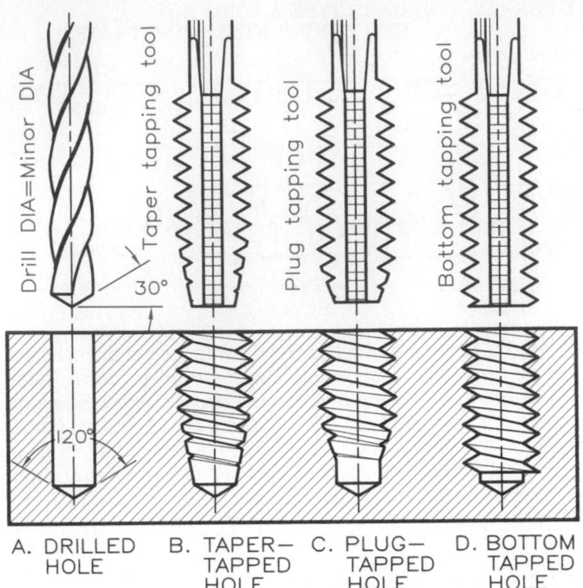

17.49 This drawing illustrates miscellaneous types of bolts and screws.

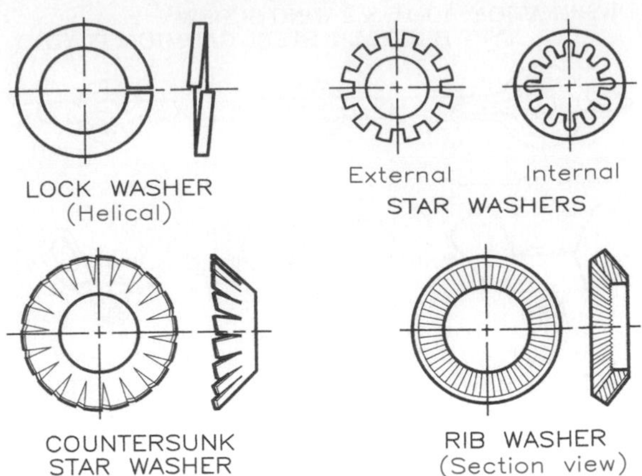

17.50 Lock washers are used to keep threaded parts from vibrating apart.

taps—taper, plug, and bottoming—are used in that sequence on the same internal threads.

Notes are added to specify the depth of a drilled hole and the depth of the threads within it. For example, a note reading 7/8 DIA-3 DEEP × 1/8 UNC-2A × 2 DEEP means that the hole is to be drilled deeper than it is threaded and that the last usable thread will be 2 in. deep in the hole.

17.16 Washers, Lock Washers, and Pins

Various types of washers are used with nuts and bolts to improve their assembly and increase their fastening strength.

Plain washers are noted on a drawing as

.938 × 1.750 × 0.134 TYPE A PLAIN WASHER,

where the numbers (left to right) represent the washer's inside diameter, outside diameter, and thickness. (See **Appendix 26**.)

Lock washers reduce the likelihood that threaded parts will loosen because of vibration and movement. **Figure 17.50** shows several common types of lock washers. **Appendix 33** contains a table of dimensions for regular and extra-heavy-duty helical-spring lock washers. Designate them with a note in the form

HELICAL-SPRING LOCK WASHER
1/4 REGULAR—PHOSPHOR BRONZE,

where the 1/4 is the washer's inside diameter. Designate tooth lock washers with a note in one of two forms:

INTERNAL-TOOTH LOCK WASHER
1/4-TYPE A—STEEL;

EXTERNAL-TOOTH LOCK WASHER
.562-TYPE B—STEEL.

Pins (**Figure 17.51**) are used to hold parts together in a fixed position. **Appendix 23** gives dimensions for straight pins. The **cotter pin** is another locking device that everyone who has had a toy wagon is familiar with. **Appendix 22** contains a table of dimensions for cotter pins.

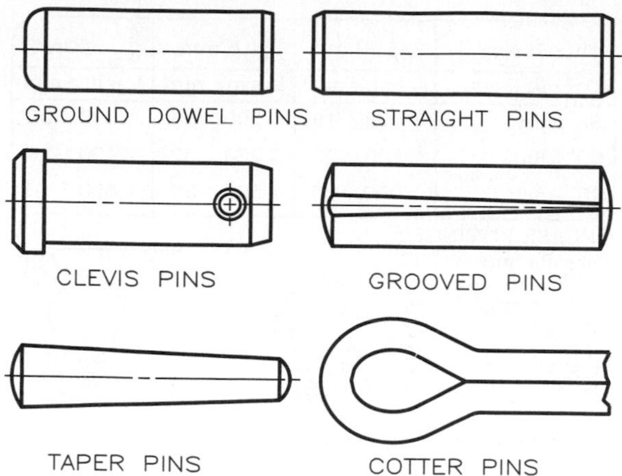

17.51 Pins are used to hold parts together in assembly.

17.17 Pipe Threads and Fittings

Pipe threads are used for connecting pipes, tubing, and various fittings including lubrication fittings. The most commonly used pipe thread is tapered at a ratio of 1 to 16 on its diameter, but straight pipe threads also are available (**Figure 17.52**). Tapered pipe threads will engage only for an effective length of

$$L = (0.80D + 6.8)P,$$

where D is the outside diameter of the threaded pipe, and P is the pitch of the thread.

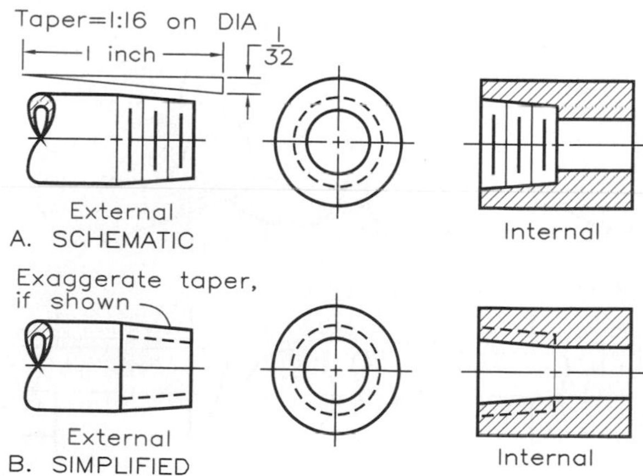

17.52 Pipe threads with schematic and simplified symbols.

The pipe threads shown in **Figure 17.52** have a taper exaggerated to 1:16 on radius (instead of on diameter) to emphasize it. Drawing them with no taper obviously is easier. You may use either schematic or simplified symbols to show the threaded features.

Use the following ANSI abbreviations in pipe thread notes. All begin with NP (for National Pipe thread).

NPT: national pipe taper

NPTF: national pipe thread (dryseal, for pressure-tight joints)

NPS: straight pipe thread

NPSC: straight pipe thread in couplings

NPSI: national pipe straight internal thread

NPSF: straight pipe thread (dryseal)

NPSM: straight pipe thread for mechanical joints

NPSL: straight pipe thread for locknuts and locknut pipe threads

NPSH: straight pipe thread for hose couplings and nipples

NPTR: taper pipe thread for railing fittings

To specify a pipe thread in note form, give the nominal pipe diameter (the common-fraction size of its internal diameter), the number of threads per inch, and the thread-type symbol:

1-1/4-11-1/2 NPT or 3-8 NPTR

Appendix 9 gives a table of dimensions for pipe threads. **Figure 17.53** shows how to present specifications for external and internal threads in note form. Dryseal threads, either straight or tapered, provide a pressure-tight joint without the use of a lubricant or sealer.

Pipe fittings and their dimensions are given in **Appendixes 42** and **43**. These fittings are connected to pipes and other fittings with pipe threads previously covered.

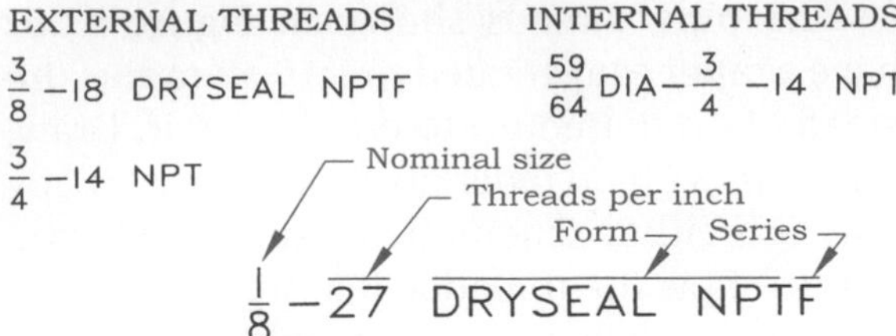

17.53 Typical pipe thread notes.

Thread size	1/8 3 mm		1/4 6 mm		3/8 10 mm	
Overall length	L = in.	mm	L = in.	mm	L = in.	mm
Straight	.625	16	1.000	25	1.200	30
90° Elbow	.800	20	1.250	32	1.400	36
45° Angle	1.000	25	1.500	38	1.600	41

GREASE FITTINGS
Threads may be NPT or UN form

L

A. STRAIGHT B. 90° ANGLE B. 45° ANGLE

17.54 Three standard types of grease fittings used to lubricate moving parts with a grease gun are shown here.

Grease Fittings

Grease fittings (**Figure 17.54**) allow the application of lubricant to moving parts. Threads of grease fittings are available as tapered and straight pipe threads. The ends where grease is inserted with a grease gun are available straight or at 90° and 45° angles. A one-way valve, formed by a ball and spring, permits grease to enter the fitting (forced through by a grease gun) but prevents it from escaping.

17.18 Keys

Keys are used to attach pulleys, gears, or crank handles to shafts, allowing them to remain assembled while moving and transmitting power. The four types of keys shown in **Figure 17.55** are the most commonly used. **Appendixes 24** and **25** contains tables of dimensions for keyways, keys, and keyseats.

17.19 Rivets

Rivets are fasteners that permanently join thin overlapping materials (**Figure 17.56**). The rivet is inserted in a hole slightly larger than the diameter of the rivet, and the application of pressure to the projecting end forms the headless end

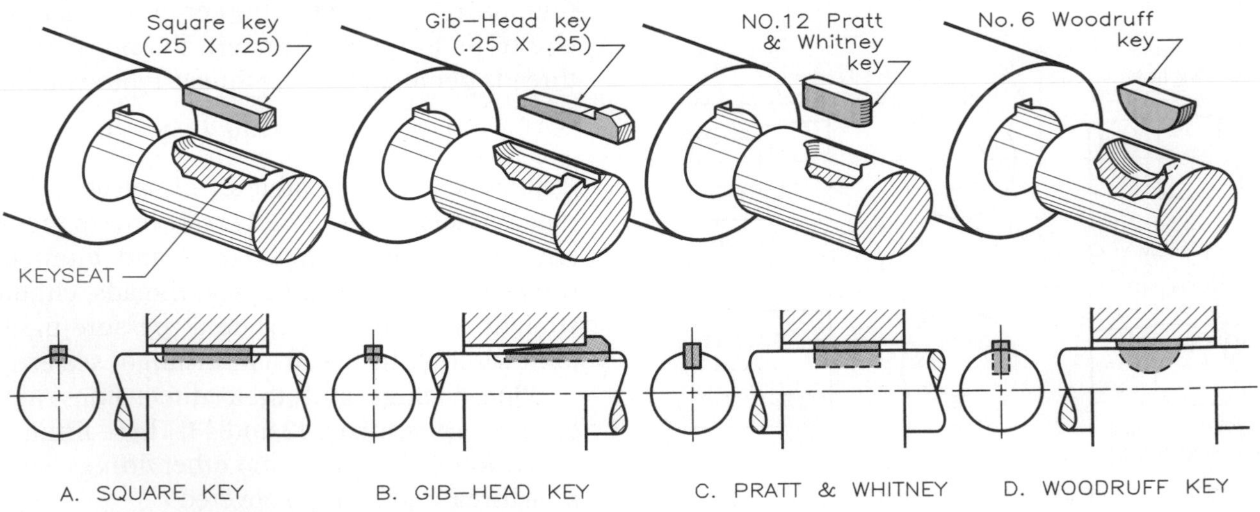

17.55 Standard types of keys used to hold parts on a shaft.

17.56 Rivets are used to permanently fasten structural elements together. *(Courtesy of Russell, Burdsall & Ward Bolt and Nut Company.)*

into shape. Forming may be done with either hot or cold rivets, depending on the application.

Figure 17.57 shows typical shapes and proportions of small rivets that vary in diameter from 1/16 to 1-3/4 in. Rivets are used extensively in pressure-vessel fabrication, heavy construction (such as bridges and buildings), and sheet-metal construction.

Figure 17.58 shows some of the standard ANSI symbols for representing rivets. Rivets that are driven in the shop are called *shop rivets,*

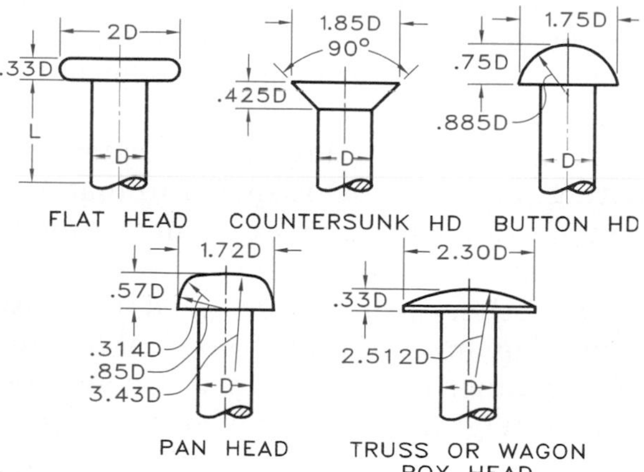

17.57 The proportions of small rivets with shanks of 1/2 in. and smaller are shown here.

17.58 Rivets are represented by these symbols in a drawing.

and those assembled at the job site are called *field rivets.*

17.20 Springs

Springs are devices that absorb energy and react with an equal force (**Figure 17.59**). Most springs are **helical**, as are bed springs, but they can also be **flat** (leaf), as in an automobile chassis. Some of the more common types of springs are **compression, torsion, extension, flat**, and **constant-force** springs. **Figures 17.60A–C** shows single-line conventional representations of the first three types. **Figures 17.60D–F** represent the types of ends used on compression springs.

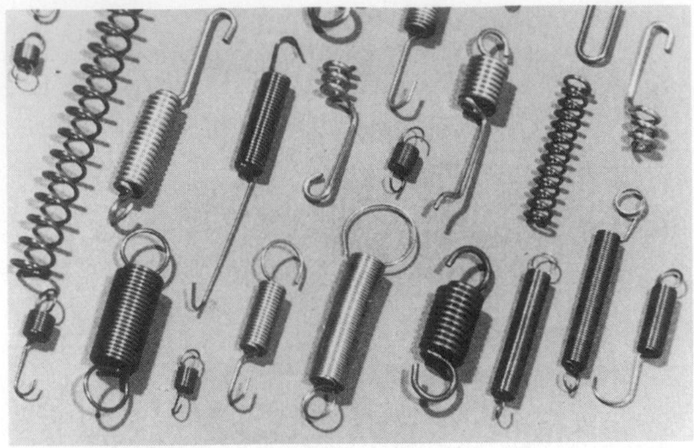

17.59 Springs are available for numerous special applications.

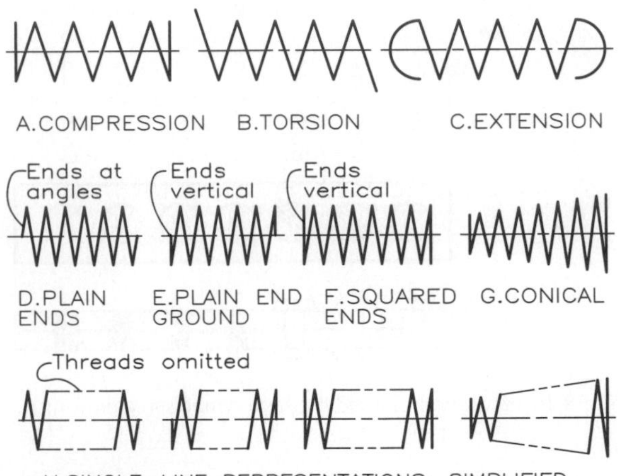

17.60 Single-line spring drawings.

A–C These are single-line representations of various types of springs.

D–G These single-line representations of springs show various types of ends.

H These are simplified single-line representations of the springs depicted in D–G.

Plain ends of springs simply end with no special modification of the coil. **Ground plain** ends are coils that have been machined by grinding to flatten the ends perpendicular to their axes. **Squared ends** are inactive coils that have been closed to form a circular flat coil at the end of a spring, which may also be ground.

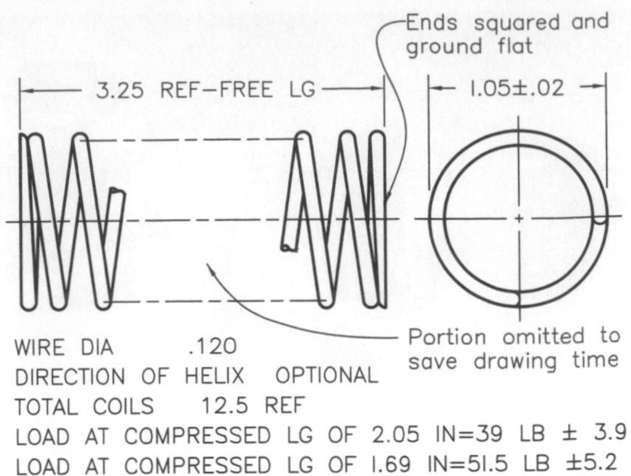

17.61 This conventional double-line drawing is of a compression spring and includes its specifications.

In **Figure 17.60G** a conical **helical spring** is shown in its simplified form. **Figure 17.60H** shows schematic single-line representations of the same types of springs depicted in **Figures 17.60D–G**, with phantom outlines instead of all the coils. This is the conventional method of drawing springs that saves time and effort.

Working drawing specifications of a compression spring drawn as a double-line representation are shown in **Figure 17.61**. Two coils are drawn at each end of the spring, and phantom lines are drawn between them to save drawing time. A dimension is given with the diameter and free length of the spring on the drawing. The remaining specifications are given in a table placed near the drawing.

A working drawing of an **extension spring** (**Figure 17.62**) is similar to that of a compression spring. An extending spring is designed to resist stretching, whereas a **compression spring** is designed to resist squeezing. In a drawing of a **helical torsion spring**, which resists and reacts to a twisting motion (**Figure 17.63**), angular dimensions specify the initial and final positions of the spring as torsion is applied. Again, dimension

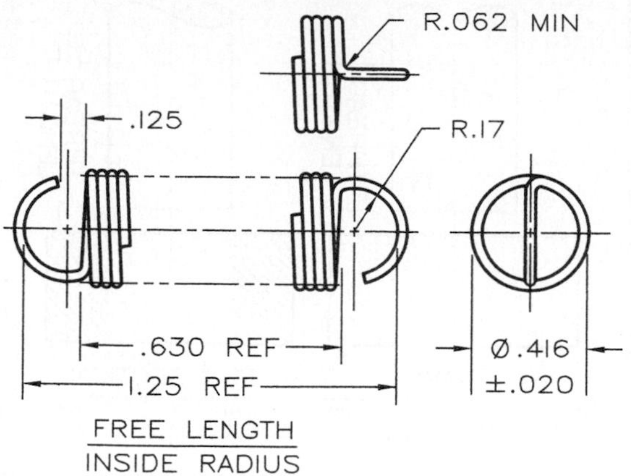

WIRE DIA	0.42
DIRECTION OF HELIX	OPTIONAL
TOTAL COILS	14 REF
RELATIVE POSITION OF ENDS	180° ±20°
EXTENDED LENGTH INSIDE ENDS WITHOUT PERMANENT SET	2.45 IN (MAX)
INITIAL TENSION	1.00 LB ±.10 LB
LOAD	4.0 LB ±.4 LB AT 1.56 IN
EXTENDED LG INSIDE ENDS	
LOAD	6.30 LB ±.63 LB AT 1.95

17.62 This conventional double-line drawing shows an extension spring and its specifications.

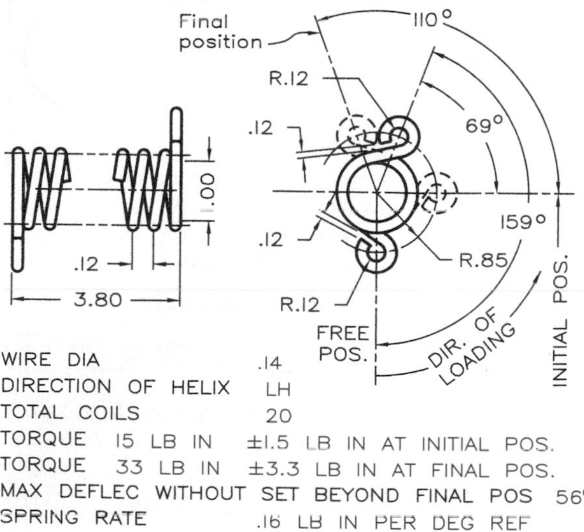

17.63 This conventional double-line drawing is of a helical torsion spring and includes its specifications.

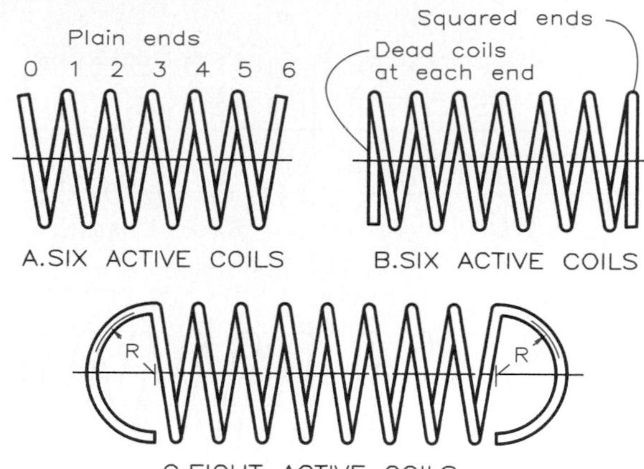

17.64 Double-line drawings of springs.

A This double-line drawing shows a spring with six active coils.

B This double-line drawing shows a spring with six coils and a "dead" coil (inactive coil) at each end.

C This double-line drawing shows an extension spring with eight active coils.

the drawing and add specifications to describe its details.

17.21 Drawing Springs

Springs may be represented with single-line drawings (**Figure 17.60**) or as more realistic double-line drawings (**Figure 17.64**). Draw each type shown by first laying out the diameters of the coils and lengths of the springs and then dividing the lengths into the number of active coils (**Figure 17.64A**). In **Figure 17.64B**, both end coils are "dead" (inactive) coils, and only six coils are active. **Figure 17.64C** depicts an extension spring with eight active coils.

The steps of drawing a double-line detailed representation of a compression spring are shown in **Figure 17.65**. Springs can be drawn right hand or left hand, but like threads, most are drawn as right-hand coils. The ends of the spring in this case are to be squared by grinding the ends to make them flat and perpendicular to the axis of the spring.

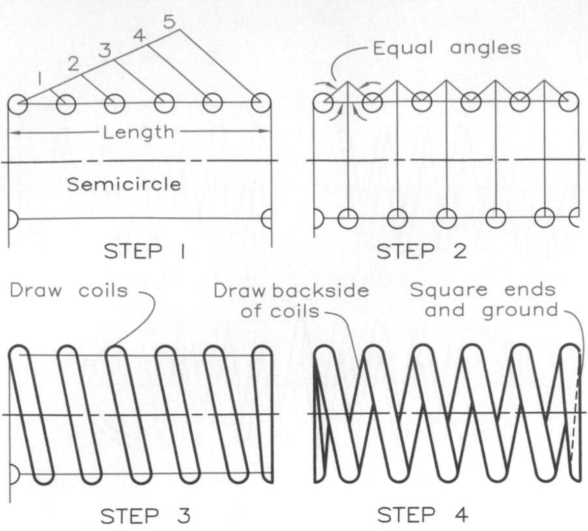

17.65 Drawing a spring in detail.

Step 1 Lay out the diameter and length of the spring and locate the five coils by the diagonal-line technique.

Step 2 Locate the coils on the lower side along the bisectors of the spaces between the coils on the upper side.

Step 3 Connect the coils on each side. This is a right-hand coil; a left-hand spring would slope in the opposite direction.

Step 4 Construct the back side of the spring and the end coils to complete the drawing. The spring has a square end that is to be ground.

Problems

Solve and draw these problems on size A sheets to apply the principles covered in this chapter. Each grid space equals 0.20 in., or 5 mm.

1. (Sheet 1) Draw detailed representations of Acme threads with major diameters of 2 in. Show both external and internal threads as views and sections. Give a thread note by referring to **Appendix 18**.

2. Repeat problem 1 with internal and external detailed representations of square threads.

3. Repeat problem 1, but draw internal and external detailed representations of UN threads. Give a thread note for a coarse thread with a class 2 fit. Refer to **Appendix 5**.

4. (Sheet 2) Using the notes given, draw detailed representations of the internal threads and holes in section. Provide thread notes on each as specified.

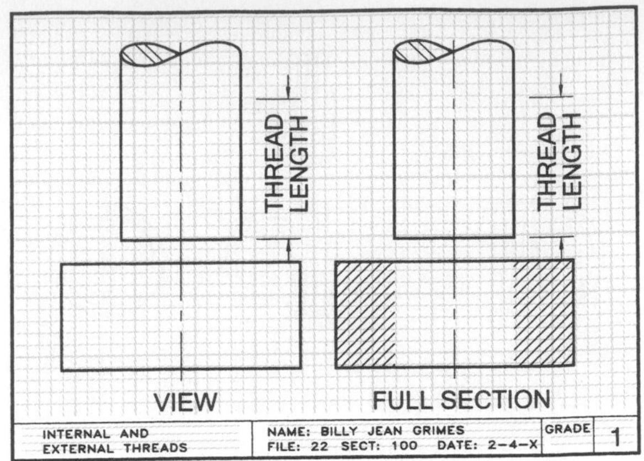

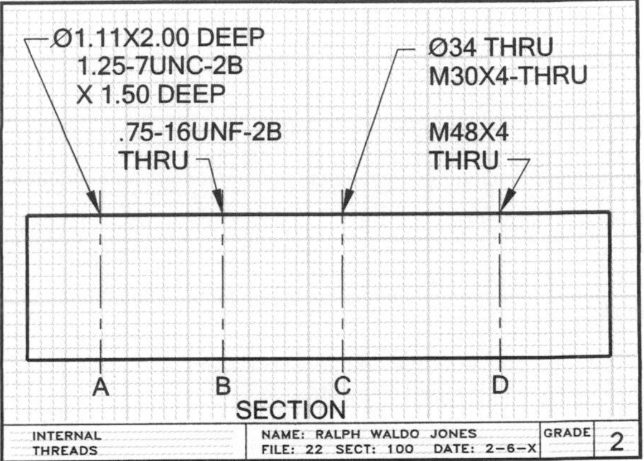

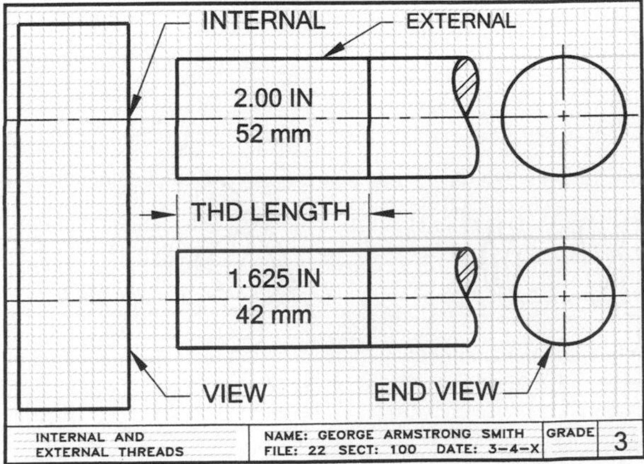

5. Repeat problem 4 but use schematic symbols to represent the threads.

6. Repeat problem 4 but use simplified symbols to represent the threads.

7. (Sheet 3) Using the partial views given and detailed thread symbols, draw external,

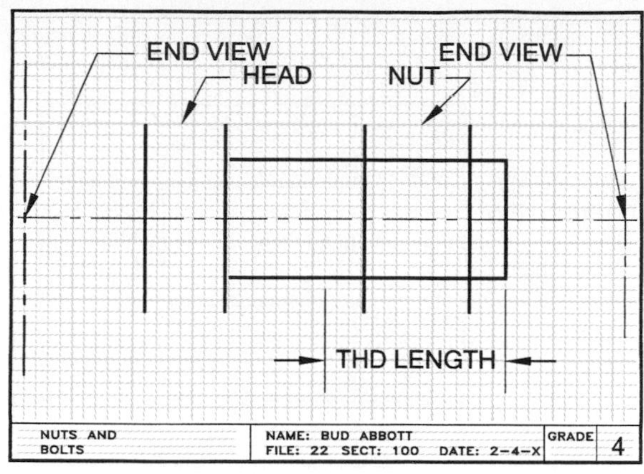

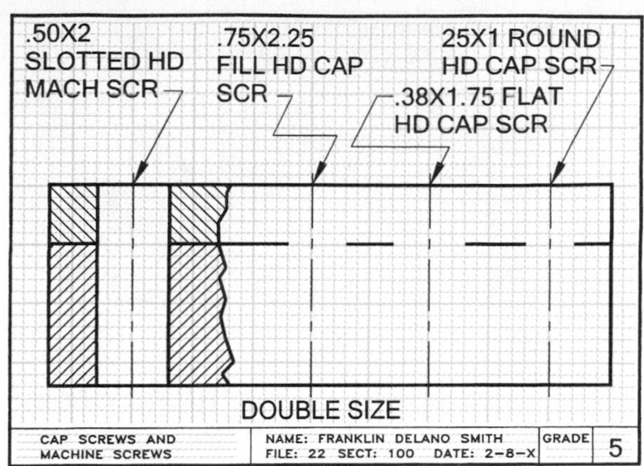

internal, and end views of the full-size threaded parts. Provide thread notes for UNC threads with a class 2 fit. Refer to **Appendix 5**.

8. Repeat problem 7, but use schematic symbols to represent the threads.

9. Repeat problem 7, but use simplified symbols to represent the threads.

10. (Sheet 4) Draw the finished hexagon-head bolt and a heavy hexagon nut. Draw the bolt head and nut across corners using detailed thread symbols. Provide thread notes in either English or metric form as assigned. Refer to **Appendixes 12** and **13**.

11. Repeat problem 10, but draw the nut and bolt as having unfinished square heads. Use schematic thread symbols. Refer to **Appendixes 10** and **11**.

12. Repeat problem 10, but draw the bolt with a regular finished hexagon head across flats, using simplified thread symbols. Draw the nut across flats also and provide thread notes for both.

13. (Sheet 5) Use the given notes and the tables in the appendix to draw the screws in section, complete the sectional view, and show the crosshatching. Use detailed thread symbols and provide thread notes for each of the parts.

14. Repeat problem 13 using schematic thread symbols to represent the threads.

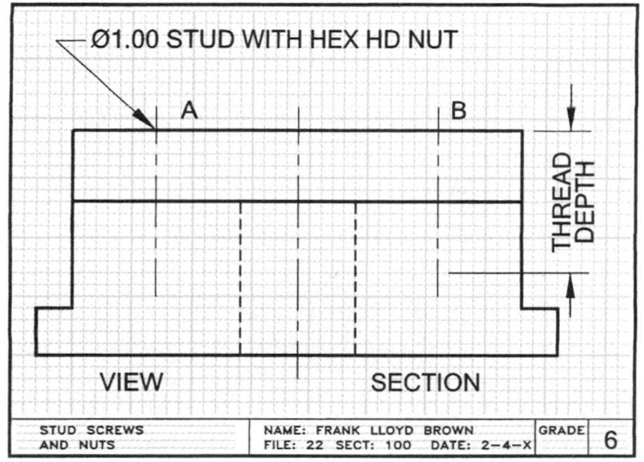

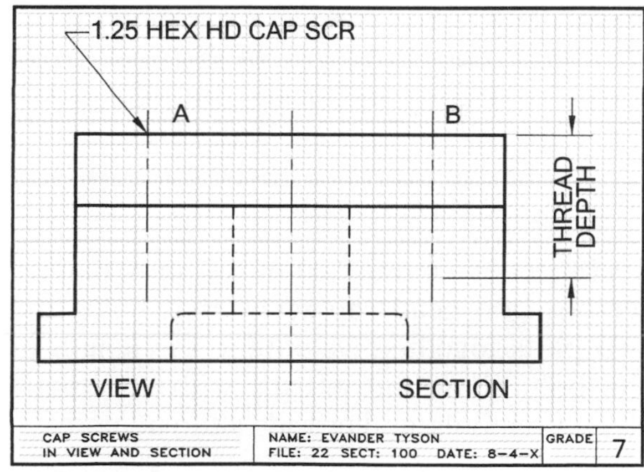

15. Repeat problem 13, using simplified thread symbols to represent the threads.

16. (Sheet 6) On axes A and B, construct hexagon-head cap screws (across flats), with UNC threads and a class 2 fit. The cap screws

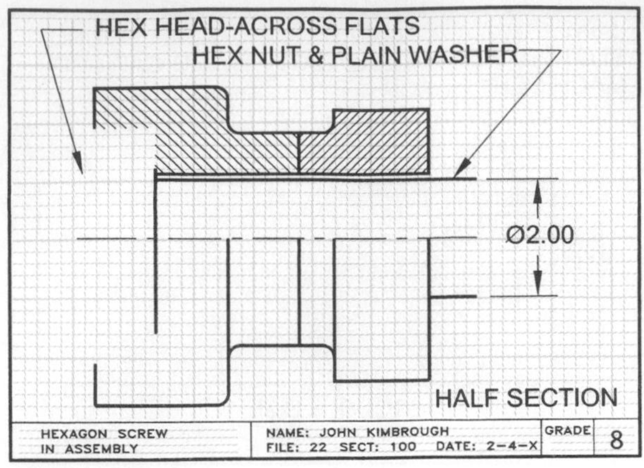

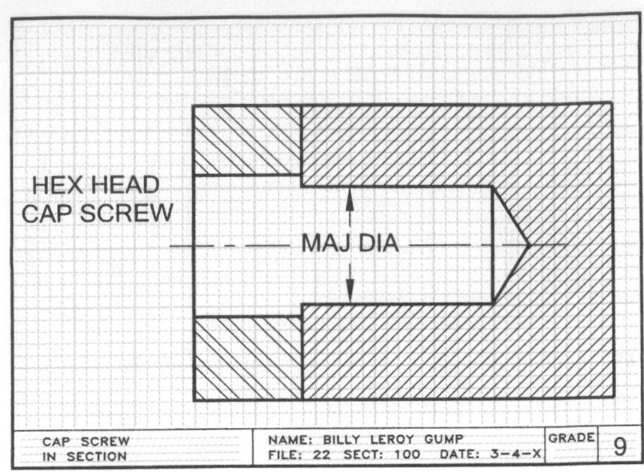

should not reach the bottoms of the threaded holes. Convert the view to a half section.

17. (Sheet 7) On axes A and B, draw studs having a hexagon-head nut (across flats) that hold the two parts together. The studs are to be fine series with a class 2 fit, and they should not reach the bottom of the threaded hole. Provide a thread note. Show the view as a half section.

18. (Sheet 8) Draw a 2.00-in. (50-mm) diameter hexagon-head bolt, with its head across flats, using schematic symbols. Draw a plain washer and regular nut (across corners) at the right end. Design the size of the opening in the part at the left end to hold the bolt head so that it will not turn. Use a UNC thread with a series 2 fit and provide a thread note. Refer to the tables in the appendix.

19. (Sheet 9) Draw a 2.00-in. (50-mm) diameter hexagon-head cap screw that holds the two parts together. Determine the length of the bolt, show the threads with schematic thread symbols, and provide a thread note.

20. (Sheet 10) Part at A is held on the shaft by a square key; Part at B is held on the shaft by a gib-head key. Using **Appendix 25**, complete the drawings and provide the necessary notes.

21. Repeat problem 20, but use Woodruff keys, one with a flat bottom and the other with a round bottom. Refer to **Appendix 24** to complete the drawings and provide the necessary notes.

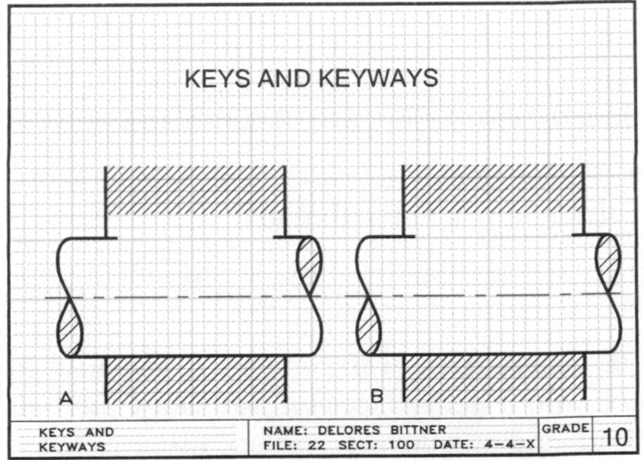

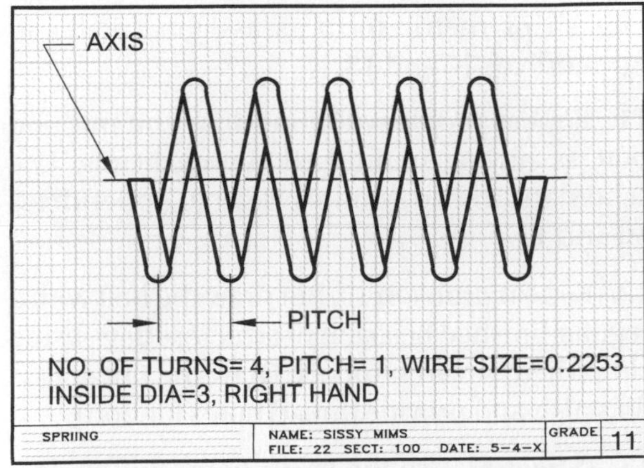

22. (Sheet 11) Make a double-line drawing of the spring with the following specifications: no. of turns 4, pitch 1, wire size no. 4 = 0.2253, inside diameter 3, right hand.

Design Problems

The following problems have a degree of design in them to see how well you can apply the principles covered in this chapter. Lay out these problems on size A sheets (if more than one sheet is needed).

DESIGN 1:
CENTERING
DEVICE

This assembly of parts is linked by threads and a pin. Draw orthographic views of the parts on size A sheets and provide thread notes based on the diameter of part 2 being 20 mm. Notice that parts 1 and 2 are joined by an interference fit. You'll astound your instructor.

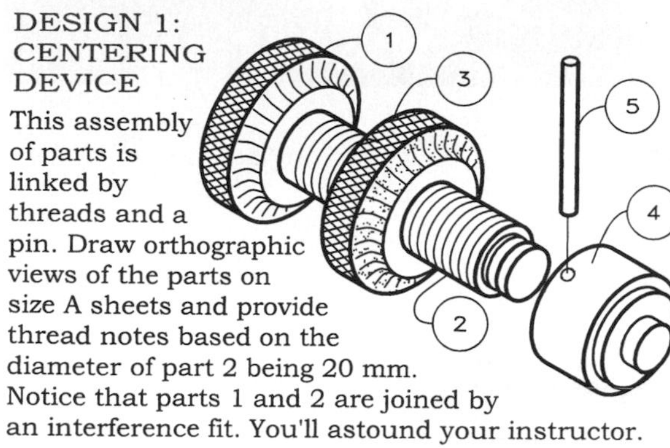

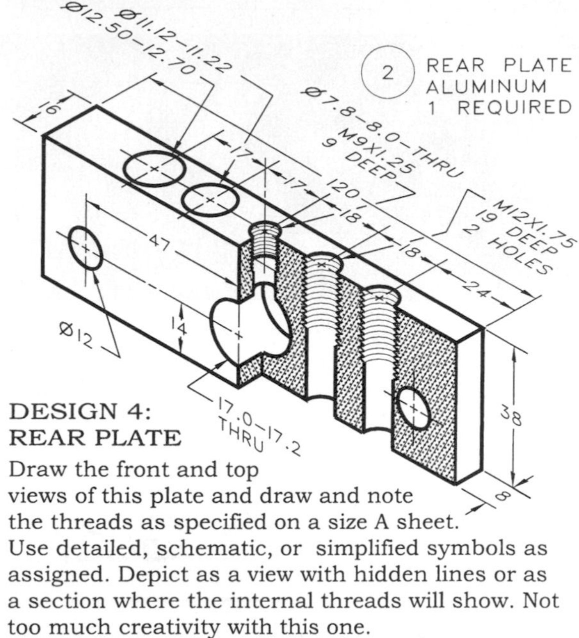

DESIGN 4:
REAR PLATE

Draw the front and top views of this plate and draw and note the threads as specified on a size A sheet. Use detailed, schematic, or simplified symbols as assigned. Depict as a view with hidden lines or as a section where the internal threads will show. Not too much creativity with this one.

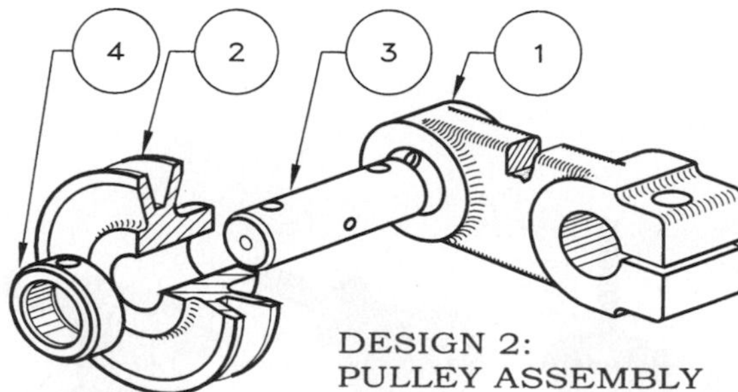

DESIGN 2:
PULLEY ASSEMBLY

Make instrument drawings of the parts and the threaded parts not shown. Notice that there will be a couple of setscrews and a bolt to clamp part 1, and it would be nice to have a grease fitting to contain the grease as the pulley turns. Can you figure out how the grease system works? The shaft has a 25 mm diameter and the pulley has an outside diameter of 100 mm. Design the rest.

DESIGN 3: JOURNAL

This journal is designed to hold a shaft. Three screws will be needed to adjust its tightness. Four base screws will be used to attach the journal to a .50-in. thick metal surface. Draw the necessary views of the journal and screws on a size A sheet.

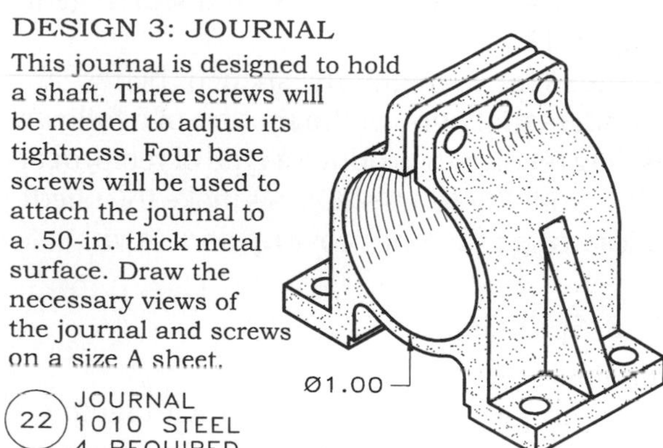

Designs 5: Pencil Pointer

The 1/4-in. shaft of the pencil pointer fits into a bracket designed to clamp to a desktop. A setscrew holds the shaft in position. Make a drawing of the bracket by estimating its dimensions. Show the details and the thread notes involved in the design.

Review Questions

1. Which thread symbol is best for drawing small threaded parts?

2. Which thread symbol gives the most realistic representation of a threaded part?

3. What is the pitch of a thread noted as 1.00–8UNC–2A?

4. What is the major diameter of a thread noted as M30 × 2?

5. Explain the difference between drawing a bolt head across flats versus across corners.

18 Gears and Cams

18.1 Introduction

Gears are toothed wheels whose circumferences mesh to transmit force and motion from one gear to the next. Multiple gears and cams in combination that mesh precisely can be seen on the multiple-spindle machine in **Figure 18.1**. The three most common types are **spur gears, bevel gears**, and **worm gears** (**Figure 18.2**).

18.2 The three basic types of gears are (A) spur gears, (B) bevel gears, and (C) worm gears. *(Courtesy of the Process Gear Company.)*

18.1 Numerous gears and cams are used in this detail of an Acme-Gridley multiple-spindle bar machine. *(Courtesy of the National Acme Company.)*

Cams are irregularly shaped plates and cylinders that control the motion of a follower as they revolve to produce a type of reciprocating action. For example, cams make the needle of a sewing machine move up and down.

18.2 Spur Gears

Terminology

The **spur gear** is a circular gear with teeth cut around its circumference. Two meshing spur

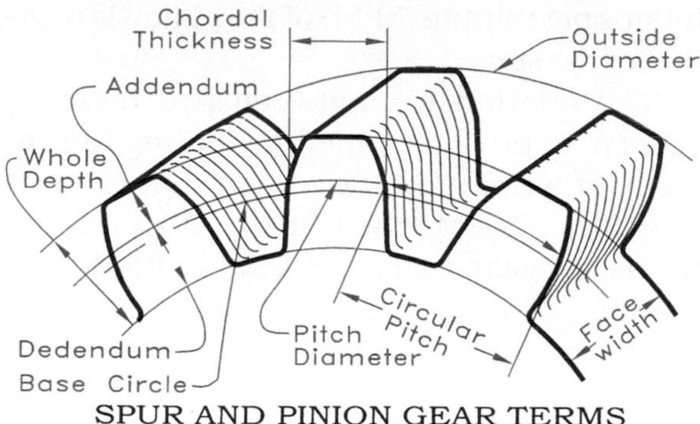

18.3 These terms apply to spur and pinion gears.

gears transmit power from one shaft to a parallel shaft. When the two meshing gears are unequal in diameter, the smaller gear is called the **pinion** and the larger one the **spur**.

The following terms and corresponding formulas describe the parts of a spur gear, several of which are shown in **Figures 18.3** and **18.4**.

Pitch circle (PC): the imaginary circle of a gear, as if it were a friction wheel without teeth that contacted another circular friction wheel.

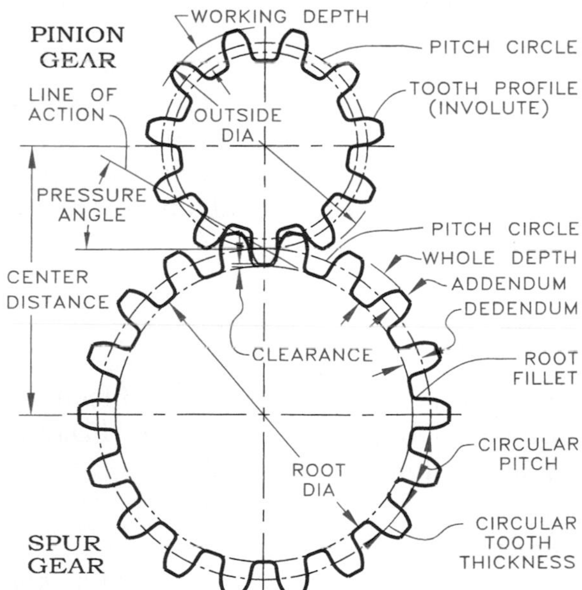

18.4 These terms apply to bevel gears. *(Courtesy of Philadelphia Gear Corporation.)*

Pitch diameter (PD): the diameter of the pitch circle; PD = N/DP, where N is the number of teeth and DP is the diametral pitch.

Diametral pitch (DP): the ratio between the number of teeth on a gear and its pitch diameter; DP = N/PD, where N is the number of teeth, and is expressed as teeth per inch of diameter.

Circular pitch (CP): the circular measurement from one point on a tooth to the corresponding point on the next tooth measured along the pitch circle; CP = 3.14/DP.

Center distance (CD): the distance from the center of a gear to its mating gear's center; CD = (NP + NS)/(2DP), where NP and NS are the number of teeth in the pinion and spur, respectively.

Addendum (A): the height of a gear above its pitch circle; A = 1/DP.

Dedendum (D): the depth of a gear below the pitch circle; D = 1.157/DP.

Whole depth (WD): the total depth of a gear tooth; WD = A + D.

Working depth (WKD): the depth to which a tooth fits into a meshing gear; WKD = 2/DP, or WKD = 2A, where A = addendum.

Circular thickness (CRT): the circular distance across a tooth measured along the pitch circle; CRT = 1.57/DP.

Chordal thickness (CT): the straight-line distance across a tooth at the pitch circle; CT = PD (sin 90°/N), where N is the number of teeth.

Face width (FW): the width across a gear tooth parallel to its axis; a variable dimension, but usually three to four times the circular pitch; FW = 3CP to 4CP.

Outside diameter (OD): the maximum diameter of a gear across its teeth; OD = PD + 2A.

Root diameter (RD): the diameter of a gear measured from the bottom of its gear teeth; RD = PD − 2D.

Pressure angle (PA): the angle between the line of action and a line perpendicular to the centerline of two meshing gears; angles of 14.5° and 20° are standard for involute gears.

Base circle (BC): the circle from which an involute tooth curve is generated or developed; BC = PD cos PA.

Number of teeth (N): the product of the pitch diameter (PD) and the diametral pitch; N = PD × DP.

Tooth Forms

The most common gear tooth is an involute tooth with a 14.5° pressure angle. The 14.5° angle is the angle of contact between two gears when the tangents of both gears are in contact. Gears with pressure angles of 20° and 25° also are used. Gear teeth with larger pressure angles are wider at the base and thus stronger than the standard 14.5° teeth.

18.3 Gear Ratios

The diameters of two meshing spur gears establish ratios that are important to their function (**Figure 18.5**). If the diameter of a gear is twice that of its pinion (the small gear), the gear has twice as many teeth as the pinion. The pinion then must make twice as many turns as the spur; therefore the speed in revolutions per minute (RPM) of the pinion is twice that of the spur.

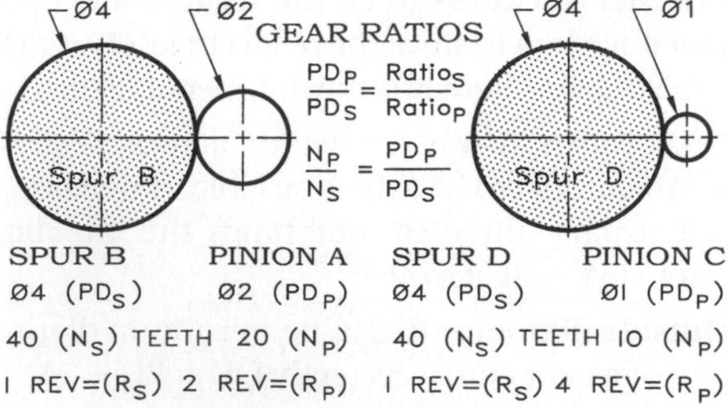

18.5 These are examples of ratios between meshing spur gears and pinion gears.

The relationship between two meshing gears may be determined by finding the velocity of a point on the pinion that is equal to $\pi/PD_P \times$ RPM. The velocity of a point on the large gear equals $\pi/PD_S \times$ RPM. The velocity of points on each gear must be equal, so

$$\pi PD_P(RPM_P) = \pi PD_S(RPM_S);$$

$$RPM_S = 10RPM.$$

Therefore,

$$\frac{PD_P}{PD_S} = \frac{RPM_S}{RPM_P}.$$

If the diameter of the pinion is 2 in., the diameter of the spur is 4 in., and the RPM of the pinion is 20, the RPM of the spur is

$$\frac{2(1)}{2(4)} = \frac{RPM_S}{20\ RPM_P}$$

or

$$RPM_S = \frac{2(20)}{2(4)} = 5\ RPM.$$

Thus the RPM of the spur (5 RPM) is one fourth that of the pinion (20 RPM).

The number of teeth on each gear is proportional to the diameters of a pair of meshing gears, or

$$\frac{N_P}{N_S} = \frac{PD_P}{PD_S},$$

where N_P and N_S are the number of teeth on the pinion and spur, respectively, and PD_P and PD_S are their pitch diameters.

Calculations

Before starting a working drawing of a gear, you have to calculate the gear's dimensions.

Problem 1 Calculate the dimensions for a spur that has a pitch diameter of 5 in., a diametral pitch of 4, and a pressure angle of 14.5°. The diametral pitch is the same for meshing gears.

Solution

Number of teeth: N = PD × DP = 5 × 4 = 20
Addendum: A = 1/DP = 1/4 = 0.25"
Dedendum: D = 1.157/DP = 1.157/4 = 0.2893"
Circular thickness: CT = 1.5708/DP = 0.3927"
Outside diameter: OD = PD + 2A = (20 + 2)/4 = 5 + 0.50 = 5.50"
Root diameter: RD = PD−2D = 5"− 2(0.2893") = 4.421"
Chordal thickness: CT = PD × sin (90°/N) = 5" × .0786) = 0.3923
Chordal addendum: CA = A + CT^2/(4 × PD) = 0.25 + 0.3927^2/(4 × 5") = 0.2577"
Face width: FW = 3.5 × CP = 3.50" × 0.79 = 2.75"
Circular pitch: CP = 3.14/DP = 3.14/4 = 0.785"
Working depth: WKD = 2A = 2 × 0.25" − 0.50"
Whole depth: WD = A + D = 0.250" + 0.289" = 0.539"

Use these dimensions to draw the spur and to provide specifications necessary for its manufacture.

Problem 2 shows the method of determining design information for two meshing gears when you know their working ratios.

Problem 2 Find the number of teeth and other specifications for a pair of meshing gears with a driving gear that turns at 100 RPM and a driven gear that turns at 60 RPM. The diametral pitch for each is 10, and the center-to-center distance between the gears is 6 in.

Solution

Step 1 Find the sum of the teeth on both gears:

$$\text{Total teeth} = 2(\text{center-to-center distance})(\text{DP}) = 2(6)(10) = 120 \text{ teeth.}$$

Step 2 Find the number of teeth for the driving gear:

$$\frac{\text{Driver RPM}}{\text{Driven RPM}} + 1 = \frac{100}{60} + 1 = 2.667,$$

so

$$\frac{\text{Total teeth}}{\frac{100}{60} + 1} = \frac{120}{2.667} = 45 \text{ teeth.}$$

(The number of teeth must be a whole number, since there cannot be fractional teeth on a gear.)

Step 3 Find the number of teeth for the driven gear:

Total teeth − teeth on driver = teeth on driven gear:

120 − 45 = 75 teeth.

Step 4 Calculate the other dimensions for the gears as in Problem 1. Adjusting the center distance to yield a whole number of teeth may be necessary.

18.4 Drawing Spur Gears

Figure 18.6 shows a conventional drawing of a spur gear. Not having to draw the gear teeth in the circular view saves a lot of time. Showing only simplified circular and sectional views of the gear and providing a table of dimensions called **cutting data** is acceptable. Circular phantom lines represent the root circle, pitch circle, and outside circle of the gear in the circular view.

A table of dimensions is a necessary part of a gear drawing (**Figure 18.7**). You may calculate these data or get them from tables of standards in gear handbooks such as *Machinery's Handbook*.

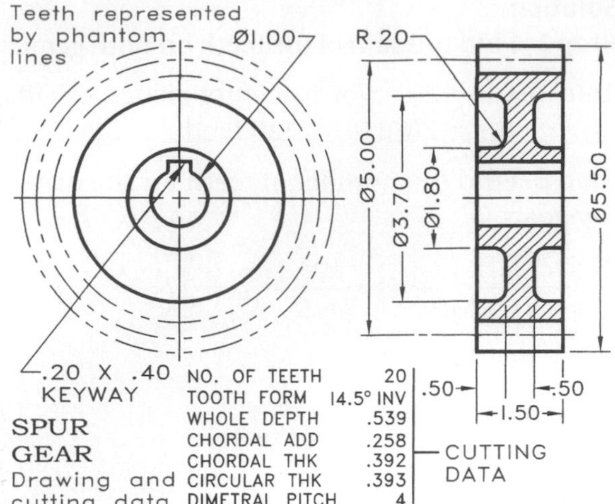

18.6 This detail drawing of a spur gear contains a table of cutting data that supplements the dimensions shown on the view and section.

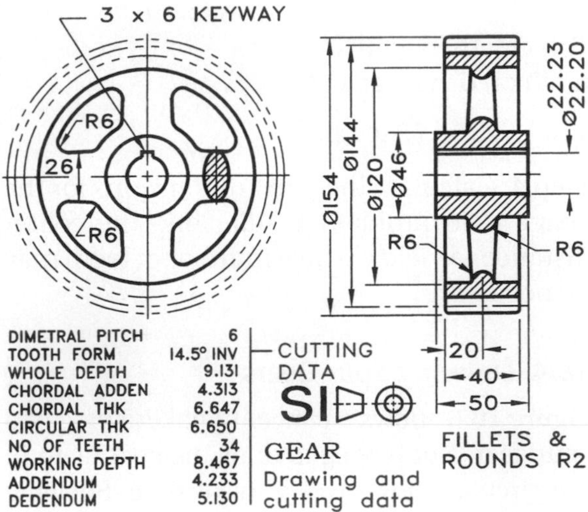

18.7 A detail drawing of a gear with its accompanying table of cutting data.

18.5 Bevel Gears

Terminology

Bevel gears have axes that intersect at angles. The angle of intersection usually is 90°, but other angles also are used. The smaller of the two bevel gears is the **pinion**, and as with spur gears, the larger is the **gear**.

Figures 18.8 and **18.9** illustrate the terminology of bevel gearing. Further explanation of and the corresponding formula for each feature follow. You may also use gear handbooks to find these dimensions.

Pitch angle of pinion (PAp): $\tan PA_p = Np/Ng$, where Ng and Np are the number of teeth on the gear and pinion, respectively.

Pitch angle of gear (PAg): $\tan PA_g = Ng/Np$.

Pitch diameter (PD): the number of teeth, N, divided by the diametral pitch, DP; PD = N/DP.

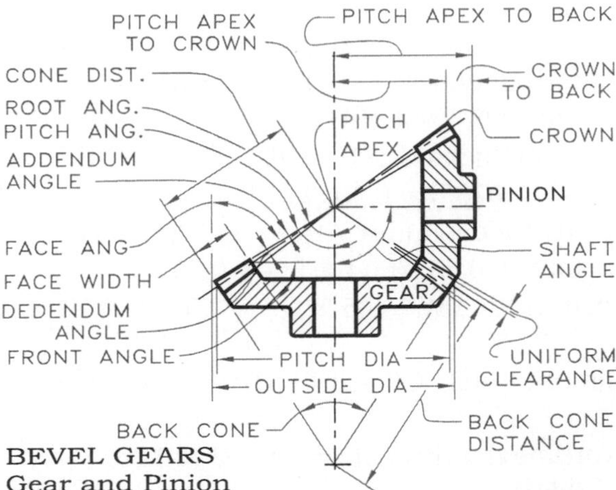

18.8 These terms apply to bevel gears. *(Courtesy of Philadelphia Gear Corporation.)*

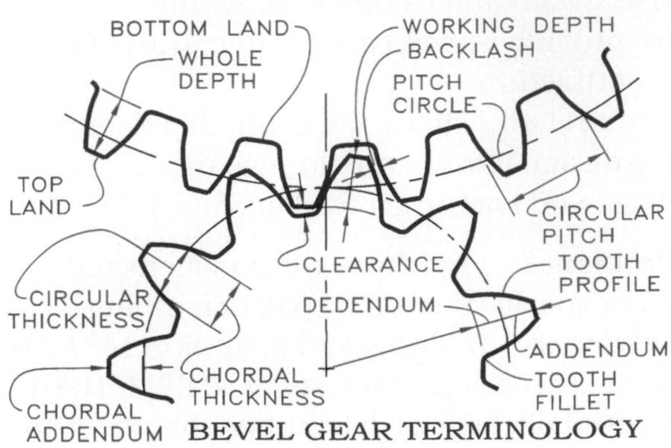

18.9 These additional definitions apply to bevel gears. *(Courtesy of Philadelphia Gear Corporation.)*

Addendum (A): measured at the large end of the tooth; A = 1/DP.

Dedendum (D): measured at the large end of the tooth; D = 1.157/DP.

Whole tooth depth (WD): WD = 2.157/DP.

Chordal thickness (CT): measured at the pitch circle; CT = 1.571/DP.

Diametral pitch: DP = N/PD, where N is the number of teeth, and PD is the pitch diameter.

Addendum angle (AA): the angle formed by the addendum and pitch cone distance; tan AA = A/PCD, where PCD is the pitch cone distance.

Angular addendum: AK = cos PA × A.

Pitch cone distance (PCD): PCD = PD/(2 sin PA).

Dedendum angle (DA): the angle formed by the dedendum and the pitch cone distance; tan DA = D/PCD.

Face angle (FA): the angle between the gear's centerline and the top of its teeth; FA = 90° − (PCD + AA).

Cutting angle (or root angle) (CA): the angle between the gear's axis and the roots of the teeth; CA = PCD − D.

Outside diameter (OD): the greatest diameter of a gear across its teeth; OD = PD + 2A.

Apex to crown distance (AC): the distance from the gear's crown to the apex of the cone measured parallel to the axis of the gear; AC = OD/(2 tan FA).

Chordal addendum (CA): CA = A + [(TT^2 cos PA)/4PD].

Chordal thickness (CT): measured at the large end of the tooth; CT = PD (sin 90°/N).

Face width (FW): can vary, but approximately equal to the pitch cone distance divided by 3.5; FW = PCD/3.5.

Calculations

The following example demonstrates use of the preceding formulas. Some of the formulas result in specifications that apply to both gear and pinion.

Problem 3 Two bevel gears intersect at right angles and have a diametral pitch of 3. The gear has 60 teeth, and the pinion has 45 teeth and a face width of 4 in. Find the dimensions of the gear and pinion.

Solution

Pitch angle of gear:
PAg = Ng/Np = 60/45 = tan 1.33; = 53°7'.

Pitch angle of pinion:
tan PAp = Np/Ng = 45/60 = 36°52'.

Pitch diameter of gear: PDg = 60/3 = 20.00 in.

Pitch diameter of pinion: PDp = 45/3 = 15.00 in.

The following calculations yield the same dimensions for both gear and pinion:

Addendum: A = 1/DP = 1/3 = 0.333".

Dedendum: D = 1.157/DP = 1.157/3 = 0.3857".

Whole depth:
WD = 2.157/DP = 2.157/3 = 0.719".

Tooth thickness on pitch circle:
W = 1.571/PD = 1.571/3 = 0.5237".

Pitch cone distance:
PCD = 20/(2 sin 53°7') = 12.5015".

Addendum angle: tan AA = tan A/PCD
tan AA = 0.333/12.5015 = 1°32'

Dedendum angle: tan DA = D/PCD tan DA = 0.3857/12.5015 = 0.0308 = 1°46'.

Face width: FW = PCD/3 = 4.00".

The following dimensions must be calculated separately for gear and pinion:

Chordal addendum of gear: CA_G = 0.333" + [(0.5237^2 cos 53°7')/(4 × 20)] = 0.338".

Chordal addendum of pinion: CA_P = 0.333" + [(0.52372 cos 36°52')/(4 × 15)] – 0.338".

Chordal thickness of gear:
$CT_G = PD_G$ (sin 90°/N_G) = 20" × sin (90°/60) = 0.5236".

Chordal thickness of pinion: $CT_P = PD_P$ (sin 90°/N) = 15" × sin (90°/45) = 0.5235".

Face angle of gear: FA_G = 90° − (PCD_G + AA) = 90° − (53°7' + 1°32') = 35° 21'.

Face angle of pinion: FA_P = 90° − (PCD_P + AA) = 90° − (36°52' + 1°32') = 51°36'.

Cutting angle of gear:
CA_G = 53°7' − 1°46' = 51°21'.

Cutting angle of pinion:
CA_P = 36°52' − 1°46' = 35°6'.

Angular addendum of gear: AK_G = cos PA_G × A = cos 53°7' × 0.333" = 0.1999".

Angular addendum of pinion: AK_P = cos PA_P × A = cos 36°52' × 0.333" = 0.2667".

Outside diameter of gear: $OD_G = PD_G$ + 2A = 20" + 2(0.1999") = 20.4000".

Outside diameter of pinion: $OD_P = PD_P$ + 2A = 15" + 2 (0.2667") = 15.533".

Apex to crown distance—gear: $AC_G = OD_G$/(2 tan FA) = (20.400"/2) × tan 35°7' = 7.173".

Apex to crown distance—pinion: AC_P = OD_P/2) × tan FA = (15.533"/2) × tan 51°36') = 9.800".

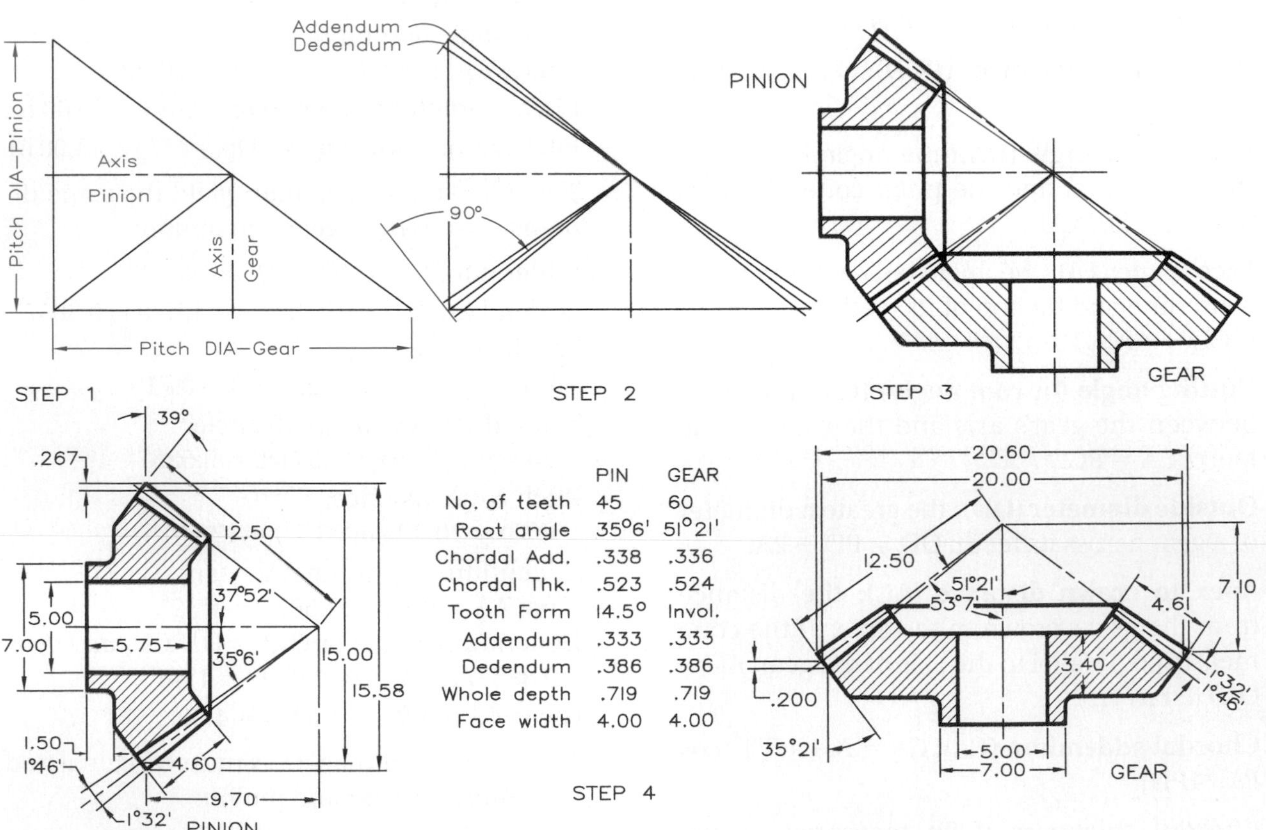

	PIN	GEAR
No. of teeth	45	60
Root angle	35°6'	51°21'
Chordal Add.	.338	.336
Chordal Thk.	.523	.524
Tooth Form	14.5°	Invol.
Addendum	.333	.333
Dedendum	.386	.386
Whole depth	.719	.719
Face width	4.00	4.00

18.10 Drawing bevel gears.

Step 1 Lay out the pitch diameters and axes of the two bevel gears with construction lines.

Step 2 Draw construction lines to establish the limits of the teeth by using the addendum and dedendum dimensions.

Step 3 Draw the pinion and gear using the specified or calculated dimensions.

Step 4 Complete the detail drawings of both gears and provide a table of cutting data.

18.6 Drawing Bevel Gears

Use the calculated dimensions to lay out bevel gears in a detail drawing. Many of these dimensions are difficult to measure with a high degree of accuracy on a drawing. Therefore, providing a table of cutting data for each gear is essential

The steps involved in drawing bevel gears are shown in **Figure 18.10**. On the final drawing, notice that dimensions on the views are supplemented by a table of additional dimensions and data.

18.7 Worm Gears

A worm gear consists of a threaded shaft called a **worm** and a circular gear called a **spider** (**Figure 18.2C**). When the worm is revolved, it causes the spider to revolve about its axis. **Figures 18.11** and **18.12** illustrate the terminology of worm gearing. The following lists further explain these terms and provide the formulas for calculating worm and spider dimensions.

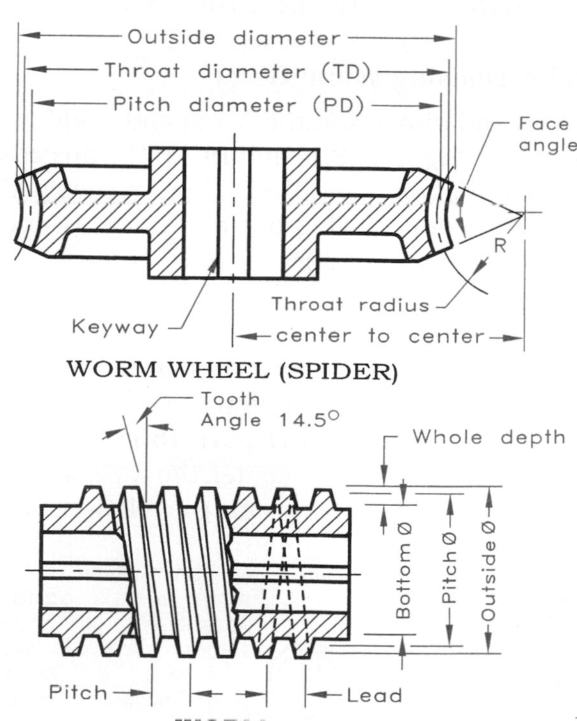

18.11 These definitions and terms of spider and worm gears must be understood to apply them to the necessary calculations.

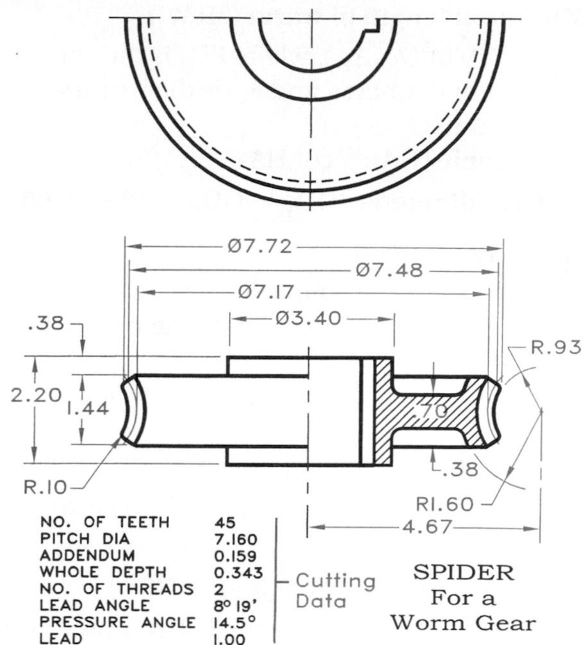

18.12 This detail drawing shows a spider gear that meshes with a worm gear, with a table of cutting data.

Worm Terminology

Linear pitch (P): the distance from one thread to the next, measured parallel to the worm's axis; $P = L/N$, where N is the number of threads (1 if a single thread, 2 if a double thread, and so on).

Lead (L): the distance a thread advances in a turn of 360°.

Addendum of worm's tooth (A_W): $A_W = 0.3183P$.

Pitch diameter (PD_W): $PD_W = OD - 2A_W$, where OD is the outside diameter.

Whole depth of tooth (WDT): $WDT = 0.6866P$.

Bottom diameter of worm (BD_W): $BD_W = OD - 2WDT$.

Width of thread at root (WT): $WT - 0.31P$.

Minimum length of worm (MLW):
$MLW = \sqrt{8PD_S\ (A_W)}$, where PD_S is the spider's pitch diameter, and A_W is the worm's addendum.
Helix angle (HA): $\cot HA = 3.14(PD_W)/L$.
Outside diameter (OD_W): $OD_W = PD_W + 2A$.

Spider Terminology

Pitch diameter of spider (PD_S):
$PD_S = N_S(P)/3.14$, where N_S is the number of teeth on the spider.

Throat diameter of spider (TD_S): $TD_S = PD_S + 2A$.

Radius of spider throat (RST):
$RST = (OD_W/2) - 2A$. (OD_W is OD of worm.)

Face angle (FA): may be selected between 60° and 80° for the average application.

Center-to-center distance (CD): measured between the worm and spider;
$CD = PD_W + PD_S/2$.

Outside diameter of spider (OD_S):
$OD_S = TD_S + 0.4775P$.

Face width of gear (FW): $FW = 2.38P + 0.25$.

Calculations

Problem 4 demonstrates use of the preceding formulas to find the dimensions for a worm gear.

Problem 4 Calculate the dimensions for a worm gear (worm and spider). The spider has 45 teeth, and the worm has an outside diameter of 2.50 in., a double thread, and a pitch of 0.5 in.

Solution

Lead: $L = P_W/N = 0.5"\ (2) = 1"$.

Worm addendum: $A_W = 0.3183 \times P_W = 0.1592"$.

Pitch diameter of worm: $PD_W = OD_W - 2A_W$
$PD_W = 2.50" - 2(0.1592") = 2.1818"$.

Pitch diameter of spider: $PD_S = (N_S \times P_W)/3.14$
$PD_S = (45 \times 0.5)/3.14 = 7.166"$.

Center distance between worm and spider: $CD = (2.182" \times 7.166")/2 = 4.674"$.

Whole depth of worm tooth: $WDT = 0.687 \times P$
$WDT = 0.687(0.5") = 0.3433"$.

Bottom diameter of worm: $BD_W = OD_W - 2(WDT)$; $BD_W = 2.50" - 2(0.3433") = 1.813"$.

Helix angle of worm: $\cot HA = (3.14 \times PD_W)/L$
$\cot HA = 3.14(2.1816)/1 = 8°19'$.

Width of thread at root: $WT = 0.31(P)$;
$WT = 0.31(.5) = 0.155"$.

Minimum length of worm:
$MLW = \sqrt{8PD_S \times A_W}$
$MLW = \sqrt{8(0.1592) \times (7.1656)} = 3.02"$

Throat diameter of spider: $TD = PD_S + 2A_W$
$TD = 7.1656" + 2(0.1592") = 7.484"$.

Radius of spider throat: $RST = (OD_W/2) - 2A_W = (2.5/2) - (2 \times 0.1592) = 0.9318"$.

Face width: $FW_S = 2.38(P) + 0.25 = 2.38(0.5) + 0.25 = 1.44"$.

Outside diameter of spider: $OD_S = TD_S + 0.4775P = 7.484 + 0.4775\ (0.5) = 7.723"$.

18.8 Drawing Worm Gears

Draw and dimension the worm and spider as shown in **Figures 18.12** and **18.13**. The preceding calculations yield the dimensions needed for scaling and laying out the drawings and providing cutting data.

18.9 Cams

Plate cams are irregularly shaped machine elements that produce motion in a single plane, usually up and down **(Figure 18.14)**. As the cam revolves about its center, the cam's shape alternately raises and lowers the follower that

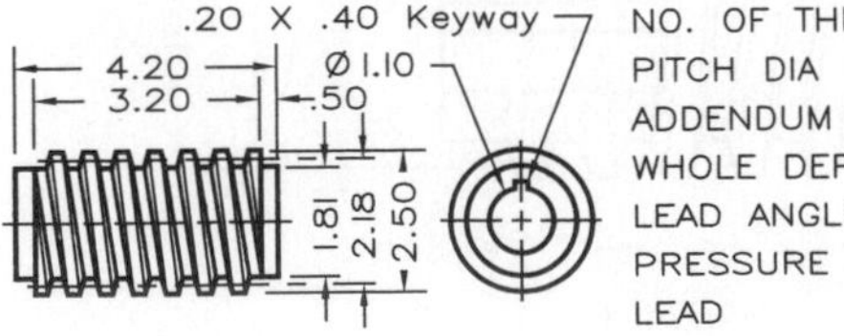

18.13 This detail drawing of a worm gear is based on calculated dimensions.

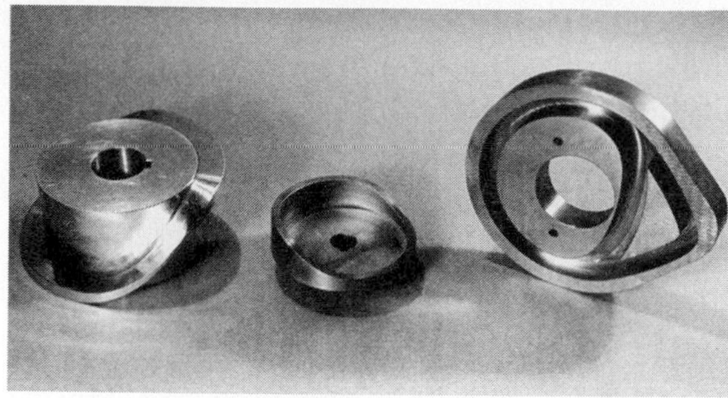

18.14 This photo shows three types of machined cams. *(Courtesy of Ferguson Machine Company.)*

is in contact with it. Cams utilize the principle of the inclined wedge, with the surface of the cam acting as the wedge, causing a change in the slope of the plane, and thereby producing the desired motion of the follower. Cams are designed primarily to produce (1) **uniform or linear motion,** (2) **harmonic motion,** (3) **gravity motion (uniform acceleration)**, or (4) **combinations of these motions.**

Uniform Motion

The uniform motion depicted in **Figure 18.15A** represents the motion of the cam follower as the cam rotates through 360°. This curve has sharp corners, indicating abrupt changes of velocity that cause the follower to bounce. Therefore, uniform motion usually is modified to smooth the changes of velocity. The radius of the modifying arc varies up to a radius of half the total displacement, depending on the speed of operation.

Harmonic Motion

The harmonic motion plotted in **Figure 18.15B** is a smooth, continuous motion based on the change of position of points on a circle. At moderate speeds this displacement gives a smooth operation.

Gravity Motion

The gravity motion (uniform acceleration) illustrated in **Figure 18.15C** is used for high-speed operation. The variation of displacement is analogous to the force of gravity, with the difference in displacement being 1, 3, 5, 5, 3, 1, based on the square of the number. For instance, $1^2 = 1; 2^2 = 4; 3^2 = 9$ give a uniform acceleration. This motion is repeated in reverse order for the remaining half of the follower's motion. Intermediate points are obtained by squaring fractional increments, such as $(2.5)^2$.

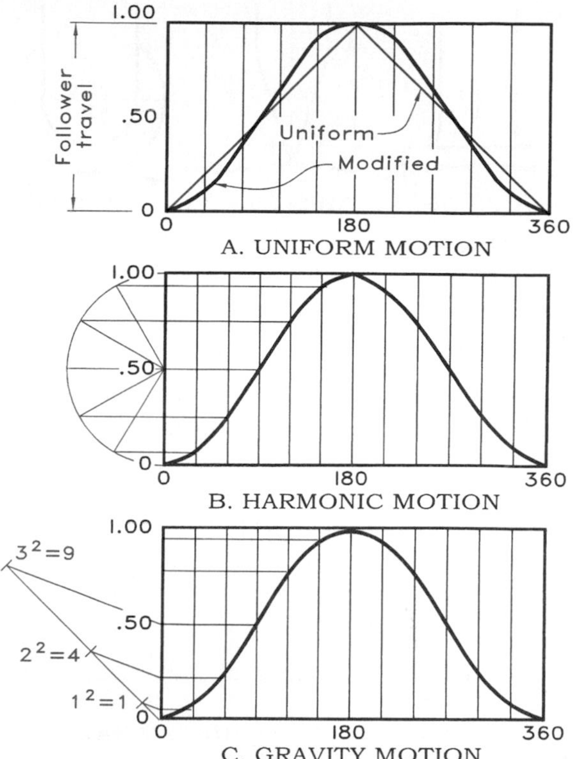

18.15 These displacement diagrams show three standard motions: uniform, harmonic, and gravity.

Cam Followers

Three basic types of cam followers are the **flat surface, roller**, and **knife edge** (**Figure 18.16**). Use of flat-surface and knife-edge followers is limited to slow-moving cams, where minor force will be exerted during rotation. The roller follower is able to withstand higher speeds.

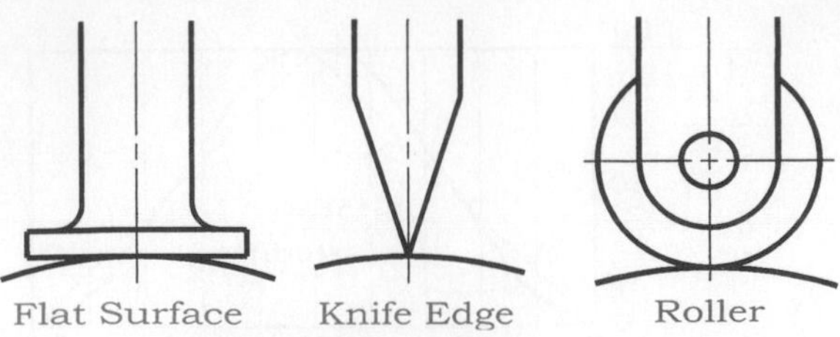

18.16 Three basic types of cam followers are the flat surface, knife edge, and roller.

18.10 Designing Plate Cams

Harmonic Motion The steps involved in designing a plate cam for harmonic motion are shown in **Figure 18.17**. Before laying out the drawing of a cam, you must know the motion of the follower, rise of the follower, diameter of the base circle, and direction of rotation. The displacement diagram shown in **Figure 18.17B** gives the specifications graphically for the cam.

Gravity Motion The steps involved in designing a cam for gravity motion (uniform acceleration) are shown in **Figure 18.18**. The same steps used in designing a cam for harmonic motion apply, but the displace-

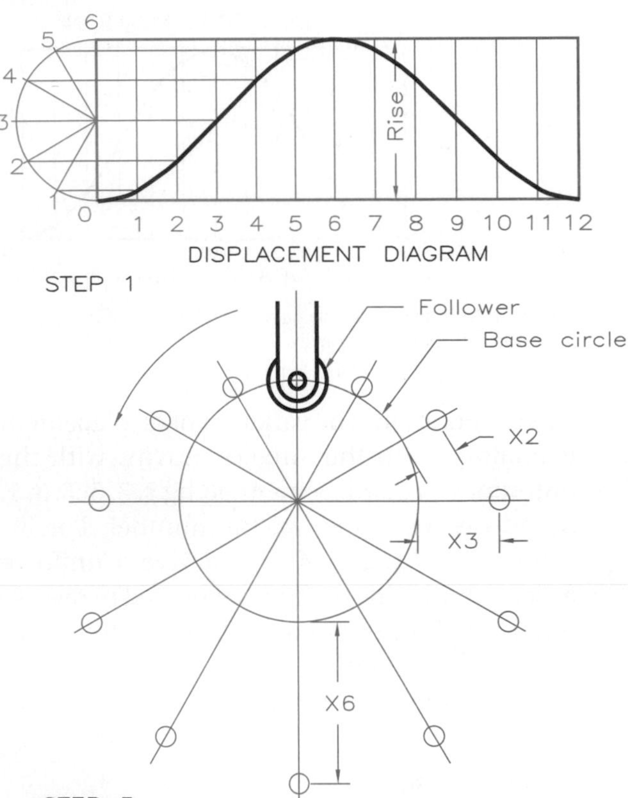

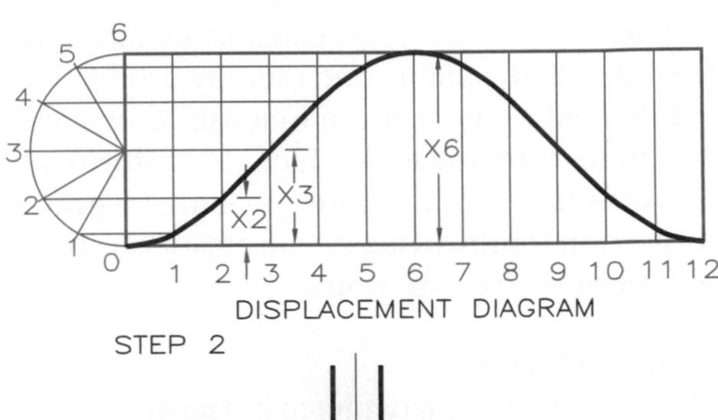

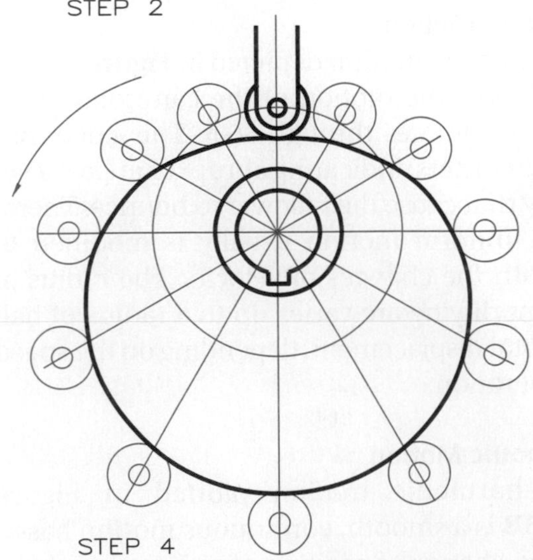

18.17 Drawing a plate cam for harmonic motion.

Step 1 Construct a semicircle on the vertical side of the displacement diagram whose diameter equals the rise of the follower. Divide the semicircle into the same number of segments as there are between 0° and 180° on the horizontal axis of the displacement diagram. Plot the displacement curve.

Step 2 Measure distances of rise and fall (X1, X2, X3, . . ., X6) at each interval from the base circle.

Step 3 Construct the base circle, draw the follower, and divide the circle into the same number of sectors as there are divisions on the displacement diagram. Transfer distances X1, X2, etc., from the displacement diagram to their respective radial lines of the circle, measuring outward from it.

Step 4 Draw circles to represent the positions of the roller as the cam revolves counterclockwise. Draw the cam profile tangent to all the rollers to complete the drawing.

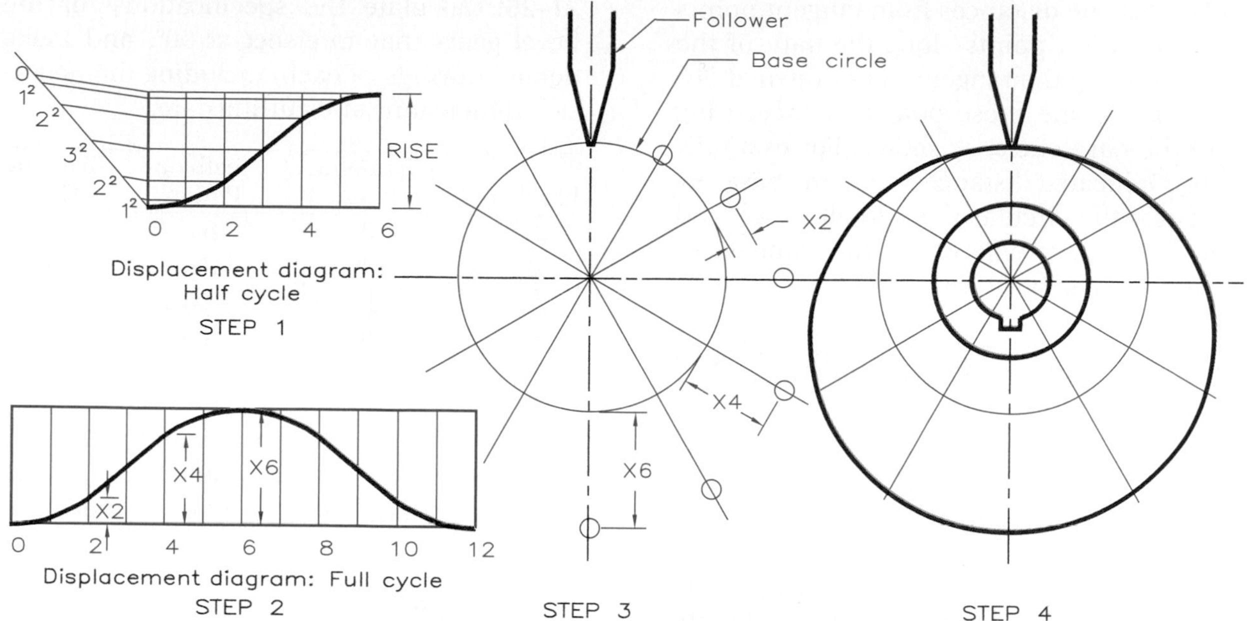

18.18 Drawing a plate cam for uniform acceleration.

Step 1 Construct a displacement diagram to represent the rise of the follower. Divide the horizontal axis into angular increments of 30°. Draw a construction line through point 0; locate the 1^2, 2^2, and 3^2 divisions and project them to the vertical axis to represent half the rise.

Step 2 Use the same construction to find the right half of the symmetrical curve.

Step 3 Construct the base circle and draw the knife-edge follower. Divide the circle into the same number of sectors as there are divisions in the displacement diagram. Transfer distances from the displacement diagram to their respective radial lines of the base circle and measure outward from the base circle.

Step 4 Connect the points found in step 3 with a smooth curve to complete the cam profile. Show the cam hub and keyway.

ment diagram and knife-edge follower are different.

Cam with an Offset Follower The cam shown in **Figure 18.19** produces harmonic motion through 360°. In this case, plot the motion directly from the follower rather than from the usual displacement diagram.

Draw a semicircle with its diameter equal to the total motion of the follower beginning at the centerline of the follower roller. Draw the base circle to pass through the center of the roller of the follower. Extend the centerline of the follower downward and draw a circle tangent to the extension with its center at the center of the base circle. Divide the small circle into 30° intervals to establish points through which to draw construction lines tangent to the circle.

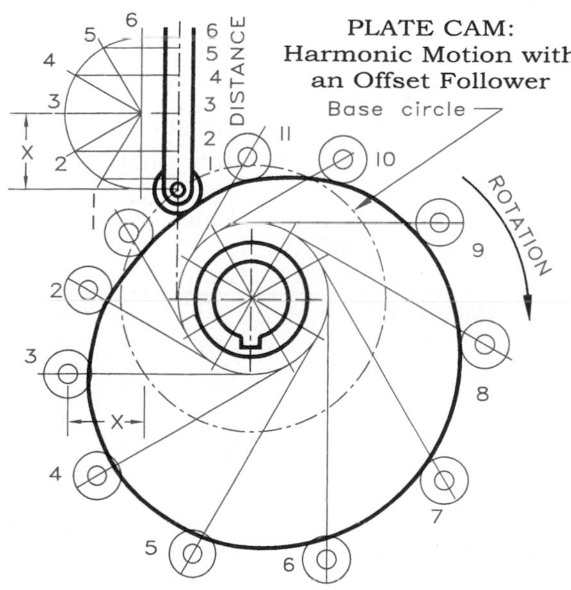

18.19 Drawing of a plate cam having an offset roller follower.

Lay out the distances from tangent points to the position points along the path of the follower along the tangent lines drawn at 30° intervals. Locate these points by measuring from the base circle, as shown. For example, point 3 is located distance X from the base circle. Draw the circular roller in all views, and then draw the profile of the cam tangent to the rollers at all positions.

Problems

Gears

Use size A sheets for the following gear problems. Select appropriate scales so that the drawings will effectively use the available space.

1–5. Calculate the dimensions for the following spur gears, and make a detail drawing of each. Give the dimensions and cutting data for each gear. Provide any other dimensions needed.

Problem	Gear Teeth	Diametral Pitch	14.5° Involute
1.	20	5	"
2.	30	3	"
3.	40	4	"
4.	60	6	"
5.	80	4	"

6–10. Calculate the gear sizes and number of teeth using the following ratios and data.

Prob.	RPM Pinion	RPM Gear	Center to Center	Diametral Pitch
6.	100 (driver)	60	6.0"	10
7.	100 (driver)	50	8.0"	9
8.	100 (driver)	40	10.0"	8
9.	100 (driver)	35	12.0"	7
10.	100 (driver)	25	14.0"	6

11–20. Make a detail drawing of each gear for which you made calculations in problems 1–10. Provide a table of cutting data and other dimensions needed to complete the specifications.

21–25. Calculate the specifications for the bevel gears that intersect at 90°, and make detail drawings of each, including the necessary dimensions and cutting data.

Problem	Diametral Pitch	Teeth on Pinion	Teeth on Gear
21.	3	60	15
22.	4	100	40
23.	5	100	60
24.	6	100	50
25.	7	100	30

26–30. Calculate the specifications for the worm gears and make a detail drawing of each, providing the necessary dimensions and cutting data.

Problem	No. of Teeth in Spider	OD of Worm	Pitch of Worm	Thread of Worm
26.	45	2.50	0.50	double
27.	30	2.00	0.80	single
28.	60	3.00	0.80	double
29.	30	2.00	0.25	double
30.	80	4.00	1.00	single

Cams

Use size B sheets for the following cam problems. The standard dimensions are base circle, 3.50 in.; roller follower, 0.60-in. diameter; shaft, 0.75-in. diameter; and hub, 1.25-in. diameter. The direction of rotation is clockwise. The follower is positioned vertically over the center of the base circle. Lay out the problems and displacement diagrams as shown in **Figure 18.20**.

31. Draw a plate cam with a knife-edge follower for uniform motion and a rise of 1.00 in.

32. Draw a displacement diagram and a cam that will give a modified uniform motion to a knife-edge follower with a rise of 1.7 in. Modify the uniform motion with an arc of one-quarter the rise in the displacement diagram.

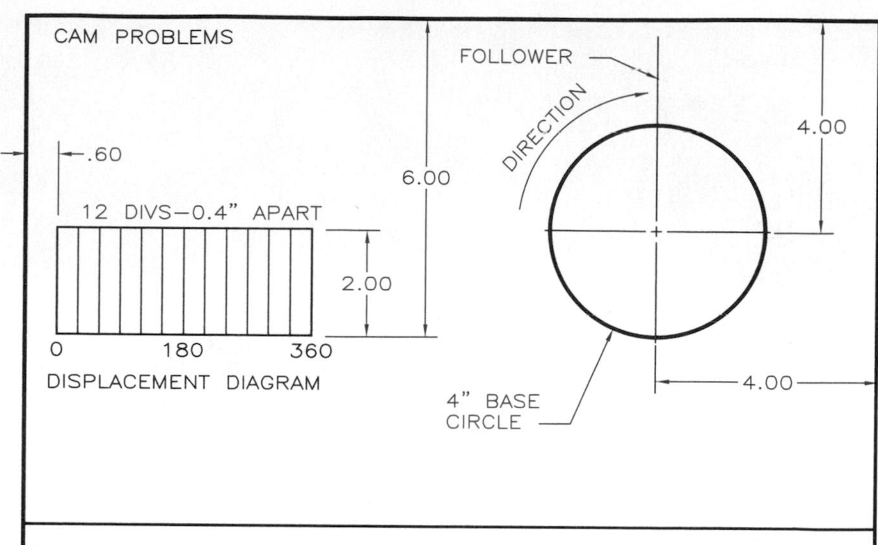

18.20 Layout for Problems 31–36 on size B sheets.

33. Draw a displacement diagram and a cam that will give a harmonic motion to a roller follower with a rise of 1.60 in.

34. Draw a displacement diagram and a cam that will give a harmonic motion to a knife-edge follower with a rise of 1.00 in.

35. Draw a displacement diagram and a cam that will give uniform acceleration to a knife-edge follower with a rise of 1.70 in.

36. Draw a displacement diagram and a cam that will give a uniform acceleration to a roller follower with a rise of 1.40 in.

37. Use the layout given in **Figure 18.20**, but use a roller follower (0.60 in. dia.) that is offset 1.10 in. to the right of the vertical centerline of the base circle. Draw a displacement diagram that will give a harmonic motion with a rise of 1.60 in. and the cam.

38. Same as problem 37, but draw a displacement diagram for a uniform motion with a rise of 1.50 in. and the cam.

39. Same as problem 37, but draw a displacement diagram for a gravity motion with a rise of 1.70 in. and the cam.

Review Questions

1. What is the difference between a spur gear and a pinion gear?

2. What is the difference between the addendum and the dedendum of a gear?

3. If one of two meshing gears has a diameter of 5 in. and the other has a diameter of 10 in., how many revolutions will the small gear make for each revolution of the larger gear?

4. What characteristic distinguishes bevel gears from standard gears?

5. What are the three standard types of cam motions and what are their applications when there are variations in speed and force?

19 Materials and Processes

19.1 Introduction

Various materials and manufacturing processes are commonly used to make parts similar to those discussed in this textbook. A large proportion of parts designed by engineers are made of metal, but other materials such as plastics, fibers, and ceramics are available to the designer in increasingly useful applications.

Metallurgy, the study of metals, is a field that is constantly changing as new processes and alloys are developed (**Figure 19.1**). These developments affect the designer's specification of metals and their proper application for various purposes and uses from appliances to large structures. Three associations have standardized and continually update guidelines for designating various types of metals: the American Iron and Steel Institute (AISI), the Society of Automotive Engineers (SAE), and the American Society for Testing Materials (ASTM). References are made to their designations in this chapter.

19.1 These workmen are assembling a sand casting mold to produce a transmission housing weighing 186 pounds of aluminum alloy. The shape in the foreground is part of the mold assembly. *(Courtesy of the Aluminum Company of America.)*

19.2 Commonly Used Metals

Iron*

Metals that contain iron, even in small quantities, are called **ferrous** metals. Three common types of iron are **gray iron, white iron**, and **ductile iron**.

Gray iron contains flakes of graphite, which result in low strength and low ductility and thus makes it easy to machine. Gray iron resists vibration better than other types of iron. **Figure 19.2** shows designations of gray iron and its typical applications.

White iron contains carbide particles that are extremely hard and brittle, enabling it to withstand wear and abrasion. Because the composition of white iron differs from one supplier to another, there are no designated grades of white iron. It is used for parts on grinding and crushing machines, digging teeth on earthmovers and mining equipment, and wear plates on reciprocating machinery used in textile mills.

Ductile iron (also called *nodular* or *spheroidized* iron) contains tiny spheres of graphite,

DESIGNATION OF GRAY IRON (450 LBS/CF)

ATSM Grade (1000 psi)	SAE Grade	Typical Uses
ASTM 25 CI	G 2500 CI	Small engine blocks, pump bodies, clutch plates, transmission cases
ASTM 30 CI	G 3000 CI	Auto engine blocks, heavy castings, flywheels
ASTM 35 CI	G 3500 CI	Diesel engine blocks, tractor transmission cases, heavy & high-strength parts
ASTM 40 CI	G 4000 CI	Diesel cylinders,

19.2 The numbering designations of gray iron and its typical uses.

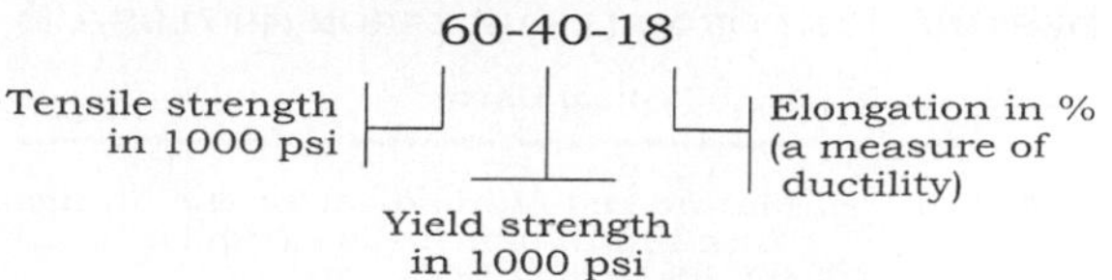

19.3 Ductile iron is specified with numerical notes in this format.

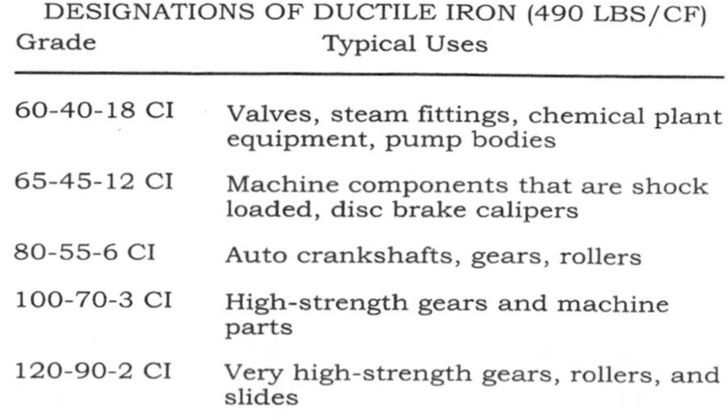

DESIGNATIONS OF DUCTILE IRON (490 LBS/CF)

Grade	Typical Uses
60-40-18 CI	Valves, steam fittings, chemical plant equipment, pump bodies
65-45-12 CI	Machine components that are shock loaded, disc brake calipers
80-55-6 CI	Auto crankshafts, gears, rollers
100-70-3 CI	High-strength gears and machine parts
120-90-2 CI	Very high-strength gears, rollers, and slides

19.4 The numbering designations of ductile iron and its typical uses.

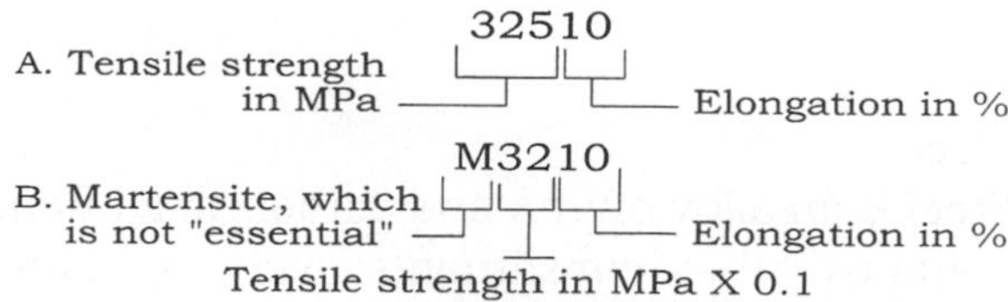

19.5 The numbering designations for malleable iron.

making it stronger and tougher than most types of gray iron and more expensive to produce. Three sets of numbers (**Figure 19.3**) describe the most important features of ductile iron. **Figure 19.4** shows the designations of and typical applications for the commonly used alloys of ductile iron.

Malleable iron is made from white iron by a heat-treatment process that converts carbides into carbon nodules (similar to ductile iron). The numbering system for designating grades of malleable iron is shown in **Figure 19.5.** Some of the commonly used grades of malleable iron and their typical applications are shown in **Figure 19.6**.

*This section on iron was developed by Dr. Tom Pollock, a metallurgist at Texas A&M University.

DESIGNATIONS OF MALLEABLE IRON (490 LBS/CF)

ASTM Grade	Typical Uses
35018 CI	Marine and railroad valves and fittings, "black-iron" pipe fittings (similar to 60-40-18 ductile cast iron)
45006 CI	Machine parts (similar to 80-55-6 ductile cast iron)
M3210 CI	Low-stress components, brackets
M4504 CI	Crankshafts, hubs
M7002 CI	High-strength parts, connecting rods, universal joints
M8501 CI	Wear-resistant gears and sliding parts

19.6 The numbering designations of malleable iron and its typical uses.

Cast iron is iron that is melted and poured into a mold to form it by casting, a commonly used process for producing machine parts. Although cheaper and easier to machine than steel, iron does not have steel's ability to withstand shock and force.

Steel

Steel is an alloy of iron and carbon that often contains other constituents such as manganese, chromium, or nickel. Carbon (usually between 0.20% and 1.50%) is the ingredient having the greatest effect on the grade of steel. The three major types of steel are **plain carbon steels, free-cutting carbon steels**, and **alloy steels. Figure 19.7** gives the types of steels and their SAE designations by four-digit numbers. The first digit indicates the type of steel: 1 is carbon steel, 2 is nickel steel, and so on. The second digit gives content (as a percentage) of the material represented by the first digit. The last two or three digits give the percentage of carbon in the alloy: 100 equals 1%, and 50 equals 0.50%.

Steel weighs about 490 lb/cu ft. Some frequently used SAE steels are 1010, 1015, 1020, 1030, 1040, 1070, 1080, 1111, 1118, 1145, 1320, 2330, 2345, 2515, 3130, 3135, 3240, 3310, 4023, 4042, 4063, 4140, and 4320.

DESIGNATIONS OF STEEL (490 LBS/CF)

Type of steel	Number	Applications
Carbon steels		
Plain carbon	10XX	Tubing, wire, nails
Resulphurized	11XX	Nuts, bolts, screws
Manganese steel	13XX	Gears, shafts
Nickel steel	23XX	Keys, levers, bolts
	25XX	Carburized parts
	31XX	Axles, gears, pins
	32XX	Forgings
	33XX	Axles, gears
Molybdenum	40XX	Gears, springs
Chromium-moly.	41XX	Shafts, tubing
Nickel-chromium	43XX	Gears, pinions
Nickel-moly.	46XX	Cams, shafts
	48XX	Roller bearings, pins
Chromium steel	51XX	Springs, gears
	52XX	Ball bearings
Chrom. vanadium	61XX	Springs, forgings
Silicon manganese	92XX	Leaf springs

19.7 The numbering designations of steel and its applications.

Copper

One of the first metals discovered, copper is easily formed and bent without breaking. Because it is highly resistant to corrosion and is highly conductive, it is used for pipes, tubing, and electrical wiring. It is an excellent roofing and screening material because it withstands the weather well. Copper weighs about 555 lb/cu ft.

Copper has several alloys, including brasses, tin bronzes, nickel silvers, and copper nickels. Brass (about 530 lb/cu ft) is an alloy of copper and zinc, and bronze (about 548 lb/cu ft) is an alloy of copper and tin. Copper and copper alloys are easily finished by buffing or plating; joined by soldering, brazing, or welding; and machined.

Wrought copper has properties that permit it to be formed by hammering. A few of the numbered designations of wrought copper are C11000, C11100, C11300, C11400, C11500, C11600, C10200, C12000, and C12200.

Aluminum

Aluminum is a corrosion-resistant, lightweight metal (approximately 169 lb/cu ft) that has

ALUMINUM DESIGNATIONS (169 LBS/CF)

Composition	Alloy Number	Application
Aluminum (99% pure)	1XXX	Tubing, tank cars
ALUMINUM ALLOYS		
Copper	2XXX	Aircraft parts, screws, rivets
Manganese	3XXX	Tanks, siding, gutters
Silicon	4XXX	Forging, wire
Magnesium	5XXX	Tubes, welded vessels
Magnesium and silicon	6XXX	Auto body, pipes
Zinc	7XXX	Aircraft structures
Other elements	8XXX	

19.8 The numbering designations of aluminum and aluminum alloys and their applications.

numerous applications. Most materials called aluminum actually are aluminum alloys, which are stronger than pure aluminum.

The types of wrought aluminum alloys are designated by four digits (**Figure 19.8**). The first digit (2 through 8) indicates the alloying element that is combined with aluminum. The second digit indicates modifications of the original alloy or impurity limits. The last two digits identify other alloying materials or indicate the aluminum's purity.

Figure 19.9 shows a four-digit numbering system used to designate types of cast aluminum and alloys. The first digit indicates the alloy group, and the next two digits identify the aluminum alloy or aluminum purity. The number to the right of the decimal point represents the aluminum form: XX.0 indicates castings, XX.1 indicates ingots with a specified chemical composition, and XX.2 indicates ingots with a specified chemical composition other than the XX.1 ingot. *Ingots* are blocks of cast metal to be remelted, and *billets* are castings of aluminum to be formed by forging.

ALUMINUM CASTINGS AND INGOT DESIGNATIONS

Composition	Alloy Number
Aluminum (99% pure)	1XX.X
Aluminum alloys	
Copper	2XX.X
Silicon with copper and/or magnesium	3XX.X
Silicon	4XX.X
Magnesium	5XX.X
Magnesium and silicon	6XX.X
Zinc	7XX.X
Tin	8XX.X
Other elements	9XX.X

19.9 The numbering designations of cast aluminum, ingots, and aluminum alloys.

Magnesium

Magnesium is a light metal (109 lb/cu ft) available in an inexhaustible supply because it is extracted from seawater and natural brines. Magnesium is an excellent material for aircraft parts, clutch housings, crankcases for air-cooled engines, and applications where lightness is desirable.

Magnesium is used for die and sand castings, extruded tubing, sheet metal, and forging. Magnesium and its alloys may be joined by bolting, riveting, or welding. Some numbered designations of magnesium alloys are M10100, M11630, M11810, M11910, M11912, M12390, M13320, M16410, and M16620.

19.3 Properties of Metals

All materials have properties that designers must utilize to the best advantage. The following terms describe these properties.

Ductility: a softness in some materials, such as copper and aluminum, that permits them to be formed by stretching (drawing) or hammering without breaking.

Brittleness: a characteristic that will not allow metals such as cast irons and hardened steels to stretch without breaking.

Malleability: the ability of a metal to be rolled or hammered without breaking.

Hardness: the ability of a metal to resist being dented when it receives a blow.

Toughness: the property of being resistant to cracking and breaking while remaining malleable.

Elasticity: the ability of a metal to return to its original shape after being bent or stretched.

Modifying Properties by Heat Treatment

The properties of metals can be changed by various types of heat treating. Although heat affects all metals, steels are affected to a greater extent than others.

Hardening: heating steel to a prescribed temperature and quenching it in oil or water.

Quenching: rapidly cooling heated metal by immersing it in liquids, gases, or solids (such as sand, limestone, or asbestos).

Tempering: reheating previously hardened steel and then cooling it, usually by air, to increase its toughness.

Annealing: heating and cooling metals to soften them, release their internal stresses, and make them easier to machine.

Normalizing: heating metals and letting them cool in air to relieve their internal stresses.

Case hardening: hardening a thin outside layer of a metal by placing the metal in contact with carbon or nitrogen compounds that it absorbs as it is heated; afterward, the metal is quenched.

Flame hardening: hardening by heating a metal to within a prescribed temperature range with a flame and then quenching the metal.

19.4 Forming Metal Shapes

Casting

One of the two major methods of forming shapes is casting, which involves preparing a mold in the shape of the part desired, pouring molten metal into it, and cooling the metal to form the part. The types of casting, which differ in the way the molds are made, are **sand casting, permanent-mold casting, die casting**, and **investment casting**.

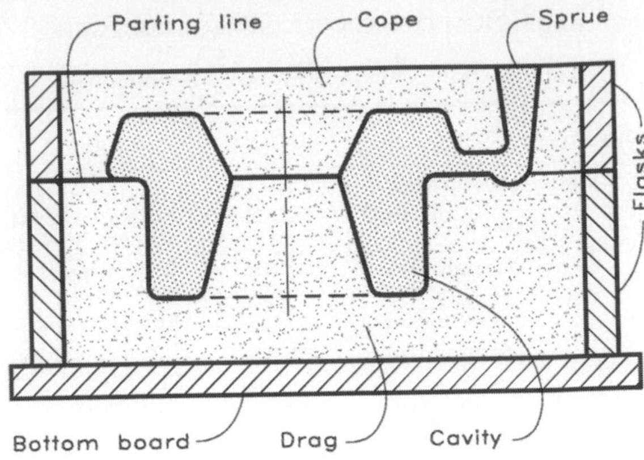

19.10 A two-section sand mold is used for casting a metal part.

Sand Casting In the first step of sand casting, a wood or metal form or pattern is made in the shape of the part to be cast. The pattern is placed in a metal box called a *flask* and molding sand is packed around the pattern. When the pattern is withdrawn from the sand, it leaves a void, forming the mold. Molten metal is poured into the mold through sprues or gates. After cooling, the casting is removed and cleaned (**Figure 19.10**).

Cores formed from sand may be placed in a mold to create holes or hollows within a casting. After the casting has been formed, the cores are broken apart and removed, leaving behind the desired void within the casting.

Because the patterns are placed in and removed from the sand before the metal is poured, the sides of the patterns must be tapered, called **draft**, for ease of withdrawal from the sand. The angle of draft depends on the depth of the pattern in the sand and varies from 2° to 8° in most applications. **Figure 19.11** shows a pattern held in the sand by a lower flask. Patterns are made oversize to compensate for the shrinkage that occurs when the casting cools.

19.11 This pattern is held in the bottom half (the drag) of a sand mold to form a mold for a casting.

Because sand castings have rough surfaces, features that come into contact with other parts must be machined by drilling, grinding, finishing, or shaping. The tailstock base of a lathe shown in **Figure 19.12** illustrates raised bosses that have been finished. The casting must be made larger than finished size where metal is to be removed by machining.

Fillets and rounds are used at the inside and outside corners of castings to increase their strength by relieving the stresses in the cast metal (**Figure 19.13**). Fillets and rounds also are used because forming square corners by the sand-casting process is difficult and because rounded edges make the finished product more attractive (**Figure 19.12**).

19.12 The tailstock casting for a lathe has raised bosses and contact surfaces that were finished to improve the effectiveness of nuts and bolts. Fillets and rounds were added to the inside and outside corners. *(Courtesy L. W. Chuck Company.)*

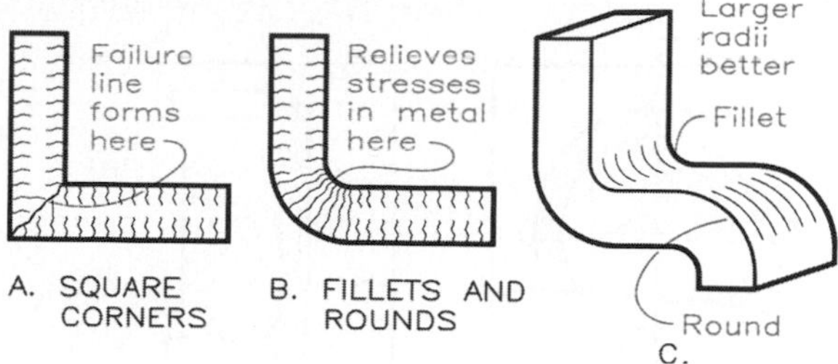

19.13 Fillets and Rounds.

A Square corners cause a failure line to form, causing a weakness at this point.

B Fillets and rounds make the corners of a casting stronger and more attractive.

C The larger the radii of fillets and rounds, the stronger the casting will be.

Permanent-Mold Casting Permanent molds are made for the mass production of parts. They are generally made of cast iron and coated to prevent fusing with the molten metal poured into them (**Figure 19.14**).

Die Casting Die castings are used for the mass production of parts made of aluminum, magnesium, zinc alloys, copper, and other materials.

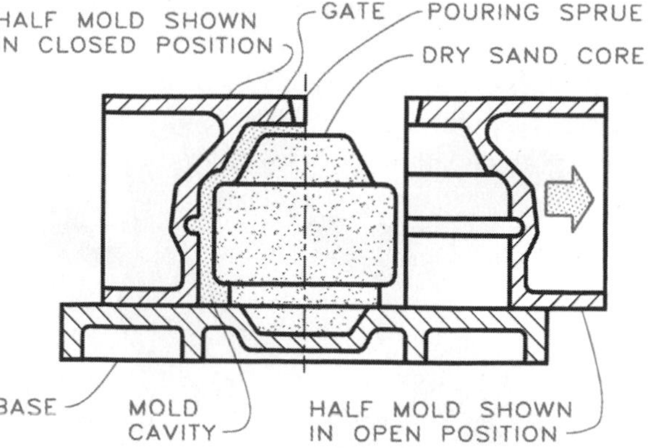

19.14 Permanent molds are made of metal for repetitive usage. Here, a sand core made from another mold is placed in the permanent mold to create a void within the casting.

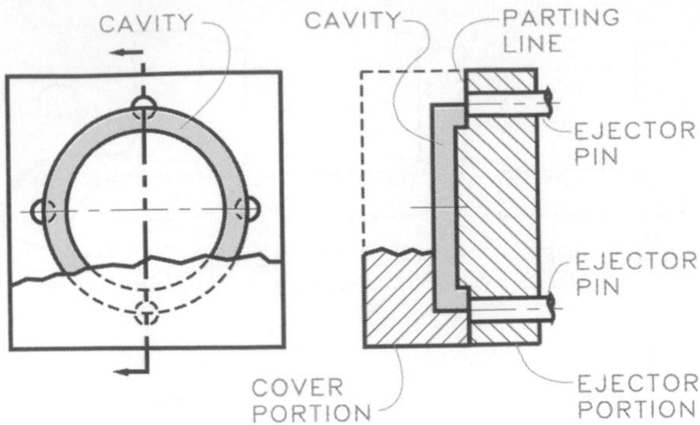

19.15 This die is used for casting a simple part. The metal is forced into the die to form the casting.

Die castings are made by forcing molten metal into dies (or molds) under pressure. They are inexpensive, meet close tolerances, and have good surface qualities. The same general principles of sand castings—using fillets and rounds, allowing for shrinkage, and specifying draft angles—apply to die castings (**Figure 19.15**).

Investment Casting Investment casting is used to produce complicated parts or artistic sculptures that would be difficult to form by other methods (**Figure 19.16**). A new pattern must be used for each investment casting, so a mold or die is made for casting a wax master pattern. The wax pattern, identical to the casting, is placed inside a container, and plaster or sand is poured (invested) around it. Once the investment has cured, the wax pattern is melted, leaving a hollow cavity to serve as the mold for the molten metal. After the casting has set, the plaster or sand is broken away from it.

19.16 An investment casting (lost-wax process) is used to produce complex metal objects and art pieces.

Forgings

The second major method of forming shapes is forging, which is the process of shaping or forming heated metal by hammering or forcing it into a die. Drop forges and press forges are used to hammer metal billets into forging dies. Forgings have the high strength and resistance to loads and impacts required for applications such as aircraft landing gears (**Figure 19.17**).

Figure 19.18 shows three types of dies. A single-impression die gives an impression on

19.17 This aircraft landing-gear component was formed by forging. *(Courtesy of Cameron Division, Cooper Cameron Corporation.)*

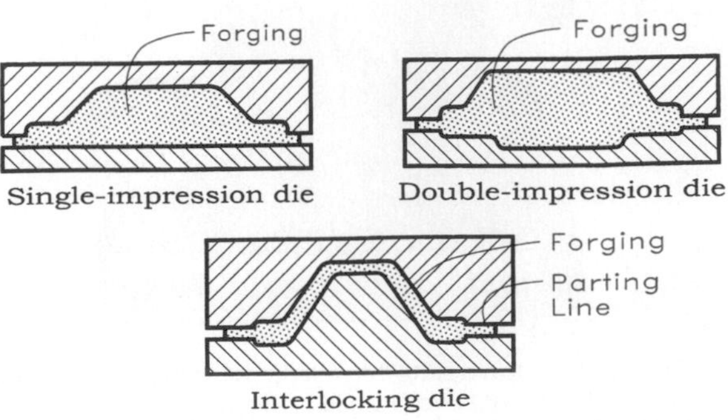

19.18 This drawing shows three types of forging dies.

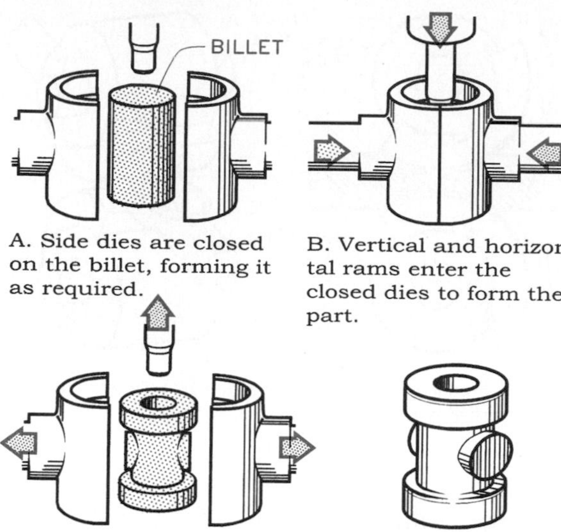

BILLET
A. Side dies are closed on the billet, forming it as required.
B. Vertical and horizontal rams enter the closed dies to form the part.
C. Rams are withdrawn, the dies open, and the forging is extracted.
D. Result: A forging having multiple planes, no flash, and no draft.

19.19 The steps involved in forging a part with external dies and an internal ram.

19.20 Steps A through G are required to forge a billet into a finished connecting rod. *(Courtesy of Forging Industry Association.)*

one side of the parting line between the mating dies; a double-impression die gives an impression on both sides of the parting line; and the interlocking dies give an impression that may cross the parting line on either side. **Figure 19.19** shows how an object is forged with horizontal dies and a vertical ram to hollow the object.

Figure 19.20 illustrates the sequence of forging a part from a billet by hammering it into different dies. It is then machined to its proper size within specified tolerances.

Figure 19.21 shows a working drawing for making a forged part. When preparing forging drawings, you must consider (1) draft angles and parting lines, (2) fillets and rounds, (3) forging tolerances, (4) extra material for machining, and (5) heat treatment of the finished forging.

Draft, the angle of taper, is crucial to the forging process. The minimum radii for inside corners (fillets) are determined by the height of

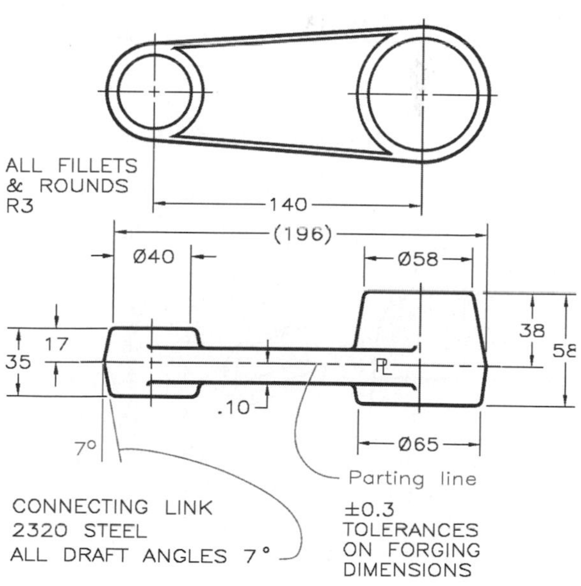

19.21 This working drawing for a forging shows draft angles and the parting line (PL) where the dies come together.

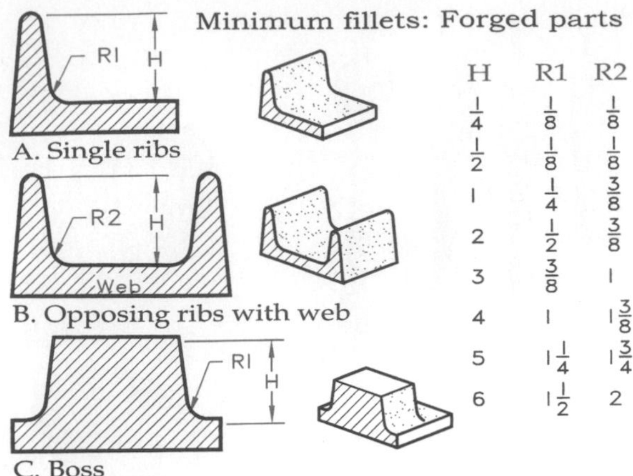

H	R1	R2
1/4	1/8	1/8
1/2	1/8	1/8
1	1/4	3/8
2	1/2	3/8
3	3/8	1
4	1	1 3/8
5	1 1/4	1 3/4
6	1 1/2	2

19.22 These guidelines are for determining the minimum radii for fillets (inside corners) on forged parts.

the feature (**Figure 19.22**). Similarly, the minimum radii for the outside corners (rounds) are related to a feature's height (**Figure 19.23**). The larger the radius of a fillet or round, the better it is for the forging process.

Some of the standard steels used for forging are designated by the SAE numbers 1015, 1020, 1025, 1045, 1137, 1151, 1335, 1340, 4620, 5120, and 5140. Iron, copper, and aluminum also can be forged.

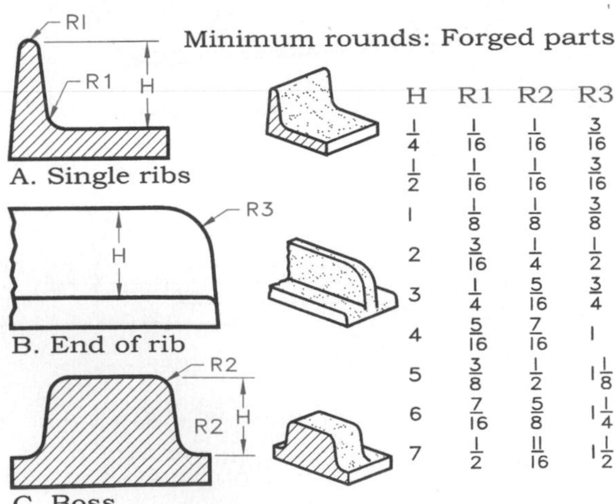

H	R1	R2	R3
1/4	1/16	1/16	3/16
1/2	1/16	1/16	3/16
1	1/8	1/8	3/8
2	3/16	1/4	1/2
3	1/4	5/16	3/4
4	5/16	7/16	1
5	3/8	1/2	1 1/8
6	7/16	5/8	1 1/4
7	1/2	11/16	1 1/2

19.23 Guidelines for determining the minimum radii of rounds (outside corners) on forged parts.

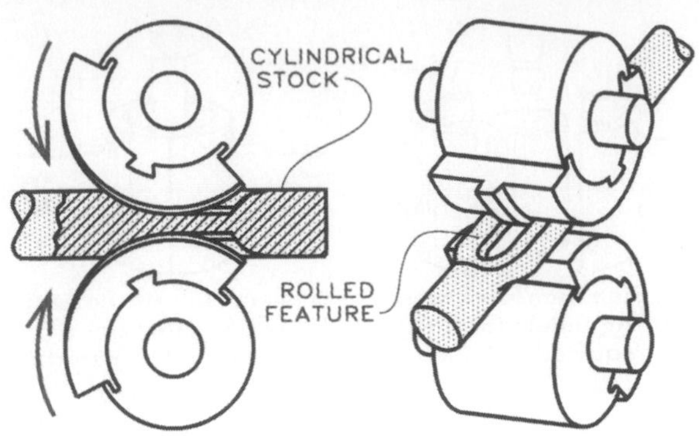

19.24 Features on parts may be formed by rolling. Here a part is being rolled parallel to its axis.

Rolling Rolling is a type of forging in which the stock is rolled between two or more rollers to shape it. Rolling can be done at right angles or parallel to the axis of the part (**Figure 19.24**). If a high degree of shaping is required, the stock usually is heated before rolling. If the forming requires only a slight change in shape, rolling can be done without heating the metal, which is called **cold rolling** (CR); CRS means cold-rolled steel. **Figure 19.25** shows a cylindrical rod being rolled.

19.25 This cylindrical rod is being rolled to shape.

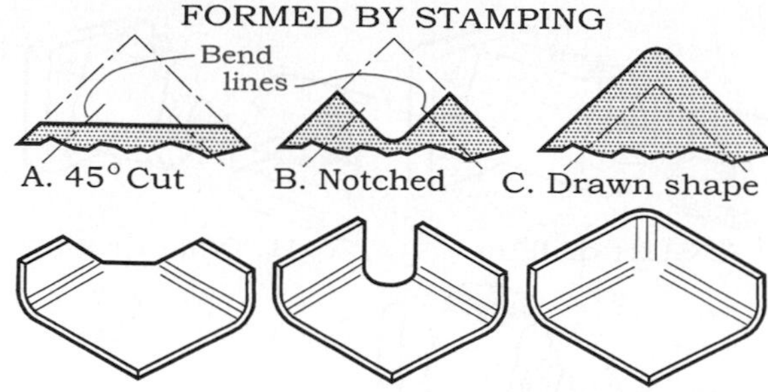
FORMED BY STAMPING
Bend lines
A. 45° Cut
B. Notched
C. Drawn shape

19.26 Box-shaped parts formed by stamping.

A A corner cut of 45° permits flanges to be folded with no further trimming.

B Notching has the same effect as the 45° cut and is often more attractive.

C A continuous-corner flange requires that the blank be developed so that it can be drawn into shape.

Stamping

Stamping is a method of forming flat metal stock into three-dimensional shapes. The first step of stamping is to cut out the shapes, called *blanks,* which are formed by bending and pressing them against forms. **Figure 19.26** shows three types of box-shaped parts formed by stamping, and **Figure 19.27** shows a design for a flange to be formed by stamping. Holes in stampings are made by punching, extruding, or piercing (**Figure 19.28**).

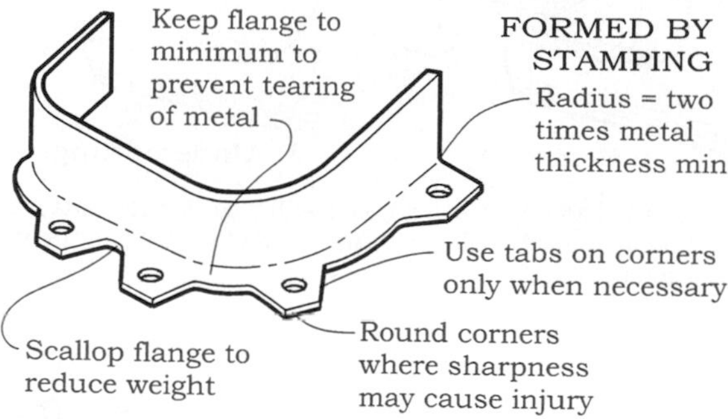
Keep flange to minimum to prevent tearing of metal
FORMED BY STAMPING
Radius = two times metal thickness min.
Use tabs on corners only when necessary
Round corners where sharpness may cause injury
Scallop flange to reduce weight

19.27 This drawing shows a sheet metal flange design with notes that explain design details.

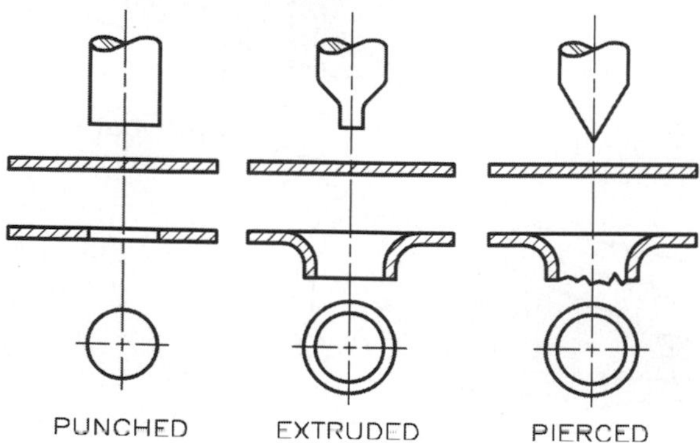
PUNCHED
EXTRUDED
PIERCED

19.28 These three methods are used to form holes in sheet metal by punching.

19.5 Machining Operations

After metal parts have been formed, machining operations must be performed to complete them. The machines used most often are the **lathe, drill press, milling machine, shaper**, and **planer**. Some of these machines require manual operation; others are computer programmed to run at high speeds automatically, and require minimal or no operator attention.

Lathe

The **lathe** shapes cylindrical parts while rotating the workpiece between its centers (**Figure 19.29**). The fundamental operations

19.29 This typical metal lathe holds and rotates the work piece between its centers for machining. *(Courtesy of the Clausing Industrial Inc.)*

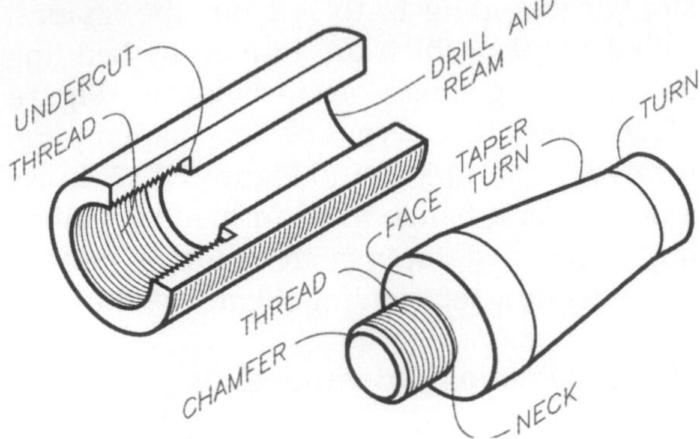

19.30 The basic operations that are performed on a lathe are shown here.

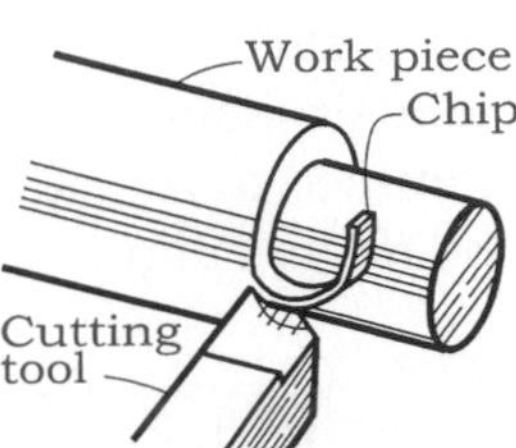

19.31 The most basic operation performed on the lathe is turning, whereby a continuous chip is removed by a cutting tool as the part rotates.

performed on the lathe are **turning, facing, drilling, boring, reaming, threading**, and **undercutting** (**Figure 19.30**).

Turning forms a cylinder with a tool that advances against and moves parallel to the cylinder being turned between the centers of the lathe (**Figure 19.31**). **Facing** forms flat surfaces perpendicular to the axis of rotation of the part being rotated.

Drilling is performed by mounting a drill in the tail stock of the lathe and rotating the work while the bit is advanced into the part (**Figures 19.32A through C**). **Boring** makes large holes by enlarging smaller drilled holes with a tool mounted on a boring bar (**Figure 19.33A**). **Undercutting** is a groove cut inside a cylindrical hole with a tool mounted on a boring bar. The groove is cut as the tool advances from the center of the axis of revolution into the part (**Figure 19.33B**). **Reaming** removes only thousandths

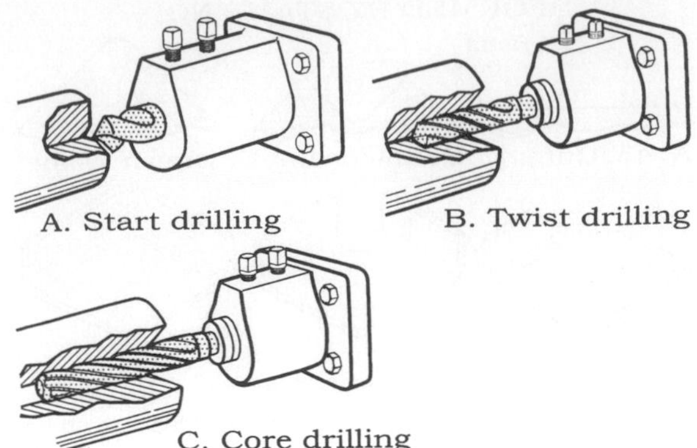

19.32 The three steps in drilling a hole in the end of a cylinder are (A) start drilling, (B) twist drilling, and (C) core drilling.

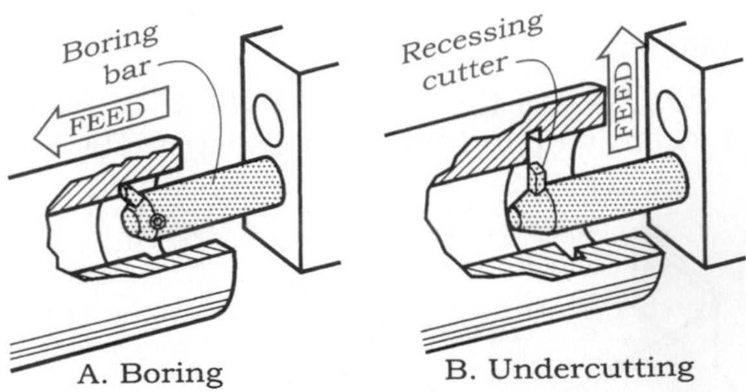

19.33 (A) This hole is being bored with a cutting tool attached to a boring bar of a lathe. (B) An undercut is being cut by the tool and boring bar.

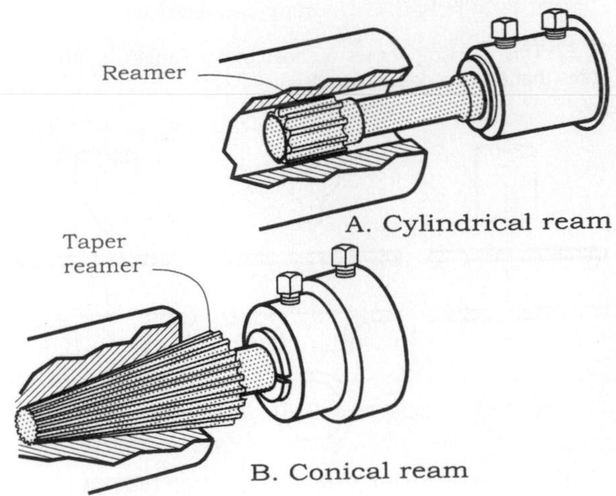

19.34 Fluted reamers can be used to finish inside (A) cylindrical and (B) conical holes within a few thousandths of an inch.

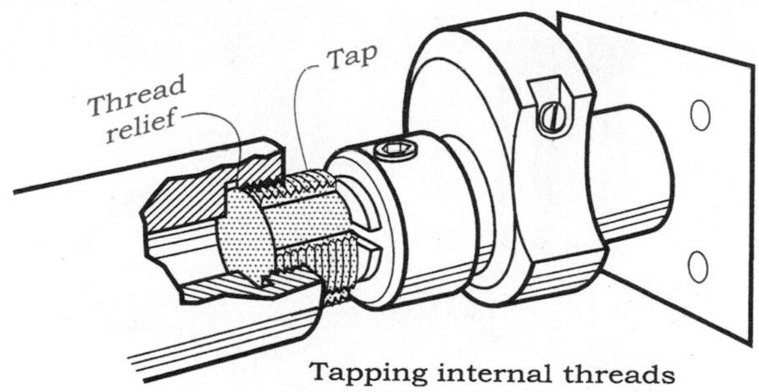

19.35 Internal threads can be cut on a lathe with a die called a **tap**. A recess, called a **thread relief**, is formed at the end of the threaded hole.

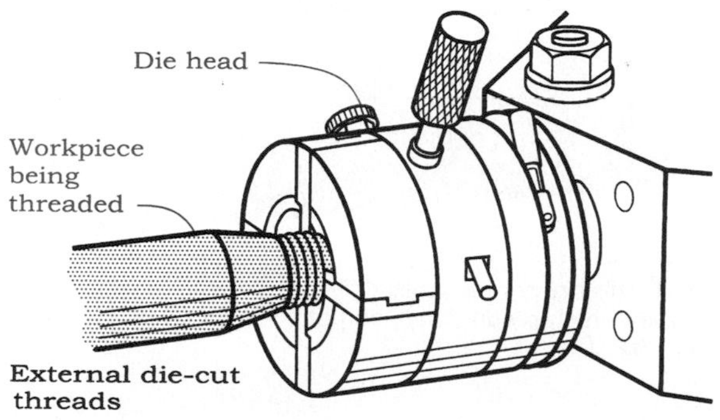

19.36 This workpiece (a shaft) is being threaded by a die head.

of an inch of material inside cylindrical and conical holes to enlarge them to their required tolerances (**Figure 19.34**).

Threading of internal holes can be done on the lathe as shown in **Figure 19.35**. The die used for cutting internal holes is called a **tap**. A threading die can be used to cut external threads on a shaft held in the chuck of a lathe as illustrated in **Figure 19.36**. Other external cuts made on a lathe are shown in **Figure 19.37**.

The **turret lathe** is a programmable lathe that can perform sequential operations, such as drilling a series of holes, boring them, and then reaming them. The turret is a multi-sided tool holder that sequentially rotates each tool into position for its particular operation (**Figure 19.38**).

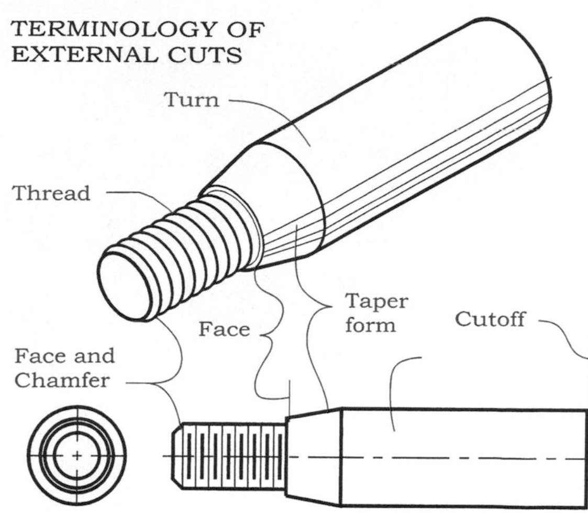

19.37 The various external cuts made on the lathe are shown here.

19.38 A turret lathe performs a sequence of operations by revolving the turret on which are mounted various tools. *(Courtesy of Clausing Industrial, Inc.)*

Drill Press

The **drill press** is used to drill small- and medium-sized holes (**Figure 19.39**). The stock being drilled is held securely by fixtures or clamps. The drill press can be used for counterdrilling, countersinking, counterboring, spotfacing, and threading (**Figure 19.40**). Large radial drills can be employed to perform a series of drilling operations for cost-effective mass-production applications (**Figure 19.41**).

19.39 This small drill press is used to make holes in parts. *(Courtesy of Clausing Industrial Inc.)*

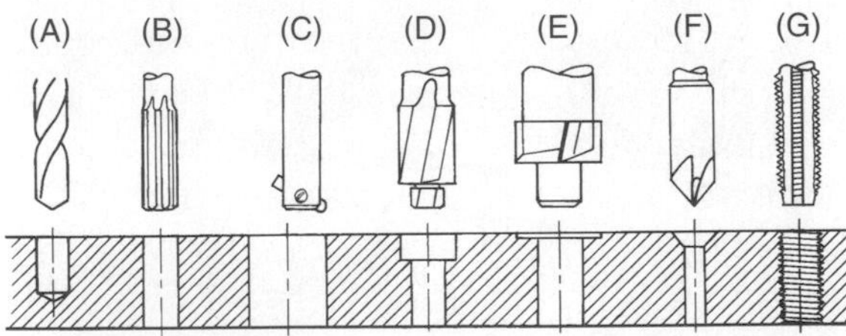

19.40 The basic operations performed on the drill press are (A) drilling, (B) reaming, (C) boring, (D) counterboring, (E) spotfacing, (F) countersinking, and (G) tapping (threading).

19.41 This heavy-duty radial drill is of the type used for large-capacity, high-productivity output. *(Courtesy of Clausing Industrial, Inc.)*

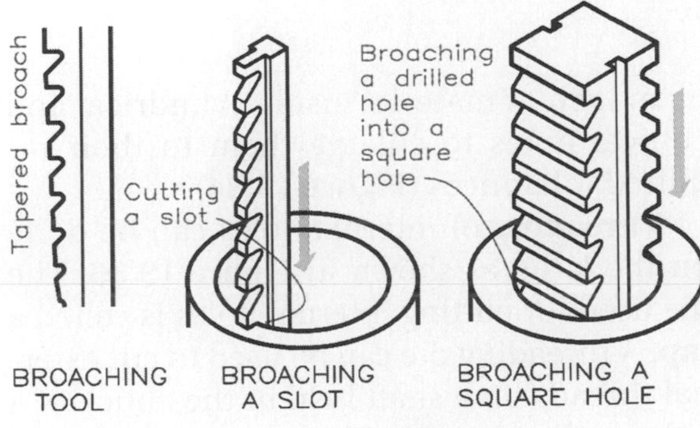

19.42 A broaching tool can be used to cut slots and holes with square corners on the interior and exterior of parts. Other shapes may be broached also.

Measuring Cylinders The diameters of cylindrical features of parts made on a drill press or a lathe are measured, not their radii, to determine their sizes. Internal and external micrometer calipers are used for this purpose to measure to within one ten-thousandth of an inch.

Broaching Machine

Cylindrical holes can be converted into square, rectangular, or hexagonal holes with a **broach** mounted on a special machine (**Figure 19.42**). A broach has a series of teeth graduated in size along its axis, beginning with teeth that are nearly the size of the hole to be broached and tapering to the final size of the hole. The broach is forced through the hole by pushing or pulling in a single pass, with each tooth cutting more from the hole as it passes through. Broaches can be used to cut external grooves, such as keyways or slots, in a part.

Milling Machine

The **milling machine** uses a variety of cutting tools, rotated about a shaft (**Figure 19.43**), to form a variety of grooved slots, threads, and gear teeth. The milling machine can cut irregular grooves in cams and finish surfaces on a part within a high degree of tolerance. The cutters revolve about a stationary axis while the workpiece on the worktable is passed beneath them.

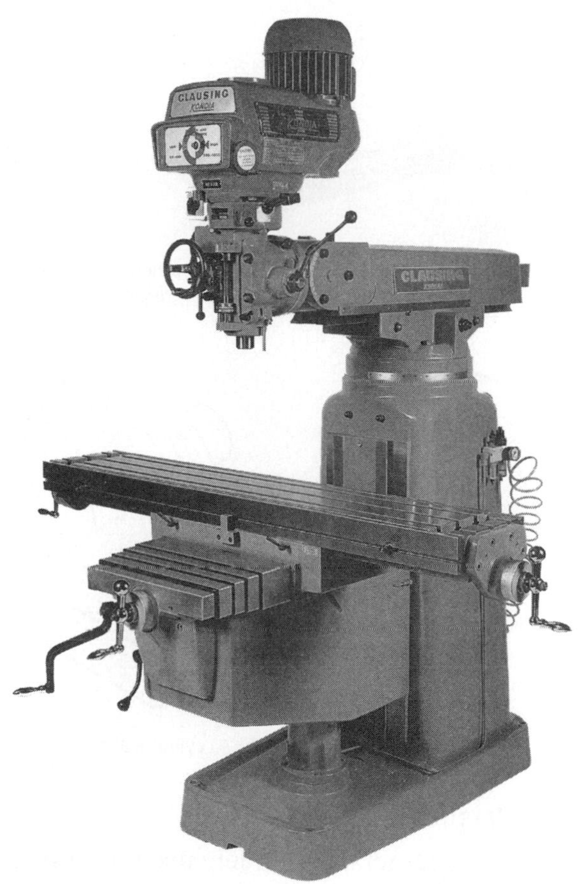

19.43 The milling machine operates by mounting the work on a bed that moves beneath revolving cutters. *(Courtesy of Clausing Industrial, Inc.)*

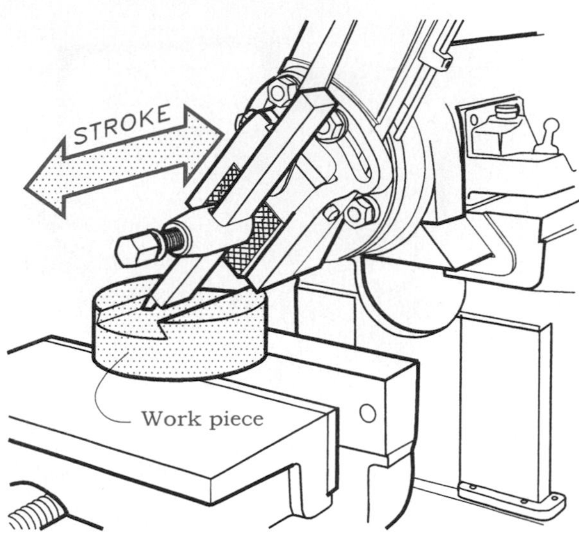

19.44 The shaper moves back and forth across the part, removing metal as it advances, to shape surfaces, cut slots, and perform other operations.

Shaper

The shaper is a machine that holds a workpiece stationary while the cutter passes back and forth across it to shape the surface or to cut a groove one stroke at a time (**Figure 19.44**). With each stroke of the cutting tool, the material is shifted slightly to align the part for the next overlapping stroke.

Planer (Mill)

Unlike the shaper, which holds the workpiece stationary, the **planer** passes the piece under the cutters to machine large flat surfaces. However, the planer has been replaced with the more efficient planer-type milling machine. Planer-type milling machines of the type shown in **Figure 19.45** are especially efficient for surfacing large areas.

19.6 Surface Finishing

Surface finishing produces a smooth, uniform surface. It may be accomplished by **grinding, polishing, lapping, buffing**, and **honing**.

Grinding involves holding a flat surface against a rotating abrasive wheel (**Figure 19.46**).

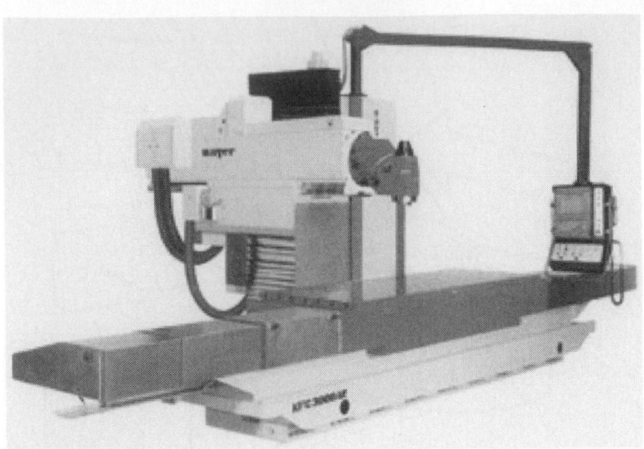

19.45 This bed-type milling machine (Model 30 KF) is capable of milling surfaces of parts weighing up to 10,000 lb. *(Courtesy of Zayer, S. A.)*

Grinding is used to smooth surfaces, both cylindrical and flat, and to sharpen edges used for cutting, such as drill bits (**Figure 19.47**). Polishing is done in the same way as grinding, except that the polishing wheel is flexible because it is made of felt, leather, canvas, or fabric.

Lapping produces very smooth surfaces. The surface to be finished is held against a lap, which is a large, flat surface coated with a fine abrasive powder that finishes a surface as the lap rotates. A surface is lapped only after it has previously been finished by a less accurate technique, such as grinding or polishing. Cylindrical parts can be lapped by using a lathe with the lap.

Buffing removes scratches from a surface with a belt or rotating buffer wheel made of wool, cotton, felt, or other fabric. To enhance the buffing, an abrasive mixture is applied to the buffed surface during the process.

Honing finishes the outside or inside of holes within a high degree of tolerance. The honing tool is rotated as it is passed through the holes to produce the types of finishes found in gun barrels, engine cylinders, and other products requiring a high degree of smoothness.

19.46 The upper surface of a part can be finished to a smooth surface with the abrasive wheel of this grinding machine. *(Courtesy of Clausing Industrial Inc.)*

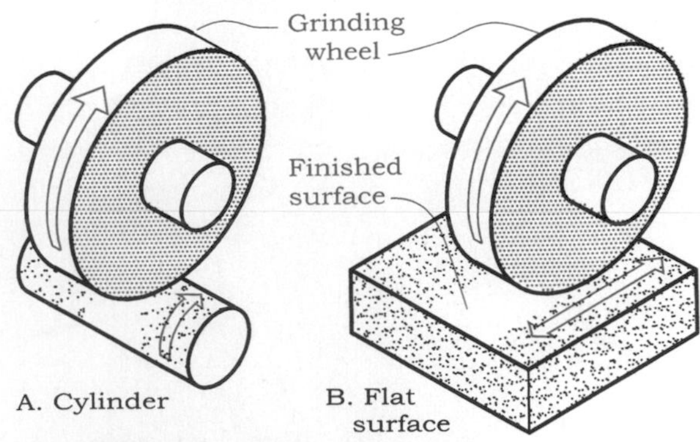

19.47 Grinding may be used to finish (A) cylindrical and (B) flat surfaces.

19.7 Plastics, Other Materials

Plastics (polymers) are widely used in numerous applications ranging from clothing, containers, and electronics to automobile bodies and components. Plastics are easily formed

E=Excellent
G=Good
F=Fair
P=Poor
A=Adhesives

	MACHINABILITY	FORMABILITY	CASTABILITY	WELDABILITY	CORROSION RES.	ABRASION RES.	LB/CU FT	YIELD: 1000 PSI	
THERMOPLASTICS									
ACRYLIC	G	G	E	A	E	F	74	9	Aircraft windows, TV parts, lenses, skylights
ABS	G	G	G	A	E	G	66	66	Luggage, boat hulls, tool handles, pipe fittings
POLYMIDES (NYLON)	E	G	G	-	G	E	73	15	Helmets, gears, drawer slides, hinges, bearings
POLYETHYLENE	G	F	G	A	F	F	58	2	Chemical tubing, containers, ice trays, bottles
POLYPROPYLENE	G	G	G	A	E	G	56	5.3	Card files, cosmetic cases, auto pedals, luggage
POLYSTYRENE	G	E	G	A	P	G	67	7	Jugs, containers, furniture, lighted signs
POLYINYL CHLORIDE	E	E	G	A	G	G	78	4.8	Rigid pipe & tubing, house siding, packaging
THERMOSETS									
EPOXY	F	G	G	-	E	G	69	17	Circuit boards, boat bodies, coatings for tanks
SILICONE	F	G	G	-	G	G	109	28	Flexible hoses, heart valves, gaskets
ELASTOMERS									
POLYURETHANE	G	G	G	A	G	E	74	6	Rigid: Solid tires, bumpers; Flexible: Foam, sponges
SBR RUBBER	-	-	E	-	F	E	39	3	Belts, handles, hoses, cable coverings
GLASSES									
GLASS	F	G	-	-	F	F	160	10+	Bottles, windows, tumblers, containers
FIBERGLASS	G	-	E	A	G	G	109	20+	Boats, shower stalls, auto bodies, chairs, signs

19.48 Characteristics of and typical applications for commonly used plastics and other materials.

into irregular shapes, have a high resistance to weather and chemicals, and are available in limitless colors. The three basic types of plastics are **thermoplastics, thermosetting plastics**, and **elastomers**.

Thermoplastics may be softened by heating and formed to the desired shape. If a polymer returns to its original hardness and strength after being heated, it is classified as a **thermoplastic**. In contrast, thermosetting plastics cannot be changed in shape by reheating after they have permanently set. **Elastomers** are rubberlike polymers that are soft, expandable, and elastic, which permits them to be deformed greatly and then return to their original size.

Figure 19.48 shows commonly used plastics and other materials, including **glass** and **fiberglass**. The weights and yields of the materials are given, along with examples of their applications.

The motorized golf cart shown in **Figure 19.49** is made of plastic. It has fewer parts and weighs less than carts made of metal. It has rounded corners and fewer joints, which makes it easy to fabricate and clean. Plastic products are as numerous and diversified as metal products. No other material is as extensively used in products from computers to trash cans as well as to wrap products from electronic gear to garbage bags.

19.49 The use of DuraShield®, a thermoplastic elastomer, in constructing the E-Z-GO® golf cart results in a body that withstands extremes of heat, cold, sunlight, and impact. *(Courtesy of E-Z-GO—a Textron Company.)*

20 Dimensioning

20.1 Introduction

Working drawings show dimensions and notes that convey sizes, specifications, and other information necessary to build a project. Drawings with their full dimensions and specifications serve as construction documents, which become legal contracts.

The techniques of dimensioning presented here are based primarily on the standards of the American National Standards Institute (ANSI), especially Y14.5M, *Dimensioning and Tolerancing for Engineering Drawings.* Standards of companies such as the General Motors Corporation also are used.

20.2 Terminology

The strap shown in **Figure 20.1** is described in **Figure 20.2** with orthographic views to which dimensions were added. Refer to this drawing as various dimensioning terms are introduced.

Dimension lines: thin lines (2H–4H pencil) with arrows at each end and numbers placed near their midpoint to specify size.

Extension lines: thin lines (2H–4H pencil) extending from the part and between which dimension lines are placed.

Centerlines: thin lines (2H–4H pencil) used to locate the centers of cylindrical parts such as holes.

Leaders: thin lines (2H–4H pencil) drawn from a note to the feature to which they apply.

Arrowheads: drawn at the ends of dimension lines and leaders and the same length as the height of the letters or numerals, usually 1/8 in., as shown in **Figure 20.3**.

Dimension numbers: placed near the middle of the dimension line and usually 1/8 in. high, with no units of measurement (", in., or mm) shown.

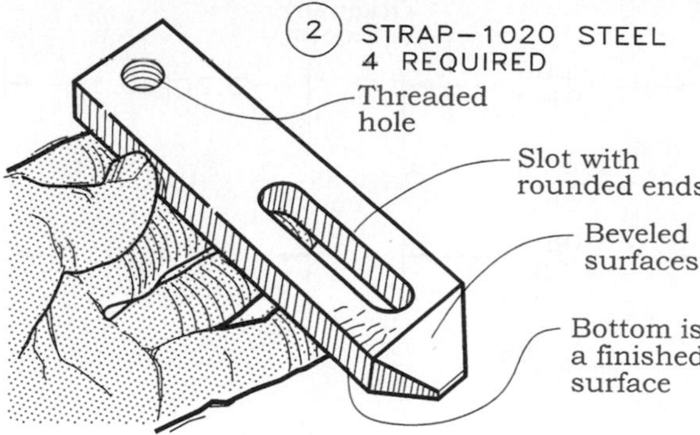

20.1 This tapered strap is a part of a clamping device that is dimensioned in **Figure 20.2**.

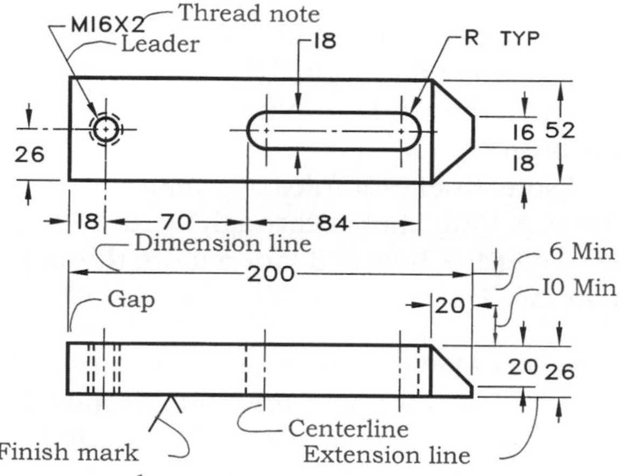

20.2 This typical dimensioned drawing of the tapered strap shown in **Figure 20.1** introduces the terminology of dimensioning.

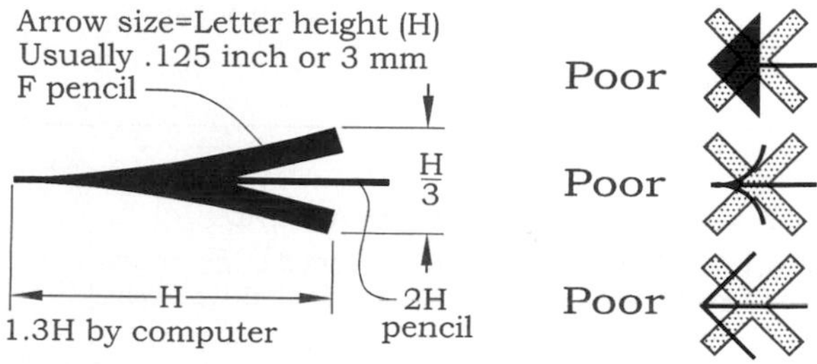

20.3 Draw arrowheads as long as the height of the letters used on the drawing and one-third as wide as they are long.

20.3 Units of Measurement

The two commonly used units of measurement are the decimal inch in the English (imperial) system, and the millimeter in the metric system (SI) (**Figure 20.4**). Giving fractional inches as decimals rather than common fractions makes arithmetic easier.

Figure 20.5 demonstrates proper and improper dimensioning techniques with millimeters, decimal inches, and fractional inches. In general, round off dimensions in millimeters to whole numbers without fractions. However, when you must show a metric dimension of less than a millimeter, use a zero before the decimal

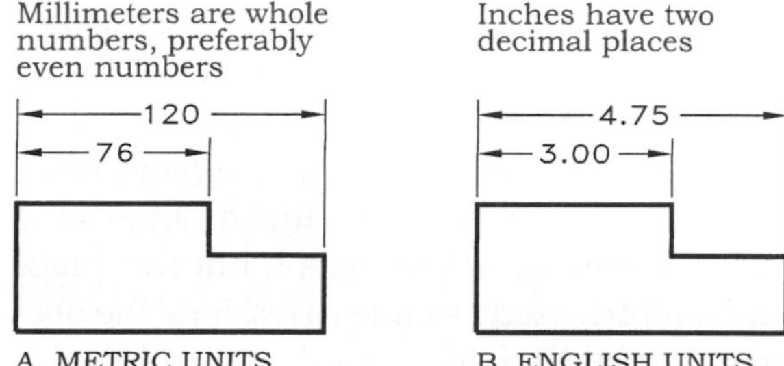

20.4 For the metric system, round millimeters to the nearest whole number. For the English system, show inches with two decimal places, even for whole numbers such as 3.00.

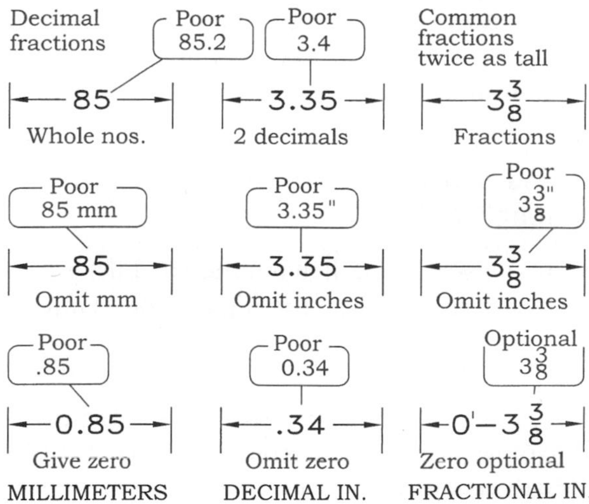

20.5 Basic principles of specifying measurements in SI and English units on a drawing.

point. Do not use a zero before the decimal point when inches are the unit.

Show decimal inch dimensions with two-place decimal fractions, even if the last numbers are zeros. Omit units of measurement from the dimension because they are understood to be in millimeters or inches. For example, use 112 (not 112 mm) and 67 (not 67" or 5'-7").

Architects use combinations of feet and inches in dimensioning and show foot marks, but usually omit inch marks, for example 7'-2. Engineers use feet and decimal fractions of feet to dimension large-scale projects such as road designs, for example, 252.7'.

20.4 English/Metric Conversions

To convert dimensions in inches to millimeters, multiply by 25.4. Similarly, to convert dimensions in millimeters to inches, divide by 25.4.

When millimeter fractions are required as a result of conversion from inches, one-place fractions usually are sufficient, but two-place fractions are used in some cases. Find the decimal digit by applying the following rules.

- Retain the last digit unchanged if it is followed by a number less than 5; for example, round 34.43 to 34.4.
- Increase the last digit retained by 1 if it is followed by a number greater than 5; for example, round 34.46 to 34.5.
- Retain the last digit unchanged if it is even and is followed by the digit 5; for example, round 34.45 to 34.4.
- Increase the last digit retained by 1 if it is odd and is followed by the digit 5; for example, round 34.75 to 34.8.

20.5 Dual Dimensioning

On some drawings you may have to give both metric and English units, called *dual dimensioning* (**Figure 20.6**). Place the millimeter equivalent either under or over the inch units,

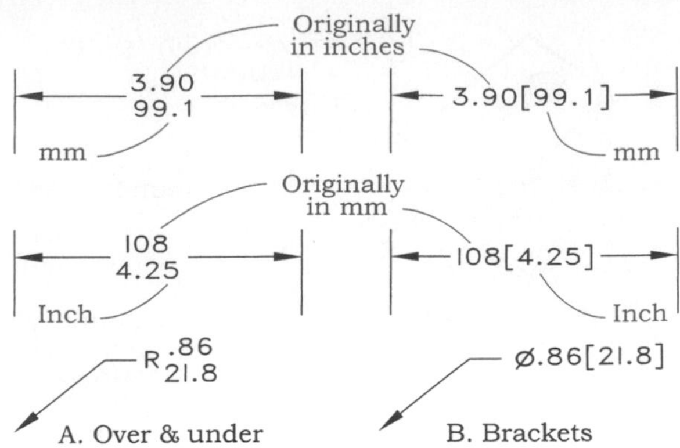

20.6 In dual dimensioning, place size equivalents in millimeters under or to the right of the inches (in brackets). Place the equivalent measurement in inches under or to the right of millimeters (in brackets). Show millimeters converted from inches as decimal fractions.

or place the converted dimension in brackets to the right of the original dimension. Be consistent in the arrangement you use on any set of drawings.

(Note: Brief examples of dimensioning by AutoCAD are shown throughout this chapter. Refer to Chapter 37 for a more thorough coverage.)

AutoCAD Method As shown in **Figure 20.7**, the dimensioning property *Dimalt* must be set to *On* to obtain alternative (dual) dimensions in brackets following the units originally

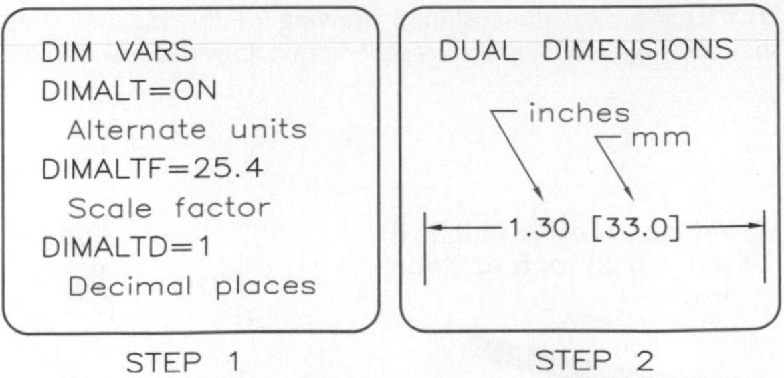

20.7 Alternate (dual) dimensions by AutoCAD.

Step 1 Type Dimalt and select On to set dual dimensioning on, type Dimaltf to assign the scale factor, and type Dimald and specify the number of decimal places.

Step 2 Find the linear dimensions by using the same steps as shown in **Figure 20.33**. The dimension in brackets is the metric equivalent of the inch dimensions.

used. Set the property *Dimaltf* (scale factor) to the value of the multiplier to be used to change the first dimension. Use *Dimaltd* to assign the desired number of decimal places for the second dimension. Then, select dimensions by using the *Dimlinear* command the same way you do to find single-value dimensions (**Figure 20.34**). Dimensioning variables can be set also from *Dimension Style* dialogue boxes.

20.6 Metric Units

Recall that in the metric system (SI), the first angle of projection positions the front view over the top view and the right-side view to the left of the front view (**Figure 20.8**). You should label metric drawings with one of the symbols shown in **Figure 20.9** to designate the angle of projection. Display either the letters SI or the word METRIC prominently in or near the title block to indicate that the measurements are metric.

20.7 Numerals and Symbols

Vertical Dimensions

Vertical numeric dimensions on a drawing may be **aligned** or **unidirectional**. In the unidirectional method, all dimensions appear in the

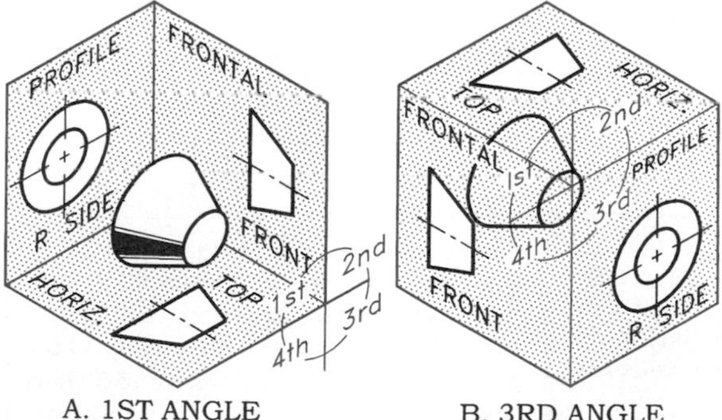

A. 1ST ANGLE

B. 3RD ANGLE

20.8 Projection systems.

A The SI system uses the first angle of orthographic projection, which places the top view under the front view.

B The American system uses the third angle of projection, which places the top view over the front view.

U.S. projection, where circle is visible here

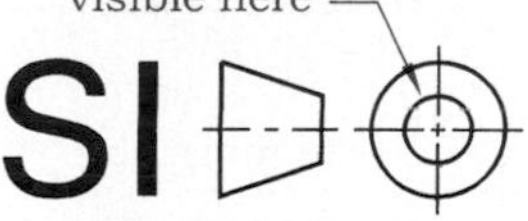

A. METRIC UNITS & 3RD ANGLE

First angle, where circle is visible, but would be hidden in U.S. system

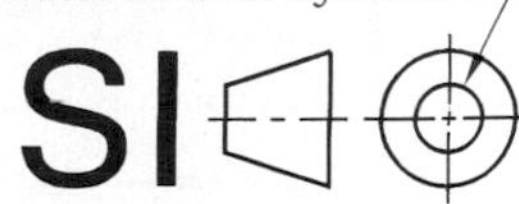

B. METRIC UNITS & 1ST ANGLE

20.9 The SI symbol.

A The SI symbol indicates that the millimeter is the unit of measurement, and the truncated cone specifies that third-angle projection was used to position the orthographic views.

B Again, the SI symbol denotes use of the millimeter, but the truncated cone designates that first-angle projection was used.

standard horizontal position (**Figure 20.10A**). In the aligned method numerals are parallel with vertical and angular dimension lines and read from the right-hand side of the drawing, never from the left-hand side (**Figure 20.10B**). Aligned dimensions are used almost entirely in architectural drawings where dimensions composed of feet, inches, and fractions are too long to fit well unidirectionally (such as 22'-10 1/2).

AutoCAD Method The variable *Dimtih* (text inside dimension lines is horizontal), a *Dim Vars* of the *Dim* AutoCAD command, must be set to *Off* for aligned dimensions and to *On* for unidirectional dimensions. The *Dimtoh* mode controls the position of text lying outside

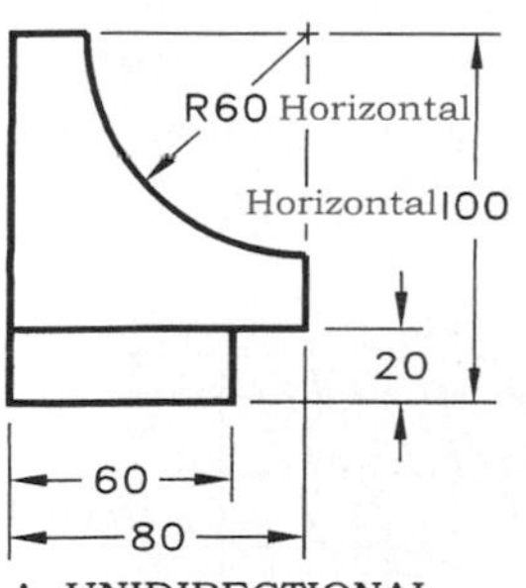

A. UNIDIRECTIONAL

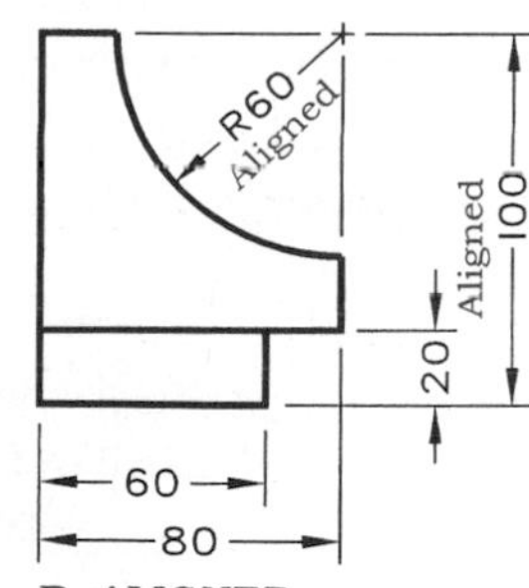

B. ALIGNED

20.10 Unidirectional and aligned dimensions.

A Dimensions are unidirectional when they are horizontal in both vertical and horizontal dimension lines.

B Dimensions are aligned when they are lettered parallel to angular and vertical dimension lines to read from the right-hand side of the drawing (not from the left).

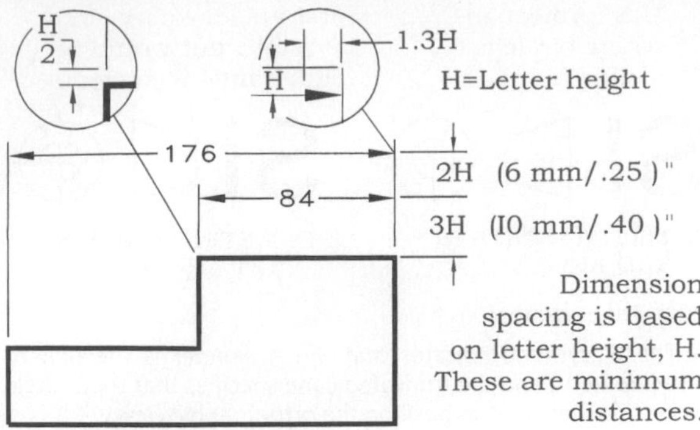

20.11 Place dimensions on a view as shown here, where all dimensioning geometry is based on the letter height (H) used.

dimension lines where the numerals do not fit within a short dimension line. When *Dimtoh* is *On,* numerals will be horizontal; when *Off,* numerals will align with the dimension line.

Placement

Dimensions should be placed on the most descriptive views of the part being dimensioned. The first row of dimensions should be at least three times the letter height (3H) from the object (**Figure 20.11**). Successive rows of dimensions should be spaced equally at least two times the letter height apart (0.25 in., or 6 mm, when 1/8-in. letters are used). Use the Braddock-Rowe lettering guide triangle to space the dimension lines (**Figure 20.12**).

Figure 20.13 illustrates how to place dimensions in limited spaces. Regardless of space limitations, do not make numerals smaller than they appear elsewhere on the drawing.

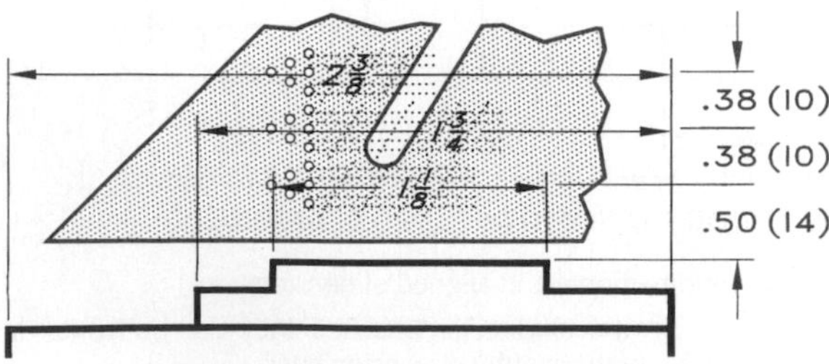

20.12 Draw guidelines for common fractions in dimensions by aligning the center holes in the Braddock-Rowe triangle with the dimension line.

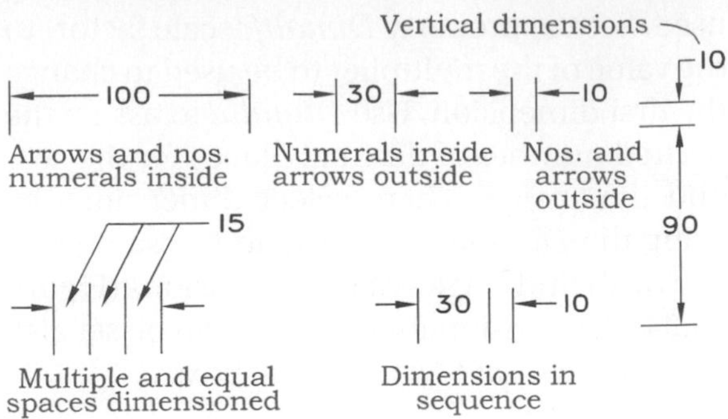

20.13 When space permits, place numerals and arrows inside extension lines. For smaller spaces use other placements, as shown.

AutoCAD Method Dimensioning variables and their minimum settings are shown in **Figure 20.14**. You may change variables set at these proportions at the same time by using *Dimscale.* For example, *Dimscale* = 25.4 would convert all dimensioning variables from inch to millimeter proportions. **Figure 20.15** shows other AutoCAD dimensioning variables. The full list of varibles and their definitions can be obtained on the screen by typing *Dim* and then *Status* (see Chapter 37 for more coverage).

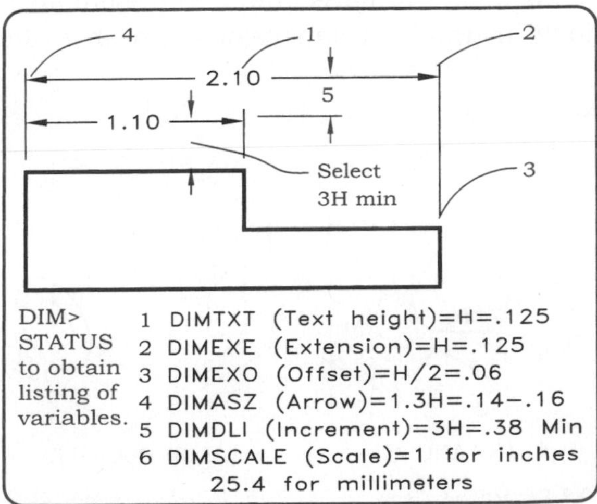

20.14 The dimensioning properties *(Dim>Status)* to be applied by AutoCAD are shown here. They remain active with the file in use. *Dimscale* can be used to enlarge or reduce all these variables.

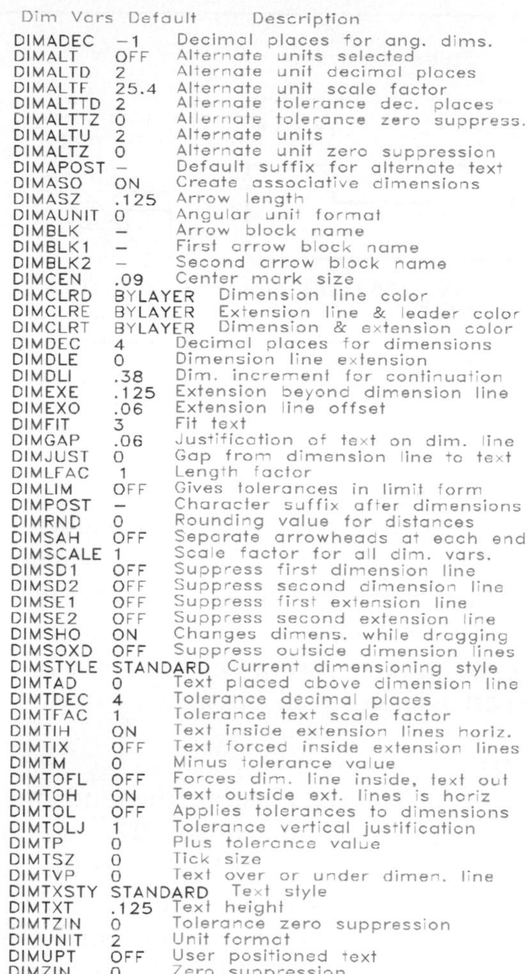

Dim Vars	Default	Description
DIMADEC	–1	Decimal places for ang. dims.
DIMALT	OFF	Alternate units selected
DIMALTD	2	Alternate unit decimal places
DIMALTF	25.4	Alternate unit scale factor
DIMALTTD	2	Alternate tolerance dec. places
DIMALTTZ	0	Alternate tolerance zero suppress.
DIMALTU	2	Alternate units
DIMALTZ	0	Alternate unit zero suppression
DIMAPOST	–	Default suffix for alternate text
DIMASO	ON	Create associative dimensions
DIMASZ	.125	Arrow length
DIMAUNIT	0	Angular unit format
DIMBLK	–	Arrow block name
DIMBLK1	–	First arrow block name
DIMBLK2	–	Second arrow block name
DIMCEN	.09	Center mark size
DIMCLRD	BYLAYER	Dimension line color
DIMCLRE	BYLAYER	Extension line & leader color
DIMCLRT	BYLAYER	Dimension & extension color
DIMDEC	4	Decimal places for dimensions
DIMDLE	0	Dimension line extension
DIMDLI	.38	Dim. increment for continuation
DIMEXE	.125	Extension beyond dimension line
DIMEXO	.06	Extension line offset
DIMFIT	3	Fit text
DIMGAP	.06	Justification of text on dim. line
DIMJUST	0	Gap from dimension line to text
DIMLFAC	1	Length factor
DIMLIM	OFF	Gives tolerances in limit form
DIMPOST	–	Character suffix after dimensions
DIMRND	0	Rounding value for distances
DIMSAH	OFF	Separate arrowheads at each end
DIMSCALE	1	Scale factor for all dim. vars.
DIMSD1	OFF	Suppress first dimension line
DIMSD2	OFF	Suppress second dimension line
DIMSE1	OFF	Suppress first extension line
DIMSE2	OFF	Suppress second extension line
DIMSHO	ON	Changes dimens. while dragging
DIMSOXD	OFF	Suppress outside dimension lines
DIMSTYLE	STANDARD	Current dimensioning style
DIMTAD	0	Text placed above dimension line
DIMTDEC	4	Tolerance decimal places
DIMTFAC	1	Tolerance text scale factor
DIMTIH	ON	Text inside extension lines horiz.
DIMTIX	OFF	Text forced inside extension lines
DIMTM	0	Minus tolerance value
DIMTOFL	OFF	Forces dim. line inside, text out
DIMTOH	ON	Text outside ext. lines is horiz
DIMTOL	OFF	Applies tolerances to dimensions
DIMTOLJ	1	Tolerance vertical justification
DIMTP	0	Plus tolerance value
DIMTSZ	0	Tick size
DIMTVP	0	Text over or under dimen. line
DIMTXSTY	STANDARD	Text style
DIMTXT	.125	Text height
DIMTZIN	0	Tolerance zero suppression
DIMUNIT	2	Unit format
DIMUPT	OFF	User positioned text
DIMZIN	0	Zero suppression

20.15 Most of AutoCAD's dimensioning variables *(Dim> Status)* are shown here. Chapter 37 covers more details of their application.

Dimensioning Symbols

Figure 20.16 shows standard dimensioning symbols and their sizes based on the letter height, usually 1/8 in. By using these symbols, lengthy notes can be replaced and drawing time saved.

20.8 Dimensioning by AutoCAD

Figure 20.17 shows several combinations of dimensioning variables that are available with the *Dim* command (type Dim).

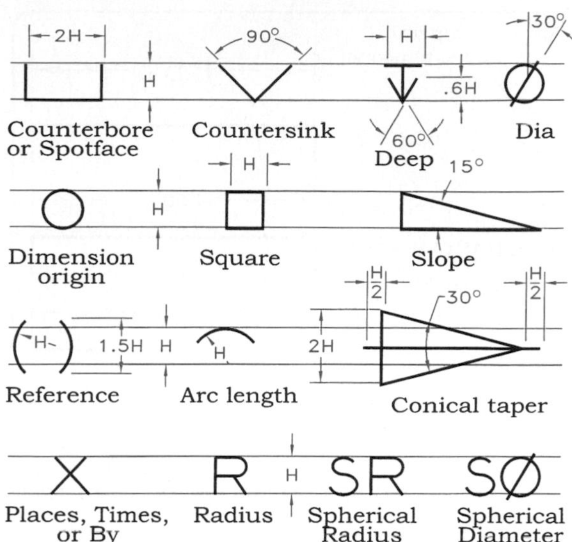

20.16 These symbols can be used instead of words to dimension parts. Their proportions are based on the letter height, H, which usually is 1/8 in.

You can place text inside the dimension line *(Dimtad: Off)* or above it *(Dimtad: On)*. You may place arrowheads at the ends of dimension lines *Dimasz*>0 or use tick marks (slashes) instead when *Dimtsz* is set to a value greater than 0, usually about half the letter height. You may select *Units* as architectural (feet and inches), metric (no decimal fractions), decimal inches (two or more decimal fractions), or engineering units (feet and decimal inches).

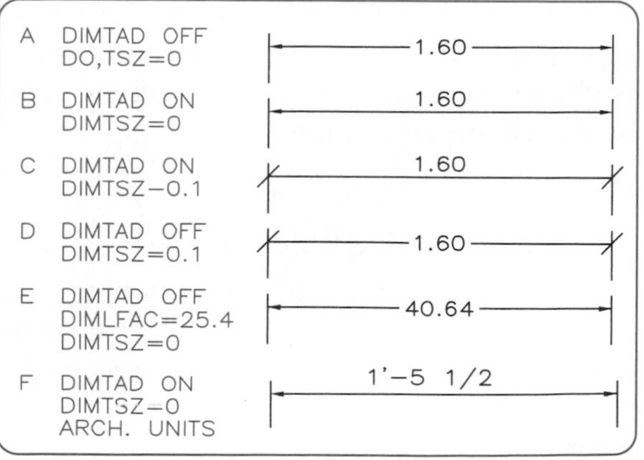

20.17 These dimension lines illustrate the effects of using the different dimensioning variables in AutoCAD.

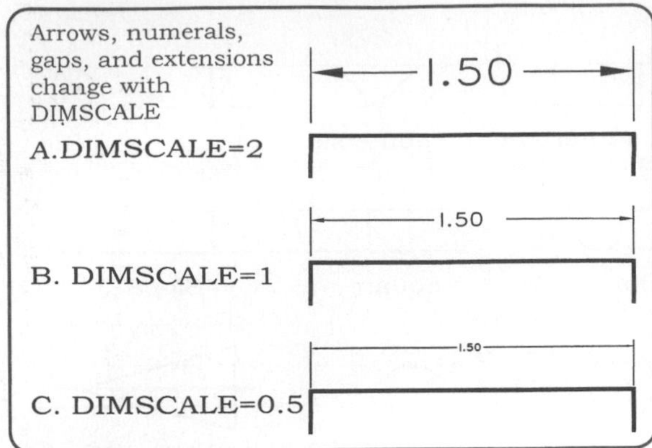

20.18 *Dimscale,* a subcommand under *Dim,* permits changing the sizes of all dimensioning variables by typing a single scale factor. It changes the text size, arrows, offsets, and extensions at the same time.

The text font (letter form) used in dimensioning is the same as the currently used text font or the font assigned by the *Dimstyle* procedure, and a *Style* is selected for dimensioning. In both cases, the text height should be set to 0 (zero) for *Dimscale* (an option with the *Dim* command) to change the text height when invoked (**Figure 20.18**).

If you set text to a specified height under the *Dimstyle* command, the text will not change with different *Dimscale* values but will remain at its constant specified height. Text size is the most critical aspect of dimensioning, since it must be sufficiently large to be readable (**Figure 20.19**). Using *Dimscale* enables text height, arrows, and extension line offsets to be changed at the same time.

20.9 Dimensioning Rules

There are many rules of dimensioning you should become familiar with to place dimensions and notes on drawings most effectively. Each geometric shape has its own set of rules: prisms, angular surfaces, cylindrical features, pyramids, cones, spheres, and arcs.

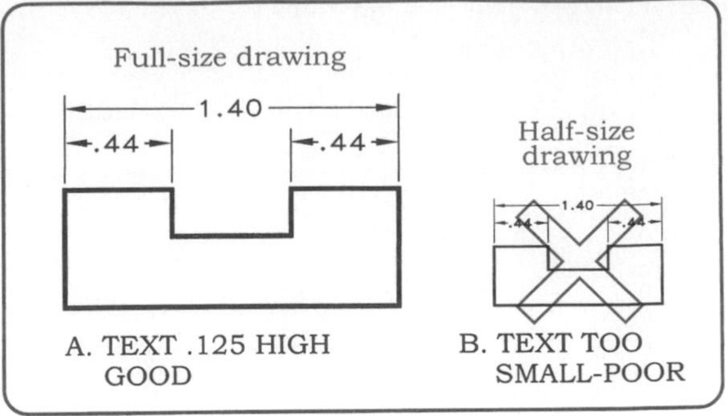

20.19 When dimensioning a drawing, be aware of its final plotted size so that you can properly size the dimensioning variables for reduction or enlargement. *Dimscale* is the most efficient command for assigning the proper scale to dimensioning variables.

Dimensioning rules are more guidelines than rules, since many drawings make it difficult to apply them rigidly. Quite often, rules of dimensioning must be violated or applied in a different manner owing to the complexity of the part or lack of available space.

Prisms

Figures 20.20–20.32 illustrate the fundamental rules of dimensioning prisms. The rules are presented in the simplest of examples to focus on the specific rules one point at a time. These generally accepted dimensioning rules were not arbitrarily arrived at, but they are based

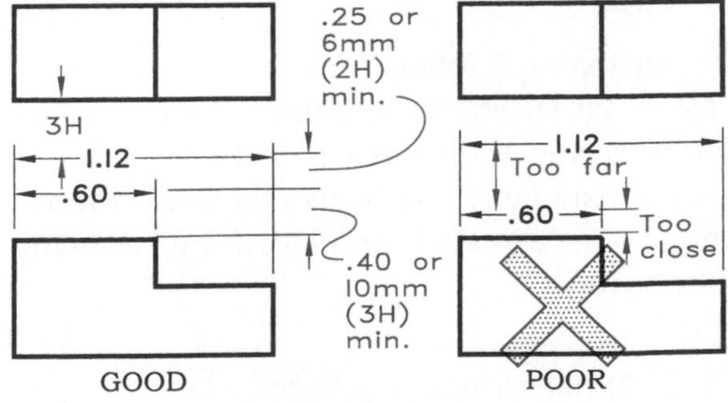

20.20 Place the first row of dimensions at least three times the letter height from the object. Successive rows should be at least two times the letter height apart.

RULE 2: **Place dimensions between the views.**

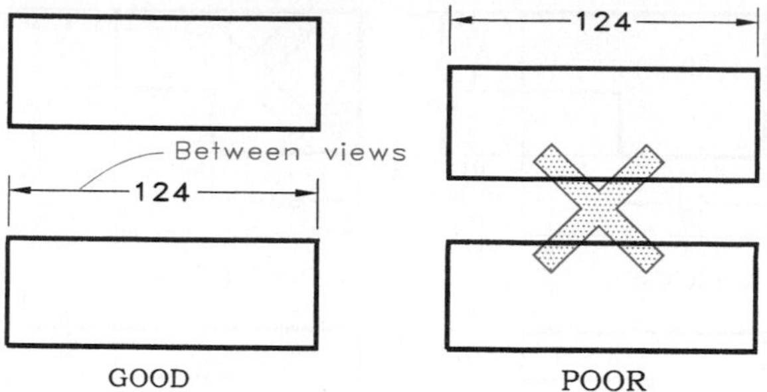

20.21 Place dimensions between the views sharing these dimensions.

RULE 3: **Dimension the most descriptive views.**

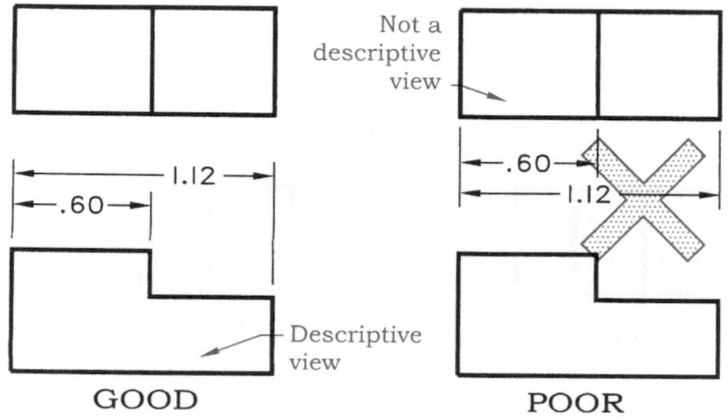

20.22 Place dimensions on the most descriptive views of an object.

RULE 4: **Dimension from visible lines, not hidden lines.**

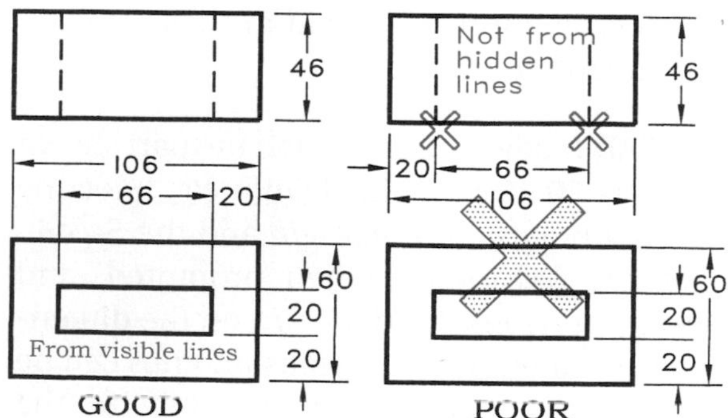

20.23 Dimension visible features, not hidden features.

RULE 5: **Give an overall dimension and omit one of the chain dimensions.**

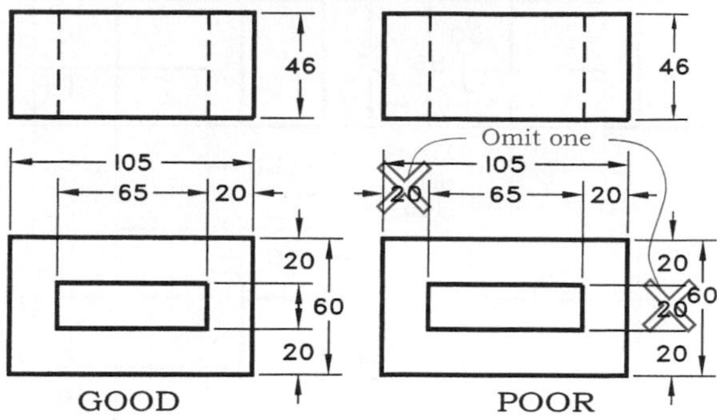

20.24 Leave the last dimension blank in a chain of dimensions and give an overall dimension.

RULE 5 (Deviation): **If all chain dimensions are given, mark one of lesser importance as a reference dimension, REF.**

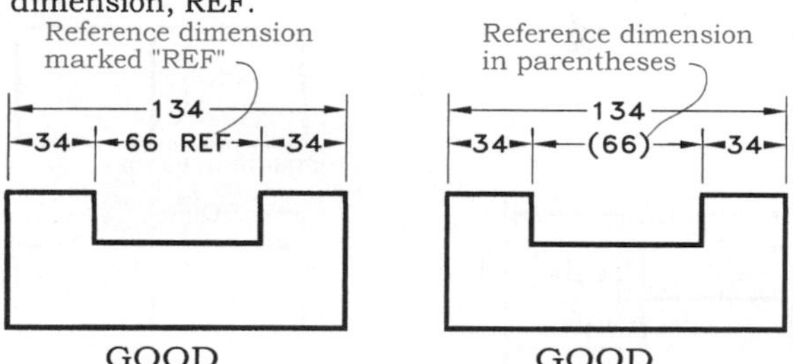

20.25 If you give all dimensions in a chain, mark the reference dimension (the one that would be omitted) with REF or place it in parentheses. Giving a reference dimension is a way of eliminating mathematical calculations in the shop.

RULE 6: **Organize and align dimensions for ease of reading.**

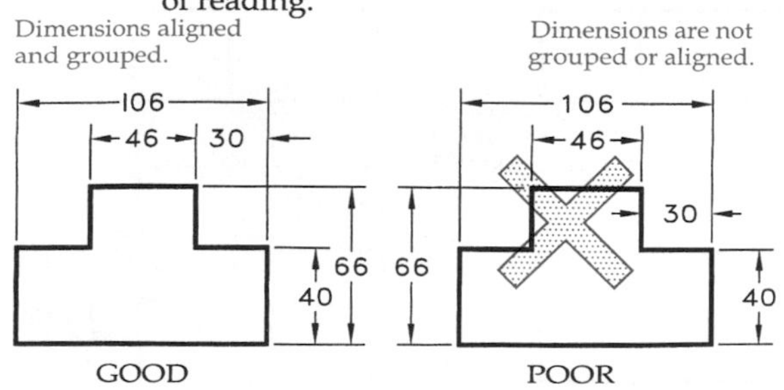

20.26 Place dimensions in well-organized lines for uncluttered drawings.

RULE 7: **Do not repeat dimensions.**

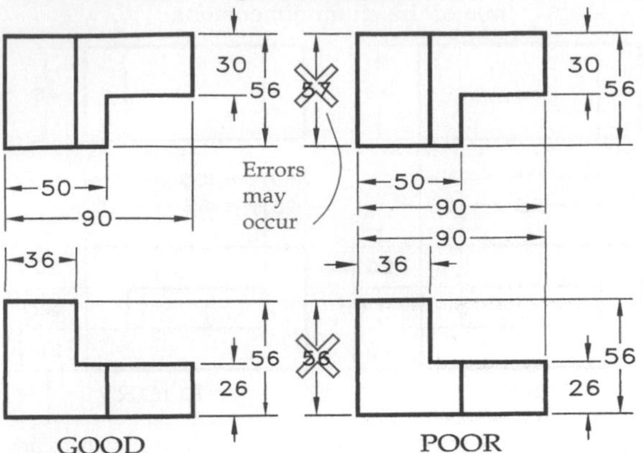

20.27 Do not duplicate dimensions on a drawing to avoid errors or confusion.

RULE 8: **Dimensions should not cross other lines.**

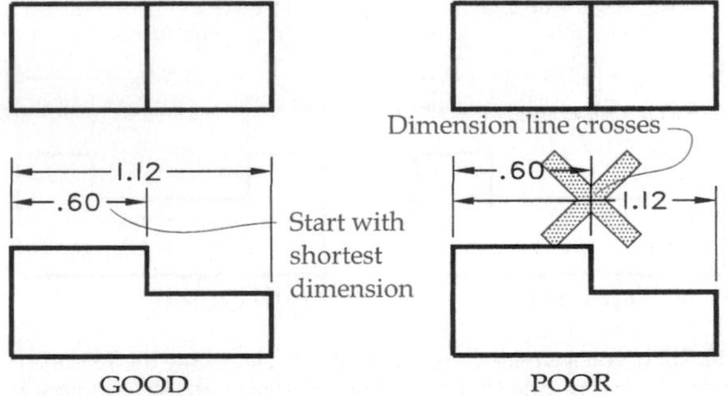

20.28 Dimension lines should not cross any other lines unless absolutely necessary.

RULE 9: Extension lines may cross other lines if they must.

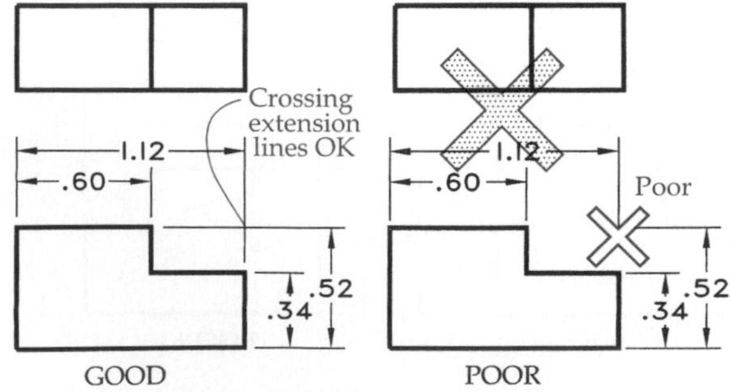

20.29 Extension lines may cross other extension lines or object lines if necessary.

RULE 9: (Continued) **Crossing extension lines.**

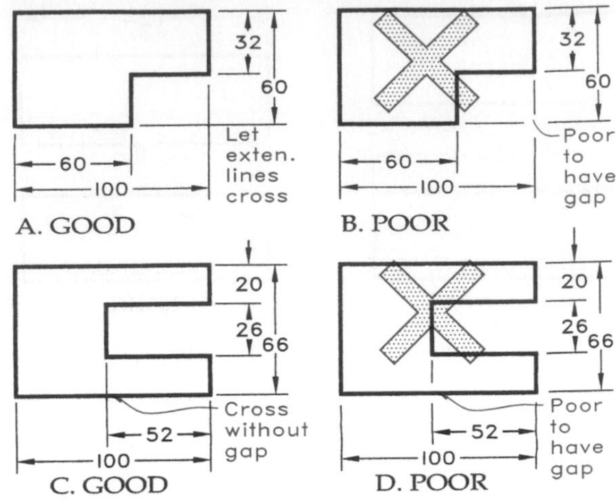

20.30 Leave a small gap between the object and the extension lines from them. Do not leave gaps where extension lines cross object lines or other extension lines.

RULE 10: **Do not place dimensions within the views unless absolutely necessary.**

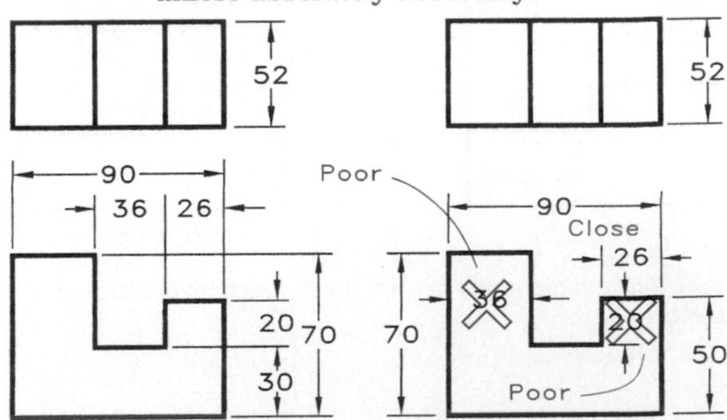

20.31 Whenever possible place dimensions outside objects rather than inside their outlines.

on a logical approach to aid in their application and interpretation.

AutoCAD Method Dimension the part shown in **Figure 20.33** by typing Dimlinear, selecting the *First extension line origin* and the *Second extension line origin* when prompted, and picking *Horizontal* and a point on the dimension line. Alternatively, extension lines can be found automatically by responding to the prompt *Select object to dimension* by selecting the line to be measured, specifying the

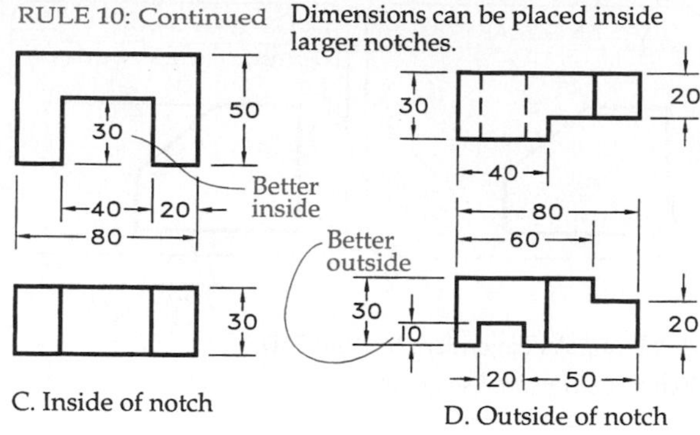

20.32

3 Dimensioning prisms.

C You may dimension large notches inside the object if doing so improves clarity.

D Small notches must be dimensioned outside the object for better clarity and because of lack of space.

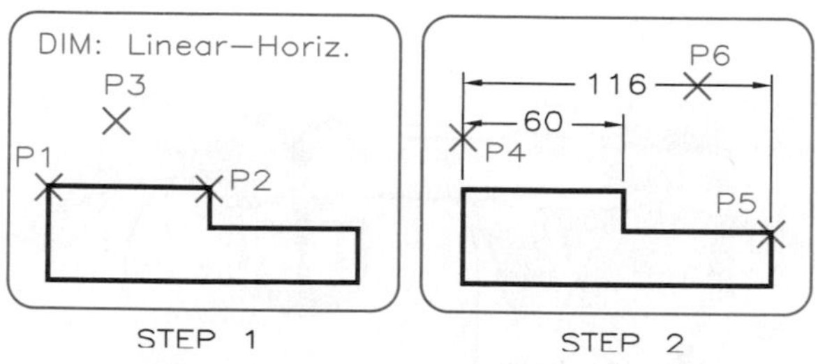

20.33 Linear dimensioning by AutoCAD.

Step 1 *Command:* Dimlinear (Enter)
Specify extension line origin or <select object >: P1
Specify second extension line origin: P2
Specify dimension line location or [Mtext/Text/Angle/Horizontal/Vertical/Rotated]: P3 (*Mtext* and *Text* can be used as options for overriding the measured distance.)

Step 2 *Command:* (Enter) (*Dimlinear* is repeated.)
Specify extension line origin or <select object>: P4
Specify second extension line origin: P5
Specify dimension line location or [Mtext/Text/Angle/Horizontal/Vertical/Rotated]: P6

direction of the dimension line, and locating the dimension line.

Setting the dimensioning variable *Dimaso* to *On,* dimensions will be associative dimensions. That is, the measurements in the dimension lines will change as the size of the objects are changed. For example, the *Stretch* command updates the dimensioning measurements as a part's size is modified (**Figure 20.34**). Associative dimensions can be erased as a unit (extension lines, dimension lines, arrows, and number). When *Dimsho* is *On,* you will be able to see the dimensioning numerals changing dynamically on the screen as you *Stretch* the part to a new size.

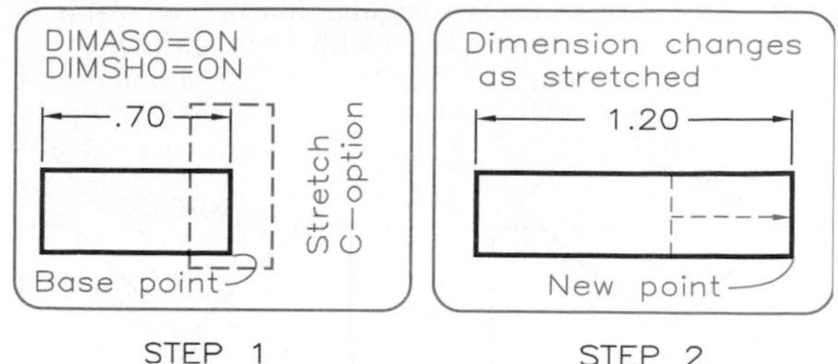

20.34 Associative dimensions.

Step 1 Set dimensioning variable *Dimaso* and *Dimsho* to *On* to associate the dimensions with the size of the part to which they apply. Use the *C* option of the *Stretch* command to window the ends of an extension line and dimension lines.

Step 2 Select a base point and a new point. Dragging the size of the part recalculates the dimensions dynamically.

Angles

You may dimension angles either by coordinates locating the ends of sloping surfaces or by angular measurements in degrees (**Figure 20.35**). Fractional angles can be specified in decimal units or in degrees, minutes, and seconds. Recall that there are 60 minutes in a degree and 60 seconds in a minute. It is seldom

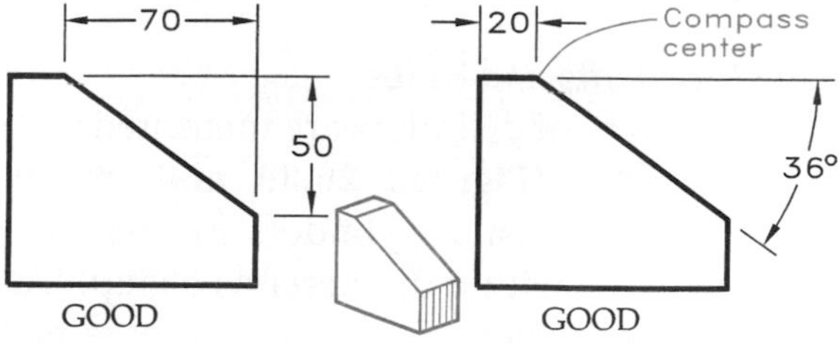

20.35 Dimensioning angles.

A Dimension angular planes by using coordinates.

B Measure angles by locating the vertex and measuring the angle in degrees. When accuracy is essential, specify angles in degrees, minutes, and seconds.

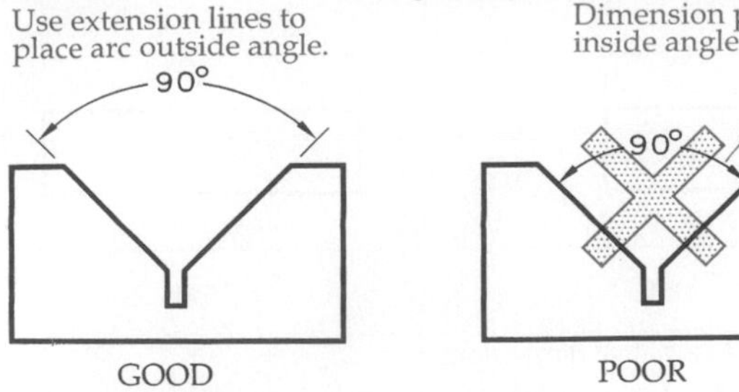

20.36 Place angular dimensions outside the object by using extension lines.

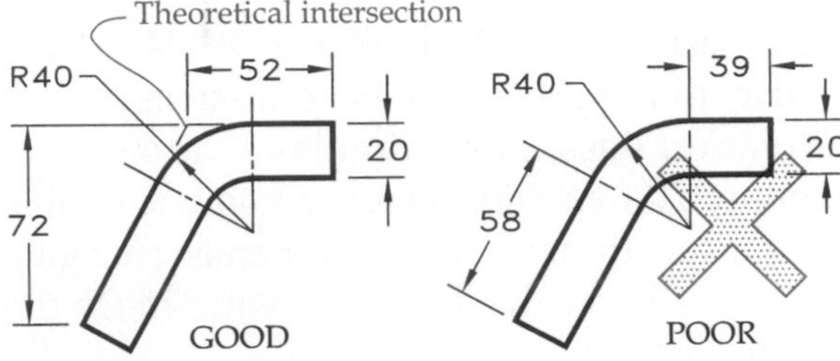

20.37 Dimension a bent surface rounded corner by locating its theoretical point of intersection with extension lines.

that you will you need to measure angles to the nearest second. **Figures 20.36** and **20.37** illustrate basic rules for dimensioning angles.

AutoCAD Method Type Dimangular at the command line to dimension angles (**Figure 20.38**). If room is not available for the arrows between the extension lines, AutoCAD will generate them outside the extension lines.

Cylindrical Parts and Holes

The diameters of cylinders are measured with a micrometer (**Figures 20.39 and 20.40**). Therefore, dimension cylinders in their rectangular views with a diameter as a graphical simulation of how the dimension is obtained (**Figures 20.41 and 20.42**). You will recall that the diametric symbol is a circle with a slash through it. In the English system the abbreviation DIA placed after the diametral dimension

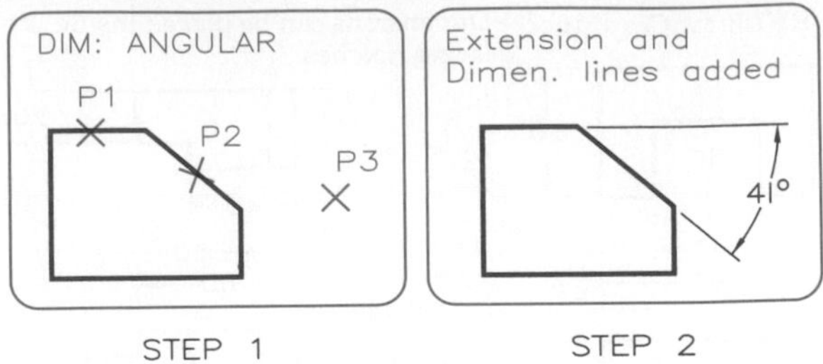

20.38 Angular dimensions by AutoCAD.

Step 1 *Command:* Dimangular (Enter)
Select arc, circle, line: P1
Select second line: P2

Step 2 *Specify dimension arc line location or (Mtext/Text/Angle):* P3 (to accept measured angle.)
Dimension text <41>:
Command: (Continue angular dimensioning or enter a new command.)

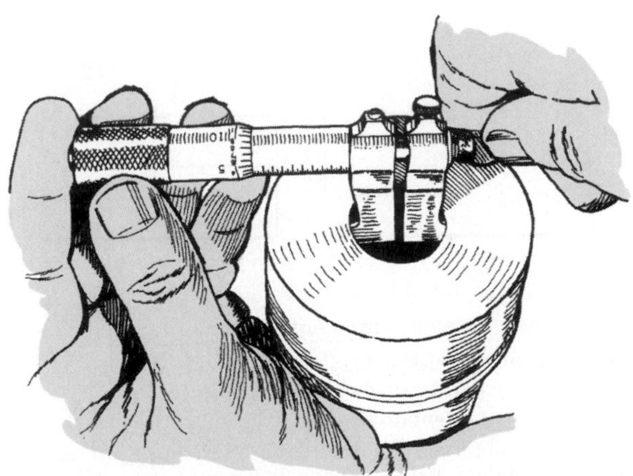

20.39 This internal micrometer caliper measures internal cylindrical diameters (radii cannot be measured).

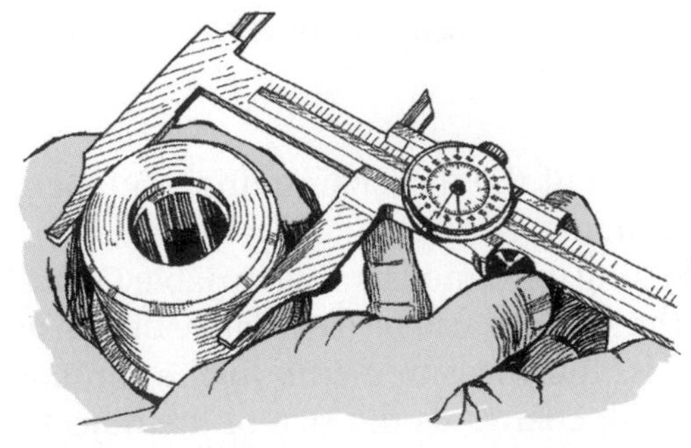

20.40 This external micrometer caliper measures the diameter of a cylinder.

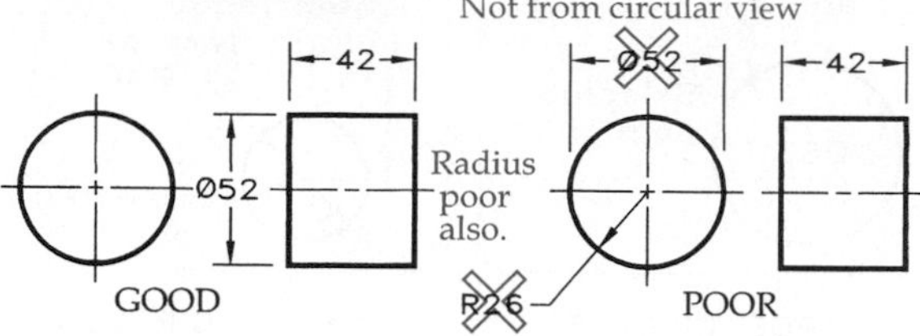

20.41 Dimension the diameter (not the radius) of a cylinder in the rectangular view.

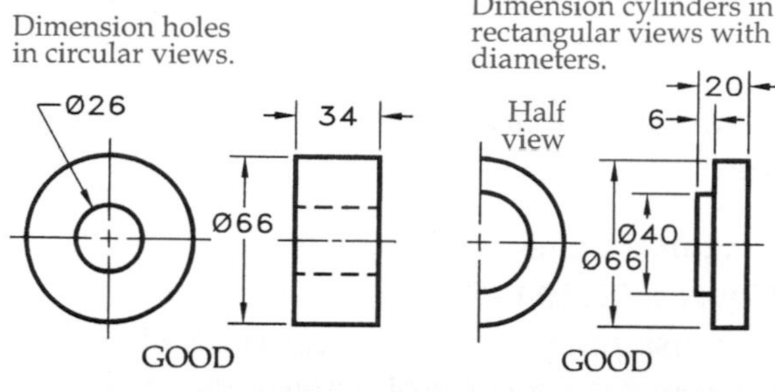

20.42 Dimension holes in their circular views with leaders. Dimension concentric cylinders with a series of diameters.

is still sometimes used, but the metric diameter symbol is preferred.

Space is almost always a problem in dimensioning, and all means of conserving space must be used. Stagger dimensions for concentric cylinders to avoid crowding, as shown in **Figure 20.43**. Dimension cylindrical holes in their circular view with leaders

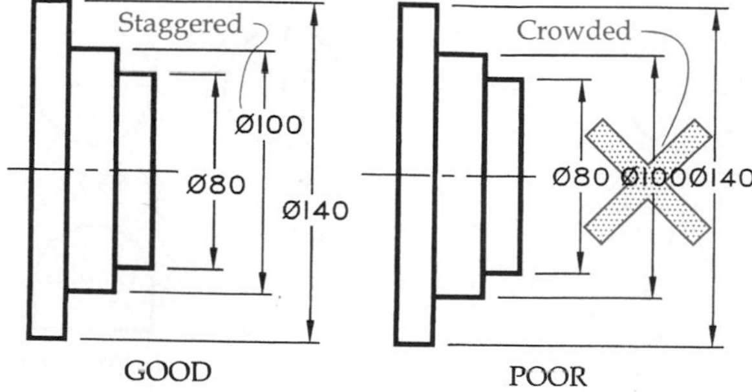

20.43 Dimensions on concentric cylinders are easier to read if they are staggered within their dimension lines.

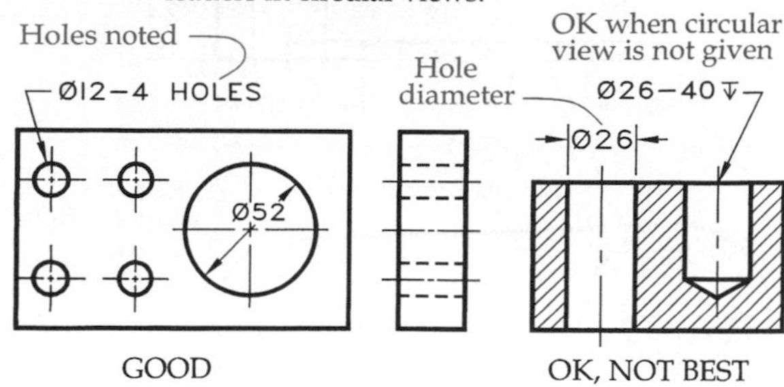

20.44 Dimension holes in their circular view with leaders whenever possible, but dimension them in their rectangular views if necessary.

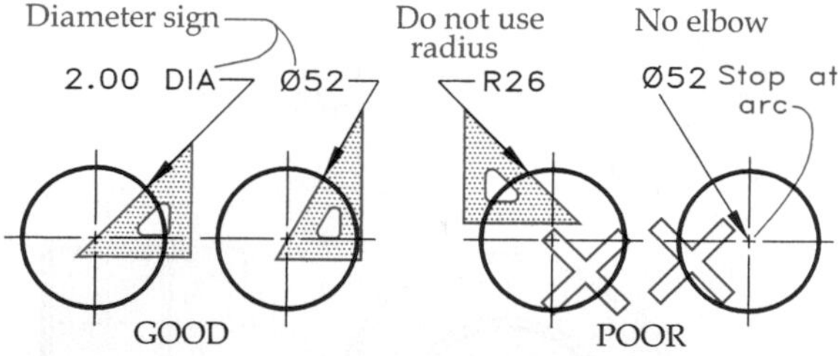

20.45 Draw leaders pointing toward the centers of holes.

(**Figure 20.44**). The circular view is the view that would be used when the hole is located and drilled. Draw leaders specifying hole sizes as shown in **Figure 20.45**. When you must place diameter notes for holes in the rectangular view instead of the circular view, draw them as shown in **Figure 20.46**. Examples of correctly dimensioned parts with cylindrical

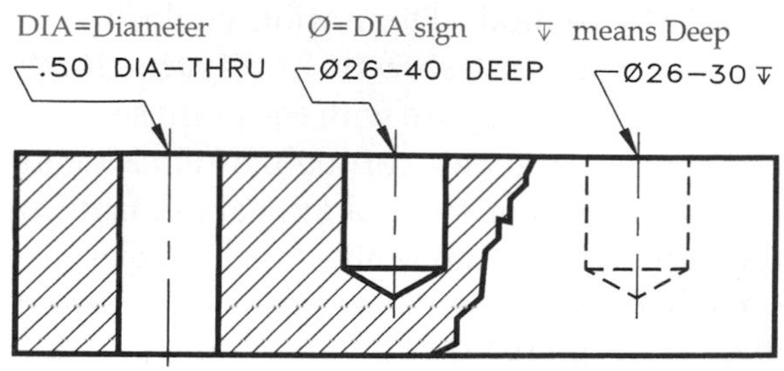

20.46 Examples of holes noted in their rectangular views.

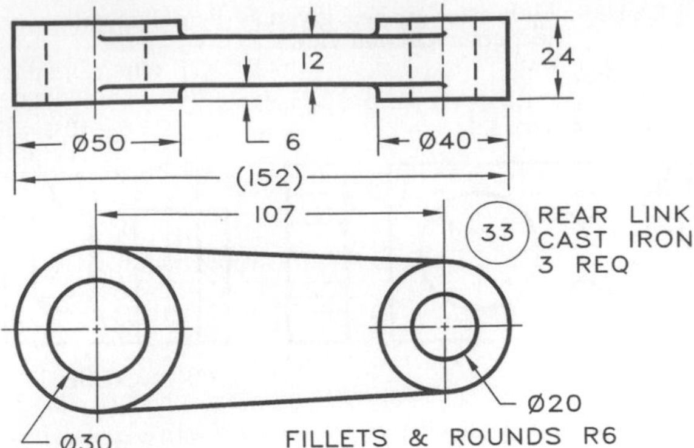

20.47 This drawing illustrates the application of dimensions to cylindrical features. (F&R R6 means that fillets and rounds have a 6-mm radius.)

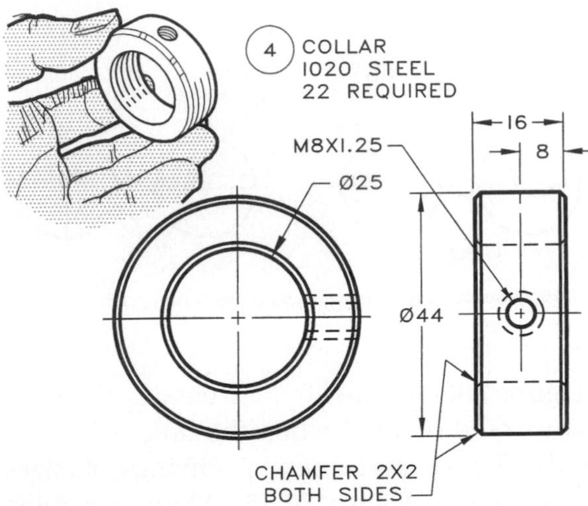

20.48 This cylindrical part, a collar, is shown drawn and dimensioned.

features are shown in **Figures 20.47** and **Figure 20.48**.

AutoCAD Method Dimension circles in the circular view as shown in **Figure 20.49**. Dimension lines begin with the point selected on the circle and pass through the circle's center. The diameter symbol appears in front of the dimension numerals. Small circles are dimensioned with the arrows inside the circle and the dimension numerals outside, connected by a leader. Circles that are smaller yet

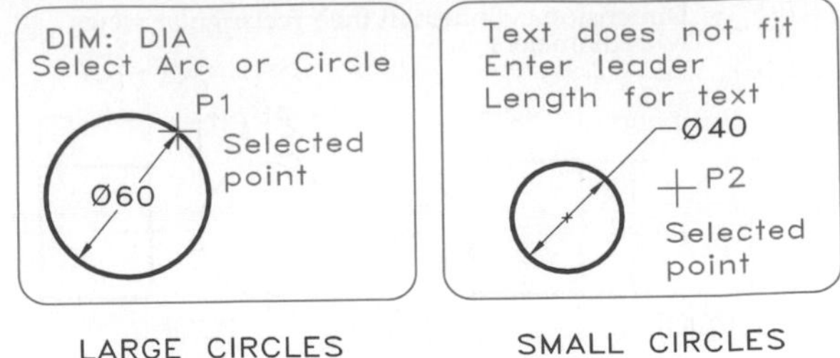

20.49 Dimensioning circles by AutoCAD.

Step 1 Type *Dimdameter* to dimension a circle. Select P1 on the arc (an endpoint of the dimension) to produce the dimension. You have the option of replacing the dimension measured by AutoCAD with a different value.

Step 2 When text does not fit, you can position it with the cursor. Select a point, P2, and the leader and dimension are drawn.

have both the arrows and dimension outside the circle.

Pyramids, Cones, and Spheres

Figures 20.50A–C show three methods of dimensioning pyramids. **Figures 20.50D** and **E** show two acceptable methods of dimensioning cones. Dimension a complete sphere by giving its diameter as shown in **Figure 20.50F**. If the spherical shape is less than a

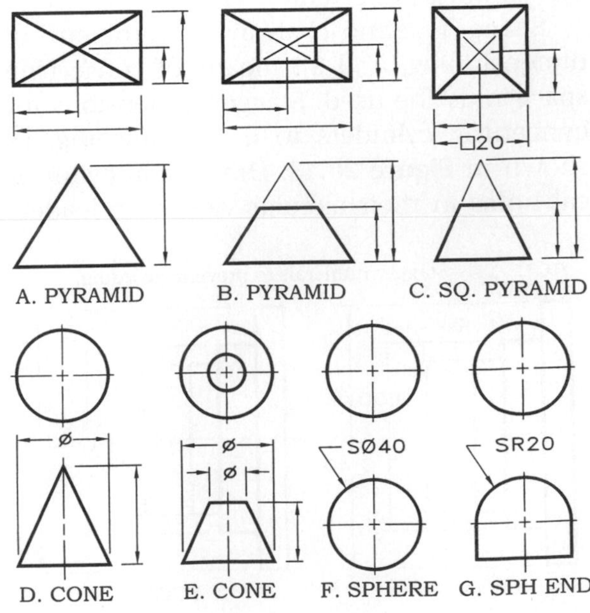

20.50 This drawing shows the proper way to dimension pyramids, cones, and spheres.

hemisphere (**Figure 20.50G**), use a spherical radius (SR). Only one view is needed to describe a sphere.

Leaders

Used to reference notes and dimensions to features, leaders most often are drawn at standard angles of triangles (**Figure 20.45**). Leaders should begin at either the first or last word of a note with a short horizontal line (elbow) from the note and extend to the feature being described as shown in **Figure 20.51**.

AutoCAD Method To produce a leader that begins with an arrow, type *Qleader* or *(Dimension> Leader)* (**Figure 20.52**). To ensure that the arrow touches the circle, use *Osnap* and *Nearest* to snap the point of the arrow to the circumference. The program will prompt you, *Specify next point* twice, allowing a leader with an angular bend prior to locating the horizontal elbow at the end of the leader. When prompted *Enter first line of annotation text,* type a note. Additional prompts will allow you to add more notes in a vertical "stack." The *Leader* command does not measure circles or lines; therefore you must type in the desired values because it applies the last number used.

If the previous option was *Dimdiameter,* the diameter symbol will precede the dimension. If the previous option was *Dimradius,* an *R,* the radius symbol, will precede the dimension.

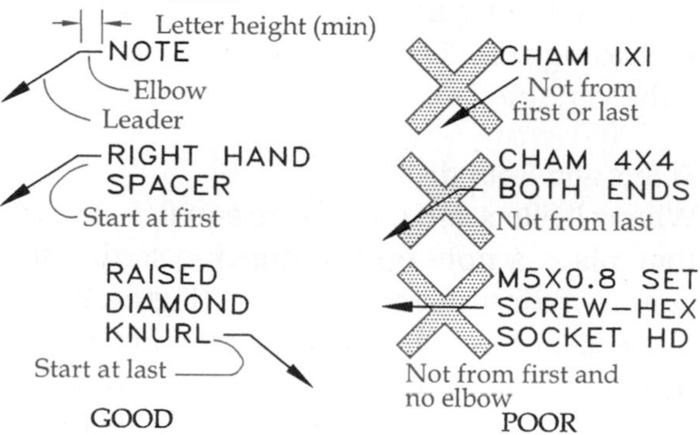

20.51 Extend leaders from the first or the last word of a note with a horizontal elbow.

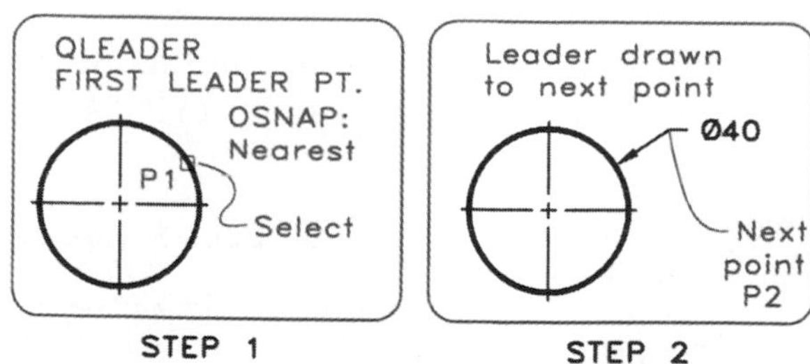

20.52 Leaders by AutoCAD.

Step 1 *Command:* Qleader (Enter)
Specify first leader point or [Settings]: P1
Step 2 *Select next point:* P2 (Enter)
Specify text width <0.00>: (Enter)
Enter first line of annotation text <Mtext>: %%C40 (Enter)
Enter next line of annotation text: (Enter)

Arcs and Radii

Full circles are dimensioned with diameters, but arcs are dimensioned with radii (**Figure 20.53**). Current standards specify that radii be dimensioned with an R preceding the dimension (for example, R10). The previous standard was for R to follow the dimension (10R, for example). Thus both methods are seen on drawings.

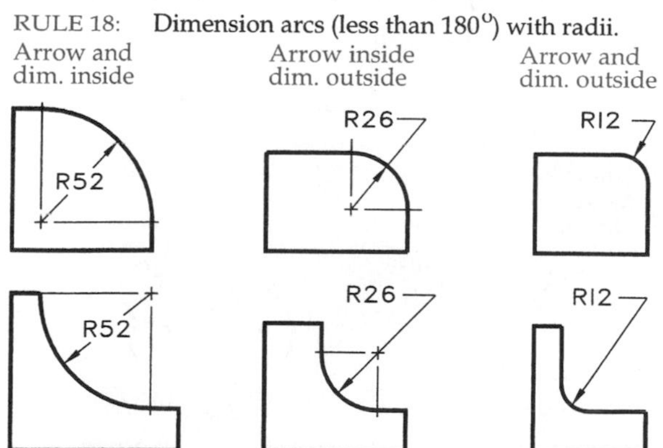

20.53 When space permits, place dimensions and arrows between the center and the arc. When the number will not fit, place it outside and the arrow inside. If the arrow will not fit inside, place both the dimension and arrow outside the arc with a leader.

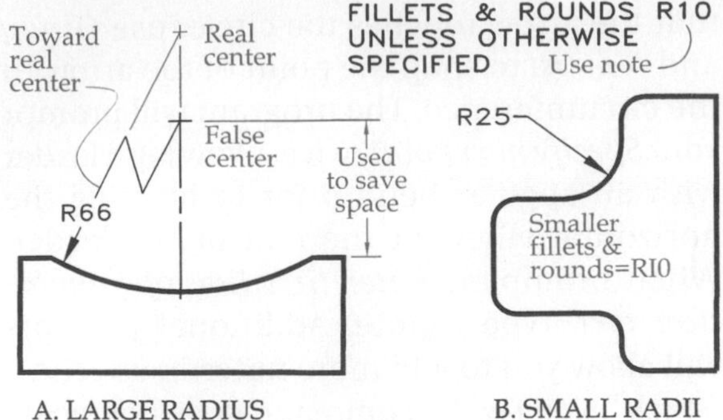

20.54 Dimensioning radii.

A Show a long radius with a false radius (a line with a zigzag) to indicate that it is not true length. Show its false center on the centerline of the true center.

B Specify fillets and rounds with a note to reduce repetitive dimensions of small arcs.

You may dimension large arcs with a false radius (**Figure 20.54**) by drawing a zigzag to indicate that the line is not the true radius. Where space is not available for radii, dimension small arcs with leaders.

AutoCAD Method Type *Dimradius* and select a point on the arc as the starting point to dimension an arc (**Figure 20.55**). If space permits, the dimension will appear between the center and the arrow. For smaller arcs, the arrows will appear inside and the dimensions outside the arc.

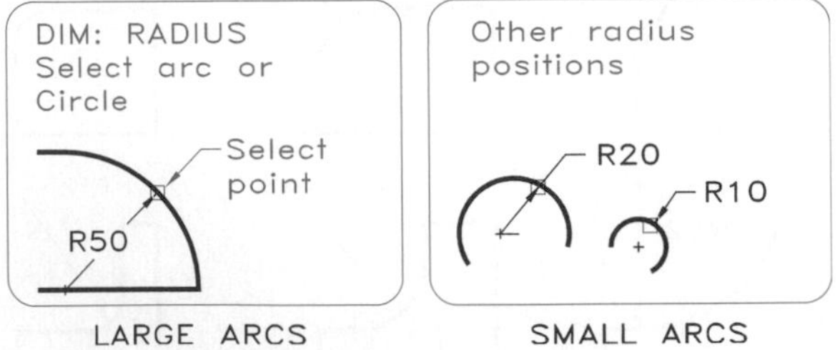

20.55 Type Dimradius to select a point on the arc. The program generates the dimension with its arrow at this point and precedes the dimension with an R. The program dimensions smaller arcs by positioning the dimension outside the arc or, because of even more limited space, by placing both the arrows and dimension outside the arc.

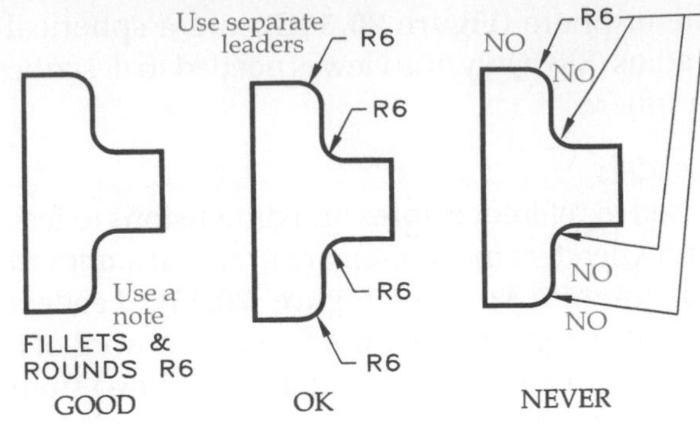

20.56 Indicate fillets and rounds by (A) notes or (B) separate leaders and dimensions. Never use confusing leaders (C).

When space is not available for arrows inside, both the arrow and dimension will appear outside the arc. Decimal values are preceded with a zero unless you override them by typing in *R* and the value without a preceding zero. Leading zeros will be omitted if the variable *Dimzin* = 4.

Fillets and Rounds

When all fillets and rounds are equal in size, you may place a note on the drawing stating that condition or use separate notes (**Figure 20.56**). If most, but not all, of the fillets and rounds have equal radii, the note may read ALL FILLETS AND ROUNDS R6 UNLESS OTHERWISE SPECIFIED (or abbreviated as F&R R6), with the fillets and rounds of different radii dimensioned separately.

You may note repetitive features as shown in **Figure 20.57** by using the notes TYPICAL, or

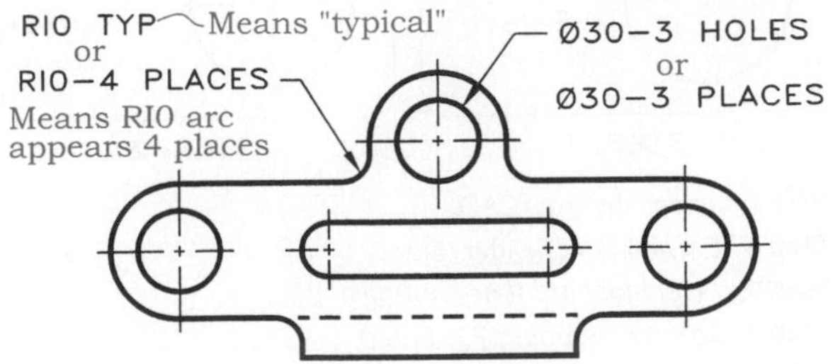

20.57 Use notes to indicate that identical features and dimensions are repeated to simplify dimensioning.

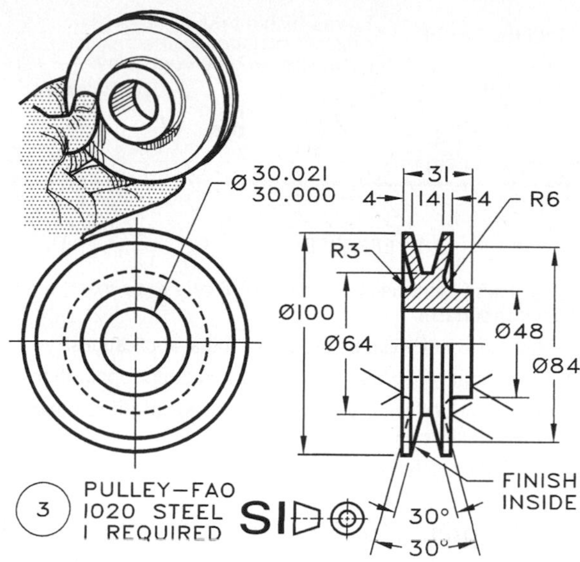

20.58 This dimensioned pulley illustrates the application of many of the rules covered in this section.

TYP, which means that the dimensioned feature is typical of those not dimensioned. You may use the note PLACES, or PL, to specify the number of places that identical features appear, although only one is dimensioned.

Figure 20.58 shows a pulley that is drawn and dimensioned. The drawing demonstrates proper application of many of the rules discussed in this section.

20.10 Curved and Symmetrical Parts

Curved Parts

You may dimension an irregular shape composed of tangent arcs of varying sizes by using a series of radii (**Figure 20.59**). Irregular curves may be dimensioned by using coordinates to locate a series of points along the curve (**Figure 20.60**). You must use your judgment in determining how many located points are necessary to define the curve. Placing extension lines at an angle provides additional space for showing dimensions.

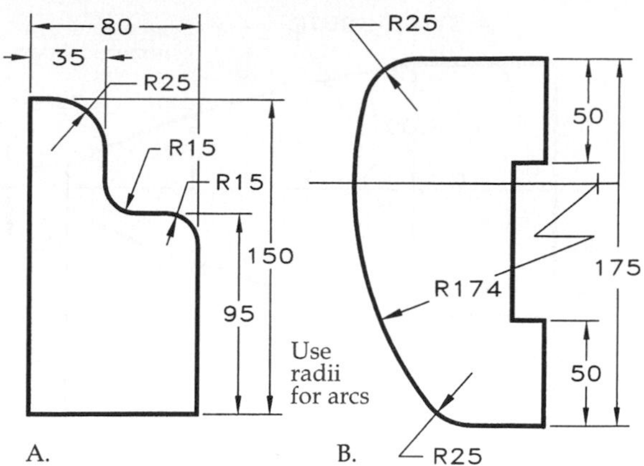

20.59 Use radii to dimension parts composed of arcs and partial circles.

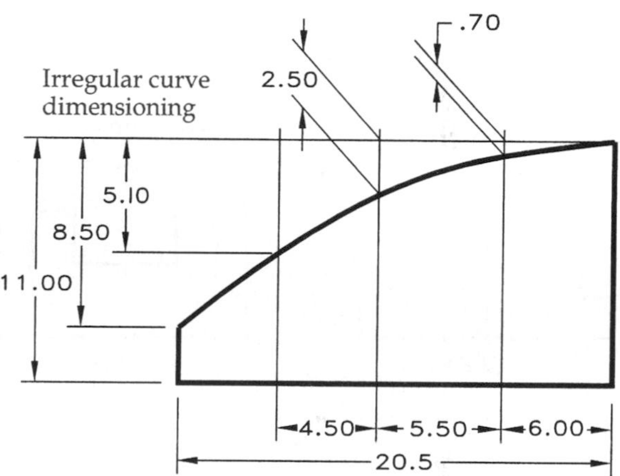

20.60 Use coordinates to dimension points along an irregular curve on a part.

Symmetrical Parts

Dimension an irregular symmetrical curve with coordinates (**Figure 20.61**). Note the use of dimension lines as extension lines, a permissible violation of dimensioning rules in this case.

Dimension symmetrical objects by using coordinates to imply that the dimensions are symmetrical about the centerline (abbreviated CL) as shown in **Figure 20.62A**. **Figure 20.62B** shows a better method of dimensioning this type of object, where symmetry is dimensioned with no interpretation required on the part of the reader.

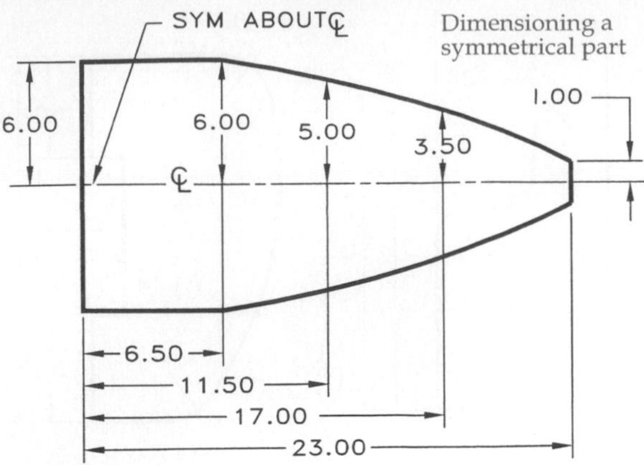

20.61 Use coordinates to dimension points along curves of a symmetrical part.

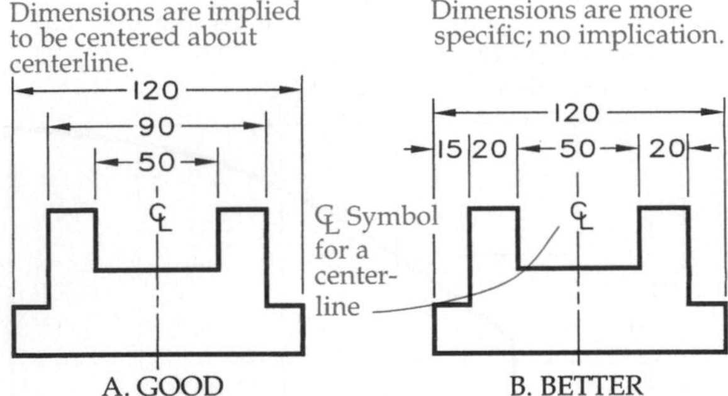

20.62 Symmetrical parts.

A You may dimension symmetrical parts implicitly about their centerlines.

B The better way to dimension symmetrical parts is explicitly about their centerlines.

20.11 Finished Surfaces

Parts formed in molds, called **castings**, have rough exterior surfaces. If these parts are to assemble with and move against other parts, they will not function well unless their contact surfaces are machined to a smooth finish by grinding, shaping, lapping, or a similar process.

To indicate that a surface is to be finished, finish marks are drawn on edge views of surfaces to be finished (**Figure 20.63**). Finish marks should be shown in every view where finished surfaces appear as edges even if they are hidden lines.

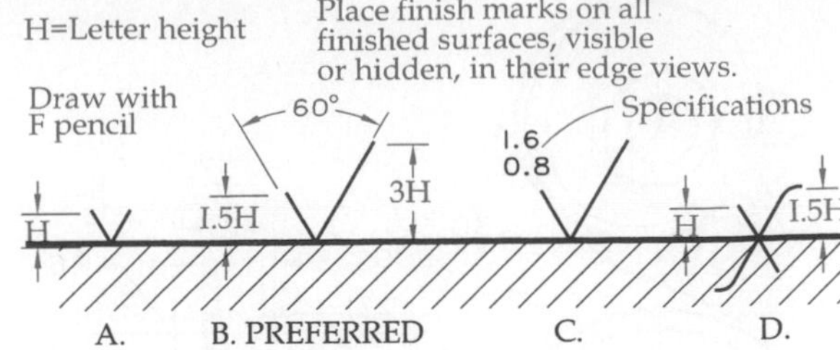

20.63 Finish marks indicate that a surface is to be machined to a smooth surface.

A The traditional V can be used for general applications.

B The unequal finish mark is the best for general applications.

C Where surface texture must be specified, this finish mark is used with texture values.

D The f-mark is the oldest and least used symbol.

The preferred finish mark for the general cases is the uneven mark shown in **Figure 20.63B**. When an object is finished on all surfaces, the note FINISHED ALL OVER (abbreviated FAO) is placed on the drawing.

20.12 Location Dimensions

Location dimensions give the positions, not the sizes, of geometric shapes (**Figure 20.64**). Locate rectangular shapes by using coordinates of their corners, and cylindrical shapes by using coordinates of their centerlines. In each case, dimension the view that shows both measurements. Always extend coordinates from any finished surfaces (even if a

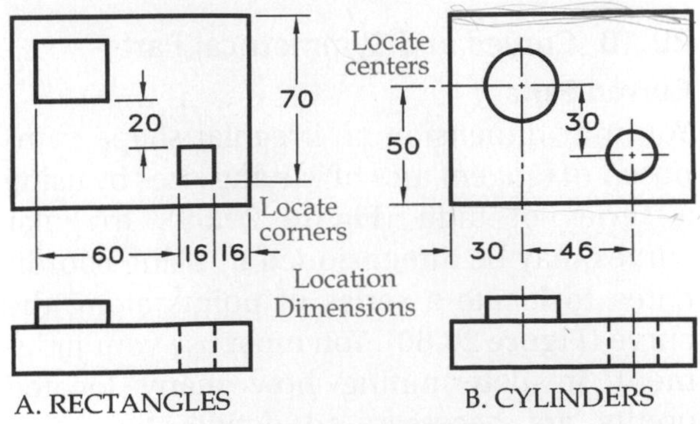

20.64 Location dimensions give the positions of geometric features with respect to other geometric features, but not their sizes.

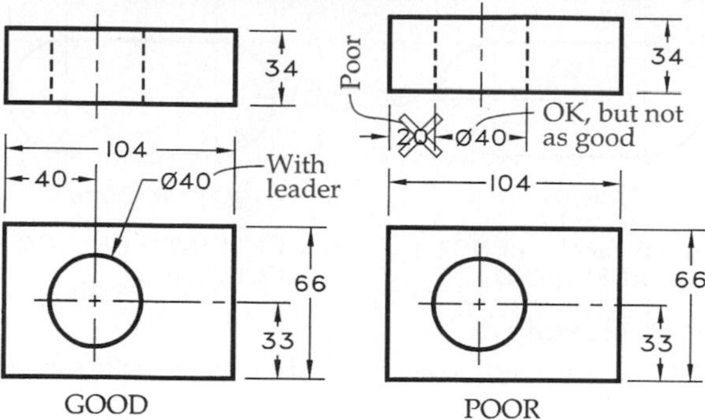

20.65 Locate cylindrical holes in their circular views by coordinates to their centers.

finished surface is a hidden line) because smooth machined surfaces allow the most accurate measurements. Locate and dimension single holes as shown in **Figure 20.65** and multiple holes as shown in **Figure 20.66**. **Figure 20.67** shows the application of location dimensions to a typical part with size dimensions omitted.

Baseline dimensions extend from two baselines in a single view (**Figure 20.68**). The use of baselines eliminates the possible accu-

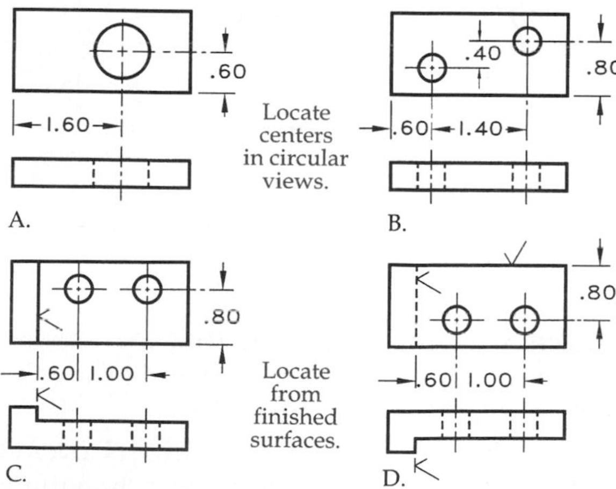

20.66 Rules in summary.

A Locate cylindrical holes in their circular views from two surfaces of the object.

B Locate multiple holes from center to center.

C Locate holes from finished surfaces, even if the finished surfaces are hidden, as in (D).

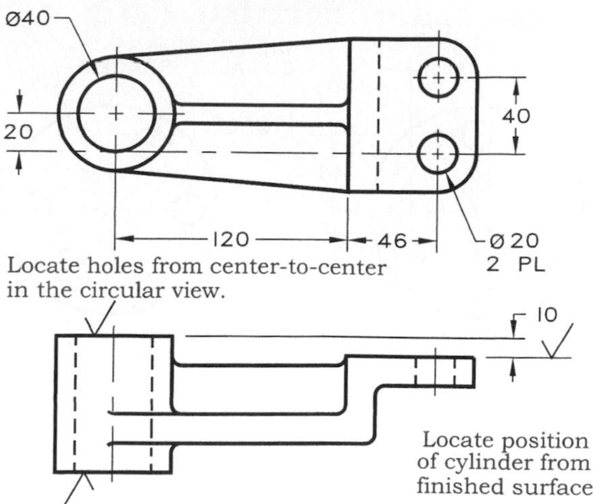

20.67 This example of a dimensioned shaft arm shows the application of location dimensions, with sizes omitted.

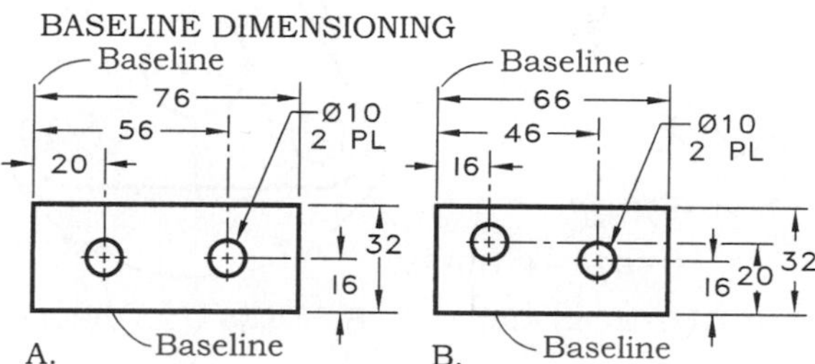

20.68 Measuring holes from two datum planes is the most accurate way to locate them and reduces the accumulation of errors possible in chain dimensioning.

mulation of errors in size that can occur from chain dimensioning.

Holes through circular plates can be located by using coordinates or a note as shown in **Figure 20.69**. Dimension the diameter of the imaginary circle passing through the centers of the holes in the circular view as a reference dimension and locate the holes by using coordinates (**Figure 20.69A**) or a note (**Figure 20.69B**). This imaginary circle is called the **bolt circle** or **circle of centers**.

You may also locate holes with radial dimensions and their angular positions in degrees (**Figure 20.70**). Holes may be located on their

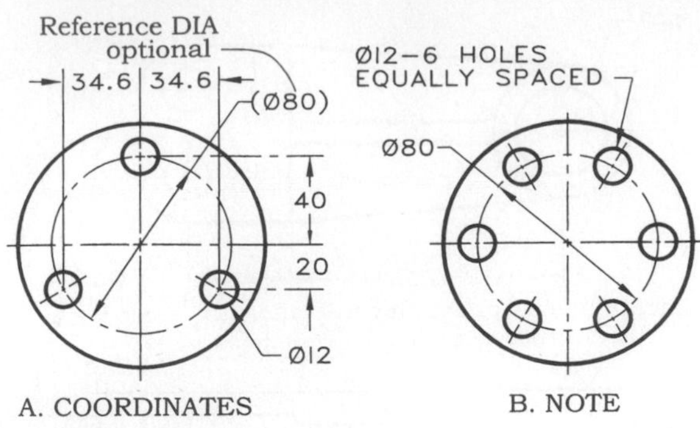

20.69 Locate holes on a bolt circle by using (A) coordinates or (B) notes.

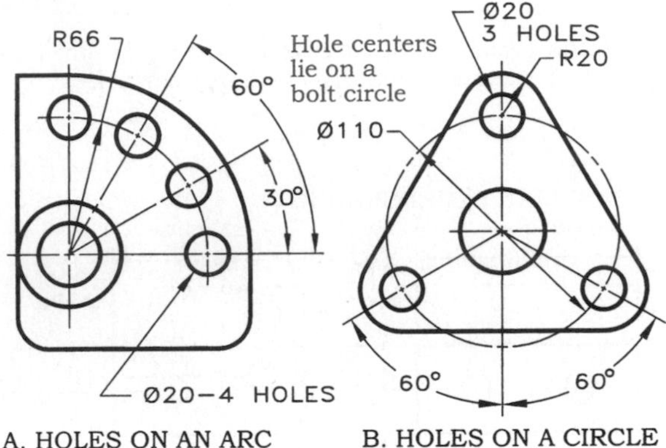

20.70 Locate centers of holes by using (A) a combination of radii and degrees or (B) a circle of centers.

bolt circle even if the shape of the object is not circular.

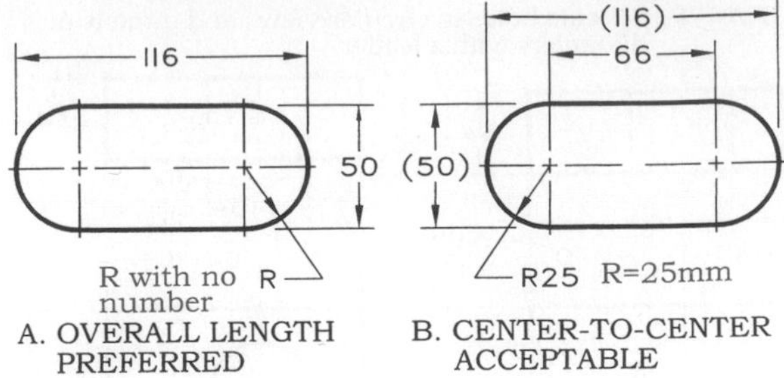

20.71 Rounded ends.

A Dimension objects having rounded ends from end to end and give the height.

B A less desirable choice is to dimension the rounded ends from center to center and give the radius.

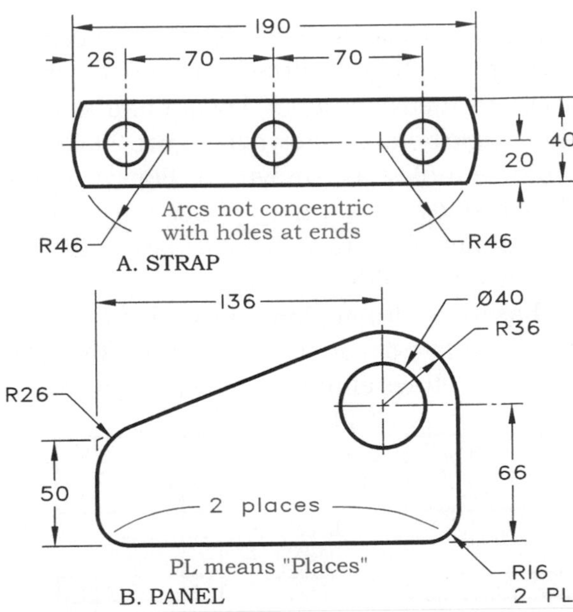

20.72 These drawings show how to dimension parts having (A) rounded ends that are not concentric with the holes and (B) rounds and cylinders.

Objects with Rounded Ends

Dimension objects with rounded ends from one rounded end to the other (**Figure 20.71A**) and show their radii as R without dimensions to specify that the ends are arcs. Obviously, the end radius is half the height of the part. If you dimension the object from center to center (**Figure 20.71B**), you must give the radius size. You may specify the overall width as a reference dimension (116) to eliminate the need for calculations.

Dimension parts with partially rounded ends as shown in **Figure 20.72A**. Dimension objects with rounded ends that are smaller than a semicircle with a radius and locate the arc's center (**Figure 20.72B**).

Dimension a single slot with its overall width and height (**Figure 20.73A**). When there are two or more slots, dimension one slot and use a note to indicate that there are other identical slots (**Figure 20.73B**).

The tool table holder shown in **Figure 20.74** illustrates dimensioning of arcs and slots. To

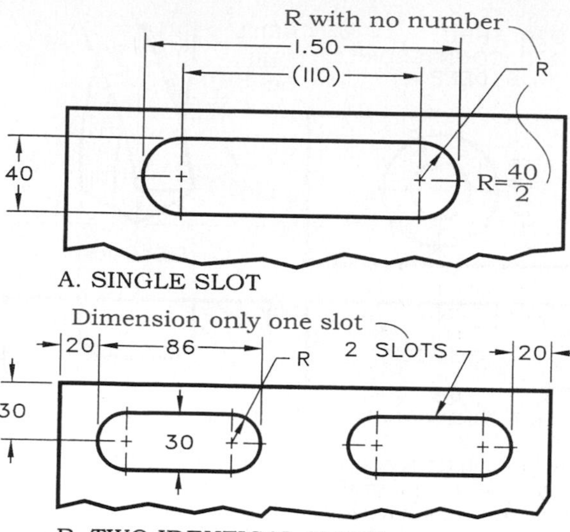

20.73 These drawings illustrate methods of dimensioning parts that have (A) one slot and (B) more than one slot.

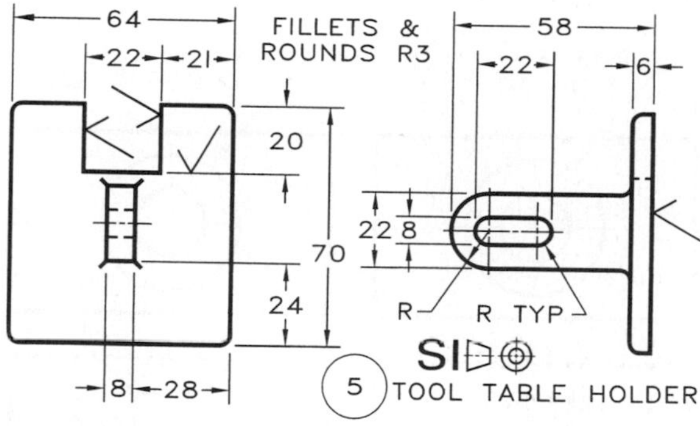

20.74 This dimensioned part has both slots and arcs.

prevent dimension lines from crossing, several dimensions are placed on a less descriptive view. Notice that the diameters of the semicircular features are given; therefore, notes of R are given to indicate radii, but the radius sizes are unnecessary, since radii are half the diameters.

20.13 Outline Dimensioning

Now that you are familiar with most of the rules of dimensioning, you can better understand outline dimensioning, which is a way of applying dimensions to a part's outline (silhouette).

20.75 Outline dimensioning is the placement of dimensions on views as if they had no internal lines. Practice in applying this concept will help you place dimensions on their most descriptive views.

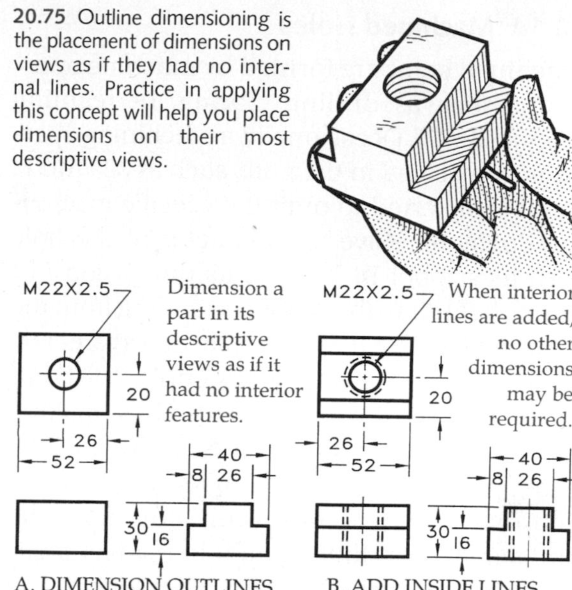

By taking this approach, you have little choice but to place dimensions in the most descriptive views of the part. For example, imagine that the T-block shown in **Figure 20.75** has no lines inside its outlines. It is dimensioned beginning with its location dimensions. When the inside lines are considered, additional dimensions are seldom needed.

Figure 20.76 shows an example of outline dimensioning. Note the extension of all dimensions from the outlines of well-defined features.

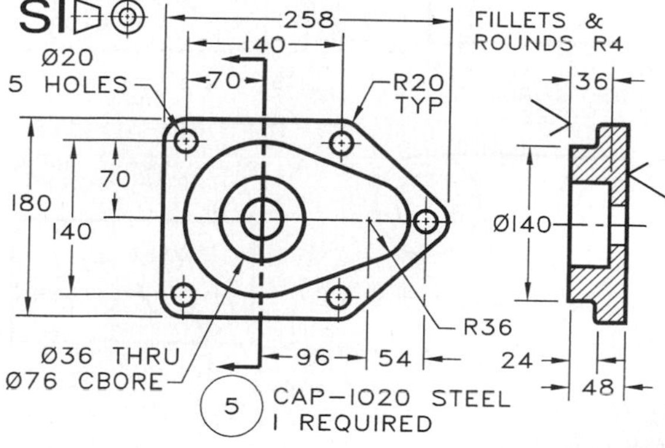

20.76 This drawing illustrates use of the outline method to dimension the cap in its most descriptive views.

20.14 Machined Holes

Machined holes are formed by machine operations such as drilling, boring, or reaming (**Figure 20.77**). Occasionally, a machining operation is specified in the note, such as 32 DRILL, but it is preferred to omit the specific machining operation. Give the diameter of the hole with its symbol in front of its dimension (for example, Ø32) with a leader extending from the circular view. You may also note hole diameters with DIA after their size (for example, 2.00 DIA).

Drilling is the basic method of making holes. Dimension the size of a drilled hole with a leader extending from its circular view. You may give its depth in the note from the circular view or dimension it in the rectangular view (**Figure 20.77B**). Dimension the depth of a drilled hole to the usable part of the hole, not to the conical point.

Counterdrilling involves drilling a large hole inside a smaller hole to enlarge it (**Figure 20.78**). The drill point leaves a 120° conical shoulder as a by-product of counterdrilling.

Countersinking is the process of forming conical holes for receiving screw heads (**Figure 20.79**). Give the diameter of a countersunk hole (the maximum diameter on the surface) and the angle of the countersink in a

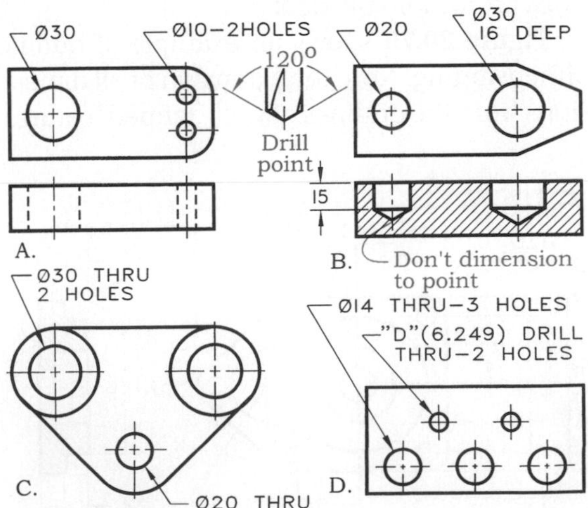

20.77 Cylindrical holes.

A–B Dimension cylindrical holes by either of these methods.

C–D When you use only one view, you have to note the THRU holes or specify their depths.

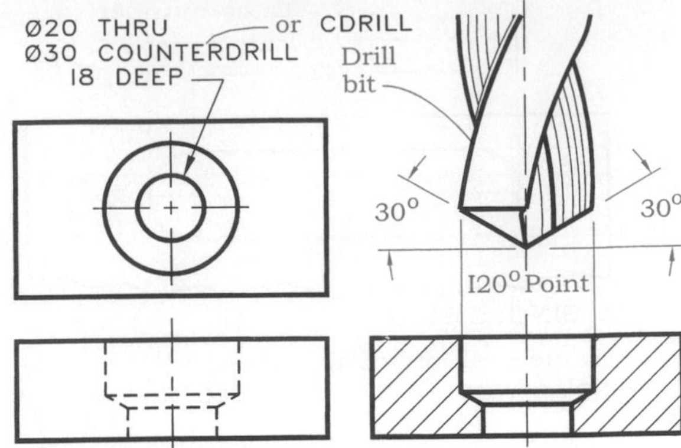

20.78 Counterdrilling notes give the specifications for drilling a larger hole inside a smaller hole. Do not dimension the 120° angle because it is a by-product of the drill point. Noting the counterdrill with a leader from the circular view is preferable.

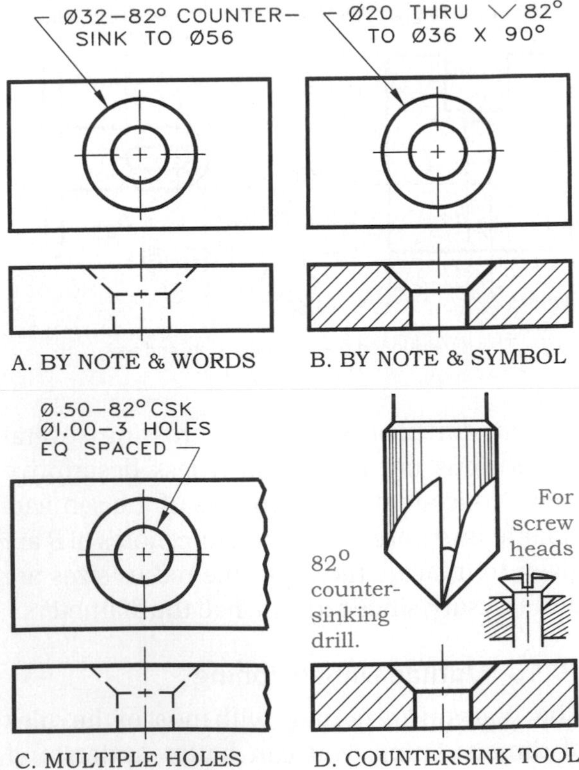

20.79 These illustrations show methods of noting and specifying countersunk holes for receiving screw heads.

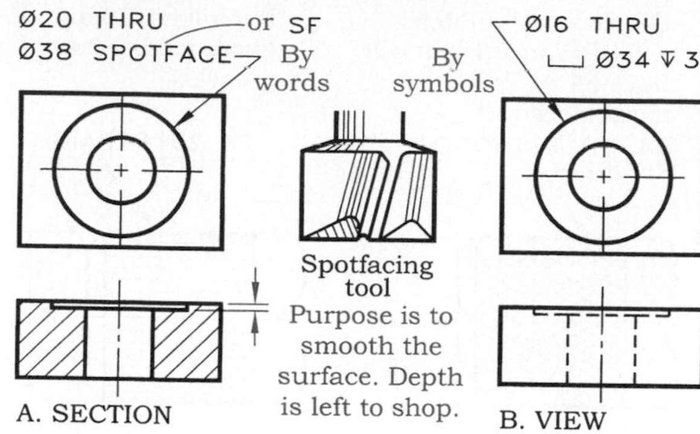

20.80 This spotfacing tool is used to finish the cylindrical boss to provide a smooth seat for a bolt head. Spotfacing is the process of smoothing the surface where it will contact a washer, nut, or bolt and is noted as shown.

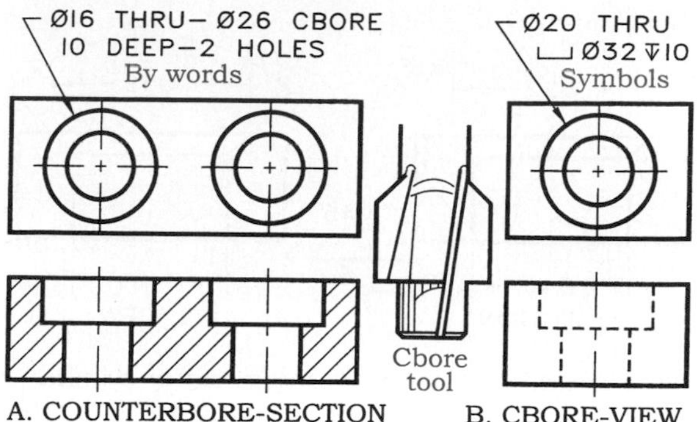

20.82 Counterbored holes are similar to counterdrilled holes but have flat bottoms instead of tapered sides. Dimension them as shown.

note. Countersunk holes also are used as guides in shafts, spindles, and other cylindrical parts held between the centers of a lathe.

Spotfacing is the process of finishing the surface around holes to provide bearing surfaces for washers or bolt heads (**Figure 20.80A**). **Figure 20.80B** shows a view of a spotfaced hole that is noted with symbols.

Boring is used to make large holes and it is usually done on a lathe with a bore or a boring bar (**Figure 20.81**).

Counterboring is the process of enlarging the diameter of a drilled hole (**Figure 20.82**) to give a flat hole bottom without the tapers as in counterdrilled holes.

Reaming is the operation of finishing or slightly enlarging drilled or bored holes within their prescribed tolerances. A ream is similar to a drill bit.

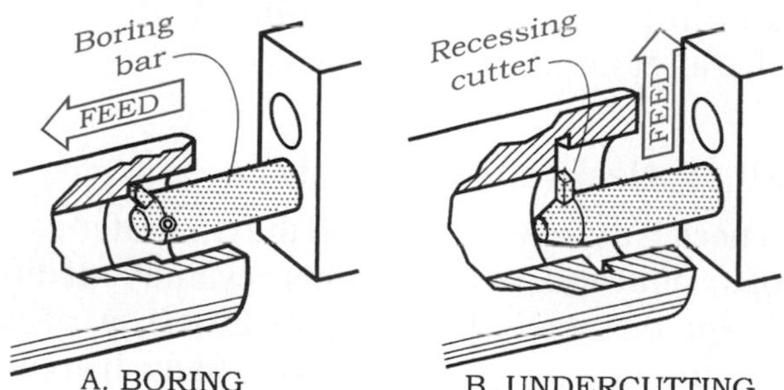

20.81 This photo shows the use of a lathe to bore a large hole or to make an undercut with a boring bar.

20.15 Chamfers

Chamfers are beveled edges cut on cylindrical parts, such as shafts and threaded fasteners, to eliminate sharp edges and to make them easier to assemble. When the chamfer angle is 45°, use a note in either of the forms shown in **Figure 20.83A**. Dimension chamfers of other angles as shown in **Figure 20.83B**. When inside openings of holes are chamfered, dimension them as shown in **Figure 20.84**.

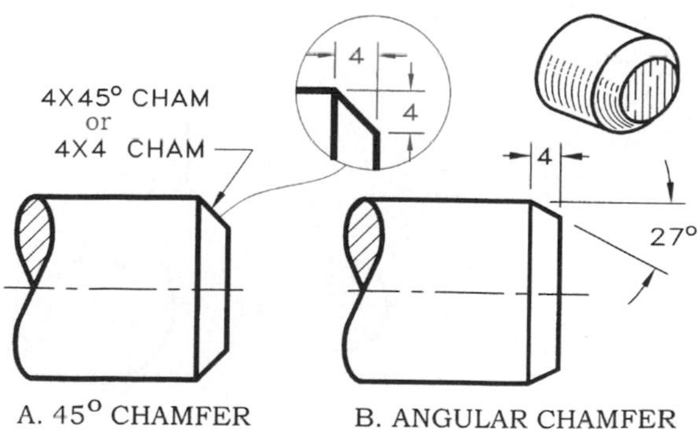

20.83 Chamfers.

A Dimension 45° chamfers by one of the methods shown.

B Dimension chamfers of all other angles as shown.

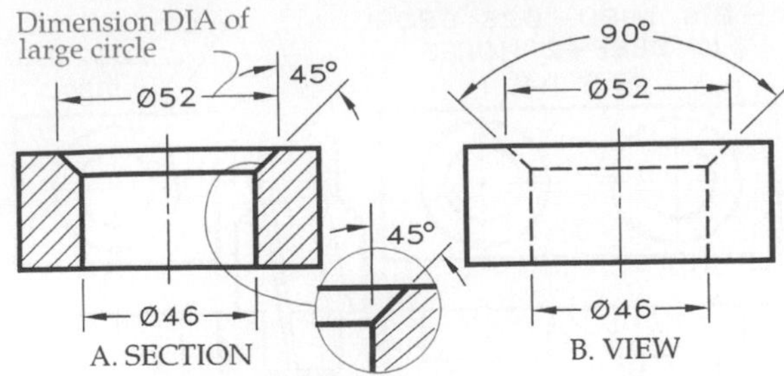

20.84 Dimension chamfers on the insides of cylinders as shown.

20.16 Keyseats

A keyseat is a slot cut into a shaft for aligning and holding a pulley or a collar on a shaft. **Figure 20.85** shows how to dimension keyways and keyseats with dimensions taken from the tables in **Appendixes 24** and **25**. The double dimensions on the diameter are tolerances (discussed in Chapter 21).

20.17 Knurling

Knurling is the operation of cutting diamond-shaped or parallel patterns on cylindrical surfaces for gripping, decoration, or press fits between mating parts that are permanently assembled. Draw and dimension diamond knurls and straight knurls as shown in **Figure 20.86**, with notes that specify type, pitch, and diameter.

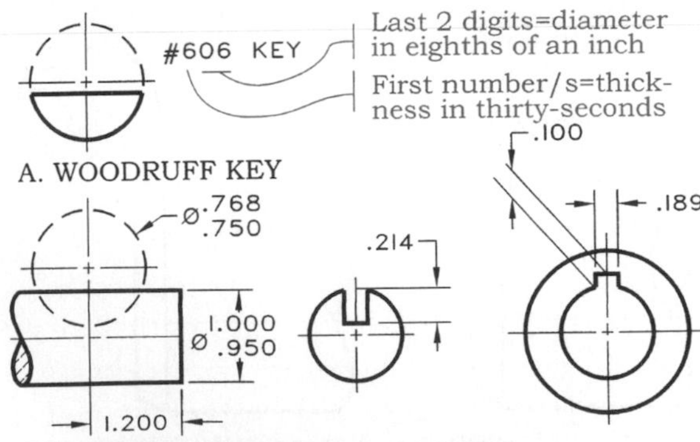

20.85 These drawings show methods of dimensioning (A) Woodruff keys and (B) keyways used to hold a part on a shaft. Appendix 24 gives their tables of sizes.

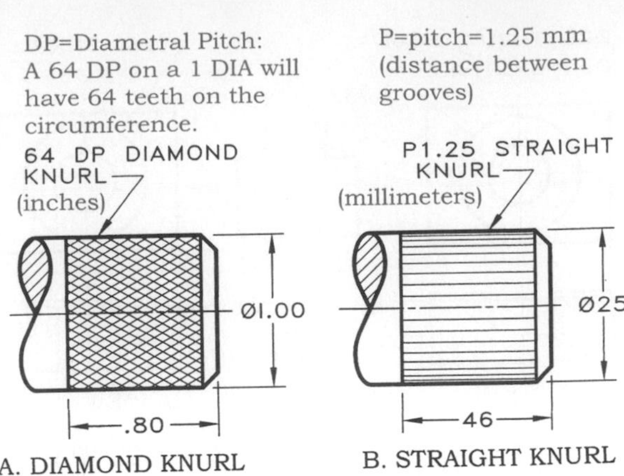

20.86 The diamond knurl has a diametral pitch, DP, of 96 and the straight knurl has a linear pitch, P, of 0.8 mm. Pitch is the distance between the grooves on the circumference.

The abbreviation DP means diametral pitch, or the ratio of the number of grooves on the circumference (N) to the diameter (D) expressed as DP = N/D. The preferred diametral pitches for knurling are 64 DP, 96 DP, 128 DP, and 160 DP.

For diameters of 1 in., knurling of 64 DP, 96 DP, 128 DP, and 160 DP will have 64, 96, 128, and 160 teeth, respectively, on the circumference. The note P0.8 means that the knurling grooves are 0.8 mm apart. Make knurling calculations in inches and then convert them to millimeters. Specify knurls for press fits with the diameter size before knurling and with the minimum diameter size after knurling.

20.18 Necks and Undercuts

A **neck** is a groove cut around the circumference of a cylindrical part. If cut where cylinders of different diameters join (**Figure 20.87**), a neck ensures that the assembled parts fit flush at the shoulder of the larger cylinder and allows trash that would cause binding to drop out of the way.

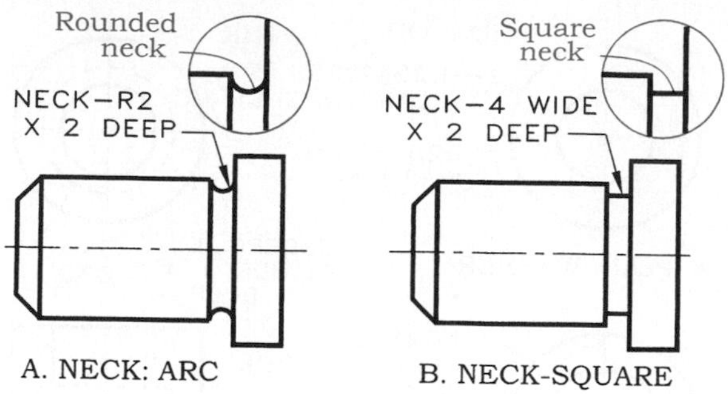

20.87 Necks are recesses cut in cylinders, with rounded or square bottoms, usually at the intersections of concentric cylinders. Dimension necks as shown.

An **undercut** is a recessed neck inside a cylindrical hole (**Figure 20.88A**). A **thread relief** is a neck that has been cut at the end of a thread to ensure that the head of the threaded part will fit flush against the part it screws into (**Figure 20.88B**).

20.19 Tapers

Tapers for both flat planes and conical surfaces may be specified with either notes or symbols. Flat taper is the ratio of the difference in the heights at each end of a surface to its length (**Figures 20.89A** and **B**). Tapers on

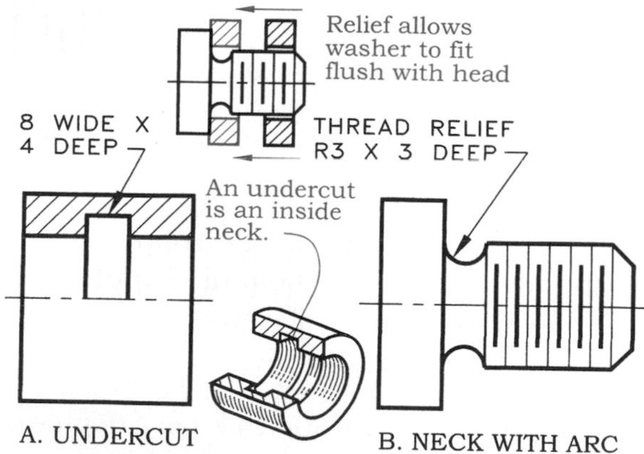

20.88 Undercuts and necks.

A An undercut is a groove cut inside a cylinder.

B A thread relief is a groove cut at the end of a thread to improve the screw's assembly. Dimension both types of necks as shown.

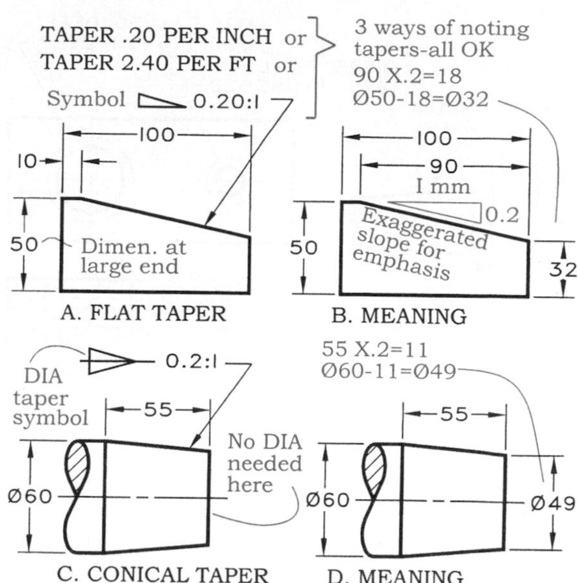

20.89 Tapers may be specified for either flat or conical surfaces: dimensioning and interpretation for (A and B) a flat taper and (C and D) for a conical taper.

flat surfaces may be expressed as inches per inch (.20 per inch), inches per foot (2.40 per foot), or millimeters per millimeter (0.20:1).

Conical taper is the ratio of the difference in the diameters at each end of a cone to its length (**Figures 20.89C** and **D**). Tapers on conical surfaces may be expressed as inches per inch (.25 per inch), inches per foot (3.00 per foot), or millimeters per millimeter (0.25:1).

20.20 Miscellaneous Notes

Notes on detail drawings provide information and specifications that would be difficult to represent by drawings alone (**Figures 20.90–20.92**). Place notes horizontally on the sheet whenever possible, because they are easier to letter and read in that position. Several notes in sequence on the same line should be separated with short dashes between them (for example, 15 DIA-30 DIA SPOTFACE). Use standard abbreviations (Appendix 1) in notes to save space and time.

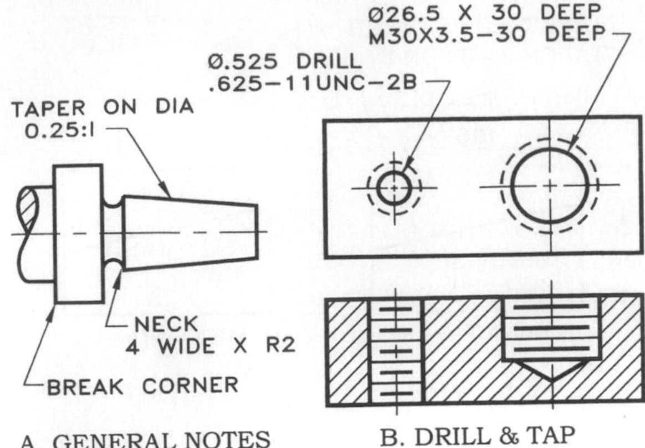

20.90 Miscellaneous dimensioning.

A The notes for this part indicate a neck, a taper, and a break corner (a slight round to remove sharpness).

B Threaded holes are sometimes dimensioned by giving the tap drill size in addition to the thread specifications, but selection of the tap drill size usually is left to the shop.

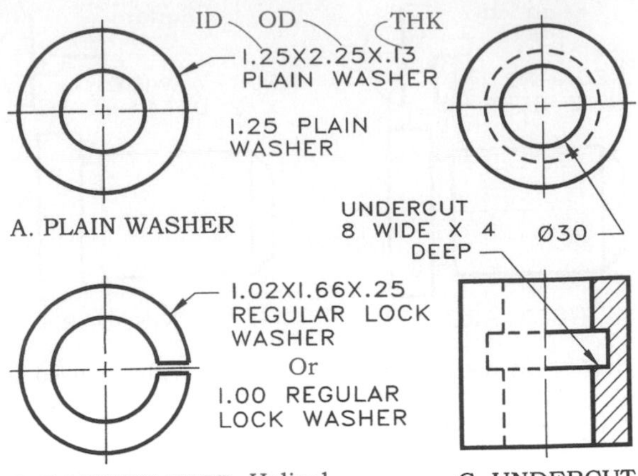

20.92 Washers and undercuts.

A and **B** Dimension washers and lock washers as shown by taking sizes from the tables in the appendix.

C Dimension an undercut with a note.

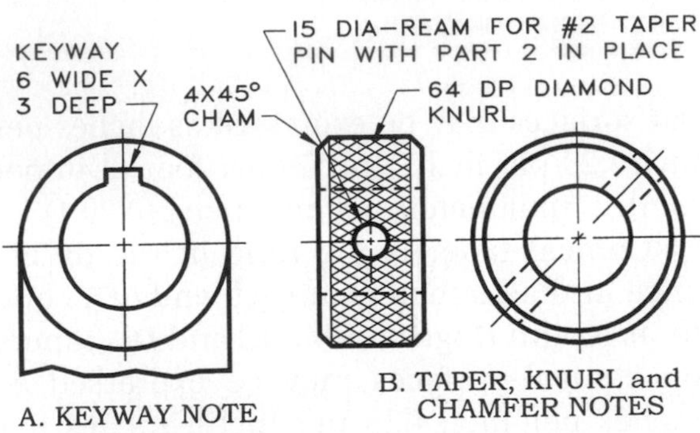

20.91 Miscellaneous dimensioning.

A This note is for dimensioning a keyway.

B The notes for this collar call for knurling, chamfering, and drilling for a #2 taper pin.

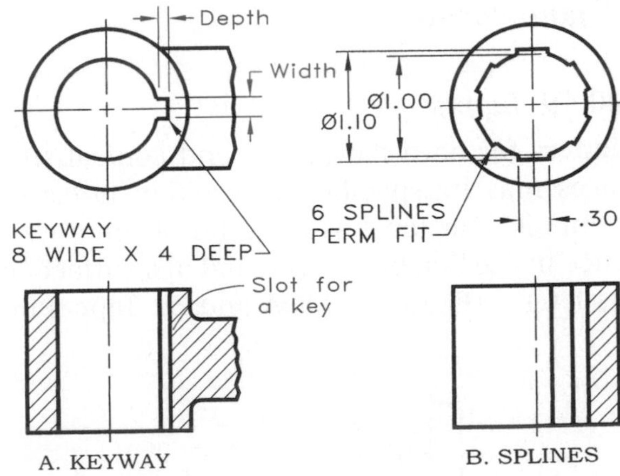

20.93 These drawings illustrate how to dimension (A) keyways and (B) splines.

Problems

1–48. (Figures 20.94 and 20.95) Solve these problems on size A paper, one per sheet, if you draw them full size. If you draw them double size, use size B paper. The views are drawn on a .20-in. (5-mm) grid. You will need to vary the spacing between views to provide adequate room for the dimensions. Sketching the views and dimensions to determine the required spacing before laying out the solutions with instruments would be helpful. Supply lines that may be missing in all views.

Layout Problems

Layout problems 1 through 4 have a degree of decision making involved in sketching a preliminary layout, selecting the scale, laying out the orthographic views with instruments, and applying dimensions. Layouts can be made on either size A or size B sheets.

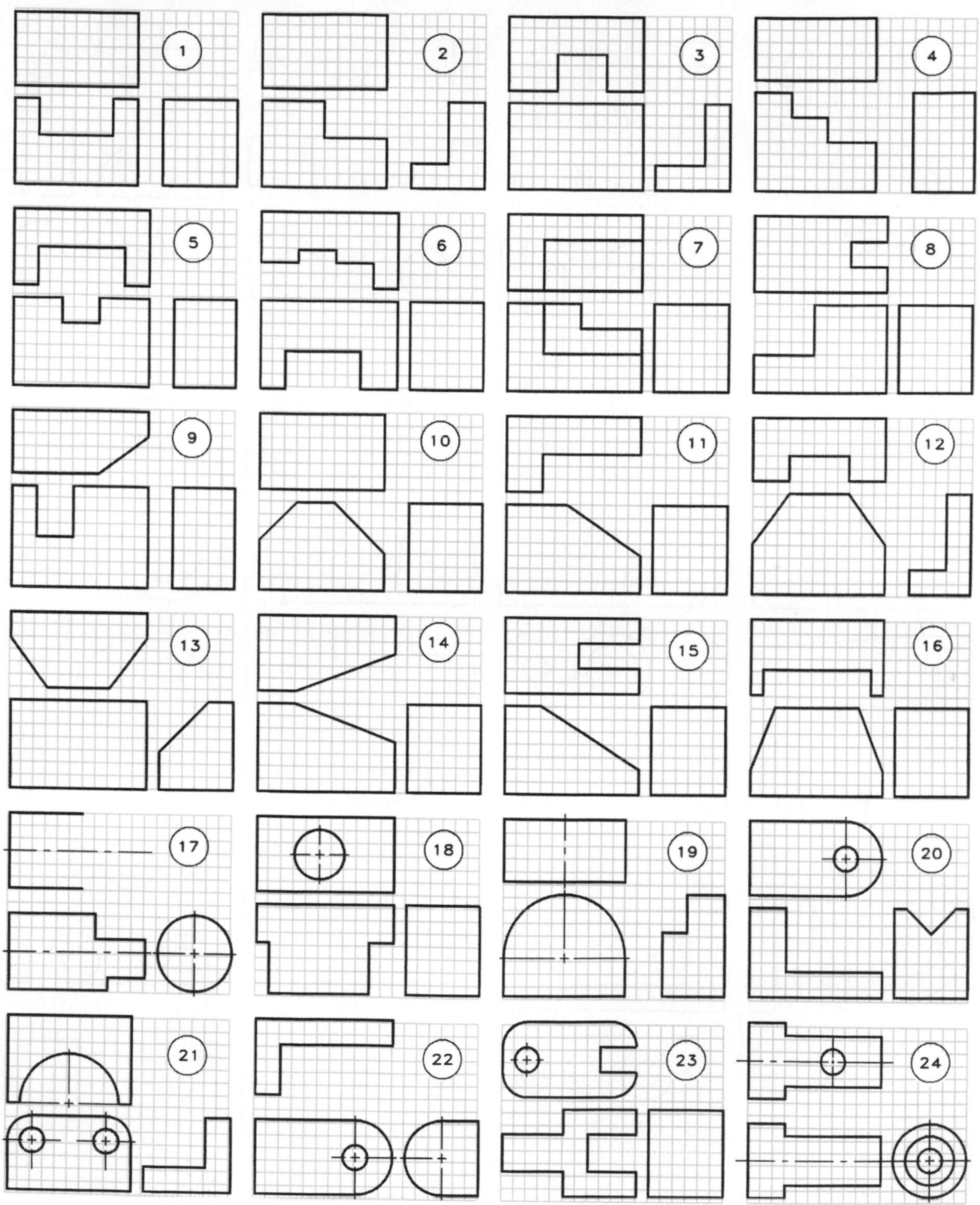

20.94 Problems 1–24.

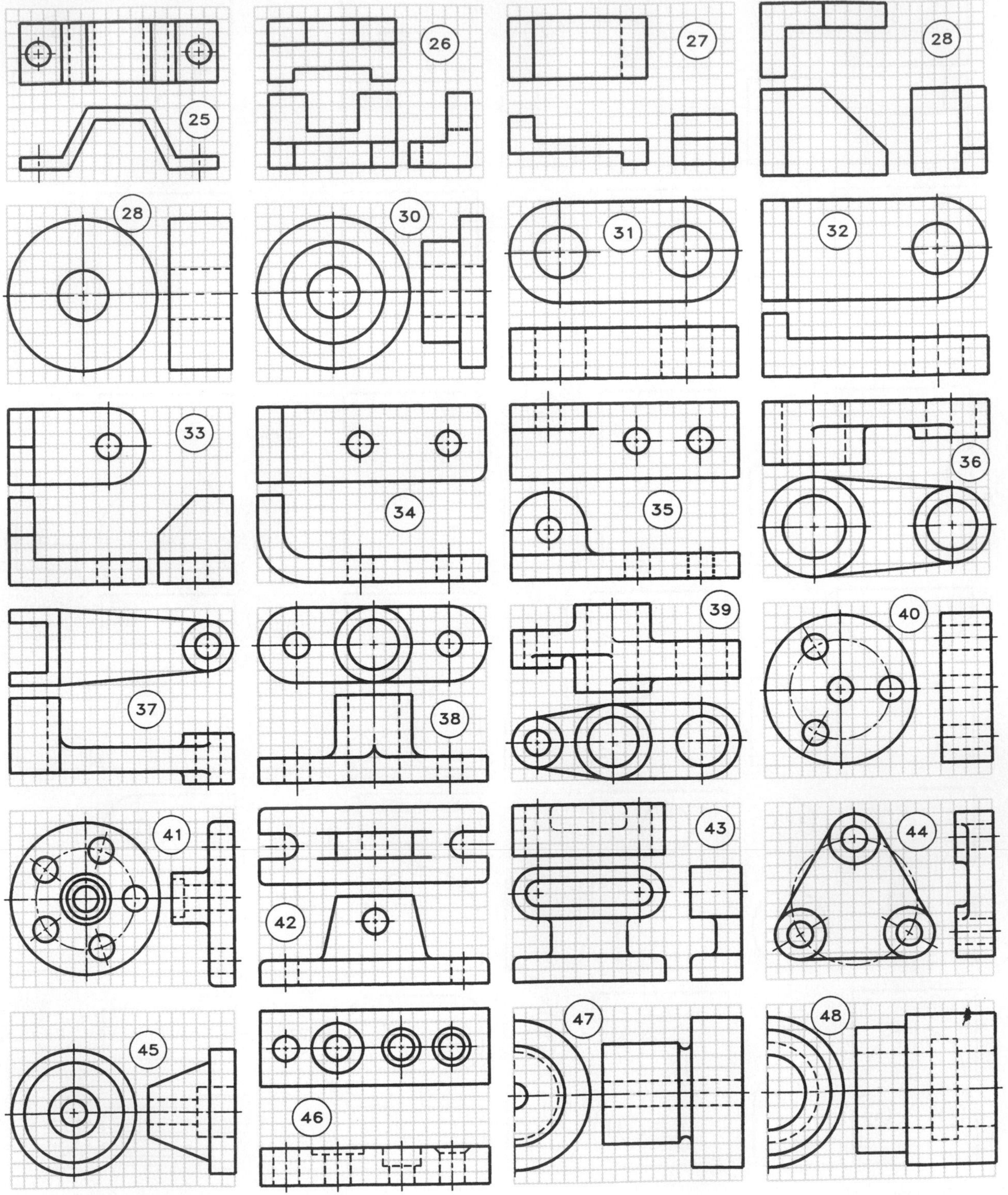

20.95 Problems 25–48.

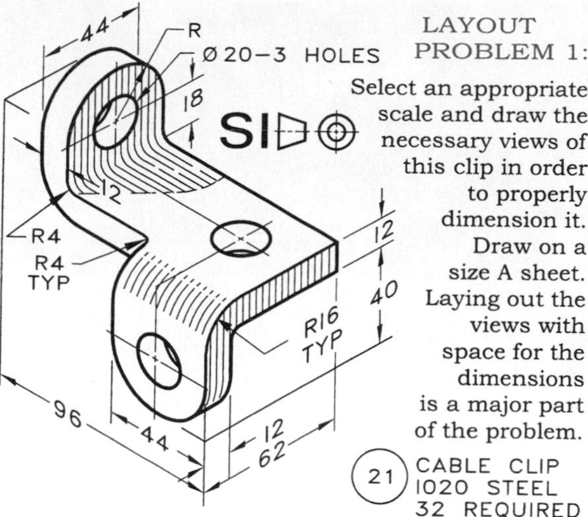

LAYOUT PROBLEM 1: Select an appropriate scale and draw the necessary views of this clip in order to properly dimension it. Draw on a size A sheet. Laying out the views with space for the dimensions is a major part of the problem.

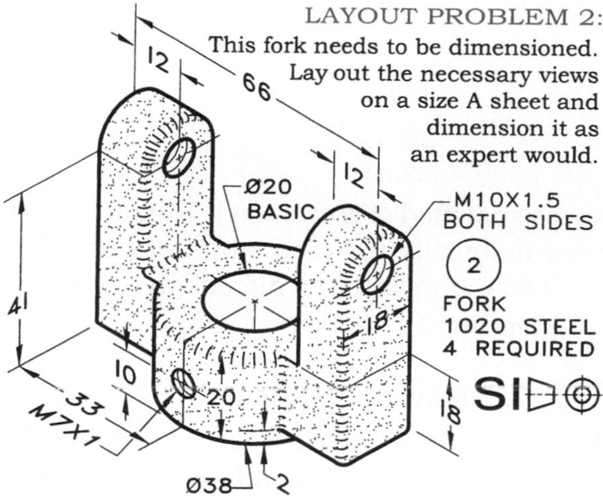

LAYOUT PROBLEM 2: This fork needs to be dimensioned. Lay out the necessary views on a size A sheet and dimension it as an expert would.

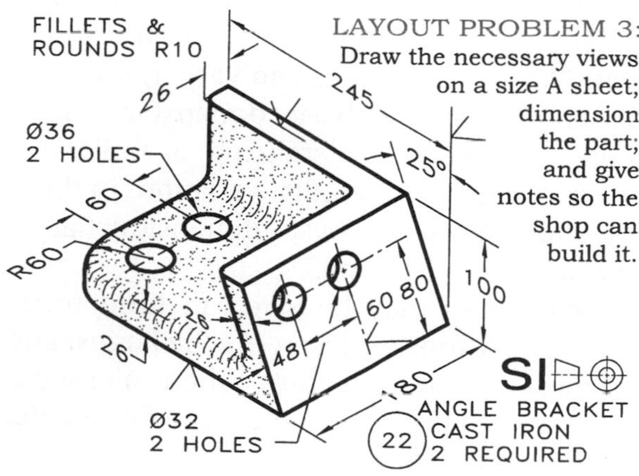

LAYOUT PROBLEM 3: Draw the necessary views on a size A sheet; dimension the part; and give notes so the shop can build it.

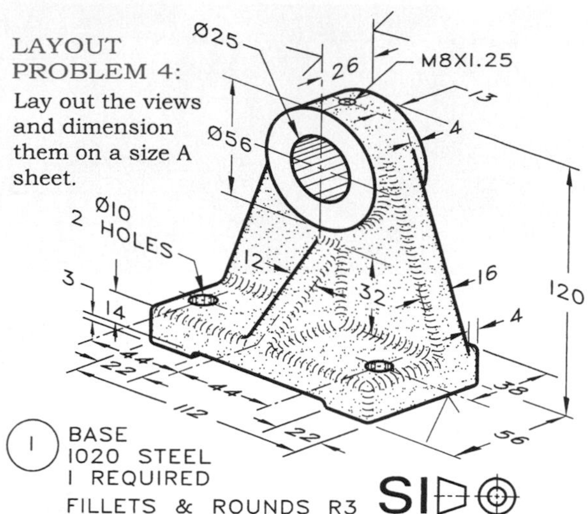

LAYOUT PROBLEM 4: Lay out the views and dimension them on a size A sheet.

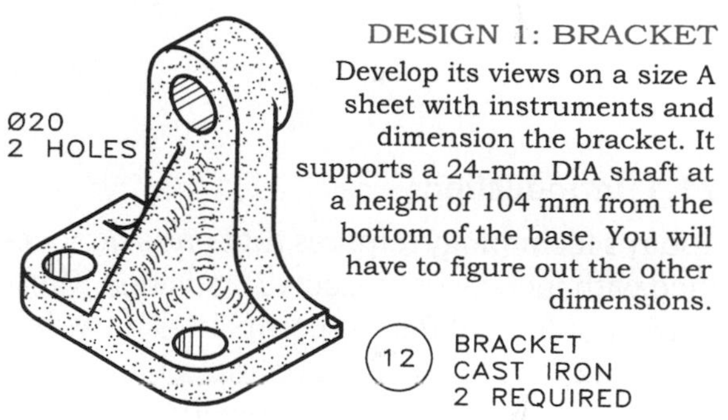

DESIGN 1: BRACKET Develop its views on a size A sheet with instruments and dimension the bracket. It supports a 24-mm DIA shaft at a height of 104 mm from the bottom of the base. You will have to figure out the other dimensions.

Design 1: Bracket

The bracket must be designed, laid out, and dimensioned using the brief specifications that are given. You must determine the needed dimensions as if you were its designer based on the given sizes of the large hole and the smaller holes. Consider surfaces that would be finished.

Supplementary Problems

Problems at the ends of Chapters 13 and 14 can be used as dimensioning exercises in which the principles covered in this chapter can be applied.

21 Tolerances

21.1 Introduction

Today's technology requires that parts be specified with increasingly exact dimensions. Many parts, made by different companies at widely separated locations, must be interchangeable, which requires precise size specifications and production.

The technique of dimensioning parts within a required range of variation to ensure interchangeability is called **tolerancing**. Each dimension is allowed a certain degree of variation within a specified zone, or tolerance. For example, a part's dimension might be expressed as 20 ± 0.50, which allows a tolerance (variation in size) of 1.00 mm.

Tolerances should be as **large as possible** without interfering with the function of the part to minimize production costs if they cannot be omitted altogether. Manufacturing costs increase as tolerances become smaller.

The parts will be carefully measured to ensure that they were made within the tolerances specified (**Figure 21.1**). Tolerances are used to specify the fabrication of parts that must function within a high degree of precision for the parts to work.

21.2 Tolerance Dimensions

Three methods of specifying tolerances on dimensions, **unilateral, bilateral**, and **limit** forms, are shown in **Figure 21.2**. When plus-or-minus tolerancing is used, it is applied to a theoretical dimension called the **basic dimension**. When dimensions can vary in only one direction from the basic dimension (either larger or smaller) tolerancing is unilateral. Tolerancing that permits variation in both directions from the basic dimension (larger and smaller) is bilateral.

Tolerances may be given in limit form, with dimensions representing the largest and smallest sizes for a feature. When tolerances are shown in limit form, the basic dimension will be unknown.

21.1 Tolerances are used only on parts where extreme accuracy and precision are required. Checking and executing tolerancing is expensive and should be limited to only these applications.

Large limit on top
22.200
22.000
A. LIMITS

Plus toleran[ce] on top
46.00 +0.4[0] −0.20
B. PLUS-MINUS

Small limit first
Ø26.00−26.40
C. LIMITS

Ø76.0 0.2
D. PLUS-MINUS

21.3 Place upper limits either above or to the right of lower limits. In plus-and-minus tolerancing, place the plus limits above the minus limits.

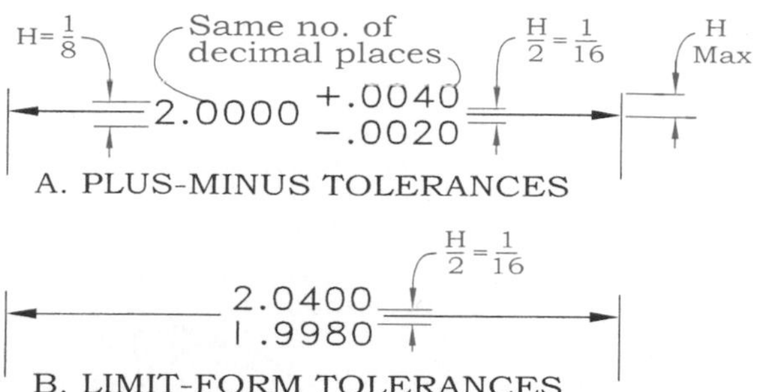

21.4 The spacing and proportions of numerals used to specify tolerances on dimensions are shown here.

The customary methods of applying tolerance values on dimension lines are shown in **Figure 21.3**. The spacing and proportions of the tolerance dimensions are shown in **Figure 21.4**.

UNILATERAL (Variation in one dir.)
2.250 +.000 −.008
General space
.650 +.040 −.000 Tight space
Ø.500 +.000 −.044 DIA form

BILATERAL (Variation in two dir.)
2.250 ±.004
General space
.650 +.020 −.020 Tight space
Ø14.000 ±.022 DIA form

LIMIT FORM (Max. & Min.)
Large on top
2.255
2.245
General space
.658
.646
Tight space
Small to large
Ø14.00−14.20
DIA form

21.2 These examples show properly applied tolerances in unilateral, bilateral, and limit forms for general and tight spaces.

21.3 Mating Parts

Mating parts must be toleranced to fit within a prescribed degree of accuracy (**Figure 21.5**). The upper part is dimensioned with limits indicating its maximum and minimum sizes. The slot in the lower part is toleranced to be slightly larger, allowing the parts to assemble with a clearance fit that allows freedom of movement.

Mating parts may be cylindrical forms, such as a pulley, bushing, and shaft (**Figure 21.6**). The bushing should force fit inside the pulley to provide a good bearing surface for the rotating shaft. At the same time, the shaft and the bushing should mate so that the pulley and bushing will rotate on the shaft with a free-running fit.

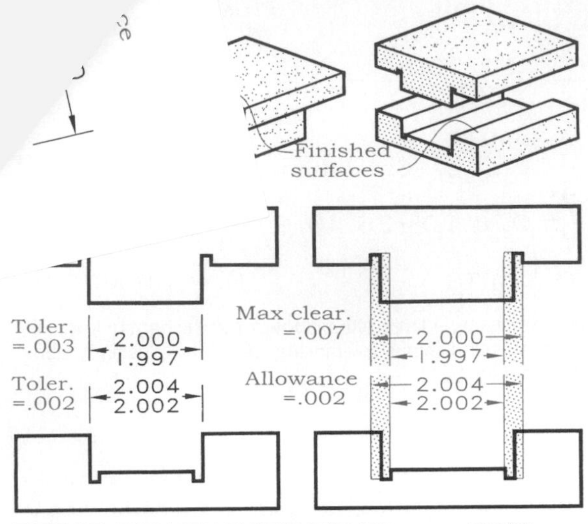

21.5 These mating parts have tolerances (variations in size) of .003″ and .002″, respectively. The allowance (tightest fit) between the assembled parts is .002″.

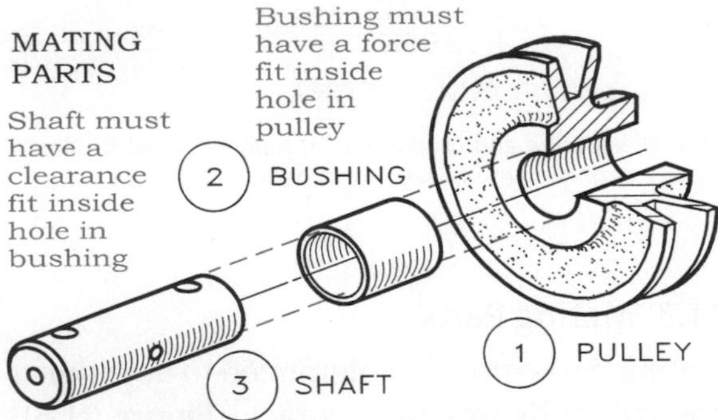

21.6 Mating parts.
These parts must be assembled with cylindrical fits that give a clearance and an interference fit.

ANSI tables (see **Appendixes 35–38**) prescribe cylindrical-fit tolerances for different applications. Familiarity with the terminology of cylindrical tolerancing is essential for applying the data from these tables.

21.4 Terminology: English Units

The following terminology and definitions of tolerancing are illustrated in **Figure 21.7**, which shows two mating cylindrical parts.

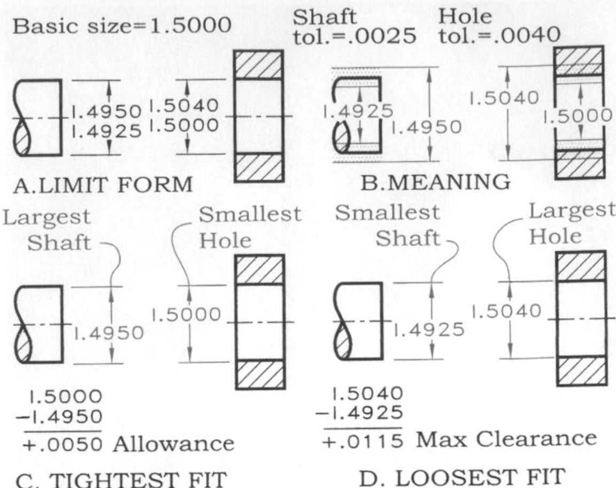

21.7 Cylindrical fits: English units.
The allowance (tightest fit) between these assembled parts is +.005″. The maximum clearance is +.0115″.

Tolerance: The difference between the limits of size prescribed for a single feature, or .0025 in. for the shaft and .0040 in. for the hole in **Figure 21.7A**.

Limits of tolerance: The maximum and minimum sizes of a feature, or 1.4925 and 1.4950 for the shaft and 1.5000 and 1.5040 for the hole in **Figure 21.7B**.

Allowance: The tightest fit between two mating parts, or +.0050 in **Figure 21.7C**. Allowance is negative for an interference fit.

Nominal size: A general size of a shaft or hole, usually expressed with common fractions, 1-1/2 in. or 1.50 in., as in **Figure 21.7**.

Basic size: The size to which a plus-and-minus tolerance is applied to obtain the limits of size, 1.5000 in **Figure 21.7**. The basic diameter cannot be determined from tolerances that are expressed in limit form.

Actual size: The measured size of the finished part.

Fit: The degree of tightness or looseness between two assembled parts, which can be one of the following: **clearance, interference, transition**, and **line**.

A *clearance fit* gives a clearance between two assembled mating parts. The shaft and

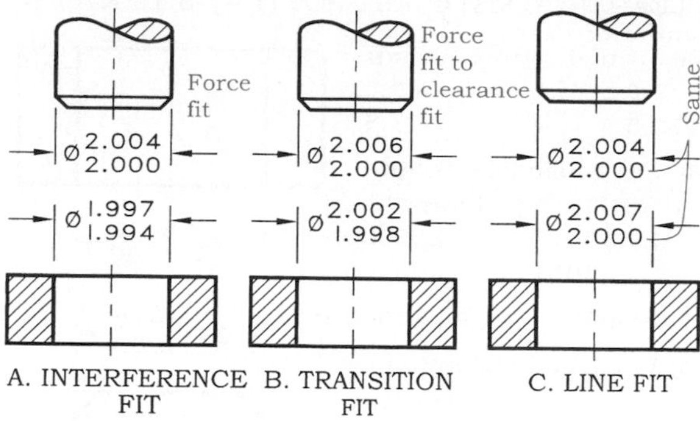

21.8 Types of cylindrical fit.
Three types of fits between mating parts are shown here in addition to the clearance fit shown in **Figure 21.7**.

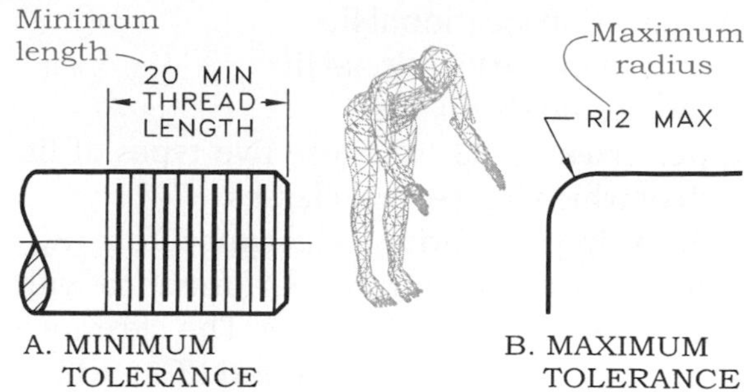

21.9 Single tolerances in maximum (MAX) or minimum (MIN) form can be given in applications of this type.

the hole in **Figures 21.7C** and **D** have a minimum clearance of .0050 in. and a maximum clearance of .0115 in.

An *interference fit* results in a binding fit that requires the parts to be forced together much as if they are welded (**Figure 21.8A**).

A *transition fit* may range from an interference to a clearance between the assembled parts. The shaft may be either smaller or larger than the hole and still be within the prescribed tolerances, as in **Figure 21.8B**.

A *line fit* results in surface contact or clearance when the limits arc reached (**Figure 21.8C**).

Selective assembly: A method of selecting and assembling parts by hand by trial and error that allows parts to be made with larger tolerances at less cost as a compromise between a high manufacturing accuracy and ease of assembly.

Single limits: Dimensions designated by either minimum (MIN) or maximum (MAX), as shown in **Figure 21.9**. Depths of holes, lengths, threads, corner radii, and chamfers are sometimes dimensioned in this manner.

21.5 Basic Hole System

The **basic hole system** uses the smallest hole size as the **basic diameter** for calculating tolerances and allowances. The basic hole system is best when drills, reamers, and machine tools are used to give precise hole sizes.

The smallest hole size is the basic diameter because a hole can be enlarged by machining but not reduced in size. If the smallest diameter of a hole is 1.500″, subtract the allowance, .0050″ (for example), from it to find the diameter of the largest shaft, 1.4950″. To find the smallest limit for the shaft diameter, subtract the tolerance from 1.4950″.

21.6 Basic Shaft System

The **basic shaft system** uses the largest diameter as the **basic diameter** to which the tolerances are applied. This system is applicable when shafts are available in uniform standard sizes.

The largest shaft size is used as the basic diameter because shafts can be machined to smaller size but not enlarged. For example, if the largest permissible shaft size is 1.500″, add the allowance to this dimension to obtain the smallest hole diameter into which the shaft fits. If the parts are to have an allowance of .0040″, the smallest hole will have a diameter of 1.5040″.

21.7 Cylindrical Fits

The *ANSI B4.1* standard gives a series of fits between cylindrical features in inches for the basic hole system. The types of fit covered in this standard are as follows:

RC: running or sliding clearance fits

LC: clearance locational fits

LT: transition locational fits
LN: interference locational fits
FN: force and shrink fits
Appendixes 29–33 list these five types of fit, each of which has several classes.

Running or **sliding clearance fits** (RC) provide a similar running performance with suitable lubrication allowance. The clearance for the first two classes (RC1 and RC2), which are used chiefly as slide fits, increases more slowly with diameter size than other classes to maintain an accurate location even at the expense of free relative motion.

Locational fits (LC, LT, LN) determine only the location of mating parts; they may provide nonmoving rigid locations (interference fits) or permit some freedom of location (clearance fits). The three locational fits are **clearance fits (LC), transition fits (LT)**, and **interference fits (LN)**.

Force fits (FN) are interference fits characterized by constant bore pressures throughout the range of sizes. There are five types of force fits: FN1 through FN5 varying from light drive to heavier drives, respectively.

The method of applying tolerance values from the tables in **Appendix 29** for an RC9 (basic hole system) fit is shown in **Figure 21.10**. The basic diameter of 2.5000″ falls between 1.97″ and 3.15″ in the *Size* column of the table. Limits are in thousandths, which requires that the decimal point be moved three places to the left. For example, +7 is +.0070″.

Add the limits to the basic diameter when a **plus sign** precedes the values, and **subtract** when a **minus sign** is given. Add the limits (+.0070″ and .0000″) to the basic diameter to find the upper and lower limits of the hole (2.5070″ and 2.5000″). Subtract the limits −.0090″ and −.0135″) from the basic diameter to find the limits of the shaft (2.4910″ and 2.4865″).

The tightest fit (the allowance) between the assembled parts (+.0090″) is the difference between the largest shaft and the smallest hole. The loosest fit, or maximum clearance (+.0205″), is the difference between the smallest shaft and the largest hole. These values appear in the *Limits* column of **Appendix 29**.

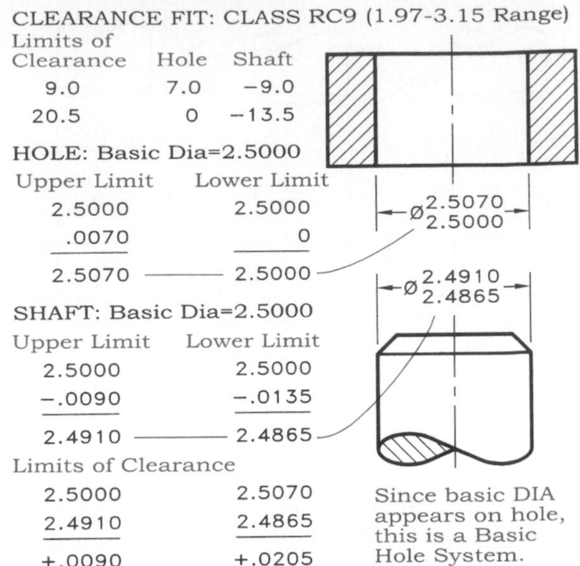

CLEARANCE FIT: CLASS RC9 (1.97-3.15 Range)
Limits of Clearance Hole Shaft
9.0 7.0 −9.0
20.5 0 −13.5
HOLE: Basic Dia=2.5000
Upper Limit Lower Limit
2.5000 2.5000
.0070 0
2.5070 2.5000
Ø2.5070 2.5000
Ø2.4910 2.4865
SHAFT: Basic Dia=2.5000
Upper Limit Lower Limit
2.5000 2.5000
−.0090 −.0135
2.4910 2.4865
Limits of Clearance
2.5000 2.5070
2.4910 2.4865
+.0090 +.0205
Since basic DIA appears on hole, this is a Basic Hole System.

21.10 Calculations: Basic hole system.
This example shows how to calculate basic hole limits and allowances for an RC9 fit between a shaft and hole with a basic diameter of 2.5000″. Values are taken from **Appendix 29**.

This method of extracting tolerancing dimensions is applied to other types of fits by using their respective tables: force fit, interference fit, transition fit, and locational fit. Subtract negative limits from the basic diameter and add positive limits to it. A **minus sign** preceding limits of clearance in the tables indicates an **interference fit** between the assembled parts, and a **positive sign** preceding the **limits** of clearance indicates a **clearance fit**.

21.8 Tolerancing: Metric Units

The system recommended by the *International Standards Organization (ISO)* in *ANSI B4.2* for metric measurements are fits that usually

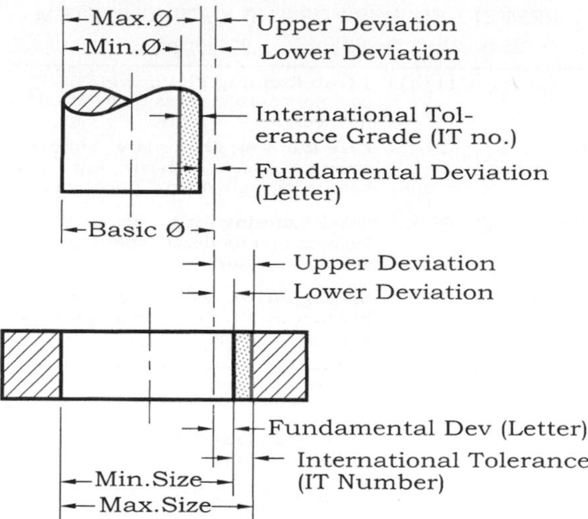

21.11 Cylintrical fits: Metric units.
The terminology and definitions of the metric system of cylindrical fits are given here.

apply to cylinders—holes and shafts—but these tables can be used to specify fits between parallel contact surfaces such as a key in a slot.

Basic size: the size, usually a diameter from which limits or deviations are calculated (**Figure 21.11**). Select basic sizes from the *First Choice* column in the table in **Figure 21.12**.

Deviation: the difference between the hole or shaft size and the basic size.

PREFERRED BASIC SIZES (Millimeters)

First Choice	Second Choice	First Choice	Second Choice	First Choice	Second Choice
1	1.1	10	11	100	110
1.2	1.4	12	14	120	140
1.6	1.8	16	18	160	180
2	2.2	20	22	200	220
2.5	2.8	25	28	250	280
3	3.5	30	35	300	350
4	4.5	40	45	400	450
5	5.5	50	55	500	550
6	7	60	70	600	700
8	9	80	90	800	900
				1000	

21.12 Basic sizes for metric fits selected first from the first-choice column are preferred over those in the second-choice column.

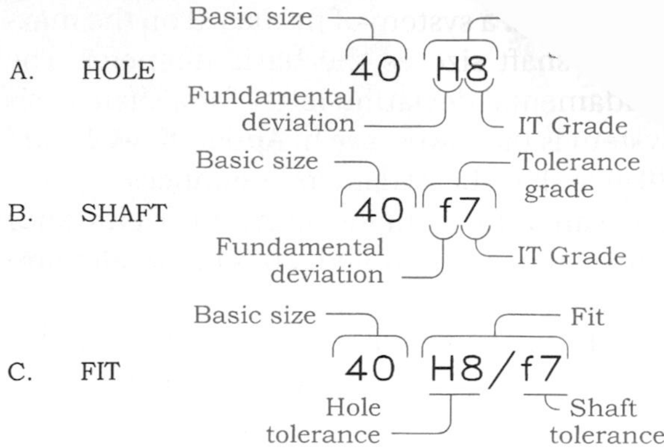

21.13 Tolerance notes.
These tolerance symbols and their definitions apply to holes and shafts.

Upper deviation: the difference between the maximum permissible size of a part and its basic size (**Figure 21.11**).

Lower deviation: the difference between the minimum permissible size of a part and its basic size (**Figure 21.11**).

Fundamental deviation: the deviation closest to the basic size (**Figure 21.11**). In the note 40 H8 in **Figure 21.13**, *H* represents the fundamental deviation for a hole, and in the note 40 f7, the *f* represents the fundamental deviation for a shaft.

Tolerance: the difference between the maximum and minimum allowable sizes of a part.

International tolerance (IT) grade: a series of tolerances that vary with basic size to provide a uniform level of accuracy within a given grade (**Figure 21.11**). In the note 40 H8 in **Figure 21.13**, the 8 represents the IT grade. There are 16 IT grades: IT01, IT0, IT1, . . . , IT16.

Tolerance zone: a combination of the fundamental deviation and the tolerance grade. The H8 portion of the 40 H8 note in **Figure 21.13** is the tolerance zone.

Hole basis: a system of fits based on the minimum hole size as the basic diameter. The fundamental deviation letter for a hole-basis system is the **uppercase H. Appendixes 35** and **36** give hole-basis data for tolerances.

...n of fits based on the max- ...s the basic diameter. The ...ation letter for a shaft-basis ...ercase h. **Appendixes 37** and ...sis data for tolerances.

... a fit resulting in a clearance ... assembled parts under all tolerance co... ...ons.

Interference fit: a force fit between two parts, requiring that they be driven together.

Transition fit: a fit that can result in either a clearance or an interference between assembled parts.

Tolerance symbols: notes giving the specifications of tolerances and fits (**Figure 21.13**). The basic size is a number, followed by the fundamental deviation letter and the IT number that give the tolerance zone.

Uppercase letters (H) indicate the fundamental deviations for **holes; lowercase letters** (h) indicate fundamental deviations for **shafts**.

Preferred Sizes and Fits

The table in **Figure 21.12** shows the preferred basic sizes for computing tolerances. Under the *First Choice* heading, each number increases by about 25% from the preceding value. Each number in the *Second Choice* column increases by about 12%. To minimize cost, select basic diameters from the first column because they correspond to standard stock sizes for round, square, and hexagonal metal products.

Figure 21.14 shows preferred clearance, transition, and interference fits for the hole-basis and shaft-basis systems. **Appendixes 35–38** contain the complete tables. **Figure 21.15** illustrates the difference among **clearance, interference**, and **transition fits**.

Preferred Fits: Hole-Basis System The preferred fits for the hole-basis system, in which the smallest hole is the basic diameter, are shown in **Figure 21.14**. Variations in fit between parts range from a clearance fit of H11/c11 to an interference fit of H7/u6.

Preferred Fits: Shaft-Basis System The preferred fits of the shaft-basis system, in which the largest shaft is the basic diameter, are

PREFERRED FITS FOR THE METRIC SYSTEM

Hole Basis		Shaft Basis	Description
H11/c11	CLEARANCE	C11/h11	**Loose Running Fit** for wide commerical tolerances on external members.
H9/d9	CLEARANCE	D9/h9	**Free Running Fit** for large temperature variations, high running speeds, or high journal pressures.
H8/f7	CLEARANCE	F8/h7	**Close Running Fit** for accurate location and moderate speeds and journal pressures.
H7/g6	CLEARANCE	G7/h6	**Sliding Fit** for accurate fit and location and free moving and turning, not free running.
H7/h6	TRANSITION	H7/h6	**Locational Clearance** for snug fits for parts that can be freely assembled.
H7/k6	TRANSITION	K7/h6	**Locational Transition Fit** for accurate locations.
H7/n6	TRANSITION	N7/h6	**Locational Transition Fit** for more accurate locations and greater interference.
H7/p6	INTERFERENCE	P7/h6	**Locational Interference Fit** for rigidity and alignment without special bore pressures.
H7/s6	INTERFERENCE	S7/h6	**Medium Drive Fit** for shrink fits on light sections; tightest fit usable for cast iron.
H7/u6	INTERFERENCE	U7/h6	**Force Fit** for parts that can be highly stressed and for shrink fits.

21.14 The preferred hole-basis and shaft-basis fits for the metric system.

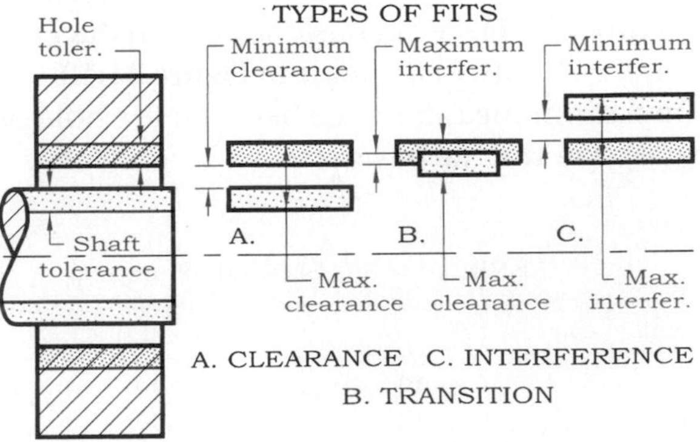

21.15 Types of fits: (A) clearance fit, where there is space between the parts; (B) transition fit, where there can be either interference or clearance; and (C) interference fit, where the parts must be forced together.

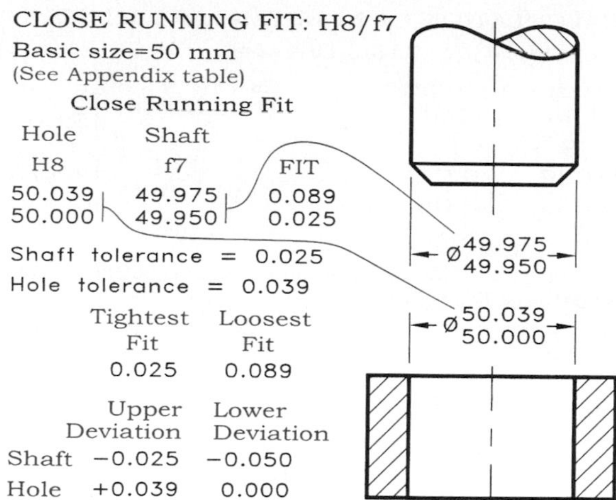

21.16 Example 1: Close running fit, hole basis.
This drawing shows how to calculate and apply metric limits and fits to a shaft and hole (Appendix 35).

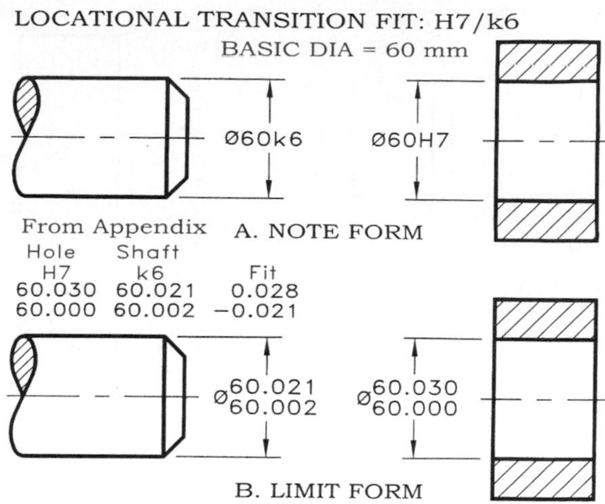

21.17 Example 2: Location transition fit, hole basis.
These methods are used to note metric tolerances for a hole and a shaft with a transition fit (Appendix 36).

shown in **Figure 21.14**. Variations in fit range from a clearance fit of C11/h11 to an interference fit of U7/h6.

Standard Cylindrical Fits

The following examples demonstrate how to calculate and apply tolerances to cylindrical parts. You must use **Figure 21.12, Figure 21.14**, and data from **Appendixes 35–38**.

Example 1 (Figure 21.16)

Required: Use the hole-basis system, a close running fit, and a basic diameter of 49 mm.

Solution: Use a preferred basic diameter of 50 mm (**Figure 21.12**) and fit of H8/f7 (**Figure 21.14**).

Hole: Find the upper and lower limits of the hole in **Appendix 35** under H8 and across from 50 mm: 50.000 mm and 50.039 mm.

Shaft: From **Appendix 35** find the upper and lower limits of the shaft under f7 and across from 50 mm: 49.950 mm and 49.975 mm.

Fit: The fit is given as 0.089 and 0.025, which means that the tightest fit (allowance) is 0.025 mm and the loosest fit is 0.089 mm.

Symbols: **Figure 21.16** shows how to apply toleranced dimensions to the hole and shaft.

Example 2 (Figure 21.17)

Required: Use the hole-basis system, a location transition fit of medium accuracy, and a basic diameter of 57 mm.

Solution: Use a preferred basic diameter of 60 mm (**Figure 21.12**) and a fit of H7/k6 (**Figure 21.14**).

Hole: Find the upper and lower limits of the hole in **Appendix 36** under H7 and across from 60 mm; 60.000 mm and 60.030 mm.

Shaft: From **Appendix 36** find the upper and lower limits of the shaft under k6 and across from 60 mm: 60.002 and 60.021 mm.

Fit: The fit between the two parts is given as 0.028 and −0.021, which means a clearance of 0.028, or an interference (force fit) of 0.021 is acceptable.

Symbols: **Figure 21.17** shows two methods of applying the tolerance symbols to a drawing, note form and limit form.

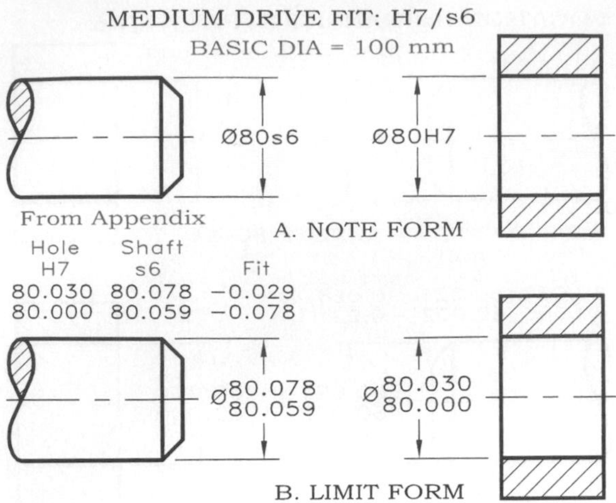

21.18 Example 3:Interference fit.
Either of these formats can be used to apply metric tolerances to a hole and shaft that have an interference fit (Appendix 36).

Example 3 (Figure 21.18)

Required: Use the hole-basis system, a medium drive fit, and a basic diameter of 96 mm.

Solution: Use a preferred basic diameter of 80 mm (**Figure 21.12**) and a fit of H7/s6 (**Figure 21.14**).

Hole: Find the upper and lower limits of the hole in **Appendix 36** under H7 and across from 80 mm to obtain limits of 80.030 mm and 80.000 mm.

Shaft: Find the upper and lower limits of the shaft under s6 and across from 80 mm in **Appendix 36**. These limits are 80.078 mm and 80.059 mm.

Fit: **Appendix 36** gives the tightest fit as an interference of −0.078 mm, and the loosest fit as an interference of −0.029 mm. Minus signs in front of these numbers in the fit column indicate interference fits.

Symbols: **Figure 21.18** shows two methods of applying toleranced dimensions to the hole and shaft.

CALCULATION OF NONSTANDARD LIMITS
FIT: H8/f7 BASIC DIA: Ø45

From Appendix

Hole	Shaft		
H8	f7	Hole Limits	45.039 45.000
0.039	-0.025	Shaft Limits	44.975 44.950
0.000	-0.050		

21.19 Nonstandard limits.
This calculation is for an H8/f7 nonstandard diameter of 45 mm (Appendixes 37 and 38).

Nonstandard Fits

Limits of tolerances for nonstandard series of the fits in **Figure 21.14** that do not appear in **Appendixes 35–38** can be calculated as shown in **Figure 21.19**. Limits of tolerances for nonstandard hole sizes are in **Appendix 39**, and limits of tolerances for nonstandard shaft sizes are in **Appendix 40**.

Figure 21.19 shows the hole and shaft limits for an H8/f7 fit and a 45-mm DIA. The tolerance limits of 0.000 and 0.039 mm for an H8 hole are taken from **Appendix 39**, across from the size range 40–50 mm. The f7 tolerance limits of −0.025 and −0.050 mm for the shaft are from **Appendix 40**. Calculate the hole limits by adding the positive tolerances to the 45-mm basic diameter and the shaft limits by subtracting the negative tolerances from the 45-mm basic diameter.

21.9 Chain versus Datum Dimensions

When parts are dimensioned to locate surfaces or geometric features by a chain of dimensions laid end to end (**Figure 21.20A**), variations may accumulate in excess of the specified tolerance. For example, the tolerance between surfaces A and B is .02, between A and C it is .04, and between A and D it is .06.

Tolerance accumulation can be eliminated by measuring from a single plane called a **datum plane** or **baseline**. A datum plane is usually on the object, but it can also be on the

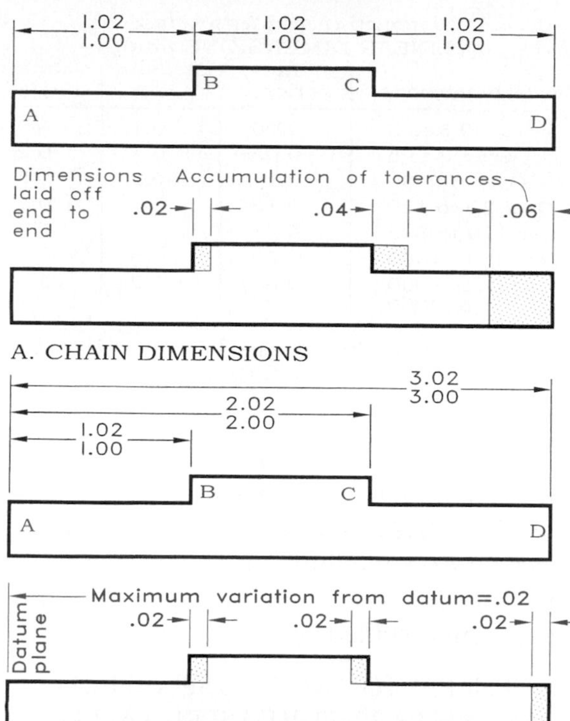

21.20 Chain versus datum dimensioning.
A Dimensions given end to end in a chain fashion may result in an accumulation of tolerances of up to .06 in. at D instead of the specified .02 in.
B When dimensioned from a single datum, the variations of B, C, and D cannot deviate more than the specified .02 in. from the datum.

machine used to make the part. Because each plane in **Figure 21.20B** is located with respect to a datum plane, the tolerances between the intermediate planes do not exceed the maximum tolerance of .02. Always base the application of tolerances on the function of a part in relationship to its mating parts.

21.10 Tolerance Notes

You should tolerance all dimensions on a drawing either by using the rules previously discussed or by placing a note in or near the title block. For example, the note

TOLERANCE ±1/64

might be given on a drawing for less critical dimensions. Some industries give dimensions in inches with two-, three-, and four-decimal-place fractions. A note for dimensions with two and three decimal places might be given on the drawing as

TOLERANCES:
XX.XX ±0.10 XX.XXX ±0.005.

Tolerances of four places would be given directly on the dimension lines. The most common method of noting tolerances is to give as large a tolerance as feasible in a note, such as

TOLERANCES ±0.05

and to give tolerances on the dimension lines for dimensions requiring closer tolerances. Give angular tolerances in a general note in or near the title block, such as

ANGULAR TOLERANCES ±0.50° or ±30′

Use one of the formats shown in **Figure 21.21** to give specific angular tolerances directly on angular dimensions.

21.11 Metric Tolerances

All dimensions on a drawing must be specified within certain tolerance ranges when they are not shown on dimension lines. Tolerances not shown on dimension lines should be specified by a general tolerance note on the drawing.

DEGREES, MINUTES, and SECONDS

28° 30′
28° 00′

28.0°±.2°

28°45′ ±0.5′

A. LIMITS B. PLUS-MINUS C. PLUS-MINUS

21.21 Angular tolerances.
Tolerances on angles can be specified by one of these methods.

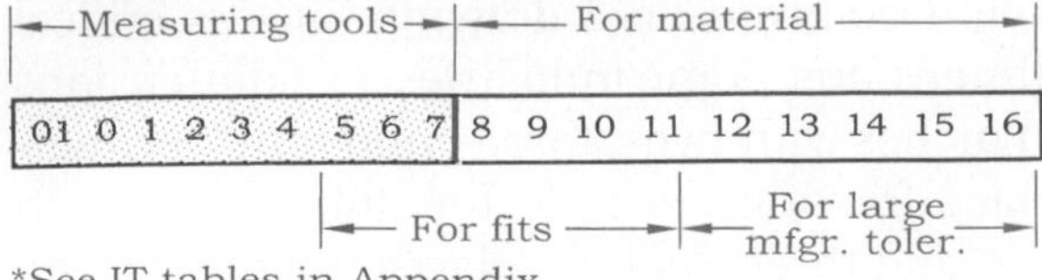

21.22 International tolerance (IT) grades and their applications are shown here. See Appendix 34 to obtain IT tolerance grade numerical values.

Linear Dimensions Tolerance linear dimensions by indicating plus and minus (±) half of an international tolerance (IT) grade, as given in **Appendix 34**. You may select the IT grade from the chart in **Figure 21.22**, where IT grades for mass-produced items range from IT12 through IT16. IT grades can be selected from **Figure 21.23** for a particular machining process.

General tolerances using IT grades may be expressed in a note as follows:

UNLESS OTHERWISE SPECIFIED
ALL UNTOLERANCED
DIMENSIONS ARE IT14.

This note means that a tolerance of ±0.700 mm is allowed for a dimension between 315 and 400 mm. The value of the tolerance, 1.400 mm, was extracted from **Appendix 34**.

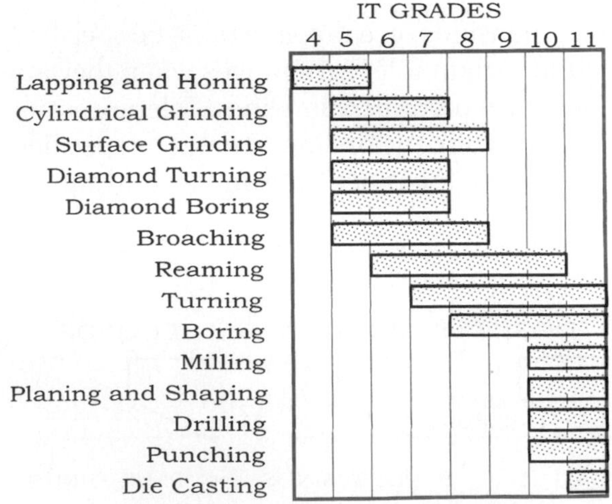

21.23 International tolerance (IT) values may be selected from this table, which is based on the general capabilities of various machining processes.

GENERAL TOLERANCES:
LINEAR DIMENSIONS (mm)

Basic Dimensions	Fine series	Medium series	Coarse series
0.5 to 3	0.05	0.1	----
Over 3 to 6	0.05	0.1	0.2
Over 6 to 30	0.1	0.2	0.5
Over 30 to 120	0.15	0.3	0.8
Over 120 to 315	0.2	0.5	1.2
Over 315 to 1000	0.3	0.8	2
Over 1000 to 2000	0.5	1.2	3

21.24 Select general tolerance values from this table for fine, medium, and coarse series. Tolerances vary with the sizes of dimensions.

Figure 21.24 shows recommended tolerances for fine, medium, and coarse series for ranges of size. A medium tolerance, for example, can be specified by the following note:

GENERAL TOLERANCES SPECIFIED
IN ANSI B4.3 MEDIUM SERIES APPLY.

Equivalent tolerances may be given in table form (**Figure 21.25**) on the drawing, the grade (medium in this example) selected from **Figure 21.24**. General tolerances may be given in a table for dimensions expressed with one or no decimal places (**Figure 21.26**). General tolerances may also be notated in the following form:

UNLESS OTHERWISE SPECIFIED
ALL UNTOLERANCED DIMENSIONS
ARE ±0.8 mm.

Get values from previous table — Specifies a Medium Series

GENERAL TOLERANCES (mm)
UNLESS OTHERWISE SPECIFIED, THE FOLLOWING TOLERANCES ARE APPLICABLE

LINEAR	Over to	0.5 6	6 30	30 120	120 315	315 1000	1000 2000
TOL.		0.1	0.2	0.3	0.5	0.8	1.2

21.25 This table for a medium series of values was extracted from **Figure 21.24** for insertion on a working drawing to provide the tolerances for a medium series of sizes.

Medium series for numbers with one decimal place

Coarse series for numbers with no decimal places

GENERAL TOLERANCES (mm) UNLESS OTHERWISE SPECIFIED, THE FOLLOWING TOLERANCES ARE APPLICABLE					
LINEAR	OVER / TO	— / 120	120 / 315	315 / 1000	1000 / —
TOL.	ONE DECIMAL ±	0.3	0.5	0.8	1.2
	NO DECIMALS ±	0.8	1.2	2	3

21.26 Placed on a drawing, this table of tolerances would indicate the tolerances for dimensions having one or no decimal places, such as 24.0 and 24, denoting medium and coarse series.

Use this method only when the dimensions on a drawing are similar in size.

Angular Tolerances Express angular tolerances as (1) an angle in decimal degrees or in degrees and minutes, (2) a taper in percentage (mm per 100 mm), or (3) milliradians. (To find milliradians, multiply the degrees of an angle by 17.45.) **Figure 21.27** shows the suggested tolerances for decimal degrees and taper, based on the length of the shorter leg of the angle. General angular tolerances may be notated on the drawing as follows:

UNLESS OTHERWISE SPECIFIED
THE GENERAL TOLERANCES
IN ANSI B4.3 APPLY.

A second method involves showing a portion of the table from **Figure 21.27** as a table of tolerances on the drawing (**Figure 21.28**). A third method is a note with a single tolerance, such as

UNLESS OTHERWISE SPECIFIED
ANGULAR TOLERANCES ARE ±0°30′

GENERAL TOLERANCES: ANGLES

Length of shorter leg (mm)	Up to 10	Over 10 to 50	Over 50 to 120	Over 120 to 400
Degrees	± 1°	± 0° 30'	± 0° 20'	± 0° 10'
mm per 100	± 1.8	± 0.9	± 0.6	± 0.3

21.27 General tolerances for angular and taper dimensions may be taken from this table of values.

ANGULAR TOLERANCES				
LENGTH OF SHORTER LEG (mm)	UP TO 10	OVER 10 TO 50	OVER 50 TO 120	OVER 120 TO 400
TOLERANCE	±1°	±0°30'	±0°20'	±0°10'

Values in degrees and minutes taken from previous table

21.28 This table, extracted from **Figure 13.27**, is placed on the drawing to indicate the general tolerance for angles in degrees and minutes.

21.12 Geometric Tolerances

Geometric tolerancing is a system that specifies tolerances that control location **form, profile, orientation, location**, and **runout** on a dimensioned part as covered by the *ANSI Y14.5M Standards* and the *Military Standards* (Mil-Std) of the U.S. Department of Defense. Before discussing those types of tolerancing, however, we need to introduce symbols, size limits, rules, three-datum-plane concepts, and applications.

Symbols

The most commonly used symbols for representing geometric characteristics of dimensioned drawings are shown in **Figure 21.29**. The proportions of feature control symbols in relation to their feature control frames, based on the letter height, are shown in **Figure 21.30**. On most drawings, a 1/8-in., or 3-mm, letter height is recommended. Examples of feature control frames and their proportions are shown in **Figure 21.31**.

Size Limits

Three conditions of size are used when geometric tolerances are applied: **maximum material condition, least material condition**, and **regardless of feature size**.

Maximum material condition (MMC) indicates that a feature contains the maximum amount of material. For example, the shaft

GEOMETRIC CHARACTERISTICS SYMBOLS

	Tolerance	Characteristic	Symbol
INDIVIDUAL FEATURES	FORM	Straightness	—
		Flatness	▱
		Circularity	○
		Cylindricity	⌭
BOTH	PROFILE	Profile: Line	⌒
		Profile: Surface	⌓
RELATED FEATURES	ORIENTATION	Angularity	∠
		Perpendicularity	⊥
		Parallelism	//
	LOCATION	Position	⌖
		Concentricity	◎
		Symmetry	⌯
	RUNOUT	Runout: Circular	↗
		Runout: Total	⌰

21.29 Symbols for geometric characteristics.
These symbols specify the geometric characteristics of a part's features.

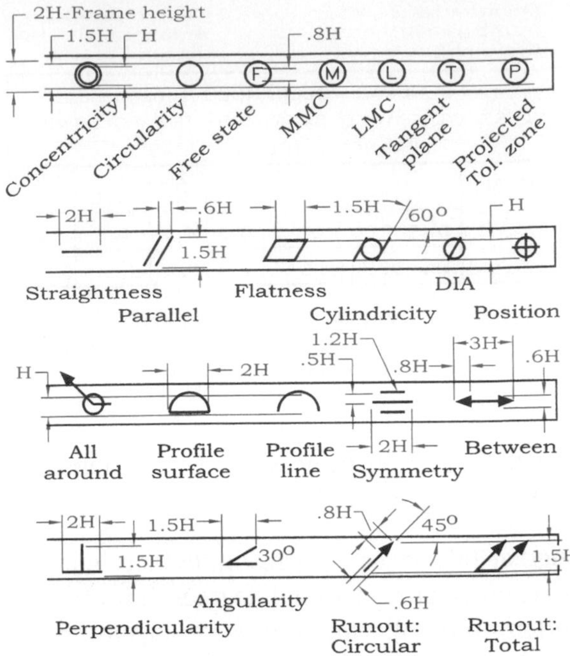

21.30 Feature control symbols.
The proportions of these feature control symbols are based on the letter height, usually 1/8 in.

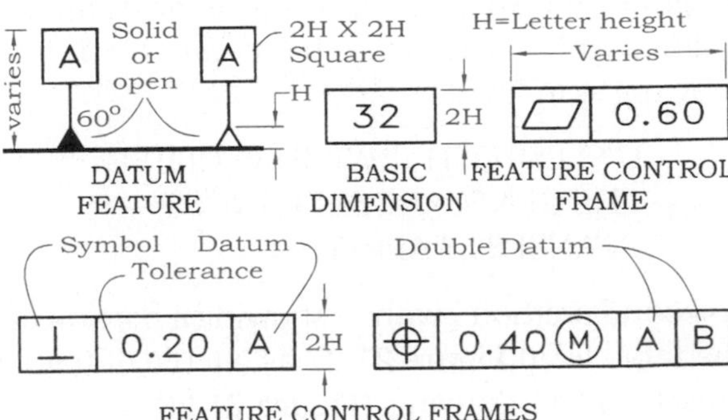

21.31 Examples of geometric tolerancing frames and feature control symbols used to indicate geometric tolerances. H is the letter height.

shown in **Figure 21.32** is at MMC when it has the largest permitted diameter of 24.6 mm. The hole is at MMC when it has the most material, or the smallest diameter, 25.0 mm.

Least material condition (LMC) indicates that a feature contains the least amount of material. The shaft in **Figure 21.32** is at LMC when it has the smallest diameter, 24.0 mm. The hole is at LMC when it has the least material, or the largest diameter, 25.6 mm.

Regardless of feature size (RFS) indicates that tolerances apply to a geometric feature regardless of its size, ranging from MMC to LMC.

21.13 Rules for Tolerancing

Two general rules of tolerancing geometric features should be followed.

Rule 1 (Individual Feature of Size) When only a tolerance of size is specified on a feature, the limits of size control the variation in its geometric form. The forms of the shaft and hole shown in **Figure 21.33** are permitted to vary within the tolerance ranges of the dimensions.

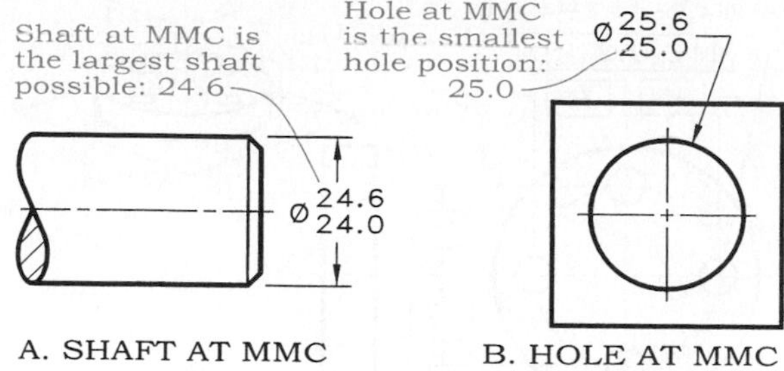

21.32 A shaft is at maximum material condition (MMC) when it is at the largest size permitted by its tolerance. A hole is at MMC when it is at its smallest size.

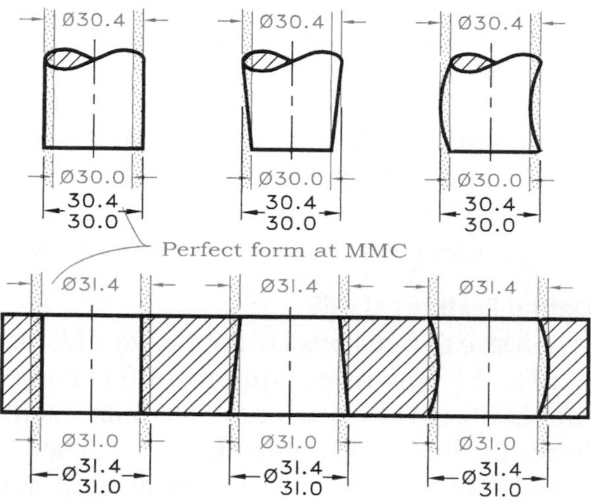

21.33 When only a tolerance of size is specified on a feature, the limits prescribe the form of the features, as shown for these shafts and holes having identical limits.

Rule 2 (All Applicable Geometric Tolerances) Where no modifying symbol is specified, RFS (regardless of features size) applies with respect to the individual tolerance, datum reference, or both. Where required on a drawing, the modifiers MMC or LMC must be specified.

Alternative Practice For a tolerance of position, RFS may be specified on the drawing with respect to the individual tolerance, datum, reference, or both.

The specification of symmetry of the part in **Figure 21.34** is based on a tolerance at RFS from the datum.

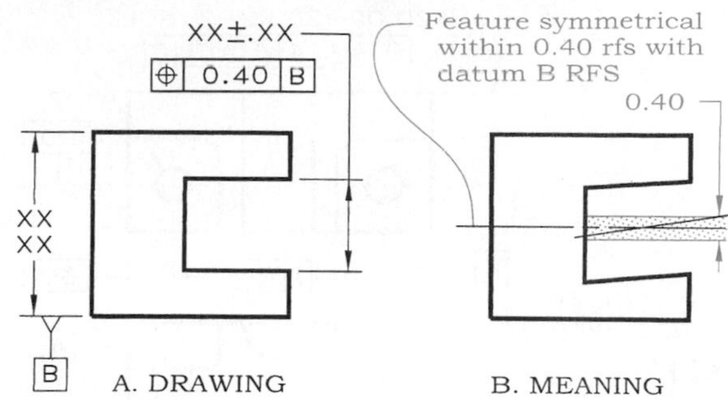

21.34 Tolerance of position, when dimensioned in this manner, indicates that a tolerance of 0.40 applies regardless of feature size (RFS).

Three-Datum-Plane Concept

A datum plane is used as the origin of a part's features that have been toleranced. Datum planes usually relate to manufacturing equipment, such as machine tables or locating pins.

Three mutually perpendicular datum planes are required to dimension a part accurately. For example, the part shown in **Figure 21.35** sits on the primary datum plane, with at least three points of its base in contact with the datum. The part is related to the secondary plane by at least two contact points. The third (tertiary) datum is in contact with at least one point on the object.

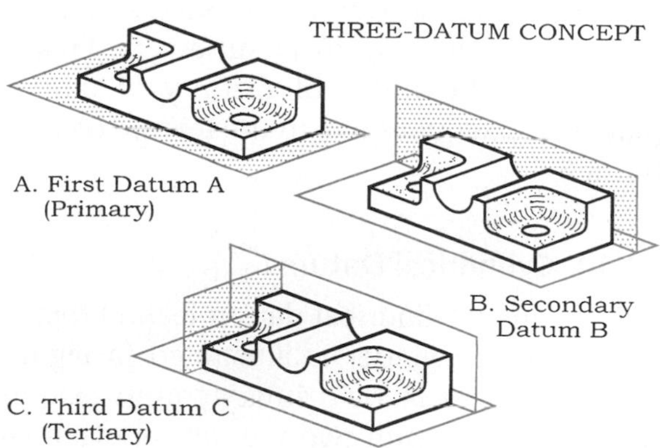

21.35 When an object is referenced to a primary datum plane, it contacts the datum at at least three points. The vertical surface contacts the secondary datum plane at at least two points. The third surface contacts the third datum at at least one point. Datum planes are listed in order of priority in the feature control frame.

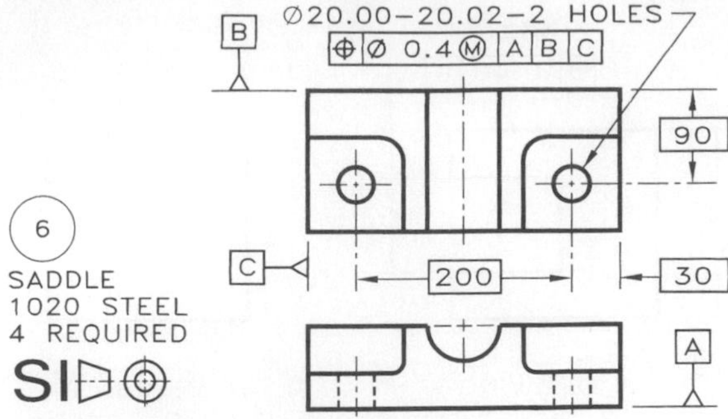

21.36 The three planes of the reference system are noted where they appear as edges. The primary datum plane (A) is given first in the feature control frame; the secondary plane (B), second; and the tertiary plane (C), third. Single numbers in frames are basic dimensions.

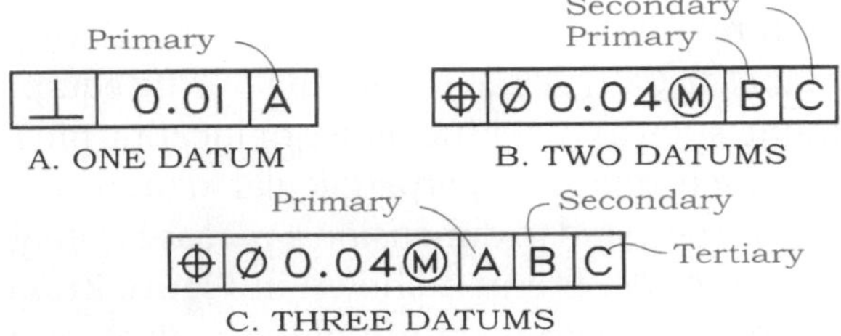

21.37 Use feature control frames to indicate from one to three datum planes in order of priority.

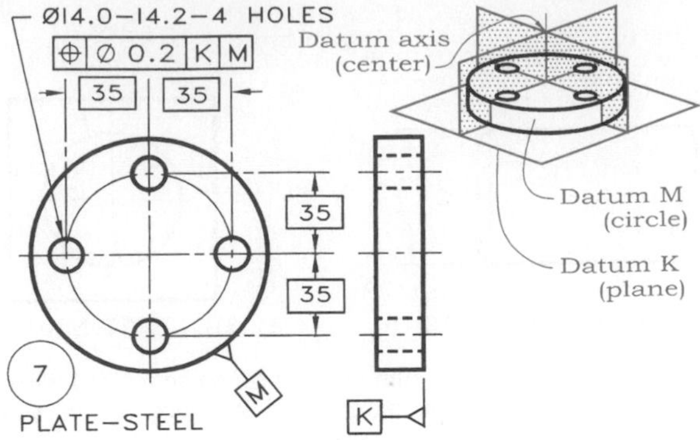

21.38 These true-position holes are located with respect to primary datum K and secondary datum M. Because datum M is a circle, the holes are located about two intersecting datum planes at the crossing centerlines in the circular view, satisfying the three-plane concept.

The priority of datum planes is presented in sequence in feature control frames. For example in **Figure 21.36**, the primary datum is surface A, the secondary datum is surface B, and the tertiary datum is surface C. **Figure 21.37** lists the order of priority of datum planes A–C sequentially in the feature control frames.

21.14 Cylindrical Datums

A part with a cylindrical datum feature that is the axis of a cylinder is illustrated in **Figure 21.38**. Datum K is the primary datum. Datum M is associated with two theoretical planes—the second and third in a three-plane relationship. The two theoretical planes are represented in the circular view by perpendicular centerlines that intersect at the point view of the datum axis. All dimensions originate from the datum axis perpendicular to datum K; the other two intersecting datum planes are used for measurements in the *x*- and *y*-directions.

Datum Features at RFS

When size dimensions are applied to a feature at RFS, the processing equipment that comes into contact with surfaces of the part establishes the datum. Variable machine elements, such as chucks or center devices, are adjusted to fit the external or internal features and establish datums.

Primary-Diameter Datums For an external cylinder (shaft) at RFS, the datum axis is the axis of the smallest circumscribed cylinder that contacts the cylindrical feature (**Figure 21.39A**). That is, the largest diameter of the part making contact with the smallest cylinder of the machine element holding the part is the datum axis.

For an internal cylinder (hole) at RFS, the datum axis is the axis of the largest inscribed cylinder making contact with the hole. That is, the smallest diameter of the hole making contact with the largest cylinder of the machine element inserted in the hole is the datum axis (**Figure 21.39B**).

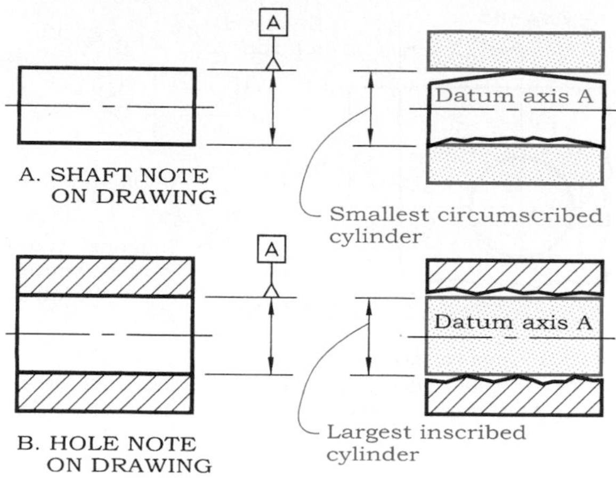

21.39 The datum axis of a shaft is the smallest circumscribed cylinder in contact with the shaft. The datum axis of a hole is the centerline of the largest inscribed cylinder in contact with the hole.

Primary External Parallel Datums The datum for external features at RFS is the center plane between two parallel planes—at minimum separation—that contact the planes of the object (**Figure 21.40A**). These are planes of a viselike device at minimum separation that holds the part.

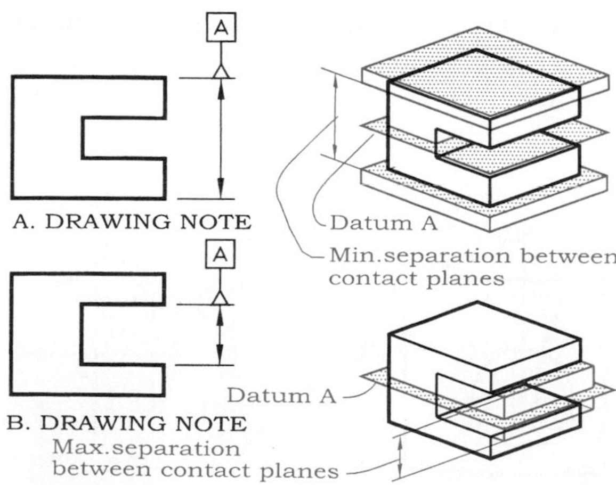

21.40 The datum plane for external parallel surfaces is the center plane between two contact parallel planes at their minimum separation. The datum plane for internal parallel surfaces is the center plane between two contact parallel surfaces at their maximum separation.

Primary Internal Parallel Datums The datum for internal features is the center plane between two parallel planes—at their maximum separation—that contact the inside planes of the object (**Figure 21.40B**).

Secondary Datums The secondary datum (axis or center plane) for both external and internal diameters (or distances between parallel planes) has the additional requirement that the cylinder in contact with the parallel elements of the hole be perpendicular to the primary datum (**Figure 21.41**). Datum axis B is the axis of cylinder B.

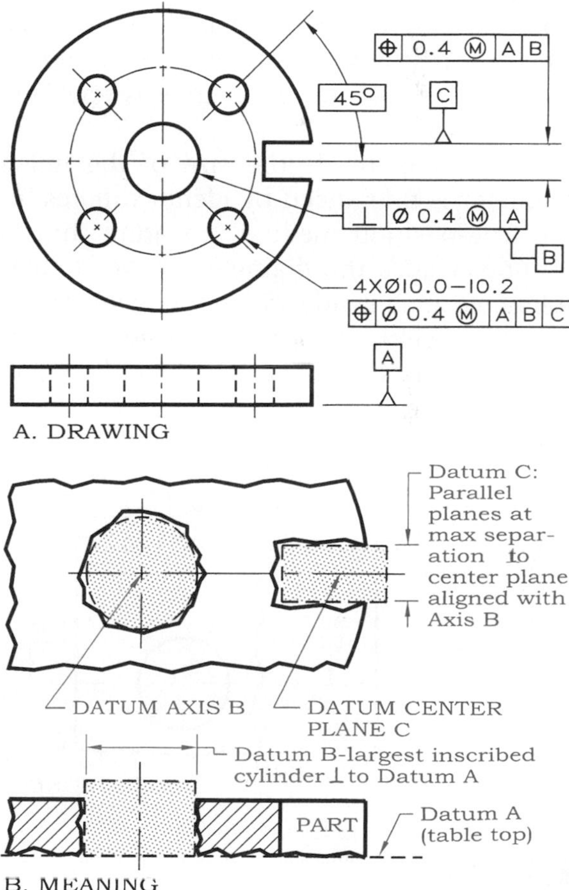

21.41 The features of this part have been dimensioned with respect to primary, secondary, and tertiary datum planes.

Tertiary Datums The third datum (axis or center plane) for both external and internal features has the further requirement that either the cylinder or parallel planes be oriented angularly to the secondary datum. Datum C in **Figure 21.41** is the tertiary datum plane.

21.15 Location Tolerancing

Tolerances of location specify **position, concentricity**, and **symmetry**.

Position Location dimensions that are toleranced result in a square (or rectangular) tolerance zone for locating the center of a hole (**Figure 21.42A**). In contrast, untoleranced location dimensions, called **basic dimensions**, locate the **true position** of a hole's center, about which a circular tolerance zone is specified (**Figure 21.42B**).

In both methods the size of the hole's diameter is toleranced by identical notes. In the true-position method, a feature control frame specifies the diameter of the circular tolerance zone inside which the hole's center must lie. A circular position zone gives a more precise tolerance of the hole's true position than a square.

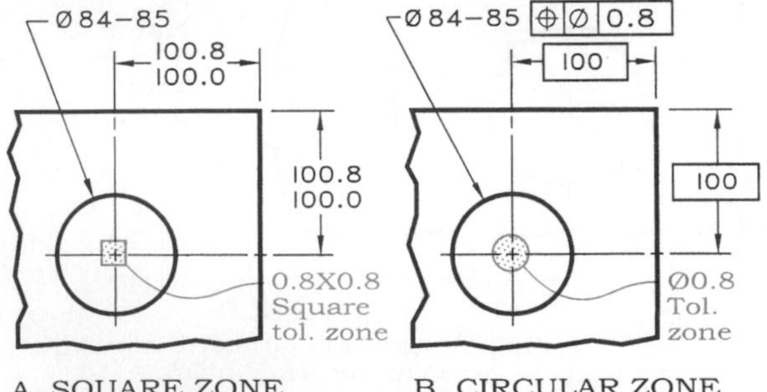

21.42 Square and circular tolerance zones.
A Toleranced location dimensions give a square tolerance zone for the axis of the hole.
B Untoleranced basic dimensions (in frames) locate the true position about which a circular tolerance zone of 0.8 mm is specified.

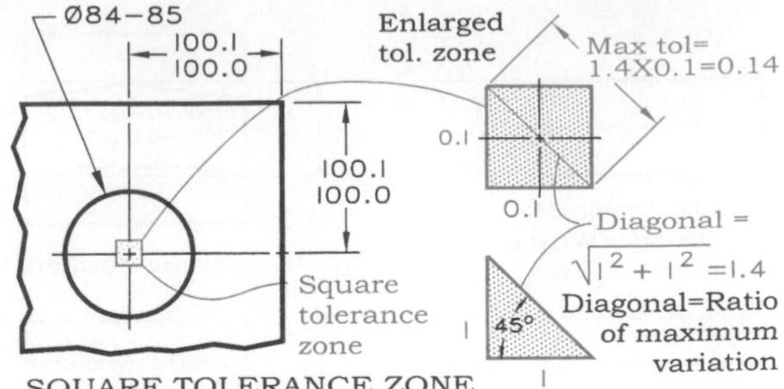

21.43 Square tolerancing.
Toleranced coordinates give a square tolerance zone with a diagonal that exceeds the specified tolerance by a factor of 1.4.

Figure 21.43 shows an enlargement of the square tolerance zone resulting from the use of toleranced location dimensions to locate a hole's center. The diagonal across the square zone is greater than the specified tolerance by a factor of 1.4. Therefore the **true-position method**, shown enlarged in **Figure 21.44**, can have a larger circular tolerance zone by a factor of 1.4 and still have the same degree of accuracy specified by the 0.1 square zone. If a variation of 0.14 across the diagonal of the square tolerance zone is acceptable in the coordinate method, a circular tolerance zone of 0.14, which is greater than the 0.1 tolerance permitted by the square zone, should be acceptable in the true-position tolerance method.

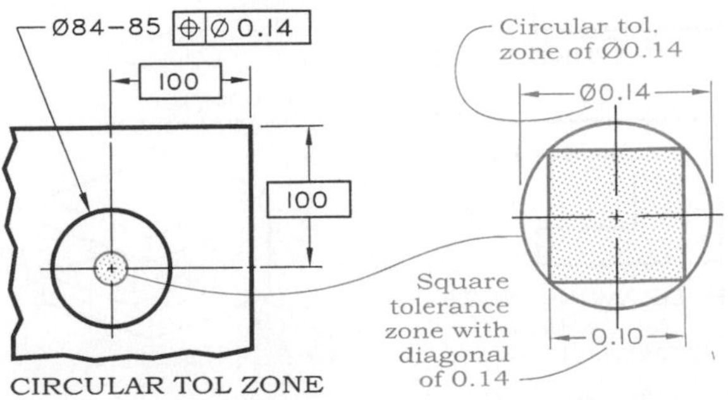

21.44 True-position tolerancing.
The true-position method of locating holes results in a circular tolerance zone. The circular zone can be 1.4 times greater than the square tolerance zone and still be as accurate.

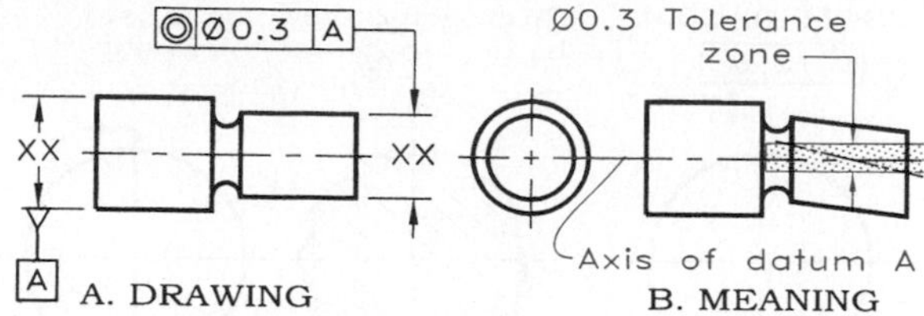

21.45 Concentricity (related to coaxiality) is a tolerance of location. This feature control frame specifies that the axis of the small cylinder be concentric to datum cylinder A, within a tolerance of a 0.3-mm diameter.

The circular tolerance zone specified in the circular view of a hole extends the full depth of the hole. Therefore, the tolerance zone for the centerline of the hole is a cylindrical zone inside which the axis must lie. Because both the size of the hole and its position are toleranced, these two tolerances establish the diameter of a gauge cylinder for checking conformance of hole sizes and their locations against specifications (**Figure 21.44**).

Concentricity Concentricity (closely related to a new term, coaxiality) is a feature of location because it specifies the location of two cylinders that share the same axis. In **Figure 21.45**, the large cylinder is labeled as datum A to be used as the datum for locating the small cylinder's axis.

Feature control frames of the type shown in **Figure 21.46** are used to specify concentricity and other geometric characteristics throughout the remainder of this chapter.

Symmetry Symmetry also is a feature of location in which a feature is symmetrical with the same contour and size on opposite sides of a central plane. **Figure 21.47A** shows how to apply a symmetry feature symbol to the notch that is symmetrical about the part's central datum plane B for a zone of 0.6 mm (**Figure 21.47B**).

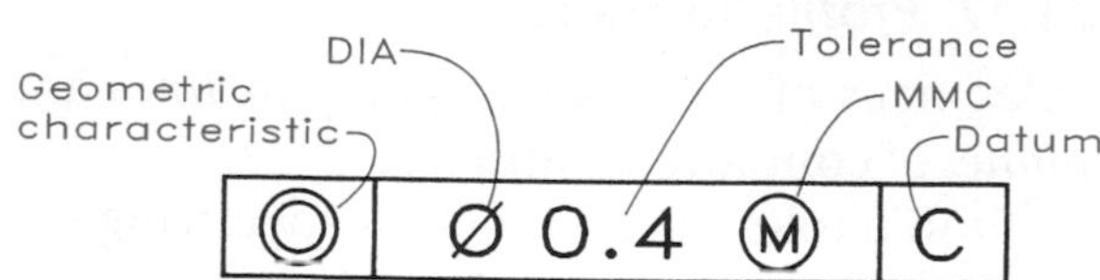

21.46 This typical feature control frame indicates that a surface is concentric to datum C within a cylindrical diameter of 0.4 mm at MMC.

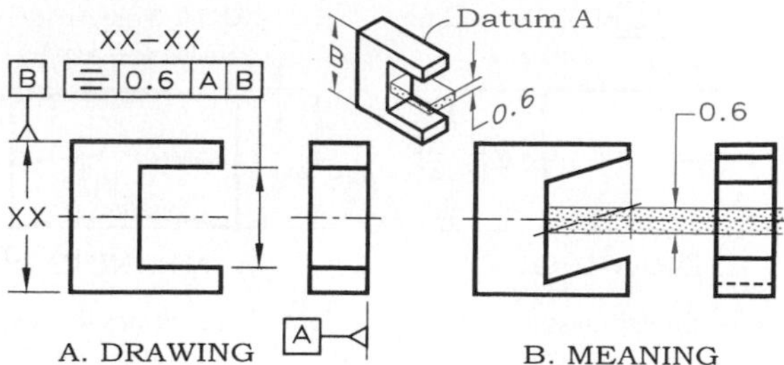

21.47 Symmetry is a tolerance of location that specifies that a part's features be symmetrical about the center plane between parallel surfaces of the part.

21.16 Form Tolerancing

The tolerances of form are **flatness, straightness, circularity**, and **cylindricity**.

Flatness A surface is flat when all its elements are in one plane. A feature control frame specifies flatness within a 0.4-mm tolerance zone in **Figure 21.48**, where no point on the surface may vary more than 0.40 from the highest to the lowest point.

Straightness A surface is straight if all its elements are straight lines within a specified tolerance zone. The feature control frame shown

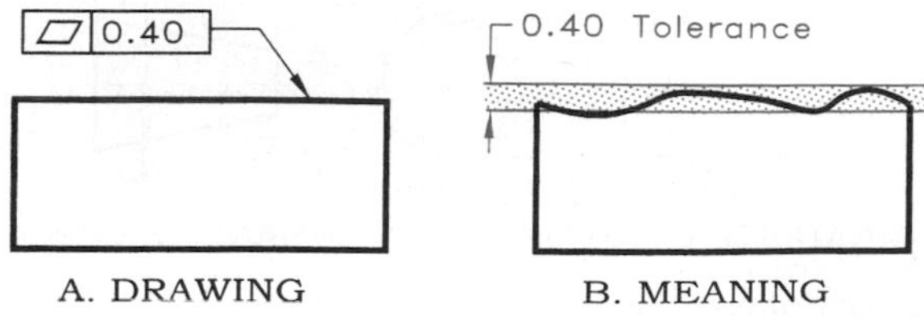

21.48 Flatness is a tolerance of form that specifies a tolerance zone within which a surface must lie.

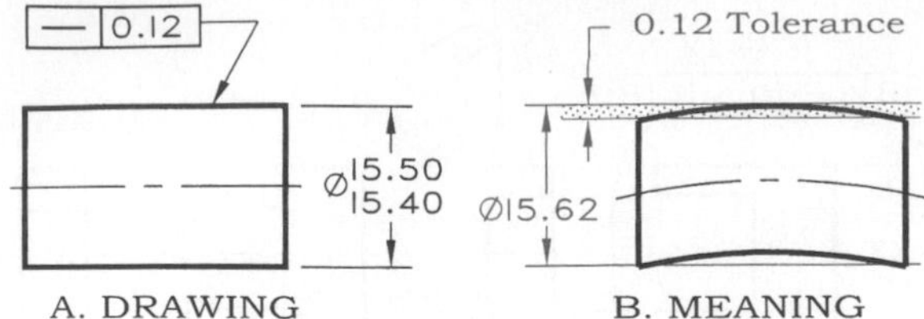

21.49 Straightness is a tolerance of form that indicates that elements of a surface are straight lines. The tolerance frame is applied to the views in which elements appear as lines, not as points.

in **Figure 21.49** specifies that the elements of a cylinder must be straight within 0.12 mm. On flat surfaces, straightness is measured in a plane passing through control-line elements, and it may be specified in two directions (usually perpendicular) if desired.

Circularity (Roundness) A surface of revolution (a cylinder, cone, or sphere) is circular when all points on the surface intersected by a plane perpendicular to its axis are equidistant from the axis. In **Figure 21.50** the feature control frame specifies circularity of a cone and cylinder, permitting a tolerance of 0.54 mm on the radius. **Figure 21.51** specifies a 0.30-mm tolerance zone for the roundness of a sphere.

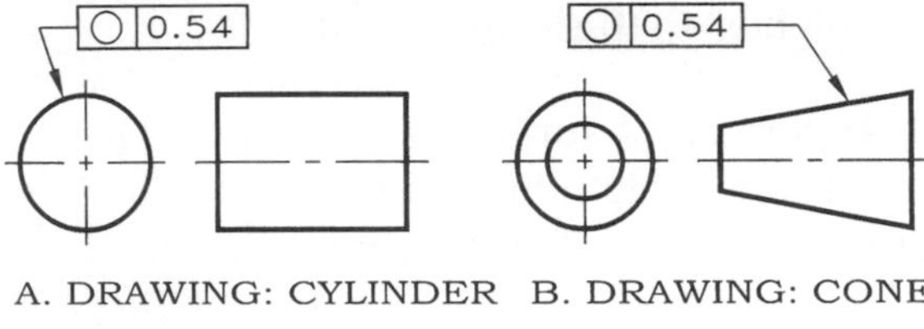

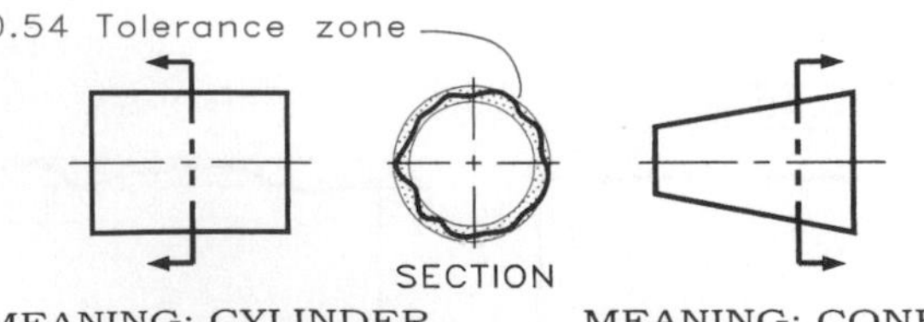

21.50 Circularity (roundness) is a tolerance of form. It indicates that a cross section through a surface of revolution is round and lies within two concentric circles.

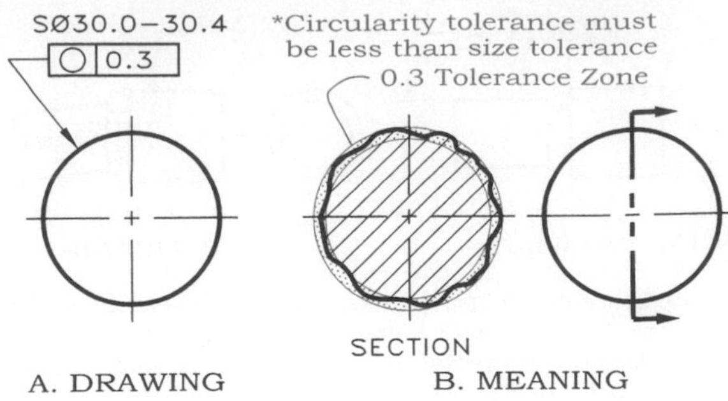

21.51 Circularity of a sphere is a tolerance of form that means that any cross section through it is round within the specified tolerance.

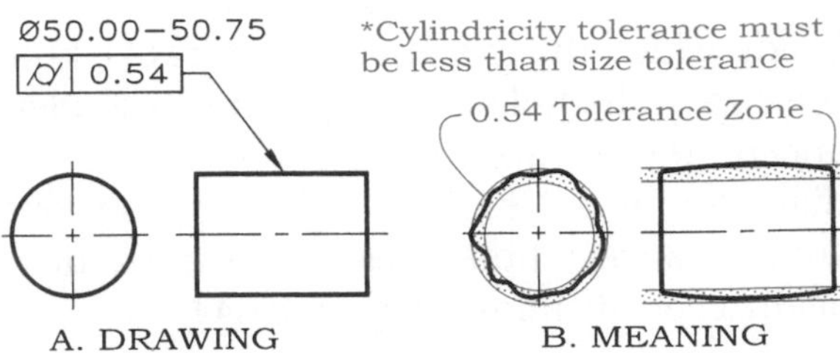

21.52 Cylindricity is a tolerance of form that is a combination of roundness and straightness. It indicates that the surface of a cylinder lies within a tolerance zone formed by two concentric cylinders that are 0.54 apart.

Cylindricity A surface of revolution is cylindrical when all its elements lie within a cylindrical tolerance zone, which is a combination of tolerances of roundness and straightness (**Figure 21.52**). Here, a cylindricity tolerance zone of 0.54 mm on the radius of the cylinder is specified.

21.17 Profile Tolerancing

Tolerances of profiles can apply to *lines* and *planes* of contoured features.

Profile tolerancing involves specifying tolerances for a contoured shape formed by arcs or irregular curves, and it can apply to a surface or a single line. The *surface* with the unilateral

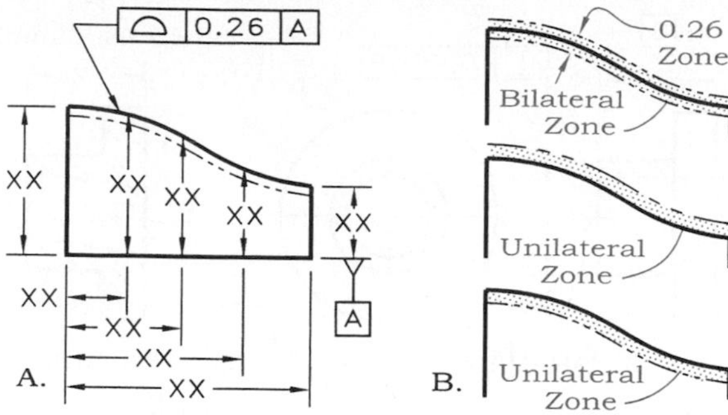

21.53 Profile is a tolerance for irregular curving planes and lines. (A) The curving plane is located by coordinates and is toleranced unidirectionally. (B) The tolerance may be applied by any of these methods.

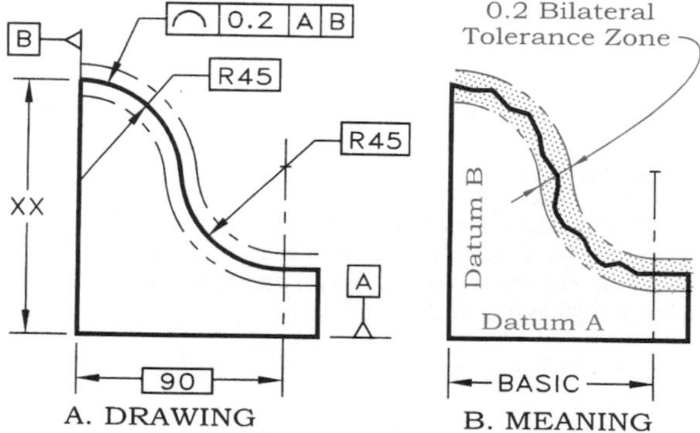

21.54 The profile of a line is a tolerance of profile that specifies the variation allowed from the path of a line. Here, the line is formed by tangent arcs. The tolerance zone may be either bilateral or unilateral, as shown in **Figure 21.53**.

profile tolerance shown in **Figure 21.53A** is defined by coordinates. **Figure 21.53B** shows how to specify bilateral and unilateral tolerance zones.

A profile tolerance for a *single line* is specified as shown in **Figure 21.54**. The curve is formed by tangent arcs whose radii are given as basic dimensions. The radii are permitted to vary ±0.10 mm from the basic radii.

21.18 Orientation Tolerancing

Tolerances of orientation include **parallelism, perpendicularity**, and **angularity**.

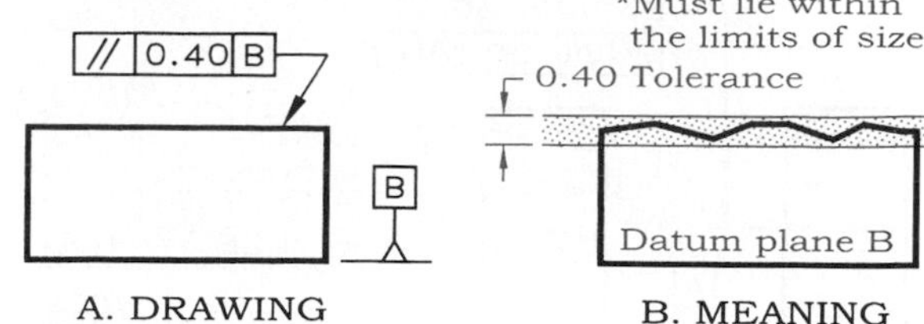

21.55 Parallelism is a tolerance of orientation indicating that a plane is parallel to a datum plane within specified limits. Here, plane B is the datum plane.

Parallelism A surface or line is parallel when all its points are equidistant from a datum plane or axis. There are two types of parallelism tolerance zones:

1. A planar tolerance zone parallel to a datum plane within which the axis or surface of the feature must lie (**Figure 21.55**). This tolerance of orientation also controls flatness.

2. A cylindrical tolerance zone parallel to a datum feature within which the axis of a feature must lie (**Figure 21.56**).

Figure 21.57 shows the effect of specifying parallelism at MMC, where the modifier M is given in the feature control frame. Tolerances of form apply at RFS when not specified. Specifying parallelism at MMC means that the axis of the cylindrical hole must vary no more

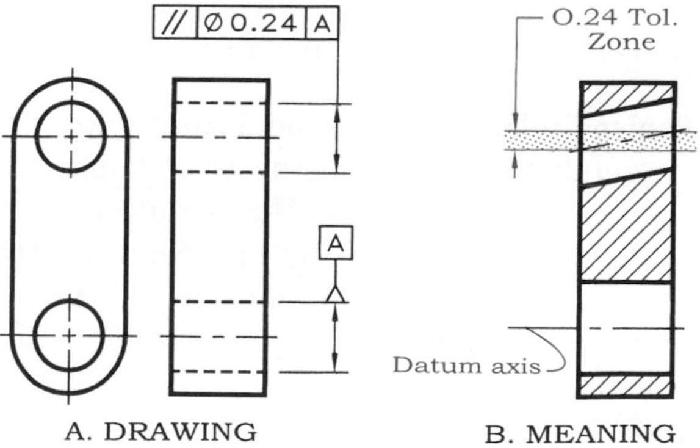

21.56 Parallelism of one centerline to another centerline can be specified by using the diameter of one of the holes as the datum.

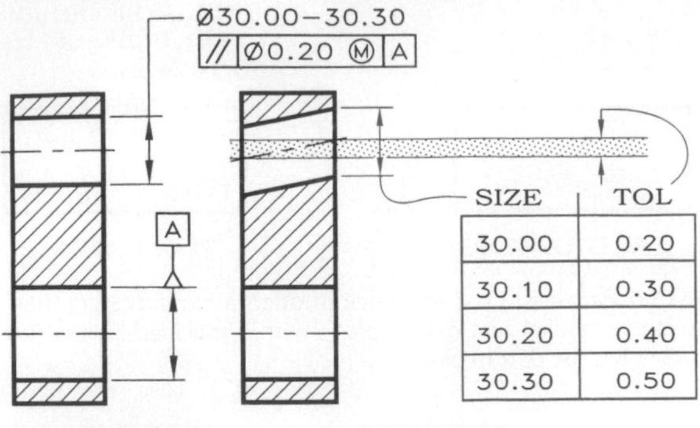

SIZE	TOL
30.00	0.20
30.10	0.30
30.20	0.40
30.30	0.50

21.57 The critical tolerance exists when features are at MMC. (A) The upper hole must be parallel to the hole used as datum A within a 0.20 DIA. (B) As the hole approaches its maximum size of 30.30 mm, the tolerance zone approaches 0.50 mm.

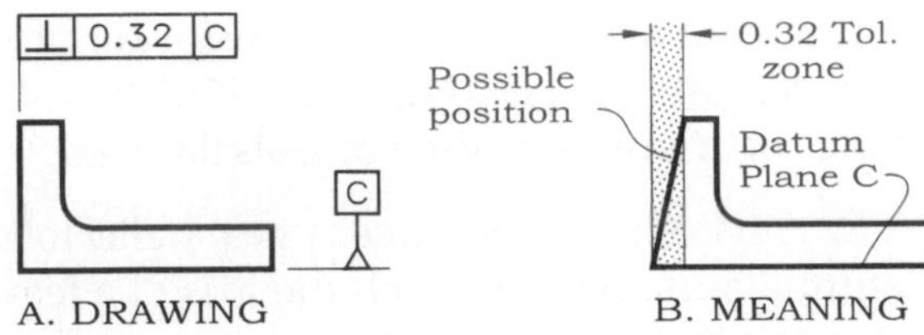

21.58 Perpendicularity is a tolerance of orientation that gives a tolerance zone of 0.32 for a plane perpendicular to a specified datum plane.

than 0.20 mm when the holes are at their smallest permissible size.

As the hole approaches its upper limit of 30.30, the tolerance zone increases to a maximum of 0.50 DIA. Therefore a greater variation is given at MMC than at RFS.

Perpendicularity The specifications for the perpendicularity of a plane to a datum are shown in **Figure 21.58**. The feature control frame shows that the surface perpendicular to datum plane C has a tolerance of 0.32 mm. In **Figure 21.59** a hole is specified as perpendicular to datum plane A.

Angularity A surface or line is angular when it is at an angle (other than 90°) from a datum or an axis. The angularity of the surface shown

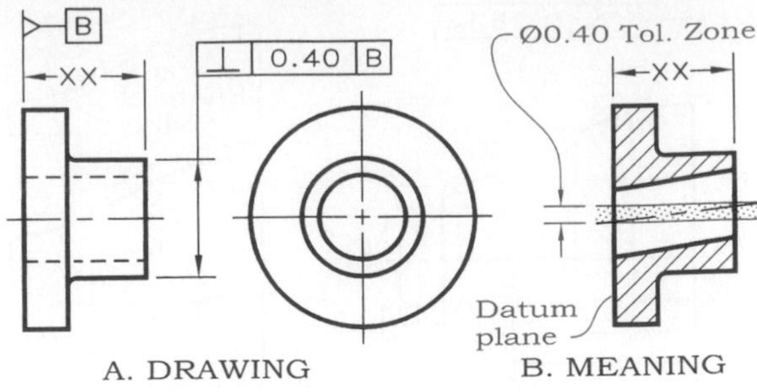

21.59 Perpendicularity is a tolerance of orientation. It can apply to the axis of a feature such as the centerline of a cylinder.

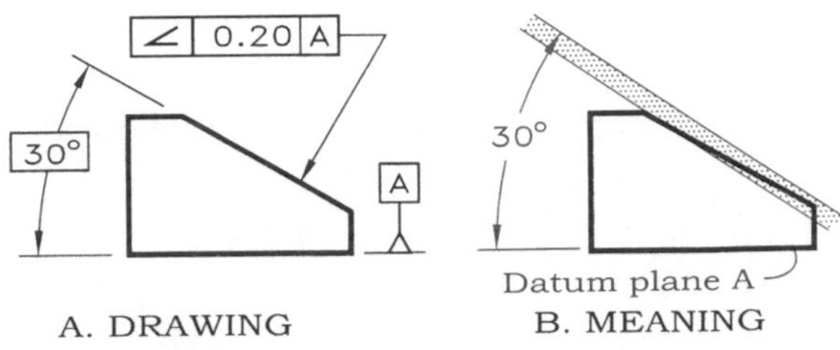

21.60 Angularity is a tolerance of orientation specifying a tolerance zone for an angular surface with respect to a datum plane. Here, the 30° angle is a true (basic) angle from which a tolerance of 0.20 mm is applied.

in **Figure 21.60** is dimensioned with a basic angle (exact angle) of 30° and an angularity tolerance zone of 0.20 mm inside which the plane must lie.

21.19 Runout Tolerancing

Runout tolerances can be **circular runouts** or **total runouts.**

Runout tolerancing is a way of controlling multiple features by relating them to a common datum axis. Features so controlled are surfaces of revolution about an axis and surfaces perpendicular to the axis.

The datum axis, such as diameter B in **Figure 21.61**, is established by a circular feature that rotates about the axis. When the part is rotated about this axis, the features of rotation must fall within the prescribed tolerance at full indicator movement (FIM).

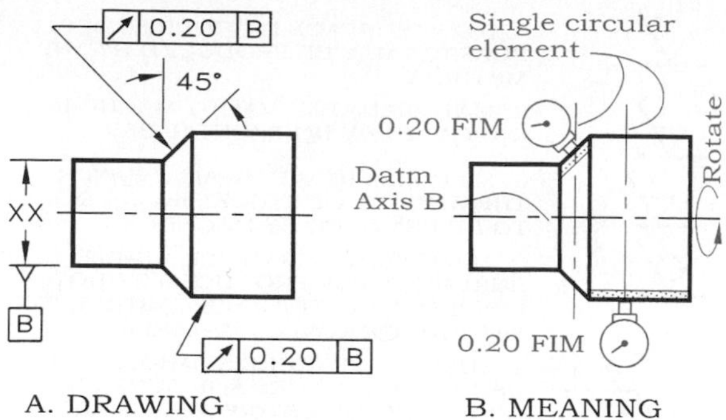

21.61 Runout tolerance, a composite of several tolerance of form characteristics, is used to specify concentric cylindrical parts. The part is mounted on the datum axis and is gauged as it is rotated.

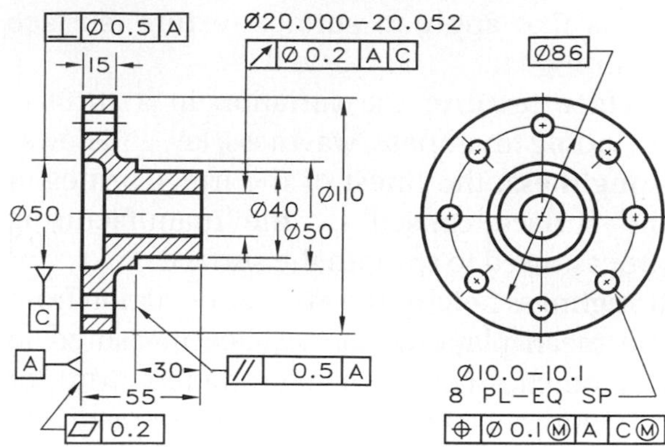

21.63 A combination of notes and symbols describes this part's geometric features.

One arrow in the feature control frame indicates **circular runout**, and two arrows indicate **total runout**.

Circular Runout Rotating an object about its axis 360° determines whether a circular cross section exceeds the permissible runout tolerance at any point (**Figure 21.62**). This same technique is used to measure the amount of wobble in surfaces perpendicular to the axis of rotation.

Total Runout Used to specify cumulative variations of circularity, straightness, concentricity, angularity, taper, and profile of a surface (**Figure 21.62**), total runout tolerances are measured for all circular and profile positions as the part is rotated 360°. When applied to surfaces perpendicular to the axis, total runout tolerances control variations in perpendicularity and flatness.

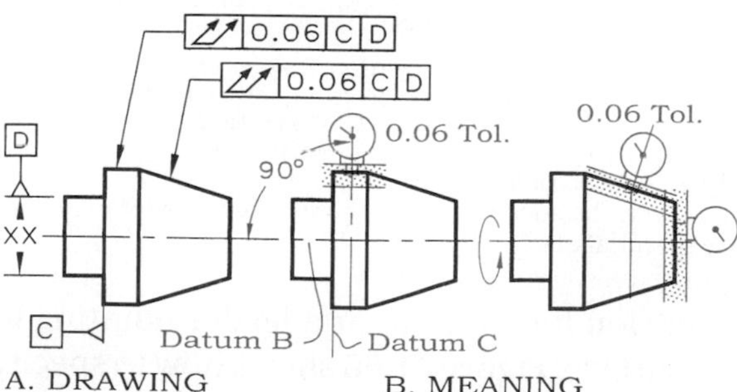

21.62 Here, runout tolerance is measured by mounting the object on the primary datum plane C and the secondary datum cylinder D. The cylinder and conical surface are gauged to check their conformity to a tolerance zone of 0.06 mm. The runout at the end of the cone could have been noted.

The dimensioned part shown in **Figure 21.63** illustrates several of the techniques of geometric tolerancing described in this and previous sections.

21.20 Surface Texture

Because the surface texture of a part affects its function, it must be precisely specified instead of being given an unspecified finished mark such as a V. **Figure 21.64** illustrates most of the

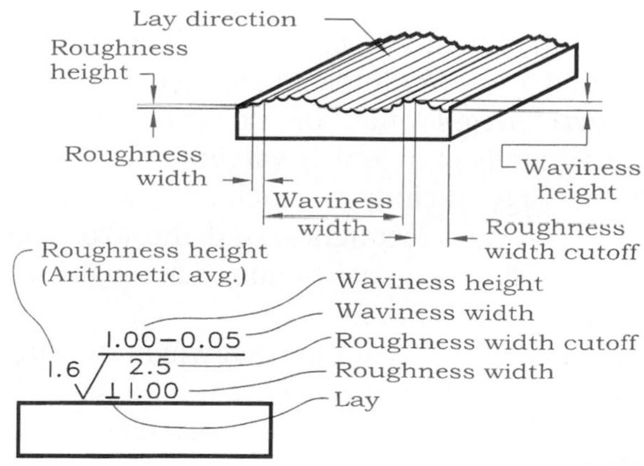

21.64 Surface texture terminology.
The definitions and terminology of surface texture for a finished surface.

terms that apply to surface texture (surface control).

Surface texture: the variation in a surface, including roughness, waviness, lay, and flaws.

Roughness: the finest of the irregularities in the surface caused by the manufacturing process used to smooth the surface.

Roughness height: the average deviation from the mean plane of the surface measured in microinches (μ in.) or micrometers (μm), or millionths of an inch and a meter, respectively.

Roughness width: the width between successive peaks and valleys forming the roughness measured in microinches or micrometers.

Roughness width cutoff: the largest spacing of repetitive irregularities that includes average roughness height (measured in inches or millimeters). When not specified, a value of 0.8 mm (.030 in.) is assumed.

Waviness: a widely spaced variation that exceeds the roughness width cutoff measured in inches or millimeters. Roughness may be regarded as a surface variation superimposed on a wavy surface.

Waviness height: the peak-to-valley distance between waves measured in inches or millimeters.

Waviness width: the spacing between wave peaks or wave valleys measured in inches or millimeters.

Lay: the direction of the surface pattern caused by the production method used.

Flaws: irregularities or defects occurring infrequently or at widely varying intervals on a surface, including cracks, blow holes, checks, ridges, scratches, and the like. The effect of flaws is usually omitted in roughness height measurements.

Contact area: the surface that will make contact with a mating surface.

Symbols for specifying **surface texture** are shown in **Figure 21.65**. The point of the V must touch the edge view of the surface, an

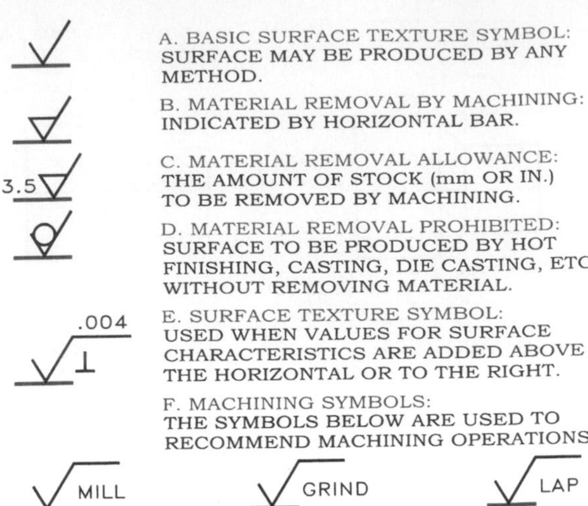

21.65 Surface texture symbols.
Use surface texture symbols to specify surface finish on the edge views of finished surfaces.

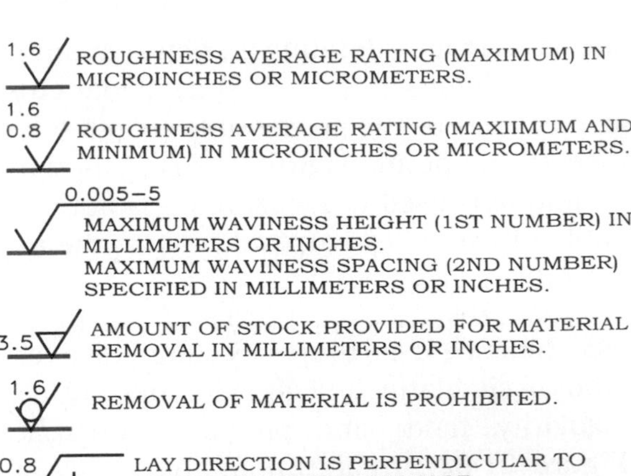

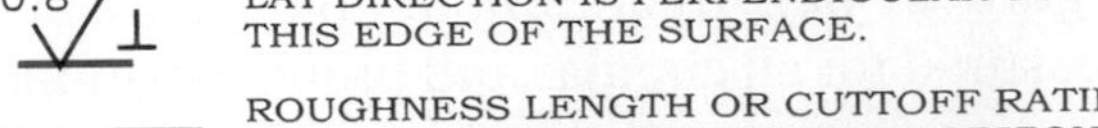

21.66 Surface control symbols.
Values may be added to surface control symbols for more precise specifications.

extension line from it, or a leader pointing to the surface. **Figure 21.66** shows how to specify values as a part of surface texture symbols. Roughness height values are related to the processes used to finish surfaces and may be

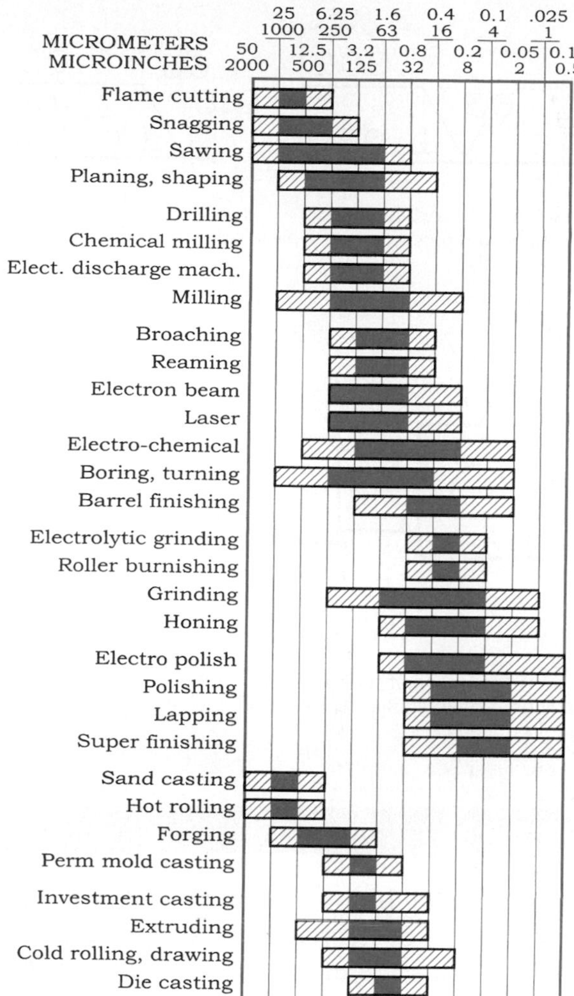

21.67 Various types of production methods result in the surface roughness heights shown in micrometers and microinches (millionths of a meter or an inch, respectively). The preferred range is in the solid portion of each bar.

taken from the table in **Figure 21.67**. The preferred values of roughness height are listed in **Figure 21.68**.

The preferred roughness width cutoff values in **Figure 21.69** are for specifying the sampling width used to measure roughness height. A value of 0.80 mm is assumed if no value is

PREFERRED ROUGHNESS AVG. VALUES

Micro-meters μm	Micro-inches μin.	Micro-meters μm	Micro-inches μin.
0.025	1	1.6	63
0.050	2	3.2	125
0.10	4	6.3	250
0.20	8	12.5	500
0.40	16	25.0	1000
0.80	32	Mircometers = 0.001 mm	

21.68 This range of roughness heights is recommended by the *ANSI Y14.36* standards for metric and English units.

ROUGHNESS WIDTH CUTOFF VALUES

Millimeters	0.08	0.25	0.80	2.5	8.0	25
Inches	.003	.010	.030	.1	.3	1

21.69 This range of roughness width cutoff values is recommended in the *ANSI Y14.36* standards. When unspecified, assume a value of 0.80 mm, or .03 in.

MAXIMUM WAVINESS HEIGHT VALUES

Millimeters	Inches	Millimeters	Inches
0.0005	.00002	0.025	.001
0.0008	.00003	0.05	.002
0.0012	.00005	0.08	.003
0.0020	.00008	0.12	.005
0.0025	.0001	0.20	.008
0.005	.0002	0.25	.010
0.008	.0003	0.38	.015
0.012	.0005	0.50	.020
0.020	.0008	0.80	.030

21.70 This range of maximum waviness height values is recommended in the *ANSI Y14.36* standards.

given. When required, maximum waviness height values may be selected from the recommended values shown in **Figure 21.70**.

Lay symbols indicating the direction of texture (markings made by the machining operation) on a surface (**Figure 21.71**) may be added to **surface texture symbols** as shown in **Figure 21.72**. The perpendicular sign indicates that lay is perpendicular to the edge view of the surface in this view (where the surface control symbol appears). **Figure 21.73**

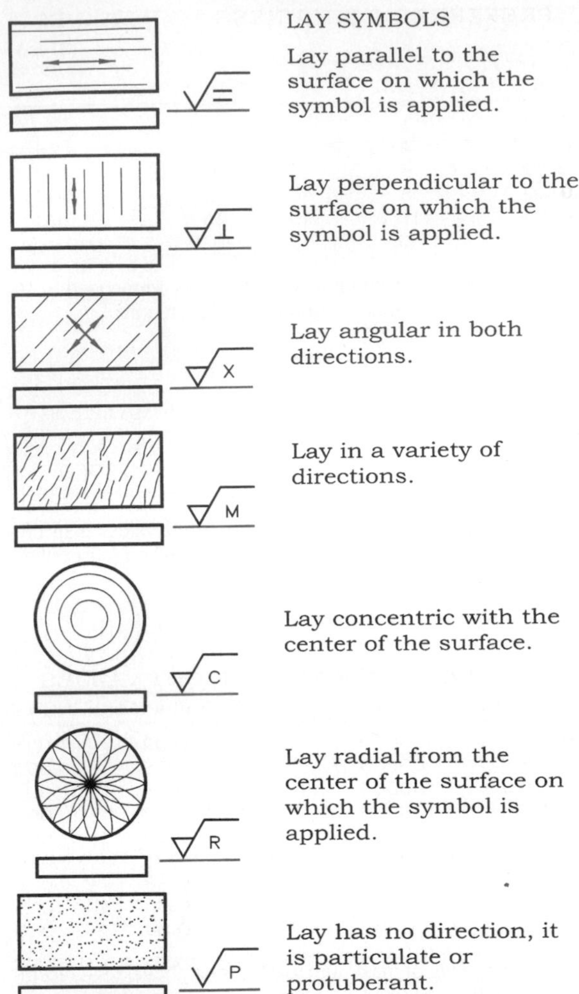

LAY SYMBOLS
Lay parallel to the surface on which the symbol is applied.
=
Lay perpendicular to the surface on which the symbol is applied.
⊥
Lay angular in both directions.
X
Lay in a variety of directions.
M
Lay concentric with the center of the surface.
C
Lay radial from the center of the surface on which the symbol is applied.
R
Lay has no direction, it is particulate or protuberant.
P

21.71 Lay symbols.
These symbols are used to indicate the direction of lay with respect to the surface where the control symbol is placed.

illustrates how to apply a variety of surface texture symbols to a part.

In Summary

The most import rule of tolerances is to **make them as large as possible** and use them only when they are absolutely essential to the function of parts. The application and verification of tolerances increases cost and time in the manufacturing process.

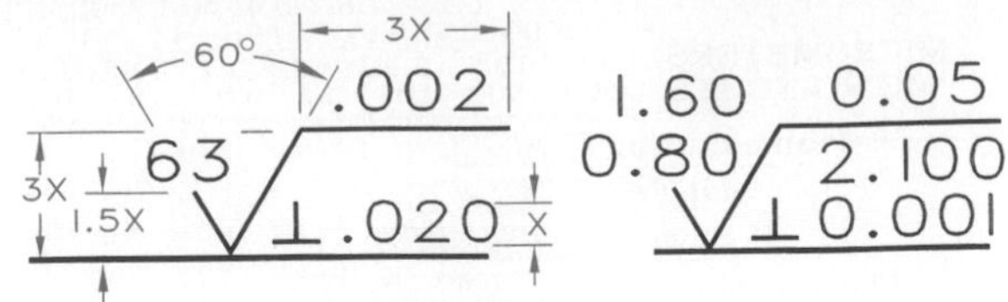

21.72 Surface texture symbols.
Examples and proportions of typical, fully specified surface texture symbols.

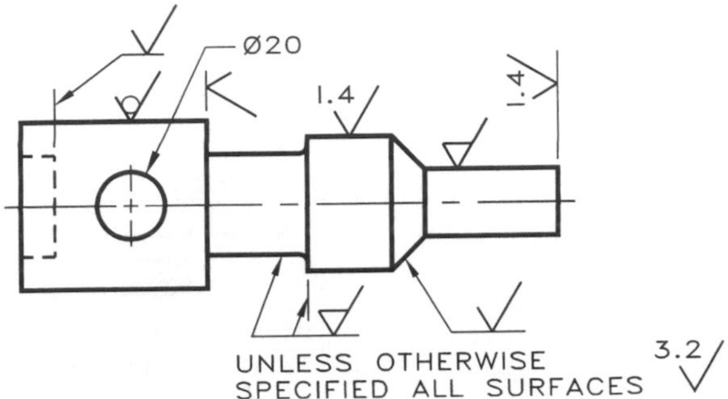

21.73 Application of surface texture symbols.
Various techniques of applying surface texture symbols to a part are illustrated here.

Problems

The following problems can be laid out (with instruments or freehand) on size A sheets by assigning a scale of .20 in., or 5 mm, to the given grid. Use 1/8-in. lettering on presenting your solutions.

Sheet 1: Cylindrical Fits

1. Draw the shaft and hole (they need not be to scale), give the limits for each diameter, and complete the table of values. Basic diameter of 1.00 in. (25 mm) and a class RC1 fit or H8/f7.

2. Repeat problem 1: Basic diameter of 1.75 in. (45 mm) and a class RC9 fit or H11/c11.

3. Repeat problem 1: Basic diameter of 2.00 in. (51 mm) and a class RC5 fit or H9/d9.

4. Repeat problem 1: Basic diameter of 12.00 in. (305 mm) and a class LC11 fit or H7/h6.

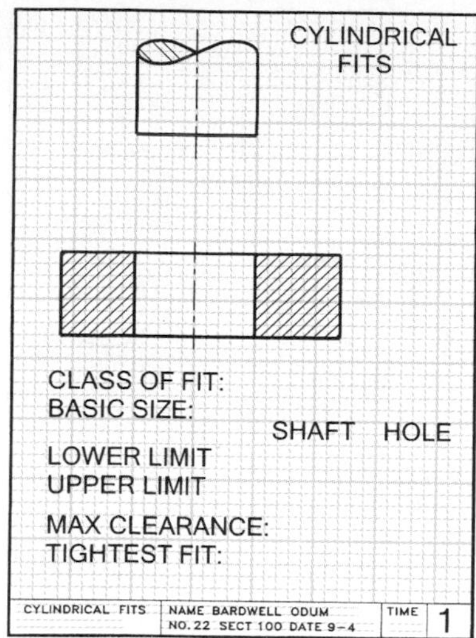

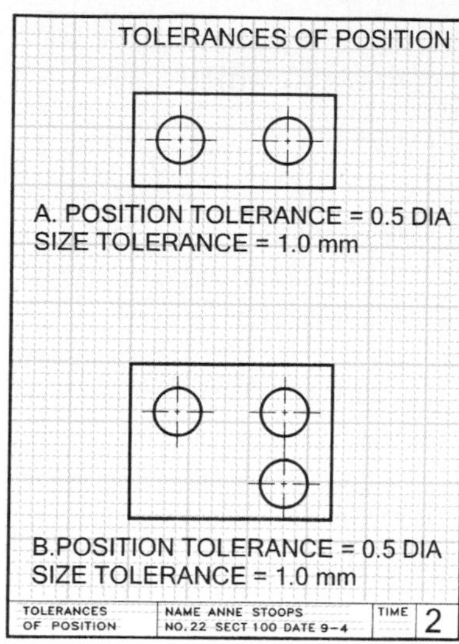

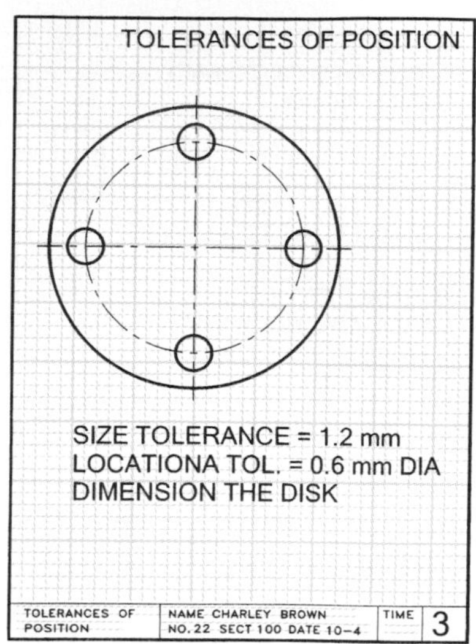

5. Repeat problem 1: Basic diameter of 3.00 in. (76 mm) and a class LC1 fit or H7/h6.

6. Repeat problem 1: Basic diameter of 8.00 in. (203 mm) and a class LC1 fit or H7/k6.

7. Repeat problem 1: Basic diameter of 102 in. (2591 mm) and a class LN3 fit or H7/n6.

8. Repeat problem 1: Basic diameter of 11.00 in. (279 mm) and a class LN2 fit or H7/p6.

9. Repeat problem 1: Basic diameter of 6.00 in. (152 mm) and a class FN5 fit or H7/s6.

10. Repeat problem 1: Basic diameter of 2.60 in. (66 mm) and a class FN1 fit or H7/u6.

Sheet 2: Tolerances of Position

A. Make a drawing of the part; locate the holes with tolerances, symbols, and dimensions.

B. Make a drawing of the part and locate and size the holes using the tolerances specified.

Sheet 3: Tolerances of Location

Make drawing of the part and locate and size the holes using the tolerances specified.

Sheet 4: Tolerances of Position

A. Make a drawing of the part and dimension it to specify symmetry of the notch with the left end of the part as specified.

B. Make a drawing of the part and dimension it to specify that the small cyclinder is symmetrical with the large cyliender.

Sheet 5: Tolerances of Form

A. Make a drawing of the part and dimension it to specify its straightness as specified.

B. Make a drawing of the part and dimension it to specify that surface A is flat as specified.

Sheet 6: Tolerances of Form

A.–C. Make drawings of the three parts and dimension them using feature control symbols to specify circularity (roundness) as noted.

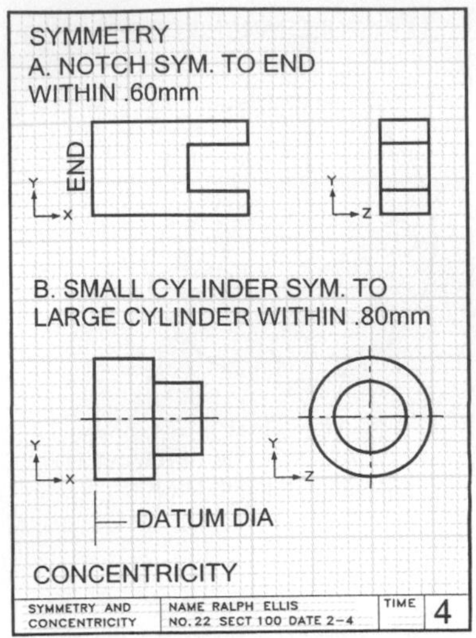

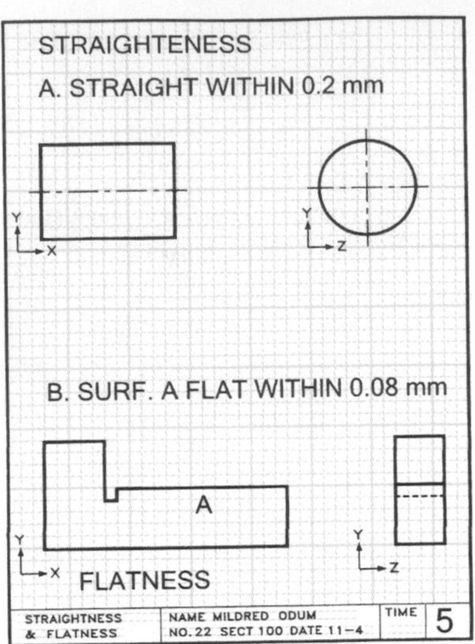

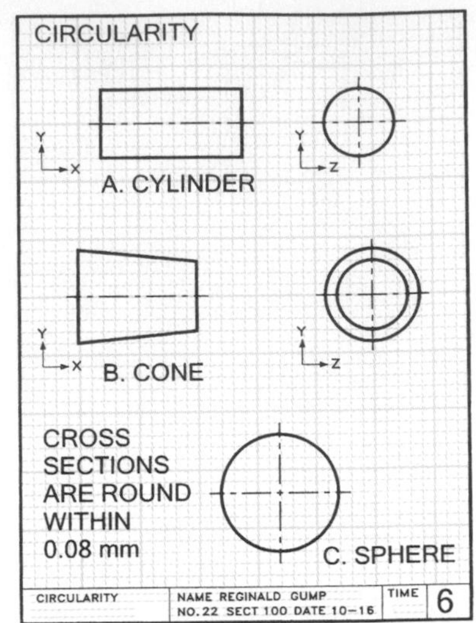

Sheet 7: Tolerances of Profile
Make drawings of the parts and give tolerance dimensions of profile on the curving lines as noted. Use a feature control symbol and the necessary dimensions.

Sheet 8: Tolerances of Orientation

A. Make a drawing of the cylinder and dimension it to specify cylindricity as noted.

B. Make a drawing of the angular part and dimension it to specify its angularity as noted.

Sheet 9: Tolerances of Orientation

A. Make a drawing of the part. Using a feature control symbol and the necessary dimensions, indicate that surface A is parallel as noted.

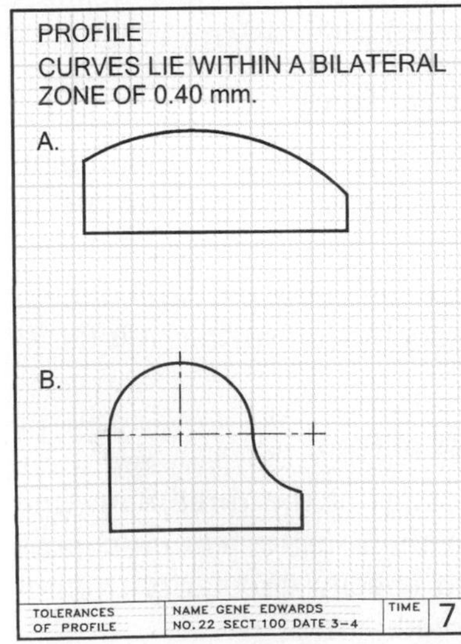

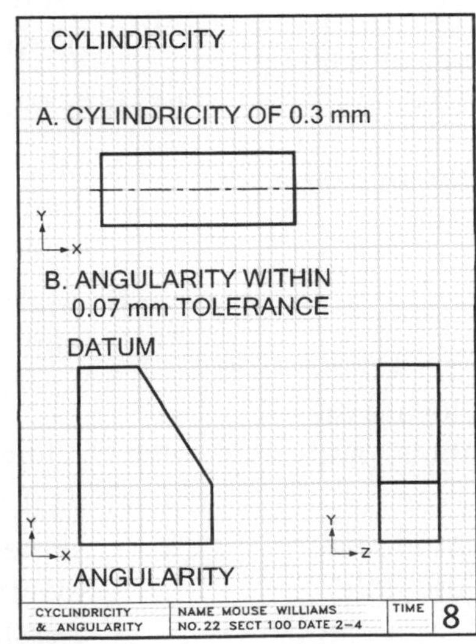

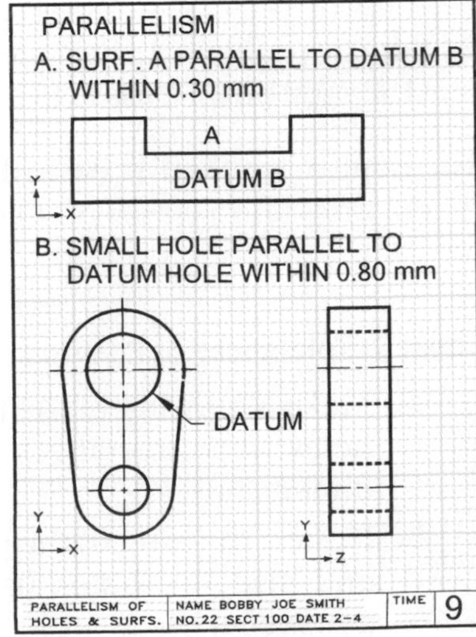

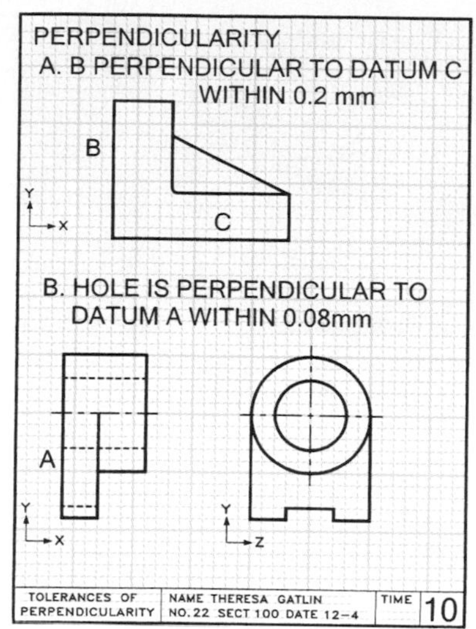

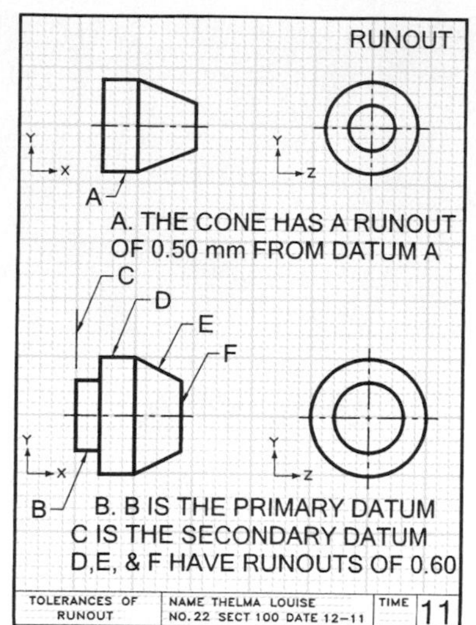

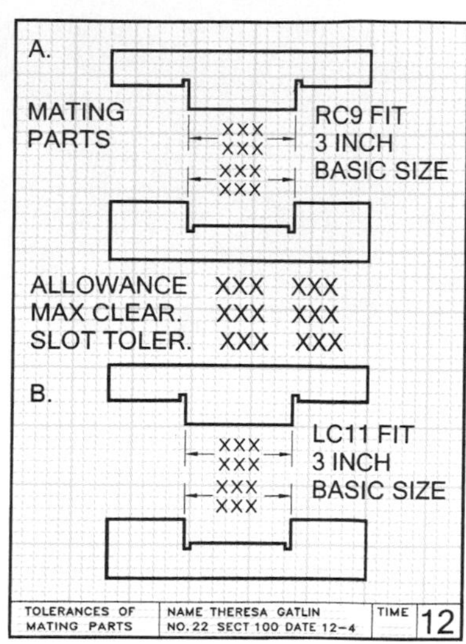

B. Make a drawing of the part. Using a feature control symbol and the necessary dimensions, indicate that the holes are parallel as noted.

Sheet 10: Tolerances of Orientation

A. and B. Make drawings of the parts. Use a feature control symbol and the necessary dimensions, and specify perpendicularity as noted.

Sheet 11: Tolerances of Runout

A. and B. Make drawings of the parts. Using the appropriate geometric tolerancing symbols and the indicated datums, dimension the conical features as noted.

Sheet 12: Mating Parts

A. and B. Make drawings of the mating parts. Using the two types of fit (RC9 and LC11) and their corresponding tables, provide the numerical values where the X's appear.

Sheet 13: Three-Plane Tolerances

A. Make a drawing of the journal base. Using metric units and the three datum planes, locate the two holes (size tolerance of 0.20) to lie within a tolerance zone of 1.6 DIA. Indicate that datum A is flat within 0.8. Indicate that datum B is perpendicular to datum A within 1.0 mm.

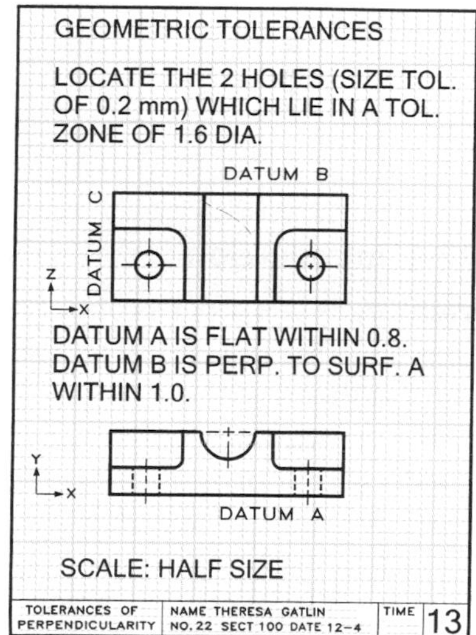

B. Same as problem A, but in addition to these specifications, give complete dimensions necessary to fully describe the part. Also indicate that the upper surface in the front view is parallel to datum A within 1.4 mm.

22 Welding

22.1 Introduction

Welding is the process of permanently joining metal by heating a joint to a suitable temperature with or without applying pressure and with or without using filler material. The welding practices described in this chapter comply with the standards developed by the American Welding Society and the American National Standards Institute (ANSI).

Welding is done in shops, on assembly lines, or in the field, as shown in **Figure 22.1**, where a welder is joining pipes. Welding is a widely used method of fabrication with its own language of notes, specifications, and symbology. You must become familiar with this system of notations to make and read drawings containing welding specifications.

Advantages of welding over other methods of fastening include (1) simplified fabrication, (2) economy, (3) increased strength and rigidity, (4) ease of repair, (5) creation of gas- and liquid-tight joints, and (6) reduction in weight and size.

22.1 This welder is joining two pipes in accordance with specifications on a set of drawings. (*Courtesy of Texas Eastern*; TE Today; *photo by Bob Thigpen.*)

22.2 Welding Processes

Figure 22.2 shows various types of welding processes. The three main types are gas welding, arc welding, and resistance welding.

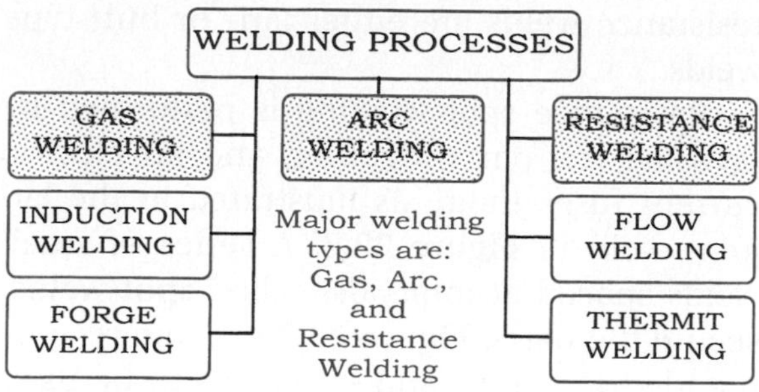

22.2 The three main types of welding processes are gas welding, arc welding, and resistance welding.

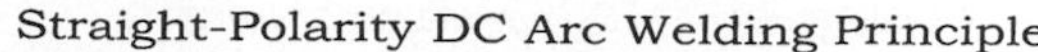

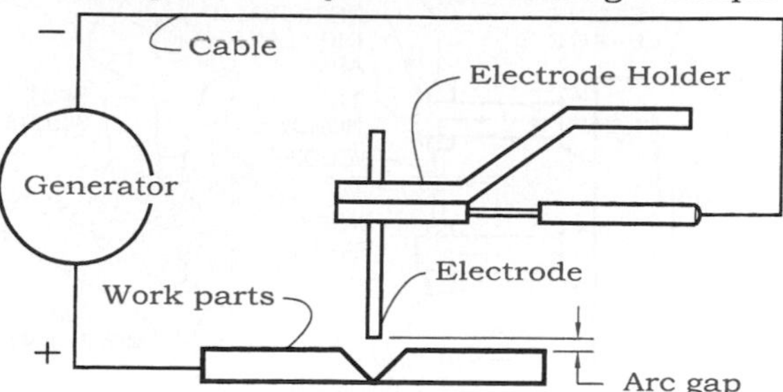

22.4 In arc welding, either AC or DC current is passed through an electrode to heat the joint.

Gas welding involves the use of gas flames to melt and fuse metal joints. Gases such as acetylene or hydrogen are mixed in a welding torch and burned with air or oxygen (**Figure 22.3**). The oxyacetylene method is widely used for repair work and field construction.

Most oxyacetylene welding is done manually with a minimum of equipment. Filler material in the form of welding rods is used to deposit metal at the joint as it is heated. Most metals, except for low- and medium-carbon steels, require fluxes to aid the process of melting and fusing the metals.

Arc welding involves the use of an electric arc to heat and fuse joints, with pressure sometimes required in addition to heat (**Figure 22.4**). The filler material is supplied by a consumable or nonconsumable electrode through which the electric arc is transmitted. Metals well suited to arc welding are wrought iron, low- and medium-carbon steels, stainless steel, copper, brass, bronze, aluminum, and some nickel alloys. In electric-arc welding, **the flux is a material coated on the electrodes that forms a coating on the metal being welded.** This coating protects the metal from oxidation so that the joint will not be weakened by overheating.

Flash welding is a form of arc welding, but it is similar to resistance welding because both pressure and electric current (**Figure 22.5**) are applied. The pieces to be welded are brought together, and an electric current is passed through them, causing heat to build up between them. As the metal burns, the current

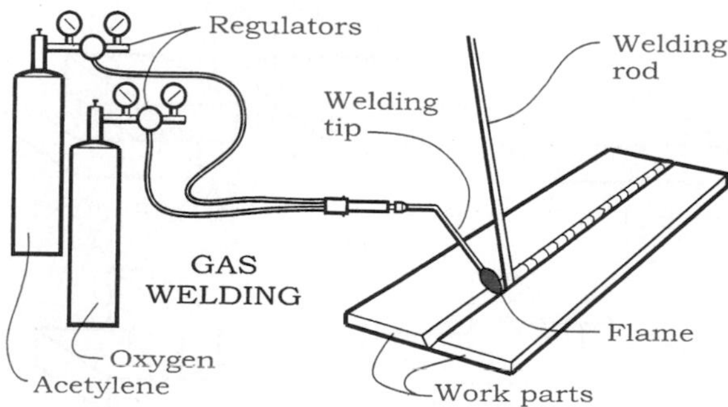

22.3 The gas welding process burns gases such as oxygen and acetylene in a torch to apply heat to a joint. The welding rod supplies the filler material.

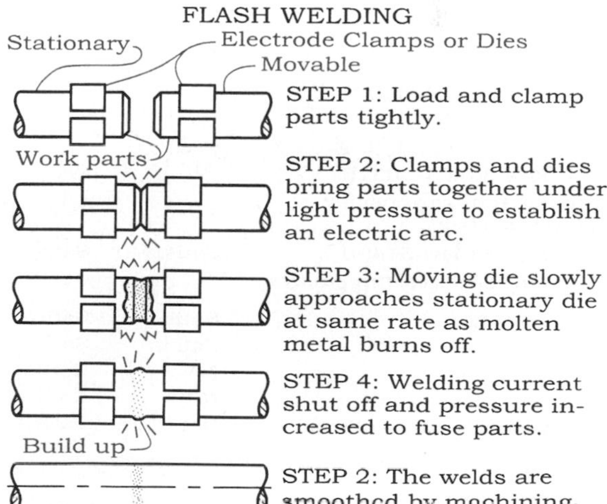

22.5 Flash welding, a type of arc welding, uses a combination of electric current and pressure to fuse two parts.

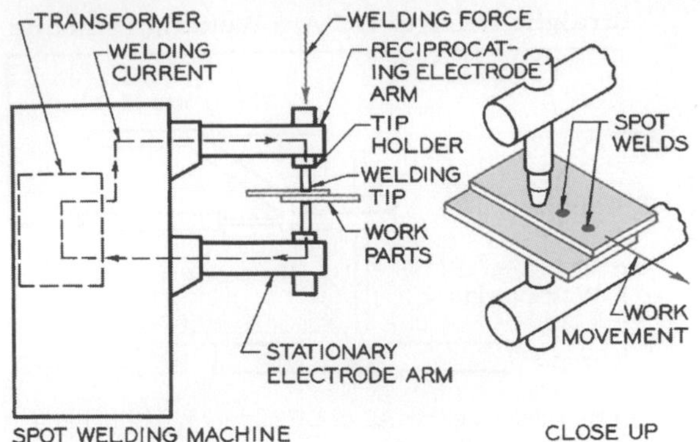

22.6 Resistance spot welding may be used to join lap and butt joints.

is turned off, and the pressure between the pieces is increased to fuse them.

Resistance welding comprises several processes by which metals are fused both by the heat produced from the resistance of the parts to an electric current and by pressure. Fluxes and filler materials normally are not used. All

RESISTANCE WELDING

Material	Spot Welding	Flash Welding
Low-carbon mild steel		
SAE 1010	Rec.	Rec.
SAE 1020	Rec.	Rec.
Medium-carbon steel		
SAE 1030	Rec.	Rec.
SAE 1050	Rec.	Rec.
Wrought alloy steel		
SAE 4130	Rec.	Rec.
SAE 4340	Rec.	Rec.
High-alloy austenitic stainless steel		
SAE 30301 -30302	Rec.	Rec.
SAE 30309-30316	Rec.	Rec.
Ferritic and martensistic stainless steel		
SAE 51410-51430	Satis.	Satis.
Wrought heat-resisting alloys		
19-9-DL	Satis.	Satis.
16-25-6	Satis.	Satis.
Cast iron	NA	Not Rec.
Gray iron	NA	Not Rec.
Aluminum & alum. alloys	Rec.	Satis.
Nickel & nickel alloys	Rec.	Satis.

REC.-Recommended SATIS.-Satisfactory
NOT REC.- Not recommended NA-Not applicable

22.7 Resistance welding processes for various materials are shown here.

resistance welds are either lap- or butt-type welds.

Resistance spot welding is performed by pressing the parts together, and an electric current fuses them, as illustrated in the lap joint weld in **Figure 22.6**. A series of small welds spaced at intervals, called **spot welds**, secure the parts. **Figure 22.7** lists the recommended materials and processes to be used for resistance welding.

22.3 Weld Joints and Welds

Figure 22.8 shows the five standard weld joints: butt joint, corner joint, lap joint, edge joint, and tee joint. The **butt joint** can be joined with square groove, V-groove, bevel groove, U-groove, and J-groove welds. The **corner joint** can be joined with these welds and with the fillet weld. The **lap joint** can be joined with bevel groove, J-groove, fillet, slot, plug, spot, projection, and seam welds. The **edge joint** uses the same welds as the lap joint along with square groove, V-groove, U-groove, and seam welds. The **tee joint** can be joined by bevel groove, J-groove, and fillet welds.

Figure 22.9 depicts commonly used welds and their corresponding ideographs (symbols). The fillet weld is a built-up weld at the intersection (usually 90°) of two surfaces. The square, bevel, V-groove, J-groove, and U-groove welds all have grooves, and the weld is made in these grooves. Slot and plug welds

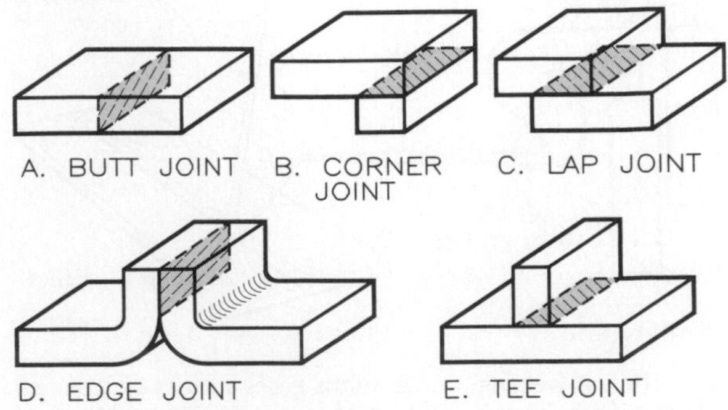

22.8 The five standard weld joints.

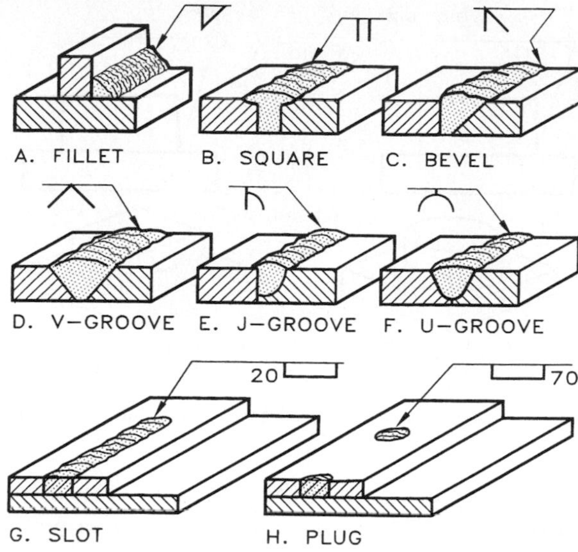

22.9 Standard welds and their corresponding ideographs.

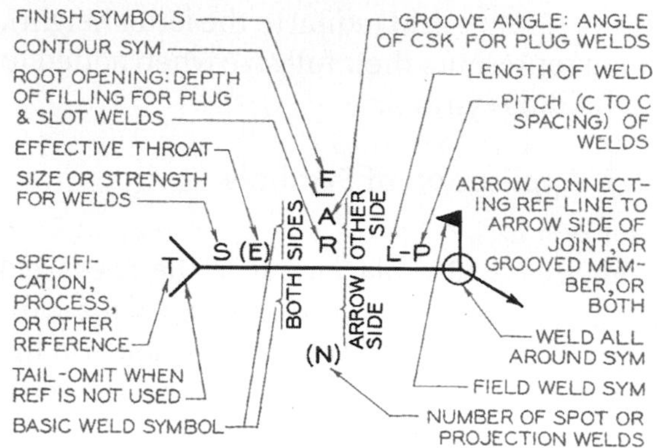

22.10 The welding symbol. It is usually modified to a simpler form for use on drawings.

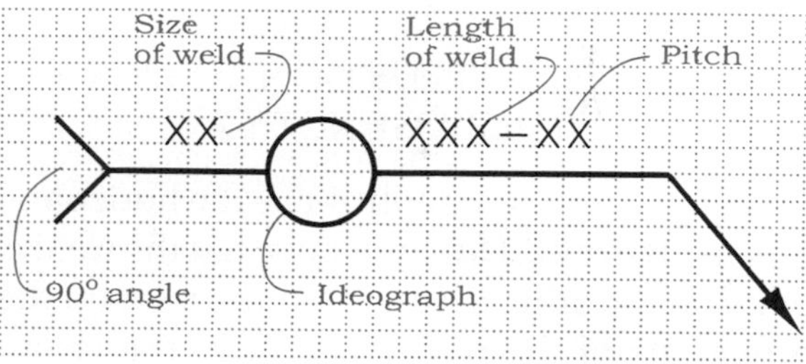

22.11 Welding symbol proportions are based on the letter height used on a drawing, usually 1/8 in., or 3 mm. This grid is equal to the letter height.

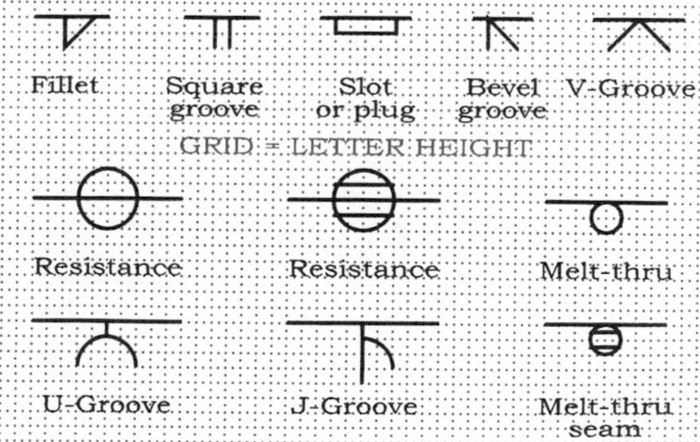

22.12 The sizes of the ideographs shown on the 1/8-in. (3-mm) grid (the letter height) are proportional to the size of the welding symbol (**Figure 22.11**).

have intermittent holes or openings where the parts are welded. Holes are unnecessary when resistance welding is used.

22.4 Welding Symbols

If a drawing has a general welding note such as ALL JOINTS ARE WELDED THROUGHOUT, the designer has transferred responsibility to the welder. Welding is too important to be left to chance and should be specified more precisely.

Symbols are used to convey welding specifications on a drawing. The complete welding symbol is shown in **Figure 22.10**, but it usually appears on a drawing in modified, more general form with less detail. The scale of the welding symbol is based on the letter height used on the drawing, which is the size of the grid on which the symbol is drawn in **Figure 22.11**. The standard height of lettering on a drawing is usually 1/8 in., or 3 mm.

The **ideograph** is the symbol that denotes the type of weld desired, and it generally depicts the cross section representation of the weld. **Figure 22.12** shows the ideographs used most often. They are drawn to scale on the

1/8-in. (3-mm) grid (equal to the letter height), which represents their full size when added to the welding symbol.

22.5 Application of Symbols

Fillet Welds

In **Figure 22.13A**, placement of the fillet weld ideograph below the horizontal line of the symbol indicates that the weld is at the joint on the arrow side—the right side in this case. The vertical leg of the ideograph is always on the left side.

A numeral (either a common fraction or a decimal value) to the right of the ideograph indicates the size of the weld. You may omit this number from the symbol if you insert a general note elsewhere on the drawing to specify the fillet size, such as

ALL FILLET WELDS 1/4 IN. UNLESS OTHERWISE NOTED.

Placing the ideograph above the horizontal line in **Figure 22.13B** indicates that the weld is to be on the other side, that is, the joint on the other side of the part, away from the arrow. When the part is to be welded on both sides, use the ideograph shown in **Figure 22.13C**. You

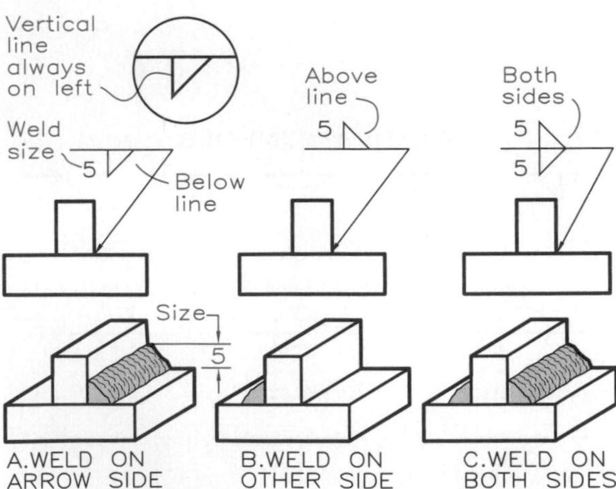

22.13 Fillet welds may be noted with abbreviated symbols. (A) When the ideograph appears below the horizontal line, it specifies a weld on the arrow side. (B) When it is above the line, it specifies a weld on the opposite side. (C) When it is on both sides of the line, it specifies a weld on each side.

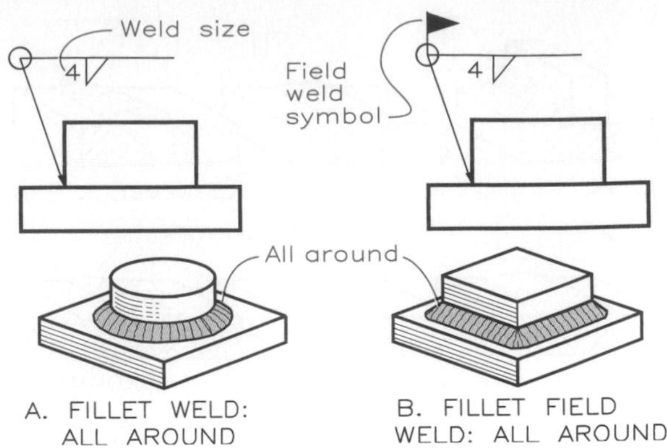

22.14 These symbols indicate fillet welds all around two types of parts.

may omit the tail and other specifications from the symbol when you provide detailed specifications elsewhere.

A single arrow often is used to specify a weld that is to be made all around two joining parts (**Figure 22.14A**). A circle of 6 mm (twice the letter height) in diameter, drawn at the bend in the leader of the symbol, denotes this type of weld. If the welding is to be done in the field rather than in the shop, a solid black triangular "flag" is added also (**Figure 22.14B**).

You may specify a fillet weld that is to run the full length of the two parts, as in **Figure 22.15A**. The ideograph is on the lower side of the horizontal line, so the weld is on the arrow side. You

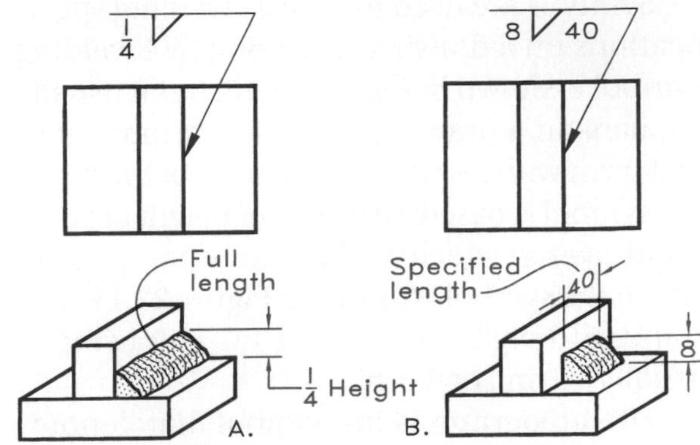

22.15 Fillet weld symbols.

A This symbol indicates full-length fillet welds.

B This symbol indicates fillet welds of specified, but less than full, length.

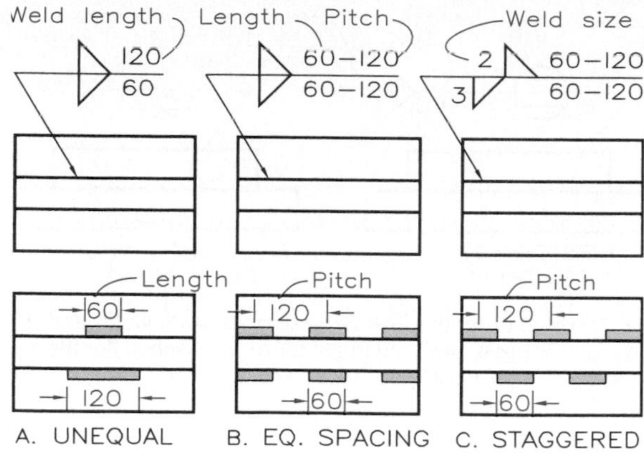

22.16 These symbols specify intermittent welds of varying lengths and alignments.

may specify a fillet weld that is to run shorter than full length, as in **Figure 22.15B**, where 40 represents the weld's length in millimeters.

You may specify fillet welds to run different lengths and be positioned on both sides of a part, as in **Figure 22.16A**. The dimension on the lower side of the horizontal gives the length of the weld on the arrow side, and the dimension on the upper side of the horizontal gives the length on the opposite side.

Intermittent welds have a specified length and are spaced uniformly, center to center, at an interval called the *pitch*. In **Figure 22.16B**, the welds are equally spaced on both sides, are 60 mm long, and have pitches of 120 mm, as indicated by the symbol shown. The symbol shown in **Figure 22.16C** specifies intermittent welds that are staggered in alternate positions on opposite sides.

Groove Welds

The standard types of groove welds are **V-groove, bevel groove, double V-groove, U-groove**, and **J-groove** (**Figure 22.17**). When you do not give the depth of the grooves, angle of the chamfer, and root openings on a symbol, you must specify them elsewhere on the drawing or in supporting documents. In **Figures 22.17A** and **B**, the angles of the V-joints

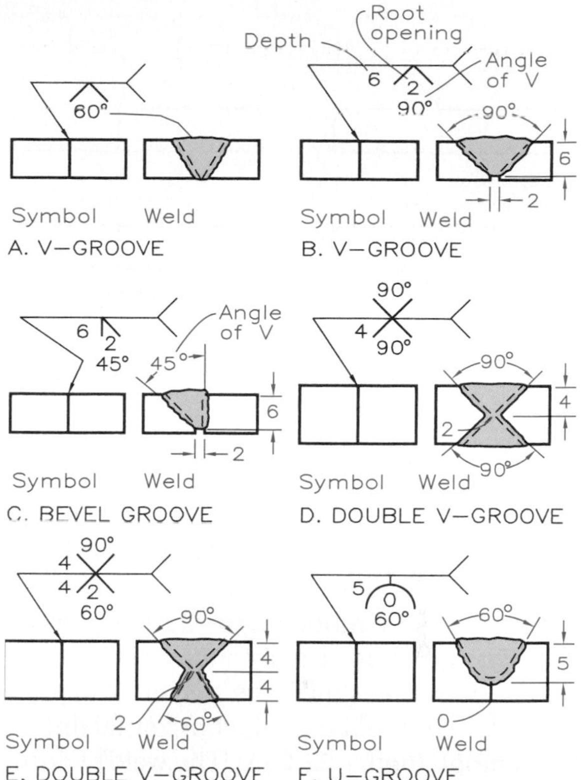

22.17 The various types of groove welds and their general specifications.

arc labeled 60° and 90° under the ideographs. In **Figure 22.17B**, the deaths of the weld (6) and the root opening (2)—the gap between the two parts—are given.

In a bevel groove weld, only one of the parts is beveled. The symbol's leader is bent and pointed toward the beveled part to call attention to it (**Figures 22.17C and 22.18B**). This practice also applies to J-groove welds, where one side is grooved and the other is not (**Figure 22.18A**).

Notate double V-groove welds by weld size, bevel angle, and root opening (**Figures 22.17D** and **E**). Omit root opening sizes or show a zero on the symbol when parts fit flush. Give the angle and depth of the groove in the symbol for a U-groove weld (**Figure 22.17F**).

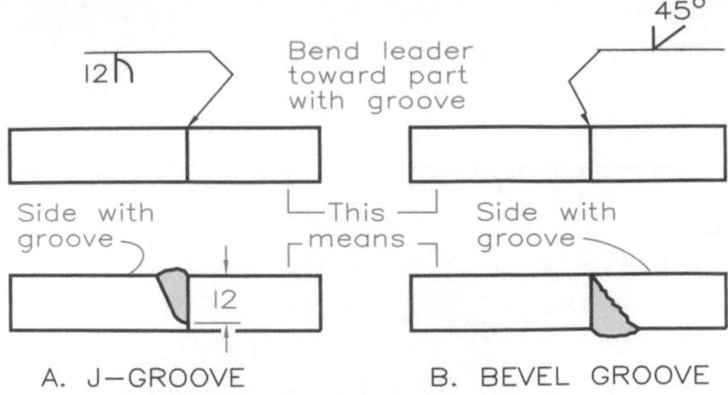

22.18 J-groove welds and bevel welds are specified by bent arrows pointing to the side of the joint to be grooved or beveled.

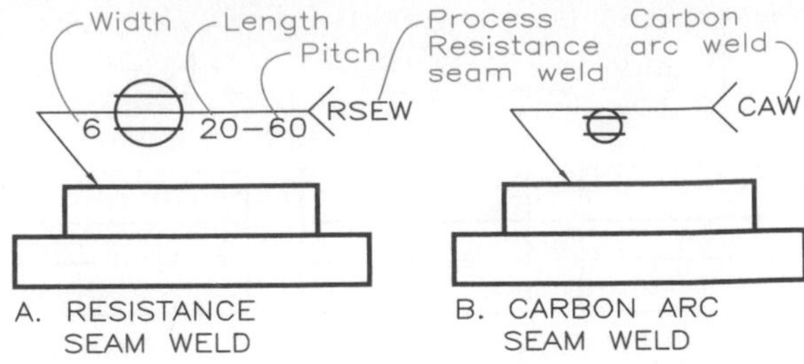

22.20 The process used for (A) resistance seam welds and (B) arc-seam welds is indicated in the tail of the symbol. For the arc weld the symbol must specify the arrow side or the other side of the piece.

Seam Welds

A **seam weld** joins two lapping parts with either a continuous weld or a series of closely spaced spot welds. The seam weld process to be used is identified by abbreviations in the tail of the weld symbol (**Figure 22.19**). The circular ideograph for a resistance weld is about 12 mm (four times the letter height) in diameter and is centered over the horizontal line of the symbol (**Figure 22.20A**). The weld's width, length, and pitch are given.

When the seam weld is to be made by arc welding (CAW), the diameter of the ideograph is about 6 mm (twice the letter height) and goes on the upper or lower side of the symbol's horizontal line to indicate whether the seam is to be applied to the arrow side or to the opposite side (**Figure 22.20B**). When the length of the weld is not shown, the seam weld is understood to extend between abrupt changes in the direction of the seam.

Spot welds are similarly specified with ideographs and specifications by diameter, number of welds, and pitch between the welds. The process of resistance spot welding (RSW) is noted in the tail of the symbol (**Figure 22.21A**). For arc welding, the arrow side or other side must be indicated by a symbol (**Figure 22.21B**).

WELDING ABBREVIATIONS

CAW	Carbon-arc w.	IB	Induction brazing
CW	Cold welding	IRB	Infrared brazing
DB	Dip brazing	OAW	Oxyacetylene w.
DFW	Diffusion welding	OHW	Oxyhydrogen w.
EBW	Electric beam w.	PGW	Pressure gas w.
ESW	Electroslag welding	RB	Resist. brazing
EXW	Explosion welding	RPW	Projection weld.
FB	Furnace brazing	RSEW	Resist. seam w.
FOW	Forge welding	RSW	Resist. spot w.
FRW	Friction welding	RW	Resist. welding
FW	Flash welding	TB	Torch brazing
GMAW	Gas metal arc w.	UW	Upset welding
GTAW	Gas tungsten w.		* w. = welding

22.19 These abbreviations represent the various types of welding processes and are used in welding symbols.

Built-Up Welds

When the surface of a part is to be enlarged, or built up, by welding, indicate this process with a symbol as shown in **Figure 22.22**. Dimension the width of the built-up weld in the view. Specify the height of the weld above the surface in the symbol to the left of the ideograph. The radius of the circular segment is 6 mm (twice the letter height).

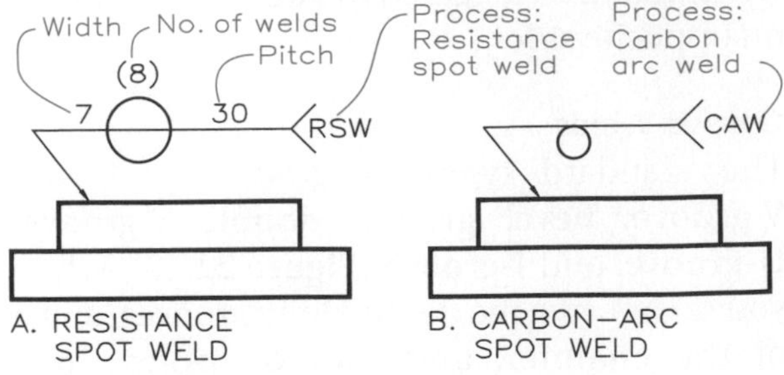

22.21 The process to be used for (A) resistance spot welds and (B) arc spot welds is indicated in the tail of the symbol. For the arc weld the symbol must specify the arrow side or the other side of the piece.

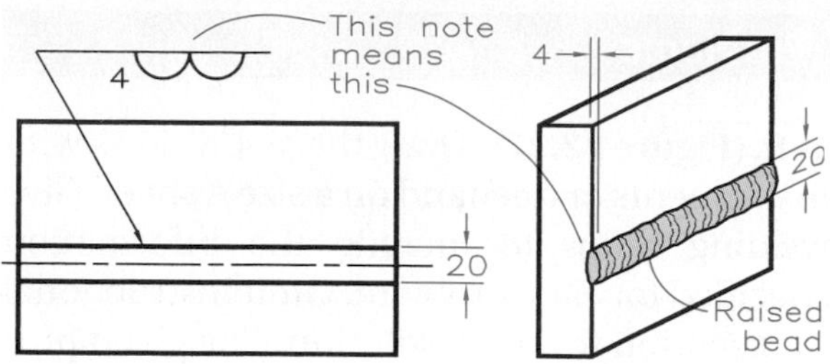

22.22 Use this method to apply a symbol to a built-up weld on a surface.

22.6 Surface Contouring

Contour symbols are used to indicate which of the three types of contours, **flush, concave**, or **convex**, is desired on the surface of the weld. Flush contours are smooth with the surface or flat across the hypotenuse of a fillet weld. Concave contours bulge inward with a curve, and convex contours bulge outward with a curve (**Figure 22.23**).

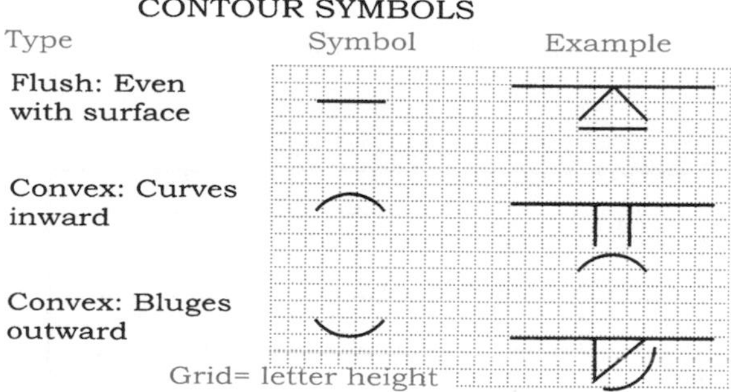

22.23 These contour symbols specify the desired surface finish of a weld.

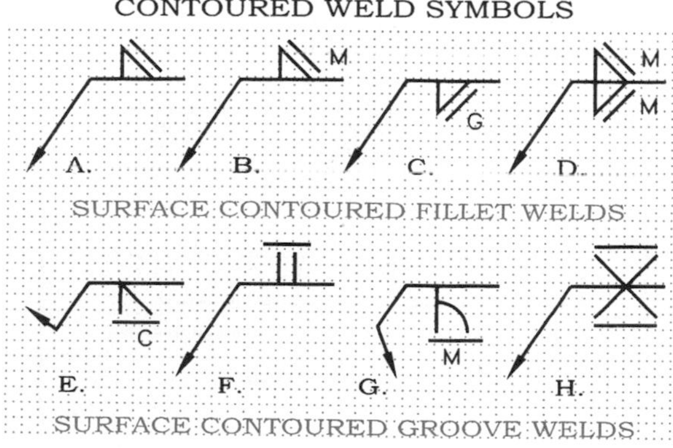

22.24 These examples of contoured weld symbols with letters added indicate the type of finishing to be applied to the weld (M, machining; G, grinding; C, chipping).

Finishing the weld by an additional process to obtain the desired contour often is necessary. These processes, which may be indicated by their abbreviations, are **chipping** (C), **grinding** (G), **hammering** (H), **machining** (M), **rolling** (R), and **peening** (P), as shown in **Figure 22.24**.

22.7 Brazing

Brazing is a method much like welding for joining pieces of metal. Brazing entails heating joints to more than 800°F and distributing by capillary action a nonferrous filler material, with a melting point below that of the base materials, between the closely fitting parts.

Before brazing, the parts must be cleaned and the joints fluxed. The brazing filler is added before or just as the joints are heated beyond the filler's melting point. After the filler material has melted, it is allowed to flow between the parts to form the joint. As **Figure 22.25** shows, there are two basic brazing joints: lap joints and butt joints.

Brazing is used to join parts, to provide gas- and liquid-tight joints, to ensure electrical

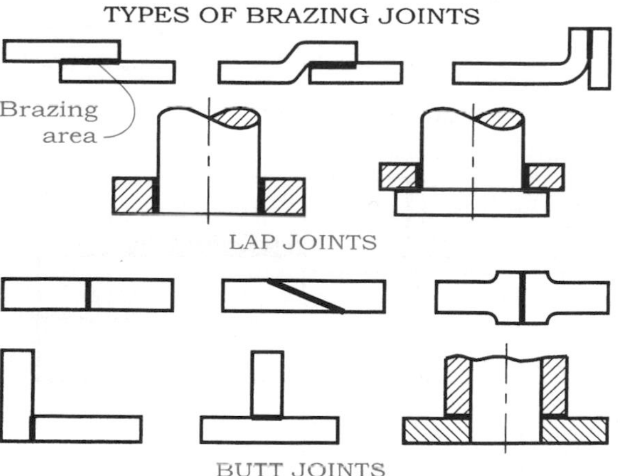

22.25 The two basic types of brazing joints are lap joints and butt joints.

conductivity, and to aid in repair and salvage. Brazed joints withstand more stress, higher temperature, and more vibration than soft-soldered joints.

22.8 Soldering

Soldering is the process of joining two metal parts with a third metal that melts below the temperature of the metals being joined. Solders are alloys of nonferrous metals that melt below 800°F. Widely used in the automotive and electrical industries, soldering is one of the basic techniques of welding and often is done by hand with a soldering iron like the one depicted in **Figure 22.26**. The iron is placed on the joint to heat it and to melt the solder. Basic soldering is noted on the drawing with a leader simply as SOLDER, and other specifications noted as needed as shown in **Figure 22.26**.

By necessity, the coverage in this chapter is introductory in nature but adequate for a basic understanding of how to specify welding on an engineering drawing. More detailed information on welding is available from the American Welding Society, 550 N.W. LeJeune Road, Miami, Florida 33126. This society maintains and publishes guidelines and standards for the technology of welding.

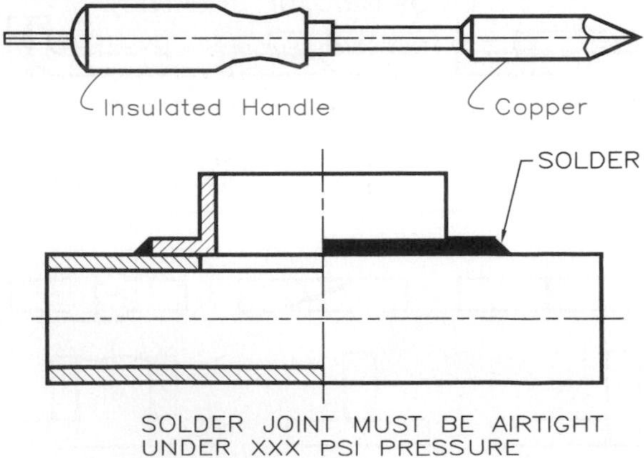

22.26 This typical handheld soldering iron is used to soft-solder two parts together. The method of notating a drawing for soldering also is shown.

Problems

1–8. (**Figure 22.27**) Draw the given views with instruments or freehand on a size A sheet. Give welding notes to include the information specified for each problem. Omit instructional information from the solution. The given problems are shown on a 0.20-in. (5-mm) grid.

Design Problems

A. Draw the necessary orthographic views of each problem to give the welding symbols as specified by the instruction accompanying each illustration. Provide the necessary welding symbols.

B. In addition to the welding symbols specifed in **A**, provide the remaining dimensions necessary to completely define the part.

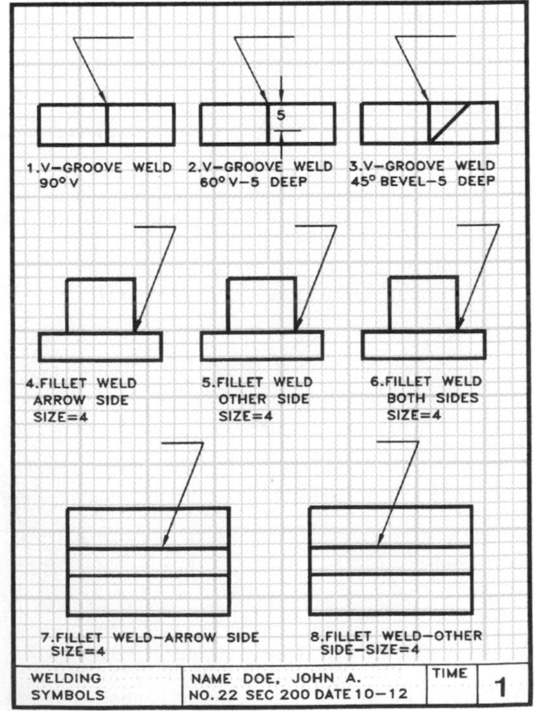

22.27 Problems 1–8.

DESIGN 1: ANGLE FIXTURE

Using your dividers, double the dimensions of the fixture and draw the orthographic views of it on a size A sheet. Give welding symbols for attaching the ribs to the vertical and horizontal surfaces.

12

ANGLE FIXTURE
1010 STEEL
6 REQUIRED

DESIGN 2: JACK BASE

Draw the necessary orthographic views of the base on a size A sheet. Show welding symbols for attaching the cylinder and ribs to the base.

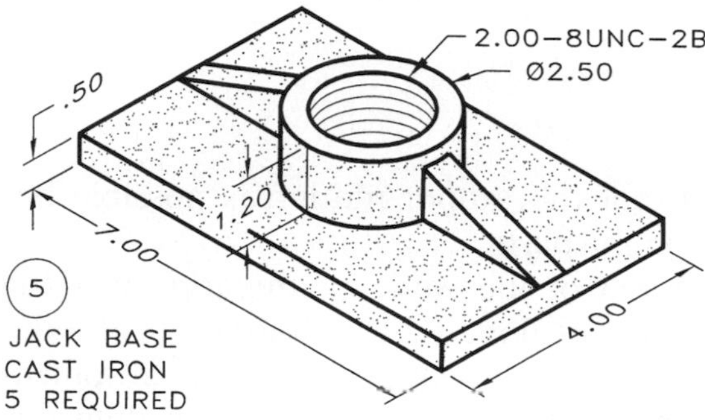

DESIGN 3: SHAFT SOCKET

Approximate the dimensions of the shaft socket based on the given diameter and draw orthographic views of it on a size A sheet. The cylinder and 4 ribs are to be welded to the 4 inch square base. Show welding symbols in the top and front views.

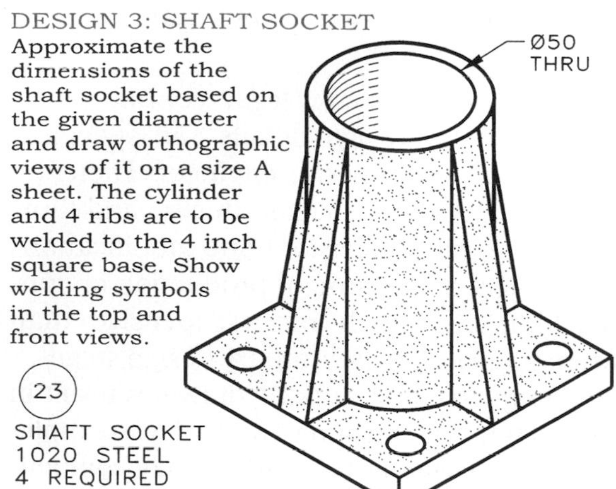

DESIGN 4: JACK BASE

Draw the necessary orthographic views of this part on a size A sheet. Each grid equals 0.2 in. or 5 mm. Show welding symbols for joining the ribs and cylinder as if they were separate parts.

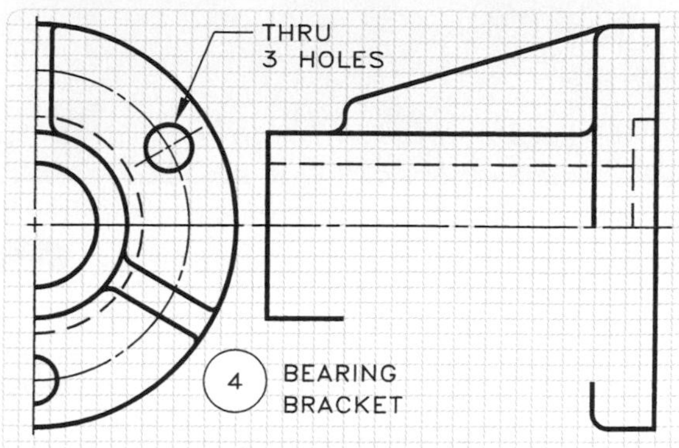

DESIGN 5: JACK BASE

Draw the necessary orthographic views of this part on a size A sheet. Each grid equals 0.2 in. or 5 mm. Show welding symbols for joining the ribs and cylinders as if they were separate parts.

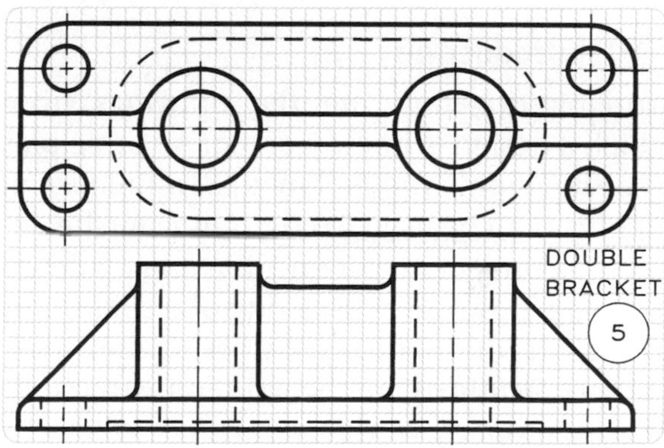

23 Working Drawings

23.1 Introduction

Working drawings are the drawings from which a design is implemented. All principles of orthographic projection and techniques of graphics can be used to communicate the details of a project in working drawings. A **detail drawing** is a working drawing of a single part (or detail) within the set of working drawings.

Specifications are the written instructions that accompany working drawings. When the design can be represented on a few sheets, the specifications are usually written on the drawings to consolidate the information into a single format.

All parts must interact with other parts to some degree to yield the desired function from a design. Before detail drawings of individual parts are made, the designer must thoroughly analyze the working drawing to ensure that the parts fit properly with mating parts, that the correct tolerances are applied, that the contact surfaces are properly finished, and that the proper motion is possible between the parts.

Much of the work in preparing working drawings is done by the drafter, but the designer, who is usually an engineer, is responsible for their correctness. Working drawings bring products and systems into being.

23.2 Working Drawings as Legal Documents

Working drawings are legal contracts that document the design details and specifications as directed by the engineer. Therefore drawings must be as clear, precise, and thorough as possible. Revisions and modifications of a project at the time of production or construction are much more expensive than when done in the preliminary design stages.

Poorly executed working drawings result in wasted time and resources and increase implementation costs. To be economically competitive, drawings must be as error-free as possible.

Working drawings specify all aspects of the design, reflecting the soundness of engineering and function of the finished product and economy of fabrication. The working drawing is the instrument that is most likely to establish the responsibility for any failure to meet specifications during implementation.

23.3 Dimensions and Units

English System

The inch is the basic unit of the English system, and virtually all shop drawings made with English units are dimensioned in inches. This practice is followed even when dimensions are several feet in length.

The base flange shown in **Figure 23.1** is an example of a relatively simple working drawing of a part. However, there are many drawings of this simplicity that must be designed, developed, and detailed for the overall projects to come into being.

The base flange is dimensioned with two-place decimal inches except where four-place decimal inches are used for toleranced dimensions. Inch marks (") are omitted from dimensions on working drawings because the units are understood to be in inches, and their omission

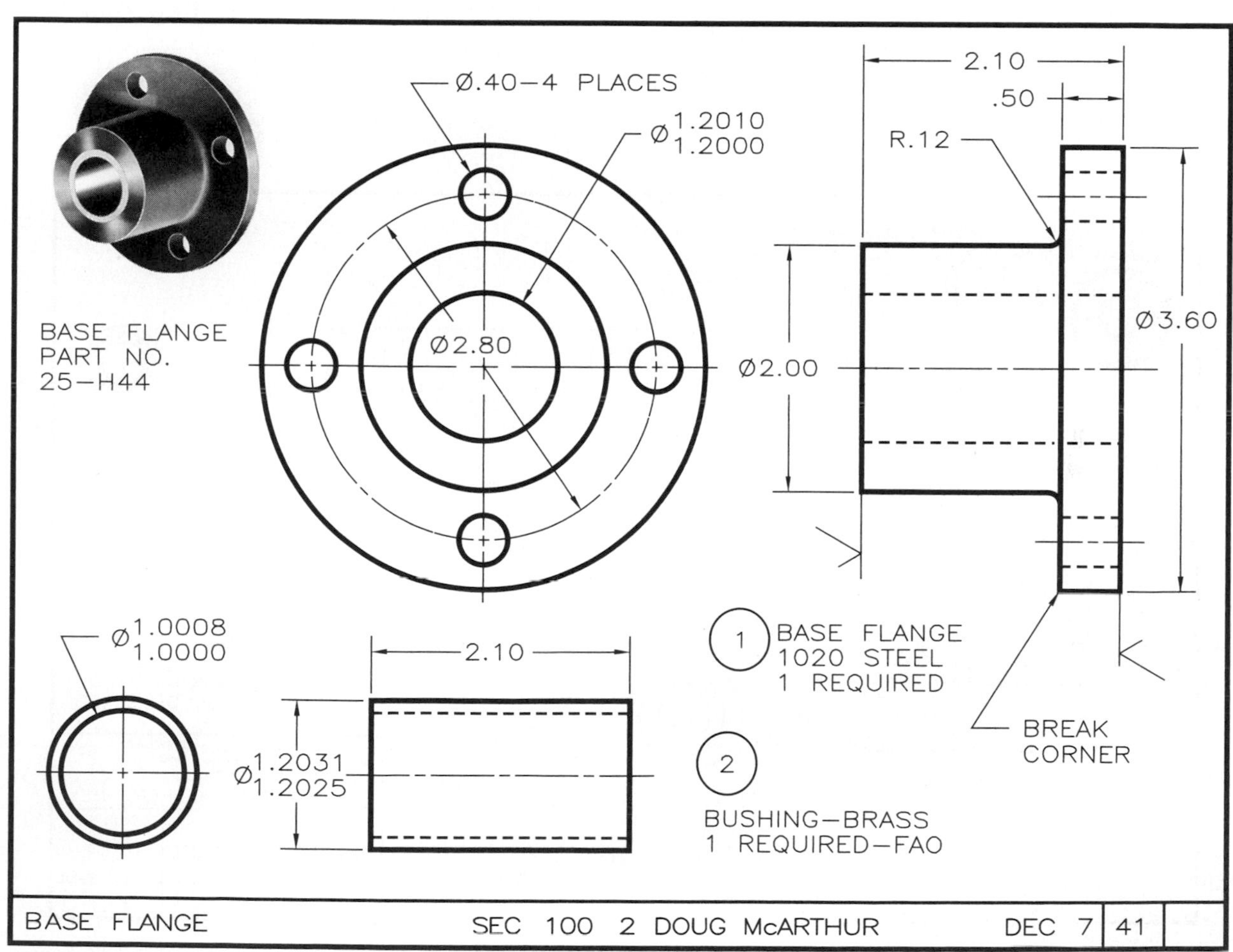

23.1 This revolving clamp assembly holds parts while they are being machined. *(Courtesy of Jergens, Inc.)*

saves drafting time. Finish marks are applied to the surfaces that must be machined smooth. Notice that the dimensions are spaced and applied in accordance with the principles covered in Chapters 13 and 14. A photograph showing a three-dimensional view of the flange has been inserted in the corner of the drawing as a raster image by using AutoCAD.

The clamp illustrated in **Figure 23.2** is detailed in three sheets of a working drawing (**Figures 23.3–23.5**), which are also dimensioned in inches. Decimal fractions are preferable to common fractions, although common fractions are still used (mostly by architects). Arithmetic can be done with greater ease with decimal fractions than with common fractions.

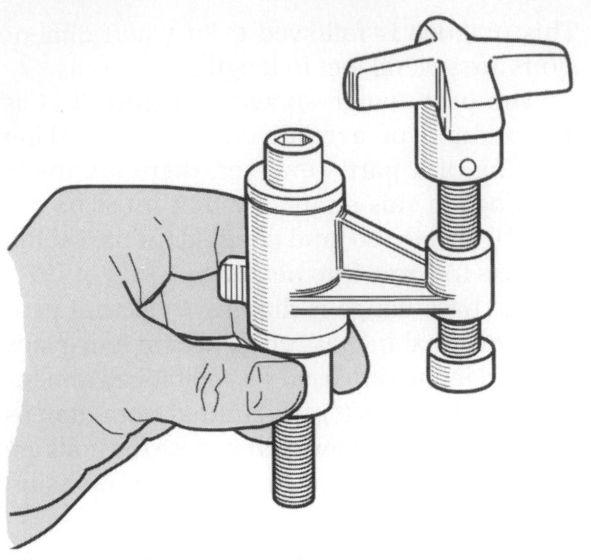

23.2 This revolving clamp assembly holds parts while they are being machined.

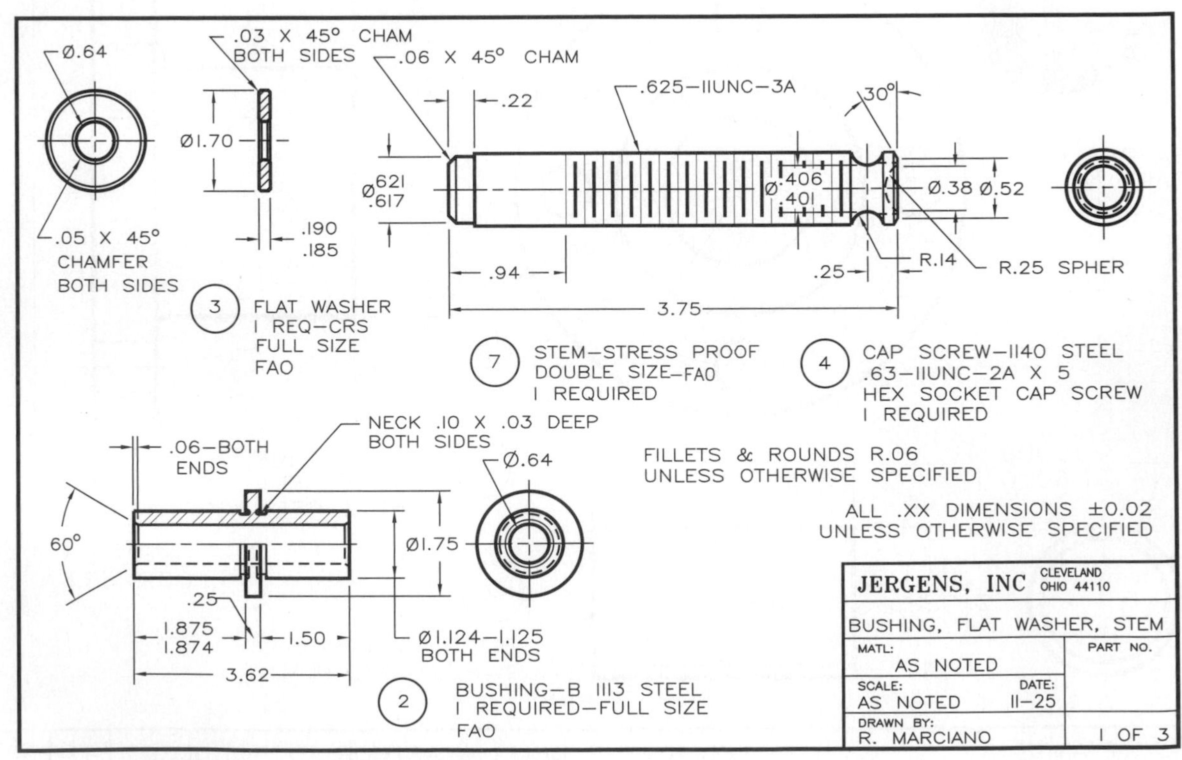

23.3 Sheet 1 of 3: A computer-drawn working drawing of parts of the clamp assembly shown in **Figure 23.2.** *(Figures 23.2–23.5 courtesy of Jergens, Inc.)*

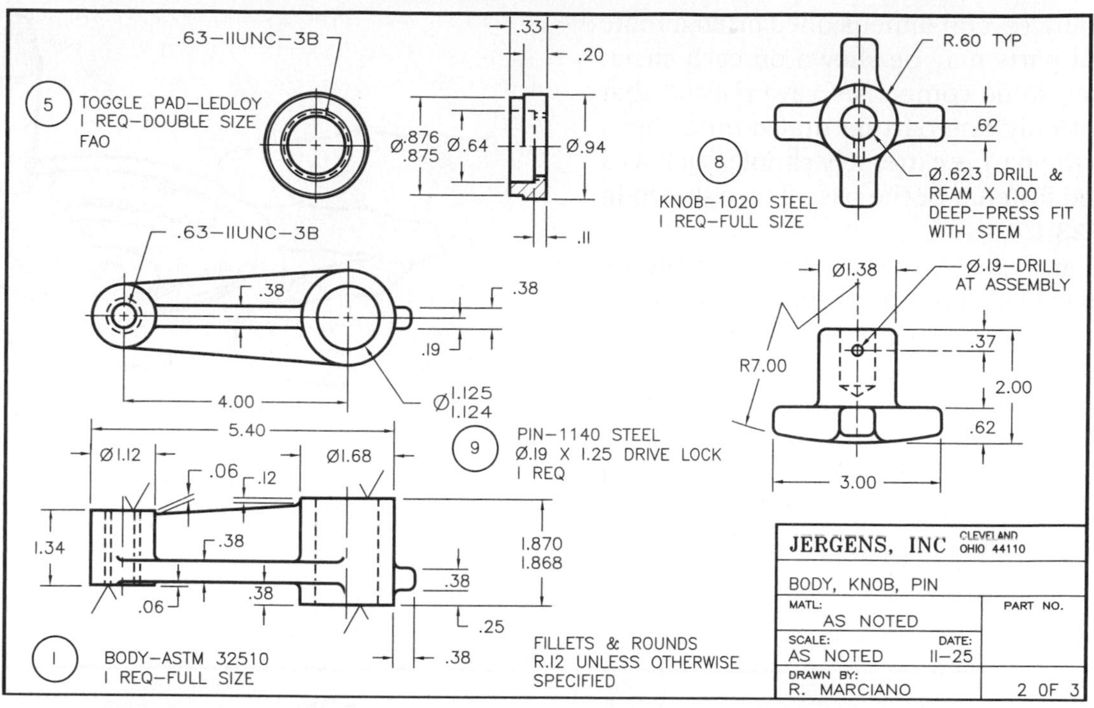

23.4 Sheet 2 of 3: This continuation of **Figure 23.3** shows other parts of the clamp assembly.

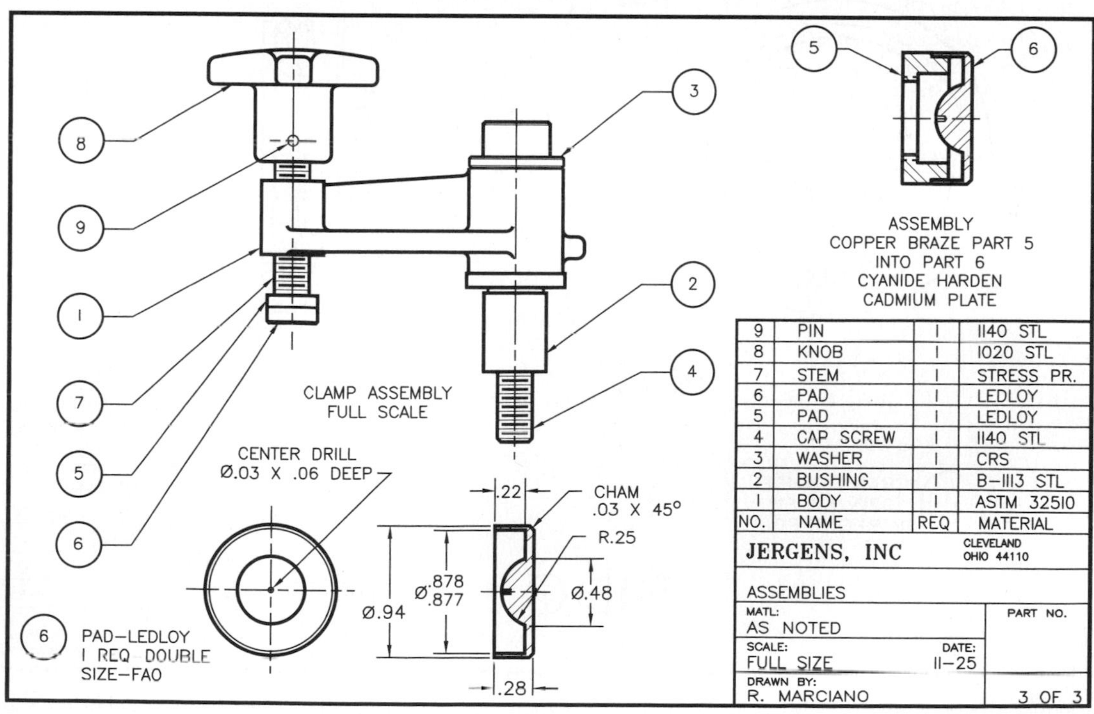

23.5 Sheet 3 of 3: A pad assembly, an overall assembly drawing, and a parts list are shown.

Usually, several dimensioned orthographic views of parts may be shown on each sheet. However, some companies have policies that views of only one part be drawn on a sheet, even if the part is extremely simple, such as a threaded fastener or the base flange shown in **Figure 23.1**.

The arrangement of views of parts on the sheet need not attempt to show the relationship of the parts when assembled; the views are simply positioned to best fit the available space on the sheet. The views of each part are labeled with a part number, a name for identification, the material it is made of, the number of the parts required, and any other notes necessary to explain manufacturing procedures.

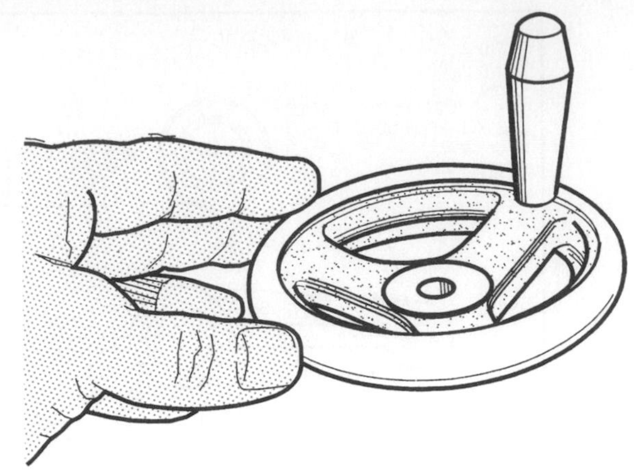

23.6 This drawing is of a left-end handcrank that is detailed in the working drawing in **Figures 23.7** and **23.8.**

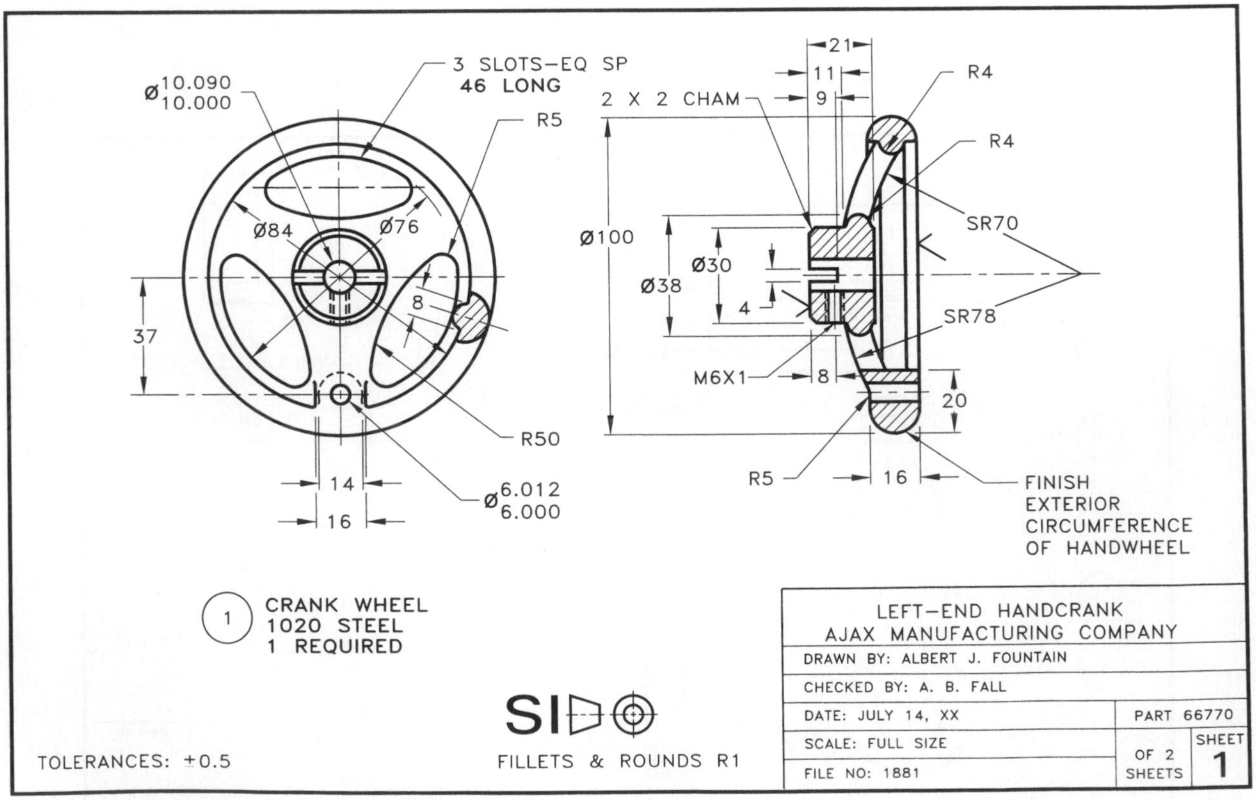

23.7 Sheet 1 of 2: This set of working drawings (dimensions in mm) depicts the crank wheel of the left-end handcrank shown in **Figure 23.6.**

The purpose of the orthographic assembly drawing shown on Sheet 3 (**Figure 23.5**) is to illustrate how the parts are to fit together. Each part is numbered and cross-referenced with the part numbers in the parts list, which serves as a bill of materials.

Metric System

The millimeter is the basic unit of the metric system, and dimensions usually are given to the nearest whole millimeter without decimal fractions (except to specify tolerances, which may require three-place decimals). Metric abbreviations (mm) after the numerals are omitted from dimensions because the SI symbol near the title block indicates that all units are metric. If you have trouble relating to the length of a millimeter, recall that the fingernail of your index finger is about 10 mm wide.

The left-end handcrank (**Figure 23.6**) is depicted and dimensioned in millimeters in the working drawings shown in **Figure 23.7** and **Figure 23.8** on two size B sheets. Dimensions and notes along with the descriptive views give the information needed to construct the four pieces.

The orthographic sectioned assembly drawing of the left-end handcrank shown in **Figure 23.8** illustrates how the parts are to be put together. The numbers in the balloons, the part numbers, provide a cross-reference to the parts list placed just above the title block.

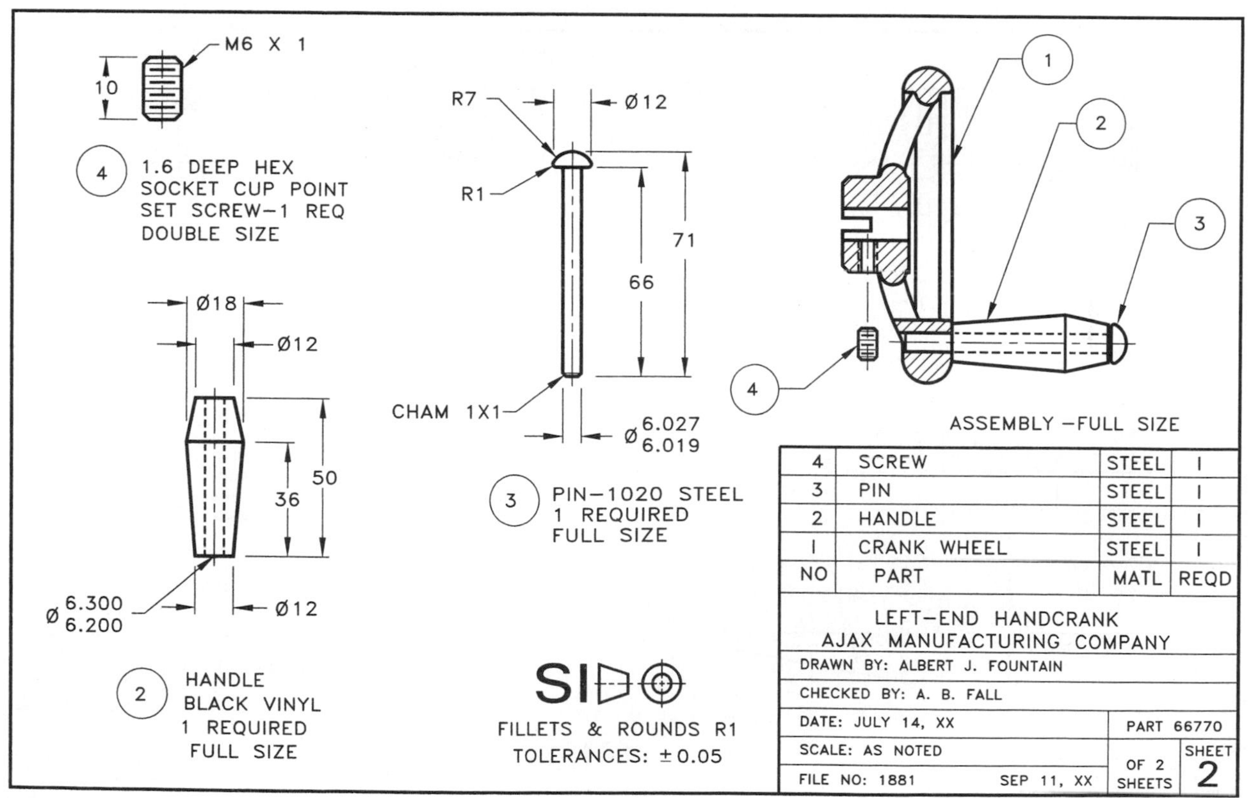

NO	PART	MATL	REQD
4	SCREW	STEEL	1
3	PIN	STEEL	1
2	HANDLE	STEEL	1
1	CRANK WHEEL	STEEL	1

23.8 Sheet 2 of 2: This continuation of **Figure 23.7** includes an assembly drawing and parts list.

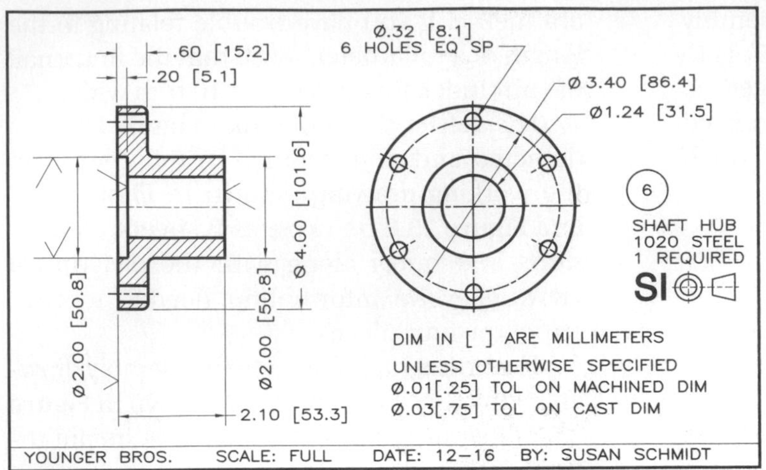

23.9 In this dual-dimensioned drawing, dimensions are shown in millimeters; their equivalents in inches are given in brackets.

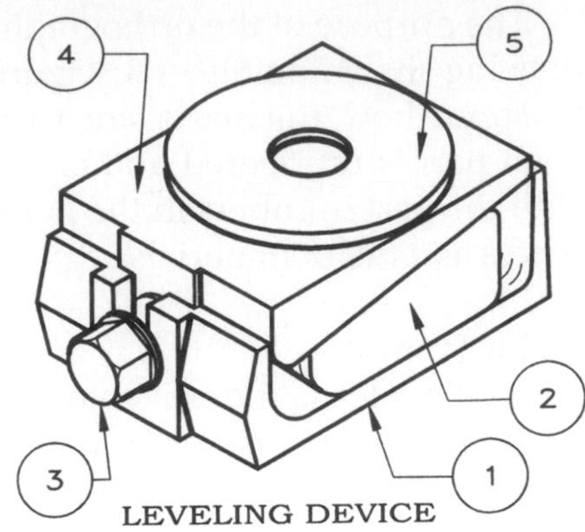

23.10 This leveling device is used to level heavy machinery.

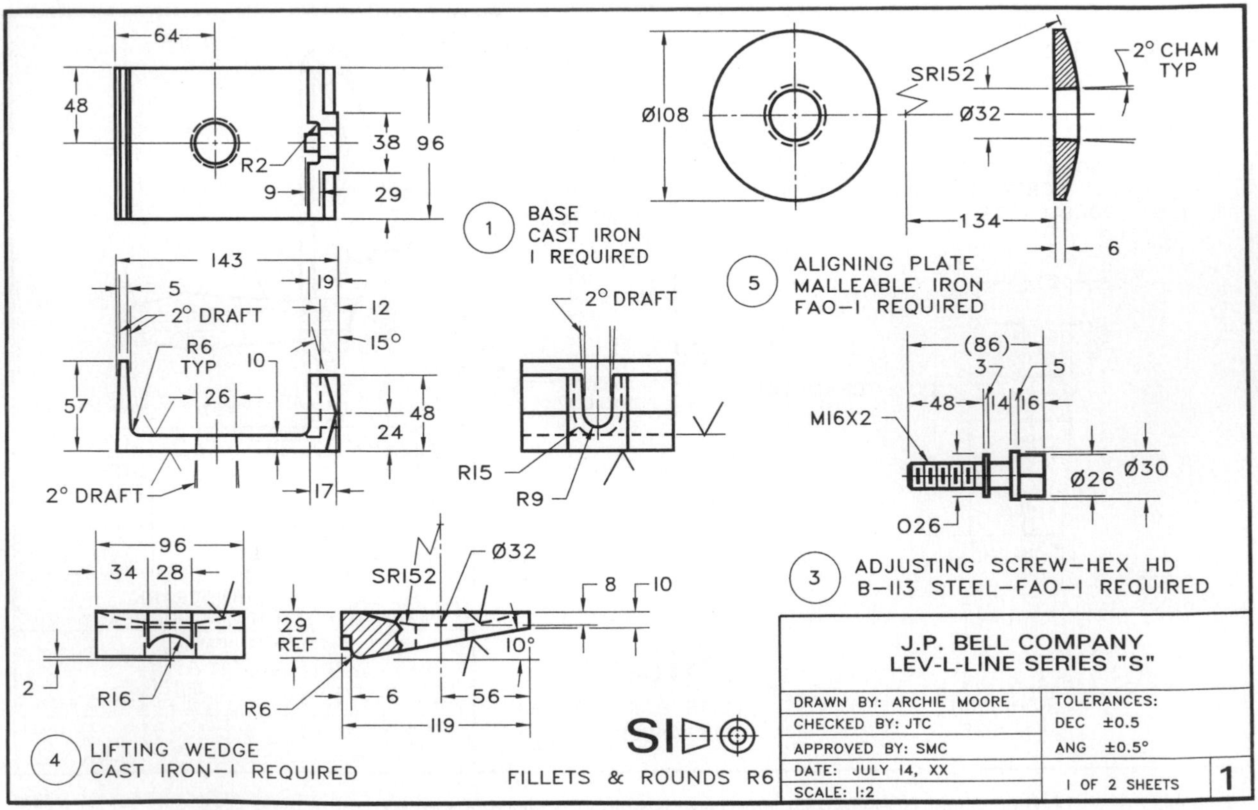

23.11 Sheet 1 of 2: This working drawing (dimensioned in SI units) is of the lifting device shown in **Figure 23.10**.

Dual Dimensions

Some working drawings carry both inch and millimeter dimensions, as shown in **Figure 23.9**, where the dimensions in parentheses or brackets are millimeters. The units may also appear as millimeters first and then be converted and shown in brackets as inches. Converting from one unit to the other results in fractional round-off errors. An explanation of the primary unit system for each drawing should be noted in the title block.

Metric Working Drawing Example

Figure 23.10 is a drawing of a leveling device used to level heavy equipment such as lathes and milling machines. The device raises or lowers the machinery when the screw is rotated, which slides two wedges together. A two-sheet working drawing that gives the details of the parts of the lifting device is shown in **Figures 23.11** and **23.12**. The SI symbol indicates that the dimensions are in millimeters, and the truncated cone indicates that the orthographic views are drawn using third-angle projection. The assembly drawing in **Figure 23.12** illustrates how the parts are to be assembled after they have been made.

23.4 Laying Out a Detail Drawing

When making a drawing with instruments on paper or film, first lay out the views and dimensions on a different sheet of paper. Then, overlay the drawing with vellum or film and trace it to obtain the final drawing. You must use guidelines for lettering for each dimension and note.

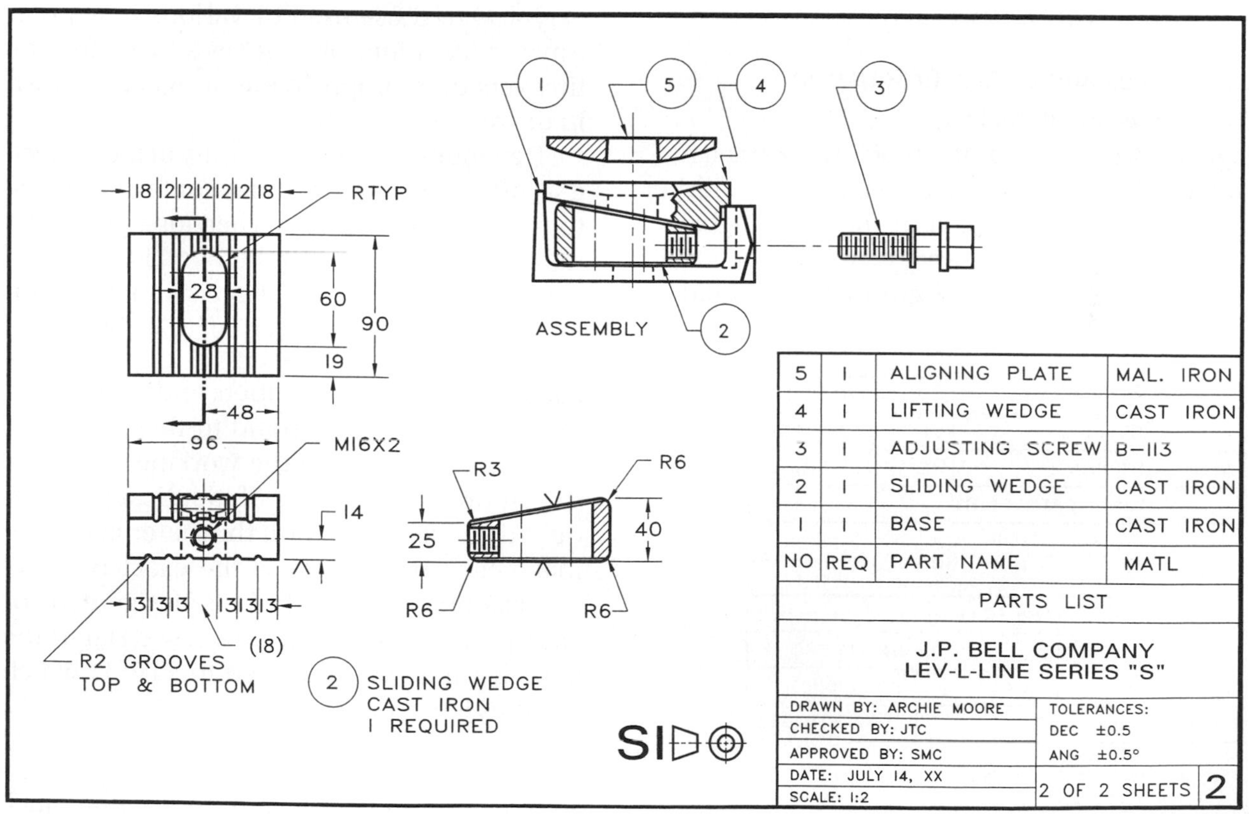

23.12 Sheet 2 of 2: This continuation of **Figure 23.11** is a further working drawing and assembly drawing of the lifting device.

DRAWING SHEET SIZES

ENGLISH SIZES		METRIC SIZES	
A	11 X 8.5	A4	297 X 210
B	17 X 11	A3	420 X 297
C	22 X 17	A2	594 X 420
D	34 X 22	A1	841 X 594
E	44 X 34	A0	1189 X 841

23.13 The standard sheet sizes for working drawings dimensioned in inches and millimeters.

Lightly draw the guidelines or underlay the drawing with a sheet containing guidelines.

Figure 23.13 shows the standard sheet sizes for working drawings. Paper, film, cloth, and reproduction materials are available in these modular sizes; good practice requires that you make drawings in one of these standard sizes. Modular-size drawings can be folded to fit standard-size envelopes, match the sizes of print paper, and fit in standard-size filing cabinets.

23.5 Notes and Other Information

Title Blocks and Parts Lists

Figure 23.14 shows a title block and parts list suitable for most student assignments. Title blocks usually are placed in the lower right-hand corner of the drawing sheet against the borders. The parts list (**Figure 23.14**) should be placed directly over the title block (see also **Figures 23.8** and **23.12**).

2	SHAFT	2	1020 STL
1	BASE	1	CAST IRON
NO	PART NAME	REQ	MATERIAL
PARTS LIST			

.38

5" (Approximately)

TITLE BLOCK	
BY: RED GRANGE	SECT: 500
DATE: MAY 2, 2XXX	SHEET 1
SCALE: FULL SIZE	OF 1 SHEETS

.38

$\frac{1}{8}$" LETTERS

23.14 This typical title block and parts list is suitable for most student assignments.

REVISIONS	COMPANY NAME Address
CHG. HEIGHT	TITLE: LEFT-END BEARING
FAO	DRAWN BY: JOHNNY RINGO
	CHECKED BY: FRED J. DODGE
	DATE: JULY 14, 2XXX
	SCALE: HALF SIZE — SHEET 1 OF 3 SHEETS

23.15 This title block, which includes a revision block, is typical of those used in industry.

Title Blocks In practice, title blocks usually contain the title or part name, drafter, date, scale, company, and sheet number. Other information, such as tolerances, checkers, and materials, also may be given. **Figure 23.15** shows another example of a title block, which is typical of those used by various industries. Any modifications or changes added after the first version to improve the design are shown in the revision blocks.

Depending on the complexity of the project, a set of working drawings may contain from one to more than 100 sheets. Therefore, giving the number of each sheet and the total number of sheets in the set on each sheet is important (for example, sheet 2 of 6, sheet 3 of 6, and so on).

Parts List The part numbers and part names in the parts list correspond to those given to each part depicted on the working drawings. In addition, the number of identical parts required is given along with the material used to make each part. Because the exact material (for example, 1020 STEEL) is designated for each part on the drawing, the material in the parts list may be shortened to STEEL, which requires less space.

Patent Rights Note

A note near the title block that names Jack Omohundro as the inventor of the part or

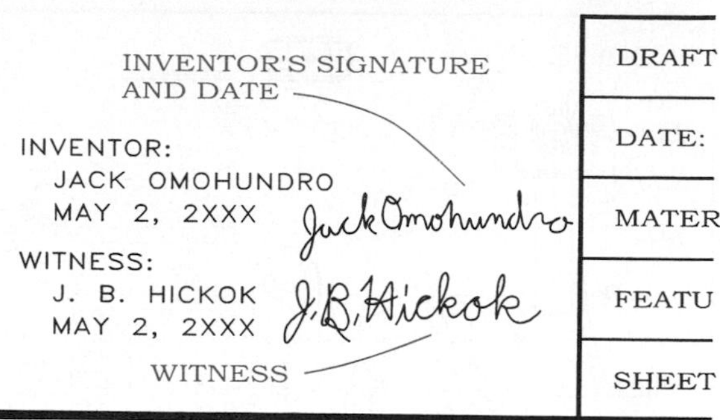

23.16 This note next to the title block names the inventor and is witnessed by an associate to establish ownership of a design for patent purposes.

process is used to establish ownership of the design (**Figure 23.16**). An associate, J. B. Hickok, signs and dates the drawing as a witness to the designer's work. This type of note establishes ownership of the ideas and dates of their development to help the inventor obtain a patent. An even better case for design ownership is made if a second witness signs and dates the drawing. As modifications to the design are made, those drawings should be documented the same way.

Scale Specification

If all working drawings in a set are the same scale, you need indicate it only once in the title block on each sheet. If several detail drawings on a working drawing are different scales, indicate them on the drawing under each set of views. In this case, write AS SHOWN in the scale area of the title block. When a drawing is not to scale, place the abbreviation NTS ("not to scale") in the title block.

Figure 23.17 shows several methods of indicating scales. Use of the colon (for example, 1:2) implies the metric system; use of the equal sign (for example, 1=2) implies the English system—but these are not absolute rules. The SI symbol or metric designation on a drawing specifies that millimeters are the units of measurement.

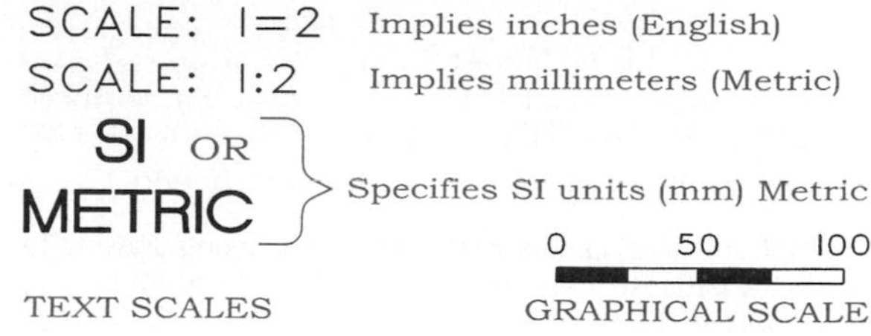

23.17 Specify scales in English and SI units on working drawings with these methods.

In some cases, you may want to show a graphical scale with calibrations on a drawing to permit the interpretation of linear measurements by transferring them with dividers from the drawing to the scale.

Tolerances

Recall from Chapter 13 that you may use general notes on working drawings to specify the dimension tolerances. **Figure 23.18** shows a table of values with boxes in which you can make a check mark to indicate whether the units are in inches or millimeters. Position plus-and-minus tolerance values under each common or decimal fraction. For example, this table specifies that each dimension with two-place decimals will have a tolerance of ±.10 in. You may also give angular tolerances in general notes (±0.5°, for example).

Part Labeling

Give each part a name and number, using letters and numbers 1/8 in. (3 mm) high (**Figure 23.19**). Place part numbers inside circles, called

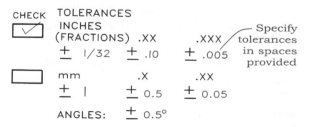

CHECK	TOLERANCES		
☑	INCHES (FRACTIONS)	.XX	.XXX
	± 1/32	± .10	± .005
☐	mm	.X	.XX
	± 1	± 0.5	± 0.05
	ANGLES:	± 0.5°	

Specify tolerances in spaces provided

23.18 General tolerance notes on working drawings specify the dimension tolerances permitted.

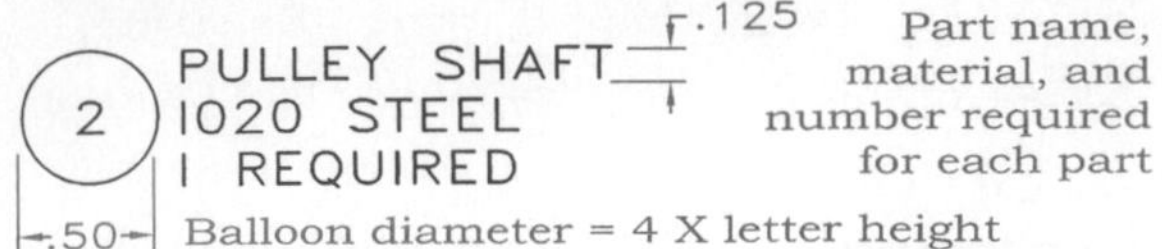

23.19 Name and number each part on a working drawing for use in the parts list, and indicate the number of parts of this particular part that are needed.

balloons, having diameters approximately four times the height of the numerals.

Place part numbers near the views to which they apply, so their association will be clear. On assembly drawings, balloons are especially important because the same parts numbers are used in the parts list. Show the number of parts required near the part name.

23.6 Drafter's Log

In addition to the individual revision records, drafters should keep a log of all changes made during a project. As the project progresses, the drafter should record the changes, dates, and people involved. Such a log allows anyone reviewing the project in the future to understand easily and clearly the process used in arriving at the final design.

Calculations often are made during a drawing's preparation. If they are lost or poorly done, they may have to be redone during a later revision; therefore, they should be a permanent part of the log to preserve previously expended work.

23.7 Assembly Drawings

After parts have been made according to the specifications of the working drawings, they will be assembled (**Figure 23.20**) in accordance with the directions of an assembly drawing. Two general types of assembly drawings are **orthographic assemblies** and **pictorial assemblies**. Dimensions usually are omitted from assembly drawings *unless they are deemed necessary.*

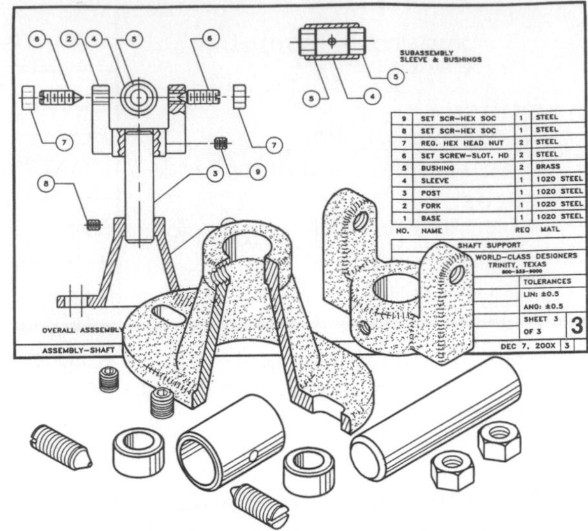

23.20 An assembly drawing explains how the parts of a product are to be assembled.

The leveling device shown in **Figure 23.10** is depicted in an isometric assembly in **Figure 23.21**. Each part is numbered with a balloon and leader to cross-reference it to the parts list, where more information about each part is given.

Figure 23.22 shows an orthographic exploded assembly drawing. In many applications, the arrangement of parts may be easier to

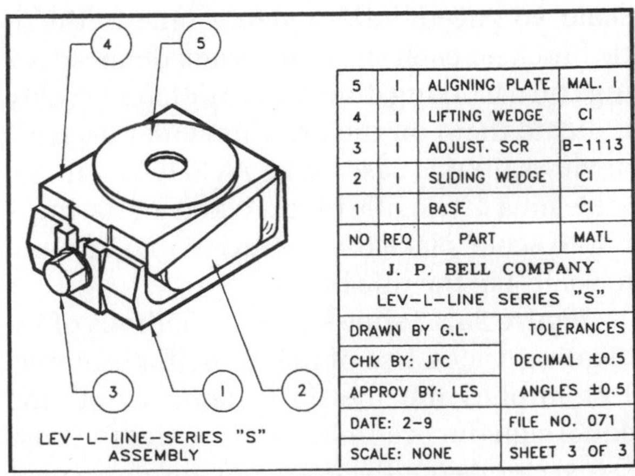

23.21 This isometric assembly drawing depicts the parts of the leveling device shown in **Figure 23.10** fully assembled. Dimensions usually are omitted from assembly drawings, and a parts list is given.

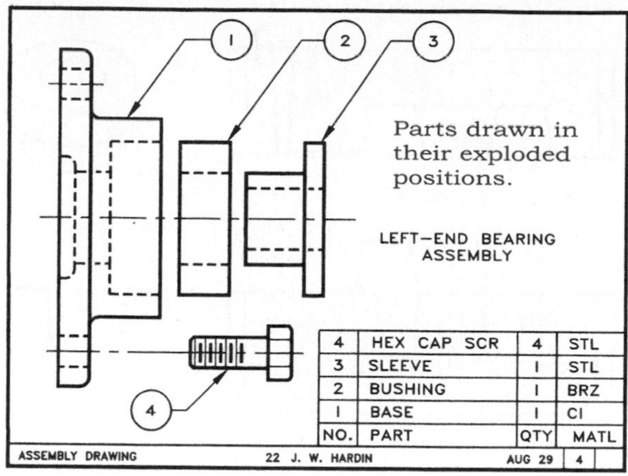

23.22 This exploded orthographic assembly illustrates how the parts shown are to be put together.

understand when the parts are shown exploded along their centerlines. These views are shown as regular orthographic views, with some lines shown as hidden lines and others omitted.

Assembly of the same part is shown in **Figure 23.23** in an orthographic assembly drawing, in which the parts are depicted in their assembled positions. The views are sectioned to make them easier to understand.

Figure 23.24 shows a pulley assembly in an exploded pictorial assembly drawing, illustrating how the parts fit together, leaving no doubt as to how the parts relate to each other. Part numbers are given in balloons to complete the drawing.

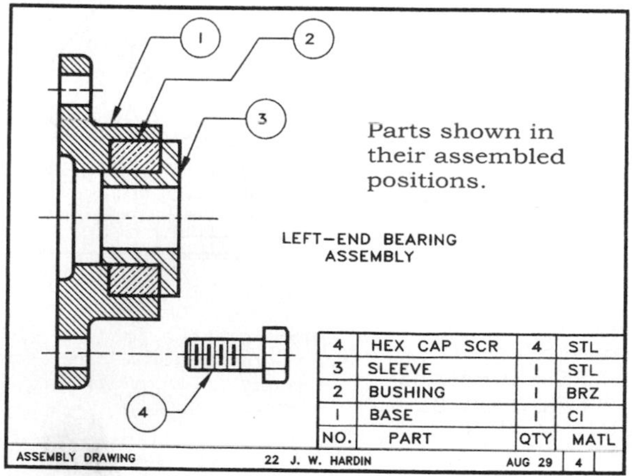

23.23 This sectioned orthographic assembly shows the parts from **Figure 23.22** in their assembled positions, except for the exploded bolt.

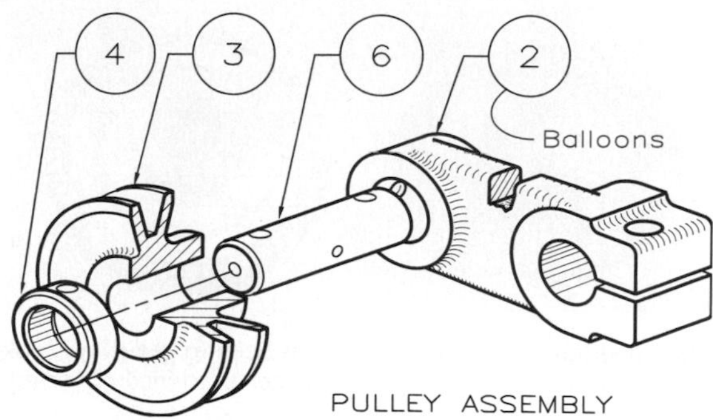

23.24 An exploded pictorial assembly drawing of a belt tensioner.

23.8 Freehand Working Drawings

A freehand sketch can serve the same purpose as an instrument drawing, provided that the part is sufficiently simple and that the essential dimensions are shown (**Figure 23.25**). Use the same principles of making working drawings with instruments when making working drawings freehand. A sketch can be made quickly, and it can be made in the field, fabrication shop, or other locations where drafting-room instruments are not readily available.

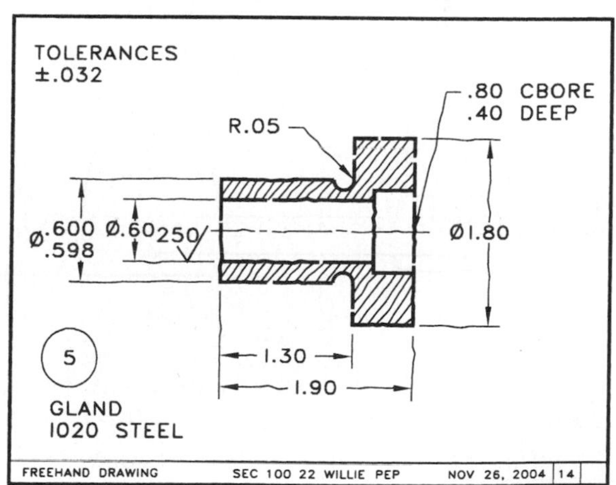

23.25 A freehand working drawing with the essential dimensions can be as adequate as an instrument-drawn detail drawing for simple parts.

23.26 The left part is a blank that has been forged. It will look like the part on the right after it has been machined. *(Courtesy of Textron Lycoming.)*

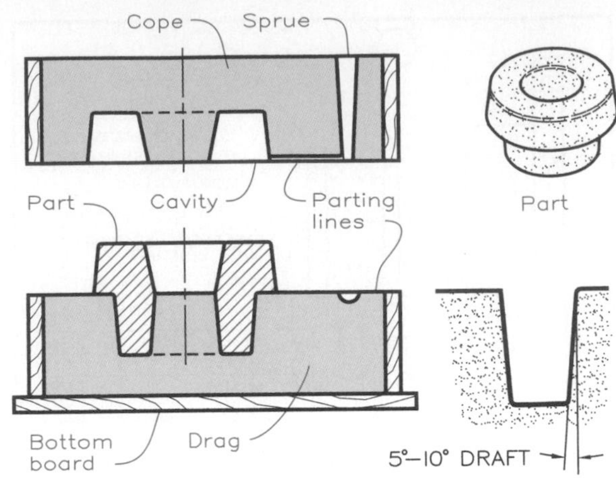

23.27 A two-part sand mold is used to produce a casting. A draft of from 5° to 10° is needed to permit withdrawal of the pattern from the sand. Some machining is usually required to finish various features of the casting within specified tolerances.

23.9 Forged Parts and Castings

The two versions of a part shown in **Figure 23.26** illustrate the difference between a part that has been forged into shape (sometimes called a **blank**) and its final state after the forging has been machined. Recall from Chapter 19 that a forging is a rough form made by hammering (forging) the metal into shape or pressing it between two forms (called *dies*). The forged part is then machined to its specified finished dimensions and tolerances so that it will function as intended.

A casting (**Figure 23.27**), like a forging, must be machined so that it too will fit and function with other parts when assembled;

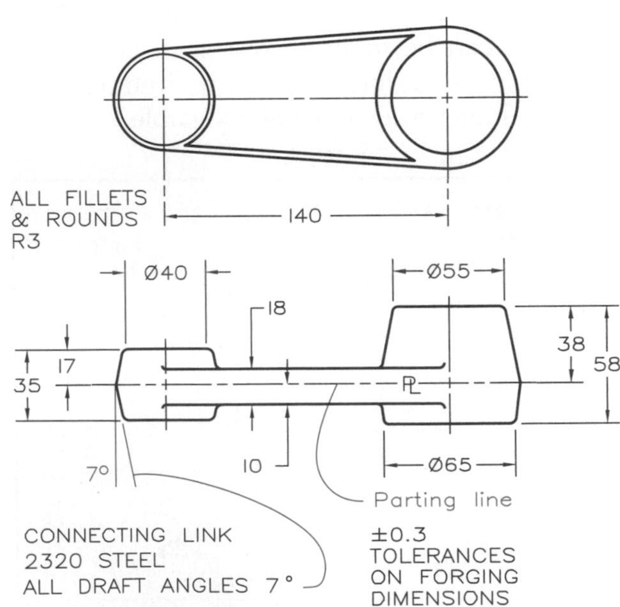

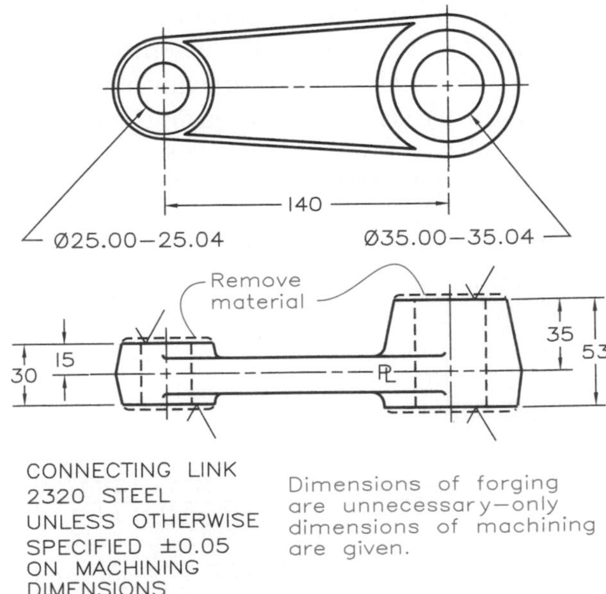

23.28 These separate working drawings, (A) a forging drawing and (B) a machining drawing, give the details of the same part. Often, this information is combined into a single drawing.

therefore, additional material is added to the areas where metal will be removed by the machining processes. As covered in Chapter 19, castings are formed by pouring molten metal into a mold formed by a pattern that is slightly larger than the finished part to compensate for metal shrinkage (**Figure 23.27**). For the pattern to be removable from the sand that forms the mold, its sides have a taper, called a **draft**, of about 5° to 10°.

Some industries require that separate working drawing be made for forged and cast parts (**Figure 23.28A**). More often, however, the parts are detailed on the regular working drawing with the understanding that the features that are to be machined by operations such as grinding or shaping are made oversize by the fabrication shop (**Figure 23.28B**)

Problems

The following problems will provide exercises in the application of the princples required in making working drawings. You should make rapid, freehand sketches of the views before drawing them with instruments or AutoCAD to determine the appropriate layout of each sheet. Material covered in all the previous chapters must be applied in completing these assignments.

Working Drawing Practice

Reproduce the drawings shown in **Figures 23.29–23.34** as directed. The purpose of these assignments is to provide experience in laying out a working drawing and improving your draftsmanship on the board or at the computer.

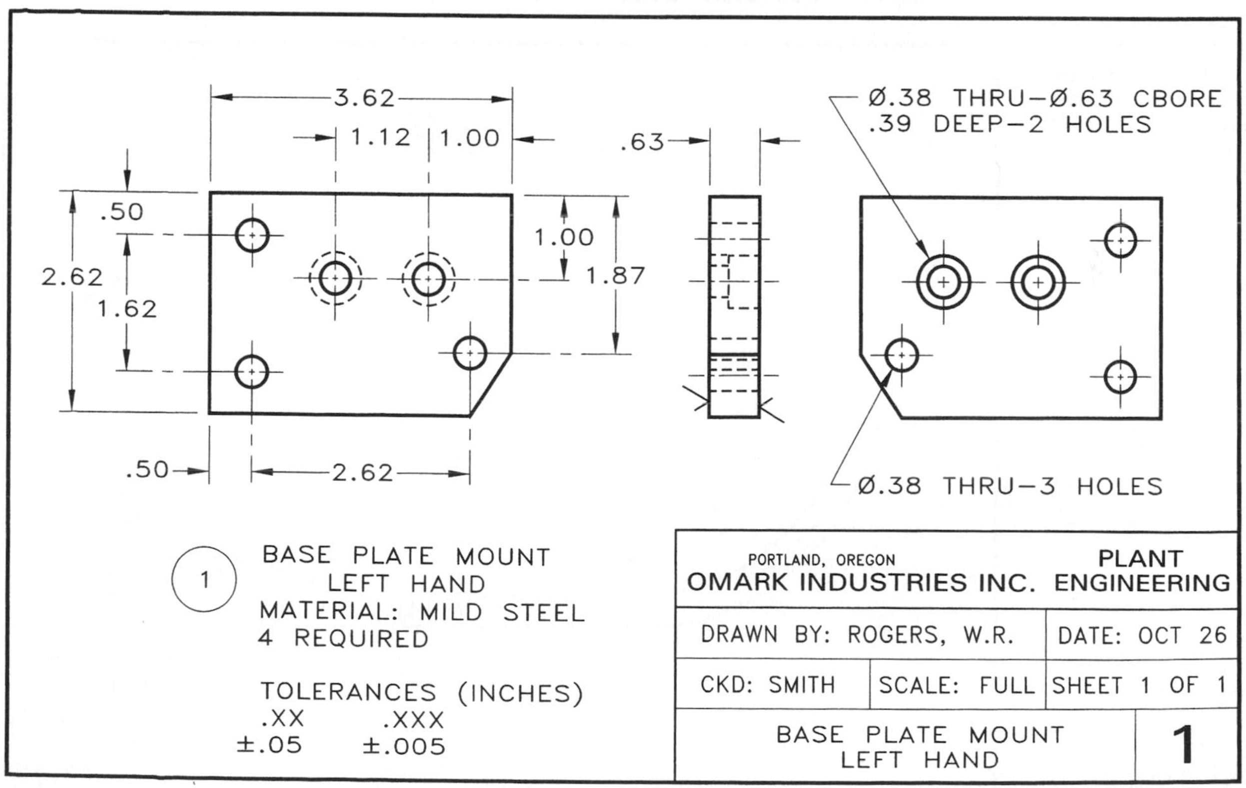

23.29 Duplicate the working drawing of the base plate mount on a size B sheet.

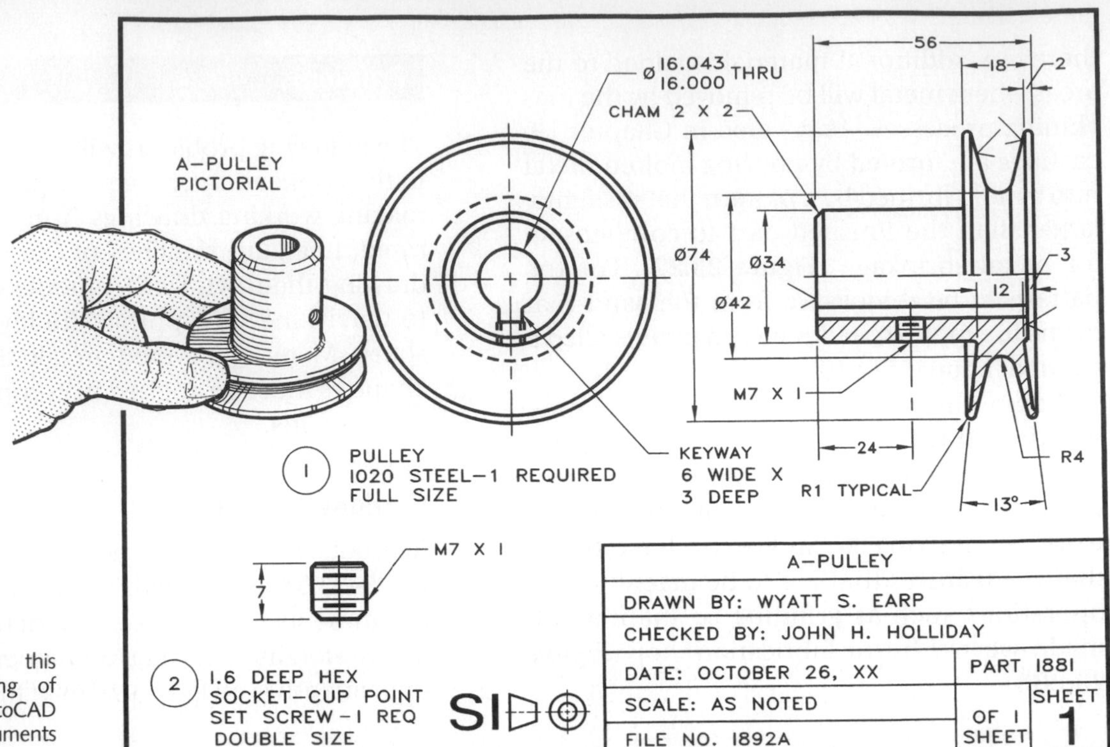

23.30 Duplicate this working drawing of the pulley by AutoCAD or drafting instruments on a size A sheet.

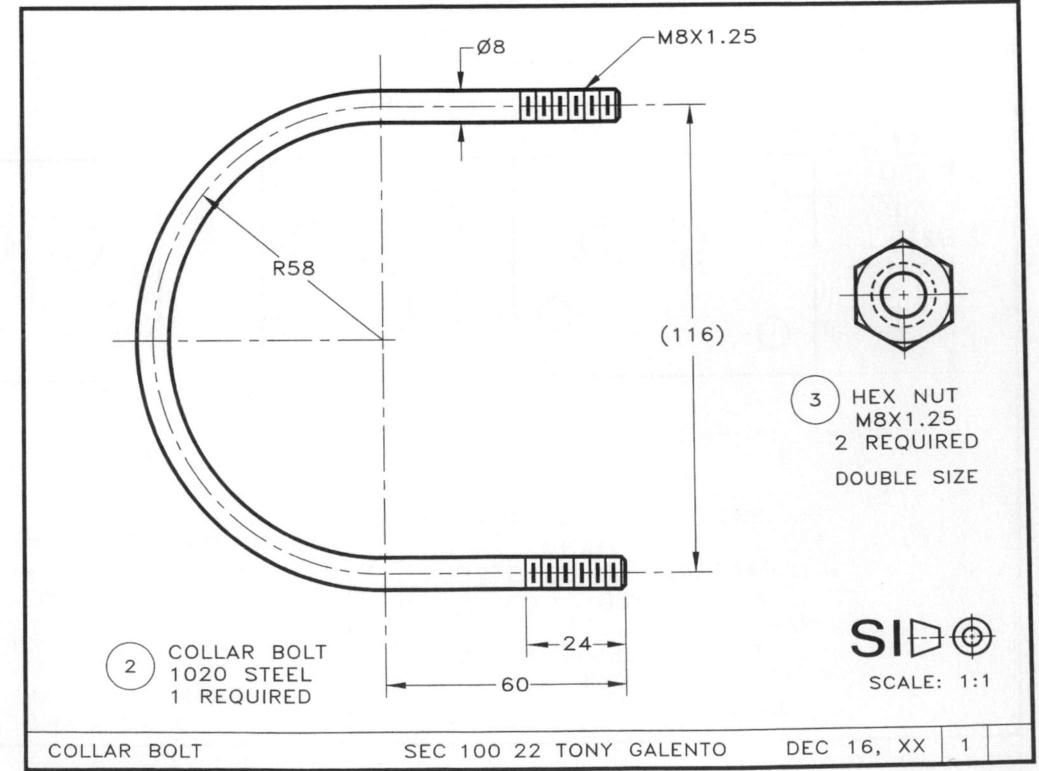

23.31 Sheet 1 of 3: Duplicate this full-size working drawing and assembly (in mm) of the pipe hanger on size A sheets.

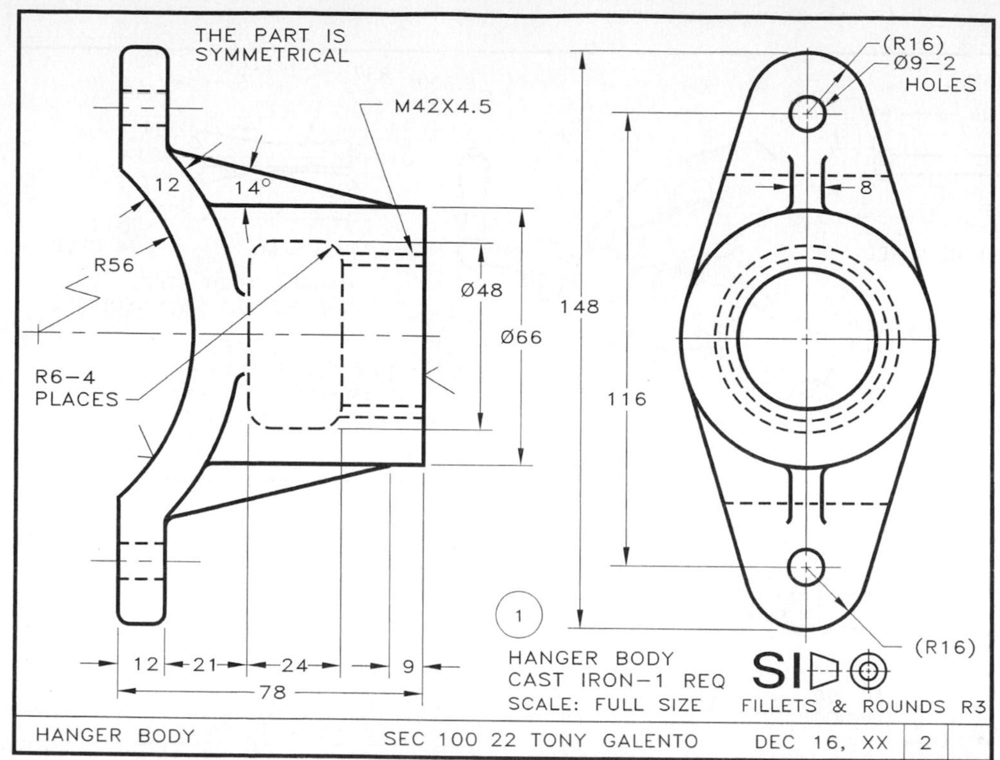

23.32 Sheet 2 of 3: Duplicate this second sheet of the pipe hanger working drawing that shows the collar bolt.

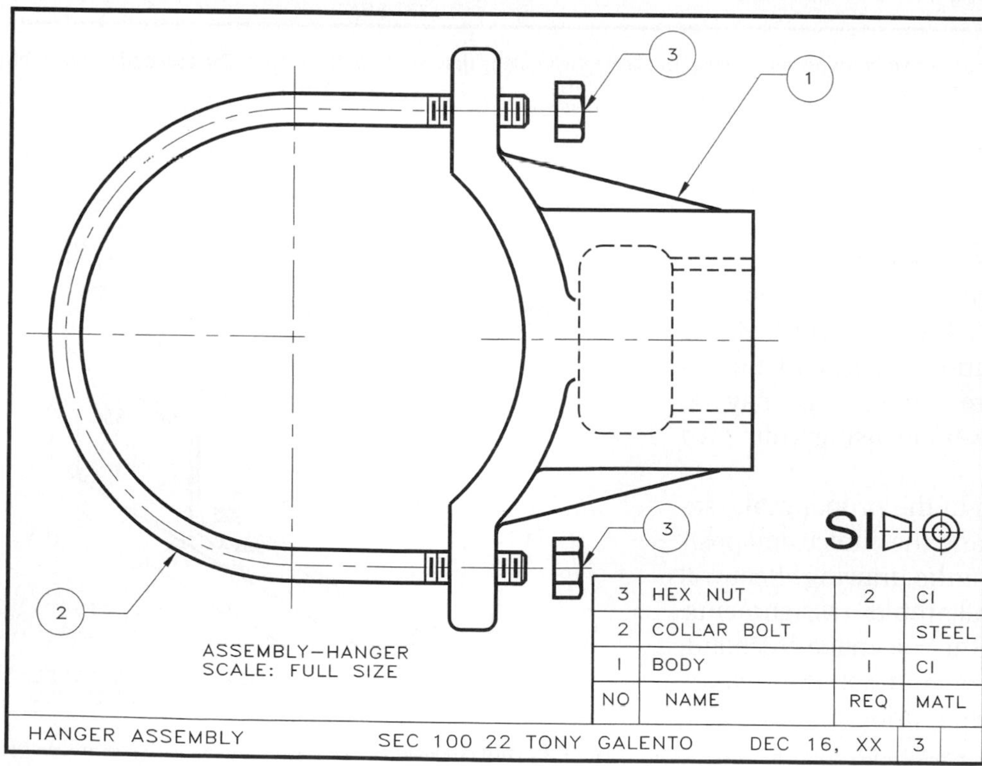

3	HEX NUT	2	CI
2	COLLAR BOLT	I	STEEL
I	BODY	I	CI
NO	NAME	REQ	MATL

23.33 Duplicate this working drawing of the switch by AutoCAD or drafting instruments on a size A sheet. Note that the views are enlarged by a factor of 4.

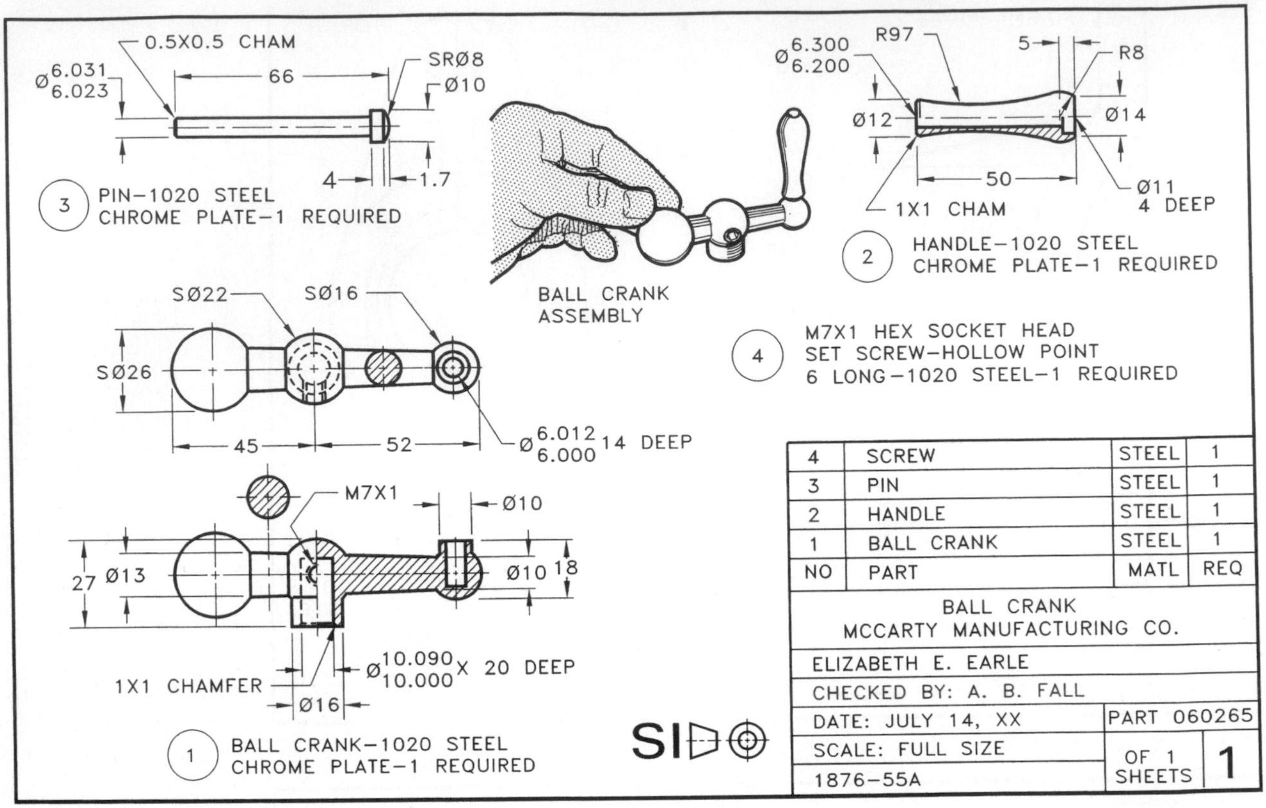

NO	PART	MATL	REQ
4	SCREW	STEEL	1
3	PIN	STEEL	1
2	HANDLE	STEEL	1
1	BALL CRANK	STEEL	1

BALL CRANK
MCCARTY MANUFACTURING CO.
ELIZABETH E. EARLE
CHECKED BY: A. B. FALL
DATE: JULY 14, XX — PART 060265
SCALE: FULL SIZE — OF 1 SHEETS — 1
1876-55A

23.34 The ball crank has been detailed in the working drawing. Duplicate the working drawing on a size B sheet. On a second size B sheet, make an assembly drawing of the parts.

Working Drawings: Single Parts

Make working drawings of the following assigned parts **(Figures 23.35–23.46)** providing the necessary information, notes, and dimensions. In cases where dimensions may be missing, approximate them using your own judgment.

The determination of the proper scale, selection of sheet sizes, and the choice and positioning of the views on the drawing sheet will be a major portion of all problem assignments. It will be very helpful if you make freehand, preliminary sketches of your solution (views, dimensions, notes, etc.) prior to beginning your final drawing.

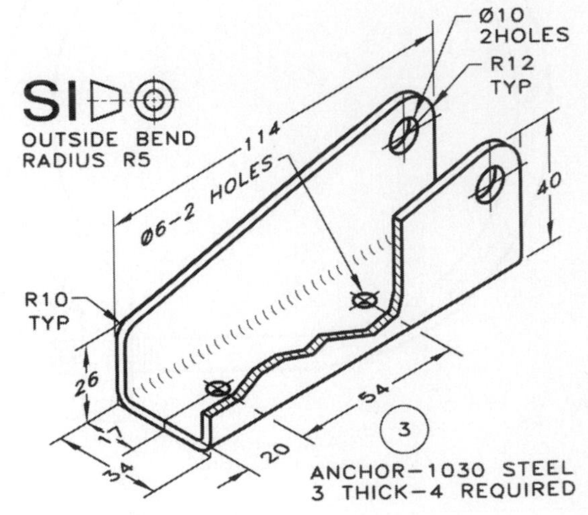

23.35 Size A sheet.

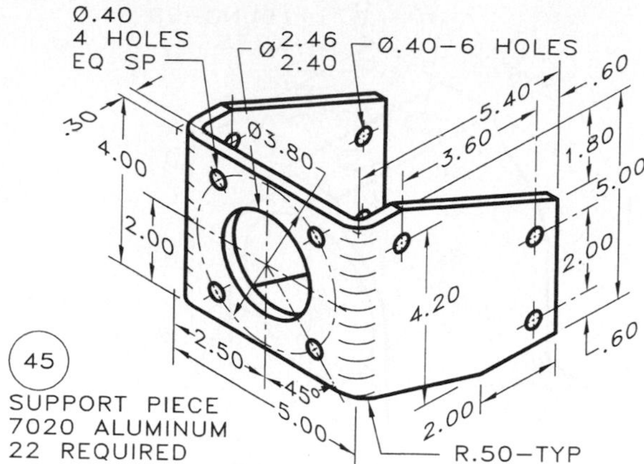

23.36 Size B sheet.

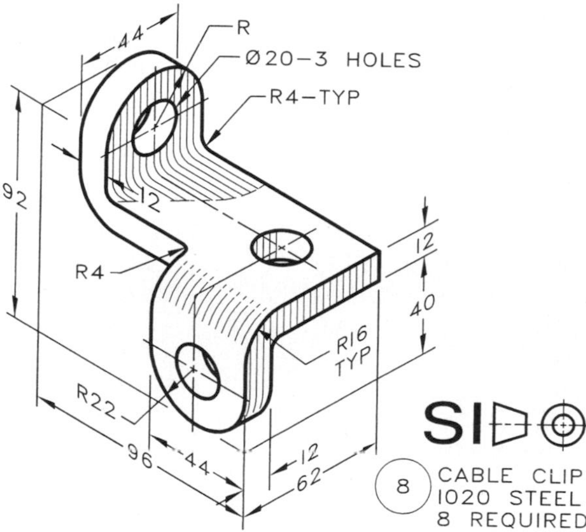

23.37 Size B sheet.

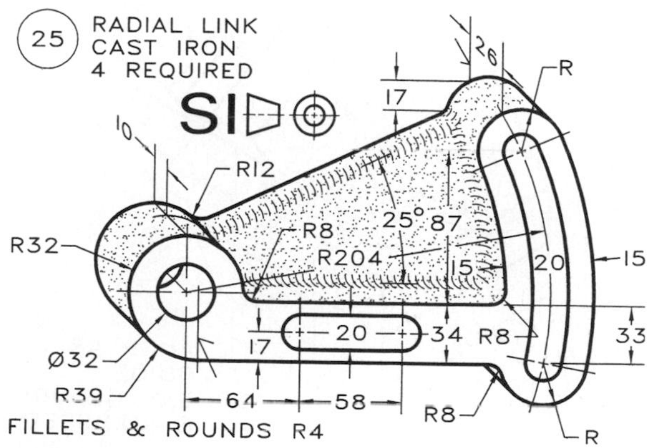

23.38 Size B sheet.

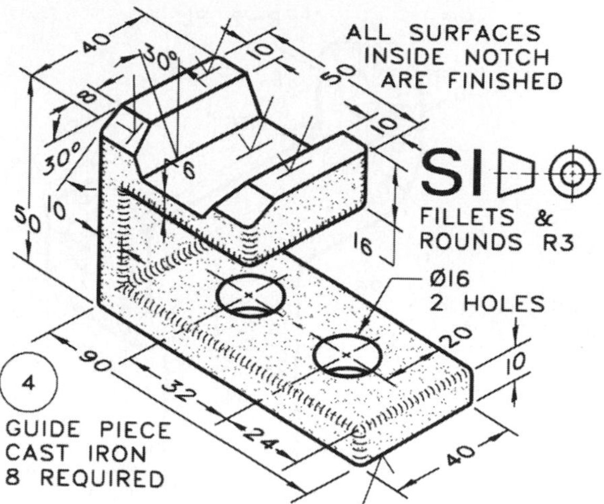

23.39 Size B sheet.

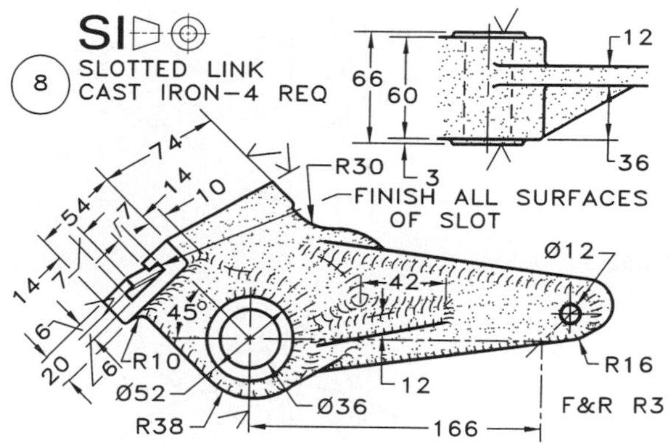

23.40 Size B sheet.

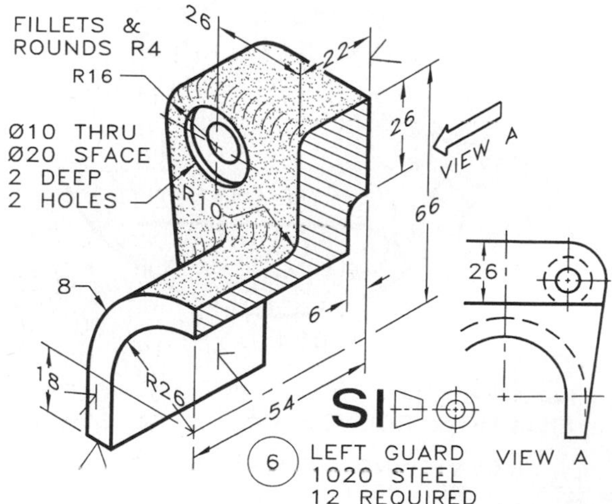

23.41 Size B sheet.

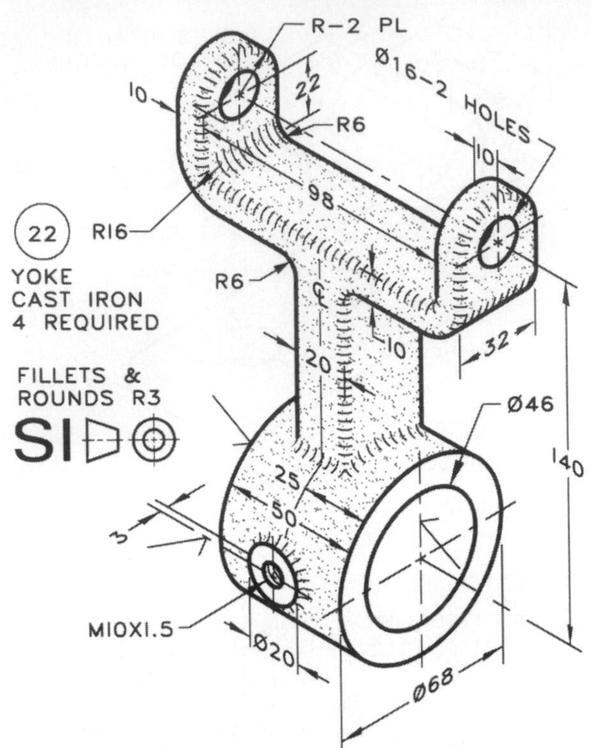

23.42 Size B sheet.

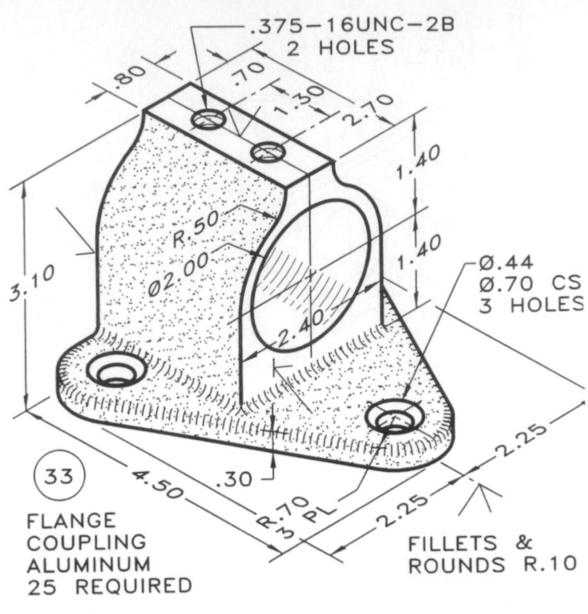

23.44 Size B sheet.

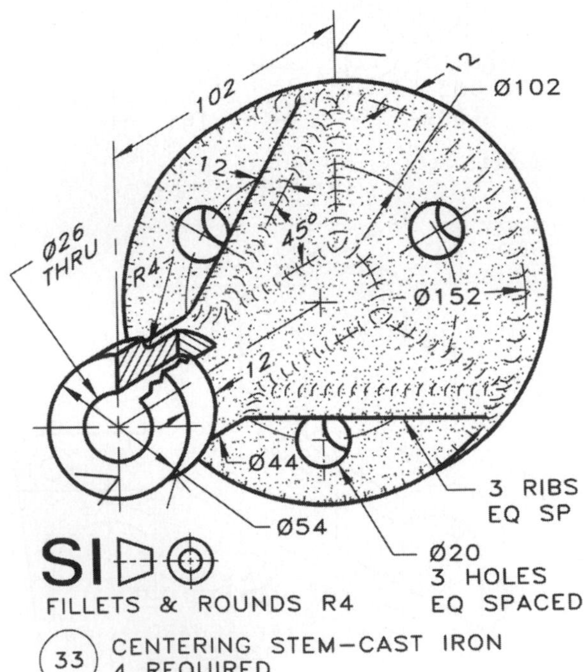

23.43 Size B sheet.

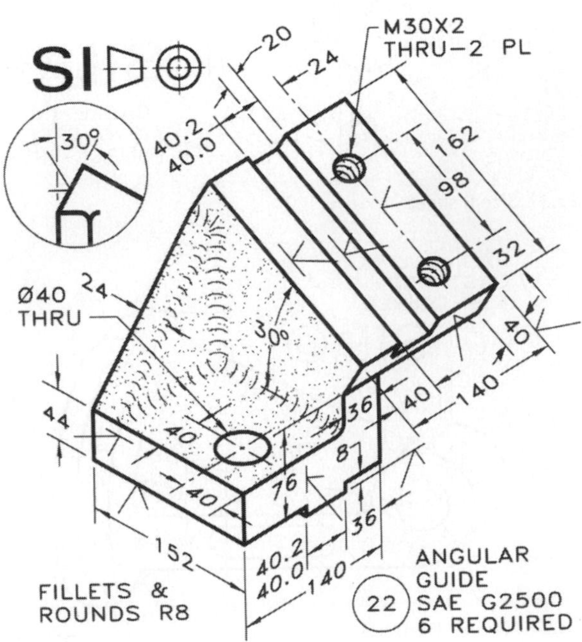

23.45 Size B sheet.

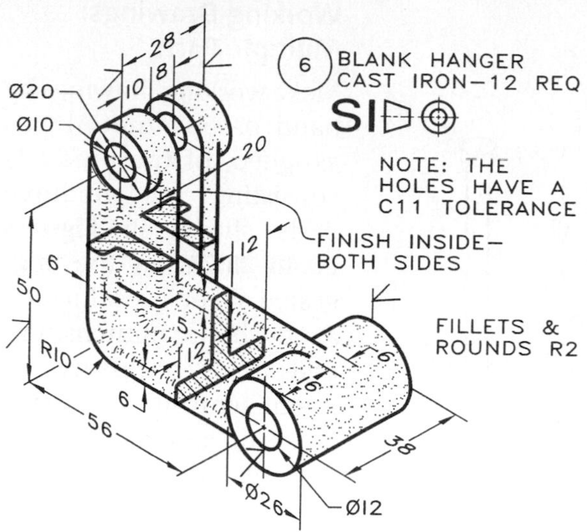

23.46 Size B sheet.

FILLETS AND ROUNDS R.125

LINES D AND E ARE PARALLEL

SURFACE A IS PARALLEL TO TO LINE B

ANGLE BETWEEN SURFACE C AND LINE B

COMPOUND BRACKET
3 REQUIRED—CAST IRON (9)

23.47 Size B sheet.

DESIGN: Compound Bracket (Figure 23.47)
(for only the best students!)

A major portion of this problem is its layout and the determination of its true-size surfaces where they can be dimensioned. Recall from Chapter 15 that partial, secondary auxiliary views are helpul in representing inclined planes. This problem can best be solved on a size C sheet.

A. Begin by drawing top and front views of the bracket, and construct the necessary auxiliary views to show its surfaces true size.

B. Dimension the views found in part A.

C. Do you have the stuff to make a model of the part? You good students will give it a shot.

D. Design a fixture to hold the slotted surfaces horizontal for forming the slot with an overhead, vertical bit.

FIXTURE DESIGN FOR CUTTING SLOTS IN THE COMPOUND BRACKET

SURFACE A

SURFACE B

This fixture prototype holds both planes A & B in a level position for milling the slots in them. Can you do the geometry and build a model like this one?

Working Drawings: Multiple Parts

Make working drawings by hand or by AutoCAD, as assigned, of the products consisting of multiple parts shown in **Figures 23.48–23.71** on the suggested sheet sizes. Include a title block, dimensions, and notes necessary for manufacturing the parts. Make an assembly drawing that shows how the parts fit together. More than one sheet may be required.

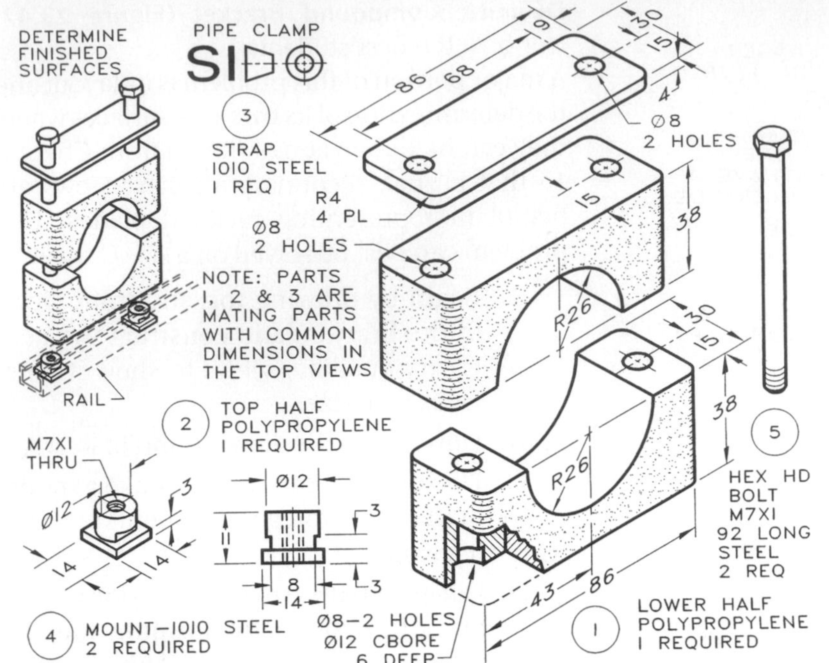

23.48 Size B sheet.

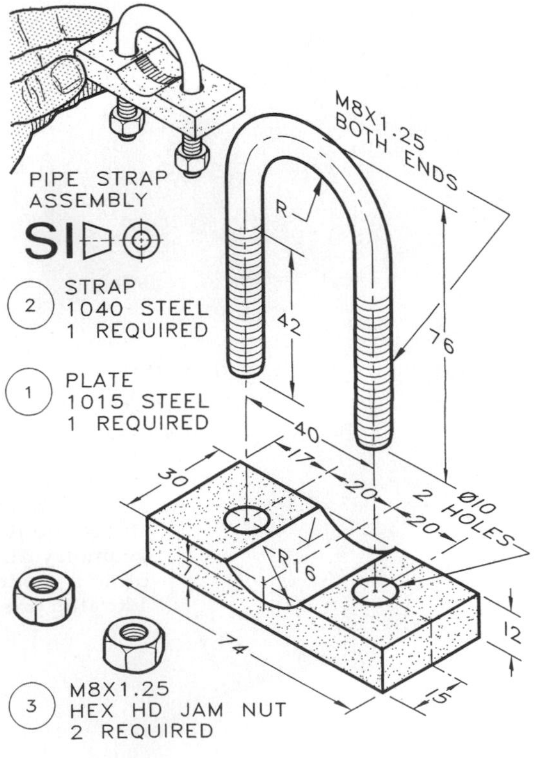

23.49 Size B sheet.

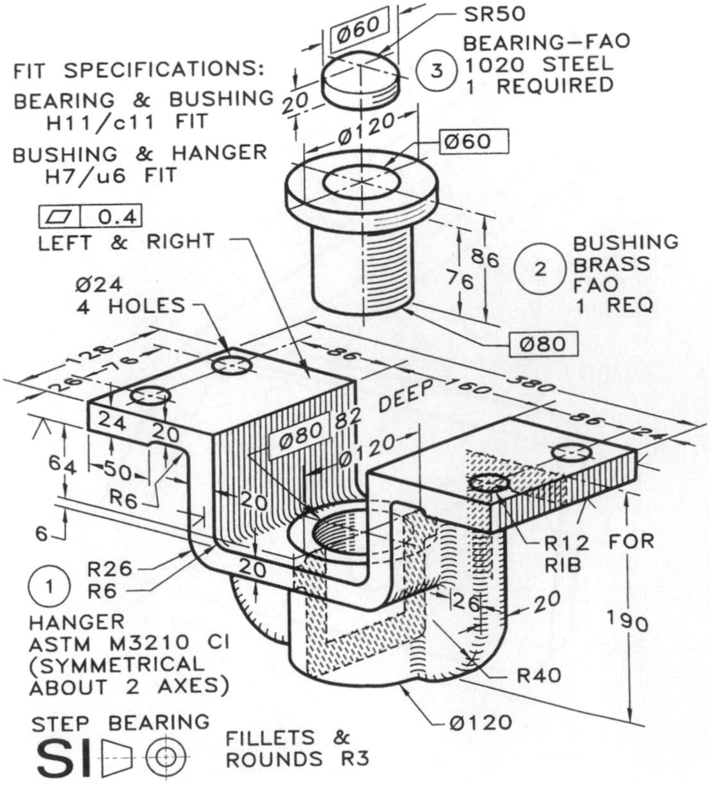

23.50 Size B sheet.

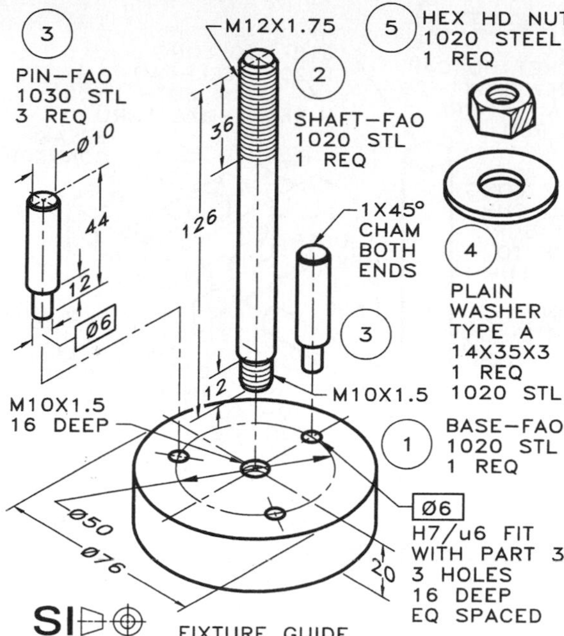

23.51 Size B sheet.

Important Points

1. Fill out the title block completely on all working drawing sheets: drafter, checker, company, sheet number, and so forth.

2. Prepare the details of each part in a very precise, accurate manner, as if you were preparing a legal contract, because that is exactly what working drawings are.

3. Provide adequate space between multiple-view drawings to avoid the crowding of dimensions and notes.

4. Check your drawing for completeness by sketching each part using your notes and dimensions.

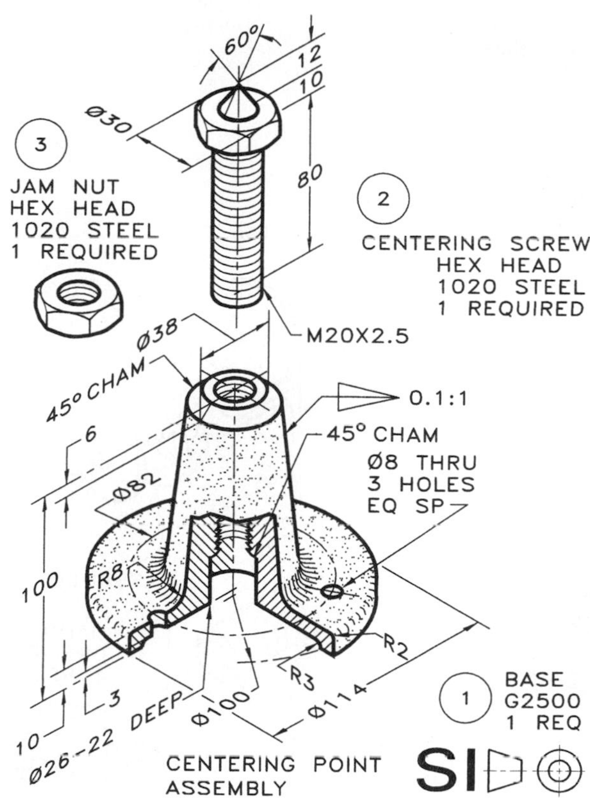

23.52 Size B sheet.

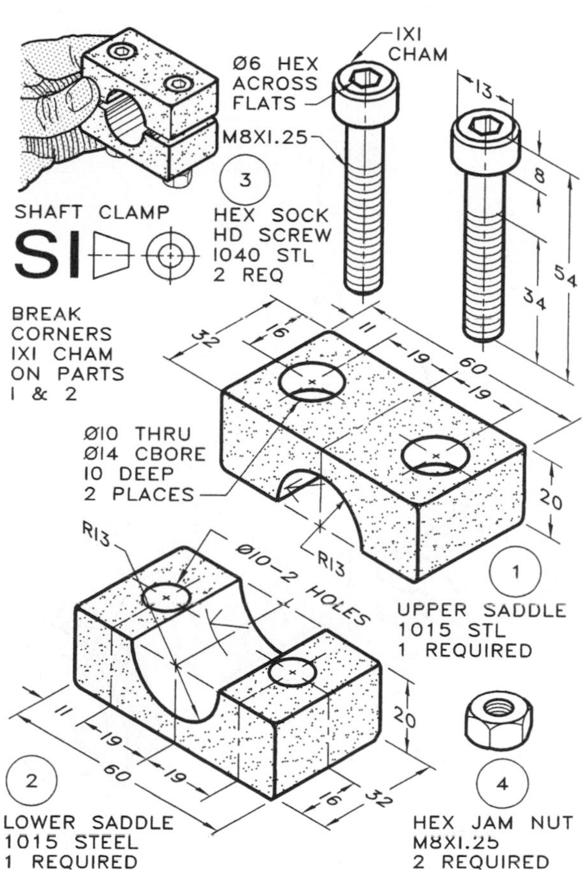

23.53 Size B sheet.

23.54 Make a working drawing with an assembly drawing of this adjustable milling stop on size B sheets. The column (part 3) that fits into the base (part 1) must be held in position with a setscrew. Select an appropriate type and size setscrew that passes through the end of the base and bears against the shaft.

23.55 Make a working drawing with an assembly drawing of the flange jig on size B sheets. Give a parts list on the assembly sheet using good drawing and dimensioning practices.

23.56 Make a working drawing with an assembly drawing of the rocker tool post on size B sheets. Give a parts list on the assembly sheet using good drawing and dimensioning practices.

23.57 Make a working drawing with an assembly drawing of the hoist ring on size B sheets. Give a parts list on the assembly sheet using good drawing and dimensioning practices.

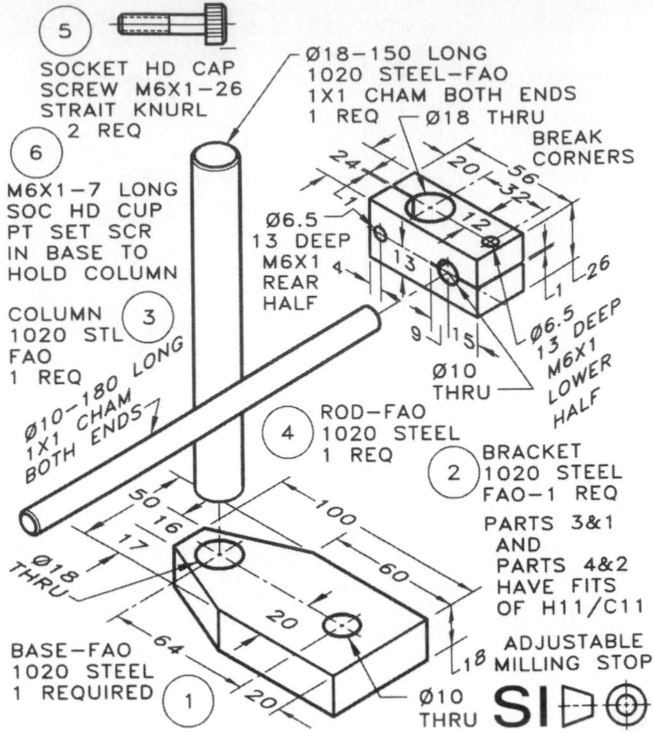

23.54 Size B sheet.

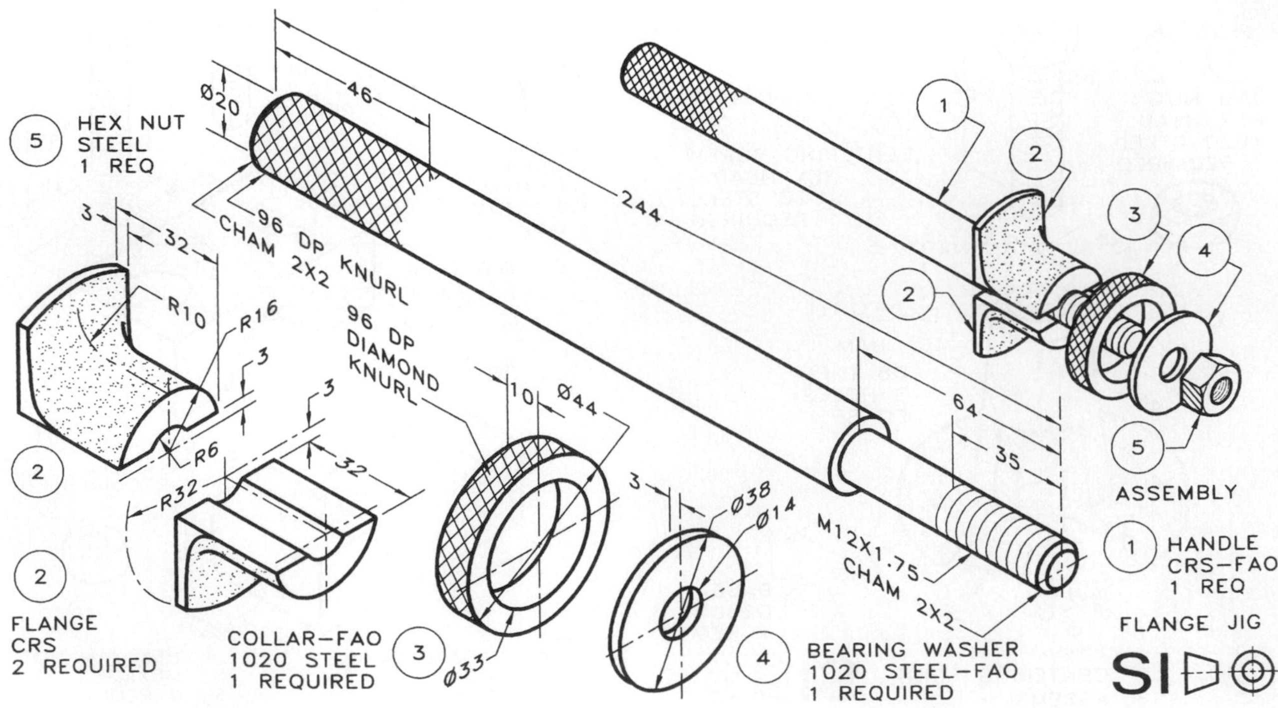

23.55 Size B sheet.

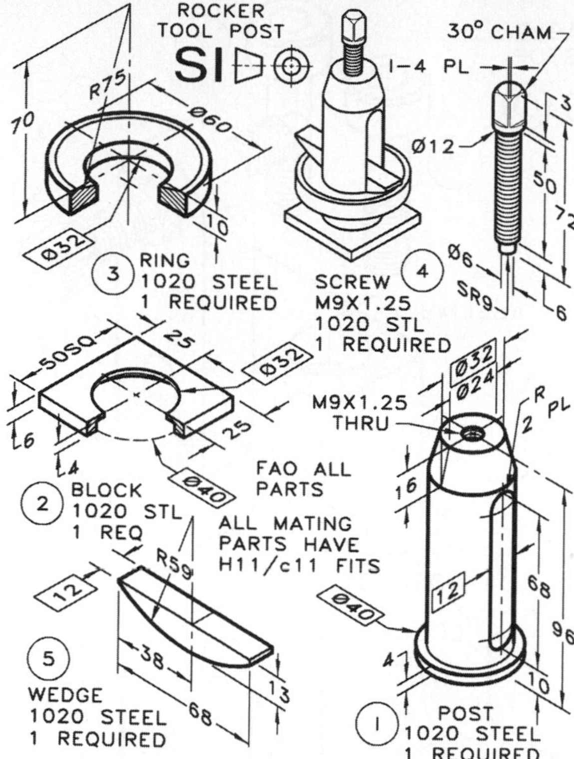

23.56 Size B sheet.

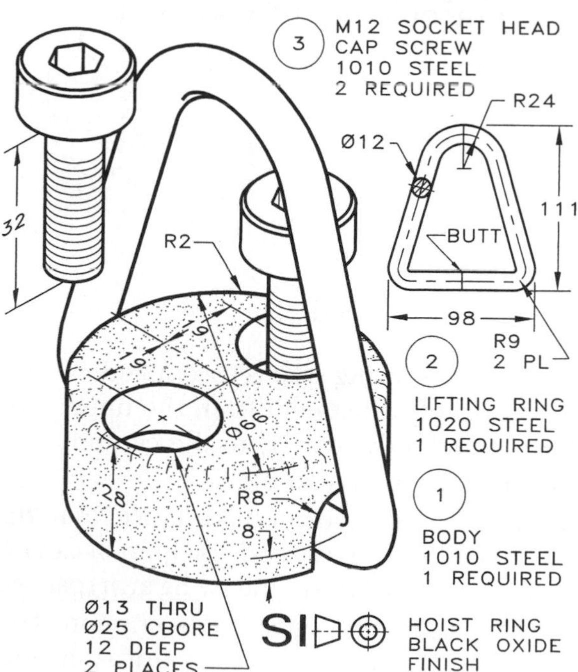

23.57 Size B sheet.

Thought Questions

1. What is *knurling* and what is its purposes?
2. What does the note "FA0" mean?
3. Which orthographic view of a cylindrical hole is best for giving its diameter with a leader and a note? Why?
4. Which orthographic view of a cylindrical hole is best for giving a location dimension to show its location? Why?
5. What does it mean when a dimension on a working drawing is enclosed in a box?
6. What does it mean when two dimensions are given on a single dimension line?
7. What term describes a hole with a flat bottom that is made partway inside a smaller hole?
8. What general information should be provided that names and identifies each part shown on a working drawing?
9. What is the variation in size of a part in a working drawing called?
10. How many types of setscrews are there? Name them.
11. Who is responsible for the correctness of a working drawing?
12. How many dimensions are necessary on an assembly drawing?

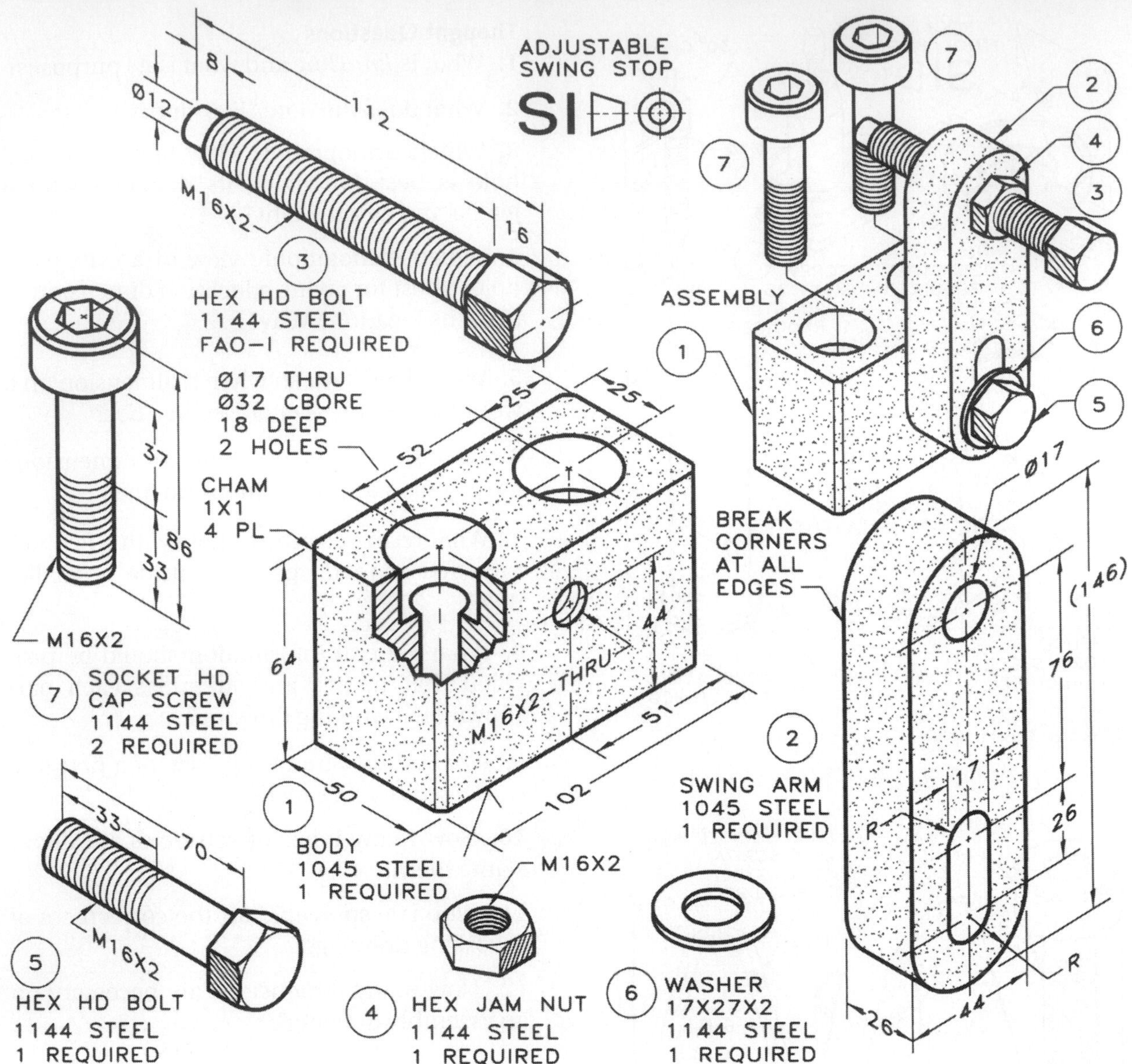

23.58 Make working drawings with an assembly drawing of this adjustable swing stop on size B sheets.

Thought Questions

1. What is the purpose of the washer (part 6) in this assembly?

2. Why is there a slot in the swing arm (part 2) instead of a circular hole?

3. Why did the designer of this assembly use both socket-head cap screws and hex-head cap screws instead of using one or the other?

4. When the swing stop is assembled, what is the range of adjustment from the upper surface of the body (part 1) to the centerline of the hex-head bolt (part 3)?

5. What is the maximum distance that the 12 DIA end of the hex-head bolt (part 3) can extend beyond the face of the swing arm (part 2)?

6. Write a paragraph giving a description of either part 1 or part 2 in the absence of a drawing.

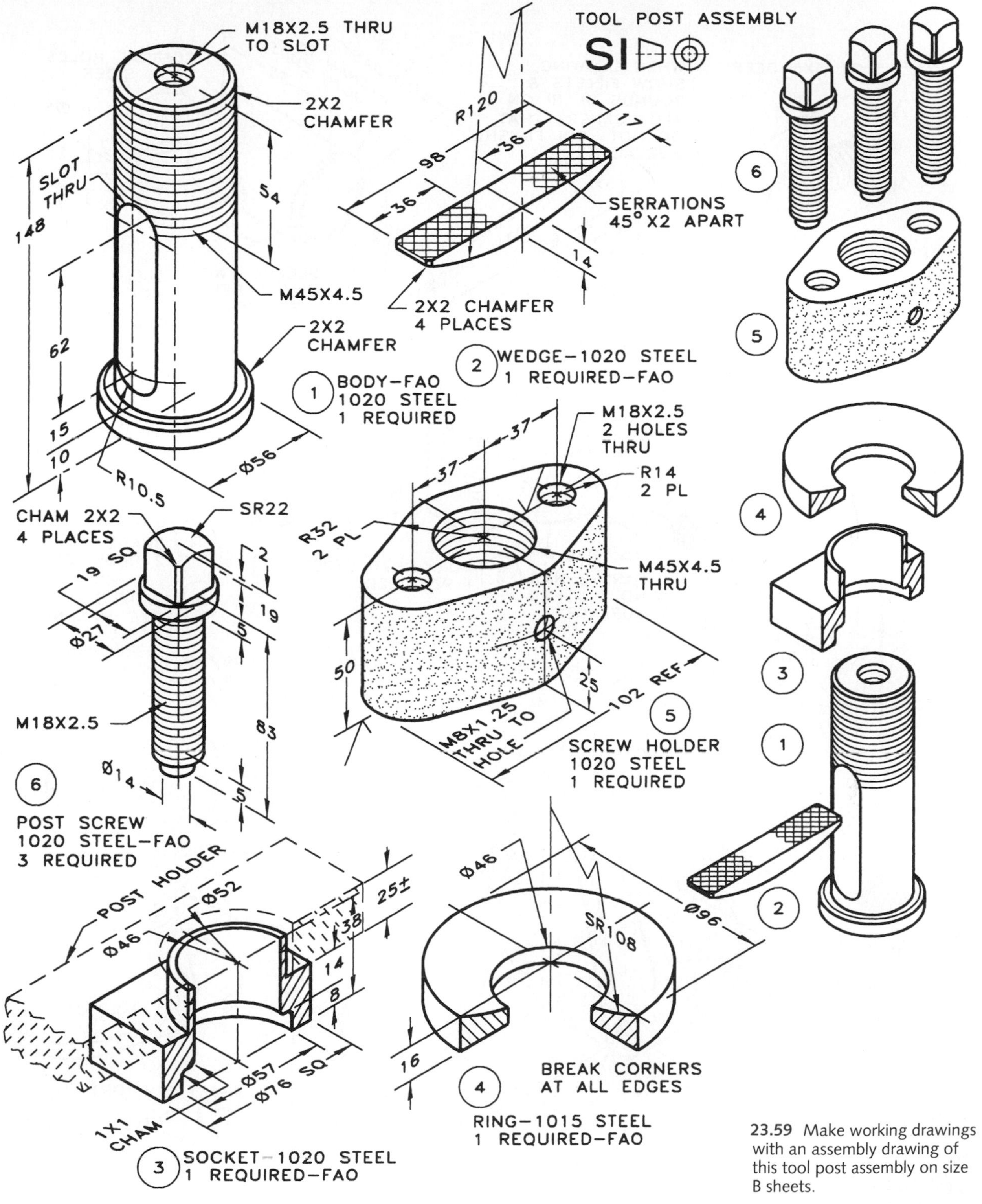

23.59 Make working drawings with an assembly drawing of this tool post assembly on size B sheets.

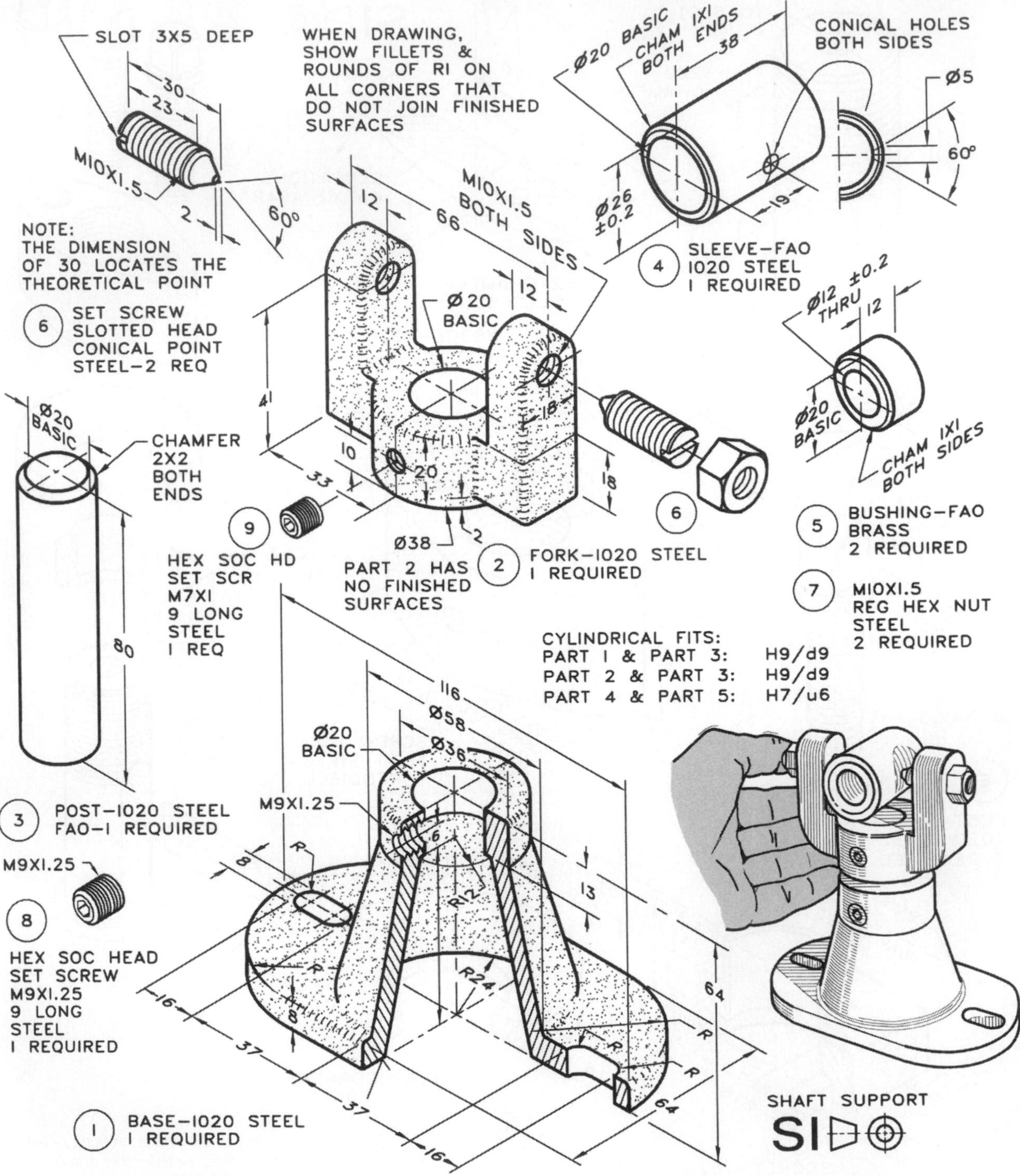
SLOT 3X5 DEEP
30
23
M10X1.5
2
60°
NOTE:
THE DIMENSION
OF 30 LOCATES THE
THEORETICAL POINT
6
SET SCREW
SLOTTED HEAD
CONICAL POINT
STEEL–2 REQ
WHEN DRAWING,
SHOW FILLETS &
ROUNDS OF R1 ON
ALL CORNERS THAT
DO NOT JOIN FINISHED
SURFACES
M10X1.5
BOTH SIDES
12
66
Ø20
BASIC
12
41
18
10
33
20
18
Ø38
2
2
PART 2 HAS
NO FINISHED
SURFACES
FORK–1020 STEEL
1 REQUIRED
Ø20 BASIC
CHAM 1X1
BOTH ENDS
38
CONICAL HOLES
BOTH SIDES
Ø5
60°
Ø26
±0.2
19
4
SLEEVE–FAO
1020 STEEL
1 REQUIRED
Ø12 ±0.2
THRU
12
Ø20
BASIC
CHAM 1X1
BOTH SIDES
6
5
BUSHING–FAO
BRASS
2 REQUIRED
7
M10X1.5
REG HEX NUT
STEEL
2 REQUIRED
Ø20
BASIC
CHAMFER
2X2
BOTH
ENDS
80
3
POST–1020 STEEL
FAO–1 REQUIRED
9
HEX SOC HD
SET SCR
M7X1
9 LONG
STEEL
1 REQ
CYLINDRICAL FITS:
PART 1 & PART 3: H9/d9
PART 2 & PART 3: H9/d9
PART 4 & PART 5: H7/u6
116
Ø58
Ø20
BASIC
Ø36
M9X1.25
6
R
8
13
R12
R24
R
64
8
16
37
37
16
R
R
R
64
M9X1.25
8
HEX SOC HEAD
SET SCREW
M9X1.25
9 LONG
STEEL
1 REQUIRED
1
BASE–1020 STEEL
1 REQUIRED
SHAFT SUPPORT
SI

23.60 Make working drawings with an assembly drawing of this shaft support on size B sheets.

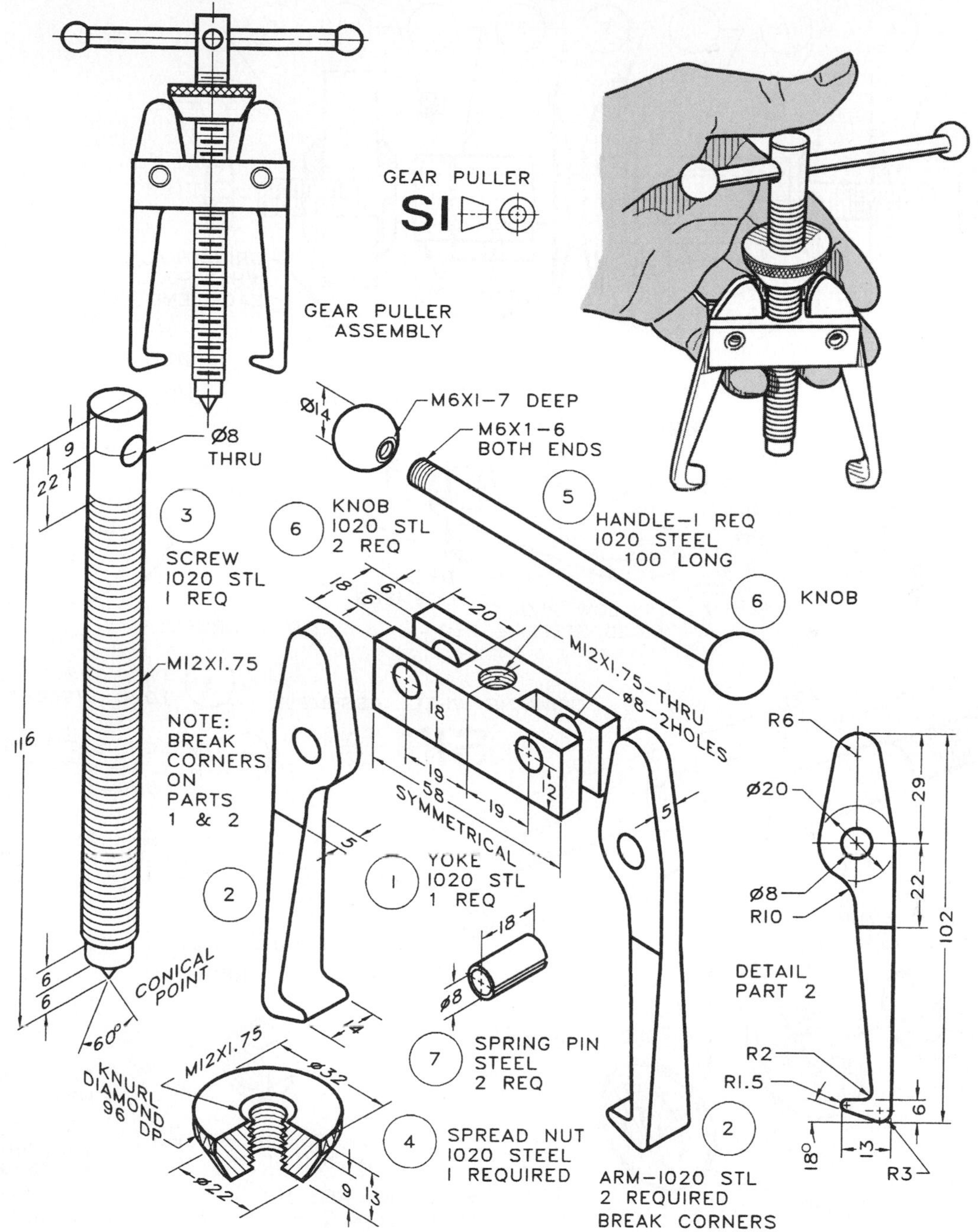

23.61 Make working drawings with an assembly drawing of this gear puller on size B sheets.

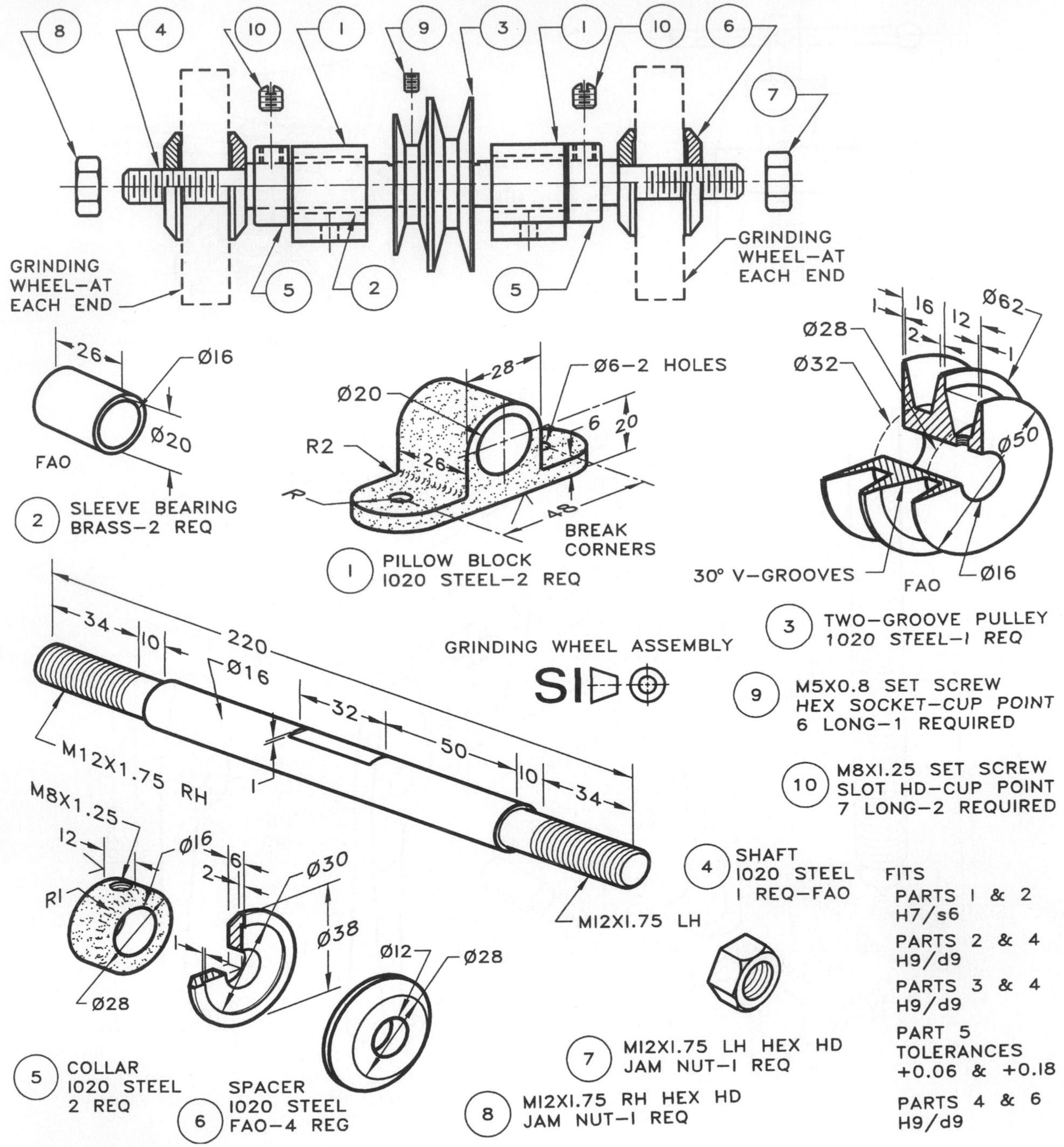

23.62 Make working drawings with an assembly drawing of this grinding wheel on size B sheets.

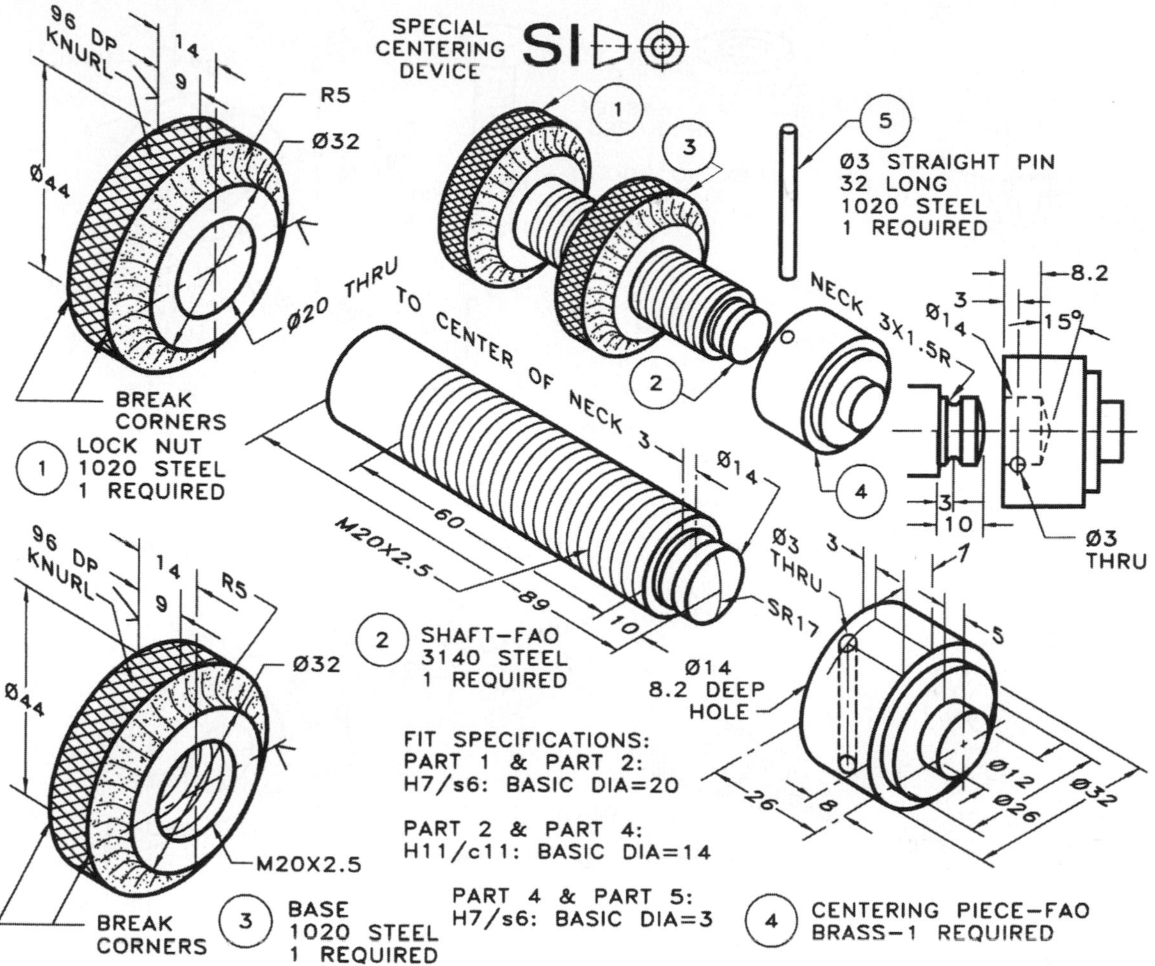

23.63 Make working drawings with an assembly drawing of this centering post on size B sheets.

Thought Questions

1. What conversion factor would you use to convert metric dimensions to English units?

2. Why is knurling specified on parts 1 and 3? Why was knurling not specified on part 4?

3. Why were parts 1 and 2 not designed with threads for attachment to each other?

4. When the centering part is assembled, will part 4 rotate about the end of part 2? Explain, and determine why it attaches as it does.

5. Why was the fit between parts 4 and 5 selected to be H7/s6 instead of H11/c11?

6. What will be the approximate weight of the total assembly if all materials are assumed to weigh 490 lb/cu ft?

7. Can you explain why parts 1 and 3 were designed with bosses as shown?

8. Which of the parts can be specified on a working drawing by a note without a drawing?

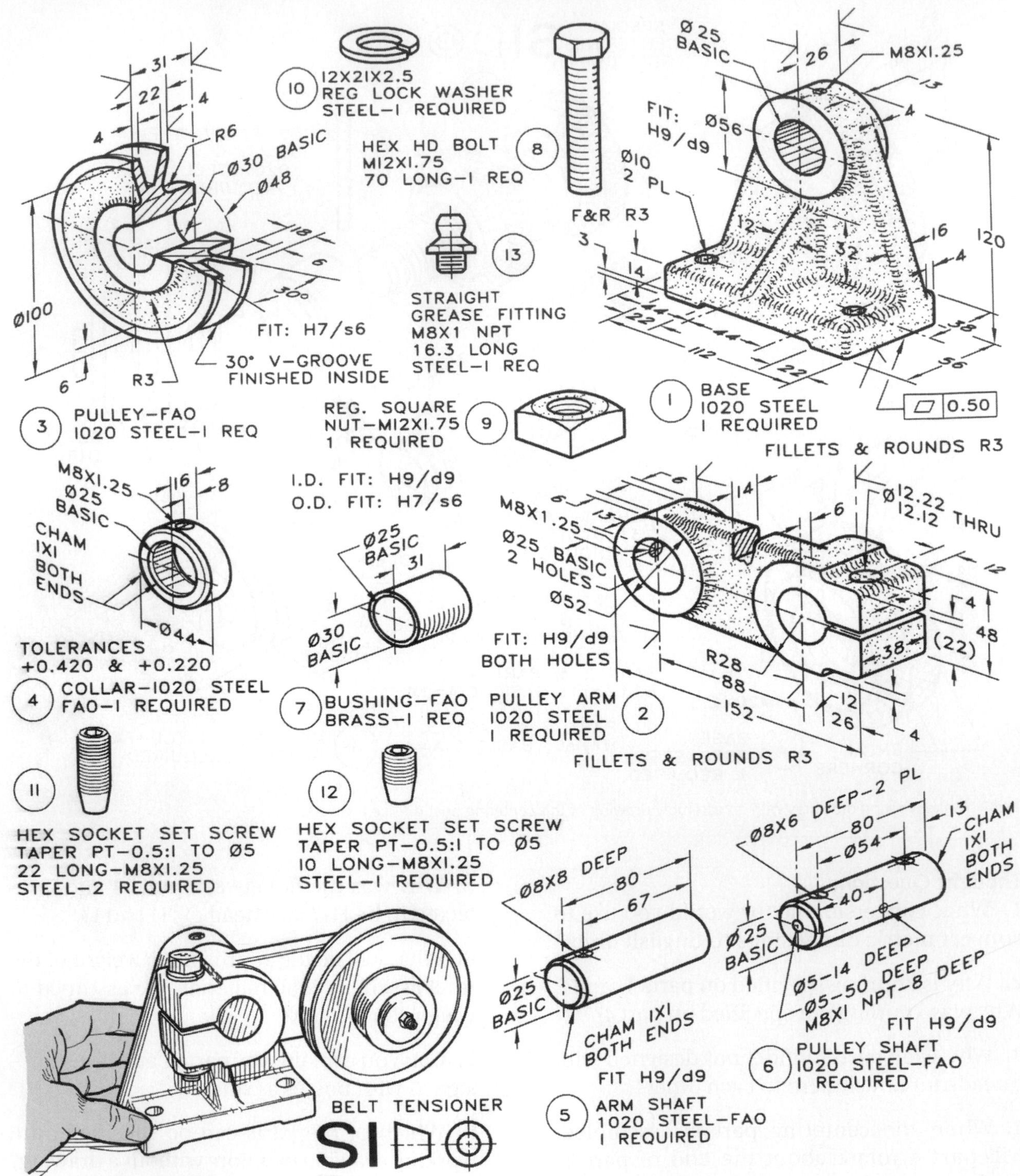

23.64 Make working drawings with an assembly drawing of this belt tensioner on size B sheets.

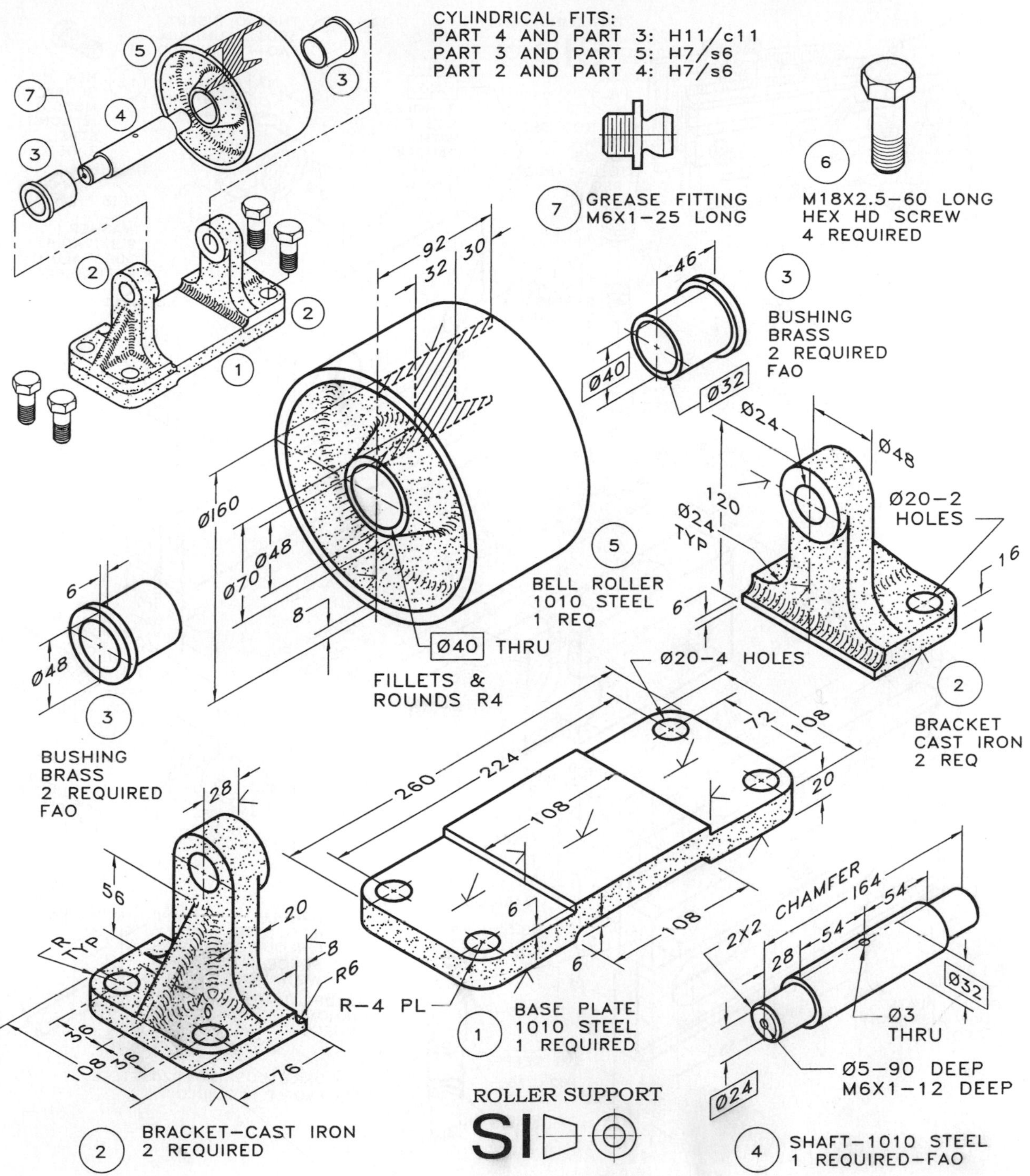

23.65 Make working drawings with an assembly drawing of this roller support on size B sheets.

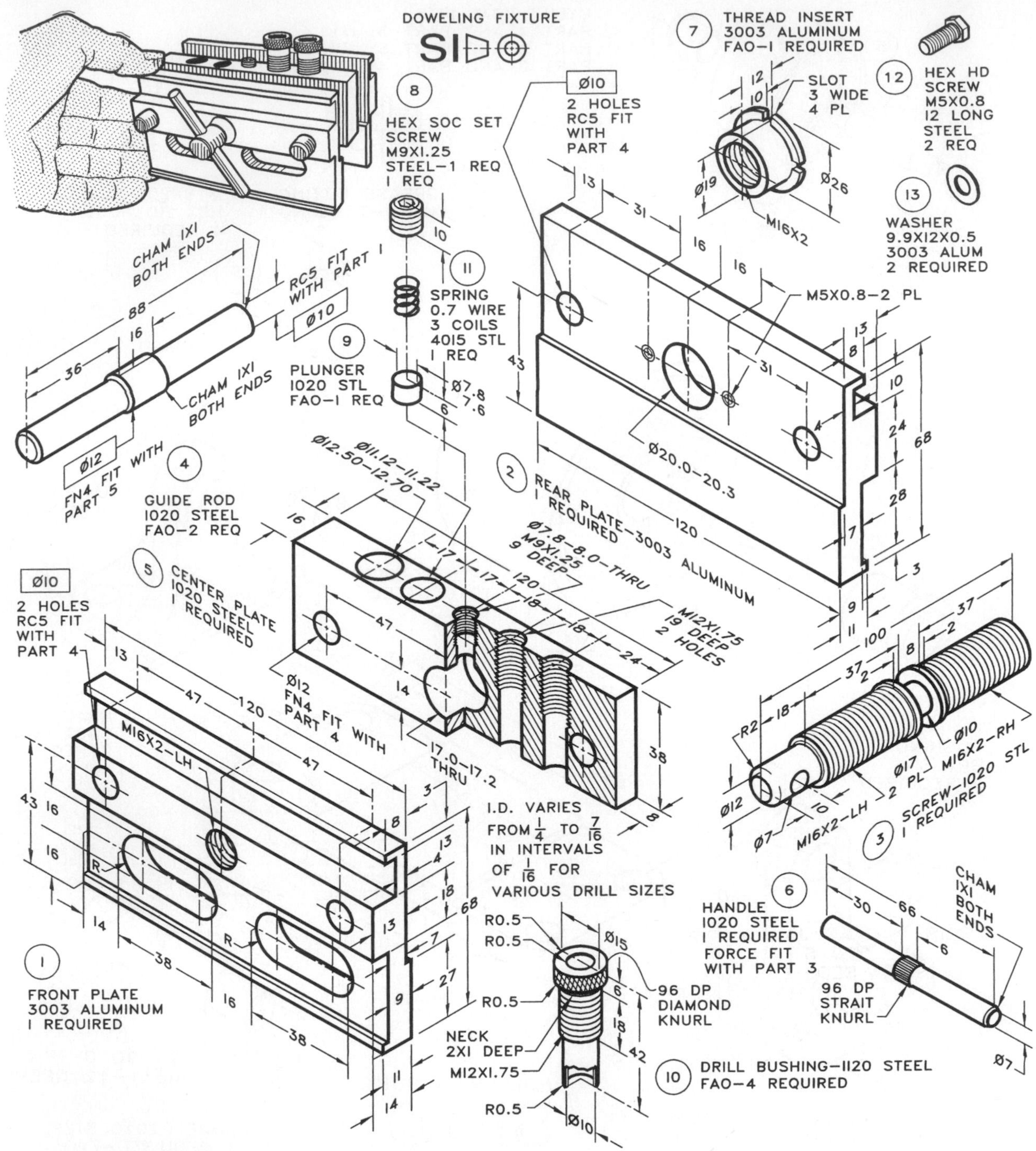

23.66 Make working drawings with an assembly drawing of this doweling fixture on size B sheets.

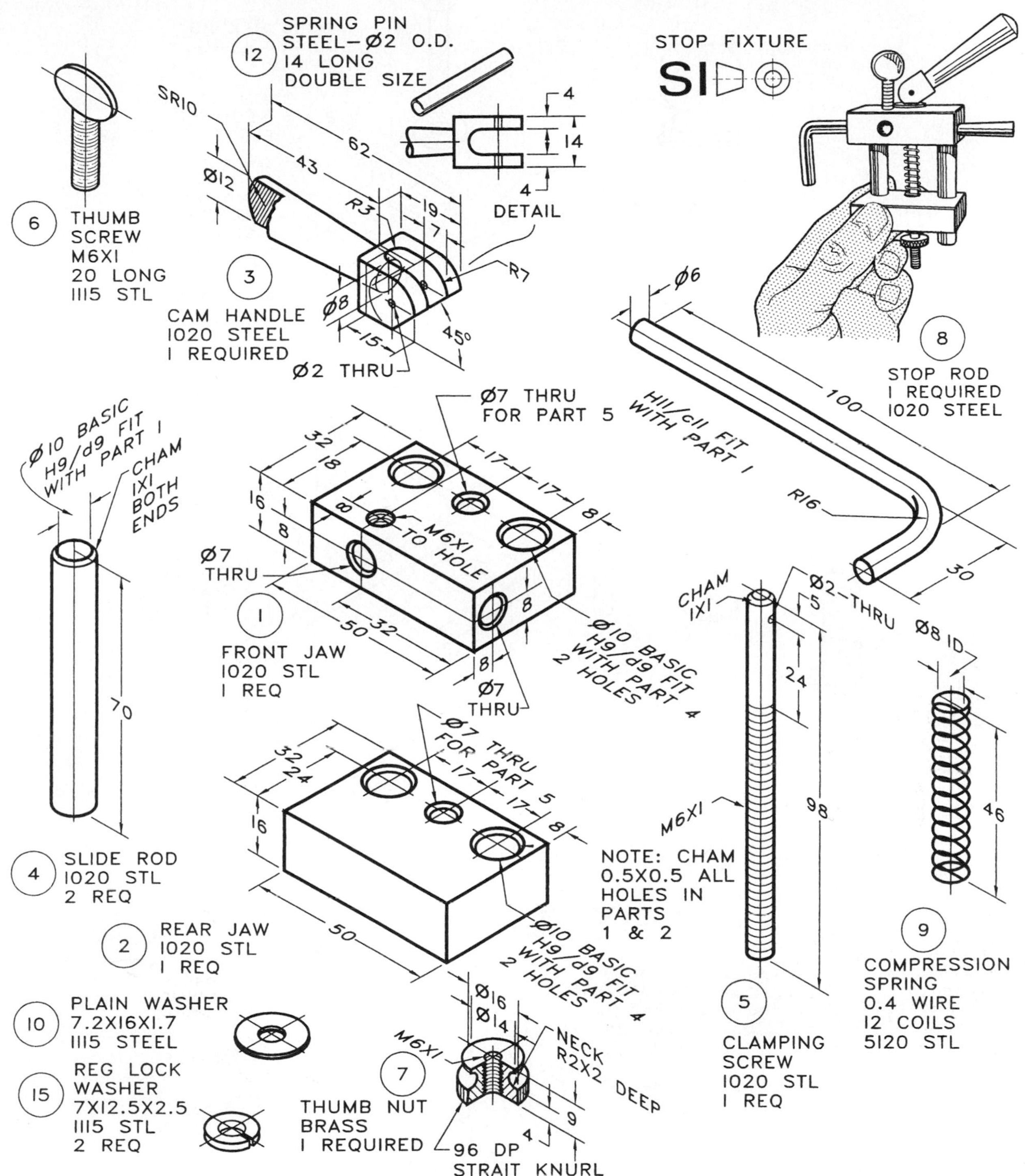

23.67 Make working drawings with an assembly drawing of this stop fixture assembly on size B sheets.

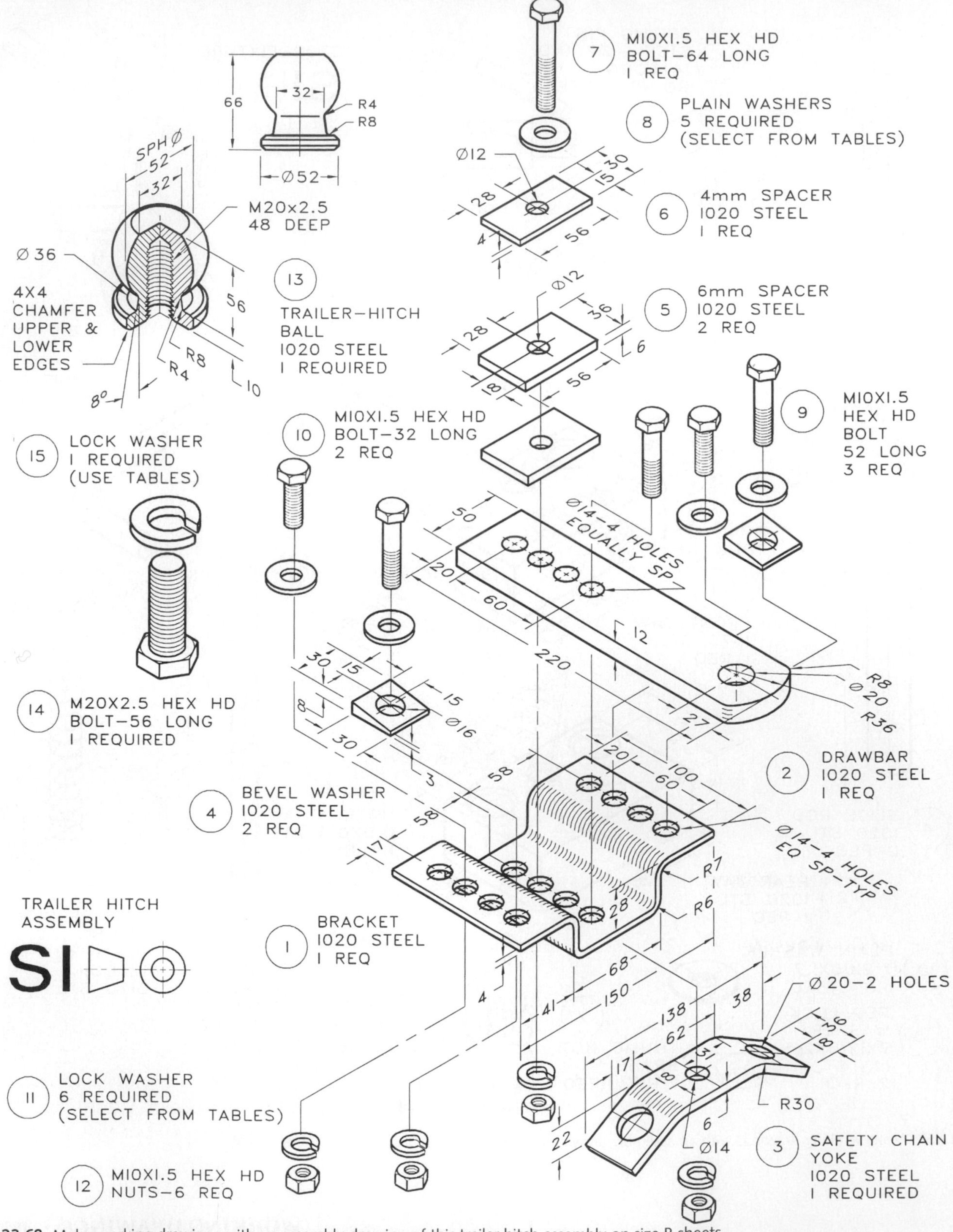

23.68 Make working drawings with an assembly drawing of this trailer hitch assembly on size B sheets.

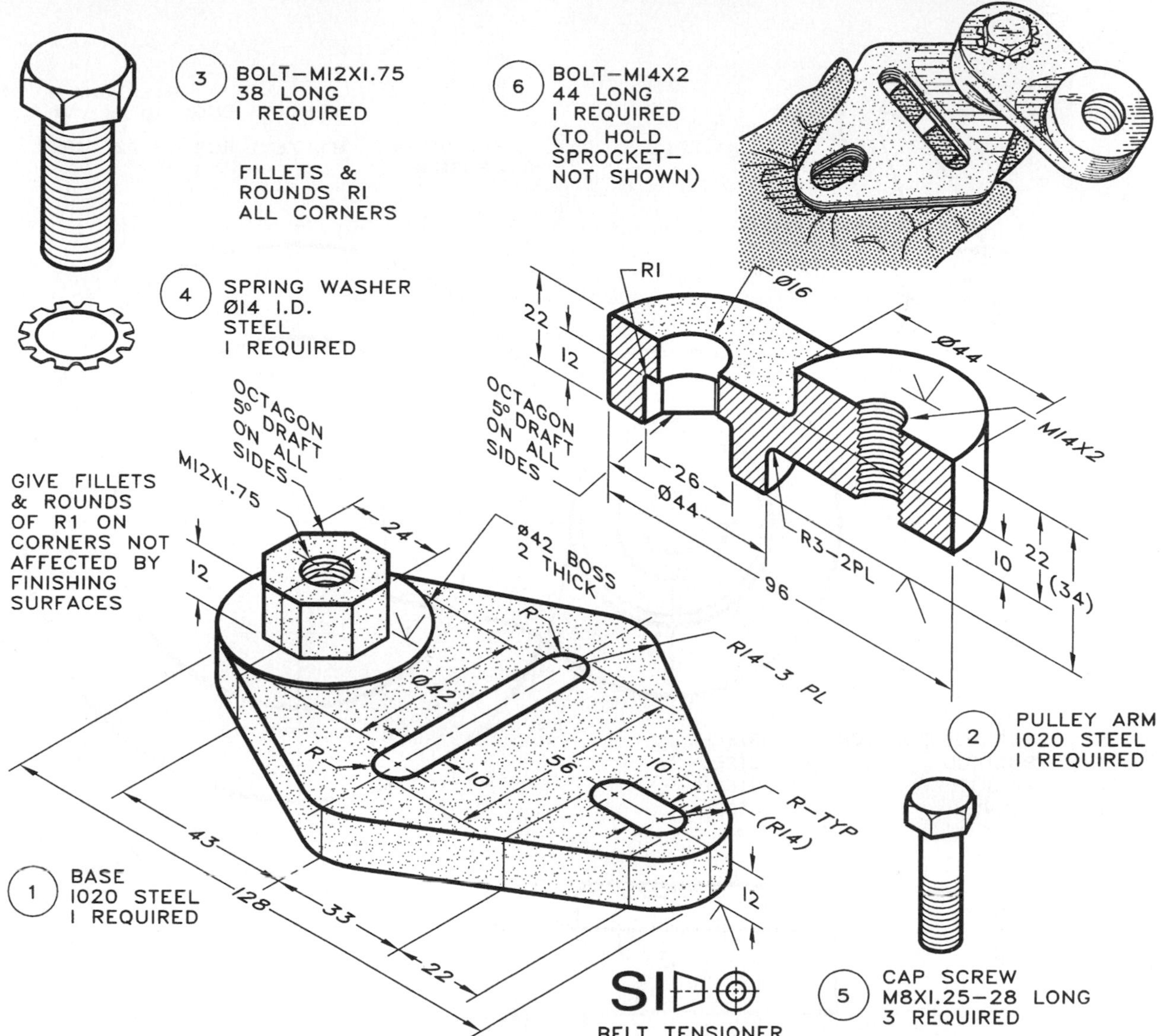

23.69 Make working drawings with an assembly drawing of this belt tensioner on size B sheets.

Working Drawings: Multiple Parts with Design Applications

Make dimensioned working drawings of the multiple parts shown in **Figures 23.70–23.71** on a sheet size of your choice with the necessary dimensions and notes to fabricate the parts. Each part is given in a general format, which requires some design on your part.

You must consider the addition of fillets and rounds, the application of finish marks, and the modification of features of the parts to make them functional and practical. Apply tolerances to the parts in limit form by using the tables of cylindrical fits in the appendix. Make an assembly drawing and parts list to show how the parts are to be put together.

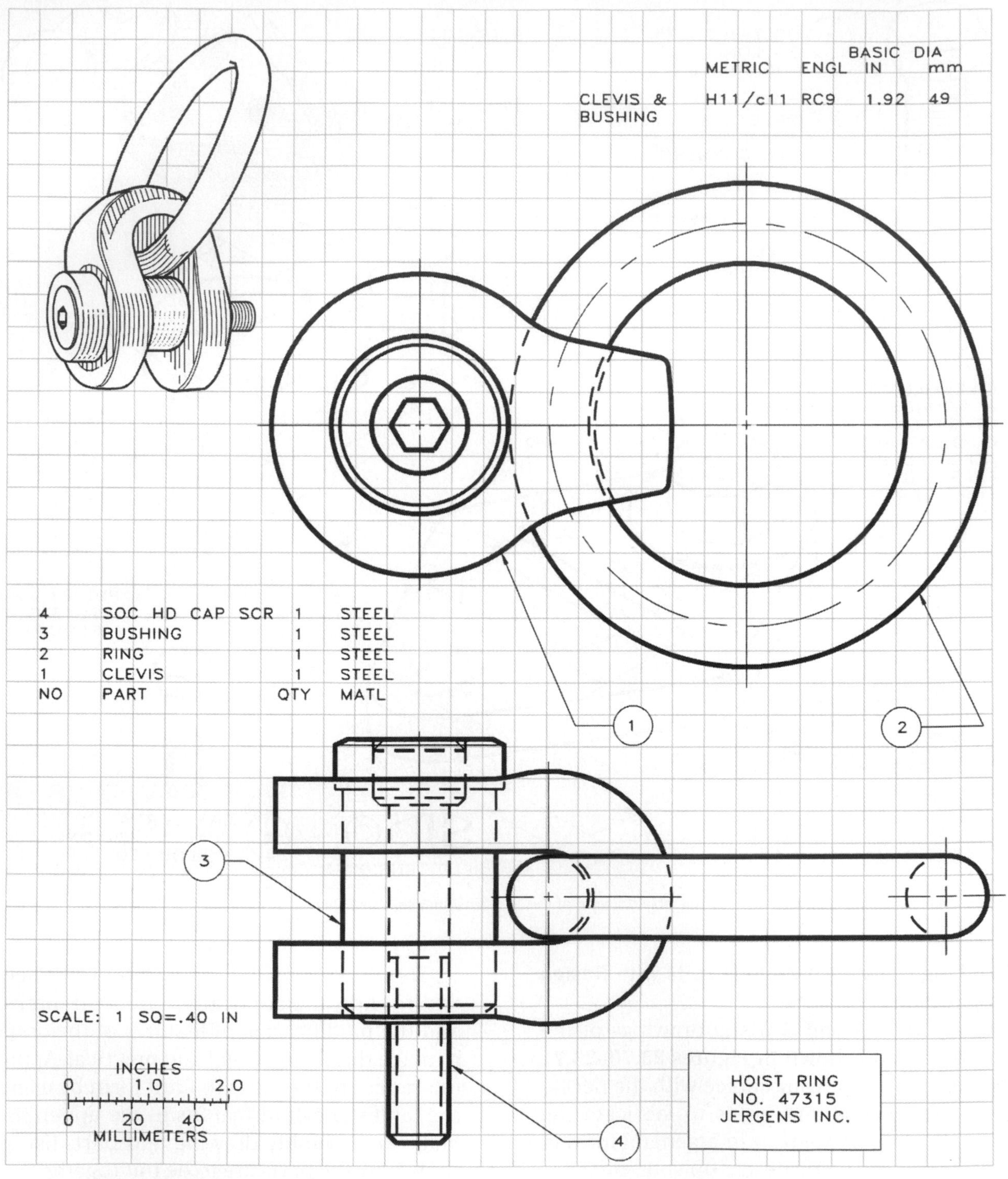
BASIC DIA
METRIC ENGL IN mm
CLEVIS & BUSHING H11/c11 RC9 1.92 49
4 SOC HD CAP SCR 1 STEEL
3 BUSHING 1 STEEL
2 RING 1 STEEL
1 CLEVIS 1 STEEL
NO PART QTY MATL
1
2
3
4
SCALE: 1 SQ=.40 IN
INCHES
0 1.0 2.0
0 20 40
MILLIMETERS
HOIST RING
NO. 47315
JERGENS INC.

23.70 Hoist ring.

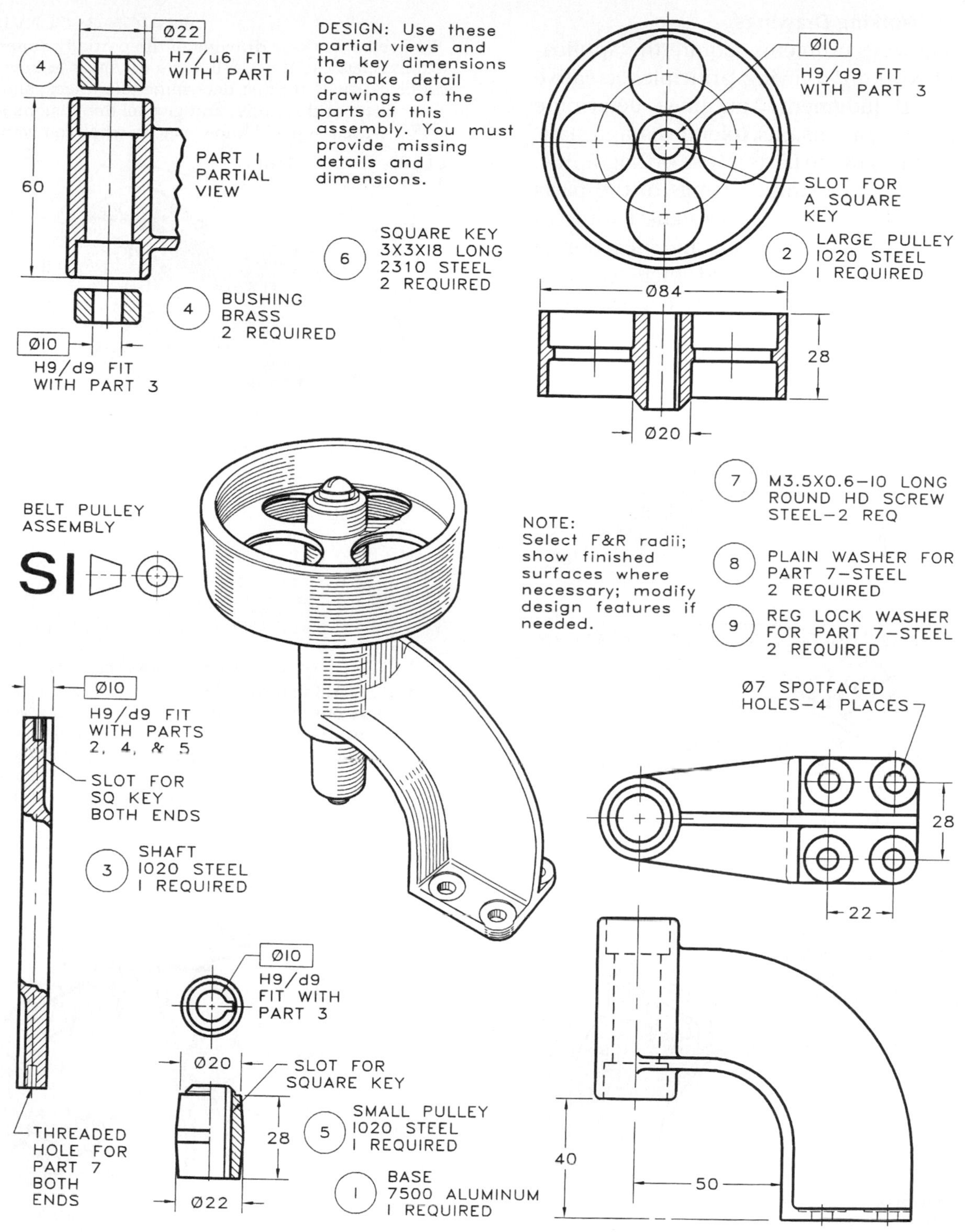
Ø22
H7/u6 FIT
WITH PART I
4
PART I
PARTIAL
VIEW
60
4
BUSHING
BRASS
2 REQUIRED
Ø10
H9/d9 FIT
WITH PART 3
DESIGN: Use these partial views and the key dimensions to make detail drawings of the parts of this assembly. You must provide missing details and dimensions.
6
SQUARE KEY
3X3X18 LONG
2310 STEEL
2 REQUIRED
Ø10
H9/d9 FIT
WITH PART 3
SLOT FOR
A SQUARE
KEY
2
LARGE PULLEY
1020 STEEL
1 REQUIRED
Ø84
28
Ø20
BELT PULLEY
ASSEMBLY
SI
7
M3.5X0.6–10 LONG
ROUND HD SCREW
STEEL–2 REQ
NOTE:
Select F&R radii; show finished surfaces where necessary; modify design features if needed.
8
PLAIN WASHER FOR
PART 7–STEEL
2 REQUIRED
9
REG LOCK WASHER
FOR PART 7–STEEL
2 REQUIRED
Ø10
H9/d9 FIT
WITH PARTS
2, 4, & 5
SLOT FOR
SQ KEY
BOTH ENDS
3
SHAFT
1020 STEEL
1 REQUIRED
Ø7 SPOTFACED
HOLES–4 PLACES
28
22
Ø10
H9/d9
FIT WITH
PART 3
Ø20
SLOT FOR
SQUARE KEY
28
5
SMALL PULLEY
1020 STEEL
1 REQUIRED
THREADED
HOLE FOR
PART 7
BOTH
ENDS
Ø22
1
BASE
7500 ALUMINUM
1 REQUIRED
40
50

23.71 Pulley assembly.

Design: Working Drawings

The following problems require the application of working drawing principles, creative skills, and judgment. You must determine many of the dimensions, tolerances, and standard features of the parts. Make orthographic, dimensioned working drawings of the parts and assemblies shown in Designs 1 through 21 on size A or size B sheets and incorporate the design features specified. Include a title block, dimensions, and notes necessary for making the part.

DESIGN 1: HINGE ASSEMBLY

Development of the working drawings for this hinge assembly will give you good exercise in figuring tolerances. Also, you need to add fillets and rounds and incorporate the given specs. Do your drawings on size A sheets and make you instructor proud.

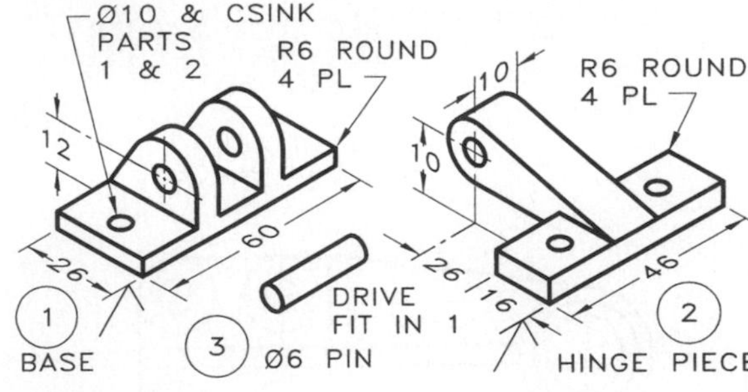

DESIGN 2: JOURNAL

We need a working drawing of this journal, but first, show fillets and rounds, give finish marks, select specs for 3 hex socket screws, select 4 hex-head base screws, and figure out other details. Draw on a size B sheet.

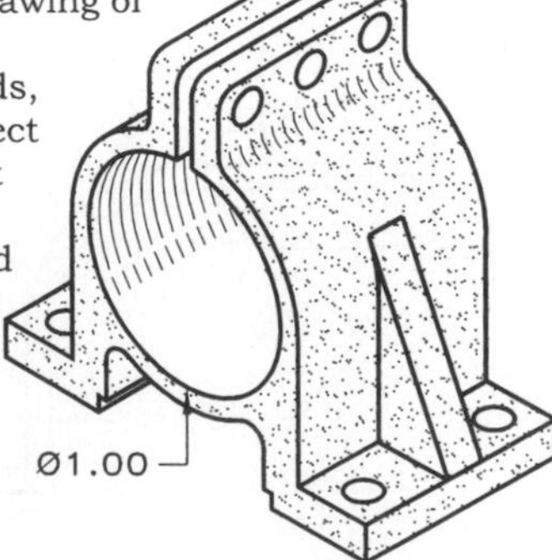

DESIGN 3: CLEVIS

We need a working drawing of the partially dimensioned clevis so there will be no doubt as to how it will be made. You must determine tolerances, show fillets and rounds, and give all dimensions so the shop will know exactly what you want.

23

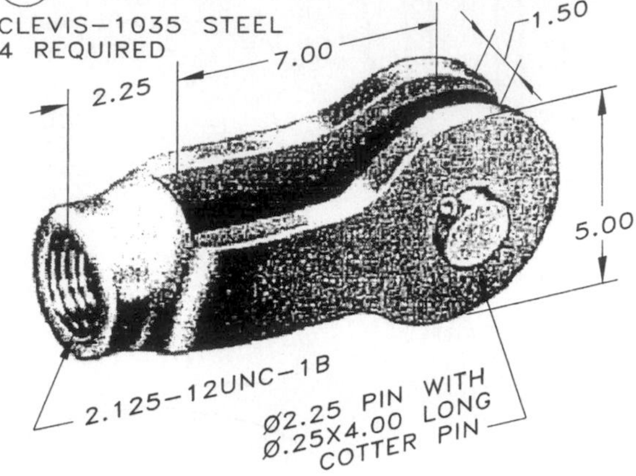

DESIGN 4: SNATCH BLOCK

Make a working drawing of the assembly, but first, figure out the appropriate tolerances in several places. Also, give thought to what materials will be best and other details. Can you develop a better design for this assembly? Give it a shot!

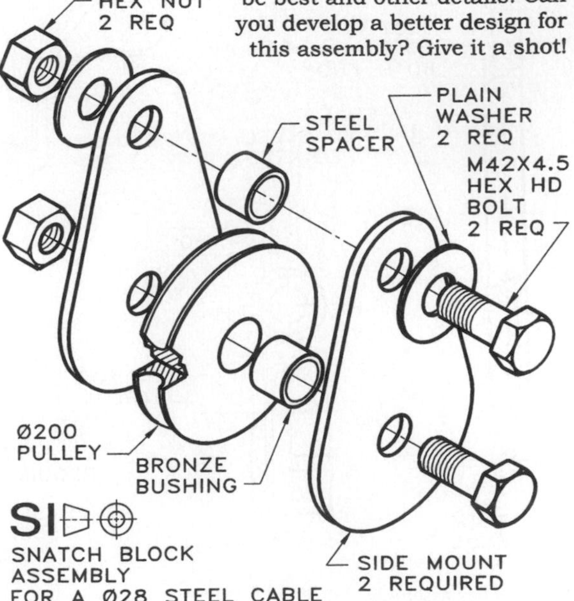

DESIGN 5: JACK BASE

How are you at following verbal instructions? This base is to be modified as specified by the notes on the drawing. Convert these specs into working drawings on a size A sheet.

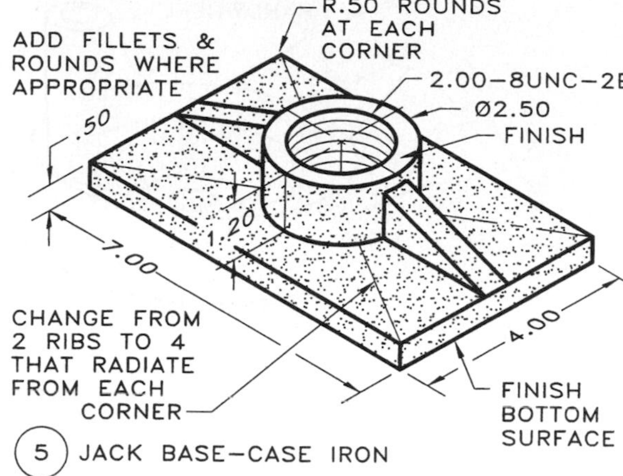

DESIGN 6: SWING HANGER

Make a working drawing of this assembly on size B sheets. Determine dimensions, fillets & rounds, tolerances, finished surfaces, and bolt lengths.

ALTERNATIVE: Redesign the hanger and make a working drawing of your design on size B sheets.

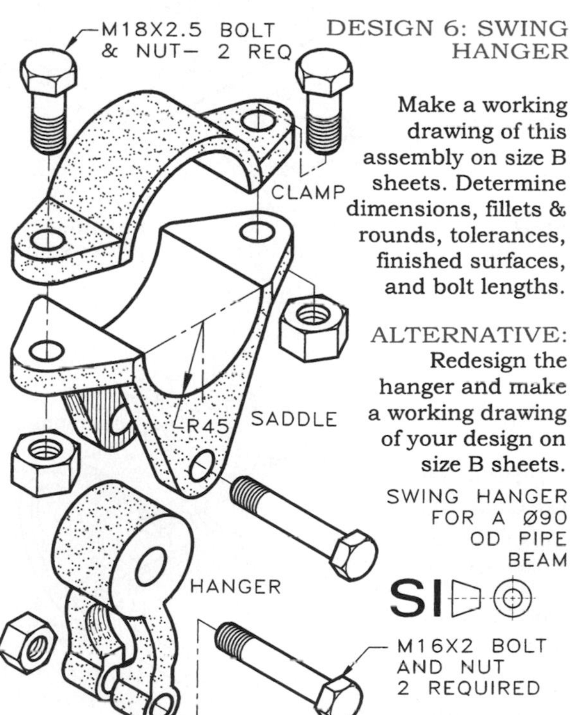

DESIGN 7: BRACKET

Make a working drawing of this bracket on a size A sheet using thc following specs:

Overall height: 10"
Base: 4" X 10" X 0.5"

Yes, yes, yes, you'll have to estimate the dimensions, but you'll be a better person for it.

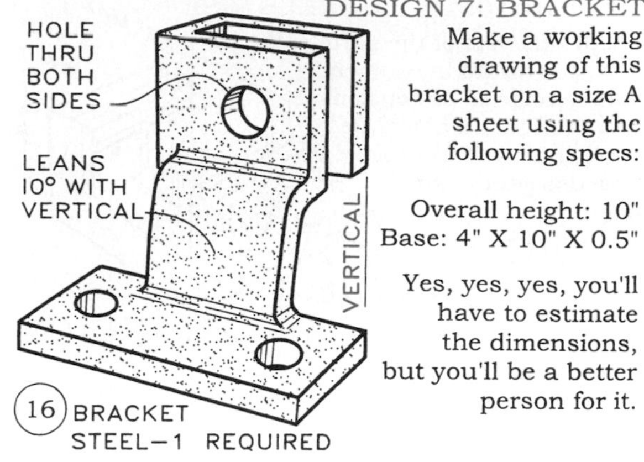

DESIGN 8: HOLD-DOWN CLAMP

Develop this concept for a clamp into a working drawing. Maybe you can improve on this design with one of your own. Draw on a size B sheet. Open up your creativity!

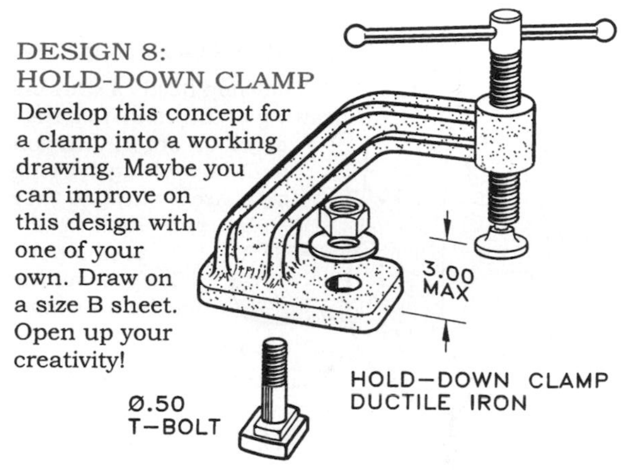

DESIGN 9: BEAM CLAMP

Sketch views of the clamp to determine its configuration and convert them into working drawings on a size B sheet.

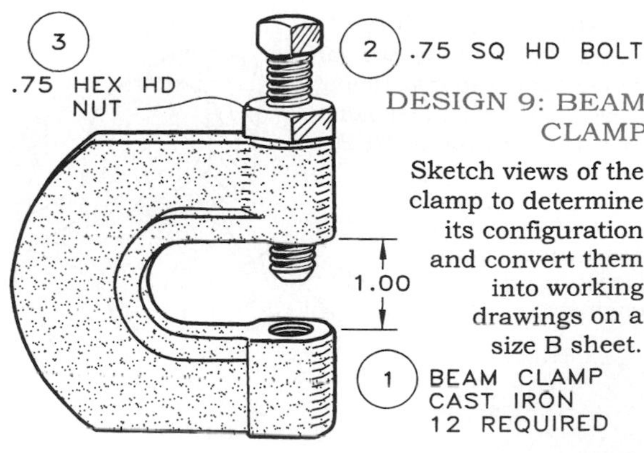

DESIGN 10: DRILL PRESS VISE

Make sketches of the parts of the vise, convert to instrument views, and add dimensions and fabrication notes. Be more than a draftsman, be a designer, a good one.

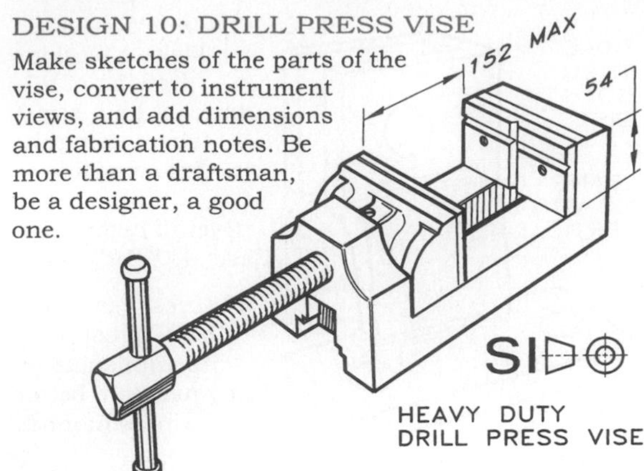

DESIGN 13: HANDWHEEL

Draw the necessary views for a dimensioned working drawing of the handwheel, handle, and pin. Draw on a size B sheet.

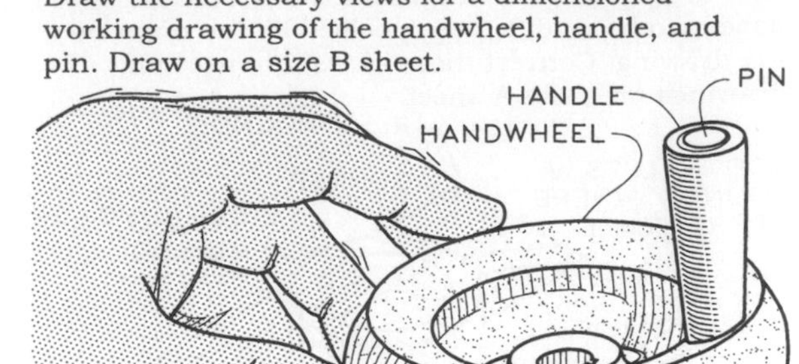

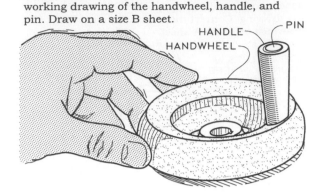

DESIGN 11: TOOL HOLDER

The shop needs a working drawing of this holder so they can fill an order. Can you make a working drawing on a size B sheet so they can crank up the production? They're waiting for the drawings.

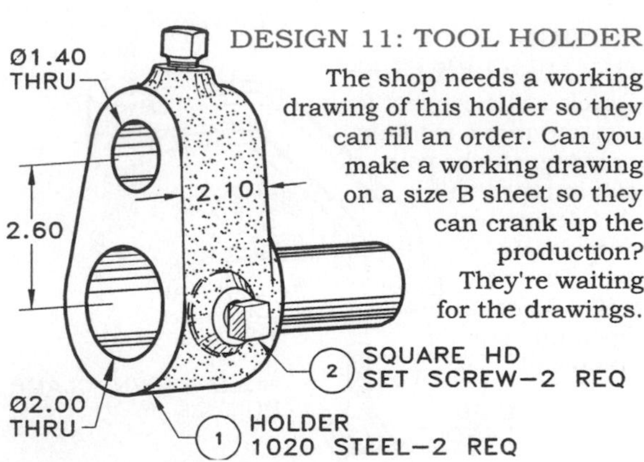

DESIGN 14: TOE CLAMP

Make working drawings of the parts of the clamp and show the true angles of the parts in auxiliary views. Estimate the dimensions that are not given in the figure. Draw on size A sheets.

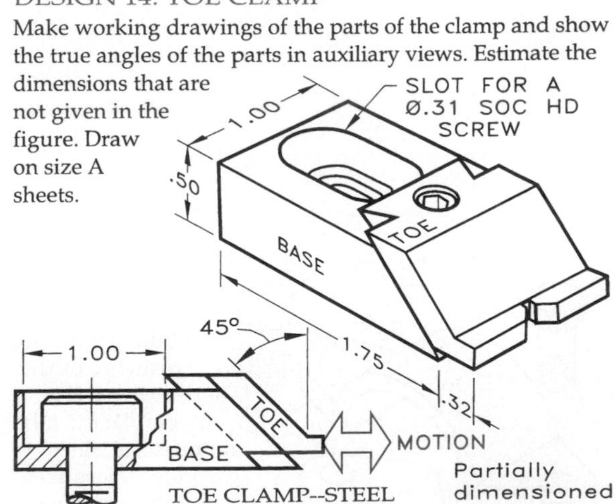

DESIGN 12: PULLEY

Sketch views of the two parts, convert them to instrument views, and give dimensions for fabrication on a size B sheet.

Turn your creativity loose; be an engineer.

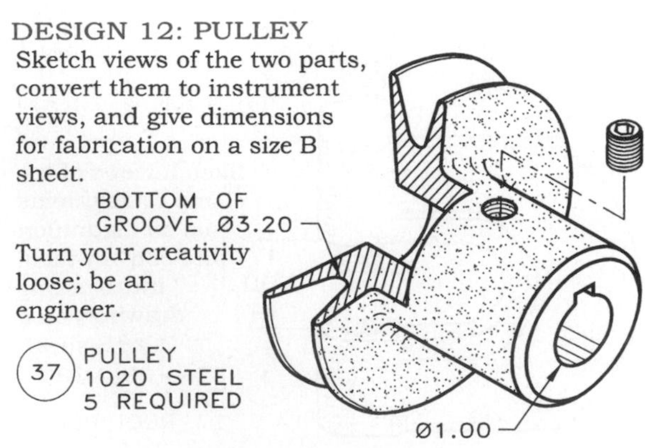

DESIGN 15: MECHANIC'S SEAT

This is a neat seat for working on a car in a garage. Make working drawings of it on a size B sheet. Bet you could do one that's maybe better. Counting on you.

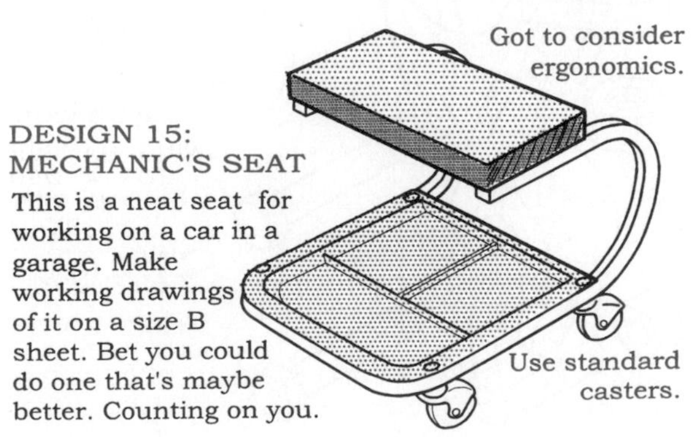

DESIGN 16: ANGLE VISE

You are familar with a standard vise. This one is adjustable up to 90°. Develop the design of each part and make a working drawing on size B sheets. You'll find this exercise a good test of your skills.

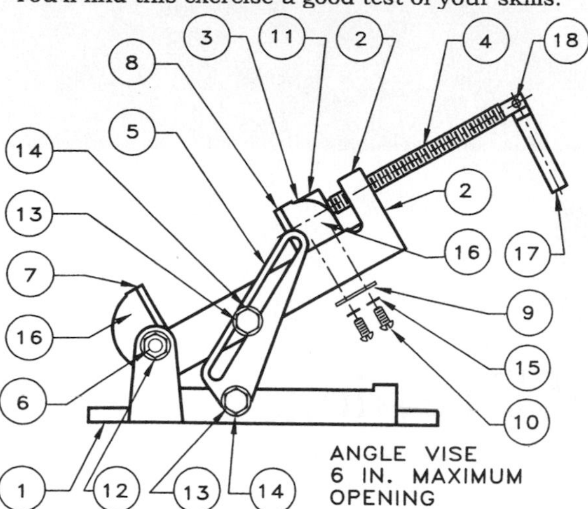

DESIGN 17: NUTCRACKER

Invent a better nutcracker and the world will beat a path to your door. Make a working drawing of your design on size B sheets. You might want to look at the patent section in Chapter 8 and select a good bank.

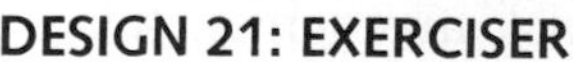

DESIGN 21: EXERCISER

A common exercise apparatus is a bicycle-type machine that is pedaled like a bicycle. How about this? We design a holder for the rear wheel of a standard bicycle so it can be used as an exerciser. It would be best if several resistance levels were provided to calibrate the exertion required for different levels. And the contraption itself? Sure would be good to make it easy to fold up and store out of the way when not in use, maybe slide it under a bed.

Begin by sketching your ideas and checking out the dimensions of a bicycle. Then, make a working drawing on size B sheets. While you're working, be thinking about the market. Where will it be sold? Will there be buyers? What is its competition?

DESIGN 18: CAN CRUSHER

This simple design serves an important purpose. Can you think of a better design that employs the same principles? Sketch some solutions and make a working drawing of your best one on size B sheets and become famous and rich.

DESIGN 19: RAPID REEL

This product fills the need for most homeowners who must care for their lawns. Do you think that you can make working drawings of it? Give it a try. Use size B sheets. What size reel will you need to reel in 100 ft of 3/4-in. hose? How much would this much hose weigh?

(Courtesy of Rapid Reel Hose Reels.)

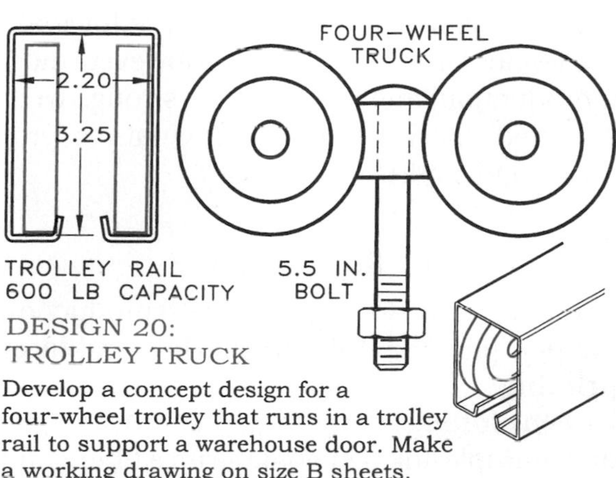

DESIGN 20: TROLLEY TRUCK

Develop a concept design for a four-wheel trolley that runs in a trolley rail to support a warehouse door. Make a working drawing on size B sheets.

24 Reproduction of Drawings

24.1 Introduction

So far we have discussed the preparation of drawings and specifications through the working-drawing stage, in which detailed drawings are completed on tracing film or paper. Now, the drawings must be reproduced, folded, and prepared for transmittal to those who will use them to prepare bids or to fabricate the parts.

Several methods of reproduction are available to engineers and technologists for making copies of their drawings. However, most reproduction methods require strong, well-executed line work on the originals to produce good copies.

24.2 Computer Reproduction

Three major types of computer reproduction are **pen plotting, ink-jet printing**, and **laser printing**.

Pen plotting is done by plotter with a single- or a multiple-ink pen holder with a fiber point that "draws" on the paper or film by moving the pen in *x*- and *y*-directions. Multiple strokes of the pen will give various thicknesses of lines.

Ink-jet printing is the process of spraying ink from tiny holes in a flat, disposable print-head onto the drawing surface as it passes through the printer. Prints can be obtained in color in addtion to black and white. Ink-jet printers vary in size from 8-1/2 × 11 in. output (**Figure 24.1**) to large engineering print sizes (**Figure 24.2**).

Laser printing is an electrophotographic process that uses a laser beam to draw an image on a photosensitive drum that is electrostatically charged to attract the toner. Then, electrostatically charged paper is rolled against the drum, the image is transferred, and toner is fused to the paper by heat (**Figure 24.3**). Laser printers make sharp drawings of the highest quality in color or black and white.

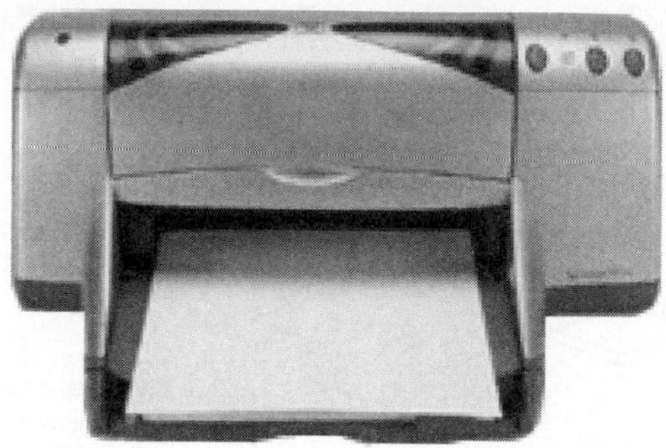

24.1 The DesignJet 995ck printer provides quiet high-speed operation and high print quality. Its letter- and legal-size format produces excellent color plots of text and graphics. *(Courtesy of Hewlett-Packard Company.)*

24.2 The DesignJet 1050c printer provides quiet high-speed operation and high print quality. This large-format color plotter can print a D-size color line drawing in less than 1 minute. *(Courtesy of Hewlett-Packard Company.)*

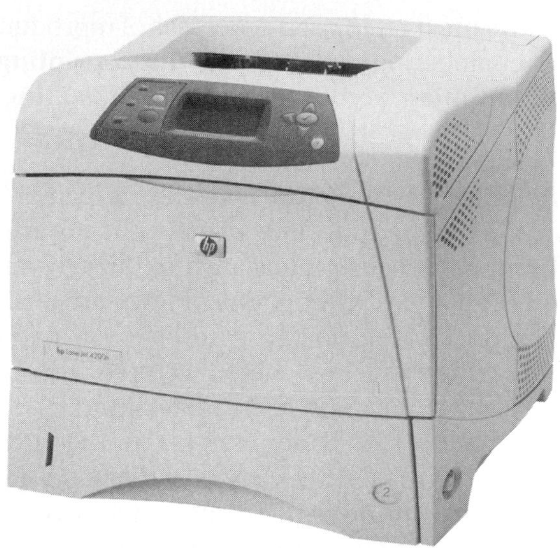

24.3 This new workgroup laser printer, the HP LaserJet 4200n has a speed of 35 pages per minute at 1200 dpi to accommodate more users and higher print volumes. *(Courtesy of Hewlett-Packard Company.)*

24.4 This HP LaserJet 1300n has a speed of 20 pages per minute and a print quality of 1200 dpi for black-and-white prints. *(Courtesy of Hewlett-Packard Company.)*

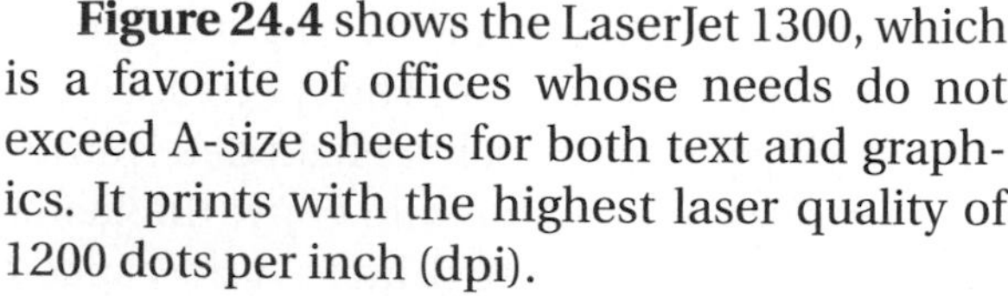

Figure 24.4 shows the LaserJet 1300, which is a favorite of offices whose needs do not exceed A-size sheets for both text and graphics. It prints with the highest laser quality of 1200 dots per inch (dpi).

24.3 Types of Reproduction

Drawings made by a drafter are of little use in their original form. If original drawings were handled by checkers and by workers in the field or shop, they would quickly be soiled and damaged, and no copy would be available as a permanent record of the job. Therefore, it is necessary to make inexpensive, expendable reproductions for use by the people who need them.

The most often used processes of reproducing engineering drawings are **diazo printing, microfilming, xerography**, and **photostating**.

Diazo Printing

The **diazo print** more correctly is called a **whiteprint** or **blue-line print** rather than a **blueprint** because it has a white background and blue lines. Other colors of lines are available, depending on the type of diazo paper used. (Blueprinting, which creates a print with white lines and a blue background, is a wet process that is almost obsolete at present.) **Figure 24.5** shows a typical diazo printer.

Diazo printing requires that original drawings be made on semitransparent tracing paper, cloth, or film that light can pass through except where lines have been drawn. The diazo paper on which the blue-line print is copied is chemically treated, giving it a yellow tint on one side. Diazo paper must be stored away from heat and light to prevent spoilage.

The sequential steps of making a diazo print are shown in **Figure 24.6**. The drawing is placed face up on the yellow side of the diazo paper and then fed through the diazo-process machine, which exposes the drawing to a built-in light. Light rays pass through the tracing paper and burn away the yellow tint on the diazo paper except where the drawing lines have shielded the paper from the light, similar to how a photographic negative is

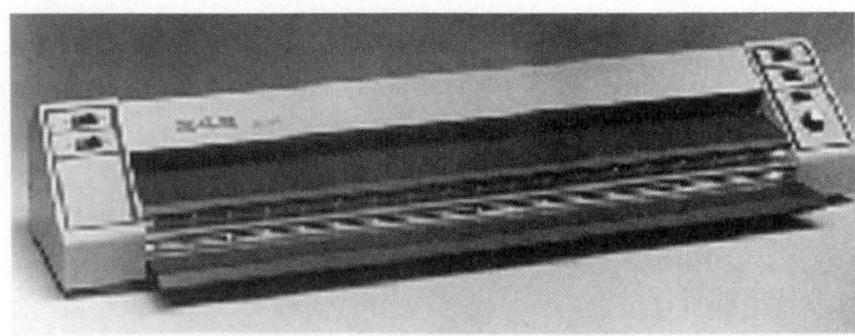

24.5 This typical whiteprinter operates on the diazo process. *(Courtesy of Blu-Ray, Incorporated, Bidwell Industrial Group, Inc.)*

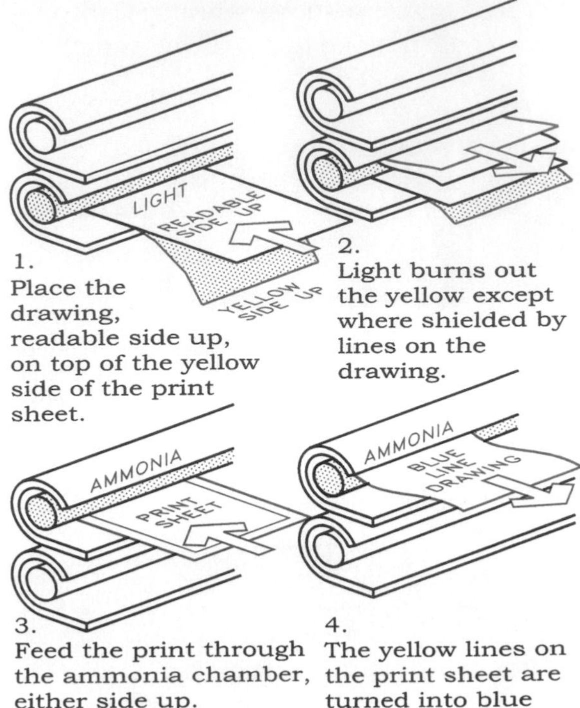

LIGHT
READABLE SIDE UP
YELLOW SIDE UP
1.
Place the drawing, readable side up, on top of the yellow side of the print sheet.
2.
Light burns out the yellow except where shielded by lines on the drawing.
AMMONIA
PRINT SHEET
AMMONIA
BLUE LINE DRAWING
3.
Feed the print through the ammonia chamber, either side up.
4.
The yellow lines on the print sheet are turned into blue lines.

24.6 Diazo (blue-line) prints are made by placing the original readable side up and on top of the yellow side of the diazo paper and feeding the two sheets under the light as shown in the steps.

used. (It is important that the lines be adequately dense to shield the diazo paper as necessary for making a good print.) The exposed diazo paper becomes a duplicate of the original drawing except that the lines are light yellow and are not permanent.

When the diazo paper is passed through the developing unit of the diazo machine, ammonia fumes develop the yellow lines on it into permanent blue lines. The speed at which the drawing passes under the light determines the darkness of the blue-line copy; the faster the speed, the darker the print is. A slow speed burns out more of the yellow and produces a clear white background, but some of the lighter lines of the drawing may be lost. Most diazo copies are made at a speed fast enough to give a light tint of blue in the background to obtain the darkest lines on the copy. Ink drawings, whether made by hand or by computer, give the best reproductions.

Diazo printing has been enhanced by the advent of the computer, since computer drawings are made in ink. Thus, the print quality is much better than that of pencil drawings. Also, drawings made by different drafters are more uniform in line weight, lettering, and technique than drawings made by hand.

Microfilming

Microfilming is a photographic process that converts large drawings into film copies—either aperture cards or roll film. Drawings are placed on a copy table and photographed on either 16 mm or 35 mm film.

The roll film or aperture cards are placed in a microfilm enlarger-printer, where the individual drawings can be viewed on a built-in screen. The selected drawings can be printed from the film in standard sizes. Microfilm copies are usually made smaller than the original drawings to save paper and make the drawings easier to use.

Microfilming eliminates the need for large, bulky files of drawings because hundreds of drawings can be stored in permanent archives in miniature on a small amount of film. This is the same process used to preserve newspapers and other large materials by libraries and archives.

Xerography

Xerography is an electrostatic process of duplicating drawings on ordinary, unsensitized paper. Originally developed for business and clerical uses, xerography is currently being used to reproduce engineering drawings. The xerographic process can also be used to reduce the sizes of the drawings being copied to more convenient and easier-to-use sizes. The Xerox 2080 can reduce a 24 × 36-in. drawing to 8 × 10 in.

Photostating

Photostating is a method of enlarging or reducing drawings photographically. The drawing is placed under the glass of the exposure table, which is lit by built-in lamps. The image appears on a glass plate inside the darkroom, where it is exposed on photographically sensitive paper. The exposed negative paper is placed in contact with receiver paper, and the two are fed through the developing solution to obtain a photostatic copy. Photostating also can be used to make reproductions on transparent films and for reproducing halftones (photographs with tones of gray).

24.4 Assembling Drawing Sets

After the original drawings have been copied, they should be stored flat and unfolded in a flat file for future use and updating. Prints made from the originals, however, usually are folded or rolled for ease of transmittal from office to office. The methods of folding size B, C, D, and E sheets so that the image will appear on the outside of the fold are shown in **Figure 24.7**. Drawings should be folded to show the title block always on the outside at the right, usually in the lower right-hand

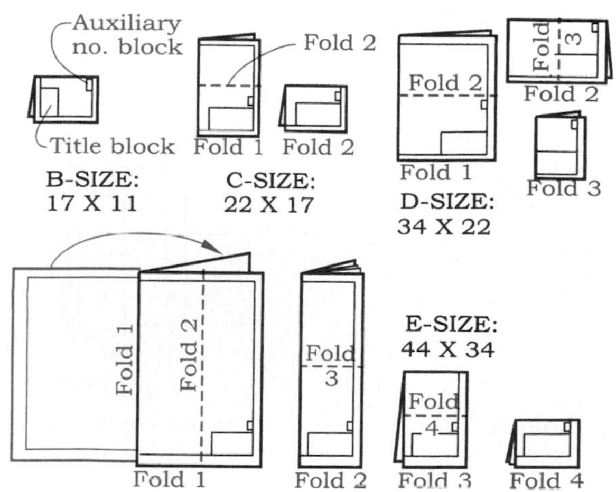

24.7 All standard drawing sheets can be folded to 8-1/2 × 11-in. size for filing and storage.

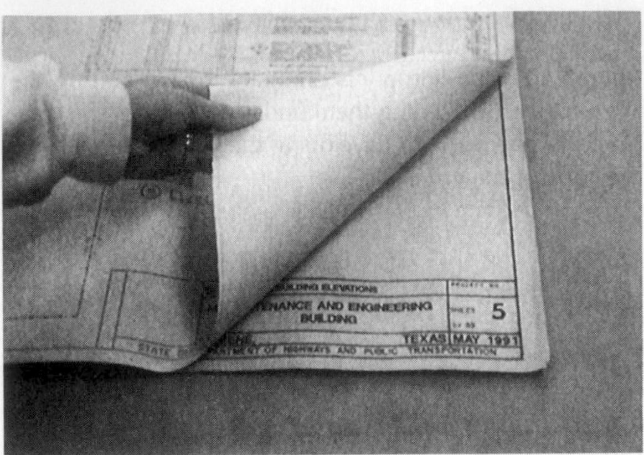

24.8 The title block should appear at the right, usually in the lower right-hand corner of the sheet.

corner of the page (**Figure 24.8**). The final size after folding is 8-1/2 × 11 in. (or 9 × 12 in.).

An alternative method of folding and stapling size B sheets often is used for student assignments so that they can be kept in a three-ring notebook (**Figure 24.9**). The basic rules of assembling drawings are listed in **Figure 24.10**.

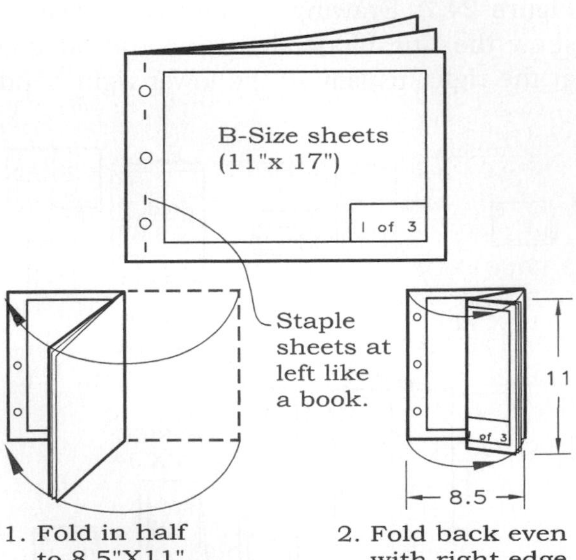

24.9 A set of size B drawings can be assembled by stapling, punching, and folding, as shown here, for safekeeping in a three-ring notebook with the title block visible on top.

WORKING DRAWING CHECKLIST

1. Staple along left edge, like a book. Use several staples, never just one.
2. Fold with drawing on outside.
3. Fold drawings as a set, not one at a time separately.
4. Fold to an 8.5 X 11 modular size.
5. The title block must be visible after folding.
6. Sheets of a set should be uniform in size.

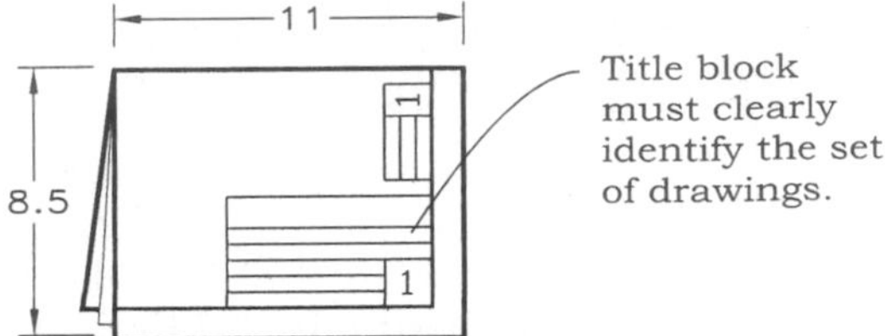

24.10 Follow these basic rules for assembling sets of working drawing prints.

24.5 Transmittal of Drawings

Prints of drawings are delivered to contractors, manufacturers, fabricators, and others who must use the drawings for implementing the project. Prints usually are placed in standard 9 × 12-in. envelopes for delivery by hand or mail. Sets of large drawings, which may be 30 × 40 in. in size and contain four or more sheets, usually are rolled and sent in a mailing tube when folding becomes impractical. It is not uncommon for a set of drawings to have 40 or 50 sheets.

An advanced method of transmitting drawings is by use of large fax machines. Within minutes, large documents can be scanned and transmitted to their destination sites.

Computer drawings can be transmitted on disk by mailing them to their destination, where hard copies can be plotted and reproduced. This procedure offers substantial savings in shipping charges.

Computer drawings can also be transmitted over the Internet in the form of data that are downloaded at their destination. The downloaded data are then printed in the form of a drawing and are stored in the computer's

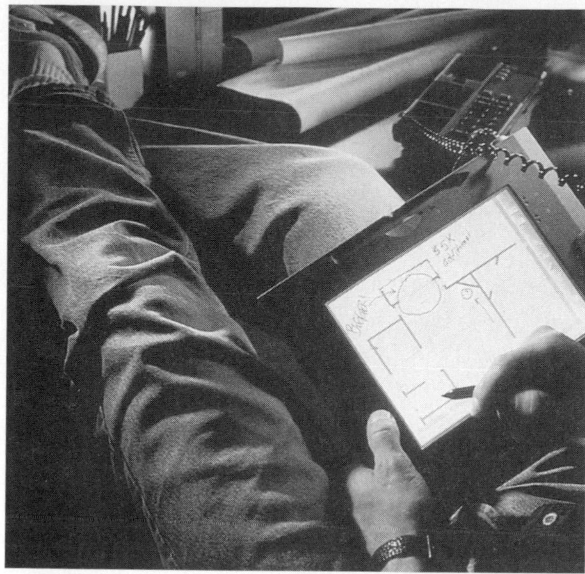

24.11 Hewlett Packard's OmniShare conferencer enables people in two locations to "meet" and collaborate on the same document, at the same time, over a single phone line. *(Courtesy of Hewlett-Packard Company.)*

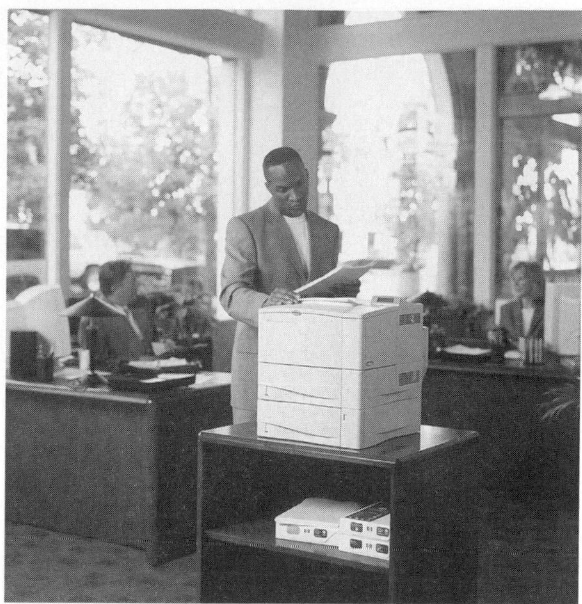

24.12 Fast, high-quality output and paper-handling flexibility required of today's business user can be found in the HP LaserJet 4100 printer. In addition, users can add copy, fax, file, and read capabilities by adding the optional LaserJet Companion printer accessory. *(Courtesy of Hewlett-Packard Company.)*

database. In the future, more drawings, documents, and photographs will be sent electronically as data and as scanned images over telephone wires, making them available instantaneously at the desired location.

Only a few years ago, transmission of information and data across the state or nation was time consuming and risky. Today, any document can be transmitted overnight with certainty of delivery, and most can be transmitted to the receiver within minutes. The OmniShare conferencer (**Figure 24.11**) lets people in two locations collaborate on the same document at the same time over a single phone line.

Hewlett Packard's LaserJet printers have accessories available for fax, copy, file, and read capabilities. Today, the communication of engineering data can be done instantaneously and easily, contributing to increased productivity (**Figure 24.12**).

Numerically controlled manufacturing systems can be actuated directly from engineering data once the designs have been digitized. Such systems can be controlled from remote sites to produce products that previously required a high intensity of work hours by individuals. The future holds many unique innovations in the manner in which business, manufacturing, and construction is done. The transfer of voice communication, hard-copy communications, working drawings, and specifications will be instantaneous.

25

Three-Dimensional Pictorials

25.1 Introduction

A three-dimensional pictorial is a drawing that shows an object's three principal planes, much as they would be captured by a camera. This type of pictorial is an effective means of illustrating a part that is difficult to visualize when only orthographic views are given. Pictorials are especially helpful when a design is complex and when the reader of the drawings is unfamiliar with orthographic drawings.

Sometimes called **technical illustrations**, pictorials are widely used to describe products in catalogs, parts manuals, and maintenance publications (**Figure 25.1**). The ability to sketch pictorials rapidly to explain a detail to an associate in the field is an important communication skill.

The four commonly used types of pictorials are **obliques, isometrics, axonometrics**, and **perspectives** (**Figure 25.2**).

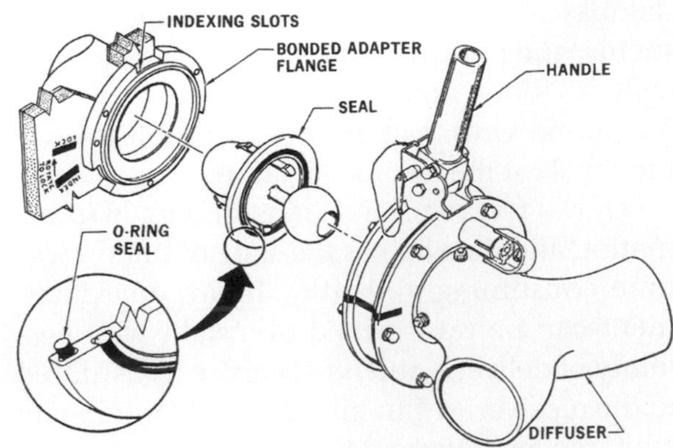

25.1 Many objects cannot be seen as well in real life as they can be seen in a drawing, as shown in this drain-line seal detail of the orbital workshop. *(Courtesy of NASA.)*

Oblique pictorials: three-dimensional drawings made by projecting from the object with parallel projectors that are oblique to the picture plane (**Figure 25.2A**).

Isometric and axonometric pictorials: three-dimensional drawings made by projecting from

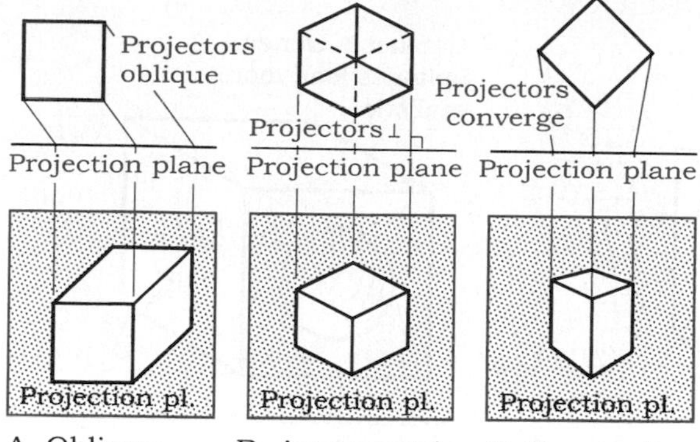

25.2 The three pictorial projection systems are (A) oblique pictorials, with parallel projectors oblique to the projection plane; (B) axonometric (including isometric) pictorials, with parallel projectors perpendicular to the projection plane; and (C) perspectives, with converging projectors that make varying angles with the projection plane.

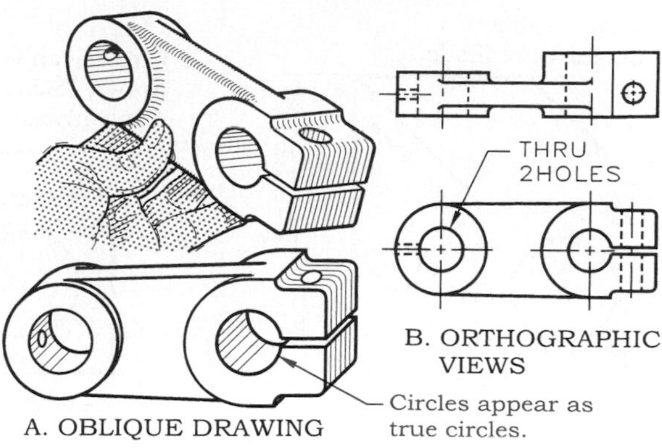

25.3 The oblique drawing of this part makes it easier to visualize it than do its orthographic views.

the object with parallel projectors that are perpendicular to the picture plane (**Figure 25.2B**).

Perspective pictorials: three-dimensional drawings made with projectors that converge at the viewer's eye and make varying angles with the picture plane (**Figue 25.2C**).

25.2 Oblique Drawings

The pulley arm shown in **Figure 25.3** is illustrated by orthographic views and an oblique pictorial. Because most parts are drawn before they are made, photographs cannot be taken; therefore, the next best option is to draw a three-dimensional pictorial of the part. Details can usually be drawn with more clarity than can be shown in a photograph.

Oblique pictorials are easy to draw. If you can draw an orthographic view of a part, you are but one step away from drawing an oblique. For example, **Figure 25.4**, shows that drawing a front view of a box twice and connecting its corners yields an oblique drawing.

Thus, an oblique is no more than an orthographic view with a receding axis, drawn at an angle to show the depth of the object. An

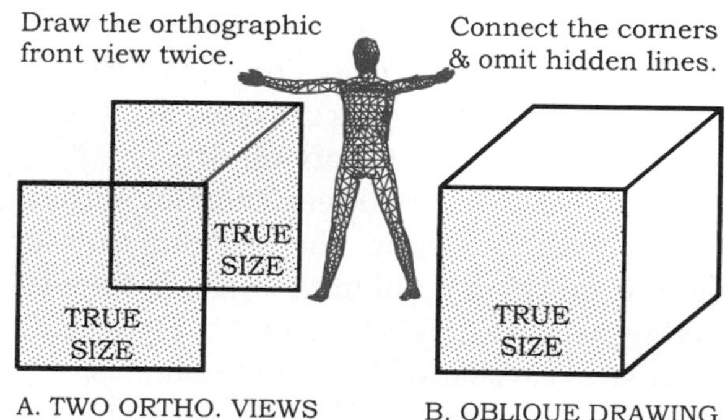

25.4 Draw two true-size surfaces of the box, connect them at the corners, and you have an oblique drawing.

oblique is a pictorial that does not exist in reality (a camera cannot give an oblique). This type of pictorial is called an *oblique* because its parallel projectors from the object are oblique to the picture plane. The underlying principles of projection are covered in Section 25.3.

Types of Obliques

The three basic types of oblique drawings are: **cavalier, cabinet**, and **general** (**Figure 25.5**). For each type, the angle of the receding axis with the horizontal can be at any angle between 0° and 90°. Measurements along the receding axes of the cavalier oblique are laid off true length, and measurements along the

TYPES OF OBLIQUES

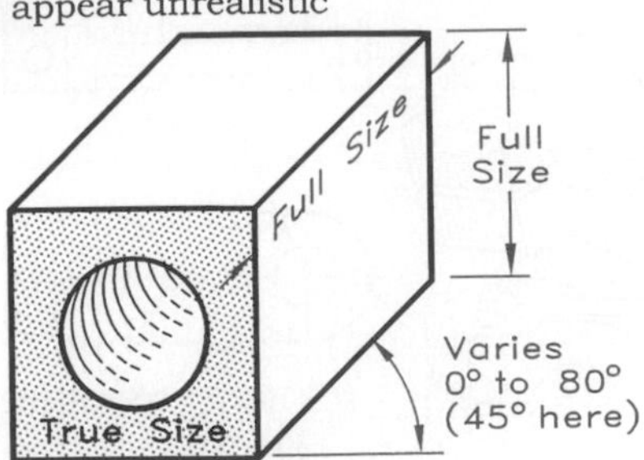

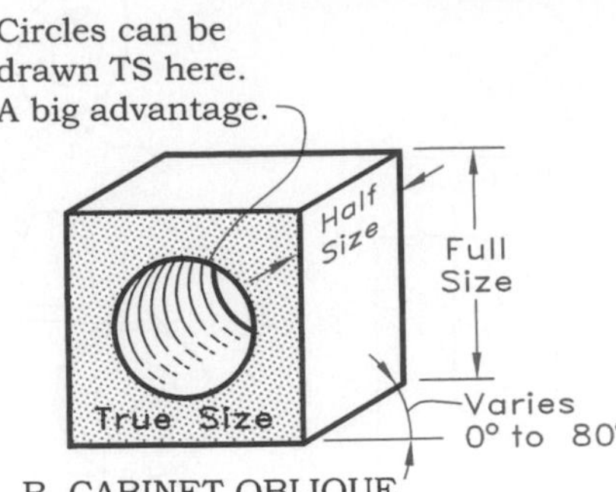

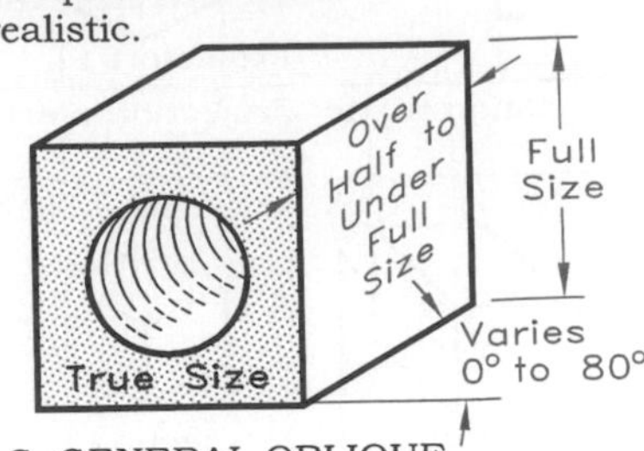

25.5 The three types of obliques.

A The cavalier oblique has a receding axis at any angle and true-length measurements on the receding axis.

B The cabinet oblique has a receding axis at any angle and half-size measurements along the receding axis.

C The general oblique has a receding axis at any angle and measurements along the receding axis larger than half size and less than full size.

receding axes of the cabinet oblique are laid off half size. The general oblique has measurements along the receding axes that are greater than half size and less than full size.

Figure 25.6 shows three examples of cavalier obliques of a cube. The receding axes for each is drawn at a different angle, but the receding axes are drawn true length. **Figure 25.7** compares cavalier with cabinet obliques.

Constructing Obliques

You can easily begin a cavalier oblique by drawing a box using the overall dimensions of height, width, and depth with light construction lines. As demonstrated in **Figure 25.8**, first draw the front view as a true-size orthographic view. Make true measurements parallel to the three axes and transfer them from the orthographic views with your dividers. Then, remove the notch from the blocked-in construction box to complete the oblique.

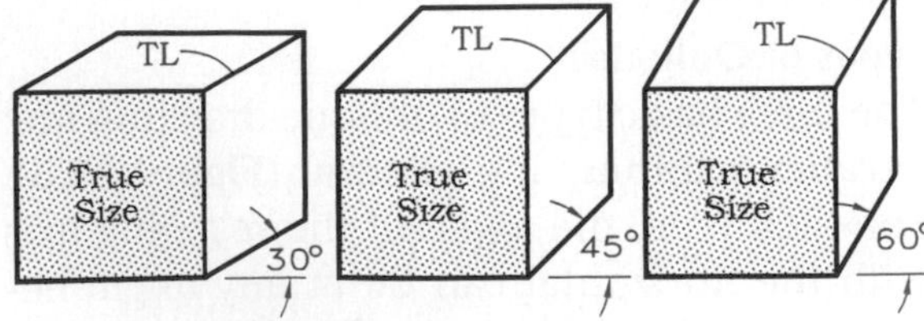

25.6 A cavalier oblique usually has its receding axis at one of the standard angles of drafting triangles. Each gives a different view of a cube.

25.7 Measurements along the receding axis of a cavalier oblique are full size, and those in a cabinet oblique are half size.

Angles

Angular measurements can be made on the true-size plane of an oblique, but not on the other two planes. Note in **Figure 25.9** that a true angle can be measured on a true-size surface, but in **Figure 25.10** angles along receding planes are either smaller or larger than their true sizes. A better, easier-to-draw oblique is obtained when angles are drawn to appear true size.

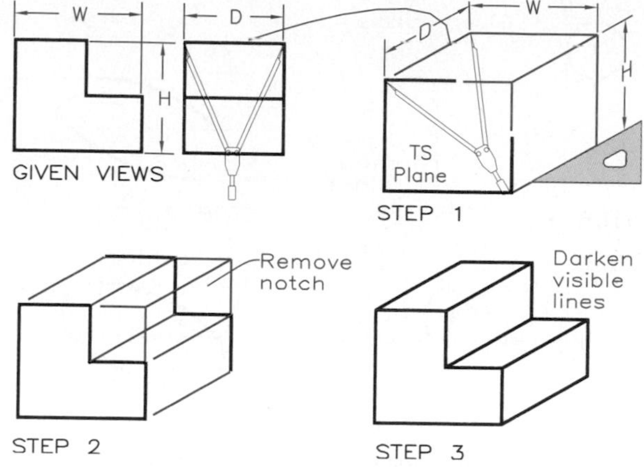

25.8 Constructing a cavalier oblique.

Step 1 Draw the front surface of the object as a true-size plane. Draw the receding axis at a convenient angle and transfer the true distance D from the side view to it with your dividers.

Step 2 Draw the notch on the front plane and project it to the rear plane.

Step 3 Darken the lines to complete the drawing.

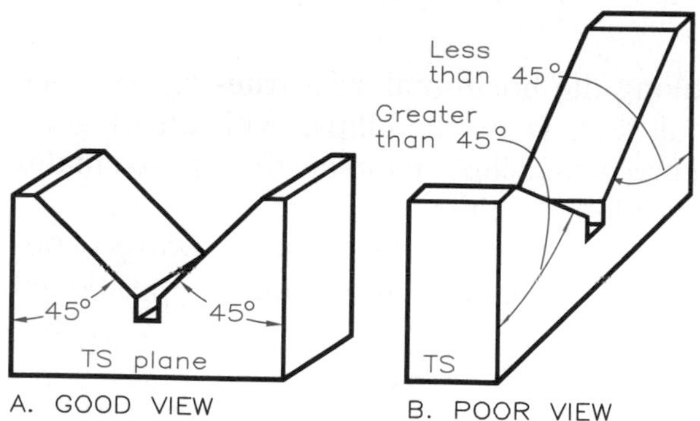

25.9 Objects with angular features should be drawn in oblique so that the angles appear true size. This results in a better pictorial and one that is easier to draw.

To construct an angle in an oblique on one of the receding planes, you must use coordinates, as shown in **Figure 25.10**. To find the surface that slopes 30° from the front surface, locate the vertex of the angle, H distance from the bottom. To find the upper end of the sloping plane, measure the distance D along the receding axis. Transfer H and D to the oblique with your dividers. The angle in the oblique is not equal to the 30° angle in the orthographic view.

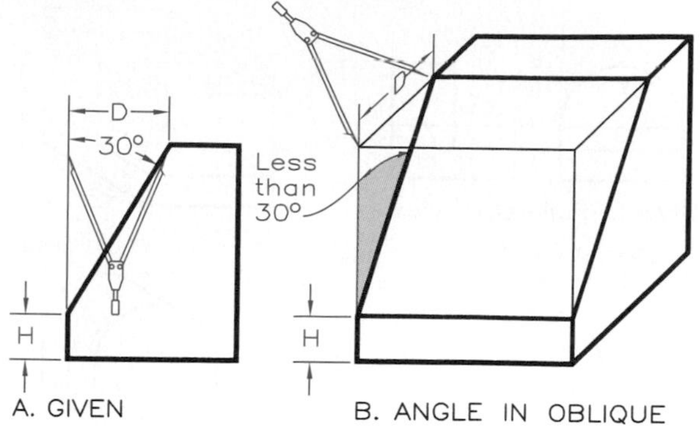

25.10 Angles that do not lie in a true-size plane of an oblique must be located with coordinates.

Cylinders

The **major advantage** of an oblique is that **circular features can be drawn as true circles** on its frontal plane (**Figure 25.11**). Draw the centerlines of the circular end at A and construct the receding axis at the desired angle. Locate the end at B by measuring along the axis, draw circles at each end at centers A and B, and draw tangents to both circles.

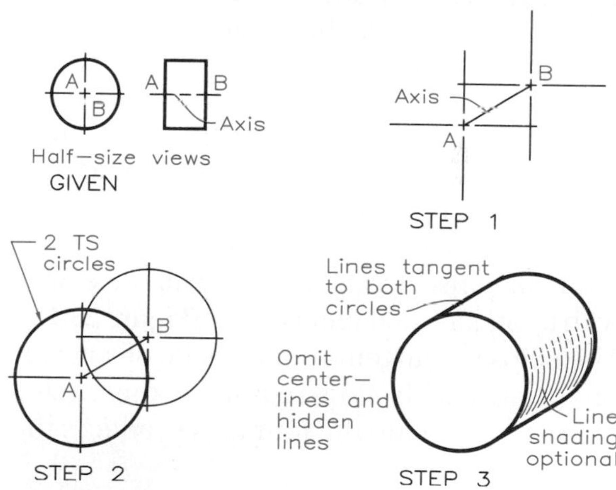

25.11 Drawing a cylinder in oblique.

Step 1 Draw axis AB and locate the centers of the circular ends of the cylinder at A and B. Because the axis is true length, this will be a cavalier oblique.

Step 2 Draw a true-size circle with its center at A by using a compass or computer-graphics techniques.

Step 3 Draw the other circular end with its center at B and connect the circles with tangent lines parallel to axis AB.

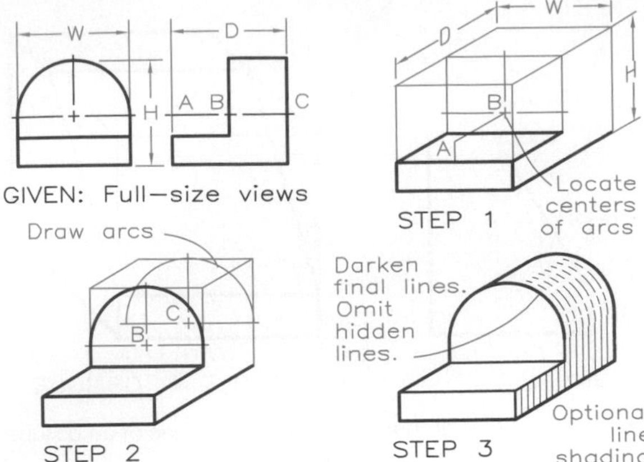

25.12 Drawing semicircular features in oblique.

Step 1 Block in the overall dimensions of the cavalier oblique with light construction lines, ignoring the semicircular feature.

Step 2 Locate centers B and C and draw arcs with a compass or by AutoCAD tangent to the sides of the construction boxes.

Step 3 Connect the arcs with lines tangent to each arc and parallel to axis BC and darken the lines.

These same principles apply to construction of the object having semicircular features shown in **Figure 25.12**. Position the oblique so that the semicircular features are true size. Locate centers A, B, and C and the two semicircles. Then, complete the cavalier oblique.

Circles

Circular features drawn as true circles on a true-size plane of an oblique pictorial appear on the receding planes as ellipses.

The four-center ellipse method is a technique of constructing an approximate ellipse with a compass and four centers (**Figure 25.13**). The ellipse is tangent to the inside of a rhombus drawn with sides equal to the circle's diameter. Drawing the four arcs produces the ellipse.

The four-center ellipse method will not work for the cabinet or general oblique; coordinates must be used. **Figure 25.14** illustrates the method of locating coordinates on the planes of cavalier and cabinet obliques. For the cabinet oblique, the coordinates along the receding axis are half size, and the coordinates along the horizontal axis (true-size axis) are full size. Draw the ellipse with an irregular curve or an ellipse template that approximates the plotted points.

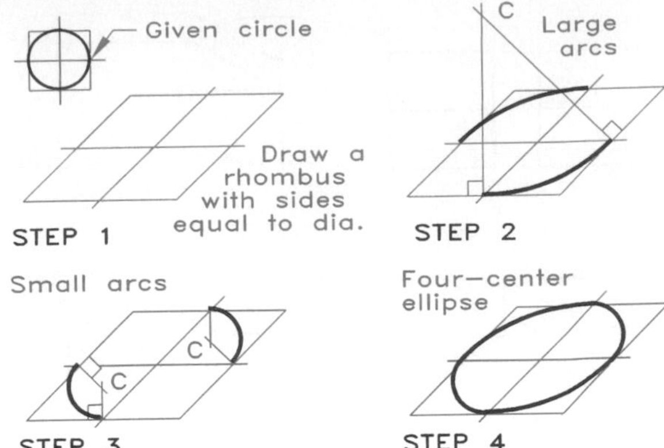

25.13 Constructing a four-center ellipse in oblique.

Step 1 Block in the circle to be drawn in oblique with a square tangent to the circle, which becomes a rhombus on the oblique plane.

Step 2 Draw construction lines perpendicular at the points of tangency to locate the centers for drawing two segments of the ellipse.

Step 3 Locate the centers for the two remaining arcs with perpendiculars drawn from adjacent tangent points.

Step 4 Draw four arcs to obtain an approximate ellipse.

Whenever possible, oblique drawings of objects with circular features should be positioned

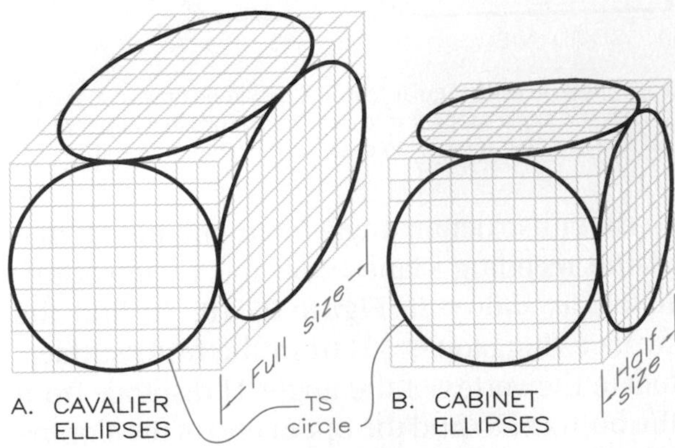

25.14 Circular features on the faces of cavalier and cabinet obliques are compared here. Ellipses on the receding planes of cabinet obliques must be plotted by coordinates. The spacing of the coordinates along the receding axis of cabinet obliques is half size.

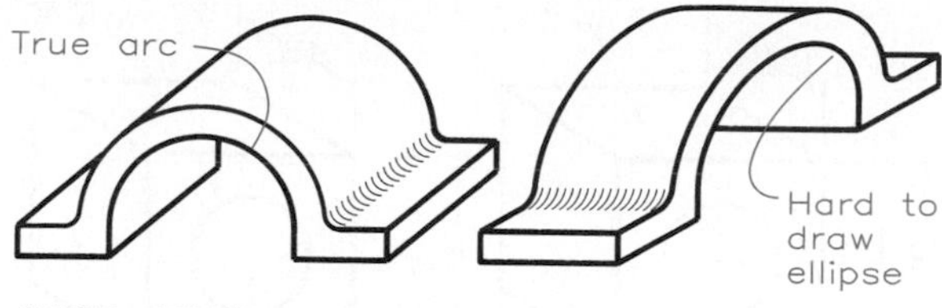

25.15 An oblique should be positioned so that circular and curving features can be drawn most easily.

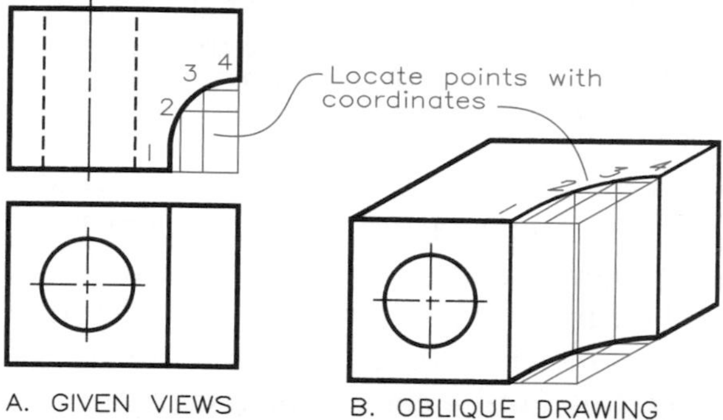

25.16 Coordinates are used to find points along irregular curves in oblique. Projecting the points downward a distance equal to the height of the object yields the lower curve.

so circles can be drawn as true circles instead of ellipses. The view in **Figure 25.15A** is better than the one in **Figure 25.15B** because it gives a more descriptive view of the part and is easier to draw.

Curves

Irregular curves in oblique pictorials must be plotted point by point with coordinates (**Figure 25.16**). Transfer the coordinates from the orthographic to the oblique view and draw the curve through the plotted points with an irregular curve. If the object has a uniform thickness, plot the points for the lower curve by projecting vertically downward from the upper points a distance equal to the object's height.

To obtain the elliptical feature on the inclined surface shown in **Figure 25.17**, use a series of coordinates to locate points along its curve. Connect the plotted points by using an irregular curve or ellipse template.

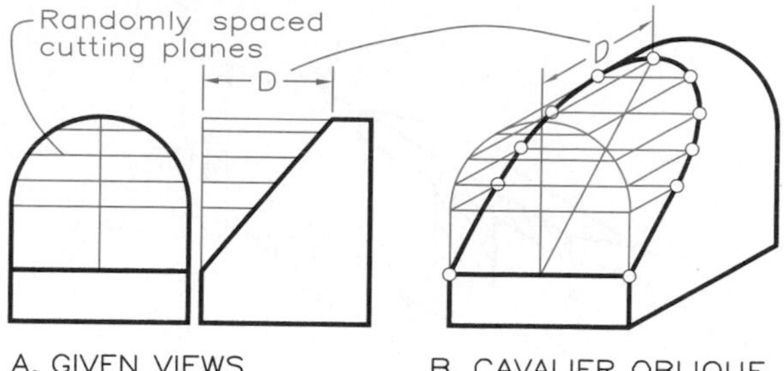

25.17 Construction of an elliptical feature on an inclined surface in oblique requires the use of three-dimensional coordinates to locate points on the curve.

Sketching

Understanding the principles of oblique construction is essential for sketching obliques freehand. The sketch of the part shown in **Figure 25.18** is based on the principles discussed, but its proportions were determined by eye instead of with scales and dividers.

Lightly drawn guidelines need not be erased when you darken the final lines. When

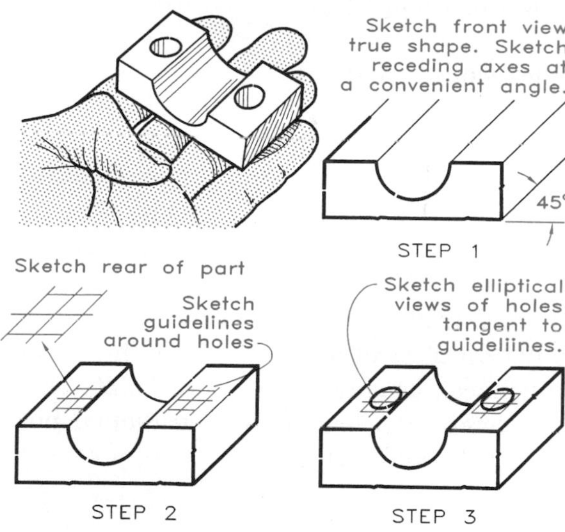

25.18 Sketching obliques.

Step 1 Sketch the front of the object as a true-size surface and draw a receding axis from each corner.

Step 2 Lay off the depth, D, along the receding axes to locate the rear of the part. Lightly sketch pictorial boxes as guidelines for drawing the holes.

Step 3 Sketch the holes inside the boxes and darken all lines.

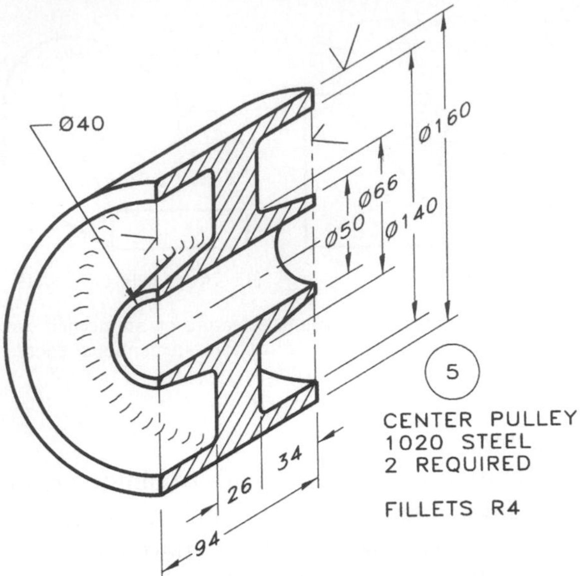

25.19 Oblique pictorials can be drawn as sections and dimensioned to serve as working drawings.

sketching on tracing vellum, you can place a printed grid under the sheet to provide guidelines. Refer to Chapter 13 to review sketching techniques if needed.

Dimensioned Obliques

Dimensioned sectional views of obliques provide excellent, easily understood depictions of objects (**Figure 25.19**). Apply numerals and lettering in oblique pictorials by using either the **aligned** method (with numerals aligned with the dimension lines) or the **unidirectional** method (with numerals positioned horizontally regardless of the direction of the dimension lines), as shown in **Figure 25.20**. Notes connected with leaders are positioned horizontally in both methods.

25.3 Oblique Projection Theory

Now that you have a general understanding of oblique pictorials, you should know the theory on which this system is based. Oblique projection, shown in **Figure 25.21**, is the basis of oblique drawings. Receding axis 1-2

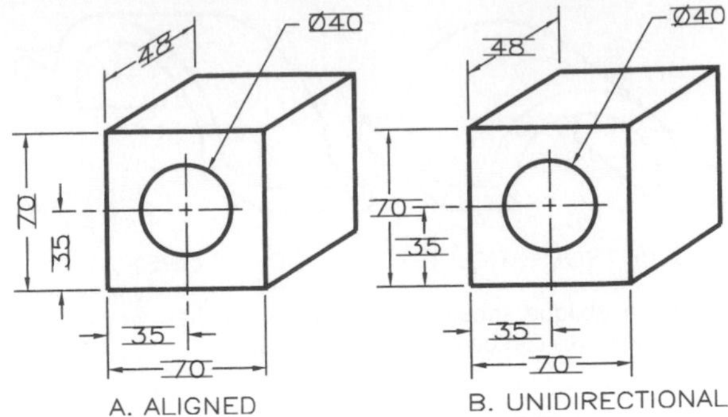

25.20 Either of these methods of lettering, aligned or unidirectional, is acceptable for dimensioning obliques.

is perpendicular to the frontal projection plane. Projectors drawn from point 2 at 45° to the projection plane yield lengths on the front surface that are the same length as 1-2 (true length, in other words). Infinitely many 45° projectors form a cone of projectors with its apex at 2.

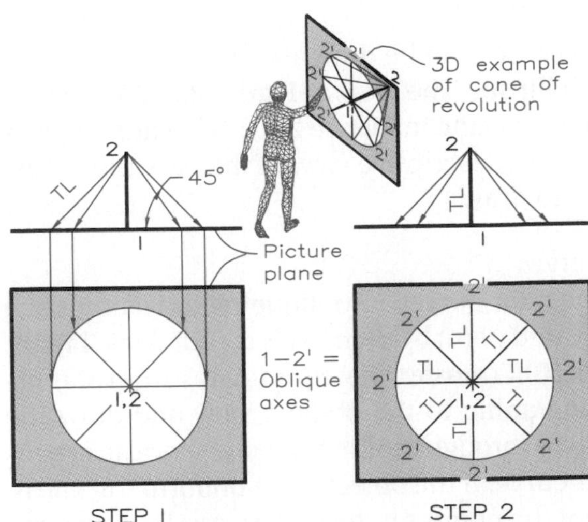

25.21 This drawing demonstrates the underlying principle of the cavalier oblique by using a series of projectors to form a cone.

Step 1 Each element from point 2 makes a 45° angle with the picture plane.

Step 2 The projected lengths of 1-2' are equal in length to line 1-2, which is perpendicular to the picture plane. Thus, the receding axis of a cavalier oblique is true length and can be drawn at any angle.

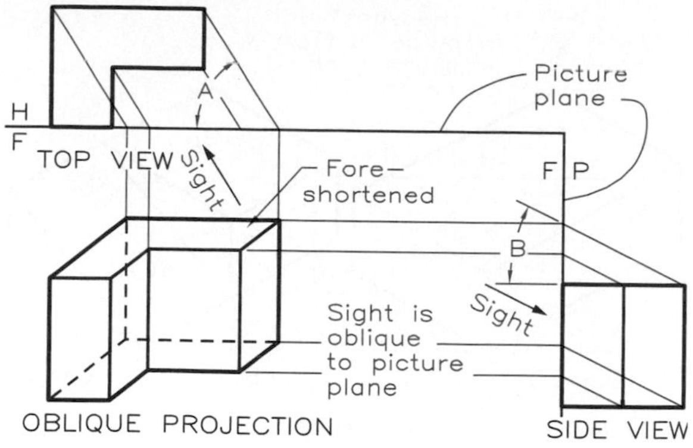

25.22 An oblique projection may be drawn at varying angles of sight. However, a line of sight making an angle of less than 45° with the picture plane would result in a receding axis longer than its true length, thereby distorting the pictorial.

The true-length projections of lines 1-2' represent receding axes that can be used for cavalier obliques, which, by definition, have true-length dimensions along their receding axes. Do not use a vertical or a horizontal receding axis, but one between those limits.

To distinguish **oblique projection** from **oblique drawing**, as described in this chapter so far, observe the top and side views of a part and the picture planes shown in **Figure 25.22**. In an oblique projection, projectors from the top and side views are oblique to the edge views of the projection planes, hence the name *oblique*.

Your line of sight can yield obliques with receding axes longer than true length (which should be avoided). Because of this shortcoming and the complexity of construction, oblique pictorials usually are *oblique drawings* rather than *oblique projections.*

25.4 Isometric Pictorials

In **Figure 25.23** the upper saddle is drawn in orthographic views and as a three-dimensional pictorial drawing. The pictorial is an isometric drawing in which the three planes of the object are equally foreshortened, representing the object more realistically than an oblique drawing can.

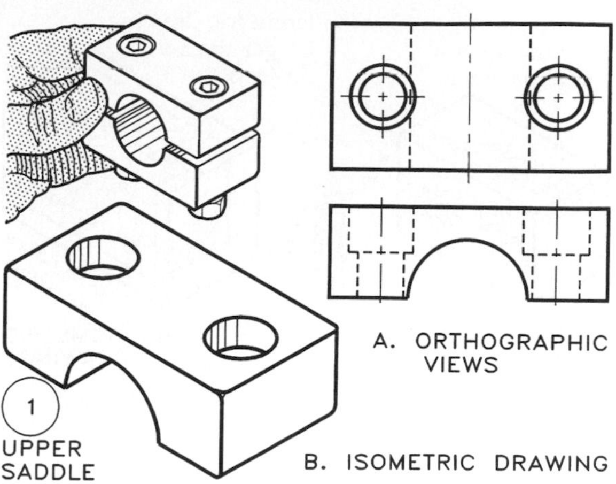

25.23 An isometric drawing gives a more realistic view of a part than an oblique drawing.

With more realism comes more difficulty of construction. In particular, circles and curves do not appear true shape on any of the three isometric planes.

Isometric Projection versus Drawing

In isometric projection, parallel projectors are perpendicular to the imaginary projection (picture) plane in which the diagonal of a cube appears as a point (**Figure 25.24**). An isometric

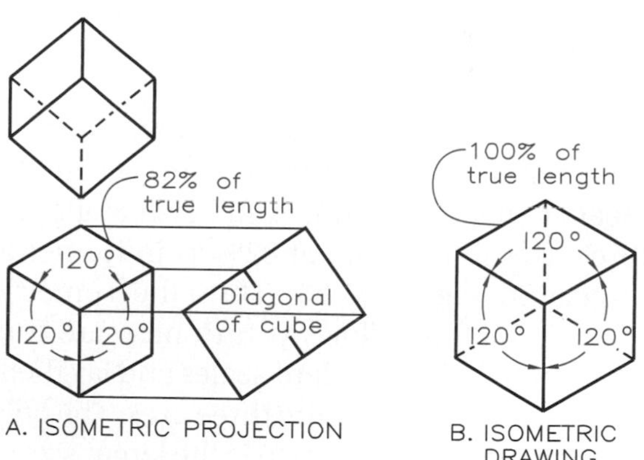

25.24 Projection versus drawing.

A A true isometric projection is found by constructing a view in which the diagonal of a cube appears as a point, and the axes are foreshortened.

B An isometric drawing is not a true projection because the dimensions are true size rather than foreshortened.

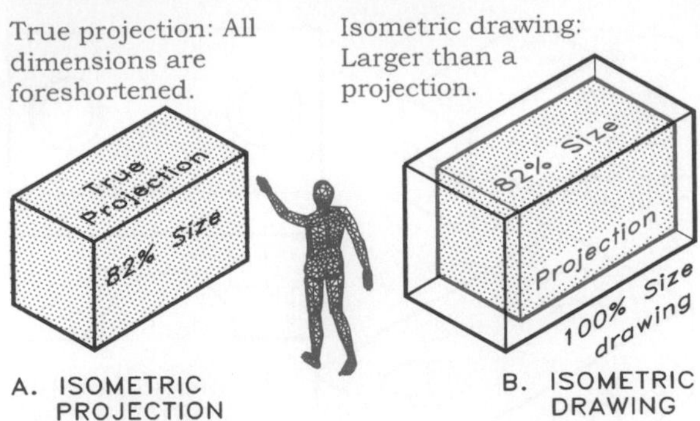

25.25 The true isometric projection is foreshortened to 82% of full size. The isometric drawing is drawn full size for convenience.

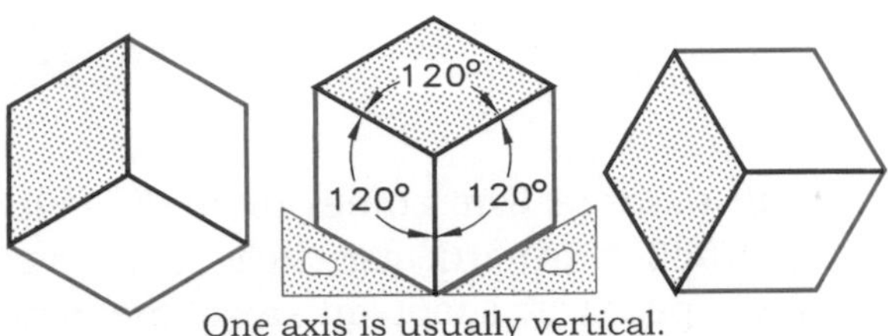

25.26 Isometric axes are spaced 120° apart, but they can be revolved into any position. Usually, one axis is vertical, but it can be at any angle with axis spacing remaining the same.

pictorial constructed by projection is called an **isometric projection**, with the three axes foreshortened to 82% of their true lengths and 120° apart. The name *isometric,* which means "equal measurement," aptly describes this type of projection because the planes are equally foreshortened.

An **isometric drawing** is a convenient approximate isometric pictorial in which the measurements are shown full size along the three axes rather than at 82% as in isometric projection (**Figure 25.25**). Thus, the isometric drawing method allows you to measure true dimensions with standard scales and lay them off with dividers along the three axes. The only difference between the two is the larger size of the drawing. Consequently, isometric drawings are used much more often than isometric projections.

The axes of isometric drawings are separated by 120° (**Figure 25.26**), but more often

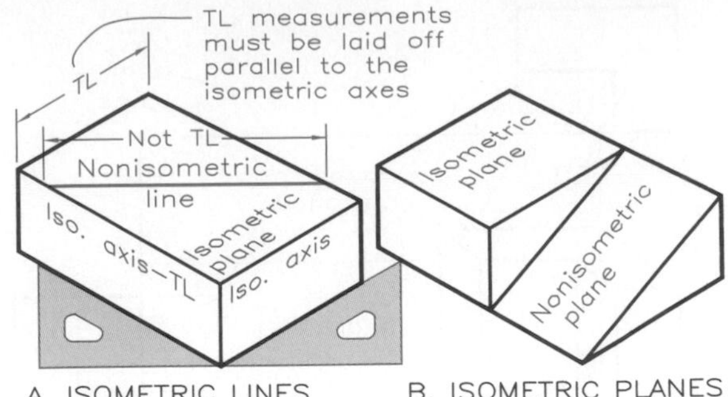

25.27 Isometric lines and planes.

A Isometric lines (parallel to the three axes) give true measurements, but nonisometric lines do not.

B Here, the three isometric planes are equally foreshortened, and the nonisometric plane is inclined at an angle to one of the isometric planes.

than not, one of the axes selected is vertical, since most objects have vertical lines. However, isometrics without a vertical axis are still isometrics.

25.5 Isometric Drawings

An isometric drawing is begun by drawing three axes 120° apart. Lines parallel to these axes are called **isometric lines** (**Figure 25.27A**). You can make true measurements along isometric lines but not along nonisometric lines. The three surfaces of a cube in an isometric drawing are called **isometric planes** (**Figure 25.27B**). Planes parallel to those planes also are isometric planes.

To draw an isometric pictorial, you need a scale, dividers, and a 30°-60° triangle (**Figure 25.28**). Begin by selecting the three axes and then constructing a plane of the isometric from the dimensions of height, H, and depth, D. Add the third dimension, width, W, and complete the isometric drawing.

Use light construction lines to block in all isometric drawings (**Figure 25.29**) and the overall dimensions W, D, and H. Take other dimensions from the given views with dividers and measure along their isometric lines to locate notches in the blocked-in drawing.

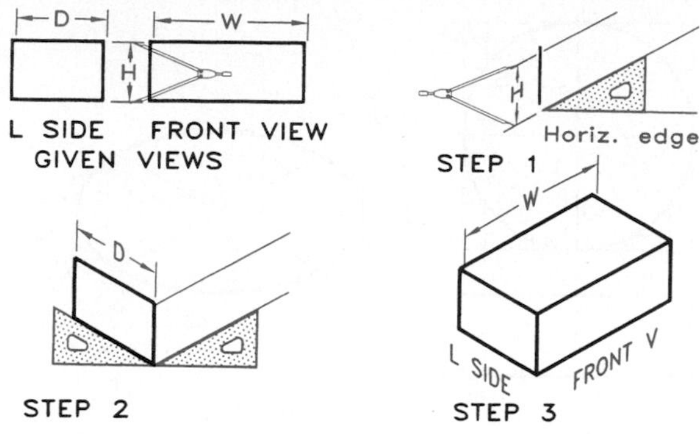

25.28 Drawing an isometric of a box.

Step 1 Use a 30°-60° triangle and a horizontal straightedge to construct a vertical line equal to the height, H, and draw two isometric lines through each end.

Step 2 Draw two 30° lines and locate the depth, D, by transferring depth from the given views with dividers.

Step 3 Locate the width, W, of the object, complete the surfaces of the isometric box, and darken the lines.

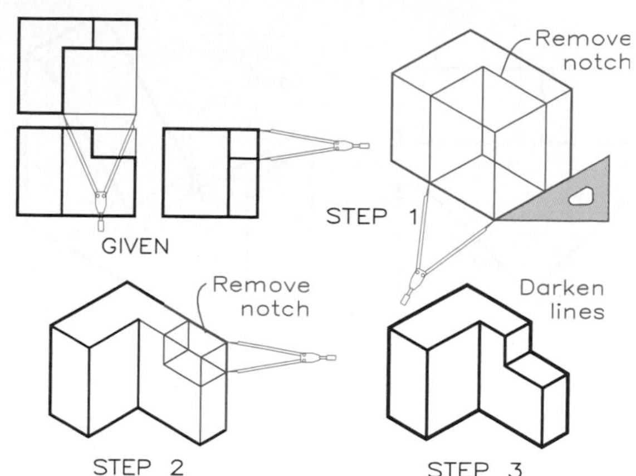

25.30 Laying out an isometric drawing.

Step 1 Use the overall dimensions given to block in the object with light lines, and remove the large notch.

Step 2 Remove the small notch.

Step 3 Darken the lines to complete the drawing.

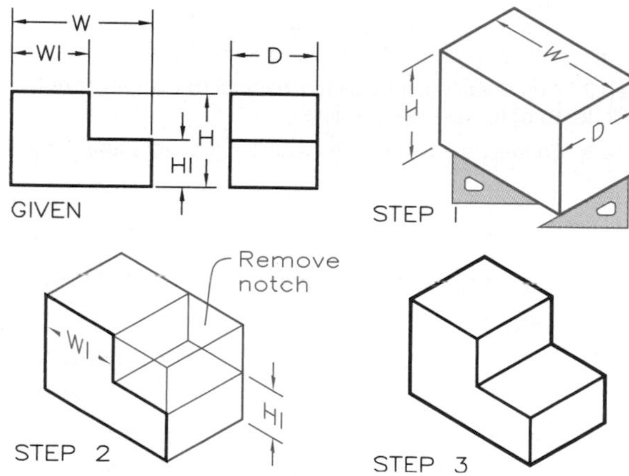

25.29 Constructing an isometric of a simple part.

Step 1 Construct an isometric drawing of a box with the overall dimensions W, D, and H from the given views.

Step 2 Locate the notch by transferring dimensions W1 and H1 from the given views with your dividers.

Step 3 Darken the lines to complete the drawing.

Figure 25.30 shows an isometric drawing of a slightly more complex object, with two notches. The object was blocked in by using the H, W, and D dimensions. Remove the notches in the block to complete the drawing.

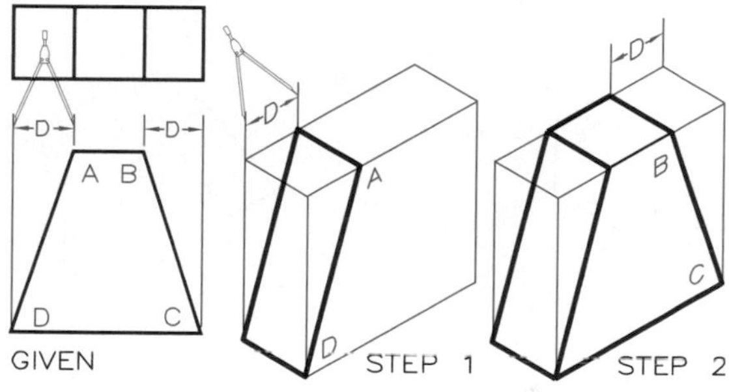

25.31 Use coordinates measured along the isometric axes to obtain inclined surfaces. Angular lines are not true length in isometric.

Angles

You cannot measure an angle's true size in an isometric drawing because the surfaces of an isometric are not true size. Instead, you must locate angles with isometric coordinates measured parallel to the axes (**Figure 25.31**). Lines AD and BC are equal in length in the orthographic view, but they are shorter and longer than true length in the isometric drawing. **Figure 25.32** shows a similar situation, in which two angles drawn in isometric are less than and greater than their true dimensions in the orthographic view.

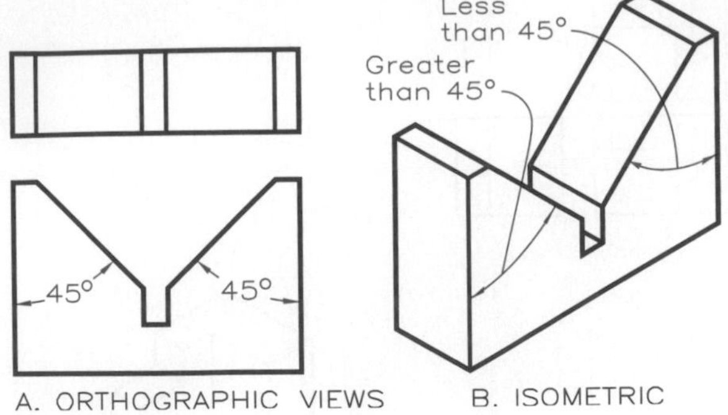

25.32 Angles in isometric may appear larger or smaller than they actually are.

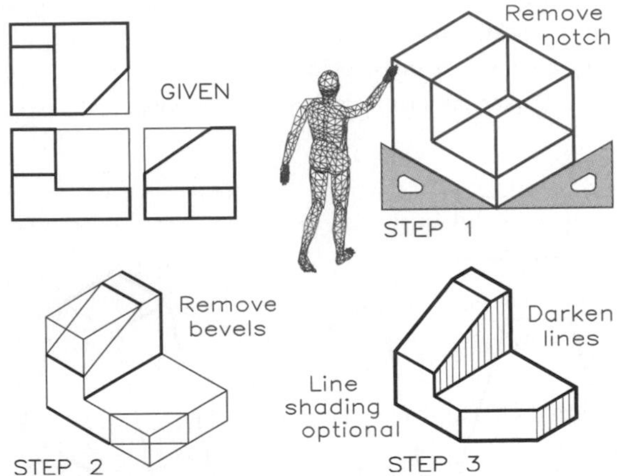

25.33 Drawing inclined planes in isometric.

Step 1 Block in the object with light lines, using the overall dimensions, and remove the notch.

Step 2 Locate the ends of the inclined planes by using measurements parallel to the isometric axes.

Step 3 Darken the lines to complete the drawing.

Figure 25.33 shows how to construct an isometric drawing of an object with inclined surfaces. Blocking in the object with its overall dimensions with light construction lines is followed by removal of the inclined portions.

Circles

Three methods of constructing circles in isometric drawings are **point plotting, four-center ellipse construction**, and **ellipse template usage**.

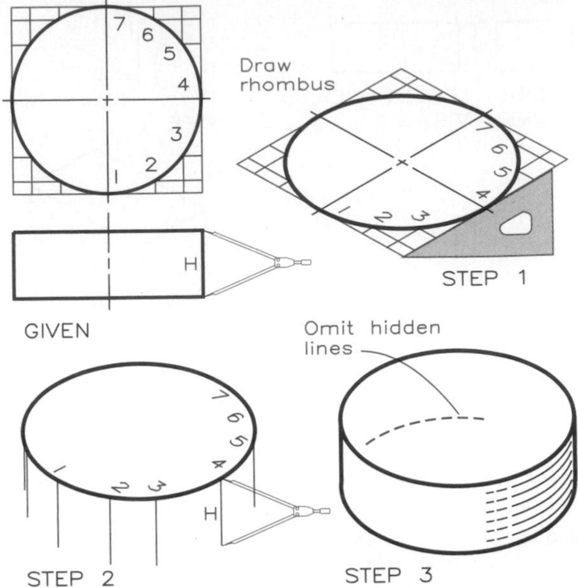

25.34 Plotting circles in isometric.

Step 1 Block in the circle by using its overall dimensions. Transfer the coordinates that locate points on the circle to the isometric plane and connect them with a smooth curve.

Step 2 Project each point a distance equal to the height of the cylinder to obtain the lower ellipse.

Step 3 Connect the two ellipses with tangent lines and darken all lines.

Point plotting is a method of using a series of *x*- and *y*-coordinates to locate points on a circle in the given orthographic views. The coordinates are then transferred with dividers to the isometric drawing to locate the points on the ellipse one at a time (**Figure 25.34**).

Block in the cylinder with light construction lines and show the centerlines. Draw coordinates on the upper plane and use the height dimension to locate the points on the lower plane. Draw the ellipses with an irregular curve or an ellipse template.

A plotted ellipse is a true ellipse and is equivalent to a 35° ellipse drawn on an isometric plane. An example of a design composed of

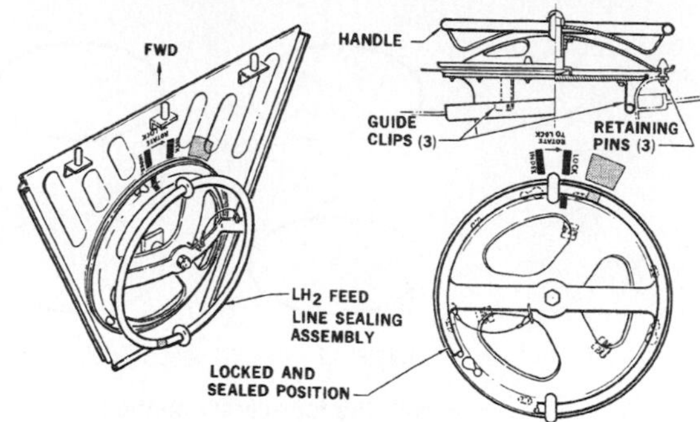

25.35 This handwheel assembly proposed for use in an orbital workshop is an example of parts with circular features drawn as ellipses in isometric. (*Courtesy of NASA.*)

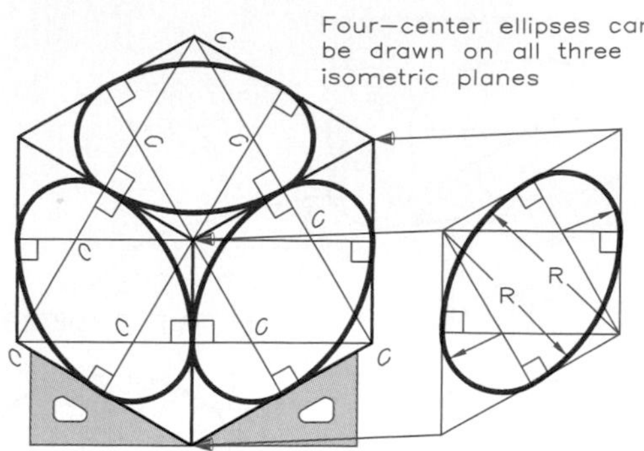

25.37 Four-center ellipses may be drawn on all three surfaces of an isometric drawing.

circular features drawn in isometric is the handwheel shown in **Figure 25.35**.

Four-center ellipse construction is the method of producing an approximate ellipse (**Figure 25.36**) by using four arcs drawn with a compass. Draw an isometric rhombus with its sides equal to the diameter of the circle to be represented. Find the four centers by constructing perpendiculars to the sides of the rhombus at the midpoints of each side, and draw the four arcs to complete the ellipse. You may draw four-center ellipses on all three isometric planes because each plane is equally foreshortened (**Figure 25.37**). Although it produces only an approximate ellipse, the four-center ellipse technique is acceptable for drawing large ellipses and as a way to draw ellipses when an ellipse template is unavailable.

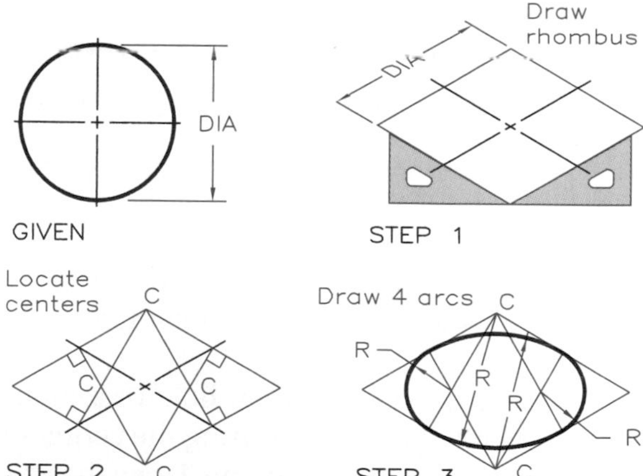

25.36 The four-center ellipse method.

Step 1 Use the diameter of the given circle to draw an isometric rhombus and the centerlines.

Step 2 Draw light construction lines perpendicularly from the midpoints of each side to locate four centers.

Step 3 Draw four arcs from the centers to represent an ellipse tangent to the rhombus.

Isometric ellipse templates are specially designed for drawing ellipses in isometric (**Figure 25.38**). The numerals on the templates represent the isometric diameters of the ellipses because diameters are measured parallel to the isometric axes of an isometric drawing

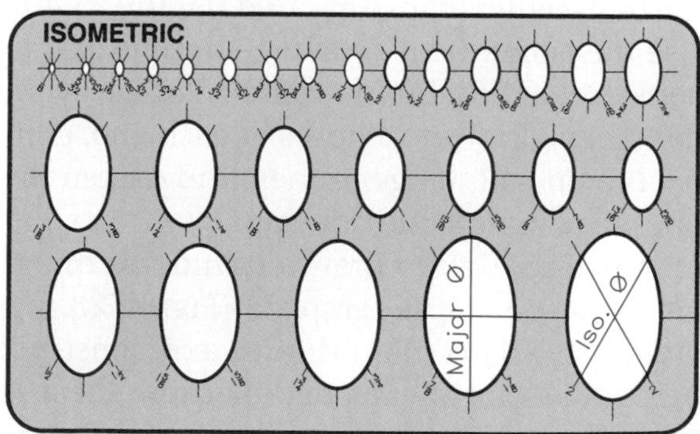

25.38 The isometric template (a 35° ellipse angle) is designed for drawing elliptical features in isometric. The isometric diameters of the ellipses are not major diameters of the ellipses but are diameters that are parallel to the isometric axes.

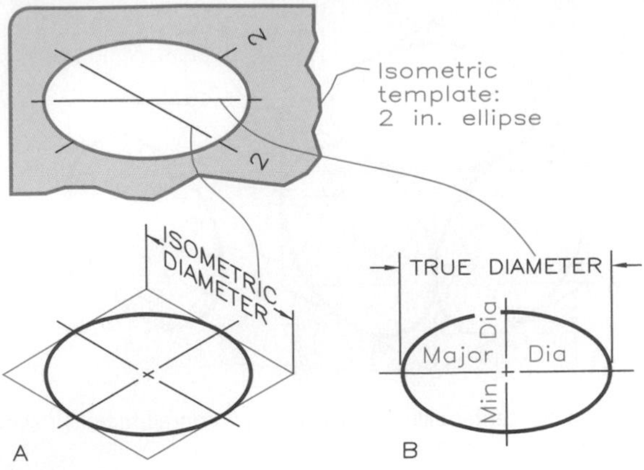

25.39 Ellipse terminology.

A Measure the diameter of a circle along the isometric axes. The major diameter of an isometric ellipse thus is larger than the measured diameter.

B The minor diameter is perpendicular to the major diameter.

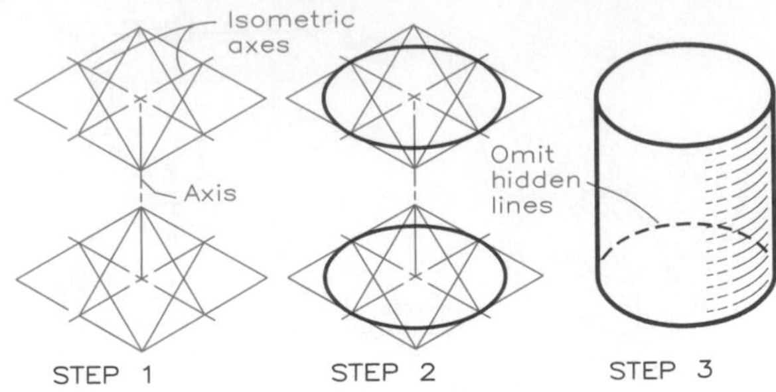

25.40 A cylinder drawn with the four-center method.

Step 1 Draw an isometric rhombus at each end of the cylinder's axis.

Step 2 Draw a four-center ellipse within each rhombus.

Step 3 Draw lines tangent to each rhombus to complete the drawing.

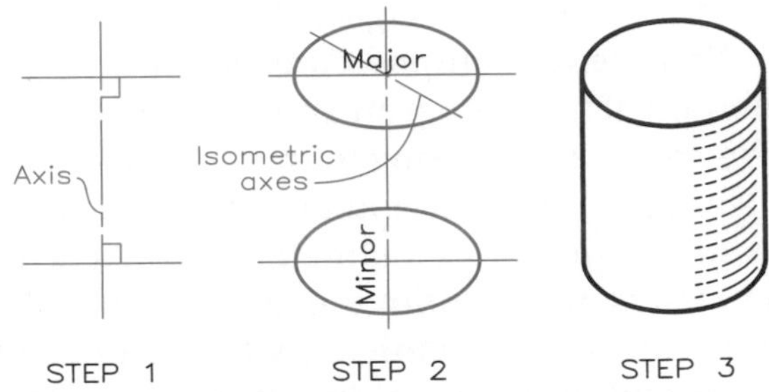

25.41 A cylinder using the ellipse template method.

Step 1 Establish the length of the axis of the cylinder and draw perpendiculars at each end.

Step 2 Draw the elliptical ends by aligning the major diameter of the ellipse template with the perpendiculars at the ends of the axis. The isometric diameters of the isometric ellipse template will align with two isometric axes.

Step 3 Connect the ellipses with tangent lines to complete the drawing, and omit hidden lines.

(**Figure 25.39**). Recall that the maximum diameter across the ellipse is its major diameter, which is a true diameter. Thus, the size of the diameter marked on the template is less than the ellipse's major diameter. You may use the isometric ellipse template to draw an ellipse by constructing centerlines of the ellipse in isometric and aligning the ellipse template with those isometric lines (**Figure 25.39**).

Cylinders

A cylinder may be drawn in isometric by using the four-center ellipse method (**Figure 25.40**). Use the isometric axes and centerline axis to construct a rhombus at each end of the cylinder. Then, draw the ellipses at each end, connect them with tangent lines, and darken the lines to complete the drawing.

An easier way to draw a cylinder is to use an isometric ellipse template (**Figure 25.41**). Draw the axis of the cylinder and construct perpendiculars at each end. Because the axis of a right cylinder is perpendicular to the major diameter of its elliptical ends, position the ellipse template with its major diameter perpendicular to the axis. Draw the ellipses at each end, connect them with tangent lines, and darken the visible lines to complete the drawing.

To construct a cylindrical hole in a block (**Figure 25.42**), begin by locating the center of the hole on the isometric plane. Draw the axis of the cylinder parallel to the isometric axis that is perpendicular to the plane of the ellipse through its center. Align the ellipse template with the major diameter, which makes a 90° angle with the cylindrical axis, and complete the elliptical view of the cylindrical hole.

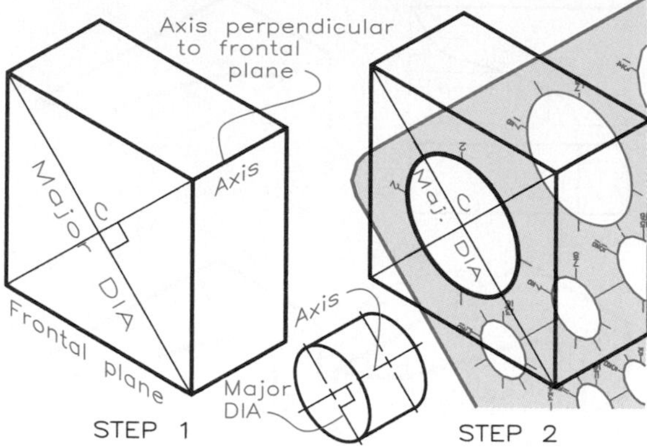

25.42 Constructing cylindrical holes through a block.

Step 1 Locate the center of the hole on a face of the isometric drawing. Draw the axis of the cylinder from the center parallel to the isometric axis perpendicular to the plane of the circle. The major diameter is perpendicular to this axis.

Step 2 Use the 2-in. ellipse template to draw the ellipse by aligning guidelines on the template with the major and minor diameters drawn on the front surface.

The isometric ellipse template can be used to draw ellipses on all three planes of an isometric drawing. On each plane, the major diameter is perpendicular to the isometric axis of the adjacent perpendicular plane. The isometric diameters marked on the template align with the isometric axes. All ellipses drawn on isometric planes must align in the directions shown in **Figure 25.43**.

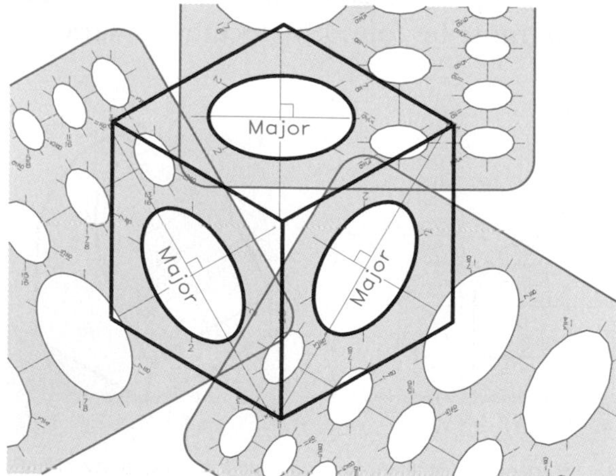

25.43 Position the isometric ellipse template as shown for drawing ellipses of various sizes on the three isometric planes.

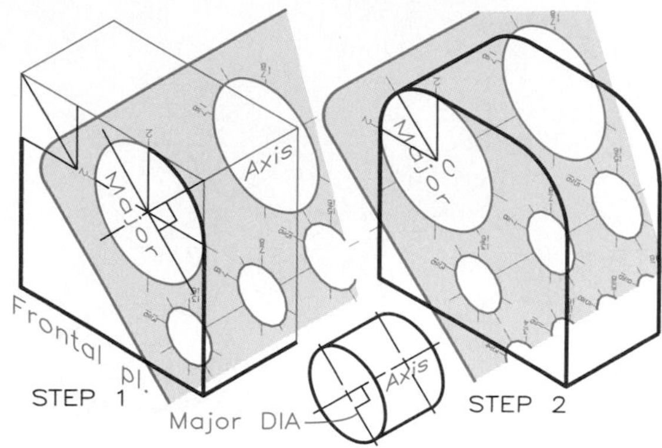

25.44 Drawing rounded corners.

Step 1 Draw the centerlines and isometric axes at the corners. Align the ellipse template with these guidelines and draw one quarter of the ellipse.

Step 2 Draw the other elliptical corner in the same manner with the same size ellipse.

Rounded Corners

The rounded corners of an object can be drawn with an ellipse template (**Figure 25.44**). Block in each corner with light construction lines, draw centerlines, draw the major diameter, and construct ellipses at each corner by positioning the template as shown. The rounded corners may also be constructed by using the four-center ellipse method (see **Figure 25.36**) or by plotting points with coordinates (see **Figure 25.34**).

A similar drawing involving the construction of ellipses is the conical shape shown in **Figure 25.45**. Block in the ellipses on the upper and lower surfaces. Then, draw the circular features by using a template or the four-center method, and draw lines tangent to each ellipse.

Inclined Planes

Inclined planes in isometric may be located by coordinates, but they cannot be measured with a protractor because they do not appear true size. **Figure 25.46** illustrates the coordinate method. Use horizontal and vertical coordinates (in the *x*- and *y*-directions) to locate key points on the orthographic views.

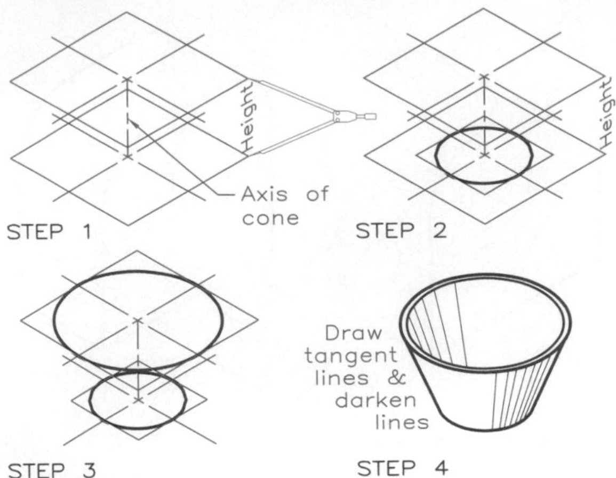

25.45 Constructing a cone in isometric.

Step 1 Draw the axis of the cone and block in the larger end at both ends.

Step 2 Block in the smaller end of the cone.

Step 3 Connect the ellipses with tangents, draw the cone's wall thickness, and darken the lines to complete the drawing.

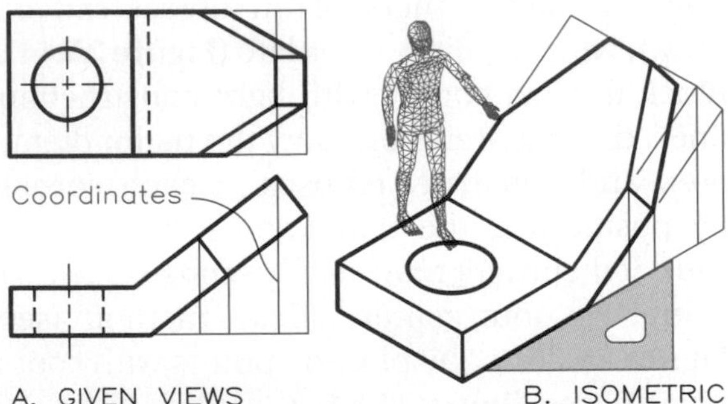

25.46 Inclined surfaces in isometric must be located with three-dimensional coordinates parallel to the isometric axes. True angles cannot be measured in isometric drawings.

Transfer these coordinates to the isometric drawing with dividers to show the features of the inclined surface.

Curves

Irregular curves in isometric must be plotted point by point, with coordinates locating each point. Locate points A through F in the orthographic view with coordinates of width and depth (**Figure 25.47**). Then, transfer them to the isometric view of the blocked-in part and connect them with an irregular curve.

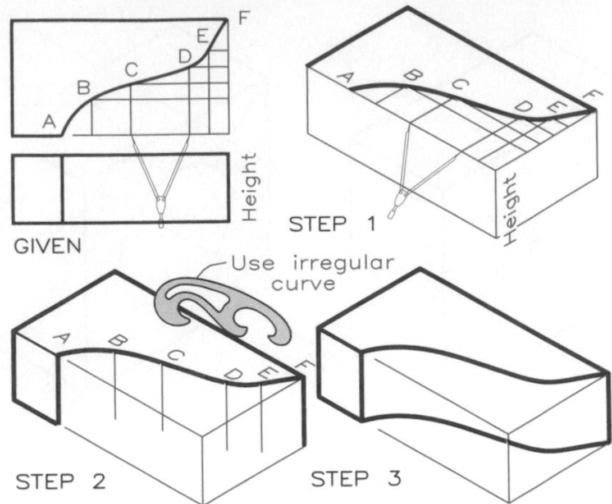

25.47 Plotting irregular curves.

Step 1 Block in the shape by using the overall dimensions. Locate points on the irregular curve with coordinates transferred from the orthographic views.

Step 2 Project these points downward the distance H (height) from the upper points to obtain the lower curve.

Step 3 Connect the points and darken the lines.

Project points on the upper curve downward a distance of H, the height of the part, to locate points on the lower curve. Connect these points with an irregular curve and darken the lines to complete the isometric.

Ellipses on Nonisometric Planes

Ellipses on nonisometric planes in an isometric drawing, such as the one shown in **Figure 25.48**, must be found by locating a series of

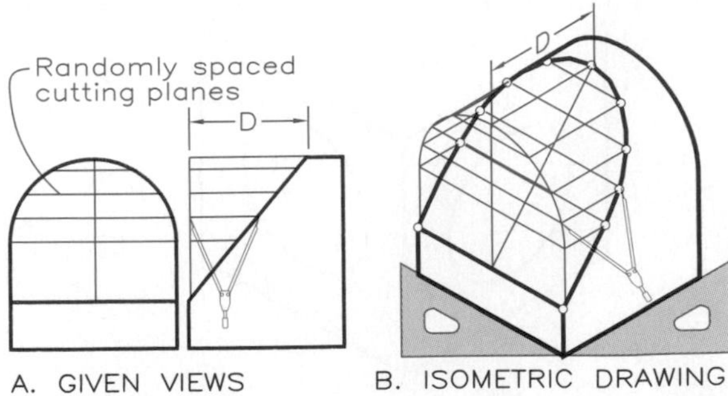

25.48 To construct ellipses on inclined planes, draw coordinates to locate points in the orthographic views. Then, transfer the three-dimensional coordinates to the isometric drawing and connect them with a smooth curve.

points on the curve. Locate three-dimensional coordinates in the orthographic views and then transfer them to the isometric with your dividers. Connect the plotted points with an irregular curve or an ellipse template selected to approximate the plotted points. The more points you select, the more accurate will be the final ellipse. It cannot be drawn by isometric ellipse template but by one that fits the plotted points.

25.6 Technical Illustration

Orthographic and isometric views of a spotface, countersink, and boss are shown in **Figure 25.49**. These features may be drawn in isometric by point-by-point plotting of the circular features, by the four-center, or by ellipse template method (the easiest method of the three).

A threaded shaft may be drawn in isometric as shown in **Figure 25.50**. First, draw the cylinder in isometric. Draw the major diameters of the crest lines equally separated by distance P, the pitch of the thread. Then, draw ellipses by aligning the major diameter of the ellipse template with the perpendiculars to the cylinder's axis. Use a smaller ellipse at the end for the 45° chamfered end.

Figure 25.51 shows how to draw a hexagon-head nut with an ellipse template. Block in

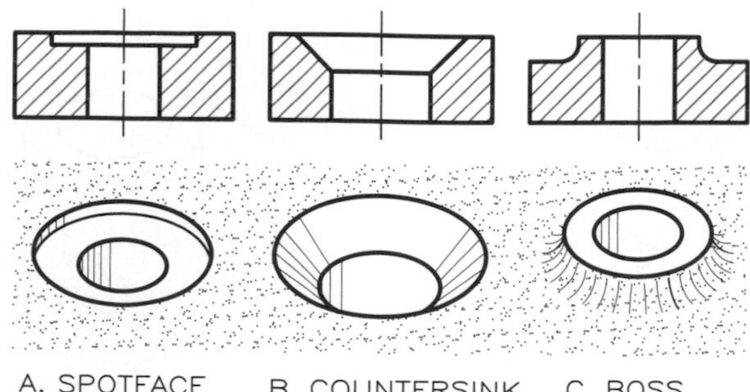

25.49 These examples of circular features in isometric may be drawn by using ellipse templates.

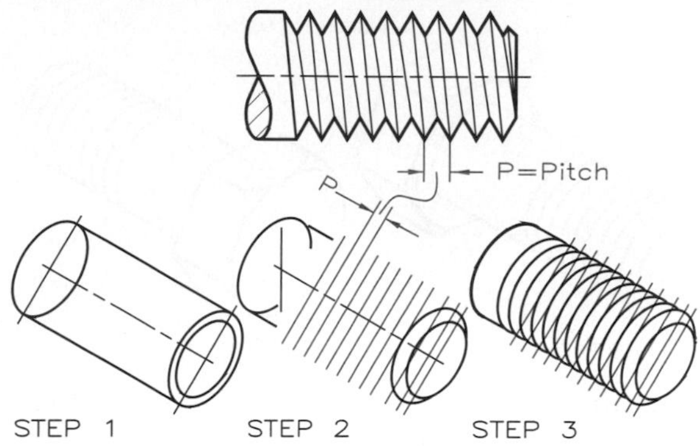

25.50 Threads in isometric.

Step 1 Using an ellipse template, draw the cylinder to be threaded.

Step 2 Lay off perpendiculars, spacing them apart a distance equal to the pitch of the thread, P.

Step 3 Draw a series of ellipses to represent the threads. Draw the chamfered end by using an ellipse whose major diameter is equal to the root diameter of the threads.

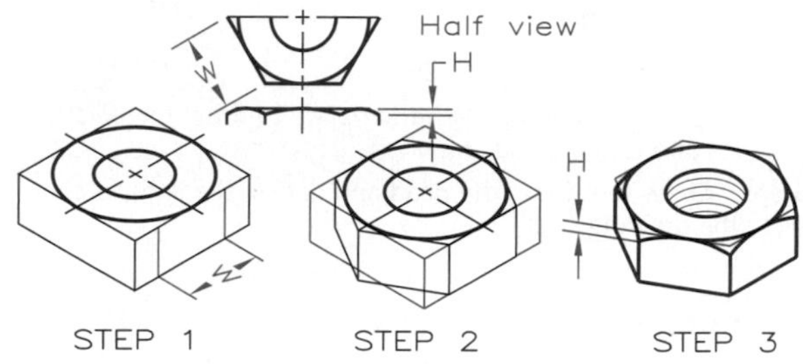

25.51 Constructing a nut.

Step 1 Use the overall dimensions of the nut to block in the nut.

Step 2 Construct the hexagonal sides at the top and bottom.

Step 3 Draw the chamfer with an irregular curve. Draw the threads to complete the drawing.

the nut and draw an ellipse tangent to the rhombus. Construct the hexagon by locating distance W across a flat parallel to the isometric axes. To find the other sides of the hexagon, draw lines tangent to the ellipse. Lay off distance H at each corner to establish the chamfers.

Figure 25.52 depicts a hexagon-head bolt in two positions. The washer face is on the lower side of the head, and the chamfer is on the upper side.

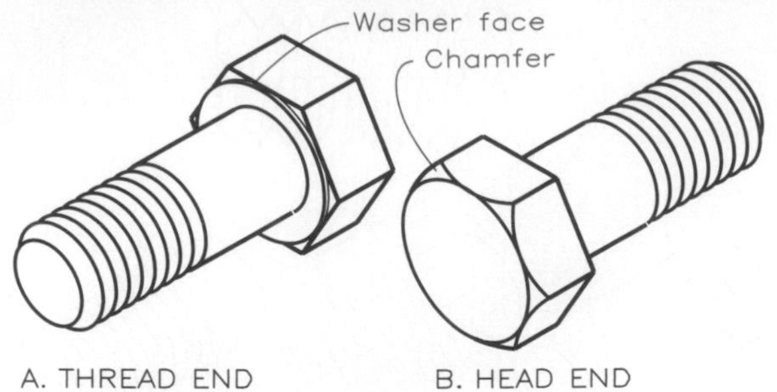

25.52 Isometric drawings of the lower and upper sides of a hexagon-head bolt.

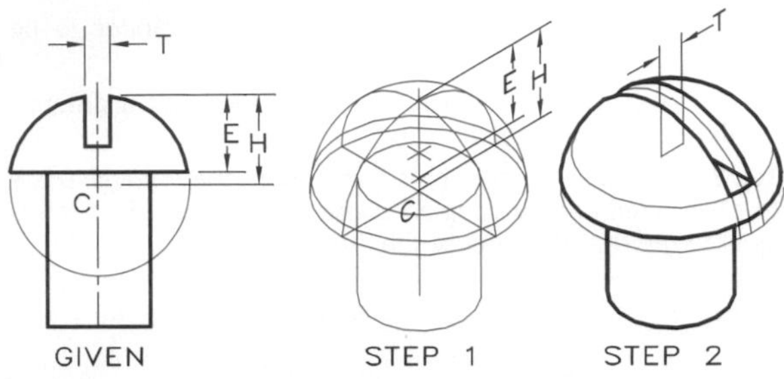

25.53 Drawing spherical features.

Step 1 Use an isometric ellipse template to draw the elliptical features of a round-head screw.

Step 2 Draw the slot in the head and darken the lines to complete the drawing.

A portion of a sphere is drawn to represent a round-head screw in **Figure 25.53**. Construct a hemisphere and locate the centerline of the slot along one of the isometric planes. Measure the head's thickness, E, from the highest point on the sphere.

Sections

A full section drawn in isometric can clarify internal details that might otherwise be overlooked (**Figure 25.54**). Half sections also may be used advantageously.

Dimensioned Isometrics

When you dimension isometric drawings, place numerals on the dimension lines, using either aligned or unidirectional numerals (**Figure 25.55**). In both cases, notes connected with leaders usually are positioned horizontally, but drawing them to lie in an isometric plane is permissible. Always use guidelines for your lettering and numerals.

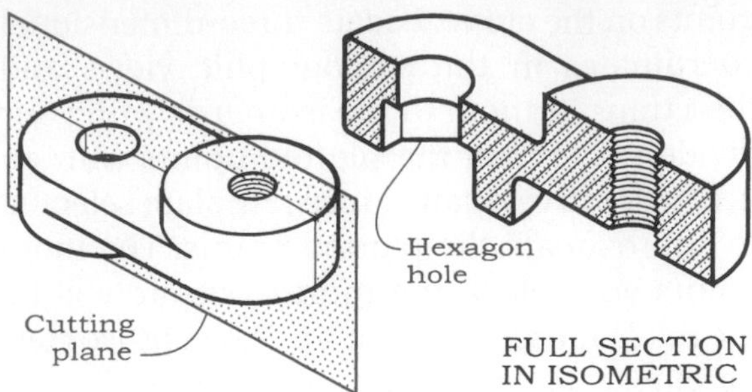

25.54 Isometric sections can be used to clarify the internal features of a part.

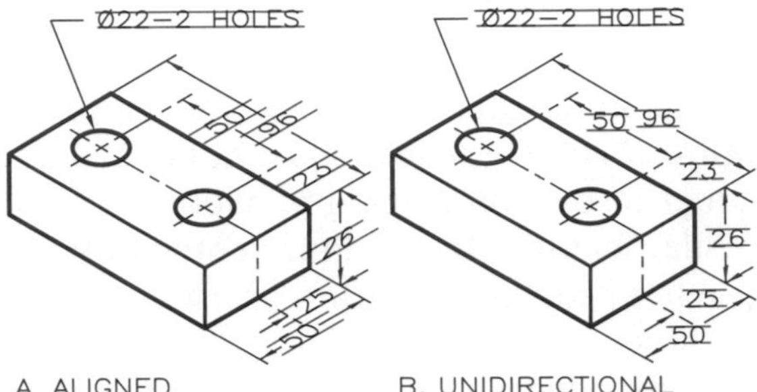

25.55 Either of the techniques shown—aligned or unidirectional—is acceptable for placing dimensions on isometric drawings. Guidelines should always be used for lettering.

Fillets and Rounds

Fillets and rounds in isometric may be represented by either of the techniques shown in **Figure 25.56** for added realism. The enlarged

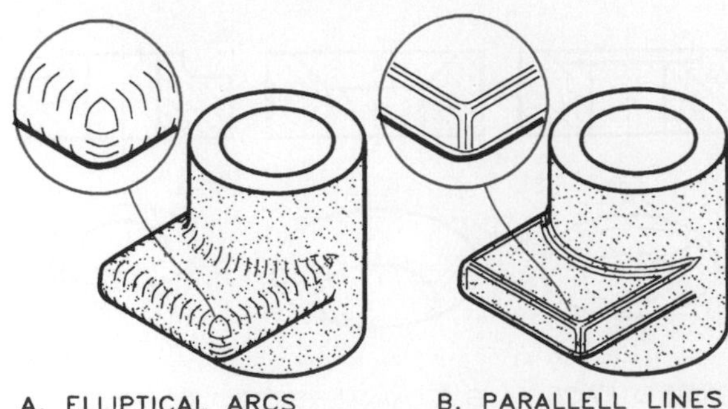

25.56 Either of these two methods may be used to represent fillets and rounds on the pictorial view of a part.

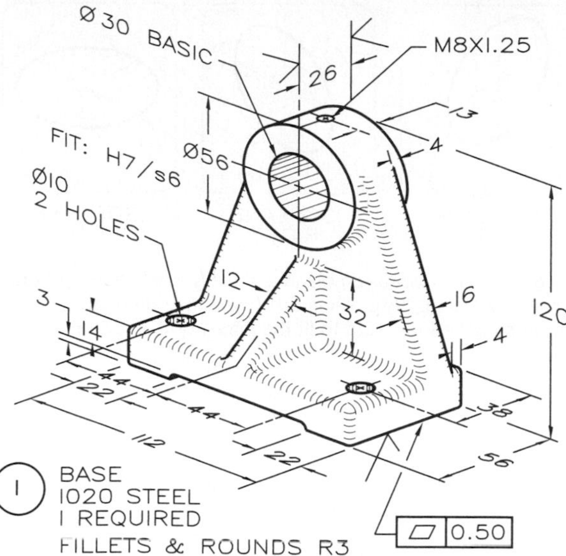

25.57 This three-dimensional pictorial has been drawn to show fillet and rounds, dimensions, and notes for its use as a working drawing.

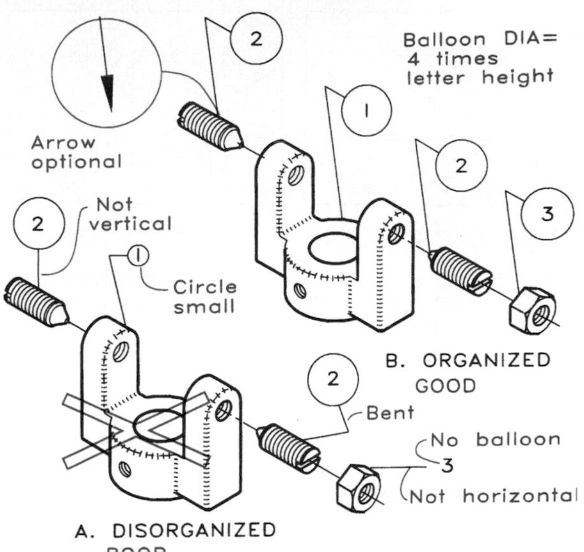

25.58 This drawing shows (A) common mistakes in applying leaders and part numbers in balloons of an assembly, and (B) acceptable techniques of applying leaders and part numbers to an assembly.

detail in the balloon shows how to draw fillets and rounds with elliptical segments (A) or with straight lines (B). These arcs are best if drawn with an ellipse template. The stipple shading was applied by using an adhesive overlay film.

When fillets and rounds of a three-dimensional part are drawn, it is much easier to understand its features than when the part is represented by orthographic views (**Figure 25.57**).

Assemblies

Assembly drawings illustrate how to put parts together. **Figure 25.58A** shows common mistakes in applying leaders and balloons to an assembly, and **Figure 25.58B** shows the correct method of applying them. The numbers in the balloons correspond to the part numbers in the parts list. **Figure 25.59** shows an exploded assembly that illustrates the relationship of four mating parts. Illustrations of this type are excellent for inclusion in parts catalogs and maintenance manuals.

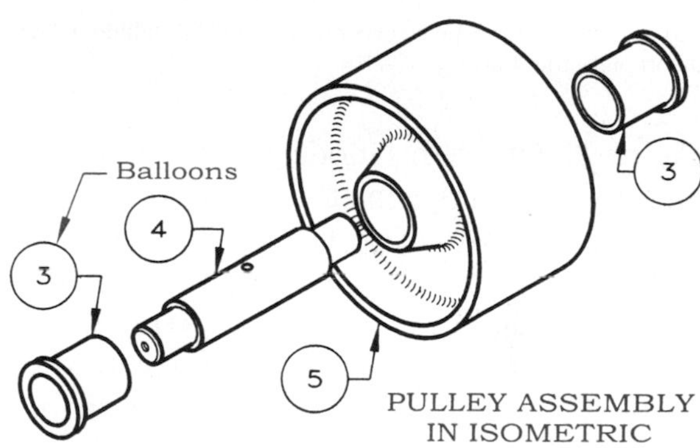

25.59 This exploded pictorial assembly shows how parts are to be put together.

25.7 Isometrics by AutoCAD

AutoCAD provides an *Isometric* grid for drawing isometrics. The *Style* option of the *Snap* command allows changing the rectangular *Grid,* called *Standard (S),* to *Isometic (I)* with dots shown vertically and at 30° to the horizontal

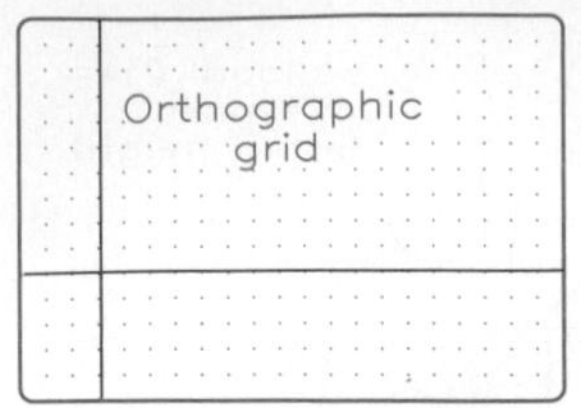

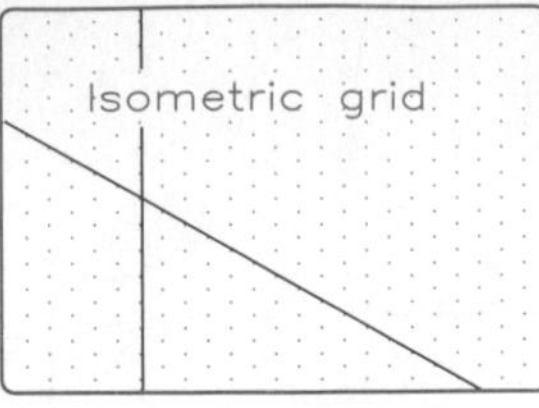

A. ORTHOGRAPHIC GRID B. ISOMETRIC GRID

25.60 The *Snap* command permits you to use the orthographic grid (*Standard*) or the isometric grid option *(I)* for drawing isometric pictorials.

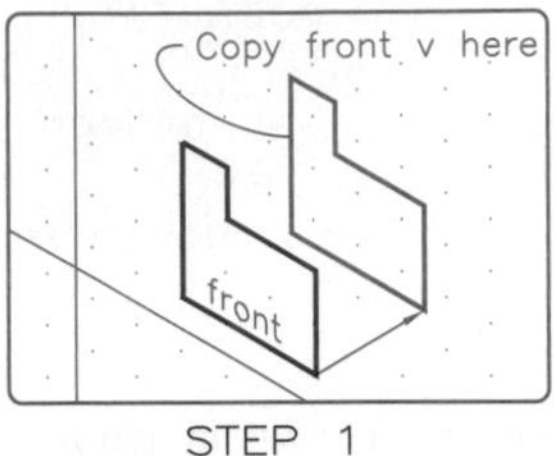

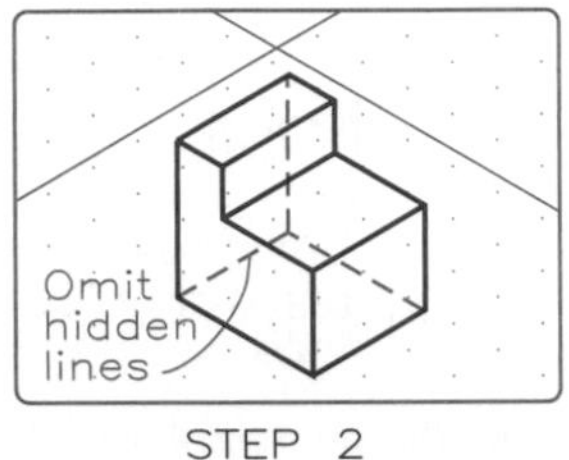

25.61 Isometrics by AutoCAD.

Step 1 Set the isometric grid on the screen (*Snap* and *I*), and set *Snap* to the grid. Draw the front view as an isometric and copy it to the back side with the *Copy* command.

Step 2 Connect the visible corner points and *Erase* hidden lines to complete the drawing.

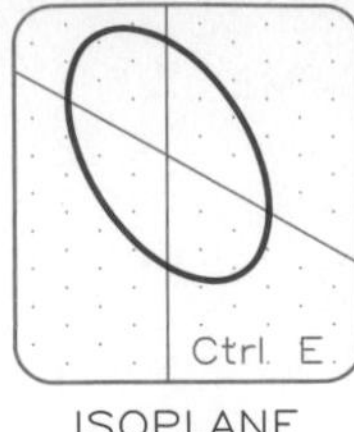

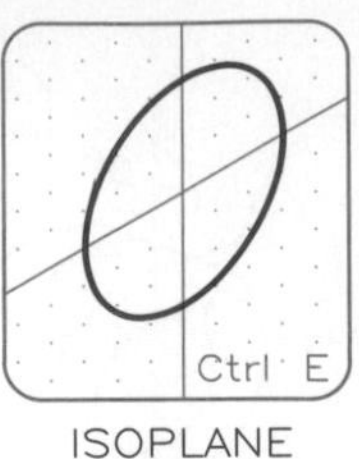

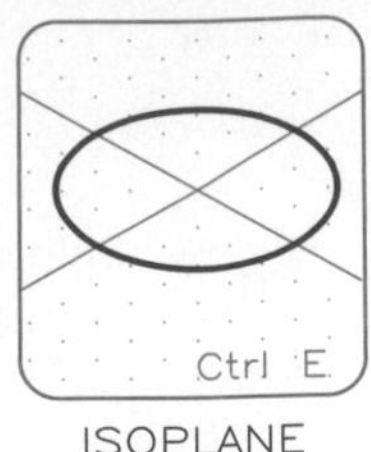

ISOPLANE LEFT ISOPLANE RIGHT ISOPLANE TOP

25.62 Use the *Ellipse* command and the *Isocircle* option to draw circles in isometric. By pressing *Ctrl-E*, you may alternatively rotate the isometric ellipses 120° to fit the three isometric planes.

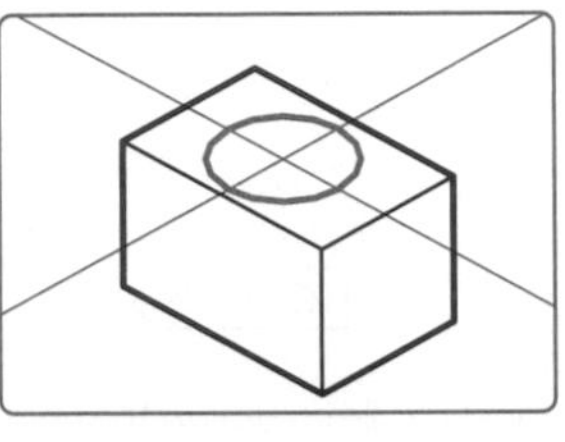

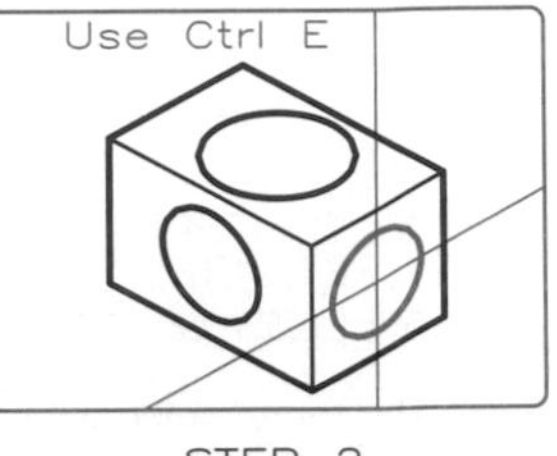

STEP 1 STEP 2

25.63 Isometric ellipses by AutoCAD.

Step 1 Use *Snap's* isometric-grid mode to draw isometric ellipses.
Command: Ellipse (Enter)
Specify axis endpoint of ellipse or [Arc/Center/Isocircle]: I (Enter).
Specify center of isocircle: (Select with cursor.)
Specify radius of isocircle or [Diameter]: (Select radius with cursor.)

Step 2 Change the orientation of the cursor for drawing isometric ellipses on the other two planes by pressing Ctrl-E. Repeat the process in step 1.

(**Figure 25.60**). In this mode, you can make the cursor's crosshairs *Snap* to the grid points and align with the axes of isometric drawings.

Isometric drawings made with this system (**Figure 25.61**) are not a true three-dimensional drawings system. Instead, they are two-dimensional isometrics that cannot be rotated to show other views.

Circles that will appear as ellipses in isometric can be drawn when *Snap* has been set to *Isometric.* From the *Draw* menu choose *Ellipse* and *I* (isometric circle). Specify the center point and the radius or diameter, and the isometric ellipse is drawn. When using this command, align the cursor with each of the three isometric planes by pressing *Ctrl-E* on the keyboard (**Figure 25.62**). When the cursor is aligned with the proper axes of an isometric plane, you may select the center of the isometric ellipse or its diameter's endpoints (**Figure 25.63**).

The *Isoplane* command changes the position of the cursor in the same way *Ctrl-E does. Isoplane* will prompt you to select from *Left/Top/Right/<Toggle>:* options. To use the *Toggle* option, press (Enter) to successively move the cursor position from plane to plane.

25.8 Axonometric Projection

An axonometric projection is a type of orthographic projection in which the pictorial view is projected perpendicularly onto the picture plane with parallel projectors. The object is positioned at an angle to the picture plane so that its pictorial projection will be a three-dimensional view. The three types

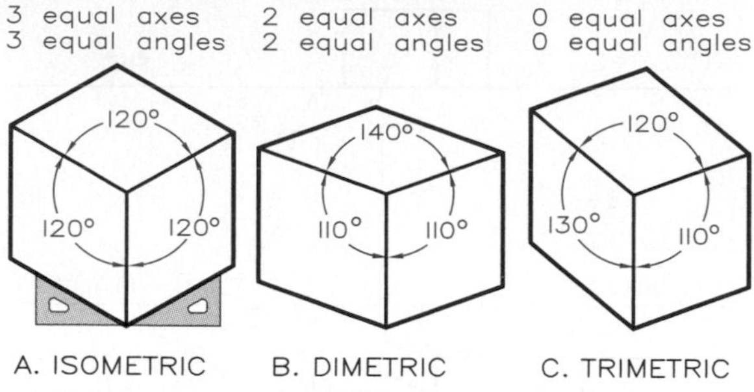

25.64 This drawing illustrates the three types of axonometric projection.

of axonometric projections are **isometric, dimetric,** and **trimetric** (**Figure 25.64**).

Recall that the **isometric projection** is the type of pictorial in which the diagonal of a cube is seen as a point, the three axes and planes of the cube are equally foreshortened, and the axes are equally spaced 120° apart. Measurements along the three axes will be equal but less than true length because the isometric projection is true projection.

A **dimetric projection** is a pictorial in which two planes are equally foreshortened and two of the axes are separated by equal angles. Measurements along two axes of the cube are equal.

A **trimetric projection** is a pictorial in which all three planes are unequally foreshortened. The lengths of the axes are unequal, and the angles between them are different.

25.9 Perspective Pictorials

A perspective pictorial most closely resembles the view seen by the eye or camera and is the most realistic form of pictorial. In a perspective, parallel lines converge at vanishing points (VPs) as the lines recede from the observer. The three basic types of perspectives are **one point, two point**, and **three point**, depending on the number of vanishing points used in their construction (**Figure 25.65**).

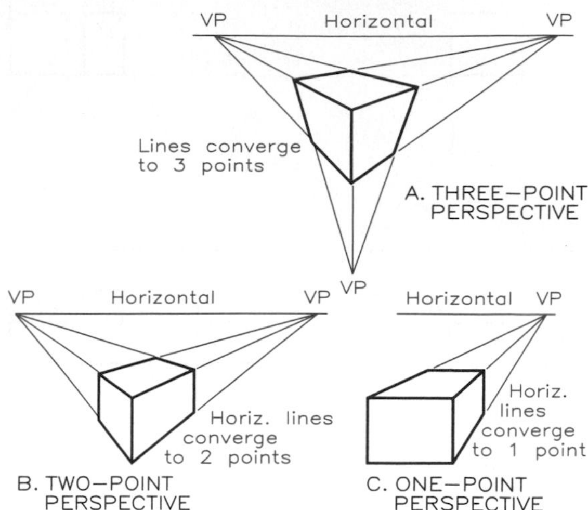

25.65 A comparison of three-point, two-point, and one-point perspectives.

One-point perspectives have one surface of the objective that is parallel to the picture plane, making it a true shape. The other sides vanish to a single vanishing point on the horizon.

Two-point perspectives are positioned with two sides at an angle to the picture plane, requiring two vanishing points. All horizontal lines converge at the vanishing points on the horizon, but vertical lines remain vertical and have no vanishing point.

Three-point perspectives have three vanishing points because the object is positioned so that all its sides make an angle with the picture plane. Three-point perspectives are used for drawing large objects, such as tall buildings. They are the most realistic perspectives and the most complex to draw. Because of their complexity, we do not show how to construct them in this section.

Construction of One-Point Perspectives

Figure 25.66 shows how to draw a one-point perspective. It shows the top and side views of the object, picture plane, station point, horizon, and ground line. The picture plane (PP)

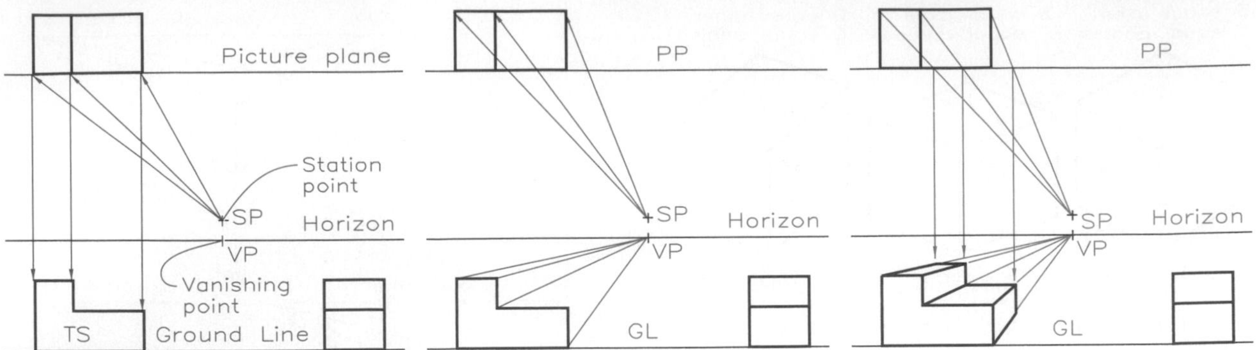

25.66 One-point perspective.

Step 1 Since the object is parallel to the picture plane, there will be only one vanishing point, located on the horizon below the station point. Projections from the top and side views establish the true-size front plane, which lies in the picture plane.

Step 2 Draw projectors from the station point to the rear points of the object in the top view and from the front view to the vanishing point on the horizon. In a one-point perspective the vanishing point is the front view of the station point on the horizon.

Step 3 Construct vertical projectors from the top view to the front view from the points where the projectors cross the picture plane. These projectors intersect the lines that are drawn to the single vanishing point VP, which is located at the back side of the perspective.

appears as an edge in the top view and is the plane onto which the perspective is projected.

The station point (SP) is the location of the observer's eye in the top view and lies on the horizon in the front view. The horizon is a horizontal line in the front view that represents an infinite horizontal, such as the surface of the ocean, and is aligned with the viewer's eye. The ground line (GL) is an infinite horizontal line parallel to the horizon from which vertical measurements are made.

Constructing Two-Point Perspectives

If two surfaces of an object are positioned at angles to the picture plane, two vanishing points are required to draw it as a perspective. Placing the horizon above the ground line and the height of the object in the front view yields an aerial view (**Figure 25.67**). Placing the ground line and horizon on top of each other in the front view gives a ground-level view (worm's-eye view). Placing the horizon above the ground line and through the object, usually at a person's height for large objects such as buildings, results in a general view.

Figure 25.67 shows how to construct a two-point perspective. Because line AB lies in the picture plane, it will be true length in the perspective. All height dimensions originate at this vertical line because it is the only true-length line of the object.

When drawing any perspective, you should position the station point far enough away from the object that the perspective can be contained in a cone of vision of 30° or less (**Figure 25.68**). A larger cone of vision will distort the perspective.

The object shown in **Figure 25.69** does not come into contact with the picture plane in the top view, as it does in **Figure 25.67**. To draw a perspective of this object, the planes of the object are extended to the picture plane. Measure the height on this line and draw an infinite plane to the right vanishing point. Locate the corner of the object on this infinite plane by projecting the object's right corner to the picture plane in the top view with a projector from the station point and then projecting this point downward to the infinite plane.

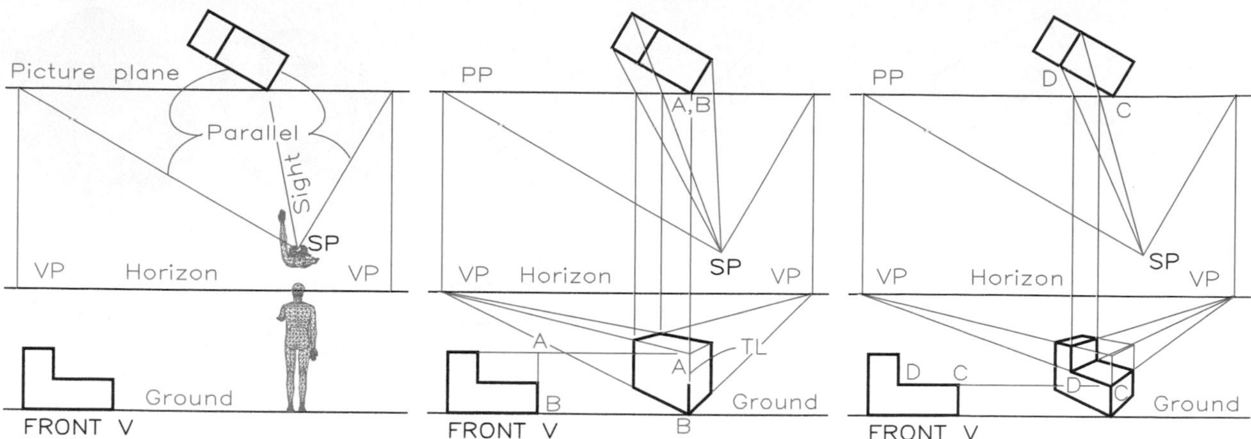

25.67 A two-point perspective.

Step 1 Extend projectors from the top view of the station point to the picture plane parallel to the forward edges of the object. Project these points vertically to the horizon in the front view to locate vanishing points. Draw the ground line below the horizon and construct the side view on the ground line.

Step 2 Lines in the picture plane are true length, so AB is true length. Project AB from the side view to determine its height. Project each end of AB to the vanishing points. Draw projectors from the station point to the exterior edges of the top view, and project the intersections of these projectors with the picture plane to the front view.

Step 3 Find point C in the front view by projecting from the side view to AB. Draw a projector from point C to the left vanishing point. Point D lies on this projector beneath the point where a projector from the station point to the top view of point D crosses the picture plane. Draw the notch by projecting to the respective vanishing points.

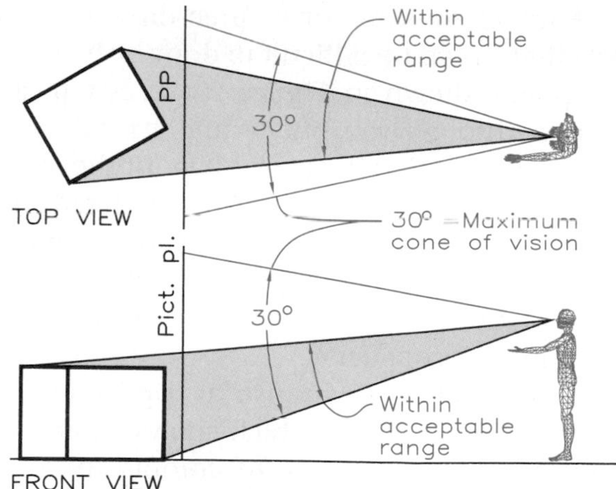

25.68 The station point should be far enough away from the object to permit the cone of vision to be less than 30° to reduce distortion.

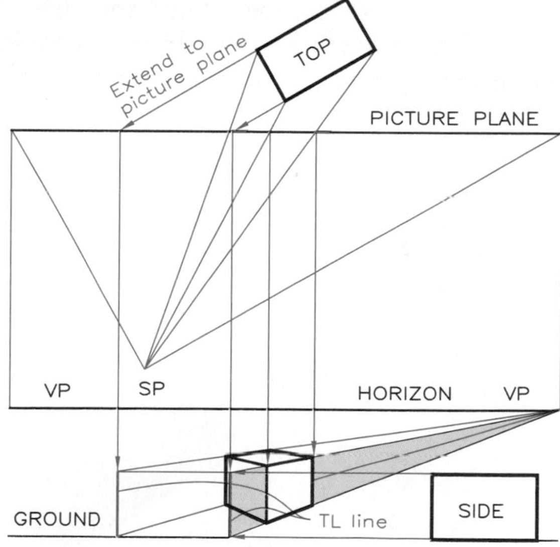

25.69 This two-point perspective is of an object that does not come into contact with the picture plane.

Arcs in Perspective

Draw arcs in perspective by using coordinates to locate points along the curves (**Figure 25.70**). Transfer points 1–7 from the semicircular arc in the orthographic view to the perspective by projecting coordinates from the top and side views. All heights are projected to the TL line from the orthographic view. These points do not form a true ellipse but an

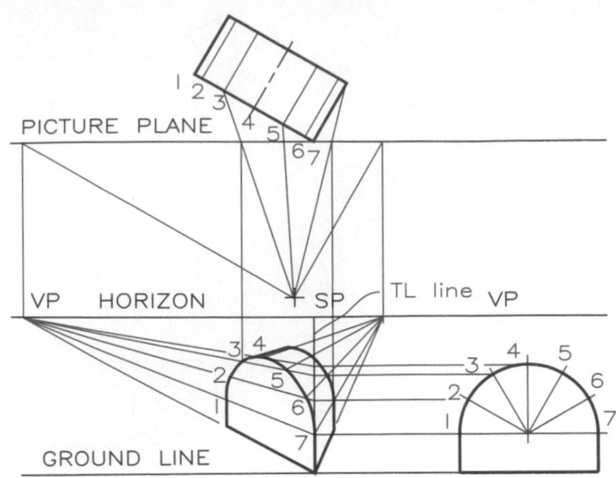

25.70 An object with a semicircular feature is drawn in this two-point perspective.

egg-shaped oval. Connect the points with an irregular curve.

25.10 Three-Dimensional Modeling

Objects drawn with AutoCAD as true three-dimensional solids can be rotated and viewed from any angle as if they were held in your hand. The object in **Figure 25.71** is an example of a

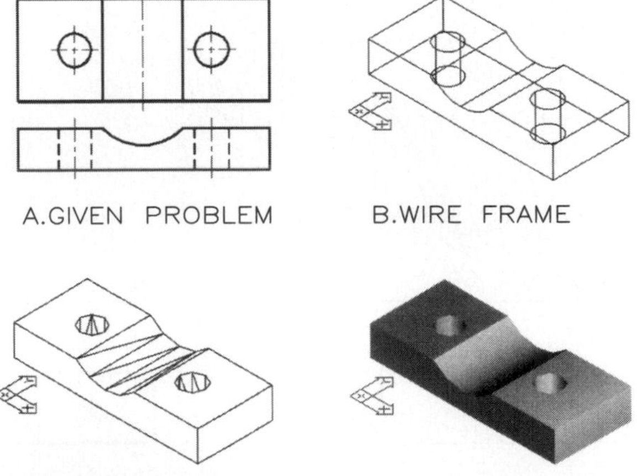

25.71 Modeling a simple part.

A The top and front orthographic views of the part are given.

B A 3-D wire-frame drawing of the part is made.

C The hidden lines are suppressed to give a three-dimensional model.

D The model is rendered to give it a realistic look.

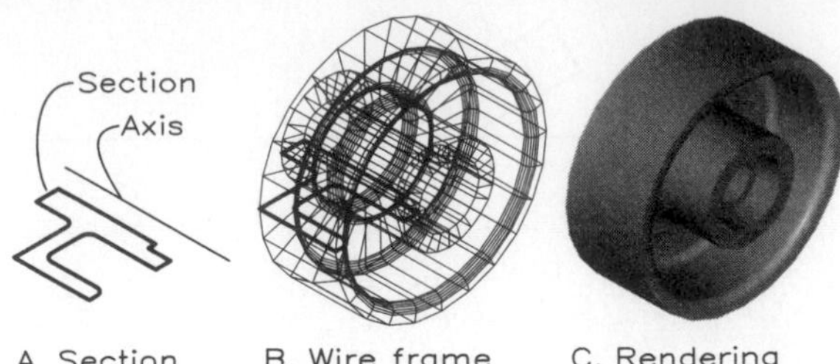

25.72 A model by revolution.

A A typical section of the pulley and its axis are drawn.

B The section is rotated about the axis to obtain a wire-frame drawing.

C The wire frame is rendered to obtain a realistic view of the pulley.

simple object represented by two orthographic views, a wire-frame drawing, a hidden-line wire-frame drawing, and a rendered solid. The capability to depict objects as rendered solids is a powerful design and communications tool.

Another example of a three-dimensional part that would be difficult to draw by hand is the pulley shown in **Figure 25.72**. A typical section through the pulley and its axis are drawn, the section is revolved about the axis, and the wire-frame diagram is rendered. In addition to being able to select various views of the pulley, you can apply different lighting combinations and materials to it in infinite combinations of effects.

An example of an industrial application is given in **Figure 25.73**, which shows an apparatus of a higher degree of complexity that would be a rigorous assignment if drawn by hand. Although it is no easy chore to draw it as a series of solids by AutoCAD, the computer drawing enables you to obtain many different views of the parts, and to replicate drawings in combination. For example, the apparatus in **Figure 25.73** is applied repetitively in the subsea production–equipment assembly in **Figure 25.74**. The savings in time and effort becomes highly significant, and the final

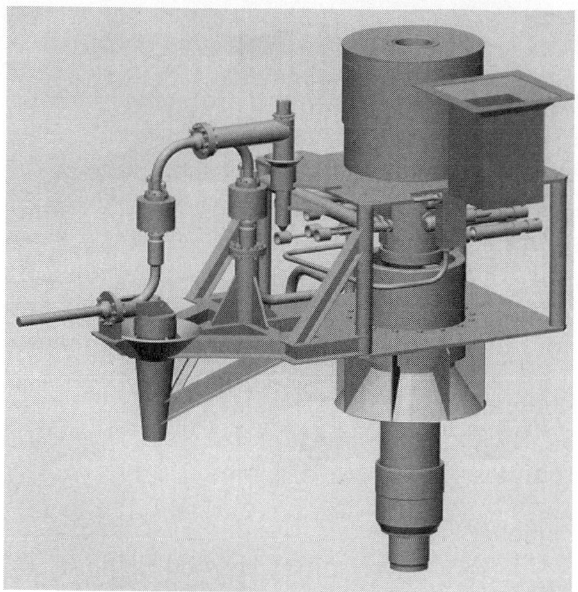

25.73 This apparatus is an example of a rendered three-dimensional model of a moderately complex application. *(Courtesy of Cameron.)*

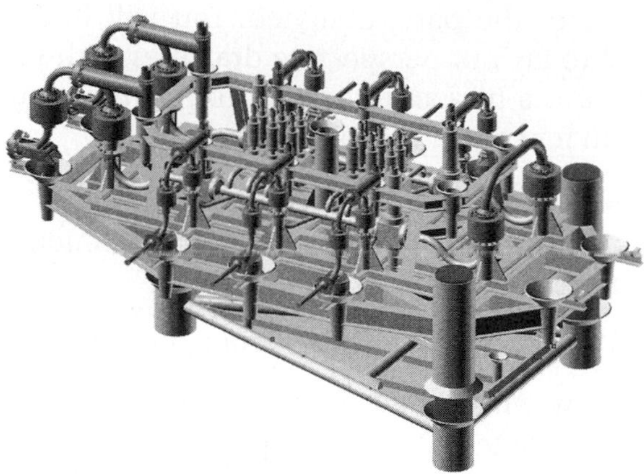

25.74 The apparatus in **Figure 25.73** is replicated a number of times in this equipment assembly used in subsea production. *(Courtesy of Cameron.)*

rendering greatly improves the understanding of the unit as a whole.

Three-dimensional modeling by several methods is introduced in Chapter 38. You will find that solid modeling begins with an understanding of the underlying fundamentals covered in this chapter. The ability to sketch three-dimensional drawings is an invaluable skill that you will use to develop and communicate design applications.

25.11 The Human Figure

An ultimate aspiration of the illustrator has always been the ability to represent the human form in a realistic manner. In addition to determining the interactions among parts, assemblies, and equipment, it is equally important to study the relationship of personnel to their working environment. An example of this type of application in **Figure 25.75** shows workers performing maintenance on a spacecraft. The figures can be moved about the work area and placed in an infinite variety of poses.

Several software packages have been developed that can be used with AutoCAD and other programs that adapt well to computer graphics. The software *Poser*® by Fractal Design offers many options for representing the human body, from stick figures to formally dressed figures

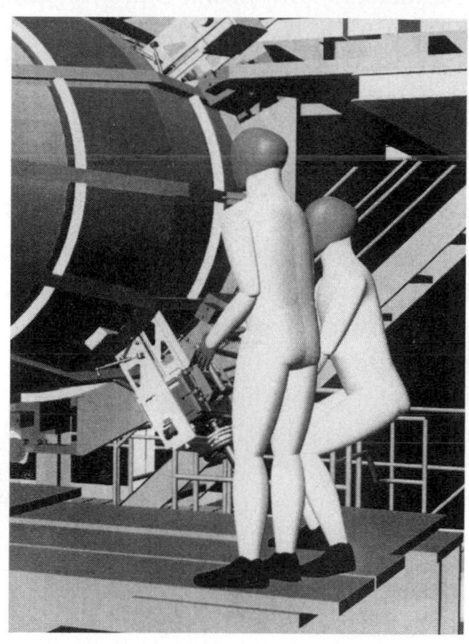

25.75 The computer-drawn scene at the Kennedy Space Center illustrates the interaction between people and equipment. *(Courtesy McDonnell-Douglas Space & Defense System—Kennedy Space Center.)*

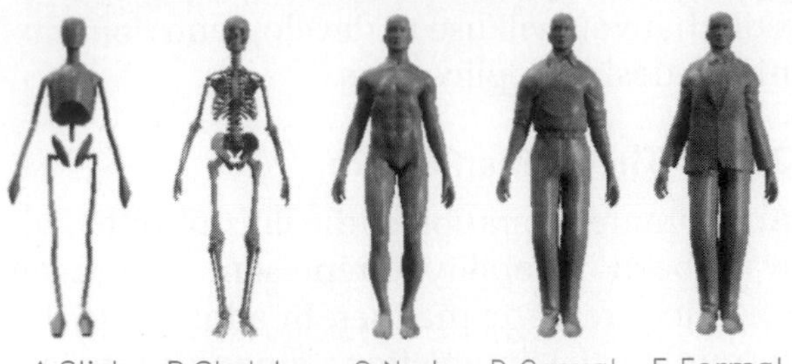

25.76 Several of the rendering options that are available as part of *Poser 2*.

(**Figure 25.76**). Choices of body styles can be made from many categories, a few of which are age, sex, weight, and pose. Bodies can be positioned and controlled to fit almost any application. Figures can be rotated to obtain orthographic, axonometric, or perspective views of them. Clothing options range from casual dress to formal for both males and females. Because all designs and projects are to fulfill the needs of people, it is important that the human body interact with design concepts at all stages of their development.

25.12 The Future

The future of 3D graphics is truly exciting. What is available today for the microcomputer was not possible even on much larger and more expensive computers just a few years ago. The capabilities of 3D programs will continue to become more powerful and easier to use. Graphics in the future will include more solid modeling, animation, and sound effects. Get ready for an exciting trip where reality will be at your fingertips!

Problems

Draw your solutions to the problems in **Figure 25.77** on size A or B sheets, as assigned. Select an appropriate scale to take advantage of the space available on each sheet. By letting each square represent 0.20 in. (5 mm), you can draw two solutions on each size A sheet. By setting each square to 0.40 inch (10 mm), you can draw one solution on each size B sheet.

Oblique Pictorials

1–24. Construct cavalier, cabinet, or general obliques of the parts assigned.

Isometric Pictorials

1–24. Construct isometrics of the parts assigned.

Perspective Pictorials

1–24. On size B sheets lay out perspective views of the parts assigned. You will find it best to lay out perspective drawings with the sheet in a horizontal format to provide more room for vanishing points.

Thought Questions

1. What is the difference between isometric projections and isometric drawings?

2. What are the three types of oblique drawings?

3. How will circular features appear on isometric planes? On oblique planes?

4. What is the major advantage of obliques over isometric drawings?

5. Of the following, which is the most realistic form of a pictorial: oblique, isometric, or perspective? Explain.

25.77 Problems 1–24.

26

Points, Lines, and Planes

26.1 Introduction

Points, lines, and planes are the basic geometric elements used in three-dimensional (3D) spatial geometry, called *descriptive geometry.* You need to understand how to locate and manipulate these elements in their simplest form because they will be applied to 3D spatial problems in Chapters 26 through 31.

The lunar landing craft in **Figure 26.1** is composed of many points, lines, and planes that represent its structural members and shapes. Its geometry had to be established one point at a time with great precision for it to function and be properly supported.

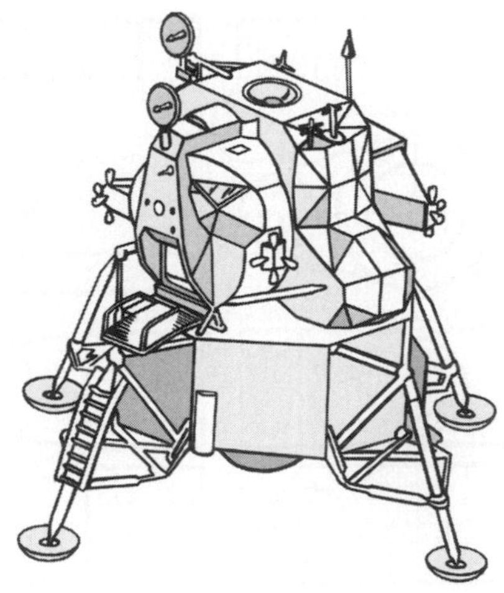

26.1 It is easy to see the numerous applications of points, lines, and planes that were encountered by the team of designers who created this lunar landing craft.

The labeling of points, lines, and planes is an essential part of 3D projection because it is your means of analyzing their spatial relationships. **Figure 26.2** illustrates the fundamental requirements for properly labeling these elements in a drawing:

Lettering: use 1/8-in. letters with guidelines for labels; label lines at each end and planes at each corner with either letters or numbers.

Points: mark with two short perpendicular dashes forming a cross, not a dot; each dash should be approximately 1/8 in. long.

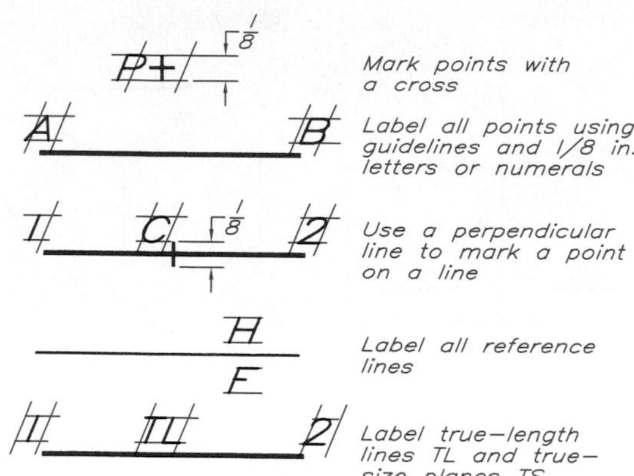

Mark points with a cross
Label all points using guidelines and 1/8 in. letters or numerals
Use a perpendicular line to mark a point on a line
Label all reference lines
Label true–length lines TL and true–size planes TS

26.2 These are standard practices for labeling points, lines, and planes.

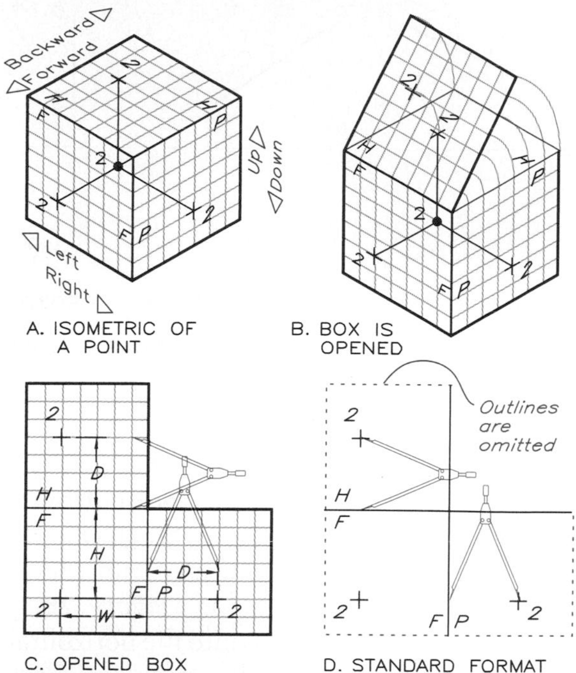

Backward
Forward
Up
Down
Left
Right
A. ISOMETRIC OF A POINT
B. BOX IS OPENED
Outlines are omitted
C. OPENED BOX
D. STANDARD FORMAT

26.3 Three views of a point.

A The point is projected to three projection planes.

B The projection planes are opened into a single plane.

C In the opened box, point 2 is 5 units to the left of the profile, 5 units below the horizontal, and 4 units behind the frontal plane.

D The outlines of the projection planes are omitted in orthographic projection.

Points on lines: mark with a short perpendicular dash crossing the line, not a dot.

Reference lines: label these thin, dark lines as described in Chapter 14.

Object lines: draw these lines used to represent points, lines, and planes twice as thick as hidden lines with an F or HB pencil; draw hidden lines twice as thick as reference lines.

True-length lines: label true length or TL.

True-size planes: label true size or TS.

Projection lines: draw precisely with a 2H or 4H pencil as thin lines, just dark enough to be visible so they need not be erased.

26.2 Projection of Points

A point is a theoretical location in space having no dimensions other than its location. However, a series of points establishes lengths, areas, and volumes of complex shapes.

A point must be located in at least two adjacent orthographic views to establish its position in 3D space (**Figure 26.3**). When the planes of the projection box (**Figure 26.3A**) are opened onto the plane of the drawing surface (**Figure 26.3C**), the projectors from each view of point 2 are perpendicular to the reference lines between the views. Letters **H, F**, and **P** represent the **horizontal, frontal**, and **profile planes**, the three principal projection planes.

A point may be located from verbal descriptions with respect to the principal planes. For example, point 2 in **Figure 26.3** may be described as being 5 units left of the profile plane, 5 units below the horizontal plane, and 4 units behind the frontal plane.

When you look at the front view of the box, the horizontal and profile planes appear as edges. In the top view, the frontal and profile planes appear as edges. In the side view, the frontal and horizontal planes appear as edges.

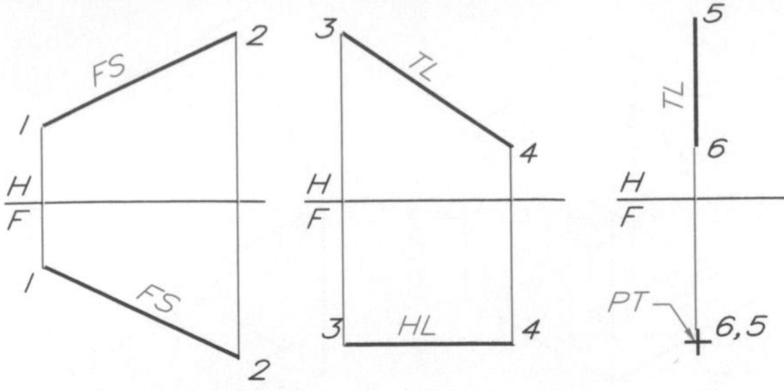

26.4 A line in orthographic projection can appear as foreshortened (FS), true length (TL), or a point (PT).

26.3 Lines

A **line** is the straight path between two points in 3D space. A line may appear as **foreshortened, true length**, or a **point** (**Figure 26.4**). Oblique lines are neither parallel nor perpendicular to a principal projection plane (**Figure 26.5**). When line 1-2 is projected onto the horizontal, frontal, and profile planes, it appears foreshortened in each view.

Principal lines are parallel to at least one of the principal projection planes. A principal line is true length in the view where the principal plane to which it is parallel appears true size. The three types of principal lines are **horizontal, frontal**, and **profile lines**.

Figure 26.6A shows a **horizontal line** (HL) that appears true length in the horizontal (top) view. Any line shown in the top view will

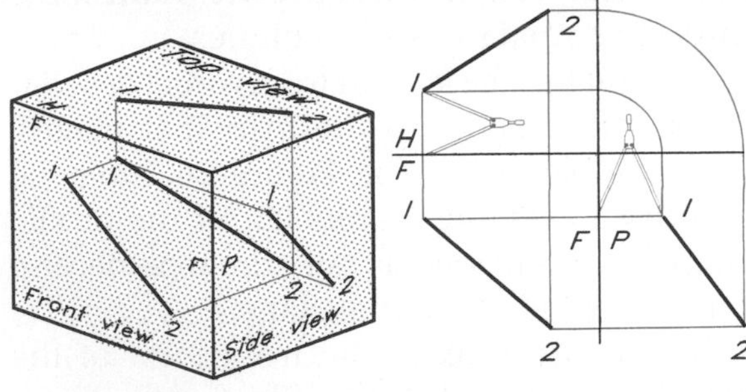

26.5 A line in space.

A Three views of a line are projected onto the three principal planes.

B These are the standard three orthographic views of a line.

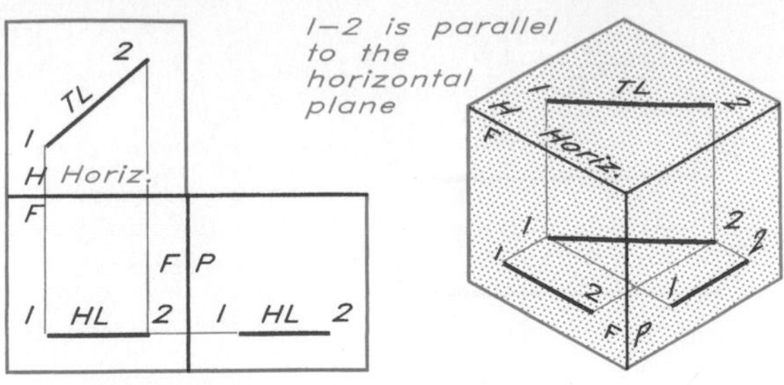

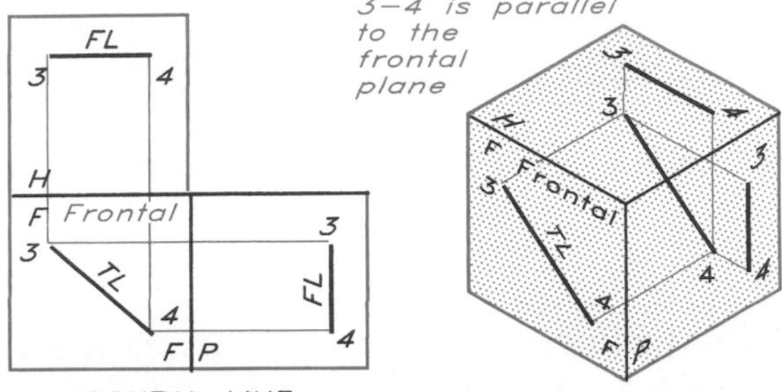

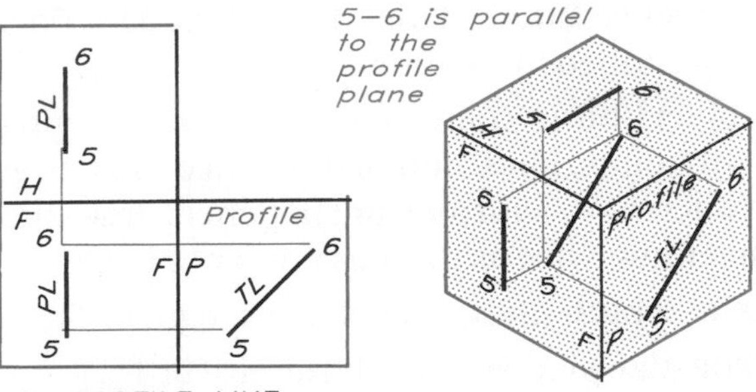

26.6 Principal lines.

A A horizontal line is true length in the horizontal (top) view. It is parallel to the edge view of the horizontal plane in the front and side views.

B The frontal line is true length in the front view. It is parallel to the edge view of the frontal plane in the top and side views.

C The profile line is true length in the profile (side) view. It is parallel to the edge view of the profile plane in the top and front views.

appear true length as long as it is parallel to the horizontal plane.

When looking at the top view, you cannot tell whether the line is horizontal. You must look at the front or side views to do so. In those views, an HL will be parallel to the edge view of the horizontal, the HF fold line (**Figure 26.7**). A line that projects as a point in the front view is a combination horizontal and profile line.

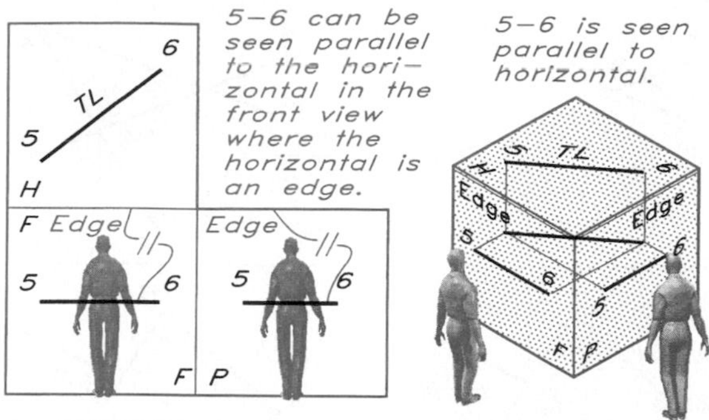
5–6 can be seen parallel to the hori–zontal in the front view where the horizontal is an edge.
5–6 is seen parallel to horizontal.
A. ORTHOGRAPHIC VIEWS
B. PICTORIAL VIEW

26.7 To determine that a line is horizontal, you must look at the front or side views in which the horizontal projection plane is an edge. Line 5-6 is seen parallel to the horizontal edge and is a horizontal line, too.

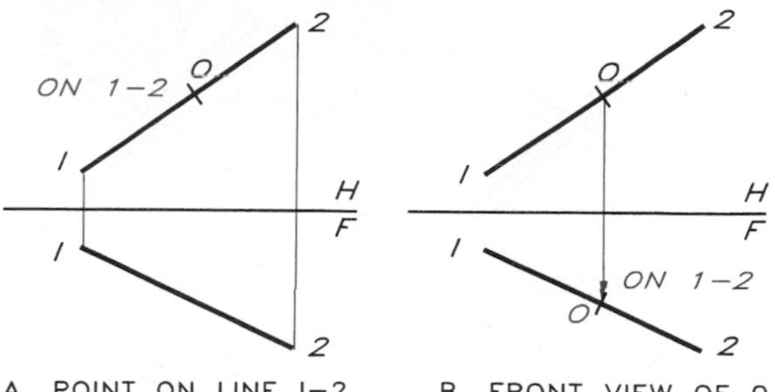
A. POINT ON LINE 1–2
B. FRONT VIEW OF O

26.8 Point O in the top view of line 1-2 can be found in the front view by projection. The projector is perpendicular to the HF reference line between the views.

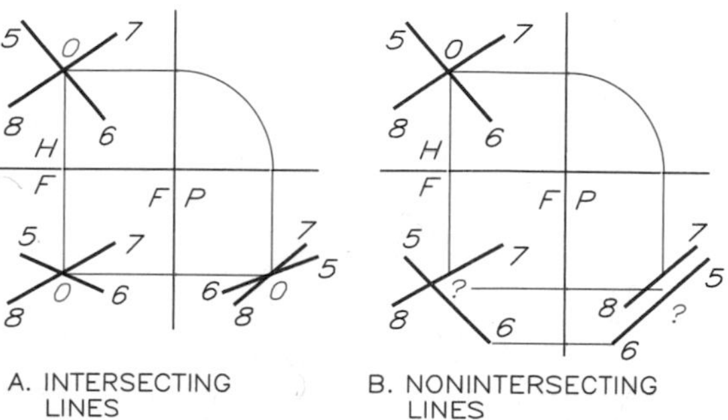
A. INTERSECTING LINES
B. NONINTERSECTING LINES

26.9 Crossing lines.

A These lines intersect because O, the point of intersection, projects as a common point of intersection in all views.

B The lines cross in the top and front views, but they do not intersect because there is no common point of intersection in all views.

A **frontal line** (FL) is parallel to the frontal projection plane. It appears true length in the front view because your line of sight is perpendicular to it in this view. In **Figure 26.6B** line 3-4 is an FL because it is parallel to the edge of the frontal plane in the top and side views.

A **profile line** (PL) is parallel to the profile projection planes and appears true length in the side (profile) views. To tell whether a line is a PL, you must look at a view adjacent to the profile view, the top or front view. In **Figure 26.6C**, line 5-6 is parallel to the edge view of the profile plane in both the top and side views.

Locating a Point on a Line

Figure 26.8 shows the top and front views of line 1-2 with point O located at its midpoint. To find the front view of the point, recall that in orthographic projection, the projector between the views is perpendicular to the HF fold line. Use that projector to project point O to line 1-2 in the front view. A point located at a line's midpoint will be at the line's midpoint in all orthographic views of the line.

Intersecting and Nonintersecting Lines

Lines that intersect have a common point of intersection lying on both lines. Point O in **Figure 26.9A** is a point of intersection because it projects to a common crossing point in all three views. However, the crossing point of the lines in **Figure 26.9B** in the top and front views is not a point of intersection. Point O does not project to a common crossing point in the top and front views, so the lines do not intersect; they simply cross, as shown in the profile view.

26.4 Visibility

Crossing Lines

In **Figure 26.10** nonintersecting lines AB and CD cross in certain views. Therefore, portions of the lines are visible or hidden at the crossing points (here, line thickness is exaggerated for purposes of illustration). Determining which line is above or in front of the other is referred to as finding a line's *visibility*, a requirement of many 3D problems.

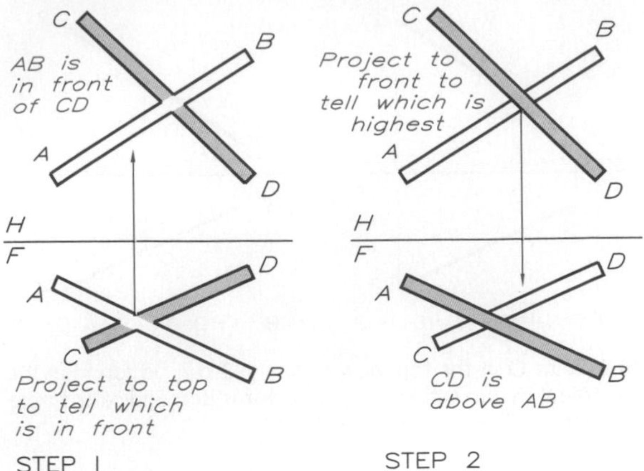

26.10 Determining visibility of lines.

Step 1 Project the crossing point from the front to the top view. This projector strikes line AB before it strikes line CD, indicating that line AB is in front and thus is visible in the front view.

Step 2 Project the crossing point from the top view to the front view. This projector strikes line CD before it strikes line AB, indicating that line CD is above line AB and thus is visible in the top view.

You have to determine line visibility by analysis. For example, select a crossing point in the front view and project it to the top view to determine which line is in front of the other. Because the projector contacts line AB first, you know that line AB is in front of CD and is visible in the front view.

Repeat this process by projecting downward from the intersection in the top view to find that line CD is above line AB and is visible in the top view. If only one view were available, visibility would be impossible to determine.

A Line and a Plane

The principles of visibility analysis also apply to determining visibility for a line and a plane (**Figure 26.11**). First, project the intersections of line AB with lines 4-5 and 5-6 to the top view to determine that the lines of the plane (4-5 and 5-6) lie in front of line AB in the front view. Therefore, line AB is a hidden line in the front view.

Similarly, project the two intersections of line AB in the top view to the front view, where line AB is found to lie above lines 4-5 and 5-6

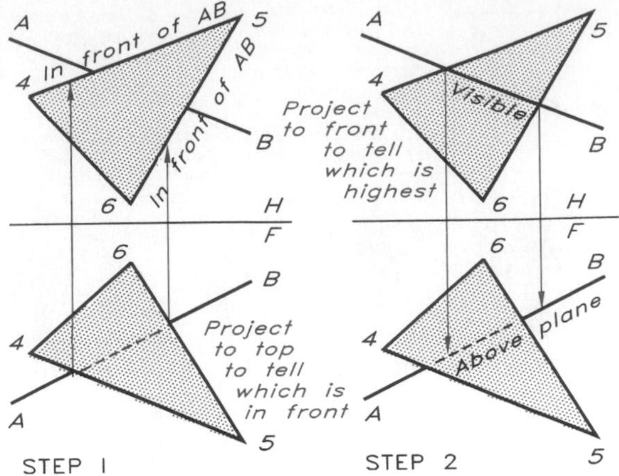

26.11 Determining visibility of a line and a plane.

Step 1 Project the points where line AB crosses the plane from the front view to the top view. These projectors intersect lines 4-6 and 5-6 of the plane first, indicating that the plane is in front of the line and making line AB hidden in the front view.

Step 2 Project the points where line AB crosses the plane in the top view to the front view. These projectors encounter line AB first, indicating that line AB is higher than the plane; thus the line is visible in the top view.

of the plane. Because line AB is above the plane, it is a visible line in the top view.

26.5 Planes

A plane may be represented in orthographic projection by any of the four combinations shown in **Figure 26.12**. In orthographic projection, a plane may appear as an **edge**, a **true-size** plane, or a **foreshortened** plane (**Figure 26.13**).

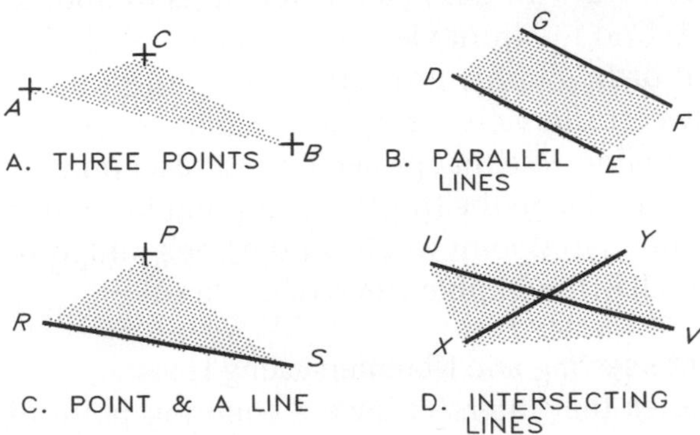

26.12 A plane can be represented as (A) three points not on a straight line, (B) two parallel lines, (C) a line and a point not on the line or its extension, and (D) two intersecting lines.

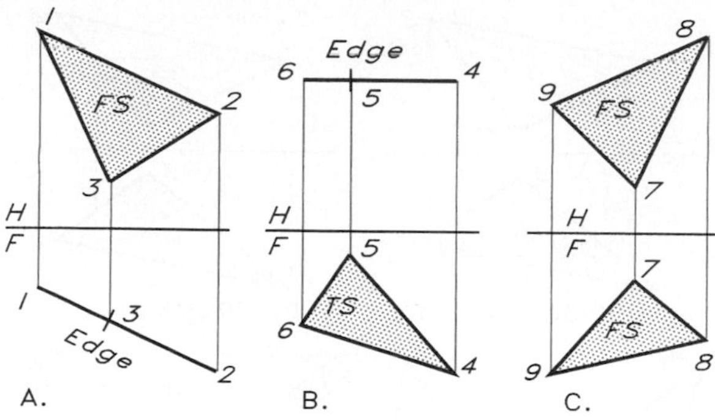

26.13 A plane in orthographic projection can appear as (A) an edge, (B) true size (TS), or (C) foreshortened (FS). A plane that is foreshortened in all principal views is an oblique plane.

Oblique planes (the general case) are not parallel to principal projection planes in any view (**Figure 26.14**). Principal planes are parallel to principal projection planes (**Figure 26.15**). The three types of principal planes are horizontal, frontal, and profile planes.

A **horizontal plane** is parallel to the horizontal projection plane and is true size in the top view (**Figure 26.15A**). To determine that the plane is horizontal, you must observe the front or profile views, where you can see its parallelism to the edge view of the horizontal plane.

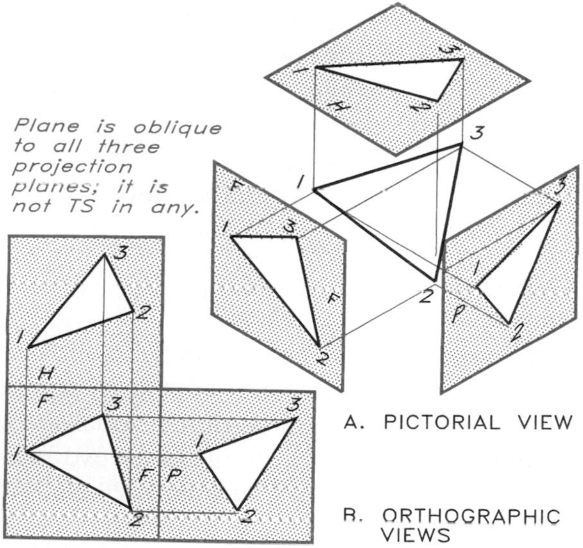

26.14 An oblique plane is neither parallel nor perpendicular to a projection plane. It is the general-case plane.

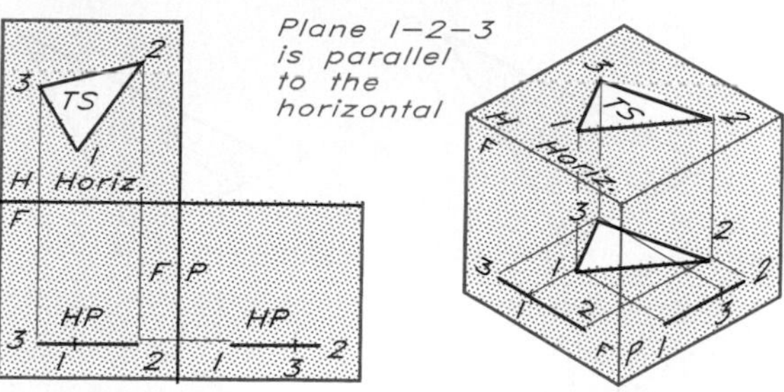

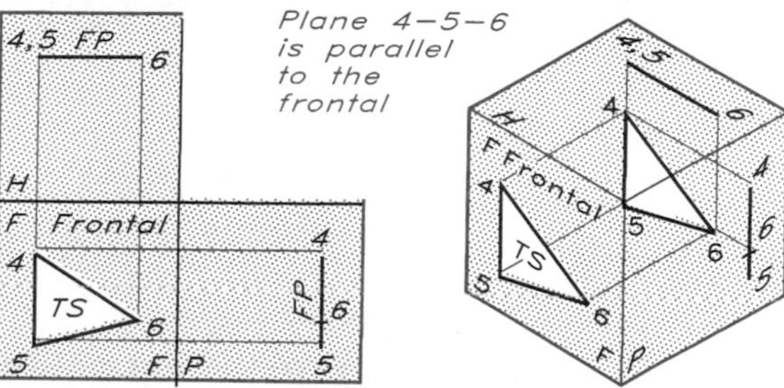

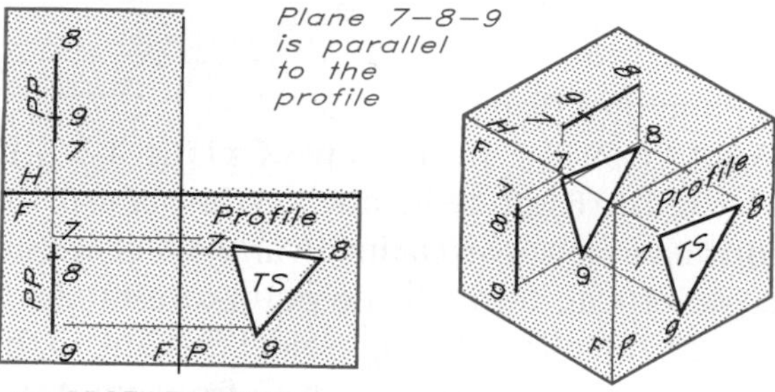

26.15 Principal planes.

A The horizontal plane is true size in the horizontal (top) view. It is parallel to the edge view of the horizontal plane in the front and profile views.

B The frontal plane is true size in the front view. It is parallel to the edge view of the frontal plane in the top and profile views.

C The profile plane is true size in the profile view. It is parallel to the edge view of the profile plane in the top and front views.

A **frontal plane** is parallel to the frontal projection plane and appears true size in the front view (**Figure 26.15B**). To determine that the plane is frontal, you must look at the top or profile views, where you can see its parallelism to the edge view of the frontal plane.

A **profile plane** is parallel to the profile projection plane and is true size in the side view (**Figure 26.15C**). To determine that the plane

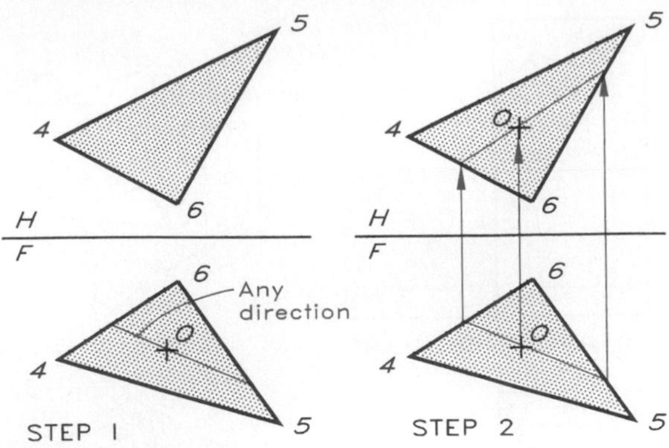

26.16 Locating a point on a plane.

Step 1 In the front view, draw a line through point O in any convenient direction except vertical.

Step 2 Project the ends of the line to the top view and draw the line. Project point O to this line.

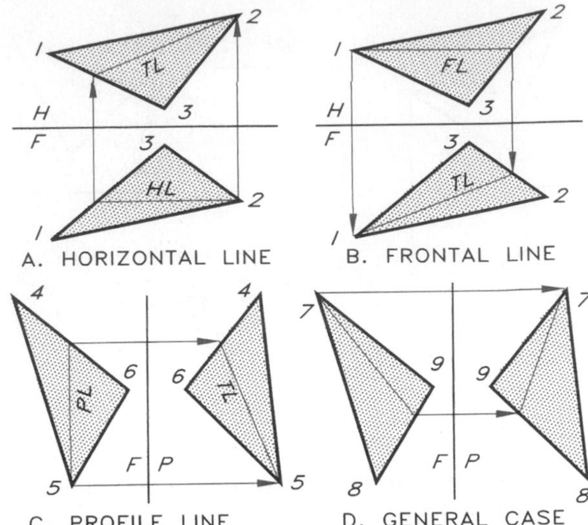

26.17 Finding principal lines on a plane.

A First, draw a horizontal line in the front view parallel to the edge view of the horizontal plane. Then, project it to the top view, where it is true length.

B First, draw a frontal line in the top view parallel to the edge view of the frontal plane. Then, project it to the front view, where it is true length.

C First, draw a profile line in the front view parallel to the edge view of the profile plane. Then, project it to the profile view, where it is true length.

D A general-case line is not parallel to the frontal, horizontal, or profile planes and is not true length in any principal view.

is profile, you must observe the top or front views, where you can see its parallelism to the edge view of the profile plane.

A Point on a Plane

Point O on the front view of plane 4-5-6 in **Figure 26.16** is to be located on the plane in the top view. First, draw a line in any direction (except vertical) through the point to establish a line on the plane. Then, project this line to the top view and project point O from the front view to the top view of the line.

Principal Lines on a Plane

Principal lines may be found in any view of a plane when at least two orthographic views of the plane are given. Any number of principal lines can be drawn on any plane.

Figure 26.17A shows a horizontal line parallel to the edge view of the horizontal projection plane in the front view. When projected to the top view, this line is true length.

Figure 26.17B shows a frontal line parallel to the edge view of the frontal projection plane in the top view. When projected to the front view, this line is true length.

Figure 26.17C shows a profile line parallel to the edge view of the profile projection plane in the front. When projected to the profile view, this line is true length.

In the general case (oblique), a line is not parallel to the edge view of any principal projection plane (**Figure 26.17D**). Therefore, it is not true length in any principal view.

26.6 Parallelism

Lines

Two parallel lines will appear parallel in all views except in views where both appear as points. Parallelism of lines in three-dimensional space cannot be determined without at least two adjacent orthographic views. In **Figure 26.18**, line AB was drawn parallel to the horizontal view of line 3-4 and through point O, which is the midpoint of AB. Line AB is drawn parallel to the

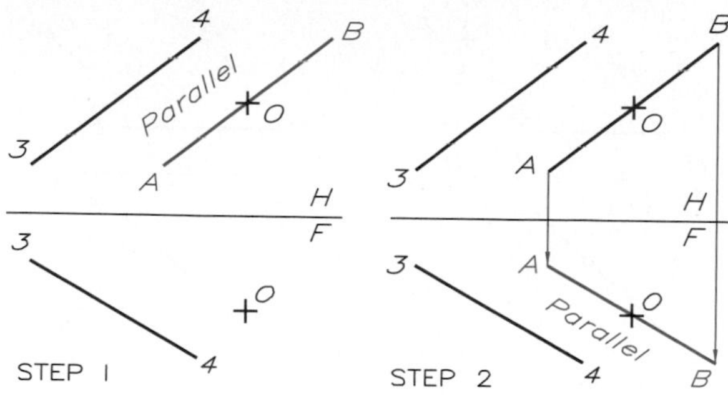

26.18 Constructing a line parallel to a line.

Step 1 Draw line AB parallel to the top view of line 3-4 with its midpoint at O.

Step 2 Draw the front view of line AB parallel to the front view of 3-4 through point O.

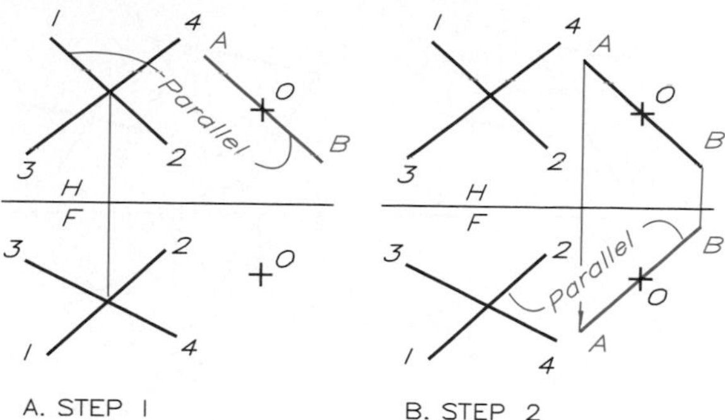

26.20 Constructing a line parallel to a plane.

Step 1 Draw line AB parallel to line 1-2 through point O.

Step 2 Draw line AB parallel to the same line, line 1-2, in the front view, which makes line AB parallel to the plane.

front view of 3-4 with its midpoint at O. The endpoints, A and B, are found in the front view by projecting points A and B to the front view from the top view with projectors perpendicular to the HF reference plane.

A Line and a Plane

A line is parallel to a plane when it is parallel to any line in the plane. In **Figure 26.19**, a line with its midpoint at point O is to be drawn parallel to plane 1-2-3. In this case line AB was drawn parallel to a line 1-3 in the plane in the top and front views. The line could have been drawn parallel to any line in the plane, making infinite solutions possible.

Figure 26.20 shows a similar example. Here, a line parallel to the plane with its midpoint at O was drawn. In this case, the plane is represented by two intersecting lines instead of an outlined area.

Planes

Two planes are parallel when intersecting lines in one plane are parallel to intersecting lines in the other (**Figure 26.21**). Determining whether planes are parallel is easy when both appear as edges in a view.

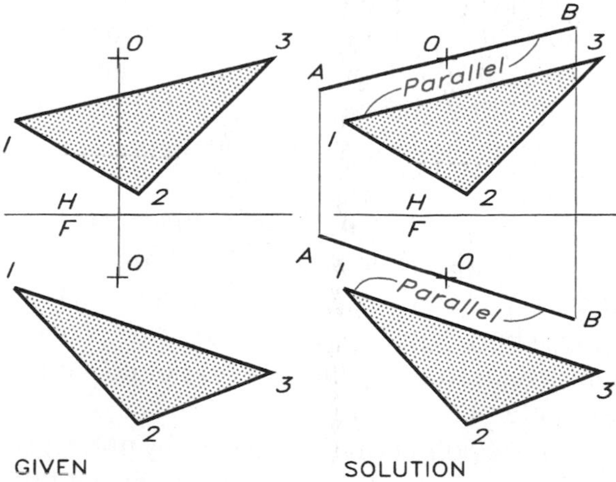

26.19 A line may be drawn through point O parallel to plane 1-2-3 if the line is parallel to any line in the plane. Draw line AB parallel to line 1-3 of the plane in the front and top views, making it parallel to the plane.

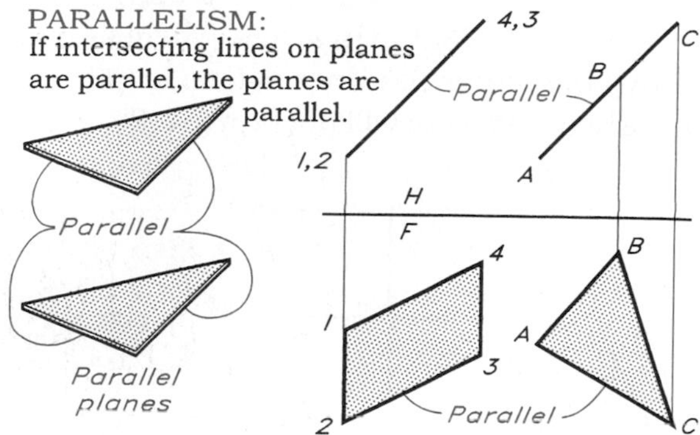

26.21 Two planes are parallel when intersecting lines in one are parallel to intersecting lines in the other. When parallel planes appear as edges, their edges are parallel.

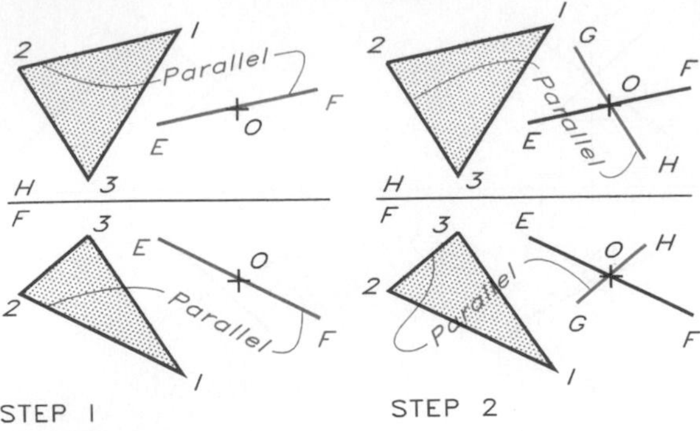

26.22 A plane through a point parallel to a plane.

Step 1 Draw EF parallel to any line in the plane (1-2 in this case). Show the line in both views.

Step 2 Draw a second line parallel to 2-3 in the top and front views. These intersecting lines passing through O represent a plane parallel to 1-2-3.

In **Figure 26.22**, a plane is to be drawn through point O parallel to plane 1-2-3. First, draw line EF through point O parallel to line 1-2 in the top and front views. Then, draw a second line through point O parallel to line 2-3 of the plane in the front and top views. These two intersecting lines form a plane parallel, to plane 1-2-3, as intersecting lines on one plane are parallel to intersecting lines on the other.

26.7 Perpendicularity

Lines

When two lines are perpendicular they can be drawn with a true 90° angle of intersection in views where one or both of them appear true length (**Figure 26.23**). In a view where neither of two perpendicular lines is true length, the angle between them will not be a true 90° angle.

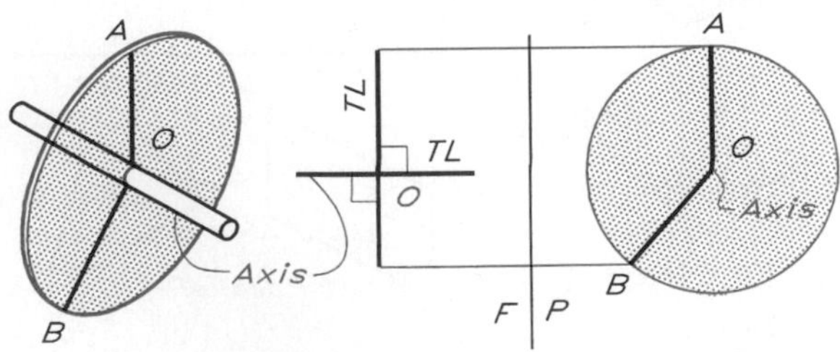

26.23 Perpendicular lines have a true angle of 90° between them in a view where one or both of them appear true length.

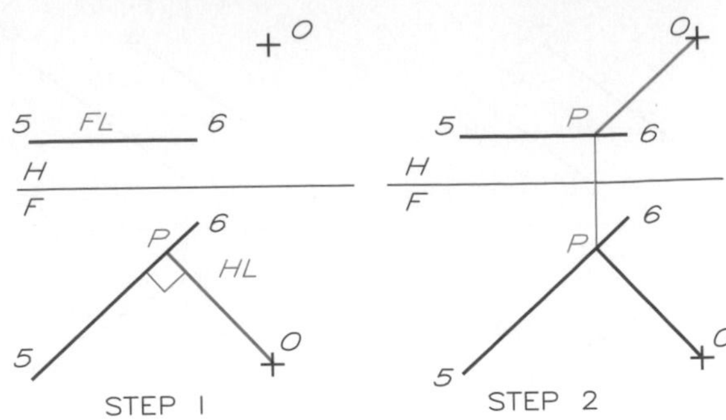

26.24 A line perpendicular to a principal line.

Step 1 Line 5-6 is a frontal line and is true length in the front view, so a perpendicular from point O makes a true 90° angle with it in the front view.

Step 2 Project point P to the top view and connect it to point O. As neither line is true length in the top view, they do not intersect at 90° in this view.

In **Figure 26.23** the axis is true length in the front view; therefore any spoke of the circular wheel is perpendicular to the axis in the front view. Spokes OA and OB are examples of true-length and foreshortened axes, respectively, in the front view.

A Line Perpendicular to a Principal Line In **Figure 26.24** a line is to be constructed through point O perpendicular to frontal line 5-6, which is true length in the front view. First, draw OP perpendicular to line 5-6 because it is true length. Then, project point P to the top view of line 5-6. In the top view, line OP cannot be drawn perpendicular to line 5-6 because neither of the lines is true length in this view.

A Line Perpendicular to an Oblique Line In **Figure 26.25**, a line is to be constructed from point O perpendicular to oblique line 1-2. First, draw a horizontal line from O to some convenient length in the front view, to point E in this example.

Locate point O in the top view by projection and draw line OE to make a 90° angle with the top view of 1-2. Line OE is true length in the top view, so it can be drawn making a true 90° angle with line 1-2.

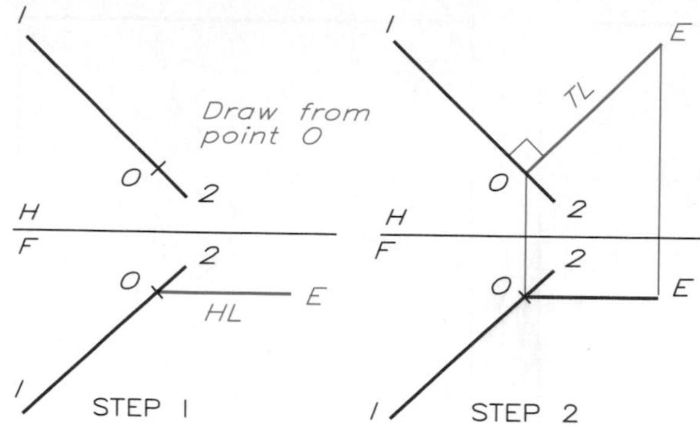

26.25 A line perpendicular to an oblique line.

Step 1 Draw a horizontal line (OE) from O in the front view.

Step 2 Horizontal line OE is true length in the top view, so draw it perpendicular to line 1-2 in this view.

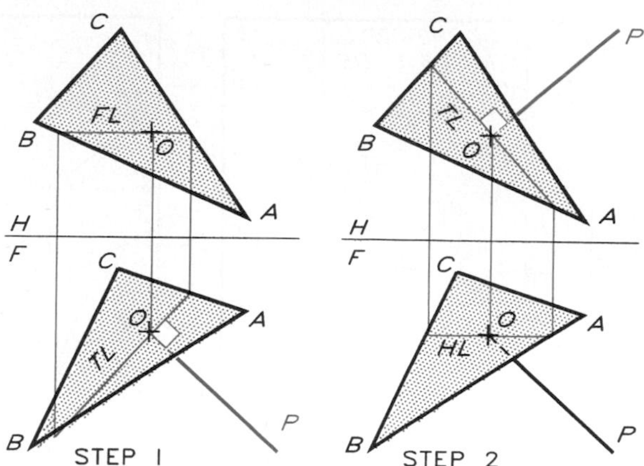

26.27 A line perpendicular to a plane.

Step 1 Draw a frontal line on the plane through O in the top view. This line is true length in the front view, so draw line OP perpendicular to this true-length line.

Step 2 Construct a horizontal line through point O in the front view. This line is true length in the top view, so draw line OP perpendicular to it.

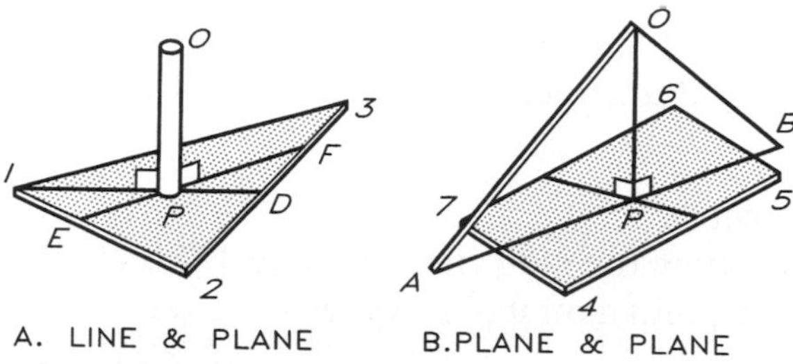

26.26 Perpendicularity of lines and planes.
A A line is perpendicular to a plane when it is perpendicular to two intersecting lines on the plane.
B A plane is perpendicular to another plane if it contains a line that is perpendicular to the other plane.

Planes

A line is perpendicular to a plane when it is perpendicular to any two intersecting lines in the plane (**Figure 26.26A**). A plane is perpendicular to another plane when a line in one plane is perpendicular to the other plane (**Figure 26.26B**).

A Line Perpendicular to a Plane

In **Figure 26.27** a line is to be drawn perpendicular to the plane from point O lying on the plane. First, draw a frontal line on the plane in the top view through O and project the line to the front view, where it is true length. Draw line OP at a convenient length and perpendicular to the true-length line.

Next, draw a horizontal line through point O in the front view and project it to the top view of the plane. Draw the top view of line OP perpendicular to this true-length horizontal line. This construction results in a line perpendicular to the plane because the line is perpendicular to two intersecting lines, a horizontal line and a frontal line in the plane.

If a plane contains a line that is perpendicular to another plane, then the two planes are perpendicular to each other. Perpendicular is the case regardless of the shape of the planes, although triangles are normally used to introduce principles owing to their clarity and simplicity.

Problems

Use size A sheets for the following problems and lay out your solutions with instruments. Each square on the grid is equal to 0.20 in., or 5 mm. Use either grid paper or plain paper. Label all reference planes and points in each problem with 1/8-in. letters and numbers using guidelines.

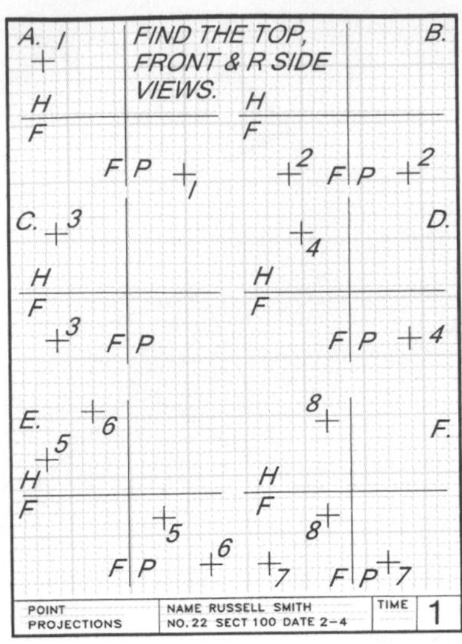

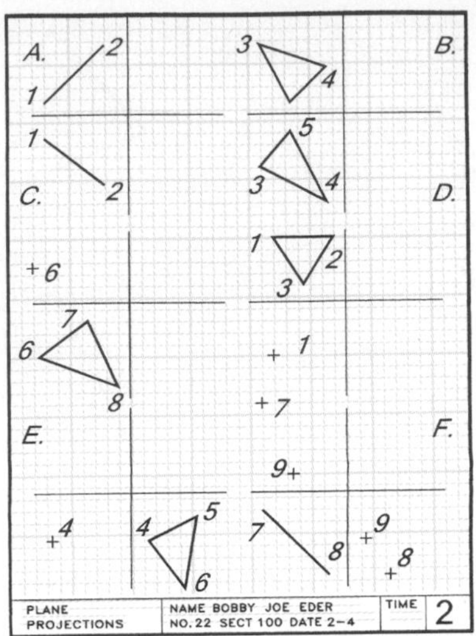

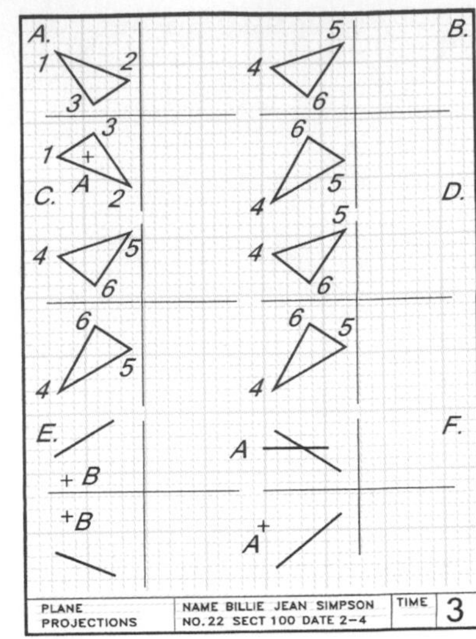

Sheet 1

A.–D. Draw three views (top, front, and right-side views) of the points.

E.–F. Draw the three views of the points and connect them to form lines.

Sheet 2

A.–B. Draw the right-side view of line 1-2 and plane 3-4-5.

C.–E. Draw the missing views of the planes so that 6-7-8 is a frontal plane, 1-2-3 is a horizontal plane, and 4-5-6 is a profile plane.

F. Complete the top and side views of the plane that appears as an edge in the front view.

Sheet 3

A. Draw the side view of plane 1-2-3 and locate point a on it in all views.

B. Draw the right-side view of plane 4-5-6 and draw two horizontal lines on it in all views.

C. Draw the right-side view of plane 4-5-6 and draw two frontal lines on it in all views.

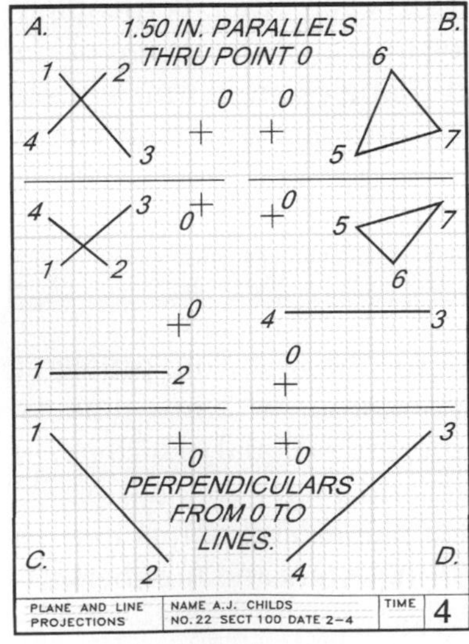

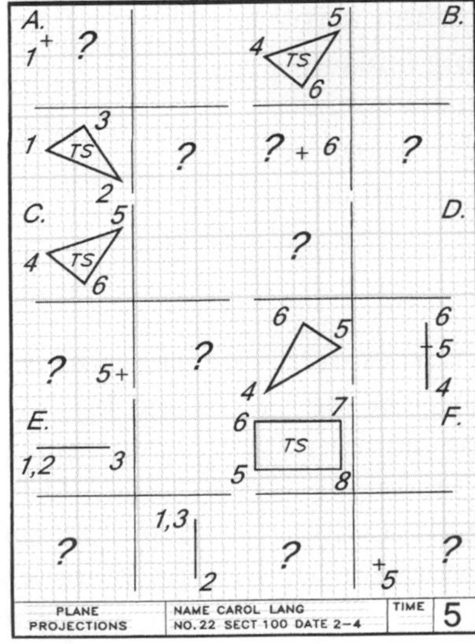

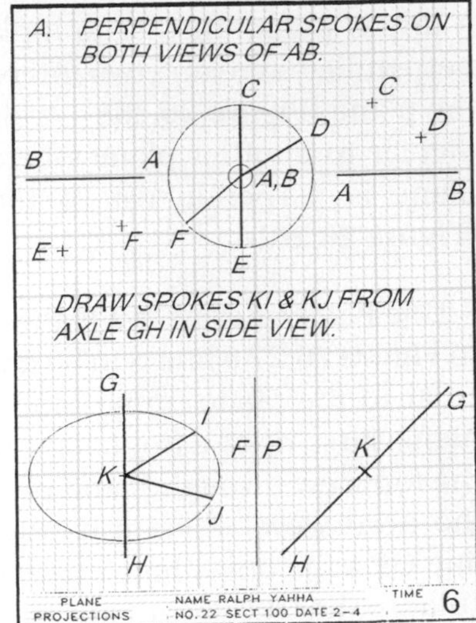

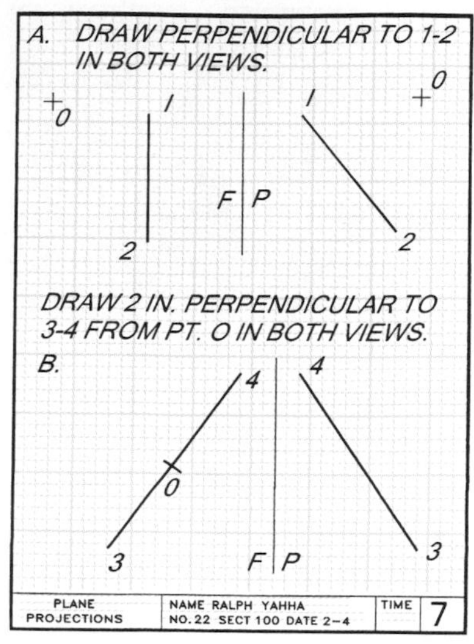
A. DRAW PERPENDICULAR TO 1-2
IN BOTH VIEWS.
DRAW 2 IN. PERPENDICULAR TO
3-4 FROM PT. O IN BOTH VIEWS.
B.
PLANE PROJECTIONS
NAME RALPH YAHHA
NO. 22 SECT 100 DATE 2-4
TIME
7

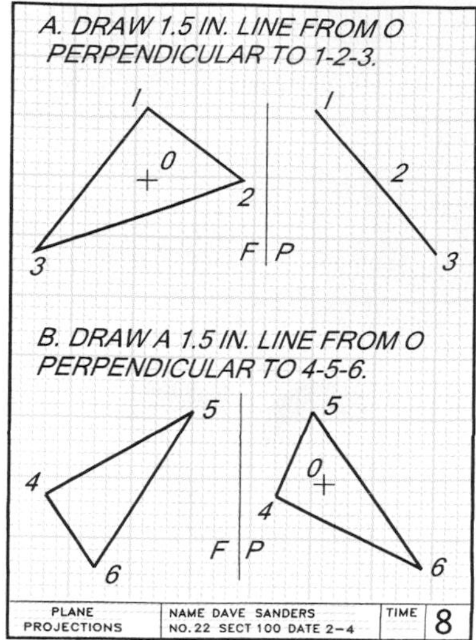
A. DRAW 1.5 IN. LINE FROM O
PERPENDICULAR TO 1-2-3.
B. DRAW A 1.5 IN. LINE FROM O
PERPENDICULAR TO 4-5-6.
PLANE PROJECTIONS
NAME DAVE SANDERS
NO. 22 SECT 100 DATE 2-4
TIME
8

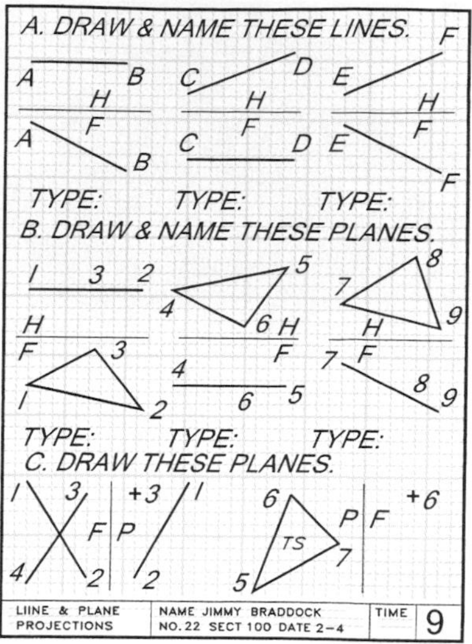
A. DRAW & NAME THESE LINES.
TYPE:
TYPE:
TYPE:
B. DRAW & NAME THESE PLANES.
TYPE:
TYPE:
TYPE:
C. DRAW THESE PLANES.
LIINE & PLANE PROJECTIONS
NAME JIMMY BRADDOCK
NO. 22 SECT 100 DATE 2-4
TIME
9

D. Draw the right-side view of plane 4-5-6 and draw two profile lines on it in all views.

E. Draw the three views of the given line and a line through B that is parallel to it.

F. Draw the three views of a plane formed by intersecting lines with A at the endpoint of one of the lines.

Sheet 4

A.–B. Draw 1.50-in. lines that pass through point O and are parallel to their respective planes.

C.–D. Through point O draw the top and front views of lines that are perpendicular to their respective lines.

Sheet 5

A.–E. Draw the missing views of the planes as three-view projections with top, front, and right-side views. Draw the missing views in the areas of the question marks.

Sheet 6

A. The views of four spokes are shown in the circular view of four wheels. Draw these spokes in their side views from their given endpoints to the axle AB.

B. Perpendicular spokes IK and JK are given in the front view. Draw them in their proper positions in the side view.

Sheet 7

A. Draw a line from O that is perpendicular to 1-2. Show it in both views.

B. Draw a 2-in.-long line that is perpendicular to 3-4. Show it in both views.

Sheet 8

A. Draw a 1.5-in.-long line from O on 1-2-3 that is perpendicular to the plane. Show it in both views.

B. Draw a 1.5-in.- (approximately) long line from O on 4-5-6 that is perpendicular to the plane. Show it in both views.

Sheet 9

A. Draw and name the type of each line that has been constructed.

B. Draw and name the type of each plane that has been constructed.

C. Draw the missing views of the two planes that are given in the front and profile views.

27

Primary Auxiliary Views: Descriptive Geometry

27.1 Introduction

Descriptive geometry is the projection of three-dimensional (3D) orthographic views onto a two-dimensional (2D) plane of paper to allow graphical determination of lengths, angles, shapes, and other geometric information. Orthographic projection is the basis for laying out and solving problems by descriptive geometry.

The primary auxiliary view, which permits analysis of 3D geometry, is essential to descriptive geometry. For example, the design of the lander frame shown in **Figure 27.1** contains many complex geometric elements (lines, angles, and surfaces) that were analyzed by descriptive geometry prior to its fabrication.

27.2 Geometry by AutoCAD

Five useful computer routines for solving descriptive geometry problems are covered in this section and documented in **Appendix 41.** The commands are *Perpline, Parallel, Transfer,*

27.1 This lunar lander was designed using the principles of descriptive geometry to determine lengths, angles, and areas. *(Courtesy of NASA.)*

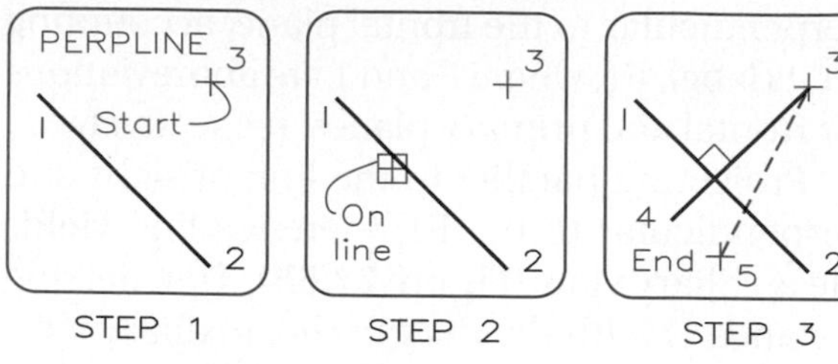

27.2 The *Perpline* command.

Step 1 *Command:* Perpline (Enter)
Select START of perpendicular line: (Select point 3.)

Step 2 *Select ANY point on line to which perp'lr:* (Select point on line.)

Step 3 *Select END point of desired perpendicular* (for length only): (Select point 5.) (3-4 is drawn.)

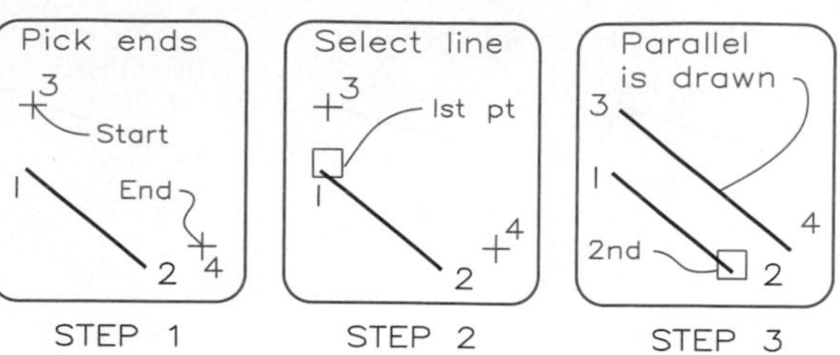

27.3 The *Parallel* command.

Step 1 *Command:* Parallel (Enter)
Select START point of parallel line: (Select point 3.)
Select END point of parallel line: (Select point 4.)

Step 2 *Select 1st point on line for parallelism:* (Select point 1.)

Step 3 *Select 2nd point on line for parallelism:* (Select point 2.) (3-4 is drawn.)

Copydist, and *Bisect** This *Lisp* program, called *Acad,* must be typed and loaded using AutoCAD's *Tools> Load Application* and its accompanying commands. To open *Acad,* type (Load "C:ACAD") at the *Command* line if the program is on the C drive, being sure to include the parentheses and quotation marks. Access the individual commands by typing their names one at a time—*Perpline,* for example.

Figure 27.2 shows how to draw line 3-4 perpendicular to line 1-2 with *Perpline.* Locate the starting point (3), select the line to which the constructed line is to be perpendicular, and pick a third point (5) in the general area of the line's endpoint (4).

In **Figure 27.3**, line 3-4 is drawn parallel to line 1-2 with *Parallel.* Locate the starting point of the parallel (point 3) and the general location of its endpoint (point 4). Select the endpoints of line 1-2 in the same order (from 1 to 2). The line is drawn.

The *Transfer* command (**Figure 27.4**) transfers distances from reference lines in the same way in which you use your dividers. Select endpoint 2 in the front view and then the reference line. Select endpoint 2 in the top view, then the auxiliary reference line, and a circle appears to locate the endpoint at its center in the auxiliary view.

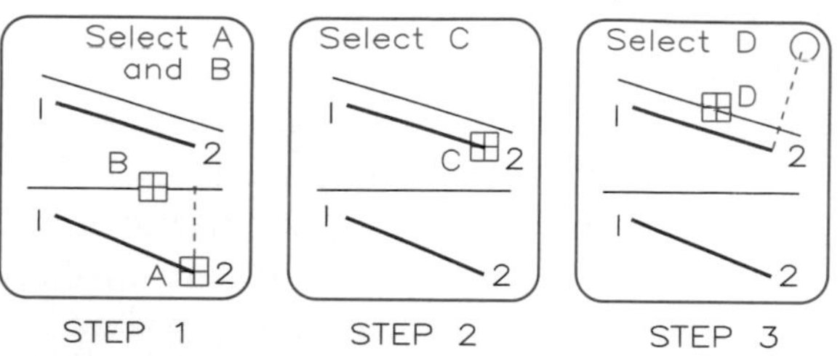

27.4 The *Transfer* command.

Step 1 *Command:* Transfer (Enter)
Select start of transfer distance: (Select point A.)
Select the reference plane: (Select point B.)

Step 2 *Select point to be projected:* (Select point C.)

Step 3 *Select other reference plane:* (Select point D.) (Point is located at the center of the circle.)

A distance may be copied from one position to another with *Copydist,* as shown in **Figure 27.5**. Select the endpoints of the line to be copied; locate its beginning point in the new position, and locate the direction of the line to be copied. A circle will appear to locate the endpoint of the line at its center the exact distance being copied.

The *Bisect* command bisects angles. It is sufficiently self-explanatory in its prompts on the screen, so we do not cover it here.

*These *LISP* commands were written by Professor Leendert Kersten of the University of Nebraska at Lincoln.

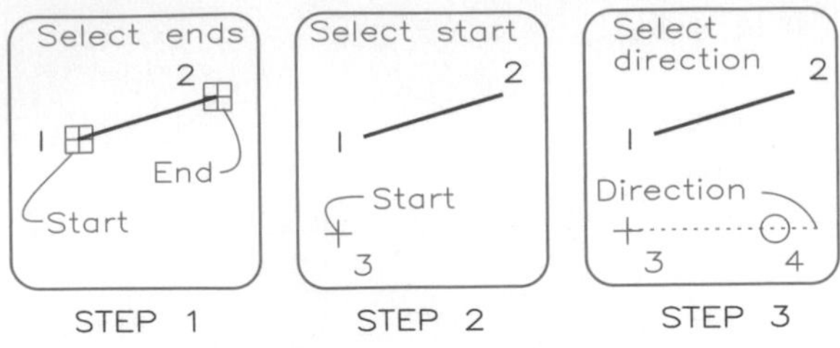

27.5 The *Copydist* command.

Step 1 *Command:* *Copydist* (Enter)
Select start point of line distance to be copied: (Select end 1.)
End point?: (Select end 2.)

Step 2 *Start point of new distance location:* (Select point 3.)

Step 3 *Which direction?:* (Select with cursor, and endpoint 4 is located at the center of the circle.)

27.3 True-Length Lines

Primary Auxiliary View

Figure 27.6 shows the top and front views of line 1-2 pictorially and orthographically. Line 1-2 is not a principal line, so it is not true length in a principal view. Therefore a primary auxiliary view is required to find its true-length view.

In **Figure 27.6A**, the line of sight is perpendicular to the front view of the line, and reference line F1 is parallel to the line's frontal view. The auxiliary plane is parallel to the line and perpendicular to the frontal plane, accounting for its label, F1, where F and 1 are abbreviations for frontal and primary planes, respectively.

Projecting parallel to the line of sight and perpendicular to the F1 reference line yields the auxiliary view (**Figure 27.6B**). Transferring distance D with dividers to the auxiliary view locates point 2 because the frontal plane appears as an edge in both the top and auxiliary views. Point 1 is located in the same manner, and the points are connected to find the true-length view of the line.

Figure 27.7 summarizes the steps of finding the true-length view of an oblique line. Letter all reference planes using the notation suggested in Chapter 26 and as shown in the examples throughout this chapter, with the

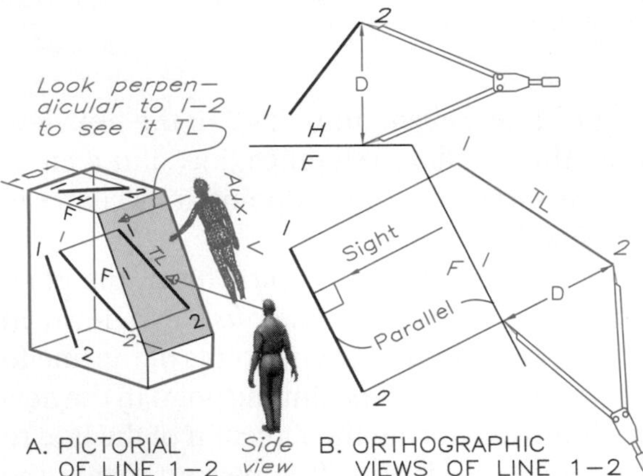

27.6 True-length line by auxiliary view.

A A pictorial of line 1-2 is shown inside a projection box where an auxiliary plane is parallel to the line and perpendicular to the frontal plane.

B The auxiliary view is projected from the front orthographic view to find 1-2 true length.

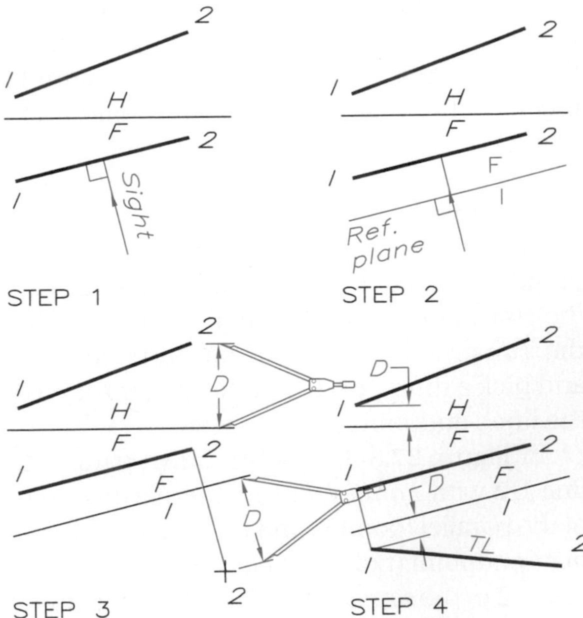

27.7 The true length of a line.

Step 1 To find the true length of line 1-2, the line of sight must be perpendicular to one of its views, the front view here.

Step 2 Draw the F1 reference line parallel to the line and perpendicular to the line of sight.

Step 3 Project point 2 perpendicularly from the front view. Transfer distance D from the top view to locate point 2 in the auxiliary view.

Step 4 Locate point 1 in the same manner to find line 1-2 true length in the auxiliary view.

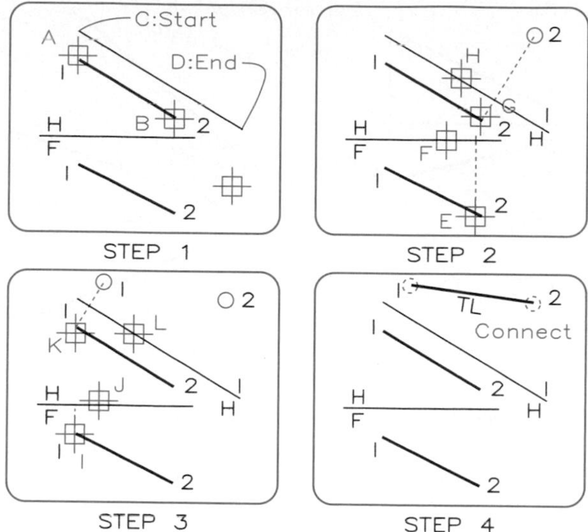

27.8 True length line by AutoCAD.

Step 1 *Command:* Parallel (Enter) (Follow the prompts in the caption of **Figure 27.3** to produce the reference line parallel to line 1-2 with *Parallel.*)

Step 2 *Command:* Transfer (Enter) (Follow the prompts in the caption of **Figure 27.4** to locate point 2 in the auxiliary view with *Transfer.*)

Step 3 Locate point 1 in the auxiliary view by using *Transfer.*

Step 4 Draw a line from the centers of the circles obtained in the preceding steps by using the *Center* option of the *Osnap* command. *Erase* the circles after this step.

exception of noted dimensions such as D. Use your dividers to transfer dimensions.

AutoCAD Method The method of using the *Parallel* and *Transfer* commands to find a line's true length by an auxiliary view is illustrated in **Figure 27.8**. Draw a line parallel to the top view of line 1-2, and *Transfer* the endpoints of the line. Use the *Center* option of the *Osnap* command to draw line 1-2 from the centers of the circles. *Erase* the circles afterward.

True Length by Analytical Geometry

The method of finding the true length of frontal line 3-4 mathematically is shown in **Figure 27.9**. The Pythagorean theorem states that the hypotenuse of a right triangle is equal to the square root of the sum of the squares of the other two sides. Because the line is true length

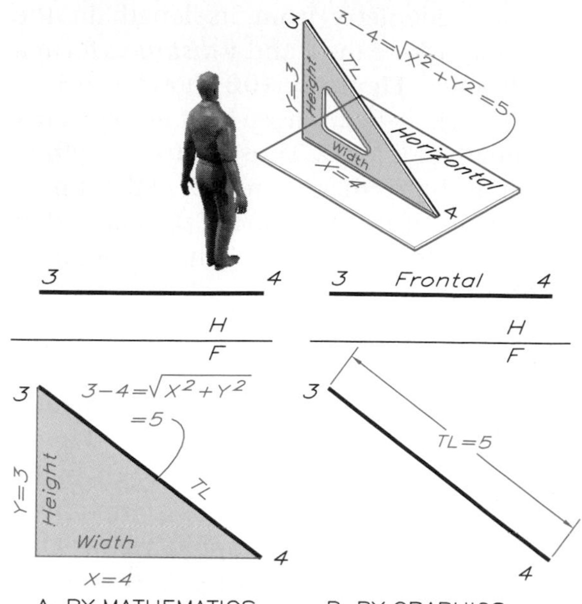

27.9 Apply the Pythagorean theorem to calculate the length of a line that appears true length in a view, the front view here. Because line 3-4 is true length in the front view, it can be measured to find its length.

in the front view, measuring that length provides a check on the mathematical solution.

The true length of a line shown pictorially in **Figure 27.10A** (line 1-2) is determined by

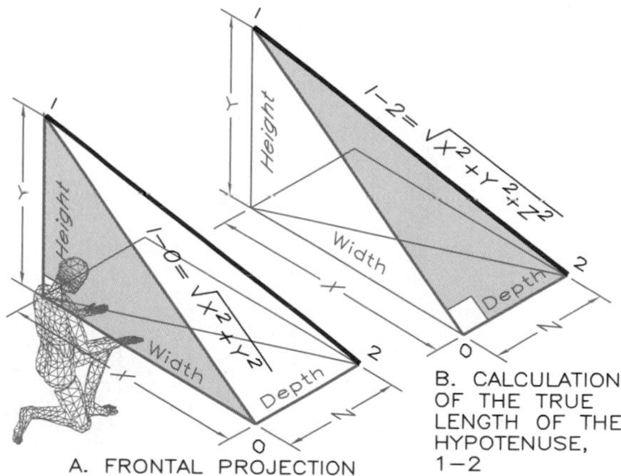

27.10 To calculate the true length of a 3D line that is not true length in the principal view, find (A) the frontal projection, line 1-O, by using the *x* and *y* distances, and (B) the hypotenuse of the right triangle 1-O-2 by using the length of line 1 O and the Z distance. Then, apply the Pythagorean theorem to find its length, 5. Orthographic views are shown in (C).

analytical geometry from its length in the front view, where the *x* and *y distances* form a right triangle. **Figure 27.10B** shows a second right triangle, 1-O-2, whose hypotenuse is the true length of line 1-2. Thus the true length of an oblique line is the square root of the sum of the squares of the *X*, *Y*, and *Z* distances that correspond to the width, height, and depth of the triangles.

True-Length Diagram

A true-length diagram is two perpendicular lines used to find a line true length (**Figure 27.11**). The two measurements laid out on the true-length diagram may be transferred from any two adjacent orthographic views. One measurement is the distance between the endpoints in one of the views. The other measurement, from the adjacent view, is the distance between the endpoints perpendicular to the reference line between the two views. Here, these dimensions are vertical, V, and horizontal, H, between points 1 and 2. This method does not give the line's direction, only its true length.

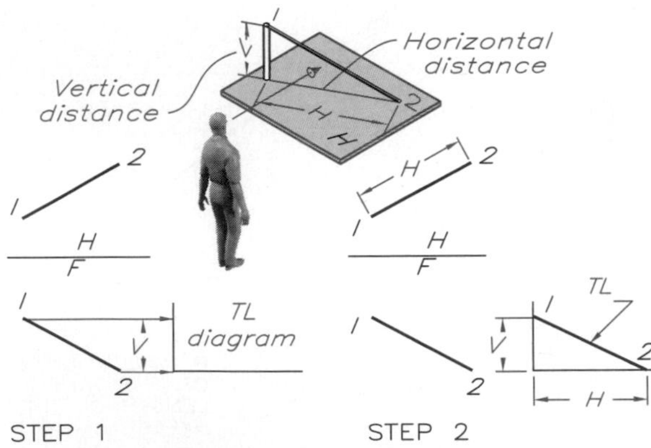

27.11 Using a true-length diagram.

Step 1 Transfer the vertical distance between the ends of line 1-2 to the vertical leg of the TL diagram.

Step 2 Transfer the horizontal length of the line in the top view to the horizontal leg of the TL diagram. The diagonal is the true length of line 1-2.

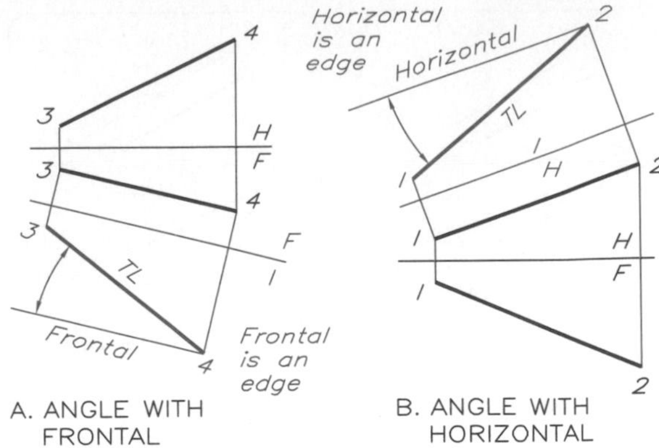

27.12 Angles between lines and principal planes.

A An auxiliary view projected from the front view that shows the line true length will show the frontal plane as an edge, where its angle with the frontal plane can be measured.

B An auxiliary view projected from the top that shows the line true length will show the horizontal plane as an edge, where its angle with the horizontal plane can be measured.

27.4 Angles between Lines and Principal Planes

To measure the angle between a line and a plane, the line must appear true length and the plane as an edge in the same view (**Figure 27.12**). A principal plane appears as an edge in a primary auxiliary view projected from it, so the angle a line makes with this principal plane can be measured if the line is true length in this auxiliary view.

27.5 Sloping Lines

Slope is the angle that a line makes with the horizontal plane when the line is true length and the plane is an edge. **Figure 27.13** shows the three methods for specifying slope: **slope angle, percent grade**, and **slope ratio**.

The **slope angle** of line AB in **Figure 27.14** is 31°. It can be measured in the front view, where the line is true length.

Percent grade is the ratio of the vertical (rise) divided by the horizontal (run) between the ends of a line, expressed as a percentage. The percent grade of line AB is determined in

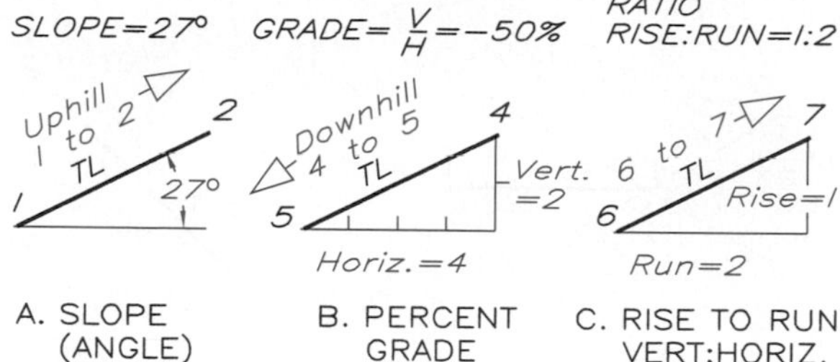

27.13 The inclination of a line with the horizontal may be measured and expressed as (A) slope angle, (B) percent grade, or (C) slope ratio.

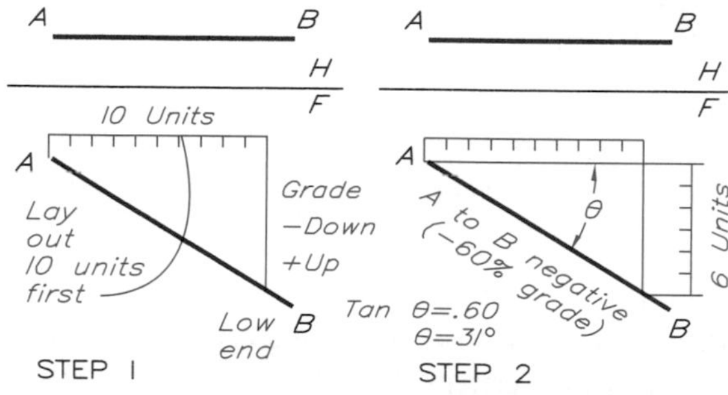

27.14 Percent grade of a line.

Step 1 The percent grade of a line can be measured in the view where the horizontal appears as an edge and the line is true length (here, the front view). Lay off 10 units parallel to the horizontal from the end of the line.

Step 2 A vertical distance from the end of the 10 units to the line measures 6 units. The percent grade is 6 divided by 10, or 60%. This is a negative grade from A to B because the line slopes downward from A. The tangent of this slope angle is 6/10, or 0.60, which can be used to verify the slope of 31° from trigonometric tables.

the front view of **Figure 27.14**, where the line is true length and the horizontal plane is an edge. Line AB has a −60% grade from A to B because the line slopes downward; it would be positive (upward) from B to A. Trigonometric tables verify that an angle whose tangent is 0.60 (6/10) is 31°.

The slope ratio is the ratio of a rise of 1 to the run. The rise is always written as 1 followed by a colon and the run (for example, 1:10, 1:200). **Figure 27.15** illustrates the graphical method of finding the slope ratio. The rise of 1 unit is laid off on the true-length view of CD. The corresponding run measures 2 units, for a slope ratio of 1:2.

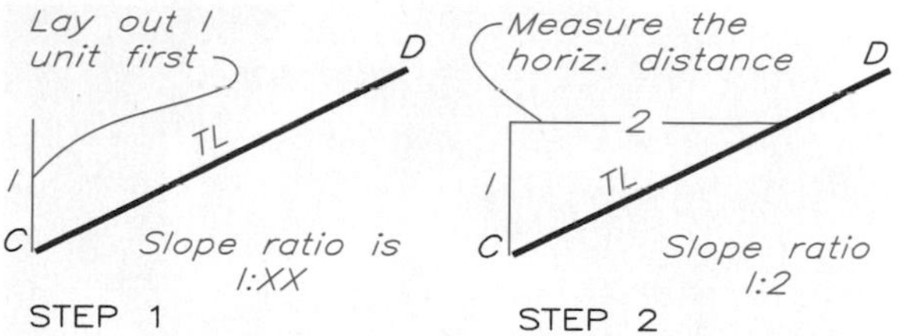

27.15 Slope ratio.

Step 1 Slope ratio always begins with 1, so lay out a vertical distance of 1 from end C.

Step 2 Lay off a horizontal distance from the end of the vertical line and measure it. It is 2, so the slope ratio (always expressed as 1:XX) of this line is 1:2.

The slopes of oblique lines are found true length in an auxiliary view projected from the top view so that the horizontal reference plane will appear as an edge (**Figure 27.16A**). The slope is expressed as an angle, or 26°.

To find the percent grade of an oblique line (**Figure 27.16B**), lay off 10 units horizontally, parallel to the H1 reference line. The corresponding vertical distance measures 4.5 units, for a −45% grade from point 3 to point 4.

The principles of true-line length and angles between lines and planes are useful in applications such as the design of aggregate conveyors (**Figure 27.17**), where slope is crucial to optimal operation of the equipment.

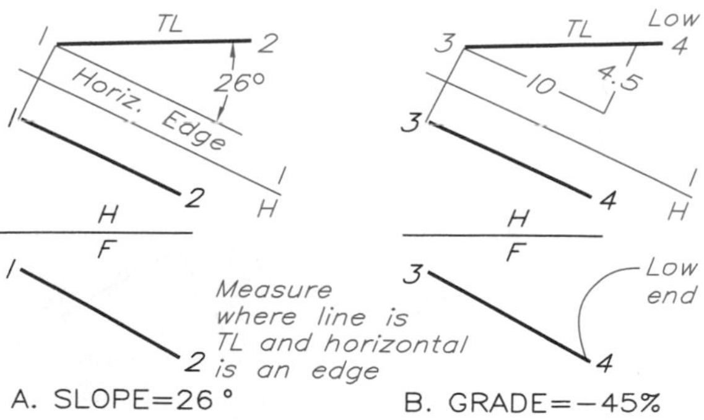

27.16 Slope of an oblique line.

A Find the slope angle of an oblique line (26° in this case) in a view where the horizontal appears as an edge and the line is true length.

B Find the percent grade in an auxiliary view projected from the top view where line 3-4 is true length (−45% from 3 to 4, the low end, in this case).

27.17 The design of these aggregate conveyors required the application of sloping-line principles to obtain their optimal slopes. *(Courtesy of Link-Belt.)*

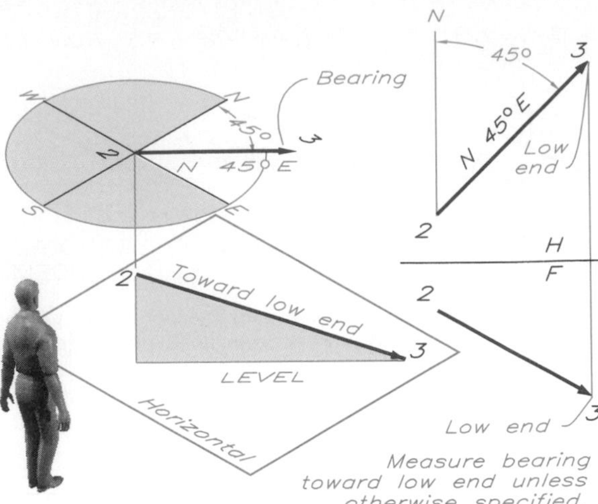

27.19 Measure the compass bearing of a line in the top view toward its low end (unless otherwise specified). Line 2-3 has a bearing of N 45° E from 2 to 3 toward the low end at point 3.

27.6 Bearings and Azimuths of Lines

Two types of bearings of a line's direction are compass bearings and azimuths. Compass bearings are angular measurements from north or south. The line in **Figure 27.18A** that makes a 30° angle with north has a bearing of N 30° W. The line making a 60° angle with south toward the east has a bearing of south 60° east, or S 60° E. Because a compass can be read only when held level, bearings of a line must be found in the top, or horizontal, view.

Azimuths are measured clockwise from north through 360° (**Figure 27.18B**). Azimuth bearings are written N 120°, N 210°, and so on, indicating that they are measured from north.

The bearing of a line is toward the low end of the line unless otherwise specified. For example, line 2-3 in **Figure 27.19** has a bearing of N 45° E because the line's low end is point 3 in the front view.

Figure 27.20 shows how to find the bearing and slope of a line. This information may be

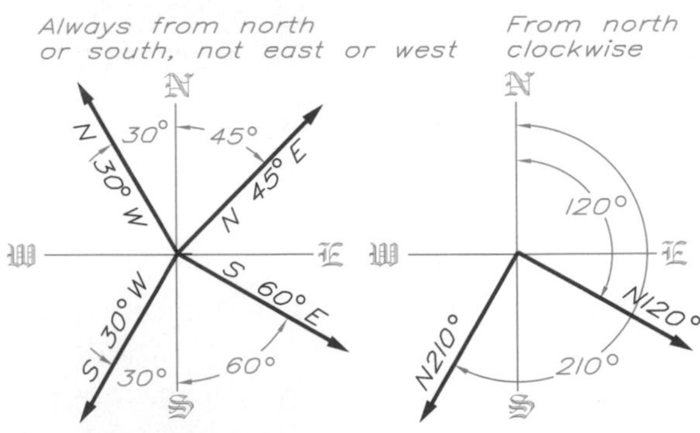

27.18 Compass directions.

A Compass bearings are measured with respect to north and south.

B Azimuths are measured clockwise from north up to 360°.

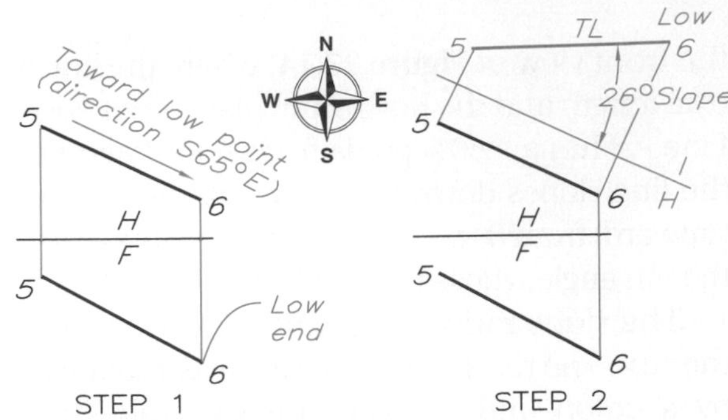

27.20 The slope and bearing of a line.

Step 1 Measure the bearing in the top view toward its low end, or S 65° E in this case.

Step 2 Measure the slope angle of 26° from the H1 reference line in an auxiliary view projected from the top view, where the line is true length.

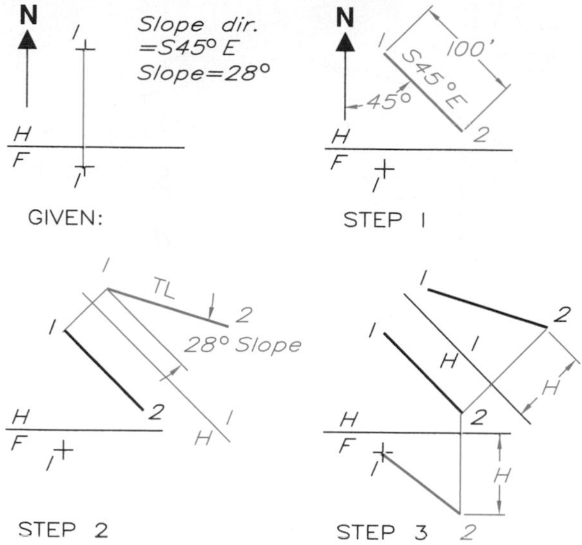

27.21 A line from slope specifications.
Required Draw a line through point 1 that bears S 45° E for 100 ft horizontally and slopes 28°.

Step 1 Draw the bearing and the horizontal distance in the top view.

Step 2 Project an auxiliary view from the top view and draw the line at a slope of 28°.

Step 3 Find the front view of line 1-2 by locating point 2 in the front view.

used verbally to describe the line as having a bearing of S 65° E and a slope of 26° from point 5 to point 6. This information and the location of one point in the top and front views is sufficient to complete a 3D drawing of a line, as illustrated in **Figure 27.21**.

27.7 Application: Plot Plans

A typical plot plan for a tract of land is shown in **Figure 27.22**. The boundary lines, their bearings, and the interior angles are used to legally define the property. AutoCAD provides two options: **Decimal** for measuring lengths and **Surveyor's Units** for measuring compass directions that are used to draw and label a plot plan.

AutoCAD Method Type *Units* (Enter) to obtain the *Drawing Units* box, select *Decimal* from the *Length Type* panel, set the decimal *Precision* to 0.00, and select *Inches* from the *Insertion scale*

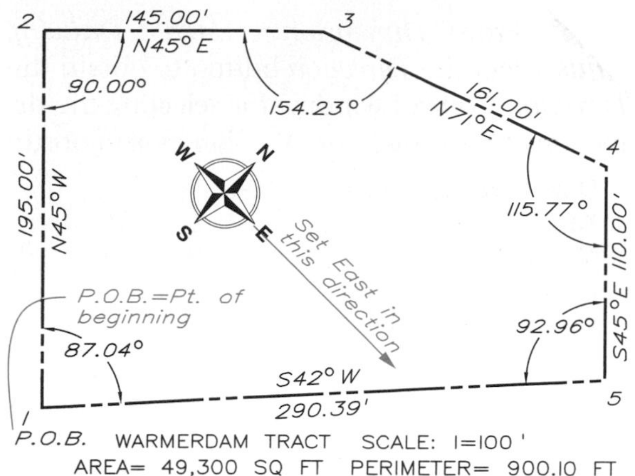

27.22 This typical plot plan shows the lengths and bearings of each side of a tract of land, the interior angles, and the north arrow by using AutoCAD's *Surveyor's units* option.

panel. (Refer to Section 37.13 to review how drawings are scaled.) From the *Angle Type* panel, the following options are available:

Decimal degrees	*45.00*
Deg/Min/Sec	*45d0'0"*
Grads	*50.0000g*
Radians	*0.7854r*
Surveyor's units	*N 45d0'0" E*

Pick *Surveyor's Units,* and select the angular units from the *Angle Precision* panel. Angles of lines will be displayed at the *Command* line with respect to north or south in east or west directions, for example, N 30d 45'10", where d = degrees, ' = minutes, and " = seconds. A line can be specified at the *Command* line and drawn from a point as @145'00"<n45d00'00"e, as was line 2-3 in **Figure 27.22**.

Lengths and directions of previously drawn lines display on the screen by typing *List* and selecting a line. Obtain length and directions for each line and type them on the outside and inside of each boundary line of the surveyor's plot. **Figure 27.22** shows the proper application of the length and direction of line 2-3 as 145.00' and N 45° E, respectively.

Interior angles are given without compass direction as 152°34'17", or as decimal fractions,

Dimension> Units> Drawing
he *Direction* button to obtain the
trol window for selecting the di-
and hence the direction of north:

angle 0:

East	*3 o'clock*	=	*0*
North	*12 o'clock*	=	*90*
West	*9 o'clock*	=	*180*
South	*6 o'clock*	=	*270*
Other	*Pick/Type*		

Select *Other* and specify the direction of east by picking two west-to-east points on your drawing and pick *OK* (**Figure 27.23**). These points establish the direction of north as well.

The default (standard) directional angle of a line is counterclockwise (**Figure 27.23**). Select the *Clockwise* button in the *Drawing Units* window to measure angles in this direction.

Use the *Dist* command to find the lengths and directions of lines by selecting endpoints of the lines clockwise about the plot from the point of beginning (P.O.B.).

27.8 Contour Maps and Profiles

A contour map depicts variations in elevation of the earth in two dimensions (**Figure 27.24**). Three-dimensional representations involve (1) conventional orthographic views of the contour map combined with profiles and (2) contoured surface views (often in the form of models).

27.23 Compass direction by AutoCAD.

Step 1 Insert the compass arrow on the plot plan. Then use the *Units* command and select 5, *Surveyor's units*. It will prompt you to give the direction for east. Select a point on the drawing with the cursor and select two points (west to east) to indicate the direction of east.

Step 2 Using the *Dist* command, select the endpoints of each side clockwise about the plot from the point of beginning (P.O.B.). Label the sides with direction inside and lengths outside the plot.

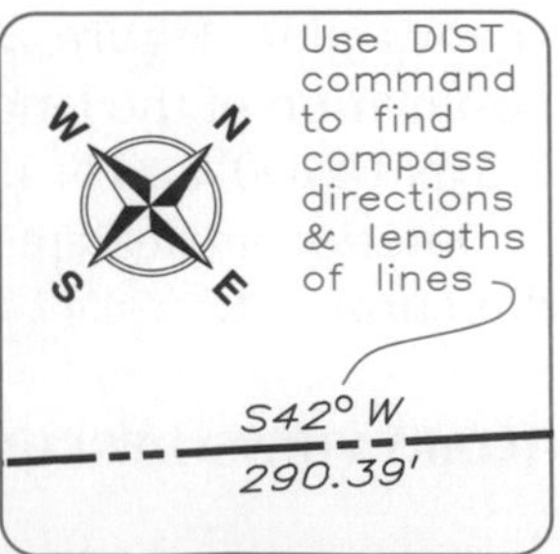

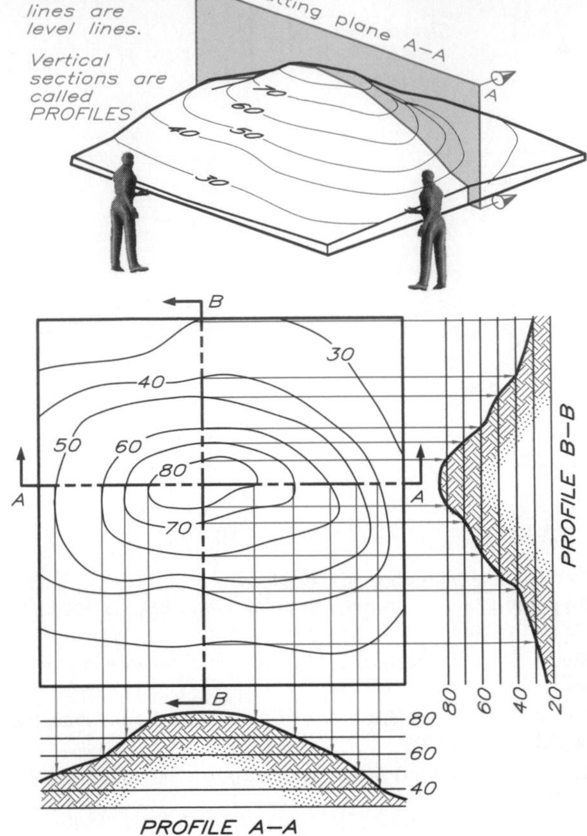

27.24 A contour map shows variations in elevation on a surface. A profile is a vertical section through the contour map. To construct a profile, draw elevation lines parallel to the cutting planes, spacing them equally to show the difference in elevations of the contours (10 ft in this case). Then, project crossing points of contours and the cutting plane to their respective elevations in the profile, and connect them.

Contour lines are horizontal (level) lines that represent constant elevations from a horizontal datum such as sea level. The vertical interval of spacing between the contours shown in **Figure 27.24** is 10 ft. Contour lines may be thought of as the intersection of horizontal planes with the surface of the earth.

Contour maps contain contour lines that connect points of equal elevation on the earth's surface and therefore are continuous (**Figure 27.24**). The closer the contour lines are to each other, the steeper the terrain is.

Profiles are vertical sections through a contour map that show the earth's surface at any

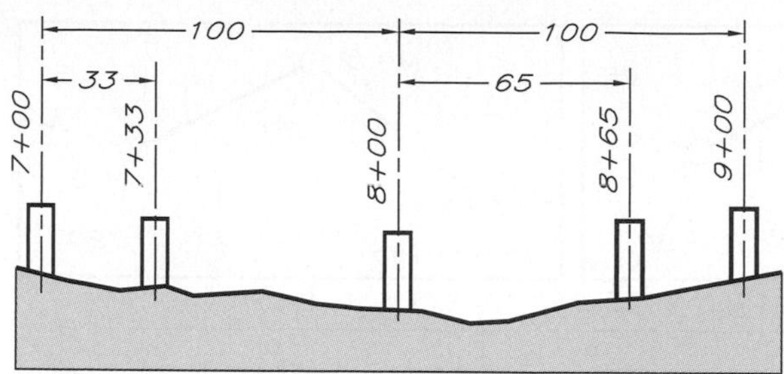

27.25 Primary station points are located 100 ft apart; for example, station 7 is 700 ft from station 0 (not shown). A point 33 ft beyond station 7 is labeled station 7 + 33. A point 865 ft from the origin is labeled station 8 + 65.

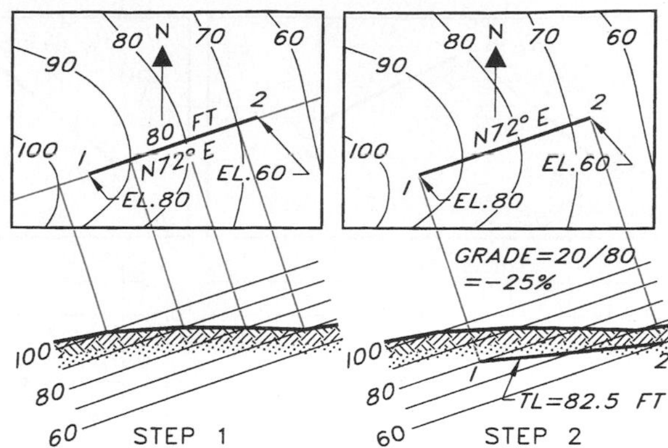

27.26 Drawing profiles (vertical sections).

Step 1 An underground pipe has elevations of 80 ft and 60 ft at its ends. Project an auxiliary view perpendicularly from the top view and draw contours at 10-ft intervals corresponding to their elevations in the plan view. Locate the ground surface by projecting from the contour lines in the plan view.

Step 2 Locate points 1 and 2 at elevations of 80 ft and 60 ft in the profile. Line 1-2 is true length in the section, so measure its slope (percent grade) here and label its bearing and slope in the top view.

desired location (**Figure 27.24**). Contour lines represent edge views of equally spaced horizontal planes in profiles. True representation of a profile involves the use of a vertical scale equal to the scale of the contour map; however, the vertical scale usually is drawn larger to emphasize changes in elevation that often are slight compared with horizontal dimensions.

Contoured surfaces also are depicted in drawings with contour lines or on models. When applied to objects other than the earth's surface—such as airfoils, automobile bodies, ship hulls, and household appliances—this technique of showing contours is called **lofting**.

Station numbers identify distances on a contour map. Surveyors use a chain (metal tape) 100 ft long, so primary stations are located 100 ft apart (**Figure 27.25**). For example, station 7 is 700 feet from the beginning point, station 0; a point 33 feet beyond station 7 is station 7 + 33.

A **plan-profile** combines a section of a contour map (a plan view) and a vertical section (a profile view). Engineers use plan-profile drawings extensively for construction projects such as pipelines, roadways, and waterways.

Application: Vertical Sections

In **Figure 27.26**, a vertical section passed through the top view of an underground pipe gives a profile view. The pipe is known to have elevations of 80 ft at point 1 and 60 ft at point 2.

27.27 Pipeline construction applies the principles of descriptive geometry, true-length lines, and slopes of 3D lines. *(Courtesy of American Gas Association, Inc.)*

Project an auxiliary view perpendicularly from the top view, locate contour lines, and draw the top of the earth over the pipe in profile. To measure the true lengths and angles of slope in the profile, use the same scale for both the contour map and the profile.

Pipeline installation (**Figure 27.27**) requires major outlays for engineering design and construction. The use of profiles, found graphically,

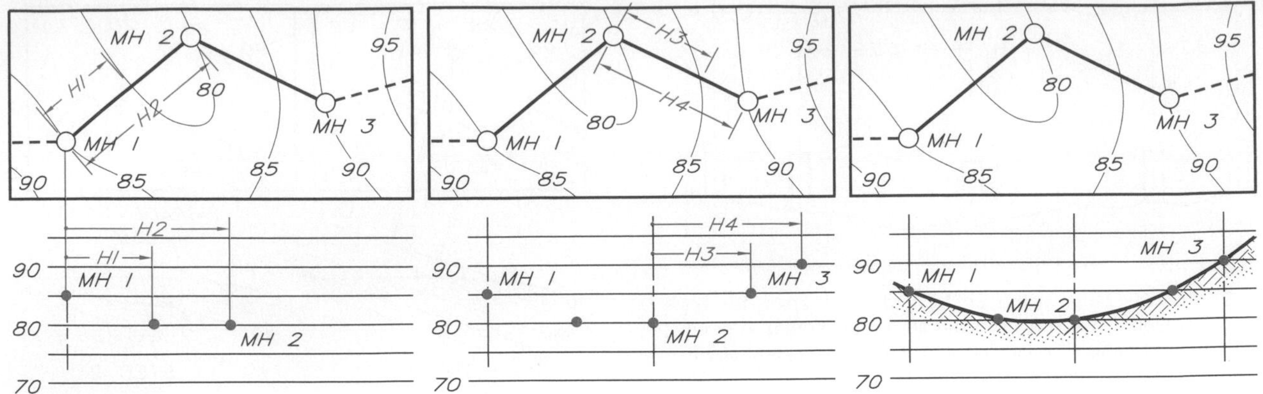

27.28 Plan-profile: Vertical section.

Required Find the profile of the earth's surface over the pipeline.

Step 1 Transfer distances H1 and H2 from MH 1 in the plan to their respective elevations in the profile view.

Step 2 Measure distances H3 and H4 from MH 2 in the plan and transfer them to their respective elevations in profile. These points represent elevations of points on the earth above the pipe.

Step 3 Connect these points with a freehand line and crosshatch the drawing to represent the earth's surface. Draw centerlines to show the locations of the three manholes.

is the best way to make cost estimations for constructing ditches for laying underground pipe.

27.9 Plan-Profiles

A plan-profile drawing shows an underground drainage system from manhole 1 to manhole 3 in **Figures 27.28** and **27.29**. The profile has a larger vertical scale to emphasize variations in the earth's surface and the grade of the pipe, although the vertical scale may be drawn at the same scale as the plan if desired.

The location of manhole 1 is projected to the profile orthographically, but the remaining points are not (**Figure 27.28**). Instead, transfer

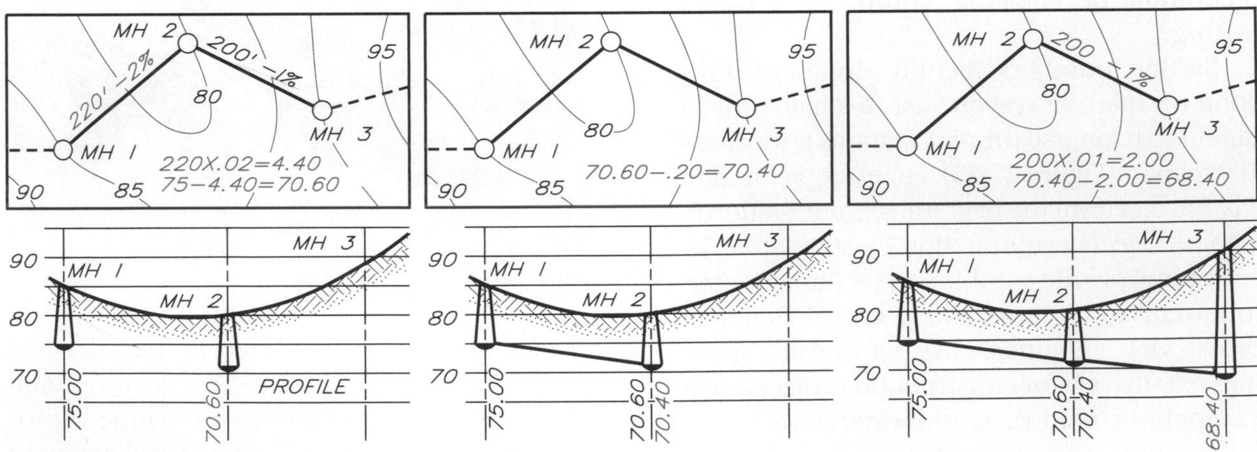

27.29 Plan-profile: Manhole location.

Step 1 Multiply the horizontal distance from MH 1 to MH 2 by −2%. Find the elevation of the bottom of MH 2 by subtracting the amount of fall from the elevation of MH 1 (70.60').

Step 2 The lower side of MH 2 is 0.20 ft lower than the inlet side to compensate for loss of head (pressure) because of the turn in the pipeline. Find the elevation on the lower side (70.40') and label it.

Step 3 Calculate the elevation of MH 3 (200 ft) at a −1% grade from MH 2 (68.40'). Draw the flow line of the pipeline from manhole to manhole and label the elevations at each manhole.

the distances where the contour lines cross the top view of the pipe to their respective elevations in the profile with your dividers to show the surface of the ground over the pipe.

Figure 27.29 shows the manholes, their elevations, and the bottom line of the pipe. Find the drop from manhole 1 to manhole 2 (4.40 ft) by multiplying the horizontal distance of 220.00 ft by a −2.00% grade. The pipes intersect at manhole 2 at an angle, so the flow of the drainage is disrupted at the turn. A drop of 0.20 ft (2.4 in.) across the bottom of the manhole compensates for the loss of pressure (head) through the manhole.

The true lengths of the pipes in the profile view cannot be measured when the vertical scale is different from the horizontal scale. Instead, trigonometry must be used to calculate them.

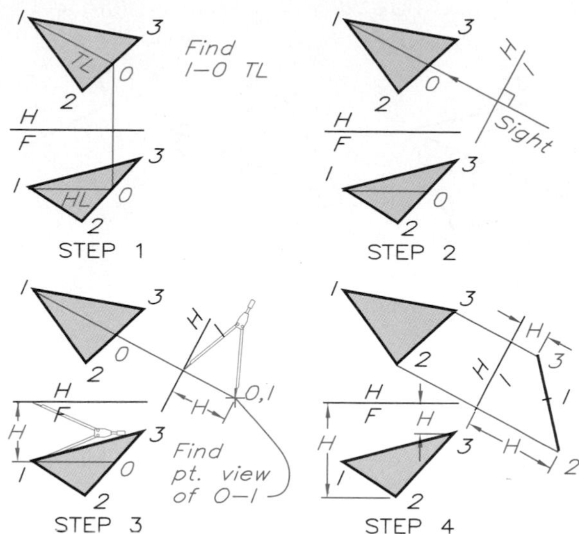

27.31 The edge view of a plane.

Step 1 To find the edge view of plane 1-2-3, draw horizontal line 1-0 on its front view of the plane and project it to the top view, where it is true length.

Step 2 Draw a line of sight parallel to the true-length line 1-0. Draw H1 perpendicular to the line of sight.

Step 3 Find the point view of 1-0 in the auxiliary view by transferring height H from the front view.

Step 4 Locate points 2 and 3 in the same manner to find the edge view of the plane.

27.10 Edge Views of Planes

The edge view of a plane appears in a view where any line on the plane appears as a point. Recall that you can find a line as a point by projecting from its true-length view (**Figure 27.30**). You may obtain a true-length line on any plane by drawing a line parallel to one of the principal planes and projecting it to the adjacent view (**Figure 27.31**). You then get the edge view of the plane in an auxiliary view by finding the point view of line 3-4 on its surface.

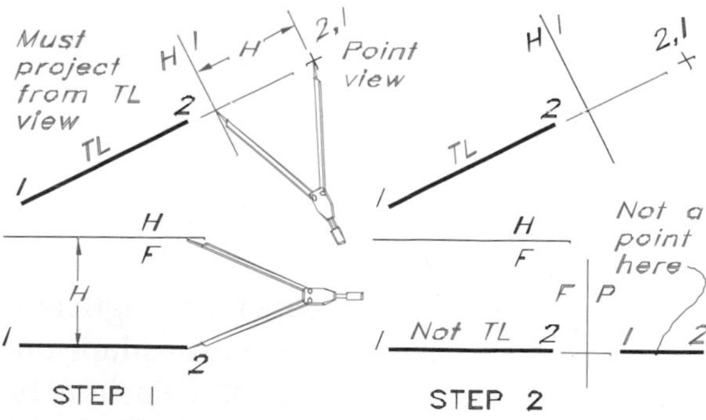

27.30 The point view of a line.

Step 1 Line 4-5 is horizontal in the front view and therefore is true length in the top view.

Step 2 Find the point view of line 4-5 by projecting parallel to its true length to the auxiliary view.

Dihedral Angle

The angle between two planes, a dihedral angle, is found in a view where the line of intersection between two planes appears as a point. In this view, both planes appear as edges, and the angle between them is true size. The line of intersection, line 1-2, between the two planes shown in **Figure 27.32** is true length in the top view. Project an auxiliary view from the top view to find the point view of line 1-2 and the edge views of both planes.

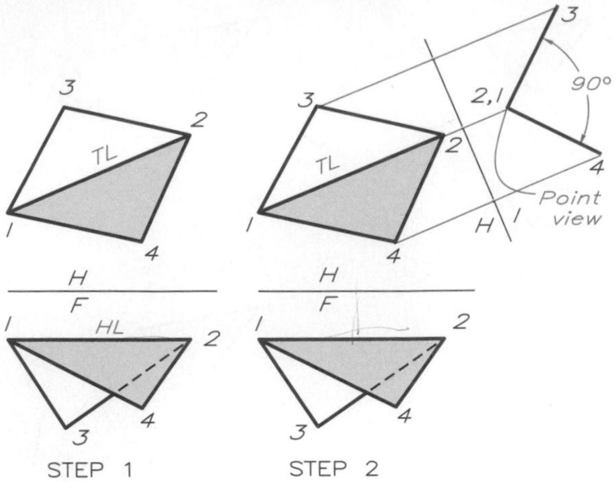

27.32 A dihedral angle.

Step 1 The line of intersection between the planes, line 1-2, is true length in the top view.

Step 2 The angle between the planes (the dihedral angle) is found in the auxiliary view where the line of intersection appears as a point, and both planes are edges.

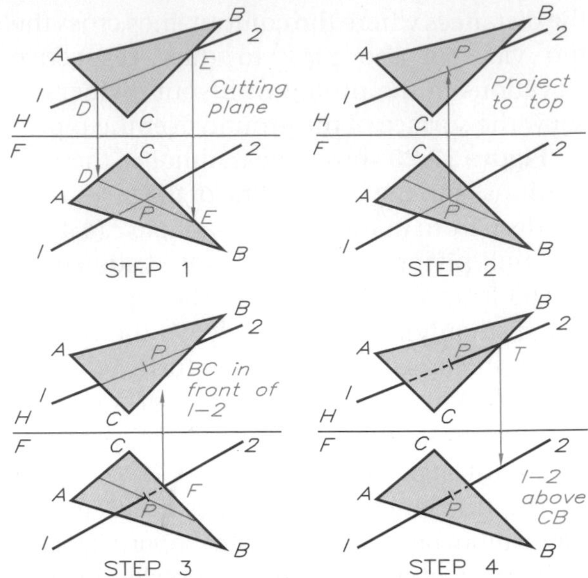

27.33 A piercing point by projection.

Step 1 Pass a vertical cutting plane through the top view of line 1-2, which cuts the plane along line DE. Project line DE to the front view to locate piercing point P.

Step 2 Project point P to the top view of line 1-2.

Step 3 Determine visibility in the front view by projecting the crossing point of lines CB and 1-2 to the top view. Because CB is encountered first, it is in front of 1-2, making segment PF hidden in the front view.

Step 4 Determine visibility in the top view by projecting the crossing point of lines CB and 1-2 to the front view. Because line 1-2 is encountered first, it is above line CB, making TP visible in the top view.

27.11 Planes and Lines

Piercing Points

By Projection Finding the piercing point of line 1-2 passing through the plane by projection is shown in **Figure 27.33**. Pass cutting planes through the line and plane in the top view. Then, project the trace of this cutting plane, line DE, to the front view to find piercing point P. Locate the top view of P and determine the visibility of the line.

By Auxiliary View You may also find the piercing point of a line and a plane by auxiliary view in which the plane is an edge (**Figure 27.34**). The location of piercing point P in step 2 is where line AB crosses the edge view of the plane. Project point P to AB in the top view from the auxiliary view, and then to the front view. To verify the location of point P in the front view, transfer dimension H from the auxiliary view with dividers.

You can easily determine visibility for the top view because you see in the auxiliary view that line AP is higher than the plane and therefore is visible in the top view. Similarly, the top view shows that endpoint A is the forwardmost point, and line AP therefore is visible in the front view.

Perpendicular to a Plane

A perpendicular line appears true length and perpendicular to a plane where the plane appears as an edge. In **Figure 27.35**, a line is to be drawn from point O perpendicular to the plane. Obtain an edge view of the plane and draw the true-length perpendicular to locate piercing point P. Locate point P in the top view by drawing line OP parallel to the H1 reference

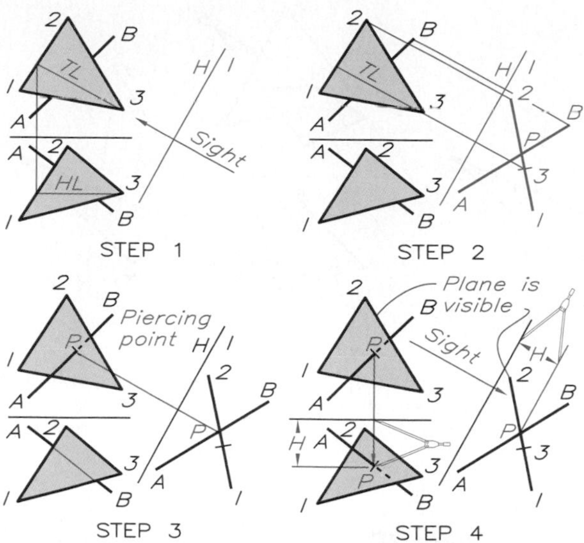

27.34 A piercing point by auxiliary view.

Step 1 Draw a horizontal line on the plane in the front view, and project it to the top view, where it is true length on the plane.

Step 2 Find the edge view of the plane in an auxiliary view and project AB to this view. P is the piercing point.

Step 3 Project point P to line AB in the top view. Line AP is nearest the H1 reference line, so it is the highest end of the line and is visible in the top view.

Step 4 Project P to line AB in the front view. AP is visible in the front view because line AP is in front of 1-2.

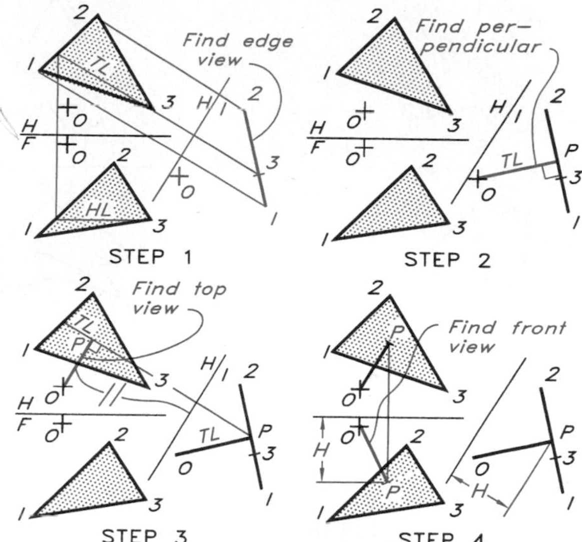

27.35 A line perpendicular to a plane.

Step 1 Find the edge view of the plane by finding the point view of a line on it in an auxiliary view. Project point O to this view, also.

Step 2 Draw line OP perpendicular to the edge view of the plane, which is true length in this view.

Step 3 Because line OP is true length in the auxiliary view, it must be parallel to the H1 reference line in the preceding view. Line OP is visible in the top view because it appears above the plane in the auxiliary view.

Step 4 Project point P to the front view and locate it by transferring height H from the auxiliary view with dividers.

line. (This principle is reviewed in **Figure 27.36**). Line OP also is perpendicular to a true-length line in the top view of the plane. Obtain the front view of point P, along with its visibility, by projection.

Intersection between Planes

To find the intersection between planes, find the edge view of one of the planes (Figure 27.37). Then, project piercing points L and M from the auxiliary view to their respective lines, 5-6 and 4-6, in the top view. Plane 4-5-L-M is visible in the top view because sight line 1 has an unobstructed view of the 4-5-L-M portion of the plane in the auxiliary view. Plane 4-5-L-M is visible in the front view because sight line 2 has an unobstructed view of the top view of this portion of the plane.

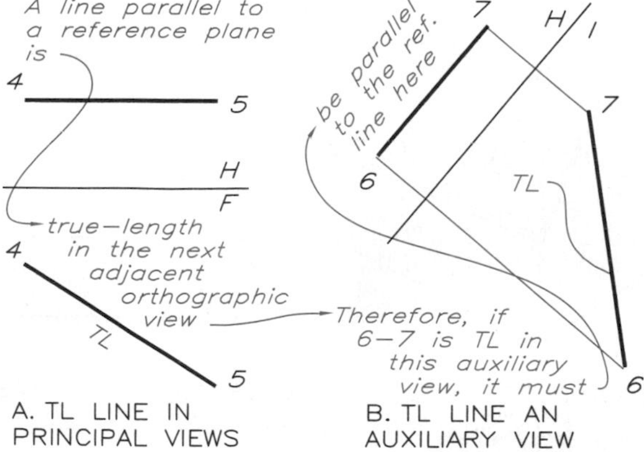

27.36 In the top view of **Figure 27.35,** line OP is parallel to the H1 reference line because it is true length in the auxiliary view. Here, lines 4-5 and 6-7 are examples of this principle: Both are true length in one view and parallel to the reference line in the preceding view.

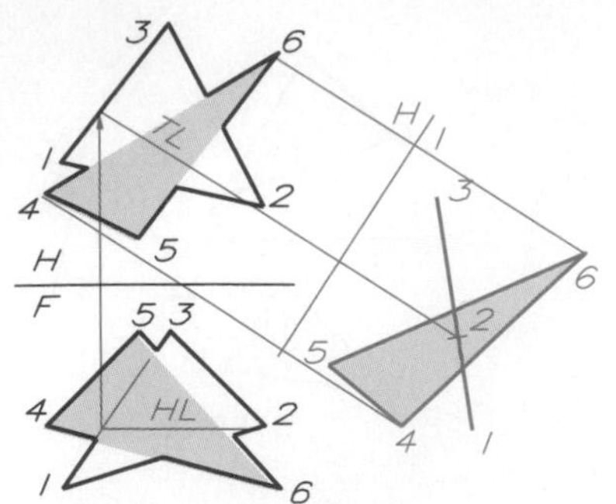

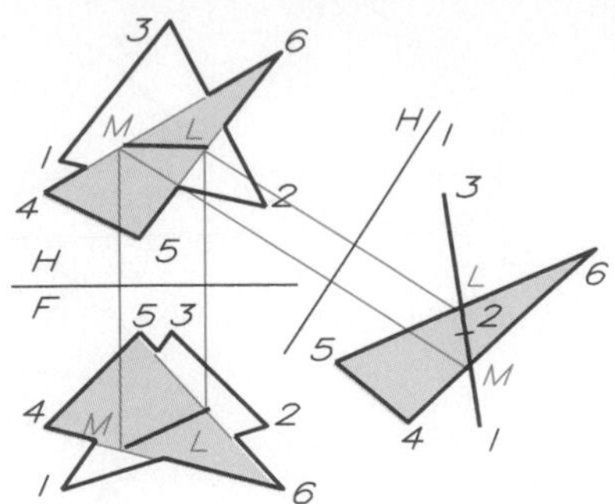

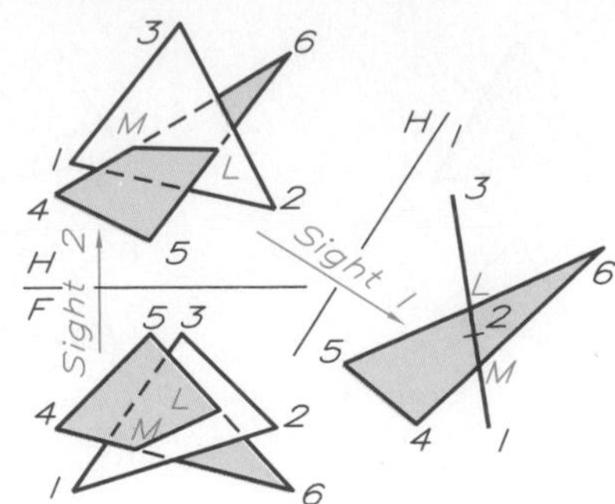

27.37 The intersection of planes by auxiliary view.

Step 1 Locate the edge view of one of the planes in an auxiliary view and project the other plane to this view.

Step 2 Piercing points L and M are found on the edge view of the plane in the auxiliary view. Project the line of intersection, LM, back to the top and front views.

Step 3 The line of sight from the top view strikes L-5 first in the auxiliary view, indicating that L-5 is visible in the top view. Line 4-5 is farthest forward in the top view and is visible in the front.

27.12 Sloping Planes

Slope and Direction of Slope

The slope of a plane is described using the following definitions:

Angle of Slope: the angle that the plane's edge view makes with the edge of the horizontal plane.

Direction of Slope: the compass bearing of a line perpendicular to a true-length line in the top view of a plane toward its low side (the direction in which a ball would roll on the plane).

As **Figure 27.38** shows, a ball would roll perpendicular to all horizontal lines on the roof toward the low side. This direction is the slope direction, and it can be measured in the top view as a compass bearing.

The steps in determining the slope and direction of slope of a plane are shown in **Figure 27.39**. Conversely, a plane can be drawn in three-dimensional space by working from slope and direction specifications as shown in **Figure 27.40**. Draw the direction of slope in the top view to locate a perpendicular true-length

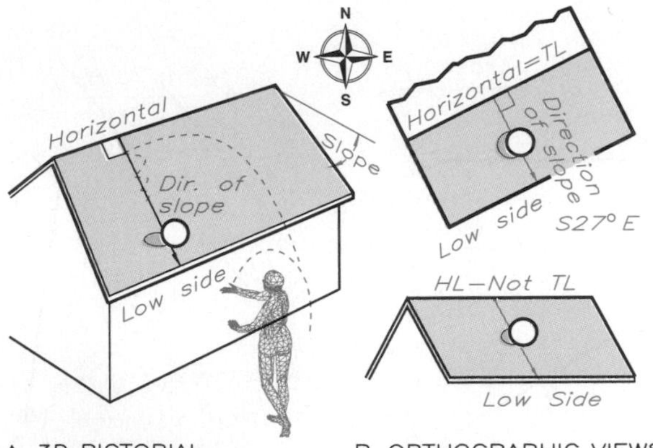

27.38 Slope definition.

A The direction of slope of a plane is the compass bearing of the direction in which a ball on the plane will roll.

B Slope direction is measured in the top view toward the low side of the plane and perpendicular to a horizontal line on the plane.

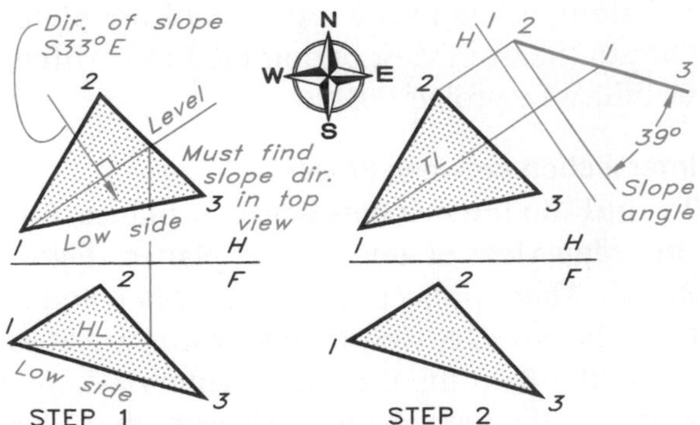

27.39 The slope and bearing of a plane.

Step 1 Slope direction is perpendicular to a true-length, level line in the top view toward the low side of the plane, or S 33° E in this case.

Step 2 Find the slope in an auxiliary view where the horizontal is an edge and the plane is an edge, or 39° in this case.

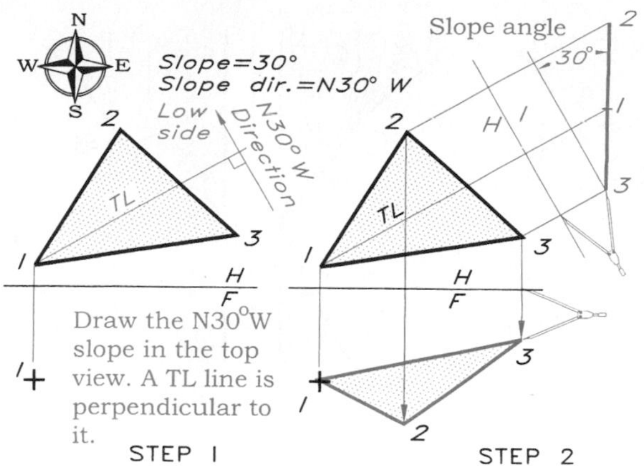

27.40 A plane from slope specifications.

Step 1 The views of a plane can be found from partial specifications. Draw the direction of slope in the top view and find a true-length horizontal line on the plane perpendicular to the slope direction.

Step 2 Find a point view of the TL line in the auxiliary view to locate point 1. Draw the edge view of the plane through point 1 at a slope of 30° as specified. Find the front view by transferring height dimensions.

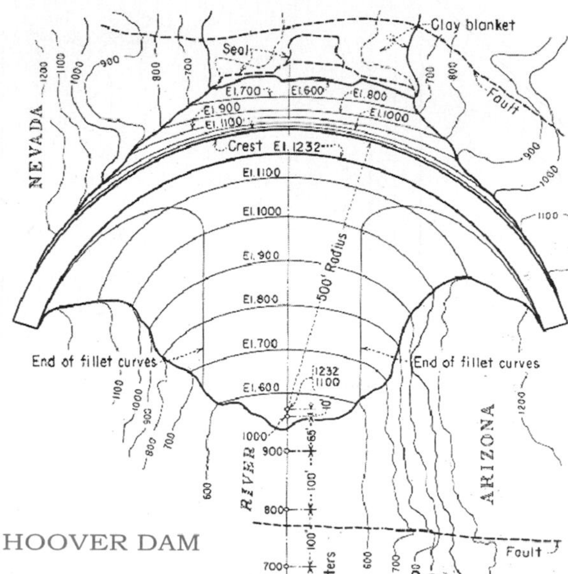

27.41 Hoover Dam was built by applying the principles of cut and fill. *(Courtesy of the Bureau of Reclamation, U.S. Department of the Interior.)*

line on the plane. Find the edge view of the plane by locating point 1 and constructing a slope of 30° through it in an auxiliary view. Transfer points 3 and 2 to the front view from the auxiliary view.

Application: Cut and Fill

The crest of Hoover Dam serves as level roadway at an elevation of 1,232 ft, while the dam forms Lake Mead (**Figure 27.41**). Its design began with the applications of the principles of cut and fill. *Cut and fill* is the process of cutting away high ground and filling low areas, generally of equal volumes.

In **Figure 27.42** a level roadway at an elevation of 60 ft is to be constructed along a specified centerline with specified angles of cut and fill. First, draw the roadway in the top view. Use contour intervals in the profile view of 10 ft to match those in the top view.

Next, measure and draw the cut angles on both sides of the roadway. Project the points where the cut angles cross each elevation line to the respective contour lines in the plan view to find the limits of cut.

Then, measure and draw the fill angles in the profile view. Project the points where the fill angles cross each elevation line to their respective contour lines in the plan view to find the limits of fill. Finally, draw new contour lines inside the areas of cut and fill parallel to the centerline.

Some of the terminology associated with the design of a dam are **crest**, or the top of the dam; **water level**; and **freeboard**, or the height of the crest above the water level. These terms are illustrated in **Figure 27.43**.

Strike and Dip

Strike and *dip* are terms used in geology and mining engineering to describe the location of strata of ore under the surface of the earth:

Strike: the compass bearings (two are possible) of a level line in the top view of a plane.

Dip: the angle that the edge view of a plane makes with the horizontal and its general compass direction, such as NW or SW.

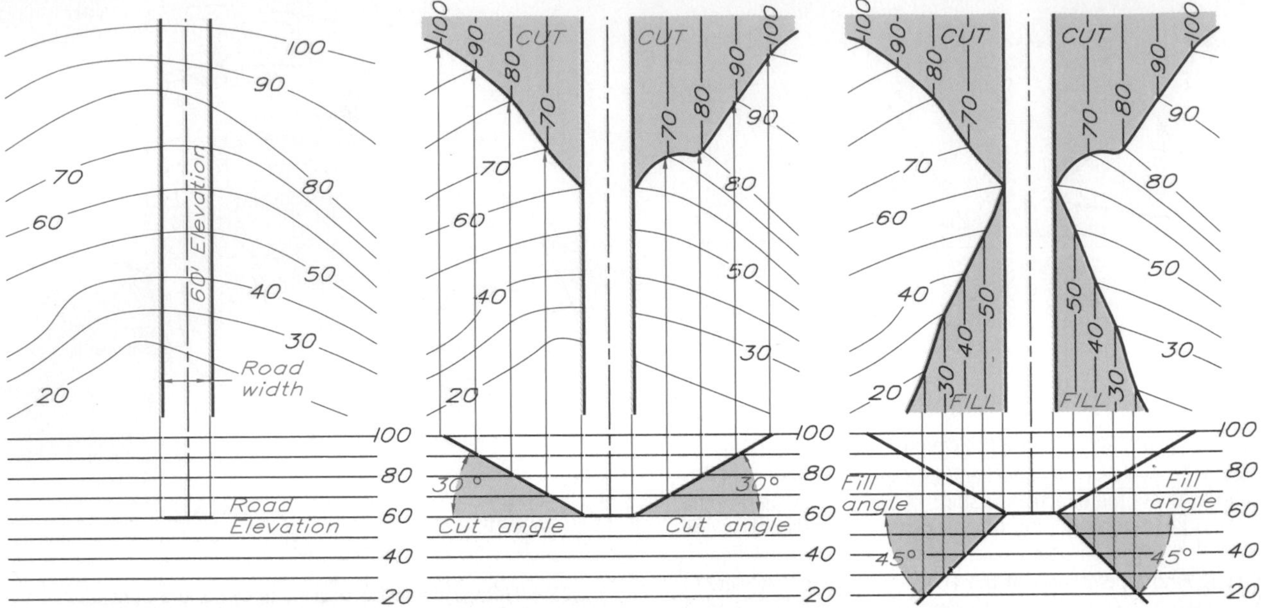

27.42 Cut and fill for a level roadway.

Step 1 Draw and label a series of elevation planes in the front view at the same scale as the contour map. Draw the width and elevation (60 ft in this case) of the roadway in the top and front views.

Step 2 Draw the cut angles on the higher sides of the road in the front view. Project the points of intersection between the cut angles and the contour lines in the front view to their respective contour lines in the top view to determine the limits of cut.

Step 3 Draw the fill angles in the front view. Project the points in the front where the fill angles cross the contour lines to their respective contour lines in the top view. Draw new contours parallel to the road in the cut-and-fill areas.

The dip angle lies in the primary auxiliary view projected from the top view. The dip direction is perpendicular to the strike and toward its low side.

Figure 27.44 demonstrates how to find the strike and dip of a plane. Here, the true-length line in the top view of the plane has a strike of N 66° W or S 66° E. The dip angle appears in an auxiliary view projected from the top view that shows the horizontal (H1) and the sloping plane as edges.

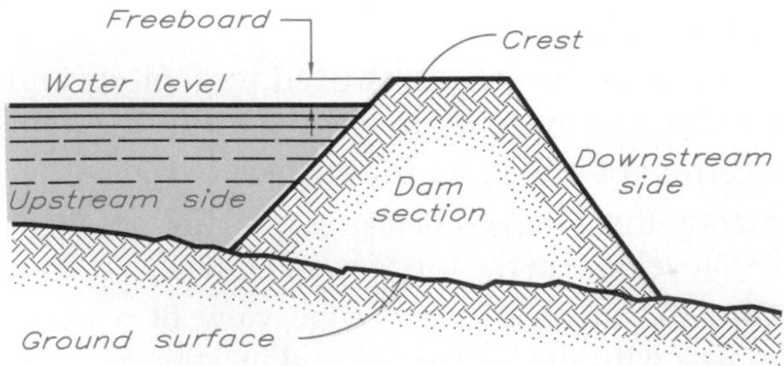

27.43 These terms and symbols are used in the design of a dam.

You can construct a plane from strike and dip specifications as shown in **Figure 27.45**. First, draw the strike as a true-length horizontal line on the plane's top view and the dip direction perpendicular to the strike. Then, find the edge view of the plane in the auxiliary view through point 1 at a dip of 30°. Locate points 2 and 3 in the front view by transferring them from the auxiliary view.

27.13 Ore-Vein Applications

The principles of descriptive geometry can be applied to find the distance from a point to a plane. Techniques of finding such distances often are used to solve mining and geological

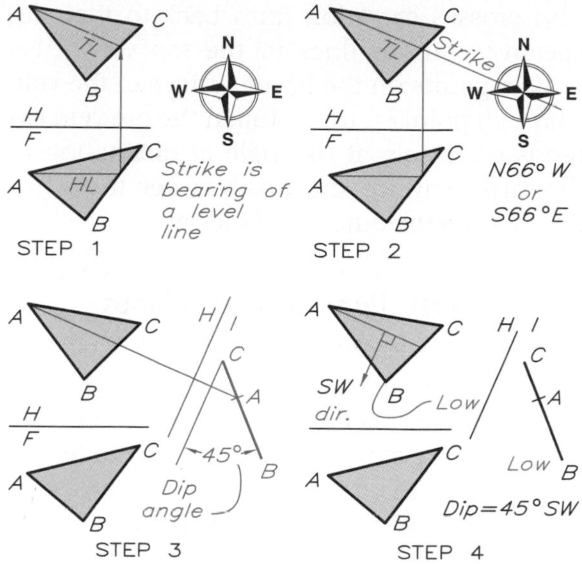

27.44 The strike and dip of a plane.

Step 1 Draw a horizontal line on the plane in the front view and project it to the top view, where it is true length.

Step 2 Strike is the compass direction of a level line on the plane in the top view, either N 66° W or S 66° E.

Step 3 Find the edge view of the plane in the auxiliary view. The dip angle of 45° is the angle between the H1 reference line and the edge view of the plane.

Step 4 The general compass direction of dip is toward the low side and perpendicular to a strike in the top view, or SW in this case. Dip direction is written as 45° SW.

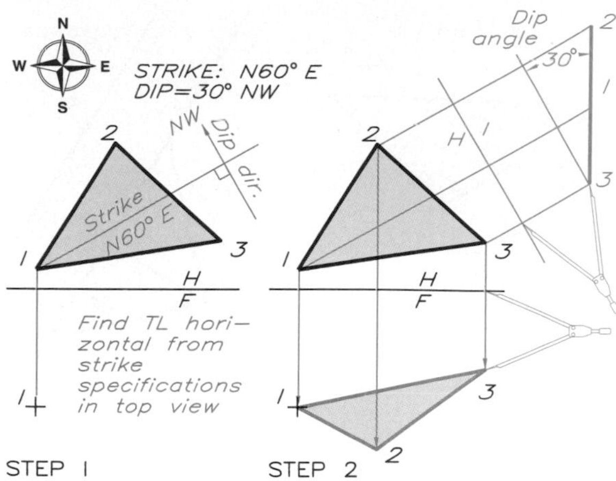

27.45 Strike and dip specifications.

Step 1 Draw the strike in the top view of the plane as a true-length horizontal line. Draw the direction of dip perpendicular to the strike toward the NW as specified.

Step 2 Find the point view of strike in the auxiliary view to locate point 1 where the edge view of the plane passes through it at a 30° dip, as specified. Complete the front view by transferring height (H) dimensions from the auxiliary to the front view.

problems. For example, test wells are drilled into coal seams to learn more about them (**Figure 27.46**).

Application: Underground Ore Veins

Geologists and mining engineers usually assume that strata of ore veins have upper and lower planes that are parallel. In **Figure 27.47**, point O is on the upper surface of the earth, and plane 1-2-3 is an underground ore vein. Point 4 is on the lower plane of the vein.

Find the edge view of plane 1-2-3 by projecting from the top view, and then draw the lower plane through point 4 parallel to the upper plane. Draw the horizontal distance from point O to the plane parallel to the H1 reference line and the vertical distance perpendicular to line H1. The shortest distance is perpendicular to the ore vein. These three lines from point O are true length in the auxiliary view, where the ore vein appears as an edge.

Application: Ore-Vein Outcrop

The same assumption is made in **Figure 27.48** that underground ore veins are defined by parallel planes that will outcrop on the earth's surface if they are inclined (nonhorizontal). When ore veins outcrop, open-pit mining can be employed to reduce costs. To find the outcrop of

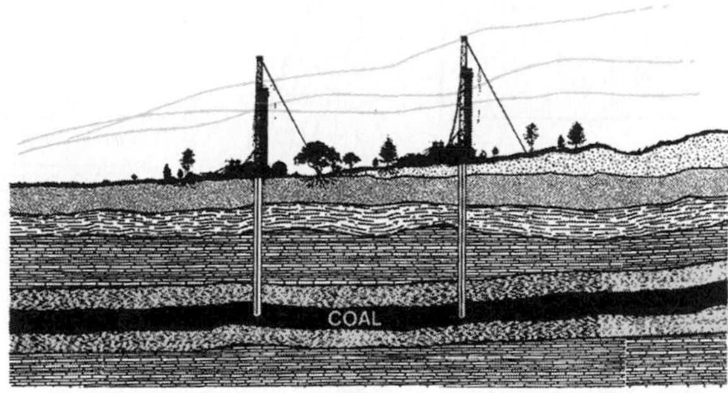

27.46 Test wells are drilled into coal zones to determine the elevations of coal seams that may contribute to the exploration for gas. (*Courtesy of Texas Eastern* News.)

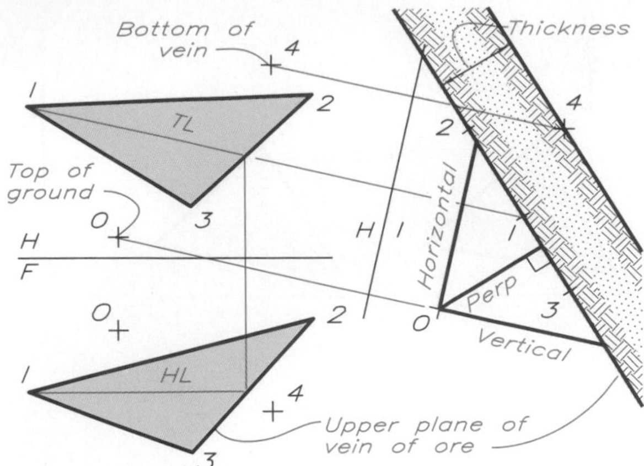

27.47 To find the vertical, horizontal, and perpendicular distances from a point to an ore vein, project an auxiliary view from the top view, where the vein appears as an edge. The thickness of an ore vein is perpendicular to the upper and lower planes of the vein.

an ore vein from the locations of sample, drillings are given on a contour map. Points A, B, and C are located on the upper plane of the ore vein, and point D is located on the lower plane of the vein. Draw them in the front view at their determined elevations.

Find the edge view of the ore vein in an auxiliary view projected from the top view. Then, project points on the upper surface where the vein crosses elevation lines back to their respective contour lines in the top view. Also project points on the lower surface of the vein (through point D) to the top. If the ore vein extends uniformly at its angle of inclination to the earth's surface, the area between these two lines will be the outcrop of the vein.

27.14 Intersections between Planes

Strike and Dip Method The method of locating the intersection of two planes located with strike and dip specifications is shown in **Figure 27.49**. The given strike lines are true-length level lines in the top view, so the edge view of the planes appear in the auxiliary views where the strikes appear as points. Draw the edge views using the given dip angles and directions.

Use the additional horizontal datum plane HRP1 to find lines on each plane at equal elevations that intersect when projected to the top view from their auxiliary views. Connect points A and B as the line of intersection between the two planes in the top view and project it to the front view to establish line AB in three dimensions.

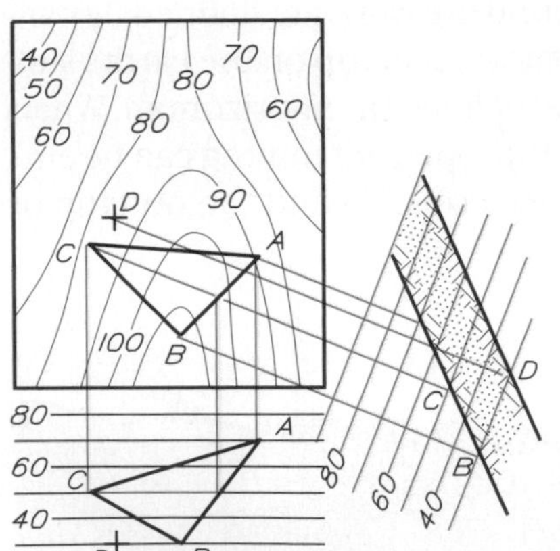

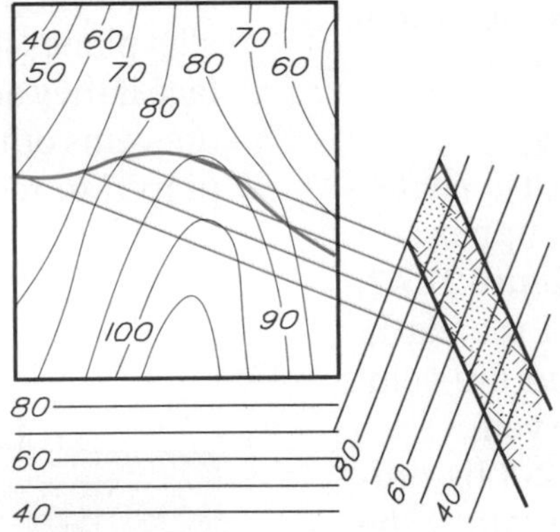

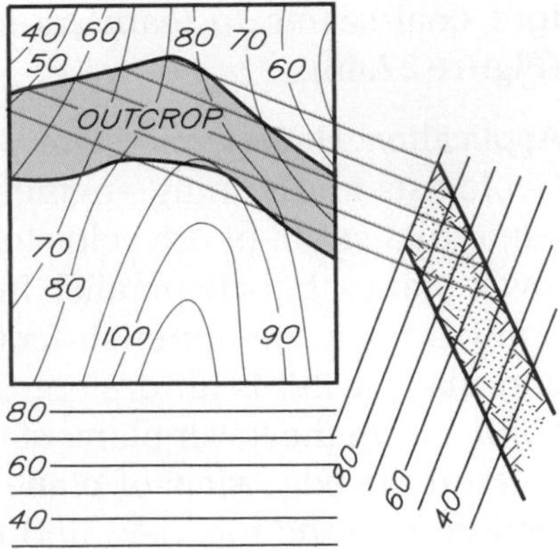

27.48 Locating an ore-vein outcrop.

Step 1 Use points A, B, and C on the upper surface of the ore vein to find its edge view by projecting an auxiliary from the top view. Draw the lower surface of the vein parallel to the upper plane through point D.

Step 2 Project points of intersection between the upper plane of the vein and their elevation lines in the auxiliary view to their respective contours in the top view to find a line of the outcrop.

Step 3 Project points from the lower plane in the auxiliary view to their respective contours in the top view to find the second line of outcrop. Crosshatch the area between the lines to depict the outcrop of the vein.

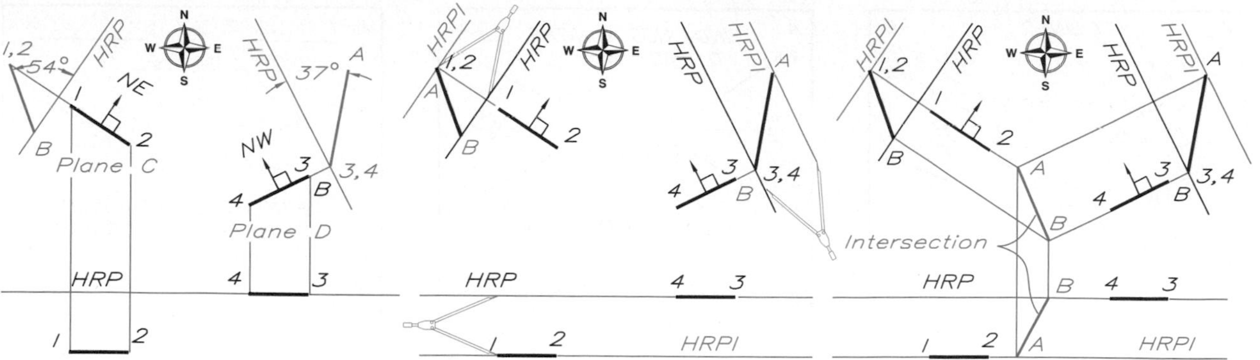

27.49 Intersection of planes: Strike and dip method.

Step 1 Lines 1-2 and 3-4 are strike lines and are true length in the top view. Use a common reference plane, HRP, to find the point view of each strike line by auxiliary views. Find the edge views by drawing the dip angles with the HRP line through the point views.

Step 2 Draw a supplementary horizontal plane, HRP1, at a convenient location in the front view. This plane, shown in both auxiliary views, is located H distance from HRP. The HRP1 cuts through each edge in both auxiliary views, locating A and B.

Step 3 Project points A from both auxiliary views on HRP1 to the top view of their intersection at A. Project points B and HRP to their intersection in the top view. Project points A and B to their respective planes in the front view. AB is the line of intersection.

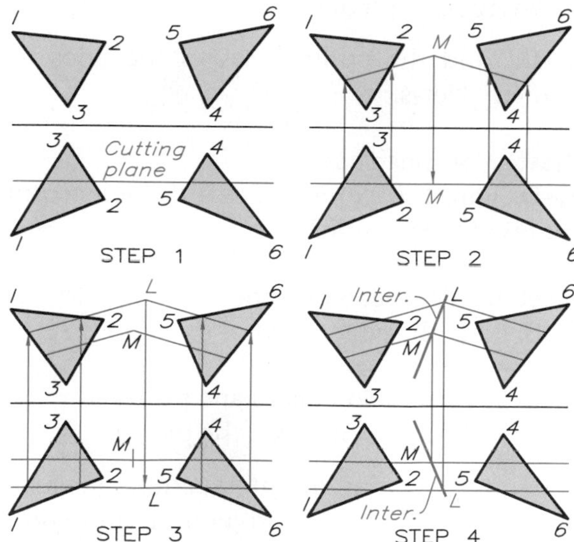

27.50 Intersection of planes by the cutting-plane method.

Step 1 Draw a cutting plane that passes through both planes in the front view in any convenient direction.

Step 2 Project the intersections of the cutting plane to the top views of the planes. Find intersection point M in the top view and project it to the front view.

Step 3 Draw a second cutting plane through the front view of the planes and project it to the top view. Find point L in the top view and project it to the front view.

Step 4 Connect L and M in the top and front views to represent the line of intersection of the extended planes.

Cutting-Plane Method In **Figure 27.50**, top and front views of two planes are given, and the line of intersection between them, if they were extended, is to be determined. Draw cutting planes through both planes in either view at any angle and project them to the top view. Find points L and M in the top view to establish the line of intersection. Find the front view of line LM, the line of intersection, by projecting its endpoints from the top view to their respective planes in the front view.

Problems

Lay out the following problems on size A sheets using instruments on either grid or plain paper. The grid is equal to 0.20 in. or 5 mm. Label all reference planes and points with 1/8-in. or 3-mm letters and numerals. Label all angles, distances, and information pertaining to your solution on the drawings in a professional manner.

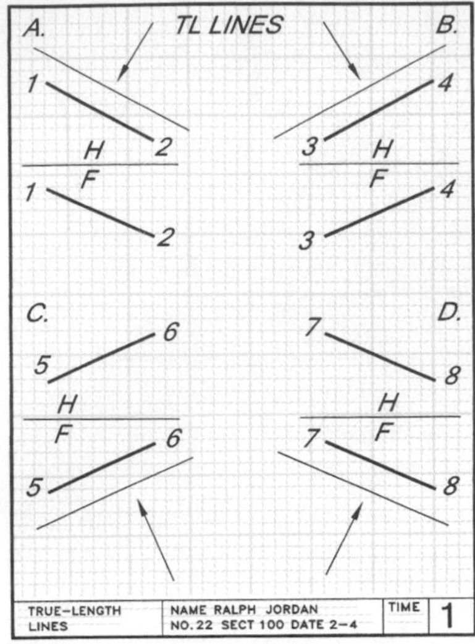

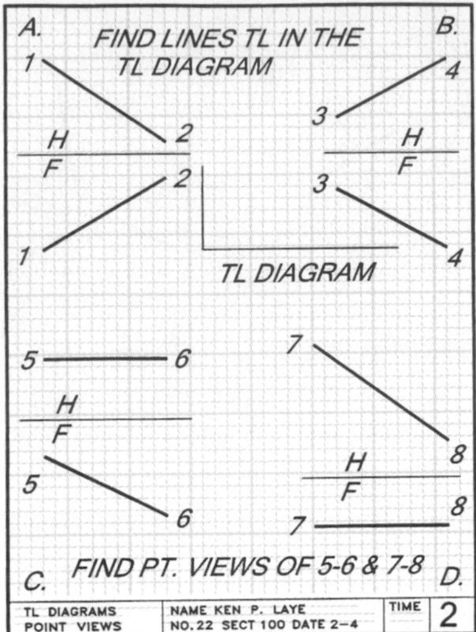

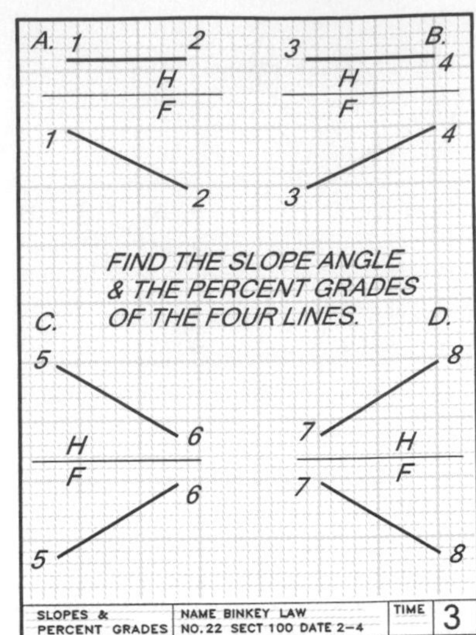

Sheet 1: True-length lines

A.–D. Find the true-length views of the lines by auxiliary view as indicated by the given lines of sight.

Alternative method:

Find the true-length of the lines by the Pythagorean theorem.

Sheet 2: True-length lines

A.–B. Find the true-length views of the lines in the true-length diagram.

C.–D. Find the point views of the lines by auxiliary views.

Sheet 3: Sloping lines

A.–D. Find the slope angles and the percent grades of the sloping lines.

Sheet 4: Edge views of planes

A.–B. Find the edge views of the planes.

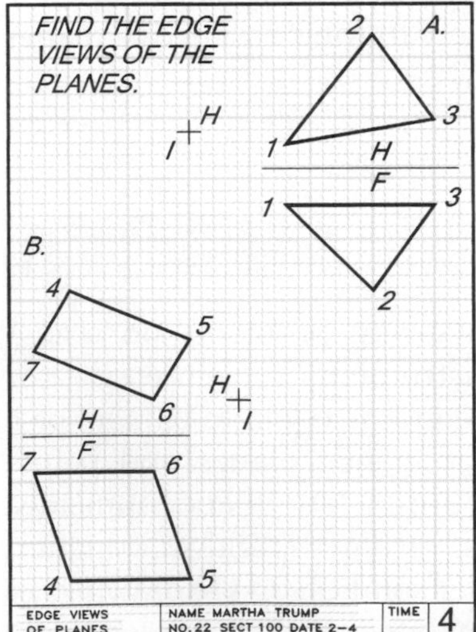

Sheet 5: Intersections: lines and planes

A. Find the angle between the planes.

B. Find the point of intersection between the line and plane by projection, and show visibility.

C. Find the point of intersection between the line and plane by the auxiliary-view method, and show visibility.

Sheet 6: Perpendiculars to planes

A. Construct a 1-in.-long line perpendicular to the plane from point O, show it in all views, and show visibility.

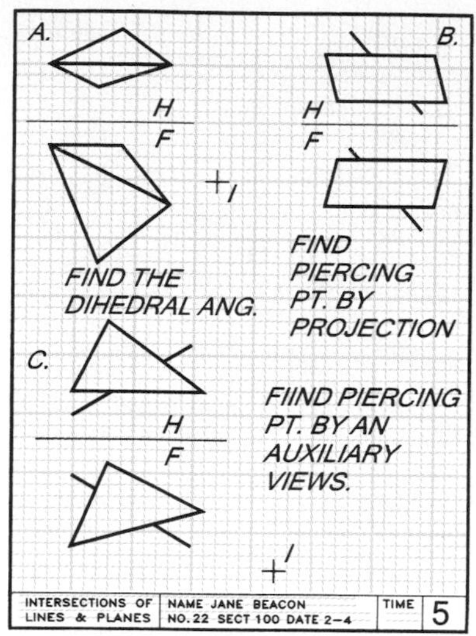

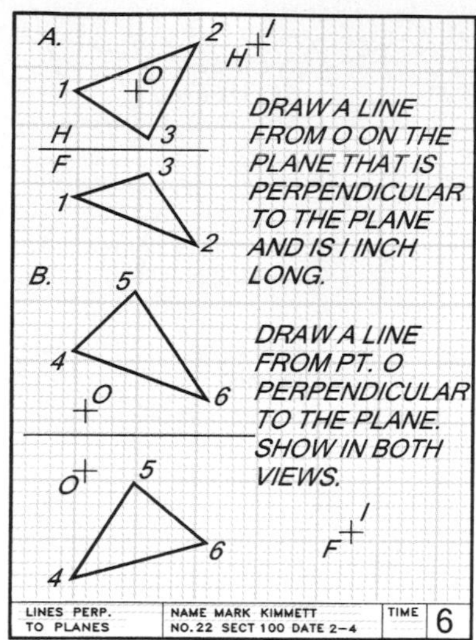

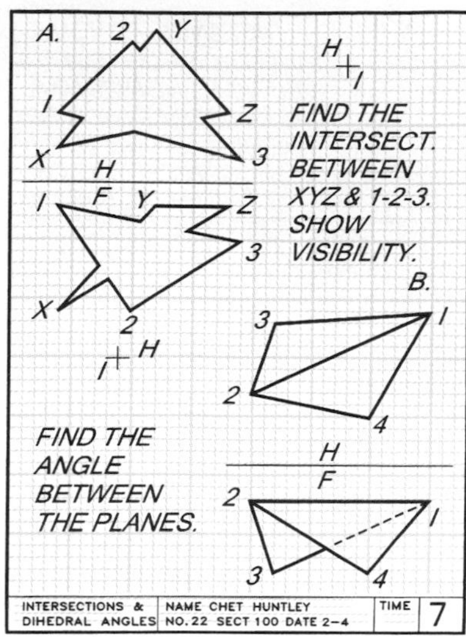

B. Draw a line perpendicular to the plane from O, find its piercing point, and show visibility.

Sheet 7: Dihedral angles

A. Find the line of intersection between the planes by the auxiliary-view method.

B. Find the angle between the planes.

Sheet 8: Slope and direction of slope

A.–B. Find the slope and direction of slope of both planes and note them where measured.

Alternative solution: Find the strike and dip of the planes.

Sheet 9: Distances to a plane

Find the distances from point O to the ore vein, plane 1-2-3. Point B is on the lower plane of the vein. Label your solutions. Scale: 1=10 ft

Sheet 10: Intersecting planes

A. Find the line of intersection between the two planes by the cutting-plane method.

B. Find the line of intersection between the two planes indicated by strikes 1-2 and 3-4.

Sheet 11: Cut and fill

Find the limits of cut and fill in the plan view of the roadway.

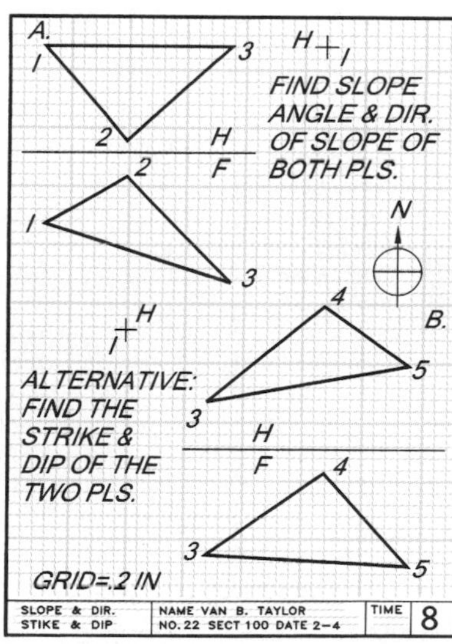

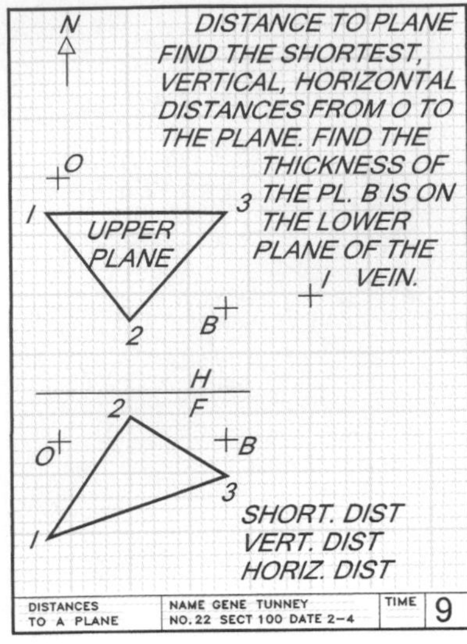

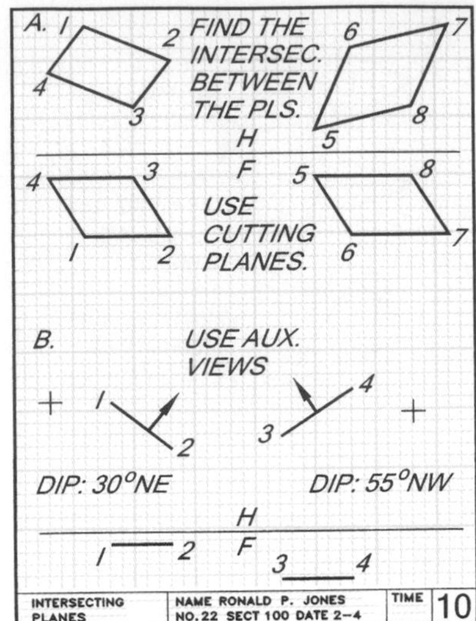

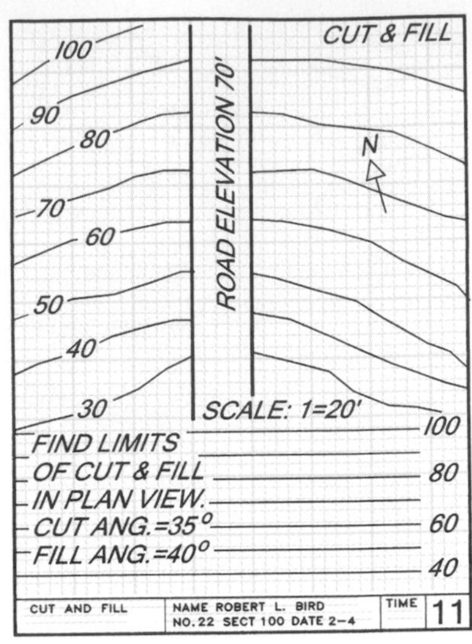

Sheet 12: Outcrop
Find the outcrop of the ore vein represented by plane 1-2-3. Scale: 1 = 20 ft

Sheet 13: Plan-profile
Complete the plan-profile drawing of the drainage system from manhole 1 through manhole 2 to manhole 3, using the grades indicated.

Sheet 14: Contour map
Draw the contour map, and give the lengths of the sides, their compass directions, interior angles, scale, and north arrow.

Sheet 15: Vertical section
Draw the contour map and construct the profile (vertical section) indicated by the cutting-plane line.

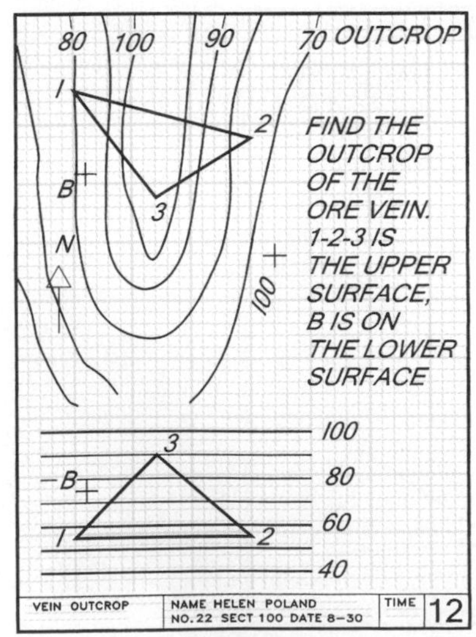

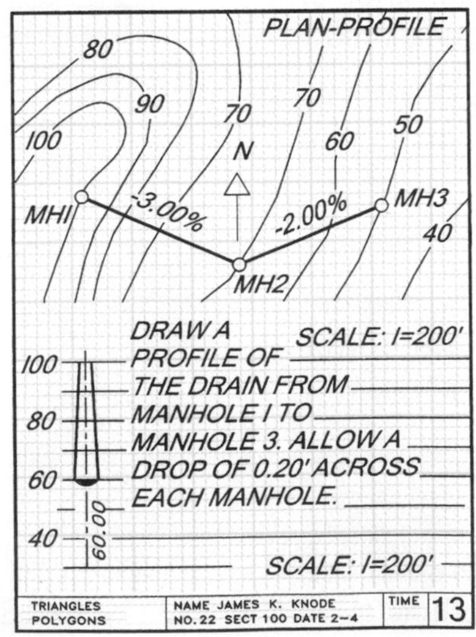

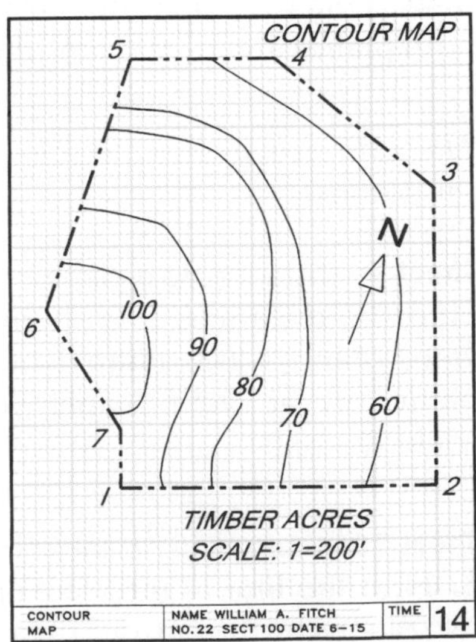

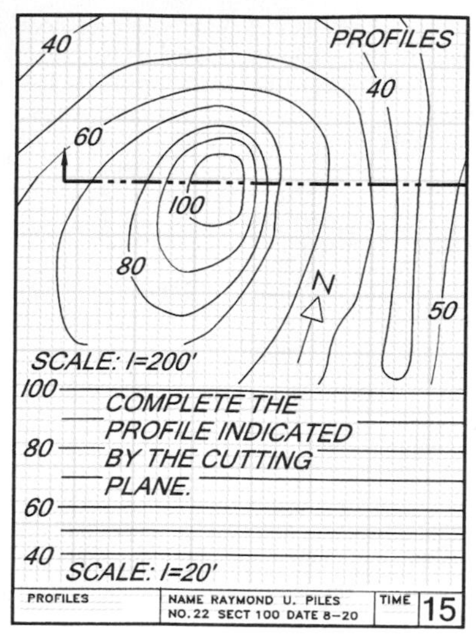

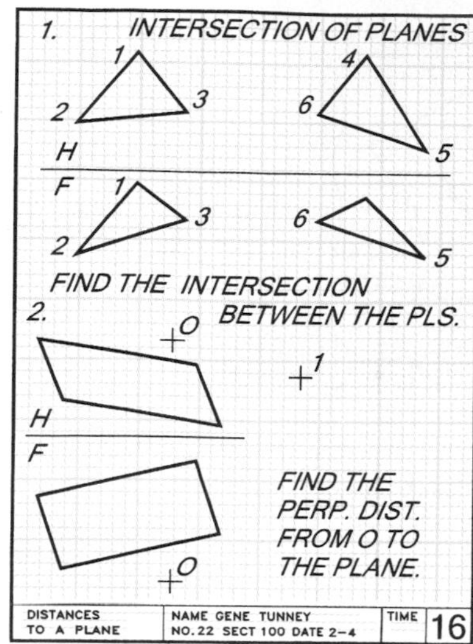

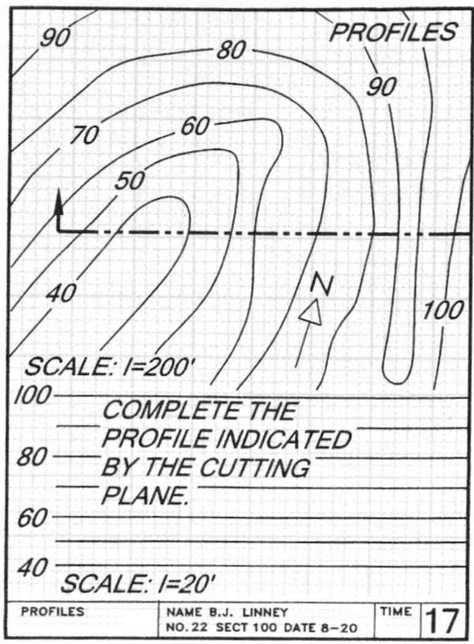

Sheet 16: Intersecting planes

A. Find the intersection between the planes.

B. Find the shortest distance from O to the plane.

Sheet 17: Vertical section

Draw the contour map and construct the vertical profile section as indicated.

Design Problems

Lay out the necessary orthographic views to solve the following problems on size A or size B sheets. *(Problems 1–4 were encountered at the Boeing Company.)*

Design 1: Bulkhead clearance

On a size B sheet, lay out the necessary orthographic views to find the clearance between the bulkhead and the electrical connector box. If necessary, relocate the connector so it will have a .50-in. clearance with the bulkhead.

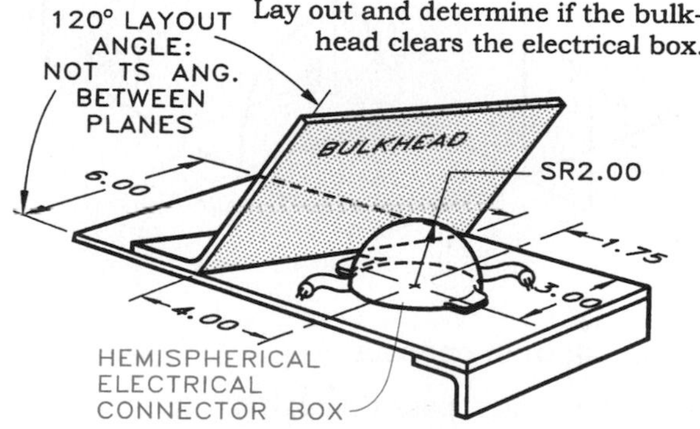

Design 2: Bolt support

A. Lay out the necessary views to find the angles the tapered washers make with the inclined block that supports an aircraft seat.

B. Make a working drawing with dimensions to describe the tapered washer.

Design 3: Fuel-tank tube

Lay out the necessary views on a size B sheet to find the length of the tube's centerline from the stubs at the fuel tank and the auxiliary fuel tank. Determine the angles between the stubs at both ends of the tube.

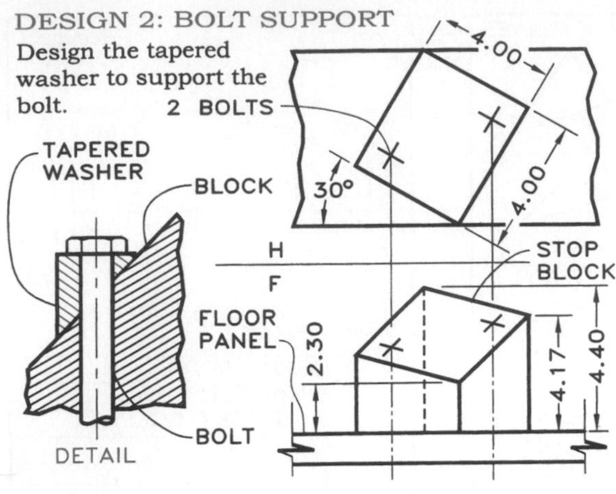

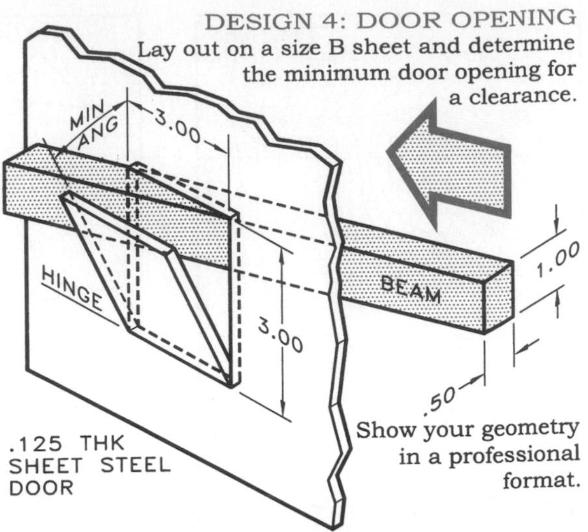

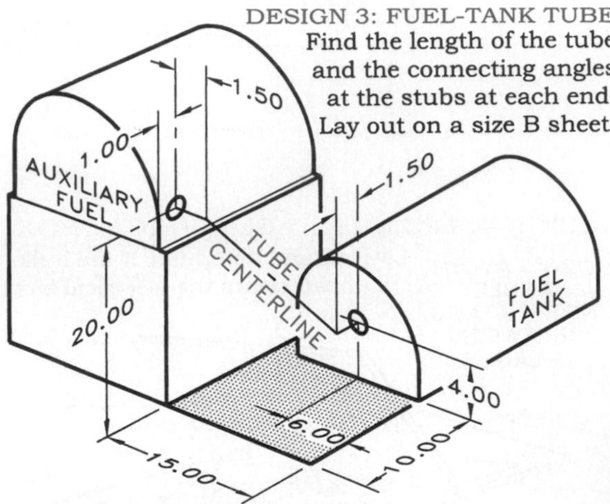

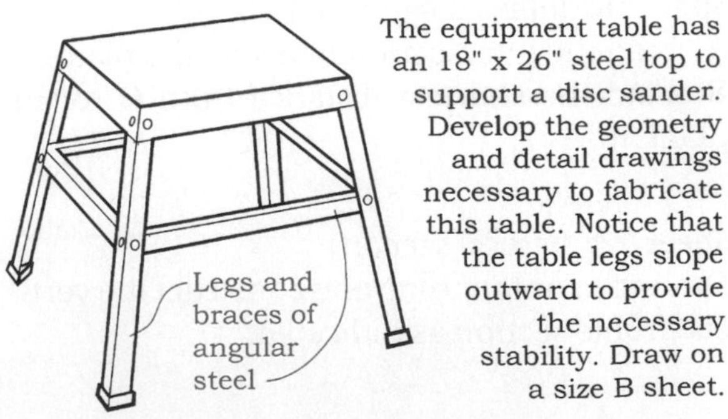

DESIGN 5: DISC SANDER TABLE
The equipment table has an 18" x 26" steel top to support a disc sander. Develop the geometry and detail drawings necessary to fabricate this table. Notice that the table legs slope outward to provide the necessary stability. Draw on a size B sheet.
Legs and braces of angular steel

Design 4: Door opening

The beam must pass through an opening in a panel installed in an airplane. The gauge of the door and structure is 0.125 in. Determine the minimum angle of the door opening to permit the beam to pass through it.

Design 5: Disc-sander table

Follow the instructions in the figure and develop a design for the sander table. Determine the geometry of the structure and details.

Design 6: Tractor sun screen

Use the given specifications and the partially dimensioned frame for a tractor sun screen and develop your design into a working drawing. Determine the pattern for the tarp cover.

Design 7: Fan base

The cage that encloses the blades of the floor fan has an outside diameter of 26 in. From this known value, can you complete the design of the fan's tubular base, its means of attachment, and its true length and the bend angles? Make your instructor proud.

Design 8: Brace fitting

The two-piece fitting is used to brace piping against sway and seismic movement. One end is attached to the building structure, and the other

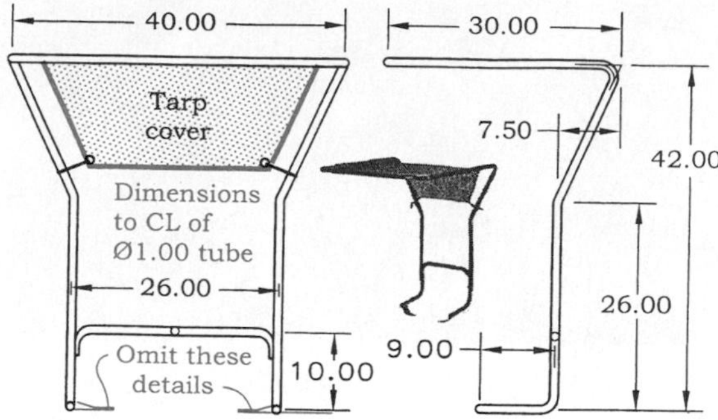

DESIGN 6: TRACTOR SUN SCREEN
Lay out the sun screen from the given dimensions and determine the details necessary for its fabrication. Determine the size of the tarpaulin screen, the length of the steel tubing, the radii of bend, and the angles of bend.

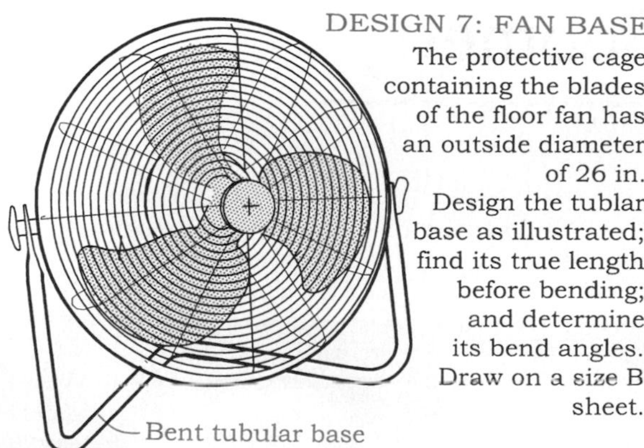

DESIGN 7: FAN BASE
The protective cage containing the blades of the floor fan has an outside diameter of 26 in. Design the tublar base as illustrated; find its true length before bending; and determine its bend angles. Draw on a size B sheet.

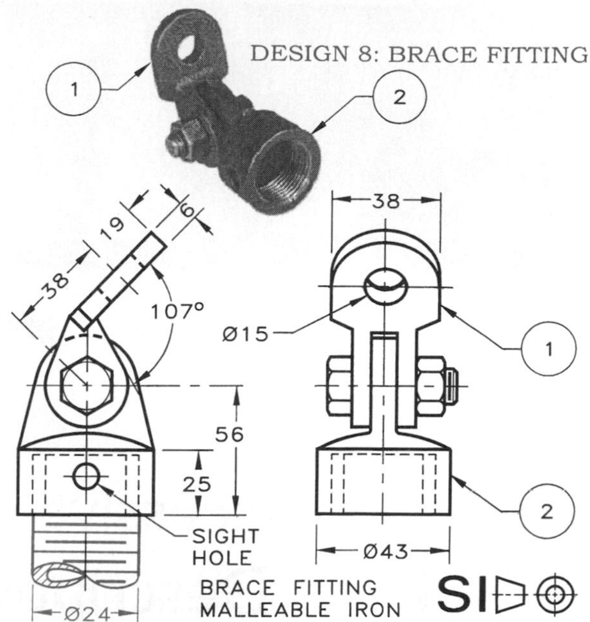

DESIGN 8: BRACE FITTING

end connects to the pipe attachment. Be the designer and provide the dimensions and details needed to fully describe the parts.

Question

What is the purpose of the sight hole in part 2?

A. Sketch freehand, orthographic views of each part on size A sheets as a preliminary step toward making an instrument drawing.

B. Convert your sketches into instrument-drawn orthographic views on size A sheets. Part 1 will require a primary auxiliary view to properly depict it. *(Courtesy of Anvil International, Inc.)*

Thought Questions

1. What conditions must exist for you to measure the angle between a line and plane?

2. In which view can you give the compass bearing of a sloping line?

3. In what direction is a sloping line assumed to slope, if not specified?

4. What is the percent grade of a line that is 100 ft long in the top view, and has a 5-ft vertical distance between its ends in the front view? What is the rise-to-run ratio of this line? What is its angle of slope?

5. From which view must an auxiliary view be projected to obtain the slope of a line?

6. What is the azimuth bearing of a line that has a compass bearing of S 30° W?

7. When given top and front views of a line, from which view must you project to find a true-length view of the line?

8. Where can you measure the slope of a line?

9. What is the difference between a level line and a contour line?

28
Successive Auxiliary Views: Descriptive Geometry

28.1 Introduction

A detailed drawing and specifications for a design cannot be completed without determining its geometry, which usually requires the application of descriptive geometry. The structural supports for the aircraft shown in **Figure 28.1** are examples of complex spatial geometry problems in which lengths must be determined, angles between lines and planes calculated, and three-dimensional connectors designed, all of which begins with descriptive geometry.

The process of determining the 3D geometry of a design requires the use of secondary and successive auxiliary views of descriptive geometry. **Secondary auxiliary views are views projected from primary auxiliary views, and successive auxiliary views are views projected from secondary auxiliary views.**

28.1 The structural support of this aircraft was designed and fabricated through the application of descriptive geometry.

28.2 Point View of a Line

Recall that when a line appears true length, you can find its point view in a primary auxiliary view projected parallel from it. In **Figure 28.2**, line 1-2 is true length in the top view because it is horizontal in the front view. To find its point view in the primary auxiliary view, first construct reference line H1 perpendicular to the true-length line. Transfer the height dimension, H, to the auxiliary view to locate the point view of 1-2.

Line 3-4 in **Figure 28.3** is not true length in either view. Finding the line's true length by a primary auxiliary view enables you to find its point view. To obtain a true-length view of line 3-4, project an auxiliary view from the front view (or from the top view). Projecting parallel from the true-length primary auxiliary view to a secondary auxiliary view gives the point view of line 3-4. Label the point view 4-3 because you see point 4 first in the secondary auxiliary view. Label the reference line between the primary and secondary planes 1-2 to represent the primary (1) and secondary (2) planes.

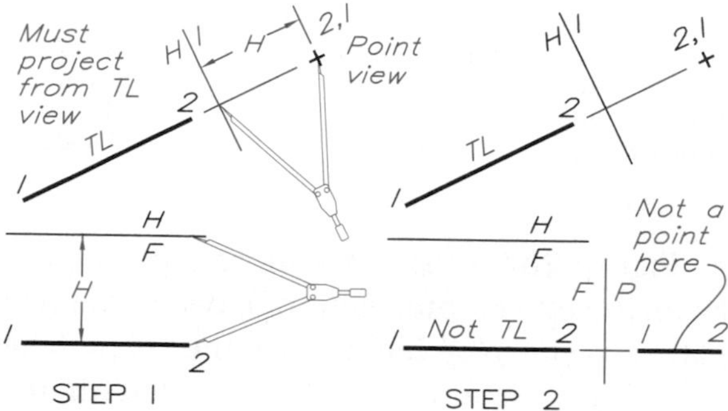

28.2 To find the point of view of a line, project an auxiliary view from the true-length view of the line.

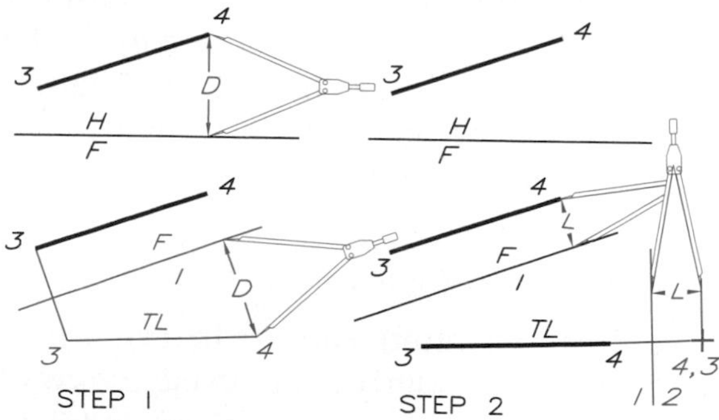

28.3 A point view of an oblique line.

Step 1 Draw a line of sight perpendicular to one of the views, the front view in this case. Line 3-4 is found true length in an auxiliary view projected perpendicularly from the front view.

Step 2 Draw a secondary reference line, 1-2, perpendicular to the true-length view of line 3-4. Find the point view by transferring dimension L from the front view to the secondary auxiliary view.

28.3 Dihedral Angles

Recall that the angle between two planes is called a **dihedral angle and can be found in a view where the line of intersection appears as a point**. The line of intersection lies on both planes, so both appear as edges when the intersection is a point view.

The planes shown in **Figure 28.4** represent a special case because their line of intersection, line 1-2, is true length in the top view. This condition permits you to find the line's point view in a primary auxiliary view and measure the true angle between the planes.

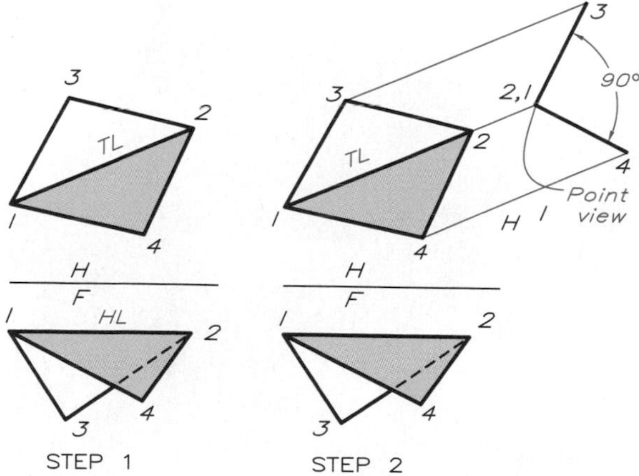

28.4 The angle between planes (the dihedral angle) appears in the view where their line of intersection projects as a point. The line of intersection, 1-2, is true length in the top view, so it can be found as a point in a view projected from the top view.

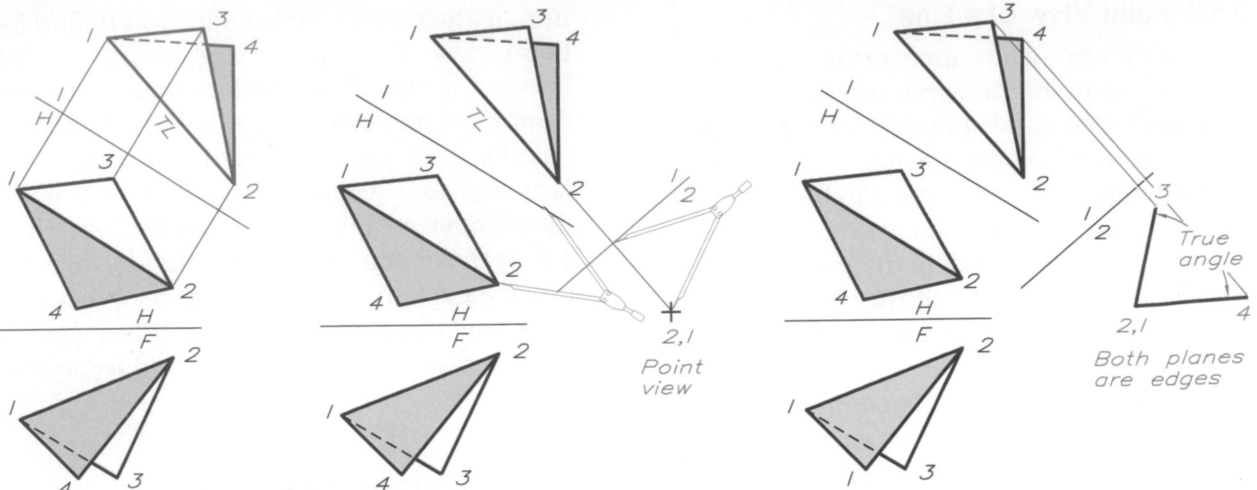

28.5 Angle between two planes.

Step 1 The angle between two planes is found in a view where the line of intersection (1-2) appears as a point. Find the true-length (TL) view of the intersection in an auxiliary view.

Step 2 Obtain the point view of the line of intersection in the secondary auxiliary view by projecting parallel to the true-length view of line 1-2 in the primary auxiliary view.

Step 3 Complete the edge views of the planes in the secondary auxiliary view by locating points 3 and 4. Measure the angle between the planes (the dihedral angle) in this view.

28.6 This Gimbal Ring, used to train astronauts, illustrates the need to determine dihedral angles to design connectors and structural members. *(Courtesy of NASA.)*

Figure 28.5 presents a more typical case. Here, the line of intersection between the two planes is not true length in either view. The line of intersection, line 1-2, is true length in a primary auxiliary view, and the point view of the line appears in the secondary auxiliary view, where you measure the dihedral angle.

This principle was applied to determine the angles between structural planes of the Gimbal Ring shown in **Figure 28.6**. That allowed the corner braces to be designed and the structure to be assembled correctly.

28.4 True Size of a Plane

A plane can be found true size in a view projected perpendicularly from an edge view of a plane. The front view of plane 1-2-3 in **Figure 28.7** appears as an edge in the front view as a special case. The plane's true size is in a primary auxiliary view projected perpendicularly from the edge view.

Figure 28.8 depicts a general case in which the true-size view of plane 1-2-3 can be

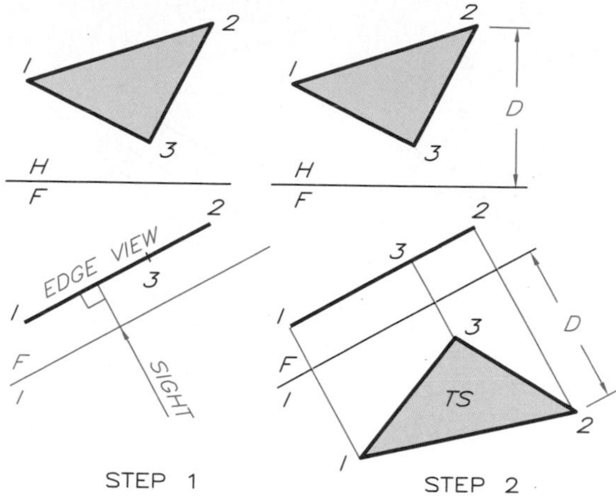

28.7 The true size of a plane (special case).

Step 1 Because plane 1-2-3 appears as an edge in the front view, it is a special case. Draw the sight line perpendicular to its edge and the F1 parallel to the edge.

Step 2 Find the true size of plane 1-2-3 in the primary auxiliary view by locating the vertex points with the depth (D) dimension.

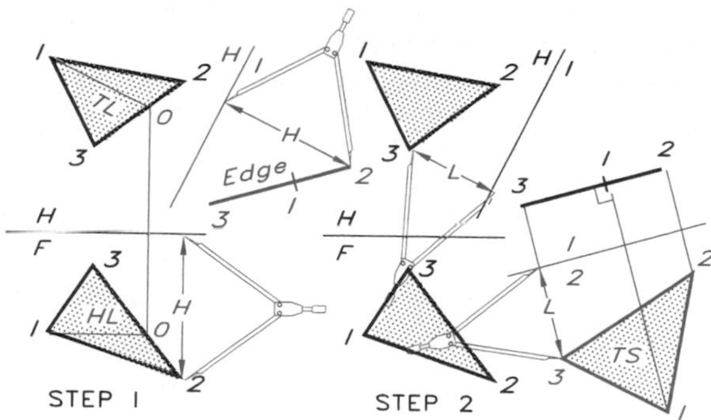

28.8 The true size of a plane: General case.

Step 1 Find the edge view of plane 1-2-3 by obtaining the point view of true-length 1-0 in an auxiliary view.

Step 2 Find a true-size view by projecting a secondary auxiliary view perpendicularly from the edge view of the plane found in the primary auxiliary view.

determined by finding the edge view of the plane and constructing a secondary auxiliary view projected perpendicularly from the edge view to find the plane's true size.

This principle can be applied to find the angle between lines such as the various components of the Mars Lander (**Figure 28.9**). The method of solving a problem of this type is shown in **Figure 28.10**. The top and front views of intersecting centerlines are given; the angles of bend and the radii of curvature must be found. Angle 1-2-3 is an edge in the primary auxiliary view and true size in the secondary view, where it can be measured and the radius of curvature drawn. The support frame of the materials conveyor (**Figure 28.11**) is an example of a design involving planes and lines in geometric combinations that was designed with applications of auxiliary views.

28.9 Many examples of geometry problems in need of solution can be seen in this early concept for the Mars Lander. *(Courtesy of NASA.)*

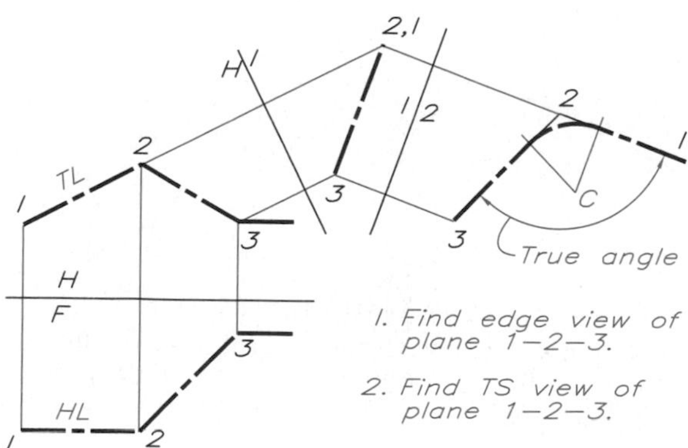

28.10 The angle between two lines is obtained by finding a true-size view of the plane formed by lines 1-2 and 2-3.

28.11 The support frame on this materials conveyor is an example of the application of determining lengths and angles during its design stages. It is used on construction sites to rapidly move cement, aggregate, and sand. *(Courtesy of Speed King Manufacturing Co.)*

28.5 Shortest Distance from a Point to a Line: Line Method

The shortest distance from a point to a line can be measured in the view where the line appears as a point. The shortest distance from point 3 to line 1-2 that appears in a primary auxiliary view in **Figure 28.12** (step 1) is a special case. The distance from point 3 to the line is true length in the auxiliary view where the line is a point, so it is parallel to reference line F1 in the front view.

Figure 28.13 shows how to solve a general-case problem of this type, where neither line appears true length in the given views.

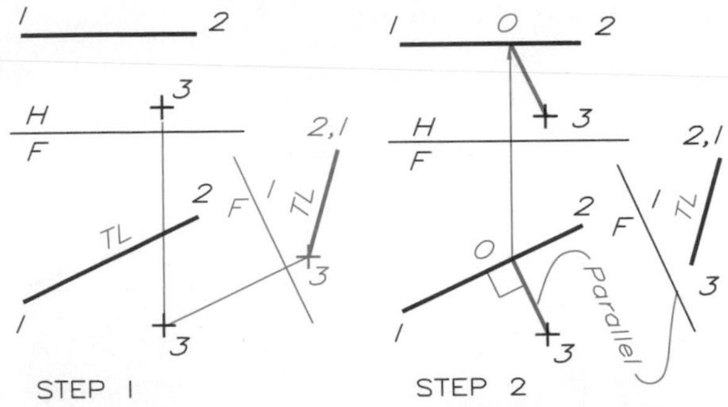

28.12 The shortest distance from a point to a line.

Step 1 The shortest distance from a point to a line is the true length where the line (1-2) appears as a point. The true-length view of the connecting line appears in the primary auxiliary view.

Step 2 When the connecting line is projected back to the front view, it must be parallel to the F1 reference line in the front view. Project line 3-O back to the top view.

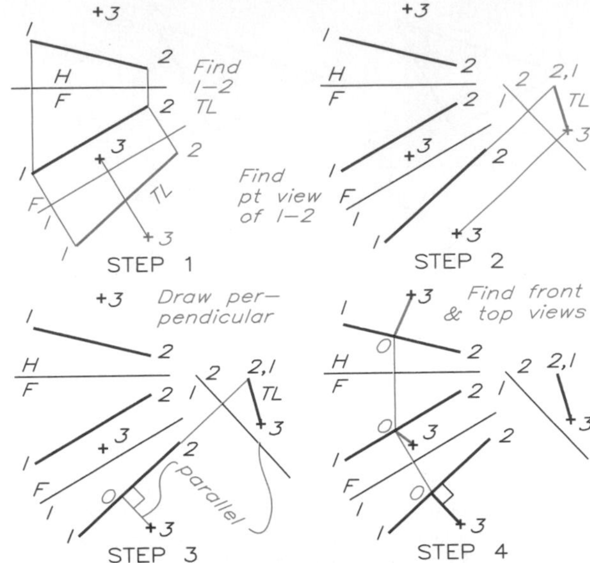

28.13 The shortest distance from a point to a line.

Step 1 The shortest distance from a point to a line is found in the view where the line appears as a point. Find the true length of line 1-2 by projecting from the front view.

Step 2 Line 1-2 is a point in a secondary auxiliary view projected from the true-length view of line 1-2. The shortest distance to it is true length in this view.

Step 3 Since 3-O is true length in the secondary auxiliary view, it is parallel to the 1-2 reference line in the primary auxiliary view and perpendicular to the line.

Step 4 Find the front and top views of 3-O by projecting from the primary auxiliary view in sequence.

Line 1-2 is true length in the primary auxiliary projected perpendicularly from the front view. The point view of line 1-2 lies in the secondary auxiliary view, where the distance from point 3 is true length. Because line O-3 is true length in this view, it will be parallel to reference line 1-2 in the preceding view, the primary auxiliary view. It is also perpendicular to the true-length view of line 1-2 in the primary auxiliary view.

28.6 Shortest Distance between Skewed Lines: Line Method

Randomly positioned (nonparallel) lines are called **skewed lines**. The shortest distance between two skewed lines is found in the

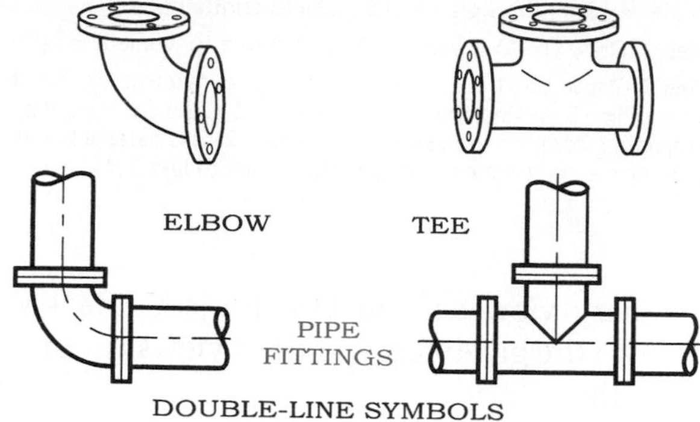

28.14 The shortest distance between two lines, the perpendicular distance, is the most economical connector bewteen them. Perpendicularity also permits the use of standard fittings, 90° tees, and elbows.

view where one of the lines appears as a point.

The shortest distance between two lines is a line perpendicular to both lines. The location of the shortest distance between lines is both functional and economical. **Figure 28.14** shows standard 90° pipe connectors (tees and elbows) that are used to make the shortest connections between skewed pipes.

Figure 28.15 illustrates how to find the shortest distance between skewed lines with the line method. Find the true length of line 3-4 and then its point view in the secondary auxiliary view, where the shortest distance is perpendicular to line 1-2. Because the distance between the lines is true length in the secondary auxiliary view, it is parallel to reference line 1-2 in the primary auxiliary view. Find point O by projection and draw OP perpendicular to line 3-4. Project the line back to the given principal views.

28.7 Shortest Distance between Skewed Lines: Plane Method

You may also determine the shortest distance between skewed lines by the plane method, which requires construction of a plane through one of the lines parallel to the other (**Figure 28.16**). The top and front views of line O-2 are parallel to their respective views of line 3-4. Therefore, plane 1-2-O is parallel to line 3-4. Both lines will appear parallel in an auxiliary view in which plane 1-2-O appears as an edge.

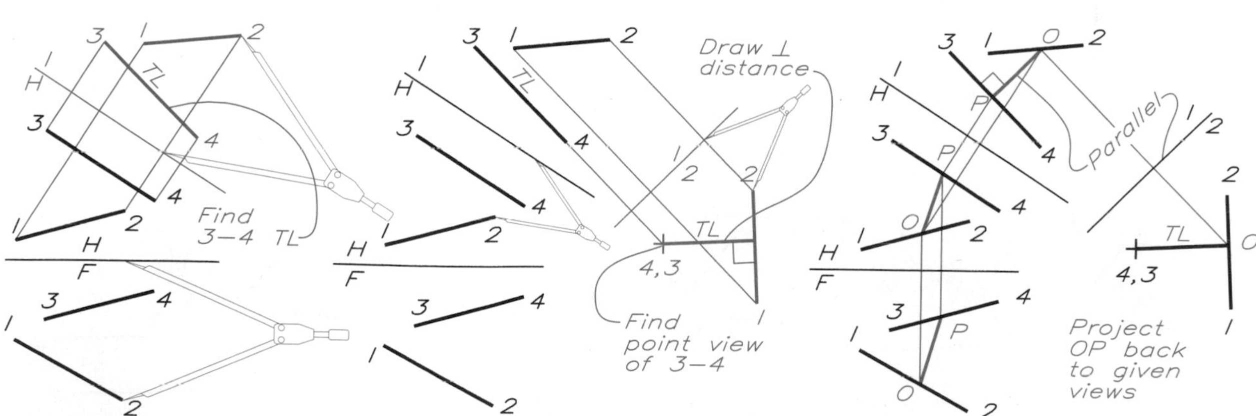

28.15 Shortest distance between skewed lines: Line method.

Step 1 The shortest distance between skewed lines appears where one of the lines is a point. Find the 3-4 true length by projecting from the top view.

Step 2 Find the point view of line 3-4 in a secondary auxiliary view projected from the true-length view of line 3-4. The shortest distance between the lines is perpendicular to line 1-2.

Step 3 The shortest distance is true length in the secondary auxiliary view, so it must be parallel to the 1-2 reference line in the preceding view. Project line OP back to the given views.

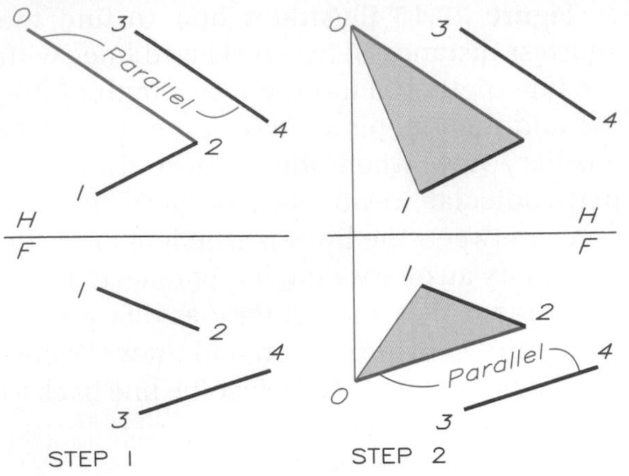

28.16 A plane through a line parallel to another line.

Step 1 Draw line O-2 parallel to line 3-4 to a convenient length.

Step 2 Draw the front view of line O-2 parallel to the front view of line 3-4. Find the length of line O-2 in the front view by projecting from the top view of O. Plane 1-2-O is parallel to line 3-4 because it contains a line that is parallel to line 3-4.

Figure 28.17 demonstrates this principle. First, construct plane 3-4-O. When its edge view is found in a primary auxiliary view, the lines appear parallel. To find the secondary auxiliary view where both lines are true length and cross, project a secondary auxiliary view perpendicularly from these parallel lines. The crossing point is the point view of the shortest distance between the lines. That distance is true length and perpendicular to both lines when projected to the primary auxiliary view as line LM. Project line LM back to the given top and front views to complete the solution.

28.8 Shortest Level Distance between Skewed Lines: Plane Method

The shortest level (horizontal) distance between two skewed lines can be found by the plane method but not by the line method. In **Figure 28.18**, plane 3-4-O is constructed parallel to line 1-2, and its edge view is found in the primary auxiliary view. Lines 1-2 and 3-4 appear parallel in this view, and the horizontal reference plane H1 appears as an edge.

A line of sight parallel to H1 is used, and the secondary reference line, 1-2, is drawn perpendicular to H1. The crossing point of the lines in

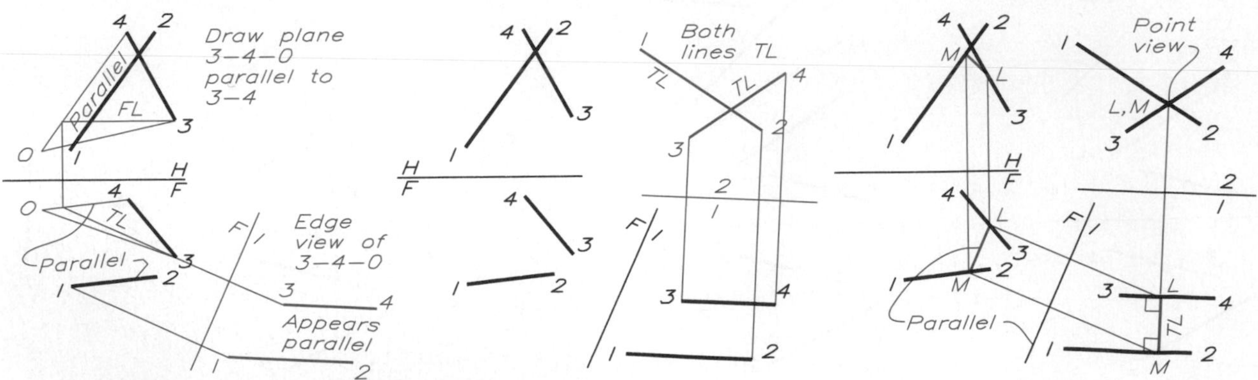

28.17 Shortest distance between skewed lines: Plane method.

Step 1 Construct a plane through 3-4 parallel to 1-2. Find plane 3-4-O as an edge by projecting it from the front view. The lines will appear parallel.

Step 2 Project a secondary auxiliary view perpendicularly from parallel lines 1-2 and 3-4 to find them true length. The shortest distance will be perpendicular to both lines in the primary auxiliary view.

Step 3 The crossing point of the two lines is the point view of the perpendicular distance (LM) between them. Project LM to the primary auxiliary view, where it is true length and parallel to F1, and back to the given views.

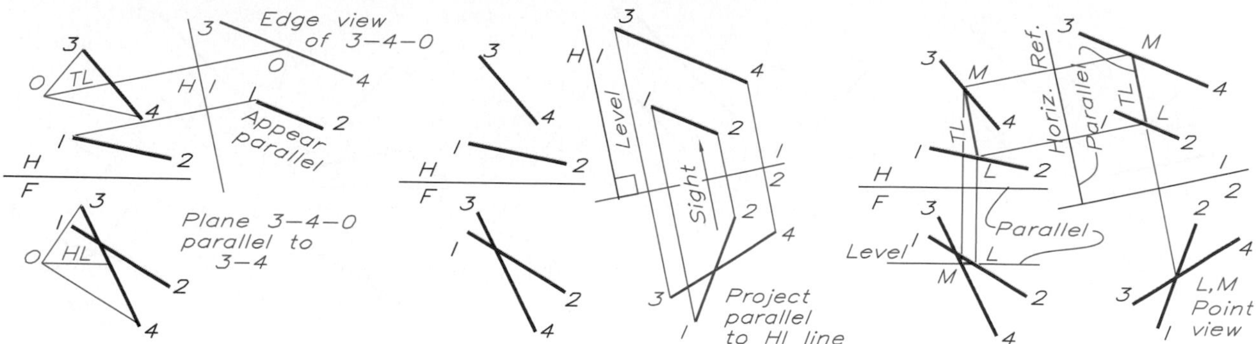

28.18 Shortest level distance between skewed lines: Plane method.

Step 1 Construct plane O-3-4 parallel to 1-2 by drawing O-4 parallel to 1-2. Find the edge view of plane O-3-4 by projecting off the top view; the lines appear parallel. When projecting from the top view, the horizontal plane is an edge.

Step 2 Infinitely many horizontal (level) lines may be drawn parallel to reference line H1 in the auxiliary view, but the shortest one appears true length. Construct the secondary auxiliary view by projecting parallel to H1 to find the point view of the shortest level line.

Step 3 The crossing point of the lines in the secondary auxiliary view is the point view of the level connector, LM. Project LM back to the given views. LM is parallel to the horizontal reference plane in the front view, verifying that it is a level line.

the secondary auxiliary view locates the point view of the shortest horizontal distance between the lines. This line, LM, is true length in the primary auxiliary view and parallel to the H1 plane. Line LM is projected back to the given views. As a check on construction, LM must be parallel to the HF line in the front view, verifying that it is a level or horizontal line.

28.9 Shortest Grade Distance between Skewed Lines: Plane Method

Features of many applications (such as highways, power lines, or conveyors) are connected to other features at specified grades other than horizontal or perpendicular. For example, the design of the highway interchange shown in **Figure 28.19** involved the application of slopes, grades, and skewed lines representing highways that were critical to its optimum design.

If you need to find a 40% grade connector between two lines (**Figure 28.20**), use the plane method. To obtain an edge view of the horizontal plane from which the 40% grade is constructed, you must project the primary auxiliary view from the top view. Construct a view in which the lines appear parallel, and draw a 40% grade line from the edge view of the horizontal (H1) by laying off rise and run units of 4 and 10, respectively. The grade line may be constructed in two directions from the H1 reference line, but the shortest distance is the direction most nearly perpendicular to both lines.

Project the secondary auxiliary view parallel to this 40% grade line to find the crossing point of the lines to locate the shortest connector,

28.19 This complex of crossing highways involved the application of principles of skewed lines at specified percent grades.

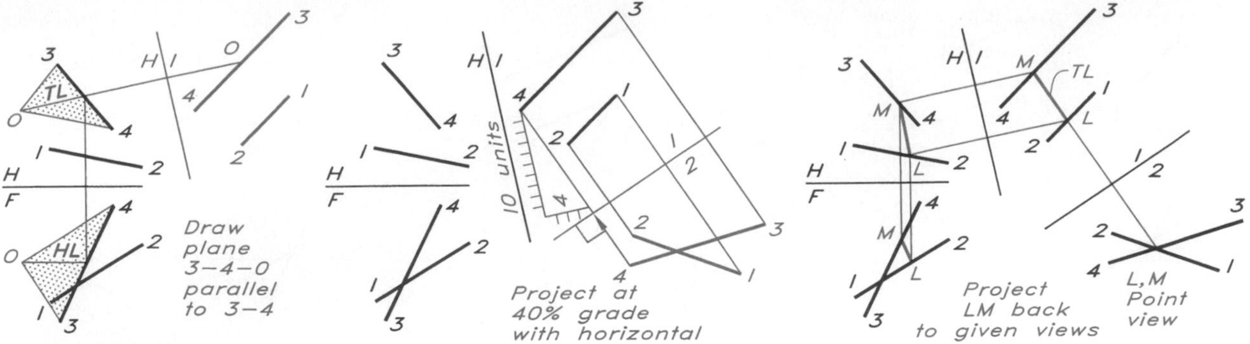

28.20 Grade distance between skewed lines.

Step 1 To find a level line or a line on a grade between two skewed lines, the primary auxiliary must be projected from the top view. Construct plane 3-4-O parallel to 1-2. Find the edge view of the plane; the lines appear parallel.

Step 2 Construct a 40% grade line from the edge view of the H1 reference line in the primary auxiliary view that is most nearly perpendicular to the lines. Project the secondary auxiliary view parallel to the grade line. The shortest grade distance appears true length in the primary auxiliary.

Step 3 The point of crossing of the two lines in the secondary auxiliary view establishes the point view of the 40% grade line, LM. Project LM back to the primary auxiliary view to find it true length. Project LM back to the top and front views to complete the problem.

LM. Project line LM back to all views; it is true length in the primary auxiliary view, where the given lines appear parallel.

The shortest distances between skewed lines—perpendicular, horizontal, and perpendicular—are true length in the view where the lines appear parallel. The plane method is the general-case method that can be used to find any shortest connector between two lines.

28.10 Angular Distance to a Line

Standard connectors used to connect pipes and structural members are available in standard angles of 90° and 45° (**Figure 28.14**). Specifying these standard connectors in a design is far more economical than calling for the fabrication of specially made connectors.

In **Figure 28.21**, a line from point O that makes an angle of 45° with line 1-2 is to be found. Connect point O with the line's endpoints, 1 and 2, to create plane 1-2-O in the top and front views, and find its edge view in a

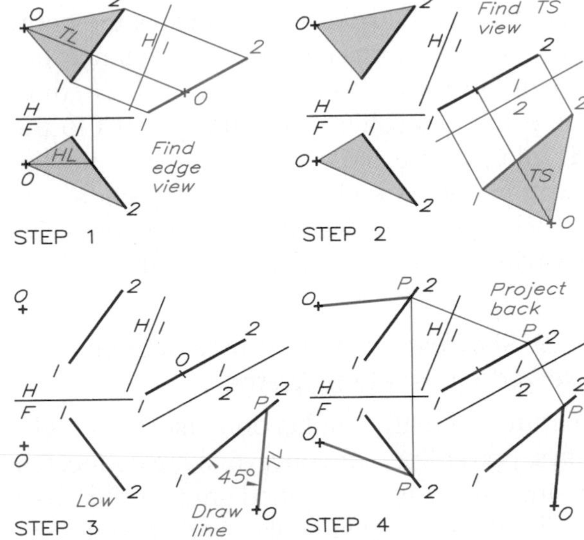

28.21 Line through a point at a given angle to a line.

Step 1 Connect O to each end of the line to form plane 1-2-O in both views. Draw a horizontal line in the front view of the plane and project it to the top view where it is true length. Find the point view of AO and the edge view of the plane.

Step 2 Find the true size of plane 1-2-O in the primary auxiliary view by projecting perpendicularly from its edge view. Omit the outline of the plane in this view and show only line 1-2 and point O.

Step 3 Construct Line OP at an angle of 45° with line 1-2. If you draw the angle toward point 2 (the low end), the line slopes downward; if toward point 1, it slopes upward.

Step 4 Project line OP back to the previous views in sequence to complete the solution.

primary auxiliary view. Find the true-size view of plane 1-2-O by projecting perpendicularly from its edge view. Measure the angle of the line from point O in this view, where the plane of the line and point is true size.

Draw the 45° connector from point O toward point 2 (the low point) if it slopes downward or toward point 1 if it slopes upward. Determine the upper and lower ends of line 1-2 by referring to the front view, where the height is easily seen. Project the 45° line, OP, back to the given views.

28.11 Angle between a Line and a Plane: Plane Method

The angle between a line and a plane can be measured in the view where the plane appears as an edge and the line appears true length. In **Figure 28.22**, the edge view of plane 1-2-3 lies in a primary auxiliary view projected from the top view and is true size (step 2) where the line appears foreshortened. Line AB is true length in a third successive auxiliary view projected perpendicularly from the secondary auxiliary view of line AB. The line appears true length and the plane appears as an edge in the third successive auxiliary view. Therefore, the angle between the line and plane can be measured here.

28.12 Angle between a Line and a Plane: Line Method

An alternative method (not illustrated here) of finding the angle between a line and a plane is the **line method**. In that method, the line, rather than the plane, is the primary geometric element that is projected. The line is found as true length in a primary auxiliary view; it is found as a point in the secondary auxiliary view; and the plane is found as an edge in the third successive auxiliary view.

Because this last view was projected from a point view of the line, the line appears true length in this view where the plane appears as an edge. Project the piercing point back to the secondary, primary, top, and front views in sequence to complete the problem.

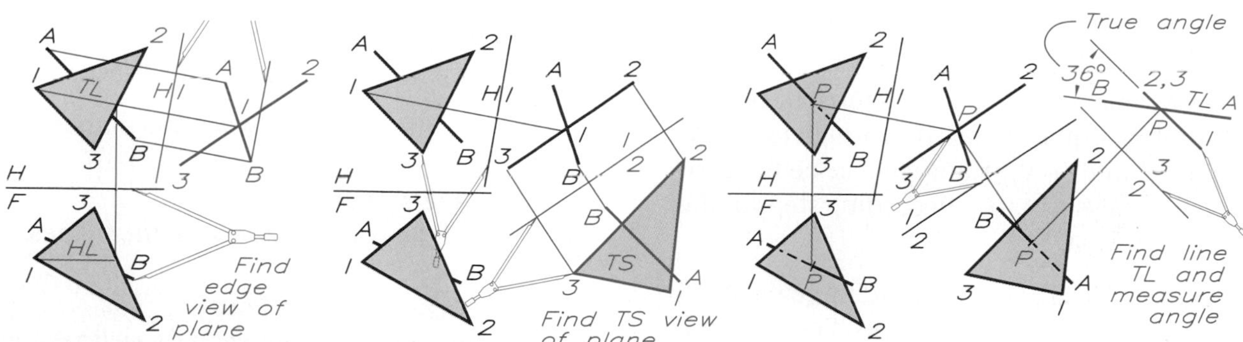

28.22 Angle between a line and plane: Plane method.

Step 1 The angle between a line and a plane is found in the view where the plane is an edge and the line is true length (TL). Find the plane as an edge by projecting it from the top view.

Step 2 To find the plane's true size, project a secondary auxiliary view perpendicularly from the edge view of the plane. A view projected in any direction from a true-size plane will show the plane as an edge.

Step 3 Project a third successive auxiliary perpendicularly from AB. The line is true length, the plane is an edge, and the angle is true size. Project AB back in sequence to the given views; find the piercing points and visibility.

Problems

General Guidelines

The following guidelines are given for the solution of geometry problems while developing preliminary ideas that are most closely associated with the refinement step of the design process. The configuration of a design may seem better in the development stage than when it is refined and its geometry established. All designs must undergo close scrutiny and evaluation throughout their development and this is the first step.

A number of points are given below as reminders of the purpose and objectives of this stage of refinement: the determination of a design's geometry. Whether designing a small, hand-held product or large industrial project, the steps are very similar.

1. Geometry begins with the determination of the lengths of elements, which may include cables, beams, or features within a design.

2. Most surfaces must be sized as true-size planes so they can be measured, fabricated, and assembled.

3. Many products are composed of intersecting planes and lines with angles that must be determined, measured, detailed, and specified in order for them to be built.

4. Lines, planes, and surfaces must be refined in combination in order for a design to be understood and so a prototype can be built for further analysis in the succeeding steps of the design process.

5. Unclear specifications regarding geometry of a design will lead to unclear specifications and, consequently, to increased development costs.

6. If there is a single universal rule of any project, it is that we all want as much as possible for as little expense as is feasible. Thoroughness in development on a drawing is much more economical than building and rebuilding a poorly planned design.

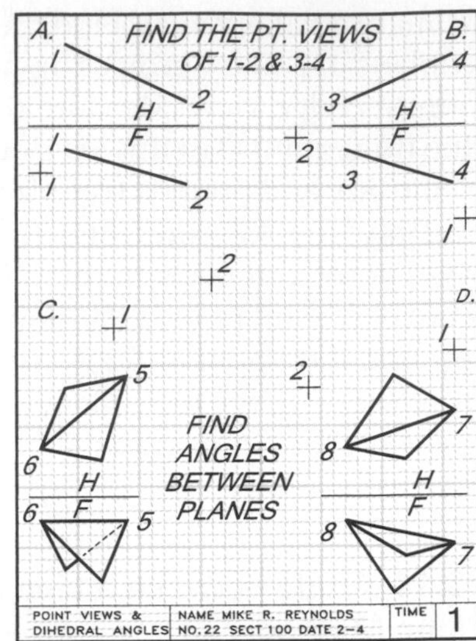

Problem Instructions

Solve the following problems on size A sheets using instruments on grid or plain paper. Each square on the grid is equal to 0.20 in. (5 mm). Label reference planes and points in each problem with 1/8-in. letters or numbers using guidelines.

Use the crosses marked "1" and "2" for positioning the primary and secondary reference lines, respectively.

Sheet 1: Lines and planes

A.–B. Find the point views of the lines.

C.–D. Find the angles between the planes.

Sheet 2: True-size planes

A.–B. Find the true-size views of the planes.

Sheet 3: Angles between lines

A.–B. Find the angles between these lines.

Sheet 4: Distance to lines

A.–B. Find the shortest distances from the points to the lines. Project the lines back into the given views.

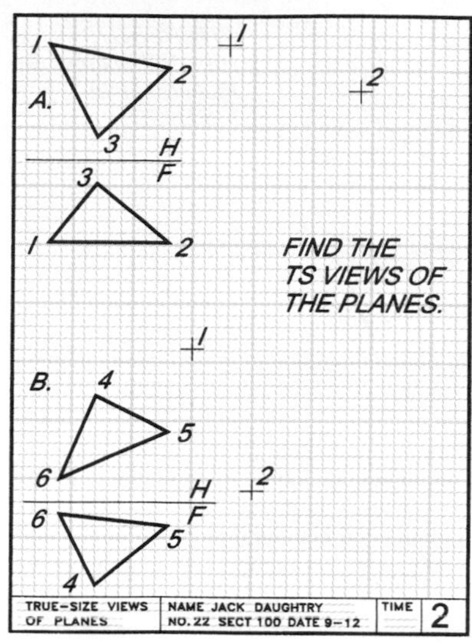

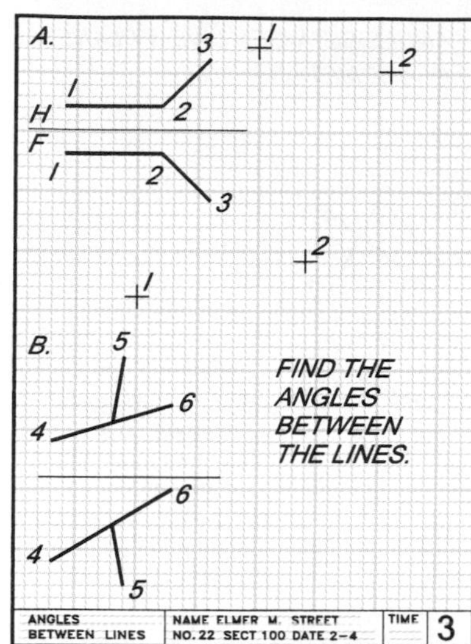

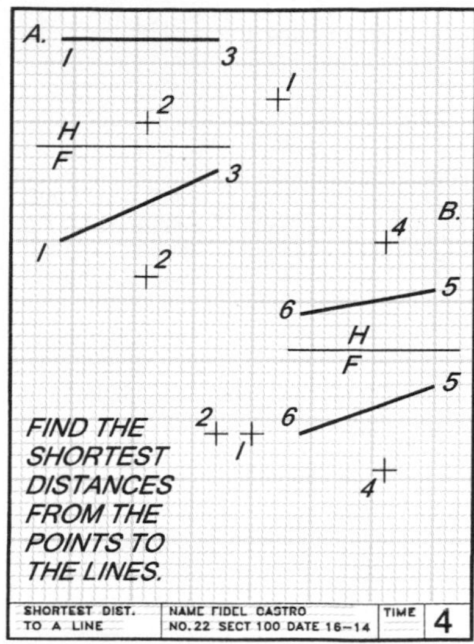

Sheet 5: Distances between lines

A.–B. Find the shortest distances between the lines by the line method. Project the lines back into the given views.

Sheet 6: Skewed line problems

Find the shortest distance between the lines by the plane method.

Alternative problem: Find the shortest horizontal distance between the two lines.

Sheet 7: Grade distance between lines

Find the shortest 20% grade distance between the two lines. Show this distance in all views.

Sheet 8: Angular distance to a line

Find the connector from point 1 that intersects intersect line 1-2 at 60°. Project from the top view and show in all views. Scale: full size.

Sheet 9: Find the angle between the line and plane by the plane method.

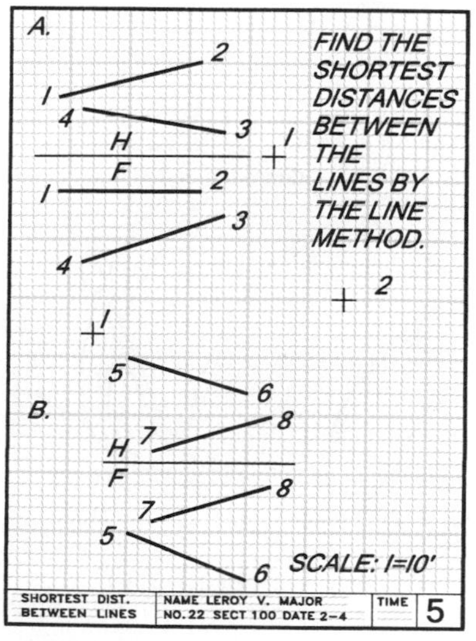

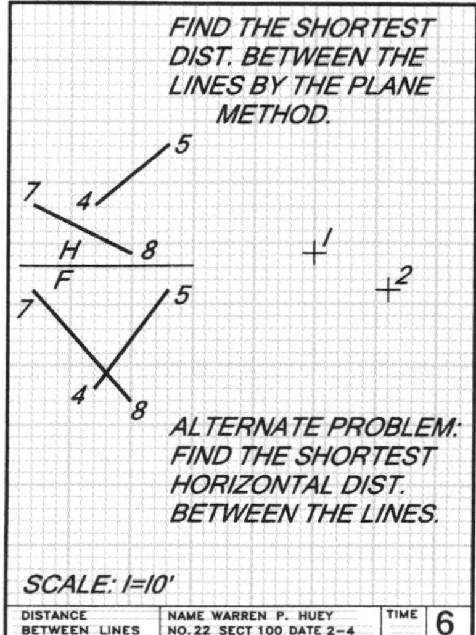

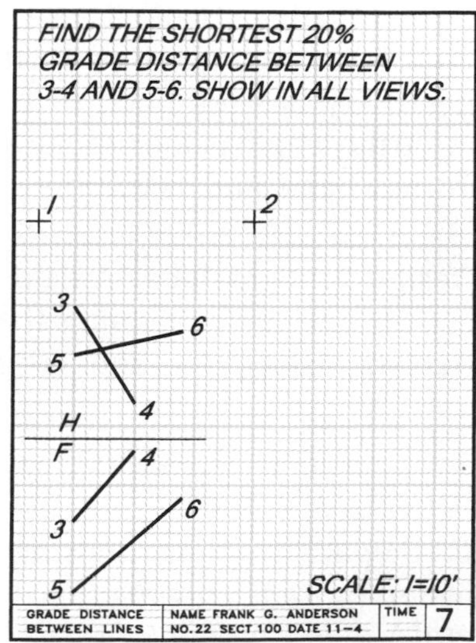

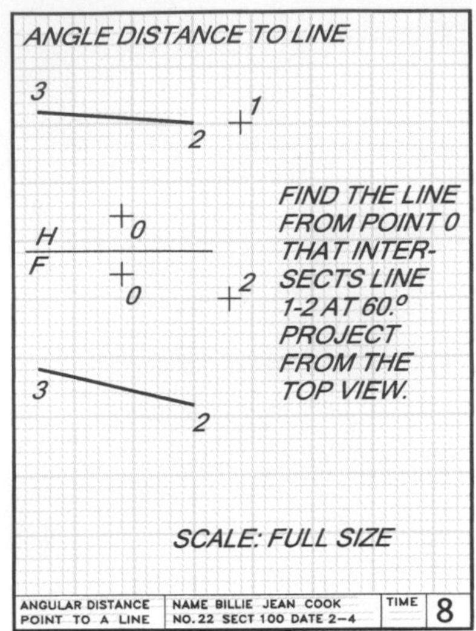

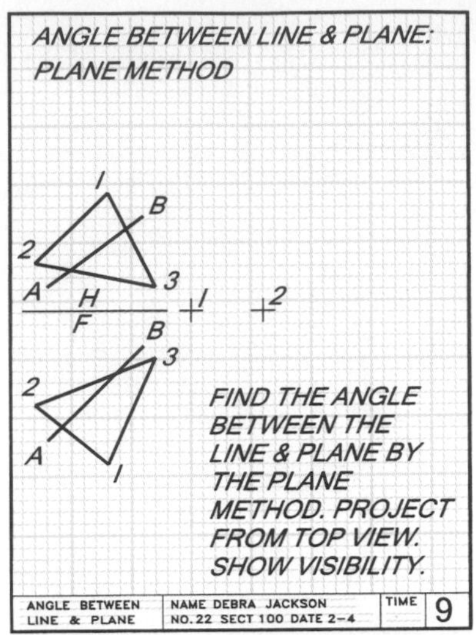

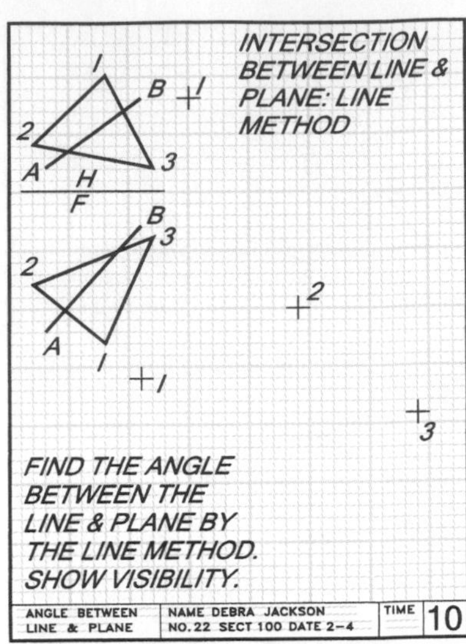

Sheet 10: Find the angle between the line and plane by the line method.

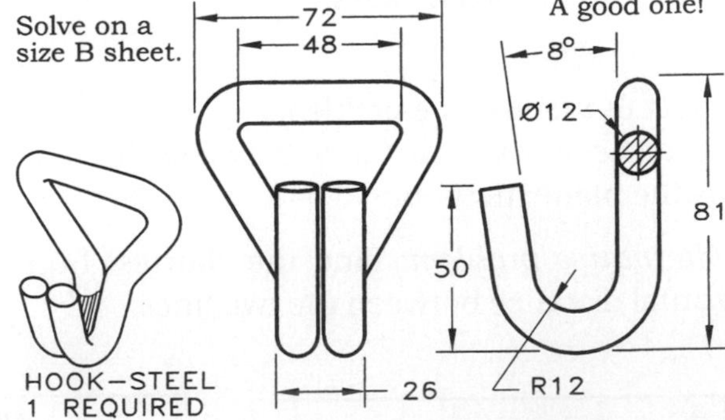

Design Problems

Lay out the necessary orthographic views to determine the specified design information. Problems can be drawn on either size A or size B sheets. (*Design problems 4–11 have been adapted from applications encountered at the Boeing Company.*)

Design 1: Lifting Hook. These views of a lifting hook have been developed, but the geometry necessary has not been determined. Determine the length of the tubular steel, the angles at each bend, and its volume.

Design 2: Rigid Tube. A rigid fuel tube for a gas turbine engine requires the calculation of the lengths of a tube and its bend angles at B and C.

A. Determine the essential geometry: angles, bending radii, and lengths on a size B sheet.

B. Prepare working drawings of the tube. *(Adapted from a problem encountered by General Motors Corporation.)*

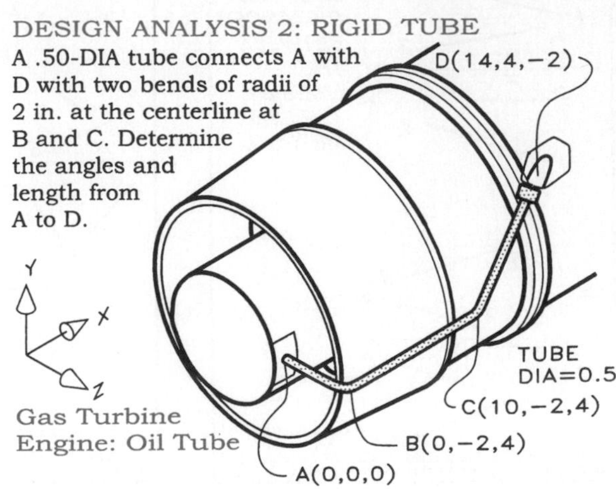

DESIGN ANALYSIS 2: RIGID TUBE
A .50-DIA tube connects A with D with two bends of radii of 2 in. at the centerline at B and C. Determine the angles and length from A to D.
D(14,4,−2)
Y
X
Z
TUBE
DIA=0.5
C(10,−2,4)
B(0,−2,4)
A(0,0,0)
Gas Turbine
Engine: Oil Tube

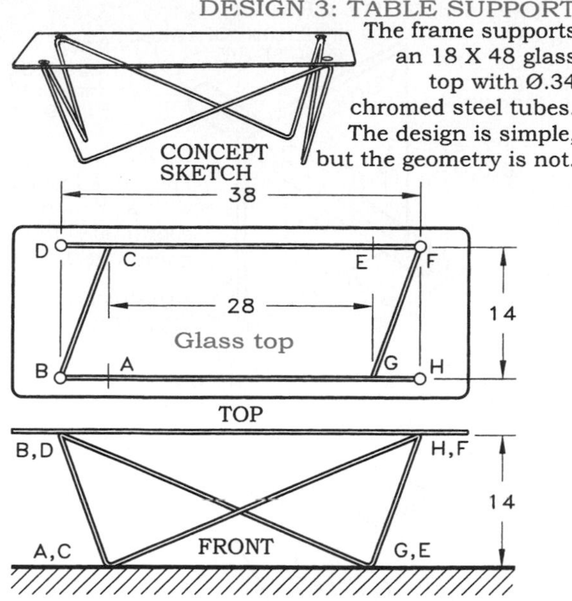

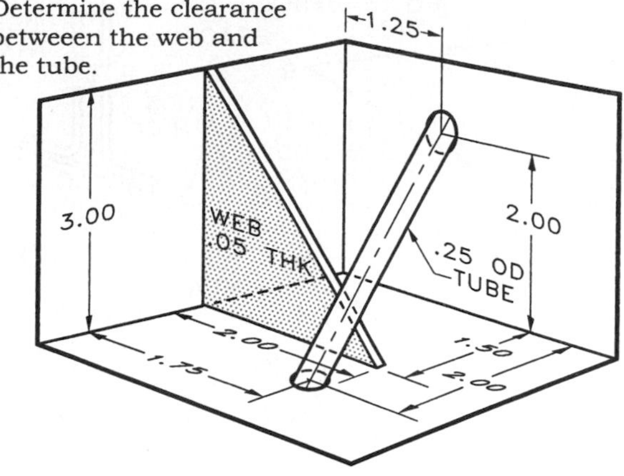

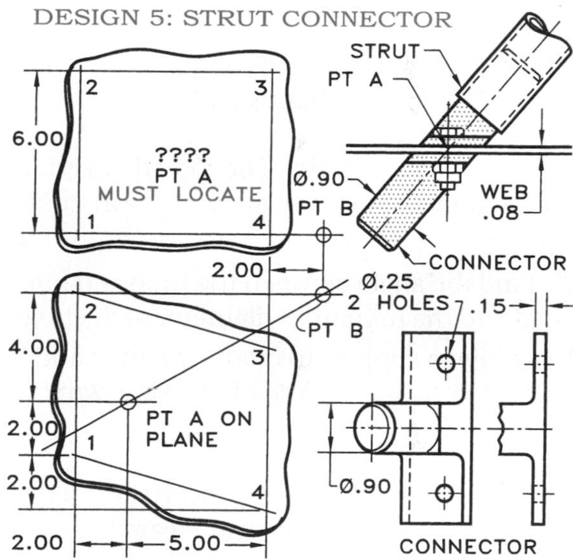

Design 3: Table Support. Convert the concept drawings into working drawings to fabricate the table design.

A. Make instrument drawings of the parts.

B. Determine the essential geometry: angles, bending radii, lengths, and weights.

C. Prepare working drawings with the necessary specifications.

Design 4: Clearance Analysis. Lay out the necessary views to determine the clearance (if any) between the web and the aircraft tube. If there is interference, modify the web accordingly.

Design 5: Strut Connector. Design a connector to support a structural strut that intersects the plane of the aircraft. Show your geometric construction and prepare detail drawings to explain your design. Use one or more size B sheets.

Design 6: Control Cable. Points A, B, and C define points on a control cable. Two brackets are to be designed to attach to the bulkhead (with 4–0.25 DIA bolts) and support a pulley that lies in the plane of the cable path. Lay out the necessary views to determine the following:

A. The angles the brackets make with the bulkhead.

B. The size of the pulley that will give the cable a clearance of .25 in. with the bulkhead.

C. Make working drawings of the pulley, brackets, and pulley axle.

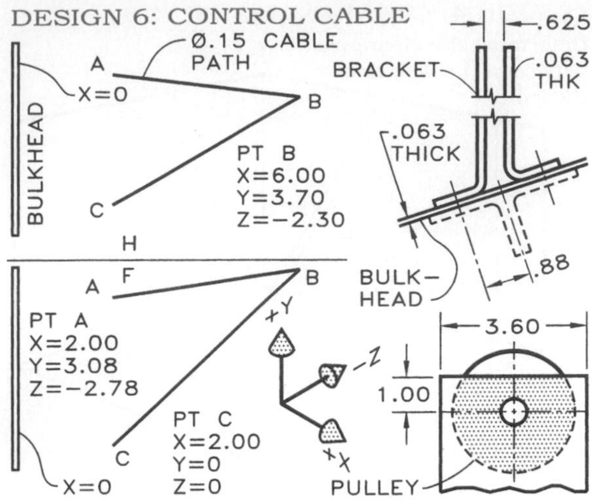

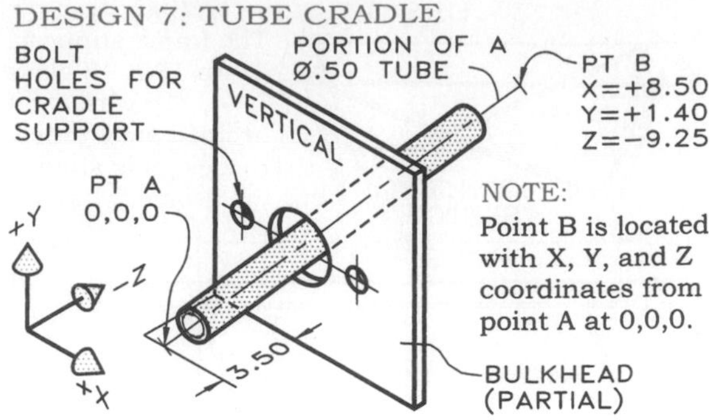

D. Make a flat-pattern development of both brackets. (Refer to Chapter 31.)

Design 7: Tube Cradle. The .50 OD overflow tube extends through an access hole in a bulkhead.

A. Find the angle between the tube and bulkhead and the minimum diameter of the hole.

B. Design a support to cradle the tube and to be bolted to the bulkhead. Make a working drawing of your design.

Design 8: Bracket. (For only the best students!) Design a bracket so the strut clears the deck, bulkhead, and brace by .10 in. The lower edge of the bracket flanges should clear the deck by .10 in. Draw a dimensioned flat pattern of your bracket design. Suggested scale: 1=5 in.

A. Determine the necessary geometry.

B. Make a working drawing of the bracket.

C. Make a flat pattern of the bracket. (Refer to Chapter 31 as needed.)

Design 9: Bracket. The bracket is made of bent flat stock. The true angle of bend at the left end is 60°, but it cannot be measured as 60° in the front view.

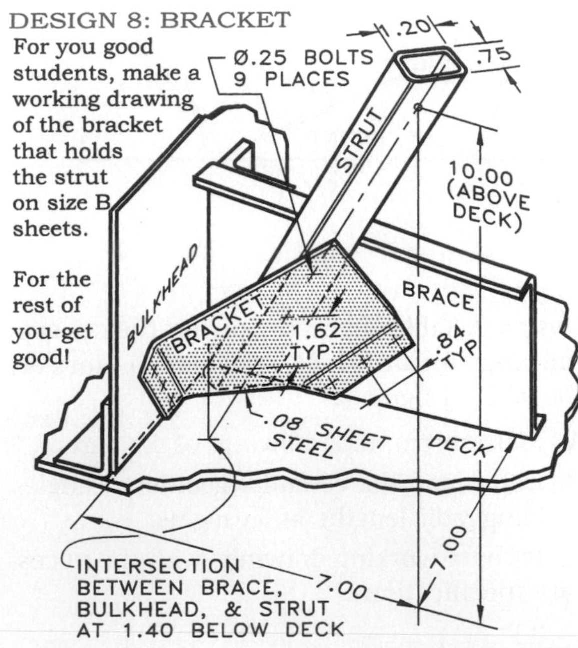

A. Determine the necessary geometry.

B. Calculate the weight of the bracket. (Steel weighs 490 lb/cu ft.)

C. Make a working drawing of it on a size A sheet.

D. Draw a developed flat view of the bracket. (Refer to Chapter 31.)

Design 10: Tube. Determine the angles in the tube at B and C and make a working drawing of the tube. What is the tube's length?

DESIGN 9: STRAP
Determine the required geometry and details.
TRUE BEND ANGLE, NOT TS IN FRONT V.
.16 THICK
2.30
3.00
45°
3.00
60°
45°
6.00
INSIDE FILLETS R.30
16
CONNECTOR STRAP
1020 STEEL–2 REQUIRED

DESIGN 10: TUBE
Determine the bend angles and the length of the aircraft tube from A to D.
D
3.00
45°
R4.00
C
B
R4.00
8.00
4.00
65°
A
TUBE 1.00 O.D.

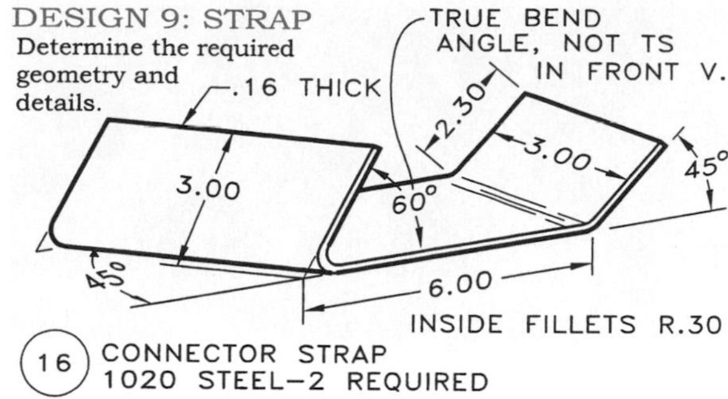

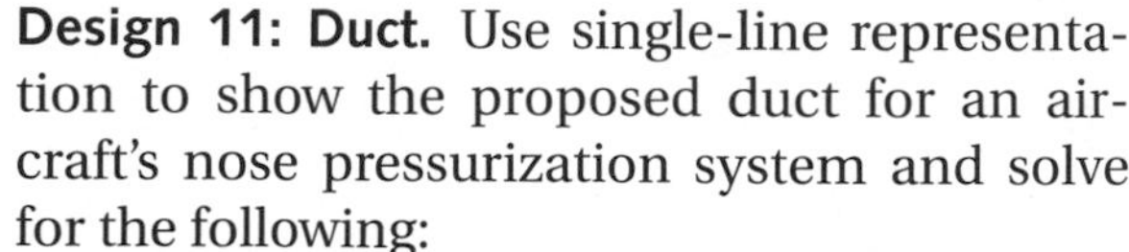

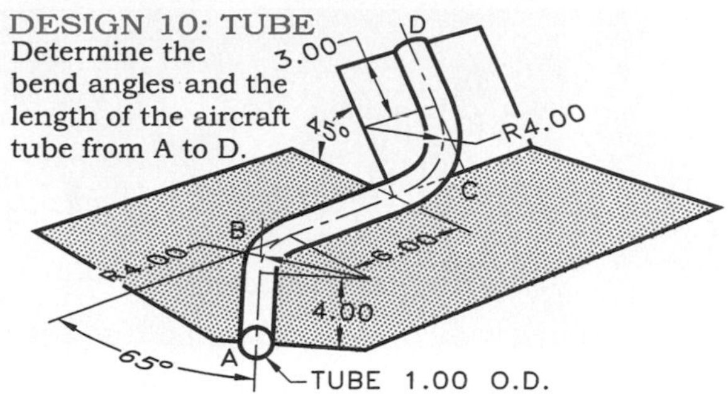

Design 11: Duct. Use single-line representation to show the proposed duct for an aircraft's nose pressurization system and solve for the following:

A. Find the lengths from point A to point F.

B. Find the angles at point C and E.

C. Give other specifications as needed.

Alternative solution: Use double-line symbols to represent the ducts; draw the components in the views where the ducts appear true length. Double-line symbols will give the most realistic representation and will require a lot more concentration, but you'll impress your instructor and, most of all, your mother.

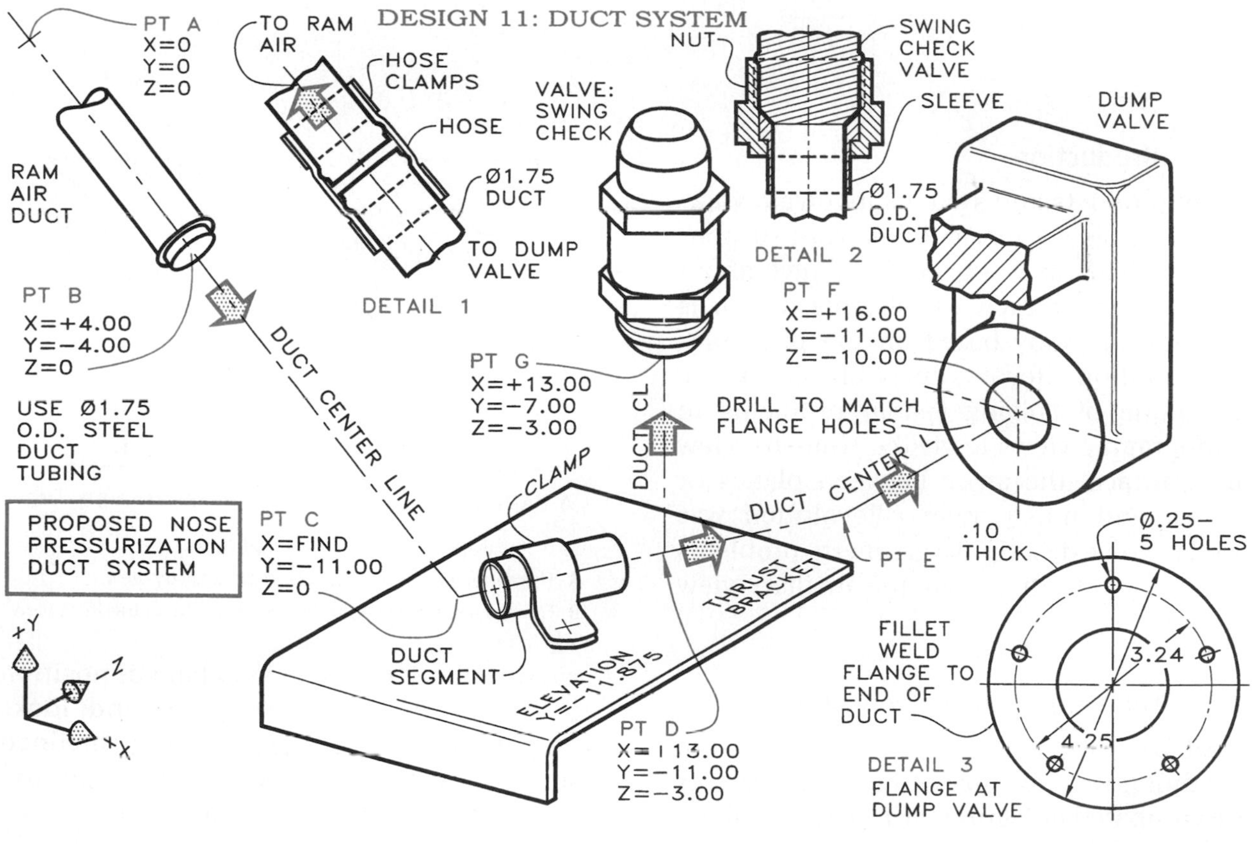

DESIGN 11: DUCT SYSTEM
PT A
X=0
Y=0
Z=0
TO RAM AIR
HOSE CLAMPS
HOSE
Ø1.75 DUCT
TO DUMP VALVE
DETAIL 1
VALVE: SWING CHECK
NUT
SWING CHECK VALVE
SLEEVE
Ø1.75 O.D. DUCT
DETAIL 2
DUMP VALVE
RAM AIR DUCT
PT B
X=+4.00
Y=−4.00
Z=0
USE Ø1.75 O.D. STEEL DUCT TUBING
DUCT CENTER LINE
PT G
X=+13.00
Y=−7.00
Z=−3.00
DUCT CL
PT F
X=+16.00
Y=−11.00
Z=−10.00
DRILL TO MATCH FLANGE HOLES
DUCT CENTER L
PROPOSED NOSE PRESSURIZATION DUCT SYSTEM
PT C
X=FIND
Y=−11.00
Z=0
CLAMP
THRUST BRACKET
PT E
.10 THICK
Ø.25– 5 HOLES
DUCT SEGMENT
ELEVATION Y=−11.875
PT D
X=+13.00
Y=−11.00
Z=−3.00
FILLET WELD FLANGE TO END OF DUCT
3.24
4.25
DETAIL 3
FLANGE AT DUMP VALVE
+Y
−Z
+X

29 Revolution: Descriptive Geometry

29.1 Introduction

Many products and systems involve revolution, such as an automobile's front suspension, which was designed to revolve about several axes at each wheel. This design is just one of many based on the principles of revolution. Revolution is an alternative technique of solving spatial problems in orthographic views to yield a true-size view of a surface, the angle between planes or a line, and many others. Revolution was used to solve descriptive geometry problems before the introduction of the auxiliary-view method.

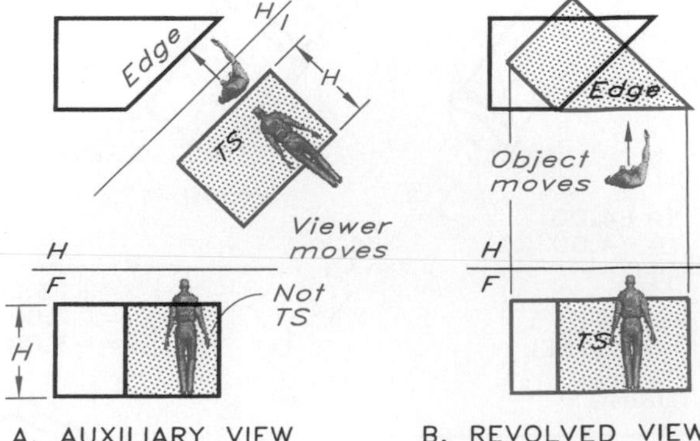

29.1 Auxiliary views versus revolved views.
A The surface is found true size in an auxiliary view.
B The surface is revolved to be seen true size in the front view.

29.2 True-Length Lines: Front View

Auxiliary view and revolution methods of obtaining the true size of inclined surfaces are compared in **Figures 29.1**. In the auxiliary view method, the observer changes position to an auxiliary vantage point and looks perpendicularly at the object's inclined surface. In the revolution method, the top view of the object is revolved about the axis until the edge view of the inclined plane is parallel to the frontal plane and perpendicular to the standard line of sight from the front view. In other words, the observer's line of sight does not change, but the object is revolved until the plane appears true size in the observer's normal line of sight.

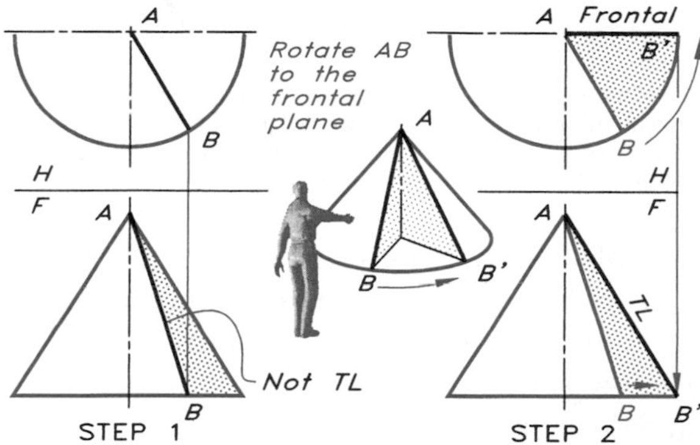

29.2 Determining true length in the front view.

Step 1 Use the top view of line AB as a radius to draw the base of a cone with point A as the apex. Draw the front view of the cone with a horizontal base through point B.

Step 2 Revolve the top view of line AB to be parallel to the frontal plane. When projected to the front view, frontal line AB′ is the outside element of the cone and is true length.

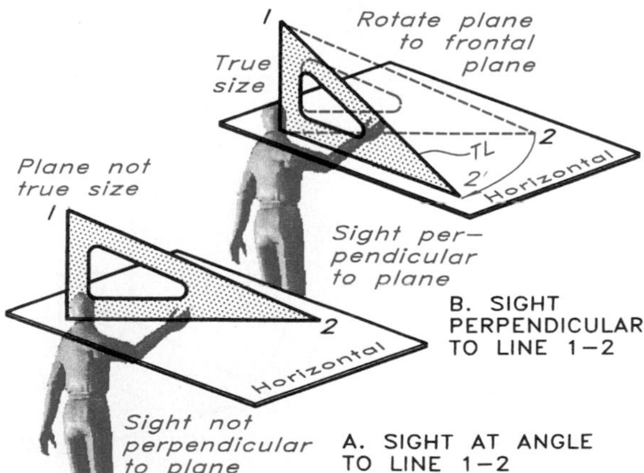

29.3 Line true length by revolution.

A Line 1-2 does not appear true length in the front view because the observer's line of sight is not perpendicular to it.

B When the triangle is revolved into the frontal plane, the observer's line of sight is perpendicular to it and line 1-2′ is seen true length.

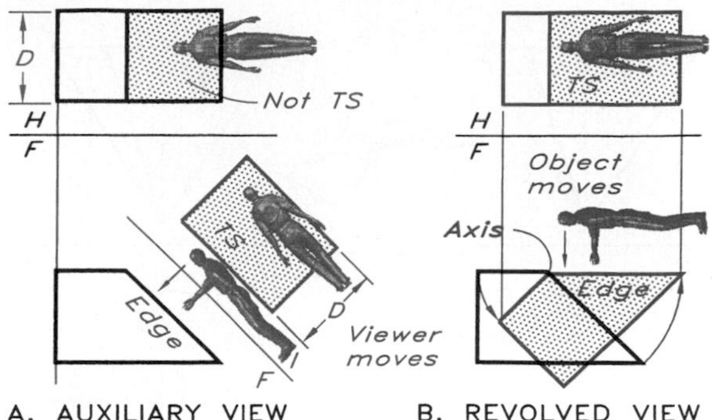

29.4 Auxiliary views versus revolved views.

A When the observer looks perpendicularly to the edge view of the plane, it appears true size in the primary auxiliary view.

B When the edge view of the plane is revolved to become horizontal, it appears true size in the top view.

To find a true-length view of line AB in the front view by revolution (**Figure 29.2**), revolve the top view of line AB into the frontal plane. The top view represents the circular base of a right cone, and the front view is the triangular view of a cone. Line AB′ is the outside element of the cone's frontal line and is true length in the front view.

Figure 29.3 illustrates the technique of finding line 1-2 true length in the front view. The observer's line of sight is not perpendicular to the triangle containing line 1-2 in its first position and therefore line 1-2 is not seen true length. When the triangle is revolved into the frontal plane in the top view, the observer's line of sight is perpendicular to the plane, and line 1-2 is seen true length in the front view.

Top View

A surface that appears as an edge in the front view may be found true size in the top view by a primary auxiliary view or by a single revolution (**Figure 29.4**). The axis of revolution is a point in the front view and true length in the top view. Revolving the edge view of the plane into the horizontal in the front view and projecting it to the top view yields the surface's

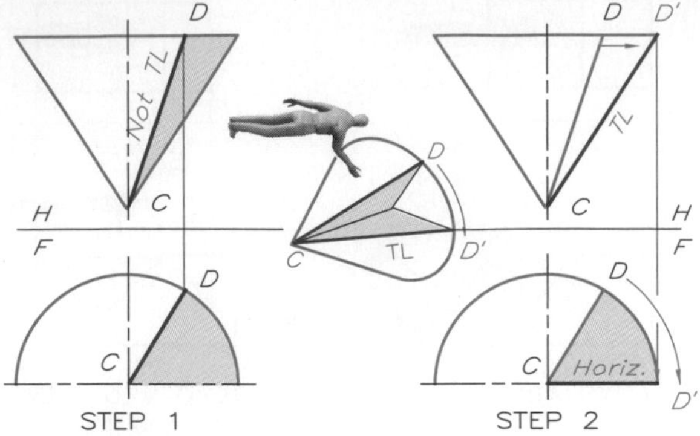

29.5 Finding the true length of a line in the top view.

Step 1 Use the front view of line CD as a radius to draw the base of a cone with C as the apex. Draw the top view of the cone with the base as a frontal plane.

Step 2 Revolve the front view of line CD into a horizontal position, CD′. When projected to the top view, CD′ is the outside element of the cone and is true length.

true size. As in the auxiliary view method, the depth dimension, D, does not change.

In **Figure 29.5**, revolving line CD into the horizontal gives its true length in the top view. The arc of revolution in the front view represents the base of the cone of revolution. Line CD′ is true length in the top view because it is horizontal and an outside element of the cone. Note that the depth in the top view does not change.

In the Profile View

In **Figure 29.6**, revolving the front view of line EF into the profile plane gives a true-length view of it. Projecting the circular view of the cone to the side view gives a triangular view of the cone. Because line EF′ is a profile line, it is true length in the side view, where it is the outside element of the cone.

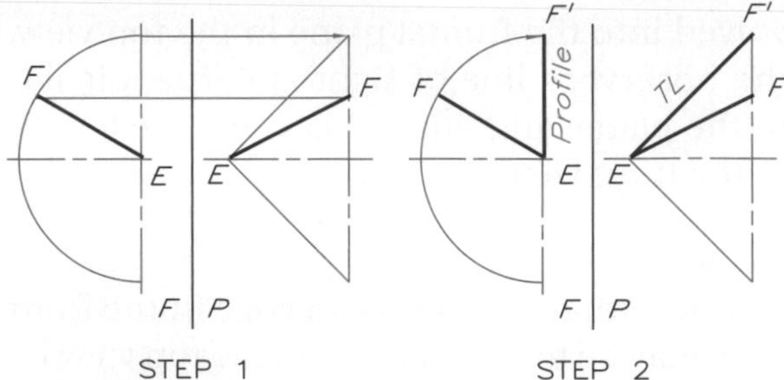

29.6 Finding the true length of a line in the side view.

Step 1 Use the front view of line EF as a radius to draw the circular view of the base of a cone. Draw the side view of the cone with its base through F.

Step 2 Revolve EF in the frontal view to position EF′, where it is a profile line, the outside element of the cone, and true length in the side view.

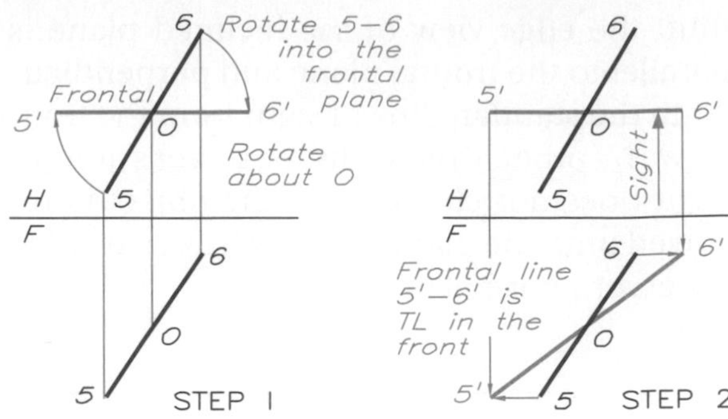

29.7 True-length views of lines may be obtained by revolving them about any point on the lines, not just their endpoints. Line 5-6 is revolved about its midpoint in the top view until it is parallel to the frontal plane and is true length in the front view.

Alternative Points of Revolution

In the preceding examples each line was revolved about one of its ends. However, a line may be revolved about any point on its length. **Figure 29.7** shows how to find line 5-6 true length by revolving it about point O and applying the previously established principles.

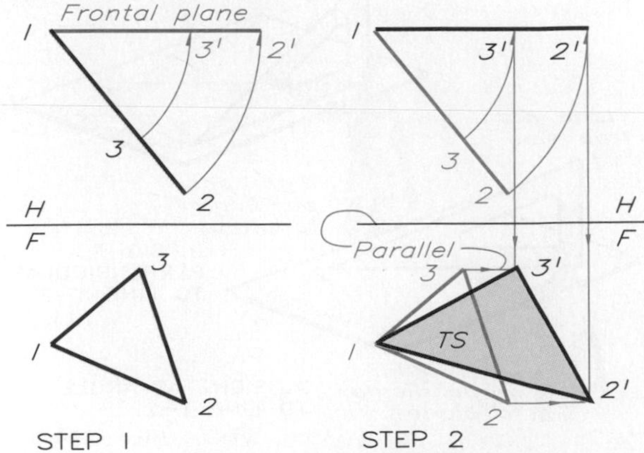

29.8 Determining the true size of a plane.

Step 1 Revolve the edge view of the plane until it is parallel to the frontal plane.

Step 2 Project points 2′ and 3′ to the horizontal projectors from points 2 and 3 in the front view.

29.3 True Size of a Plane

When a plane appears as an edge in a principal view (the top view in **Figure 29.8**), it can be revolved to be parallel to the frontal reference plane. The new front view is true size when projected horizontally across from its original front view.

The combination of an auxiliary view and a single revolution finds the plane in **Figure 29.9** true size. After finding the plane as an edge by finding the point of view of a true-length line in the plane, revolve the edge view to be parallel to the F1 reference line. To find the true size of the plane, project the original points (1, 2, and 3) in the front view parallel to the F1 line to intersect the projectors from 1′ and 2′. The true size of the plane also may be found by projecting from the top view to find the edge view.

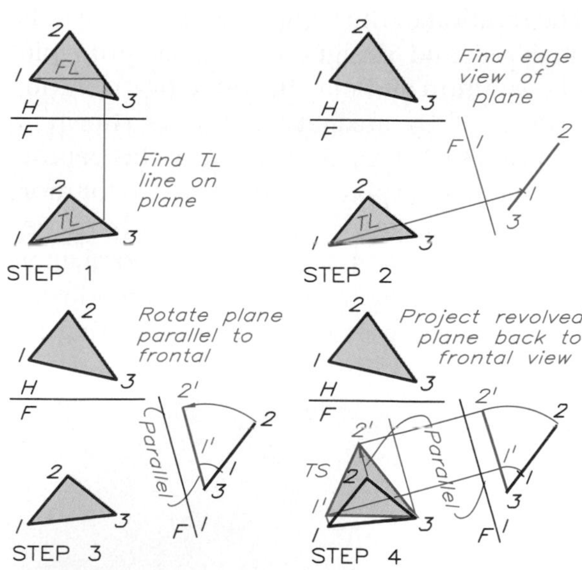

29.9 Obtaining the true size of a plane by revolution.

Step 1 To find the edge view of the plane by revolution, draw a frontal line on the plane that is true length in the front view.

Step 2 Find the edge view of the plane by finding the point view of the frontal line.

Step 3 Revolve the edge view of the plane until it is parallel to the F1 reference line.

Step 4 Project the revolved points 1′ and 2′ to the front view to the projectors from points 1 and 2 that are parallel to the F1 reference line.

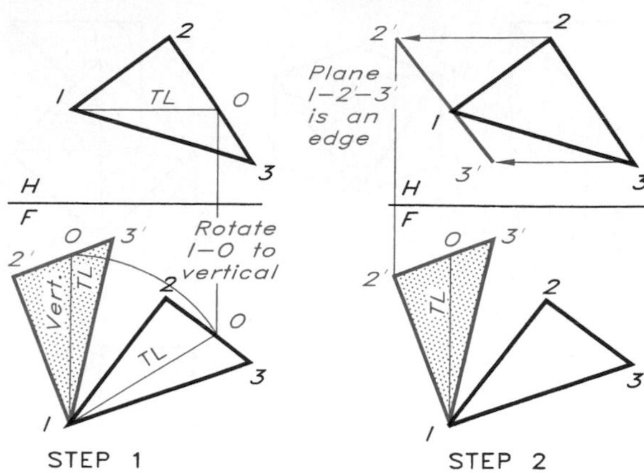

29.10 Finding the edge view of a plane.

Step 1 Draw a true-length frontal line on the plane. Revolve the front view until the true-length line is vertical.

Step 2 Locate points 2′ and 3′ by projecting in the top view. Plane 1-2′-3′ appears as an edge in the top view.

By Double Revolution

The edge view of a plane can be found by revolution without using auxiliary views (**Figure 29.10**). Draw a frontal line on plane 1-2-3, and project it to the front view, where it is true length. Revolve the plane until the true-length line is vertical in the front view. The true-length line projects as a point in the top view;

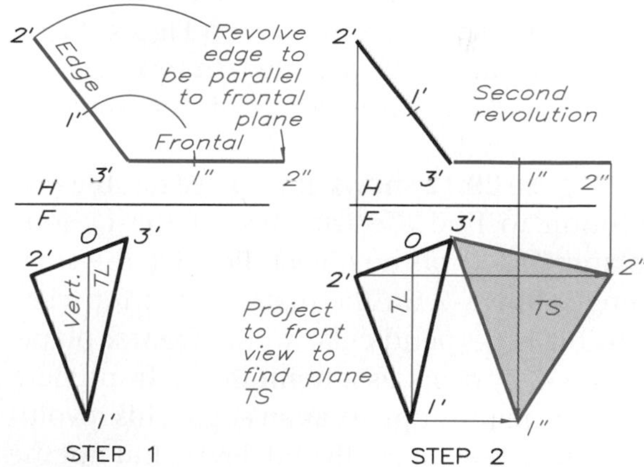

29.11 Finding the true size of a plane.

Step 1 The plane in the top view of **Figure 29.12** is revolved to a position parallel to the frontal line.

Step 2 Project points 1″ and 2″ to the front view to intersect with the horizontal projectors from the original points 1′ and 2′. Plane 1″-2″-3′ is true size in this view.

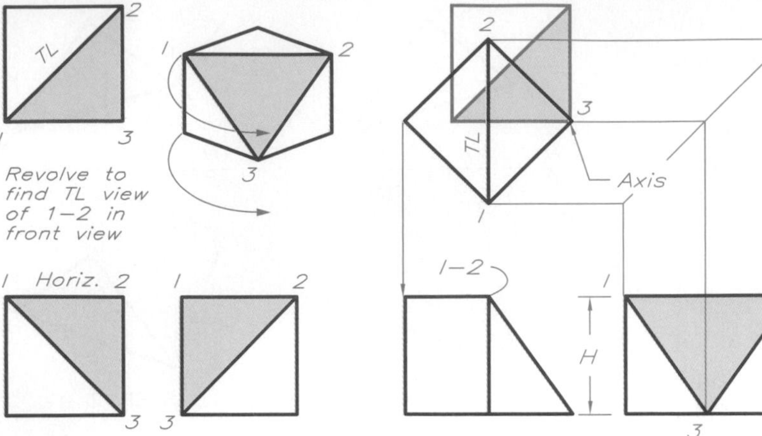

29.12 True size of a plane by double revolution.
Required Find the true size of the plane by revolution.

Step 1 Line 1-2 is horizontal in the frontal view and true length in the top view. Revolve the top view so that line 1-2 appears as a point in the front view.

Step 2 Plane 1-2-3 is an edge; revolve it into a vertical position in the front view to find its true size in the side view. The depth does not change.

therefore, the plane appears as an edge in this view. Projectors from points 2 and 3 from the top view are parallel to the HF reference line.

A second revolution, called a *double revolution,* positions this edge view of the plane parallel to the frontal plane, as shown in step 1 of **Figure 29.11**. Projecting the top views of points 1″ and 2″ to the front view gives a true-size plane 1″-2″-3″ (step 2). We could have shown this second revolution in **Figure 29.10**, but it would have resulted in overlapping views, making observation of the separate steps difficult.

Figure 29.12 shows how to use double revolution to find the true size of the oblique plane (1-2-3) of the object. Revolve the true-length line 1-2 on the plane in the top view until it is perpendicular to the frontal plane. Line 1-2 appears as a point in the front view, and the plane appears as an edge. This revolution changes the width and depth, but not the height. Then, revolve the edge view of the plane into a vertical position parallel to the profile plane. To find the plane in true size, project to the profile view, where the depth remains unchanged, but the height is greater.

29.4 Angle between Planes

The rotation of the wings of an aircraft can be analyzed and designed by using principles of revolution and may be found by revolution instead of by auxiliary views, as shown in **Figure 29.13**. This application of this geometry enabled the planes to be designed for more convenient storage below the deck of a carrier.

In **Figure 29.14**, finding the dihedral angle involves drawing its edge view perpendicular to the line of intersection and projecting the

29.13 The principles of revolution were used to determine the wing configuration of this naval aircraft.

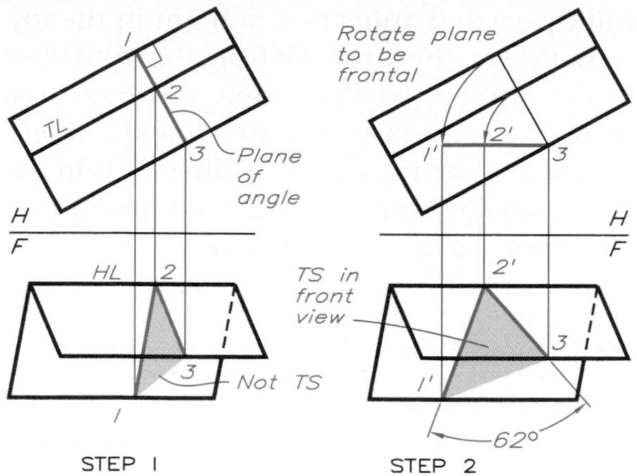

29.14 Finding the angle between planes.

Step 1 Draw the edge of the angle perpendicular to the true-length line of intersection between the planes in the top view; project it to the front view.

Step 2 Revolve the edge view of the plane of the angle to position angle 1′-2′-3 in the top view parallel to the frontal plane. Project this angle to the frontal view, where it is true size.

plane of the angle to the front view. When the edge view of the angle is revolved into a frontal plane and projected to the front view, the angle appears true size and can be measured.

Figure 29.15 shows how to solve a similar problem. Here, the line of intersection does not appear true length in the given views; therefore, an auxiliary view is needed to find its true length. Draw the plane of the dihedral angle as an edge perpendicular to the true-length line of intersection. Project the edge view of plane 1-2-3 to the top view. Then, revolve the edge view of plane 1-2-3 in the primary auxiliary view until it is parallel to the H1 reference line. Project the revolved edge view of the angle back to the top view, where it is true size.

29.5 Determining Direction

To solve more advanced problems of revolution, you must be able to locate the basic directions of up, down, forward, and backward in any given view. In **Figure 29.16A**, directional arrows in the top and front views identify the directions of backward and up. Pointing backward in the top

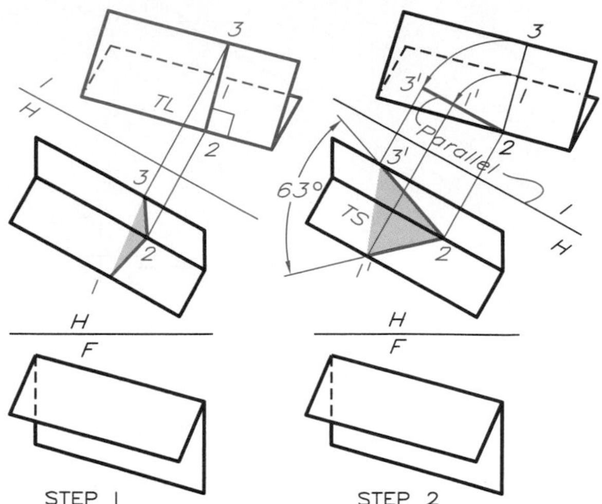

29.15 Finding the angle between oblique planes.

Step 1 Find the true-length view of the line of intersection by projecting perpendicularly from its top view. Draw the edge of the angle perpendicular to the true length of the line of intersection; project it to the top view.

Step 2 Revolve the edge view of the plane of the angle (plane 2-1′-3′) until it is parallel to the H1 reference line so that it appears true size in the top view.

view, line 4-5 appears as a point in the front view. Projecting arrow 4-5 to the auxiliary view as you would any other line determines the direction of backward. By drawing the arrow on the other end of the line, you would find the direction of forward.

Locate the direction of up in **Figure 29.16B** by drawing line 4-6 in the direction of up in

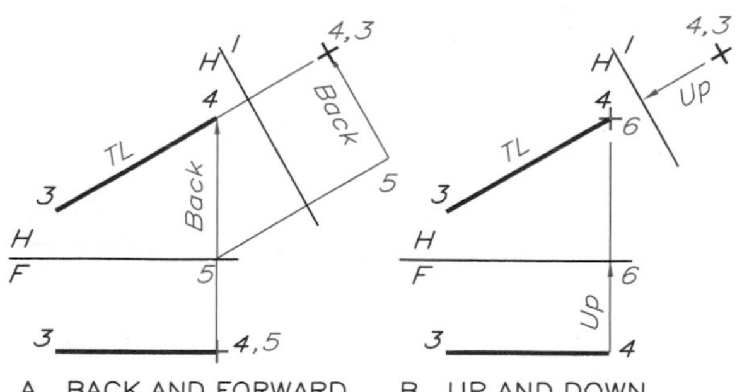

29.16 The directions of backward, forward, up, and down can be identified in the given views with arrows pointing in these directions. Directional arrows can be projected to successive auxiliary views. This drawing shows the directions of (A) backward and (B) up.

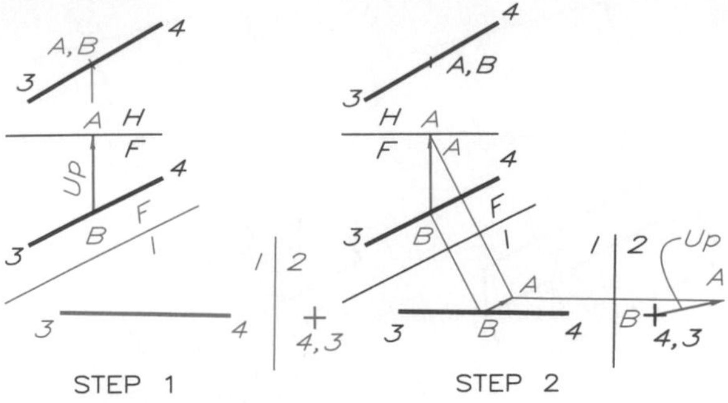

29.17 Direction in a secondary auxiliary view.

Step 1 To find the direction of up in the secondary auxiliary view, draw arrow AB pointing up in the front view. It appears as a point in the top view.

Step 2 Project arrow AB to the primary and secondary auxiliary views to show the direction of up.

the front view and as a point in the top view. Then, find the arrow in the primary auxiliary by the usual projection method. The direction of down is in the opposite direction.

You find the location of directions in secondary auxiliary views in the same way. To determine the direction of up in **Figure 29.17**, begin with an arrow that points up in the front view and appears as a point in the top view. Project the arrow AB from the front view to the primary auxiliary view and then to a secondary auxiliary view to show the direction of up. Identify the other directions in the same way by beginning with the two principal views of a known direction.

29.6 Revolution: Point about an Axis

In **Figure 29.18**, point O is to be revolved about axis 3-4 to its most forward position. Find the axis as a point in the primary auxiliary view and draw the circular path of revolution. Draw the direction of forward and find the new location of point O at O′. Project back through the successive views to find point O′ in each view. Note that point O′ lies on the line in the front view, verifying that point O′ is in its most forward position.

In **Figure 29.19** an additional auxiliary view is needed to rotate a point about an axis because axis 3-4 is not true length in the given views. You must find the true length of the axis

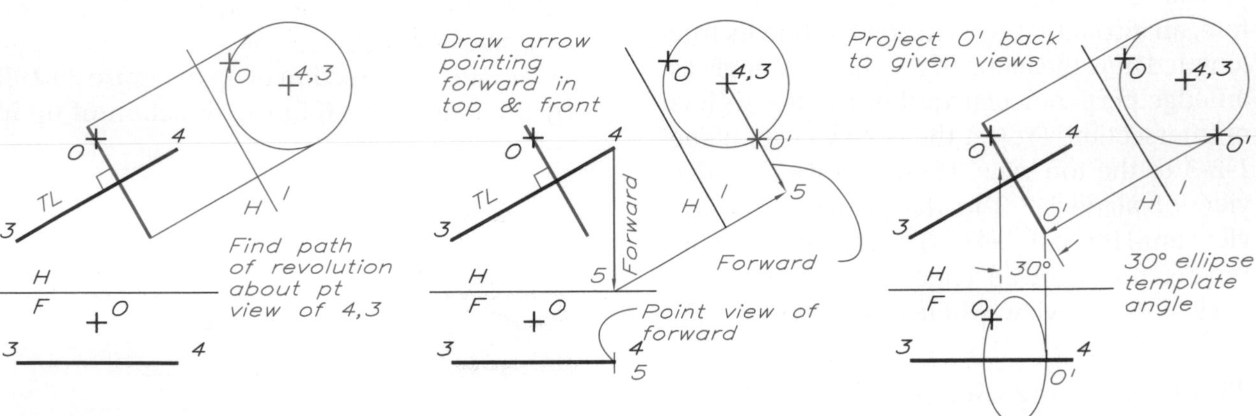

29.18 A point about an axis.

Step 1 To rotate O about axis 3-4 to its most forward position, find the point view of 3-4. The path of revolution is a circle in the auxiliary view and an edge perpendicular to 3-4 in the top view.

Step 2 Locate the most forward position of point O by drawing an arrow pointing forward in the top view that appears as a point in the front view. Find the arrow, 4-5, in the auxiliary view to locate point O′ on the circular path of revolution.

Step 3 Project O′ to the given views. The path of revolution appears as an ellipse in the front view because the axis is not true length in this view. Draw a 30° ellipse; this is the angle your line of sight makes with the circular path in the front view.

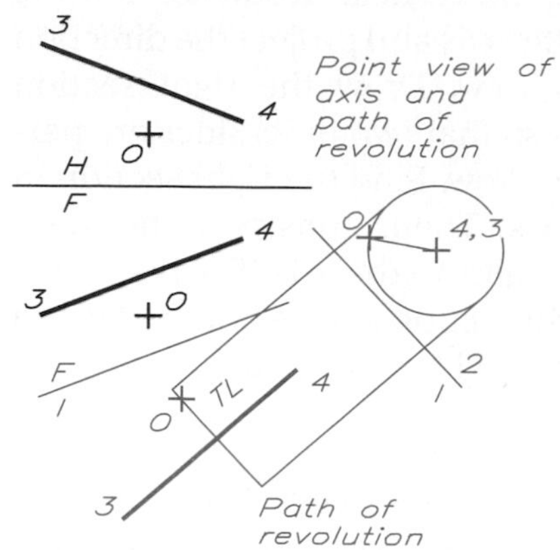

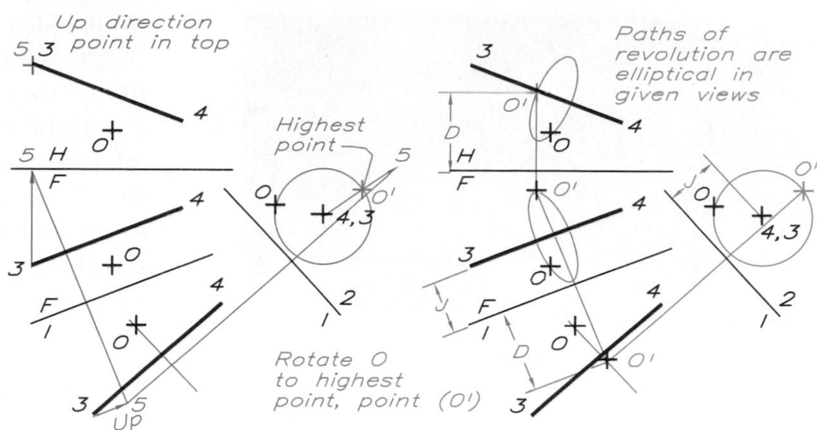

29.19 A point about an oblique axis.

Step 1 To rotate O about axis 3-4 to its highest position, find the point view of 3-4 and draw the circular path. The path of revolution is perpendicular to 3-4 in the primary auxiliary views.

Step 2 To locate the highest position on the path of revolution, draw arrow 3-5 pointing up in the front view and as a point in the top view and project it to the secondary auxiliary view to find O′.

Step 3 Project point O′ back to the given views by transferring the dimensions J and D with your dividers. The highest point lies over the line in the top view. The path of revolution is elliptical where the axis is not true length.

before you can find it as a point in the secondary auxiliary view, where the path of revolution appears as a circle. Revolve point O into its highest position, O′, and locate the up arrow, 3-5, in the secondary auxiliary view. Project back to the given views to locate O′ in each view. Its position in the top view is over the axis, which verifies that the point is at its highest position.

The paths of revolution appear as edges when their axes are true length and as ellipses when their axes are not true length. The angle of the ellipse template for drawing the ellipse in the front view is the angle the projectors from the front view make with the edge view of the revolution in the primary auxiliary view. To find the ellipse in the top view, project an auxiliary view from the top view to obtain the path of revolution as an edge perpendicular to the true-length axis.

The handcrank of a casement window (**Figure 29.20**) is an example of the application of revolution techniques. The designer must determine the clearances between the sill and the window frame when designing the crank for it to operate properly.

A Right Prism

The aggregate conveyors shown in **Figure 29.21** move materials continuously between various locations. The sides of the enclosed chute must be vertical and the bottom of the

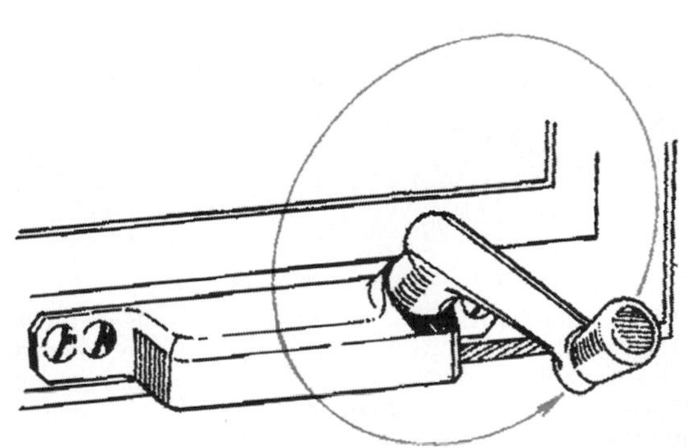

29.20 The handcrank on a casement window was analyzed and designed by applying principles of revolution for it to properly function.

29.21 A conveyor chute must be installed so that two edges of its right section are vertical for the conveyors to function properly.

chute's right section must be horizontal. Design of the chute required application of the technique of revolving a prism about its axis.

In **Figure 29.22**, the right section is to be positioned about centerline AB so that two of its sides will be vertical. To do so, find the point view of the axis and project the direction of up to this view. Draw the right section about the axis so that two of its sides are parallel to the up arrow. Find the right section in the other views. Then, construct the sides of the chute parallel to the axis. The bottom of the chute's right section will be horizontal and properly positioned for conveying material.

29.7 A Line at Specified Angles

In **Figure 29.23**, a line is to be drawn through point O that makes angles of 35° with the frontal plane and 44° with the horizontal plane and slopes forward and down. First, draw the cone containing elements making 35° with the frontal plane and then the cone with elements making 44° with the horizontal plane. The length of the elements of both cones must be equal so that the cones will intersect with equal elements. Finally, find lines O-1 and O-2, which are elements that lie on each cone and make the specified angles with the principal planes.

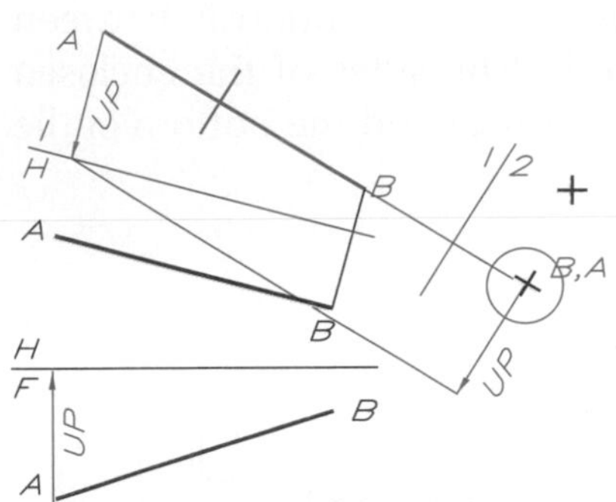

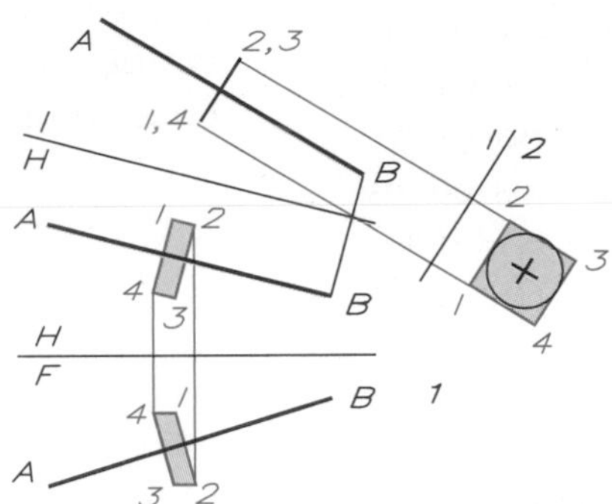

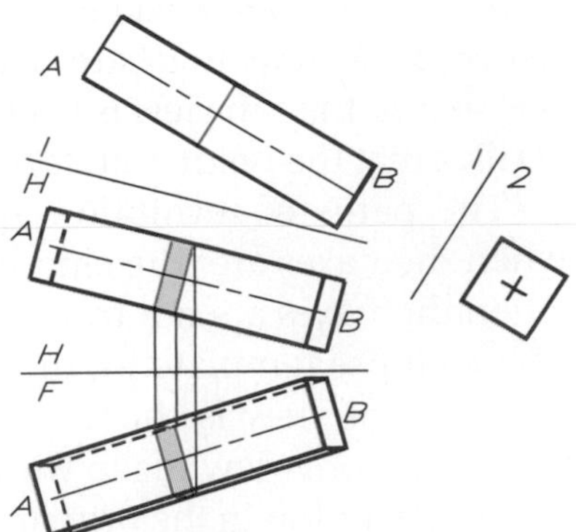

29.22 A prism about its axis.

Step 1 To draw a square chute with two vertical sides, find the point view of centerline AB in the secondary auxiliary view. Draw a circle about the axis with a diameter equal to the square section. Draw the front and top views of a vertical arrow; project it to the secondary auxiliary view to show the direction of vertical.

Step 2 Draw the right section, 1-2-3-4, in the secondary auxiliary view with two sides parallel to the vertical directional arrow. Project this section back to the previous views by transferring measurements with dividers. Locate the edge view of the section anywhere along AB in the primary auxiliary view.

Step 3 Draw the edges of the prism through the corners of the right section parallel to AB in all views. Draw the ends of the prism perpendicular to the centerline in the primary auxiliary view, where they appear as edges. Project the corner points of the ends to the top and front views.

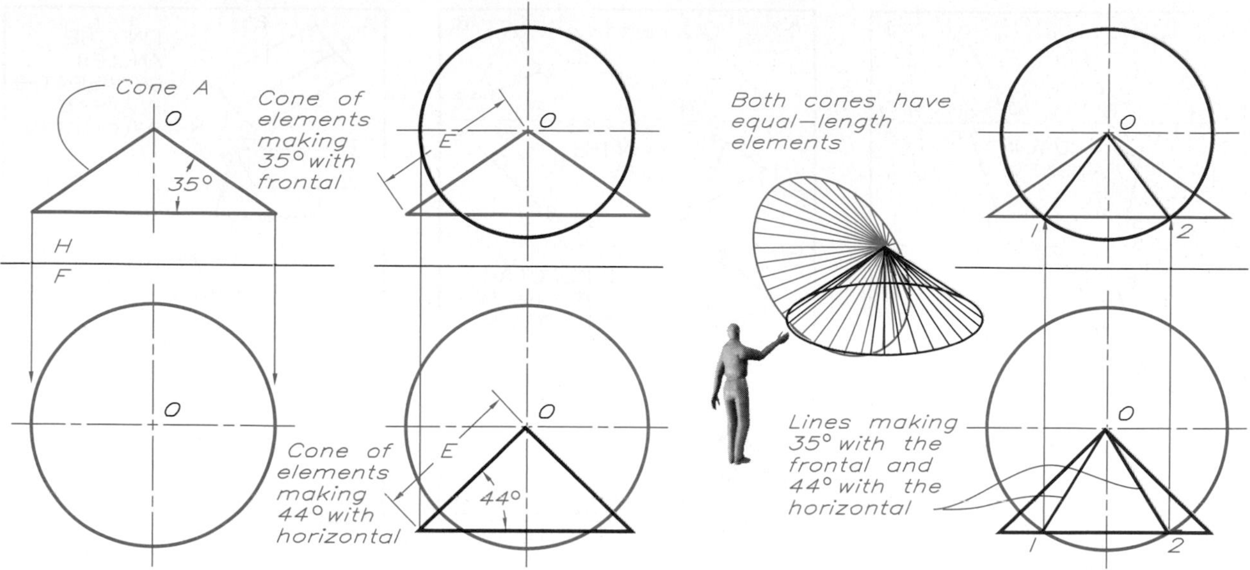

29.23 A line at specified angles.

Step 1 To draw lines at angles of 35° with the frontal and 44° with the horizontal, draw a cone in the top view with elements at 35° with the frontal plane. Draw the circular view of the cone in the front with O as the apex. All elements of the cone are 35° with the frontal plane.

Step 2 Draw a second cone in the front view with outside elements that make an angle of 44° with the horizontal plane. Draw the elements of this cone equal in length to element E of cone A. All elements of cone B are 44° with the horizontal plane.

Step 3 Because the elements are equal in length, two elements lie on the surface of each cone: lines O-1 and O-2. Locate points 1 and 2 where the bases of the cones intersect in both views. These lines slope forward and down from point O at the specified angles.

Problems

Lay out the problems on size A sheets with instruments. Each grid is equal to .20 in. (5 mm). Label all reference planes and points in each problem with 1/8-in. letters. Primary and secondary reference lines should pass through the crosses marked "1" and "2," respectively.

Sheet 1: True-length lines
A.–D. Find the true-length views of the lines by revolution as specified.

Sheet 2: True-size planes
A.–C. Find the true-size views of planes true size as specified.

Sheet 3: Angles between planes
A.–B. Find the angles between the planes by revolution.

Sheet 4: Revolution of a point
A.–B. Revolve the points about their axes as specified.

Sheet 5: Chute design
Construct a chute from A to B making the longer sides of its cross section vertical.

Sheet 6: Lines at specified angles
Draw the views of the line in accordance with the given specifications.

Sheet 7: General revolution
A.–B. Find the edge views of the planes by revolving them about their axes.
C.–D. Find the angles with the horizontal and frontal planes.

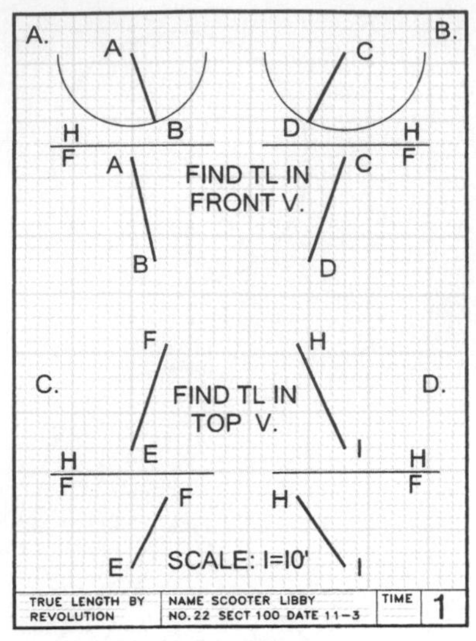

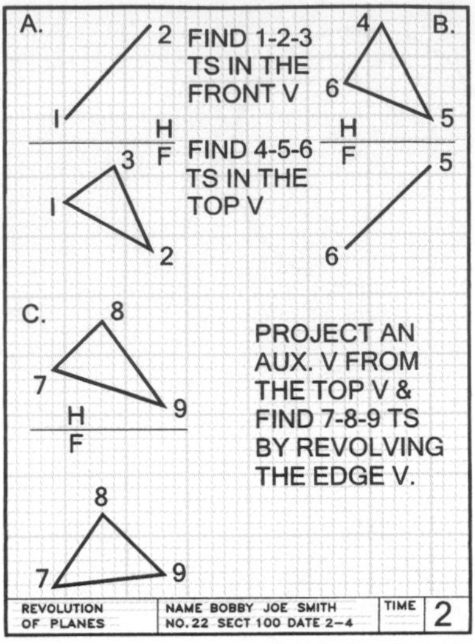

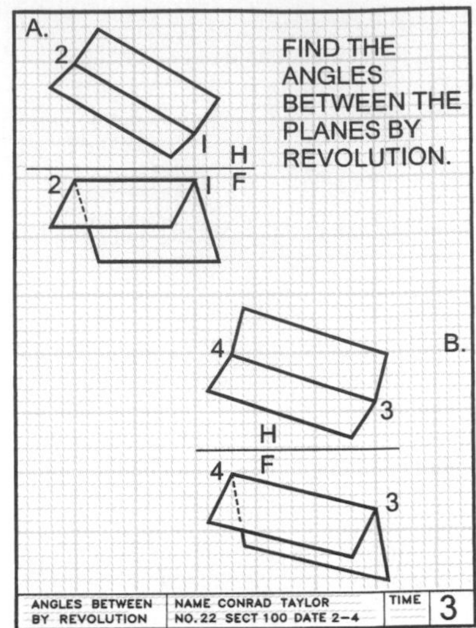

Design Problems

Design 1: Speaker mount

This concept for a proposed speaker mount provides for revolution about two axes for achievement of the best sound. Lay out on a size B sheet.

Design 2: Valve clearance

The shut-off valve must be located in the pipe so its handle will clear the bulkhead by 1 in. Lay out the necessary views on a size B sheet.

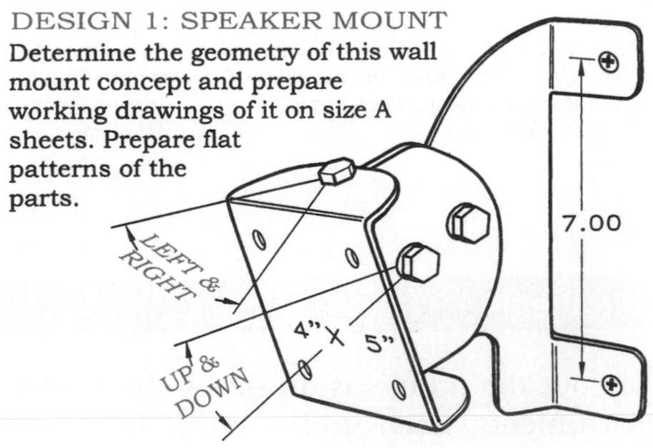

DESIGN 1: SPEAKER MOUNT
Determine the geometry of this wall mount concept and prepare working drawings of it on size A sheets. Prepare flat patterns of the parts.
LEFT & RIGHT
UP & DOWN
4"
5"
7.00

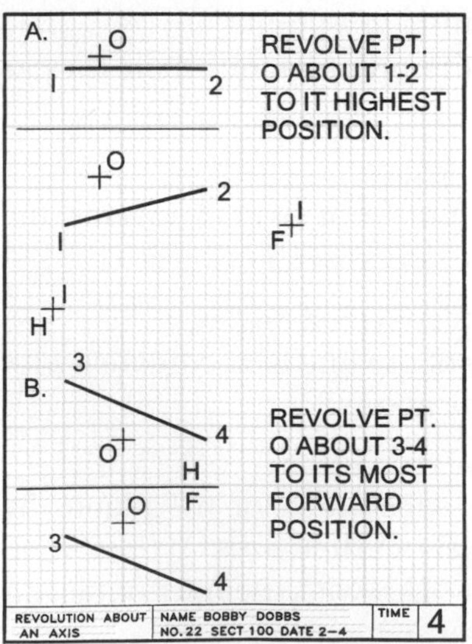

A. Determine the range of revolutions about the two axes that would be sufficient in most applications.

B. Make sketches of each part.

C. Make working drawings of the final design of the mount.

D. Make flat-pattern developments of each part. (Refer to Chapter 31.)

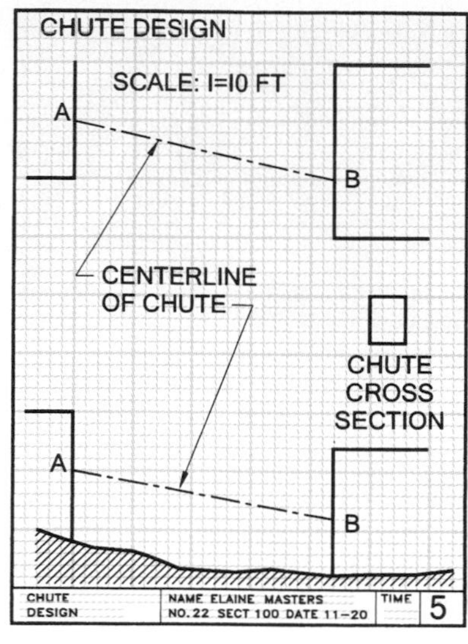

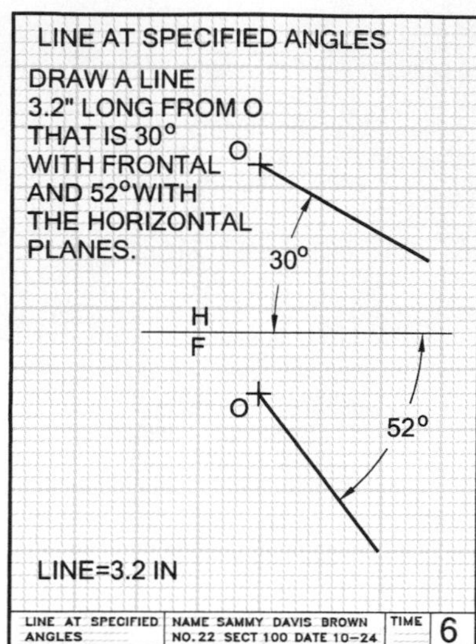

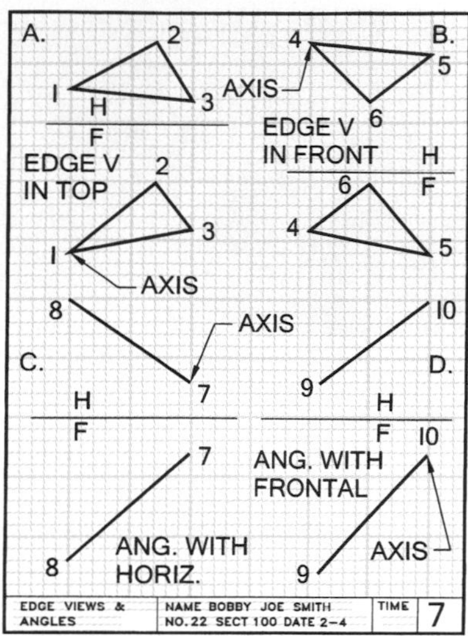

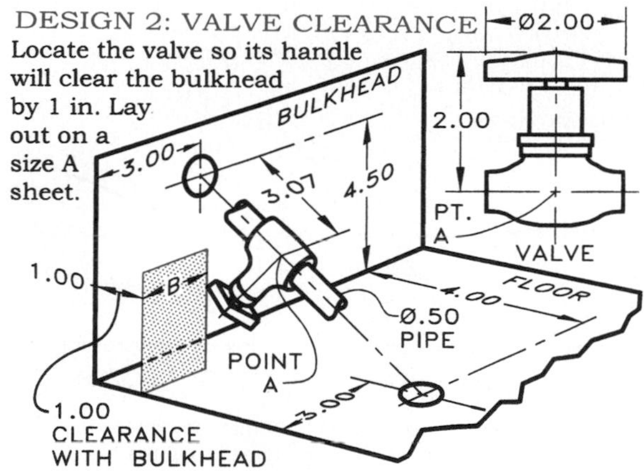

Thought Questions

1. Explain the difference between finding a line or a plane true size by revolution instead of by auxiliary views.

2. To find a line true length in the front view, in which view must the line be revolved: front, top, or side?

3. A surface that appears as an edge in the front view can be found true size by revolution in which views?

4. For a true-size view of a plane to be found, how must the preceding view of the plane appear?

5. When a plane does not appear as an edge in a principal view, how many revolutions will be required to find a true-size view of it?

6. To find a true-size view of an angle between two planes, how must the plane of the angle be positioned with regard to the line of intersection between the planes?

7. In what view must the directions of forward and backward be drawn for revolving a point about a line to its most forward position?

8. How does the circular path of revolution about an axis appear in the view where the axis is true length?

9. How must the line that is the axis of revolution appear to show the true, circular path of revolution?

10. Sketch the setup geometry for a line that makes 35° with horizontal and 45° with the front. Sketch its solution.

30 Vector Graphics

30.1 Introduction

Design of a structural system requires analysis of each member to determine the loads each must support and whether those loads are in tension or compression. Forces may be represented graphically by vectors and their magnitudes and directions determined in 3D space. Graphical methods are useful in the solution of vector problems as alternatives to conventional trigonometric and algebraic methods. Quantities such as distance, velocity, and electrical properties also may be represented as vectors for graphical solution.

30.2 Definitions

To help you understand more easily the discussion of vectors in this chapter, the following terms are defined:

Force: a push or pull tending to produce motion. All forces have magnitude, direction, and a point of application. The person shown pulling the rope in **Figure 30.1A** is applying a force to the weight W.

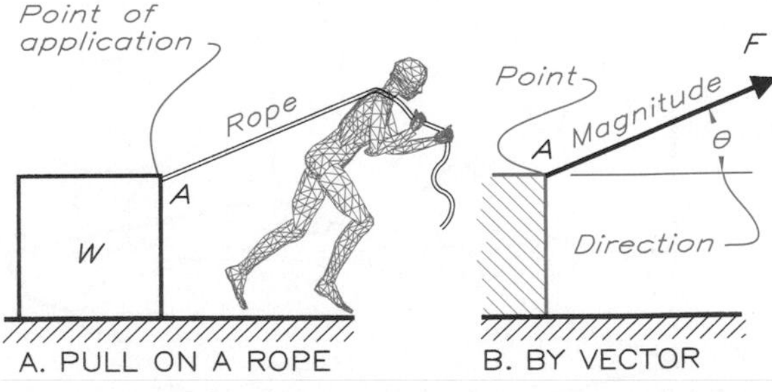

30.1 A force applied to an object (A) may be represented by a vector depicting the magnitude and direction of the force (B).

Vector: a graphical representation of a force drawn to scale and depicting magnitude, direction, and point of application. The vector in **Figure 30.1B** represents the force applied through the rope to pull the weight W.

Magnitude: the amount of push or pull represented by the length of the vector line, usually measured in pounds or kilograms.

Direction: the inclination of a force (with respect to a reference coordinate system) indicated by a line with an arrow at one end.

Point of application: the point through which the force is applied on the object or member (point A in **Figure 30.1A**).

Compression: the state created in a member by forces that tend to shorten it. Compression is represented by the letter C or a plus sign (+).

Tension: the state created in a member by pulling forces that tend to stretch it. Tension is represented by the letter T or a minus sign (−).

System of forces: the combination of all forces acting on an object as shown (forces A, B, and C in **Figure 30.2**).

Resultant: a single force that can replace all the forces of a force system and have the same effect (force R in **Figure 30.2**).

Equilibrant: the opposite of a resultant; the single force that can be used to counterbalance all forces of a force system.

Components: separate forces that if combined would result in a single force; forces A and B are components of resultant R1 in **Figure 30.2**.

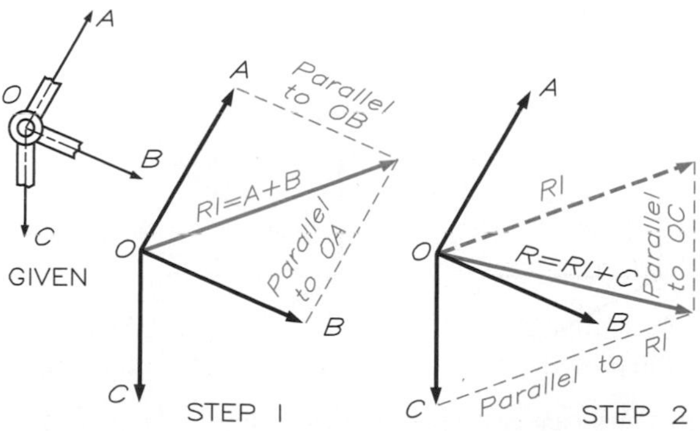

30.2 Determining the resultant by the parallelogram method.

Step 1 Draw a parallelogram with its sides parallel to vectors A and B. The diagonal R1 is the resultant of forces A and B.

Step 2 Draw a parallelogram using vectors R1 and C to find diagonal R, or the overall resultant that can replace forces A, B, and C.

Space diagram: a diagram depicting the physical relationship between structural members, as given in **Figure 30.2**.

Vector diagram: a diagram of vectors representing the forces in a system and used to solve for unknown vectors in the system.

Metric units: standard units of weights and measures. The kilogram (kg) is the unit of mass (load); and one kilogram is approximately 2.2 lb.

30.3 Coplanar, Concurrent Forces

When several forces, represented by vectors, act through a common point of application, the system is **concurrent**. In **Figure 30.2** vectors A, B, and C act through a single point; therefore this system is concurrent. When all vectors lie in the same plane, the system is **coplanar**, and only one view is necessary to show them true length.

The **resultant** is the single vector that can replace all forces acting on the point of application. Resultants may be found graphically by the **parallelogram method** and the **polygon method**.

An **equilibrant** has the same magnitude, orientation, and point of application as the resultant in a system of forces, but in the opposite direction. The resultant of the system of forces shown in **Figure 30.3** is balanced by the equilibrant applied at point O, thereby causing the system to be in equilibrium.

Resultant: Parallelogram Method

In **Figure 30.2**, the vectors lie in the same plane, act through a common point, and are drawn to scale using their known magnitudes. Use of the parallelogram method to determine resultants requires that the vectors be drawn to scale. Vectors A and B form two sides of a parallelogram. Constructing parallels to these vectors completes the parallelogram. Diagonal R1 is the resultant of forces A and B; that is, resultant R1 is the vector sum of vectors A and B and can be used to replace A and B.

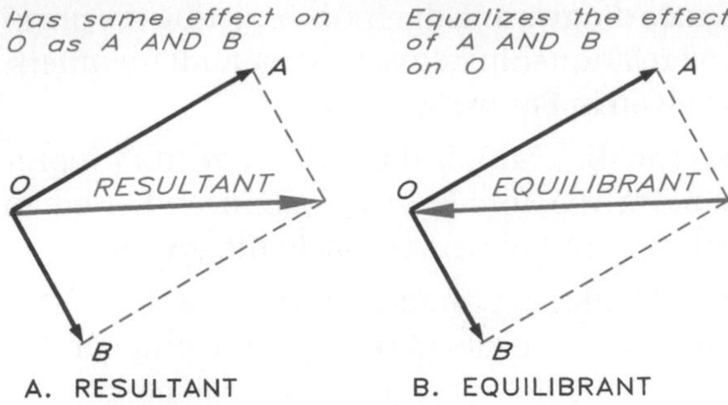

30.3 The (A) resultant and (B) equilibrant are equal in all respects except in direction (shown by arrowhead).

Replaced by R1, vectors A and B now may be disregarded. Resultant R1 and vector C form two sides of a second parallelogram. Its diagonal, R, is the vector sum of R1 and C and is the resultant of the entire system. Resultant R may be thought of as the only force acting on the point of application, thereby simplifying further analysis by replacing three forces, A, B, and C.

Resultant: Polygon Method

Figure 30.4 shows the same system of forces, but here the resultant is determined by the polygon method. Again, the vectors are drawn to scale but in this case head-to-tail, in their true directions to form the polygon. The vectors are laid out in a clockwise sequence beginning with vector A. The polygon does not close, so the system is not in equilibrium but tends to be in motion. The resultant (from the tail of vector A to the head of vector C) closes the polygon.

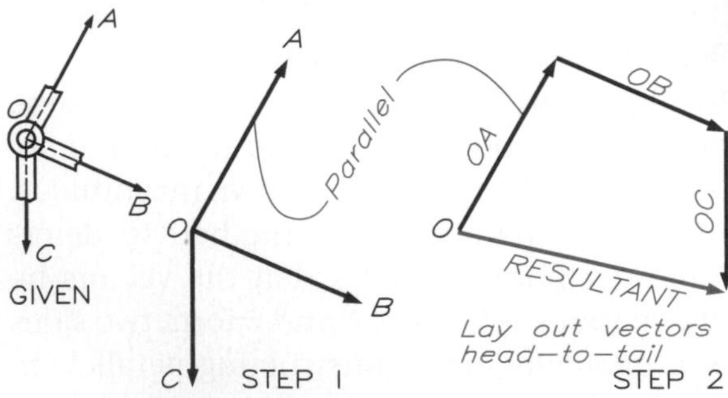

30.4 The resultant of a coplanar, concurrent system may be determined by the polygon method, in which the vectors are drawn head-to-tail. The vector that closes the polygon is the resultant.

30.4 Noncoplanar, Concurrent Forces

When vectors lie in more than one plane of projection, they are noncoplanar, requiring 3D views for analysis of their spatial relationships. The resultant of a system of noncoplanar forces may be obtained by the parallelogram method if their projections are given in two adjacent orthographic views.

Resultant: Parallelogram Method

In **Figure 30.5** vectors 1 and 2 were used to construct the top and front views of a parallelogram and its diagonal R1 in both views. The front view of R1 must be an orthographic projection of its top view.

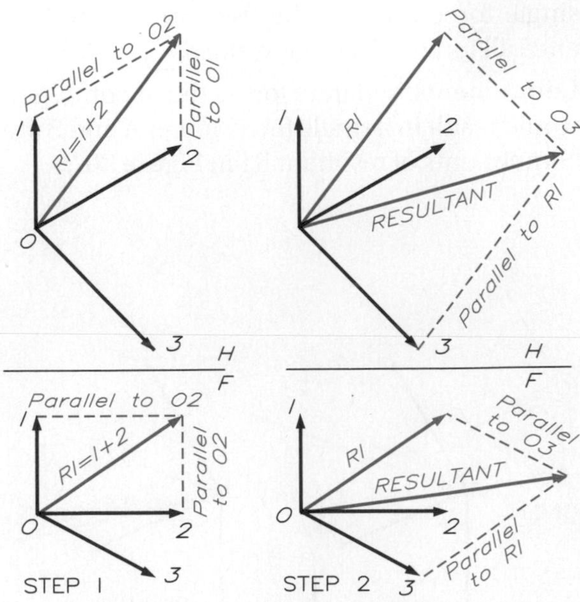

30.5 Resultant by the parallelogram method.

Step 1 Use vectors 1 and 2 to construct a parallelogram in the top and front views. Diagonal R1 is the resultant of vectors 1 and 2.

Step 2 Use vectors 3 and R1 to construct a second parallelogram to find the overall resultant, R.

Then, resultant R1 and vector 3 are resolved to form the overall resultant in both views. The top and front views of the resultant must project orthographically. The overall resultant replaces vectors 1, 2, and 3. However, it is an oblique line, so an auxiliary view (**Figure 30.6**) or revolution must be used to obtain its true length.

Resultant: Polygon Method

Figure 30.6 shows the solution of the same system of forces for the resultant by the polygon method. **Each vector is laid off head-to-tail clockwise, beginning with vector 1 in the front view.**

Then, the vectors are projected orthographically from the front view to the top view of the vector polygon. The vector polygon does not close, so the system is not in equilibrium. In both views the resultant (from the tail of vector 1 to the head of vector 3) closes the polygon. However, the resultant is an oblique line, requiring an auxiliary view to obtain its true length.

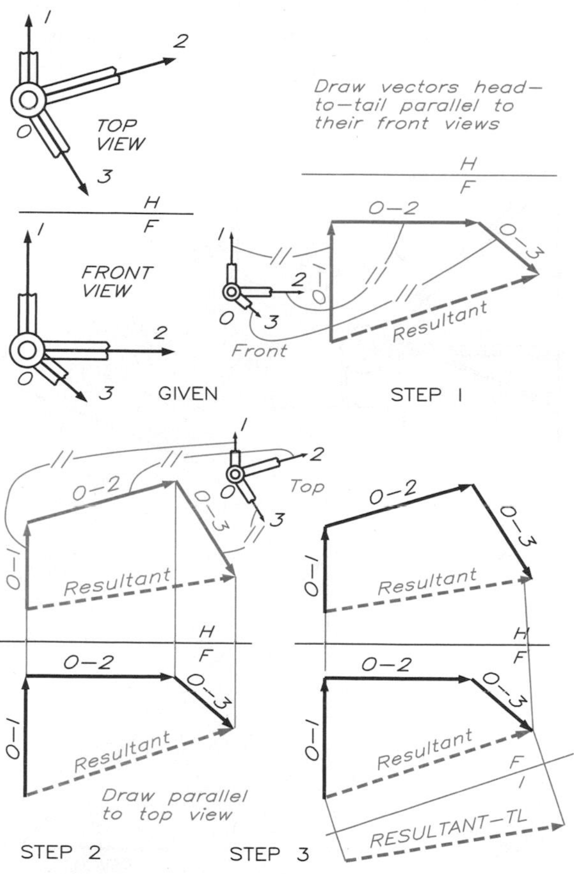

30.6 Resultant by the polygon method.
Find the resultant of the forces by the polygon method.

Step 1 Lay off each vector head-to-tail parallel to the given view and find the front view of the resultant.

Step 2 Draw the top view of the same vectors head-to-tail in the top view as a 3D polygon projected above the front view.

Step 3 The resultant is found true length in an auxiliary view projected from the front view.

30.5 Forces in Equilibrium

The manufacturing hoist shown in **Figure 30.7** can be analyzed graphically to determine the loads carried by each member and cable, since it is a coplanar, concurrent structure in equilibrium. **A structure in equilibrium is one that is static with no motion taking place; the forces balance each other.** If the forces in a system are not in balance, it is not static, but instead it is a **dynamic** system that is in motion.

30.7 The loads in the members of this crane can be determined by vector graphics as a coplanar system in equilibrium. *(Courtesy of Pacific Hoist Company.)*

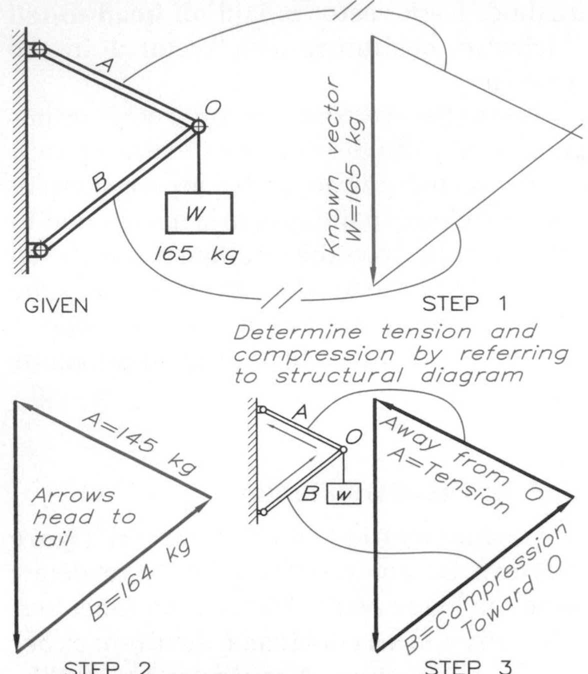

30.8 Coplanar forces in equilibrium: Find the forces in the structural members supporting the 165-kg load.

Step 1 Draw the load of 165 kg as a vector. Draw vectors A and B parallel to their directions from the ends of the 165 kg and extend them to their intersection.

Step 2 The direction of the 165-kg vector is known. Draw the arrows on the triangular polygon head-to-tail to find the directions of A and B.

Step 3 Vector A points away from point O when transferred to the structural diagram and thus is in tension. Vector B points toward point O and is in compression.

The coplanar, concurrent structure depicted in **Figure 30.8** is designed to support a load of W = 165 kg. The maximum loading of each structural member determines the material and size of the members to be used in the design.

A single view of a vector polygon in equilibrium allows you to find only two unknown values. (Later, we show how to solve for three unknowns by using descriptive geometry.) Lay off the only known force, W = 165 kg, parallel to its given direction (here pointing vertically downward). Then, draw the unknown forces A and B parallel to the supports to form the vector polygon and scale (or calculate) the magnitude of these forces.

Analyze vectors A and B to determine whether they are in tension or compression and thus find their direction. Vector B points upward to the right, which is toward point O when transferred to the structural diagram shown in the small drawing. Vectors that act *toward* their point of application are in compression. Vector A points away from point O when transferred to the structural diagram and is in tension.

Figure 30.9 is a similar example involving determination of the loads in the structural members caused by the weight of 110 lb acting over a pulley. The only difference between this solution and the previous one is the

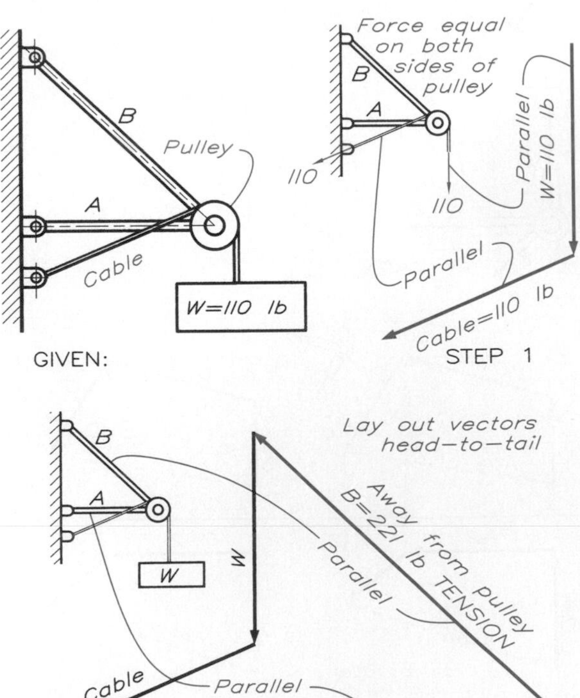

30.9 Forces in equilibrium: Pulley application. Find the forces in the members.

Step 1 The force in the cable is equal to 110 lb on both sides of the pulley. Draw these two forces as vectors head-to-tail and parallel to their directions in the space diagram.

Step 2 Draw A and B head-to-tail to close the polygon. Vector A points toward the point of application and thus is in compression. Vector B points away from the point and is in tension.

construction of two equal vectors at the outset to represent the cable loads on both sides of the pulley. These two vectors are laid off first, since their values and directions are known, leaving only the unknown vectors to be determined.

30.6 Coplanar Truss Analysis

Designers use vector polygons to determine the loads in each member of a truss by two graphical methods: (1) joint-by-joint analysis and (2) Maxwell diagrams.

Joint-by-Joint Analysis

In the **Fink truss** shown in **Figure 30.10**, 3000-lb loads are applied at its joints. The exterior forces on the truss are labeled with letters placed between them, and numerals are placed between the interior members. Each vector is referred to by the number on each of its sides clockwise about its joint. For example, the vertical load at the left is denoted AB, with A at the tail and B at the head of the vector. This method of designating forces is called **Bow's notation**.

First analyze the joint at the left end with a reaction of 4500 lb. When you read clockwise about the joint, the force is EA, where E is the tail and A is the head of the vector. Continuing clockwise, the next forces are A-1 and 1-E, which close the polygon at E, the beginning letter. Place arrowheads in a head-to-tail sequence beginning with the known vector EA.

Determine tension and compression by relating the directions of each vector to the original joint. For example, A-1 points toward the joint and is in compression, whereas 1-E points away and is in tension. The truss is symmetrical and equally loaded, so the loads in the members on the right will be equal to those on the left.

Analyze the other joints in the same way. The directions of the vectors are opposite at each end. For example, vector A-1 is toward the left in step 1 and toward the right in step 2.

Maxwell Diagrams

The **Maxwell diagram** is virtually the same as the joint-by-joint analysis, with the exception that the polygons overlap, with some vectors common to more than one polygon.

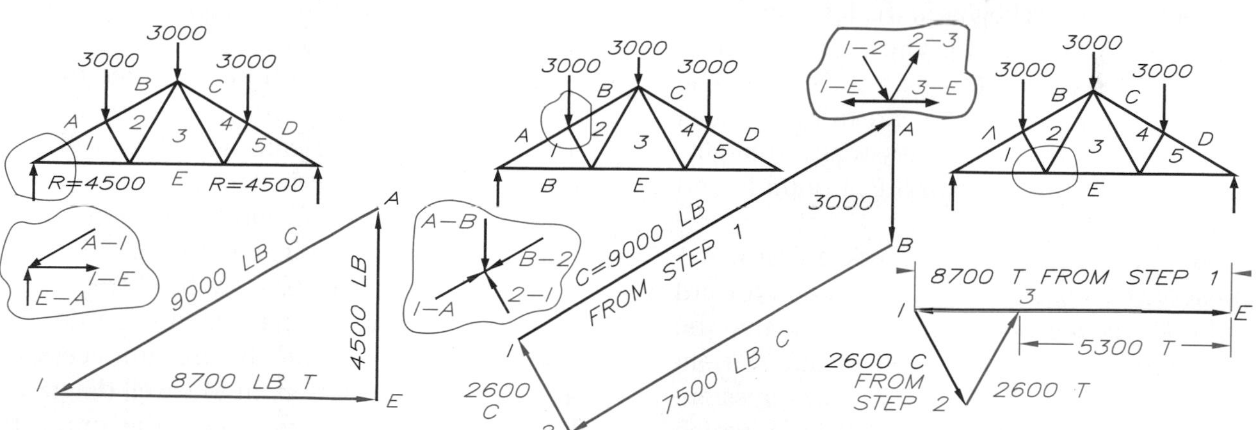

30.10 Truss analysis: Joint-by-joint.

Step 1 Label the truss, with letters between the exterior loads and numbers between interior members. Analyze the left joint with two unknowns, A-1 and 1-E. Draw vectors A-1 and 1-E, parallel to their directions from both ends of EA in a head-to-tail sequence.

Step 2 Use vector 1-A and load AB from step 1 to find B-2 and 2-1. Draw 1-A first, then AB, and draw B-2 and 2-1 to close the polygon, moving clockwise about the joint. A vector pointing toward the point of application is in compression. A vector pointing away from the point of application is in tension.

Step 3 Lay out vectors E-1 and 1-2 from the preceding steps. Vectors 2-3 and 3-E close the polygon and are parallel to their directions in the space diagram. Vectors 2-3 and 3-E point away from the point of application and thus are in tension

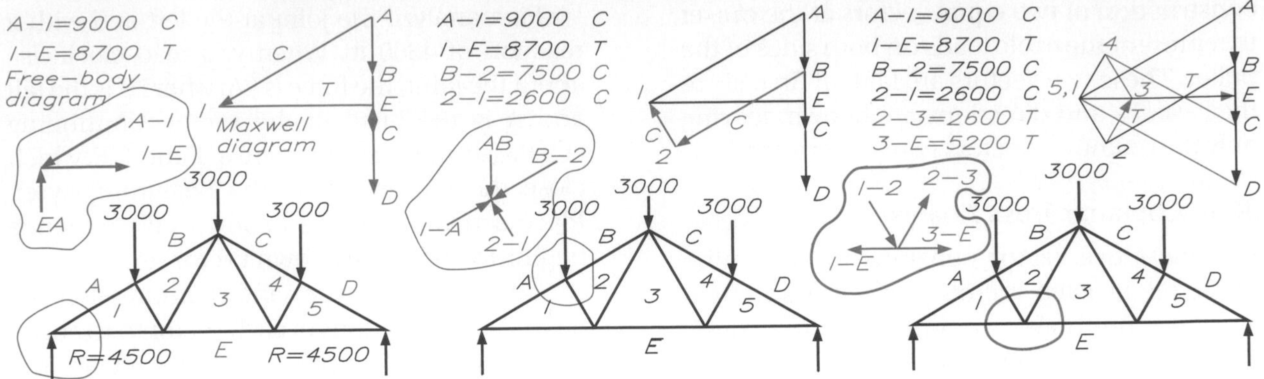

30.11 Truss analysis: Maxwell diagram.

Step 1 Label the outer spaces with letters and the internal spaces with numbers. Draw the loads head-to-tail in a Maxwell diagram; sketch a free-body diagram of the first joint. Use EA, A-1, and 1-E (head-to-tail) to draw a vector diagram. A-1 is in compression because it points toward the joint;1-E is in tension because it points away from it.

Step 2 Sketch the next joint to be analyzed. Because AB and A-1 are known, only 2-1 and B-2 are unknown. Draw them parallel to their direction (head-to-tail) in the Maxwell diagram using the previously found vector. Vectors B-2 and 2-1 are in compression, since each points toward the joint. Vector A-1 becomes vector 1-A when read in a clockwise direction.

Step 3 Sketch a free-body diagram of the next joint to be analyzed, where the unknowns are 2-3 and 3-E. Draw their vectors in the Maxwell diagram parallel to their given members to find point 3. Vectors 2-3 and 3-E are in tension because they point away from the joint. Repeat this process to find the vectors on the opposite side.

In **Figure 30.11** (step 1) the exterior loads are laid out head-to-tail in a clockwise sequence—AB, BC, CD, DE, and EA—with a letter placed at each end of each vector. The forces are parallel, so this force diagram is a vertical line.

Vector analysis begins at the left end where the force EA of 4500 lb is known. A free-body diagram is sketched to isolate this joint. The two unknowns, A-1 and 1-E, are drawn parallel to their directions in the truss, with A-1 beginning at point A, 1-E beginning at point E, and both extended to point 1.

Because resultant EA points upward, A-1 must have its tail at A and its direction toward point 1. The free-body diagram shows that the direction is toward the point of application, which means that A-1 is in compression. Vector 1-E points away from the joint, which means that it is in tension. The vectors are coplanar and may be scaled to determine their magnitudes.

In step 2, where vectors 1-A and AB are known, the unknown vectors, B-2 and 2-1, may be determined. Vector B-2 is drawn parallel to its structural member through point B in the Maxwell diagram, and the line of vector 2-1 is extended from point 1 to intersect with B-2 at point 2. The arrows of each vector are drawn head-to-tail. Vectors B-2 and 2-1 point toward the joint in the free-body diagram and therefore are in compression.

In step 3, the next joint is analyzed to find the forces in 2-3 and 3-E. The truss and its loading are symmetrical, so the Maxwell diagram will be symmetrical when completed.

If the last force polygon in the series does not close perfectly, an error in construction has occurred. A slight error may be disregarded, as a rounding error may be disregarded in mathematics. Arrowheads are unnecessary and usually are omitted on Maxwell diagrams because each vector will have the opposite direction when applied to a different joint.

A table is usually prepared that gives a listing of the structural members and their forces, with a C or T indicating whether they are in compression or tension. It is possible that under a particular loading, a member will be redundant and carry no load at all. It will be listed as a zero value.

30.7 Noncoplanar Vectors: Special Cases

The solution of three-dimensional vector systems requires the use of descriptive geometry because the system must be analyzed in three-dimensional space. An example is the manned flying system (MFS) shown in **Figure 30.12**, which was analyzed to determine the loads on its support members. Weight on the moon is 0.165 of weight on the earth. Thus a tripod that must support 182 lb on earth needs to support only 30 lb on the moon.

In general, only two unknown vectors can be determined in a single view of a vector polygon that is in equilibrium. However, the system shown in **Figure 30.13** is a special case because members B and C lie in the same edge view of the plane in the front view and appear as a single vector. Therefore, solving for three unknowns is possible in this case.

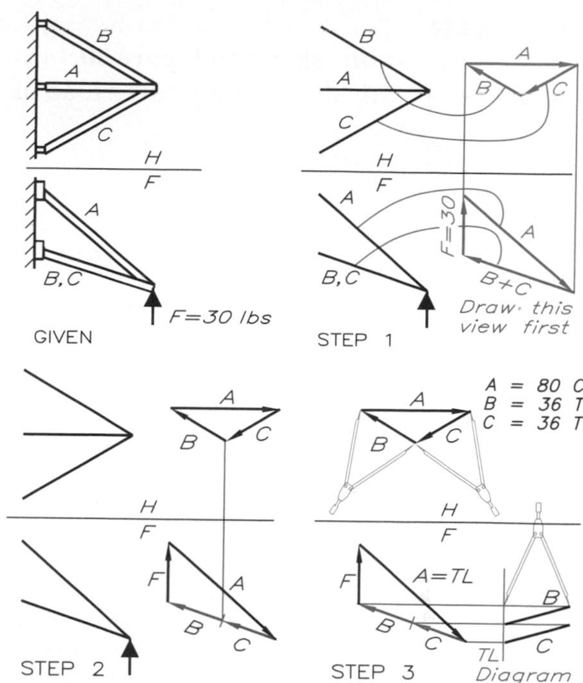

30.13 Noncoplanar structural analysis: Special case.

Step 1 Forces B and C coincide in the front view, resulting in only two unknowns. Draw vector F (30 lb) and the two unknown forces parallel to their front view in the front view of the vector polygon. Find the top view of A by projecting from the front. Draw vectors B and C parallel to their top views.

Step 2 Project the point of intersection of vectors B and C in the top view to the front view to separate the head-to-tail vectors.

Step 3 Vectors B and C are in tension because they point away from the point of application in the space diagram. Vector A is in compression because it points toward the point of application.

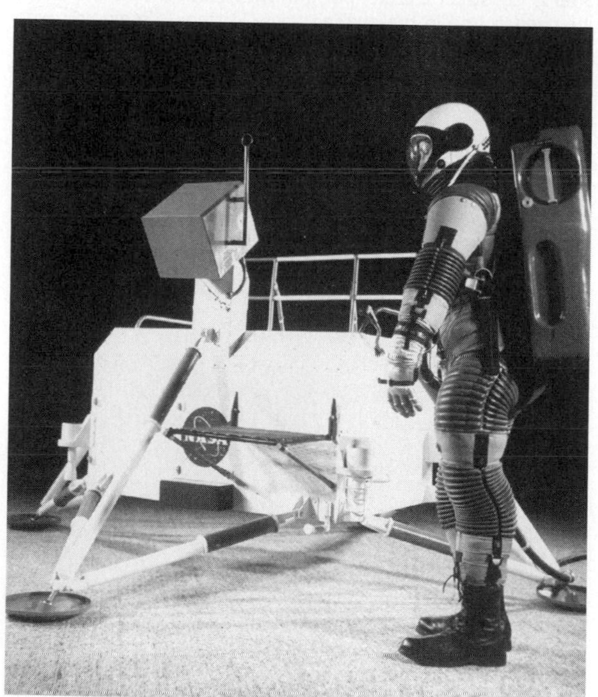

30.12 The structural members of this tripod support for a moon vehicle may be analyzed graphically to determine design load requirement. *(Courtesy of NASA.)*

Construct a vector polygon in the front view by drawing force F as a vector and using the other vectors as the sides of the polygon. Draw the top view using vectors B and C to form the polygon that closes at each end of vector A. Then, find the front view of vectors B and C.

A true-length diagram gives the lengths of the vectors where they can be measured to determine their magnitudes. Vector A is in compression because it points toward the point of application. Vectors B and C are in tension because they point away from the point.

General Case

The structural frame shown in **Figure 30.14** is attached to a vertical wall to support a load of W = 1200 lb. There are three unknowns in each of the views, so begin by projecting an auxiliary view from the top view to obtain the

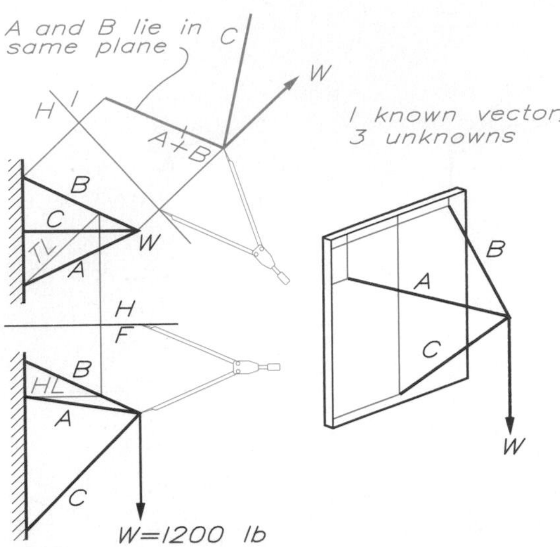

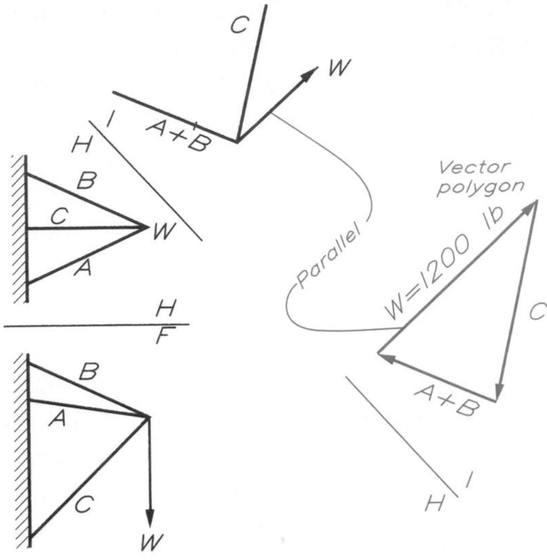

30.14 Noncoplanar analysis: General case.

Step 1 Draw an auxiliary view to show the edge view of the plane containing vectors A and B, which are both unknowns. The load W = 120 lb is true length and the only known vector in this view.

Step 2 Construct a vector polygon with its vectors parallel to the members found in the auxiliary view in step 1. Beginning with true-length vector W, draw the vector polygon head-to-tail using the two unknown vectors (Refer to the solution in **Figure 30.13**.)

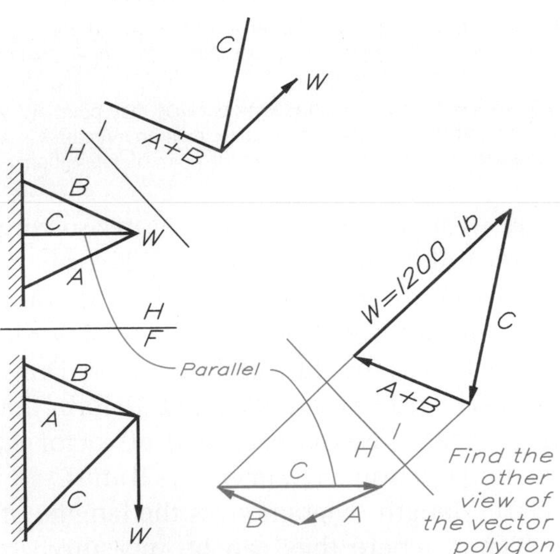

Step 3 Draw the adjacent orthographic view of the vector polygon by projecting perpendicularly to the H1 reference line. Load W appears as a point in this view, and vectors A and B are parallel to their corresponding members in the top view of the space diagram.

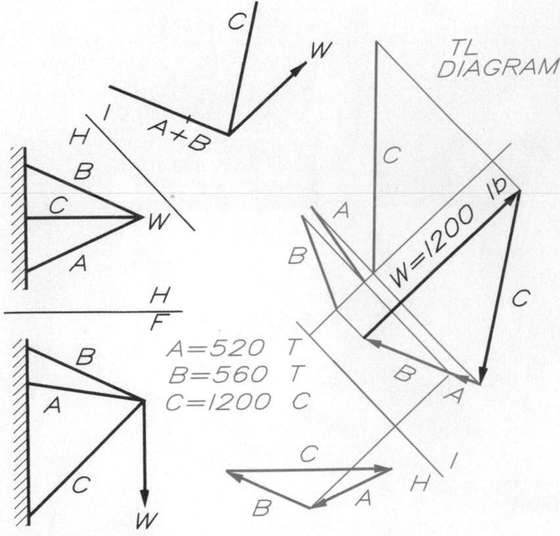

Step 4 Project the intersection of A and B to the adjacent vector polygon. A and B are in tension, since they point toward the application point when transferred to the space diagram. The magnitudes of vectors A, B, and C are found in a time-length diagram and are listed in a table.

edge view of a plane containing vectors A and B, thereby reducing the number of unknowns to two. Doing so converts the frame into a special case of the type covered in the previous example. You no longer need to refer to the front view.

Draw a vector polygon with vectors parallel to their members in the auxiliary view. Then, draw an adjacent orthographic view of the vector polygon with vectors parallel to their members in the top view. Use a true-length diagram to find the true length of the vectors and measure their magnitudes.

30.8 Resultant of Parallel, Nonconcurrent Forces

The beam in **Figure 30.15** supports the three loads shown. It is necessary to determine the magnitude of supports R1 and R2, the magnitude of the resultant of the loads, and the resultant's location. Begin by labeling the spaces between all vectors clockwise with Bow's notation and draw a vector diagram.

Extend the lines of force in the space diagram and draw the strings from the vector diagram in their respective spaces, parallel to their original directions. For example, string oa is parallel to string oA in space A between forces EA and AB, and string ob is in space B, beginning at the intersection of oa with vector AB. The last string, oe, closes the diagram, called a **funicular diagram**.

Transfer the direction of string oe to the vector diagram, and lay it off through point O to intersect the load line at E (step 2). Vector DE represents R2 (refer to Bow's notation as it was applied in step 1), and vector EA represents R1. It is easy to see that DE and EA are equal to the sum of the downward loads represented by AD.

To find the location of the resultant from R1, extend the outside strings of the funicular diagram, oa and od, to their intersection. The resultant will pass downward through this point of intersection. The resultant has a magnitude of 500 lb, a vertical downward direction, and a point of application at X = 6.1 ft. Notice that two scales are used in this problem: one for the vectors in pounds, and one in feet for the space diagram.

30.9 Resultant of Cantilever Forces

The beam in **Figure 30.16** is on a rotational crane used to move building materials. The magnitude of the weight W is unknown, but

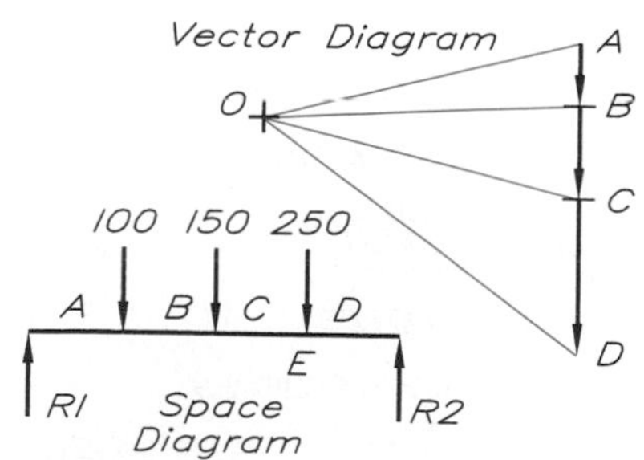

30.15 Parallel, nonconcurrent loads.

Step 1 Letter the spaces between the loads using Bow's notation. Draw the vertical loads head-to-tail in a vector diagram. Locate pole point O at a convenient location and draw strings from O to the ends of each vector.

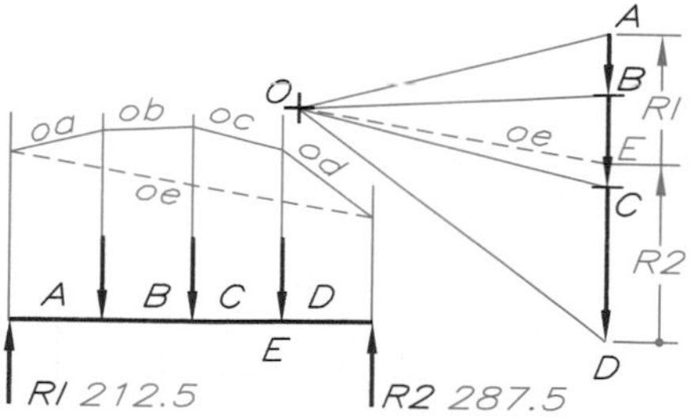

Step 2 Extend the lines of the vertical loads and draw a funicular diagram with string oa in the A space, ob in the B space, oc in the C space, and so on. The last string, oe, closes the diagram. Transfer oe to the vector diagram to locate E, thus establishing R1 and R2, which are EA and DE, respectively.

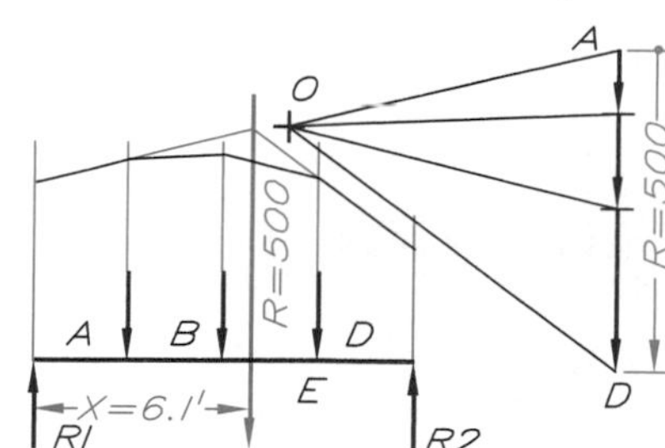

Step 3 The resultant of the three downward forces equals their graphical summation, line AD. Locate the resultant by extending strings oa and od in the funicular diagram to their intersection. The resultant, R = 500 lb, acts through this point in a downward direction X = 6.1 ft. from the left end.

CONSTRUCTION CRANE

A B

Find W necessary to balance F=2000 lb

F=2000 lb R W=? 2000 LB

O W=1000 lb

30.16 The determination of the balancing load of nonconcurrent parallel forces applied to a construction crane.

the counterbalance weight is 2000 lb; column R supports the beam as shown. Assuming the support cables have been omitted, find the weight W that would balance the beam.

The graphical solution is found by constructing a line representing the total distance between the forces F and W. Point O, the point of balance where the summation of the moments will be equal to zero, is projected from the space diagram to this line. Vectors F and W are drawn to scale at each end of the line by transposing them to the opposite ends of the beam. A line is drawn from the end of vector F through point O and extended to intersect the direction of vector W. This point represents the end of vector W, which can be scaled to have a magnitude of 1000 lb.

Problems

Draw your solutions to these problems with instruments on size A grid or plain sheets. Each grid represents 0.20 in. (5 mm). Letter written matter legibly, using 1/8-in. (3 mm) letters with guidelines.

Sheet 1: Resultants

A.–B. Find the resultants of the force systems by the parallelogram and polygon methods. Scale: 1" = 100 lb.

Sheet 2: Resultants

A.–B. Find the resultants of the force systems as specified. Scale: 1" = 100 lb.

Sheet 3: Concurrent, coplanar

A.–B. Find the forces in the coplanar force systems. Scale: 1" = 100 lb.

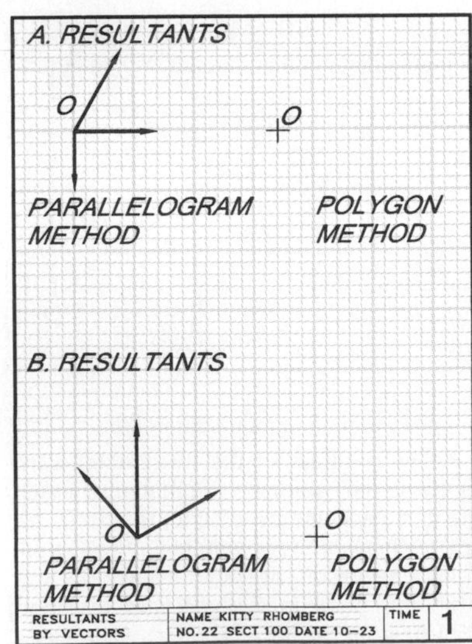

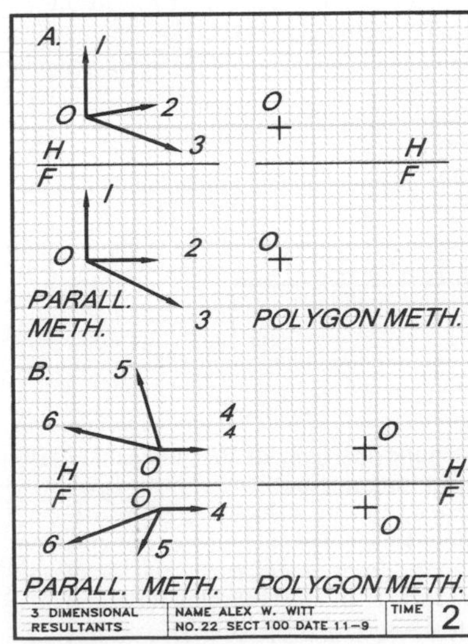

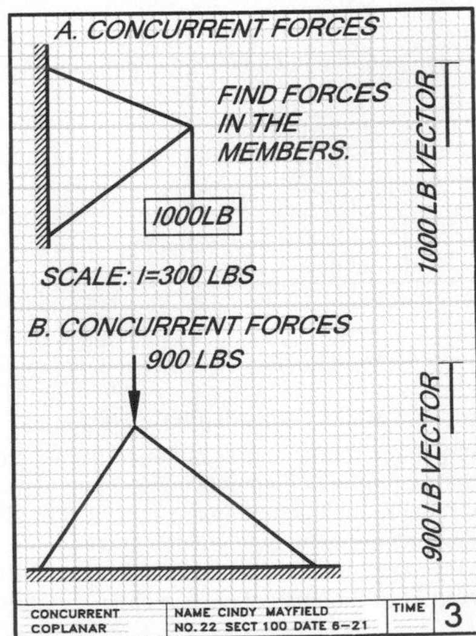

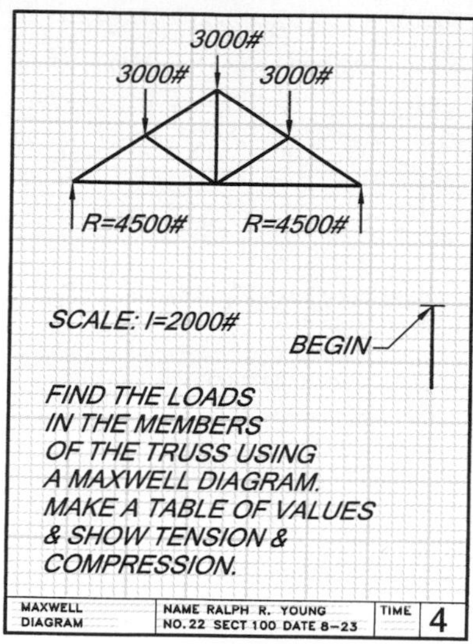

3000#
3000#
3000#
R=4500#
R=4500#
SCALE: I=2000#
BEGIN
FIND THE LOADS IN THE MEMBERS OF THE TRUSS USING A MAXWELL DIAGRAM. MAKE A TABLE OF VALUES & SHOW TENSION & COMPRESSION.
MAXWELL DIAGRAM
NAME RALPH R. YOUNG
NO. 22 SECT 100 DATE 8-23
TIME
4

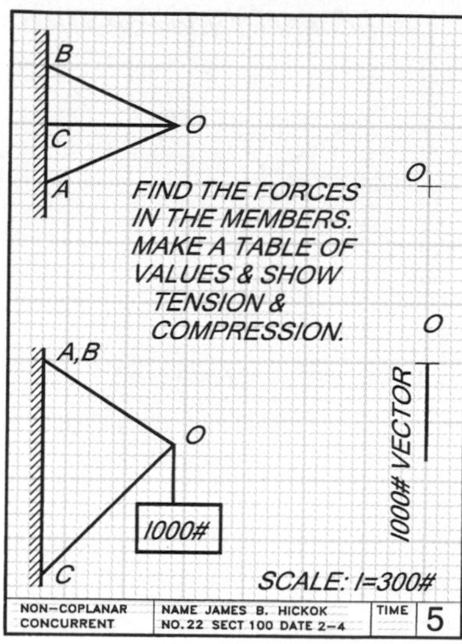

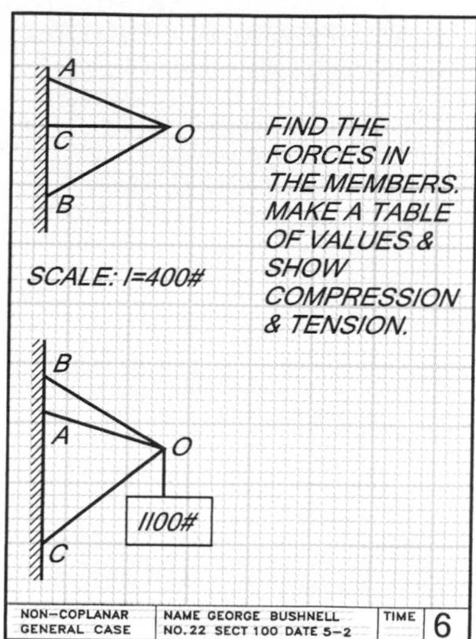

Sheet 4: Truss analysis
Find the loads in the members of the truss using a Maxwell diagram. Make a table of forces as shown in **Figure 30.11**.

Sheet 5: Noncoplanar, special case
Find the forces in the members of the concurrent noncoplanar system. Make a table of forces as shown in **Figure 30.13**.

Sheet 6: Noncoplanar, general case
Find the forces in the members of the concurrent noncoplanar system. Make a table of forces as shown in **Figure 30.14**.

Sheet 7: Beam analysis

A. Find forces R1 and R2.

B. Find the magnitude and location of the single support to replace R1 and R2.

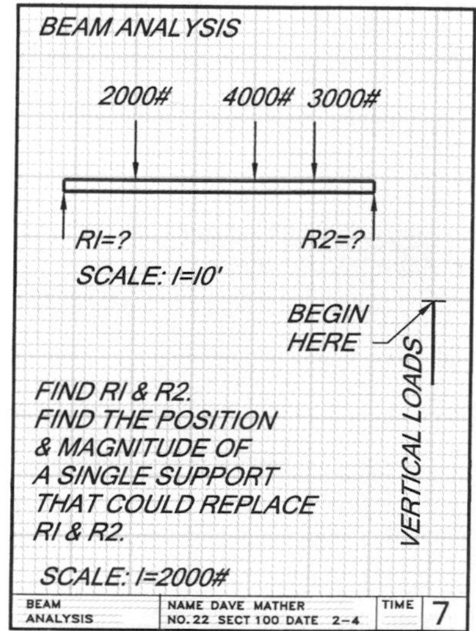

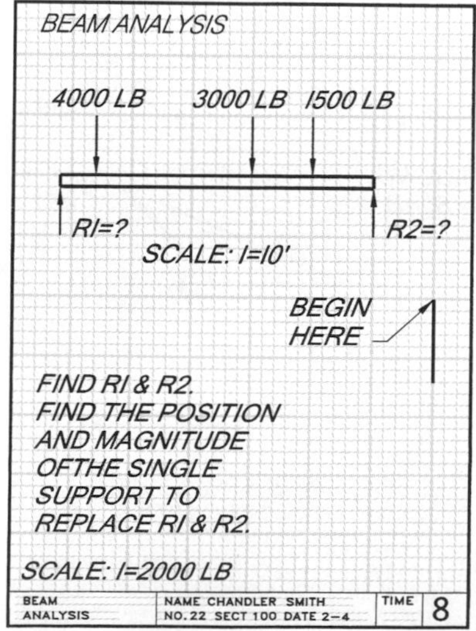

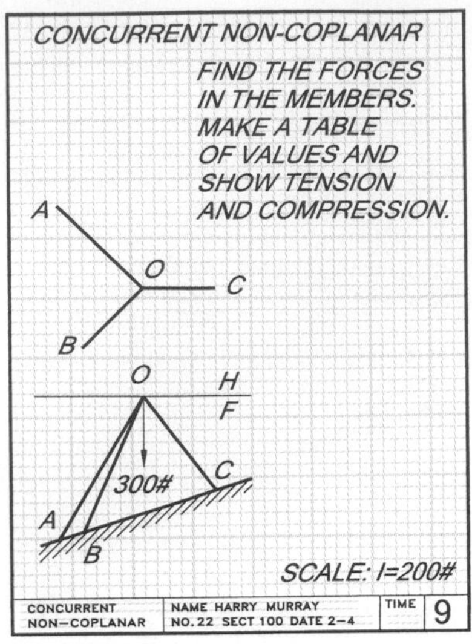
CONCURRENT NON-COPLANAR
FIND THE FORCES IN THE MEMBERS. MAKE A TABLE OF VALUES AND SHOW TENSION AND COMPRESSION.
300#
SCALE: I=200#
CONCURRENT NON-COPLANAR
NAME HARRY MURRAY
NO. 22 SECT 100 DATE 2-4
TIME
9

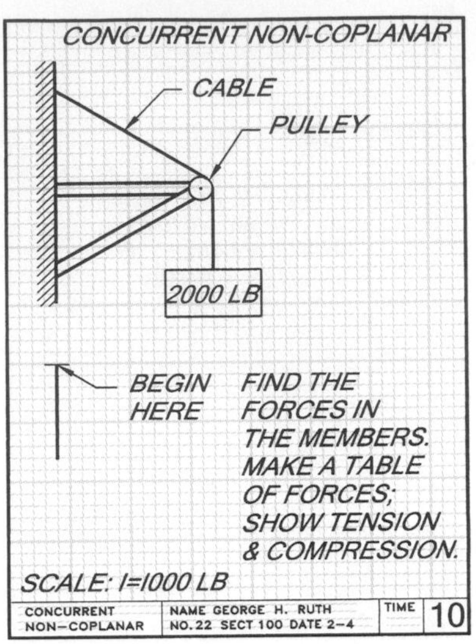
CONCURRENT NON-COPLANAR
CABLE
PULLEY
2000 LB
BEGIN HERE
FIND THE FORCES IN THE MEMBERS. MAKE A TABLE OF FORCES; SHOW TENSION & COMPRESSION.
SCALE: I=1000 LB
CONCURRENT NON-COPLANAR
NAME GEORGE H. RUTH
NO. 22 SECT 100 DATE 2-4
TIME
10

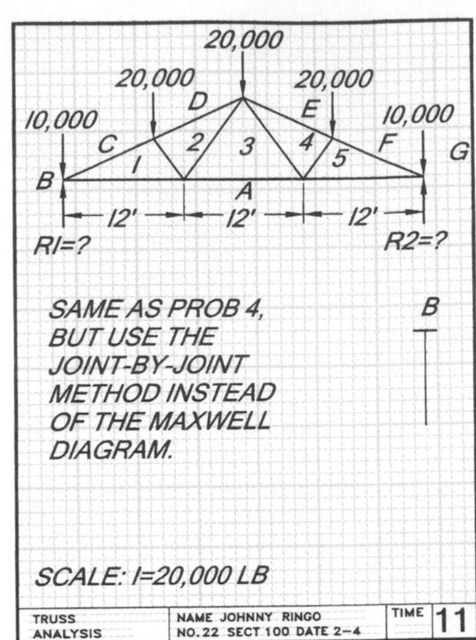
20,000
20,000
20,000
10,000
10,000
R1=?
R2=?
SAME AS PROB 4, BUT USE THE JOINT-BY-JOINT METHOD INSTEAD OF THE MAXWELL DIAGRAM.
SCALE: I=20,000 LB
TRUSS ANALYSIS
NAME JOHNNY RINGO
NO. 22 SECT 100 DATE 2-4
TIME
11

Sheet 8: Beam analysis
Repeat problem 7 for this configuration.

Sheet 9: Concurrent, noncoplanar
Find the forces in the support members and make a table of forces of your findings.

Sheet 10: Concurrent, coplanar
Find the forces in the coplanar system and make a table of your findings.

Sheet 11: Truss analysis
Using joint-by-joint analysis, find the magnitudes of the forces in the truss members. Prepare a table of values.

Sheet 12: Concurrent, noncoplanar
Determine the forces in the tripod frame used to lift a concrete slab into an upright position as illustrated.

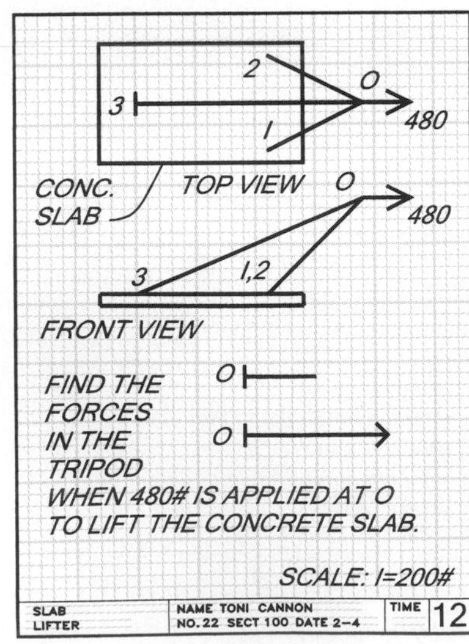
480
CONC. SLAB
TOP VIEW
FRONT VIEW
FIND THE FORCES IN THE TRIPOD WHEN 480# IS APPLIED AT O TO LIFT THE CONCRETE SLAB.
SCALE: I=200#
SLAB LIFTER
NAME TONI CANNON
NO. 22 SECT 100 DATE 2-4
TIME
12

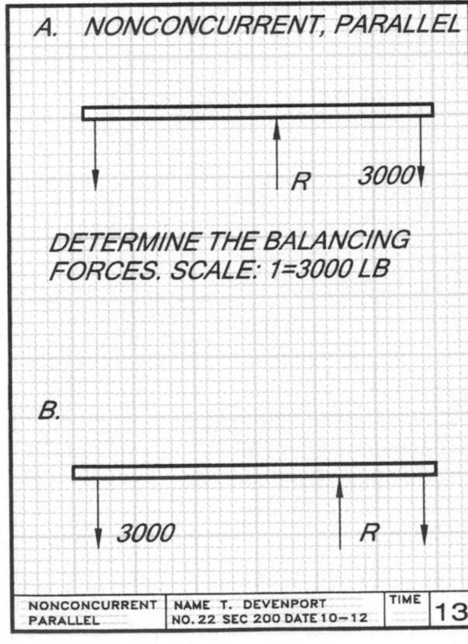
A. NONCONCURRENT, PARALLEL
3000
DETERMINE THE BALANCING FORCES. SCALE: 1=3000 LB
B.
3000
NONCONCURRENT PARALLEL
NAME T. DEVENPORT
NO. 22 SEC 200 DATE 10-12
TIME
13

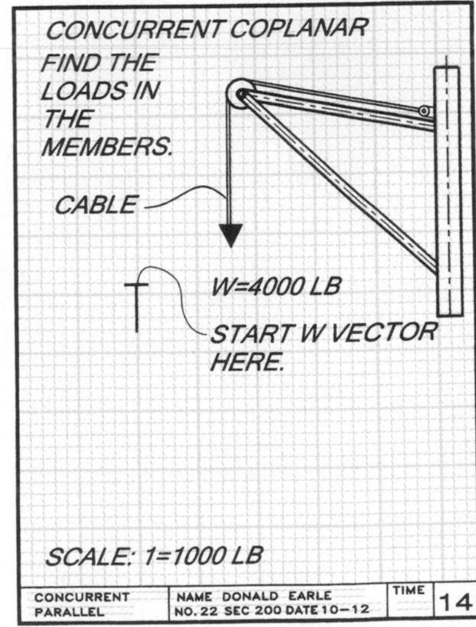
CONCURRENT COPLANAR
FIND THE LOADS IN THE MEMBERS.
CABLE
W=4000 LB
START W VECTOR HERE.
SCALE: 1=1000 LB
CONCURRENT PARALLEL
NAME DONALD EARLE
NO. 22 SEC 200 DATE 10-12
TIME
14

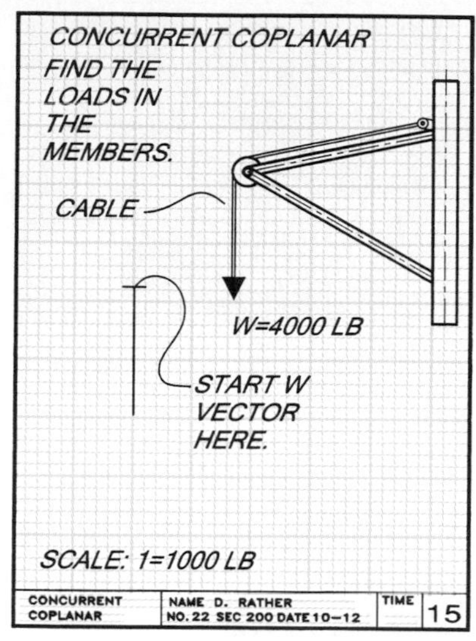

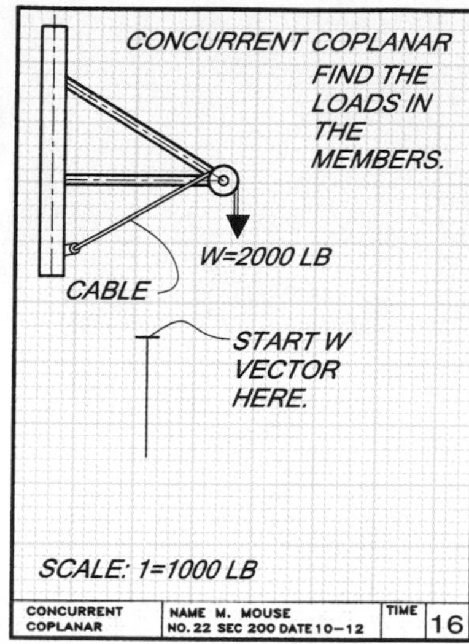

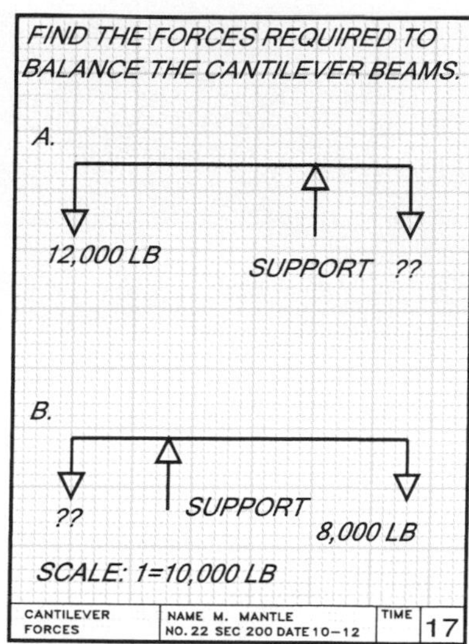

Sheet 13: Nonconcurrent, coplanar
A.–B. Find the balancing force for both nonconcurrent, coplanar, parallel systems of forces and determine the magnitude of resultants R.

Sheet 14: Concurrent, coplanar
Find the loads in the members of this coplanar crane and prepare a table of loads and show compression and tension.

Sheet 15: Concurrent, coplanar
Find the loads in the members of this coplanar crane and prepare a table of loads and show compression and tension.

Sheet 16: Concurrent, coplanar
Find the loads in the members of this coplanar crane, prepare a table of loads, and show compression and tension.

Sheet 15: Cantilever beam
Find the loads in the members of the cantilever beams.

Thought Questions

1. Explain the difference between tension and compression. How do these difference affect the selection of structural members?

2. What is the difference between force systems that are in equilibrium and those that are not?

3. What is Bow's notation and how is it used to analyze members in a truss?

4. If a tripod is loaded at its apex with a 1,200-lb force, what is the maximum load in each leg of the tripod: 400 lb, 1,200 lb, greater than 1,200 lb? Sketch possibilities to determine your answer.

5. How does the physical length of a structural member affect the force in it when loaded? Explain.

6. If a horizontal beam is loaded with several forces, such as the one shown in **Figure 30.15**, what is the maximum sum of the resultants at both ends?

7. What is the maximum number of members in a concentric, noncoplanar system, as shown in **Figure 30.14**, that can be solved for the forces in each of them?

31 Intersections and Developments: Descriptive Geometry

31.1 Introduction

Several methods may be used to find lines of intersection between parts that join. Usually, such parts are made of sheet metal, or of plywood if used as forms for concrete. After **intersections** are found, **developments**, or flat patterns, can be laid out on sheet metal and cut to the desired shape. You will see examples of intersections and developments ranging from air-conditioning ducts to massive refineries.

31.2 Intersections: Lines and Planes

Figure 31.1 illustrates the fundamental principle of finding the intersection between a line and a plane. This example is a special case in which the point of intersection clearly shows in the view where the plane appears as an edge. Projecting the piercing point P to the front view completes the visibility of the line.

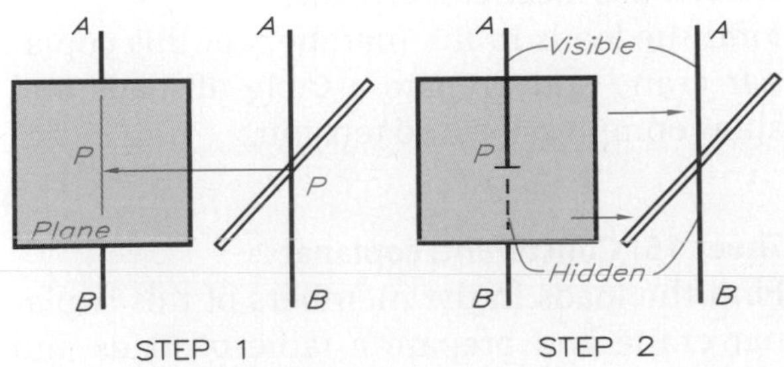

31.1 Intersection: Line and plane.

Step 1 Find the point of intersection in the view where the plane appears as an edge, the side view in this case, and project it to the front view.

Step 2 Determine visibility in the front view by looking from the front view to the right-side view.

This same principle is applied to finding the line of intersection between two planes (**Figure 31.2**). By locating the piercing points of lines AB and DC and connecting these points, the line of intersection is found.

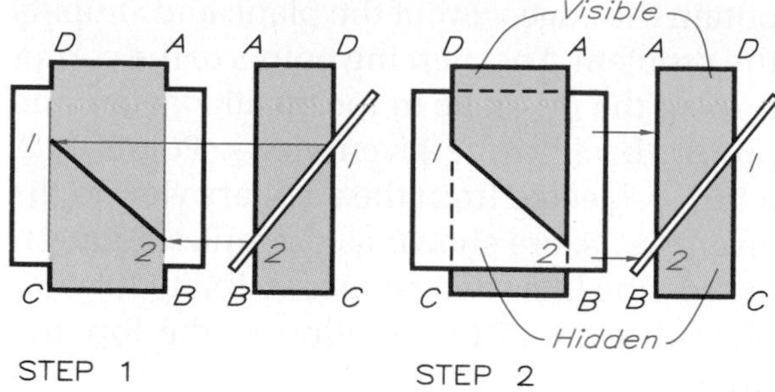

31.2 Intersections: Planes.

Step 1 Find the piercing points of lines AB and DC with the plane where the plane appears as an edge and project them to the front view, points 1 and 2.

Step 2 Line 1-2 is the line of intersection. Determine visibility by looking from the front view to the right-side view.

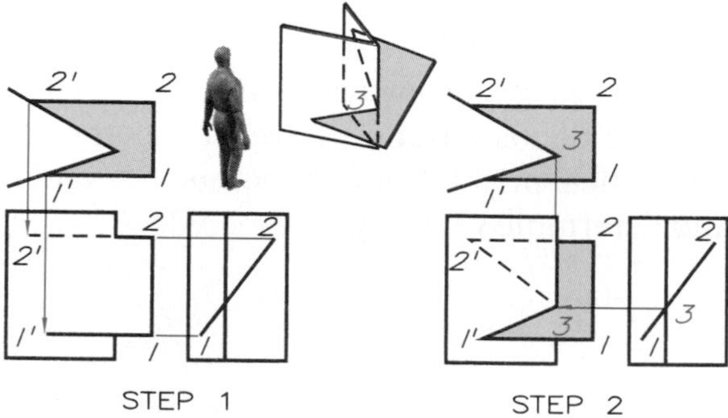

31.3 Intersections: A plane around a corner.

Step 1 The intersecting plane appears as an edge in the side view. Project intersection points 1′ and 2′ from the top and side views to the front view.

Step 2 The line of intersection from 1′ to 2′ must bend around the vertical corner at 3 in the top and side views. Project point 3 to the front view to locate line 1′-3-2′.

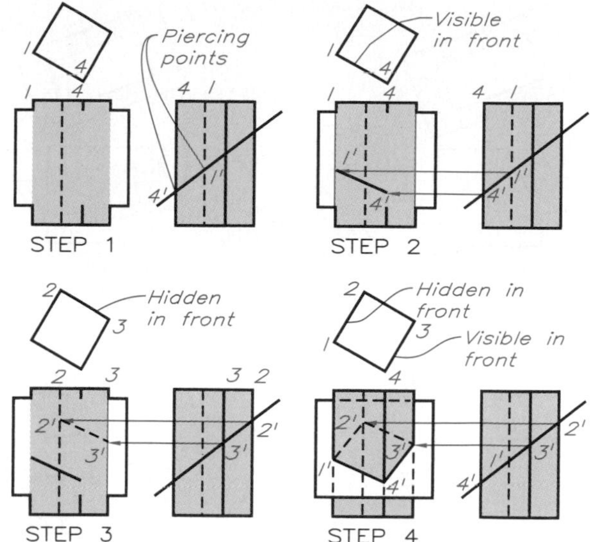

31.4 Intersections: Plane and prism.

Step 1 Vertical corners 1 and 4 intersect the edge view of the plane in the side view at points 1′ and 4′.

Step 2 Project points 1' and 4' from the side view to lines 1 and 4 in the front view. Connect them to form a visible line of intersection.

Step 3 Vertical corners 2 and 3 intersect the edge view of the plane at points 2′ and 3′ in the side view. Project points 2′ and 3' to the front view to form a hidden line of intersection.

Step 4 Connect points 1′,-2′,-3′,-and-4′ and determine visibility by analyzing the top and side views.

The angular intersection of two planes at a corner gives a line of intersection that bends around the corner (**Figure 31.3**). First, find piercing points 2' and 1'. Then, project corner point 3 from the side view where the vertical corner pierces the plane to the front view of the corner. Point 2' is hidden in the front view because it is on the back side.

Figure 31.4 shows how to find the intersection between a plane and prism where the plane appears as an edge. Obtain the piercing points for each corner line and connect them to form the line of intersection. Show visibility to complete the intersection.

Figure 31.5 depicts a more general case of an intersection between a plane and prism. Passing vertical cutting planes through the planes of the prism in the top view yields traces (cut lines) on the front view of the oblique plane on which the piercing points of the vertical corner lines lie. Connect the points and determine visibility to complete the solution.

In **Figure 31.6**, finding the intersection between a foreshortened plane and an oblique prism involves finding an auxiliary view to

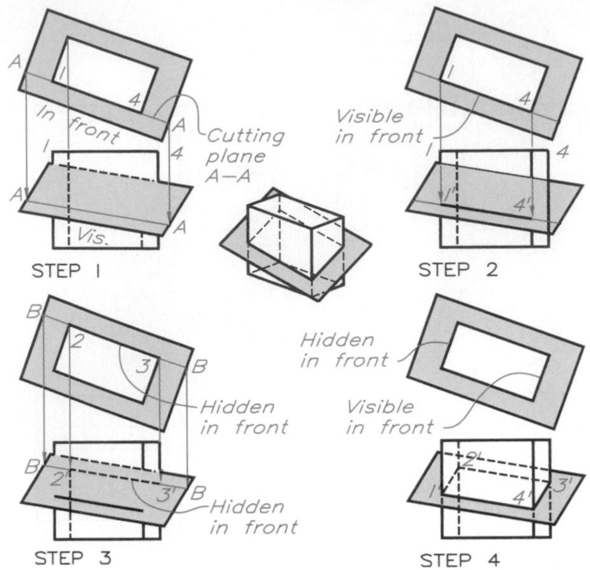

31.5 Intersections: Oblique plane and prism.

Step 1 Pass vertical cutting plane A-A through corners 1 and 4 in the top view and project endpoints to the front view.

Step 2 Locate piercing points 1′ and 4′ in the front view where line AA crosses lines 1 and 4.

Step 3 Pass vertical cutting plane B-B through corners 2 and 3 in the top view and project them to the front view to locate piercing points 2′ and 3′.

Step 4 Connect the four piercing points and determine visibility by analysis of the top view.

obtain the edge view of the plane and simplify the problem. The piercing points of the corner lines of the prism lie in the auxiliary view and project back to the given views. Points 1, 2, and 3, projected from the auxiliary view to the given views, are shown as examples. Analysis of crossing lines determines visibility to complete the line of intersection in the top and front views.

31.3 Intersections: Prisms

The techniques used to find the intersections between planes and lines also apply to finding the intersections between two prisms (**Figure 31.7**). Project piercing points 1, 2, and 3 from the side and top views to the front view. Point X lies in the side view where line of intersection 1-2 bends around the vertical corner of the vertical prism. Connect points 1, X, and 2 and determine visibility.

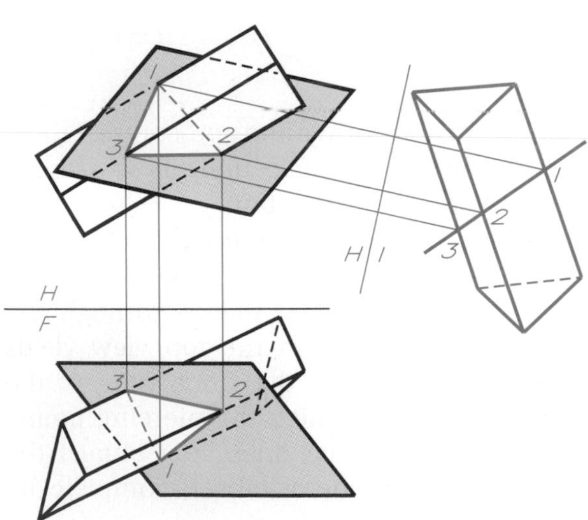

31.6 Intersections: Plane and prism.
To find the intersection between a plane and a prism, construct a view in which the plane appears as an edge. Project piercing points 1, 2, and 3 back to the top and front views.

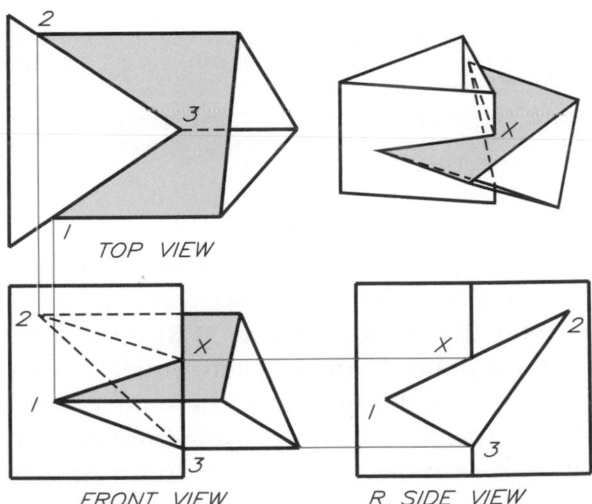

31.7 Intersections: Prisms at corner.
These are three views of intersecting prisms. The points of intersection are best found where intersecting planes appear as edges.

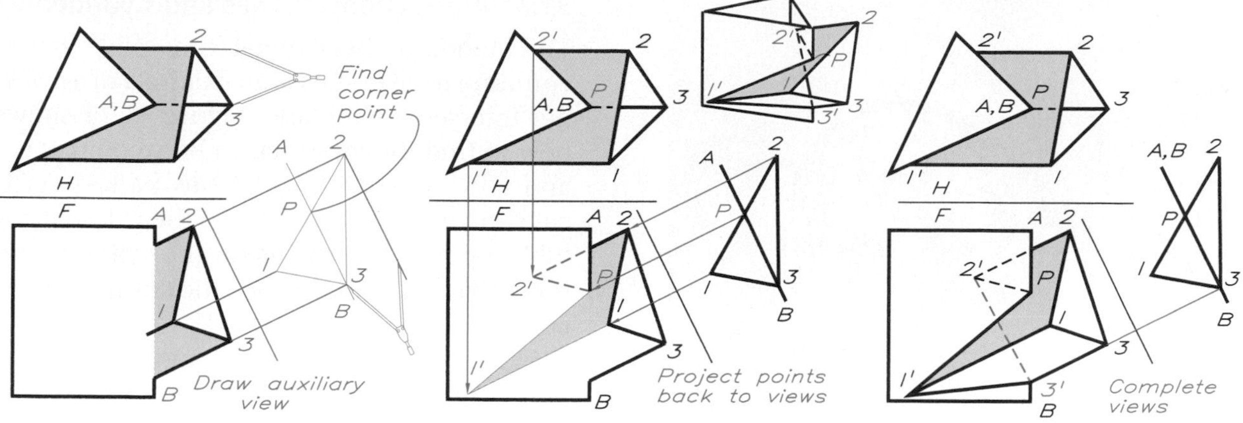

31.8 Intersections: Prisms by auxiliary view.

Step 1 Draw the end view of the inclined prism in an auxiliary view from the front view. Show line AB of the vertical prism in the auxiliary view.

Step 2 Locate piercing points 1′ and 2′ in the top and front views. Intersection line 1′-2′ bends around corner AB at P projected from the auxiliary view.

Step 3 The intersection lines from 2′ and 1′ to 3′ do not bend around the corner but are straight lines. Line 1′-3′ is visible, and line 2′-3′ is invisible.

Figure 31.8 illustrates how to find the line of intersection between an inclined prism and a vertical prism. An auxiliary view reveals the end view of the inclined prism where its planes appear as edges. In the auxiliary view, plane 1-2 bends around corner AB at point P. Project points of intersection 1′ and 2′ from the top and auxiliary to their intersections in the front view. Then draw the line of intersection 1′-P-2′ for this portion of the line of intersection. Connect the remaining lines, 1′-3′ and 2′-3′ to complete the solution.

Figure 31.9 shows an alternative method of solving this type of problem. Piercing points 1′ and 2′ appear in the front view as projections from the top view. Point 5 is the point where line 1′-5-2′ bends around vertical corner AB. To find point 5 in the front view, pass a frontal plane through corner AB in the top view and project its trace (4-5) to the front view. Draw the lines of intersection, 1′-5-2′.

Some applications of intersections and developments vary in size from massive to relatively small, as shown in **Figure 31.10**, where the headlight of an automobile intersects with its fender. It intersects with both regular and irregular surfaces.

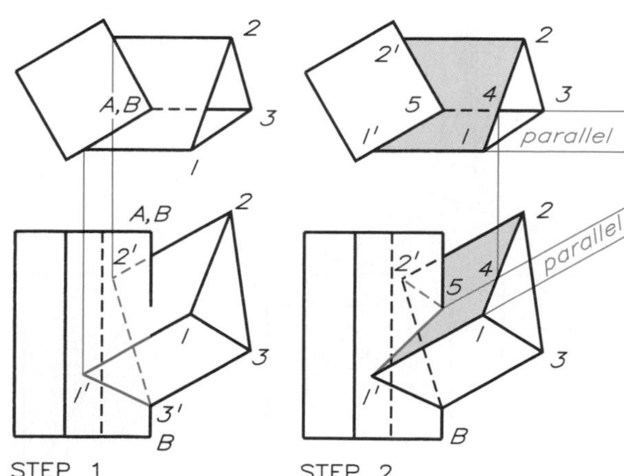

31.9 Intersections: Prisms by projection.

Step 1 Project the piercing points of lines 1, 2, and 3 from the top view to the front view to locate piercing points 1′, 2′, and 3′.

Step 2 Pass a plane through corner AB in the top view to locate point 5, where intersection line 1′-2′ bends around the vertical prism. Find point 5 in the front view and draw line 1′-5-2′.

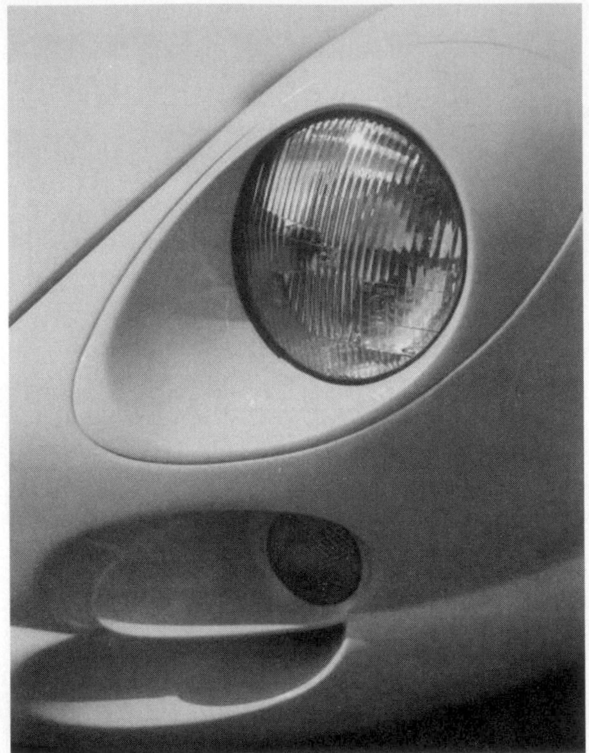

31.10 The design of this headlight and automobile fender required the applications of principles of intersections and developments.

31.4 Intersections: Planes and Cylinders

The standard sheet-metal vent pipe that is common to all homes is an example of a cylinder intersecting a plane. **Figure 31.11** shows how to find the intersection between a plane and a cylinder. Cutting planes passed vertically through the top view of the cylinder establish pairs of elements on the cylinder and their piercing points. Space the cutting planes conveniently apart by eye. Then, project the piercing points to each view and draw the elliptical line of intersection.

Figure 31.12 shows the solution of a more general problem. Here, the cylinder is vertical, and the plane is oblique and does not appear as an edge. Passing vertical cutting planes through the cylinder and the plane in the top view gives elements on the cylinder and their piercing points on the plane. Projecting these points to the front view completes the elliptical line of intersection (step 2). The more cutting planes used, the more accurate the line of intersection will be.

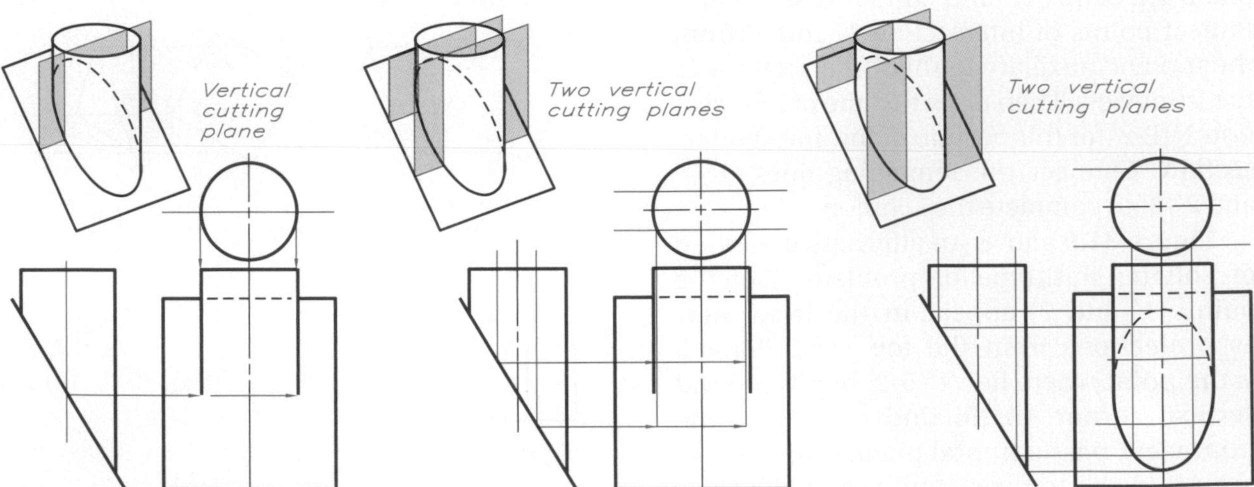

31.11 Intersections: Cylinder and plane.

Step 1 Pass a vertical cutting plane through the cylinder parallel to its axis to find two points of intersection on this plane in the front view.

Step 2 Use two more cutting planes to find four additional points in the top and left-side views. Project these points to the front view.

Step 3 Use additional cutting planes to find more points. Determine visibility and connect these points to give an elliptical line of intersection.

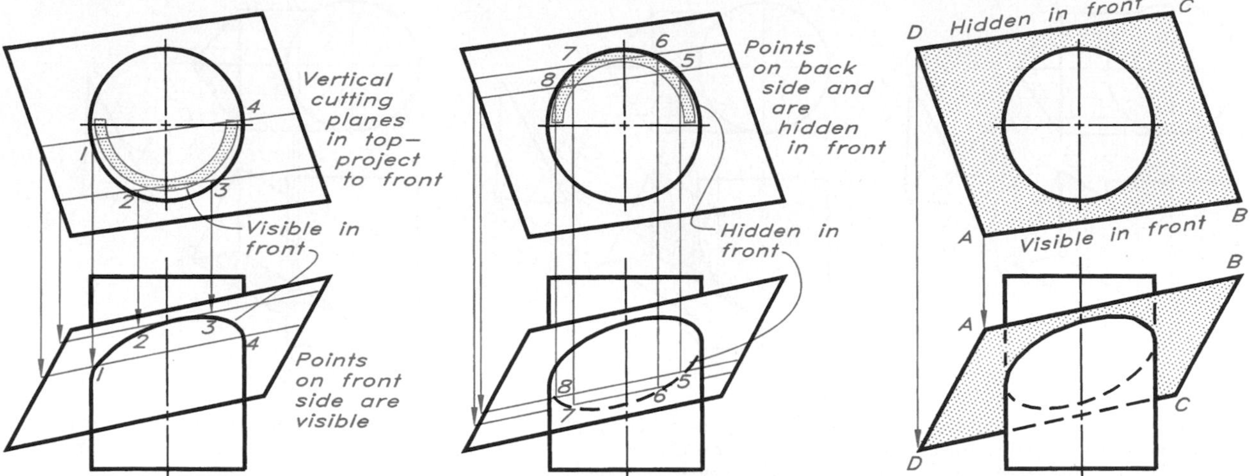

31.12 Intersection: Cylinder and oblique plane.

Step 1 Pass vertical cutting planes through the cylinder in the top view to find elements on it and the plane. Project points 1, 2, 3, and 4 to the front view of their respective lines and connect them with a visible line.

Step 2 Use additional cutting planes to find piercing points 5, 6, 7, and 8; project them to the front view of their respective lines on the plane. The points are on the back side and are hidden; connect them with a hidden line.

Step 3 Determine visibility of the plane and cylinder in the front view. Line AB is visible by inspection of the top view, since it is the farthest out in front. Line CD is the farthest back in the top view and is hidden in the front view.

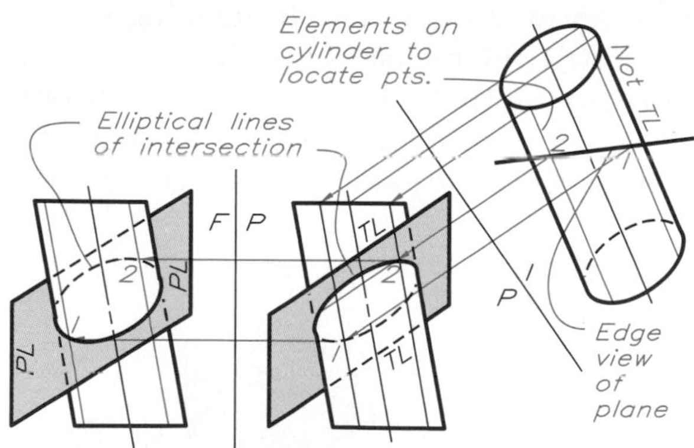

31.13 Intersection: Cylinder and plane by auxiliary view. To find the intersection between an oblique cylinder and an oblique plane, construct a view that shows the plane as an edge. Cutting planes passed through the cylinder locate points on the line of intersection.

Figure 31.13 demonstrates the general case of the intersection between a plane and cylinder, where both the plane and cylinder are oblique in the given views. An auxiliary view is used to show the edge view of the plane. Cutting planes passed through the cylinder parallel to its axis in the auxiliary view establish elements on the cylinder and their piercing points. The points are projected back to the given views and connected to give an elliptical line of intersection in the front and side views.

31.5 Intersections: Cylinders and Prisms

An inclined prism intersects a vertical cylinder in **Figure 31.14**. A primary auxiliary view is drawn to show the end view of the inclined prism where its planes appear as edges. A series of vertical cutting planes in the top view establish lines lying on the surfaces of the cylinder and prism. The cutting planes, also shown in the auxiliary view, are the same distance apart as in the top view.

Projecting the line of intersection from 1 to 3 from the auxiliary view to the front view yields an elliptical line of intersection. The

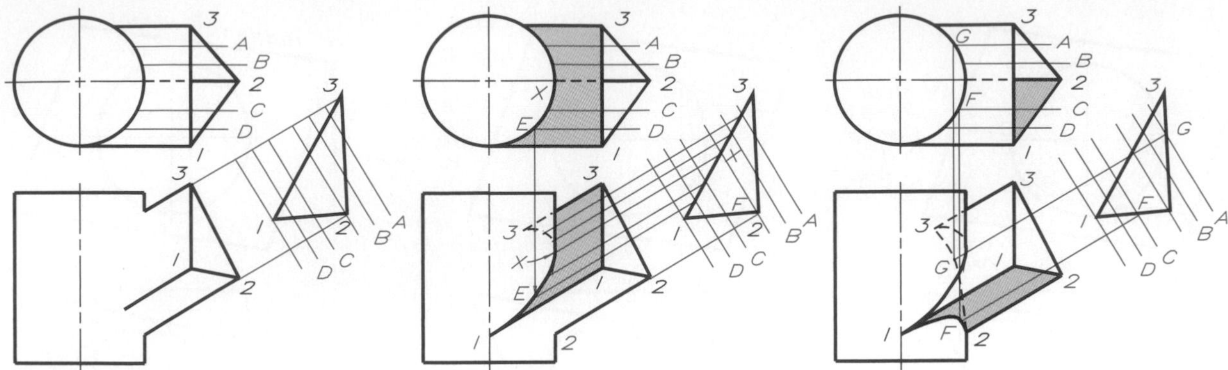

31.14 Intersection: Cylinder and inclined prism.

Step 1 Find the edge views of the planes of the triangular prism in an auxiliary view projected from the front view. Draw frontal cutting planes through the top view and locate them in the auxiliary view with dividers.

Step 2 Locate points along intersection line 1-3 in the top view and project them to the front view. For example, find point E on cutting plane D in the top and auxiliary views and project it to the front view where the projectors intersect. Visibility changes in the front view at point X.

Step 3 Determine the remaining points of intersection by using the other cutting planes. Project point F, shown in the top and auxiliary views, to the front view of line 1-2. Connect the points and determine visibility.

visibility of this line changes from visible to hidden at point X, which appears in the auxiliary view and is projected to the front view. Continuing this process gives the lines of intersection of the other two planes of the prism.

31.6 Intersections: Cylinders

To find the line of intersection between two perpendicular cylinders, pass cutting planes through them parallel to their centerlines (**Figure 31.15**). Each cutting plane locates a pair of elements on both cylinders that intersect at a piercing point. Connecting the points and determining visibility completes the solution. An example of an air-handling system fabricated with intersecting cylinders is shown in **Figure 31.16**. Each cylinder had to be precisely cut to form accurate intersections for tight joints before joining them together.

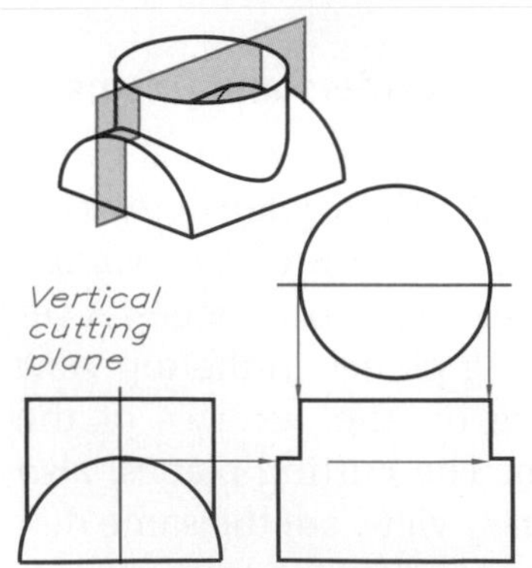

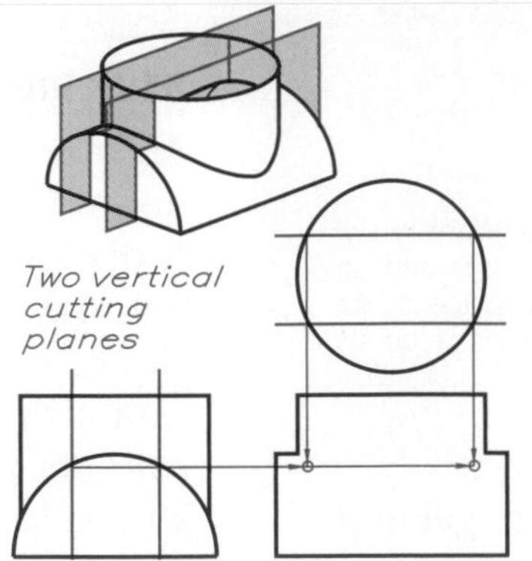

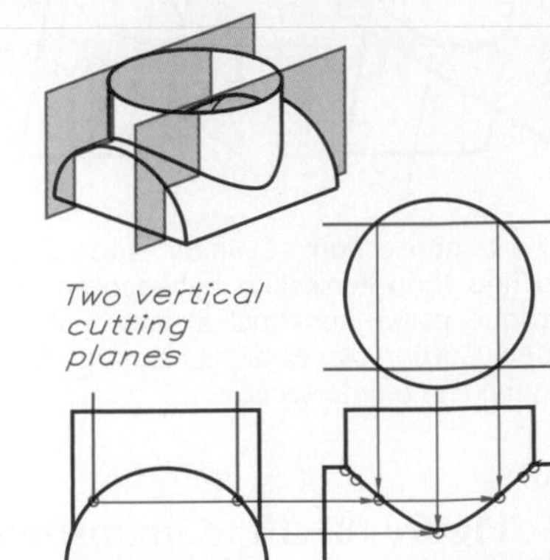

31.15 Intersection: Perpendicular cylinders.

Step 1 Pass a cutting plane through the cylinders parallel to their axes, locating two points of intersection.

Step 2 Use two more cutting planes to find four additional points on the line of intersection.

Step 3 Use two more cutting planes to locate four more points. Connect the points with a smooth curve to complete the line of intersection.

31.16 Intersecting cylindrical ducts of this air-handling system were designed to gather and exhaust contaminants. *(Courtesy of Kirk & Blum, a CECO Environmental Company.)*

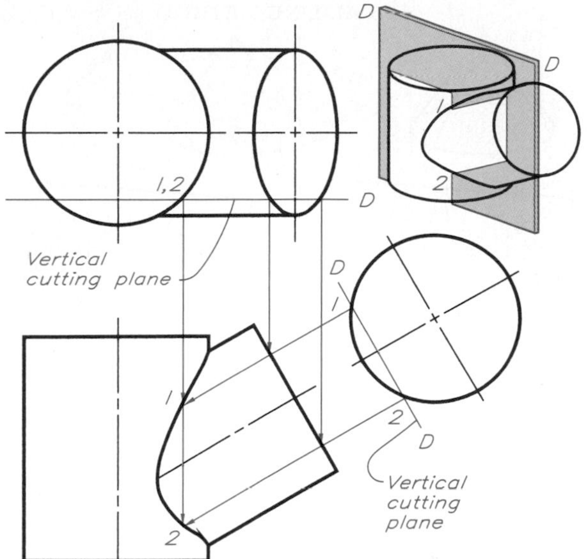

31.17 Intersection: Inclined cylinders.
To find this intersection, find the end view of the inclined cylinder in an auxiliary view. Use a series of vertical cutting planes to find the piercing points of the cylindrical elements and the line of intersection.

Figure 31.17 illustrates how to find the intersection between nonperpendicular cylinders. This method involves passing a series of vertical cutting planes through the cylinders parallel to their centerlines. Points 1 and 2, labeled on cutting plane D, are typical of points on the line of intersection. Other points may be found in the same manner. Although the auxiliary view is not essential to the solution, it is an aid in visualizing the problem. Projecting points 1 and 2 on cutting plane D in the auxiliary view to the front view provides a check on the projections from the top view.

31.7 Intersections: Planes and Cones

To find points of intersection on a cone, use cutting planes that are (1) perpendicular to the cone's axis or (2) parallel to the cone's axis. The vertical planes in the top view of **Figure 31.18A** cut radial lines on the cone and establish elements on its surface. The

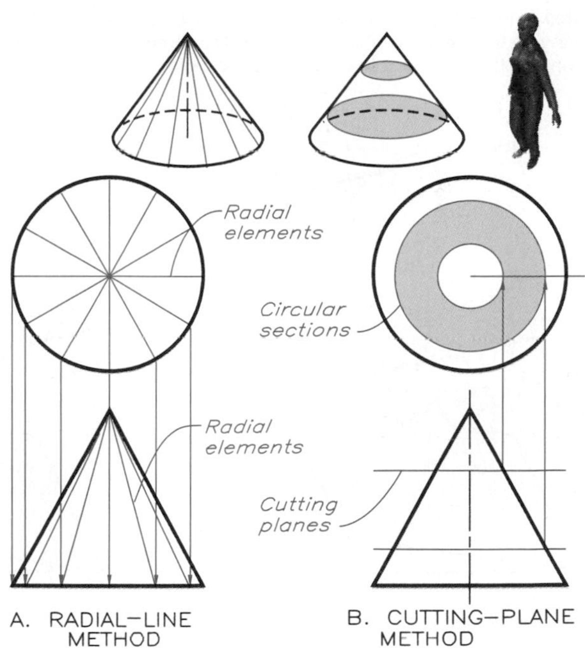

31.18 Cutting-plane methods.
To find intersections on conical surfaces, use (A) radial cutting planes that pass through the cone's centerline and are perpendicular to its base, or (B) cutting planes that are parallel to the cone's base.

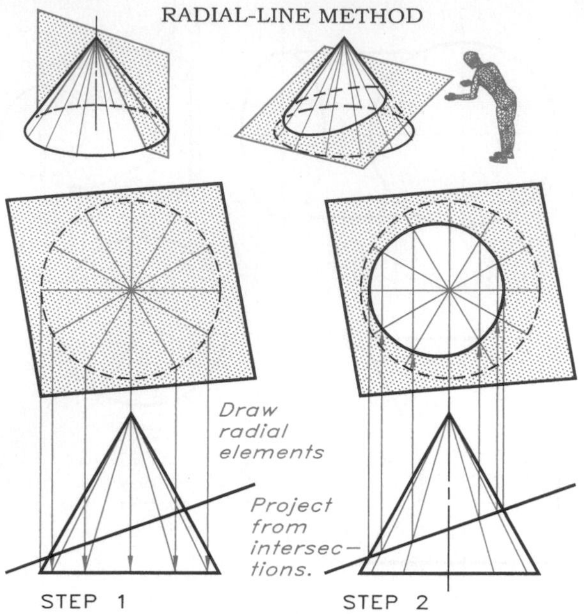

31.19 Intersection: Plane and a cone.

Step 1 Divide the base evenly in the top view and connect these points with the apex to establish elements on the cone. Project these elements to the front view.

Step 2 Project the piercing point of each element on the edge view of the plane to the top view of the same elements, and connect them to form the line of intersection.

horizontal planes in **Figure 31.18B** cut circular sections that appear true size in the top view of a right cone.

A series of radial cutting planes define elements on a cone (**Figure 31.19**). These elements cross the edge view of the plane in the front view to locate piercing points of each element that when projected to the top view of the same elements lie on the line of intersection.

A series of horizontal cutting planes may be used to determine the line of intersection between a cone and an oblique plane (**Figure 31.20**). The sections cut by these imaginary planes are circles in the top view. The cutting planes also locate lines on the oblique plane that intersect the circular sections cut by each respective cutting plane. The points of intersection found in the top view project to the front view. We could have used the radial-line method shown in **Figure 31.19** to obtain the same results.

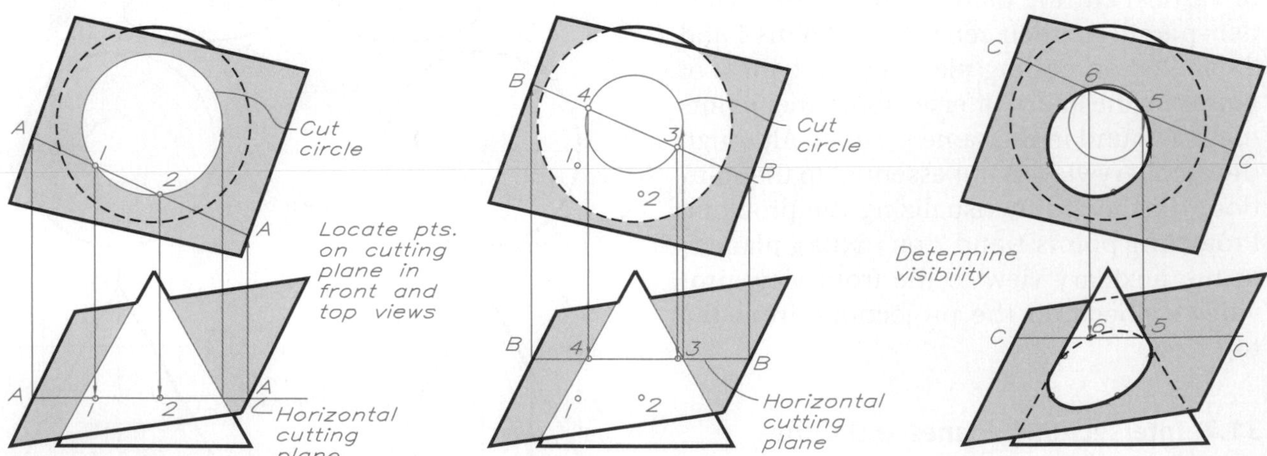

31.20 Intersection: Oblique plane and cone.

Step 1 Pass a horizontal cutting plane through the front view to find a circular section on the cone and a line on the plane in the top view. The piercing points of this line are on the circle. Project points 1 and 2 to the front view.

Step 2 Pass horizontal cutting plane B-B through the front view in the same manner to locate piercing points 3 and 4 in the top view. Project these points to the horizontal plane in the front view from the top view.

Step 3 Use additional horizontal planes to find a sufficient number of points to complete the line of intersection in the same manner as covered in the previous steps. Draw the intersection and determine visibility.

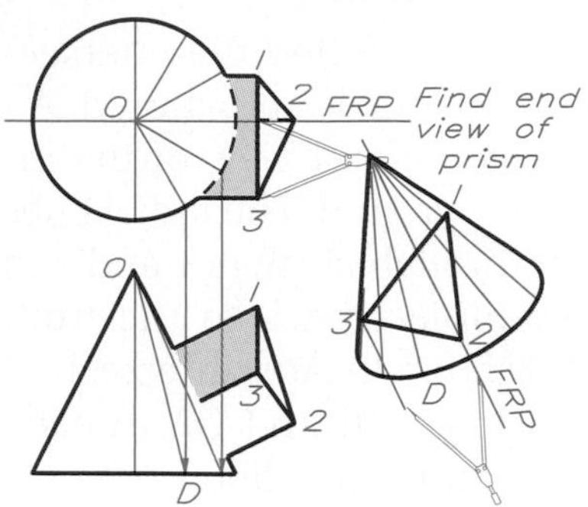

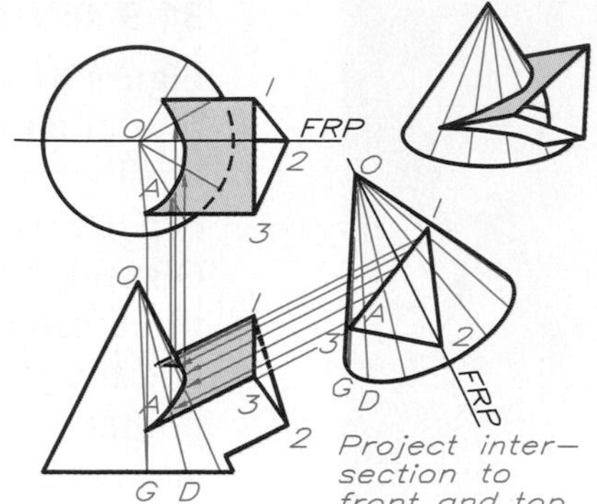

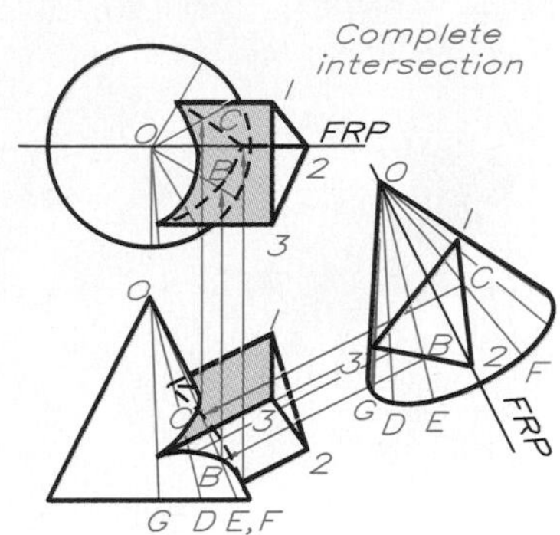

31.21 Intersection: Cone and prism.

Step 1 Draw an auxiliary view to obtain the edge views of the planes of the prism. In the top view, pass vertical cutting planes through the cone through apex O. Project these elements to the front and auxiliary views.

Step 2 Find the piercing points of the cone's elements with the edge view of plane 1-3 in the auxiliary view and project them to the front and top views. For example, point A lies on element OD in the auxiliary view, so project it to the front and top views of OD.

Step 3 Locate the piercing points where the conical elements intersect the edge views of the planes of the prism in the auxiliary view. For example, find point B on OE in the primary auxiliary view and project it to the front and top views of OE.

31.8 Intersections: Cones and Prisms

A primary auxiliary view gives the end view of the inclined prism that intersects the cone in **Figure 31.21**. Cutting planes that radiate from the apex of the cone in the top view locate elements on the cone's surface that intersect the edge view of the prism in the auxiliary view. These elements are projected to the front view.

Wherever the edge view of plane 1-3 intersects an element in the auxiliary view, the piercing points project to the same element in the front and top views. Passing an extra cutting plane through point 3 in the auxiliary view locates an element that projects to the front and top views. Piercing point 3 projects to this element in sequence from the auxiliary view to the top view.

This same procedure yields the piercing points of the other two planes of the prism. All projections of points of intersection originate in the auxiliary view, where the planes of the prism appear as edges.

In **Figure 31.22**, horizontal cutting planes passed through the front view of the cone and cylinder give a series of circular sections in the top view. Points 1 and 2, shown on cutting plane C in the top view, are typical and project to the front view. The same method produces other points.

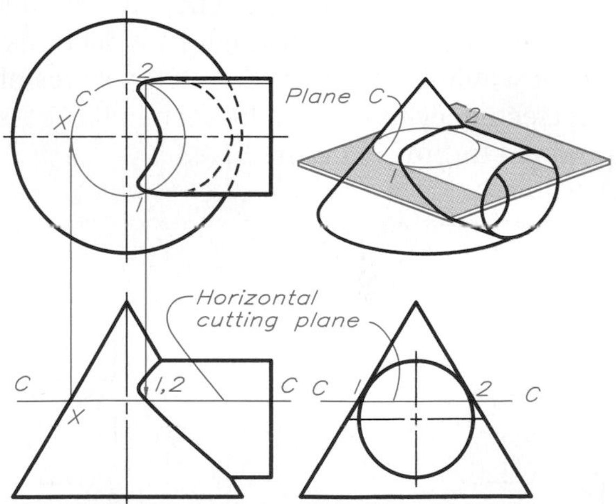

31.22 Intersection: Horizontal planes.
Horizontal cutting planes are used to find the intersection between the cone and the cylinder. The cutting planes cut circles in the top view. Only one cutting plane is shown here as an example.

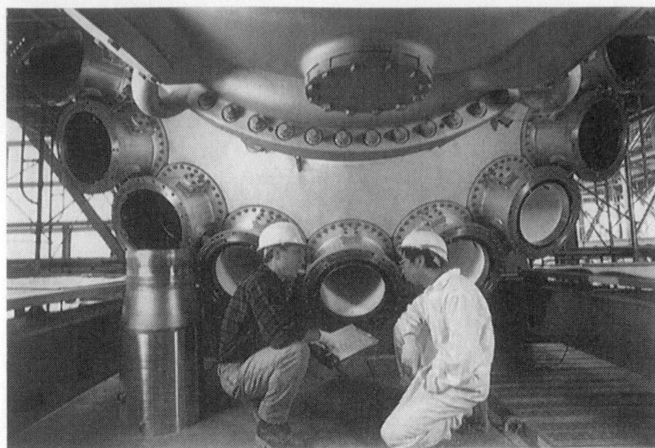

31.23 Examples of intersecting cylinders are shown in this gas turbine power plant in Hong Kong. *(Courtesy of General Electric Company.)*

This method is feasible only when the centerline of the cylinder is perpendicular to the axis of the cone, producing circular sections in the top view (rather than elliptical sections, which would be difficult to draw). A series of intersecting cylinders can be seen in this gas-powered turbine in **Figure 31.23**.

31.9 Intersections: Pyramids

Figure 31.24 shows how to find the intersection of an inclined prism with a pyramid. An auxiliary view shows the end view of the inclined prism and the pyramid. The radial lines OB and OA drawn through corners 1 and 2 in the auxiliary view project back to the front and top views. Projection locates intersecting points 1 and 2 on lines OB and OA in each view. Point P is the point where line 1-2 bends around corner OC. Finding lines of intersection 1-3 and 2-3 and determining visibility complete the solution.

Figure 31.25 shows a horizontal prism that intersects a pyramid. An auxiliary view depicts the end view of the horizontal prism with its planes as edges. Passing a series of horizontal cutting planes through the corner points of the horizontal prism and the pyramid in the auxiliary view gives the lines of intersection, which form triangular sections in the top view.

The cutting plane through corner point P in the auxiliary view is an example of a

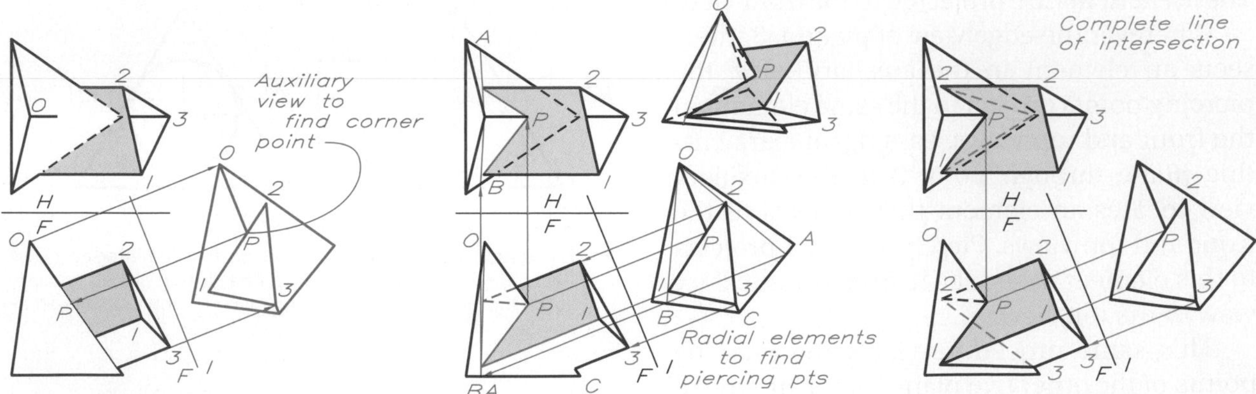

31.24 Intersection: Prism and pyramid.

Step 1 Find the edge views of the planes of the prism in an auxiliary view. Project the pyramid into this view also, showing only the visible surfaces.

Step 2 Pass planes A and B through O and points 1 and 3 in the auxiliary view. Project OA and OB to the front and top views; project 1 and 3 to them. Point 2 lies on OC. Connect 1, 2, and 3 for the intersection of this plane.

Step 3 Point 3 lies on OC in the auxiliary view. Project this point to the principal views. Connect 3 to points 1 and 2 to complete the intersections and show visibility. Assume that these shapes are constructed of sheet metal.

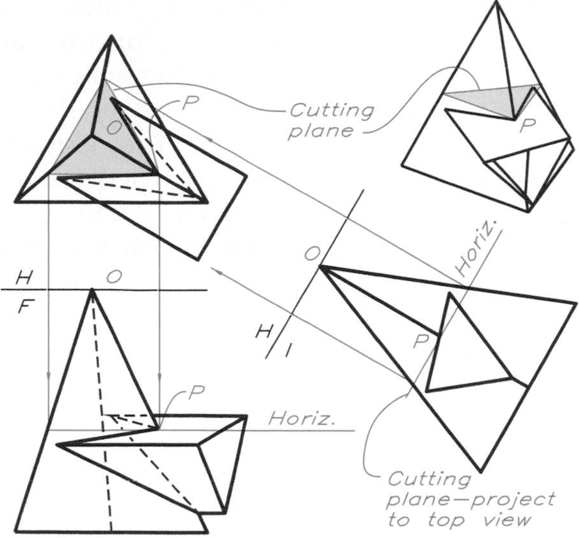

31.25 Intersection: Pyramid and prism.
The intersection of this pyramid and prism is found by obtaining the end view of the prism in an auxiliary view. Horizontal cutting planes are passed through the fold lines of the prism to find the piercing points on the line of intersection. One cutting plane that is used to find corner point P is shown.

31.26 Principles of intersections and development are applied to industrial projects varying in scope from handheld devices to massive installations such as this one, but the principles are the same.

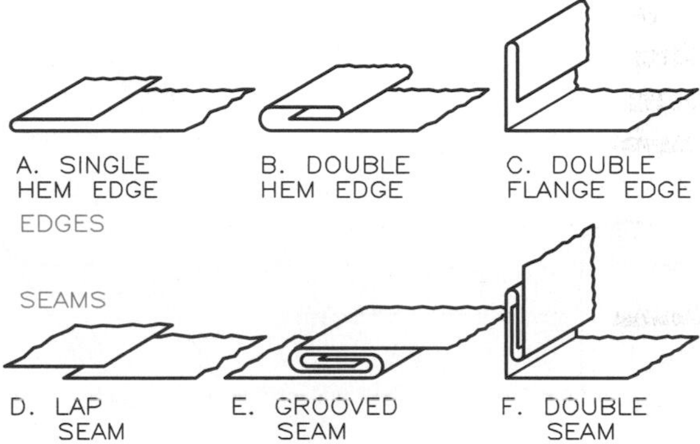

31.27 Examples of several types of edges and seams used to join sheet-metal developments. Other seams are joined by riveting and welding.

typical cutting plane. At point P the line of intersection of this plane bends around the corner of the pyramid. Other cutting planes are passed through the corner lines of the prism in the auxiliary and front views. Each corner line of the prism extends in the top view to intersect the triangular section formed by the cutting plane in the same manner P was found.

31.10 Principles of Developments

Both massive and small projects (**Figure 31.26**) are designed to be fabricated from sheet-metal stock that is formed into shape using the same principles. Although the design of an aircraft is one of the most advanced applications of **developments**, the principles are the same as for the design of a garbage can. **Figure 31.27** illustrates some of the standard edges and joints for sheet metal. The application determines the type of seam that is used.

The development of patterns for four typical shapes is shown in **Figure 31.28**. The sides of a box are unfolded into a common plane. The cylinder is rolled out along a **stretch-out line** equal in length to its circumference. The pattern of a right cone and right pyramid are developed with the length of an element serving as a radius for drawing the base arc.

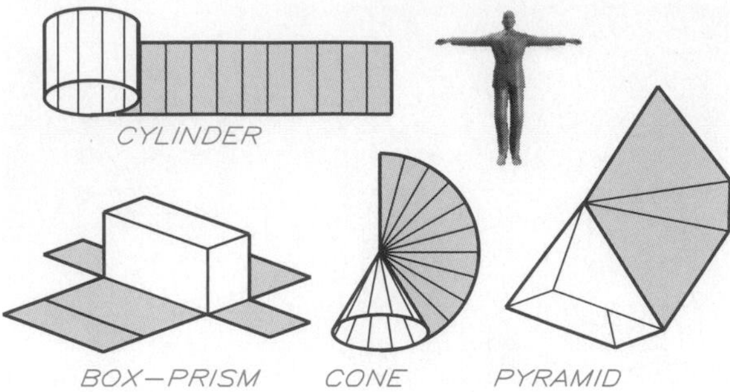

31.28 Types of developments.
Three standard types of developments are the box, cylinder, pyramid, and cone.

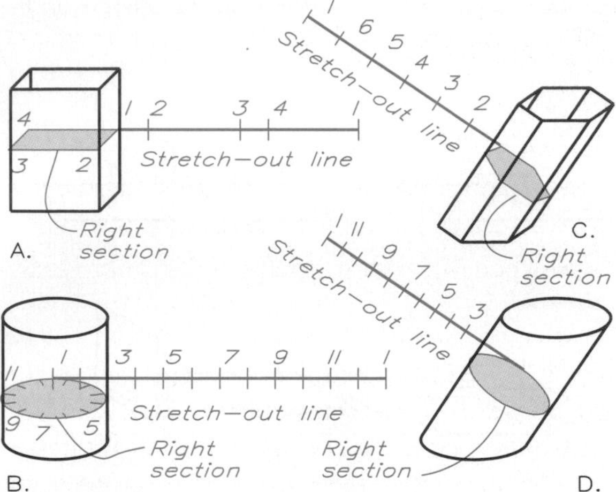

31.29 Stretch-out lines.
A–B Obtain the developments of right prisms and right cylinders by rolling out the right sections along a stretch-out line.
C–D Draw stretch-out lines parallel to the edge views of the right section of cylinders and prisms and perpendicular to their true-length elements.

The construction of patterns for geometric shapes with parallel elements, such as the prisms and cylinders shown in **Figures 31.29A** and **31.29B**, begins with drawing stretch-out lines parallel to the edge views of the shapes' right sections. The distance around the right section becomes the length of the stretch-out line. The prism and cylinder in **Figures 31.29C** and **31.29D** are inclined, so their right sections are perpendicular to their sides, not parallel to their bases.

In development, an inside pattern is preferable to an outside pattern for two reasons: (1) most bending machines are designed to fold metal inward, and (2) markings and scribings will be hidden. The designer labels patterns with a series of lettered or numbered points on the layouts. **All lines on developments must be true length. Patterns should be laid out so that the seam line (a line where the pattern is joined) is the shortest line in order to reduce the expense of riveting or welding the seams.**

31.11 Developments: Rectangular Prisms

The development of a flat pattern for a rectangular prism is illustrated in **Figure 31.30**. The edges of the prism are vertical and true length in the front view. The right section is perpendicular to these sides, and the right section is true size in the top view. The stretch-out line begins with point 1 and is drawn parallel to the edge view of the right section.

If an inside pattern is to be laid out to the right, you must determine which point is to the right of the beginning point, point 1. Let's assume that you are standing inside the top

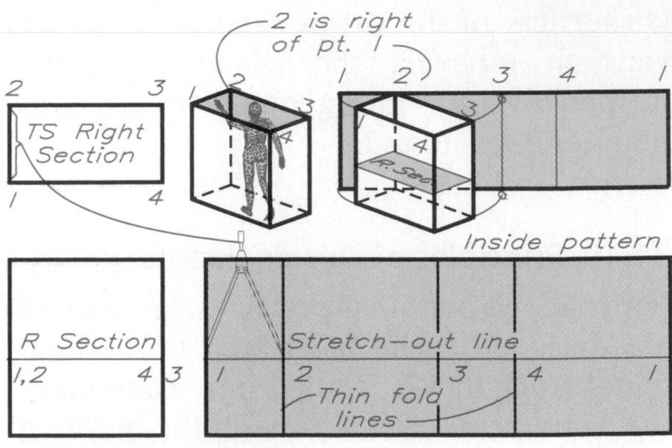

31.30 Development: Prism.
Develop the inside pattern of a rectangular prism by drawing the stretch-out line parallel to the edge view of the right section. Transfer the distances between the fold lines from the true-size right section to the stretch-out line.

view and are looking at point 1: You will see point 2 to the right of point 1.

To locate the fold lines of the pattern, transfer lines 2-3, 3-4, and 4-1 with your dividers from the right section in the top view to the stretch-out line. The length of each fold line is its projected true length from the front view. Connect the ends of the fold lines to form the boundary of the developed surface. Draw the fold lines as thin dark lines and the outside lines as thicker, visible object lines.

The chapel at the United States Air Force Academy in **Figure 31.31** was designed using the principles of intersections and developments. Development of the prism depicted in **Figure 31.32** is similar to that shown in **Figure 31.30**, although here, one of its ends is beveled (truncated) rather than squared off perpendicular to its fold lines. The stretch-out line is parallel to the edge view of the right section in the front view. Lay off the true-length distances around the right section along the stretch-out line (beginning with the shortest one) and locate the fold lines. Find the lengths of the fold lines by projecting from the front view of these lines.

31.31 The structure of the chapel of the U.S. Air Force Academy was designed using many principles of intersections and developments.

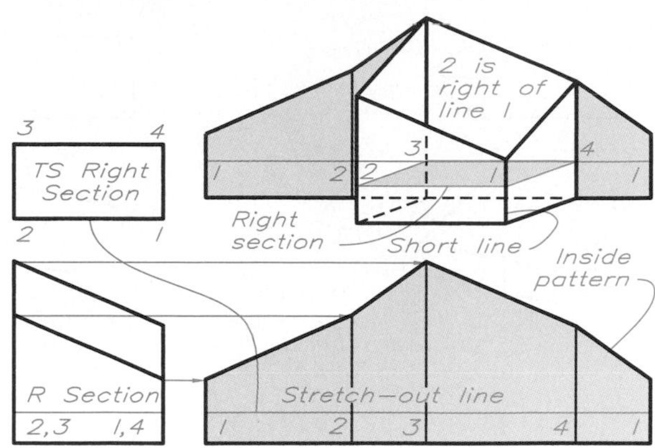

31.32 Development: Truncated prism.
Develop an inside pattern of a rectangular prism with a beveled end by drawing the stretch-out line parallel to the right section. Find the fold lines by transferring distances between the fold lines from the true-size right section to the stretch-out line.

31.12 Developments: Oblique Prisms

The prism shown in **Figure 31.33** is inclined to the horizontal plane, but its fold lines are true length in the front view. The right section is an edge perpendicular to these true-length fold lines, and the stretch-out line is parallel to the edge of the right section. A true-size view of the right section is found in the auxiliary view.

Transfer the distances between the fold lines from the true-size right section to the stretch-out line. Find the lengths of the fold lines by projecting from the front view. Determine the ends of the prism and attach them to the pattern so that they can be folded into position.

In **Figure 31.34**, the fold lines of the prism are true length in the top view, and the edge view of the right section is perpendicular to them. The stretch-out line is parallel to the edge view of the right section, and the true size of the right section appears in an auxiliary view projected from the top view. Transfer the distances about the right section to the stretch-out line to locate the fold lines, beginning with the shortest line. Find the lengths of the fold lines by projecting from the top view. Attach the end portions to the pattern to complete the construction.

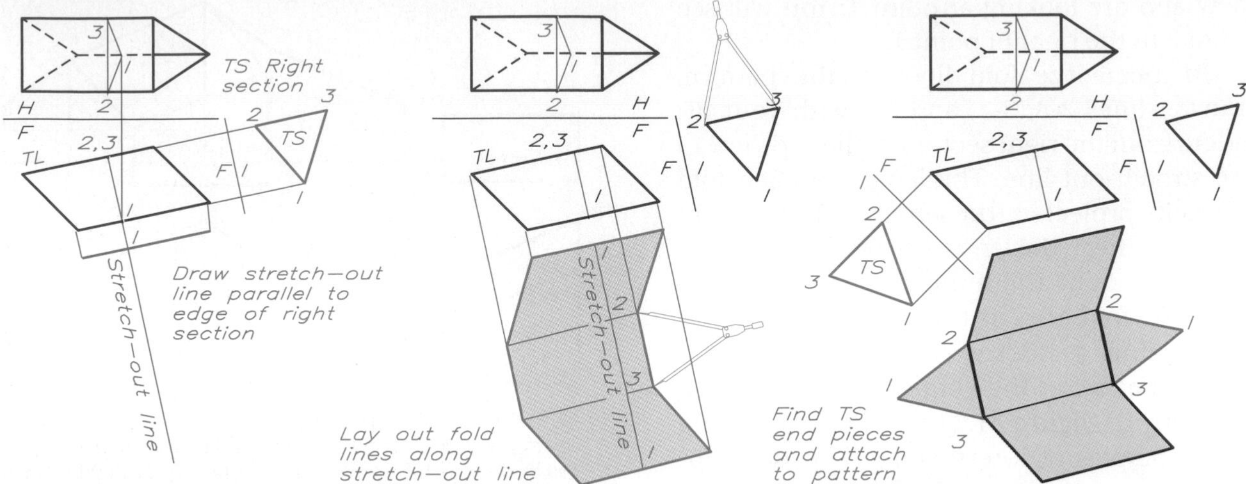

31.33 Development: Oblique prism.

Step 1 Draw the edge view of the right section perpendicular to the true-length axis in the front view. Find the true-size view of the right section in the auxiliary view. Draw the stretch-out line parallel to the edge of the right section. The line through point 1 is the first line of the development.

Step 2 Because the pattern is to be laid out to the right from line 1, the next point is line 2 (from the auxiliary view). Transfer true-length lines 1-2, 2-3, and 3-1 from the right section to the stretch-out line to locate fold lines. Determine the lengths of bend lines by projection.

Step 3 Find true-size views of the end pieces by projecting auxiliary views from the front view. Connect these ends to the development to form the completed pattern. Draw fold lines as thin dark lines and outside lines as thicker, visible object lines.

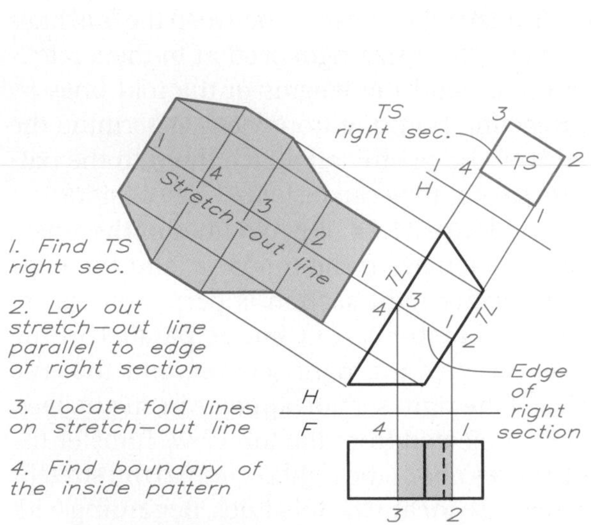

31.34 Development: Inclined prism.
Develop this oblique chute by locating the true-size right section in the auxiliary view. Draw the stretch-out line parallel to its right section. Find fold lines by transferring their spacings from the true-size right section to the stretch-out line.

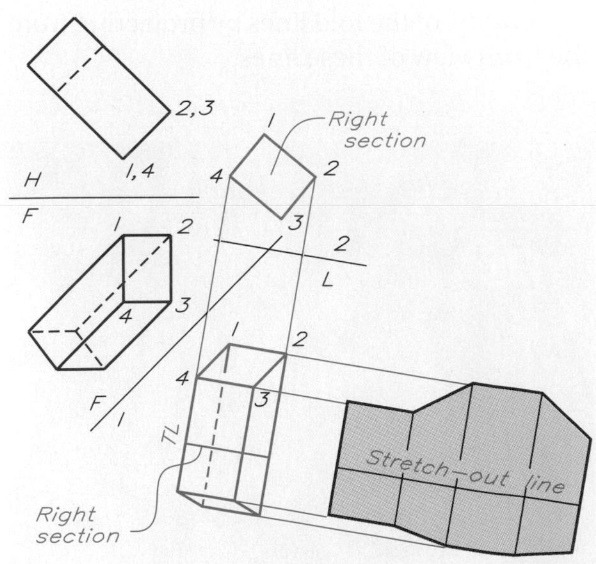

31.35 Develpment: Prism with a secondary auxiliary.
Develop an oblique prism by drawing a primary auxiliary view to find the fold lines true length and a secondary auxiliary view to find the true-size view of the right section. Use these views to develop the pattern the same way as in **Figure 31.34**.

A prism that does not project true length in either view may be developed as shown in **Figure 31.35**. The fold lines are true length in an auxiliary view projected from the front view. The right section appears as an edge perpendicular to the fold lines in the primary auxiliary view and true size in a secondary auxiliary view.

Draw the stretch-out line parallel to the edge view of the right section. Locate the fold lines on the stretch-out line by measuring around the right section in the secondary auxiliary view, beginning with the shortest one. Then, project the lengths of the fold lines to the development from the primary auxiliary view.

31.13 Developments: Cylinders

Figure 31.36 illustrates how to develop a flat pattern of a right cylinder. The elements of the cylinder are true length in the front view, so the right section appears as an edge in this view and true size in the top view. The stretch-out line is parallel to the edge view of the right section, and point 1 is the beginning point because it lies on the shortest element.

Let's assume that you are standing inside the cylinder in the top view and are looking at point 1: You will see that point 2 is to the right

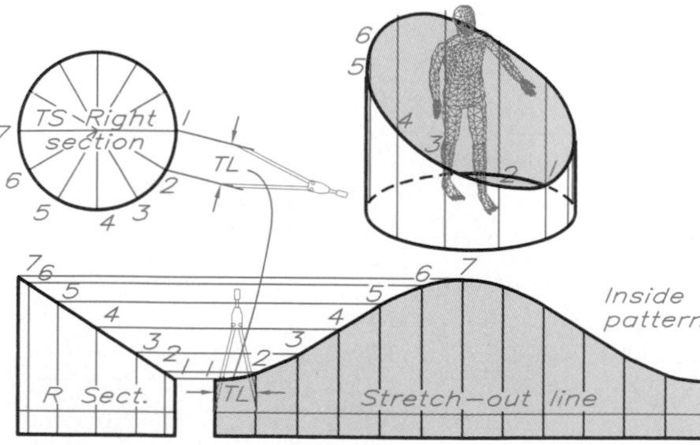

31.36 Development: Truncated cylinder.
Develop an inside pattern of a truncated right cylinder by drawing the stretch-out line parallel to the right section. Transfer points 1 through 7 from the top view to the stretch-out line that is parallel to the right section. Point 2 is to the right of point 1 for an inside pattern.

31.37 Examples of a large cylindrical component of an oil refinery is shown being installed. *(Courtesy of Exxon Mobil Corporation.)*

of point 1. Therefore, lay off point 2 to the right of point 1 for developing an inside pattern.

By drawing radial lines at 15° or 30° intervals you can equally space the elements in the top view and conveniently lay them out along the stretch-out line as equal measurements. To complete the pattern, find the lengths of the elements by projecting from the front view. An application of a large cylindrical component of an oil refinery that required the application of these principles is shown in **Figure 31.37**.

31.14 Developments: Oblique Cylinders

The pattern for an oblique cylinder (**Figure 31.38**) involves the same determinations as the preceding cases, but with the additional step of finding a true-size view of the right section in an auxiliary view. First, locate a right section in the auxiliary view and project

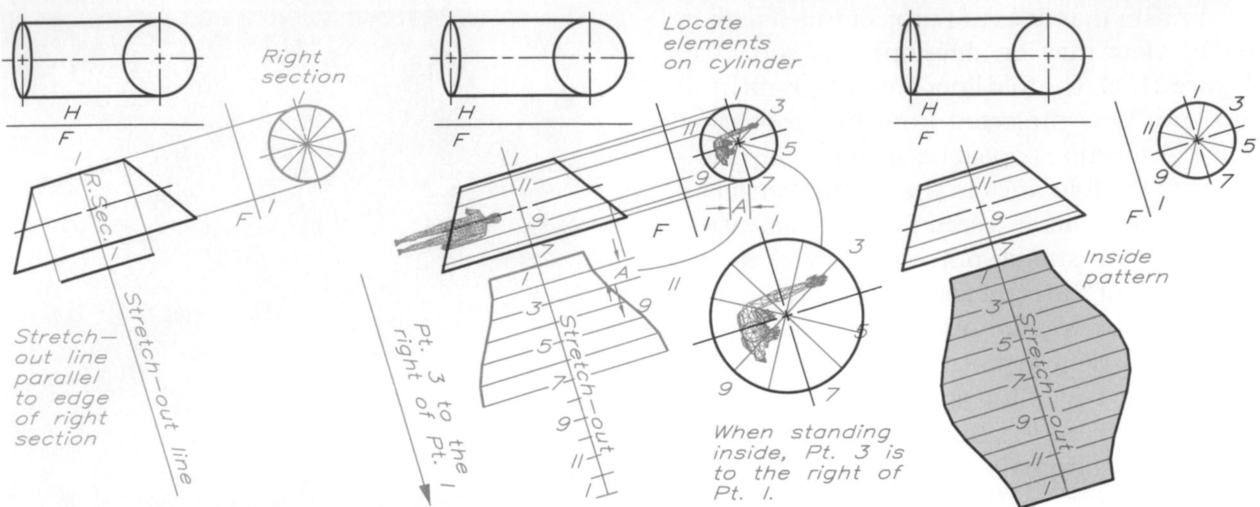

31.38 Development: Oblique cylinder.

Step 1 Draw the right section perpendicular to the true-length axis in the front view. Draw an auxiliary view to find the right section true size; divide it into equal chords. Draw a stretch-out line parallel to the edge of the right section. Locate the shortest line at 1.

Step 2 Project elements from the right section to the front view. Transfer the chordal measurements in the auxiliary view to the stretch-out line to locate cylindrical elements and determine their lengths by projection.

Step 3 Locate the remaining elements to complete the construction as begun in step 2. Connect the ends of the elements with a smooth curve. This is an inside pattern with a seam along its shortest element.

it back to the true-length view. Draw the stretch-out line parallel to the edge view of the right section in the front view.

Lay out the spacing between the elements along the stretch-out line, and draw the elements through these points perpendicular to the stretch-out line. Find the lengths of the elements by projecting from the front view, and complete the pattern.

A more general case is the oblique cylinder shown in **Figure 31.39**, where the elements are not true length in the given views. A primary auxiliary view gives the element's true length, and a secondary auxiliary view yields a true-size view of the right section. Draw the stretch-out line parallel to the edge view of the right section in the primary auxiliary view. Transfer the elements to the stretch-out line from the true-size right section.

Draw the elements perpendicular to the stretch-out line and find their lengths by

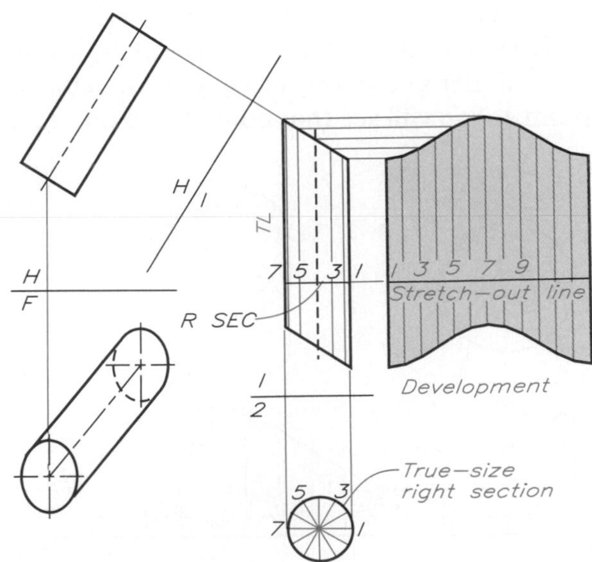

31.39 Development: Cylinder—secondary auxiliary. Develop an oblique cylinder by drawing a primary auxiliary view showing its elements true-length. Find the right section true size in a secondary auxiliary view. Complete the construction as shown in **Figure 31.38**.

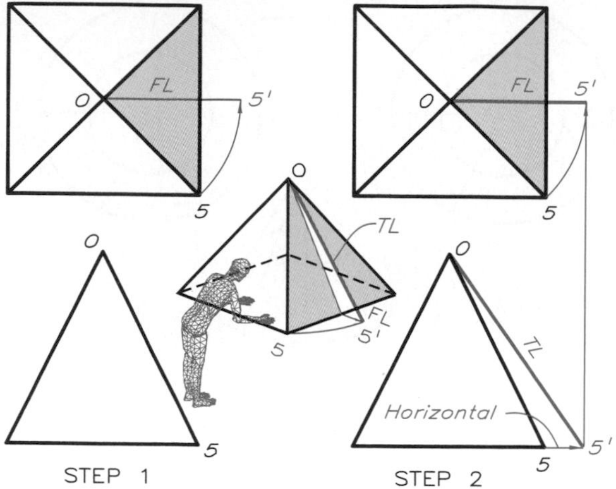

31.40 Elements true length by revolution: Pyramid.

Step 1 Find the true length of corner line O-5 of the pyramid by revolving it into the frontal plane in the top view to O-5′.

Step 2 Project point 5′ to the front view, where frontal line O-5′ is true length.

projecting from the primary auxiliary view. Connect the endpoints with a smooth curve to complete the pattern.

31.15 Developments: Pyramids

All lines used to draw patterns must be true length, but pyramids have few lines that are true length in the given views. For this reason you must find the sloping corner lines' true length before drawing a development.

Figure 31.40 shows the method of finding the corner lines of a pyramid true length by revolution. Revolve line O-5 into the frontal plane to line O-5′ in the top view so that it will be true length in the front view. An application of the development of a pyramid is the sheet-metal hopper shown in **Figure 31.41**.

Figure 31.42 shows the development of a right pyramid. Line O-1 is revolved into the frontal plane in the top view to find its true length in the front view. Because it is a right pyramid, all corner lines are equal in length. Line O-1′ is the radius for the base circle of the

31.41 This sheet-metal hopper was designed by applying the principles of the development of a pyramid.

development. When you transfer distance 1-2 from the base in the top view to the development, it forms a chord on the base circle. Find lines 2-3, 3-4, and 4-1 in the same manner and in sequence. Draw the fold lines as thin lines from the base to the apex, point O.

A variation of this case is the truncated pyramid (**Figure 31.43**). Development of the inside pattern proceeds as in the preceding case, but establishing the upper lines of the development requires an additional step. Revolution

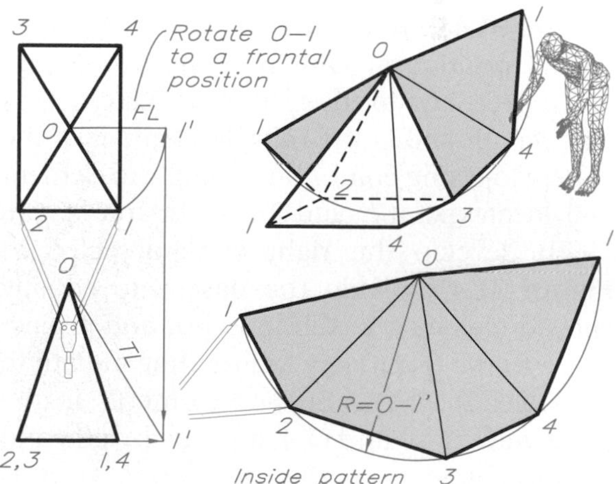

31.42 Development: Pyramid.
Develop this right pyramid by laying out an arc by using the true length of corner line O-1′ as the radius. Transfer true-length distances around the base in the top view to the arc by triangulation, and darken the lines.

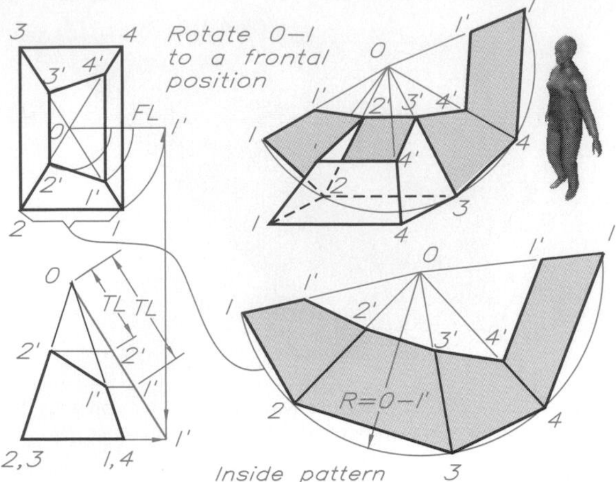

31.43 Development: Truncated pyramid.
Develop an inside pattern of a truncated right pyramid by using the method shown in **Figure 31.42**. Find the true lengths of elements O-1′, O-2′, O-3′, and O-4′ in the front view by revolution. Lay them off along their respective elements to find the upper boundary of the pattern.

yields the true-length lines from the apex to points 1′, 2′, 3′, and 4′. Lay off these distances along their fold lines on the pattern to find the upper boundary of the pattern.

31.16 Developments: Cones

All elements of a right cone are equal in length (**Figure 31.44**). Revolving element O-6 into its frontal position at O-6′ gives its true length when projected to the front view. Line O-6′ is true length and is the outside element of the cone. Projecting point 7 horizontally to element O-6′ locates point 7′, and O-7′ is also true length.

To develop the right cone depicted in **Figure 31.45**, divide the base into equally spaced elements in the top view and project them to the front view, where they radiate to the apex at O. The outside elements in the front view, O-10 and O-4, are true length, and all the elements of this right cone are this same true length.

Using element O-10 as a radius, draw the base arc of the development. The spacing of the elements along the base circle is equal to

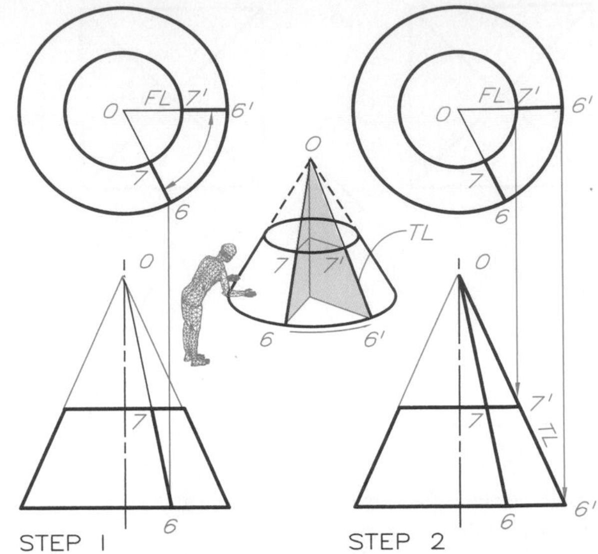

31.44 True length by revolution: Cone.

Step 1 Revolve an element of a cone, O-6, into a frontal plane in the top view, O-6′.

Step 2 Project point 6′ to the front view, where it is a true-length outside element of the cone. Find the true length of line O-7 by projecting point 7 to the outside element in the front view, 7′.

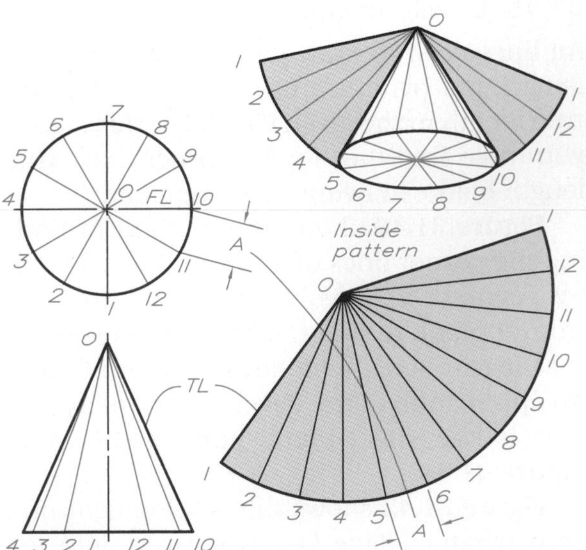

31.45 Development: Cone.
Develop an inside pattern of a right cone by usimg a true-length element (O-4 or O-10 in the front view) as the radius. Transfer chordal distances from the true-size base in the top view and mark them off along the arc.

the true-length chordal distances between them on the circular base in the top view. Inspection of the top view from the inside, where point 2 is to the right of point 1, indicates that this is an inside pattern. The body of the crew module for the space shuttle in **Figure 31.46** is an example of developed panels that were welded together.

Figure 31.47 shows the development of a truncated cone. To find its pattern, lay out the entire cone by using the true-length element O-1 as the radius, ignoring the portion removed from it. Locate the hyperbolic section formed by the inclined plane through the front view of the cone in the top view by projecting points on each element of the cone to the top view of these elements. For example, determine the true length of line O-3′ by projecting point 3′ horizontally to the true-length element O-1 in the front view. Lay off these distances, and others, along their respective elements to establish points on a curve. Connect these point to form a smooth curve. Greater accuracy can be achieved in plotting the curve if more elements of construction are used using these same principles. The conical development of the Mercury capsule is an example of the application of developments (**Figure 31.48**).

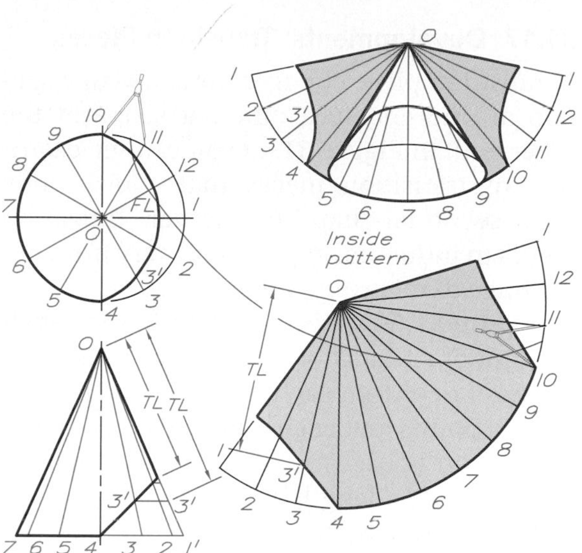

31.47 Development: Truncated cone.
To develop a conical surface with a side opening, begin by laying it out as in **Figure 31.47**. Find true-length elements by revolution in the front view, and transfer them to their respective elements in the pattern.

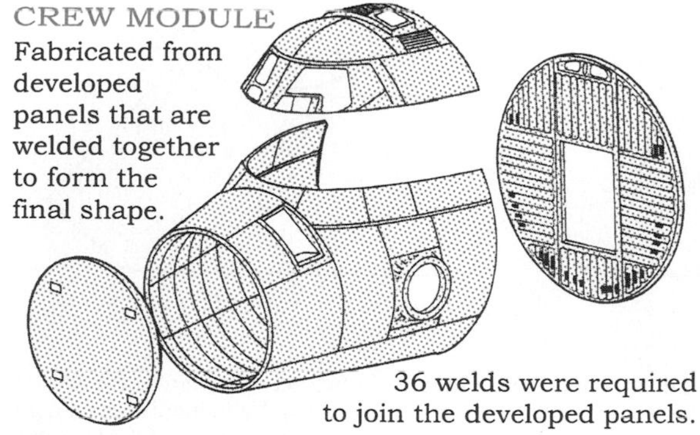

CREW MODULE
Fabricated from developed panels that are welded together to form the final shape.
36 welds were required to join the developed panels.

31.46 Applications of developments and intersections of cones and cylinders can be seen in the crew module for the space shuttle. *(Courtesy of NASA)*

31.48 Applications of developments and intersections of cones and cylinders can be seen in the Mercury capsule #2. *(Courtesy of NASA)*

31.17 Developments: Transition Pieces

A transition piece changes the shape of a section at one end to a different shape at the other end. In **Figure 31.49** you can see examples of transition pieces that convert one cross-sectional shape to another. Transition pieces in industrial applications vary from being huge to relatively small.

Figure 31.50 shows the steps in the development of a transition piece. Radial elements are extended from each corner to the equally spaced points on the circular end of the piece. Revolution is used to find the true length of each line. True-length lines 2-D, 3-D, and 2-3 yield the inside pattern of 2-3-D.

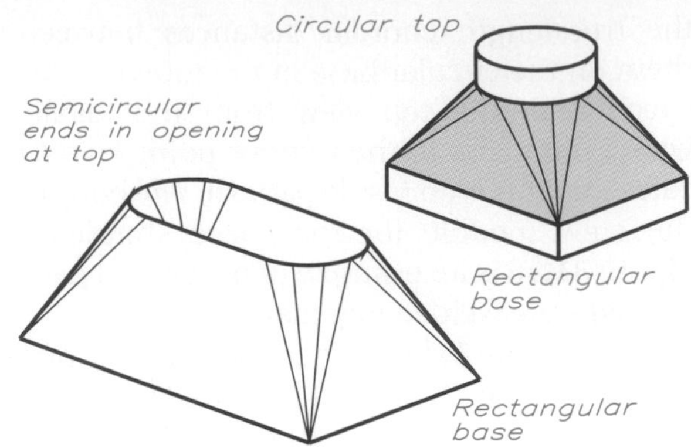

31.49 Transition pieces.
These are examples of transition pieces that connect parts having different cross sections.

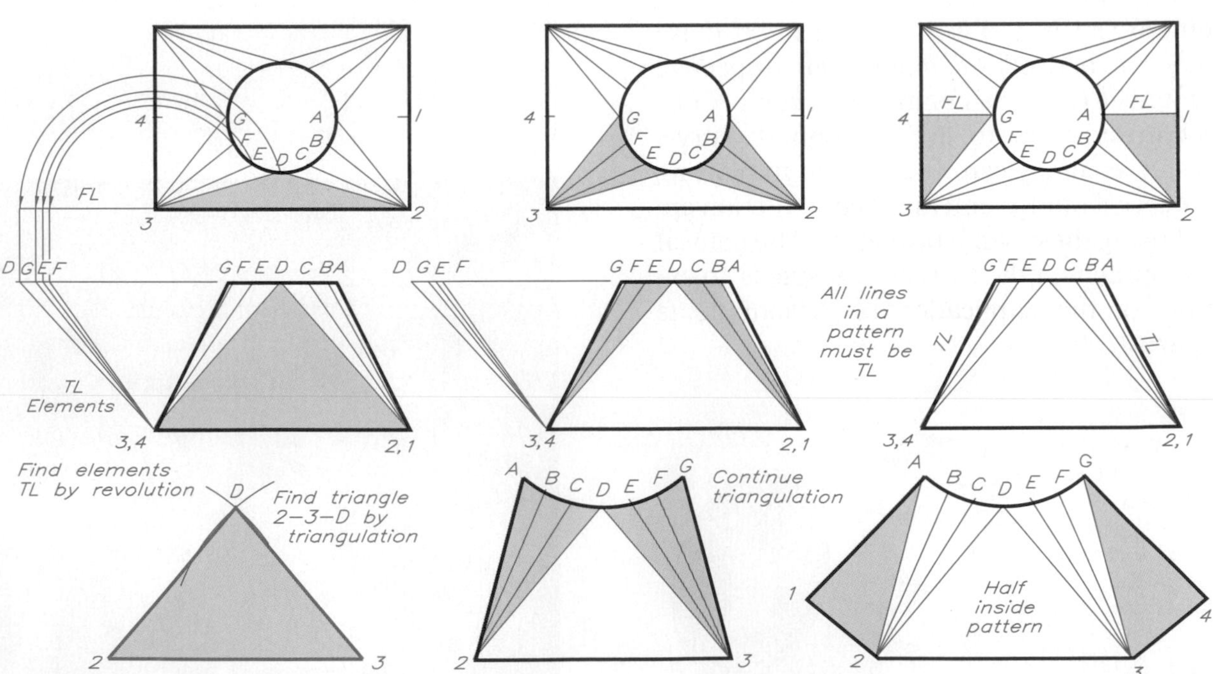

31.50 Development: Transition piece.

Step 1 Divide the circular end into equal parts in the top view, and connect these points with lines to corner points 2 and 3. Find the true length of these lines by revolving and projecting them to the front view. Using the true-length lines, draw triangle 2-3-D.

Step 2 Using other true-length lines and the chord distances on the circular end in the top view, draw a series of triangles joined at common sides. For example, draw arc 2-C from point 2. To find point C, draw arc DC from D. Chord DC is true length in the top view.

Step 3 Construct the remaining planes, A-1-2 and G-3-4, by triangulation to complete the inside half-pattern of the transition piece. Draw the fold lines, where the surface is to be bent, as thin lines. The seam line for the pattern is line A-1, the shortest line.

The true-length radial lines, used in combination with the true-length chordal distances in the top view, give a series of abutting triangles to form the pattern beginning with element D2. Adding the triangles A-1-2 and G-3-4 at each end of the pattern completes the development of a half-pattern. Only a half-pattern is shown in this example.

Problems

Two solutions can be drawn on a size A sheet when using a grid size of 0.20 in. (5 mm). One solution can be drawn on a size A sheet by using a grid size of 0.40 in. (10 mm). Use instruments, number the points, and show construction in a professional manner.

1.–24. (**Figure 31.51**) **Intersections** Lay out the given views of the problems and find the intersections between the shapes that are necessary to complete the views.

25.–48. (**Figure 31.52**) **Developments** Lay out the problems and draw their inside developments. Orient the long side of the size A sheet horizontally to allow space at the right of the given views for the development.

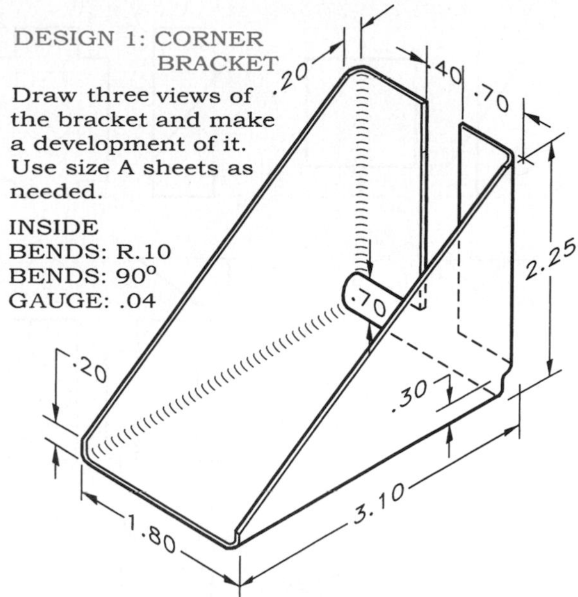

Design 1: Corner Bracket

A. Draw three views of the corner bracket with instruments on a size A sheet.

B. Draw a flat-pattern development of the corner bracket on a size A sheet.

Thought Questions

1. Which construction should come first when detailing the sheet-metal parts of a part with intersecting elements: intersection or development construction? Explain your response.

2. Describe the resulting lines of intersections between flat planes, two cylindrical surfaces, and between cylindrical surfaces and flat planes.

3. Why is a development constructed as an inside pattern rather than an outside pattern? Explain.

4. Explain the difference between the radial-line and cutting-plane methods of constructing intersections on the surface of a cone.

5. What is a stretch-out line and how is it used in the development of a cylinder? How must it be positioned?

6. Explain why all lines of development must be true length.

7. In general, which line of a development must be used as the splice line of the flat pattern being constructed? Explain.

8. What is the significance of a right section of a cylinder and how is it used in the development of a cylinder?

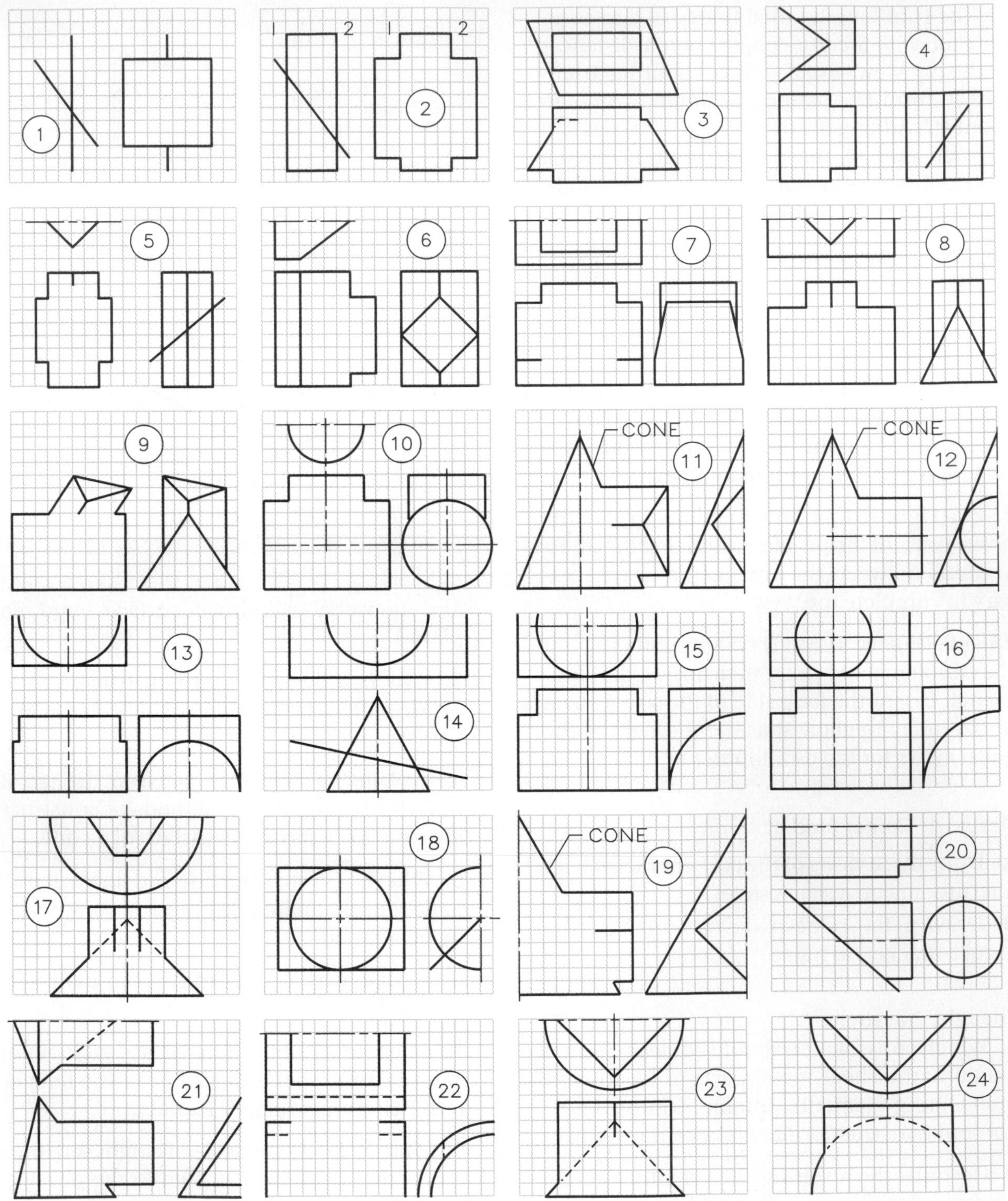

31.51 (Problems 1–24) Intersections.

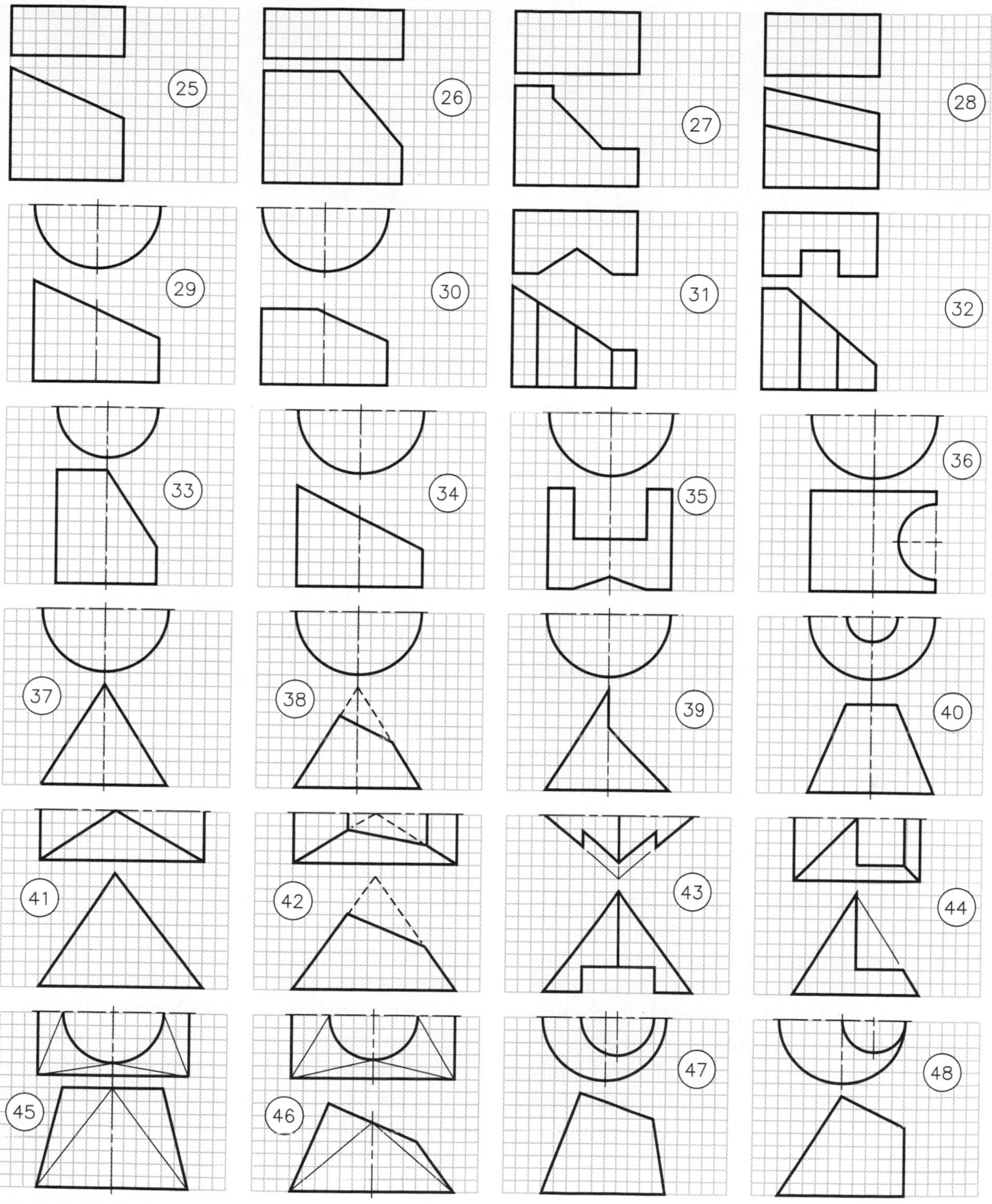

31.52 (Problems 25–48) Developments.

32 Graphs

32.1 Introduction

Data and information expressed as numbers and words are usually difficult to analyze or evaluate unless transcribed into graphical form, or as a **graph**. The term **chart** is an acceptable substitute for graph, but it is more appropriate when applied to maps, a specialized form of graphs.

Graphs are especially useful in presenting data at briefings where the data must be interpreted and communicated quickly to those in attendance. Graphs are convenient ways to condense and present data visually, allowing the data to be grasped much more easily than when presented as tables of numbers or verbally.

Several different types of graphs are widely used. Their application depends on the data and the nature of the presentation required. The most common types of graphs are:

1. Pie graphs
2. Bar graphs
3. Linear coordinate graphs
4. Logarithmic coordinate graphs
5. Semilogarithmic coordinate graphs
6. Schematics and diagrams

Proportions

Graphs are used on large display boards, and in technical reports, as slides for a projector, or as transparencies for an overhead projector. Consequently, the proportion of the graph must be determined before it is constructed to match the page, slide, or transparency.

A graph that is to be photographed with a 35 mm camera must be drawn to the proportions of the film, or approximately 3 × 2 (**Figure 32.1**). This area may be enlarged or reduced proportionally by using the diagonal-line method.

The proportions of an overhead projector transparency are approximately 10 × 8. The image size should not exceed 9.5 in. × 7.5 in.

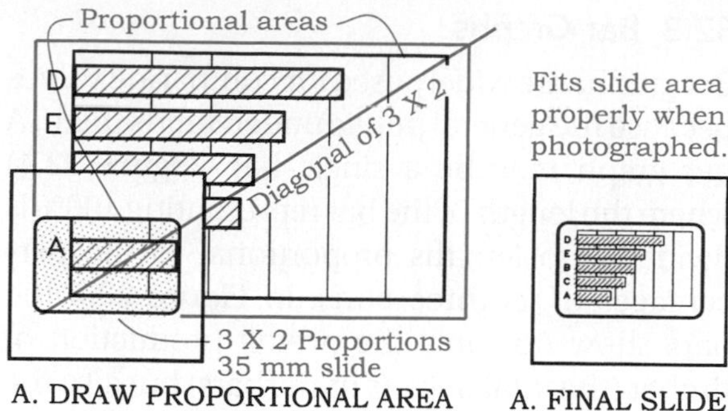

32.1 This diagonal-line method may be used to lay out drawings that are proportional to the area of a 35 mm slide.

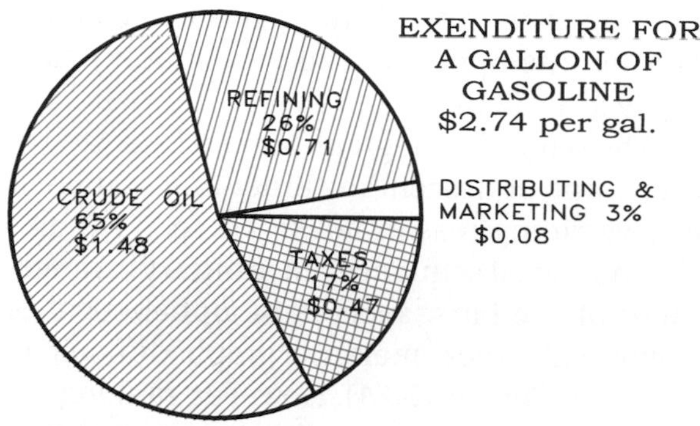

32.2 A pie graph shows the relationship of parts to a whole. It is most effective when there are only a few parts.

to allow an adequate margin for mounting the transparency on a frame of plastic or cardboard.

32.2 Pie Graphs

Pie graphs compare the relationship of parts to a whole. For example, **Figure 32.2** shows a pie graph that compares costs of producing a gallon of gasoline at a given point in time. This information would be difficult to convey verbally.

Figure 32.3 illustrates the steps involved in drawing a pie graph. The data in this example, as simple as they are, are not as easily compared in numerical form as when drawn as a pie graph. Position thin sectors of a pie graph as nearly horizontal as possible to provide more space for labeling. When space is not available within the sectors, place labels outside the pie graph and, if necessary, use leaders (**Figure 32.2**). Showing the percentage represented by each sector is important, and giving the actual numbers or values as part of the label is also desirable.

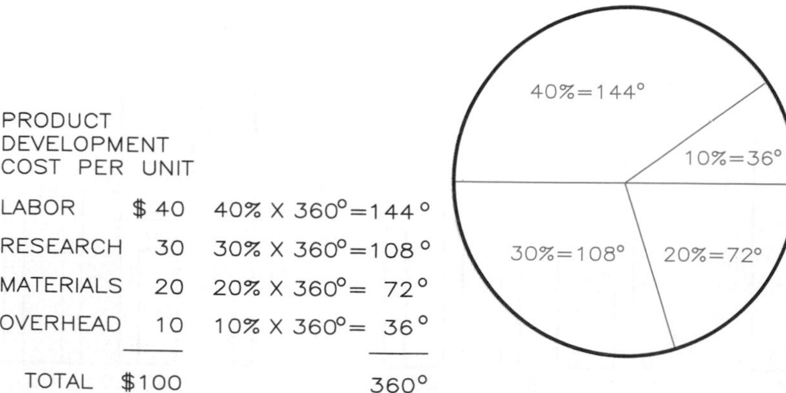

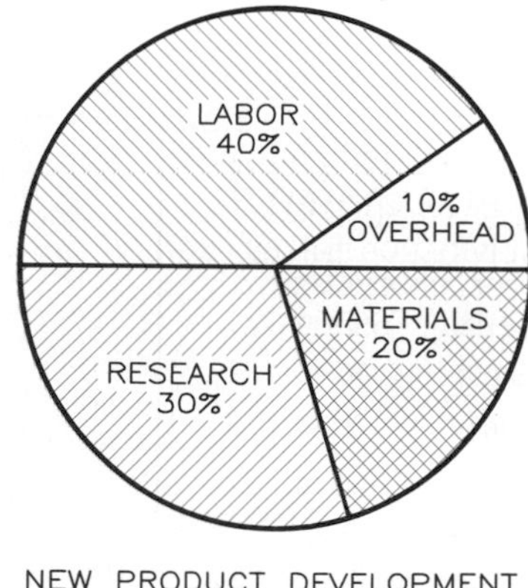

32.3 Pie graphs.

Step 1 Find the sum of the parts and the percentage that each is of the total. Multiply each percentage by 360° to obtain the angle of each sector.

Step 2 Draw the circle and construct each sector using the degrees of each from step 1. Place small sectors as nearly horizontal as possible.

Step 3 Label sectors with their proper names and percentages. Exact numbers also may be included in each sector to add more clarity.

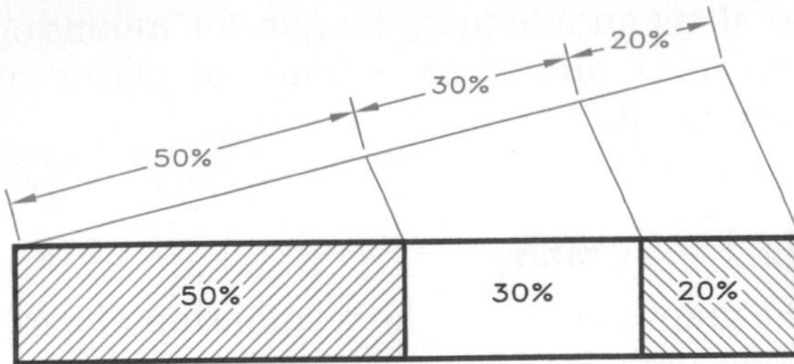

32.4 The diagonal-line method may be used to find the percentages of the parts to the whole, where the total bar represents 100%.

32.3 Bar Graphs

Bar graphs are widely used for comparing values because the general public understands them. A bar graph may be a single bar (**Figure 32.4**) where the length of the bar representing 100% is divided into lengths proportional to the percentages of its three parts. In **Figure 32.5** the bars show not only the overall production of timber (the total heights of the bars) but also the percentages of the total devoted to three uses of the timber.

Figure 32.6 shows how to convert data into a bar graph that can be used in a report or briefing. The axes of the graph carry labels, and its title appears inside the graph where space is available.

The bars of a bar graph should be sorted in ascending or descending order unless there is an overriding reason not to do so, such as a chronological sequence. An arbitrary arrangement of the bars, such as in alphabetical or numerical order, makes a graph difficult to evaluate (**Figure 32.7A**). However, ranking the categories by bar length allows easier comparisons from smallest to largest (**Figure 32.7B**). If the data are sequential and involve time, such as sales per month, a better arrangement

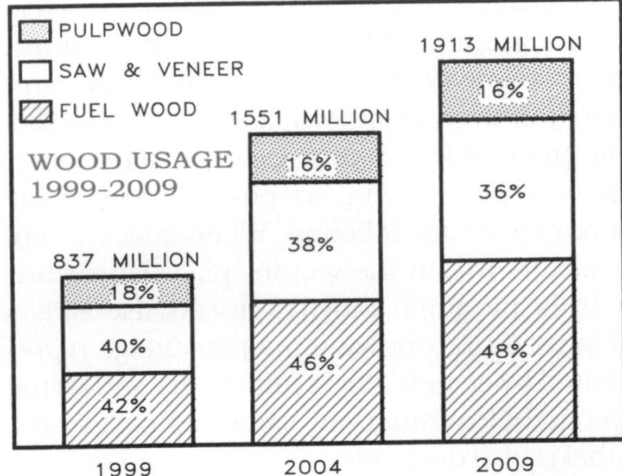

32.5 In this bar graph, each bar represents 100% of the total amount and shows the percentages of the parts to the total.

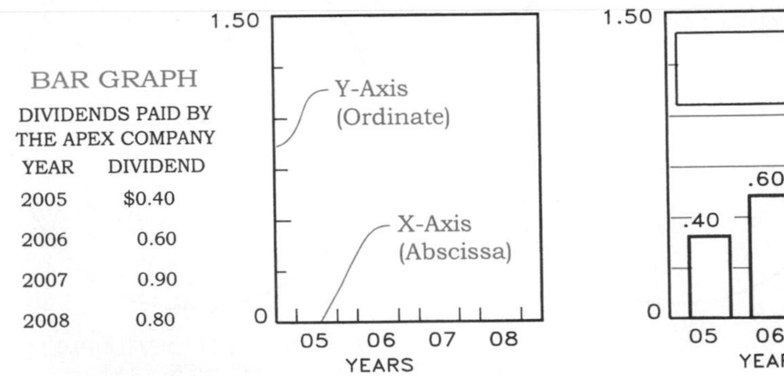

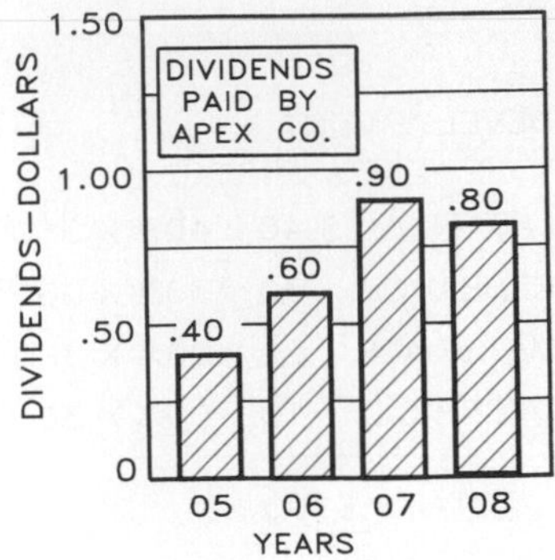

32.6 Drawing a bar graph.

Step 1 Scale the vertical and horizontal axes so that the data will fit on the grid. Begin the bars at zero.

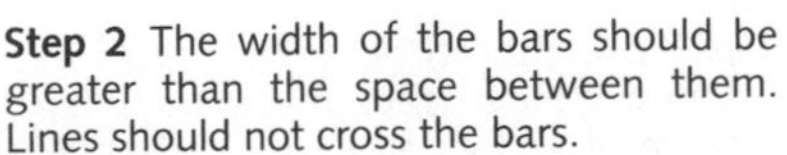

Step 2 The width of the bars should be greater than the space between them. Lines should not cross the bars.

Step 3 Strengthen lines, place a title in the graph, label the axes, and crosshatch the bars.

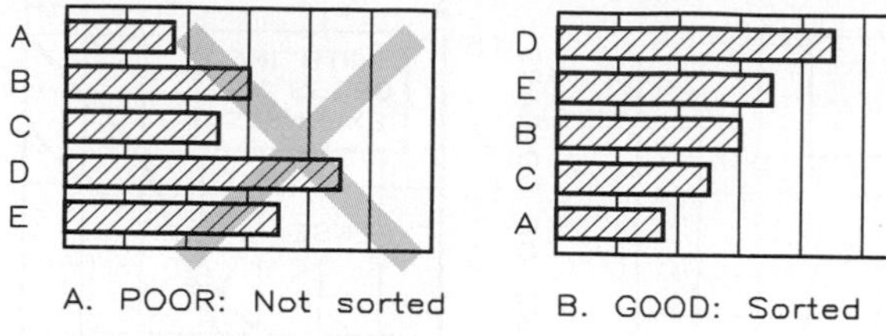

32.7 Arranging bars by length.

A When bars are arbitrarily arranged, such as alphabetically, the bar graph is difficult to interpret.

B When the bars are sorted by length, the graph is much easier to interpret.

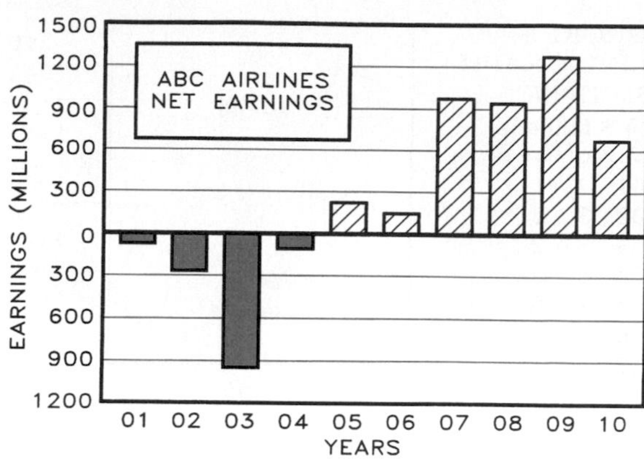

32.9 Bar graphs may be drawn with bars in both negative and positive directions.

of the bars is chronologically, to show the effect of time.

Bars in a bar graph may be horizontal (**Figure 32.8**) or vertical. Data cannot be compared accurately unless each bar is full length and originates at zero. Also, bars should not extend beyond the limits of the graph (giving the impression that the data were "too hot" to hold). Another form of bar graph shows plus and minus changes from a base value (**Figure 32.9**).

32.4 Linear Coordinate Graphs

Figure 32.10 shows a typical linear coordinate graph, with notes explaining its important features. Divided into equal divisions, the axes are referred to as *linear scales.* Data points are plotted on the grid by using measurements, called *coordinates,* along each axis from zero. The plotted points are marked with symbols such as circles or squares that may be easily drawn with a template. The horizontal scale of the graph is called the **abscissa** or *x*-axis. The vertical scale is called the **ordinate** or *y*-axis.

When the points have been plotted, a curve is drawn through them to represent the data. The line drawn to represent data points is called

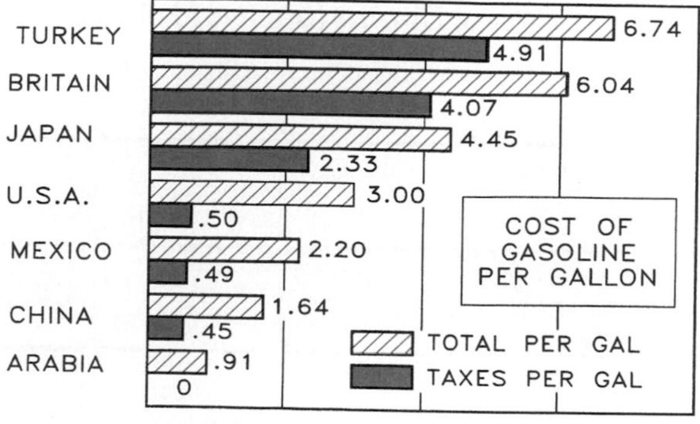

32.8 The horizontal bars of this graph are arranged in descending order to show the cost of gasoline and its associated taxation.

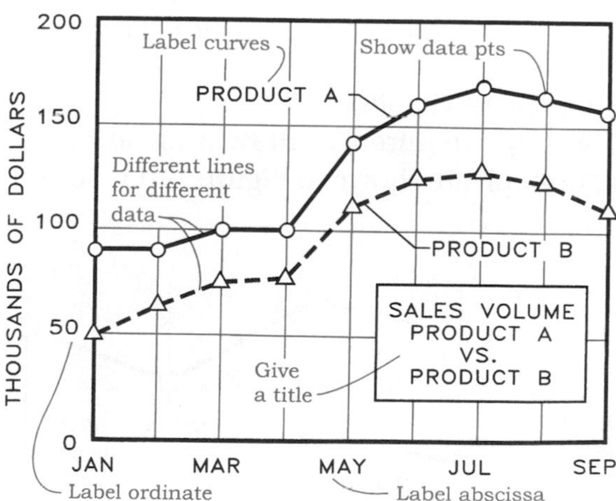

32.10 This basic linear coordinate graph illustrates the important features on a graph.

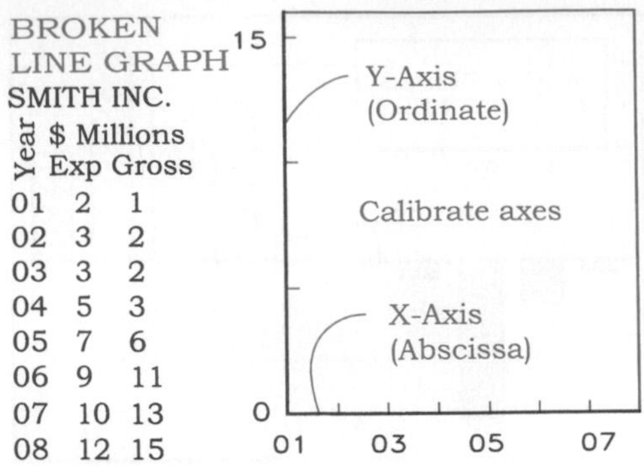

BROKEN
LINE GRAPH
SMITH INC.
Year
$ Millions
Exp Gross
01 2 1
02 3 2
03 3 2
04 5 3
05 7 6
06 9 11
07 10 13
08 12 15
15
Y-Axis
(Ordinate)
Calibrate axes
X-Axis
(Abscissa)
0
01
03
05
07

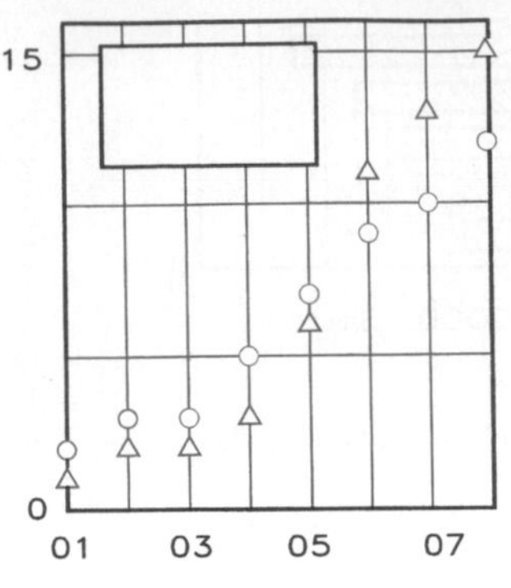

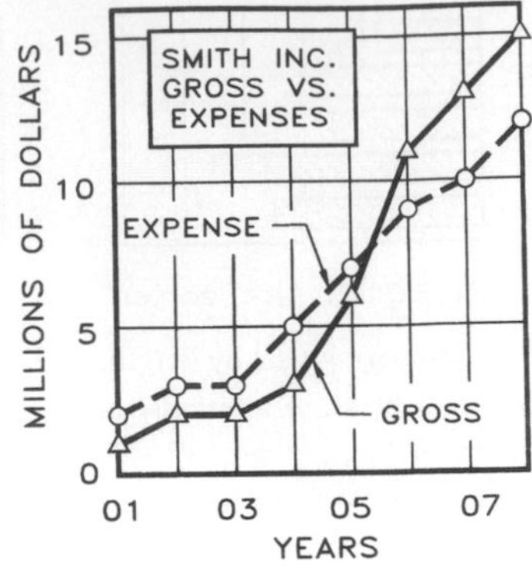

32.11 Broken-line graph.

Step 1 Using the given data, lay off the vertical (ordinate) and horizontal (abscissa) axes to provide space for the largest values.

Step 2 Draw division lines and plot the data, using different symbols for each set of data.

Step 3 Connect points with straight lines, label the axes, title the graph, darken lines, and label the curves.

a **curve** regardless whether it is a straight line, smooth curve, or broken line. The curve should not extend through the plotted points; rather, the points should be left as open circles or other symbols.

The curve is the most important part of the graph, so it should be drawn as the most prominent (thickest) line. If there are two curves in a graph, they should be drawn as different line types and labeled. The title of the graph is placed in a box inside the graph and units are given along the *x*- and *y*-axes with labels identifying the scales of the graph.

Broken-Line Graphs

The steps required to draw a linear coordinate graph are shown in **Figure 32.11**. Because the data points represent sales, which have no predictable pattern, the data do not give a smooth progression from point to point. Therefore the points are connected with a **broken-line curve** drawn as an angular line from point to point.

Again, leave the symbols used to mark the data points open rather than extending grid lines or the data curve through them (**Figure 32.12**). Each circle or symbol used to plot points should be about 1/8 in. (3 mm) in diameter. **Figure 32.13** shows typical data-point symbols and lines.

AutoCAD Method Data points may be produced as *Circles, Donuts* (open and closed), or

TEXT HEIGHT
Circles a little smaller than the lettering height.
A. GOOD: No lines thru circles
Plotted curves boldest lines
B. POOR: Lines thru circles

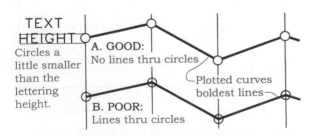

32.12 The curve of a graph drawn from point to point should not extend through the symbols used to represent data points.

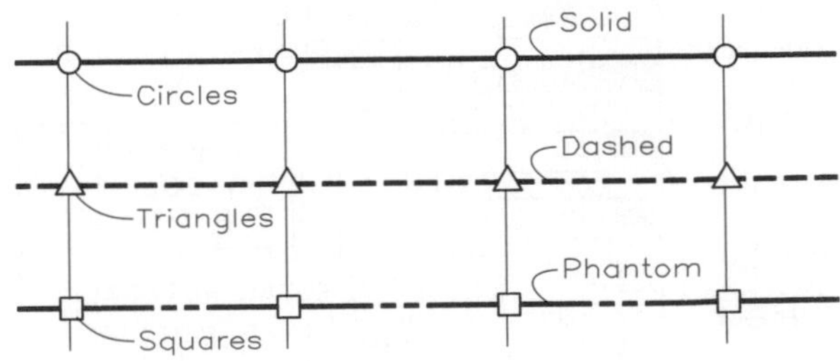

32.13 Symbols and lines such as these may be used to represent different curves on a graph. The data-point symbols should be drawn about the same size as the letter height being used, usually a little less than 1/8 in. (3 mm) in diameter.

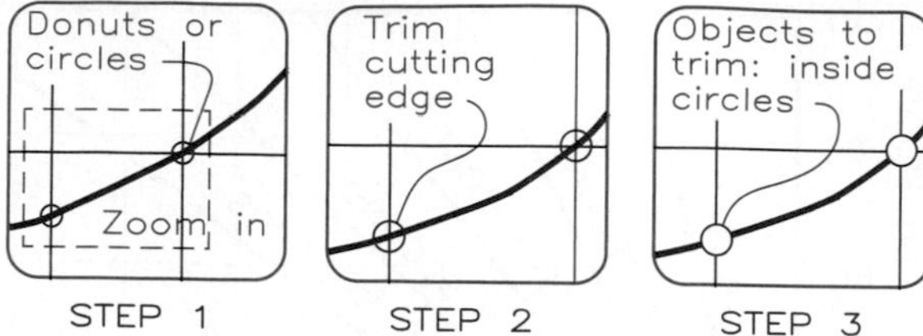

32.14 Editing data points.

Step 1 Open data points may be plotted on a graph as *Circles, Donuts,* or *Polygons.* To remove lines from inside the open points, *Zoom* in on several points.

Step 2 *Command:* Trim (Enter)
Select cutting edge (s): . . .
Select objects: (Select the circle.) (Enter)

Step 3 *Select object to trim:* (Select the lines inside the circle, and they will be removed.)
Continue this process for all points.

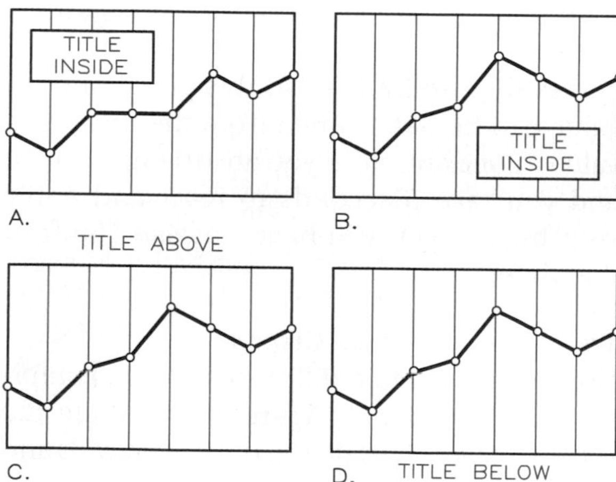

32.15 Placement of titles on a graph.

A and **B** The title of a graph may be placed inside a box within the graph. Box perimeter lines should not coincide with grid lines.

C Titles may be placed over the graph.

D Titles may be placed under the graph.

Polygons. The grid lines and curves that pass through the open symbols may be removed easily with the *Trim* command (**Figure 32.14**).

Titles The title of a graph may be located in any of the positions shown in **Figure 32.15**. A graph's title should never be as meaningless as "graph" or "coordinate graph." Instead, it should identify concisely what the graph shows.

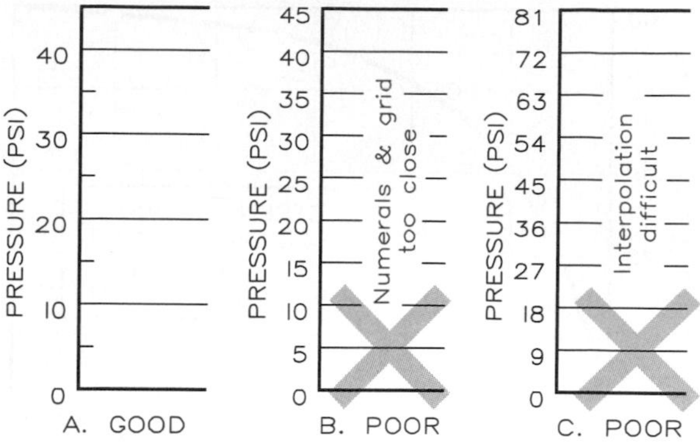

32.16 Calibrating graph scales.

A The scale is properly labeled and calibrated. It has about the right number of grid lines and divisions, and the numbers are well spaced and easy to interpolate.

B The numbers are too close together, and there are too many grid lines.

C The increments selected make interpolation difficult.

Scale and Labeling The calibration and labeling of the axes affect the appearance and readability of a graph. **Figure 32.16A** shows a properly calibrated and labeled axis. **Figures 32.16B** and **32.16C** illustrate common mistakes: placing the grid lines too close together and labeling too many divisions along the axis. In **Figure 32.16C**, the choice of the interval between the labeled values (9 units) makes interpolation between them difficult. For example, locating the value 22 by eye is more difficult on this scale than on the one shown in **Figure 32.16A**.

Smooth-Line Graphs

The strength of concrete related to its curing time is plotted in **Figure 32.17**. The strength of concrete changes gradually and continuously in relation to curing time. Therefore, the data points are connected with a smooth-line curve rather than a broken-line curve. These relationships are represented by the **best-fit curve**, a smooth curve that is an average representation of the points.

There is a smooth-line curve relationship between miles per gallon and the speed at

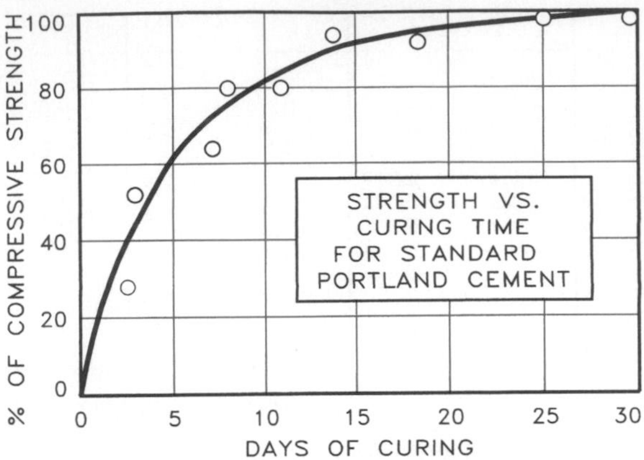

32.17 When the data being graphed involve gradual, continuous changes in relationships, the curve is drawn as a smooth line.

which a car is driven. **Figure 32.18** compares the results for two engines.

A smooth-line curve on a graph implies that interpolations between data points can be made to estimate other values. Data points connected by a broken-line curve imply that interpolations between the plotted points cannot be made.

Straight-Line Graphs

Some graphs have neither broken-line curves nor smooth-line curves, but straight-line curves (**Figure 32.19**). On this graph, a third value can be determined from the two given values. For example, if you are driving 70 mi/h and you take 5 seconds to react and apply your brakes, you will have traveled 550 ft in that time.

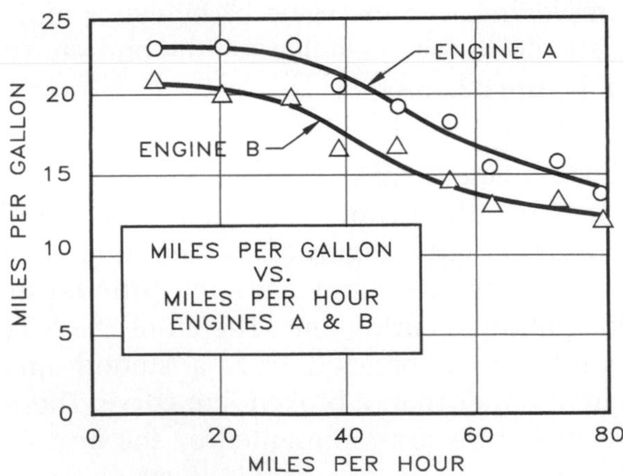

32.18 These data are represented by best-fit curves that approximate the data without necessarily passing through each point. The relationship of these data indicates that this curve should be a smooth-line curve rather than a broken-line curve.

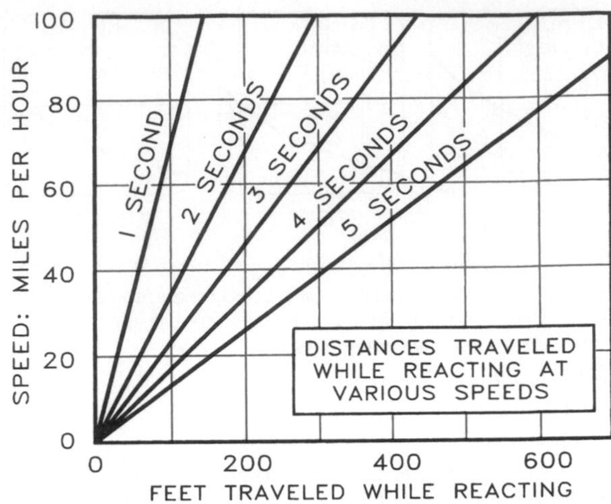

32.19 This graph may be used to determine a third value from the other two variables. For example, select a speed of 70 mi/h and a time of 5 seconds to find a distance traveled of 550 ft.

Two-Scale Coordinate Graphs

Graphs may contain different scales in combination, as shown in **Figure 32.20**, where the vertical scale at the left is in units of pounds and

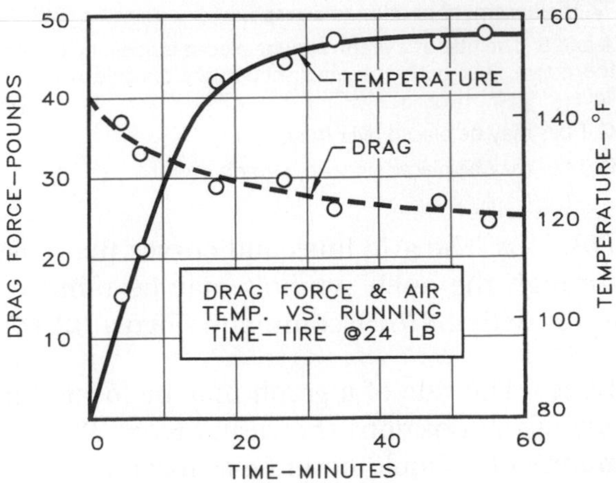

32.20 A two-scale graph has different scales along each y-axis, and labels identify which scale applies to which curve.

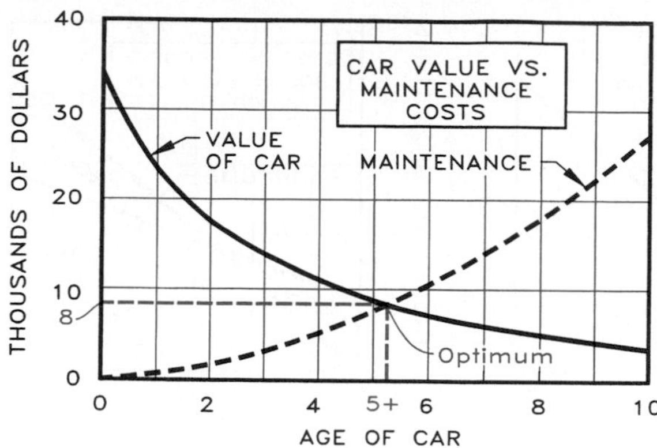

32.21 This graph shows the approximate optimum time to sell a car based on the intersection of curves representing the depreciating value of the car and its increasing maintenance costs.

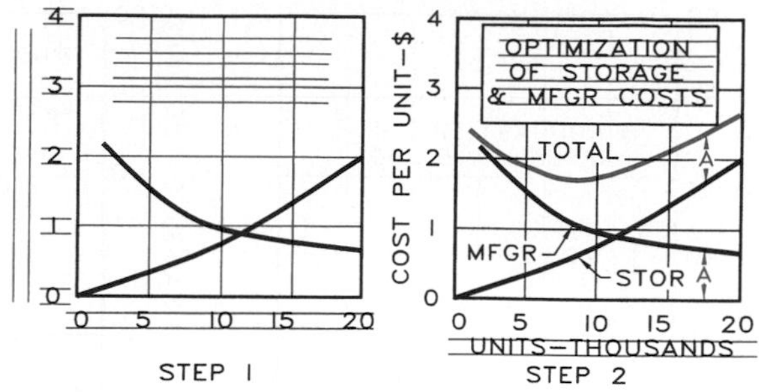

32.22 Constructing an optimization graph.

Step 1 Lay out the graph and plot the curves from the data given.

Step 2 Graphically add the two curves to find a third curve. For example, transfer distance A to locate a point on the third curve. The lowest point of the "total" curve is the optimum point, or 8000 units.

the one at the right is in degrees of temperature. Both curves are drawn with respect to their *y* axes and each curve is labeled. Two-scale graphs of this type may be confusing unless they are clearly labeled. Two-scale graphs are effective for comparing related variables, as shown here.

Optimization Graphs

Figure 32.21 depicts the optimization of an automobile's depreciation in terms of maintenance cost increases. These two sets of data cross at an *x*-axis value of slightly more than 5 years, or the optimum point. At that time the cost of maintenance is equal to the value of the car, indicating that it might be a desirable time to buy a new car.

The steps involved in drawing an optimization graph are illustrated in **Figure 32.22**. Here, the manufacturing cost per unit is reduced as more units are made, causing warehousing costs to increase. Adding the two curves to get a third (total) curve indicates that the optimum number to manufacture at a time is about 8000 units (the low point on the total curve). When more or fewer units are manufactured, the total cost per unit is greater.

Composite Graphs

The graph shown in **Figure 32.23** is a composite (or combination) of an area graph and a coordinate graph. The upper curve is a plot of the company's gross income. The lower curve is a plot of the company's expenses. The difference between the two is the company's profit. Crosshatching the areas emphasizes the relative values of expenses and profits.

Break-Even Graphs

Break-even graphs help in evaluating marketing and manufacturing costs to determine the

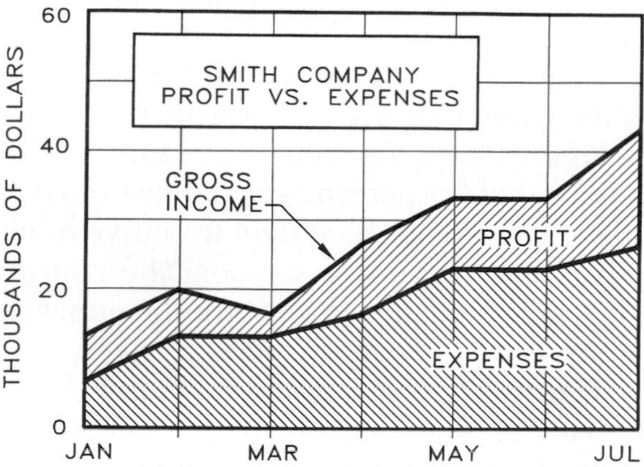

32.23 This composite graph is a combination of a coordinate graph and an area graph. The upper area represents the difference between the two plotted curves.

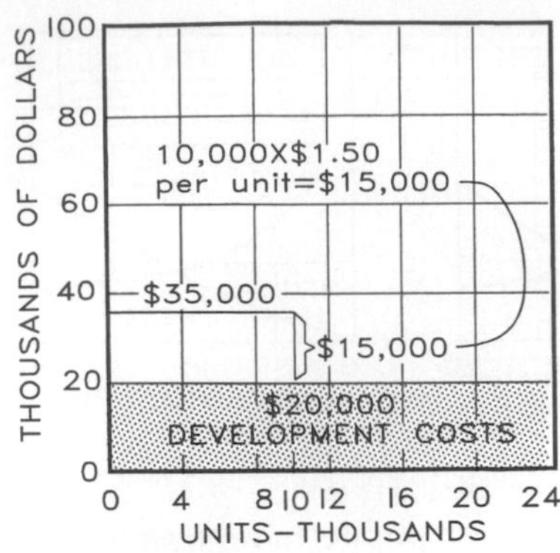

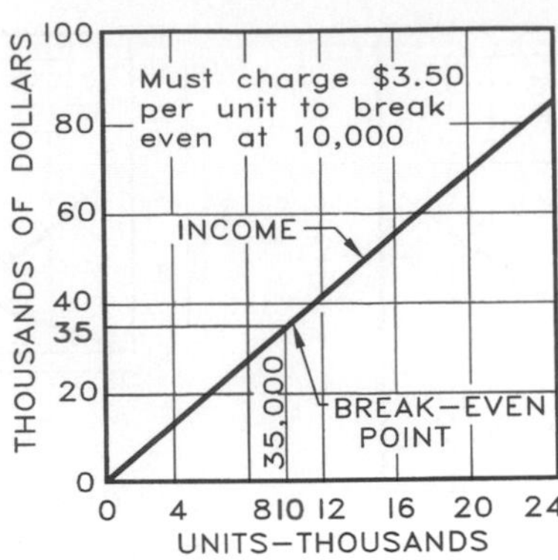

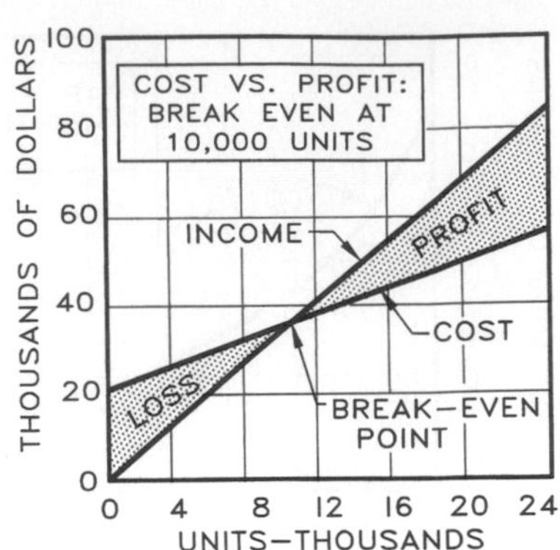

32.24 Drawing a break-even graph.

Step 1 Plot the development cost ($20,000). At $1.50 per unit to make, the total cost would be $35,000 for 10,000 units, the break-even point.

Step 2 To break even at 10,000, the manufacturer must sell each unit for $3.50. Draw a line from zero through the break-even point of $35,000 to represent income.

Step 3 There is a loss of $20,000 at zero units, but progressively less until the break-even point is reached. Profit is the difference between the curves to the right of the break-even point.

selling price of a product. As **Figure 32.24** shows, if the desired break-even point for a product is 10,000 units, it must sell for $3.50 each to cover the costs of manufacturing and development.

32.5 Semilogarithmic Graphs

Semilogarithmic graphs, usually referred to as semilog graphs, are called *ratio graphs* because they graphically represent ratios. One scale, usually the vertical scale, is logarithmic, and the other is linear (divided into equal divisions).

The same data plotted on a linear grid and on a semilogarithmic grid are compared in **Figure 32.25**. The semilogarithmic graph reveals that the percentage change from 0 to 5 is greater for curve B than for curve A because here curve B is steeper. The plot on the linear grid appears to show the opposite result.

Figure 32.26 shows the relationship between the linear scale and the logarithmic scale. Equal divisions along the linear scale have unequal ratios, but equal divisions along the log scale have equal ratios.

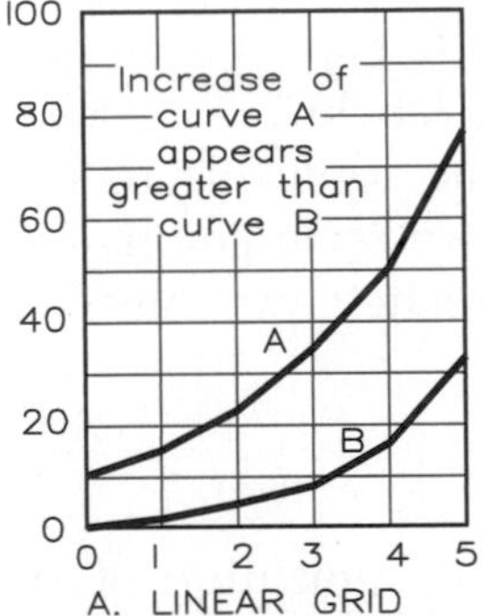

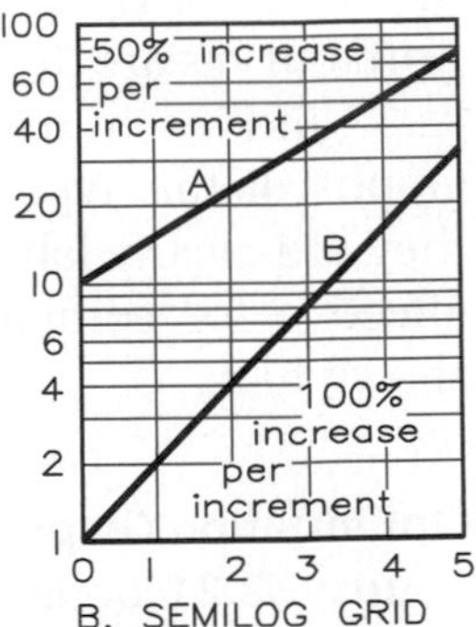

32.25 When plotted on a linear grid, curve A appears to be increasing at a greater rate than curve B. However, plotting the data on a semilogarithmic grid reveals the true rate of change.

Log scales may have one or many cycles. Each cycle increases by a factor of 10. For example, the scale shown in **Figure 32.27A** is a three-cycle scale, and the one shown in **Figure 32.27B** is a two-cycle scale. When scales must be drawn to a certain length, commercially printed log scales may be used to transfer graphically the calibrations to the scale being used (**Figure 32.27C**).

An application of a semilogarithmic graph for presenting industrial data is illustrated in **Figure 32.28**. People who do not realize that

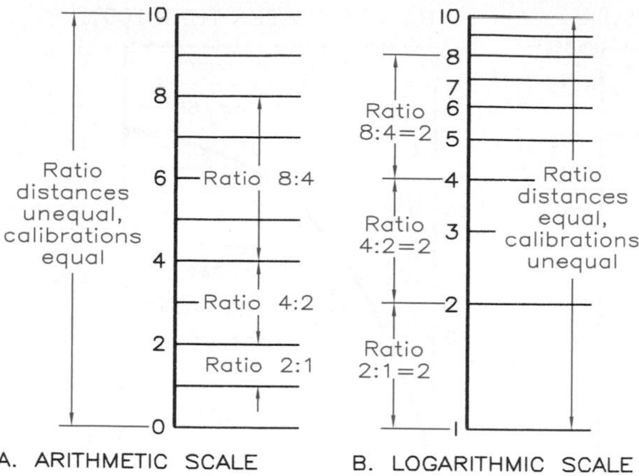

32.26 The divisions on an arithmetic scale are equal and represent unequal ratios between points. The divisions on logarithmic scales are unequal and represent equal ratios.

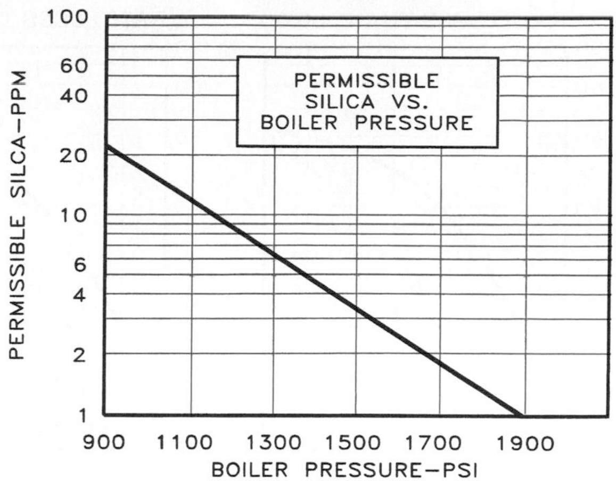

32.28 This semilogarithmic graph relates permissible silica (parts per million) to boiler pressure.

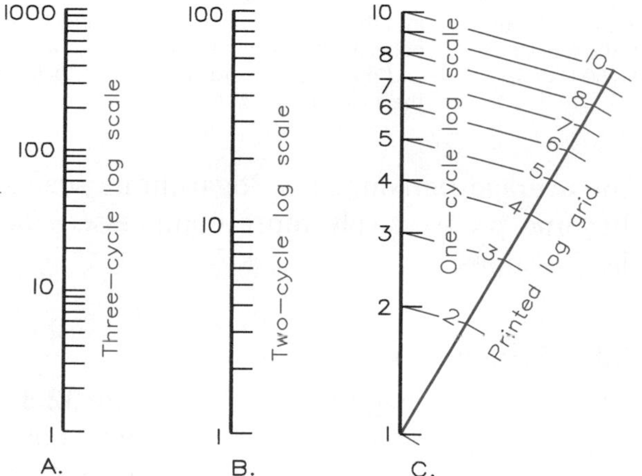

32.27 Logarithmic scales may have several cycles: (A) three-cycle scales, (B) two-cycle scales, and (C) one-cycle scales. Calibrations may be projected to a scale of any length from a printed scale as shown here (C).

semilog graphs are different from linear coordinate graphs may misunderstand them. Also, zero values cannot be shown on log scales.

Percentage Graphs

The percentage that one number is of another, or the percentage increase of one number to a greater number, can be determined on a semilogarithmic graph. Data plotted in **Figure 32.29A** are used to find the percentage that 30 is of 60 (two points on the curve) by arithmetic. The vertical distance between them is the difference between their logarithms, so the percentage can be found graphically in **Figure 32.29B**. The distance from 30 to 60 is transferred to the log scale at the right of the graph and subtracted from the log of 100 to find the value of 50% as a direct reading of percentage.

In **Figure 32.29C**, the percentage increase between two points is transferred from the grid to the lower end of the log scale and measured upward because the increase is greater than zero. These methods may be used to find percentage increases or decreases for any set of points on the grid.

32.6 Log-Log Graphs

The logarithmic graph, usually referred to as a log-log graph, has a logarithmic grid plotted on both the *x*- and *y*-axes, and the scales are usually equal. An example of a log-log graph is given in **Figure 32.30**, where the strength characteristics of gray iron are plotted. Notice that the zero value never appears on a log scale, which was the case with the logarithmic scale on the semilog graph.

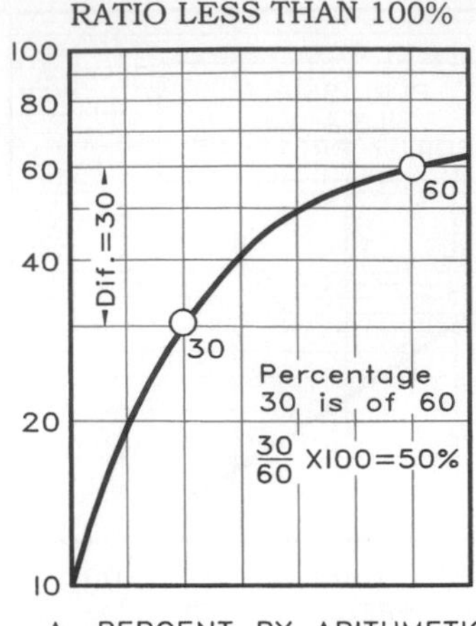

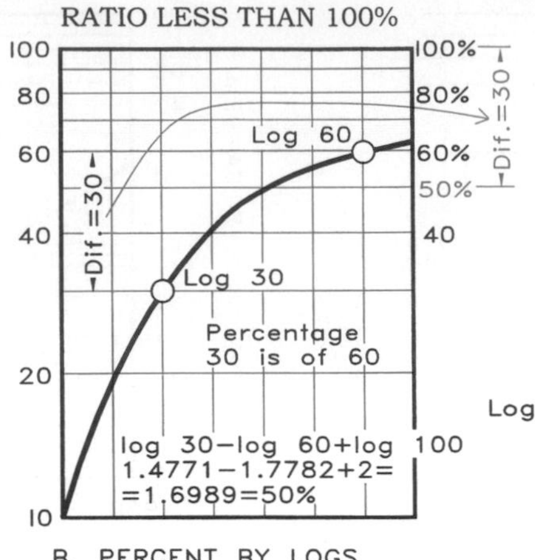

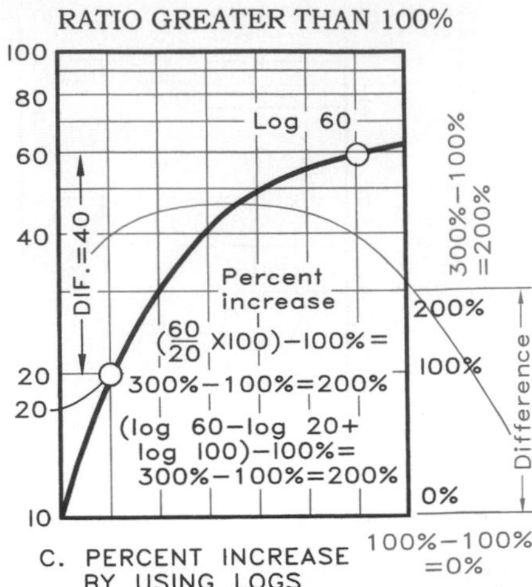

32.29 Percentage graphs.

A To find the percentage that one data point is of another point (the percentage that 30 is of 60, for example), you may calculate it mathematically: (30/60)(100) = 50%.

B Find the percentage that 30 is of 60 by using the logarithms of the numbers. Or find it graphically by transferring the distance between 30 and 60 to the scale at the right, which shows that 30 is 50% of 60.

C To find a percentage increase greater than 100%, divide the smaller number into the larger number. Find the difference between the logs of 60 and 20 with dividers and measure upward from 100% to find the increase, 200%.

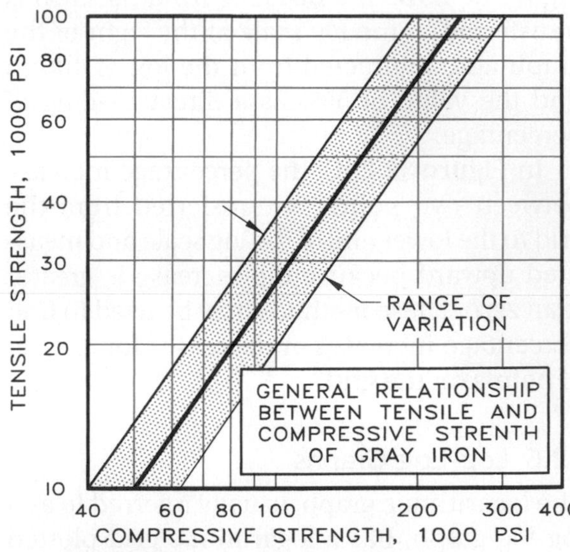

32.30 This logarithmic graph has log scales on both the vertical and horizontal axes.

Log-log graphs will used in Chapter 34 to determine the equations for empirical data that plot as straight lines on them. Again, interpretation of log-log graphs can be confusing to the average person, since logarithmic scales become progressively more compressed for larger values.

32.7 Schematics

The schematic diagram shown in **Figure 32.31** depicts the steps required to complete a construction project. Each step is blocked in and connected with arrows to give the sequence.

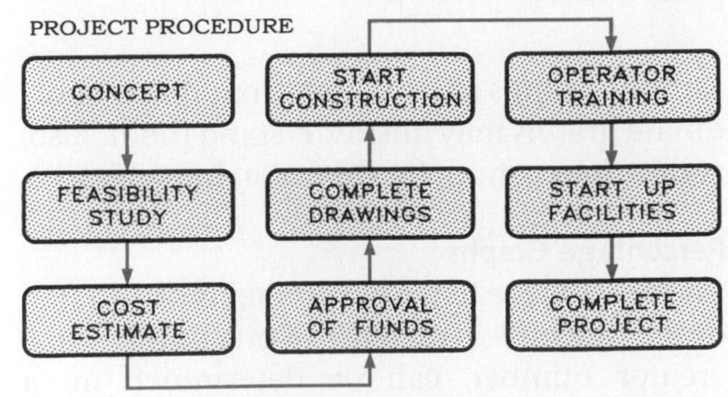

32.31 A computer-drawn organizational chart clearly outlines the lines of responsibility.

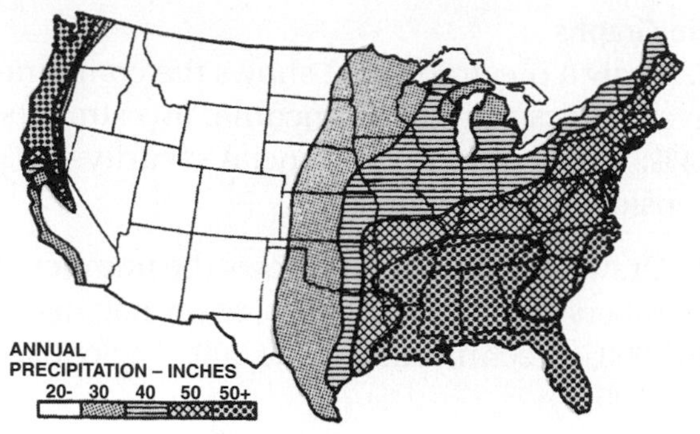

32.32 This graph shows the annual rain for various parts of the nation. *(Courtesy of the Structural Clay Products Institute.)*

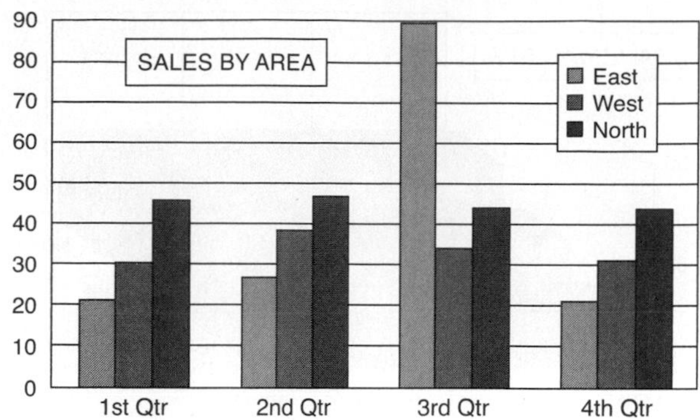

32.34 A computer-drawn three-dimensional bar graph.

The organization of a group of people can be represented in an organizational graph (usually called an *organization chart*).

Geographic charts are used to combine maps and other relationships, such as weather (**Figure 32.32**). Here, different hatching symbols represent the annual rainfall in various parts of the nation. The graph in **Figure 32.33** shows the expected changes in worldwide usage of energy from 2000 until 2030. The bars in conjunction with the map are effective in summarizing this information.

32.8 Graphs by Computer

Many computer programs are available for converting numerical data into various types of graphs to improve comprehension and interpretation. These programs vary from data representation as bar graphs, coordinate graphs, and pie graphs to 3D mathematical models.

Computer-produced graphs are especially useful for preparing visual aids for projection on a screen for a presentation and for technical reports. **Figure 32.34** is a example of a 3D bar graph printed from data that were input in tabular form. These same data can be instantaneously plotted in a different 3D form as shown in **Figure 32.35**, and plotted in yct a different format as shown in **Figure 32.36**.

It is up to you, the user, to determine which format is best in communicating a particular type of data to your audience, whether by an

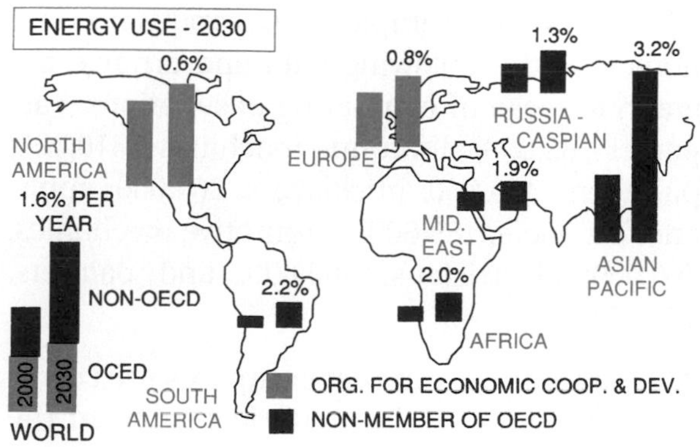

32.33 This map shows the worldwide energy use change from 2000 until 2030. *(Courtesy of Exxon Mobil Corporation.)*

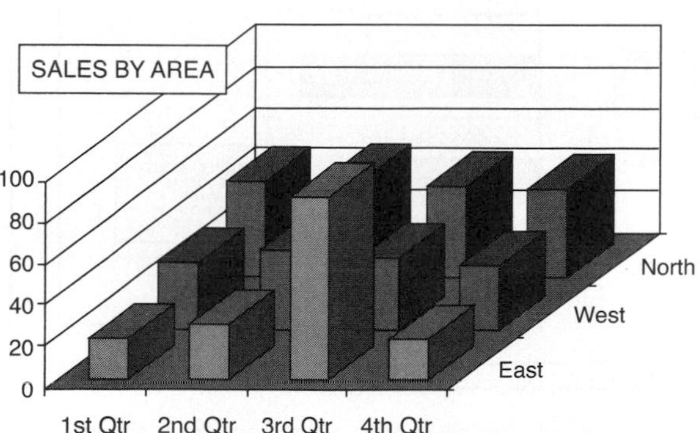

32.35 A three-dimensional plot of the data shown in **Figure 32.34**, drawn by a computer program.

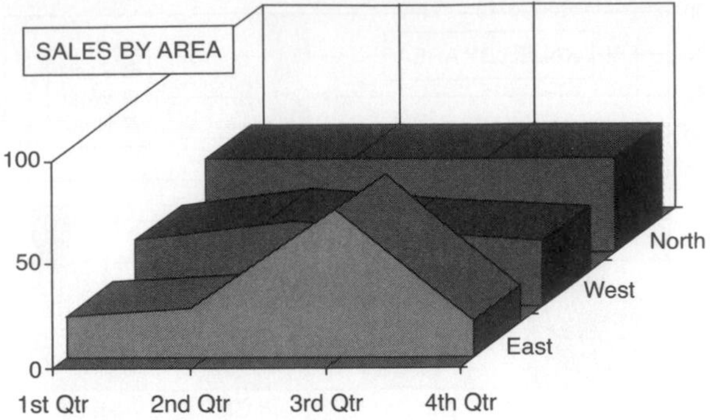

32.36 Another three-dimensional version of the data from **Figure 32.34** drawn by a computer program.

illustration in a written report or by a visual aid during an oral presentation. The principles of preparing effective graphs are the same, whether they are drawn by hand or by computer.

Problems

Draw your solutions to these problems on size A sheets as shown in **Figure 32.37** and apply the techniques and principles covered in this chapter.

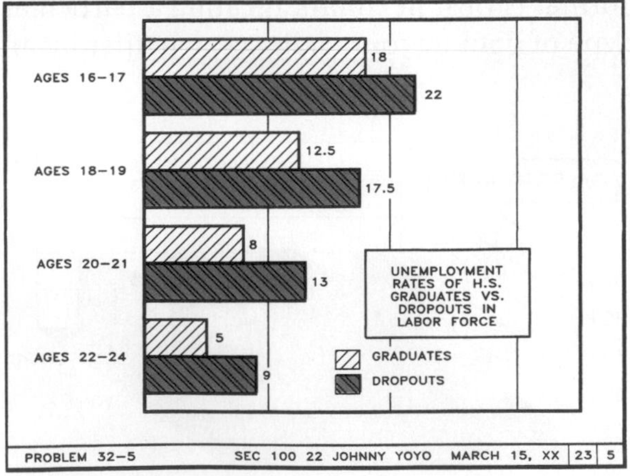

32.37 Lay out the following problems on size A sheets in the horizontal format shown here.

Pie Graphs

1. Draw a pie graph that shows the comparative sources of retirees' income: investments, 34%; employment, 24%; social security, 21%; pensions, 19%; other, 2%.

2. Draw a pie graph that shows the number of members of the technological team: engineers, 985,000; technicians, 932,000; scientists, 410,000.

3. Construct a pie graph of the employment status of graduates of 2-year technician programs a year after graduation: employed, 63%; continuing full-time study, 23%; considering job offers, 6%; military, 6%; other, 2%.

4. Draw a pie graph showing the types of degrees held by aerospace engineers: BS, 65%; MS, 29%; PhD, 6%.

Bar Graphs

5. Draw a bar graph that shows the expected job growth per year by city: Austin, 1.3%; San Antonio, 0.8%; Houston, 1.6%; Fort Worth, 0%; Dallas, 0.4%; all of Texas, 0.8%.

6. Draw a single-bar bar graph that represents 100% of a die casting alloy. The proportional parts of the alloy are tin, 16%; lead, 24%; zinc, 38.8%; aluminum, 16.4%; copper, 4.8%.

7. Draw a bar graph that compares the number of skilled workers employed in various occupations. Use the following data and arrange the graph for ease of comparing occupations: carpenters, 82,000; all-around machinists, 310,000; plumbers, 350,000; bricklayers, 200,000; appliance servicers, 185,000; automotive mechanics, 760,000; electricians, 380,000; and painters, 400,000.

8. Draw a bar graph that compares the corrosion resistance of the materials listed in the following table.

	Loss in Weight (%)	
	In atmosphere	In seawater
Common steel	100	100
10% nickel steel	70	80
25% nickel steel	20	55

9. Draw a bar graph that shows the characteristics of a typical U.S. family's spending: housing, 29.6%; food, 15.1%; transportation, 16.7%; clothing, 5.9%; retirement, 8.6%; entertainment, 4.9%; insurance, 5.2%; health care, 3.0%; charity, 3.1%; other, 7.9%.

10. Draw a bar graph of the data from problem 1.

11. Draw a bar graph of the data from problem 2.

12. Draw a bar graph of the data from problem 3.

13. Construct a bar graph comparing sales and earnings of Awesome Computers from 1999 through 2008. Data are by year for sales and earnings (profit) in billions of dollars: 1999, 0 and 0; 2000, 0.33 and 0.05; 2001, 0.60 and 0.07; 2002, 1.00 and 0.09; 2003, 1.51 and 0.08; 2004, 1.90 and 0.07; 2005, 1.85 and 0.12; 2006, 2.70 and 0.25; 2007, 4.15 and 0.40; 2008, 5.50 and 0.45.

Linear Coordinate Graphs

14. Draw a linear coordinate graph to show worldwide commerce in billions on the Internet (W) and USA Internet commerce (U) from 1998 to 2003. 1998: $20 U and $22 W, 1999: $25 U and $35 W, 2000: $45 U and $62 W, 2001: $60 U and $150 W, 2002: $100 U and $250 W, 2003: $147 U and $380 W.

15. Construct a linear coordinate graph that shows the relationship of energy costs (mills per kilowatt-hour) on the *y*-axis to the percent capacity of a nuclear power plant and a gas- or oil-fired power plant on the *x*-axis. Gas- or oil-fired plant data: 17 mills, 10%; 12 mills, 20%; 8 mills, 40%; 7 mills, 60%; 6 mills, 80%; 5.8 mills, 100%. Nuclear plant data: 24 mills, 10%; 14 mills, 20%; 7 mills, 40%; 5 mills, 60%; 4.2 mills, 80%; 3.7 mills, 100%.

16. Plot the data from problem 13 as a linear coordinate graph.

17. Construct a linear coordinate graph to show the relationship between the transverse resilience in inch-pounds (ip) on the *y*-axis and the single-blow impact in foot-pounds (fp) on the *x*-axis of gray iron. Data: 21 fp, 375 ip; 22 fp, 350 ip; 23 fp, 380 ip; 30 fp, 400 ip; 32 fp, 420 ip; 33 fp, 410 ip; 38 fp, 510 ip; 45 fp, 615 ip; 50 fp, 585 ip; 60 fp, 785 ip; 70 fp, 900 ip; 75 fp, 920 ip.

18. Draw a linear coordinate graph to show the estimated cost per year of colonizing the moon. The *y*-axis is systems cost in billions of dollars, and the *x*-axis is duration of the project in years. 10 years, $250; 15 years, $125; 20 years, $110; 25 years, $100; 30 years, $95.

19. Draw a linear coordinate graph for the centrifugal pump test data in the following table. The units along the *x*-axis are to be gallons per minute. Use two curves to represent the variables given.

Gallons per Minute	Water HP	Electric HP
0	0.00	1.36
75	0.72	2.25
115	1.00	2.54
154	1.00	2.74
185	0.74	2.80
200	0.63	2.83

20. Draw a graph with two curves, one comparing the efficiencey of trip speed (miles per hour) and the other comparing the efficiency of fuel consumption (miles per gallon) of a truck with engine horsepower (hp) as shown in the given data. Lay out the *y*-axis from 80% to 110% efficiency and the *x*-axis from 180 to 240 hp. Data: 184 hp, 100 mph, 100 mpg; 190 hp, 101 mph, 99.5 mpg; 200 hp, 103 mph, 98 mpg; 210 hp, 104 mph, 97 mpg; 220 hp, 105 mph, 95 mpg; 230 hp, 106 mph, 90 mpg.

21. Draw a linear coordinate graph that compares two of the values shown in the table of the relationship of ultimate strength and elastic limit (pounds) to temperature (*x*-axis). Calibrate the *x*-axis from 400 to 1300 and the *y*-axis from 0 to 300.

°F	Ultimate Strength (lb)	Elastic Limit (lb)
400	257,500	208,000
500	247,000	224,500
600	232,500	214,000
700	207,500	193,500
800	180,500	169,000
900	159,500	146,500
1000	142,500	128,500
1100	126,500	114,000
1200	114,500	96,500
1300	108,000	85,500

Break-Even Graphs

22. Draw a break-even graph that shows the earnings for a new product that has a development cost of $12,000. The break-even point is at 8000 units, and each costs $0.50 to manufacture. What will be the profit at volumes of 20,000 and 25,000?

23. Repeat problem 22 except that the development costs are $80,000, the manufacturing cost of the first 10,000 units is $2.30 each, and the desired break-even point is 10,000 units. What is the profit at volumes of 20,000 and 30,000?

Logarithmic Graphs

24. Construct a logarithmic graph. Plot the vibration amplitudes (A1 and A2) as the ordinates and the vibration frequency (F) as the abscissa. The data for curve A1 represent the maximum limits of machinery in good condition with no danger from vibration. The data for curve A2 are the lower limits of machinery that is being vibrated excessively to the danger point. The vertical scale is three cycles (0.0001 to 0.1), and the horizontal scale is two cycles (100 to 10,000). Data for A1: F = 100, A1 = 0.0028; F = 200, A1 = 0.002; F = 500, A1 = 0.0015; F = 1000, A1 = .001; F = 2000, A1 = .0006; F = 5000, A1 = 0.0003; F = 10,000, A1 = 0.00013. Data for A2: F = 100, A2 = 0.06; F = 200, A2 = 0.05; F = 500, A2 = 0.04; F = 1000, A2 = 0.03; F = 2000, A2 = 0.018; F = 5000, A2 = 0.005; F = 10,000, A2 = 0.001.

25. Plot the following data on a two-cycle log graph to show the current in amperes (*y*-axis) versus the voltage in volts (*x*-axis) of precision temperature-sensing resistors. Data: 1 volt, 1.9 amps; 2 volts, 4 amps; 4 volts, 8 amps; 8 volts, 17 amps; 10 volts, 20 amps; 20 volts, 30 amps; 40 volts, 36 amps; 80 volts, 31 amps; 100 volts, 30 amps.

26. Plot the data in problem 21 as a logarithmic graph.

27. Construct a two-cycle log-log graph (1 to 100 on both axes) that gives the life expectancy for two sizes of ball-bearing screws, B1 and B2. Plot life expectancy in millions of inches along the *x*-axis, and axial loads in pounds along the *y*-axis. Data for B1:

$x = 1$, $y = 20$; $x = 3$, $y = 14$; $x = 6$, $y = 11$; $x = 8$, $y = 10$; $x = 10$, $y = 9.5$; $x = 20$, $y = 7.2$; $x = 40$, $y = 6$; $x = 70$, $y = 5$; $x = 100$, $y = 4.2$. Data for B2: $x = 1$, $y = 45$; $x = 3$, $y = 31$; $x = 6$, $y = 23$; $x = 8$, $y = 22$; $x = 10$, $y = 21$; $x = 20$, $y = 18$; $x = 40$, $y = 13$; $x = 70$, $y = 11$; $x = 100$, $y = 10$.

Semilogarithmic Graphs

28. Construct a semilogarithmic graph with the y-axis a two-cycle log scale from 1 to 100 and the x-axis a linear scale from 1 to 7 to show the survivability of a shelter at varying distances from the atmospheric detonation of a 1-megaton thermonuclear bomb. Plot overpressure in psi along the y-axis and distance from ground zero in miles along the x-axis. The data points represent an 80% chance of survival of the shelter. Data: 1 mi, 55 psi; 2 mi, 11 psi; 3 mi, 4.5 psi; 4 mi, 2.5 psi; 5 mi, 2.0 psi; 6 mi, 1.3 psi.

29. The growth of Division A and Division B of a company is to be plotted on a semilog graph with a one-cycle log scale on the y-axis for sales in thousands of dollars and a linear scale on the x-axis for years. Data: first year, A = \$11,700 and B = \$44,000; second year, A = \$19,500 and B = \$50,000; third year, A = \$25,000 and B = \$55,000; fourth year, A = \$32,000 and B = \$64,000; fifth year, A = \$42,000 and B = \$66,000; sixth year, A = \$48,000 and B = \$75,000. Which division has the better growth rate?

30. Draw a semilog chart showing probable engineering progress based on the following indices: 40,000 B.C., 21; 30,000 B.C., 21.5; 20,000 B.C., 22; 16,000 B.C., 23; 10,000 B.C., 27; 6000 B.C., 34; 4000 B.C., 39; 2000 B.C., 49; 500 B.C., 60; A.D. 1900, 100. Use a horizontal scale of 1 in. = 10,000 years, a height of about 5 in., and two-cycle printed paper, if available.

31. Plot the data in problem 19 as a semilogarithmic graph.

32. Plot the data in problem 21 as a semilogarithmic graph.

Percentage Graphs

33. Using the graph plotted in problem 29, determine the percentage of increase of Division A and Division B growth from year 1 to year 4. What percentage of sales of Division A are the sales of Division B at the end of year 2? At the end of year 6?

34. Plot the values for water horsepower and electric horsepower from problem 19 on semilog paper. What percentage of electric horsepower is water horsepower when 75 gallons per minute are being pumped?

Thought Questions

1. What type of graph is best for depicting the relationship of your usage of the hours of a day for sleep, class, study, relaxation, and sports?

2. When should the bars of a bar graph be arranged by length? Explain.

3. Explain how the grid lines of a linear coordinate should be spaced for the best effect.

4. Is the title of a graph optional? If a title is used, where should it be placed on the graph?

5. Explain the difference between a coordinate graph, in which the data points are connected with straight-line segments, versus one connected with a smooth curve.

6. Which lines used to draw a graph should be the most prominent (boldest) for the best effect?

7. Explain why data depicted on a graph is better than a table of data in numerical form. Or is it better? Explain.

8. Explain the difference between a log-log grid and a semi-log grid. What are the advantages of each of them?

9. Explain the difference in log scales designatged as a one-cycle log, two-cycle, three-cycle, and so forth. If the lowest value on a three-cycle log scale is 10, what is it highest value?

10. Which type of graph lends itself to the determination of the percentages between data points? What type of grid makes this possible?

33
Nomography

33.1 Introduction

An additional aid in analyzing data is a graphical computer called a **nomogram, nomograph**, or "number chart." Basically, it is any graphical arrangement of calibrated scales and lines that may be used for calculations, usually those of a repetitive nature. Its primary value is the rapidity of finding solutions to equations in nomogram form without the application of numerical computation.

The term *nomogram* frequently denotes a specific type of scale arrangement called an **alignment graph**. Two examples of alignment graphs are shown in **Figure 33.1**. Other types have curved scales or different scale arrangements for use with more complex problems.

An alignment graph usually is constructed to solve for one or more unknowns in a formula or empirical relationship between two or more quantities. For example, such a graph can be used to convert degrees Celsius to degrees Fahrenheit or to find the size of a structural member to sustain a certain load. To read an alignment graph, **place a straightedge or draw a line, called an isopleth**, across the scales of the graph and read corresponding values from the scale on this line. **Figure 33.2** is an example nomogram that shows readings for the formula $W = U + V$.

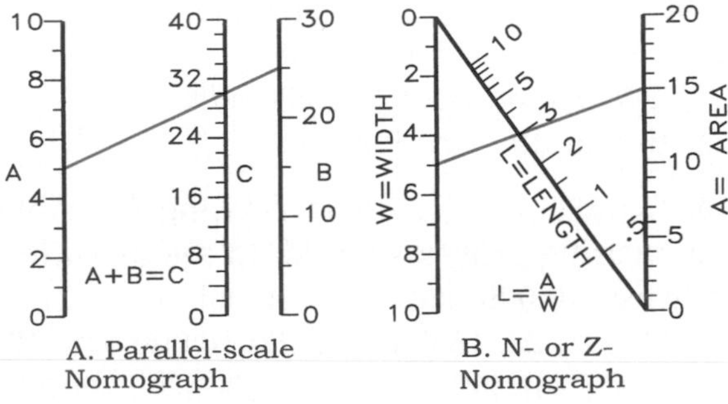

33.1 These two types of alignment graphs are typical nomographs.

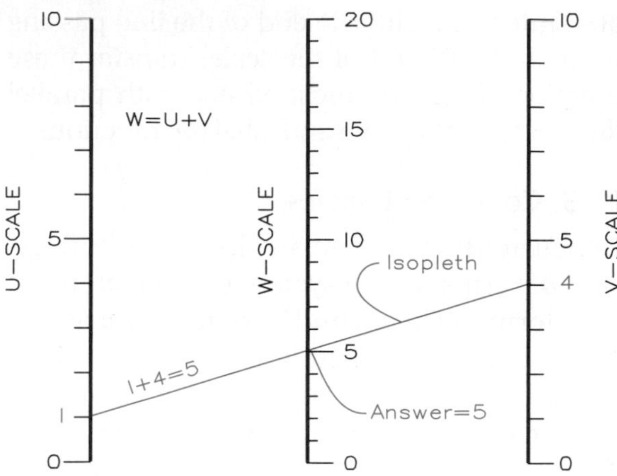

33.2 This graph illustrates the use of an isopleth to solve graphically for unknowns in an equation, $W = U + V$.

33.2 Alignment Graph Scales

To construct any alignment graph, you must first determine the graduations of the scales that give the desired relationships. Alignment graph scales, called **functional scales**, are graduated according to values of some function of a variable. **Figure 33.3** illustrates a functional scale for $F(U) = U^2$. Substituting a value of $U = 2$ into the equation gives the position of U on the functional scale 4 units ($2^2 = 4$) from zero. Repeating this procedure for as many values of U as required yields a scale for finding all corresponding values of the function.

The Scale Modulus

Because the graduations on a functional scale are spaced in proportion to values of the

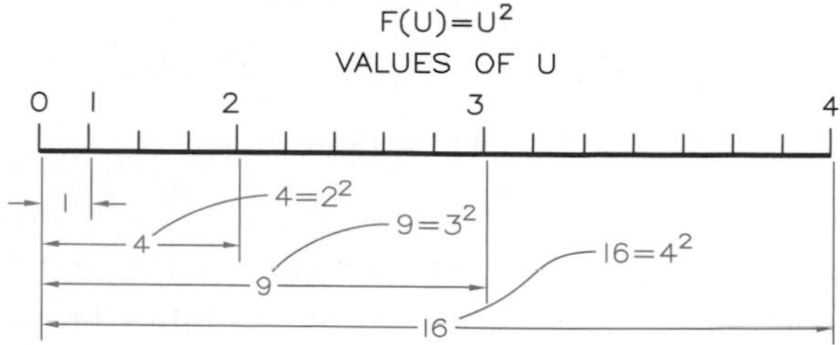

33.3 This functional scale contains units of measurement proportional to $F(U) = U^2$.

function, a proportionality, or scaling factor, is needed. This constant of proportionality is called the **scale modulus**, m:

$$m = \frac{L}{F(U_2) - F(U_1)} \qquad \text{(Eq. 1)}$$

where

m = scale modulus, in inches per functional unit,

L = desired length of the scale in inches,

$F(U_2)$ = functional value at the end of the scale,

$F(U_1)$ = functional value at the start of the scale.

For example, suppose that you are to construct a functional scale for $F(U) = \sin U$ from 0° to 45° and a scale 6 in. in length. Thus, $L = 6$ in., $F(U_2) = \sin 45° = 0.707$, $F(U_1) = \sin 0° = 0$. Substituting these values into Eq. (1), we get

$$m = \frac{6}{0.707 - 0} = 8.49 \text{ in. per sine unit.}$$

The Scale Equation

A scale equation makes possible graduation and calibration of functional scales. The general form of this equation is a variation of Eq. (1):

$$X = m[F(U) - F(U_1)], \qquad \text{(Eq. 2)}$$

where

X = distance from the measuring point of the scale to any graduation point,

m = scale modulus,

$F(U)$ = functional value at the graduation point,

$F(U_1)$ = functional value at the measuring point of the scale.

For example, let's construct a functional scale for the equation $F(U) = \sin U$ (0° ≤ 45°). We have already determined that $m = 8.49$, $F(U) = \sin U$,

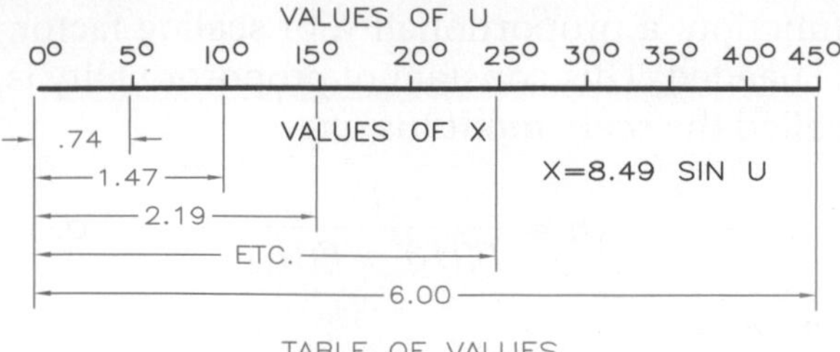

TABLE OF VALUES

U	0°	5°	10°	15°	20°	25°	30°	35°	40°	45°
X	0	.74	1.47	2.19	2.90	3.58	4.24	4.86	5.45	6.00

33.4 This functional scale is calibrated with values from the table, which were derived from the scale equation, $X = 8.49 \sin U$.

and $F(U_1) = \sin 0° = 0$. By substitution, Eq. (2) becomes

$$X = 8.49(\sin U - 0) = 8.49 \sin U.$$

Using this equation, we can substitute values of U and construct a table of positions at 5° intervals as shown in **Figure 33.4**. The values of X give the positions in inches for the corresponding graduations measured from $U = 0°$. The initial measuring point does not have to be at one end of the scale, but an end is usually the most convenient point, especially if the functional value is zero at that point.

Figure 33.5 shows how to locate functional values along a scale with the proportional-line method. Measure the sine functions along a line at 5° intervals, with the end of the line passing through the 0° end of the scale. Transfer these functions from the inclined line with parallel lines back to the scale and label the functions.

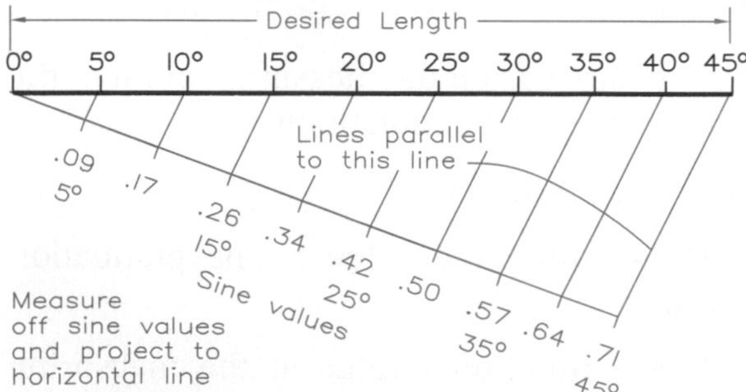

33.5 This functional scale shows the sine of the angles from 0° to 45° drawn by the proportional-line method. Draw the scale to a desired length and lay off the sine values of angles at 5° intervals along a construction line passing through the 0° end of the scale.

33.3 Concurrent Scales

Concurrent scales aid in the rapid conversion of terms in one system of measurement into terms of a second system of measurement. Formulas of the type $F_1 = F_2$, which relate two variables, may be adapted to the concurrent scale format. An example is the Fahrenheit–Celsius temperature relationship:

$$°F = \frac{9}{5}°C + 32.$$

Another is the area of a circle:

$$A = \pi r^2$$

Construction of a concurrent scale chart involves determining a functional scale for each side of the mathematical formula so that the position and lengths of each scale coincide. To construct a conversion chart 5 in. long that gives the areas of circles whose radii range from 1 to 10, we first write $F_1(A) = A$, $F_2(r) = \pi r^2$, $r_1 = 1$, and $r_2 = 10$. The scale modulus for r is

$$m_R = \frac{L}{F_2(r_2) - F_2(r_1)}$$

$$= \frac{5}{\pi(10)^2 - \pi(1)^2} = 0.0161.$$

Thus, the scale equation for r becomes

$$X_R = m_R[F_2(r) - F_2(r1)]$$
$$= 0.0161[\pi r^2 - \pi(1)^2]$$
$$= 0.0161\,\pi(r^2 - 1)$$
$$= 0.0505\,(r^2 - 1).$$

Figure 33.6 shows a table of values for X_r and r. The r-scale values come from this table. From the original formula, $A = \pi r^2$, the limits of A are found to be $A_1 = \pi = 3.14$, and $A_2 = 100\,\pi = 314$. The scale modulus for concurrent scales is

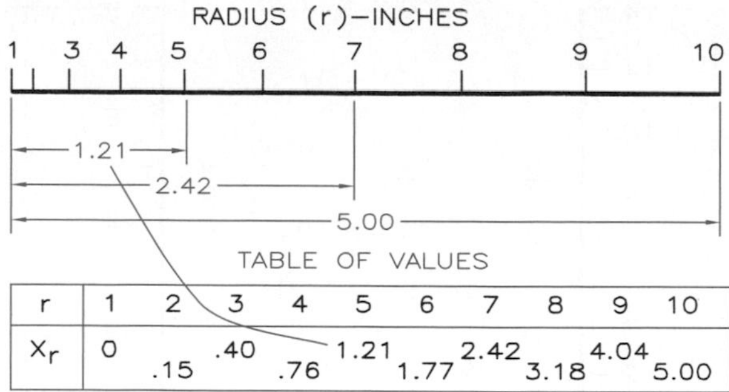

r	1	2	3	4	5	6	7	8	9	10
X_r	0	.15	.40	.76	1.21	1.77	2.42	3.18	4.04	5.00

33.6 Calibrate one scale of a concurrent scale chart by using calculated values from the table.

always the same for equal-length scales; therefore, $m_A = m_R = 0.0161$, and the scale equation for A becomes

$$\begin{aligned} X_A &= m_A[F_1(A) - F_1(A_1)] \\ &= 0.0161(A - 3.14). \end{aligned}$$

We then compute the corresponding table of values for selected values of A, as shown in **Figure 33.7**. We superimposed the A-scale on the r-scale and placed its calibrations on the other side of the line to facilitate reading.

To expand or contract one of the scales, use the technique shown in **Figure 33.8**. Draw the scales parallel at any distance apart and calibrate them in opposite directions. If they have different lengths, a different scale modulus and scale equation must be calculated for each scale.

To draw concurrent scales, use the proportional line method shown in **Figure 33.9**.

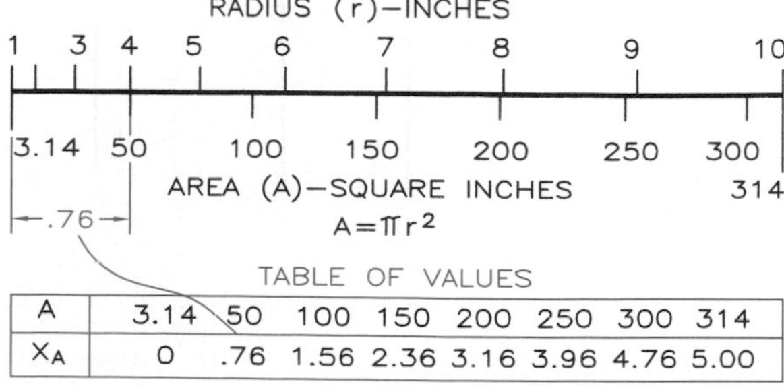

A	3.14	50	100	150	200	250	300	314
X_A	0	.76	1.56	2.36	3.16	3.96	4.76	5.00

33.7 This completed concurrent scale chart is for the formula $A = \pi R^2$. Values for the A-scale are from the table.

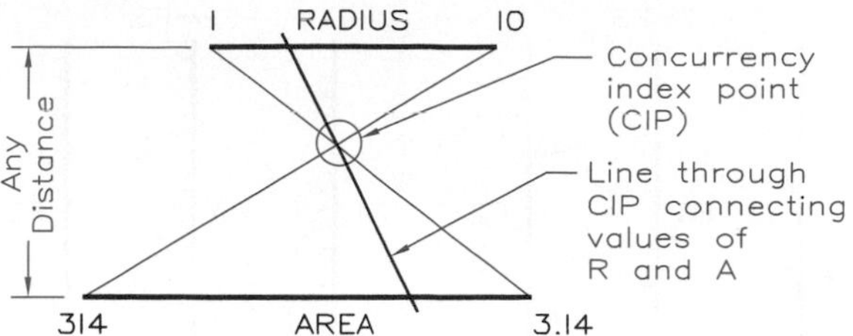

33.8 This construction is used to draw a concurrent graph with unequal scales.

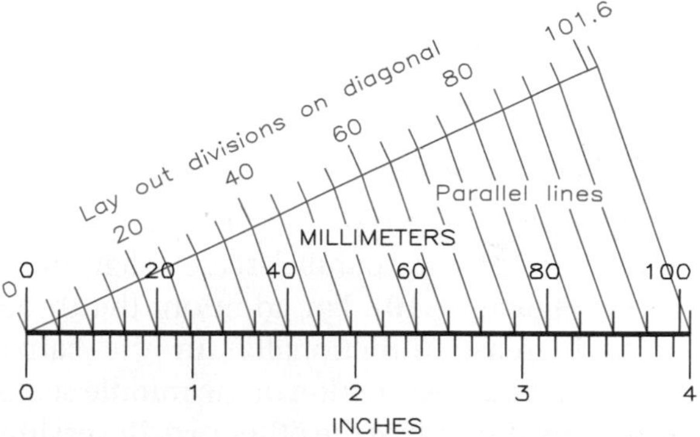

33.9 The proportional-line method can be used to construct an alignment graph that converts inches to millimeters. The units at each end of the scales must be known—101.6 mm and 4 in., in this case.

There are 101.6 mm in 4 in. Project millimeters to the upper side of the inch scale with a series of parallel projectors.

33.4 Alignment Graphs: Three Variables

For a formula containing three functions (of one variable each), draw a nomograph by selecting the lengths and positions of two scales according to the size of the graph desired. Calibrate these scales by using the scale equations presented in **Section 33.3**. Mathematical relationships may be used to locate the third scale, but graphical methods are simpler and less subject to error. Examples of the various forms of nomographs are shown in the following sections.

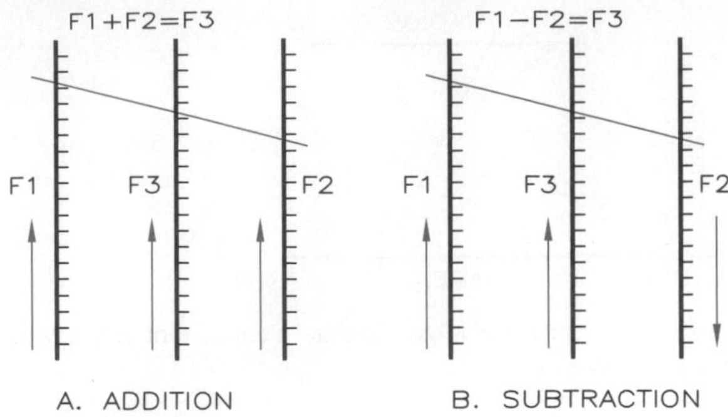

33.10 These two common forms of parallel-scale alignment nomographs show the directions in which the scales increase for addition and subtraction.

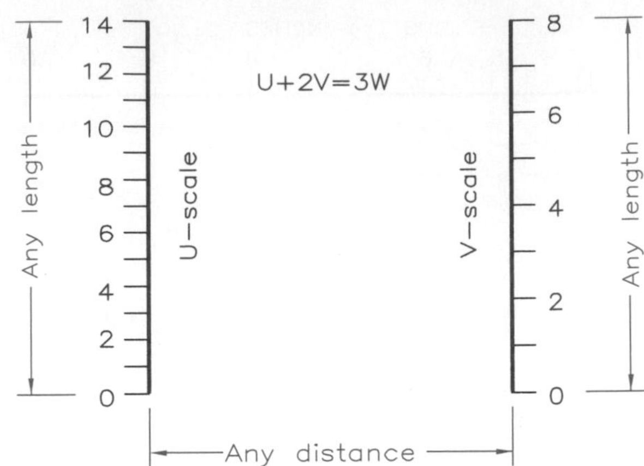

33.12 This calibration is of the outer scales for the formula $U + 2V = 3W$, where $U =$ 0 to 12, and $V =$ 0 to 8.

33.5 Parallel-Scale Graphs: Linear Scales

Any formula of the type $F_3 = F_1 + F_2$ may be represented as a parallel-scale alignment graph (**Figure 33.10**). For addition, the three scales increase (functionally) in the same direction, and the function of the middle scale represents the sum of the other two. Reversing the direction of any scale changes the sign of its function in the formula, as for $F_1 - F_2 = F_3$.

The formula $Z = X + Y$ is used to illustrate this type of alignment graph (**Figure 33.11**). Draw and calibrate the outer scales for *X* and *Y*, then use two sets of data that yield a *Z* of 8 to locate the parallel *Z*-scale. Divide the *Z*-scale into 16 units. Add various values of *X* and *Y* with an isopleth to find their sums along the *Z*-scale.

Figure 33.12 illustrates how to calibrate the outer scales of a parallel-scale nomograph for the equation $U + 2V = 3W$. The scales are placed any distance apart and are divided into linear divisions from 0 to 14 for *U*

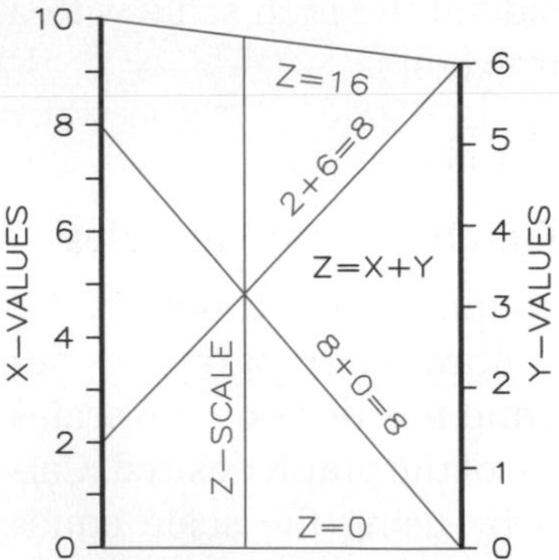

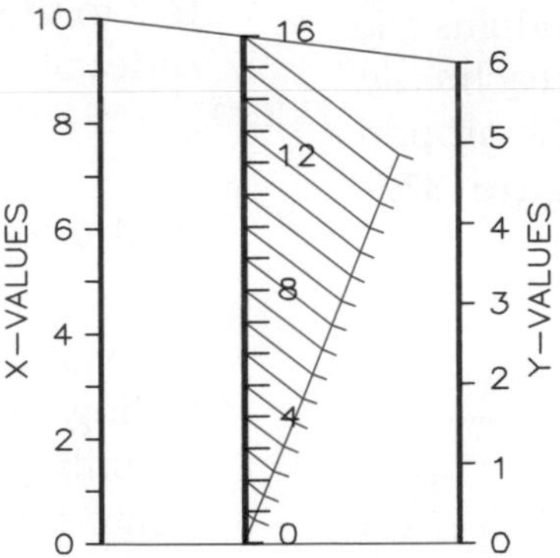

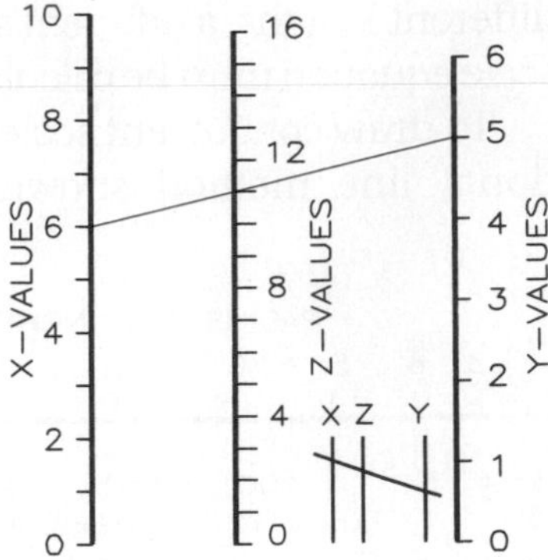

33.11 Parallel-scale nomograph (linear scales).

Step 1 Draw and calibrate two parallel scales of any length. Locate the parallel *Z*-scale by using two sets of values that give the same value (8 in this case). The ends of the *Z*-scale are 0 and 16, the sum of the end values of *X* and *Y*.

Step 2 Draw the *Z*-scale through the point located in step 1 parallel to the other scales. Calibrate the scale from 0 to 16 by using the proportional-line method.

Step 3 Calibrate and label the *Z*-scale. Draw a key to show how to use the nomograph. If the *Y*-scale were calibrated with 0 at the upper end instead of at the bottom, a different *Z*-scale could be computed for $Z = X - Y$.

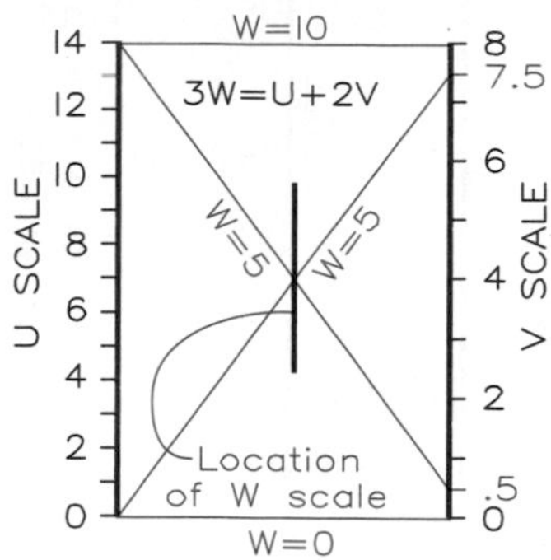

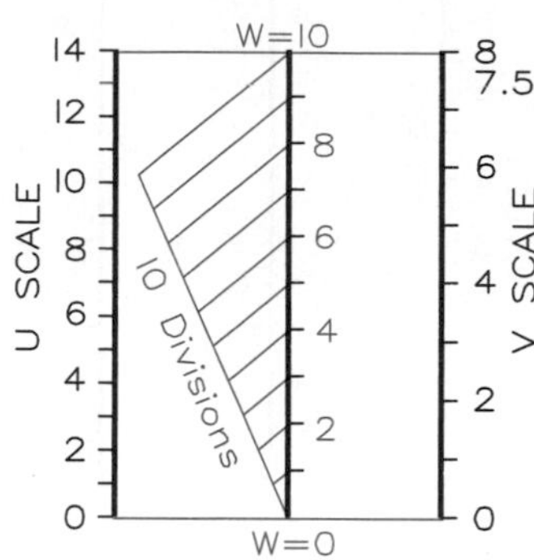

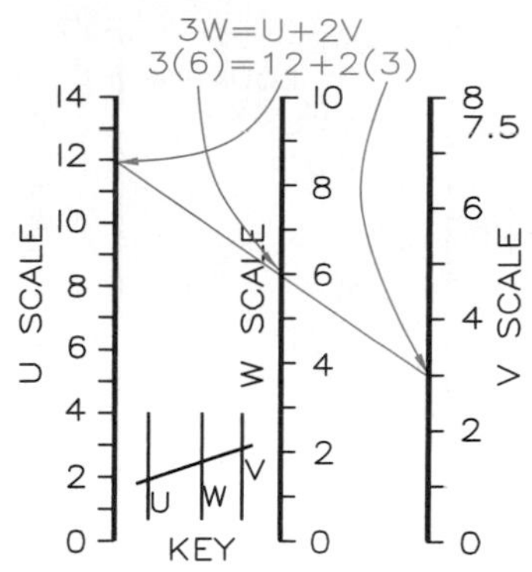

33.13 Parallel-scale nomograph (linear scales).

Step 1 Substitute the end values of U and V into the formula to find end values of W: 0 and 10. Use any two sets of U and V that give the same W ($U = 0$ and $V = 7.5$, $W = 5$, and $U = 14$ and $V = 0.5$, $W = 5$) to locate the W scale.

Step 2 Draw the W scale parallel to the outer scales to the limit lines of $W = 10$ and $W = 0$. This scale is 10 linear divisions long, so divide it graphically into 10 units. The W scale is a linear scale; construct it as shown in **Figure 33.11.**

Step 3 Connect any values of U and V with an isopleth to determine the resulting value of W. Draw a key that shows how to use the nomograph. The example values of $U = 12$ and $V = 3$ verify the graph's accuracy.

and 0 to 8 for V. These scales are used to complete the nomograph that is explained in **Figure 33.13**.

Obtain the end calibrations for the middle scale by connecting the endpoints of the outer scales and substituting these values into the formula. W is 0 and 10 at its ends. Select two pairs of corresponding values of U and V that give the same value of W. For example, $U = 0$ and $V = 7.5$ give $W = 5$. Also, $W = 5$ where $U = 14$ and $V = 0.5$. Because the W-scale is linear ($3W$ is a linear function), it can be subdivided into uniform intervals of equal parts. For a nonlinear scale, find the scale modulus and equation by substituting length and end values into Eq. (1).

Logarithmic Scales

Problems involving equations of the type $F_3 = (F_1)(F_2)$ can be solved in the manner described in **Figure 33.11** by using logarithmic scales instead of linear scales. The first step in drawing a nomograph with logarithmic scales is to transfer the logarithmic functions to the scales. **Figure 33.14** shows the graphical method where units are projected from a printed logarithmic scale to the nomographic scale.

Figure 33.15 illustrates the conversion of the formula $Z = XY$ into a nomograph. The desired end values of the X- and Y-scales are 1 and 10. Sets of values of X and Y that give the same value of Z (10 in this case) are used to locate the Z-axis with end values of 1 and 100.

The Z-axis is drawn and calibrated as a two-cycle log scale. A key explains how to use an isopleth to add the logarithms of X and Y to give the log of Z. The addition of logarithms performs multiplication. Had the Y-axis been calibrated in the opposite direction with 1 at the upper end and 10 at the lower end, a new Z-axis could have been calibrated for the

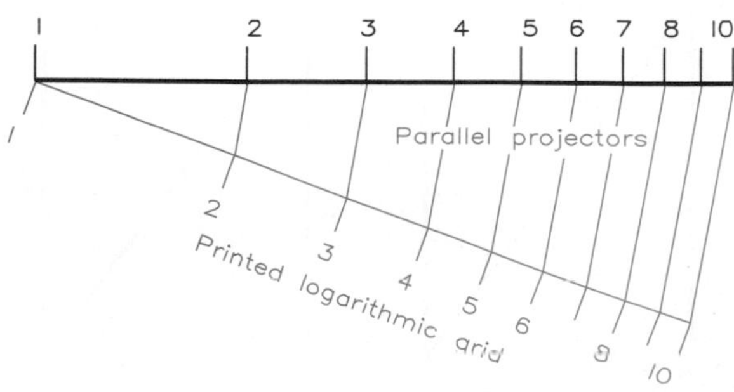

33.14 Here, a scale is calibrated graphically by projection from a printed logarithmic scale.

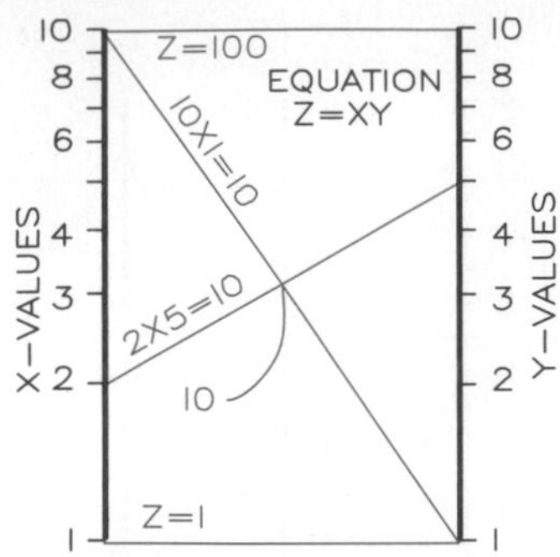

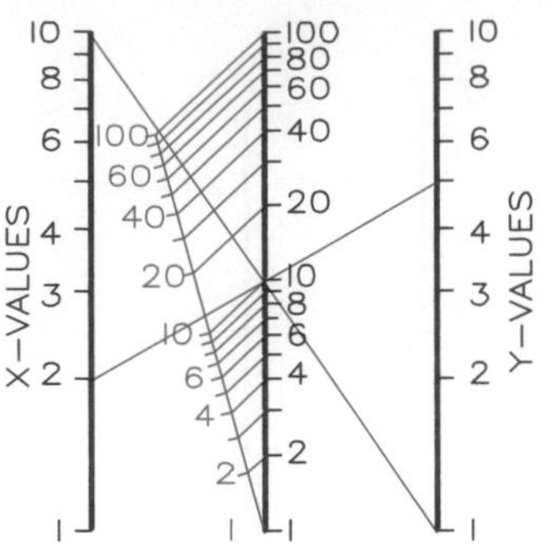

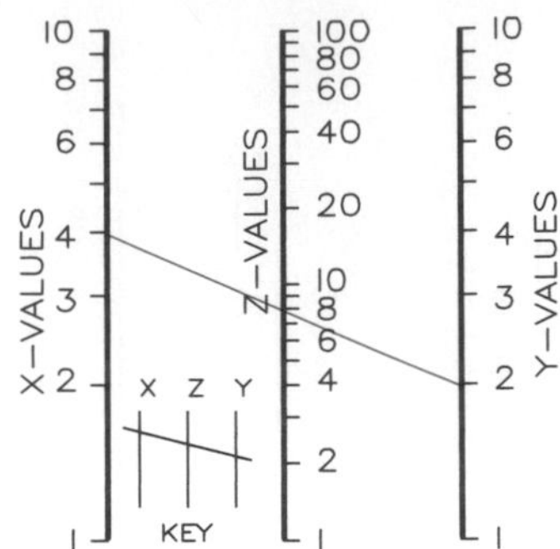

33.15 Parallel-scale nomograph (logarithmic scales).

Step 1 For the equation $Z = XY$ draw parallel log scales. Construct sets of X and Y points that give the same value of Z (10 in this case) to locate the Z-scale with end values of 1 and 100.

Step 2 Graphically calibrate the Z-axis as a two-cycle logarithmic scale from 1 to 100 by projection from a printed log scale. The Z-scale is parallel to the X- and Y-scales.

Step 3 Draw a key showing how to use the nomograph. Reversing the Y-value scale from 1 to 10 downward and computing a different Z-scale would allow the nomograph to be used for $Z = Y/X$.

formula $Z = Y/X$ for division by subtracting logarithms.

33.6 N- or Z-Nomographs

Whenever F_2 and F_3 are linear functions, we can avoid using logarithmic scales for formulas of the type

$$F_1 = \frac{F_2}{F_3}$$

We use an N-graph (**Figure 33.16**), where the outer scales are functional scales and are linear if F_2 and F_3 are linear. If a parallel-scale graph were used for the same formula, all its scales would be logarithmic. Main features of N graphs are as follows:

1. The outer scales are parallel functional scales of F_2 and F_3.

2. The outer scales increase functionally in opposite directions.

3. The diagonal scale connects the functional zeros of the outer scales.

4. The diagonal scale is not a functional scale for the function F_1 and is nonlinear.

Construction of an N-nomograph is simplified because locating the middle (diagonal) scale is usually less of a problem than it is for a parallel-scale graph. Calibration of the diagonal scale is most easily accomplished graphically.

Figure 33.17 shows how to construct a basic N-graph of the equation $Z = Y/X$. Draw the diagonal to connect the zero ends of the scales, then locate whole values along the diagonal by using combinations of X- and Y-values. Use whole-value units along the diagonal that are easy to interpolate. Label the diagonal and give a key explaining how to use the nomograph. A sample isopleth verifies the correctness of the graphical relationship of the scales.

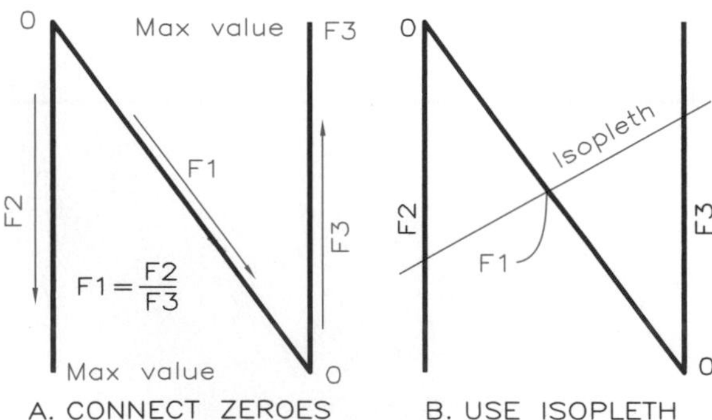

33.16 This N-graph solves an equation of the form $F_1 = F_2/F_3$.

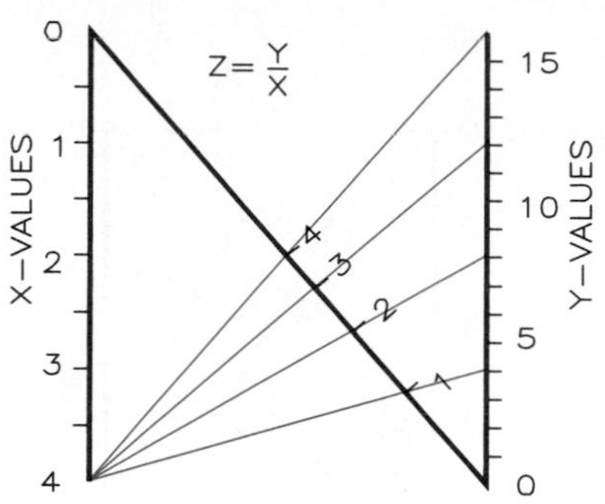

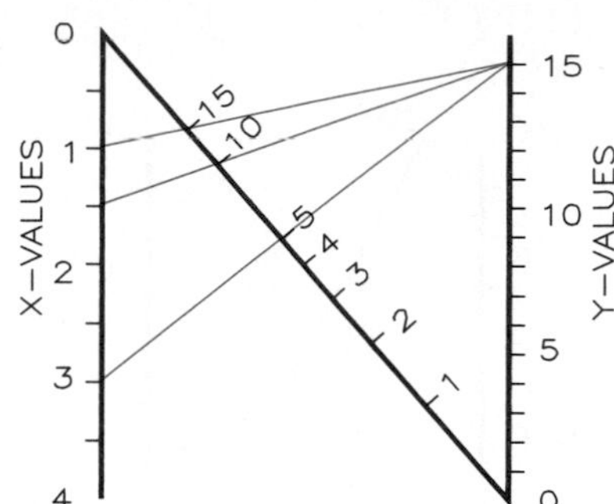

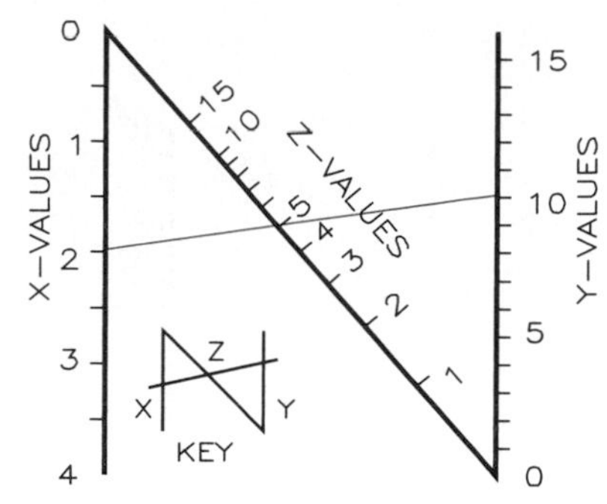

33.17 Constructing an N-graph.

Step 1 Draw an N-graph for the equation $Z = Y/X$ and connect the zero ends of each scale with a diagonal scale. Draw isopleths to locate units along the diagonal scale.

Step 2 Draw additional isopleths to locate other units along the diagonal. The units on the diagonal should be whole units to make interpolation between them easy.

Step 3 Label the diagonal scale and draw a key. An isopleth confirms that 10/2 = 5. The accuracy of the N-graph is greatest at the 0 end of the diagonal; the other end approaches infinity.

A more advanced N-graph can be drawn for the equation

$$A = \frac{B + 2}{C + 5}, \text{ where } B = 0 \text{ to } 8, \text{ and } C = 0 \text{ to } 15.$$

This equation takes the form

$$F_1 = \frac{F_2}{F_3},$$

where $F_1(A) = A$, $F_2(B) = B + 2$, and $F_3(C) = C + 5$.

Thus, the outer scales will represent $B + 2$ and $C + 5$, and the diagonal scale will represent A.

Begin the construction in the same manner as for a parallel-scale graph by selecting the layout of the outer scales (**Figure 33.18**). Determine the limits of the diagonal scale by connecting the endpoints on the outer scales, giving $A = 0.1$ for $B = 0$, $C = 15$, and $A = 2.0$ for $B = 8$, and $C = 0$. **Figure 33.19** shows these relationships and gives the remainder of the construction.

Locate the diagonal scale by finding the function zeros of the outer scales (that is, the points where $B + 2 = 0$, or $B = -2$, and $C + 5 = 0$, or $C = -5$). Then, draw the diagonal scale by connecting these points. Calibrating the diagonal scale is most easily accomplished by substituting into the formula. Selecting the upper limit of an outer scale, say, $B = 8$, gives the formula

$$A = \frac{10}{C + 5}.$$

Then, solve this equation for the other outer scale variable:

$$C = \frac{10}{A} - 5$$

Using it as a "scale equation," make a table of values for the desired values of A and

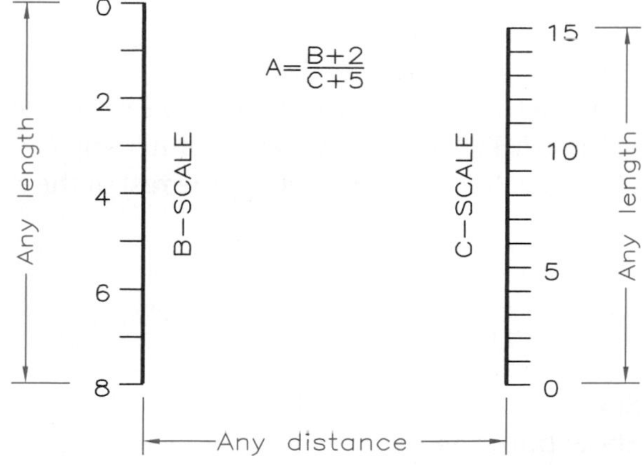

33.18 This calibration of the outer scales of an N-graph is for the equation $A = (B + 2)/(C + 5)$.

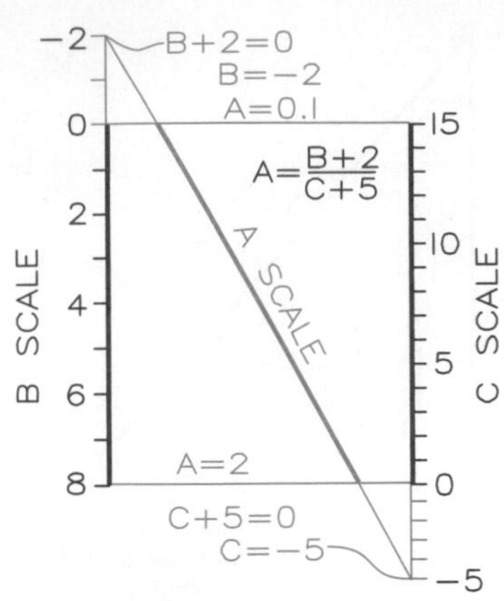

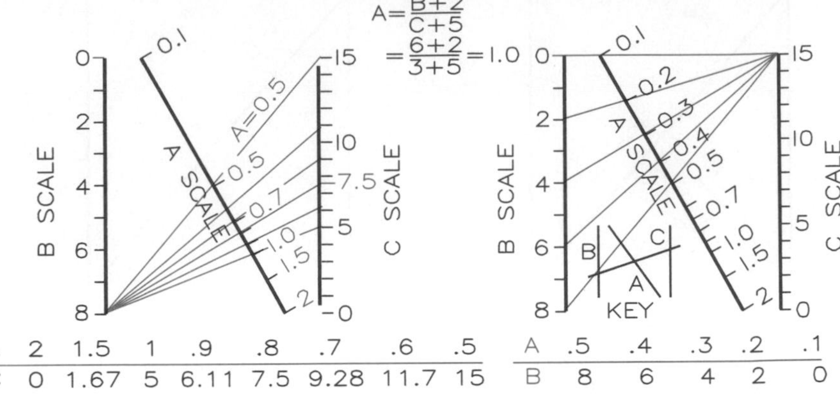

33.19 Constructing an N-graph.

Step 1 Locate the diagonal scale by finding the functional zeros of the outer scales. Set $B + 2 = 0$ and $C + 5 = 0$, which gives a zero value for *A*. Therefore, $B = -2$ and $C = -5$.

Step 2 Select the upper limit of an outer scale ($B = 8$ in this case), substitute it into the equation, and obtain values of *C* for whole values of *A*. Draw isopleths from $B = 8$ to the values of *C* to calibrate the *A*-scale.

Step 3 Calibrate the rest of the *A*-scale by substituting $C = 15$ into the equation to determine values on the *B*-scale for whole values on the *A*-scale. Draw isopleths from $C = 15$ to calibrate the *A*-scale.

corresponding values of *C* (up to the limit of *C* in the graph), as shown in **Figure 33.19**. Connect isopleths from $B = 8$ to the tabulated values of *C*. Their intersections with the diagonal scale give the required calibrations for approximately half the diagonal scale. Calibrate the rest of the diagonal scale by substituting the end value of the other outer scale ($C = 15$) into the formula, giving

$$A = \frac{B + 2}{20}.$$

Solving for *B* yields $B = 20A - 2$.

Construct a table for the desired values of *A* (**Figure 33.19**) with isopleths connecting $C = 15$ with values of *B*, calibrating the rest of the *A* scale.

Problems

Solve the following problems on size A sheets. Show both the construction and calculations used in the solutions. If the calculations are extensive, show them on a separate sheet.

Concurrent Scales

Draw concurrent scales for converting one type of unit to the other using the ranges given.

1. Kilometers and miles:
   1.609 km = 1 mi; from 10 to 100 mi
2. Liters and U.S. gallons:
   1 L = 0.2692 U.S. gal; from 1 to 10 L
3. Knots and miles per hour:
   1 knot = 1.15 mph; from 0 to 45 knots
4. Horsepower and British thermal units:
   1 hp = 42.4 Btu; from 0 to 1200 hp
5. Radius and area of a circle:
   $A = \pi r^2$; from $r = 0$ to 10
6. Inches and millimeters:
   1 in. = 25.4 mm; from 0 to 5 in.
7. Numbers and their logarithms:
   Use log tables; numbers from 1 to 10

Addition and Subtraction Nomographs

Construct parallel-scale nomographs to solve the following problems.

8. $A = B + C$, where $B = 0$ to 10, and $C = 0$ to 5.

9. $Z = X + Y$, where $X = 0$ to 8, and $Y = 0$ to 12.

10. $Z = Y - X$, where $X = 0$ to 6, and $Y = 0$ to 24.

11. $A = C - B$, where $C = 0$ to 30, and $B = 0$ to 6.

12. $W = 2V + U$, where $U = 0$ to 12, and $V = 0$ to 9.

13. $W = 3U + V$, where $U = 0$ to 10; $V = 0$ to 10.

Multiplication and Division: Parallel Scales

Construct parallel-scale nomographs with logarithmic scales for performing the following multiplication and division operations.

14. Area of a rectangle: $A = H \times W$, where $H =$ 1 to 10, and $W =$ 1 to 12.

15. Area of a triangle: $A = 1/2B \times H$, where $B =$ 1 to 10, and $H =$ 1 to 5.

16. Use the equation $3Z = X + 2Y$, where $X = 0$ to 14, and $Y = 0$ to 8. Show the tabulation of your calculations in addition to drawing the nomograph.

17. Pythagorean theorem:
$C^2 = A^2 + B^2$, where
$C =$ hypotenuse of a right triangle (in cm),
$A =$ one leg of the right triangle, 5 to 50 cm,
$B =$ second leg of the triangle, 20 to 80 cm.

18. Miles per gallon (mi/gal) an automobile gets. Miles vary from 1 to 500; gallons from 1 to 24.

19. Cost per mile (cpm) of an automobile. Miles vary from 1 to 500; cost varies from $1 to $28.

N-Nomographs

Construct *N*-graphs that will solve the following equations.

20. Stress $= P/A$, where P varies from 0 to 1000 psi, and A varies from 0 to 15 in.^{2}

21. Volume of a cylinder: $V = \pi r^2 h$, where $V =$ volume in in.^{3}; $r =$ radius (5 to 10 ft); and $h =$ height (2 to 20 in.).

22. From the equation $Z = (X + 2) / (Y + 5)$, draw an N-graph where $X = 8$ and $Y = 15$. Show tabular values used to solve the problem.

23. Repeat problem 14 as an N-graph nomograph.

24. Repeat problem 15 as an N-graph nomograph.

25. Repeat problem 16 as an N-graph nomograph.

26. Repeat problem 17 as an N-graph nomograph.

27. Repeat problem 18 as an N-graph nomograph.

Thought Questions

1. When does the construction of a nomograph become advantageous over the mathematical method? Explain.

2. What type of nomograph is effective in converting one system of measurement into another, for example, Fahrenheit into Celsius temperatures?

3. Parallel-scale nomographs can be used to solve equations in the forms of $Z = X + Y$ and $Z = (X)(Y)$. Explain the difference in the scales used to construct a nomograph for each of these types of equations.

4. Explain the layout of the scales of parallel-scale nomographs that would be used for the equations of $A = B + C$ and $A = B - C$.

5. What construction techniques of drawing logarithmic scales for a nomograph can be used? Explain.

6. Explain which variables of a parallel-scale alignment graph (with three parallel scales) should be placed on the outside scales.

34 Empirical Equations and Calculus

34.1 Introduction

Graphical methods are useful supplements to mathematical techniques of solving problems dealing with experimental data. Graphics can be used to determine the mathematical equation of data obtained from laboratory testing and experimentation. Data from laboratory experiments and field tests are called **empirical data**. Empirical data often are expressed as one of three types of equations: **linear, power**, or **exponential**.

Analysis of empirical data begins by plotting the data on three types of standard grids: **rectangular (linear), logarithmic**, or **semilogarithmic**. When the data plot as a straight line on one of these grids, its mathematical equation can be determined by using the characteristics of that particular grid (**Figure 34.1**).

To find the equation of a straight-line plot of data, you will need to know the **slope (M)**

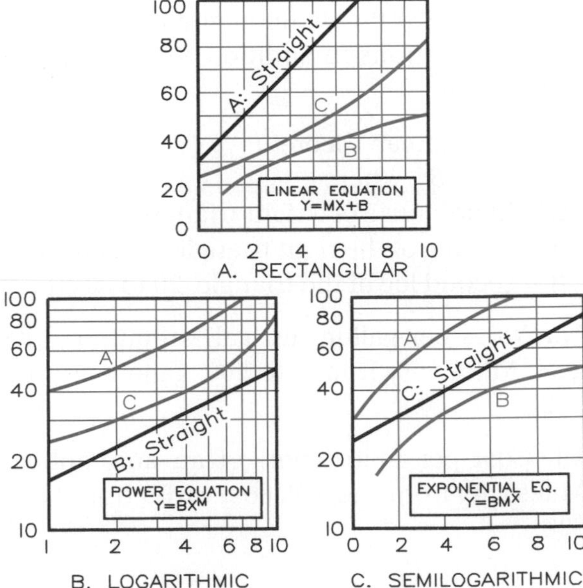

34.1 Plotting empirical data on each type of grid determines which one yields a straight-line plot. A straight-line plot on one of these grids means that a mathematical equation can be derived to describe the data.

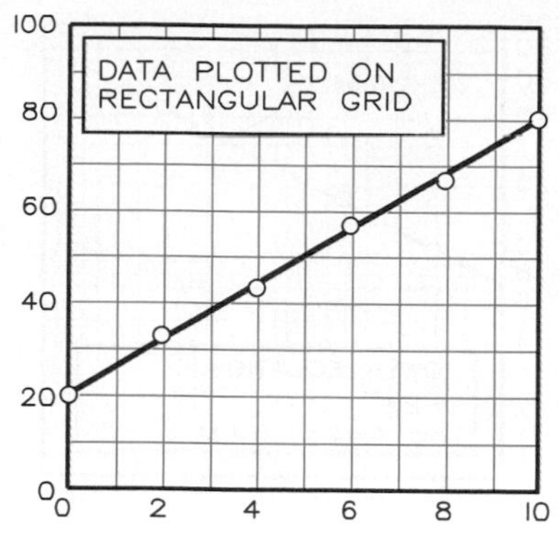

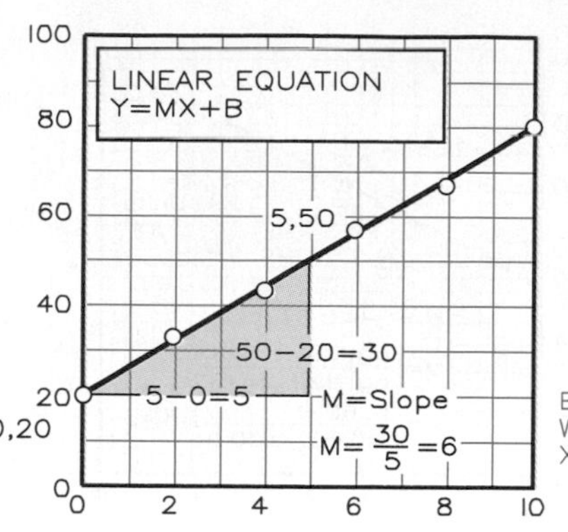

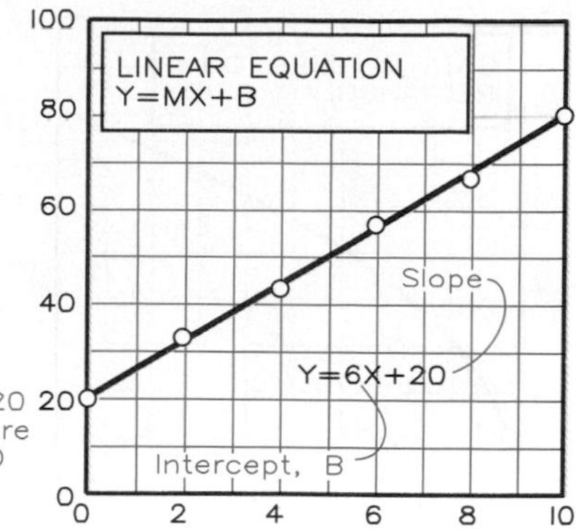

34.2 The linear equation, $Y = MX + B$.

Step 1 When plotted on a linear grid, the data lie on a straight line described by the equation $Y = MX + B$.

Step 2 Two points (0, 20) and (5, 50) are selected on the data curve to find the slope, M, which is dY/dX. The slope is found to be 6.

Step 3 The intercept, B, where the curve crosses the Y-axis where $X = 0$, is found to be 20. The equation of the data is found to be $Y = 6X + 20$.

of the curve, and its **intercept (B)** and apply them to the **slope-intercept** equation, $Y = MX + B$.

Slope is found by taking any two widely separated points on the curve and drawing a triangle to find the ratio of the height (dY) to the width (dX), which is the tangent of the curve's angle with the horizontal. The slope in **Figure 34.2** is found to be 6 by using this construction.

The intercept (B) is the point where the curve intersects the Y-axis at $X = 0$. The intercept in **Figure 34.2** is $B = 20$. The values of slope and intercept can be combined with variables X and Y to find the equations of the data, as will be shown in the following examples.

34.2 Linear Equation: $Y = MX + B$

The curve representing empirical data in **Figure 34.3** plots as a straight line on a rectangular graph, which identifies the data as linear. Each measurement along the Y-axis is directly proportional to the measurement along the X-axis.

The first step in determing the equation of the curve is to select two points to find the slope and the intercept. The vertical and horizontal differences between the coordinates of each point establish the adjacent sides of a right triangle in step 2. In the slope-intercept equation $Y = MX + B$, the slope M is the tangent of the angle between the curve and the horizontal; B is the Y-intercept of the curve (where $X = 0$); and X and Y are variables. Here, $M = 30/5 = 6$, and the intercept is at 20.

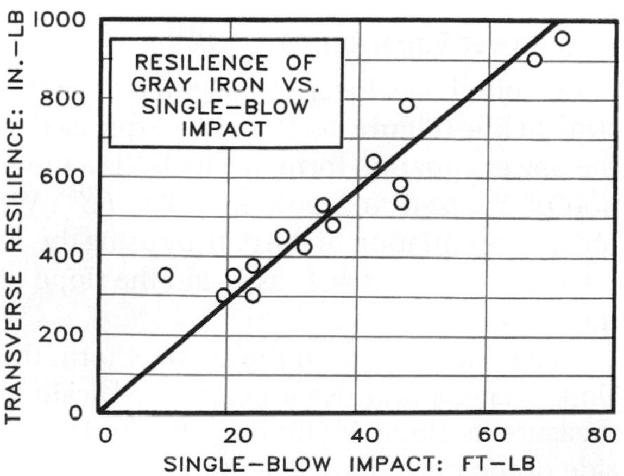

34.3 The relationship between the transverse strength of gray iron and impact resistance plots as a straight line yielding an equation of the form $Y = MX + B$, or $Y = 13.3X$.

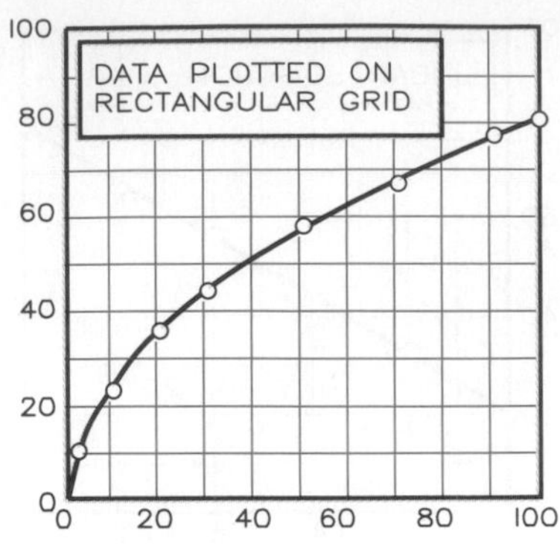

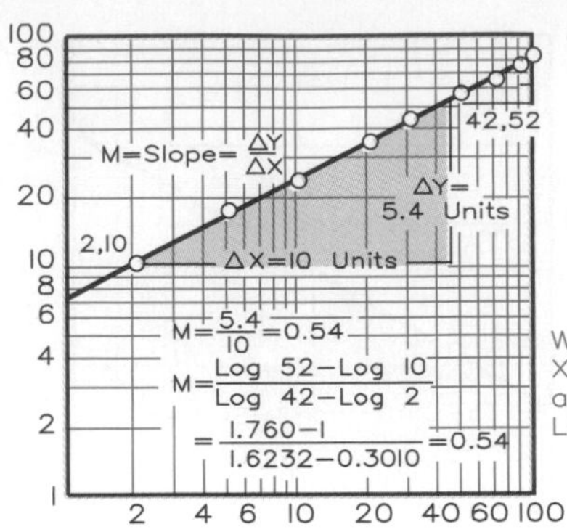
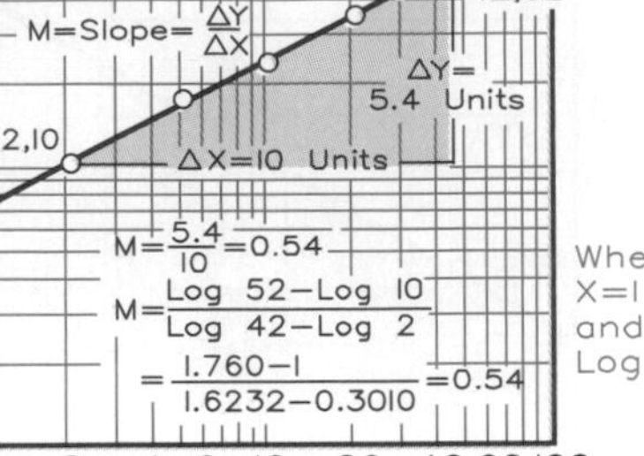

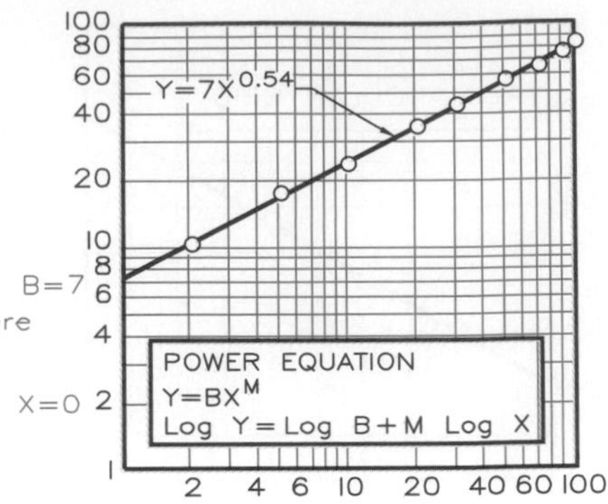

34.4 Power equation, $Y = BX^M$.

Step 1 Data plotted on a rectangular (linear) grid give a parabolic curve. Because the curve is not a straight line on this grid, its equation is not linear.

Step 2 The data plot as a straight line on a logarithmic grid. Find the slope, M, graphically with an engineers' scale by setting dX at 10 units and measuring dY as 5.4 units. $M = 5.4/10$, or 0.54.

Step 3 The intercept $B = 7$ lies at $X = 1$. Substitute the slope (0.54) and intercept (7) into the equation form of $Y = BX^M$ to obtain the equation of the data: $Y = 7X^{0.54}$.

Substituting these values into the slope-intercept equation, we obtain $Y = 6X + 20$, from which we may determine values of Y by substituting any value of X into the equation. If the curve had sloped downward to the right, the slope would have been negative.

Figure 34.3 shows the relationship between the transverse strength and impact resistance of gray iron obtained from empirical data. The data plot as a stright line on a linear grid, so its equation takes the linear form.

34.3 Power Equation: $Y = BX^M$

Data plotted on a logarithmic grid that yield a straight line (**Figure 34.4**) may be expressed in the power equation form in which Y is a function of X raised to a power, or $Y = BX^M$. We obtain the equation of the data by using the Y-intercept (where $X = 1$) as B and the slope of the curve as M.

Select two points on the curve to form the slope triangle and use an engineers' scale to measure its slope. If you draw the horizontal side of the right triangle as 1 or a multiple of 10, the vertical distance can be read directly. Here, the slope M (tangent of the angle) is 0.54 and the Y-intercept, B, is 7; thus the equation is $Y = 7X^{0.54}$, which in logarithmic form is

$$\log Y = \log B + M \log X,$$
$$= \log 7 + 0.54 \log X.$$

We used base-10 logarithms in these examples, but natural logs may be used with e (2.718) as the base. In **Figure 34.5** the intercept, B, lies on the Y-axis where $X = 1$ because the curve is plotted on a logarithmic grid. The Y-intercept

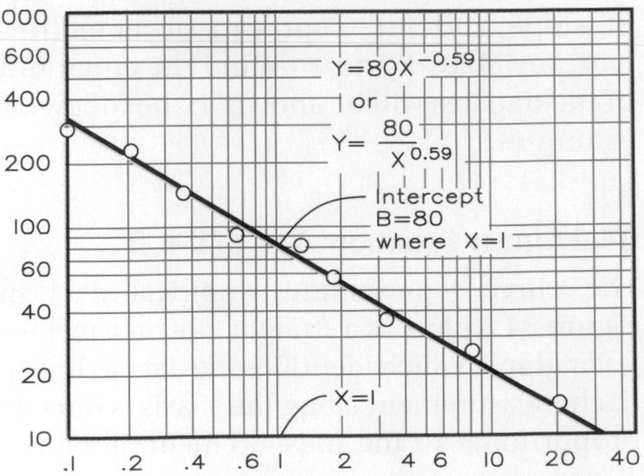

34.5 When using the slope-intercept method on a logarithmic grid, the intercept must be selected where $X = 1$. In this case the intercept lies at 80 (near the middle of the graph).

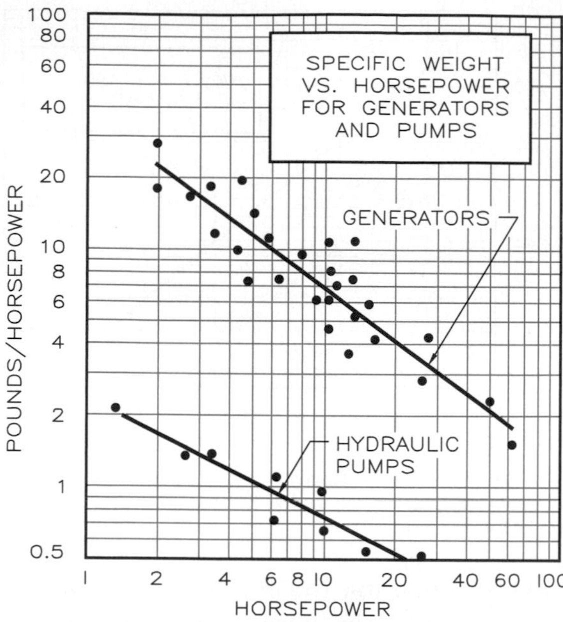

34.6 Empirical data plotted on a logarithmic grid showing the specific weight versus horsepower of electric generators and hydraulic pumps are straight lines. Their equations take the power form, $Y = BX^M$.

($B = 80$) is found where $X = 1$. Recall that the intercept at this point is analogous to the linear form of the equation because the log of 1 is 0. The curve slopes downward to the right making the slope, M, negative.

Figure 34.6 shows plots of empirical data that relate the specific weight (pounds per horsepower) of generators and hydraulic pumps to horsepower. The plots of the data are represented by straight lines on a logarithmic grid, which means that their equations take the power form.

34.4 Exponential Equation: $Y = BM^X$

When data plotted on a semilogarithmic grid (**Figure 34.7**) yield a straight line, the equation takes the form $Y = BM^X$, where B is the Y-intercept, and M is the slope of the curve. Select two points along the curve, draw a right triangle, and find its slope, M. The slope of the curve is

$$\log M = \frac{\log 40 - \log 6}{8 - 3} = 0.1648,$$

or

$$M = (10)^{0.1648} = 1.46.$$

Substitute this value of M into the exponential equation:

$$Y = BM^X \quad \text{or} \quad Y = 2(1.46)^X,$$
$$Y = B(10)^{MX} \quad \text{or} \quad Y = 2(10)^{0.1648X},$$

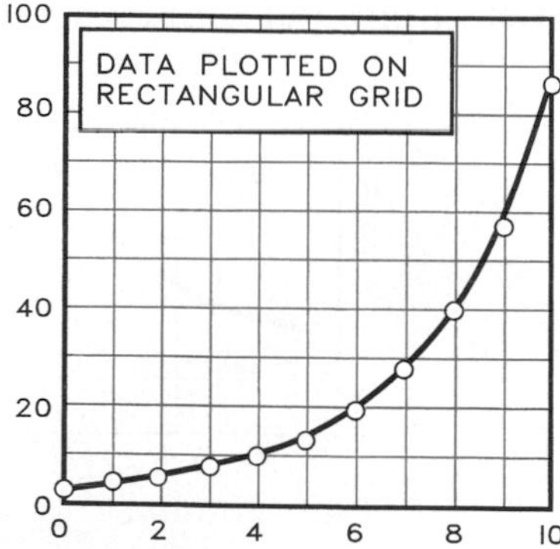

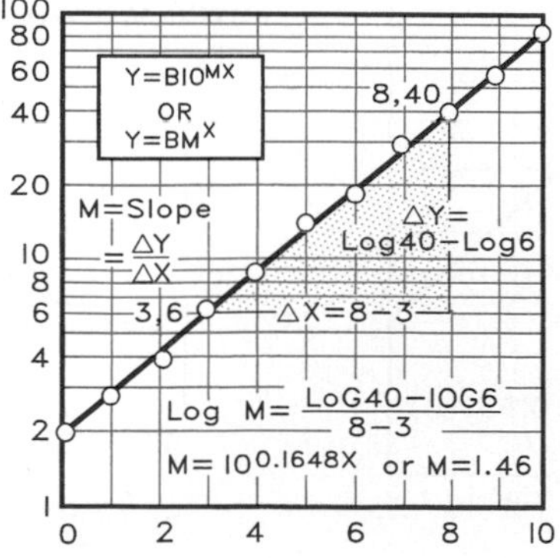

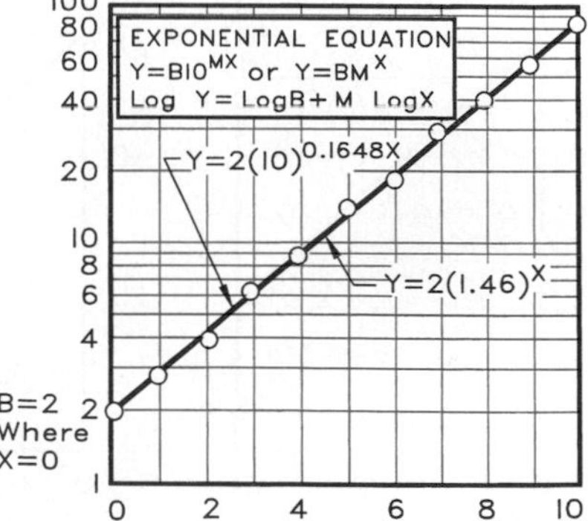

34.7 Exponential equation, $Y = BM^X$.

Step 1 These data plotted on a rectangular grid plot as a straight line on a semilogarithmic grid. The equation takes the form $Y = BM^X$.

Step 2 The slope must be found mathematically because the X- and Y-scales are unequal. Write the slope equation in either of the forms shown. The slope is found to be $M = 1.46$.

Step 3 Find the intercept, $B = 2$, on the Y-axis where $X = 0$. Substitute the values for $M(1.46)$ and $B(2)$ into the equation to get the equation $Y = 2(10)^{0.1648X}$, or $Y = 2(1.46)^X$.

where X is a variable that can be substituted into the equation to give infinitely many values for Y. In logarithmic form, the equation is

$\log Y = \log B + X \log M,$

or

$\log Y = \log 2 + X \log 1.46.$

The same methods give the negative slope of a curve. The curve shown in **Figure 34.8** slopes downward to the right and has a negative slope. M is the antilog of -0.0274. The intercept of 70 and the slope yield the equation for the curve.

The half-life decay of radioactivity plotted in **Figure 34.9** compares decay to time. The half-life of different isotopes varies, so different values would be assigned along the X-axis for them. However, the curves for all isotopes would be straight lines with the exponential equation form.

34.5 Graphical Calculus

If the equation of a curve is known, calculus may be used to perform various types of calculations. However, experimental data often do not fit standard mathematical equations,

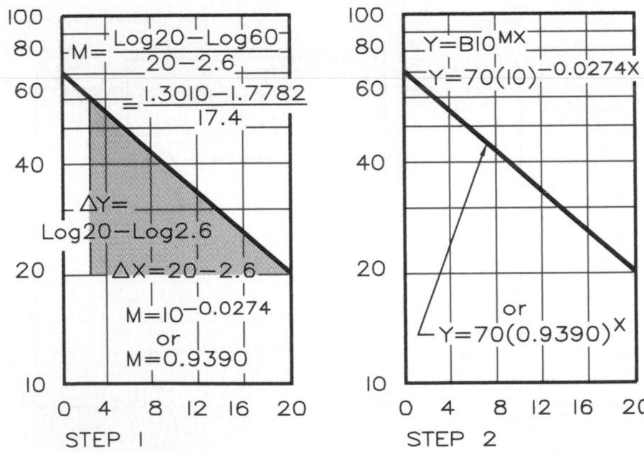

34.8 Negative slope (M).

A When a curve slopes downward to the right, its slope is negative.

B Substitution gives these two forms of the equation shown for the curve.

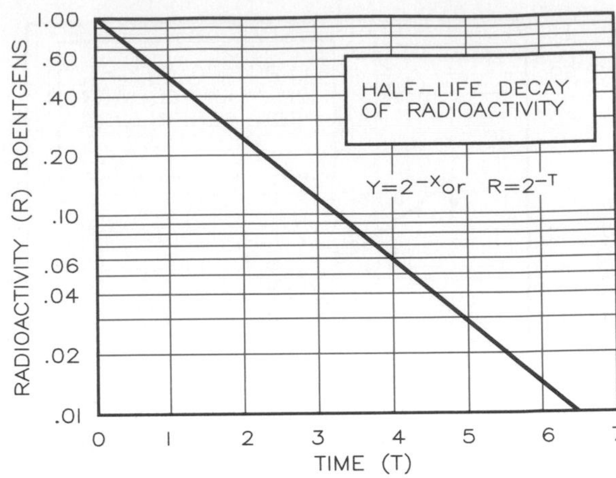

34.9 The decay of radioactivity is represented by a straight line on a semilog grid, indicating that its equation takes the exponential form, $Y = BM^X$ or $R = 2^{-T}$.

making impossible the mathematical application of calculus. In these cases, graphical calculus can be used. The two basic forms of calculus are (1) **differential calculus** and (2) **integral calculus.**

Differential calculus is used to determine the rate of change of one variable with respect to another (**Figure 34.10A**). The rate of change at any instant along the curve is the slope of a line tangent to the curve at that point. Constructing a chord at any interval allows approximation of this slope. The tangent, dY/dX, may represent miles per hour, weight

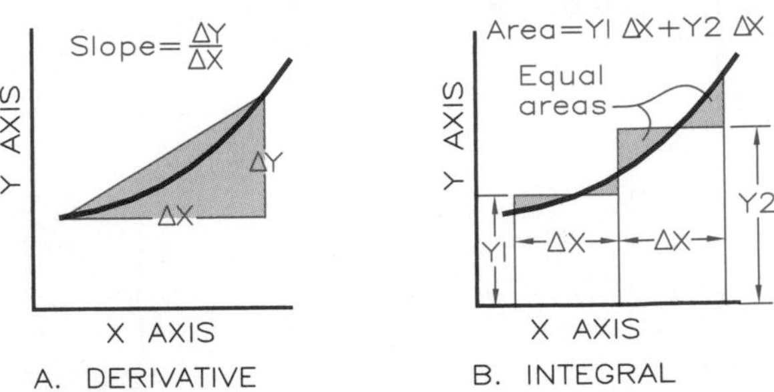

34.10 Derivatives and integrals.

A The derivative of a curve is the rate of change at any point on the curve, or its slope, $\Delta Y/\Delta X$.

B The integral of a curve is the cumulative area enclosed by the curve, or the summation of the incremental areas constituting the whole.

versus length, or various other rates of change important in the analysis of data.

Integral calculus is the reverse of differential calculus. Integration is used to find the area under a curve (the product of the variables plotted on the *X*- and *Y*-axes). The area under a curve is approximated by dividing one of the variables into a number of very small rectangular bars under the curve (**Figure 34.10B**). Each bar is drawn so that equal areas lie above and below the curve, and the average height of the bar is near its midpoint.

34.6 Graphical Differentiation

Graphical differentiation is used to determine the rate of change of two variables with respect to each other at any given point. **Figure 34.11** illustrates the preliminary construction of a derivative scale and the pole point for plotting a derivative curve.

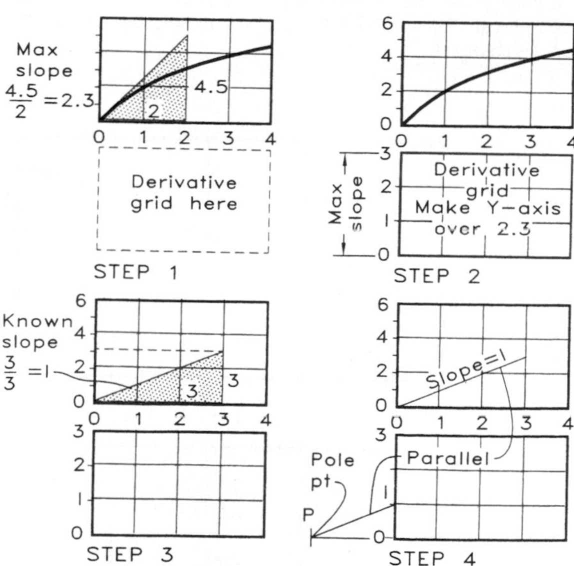

34.11 Scales for graphical differentiation.

Step 1 Estimate the maximum slope of the curve (here, 2.3) by drawing a line tangent to the curve where it is steepest.

Step 2 Draw the derivative grid with a maximum ordinate of 3.0 to accommodate the slope of 2.3.

Step 3 Find a known slope of 1 on the given grid. The slope has no relationship to the data curve.

Step 4 Draw a line from 1 on the *Y*-axis of the derivative grid parallel to the slope of the triangle drawn in the given grid. This locates the pole point on the extension of the *X*-axis.

The graphical differentiation process is illustrated in **Figure 34.12**. The maximum slope of the data curve is estimated to be slightly less than 12; an ordinate scale long enough to accommodate the maximum slope is selected. To locate the pole point, a line is drawn from point 4 on the ordinate axis of the derivative grid parallel to the known slope of 12/3 = 4 found on the given curve grid, and the line is extended to the *X*-axis.

A series of chords is constructed on the given curve. The interval between 0 and 1, where the curve is steepest, is divided in half to obtain a more accurate plot. After other bars are found, a smooth curve is drawn through the top of them so that the area above and under the top of each bar is equal. The rate of change, dY/dX, can be found for any value of *X* in the derivative graph.

Applications

The mechanical handling shuttle shown in **Figure 34.13** converts rotational motion into linear motion. The drawing of the linkage shows the end positions of point P, which is the zero point for plotting travel versus degrees of revolution. Rotation is constant at one revolution every 3 seconds, so the degrees of revolution may be converted to time (**Figure 34.14**). The drive crank, R1, is revolved at 30° intervals, and the distance that point P travels from its end position is plotted on the graph to give the distance-time relationship.

The ordinate scale of the derivative grid is scaled with an end value of 100 in./sec, or slightly larger than the estimated maximum slope of the curve. A slope of 40 is drawn on the given data grid. Pole point P is found by drawing a line from 40 on the derivative ordinate scale parallel to the slope of 40 in the

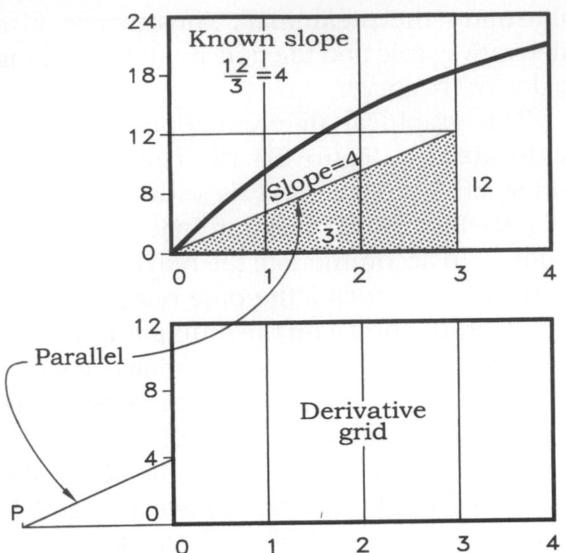

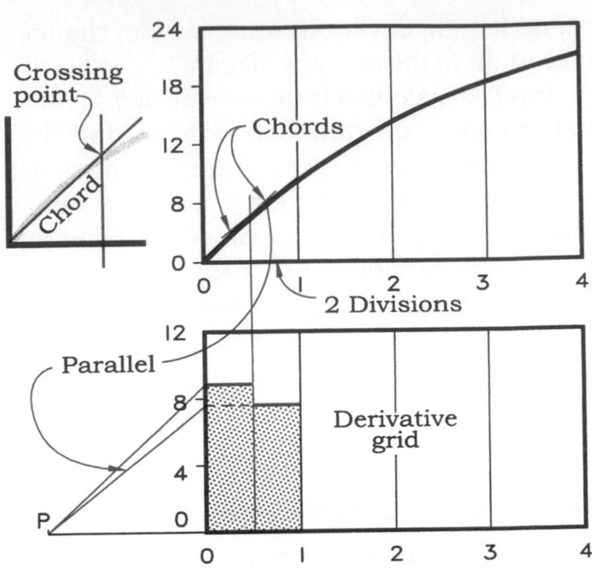

34.12 Graphical differentiation.

Step 1 Find the derivative grid and the pole point by using the steps introduced in **Figure 34.11.** A slope of 4 is found ($M = Y/X = 12/3 = 4$) in the given grid. Draw a parallel line from 4 on the Y-axis of the derivative grid to the extension of the X-axis to find pole point P.

Step 2 Construct chords between intervals on the given curve and draw lines parallel to them through point P on the derivative grid. These lines locate the heights of bars in their respective intervals. Divide the first interval into two bars where the curve is sharpest.

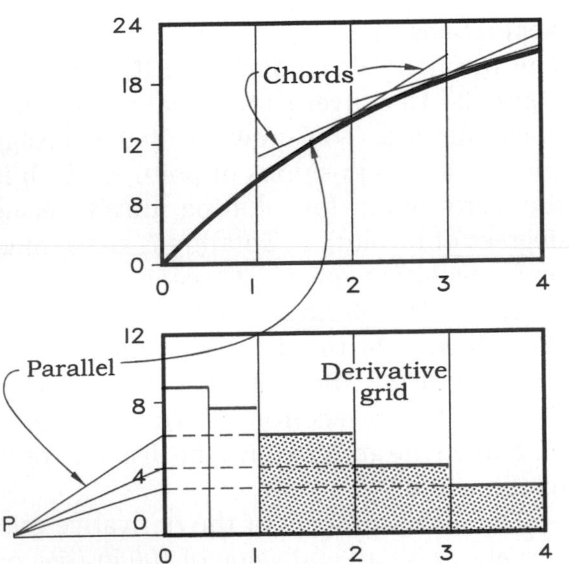

Step 3 Draw additional chords on the curve in the last three intervals. Draw lines parallel to the chords through point P to the Y-axis. This construction locates the remainder of the bars needed to draw the derivative curve.

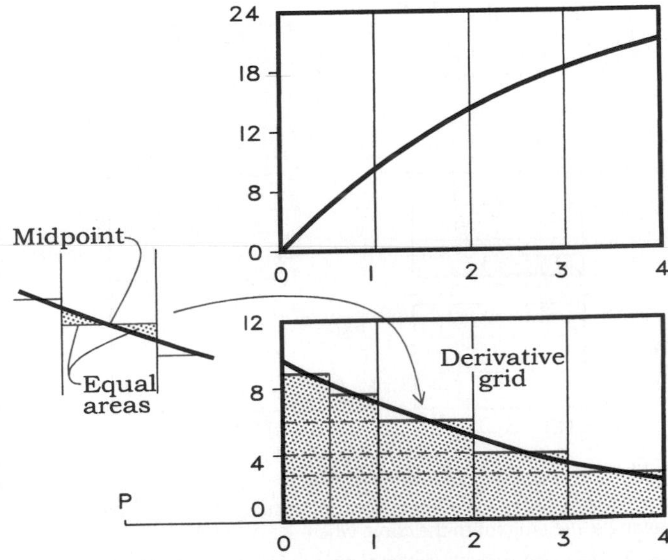

Step 4 The vertical bars represent the slopes of the curve at different intervals. Draw the derivative curve through the midpoints of the bars so that the areas below and above the bars are equal.

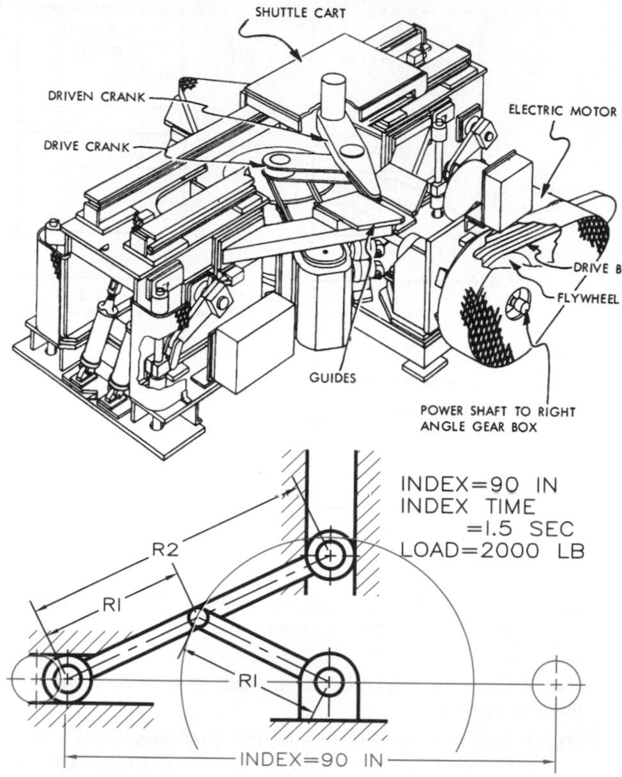

34.13 Drawings of a mechanical handling shuttle used to move automobile parts on an assembly line. *(Courtesy of General Motors Corporation.)*

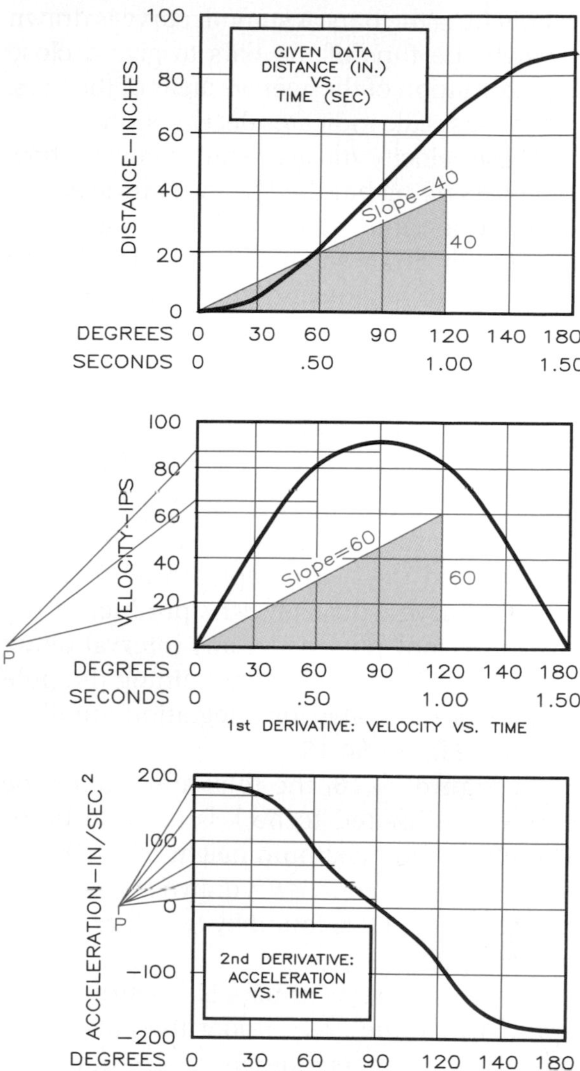

34.14 Velocity and acceleration of the mechanical handling shuttle may be obtained with graphical differential calculus.

given data graph to the extension of the *X*-axis of the derivative graph.

Chords drawn on the curve approximate the slope at various points. Draw lines from point P of the derivative scale parallel to the chordal lines to the ordinate axis. These intersections on the *Y*-axis are projected horizontally to their respective intervals to form vertical bars. A curve is drawn through the tops of the bars to give an average of the bars. This curve shows the velocity of the shuttle in inches per second at any time interval.

The second-derivative curve, acceleration versus time, is drawn in the same manner as the first-derivative curve. Inspection of the first-derivative curve shows that the maximum slope is about 200 in./sec/sec. An easily measured scale for the ordinate is chosen. Pole point P is found in the same manner as in the previous examples.

Chords are drawn at intervals on the first-derivative curve. Lines drawn from P parallel to these chords intersect the *Y*-axis of the second derivative graph, where they are projected horizontally to their respective intervals, establishing the bars. A smooth curve is drawn through the tops of the bars to give a close approximation of the average areas of the bars. The minus scale indicates deceleration.

These velocity and acceleration graphs show that parts being handled by the shuttle accelerate at a rapid rate until the maximum velocity is attained at 90°, at which time deceleration begins and continues until the parts come to rest.

34.7 Graphical Integration

Graphical **integration** is used to determine the area (product of two variables) under a curve. For example, if the *Y*-axis represented pounds and the *X*-axis represented feet, the integral curve would give the product of the variables, foot-pounds, at any interval along the *X*-axis. The steps in determining the pole point and the scales for integration are illustrated in **Figure 34.15**.

In **Figure 34.16**, the total area under the curve is estimated to be less than 80 units. Therefore, the maximum height of the *Y*-axis on the integral curve is 80, drawn at a convenient scale. Pole P is found by the steps shown in **Figure 34.15**.

A series of vertical bars is constructed to approximate the areas under the curve. The narrower the bars, the more accurate will be the resulting plotted curve. The interval between 2 and 3 is divided into two bars to obtain more accuracy where the curve is sharpest. The tops of the bars are extended horizontally to the *Y*-axis and are connected to point P.

Lines are drawn parallel to AP, BP, CP, DP, and EP in the integral grid to correspond to the respective intervals in the given grid. The intersection points of the chords are connected by a smooth curve—the integral curve—to give the cumulative product of the *X*- and *Y*-variables along the *X*-axis.

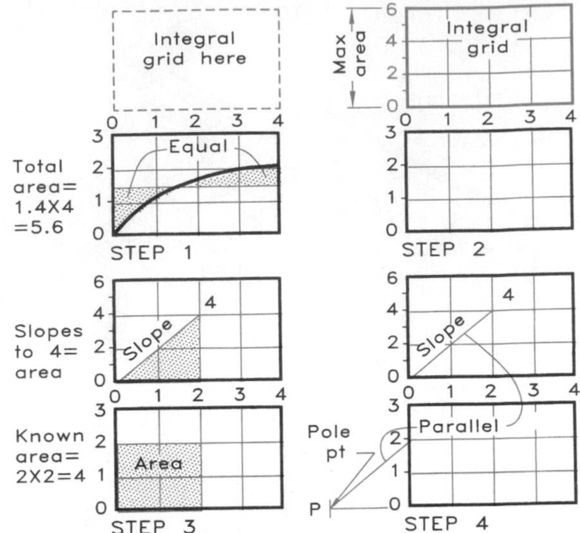

34.15 Scales for graphical integration.

Step 1 To determine the maximum value on the *Y*-axis, draw a line to approximate the area under the given curve (5.6 rectangular units here).

Step 2 Draw the integral with a *Y*-axis of 6 to accommodate the maximum area.

Step 3 Find a known area of 4 on the given grid. Draw a slope from 0 to 4 on the integral grid directly above the known area to establish the integral.

Step 4 Draw a line from 2 on the *Y*-axis of the given grid parallel to the slope line in the integral grid. Locate the pole point on the extension of the *X*-axis.

Problems

Use size A sheets to solve the following problems. Show mathematical calculations either on the same or on a separate sheet if space is not available next to the graphical solutions.

Empirical Equations: Linear

1. Construct a linear graph and determine the equation for the annual cost of a compressor (*Y*-axis from 0 to 12,000) in relation to the compressor's size in horsepower (*X*-axis from 0 to 300). Data: 0 hp, \$0; 50 hp, \$2100; 100 hp, \$4500; 150 hp, \$6700; 200 hp, \$9000; 250 hp, \$11,400.

2. Construct a linear graph on which the *X*-axis is the mat depth from 0 to 4 in., and the *Y*-axis is

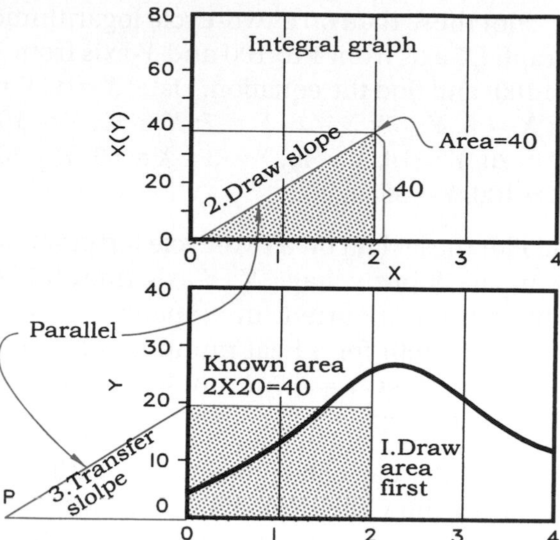

34.16 Graphical integration.
Required Plot the integral curve of the given data.

Step 1 Find pole point P by using the technique described in **Figure 34.15.**

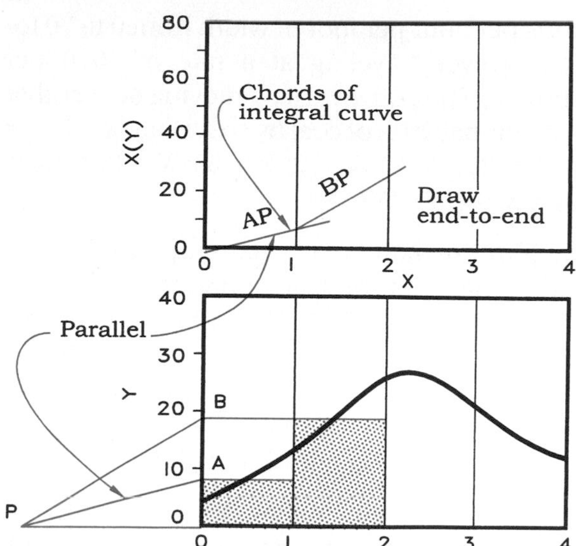

Step 2 Construct bars in the given graph to approximate the areas under the curve. Project the heights of the bars to the Y-axis and draw lines to pole P. Draw sloping lines AP and BP in their respective intervals parallel to the lines drawn to P in the integral graph.

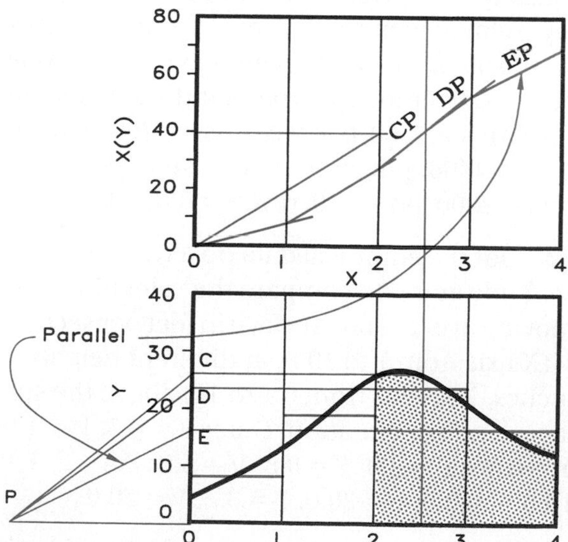

Step 3 Draw additional bars from 2 to 4 on the X-axis of the given curve. Project the heights of the bars to the Y-axis and draw rays to pole P. Draw lines CP, DP, and EP at their respective intervals and parallel to their rays in the integral grid.

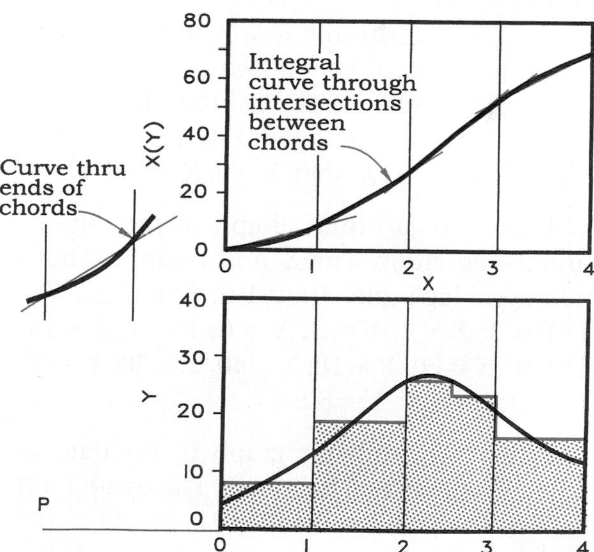

Step 4 The lines connected in the integral grid are chords of the integral curve. Draw the curve to pass through the intersections of the chords. An ordinate value on the integral curve represents the cumulative area under the given curve from zero to that point on the X-axis.

tons per hour per foot of width from 0 to 70 for a conveyor traveling at a rate of 50 ft per minute. The conveyor is a moving shaker that screens particles of coal by size. Data: $X = 0$, $Y = 0$; $X = 1$, $Y = 13$; $X = 2$, $Y = 25$; $X = 3$, $Y = 38$; and $X = 4$, $Y = 50$.

3. Plot the data on a linear graph and determine the equation that shows the deflection in centimeters of a spring, D (Y-axis from 0 to 4), when it is loaded with different weights in kilograms, W (X-axis from 0 to 4). Data: $W = 0$, $D = 0.45$; $W = 1$, $D = 1.10$; $W = 2$, $D = 1.45$; $W = 3$, $D = 2.03$, $W = 4$, $D = 2.38$; $W = 2.38$, $D = 3.09$.

4. Plot the empirical data on a linear graph and determine the equation for temperatures on a Fahrenheit thermometer, °F (Y-axis from 0 to 180), and a Celsius thermometer, °C (X-axis from -10 to 80). Data: $C = -6.8$, $F = 20$; $C = 6$, $F = 43$; $C = 16$, $F = 60.8$; $C = 32.2$, $F = 90$; $C = 52$, $F = 125.8$; $C = 76$, $F = 169$.

Empirical Equations: Logarithmic

5. Draw a logarithmic graph of the data to find the equation. The X- and Y-axes are both two-cycle log scales from 1 to 100. Data: $X = 1$, $Y = 40$; $X = 4$, $Y = 18$; $X = 7$, $Y = 12$; $X = 10$, $Y = 10$; $X = 20$, $Y = 7$; $X = 40$, $Y = 5$; $X = 100$, $Y = 3$.

6. Draw a logarithmic graph of the data to find the equation. The X- and Y-axes are both two-cycle log scales from 1 to 100. Data: $X = 1$, $Y = 2$; $X = 2$, $Y = 3$; $X = 6$, $Y = 7$; $X = 10$, $Y = 10$; $X = 20$, $Y = 18$; $X = 40$, $Y = 30$; $X = 60$, $Y = 40$; $X = 100$, $Y = 60$.

7. Draw a logarithmic graph of the data to find the equation. The X- and Y-axes are both two-cycle log scales; the X-axis is from 1 to 100 and the Y-axis from 10 to 1000. Data: $X = 1$, $Y = 50$; $X = 4$, $Y = 92$; $X = 6$, $Y = 110$; $X = 10$, $Y = 150$; $X = 30$, $Y = 215$; $X = 60$, $Y = 310$; $X = 100$, $Y = 400$.

8. Plot these data on a two-cycle logarithmic graph (X-axis from 1 to 100 and Y-axis from 1 to 100) and find the equation. Data: $X = 1$, $Y = 2$; $X = 2$, $Y = 3$; $X = 6$, $Y = 7$; $X = 10$, $Y = 10$; $X = 20$, $Y = 18$; $X = 40$, $Y = 30$; $X = 60$, $Y = 40$; $X = 100$, $Y = 60$.

9. Plot these data on a two-cycle log graph to compare input voltage V (Y-axis from 0.1 to 10) with input current in amperes, I (X-axis from 1 to 100) for a heat pump and find the equation. Data: $V = 0.7$, $I = 8$; $V = 1.1$, $I = 20$; $V = 1.6$, $I = 30$; $V = 1.8$, $I = 40$; $V = 2.1$, $I = 60$.

10. Plot the data on a two-cycle logarithmic graph to show the peak allowable current in amperes, I (Y-axis from 100 to 10,000), and the overload operating time in cycles at 60 cycles per second, C (X-axis from 1 to 100). Find the equation. Data: $I = 2000$, $C = 1$; $I = 1840$, $C = 2$; $I = 1640$, $C = 5$; $I = 1480$, $C = 10$; $I = 1300$, $C = 20$; $I = 1200$, $C = 50$; $I = 1000$, $C = 100$.

11. Plot the data on a two-cycle log graph of a low-voltage circuit breaker used on a welding machine that gives the maximum loading during welding in amperes, rms (Y-axis from 1000 to 100,000), for the percentage of duty cycle, pdc (X-axis from 1 to 100). Find the equation. Data: rms = 7500, pdc = 3; rms = 5200, pdc = 6; rms = 4400, pdc = 9; rms = 3400, pdc = 15; rms = 2300, pdc = 30; rms = 1700, pdc = 60.

12. Plot the empirical data on a two-cycle logarithmic graph to compare the velocities of air moving over a plane surface in feet per second, V (X-axis from 1 to 100), at different heights in inches, Y (Y-axis from 0.1 to 10) above the surface. Find the equation. Data: $Y = 0.3$, $V = 1.0$; $Y = 0.46$, $V = 2.0$; $Y = 0.8$, $V = 5.0$; $Y = 1.2$, $V = 10.0$; $Y = 2.0$, $V = 20.0$, $Y = 3.2$, $V = 50.0$.

13. Plot the data on a two-cycle logarithmic graph to compare the distance traveled in feet, S (Y-axis from 10 to 1000), at various times in seconds, T (X-axis from 1 to 100), of a test vehicle.

Find the equation. Data: $T = 1$, $S = 15.8$; $T = 2$, $S = 63.3$; $T = 3$, $S = 146$; $T = 4$, $S = 264$; $T = 5$, $S = 420$; $T = 6$, $S = 580$.

Empirical Equations: Semilogarithmic

14. Draw a semilogarithmic graph of the data to find its equation. The Y-axis is a two-cycle log scale from 1 to 100, and the X-axis is from 0 to 10. Data: $X = 0$, $Y = 5$; $X = 2$, $Y = 8$; $X = 4$, $Y = 12$; $X = 6$, $Y = 21$; $X = 8$, $Y = 36$; $X = 10$, $Y = 60$.

15. Draw a semilog graph of the data to find its equation. The Y-axis is a two-cycle log scale from 1 to 100, and the X-axis is from 0 to 10. Data: $X = 0$, $Y = 60$; $X = 2$, $Y = 30$; $X = 4$, $Y = 15$; $X = 6$, $Y = 8$; $X = 8$, $Y = 4$; $X = 10$, $Y = 2$.

16. Plot the following empirical data on a two-cycle (Y-axis from 10 to 1000) semilogarithmic graph (X-axis from 0 to 10) to obtain the equation of the following data: $X = 0$, $Y = 20$; $X = 2$, $Y = 39$; $X = 4$, $Y = 70$; $X = 6$, $Y = 130$; $X = 8$, $Y = 270$; $X = 10$, $Y = 500$.

17. Plot the following empirical data on a semilogarithmic graph and find its equation. The Y-axis is a two-cycle log scale from 0.1 to 10 for V (voltage), and the linear X-axis, from 0 to 10 for T (time) in sixteenths of a second, represents resistor voltage during capacitor charging. Data: 0 sec, 10 V; 2 sec, 6 V; 4 sec, 3.6 V; 6 sec, 2.2 V; 8 sec, 1.4 V; 10 sec, 0.8 V.

18. Plot the following data on a semilogarithmic graph and find the equation. Make the Y-axis a three-cycle log scale from 0.001 to 1.0 for the reduction factor, R, and the X-axis a linear scale from 0 to 360 for mass thickness per square foot (M) of a nuclear protection barrier. Data: $M = 0$, $R = 1.0$; $M = 100$, $R = 0.9$; $M = 150$, $R = 0.028$; $M = 200$, $R = 0.009$; $M = 300$, $R = 0.0011$.

19. Plot the following data of the ABC Company as a semilogarithmic graph with a three-cycle Y-axis from 0.01 to 10 and linear X-axis from 0 to 10. Show their years of operation on the X-axis, and their annual income in tens of thousands of dollars on the Y-axis. Data: $X = 1$, $Y = 0.05$; $X = 2$, $Y = 0.08$; $X = 3$, $Y = 0.12$; $X = 4$, $Y = 0.2$; $X = 5$, $Y = 0.32$; $X = 6$, $Y = 0.51$; $X = 7$, $Y = 0.8$; $X = 8$, $Y = 1.3$; $X = 9$, $Y = 2.05$; $X = 10$, $Y = 3.25$.

Calculus: Graphical Differentiation

20. Plot the equation $Y = X^2/6$ as a linear graph. Plot its first derivative curve.

21. Plot the equation $Y = 2X^2$; find its derivative curve on a graph placed below the first.

22. Plot the equation $4Y = 8 - X^2$; find its derivative curve on a graph placed below the given grid.

23. Plot the equation $3Y = X^2 + 16$; find its derivative curve on a graph placed below the given grid.

24. Plot the equation $X = 3Y^2 - 5$; find the derivative curve on a graph placed below the first.

Calculus: Graphical Integration

25. Plot the equation $Y = X^2$; find its integral curve on a graph above the given grid.

26. Plot the equation $Y = 9 - X^2$; find its integral curve on a graph above the given grid.

27. Plot the equation $Y = X$ on a graph; find its integral curve on a graph above the given grid.

35 Pipe Drafting

35.1 Introduction

An understanding of pipe drafting begins with a familiarity with the types of pipe that are available. The commonly used types of pipe are (1) steel pipe; (2) cast-iron pipe; (3) copper, brass, and bronze pipe and tubing; and (4) plastic pipe. The use of all these types of pipes can be seen in ExxonMobil's refinery in **Figure 35.1**.

The standards for the grades and weights for pipe and pipe fittings are specified by several organizations to ensure the uniformity of size and strength of interchangeable components. Several of these organizations are the American National Standards Institute (ANSI), the American Society for Test Materials (ASTM), the American Petroleum Institute (API), and the Manufacturers Standardization Society (MSS).

35.1 Nowhere is the application of pipes and vessels more impressive than in an oil refinery.

35.2 Welded and Seamless Steel Pipe

Traditionally, steel pipe has been specified in three weights **standard (STD), extra strong (XS)**, and **double extra strong (XXS)**. These designations and their specifications are listed in the *ANSI B 36.10* standards. However, additional designations for pipe, called *schedules,* have been introduced to provide the pipe designer with a wider selection of pipe to cover more applications.

The 10 schedules are Schedule 10, Schedule 20, Schedule 30, Schedule 40, Schedule 60, Schedule 80, Schedule 100, Schedule 120, Schedule 140, and Schedule 160. The wall thicknesses of the pipes vary from the thinnest, in Schedule 10, to the thickest, in Schedule 160. The outside diameters are of a constant size for pipes of the same nominal size in all schedules. Schedule designations correspond to STD, XS, and XXS specifications in some cases (**Table 35.1**). This table has been abbreviated from the *ANSI B 36.10* tables

Table 35.1 Dimensions and weights of welded and seamless steel pipe (ANSI B 36.10)

Inch Units				Identification		SI Units		
Inch Nominal Size	O.D. (in.)	Wall Thk. (in.)	Weight lbs/ft	*STD XS XXS	Sch. no.	O.D. (mm)	Wall Thk. (mm)	Weight kg/m
½	0.84	0.11	0.85	STD	40	21.3	2.8	1.3
1	1.32	0.13	1.68	STD	40	33.4	3.4	2.5
1	1.3	0.18	2.17	XS	80	33.4	4.6	3.2
1	1.3	0.36	3.66	XXS		33.4	9.1	5.5
2	2.38	0.22	3.65	STD	40	60.3	3.9	5.4
2	2.38	0.22	5.02	XS	80	60.3	5.5	7.5
2	2.38	0.44	9.03	XXS		60.3	11.1	13.4
4	4.50	0.23	10.79	STD	40	114.3	6.0	16.1
4	4.50	0.34	14.98	XS	80	114.3	8.6	42.6
4	4.50	0.67	27.54	XXS		114.3	17.1	41.0
8	8.63	0.32	28.55	STD	40	219.1	8.2	42.6
8	8.63	0.50	43.39	XS	80	219.1	12.7	64.6
8	8.63	0.88	74.40	XXS		219.1	22.2	107.9
12	12.75	0.38	49.56	STD		323.0	9.5	67.9
12	12.75	0.50	65.42	XS		323.0	12.7	97.5
12	12.75	1.00	125.4	XXS	120	133.9	25.4	187.0
14	†14.00	0.38	54.57	STD	30	355.6	9.5	87.3
14	14.00	0.50	72.08	XS		355.6	12.7	107.4
18	18.00	0.38	70.59	STD		457	9.5	106.2
18	18.00	0.50	93.45	XS		457	12.7	139.2
24	24.00	0.38	94.62	STD	20	610	9.5	141.1
24	24.00	0.50	125.49	XS		610	12.7	187.1
30	30.00	0.38	118.65	STD		762	9.5	176.8
30	30.00	0.50	157.53	XS	20	762	12.7	234.7
40	40.00	0.38	158.70	STD		1016	9.5	236.5
40	40.00	0.50	210.90	XS		1016	12.7	314.2

*Standard (STD); X-strong (XS); XX-strong (XXS).

†Beginning with 14-in. DIA pipe, the nominal size represents the outside diameter (O.D.).

This table has been compressed by omitting many of the available pipe sizes. The nominal sizes of pipes that are listed in the complete table are ⅛″, ¼″, ⅜″, ½″, ¾″, 1″, 1¼″, 1½″, 2″, 2½″, 3″, 3½″, 4″, 5″, 6″, 8″, 10″, 12″, 14″, 16″, 18″, 20″, 22″, . . . (in 2″ increments up to 60″).

by omitting a number of the pipe sizes and schedules. The most often used schedules are 40, 80, and 120.

Pipes from the smallest size up to and including 12-in. pipes are specified by their inside diameter (ID), which means that the outside diameter (OD) is larger than the specified size. The inside diameters are the same size as the nominal sizes of the pipe for STD weight pipe. For XS and XXS pipe, the inside diameters are slightly different in size from the nominal size. Beginning with the 14-in. diameter pipes, the nominal sizes represent the outside diameters of the pipe.

The standard lengths for steel pipe are 20 ft and 40 ft. **Seamless steel (SMLS STL)** pipe is a smooth pipe with no weld seams along its length. Welded pipe is formed into a cylinder and is butt-welded (BW) at the seam, or it is joined with an electric resistance weld (ERW).

35.3 Cast-Iron Pipe

Cast-iron pipe is used for the transportation of liquids, water, gas, and sewage. When used as a sewage pipe, cast-iron pipe is referred to as soil pipe. Cast-iron pipe is available in diameter sizes from 3 in. to 60 in.

The standard lengths of cast-iron pipe are 5 ft and 10 ft. Cast iron is more brittle and more subject to cracking when loaded than is steel pipe. Therefore, cast-iron pipe should not be used where high pressures or weights will be applied to it.

35.4 Copper, Brass, and Bronze Piping

Copper, brass, and bronze are used to manufacture piping and tubing for use in applications where there must be a high resistance to corrosive elements, such as acidic soils and chemicals transmitted through the pipes. Copper pipe is used when the pipes are placed within or under concrete slab foundations of buildings to ensure that they will resist corrosion. The standard length of pipes made of these nonferrous materials is 12 ft.

Tubing is a smaller-size pipe that can be easily bent when it is made of copper, brass, or bronze. The term **piping** refers to rigid pipes that are larger than tubes, usually in excess of 2 in. in diameter.

35.5 Miscellaneous Pipes

Other materials that are used to manufacture pipes are aluminum, concrete, polyvinyl chloride (PVC), and various other plastics. Each of these materials has its special characteristics that make it desirable or economical for certain applications. The method of designing and detailing piping systems by the pipe drafter is essentially the same regardless of the piping material used.

35.6 Pipe Joints

The basic connection in a pipe system is the joint where two straight sections of pipe fit together. Three types of joints are illustrated in **Figure 35.2: screwed, welded**, and **flanged**.

Screwed joints are joined by pipe threads of the type covered in Chapter 10 and **Appendix 9**. Pipe threads are tapered at a ratio of 1 to 16 along the outside diameter (**Figure 35.3**). As the pipes are screwed together, the threads bind to form a snug, locking fit. A cementing compound is applied to the threads before joining, to improve the seal.

Flanged joints, shown in **Figure 35.4**, are welded to the straight sections of pipe, which are then bolted together around the perimeter of the flanges. Flanged joints form strong rigid joints that can withstand high pressure and permit disassembly of the joints when needed. Several types of flange faces are shown in **Figure 35.5** and in **Appendix 43**.

Welded joints are joined by welded seams around the perimeter of the pipe to form butt

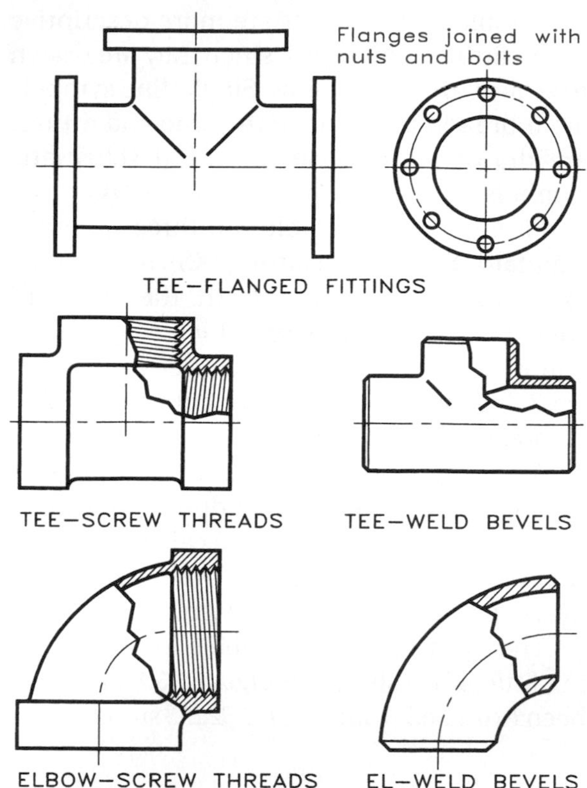

35.2 Examples of some of the types of fittings that are used to connect pipes.

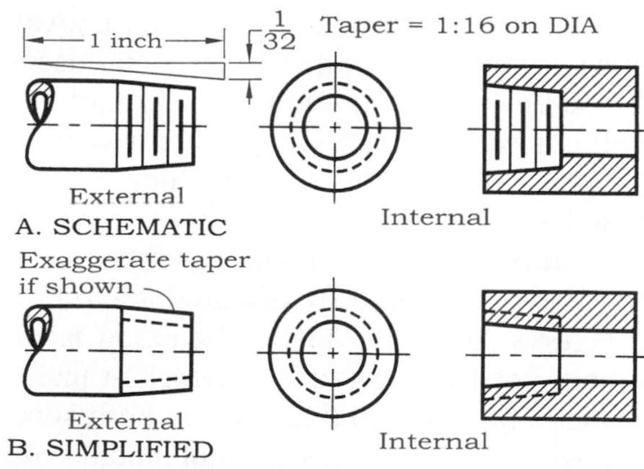

35.3 Pipe threads have a slight taper and are used to connect screwed pipe fittings.

welds. Welded joints are used extensively in "big inch" pipelines that are used for transporting petroleum products cross-country.

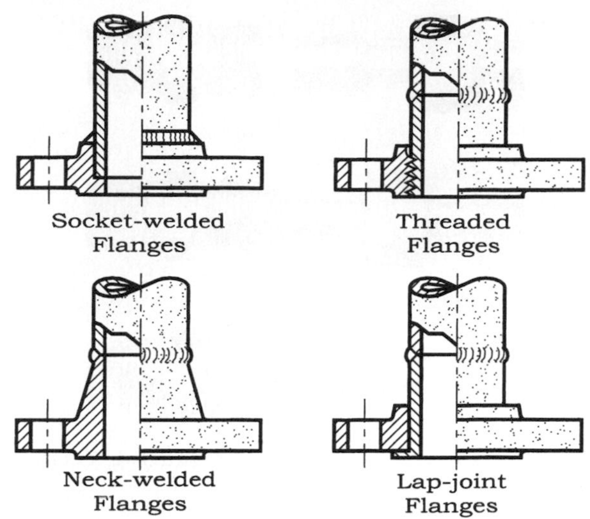

35.4 Types of flanged joints and the methods of attaching the flanges to the pipes are shown here.

Bell and spigot (B&S) joints are used to join cast-iron pipes (**Figure 35.6**). The spigot is placed inside the bell and the two are sealed with molten lead or a sealing ring that snaps into position to form a sealed joint.

Soldering is used to connect smaller pipes and tubes, especially nonferrous tubing.

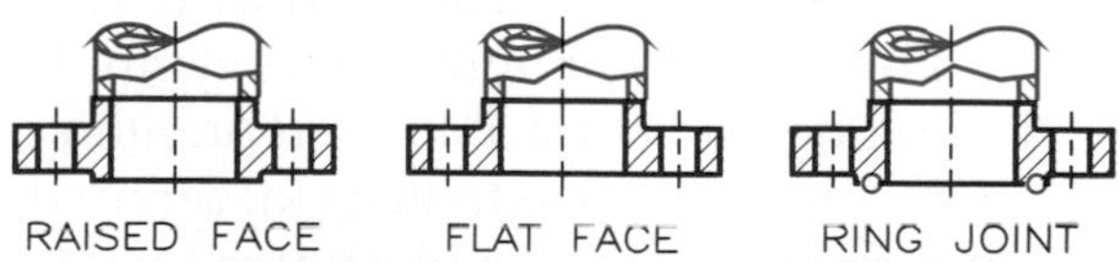

35.5 Three types of flange faces are the raised face (RF), the flat face (FF), and the ring joint (RJ).

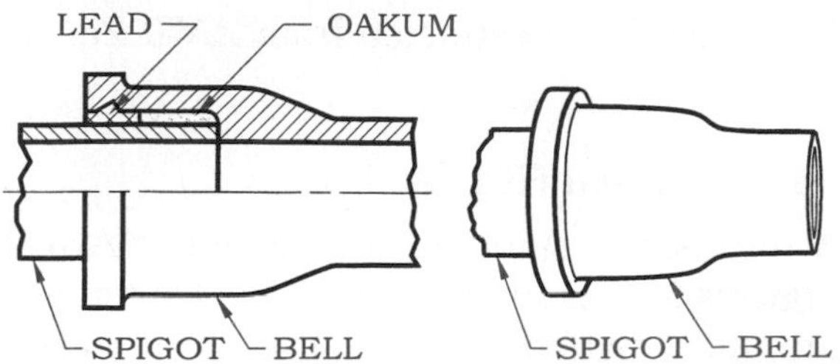

35.6 A bell and spigot joint (B&S) is used to connect cast-iron pipes.

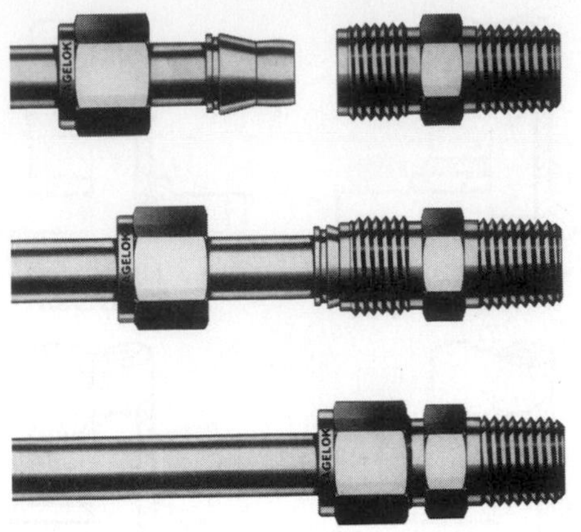

35.7 Screwed joints can be used to join small tubing. *(Courtesy of Crawford Fitting Co.)*

Screwed fittings are available to connect tubing, as shown in **Figure 35.7**.

35.7 Pipe Fittings

Pipe fittings are placed within a pipe system to join pipes at various angles, to transform the pipe diameter to a different size, or to control the flow and its direction within the system. Fittings are placed in the system using any of the previously covered joints. A pipe system can be drawn with single-line symbols or double-line symbols.

The fittings in **Figure 35.8** are represented as single-line symbols with flanged, screwed, bell and spigot, welded, and soldered joints. Most symbols have been shown as they would be drawn to appear in various orthographic views—top, front, and side views. These symbols have been extracted from *ANSI Z32.2.3* standards.

35.8 Screwed Fittings

A number of standard fittings are shown in **Figures 35.9** through **35.12**. The two types of graphical symbols that are used to represent fittings and pipe are **double-line symbols** and **single-line symbols**.

Double-line symbols are more descriptive of the fittings and pipes, since they are drawn to scale with double lines. Single-line symbols are more symbolic, since the pipe and fittings are drawn with single lines and schematic symbols.

Fittings are available in three weights: standard (STD), extra strong (XS), and double extra strong (XXS) to match the standard weights of the pipes with which they will be connnected. Other weights of fittings are available, but these three weights are stocked by practically all suppliers.

A piping system of screwed fittings is shown in **Figure 35.13** with double-line symbols in a single-line system to call attention to them. These could just as well have been drawn using the single-line symbols.

The most common symbols for representing fittings are shown in **Figure 35.8** and have been extracted from *ANSI Z 32.2.3* standards.

35.9 Flanged Fittings

Flanges are used to connect fittings into a piping system when heavy loads are supported in large pipes and where pressures are great. Since flanges are expensive, their usage should be kept to a minimum if other joining methods can be used. Flanges are welded to straight pipe sections so that they can be bolted together.

Examples of several flanged fittings are drawn as double-line and single-line symbols in **Figures 35.14** and **35.15**. The elbow is commonly referred to as an "ell" and it is available in angles of turn of 90° and 45° in both short and long radii. The radius of a short-radius (SR) ell is equal to the diameter of the larger end. The long-radius (LR) ells have radii that are approximately 1.5 times the nominal diameter of the large end of the ell. A table of dimensions for 125-lb cast-iron fittings is given in **Appendixes 42** and **43**.

	FLANGED	SCREWED	BELL & SPIGOT	WELDED	SOLDERED
1. JOINT					
2. 90° ELBOW					
TOP VIEW					
FRONT VIEW					
BOTTOM VIEW					
3. ELBOW-LONG RADIUS	LR	LR			
4. ELBOW-REDUCING	2 3	2 3			2 3
5. TEE					
TOP VIEW					
FRONT VIEW					
BOTTOM VIEW					
6. 45° ELBOW					
TOP VIEW					
FRONT VIEW					
BOTTOM VIEW					
7. 45° LATERAL					
TOP VIEW					
FRONT VIEW					
8. REDUCER					
9. GATE VALVE					
10. GLOBE VALVE					
11. CHECK VALVE					
12. UNION					

35.8 These single-line pipe fitting symbols are extracted from the *ANSI Z32.2* standards.

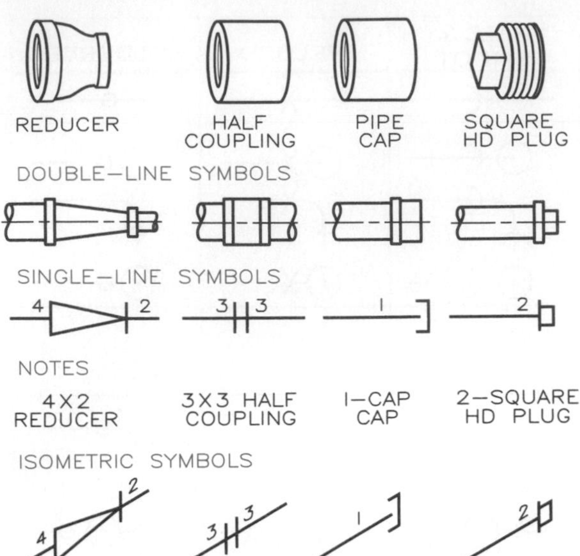

35.9 Examples of standard fittings for screwed connections along with the single-line and double-line symbols that are used to represent them are shown here. Nominal pipe sizes can be indicated by numbers placed near the joints. The major flow direction is labeled first, with the branches labeled second. The large openings are labeled to precede the smaller openings.

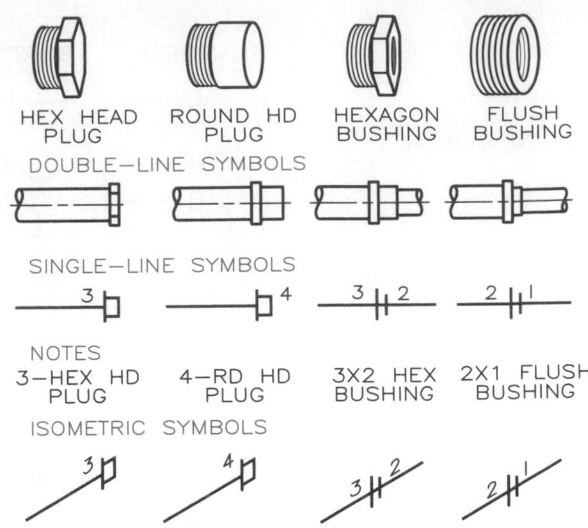

35.10 Single-line, double-line, and isometric drawings of plugs and bushings with screwed connections.

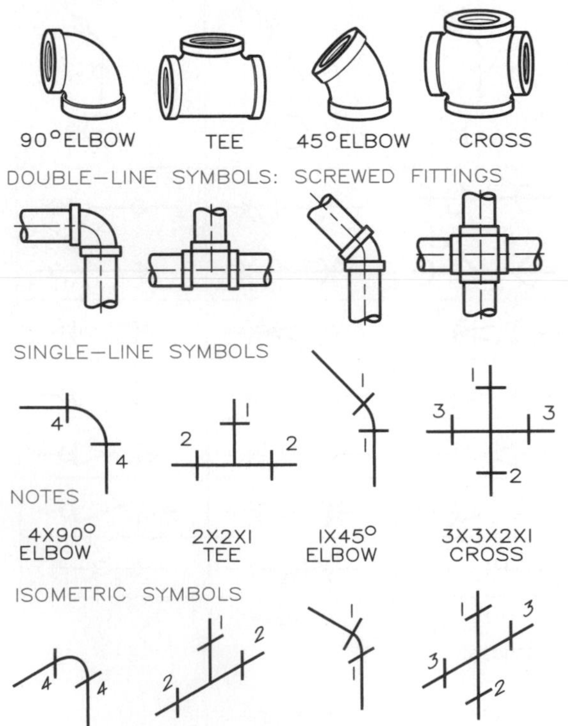

35.11 Examples of standard fittings for screwed connections.

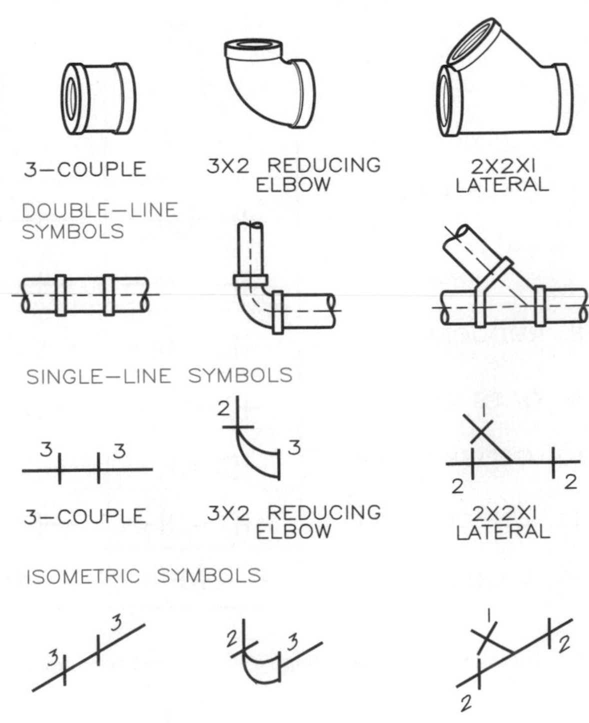

35.12 Single-line, double-line, and isometric drawings of couples, elbows, and laterals with screwed connections.

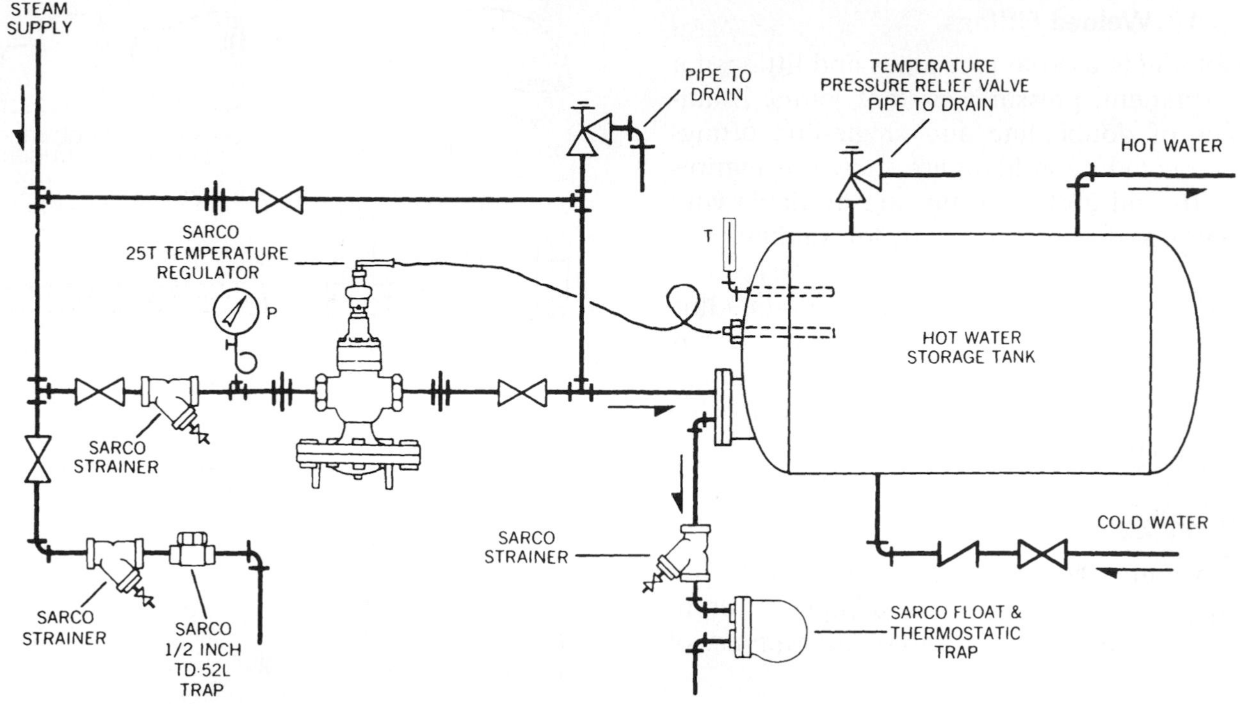

35.13 A single-line piping system with the major valves represented with double-line symbols. *(Courtesy of Sarco Inc.)*

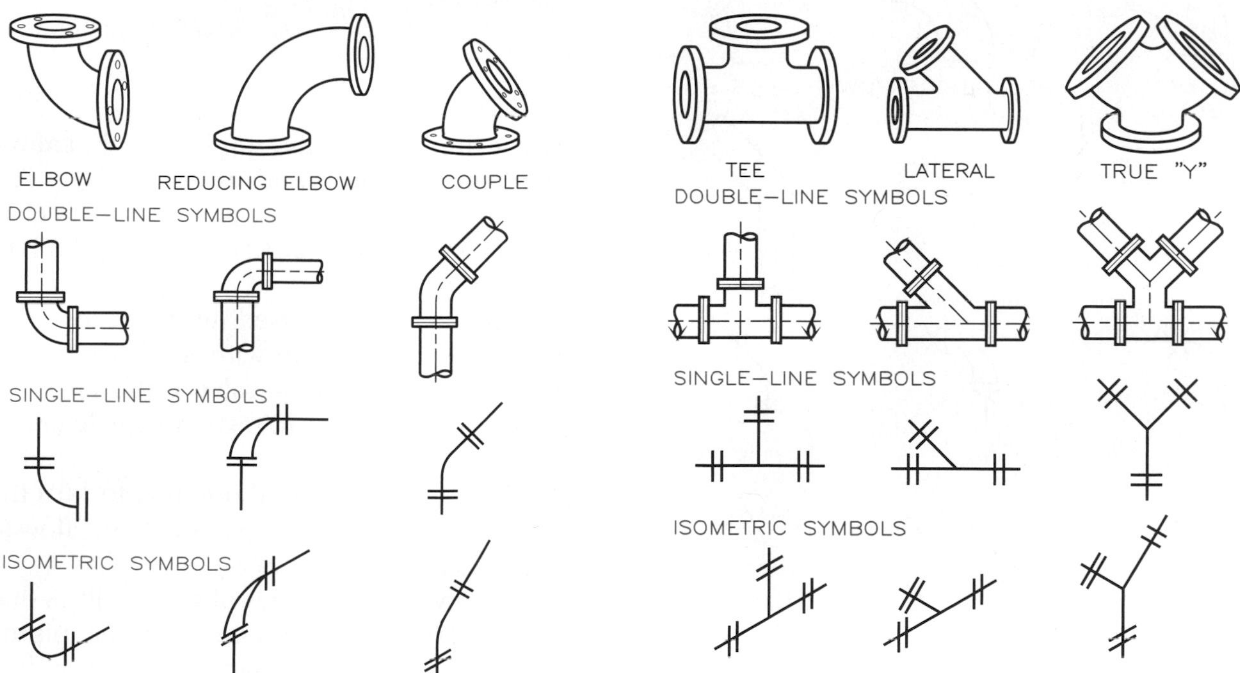

35.14 Examples of standard flanged fittings along with the single-line and double-line symbols that are used to represent them.

35.15 Examples of standard flanged fittings along with the single-line and double-line symbols that are used to represent them.

35.10 Welded Fittings

Welding is used to join pipes and fittings for permanent, pressure-resistant joints. Examples of double-line and single-line fittings connected by welding are shown in **Figures 35.16** and **35.17**. Fittings are available with beveled edges that are ready for welding.

A piping layout in **Figure 35.18** illustrates a series of welded joints with a double-line drawing. The location of the welded joints has been dimensioned. Several flanged fittings have been welded into the system for the flanges to be used.

35.11 Valves

Valves are used to regulate the flow of gas and liquid transported within a pipeline or to turn off the flow completely. Several types of valves are **gate, globe, angle, check, safety, diaphragm**, **float**, and **relief** valves. The three basic valves—gate, globe, and check—are shown in **Figure 35.19** drawn with double-line symbols.

Gate valves are used to turn the flow within a pipe on or off with the least restriction of flow through the valve. Gate valves are not meant to be used to regulate the degree of flow.

Globe valves are used not only to turn the flow on and off but also to regulate the flow to a desired level.

Angle valves are types of globe valves that turn at 90° angles at bends in the piping system. They have the same controlling features as the straight globe valves.

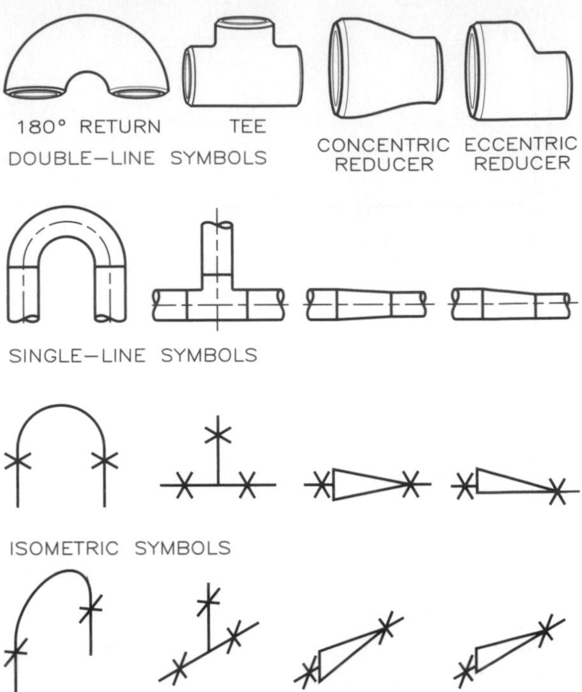

35.17 Additional examples of standard welded fittings along with the single-line and double-line symbols that are used to represent them.

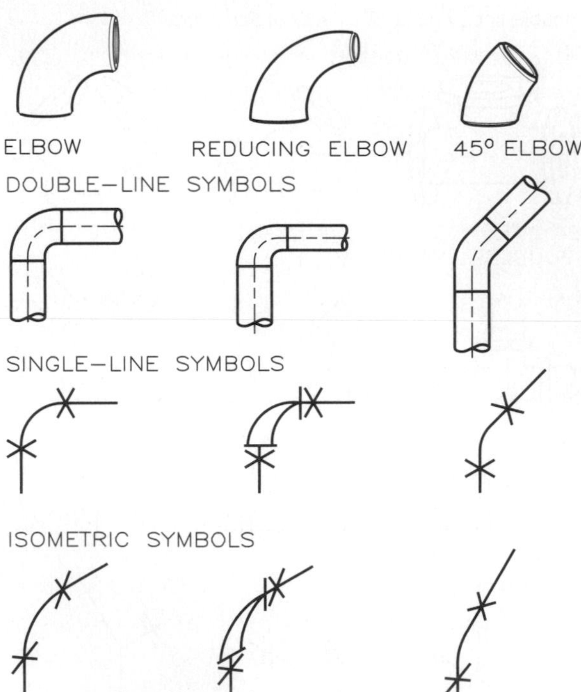

35.16 Examples of welded fittings along with the single-line and double-line symbols that are used to represent them.

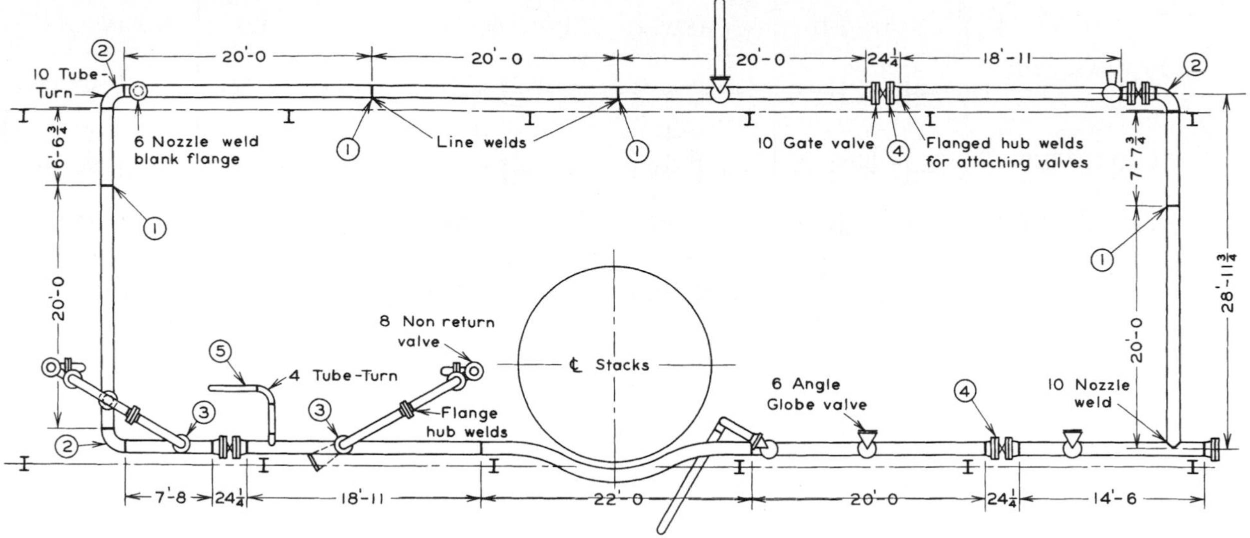

35.18 This piping layout uses a series of welded and flanged joints and is drawn using double-line symbols.

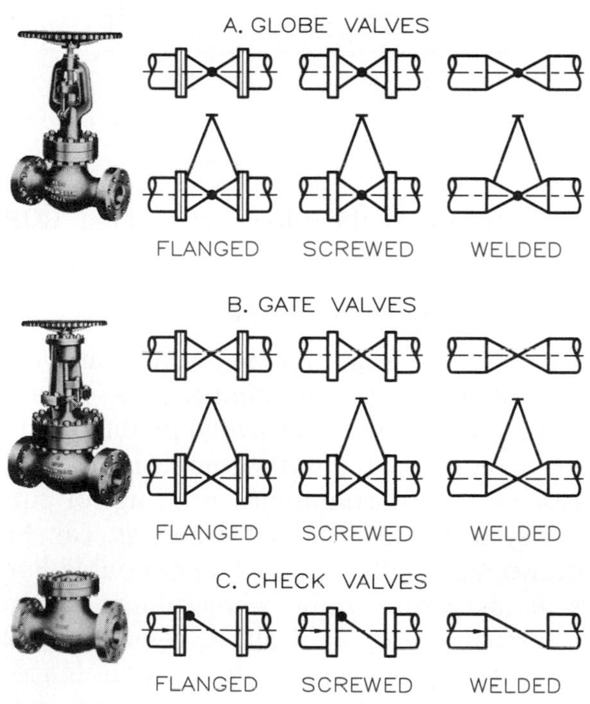

35.19 The three basic types of valves are gate, globe, and check valves. *(Photographs courtesy of Walworth/Aloyco.)*

Check valves restrict the flow in the pipe to only one direction. A backward flow is prevented by either a movable piston or a swinging washer activated by a reverse in the flow (**Figure 35.19**).

Orthographic symbols for types of valves are shown in **Figure 35.20**. These symbols can be converted to isometric as shown in **Figure 35.22**.

35.12 Fittings in Orthographic Views

Fittings and valves must be shown from any view in orthographic projection. Two and three views of typical fittings are shown in **Figure 35.8** as single-line screwed fittings. The same general principles are used to represent joints as double-line drawings. Observe the various views of the fittings and notice how the type of elbow can be shown by a slight variation in the adjacent views. The

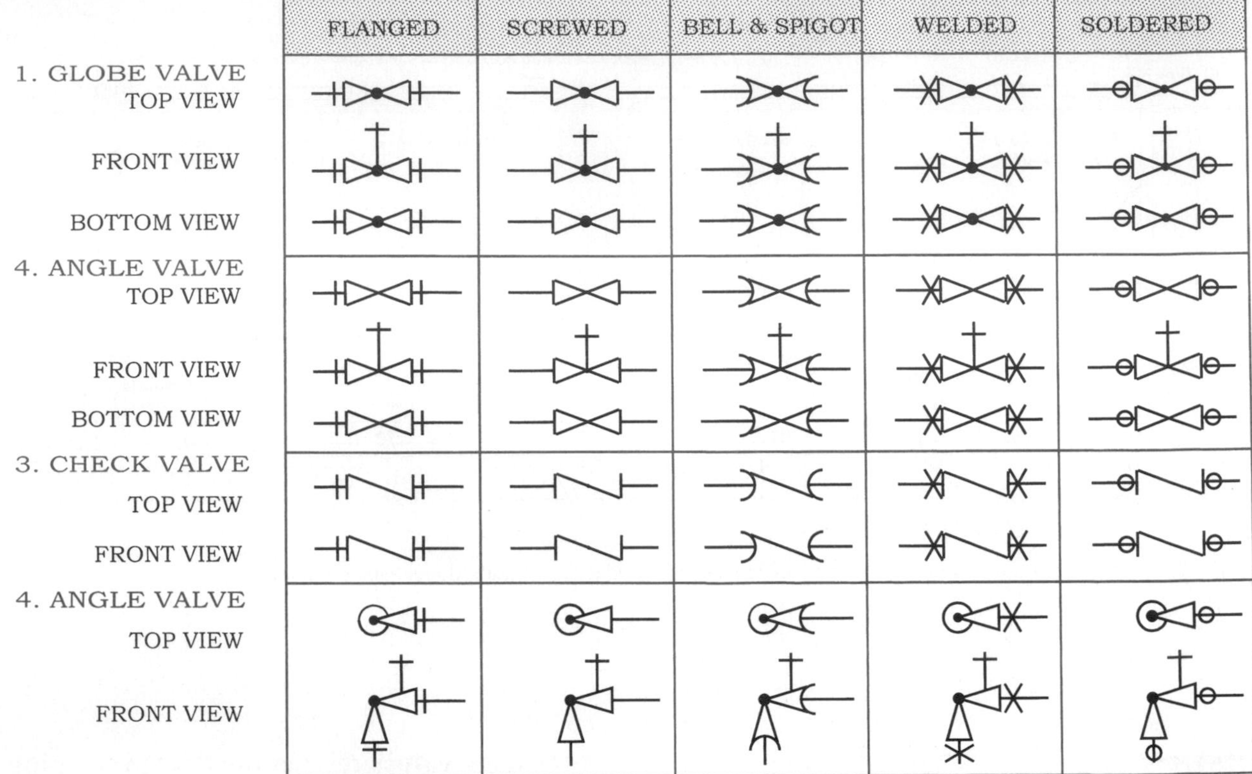

35.20 Examples of orthographic views of valves drawn as single-line symbols.

same techniques are used to represent tees and laterals.

A piping system is shown in a single orthographic view in **Figure 35.21**, where a combination of double-line and single-line symbols are drawn. Note that arrows are used to give the direction of flow in the system. Joints are screwed, welded, and flanged.

Horizontal elevation lines are given to dimension the heights of each horizontal pipe. Station 5 + 12-0-1/4″ represents a distance of 500 feet plus 12′-0-1/4″, or 512′-0-1/4″ from the beginning station point of 0 + 00.

The dimensions in **Figure 35.21** are measured from the centerlines of the pipes; this is indicated by the **CL** symbols. In some cases, the elevations of the pipes are dimensioned to the bottom of the pipe, abbreviated **BOP** (**Figure 35.25**).

35.13 Piping Systems in Pictorial

Isometric drawings of piping systems are very helpful in the representation of three-dimensional installations that would be difficult to interpret if drawn in orthographic projection. Isometric and axonometric drawings of piping systems, called **spool drawings**, can be drawn using either single-line or double-line symbols. A three-dimensional piping system is drawn orthographically in **Figure 35.22** with top and front views. Although this is a relatively simple three-dimensional system, a thorough understanding of orthographic projection is required to read the drawing.

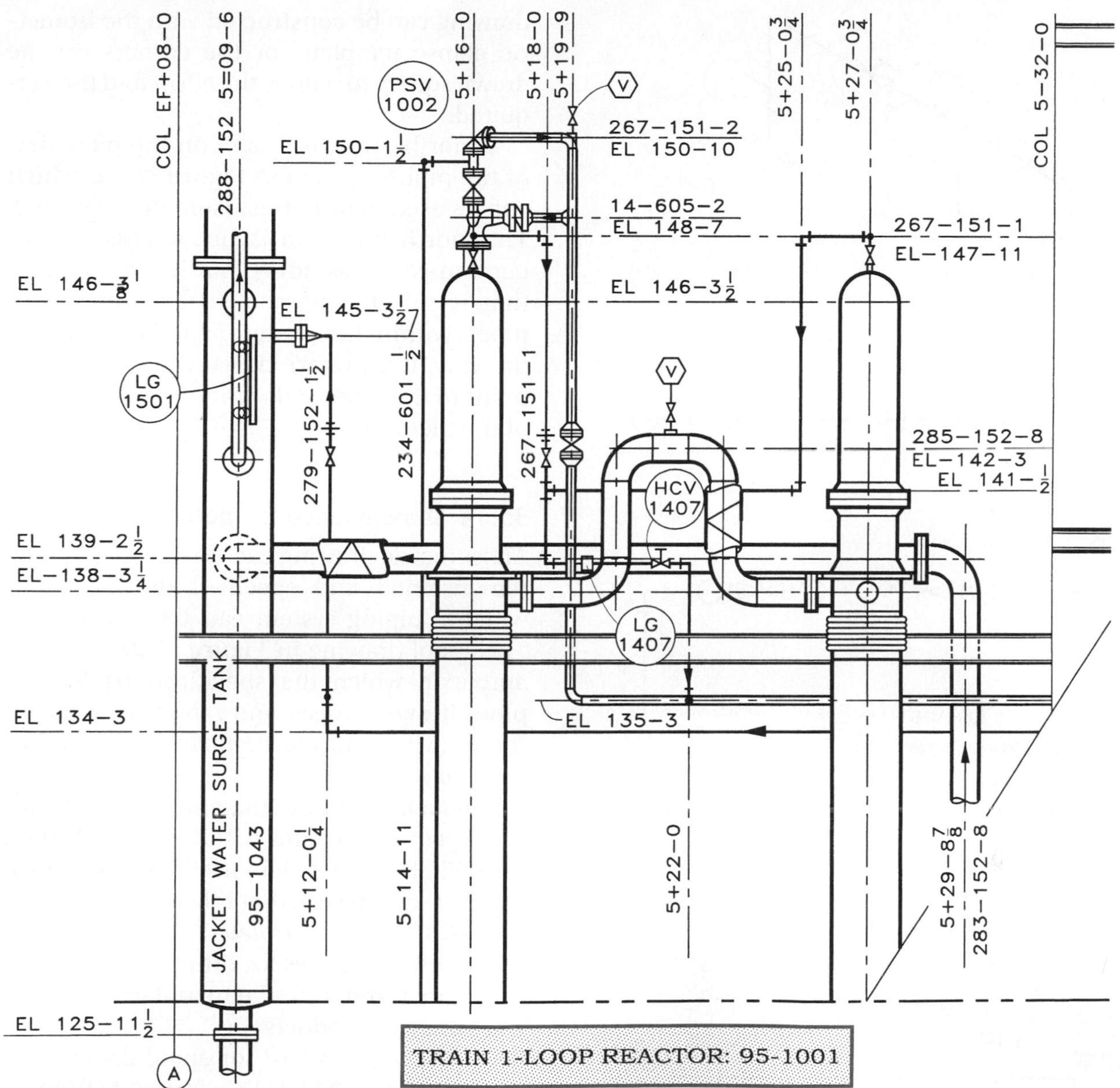

35.21 This piping system is drawn using a combination of single-line and double-line symbols. The connections are shown as screwed, welded, and flanged. *(Courtesy of Bechtel Corporation.)*

In **Figure 35.23**, the piping system is drawn with all the pipes revolved into the same horizontal plane. You will notice that the vertical pipes and their fittings are drawn true size in the top view. This is called a **developed pipe drawing**. The fittings and pipe sizes are noted on this preliminary sketch from which the finished drawing will be made in **Figure 35.24**.

An isometric schematic is drawn in **Figure 35.22** to explain the three-dimensional relationship of the parts of the system. The rounded bends in the elbows in an isometric

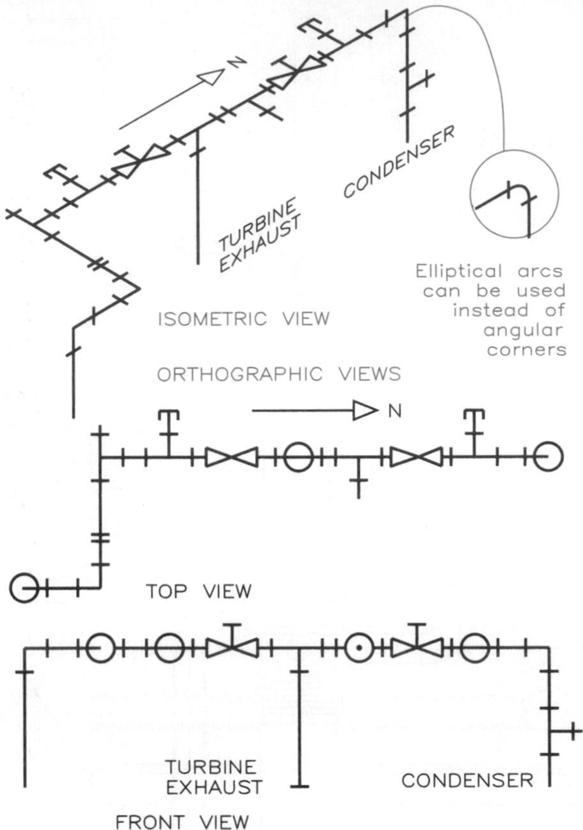

35.22 Top and front orthographic views are used as the basis for drawing a three-dimensional piping system using single-line symbols.

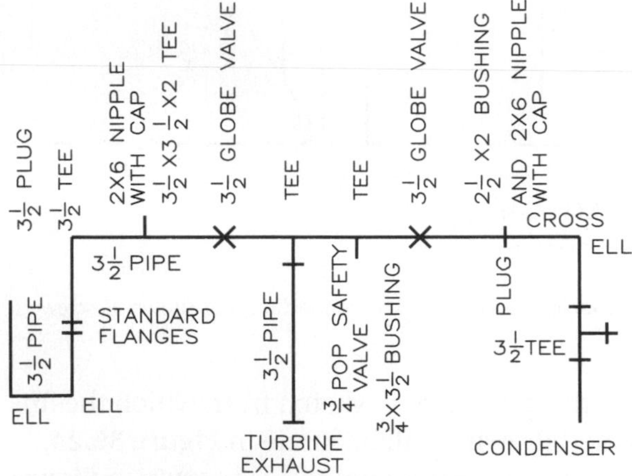

35.23 The vertical pipes shown in **Figure 35.22** are revolved into the horizontal plane to form a developed drawing. The fittings and valves are noted on the sketch.

drawing can be constructed with the isometric ellipse template, or the corners can be drawn square to reduce the effort and time required.

A north arrow is drawn on the plan view of the piping system in **Figure 35.22**, which can be used to orient the isometric pictorial. This north direction is not necessarily related to compass north, but it is a direction that is selected parallel to a major set of pipes within the system. In the isometric drawing, it is preferred that the north arrow point to the upper-left or upper-right corner of the pictorial.

35.14 Dimensioned Isometrics

An isometric drawing can be drawn as a fully dimensioned and specified drawing from which a piping system can be constructed. The spool drawing in **Figure 35.25** is an example in which the specifications for the pipe, fittings, flanges, and valves are noted on the drawing and are itemized in the bill of materials.

Under the column "materials," you will notice a code that begins with the letter A, such as A-53. The letter A is used to represent a grade of carbon steel that is listed in Table A of the *ANSI B31.3: Petroleum Refinery Piping Standards*. The codes for fittings, flanges, and valves are taken from the manufacturers' catalogs of these products.

A suggested format for spool drawings is given in **Figure 35.26**. This format is used by the Bechtel Corporation, a major construction company, in designing and constructing pipelines and refineries.

A number of abbreviations are used to specify piping components and fittings, as you can see by referring to the bill of materials. Many of the standard abbreviations associated with pipe drawings and specifications are given in **Table 35.2**. Part number 1, for example, is an

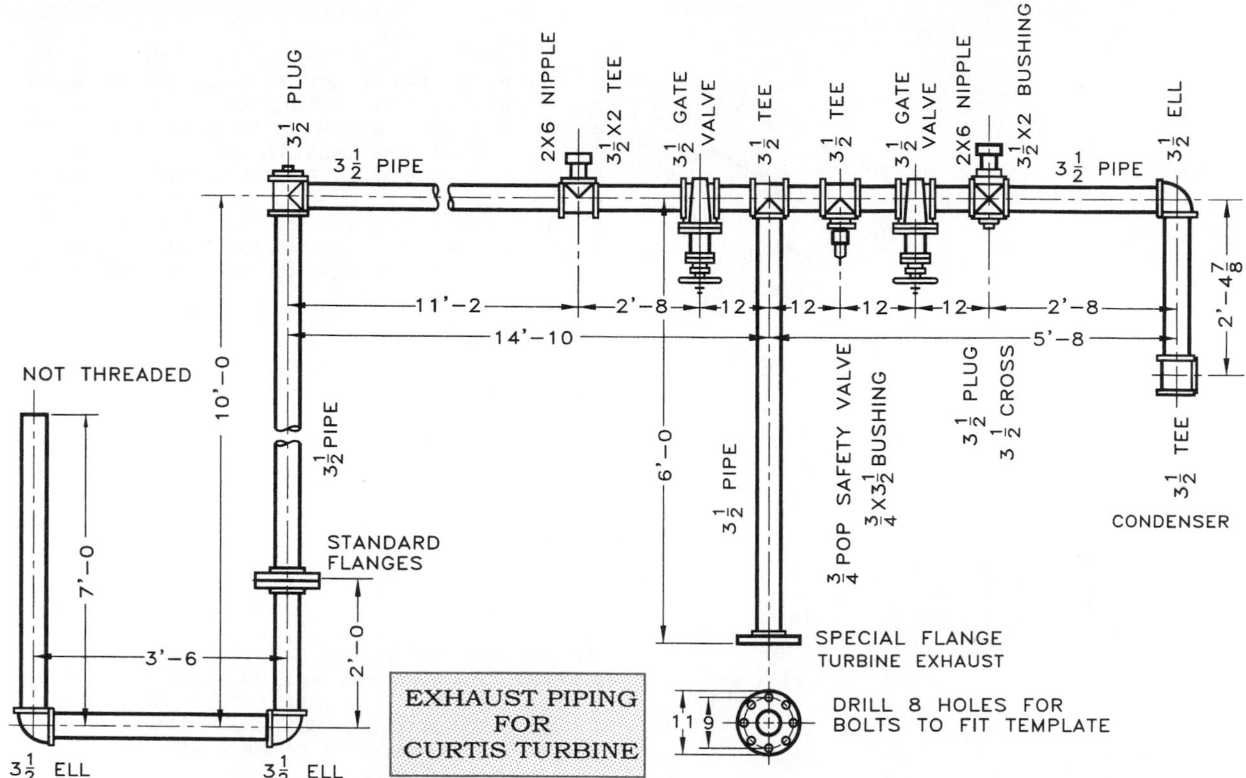

35.24 A finished developed drawing that shows all the components in the system true size with double-line symbols.

8-in. diameter pipe of a Schedule 40 weight that is made of seamless steel by the open hearth (OH) process. Instead of OH, the abbreviation EF may be used, which is the abbreviation for electric furnace.

35.15 Vessel Detailing

Vessels are containers, usually cylindrical in shape, that are used to contain petroleum products and other chemicals. The cylinders can be installed in vertical or horizontal positions. Vessels can also be spherical or ellipsoidal.

A detailed drawing of a cylindrical vessel is drawn and dimensioned with specifications by following the general rules of working drawings. In addition, the types of welded joints required are specified to ensure that the vessel is properly fabricated to withstand the pressures and weights to which it will be subjected.

35.16 Computer Drawings

Pipe drawings range from plumbing drawings of typical homes to offshore oil wells and similar large-scale applications. Due to the broadness of this field, several software packages have been developed for use by engineers and technicians who are responsible for the preparation of pipe drawings.

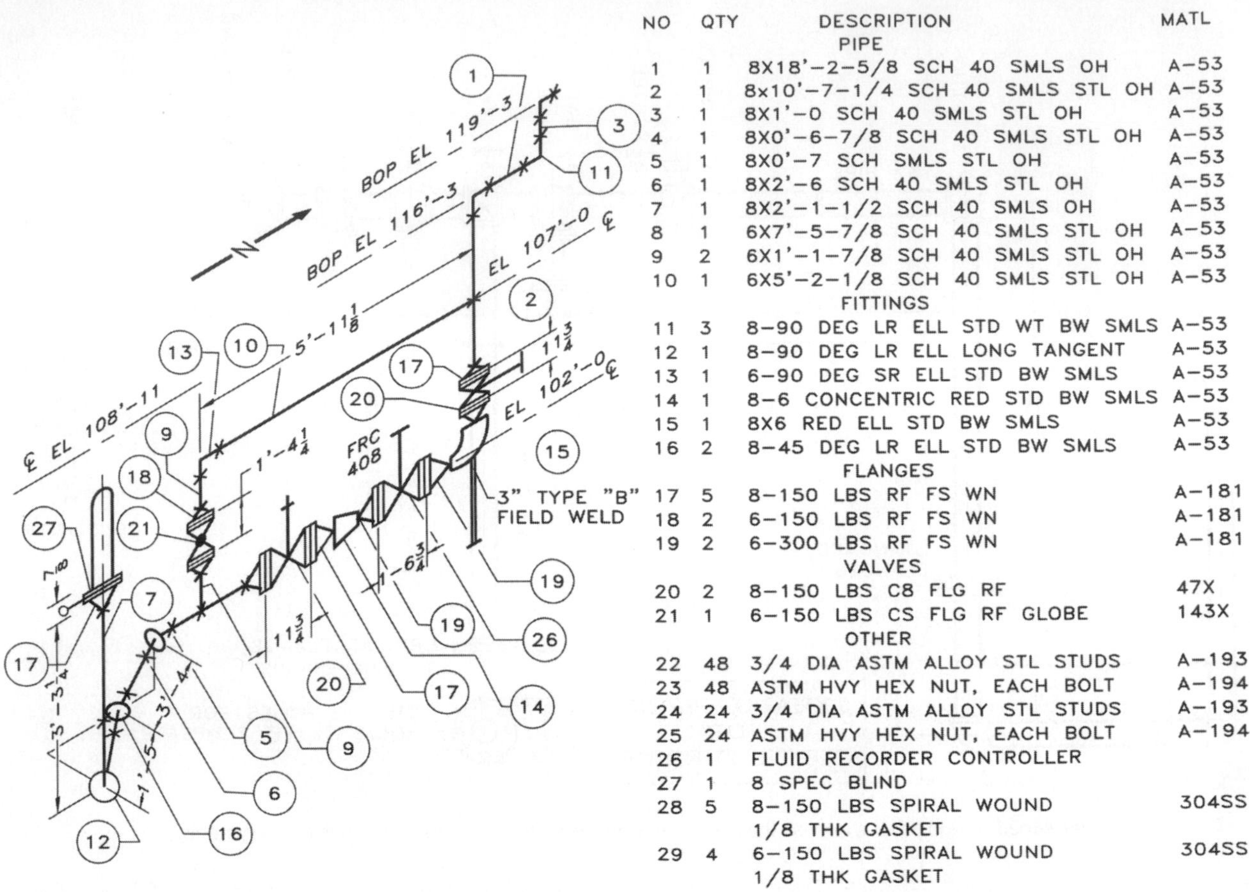

NO	QTY	DESCRIPTION	MATL
		PIPE	
1	1	8X18'-2-5/8 SCH 40 SMLS OH	A-53
2	1	8x10'-7-1/4 SCH 40 SMLS STL OH	A-53
3	1	8X1'-0 SCH 40 SMLS STL OH	A-53
4	1	8X0'-6-7/8 SCH 40 SMLS STL OH	A-53
5	1	8X0'-7 SCH SMLS STL OH	A-53
6	1	8X2'-6 SCH 40 SMLS STL OH	A-53
7	1	8X2'-1-1/2 SCH 40 SMLS OH	A-53
8	1	6X7'-5-7/8 SCH 40 SMLS STL OH	A-53
9	2	6X1'-1-7/8 SCH 40 SMLS STL OH	A-53
10	1	6X5'-2-1/8 SCH 40 SMLS STL OH	A-53
		FITTINGS	
11	3	8-90 DEG LR ELL STD WT BW SMLS	A-53
12	1	8-90 DEG LR ELL LONG TANGENT	A-53
13	1	6-90 DEG SR ELL STD BW SMLS	A-53
14	1	8-6 CONCENTRIC RED STD BW SMLS	A-53
15	1	8X6 RED ELL STD BW SMLS	A-53
16	2	8-45 DEG LR ELL STD BW SMLS	A-53
		FLANGES	
17	5	8-150 LBS RF FS WN	A-181
18	2	6-150 LBS RF FS WN	A-181
19	2	6-300 LBS RF FS WN	A-181
		VALVES	
20	2	8-150 LBS C8 FLG RF	47X
21	1	6-150 LBS CS FLG RF GLOBE	143X
		OTHER	
22	48	3/4 DIA ASTM ALLOY STL STUDS	A-193
23	48	ASTM HVY HEX NUT, EACH BOLT	A-194
24	24	3/4 DIA ASTM ALLOY STL STUDS	A-193
25	24	ASTM HVY HEX NUT, EACH BOLT	A-194
26	1	FLUID RECORDER CONTROLLER	
27	1	8 SPEC BLIND	
28	5	8-150 LBS SPIRAL WOUND 1/8 THK GASKET	304SS
29	4	6-150 LBS SPIRAL WOUND 1/8 THK GASKET	304SS

35.25 This dimensioned isometric pictorial is called a "spool drawing." It is sufficiently complete that it can serve as a working drawing when used with the bill of materials.

Models have been extensively used for the design and layout of complex systems—refineries, processing plants, and similar installations—because of the difficulty in representing the intricate details of three-dimensional piping systems in two-dimensional drawings. Models (by computer and by hand) are used to design, develop, and explain these projects with the supplementation of drawings (**Figure 35.26**).

The ability to use three-dimensional models made by computer has alleviated some of the need for shop-made models. Computer programs are available that enable the piping layout to be designed as a three-dimensional model on the screen, which permits the generation of views from any angle. An example of a pipe layout program is shown in **Figure 35.27**, where a pipe is shown being drawn as a rendered, three-dimensional model.

The area of pipe drafting is a complex study in graphics and technology worthy of a sizable textbook on this field alone. The coverage here was limited to a brief introduction to the basics of piping. The standards of pipe drafting vary to a notable degree from company to company.

Table 35.2 Standard Abbreviations Associated with Pipe Specifications

AVG	average	FS	forged steel	SPEC	specification
BC	bolt circle	FSS	forged stainless steel	SR	short radius
BE	beveled ends	FW	field weld	SS	stainless steel
BF	blind flange	GALV	galvanized	STD	standard
BM	bill of materials	GR	grade	STL	steel
BOP	bottom of pipe	ID	inside diameter	STM	steam
B&S	bell & spigot	INS	insulate	SW	socketweld
BWG	Birmingham wire gauge	IPS	iron pipe size	SWP	standard working pressure
CAS	cast alloy steel	LR	long radius	TC	test connection
CI	cast iron	LW	lap weld	TE	threaded end
CO	clean out	MI	malleable iron	TEMP	temperature
CONC	concentric	MFG	manufacture	T&G	tongue & groove
CPLG	coupling	OD	outside diameter	TOS	top of steel
CS	carbon steel, cast steel	OH	open hearth	TYP	typical
DWG	drawing	PE	plain end—not beveled	VC	vitrified clay
ECC	eccentric	PR	pair	WE	weld end
EF	electric furnace	RED	reducer	WN	weld neck
EFW	electric fusion weld	RF	raised face	WB	welded bonnet
ELEV	elevation	RTG or RJ	ring type joint	WT	weight
ERW	electric resistance weld	SCH	schedule	XS	extra strong
FF	flat face	SCRD	screwed	XXS	double extra strong
FLG	flange	SMLS	seamless		
FOB	flat on bottom	SO	slip-on		

Problems

1.–6. On a size A sheet, draw five orthographic views of the fittings listed below, including the front, top, bottom, and the left- and right-side views. Draw two per sheet using the following specifications.

1. Single-line, screwed fittings. Draw the following fittings: 90° ell, 45° ell, tee, lateral, cap, reducing ell, cross, concentric reducer, check valve, union, globe valve, gate valve, and bushing as single-line, screwed fittings.

2. Single-line, flanged fittings. Same as problem 1, but draw the fittings as flanged fittings.

3. Single-line, welded fittings. Same as problem 1, but draw the fittings as welded fittings.

4. Double-line, screwed fittings. Same as problem 1, but draw the fittings as double-line, screwed fittings.

5. Double-line, flanged fittings. Same as problem 1, but draw the fittings as double-line, flanged fittings.

6. Double-line, welded fittings. Same as problem 1, but draw the fittings as double-line, welded fittings.

7. Two-view, single-line drawing. Convert the single-line sketch in **Figure 35.28** into a two-view, single-line drawing that will fit on a size A sheet.

8. Two-view, double-line drawing.

A. Convert the single-line pipe system in **Figure 35.29** into a double-line drawing with screwed fittings that will fit on a size B sheet,

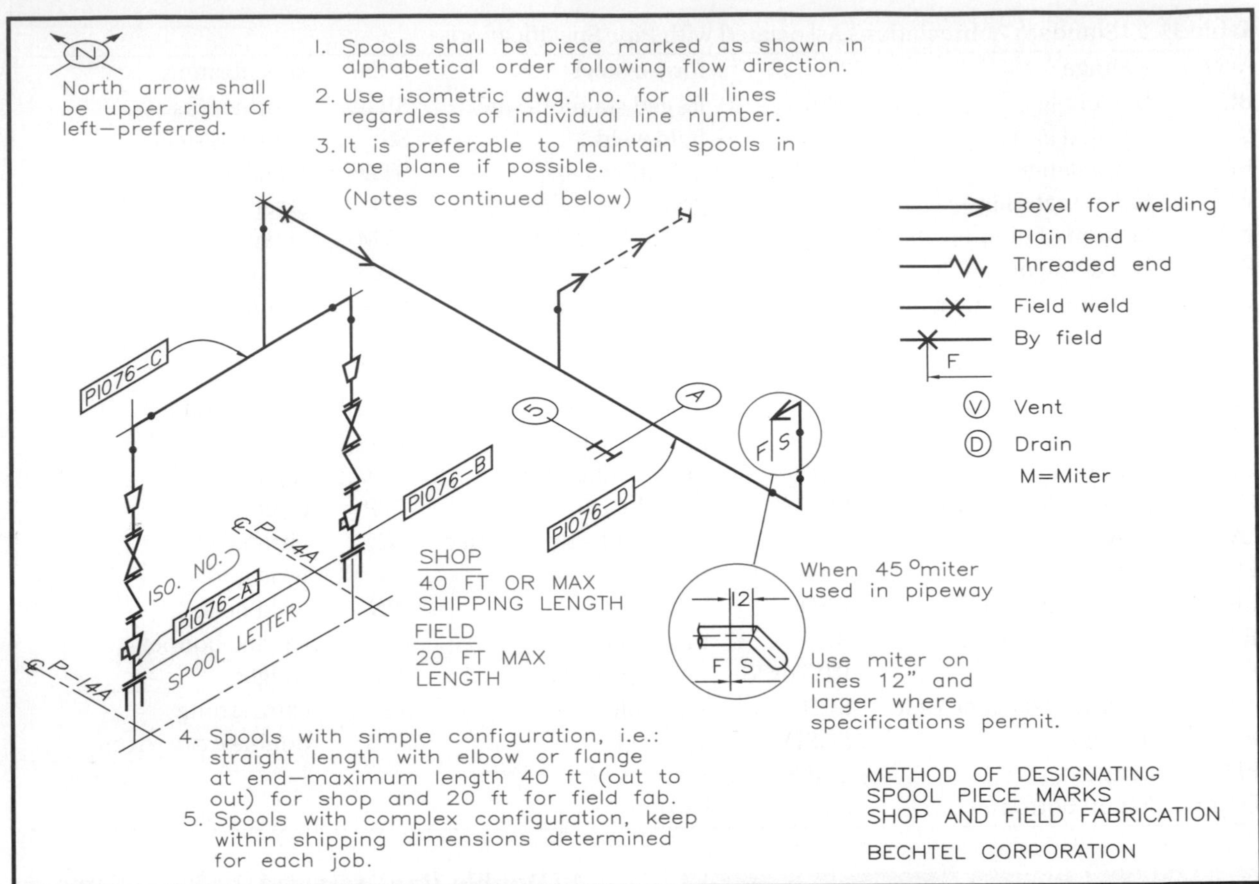

North arrow shall be upper right of left—preferred.
I. Spools shall be piece marked as shown in alphabetical order following flow direction.
2. Use isometric dwg. no. for all lines regardless of individual line number.
3. It is preferable to maintain spools in one plane if possible.
(Notes continued below)
Bevel for welding
Plain end
Threaded end
Field weld
By field
F
Vent
Drain
M=Miter
PI076–C
PI076–B
PI076–D
PI076–A
ISO. NO.
SPOOL LETTER
SHOP
40 FT OR MAX SHIPPING LENGTH
FIELD
20 FT MAX LENGTH
When 45° miter used in pipeway
Use miter on lines 12" and larger where specifications permit.
4. Spools with simple configuration, i.e.: straight length with elbow or flange at end—maximum length 40 ft (out to out) for shop and 20 ft for field fab.
5. Spools with complex configuration, keep within shipping dimensions determined for each job.
METHOD OF DESIGNATING SPOOL PIECE MARKS SHOP AND FIELD FABRICATION
BECHTEL CORPORATION

35.26 A suggested format for preparing spool drawings from a company standard. *(Courtesy of the Bechtel Corporation.)*

using the graphical scale given in the drawing to select the best scale for the system.

B. Same as A but draw the layout with single-line, welded joints.

9. Single-line, screwed fittings. Convert the pipe system in **Figure 35.30** into a single-line orthographic (screwed joints) drawing that will fit on a size A sheet.

10. Double-line, screwed fittings. Convert the pipe system given in **Figure 35.22** into a two-view orthographic drawing using double-line symbols that will fit on a size B sheet.

11. Single-line, screwed fittings. Convert the isometric drawing of the pipe system in **Figure 35.25** into a two-view orthographic drawing that will fit on a size B sheet. Take the measurements from the given drawing, and select a convenient scale.

12. Double-line, welded fittings. Convert the isometric drawing of the pipe system in **Figure 35.26** into a two-view, double-line orthographic drawing that will fit on a size B sheet.

13. Single-line isometric drawing. Convert the orthographic pipe system in **Figure 35.13** into a single-line isometric drawing that will fit on a size B sheet. Estimate the dimensions.

14. Double-line orthographic drawing. Convert the orthographic pipe system in **Figure 35.13** into a double-line orthographic view that will fit on a size B sheet.

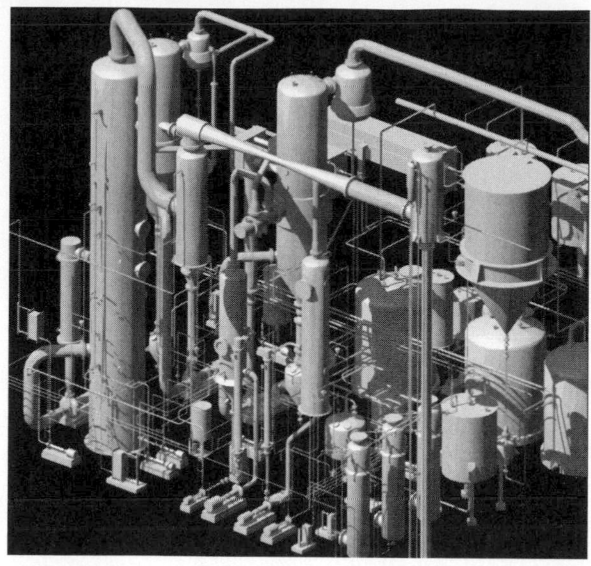

35.27 Models (by computer or by hand) are often necessary in the design, development, and explanation of piping installations. *(Courtesy of Coade, Inc.)*

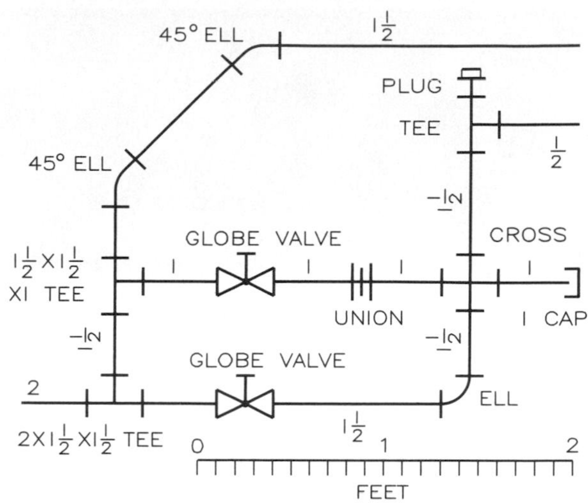

35.29 Problem 8.

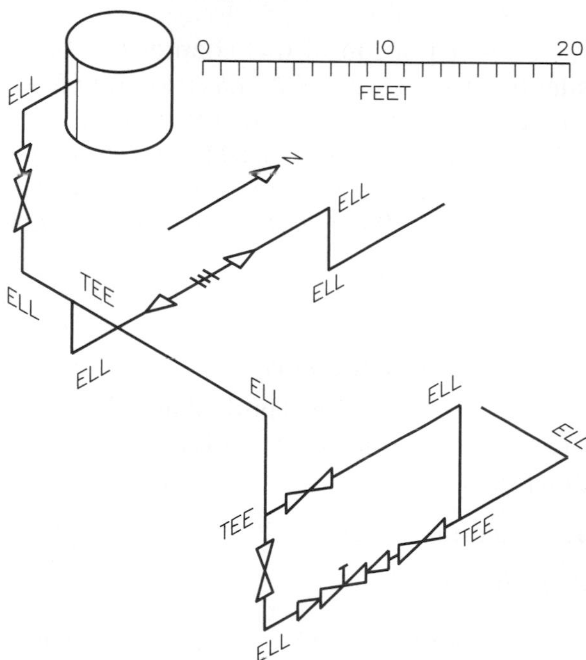

35.28 Problem 7.

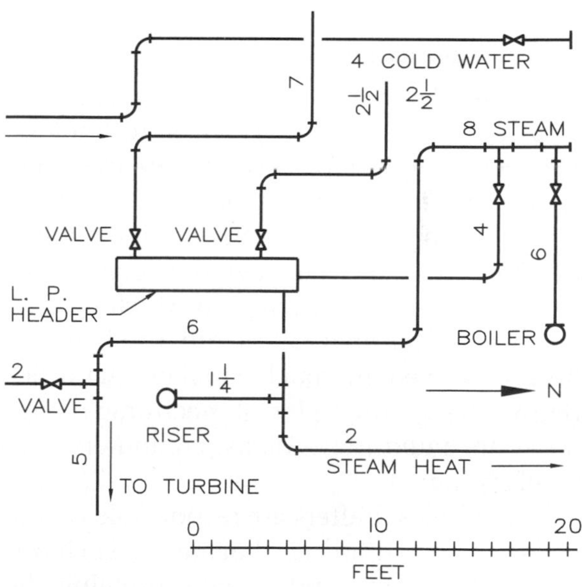

35.30 Problem 9.

36 Electrical/Electronics Graphics

36.1 Introduction

Electrical/electronics graphics is a specialty area of the field of graphics technology. **Electrical** graphics is related to the transmission of electrical power that is used in large quantities in homes and industry for lighting, heating, and equipment operation. **Electronics** graphics deals with circuits in which transistors and electronic tubes are used, where power is used in much smaller quantities (**Figure 36.1**). Examples of electronic equipment are radios, televisions, computers, and similar products.

Electronics drafters are responsible for the preparation of drawings that are used in fabricating the circuit and thereby bringing the product into being. They work from sketches and specifications developed by the engineer or electronics technologist. This chapter reviews the practices that are necessary for the preparation of electronics diagrams.

A major portion of this chapter has been adapted from *ANSI Y14.15, Electrical and Electronics Diagrams,* the standards that regulate the graphics techniques used in this area. The symbols used were taken from *ANSI Y32.2, Graphic Symbols for Electrical and Electronics Diagrams.*

36.2 Types of Diagrams

Electronic circuits are classified and drawn in the format of one of the following types of diagrams:

1. Single-line diagrams
2. Schematic diagrams
3. Connection diagrams

The suggested line weights for drawing these types of diagrams are shown in **Figure 36.2**.

36.1 The typical electronic installation comprises printed circuit boards, transistors, and microchips.

APPLICATION	LINE THICKNESS
General use	Medium
Mechanical connection: shielding and future circuits line	Medium (dashed)
Bracket connecting dashed line	Medium (dashed)
Brackets, leader lines, etc.	Thin
Mechanical-grouping boundary lines	Thin (dashed)
For emphasis	Thick

(Brackets, leader lines, mechanical-grouping boundary lines, and for emphasis: Optional thicknesses)

36.2 The recommended line weights for drawing electronics diagrams.

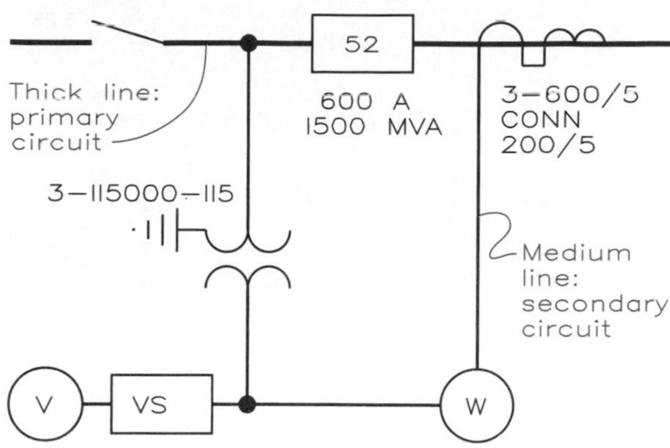

36.3 A portion of a single-line diagram where heavy lines represent the primary circuits, and medium lines represent the connections to the current and potential sources.

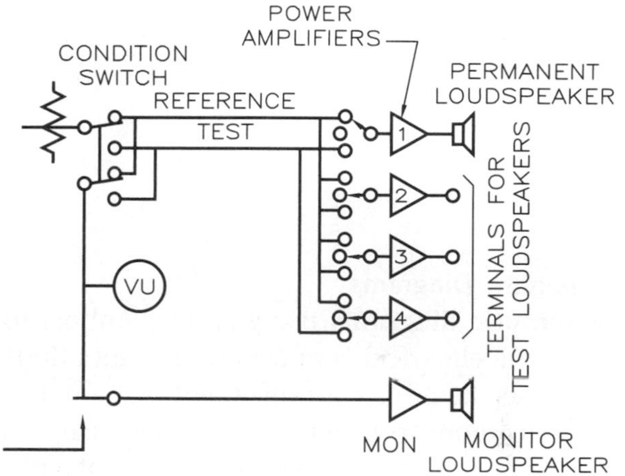

36.4 A typical single-line diagram for illustrating a circuit. Its basic functions are shown, but many of the details, components, and their ratings that are shown in a schematic, are omitted.

Single-Line Diagrams

Single-line diagrams are drawn with single lines and general symbols that are adequate to trace the flow of current through the circuit and obtain a basic understanding of the parts and devices within it. Descriptions of the circuit components are not specified in detail. Single lines are used to represent both AC and DC systems, as illustrated in **Figure 36.3**. An example of a single-line diagram of an audio system is shown in **Figure 36.4**. Primary circuits are indicated by thick connecting lines, and medium lines are used to represent connections to the current and potential sources.

Single-line diagrams show the connections of meters, major equipment, and instruments. Ratings are often given to supplement the graphic symbols to provide such information as kilowatts, voltages, cycles and revolutions per minute, and generator ratings (**Figure 36.5**).

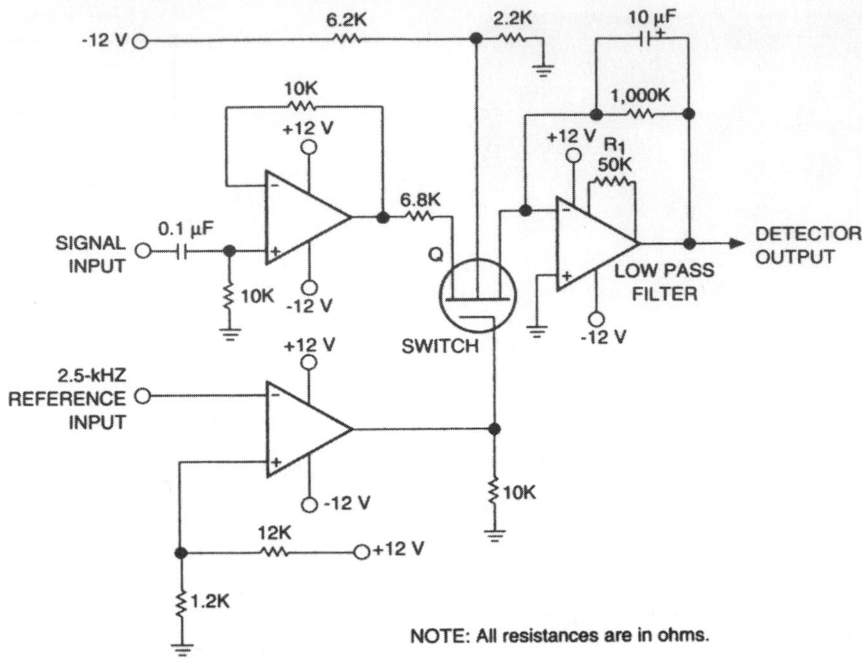

36.5 A single-line diagram illustrates a switching circuit complete with notation of device designations. *(Courtesy of NASA.)*

Schematic Diagrams

Schematic diagrams use graphic symbols to show the electrical connections and functions of a specific circuit arrangement. Schematics provide more information and specifications that are necessary for the composition of a circuit than do single-line diagrams. Although a schematic diagram enables one to trace the circuit and its functions, physical sizes, shapes, and locations of various components are not shown. The schematic diagram in **Figure 36.6** can be referred to for many applications of the principles covered in this chapter.

Connection Diagrams

Connection diagrams show the connections and installations of the parts and devices of the system. In addition to showing the internal connections, external connections, or both, they show the physical arrangement of the parts. Such a diagram can be described as an *installation diagram,* such as the one shown in **Figure 36.7**.

36.3 Schematic Diagram Connecting Symbols

The most basic symbols of a circuit are those used to represent connections of parts within the circuit. Connections, or junctions, are indicated by abutting lines with no dots or with dots at the junctions (**Figure 36.8**). The dots emphasize points of junction between connecting lines and those that simply pass over another. The use of dots to show connections is optional, but it is preferable to omit them if clarity is not sacrificed.

When crossover lines have a loop at the crossing point, it very clear that there is not a junction. However, the lines are assumed to be nonintersecting when a loop is not given.

When the layout of a circuit does not permit the use of no-dot junctions, and lines within

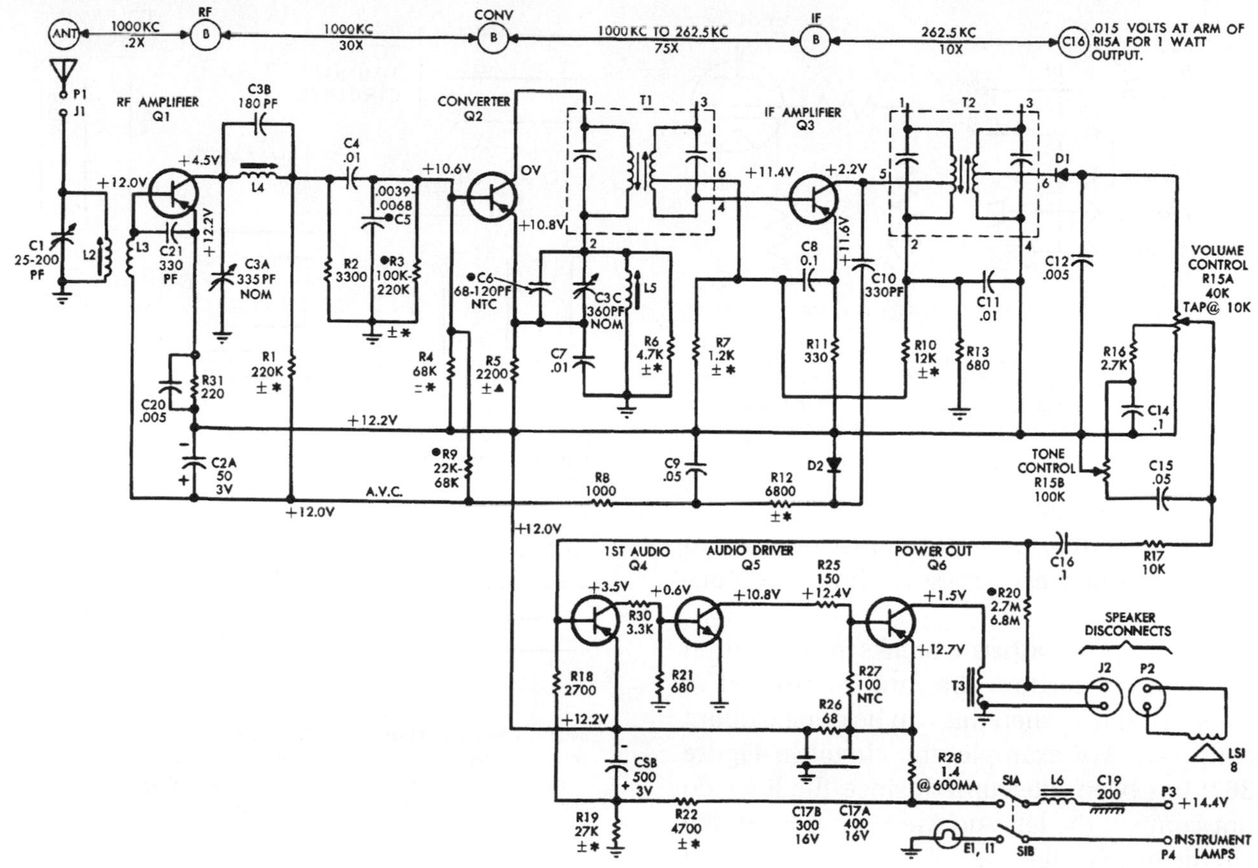

36.6 A typical schematic diagram of an AM radio circuit with all parts of the system labeled. *(Courtesy of Ford Motor Company.)*

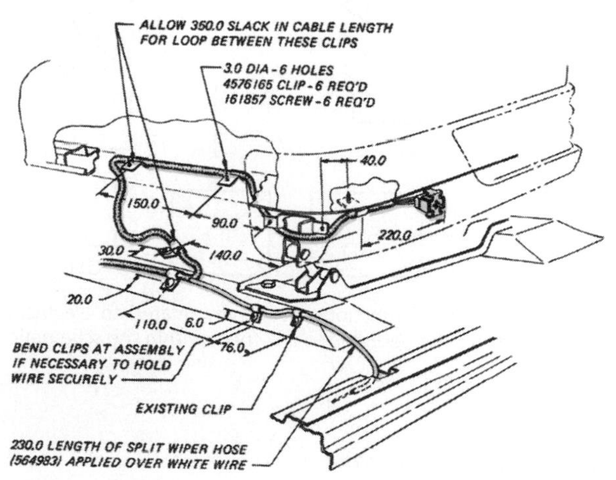

36.7 This three-dimensional connection diagram shows the circuit and its components with the necessary details to explain how it is connected or installed. *(Courtesy of the General Motors Corporation.)*

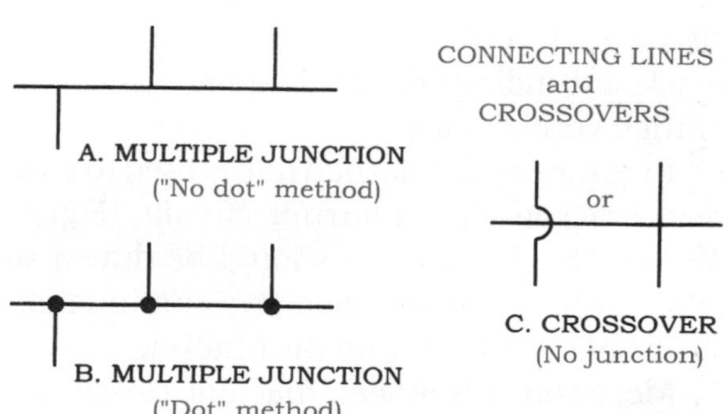

36.8 Connections can be shown with no dots at junctions, as shown at (A), or dots may be used to emphasize connections, as shown at (B). Crossovers with loops clarify that the lines do not intersect, as shown at (C), but crossovers with no dots are meant to indicate no junction, too, and are preferred if clarity is not compromised.

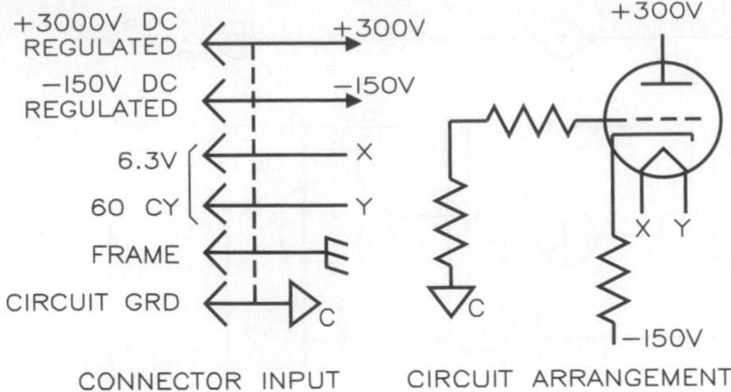

36.9 Circuits may be interrupted and connections not shown by lines if they are properly labeled to clarify their relationship to the removed part of the circuit. The connections here are labeled to match those on the left and right sides of the illustration.

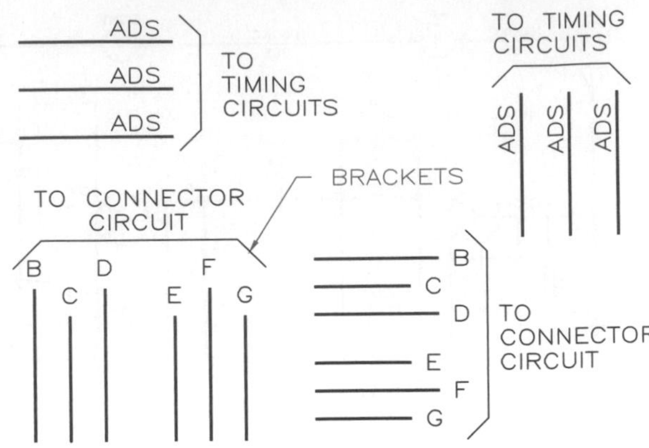

36.10 Brackets and notes may be used to specify the destinations of interrupted circuits, as shown in this illustration.

the circuit cross, then dots must be used to distinguish between crossover lines and connecting lines.

Interrupted paths are breaks in lines within a schematic diagram that are interrupted to conserve space when this can be done without confusion. For example, the circuit in **Figure 36.9** has been interrupted, since the lines do not connect the left and the right sides of the circuit. Instead, the ends of the lines are labeled to correspond to the matching notes at the other side of the interrupted circuit.

Sometimes, sets of lines in a horizontal or vertical direction will be interrupted (**Figure 36.10**). Brackets will be used to interrupt the circuit and notes will be placed outside the brackets to indicate the destinations of the wires or their connections.

In some cases, a dashed line is used to connect brackets that interrupt circuits (**Figure 36.11**). The dashed line should be drawn so that it will not be mistaken as a continuation of one of the lines within the bracket.

Mechanical linkages that are closely related to electronic functions may be shown as part of a schematic diagram (**Figure 36.12**). An arrangement of this type helps clarify the relationship of the electronics circuit with the mechanical components.

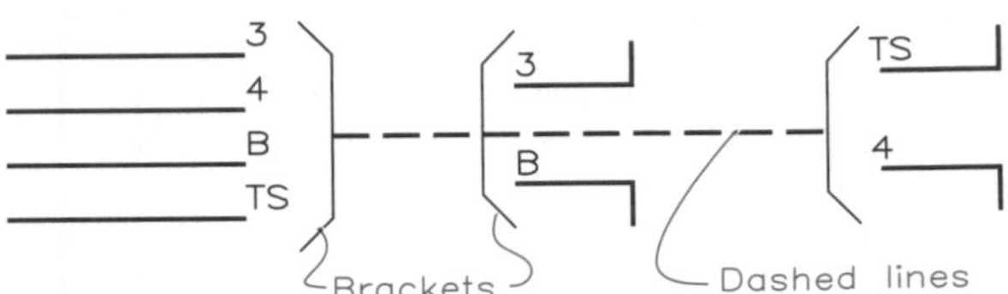

36.11 The connections of interrupted circuits can be indicated by using brackets and a dashed line in addition to labeling the lines. The dashed line should not be drawn to appear as an extension of one of the lines in the circuit.

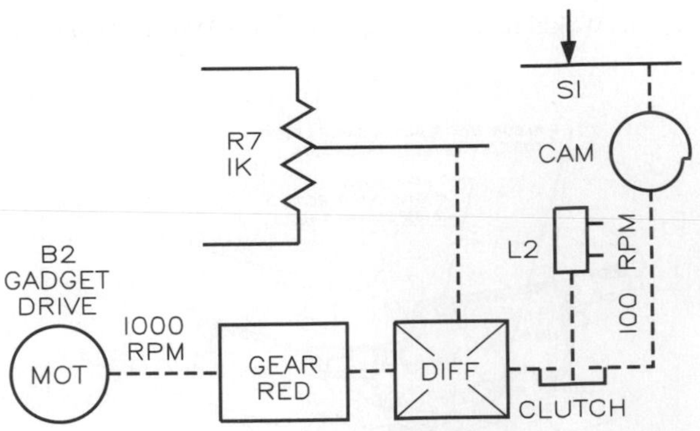

36.12 If mechanical functions are closely related to electrical functions, it may be desirable to link them within the schematic diagram.

36.4 Graphic Symbols

The electronics drafter must be familiar with the basic graphic symbols that are used to represent the parts and devices within the

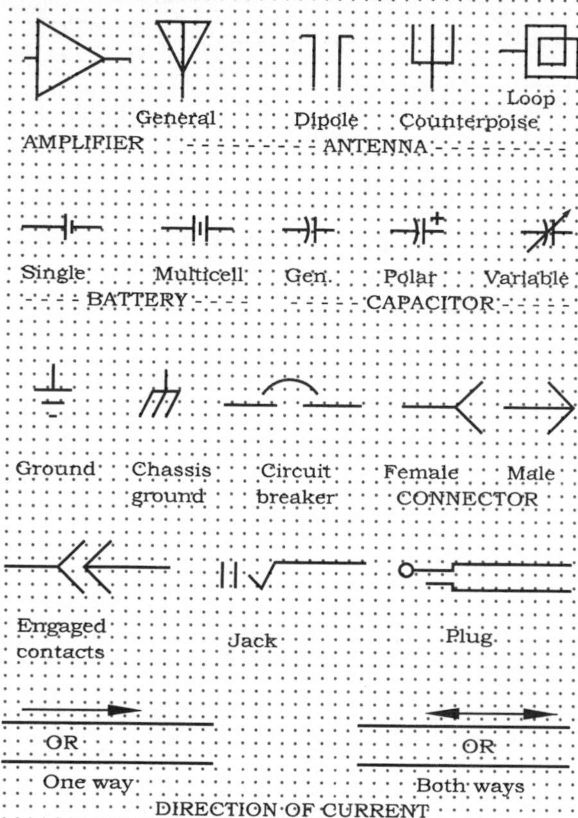

36.13 The proportions of these symbols are drawn on a 3-mm (.13-in.) grid that gives their sizes when enlarged to full size.

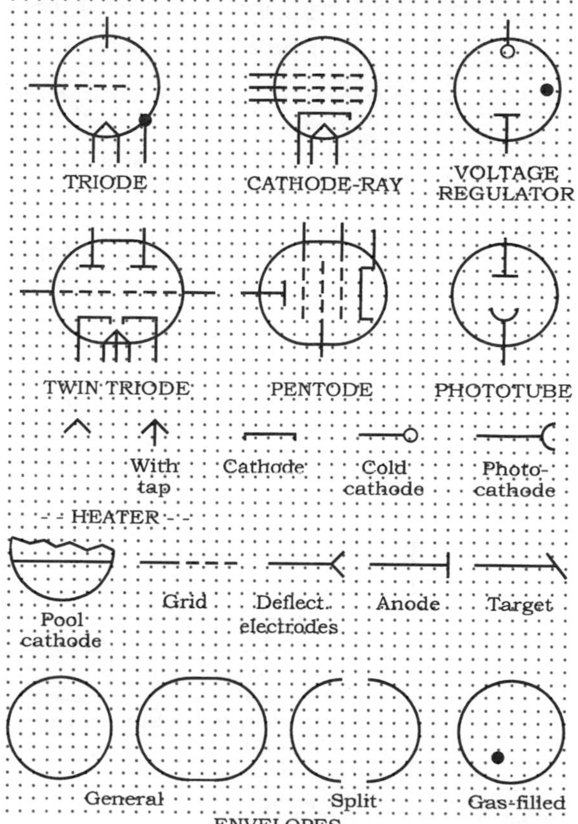

36.14 The upper six symbols are used to represent often-used types of electron tubes drawn on a 3-mm (0.13-in.) grid. An explanation of the parts that make up each symbol is given in the lower half of the figure. (Electron tubes have been mostly replaced by transistors.)

electrical and electronics circuits shown in **Figures 36.13–36.17**. These symbols, extracted from the *ANSI Y32.2* standard, are adequate for practically all diagrams. However, when a highly specialized part needs to be shown and a symbol for it is not provided in these standards, it is permissible for the drafter to develop his or her own symbol provided it is properly labeled and its meaning clearly conveyed.

The symbols shown in **Figures 36.13–36.17** are drawn on a grid of 3-mm (0.13-in.) squares that have been reduced. The size of this grid is equal to the letter height used on the final drawing. It is general practice to size graphic symbols based on letter height, since text and numerals cannot be enlarged or reduced as easily as graphic symbols without affecting readability. Symbols may be drawn larger or smaller to fit the size of your layout provided the relative proportions of the symbols are kept about the same.

The symbols in **Figures 36.13–36.17** are but a few of the more commonly used symbols. There are between 500 and 600 different symbols in the ANSI standards for variations of the basic electrical/electronics symbols.

Preparation of a schematic diagram begins with drawing a freehand sketch to show the circuit and the placement of its components

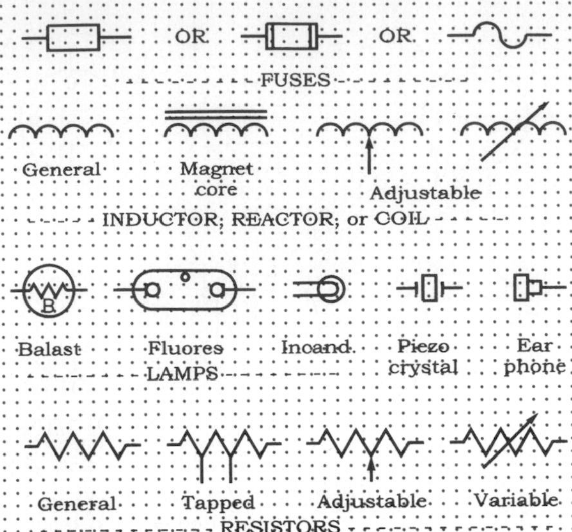

36.15 Graphics symbols of standard circuit components drawn on a 3-mm (0.13-in.) grid.

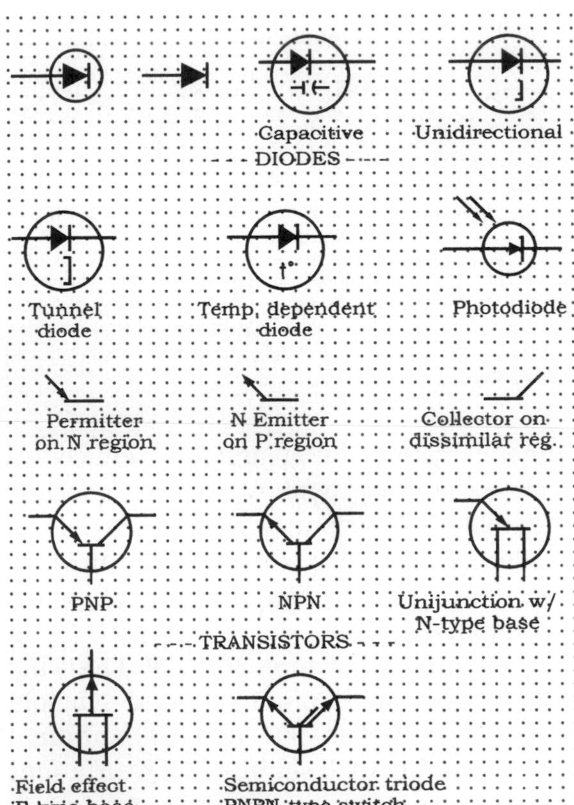

36.16 Graphic symbols for semiconductor devices and transistors drawn on a 3-mm (.13-in.) grid. The arrows in the middle of the figure illustrate the meanings of the arrows used in the transistor symbols shown below them.

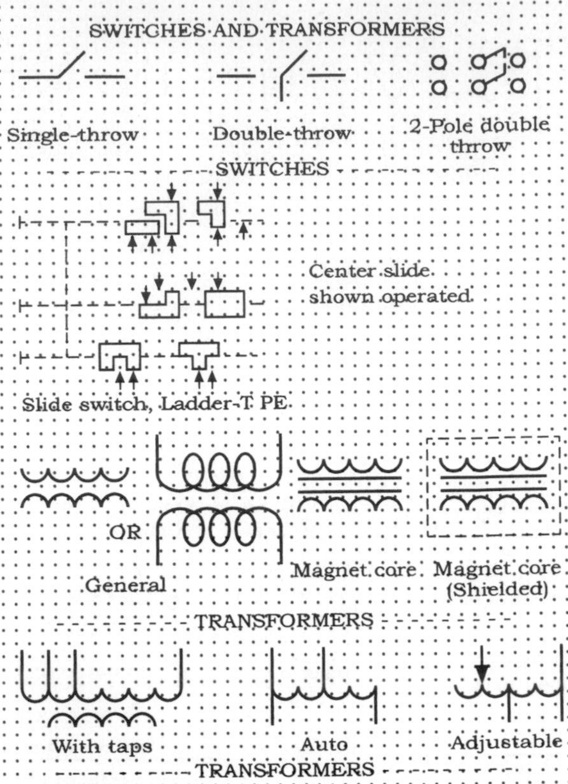

36.17 Graphic symbols for representing switches and transformers drawn on a 3-mm (.13-in.) grid.

(**Figure 36.18A**). Next, an instrument drawing can be made by hand or by computer showing the components at the proper scale and designations added (**Figure 36.18B**).

Some of the symbols have been noted to provide designations of their sizes or ratings. The need for this additional information depends on the requirements and the usage of the schematic diagrams.

36.5 Terminals

Terminals are the ends of the circuit where devices are attached with connecting wires. Examples of devices with terminals that are specified in circuit diagrams are switches, relays, and transformers. The graphic symbol for a terminal is an open circle that is the same size as the solid circle used to indicate a connection.

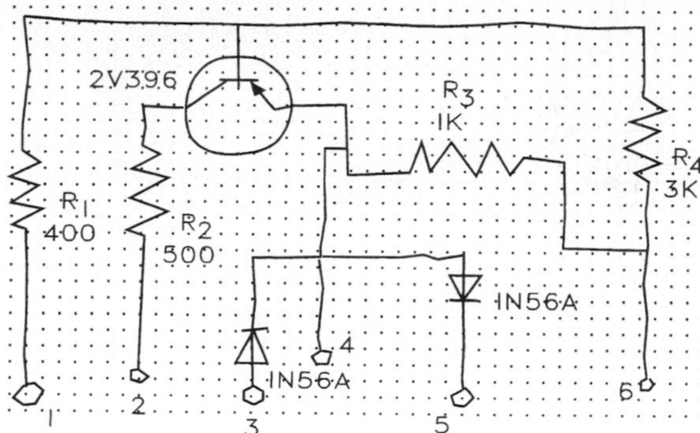

A. A RAPID FREEHAND SKETCH

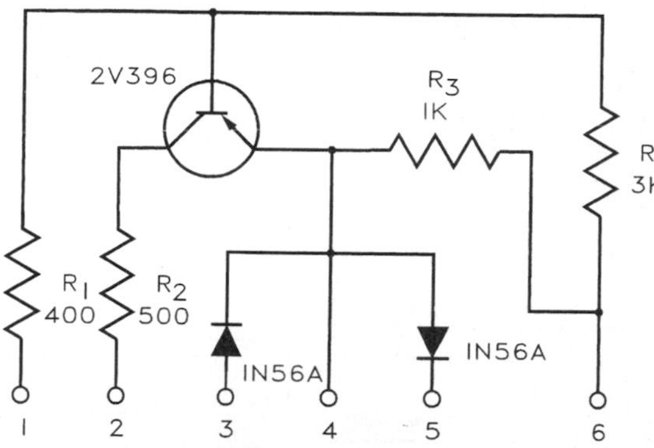

B. AN INSTRUMENT DRAWING

36.18 Drawing a diagram from a sketch.

Step 1 The circuit designer can make a freehand sketch of a circuit as a preliminary drawing.

Step 2 The final drawing of the circuit is made using the proper symbols and lines.

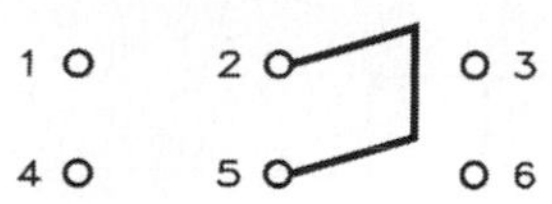

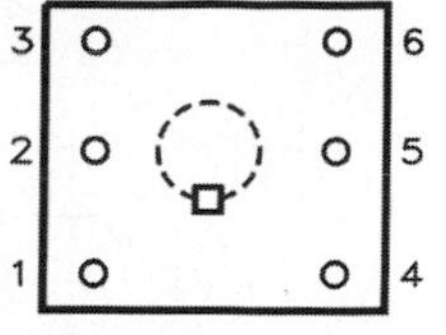

A. Schematic diagram symbol

B. Diagram showing the terminal orientation associated with note

36.19 An example of a method of labeling the terminals of a toggle switch on a schematic diagram (left) and a diagram that illustrates the toggle switch when it is viewed from its rear (right).

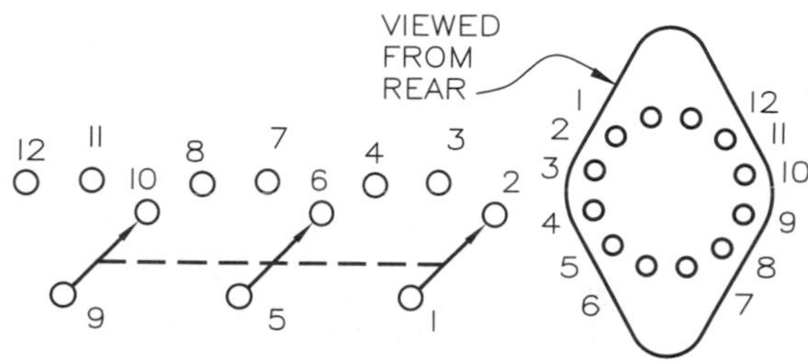

A. SYMBOL ON SCHEMATIC DIAGRAM

B. TERMINAL ORIENTATION DIAGRAM ASSOCIATED WITH NOTE

36.20 An example of a rotary switch as it would appear on a schematic diagram (left) and a diagram that shows the numbered terminals of the switch when viewed from its rear.

Switches are used to turn a circuit on or off, or else to actuate a certain part of it while turning another off (**Figure 36.17**). Examples of switches, labeled S1A and S1B, are shown in the lower right of **Figure 36.6**.

When a group of parts is enclosed or shielded (drawn enclosed with dashed lines) and the terminal circles have been omitted, the terminal markings should be placed immediately outside the enclosure, as shown in **Figure 36.6** at T1 and T2 at the upper side. The terminal identifications should be added to the graphic symbols that correspond to the actual physical markings that appear on or near the terminals of the part (not given in this diagram). Several examples of notes and symbols that explain the parts of a circuit diagram are shown in **Figures 36.19–36.21**.

When colored wires, numbers, or geometric symbols are used to identify the various leads or terminals of multilead parts, show this identification near the connecting line adjacent to the symbol. Colored wires can be identified on a diagram with color abbreviations to denote their color.

Rotary terminals are used to regulate the resistance in some circuits, and the direction of rotation of the dial is indicated on the schematic diagram. The abbreviations CW (clockwise) or CCW (counterclockwise) are placed adjacent to the movable contact when it is in its extreme clockwise position, as shown in **Figure 36.22A**. The movable contact can be identified by an arrow at its end.

If the device terminals are not marked, numbers may be used with the resistor symbol

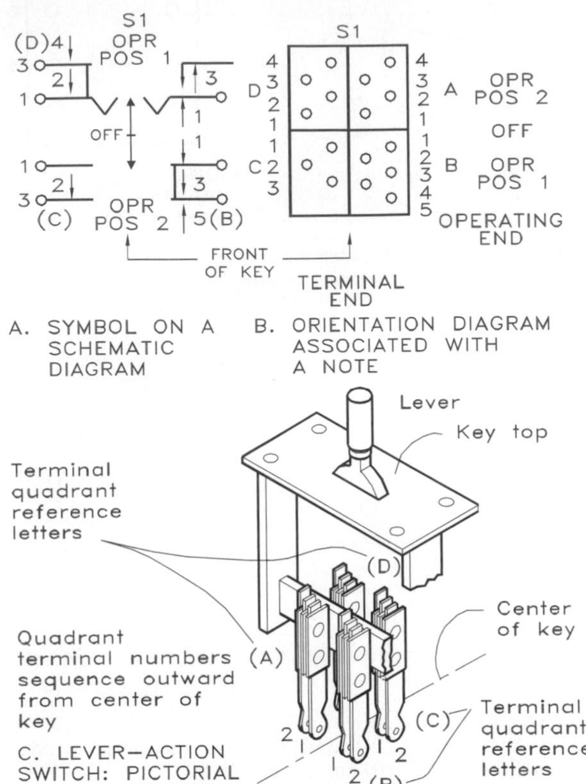

36.21 (A) An example of a typical lever switch as it would appear on a schematic diagram. (B) An orientation diagram that shows the terminal end and the numbered terminals of the switch when viewed from its operating end. (C) A pictorial of the lever switch and its four quadrants.

and the number 2 assigned to the adjustable contact (**Figure 36.22B**). Other fixed taps may be sequentially numbered and added as shown in part C.

The position of a switch as it relates to the function of a circuit should be indicated on a schematic diagram. A method of showing functions of a variable switch is shown in **Figure 36.23**. The arrow, representing the movable end of the switch, can be positioned to connect with several circuits. The different functional positions of the rotary switch are shown both by symbol and by table.

Another method of representing a rotary switch is shown in **Figure 36.24** by symbol

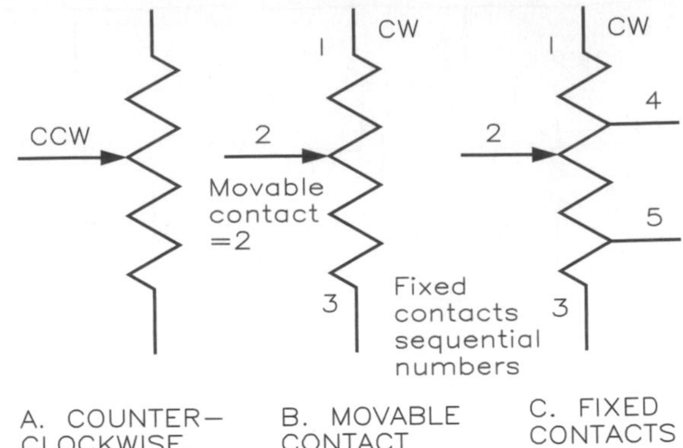

36.22 To indicate the direction of rotation of rotary switches on a schematic diagram, the abbreviations CW (clockwise) and CCW (counterclockwise) are placed near the movable contact (A). If the device terminals are not marked, numbers may be used with the resistor symbols and the number 2 assigned to the adjustable contact (B). Additional contacts may be labeled as shown at (C).

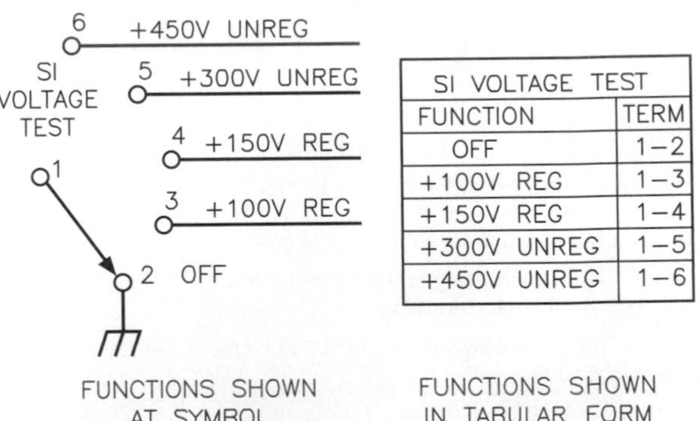

SI VOLTAGE TEST	
FUNCTION	TERM
OFF	1–2
+100V REG	1–3
+150V REG	1–4
+300V UNREG	1–5
+450V UNREG	1–6

36.23 For more complex switches, position-to-position function relations may be shown using symbols on the schematic diagram or by a table of values located elsewhere on the diagram.

and table. The tabular form is preferred due to the complexity of this particular switch. The dashes between the numbers in the table indicate that the numbers have been connected. For example, when the switch is in position 2, the following terminals are connected: 1 and 3, 5 and 7, and 9 and 11. A table of this type should be placed at the bottom of a schematic diagram, if applicable.

Electron tubes have pins that fit into sockets that have terminals connecting into circuits.

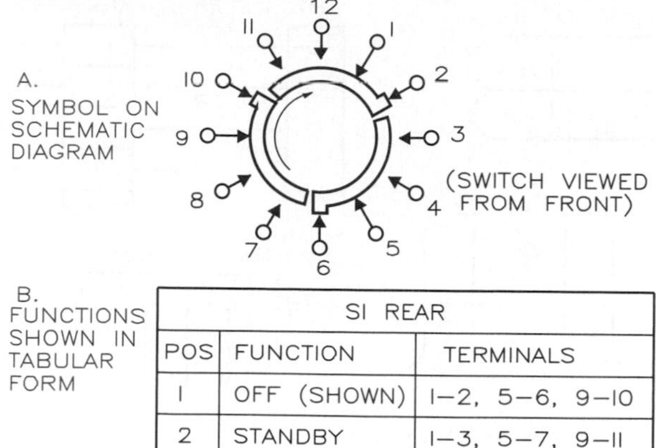

SI REAR		
POS	FUNCTION	TERMINALS
1	OFF (SHOWN)	1–2, 5–6, 9–10
2	STANDBY	1–3, 5–7, 9–11
3	OPERATE	1–4, 5–8, 9–12

36.24 A rotary switch may be shown on a schematic diagram with its terminals labeled as shown, or its functions can be given in a table placed elsewhere on the drawing as shown. Dashes are used to indicate the linkage of the numbered terminals. For example, 1-2 means that terminals 1 and 2 are connected in the "off" position.

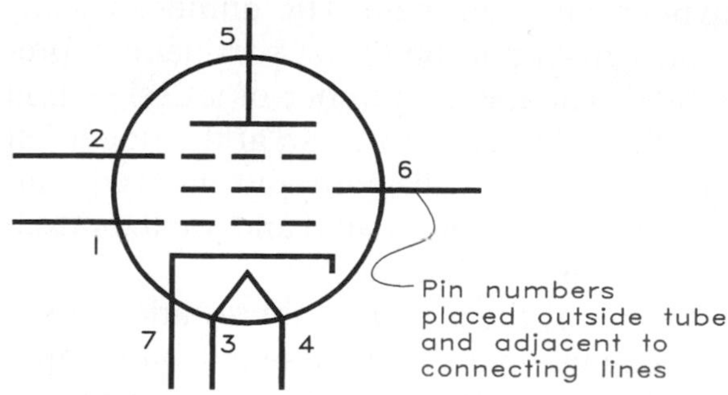

36.25 Tube pin numbers should be placed outside the tube envelope and adjacent to the connecting lines. *(Courtesy of ANSI.)*

Pins are labeled with numbers placed outside the symbol used to represent the tube, as shown in **Figure 36.25**, and are numbered in a clockwise direction with the tube viewed from its bottom.

36.6 Separation of Parts

In complex circuits, it is often advantageous to separate elements of a multielement part with portions of the graphic symbols drawn in different locations on the drawing. An example of this method of separation is the switch labeled S1A and S1B in **Figure 36.6**. The switch is labeled S1 and the letter that follows, called a suffix, is used to designate different parts of the same switch. Suffix letters may also be used to label subdivisions of an enclosed unit that is made up of a series of internal parts, such as the crystal unit shown in **Figure 36.26**. These crystals are referred to as Y1A and Y1B.

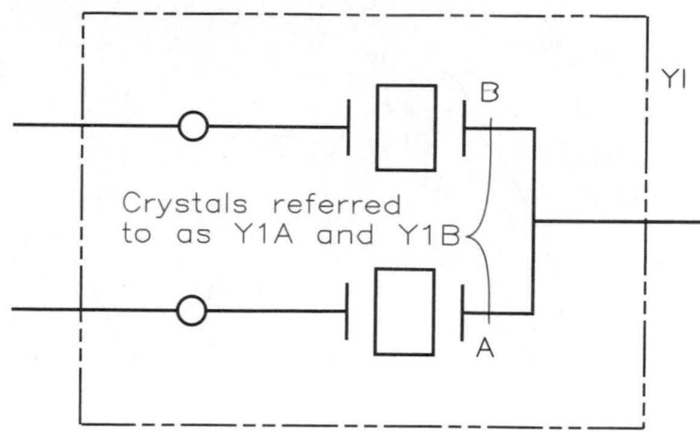

36.26 As subdivisions within the complete part, crystals A and B are referred to as Y1A and Y1B.

Rotary switches of the type shown in **Figure 36.27** are designated as S1A, S1B, etc. The suffix letters A, B, etc., are labeled in sequence beginning with the knob and working away from it. Each end of the various sections of the switch should be viewed from the same end. When the rear and front of the switches need to be used, the words FRONT and REAR are added to the designations.

Portions of items such as terminal boards, connectors, or rotary switches may be separated on a diagram. The words PART OF may precede the identification of the portion of the circuit of which it is a part, as shown in **Figure 36.28A**. A second method of showing a part of a system is by using conventional break lines that make the note PART OF unnecessary.

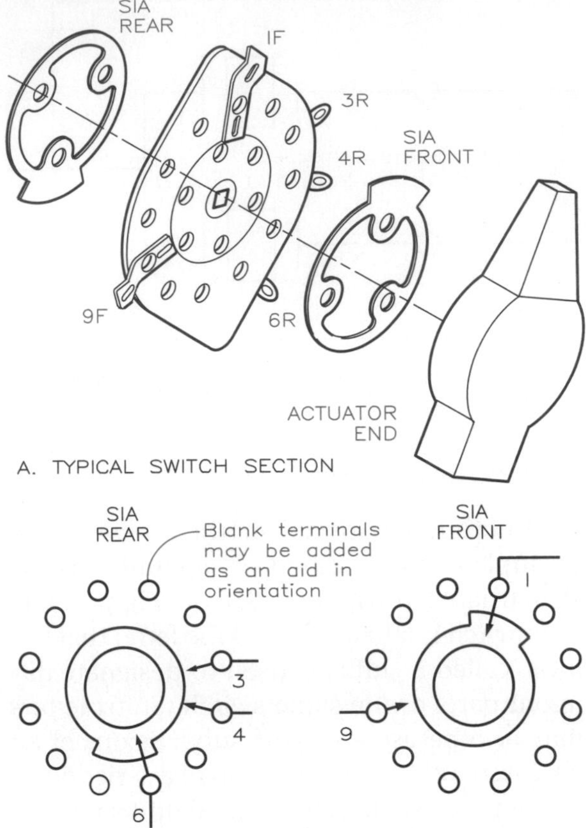

36.27 Parts of rotary switches are designated with suffix letters A, B, C, etc., and are referred to as S1A, S1B, S1C, etc. The words FRONT and REAR are added to these designations when both sides of the switch are used. *(Courtesy of ANSI.)*

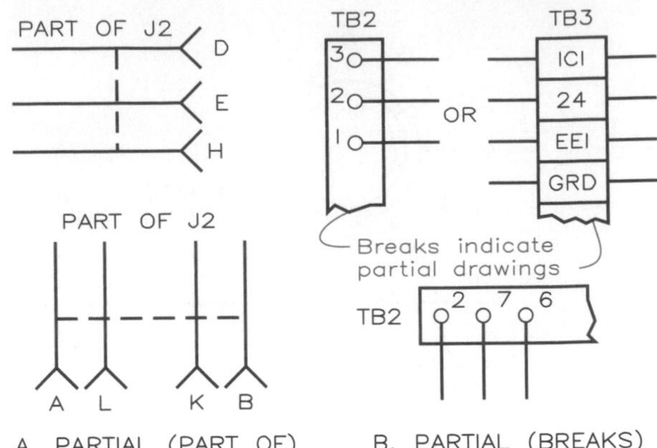

36.28 The portions of connectors or terminal boards are functionally separated on a diagram; the words PART OF may precede the reference designation of the entire portion. Or conventional breaks may be used to indicate graphically that the part is only a portion of the whole.

36.7 Reference Designations

A combination of letters and numbers that identify items on a schematic diagram are called **reference designations**. These designations are used to identify the components not only on the drawing but in the related documents that refer to them. Reference designations should be placed close to the symbols that represent the replaceable items of a circuit on a drawing. Items that are not separately replaceable may be identified if this is considered necessary. Mounting devices for electron tubes, lamps, fuses, and so forth, are seldom identified on schematic diagrams.

It is standard practice to begin each reference designation with an uppercase letter that may be followed by a numeral with no hyphen between them. The number usually represents a portion of the part being represented. The lowest number of a designation should be assigned to begin at the upper left of the schematic diagram and proceed consecutively from left to right and top to bottom throughout the drawing.

Some of the standard abbreviations used to designate parts of an assembly are amplifier-A, battery-BT, capacitor-C, connector-J, piezoelectric crystal-Y, fuse-F, electron tube-V, generator-G, rectifier-CR, resistor-R, transformer-T, and transistor-Q.

As the circuit is being designed, some of the numbered elements may be deleted from the circuit drawing. The numbered elements that remain should not be renumbered even though there is a missing element within the sequence of numbers used to label the parts. Instead, a table of the type shown in **Figure 36.29** can be used to list the parts that have been omitted from the circuit. The highest designations are also given in the table as a check to be sure that all parts were considered.

HIGHEST REFERENCE DESIGNATIONS	
R72	C40
REFERENCE DESIGNATIONS NOT USED	
R8, R10, R61 R64, R70	C12, C15, C17 C20, C22

36.29 Reference designations are used to identify parts of a circuit. They are labeled in a numerical sequence from left to right beginning at the upper left of the diagram. If parts are later deleted from the system, the ones deleted should be listed in a table, along with the highest reference number designations.

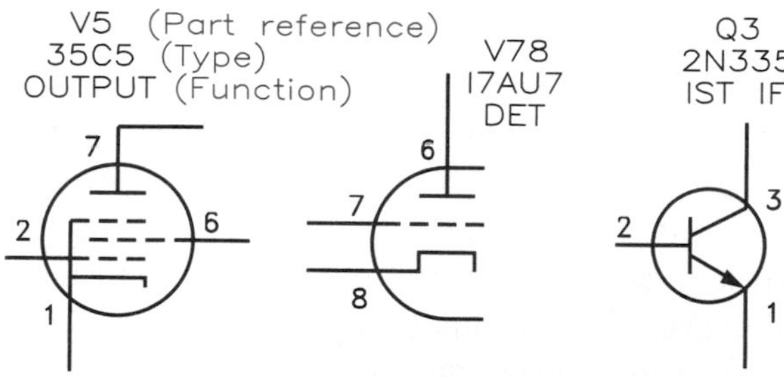

A. ELECTRON TUBES B. TRANSISTOR

36.30 Three lines of notes can be used with electron tubes and transistors to specify reference designation, type designation, and function. This information should be located adjacent to and preferably above the symbol.

Electron tubes are labeled not only with reference designations but with type designation and circuit function as shown in **Figure 36.30**. This information is labeled in three lines, such as V5/35C5/OUTPUT, which are located adjacent to the symbol.

36.8 Numerical Units of Function

Functional units such as the values of resistance, capacitance, inductance, and voltage should be specified with the fewest number of zeros by using the multipliers in **Figure 36.31A** as prefixes. Examples using this method of expression are shown in parts B and C, where units of resistance and capacitance are given. When four-digit numbers are given, omit the commas; write one thousand as 1000, not as 1,000. You should recognize and use the lowercase or uppercase prefixes as indicated in the table of **Figure 36.31**.

A. MULTIPLIERS

MULTIPLIER	PREFIX	SYMBOL Method 1	SYMBOL Method 2
10^{12}	TERA	T	T
10^{9}	GIGA	G	G
10^{6} (1,000,000)	MEGA	M	M
10^{3} (1,000)	KILO	k	K
10^{-3} (0.001)	MILLI	m	MILLI
10^{-6} (0.000,001)	MICRO	μ	U
10^{-9}	NANO	n	N
10^{-12}	PICO	p	P
10^{-13}	FEMTO	f	F
10^{-16}	ATTO	a	z

B. RESISTANCE UNITS

RANGE IN OHMS	EXPRESS AS	EXAMPLE
LESS THAN 1,000	OHMS	0.031 470
1,000 TO 99,999	OHMS OR KILOHMS	1800 15,853 10k
100,000 to 999,999	KILOHMS OR MEGOHMS	220k 0.22M
1,000,000 OR MORE	MEGOHMS	3.3M

C. CAPACITANCE UNITS

RANGE IN PICOFARADS	EXPRESS AS	EXAMPLE
LESS THAN 10,000	PICOFARADS	152.4pF 4700pF
10,000 OR MORE	MICROFARADS	0.015μF 30μF

36.31 (A) Multipliers should be used to reduce the number of zeros in a number. (B, C) Examples of units of capacitance and resistance.

A general note can be used where certain units are repeated on a drawing, to reduce time and effort:

UNLESS OTHERWISE SPECIFIED:

RESISTANCE VALUES ARE IN OHMS.

CAPACITANCE VALUES ARE IN MICROFARADS.

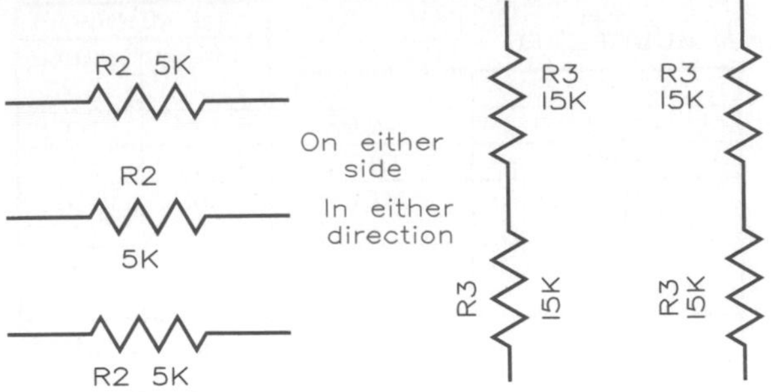

36.32 Methods of labeling the units of resistance on a schematic diagram.

or

CAPACITANCE VALUES ARE IN PICOFARADS.

A note for specifying capacitance values is:

CAPACITANCE VALUES SHOWN AS NUMBERS EQUAL TO OR GREATER THAN UNITS ARE IN pF AND NUMBERS LESS THAN UNITY ARE IN µF.

Examples of the placement of the reference designations and the numerical values of resistors are shown in **Figure 36.32**.

36.9 Functional Identification of Parts

The readability of a circuit is improved if parts are labeled to indicate their functions. Test points are labeled on drawings with the letters "Tp" and their suffix numbers. The sequence of the suffix numbers should be the same as the sequence of troubleshooting the circuit when it is defective. As an alternative, the test function can be indicated on the diagram below the reference designation.

Additional information may be included on a schematic diagram to aid in the maintenance of the system:

DC resistance of windings and coils.

Critical input and output impedance values.

Wave shapes (voltage or current) at significant points.

Wiring requirements for critical ground points, shielding, pairing, etc.

Power or voltage ratings of parts.

Caution notation for electrical hazards at maintenance points.

Circuit voltage values at significant points (tube pins, test points, terminal boards, etc.).

Zones (grid system) on complex schematics.

Signal flow direction in main signal paths shall be emphasized.

36.10 Printed Circuits

Printed circuits are universally used for miniature electronic components and computer systems. For years the vacuum tube was the best means of controlling electrical current; however, it was bulky, fragile, and unreliable, and consumed large amounts of power. In 1947 the transistor replaced the vacuum tube, eliminated the disadvantages of the tube, and reduced its size to fit on the head of pin.

In 1958 Jack Kilby of Texas Instruments (**Figure 36.33**) advanced miniaturization further with his integrated circuit in which resistors, capacitors, transistors, and other components were merged on a slice of silicon called a chip.

36.33 Jack Kilby's invention of the integrated circuit began the digital revolution. Today's chips integrate millions of transistors onto a single chip with unprecedented levels of integration, performance, and power. *(Courtesy of Texas Instruments.)*

36.34 A microchip lying on a penny gives an example of the degree of miniaturization of electronic components. *(Courtesy of Oak Ridge National Laboratory, U.S. Department of Energy.)*

With each advancement in electronics have come even more breakthroughs that have offered more productivity, at greater speeds and at lower costs. The dramatic degree of miniaturization that has occurred can be seen in **Figure 36.34**, where a complex circuit fits on a one-square-centimeter chip.

Printed circuit boards, on which chips and other devices are assembled, are drawn at up to four times their final size. The drawings are precisely drawn in ink on a highly stable acetate film and are photographically reduced to the desired size. The circuit is "printed" onto an insulated board made of plastic or ceramics, and the devices within the circuit are connected and soldered (**Figure 36.35**).

Some printed circuits are printed on both sides of the circuit board, requiring two photographic negatives, as shown in **Figure 36.36**, that are made from positive drawings (black lines on a white background). The drawing for each side can be made on separate sheets of acetate that are laid over each other when the second diagram is drawn. However, a more efficient method uses red and blue tape that can be used for making a single drawing (**Figure 36.37**) from which two negatives are photographically made. Filters are used on the process camera to drop out the red for one negative and a different filter to drop out the blue for the second negative.

36.35 A magnified view of a circuit that has been printed and etched on a board and the devices soldered in position. *(Courtesy of Bishop Industries Corp.)*

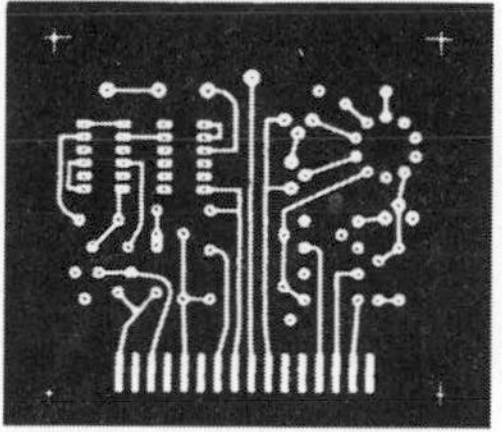

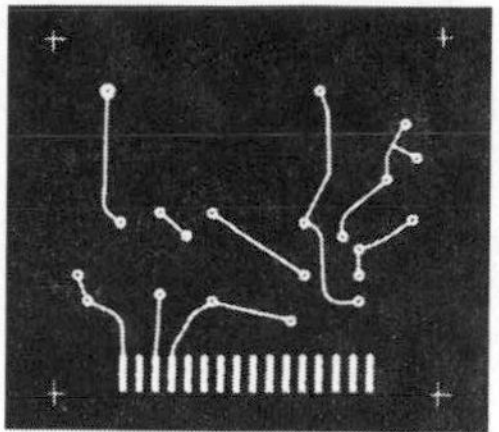

36.36 A printed circuit applied to both sides of the circuit board requires two drawings, one for each side, that are photographically converted to negatives for printing. *(Courtesy of Bishop Industries Corp.)*

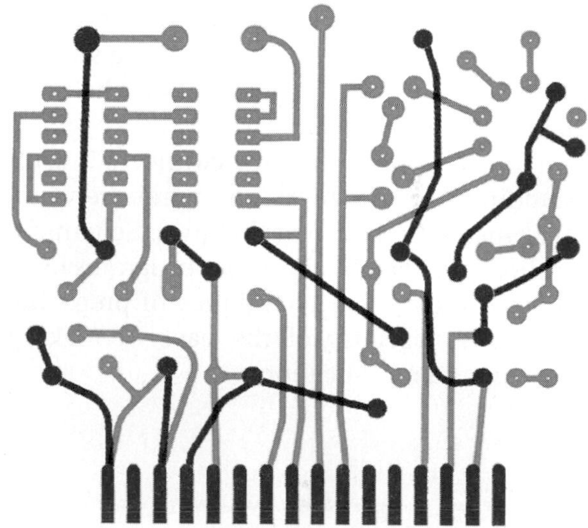

36.37 Using two colors, such as blue and red, allows one circuit drawing to be made, and two negatives to be made from the same drawing by using camera filters that screen out one of the colors with each shot. The circuits are then printed on each side of the board. *(Courtesy of Bishop Industries Corp.)*

Printed circuits are usually coated with silicone varnish to prevent malfunction because of the collection of moisture or dust on the surface. They may also be enclosed in protective shells.

36.11 Shortcut Symbols

Preprinted symbols are available commercially that can be used for "drawing" high-quality electronic circuits and printed circuits. The symbols are available on sheets or on tapes that can be burnished onto the surface of the drawing to form a permanent schematic diagram (**Figure 36.38**).

The symbols can be connected with matching tape to represent wires between them instead of drawing the lines. Schematic symbols provided by computer programs have replaced most other techniques of preparing schematics because of the ease of making changes and modifications.

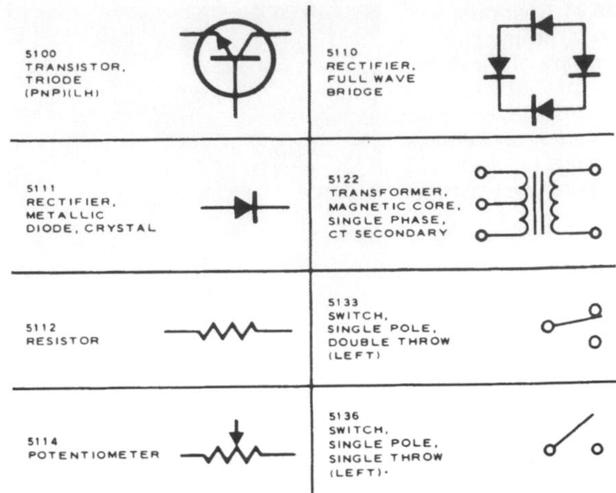

36.38 Stick-on symbols are available for laying out schematic diagrams rather than drawing them. They give a higher contrast and sharpness that improves their reproducibility. *(Courtesy of Bishop Industries Corp.)*

36.12 Installation Drawings

Many types of electrical/electronics drawings are used to produce the finished installation, in the process that starts with the designer who visualizes the system at the outset of the

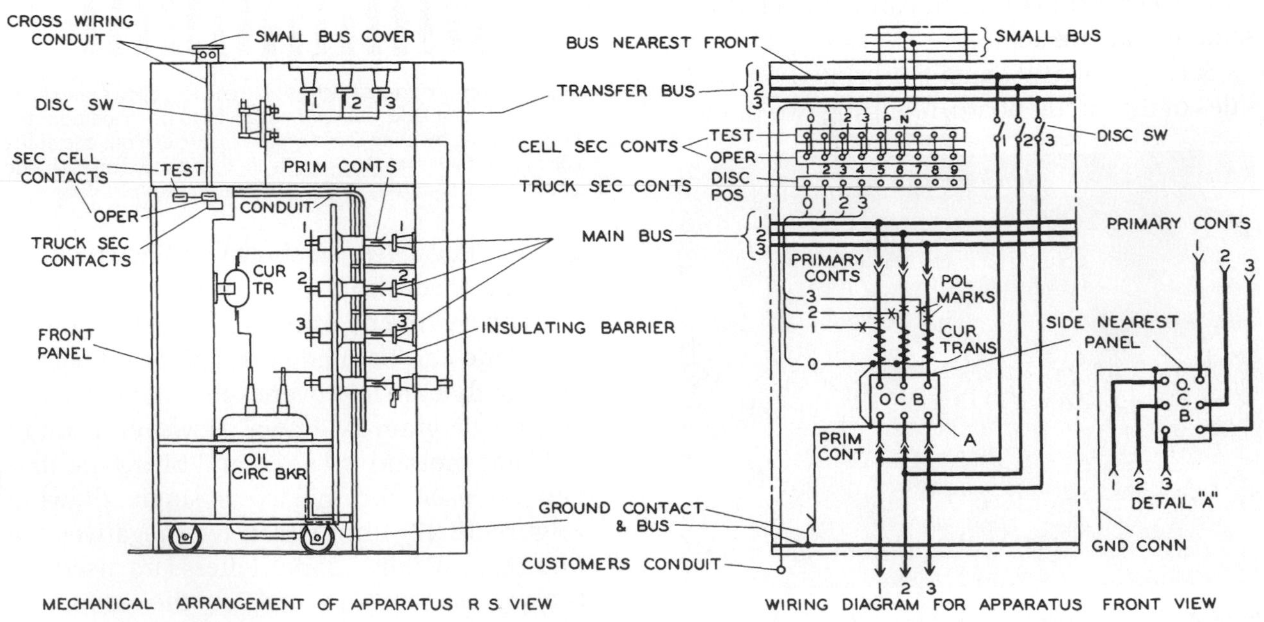

36.39 This drawing shows views of a metal-enclosed switchgear to describe the arrangement of the apparatus; it also gives the wiring diagram for the unit.

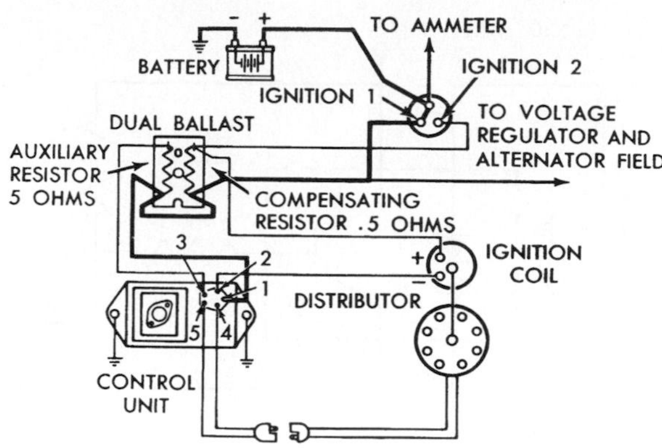

36.40 An installation/circuit diagram that describes how to troubleshoot a circuit. *(Courtesy of Chrysler Corporation.)*

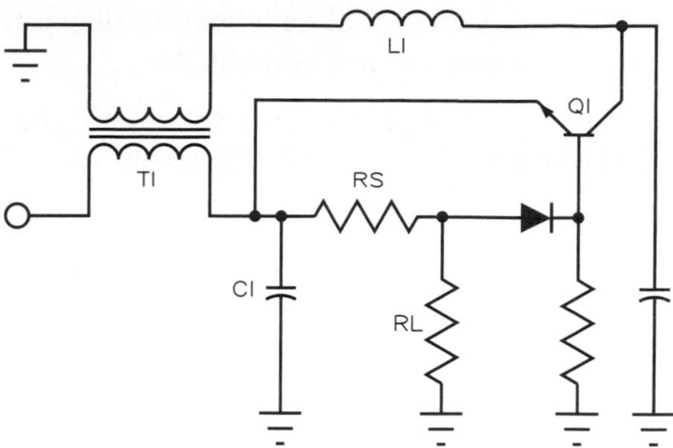

36.41 Problem 1: A low-pass inductive-input filter. *(Courtesy of NASA.)*

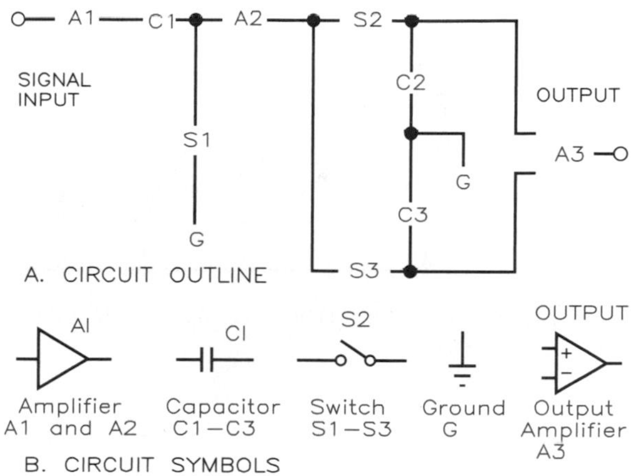

36.42 Problem 2: A quadruple-sampling processor. *(Courtesy of NASA.)*

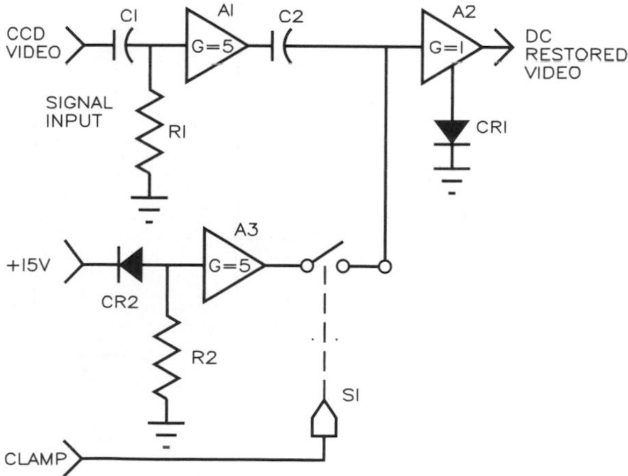

36.43 Problem 3: A temperature-compensating DC restorer circuit. *(Courtesy of NASA.)*

project and ends with the contractor who builds it (**Figure 36.39**). Drawings are used to design the circuit, detail its parts for fabrication, specify the arrangement of the devices within the system, and instruct the contractor how to install the project.

A combination arrangement and wiring diagram is shown in **Figure 36.39**, where the system is shown in a front and a right-side view. The wiring diagram explains how the wires and components within the system are connected for the metal-encased switchgear. Bus bars are conductors for the primary circuits.

An installation/circuit diagram in **Figure 36.40** is a drawing used in a maintenance manual to show how to troubleshoot a defective circuit. It is a combination drawing that shows physical arrangement and the circuit as well.

Problems

1. On a size A sheet, make a schematic diagram of the circuit shown in **Figure 36.41**.

2. On a size A sheet, make a schematic diagram of the circuit shown in **Figure 36.42**.

3. On a size A sheet, make a schematic diagram of the circuit shown in **Figure 36.43**.

4. On a size A sheet, make a schematic diagram of the circuit shown in **Figure 36.44**.

5. On a size A sheet, make a schematic diagram of the circuit shown in **Figure 36.45**.

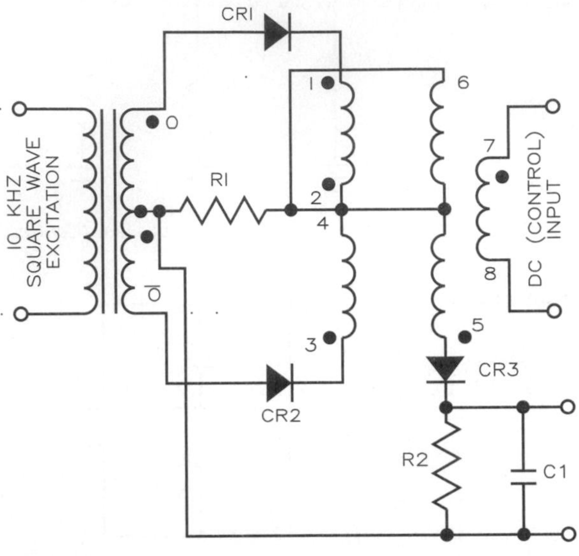

36.44 Problem 4: A magnetic amplifier DC transducer. *(Courtesy of NASA.)*

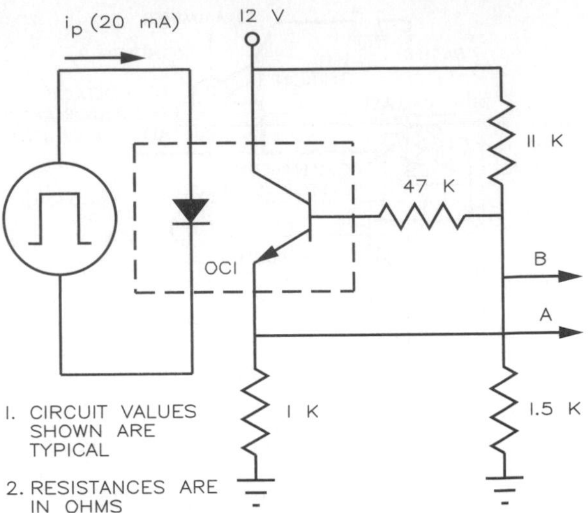

36.45 Problem 5: An improved power-factor controller. *(Courtesy of NASA.)*

6. On a size B sheet, make a schematic diagram of the circuit shown in **Figure 36.46**.

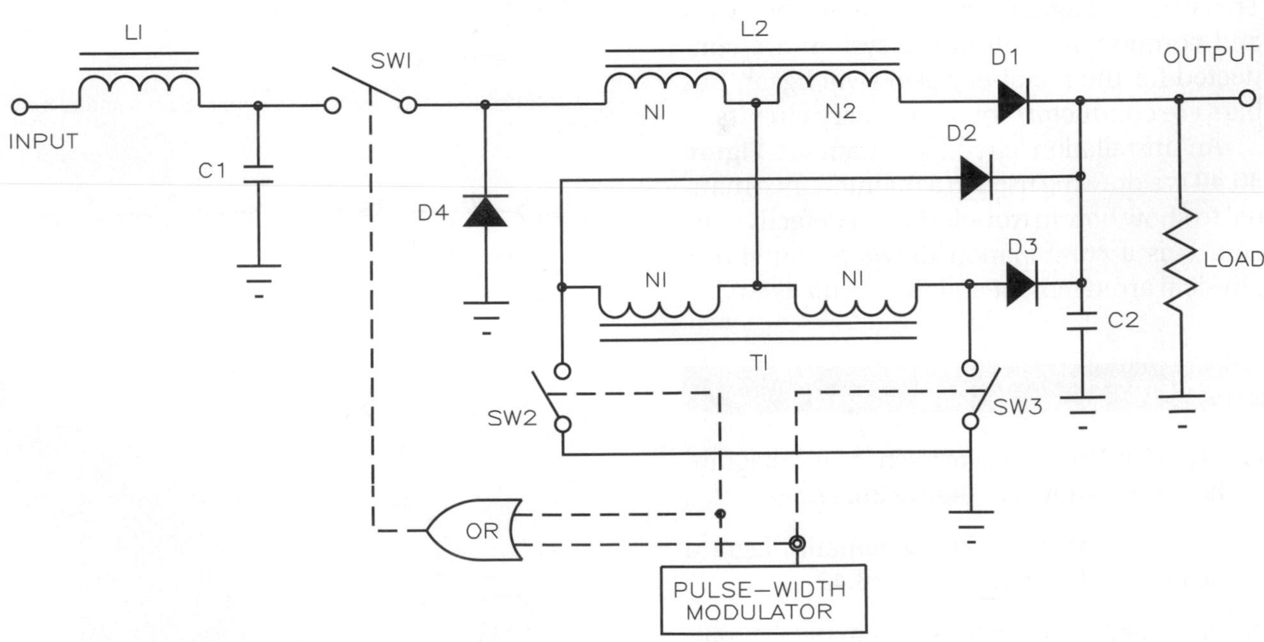

36.46 Problem 6: A "buck/boost" voltage regulator. *(Courtesy of NASA.)*

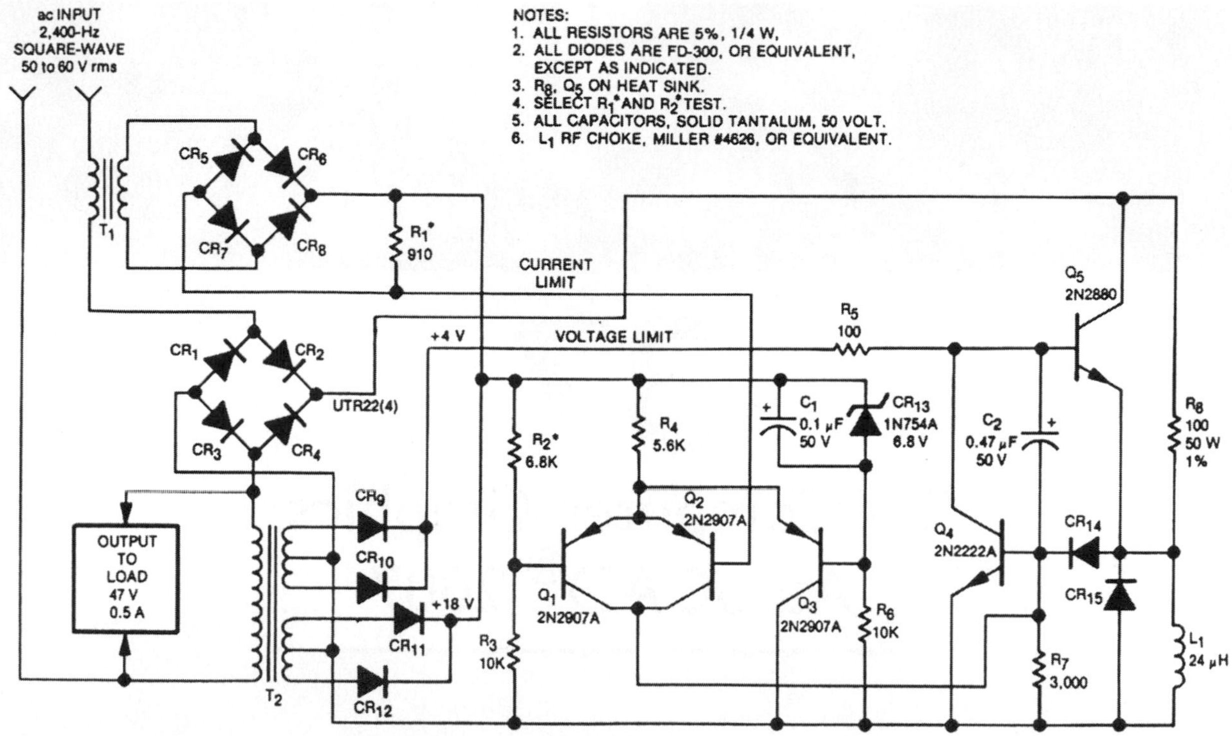

36.47 Problem 7: An overload protection circuit. *(Courtesy of NASA.)*

7. On a size C sheet, draw a schematic diagram of the circuit shown in **Figure 36.47**.

8. On a size B sheet, draw a schematic diagram of the circuit shown in **Figure 36.48** and give a parts list.

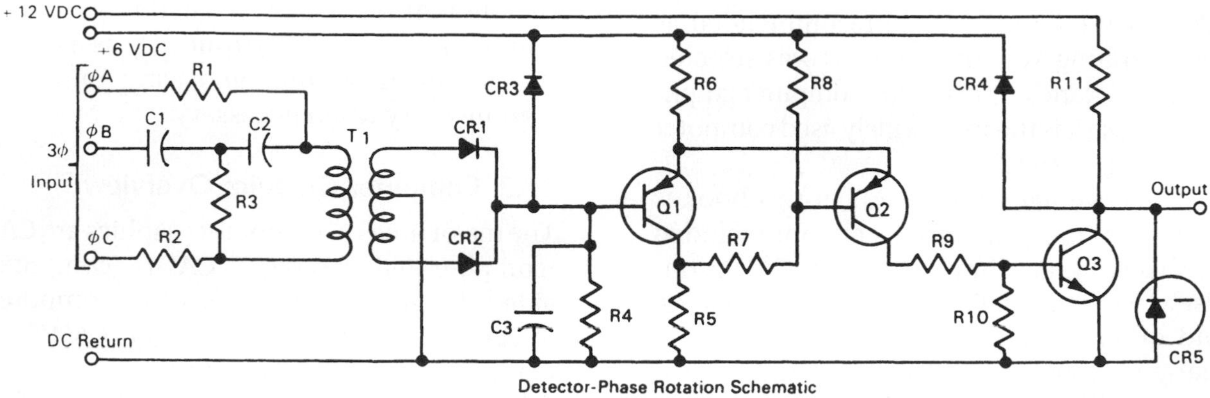

36.48 Problem 8: A schematic of a phase detector circuit. *(Courtesy of NASA.)*

37 2D Computer Graphics: AutoCAD® 2007

37.1 Introduction

This chapter provides an introduction to computer graphics using AutoCAD 2007 running on an Intel 486 or Pentium processor with 32 MB (64 MB preferred) of RAM, at least 200 MB of hard disk space, a mouse (or tablet), an A-B plotter, and/or printer. Windows® 2000, or Windows® XP are recommended as the operating system. AutoCAD was selected as the software for presenting computer graphics because it is the most widely used computer graphics program.

The coverage of AutoCAD in this book is brief, and many operations are not included because of space limitations. AutoCAD's concisely written *User's Guide* has 1235 pages, and other manuals on the market have as many as 1500 pages. However, AutoCAD is covered here sufficiently well enough to guide you through the applications necessary for a typical engineering design graphics course.

You will find that the learning of computer graphics and its successive upgrades will be a career-long experience. We recommend that you begin this self-teaching process by experimenting with the peripheral commands and options that are not covered in this book. Also, you should refer to *Help* routinely as a means of learning new commands and refreshing your memory when necessary.

37.2 Computer Graphics Overview

The major areas of computer graphics are **CAD** (computer-aided design), **CADD** (computer-aided design and drafting), **CIM** (computer-integrated manufacturing), and **CAD/CAM** (computer-aided manufacturing).

CAD (computer-aided design) is used to solve design problems, analyze design data, and store design information for easy retrieval. Many CAD systems perform these functions in an integrated manner, greatly increasing the designer's productivity.

CADD (computer-aided design and drafting) is the computer process of making engineering drawings and technical documents more closely related to drafting than is CAD.

CAD/CAM (computer-aided design/computer-aided manufacturing) is a system that can be used to design a part or product, devise the production steps, and electronically communicate this data to control the operation of manufacturing equipment and robots.

CIM (computer-integrated manufacturing) is a more advanced system of CAD/CAM that coordinates and operates all stages of manufacturing from design to finished product.

Advantages of CAD and CADD

Computer-graphics systems offer the designer and drafter some or all of the following advantages.

1. Increased accuracy. CAD systems are capable of producing drawings that are essentially 100% accurate in size, line quality, and uniformity.

2. Increased drawing speed. Engineering drawings and documents can be prepared more quickly, especially when standard details from existing libraries are incorporated into new drawings.

3. Easy to revise. Drawings can be more easily modified, scaled, and revised than is possible by hand techniques.

4. Better design analysis. Alternative designs can be analyzed quickly and easily. Software is available to simulate a product's operation and test it under a variety of conditions, which lessens the need for models and prototypes.

5. Better presentation. Drawings can be presented in 2D or 3D and rendered as technical illustrations to better communicate designs.

6. Libraries of drawing aids. Databases of details, symbols, and figures that are used over and over can be archived for immediate use in making drawings.

7. Improved filing. Drawings can be conveniently filed, retrieved, and transmitted on disks and tapes.

37.3 Hardware

The hardware of a computer graphics system includes the **computer, monitor, input device** (keyboard, digitizer, mouse, or light pen), and **output device** (plotters and printers).

Computer

The computer, with an installed **program**, receives input from the user through the keyboard, executes the instructions, and produces output. The part of the computer that follows the program's instructions is the **CPU** (central processing unit). The computer graphics computer should have at least 32 MB of RAM, and its hard disk storage should be large, preferably 6 to 8 gigabytes and larger (**Figure 37.1**).

The monitor is a **CRT (cathode-ray tube)** and has an electron gun that emits a beam that sweeps rows of raster lines onto the screen. Each line consists of dots called **pixels**. Raster-scanned CRTs refresh the picture display many times per second. A measure of monitor quality

37.1 The basic components of a desktop computer system are the CPU (central processing unit), monitor (screen), keyboard, and mouse. *(Courtesy of Dell Inc.)*

37.2 Current technology enables computers to send 3D graphics over networks for instantaneous communication. *(Courtesy of Hewlett Packard Company.)*

37.3 The DeskJet 990c series of printers produces photo-quality color images that are as close to traditional photographs as desktop printers have ever come. *(Courtesy of Hewlett Packard Company.)*

is **resolution**, which is the number of pixels per inch that can be produced on the screen. The greater the number of pixels, the greater will be the clarity of the image on the screen (**Figure 37.2**).

Input Devices

In addition to the standard keyboard, the **digitizer** is used to enter graphic data to the computer. The **mouse**, a handheld device that is moved about the table top to transmit information to the computer, is the most commonly used input device. Variations of the mouse are **thumbwheels** operated by fingertips, **joysticks** that let the user "steer" about the screen by tilting a lever, and **spherical balls** that can be rotated to input 3D data to the screen.

A **tablet** and digitizer used in combination are an alternative to the mouse. The digitizer (stylus) can be used to select commands from the menu attached to the tablet. Also, drawings can be attached to tablets and "traced" with the stylus to convert it to *x*- and *y*-coordinates. The **light pen** enables the user to "draw" on the screen with it to select points and lines.

Output Devices

Plotters make drawings on paper or film with a pen in the same manner a drawing is made by hand. Plotter types are **flatbed plotters, drum plotters**, and **sheet-fed plotters**. In flatbed plotters, the drawing paper is held stationary while pens are moved about its surface. Drum plotters roll the paper up and down over a cylinder while the pen moves left and right to make the drawing. Sheet-fed pen plotters hold the paper with grit wheels in a flat position as the sheet is moved forward and backward, and the pen moves left and right to make the drawing.

Printers are of the impact type (much like typewriters) or nonimpact type in which images are formed by sprays, laser beams, photography, or heat (**Figure 37.3**). The laser printer gives an excellent resolution of dense, accurately drawn lines in color, as well as in black and white. Ink-jet technology has enabled images to be sprayed onto the drawing surface in color or in black that approaches the quality of the laser. Larger nonimpact printers (24 × 36 in. and larger) are most often ink-jet printers, since large lasers are much more expensive.

37.4 Your First Session

AutoCAD Classic

When AutoCAD 2007 is opened, two workspace options are displayed: **AutoCAD Classic** and **3D**

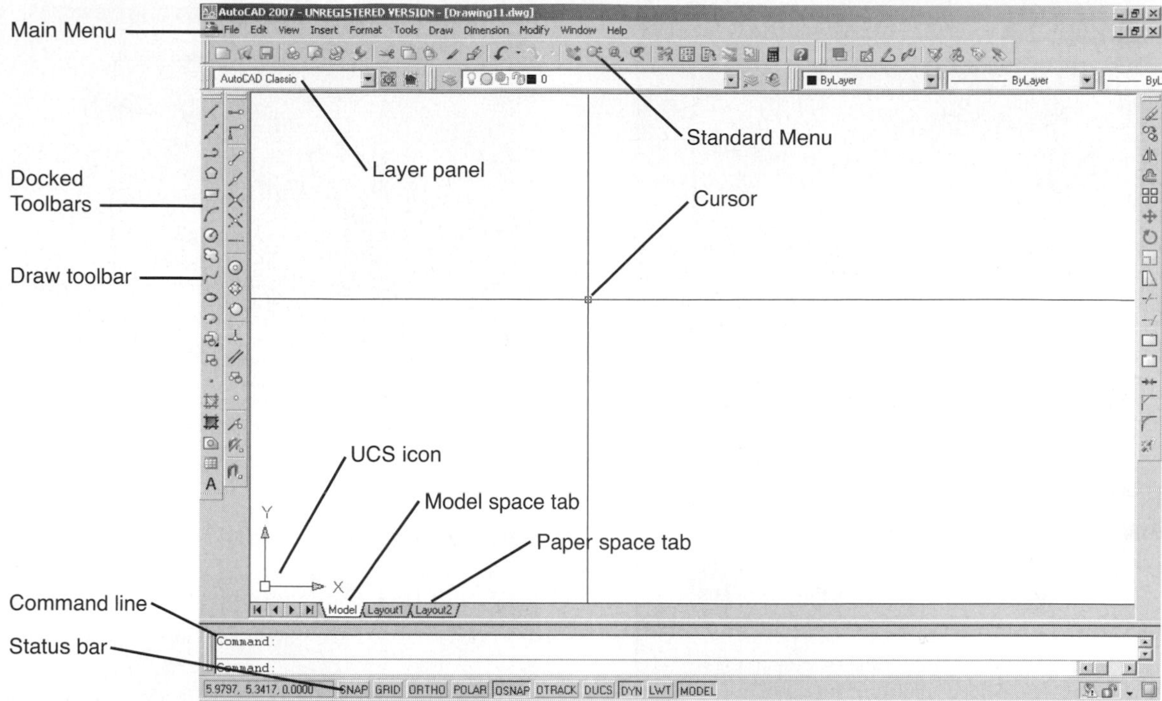

37.4 This is a typical view of the AutoCAD 2007 main screen. Additional toolbars can added to and removed from the screen by the user.

Modeling. The examples in this chapter can be effectively executed using AutoCAD Classic.

Format of Presentation

The progression from one step of a command to the next level will be separated by an angle pointing to the right (>) to simplify presentation and reduce explanatory text. Since there are about three different ways of actuating most commands, these methods will be used alternatively in the following examples. The commands and prompts that appear on the screen will be given in italics to distinguish them from supplementary notes of explanation. (Enter) is the keyboard key with this name. Once a command is selected, additional prompts will be given at the *Command* line at the bottom of the screen or in dialog boxes and menus that must be followed.

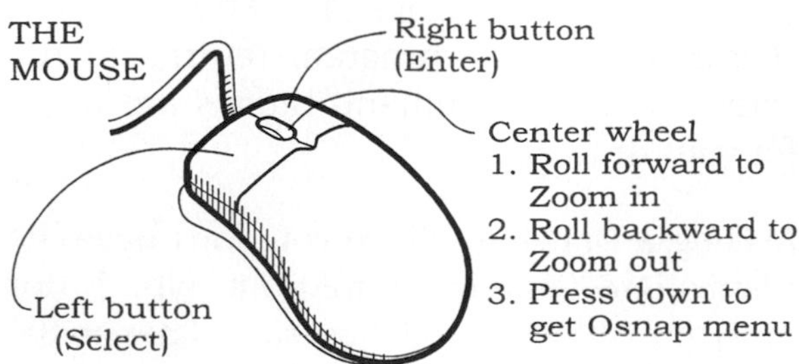

37.5 The left mouse button is used for picking points when drawing and for selecting operational buttons. The right mouse button has the same effect as pressing the (Enter) button on the keyboard.

Booting Turn on the computer and boot the system by typing ACAD2007 (or the command used by your system) to activate the program (**Figure 37.4**). Experiment by moving the cursor around the screen with your mouse, select items, and try the pull-down menu.

Mouse Most interactions with the computer will be accomplished with a mouse (**Figure 37.5**), but many commands can be entered at

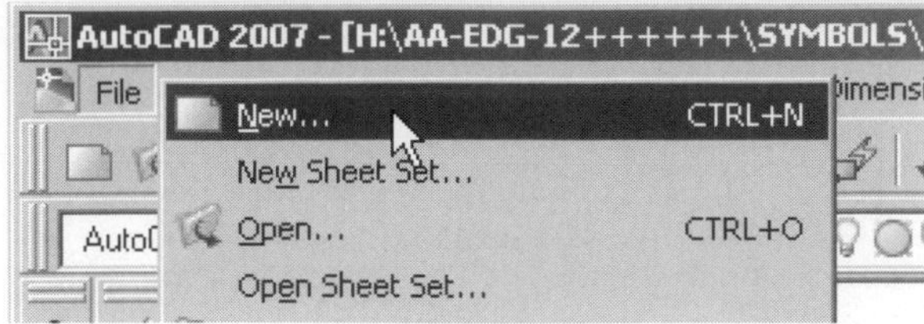

37.6 To begin a new drawing, select *Main Menu> File> New* to obtain the *New* box.

37.7 In the *Create New Drawing* box, select *Use a Wizard* icon button> *Quick Setup*> and *Ok.*

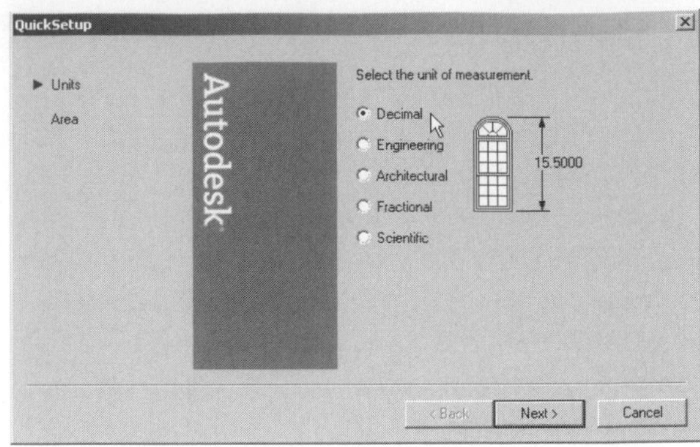

37.8 In the *QuickSetup* box, specify the type of *Units* you want (*Decimal* units in this example) and select *Next.*

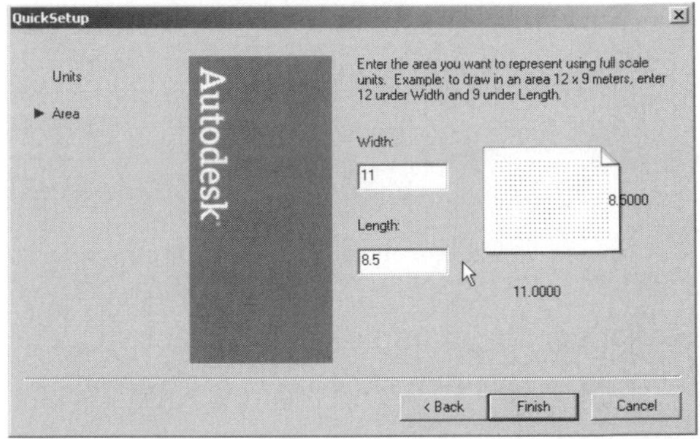

37.9 Type the values for *Width* and *Length* (11 and 8.5 for a size A sheet) and select *Finish.*

the keyboard (maybe more quickly after you learn them). Press the left mouse button to click on, select, or pick a command or object; a double click is needed in some cases. The right button has the same effect as pressing (Enter) on the keyboard.

Creating a File To create a new file on a disk, place your formatted disk in its slot, from the *Main menu* bar pick *Files* and *New* from the dialog box (**Figure 37.6**), and the *New* option appears; select it and the *Create New Drawing* dialog box appears on the screen (**Figure 37.7**). Select the *Use a Wizard* icon button, *Quick Setup,* and *OK,* and the *Quick Setup* box appears where size *Units* can be specified (**Figure 37.8**). Select *Decimal* units and the *Next* button. When the *Area* box appears on the screen, insert the *Width* and *Length* (11 × 8.5) and select the *Finish* button (**Figure 37.9**). The program returns to the screen, and its command menus are ready for your drawing.

Making a Drawing Since you don't have the menus and toolbars figured out, type L (for *Line*), press (Enter), and draw some lines on the screen with the mouse for the fun of it by selecting endpoints with the left button as shown in **Figure 37.10**. A line on the screen "rubber bands" from point to point. To disengage the

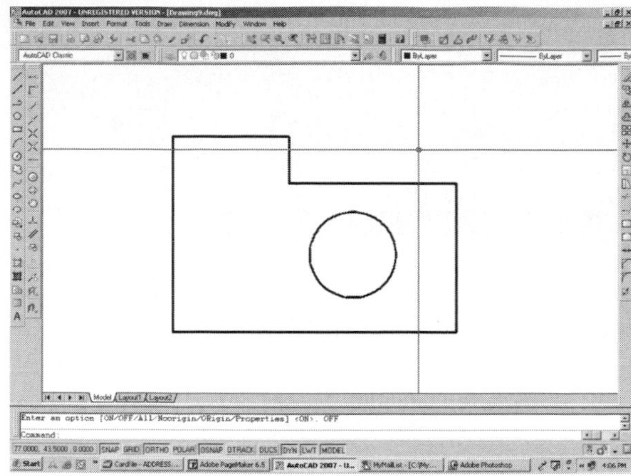

37.10 Using *Command:* L (for *Line*), or selecting *Main Menu> Draw> Line,* allows endpoints of lines to be selected on the screen with the left mouse button to draw a figure.

rubber band, press the right mouse button, which is the same as pressing (Enter) on the keyboard. Press the right button again to return to the *Line* command.

Instead of typing L to enter the *Line* command, pick the *Main Menu> Draw* and select the *Line* option to get the prompt *Specify first point:* at the *Command* line at the bottom of the screen. Now, use your mouse to draw on the screen. The *Line* command can also be selected from the *Draw* toolbar that you will learn about soon. Try drawing circles and other objects on the screen by selecting icons from the *Main Menu> Draw* pull-down menu.

Repeat Commands By pressing (Enter) on the keyboard (or the right mouse button) twice after the previous command, you can repeat the command. For example, *Line* will appear in the *Command* line at the bottom of the screen after you press (Enter) twice, if *Line* was the previous command.

Saving Your File. Click on *File* on the *Main Menu* bar and pick *Save As* from the pull-down menu to get the menu box shown in

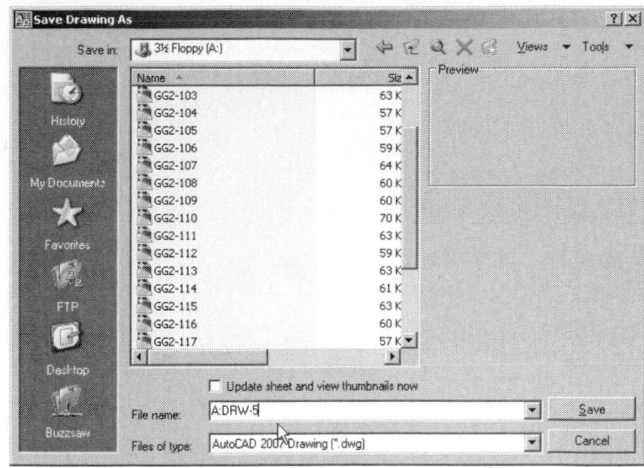

37.11 Select *Main Menu> File> Save As* to obtain the *Save Drawing As* box; type the drawing drive (A:) and the file name DRW-5 in the *File name* box and select *Save.* File *A:DRW-5* is saved.

Figure 37.11. Type A:DRW-5 (if your disk is in Drive A) and select the *Save* button; the light over drive A will blink briefly, and the drawing named *DRW-5* is saved to the disk in the A drive.

Plotting Your Drawing. Select *File* (**Figure 37.12**) and the *Plot* option from its pull-down menu to get the *Plot-Model* dialog box (**Figure 37.13**). Select the printer from the *Printer/plotter* area in the *Name:* window, an HP LaserJet

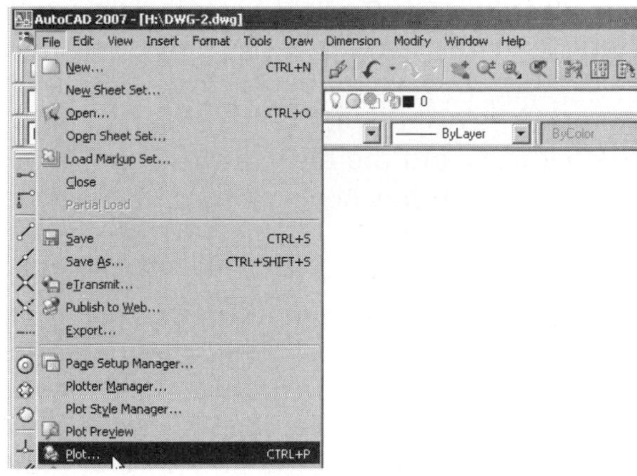

37.12 Select *Main Menu> File> Plot* to pick plotter settings.

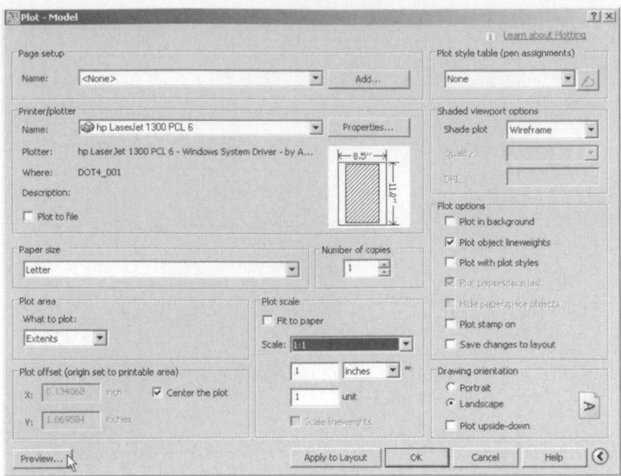

37.13 In the *Plot-Model* box, select the plotter or printer that you will use, *Paper size* (8.5 × 11), *Drawing orientation* (Landscape), *Plot area* (Extents), *Plot scale* (1:1), *Plot offset (Center the plot),* and click on *Preview* to obtain a view of what will be plotted. If it looks correct, select *OK,* and the drawing is printed.

in this case. Select the *Paper size* tab, set the *What to plot:* box to *Extents,* check the *Center the plot* button, and set the *Scale* to 1:1. Load the size A paper sheet in the printer or plotter; pick the *Preview* button to see how the drawing will appear when plotted. If it appears correct, press the *OK* button and the drawing is printed.

Quitting AutoCAD To be sure that your latest changes have been saved to disk, select *File* from the *Main Menu* and pick *Save* from the pull-down menu to update *A:DRW-5.* To quit AutoCAD, close the active file *(Main Menu> File> Close)* and the file will close and leave the screen if it has been *Saved* in its current form (**Figure 37.14**). If changes have been made to it since its last *Save,* the pop-up box in **Figure 37.15** lets you decide to *Save* it or not (*Yes* or *No*) or *Cancel.* To quit your session *Main Menu> File> Exit,* and AutoCAD closes (**Figure 37.16**). If you intend to continue your drawing session, do not *Exit* now but continue with other drawings. When working from a

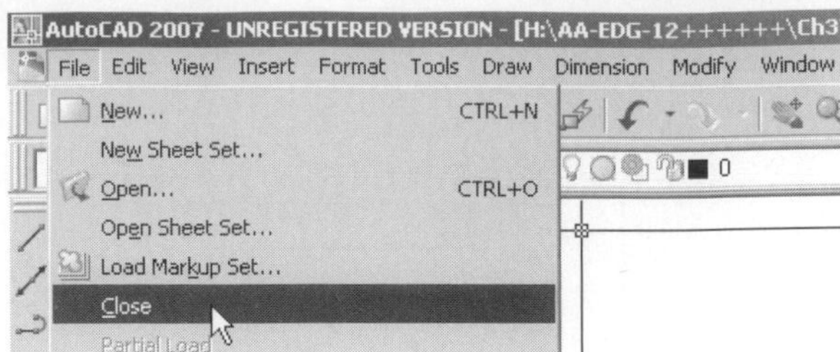

37.14 Select *Main Menu> File> Close* to close the current file; you will be prompted to save it if it has not been saved.

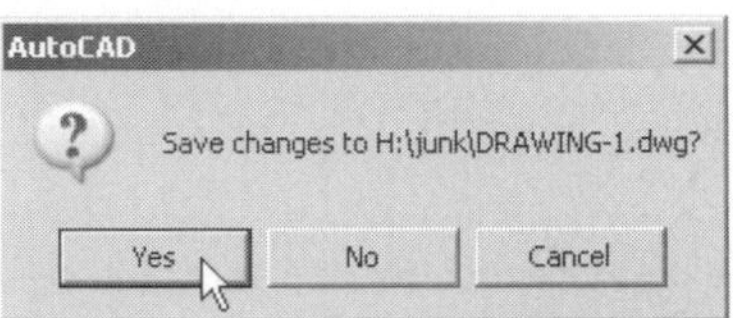

37.15 If the file has not been *Saved,* this dialog box prompts you to decide whether you want to save (*Yes, No,* or *Cancel).*

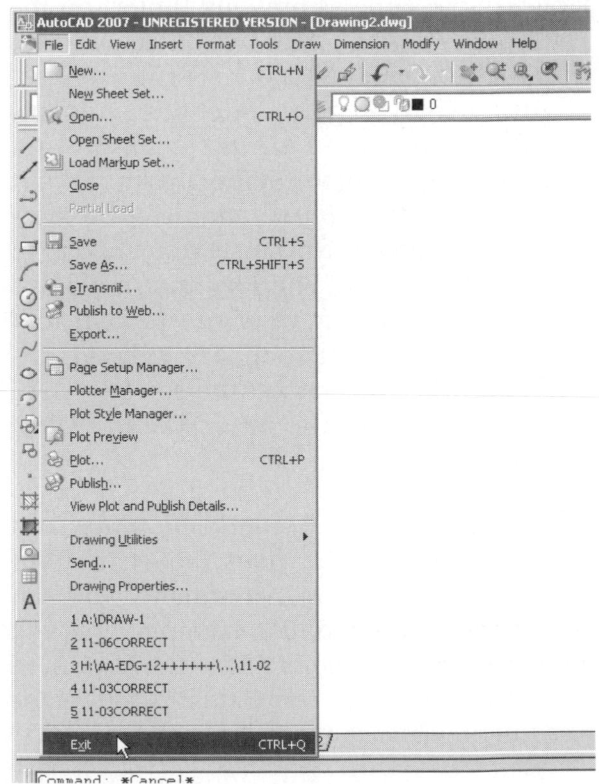

37.16 If you wish to quit AutoCAD completely: *Main Menu> File> Exit.* It is always good practice to save your drawing again before exiting the program, just to be safe.

removable disk, do not remove it from its drive until it has been saved with either the *Save* or *Save As* options.

That's how it works. Now, let's get into the details and learn more.

37.5 Introduction to Windows

The recommended operating system for AutoCAD 2007 for a single user is Windows XP, which allows several programs to be open and running at the same time. For example, a word-processing program can be running in addition to AutoCAD.

A drawing file can be manipulated with the three buttons in the upper-right corner of the window (**Figure 37.17**). The "overlapping-boxes" button is selected to display the file covering only a portion of the screen and to allow other files or programs to share the screen. The "X" button closes the current file. The dash button minimizes a file to an icon box (that retains the three buttons of the original) located above the *Command* line (**Figure 37.18**). Maximize the minimized file to fill the screen by selecting the "box" button (**Figure 37.19**) and it will return to the screen and cover the images displayed on the screen.

Windows can be resized by selecting a border, or the corner of the border, while holding down the left mouse button and "dragging" the window to size (**Figure 37.20**). When several active programs are displayed on the screen, select any point on one and it moves to the front and becomes the current program.

37.17 The icons in the upper right of the screen can be used to minimize a drawing to an icon (dash), reduce it to partial size (two boxes), or exit from the file (X).

37.18 Minimized files are displayed as an icon box above the *Command* line.

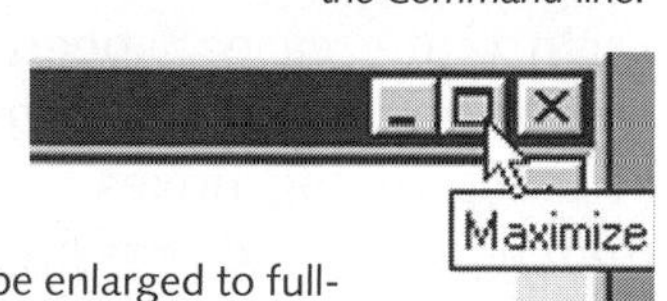

37.19 A partial screen can be enlarged to full-screen size by selecting the box button.

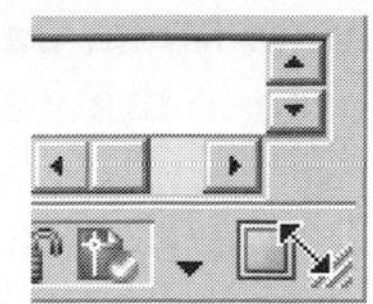

37.20 Select the lower right corner, hold down the left mouse button, and "drag" the border to size the screen as you desire.

37.6 Format of Presentation

AutoCAD has several ways of using a command in almost all cases. For example, a circle can be drawn by typing C at the *Command* line; selecting the *circle icon* from the *Draw* toolbar; or using the *Main Menu> Draw> Circle* on the drop-down menu. In each of these examples, you must select from options—*Center, radius; Center, diameter;* and others—before drawing the circle.

In this chapter the progression from one step of a command to the next level will be separated by an angle pointing to the right (>) to simplify presentation and reduce explanatory text. The commands and prompts that appear on the screen will be given in *italics* to distinguish them from supplementary notes of explanation. (Enter) is the keyboard key with this name. Once a command is selected, additional prompts given at the *Command* line at the bottom of the screen and/or in dialog boxes must be responded to.

Command Line When a circle is drawn by typing at the *Command* line, it will be presented as follows: *Command:* Circle (or C)> *Center point*> P1> *Radius*> 4 (Enter). Entries that are typed in response to prompts are underlined. The underlined P1 is a point selected on the screen, and the underlined 4 is the radius, which is typed at the *Command* line in response to the prompt *Radius.*

Main Menu Bar When the *Main Menu* bar is used to draw a circle, the sequence of steps is presented as *Main Menu> Draw> Circle> Center, radius> Center point>* P1*> Radius>* Drag to a radius of 4.

Draw Toolbar When the *Draw* toolbar is used to draw a circle, the steps are presented as *Draw* toolbar> *Circle* icon> P1, *Specify radius of circle or [Diameter]:* D, *Specify diameter of circle:* 8

37.7 Using Dialog Boxes

AutoCAD 2007 has many dialog boxes with names beginning with *DD (DDPTYPE,* for example) to interact with the user. The command *Filedia* can be used to turn off (0 = off and 1 = on) the dialog boxes if you prefer to type the commands without dialog boxes. When a command on a menu followed by three dots (...) or an arrow (>) is selected, supplemental dialog boxes will be displayed, and some of these boxes have subdialog boxes (**Figure 37.21**).

Definition boxes are provided to identify the functions of each box on the screen. Resting the cursor on a box causes a *flyout* to appear to define its function, as shown in **Figure 37.22**.

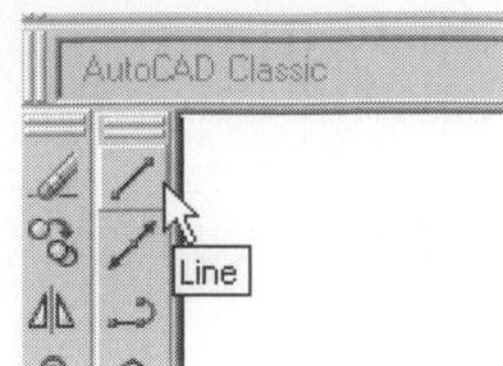

37.22 *Definition boxes* are flyout boxes that explain the functions of the various icons when the cursor is rested on them briefly.

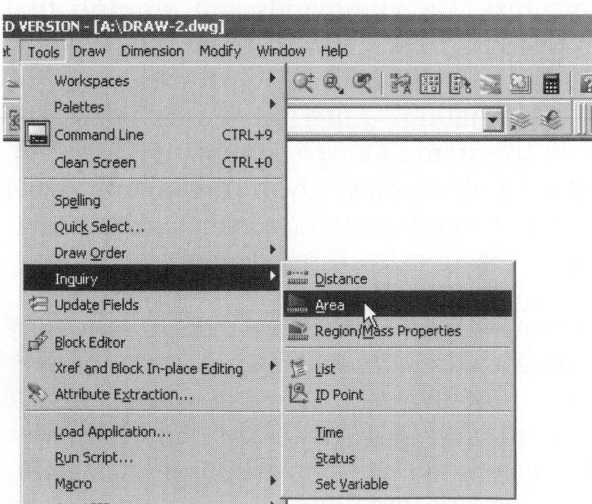

37.21 The *Main Menu* has many pull-down menus. Commands in the pull-down menu followed by black arrows have subdialog boxes. The sequence in this example is *Main Menu> Tools> Inquiry> Area.*

Double clicking the mouse (quickly pressing the left button twice) selects a file from a list and displays it. Single clicking followed by *OK* is an alternative for activating a selection. With experimentation you will soon learn where double clicking can be best applied.

Right clicking when the cursor (right mouse key) is placed over an icon displays a set of commands that are related to that particular command.

The *Select File* box in **Figure 37.23** has dialog boxes, lists, blanks, and buttons that have to be selected by the cursor. When a file is selected, it is darkened by a gray bar, and a thumbnail illustration of it is shown in the window. To find a file for which you have a name, from the *Select File* box select *Tools> Find,* click on *Find* to display the *Find:* box, and enter the name of the file (**Figure 37.24**). Pick the *Name & Location* tab> type the file name in the *Named* window> specify the file type from the *Type* window> *Browse* to select the drive or folder to search> *Find Now.* The matching files will appear in a window at the bottom of the *Find* box.

When the name of the file has been forgotten, set the *Views* option of the *Select File* menu to *Thumbnails* to obtain small views of the drawings in the current folder (**Figure 37.25**).

In many cases, speed is increased if you type commands at the *Command* line instead of using dialog boxes. What could be easier than typing L and pressing (Enter) for drawing a *Line*?

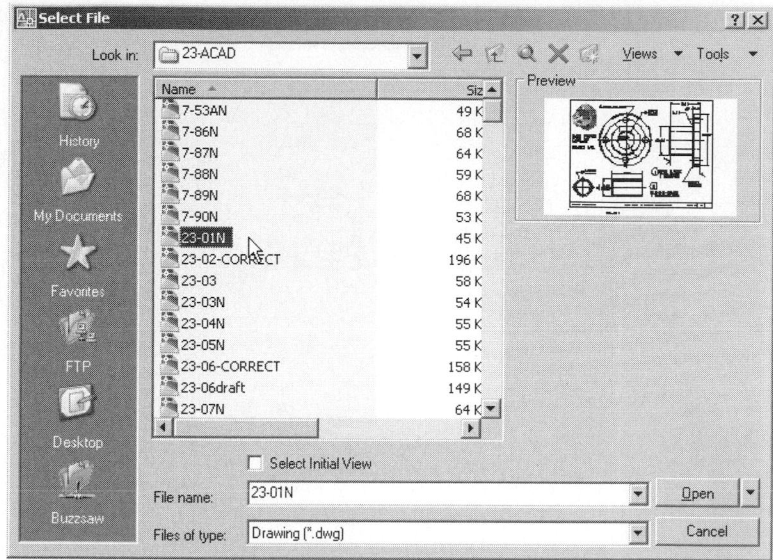

37.23 *Main Menu> File> Open* gives the *Select File* box, which displays a list of the files that can be opened. A thumbnail view of the selected file is previewed in the window for verification.

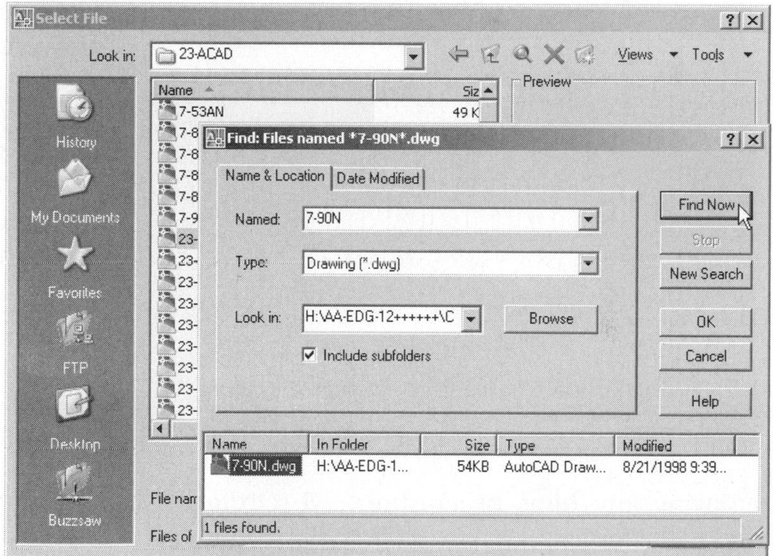

37.24 To locate a file for which you have a name, select *Tools> Find> Find* box> *Name & Location* tab> type the file name in *Named* window> select file type in *Type* window> *Browse* to select drive or folder to search> *Find Now* and the matching files appear in the window at the bottom of the *Find* box.

37.8 Drawing Aids

Function Keys

Convenient drawing aids are available from the function keys on the keyboard, which can be used to turn settings on and off (**Figure 37.26**). *F1 (Help)* can be pressed to open the help screen for instant troubleshooting. *F2 (Flip screen)* alternates between the graphics on the screen and its corresponding text mode. *F3* controls *Snap,* and *F5* controls *Isoplane. F4 (Tablet)* activates a digitizing tablet if one is attached to your computer. *F6 (Coordinates)* shows numerical coordinates of the cursor in the S*tatus* bar at the bottom of the screen as the cursor is moved. *F7 (Grid)* turns the grid on or off and refreshes the screen in the process,

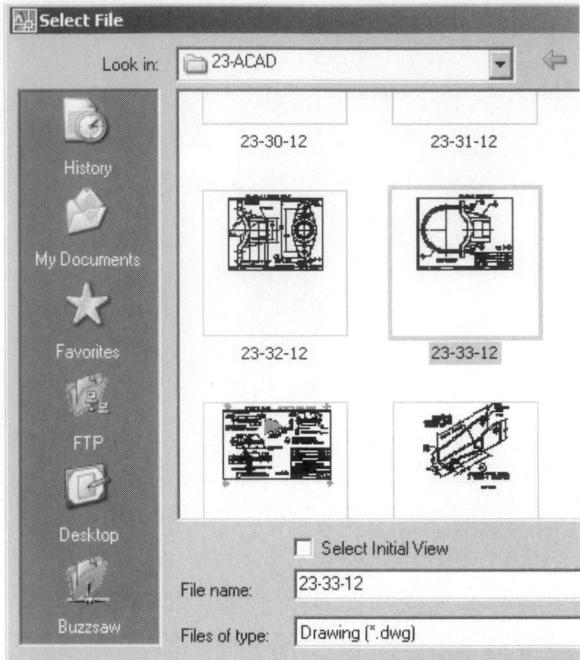

37.25 Selecting *Views* on the *Select File* menu and picking *Thumbnails* displays drawings in the folders.

37.26 These function keys on the keyboard control the options as indicated by the notes.

removing any blips or erasures. *F8 (Ortho)* forces all lines to be drawn either in horizontal or vertical directions. *F9 (Snap),* when on, makes all object points lie on points defined by an invisible grid.

One of the first settings to make when beginning a drawing is that of the area size, called *Limits,* in which the drawing will be made. To set, type Limits at the *Command* line and respond to the prompts by typing the coordinates of the diagonal across the area. The *Limits* command can also be accessed by *Main Menu> Format> Drawing Limits.* A drawing that fills an A-size sheet (11 × 8.5 in.) has a plotting area of about 10.6 × 8.1 in., or 269 × 206 mm. The drawing area is specified with the *Limits* command as follows:

Command: Limits (Enter)

Specify lower left corner [ON/OFF] <0.00,0.00>: (Enter) to accept the default value of 0,0

Specify upper right corner <12.00,9.00>: 11, 8.5 (Enter)

Press F7 *(Grid)* to see the dot pattern of the grid fill the *Limits.*

Command: Zoom (Enter)> type All (Enter) and the drawing *Limits* and *Grid* will fill the screen.

Limits can be reset at any time during the drawing session by repeating these steps.

Drafting Settings

The *Drafting Settings* box is found by *Main Menu Tools> Drafting Settings* or by typing DDrmodes (**Figure 37.27**). *Snap and Grid* is a tab with buttons for checking and blanks for filling in to activate these settings.

Snap forces the cursor to stop only at points on an imaginary grid of a specified spacing. The *Snap X* and *Snap Y* spacings can be set by typing values in the blanks. *Snap* can also be set by *Command:* Snap and specifying the spacing interval desired. When *On,* the *Snap* button in the *Status* bar at the bottom of the screen is highlighted. *Snap* can be toggled on and off by clicking on this button or by pressing *F9.*

Grid of the *Drafting Settings* box fills the *Limits* area with dots spaced apart according to typed values in the *Grid X spacing* and *Grid Y spacing* boxes. When *Snap type> Grid snap> Rectangular snap* is selected, the cursor snaps to the grid if the *Snap* and *Grid* spacings are equal.

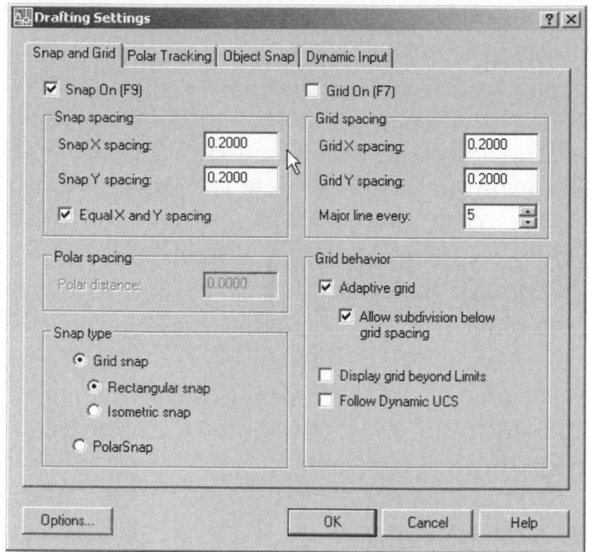

37.27 *Main Menu> Tools* menu> *Drafting Settings* dialog box (or *Comand:* DDrmodes (Enter)) has four tabs from which to make settings: *Snap and Grid, Polar Tracking, Object Snap,* and *Dynamic Input.*

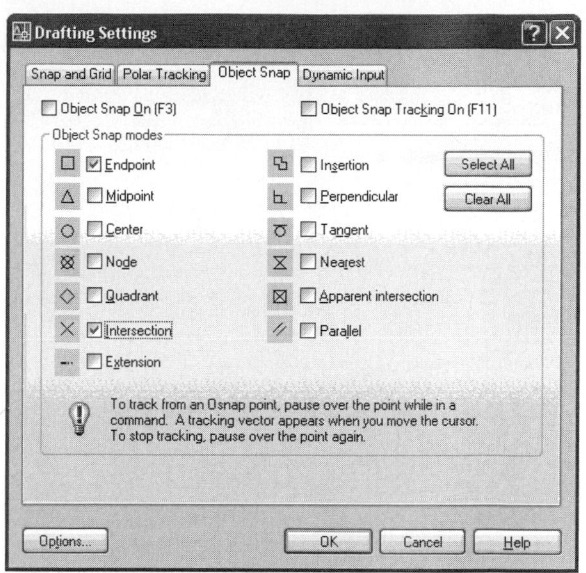

37.28 *Osnap* settings can be made from the *Object Snap* tab of the *Drafting Settings* dialog box *(DDrmodes).*

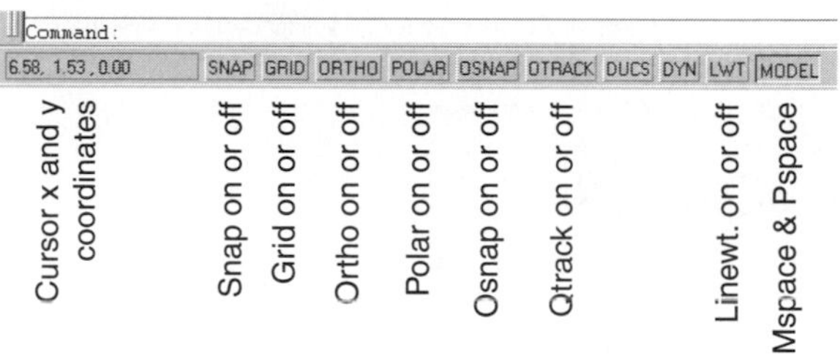

37.29 *Drawing Aids* boxes in the *Status* bar beneath the *Command* line at the bottom of the screen display the current settings. Click on these buttons to turn them on or off.

The ***Object Snap*** tab (**Figure 37.28**) gives options for making lines and other geometry of a drawing snap to previously drawn objects at specified points.

The ***Dynamic Input*** tab provides options for drawing in which points and distances are shown numerically in boxes on the screen as points and lengths are chosen.

The ***Status*** bar at the bottom of the screen displays several of the settings discussed above when they are turned *On* (**Figure 37.29**). Single clicking on these buttons toggles them off or on.

Blips (*Command:* Blipmode) are temporary markers made on the screen when selections are made with the mouse. They are removed by refreshing the screen by pressing *F7 (Grid).*

37.9 Help and Helpful Commands

Several examples of helpful commands that can be typed at the *Command* line are shown here.

Main Menu> Help> Help> AutoCAD 2007 Help gives tabs labeled *Contents, Index,* and *Search* to help you with different aspects of AutoCAD. By typing a word or phrase in the *keyword* blank as shown in **Figure 37.30** and picking the *Display* button, you will obtain detailed assistance on the screen. When a topic, *Circle,* for example, is selected and *Display* is picked, a screen of instructions will appear to help you with using the *Circle* command (**Figure 37.31**). Additional options are provided under *Help* that are self-explanatory when you experiment with them.

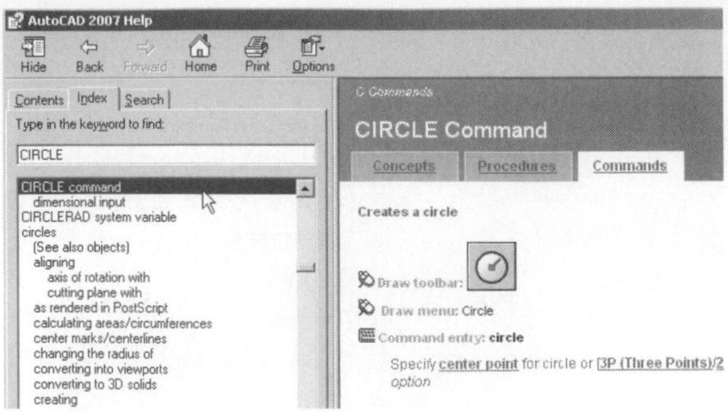

37.30 By selecting *Help* from the *Main Menu,* the *AutoCAD 2007 Help* box with three tabs appears on the screen. Select *Index* tab, type the keyword in the blank, and you will get a list of related options from which to get help, or type the name of the subject for which you need help.

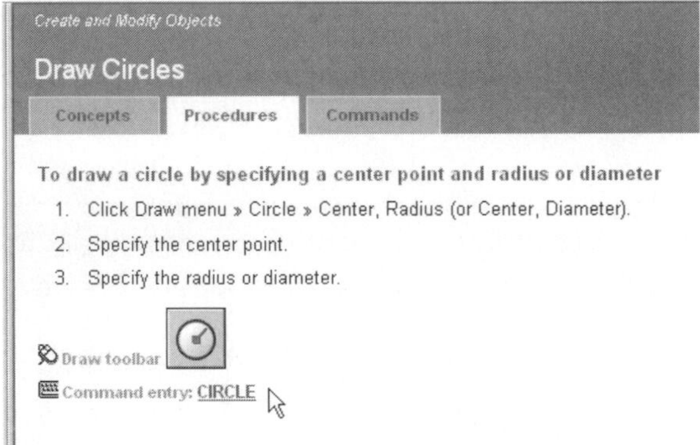

37.31 The *Help* box can be obtained by *Main Menu> Help> AutoCAD 2007 User Help>* type subject Circle> Select *CIRCLE* from list (all caps for a command)> Select tab labeled *Procedures>* Select the option *To draw a circle by specifying a center point and a radius or diameter* to get the help screen shown here.

The *Purge* command *(Main Menu> File> Drawing Utilities> Purge> All)* can be used at any time to remove unused layers, blocks, and other attributes from files. *Purge* can be activated by using *Command:* Purge (Enter) to obtain the *Purge* box, where you can select *All items* or *Blocks/ Dimension styles/ Layers/ Linetypes/ Materials/ Mline styles/ Plot styles/ Shapes/ Table styles/ Text styles/ Visual styles.* The *All* option is used to eliminate all unused references one at a time as prompted. The other purge options remove selected features of a drawing. Purging unused attributes of a file eliminates clutter and saves disk space.

Main Menu> Tools> Inquiry> List (or *Command:* List) and select any object drawn on the screen to obtain information about it. For example, when a circle is selected, its radius, circumference, and area plus the coordinates of its center point are displayed.

Modify toolbar> Copy icon> is used to select objects on the screen (single objects or groups of objects) with the cursor, pick a new position, and make a duplicate of the selection. Multiple copies will continue to be made until (Enter) is pressed.

37.10 Drawing Layers

An almost infinite number of layers can be created, each assigned a *Name, Color, Linetype, Lineweight,* and *Plot Style,* on which to draw. For example, a yellow layer named *Hidden* for drawing dashed lines may be created.

Architects use separate copies of the same floor plan for different applications: dimensions, floor finishes, electrical details, and so forth. The same basic plan is used for all these applications by turning on the needed layers and turning off others.

Working with Layers Layers and their settings are created and manipulated in the *Layer Properties Manager* box, which is displayed by selecting the paper-stack icon next to the *Layer Control* panel (**Figure 37.32**). For most working drawings, the layers shown in the *Layer Properties Manager* box in **Figure 37.33** are sufficient. Layers are assigned linetypes, lineweights, and different colors so they can easily be distinguished from one another. The 0 (zero) layer is the default layer, which can be turned off or frozen but not deleted.

Layers can be created by selecting the starburst box to obtain *Layer1,* the default name, which can be replaced with a new name

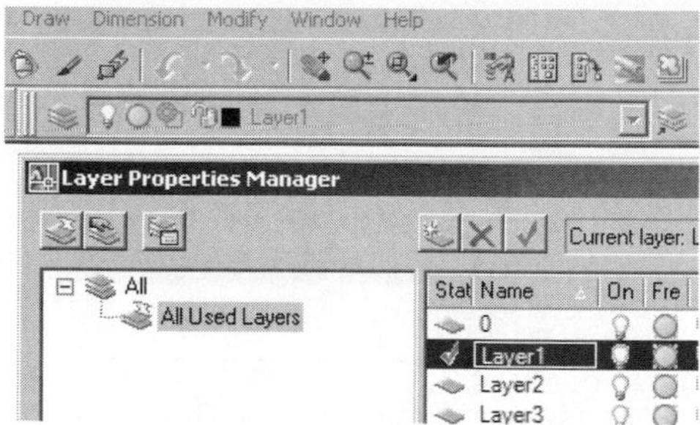

37.32 Select the paper stack next to *Layer Control* panel to display the *Layer Properties Manager* box for setting all layer properties.

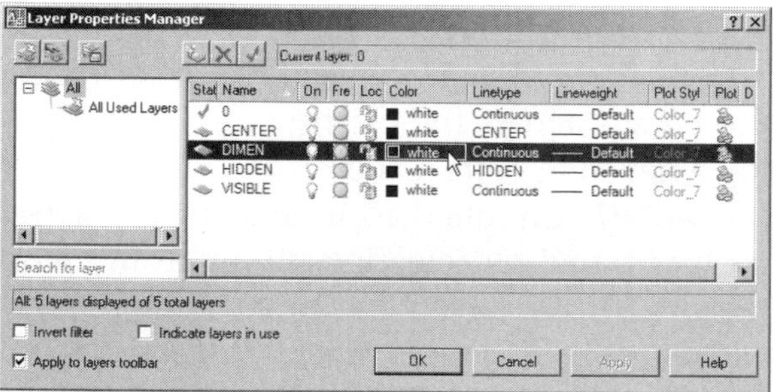

37.33 *Main Menu> Format> Layer. . .> Layer Properties Manager* box (or *Command:* Layer) lists the layers and their properties. From this box, layers can be created and deleted, linetypes and colors assigned, and other settings made.

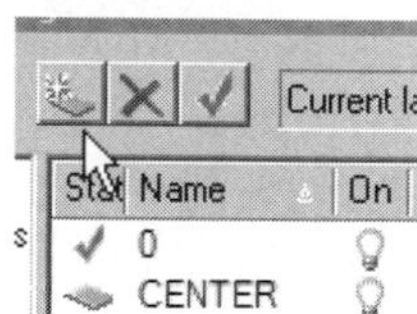

37.34 The starburst icon creates a new layer named Layer1 that can be renamed. The X deletes a layer, and the check makes the selected layer the current layer on which drawings are made.

(**Figure 37.34**). The new layer will appear in the listing of layers with a default color of white and a continuous linetype, all of which can be changed to your specifications.

Color for a new layer can be changed from its default color of white by selecting its current color name in the *Color* column to display the *Select Color* menu. From this menu, pick a color and pick the *OK* button to finalize the color change (**Figure 37.35**).

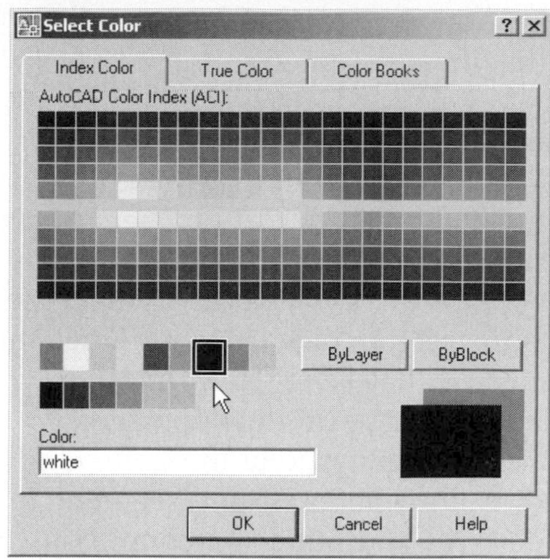

37.35 To obtain the *Select Color* box, *Main Menu> Format> Color> Select Color* box (or select the current color to be changed that is listed under *Color* of the *Layer Properties Manager* box).

Linetypes are found by clicking on the default linetype of the new layer in the *Layer Properties Manager* box. The *Select Linetype* box appears. Select *Load . . .* and the *Load or Reload Linetypes* box appears with a list of linetypes from which to select (**Figure 37.36**). To assign a hidden *Linetype* to a layer named *Hidden,* select the linetype of that layer, select

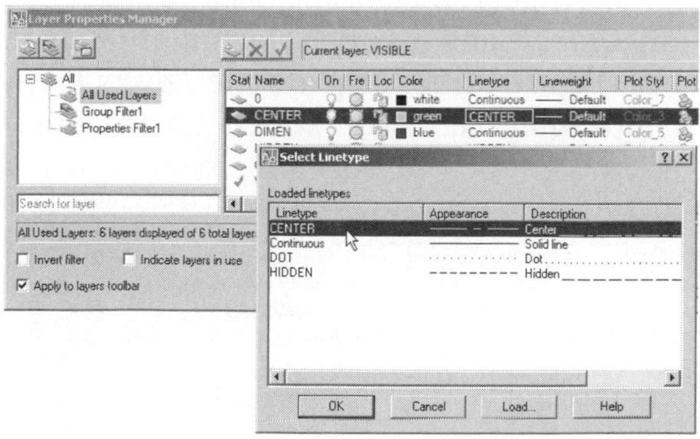

37.36 In *Main Menu> Format> Layer. . .> Layer Properties Manager* box> select *Linetype* of the selected layer (or *Command:* DDltype) (Enter) to display the *Select Linetype* box. Pick *Load* to display a list of linetypes from which to select, and select *OK*.

Hidden from the *Select Linetype* box, pick *OK*, and the line is assigned to the layer. Now, all lines drawn on the *Hidden* layer will be dashed lines.

Lineweights are found by clicking on the current lineweight of a layer in the *Layer Properties Manager* box. The *Lineweight* box appears with a list of lineweights. Select the desired lineweight, pick *OK*, and the line is assigned to that layer. Now, lines drawn on this layer will have this line thickness.

Ltscale, when typed at the *Command* line, modifies the lengths of line segments of *all* hidden lines and other noncontinuous linetypes at one time.

Layers Toolbar

A layer must be selected as the current layer to draw on it using the assigned color and linetypes. The *Layers* toolbar offers the quickest method of setting a layer (**Figure 37.37**). Picking a point anywhere within the *Layers* toolbar panel displays a listing of the named layers and their properties, from which a layer can be selected to make it the current layer (**Figure 37.38**). Now, you can draw on this current layer.

This same portion of the *Layer Control* panel can also be used to make other layer assignments: *On* and *Off, Freeze* and *Thaw, Lock* and *Unlock,* and others. Selecting the *Layers* icon (**Figure 37.37**) displays the *Layers Properties Manager* box, from which the previously covered setting can be made. This box can also be displayed by *Command:* LA (Enter).

Renaming a layer can be done from the *Layers Properties Manager* box by dragging the cursor across the existing name and typing a new one in its place.

On/Off is applied to a layer in the *Layer* toolbar panel by selecting the lightbulb icon (**Figure 37.38**). Layers can be turned on or off with buttons from the *Layers Properties Manager* box (**Figure 37.36**) or *Command:* LA and picking *Off.* An *Off* layer that is selected as the current layer can be drawn on, but this is seldom done.

Freeze and ***Thaw*** options (sun icon) under the *Layer* toolbar are used like the *On* and *Off* options (**Figure 37.38**). *Freeze* a layer and it will (unlike an *Off* layer) be ignored by the computer until it has been *Thawed,* which makes regeneration faster than when *Off* is used.

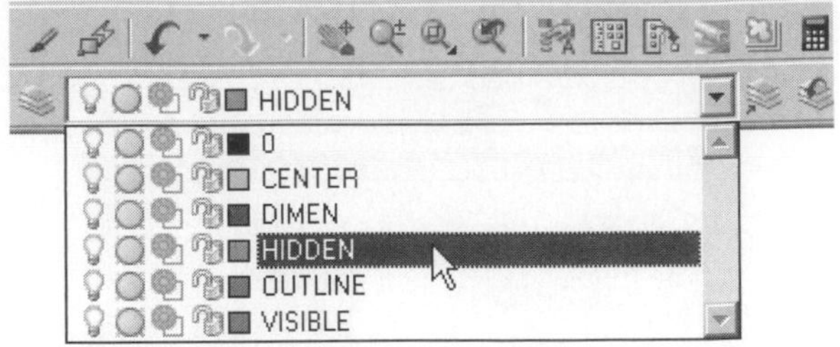

37.38 Select any point on the *Layers* toolbar panel where the name of the active layer's name appears, or select the down-arrow button, and this drop-down list of the layers appears.

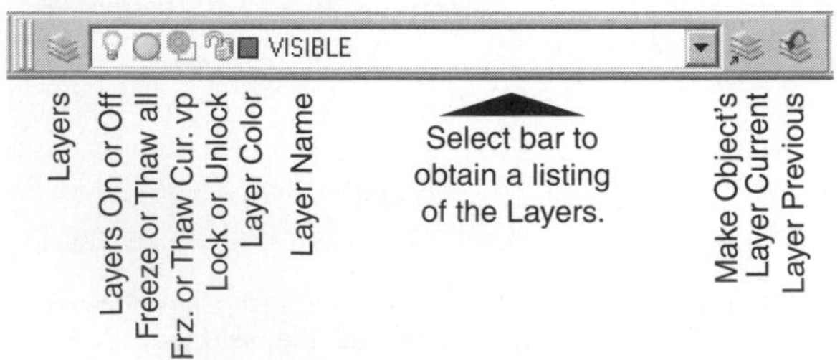

37.37 The *Layers* toolbar offers easy access to layers and their properties by selecting one of the icons shown here.

37.11 Toolbars

Right clicking on any toolbar displayed on the screen displays a listing of all toolbars with check marks to identify those currently displayed on the screen (**Figure 37.39**). Toolbars are selected by right clicking on any toolbar that is currentely displayed and selecting from a list of toolbars. A portion of the *Standard* toolbar (**Figure 37.40**) gives a sequence of icons for commands from *Qview* to *Redo.* The

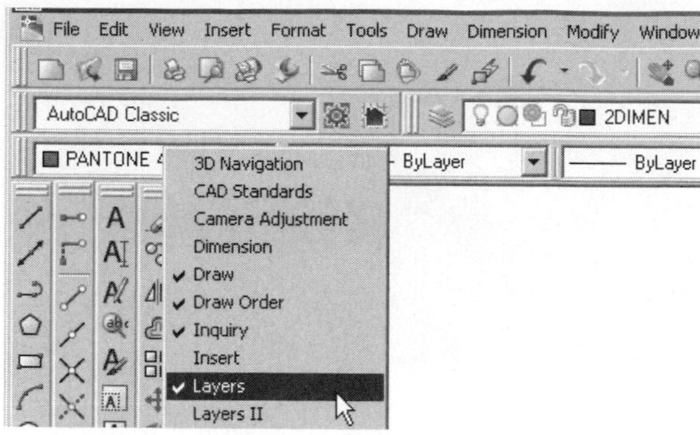

37.39 Right click on any toolbar displayed on the screen and a listing of all toolbars will appear with check marks next to those currently displayed. Only a partial listing is shown here.

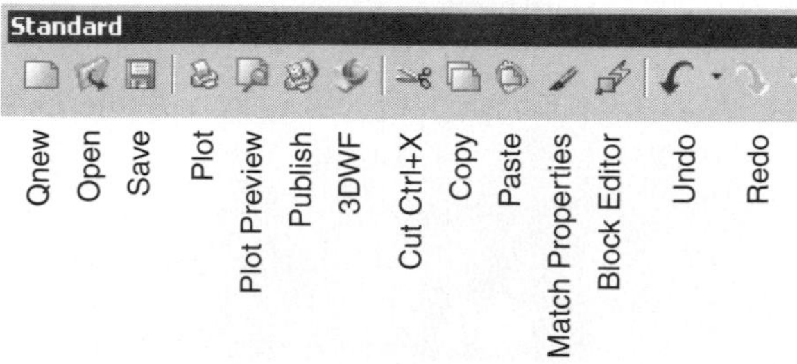

37.40 The left half of the *Standard* toolbar provides many routine operations that can be accessed with the cursor.

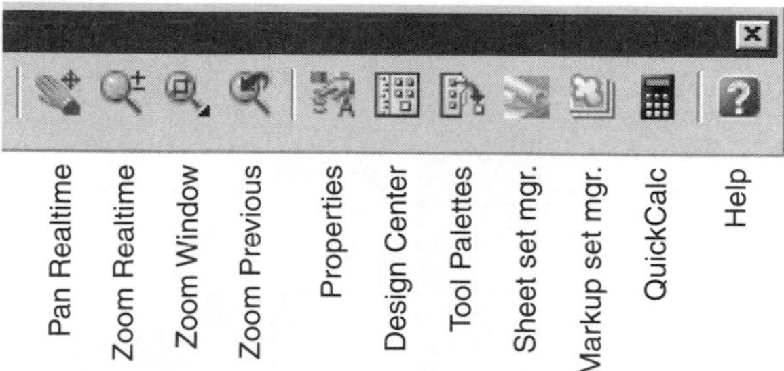

37.41 The right half of the *Standard* toolbar has additional helpful commands that you will need for most drawings.

remainder of the *Standard* toolbar is shown from *Pan Realtime* to *Help* in **Figure 37.41**.

Toolbars can be moved about the screen by selecting a point on their blue title bar, holding down the select button of the mouse, and moving the cursor to a new position. *Toolbars* can be *docked* by moving them into contact

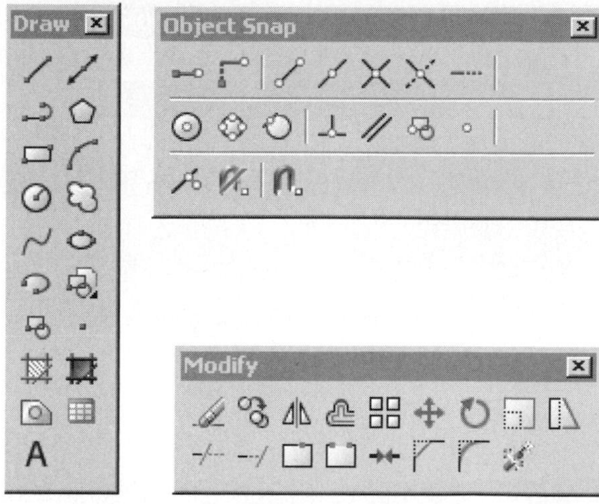

37.42 *Toolbars* can be configured by dragging their corners to make single, double, or triple strips that are horizontal or vertical. They can be docked at the borders or left "floating" on the screen. They can be undocked by selecting the double-line symbol at their ends with the select button held down.

with a border on the screen. They can be changed from single strips to double and triple blocks by moving the corners of the toolbars, or into vertical or horizontal strips depending on the border of the screen to which they are moved (**Figure 37.42**). When located in the open area of the screen, toolbars will appear as *floating menus.* When a small icon needs explanation, place the pointer on the icon, and a flyout box will appear with its definition.

37.12 A New Drawing

To create a new drawing, select *Main Menu> File> New>* (**Figure 37.43**) and the *Create New Drawing* box appears giving two options: *Advanced Setup* or *Quick Setup* (**Figure 37.44**). Pick *Advanced Setup,* set the *Units* to *Decimal* with a *Precision* (decimal places) of 0.00, and select *Next* (**Figure 37.45**). In the following screen (**Figure 37.46**), set the *Angle* to *Decimal Degrees* with a *Precision* of 0 and pick *Next.* In the *Angle Measure* box (**Figure 37.47**),

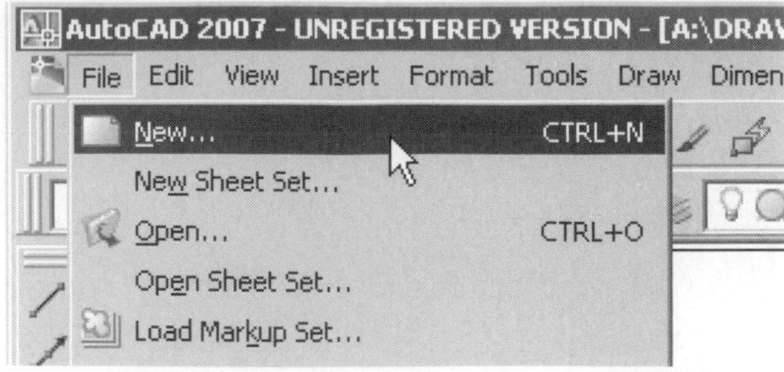

37.43 Begin the creation of a new drawing using these steps: *Main Menu> File> New.*

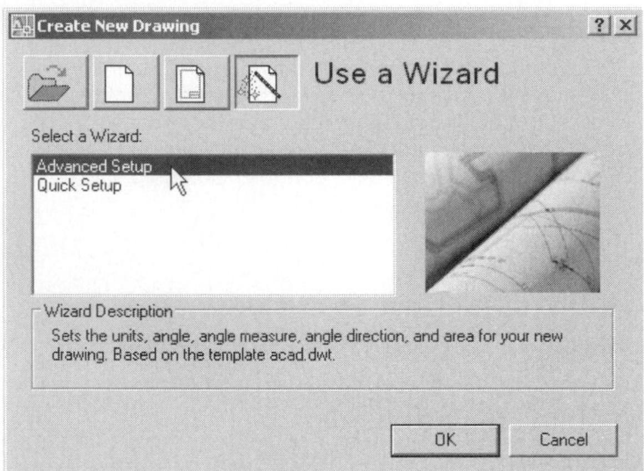

37.44 The *Create New Drawing* box appears and offers three options for a new drawing. Select *Use a Wizard> Advanced Setup>* and *OK.*

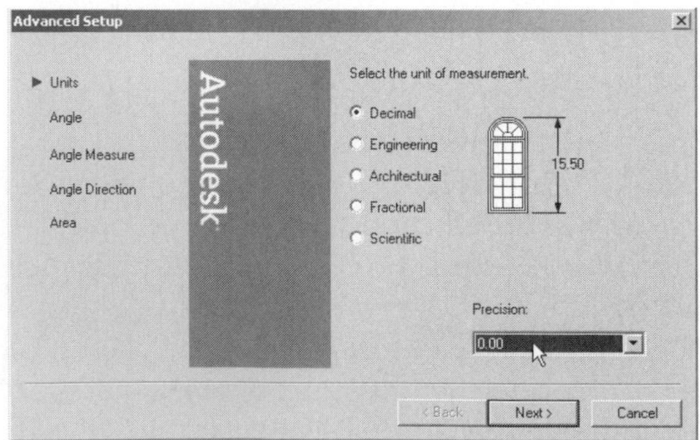

37.45 Set *Units* to *Decimal* and set *Precision to* 0.00 (two decimal places: X.00, for example).

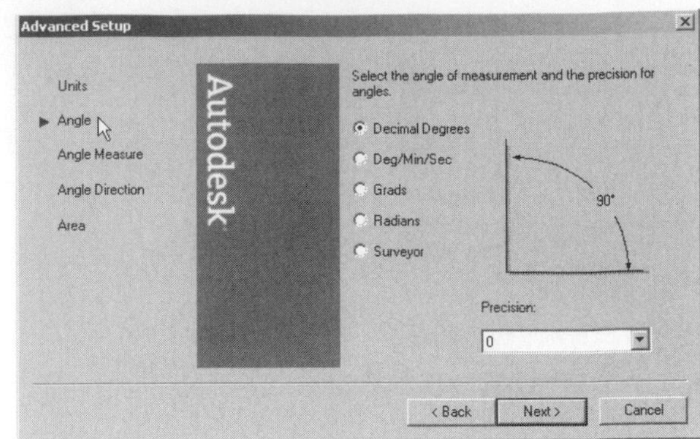

37.46 For *Angle,* select *Decimal Degrees* with a *Precision* of 0 and pick *Next.*

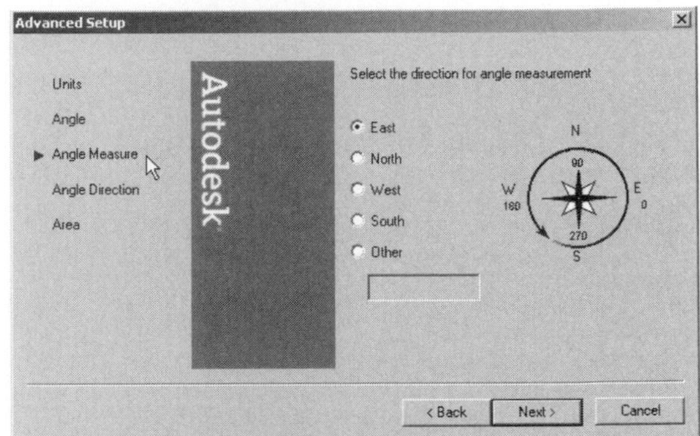

37.47 For *Angle Measure,* select the *East* and *Next* buttons.

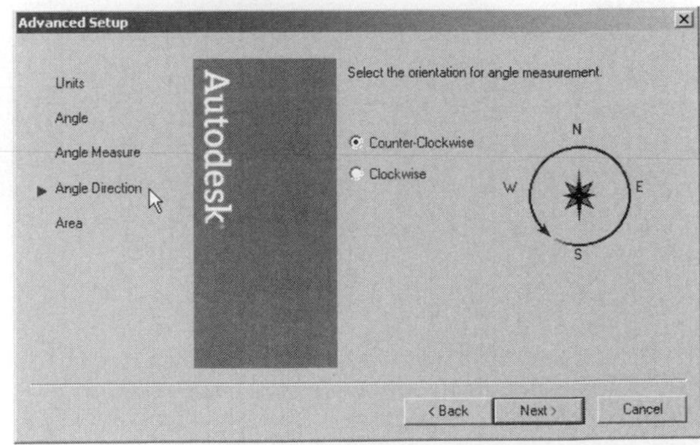

37.48 For *Angle Direction* select *Counter-Clockwise* and *Next.*

set the angle measurement to *East* and pick *Next.* In the *Angle Direction* box (**Figure 37.48**), set the angle direction to *Counter-Clockwise* and pick *Next.* In the *Area* box

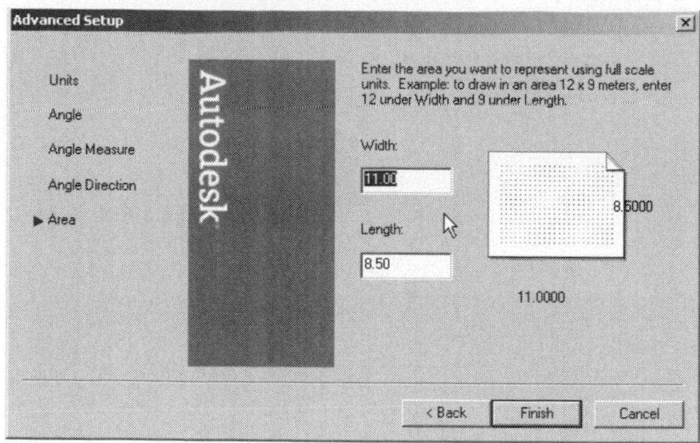

37.49 For the drawing *Area* type values of 11 and 8.5 for *Width* and *Length,* respectively, for an 8.5 × 11 sheet size and pick *Finish.*

(**Figure 37.49**), set the values for *Width* (11) and *Length* (8.5) and pick *Finish.*

Prototype Drawing

The drawing screen appears ready for drawing. If the grid dots do not appear, press *F7* to show them; the upper right dot has coordinates of about 11 and 8.5, the sheet size that was assigned. Draw a border using *Line*> 0,0> 10.4, 0> 10.4, 7.8> 0, 7.8> 0,0 to get a 10.4 × 7.8 border (**Figure 37.50**). Save this size

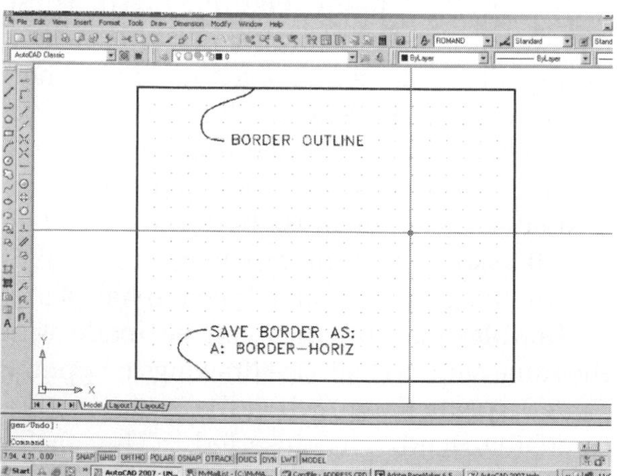

37.50 In the new screen, press *F7* to turn the grid on and *Command:* Zoom> (Enter)> All (Enter) to make the grid fill the drawing area. Draw a border (10.4 × 7.8), *Save As* A:ABORD-HORIZ, and close the file.

A border for future use as a prototype file for making drawings with these same settings (*Main Menu*> *File*> *Save As*> A:ABORD-HORIZ (Enter)). Close this file (*Main Menu*> *File*> *Close*), and the drawing leaves the screen.

Using the Prototype Drawing

So far, you have been working entirely in *Model Space,* which is preferred for the two-dimensional drawing covered in this chapter. The application of *Model Space* and *Paper Space* in combination will be covered in Chapter 38.

To make a drawing using the settings and border made in the previous sequence, open the prototype file (*Main Menu*> *File*> *Open*> A:ABORD-HORIZ), and the border and grid appear on the screen as it did at the end of the last drawing (**Figure 37.51**). Save the file with a new name (*Main Menu*> *File*> *Save As*> DWG5> (Enter)), and DWG5 becomes the current file and replaces the prototype file on the screen. (This same procedure can be used to create a new file by saving the prototype file to a new name while preserving the prototype file in its original form.)

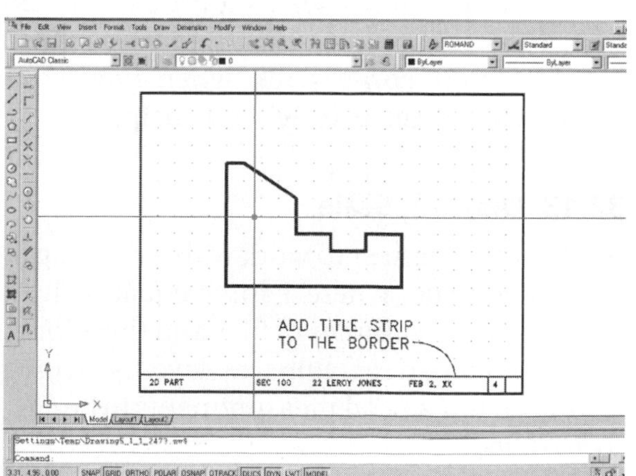

37.51 Open A:ABORD-HORIZ, save the file (*Main Menu*> *Save As*> DWG5 (Enter)), and DWG5 becomes the current drawing. Make your drawing, add a title strip to the border, and save the file (*Main Menu*> *File*> *Save*).

37.52 When saving a drawing file with *Save As*, you will be asked by this box if you want to update the existing file. Selecting *Yes* replaces the named file with the current file.

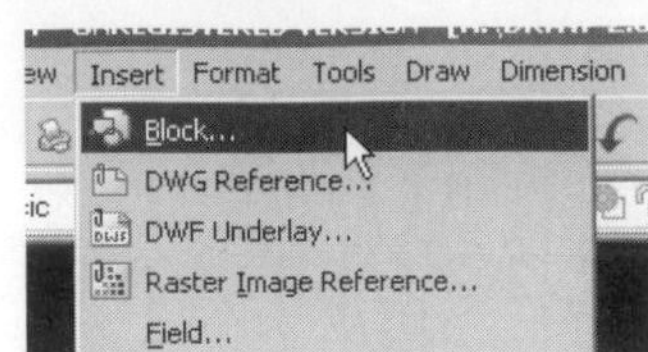

37.53 To insert a file into another file, from *Main Menu* select *Insert* and *Block*.

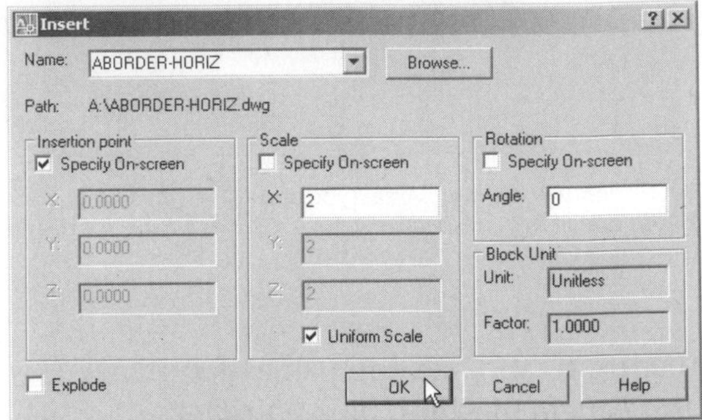

37.54 Type the name of the file to insert, A:ABORD-HORIZ, select *Uniform Scale*, assign a *Scale* factor of 2, select *OK*, and insert the file at 0,0 at the *Command* line when prompted.

Add a title strip to the border for your name, date, and other information required by your instructor. You may consider making this information part of your prototype file so it will be displayed every time it is used: *File> Save As>* A:ABORD-HORIZ. Since you are saving to an existing file, the *Save Drawing As* box in **Figure 37.52** will ask you if you want to replace it; select *Yes*. Prototype file ABORD-HORIZ is updated so the title strip will be included when it is used next.

Make your drawing within the border and save it *(Main Menu> File> Save As> DWG5)*, and your drawing is ready to be plotted.

Section 37.70 covers the techniques of customizing your title block for classroom drawings, but first, you must learn more about the operation of AutoCAD. **If the discussion of making a title block seems a little advanced for you at this point, omit the text portion, leave it, and come back when you have learned a few more drawing principles**.

37.13 Drawing Scale

It is best and easiest to work with a drawing at a full-size scale, where 1 in. is equal to 1 in. The previous examples of files and title blocks were developed as full-size layouts, which permits text size and measurements to be easily handled.

Half-size drawings can be made by creating a new drawing, DWG6, by using the *Advanced Setup* steps covered in the last section. As shown in **Figure 37.53**, insert the prototype drawing, A:ABORD-HORIZ. Use the following steps: *(Main Menu> Insert> Block> File>* A:ABORD-HORIZ> set parameters: check *Uniform Scale,* type 2 in the *X-Scale window> OK>* type 0,0 at the *Command* line as the insertion point (**Figure 37.54**)). These commands insert the border and title strip at double size (scale = 2). For a double-size metric drawing, the scale would be 25.4 × 2 = 50.8 for millimeters. A full-size drawing is made within the double-size border. At plot time the double-size border must be reduced to half size (0.5) so it will fit on its sheet, and the full-size drawing within it is reduced to half size.

Double-size drawings can be made with the same steps as half-size drawings except the *Scale* is 0.5 (half size) when the prototype file, A:ABORD-HORIZ, is inserted. (The factor would be 25.4 × 0.5 = 12.7 for millimeters.) At plot time, the half-size border must be enlarged by a factor of 2 so it will fill the sheet, and the full-size drawing within it is doubled in size.

Using this logic, you can determine other combinations of scale factors for drawings of any scale. The important point to remember is that you are better off working with full-size drawings and scaling at plot time.

37.14 Saving and Exiting

The pull-down file *(Main Menu> File)* gives options for saving a drawing—*Save* and *Save As*—that can be selected from the pull-down menu, the *Standard* toolbar, or by typing one of these commands at the *Command* line.

Saving

At the *Command:* Save (Enter) to "quick save" to the current file's name if it has been previously named and saved. If the file is unnamed, the *Save* command prompts for a file name by displaying the *Save Drawing As* dialog box in **Figure 37.55**. Select the directory and name the file (A:NEW 7) to save it on the disk in drive A. The new drawing, *A:NEW7,* becomes the current file on the screen.

Exiting

To exit the drawing session and close AutoCAD, select *Main Menu> File> Exit.* If you have not saved immediately before selecting *Exit,* the dialog box shown in **Figure 37.52** asks if you want to save the updated drawing. Select *Yes,* and the *Save Drawing As* menu box appears for assigning the drive, directory, file name, and file type. To exit without saving, respond to *Save Changes?* with *No,* and the latest changes made since the last *Save* will be discarded.

The command *Close* saves the current drawing but does not close AutoCAD. When using *Command:* Close (Enter) you will be prompted to *Save* the drawing if it has been changed since the last *Save.* If the drawing has not been previously named, the *Save Drawing As* dialog box will prompt you for a file name. The previous version of the drawing is automatically saved as a backup file with a *.bak* extension, and the current drawing is saved with a *.dwg* extension. Several drawing files can be open at the same time during a session.

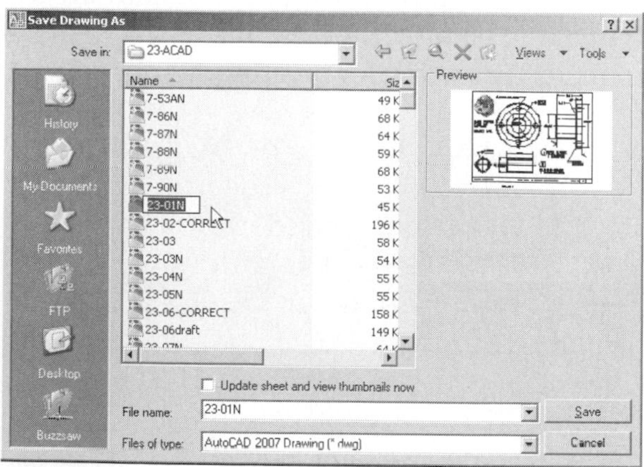

37.55 Name and save the file with the following steps: *Main Menu> File> Save As* (give its name in the *File name:* window).

37.15 Plotting and Plotting Setups

To plot a drawing before ending a drawing session, select *File> Plot* to display the *Plot – Model* box (**Figure 37.56**). Select the *Plot Device* tab to obtain the subdialog box for selecting

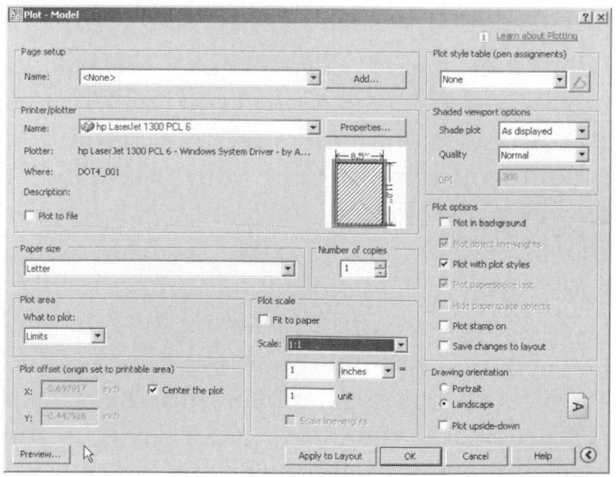

37.56 The printing options for a laser printer (without physical pens) are specified in this box *(Main Menu> File> Plot> Plot-Model* tab). Select the printer to be used from the pull-down window across from *Name:* under *Printer/plotter.*

HP 7475 plotter to make a pen drawing. (A *plotter* has pens that plot a drawing, whereas a *printer* has no pens but sprays the ink onto the drawing.)

Plotter Settings

Main Menu> File> Plot> Printer/Plotter tab> *Name> HP 7475A>* and the physical pens can be set for a Hewlett Packard 7475A pen plotter (**Figure 37.56**). Since plotters use physical pens, the pens to be used by each color on the screen must be specified and properly located in the pen holder. The colors of the lines on the paper plot depend on the colors of the physical pens, which may be all one color, and lineweights will be determined by the lineweights of the physical pens, usually 0.3 and 0.7 mm.

A *Color* of red, a pen *Speed* of 9 in. per sec (228 mm per sec), and a *Width* of .01 (0.25 mm) is assigned to pen 1 (the slot occupied by the pen in the pen holder). All lines drawn in red on the screen will plot with pen 1 at this speed. Select *Save As> Pen Plotter HP7475* and the settings are saved with a *.pc3* extension for this setup.

Printer Settings

Use *Main Menu> Plot> File> Plot-Model* box> *Printer/plotter-Name:> hp LaserJet 1300 PCL 6* to select the configured printer that you intend to use for plotting your drawing. Set *Drawing orientation* to *Landscape,* specify *Plot area (Limits, Display,* or *Window),* assign a *Plot scale,* set *Plot offset* to *Center the plot.* Save this *Page setup* by selecting the *Add* button (**Figure 37.56**) and naming it in the *Add Page Setup* box that appears on the screen (**Figure 37.57**), then pick *OK.* A listing of the available setups is obtained by picking a point in the *Name* window (**Figure 37.58**). These settings will be saved with the drawing when the file is saved.

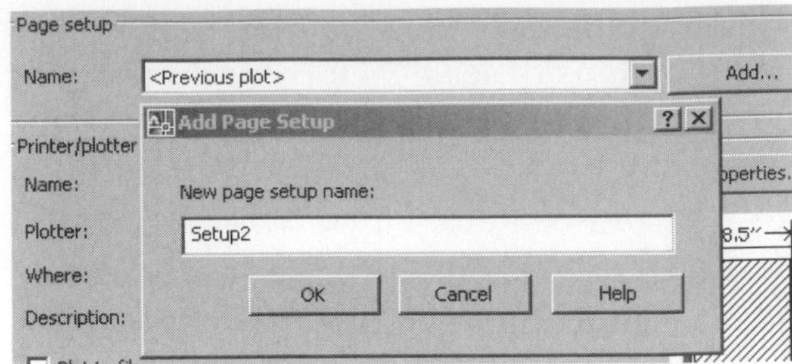

37.57 Select the *Add...* button to obtain this *Add Page Setup* box to assign a name to the current setup.

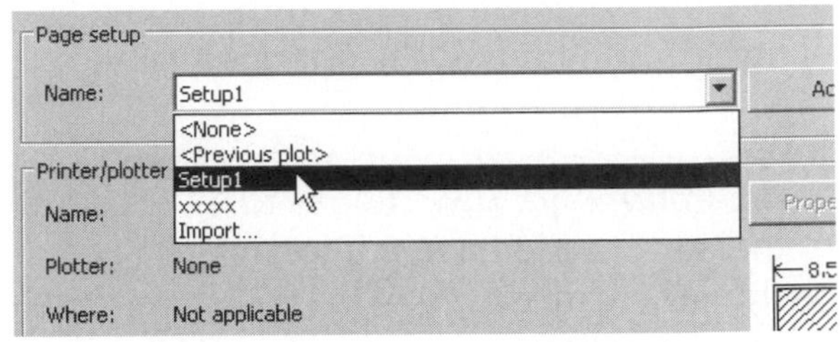

37.58 Pick the down arrow left of the *Add...* button, and the names of the available *Page setups* scroll down.

Plot Settings Definitions

Plot settings applicable to both pen plotters and printers are set in the *Plot-Model* box shown in **Figure 37.56.**

Plot area (Figure 37.59):

Display plots the portion of the drawing shown on the screen.

Extents plots a drawing to its maximum extents. It is good practice to use *Zoom Extents* to ready a drawing for printing.

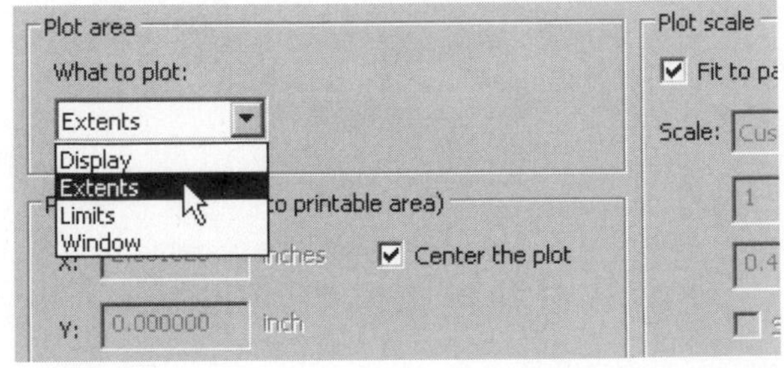

37.59 The *Plot area* section of the *Plot-model* box is used to specify the portion of the drawing that will be plotted: *Display, Extents, Limits,* or *Window.*

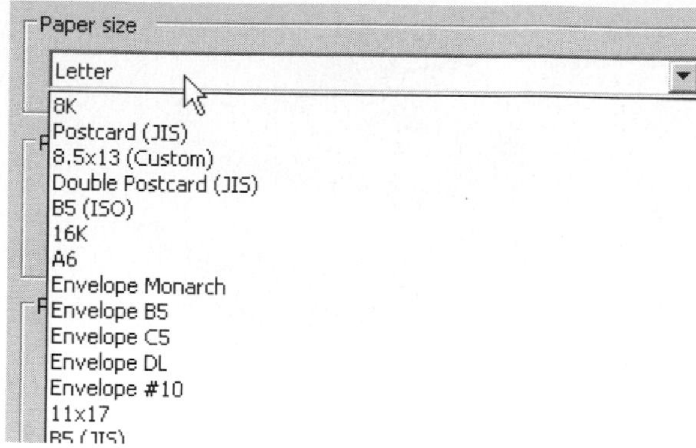

37.60 The *Paper size* window gives a listing of the standard plot sizes.

Limits is used to plot the portion of the drawing bounded by the grid pattern defined by its *Limits.*

Window specifies the portion of a drawing to be plotted when the window is sized with the cursor or coordinates typed from the keyboard.

Paper size area (Figure 37.60):

Paper size lists standard and user-specified plot sizes

Drawing orientation area:

Drawing orientation offers *Portrait* and *Landscape* options.

Plot scale area (Figure 37.61):

Scale can be typed in the edit boxes or selected from the pull-down window where 1:2 appears. The scale 1 = 1 is full size, 1 = 2 is half size, and 2 = 1 is double size.

37.61 Select the desired scale (1 = 2, half size in this case). If *Fit to paper* is selected, the drawing fills the sheet if the placement of the orgin permits.

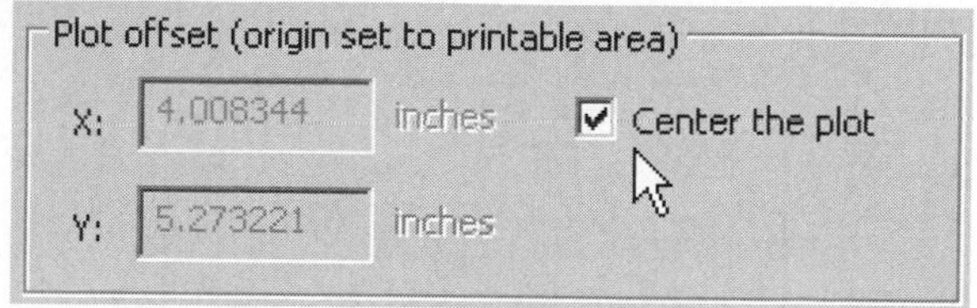

37.62 Select the *Center the plot* box to position the plot at the center of the sheet with equal margins. The X- and Y-coordinates of the drawing's origin are given.

Fit to paper calculates the scale that makes the drawing's extent fill the plotting area and be as large as possible.

Plot offset area (Figure 37.62):

Center the plot is picked to specify that the drawing will be centered on the sheet.

Plot offset can be set with X- and Y-coordinates to locate a plot on a sheet.

Preview button:

A general preview showing the relationship of the drawing area to the sheet size is shown after the *Paper size* has been selected and the *Plot scale* specified to verify whether the drawing will fit properly (**Figure 37.63**). The part of the drawing area that exceeds the paper size cannot be plotted unless the scale, origin, or both are adjusted.

Select the *Preview...* button to display the entire drawing on the screen as it will appear when plotted (**Figure 37.64**). Right click to *Pan* and *Zoom* about the preview drawing. Pick *Exit* to return to the *Plot* dialog box, or pick *Plot* to print the drawing.

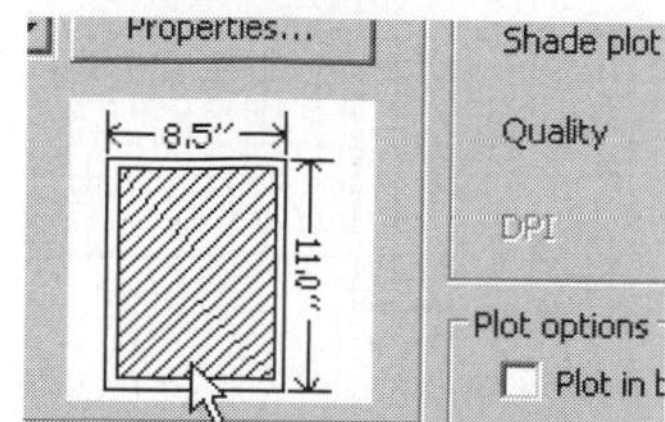

37.63 Once the *Paper size* is specified, a graphic preview of the general appearance of the page will appear in the *Printer/plotter* area.

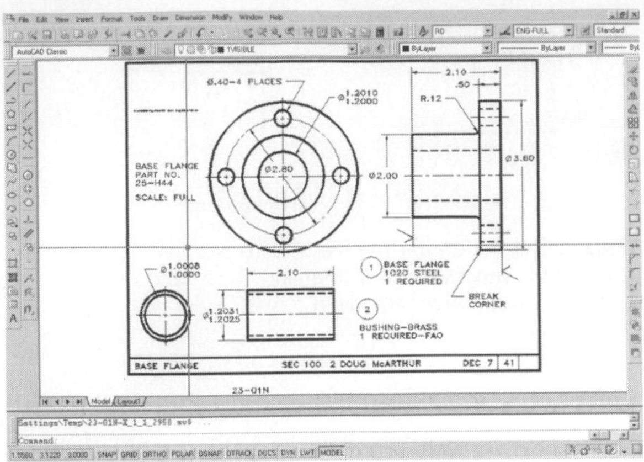

37.64 Select *Preview* to display this view of the drawing that is to be printed when *Plot* is selected.

37.16 Readying the Printing Device

Plotter

Load paper in the plotter, as shown in **Figure 37.65** with the thick pen (P.7) in slot 1 and the thin pen (P.3) in slot 2 as specified by *Pen assignments* in **Figure 37.56**. Press (Enter), and the plot will begin. Plotting can be canceled by pressing (Esc), but it may take almost a minute for it to take effect. When the plot is completed, select *File> Exit* to close AutoCAD and end the session.

1. Load paper, lower lever
2. Pens: P.7 (Slot 1); P.3 (Slot 2)
3. Set for A-Size
4. Press P1 and P2

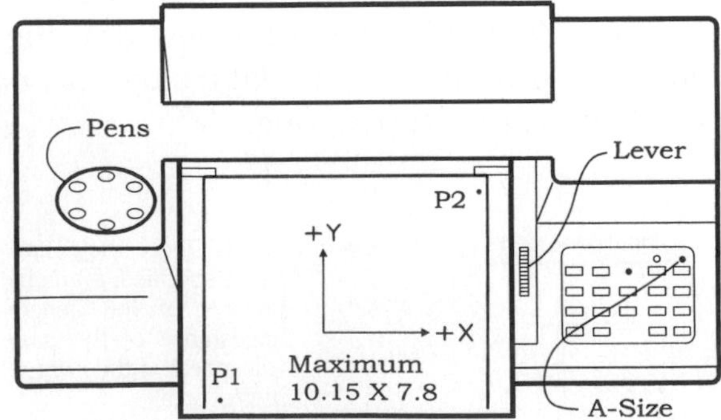

37.65 The Hewlett-Packard 7475A plotter is often the plotter of choice for size A and size B plots with pens.

37.66 The Hewlett-Packard LaserJet 1300 printer has no physical pens; the ink is sprayed onto the paper. *(Courtesy Hewlett-Packard Company.)*

Printer

Load the printer with the necessary sheets of paper, be sure the printer is turned on, display the drawing to be plotted on the screen, select *Main Menu> File> Plot> Plot-Model* menu, select the name of the *Page setup,* select the printer, and pick *Preview.* If it appears correct, pick *OK,* and the drawing file is sent to the printer, where it is printed. A laser printer has no physical pens, since the ink is transferred onto the paper (**Figure 37.66**).

Now that we know how to set a few drawing aids, save files, and plot, let's learn how to make drawings.

37.17 Lines

Open your prototype drawing, *Main Menu> File> Open>* A:ABORD-HORIZ, and use *Save As* to name the drawing A:NO1, which becomes the current drawing with the same settings as A:ABORD-HORIZ.

A *Line* (called an object) can be drawn by using the *Draw* toolbar, the *Main Menu (Main Menu> Draw> Line>* select endpoints) or *Command:* Line (or L) and responding to the prompts as shown in **Figure 37.67**. Draw lines by picking endpoints with the left button of the mouse. The current line will rubber-band from the last point, and lines are drawn in succession until (Enter) or the right button of

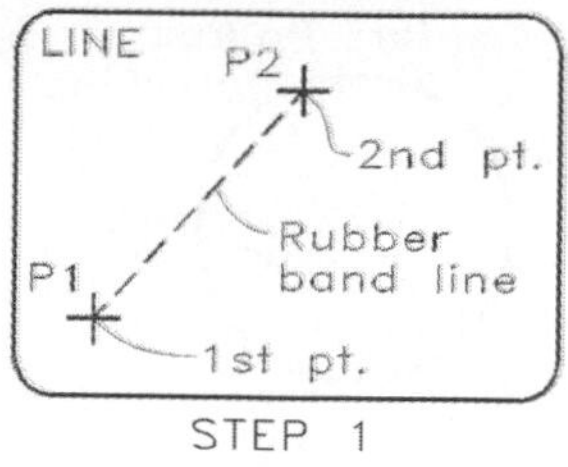

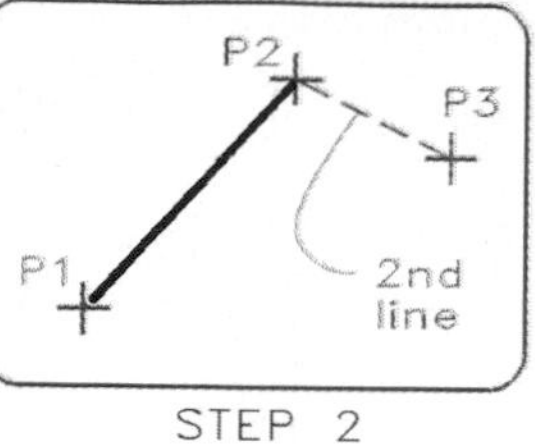

37.67 *Line.*

Step 1 *Command: > Line> Specify first point:* P1 *Specify next point or [Undo]:* P2

Step 3 *Specify next point or [Close/Undo]:* P3. (Enter)

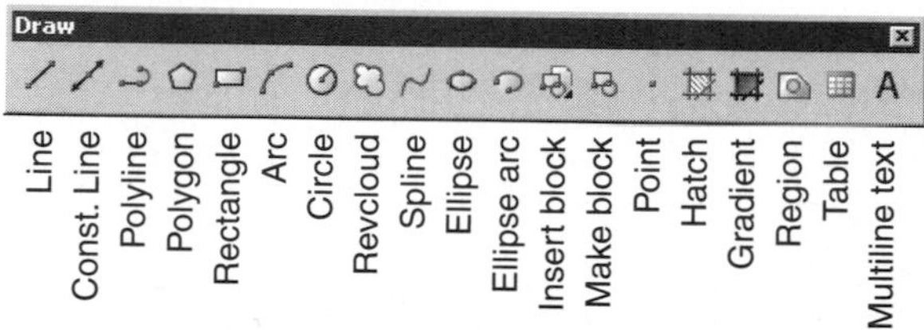

37.68 The *Draw* toolbar makes it easy to select commands with the cursor. Right click on any displayed toolbar to display a list of the toolbars, and select *Draw*.

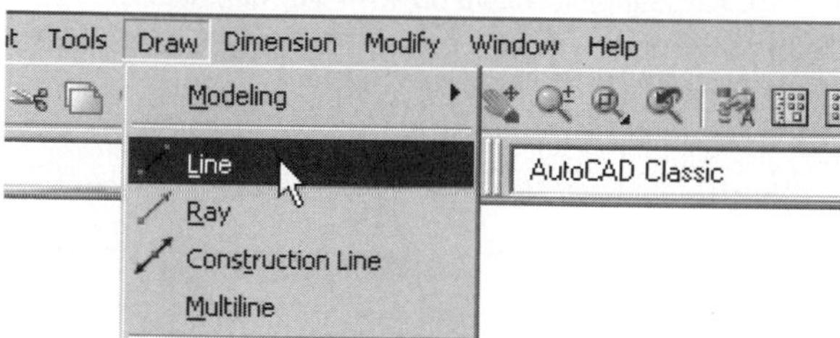

37.69 These types of lines can be selected from the *Draw* drop-down menu or from the *Main Menu* toolbar.

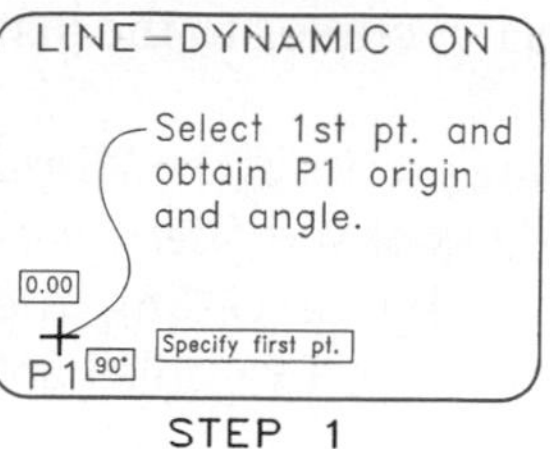

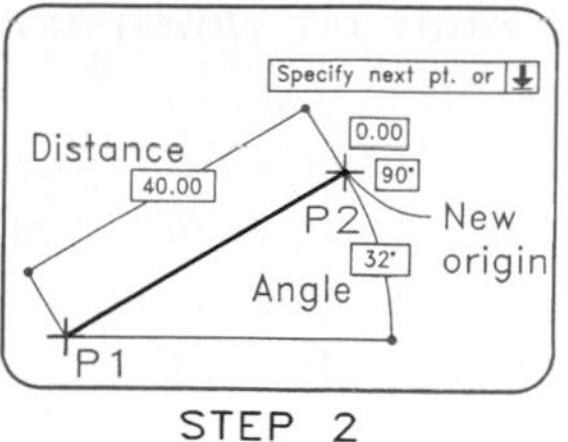

37.70 Line: *Dynamic* on. Selecting the *DYN* tab on the *Status* bar below the *Command* line sets commands to *Dynamic,* so that numerical data will be displayed as the cursor is moved about the screen. Values can be inserted into the data boxes.

your mouse is pressed. Press (Enter) again and you will be returned to *Line* command with the last point drawn as the active point.

The *Draw* toolbar shown in **Figure 37.68** can be displayed and used for drawing lines and other elements of a drawing. Four types of lines, *Line, Ray, Construction,* and *Multilines,* can be selected and drawn using this toolbar. These types of lines can also be selected from *Main Menu> Draw* (**Figure 37.69**). A *Construction line* is drawn totally across the screen, and a *Ray* is drawn from the selected point to the edge of the screen.

Lines can be specified by entering numeric values in the data boxes that appear when the *Dynamic* option is activated by selecting the *DYN* tab on the *Status* bar below the *Command* line (**Figure 37.70**). This option applies to most commands that you will be using.

A comparison of absolute and polar coordinates is shown in **Figure 37.71**. *Delta coordinates* can be typed as @2,4 to specify the end of a line 2 units in the *x*-direction and 4 units in the *y*-direction from the current end.

Polar coordinates are *2D* coordinates that are typed as @3.6 < 56 to draw a 3.6-long line from the current (and active) end of a line at an angle of 56° with the *x*-axis. *Last coordinates* are found by typing @ while in the *Line*

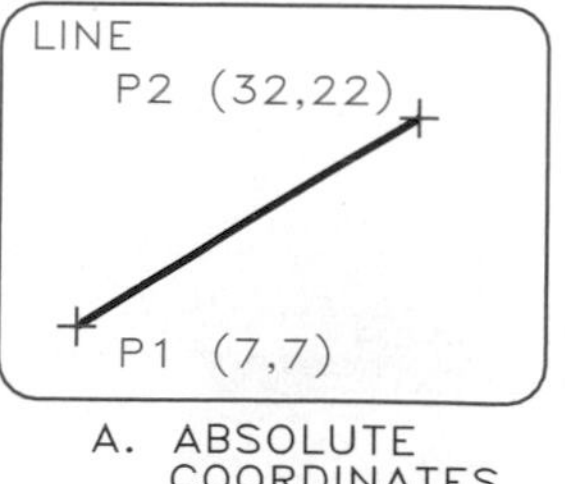

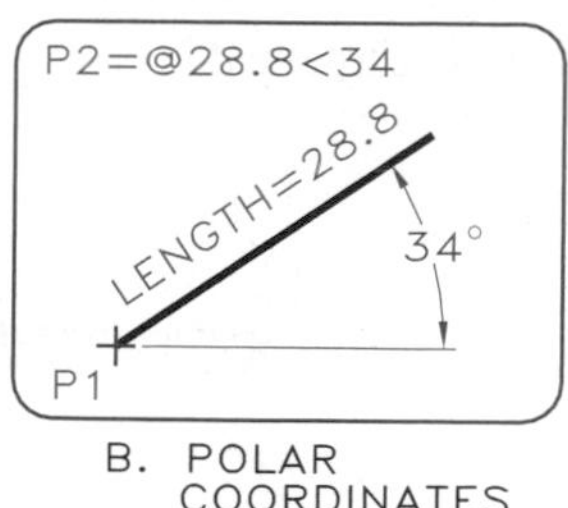

37.71 Lines by coordinates.

A Absolute coordinates can be typed (7,7 and 32,22) at the *Command* line to establish the ends of a line.

B Polar coordinates are relative to the current point and are specified with a length and the angle measured clockwise from the horizontal (@28.8 <34).

command, which moves the cursor to the last point.

World coordinates locate points in the *World Coordinate System* regardless of the *User Coordinate System* being used by preceding the coordinates with an asterisk (*). Examples are *4,3; *90 < 44; and @*1,3.

The *Status* line at the bottom of the screen shows the length of the line and its angle from the last point as it is rubber-banded from point to point. The *Close* command will close a continuous series of lines from the last to first point selected.

37.18 Circles

The *Circle* command (*Main Menu> Draw> Circle*) draws circles when you select a center and radius, a center and diameter, or three points (**Figure 37.72**). Using *Command:* Circle (or C) (Enter) is the fastest means of activating the *Circle* command, but the *Circle* icon on the *Draw* toolbar (**Figure 37.68**) can also be selected. **Figure 37.73** illustrates how a circle is drawn.

The *Tan, Tan, Radius* option of *Circle* draws a circle tangent to a circle and a line, two lines, or two circles. A circle is drawn tangent to a line and a circle by selecting the circle, the line, and giving the radius (**Figure 37.74**). The *Tan, Tan, Tan* option calculates the radius length and draws a circle tangent to three lines (**Figure 37.75**).

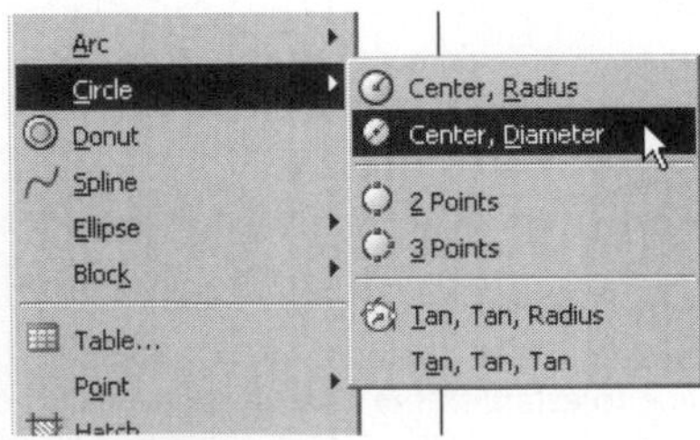

37.72 The *Circle* command (*Main Menu> Draw> Circle*) has a flyout menu with these options for drawing circles.

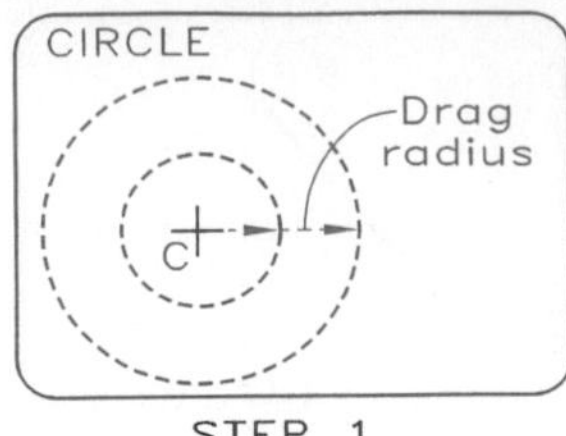

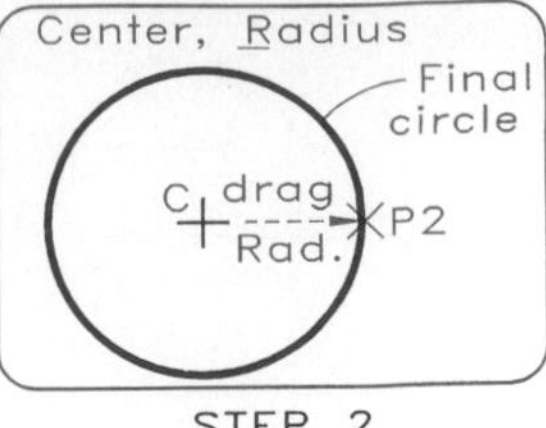

37.73 Circle.

Step 1 *Main Menu> Draw> Circle> Center, Radius> Specify center point for circle or [3P/2P/Ttr (tan tan radius)]:* Pick C (center)
Specify radius of circle or [Diameter] <0.00>:

Step 2 Drag the radius to P2 to enlarge the circle, click the left mouse button, (Enter), and the final circle is drawn. Or enter the numerical value for the radius.

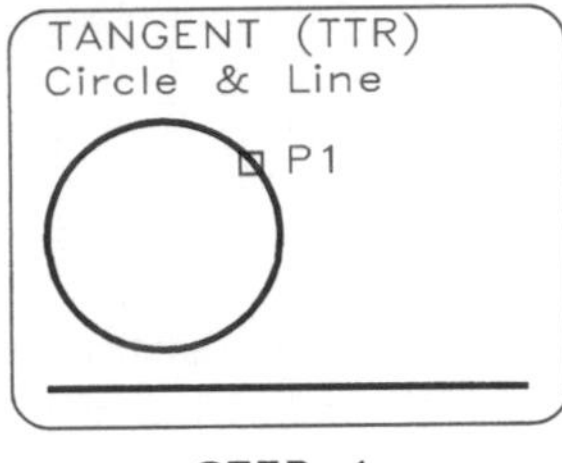

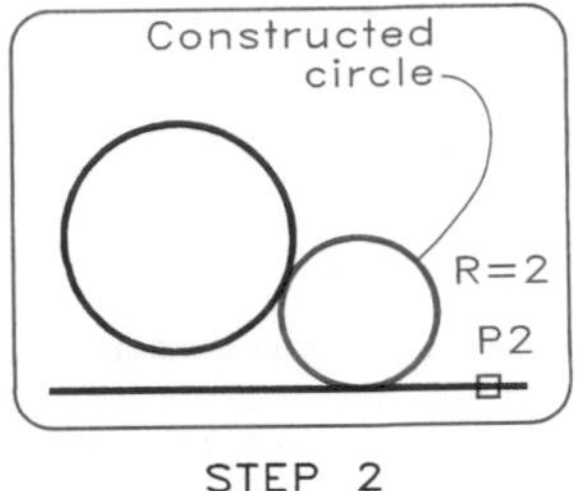

37.74 Circle: Tangent to two objects (Tan, Tan, Radius).

Step 1 *Main Menu> Draw> Circle> Tan, Tan, Radius> Specify point on object for first tangent of circle:* P1

Step 2 *Specify point on object for second tangent of circle:* P2
Specify radius of circle <0.00>: 2 (Enter)

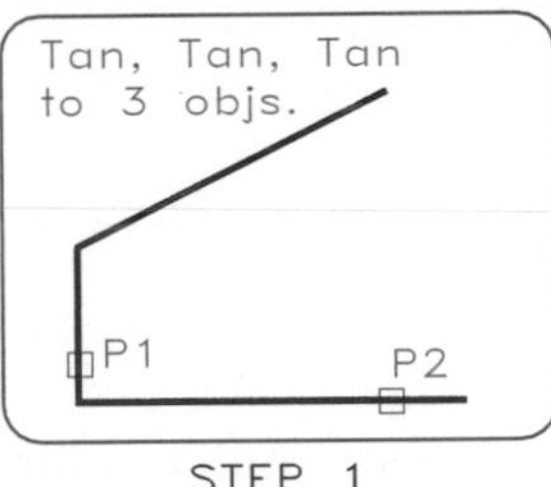

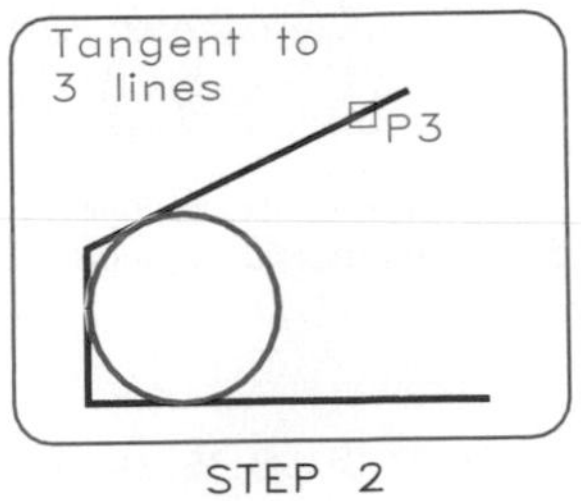

37.75 Circle: Tangent to 3 lines (Tan, Tan, Tan).

Step 1 *Main Menu> Draw> Circle> Tan, Tan, Tan> Specify first point on circle: tan to* P1
Specify second point on circle: tan to P2

Step 2 *Specify third point on circle: tan to* P3

37.19 Arcs

The *Arc* command *(Main Menu> Draw> Arc> options)* (**Figure 37.76**) or the *Arc* icon in the *Draw* toolbar (**Figure 37.68**) has 11

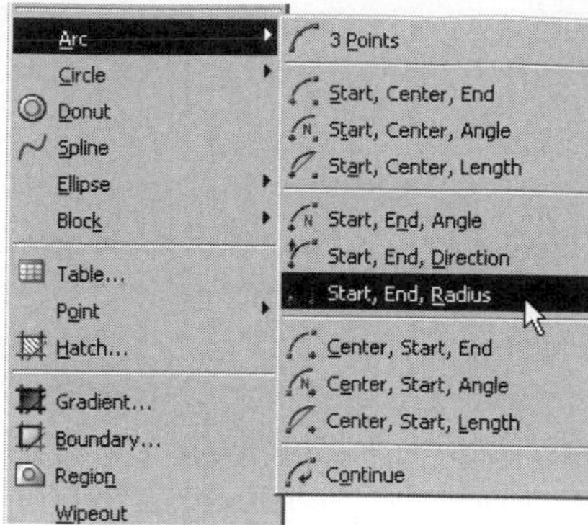

37.76 To draw an arc, select *Main Menu> Draw> Arc>* and these options are given. When using the *Start, End, Radius,* for example, these elements you must specify in this order. Arcs can be drawn by using the *Draw* toolbar or the *Command* line.

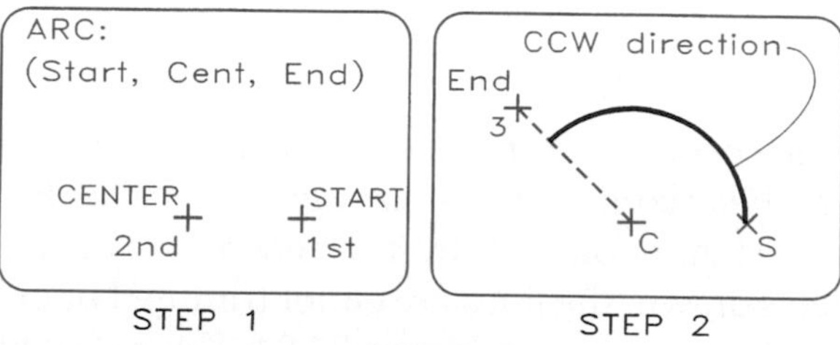

37.77 Arc: Start, Center, End option (SCE).

Step 1 *Main Menu> Draw> Arc> Start, Center, End> Specify start point of arc or [Center]:* Start point (Enter)
Specify center point of arc: Center point (Enter)

Step 2 *Specify end point of arc or [Angle/chord Length]:* 3 Drag the arc to the end on the radial line 3, click the left mouse button (Enter), and the arc is drawn.

combinations of variables that use abbreviations for starting point, center, angle, ending point, length of chord, and radius. The *S, C, E* version requires that you locate the starting point S, the center C, and the ending point E (**Figure 37.77**). The arc begins at point S and is drawn counterclockwise by default to a point on line CE.

A line can be continued as an arc drawn from its last point and tangent to it for drawing runouts of fillets and rounds (**Figure 37.78**). The reverse of this procedure can be used to draw a tangent line from an arc and tangent to it and dragging the line to its final length.

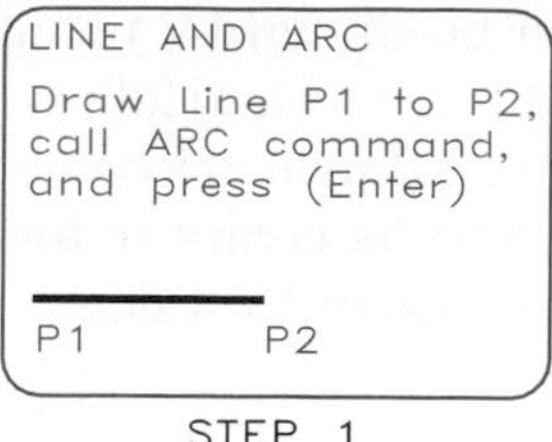

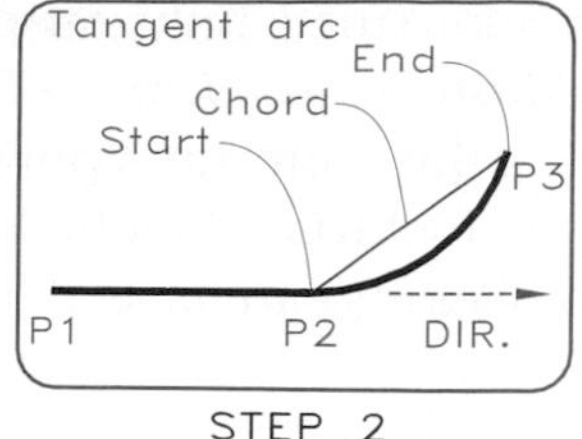

37.78 Arc: Tangent at the end of a line.

Step 1 *Draw* toolbar> *Line> Specify first point:* P1
Specify next point or [Undo]: P2

Step 2 *Draw* toolbar> *Arc> Continue> Specify end point of arc:* P3. The arc is drawn tanget to the line from P2.

37.20 Polygons

A *Polygon* and other objects can be drawn by selecting their icons from the *Draw* toolbar (**Figure 37.79**). The steps of drawing inscribed and circumscribed *Polygons* from the *Draw* toolbar are shown in **Figure 37.80.** An

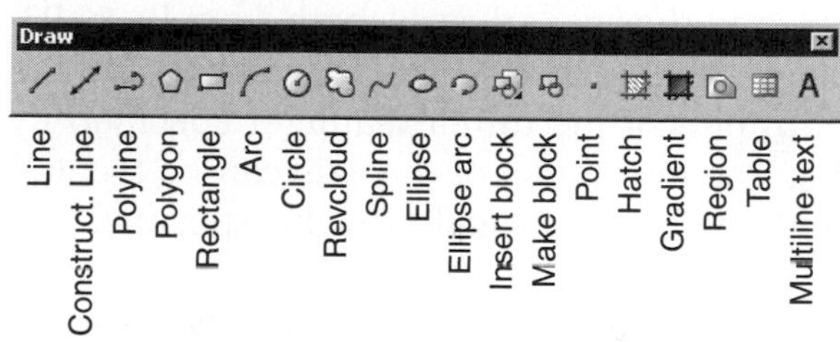

37.79 Right click on any toolbar on the screen to obtain a list of the toolbars. Select the *Draw* toolbar and pick *Polygon* from it to draw a polygon as shown in **Figure 37.80.**

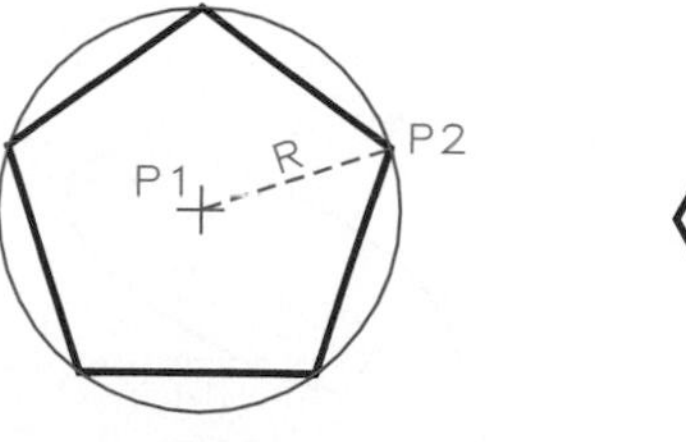

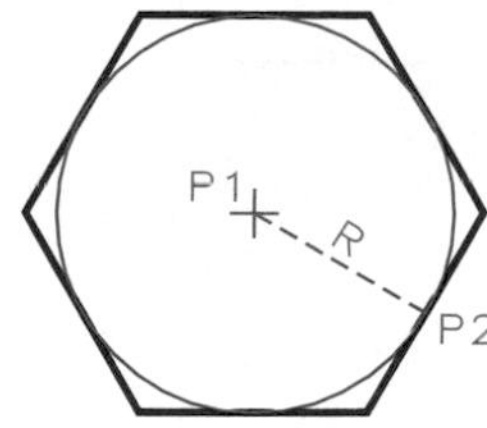

37.80 Polygons: Inscribed and circumscribed.

A *Draw* toolbar> *Polygon> Enter number of sides <4>:* 5 (Enter)> *Specify center of polygon or [Edge]:* P1
Enter an option [Inscribed in circle/Circumscribed about circle] <I>: I (Enter) (Or circumscribed as at B.)

B Select *Circumscribed* option. *Specify radius of circle:* Drag radius to P2 to size the circumscribed circle.

equal-sided polygon can be drawn by using *Main Menu> Draw> Polygon* icon and following the prompts. A polygon is drawn in a counterclockwise direction about its center point. Polygons can have a maximum of 1024 sides.

37.21 Ellipses

The *Ellipse* command in the *Main Menu> Draw* gives icons for three types of ellipses (**Figure 37.81**). An ellipse is drawn by selecting the endpoints of the major axis and a third point P3 to give the length of the minor radius (**Figure 37.82**). P3 need not lie on the ellipse; the distance from the midpoint of the axes to P3 merely gives the length of the minor axis, which is perpendicular to the major diameter, regardless of the direction in which the distance is specified.

In **Figure 37.83** points are picked at the center of the ellipse at P1, one axis endpoint at P2, and the second axis length from P1 to P3. The ellipse is drawn through points P2 and the endpoint of the minor diameter specified by P3. The endpoints of the axis can be located and the rotation angle can be specified. An angle of 0° gives an ellipse as a full circle, and an angle of 90° gives an edge view of the circle.

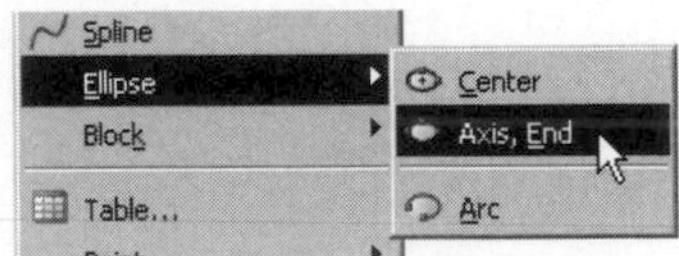

37.81 *Draw* toolbar> *Ellipse> Axis, End* can be used for drawing ellipses.

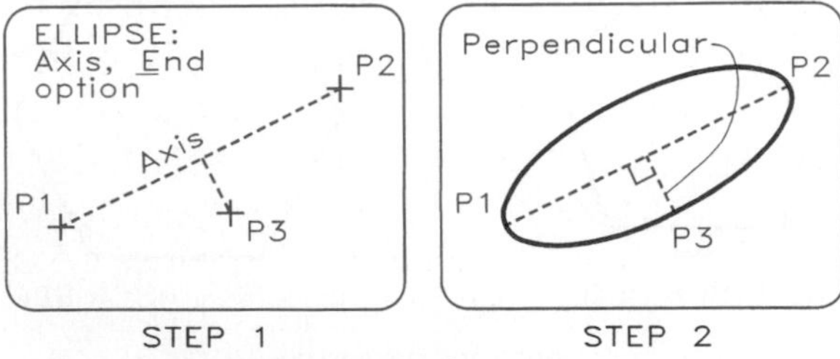

37.82 Ellipse: Axis, End option.

Step 1 *Main Menu> Draw> Ellipse> Axis, End>*
Specify axis endpoint of ellipse or [Arc/Center]: P1
Specify other endpoint of axis: P2

Step 2 *Specify distance to other axis or [Rotation]:* P3. The ellipse is drawn through P1, P2, and the point established by P3.

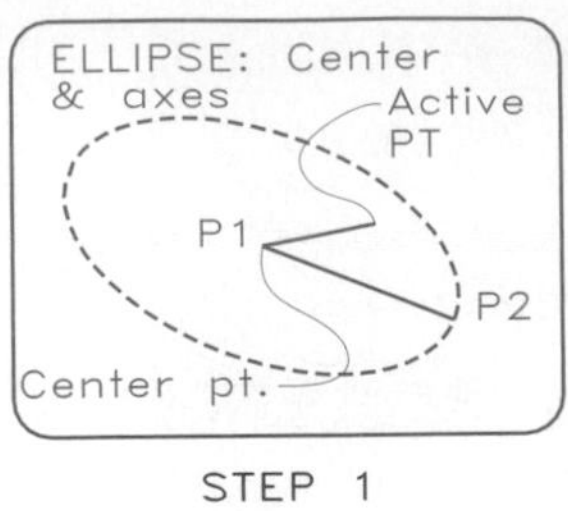

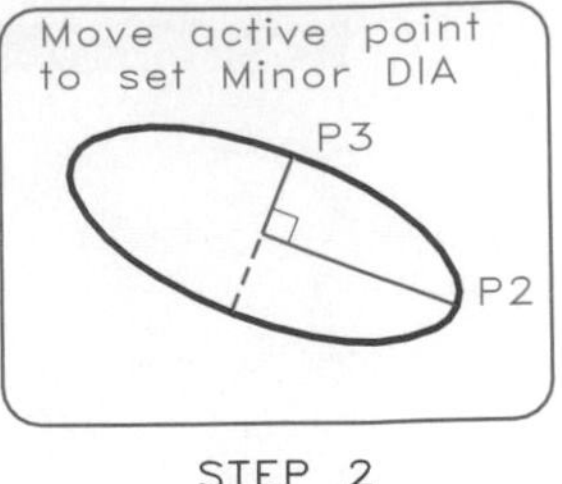

37.83 Ellipse: Center option.

Step 1 *Draw* toolbar> *Ellipse> Center*
Specify axis endpoint of ellipse or [Arc/Center]: C (Enter)
Specify center of ellipse: P1> *Specify endpoint of axis:* P2

Step 2 *Specify distance to other axis or [Rotation]:* P3
The ellipse is drawn.

37.22 Fillets

The corners of two lines can be rounded with the *Fillet* command *(Main Menu> Modify> Fillet)* whether or not they intersect. When the fillet is drawn, the lines are either trimmed or extended as shown in **Figure 37.84.** The assigned radius is remembered until it is changed. Setting the radius to 0 extends lines to a perfect intersection. This change can be made automatically by holding down the Shift key when selecting the second line, which sets the radius to zero. Fillets of a specified radius

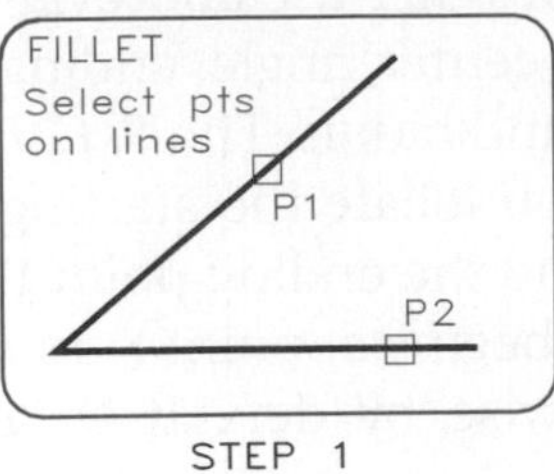

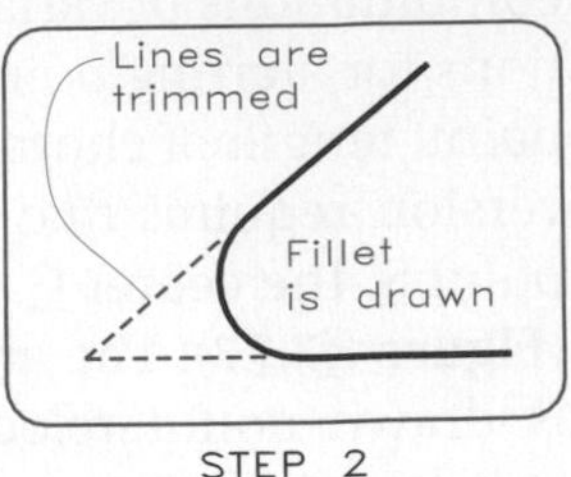

37.84 Fillet.

Step 1 *Command:>* Fillet (Enter)
Current settings: Mode = TRIM, Radius = 0.0000
Select first object or [Undo/Polyline/Radius/Trim/Multiple]: R (Enter)> *Specify fillet radius* <0.0000>: 1.00 (Enter) (Enter)
Select first object or [Undo/Polyline/Radius/Trim/Multiple]: P1

Step 2 *Select second object or shift-select to apply corner:* P2
The tanget arc is drawn and the lines are trimmed.

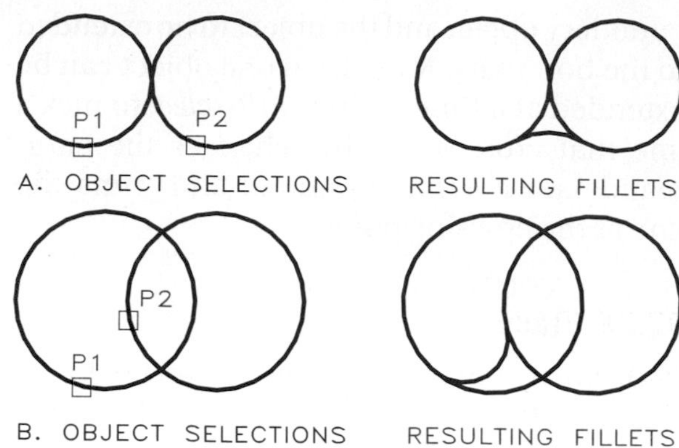

37.85 Fillets: Selection of arcs.

A. When nonintersecting arcs are selected, only one resulting fillet is possible.

B When two circles intersect, fillets can be be drawn in several locations depending on the arcs that are selected.

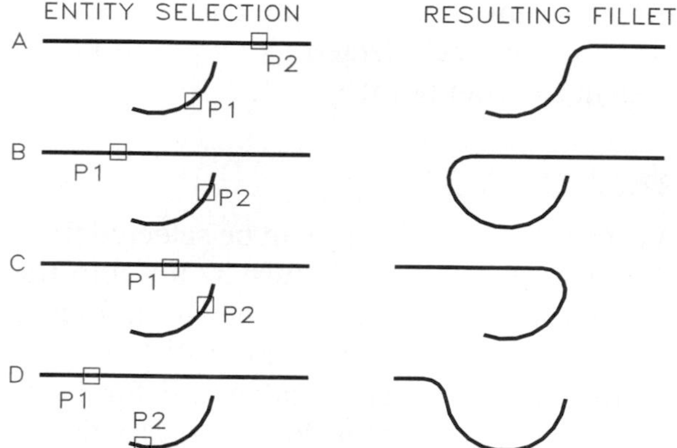

37.86 The applications of fillets between lines and arcs are determined by the positions of the selection points.

can be drawn tangent to circles or arcs as shown in **Figures 37.85** and **37.86**.

The *Fillet* command can also be selected by typing Fillet at the *Command* line or selecting the icon from the *Draw* toolbar. Practically all commands can be entered from the *Command* line, *Main Menu,* and toolbars in this manner.

37.23 Chamfer

The *Chamfer* command *(Main Menu> Modify> Chamfer)* draws angular bevels at intersections of lines or polylines. Two chamfer

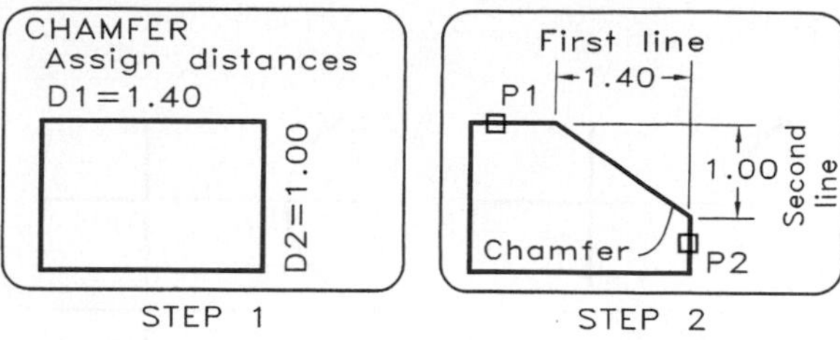

37.87 Chamfer.

Step 1 *Main Menu> Modify> Chamfer>*
Select first line or [Polyline/Distance/Angle/Trim/Method/mUltiple]: D (Enter)
*Specify first chamfer distance <0.50>:*1.40 (Enter)
Specify second chamfer distance <1.40>: 1.00 (Enter)

Step 2 (Enter) *Chamfer (TRIM mode) Current chamfer Dist1=1.4000, Dist2=1.0000*
Select first line or [Undo/Polyline/Distance/Angle/Trim/mEthod/Multiple]: P1>
Select second line or shift-select to apply corner: P2

distances can be assigned if the bevel has unequal distances. After assigning chamfer distances D1 and D2, select two lines and they are trimmed or extended and the chamfer is drawn (**Figure 37.87**). To repeat this command using the previous settings, press (Enter). By setting the chamfer distance to zero (or using the *shift-select* option when selecting the second line) you can use this command to trim nonparallel lines to perfect intersections.

37.24 Trim

The *Trim* command *(Main Menu> Modify> Trim)* selects cutting edges for trimming selected lines, arcs, or circles that cross the cutting edges (**Figure 37.88**). A series of objects can be selected one at a time or selected as a group by a window. A *Crossing* window is used to select four cutting edges for trimming four lines in **Figure 37.89**.

37.25 Extend

The *Extend* command lengthens lines, plines, and arcs to intersect a selected boundary (**Figure 37.90**). You are prompted to select the

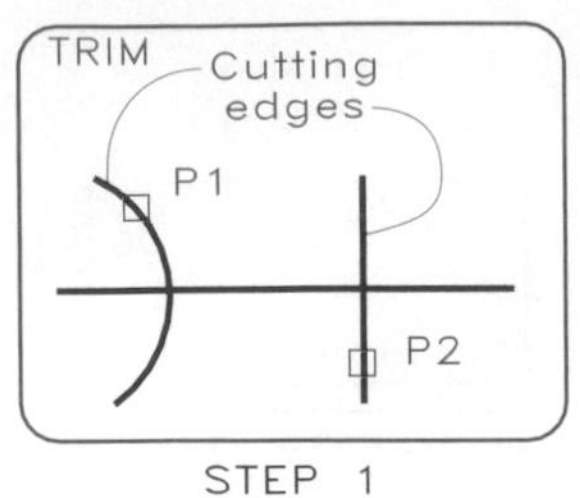

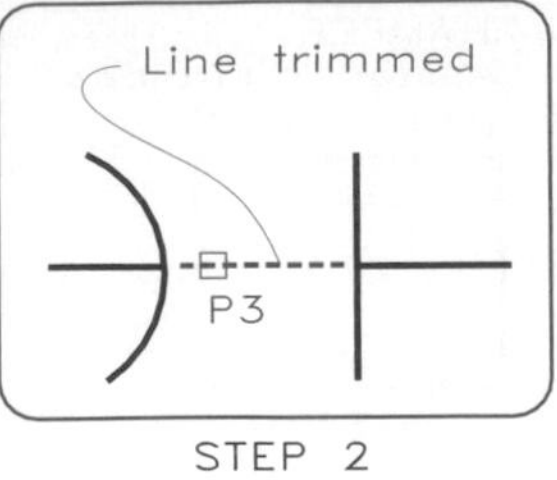

37.88 Trim: Cutting edges.

Step 1 *Modify* toolbar> *Trim> Current settings: Projection= UCS Edge=None*
Select cutting edges...
Select objects or <select all>: P1 *1 found*
Select objects: P2 *1 found, 2 total> Select objects:* (Enter)

Step 2 *Select object to trim or [Fence/ Crossing/ Edge/ eRase/ Undo]:* P3 (Enter) Line between the cutting edges is removed.

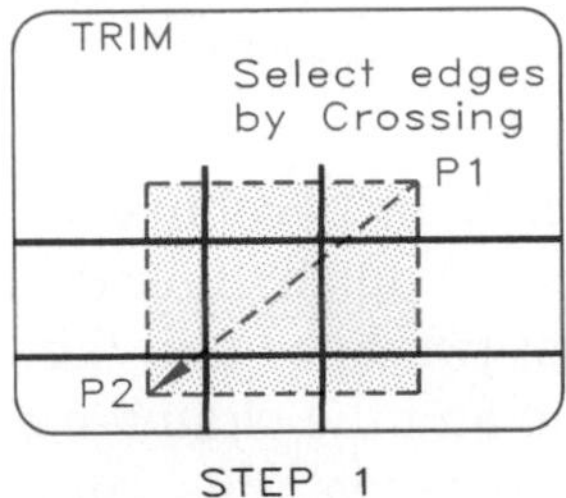

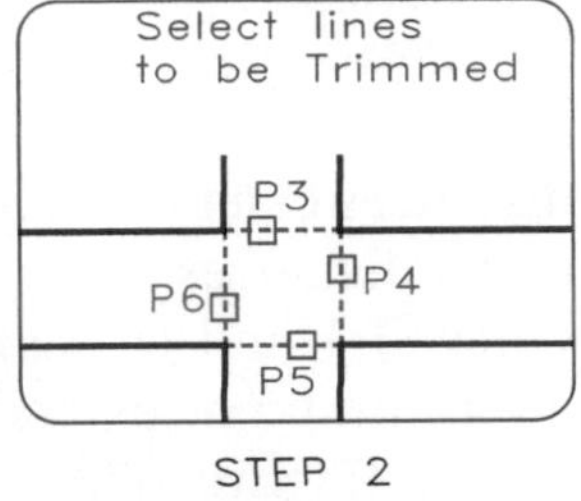

37.89 Trim: Crossing window.

Step 1 *Main Menu> Modify> Trim> Current settings: Projection=UCS, Edge=None, Select cutting edges or <select all>: Select objects:* P1> Specify opposite corner: P2 *4 found (Enter)*

Step 2 *Select object to trim or shift-select to extend or [Fence/Crossing/Project/ Project/ Edge/eRase/Undo]:* P3
Select object to trim . . . /Edge/ eRase/ Undo]: P4
Select object to trim . . . /Edge/ eRase/ Undo]: P5
Select object to trim . . . or [Project/Edge/Undo]: P6 (Enter)

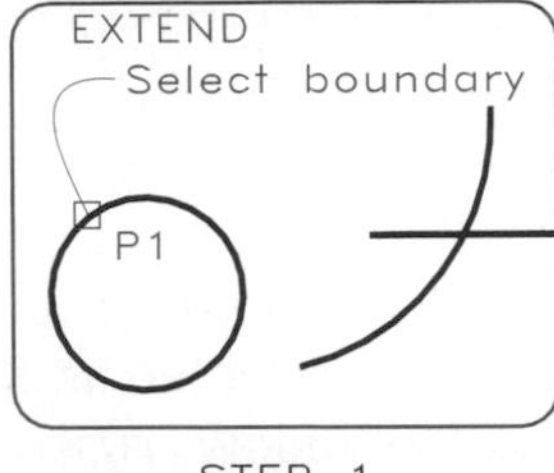

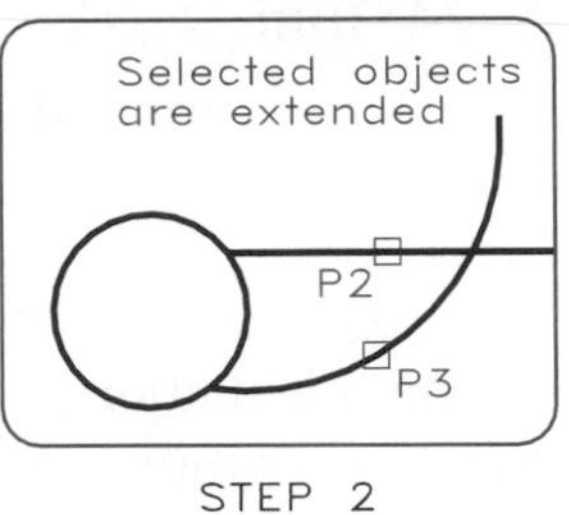

37.90 Extend.

Step 1 *Main Menu> Modify> Extend*
Current settings: Projection=UCS, Edge=None
Select boundary edges... Select objects or <select all>: P1 *1 found > Select objects:>* (Enter)

Step 2 *Select objects: Select object to extend or shift-select to trim [Fence/ Crossing/Project/Edge/Undo]:* P2
Select object to extend or shift-select to trim [Fence/ Crossing/ Project/Edge/Undo]: P3

boundary object and the object to be extended to the boundary. More than one object can be extended at a time. Using s*hift-select* to pick a line that crosses another changes the command into a *Trim* command and trims the line at the crossing point.

37.26 Trace

Wide lines (either solid or open) can be drawn with the *Trace* command. For solid lines, select *Command:* Fill (Enter) pick On (Enter). To draw trace lines, *Command*: Trace (Enter) as shown in **Figure 37.91A**. When *Fill* is *Off*, the lines will be drawn as open, parallel lines with "mitered" angles at their corners (**Figure 37.91B**). Notice that the poor corner joint of the *Trace* lines can be omitted if the line's beginning point is selected along a line rather than at a corner point.

37.27 QuickCalc

A calculator *(QuickCalc)* can be selected from the *Standard* toolbar (**Figure 37.92**) and the calculator will appear as shown in **Figure 37.93**. It is shown in this figure in its *Basic Calculator Mode,* which is adequate for basic arithmetic. Selecting the down arrows activates

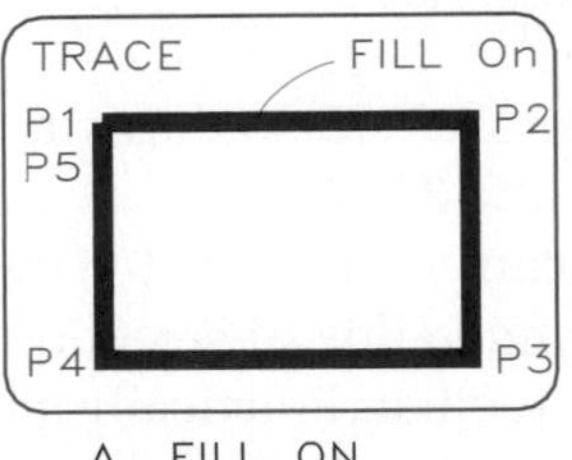

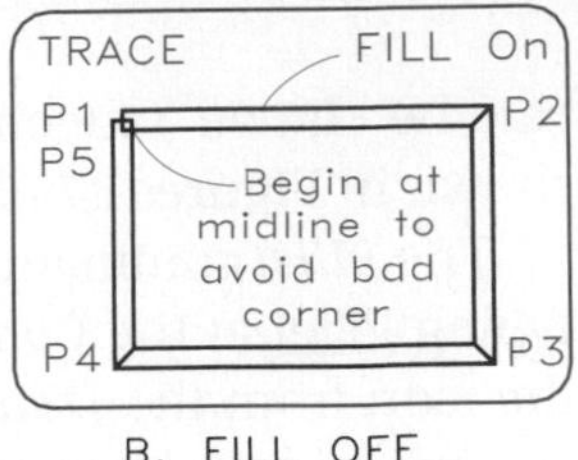

37.91 Trace.

A. *Command:* Fill, *Enter mode [On/Off]: <On>* On (Enter)
Command: Trace (Enter), *Specify trace width <0.00>:* 0.20, *Specify start point:* P1, *Select next point:* P2 *Select next point:* Continue point selection; (Enter) to end.

B. To obtain a *Trace* with unfilled lines: *Command*: Fill, (Enter) *Enter mode [On/Off]: <On>* Off (Enter)
Command: Regen (Enter) Draw the trace as in (B).

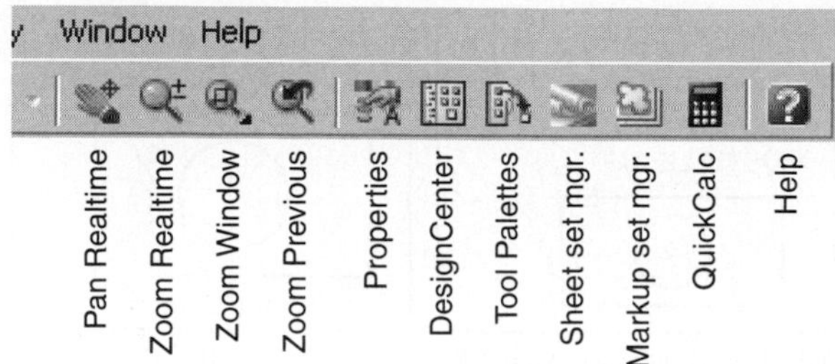

37.92 This part of the *Standard* toolbar contains options for *Panning* and *Zooming* on the screen.

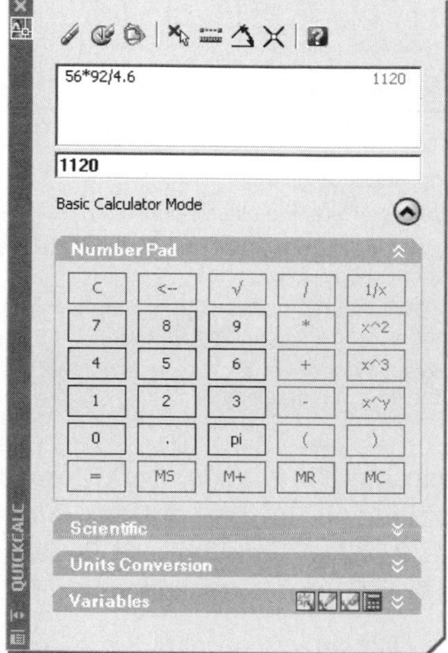

37.93 From the *Standard* toolbar, the calculator icon can be selected to obtain an on-screen calculator for making computations. It includes *Scientific, Units Conversion,* and *Variables* panels for advanced calculations.

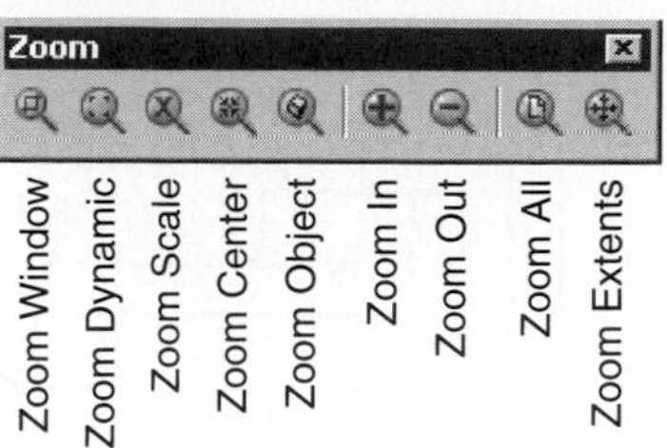

37.94 The *Zoom* toolbar contains these options for sizing images on the screen.

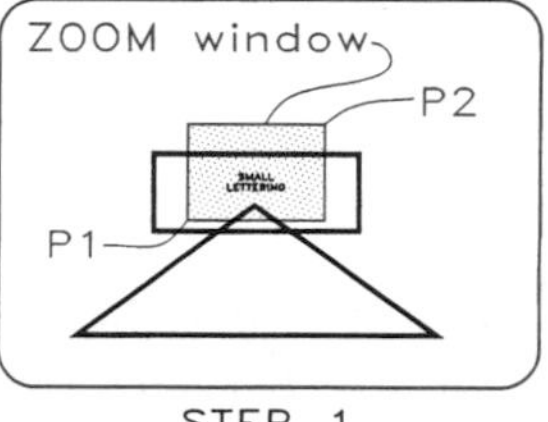

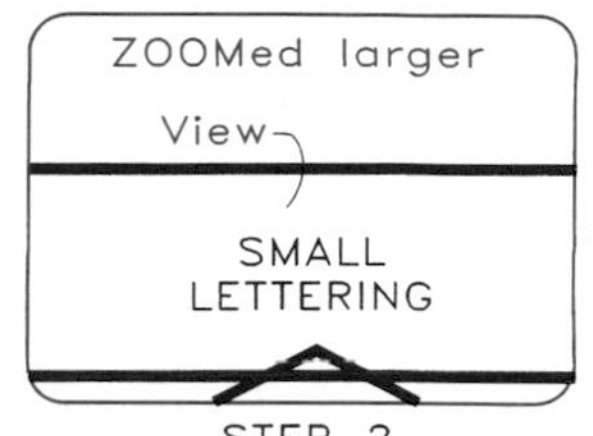

37.95 Zoom: Window.

Step 1 *Zoom* toolbar> *Zoom Window* icon> Pick P1 and P2 to form a zoom window.

Step 2 The area of the window is expanded to fill the screen as much as the proportions allow.

three modes: *Scientific, Units of Conversion,* and *Variables,* which are useful for more advanced computations. Explanation of these applications can be accessed from the *Help* key (?) on the calculator's panel.

37.28 Zoom and Pan

Drawings can be enlarged or reduced from the *Zoom* toolbar using the *Zoom* options shown in **Figure 37.92**. Other options can be selected from the *Zoom* toolbar shown in **Figure 37.94**. The same options are available in a pull-down menu *(Main Menu> View> Zoom)*. An example of a *Zoom Window* used to enlarge part of a drawing is shown in **Figure 37.95**.

The *Zoom* (*Command:>* Z) gives the following options: *All, Center, Dynamic, Extents, Previous, Scale, Window, Object,* and *Real time.*

All expands the drawing's *Limits* (dot pattern) to fill the screen.

Center is picked to select the center of the *Zoomed* image and to specify its magnification or reduction.

Dynamic lets you *Zoom* and *Pan* by selecting points with the cursor.

Extents enlarges the drawing to its maximum size on the screen.

Previous displays the last *Zoomed* view.

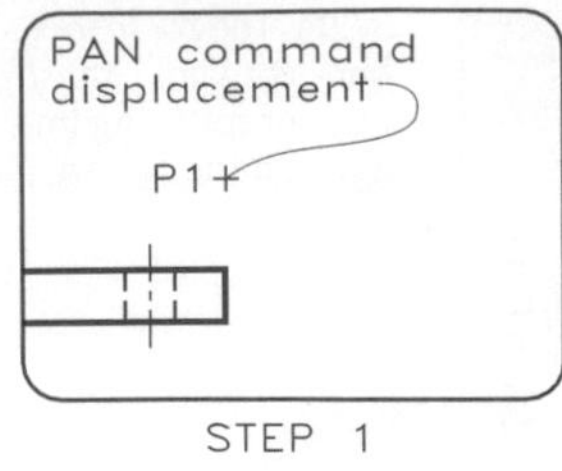

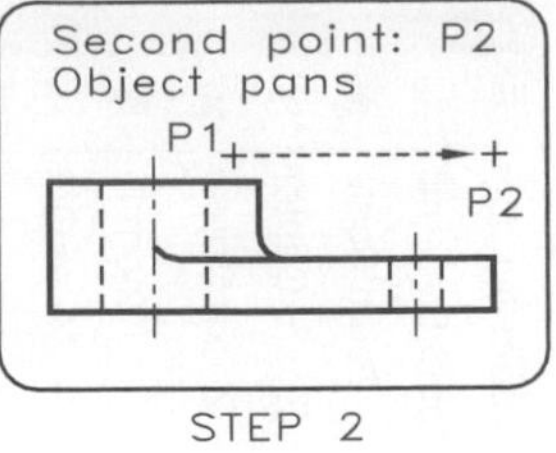

37.96 Pan.

Step 1 *Standard* toolbar> *Pan* icon

Step 2 Pick P1, hold down the left button, and drag to P2 to change your view of the screen.

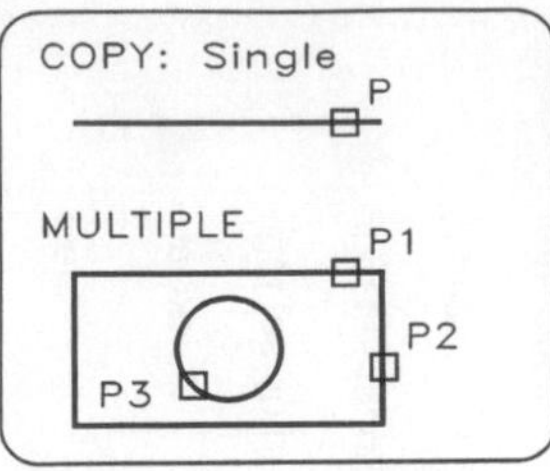

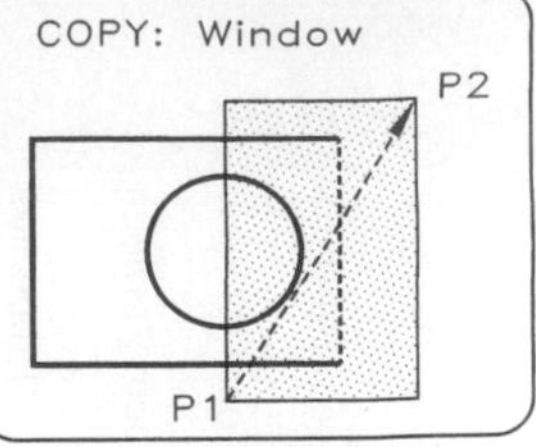

COPY: Crossing

P1

P2

C. CROSSING

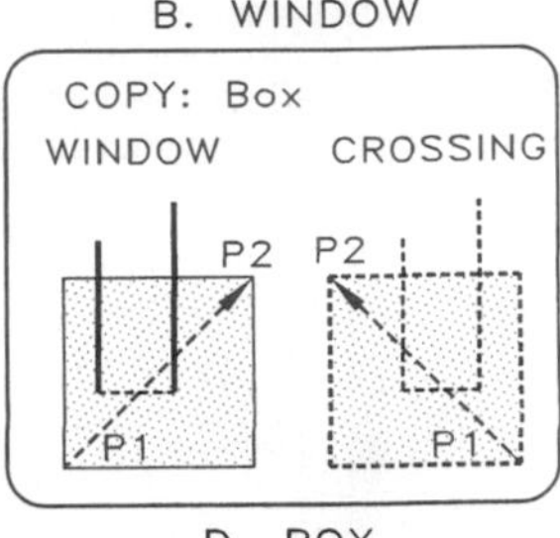

37.97 Copy: Selection options.

A *Select objects:* selects the objects one at a time.

B *Window (W)* selects only objects lying completely within the window; drag window left to right.

C *Crossing Window (C)* selects objects lying within or crossed by the window; drag window right to left.

D *Box* makes a *Window* or a *Crossing Window* that is determined by the direction dragging.

Scale X/XP magnifies a drawing relative to paper space. Typing 1/4XP or .25XP scales the drawing so that .25 in. equals 1 in.

Window lets you pick the diagonal corners of a window to fill the screen.

Object fills the screen with objects that have been selected.

Real time (the default) lets you drag to the left to make a crossing window, or to the right to make a window to specify the area to be enlarged.

The *Pan (P)* command (**Figure 37.96**) is used to pan the view across the screen by selecting a handle point and its final position. The drawing is not relocated as with the *Move* command; only your viewpoint of it is changed.

37.29 Selecting Objects

A recurring prompt, *Select objects:*, asks you to select an object or objects that are to be *Erased, Changed,* or modified in some way. Type *Select* when in a current command that requires a selection *(Move,* for example) and the options will be displayed: *Window, Last, Crossing, BOX, ALL, Fence, WPolygon, CPolygon, Group, Add, Remove, Multiple, Previous, Undo, AUto, SIngle, SUbobject,* and *Object.* **Figure 37.97** shows ways of selecting objects for applicable commands, *Copy,* for example. The application of the options *Single* and *Multiple, Window, Crossing,* and *Box* are shown in parts A, B, C, and D, respectively.

Window (W) selects objects lying completely within it.

Crossing (C) selects objects lying within or crossed by the window.

Last (L) picks the most recently drawn object.

Box (B) lets you make a window by selecting a point and dragging to the right. A crossing window can be made by dragging to the left.

Other techniques for selecting objects are shown in **Figure 37.98**.

WPolygon (WP) forms a solid-line polygon that has the same effect as a window.

CPolygon (CP) forms a dotted-line polygon that has the same effect as a crossing window.

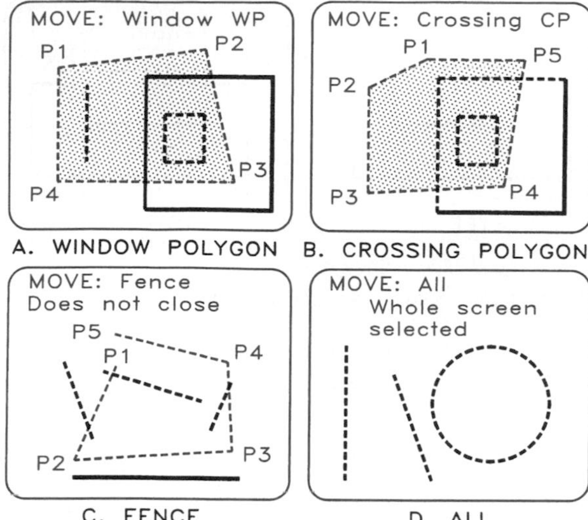

37.98 Move: Selection options.

A *Window Polygon (WP)* selects only objects inside it.

B *Crossing Polygon (CP)* selects objects inside it and crossed by the polygon.

C *Fence (F)* is a nonclosing polyline that erases objects crossed by it.

D *All* selects all objects on the screen.

Fence (F) selects corner points of a polyline that will select any object it crosses the same as a crossing window.

ALL selects everything on the screen.

Remove and *Add* are used while selecting objects to remove by typing R (Remove) or to add one by typing A *(Add)*. Press (Enter) when finished.

Multiple (M) selects multiple points (without highlighting) to speed up the selection process.

Previous (P) recalls the previously selected set of objects. For example, enter *Move,* and type P, and the last selected objects are recalled.

Undo (U) removes objects in reverse order one at a time as U (undo) is typed repetitively.

Single (SI) causes the program to act on the object or sets of objects without pausing for a response.

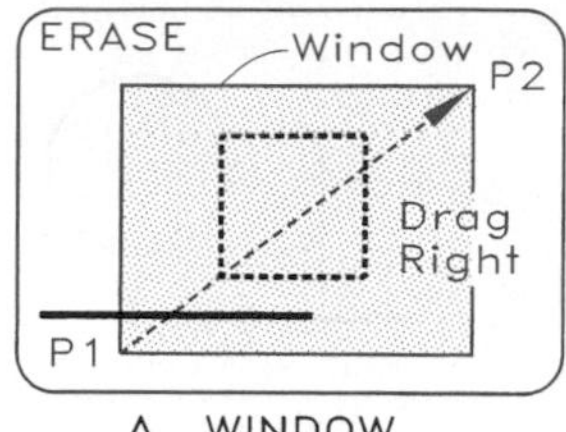

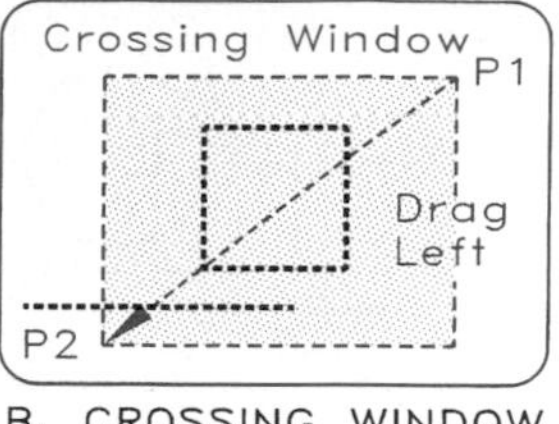

37.99 Erase: Selection of windows.

A A *Window* is formed by holding down the select button while dragging a diagonal corner to the **right**.

B A *Crossing Window* is formed in the same manner, but dragged to the **left**.

A *Window (W)* or a *Crossing Window* can be obtained automatically by pressing the pick button, holding it down, and selecting the diagonal of a window. Dragging it to the right displays a window; dragging it to the left displays a crossing window (**Figure 37.99**).

37.30 Erase, Break, and Join

The *Erase* command (*Command:* E) (**Figure 37.100**) deletes specified parts of a drawing. The selection techniques described previously can be used to select objects to be erased as shown in **Figures 37.101** and **37.102**. The default of the *Erase* command, *Select Objects,* allows you to pick one or more objects and delete them by pressing (Enter). Type Oops to restore the last erasure, but only the last one can be restored.

The *Break* command (*Modify* toolbar> *Break* icon) removes part of a line, pline, arc,

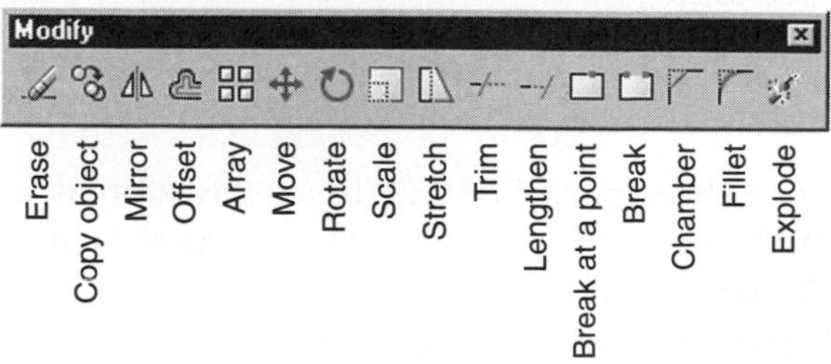

37.100 The *Modify* toolbar, a portion of which is shown here, has options for making changes in a drawing.

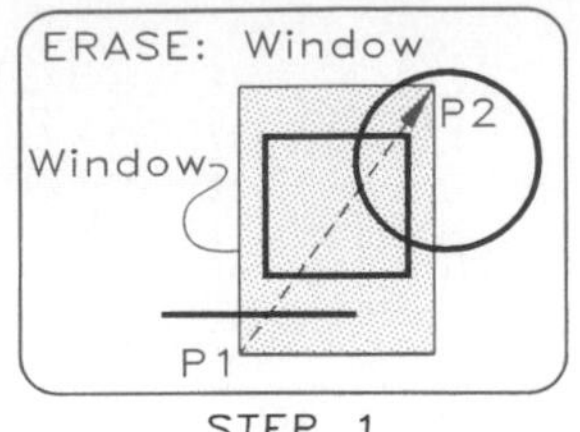

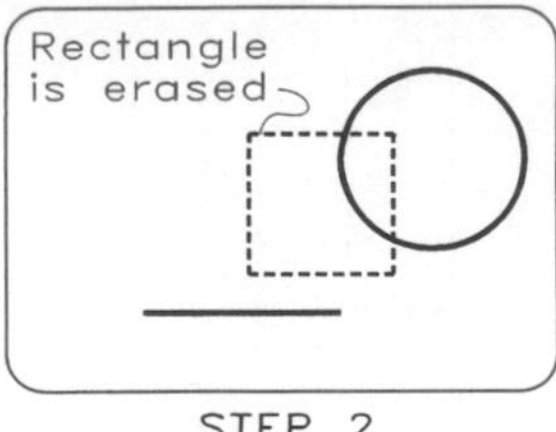

37.101 Erase: Window option.

Step 1 *Modify* toolbar> *Erase* icon
Select objects: P1, *Other corner:* P2 (left to right)

Step 2 *Select objects:* (Enter) The box completely within the erasing window is removed.

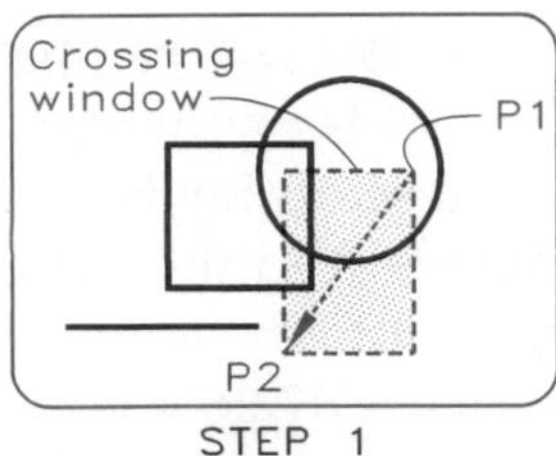

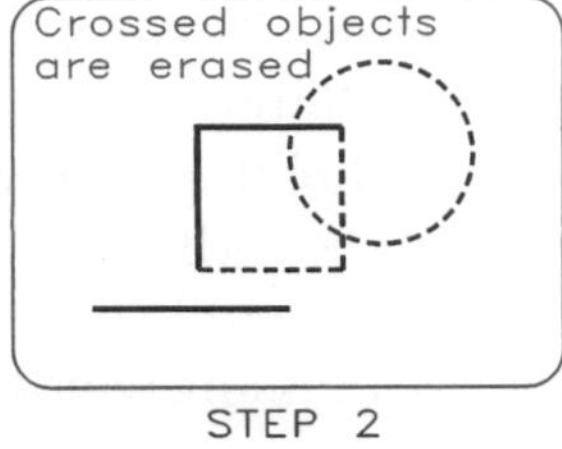

37.102 Erase: Crossing option.

Step 1 *Modify* toolbar> *Erase* icon
Select objects: P1, *Other corner:* P2 (right to left for a crossing window).

Step 2 *Select objects:* (Enter) The objects crossed by or completely within the window are removed.

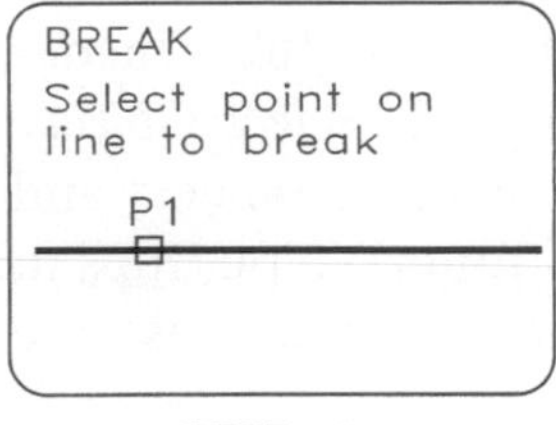

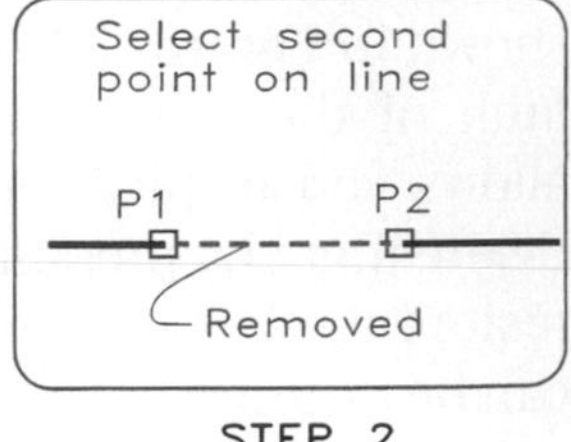

37.103 Break.

Step 1 *Modify* toolbar> *Break* icon
Select object: P1,

Step 2 *Specify second break point or [First point]:* P2,
Line between P1 and P2 is removed.

or circle (**Figure 37.103**). To specify a break at an intersection with another line as shown in **Figure 37.104**, select the line to be broken, select the *F*option, and pick the two endpoints of the line to be removed. Endpoints can be selected without fear of selecting the wrong lines.

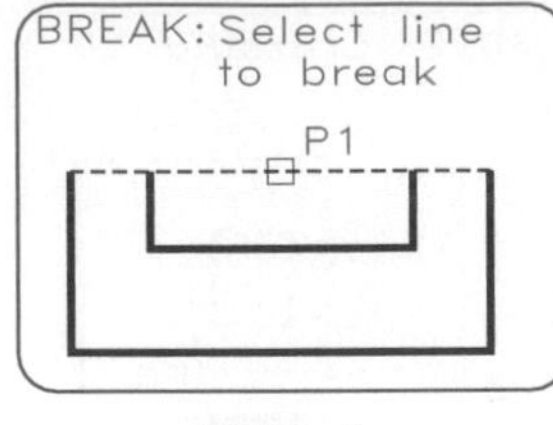

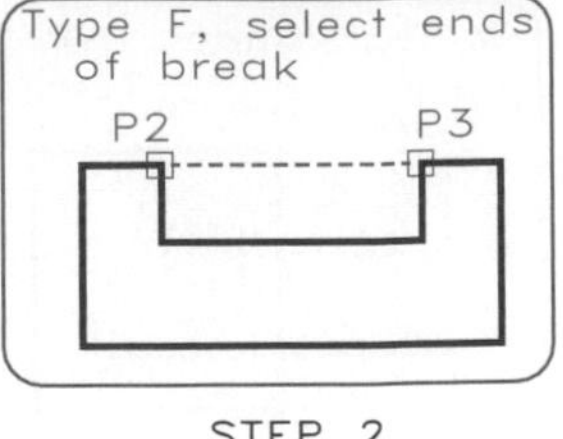

37.104 Break: First point option.

Step 1 *Modify* toolbar> *Break icon*
Select object: P1,
Specify second break point or [First point]: F (Enter)

Step 2 *Specify first break point:* P2,
Specify second break point: P3, Line P2-P3 is removed.

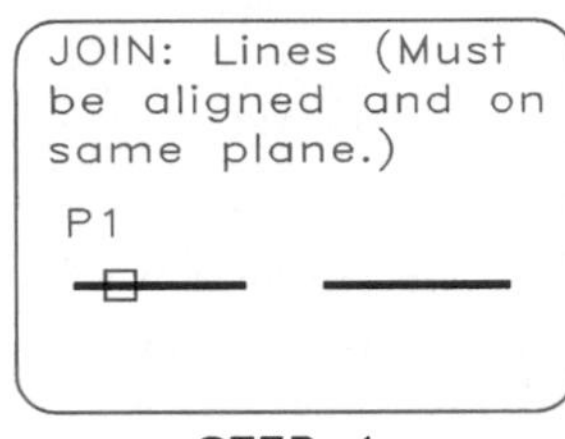

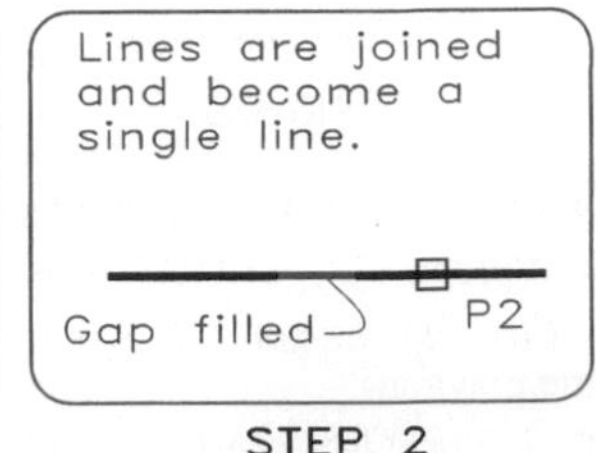

37.105 Join command.

Step 1 *Command:> Select source object:* P1

Step 2 *Select objects to join to source:* P2 (Enter)

This command can be used to join lines, polylines, arcs, elliptical arcs, splines, and helixes that will abut when extended.

Lines can be joined by using the *Join* command, illustrated in **Figure 37.105**. Only lines, arcs, and other linetypes that are segments of the same continuous lines (lines with gaps) can be joined.

37.31 Move and Copy

The *Move* command (*Modify* toolbar> *Move* icon) repositions a drawing (**Figure 37.106**), and the *Copy* command duplicates and moves a drawing, leaving the original in its same position. The *Copy* command makes multiple copies of the selected drawing in different positions.

37.32 Undo

The *Undo* command *(Command:* Undo, or U) can reverse the previous command, and the process can be continued until all objects

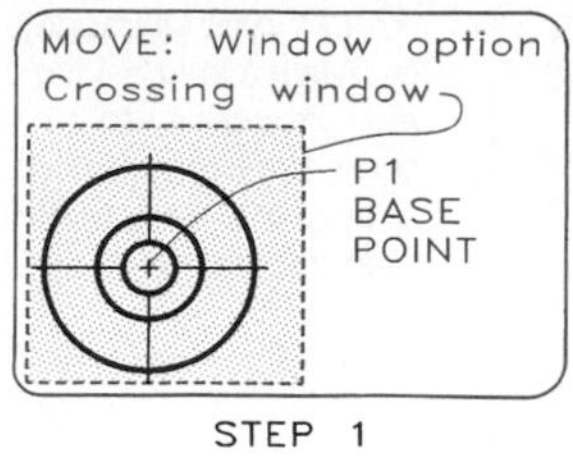

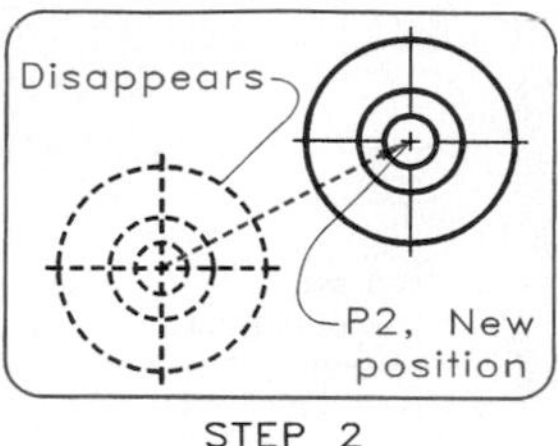

37.106 Move.

Step 1 *Modify* toolbar> *Move* icon
Select objects: W, *Window* the drawing.
Specify base point or [Displacement] <displacement>: P1

Step 2 *Specify second point of displacement or <use first point as displacement>:* Drag to new posiiton of P2.

have been erased. The *Redo* command reverses the last *Undo.* The *Undo* command has options of *Auto, Control, Begin, End, Mark,* and *Back.*

Command: Undo (Enter)
[Auto/ Control/ BEgin/End/Mark/Back] <1>: 4 (Enter)

Entering 4 has the same effect as using the U command four separate times.

Mark identifies a point in the drawing process to which subsequent additions can be undone by the *Back* option. Only the part of the drawing added after placing the *Mark* will be undone at the prompt:

This will undo everything.
OK? <Y>: Y (Enter)

Responding Y will remove the *Mark,* making it possible for the next *Undo (U)* to proceed backward past the mark.

The *BEgin* and *End* options group a sequence of operations until *End* terminates the group. *Undo* treats the group as a single operation. The *Control* subcommand has three options: *All, None,* and *One. All* turns on the full features of the *Undo* command, *None* turns them off, and *One* uses *Undo* commands for single operations and requires the least disk space.

37.33 Change

Command: Change is used to modify features: *Lines, Circles, Text, Attribute Definitions, Blocks, Color, Layers, Linetypes,* and *Thickness.* The position of an endpoint of a *Line* is changed by selecting one end and locating a new endpoint (**Figure 37.107**). *Change* varies the size of a circle when you pick a point on its arc and a second point to establish the size of a new radius (**Figure 37.108**).

Text can be modified with the *Change* command by pressing (Enter) until the prompts *Insertion point, Style, Height, Rotation Angle,* and *New Text* appear in sequence (**Figure 37.109**). *Attribute Definitions,* including *Tag, Prompt String,* and *Default Value,* can be revised with the *Change* command.

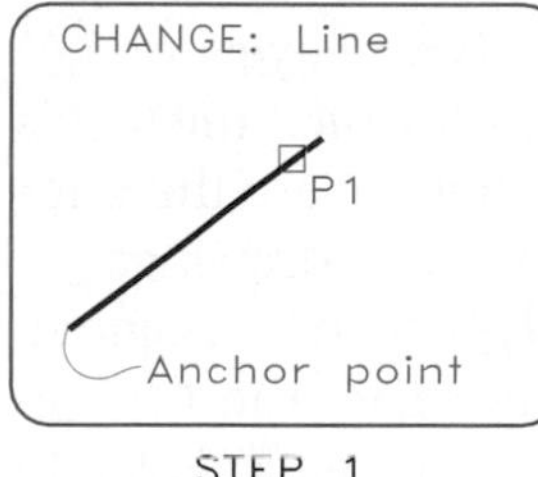

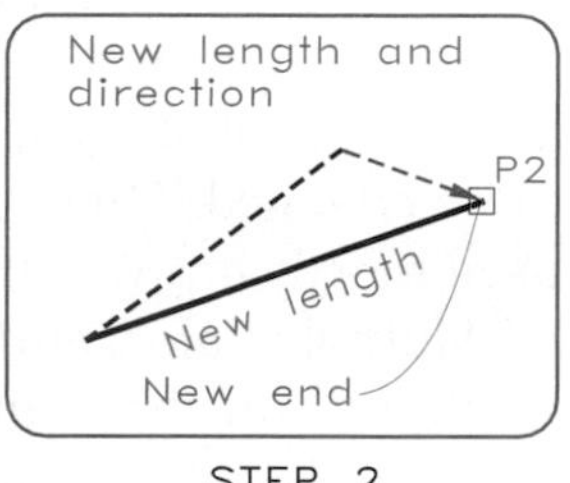

37.107 Change: Line.

Step 1 *Command:* Change> (Enter)
Select objects: P1, *1 found> Select objects:* (Enter)

Step 2 *Specify change point or [Properties]:* Select the new end of the line P2.

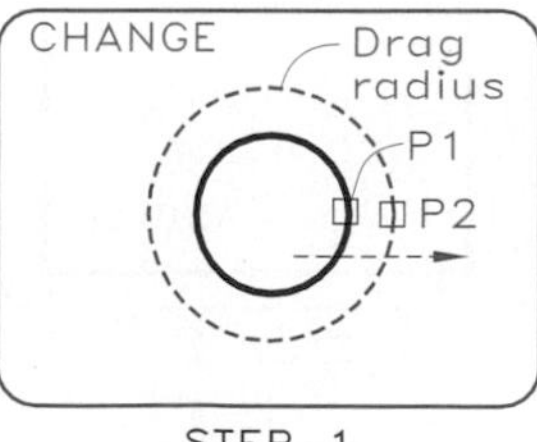

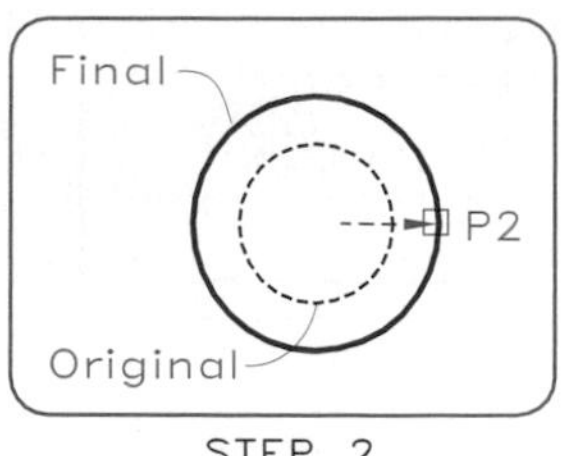

37.108 Change: Circle.

Step 1 *Command:* Change> (Enter)
Select objects: P1, *1 found*
Select objects: (Enter)

Step 2 *Specify change point or [Properties]:* P2, to pick a new radius.

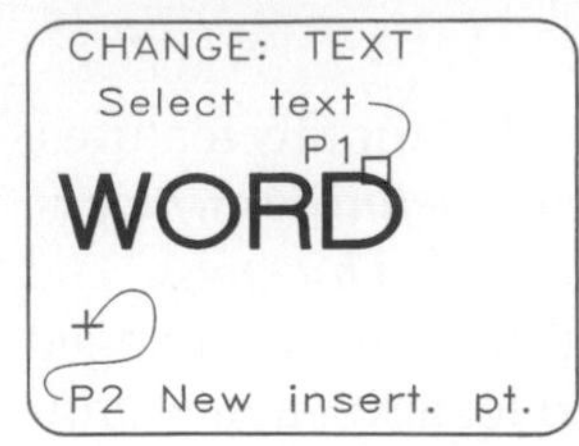

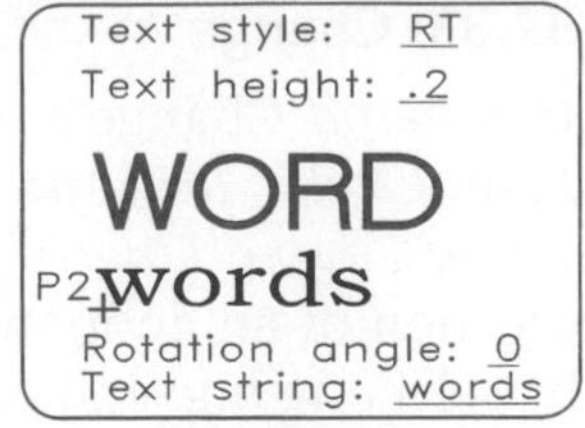

37.109 Change: Text.

Step 1 *Command:* <u>Change</u> (Enter)
Select objects: <u>P1</u>, *1 found, Select objects:* (Enter)
Specify change point or [Properties]: (Enter)
Specify new text insertion point <no change>: <u>P2</u>

Step 2 *Enter new text style <Outline>:* <u>RT</u> (Enter)
Specify new height <0.00>: <u>.20</u> (Enter)
Specify new rotation angle <0>: (Enter)
Enter new text <WORD>: <u>words</u> (Enter)

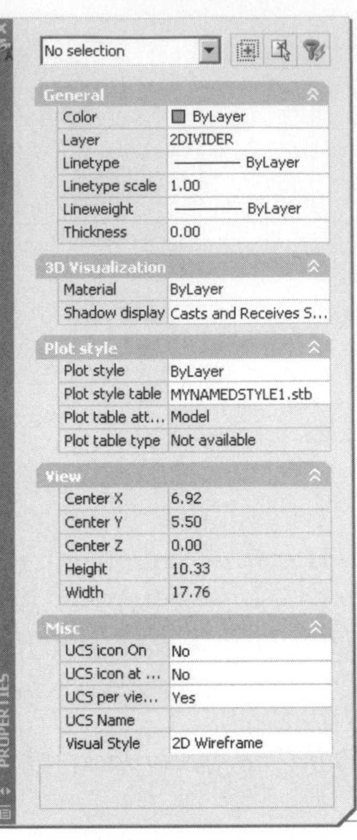

37.111 Type <u>DDmodify</u> or *(Main Menu> Modify> Properties)* to observe the properties of a drawing and make changes if desired.

Property changes of the *Change* command, *Color, LAyer, LType,* and *LWeight* are made by selecting objects and typing *P (Properties)* as shown in **Figure 37.110**. Type <u>Layer</u> (or <u>LA</u>) and the name of the layer on which the text is to be changed. These properties are the ones used mostly in two-dimensional drawings.

Multiple *Colors* and *LTypes* can be assigned to objects on the same layer by the *Change* command, but it is better for each layer to have only one layer and linetype.

At the *Command* line, type <u>DDmodify</u> or *(Main Menu> Modify> Properties)* and select an object when prompted to obtain a *Properties* box (**Figure 37.111**) to change colors, layers, linetypes, thickness, linetype scale, and ends of lines as well as the properties of other objects.

37.34 Grips

Grips are small squares that appear when objects are selected at midpoints and ends of lines, centers and quadrant points of circles, and at insertion points of text. *Grips* are used to *Stretch, Move, Rotate, Scale,* and *Mirror.*

The *Grips* dialog box is found under the *Standard* menu> *Tools> Options> Selection* tab (or *Command:* <u>DDgrips</u>) (**Figure 37.112**). The *Enable grips* check box turns on grips for all objects. *Enable grips within blocks* turns on grips for objects in a *Block;* when *Off,* a single grip is given at the insertion point of the *Block.*

Colors for *Grips* can be assigned for unselected, selected, and hover grips (unselected

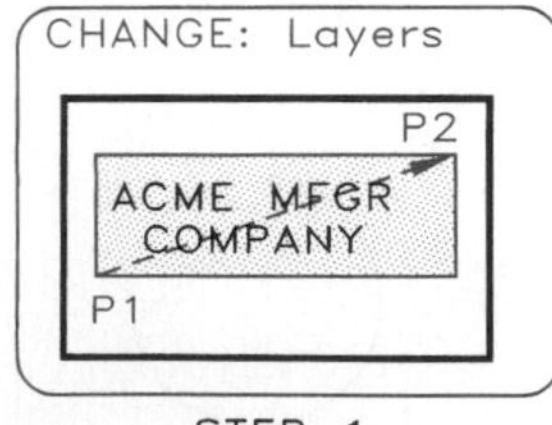

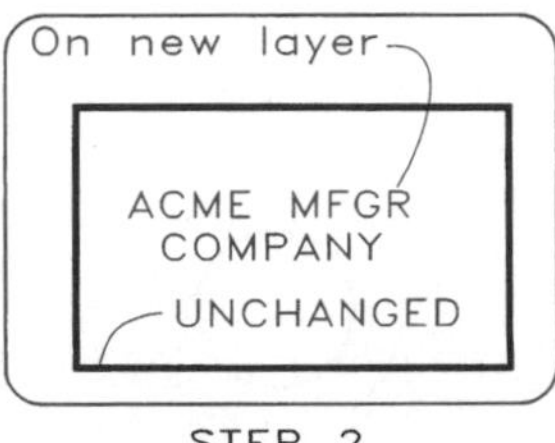

37.110 Change: Layers.

Step 1 *Command:* <u>Change</u>> *Select objects:* <u>W</u>
Pick points <u>P1</u> and <u>P2</u> to make window.
1 found, Select objects:
Specify change point or [Properties]: <u>P</u> (Enter)

Step 2 *Enter property to change [Color/Elev/LAyer/LType/ltScale/LWeight/Thickness/Material]:* <u>Layer</u> (Enter)
Enter new layer name <0>:<u>Visible</u> (Enter)

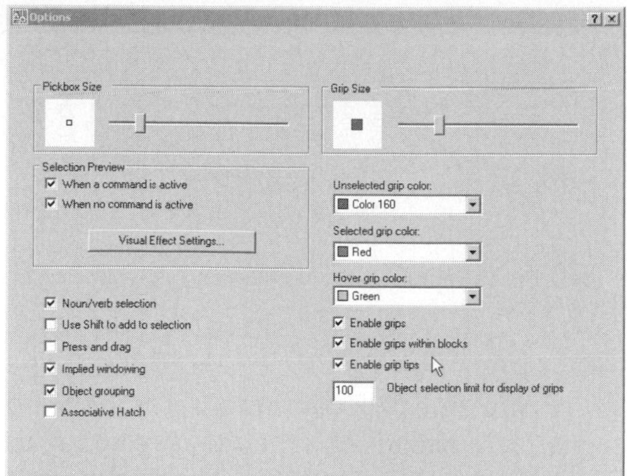

37.112 Use *Main Menu> Tools> Options> Selection* tab to obtain this box for *Enabling Grips,* setting *Grip size,* selecting *Grip color,* and other options.

grips are not filled in). *Grip Size* sets the size of grip boxes with a slider box.

Using Grips

Selecting an object with the cursor makes grips appear on it as open boxes. A grip that is picked and made a "hot" point is filled with color. Holding down the *Shift* key allows more than one grip to be picked as a hot point, but the last grip of a series must be selected without pressing *Shift.* Press the *Esc* key to remove grips. Turning grips on and successively pressing (Enter) sequentially activates the options *Stretch, Move, Rotate, Scale,* and *Move,* each with its own subcommands.

Stretch selects the endpoint grip of a line as a hot point, and a second point as the new end of the modified line (**Figure 37.113A**). This option can also be used to move a line using its midpoint grip as the hot point (**Figure 37.113B**). Select the midpoint grip to *Move* the line to a new position.

Move the *Block* in **Figure 37.114** by selecting the block, and its insertion point becomes the hot point. Options of *Base Point, Copy, Undo,* and *eXit* can be used for these applications.

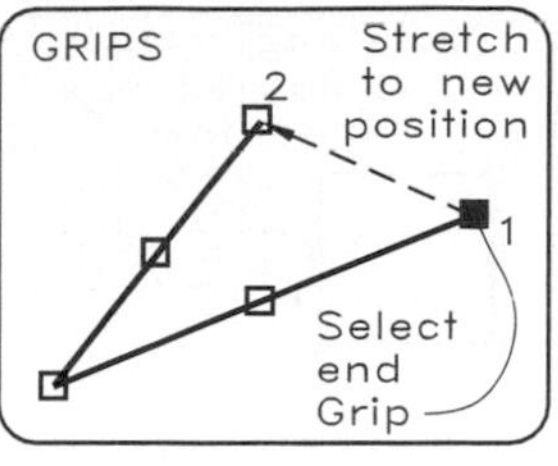

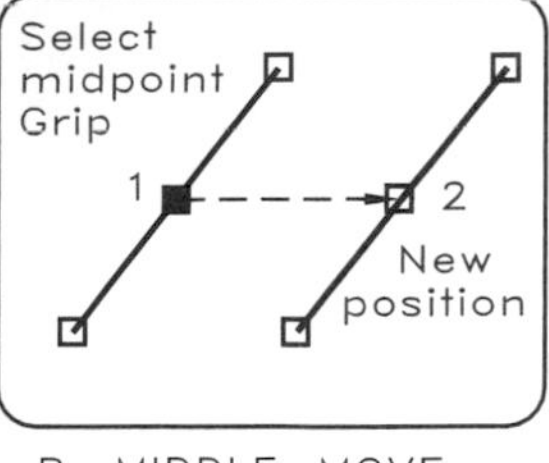

37.113 Grips: Stretch.

A Select the line and grips will appear; click on the end grip: 1 and select a new position at 2.

B Select the midpoint grip: 1, pick the second point: 2, and the line is moved. The color-filled grip is the hot point.

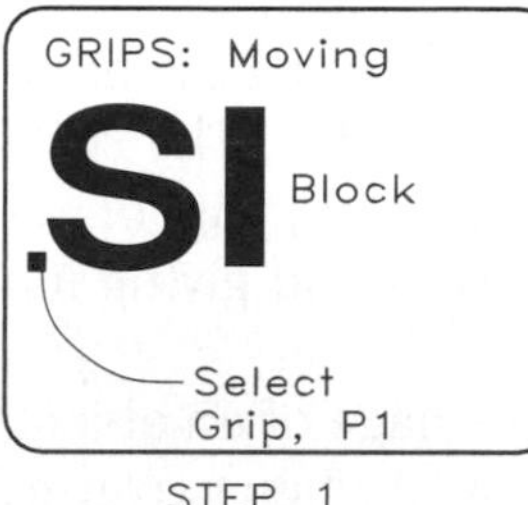

37.114 Grips: Move.

Step 1 Select the *Block* and a grip appears at the insertion point. Click on this grip as the hot point.

Step 2 Move the cursor to a new position and the *Block* is moved.

Rotate revolves an object about a selected grip. Dragging or typing a number in the *Reference* option rotates an object about a selected grip. The object in **Figure 37.115** is rotated 60° from the reference line by typing 50.

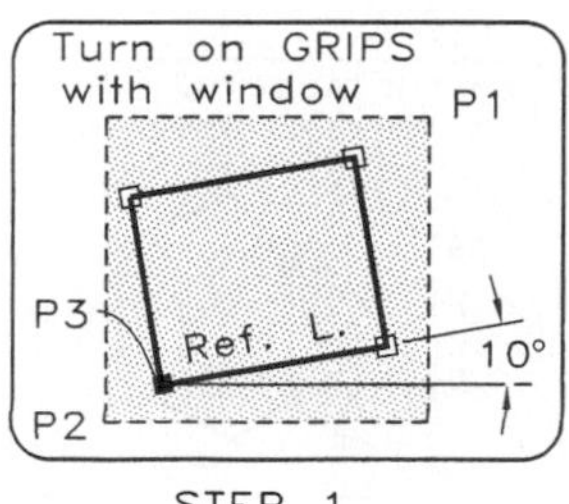

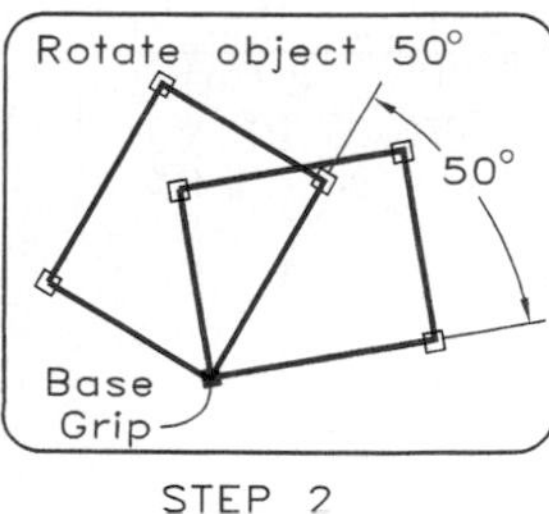

37.115 Grips: Rotation.

Step 1 Turn on grips by windowing the object (P1 and P2); select P3 as the pivot point> press (Enter) until **ROTATE** appears.

Step 2 *Specify rotation angle or [Base point/Copy/Undo/Reference/eXit]:* 50 (Enter) (Esc) The object is rotated.

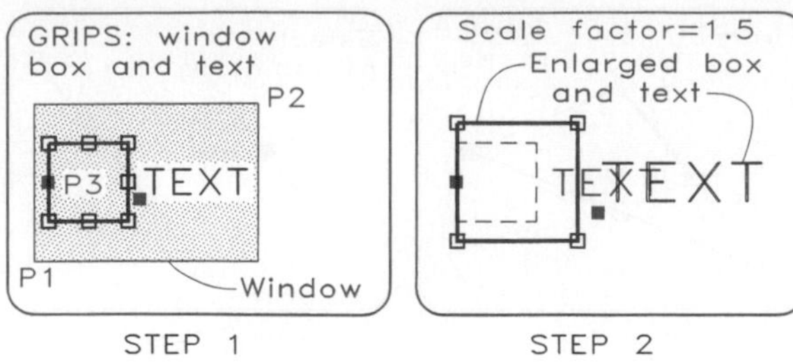

37.116 Grips: Scale.

Step 1 Turn on grips by windowing the object (P1 and P2); select P3 as the base, press (Enter) until ***SCALE*** appears.

Step 2 *Specify scale factor or [Base point/Copy/Undo/Reference/eXit]:* 1.5 (Enter) (Esc)

Scale uses the grip selected as a base point to size the object (**Figure 37.116**). The scale factor is assigned by typing, dragging, or selecting a reference dimension and giving it a new dimension.

Mirror makes a mirror image of an object. The original object is removed when two grips are selected to specify a mirror line (**Figure 37.117**). Hold down the *Shift* key while selecting the second grip point on the mirror line and the initial drawing will not be removed. The mirror line need not be a line of the view being mirrored.

37.35 Polyline

Select the *Polyline (PL)* icon from the *Draw* toolbar (**Figure 37.118**) to draw 2D polylines,

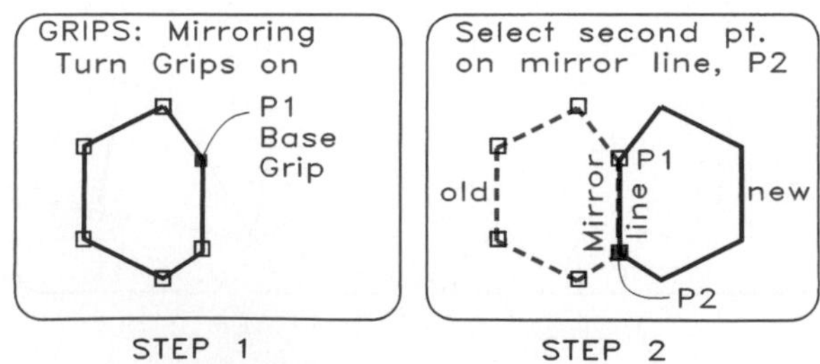

37.117 Grips: Mirror.
Step 1 Turn on grips by windowing object>; select P1 as the base grip> press (Enter) until ***MIRROR*** appears.
Step 2 *Specify second point or [Base point/Copy/Undo/eXit]:* P2. The object is mirrored. (Enter) (Esc)

37.118 The *Polyline* icon on the *Draw* toolbar is selected for drawing polylines.

which are lines of continuously connected segments instead of separate segments as drawn by the *Line* command. The thickness of a *Pline* can be varied as well, which requires the pen to plot with multiple strokes when plotting with a pen plotter instead of printing (**Figure 37.119**).

The *Pline* options are *Arc, Close, Halfwidth, Length, Undo,* and *Width. Close* automatically connects the last end of the polyline with its beginning point and ends the command. *Halfwidth* specifies the width of the line measured on both sides of its centerline. *Length* continues a *Pline* in the same direction when you type the length of the segment. If the first line was an arc, a line is drawn tangent to the arc. *Undo* erases the last segment

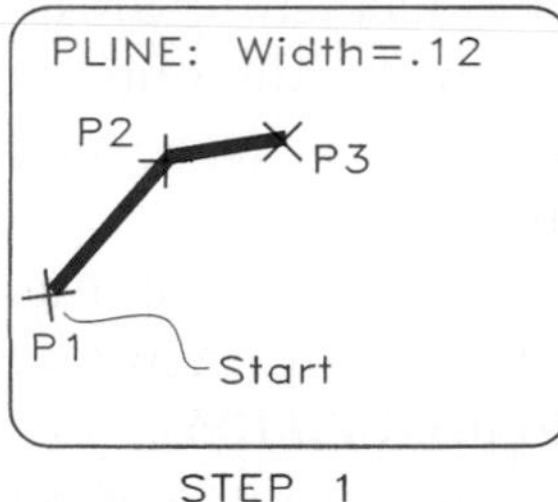

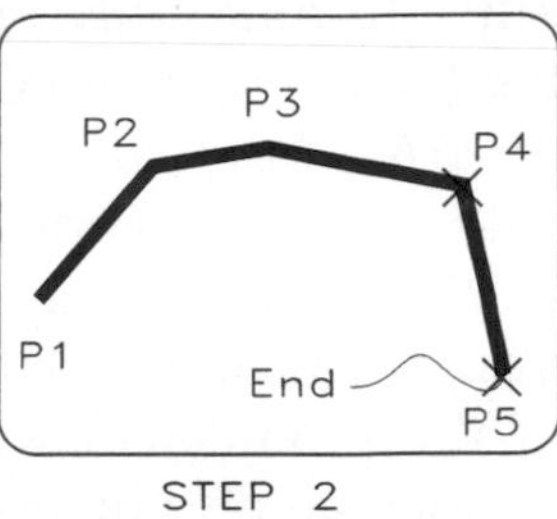

37.119 Polyline: Width option.

Step 1 *Draw* toolbar> *Polyline* icon> *Specify start point:* P1> *Current line-width is 0.00> Specify next point or [Arc/Close/Halfwidth/Length/Undo/Width]:* W > *Specify starting width* <0.00>*:* .12 (Enter)> *Specify ending width* <0.12>*:* (Enter), *Specify next point, or [Arc/Close/Halfwidth/Length/Undo/Width]:* P2 *Specify next point, or [Arc/Close . . . /Width]:* P3

Step 2 *Specify next point, or [Arc/Close . . . /Width]:* P4 *Specify next point, or [Arc/Close . . . /Width]:* P5 (Enter)

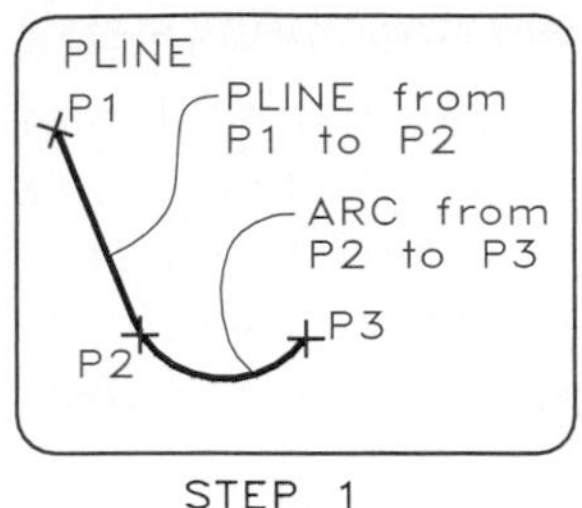

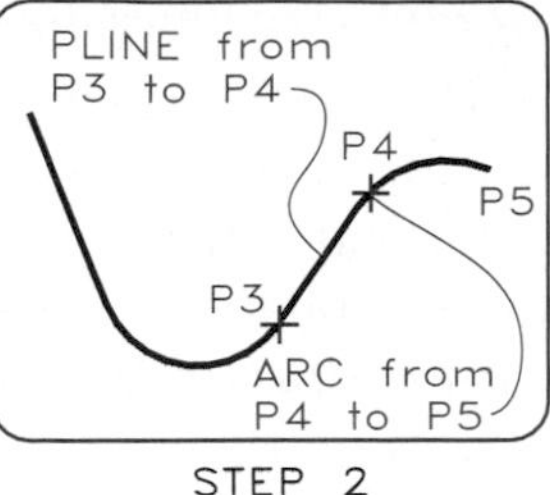

37.120 Polyline: Lines and arcs.

Step 1 *Draw* toobar> Select *Polyline* icon> *Specify start point:>* P1 (Enter)> *Current line-width is 0.12> Specify next point or [Arc/Close/Halfwidth/Length/Undo/Width]:* P2
Specify next point or [Arc/Close . . . /Width]: Arc
Specify endpoint of arc or [Arc/Close . . . /Width]: P3

Step 2 *Specify endpoint of arc or [Arc/Close . . . /Width]:* Line (Enter)
Specify next point or [Arc/ Close . . . /Width]. Length
Specify length of line: P4
Specify endpoint of arc or [Arc/Close . . . /Width]: Arc
Specify endpoint of arc or [Arc/Close . . . /Width]: P5
Specify endpoint of arc or [Arc/Close . . . /Width]: (Enter)

of the polyline, and it can be repeated to continue erasing segments.

The *Arc* option of *Pline* is selected to obtain the prompts shown in **Figure 37.120**. The default draws the arc tangent from the endpoint of the last line and through the next selected point. *Angle* gives the prompt *Included angle:*, to which a positive or negative value is given. The next prompt asks for *Center/Radius/<Endpoint>:* to draw an arc tangent to the previous line segment. Select *Center* and you will be prompted for the center of the next arc segment.

The next prompt is *Angle/Length/<Endpoint>:*, where *Angle* is the included angle, and *Length* is the chordal length of the arc. *Close* causes the *Pline*'s arc segment to close to its beginning point.

Direction lets you override the default, which draws the next arc tangent to the last *Pline* segment. When prompted with *Direction from starting point:*, pick the beginning point and respond to the next prompt, *Endpoint*, by picking a second point to give the direction of the arc.

Line switches the *Pline* command back to the straight-line mode. *Radius* gives the prompt *Radius:* for specifying the size of the next arc. The next prompt, *Angle/Length/<Endpoint>:*, lets you specify the included angle or the arc's chordal length. *Second Pt* gives two prompts, *Second point:* and *Endpoint:*, for selecting points on an arc.

37.36 Pedit

The *Pedit* command (*Command:* Pedit> (Enter)) modifies *Plines* with the following options: *Close, Join, Width, Edit vertex, Fit, Spline, Decurve, Ltype gen,* and *Undo.*

Close connects the last point of a series of lines with the first point. If the *Pline* is already closed, the *Close* command will be replaced by the *Open* option.

Join (J) gives the prompt *Select objects* for selecting segments to be joined into a polyline. *Segments* must have exact meeting points to be joined.

Width (W) gives the prompt *Specify new width for all segments:* for assigning a new width to a *Pline.*

Fit (F) converts a polyline into a line composed of circular arcs that pass through each point (**Figure 37.121**).

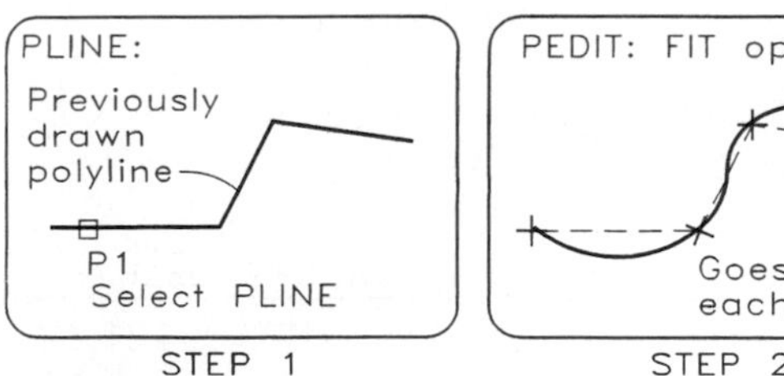

37.121 Pedit: Fit curve.

Step 1 *Modify II* toolbar> *Select Pedit* icon> *Select polyline:* P1 (Enter)

Step 2 *[Close/Join/Width/Edit vertex/Fit/ . . . Undo/ eXit <X>]:* Fit (Enter) The curve is drawn as a series of arcs passing through all polyline points.

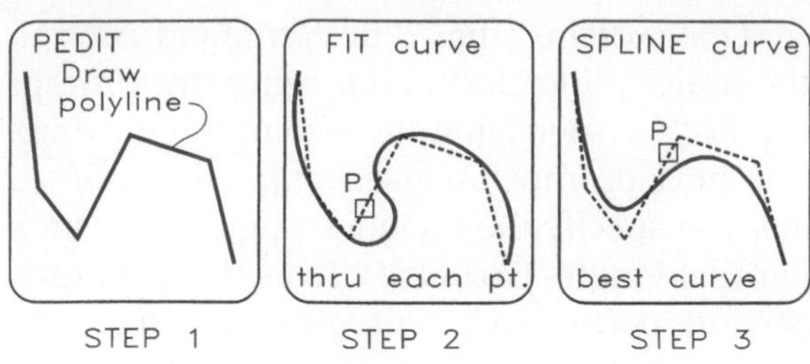

37.122 Pedit: Fit and Spline curve.
Step 1 Draw a polyline *(Pline).*
Step 2 *Modify II toolbar> Select Pedit* icon> *Select polyline:* P (Select line)
Close/Join/Width/Edit vertex/Fit/ . . . Undo/eXit <X>: Fit (Enter). The curve of arcs passes through all points.
Step 3 *Pedit* in the same way, but use the *Spline* option to obtain a "best curve" that may not pass through the selected points.

Spline (S) modifies the polyline as did the *Fit* curve, but it draws cubic curves passing through the first and last points, not necessarily through the other points (**Figure 37.122**). *Decurve (D)* converts *Fit* or *Spline* curves to their original straight-line forms.

Ltype gen (L) applies dashed lines (such as hidden lines) in a continuous pattern on curved polylines. Without application of this option, dashed lines may omit gaps in curved lines (**Figure 37.123**). Setting *Plinegen* on *(Command:* Plinegen (Enter) 1 (Enter)) will apply linetype generation *(Ltype gen)* as *Plines* are drawn.

Undo (U) reverses the last *Pedit* editing step.

Edit vertex (E) selects vertexes of the *Pline* for editing by placing an X on the first vertex when the polyline is picked. The following options appear: *Next/Previous/Break/Insert/Move/Regen/Straighten/Tangent/Width/eXit/<N>:* Next (Enter).

Next (N) and *Previous (P)* options move the X marker to next or previous vertexes when you press (Enter). *Break (B)* prompts you to select a vertex with the X marker. Then, use *Next* or *Previous* to move to a second point, and pick *Go* to remove the line between the vertexes. Select *eXit* to leave the *Break* command and return to *Edit Vertex.*

Insert adds a new vertex to the polyline between a selected vertex and the next vertex (**Figure 37.124**). *Move (M)* relocates a selected vertex (**Figure 37.125**).

Straighten (S) converts the polyline into a straight line between two selected points. An X marker appears at the current vertex and the prompt, *Next/Previous/Go/eXit/<N>*, appears. Move the X marker to a new vertex with *Next* or *Previous,* select *Go,* and the line is straightened between the vertices (**Figure 37.126**). Enter X to *eXit* and return to the *Edit vertex* prompt.

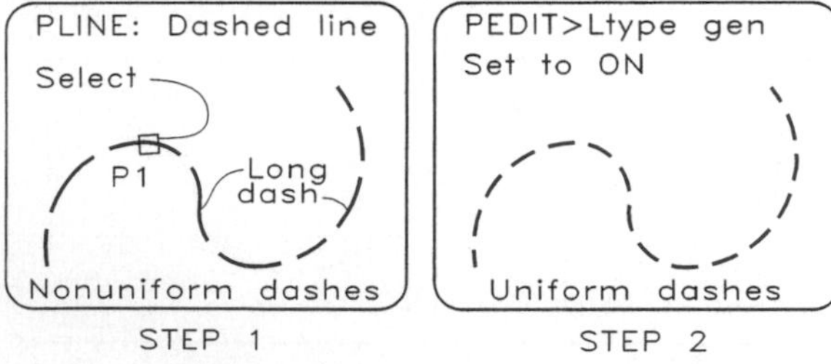

37.123 Pedit: Ltype generate.

Step 1 *Modify II* toolbar> *Select Pedit* icon> *Select polyline:* P1 (Select polyline) (Enter)

Step 2 *Enter an option [Close/Join/Width/Edit vertex/Fit/ . . . Ltype gen/Undo/eXit <X>]:* Ltype gen (Enter)
Enter polyline linetype generation option [ON/OFF] <Off>: On (Enter) Dashes become uniform around curves.

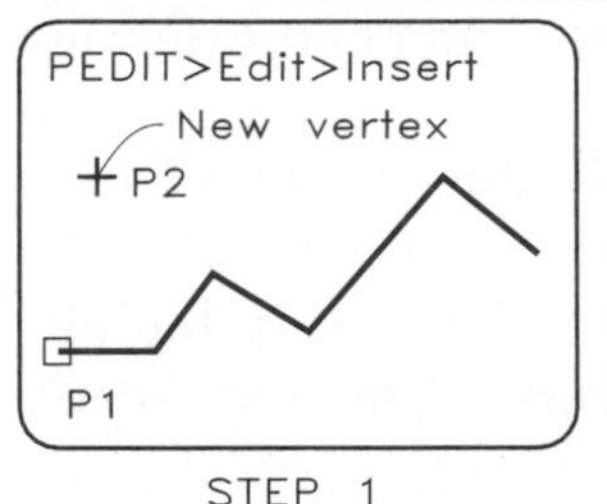

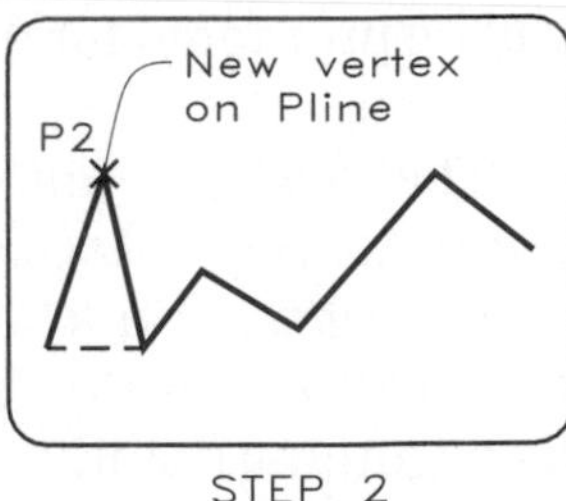

37.124 Pedit: Edit vertex—Insert.

Step 1 *Modify II* toolbar> Select *Pedit* icon> *Select polyline:* P1 > Select polyline (Enter)
Enter an option [Close/Join/Width/Edit vertex . . . Undo]: E (Enter) *Enter a vertex editing option [Next/ . . . /Insert/ . . . / eXit] <N>:* Insert (Enter) *Specify location for new vertex:* P2

Step 2 *Enter a vertex editing option* [Next/. . . /Insert/. . . /eXit] <N>: X (Enter)

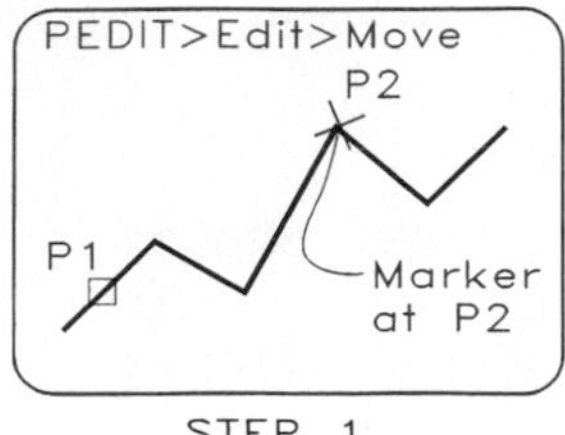

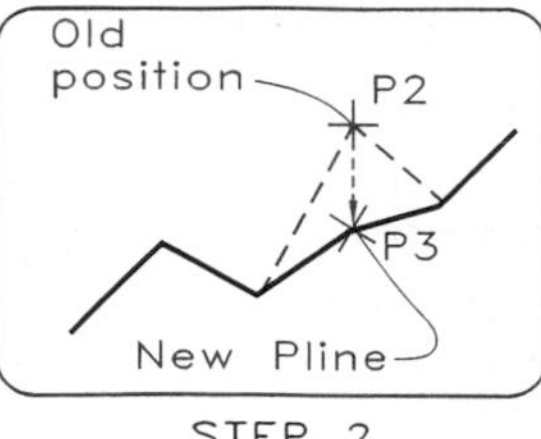

37.125 Pedit: Edit vertex—Move.

Step 1 *Modify II* toolbar> Select *Pedit* icon> *Select polyline:* P1 *Enter an option [Close/Join/Width/Edit vertex . . . Undo]:* E (Enter) (Enter) (Enter) (Enter) to place cursor on P2.
Enter a vertex editing option [Next . . . /Move/. . ./eXit] <N>: Move (Enter)

Step 2 *Specify a new location for marked vertex:* P3. *Enter a vertex editing option* [Next/ . . . /Insert/ . . . /eXit] <N>: X (Enter)

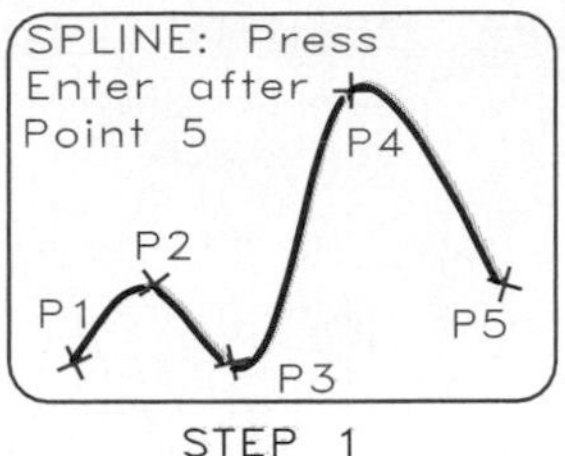

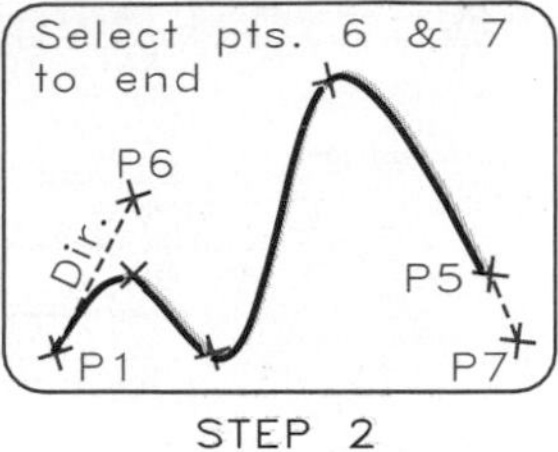

37.127 Spline.
Step 1 *Draw* toolbar> *Spline* icon> *Specify first point or [Object]:* P1> *Specify next point:* P2
Specify next point or [Close/Fit tolerance] <start tangent>: P3> Continue specifying points until P5 (Enter)
Step 2 *Specify start tangent:* Rubber-band to P6 (Enter)
Specify end tangent: Rubber-band to P7 (Enter)

37.128 *Draw* toolbar> Select the *Hatch* icon to open the *Hatch and Gradient* menu for selecting a hatch setting.

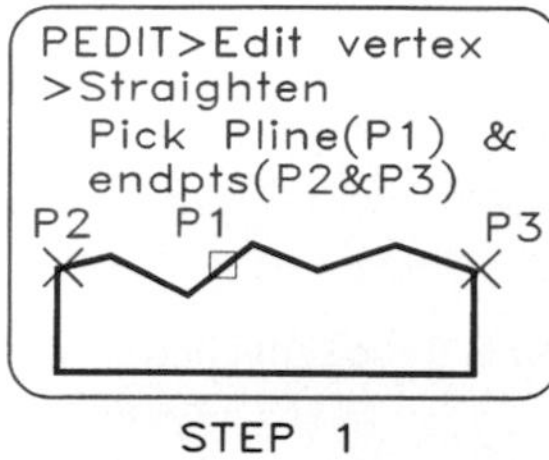

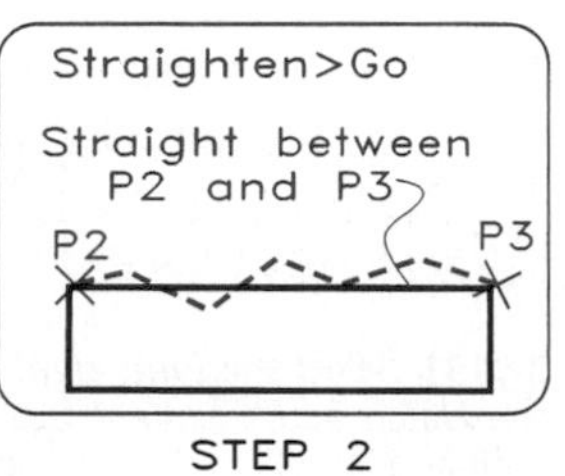

37.126 Pedit: Edit vertex—Straighten.

Step 1 *Modify II* toolbar> *Select Pedit* icon> *Select polyline or [Multiple]:* P1 to pick the polyline
Enter an option [Close/ . . . /Edit vertex/ . . . /Undo]: E (Enter)
Enter a vertex editing option [Next . . . /Straighten/ . . . /eXit] <N>: Straighten (Enter) P2 is selected.
Enter an option [Next/Previous/Go/eXit] <N>: Press (Enter) until X is on P3.

Step 2 *Next/Previous/Go/eXit* <N>: Go (Enter) Line is straightened between P2 and P3.

Tangent (T) lets you select a tangent direction at the vertex marked by the X for curve fitting by responding to the prompt, *Direction of tangent.* Enter the angle from the keyboard or by cursor.

Width (W) sets the beginning and ending widths of an existing line segment from the X-marked vertex. Use *Next* and *Previous* to confirm in which direction the line will be drawn from the X marker. The polyline will be changed to its new thickness when the screen is regenerated with *Regen (R).* Use *eXit* to leave the *Pedit* command.

37.37 Spline

The *Spline* command (*Draw* toolbar> *Spline* icon) draws a smooth curve with a sequence of points within a specified tolerance as shown in **Figure 37.127**. When *Fit Tolerance* is set to 0, the curve will pass through the points; when set to a value greater than 0, it will pass within a tolerance of each point.

Once the points of the spline are selected, press (Enter) and you will be prompted for tangent directions to be specified at each end. The *Endpoint tangent* determines the angle of the spline at each end.

37.38 Hatching

Hatching is a pattern of lines that fills sectioned areas, bars on graphs, and similar applications. From the *Draw* toolbar (**Figure 37.128**) pick the *Hatch* button and the *Hatch and Gradient* menu is displayed (**Figure 37.129**). Selecting the down arrow at the *Pattern* box displays a listing of pattern names from which to select. When one is selected, a view of the pattern will appear in the

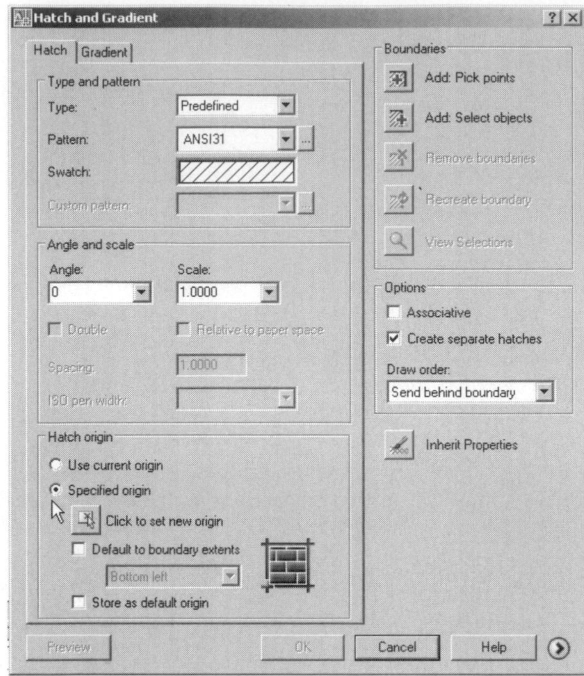

37.129 When the *Hatch* icon is selected, this *Hatch and Gradient* box appears on the screen for making selections.

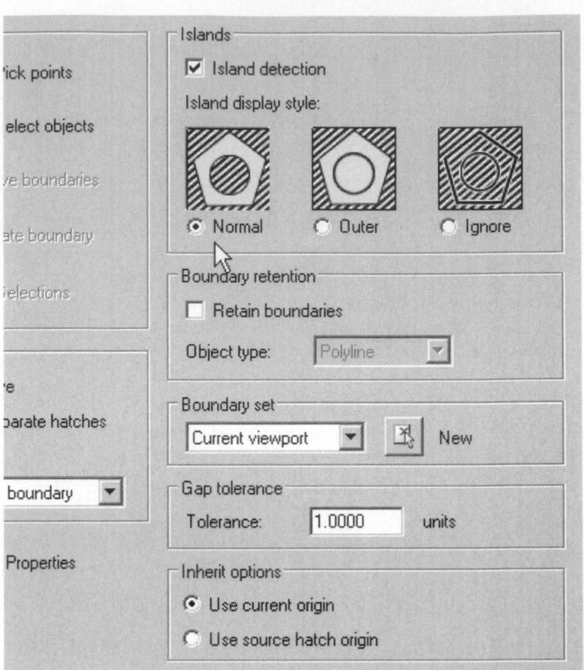

37.131 Select the *blue, right arrow* in the lower right corner of the *Hatch and Gradient* box to obtain this extended portion with additional hatching options.

Swatch window. Examples of several predefined patterns are shown in **Figure 37.130**. *Scale* sets the spacing between the lines of a pattern, and *Angle* assigns their direction.

Picking the right arrow in the lower right of the *Hatch and Gradient* menu expands the menu to display the options shown in **Figure 37.131**, from which choices of *Normal, Outer,* or *Ignore* can be made. A square with a pentagon and a circle inside it illustrates the effect of each choice. *Normal* hatches every other nested area beginning with the outside. *Outer* hatches the outside area, and *Ignore* hatches the entire area within the outer boundary. When text within the hatching area is selected, it will appear in an opening in the hatching, and hatch lines will not pass through it.

Options of *Add: Pick points* and *Add: Select Objects* (**Figure 37.129**) are used to select areas inside boundaries and the boundaries themselves, respectively, as shown in **Figure 37.132**. When points are selected outside the boundary or if the boundary is not closed, error messages will appear. Under *Options,* boxes can be checked for *Associative* and *Create separate hatches. Associative* hatching is automatically updated when the size of the hatching area is changed, as by using the *Stretch* command.

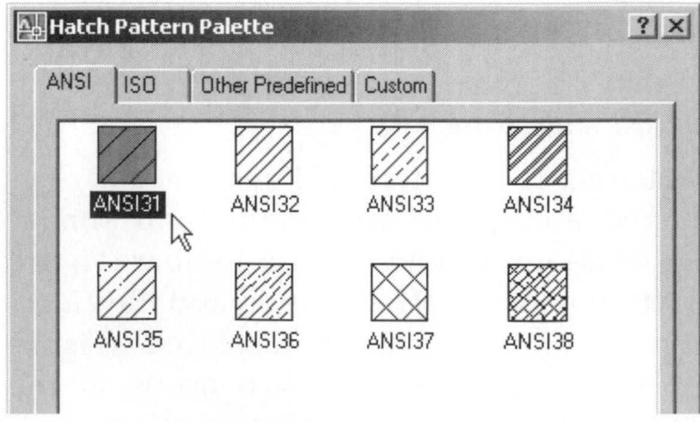

37.130 When the *Pattern* button in the *Boundary Hatch and Fill* box is selected, the hatch patterns and their names are displayed in this *Hatch Pattern Palette* box.

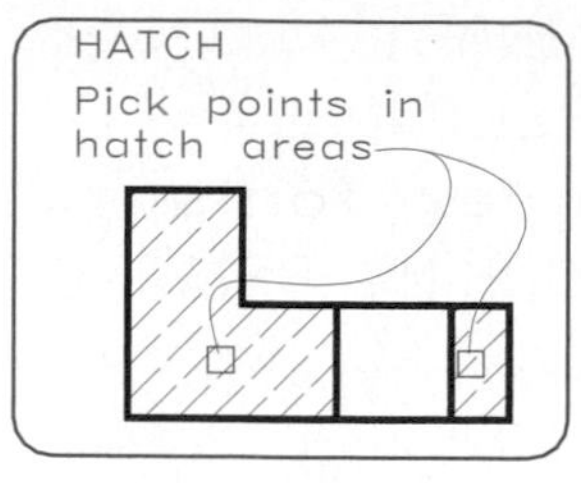

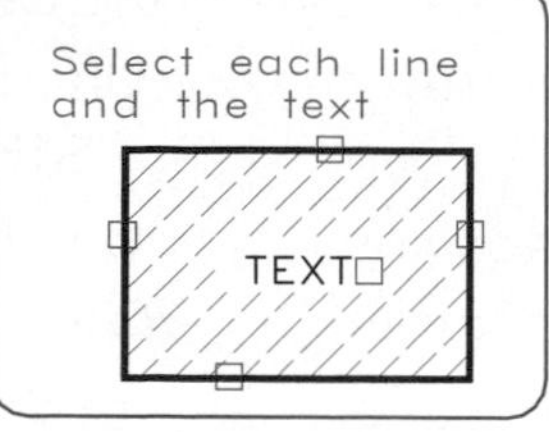

37.132 Hatching areas.

A The *Add: Pick Points* option (**Figure 37.129**) of *Hatch and Gradient* prompts for points inside the boundaries for hatching.

B The *Add: Select Objects* option requires that boundary lines be selected, including text.

37.133 The *Draw Order* toolbar positions objects with respect to others on the screen. Options are (left to right): In front of all, behind all, in front of selected object, and behind selected object.

When *Create separate hatches* is checked, you can select several areas to be hatched at one time and they will remain as separate hatches. Select the *Inherit Properties* icon, pick the symbols within a hatched area, and select the new area to be hatched. Then, it is filled with the same hatching symbols.

37.39 Draw Order

Drawings elements that overlap in a distracting manner can be improved by using the *Draw Order* toolbar shown in **Figure 37.133**. For example, objects of one color that lie partially on top of an object of a different color can be moved behind it. Select the icon with the single dark box behind the lighter box, select the object to be moved behind, and then pick the object that you want in front. Icons with a dark box and two lighter boxes are used to bring the selected object in front of all objects. Experiment with these options to better understand their applications.

37.40 Text and Numerals

The *Text* toolbar is a convenient means for accessing various text commands (**Figure 37.134**). Text and numerals can be added to

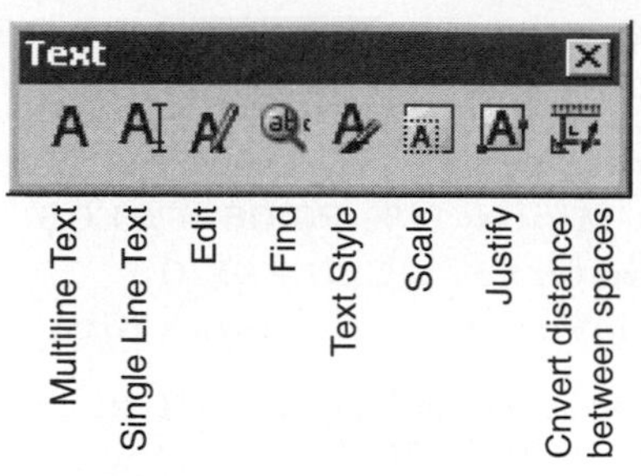

37.134 The *Text* toolbar offers these options for letters and numbers. The *Text* command can be accessed from *Main Menu> Draw> Text,* or *Command:* Dtext.

a drawing with the *Dtext* command. *Command:* Dtext> *Specify start point of text or [Justify/Style]:* Justify (Enter) *Enter an option [Align/Fit/Center/Middle/Right/TL/TC/TR/ML/MC/MR/BL/BC/BR]:* specify the insertion point for the text you are entering (**Figure 37.135**). For example, *BC* means bottom center, *RT* means right top, and so forth.

Figure 37.136 illustrates how multiple lines of *Dtext* are automatically spaced by

37.135 Text can be added to a drawing by using any of the insertion points above. For example, *BC* means the bottom center of a word or sentence that will be located at the cursor point.

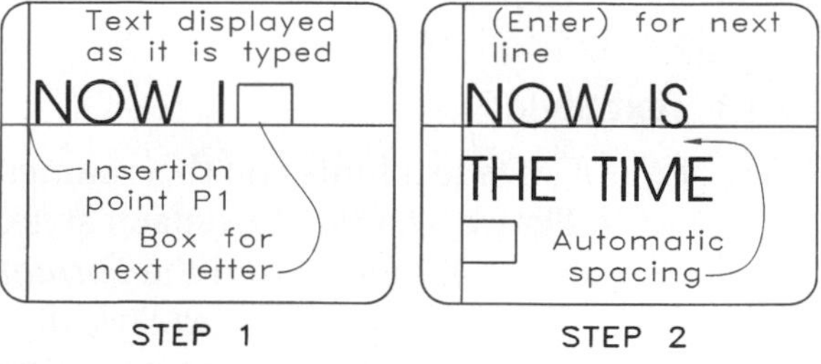

37.136 Dtext.

Step 1: *Command:* Dtext (Enter)
Current text style: "standard" Text height 0.50
Specify start point of text or [Justify/Style]: P1
Specify height <0.50>: .125. *Specify rotation angle of text <0>:* (Enter) *Enter text:* NOW IS

Step 2 (Enter) *Enter text:* THE TIME (Enter) (Enter)

%%O	Start or stop of Overline text
%%U	Start or stop of Underline of text
%%D	Degree symbol: 45%% D = 45°
%%P	Plus-Minus: %% P0.05 = ±0.05
%%C	Diameter: %% C20 = Ø20
%%nnn	Special character number nnn

37.137 The special characters that begin with %% are used with the *Text* command to obtain these symbols.

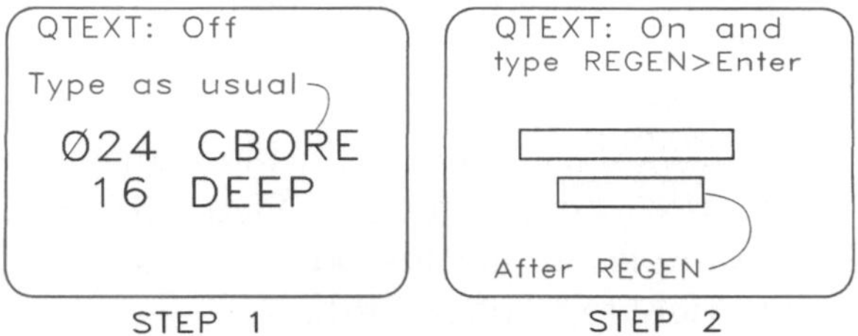

37.138 Qtext.

Step 1 *Command:* Qtext (Enter), *On/Off:* On (Enter)

Step 2 *Command:* Regen (Enter) Text is shown as boxes to speed up regeneration.

pressing (Enter) at the end of each line. The special characters shown in **Figure 37.137** can be inserted by typing a double percent sign (%%) in front of them.

Type Qtext and select *On* to reduce screen regeneration time by drawing text as boxes (**Figure 37.138**). When *Qtext* is *Off*, the full text will be restored after regeneration. Type *Command:* Regen.

37.41 Text Style

A few of AutoCAD's text fonts and their names are shown in **Figure 37.139**. The default style, *Standard*, uses the *Txt* font. From the *Format* menu, select *Text Style*, and the *Text Style* dialog box appears, where you can assign a *New Style Name* (**Figure 37.140**). Select the *New* button, get the *New Style* box, type the name (ROMAND), and the style is named. Pick the down arrow at the *Font Name* panel, and pick the font that you want to assign to the new style. Other options can be assigned: *Height* (0 is recommended), *Width Factor*, and *Oblique Angle*. A preview of your preferences is shown in the *Preview* window.

The *Style* names are listed in a drop-down menu in the window beneath the heading *Style Name* of the *Text Style* dialog box. An example of the text font is displayed when a *Style* is selected (**Figure 37.141**). A defined *Style* will retain its settings until they are changed.

TXT	PRELIMINARY PLOTS
MONOTXT	FOR SPEED ONLY
	Simplex fonts
ROMANS	FOR WORKING DRAWINGS
SCRIPTS	Handwritten Style, 1234
GREEKS	ΓΡΕΕΚ ΣΙΜΠΛΕΞ, 12345
	Duplex fonts
ROMAND	THICK ROMAN TEXT
	Complex fonts
ROMANC	ROMAN WITH SERIFS
ITALICC	*ROMAN ITALICS TEXT*

37.139 Examples of some of the available fonts are shown here. *Main Menu> Format> Text Style>* pick down arrow in *Font Name:* panel.

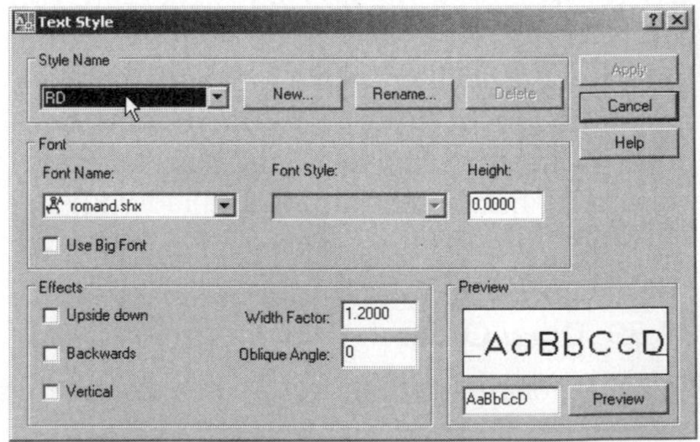

37.140 *Main Menu> Format> Text Style* (or *Command:* Style) to display this *Text Style* box. From here, a *New style* can be named, *Fonts* assigned, *Width Factors* specified, and other assignments made.

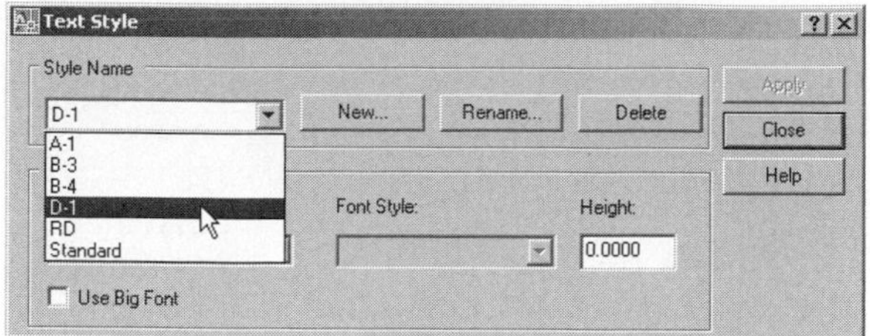

37.141 The style names are displayed when the down arrow is picked at the *Style Name* window, where they can be selected for application.

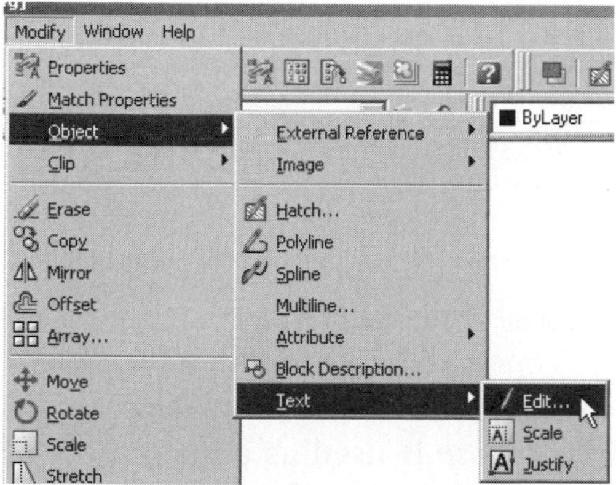

37.142 *Main Menu> Modify> Object> Text> Edit* (or select from the *Text* toolbar) select a line of text on the screen to be edited as a whole or in parts.

Figure 37.142 illustrates how text can edited from the *Main Menu.* A more direct way is by using the *Text* toolbar, shown in **Figure 37.134.**

If you later change a named *Style* with new settings or fonts and select *Apply* in the *Text Style* box, all text previously entered under this style name will be updated with the new properties. This technique is used to change the *Txt* and *Monotxt* fonts to more attractive fonts at plot time. Beforehand, time is saved by using *Txt* and *Monotxt* fonts because they regenerate quickly.

37.42 Multiline Text

From the *Text* Toolbar> *Draw> A* icon *(Multiline Text),* pick a point and drag a diagonal to

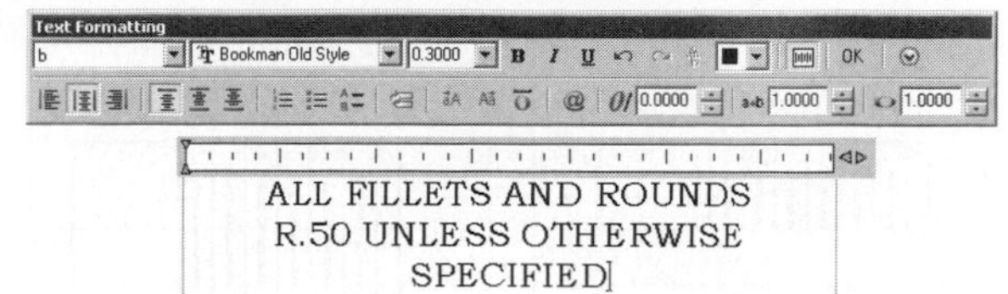

37.143 *Text* toolbar> *Multiline Text* icon> and pick two diagonal corners to specify the area for the lines of text on the screen and this *Text Formatting* bar appears. Type your lines of text in the box, pick *OK,* and the lines of text are drawn in the specified area. Windows in the *Text Formatting* box let you specify text *Style, Font, Height,* and *Color.* Text can also be changed to *bold, italics,* or *underlined* and other options.

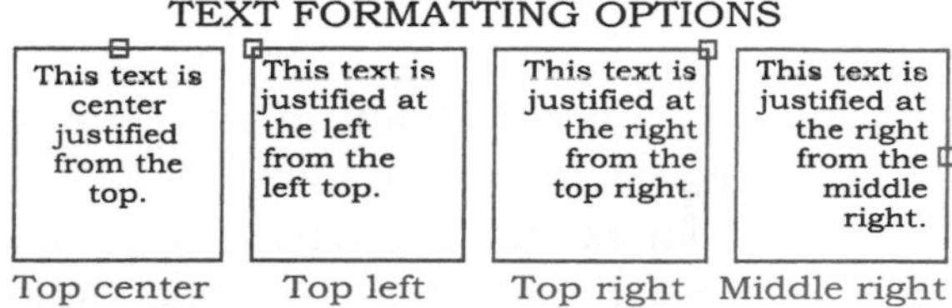

37.144 While the *Text Formatting* bar is active, select the text and right click your mouse to get a list of justification options, and pick the one desired. Several examples are shown here.

size the boundary of the lines of text. The *Text Formatting* panel will appear on the screen ready for your specifications (**Figure 37.143**). Select text *Height, Font, Style,* and other factors listed in the *Text Formatting* dialog box. Select *OK* to attach the paragraph to the drawing and close the dialog box.

Windows on the *Text Formatting* bar enable you to specify text *Style, Fonts, Height,* and *Color.* Click your mouse to display other formatting options from which to select. Try the a/b option, which will convert 2/3 into a fraction stacked vertically. Most of these options are easy to learn after a degree of experimentation and the use of the *Help* command when needed. Examples of formatted text are shown in **Figure 37.144**.

37.43 Mirror

Select the *Mirror* icon (*Modify* toolbar> *Mirror* icon) or *(Command:* Mirror (Enter)) to

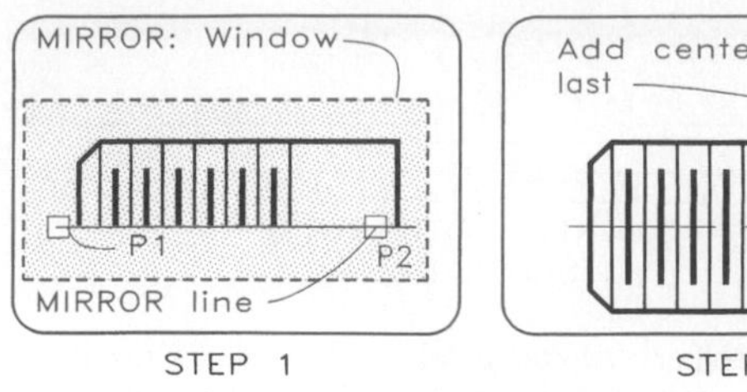

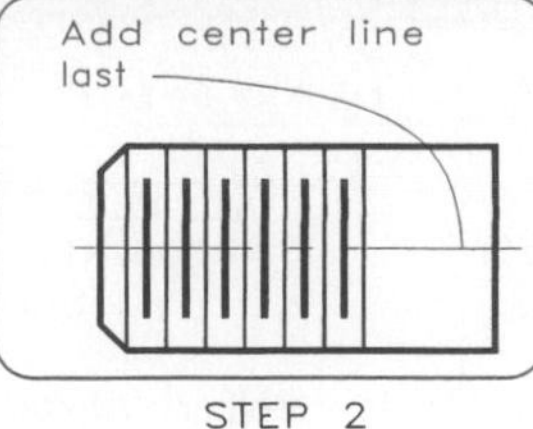

37.145 Mirror.

Step 1 Draw the half to be mirrored. *Modify* toolbar> *Mirror* icon> *Select objects:* W (Enter) Window the drawing. *Select objects:* (Enter) *First point of mirror line:* P1, *Second point:* P2

Step 2 *Delete old objects? <N>:* No (Enter) The drawing is mirrored. Draw the centerline.

mirror partial figures about an axis (**Figure 37.145**). A line that coincides with the *Mirror line* (P1-P2, for example) will be drawn twice when mirrored; therefore, parting lines should not be selected for mirroring.

The system variable *Mirrtext (Command: Setvar> Mirrtext)* mirrors text. Setting *Mirrtext* to 0 sets it to *Off,* and text will not be mirrored. Set *Mirrtext* to 1 *(On)* and the text will be mirrored along with the drawing.

37.44 Osnap

By using *Osnap (Object Snap),* you can snap to objects of a drawing rather than to the *Snap* grid. *Osnap* icons from the *Object snap* toolbar (**Figure 37.146**) give the following options: *Endpoint, Midpoint, Intersection, Apparent Intersection, Center, Quadrant, Perpendicular, Tangent, Node, Intersection, Nearest, Quick,* and *None. Osnap* is used as an accessory to other commands: *Line, Move, Break,* and so forth.

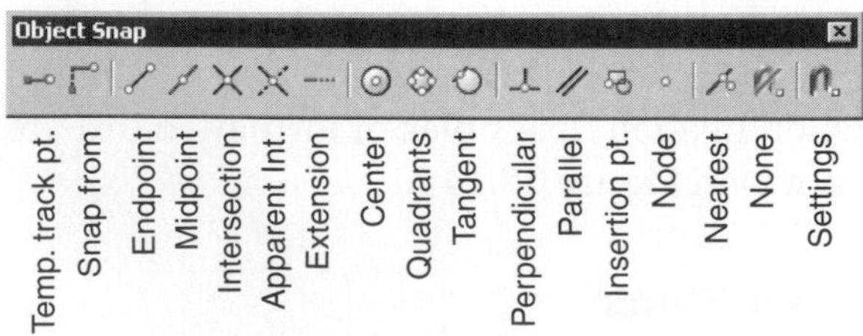

37.146 The *Object Snap* toolbar has these options for drawing to and from object features on the screen.

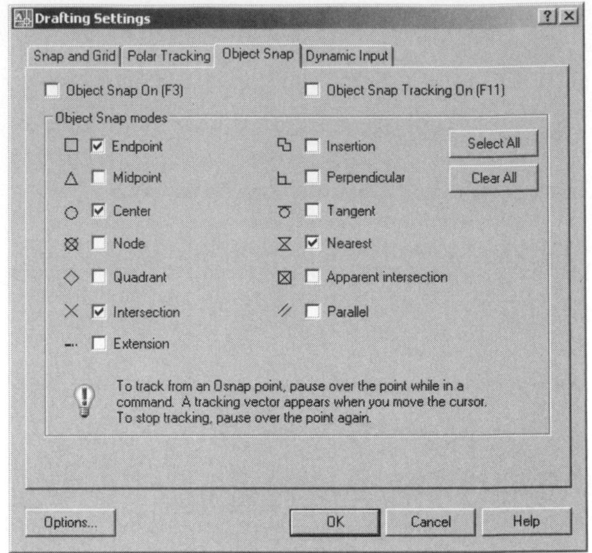

37.147 *Object Snap* toolbar> *Settings* icon to obtain the *Drafting Settings> Object Snap,* where the various snap modes can be turned on or off by checking the boxes.

Selections made from these icons must be picked anew for every application. To permanently set various *Osnap* settings, select *Settings* from the *Object Snap* toolbar to open the *Drafting Settings* menu, where the *Object Snap* tab shows the options for selection (**Figure 37.147**).

Figure 37.148 shows how a line is drawn from an intersection to the endpoint of a line. In **Figure 37.149** a line is drawn from P1 tangent to the circle by using the *Tangent* option of *Osnap.* The *Tangent* option can also be used to draw a line between and tangent to two arcs.

The *Node* option snaps to a *Point,* the *Quadrant* option snaps to one of the four compass points on a circle, the *Insert* option snaps to the intersection point of a *Block,* and the *None* option turns off *Osnap* for the next selection. The *Quick* option reduces searching

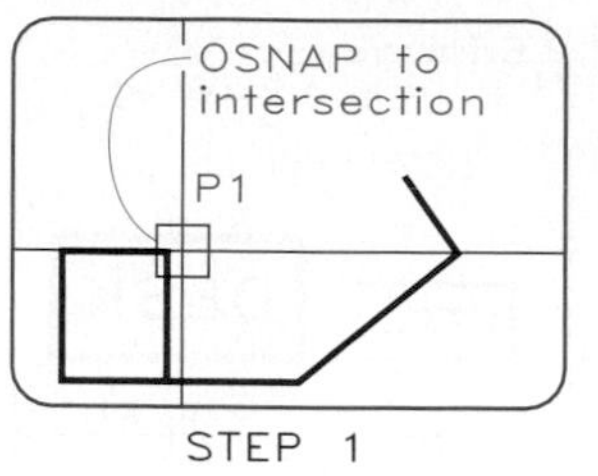

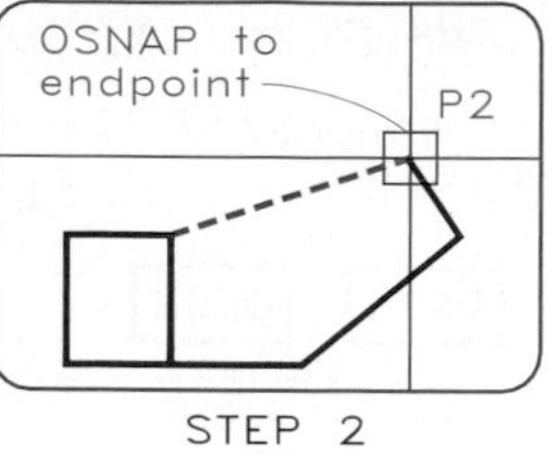

37.148 Osnap: Intersection and end.

Step 1 *Draw* toolbar> *Line* icon> *Line from point:*> *Intersection* icon> *Int of:* P1

Step 2 *To point:*> *Endpoint* icon on *Osnap* toolbar. *To point:* P2. The line snaps to the endpoint and is drawn.

time by selecting the first object encountered rather than searching for the one closest to the aperture's center.

Osnap settings can be temporarily retained as "running" *Osnaps* for repetitive use. One way to set running *Osnaps* is to click on *OSnap* tab in the *Status* line at the bottom of the screen, which activates the previously set *Osnaps.* Now, the cursor has an aperture target at its intersection for picking endpoints and centers of arcs. The *Osnap* command can be turned on or off by selecting the *OSnap* button in the *Status* line at the bottom of the screen. From the *Object Snap* box> *Osnap Settings*> *Drafting Settings*> *Object Snap* tab> select *Object Snap Modes* and your settings will remain until they are changed in the same manner.

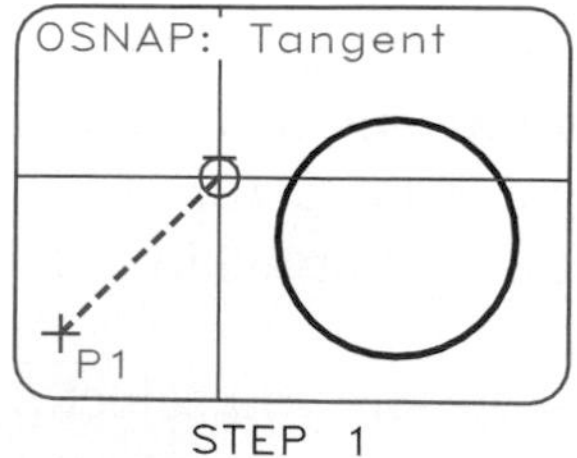

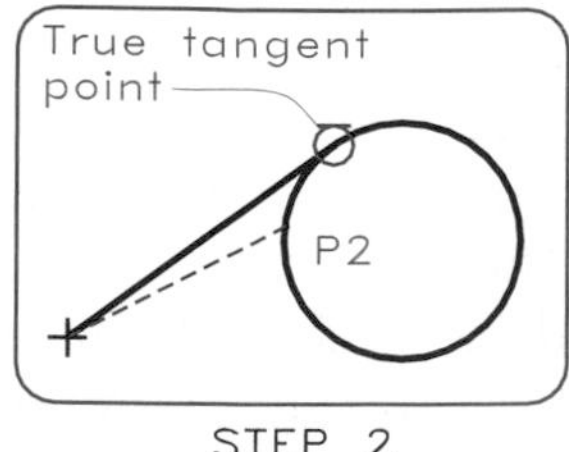

37.149 Osnap: Tangent.

Step 1 *Draw* toolbar> *Line* icon> *Line from point:* P1 *Specify next point or [Undo]:*> *Tangent* icon>

Step 2 *Tan to:* P2. The line is drawn from P1 tangent at the true tanget point on the circle nearest P2.

37.45 Array

The *Modify* tollbar> *Array* icon is used to draw rectangular patterns (rows and columns) or polar layouts of selected drawings using the *Array* dialog box (**Figure 37.150**). A series of holes can be drawn on a bolt circle by drawing the first hole and arraying it as a polar array (**Figure 37.151**).

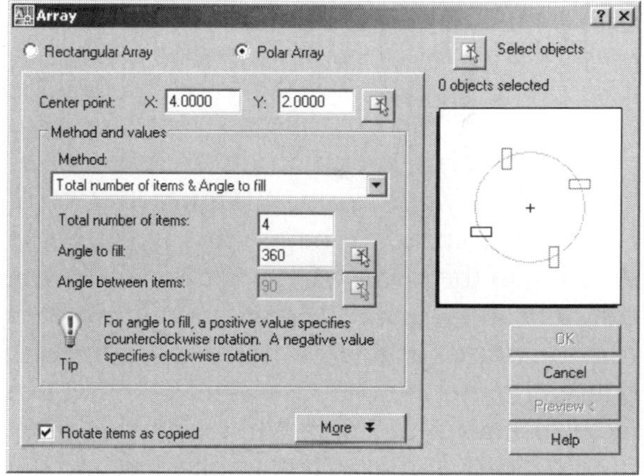

37.150 Select the *Modify* toolbar> *Array* icon to obtain the *Array* box in which to specify *Rectangular* or *Polar* arrays.

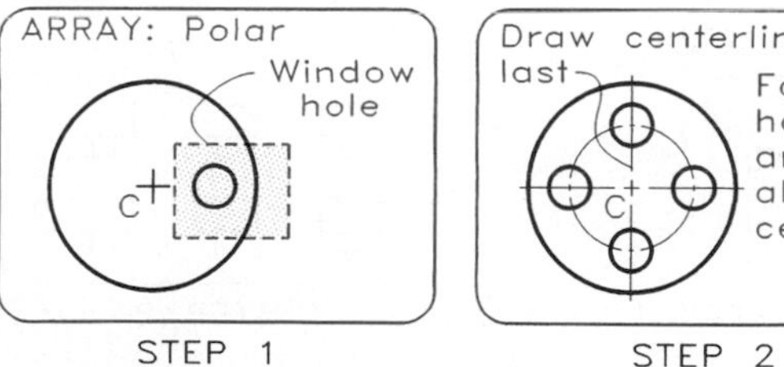

37.151 Array: Polar.

Step 1 *Modify* toolbar> *Array* icon> *Select objects:* W (Enter) Window the hole> *Select objects: Enter the type of array [Rectangular/Polar] <R>:* P (Enter) *Specify center point of array:* C (Enter)

Step 2 *Enter the number of items in the array:* 4 (Enter) *Specify the angle to fill (+ = ccw, − = cw) <360>:* 360 (Enter) *Rotate arrayed objects? [Yes/No] <Y>:* (Enter)

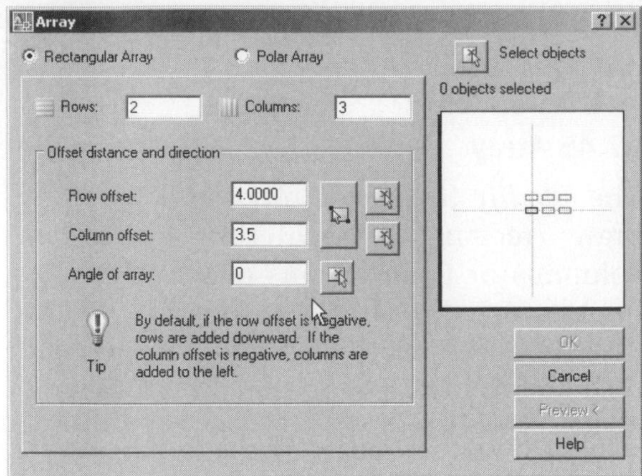

37.152 Select the *Modify* toolbar> *Array* icon to obtain the *Array* box in which to specify *Rectangular* array.

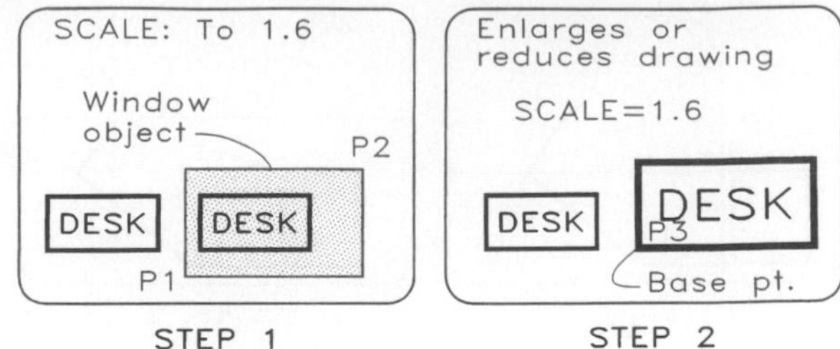

37.154 Scale: Numeric.

Step 1 *Modify* toolbar> *Scale* icon> *Select objects:* W (Enter) Window the desk with P1 and P2.

Step 2 *Specify base point:* P3 *Specify scale factor or [Reference]:* 1.6 (Enter) The desk is drawn 60% larger. Scaling can also be done by dragging with P3 as the anchor point.

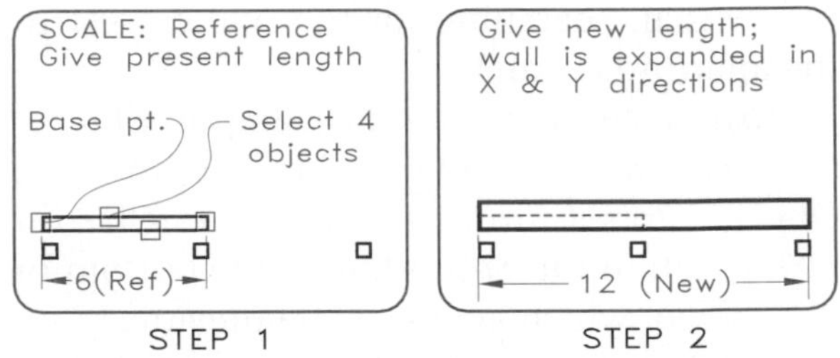

37.155 Scale: Reference.

Step 1 *Modify* toolbar> *Scale* icon> *Select objects:* Select 4 objects,
Base point: Select <Scale factor>/Reference: R (Enter)
Reference length <1>: 6 (Enter) Or specify with the mouse.

Step 2 *New length:* 12 (Enter) Or specify with the mouse. The drawing is enlarged in all directions.

Select the *Modify* tollbar> *Array* icon to display the *Array* menu on the screen and select the *Rectangular* option (**Figure 37.152**). A rectangular array is begun by making the drawing in the lower left corner and following the steps in **Figure 37.153**. Rectangular arrays may be drawn at angles by using *Command:* Snap> Rotate to rotate the grid. The first object is drawn in the lower left corner of the array, and the number of rows, columns, and the cell distances are specified when prompted.

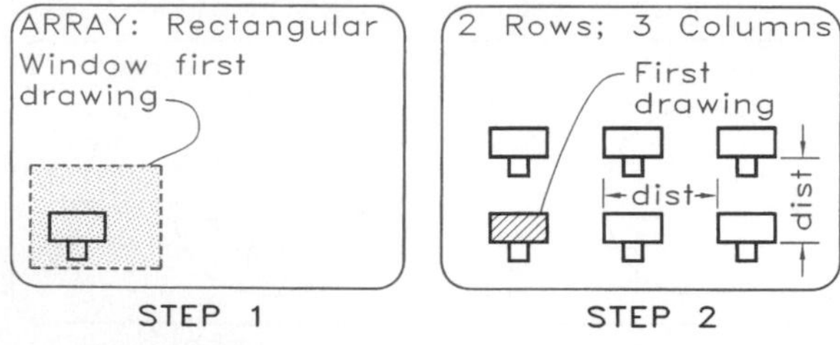

37.153 Array: Rectangular.

Step 1 *Modify* toolbar> *Array* icon> (obtain *Array* box in **Figure 37.152**). Check the *Rectangular Array* circle. Pick the *Select objects* button and window the desk on the screen.

Step 2 *Enter the number of rows (—) <1>:* 2 (Enter)
Enter the number of columns (|||) <1>: 3 (Enter)
Enter the distance between rows or specify unit cell (—) <1>: 4 (Enter),
Specify the distance between columns (|||) <1>: 3.5 (Enter)

37.46 Scale

The *Scale* command reduces or enlarges previously drawn objects. The desk in **Figure 37.154** is enlarged by windowing it, selecting a base point, and typing a scale factor of 1.6. The drawing and its text are enlarged in both the *x*- and *y*-directions.

A second option of *Scale* lets you select a length of a given object, specify its present length, and assign a length as a ratio of the first dimension (**Figure 37.155**). The lengths can be specified by the cursor or typed at the keyboard in numeric values.

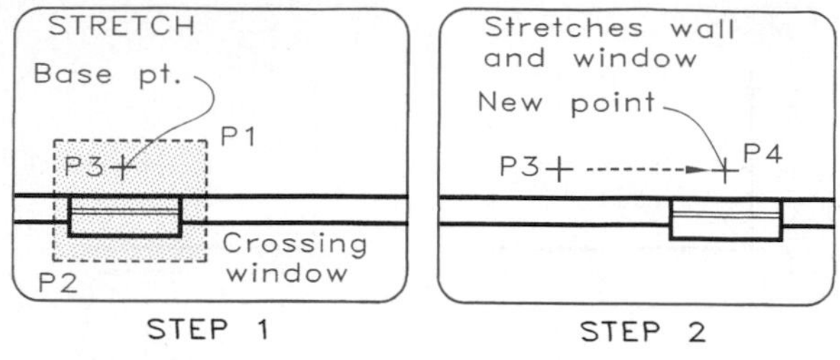

37.156 Stretch.

Step 1 *Modify* toolbar> *Stretch* icon> *Select objects:* Use P1 and P2 to form a crossing window.
Specify base point or [Displacement] <Displacement>: P3

Step 2 *Specify second point of displacement:* P4 The windowed portion of the drawing is repositioned.

37.47 Stretch

The *Stretch* command *(Modify* toolbar> *Stretch* icon) lengthens or shortens a portion of a drawing while one end is left stationary. The window symbol in the floor plan in **Figure 37.156** is *Stretched* to a new position, leaving the lines of the wall unchanged. A *Crossing Window* must be used to select lines that will be stretched.

37.48 Rotate

A drawing can be rotated about a base point by using the *Rotate* command (*Modify* toolbar> *Rotate* icon) as shown in **Figure 37.157.** *Window* the drawing, select a base point, and type the rotation angle or select the angle with the cursor. Drawings made on multiple layers can be rotated also.

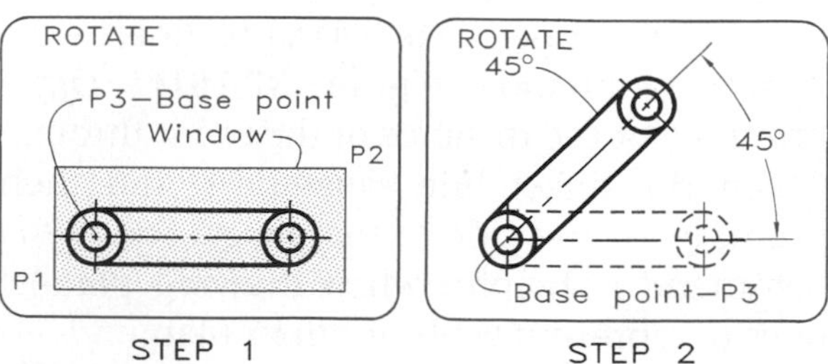

37.157 Rotate.

Step 1 *Modify* toolbar> *Rotate* icon> *Select objects:* Window the part with P1 and P2. *Specify base point:* P3

Step 2 *Specify rotation angle or [Copy/Reference]:* 45 (Enter) Object is rotated 45° counterclockwise.

37.49 Setvar

Many system variables (several hundred) can be inspected and changed from *Command:* Setvar and ? if they are not read-only commands. To change one or more variables (*Textsize,* for example), respond as follows:

Command: Setvar (Enter)

Variable name or ?: Textsize (Enter)

Enter new value for TEXTSIZE <0.18>: 0.12 (Enter)

By entering the *Setvar* command with an apostrophe in front of it *('Setvar),* you can use it transparently without exiting from the command in progress.

37.50 Divide

The *Divide* command *(Main Menu> Draw> Point> Divide)* places markers on a line to show a specified number of equal divisions. The line in **Figure 37.158** is selected by the cursor, the number of divisions is specified, and markers are equally spaced along it. The markers will be of the type and size currently

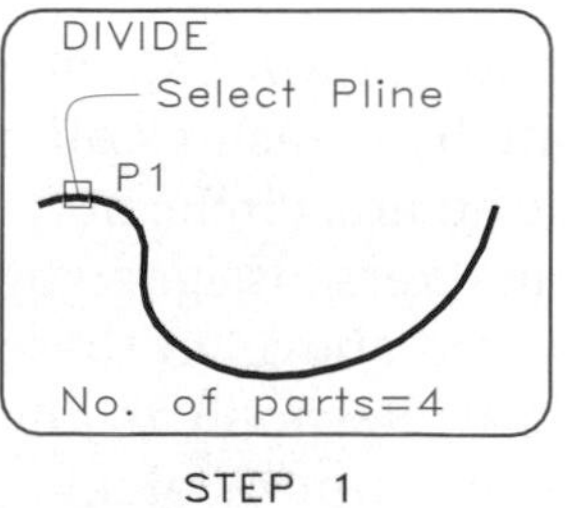

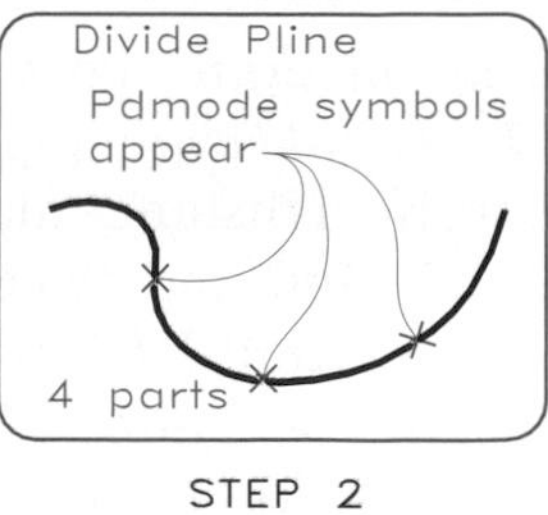

37.158 Divide.

Step 1 *Command:* Divide (Enter)
Select object to divide: P1
Enter the number of segments or [Block]: 4 (Enter)

Step 2 Four *Pdmode* symbols are placed along the line, dividing it into equal divisions.

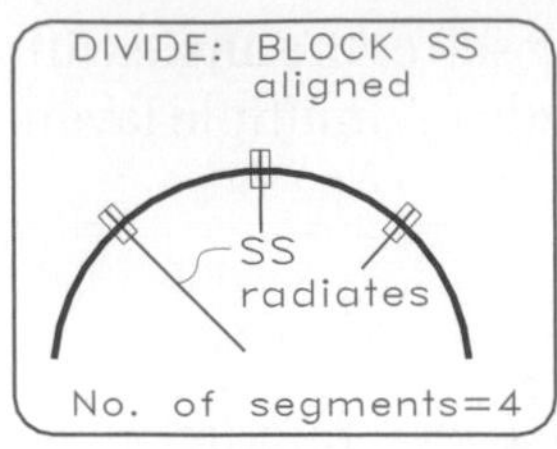

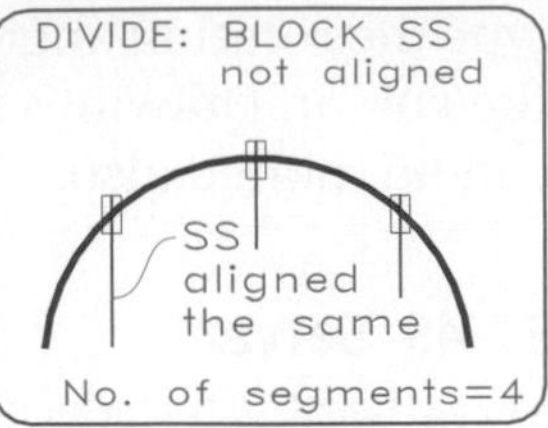

A. ALIGNED B. NOT ALIGNED

37.159 Divide.

A. *Command:* Divide (Enter)
Select object to divide: Select arc.
Enter the number of segments or [Block]: B (Enter)
Enter the name of block to insert: SS (Enter)
Align block with object? [Yes/No]:<Y>: Y (Enter)
Enter the number of segments: 4 (Enter)

B. *Align block with object? <Y>:* N (Enter) Blocks are drawn to be vertical and parallel.

set by the *Pdmode* and *Pdsize* variables under the *Setvar* command. Set *Pdmode* to 3 to get an X when the *Point* command is used.

Pdmode and *Pdsize* define symbols used to mark points. *Main Menu> Help> Point* to obtain a display of symbols to use as markers from which to select and assign as *Setvars* (system variables). The *Block* option of *Divide* allows saved *Blocks* (rectangles, used here) to be used as markers on the line (**Figure 37.159**). *Blocks* can be either *Aligned* or *Not Aligned* as shown.

37.51 Measure

The *Measure* command *(Main Menu> Draw> Measure)* repeatedly measures off a specified distance along an arc, circle, polyline, or line and places markers (assigned by *Pdmode* and *Pdsize* covered above) at these distances (**Figure 37.160**). Respond to the *Select object to measure* prompt by picking a point near the end where measuring is to begin. When prompted, give the segment length, and markers are displayed along the line. The last segment is usually a shorter length.

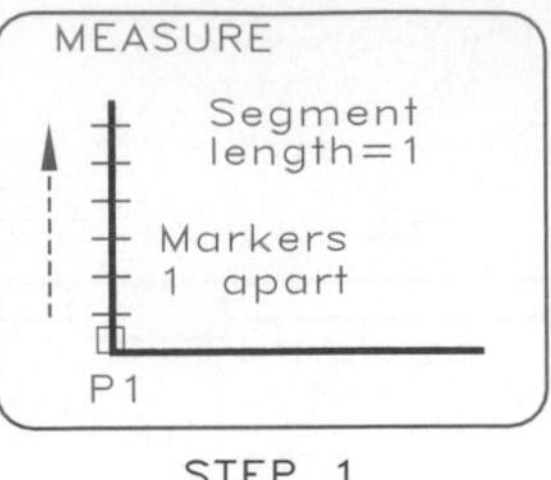

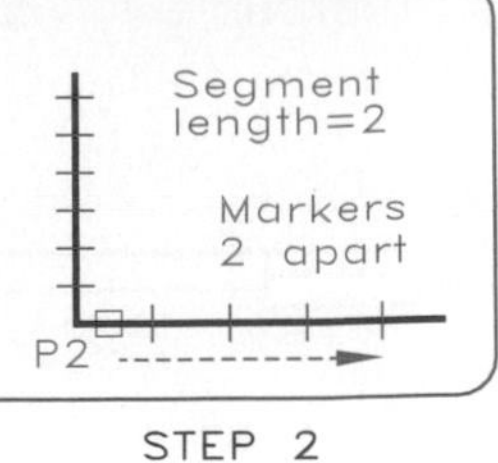

STEP 1 STEP 2

37.160 Measure.

Step 1 *Command:* Measure (Enter)
Select object to measure: P1
Specify length of segment or [Block]: 1 (Enter)
Markers are placed 1 apart starting at the end nearest P1.

Step 2 *Command:* Measure (Enter)
Specify length of segment or [Block]: 2 (Enter)
Markers are placed 2 units apart starting at the end nearest P2.

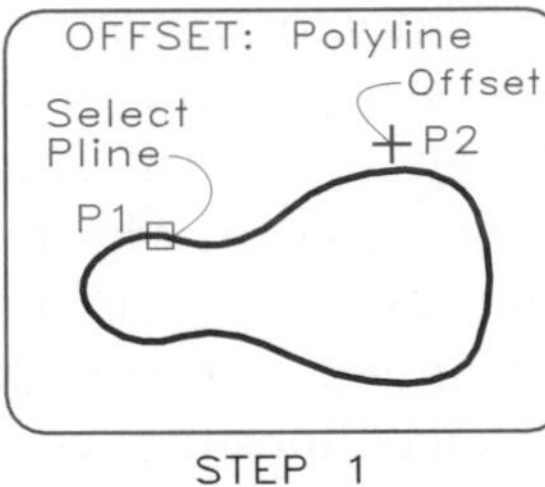

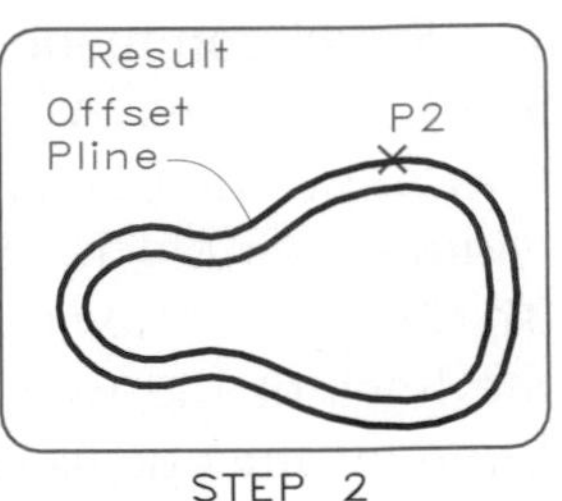

STEP 1 STEP 2

37.161 Offset.

Step 1 *Command:* Offset (Enter)
Specify offset distance or [Through] <1>: T (Enter)
Select object to offset or <exit>: P1 (Enter)

Step 2 *Specify through point:* P2 (Enter).
An enlarged *Pline* is drawn that passes through P2.

37.52 Offset

An object can be drawn parallel to and offset from another object, such as a polyline, by the *Offset* command (**Figure 37.161**). *Offset* prompts for the distance or the point through which the offset line must pass and then prompts for the side of the offset. The *Offset* command is helpful when drawing parallel lines to represent walls of a floor plan.

37.53 Blocks

One of the most productive features of computer graphics is the capability to create draw-

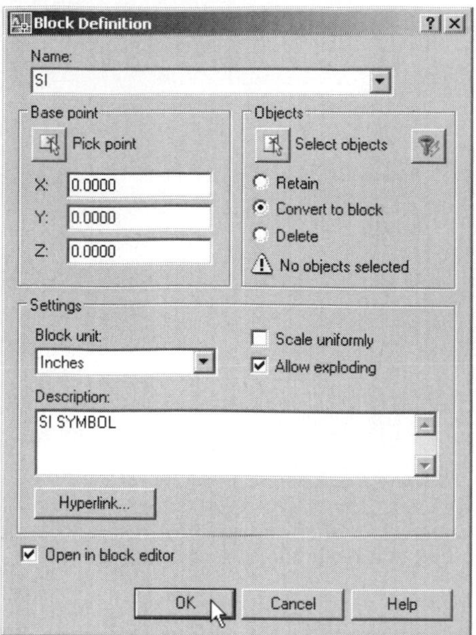

37.162 A *Block* can be defined from this window by selecting the drawing to be blocked, assigning insertion points, and other information.

ings for repetitive use called *Blocks. Draw Menu> Block> Make> Block definition* box is used to make a block (**Figure 37.162**). The SI symbol in **Figure 37.163** is a typical drawing that is made into a *Block* and inserted into drawings using icons from *Main Menu> Insert* shown in **Figure 37.164**. *Main Menu>*

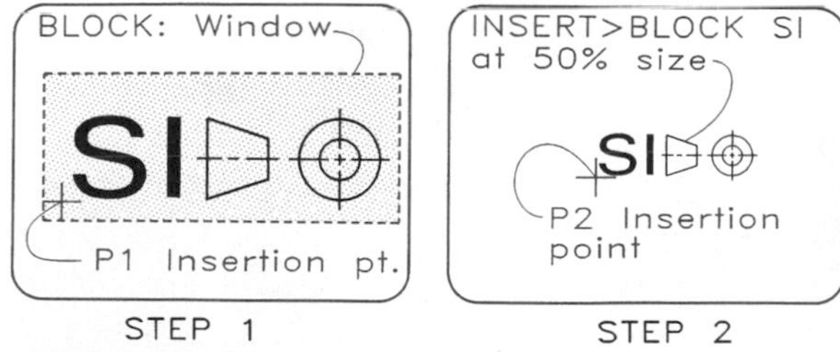

37.163 Block.

Step 1 *Main Menu> Draw> Block> Make>* Get *Block Definition* box> *Name:* SI> Select *Pick point* button> P1
Pick *Select objects* button> Window drawing (Enter)

Step 2 *Command:>* Insert (Enter)> *Insert* box> *Name:* SI> *Scale:* .50> Check *Uniform Scale* box> OK> *Specify insertion point:* P2. The block is inserted.

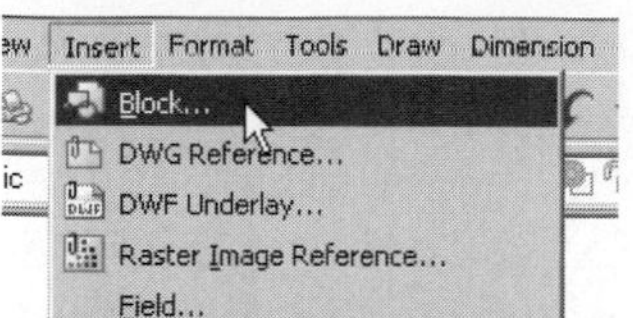

37.164 The *Make block* and *Insert block* icons can be selected from the *Draw* toolbar.

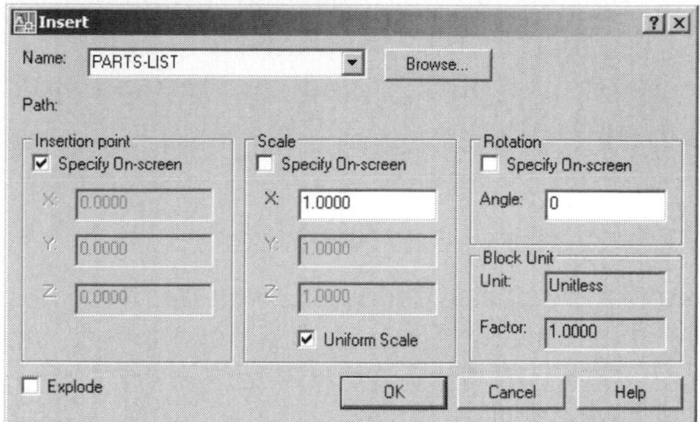

37.165 Select *Main Menu> Insert>* to get *Insert* box to specify *Blocks* or *Files (Wblocks)* for insertion in a drawing.

Insert> Block gives the *Insert* dialog box (**Figure 37.165**) for inserting *Blocks*. You can select a *Block* from the window or *Browse* for other files to insert as *Blocks* (**Figure 37.166**).

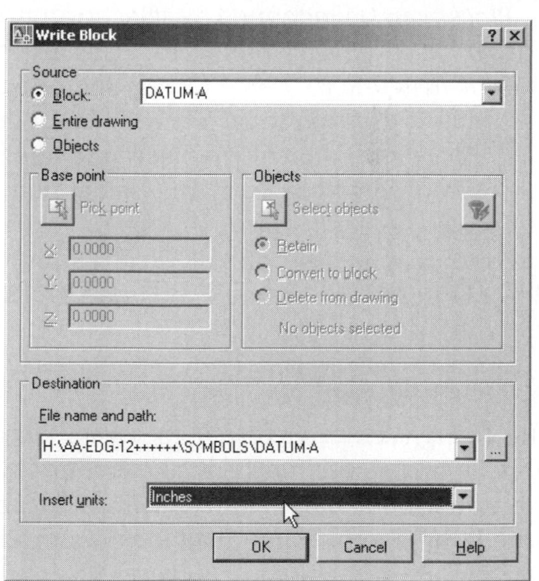

37.166 *Command*: Wblock (Enter) and the *Write Block* box enables you to select a *Block* as the *Source* and convert it to a *Wblock* with its destination *File name and path* specified in the lower window. Non-*Block* drawings can also be made into *Wblocks* by checking the *Objects* box under *Source*.

When a *Block* is selected on the screen (to be *Moved,* for example), it is selected as a total unit. However, *Blocks* that were *Inserted* by selecting the *Explode* box first, or by typing a star in front of the *Block* name (**SI,* for example), can be selected one object at a time. An inserted *Block* can be separated into individual entities by typing Explode at the *Command* line and selecting the *Block.*

37.54 Write Blocks (Wblocks)

Blocks are parts of files that can be used only in the current drawing file unless they are converted to *Wblocks (Write Blocks),* which are independent files, not parts of files. This conversion is performed by typing Wblock at the *Command* line to get the *Write Block* dialog box (**Figure 37.166**). Select the *Block* button and type the name of the *Block* that is to be converted to a file in the window of the *Source* area. Give the *File name and path* in the *Destination* area, and press *OK.*

Blocks can be redefined by selecting a previously used *Block* name to receive the prompt *Redefine it?* <N>*:* Y *(Yes)* and selecting the new drawing to be blocked. The redefined *Block* automatically replaces the one in the current drawing with the same name. *Command:* Insert> *Block> Browse* can be used to display thumbnail illustrations of *Wblocks (Files)* as illustrated in **Figure 37.167**.

37.55 DesignCenter

The DesignCenter (referred to as DC occasionally in this section) is a convenient storage unit where *Blocks* and drawings can be stored, retrieved, and applied to your current drawing. From here you can access files and content of your own and from commercial sources on the Internet.

To open the *DesignCenter,* select the *DesignCenter* icon from the *Standard* toolbar and the DC appears as shown in **Figure 37.168**. The DC can also be opened by *Command:* Adcenter (Enter). Initialize the DC with the *Home* button (house icon) and the *Tree View Toggle* as shown in **Figure 37.169**. The right portion of the DC is called the *Content area,* the area where files are listed that can be operated on by clicking and double clicking on them. For example, a file listed in the *Contact area* can be selected and dragged with the mouse into the current drawing.

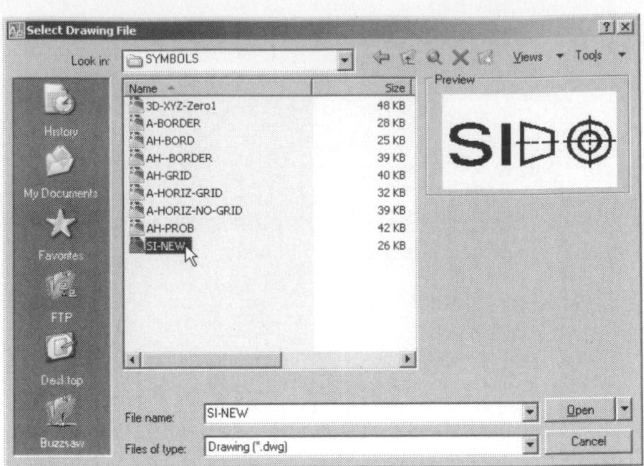

37.167 To find a *Block* for insertion, select the *Browse* button in the *Insert box.* (*Command*: Insert (Enter)> *Browse>* then select a defined block from the list> *Open>* select an insertion point on the screen with the cursor.)

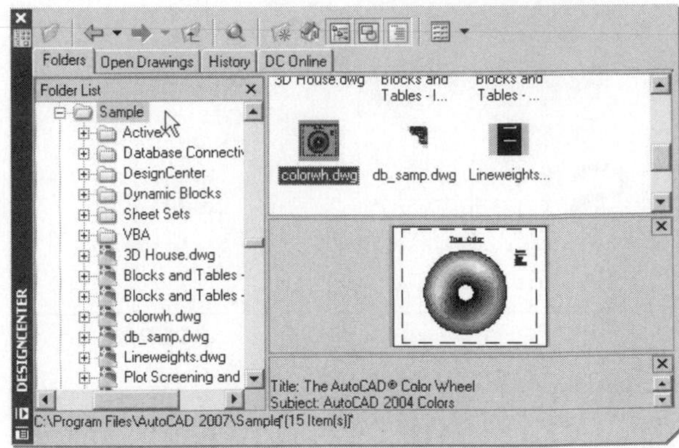

37.168 To open the *DesignCenter,* select the *DesignCenter* icon on the *Standard* toolbar. Experiment with it; notice that several of its areas can be resized and moved about with your mouse.

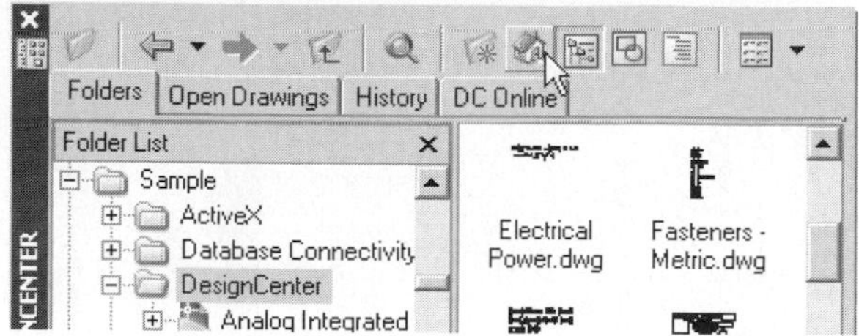

37.169 Initialize the *DesignCenter* by selecting the *Home* (house icon) and the *Tree View Toggle*. The *Folder List* opens at the left and the content area at the right of the *DesignCenter*.

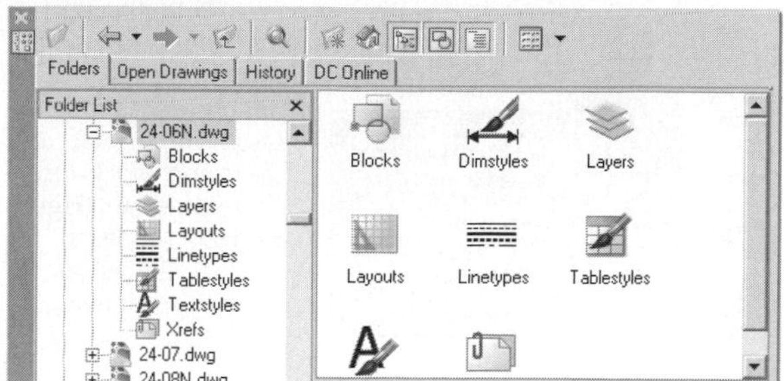

37.171 When a drawing file is double clicked, these eight options are displayed and can be picked to provide more information about the file.

The *DesignCenter* can be reduced to its title bar labeled *DesignCenter* and docked or undocked on the screen. When undocked, the DC is movable by the cursor at all times. Set *Auto-hide* to on, and the *DesignCenter* will disappear from the screen leaving only the vertical title bar to make room for drawing. Click anywhere on the title bar and the DC will reappear. *Auto-hide* and other options are found when you right click on the icon at the upper end of the title bar.

The icons and tabs of the *DesignCenter* are given in **Figure 37.170**. The *Folders* tab displays the files stored on your computer. The *Open Drawings* tab lists the drawings that are presently open, and the *History* tab lists the last 20 files that were opened. The *DC Online* tab gives access to content from commercial sources on the Web.

Content is added to a drawing from the *DesignCenter*'s content area, the area to the right of the *Tree View* at the left of the box. Once a folder is selected and a file is double clicked, eight option icons appear that can be selected to obtain more information about the file in **Figure 37.171**.

The steps of locating a *Block* drawing, obtaining an enlarged view of it with a verbal description, are discussed in **Figure 37.172**.

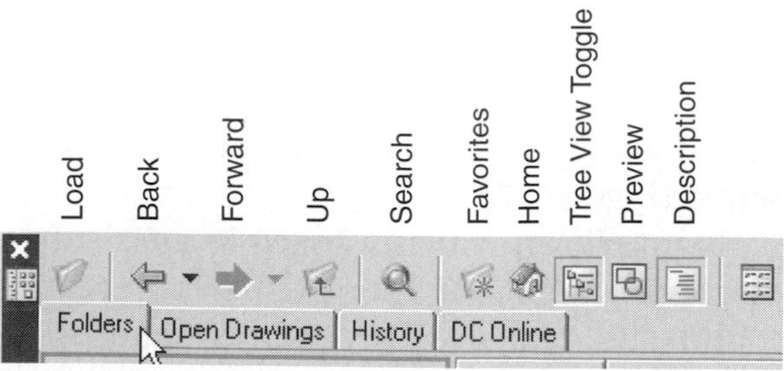

37.170 The icons of the *DesignCenter* are defined here. The *Folders* tab shows navigational icons. The *Open Drawings* tab displays the drawings that are presently open, and the *History* tab displays previously opened files. *DC Online* connects to the Web page, where material can be accessed from manufacturers and their catalogs.

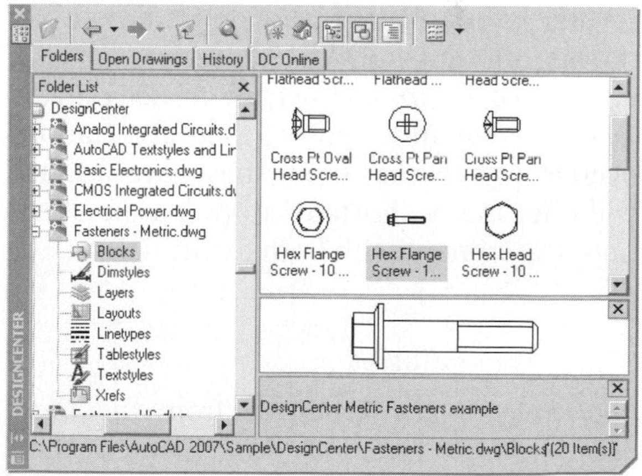

37.172 In this example, the *Fasteners* folder has been opened and the *Blocks* option selected to fill the content area with a selection of fasteners. The *Hex Flange Screw* is picked and the *Preview* and *Description* icons at the top of the DC are clicked to give an enlarged view of the screw beneath the content area with a word description beneath it.

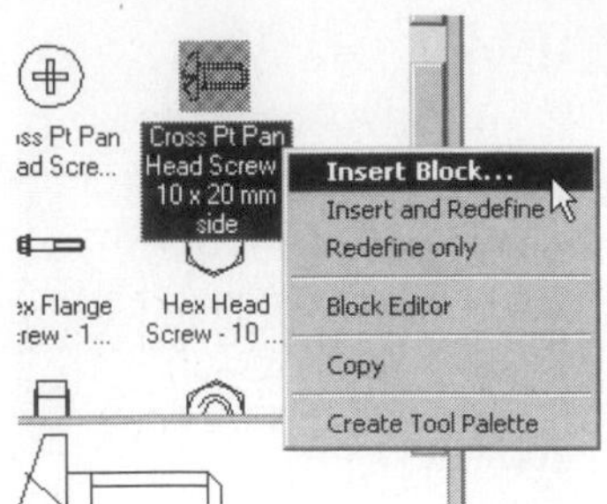

37.173 Right click on the *Block* to be inserted and this box of options appears. Select *Insert Block . . .* and the same *Block Insertion* window (**Figure 37.165**) appears for placing the *Block* in the current drawing.

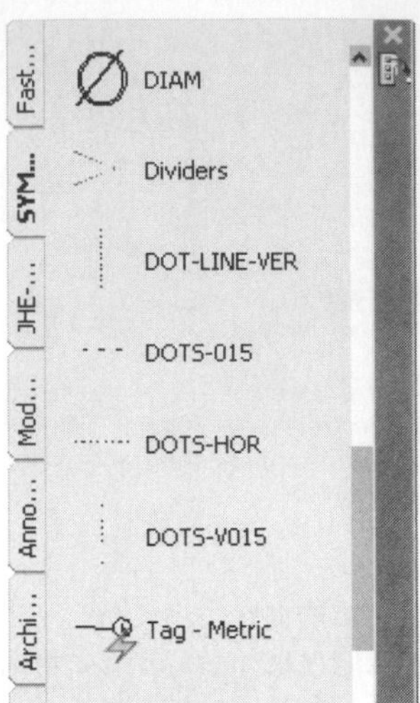

37.174 Press *Ctrl+3* to display this panel, which shows all *Tool Palettes* that are available for selection. The tabs can be clicked to open their contents for application to the current drawing. Only a portion of the panel is shown here. In this example, the *Symbol* tab has been opened to reveal a variety of drawing symbols.

Occasionally, you will find it necessary to enlarge portions of the *DesignCenter* by dragging the border lines that separate its areas to make room for the various displays, the *Preview* area, for example.

From the content area where *Blocks* are shown (not the *Preview* area), you can click on a *Block,* hold down the left key, and drag it into the current drawing, or, right click on the *Block* (**Figure 37.173**).

Coverage of the *DesignCenter* presented here is necessarily brief due to the extensiveness of the topic. Use the *Help* commands that accompany many of the DC commands with tutorials. Experiment with clicking, double clicking, and right clicking, and you will find several layers of depth assigned to many of the options that you will choose.

The *Tool Palette* is closely associated with the *DesignCenter* and many of their applications overlap. When mastered, these two options will offer many shortcuts to preparing drawings. Experiment with both features.

37.56 Tool Palettes

Tool Palettes are displayed from the *Main Menu> Tools> Palettes> Tool Palettes,* or simply *Ctrl+3* (**Figure 37.174**). A tab, the *Symbol* tab in this example, can be clicked to show the individual symbols stored there that can be dragged into the drawing in progress. A flathead screw was selected and dragged left to the current drawing and sized with the *Scale* command (**Figure 37.175**).

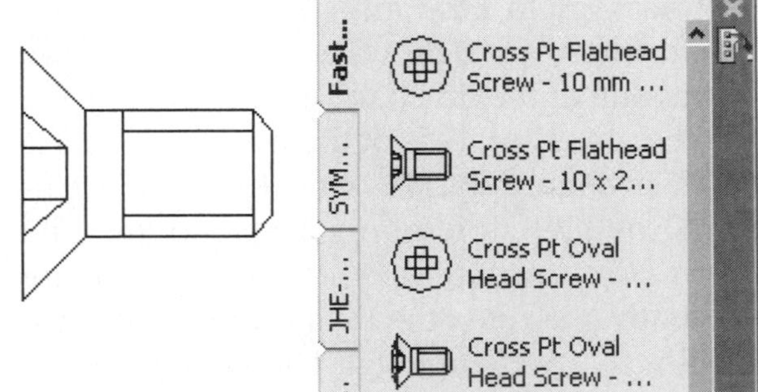

37.175 Samples of *Blocks* are displayed in the *Fasteners* tab section of *Tool Palettes,* which can clicked on and dragged to the current drawing, as was this *Flathead Screw.* It can be scaled and edited like any other *Block*.

Right click in a blank space in a *Palette* to display the menu of options shown in **Figure 37.176**. As with the *DesignCenter,* the *Auto-hide* option, if on, lets you turn on palettes by selecting the vertical name bar with the cursor. When the cursor is removed from the *Tool Palette,* it is automatically hidden. *Auto-hide> On* leaves the palette on.

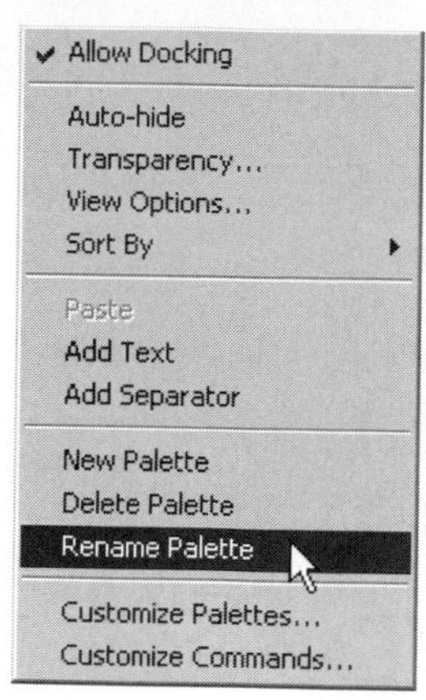

37.176 Right click a blank space in the *Tools Palette* and this menu is displayed from which these commands can be used: *Rename, Delete,* or make a *New Palette,* plus other options. The *Allow Docking* command lets the panel of *Tool Palettes* be anchored at the edge of the drawing area. *Auto-hide* is a feature that causes the panel to disappear, leaving only the veritcal title bar when the cursor is moved from it. It reappears when the cursor is placed on the title bar.

Tool Palettes will be most convenient and beneficial when you customize them to contain items that you use most often and perhaps have developed yourself. When added to a *Tool Palette,* items are called *Tools* that can be used in a drawing by *Ctrl+3> Tool tab> pick Block>* and drag to the current drawing. Items that can be assigned tab areas are *Blocks, Dimensions, Hatches, Raster images, Geometric objects,* and *Solid fills.* This procedure works best if *Grips* are turned off (*Command:* <u>Grips</u> *Enter new value for GRIPS:* <u>0</u> (Enter)).

An example *Block* is dragged to the *Tool Palette Symbol* tab as shown in **Figure 37.177**, where it will remain as a *Tool* as long as you like for convenience of use. Resting the cursor on the icon representing a *Tool* produces a *flyout* that helps identify the item. You will find it desirable to create new tab areas in which to place tools by category. To create a new *Tool Palette,* right click in the blank area of the *Tool Palettes* window and pick *New Palette.* A text window will appear. Type the name of the *New Palette,* and change its location in the upper or lower part of the list by selecting the *Move Up* or *Move Down* options.

A listing of the available *Tool Palettes* can be obtained by picking the multiple-tab symbol (beneath the last tab) from which to pick for display. Also, the *Tool Properties* box can be opened to provide information about items listed in a palette. An example is shown in **Figure 37.178** for a hex socket bolt. Properties in the *Tool Properties* box can be edited; for

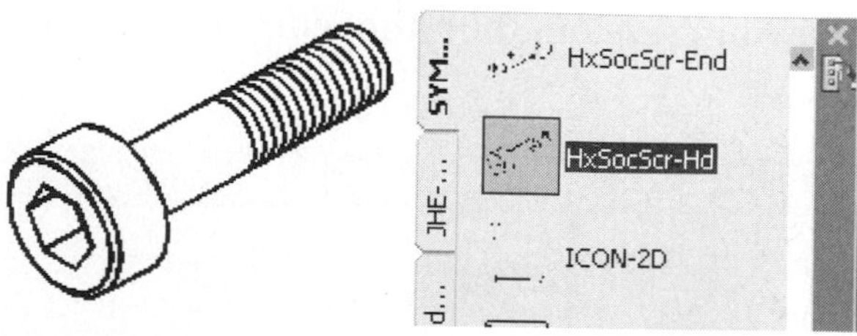

37.177 An isometric of a socket screw drawn and made into a *Block* can be added to the *Symbol* tab by selecting the image, holding the select button down, and dragging it to the desired position. A heavy line will appear in the listing of blocks to show where it will be positioned; then, release the left button to place the isometric block.

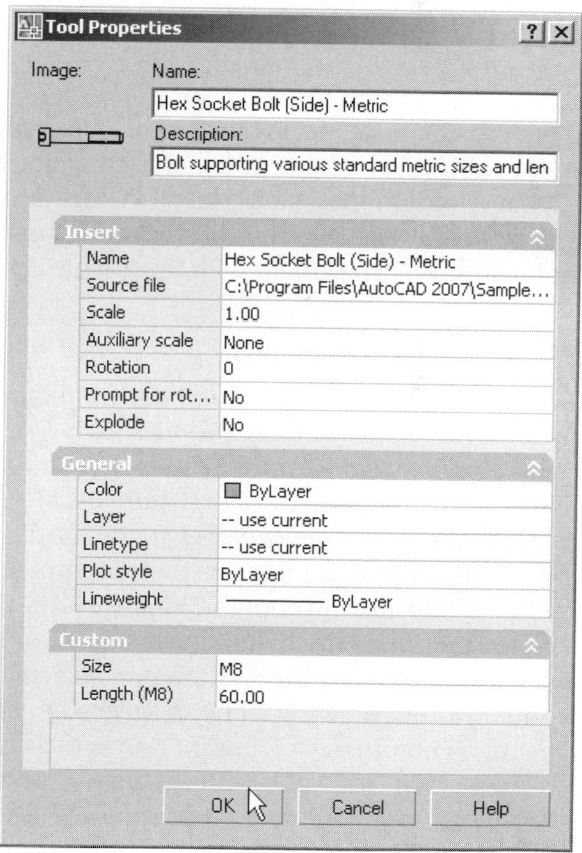

37.178 By clicking on the *Mechanical* tab and right clicking on the *Hex Socket Bolt* icon, you will obtain this *Tool Properties* box that gives information about the *Block* and enables you to edit these values.

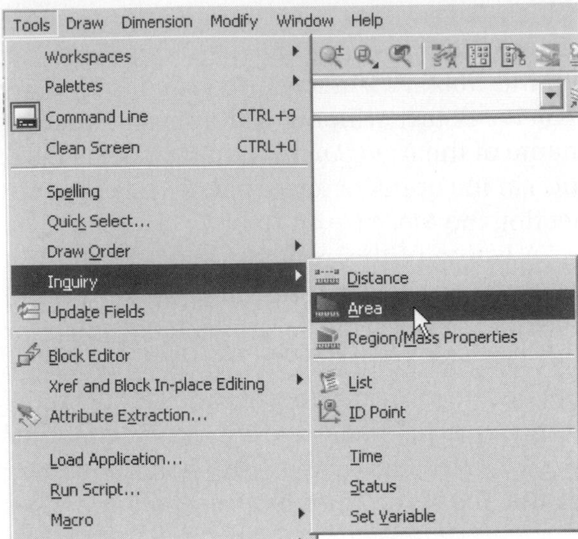

37.179 *Main Menu> Tools> Inquiry Menu* offers these options to assist you in learning more about a selected drawing.

example, the scale of the bolt can be changed in the table and inserted at the revised scale.

Many additional embedded menus are available for clicking, double clicking, and right clicking. Experiment with these features.

37.57 Inquiry Commands

From *Main Menu> Tools> Inquiry* to obtain information about objects and files with *Dist, Area, Region/ Mass Properties, List, ID Point, Time, Status,* and *Set Variable* (**Figure 37.179**). *List* is selected (or *Command:* List) and the circle (or any object) is selected when prompted to obtain information about it (**Figure 37.180**).

Dist measures the distance, its angle, and its Δx and Δy distances between selected points without drawing a line. *ID* gives the *x*-, *y*-, and *z*-coordinates of a point that is picked on the screen. *Area* gives the perimeter of a space enclosed on the screen. Prompts request *First point:, Next point:, Next point:,* and so on, to pick all points, then press (Enter). *Areas* can be added and removed when they are being selected as shown in **Figure 37.181**.

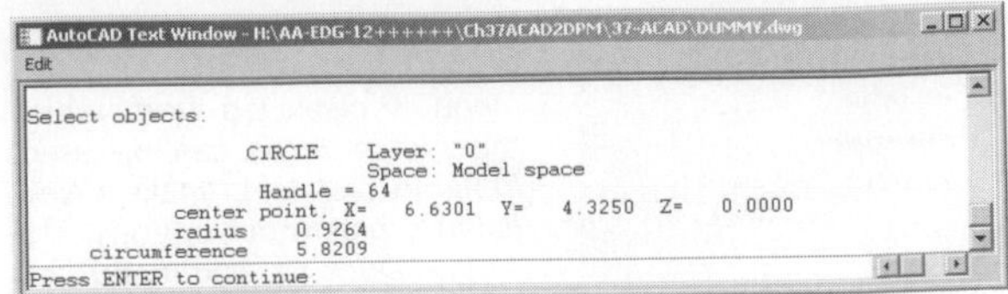

37.180 Use *Main Menu> Tools> Inquiry* toolbar> *List* icon> (or *Command:* List) and select a circle on the screen. This data box appears and gives the center of the circle, its radius, circumference, and area.

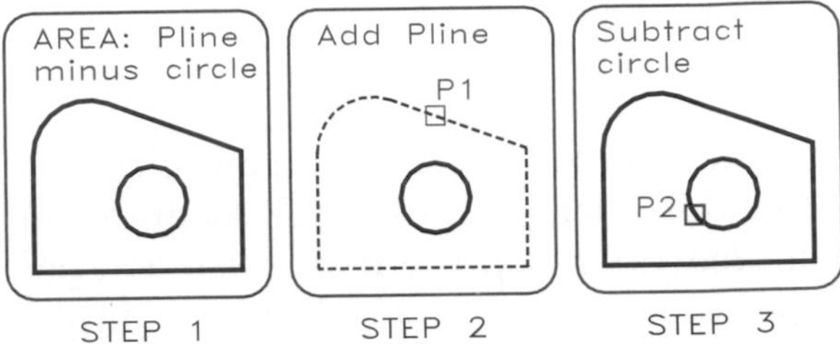

37.181 Area.

Step 1 Draw the object with a *Polyline* outline and a circular hole in it.

Step 2 *Main Menu> Tools> Inquiry> Area>* <First point>/ *Specify first corner point or [Object/..../Subtract]:* Area (Enter) *Specify first corner point or [Object/Subtract]:* O (Enter) *(ADD mode) Select objects:* P1
Area= 4.0300, Perimeter = 24.8560, Total area = 4.0300

Step 3 *Specify first corner point or [Object/Subtract]:* S (Enter), *Specify first corner point or [Object/Add]:* O (Enter) *(SUBTRACT mode) Select objects:* P2
Area = 0.4910, Perimeter = 7.8540, Total area = 3.5400

The *Status* option gives information about the settings, layers, coordinates, and disk space. *Time* displays information about the time spent on a drawing (**Figure 37.182**). The timer can be *Reset* and turned *On* to record the time of a drawing session, but the cumulative time

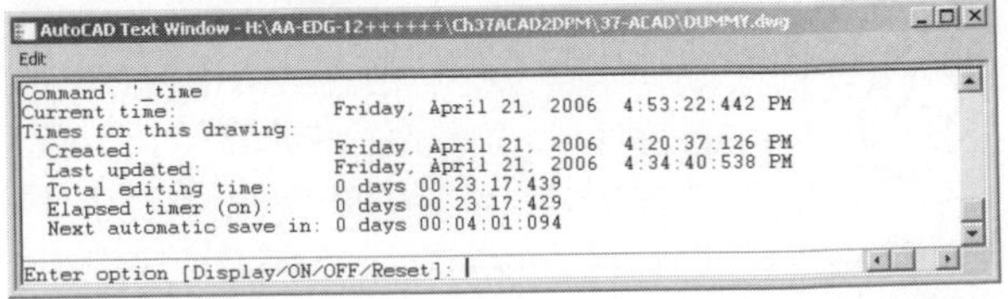

37.182 The *Time* option of the *Inquiry menu* can be used for inspecting the time spent on a drawing and for setting the time for an assignment.

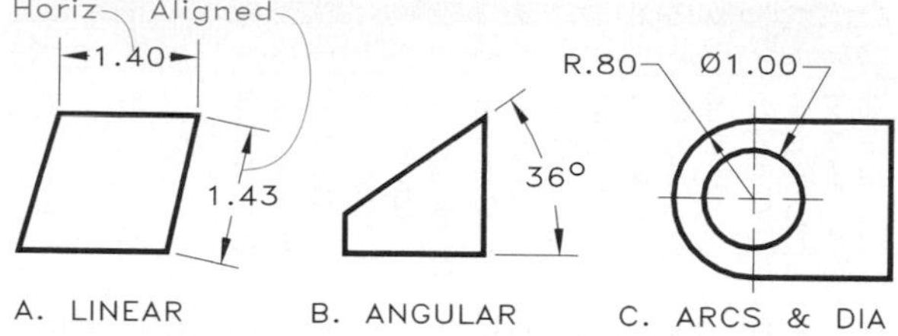

37.183 The basic types of dimensions that may appear on a drawing are shown here.

cannot be erased without deleting the drawing file. After *Resetting, Display* shows the time of the current session at the heading *Elapsed time:*.

37.58 Dimensioning Basics

Figure 37.183 shows common types of dimensions that are typical of those applied to drawings. Since dimensions are determined by the size of the objects being dimensioned, the process is greatly simplified if the **drawings are drawn full size on the screen** to simplify their measurements and dimensions. Scaling should be done at plotting time.

Dimensions can be applied as *Associative* or as *Nonassociative (Exploded)* dimensions. *Associative* dimensions (when *Dimaso* is *On*) are inserted as if the dimension line, extension lines, text, and arrows are parts of a single *Block*. Exploded dimensions *(Dimaso* set to *Off)* are applied as individual objects that can be modified independently. Most of the examples that follow are associative dimensions.

37.59 Dimension Style Variables

Dimensions cannot be appropriately applied without specifying text height, arrowhead size, decimal values, and other variables. For example, six of the fundamental dimensioning variables are shown in **Figure 37.184** along with their proportions, which are based on the letter height (H) that is assigned to the drawing. These variables are called *Dimension Style*

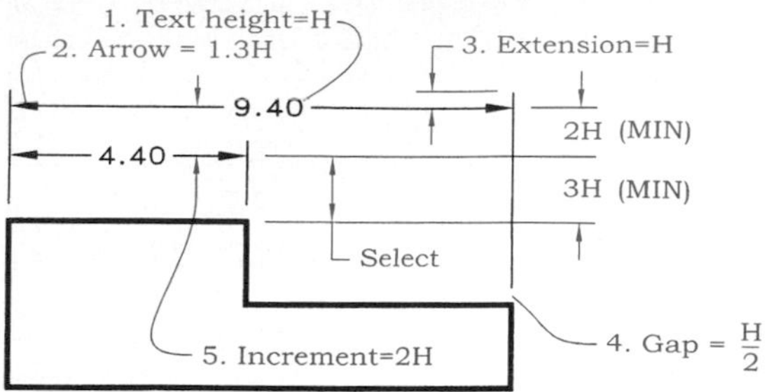

DIM VARS
Based on the letter height, H, which is usually .125 in.

1 DIMTXT (TEXT HT.)=H=.125
2 DIMASZ (ARROW)=1.3H=.125–.160
3 DIMEXE (EXTENSION)=H=.125
4 DIMEXO (OFFSET)=H/2=.06
5 DIMDLI (INCREMENT)=2H=.25 MIN.
6 DIMSCALE (SCALE) = 1 for INCHES
25.4 for MILLIMETERS

37.184 Dimensioning variables are based on the height of the lettering (text), which is usually about 1/8 in. high.

variables and are accessible from the *Command* line or from the *Dimension Style Manager* menu box.

Before we go further in dimensioning, we must become familiar with both of these systems of assigning variables.

37.60 Dimension Variables from the Command Line

To get a list of the current dimensioning variables as shown in **Figure 37.185**, *Command:* Dim> *Dim:* Status (Enter). Sizes of dimensioning variables are based on the letter height, which most often is 0.125 in.

To set and save variables needed for basic applications, *Open* (or *Create)* the file

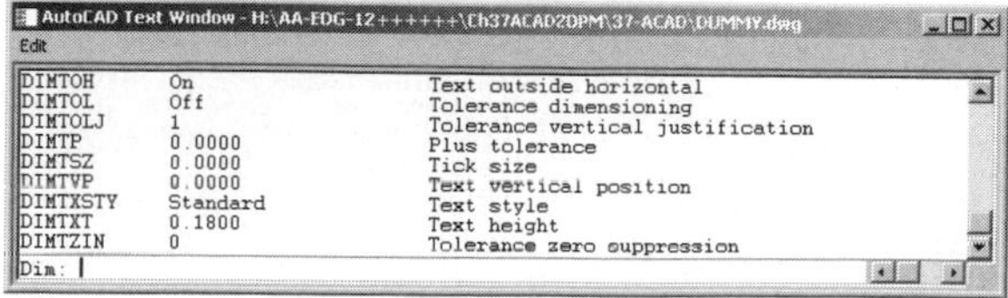

37.185 Use *Command:* Dim> Dim: Status (Enter) to obtain a listing of the dimension system variables. Only the first of the list is shown here.

```
AutoCAD Text Window - Drawing11.dwg
Edit
DIMASO       Off            Create dimension objects
DIMSTYLE     Standard       Current dimension style (read-only)

DIMADEC      0              Angular decimal places
DIMALT       Off            Alternate units selected
DIMALTD      2              Alternate unit decimal places
DIMALTF      25.4000        Alternate unit scale factor
DIMALTRND    0.0000         Alternate units rounding value
DIMALTTD     2              Alternate tolerance decimal places
DIMALTTZ     0              Alternate tolerance zero suppression
DIMALTU      2              Alternate units
DIMALTZ      0              Alternate unit zero suppression
DIMAPOST                    Prefix and suffix for alternate text
DIMARCSYM    0              Arc length symbol
DIMASZ       0.1800         Arrow size
DIMATFIT     3              Arrow and text fit
DIMAUNIT     0              Angular unit format
DIMAZIN      0              Angular zero supression
DIMBLK       ClosedFilled   Arrow block name
DIMBLK1      ClosedFilled   First arrow block name
DIMBLK2      ClosedFilled   Second arrow block name
DIMCEN       0.0900         Center mark size
DIMCLRD      BYBLOCK        Dimension line and leader color
DIMCLRE      BYBLOCK        Extension line color
DIMCLRT      BYBLOCK        Dimension text color
DIMDEC       4              Decimal places
DIMDLE       0.0000         Dimension line extension
DIMDLI       0.3800         Dimension line spacing
DIMDSEP      .              Decimal separator
DIMEXE       0.1800         Extension above dimension line
DIMEXO       0.0625         Extension line origin offset
DIMFRAC      0              Fraction format
DIMFXL       1.0000         Fixed Extension Line
DIMFXLON     Off            Enable Fixed Extension Line
DIMGAP       0.0900         Gap from dimension line to text
DIMJOGANG    45             Radius dimension jog angle
DIMJUST      0              Justification of text on dimension line
Dim:
```

37.186 Use *Command*: Dim> *Dim>* Status (Enter) to obtain a listing of the dimension variables, their settings, and definitions.

A:PROTO1. Each variable is set by typing Setvar and the name of the dimensioning variable (*Dimtxt* for text height, for example) and assigning a numerical value. A list of the dimensioning variables is given in **Figures 37.186** and **37.187**. Assign the basic variable values, one at

```
AutoCAD Text Window - Drawing11.dwg
Edit
DIMJUST      0              Justification of text on dimension line
DIMLDRBLK    ClosedFilled   Leader block name
DIMLFAC      1.0000         Linear unit scale factor
DIMLIM       Off            Generate dimension limits
DIMLTEX1     BYBLOCK        Linetype extension line 1
DIMLTEX2     BYBLOCK        Linetype extension line 2
DIMLTYPE     BYBLOCK        Dimension linetype
DIMLUNIT     2              Linear unit format
DIMLWD       -2             Dimension line and leader lineweight
DIMLWE       -2             Extension line lineweight
DIMPOST                     Prefix and suffix for dimension text
DIMRND       0.0000         Rounding value
DIMSAH       Off            Separate arrow blocks
DIMSCALE     1.0000         Overall scale factor
DIMSD1       Off            Suppress the first dimension line
DIMSD2       Off            Suppress the second dimension line
DIMSE1       Off            Suppress the first extension line
DIMSE2       Off            Suppress the second extension line
DIMSOXD      Off            Suppress outside dimension lines
DIMTAD       0              Place text above the dimension line
DIMTDEC      4              Tolerance decimal places
DIMTFAC      1.0000         Tolerance text height scaling factor
DIMTFILL     0              Text background enabled
DIMTFILLCLR  BYBLOCK        Text background color
DIMTIH       On             Text inside extensions is horizontal
DIMTIX       Off            Place text inside extensions
DIMTM        0.0000         Minus tolerance
DIMTMOVE     0              Text movement
DIMTOFL      Off            Force line inside extension lines
DIMTOH       On             Text outside horizontal
DIMTOL       Off            Tolerance dimensioning
DIMTOLJ      1              Tolerance vertical justification
DIMTP        0.0000         Plus tolerance
DIMTSZ       0.0000         Tick size
DIMTVP       0.0000         Text vertical position
DIMTXSTY     Standard       Text style
DIMTXT       0.1800         Text height
DIMTZIN      0              Tolerance zero suppression
DIMUPT       Off            User positioned text
DIMZIN       0              Zero suppression
Dim:
```

37.187 Additional dimension variables are shown here as a continuation of **Figure. 37.186.**

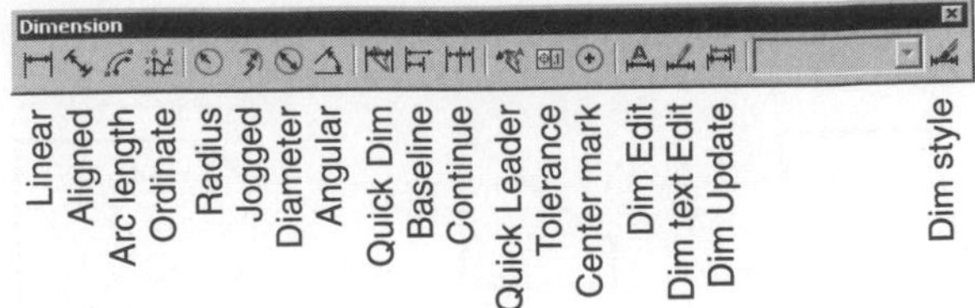

37.188 The *Dimension* toolbar has these dimensioning options from which to select.

a time, of *Dimtxt, Dimasz, Dimexe, Dimexo, Dimtad, Dimdli, Dimaso,* and *Dimscale* shown in **Figure 37.184** to A:PROTO1, since they apply to most applications. *Command:* Units and set to decimal units. *Save* these settings to A:PROTO1 as an empty file with no drawing on it for use as the prototype with its dimensioning settings. Open A:PROTO1 and create a new file by *Save As:* A:DWG-3, for example, which becomes the current file with the same settings as A:PROTO1.

Once variables have been set, open the *Dimension* toolbar shown in **Figure 37.188** to conveniently select types of dimensions.

37.61 Dimension Variables from the Dimension Style Manager

Dimensioning variables can also be set from the *Dimension Style Manager* and its seven tabs, which is activated from the icon at the right end of the *Dimension* toolbar (**Figure 37.189**). Or select *Main Menu> Format> Dimension Style* to display the *Dimension Style Manager* box from which dimension variables can be set or modified from different tabs.

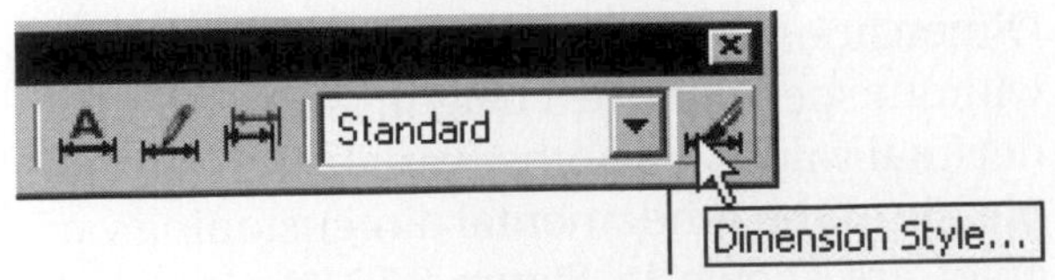

37.189 Use *Dimension* toolbar> *Dimension Style* icon to display the *Dimension Style Manager* box from which to create a new *Dimension Style* that will appear in the window with the *Standard* style.

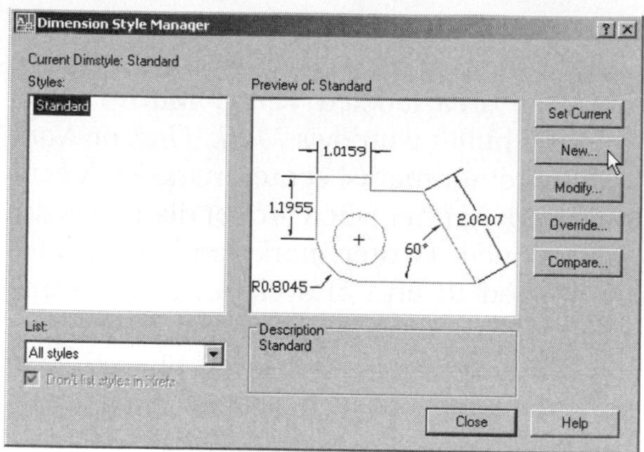

37.190 Use *Dimension* toolbar> *Dimension Style* icon> to display the *Dimension Style Manager* box for setting dimensioning variables. Pick the *New* button to create a new *Dimension Style.*

The five tabs at the right side of the *Dimension Style Manager* box are *Set Current, New, Modify, Override,* and *Compare* (**Figure 37.190**). Select *New* to define a new style (**Figure 37.191**). (Pick the *Help* button to get a definition of other buttons.) Each group of settings can be made and saved by style name (*DEC DIM-2,* for example) for future use to eliminate the time and effort required to make new settings for each drawing.

Click on the *New* box (**Figure 37.190**) to get the *Create New Dimension Style* box (**Figure 37.191**), in which you can make modifications to the *DEC DIM-2* style.

Lines Tab

Select the *Lines* tab shown in **Figure 37.192** to make settings for *Dimension lines, Extension*

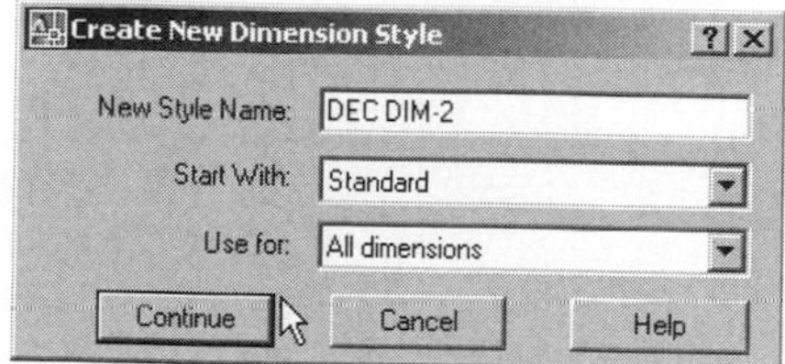

37.191 In the *New Style Name* window, type the name of the new style, DEC DIM-2, and pick the *Continue* button.

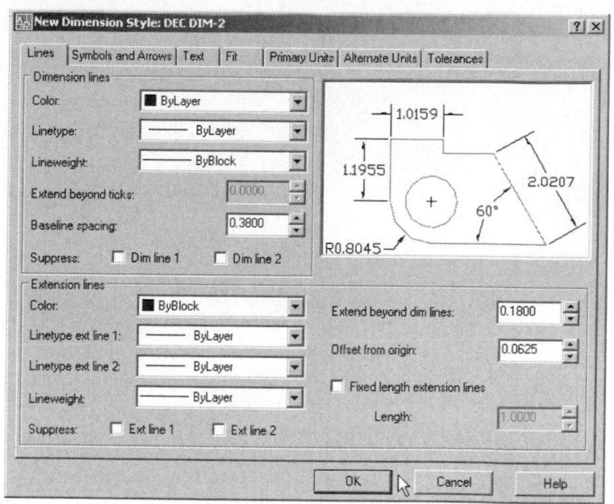

37.192 Select the *Lines* tab and make settings in the windows. Select the *Symbols and Arrows* tab to continue setting variables, or select *OK* to return to the *Dimension Style Manager.*

lines, Arrowheads, and *Center marks.* When *Oblique-Stroke* arrows are used, the value placed in the *Arrow size* box specifies the distance the dimension line extends beyond the extension line. The *Baseline spacing* box is used to set *Dimdli,* which controls the spacing between baseline dimensions. The *Color* button displays the color menu from which to select a color for the dimension line *(Dimclrd).*

The options of the *Extension Lines* group (**Figure 37.192**) control the variables *Lineweight, Extend beyond dim lines, Color,* and *Offset from origin.* The *Suppress 1st* and *2nd* boxes turn *On* the *Dimse1* and *Dimse2* variables to suppress the first and second extension lines. The value typed in the *Extension* box specifies the distance the extension line extends beyond the dimensioning arrowhead *(Dimexe).* The *Offset from origin* option is used to specify the size of the gap between the object and the extension line *(Dimexo).* The *Color* button lets you select the color of the extension lines *(Dimclre).*

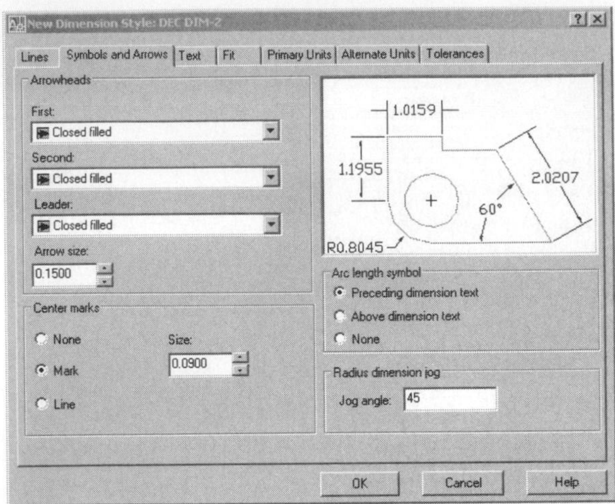

37.193 Select the *Symbols and Arrows* tab and assign variables for the arrowheads and the symbols. Press the *Text* tab to select more variables, or pick *OK* to return to the *Dimension Style Manager* box.

Symbols and Arrows Tab

The options of the *Arrowheads* group (**Figure 37.193**) control the following variables: *Dimasz, Dimtsz, Dimblk1,* and *Dimblk2.* The value typed in the *Size* box sizes the arrowhead (the *Dimasz* variable). Selecting scroll arrows next to the *1st* or *2nd* boxes lists the types of arrowheads for each end of the dimension (**Figure 37.194**). If only the *1st* arrow type is selected, it is automatically applied to the second end unless a *2nd* arrow type is specified. *Tick marks* are given when *Oblique* is selected, the *Dimtsz* variable. The *User Arrow* is selected for inserting custom-made arrows (*Dimblk1* and *Dimblk2*).

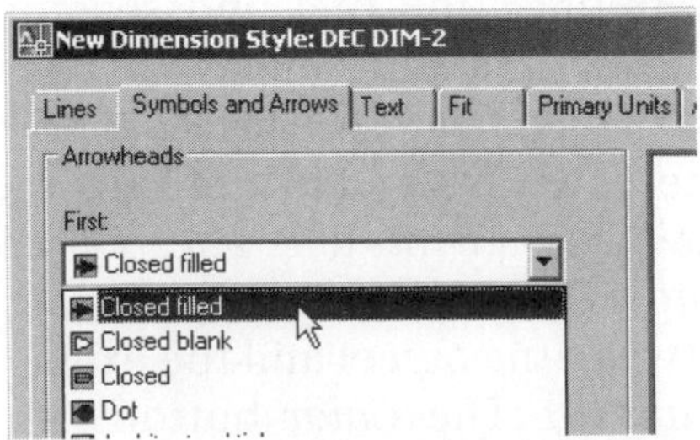

37.194 From the *Arrowheads* area, a drop-down listing of *Symbols and Arrows* is given from which to select.

In the area labeled *Center Marks,* select from the bullet windows *Mark, Line,* or *None* to draw center marks, center marks with centerlines, or neither when arcs or diameters are dimensioned. Center marks and centerlines are applied to arcs and circles in the same manner without dimensions by *Command:* Dim> *Dim>* Center> select the object.

Text Tab

Select the *Text* tab to get the menu shown in **Figure 37.195**, which controls the text used in dimensioning. The *Text appearance* area includes settings for *Text style, Text color, Fill color,* and *Text height.* The *Text placement* area gives windows for specifying *Vertical* and *Horizontal* text placement and the *Offset from dim line.* The *Text alignment* section lets you set text as *Horizontal* (unidirectional), *Aligned with dimension line,* or *ISO,* which aligns text with the dimension line when text is inside the extension lines but aligns it horizontally when text is outside

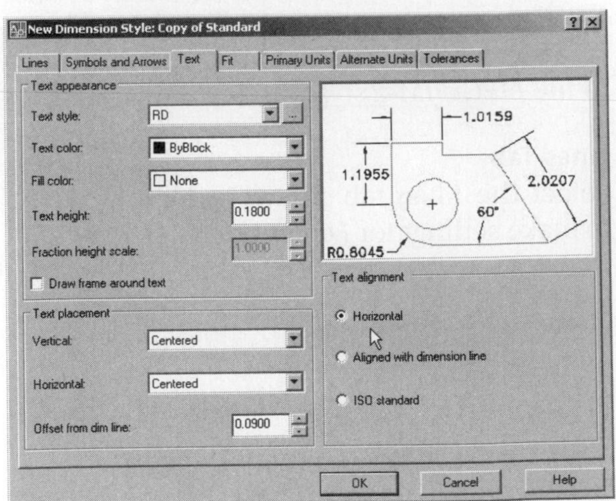

37.195 Select the *Text* tab and assign values to these variables. Select the *Fit* tab when finished and move to it, or select *OK* to return to the *Dimension Style Manager* box.

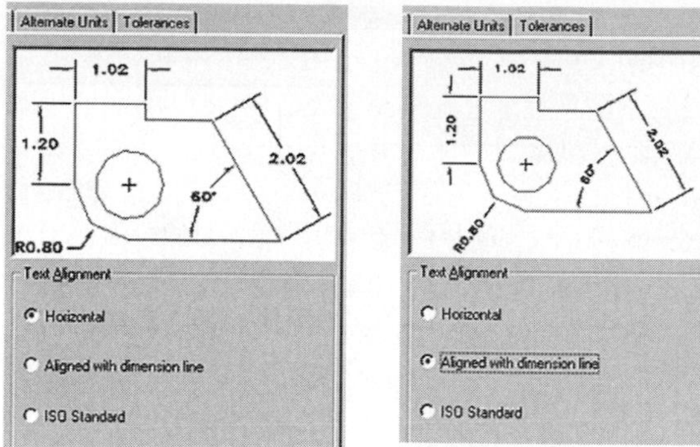

37.196 These examples show a comparison of *Unidirectional (Horizontal)* and *Aligned* text in dimension lines.

(**Figure 37.196**). *Text styles* can be selected from the pull-down window or created by pressing the button next to the style window. *Text placement* options let dimensioning text be positioned as shown in **Figures 37.197** through **37.199**.

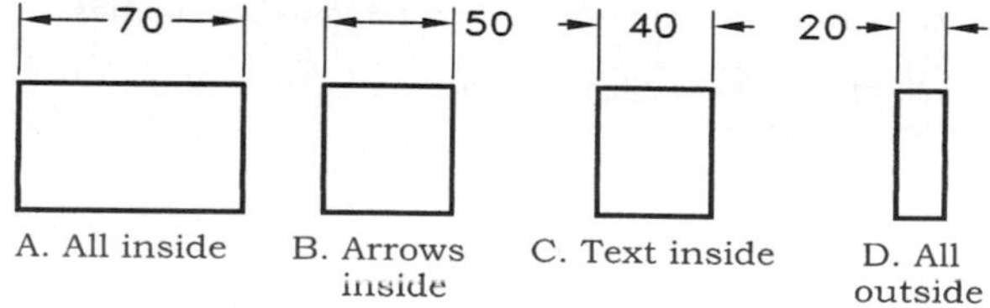

37.197 Examples of dimension applications when the *Best Fit* option is used.

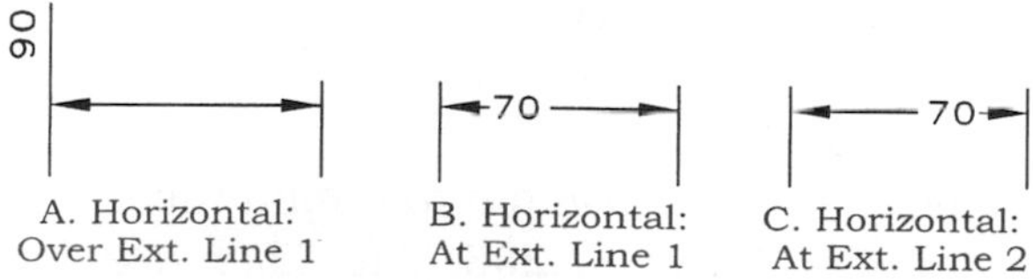

37.198 Examples of *Text Placement* settings.

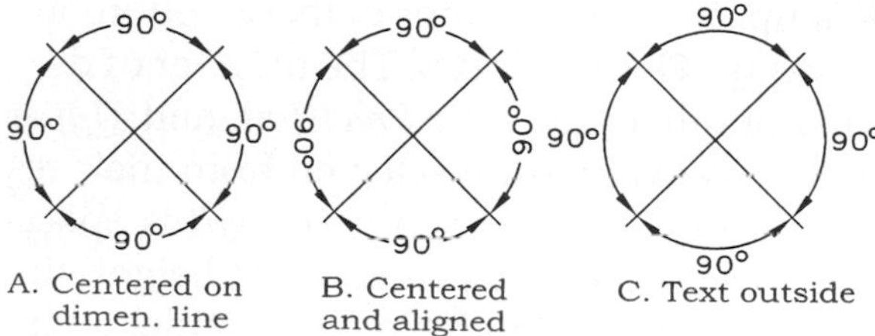

37.199 Examples of *Text Placement* settings on arcs.

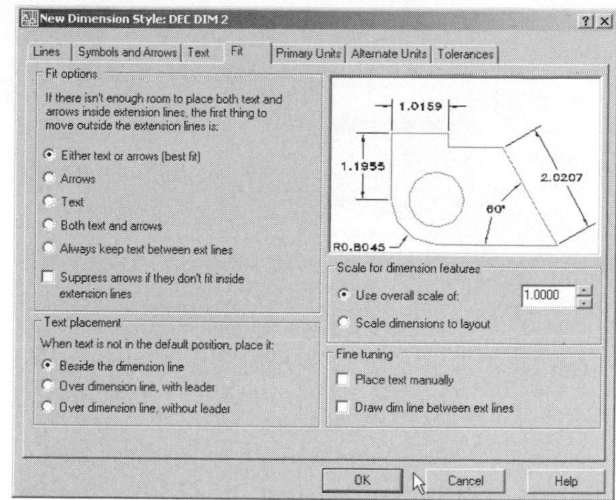

37.200 Pick the *Fit* tab and assign values to the variables. Select the *Primary Units* tab to move to it or select *OK* to return to the *Dimension Style Manager* box.

Fit Tab

Under the *Fit* tab, *Fit options, Text placement, Scale for dimension features,* and *Fine tuning* areas enable you to make dimensioning adjustments (**Figure 37.200**). The *Use overall scale of:* box controls the scale of all the dimensioning variables on the screen: arrow size, text height, extension-line offsets, center size, and others. It is very useful in changing the units of dimensioning from English to metric by entering a scale factor of 25.4.

Primary Units Tab

Select the *Primary Units* tab to obtain options for *Linear dimensions, Measurement scale, Zero suppression,* and *Angular dimensions* (**Figure 37.201**). Use the scroll arrow of *Precision,* and select the number of decimal places (or fractions) desired. From the *Angular dimensions* area, the *Units format* of degrees and their *Precision* can be specified.

Entries in the *Zero suppression (Dimzin)* boxes suppress zeros that are leading or trailing decimal points. Select *Leading* to make 0.20 become .20. **Figure 37.202** shows the results of applying the four options to architectural

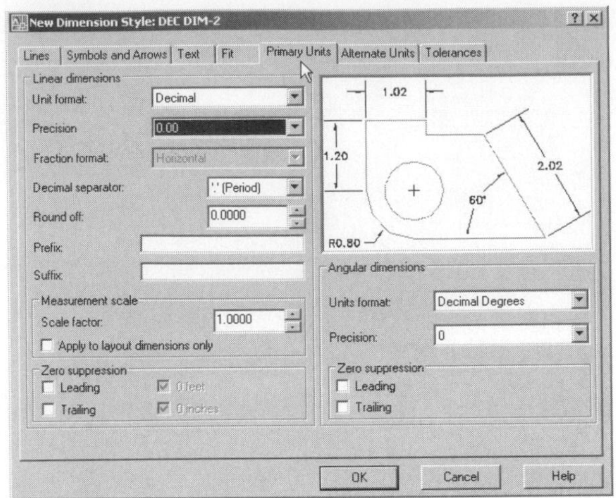

37.201 Pick the *Primary Units* tab and assign values to the variables. Select the *Alternate Units* tab to move to it or select *OK* to return to the *Dimension Style Manager* box.

ZERO SUPPRESSION FOR FEET & INCHES

0 Feet 0 Inches	1/4"	4"	1'	1'-01/4"
No options	0'-01/4"	0'-6"	2'-0"	1'-01/4"
0 In	0'-01/4"	0'-4"	1'	1'-01/4"
0 Ft	1/2"	4"	1'-0"	1'-01/4"

37.202 The *Zero suppression (Dimzin)* options control the leading and trailing zeros in dimensioning, especially when applied to architectural dimensions.

units. From under *Measurement Scale factor (Dimlfac)* units for measurements can be specified.

Alternate Units Tab

Select the *Alternate Units* tab to obtain the menu shown in **Figure 37.203**. Select the *Display alternate units* button, and two dimensions will appear on each dimension as in the example drawing in **Figure 37.204**. *Unit format* and *Precision* are used to define units and decimal points. If *Multiplier for all units* is set to 25.4, the millimeter equivalents for inches are given as the alternate dimension.

Values can be entered in the *Prefix* and *Suffix* panels (**Figure 37.203**) to place text

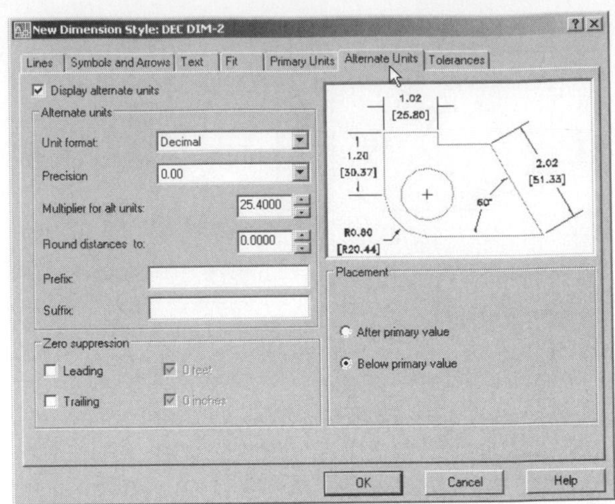

37.203 Pick the *Alternate Units* tab and assign values to the variables. Select the *Tolerance* tab to move to it or select *OK* to return to the *Dimension Style Manager* box.

ALTERNATIVE UNITS

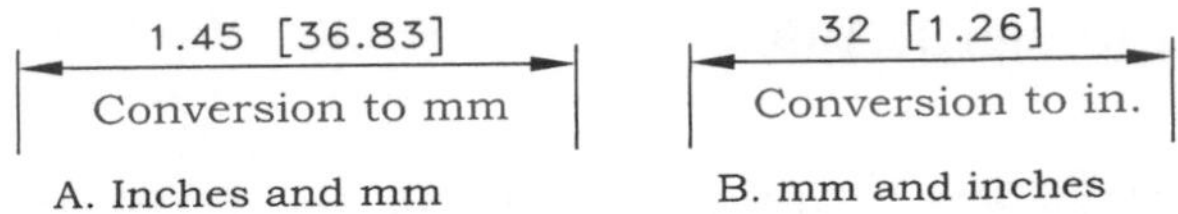

A. Inches and mm   B. mm and inches

37.204 Examples of alternate units (dual dimensions) made in inches and millimeters.

(such as inches) before or after the dimensions (such as 26 mm or 42 in.). *Placement* options allow alternate dimensions to be placed over or after primary units.

Tolerances Tab

Select the *Tolerances* tab to obtain the menu shown in **Figure 37.205**. The *Tolerance format* area offers *Method* options of *None, Symmetrical, Deviation, Limits,* and *Basic.* Examples of applications of these options are shown in **Figure 37.206**. The number of decimal points is set with *Precision,* and *Upper* and *Lower* values are selected from their respective pull-down menus. *Height* is specified as a ratio of the primary text height, the basic dimension, and is recommended to be about 80%.

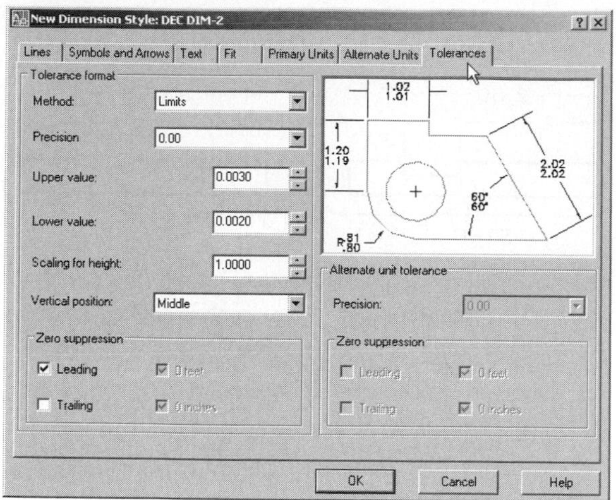

37.205 Pick the *Tolerance* tab and assign values to the variables. Select any other tab to move to it or select *OK* to return to the *Dimension Style Manager* box.

FORMATS FOR TOLERANCING

2.0000 ±.0020	2.0000 +.0030 −.0020	2.0030 1.9980
DIMTP & DIMTM Same	DIMTP & DIMTM Different	DIMLIM

37.206 Examples of various formats for tolerancing using the names of the dimensioning variables.

37.62 Saving Dimension Styles

When the settings of this new *Dimension Style* are complete, press the *OK* button at the current tab and the first menu of the *Dimension Style Manager* will be saved and will appear on the screen showing the new style, DEC DIM-2, along with the *Standard* style. Options of *Modify* (change any settings), *Override* (make temporary changes in a style), and *Compare* (list the settings of any two selected styles side by side) are available (**Figure 37.207**). An often-used override is the change of the *overall scale factor (Dimscale)* by changing a single

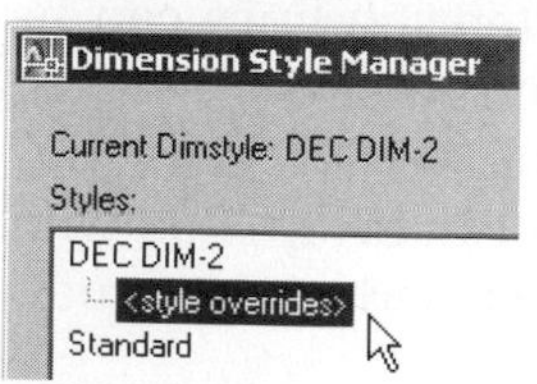

37.207 The new style, DEC DIM-2, is displayed in the list of *Styles*. When a style is *Overridden* (values changed), a *<style overrides>* subheading is displayed beneath the primary style.

THE DIMSCALE FACTOR

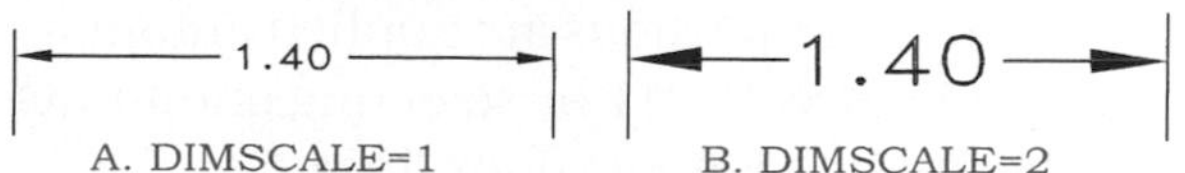

37.208 When *Dimscale* is changed from 1 to 2 and *Override* is used, the selected dimension is updated.

multipler (**Figure 37.208**). This text style can be used in the future with the various scale factors.

Now, let's apply the settings to the general types of drawing that are encountered and dimensioned.

37.63 Dimensioning Lines

The *Dimension* toolbar (**Figure 37.209**) provides a convenient means of selecting dimensioning commands. Select the *Linear* icon, the points as prompted, and the dimension is placed as shown in **Figure 37.210**

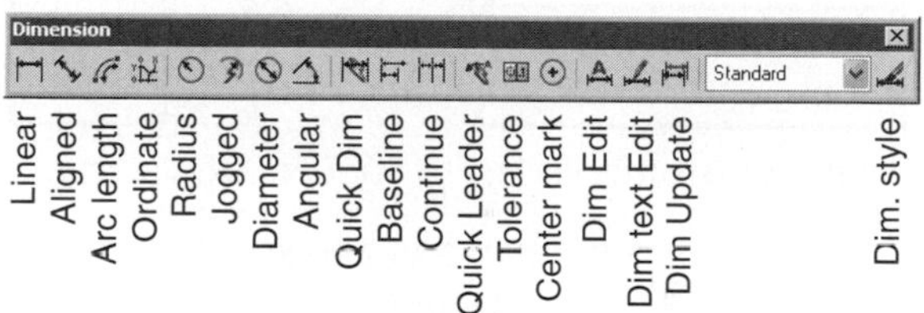

37.209 The *Dimension* toolbar has these dimensioning options from which to select.

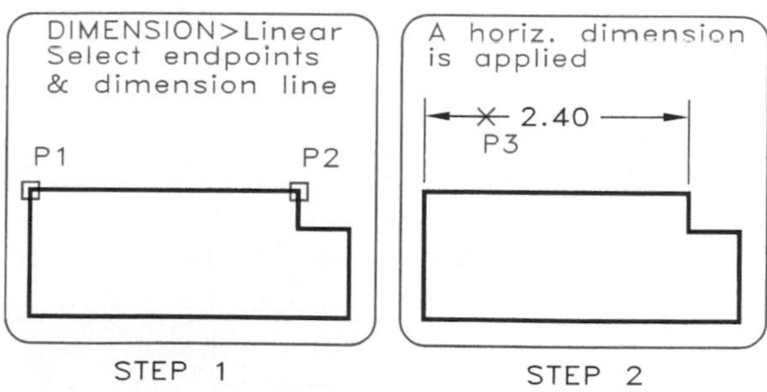

37.210 Dimensioning: Linear—Horizontal.

Step 1 *Dimension* toolbar> *Linear* icon> *Specify first extension line origin or <select object>:* P1 *Specify second extension line origin:* P2

Step 2 *Specify dimension line location or [Mtext/Text/Angle]:* P3 (Enter)> *Dimension text = 2.40*> (Enter) to accept the dimension.

to apply a horizontal dimension. Horizontal and vertical dimensions are applied automatically in **Figure 37.211** by selecting endpoints and locating the dimensions lines.

Select *Main Menu> Dimension> Continue* (or type *Dimcontinue* at the *Command* line) to continue a chain of linear, angular, or ordinate dimensions from the last extension line (**Figure 37.212**). *Baseline* applies dimensions from a single endpoint, and each dimension is offset incrementally by the dimension line increment variable *Dimdli* (**Figure 37.213**).

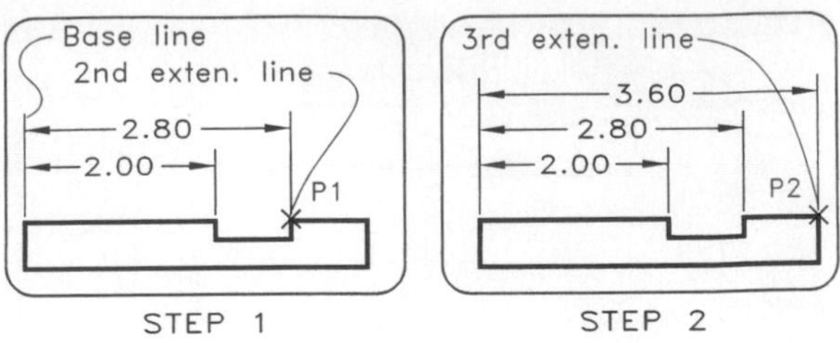

37.213 Dimensioning: Baseline option.

Step 1 *Dimension* toolbar:> *Linear* icon> place a 2.00 *Linear* dimension. (The first extension line becomes the baseline.) *Dimension* toolbar> *Baseline* icon> *Specify a second extension line origin or [Undo/Select] <Select>:* P1
Dimension text = 2.80 (Enter) The 2.80 dimension is drawn.

Step 2 *Specify a second extension line origin or [Undo/Select] <Select>:* P2 *>Dimension text = 3.60* (Enter) The 3.60 dimension is drawn. (Enter) to exit from the last dimension.

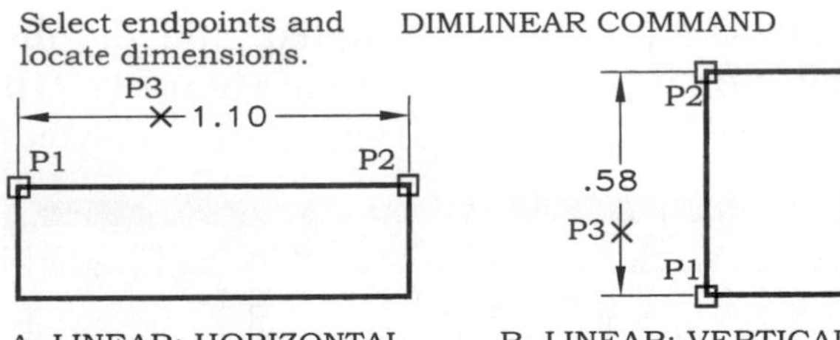

37.211 Dimensioning: Linear—Semiautomatic.

A *Dimensioning* toolbar> *Aligned> Specify first extension line origin or <Select object>:* (Enter)
Select object to dimension: P1
[Mtext/Text/Angle ...Rotated]: P2; *Dimension text = 1.10*

B Use these same steps and select a point on the circle P1 and P2 to locate the dimension of its diameter.

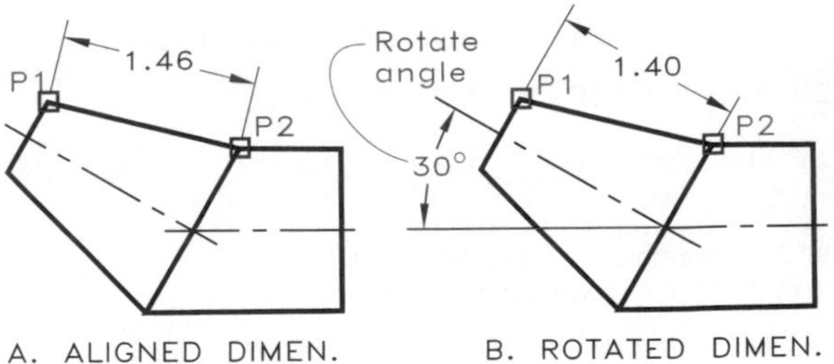

37.214 Dimensioning: Oblique lines.

A Linear dimensions can be aligned by selecting the *Align* icon and selecting endpoints P1 and P2.

B Linear dimensions can be rotated by selecting the *Linear* icon and the *Rotate* option, assigning the angle (150°), and picking endpoints P1 and P2.

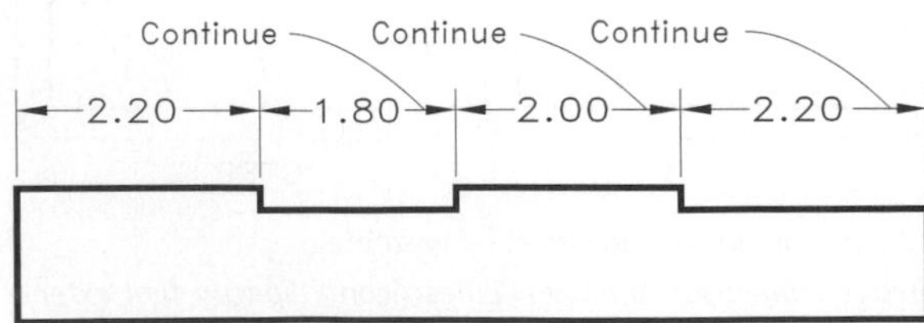

37.212 When dimensions are placed end to end, use the *Continue Dimension* option from the *Dimension* toolbar to specify the successive second extension line origins after the first dimension line has been drawn.

Select the *Aligned* command from the *Dimension* toolbar and you will be prompted to select the *1st* and *2nd* extension lines and the position of the dimension line (**Figure 37.214**). The dimension line will be inserted aligned with line 1-2. Extension lines can be automatically drawn by pressing (Enter) at the first prompt and selecting the line to be dimensioned. A dimension can be applied with the *Rotate* option at an assigned angle of rotation (**Figure 37.214**).

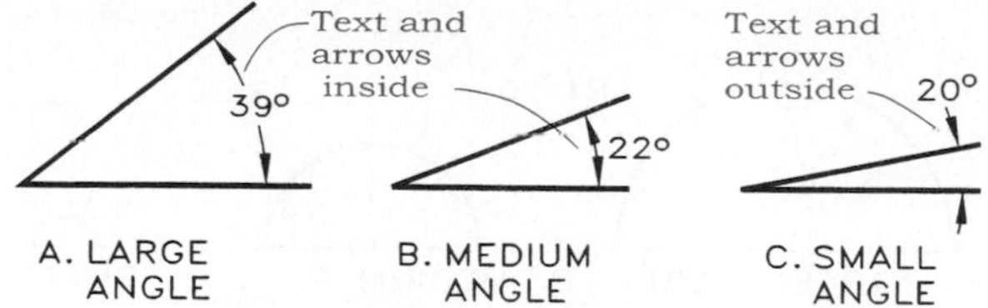

37.215 Angles will be dimensioned in one of these three formats depending on the size of the angle.

37.64 Dimensioning Angles

Figure 37.215 shows variations for dimensioning angles depending on the space available. In **Figure 37.216** an angle is dimensioned by selecting the *Angular* icon, selecting lines of the angle, and locating the dimension line arc as shown in step 1. If space permits, the dimension text will be centered in the arc between the arrows (step 2).

An angular dimension can be applied by selecting its vertex and points on each line when prompted. **Figure 37.217** shows how angles over 180° can be dimensioned by drawing an arc with its center at the vertex and with its ends abutting each line. Use *Dimension* toolbar> *Select arc, circle, line, or <specify vertex>:* P1> *Specify dimension arc line location or [Mtext/Text/Angle]:* P2> *Dimension text = 280* (Enter) to accept the angle of 280°.

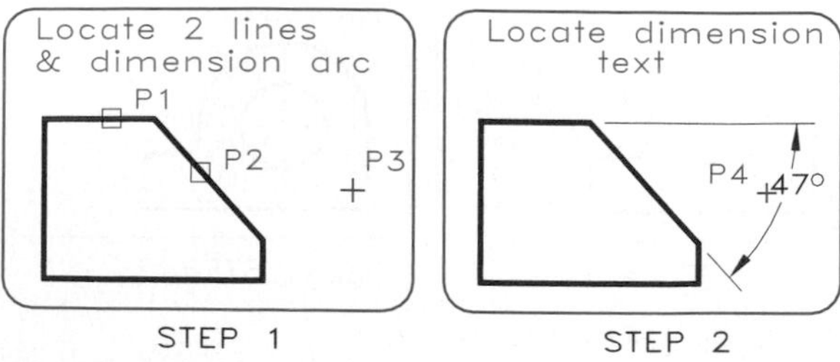

37.216 Dimensioning: Angles.

Step 1 Use *Dimension* toolbar> *Angular* icon> *Select arc, circle, line, or <specify vertex>:* P1 > *Select second line:* P2 *Specify dimension arc line location or [Mtext/Text/Angle]:* P3

Step 2 *Enter dimension text <47>:* (Enter) *Enter text location (or press ENTER):* (Enter)

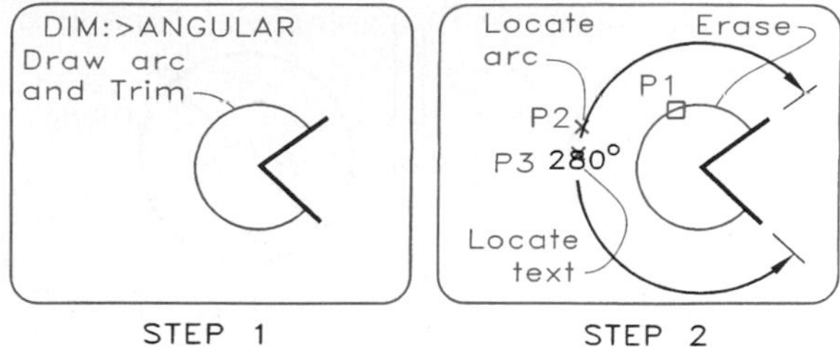

37.217 Dimensioning: Arcs.

Step 1 Draw an arc with its center at the vertex and *Trim* it to end at the lines.

Step 2 *Select Angular* icon> *Select arc, circle, line, or <specify vertex>:* P1 > *Specify dimension arc line location or [Mtext/Text/Angle]:* P2> *Dimension text = 280* (Enter)

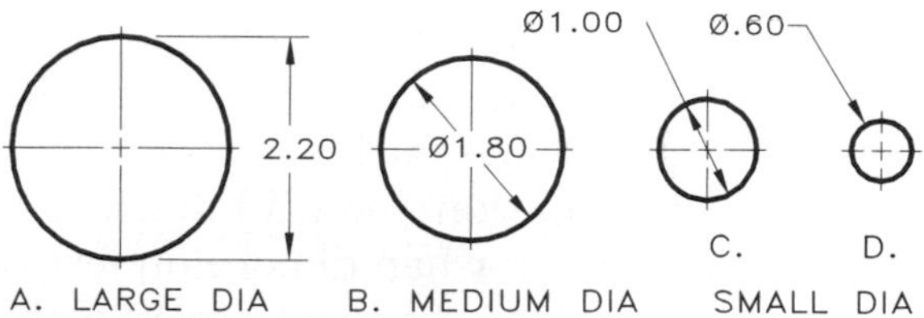

37.218 Examples of methods of dimensioning circles of different sizes.

37.65 Dimensioning Diameters

Diameters of circles can be placed as shown in **Figure 37.218** depending on the available space. By changing system variables *Dimatfit, Dimtofl,* and *Dimtmove* circles can be dimensioned as shown in **Figures 37.219**

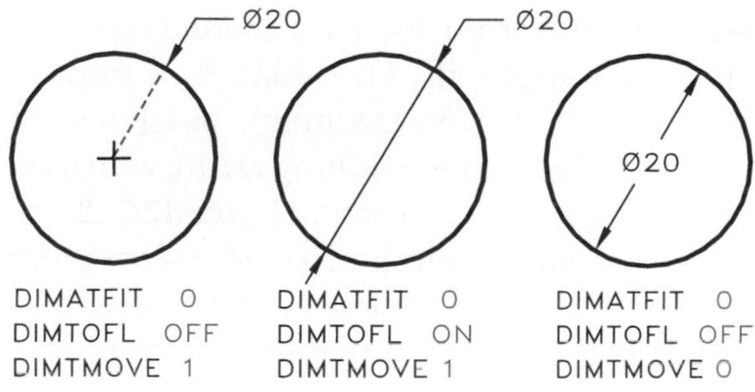

37.219 Examples of circle diameters with their associated dimensioning variables. Assign variables by *Command:* Dim> *Dim>* type name of variable (Enter).

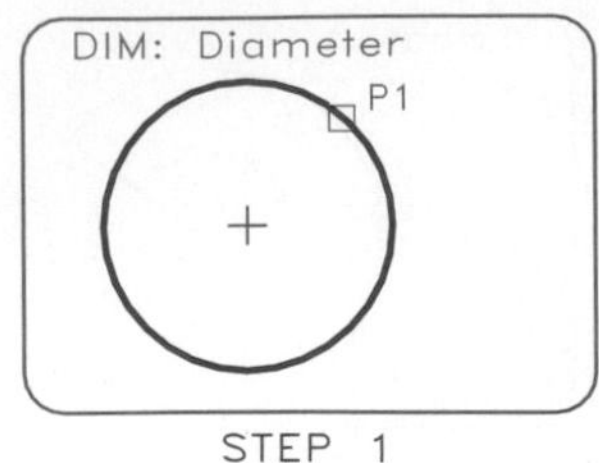

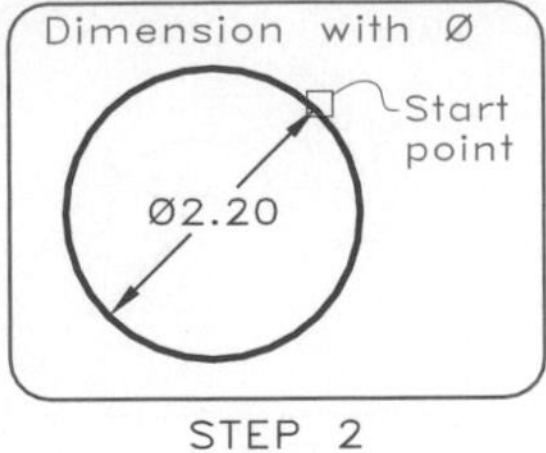

37.220 Dimensioning: Circle.

Step 1 *Dimension* toolbar> *Diameter* icon> *Select arc or circle:* P1

Step 2 *Dimension text* = <2.20> (Enter)
Specify dimension line location or [Mtext/Text/Angle]: Select start point (Enter)

and **37.220.** Setting the *Dimtix* system variable *On* forces the text inside the extension lines regardless of the available space. The *Dimtmove* variable has the following options: *0* moves the dimension line with dimension text; *1* adds a leader when dimension text is moved; *2* allows text to be moved freely without a leader.

The *Dimatfit* variable has the following options: *0* places both text and arrows outside extension lines; *1* moves arrows first, then text; *2* moves text first, then arrows; *3* moves either text or arrows, whichever fits best. The *Dimtofl (On)* dimension variable forces a dimension line to be drawn between the arrows when the text is located outside. To specify whether a dimension has a leader, use *Command:* Dim> *Dim*> Dimtmove> 1 (Enter).

37.66 Dimensioning Radii

Select *Radius* from the *Dimension* toolbar to dimension arcs with an *R* placed in front of the text (R1.00, for example), as shown in **Figure 37.221.** Dimensioning an arc with a radius and leader is shown in **Figure 37.222.**

The *Leader* command (*Dimension Quick Leader* on the *Dimension* toolbar) is used to add a leader with a dimension or note to a drawing, but it cannot measure the circle; it inserts the value of the last measurement made (**Figure 37.223**). The arc's diameter or radius must be known and typed to override this measurement. Notes can be added in multiple lines at a specified length by using the *text width* option.

When the lack of space does not permit an arc's radius to be drawn full size, it can be drawn with a jog as a conventional practice. From the *Dimension* toolbar, select the *Jogged*

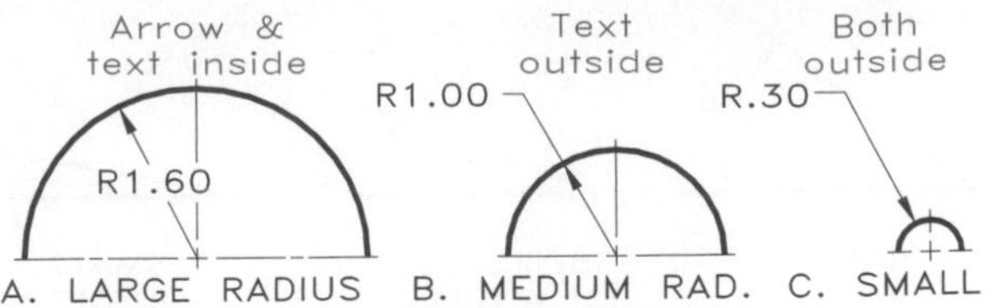

37.221 Arcs are dimensioned by one of the formats given here depending on the size of the radius.

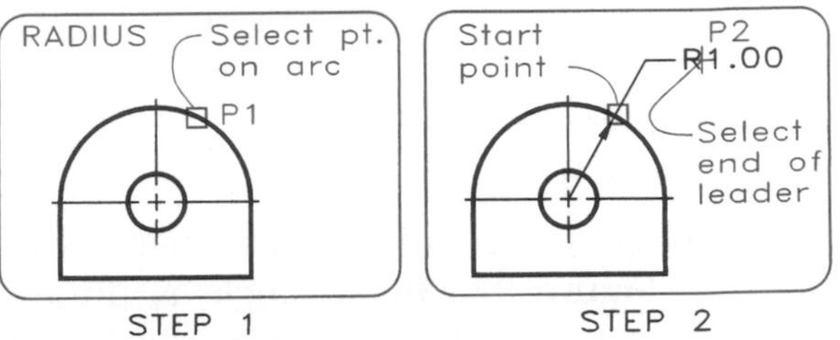

37.222 Dimensioning: Radius.

Step 1 *Command:* Dim (Enter)
Dim: Radius (Enter) *Select arc or circle:* P1

Step 2 *Enter dimension text <1.00>:* (Enter)
Specify dimension line location or [Mtext/Text/Angle]: P2
The leader is drawn and the measurement given.

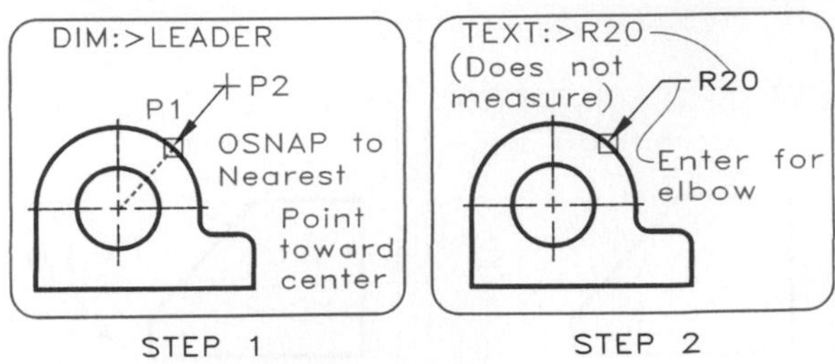

37.223 Dimensioning: Quick Leader.

Step 1 *Dimension* toolbar>*Quick Leader* icon> *Specify first leader point, or [Settings] <Settings>:* P1
Specify next point: P2> (Enter)
Specify text width <1.00>: (Enter)

Step 2 *Enter first line of annotation text <Mtext>:* R20 (Enter)
Enter next line of annotation text: (Enter) Note: The *Leader* command does not make measurements; you must insert them.

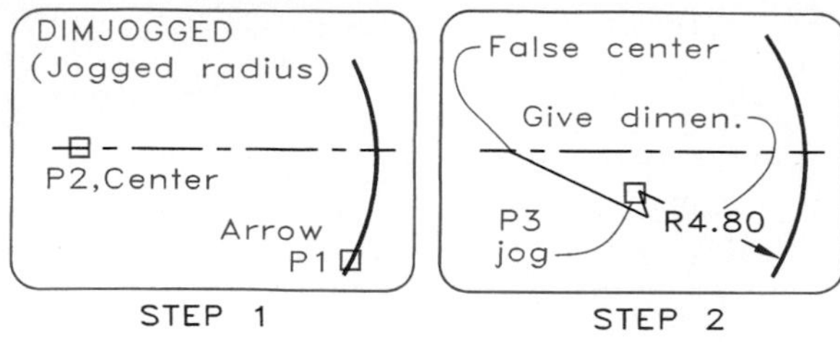

37.224 Dimensioning: Jogged radius.

Step 1 *Dimension* toolbar> *Jogged* icon> *Select arc or circle:* P1, *<specify center location override>:* P2

Step 2 *Specify dimension line location of [Mtext/Text/Angle] <00>:* R 4.80 (Enter)
Specify jog location: P3

icon and follow the instructions as shown in **Figure 37.224**.

37.67 Editing Dimensions

When the dimensioning variable *Dimaso* is set to *On,* the dimensioning entities (arrows, text, extension lines, etc.) become a single unit *(Associative)* once a dimension has been inserted into a drawing.

A related dimensioning variable, *Dimsho,* can be set *On* to show the dimensioning numerals being dynamically changed on the screen as the dimension line is *Stretched.* When *Dimaso* is *On* and *Dimsho* is *Off,* the numerals will be changed after the *Stretch* (**Figure 37.225**) but not dynamically during the *Stretch.*

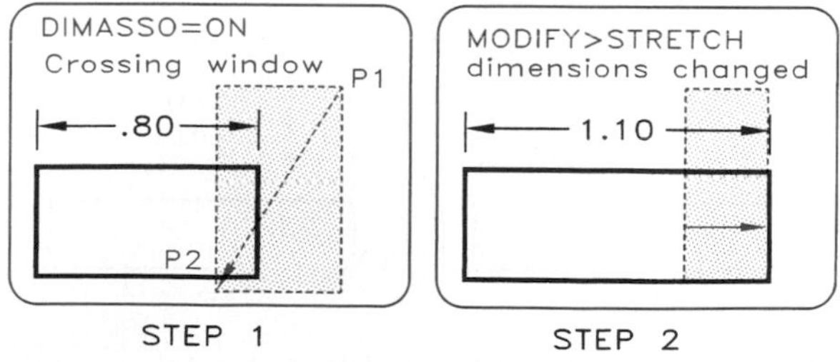

37.225 Dimensiong: Associative—Dimassoc.

Step 1 *Command:* Dim> *Dim>* Dimassoc> *Enter new value for DIMASSOC <1>:* 1 (On) and apply dimensions to the part. Use the *Stretch* command with a *Crossing window* at the end of the part.

Step 2 *Stretch* the side of the window to a new position; the object will be lengthened, a new dimension will be dynamically calculated, and the object will be shown in its final position.

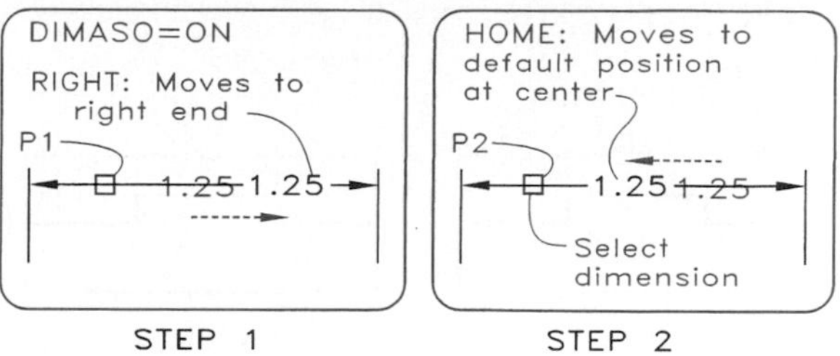

37.226 Dimensioning: Associative—Left, right, home.

Step 1 *Dimension* toolbar> *Dimension text edit* icon> *Select dimension* P1, *Specify new location for dimension text or (Left/ Right/ Home/ Angle):* Right (Enter) Numeral moves to right.

Step 2 *Command:* (Enter) *Select dimension:* P2
Specify new location for dimension text or [Left/Right/Center/ Home/Angle]: Home (Enter) Numeral moves to the midpoint of the dimension line.

In the associative dimensioning mode, the *Dimension edit* can be selected from the *Dimension* toolbar to obtain the options *Home, New, Rotate,* and *Oblique* for changing existing dimensions. *Home* repositions text to its standard position at the center of the dimension line after being changed by the *Stretch* commands (**Figure 37.226**). *New* changes text within a dimension line (**Figure 37.227**) when you press (Enter) when prompted and insert the new text. *Rotate* positions dimension text

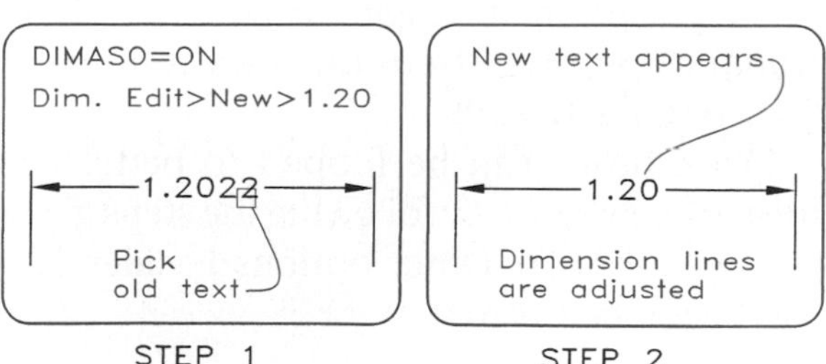

37.227 Dimensiong: Associative—New text.

Step 1 *Dimension* toolbar> *Dimension Edit* icon>
Enter type of dimension editing [Home/New/Rotate/Oblique] <Home>: New (Enter)> *Select objects:* pick text

Step 2 Type new text inside the shaded area beneath the existing dimension and pick *OK* in the *Text Formatting* bar. *Select objects:* Pick a point on the dimension line and the text is changed.

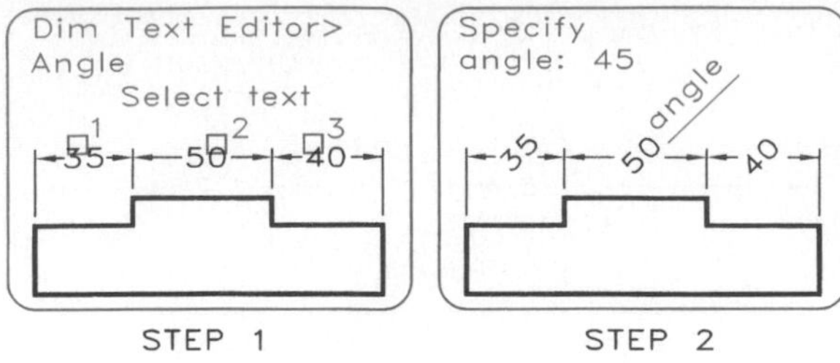

37.228 Dimensioning: Associative—Oblique text.

Step 1 Dimension as usual with vertical extension lines.
Dimension toolbar> *Dimension Text Edit* icon>
Select dimension: pick 1, 2, and 3 (Enter)
Specify new location for dimension text or [Left/Right/Center/Home/Angle]: Angle (Enter)

Step 2 *Specify angle for dimension text:* 45 (Enter)
Text is angled at 45° counterclockwise.

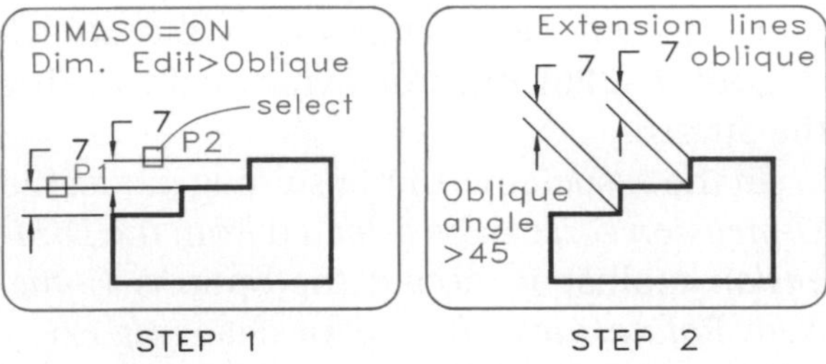

37.229 Dimensioning: Associative—Oblique extension lines.

Step 1 Dimension as usual with vertical extension lines.
Dimension toolbar> *Dimension Edit* icon>
Enter type of dimension editing [Home/New/Rotate/Oblique] <Home>: Oblique (Enter)
Select objects: P1 and P2 (Enter)> *Select objects: 2 found*

Step 2 *Enter obliquing angle (press ENTER for none):* –45 (Enter) The text is rotated 45° counterclockwise.

at any specified angle (**Figure 37.228**). *Oblique* converts extension lines to angular lines (**Figure 37.229**).

Arrowheads can be flipped to better use the available space by following the steps given in **Figure 37.230**. Other options besides *Flip* can be applied as well.

37.68 Dimensions with Tolerances

Dimensions can be toleranced automatically using the *Dimension Styles* defined previously in which the settings shown in **Figure 37.231** were made: *Dimtol* (tolerance on), *Dimtp* (plus tolerance), and *Dimtm* (minus tolerance). When *Dimlim* is *On,* the upper and lower limits of the dimension are given (**Figure 37.232**).

Dimtfac is a scale factor that controls the text height of the tolerance values, which is usually about 80% of the basic dimension height.

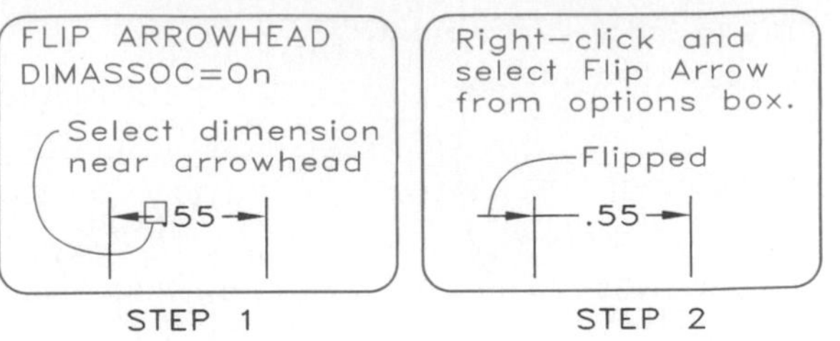

37.230 Dimensioning: Flip arrow.

Step 1 *Command:>* Select the associate dimension near the arrowhead to be flipped.

Step 2 *Right click* (*Options* box appears)> Pick *Flip Arrow* and the arrowhead is flipped. The opposite arrowhead can be flipped by selecting the dimension near it.

Tolerancing Formats

2.0000 ±.0020	2.0000 $^{+.0030}_{-.0020}$	2.0030 1.9980
DIMTP & DIMTM Same	DIMTP & DIMTM Different	DIMLIM

37.231 Dimensions can be toleranced in any of these three formats.

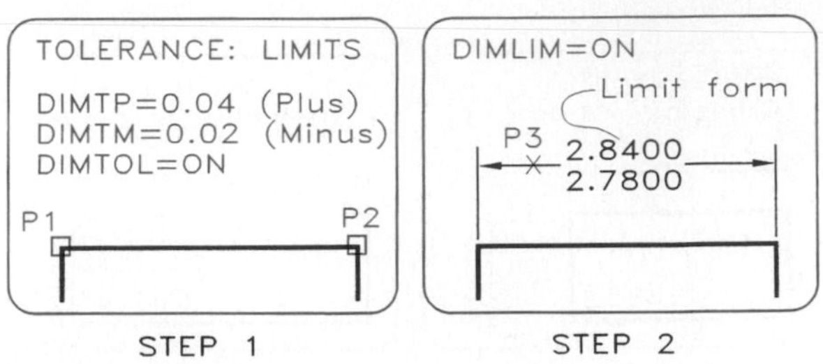

37.232 Dimensioning: Tolerance—Limit form.

Step 1 *Dimension* toolbar> *Dimension Style* icon> pick *DEC DIM-2*> *Modify*> *Tolerances* tab> set *Method* to Limits> set *Upper value (Dimtp)* and *Lower value (Dimtm)*.
Apply the dimension line by selecting the endpoints P1 and P2 when prompted.

Step 2 Locate the dimension line, P3. The dimension is shown with its upper and lower limits based on the values of *Dimtp* (tolerance plus) and *Dimtm* (tolerance minus).

37.69 Geometric Tolerances

Geometric tolerances specify the permissible variations in form, profile, orientation, location, and runout. A typical geometric tolerance feature control frame is given in **Figure 37.233**.

From the *Dimension* toolbar, select the *Tolerance* icon to obtain the *Geometric Tolerance* box (**Figure 37.234**); pick the *Symbol* icon to display the *Symbol* menu (**Figure 37.235**); select the desired symbol, and pick *OK*. Continue the process of responding to the prompts and icons to complete the geometric tolerance frame necessary for it to comply with the guidelines covered in Chapter 21. Examples of completed feature control frames as they would appear on a drawing are shown in **Figure 37.236**.

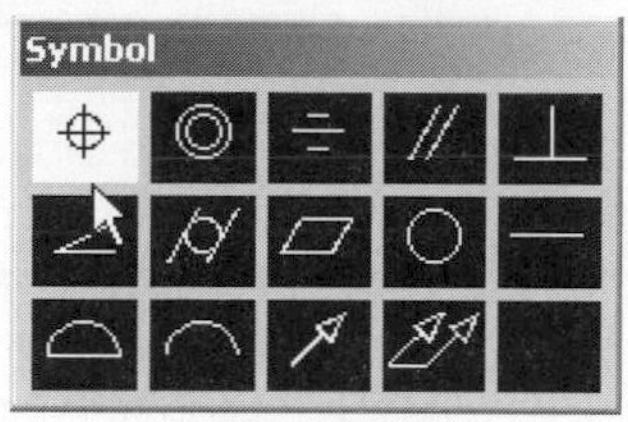

37.235 The symbols of geometric tolerance are found in the *Symbol* box.

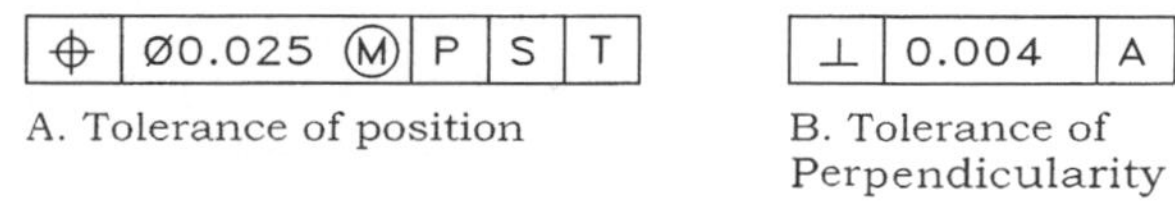

37.236 Applications of *Geometric Tolerances* in feature control frames are shown here.

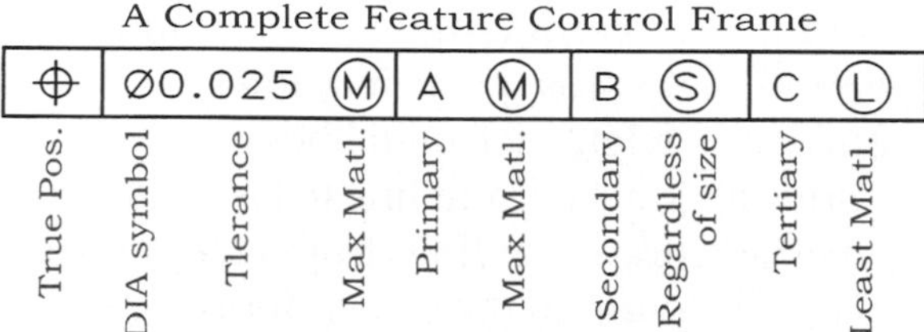

37.233 The parts of the feature control frame that give geometric tolerance specifications are defined here.

37.70 Custom Border and Title Block

Having covered most of the basics of 2D drawing, you may wish to make your own customized title blocks with their own unique parameters that can be used to start up new

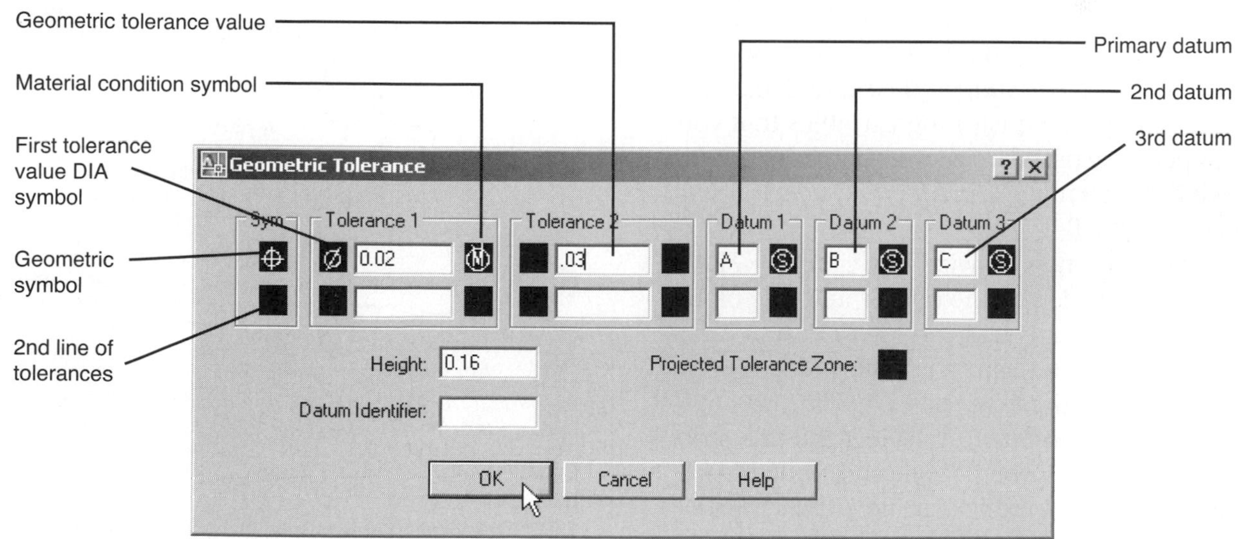

37.234 The *Geometric Tolerance box* (*Dimension* toolbar> *Tolerance* icon) is used to specify geometric tolerances.

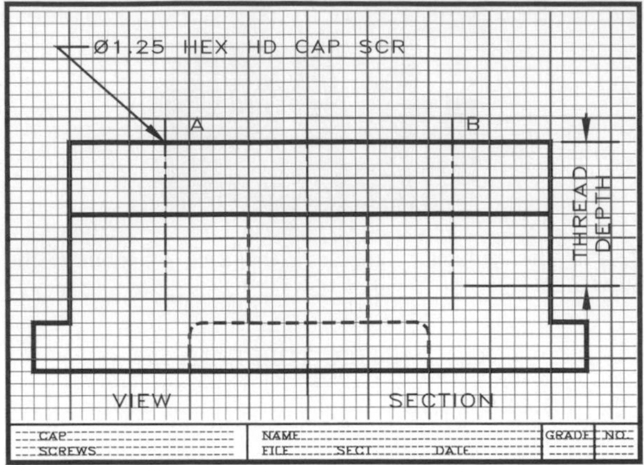

37.237 This is an example of a problem sheet border and title block that you can draw and save as a template file.

drawings as introduced in Section 37.12. The format shown in **Figure 37.237** is used for laying out many problems given at the ends of the chapters in this book.

To make a border identical to the one used in this example, draw the border 10.3 in. wide × 7.6 in. high, with its lower left corner at 0,0 and a polyline that is .03 thick. Draw a title strip across the bottom that has two rows of 1/8-in. text with spacing of 1/8 in. above and below each line. Fill out the title strip using the *Romand* font (single-stroke Gothic) and fill in all blanks (name, date, etc.); they will be changed later. Set *Snap* and *Grid* to .2 in., and set any other dimensioning variables that you expect to use based on a letter height of 1/8 in. Save the drawing *(Main Menu> Save As> File Name>:* PROB-1.DWG).

To create a new drawing *Main Menu> File> Open>* PROB-1, and the border and title block appear on the screen. *Main Menu> File> Save As>* NEW-1 (Enter), and a new file named NEW-1 is ready for drawing. Use *DDedit* (*Modify II* toolbar> *Text edit* icon) to select the title strip text that needs to be edited, and update each entry. Save this setup to a file *(Main Menu> File> Save>*, and the drawing is updated and saved again as NEW-1, ready for drawing.

37.71 Sketch and Skpoly

The *Sketch* command can be used with the tablet for tracing drawings composed of irregular lines (**Figure 37.238**). Tape the drawing to the tablet and calibrate it as follows:

Command: Sketch (Enter)

Record increment <0.1>: 0.01 (Enter)

Sketch. Pen eXit Quit Record Erase Connect.

The record increment specifies the distances between the endpoints of the connecting lines that are sketched. Other command options are:

Pen	raises or lowers pen.
eXit	records lines and exits.
Quit	discards temporary lines and exits.
Record	records temporary lines.
Erase	deletes selected lines.
Connect	joins current line to last endpoint.
. *(period)*	draws a line from the current point to the last endpoint.

Begin sketching by moving your pointer to the first point, lower the pen (type P), trace

APPLICATION OF THE SKETCH COMMAND

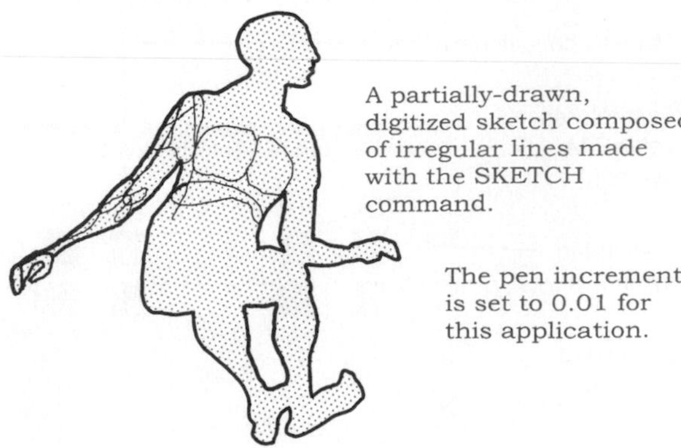

A partially-drawn, digitized sketch composed of irregular lines made with the SKETCH command.
The pen increment is set to 0.01 for this application.

37.238 This drawing was made with the *Sketch* command and a tablet instead of with a mouse. The drawing was taped to the tablet and traced with the stylus at increments of .01 in.

over the line with the stylus, and the line is displayed on the screen. To *Erase,* raise the pen (type P), enter *Erase* (type E), move the stylus backward from the current point, and select the point where the erasure is to stop. All lines are temporary until you select *Record* (type R) or *eXit* (type X) to save them. Begin new lines by repeating these steps. A series of lines drawn with the *Sketch* command can be erased one at a time. These segments can be converted to a polyline by linking them with the *Join* option of the *Pedit* command.

A series of lines drawn using the *Skpoly* variable and *Sketch* command are drawn in the same manner, but the lines are linked as if they were a single, continuous polyline. *Command:* Setvar> *Skpoly>* 1 *(On).* Since a sketched line is a polyline, it can be edited by using *Fit, Spline, Width,* and the other options of this command.

37.72 Oblique Pictorials

An oblique pictorial can be constructed as shown in **Figure 37.239**. The front orthographic view is drawn and duplicated behind the front view at the angle for the receding axis with the *Copy* command. The visible endpoints are connected with *Osnap Endpoint,* and the invisible lines are erased. Circles are drawn as true circles on the true-size front surface, but circular features should be avoided on the receding planes, since their construction is complex.

This oblique is not a true three-dimensional drawing that can be rotated to view its different sides. It is merely a two-dimensional drawing with a single point of view.

37.73 Isometric Pictorials

To set the isometric grid *Command:* Snap> *Style>* Isometric. By using the same sequence of commands and typing S for *Standard,* you can convert the grid back to the rectangular grid. The Isometric style shows the grid dots in an isometric pattern—vertically and at 30° with the horizontal (**Figure 37.240**). The cursor will align with two of the isometric axes and can be made to *Snap* to the grid if you activate the *Snap* command *(F9).* The axes of the cursor are rotated 120° when you press *Ctrl E* or by *Command:* Isoplane (Enter). When *Ortho* is *On,* lines are forced to be drawn parallel to the isometric axes. **Figure 37.241** illustrates the steps for constructing an isometric drawing.

When the *Grid* is set to the *Isometric* mode, the *Ellipse* command displays the following options: *<Axis endpoint 1>/Center/Isocircle:* Isocircle (Enter). Selection of the *Isocircle* option enables isometric ellipses to be posi-

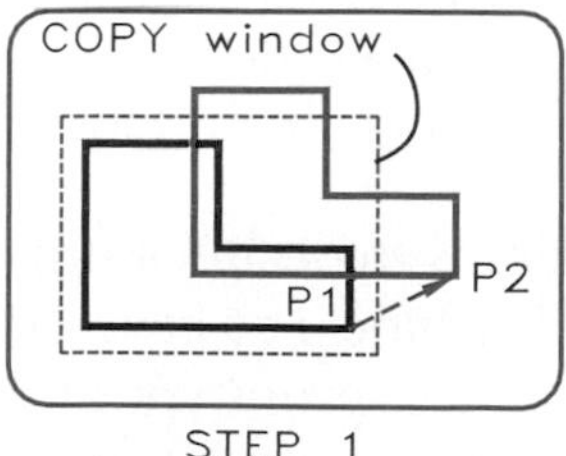

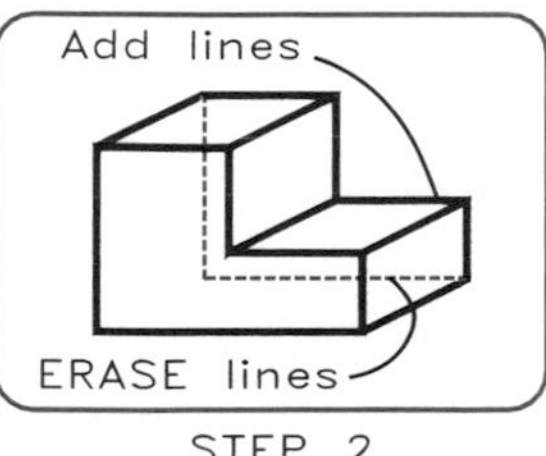

37.239 Pictorial: Oblique.

Step 1 Draw the front surface of the oblique and *Copy* the view from P1 to P2.

Step 2 Connect the corner points with oblique lines from front to back and erase the invisible lines to complete the oblique. This is not a true 3D drawing but a 2D drawing with only one viewpoint.

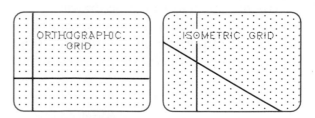

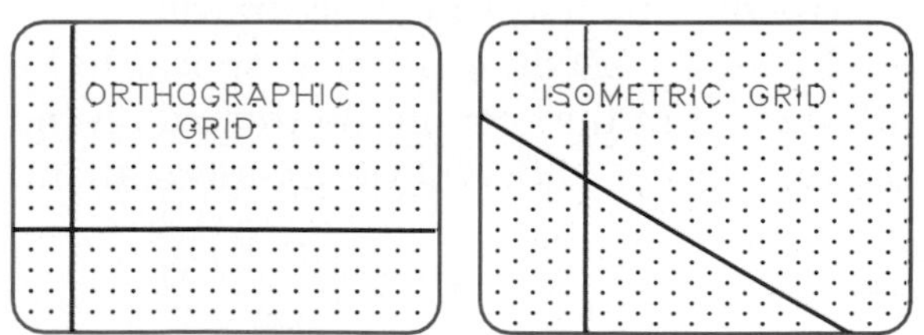

37.240 Screen grids.

A The orthographic grid is called the *Standard* style. *(Command:* Snap> *Style> Standard>* (Enter))

B The isometric grid is specified as follows: *Command:* Snap> *Style> Isometric* (Enter)

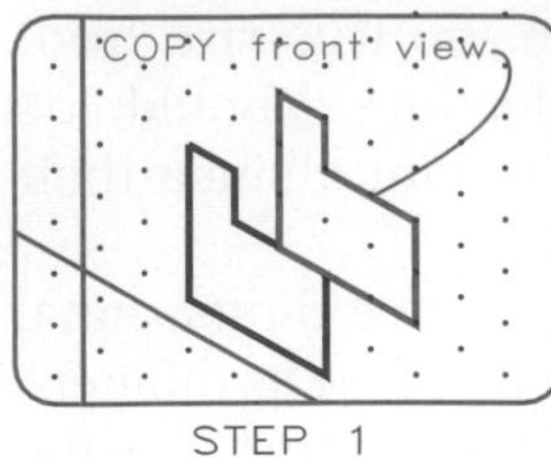

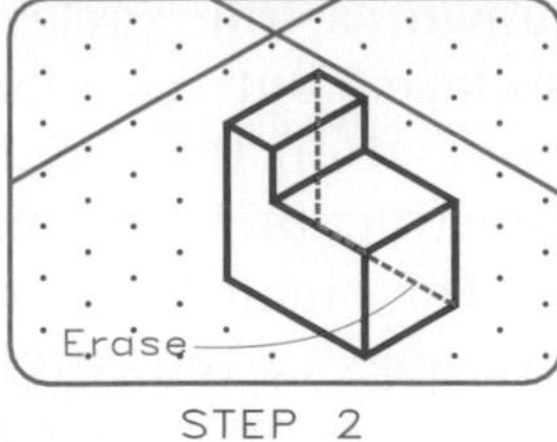

37.241 Pictorial: Isometric.

Step 1 Draw the front view of the object with the grid set to the *Isometric* style and *Copy* the view at its proper depth.

Step 2 Connect the corner points and erase the invisible lines. The cursor lines can be rotated into three positions using *Ctrl E* or by *Command:* Isoplane (Enter)

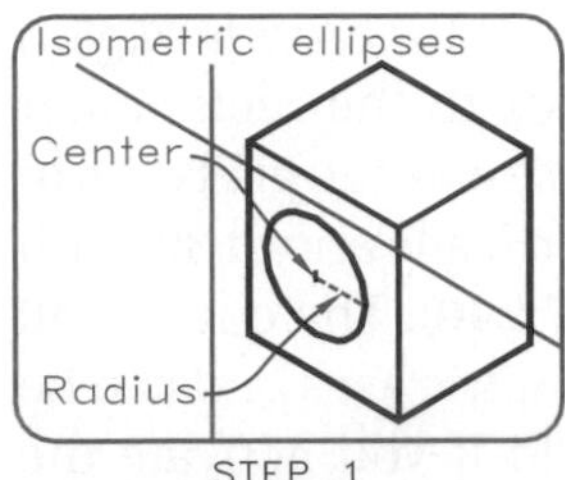

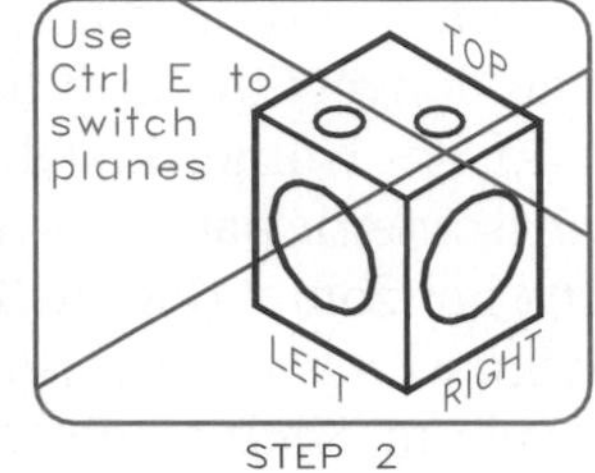

37.242 Pictorial: Isometric—isocircle.

Step 1 When in the isometric *Snap* mode:
Command: *Ellipse* (Enter)
<Axis endpoint 1>/Center/Isocircle: Isocircle (Enter)
Center of circle: Select center.
<Circle radius>/Diameter: Drag or type radius size.

Step 2 Other isocircle ellipses are drawn using these same steps and by changing the cursor to corespond to each isoplane of the box (Ctrl E).

tioned in each of the isometric orientations shown in **Figure 37.242** by using *Ctrl E.* An example of an isometric with partial ellipses is shown in **Figure 37.243**.

The oblique and isometric drawings covered here are 2D drawings that appear to be 3D views, but they cannot be rotated on the screen to obtain different viewpoints of them.

Summary

The coverage of two-dimensional computer graphics and AutoCAD fundamentals has been presented in this chapter to enable you to prepare working drawings. However, this coverage is, of necessity, very brief and is meant to serve as an introduction to the basics of computer graphics. Many options of menus, dialog boxes, and toolbars could not be covered in this limited space. Therefore, you should experiment on your own with various options and commands as you progress in learning and applying the fundamentals.

The *Help* command on the *Main Menu* provides a valuable on-screen reference manual that will provide the answers to many of your questions. This is one of the first menus with which you should become familiar. You will soon find that most of your knowledge of computer graphics will be self-taught.

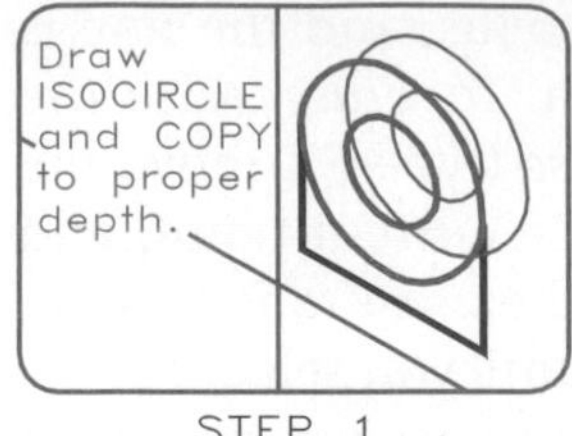

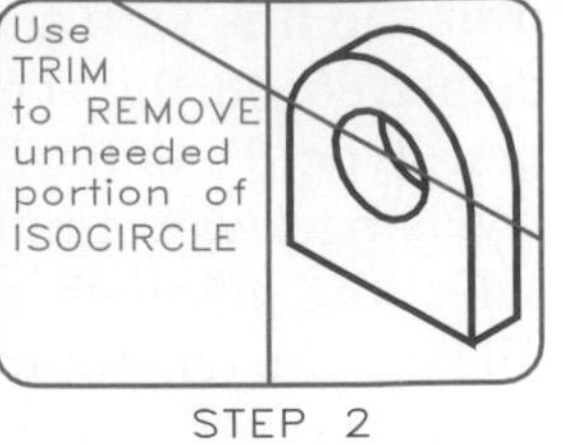

37.243 Pictorial: Isometric—partial isocircles.

Step 1 *Command* line: Ellipse (Enter)
<Axis endpoint 1> /Center/Isocircle: Isocircle (Enter)
Center of circle: Select center.
<Circle radius>/Diameter: Drag or type radius size.
Draw the outside and inside *Isocircles*.

Step 2 Use the *Trim* command to remove the unneeded portions of the *Isocircles*. If the *Trim* fails to respond in some cases, use the *Break* command to select points on the *Isocircle* for line removal. Add missing lines.

Problems

It is suggested that problems be solved in a professional format within a border with a title block similar to the one illustrated in **Figure 37.237**.

1. A good first assignment is to design a prototype of a border and title block, as covered in Section 37.70. As you use this prototype and introduce more variables, you can add them to the prototype file to save the time and effort required to make these settings.

2. Orthographic Views: Select a problem from Figure 13.41 at the end of **Chapter 13** and draw its three views using orthographic projection. Draw on a size A sheet with the border and title strip.

3. Orthographic Views: Same as problem 2 except select problems from **Figures 13.42** and **13.43.**

4. Single Views: Select a problem from those offered at the end of Chapter 12 beginning with **Figure 12.47.** Scale to fit on a size A sheet with a border and title strip.

5. Single Views: Same as problem 4, except select problems from those at the end of Chapter 10.

6. Text Exercise: Three often-used fonts in preparing working drawings and notes are **romans, romand,** and **romant**. Write the following note three times using each of these fonts with a text height of 0.20 in. and capital letters on a size A sheet: HOLES ON BASIC LOCATING DIMENSIONS MUST FREELY ADMIT BASICALLY LOCATED GAGE PINS .300 UNDER MINIMUM HOLE SIZE.

7. Oblique Drawings: Select one from problems 1 to 7 at the end of Chapter 14 and convert the given views into an isometric drawing following the steps in Section 37.72. Draw on a size A sheet.

8. Isometric Drawings: Select one from problems 1 to 7 at the end of Chapter 14 and convert the given views into an isometric drawing following the steps in Section 37.73. Draw on a size A sheet.

9. General: Problems can be selected from the ends of all chapters and solved using the AutoCAD approach introduced in the chapter. Begin with the easy ones first and develop your basic skills to avoid the frustration that may come from attempting more difficult problems.

Design 4: **Logo Design**

Determine the name of the engineering firm that you intend to establish upon graduation

DESIGN 1: FILM REEL

Draw a view of the film reel that generally appears as shown here with the given dimensions on a size A sheet.

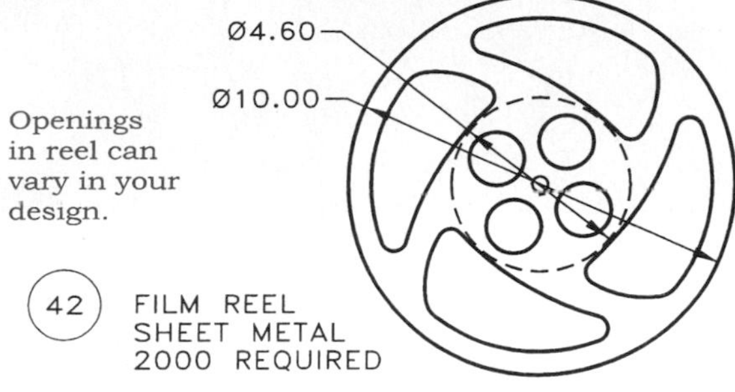

DESIGN 2: JOURNAL

We need a working drawing of this journal, but first, show fillets and rounds, give finish marks, select specs for 3 hex socket screws, select 4 hex-head base screws, and figure out other details. Draw on a size B sheet.

22 JOURNAL
1010 STEEL
4 REQUIRED

Ø1.00

DESIGN 3: FLAT CLAMP

Draw orthographic views that would be necessary to describe each part of this assembly by using the length of the 3.50 in. strap as the basis for all other dimensions. Draw on size A sheets with a border and a title strip.

MORE:

Give the necessay dimensions on each part required for fabrication.

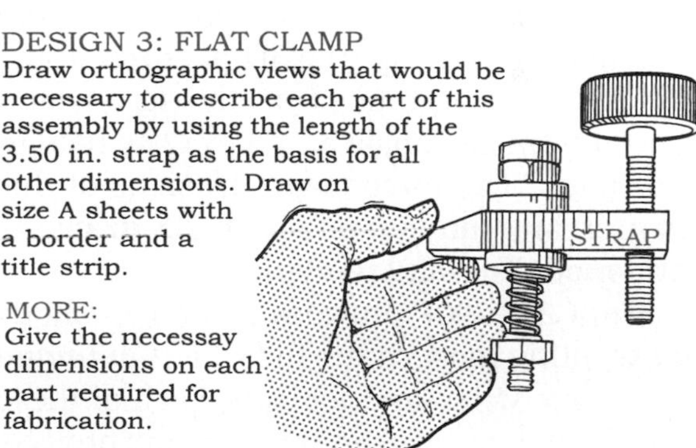

and develop a logo (a symbol) that can be used as your trademark. Logos should be unique, identifiable, and memorable to the observer who may see it on your stationery, office sign, or product. Develop several logos on a size A sheet.

38 3D Computer Graphics: AutoCAD® 2007

38.1 Introduction

This chapter provides an introduction to the principles of making true 3D pictorial drawings that can be rotated on the screen and viewed from any angle as if they were held in your hand. The three major divisions of this chapter are **fundamentals of 3D drawing, solid modeling**, and **rendering**.

AutoCAD 2007 provides several methods of executing most commands: the *Command* line, *Main Menu,* and *toolbars.* Each of these techniques is used in the examples and projects in this chapter. You are encouraged to use the online *Help* screen for each command and to experiment with various options.

38.2 Classic versus 3D Modeling

AutoCAD 2007 is a major modification that introduces two major workspaces that can be used separately or in combination: **AutoCAD Classic** and **3D Modeling**. Each of these workspaces can be accessed by picking them from the *Workspaces* toolbar shown in **Figure 38.1**. Customized workspaces can be added to the list.

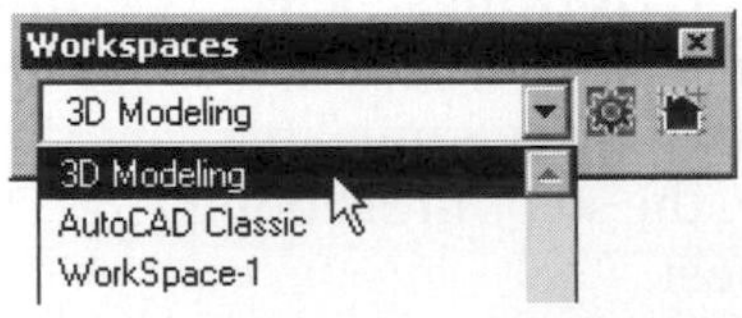

38.1 Two major workspaces can be accessed from the Workspaces toolbar: *3D Modeling* and *AutoCAD Classic.*

38.3 Paper Space and Model Space

The two distinctly different ways of obtaining views of objects are from *Model Space* (*Model* tab) or *Paper Space* (*Layout* tab), which are found in the *Status* bar at the bottom of the

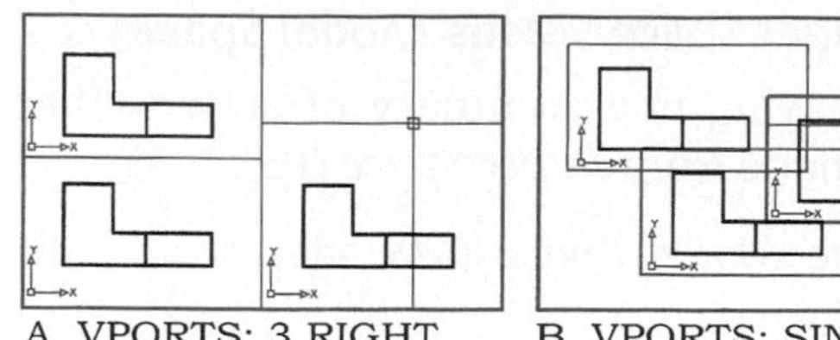

38.2 Viewports: Abutting and floating.

A When the *Layout* tab is current, *Command:* Vports> *Three: Right*> specifies the corners of the space to be filled (Enter) to obtain the three abutting viewports.

B When the *Layout* tab is current, *Command:* Vports> *Single*> specifies the corners of three separate, floating viewports.

screen. In *Paper Space* the screen can be divided into predefined 3D *Viewports (Vports)* that abut each other in standard arrangements (**Figure 38.2A**). The viewports also can be created with *Command:* Vports in nonstandard positions (floating viewports) as shown in **Figure 38.2B** by using the *Single* option. To establish one or several 3D viewports within the paper space area use *Command:* Mview (Enter) and specify viewport corners. These viewports can either overlap or be separated.

Model Space (Model tab)

Previous examples in this book have been given in *Model Space,* where, by default, drawings can be made in two dimensions (2D) and three dimensions (3D). The *Vports* (viewports) command lets you create abutting viewports on the screen. Drawings made before the *Vports* command is applied will be duplicated in each viewport as if multiple monitors were wired to your computer (**Figure 38.3**). Only the active viewport, shown with a heavy outline, can be plotted from *Model Space.*

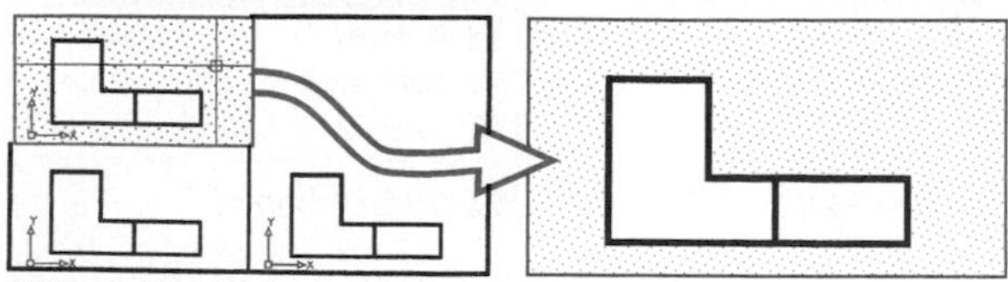

When the Model tab has been selected, only the active 3D viewport will be printed to paper.

38.3 When the *Model* tab (bottom of screen) is current, only the active viewport can be plotted to paper.

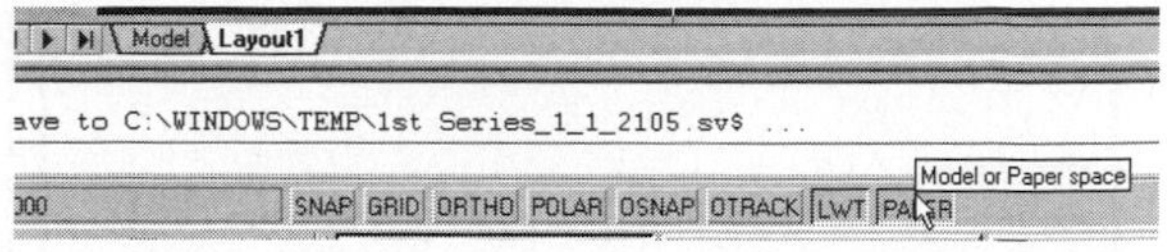

38.4 When in AutoCAD Classic, select the *Layout1* tab and you are in *Paper Space,* where a plotter and page layout can be specified. By alternately picking a *Model/Layout* button in the *Status line,* you can move from *Paper Space (PS)* to *Model Space (MS)* for drawing in either 2D or 3D.

Paper Space (Layout tab)

Select the *Layout1* tab at the bottom of the screen to move into *Paper Space,* where a *Model Space* window appears and where a 3D drawing will appear (**Figure 38.4**). A triangle icon appears at the lower left of the screen to signify that you are in 2D *Paper Space.* You can move between *Paper Space* and *Model Space* by typing MS or PS or by clicking on the *Model* or *Layout* button above the *Command* line. Since drawings made in *Paper Space (PS)* are 2D drawings, toggle to *PS* and insert or draw a 2D border to define the drawing area (**Figure 38.5A**).

While in *Paper Space,* erase the default *Model Space* port. In its place, create two *Model Space* views by typing Mview and defining their corners with a diagonal when prompted (**Figure 38.5B**). Type MS or toggle the *Paper/Model* button at the bottom of the screen in the *Status* bar to set it to *MS* (*Model*

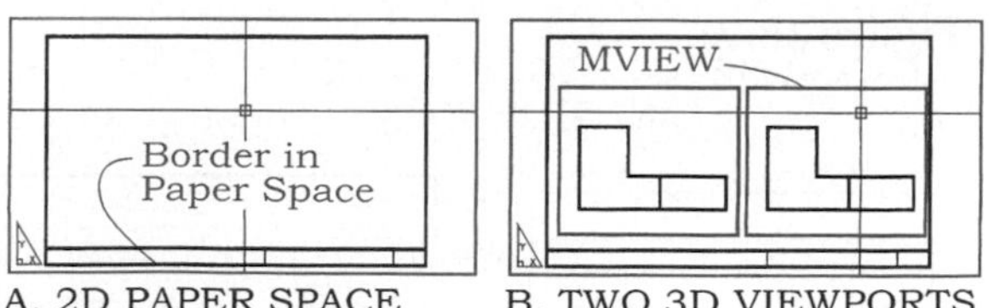

38.5 *Layout* tab: *Paper Space.*

A When the *Layout1* tab (bottom of screen) is picked, the screen is set to *Paper Space,* where a 2D border can be inserted or drawn.

B Use the *Mview (Makeview)* or *Vports (Viewports)* command to define the diagonal corners of two viewports in 3D space to create a combination of a *Model-* and a *Paper-Space* drawing.

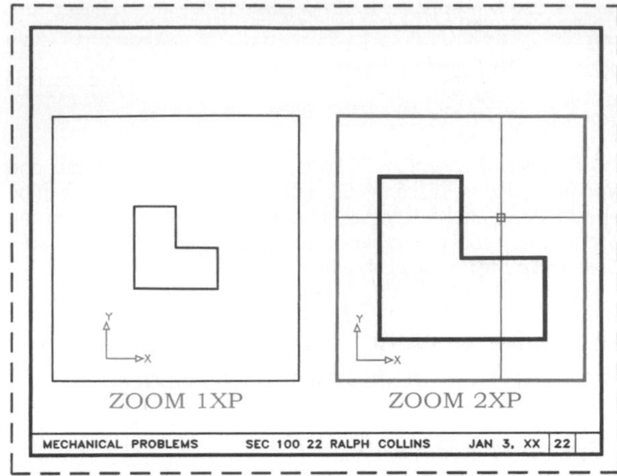

38.6 Select the *Model* button (in the *Status* bar above the *Command* line) to enter *Model Space*. Use *Command:* Zoom (Enter)>1XP to show the drawing full size in that viewport. Select the other viewport, *Command:* Zoom (Enter)> 2XP to obtain a double-size view in that viewport.

Space), and the cursor will appear in the active viewport (**Figure 38.6**). Move to a new viewport and select it with the cursor. The drawing in the *Model-Space* port can be scaled by typing Zoom> 1XP for a full-size drawing, 2XP for a double-size drawing, and 0.5XP for a half-size drawing (**Figure 38.6**).

To make a plot, return to *Paper Space* with the *Model/Paper* button; the triangular paper space icon reappears, and *Paper* replaces *Model* in the *Paper/Model* button at the bottom of the screen in the *Status* bar. Plot from *Paper Space,* and both the 2D and 3D drawings will plot as they appear on the screen (**Figure 38.7**).

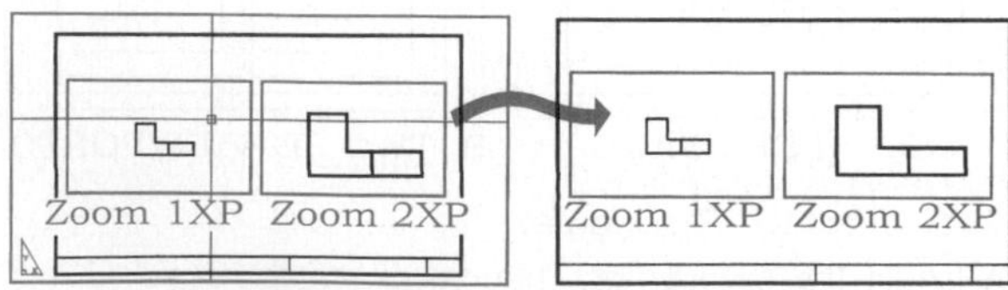

38.7 Plotting from *Paper Space*.

A Select *PS* to enter *Paper Space* for plotting a drawing.

B Both *Paper Space* and *Model Space* drawings are plotted when plotting from *Paper Space*.

38.4 Paper Space versus Model Space

The following is a summary of actions that can be made from *Paper Space (PS):*

1. Create *Model Space (MS)* viewports with *Vports*
2. *Stretch, Move,* and *Scale MS* viewports
3. *Erase MS* viewports
4. *Freeze MS* outlines
5. *Insert* 2D drawings
6. Remove invisible lines from selected viewports with *Hide*
7. Add *Text* across *MS* viewports

The following is a summary of actions that can be made from *Model Space (MS):*

1. *Modify* a 3D drawing
2. *Rotate* the *User Coordinate System (UCS)*
3. *Pan, Zoom, Scale,* etc., *MS* drawings
4. *Attach* dimensions to an *MS* drawing
5. *Erase* the contents of an *MS* viewport

38.5 Setting Up for 3D Drawing

To begin drawing in 3D, you will find it convenient to use the *Dashboard (Tools> Palettes> Dashboard)* as shown in **Figure 38.8**. The

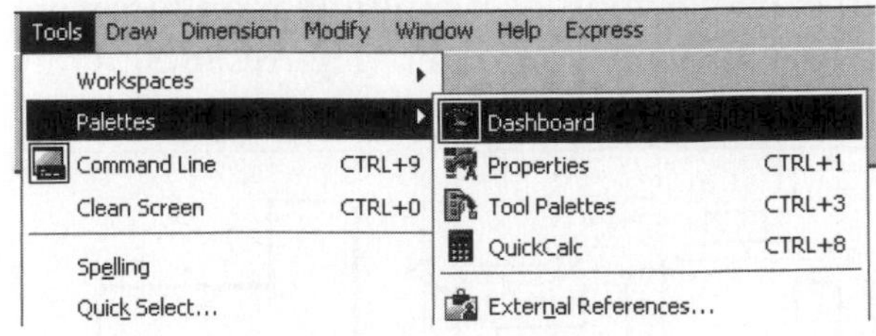

38.8 *Main Menu> Tools> Palettes>* displays the *Dashboard, Properties, Tool Palettes,* and *QuicCalc* palettes from which to select. Notice the two-key combinations that can be used to open three of them. *Ctrl+2* opens the *DesignCenter,* which is farther down on the list.

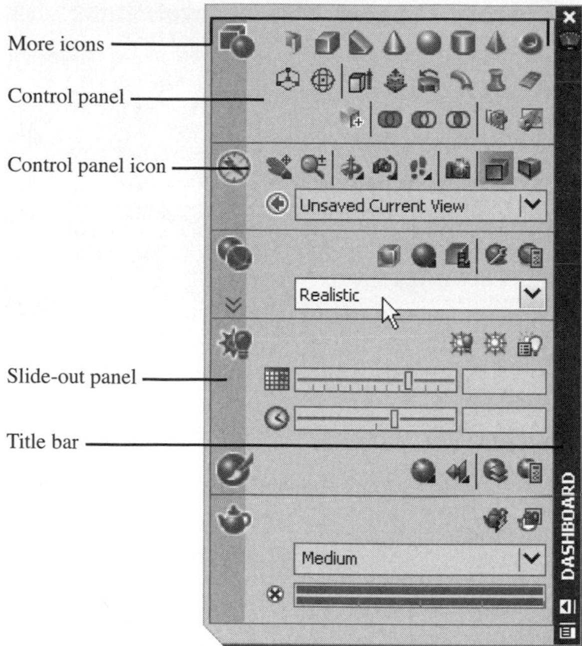

38.9 *Main Menu> Tools> Palettes> Dashboard* displays the *Dashboard* on the screen. It can be docked against either side of the screen or left as a floating palette. Right click on the double line (or the icon on the title bar) and select *Allow Docking* to free it.

Dashboard is displayed automatically when you enter the *3D Modeling* workspace and will appear as shown in **Figure 38.9**. The number of control panels displayed in the *Dashboard* can be increased or decreased by picking the bottommost icon on the title bar and choosing *Control panels* to obtain a listing of those from which to select (**Figure 38.10**).

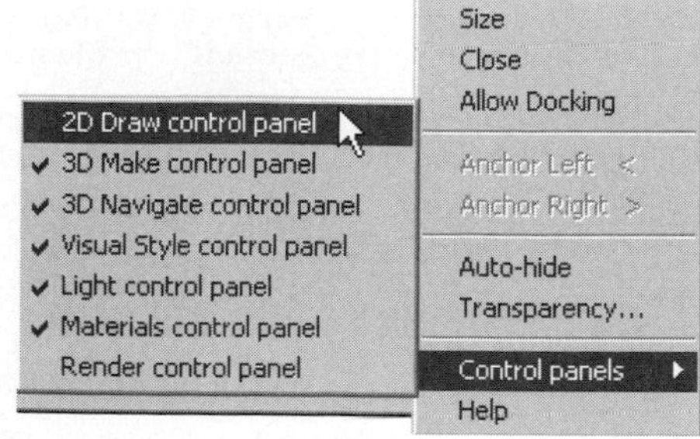

38.10 Pick the *Properties* icon at the bottom of the *Dashboard* title bar and select *Control panels* to display a list of control panels that can be turned off or on.

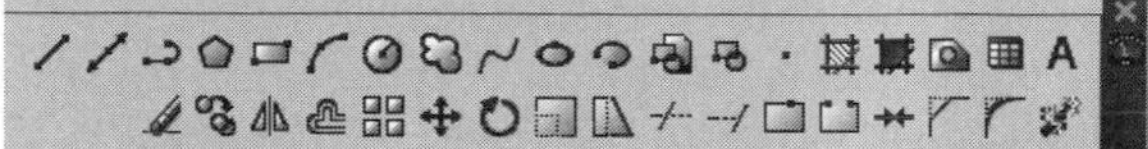

38.11 Checking the *2D Draw Control Panel* as described in **Figure 38.9** displays it at the top of the *Dashboard*. These icons represent commands that are most often used in 2D construction, which is covered in Chapter 37.

38.12 Selecting the slide-out panel enlarges the *3D Make* control panel to reveal hidden options. Most other panels have additional information that can be accessed in this same manner. The panel is reduced to its original size by the up arrow.

The *2D Draw* control panel was selected in **Figure 38.11** to be displayed on the *Dashboard*. Most panels on the *Dashboard* must be widened by dragging for them to show in their entirety (**Figure 38.12**). You will be familiar with the icons and their commands because they are the same as those on the toolbars that you used in Chapter 37.

You can toggle between the *AutoCAD Classic* workspace and the *3D Modeling* workspace from the *Workspaces* toolbar (or *Tools> Workspaces*). Workspaces can be modified or accessed as shown in **Figure 38.13**.

The *Quick Help* panel can be displayed *(Help Menu> Info Palette* or *Ctrl+5)* to provide

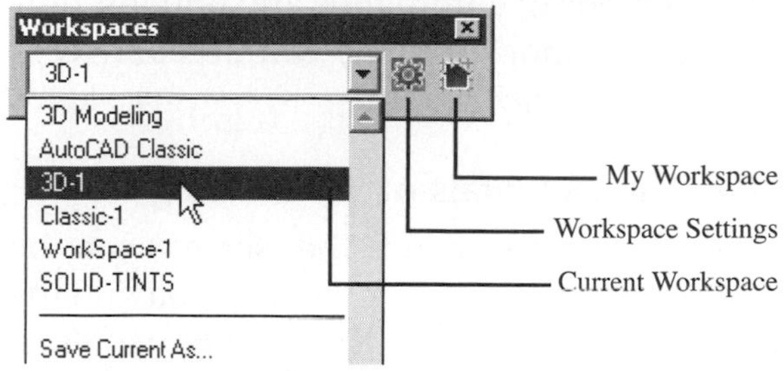

38.13 *Workspaces* can be selected, created, and customized by beginning with this *Workspaces* toolbar.

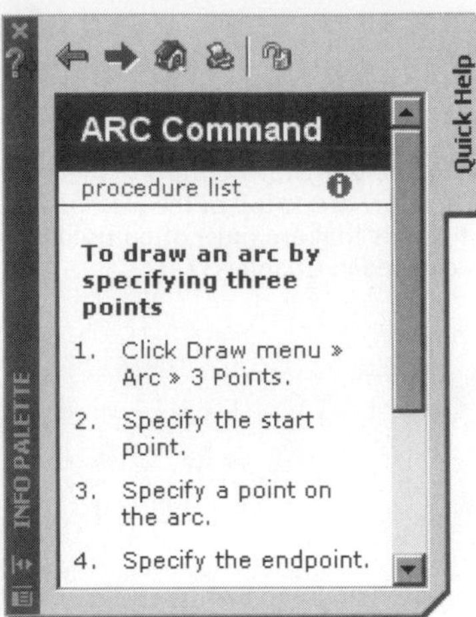

38.14 *Quick Help (Help> Info Palette)* gives instructions while you are in the process of using a command.

information about commands while you are in the process of applying them (**Figure 38.14**).

Toolbars, in addition to those in the *Dashboard,* are helpful in providing icons for commands that can be selected by the cursor. *Toolbars* are opened by right clicking on any other *toolbar* that is open on the screen. They can be docked or left floating and positioned as horizontal or vertical strips.

The *Options* panel offers 10 tabs of multiple options that can be manipulated to suit your needs, as shown in **Figure 38.15**. It can be conveniently displayed on the screen by right clicking in a blank area of a current drawing.

Be prepared to experiment as you learn AutoCAD's commands and procedures and use the help features that are provided. There are hundreds of commands and options; only the more important ones can be covered in this limited space.

38.6 Fundamentals of 3D Drawing

Icons that appear on the screen can be thought of as road signs that help you find the way while drawing. The icons in **Figures 38.16** and **38.17** are basic symbols that you will become familiar with.

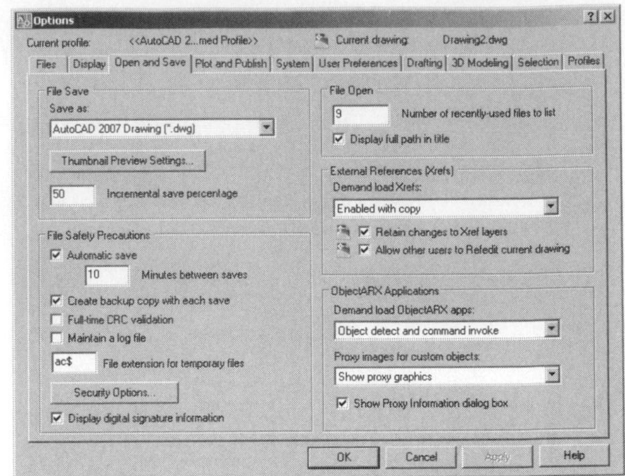

38.15 Both major settings and fine tunings can be made from the *Options* panel. Right click on a blank space of an active drawing and select *Options* from the menu that appears. Settings can be selected from 10 tabs at the top of the panel.

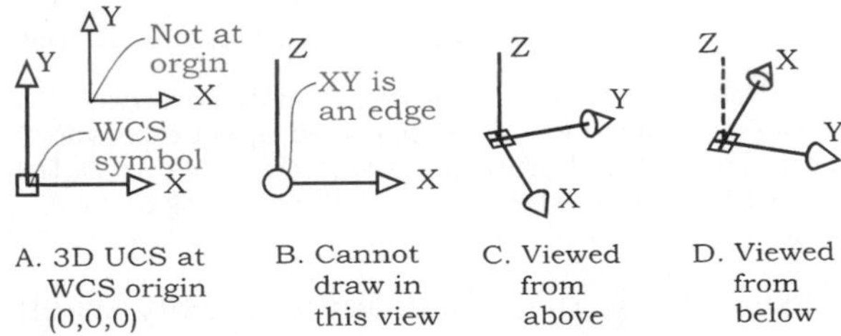

38.16 Select *Command:* <u>Ucsicon</u> (Enter)> *Properties*> *3D* and these icons appear on the screen. Point the thumb of your right hand in the positive x-direction, your index finger in the positive y-direction. Your middle finger will point in the positive z-direction.

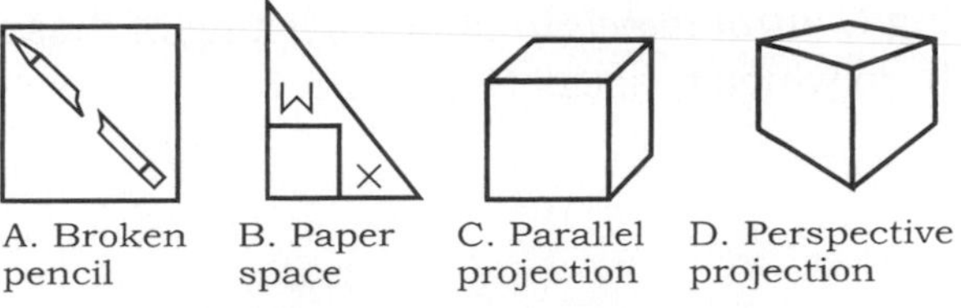

38.17 These icons appear on the screen or in the *Dashboard*. (A) The plane to be drawn on appears as an edge. (B) You are in *Paper Space* (*Layout* tab). (C) The pictorial view is axonometric. (D) The pictorial is a perspective.

Essentially all 3D drawing must be done on the X-Y plane of the *User Coordinate System (UCS),* which is identified by an icon (**Figure 38.16**). Therefore, it is necessary to learn to manipulate the UCS before making a drawing.

Experiment with 3D drawing; toggle the *Model/Paper* button to *Model,* type Ucsicon, set it to *On,* and the X-Y icon will appear as shown in **Figure 38.6**. *Command:* Ucsicon (Enter)> *Properties*> *3D* and the icons will appear as shown in **Figure 38.16**. *Command:* Ucsicon (Enter)> *ORigin* to make the *UCS* icon appear at the origin of the *UCS* with a plus sign in its corner. You may need to *Pan* the 0,0 origin up and to the right of the screen's corner so the *UCS* icon has room to sit on the origin. When a small box appears on the *2D* icon, it is in the *World Coordinate System (WCS).* Without the *box,* the icon is in the *User Coordinate System (UCS).*

In **Figure 38.17**, a *broken-pencil* icon warns that the projection plane appears as an edge, making it impractical to draw in that viewpoint. The *triangular icon* indicates that the screen is in 2D *Paper Space.* The *parallel projection box* icon indicates that the current drawing is an isometric (a type of axonometric). The *perspective projection box* icon tells you that the current drawing is a perspective.

The standard *Vports* are shown in the *Vports* menu in **Figure 38.18**. You must name a *Vports* arrangement to *Save* it by typing a name in the panel of the *Vports* menu.

38.7 Introductory Tutorial

The coverage of extrusion principles in this section is intended to be an introductory tutorial for working in 3D space and learning necessary UCS fundamentals.

The *extrusion* technique is an elementary method of drawing 3D objects with the *Vpoint, Plan, Elev, Thickness,* and *Hide* commands. *Vpoint* (viewpoint) selects the direction in which an object is viewed. *Plan* changes the *UCS* to give a true-size view of the *XY* icon and the surfaces parallel to it. *Elev* (elevation) sets the level of the base plane of the drawing. *Thickness* is the distance of the extrusion in a direction parallel to the *z*-axis. *Hide* removes the invisible lines of the extruded surfaces.

Select *Command:* UCSicon (Enter)> On (Enter) to obtain the *XY* icon, type Elev (Enter)> 0 (zero) (Enter), type Thickness (Enter)> 4 (Enter), and draw the *Plan* view of the base of the block with the *Line* command as illustrated in **Figure 38.19**. The finished box is shown in **Figure 38.20** with sides but no bottom or top.

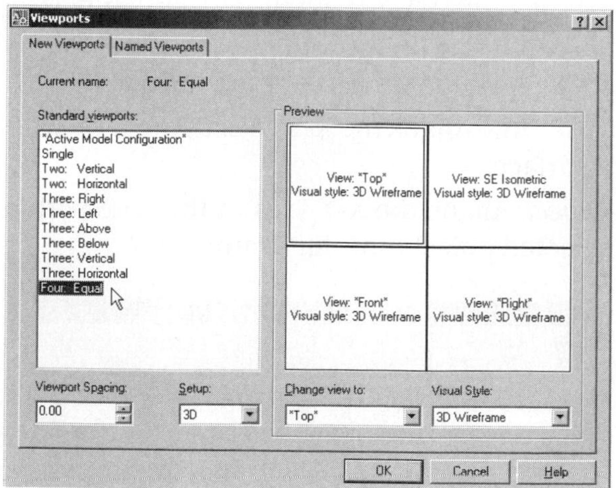

38.18 Select *Main Menu*> *View*> *Viewports*> *New Viewports*> to obtain the *Viewports* dialog box for setting viewports on the screen. In the *Setup* window, select 3D to display this arrangement.

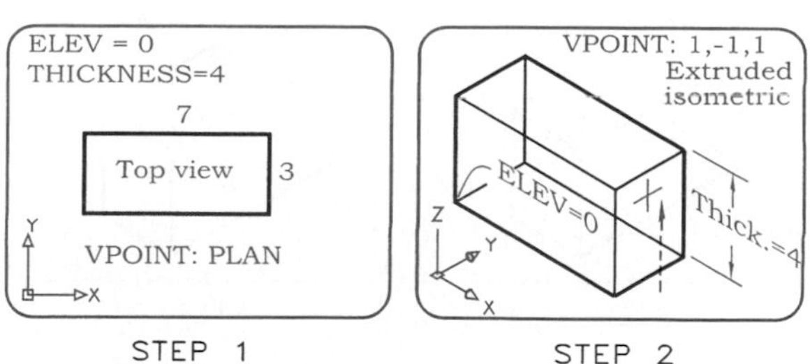

38.19 Elevation and Thickness commands.

Step 1 *Command:* Elev (Enter)
Specify new default elevation <0.00>: 0 (Enter)
Specify new default thickness <0.00>: 4 (Enter)
Command: Line (Enter)
Specify first point: (Draw a 7 × 3 rectangle as a top view.)

Step 2 *Command:* Vpoint (Enter)
Specify a view point or [Rotate] <display compass and tripod>: 1,−1,1 (Enter) An isometric view of the extruded box appears.

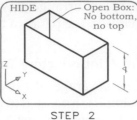

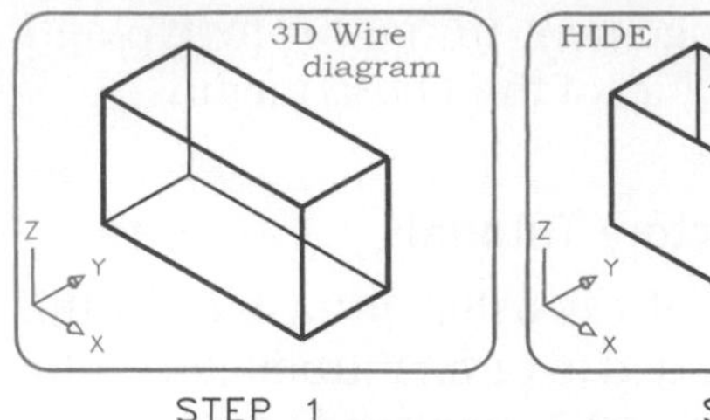

38.20 Elevation and Thickness: Hiding.

Step 1 After the box is drawn, it appears as a wire frame on the screen.

Step 2 *Command:* Hide (Enter) The vertical surfaces become opaque (solid) planes, and the top appears open.

You can use most of the regular *Draw* commands such as *Line, Circle,* and *Arc* to draw features, all of which will be extruded 4 units in the *z*-direction. The extrusion value of 4 units will remain in effect until reset with another value.

Add *3D Faces* to the box as shown in **Figure 38.21** and use the *Command:* Hide (Enter) to remove hidden lines from the view of the box.

The *Solid* command can be used to make the top surface opaque by assigning it an *Elev* equal to the *Thickness* (4), setting its *Thickness* to zero, and applying a solid area to the top by selecting the four corners. Type *Hide* and the top appears opaque.

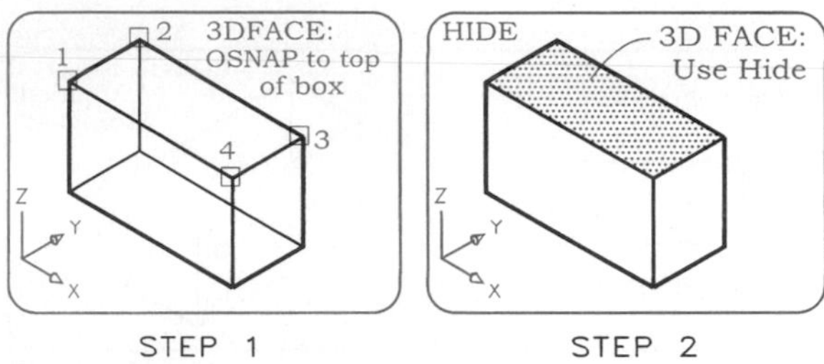

38.21 3DFace.

Step 1 *Command:* Osnap (Enter)
Object snap modes: End (Enter)
Command: 3Dface (Enter)
Specify first point or [Invisible]: 1 > *Specify second point or [Invisible]:* 2 > *Specify third point or [Invisible]:* 3 > *Specify fourth point or [Invisible] <created three-sided face>:* 4 > *Specify first point or [Invisible]:* (Enter)

Step 2 *Command:* Hide (Enter) The top surface appears as an opaque surface.

38.8 Coordinate System

Almost all drawing is done in the plane of the active coordinate system indicated by the *XY* icon. The two coordinate systems are the *World Coordinate System (WCS)* and the *User Coordinate System (UCS).*

The *WCS* has an origin where X, Y, and Z are 0, and, usually, the *x*- and *y*-axes are true length in the top view, the plan view.

A *UCS* can be located within the *WCS* with its *x*- and *y*-axes positioned in any direction and its origin at any selected point. *Command:* Ucsicon> On, select *ORigin* to move it to its origin, and establish a *User Coordinate System* in the following manner:

Command: UCS (Enter)

The default option is *Specify origin of UCS>* move the cursor to the desired position, select the point, and press (Enter).

The options of the *UCS* command are given in the *UCS* toolbar (**Figure 38.22**). Resting the cursor on one of these icons displays a flyout box to identify it. These options are as follows:

UCS: Pick an origin with the cursor and the *UCS* icon moves to the new origin.

World: The *WCS* is identified and the *UCS* icon moves to it.

UCS Previous: Returns to the previous *UCS*.

Face UCS: Aligns the X-Y axes of the *UCS* with a surface.

Object: Aligns the X-Y axes of the *UCS* with a selected object (line, for example).

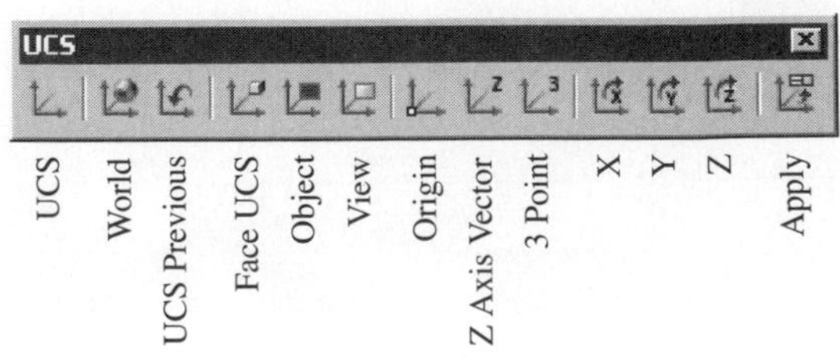

38.22 The *UCS* toolbar gives the options shown above. Most of these options can be accessed from the *Command* line.

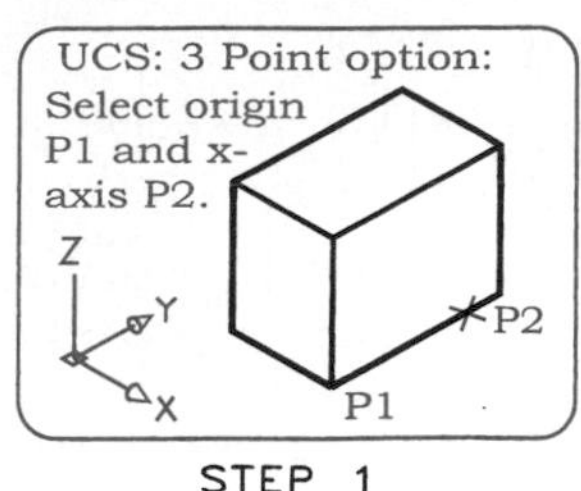

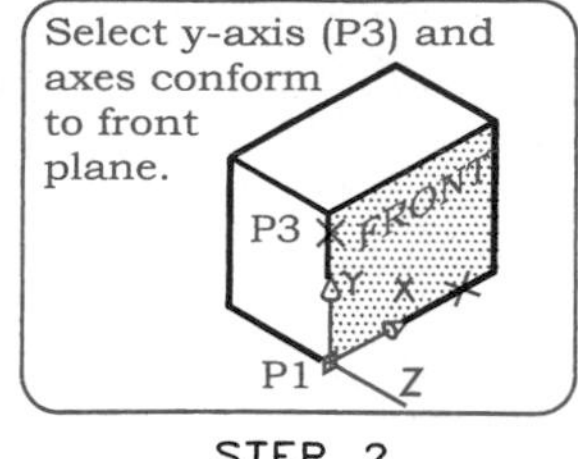

38.23 UCS: 3 Point option.

Step 1 *Main Menu> Tools> New UCS> 3 Point> Specify new origin point <(0,0,0)>:* P1

Specify point on positive portion of the x-axis: P2

Step 2 *Specify point on the positive Y portion of the UCS XY plane:* P3 The *UCS* icon is transferred to the origin, P1. The plus sign at its corner box indicates that it is at the origin.

View: Aligns the X-Y axes of the *UCS* with the plane of the viewing screen.

Origin: Sets a new origin.

Z Axis Vector: Sets the direction of the Z-axis.

3 Point: Sets the *UCS* by selecting an origin, *x*-axis, and *y*-axis (**Figure 38.23**).

X: Rotates the *UCS* about the *x*-axis a specified angle.

Y: Rotates the *UCS* about the *y*-axis a specified angle.

Z: Rotates the *UCS* about the *z*-axis a specified angle.

Apply: Applies the current *UCS* to a selected *Viewport* or to *All Viewports* in a multiview layout.

The UCS II toolbar (**Figure 38.24**) gives the following options:

Setting the *UCS* and a *UCS box* with tabs for using *Named UCSs,* selecting *Orthographic UCSs,* and making *Settings.*

Save: Saves the current *UCS* to a specified name.

Delete: Removes a saved *UCS* from a list of saved *UCSs.*

Apply: Assigns the current *UCS* to a specified *Viewport* or *Viewports.*

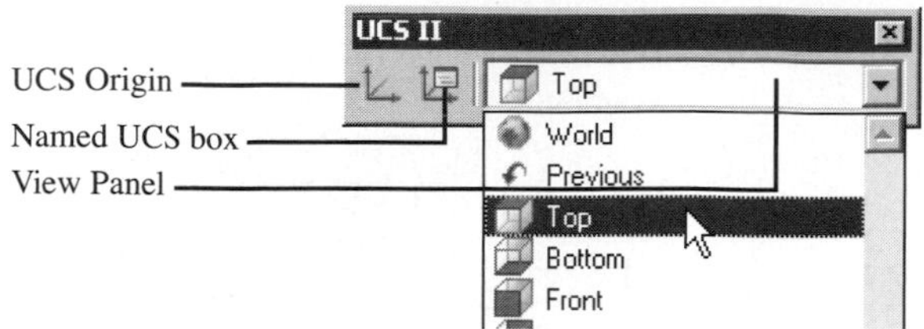

38.24 From the *UCS II* toolbar, select the panel to reveal a listing of orthographic views that can be selected to display 3D objects.

?: List names of *UCSs* and their origins and *x*-, *y*-, and *z*-axes for each.

World: Set the *UCS* to the *World Coordinate System.*

Save a *UCS* as follows: *Command:* UCS (Enter)> Save> type a name when prompted. Select *Main Menu> Tools> UCS* box> *Named UCSs* tab to obtain a list of the saved coordinate systems. Delete a *UCS* by right clicking on it and selecting *Delete,* or *Rename* it by right clicking on it and typing a new name. Three tabs are given in the *UCS* box: *Named UCSs, Orthographic UCSs,* and *Settings.*

The *UCS* icon is turned on in the following manner:

Command:> UCSicon (Enter)> *Enter an option [ON/ OFF/ All/ Noorigin/ ORigin] <ON>:>* ON (Enter)

The functions of these *UCSicon* options are as follows:

ON/ OFF turns the icon on and off.

All displays the icon in all viewports.

Noorigin displays the icon at the lower left corner regardless of the *UCS's* location.

ORigin places the icon at the origin of the current coordinate system if space permits, or at the lower left if space is unavailable.

38.9 Setting Viewpoints

Use *Vpoint* (*Command:* Vpoint) to set the viewpoint of a *UCS* by typing the three-dimensional coordinates or by using the tripod axes

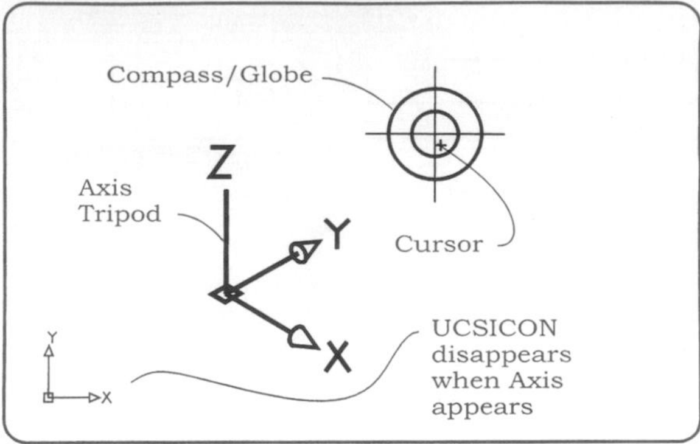

38.25 *Command:* Vpoint (Enter) (Enter) displays a compass globe and axes on the screen for selecting a viewpoint.

(**Figure 38.25**). Predefined *Viewpoints* can also be selected from the *Dashboard* or from the *View* toolbar. For example, select the top view icon, and *x*- and *y*-axes along with the constructed object will rotate, showing its top view and the plane of the *x-y* axes true size.

When *UCSicon* is *On,* from *Command:* Vpoint (Enter), the *display compass and tripod* option (a set of *x*-, *y*-, and *z*-axes) appears on the screen (**Figure 38.25**). A viewpoint of the object is found by selecting a point on the *compass globe* as described in **Figure 38.26**. Repeat this command by pressing (Enter) and selecting other views until the desired view is found.

Figure 38.27 compares the viewpoints found on the compass globe with those specified with numbers at the keyboard. A *Vpoint* of 1,−1,1 means that the origin (0,0,0) is viewed

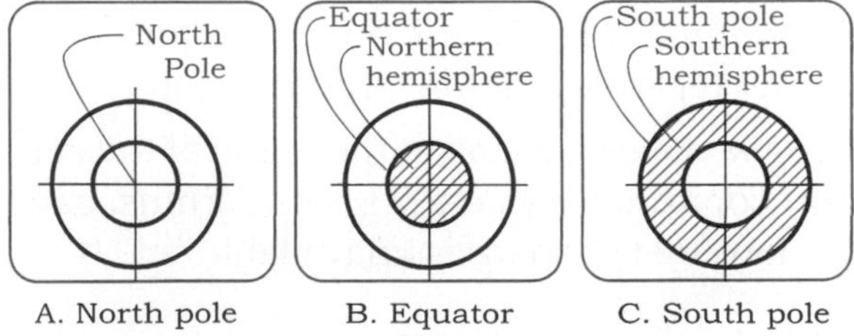

38.26 The compass globe.

A. The North Pole is at the intersection of the crosshairs.

B. The small circle locates viewpoints on the equator.

C. The large circle locates the viewpoint at the South Pole.

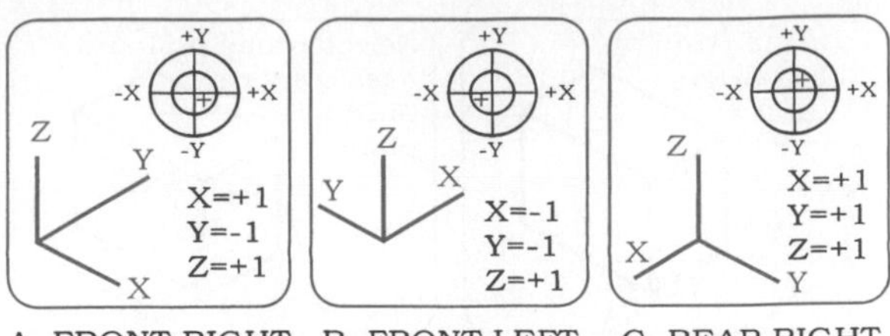

38.27 Examples of the relationship between the points on the *Vpoint globe* and the *Vpoint values* selected from the keyboard.

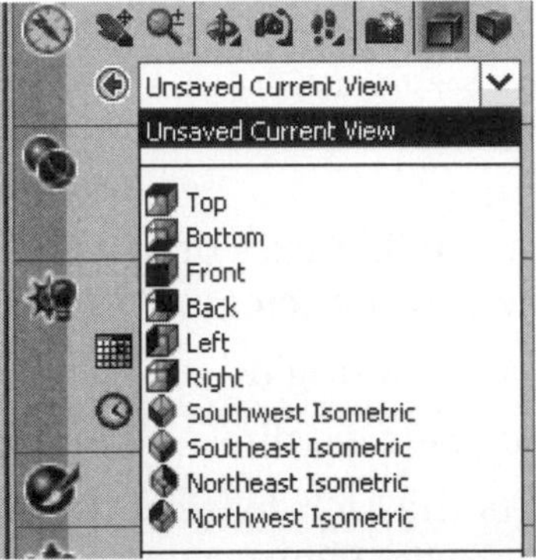

38.28 Preset views can be selected from the *Dashboard's 3D Navigate* control panel. When selected the *UCS* is automatically established.

from a point that is 1 unit in the *x*-direction, 1 unit in the negative *y*-direction, and 1 unit in the positive *z*-direction from 0,0,0.

Preset views can be selected from the *Dashboard,* which includes four isometric UCS views (**Figure 38.28**). (Open the *Dashboard* on the screen by *Command* line> Dashboard.) The six principal orthographic views can be picked from *3D Viewport Presets* under *View,* or by typing *Vpoint* at the *Command* line, as follows:

Presets	*By Typing*
Top view	0,0,1
Front view	0, −1,0
Right-side view	1,0,0
Left-side view	−1,0,0
Rear view	0,1,0
Bottom view	0,0,−1

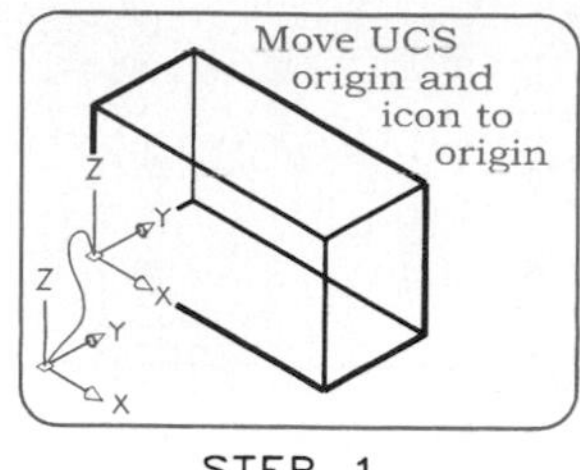

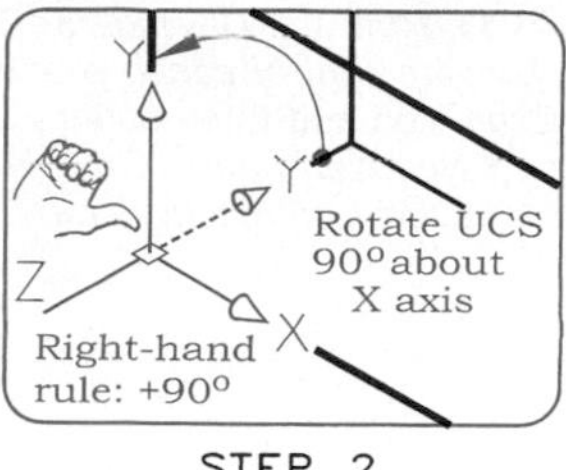

38.29 Setting the UCS.

Step 1 *Command:* UCSicon (Enter)

Enter an option [On/ . . . /ORigin] <ON>: OR (Enter) *Command:* UCS (Enter)

Enter an option [New/Move/orthoGraphic/Prev/Restore/ Save/ Del/Apply/?/World] <World>: N (Enter) *Specify origin of new UCS or [ZAxis/3point/OBject/Face/View/X/Y/Z]:* OB Icon moves to selected object.

Step 2 *Command:* UCS (Enter)

Enter an option [New/Move . . . /?/World] <World>: N (Enter)

Specify origin of new UCS or [ZAxis/ . . . /X/Y/Z]: X (Enter)

Specify rotation angle about X axis: 90. The UCS icon rotates 90° about the x-axis.

38.10 Basic Extrusions

An extruded box similar to the one in **Figure 38.19** is shown in isometric by typing Vpoint (Enter) and giving coordinates of 1,−1,1, as in **Figure 38.29**. The *UCS* icon is moved to the object's lower left corner by the *UCS* command and rotated 90° about the *x*-axis to lie in the frontal plane of the box. The right-hand rule is used to determine the direction of rotation by pointing the right thumb in the positive direction of the axis of rotation (**Figure 38.30**). Typing Plan makes the *x-y* view of the *UCS* icon (the front view) appear true size.

The circle is drawn as an extrusion by setting the *Elev* to 0 and *Thickness* to −3 (the depth of the box) and drawing a cylindrical hole on the frontal plane (**Figure 38.31**). Apply *3Dfaces* to the upper and lower planes of the box and *Hide* invisible lines.

38.11 Viewpoint Options

Once a three-dimensional object has been constructed, it can be viewed from any angle, as a pictorial or as an orthographic view.

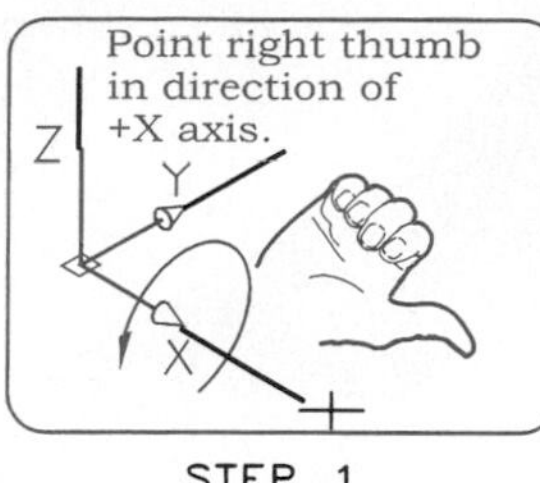

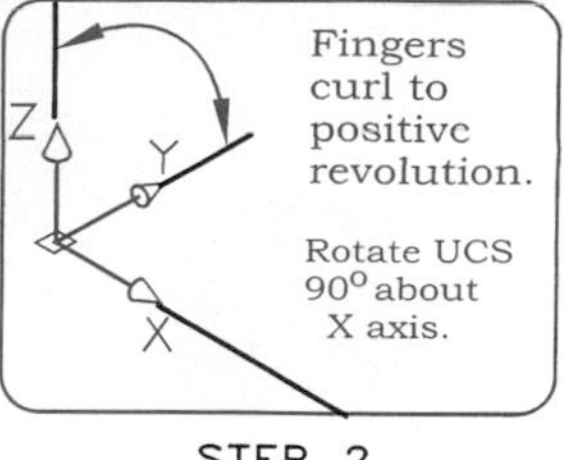

38.30 Rotating the UCS.

Step 1 *Command:* UCS (Enter)

Enter an option [New/Move . . . /?/World] <World>: N (Enter)

Specify origin of new UCS or [ZAxis/ . . . /X/Y/Z]: X (Enter)

Step 2 *Specify rotation angle about X axis:* 90 The UCS icon rotates.

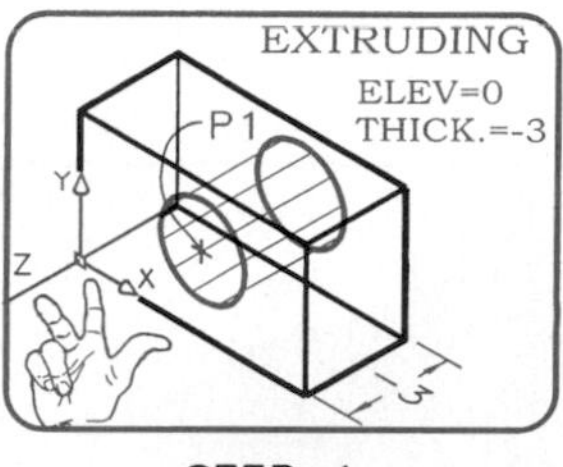

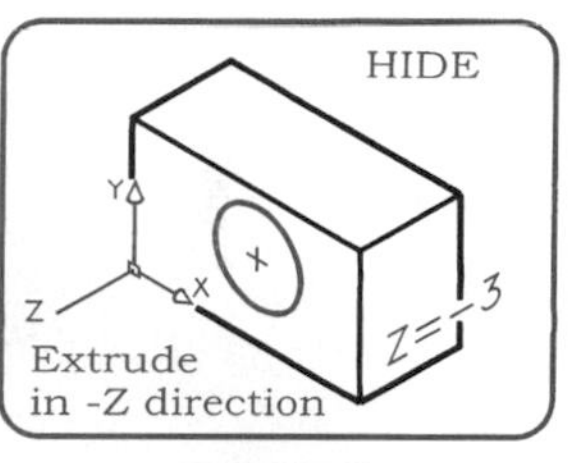

38.31 Extruding a hole.

Step 1 *Command:* Elev (Enter)

Specify new default elevation <0>: 0 (Enter)

Specify new default thickness <4>: −3 (Enter)

Command: Circle (Enter) *CIRCLE specifies center point for circle or [3P/2P/Ttr (tan tan radius)]:* P1

Specify radius of circle or [Diameter]: .5 (Enter)

A 1-in.-diameter cylinder is extruded 3 in. deep into the box.

Step 2 *Command:* Hide (Enter) The outline of the hole is shown, but it cannot be seen through.

Figure 38.32 displays the options that are available. The *Orbit, Swivel,* and *Walk* icons have additional pull-down options when they are picked.

38.32 The *3D Navigate control panel* of the *Dashboard* gives the commands (l to r) *Pan, Zoom, Orbit, Swivel, Walk, Camera, Parallel Projection,* and *Perspective Projection.* The window contains orthographic and isometric views that can be selected.

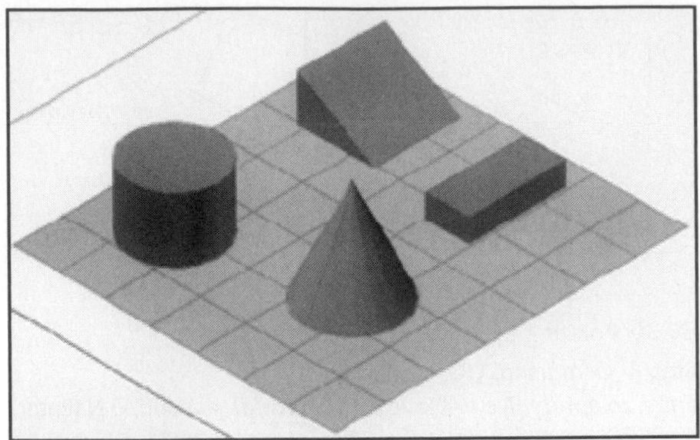

PARALLEL PROJECTION: ISOMETRIC

38.33 From the *Dashboard's 3D Navigate control panel,* select the *Parallel Projection* icon to obtain a pictorial where parallel lines project as parallel.

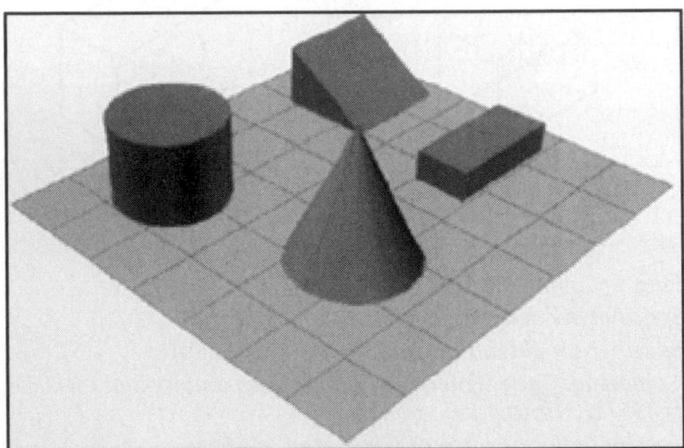

PERSPECTIVE PROJECTION

38.34 From the *Dashboard's 3D Navigate control panel,* select the *Perspective Projection* icon to obtain a perspective in which parallel lines converge to vanishing points.

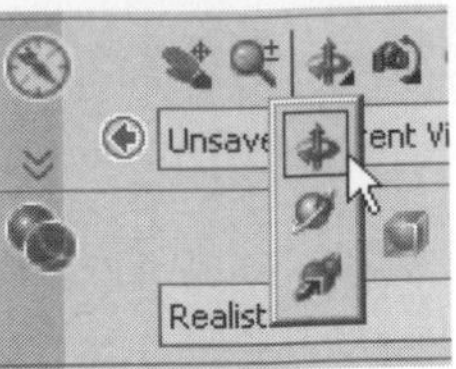

38.35 From the *Dashboard's 3D Navigate control panel,* pick the *Orbit* icon and three options are displayed: *Constrained Orbit, Free Orbit,* and *Continuous Orbit.*

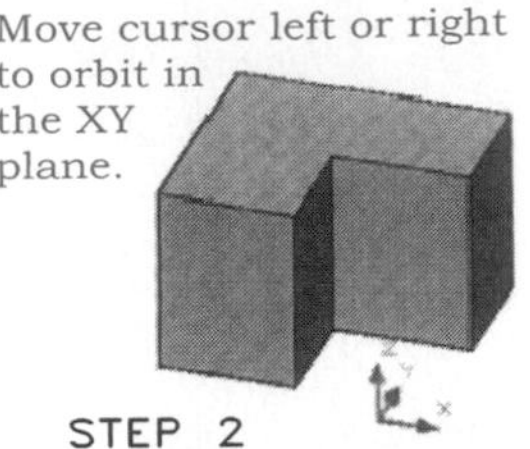

38.36 Constrained Orbit.

Step 1 From the *Dashboard's 3D Navigate control panel,* select the *Constrained Orbit* icon, and select the object.

Step 2 Move the cursor left or right to orbit in the *x-y* plane. Move up or down to orbit in the *z*-direction.

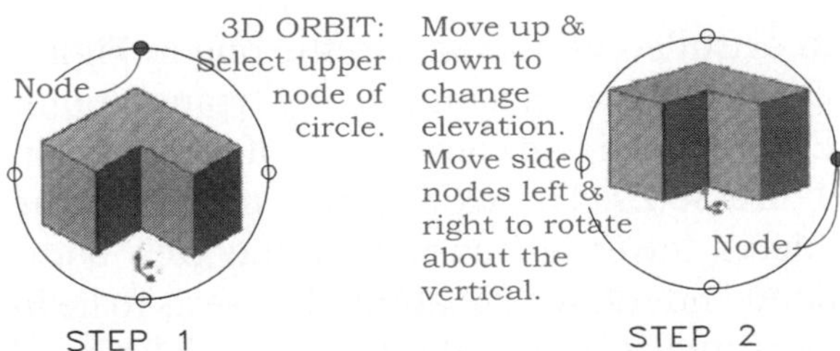

38.37 Free Orbit.

Step 1 From the *Dashboard's 3D Navigate control panel,* select the *Free Orbit* icon, and select the object.

Step 2 Move the upper node up or down to rotate about the horizontal axis. Move a side node left or right to rotate about the vertical axis.

Examples of *Parallel* and *Perspective* projections are shown in **Figures 38.33** and **38.34**. A perspective view is the most realistic view of an object.

From the *Dashboard,* hold down the *Orbit* icon and select the *Constrained Orbit* icon in the drop-down menu shown in **Figure 38.35**. Move the cursor as described in **Figure 38.36** to change your point of view.

Select the *Free Orbit* icon located below the *Constrained Orbit* icon and follow the steps shown in **Figure 38.37** to manipulate your view of the part. Use the nodes on the orbit circle as handles to control the rotation.

Select the *Create Camera* icon located in the *3D Navigate control panel* and follow the steps shown in **Figure 38.38** to set the camera and retrieve its view of the part. By default, the resulting view is a perspective. The *Create Camera* command is one that must be experimented with in order to become proficient. The *Create Camera* command has an option

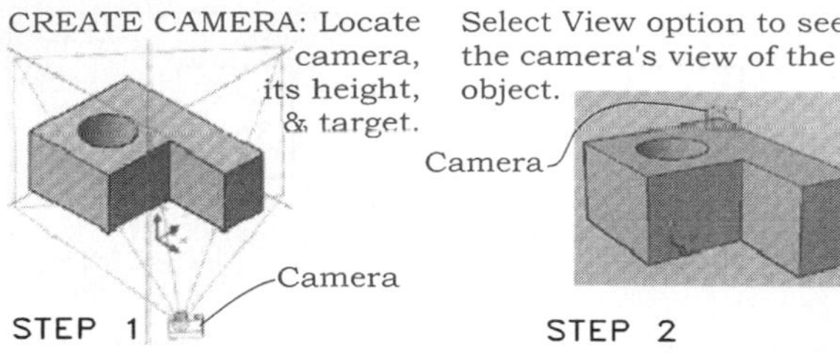
CREATE CAMERA: Locate camera, its height, & target.
Camera
STEP 1
Select View option to see the camera's view of the object.
Camera
STEP 2

38.38 Create Camera.

Step 1 From the *Dashboard's 3D Navigate control panel*, select the *Create Camera* icon, locate the camera, specify its height, and pick the target.

Step 2 Pick the *View* option to obtain the view seen by the camera.

38.39 Solid primitives can be chosen from the *Dashboard*. The *Extrude* command has been selected.

for *Clipping*, which is used to remove portions of the image that are placed in front of or behind specified planes. Experiment with this command.

38.12 Solid Modeling: Introduction

AutoCAD 2007 provides solid modeling capabilities of *Regions* (2D solids) and *Solids* (3D solids). The commands for solid modeling found in the *Dashboard* (**Figure 38.39**) are used to create solid primitives—*boxes, cylinders, spheres,* and others—that can be added to or subtracted from each other to form composite objects.

Regions

Region modeling is a 2D version of solid modeling in which a closed surface can be converted into a solid plane called a **Region** (**Figure 38.40**). The upper plane of a wire frame enclosed by a *Pline* is made into a 2D solid by typing Region and selecting the polyline. The circle is made into a *Region* and is removed from the rectangular *Region* by the *Subtract* command.

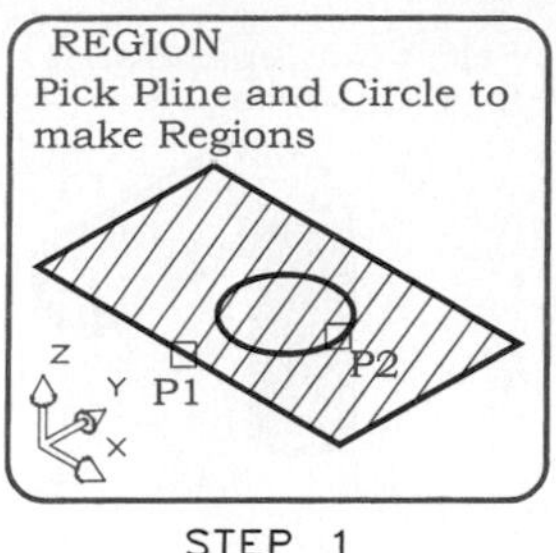
REGION
Pick Pline and Circle to make Regions
P1
P2
STEP 1

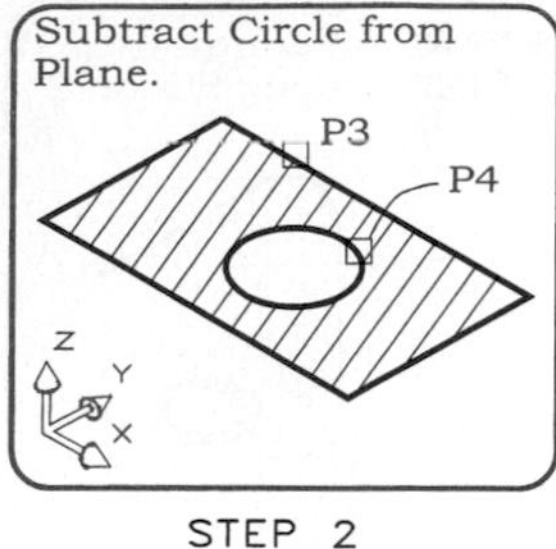
Subtract Circle from Plane.
P3
P4
STEP 2

38.40 2D Regions.

Step 1 *Command:* Region (Enter) *Select objects:* P1 *1 found*> *Select objects:* P2 (Enter) *2 Regions created.*

Step 2 *Command:* Subtract (Enter) *Select solids and regions to subtract from . . .*> *Select objects:* P3 *1 found*> *Select objects:* (Enter)> *Select solids and regions to subtract . . .*
Select objects: P4> *1 found*> *Select objects:* (Enter)

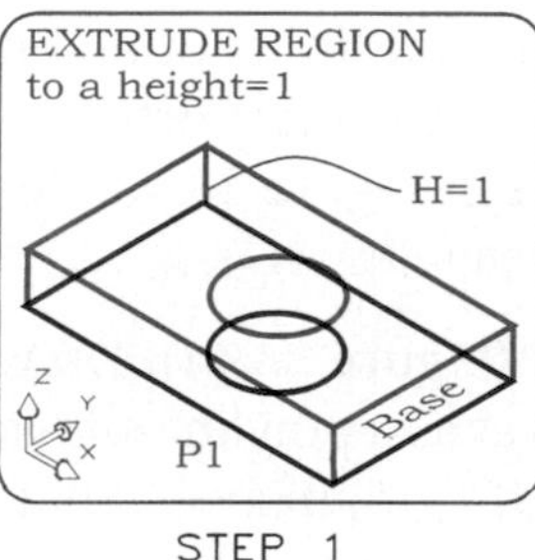
EXTRUDE REGION to a height=1
H=1
Base
P1
STEP 1

Select Realistic style from Dashboard to hide.
Solid
STEP 2

38.41 Extruding a Region.

Step 1 *Command:* Extrude (Enter) *Select objects:* P1> *1 found*> *Select objects:* (Enter)

Step 2 *Specify height of extrusion or [Path]:* 2 (Enter)
Specify angle of taper for extrusion<*0*>*:* (Enter)
Region is extruded a vertical distance of 2 units.

Extrude

The *Extrude* command picked from the *Dashboard* (**Figure 38.39**) is used with closed polylines, polygons, circles, ellipses, and 3D entities to extrude them to a specified height (with tapered sides if desired). **Figure 38.41** shows the extrusion of the 2D *Region* developed in **Figure 38.40** to an assigned height of 1. Polylines with crossing or intersecting segments cannot be extruded.

Regions can be extruded along paths (usually a polyline) to form a 3D shape as illustrated in **Figure 38.42**. Extruded shapes can be hidden and rendered.

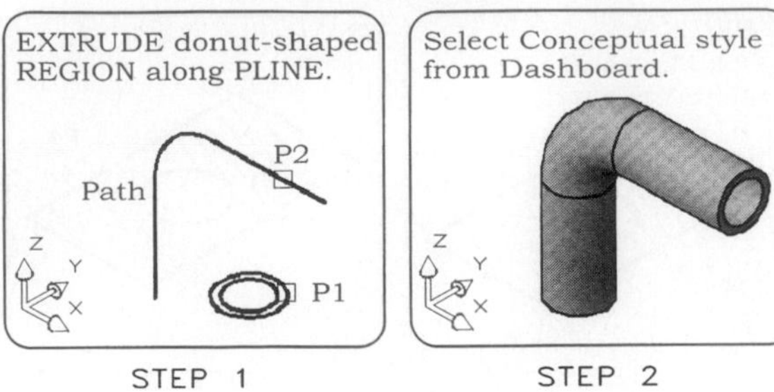

38.42 Extruding a Region.

Step 1 *Command*: Extrude (Enter) *Select objects:* P1> *1 found> Select objects:* (Enter)
Specify height of extrusion or [Path]: Path (Enter)

Step 2 *Select extrusion path:* P2. Type Hide to show visibility.

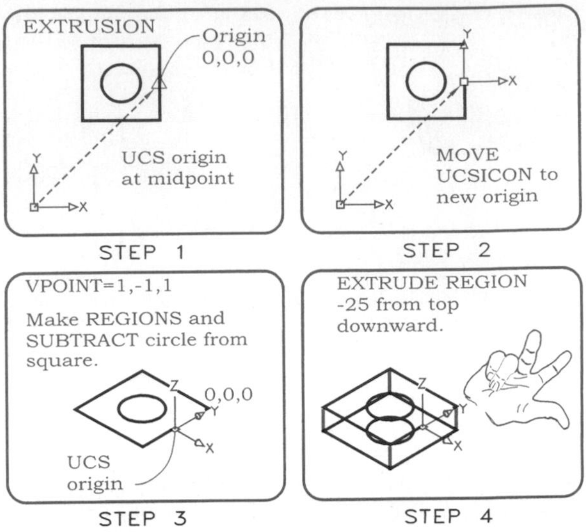

38.44 Part 1: First extrusion.

Step 1 Draw the top view of the bracket and set the *UCS* origin at the midpoint of the line as shown.

Step 2 Use *Ucsicon* and *ORigin* to place the icon at the origin.

Step 3 *Command:* Vpoint> 1,−1,1 to obtain an isometric view of the plane. Make the plane into a *Region* with a hole in it.

Step 4 *Extrude* the *Region* to a height of −25.

38.13 An Extrusion Example

While in *Model Space,* assign limits of about 200 × 180 in which to draw the first portion of the angle bracket shown in **Figure 38.43**. Begin drawing the bracket as follows:

Part 1—First Extrusion (Figure 38.44): Draw the top view of the bracket as a polyline with a circle in it, and set the *UCS* origin at the midpoint of the line shown. *Move* the *UCS* icon to the *UCS* origin, convert the plane into a *Region,* and *Subtract* the circle from the rectangular plane. Obtain an isometric view (*Vpoint*= 1,−1,1), and *Extrude* the *Region* to −25 mm below the upper surface.

Part 2—Draw the Inclined Centerline (Figure 38.45): Rotate the UCS 90° about the *x*-axis and 90° about the *y*-axis. Draw a line from 0,0,0 (the UCS origin) to 0,−80,80 to find the centerline of the inclined surface.

Part 3—Draw the Inclined Surface (Figure 38.46): Rotate the UCS −45° about the *x*- axis so that it lies in the plane of the inclined surface. Draw a closed *Polyline* using the coordinates of the inclined plane to locate its corners. Convert this plane into a *Region.*

Part 4—Extrude the Inclined Surface (Figure 38.47): *Command: Extrude* (Enter) and enter an extrusion height of −25 when prompted. Use the *Union* command, select the two extrusions, and join them together into a single solid.

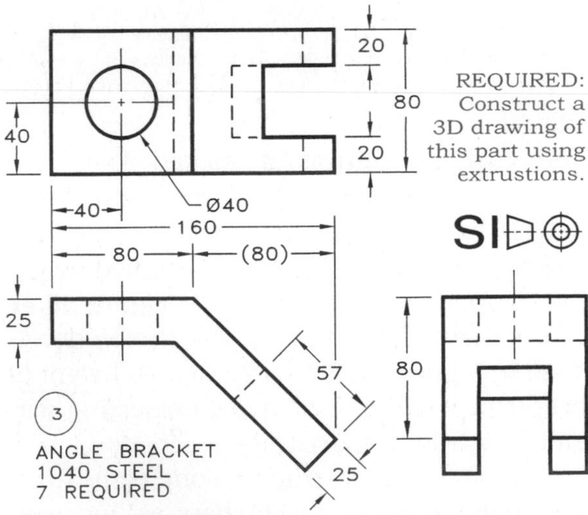

38.43 This angle bracket will be used as the orthographic drawing from which an extruded solid will be developed in the following steps.

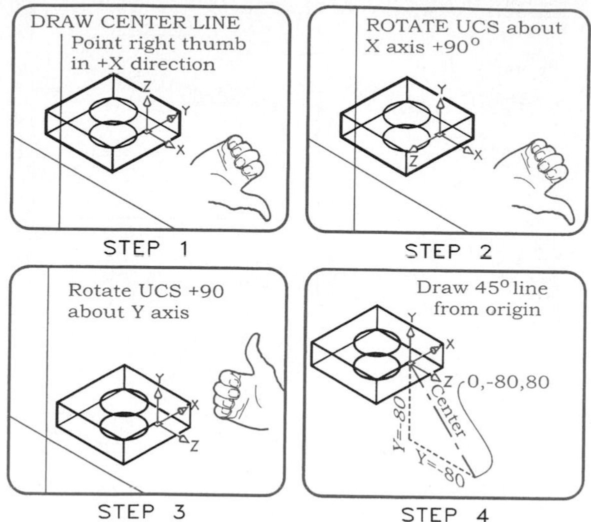

38.45 Part 2: Draw the centerline.

Step 1 *Command:* UCS (Enter) *Enter an option [New/ Move/ . . . /World]:* New (Enter) *Specify origin of new UCS:* X (Enter)

Step 2 *Specify rotation angle about X axis:* 90 (Enter)

Step 3 *Command:* UCS (Enter) *Enter an option [New/ Move/ . . . / World]:* New (Enter)
Specify origin of new UCS: Y (Enter)
Specify rotation angle about Y axis: 90 (Enter)

Step 4 *Command:* Line (Enter) *Specify first point:* 0,0,0 (Enter) *Specify next point:* 0,−80,80 (Enter) Centerline is drawn.

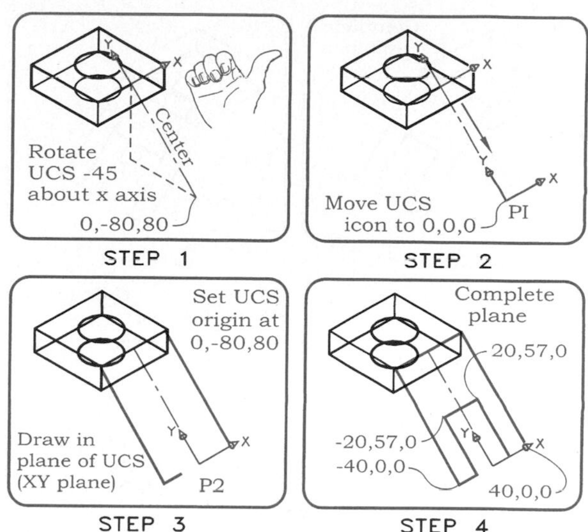

38.46 Part 3: Draw the inclined plane.

Step 1 *Command:* UCS (Enter) *Enter an option [New/ Move/ . . . / World]:* New (Enter) *Specify origin of new UCS:* X (Enter) *Specify rotation angle about X axis:* −45 (Enter)

Step 2 *Command:* UCS (Enter) *Enter an option [New/Move/ . . . / World]:* Move (Enter) *Specify origin of new UCS:* P1 (Enter) Endpoint of centerline.

Step 3 *Command:* Line (Enter) *Specify first point:* 0,0,0 (Enter) *Specifiy next point:* P2

Step 4 *Command:* Pline (Enter) Draw the inclined plane.

Part 5—Four Equal Views (Figure 38.48): Pick the *Layout1* tab at the bottom of the screen to display a dialog box that will let you open a single viewport. Erase this viewport, which leaves no viewport. Select *Four Equal* (3D) ports from the *Viewports* box (**Figure 38.48**); when prompted select the diagonal corner of the area for the four ports. Select *3D* under *Setup* and pick *OK*. The four viewports will appear as shown in **Figure 38.49** with top, front, side, and isometric views. It is usually necessary to size the views to a uniform scale by using *Zoom>* nXP (.3XP, for example). Type Hide in each *Model Space* viewport to remove hidden lines. Return to *Paper Space,* and *Main Menu> File> Plot* to obtain the *Plot* menu for making final settings before plotting.

38.14 Solid Modeling: Primitives

Solid primitives—*box, sphere, wedge, cone, cylinder,* and *torus*—can be selected from the *Solids* toolbar shown in **Figure 38.50**. From the *Dashboard's Visual Style* control panel shown in **Figure 38.51**, solids can be created in five different styles depending on the result desired. The *Hide* command can be applied to a solid to convert it to a line drawing and remove its hidden lines. Now, let's draw solids.

Box (**Figure 38.52**): A box is drawn beginning with the base in the *x-y* plane of the current *UCS*. The dimensions of the box can be created with separate widths and depths, diagonal corners of the base, or as a cube by typing values at the keyboard or by selecting them with the cursor.

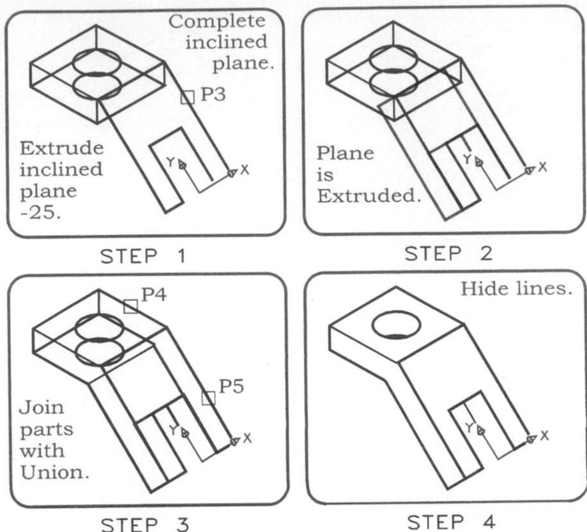

38.47 Part 4: Extrude the inclined surface.

Step 1 *Command:* Region (Enter) *Select object:* P3 (Enter) *Command:* Extrude (Enter)

Step 2 *Specify height of extrusion or [path]:* −25 (Enter)

Step 3 *Command:* Union (Enter) *Select object:* P4 *Select object:* P5 (Enter) The parts are joined.

Step 4 *Command:* Hide (Enter) Hidden lines are removed.

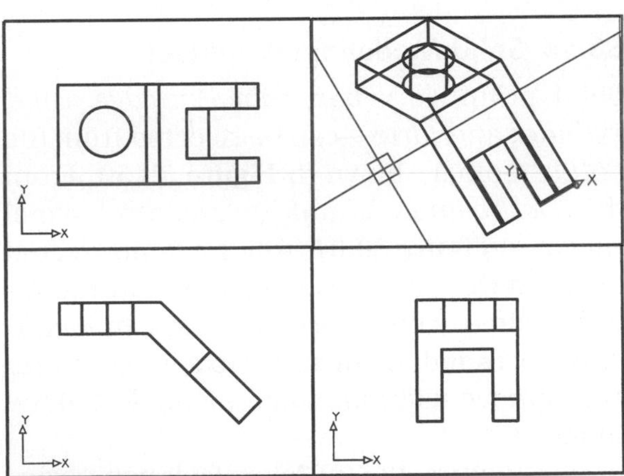

38.48 Part 5: Four equal views.

Select the *Layout1* tab (Enter) to obtain a single viewport in *Paper Space. Erase* the window. *Main Menu> View> Viewports> New Viewports>* Select *3D* under *Setup>* Select *Four: Equal* under viewports. Four viewports appear (top, front, side, and isometric views). The 3D view of the bracket appears in the upper right port along with its three principal orthographic views: top, front, and right-side views.

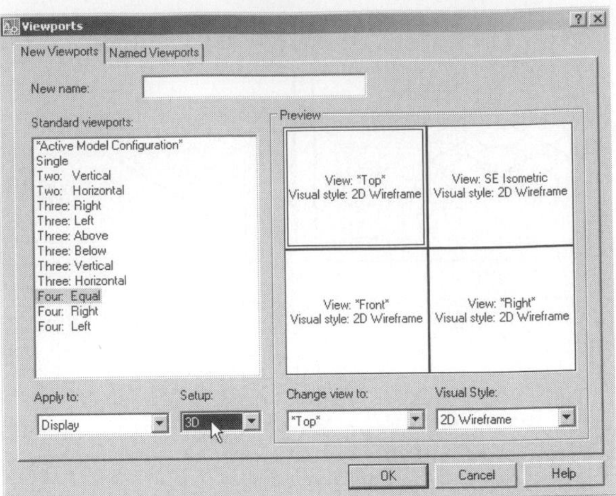

38.49 *Main Menu> View> Viewports> New viewports* to obtain this *Viewports* dialog box, select *Four Equal* windows as your viewports option, and select *3D* under *Setup.*

38.50 From the *Dashboard,* you can select *3D Solids* to draw.

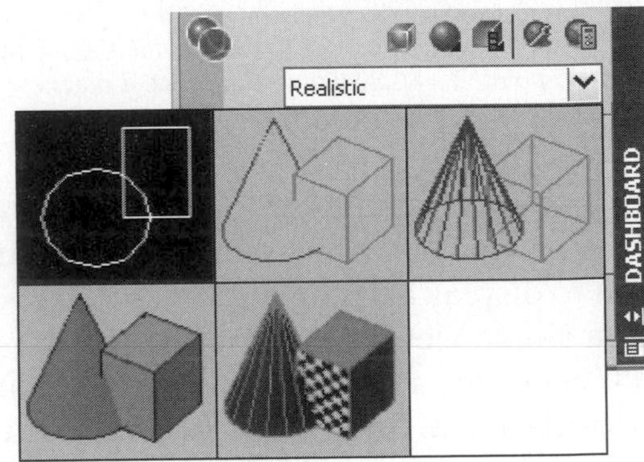

38.51 Visual Style Control Panel.

From the *Dashboard* the *Visual Style* can be selected from five options: *2D Wireframe, 3D Hidden, 3D Wireframe, Conceptual,* and *Realistic.* The *Hide* command can be applied to each of these styles as well.

Wedge (**Figure 38.53**): A wedge is drawn beginning with the base in the *x-y* plane of the current *UCS* with the upper plane sloping toward the second point selected. Prompts ask for the length, width, and height of the wedge.

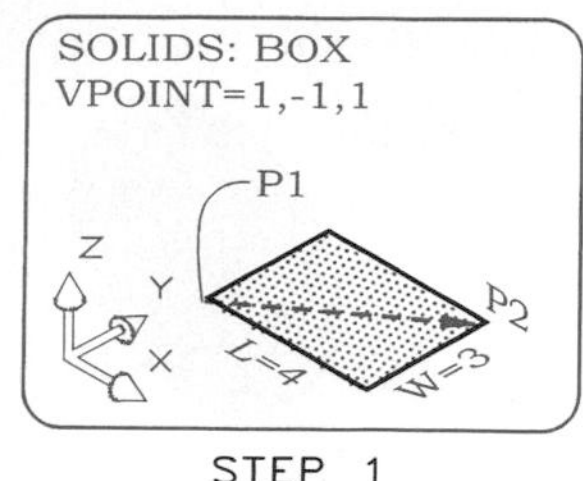

STEP 1

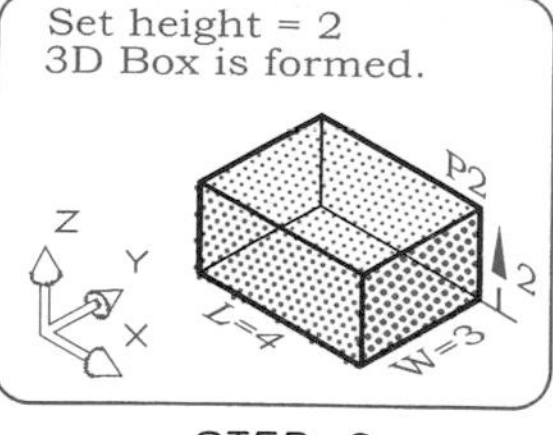

STEP 2

38.52 Solids: Box.

Step 1 *Command:* Box (Enter)
Specify corner of box or [Center] <0,0,0>: P1 (Enter)
Specify corner or [Cube/Length]: P2 (Enter)

Step 2 *Specify height:* 2 (Enter) If the *3D Wireframe* style was selected from the *Dashboard,* this is how the box would appear. Experiment with the *Conceptual* and *Realistic styles*.

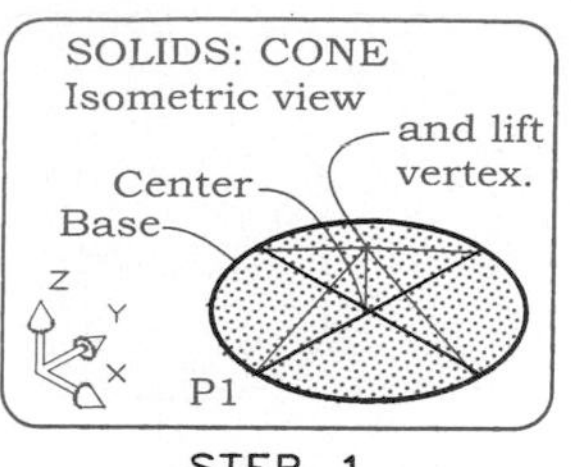

STEP 1

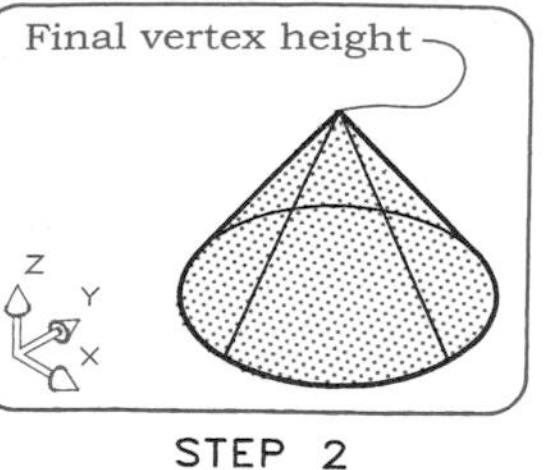

STEP 2

38.54 Solids: Cone.

Step 1 *Command:* Cone (Enter)
Specify center point for base of cone or [Elliptical]: <0,0,0>: Center (Enter)
Specify radius for base of cone or [Diameter]: P1 (Enter)

Step 2 *Specify height of cone or [Apex]:* 3 (Enter) Convert to the *Conceptual* style to suppress hidden lines.

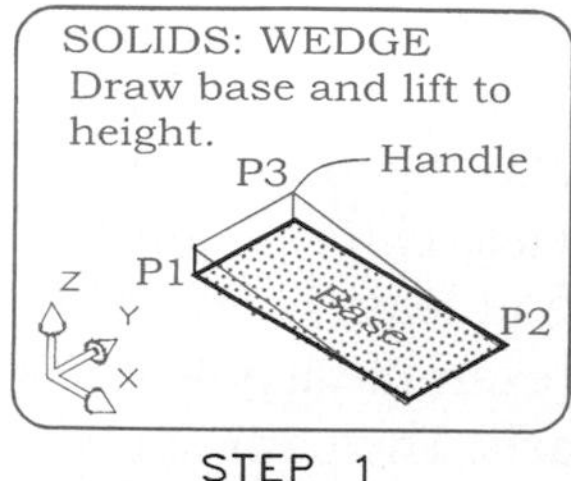

STEP 1

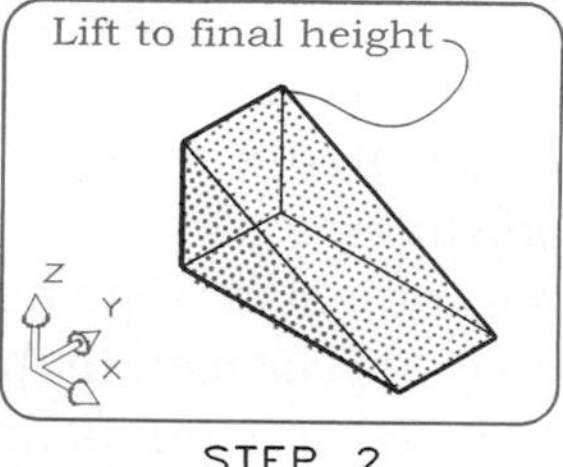

STEP 2

38.53 Solids: Wedge.

Step 1 *Command:* Wedge (Enter)
Specify first corner of wedge or [Center]<0,0,0>: P1 (Enter)
Specify corner or [Cube/Length]: P2 (Enter)

Step 2 *Specify height:* 2 (Enter) Shown as *3D Wireframe*. Try it as a *Realistic* style.

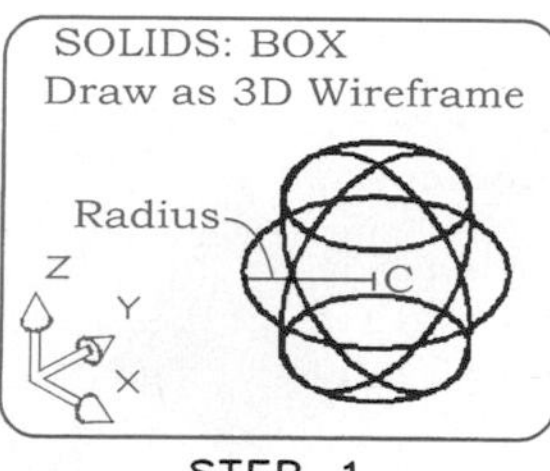

STEP 1

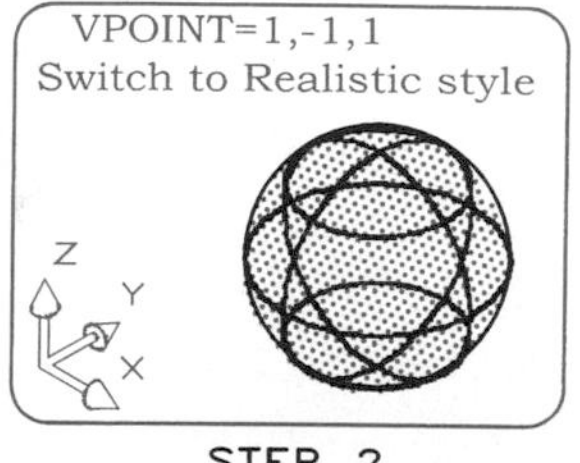

STEP 2

38.55 Solids: Sphere.

Step 1 *Command:* Sphere (Enter)
Specify center of sphere <0,0,0>: Center (Enter)
Specify radius of sphere or [Diameter]: 2 (Enter)

Step 2 *Command:* Vpoint (Enter)
Specify a viewpoint or [Rotate] <display compass and tripod>: 1,−1,1 (Enter) 3D view of the sphere is obtained.
Command: Hide (Enter) to suppress invisible lines.

Cone (**Figure 38.54**): A cone is drawn beginning with a circular or elliptical base in the *x-y* plane of the current *UCS*. This example illustrates a cone drawn with a circular base and its center, axis endpoints, and height specified when prompted.

Sphere (**Figure 38.55**): A sphere is drawn by drawing its equator in the *x-y* plane of the current *UCS* and responding to the prompts with the center and radius, or center and diameter. The axis of the sphere connecting its north and south poles is parallel to the *z*-axis of the current *UCS*, and its center is on the *x-y* plane of the *UCS*.

Cylinder (**Figure 38.56**): A cylinder is drawn by drawing its circular or elliptical base on the *x-y* plane of the current *UCS* and giving its height when prompted. The steps of drawing a cylinder with a circular base are given in this example.

Pyramid (**Figure 38.57**): A pyramid is drawn by locating the corners of the base on the *x-y* plane of the current *UCS* and specifying its height in either the plus or minus direction.

Torus (**Figure 38.58**): A torus (a donut) is drawn by giving its center, diameter or radius of the tube, and diameter or radius of

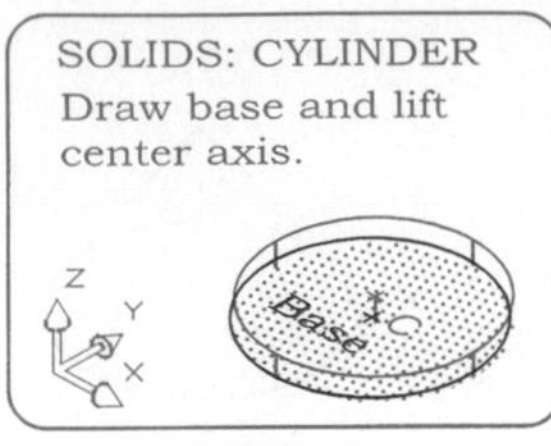

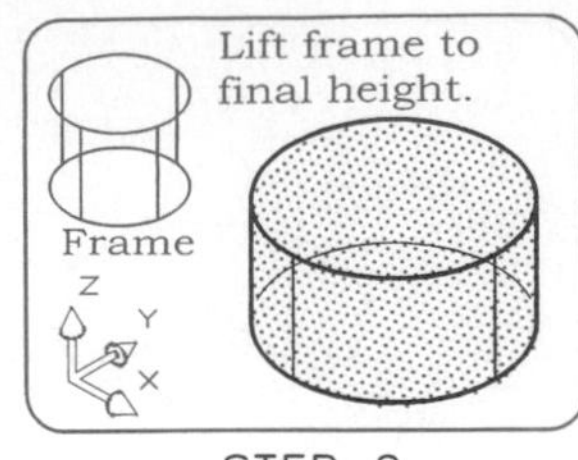

38.56 Solids: Cylinder.

Step 1 *Command:* Cylinder (Enter)
Specify center point for base of cylinder or [Elliptical]<0,0,0>: Center (Enter)
Specify radius for base of cylinder or [Diameter]: 2.5 (Enter)

Step 2 *Specify height of cylinder or [Center of]:* 3 (Enter) Remove hidden lines by converting to the *Conceptual* style.

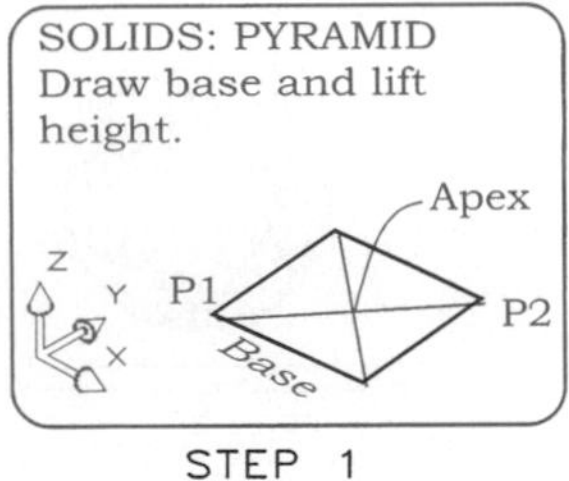

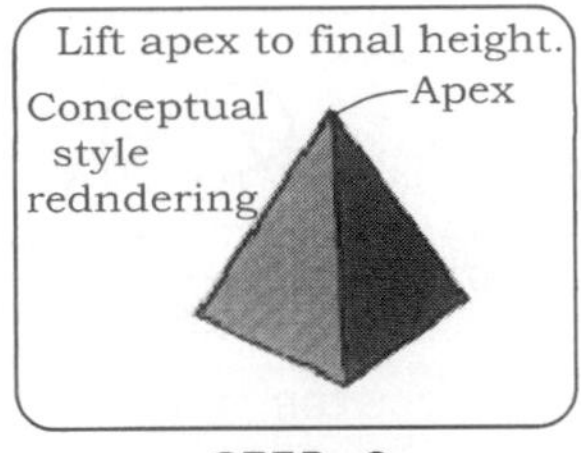

38.57 Solids: Pyramid

Step 1 *Command:* Pyramid (Enter) *Specify center point of base of [Edge/Sides]:* P1 (Enter)
Specify base radius or [Inscribed]: P2 (Enter)

Step 2 *Specify height or [2Point/ . . . Top radius]:* Drag apex to the desired height. (Shown as a *Conceptual* style drawing.)

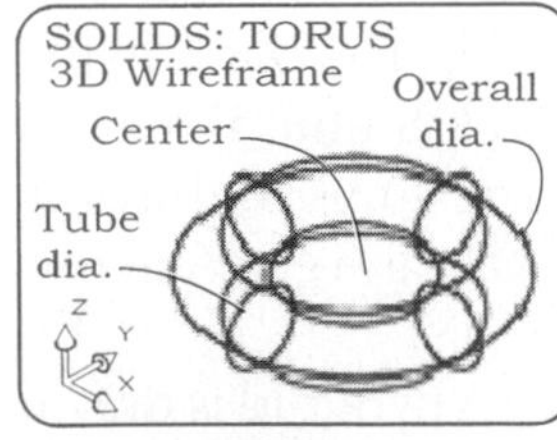

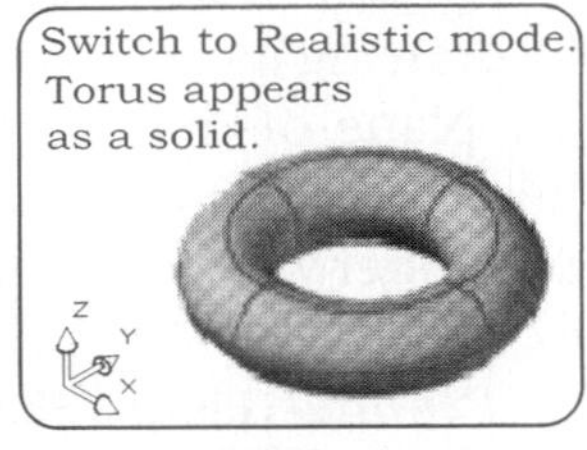

38.58 Solids: Torus.

Step 1 *Command:* Torus (Enter) *Specify center of torus <0,0,0>:* C (Enter)
Specify radius or [Diameter]: 6 (Enter)

Step 2 *Specify radius of tube or [Diameter]:* 2 (Enter)
The *Realistic* style is used to depict the final drawing.

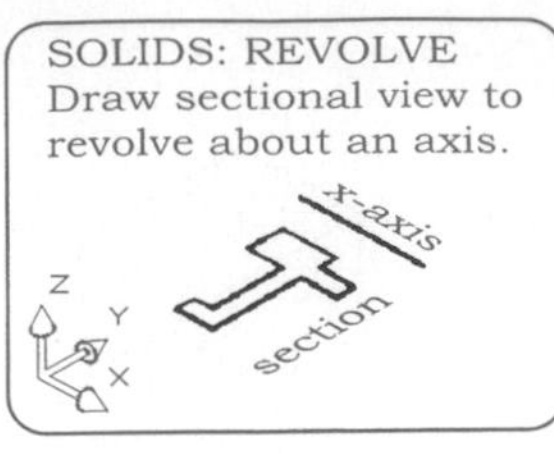

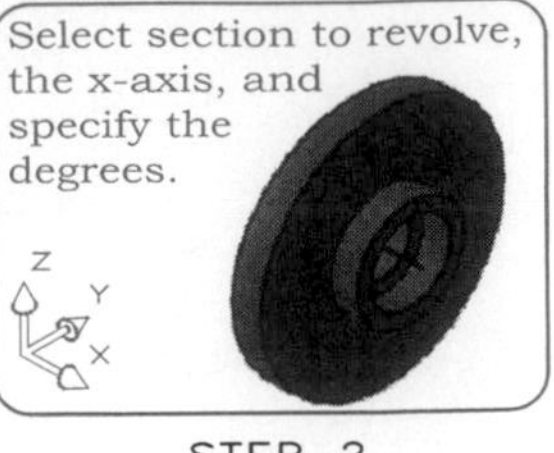

38.59 Solids: Revolve.

Step 1 *Command:* Revolve (Enter) Specify object to revolve: P1
Specify axis start point or define axis by [Object/X/Y/Z/]: Pick X axis.

Step 2 *Specify angle of revolution or [STart angle]:* 360 (Enter)
Disk is drawn using the *Conceptual* style.

revolution. The diameter of the torus will lie in the *x-y* plane of the current *UCS*.

Revolve (**Figure 38.59**): Cross sections of parts can be rotated about an axis in the *x-y* plane of the current *UCS*. Sections can be polylines, polygons, circles, ellipses, and 3D poly objects if they have at least 3, but fewer than 300 vertices. In this example, a polyline is revolved 360° about an axis. The path of revolution can start and end at any point between 0 and 360°. Polylines that have been *Fit* or *Splined* will require extensive computations by the computer when revolved.

Helix (**Figure 38.60**): The helix is the geometric figure that is applied to the formation

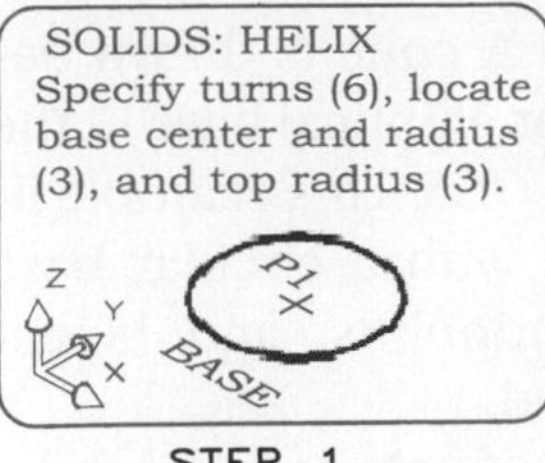

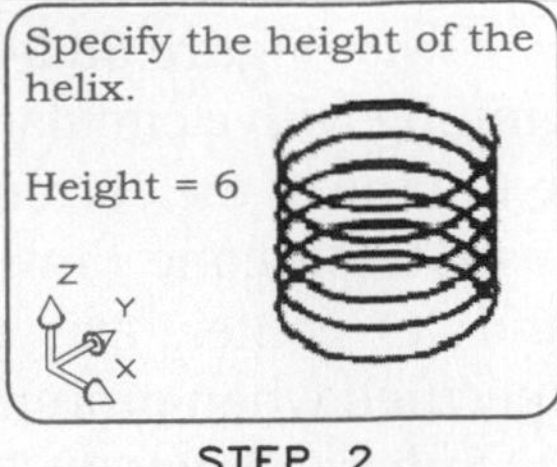

38.60 Solids: Helix.

Step 1 *Command:* Helix (Enter) *Number of turns:* 6 (Enter)
Specify center point of base: P1 (Enter)
Specify base radius or [Diameter]: 3 (Enter)
Specify top radius or [Diameter]: 3 (Enter)
Specify helix height or [Axis . . . /Turns/ . . . tWist]: T *(Enter)*
Enter number of turns: 6 (Enter)

Step 2 *Specify helix height or [Axis endpoint/ . . . / tWist]:* 6 *(Enter)* (7 is the height of the helix.)

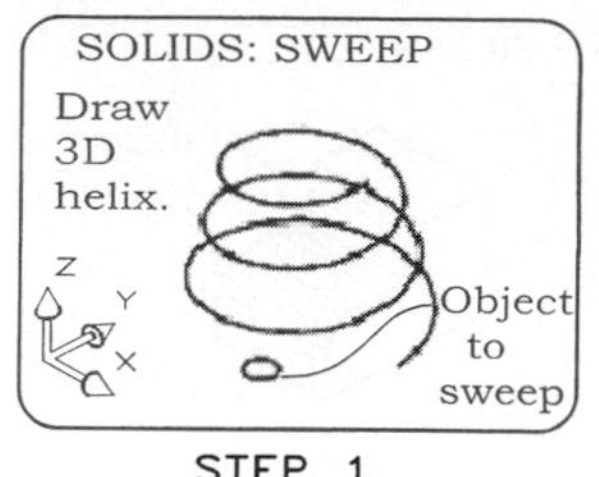
SOLIDS: SWEEP
Draw 3D helix.
Object to sweep
STEP 1

Command: SWEEP
Select object to sweep and select sweep path.
STEP 2

38.61 Solids: Sweep.

Step 1 Draw the helix as shown in **Figure 38.60**, except this helix is tapered with unequal bases. Draw the circular cross section to be applied to the coil.

Step 2 Select *Sweep* from the *Dashboard. Command: Sweep* (Enter) *Select objects to sweep:* Pick the circular cross section. *Select sweep path:* Pick the helix. The cross section is applied to the coil in the *Conceptual* style.

of springs. The first circle of the helix is drawn in the *x-y* plane of the current *UCS.* In this example, the diameters of both ends are equal, but this command can be used to draw tapered helixes with unequal end diameters as well.

Sweep (**Figure 38.61**): Helixes can be made more realistic by giving the coils a circular or rectangular cross section with the *Sweep* command. The section is drawn in the *x-y* plane of the current *UCS.*

38.15 Editing Solids

Once drawn, *Solids* have a number of editing options that can be used to edit them. The most basic and often-used ones are *Subtract, Union, Explode, Chamfer, Fillet, Extend,* and *Trim.* These tools can be accessed from the *Solids Editing* toolbar (**Figure 38.62**).

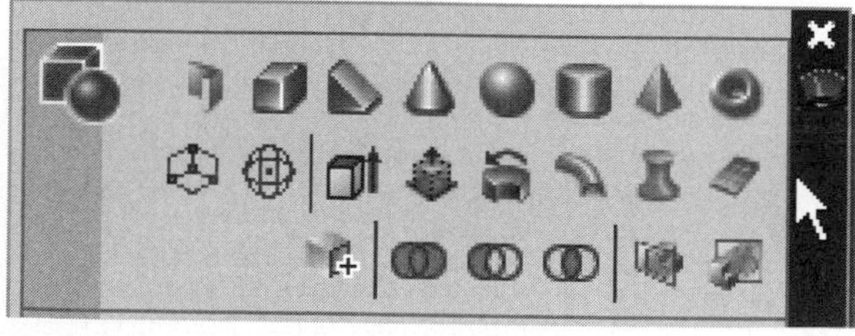

38.62 Several of the *Solids* editing commands can be picked from the *Dashboard*. By resting the cursor on an icon, its name wil be displayed on a flyout.

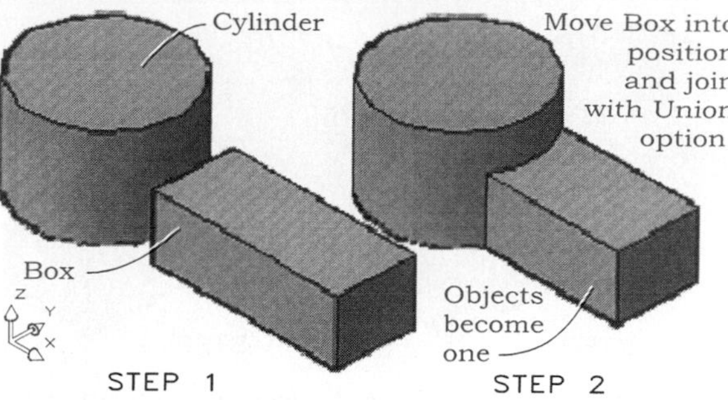
SOLIDS IN COMBINATION: UNION
Cylinder
Move Box into position and join with Union option.
Box
Objects become one
STEP 1
STEP 2

38.63 Union: Joining solids.

Step 1 From the *Dashboard,* select *Cylinder*, and follow the prompts to construct the cylinder. Draw the *Box* in the same manner.

Step 2 Position the *Box* to intersect the *Cylinder* and use the *Union* command to select the two objects and merge them into a single solid.

Union is used to join intersecting solids to form a single composite solid model. **Figure 38.63** shows how a *Box* and a *Cylinder* are unified into a single solid.

Subtract is used to remove one intersecting solid from another as illustrated in **Figures 38.64** and **38.65**.

Interfere is used to obtain a solid that is common to two intersecting solids. An interference solid is found with this command in **Figure 38.66**.

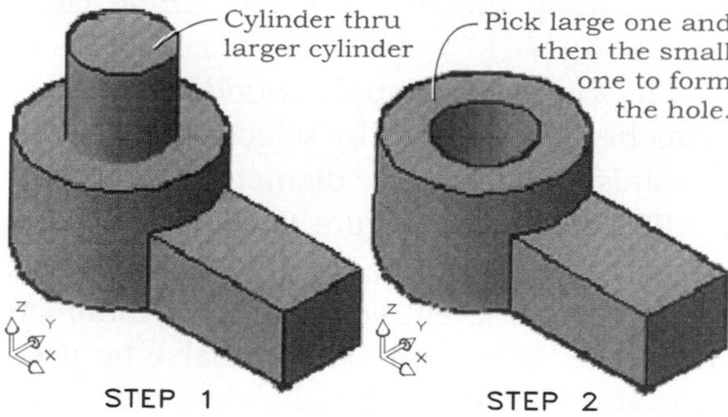
SOLIDS IN COMBINATION: SUBTRACTION
Cylinder thru larger cylinder
Pick large one and then the small one to form the hole.
STEP 1
STEP 2

38.64 Subtract.
Step 1 Draw a cylinder representing the hole inside the larger cylinder with the *Cylinder* command from the *Dashboard*.
Step 2 Use the *Subtract* command from the *Dashboard* to remove the small cylinder making the hole.

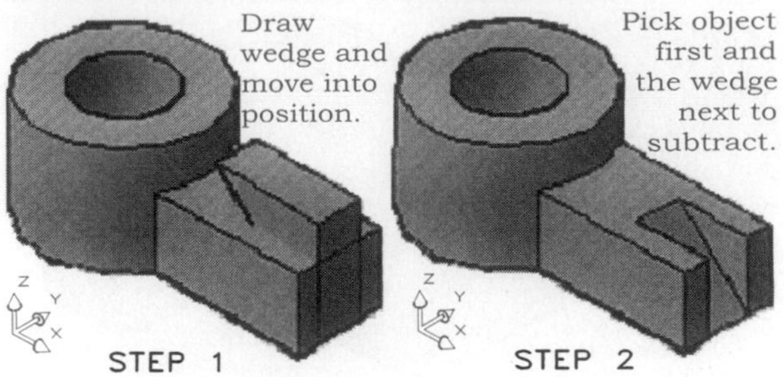

38.65 The last feature of the part is formed by subtracting the *Wedge* from the *Box* to form the sloping surface.

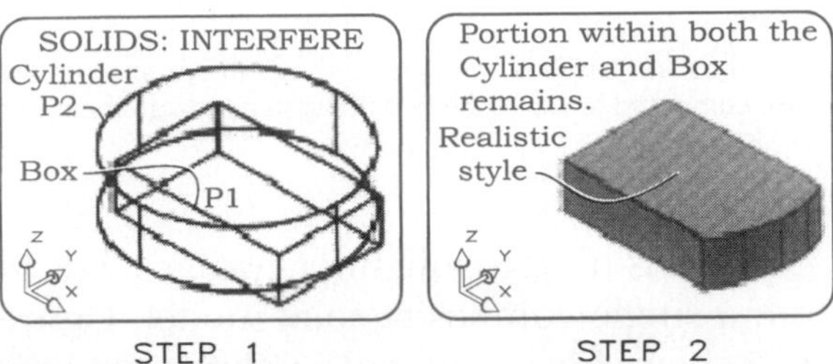

38.66 Solids: Interfere.

Step 1 *Command:* Interfere (Enter)
Select first set of solids: Select objects: P1 (Enter)
Select second set of solids:

Step 2 *Select objects:* P2 (Enter)
Create interference solids? <N>: Yes (Enter) The interference solid is created.

Explode is used to separate solids or regions that were combined by the *Subtract* and *Union* commands to permit editing or correcting before redoing the *Subtract* and *Union* commands.

Fillet is used to apply rounded intersections between planes by selecting the edges of solids and giving the diameter or radius of the fillet as shown in **Figure 38.67**. The *mUltiple* option of *Fillet* can be used for applying the same radius to several edges using the same settings. The *Fillet* command can also be used to round the edges of cylindrical or curved objects.

Chamfer is used to apply beveled edges by selecting the base surface, the adjoining surface, and the edges to be chamfered, giving

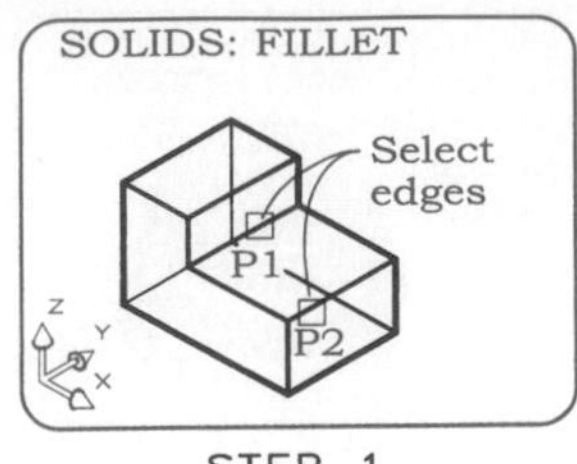

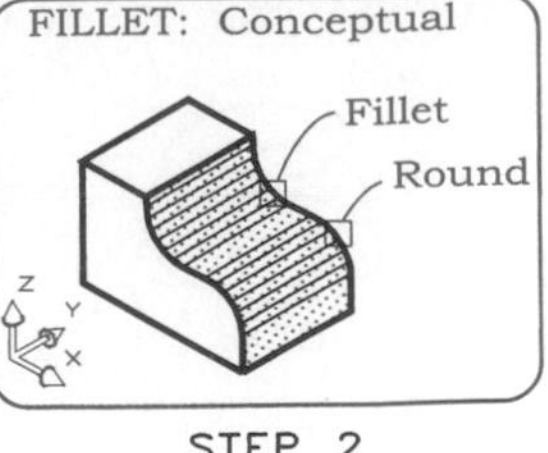

38.67 Solids: Fillet.

Step 1 *Command:* Fillet (Enter) > *Select first object or [Polyline/Radius/Trim/mUltiple]:* R > *Enter fillet radius <0>:* .50 (Enter)
Select an edge or [Chain/Radius]: P1,
1 edge(s) selected for fillet. (Enter)

Step 2 The *Fillet* is drawn. Repeat these commands; select P2 for drawing the *round*.

the first and second chamfer distances (**Figure 38.68**). When these prompts have been satisfied, the chamfers are automatically drawn.

Sweep is a form of the *Extrusion* command in that it forms a solid or a hollow form by "sweeping" a region along a 3D path. An application of *Sweep* is shown in **Figure 38.69**, where a hollow pipe is formed and rendered in the conceptual style.

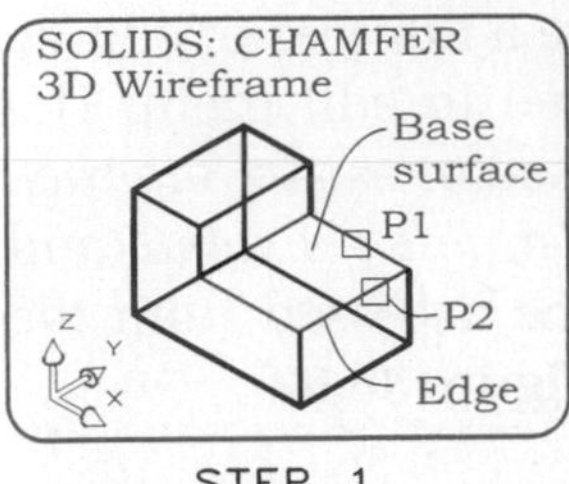

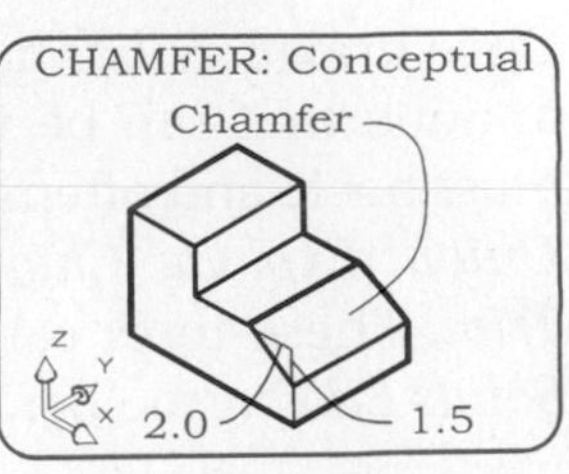

38.68 Solids: Chamfer.

Step 1 *Command:* Chamfer (Enter) > *Select first line or [Polyline/ . . . /mUltiple]:* P1
Base surface selections . . . Enter surface selection option [Next/OK (current)] <OK>: Next (Enter) to activate upper plane of object.
Base surface selection . . . Enter surface selection option [Next/OK (current)] <OK>: OK (Enter) to accept top plane as base.
Specify base surface chamfer dist. <1.000>: 2.0 (Enter)
Specify other surface chamfer dist. <1.000>: 1.5 (Enter)
Select an edge or [Loop]: P2

Step 2 The *Chamfer* is drawn.

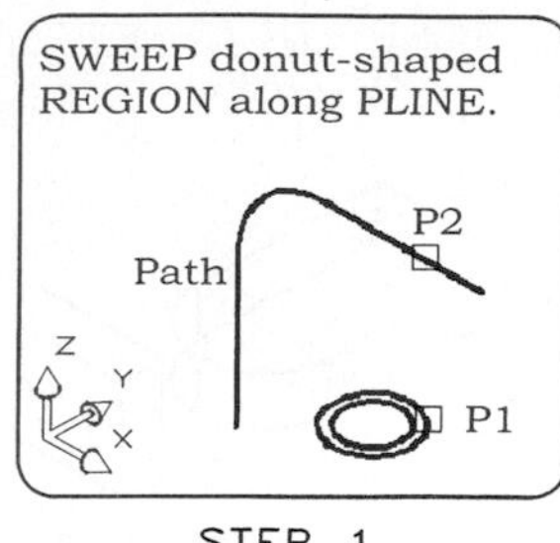

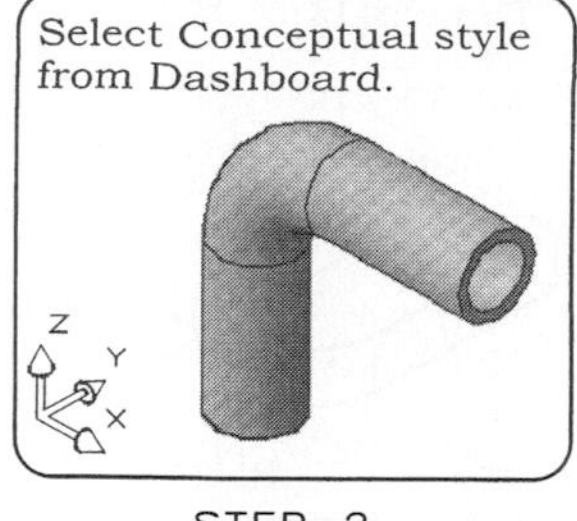

38.69 Sweep.

Step 1 Draw the pipe's section in the plane of the *x-y* UCS. *Command:* Sweep (Enter) *Select objects to sweep:* P1 (Enter) *Select sweep path or [Alignment/Base point/Scale/Twist]:*. P2

Step 2 Select the *Conceptual* style from the *Visual Style control panel* of the *Dashboard* to render the pipe.

38.16 Solids: Sections

Section is used to pass a cutting plane through a 3D solid to show a *Region* that outlines its internal features. *Bhatch* (hatch pattern) can be used to assign the hatching pattern to the *Region* if it lies in the plane of the *UCS*. In **Figure 38.70**, the hatch pattern is set to ANSI31, a symbol used for representing cast iron or general applications.

The *UCS* icon is placed on the object to establish the plane of the section, Section is typed, the first point is selected, and the section plane appears. The section plane can be moved as shown in this example. Other sections through the object are found in this same manner by positioning the icon in the cutting plane or by selecting from one of the following options: *3point, Object, Zaxis, View, XY, YZ,* or *ZX*.

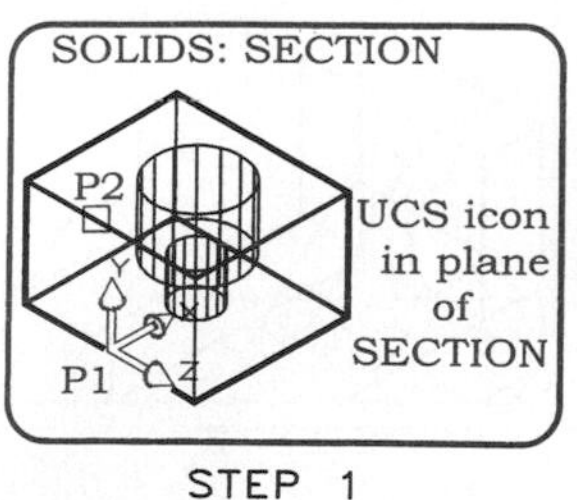

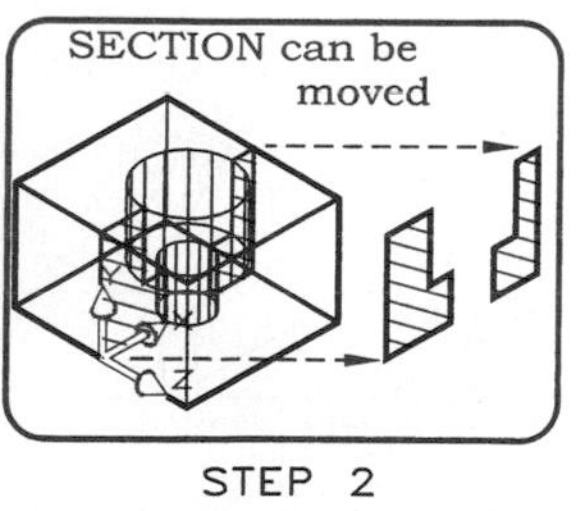

38.70 Solids: Section.

Step 1 Position the *UCS* in the plane of the section. *Command:* Section (Enter) *Select objects:* P1 *Specify the first point on Section plane by [Object/ . . . / XY/YZ/ZX/3points]:* XY (Enter) *Specify a point on the XY plane <0,0,0>:* P2 This section establishes a *Region* in the plane of the *UCS* icon.

Step 2 *Command:* Move (Enter) *Move* the *Region* outside the part; apply section lines to it if you like.

38.17 Slice

With the *Slice* command, an object can be cut through and made into separate parts, either or both of which can be retained as shown in **Figure 38.71**. The *Slice* command has the following options:

3points defines three points on the slice plane.

Object aligns the cutting plane with a circle, ellipse, 2D spline, or 2D polyline element.

Zaxis defines a plane when an origin point on the *z*-axis is picked that is perpendicular to the selected points.

View makes the cutting plane parallel with the viewport's viewing plane when a single point is selected.

XY, YZ, or *ZX* aligns the cutting plane with the planes of the *UCS* when only one point is selected.

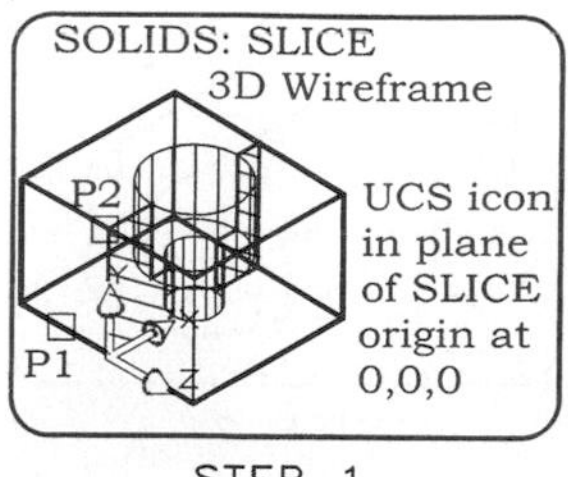

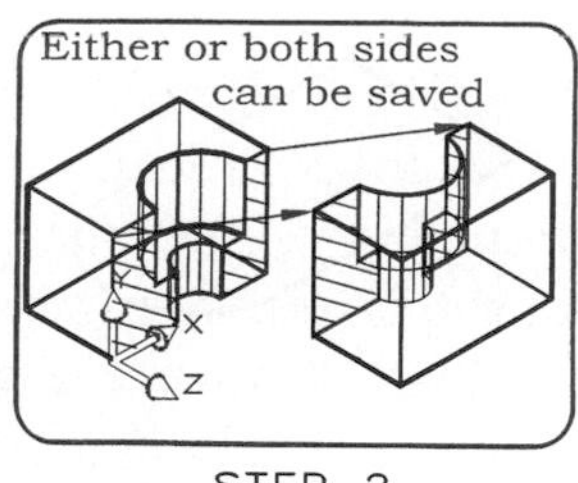

38.71 Solids: Slice.

Step 1 Move the *UCS* to the desired plane of the *Slice*. *Command* line: Slice (Enter) *Select objects:* P1 *Specify first point on slicing plane by [planar Object/ . . . ZX/3 points]:* XY (Enter) > *Specify a point on the XY-plane <0,0,0>:* P2

Step 2 *Specify a point on the desired side of the plane or [keep Both sides]:* Both (Enter) Halves can be moved apart and hatched.

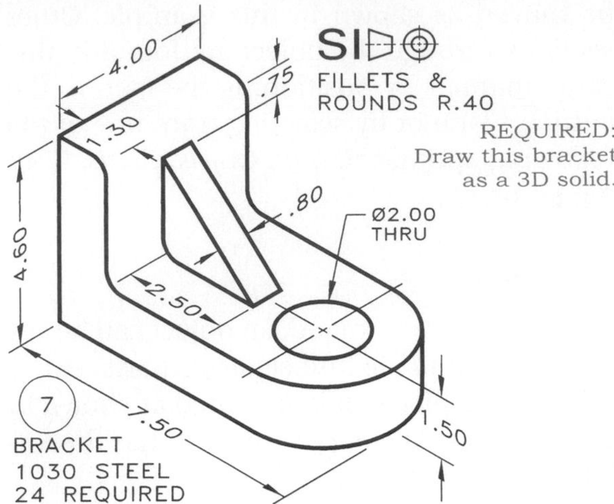
SI
FILLETS &
ROUNDS R.40
REQUIRED:
Draw this bracket
as a 3D solid.
4.00
.75
1.30
.80
Ø2.00
THRU
4.60
2.50
7
7.50
1.50
BRACKET
1030 STEEL
24 REQUIRED

38.72 This bracket is drawn in the following steps as an example of 3D solid construction.

38.18 A Solid Model Example

The bracket shown in **Figure 38.72** is to be drawn as a solid model by using the commands from the *Solids* toolbar.

Part 1 (Figure 38.73): Create the outline of the base with a *Polyline* and obtain an isometric view of it by *Command: Vpoint* (Enter) 1 − 1,1. Type Extrude and specify an extrusion height of 1.50 units.

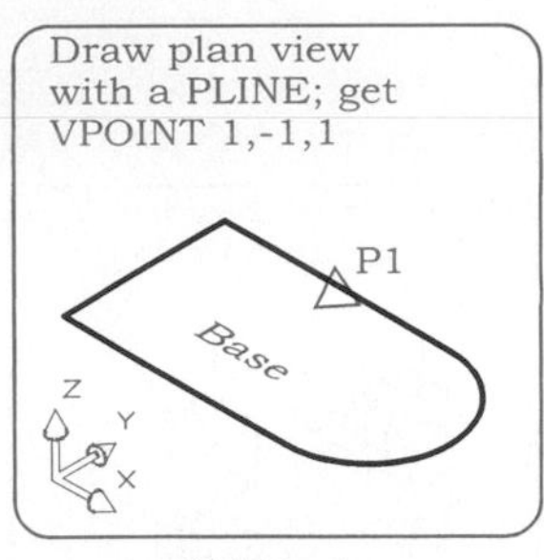
Draw plan view
with a PLINE; get
VPOINT 1,-1,1
P1
Base
STEP 1

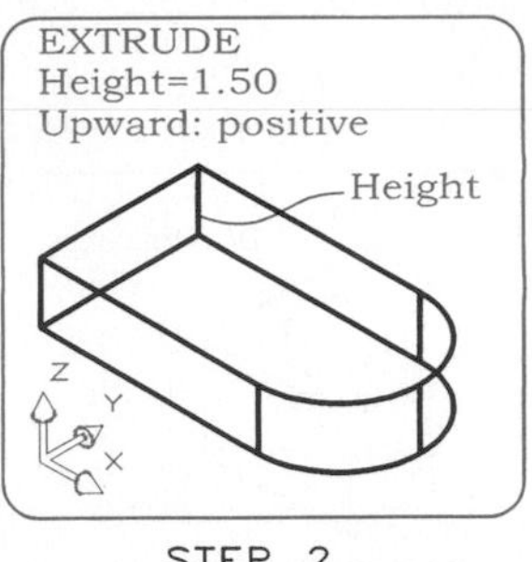
EXTRUDE
Height=1.50
Upward: positive
Height
STEP 2

38.73 Solids—Part 1: Extrude base.

Step 1 Draw the base with a closed *Polyline. Command:* Vpoint (Enter)
Specify a view point or [Rotate] <display compass and tripod>: 1,−1,1 (Enter) Get isometric view of the base.
Command line: Extrude (Enter) *Select objects:* P1

Step 2 *Specify height of extrusion or [Path]:* 1.50 (Enter)
Specify angle of taper for extrusion <0>: (Enter)
The base is extruded 1.50 in. in the positive *y*-direction.

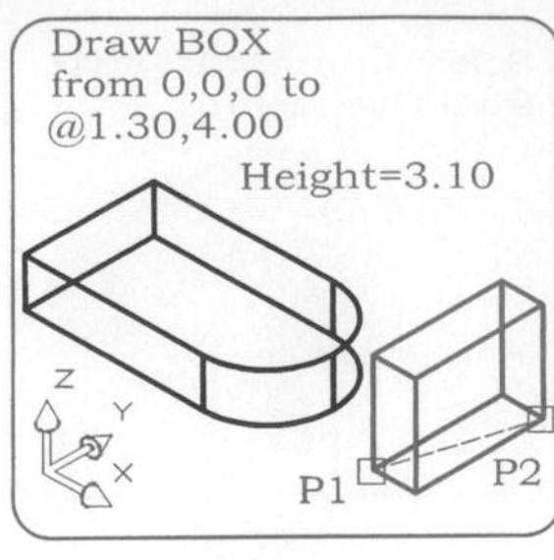
Draw BOX
from 0,0,0 to
@1.30,4.00
Height=3.10
P1
P2
STEP 1

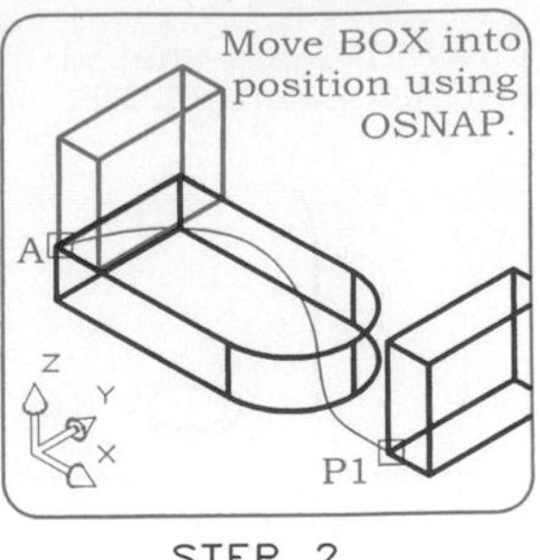
Move BOX into
position using
OSNAP.
A
P1
STEP 2

38.74 Solids—Part 2: Draw box.

Step 1 *Command* line: Box (Enter)
Specify corner of box or [Center]: P1 (Enter)
Specify corner or [Cube/Length]: @1.30,4.00 (Enter)
Specify height: 3.1 (Enter) The box is drawn.

Step 2 Set *Osnap* to *End. Command* line: Move (Enter)
Select objects: Pick box.
Specify base point or displacement: P1 (Enter)
Second point of displacement: A (Enter) The box is moved.

Part 2 (Figure 38.74): A *Box* of 1.30 × 4.00 × 3.10 is drawn. *Snap* to P1 on the box, and drag it to the *Endpoint* at A.

Part 3 (Figure 38.75): Use the *Wedge* command to draw the bracket's rib. *Move* the rib to join the base and the upright box by using the *Midpoint* option of *Osnap.*

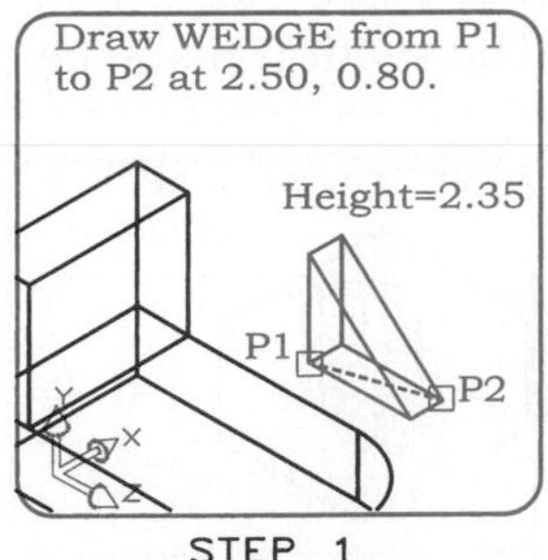
Draw WEDGE from P1
to P2 at 2.50, 0.80.
Height=2.35
P1
P2
STEP 1

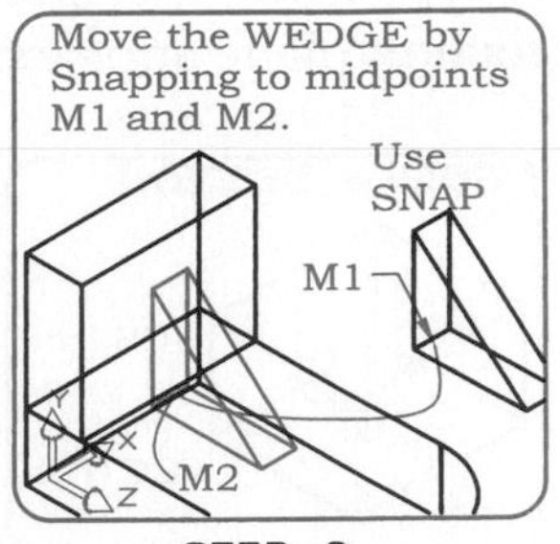
Move the WEDGE by
Snapping to midpoints
M1 and M2.
Use
SNAP
M1
M2
STEP 2

38.75 Solids—Part 3: Draw the wedge.

Step 1 *Command:* Wedge (Enter)
Specify first corner of wedge or [Center]: P1
Specify corner or [Cube/Length]: @2.50,0.80 (Enter)
Specify height: 2.35 The wedge is drawn.

Step 2 Set *Osnap* to *Midpoint> Command:* Move (Enter)
Select objects: Pick wedge.
Specify base point or displacement: M1
Specify second point or displacement or <use first point as displacement>: M2 (Enter) The wedge is moved to the base.

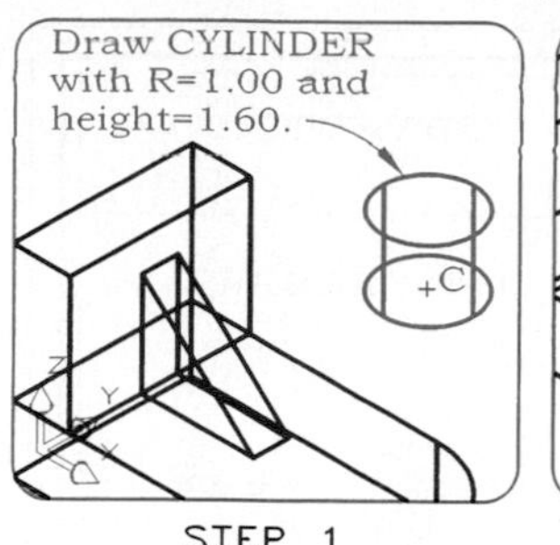

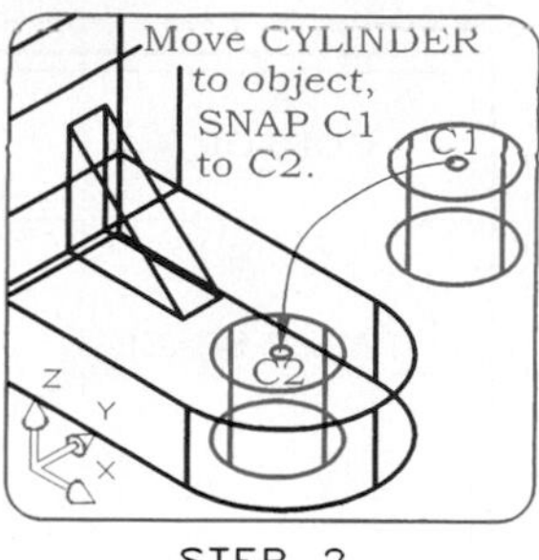

38.76 Solids—Part 4: Draw the cylinder.

Step 1 *Command:* Cylinder (Enter)
Specify center point for base of cylinder or [Elliptical] <0,0,0>: C
Specify radius for base of cylinder or [Diameter]: 1.00 (Enter)
Specify height for base of cylinder or [Center of other end]: 1.60 (Enter) The cylinder is drawn.

Step 2 Set *Osnap* to *Center. Command* line: Move (Enter)
Select objects: Pick cylinder.
Specify base point or displacement: C1
Specify second point of displacement: C2. The hole is placed.

Part 4 (Figure 38.76): Draw a *Cylinder* to represent the hole and *Move* it to the center of the semicircular end of the base using the *Center* option of *Osnap.*

Part 5 (Figure 38.77): Use *Subtract* to create the hole in the base. Use the *Union* command to join the base, upright box, and wedge together into a composite solid.

Part 6 (Figure 38.78): *Fillet* is used to select the edges to be rounded with a radius of .40.

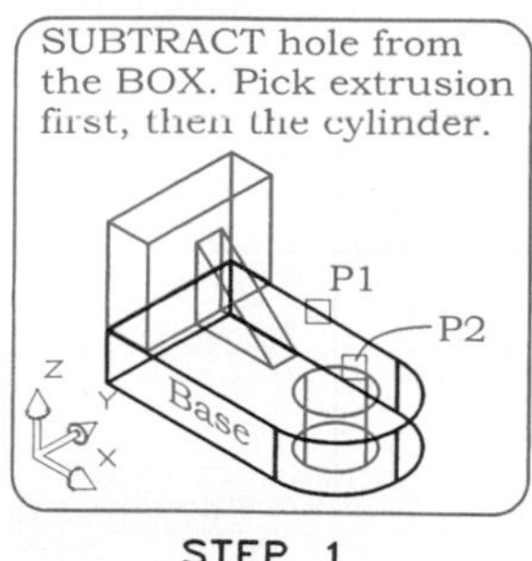

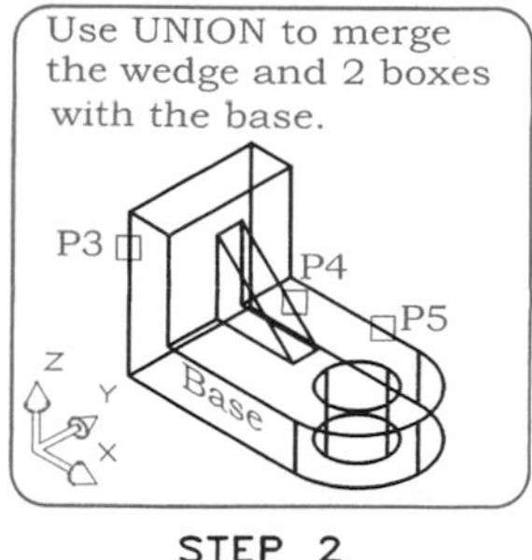

38.77 Solids—Part 5: Subtract and Union.

Step 1 *Command:* Subtract (Enter) *Select solids and regions to subtract from . . . Select objects:* P1 (Enter)
Select objects: P2 (Enter) Hole is subtracted from base.

Step 2 *Command:* Union (Enter)
Select objects: P3, P4, P5 (Enter) *Select objects:* (Enter)
The bracket is unified into one solid.

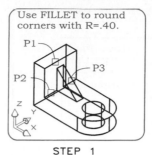

Use FILLET to round
corners with R=.40.
P1
P2
P3
STEP 1

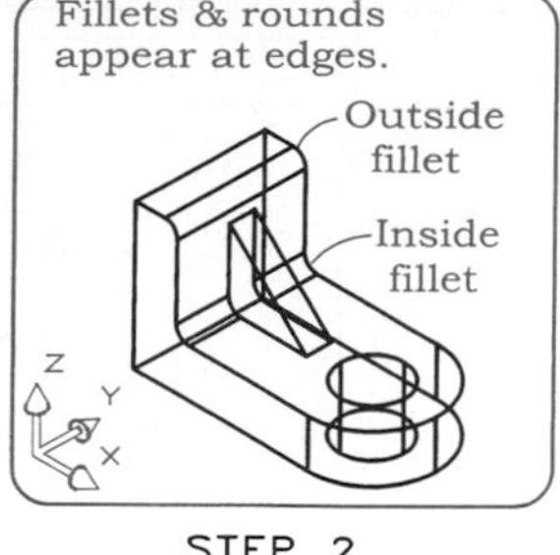

38.78 Solids—Part 6: Fillets.

Step 1 *Command:* Fillet (Enter) (*Trim* mode)
Select first object or [Polyline/Radius/Trim]<Select first object>: P1 *Enter fillet radius:.* .40 (Enter)

Step 2 *Command:* Fillet (Enter)
Select an edge or [Chain/Radius]: P2
Select an edge or [Chain/Radius]: P3
Select an edge or [Chain/Radius]: P4
Select an edge or [Chain/Radius]: P5 (Enter)

Part 7 (Figure 38.79): Use the *Hide* command to suppress the invisible lines

An infinite number of views of the bracket can be obtained with *Vpoint* or *Dview.*

38.19 Three-View Drawing

A drawing composed of three orthographic views (top, front, and side) with an isometric view is a classic arrangement of an engineering drawing suitable for depicting most parts. This layout can be obtained by drawing an

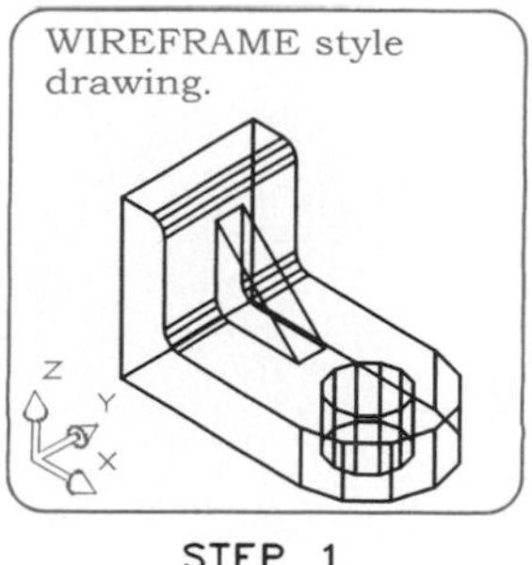

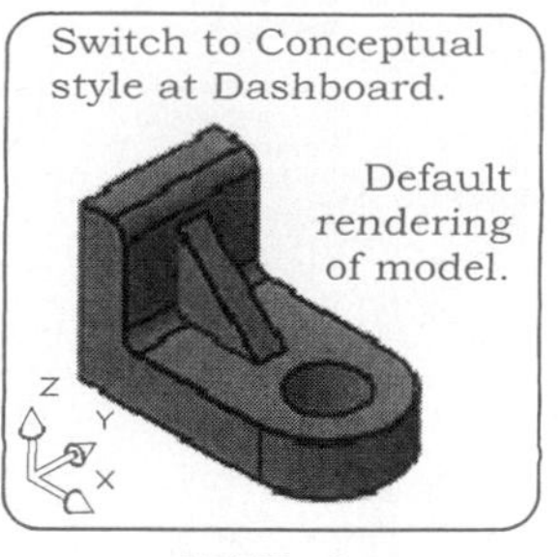

38.79 Solids—Part 7: Conceptual style.

Step 1 From the *Dashboard* convert the solid to the *Conceptual* style.

Step 2 The hidden lines are suppressed, and the bracket becomes a realistic-appearing solid.

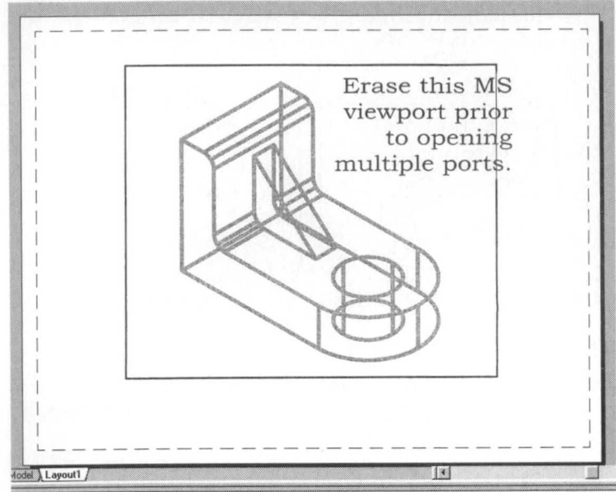

38.80 A single *Model Space* viewport is opened in the *Paper Space (Layout1* tab*)* showing the isometric view of the bracket that was originally drawn in *Model Space*. Erase this *MS* viewport.

object in *Model Space,* as the bracket in **Figure 38.72** was drawn in the previous examples.

Select the *Layout1* tab at the bottom of the screen to open a dialog box. A single viewport in *Paper Space* is displayed that shows the bracket (**Figure 38.80**). Once the single view window is displayed, erase it. Use the steps outlined in **Figure 38.81** to insert a title block into *Paper Space* as shown in **Figure 38.82**.

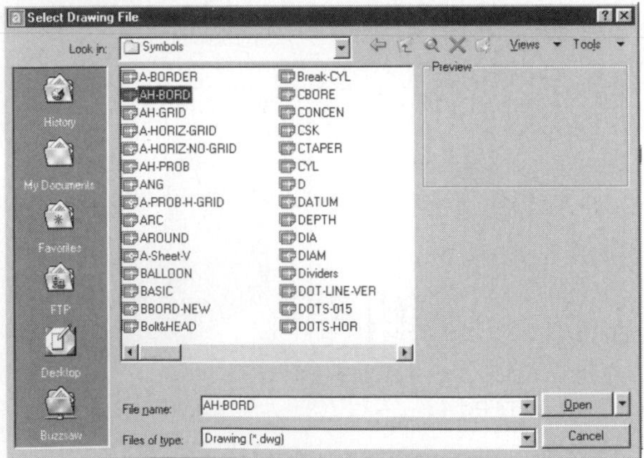

38.81 Use *Main Menu> Insert> Block> Browse>* select ABORD-HOR and insert it into *Paper Space (Layout1* tab*)*. This previously saved title block establishes the full-size border and the drawing area.

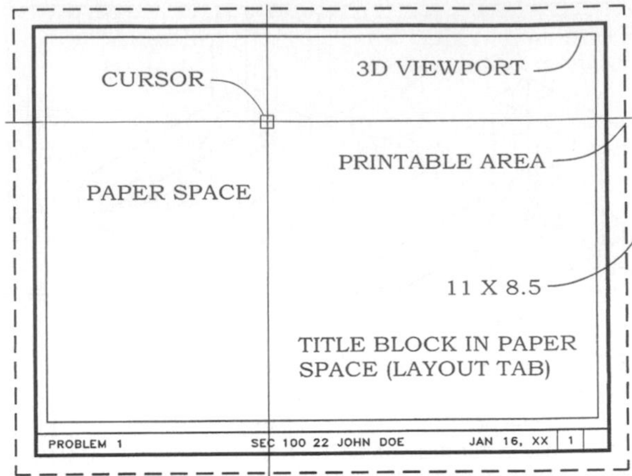

38.82 The title block is in *Paper Space (Layout1* tab*)*, and no viewports are defined in *Model Space* at this point.

Specify four 3D viewports following the steps given in **Figure 38.83**. The four *Model Space* viewports will appear within the *Paper Space* of the *Layout1* tab as illustrated in **Figure 38.84**, but the views of the bracket may not be displayed at a uniform scale. Double click on a viewport (*UCS* icons will appear) to enter the *Model Space* of that viewport, where

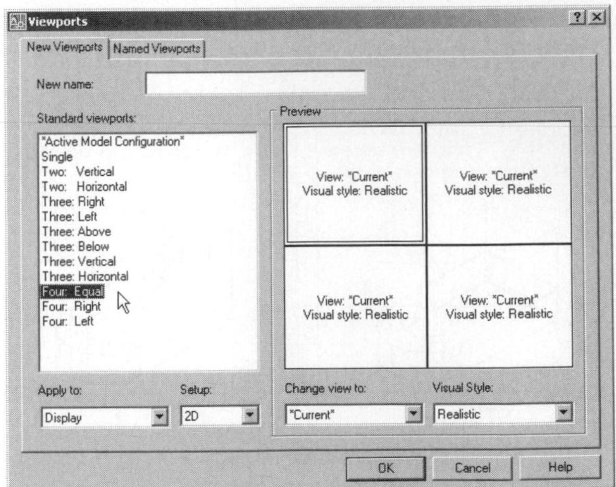

38.83 *Use Main Menu> View> Viewports> New Viewports> Four: Equal* and select *3D* under *Setup* to obtain this *Preview* of the four 3D viewports. Select *OK* and specify the diagonal of the window into which the four viewports are to fit within the border.

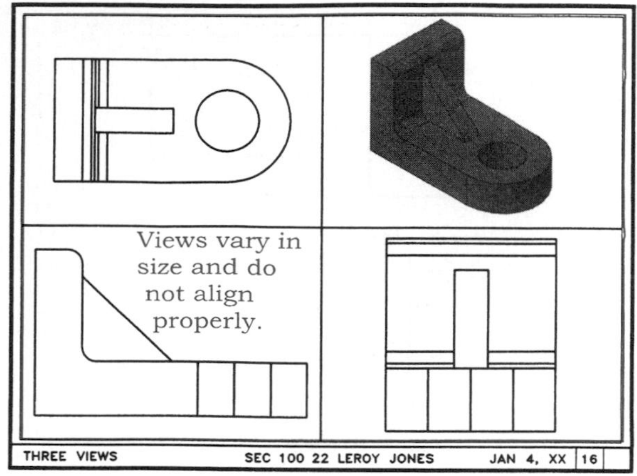

38.84 Four *Model Space* viewports appear in the *Paper Space (Layout1* tab) window when its area is defined by diagonal corners.

you can use a *Zoom* factor to size that view of the bracket (*Zoom* .5XP, for example). Select the other viewports by double clicking on them, and assigning the same *Zoom* factor to them to size them uniformly (**Figure 38.85**).

If the views need to be aligned vertically and/or horizontally, enter *Paper Space* and draw a horizontal and vertical line that can be used to align the top, front, and side views.

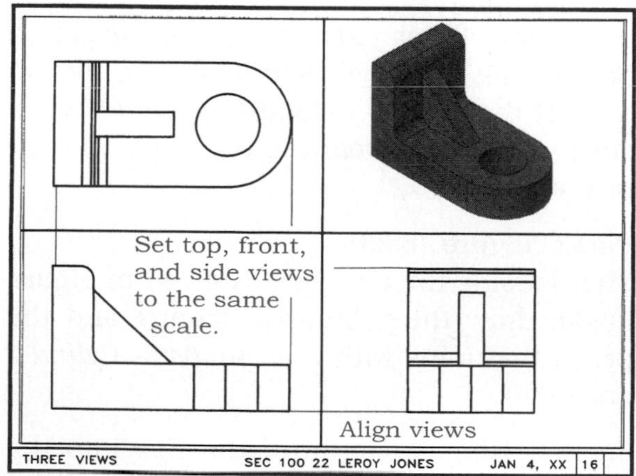

38.85 Size each view with the same *Zoom* factor. For example, use *Zoom* nXP (.5XP—half size, perhaps) to match the views orthographically in size.

Enter *Model Space* and align the views in each port with the alignment lines as shown in **Figure 38.85**.

Double click on a *Paper Space* area (the title block) to return to *Paper Space,* and the triangular icon reappears. A plot can be made from *Paper Space* that will show the four viewports, but the outlines of the viewports will plot, and hidden lines will plot as solid lines.

To remove the viewport outlines, create a new layer by selecting the viewport outlines from *Paper Space* and *Change* them to the new layer. *Freeze* the new layer at plot time, and the outlines will not be plotted.

The hidden lines can be suppressed if you double click in a viewport to enter its *Model Space* and *Command:* Hide. Repeat these steps for each viewport. Double click on a *Paper Space* area or select the *Paper* button in the *Status* line, and the four viewports can be plotted as a set, as displayed.

However, it is preferable to show invisible lines as dashed lines rather than omit them. *Main Menu> Draw> Modeling> Setup> Profile* (**Figure 38.86**) and click on the front view of the bracket in *Model Space* (Enter) to get the following prompts:

Display hidden profile lines on separate layer? <Y>: (Enter)

Project profile lines onto a plane? <Y>: (Enter)

Delete tangential edges? <Y>: (Enter)

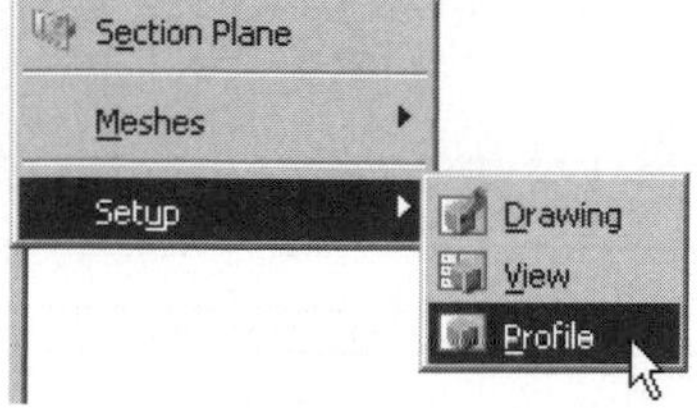

38.86 *Main Menu> Draw> Modeling> Setup> Profile* and profile planes will be created and placed in front of the 3D views.

When each viewport with hidden lines has been manipulated in this manner, two profile planes, one representing the hidden lines (*PH-43, Profile Hidden*) and the other representing visible lines (*PV-43, Profile Visible*), are created. Two 2D views are placed in front of the 3D solid. Therefore, it is necessary to *Freeze* the 3D solid in each view, leaving only the two newly created profiles. Select *Main Menu> Format> Layer> Layer Properties Manager*, pick the layer whose name begins with "PH" *(Profile Hidden)*, and *Change* its *Linetype* to *Hidden* to assign hidden-line symbols to the lines drawn on this layer.

Double click on a *Paper Space* area to return to *Paper Space;* turn off the *Layer* on which the solid model was drawn to leave only the profile planes, *PH* and *PV*, turned on to represent the views of the bracket. The variable *Dispsilh* (Display Silhouette Hidden) can be used to display the silhouette (outline) of features of the isometric view and omit its unnecessary hidden lines or meshes. *Command:* Dispsilh (Enter) 1 (Enter) to set *On. Command:* Hide so the hidden lines appear as dashed lines, and the visible lines appear as solid lines (**Figure 38.87**).

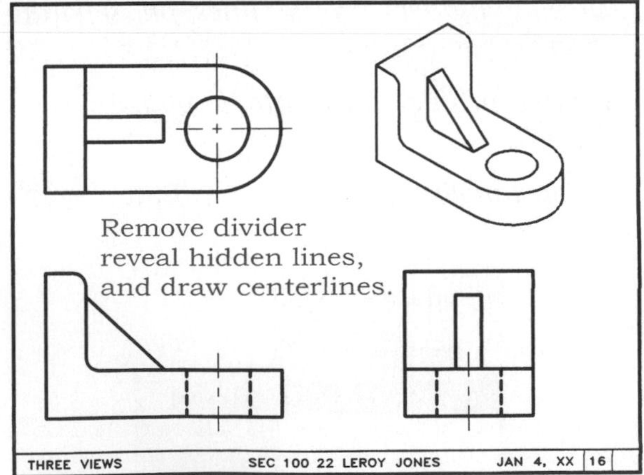

38.87 The viewport outlines can be removed and hidden lines generated by the *Setup Profile* command to make the layout and the views appear in the standard format.

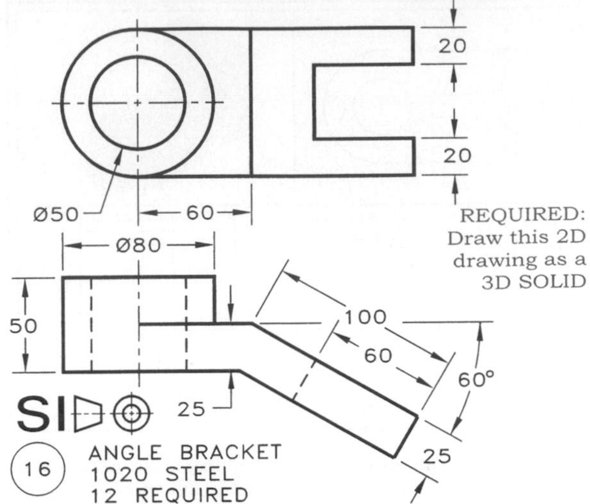

38.88 This angle bracket with an inclined surface is drawn as a 3D object in the following figures.

38.20 3D with Inclined Plane Tutorial

The angle bracket in **Figure 38.88** is shown as a dimensioned two-view orthographic view drawing, a traditional depiction of a part. This object will be converted into a 3D solid by joining and subtracting solid primitives that were used to form the object. It would be a good exercise for you to follow along with these steps of construction as a tutorial at your computer.

Setup: Enter *Model Space,* select a *Southeast Isometric* view from the *Dashboard,* and set the display style to *Conceptual* while you're at the *Dashboard* so the solids will appear realistic.

Part 1 (Figure 38.89):

Step 1 Using the dimensions given in **Figure 38.88**, draw the cylindrical feature and the prism that joins with it as solids: a *Cylinder* and a *Box.*

Step 2 Using *Snap,* move the *Box* into the *Cylinder* according to the dimension given. With the *Union* command, merge the two parts together.

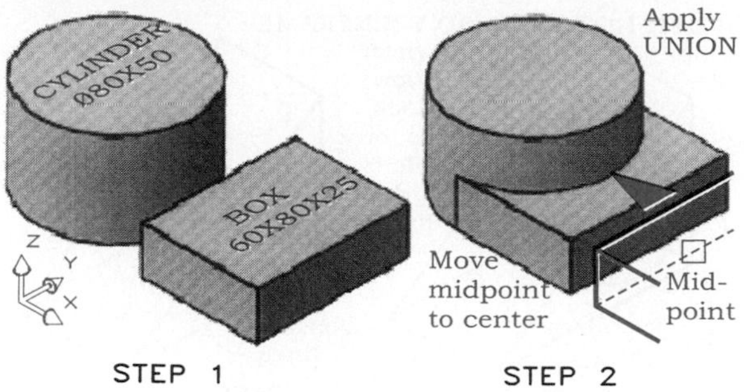

38.89 Part 1—Union: Merging solids.

Step 1 From the *Dashboard* select the *Cylinder* and *Box* icons and draw them one at a time using the dimensions from **Figure 38.88**.

Step 2 Using *Osnap*, pick the lower line of the box and drag it to the center of the cylinder. Enter the *Union* command, select both parts, and (Enter) to merge them into a single solid.

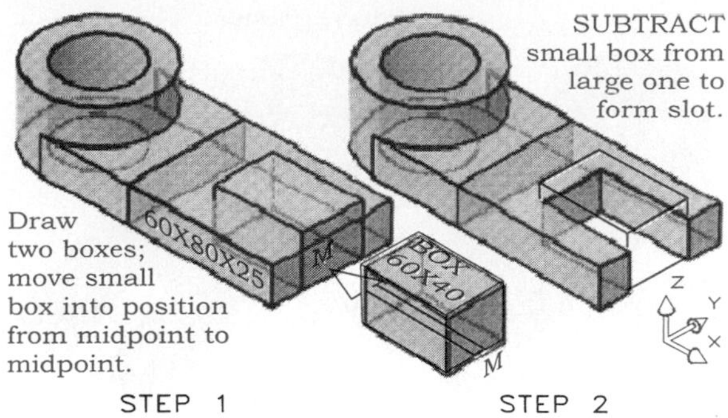

38.91 Part 3—Subtract: Forming the slot.

Step 1 Use the *Box* command to create a box representing the dimensions of the slot, but make it a little taller. *Osnap* to the midpoints (M) of the parts and drag the box into position.

Step 2 Select *Subtract*, pick the larger part, pick the inserted box (Enter), and the slot is formed.

Part 2 (Figure 38.90):

Step 1 The cylindrical hole must be formed by drawing a cylinder with a 50 diameter.

Step 2 Using the *Subtract* command removes the 50 diameter cylinder to leave a hole in the cylindrical feature.

Part 3 (Figure 38.91):

Step 1 Draw the inclined surface to the bracket in a horizontal position for ease of construction, but do not join it to the first part of the object.

Step 2 Construct a *Box* with the dimensions of the slot, but make it a little taller. *Osnap* it into position, and with the *Subtract* command create the slot.

Part 4 (Figure 38.92):

Step 1 Let's concentrate on the plane to incline it by itself. Select the *Rotate* command from

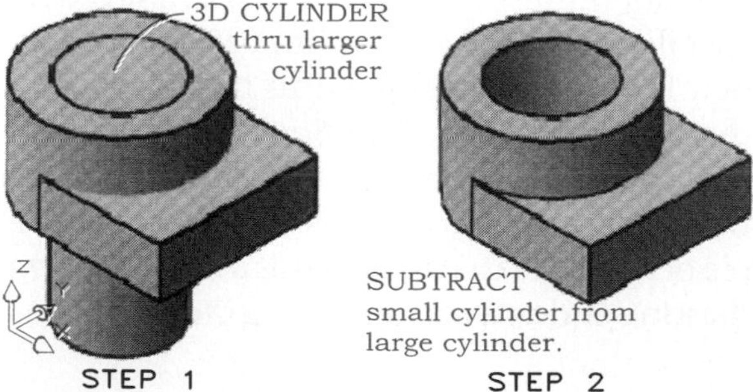

38.90 Part 2—Subtract: Forming the hole.

Step 1 Using *Osnap*, construct a *Cylinder* at the center of the larger cylinder. Give it an additional height.

Step 2 From the *Dashboard*, select *Subtract*, pick the object, pick the cylinder that represents the hole, and (Enter). The hole is formed.

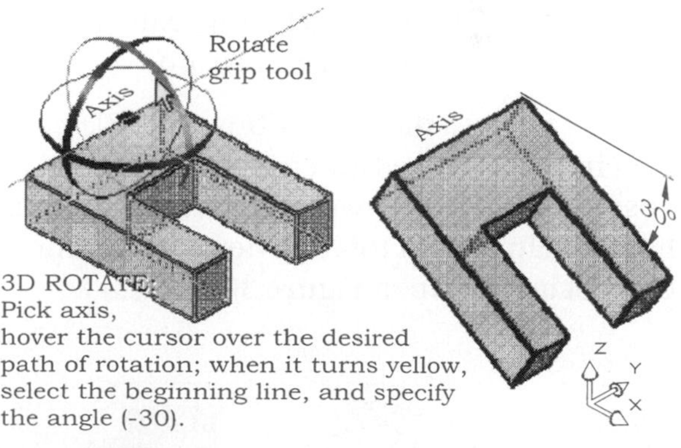

38.92 Part 4—Rotate: The inclined feature.

Step 1 From the *Dashboard* select the *Rotate* icon, and pick a point on the axis of rotation. The *Rotate grip tool* appears with 3D paths of rotation.

Step 2 Rest the cursor on the appropriate rotation path until it turns yellow, specify the starting line and the angle of rotation, and the feature is inclined.

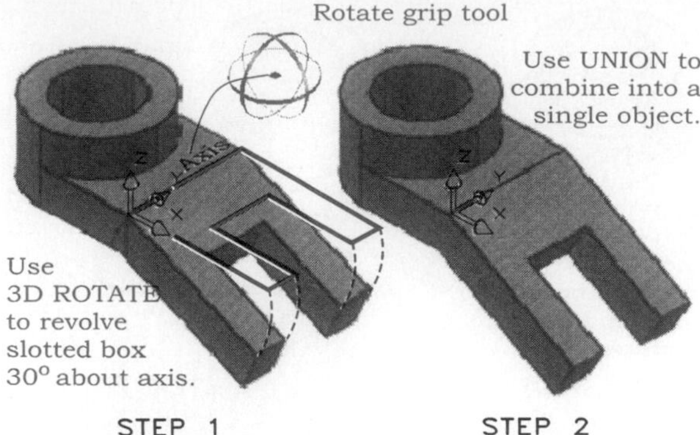

38.93 Part 5: Union—Finalizing the solid.

Step 1 Using *Osnap* join the inclined feature with the first-drawn portion of the object.

Step 2 With the *Union* command, select the two parts, and (Enter) to form a single solid.

the *Dashboard* and select the axis of rotation. A *Rotate grip tool* appears on the axis.

Step 2 Rest the cursor on the path of revolution that will hinge the surface about the axis and enter the angle, 30° in this case, and the rotation is done.

Part 5 (Figure 38.93):
Step 1 Move the inclined plane into position.

Step 2 Merge the inclined feature with its mating part using the *Union* command.

This finishes the formation of the 3D part, which can be viewed and rotated as needed to observe it as if you were holding it in your hand. Examples of rotated views of the angle bracket are shown in **Figure 38.94**.

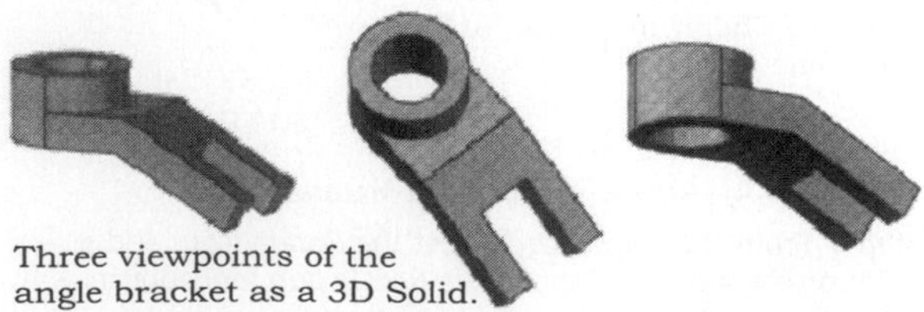

Three viewpoints of the angle bracket as a 3D Solid.

38.94 Now that you have a 3D solid of the angle bracket, you can look at it from any viewpoint as if you were holding it in your hand.

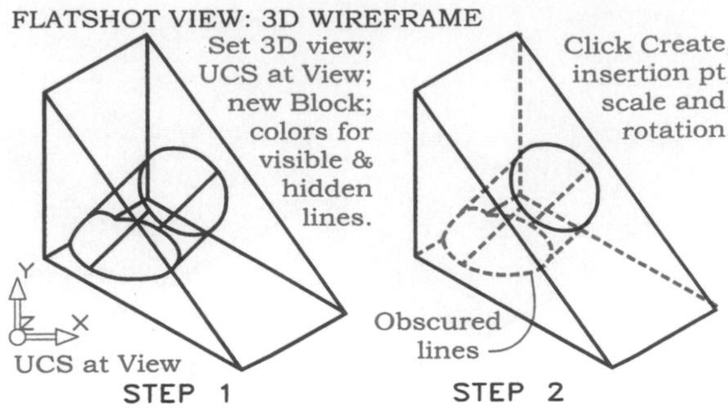

38.95 Flatshot

Step 1 *Command:* UCS (Enter) Select *View* to set the *UCS* icon parallel to the screen.
Command: Flatshot (Enter) *Flatshot* box appears on the screen. Check *Insert as new block*, assign colors to *foreground* and *obscured lines*, check *Show* box under *Obscured lines*, and pick *Create*.

Step 2 Specify *insertion point;* specify *scale;* specify *rotation* (Enter) The *Flatshot* view is displayed with obscured lines shown as hidden lines.

38.21 Flatshots of Solids

The *Flatshot* command can be activated from the *Dashboard* or *Command:* Flatshot. Its purpose is to create 2D flattened views of 3D solids with their hidden lines shown, which have applications as technical illustrations.

In **Figure 38.95**, the *UCS* of a *3D Wireframe* drawing is set to *View* since *Flatshots* are projected onto the *x-y* plane. By *Command:* Flatshot (Enter) a *Flatshot* box is displayed for specification entries. It is important that hidden linetypes be assigned to the layers with the obscured lines. The *Show* option under *Obscured lines* is checked so that hidden lines will be shown. **Figure 38.96** is another example of a bracket that is shown as a *3D Wireframe* drawing and as a converted *Flatshot* figure.

38.22 Views of Solids

Two commands, *Solview* and *Soldraw,* are used together to convert a 3D solid into orthographic views, auxiliary views, or sections. Once a 3D solid has been drawn in *Model*

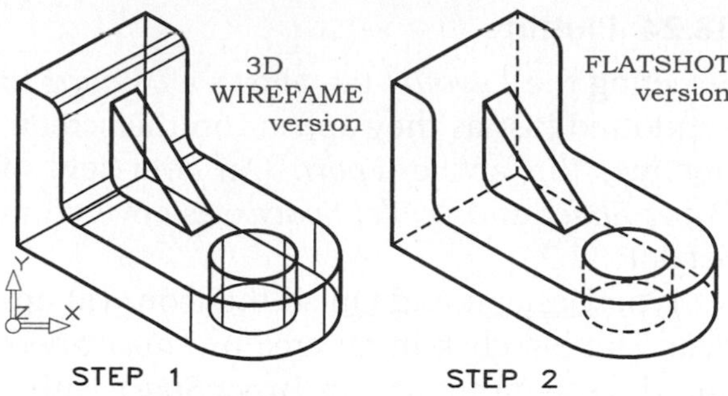

38.96 Flatshot conversion.

Step 1 The *3D Wireframe* version of the bracket is drawn and its *UCS* is set to *View*.

Step 2 Enter the *Flatshot* command to obtain a view with the obscured lines shown as hidden lines.

Space, select the *Layout1* tab, erase the *MS* window, and with *MView* select the corners of a viewport to fill the screen. Select *Draw Menu> Modeling> Setup> View* (**Figure 38.97**) (or *Command:* Solview); the screen will enter *Paper Space* and you will be given the options *UCS, Ortho, Auxiliary,* and *Section.* Select Auxiliary and follow the prompts as shown in **Figure 38.98.**

Since the object has an inclined plane (Part 2), specify the next view as an *Auxiliary,* and select two points on the inclined plane in the front view. Pick the side of the inclined plane where the auxiliary is to be drawn, pick the view's center, and the auxiliary view is drawn. Select the diagonal corners of the viewport that contains the auxiliary view.

Solview automatically creates four layers for each named view. The name of the view is

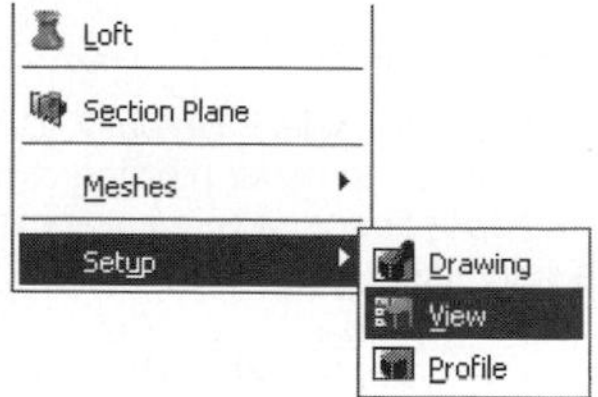

38.97 *Draw Menu> Modeling> Setup> View* to access the *Solview* command for drawing auxiliary and other orthograhic views.

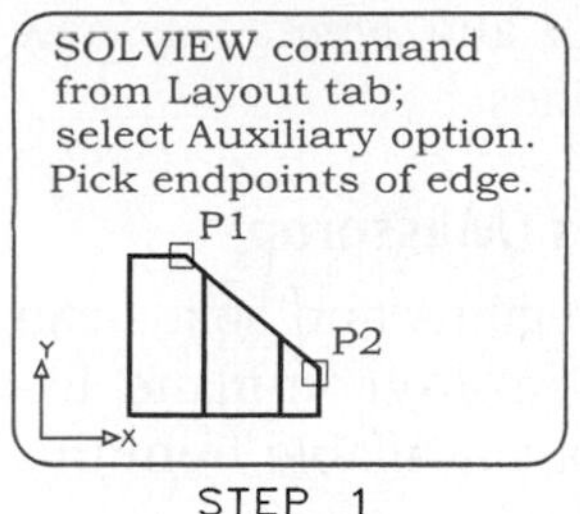

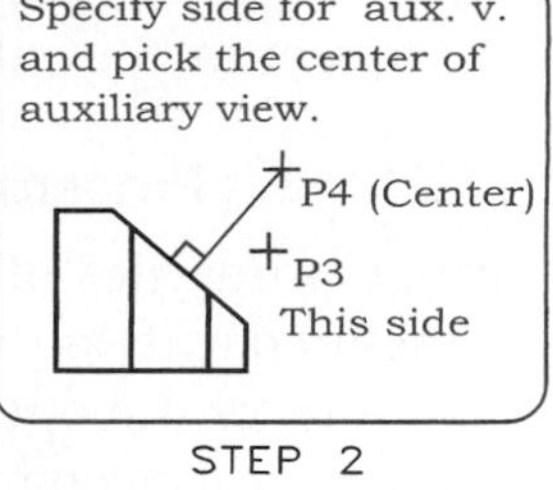

38.98 Part 1—Solview: Auxiliary view.

Step 1 *Command:* Solview (Enter)
[Ucs/ Ortho/ Auxiliary/ Section]: Auxiliary (Enter)
Specify first point on inclined plane: P1
Specify second point on inclined plane: P2

Step 2 *Specify side to view from:* P3
Specify view center <specify viewport>: P4

followed by a dash and these abbreviations, *-VIS, -HID, -DIM,* and *-VPORTS* (for visible, hidden, dimension, and viewport, respectively) on which these features can be drawn.

In **Figure 38.99** select the *Drawing* icon (**Figure 38.97**) or *Command:* Soldraw (Enter) and you will be prompted for *Viewports to draw.* Select points on the *MS* windows, and invisible lines will be converted to hidden (dashed) lines. It is necessary that *Linetype Hidden* be loaded and assigned to the *Layers* whose names are followed by *-Hid* (*Aux1-Hid,* for example) so invisible lines will appear as dashed lines. From *Paper Space, Change* the *MS* outlines of the viewports

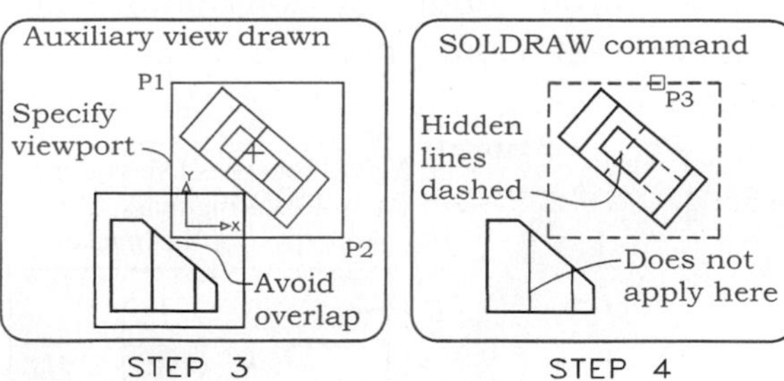

38.99 Part 2—Soldraw: Auxiliary view.

Step 1 *Continued: Specify first corner of viewport:* P1
Specify opposite corner of viewport: P2
Enter view name: Aux-1 (Enter)

Step 2 Command: Soldraw (Enter)
Select objects: P3 (Enter) (*You must first set the linetype of *aux-1-HID* to *Hidden* so a dashed line will be displayed when *Soldraw* is applied.)

to a newly created layer and *Freeze* this new layer to remove the outlines.

38.23 Mass Properties (Massprop)

Various properties of regions and solids can be obtained with the *Massprop* command. Explanations of the options available from this command are given next:

Mass calculates the weight of a solid.

Volume gives the 3D space enclosed in a solid.

Bounding Box gives coordinates of the diagonal corners of a region's enclosing rectangle. For a solid, coordinates of the diagonal and opposite corners of a 3D box are given.

Centroid gives the coordinates of the center of a region or the 3D center of a solid.

Moments of Inertia are calculated for regions and solids.

Products of Inertia are calculated for regions and solids.

Radii of Gyration are calculated for regions and solids.

Principal moments and X-Y-Z directions about the centroid.

Mass Properties are shown in a table of values obtained by applying the command, as in **Figure 38.100**. Hours of computation are saved with this command.

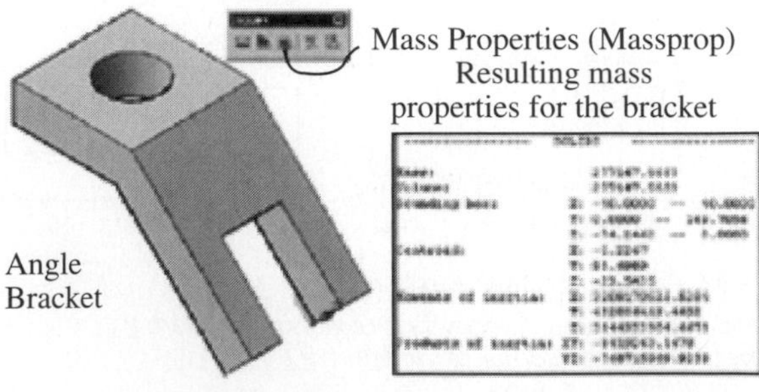

38.100 Mass Properties (Massprop).
A *3D Solid* is more than just a pretty picture. Its mass properties can be determined by selecting the *Mass Properties* icon from the *Inquiry* toolbar and selecting the solid.

38.24 Plotting

Selecting the *Layout1* tab allows all *Vports* to be plotted just as they appear on the screen, not just the active *Vport.* (An overview of *Paper Space* and *Model Space* was covered in Section 38.3.)

Type Ucsicon and On so the icon will appear. Double click in an area of *Paper Space* and the screen returns to *Paper Space* with a *PS* icon (a triangle) in its lower left corner, and *Paper* appears in the *Status* line (**Figure 38.101**). The *Paper Space Limits* are determined by the maximum size permitted by the printer being used, usually 11 × 8.5 in. Insert a size-A border. You may design your own border and save it as a *Wblock.*

From *Paper Space,* use *Command:* Vports, create the diagonal corners of a *MS* viewport with the cursor, *Copy* this viewport, and double click in one of the viewports to enter *Model Space* in that particular port (**Figure 38.102**). Set the *Limits* in this *MS* viewport to 24 × 20, large enough to contain the drawing. Move between *MS* and *PS* by double clicking on the button in the *Status* line beneath the *Command* line that will display as either *MODEL* or *PAPER.*

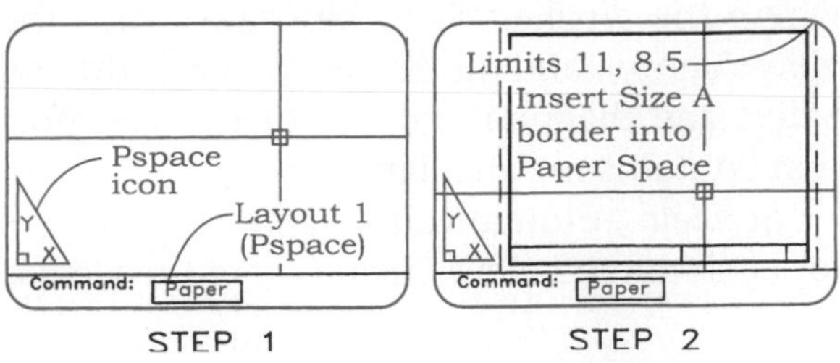

38.101 Paper Space: Layout1.

Step 1 From *Model Space,* select *Layout1,* click *File> Page Setup Manager* from which to make plotting assignments, and pick *OK*. You are in *Paper Space,* where a viewport into 3D is a box outlined with solid lines. *Erase* this box to close it.

Step 2 *Command:* Insert (Enter)
Block name (or ?): Border-A (Enter)
Specify Insertion point or [Scale/X/Y/Z./Rotate/ PScale/PX/ PY/PZ/PRotate]: 0,0 (Enter)
The title block is inserted into *Paper Space* at the scale to which it was drawn, full size in this case.

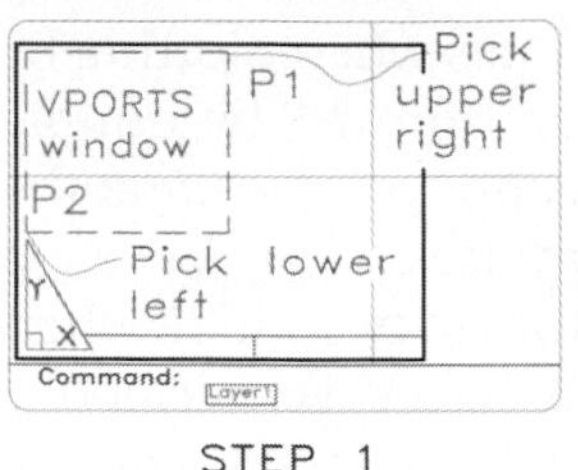

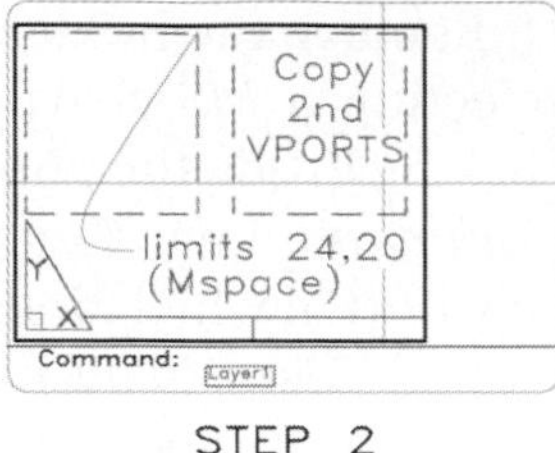

38.102 Paper Space: Vports.

Step 1 While in *Paper Space,* select *Main Menu> View> Viewports> New Viewports* to obtain the *Viewports* dialog box. Select *Single* and P1 and P2 to form a floating viewport into 3D space.

Step 2 Copy this viewport to form a second one. Return to *Model Space* by selecting the *MODEL* button in the *Status* line and set the viewports *Limits* to 24,20. A *Model Space* viewport can be made current by double clicking inside it, and *Paper Space* entered by double clicking outside the viewport.

Use *Command:* *-Vports* to obtain the following prompts:

On/ Off: Selects and turns off viewports to save regeneration time, but leave at least one on.

Fit: Makes a viewport fill the current screen.

Shadeplot: Gives options for rendering a 3D solid.

Lock: Locks the current viewport.

Object: Specifies a closed polyline, ellipse, spline, region, or circle to convert into a viewport.

Polygonal: Creates an irregularly shaped viewport.

Restore: Recalls a saved viewport configuration.

2/ 3/ 4: Give options for specifying the number of viewports.

Figure 38.103 shows a 3D object drawn by *Solids* toolbar> *Extrude* in one of the *MS* viewports and displayed simultaneously in a second port. *Command:* Vpoint (Enter)> Select an isometric viewpoint (1,−1,1) and double click on a *Paper Space* area to enter *Paper Space.* The cursor spans the screen in *Paper Space.* Now, the drawing must be scaled.

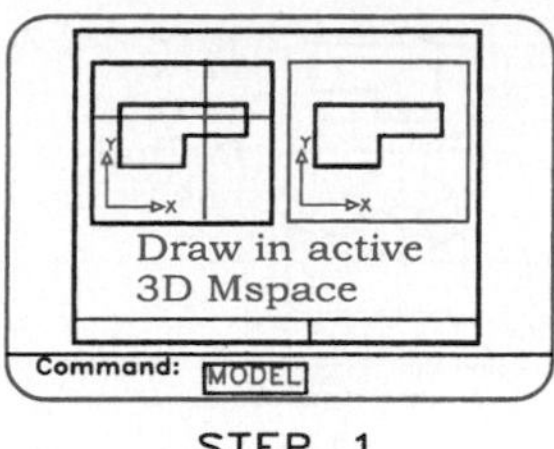

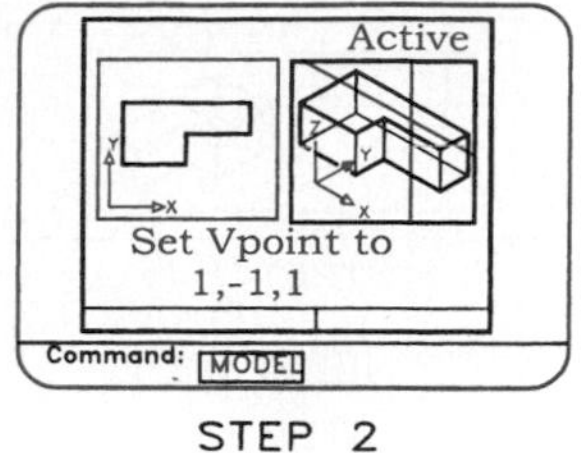

38.103 Paper Space: Drawing in Model Space.

Step 1 Double click inside one of the *Model Space* viewports to make it current and draw an extruded 3D part. It will show in both views.

Step 2 Click in the right viewport to make it active.
Command: Vpoint (Enter)> *Specify viewpoint:* 1, −1, 1 (Enter)
An isometric drawing is obtained.

The *Paper Space Limits* are 11 × 8.5 in., inside which two *MS* viewports must fit, each with *Limits* of 24,20. These *MS* viewports must be sized to fit, which requires calculations. The combined width of the two 24-in.-wide *Model Spaces* is 48 in. When scaled to half size (0.50), their width is 24 in. and too wide to fit. If scaled to 0.20 (20% size), their width is 9.6 in. and small enough to fit inside the A-size border.

From *Model Space* type Zoom and use the *X/ XP* option (2/ 10XP or 0.2XP) to size the contents of each viewport (**Figure 38.104**). This factor changes the width limit of each viewport

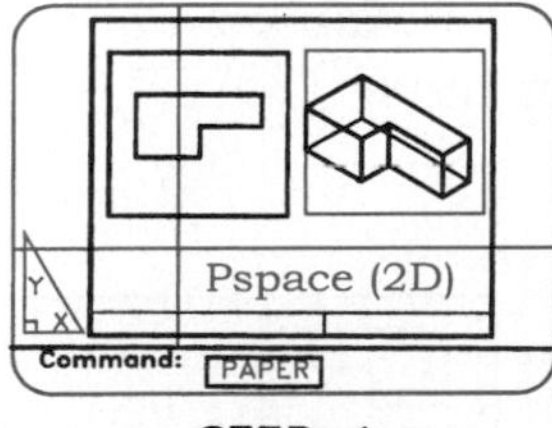

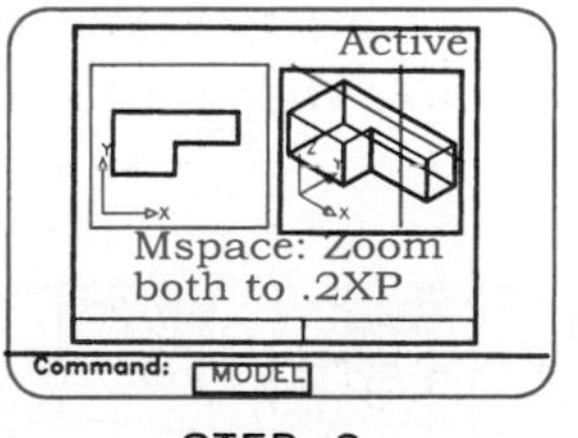

38.104 Paper Space: Zoom to Scale.

Step 1 Double click in the *Paper Space* area (or select the *Paper Space* button in the *Status* bar) to enter *Paper Space,* and the cursor spans the screen. Since *PS* had limits of 12,0 and *MS* had limits of 24,20, the *MS* ports must be *Zoomed* to about 0.20 size for both to fit inside the border.

Step 2 Double click on one of the *MS viewports* to make it active. Command: Zoom (Enter)
All/Center/ ... /<Scale (X/XP)>: .2XP (Enter)
The active port is scaled to a 0.2 size to fit in the *PS* border. *Zoom* the other viewport to .2XP also.

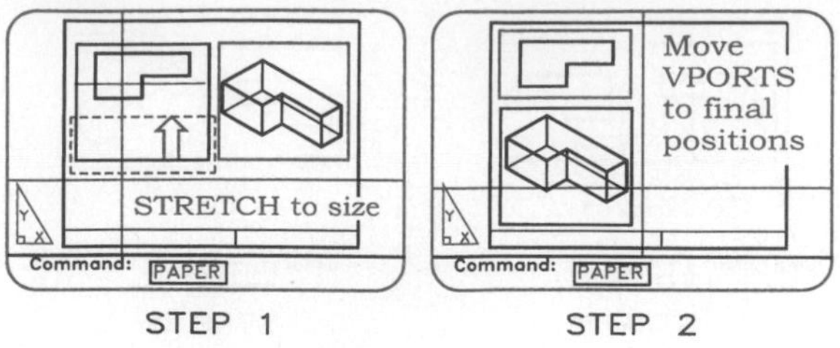

38.105 Paper Space: Stretch.

Step 1 Double click in a *Paper Space* area to switch to *Paper Space.* Use *Stretch* to reduce the size of the *MS* viewport.

Step 2 *Move* the viewports to their final positions within the *Paper Space* border.

from 24 to 4.8 in., with both drawings having the same scale on the screen. In other words, you may scale viewports with width limits of 24 in. to a full-size width of 4.8 in. in *Paper Space.*

Double click on a *Paper Space* area to enter *Paper Space* and use *Stretch* to reduce the size of the *MS* viewport outlines (**Figure 38.105**). Reposition the *MS* viewports for plotting with *Move.*

Plotting must be performed from *Paper Space;* both the *PS* and *MS* drawings are plotted at the same time, including the outlines of the *MS* viewports (**Figure 38.106**). To remove the *MS* viewport outlines, *Change* them to a separate *Layer* (*Window,* for example), *Freeze* it, and *Plot* in the usual manner.

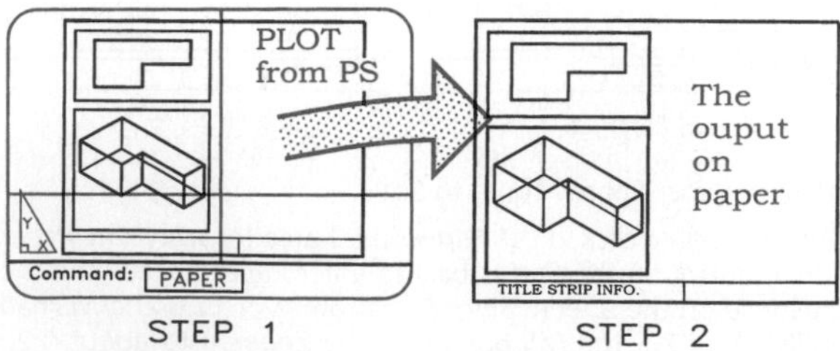

38.106 Paper Space: Plot.

Step 1 Select *Main Menu> File> Plot* and give specifications for plotters and plotting from *Paper Space.*

Step 2 The size A layout is plotted to show both 2D (*Paper Space*) and 3D (*Model Space*) drawings in the same plot.

Remove the hidden lines when plotting by selecting a *MS* viewport from *PS* by double clicking inside the port, and typing *Hide* at the *Command* line. Repeat this step for each viewport in which lines are to be hidden when plotted. Use *Vplayer* to select *MS viewports* from *Paper Space* in which layers can be turned *Off* or *Frozen* while remaining *On* or *Thawed* in other viewports.

38.25 Rendering: Introduction

Rendering is the process of giving 3D objects a realistic appearance by adding color, lighting, and materials to them. The following examples illustrate how 3D drawings are rendered.

The bracket from **Figure 38.72** is displayed in two viewports as an axonometric and a perspective (**Figure 38.107**). The *Render* toolbar, shown in **Figure 38.108**, gives eight options, each of which has pull-down panels of additional settings.

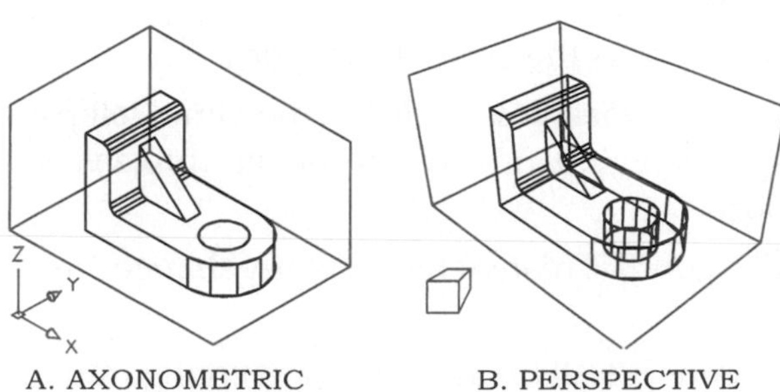

38.107 This part is used to illustrate rendering techniques in the following examples.

38.108 The icons on the *Render* toolbar are (l to r): *Hide, Render, Lights, Light List, Materials, Planar Mapping, Render Environment,* and *Advanced Render Settings.*

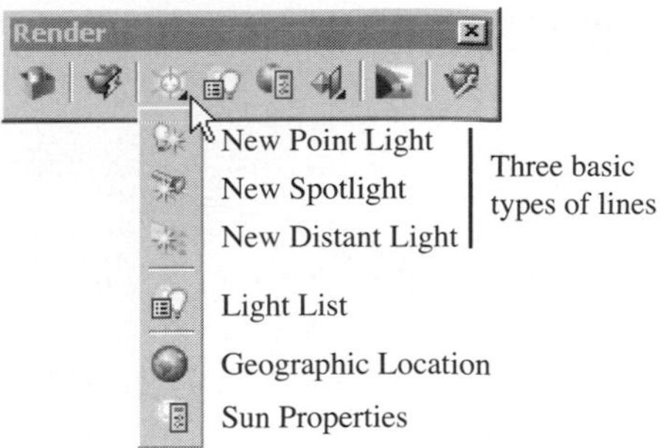

38.109 The *Lights* icon can be pressed and held to give these options for lighting a model.

38.26 Rendering: Lights

Lighting is an important aspect of rendering a 3D model because it controls brightness, shades, and shadows to enhance its realism. From the *Render* toolbar (**Figure 38.109**) the *Lights* icon is picked to display a pull-down list of icons that includes three types of lights: *New Point Light, New Spotlight,* and *New Distant Light.* Each of these types of lights has its own set of pull-down dialog boxes and action icons.

Point Lights emits rays in all directions from a point source. *Spotlights* emit cones of light directed toward a target. *Distant Lights* emit parallel beams of light like those of sunlight.

Default lighting (as its name implies) is used to cast a neutral light on a model on the screen prior to the selection of customized lighting. When the user adds lighting, the *Default* lighting can be set to turn off automatically, as indicated in the *Viewport Lighting Mode* box shown in **Figure 38.110**.

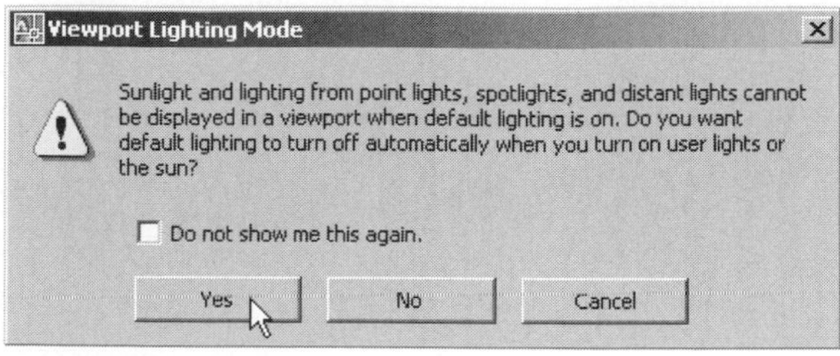

38.110 Default lighting must be turned off to display other specified lighting. Select the *Yes* button.

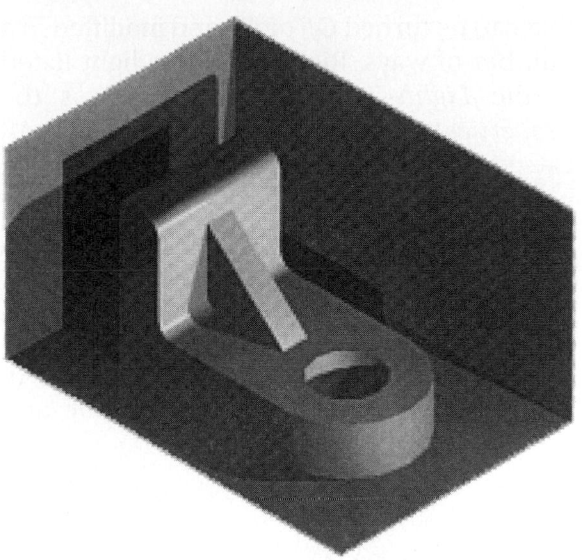

38.111 A sample rendering of the bracket that shows shades and shadows.

The bracket that has been used as an example previously in this chapter will be used to demonstrate applications of the *Lights* and *Render* command (**Figure 38.111**). In this view, the bracket is rendered with three light sources and the application of *Shadows* for added realism. After the lighting has been set for the bracket, select *Render* from the *Render* toolbar, or *Command:* Render (Enter), and the bracket is rendered.

Lights that are assigned to a model become part of a list of lights shown in **Figure 38.112**

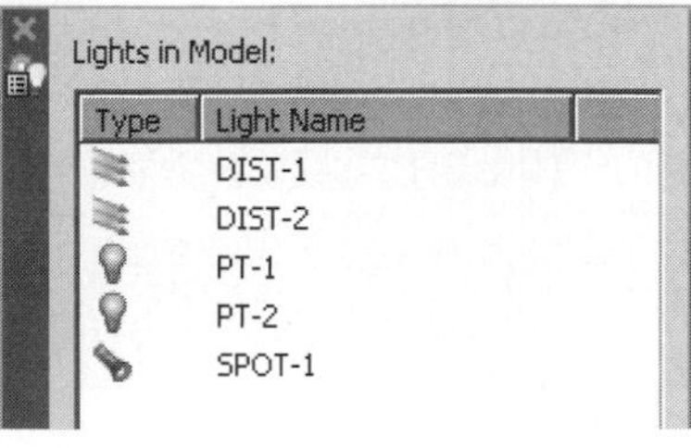

38.112 From the *Render* toolbar, select the *Lights List* icon to obtain the *Lights in Model* panel that lists the light sources that have been assigned to the model. Right click on a *Light Name* in the list and select *Properties,* which appears in **Figure 38.113**.

that can be turned *Off* or *On* and modified in a number of ways. Right click on a light listed in the *Lights in Model* list to access the *Properties* toolbar shown in **Figure 38.113**. All categories listed in this panel of options can be clicked on to obtain selections for modifying the current lighting setup. For example, lights can be turned on or off, varied in intensity, or colors of lighting changed from the pop-up *Select Color* box shown in **Figure 38.114**. Tabs are available for selecting three types of color: *Index Color, True Color,* and *Color Books.*

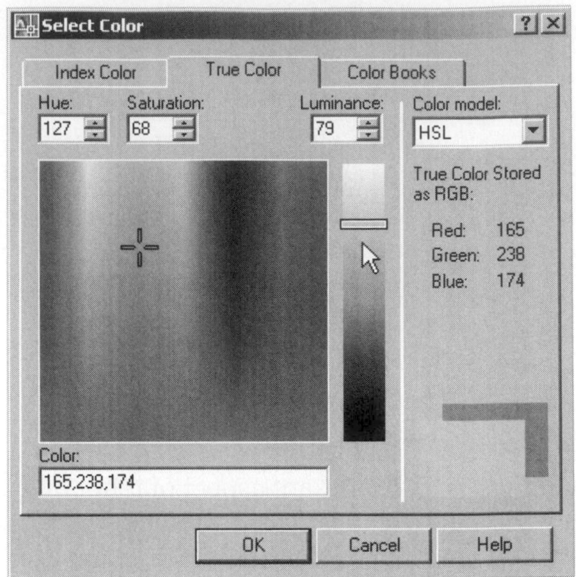

38.114 Select Color.
From the *Lights in Model* box> right click on *New Distant Light*> pick *Color*> *Select Color ...*> *True Color* tab to display this panel from which to select a color. Other tabs available are *Index Color* and *Color Books.*

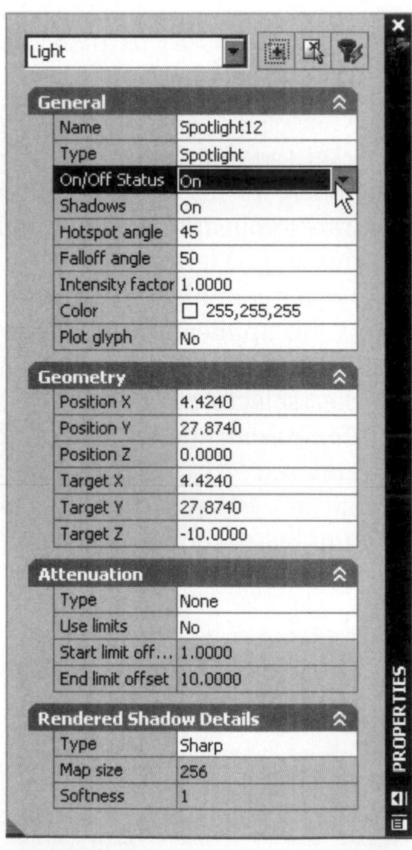

38.113 Right clicking on a light shown in **Figure 30.112** and selecting *Properties* displays these characteristics for editing. Light sources can be turned on and off from here, and so can shadows and other modifications, which enables you to fine-tune the appearance of your model.

38.27 Rendering: Types of Lights

The three major types of lights are *Point Lights, Spotlights,* and *Distant Lights.* Each type of light, except for *Distant Lights,* has an icon to identify it on a drawing (**Figure 38.115**). Both the *Point Light* and *Spotlight* have a falloff, which means that their intensity diminishes as the distance from the light source increases, just as in nature. *Distant Lights* cast parallel rays with a constant intensity in the direction that you prescribe, which simulates rays of light from the sun.

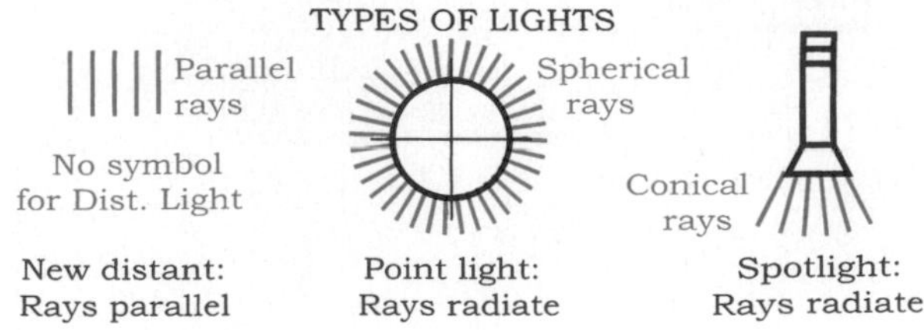

38.115 Light symbols.
Distant Light, Point Light, and *Spotlight* symbols are placed on drawings to indicate the positions for lighting.

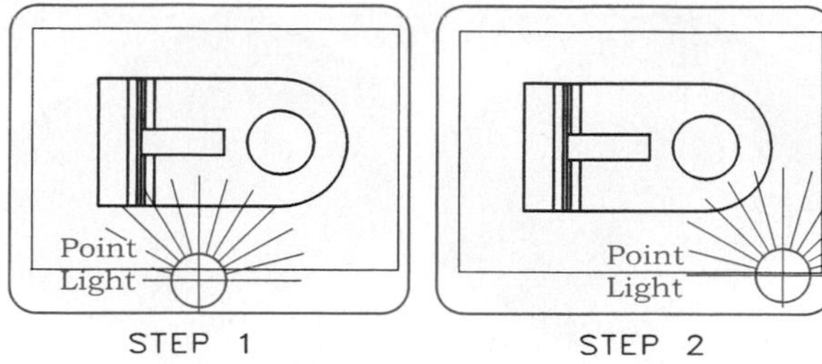

38.116 Moving a light: *Spotlight* or *Point Light*.

Step 1 With the *Move* command, select the *Point Light* icon.

Step 2 Move the light source to its new position.

Point Light: A single *Point Light* in **Figure 38.116** is shown in two positions, prior to and after being moved. The results are shown in the rendered model in **Figure 38.117**. The effects of lighting angle and falloff can be seen in this example.

Distant Light: A light source casting parallel, sunlike rays is a *Distant Light*.

In this example the light is assigned its direction as shown in **Figure 38.118**. From the *Properties* box, *Shadows* are set to *On* to obtain a small shadow, but one that effectively defines the model.

Spotlight: A *Spotlight* emits a cone of light as does a flashlight, which is the icon used to show the source of light from a *Spotlight*. Its characteristics that can be set and modified are identified in **Figure 38.119**. Select the *Spotlight* icon from the *Render* toolbar, and position the light by following the prompts. An example of an applied *Spotlight* is shown in **Figure 38.120**. After a *Spotlight* has been set, its parameters are shown when the cursor is rested on its icon, as shown in **Figure 38.120A**. These factors and

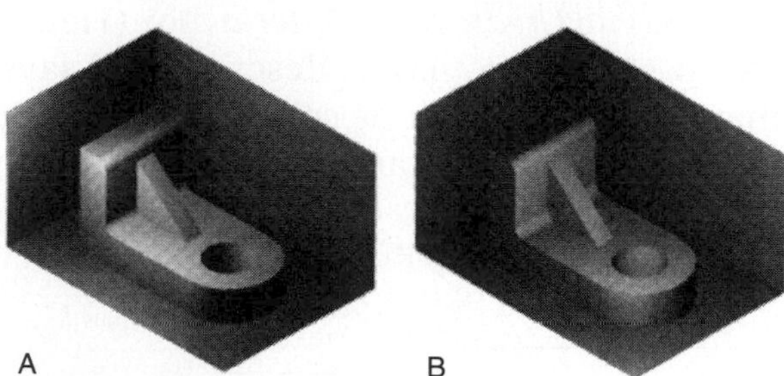

38.117 The results of moving the *Point Light* from position A to position B as shown in **Figure 38.116**.

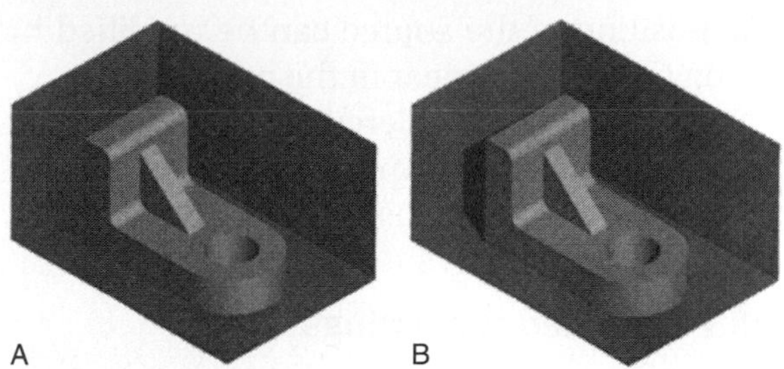

38.118 New *Distant Light*.

A From *Lights* toolbar> *New Distant Light*> position source and direction to obtain the view at the left.

B From the *Lights in Model* box, right click the *Distant Light* to obtain the *Properties* box. Set *Shadows On* to obtain a better defined view at the right.

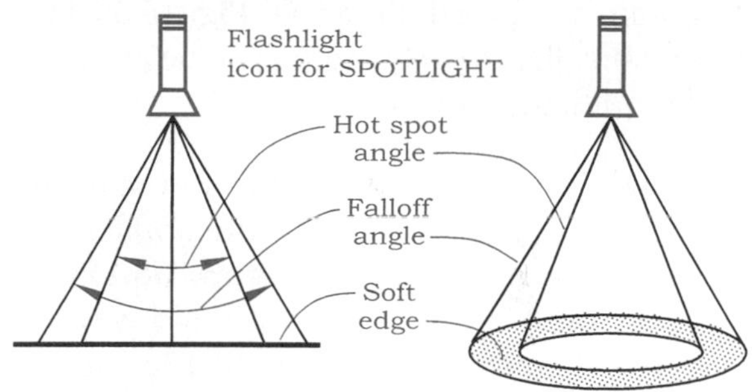

38.119 The definitions of the characteristics of a spotlight are shown here.

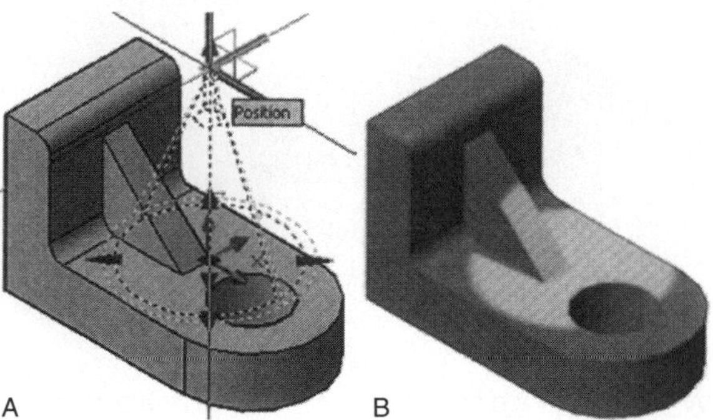

38.120 An example of a *Spotlight* applied to the rendered bracket.

the position of the source can be modified by using *Grips* that appear in the preview.

The resulting rendered view is shown in **Figure 38.120B**. As expected, it gives the impression of a spotlight shining on the model.

38.28 Rendering: Settings

All lights have settings that can be made from the start after selecting a type of light from the *Render* toolbar. Prompts appear asking for specifications in lighting that you wish to make. One of the first options is lighting *Intensity,* which is the brightness of the light that is best suited to your model.

Intensity: The effect of lighting of two intensities is shown in **Figure 38.121**. *Intensity* can be changed by selecting the *Lights List* from the *Render* toolbar, right clicking on the name of the light to change, and picking *Properties* to obtain the panel shown in **Figure 38.113**. From here, the *Intensity* value can be assigned and modified.

Shadows: Realism and definition can be added to rendered models by the application of *Shadows,* as shown in **Figure 38.111**. A comparison of the bracket with and without shadows is shown in **Figure 38.122**. Assign *Shadows* to a model by picking the *shadoW* option from the prompts after placing the *Point Light* or *Spotlight.*

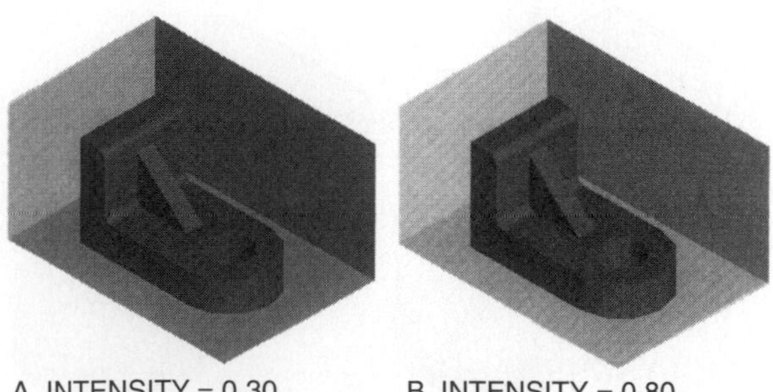

38.121 A comparison of *Ambient light* set at two intensities is shown here.

38.122 *Shadows.*

A *Lights Menu> New Point Light>* position light to obtain the view at A with no shadows.

B *Lights Menu> New Point Light>* position light> shadoW option to obtain the view at B with full shadows.

Many other changes can be made from the *Properties* panel under the headings of *General, 3D Visualization, Plot Style, View,* and *Miscellaneous.* Experiment with these alternatives to broaden your skills.

38.29 Rendering: Materials

Select the *Materials* icon from the *Render* toolbar (**Figure 38.123**) to display the *Materials* dialog box shown in **Figure 38.124**. The box will require experimentation to become acquainted with its many options. The material of an object determines the reflective quality of its surfaces, from dull to shiny. To add a material to the *Current Drawing* list for future use, pick the *Create New Material* at the center of the icon strip under the pictorial window at the top of the *Materials* palette shown in **Figure 38.125**. The *Create New Material* box **(Figure 38.126)** is used to name, describe, and save materials. Colors can be selected by picking the *Edit Map* button and clicking on a color

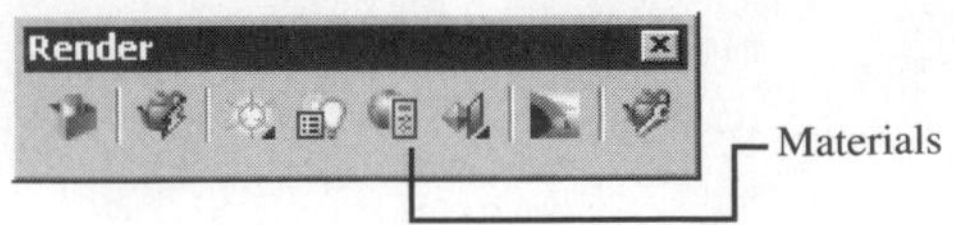

38.123 The *Materials* and *Materials Library* icons are used in assigning materials that are applied to 3D objects.

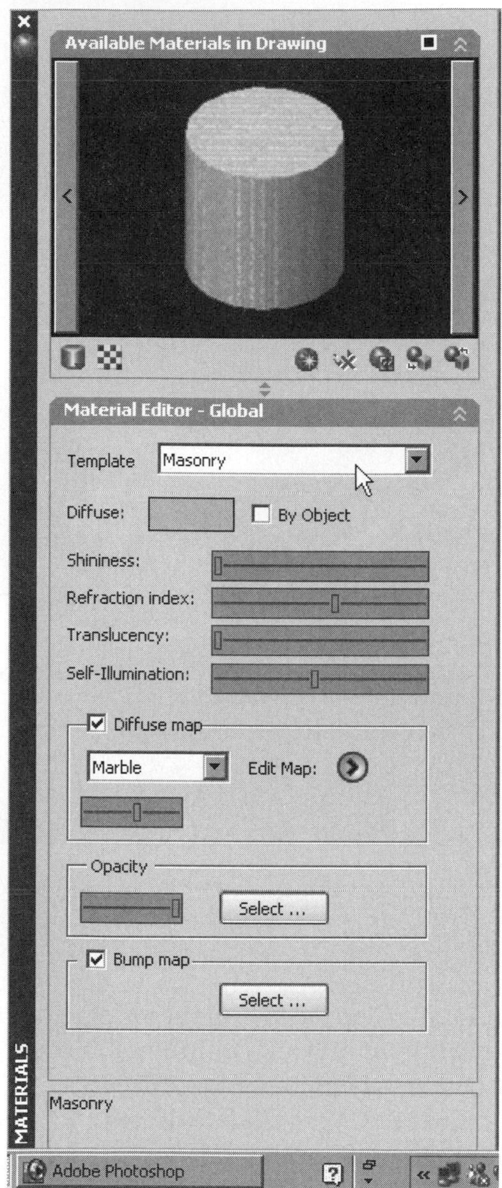

38.124 From the *Render* toolbar> *Materials* to obtain this dialog box from which materials can be specified, modified, and applied to models. Examples of the materials can be shown on box, sphere, or cylinder (as shown here).

box to display the *Select Color* box shown in **Figure 38.114**. Multiple materials can be created in this manner and displayed in the *Available Materials in Drawing* area as shown in **Figure 38.127**.

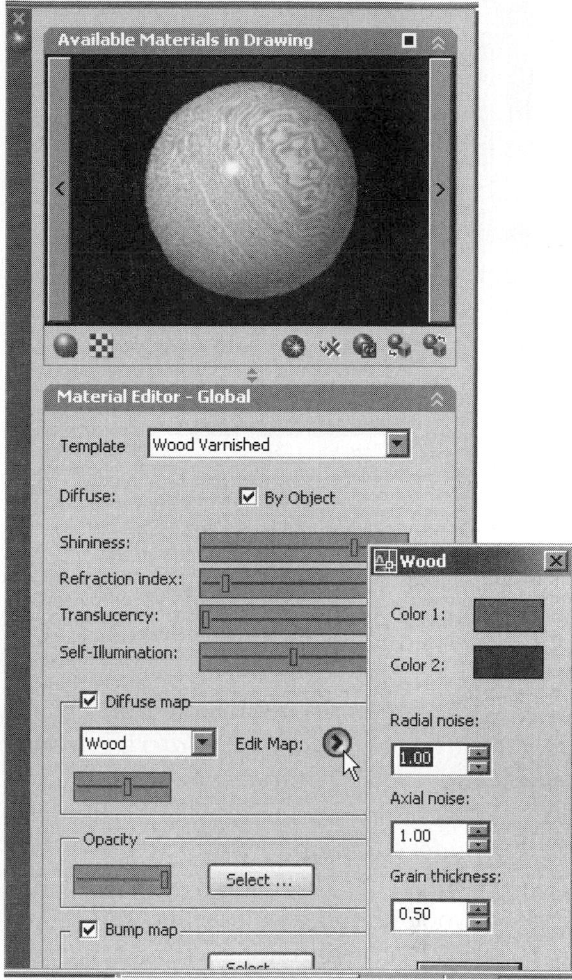

38.125 From the *Materials* palette, pick the *Edit Map* button to obtain this supplementary box from which to select two colors to represent the wood grain. In this case the material is displayed on a sphere in the upper window.

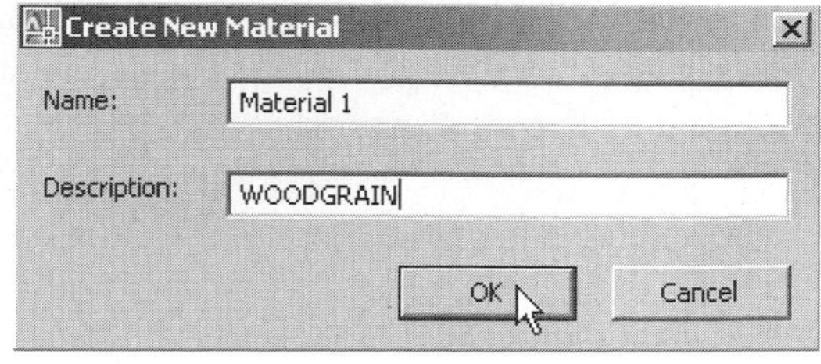

38.126 When a material has been edited, pick the *Create New Material* icon to obtain this box and name the material.

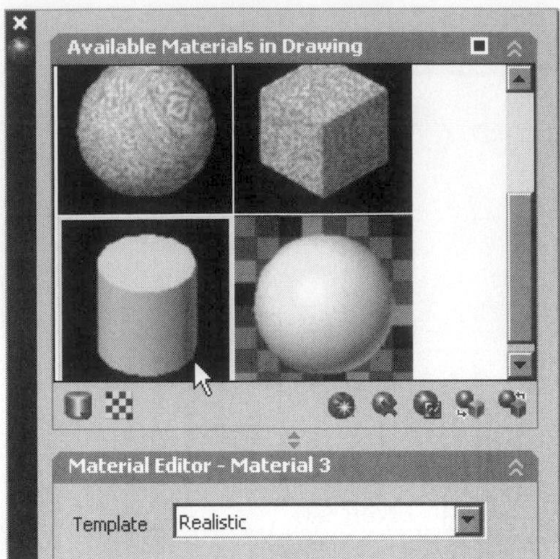

38.127 An assortment of material combinations can be created, saved, and displayed in the *Available Materials in Drawing* portion of the *Materials* palette. These material representations can be dragged onto a solid model with the cursor and revealed by the *Render* command.

A created material representation can be selected from the *Available Materials* by the cursor and dragged onto a *3D Solid,* where it becomes part of its surface. It is not visible until the *Render* command is activated.

An example of a rendered 3D model with a created wood grain applied to it is illustrated in **Figure 38.128**. With added shadows and a wood grain surface in two colors, the final model gives a highly realistic representation of the part.

This chapter on 3D modeling has been introductory in nature, with many areas left unexplored. You must experiment with all options, use the *Help* command, and pursue the learning of AutoCAD with the same intensity that you apply to computer games. This is the technique used by the most experienced users.

38.128 Our example part is shown here with the application of a *Wood* material and *Shadows* applied.

Problems

Most problems can be solved and plotted on size A sheets using a text height of no smaller than 0.10 in.

1. *Exercises:* Repeat each of the example figures in this chapter on your computer following the instructions given in the legends, and plot the examples. This technique will help you learn the fundamental commands.

2. *Problems:* The problems at the ends of the previous chapters can be drawn and plotted using the computer-graphics techniques covered in this and previous chapters.

DECIMAL EQUIVALENTS—INCH-MILLIMETER CONVERSION TABLE

1/2	1/4	1/8	1/16	1/32	1/64	Decimals	Millimeters	1/2	1/4	1/8	1/16	1/32	1/64	Decimals	Millimeters
					1	.015625	.396875						33	.515625	13.096875
				1		.031250	.793750					17		.531250	13.493750
					3	.046875	1.190625						35	.546875	13.890625
			1			.062500	1.587500				9			.562500	14.287500
					5	.078125	1.984375						37	.578125	14.684375
				3		.093750	2.381250					19		.593750	15.081250
					7	.109375	2.778125						39	.609375	15.478125
		1				.125000	3.175000			5				.625000	15.875000
					9	.140625	3.571875						41	.640625	16.271875
				5		.156250	3.968750					21		.656250	16.668750
					11	.171875	4.365625						43	.671875	17.065625
			3			.187500	4.762500				11			.687500	17.462500
					13	.203125	5.159375						45	.703125	17.859375
				7		.218750	5.556250					23		.718750	18.256250
					15	.234375	5.953125						47	.734375	18.653125
	1					.250000	6.350000		3					.750000	19.050000
					17	.265625	6.746875						49	.765625	19.446875
				9		.281250	7.143750					25		.781250	19.843750
					19	.296875	7.540625						51	.796875	20.240625
			5			.312500	7.937500				13			.812500	20.637500
					21	.328125	8.334375						53	.828125	21.034375
				11		.343750	8.731250					27		.843750	21.431250
					23	.359375	9.128125						55	.859375	21.828125
		3				.375000	9.525000			7				.875000	22.225000
					25	.390625	9.921875						57	.890625	22.621875
				13		.406250	10.318750					29		.906250	23.018750
					27	.421875	10.715625						59	.921875	23.415625
			7			.437500	11.112500				15			.937500	23.812500
					29	.453125	11.509375						61	.953125	24.209375
				15		.468750	11.906250					31		.968750	24.606250
					31	.484375	12.303125						63	.984375	25.003125
1						.500000	12.700000	2	4	8	16	32	64	1.00000	25.400000

LENGTH

1 millimeter (mm) = 0.03937 inch
1 centimeter (cm) = 0.39370 inch
1 meter (m) = 39.37008 inches
1 meter = 3.2808 feet
1 meter = 1.0936 yards
1 kilometer (km) = 0.6214 miles
1 inch = 25.4 millimeters
1 inch = 2.54 centimeters
1 foot = 304.8 millimeters
1 foot = 0.3048 meters
1 yard = 0.9144 meters
1 mile = 1.609 kilometers

DRY CAPACITY

1 cubic centimeter (cm^3) = 0.061 cubic inches
1 liter = 0.0353 cubic foot
1 liter = 61.023 cubic inches
1 cubic meter (m^3) = 35.315 cubic feet
1 cubic meter = 1.308 cubic yards
1 cubic inch = 16.38706 cubic centimeters
1 cubic foot = 0.02832 cubic meter
1 cubic foot = 28.317 liters
1 cubic yard = 0.7646 cubic meter

AREA

1 square millimeter = 0.00155 square inch
1 square centimeter = 0.155 square inch
1 square meter = 10.764 square feet
1 square meter = 1.196 square yards
1 square kilometer = 0.3861 square mile
1 square inch = 645.2 square millimeters
1 square inch = 6.452 square centimeters
1 square foot = 929 square centimeters
1 square foot = 0.0929 square meter
1 square yard = 0.836 square meter
1 square mile = 2.5899 square kilometers

LIQUID CAPACITY

1 liter = 1.0567 U.S. quarts
1 liter = 0.2642 U.S. gallons
1 liter = 0.2200 Imperial gallon
1 cubic meter = 264.2 U.S. gallons
1 cubic meter = 219.969 Imperial gallons
1 U.S. quart = 0.946 liters
1 Imperial quart = 1.136 liters
1 U.S. gallon = 3.785 liters
1 Imperial gallon = 4.546 liters

WEIGHT

1 gram (g) = 15.432 grains
1 gram = 0.03215 ounce troy
1 gram = 0.03527 ounce avoirdupois
1 kilogram (kg) = 35.274 ounces avoirdupois
1 kilogram = 2.2046 pounds
1000 kilograms = 1 metric ton (t)
1000 kilograms = 1.1023 tons of 2000 pounds
1000 kilograms = 0.9842 tons of 2240 pounds
1 ounce avoirdupois = 28.35 grams
1 ounce troy = 31.103 grams
1 pound = 453.6 grams
1 pound = 0.4536 kilogram
1 ton of 2240 pounds = 1016 kilograms
1 ton of 2240 pounds = 1.016 metric tons
1 grain = 0.0648 gram
1 metric ton = 0.9842 tons of 2240 pounds
1 metric ton = 2204.6 pounds

APPENDIX 3 • Logarithms of Numbers

N	0	1	2	3	4	5	6	7	8	9
1.0	.0000	.0043	.0086	.0128	.0170	.0212	.0253	.0294	.0334	.0374
1.1	.0414	.0453	.0492	.0531	.0569	.0607	.0645	.0682	.0719	.0755
1.2	.0792	.0828	.0864	.0899	.0934	.0969	.1004	.1038	.1072	.1106
1.3	.1139	.1173	.1206	.1239	.1271	.1303	.1335	.1367	.1399	.1430
1.4	.1461	.1492	.1523	.1553	.1584	.1614	.1644	.1673	.1703	.1732
1.5	.1761	.1790	.1818	.1847	.1875	.1903	.1931	.1959	.1987	.2014
1.6	.2041	.2068	.2095	.2122	.2148	.2175	.2201	.2227	.2253	.2279
1.7	.2304	.2330	.2355	.2380	.2405	.2430	.2455	.2480	.2504	.2529
1.8	.2553	.2577	.2601	.2625	.2648	.2672	.2695	.2718	.2742	.2765
1.9	.2788	.2810	.2833	.2856	.2878	.2900	.2923	.2945	.2967	.2989
2.0	.3010	.3032	.3054	.3075	.3096	.3118	.3139	.3160	.3181	.3201
2.1	.3222	.3243	.3263	.3284	.3304	.3324	.3345	.3365	.3385	.3404
2.2	.3424	.3444	.3464	.3483	.3502	.3522	.3541	.3560	.3579	.3598
2.3	.3617	.3636	.3655	.3674	.3692	.3711	.3729	.3747	.3766	.3784
2.4	.3802	.3820	.3838	.3856	.3874	.3892	.3909	.3927	.3945	.3962
2.5	.3979	.3997	.4014	.4031	.4048	.4065	.4082	.4099	.4116	.4133
2.6	.4150	.4166	.4183	.4200	.4216	.4232	.4249	.4265	.4281	.4298
2.7	.4314	.4330	.4346	.4362	.4378	.4393	.4409	.4425	.4440	.4456
2.8	.4472	.4487	.4502	.4518	.4533	.4548	.4564	.4579	.4594	.4609
2.9	.4624	.4639	.4654	.4669	.4683	.4698	.4713	.4728	.4742	.4757
3.0	.4771	.4786	.4800	.4814	.4829	.4843	.4857	.4871	.4886	.4900
3.1	.4914	.4928	.4942	.4955	.4969	.4983	.4997	.5011	.5024	.5038
3.2	.5051	.5065	.5079	.5092	.5105	.5119	.5132	.5145	.5159	.5172
3.3	.5185	.5198	.5211	.5224	.5237	.5250	.5263	.5276	.5289	.5302
3.4	.5315	.5238	.5340	.5353	.5366	.5378	.5391	.5403	.5416	.5428
3.5	.5441	.5453	.5465	.5478	.5490	.5502	.5514	.5527	.5539	.5551
3.6	.5563	.5575	.5587	.5599	.5611	.5623	.5635	.5647	.5658	.5670
3.7	.5682	.5694	.5705	.5717	.5729	.5740	.5752	.5763	.5775	.5786
3.8	.5798	.5809	.5821	.5832	.5843	.5855	.5866	.5877	.5888	.5899
3.9	.5911	.5922	.5933	.5944	.5955	.5966	.5977	.5988	.5999	.6010
4.0	.6021	.6031	.6042	.6053	.6064	.6075	.6085	.6096	.6107	.6117
4.1	.6128	.6138	.6149	.6160	.6170	.6180	.6191	.6201	.6212	.6222
4.2	.6232	.6243	.6253	.6263	.6274	.6284	.6294	.6304	.6314	.6325
4.3	.6335	.6345	.6355	.6365	.6375	.6385	.6395	.6405	.6415	.6425
4.4	.6435	.6444	.6454	.6464	.6474	.6484	.6493	.6503	.6513	.6522
4.5	.6532	.6542	.6551	.6561	.6571	.6580	.6590	.6599	.6609	.6618
4.6	.6628	.6637	.6646	.6656	.6665	.6675	.6684	.6693	.6702	.6712
4.7	.6721	.6730	.6739	.6749	.6758	.6767	.6776	.6785	.6794	.6803
4.8	.6812	.6821	.6830	.6839	.6848	.6857	.6866	.6875	.6884	.6893
4.9	.6902	.6911	.6920	.6928	.6937	.6946	.6955	.6964	.6972	.6981
5.0	.6990	.6998	.7007	.7016	.7024	.7033	.7042	.7050	.7059	.7067
5.1	.7076	.7084	.7093	.7101	.7110	.7118	.7216	.7135	.7143	.7152
5.2	.7160	.7168	.7177	.7185	.7193	.7202	.7210	.7218	.7226	.7235
5.3	.7243	.7251	.7259	.7267	.7275	.7284	.7292	.7300	.7308	.7316
5.4	.7324	.7332	.7340	.7348	.7356	.7364	.7372	.7380	.7388	.7396
N	0	1	2	3	4	5	6	7	8	9

APPENDIX 3 • Logarithms of Numbers (continued)

N	0	1	2	3	4	5	6	7	8	9
5.5	.7404	.7412	.7419	.7427	.7435	.7443	.7451	.7459	.7466	.7474
5.6	.7482	.7490	.7497	.7505	.7513	.7520	.7528	.7536	.7543	.7551
5.7	.7559	.7566	.7574	.7582	.7589	.7597	.7604	.7612	.7619	.7627
5.8	.7634	.7642	.7649	.7657	.7664	.7672	.7679	.7686	.7694	.7701
5.9	.7709	.7716	.7723	.7731	.7738	.7745	.7752	.7760	.7767	.7774
6.0	.7782	.7789	.7796	.7803	.7810	.7818	.7825	.7832	.7839	.7846
6.1	.7853	.7860	.7868	.7875	.7882	.7889	.7896	.7903	.7910	.7917
6.2	.7924	.7931	.7938	.7945	.7952	.7959	.7966	.7973	.7980	.7987
6.3	.7993	.8000	.8007	.8014	.8021	.8028	.8035	.8041	.8048	.8055
6.4	.8062	.8069	.8075	.8082	.8089	.8096	.8102	.8109	.8116	.8122
6.5	.8129	.8136	.8142	.8149	.8156	.8162	.8169	.8176	.8182	.8189
6.6	.8195	.8202	.8209	.8215	.8222	.8228	.8235	.8241	.8248	.8254
6.7	.8261	.8267	.8274	.8280	.8287	.8293	.8299	.8306	.8312	.8319
6.8	.8325	.8331	.8338	.8344	.8351	.8357	.8363	.8370	.8376	.8382
6.9	.8388	.8395	.8401	.8407	.8414	.8420	.8426	.8432	.8439	.8445
7.0	.8451	.8457	.8453	.8470	.8476	.8482	.8488	.8494	.8500	.8506
7.1	.8513	.8519	.8525	.8531	.8537	.8543	.8549	.8555	.8561	.8567
7.2	.8573	.8579	.8585	.8591	.8597	.8603	.8609	.8615	.8621	.8627
7.3	.8633	.8639	.8645	.8651	.8657	.8663	.8669	.8675	.8681	.8686
7.4	.8692	.8698	.8704	.8710	.8716	.8722	.8727	.8733	.8739	.8745
7.5	.8751	.8756	.8762	.8768	.8774	.8779	.8785	.8791	.8797	.8802
7.6	.8808	.8814	.8820	.8825	.8831	.8837	.8842	.8848	.8854	.8859
7.7	.8865	.8871	.8876	.8882	.8887	.8893	.8899	.8904	.8910	.8915
7.8	.8921	.8927	.8932	.8938	.8943	.8949	.8954	.8960	.8965	.8971
7.9	.8976	.8982	.8987	.8993	.8998	.9004	.9009	.9015	.9020	.9025
8.0	.9031	.9036	.9042	.9047	.9053	.9058	.9063	.9069	.9074	.9079
8.1	.9085	.9090	.9096	.9101	.9106	.9112	.9117	.9122	.9128	.9133
8.2	.9138	.9143	.9149	.9154	.9159	.9165	.9170	.9175	.9180	.9186
8.3	.9191	.9196	.9201	.9206	.9212	.9217	.9222	.9227	.9232	.9238
8.4	.9243	.9248	.9253	.9258	.9263	.9269	.9274	.9279	.9284	.9289
8.5	.9294	.9299	.9304	.9309	.9315	.9320	.9325	.9330	.9335	.9340
8.6	.9345	.9350	.9355	.9360	.9365	.9370	.9375	.9380	.9385	.9390
8.7	.9395	.9400	.9405	.9410	.9415	.9420	.9425	.9430	.9435	.9440
8.8	.9445	.9450	.9455	.9460	.9465	.9469	.9474	.9479	.9484	.9489
8.9	.9494	.9499	.9504	.9509	.9513	.9518	.9523	.9528	.9533	.9538
9.0	.9542	.9547	.9552	.9557	.9562	.9566	.9571	.9576	.9581	.9586
9.1	.9590	.9595	.9600	.9605	.9609	.9614	.9619	.9624	.9628	.9633
9.2	.9638	.9643	.9647	.9652	.9657	.9661	.9666	.9671	.9675	.9680
9.3	.9685	.9689	.9694	.9699	.9703	.9708	.9713	.9717	.9722	.9727
9.4	.9731	.9736	.9741	.9745	.9750	.9754	.9759	.9763	.9768	.9773
9.5	.9777	.9782	.9786	.9791	.9795	.9800	.9805	.9809	.9814	.9818
9.6	.9823	.9827	.9832	.9836	.9841	.9845	.9850	.9854	.9859	.9863
9.7	.9868	.9872	.9877	.9881	.9886	.9890	.9894	.9899	.9903	.9908
9.8	.9912	.9917	.9921	.9926	.9930	.9934	.9939	.9943	.9948	.9952
9.9	.9956	.9961	.9965	.9969	.9974	.9978	.9983	.9987	.9991	.9996
N	0	1	2	3	4	5	6	7	8	9

ANGLE in DEGREES	SINE	COSINE	TAN	COTAN	ANGLE in DEGREES
0	0.0000	1.0000	0.0000		90
1	.0175	.9998	.0175	57.290	89
2	.0349	.9994	.0349	28.636	88
3	.0523	.9986	.0524	19.081	87
4	.0698	.9976	.0699	14.301	86
5	.0872	.9962	.0875	11.430	85
6	.1045	.9945	.1051	9.5144	84
7	.1219	.9925	.1228	8.1443	83
8	.1392	.9903	.1405	7.1154	82
9	.1564	.9877	.1584	6.3138	81
10	.1736	.9848	.1763	5.6713	80
11	.1908	.9816	.1944	5.1446	79
12	.2079	.9781	.2126	4.7046	78
13	.2250	.9744	.2309	4.3315	77
14	.2419	.9703	.2493	4.0108	76
15	.2588	.9659	.2679	3.7321	75
16	.2756	.9613	.2867	3.4874	74
17	.2924	.9563	.3057	3.2709	73
18	.3090	.9511	.3249	3.0777	72
19	.3256	.9455	.3443	2.9042	71
20	.3420	.9397	.3640	2.7475	70
21	.3584	.9336	.3839	2.6051	69
22	.3746	.9272	.4040	2.4751	68
23	.3907	.9205	.4245	2.3559	67
24	.4067	.9135	.4452	2.2460	66
25	.4226	.9063	.4663	2.1445	65
26	.4384	.8988	.4877	2.0503	64
27	.4540	.8910	.5095	1.9626	63
28	.4695	.8829	.5317	1.8807	62
29	.4848	.8746	.5543	1.8040	61
30	.5000	.8660	.5774	1.7321	60
31	.5150	.8572	.6009	1.6643	59
32	.5299	.8480	.6249	1.6003	58
33	.5446	.8387	.6494	1.5399	57
34	.5592	.8290	.6745	1.4826	56
35	.5736	.8192	.7002	.14281	55
36	.5878	.8090	.7265	1.3764	54
37	.6018	.7986	.7536	1.3270	53
38	.6157	.7880	.7813	1.2799	52
39	.6293	.7771	.8098	1.2349	51
40	.6428	.7660	.8391	1.1918	50
41	.6561	.7547	.8693	1.1504	49
42	.6691	.7431	.9004	1.1106	48
43	.6820	.7314	.9325	1.0724	47
44	.6947	.7193	.9657	1.0355	46
45	.7071	.7071	1.0000	1.0000	45

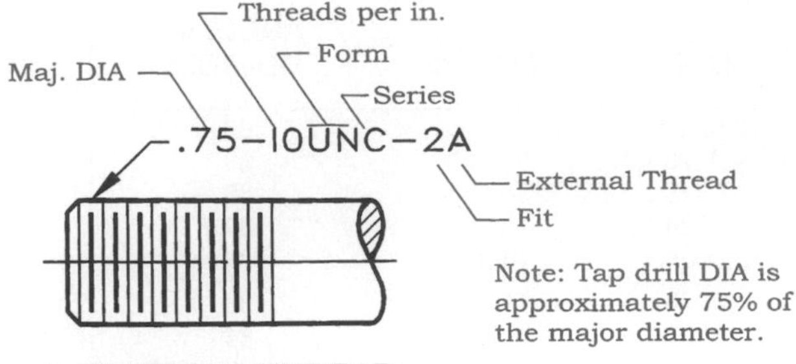

A. EXTERNAL THREAD

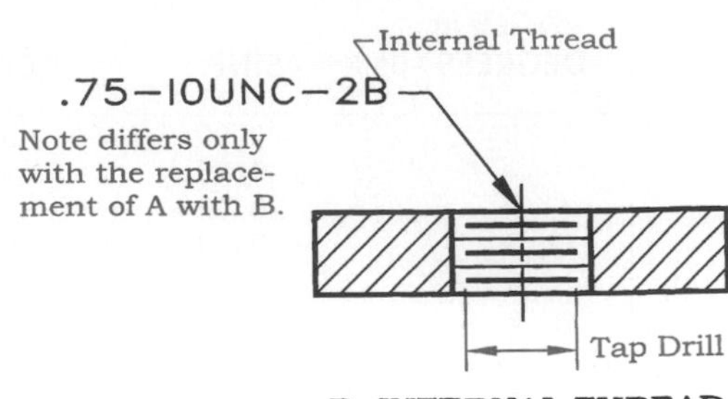

B. INTERNAL THREAD

Nominal Diameter	Basic Diameter	Coarse NC & UNC		Fine NF & UNF		Extra Fine NEF/UNEF	
		Thds per in.	Tap Drill DIA	Thds per in.	Tap Drill DIA	Thds per in.	Tap Drill DIA
0	.060			80	.0469		
1	.073	64	No. 53	72	No. 53		
2	.086	56	No. 50	64	No. 50		
3	.099	48	No. 47	56	No. 45		
4	.112	40	No. 43	48	No. 42		
5	.125	40	No. 38	44	No. 37		
6	.138	32	No. 36	40	No. 33		
8	.164	32	No. 29	36	No. 29		
10	.190	24	No. 25	32	No. 21		
12	.216	24	No. 16	28	No. 14	32	No. 13
1/4	.250	20	No. 7	28	No. 3	32	.2189
5/16	.3125	18	F	24	I	32	.2813
3/8	.375	16	.3125	24	Q	32	.3438
7/16	.4375	14	U	20	.3906	28	.4062
1/2	.500	13	.4219	20	.4531	28	.4688
9/16	.5625	12	.4844	18	.5156	24	.5156
5/8	.625	11	.5313	18	.5781	24	.5781
11/16	.6875	...	...	...	...	24	.6406
3/4	.750	10	.6563	16	.6875	20	.7031
13/16	.8125	...	...	...	...	20	.7656
7/8	.875	9	.7656	14	.8125	20	.8281
15/16	.9375	...	...	...	...	20	.8906

Nominal Diameter	Basic Diameter	Coarse NC & UNC		Fine NF & UNF		Extra Fine NEF/UNEF	
		Thds per in.	Tap Drill DIA	Thds per in.	Tap Drill DIA	Thds per in.	Tap Drill DIA
1	1.000	8	.875	12	.922	20	.953
1-1/16	1.063	...	...	...	...	18	1.000
1-1/8	1.125	7	.904	12	1.046	18	1.070
1-3/16	1.188	...	...	...	...	18	1.141
1-1/4	1.250	7	1.109	12	1.172	18	1.188
1-5/16	1.313	...	...	...	...	18	1.266
1-3/8	1.375	6	1.219	12	1.297	18	1.313
1-7/16	1.438	...	...	...	...	18	1.375
1-1/2	1.500	6	1.344	12	1.422	18	1.438
1-9/16	1.563	...	...	...	...	18	1.500
1-5/8	1.625	...	...	...	...	18	1.563
1-11/16	1.688	...	...	...	...	18	1.625
1-3/4	1.750	5	1.563	...	...	...	...
2	2.000	4.5	1.781	...	...	...	...
2-1/4	2.250	4.5	2.031	...	...	...	...
2-1/2	2.500	4	2.250	...	...	...	...
2-3/4	2.750	4	2.500	...	...	...	...
3	3.000	4	2.750	...	...	...	...
3-1/4	3.250	4	...	...	...	...	...
3-1/2	3.500	4	...	...	...	...	...
3-3/4	3.750	4	...	...	...	...	...
4	4.000	4	...	...	...	...	...

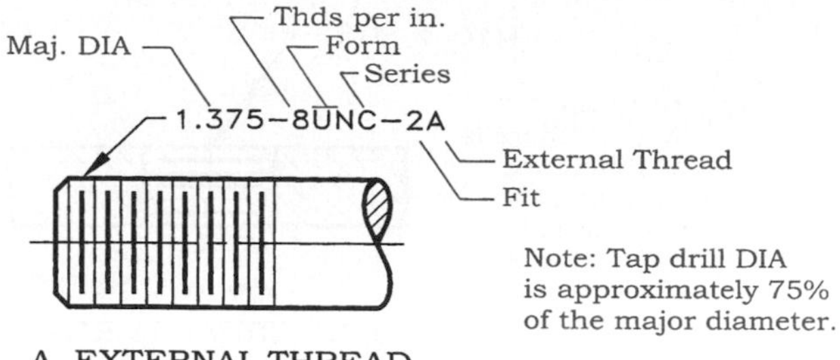

A. EXTERNAL THREAD

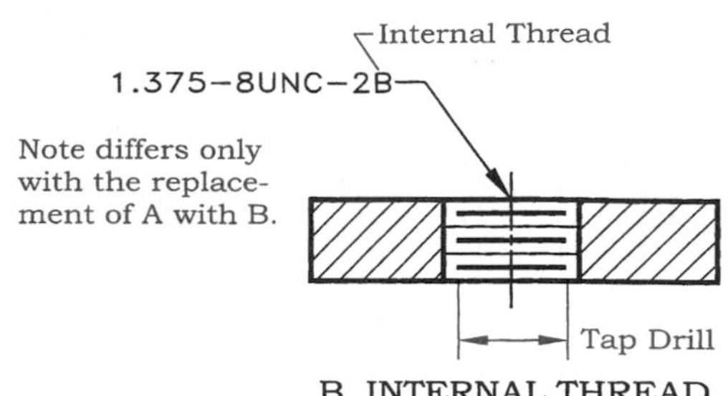

B. INTERNAL THREAD

Nominal Diameter	8 Pitch 8N & 8UN		12 Pitch 12N & 12UN		16 Pitch 16N & 16UN	
	Thds per in.	Tap Drill DIA	Thds per in.	Tap Drill DIA	Thds per in.	Tap Drill DIA
.500	...	...	12	.422	...	...
.563	...	...	12	.484	...	...
.625	...	...	12	.547	...	...
.688	...	...	12	.609	...	...
.750	...	...	12	.672	16	.688
.813	...	...	12	.734	16	.750
.875	...	...	12	.797	16	.813
.934	...	...	12	.859	16	.875
1.000	8	.875	12	.922	16	.938
1.063	...	...	12	.984	16	1.000
1.125	8	1.000	12	1.047	16	1.063
1.188	...	...	12	1.109	16	1.125
1.250	8	1.125	12	1.172	16	1.188
1.313	...	...	12	1.234	16	1.250
1.375	8	1.250	12	1.297	16	1.313
1.434	...	...	12	1.359	16	1.375
1.500	8	1.375	12	1.422	16	1.438
1.563	...	...	...	...	16	1.500
1.625	8	1.500	12	1.547	16	1.563
1.688	...	...	...	...	16	1.625
1.750	8	1.625	12	1.672	16	1.688
1.813	...	...	...	...	16	1.750
1.875	8	1.750	12	1.797	16	1.813
1.934	...	...	...	...	16	1.875
2.000	8	1.875	12	1.922	16	1.938

Nominal Diameter	8 Pitch 8N & 8UN		12 Pitch 12N & 12UN		16 Pitch 16N & 16UN	
	Thds per in.	Tap Drill DIA	Thds per in.	Tap Drill DIA	Thds per in.	Tap Drill DIA
2.063	...	...	...	...	16	2.000
2.125	...	...	12	2.047	16	2.063
2.188	...	...	...	...	16	2.125
2.250	8	2.125	12	2.172	16	2.188
2.313	...	...	...	...	16	2.250
2.375	...	...	12	2.297	16	2.313
2.438	...	...	...	...	16	2.375
2.500	8	2.375	12	2.422	16	2.438
2.625	...	...	12	2.547	16	2.563
2.750	8	2.625	12	2.717	16	2.688
2.875	...	...	12	...	16	...
3.000	8	2.875	12	...	16	...
3.125	...	...	12	...	16	...
3.250	8	...	12	...	16	...
3.375	...	...	12	...	16	...
3.500	8	...	12	...	16	...
3.625	...	...	12	...	16	...
3.750	8	...	12	...	16	...
3.875	...	...	12	...	16	...
4.000	8	...	12	...	16	...
4.250	8	...	12	...	16	...
4.500	8	...	12	...	16	...
4.750	8	...	12	...	16	...
5.000	8	...	12	...	16	...
5.250	8	...	12	...	16	...

Source: ANSI/ASME B1.1—1989.

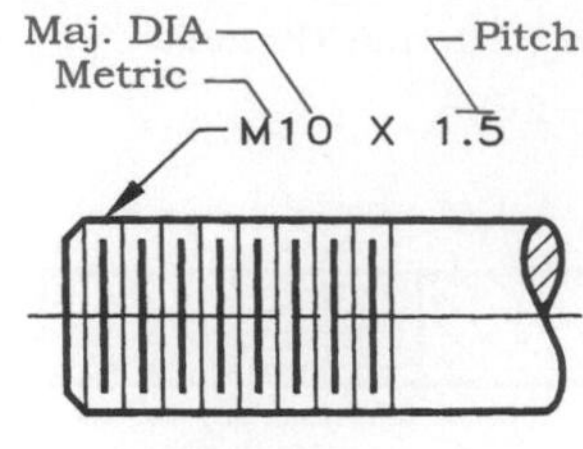

A. EXTERNAL THREAD

Note: Tap drill DIA is approximately 75% of the major diameter.

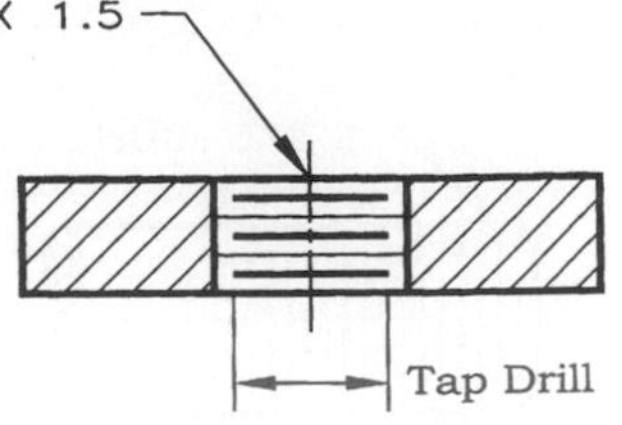

In the metric system, there is no difference between notes for internal and external threads.

B. INTERNAL THREAD

COARSE		FINE	
MAJ. DIA & THD PITCH	TAP DRILL	MAJ. DIA & THD PITCH	TAP DRILL
M1.6 × 0.35	1.25		
M1.8 × 0.35	1.45		
M2 × 0.4	1.6		
M2.2 × 0.45	1.75		
M2.5 × 0.45	2.05		
M3 × 0.5	2.5		
M3.5 × 0.6	2.9		
M4 × 0.7	3.3		
M4.5 × 0.75	3.75		
M5 × 0.8	4.2		
M6 × 1	5.0		
M7 × 1	6.0		
M8 × 1.25	6.8	M8 × 1	7.0
M9 × 1.25	7.75		
M10 × 1.5	8.5	M10 × 1.25	8.75
M11 × 1.5	9.5		
M12 × 1.75	10.3	M12 × 1.25	10.5
M14 × 2	12.0	M14 × 1.5	12.5
M16 × 2	14.0	M16 × 1.5	14.5
M18 × 2.5	15.5	M18 × 1.5	16.5

COARSE		FINE	
MAJ. DIA & THD PITCH	TAP DRILL	MAJ. DIA & THD PITCH	TAP DRILL
M20 × 2.5	17.5	M20 × 1.5	18.5
M22 × 2.5	19.5	M22 × 1.5	20.5
M24 × 3	21.0	M24 × 2	22.0
M27 × 3	24.0	M27 × 2	25.0
M30 × 3.5	26.5	M30 × 2	28.0
M33 × 3.5	29.5	M33 × 2	31.0
M36 × 4	32.0	M36 × 3	33.0
M39 × 4	35.0	M39 × 3	36.0
M42 × 4.5	37.5	M42 × 3	39.0
M45 × 4.5	40.5	M45 × 3	42.0
M48 × 5	43.0	M48 × 3	45.0
M52 × 5	47.0	M52 × 3	49.0
M56 × 5.5	50.5	M56 × 4	52.0
M60 × 5.5	54.5	M60× 4	56.0
M64 × 6	58.0	M64 × 4	60.0
M68 × 6	62.0	M68 × 4	64.0
M72 × 6	66.0	M72 × 4	68.0
M80 × 6	74.0	M80 × 4	76.0
M90 × 6	84.0	M90 × 4	86.0
M100 × 6	94.0	M100 × 4	96.0

Source: ANSI/ASME B1.13.

APPENDIX 8 • Square and Acme Threads

2.00−2.5 SQUARE

A typical thread note of a square thread

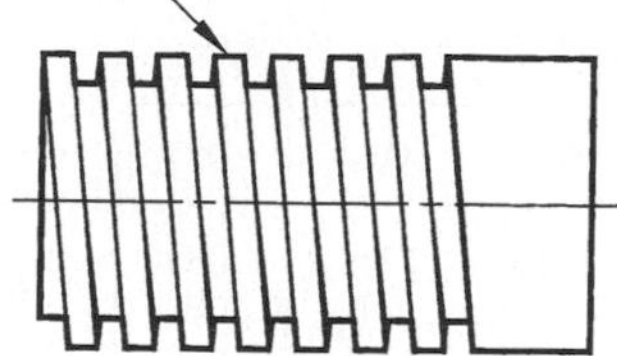

Size	Size	Thds per inch
3/8	.375	12
7/16	.438	10
1/2	.500	10
9/16	.563	8
5/8	.625	8
3/4	.75	6
7/8	.875	5
1	1.000	5
1-1/8	1.125	4
1-1/4	1.250	4
1-1/2	1.500	3
1-3/4	1.750	2-1/2
2	2.000	2-1/2
2-1/4	2.250	2
2-1/2	2.500	2
2-3/4	2.750	2
3	3.000	1-1/2
3-1/4	3.125	1-1/2
3-1/2	3.500	1-1/3
3-3/4	3.750	1-1/3
4	4.000	1-1/3
4-1/4	4.250	1-1/3
4-1/2	4.500	1
Larger		1

Dimensions are in inches.

APPENDIX 9 • American Standard Taper Pipe Threads (NPT)

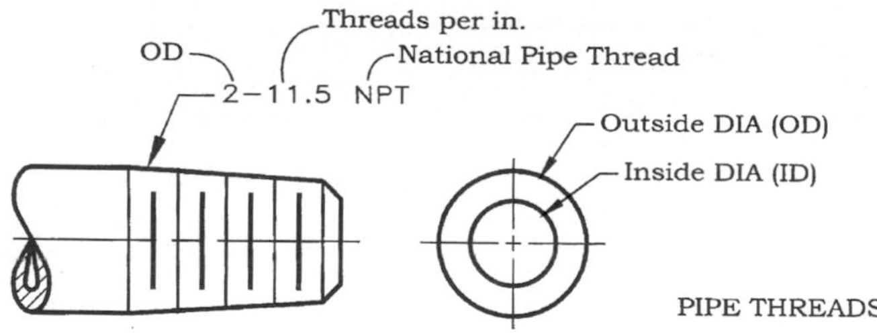

Pipes through 12 inches in diameter are specified by their inside diameters (ID). Larger pipes are specified by their outside diameters (OD).

$\frac{1}{16}$ DIA to $1\frac{1}{4}$ DIA

Nominal ID	$\frac{1}{16}$	$\frac{1}{8}$	$\frac{1}{4}$	$\frac{3}{8}$	$\frac{1}{2}$	$\frac{3}{4}$	1	1-1/4
Outside DIA	0.313	0.405	0.540	0.675	0.840	1.050	1.315	1.660
Thds/Inch	27	27	18	18	14	14	$11\frac{1}{2}$	$11\frac{1}{2}$

$1\frac{1}{2}$ DIA to 6 DIA

Nominal ID	$1\frac{1}{2}$	2	$2\frac{1}{2}$	3	$3\frac{1}{2}$	4	5	6
Outside DIA	1.900	2.375	2.875	3.500	4.000	4.500	5.563	6.625
Thds/Inch	$11\frac{1}{2}$	$11\frac{1}{2}$	8	8	8	8	8	8

8 DIA to 24 DIA

Nominal ID	8	10	12	14 OD	16 OD	18 OD	20 OD	24 OD
Outside DIA	8.625	10.750	12.750	14.000	16.000	18.000	20.000	24.000
Thds/Inch	8	8	8	8	8	8	8	8

Source: ANSI B2.1.
Dimensions are in inches.

APPENDIX 10 • Square Bolts (inches)

DIA	E Max.	F Max.	G Avg.	H Max.	R Max.
1/4	.250	.375	.530	.188	.031
5/16	.313	.500	.707	.220	.031
3/8	.375	.563	.795	.268	.031
7/16	.438	.625	.884	.316	.031
1/2	.500	.750	1.061	.348	.031
5/8	.625	.938	1.326	.444	.062
3/4	.750	1.125	1.591	.524	.062
7/8	.875	1.313	1.856	.620	.062
1	1.000	1.500	2.121	.684	.093
1-1/8	1.125	1.688	2.386	.780	.093
1-1/4	1.250	1.875	2.652	.876	.093
1-3/8	1.375	2.625	2.917	.940	.093
1-1/2	1.500	2.250	3.182	1.036	.093

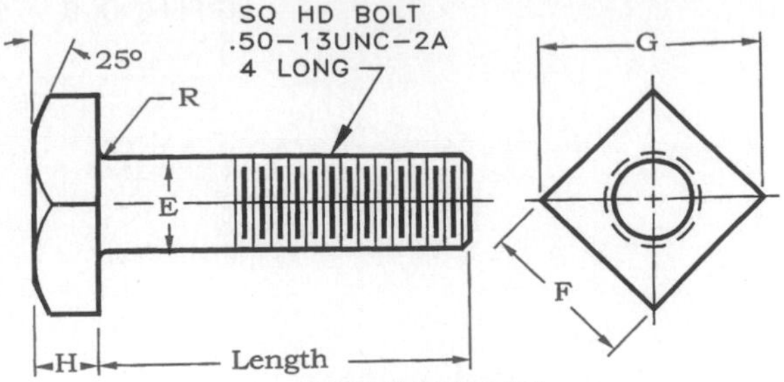

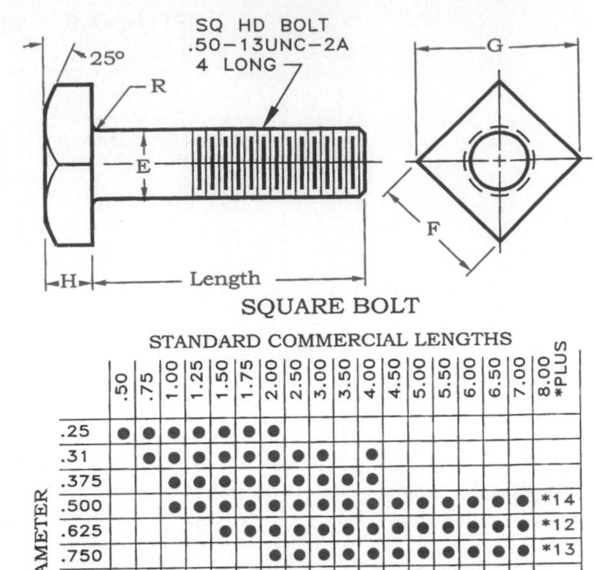

SQUARE BOLT

STANDARD COMMERCIAL LENGTHS

DIAMETER	.50	.75	1.00	1.25	1.50	1.75	2.00	2.50	3.00	3.50	4.00	4.50	5.00	5.50	6.00	6.50	7.00	8.00 *PLUS
.25	●	●	●	●	●	●	●											
.31		●	●	●	●	●	●	●	●		●							
.375			●	●	●	●	●	●	●	●	●							
.500			●	●	●	●	●	●	●	●	●	●	●	●	●	●	●	*14
.625					●	●	●	●	●	●	●	●	●	●	●	●	●	*12
.750							●	●	●	●	●	●	●	●	●	●	●	*13
.875										●	●	●	●	●				
1.00															●	●	●	*12
1.25															●	●	●	●

*14 MEANS THAT LENGTHS ARE AVAILABLE AT 1 INCH INCREMENTS UP 14 INCHES.

APPENDIX 11 • Square Nuts

DIA	DIA	F Max.	G Avg.	H Max.
1/4	.250	.438	.619	.235
5/16	.313	.563	.795	.283
3/8	.375	.625	.884	.346
7/16	.438	.750	1.061	.394
1/2	.500	.813	1.149	.458
5/8	.625	1.000	1.414	.569
3/4	.750	1.125	1.591	.680
7/8	.875	1.313	1.856	.792
1	1.000	1.500	2.121	.903
1-1/8	1.125	1.688	2.386	1.030
1-1/4	1.250	1.875	2.652	1.126
1-3/8	1.375	1.063	2.917	1.237
1-1/2	1.500	2.250	3.182	1.348

Dimensions are in inches.

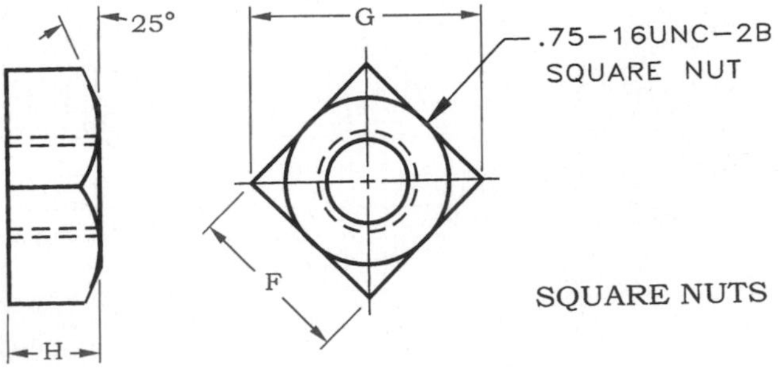

SQUARE NUTS

APPENDIX 12 • Hexagon Head Bolts

DIA	E Max.	F Max.	G Avg.	H Max.	R Max.
1/4	.250	.438	.505	.163	.025
5/16	.313	.500	.577	.211	.025
3/8	.375	.563	.650	.243	.025
7/16	.438	.625	.722	.291	.025
1/2	.500	.750	.866	.323	.025
9/16	.563	.812	.938	.371	.045
5/8	.625	.938	1.083	.403	.045
3/4	.750	1.125	1.299	.483	.045
7/8	.875	1.313	1.516	.563	.065
1	1.000	1.500	1.732	.627	.095
1-1/8	1.125	1.688	1.949	.718	.095
1-1/4	1.250	1.875	2.165	.813	.095
1-3/8	1.375	2.063	2.382	.878	.095
1-1/2	1.500	2.250	2.598	.974	.095
1-3/4	1.750	2.625	3.031	1.134	.095
2	2.000	3.000	3.464	1.263	.095
2-1/4	2.250	3.375	3.897	1.423	.095
2-1/2	2.500	3.750	4.330	1.583	.095
2-3/4	2.750	4.125	4.763	1.744	.095
3	3.000	4.500	5.196	1.935	.095

Dimensions are in inches.

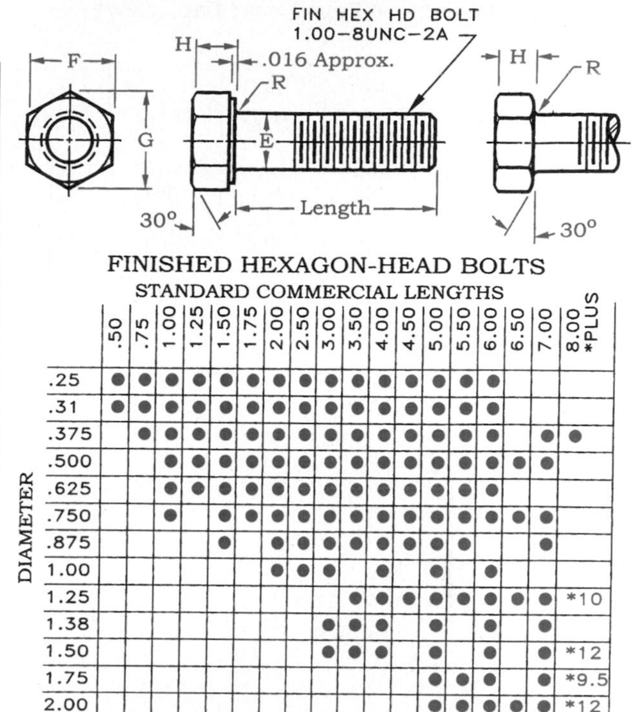

FINISHED HEXAGON-HEAD BOLTS

STANDARD COMMERCIAL LENGTHS

DIAMETER	.50	.75	1.00	1.25	1.50	1.75	2.00	2.50	3.00	3.50	4.00	4.50	5.00	5.50	6.00	6.50	7.00	8.00 *PLUS
.25	●	●	●	●	●	●	●	●	●	●	●	●	●	●	●			
.31	●	●	●	●	●	●	●	●	●	●	●	●	●	●	●			
.375		●	●	●	●	●	●	●	●	●	●	●	●	●	●		●	●
.500			●	●	●	●	●	●	●	●	●	●	●	●	●	●	●	
.625			●	●	●	●	●	●	●	●	●	●	●	●	●			
.750			●		●	●	●	●	●	●	●	●	●	●	●	●	●	
.875					●		●	●	●	●	●	●	●	●			●	
1.00							●	●	●		●		●		●			
1.25										●	●	●	●	●	●	●	●	*10
1.38									●	●	●		●		●		●	
1.50									●	●	●		●		●		●	*12
1.75													●	●	●		●	*9.5
2.00													●	●	●	●	●	*12

*10 MEANS THAT LENGTHS ARE AVAILABLE AT 1 INCH INCREMENTS UP TO 10 INCHES.

APPENDIX 13 • Hex Nuts and Hex Jam Nuts

MAJOR DIA		F Max.	G Avg.	H1 Max.	H2 Max.
1/4	.250	.438	.505	.226	.163
5/16	.313	.500	.577	.273	.195
3/8	.375	.563	.650	.337	.227
7/16	.438	.688	.794	.385	.260
1/2	.500	.750	.866	.448	.323
9/16	.563	.875	1.010	.496	.324
5/8	.625	.938	1.083	.559	.387
3/4	.750	1.125	1.299	.665	.446
7/8	.875	1.313	1.516	.776	.510
1	1.000	1.500	1.732	.887	.575
1-1/8	1.125	1.688	1.949	.899	.639
1-1/4	1.250	1.875	2.165	1.094	.751
1-3/8	1.375	2.063	2.382	1.206	.815
1-1/2	1.500	2.250	2.589	1.317	.880

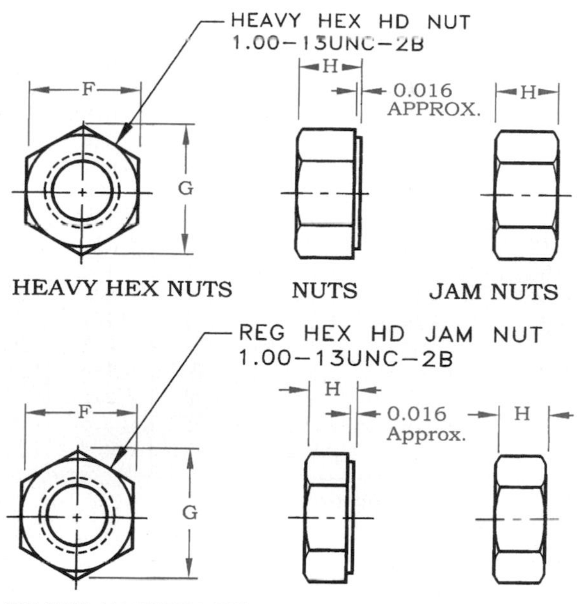

APPENDIX 14 • Round Head Cap Screws

DIA	D Max.	A Max.	H Avg.	J Max.	T Max.
1/4	.250	.437	.191	.075	.117
5/16	.313	.562	.245	.084	.151
3/8	.375	.625	.273	.094	.168
7/16	.438	.750	.328	.094	.202
1/2	.500	.812	.354	.106	.218
9/16	.563	.937	.409	.118	.252
5/8	.625	1.000	.437	.133	.270
3/4	.750	1.250	.546	.149	.338

Dimensions are in inches.

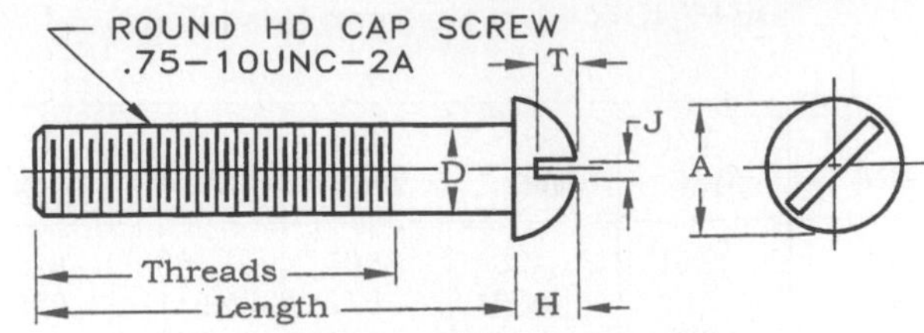

ROUND HEAD CAP SCREW

STANDARD COMMERCIAL LENGTHS

Dimensions are in inches.

DIAMETER	.50	.75	1.00	1.25	1.50	1.75	2.00	2.50	3.00	3.50	4.00
.25	●	●	●	●	●	●	●				
.31		●	●	●	●	●	●	●	●	●	●
.375			●	●	●	●	●	●	●	●	●
.500			●	●	●	●	●	●	●	●	●
.625					●	●	●	●	●	●	●
.750							●	●	●	●	●

OTHER LENGTHS AND DIAMETERS ARE AVAILABLE, BUT THESE ARE THE MORE STANDARD ONES.

APPENDIX 15 • Flat Head Cap Screws

DIA	D Max.	A Max.	H Avg.	J Max.	T Max.
1/4	.250	.500	.140	.075	.068
5/16	.313	.625	.177	.084	.086
3/8	.375	.750	.210	.094	.103
7/16	.438	.813	.210	.094	.103
1/2	.500	.875	.210	.106	.103
9/16	.563	1.000	.244	.118	.120
5/8	.625	1.125	.281	.133	.137
3/4	.750	1.375	.352	.149	.171
7/8	.875	1.625	.423	.167	.206
1	1.000	1.875	.494	.188	.240
1-1/8	1.125	2.062	.529	.196	.257
1-1/4	1.250	2.312	.600	.211	.291
1-3/8	1.375	2.562	.665	.226	.326
1-1/2	1.500	2.812	.742	.258	.360

Dimensions are in inches.

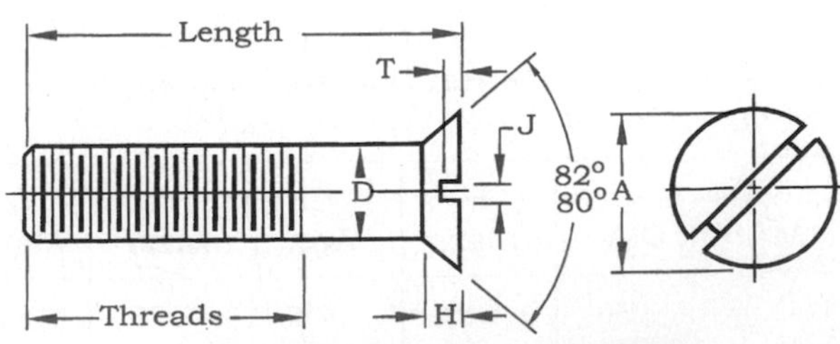

FLAT-HEAD CAP SCREWS

STANDARD COMMERCIAL LENGTHS

Dimensions are in inches.

DIAMETER	.50	.75	1.00	1.25	1.50	1.75	2.00	2.50	3.00	3.50	4.00
.25	●	●	●	●	●	●	●				
.31		●	●	●	●	●	●	●	●	●	●
.375			●	●	●	●	●	●	●	●	●
.500			●	●	●	●	●	●	●	●	●
.625					●	●	●	●	●	●	●
.750							●	●	●	●	●
.875								●	●	●	●
1.00									●	●	●
1.50									●	●	●

OTHER LENGTHS AND DIAMETERS ARE AVAILABLE, BUT THESE ARE THE MORE STANDARD ONES.

APPENDIX 16 • Fillister Head Cap Screws

DIA	D Max.	A Max.	H Avg.	J Max.	T Max.
1/4	.250	.375	.172	.075	.097
5/16	.313	.437	.203	.084	.115
3/8	.375	.562	.250	.094	.142
7/16	.438	.625	.297	.094	.168
1/2	.500	.750	.328	.106	.193
9/16	.563	.812	.375	.118	.213
5/8	.625	.875	.422	.133	.239
3/4	.750	1.000	.500	.149	.283
7/8	.875	1.125	.594	.167	.334
1	1.000	1.312	.656	.188	.371

Source: ANSI B18.6.2.

Dimensions are in inches.

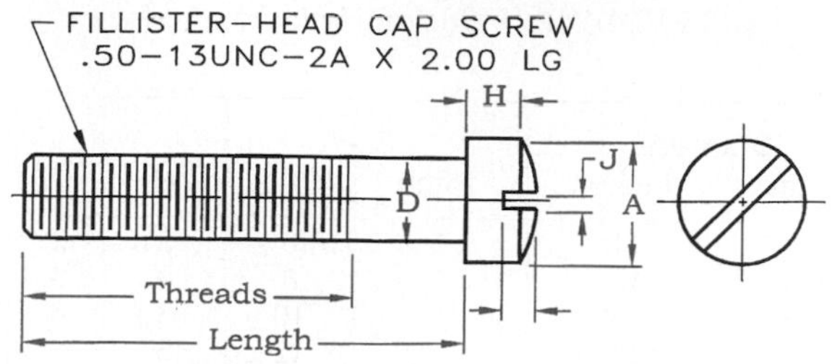

FILLISTER-HEAD CAP SCREW

Dimensions are in inches.

STANDARD LENGTHS

DIAMETER	.50	.75	1.00	1.25	1.50	1.75	2.00	2.50
.25	●	●	●	●	●	●	●	●
.313	●		●	●			●	
.375		●	●	●		●	●	
.500		●	●				●	●
.625			●		●		●	●
.750			●		●		●	●
.875				●	●		●	●
1.00				●	●	●	●	●

APPENDIX 17 • Flat Socket Head Cap Screws

Diameter mm	Diameter inches	Pitch	A	Ang.	W
M3	.118	.5	6	90	2
M4	.157	.7	8	90	2.5
M5	.197	.8	10	90	3
M6	.236	1	12	90	4
M8	.315	1.25	16	90	5
M10	.394	1.5	20	90	6
M12	.472	1.75	24	90	8
M14	.551	2	27	90	10
M16	.630	2	30	90	10
M20	.787	2.5	36	90	12

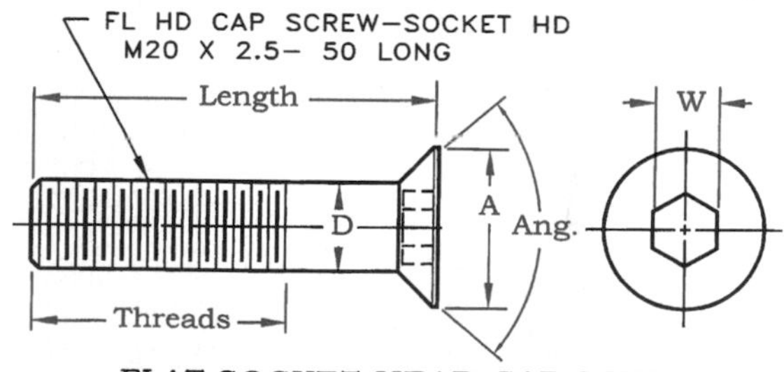

FLAT SOCKET-HEAD CAP SCREW

STANDARD COMMERCIAL LENGTHS

Dimensions in mm

DIAMETER	8–30	8–40	8–50	10–70	12–100	20–100	25–100	30–100	35–100		
M3	●										
M4		●									
M5			●								
M6			●								
M8				●							
M10					●						
M12						●					
M16								●			
M20									●		

DIA 8-16: LENGTHS AT INTERVALS OF 2 MM
DIA 20-100: LENGTHS AT INTERVALS OF 5 MM

APPENDIX 18 • Socket Head Cap Screws

Diameter mm	Diameter inches	Pitch	A	H	W
M3	.118	.5	6	3	2
M4	.157	.7	8	4	3
M5	.187	.8	10	5	4
M6	.236	1	12	6	6
M8	.315	1.25	16	8	6
M10	.394	1.5	20	10	8
M12	.472	1.75	24	12	10
M14	.551	2	27	14	12
M16	.630	2	30	16	14
M20	.787	2.5	36	20	17

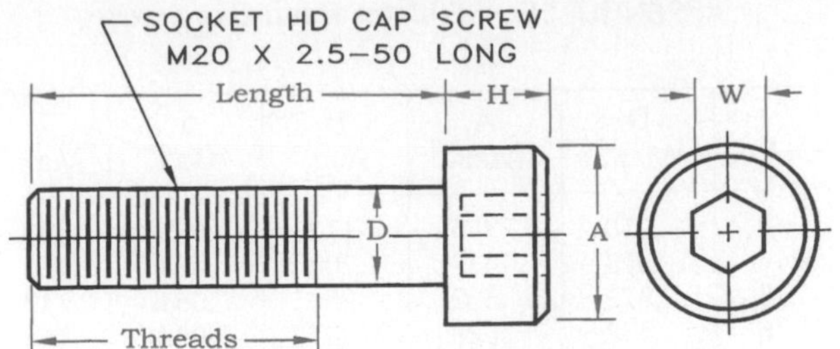

SOCKET-HEAD CAP SCREW

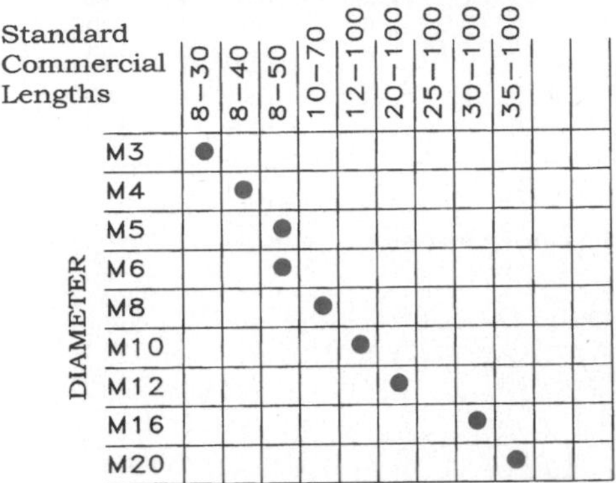

Standard Commercial Lengths

DIAMETER	8–30	8–40	8–50	10–70	12–100	20–100	25–100	30–100	35–100		
M3	●										
M4		●									
M5			●								
M6			●								
M8				●							
M10					●						
M12						●					
M16								●			
M20									●		

DIA 8-16: LENGTHS AT INTERVALS OF 2 MM
DIA 20-100: LENGTHS AT INTERVALS OF 5 MM

APPENDIX 19 • Round Head Machine Screws

DIA	D Max.	A Max.	H Avg.	J Max.	T Max.
0	.060	.113	.053	.023	.039
1	.073	.138	.061	.026	.044
2	.086	.162	.069	.031	.048
3	.099	.187	.078	.035	.053
4	.112	.211	.086	.039	.058
5	.125	.236	.095	.043	.063
6	.138	.260	.103	.048	.068
8	.164	.309	.120	.054	.077
10	.190	.359	.137	.060	.087
12	.216	.408	.153	.067	.096
1/4	.250	.472	.175	.075	.109
5/16	.313	.590	.216	.084	.132
3/8	.375	.708	.256	.094	.155
7/16	.438	.750	.328	.094	.196
1/2	.500	.813	.355	.106	.211
9/16	.563	.938	.410	.118	.242
5/8	.625	1.000	.438	.133	.258
3/4	.750	1.250	.547	.149	.320

Dimensions are in inches.

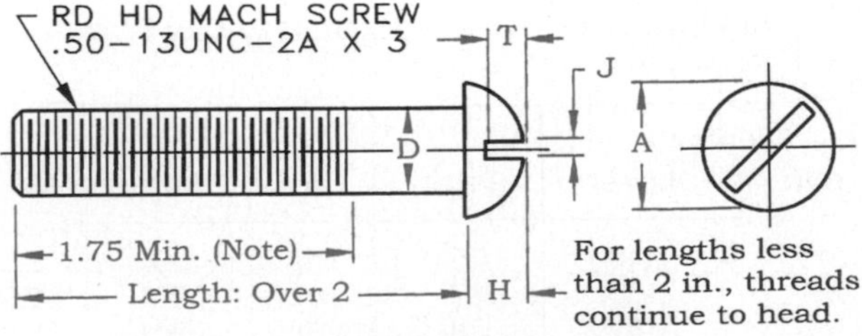

ROUND-HEAD MACHINE SCREW

Standard Lengths

DIAMETER	.25	.50	.75	1.00	1.25	1.50	1.75	2.00	2.50	3.00
0	●	●								
1	●	●								
2	●	●	●	●						
4	●	●	●	●	●	●				
6	●	●	●	●	●	●	●	●	●	
.125	●	●	●	●	●	●	●	●	●	
.250	●	●	●	●	●	●	●	●	●	
.375		●	●	●	●	●	●	●	●	
.500		●	●	●	●	●	●	●	●	●
.625		●	●	●	●	●	●	●	●	●
.750		●	●	●	●	●	●	●	●	●

OTHER LENGTHS AND DIAMETERS ARE AVAILABLE; THESE ARE THE MORE STANDARD ONES.

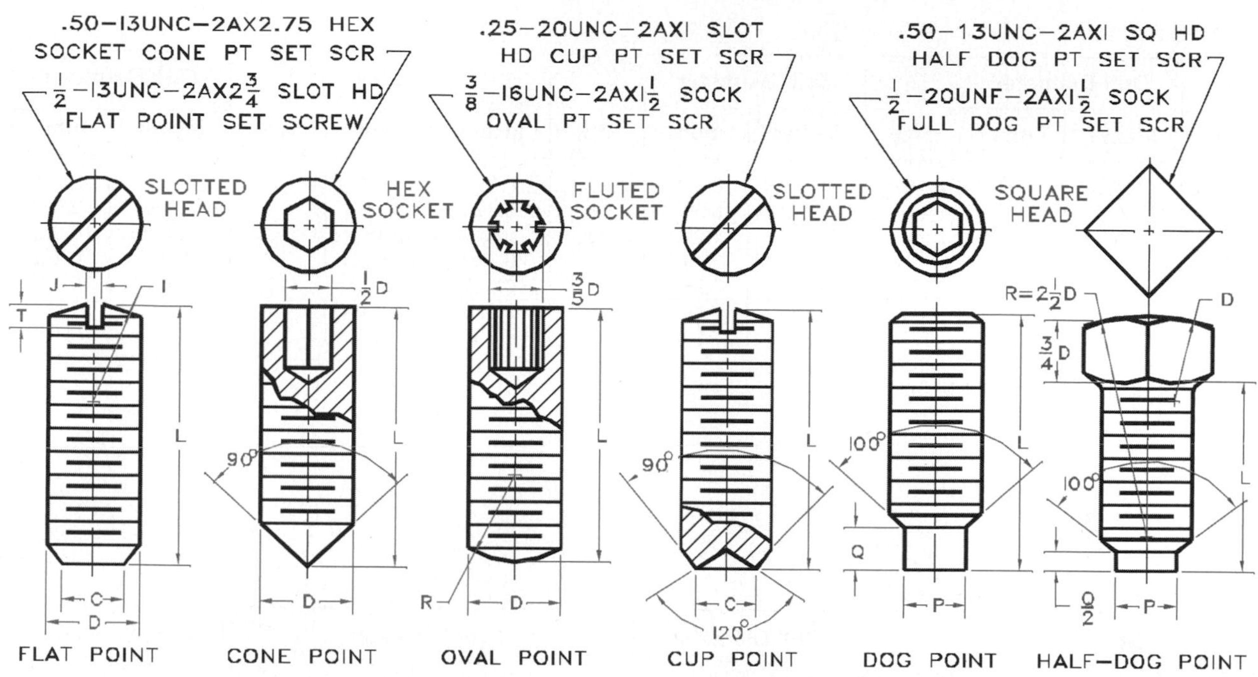

D	I	J	T	R	C		P		Q	q
Nominal Size	Radius of Headless Crown	Width of Slot	Depth of Slot	Oval Point Radius	Diameter of Cup and Flat Points		Diameter of Dog Point		Length of Dog Point	
					Max	Min	Max	Min	Full	Half
5 0.125	0.125	0.023	0.031	0.094	0.067	0.057	0.083	0.078	0.060	0.030
6 0.138	0.138	0.025	0.035	0.109	0.047	0.064	0.092	0.087	0.070	0.035
8 0.164	0.164	0.029	0.041	0.125	0.087	0.076	0.109	0.103	0.080	0.040
10 0.190	0.190	0.032	0.048	0.141	0.102	0.088	0.127	0.120	0.090	0.045
12 0.216	0.216	0.036	0.054	0.156	0.115	0.101	0.144	0.137	0.110	0.055
1/4 0.250	0.250	0.045	0.063	0.188	0.132	0.118	0.156	0.149	0.125	0.063
5/16 0.3125	0.313	0.051	0.076	0.234	0.172	0.156	0.203	0.195	0.156	0.078
3/8 0.375	0.375	0.064	0.094	0.281	0.212	0.194	0.250	0.241	0.188	0.094
7/16 0.4375	0.438	0.072	0.190	0.328	0.252	0.232	0.297	0.287	0.219	0.109
1/2 0.500	0.500	0.081	0.125	0.375	0.291	0.270	0.344	0.344	0.250	0.125
9/16 0.5625	0.563	0.091	0.141	0.422	0.332	0.309	0.391	0.379	0.281	0.140
5/8 0.625	0.625	0.102	0.156	0.469	0.371	0.347	0.469	0.456	0.313	0.156
3/4 0.750	0.750	0.129	0.188	0.563	0.450	0.425	0.563	0.549	0.375	0.188

Source: Courtesy of ANSI; B18.6.2.
Dimensions for the set screws shown in ANSI Fig. 18.44 (dimensions in inches).

APPENDIX 21 • Twist Drill Sizes

Letter Size Drills

Size	Drill Diameter		Size	Drill Diameter		Size	Drill Diameter		Size	Drill Diameter	
	inches	mm		inches	mm		inches	mm		inches	mm
A	0.234	5.944	H	0.266	6.756	O	0.316	8.026	V	0.377	9.576
B	0.238	6.045	I	0.272	6.909	P	0.323	8.204	W	0.386	9.804
C	0.242	6.147	J	0.277	7.036	Q	0.332	8.433	X	0.397	10.084
D	0.246	6.248	K	0.281	7.137	R	0.339	8.611	Y	0.404	10.262
E	0.250	6.350	L	0.290	7.366	S	0.348	8.839	Z	0.413	10.490
F	0.257	6.528	M	0.295	7.493	T	0.358	9.093			
G	0.261	6.629	N	0.302	7.601	U	0.368	9.347			

Source: Courtesy of General Motors Corporation.

Number Size Drills

Size	Drill Diameter		Size	Drill Diameter		Size	Drill Diameter		Size	Drill Diameter	
	inches	mm		inches	mm		inches	mm		inches	mm
1	0.2280	5.7912	21	0.1590	4.0386	41	0.0960	2.4384	61	0.0390	0.9906
2	0.2210	5.6134	22	0.1570	3.9878	42	0.0935	2.3622	62	0.0380	0.9652
3	0.2130	5.4102	23	0.1540	3.9116	43	0.0890	2.2606	63	0.0370	0.9398
4	0.2090	5.3086	24	0.1520	3.8608	44	0.0860	2.1844	64	0.0360	0.9144
5	0.2055	5.2197	25	0.1495	3.7973	45	0.0820	2.0828	65	0.0350	0.8890
6	0.2040	5.1816	26	0.1470	3.7338	46	0.0810	2.0574	66	0.0330	0.8382
7	0.2010	5.1054	27	0.1440	3.6576	47	0.0785	19.812	67	0.0320	0.8128
8	0.1990	5.0800	28	0.1405	3.5560	48	0.0760	1.9304	68	0.0310	0.7874
9	0.1960	4.9784	29	0.1360	3.4544	49	0.0730	1.8542	69	0.0292	0.7417
10	0.1935	4.9149	30	0.1285	3.2639	50	0.0700	1.7780	70	0.0280	0.7112
11	0.1910	4.8514	31	0.1200	3.0480	51	0.0670	1.7018	71	0.0260	0.6604
12	0.1890	4.8006	32	0.1160	2.9464	52	0.0635	1.6129	72	0.0250	0.6350
13	0.1850	4.6990	33	0.1130	2.8702	53	0.0595	1.5113	73	0.0240	0.6096
14	0.1820	4.6228	34	0.1110	2.8194	54	0.0550	1.3970	74	0.0225	0.5715
15	0.1800	4.5720	35	0.1100	2.7940	55	0.0520	1.3208	75	0.0210	0.5334
16	0.1770	4.4958	36	0.1065	0.7051	56	0.0465	1.1684	76	0.0200	0.5080
17	0.1730	4.3942	37	0.1040	2.6416	57	0.0430	1.0922	77	0.0180	0.4572
18	0.1695	4.3053	38	0.1015	2.5781	58	0.0420	1.0668	78	0.0160	0.4064
19	0.1660	4.2164	39	0.0995	2.5273	59	0.0410	1.0414	79	0.0145	0.3638
20	0.1610	4.0894	40	0.0980	2.4892	60	0.0400	1.0160	80	0.0135	0.3428

APPENDIX 21 • Twist Drill Sizes (continued)

Metric Drill Sizes Decimal-inch equivalents are for reference only.

Drill Diameter		Drill Diameter		Drill Diameter		Drill Diameter		Drill Diameter		Drill Diameter		Drill Diameter	
mm	in.	mm	in.	mm	in.	mm	in.	mm	in.	mm	in.	mm	in.
.40	.0157	1.03	.0406	2.20	.0866	5.00	.1969	10.00	.3937	21.50	.8465	48.00	1.8898
.42	.0165	1.05	.0413	2.30	.0906	5.20	.2047	10.30	.4055	22.00	.8661	50.00	1.9685
.45	.0177	1.08	.0425	2.40	.0945	5.30	.2087	10.50	.4134	23.00	.9055	51.50	2.0276
.48	.0189	1.10	.0433	2.50	.0984	5.40	.2126	10.80	.4252	24.00	.9449	53.00	2.0866
.50	.0197	1.15	.0453	2.60	.1024	5.60	.2205	11.00	.4331	25.00	.9843	54.00	2.1260
.52	.0205	1.20	.0472	2.70	.1063	5.80	.2283	11.50	.4528	26.00	1.0236	56.00	2.2047
.55	.0217	1.25	.0492	2.80	.1102	6.00	.2362	12.00	.4724	27.00	1.0630	58.00	2.2835
.58	.0228	1.30	.0512	2.90	.1142	6.20	.2441	12.50	.4921	28.00	1.1024	60.00	2.3622
.60	.0236	1.35	.0531	3.00	.1181	6.30	.2480	13.00	.5118	29.00	1.1417		
.62	.0244	1.40	.0551	3.10	.1220	6.50	.2559	13.50	.5315	30.00	1.1811		
.65	.0256	1.45	.0571	3.20	.1260	6.70	.2638	14.00	.5512	31.00	1.2205		
.68	.0268	1.50	.0591	3.30	.1299	6.80	.2677	14.50	.5709	32.00	1.2598		
.70	.0276	1.55	.0610	3.40	.1339	6.90	.2717	15.00	.5906	33.00	1.2992		
.72	.0283	1.60	.0630	3.50	.1378	7.10	.2795	15.50	.6102	34.00	1.3386		
.75	.0295	1.65	.0650	3.60	.1417	7.30	.2874	16.00	.6299	35.00	1.3780		
.78	.0307	1.70	.0669	3.70	.1457	7.50	.2953	16.50	.6496	36.00	1.4173		
.80	.0315	1.75	.0689	3.80	.1496	7.80	.3071	17.00	.6693	37.00	1.4567		
.82	.0323	1.80	.0709	3.90	.1535	8.00	.3150	17.50	.6890	38.00	1.4961		
.85	.0335	1.85	.0728	4.00	.1575	8.20	.3228	18.00	.7087	39.00	1.5354		
.88	.0346	1.90	.0748	4.10	.1614	8.50	.3346	18.50	.7283	40.00	1.5748		
.90	.0354	1.95	.0768	4.20	.1654	8.80	.3465	19.00	.7480	41.00	1.6142		
.92	.0362	2.00	.0787	4.40	.1732	9.00	.3543	19.50	.7677	42.00	1.6535		
.95	.0374	2.05	.0807	4.50	.1772	9.20	.3622	20.00	.7874	43.50	1.7126		
.98	.0386	2.10	.0827	4.60	.1811	9.50	.3740	20.50	.0871	45.00	1.7717		
1.00	.0394	2.15	.0846	4.80	.1890	9.80	.3858	21.00	.8268	46.50	1.8307		

APPENDIX 22 • Cotter Pins: American National Standard (inches)

Nominal Diameter	Maximum DIA A	Minimum DIA B	Hole Size
0.031	0.032	0.063	0.047
0.047	0.048	0.094	0.063
0.062	0.060	0.125	0.078
0.078	0.076	0.156	0.094
0.094	0.090	0.188	0.109
0.109	0.104	0.219	0.125
0.125	0.120	0.250	0.141
0.141	0.176	0.281	0.156
0.156	0.207	0.313	0.172
0.188	0.176	0.375	0.203
0.219	0.207	0.438	0.234
0.250	0.225	0.500	0.266
0.312	0.280	0.625	0.313
0.375	0.335	0.750	0.375
0.438	0.406	0.875	0.438
0.500	0.473	1.000	0.500
0.625	0.598	1.250	0.625
0.750	0.723	1.500	0.750

Source: Courtesy of ANSI: B18.8.1—1983.

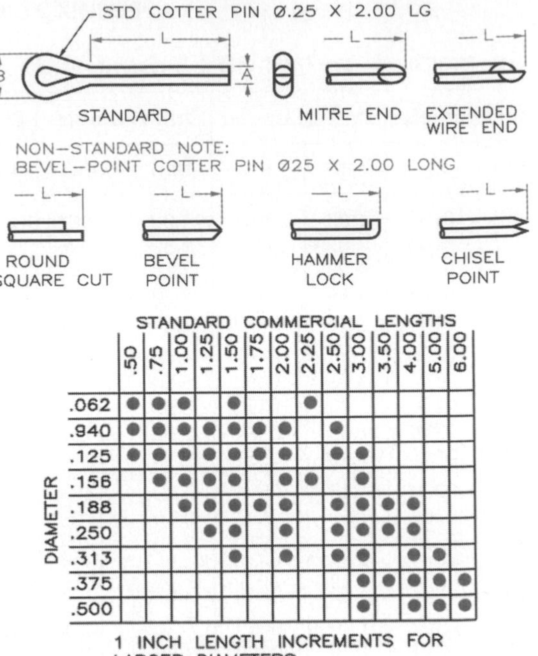

STANDARD COMMERCIAL LENGTHS

DIAMETER	.50	.75	1.00	1.25	1.50	1.75	2.00	2.25	2.50	3.00	3.50	4.00	5.00	6.00
.062	●	●	●		●			●						
.940	●	●	●	●	●	●	●		●					
.125	●	●	●	●	●	●	●		●	●				
.156		●	●	●	●		●	●		●				
.188			●	●	●	●	●		●	●	●	●		
.250				●	●		●		●	●	●	●		
.313					●		●		●	●		●	●	
.375										●	●	●	●	●
.500										●		●	●	●

1 INCH LENGTH INCREMENTS FOR LARGER DIAMETERS

APPENDIX 23 • Straight Pins (inches)

Nominal DIA	Diameter A Max	Diameter A Min	Chamfer B
0.062	0.0625	0.0605	0.015
0.094	0.0937	0.0917	0.015
0.109	0.1094	0.1074	0.015
0.125	0.1250	0.1230	0.015
0.156	0.1562	0.1542	0.015
0.188	0.1875	0.1855	0.015
0.219	0.2187	0.2167	0.015
0.250	0.2500	0.2480	0.015
0.312	0.3125	0.3095	0.015
0.375	0.3750	0.3720	0.030
0.438	0.4345	0.4345	0.030
0.500	0.4970	0.4970	0.030

Source: Courtesy of ANSI: B5.20.

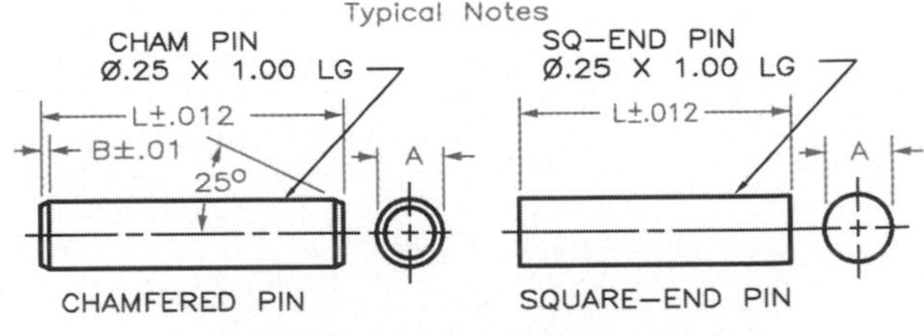

STANDARD COMMERCIAL LENGTHS

DIAMETER	.188	.25	.38	.50	.63	.75	.88	1.00	1.25	1.50	1.75	2.00	2.25	2.50	3.00	3.50
.062	●	●	●	●		●		●								
.940	●	●	●	●		●		●								
.125			●	●	●	●	●	●	●	●	●	●				
.156			●	●	●	●	●	●	●	●	●	●				
.188			●	●	●	●	●	●	●	●	●	●				
.219																
.250				●	●	●	●	●	●	●	●	●		●		
.312				●	●	●	●	●	●	●	●	●	●	●	●	●
.375				●	●	●	●	●	●	●	●	●	●	●	●	
.438								●				●		●	●	
.500								●		●		●		●		●

1 INCH LENGTH INCREMENTS FOR LARGER DIAMETERS

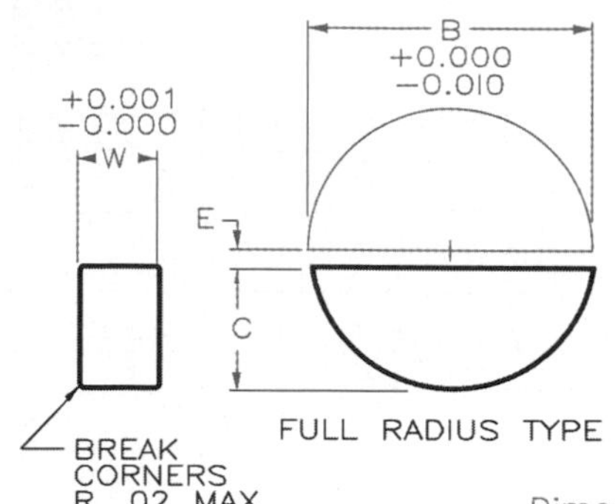

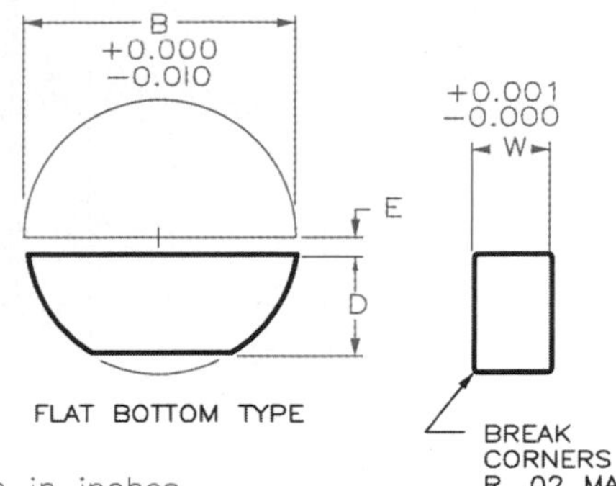

Dimensions are in inches

Key No.	W × B	C Max.	D Max.	E
204	1/16 × 1/2	.203	.194	.047
304	3/32 × 1/2	.203	.194	.047
404	1/8 × 1/2	.203	.194	.047
305	3/32 × 5/8	.250	.240	.063
405	1/8 × 5/8	.250	.240	.063
505	5/32 × 5/8	.250	.240	.063
406	1/8 × 3/4	.313	.303	.063

Key No.	W × B	C Max.	D Max.	E
506	5/32 × 3/4	.313	.303	.063
606	3/16 × 3/4	.313	.303	.063
507	5/32 × 7/8	.375	.365	.063
607	3/16 × 7/8	.375	.365	.063
807	1/4 × 7/8	.375	.365	.063
608	3/16 × 1	.438	.428	.063
609	3/16 × 1-1/8	.484	.475	.078

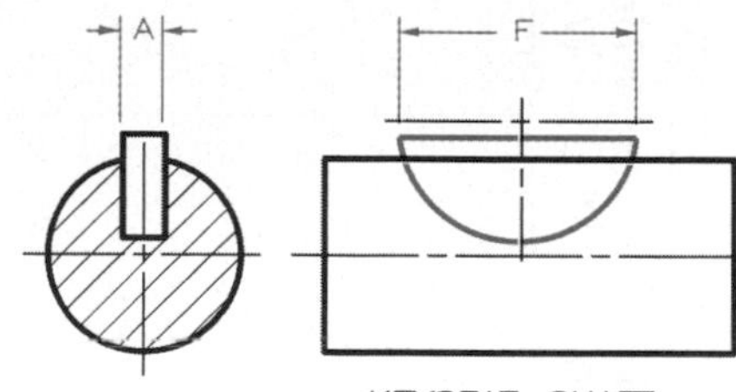

KEYSEAT—SHAFT

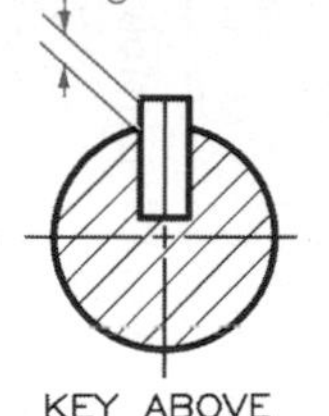

KEY ABOVE SHAFT

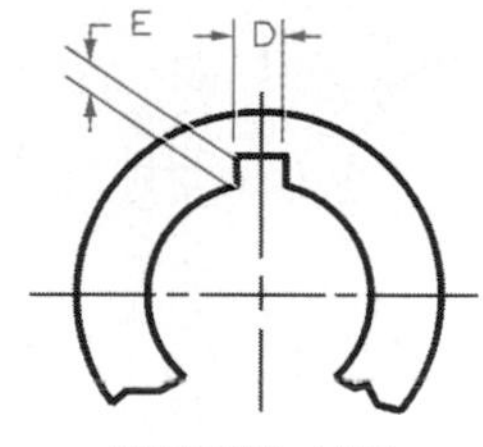

KEYSEAT—HUB

Key No.	A Min.	C +.005 −.000	F	D +.005 −.000	E +.005 −.000
204	.0615	.0312	.500	.0635	.0372
304	.0928	.0469	.500	.0948	.0529
404	.1240	.0625	.500	.1260	.0685
305	.0928	.0625	.625	.0948	.0529
405	.1240	.0469	.625	.1260	.0685
505	.1553	.0625	.625	.1573	.0841
406	.1240	.0781	.750	.1260	.0685

Key No.	A Min.	C +.005 −.000	F	D +.005 −.000	E +.005 −.000
506	.1553	.0781	.750	.1573	.0841
606	.1863	.0937	.750	.1885	.0997
507	.1553	.0781	.875	.1573	.0841
607	.1863	.0937	.875	.1885	.0997
807	.2487	.1250	.875	.2510	.1310
608	.1863	.3393	1.000	.1885	.0997
609	.1863	.3853	1.125	.1885	.0997

KEY SIZES VS. SHAFT SIZES

Shaft DIA	to .375	to .500	to .750	to 1.313	to 1.188	to 1.448	to 1.750	to 2.125	to 2.500
Key Nos.	204	304 305	404 405 406	505 506 507	606 607 608 609	807 808 809	810 811 812	1011 1012	1211 1212

APPENDIX 25 • Standard Keys and Keyways

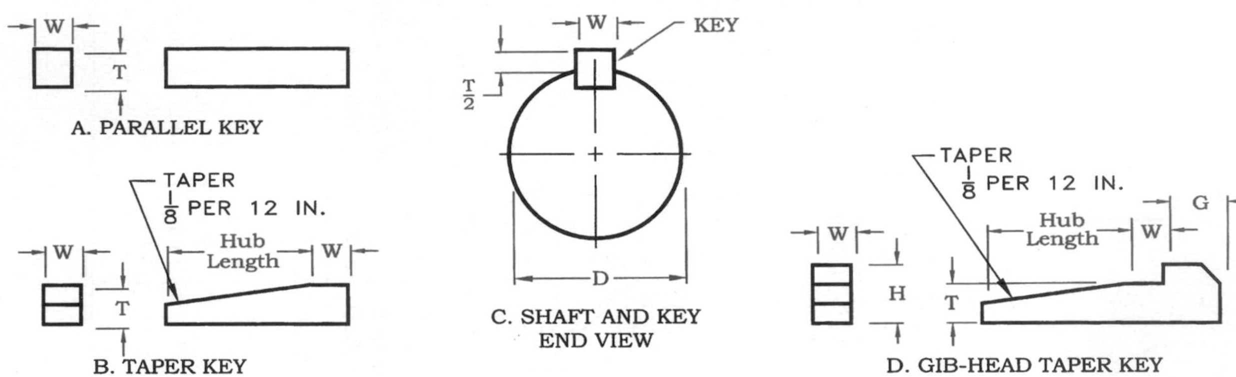

Sprocket Bore (= Shaft Diam.)	Keyway Dimensions—Inches		Key Dimensions—Inches		Tolerance on W and T (−)	Gib Head Dimensions–Inches				Key Tolerances Taper and Gib Head	
	For Square Key	For Flat Key	Square	Flat		Square Key		Flat Key			
Inches D	Width W × Depth T/2	Width W × Depth T/2	Width W × Height T	Width W × Height T		H	G	H	G	W (−)	T (−)
1/2—9/16	1/8 × 1/16	1/8 × 3/64	1/8 × 1/8	1/8 × 3/32	0.002	1/4	7/32	3/16	1/8	0.002	0.002
5/8—7/8	3/16 × 3/32	3/16 × 1/16	3/16 × 3/16	3/16 × 1/8	0.002	5/16	9/32	1/4	3/16	0.002	0.002
13/16—1 1/4	1/4 × 1/8	1/4 × 3/32	1/4 × 1/4	1/4 × 3/16	0.002	7/16	11/32	5/16	1/4	0.002	0.002
1 5/16—1 3/8	5/16 × 5/32	5/16 × 1/8	5/16 × 5/16	5/16 × 1/4	0.002	9/16	13/32	3/8	5/16	0.002	0.002
1 7/16—1 3/4	3/8 × 3/16	3/8 × 1/8	3/8 × 3/8	3/8 × 1/4	0.002	11/16	15/32	7/16	3/8	0.002	0.002
1 13/16—2 1/4	1/2 × 1/4	1/2 × 3/16	1/2 × 1/2	1/2 × 3/8	0.0025	7/8	19/32	5/8	1/2	0.0025	0.0025
2 5/16—2 3/4	5/8 × 5/16	7/8 × 7/32	5/8 × 5/8	5/8 × 7/16	0.0025	1 1/16	23/32	3/4	5/8	0.0025	0.0025
2 7/8—3 1/4	3/4 × 3/8	3/4 × 1/4	3/4 × 3/4	3/4 × 1/2	0.0025	1 1/4	7/8	7/8	3/4	0.0025	0.0025
3 3/8—3 3/4	7/8 × 7/16	7/8 × 5/16	7/8 × 7/8	7/8 × 5/8	0.003	1 1/2	1	1 1/16	7/8	0.003	0.003
3 7/8—4 1/2	1 × 1/2	1 × 3/8	1 × 1	1 × 3/4	0.003	1 3/4	1 3/16	1 1/4	1	0.003	0.003
4 3/4—5 1/2	1 1/4 × 5/8	1 1/4 × 7/16	1 1/4 × 1 1/4	1 1/4 × 7/8	0.003	2	1 7/16	1 1/2	1 1/4	0.003	0.003
5 3/4—7 3/8	1 1/2 × 3/4	1 1/2 × 1/2	1 1/2 × 1 1/2	1 1/2 × 1	0.003	2 1/2	1 3/4	1 3/4	1 1/2	0.003	0.003
7 1/2—9 7/8	1 3/4 × 7/8	- - -	1 3/4 × 1 3/4	- - -	0.004	3	2	1 3/4	1 1/2	0.004	0.004
10—12 1/2	2 × 1	- - -	2 × 2	- - -	0.004	3 1/2	2 3/8	1 3/4	1 1/2	0.004	0.004

Standard Keyway Tolerances: Straight Keyway—Width (W) + .005 −.000 Depth (T/2) + .010 −.000

Taper Keyway—Width (W) + .005 −.000 Depth (T/2) + .000 −.010

APPENDIX 26 • Plain and Wide Washers (inches)

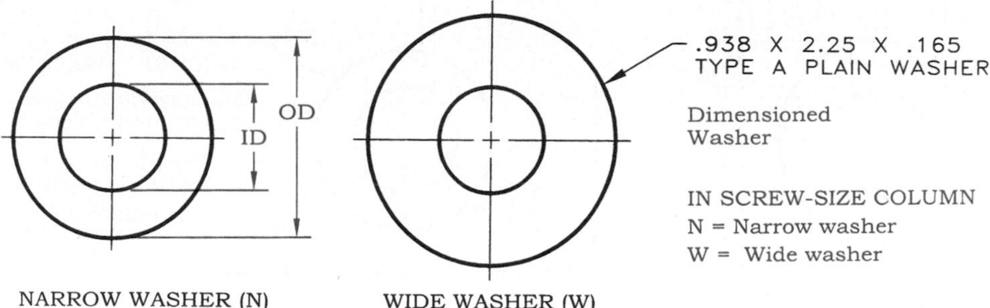

TYPE A PLAIN WASHERS

Screw Size	ID Size	OD Size	Thick-ness
0.138	0.156	0.375	0.049
0.164	0.188	0.438	0.049
0.190	0.219	0.500	0.049
0.188	0.250	0.562	0.049
0.216	0.250	0.562	0.065
0.250 N	0.281	0.625	0.065
0.250 W	0.312	0.734	0.065
0.312 N	0.344	0.688	0.065
0.312 W	0.375	0.875	0.083
0.375 N	0.406	0.812	0.065
0.375 W	0.438	1.000	0.083
0.438 N	0.469	0.922	0.065
0.438 W	0.500	1.250	0.083
0.500 N	0.531	1.062	0.095
0.500 W	0.562	1.375	0.109
0.562 N	0.594	1.156	0.095
0.562 W	0.594	1.469	0.190
0.625 N	0.625	1.312	0.095
0.625 N	0.625	1.750	0.134
0.750 W	0.812	1.469	0.134
0.750 W	0.812	2.000	0.148

Screw Size	ID Size	OD Size	Thick-ness
0.875 N	0.938	1.750	0.134
0.875 W	0.938	2.250	0.165
1.000 N	1.062	2.000	0.134
1.000 W	1.062	2.500	0.165
1.125 N	1.250	2.250	0.134
1.125 W	1.250	2.750	0.165
1.250 N	1.375	2.500	0.165
1.250 W	1.375	3.000	0.165
1.375 N	1.500	2.750	0.165
1.375 W	1.500	3.250	0.180
1.500 N	1.625	3.000	0.165
1.500 W	1.625	3.500	0.180
1.625	1.750	3.750	0.180
1.750	1.875	4.000	0.180
1.875	2.000	4.250	0.180
2.000	2.125	4.500	0.180
2.250	2.375	4.750	0.220
2.500	2.625	5.000	0.238
2.750	2.875	5.250	0.259
3.000	3.125	5.500	0.284

Dimensions are in inches.

APPENDIX 27 • Metric Flat and Wrought Washers (millimeters)

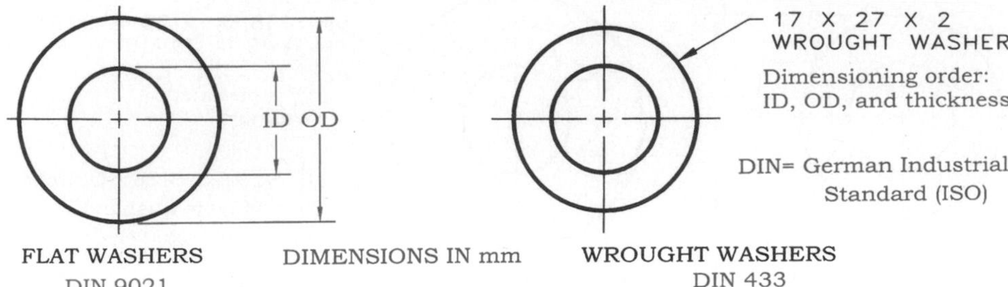

Screw Size	ID Size	OD Size	Thick-ness	
3	3.2	9	0.8	FLAT WASHERS
4	4.3	12	1	
5	5.3	15	1.5	
6	6.4	18	1.5	
8	8.4	25	2	
10	10.5	30	2.5	
12	13	40	3	
14	15	45	3	
16	17	50	3	
18	19	56	4	
20	21	60	4	
2.6	2.8	5.5	0.5	WROUGHT WASHERS
3	3.2	6	0.5	
4	4.3	8	0.5	
5	5.3	10	1.0	
6	6.4	11	1.5	
8	8.4	15	1.5	
10	10.5	18	1.5	
12	13	20	2.0	
14	15	25	2.0	
16	17	27	2.0	
18	19	30	2.5	
20	21	33	2.5	

APPENDIX 28 • Regular Helical Spring Lock Washers (inches and millimeters)

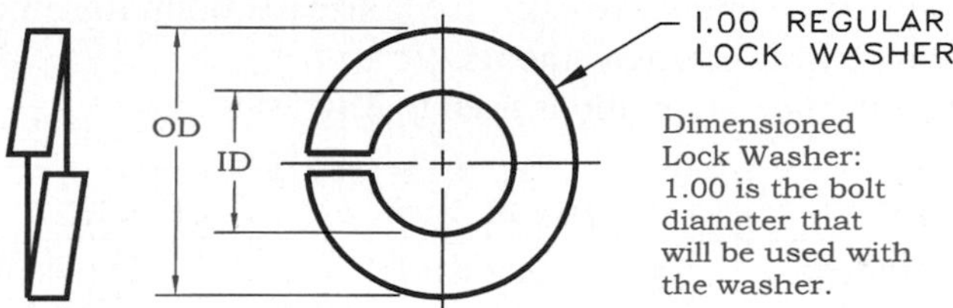

Lock Washers—inches

Screw Size	ID Size	OD Size	Thick-ness
0.164	0.168	0.175	0.040
0.190	0.194	0.202	0.047
0.216	0.221	0.229	0.056
0.250	0.255	0.263	0.062
0.312	0.318	0.328	0.078
0.375	0.382	0.393	0.094
0.438	0.446	0.459	0.109
0.500	0.509	0.523	0.125
0.562	0.572	0.587	0.141
0.625	0.636	0.653	0.156
0.688	0.700	0.718	0.172
0.750	0.763	0.783	0.188
0.812	0.826	1.367	0.203
0.875	0.890	1.464	0.219
0.938	0.954	1.560	0.234
1.000	1.017	1.661	0.250
1.062	1.080	1.756	0.266
1.125	1.144	1.853	0.281
1.188	1.208	1.950	0.297
1.250	1.271	2.045	0.312
1.312	1.334	2.141	0.328
1.375	1.398	2.239	0.344
1.438	1.462	2.334	0.359
1.500	1.525	2.430	0.375

Metric Lock Washers—Din 127 (Millimeters)

Screw Size	ID Size	OD Size	Thick-ness
4	4.1	7.1	0.9
5	5.1	8.7	1.2
6	6.1	11.1	1.6
8	8.2	12.1	1.6
10	10.2	14.2	2
12	12.1	17.2	2.2
14	14.2	20.2	2.5
16	16.2	23.2	3
18	18.2	26.2	3.5
20	20.2	28.2	3.5
22	22.5	34.5	4
24	24.5	38.5	5
27	27.5	41.5	5
30	30.5	46.5	6
33	33.5	53.5	6
36	36.5	56.5	6
39	39.5	59.5	6
42	42.5	66.5	7
45	45.5	69.5	7
48	49	73	7

Limits are in thousandths of an inch.
Limits for hole and shaft are applied algebraically to the basic size to obtain the limits of size for the parts.
Data in boldface are in accordance with ABC agreements.
Symbols H5, g5, etc., are Hole and Shaft designations used in ABC System.

Nominal Size Range Inches		Class RC 1			Class RC 2			Class RC 3			Class RC 4		
		Limits of Clearance	Standard Limits		Limits of Clearance	Standard Limits		Limits of Clearance	Standards Limits		Limits of Clearance	Standard Limits	
Over	To		Hole H5	Shaft g4		Hole H6	Shaft g5		Hole H7	Shaft f6		Hole H8	Shaft f7
0	−0.12	0.1	+0.2	−0.1	0.1	+0.25	−0.1	0.3	+0.4	−0.3	0.3	+0.6	−0.3
		0.45	0	−0.25	0.55	0	−0.3	0.95	0	−0.55	1.3	0	−0.7
0.12	−0.24	0.15	+0.2	−0.15	0.15	+0.3	−0.15	0.4	+0.5	−0.4	0.4	+0.7	−0.4
		0.5	0	−0.3	0.65	0	−0.35	1.12	0	−0.7	1.6	0	−0.9
0.24	−0.40	0.2	0.25	−0.2	0.2	+0.4	−0.2	0.5	+0.6	−0.5	0.5	+0.9	−0.5
		0.6	0	−0.35	0.85	0	−0.45	1.5	0	−0.9	2.0	0	−1.1
0.40	−0.71	0.25	+0.3	−0.25	0.25	+0.4	−0.25	0.6	+0.7	−0.6	0.6	+1.0	−0.6
		0.75	0	−0.45	0.95	0	−0.55	1.7	0	−1.0	2.3	0	−1.3
0.71	−1.19	0.3	+0.4	−0.3	0.3	+0.5	−0.3	0.8	+0.8	−0.8	0.8	+1.2	−0.8
		0.95	0	−0.55	1.2	0	−0.7	2.1	0	−1.3	2.8	0	−1.6
1.19	−1.97	0.4	+0.4	−0.4	0.4	+0.6	−0.4	1.0	+1.0	−1.0	1.0	+1.6	−1.0
		1.1	0	−0.7	1.4	0	−0.8	2.6	0	−1.6	3.6	0	−2.0
1.97	−3.15	0.4	+0.5	−0.4	0.4	+0.7	−0.4	1.2	+1.2	−1.2	1.2	+1.8	−1.2
		1.2	0	−0.7	1.6	0	−0.9	3.1	0	−1.9	4.2	0	−2.4
3.15	−4.73	0.5	+0.6	−0.5	0.5	+0.9	−0.5	1.4	+1.4	−1.4	1.4	+2.2	−1.4
		1.5	0	−0.9	2.0	0	−1.1	3.7	0	−2.3	5.0	0	−2.8
4.73	−7.09	0.6	+0.7	−0.6	0.6	+1.0	−0.6	1.6	+1.6	−1.6	1.6	+2.5	−1.6
		1.8	0	−1.1	2.3	0	−1.3	4.2	0	−2.6	5.7	0	−3.2
7.09	−9.85	0.6	+0.8	−0.6	0.6	+1.2	−0.6	2.0	+1.8	−2.0	2.0	+2.8	−2.0
		2.0	0	−1.2	2.6	0	−1.4	5.0	0	−3.2	6.6	0	−3.8
9.85	−12.41	0.8	+0.9	−0.8	0.8	+1.2	−0.8	2.5	+2.0	−2.5	2.5	+3.0	−2.5
		2.3	0	−1.4	2.9	0	−1.7	5.7	0	−3.7	7.5	0	−4.5
12.41	−15.75	1.0	+1.0	−1.0	1.0	+1.4	−1.0	3.0	+	−3.0	3.0	+3.5	−3.0
		2.7	0	−1.7	3.4	0	−2.0	6.6	0	−4.4	8.7	0	−5.2
15.75	−19.69	1.2	+1.0	−1.2	1.2	+1.6	−1.2	4.0	+1.6	−4.0	4.0	+4.0	−4.0
		3.0	0	−2.0	3.8	0	−2.2	8.1	0	−5.6	10.5	0	−6.5
19.69	−30.09	1.6	+1.2	−1.6	1.6	+2.0	−1.6	5.0	+3.0	−5.0	5.0	+5.0	−5.0
		3.7	0	−2.5	4.8	0	−2.8	10.0	0	−7.0	13.0	0	−8.0
30.09	−41.49	2.0	+1.6	−2.0	2.0	+2.5	−2.0	6.0	+4.0	−6.0	6.0	+6.0	−6.0
		4.6	0	−3.0	6.1	0	−3.6	12.5	0	−8.5	16.0	0	−10.0
41.49	−56.19	2.5	+2.0	−2.5	2.5	+3.0	−2.5	8.0	+5.0	−8.0	8.0	+8.0	−8.0
		5.7	0	−3.7	7.5	0	−4.5	16.0	0	−11.0	21.0	0	−13.0
56.19	−76.39	3.0	+2.5	−3.0	3.0	+4.0	−3.0	10.0	+6.0	−10.0	10.0	+10.0	−10.0
		7.1	0	−4.6	9.5	0	−5.5	20.0	0	−14.0	26.0	0	−16.0
76.39	−100.9	4.0	+3.0	−4.0	4.0	+5.0	−4.0	12.0	+8.0	−12.0	12.0	+12.0	−12.0
		9.0	0	−6.0	12.0	0	−7.0	25.0	0	−17.0	32.0	0	−20.0
100.9	−131.9	5.0	+4.0	−5.0	5.0	+6.0	−5.0	16.0	+10.0	−16.0	16.0	+16.0	−16.0
		11.5	0	−7.5	15.0	0	−9.0	32.0	0	−22.0	36.0	0	−26.0
131.9	−171.9	6.0	+5.0	−6.0	6.0	+8.0	−6.0	18.0	+8.0	−18.0	18.0	+20.0	−18.0
		14.0	0	−9.0	19.0	0	−11.0	38.0	0	−26.0	50.0	0	−30.0
171.9	−200	8.0	+6.0	−8.0	8.0	+10.0	−8.0	22.0	+16.0	−22.0	22.0	+25.0	−22.0
		18.0	0	−12.0	22.0	0	−12.0	48.0	0	−32.0	63.0	0	−38.0

Source: Courtesy of USASI; B4.1—1955.

Class RC 5			Class RC 6			Class RC 7			Class RC 8			Class RC 9			Nominal Size Range Inches	
Limits of Clearance	Standard Limits		Limits of Clearance	Standard Limits		Limits of Clearance	Standard Limits		Limits of Clearance	Standard Limits		Limits of Clearance	Standard Limits			
	Hole H8	Shaft e7		Hole H9	Shaft e8		Hole H9	Shaft d8		Hole H10	Shaft c9		Hole H11	Shaft	Over	To
0.6	+0.6	−0.6	0.6	+1.0	−0.6	1.0	+1.0	−1.0	2.5	+1.6	−2.5	4.0	+2.5	−4.0	0	0.12
1.6	−0	−1.0	2.2	−0	−1.2	2.6	0	−1.6	5.1	0	−3.5	8.1	0	−5.6		
0.8	+0.7	−0.8	0.8	+1.2	−0.8	1.2	+1.2	−1.2	2.8	+1.8	−2.8	4.5	+3.0	−4.5	0.12	0.24
2.0	−0	−1.3	2.7	−0	−1.5	3.1	0	−1.9	5.8	0	−4.0	9.0	0	−6.0		
1.0	+0.9	−1.0	1.0	+1.4	−1.0	1.6	+1.4	−1.6	3.0	+2.2	−3.0	5.0	+3.5	−5.0	0.24	0.40
2.5	−0	−1.16	3.3	−0	−1.9	3.9	0	−2.5	6.6	0	−4.4	10.7	0	−7.2		
1.2	+1.0	−1.2	1.2	+1.6	−1.2	2.0	+1.6	−2.0	3.5	+2.8	−3.5	6.0	+4.0	−6.0	0.40	0.71
2.9	−0	−1.9	3.8	−0	−2.2	4.6	0	−3.0	7.9	0	−5.1	12.8	−0	−8.8		
1.6	+1.2	−1.6	1.6	+2.0	−1.6	2.5	+2.0	−2.5	4.5	+3.5	−4.5	7.0	+5.0	−7.0	0.71	1.19
3.6	−0	−2.4	4.8	−0	−2.8	5.7	0	−3.7	10.0	0	−6.5	15.5	0	−10.5		
2.0	+1.6	−2.0	2.0	+2.5	−2.0	3.0	+2.5	−3.0	5.0	+4.0	−5.0	8.0	+6.0	−8.0	1.19	1.97
4.6	−0	−3.0	6.1	−0	−3.6	7.1	0	−4.6	11.5	0	−7.5	18.0	0	−12.0		
2.5	+1.8	−2.5	2.5	+3.0	−2.5	4.0	+3.0	−4.0	6.0	+4.5	−6.0	9.0	+7.0	−9.0	1.97	3.15
5.5	−0	−3.7	7.3	−0	−4.3	8.8	0	−5.8	13.5	0	−9.0	20.5	0	−13.5		
3.0	+2.2	−3.0	3.0	+3.5	−3.0	5.0	+3.5	−5.0	7.0	+5.0	−7.0	10.0	+9.0	−10.0	3.15	4.73
6.6	−0	−4.4	8.7	−0	−5.2	10.7	0	−7.2	15.5	0	−10.5	24.0	0	−15.0		
3.5	+2.5	−3.5	3.5	+4.0	−3.5	6.0	+4.0	−6.0	8.0	+6.0	−8.0	12.0	+10.0	−12.0	4.73	7.09
7.6	−0	−5.1	10.0	−0	−6.0	12.5	0	−8.5	18.0	0	−12.0	28.0	0	−18.0		
4.0	+2.8	−4.0	4.0	+4.5	−4.0	7.0	+4.5	−7.0	10.0	+7.0	−10.0	15.0	+12.0	−15.0	7.09	9.85
8.6	−0	−5.8	11.3	0	−6.8	14.3	0	−9.8	21.5	0	−14.5	34.0	0	−22.0		
5.0	+3.0	−5.0	5.0	+5.0	−5.0	8.0	+5.0	−8.0	12.0	+8.0	−12.0	18.0	+12.0	−18.0	9.85	12.41
10.0	0	−7.0	13.0	0	−8.0	16.0	0	−11.0	25.0	0	−17.0	38.0	0	−26.0		
6.0	+3.5	−6.0	6.0	+6.0	−6.0	10.0	+6.0	−10.0	14.0	+9.0	−14.0	22.0	+14.0	−22.0	12.41	15.75
11.7	0	−8.2	15.5	0	−9.5	19.5	0	13.5	29.0	0	−20.0	45.0	0	−31.0		
8.0	+4.0	−8.0	8.0	+6.0	−8.0	12.0	+6.0	−12.0	16.0	+10.0	−16.0	25.0	+16.0	−25.0	15.75	19.69
14.5	0	−10.5	18.0	0	−12.0	22.0	0	−16.0	32.0	0	−22.0	51.0	0	−35.0		
10.0	+5.0	−10.0	10.0	+8.0	−10.0	16.0	+8.0	−16.0	20.0	+12.0	−20.0	30.0	+20.0	−30.0	19.69	30.09
18.0	0	−13.0	23.0	0	−15.0	29.0	0	−21.0	40.0	0	−28.0	62.0	0	−42.0		
12.0	+6.0	−12.0	12.0	+10.0	−12.0	20.0	+10.0	−20.0	25.0	+16.0	−25.0	40.0	+25.0	−40.0	30.09	41.49
22.0	0	−16.0	28.0	0	−18.0	36.0	0	−26.0	51.0	0	−35.0	81.0	0	−56.0		
16.0	+8.0	−16.0	16.0	+12.0	−16.0	25.0	+12.0	−25.0	30.0	+20.0	−30.0	50.0	+30.0	−50.0	41.49	56.19
29.0	0	−21.0	36.0	0	−24.0	45.0	0	−33.0	62.0	0	−42.0	100	0	−70.0		
20.0	+10.0	−20.0	20.0	+16.0	−20.0	30.0	+16.0	−30.0	40.0	+25.0	−40.0	60.0	+40.0	−60.0	56.19	76.39
36.0	0	−26.0	46.0	0	−30.0	56.0	0	−40.0	81.0	0	−56.0	125	0	−85.0		
25.0	+12.0	−25.0	25.0	+20.0	−25.0	40.0	+20.0	−40.0	50.0	+30.0	−50.0	80.0	+50.0	−80.0	76.39	100.9
45.0	0	−33.0	57.0	0	−37.0	72.0	0	−52.0	100	0	−70.0	160	0	−110		
30.0	+16.0	−30.0	30.0	+35.0	−30.0	50.0	+25.0	−50.0	60.0	+40.0	−60.0	100	+60.0	−100	100.9	131.9
56.0	0	−40.0	71.0	0	−46.0	91.0	0	−66.0	125	0	−85.0	200	0	−140		
35.0	+20.0	−35.0	35.0	+30.0	−35.0	60.0	+30.0	−60.0	80.0	+50.0	−80.0	130	+80.0	−130	131.9	171.9
57.0	0	−47.0	85.0	0	−55.0	110.0	0	−80.0	160	0	−110	260	0	−180		
45.0	+25.0	−45.0	45.0	+40.0	−45.0	80.0	+40.0	−80.0	100	+60.0	−100	150	+100	−150	171.9	200
86.0	0	−61.0	110.0	0	−70.0	145.0	0	−105.0	200	0	−140	310	0	−210		

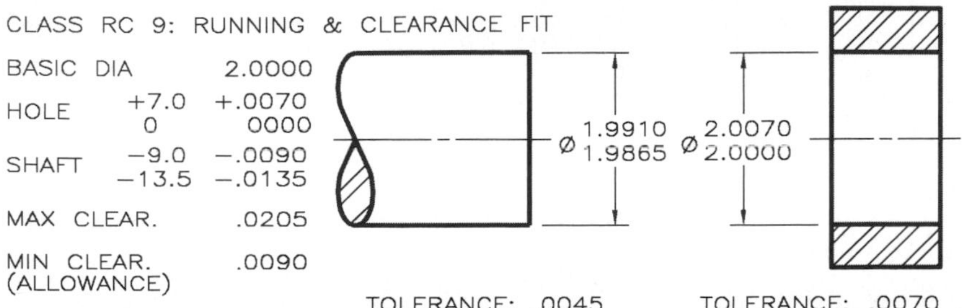

Limits are in thousandths of an inch.
Limits for hole and shaft are applied algebraically to the basic size to obtain the limits of size for the parts.
Data in boldface are in accordance with ABC agreements.
Symbols H9, f8, etc., are Hole and Shaft designations used in ABC System.

Nominal Size Range Inches		Class LC 1			Class LC 2			Class LC 3			Class LC 4			Class LC 5		
Over	To	Limits of Clearance	Standard Limits Hole H6	Standard Limits Shaft h5	Limits of Clearance	Standard Limits Hole H7	Standard Limits Shaft h6	Limits of Clearance	Standard Limits Hole H8	Standard Limits Shaft h7	Limits of Clearance	Standard Limits Hole H10	Standard Limits Shaft h9	Limits of Clearance	Standard Limits Hole H7	Standard Limits Shaft g6
0	−0.12	**0**	**+0.25**	**+0**	**0**	**+0.4**	**+0**	**0**	**+0.6**	**+0**	**0**	**+1.6**	**+0**	**0.1**	**+0.4**	**−0.1**
		0.45	**−0**	**−0.2**	**0.65**	**−0**	**−0.25**	**1**	**−0**	**−0.4**	**2.6**	**−0**	**−1.0**	**0.75**	**−0**	**−0.35**
0.12	−0.24	**0**	**+0.3**	**+0**	**0**	**+0.5**	**+0**	**0**	**+0.7**	**+0**	**0**	**+1.8**	**+0**	**0.15**	**+0.5**	**−0.15**
		0.5	**−0**	**−0.2**	**0.8**	**−0**	**−0.3**	**1.2**	**−0**	**−0.5**	**3.0**	**−0**	**−1.2**	**0.95**	**−0**	**−0.45**
0.24	−0.40	**0**	**+0.4**	**+0**	**0**	**+0.6**	**+0**	**0**	**+0.9**	**+0**	**0**	**+2.2**	**+0**	**0.2**	**+0.6**	**−0.2**
		0.65	**−0**	**−0.25**	**1.0**	**−0**	**−0.4**	**1.5**	**−0**	**−0.6**	**3.6**	**−0**	**−1.4**	**1.2**	**−0**	**−0.6**
0.40	−0.71	**0**	**+0.4**	**+0**	**0**	**+0.7**	**+0**	**0**	**+1.0**	**+0**	**0**	**+2.8**	**+0**	**0.25**	**+0.7**	**−0.25**
		0.7	**−0**	**−0.3**	**1.1**	**−0**	**−0.4**	**1.7**	**−0**	**−0.7**	**4.4**	**−0**	**−1.6**	**1.35**	**−0**	**−0.65**
0.71	−1.19	**0**	**+0.5**	**+0**	**0**	**+0.8**	**+0**	**0**	**+1.2**	**+0**	**0**	**+3.5**	**+0**	**0.3**	**+0.8**	**−0.3**
		0.9	**−0**	**−0.4**	**1.3**	**−0**	**−0.5**	**2**	**−0**	**−0.8**	**5.5**	**−0**	**−2.0**	**1.6**	**−0**	**−0.8**
1.19	−1.97	**0**	**+0.6**	**+0**	**0**	**+1.0**	**+0**	**0**	**+1.6**	**+0**	**0**	**+4.0**	**+0**	**0.4**	**+1.0**	**−0.4**
		1.0	**−0**	**−0.4**	**1.6**	**−0**	**−0.6**	**2.6**	**−0**	**−1**	**6.5**	**−0**	**−2.5**	**2.0**	**−0**	**−1.0**
1.97	−3.15	**0**	**+0.7**	**+0**	**0**	**+1.2**	**+0**	**0**	**+1.8**	**+0**	**0**	**+4.5**	**+0**	**0.4**	**+1.2**	**−0.4**
		1.2	**−0**	**−0.5**	**1.9**	**−0**	**−0.7**	**3**	**−0**	**−1.2**	**7.5**	**−0**	**−3**	**2.3**	**−0**	**−1.1**
3.15	−4.73	**0**	**+0.9**	**+0**	**0**	**+1.4**	**+0**	**0**	**+2.2**	**+0**	**0**	**+5.0**	**+0**	**0.5**	**+1.4**	**−0.5**
		1.5	**−0**	**−0.6**	**2.3**	**−0**	**−0.9**	**3.6**	**−0**	**−1.4**	**8.5**	**−0**	**−3.5**	**2.8**	**−0**	**−1.4**
4.73	−7.09	**0**	**+1.0**	**+0**	**0**	**+1.6**	**+0**	**0**	**+2.5**	**+0**	**0**	**+6.0**	**+0**	**0.6**	**+1.6**	**−0.6**
		1.7	**−0**	**−0.7**	**2.6**	**−0**	**−1.0**	**4.1**	**−0**	**−1.6**	**10**	**−0**	**−4**	**3.2**	**−0**	**1.6**
7.09	−9.85	**0**	**+1.2**	**+0**	**0**	**+1.8**	**+0**	**0**	**+2.8**	**+0**	**0**	**+7.0**	**+0**	**0.6**	**+1.8**	**−0.6**
		2.0	**−0**	**−0.8**	**3.0**	**−0**	**−1.2**	**4.6**	**−0**	**−1.8**	**11.5**	**−0**	**−4.5**	**3.6**	**−0**	**−1.8**
9.85	−12.41	**0**	**+1.2**	**+0**	**0**	**+2.0**	**+0**	**0**	**+3.0**	**+0**	**0**	**8.0**	**+0**	**0.7**	**+2.0**	**−0.7**
		2.1	**−0**	**−0.9**	**3.2**	**−0**	**−1.2**	**5**	**−0**	**−2.0**	**13**	**−0**	**−5**	**3.9**	**−0**	**−1.9**
12.41	−15.75	**0**	**+1.4**	**+0**	**0**	**+2.2**	**+0**	**0**	**+3.5**	**+0**	**0**	**+9.0**	**+0**	**0.7**	**+2.2**	**−0.7**
		2.4	**−0**	**−1.0**	**3.6**	**−0**	**−1.4**	**5.7**	**−0**	**−2.2**	**15**	**−0**	**−6**	**4.3**	**−0**	**−2.1**
15.75	−19.69	**0**	**+1.6**	**+0**	**0**	**+2.5**	**+0**	**0**	**+4**	**+0**	**0**	**+10.0**	**+0**	**0.8**	**+2.5**	**−0.8**
		2.6	**−0**	**−1.0**	**4.1**	**−0**	**−1.6**	**6.5**	**−0**	**−2.5**	**16**	**−0**	**−6**	**4.9**	**−0**	**−2.4**
19.69	−30.09	0	+2.0	+0	0	+3	+0	0	+5	+0	0	+12.0	+0	0.9	+3.0	−0.9
		3.2	−0	−1.2	5.0	−0	−2	8	−0	−3	20	−0	−8	5.9	−0	−2.9
30.09	−41.49	0	+2.5	+0	0	+4	+0	0	+6	+0	0	+16.0	+0	1.0	+4.0	−1.0
		4.1	−0	−1.6	6.5	−0	−2.5	10	−0	−4	26	−0	−10	7.5	−0	−3.5
41.49	−56.19	0	+3.0	+0	0	+5	+0	0	+8	+0	0	+20.0	+0	1.2	+5.0	−1.2
		5.0	−0	−2.0	8.0	−0	−3	13	−0	−5	32	−0	−12	9.2	−0	−4.2
56.19	−76.39	0	+4.0	+0	0	+6	+0	0	+10	+0	0	+25.0	+0	1.2	+6.0	−1.2
		6.5	−0	−2.5	10	−0	−4	16	−0	−6	41	−0	−16	11.2	−0	−5.2
76.39	−100.9	0	+5.0	+0	0	+8	+0	0	+12	+0	0	+30.0	+0	1.4	+8.0	−1.4
		8.0	−0	−3.0	13	−0	−5	20	−0	−8	50	−0	−20	14.4	−0	−6.4
100.9	−131.9	0	+6.0	+0	0	+10	+0	0	+16	+0	0	+40.0	+0	1.6	+10.0	−1.6
		10.0	−0	−4.0	16	−0	−6	26	−0	−10	65	−0	−25	17.6	−0	−7.6
131.9	−171.9	0	+8.0	+0	0	+12	+0	0	+20	+0	0	+50.0	+0	1.8	+12.0	−1.8
		13.0	−0	−5.0	20	−0	−8	32	−0	−12	8	−0	−30	21.8	−0	−9.8
171.9	−200	0	+10.0	+0	0	+16	+0	0	+25	+0	0	+60.0	+0	1.8	+16.0	−1.8
		16.0	−0	−6.0	26	−0	−10	41	−0	−16	100	−0	−40	27.8	−0	−11.8

Source: Courtesy of USASI; B4.1.

APPENDIX 30 • American Standard Clearance Locational Fits (hole basis) (continued)

Class LC 6			Class LC 7			Class LC 8			Class LC 9			Class LC 10			Class LC 11			Nominal Size Range Inches	
Limits of Clearance	Standard Limits		Limits of Clearance	Standard Limits		Limits of Clearance	Standard Limits		Limits of Clearance	Standard Limits		Limits of Clearance	Standard Limits		Limits of Clearance	Standard Limits			
	Hole H9	Shaft f8		Hole H10	Shaft e9		Hole H10	Shaft d9		Hole H11	Shaft c10		Hole H12	Shaft		Hole H13	Shaft	Over	To
0.3	+1.0	−0.3	0.6	+1.6	−0.6	1.0	+0.6	−1.0	2.5	+2.5	−2.5	4	+4	−4	5	+6	−5	0 –	0.12
1.9	0	−0.9	3.2	0	−1.6	3.6	−0	−2.0	6.6	−0	−4.1	12	−0	−8	17	−0	−11		
0.4	+1.2	−0.4	0.8	+1.8	−0.8	1.2	+1.8	−1.2	2.8	+3.0	−2.8	4.5	+5	−4.5	6	+7	−6	0.12 –	0.24
2.3	0	−1.1	3.8	0	−2.0	4.2	−0	−2.4	7.6	−0	−4.6	14.5	−0	−9.5	20	−0	−13		
0.5	+1.4	−0.5	1.0	+2.2	−1.0	1.6	+2.2	−1.6	3.0	+3.5	−3.0	5	+6	−5	7	+9	−7	0.24 –	0.40
2.8	0	−1.4	4.6	0	−2.4	5.2	−0	−3.0	8.7	−0	−5.2	17	−0	−11	25	−0	−16		
0.6	+1.6	−0.6	1.2	+2.8	−1.2	2.0	+2.8	−2.0	3.5	+4.0	−3.5	6	+7	−6	8	+10	−8	0.40 –	0.71
3.2	0	−1.6	5.6	0	−2.8	6.4	−0	−3.6	10.3	−0	−6.3	20	−0	−13	28	−0	−18		
0.8	+2.0	−0.8	1.6	+3.5	−1.6	2.5	+3.5	−2.5	4.5	+5.0	−4.5	7	+8	−7	10	+12	−10	0.71 –	1.19
4.0	0	−2.0	7.1	0	−3.6	8.0	−0	−4.5	13.0	−0	−8.0	23	−0	−15	34	−0	−22		
1.0	+2.5	−1.0	2.0	+4.0	−2.0	3.0	+4.0	−3.0	5	+6	−5	8	+10	−8	12	+16	−12	1.19 –	1.97
5.1	0	−2.6	8.5	0	−4.5	9.5	−0	−5.5	15	−0	−9	28	−0	−18	44	−0	−28		
1.2	+3.0	−1.2	2.5	+4.5	−2.5	4.0	+4.5	−4.0	6	+7	−6	10	+12	−10	14	+18	−14	1.97 –	3.15
6.0	0	−3.0	10.0	0	−5.5	11.5	−0	−7.0	17.5	−0	−10.5	34	−0	−22	50	−0	−32		
1.4	+3.5	−1.4	3.0	+5.0	−3.0	5.0	+5.0	−5.0	7	+9	−7	11	+14	−11	16	+22	−16	3.15 –	4.73
7.1	0	−3.6	11.5	0	−6.5	13.5	−0	−8.5	21	−0	−12	39	−0	−25	60	−0	−38		
1.6	+4.0	−1.6	3.5	+6.0	−3.5	6	+6	−6	8	+10	−8	12	+16	−12	18	+25	−18	4.73 –	7.09
8.1	0	−4.1	13.5	0	−7.5	16	−0	−10	24	−0	−14	44	−0	−28	68	−0	−43		
2.0	+4.5	−2.0	4.0	+7.0	−4.0	7	+7	−7	10	+12	−10	16	+18	−16	22	+28	−22	7.09 –	9.85
9.3	0	−4.8	15.5	0	−8.5	18.5	−0	−11.5	29	−0	−17	52	−0	−34	78	−0	−50		
2.2	+5.0	−2.2	4.5	+8.0	−4.5	7	+8	−7	12	+12	−12	20	+20	−20	28	+30	−28	9.85 –	12.41
10.2	0	−5.2	17.5	0	−9.5	20	−0	−12	32	−0	−20	60	−0	−40	88	−0	−58		
2.5	+6.0	−2.5	5.0	+9.0	−5	8	+9	−8	14	+14	−14	22	+22	−22	30	+35	−30	12.41 –	15.75
12.0	0	+6.0	20.0	0	−11	23	−0	−14	37	−0	−23	66	−0	−44	100	−0	−65		
2.8	+6.0	−2.8	5.0	+10.0	−5	9	+10	−9	16	+16	−16	25	+25	−25	35	+40	−35	15.75 –	19.69
12.8	0	−6.8	21.0	0	−11	25	−0	−15	42	−0	−26	75	−0	−50	115	−0	−75		
3.0	+8.0	−3.0	6.0	+12.0	−6	10	+12	−10	18	+20	−18	28	+30	−28	40	+50	−40	19.69 –	30.09
16.0	0	−8.0	26.0	−0	−14	30	−0	−18	50	−0	−30	88	−0	−58	140	−0	−90		
3.5	+10.0	−3.5	7.0	+16.0	−7	12	+16	−12	20	+25	−20	30	+40	−30	45	+60	−45	30.09 –	41.49
19.5	0	−9.5	33.0	−0	−17	38	−0	−22	61	−0	−36	110	−0	−70	165	−0	−105		
4.0	+12.0	−4.0	8.0	+20.0	−8	14	+20	−14	25	+30	−25	40	+50	−40	60	+80	−60	41.49 –	56.19
24.0	0	−12.0	40.0	−0	−20	46	−0	−26	75	−0	−45	140	−0	−90	220	−0	−140		
4.5	+16.0	−4.5	9.0	+25.0	−9	16	+25	−16	30	+40	−30	50	+60	−50	70	+100	−70	56.19 –	76.39
30.5	0	−14.5	50.0	−0	−25	57	−0	−32	95	−0	−55	170	−0	110	270	−0	−170		
5.0	+20.0	−5	10.0	+30.0	−10	18	+30	−18	35	+50	−35	50	+80	−50	80	+125	−80	76.39 –	100.9
37.0	0	−17	60.0	−0	−30	68	−0	−38	115	−0	−65	210	−0	−130	330	−0	−205		
6.0	+25.0	−6	12.0	+40.0	−12	20	+40	−20	40	+60	−40	60	+100	−60	90	+160	−90	100.9 –	131.9
47.0	0	−22	67.0	−0	−27	85	−0	−45	140	−0	−80	260	−0	−160	410	−0	−250		
7.0	+30.0	−7	14.0	+50.0	−14	25	+50	−25	50	+80	−50	80	+125	−80	100	+200	−100	131.9 –	171.9
57.0	0	−27	94.0	−0	−44	105	−0	−55	180	−0	−100	330	−0	−205	500	−0	−300		
7.0	+40.0	−7	14.0	+60.0	−14	25	+60	−25	50	+100	−50	90	+160	−90	125	+250	−125	171.9 –	200
72.0	0	−32	114.0	−0	−54	125	−0	−65	210	−0	−110	410	−0	−250	625	−0	−375		

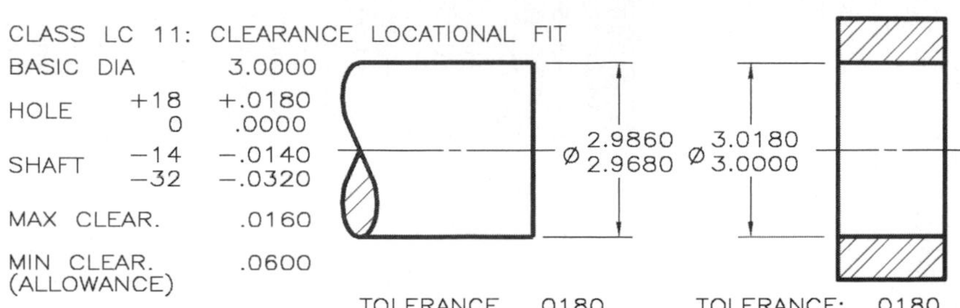

APPENDIX 31 • American Standard Transition Locational Fits (hole basis)

Limits are in thousandths of an inch.
Limits for hole and shaft are applied algebraically to the basic size to obtain the limits of size for the mating parts.
Data in boldface are in accordance with ABC agreements.
"Fit" represents the maximum interference (minus values) and the maximum clearance (plus values).
Symbols H7, js6, etc., are Hole and Shaft designations used in ABC System.

		Class LT 1			Class LT 2			Class LT 3			Class LT 4			Class LT 5			Class LT 6		
Nominal Size Range Inches		Fit	Standard Limits		Fit	Standard Limits		Fit	Standard Limits		Fit	Standard Limits		Fit	Standard Limits		Fit	Standard Limits	
Over	To		Hole H7	Shaft js6		Hole H8	Shaft js7		Hole H7	Shaft k6		Hole H8	Shaft k7		Hole H7	Shaft n6		Hole H7	Shaft n7
0	−0.12	−0.10	+0.4	+0.10	−0.2	+0.6	+0.2							−0.5	+0.4	+0.5	−0.65	+0.4	−0.65
		+0.50	−0	−0.10	+0.8	−0	−0.2							+0.15	−0	+0.25	+0.15	−0	+0.25
0.12	−0.24	−0.15	+0.5	+0.15	−0.25	+0.7	+0.25							−0.6	+0.5	+0.6	−0.8	+0.5	+0.8
		+0.65	−0	−0.15	+0.95	−0	−0.25							+0.2	−0	+0.3	+0.2	−0	+0.3
0.24	−0.40	−0.2	+0.6	+0.2	−0.3	+0.9	+0.3	−0.5	+0.6	+0.5	−0.7	+0.9	+0.7	−0.8	+0.6	+0.8	−1.0	+0.6	+1.0
		+0.8	−0	−0.2	+1.2	−0	−0.3	+0.5	−0	+0.1	+0.8	−0	+0.1	+0.2	−0	+0.4	+0.2	−0	+0.4
0.40	−0.71	−0.2	+0.7	+0.2	−0.35	+1.0	+0.35	−0.5	+0.7	+0.5	−0.8	+1.0	+0.8	−0.9	+0.7	+0.9	−1.2	+0.7	+1.2
		+0.9	−0	−0.2	+1.35	−0	−0.35	+0.6	−0	+0.1	+0.9	−0	+0.1	+0.2	−0	+0.5	+0.2	−0	+0.5
0.71	−1.19	−0.25	+0.8	+0.25	−0.4	+1.2	+0.4	−0.6	+0.8	+0.6	−0.9	+1.2	+0.9	−1.1	+0.8	+1.1	−1.4	+0.8	+1.4
		+1.05	−0	−0.25	+1.6	−0	−0.4	+0.7	−0	+0.1	+1.1	−0	+0.1	+0.2	−0	+0.6	+0.2	−0	+0.6
1.19	−1.97	−0.3	+1.0	+0.3	−0.5	+1.6	+0.5	−0.7	+1.0	+0.7	−1.1	+1.6	+1.1	−1.3	+1.0	+1.3	−1.7	+1.0	+1.7
		+1.3	−0	−0.3	+2.1	−0	−0.5	+0.9	−0	+0.1	+1.5	−0	+0.1	+0.3	−0	+0.7	+0.3	−0	+0.7
1.97	−3.15	−0.3	+1.2	+0.3	−0.6	+1.8	+0.6	−0.8	+1.2	+0.8	−1.3	+1.8	+1.3	−1.5	+1.2	+1.5	−2.0	+1.2	+2.0
		+1.5	−0	−0.3	+2.4	−0	−0.6	+1.1	−0	+0.1	+1.7	−0	+0.1	+0.4	−0	+0.8	+0.4	−0	+0.8
3.15	−4.73	−0.4	+1.4	+0.4	−0.7	+2.2	+0.7	−1.0	+1.4	+1.0	−1.5	+2.2	+1.5	−1.9	+1.4	+1.9	−2.4	+1.4	+2.4
		+1.8	−0	−0.4	+2.9	−0	−0.7	+1.3	−0	+0.1	+2.1	−0	+0.1	+0.4	−0	+1.0	+0.4	−0	+1.0
4.73	−7.09	−0.5	+1.6	+0.5	−0.8	+2.5	+0.8	−1.1	+1.6	+1.1	−1.7	+2.5	+1.7	−2.2	+1.6	+2.2	−2.8	+1.6	+2.8
		+2.1	−0	−0.5	+3.3	−0	−0.8	+1.5	−0	+0.1	+2.4	−0	+0.1	+0.4	−0	+1.2	+0.4	−0	+1.2
7.09	−9.85	−0.6	+1.8	+0.6	−0.9	+2.8	+0.9	−1.4	+1.8	+1.4	−2.0	+2.8	+2.0	−2.6	+1.8	+2.6	−3.2	+1.8	+3.2
		+2.4	−0	−0.6	+3.7	−0	−0.9	+1.6	−0	+0.2	+2.6	−0	+0.2	+0.4	−0	+1.4	+0.4	−0	+1.4
9.85	−12.41	−0.6	+2.0	+0.6	−1.0	+3.0	+1.0	−1.4	+2.0	+1.4	−2.2	+3.0	+2.2	−2.6	+2.0	+2.6	−3.4	+2.0	+3.4
		+2.6	−0	−0.6	+4.0	−0	−1.0	+1.8	−0	+0.2	+2.8	−0	+0.2	+0.6	−0	+1.4	+0.6	−0	+1.4
12.41	−15.75	−0.7	+2.2	+0.7	−1.0	+3.5	+1.0	−1.6	+2.2	+1.6	−2.4	+3.5	+2.4	−3.0	+2.2	+3.0	−3.8	+2.2	+3.8
		+2.9	−0	−0.7	+4.5	−0	−1.0	+2.0	−0	+0.2	+3.3	−0	+0.2	+0.6	−0	+1.6	+0.6	−0	+1.6
15.75	−19.69	−0.8	+2.5	+0.8	−1.2	+4.0	+1.2	−1.8	+2.5	+1.8	−2.7	+4.0	+2.7	−3.4	+2.5	+3.4	−4.3	+2.5	+4.3
		+3.3	−0	−0.8	+5.2	−0	−1.2	+2.3	−0	+0.2	+3.8	−0	+0.2	+0.7	−0	+1.8	+0.7	−0	+1.8

Source: Courtesy of ANSI; B4.1.

Limits are in thousandths of an inch.
Limits for hole and shaft are applied algebraically to the basic size to obtain the limits of size for the parts.
Data in boldface are in accordance with ABC agreements.
Symbols H7, p6, etc., are Hole and Shaft designations used in ABC System.

Nominal Size Range Inches		Class LN 1			Class LN 2			Class LN 3		
		Limits of Interference	Standard Limits		Limits of Interference	Standard Limits		Limits of Interference	Standard Limits	
Over	To		Hole H6	Shaft n5		Hole H7	Shaft p6		Hole H7	Shaft r6
0	−0.12	0	+0.25	+0.45	0	+0.4	+0.65	0.1	+0.4	+0.75
		0.45	−0	+0.25	0.65	−0	+0.4	0.75	−0	+0.5
0.12	−0.24	0	+0.3	+0.5	0	+0.5	+0.8	0.1	+0.5	+0.9
		0.5	−0	+0.3	0.8	−0	+0.5	0.9	0	+0.6
0.24	−0.40	0	+0.4	+0.65	0	+0.6	+1.0	0.2	+0.6	+1.2
		0.65	−0	+0.4	1.0	−0	+0.6	1.2	−0	+0.8
0.40	−0.71	0	+0.4	+0.8	0	+0.7	+1.1	0.3	+0.7	+1.4
		0.8	−0	+0.4	1.1	−0	+0.7	1.4	−0	+1.0
0.71	−1.19	0	+0.5	+1.0	0	+0.8	+1.3	0.4	+0.8	+1.7
		1.0	−0	+0.5	1.3	−0	+0.8	1.7	−0	+1.2
1.19	−1.97	0	+0.6	+1.1	0	+1.0	+1.6	0.4	+1.0	+2.0
		1.1	−0	+0.6	1.6	−0	+1.0	2.0	−0	+1.4
1.97	−3.15	0.1	+0.7	+1.3	0.2	+1.2	+2.1	0.4	+1.2	+2.3
		1.3	−0	+0.7	2.1	−0	+1.4	2.3	−0	+1.6
3.15	−4.73	0.1	+0.9	+1.6	0.2	+1.4	+2.5	0.6	+1.4	+2.9
		1.6	−0	+1.0	2.5	−0	+1.6	2.9	−0	+2.0
4.73	−7.09	0.2	+1.0	+1.9	0.2	+1.6	+2.8	0.9	+1.6	+3.5
		1.9	−0	+1.2	2.8	−0	+1.8	3.5	−0	+2.5
7.09	−9.85	0.2	+1.2	+2.2	0.2	+1.8	+3.2	1.2	+1.8	+4.2
		2.2	−0	+1.4	3.2	−0	+2.0	4.2	−0	+3.0
9.85	−12.41	0.2	+1.2	+2.3	0.2	+2.0	+3.4	1.5	+2.0	+4.7
		2.3	−0	+1.4	3.4	−0	+2.2	4.7	−0	+3.5
12.41	−15.75	0.2	+1.4	+2.6	0.3	+2.2	+3.9	2.3	+2.2	+5.9
		2.6	−0	+1.6	3.9	−0	+2.5	5.9	−0	+4.5
15.75	−19.69	0.2	+1.6	+2.8	0.3	+2.5	+4.4	2.5	+2.5	+6.6
		2.8	−0	+1.8	4.4	−0	+2.8	6.6	−0	+5.0
19.69	−30.09		+2.0		0.5	+3	+5.5	4	+3	+9
			−0		5.5	−0	+3.5	9	−0	+7
30.09	−41.49		+2.5		0.5	+4	+7.0	5	+4	+11.5
			−0		7.0	−0	+4.5	11.5	−0	+9
41.49	−56.19		+3.0		1	+5	+9	7	+5	+15
			−0		9	−0	+6	15	−0	+12
56.19	−76.39		+4.0		1	+6	+11	10	+6	+20
			−0		11	−0	+7	20	−0	+16
76.39	−100.9		+5.0		1	+8	+14	12	+8	+25
			−0		14	−0	+9	25	−0	+20
100.9	−131.9		+6.0		2	+10	+18	15	+10	+31
			−0		18	−0	+12	31	−0	+25
131.9	−171.9		+8.0		4	+12	+24	18	+12	+38
			−0		24	−0	+16	38	−0	+30
171.9	−200		+10.0		4	+16	+30	24	+16	+50
			−0		30	−0	+20	50	−0	+40

Source: Courtesy of ANSI; B4.1.

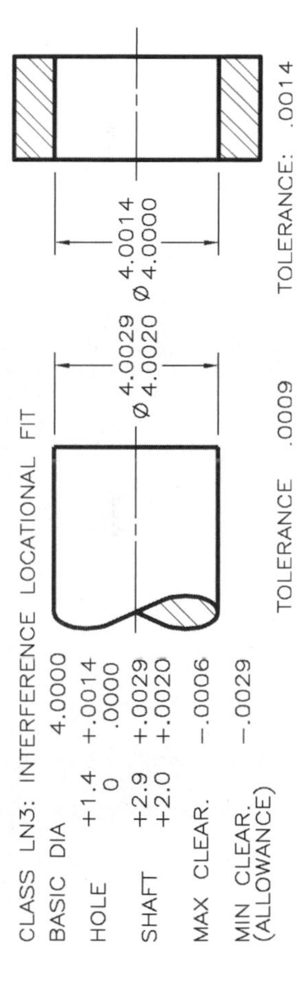

Limits are in thousandths of an inch.
Limits for hole and shaft are applied algebraically to the basic size to obtain the limits of size for the parts.
Data in boldface are in accordance with ABC agreements.
Symbols H7, s6, etc., are Hole and Shaft designations used in ABC System.

Nominal Size Range Inches		Class FN 1			Class FN 2			Class FN 3			Class FN 4			Class FN 5		
		Limits of Interference	Standard Limits		Limits of Interference	Standard Limits		Limits of Interference	Standards Limits		Limits of Interference	Standard Limits		Limits of Interference	Standard Limits	
Over	To		Hole H6	Shaft h5		Hole H7	Shaft s6		Hole H7	Shaft t6		Hole H7	Shaft u6		Hole H8	Shaft x7
0	−0.12	0.05	+0.25	+0.5	0.2	+0.4	+0.85				0.3	+0.4	+0.95	0.3	+0.6	+1.3
		0.5	−0	+0.3	0.85	−0	+0.6				0.95	−0	+0.7	1.3	−0	+0.9
0.12	−0.24	0.1	+0.3	+0.6	0.2	+0.5	+1.0				0.4	+0.5	+1.2	0.5	+0.7	+1.7
		0.6	−0	+0.4	1.0	−0	+0.7				1.2	−0	+0.9	1.7	−0	+1.2
0.24	−0.40	0.1	+0.4	+0.75	0.4	+0.6	+1.4				0.6	+0.6	+1.6	0.5	+0.9	+2.0
		0.75	−0	+0.5	1.4	−0	+1.0				1.6	−0	+1.2	2.0	−0	+1.4
0.40	−0.56	0.1	−0.4	+0.8	0.5	+0.7	+1.6				0.7	+0.7	+1.8	0.6	+1.0	+2.3
		0.8	−0	+0.5	1.6	−0	+1.2				1.8	−0	+1.4	2.3	−0	+1.6
0.56	−0.71	0.2	+0.4	+0.9	0.5	+0.7	+1.6				0.7	+0.7	+1.8	0.8	+1.0	+2.5
		0.9	−0	+0.6	1.6	−0	+1.2				1.8	−0	+1.4	2.5	−0	+1.8
0.71	−0.95	0.2	+0.5	+1.1	0.6	+0.8	+1.9				0.8	+0.8	+2.1	1.0	+1.2	+3.0
		1.1	−0	+0.7	1.9	−0	+1.4				2.1	−0	+1.6	3.0	−0	+2.2
0.95	−1.19	0.3	+0.5	+1.2	0.6	+0.8	+1.9	0.8	+0.8	+2.1	1.0	+0.8	+2.3	1.3	+1.2	+3.3
		1.2	−0	+0.8	1.9	−0	+1.4	2.1	−0	+1.6	2.3	−0	+1.8	3.3	−0	+2.5
1.19	−1.58	0.3	+0.6	+1.3	0.8	+1.0	+2.4	1.0	+1.0	+2.6	1.5	+1.0	+3.1	1.4	+1.6	+4.0
		1.3	−0	+0.9	2.4	−0	+1.8	2.6	−0	+2.0	3.1	−0	+2.5	4.0	−0	+3.0
1.58	−1.97	0.4	+0.6	+1.4	0.8	+1.0	+2.4	1.2	+1.0	+2.8	1.8	+1.0	+3.4	2.4	+1.6	+5.0
		1.4	−0	+1.0	2.4	−0	+1.8	2.8	−0	+2.2	3.4	−0	+2.8	5.0	−0	+4.0
1.97	−2.56	0.6	+0.7	+1.8	0.8	+1.2	+2.7	1.3	+1.2	+3.2	2.3	+1.2	+4.2	3.2	+1.8	+6.2
		1.8	−0	+1.3	2.7	−0	+2.0	3.2	−0	+2.5	4.2	−0	+3.5	6.2	−0	+5.0
2.56	−3.15	0.7	+0.7	+1.9	1.0	+1.2	+2.9	1.8	+1.2	+3.7	2.8	+1.2	+4.7	4.2	+1.8	+7.2
		1.9	−0	+1.4	2.9	−0	+2.2	3.7	−0	+3.0	4.7	−0	+4.0	7.2	−0	+6.0
3.15	−3.94	0.9	+0.9	+2.4	1.4	+1.4	+3.7	2.1	+1.4	+4.4	3.6	+1.4	+5.9	4.8	+2.2	+8.4
		2.4	−0	+1.8	3.7	−0	+2.8	4.4	−0	+3.5	5.9	−0	+5.0	8.4	−0	+7.0
3.94	−4.73	1.1	+0.9	+2.6	1.6	+1.4	+3.9	2.6	+1.4	+4.9	4.6	+1.4	+6.9	5.8	+2.2	+9.4
		2.6	−0	+2.0	3.9	−0	+3.0	4.9	−0	+4.0	6.9	−0	+6.0	9.4	−0	+8.0
4.73	−5.52	1.2	+1.0	+2.9	1.9	+1.6	+4.5	3.4	+1.6	+6.0	5.4	+1.6	+8.0	7.5	+2.5	+11.6
		2.9	−0	+2.2	4.5	−0	+3.5	6.0	−0	+5.0	8.0	−0	+7.0	11.6	−0	+10.0
5.52	−6.30	1.5	+1.0	+3.2	2.4	+1.6	+5.0	3.4	+1.6	+6.0	5.4	+1.6	+8.0	9.5	+2.5	+13.6
		3.2	−0	+2.5	5.0	−0	+4.0	6.0	−0	+5.0	8.0	−0	+7.0	13.6	−0	+12.0
6.30	−7.09	1.8	+1.0	+3.5	2.9	+1.6	+5.5	4.4	+1.6	+7.0	6.4	+1.6	+9.0	9.5	+2.5	+13.6
		3.5	−0	+2.8	5.5	−0	+4.5	7.0	−0	+6.0	9.0	−0	+8.0	13.6	−0	+12.0
7.09	−7.88	1.8	+1.2	+3.8	3.2	+1.8	+6.2	5.2	+1.8	+8.2	7.2	+1.8	+10.2	11.2	+2.8	+15.8
		3.8	−0	+3.0	6.2	−0	+5.0	8.2	−0	+7.0	10.2	−0	+9.0	15.8	−0	+14.0
7.88	−8.86	2.3	+1.2	+4.3	3.2	+1.8	+6.2	5.2	+1.8	+8.2	8.2	+1.8	+11.2	13.2	−2.8	+17.8
		4.3	−0	+3.5	6.2	−0	+5.0	8.2	−0	+7.0	11.2	−0	+10.0	17.8	−0	+16.0
8.86	−9.85	2.3	+1.2	+4.3	4.2	+1.8	+7.2	6.2	+1.8	+9.2	10.2	+1.8	+13.2	13.2	+2.8	+17.8
		4.3	−0	+3.5	7.2	−0	+6.0	9.2	−0	+8.0	13.2	−0	+12.0	17.8	−0	+16.0
9.85	−11.03	2.8	+1.2	+4.9	4.0	+2.0	+7.2	7.0	+2.0	+10.2	10.0	+2.0	+13.2	15.0	+3.0	+20.0
		4.9	−0	+4.0	7.2	−0	+6.0	10.2	−0	+9.0	13.2	−0	+12.0	20.0	−0	+18.0
11.03	−12.41	2.8	+1.2	+4.9	5.0	+2.0	+8.2	7.0	+2.0	+10.2	12.0	+2.0	+15.2	17.0	+3.0	+22.0
		4.9	−0	+4.0	8.2	−0	+7.0	10.2	−0	+9.0	15.2	−0	+14.0	22.0	−0	+20.0
12.41	−13.98	3.1	+1.4	+5.5	5.8	+2.2	+9.4	7.8	+2.2	+11.4	13.8	+2.2	+17.4	18.5	+3.5	+24.2
		5.5	−0	+4.5	9.4	−0	+8.0	11.4	−0	+10.0	17.4	−0	+16.0	24.2	+0	+22.0
13.98	−15.75	3.6	+1.4	+6.1	5.8	+2.2	+9.4	9.8	+2.2	+13.4	15.8	+2.2	+19.4	21.5	+3.5	+27.2
		6.1	−0	+5.0	9.4	−0	+8.0	13.4	−0	+12.0	19.4	−0	+18.0	27.2	−0	+25.0
15.75	−17.72	4.4	+1.6	+7.0	6.5	+2.5	+10.6	9.5	+2.5	+13.6	17.5	+2.5	+21.6	24.0	+4.0	+30.5
		7.0	−0	+6.0	10.6	−0	+9.0	13.6	−0	+12.0	21.6	−0	+20.0	30.5	−0	+28.0
17.72	−19.69	4.4	+1.6	+7.0	7.5	+2.5	+11.6	11.5	+2.5	+15.6	19.5	+2.5	+23.6	26.0	+4.0	+32.5
		7.0	−0	+6.0	11.6	−0	+10.0	15.6	−0	+14.0	23.6	−0	+22.0	32.5	−0	+30.0

Courtesy of ANSI; B4.1

APPENDIX 34 • The International Tolerance Grades (ANSI B4.2)

Basic sizes		Tolerance grades[1]																	
Over	Up to and including	IT01	IT0	IT1	IT2	IT3	IT4	IT5	IT6	IT7	IT8	IT9	IT10	IT11	IT12	IT13	IT14	IT15	IT16
0	3	0.0003	0.0005	0.0008	0.0012	0.002	0.003	0.004	0.006	0.010	0.014	0.025	0.040	0.060	0.100	0.140	0.250	0.400	0.600
3	6	0.0004	0.0006	0.001	0.0015	0.0025	0.004	0.005	0.008	0.012	0.018	0.030	0.048	0.075	0.120	0.180	0.300	0.480	0.750
6	10	0.0004	0.0006	0.001	0.0015	0.0025	0.004	0.006	0.009	0.015	0.022	0.036	0.058	0.090	0.150	0.220	0.360	0.580	0.900
10	18	0.0005	0.0008	0.0012	0.002	0.003	0.005	0.008	0.011	0.018	0.027	0.043	0.070	0.110	0.180	0.270	0.430	0.700	1.100
18	30	0.0006	0.001	0.0015	0.0025	0.004	0.006	0.009	0.013	0.021	0.033	0.052	0.084	0.130	0.210	0.330	0.520	0.840	1.300
30	50	0.0006	0.001	0.0015	0.0025	0.004	0.007	0.011	0.016	0.025	0.039	0.062	0.100	0.160	0.250	0.390	0.620	1.000	1.600
50	80	0.0008	0.0012	0.002	0.003	0.005	0.008	0.013	0.019	0.030	0.046	0.074	0.120	0.190	0.300	0.460	0.740	1.200	1.900
80	120	0.001	0.0015	0.0025	0.004	0.006	0.010	0.015	0.022	0.035	0.054	0.087	0.140	0.220	0.350	0.540	0.870	1.400	2.200
120	180	0.0012	0.002	0.0036	0.005	0.008	0.012	0.018	0.025	0.040	0.063	0.100	0.160	0.250	0.400	0.630	1.000	1.600	2.500
180	250	0.002	0.003	0.0045	0.007	0.010	0.014	0.020	0.029	0.046	0.072	0.115	0.185	0.290	0.460	0.720	1.150	1.850	2.900
250	315	0.0025	0.004	0.006	0.008	0.012	0.016	0.023	0.032	0.052	0.081	0.130	0.210	0.320	0.520	0.810	1.300	2.100	3.200
315	400	0.003	0.005	0.007	0.009	0.013	0.018	0.025	0.036	0.057	0.089	0.140	0.230	0.360	0.570	0.890	1.400	2.300	3.600
400	500	0.004	0.006	0.008	0.010	0.015	0.020	0.027	0.040	0.063	0.097	0.156	0.250	0.400	0.630	0.970	1.550	2.500	4.000
500	630	0.0045	0.006	0.009	0.011	0.016	0.022	0.030	0.044	0.070	0.110	0.175	0.280	0.440	0.700	1.100	1.750	2.800	4.400
630	800	0.005	0.007	0.010	0.013	0.018	0.025	0.035	0.050	0.080	0.125	0.200	0.320	0.500	0.800	1.250	2.000	3.200	5.000
800	1000	0.0055	0.008	0.011	0.015	0.021	0.029	0.040	0.056	0.090	0.140	0.230	0.360	0.560	0.900	1.400	2.300	3.600	5.600
1000	1250	0.0065	0.009	0.013	0.018	0.024	0.034	0.046	0.066	0.105	0.165	0.260	0.420	0.660	1.050	1.650	2.600	4.200	6.600
1250	1600	0.008	0.011	0.015	0.021	0.029	0.040	0.054	0.078	0.125	0.195	0.310	0.500	0.780	1.250	1.950	3.100	5.000	7.800
1600	2000	0.009	0.013	0.018	0.025	0.035	0.048	0.065	0.092	0.150	0.230	0.370	0.600	0.920	1.500	2.300	3.700	6.000	9.200
2000	2500	0.011	0.015	0.022	0.030	0.041	0.057	0.077	0.110	0.175	0.280	0.440	0.700	1.100	1.750	2.800	4.400	7.000	11.000
2500	3150	0.013	0.018	0.026	0.036	0.050	0.069	0.093	0.135	0.210	0.330	0.540	0.860	1.350	2.100	3.300	5.400	8.600	13.500

[1] IT Values for tolerance grades larger than IT16 can be calculated by using the following formulas:
IT17 = IT12 × 10; IT18 = IT13 × 10; etc.

Dimensions are in mm.

APPENDIX 35 • Preferred Hole-Basis Clearance Fits—Cylindrical Fits (ANSI B4.2)

AMERICAN NATIONAL STANDARD PREFERRED METRIC LIMITS AND FITS ANSI B4.2

Dimensions are in mm.

Basic Size		Loose Running			Free Running			Close Running			Sliding			Locational Clearance		
		Hole H11	Shaft c11	Fit	Hole H9	Shaft d9	Fit	Hole H8	Shaft f7	Fit	Hole H7	Shaft g6	Fit	Hole H7	Shaft h6	Fit
1	MAX	1.060	0.940	0.180	1.025	0.980	0.070	1.014	0.994	0.030	1.010	0.998	0.018	1.010	1.000	0.016
	MIN	1.000	0.880	0.060	1.000	0.955	0.020	1.000	0.984	0.006	1.000	0.992	0.002	1.000	0.994	0.000
1.2	MAX	1.260	1.140	0.180	1.225	1.180	0.070	1.214	1.194	0.030	1.210	1.198	0.018	1.210	1.200	0.016
	MIN	1.200	1.080	0.060	1.200	1.155	0.020	1.200	1.184	0.006	1.200	1.192	0.002	1.200	1.194	0.000
1.6	MAX	1.660	1.540	0.180	1.625	1.580	0.070	1.614	1.594	0.030	1.610	1.598	0.018	1.610	1.600	0.016
	MIN	1.600	1.480	0.060	1.600	1.555	0.020	1.600	1.584	0.006	1.600	1.592	0.002	1.600	1.594	0.000
2	MAX	2.060	1.940	0.180	2.025	1.980	0.070	2.014	1.994	0.030	2.010	1.998	0.018	2.010	2.000	0.016
	MIN	2.000	1.880	0.060	2.000	1.955	0.020	2.000	1.984	0.006	2.000	1.992	0.002	2.000	1.994	0.000
2.5	MAX	2.560	2.440	0.180	2.525	0.480	0.070	2.514	2.494	0.030	2.510	2.498	0.018	2.510	2.500	0.016
	MIN	2.500	2.380	0.060	2.500	2.455	0.020	2.500	2.484	0.006	2.500	2.492	0.002	2.500	2.494	0.000
3	MAX	3.060	2.940	0.180	3.025	2.980	0.070	3.014	2.994	0.030	3.010	2.998	0.018	3.010	3.000	0.016
	MIN	3.000	2.880	0.060	3.000	2.955	0.020	3.000	2.984	0.006	3.000	2.992	0.002	3.000	2.994	0.000
4	MAX	4.075	3.930	0.220	4.030	3.970	0.090	4.018	3.990	0.040	4.012	3.996	0.024	4.012	4.000	0.020
	MIN	4.000	3.855	0.070	4.000	3.940	0.030	4.000	3.978	0.010	4.000	3.988	0.004	4.000	3.992	0.000
5	MAX	5.075	4.930	0.220	5.030	4.970	0.090	5.018	4.990	0.040	5.012	4.996	0.024	5.012	5.000	0.020
	MIN	5.000	4.855	0.070	5.000	4.940	0.030	5.000	4.978	0.010	5.000	4.988	0.004	5.000	4.992	0.000
6	MAX	6.075	5.930	0.220	6.030	5.970	0.090	6.018	5.990	0.040	6.012	5.996	0.024	6.012	6.000	0.020
	MIN	6.000	5.855	0.070	6.000	5.940	0.030	6.000	5.978	0.010	6.000	5.988	0.004	6.000	5.992	0.000
8	MAX	8.090	7.920	0.260	8.036	7.960	0.112	8.022	7.987	0.050	8.015	7.995	0.029	8.015	8.000	0.024
	MIN	8.000	7.830	0.080	8.000	7.924	0.040	8.000	7.972	0.013	8.000	7.986	0.005	8.000	7.991	0.000
10	MAX	10.090	9.920	0.260	10.036	9.960	0.112	10.022	9.987	0.050	10.015	9.995	0.029	10.015	10.000	0.024
	MIN	10.000	9.830	0.080	10.000	9.924	0.040	10.000	9.972	0.013	10.000	9.986	0.005	10.000	9.991	0.000
12	MAX	12.110	11.905	0.315	12.043	11.950	0.136	12.027	11.984	0.061	12.018	11.994	0.035	12.018	12.000	0.029
	MIN	12.000	11.795	0.095	12.000	11.907	0.050	12.000	11.966	0.016	12.000	11.983	0.006	12.000	11.989	0.000
16	MAX	16.110	15.905	0.315	16.043	15.950	0.136	16.027	15.984	0.061	16.018	15.994	0.035	16.018	16.000	0.029
	MIN	16.000	15.795	0.095	16.000	15.907	0.050	16.000	15.966	0.016	16.000	15.983	0.006	16.000	15.989	0.000
20	MAX	20.130	19.890	0.370	20.052	19.935	0.169	20.033	19.980	0.074	20.021	19.993	0.041	20.021	20.000	0.034
	MIN	20.000	19.760	0.110	20.000	19.883	0.065	20.000	19.959	0.020	20.000	19.980	0.007	20.000	19.987	0.000
25	MAX	25.130	24.890	0.370	25.052	24.935	0.169	25.033	24.980	0.074	25.021	24.993	0.041	25.021	25.000	0.034
	MIN	25.000	24.760	0.110	25.000	24.883	0.065	25.000	24.959	0.020	25.000	24.980	0.007	25.000	24.987	0.000
30	MAX	30.130	29.890	0.370	30.052	29.935	0.169	30.033	29.980	0.074	30.021	29.993	0.041	30.021	30.000	0.034
	MIN	30.000	29.760	0.110	30.000	29.883	0.065	30.000	29.959	0.020	30.000	29.980	0.007	30.000	29.987	0.000

Source: American National Standard Preferred Metric Limits and Figs, ANSI B4.2.

APPENDIX 35 • Preferred Hole-Basis Clearance Fits—Cylindrical Fits (ANSI B4.2) (continued)

Basic Size		Loose Running			Free Running			Close Running			Sliding			Locational Clearance		
		Hole H11	Shaft c11	Fit	Hole H9	Shaft d9	Fit	Hole H8	Shaft f7	Fit	Hole H7	Shaft g6	Fit	Hole H7	Shaft h6	Fit
40	MAX	40.160	39.880	0.440	40.062	39.920	0.204	40.039	39.975	0.089	40.025	39.991	0.050	40.025	40.000	0.041
	MIN	40.000	39.720	0.120	40.000	39.858	0.080	40.000	39.950	0.025	40.000	39.975	0.009	40.000	39.984	0.000
50	MAX	50.160	49.870	0.450	50.062	49.920	0.204	50.039	49.975	0.089	50.025	49.991	0.050	50.025	50.000	0.041
	MIN	50.000	49.710	0.130	50.000	49.858	0.080	50.000	49.950	0.025	50.000	49.975	0.009	50.000	49.984	0.000
60	MAX	60.190	59.860	0.520	60.074	59.900	0.248	60.046	59.970	0.106	60.030	59.990	0.059	60.030	60.000	0.049
	MIN	60.000	59.670	0.140	60.000	59.826	0.100	60.000	59.940	0.030	60.000	59.971	0.010	60.000	59.981	0.000
80	MAX	80.190	79.850	0.530	80.074	70.900	0.248	80.046	79.970	0.106	80.030	79.990	0.059	80.030	80.000	0.049
	MIN	80.000	79.660	0.150	80.000	79.826	0.100	80.000	79.940	0.030	80.000	79.971	0.010	80.000	79.981	0.000
100	MAX	100.220	99.830	0.610	100.087	99.880	0.294	100.054	99.964	0.125	100.035	99.988	0.069	100.035	100.000	0.057
	MIN	100.000	99.610	0.170	100.000	99.793	0.120	100.000	99.929	0.036	100.000	99.966	0.012	100.000	99.978	0.000
120	MAX	120.220	119.820	0.620	120.087	119.880	0.294	120.054	119.964	0.125	120.035	119.988	0.069	120.035	120.000	0.057
	MIN	120.000	119.600	0.180	120.000	119.793	0.120	120.000	119.929	0.036	120.000	119.966	0.012	120.000	119.978	0.000
160	MAX	160.250	159.790	0.710	160.100	159.855	0.345	160.063	159.957	0.146	160.040	159.986	0.079	160.040	160.000	0.065
	MIN	160.000	159.540	0.210	160.000	159.755	0.145	160.000	159.917	0.043	160.000	159.961	0.014	160.000	159.975	0.000
200	MAX	200.290	199.760	0.820	200.115	199.830	0.400	200.072	199.950	0.168	200.046	199.985	0.090	200.046	200.000	0.075
	MIN	200.000	199.470	0.240	200.000	199.715	0.170	200.000	199.904	0.050	200.000	199.956	0.105	200.000	199.971	0.000
250	MAX	250.290	249.720	0.860	250.115	249.830	0.400	250.072	249.950	0.168	250.046	249.985	0.090	250.046	250.000	0.075
	MIN	250.000	249.430	0.280	250.000	249.715	0.170	250.000	249.904	0.050	250.000	249.956	0.015	250.000	249.971	0.000
300	MAX	300.320	299.670	0.970	300.130	299.810	0.450	300.081	299.944	0.189	300.052	299.983	0.101	300.052	300.000	0.084
	MIN	300.000	299.350	0.330	300.000	299.680	0.190	300.000	299.892	0.056	300.000	299.951	0.017	300.000	299.968	0.000
400	MAX	400.360	399.600	1.120	400.140	399.790	0.490	400.089	399.938	0.208	400.057	399.982	0.111	400.057	400.000	0.093
	MIN	400.000	399.240	0.400	400.000	399.650	0.210	400.000	399.881	0.062	400.000	399.946	0.018	400.000	399.964	0.000
500	MAX	500.400	499.520	1.280	500.155	499.770	0.540	500.097	499.932	0.228	500.063	499.980	0.123	500.063	500.000	0.103
	MIN	500.000	499.120	0.480	500.000	499.615	0.230	500.000	499.869	0.068	500.000	499.940	0.020	500.000	499.960	0.000

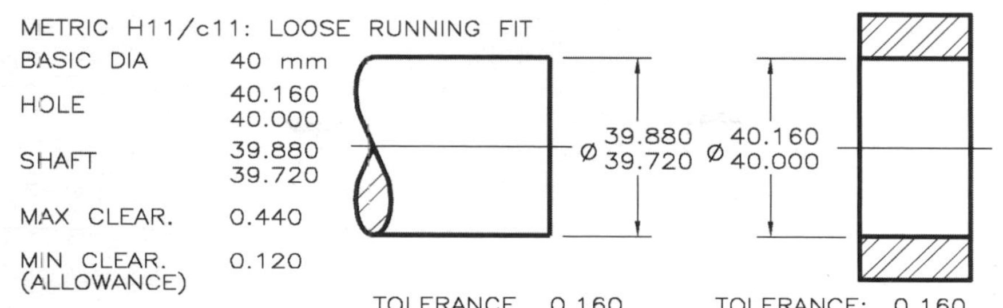

APPENDIX 36 • Preferred Hole-Basis Transition and Interference Fits—Cylindrical Fits (ANSI B4.2)

Basic Size		Locational Transn.			Locational Transn.			Locational Interf.			Medium Drive			Force		
		Hole H7	Shaft k6	Fit	Hole H7	Shaft n6	Fit	Hole H7	Shaft p6	Fit	Hole H7	Shaft s6	Fit	Hole H7	Shaft u6	Fit
1	MAX	1.010	1.006	0.010	1.010	1.010	0.006	1.010	1.012	0.004	1.010	1.020	−0.004	1.010	1.024	−0.008
	MIN	1.000	1.000	−0.006	1.000	1.004	−0.010	1.000	1.006	−0.012	1.000	1.014	−0.020	1.000	1.018	−0.024
1.2	MAX	1.210	1.206	0.010	1.210	1.210	0.006	1.210	1.212	0.004	1.210	1.220	−0.004	1.210	1.224	−0.008
	MIN	1.200	1.200	−0.006	1.200	1.204	−0.010	1.200	1.206	−0.012	1.200	1.214	−0.020	1.200	1.218	−0.024
1.6	MAX	1.610	1.606	0.010	1.610	1.610	0.006	1.610	1.612	0.004	1.610	1.620	−0.004	1.610	1.624	−0.008
	MIN	1.600	1.600	−0.006	1.600	1.604	−0.010	1.600	1.606	−0.012	1.600	1.614	−0.020	1.600	1.618	−0.024
2	MAX	2.010	2.006	0.010	2.010	2.010	0.006	2.010	2.010	0.004	2.010	2.020	−0.004	2.010	2.024	−0.008
	MIN	2.000	2.000	−0.006	2.000	2.004	−0.010	2.000	2.006	−0.012	2.000	2.014	−0.020	2.000	2.018	−0.024
2.5	MAX	2.510	2.506	0.010	2.510	2.510	0.006	2.510	2.512	0.004	2.510	2.520	−0.004	2.510	2.524	−0.008
	MIN	2.500	2.500	−0.006	2.500	2.504	−0.010	2.500	2.506	−0.012	2.500	2.514	−0.020	2.500	2.518	−0.024
3	MAX	3.010	3.006	0.010	3.010	3.010	0.006	3.010	3.012	0.004	3.010	3.020	−0.004	3.010	3.024	−0.008
	MIN	3.000	3.000	−0.006	3.000	3.004	−0.010	3.000	3.006	−0.012	3.000	3.014	−0.020	3.000	3.018	−0.024
4	MAX	4.012	4.009	0.011	4.012	4.016	0.004	4.012	4.020	0.000	4.012	4.027	−0.007	4.012	4.031	−0.011
	MIN	4.000	4.001	−0.009	4.000	4.008	−0.016	4.000	4.012	−0.020	4.000	4.019	−0.027	4.000	4.023	−0.031
5	MAX	5.012	5.009	0.011	5.012	5.016	0.004	5.012	5.020	0.000	5.012	5.027	−0.007	5.012	5.031	−0.011
	MIN	5.000	5.001	−0.009	5.000	5.008	−0.016	5.000	5.012	−0.020	5.000	5.019	−0.027	5.000	5.023	−0.031
6	MAX	6.012	6.009	0.011	6.012	6.016	0.004	6.012	6.020	0.000	6.012	6.027	−0.007	6.012	6.031	−0.011
	MIN	6.000	6.001	−0.009	6.000	6.008	−0.016	6.000	6.012	−0.020	6.000	6.019	−0.027	6.000	6.023	−0.031
8	MAX	8.015	8.010	0.014	8.015	8.019	0.005	8.015	8.024	0.000	8.015	8.032	−0.008	8.015	8.037	−0.013
	MIN	8.000	8.001	−0.010	8.000	8.010	−0.019	8.000	8.015	−0.024	8.000	8.023	−0.032	8.000	8.028	−0.037
10	MAX	10.015	10.010	0.014	10.015	10.019	0.005	10.015	10.024	0.000	10.015	10.032	−0.008	10.015	10.037	−0.013
	MIN	10.000	10.001	−0.010	10.000	10.010	−0.019	10.000	10.015	−0.024	10.000	10.023	−0.032	10.000	10.028	−0.037
12	MAX	12.018	12.012	0.017	12.018	12.023	0.006	12.018	12.029	0.000	12.018	12.039	−0.010	12.018	12.044	−0.015
	MIN	12.000	12.001	−0.012	12.000	12.012	−0.023	12.000	12.018	−0.029	12.000	12.028	−0.039	12.000	12.033	−0.044
16	MAX	16.018	16.012	0.017	16.018	16.023	0.006	16.018	16.029	0.000	16.018	16.019	−0.010	16.018	16.044	−0.015
	MIN	16.000	16.001	−0.012	16.000	16.012	−0.023	16.000	16.018	−0.029	16.000	16.028	−0.039	16.000	16.033	−0.044
20	MAX	20.021	20.015	0.019	20.021	20.028	0.006	20.021	20.035	−0.001	20.021	20.048	−0.014	20.021	20.054	−0.020
	MIN	20.000	20.002	−0.015	20.000	20.015	−0.028	20.000	20.022	−0.035	20.000	20.035	−0.048	20.000	20.041	−0.054
25	MAX	25.021	25.015	0.019	25.021	25.028	0.006	25.021	25.035	−0.001	25.021	25.048	−0.014	25.021	25.061	−0.027
	MIN	25.000	25.002	−0.015	25.000	25.015	−0.028	25.000	25.022	−0.035	25.000	25.035	−0.048	25.000	25.048	−0.061
30	MAX	30.021	30.015	0.019	30.021	30.028	0.006	30.021	30.035	−0.001	30.021	30.048	−0.014	30.021	30.061	−0.027
	MIN	30.000	30.002	−0.015	30.000	30.015	−0.028	30.000	30.022	−0.035	30.000	30.035	−0.048	30.000	30.048	−0.061

Source: American National Standard Preferred Metric Limit and Fits, ANSI B4.2.

Dimensions are in mm.

APPENDIX 36 • Preferred Hole-Basis Transition and Interference Fits—Cylindrical Fits (ANSI B4.2) (continued)

Basic Size		Locational Transn.			Locational Transn.			Locational Interf.			Medium Drive			Force		
		Hole H7	Shaft k6	Fit	Hole H7	Shaft n6	Fit	Hole H7	Shaft p6	Fit	Hole H7	Shaft s6	Fit	Hole H7	Shaft u6	Fit
0	MAX	40.025	40.018	0.023	40.025	40.033	0.008	40.025	40.042	−0.001	40.025	40.059	−0.018	40.025	40.076	−0.035
	MIN	40.000	40.002	−0.018	40.000	40.017	−0.033	40.000	40.026	−0.042	40.000	40.043	−0.059	40.000	40.060	−0.076
50	MAX	50.025	50.018	0.023	50.025	50.033	0.008	50.025	50.042	−0.001	50.025	50.059	−0.018	50.025	50.086	−0.045
	MIN	50.000	50.002	−0.018	50.000	50.017	−0.033	50.000	50.026	−0.042	50.000	50.043	−0.059	50.000	50.070	−0.086
60	MAX	60.030	60.021	0.028	60.030	60.039	0.010	60.030	60.051	−0.002	60.030	60.072	−0.023	60.030	60.106	−0.057
	MIN	60.000	60.002	−0.021	60.000	60.020	−0.039	60.000	60.032	−0.051	60.000	60.053	−0.072	60.000	60.087	−0.106
80	MAX	80.030	80.021	0.028	80.030	80.039	0.010	80.030	80.051	−0.002	80.030	80.078	−0.029	80.030	80.121	−0.072
	MIN	80.000	80.002	−0.021	80.000	80.020	−0.039	80.000	80.032	−0.051	80.000	80.059	−0.078	80.000	80.102	−0.121
100	MAX	100.035	100.025	0.032	100.035	100.045	0.012	100.035	100.059	−0.002	100.035	100.093	−0.036	100.035	100.146	−0.089
	MIN	100.000	100.003	−0.025	100.000	100.023	−0.045	100.000	100.037	−0.059	100.000	100.071	−0.093	100.000	100.124	−0.146
120	MAX	120.035	120.025	0.032	120.035	120.045	0.012	120.035	120.059	−0.002	120.035	120.101	−0.044	120.035	120.166	−0.109
	MIN	120.000	120.003	−0.025	120.000	120.023	−0.045	120.000	120.037	−0.059	120.000	120.079	−0.101	120.000	120.144	−0.166
160	MAX	160.040	160.028	0.037	160.040	160.052	0.013	160.040	160.068	−0.003	160.040	160.125	−0.060	160.040	160.215	−0.150
	MIN	160.000	160.003	−0.028	160.000	160.027	−0.052	160.000	160.043	−0.068	160.000	160.100	−0.125	160.000	160.190	−0.215
200	MAX	200.046	200.033	0.042	200.046	200.060	0.015	200.046	200.079	−0.004	200.046	200.151	−0.076	200.046	200.265	−0.190
	MIN	200.000	200.004	−0.033	200.000	200.031	−0.060	200.000	200.050	−0.079	200.000	200.122	−0.151	200.000	200.236	−0.265
250	MAX	250.046	250.033	0.042	250.046	250.060	0.015	250.046	250.079	−0.004	250.046	250.169	−0.094	250.046	250.313	−0.238
	MIN	250.000	250.004	−0.033	250.000	250.031	−0.060	250.000	250.050	−0.079	250.000	250.140	−0.169	250.000	250.284	−0.313
300	MAX	300.052	300.036	0.048	300.052	300.066	0.018	300.052	300.088	−0.004	300.052	300.202	−0.118	300.052	300.382	−0.298
	MIN	300.000	300.004	−0.036	300.000	300.034	−0.066	300.000	300.056	−0.088	300.000	300.170	−0.202	300.000	300.350	−0.382
400	MAX	400.057	400.040	0.053	400.057	400.073	0.020	400.057	400.098	−0.005	400.057	400.244	−0.151	400.057	400.471	−0.378
	MIN	400.000	400.004	−0.040	400.000	400.037	−0.073	400.000	400.062	−0.098	400.000	400.208	−0.244	400.000	400.435	−0.471
500	MAX	500.063	500.045	0.058	500.063	500.080	0.023	500.063	500.108	−0.005	500.063	500.292	−0.189	500.063	500.580	−0.477
	MIN	500.000	500.005	−0.045	500.000	500.040	−0.080	500.000	500.068	−0.108	500.000	500.252	−0.292	500.000	500.540	−0.580

METRIC H7/u6:	FORCE FIT
BASIC DIA	40 mm
HOLE	40.025 40.000
SHAFT	40.076 40.060
MAX CLEAR.	−0.035
MIN CLEAR. (ALLOWANCE)	−0.076

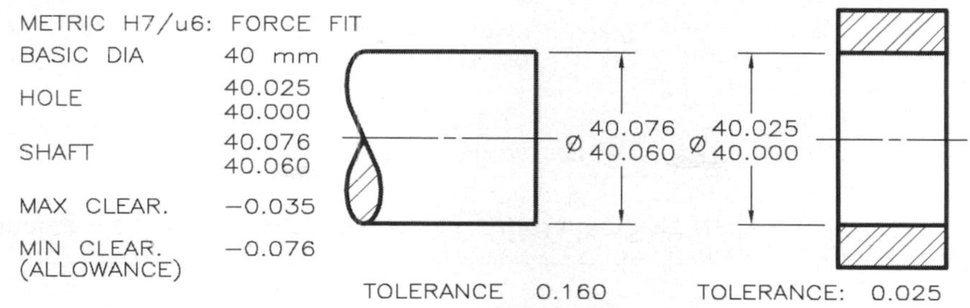

APPENDIX 37 • Preferred Shaft-Basis Clearance Fits—Cylindrical Fits (ANSI B4.2)

Basic Size		Loose Running			Free Running			Close Running			Sliding			Locational Clearance		
		Hole C11	Shaft h11	Fit	Hole D9	Shaft h9	Fit	Hole F8	Shaft h7	Fit	Hole G7	Shaft h6	Fit	Hole H7	Shaft h6	Fit
1	MAX	1.120	1.000	0.180	1.045	1.000	0.070	1.020	1.000	0.030	1.012	1.000	0.018	1.010	1.000	0.016
	MIN	1.060	0.940	0.060	1.020	0.975	0.020	1.006	0.990	0.006	1.002	0.994	0.002	1.000	0.994	0.000
1.2	MAX	1.320	1.200	0.180	1.245	1.200	0.070	1.220	1.200	0.030	1.212	1.200	0.018	1.210	1.200	0.016
	MIN	1.260	1.140	0.060	1.220	1.175	0.020	1.206	1.190	0.006	1.202	1.194	0.002	1.200	1.194	0.000
1.6	MAX	1.720	1.600	0.180	1.656	1.600	0.070	1.620	1.600	0.030	1.612	1.600	0.018	1.610	1.600	0.016
	MIN	1.660	1.540	0.060	1.620	1.575	0.020	1.606	1.590	0.006	1.602	1.595	0.002	1.600	1.594	0.000
2	MAX	2.120	2.000	0.180	2.045	2.000	0.070	2.020	2.000	0.030	2.012	2.000	0.018	2.010	2.000	0.016
	MIN	2.060	1.940	0.060	2.020	1.975	0.020	2.006	1.990	0.006	2.002	1.994	0.002	2.000	1.994	0.000
2.5	MAX	2.620	2.500	0.180	2.545	2.500	0.070	2.520	2.500	0.030	2.512	2.500	0.018	2.510	2.500	0.016
	MIN	2.560	2.440	0.060	2.520	2.475	0.020	2.506	2.490	0.006	2.502	2.494	0.002	2.500	2.494	0.000
3	MAX	3.120	3.000	0.180	3.045	3.000	0.070	3.020	3.000	0.030	3.012	3.000	0.018	3.010	3.000	0.016
	MIN	3.060	2.940	0.060	3.020	2.975	0.020	3.006	2.990	0.006	3.002	2.994	0.002	3.000	2.994	0.000
4	MAX	4.145	4.000	0.220	4.060	4.000	0.090	4.028	4.000	0.040	4.016	4.000	0.024	4.012	4.000	0.020
	MIN	4.070	3.925	0.070	4.030	3.970	0.030	4.010	3.988	0.010	4.004	3.992	0.004	4.000	3.992	0.000
5	MAX	5.145	5.000	0.220	5.060	5.000	0.090	5.028	5.000	0.040	5.016	5.000	0.024	5.012	5.000	0.020
	MIN	5.070	4.925	0.070	5.030	4.970	0.030	5.010	4.988	0.010	5.004	4.992	0.004	5.000	4.992	0.000
6	MAX	6.145	6.000	0.220	6.060	6.000	0.090	6.028	6.000	0.040	6.016	6.000	0.024	6.012	6.000	0.020
	MIN	6.070	5.925	0.070	6.030	5.970	0.030	6.010	5.988	0.010	6.004	5.992	0.004	6.000	5.992	0.000
8	MAX	8.170	8.000	0.260	8.076	8.000	0.112	8.035	8.000	0.050	8.020	8.000	0.029	8.015	8.000	0.024
	MIN	8.080	7.910	0.080	8.040	7.964	0.040	8.013	7.985	0.013	8.005	7.991	0.005	8.000	7.991	0.000
10	MAX	10.170	10.000	0.260	10.076	10.000	0.112	10.035	10.000	0.050	10.020	10.000	0.029	10.015	10.000	0.024
	MIN	10.080	9.910	0.080	10.040	9.964	0.040	10.013	9.985	0.013	10.005	9.991	0.005	10.000	9.991	0.000
12	MAX	12.205	12.000	0.315	12.093	12.000	0.136	12.043	12.000	0.061	12.024	12.000	0.035	12.018	12.000	0.029
	MIN	12.095	11.890	0.095	12.050	11.957	0.050	12.016	11.982	0.016	12.006	11.989	0.006	12.000	11.989	0.000
16	MAX	16.205	16.000	0.315	16.093	16.000	0.136	16.043	16.000	0.061	16.024	16.000	0.035	16.018	16.000	0.029
	MIN	16.095	15.890	0.095	16.050	15.957	0.050	16.016	15.982	0.016	16.006	15.989	0.006	16.000	15.989	0.000
20	MAX	20.240	20.000	0.370	20.117	20.000	0.169	20.053	20.000	0.074	20.028	20.000	0.041	20.021	20.000	0.034
	MIN	20.110	19.870	0.110	20.065	19.948	0.065	20.020	19.979	0.020	20.007	19.987	0.007	20.000	19.987	0.000
25	MAX	25.240	25.000	0.370	25.117	25.000	0.169	25.053	25.000	0.074	25.028	25.000	0.041	25.021	25.000	0.034
	MIN	25.110	24.870	0.110	25.065	24.948	0.065	25.020	24.979	0.020	25.007	24.987	0.007	25.000	24.987	0.000
30	MAX	30.240	30.000	0.370	30.117	30.000	0.169	30.053	30.000	0.074	30.028	30.000	0.041	30.021	30.000	0.034
	MIN	30.110	29.870	0.110	30.065	29.948	0.065	30.020	29.979	0.020	30.007	29.987	0.007	30.000	29.987	0.000

Source: American National Standard Preferred Metric Limits and Fits, ANSI B4.2.
Dimensions are in mm.

APPENDIX 37 • Preferred Shaft-Basis Clearance Fits—Cylindrical Fits (ANSI B4.2) (continued)

Basic Size		Loose Running			Free Running			Close Running			Sliding			Locational Clearance		
		Hole C11	Shaft h11	Fit	Hole D9	Shaft h9	Fit	Hole F8	Shaft h7	Fit	Hole G7	Shaft h6	Fit	Hole H7	Shaft h6	Fit
40	MAX	40.280	40.000	0.440	40.142	40.000	0.204	40.064	40.000	0.089	40.034	40.000	0.050	40.025	40.000	0.041
	MIN	40.120	39.840	0.120	40.080	39.938	0.080	40.025	39.975	0.025	40.009	39.984	0.009	40.000	39.984	0.000
50	MAX	50.290	50.000	0.450	50.142	50.000	0.204	50.064	50.000	0.089	50.034	50.000	0.050	50.025	50.000	0.041
	MIN	50.130	49.840	0.130	50.080	49.938	0.080	50.025	49.975	0.025	50.009	49.984	0.009	50.000	49.984	0.000
60	MAX	60.330	60.000	0.520	60.174	60.000	0.248	60.076	60.000	0.106	60.040	60.000	0.059	60.030	60.000	0.049
	MIN	60.140	59.810	0.140	60.100	59.926	0.100	60.030	59.970	0.030	60.010	59.981	0.010	60.000	59.981	0.000
80	MAX	80.340	80.000	0.530	80.174	80.000	0.248	80.076	80.000	0.106	80.040	80.000	0.059	80.030	80.000	0.049
	MIN	80.150	79.810	0.150	80.100	79.926	0.100	80.030	79.970	0.030	80.010	79.981	0.010	80.000	79.981	0.000
100	MAX	100.390	100.000	0.610	100.207	100.000	0.294	100.090	100.000	0.125	100.047	100.000	0.069	100.035	100.000	0.057
	MIN	100.170	99.780	0.170	100.120	99.913	0.120	100.036	99.965	0.036	100.012	99.979	0.012	100.000	99.979	0.000
120	MAX	120.400	120.000	0.620	120.207	120.000	0.294	120.090	120.000	0.125	120.047	120.000	0.069	120.035	120.000	0.057
	MIN	120.180	119.780	0.180	120.120	119.913	0.120	120.036	119.965	0.036	120.012	119.978	0.012	120.000	119.978	0.000
160	MAX	160.460	160.000	0.710	160.245	160.000	0.345	160.106	160.000	0.146	160.054	160.000	0.079	160.040	160.000	0.065
	MIN	160.210	159.750	0.210	160.145	159.900	0.145	160.043	159.960	0.043	160.014	159.975	0.014	160.000	159.975	0.000
200	MAX	200.530	200.000	0.820	200.285	200.000	0.400	200.122	200.000	0.168	200.061	200.000	0.090	200.046	200.000	0.075
	MIN	200.240	199.710	0.240	200.170	199.885	0.170	200.050	199.954	0.050	200.015	199.971	0.015	200.000	199.971	0.000
250	MAX	250.570	250.000	0.860	250.285	250.000	0.400	250.122	250.000	0.168	250.061	250.000	0.090	250.046	250.000	0.075
	MIN	250.280	249.710	0.280	250.170	249.885	0.170	250.050	249.954	0.050	250.015	249.971	0.015	250.000	249.971	0.000
300	MAX	300.650	300.000	0.970	300.320	300.000	0.450	300.137	300.000	0.189	300.069	300.000	0.101	300.052	300.000	0.084
	MIN	300.330	299.680	0.330	300.190	299.870	0.190	300.056	299.948	0.056	300.017	299.968	0.017	300.000	299.968	0.000
400	MAX	400.760	400.000	1.120	400.350	400.000	0.490	400.151	400.000	0.208	400.075	400.000	0.111	400.057	400.000	0.983
	MIN	400.400	399.640	0.400	400.210	399.860	0.210	400.062	399.943	0.062	400.018	399.964	0.018	400.000	399.964	0.000
500	MAX	500.880	500.000	1.280	500.385	500.000	0.540	500.165	500.000	0.228	500.083	500.000	0.123	500.063	500.000	0.103
	MIN	500.480	499.600	0.480	500.230	499.845	0.230	500.068	499.937	0.068	500.020	499.960	0.020	500.000	499.960	0.000

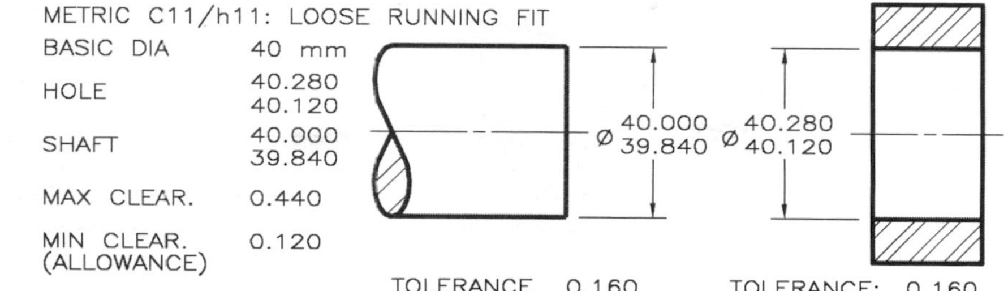

APPENDIX 38 • Preferred Shaft-Basis Transition and Interference Fits—Cylindrical Fits (ANSI B4.2)

Basic Size		Locational Transn.			Locational Transn.			Locational Interf.			Medium Drive			Force		
		Hole K7	Shaft h6	Fit	Hole N7	Shaft h6	Fit	Hole P7	Shaft h6	Fit	Hole S7	Shaft h6	Fit	Hole U7	Shaft h6	Fit
1	MAX	1.000	1.000	0.006	0.996	1.000	0.002	0.994	1.000	0.000	0.986	1.000	−0.008	0.982	1.000	−0.012
	MIN	0.990	0.994	−0.010	0.986	0.994	−0.014	0.984	0.994	−0.016	0.976	0.994	−0.024	0.972	0.994	−0.028
1.2	MAX	1.200	1.200	0.006	1.196	1.200	0.002	1.194	1.200	0.000	1.186	1.200	−0.008	1.182	1.200	−0.012
	MIN	1.190	1.194	−0.010	1.186	1.194	−0.014	1.184	1.194	−0.016	1.176	1.194	−0.024	1.172	1.194	−0.028
1.6	MAX	1.600	1.600	0.006	1.596	1.600	0.002	1.594	1.600	0.000	1.586	1.600	−0.008	1.582	1.600	−0.012
	MIN	1.590	1.594	−0.010	1.586	1.594	−0.014	1.584	1.594	−0.016	1.576	1.594	−0.024	1.572	1.594	−0.028
2	MAX	2.000	2.000	0.006	1.996	2.000	0.002	1.994	2.000	0.008	1.986	2.000	−0.008	1.982	2.000	−0.012
	MIN	1.990	1.994	−0.010	1.986	1.994	−0.014	1.984	1.994	−0.016	1.976	1.994	−0.024	1.972	1.994	−0.028
2.5	MAX	2.500	2.500	0.006	2.496	2.500	0.002	2.494	2.500	0.000	2.486	2.500	−0.008	2.482	2.500	−0.012
	MIN	2.490	2.494	−0.010	2.486	2.494	−0.014	2.484	2.494	−0.016	2.476	2.494	−0.024	2.472	2.494	−0.028
3	MAX	3.000	3.000	0.006	2.996	3.000	0.002	2.994	3.000	0.000	2.986	3.000	−0.008	2.982	3.000	−0.012
	MIN	2.990	2.994	0.010	2.986	2.994	−0.014	2.984	2.994	−0.016	2.976	2.994	−0.024	2.972	2.994	−0.028
4	MAX	4.003	4.000	0.011	3.996	4.000	0.004	3.992	4.000	0.000	3.985	4.000	−0.007	3.981	4.000	−0.011
	MIN	3.991	3.992	−0.009	3.984	3.992	−0.016	3.980	3.992	−0.020	3.973	3.992	−0.027	3.969	3.992	−0.031
5	MAX	5.003	5.000	0.011	4.996	5.000	0.004	4.992	5.000	0.000	4.985	5.000	−0.007	4.981	5.000	−0.011
	MIN	4.991	4.992	−0.009	4.984	4.992	−0.016	4.980	4.992	−0.020	4.973	4.992	−0.027	4.969	4.992	−0.031
6	MAX	6.003	6.000	0.011	5.996	6.000	0.004	5.992	6.000	0.000	5.985	6.000	−0.007	5.981	6.000	−0.011
	MIN	5.991	5.992	−0.009	5.984	5.992	−0.016	5.980	5.992	−0.020	5.973	5.992	−0.027	5.969	5.992	−0.031
8	MAX	8.005	8.000	0.014	7.986	8.000	0.005	7.991	8.000	0.000	7.983	8.000	−0.008	7.978	8.000	−0.013
	MIN	7.990	7.991	−0.010	7.981	7.991	−0.019	7.976	7.991	−0.024	7.968	7.991	−0.032	7.963	7.991	−0.037
10	MAX	10.005	10.000	0.014	9.996	10.000	0.005	9.991	10.000	0.0000	9.983	10.000	−0.008	9.978	10.000	−0.013
	MIN	9.990	9.991	−0.010	9.981	9.991	−0.019	9.976	9.991	−0.024	9.968	9.991	−0.032	9.963	9.991	−0.037
12	MAX	12.006	12.000	0.017	11.995	12.000	0.006	11.989	12.000	0.000	11.979	12.000	−0.010	11.974	12.000	−0.015
	MIN	11.988	11.989	−0.012	11.977	11.989	−0.023	11.971	11.989	−0.029	11.961	11.989	−0.039	11.956	11.989	−0.044
16	MAX	16.006	16.000	0.017	15.995	16.000	0.006	15.989	16.000	0.000	15.979	16.000	−0.010	15.974	16.000	−0.015
	MIN	15.988	15.989	−0.012	15.977	15.989	−0.023	15.971	15.989	−0.029	15.961	15.989	−0.039	15.956	15.989	−0.044
20	MAX	20.006	20.000	0.019	19.993	20.000	0.006	19.986	20.000	−0.001	19.973	20.000	−0.014	19.967	20.000	−0.020
	MIN	19.985	19.987	−0.015	19.972	19.987	−0.028	19.965	19.987	−0.035	19.952	19.987	−0.048	19.946	19.987	−0.054
25	MAX	25.006	25.000	0.019	24.993	25.000	0.006	24.986	25.000	−0.001	24.973	25.000	−0.014	24.960	25.000	−0.027
	MIN	24.985	24.987	−0.015	24.972	24.987	−0.028	24.965	24.987	−0.035	24.952	24.987	−0.048	24.939	24.987	−0.061
30	MAX	30.006	30.000	0.019	29.993	30.000	0.006	29.986	30.000	−0.001	29.973	30.000	−0.014	29.960	30.000	−0.027
	MIN	29.985	29.987	−0.015	29.972	29.987	−0.028	29.965	29.987	−0.035	29.952	29.987	−0.048	29.939	29.987	−0.061

Source: American National Standard Preferred Metric Limits and Fits, ANSI B4.2.
Dimensions are in mm.

APPENDIX 38 • Preferred Shaft-Basis Transition and Interference Fits—Cylindrical Fits (ANSI B4.2) (continued)

Basic Size		Locational Transn.			Locational Transn.			Locational Interf.			Medium Drive			Force		
		Hole K7	Shaft h6	Fit	Hole N7	Shaft h6	Fit	Hole P7	Shaft h6	Fit	Hole S7	Shaft h6	Fit	Hole U7	Shaft h6	Fit
40	MAX	40.007	40.000	0.023	39.992	40.000	0.008	39.983	40.000	−0.001	39.966	40.000	−0.018	39.949	40.000	−0.035
	MIN	39.982	39.984	−0.018	39.967	39.984	−0.033	39.958	39.984	−0.042	39.941	39.984	−0.059	39.924	39.984	−0.076
50	MAX	50.007	50.000	0.023	49.992	50.000	0.008	49.983	50.000	−0.001	49.966	50.000	−0.018	49.939	50.000	−0.045
	MIN	49.982	49.984	−0.018	49.967	49.984	−0.033	49.958	49.984	−0.042	49.941	49.984	−0.059	49.914	49.984	−0.086
60	MAX	60.009	60.000	0.028	59.991	60.000	0.010	59.979	60.000	−0.002	59.958	60.000	−0.023	59.924	60.000	−0.057
	MIN	59.979	59.981	−0.021	59.961	59.981	−0.039	59.949	59.981	−0.051	59.928	59.981	−0.072	59.894	59.981	−0.106
80	MAX	80.009	80.000	0.028	79.991	80.000	0.010	79.979	80.000	−0.002	79.952	80.000	−0.029	79.909	80.000	−0.072
	MIN	79.979	79.981	−0.021	79.961	79.981	−0.039	79.949	79.981	−0.051	79.922	79.981	−0.078	79.879	79.981	−0.121
100	MAX	100.010	100.000	0.032	99.990	100.000	0.012	99.976	100.000	−0.002	99.942	100.000	−0.036	99.889	100.000	−0.089
	MIN	99.975	99.978	−0.025	99.955	99.978	−0.045	99.941	99.978	−0.059	99.907	99.978	−0.093	99.854	99.978	−0.146
120	MAX	120.010	120.000	0.032	119.990	120.000	0.012	119.976	120.000	−0.002	119.934	120.000	−0.044	119.869	120.000	−0.109
	MIN	119.975	119.978	−0.025	119.955	119.978	−0.045	119.941	119.978	−0.059	119.899	119.978	−0.101	119.834	119.978	−0.166
160	MAX	160.012	160.000	0.037	159.988	160.000	0.013	159.972	160.000	−0.003	159.915	160.000	−0.060	159.825	160.000	−0.150
	MIN	159.972	159.975	−0.028	159.948	159.975	−0.052	159.932	159.975	−0.068	159.875	159.975	−0.125	159.785	159.975	−0.215
200	MAX	200.013	200.000	0.042	199.986	200.000	0.015	199.967	200.000	−0.004	199.895	200.000	−0.076	199.781	200.000	−0.190
	MIN	199.967	199.971	−0.033	199.940	199.971	−0.060	199.921	199.971	−0.079	199.849	199.971	−0.151	199.735	199.971	−0.265
250	MAX	250.013	250.000	0.042	249.986	250.000	0.015	249.967	250.000	−0.004	249.877	250.000	−0.094	249.733	250.000	−0.238
	MIN	249.967	249.971	−0.033	249.940	249.971	−0.060	249.921	249.971	−0.079	249.831	249.971	−0.169	249.687	249.971	−0.313
300	MAX	300.016	300.000	0.048	299.986	300.000	0.018	299.964	300.000	−0.004	299.850	300.000	−0.188	299.670	300.000	−0.298
	MIN	299.964	299.968	−0.036	299.934	299.968	−0.066	299.912	299.968	−0.088	299.798	299.968	−0.202	299.618	299.968	−0.382
400	MAX	400.017	400.000	0.053	399.984	400.000	0.020	399.959	400.000	−0.005	399.813	400.000	−0.151	399.586	400.000	−0.378
	MIN	399.960	399.964	−0.040	399.927	399.964	−0.073	399.902	399.964	−0.080	399.756	399.964	−0.244	399.529	399.964	−0.471
500	MAX	500.018	500.000	0.058	499.983	500.000	0.023	499.955	500.000	−0.005	499.771	500.000	−0.189	499.483	500.000	−0.477
	MIN	499.955	499.960	−0.045	499.920	499.960	−0.080	499.892	499.960	−0.180	499.708	499.960	−0.292	499.420	499.960	−0.580

Dimensions are in mm.

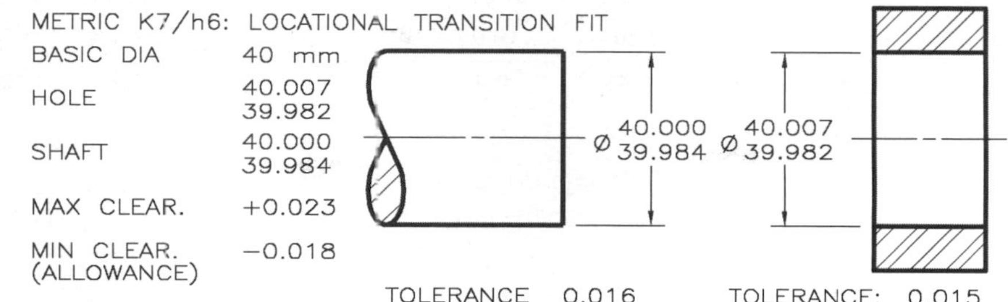

APPENDIX 39 • Hole Sizes for Nonpreferred Diameters (millimeters)

Basic Size		C11	D9	F8	G7	H7	H8	H9	H11	K7	N7	P7	S7	U7
OVER	0	+0.120	+0.045	+0.020	+0.012	+0.010	+0.014	+0.025	+0.060	0.000	−0.004	−0.006	−0.014	−0.018
TO	3	+0.060	+0.020	+0.006	+0.002	0.000	0.000	0.000	0.000	−0.010	−0.014	−0.016	−0.024	−0.028
OVER	3	+0.145	+0.060	+0.028	+0.016	+0.012	+0.018	+0.030	+0.075	+0.003	−0.004	−0.008	−0.015	−0.019
TO	6	+0.070	+0.030	+0.010	+0.004	0.000	0.000	0.000	0.000	−0.009	−0.016	−0.020	−0.027	−0.031
OVER	6	+0.170	+0.076	+0.035	+0.020	+0.015	+0.022	+0.036	+0.090	+0.005	−0.004	−0.009	−0.017	−0.022
TO	10	+0.080	+0.040	+0.013	+0.005	0.000	0.000	0.000	0.000	−0.010	−0.019	−0.024	−0.032	−0.037
OVER	10	+0.205	+0.093	+0.043	+0.024	+0.018	+0.027	+0.043	+0.110	+0.006	−0.005	−0.011	−0.021	−0.026
TO	14	+0.095	+0.050	+0.016	+0.006	0.000	0.000	0.000	0.000	−0.012	−0.023	−0.029	−0.039	−0.044
OVER	14	+0.205	+0.093	+0.043	+0.024	+0.018	+0.027	+0.043	+0.110	+0.006	−0.005	−0.011	−0.021	−0.026
TO	18	+0.095	+0.050	+0.016	+0.006	0.000	0.000	0.000	0.000	−0.012	−0.023	−0.029	−0.039	−0.044
OVER	18	+0.240	+0.117	+0.053	+0.028	+0.021	+0.033	+0.052	+0.130	+0.006	−0.007	−0.014	−0.027	−0.033
TO	24	+0.110	+0.065	+0.020	+0.007	0.000	0.000	0.000	0.000	−0.015	−0.028	−0.035	−0.048	−0.054
OVER	24	+0.240	+0.117	+0.053	+0.028	+0.021	+0.033	+0.052	+0.130	+0.006	−0.007	−0.014	−0.027	−0.040
TO	30	+0.110	+0.065	+0.020	+0.007	0.000	0.000	0.000	0.000	−0.015	−0.028	−0.035	−0.048	−0.061
OVER	30	+0.280	+0.142	+0.064	+0.034	+0.025	+0.039	+0.062	+0.160	+0.007	−0.008	−0.017	−0.034	−0.051
TO	40	+0.120	+0.080	+0.025	+0.009	0.000	0.000	0.000	0.000	−0.018	−0.033	−0.042	−0.059	−0.076
OVER	40	+0.290	+0.142	+0.064	+0.034	+0.025	+0.039	+0.062	+0.160	+0.007	−0.008	−0.017	−0.034	−0.061
TO	50	+0.130	+0.080	+0.025	+0.009	0.000	0.000	0.000	0.000	−0.018	−0.033	−0.042	−0.059	−0.086
OVER	50	+0.330	+0.174	+0.076	+0.040	+0.030	+0.046	+0.074	+0.190	+0.009	−0.009	−0.021	−0.042	−0.076
TO	65	+0.140	+0.100	+0.030	+0.010	0.000	0.000	0.000	0.000	−0.021	−0.039	−0.051	−0.072	−0.106
OVER	65	+0.340	+0.174	+0.076	+0.040	+0.030	+0.046	+0.074	+0.190	+0.009	−0.009	−0.021	−0.048	−0.091
TO	80	+0.150	+0.100	+0.030	+0.010	0.000	0.000	0.000	0.000	−0.021	−0.039	−0.051	−0.078	−0.121
OVER	80	+0.390	+0.207	+0.090	+0.047	+0.035	+0.054	+0.087	+0.220	+0.010	−0.010	−0.024	−0.058	−0.111
TO	100	+0.170	+0.120	+0.036	+0.012	0.000	0.000	0.000	0.000	−0.025	−0.045	−0.059	−0.093	−0.146

APPENDIX 39 • Hole Sizes for Nonpreferred Diameters (millimeters) (continued)

Basic Size		C11	D9	F8	G7	H7	H8	H9	H11	K7	N7	P7	S7	U7
OVER	100	+0.400	+0.207	+0.090	+0.047	+0.035	+0.054	+0.087	+0.220	+0.010	−0.010	−0.024	−0.066	−0.131
TO	120	+0.180	+0.120	+0.036	+0.012	0.000	0.000	0.000	0.000	−0.025	−0.045	−0.059	−0.101	−0.166
OVER	120	+0.450	+0.245	+0.106	+0.054	+0.040	+0.063	+0.100	+0.250	+0.012	−0.012	−0.028	−0.077	−0.155
TO	140	+0.200	+0.145	+0.043	+0.014	0.000	0.000	0.000	0.000	−0.028	−0.052	−0.068	−0.117	−0.195
OVER	140	+0.460	+0.245	+0.106	+0.054	+0.040	+0.063	+0.100	+0.250	+0.012	−0.012	−0.028	−0.085	−0.175
TO	160	+0.210	+0.145	+0.043	+0.014	0.000	0.000	0.000	0.000	−0.028	−0.052	−0.068	−0.125	−0.215
OVER	160	+0.480	+0.245	+0.106	+0.054	+0.040	+0.063	+0.100	+0.250	+0.012	−0.012	−0.028	−0.093	−0.195
TO	180	+0.230	+0.145	+0.043	+0.014	0.000	0.000	0.000	0.000	−0.028	−0.052	−0.068	−0.133	−0.235
OVER	180	+0.530	+0.285	+0.122	+0.061	+0.046	+0.072	+0.115	+0.290	−0.013	−0.014	−0.033	−0.105	−0.219
TO	200	+0.240	+0.170	+0.050	+0.015	0.000	0.000	0.000	0.000	−0.033	−0.060	−0.079	−0.151	−0.265
OVER	200	+0.550	+0.285	+0.122	+0.061	+0.046	+0.072	+0.115	+0.290	+0.013	−0.014	−0.033	−0.113	−0.241
TO	225	+0.260	+0.170	+0.050	+0.015	0.000	0.000	0.000	0.000	−0.033	−0.060	−0.079	−0.159	−0.287
OVER	225	+0.570	+0.285	+0.122	+0.061	+0.046	+0.072	+0.115	+0.290	+0.013	−0.014	−0.033	−0.123	−0.267
TO	250	+0.280	+0.170	+0.050	+0.015	0.000	0.000	0.000	0.000	−0.033	−0.060	−0.079	−0.169	−0.313
OVER	250	+0.620	+0.320	+0.137	+0.069	+0.052	+0.081	+0.130	+0.320	+0.016	−0.014	−0.036	−0.138	−0.295
TO	280	+0.300	+0.190	+0.056	+0.017	0.000	0.000	0.000	0.000	−0.036	−0.066	−0.088	−0.190	−0.347
OVER	280	+0.650	+0.320	+0.137	+0.069	+0.052	+0.081	+0.130	+0.320	+0.016	−0.014	−0.036	−0.150	−0.330
TO	315	+0.330	+0.190	+0.056	0.017	0.000	0.000	0.000	0.000	−0.036	−0.066	−0.088	−0.202	−0.382
OVER	315	+0.720	+0.350	+0.151	+0.075	+0.057	+0.089	+0.140	+0.360	+0.017	−0.016	−0.041	−0.169	−0.369
TO	355	+0.360	+0.210	+0.062	+0.018	0.000	0.000	0.000	0.000	−0.040	−0.073	−0.058	−0.226	−0.426
OVER	355	+0.760	+0.350	+0.151	+0.075	+0.057	+0.089	+0.140	+0.360	+0.017	−0.016	−0.041	−0.187	−0.414
TO	400	+0.400	+0.210	+0.062	+0.018	0.000	0.000	0.000	0.000	−0.040	−0.073	−0.058	−0.244	−0.471
OVER	400	+0.840	+0.385	+0.165	+0.083	+0.063	+0.097	+0.155	+0.400	+0.018	−0.017	−0.045	−0.209	−0.467
TO	450	+0.440	+0.230	+0.068	+0.020	0.000	0.000	0.000	0.000	−0.045	−0.080	−0.108	−0.272	−0.530
OVER	450	+0.880	+0.385	+0.165	+0.083	+0.063	+0.097	+0.155	+0.400	+0.018	−0.017	−0.045	−0.229	−0.517
TO	500	+0.480	+0.230	+0.068	+0.020	0.000	0.000	0.000	0.000	−0.045	−0.080	−0.108	−0.292	−0.580

APPENDIX 40 • Shaft Sizes for Nonpreferred Diameters (millimeters)

Basic Size		c11	d9	f7	g6	h6	h7	h9	h11	k6	n6	p6	s6	u6
OVER	0	−0.060	−0.020	−0.006	−0.002	0.000	0.000	0.000	0.000	+0.006	+0.010	+0.012	+0.020	+0.024
TO	3	−0.120	−0.045	−0.016	−0.008	−0.006	−0.010	−0.025	−0.060	0.000	+0.004	+0.006	+0.014	+0.018
OVER	3	−0.070	−0.030	−0.010	−0.004	0.000	0.000	0.000	0.000	+0.009	+0.016	+0.020	+0.027	+0.031
TO	6	−0.145	−0.060	−0.022	−0.012	−0.008	−0.012	−0.030	−0.075	+0.001	+0.008	+0.012	+0.019	+0.023
OVER	6	−0.080	−0.040	−0.013	−0.005	0.000	0.000	0.000	0.000	+0.010	+0.019	+0.024	+0.032	+0.037
TO	10	−0.170	−0.076	−0.028	−0.014	−0.009	−0.015	−0.036	−0.090	+0.001	+0.010	+0.024	+0.023	+0.028
OVER	10	−0.095	−0.050	−0.016	−0.006	0.000	0.000	0.000	0.000	+0.012	+0.023	+0.029	+0.039	+0.044
TO	14	−0.205	−0.093	−0.034	−0.017	−0.011	−0.018	−0.043	−0.110	+0.001	+0.012	+0.018	+0.028	+0.033
OVER	14	−0.095	−0.050	−0.016	−0.006	0.000	0.000	0.000	0.000	+0.012	+0.023	+0.029	+0.039	+0.044
TO	18	−0.205	−0.093	−0.034	−0.017	−0.011	−0.018	−0.043	−0.110	+0.001	+0.012	+0.018	+0.028	+0.033
OVER	18	−0.110	−0.065	−0.020	−0.007	0.000	0.000	0.000	0.000	+0.015	+0.028	+0.035	+0.048	+0.054
TO	24	−0.240	−0.117	−0.041	−0.020	−0.013	−0.021	−0.052	−0.130	+0.002	+0.015	+0.022	+0.035	+0.041
OVER	24	−0.110	−0.065	−0.020	−0.007	0.000	0.000	0.000	0.000	+0.015	+0.028	+0.035	+0.048	+0.061
TO	30	−0.240	−0.117	−0.041	−0.020	−0.013	−0.021	−0.052	−0.130	+0.002	+0.015	+0.022	+0.035	+0.048
OVER	30	−0.120	−0.080	−0.025	−0.009	0.000	0.000	0.000	0.000	+0.018	+0.033	+0.042	+0.059	+0.076
TO	40	−0.280	−0.142	−0.050	−0.025	−0.016	−0.025	−0.062	−0.160	+0.002	+0.017	+0.026	+0.043	+0.060
OVER	40	−0.130	−0.080	−0.025	−0.009	0.000	0.000	0.000	0.000	+0.018	+0.033	+0.042	+0.059	+0.086
TO	50	−0.290	−0.142	−0.050	−0.025	−0.016	−0.025	−0.062	−0.160	+0.002	+0.017	+0.026	+0.043	+0.070
OVER	50	−0.140	−0.100	−0.030	−0.010	0.000	0.000	0.000	0.000	+0.021	+0.039	+0.051	+0.072	+0.106
TO	65	−0.330	−0.174	−0.060	−0.029	−0.019	−0.030	−0.074	−0.190	+0.002	+0.020	−0.032	+0.053	+0.087
OVER	65	−0.150	−0.100	−0.030	−0.010	0.000	0.000	0.000	0.000	+0.021	+0.039	+0.051	+0.078	+0.121
TO	80	−0.340	−0.174	−0.060	−0.029	−0.019	−0.030	−0.074	−0.190	+0.002	+0.020	+0.032	+0.059	+0.102
OVER	80	−0.170	−0.120	−0.036	−0.012	0.000	0.000	0.000	0.000	+0.025	+0.045	+0.059	+0.093	+0.146
TO	100	−0.390	−0.207	−0.071	−0.034	−0.022	−0.035	−0.087	−0.220	+0.003	+0.023	+0.037	+0.071	+0.124

APPENDIX 40 • **Shaft Sizes for Nonpreferred Diameters (millimeters) (continued)**

Basic Size		c11	d9	f7	g6	h6	h7	h9	h11	k6	n6	p6	s6	u6
OVER	100	−0.180	−0.120	−0.036	−0.012	0.000	0.000	0.000	0.000	+0.025	+0.045	+0.059	+0.101	+0.166
TO	120	−0.400	−0.207	−0.071	−0.034	−0.022	−0.035	−0.087	−0.220	+0.003	+0.023	+0.037	+0.079	+0.144
OVER	120	−0.200	−0.145	−0.043	−0.014	0.000	0.000	0.000	0.000	+0.028	+0.052	+0.068	+0.117	+0.195
TO	140	−0.450	−0.245	−0.083	−0.039	−0.025	−0.040	−0.100	−0.250	+0.003	+0.027	+0.043	+0.092	+0.170
OVER	140	−0.210	−0.145	−0.043	−0.014	0.000	0.000	0.000	0.000	+0.028	+0.052	+0.068	+0.125	+0.215
TO	160	−0.460	−0.245	−0.083	−0.039	−0.025	−0.040	−0.100	−0.250	+0.003	+0.027	+0.043	+0.100	+0.190
OVER	160	−0.230	−0.145	−0.043	−0.014	0.000	0.000	0.000	0.000	+0.028	+0.052	+0.068	+0.133	+0.235
TO	180	−0.480	−0.245	−0.083	−0.039	−0.025	−0.040	−0.100	−0.250	+0.003	+0.027	+0.043	+0.108	+0.210
OVER	180	−0.240	−0.170	−0.050	−0.015	0.000	0.000	0.000	0.000	+0.033	+0.060	+0.079	+0.151	+0.265
TO	200	−0.530	−0.285	−0.096	−0.044	−0.029	−0.046	−0.115	−0.290	+0.004	+0.031	+0.050	+0.122	+0.236
OVER	200	−0.260	−0.170	−0.050	−0.015	0.000	0.000	0.000	0.000	+0.033	+0.060	+0.079	+0.159	+0.287
TO	225	−0.550	−0.285	−0.096	−0.044	−0.029	−0.046	−0.115	−0.290	+0.004	+0.031	+0.050	+0.130	+0.258
OVER	225	−0.280	−0.170	−0.050	−0.015	0.000	0.000	0.000	0.000	+0.033	+0.060	+0.079	+0.169	+0.313
TO	250	−0.570	−0.285	−0.096	−0.044	−0.029	−0.046	−0.115	−0.290	+0.004	+0.031	+0.050	+0.140	+0.284
OVER	250	−0.300	−0.190	−0.056	−0.017	0.000	0.000	0.000	0.000	+0.036	+0.066	+0.088	+0.190	+0.347
TO	280	−0.620	−0.320	−0.108	−0.049	−0.032	−0.052	−0.130	−0.320	+0.004	+0.034	+0.056	+0.158	+0.315
OVER	280	−0.330	−0.190	−0.056	−0.017	0.000	0.000	0.000	0.000	+0.036	+0.066	+0.088	+0.202	+0.382
TO	315	−0.650	−0.320	−0.108	−0.049	−0.032	−0.052	−0.130	−0.320	+0.004	+0.034	+0.056	+0.170	+0.350
OVER	315	−0.360	−0.210	−0.062	−0.018	0.000	0.000	0.000	0.000	+0.040	+0.073	+0.098	+0.226	+0.426
TO	355	−0.720	−0.350	−0.119	−0.054	−0.036	−0.057	−0.140	−0.360	+0.004	+0.037	+0.062	+0.190	+0.390
OVER	355	−0.400	−0.210	−0.062	−0.018	0.000	0.000	0.000	0.000	+0.040	+0.073	+0.098	+0.244	+0.471
TO	400	−0.760	−0.350	−0.119	−0.054	−0.036	−0.057	−0.140	−0.360	+0.004	+0.037	+0.062	+0.208	+0.435
OVER	400	−0.440	−0.230	−0.068	−0.020	0.000	0.000	0.000	0.000	+0.045	+0.080	+0.108	+0.272	+0.530
TO	450	−0.840	−0.385	−0.131	−0.060	0.040	0.063	−0.155	0.400	+0.005	+0.040	+0.068	+0.232	+0.490
OVER	450	−0.480	−0.230	−0.068	−0.020	0.000	0.000	0.000	0.000	+0.045	+0.080	+0.108	+0.292	+0.580
TO	500	−0.880	−0.385	−0.131	−0.060	−0.040	−0.063	−0.155	−0.400	+0.005	+0.040	+0.068	+0.252	+0.540

The following LISP programs were written by Professor Leendert Kersten of the University of Nebraska and are given here with his permission These programs were introduced in Chapter 27, in which the principles of descriptive geometry are covered. These very valuable programs can be duplicated and added as supplements to your AutoCAD software.

```
)
(defun C: PARALLEL ( )
 (setvar "aperture" 5)
   (setq sp (getpoint "\nSelect START point of
     parallel line:") )
   (setq ep (getpoint "\nSelect END point of
     parallel line:") )
   (setvar "osmode" 1)
   (setq s1 (getpoint "\nSelect 1st point on
     line for parallelism:") )
   (setq e1 (getpoint "\nSelect 2nd point on
     line for parallelism:") )
   (setvar "osmode" 0)
   (setq pa (angle s1 e1) )
   (setq 1a (angle sp ep) )
   (setq 11 (distance sp ep) )
   (setq m -1)
   (setq d 0)
   (if (> pa d) (setq m 1) )
   (if (> la d) (setq d 1) )
   (if (/= m d) (setq pa (+ pa 3.141593) ) )
   (setq ep (polar sp pa 11) )
   (setvar "cmdecho" 0)
   (command line sp en "")
   (restore)
)
(defun C: PERPLINE ( )
   (setvar "aperture" 5) (setvar "cmdecho" 0)
   (setq sp (getpoint "\nSelect START point of
     perpendicular line:") )
   (setvar "osmode" 128)
   (setq cc (getpoint sp "\nSelect ANY point on
     line to which perp'1r:") )
   (setq beta (angle sp cc) ) (setvar "osmode" 0)
(setq ep
(getpoint "\nSelect END point of desired
perpendicular (for length only): ") )
   (setq length (distance sp ep) )
   (setq ep (polar sp beta length) )
   (command "line sp ep " ")
   (restore)
)
(defun C: TRANSFER ( )
   (setvar "aperture" 5) (setvar "cmdecho" 0)
   (setvar "osmode" 1)
   (setq aa (getpoint "\nSelect start of
     transfer distance:") )
   (setvar "osmode" 128)
   (setq bb (getpoint aa "\nSelect the reference
     plane:") )
   (setq length (distance aa bb) )
   (setvar "osmode" 1)
   (setq cc (getpoint "\nSelect point to be
     projected: ") )
   (setvar "osmode" 128)
   (setq dd (getpoint oc "\nSelect other
     reference plane:") )
 (setvar "osmode" 0)
   (setq alpha (angle cc dd) )
   (setq ep (polar dd alpha length) )
   (COMMAND "CIRCLE" EP 0.05)
   (restore)
)
(defun RESTORE ( )
   (setvar "aperture" 10)
   (setvar "cmdecho" 1)
   (setvar "osmode" 0)
)
(DEFUN *ERROR* (MSG)
(SETVAR "OSMODE" 0)
(setvar "aperture" 10)
( setvar "cmdecho" 1)
(PRINC "error: ")
(princ msg)
(terpri)
)
(defun C: COPYDIST ( )
     (setvar "aperture" 5)
     (setvar "cmdecho" 0)
   (setvar "osmode" 1)
     (setq p1 (getpoint "\nSelect start point of
      line distance to be copied: ") )
     (setq p2 (getpoint "\nEnd point?: ") )
   (setvar "osmode" 0)
     (setq dist (distance p1 p2) )
     (setq p1 (getpoint "\nStart point of new
     distance location:") )
     (setq ang (getangle p1 "\nWhich
      direction?: ") )
     (setq p2 (polar p1 ang diet) )
   (setvar "osmode" 0)
     (command "circle" p2 0.05)
     (restore)
)
(defun C:BISECT ( )
   (setvar "aperture" 5)
   (setvar "osmode" 32)
   (setq sp (getpoint "\nSelect Corner of
     angle: ") )
   (setvar "osmode" 2)
   (setq aa (getpoint "\nSelect first side
     (remember CCW) :") )
   (setq alpha (angle sp aa) )
   (setq bb (getpoint "\nSelect other side:") )
   (setvar "osmode" 0)
   (setq beta (angle sp bb) )
   (setq m (/ (+ alpha beta) 2) )
   (if (> alpha beta) (setq ang (+ pi m) )
     (setq ang m) )
 (setq ep
   (getpoint "\nSelect endpoint of bisecting
     line (for length only): ") )
   (setq length (distance sp ep) )
   (setq ep (polar sp ang length) )
   (setvar "cmdecho" 0)
   (command "line sp ep " ")
   (restore)
}
```

APPENDIX 42 • American National Standard 125-lb Cast-Iron Screwed Fittings (inches)

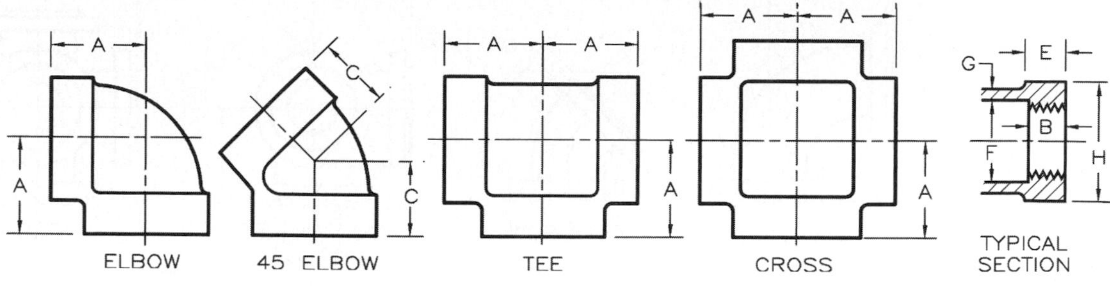

Nominal Pipe Size	A	C	B	E	F		G	H
			Min	Min	Min	Max	Min	Min
¼	0.81	0.73	0.32	0.38	0.540	0.584	0.110	0.93
⅜	0.95	0.80	0.36	0.44	0.675	0.719	0.120	1.12
½	1.12	0.88	0.43	0.50	0.840	0.897	0.130	1.34
¾	1.31	0.98	0.50	0.56	1.050	1.107	0.155	1.63
1	1.50	1.12	0.58	0.62	1.315	1.385	0.170	1.95
1¼	1.75	1.29	0.67	0.69	1.660	1.730	0.185	2.39
1½	1.94	1.43	0.70	0.75	1.900	1.970	0.200	2.68
2	2.25	1.68	0.75	0.84	2.375	2.445	0.220	3.28
2½	2.70	1.95	0.92	0.94	2.875	2.975	0.240	3.86
3	3.08	2.17	0.98	1.00	3.500	3.600	0.260	4.62
3½	3.42	2.39	1.03	1.06	4.000	4.100	0.280	5.20
4	3.79	2.61	1.08	1.12	4.500	4.600	0.310	5.79
5	4.50	3.05	1.18	1.18	5.563	5.663	0.380	7.05
6	5.13	3.46	1.28	1.28	6.625	0.725	0.430	8.28
8	6.56	4.28	1.47	1.47	8.625	8.725	0.550	10.63
10	8.08	5.16	1.68	1.68	10.750	10.850	0.690	13.12
12	9.50	5.97	1.88	1.88	12.750	12.850	0.800	15.47
14 O.D.	10.40	—	2.00	2.00	14.000	14.100	0.880	16.94
16 O.D.	11.82	—	2.20	2.20	16.000	16.100	1.000	19.30

Source: Extracted from American National Standards, "Cast-Iron Screwed Fittings, 125- and 250-lb" (ANSI B16.4), with the permission of the publisher, The American Society of Mechanical Engineers.

APPENDIX 43 • American National Standard 250-lb Cast-Iron Flanged Fittings (inches)

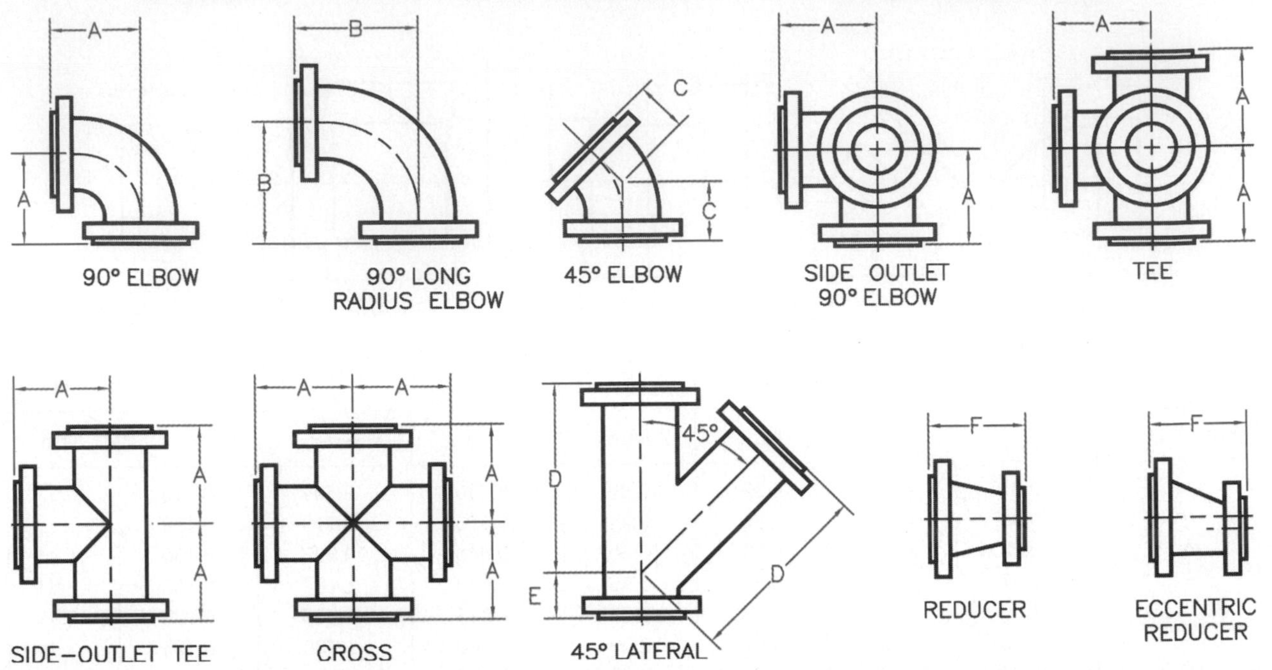

Nominal Pipe Size	Flanges: Dia of Flange	Flanges: Thickness of Flange (Min)	Flanges: Dia of Raised Face	Fittings: Inside Dia of Fittings (Min)	Fittings: Wall Thickness	Straight: Center to Face 90 Deg Elbow Tees, Crosses and True "Y" A	Straight: Center to Face 90 Deg Long Radius Elbow B	Straight: Center to Face 45 Deg Elbow C	Straight: Center to Face Lateral D	Straight: Short Center to Face True "Y" and Lateral E	Straight: Face to Face Reducer F
1	4⅞	11/16	2 11/16	1	7/16	4	5	2	6½	2	—
1¼	5¼	¾	3 1/16	1¼	7/16	4¼	5½	2½	7¼	2¼	—
1½	6⅛	13/16	3 9/16	1½	7/16	4½	6	2¾	8½	2½	—
2	6½	⅞	4 3/16	2	7/16	5	6½	3	9	2½	5
2½	7½	1	4 15/16	2½	½	5½	7	3½	10½	2½	5½
3	8¼	1⅛	5 11/16	3	9/16	6	7¾	3½	11	3	6
3½	9	1 3/16	6 5/16	3½	9/16	6½	8½	4	12½	3	6½
4	10	1¼	6 15/16	4	⅝	7	9	4½	13½	3	7
5	11	1⅜	8 5/16	5	11/16	8	10¼	5	15	3½	8
6	12½	1 7/16	9 11/16	6	¾	8½	11½	5½	17½	4	9
8	15	1⅝	11 15/16	8	13/16	10	14	6	20½	5	11
10	17½	1⅞	14 1/16	10	15/16	11½	16½	7	24	5½	12
12	20½	2	16 7/16	12	1	13	19	8	27½	6	14
14	23	2⅛	18 15/16	13¼	1⅛	15	21½	8½	31	6½	16
16	25½	2¼	21 1/36	15¼	1¼	16½	24	9½	34½	7½	18
18	28	2⅜	23 5/16	17	1⅜	18	26½	10	37½	8	19
20	30½	2½	25 9/16	19	1½	19½	29	10½	40½	8½	20
24	36	2¾	30 5/16	23	1⅝	22½	34	12	47½	10	24
30	43	3	37 3/16	29	2	27½	41½	15	—	—	30

Source: Courtesy of ANSI; B16.1.

This graph can be used to determine the individual grades of members of a team and to compute grade averages for those who do extra assignments.

The percent participation of each team member should be determined by the team as a whole (see Chapter 2 problems).

Example: Written or oral report grades

Overall team grade: 82

Team members N=5	Contribution C=%	F=CN	Grade (graph)
J. Doe	20%	100	82.0
H. Brown	16%	80	75.8
L. Smith	24%	120	86.0
R. Black	20%	100	82.0
T. Jones	20%	100	82.0
	100%		

Example: Quiz or problem sheet grades

Number assigned: 30
Number extra: 6
Total 36

Average grade for total (36): 82

$$F = \frac{\text{No. completed} \times 100}{\text{No. assigned}} = \frac{36 \times 100}{30} = 120$$

Final grade (from graph): 86.0

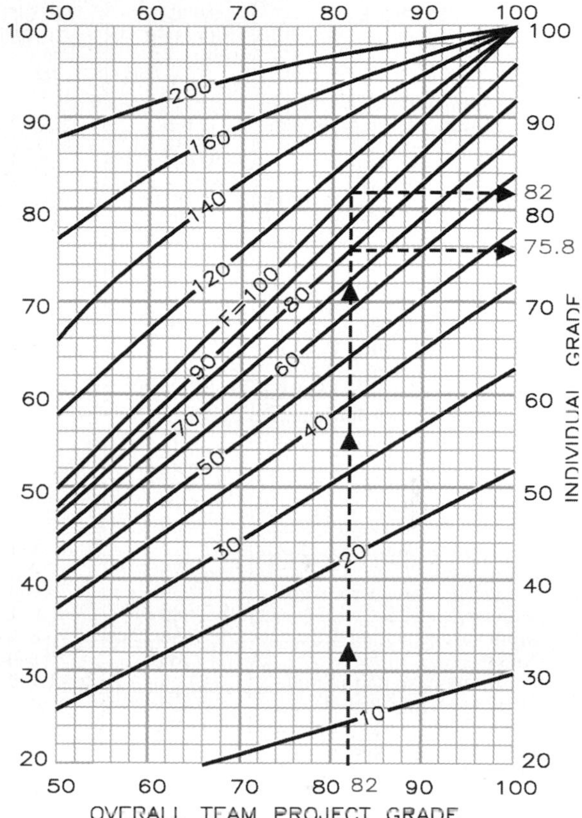

APPENDIX 45 • Weights and Specific Gravities

SUBSTANCE	WEIGHT LB. PER CU. FT.	SPECIFIC GRAVITY	SUBSTANCE	WEIGHT LB. PER CU. FT.	SPECIFIC GRAVITY
METALS, ALLOYS, ORES			TIMBER, U.S. SEASONED		
Aluminum, cast, hammered	165	2.55–2.75	Moisture Content by Weight		
Brass, cast, rolled	534	8.4–8.7	Seasoned timber 15 to 20%		
Bronze, 7.9 to 14% Sn	509	7.4–8.9	Green timber up to 50%		
Bronze, aluminum	481	7.7	Ash, white, red	40	0.62–0.65
Copper, cast, rolled	556	8.8–9.0	Cedar, white, red	22	0.32–0.38
Copper ore, pyrites	262	4.1–4.3	Chestnut	41	0.66
Gold, cast, hammered	1205	19.25–19.3	Cypress	30	0.48
Iron, cast, pig	450	7.2	Fir, Douglas spruce	32	0.51
Iron, wrought	485	7.6–7.9	Fir, eastern	25	0.40
Iron, spiegel-eisen	466	7.5	Elm, white	45	0.72
Iron, ferro-silicon	437	6.7–7.3	Hemlock	29	0.42–0.52
Iron ore, hematite	325	5.2	Hickory	49	0.74–0.84
Iron ore, hematite in bank	160–180	—	Locust	46	0.73
Iron ore, hematite loose	130–160	—	Maple, hard	43	0.68
Iron ore, limonite	237	3.6–4.0	Maple, white	33	0.53
Iron ore, magnetite	315	4.9–5.2	Oak, chestnut	54	0.86
Iron slag	172	2.5–3.0	Oak, live	59	0.95
Lead	710	11.37	Oak, red, black	41	0.65
Lead ore, galena	465	7.3–7.6	Oak, white	46	0.74
Magnesium, alloys	112	1.74–1.83	Pine, Oregon	32	0.61
Manganese	475	7.2–8.0	Pine, red	30	0.48
Manganese ore, pyrolusite	259	3.7–4.6	Pine, white	26	0.41
Mercury	849	13.6	Pine, yellow, long-leaf	44	0.70
Monel Metal	556	8.8–9.0	Pine, yellow, short-leaf	38	0.61
Nickel	565	8.9–9.2	Poplar	30	0.48
Platinum, cast, hammered	1330	21.1–21.5	Redwood, California	26	0.42
Silver, cast, hammered	656	10.4–10.6	Spruce, white, black	27	0.40–0.46
Steel, rolled	490	7.85	Walnut, black	38	0.61
Tin, cast, hammered	459	7.2–7.5			
Tin ore, cassiterite	418	6.4–7.0			
Zinc, cast, rolled	440	6.9–7.2	VARIOUS LIQUIDS		
Zinc ore, blends	253	3.9–4.2	Alcohol, 100%	49	0.79
			Acids, muriatic 40%	75	1.20
VARIOUS SOLIDS			Acids, nitric 91%	94	1.50
Cereals, oats ... bulk	32	—	Acids, sulphuric 87%	112	1.80
Cereals barley ... bulk	39	—	Lye, soda	106	1.70
Cereals, corn, rye ... bulk	48	—	Oils, vegetable	58	0.91–0.94
Cereals, wheat ... bulk	48	—	Oils, mineral, lubricants	57	0.90–0.93
Hay and Straw ... bales	20	—	Water, 4°C. max, density	62.428	1.0
Cotton, Flax, Hemp	93	1.47–1.50	Water, 100°C	59.830	0.9584
Fats	58	0.90–0.97	Water, ice	56	0.88–0.92
Flour, loose	28	0.40–0.50	Water, snow, fresh fallen	8	.125
Flour, pressed	47	0.70–0.80	Water, sea water	64	1.02–1.03
Glass, common	156	2.40–2.60			
Glass, plate or crown	161	2.45–2.72			
Glass, crystal	184	2.90–3.00	GASES		
Leather	59	0.86–1.02			
Paper	58	0.70–1.15	Air, 0°C 760 mm	.08071	1.0
Potatoes, piled	42	—	Ammonia	.0478	0.5920
Rubber, caostchouc	59	0.92–0.96	Carbon dioxide	.1234	1.5291
Rubber goods	94	1.0–2.0	Carbon monoxide	.0781	0.9673
Salt, granulated, piled	48	—	Gas, illuminating	.028–.036	0.35–0.45
Saltpeter	67	—	Gas, natural	.038–.039	0.47–0.48
Starch	96	1.53	Hydrogen	.00559	0.0693
Sulphur	125	1.93–2.07	Nitrogen	.0784	0.9714
Wool	82	1.32	Oxygen	.0892	1.1056

The specific gravities of solids and liquids refer to water at 4°C., those of gases to air at 0°C. and 760 mm. pressure. The weights per cubic foot are derived from average specific gravities, except where stated that weights are for bulk, heaped or loose materials, etc.

(Courtesy of the American Institute of Steel Construction.)

INDEX

A

B

C

D

E

F

G

H

I

J

K

L

M

N

O

P

Q

R

S

T

U

V

Z